R. Gupta's®

Popular Master Guide

NATIONAL TESTING AGENCY (NTA)

CUET-UG

Common University Entrance Test for
Under Graduate Courses/Programmes

B.A. (Hons.)

POLITICAL SCIENCE HISTORY

Entrance Exam

by

RPH Editorial Board

2026-27
EDITION

RAMESH PUBLISHING HOUSE, NEW DELHI

CUET Guidance Note For B.A. (Hons.) POLITICAL SCIENCE/B.A. (Hons.) HISTORY Aspirants

Dear students choosing the Right CUET paper combination is paramount for your chosen career. The distinction between a correct combination and a hasty choice can influence your chances of admission. This book specifically contains the CUET paper combinations which as per our editorial board is vital for your admission as most of the students/Universities will go with same paper combination only. However also note that different Universities can also have slightly different combinations or you can also choose different paper combinations, in that scenario other subjects so opted are to be studied by you from your own resources.

Published by

O.P. Gupta *for* Ramesh Publishing House

Admin. Office

12-H, New Daryaganj Road, Opp. Officers' Mess,
New Delhi-110002 ✆ 23275224, 23245124

E-mail: info@rameshpublishinghouse.com
For Online Shopping: www.rameshpublishinghouse.com

Showroom

- Balaji Market, Nai Sarak, Delhi-6 ✆ 23282525 📱 9354373464
- 4457, Nai Sarak, Delhi-110006

Book Code: R-2595

ISBN: 978-93-5477-671-7

Price: ₹ 925

Printed at: Deepak Offset, Delhi

CONTENTS

PREVIOUS YEARS' PAPERS (With explanatory answers)

ENGLISH

HISTORY

POLITICAL SCIENCE

SOCIOLOGY

GENERAL TEST

★★★★★

Previous Years' Paper

Common University Entrance Test for UG Programmes

CUET-UG—ENGLISH LANGUAGE

Entrance Exam, 2025

(Exam held on 27-05-2025)

Subject Code: 101

Directions (Qs. No. 1-4): *Read the given passage and answer the questions that follow:*

Virtues are the result of repeated actions, as habits lay the foundation of moral excellence. Right from the beginning of their lives, children are taught good habits by their parents and teachers. Magnanimity, helpfulness and sacrifice are great virtues which need to be well cultivated in human beings. Trees give shade for the benefit of others, while they themselves stand enduring the scorching heat of the sun. They selflessly bear the fruit which is consumed by birds, animals and human beings. Rivers travel hundreds of kilometers, irrigating the land and providing water for all living beings. Flowers spread their scent to make the environment pleasant. Nature teaches us to tolerate pain for the sake of service to others. Henna yields its reddish hue when ground into a paste. Sugarcane yields sweet juice when it is pressed. Flowers get pierced through with a needle to embellish us with garlands.

The character of virtuous men and women is also like the above things and elements of Nature. What is the use of this perishable and mortal frame if it is not used for the benefit of others? To live our life only for ourselves is to live like cats and dogs. People who are noble at heart do not abandon human virtues even if they have to lose their lives. A Sanskrit couplet says—"Whether men praise them or no, whether they get riches or no, whether they live long or soon die, the virtuous will never waver from the path of righteousness."

1. Which of the following is NOT mentioned in the passage?
1. Being truthful is the most important sign of virtuosity.
2. Nature teaches us to endure pain and serve others.
3. A self-centred existence is a bestial existence.
4. Not abandoning the right path even in the face of death.

2. In the passage, what is meant by "mortal frame"?
1. Nature
2. Animals
3. Land
4. Human body

3. According to the passage, which of the following is NOT true?
1. Parents and teachers inculcate good habits in children from the early stages.
2. There are parallels between the character of virtuous human beings and Nature.
3. Ethical behaviour is not dependent upon praise or reward.
4. The virtuous deviate from their path, if they aren't duly acknowledged.

4. Which of the following does not exemplify 'endurance', according to the passage?
1. Trees enduring the scorching heat of the Sun.
2. Sugarcane getting pressed to yield juice.
3. Trees bearing fruit and flowers spreading fragrance.
4. Henna being ground and turned into a paste.

Directions (Qs. No. 5-8): *Read the given passage and answer the questions that follow:*

Uma could not sing; but since learning to write, she had developed the habit of writing down any song she heard, to lessen the pain of not being able to sing it. Today the beggar woman was singing...

Resentful anguish welled up in Uma's heart. She called the singer secretly to her room, shut the door and began to write down the song in her eccentric spelling.

Tilakmanjari, Kanakmanjari and Anangamanjari observed everything through the crack in the door, and burst out, clapping their hands, "Boudidi, we've seen what you're doing!"

Uma quickly unfastened the door and began to plead with them, "Darling sisters, please don't tell anybody. I beg you, please don't. I'll never do it again. I'll never write again..."

1. 1	**2.** 4	**3.** 4	**4.** 3

At length, Uma noticed that Tilakmanjari was eyeing her exercise-book. She ran and clutched the book to her chest. Her sisters-in-law tried to take it away from her by force, but when they did not succeed, Anangamanjari went to summon her brother.

Pyarimohan arrived and sat down grimly on the bed. He said in a voice like thunder, "Give me the exercise-book."

The little girl clasped the exercise-book to her chest and directed a glance of utter supplication at her husband's face. But when she saw Pyarimohan was getting up to snatch the book from her, she flung it down, covered her face with her hands and collapsed on the floor.

5. Pyarimohan is bound to Uma by ....
1. paternal-ties
2. the bond of friendship
3. marital-ties
4. fraternal-ties

6. What is meant by "eccentric" in the passage?
1. neat and beautiful
2. strange and incorrect
3. written in the upper case
4. written in European languages

7. Why did Uma develop the habit of writing down any song she heard?
1. To alleviate her anguish at her lack of skill at singing.
2. To work upon and enhance her recently acquired skill at writing.
3. To compile all the songs in her exercise book.
4. To be able to learn to sing the song later.

8. What does the phrase 'a glance of utter supplication' mean in the passage?
1. an extremely angry and irritated look
2. a look of total excitement
3. a look showing celebration
4. a look of request and prayer

Directions (Qs. No. 9-12): *Read the given passage and answer the questions that follow:*

Solace. He turned the roll of paper between his fingers and wondered if that had not been his error—to search always for solace when there was other game to hunt in the forest. Had he had more spirit, more nerve, more desire and ambition, then perhaps he would have instead hunted for success, distinction, magic. Perhaps he would have followed in pursuit of an art, published a book of poetry, earned a name for himself, a little fame, even gold bangles for Sarla...

But the thought was puerile that it was made him spit out a bitter shred of tobacco. Every effort he had made had ended in defeat: most of the poems he had written and sent to Murad had been rejected, his monograph never published; his wife and son eyed him with blatant disappointment; nor had he won the regard of his colleagues or students. The inherent weakness in his father that had made him an ineffectual, if harmless, teacher and householder, had been passed on to him. He felt it inside him like an empty hole, one he had been staring at all his years, intimidated by its blackness and blankness. Even his attempt to fill it with a genuine and heartfelt homage to a true poet, a man who had distinguished himself as he would have liked to do, had been defeated by all the obstacles that sprang up in his life like shards and pebbles sent up at every step. It was one more blow, and perhaps the bitterest of all.

9. Choose a word similar in meaning to the word- Puerile
1. childish
2. melancholy
3. cosmopolitan
4. precocious

10. What does the word 'game' in the given phrase symbolise, 'other games to hunt in the forest'
1. Wild animals in the forest
2. Desires or goals being pursued
3. Playful activities
4. Rules of a competition.

11. On the basis of your reading identify the tone of the passage.
1. Contemptuous
2. Mournful
3. Satarical
4. Disillusioned

12. Who does Deven blame for his failure in life?
1. His wife and son
2. His lack of creativity
3. His father's submissive and timid nature
4. His inherited activism and assertiveness

13. Arrange the parts in the correct sequence to form a meaningful sentence:

(A) peeps into the dark abyss of human consciousness,
(B) Neruda conceives poetry not as something which has
(C) its deliberate relation with things of beauty, but rather as an art which
(D) something which has the ability to perceive suffering

Choose the **correct** answer from the options given below:
1. (B), (C), (A), (D)
2. (A), (D), (C), (B)
3. (C), (A), (B), (D)
4. (D), (B), (C), (A)

5. 3	**6.** 2	**7.** 1	**8.** 4	**9.** 1	**10.** 2	**11.** 2, 4	**12.** 3	**13.** 1

14. Select the correct antonym for the word: HEGEMONY

1. Supremacy
2. Leadership
3. Prosperity
4. Independence

15. Arrange the following parts in the correct sequence to form a meaningful sentence:

(A) the three best hypotheses
(B) ask them to get together
(C) the group has come up with
(D) in fours and decide on

Choose the **correct** answer from the options given below:

1. (A), (D), (C), (B)
2. (C), (B), (D), (A)
3. (B), (D), (A), (C)
4. (D), (B), (C), (A)

16. Complete the idioms given in List-I with their second part given in List-II:

List-I (Idiom's first part)	List-II (Idiom's second part)
(A) To hit the nail	(I) to injury
(B) To add insult	(II) before the horse
(C) To put the cart	(III) in the air
(D) To build castles	(IV) on the head

Choose the **correct** answer from the options given below:

1. (A) - (I), (B) - (III), (C) - (II), (D) - (IV)
2. (A) - (II), (B) - (IV), (C) - (III), (D) - (I)
3. (A) - (IV), (B) - (I), (C) - (II), (D) - (III)
4. (A) - (III), (B) - (IV), (C) - (I), (D) - (II)

17. Select the correct synonym for the word: DISCONCERTING

1. Embarrasing
2. Comfortable
3. Suave
4. Adroit

18. Select the correct antonym for the word: Valiant

1. Nervous
2. Kind
3. Coward
4. Brave

19. Arrange the following parts in the correct sequence to form a meaningful sentence:

(A) tell a lie to the teacher
(B) he is between the devil
(C) neither betray his friend nor
(D) and the deep sea as he can

Choose the **correct** answer from the options given below:

1. (A), (C), (B). (D)
2. (B), (D), (C), (A)
3. (C), (B), (D), (A)
4. (D), (A), (B), (C)

20. Rearrange the following parts in the correct sequence to form a meaningful sentence

(A) better known as the shifting cultivation
(B) garia is a folk dance performed in
(C) Tripura revolves around the Jhum culture,
(D) Tripura where the life and culture of the people of

Choose the **correct** answer from the options given below:

1. (C), (A), (B), (D)
2. (D), (C), (B), (A)
3. (A), (B), (D), (C)
4. (B), (D), (C), (A)

21. Fill in the blank in the given sentence with the correct option:

The person who studies the structure and composition of the earth to know about its history and antiquity is called a ....

1. Botanist
2. Geologist
3. Cartographer
4. Geographer

22. The little priest was not an interesting man to look at, having stubby brown hair and a round and stolid face which did not give away anything.

The word STOLID in the above sentence means:

1. Frowning
2. Darkish
3. Emotionless
4. Hateful

23. Fill in the blanks in the sentences given in List-I with the appropriate words given in List-II.

List-I (Sentences)	List-II (Words)
(A) The .... silence in the courtroom was broken only by the sound of a pen tapping.	(I) eccentric
(B) Her .... behaviour raised eyebrows at the otherwise formal event.	(II) penetrating
(C) The .... weather made the trek arduous for the beginners.	(III) oppressive
(D) The professor gave a .... analysis of the painting, revealing hidden layers of meaning.	(IV) inclement

Choose the **correct** answer from the options given below:

1. (A) - (I), (B) - (III), (C) - (II), (D) - (IV)
2. (A) - (III), (B) - (I), (C) - (IV), (D) - (II)
3. (A) - (II), (B) - (IV), (C) - (I), (D) - (III)
4. (A) - (IV), (B) - (II), (C) - (III), (D) - (I)

24. Which of the following words does not refer to one of the movements of a horse?

1. Trotting
2. Cantering
3. Galloping
4. Spinning

14. 4 **15.** 3 **16.** 3 **17.** 1 **18.** 3 **19.** 2 **20.** 4 **21.** 2 **22.** 3 **23.** 2 **24.** 4

25. Match the words given in List-I with the appropriate definitions in List-II.

List-I (Words)	List-II (Definitions)
(A) Neurologist	(I) one who treats heart diseases
(B) Orthodontist	(II) one who studies causes and diagnosis of diseases
(C) Cardiologist	(III) one who corrects and straightens irregular teeth
(D) Pathologist	(IV) one who cures nerve-related diseases

Choose the **correct** answer from the options given below:

1. (A) - (I), (B) - (III), (C) - (IV), (D) - (II)
2. (A) - (IV), (B) - (III), (C) - (I), (D) - (II)
3. (A) - (II), (B) - (IV), (C) - (I), (D) - (III)
4. (A) - (III), (B) - (I), (C) - (II), (D) - (IV)

26. Rearrange the following parts in the correct sequence to form a meaningful sentence

(A) the lives of labourers
(B) *Pahala Pandhav* is
(C) Shrilal Shukla's
(D) a realistic portrayal of

Choose the **correct** answer from the options given below:-

1. (A), (B), (C), (D) 2. (A), (B), (D), (C)
3. (B), (A), (D), (C) 4. (C), (B), (D), (A)

27. Arrange the following parts in the correct sequence to form a meaningful sentence:

(A) who is a doctor, (B) for his higher studies (C) has gone to America (D) my brother Jagan,

Choose the **correct** answer from the options given below:

1. (A), (D), (B), (C) 2. (B), (C), (D), (A)
3. (D), (A), (C), (B) 4. (C), (A), (D), (B)

28. Select the word closest in meaning to the word 'ARDUOUS' from the options given below:

1. Mysterious 2. Continuous
3. Supportive 4. Difficult

29. Match the words given in List-I with their corresponding definitions in List-II.

List-I (Words)	List-II (Definitions)
(A) Meteorologist	(I) One who studies election and trends in voting
(B) Cosmologist	(II) One who studies fossils and the history of life forms on the earth
(C) Psephology	(III) One who studies and predicts atmospheric phenomena
(D) Paleontologist	(IV) One who studies the universe, its origin, expanse etc.

Choose the **correct** answer from the options given below:

1. (A) - (II), (B) - (I), (C) - (IV), (D) - (III)
2. (A) - (IV), (B) - (II), (C) - (III), (D) - (I)
3. (A) - (I), (B) - (III), (C) - (II), (D) - (IV)
4. (A) - (III), (B) - (IV), (C) - (I), (D) - (II)

30. Rearrange the following parts in the correct sequence to form a meaningful sentence:

(A) technology, political opinions, military capacities, education, lifestyle, inter alia
(B) there has been growing awareness and rise in urge to be at par with
(C) with increasing purchasing power and larger disposable incomes
(D) current trends in different countries across the world in terms of science,

Choose the **correct** answer from the options given below:-

1. (D), (B), (C), (A) 2. (A), (B), (C), (D)
3. (C), (B), (D), (A) 4. (C), (A), (B), (D)

31. Select the correct antonym for the word: PLACATE

1. Provoke 2. Appease
3. Hate 4. Nullify

32. Select the correct antonym for the word: PURGE

1. Contaminate 2. Truncate
3. Conceal 4. Complicate

33. Choose the correct synonym for the word: DISDAIN

1. Astonish 2. Contempt
3. Destruction 4. Exhaustion

34. Select the correct expression to complete the sentence: It .... since morning.

1. has been raining 2. has raining
3. will raining 4. rain

35. Rearrange the following parts in the correct sequence to form a meaningful sentence:

(A) culture is a characteristic
(B) the vision
(C) way of life inspired by
(D) and values of life.

Choose the **correct** answer from the options given below:

1. (A), (C), (B), (D) 2. (A), (B), (C), (D)
3. (B), (A), (D), (C) 4. (C), (B), (D), (A)

25. 2 **26.** 4 **27.** 3 **28.** 4 **29.** 4 **30.** 3 **31.** 1 **32.** 1 **33.** 2 **34.** 1 **35.** 1

36. Select the correct antonym for the word: BELLIGERENT

1. Brave
2. Friendly
3. Hostile
4. Bemused

37. Match the words given in List-I with the appropriate definitions in List-II.

List-I (Words)	List-II (Definitions)
(A) Aviator	(I) controls and operates the flight of an aircraft
(B) Jurist	(II) knows several languages, mainly foreign
(C) Lexicographer	(III) an expert in the legal field
(D) Linguist	(IV) writer of a dictionary

Choose the **correct** answer from the options given below:

1. (A) - (I), (B) - (II), (C) - (IV), (D) - (III)
2. (A) - (II), (B) - (IV), (C) - (III), (D) - (I)
3. (A) - (I), (B) - (III), (C) - (IV), (D) - (II)
4. (A) - (III), (B) - (I), (C) - (II), (D) - (IV)

38. Select the correct antonym for the word: Zenith

1. Horizon
2. Nadir
3. Savage
4. Sober

39. Select the correct expression to complete the sentence What is the time ………… ?

1. for your watch
2. at your watch
3. by your watch
4. from your watch

40. Choose the appropriate word to fill in the blank in the given sentence:

………… they had been waiting in line all night, I was sure they'd get the tickets for the show.

1. As though
2. Because of
3. Since
4. Until

41. Select the correct antonym for the word: INIQUITOUS

1. Unfair
2. Wicked
3. Virtuous
4. Hilarious

42. Choose the correct word from the given options to fill the blank in the sentence given below:

"Pakhom ………… with him and the deal was closed at one thousand Rupees."

1. played
2. negotiated
3. disagreed
4. fought

43. Match the words given in List-I with their definitions in List-II.

List-I (Words)	List-II (Definitions)
(A) Theology	(I) A branch of philosophy that deals with the nature of existence
(B) Epistemology	(II) The study of the origin of the human race, its customs, beliefs and development
(C) Ontology	(III) A part of philosophy that deals with knowledge
(D) Anthropology	(IV) The study of religion and beliefs

Choose the **correct** answer from the options given below:

1. (A) - (I), (B) - (II), (C) - (III), (D) - (IV)
2. (A) - (I), (B) - (III), (C) - (II), (D) - (IV)
3. (A) - (IV), (B) - (III), (C) - (I), (D) - (II)
4. (A) - (III), (B) - (IV), (C) - (I), (D) - (II)

44. Match the idioms given in List-I with the underlined part of the sentences given in List-II.

List-I (Idioms)	List-II (Sentences)
(A) turned over a new leaf	(I) This unexpected new difficulty <u>roused me to do my best.</u>
(B) set his face against	(II) It is a matter of gratification that he <u>changed for the better.</u>
(C) put me on my mettle	(III) It is pointless to <u>worry about</u> the result before it's declared.
(D) to meet trouble half-way	(IV) As a social reformer, he <u>sternly opposed</u> child labour.

Choose the **correct** answer from the options given below:-

1. (A) - (I), (B) - (II), (C) - (III), (D) - (IV)
2. (A) - (II), (B) - (IV), (C) - (I), (D) - (III)
3. (A) - (II), (B) - (I), (C) - (IV), (D) - (III)
4. (A) - (III), (B) - (IV), (C) - (I), (D) - (II)

45. Select the correct synonym for the word: BENEDICTION

1. benefit
2. forgiveness
3. blessing
4. calmness

46. Select the correct synonym for the word: EPHEMERAL

1. Putrid
2. Invisible
3. Temporary
4. Permanent

36. 2 **37.** 3 **38.** 2 **39.** 3 **40.** 3 **41.** 3 **42.** 2 **43.** 3 **44.** 2 **45.** 3 **46.** 3

47. Rearrange the following parts in the correct sequence to form a meaningful sentence

(A) producing harmones, proteins lend satiety, prevent

(B) hunger pangs at bay, managing both weight and calories

(C) apart from building muscle, repair tissues and

(D) quick breakdown of sugar in the blood and keep

Choose the **correct** answer from the options given below:

1. (C), (A), (D), (B)
2. (A), (B), (C), (D)
3. (D), (C), (A), (B)
4. (D), (B), (C), (A)

48. Select the correct meaning of the underlined word in the sentence given below:

His desultory efforts at studying made it clear that he was not serious about passing the exam.

1. cautious
2. impetuous
3. guileful
4. unenthusiastic

49. Match the sentences given in List-I with the correct figures of speech given in List-II:

List-I (Sentences)	List-II (Figures of speech)
(A) The wind whispered through the trees.	(I) Alliteration
(B) A plumber's house always has a leaking tap.	(II) Oxymoron
(C) She opened her eyes to the deafening silence	(III) Irony
(D) The buzzing bees drew attention.	(IV) Personification

Choose the **correct** answer from the options given below:

1. (A) - (IV), (B) - (III), (C) - (II), (D) - (I)
2. (A) - (III), (B) - (I), (C) - (II), (D) - (IV)
3. (A) - (I), (B) - (IV), (C) - (III), (D) - (II)
4. (A) - (II), (B) - (III), (C) - (IV), (D) - (I)

50. Rearrange the following parts in the correct sequence to form a meaningful sentence:

(A) had left before Namita

(B) the large group

(C) reached the venue for her performance

(D) of Sattriya dancers

Choose the **correct** answer from the options given below:

1. (B), (C), (A), (D)
2. (B), (A), (D), (C)
3. (B), (D), (A), (C)
4. (C), (B), (D), (A)

EXPLANATORY ANSWERS

1. (1): Being truthful is the most important sign of virtuosity: This point is not found in the passage. The author emphasizes virtues like magnanimity, helpfulness, sacrifice, and righteousness, but never mentions truthfulness as a key virtue. Therefore, this option is correctly identified as not mentioned.

2. (4): The term "mortal frame" refers to the human body, which is described as perishable. The passage suggests that if the body is not used for the benefit of others, it serves no noble purpose. Thus, using one's life selflessly is seen as true virtue.

3. (4): The virtuous deviate from their path, if they aren't duly acknowledged: This is not true as per the passage. It clearly states that virtuous people stay committed to righteousness, regardless of praise, wealth, or life span. The Sanskrit couplet confirms this idea strongly.

4. (3): Trees bearing fruit and flowers spreading fragrance: These acts are beneficial but do not show "endurance" or suffering. The passage defines endurance through actions like facing the sun's heat or being pressed or pierced. Hence, this option does not truly reflect endurance.

5. (3): The passage identifies Pyarimohan as Uma's husband, especially when it says "a glance of utter supplication at her husband's face." This clearly establishes that the bond between them is marital, not paternal or fraternal. His commanding tone and her pleading reaction further indicate a traditional husband-wife relationship.

6. (2): The word "eccentric" in "eccentric spelling" means that Uma wrote words in a peculiar and incorrect manner. Since she was newly literate, her spellings were likely unconventional. The passage implies she spelled words phonetically or in her own unique way, not neatly or correctly.

7. (1): Uma couldn't sing and felt deep pain because of it. She started writing songs she heard as a way to reduce this sorrow. The passage clearly states she developed this habit "to lessen the pain of not being able to sing," which makes option 1 the accurate reason.

8. (4): "Utter supplication" means a deep and humble plea. Uma looks at her husband with such a pleading expression, silently begging him not to take away her book. The tone is one of desperation and emotional appeal, fitting the meaning of request and prayer.

9. (1): The word "puerile" means childish or immature. In the passage, the thought that achieving fame and success could still be possible is called "puerile," indicating that Deven himself sees it as naive or juvenile, not grounded in reality.

10. (2): The phrase "other game to hunt in the forest" is metaphorical. Here, "game" symbolizes ambitions or goals like success, art, poetry, and fame that Deven feels he failed to pursue due to his constant search for solace or comfort.

47. 1	**48.** 4	**49.** 1	**50.** 3

11. (2, 4): Both "mournful" and "disillusioned" tones are present in the passage. The narrator expresses mournful regret over missed opportunities and failed ambitions. At the same time, there is a clear sense of disillusionment—he once hoped for recognition, poetry, success, and meaning, but now sees all those dreams shattered. He even calls his hope "puerile," showing that he no longer believes in it. Therefore, the combined tone is rightly described as mournful and disillusioned, and 2 & 4 is the correct answer.

12. (3): Deven blames his father's weakness, which he believes was passed on to him. He feels this inherited trait made both of them ineffectual in life. He sees it as a black hole inside him that prevented him from achieving anything meaningful.

13. (1): The correct sequence is: Neruda conceives poetry not as something which has (B), its deliberate relation with things of beauty, but rather as an art which (C), peeps into the dark abyss of human consciousness, (A), something which has the ability to perceive suffering (D). This order forms a logical and grammatically correct sentence describing Neruda's view of poetry.

14. (4): Hegemony means dominance or leadership, especially by one state or group over others. The opposite of dominance is independence, where no control or influence is exerted by another power. Hence, Independence is the correct antonym.

15. (3): The meaningful sentence is: Ask them to get together (B), in fours and decide on (D), the three best hypotheses (A), the group has come up with (C). This sequence maintains proper structure and meaning in a collaborative task context.

16. (3): (A) - (IV), (B) - (I), (C) - (II), (D) - (III)
(A) To hit the nail on the head (IV) – means to describe exactly what is causing a situation.
(B) To add insult to injury (I) – means to make a bad situation worse.
(C) To put the cart before the horse (II) – means to do things in the wrong order.
(D) To build castles in the air (III) – means to make unrealistic plans or dreams.

17. (1): The word "disconcerting" refers to something that causes discomfort, confusion, or embarrassment. It unsettles a person and makes them feel uneasy or awkward. Among the given options, "embarrassing" is the closest synonym in both tone and meaning.

18. (3): "Valiant" means showing courage, bravery, or heroism. Its direct opposite would be someone who lacks courage, i.e., a "coward." A coward avoids danger or challenge due to fear, which is the antonym of being valiant.

19. (2): The correct sentence is: He is between the devil (B), and the deep sea as he can (D), neither betray his friend nor (C), tell a lie to the teacher (A). This describes a dilemma with no good outcome.

20. (4): The meaningful sentence is: Garia is a folk dance performed in (B), Tripura where the life and culture of the people of (D), Tripura revolves around the Jhum culture, (C), better known as the shifting cultivation (A). This forms a coherent and informative statement.

21. (2): A geologist studies the Earth's structure, materials, and processes to understand its history and formation. The question mentions learning about the Earth's structure and antiquity, which directly relates to the work of a geologist, not a geographer or cartographer.

22. (3): The term "stolid" means showing little or no emotion. In the sentence, the priest's face "did not give away anything," which supports the meaning of being unexpressive or emotionless.

23. (2): (A) - (III), (B) - (I), (C) - (IV), (D) - (II)
(A) **Oppressive silence:** Refers to a tense, heavy quietness, often making people feel uncomfortable or pressured—common in intense places like courtrooms.
(B) **Eccentric behaviour:** Means odd or unusual conduct; at a formal event, such behaviour would naturally draw attention.
(C) **Inclement weather:** Describes harsh or severe weather—like rain, storms, or cold—making physical activity like trekking difficult.
(D) **Penetrating analysis:** Means a deep and insightful examination that uncovers hidden details or meanings, often used in intellectual or academic contexts.

24. (4): Trotting, cantering, and galloping are standard horse gaits, each indicating a specific speed or movement pattern. Spinning, however, is not a recognized horse gait and does not describe movement used in equestrian contexts.

25. (2): (A) - (IV), (B) - (III), (C) - (I), (D) - (II)
(A) **Neurologist:** treats nervous system disorders (IV)
(B) **Orthodontist:** specializes in correcting teeth alignment (III)
(C) **Cardiologist:** deals with heart-related issues (I)
(D) **Pathologist:** studies disease causes and diagnosis (II)

26. (4): The correct sequence is: Shrilal Shukla's (C), *Pahala Pandhav* is (B), a realistic portrayal of (D), the lives of labourers (A). This forms a clear and meaningful sentence introducing the author and theme of the work.

27. (3): The sentence becomes: My brother Jagan, (D) who is a doctor, (A) has gone to America (C) for his higher studies (B). This flows smoothly and logically describes the subject and his action.

28. (4): The word "arduous" means something that is difficult, strenuous, or requiring great effort. It does not relate to mystery, supportiveness, or continuity, making "difficult" the correct synonym.

29. (4): (A) - (III), (B) - (IV), (C) - (I), (D) - (II)
(A) Meteorologist – (III): A meteorologist studies and predicts weather and atmospheric conditions such as rainfall, storms, and temperature changes.
(B) Cosmologist – (IV): A cosmologist is concerned with the study of the universe, including its origin, structure, and overall dynamics like the Big Bang theory.
(C) Psephology – (I): Psephology is the branch of political science that deals with the study of elections and voting trends.
(D) Paleontologist – (II): A paleontologist examines fossils and ancient life forms to understand Earth's biological history.

Each word is matched with its correct scientific field, making Option 4 the correct answer.

30. **(3):** The sentence reads: With increasing purchasing power and larger disposable incomes (C), there has been growing awareness and rise in urge to be at par with (B), current trends in different countries across the world in terms of science, (D), technology, political opinions, military capacities, education, lifestyle, inter alia (A).
This sequence builds logically from cause to effect and covers all aspects clearly.

31. **(1):** Placate means to calm, pacify, or soothe someone who is angry. The opposite of calming is to provoke, which means to stir up anger or annoyance. Therefore, provoke is the correct antonym.

32. **(1):** Purge means to cleanse or remove impurities. The opposite would be to make something impure or dirty, which is contaminate. So, contaminate is the correct antonym.

33. **(2):** Disdain means a strong feeling of dislike or contempt for someone or something considered unworthy. It does not relate to astonishment or exhaustion. Hence, contempt is the correct synonym.

34. **(1):** The sentence refers to a continuous action starting in the past and still ongoing, which calls for the present perfect continuous tense. So, "It has been raining since morning" is grammatically correct.

35. **(1):** The sentence reads: Culture is a characteristic (A), way of life inspired by (C), the vision (B), and values of life (D). This sequence is grammatically logical and meaningful.

36. **(2):** Belligerent means hostile or aggressive, especially in a confrontational way. The opposite of being aggressive is friendly, which indicates a peaceful and kind attitude. Hence, friendly is the correct antonym.

37. **(3):** (A) - (I), (B) - (III), (C) - (IV), (D) - (II)
(A) **Aviator – (I):** One who operates or flies aircraft.
(B) **Jurist – (III):** A legal expert or authority in law.
(C) **Lexicographer – (IV):** A person who writes or compiles dictionaries.
(D) **Linguist – (II):** Someone who knows or studies multiple languages, especially foreign ones.

38. **(2):** Zenith means the highest point or peak. Its antonym is nadir, which means the lowest point. The two are direct opposites in figurative and literal usage, making nadir the correct answer.

39. **(3):** The correct phrase is "What is the time by your watch?", which is the standard and idiomatic way of asking someone the time based on their watch. Other options are grammatically or idiomatically incorrect.

40. **(3):** The sentence is giving a reason for the speaker's certainty that the people would get the tickets. "Since" means because, which fits perfectly: "Since they had been waiting in line all night..." conveys both cause and context.

41. **(3):** Iniquitous means extremely wicked, immoral, or unjust. The correct antonym is virtuous, which refers to someone who is morally good, righteous, or ethical. Hence, virtuous is the correct opposite.

42. **(2):** The sentence "Pakhom .... with him and the deal was closed at one thousand Rupees" refers to reaching a deal. The word negotiated best fits here, as it means discussing terms to arrive at an agreement. Other options do not suit the context of closing a deal.

43. **(3):** (A) - (IV), (B) - (III), (C) - (I), (D) - (II)
(A) **Theology – (IV):** Theology is the study of religion and beliefs, focusing on divine concepts, scriptures, and spiritual matters.
(B) **Epistemology – (III):** Epistemology is a branch of philosophy that deals with knowledge—its nature, sources, and limits.
(C) **Ontology – (I):** Ontology studies the nature of existence and being, examining what entities exist and how they relate.
(D) **Anthropology – (II):** Anthropology is the study of human beings, including their origins, development, cultural customs, and evolution.

44. **(2):** (A) - (II), (B) - (IV), (C) - (I), (D) - (III)
(A) **Turned over a new leaf – (II):** This idiom means to reform or start afresh, which matches the sentence where someone changed for the better.
(B) **Set his face against – (IV):** This means to firmly oppose something, matching the context of sternly opposing child labour.
(C) **Put me on my mettle – (I):** Means to test someone's strength or ability, as in the sentence about a difficulty that made someone do their best.
(D) **To meet trouble half-way – (III):** Refers to anticipating or worrying about trouble before it happens, matching the idea of worrying before results are declared.

45. **(3):** Benediction means a blessing or expression of good wishes, especially at the end of a religious service. Among the options, blessing is the most accurate synonym.

46. **(3):** Ephemeral means lasting for a very short time. The best synonym among the options is temporary, which also refers to something not permanent or enduring.

47. **(1):** The sentence becomes:
(C) Apart from building muscle, repair tissues and
(A) producing hormones, proteins lend satiety, prevent
(D) quick breakdown of sugar in the blood and keep
(B) hunger pangs at bay, managing both weight and calories.
This arrangement logically explains the multiple roles of proteins in the body.

48. **(4):** Desultory means lacking a plan, purpose, or enthusiasm. In the sentence, it reflects that his studying was aimless and showed no real effort, making unenthusiastic the correct meaning.

49. **(1):** (A) - (IV), (B) - (III), (C) - (II), (D) - (I)
(A) The wind whispered... – Personification (IV): giving human traits to wind
(B) A plumber's house always has a leaking tap – Irony (III): unexpected contradiction
(C) Deafening silence – Oxymoron (II): two opposite terms used together
(D) Buzzing bees... – Alliteration (I): repetition of initial consonant sounds

50. **(3):** The correct sequence is:
(B) The large group
(D) of Sattriya dancers
(A) had left before Namita
(C) reached the venue for her performance.
This order forms a clear, grammatically correct sentence.

Previous Years' Paper

Common University Entrance Test for UG Programmes

CUET–UG—HISTORY*

Entrance Exam, 2025

(Exam held on 13-05-2025)

Subject Code: 314

1. Arrange the major developments in Harappan Archaeology in a chronological order

A. Report of Alexander Cunningham on Harappan seal.

B. S.R. Rao begins excavations at Lothal.

C. Daya Ram Sahni begins excavations at Harappa.

D. Vasant Shinde begins archaeogenetic research at Rakhigarhi.

Choose the ***correct*** answer from the options given below:

1. A, B, C, D 2. A, C, B, D
3. B, A, D, C 4. C, B, D, A

2. Traces of canals have been found at the Harappan site of _____.

1. Shortughai in Afghanistan
2. Banawali in Haryana
3. Harappa
4. Mohenjodaro

3. Which of the following rulers adopted the title *devaputra*, or "Son of God"?

1. Kushanas 2. Sakas
3. Mauryas 4. Satavahanas

4. The *Gandatindu Jataka* describes:

A. Cordial relationship between a king and his subjects.

B. The plight of the subjects of a wicked king.

C. The strained relationship, especially with the rural population.

D. That kings frequently fill their coffers by demanding high and oppressive taxes.

Choose the ***correct*** answer from the options given below:

1. A, B and D only 2. A, B and C only
3. A, B, C and D 4. B, C and D only

5. Match List-I with List-II.

	List-I (Meanings)		List-II (Terms)
A.	When descent is traced through the mother	I.	Adi-Parvan
B.	Barbarians or outsiders of the Brahmanical order	II.	Endogamy
C.	The first section of Mahabharata	III.	Matriliny
D.	Marriage within a kin group, caste, or a group living in the same locality	IV.	Mlechchhas

Choose the ***correct*** answer from the options given below:

1. A-I, B-II, C-III, D-IV
2. A-I, B-III, C-II, D-IV
3. A-I, B-II, C-IV, D-III
4. A-III, B-IV, C-I, D-II

6. In play the *Mrichchhakatika*, the hero Charudatta was described as both a Brahmana and a _____.

1. Nishada
2. Kshatriya
3. Sarthavaha
4. Mlechchha

7. Which ruler of the Satavahana dynasty claimed to be a unique Brahmana (*eka bamhana*)?

1. Gotami-puta Siri-Satakani
2. Gotami-puta Siri-Vijay-Satakani
3. Vashisti-puta Pulmayi
4. Madhari-puta-Svami Sakasena

8. The Buddha regarded the 'social world' as the creation of:

1. Humans 2. Planets
3. Lord Brahma 4. Lord Vishnu

1. 2	**2.** 1	**3.** 1	**4.** 4	**5.** 4	**6.** 3	**7.** 1	**8.** 1

9. Who persuaded Buddha to allow women into the *sangha*?
1. Ajatasattu 2. Makkhali Gosala
3. Mahapajapati Gotami 4. Ananda

10. If you are reading the traveller's accounts, which of the following would be of Al-Biruni:
1. Explanation of the caste system by looking for parallels in ancient Persia.
2. Description of Delhi and Daulatabad (in Maharashtra) as vast cities.
3. Finding the lack of private property in India.
4. Description of the coconut and the *paan*, two kinds of plant produced in Medieval India.

11. Which of the following is **not** true about the *Lingayats*?
1. On death, the devotee will be united with Vishnu.
2. They ceremonially bury their dead.
3. They worship Shiva in his manifestation as a 'linga'.
4. Lingayats wear a small linga in a silver case on a loop strung over the left shoulder.

12. Match List-I with List-II.

List-I (Meaning/Characteristics)	List-II (Sufi-Terms)
A. Sufi lineages	I. Ziyarat
B. Established rules for spiritual conduct and interaction between inmates/laypersons and the master	II. Langar
C. The practice of pilgrimage to the grave of the Shaikh	III. Silsila
D. Open kitchen which runs on *futuh* (unasked-for charity)	IV. Murshid

Choose the ***correct*** answer from the options given below:
1. A-I, B-II, C-III, D-IV
2. A-I, B-III, C-II, D-IV
3. A-I, B-II, C-IV, D-III
4. A-III, B-IV, C-I, D-II

13. Why were agricultural tracts incorporated within the fortified area of the Vijayanagara Empire?
1. To protect the agricultural belt itself.
2. To beautify the capital with greenery.
3. To provide fresh fruits and vegetables to the royal family.
4. To use agricultural fields as line of defense.

14. In Vijayanagara, water from which one of the following structures was conducted through the channel to the "royal centre"?
1. Lotus tank
2. Hiriya canal
3. Vijaya canal
4. Kamalapuram tank

15. Which of the following is **not** true about the *Ain-i Akbari*?
1. It was completed in 1598.
2. This is a view of the regions from the centre.
3. It provides quantitative information of various provinces.
4. Undertaken at the order of Emperor Akbar and completed at the time of Shah Jahan.

16. Match List-I with List-II.

List-I (Revenue-Collection)	List-II (Terms)
A. The crops are reaped and stacked and divided by agreement in the presence of the parties	I. bhaoli
B. After the crops are cut and estimated in three lots; the good, the middling, and the inferior	II. lang-batai
C. After cutting the grain, heaps are divided among themselves	III. kankut
D. When the fields are divided after they are sown	IV. khet-batai

Choose the ***correct*** answer from the options given below:
1. A-I, B-II, C-III, D-IV
2. A-I, B-III, C-II, D-IV
3. A-I, B-II, C-IV, D-III
4. A-III, B-IV, C-I, D-II

17. In the seventeenth-century agrarian society, women of Rajasthan could send petitions to _____ seeking justice.
1. Village panchayat 2. Amin
3. Diwan 4. Subedar

18. Arrange the following events in a chronological order:
A. Santhals begin to come and settle in the Rajmahal hills
B. Permanent Settlement in Bengal
C. Cotton boom begins
D. Santhal rebellion

Choose the ***correct*** answer from the options given below:
1. A, B, C, D 2. A, C, B, D
3. B, A, D, C 4. C, B, D, A

9. 4	**10.** 1	**11.** 1	**12.** 4	**13.** 1	**14.** 4	**15.** 4	**16.** 2	**17.** 1	**18.** 3

19. Arrange the following events of 1857 chronologically:

A. Mutiny turned into a general revolt of the people
B. Mutiny started in Meerut
C. Delhi garrisons revolt
D. British forces under Havelock and Outram entered the Residency in Lucknow

Choose the ***correct*** answer from the options given below:

1. A, B, C, D
2. B, C, A, D
3. B, A, D, C
4. C, B, D, A

20. Who was approached for leadership by the sepoys of Meerut who broke out in mutiny against the British in 1857?

1. Rani Lakshmi Bai
2. Nana Sahib
3. Mughal emperor Bahadur Shah
4. Kunwar Singh

21. Which movement was withdrawn by Gandhiji after a group of peasants attacked and torched a police station in the hamlet of Chauri Chaura (United Provinces)?

1. Non-Cooperation Movement
2. Civil Disobedience Movement
3. Quit India Movement
4. Ahmedabad Labour Strike

22. Arrange the following events in a chronological order:

A. Ryots in Deccan villages rebel
B. Slow process of agrarian expansion in the Bombay Deccan
C. First revenue settlement in the Bombay Deccan
D. Regulating Act passed by the British Parliament

Choose the ***correct*** answer from the options given below:

1. D, C, B, A
2. A, B, C, D
3. B, A, D, C
4. C, B, D, A

23. Arrange the following events in a chronological order:

A. Babur defeats Ibrahim Lodi, the Delhi Sultan, at Panipat, and becomes the first Mughal emperor
B. Humayun is defeated by Sher Shah, in exile at the Safavid court
C. Nadir Shah invades India and sacks Delhi
D. The 'diwani' of Bengal was transferred to the English East India Company

Choose the ***correct*** answer from the options given below:

1. A, B, C, D
2. A, C, D, B
3. B, A, D, C
4. C, B, D, A

24. In the eighteenth-century, which of the following was **not** the reason for the defaults on payments by the *zamindars*?

1. The initial demands were very high.
2. The *zamindars*' were allowed to organise troops and "cutcheries", for increasing their authority in the rural areas.
3. High demand was imposed at a time when the prices of agricultural produce were depressed.
4. The revenue was invariable, regardless of the harvest and had to be paid punctually.

25. What is the meaning of the term *Benami*?

1. Transactions made in the name of a fictitious or relatively insignificant person, whereas the real beneficiary remains unnamed.
2. In the name of a person called 'Benam'.
3. Transaction is done by and in the name of the real owner.
4. The special transactions where the real beneficiary remains traceable and accountable.

26. Match List-I with List-II.

List-I (Leaders)	List-II (Regions)
A. Shah Mal	I. Pargana Barout in Uttar Pradesh
B. Gonoo	II. Singhbhum in Chotanagpur
C. Birjis Qadr	III. Awadh
D. Kunwar Singh	IV. Arrah in Bihar

Choose the ***correct*** answer from the options given below:

1. A-I, B-III, C-II, D-IV
2. A-I, B-II, C-III, D-IV
3. A-II, B-I, C-IV, D-III
4. A-III, B-IV, C-I, D-II

27. The total time span of the Harappan Civilisation ranges:

1. From 2000 BCE to 1000 BCE
2. From 6000 BCE to 1300 BCE
3. From 1500 BCE to 900 BCE
4. From Post Vedic Civilisation

28. Who deciphered 'Brahmi' and 'Kharosthi' scripts in 1838?

1. James Prinsep
2. Alexander Cunningham
3. D.C. Sircar
4. R.E.M. Wheeler

19. 2	**20.** 3	**21.** 1	**22.** 1	**23.** 1	**24.** 2	**25.** 1	**26.** 2	**27.** 2	**28.** 1

29. Identify the correct statements about the 'Inscriptions':

A. Routine agricultural practices and events of daily life are the subject-matter of inscriptions.

B. Record the achievements, activities or ideas of those who commissioned them.

C. Writings are engraved on hard surfaces such as stone, metal or pottery.

D. The earliest inscriptions were in Prakrit.

Choose the ***correct*** answer from the options given below:

1. A, B and D only
2. A, B and C only
3. A, B, C and D
4. B, C and D only

30. In which language were the Ashokan inscriptions written in Afghanistan?

1. Sanskrit
2. Prakrit
3. Aramaic and Greek
4. Latin and Greek

31. Match List-I with List-II.

List-I (Meanings)	List-II (Terms)
A. Term used by the Sanskrit texts to designate families	I. Kula
B. Tracing descent from father to son	II. Polygyny
C. The practice of a man having several wives	III. Patriliny
D. The gift of a daughter in marriage	IV. Kanyadana

Choose the ***correct*** answer from the options given below:

1. A-I, B-II, C-III, D-IV
2. A-I, B-III, C-II, D-IV
3. A-I, B-II, C-IV, D-III
4. A-III, B-IV, C-I, D-II

32. In Sanskrit texts and inscriptions, the term '*Vanik*' refers to:

1. Peasants
2. Merchants
3. Guilds
4. Kings

33. Match List-I with List-II.

List-I (Origin-Country)	List-II (Thinker)
A. Iran	I. Plato and Aristotle
B. China	II. Mahavira and Gautama Buddha
C. Greece	III. Zarathustra
D. India	IV. Kong Zi

Choose the ***correct*** answer from the options given below:

1. A-I, B-II, C-III, D-IV
2. A-I, B-III, C-II, D-IV
3. A-I, B-II, C-IV, D-III
4. A-III, B-IV, C-I, D-II

34. According to which Buddhist text, Asoka distributed portions of the Buddha's relics to every important town and ordered the construction of stupas over them?

1. Ashokavadana
2. Sutta Pitaka
3. Vinaya Pitaka
4. Mahaparinibbana Sutta

35. Match List-I with List-II.

List-I (Incident/ Characteristics)	List-II (Traveller)
A. He arrived in Ghazni as a hostage, but gradually developed a liking for this city	I. Al-Biruni
B. He reached Sind in 1333 and was later appointed as the *qazi* of Delhi	II. Francois Bernier
C. Physician to Prince Dara Shukoh	III. Ibn Battuta
D. Wrote a detailed account of trade and society in South India	IV. Duarte Barbosa

Choose the ***correct*** answer from the options given below:

1. A-I, B-II, C-III, D-IV
2. A-I, B-III, C-II, D-IV
3. A-I, B-II, C-IV, D-III
4. A-III, B-IV, C-I, D-II

36. Which of the following is **not** true about Ibn Battuta?

1. Wrote *Rihla*, book of travels, in Arabic
2. He was born in Tangier, into an educated family known for its expertise in Islamic religious law or *shari'a*.
3. He describes that certain varieties of fine muslin were too expensive to be worn by ordinary people.
4. He was ordered in 1342 to proceed to Persia as the envoy of Muhammad bin Tughlaq.

37. The terms "great and little traditions" were coined by:

1. John Marshall
2. R.E.M. Wheeler
3. Robert Redfield
4. M.N. Srinivas

38. *Saguna* bhakti traditions do **not** include:

1. Traditions that focused on the worship of specific deities such as Shiva, Vishnu and his *avatars* (incarnations)
2. Forms of the goddess or Devi, all often conceptualized in anthropomorphic forms
3. Worship of an abstract form of god
4. Worship of a form of god with attributes

39. The rulers of Vijayanagara empire called themselves _____.

1. Rayas
2. Nayakas
3. Kudirais
4. Samrajyapatis

29. 4	**30.** 3	**31.** 2	**32.** 2	**33.** 4	**34.** 1	**35.** 2	**36.** 4	**37.** 3	**38.** 3	**39.** 1

40. Who was appointed as the first Surveyor General of India in 1815?

1. George Michell 2. John Marshall
3. R.E.M. Wheeler 4. Colin Mackenzie

Directions (Q.No. 41-45): *Read the passage and answer the questions:*

"The British element is gone, but they have left the mischief behind"

It is no use saying that we ask for separate electorates, because it is good for us. We have heard it long enough. We have heard it for years, and as a result of this agitation we are now a separate nation ... Can you show me one free country where there are separate electorates? If so, I shall be prepared to accept it. But in this unfortunate country if this separate electorate is going to be persisted in, even after the division of the country, woe betide the country; it is not worth living in. Therefore, I say, it is not for my good alone, it is for your own good that I say it, forget the past. One day, we may be united ... The British element is gone, but they have left the mischief behind. We do not want to perpetuate that mischief. (Hear, hear). When the British introduced this element they had not expected that they will have to go so soon. They wanted it for their easy administration. That is all right. But they have left the legacy behind. Are we to get out of it or not?

41. Who is the speaker of this passage?

1. Mahatma Gandhi 2. Sardar Vallabhbhai Patel
3. B. Pocker Bahadur 4. R.V. Dhulekar

42. According to the speaker, what was the consequence of the policy of a separate electorates?

1. Free and fair election
2. Increase in nationalism in India
3. Freedom for India
4. The partition of India

43. What is opposed by the speaker in the above passage?

1. The division of the country
2. The demand for separate electorate
3. The lapse of the British element
4. The demand for easy administration

44. The mischief of separate electorates was left behind by:

1. The Muslim League
2. The British Government
3. People leaving due to partition
4. The Nawabs and the Rajas

45. Why, according to the speaker, the British introduced the separate electorates?

1. For their easy administration
2. To strengthen the Indian polity
3. To protect the rights of the Indians
4. To provide a balanced political framework

Directions (Q.No. 46-50): *Read the passage and answer the questions:*

Charkha

What I object to, is the craze for machinery as such. The craze is for what they call labour-saving machinery. Men go on "saving labour", till thousands are without work and thrown on the open streets to die of starvation. I want to save time and labour, not for a fraction of mankind, but for all; I want the concentration of wealth, not in the hands of few, but in the hands of all.

YOUNG INDIA, 13 NOVEMBER 1924

Khaddar does not seek to destroy all machinery but it does regulate its use and check its weedy growth. It uses machinery for the service of the poorest in their own cottages. The wheel is itself an exquisite piece of machinery.

YOUNG INDIA, 17 MARCH 1927

46. Who is the author of the passage?

1. Mahatma Gandhi 2. Jawaharlal Nehru
3. Subhash Chander Bose 4. Vallabhbhai Patel

47. What is the writer opposing in the passage?

1. Quest for modernisation
2. Setting up of factories
3. Changing trends in modern times
4. Mindless craze for machinery

48. What does the writer mean by 'saving labour'?

1. Saving the lives of humans
2. Saving humans from hard labour
3. Employing machines instead of human beings
4. Giving honor to human labour

49. What fear is expressed in this paragraph?

1. Men will start loving machinery
2. Machines will replace human labor and thousands will go unemployed
3. Machines will rule the world
4. Machine labour will get respect

50. What are the views of the writer about the role of machines and the concentration of wealth?

1. Industrialisation should not result in the concentration of wealth in the hands of a few elites
2. Humans should get employment and not machines
3. Machines should not be employed to replace humans
4. Time and labour should be saved

40. 4	**41.** 2	**42.** 4	**43.** 2	**44.** 2	**45.** 1	**46.** 1	**47.** 4	**48.** 3	**49.** 2	**50.** 1

EXPLANATORY ANSWERS

1. The major developments in Harappan Archaeology can be arranged as follows:
   A. Alexander Cunningham reported the Harappan seal in the 1870s, marking the first scholarly reference.
   C. Daya Ram Sahni began excavations at Harappa in 1921, formally bringing the Indus Valley Civilization into archaeological history.
   B. S.R. Rao started excavations at Lothal in 1954, which became significant for maritime trade studies.
   D. Vasant Shinde initiated archaeogenetic research at Rakhigarhi in the 21st century, providing DNA insights.

2. At the Harappan site of Shortughai (Afghanistan), archaeologists found evidence of irrigation canals, which is unique among Harappan settlements. Located near the Amu Darya river, this site was important for trade, especially in lapis lazuli from Badakhshan. The canals show that Harappans practiced irrigation agriculture even in distant colonies, adapting their water-management skills outside the Indus core region. Other sites like Harappa, Mohenjodaro, or Banawali do not provide such clear evidence.

3. The title Devaputra ("Son of God") was adopted by the Kushanas, particularly by rulers like Kanishka. The Kushanas, originally of Central Asian origin, used this divine title to legitimize their authority over a vast and diverse empire. It emphasized that their kingship had divine sanction, similar to the Chinese concept of the "Son of Heaven." Inscriptions and coins confirm its frequent use, while other dynasties like Mauryas, Sakas, and Satavahanas did not employ this title.

4. The *Gandatindu Jataka* describes the sufferings of the subjects under an oppressive ruler. It highlights:
   B. The plight of the subjects of a wicked king.
   C. The strained relationship between rulers and rural people.
   D. The tendency of kings to impose heavy and exploitative taxes.

5. Matching the terms with meanings:
   A. When descent is traced through the mother → III. Matriliny
   B. Barbarians or outsiders of the Brahmanical order → IV. Mlechchhas
   C. The first section of Mahabharata → I. Adi-Parvan
   D. Marriage within a kin group, caste, or locality → II. Endogamy

6. In the Sanskrit play *Mrichchhakatika* (The Little Clay Cart), written by Shudraka, the hero Charudatta is described as a Brahmana by birth but also as a Sarthavaha (merchant/caravan leader). This shows the flexible and sometimes overlapping social roles in early Indian society, where a Brahmana could also engage in trade.

7. Among the Satavahana rulers, Gotami-puta Siri-Satakani (Satakarni II) claimed to be an eka bamhana ("unique Brahmana"). This title indicated that although he was a king, he identified himself with Brahmanical ideals and upheld Vedic traditions, thereby combining political power with religious authority.

8. The Buddha explained that the social world was created by Humans themselves, not by divine will. He emphasized that social divisions like caste were man-made conventions, which could be changed or reformed, and not eternal or divinely ordained.

9. Ananda, a close disciple and cousin of the Buddha, persuaded him to allow women into the Buddhist monastic community (*sangha*). Although Buddha was initially reluctant, Ananda's request and the devotion of Mahapajapati Gotami (Buddha's foster mother) led to women's admission under specific conditions.

10. The Persian scholar Al-Biruni (11th century) wrote Kitab-ul-Hind after studying Indian society. He explained the caste system by comparing it with divisions in ancient Persia, showing his analytical and comparative method. His work remains one of the most detailed accounts of early Indian society by a foreign traveller.

11. The *Lingayats* were a Shaiva devotional movement founded by Basavanna in the 12th century.
    - They worship Shiva in the form of a linga, worn in a small silver case on the body.
    - They reject elaborate Brahmanical rituals and believe in equality.
    - They bury their dead (instead of cremation), showing distinct practices.
    - However, it is not true that they believe in uniting with Vishnu after death—they seek union with Shiva.

12. Let's match the Sufi terms:
    A. Sufi lineages → III. Silsila (chain of spiritual succession).
    B. Established rules for conduct between disciples and master → IV. Murshid (spiritual guide).
    C. Pilgrimage to the grave of the Shaikh → I. Ziyarat.
    D. Open kitchen based on futuh (charity) → II. Langar.

13. In Vijayanagara, agricultural tracts were deliberately incorporated within fortified areas. The main purpose was to protect the agricultural belt itself, ensuring that food supply remained safe during times of war. This made the capital siege-proof, since inhabitants could rely on crops, orchards, and gardens inside the walls. Foreign travellers like Abdur Razzaq noted this unique feature, which was uncommon in other medieval cities where farmland usually lay outside the fortifications.

14. The Kamalapuram tank, situated close to the royal centre, was an important water reservoir. Water from this tank was conducted via channels to supply the royal centre of Vijayanagara, ensuring regular water for the palace and surrounding elite quarters.

15. The Ain-i Akbari was written by Abul Fazl and completed in 1598 under Akbar's reign. It provides a detailed statistical account of provinces, administration, and society, presenting a "view from the centre." It was not completed during Shah Jahan's reign—it was finished under Akbar himself.

16. In medieval India, several systems of revenue collection were practiced depending on crops and regions:

- Bhaoli (A-I): Crops were reaped, stacked, and then divided between cultivator and state in the presence of both parties.
- Kankut (B-III): The crop was cut and divided into three lots—good, medium, and inferior—for revenue estimation.
- Lang-batai (C-II): After cutting, the grain heaps were shared among cultivators and officials.
- Khet-batai (D-IV): The field itself was divided after sowing, and each party cultivated their share.

These methods ensured fairness and adaptability in collection.

17. In the seventeenth-century agrarian society of Rajasthan, women could seek justice by submitting petitions to the village panchayat. The panchayat, made up of local elders, was the primary judicial body at the village level. It resolved disputes concerning land, family issues, and social conflicts. This shows that even women had recognized access to community-level justice.
- Amin: dealt with land revenue assessment, not petitions.
- Diwan: was a provincial revenue head, above village matters.
- Subedar: was a governor representing the central Mughal authority.

18. Chronology of events:
B. Permanent Settlement in Bengal (1793) established a fixed revenue system.
A. Santhals began settling in Rajmahal Hills (c. 1830s) as forest clearers and cultivators.
D. Santhal rebellion (1855–56) broke out against oppressive landlords and moneylenders.
C. Cotton boom (1860s) occurred during the American Civil War, boosting Indian cotton exports.
Thus, the order is B → A → D → C.

19. Key events of the 1857 revolt:
B. Meerut mutiny (10 May 1857) triggered the uprising.
C. Delhi garrison revolted (11 May 1857), declaring Bahadur Shah Zafar their leader.
A. Mutiny turned into a general revolt, spreading across north India.
D. British forces under Havelock and Outram relieved Lucknow Residency (Sept 1857).
This sequence marks the transformation from mutiny to widespread rebellion.

20. When the sepoys of Meerut mutinied, they marched to Delhi and sought legitimacy by declaring Mughal emperor Bahadur Shah Zafar as their leader. Though old and powerless, his symbolic authority as the last Mughal emperor gave the revolt a unifying banner, turning a mutiny into a general rebellion.

21. In 1922, Gandhiji abruptly withdrew the Non-Cooperation Movement after the Chauri Chaura incident in the United Provinces, where protesting peasants clashed with police, leading to the burning of a police station and the death of 22 policemen. Gandhi felt the movement had turned violent, which contradicted his principle of ahimsa (non-violence). This decision disappointed many nationalists but reflected Gandhi's insistence on moral discipline in mass movements.

22. The events in the Bombay Deccan followed this chronology:
D. Regulating Act (1773): First step by the British Parliament to control the East India Company.
C. First revenue settlement in the Bombay Deccan (early 19th century): Introduced new land revenue systems that increased pressure on peasants.
B. Slow agrarian expansion: After settlements, peasants cleared new lands, but burden of debt and revenue demand persisted.
A. Deccan Riots (1875): Ryots rebelled against moneylenders due to mounting debts and land loss, marking a major agrarian uprising.
This makes the correct sequence D → C → B → A.

23. Chronology of key Mughal-era events:
A. Babur defeated Ibrahim Lodi at Panipat (1526) beginning of Mughal rule.
B. Humayun defeated by Sher Shah (1540) and went into exile at the Safavid court.
C. Nadir Shah invaded and sacked Delhi (1739), a major Mughal setback.
D. Diwani of Bengal transferred to the Company (1765) after Battle of Buxar.
So the sequence is A → B → C → D.

24. In the 18th century, many zamindars defaulted on payments due to revenue pressures: • Demands were very high initially. • Revenue was rigid and invariable, regardless of harvest outcomes. • Prices of crops were depressed, worsening the crisis. • However, the claim that zamindars were allowed to organize troops and "cutcheries" is not a reason for default—this increased their local power, not financial weakness.

25. The term Benami refers to transactions carried out in the name of another person (fictitious or minor) while the real owner/beneficiary remains hidden. This allowed elites and landlords to conceal property ownership to avoid detection, taxation, or legal complications. The front person's name is used, but they have no real claim.

26. Match the leaders with their regions during the revolt of 1857:
A. Shah Mal → I. Pargana Barout in Uttar Pradesh, a leader who mobilized peasants against the British.
B. Gonoo → II. Singhbhum in Chotanagpur, a tribal leader of Kol rebels.
C. Birjis Qadr → III. Awadh, son of Begum Hazrat Mahal, declared Nawab of Awadh during 1857.
D. Kunwar Singh → IV. Arrah in Bihar, a zamindar who fought bravely against the British.

27. The Harappan Civilization's time span is estimated between 6000 BCE to 1300 BCE. Early farming communities like Mehrgarh date back to c. 6000 BCE, leading into the Early Harappan phase (c. 3300 BCE), the Mature Harappan phase (2600–1900 BCE), and the Late Harappan phase (till 1300 BCE). This broad span reflects its long evolution from pre-urban to urban and post-urban phases.

28. In 1838, James Prinsep, an officer of the East India Company, successfully deciphered the Brahmi and Kharosthi scripts. This breakthrough allowed scholars to read Ashokan inscriptions and reconstruct early Indian history. It was a turning point in Indian epigraphy, connecting archaeological findings with historical records.

29. About inscriptions:
- A is incorrect (routine agricultural practices were usually not inscribed).
- B is correct: inscriptions record achievements and ideas of patrons.

- C is correct: they are engraved on stone, metal, pottery.
- D is correct: earliest inscriptions (like Ashokan edicts) were in Prakrit.

Thus, inscriptions were not about daily life but about rulers, donors, and religious messages.

30. Ashokan inscriptions in Afghanistan were written in Aramaic and Greek, reflecting the linguistic diversity of the northwestern region, which had strong Hellenistic and Persian influences after Alexander's invasion. These inscriptions show how Ashoka tailored his messages to local populations.

31. Match the meanings with terms:
A. Families (Sanskrit texts) → I. Kula.
B. Descent traced from father to son → III. Patriliny.
C. A man having several wives → II. Polygyny.
D. Gift of a daughter in marriage → IV. Kanyadana.
These terms reflect family structures, kinship, and marriage practices in early Indian society.

32. The Sanskrit term Vanik refers to merchants. Vaniks were traders who formed part of the larger economic structure, sometimes organized into shrenis (guilds). They played a crucial role in long-distance and local trade, ensuring the circulation of goods in early Indian society.

33. Match the thinkers with their origin:
A. Iran → III. Zarathustra (founder of Zoroastrianism).
B. China → IV. Kong Zi (Confucius).
C. Greece → I. Plato and Aristotle (classical philosophers).
D. India → II. Mahavira and Gautama Buddha.
This shows the diverse intellectual traditions of the ancient world.

34. According to the Ashokavadana, Emperor Ashoka distributed portions of the Buddha's relics across major towns and ordered the construction of stupas over them. This was part of Ashoka's effort to popularize Buddhism and establish a sacred geography across his empire.

35. Match the travellers with their accounts:
A. Arrived in Ghazni as a hostage, later admired the city → I. Al-Biruni.
B. Reached Sind in 1333, later Qazi of Delhi → III. Ibn Battuta.
C. Physician to Prince Dara Shukoh → II. Francois Bernier.
D. Wrote about South Indian trade and society → IV. Duarte Barbosa.

36. Ibn Battuta, a Moroccan traveller, wrote Rihla in Arabic and was born in Tangier to a family of Islamic legal scholars. He described Indian products like fine muslin, noting their high cost. However, the statement that in 1342 he was ordered to Persia as Muhammad bin Tughlaq's envoy is incorrect—he was actually sent as an envoy to the Chinese Yuan court.

37. The terms "great tradition" and "little tradition" were coined by Robert Redfield, an American anthropologist. They describe the relationship between elite, literate, classical traditions (great) and localized, folk-based cultural practices (little) in a society. Indian historians later applied this concept to study the interaction between Sanskritic and local traditions.

38. Saguna bhakti emphasizes worship of a god with attributes, often in personal forms like Shiva, Vishnu, avatars, and goddesses. In contrast, Nirguna bhakti focuses on worship of a formless, abstract god (as in Kabir's teachings). Hence, worship of an abstract form of god does not belong to Saguna traditions.

39. The rulers of the Vijayanagara Empire styled themselves as Raya (e.g., Krishnadevaraya). This title signified sovereign authority and royal dignity, distinguishing them from subordinate chiefs called Nayakas, who ruled smaller territories within the empire.

40. In 1815, Colin Mackenzie was appointed as the first Surveyor General of India. A Scottish officer and orientalist, he collected extensive manuscripts, inscriptions, and monuments, creating one of the earliest systematic surveys of Indian history and culture.

41. The speech was made in the Constituent Assembly Debates by Sardar Vallabhbhai Patel, where he criticized the continuation of separate electorates. Patel argued that this system had already led to the partition of India and should not be retained in independent India.

42. The speaker clearly states that due to the agitation for separate electorates, Indians "are now a separate nation." This is a direct reference to the partition of India in 1947, which was a result of communal political divisions encouraged by this policy.

43. The passage shows Patel strongly opposing the demand for separate electorates. He calls it a divisive "mischief" introduced by the British and insists it must not continue in free India, otherwise the nation's unity would be at risk.

44. The "mischief" of separate electorates was a British innovation. It began with the Indian Councils Act of 1909 (Morley-Minto Reforms), which introduced separate representation for Muslims, later extended to other communities. Patel calls it a colonial legacy left behind.

45. According to the speaker, the British introduced separate electorates only "for their easy administration." It was a classic "divide and rule" tactic to weaken Indian unity and make governing simpler, not to empower Indians.

46. The extracts are from Young India, a journal edited and published by Mahatma Gandhi. He often wrote on the role of charkha, khadi, machinery, and the need for decentralized village industries.

47. The writer is not rejecting all machinery but is opposing the mindless craze for machinery. Gandhi believed that machines should serve the poorest, not displace them. He wanted balanced use of technology, not blind industrialisation that caused mass unemployment.

48. By 'saving labour', Gandhi refers to the practice of employing machines in place of human beings, which saves effort for some but displaces thousands of workers. He opposed this form of labour-saving that benefited only a small elite while harming the poor.

49. The fear expressed is that machines will replace human labour, leading to unemployment, poverty, and starvation. Gandhi saw this as a social danger of modern industrialisation where efficiency for a few meant misery for many.

50. The writer's view is that industrialisation should not lead to concentration of wealth in the hands of a few. Machinery must be used carefully, to save labour for all and to uplift the poorest in their cottages, not to enrich only the elites.

Previous Years' Paper

Common University Entrance Test for UG Programmes

CUET–UG—POLITICAL SCIENCE

Entrance Exam, 2025

(Exam held on 15-05-2025)

Subject Code: 323

1. Which commission of inquiry was appointed by the Janata Party government to inquire into several aspects of allegations of abuse of authority during the Emergency?

1. Shah Commission 2. Sarkaria Commission
3. Kamraj Commission 4. Sinha Commission

2. From 1964 to 1966 the country faced two major challenges, namely the war with China and failed monsoons. In this context, which of the following slogans symbolized the country's resolve to face both these challenges?

1. Sampoorna Kranti 2. Save Democracy
3. Jai Jawan Jai Kisan 4. Karo ya Maro

3. In 1972, a global think tank published a book that cautioned about the potential depletion of the Earth's resources against the backdrop of a rapidly growing world population. What is the name of the think tank and the title of the book?

1. Consortium of Madrid, The Environment and the Earth
2. Greenpeace, Take Action Now
3. Club of Rome, Limits to Growth
4. Survival Summit, The Silent Spring

4. In 1944, a group of big industrialists drafted a joint proposal for setting up a planned economy in India. Name the Plan.

1. K.N. Raj Plan
2. Calcutta Plan
3. Bombay Plan
4. Mahalanobis Plan

5. In 1973, who among the following was appointed as the Chief Justice of the Supreme Court of India by the then central government superseding three senior judges?

1. Justice A.N. Ray
2. Justice J.C. Shah
3. Justice P.N. Bhagwati
4. Justice A.N. Verma

6. Which of the following regions within Indian territory were claimed by China?

1. Meghalaya
2. Tripura
3. NEFA
4. Sikkim

7. Which of the following years was labelled as the 'Dangerous Decade' in India?

1. 1940s
2. 1950s
3. 1960s
4. 1970s

8. Who among the following were the leaders of the United Front government that was formed in June 1996?

1. H.D. Deve Gowda, I.K. Gujral
2. V.P. Singh, Chandra Shekhar
3. A.B. Vajpayee, L.K. Advani
4. P.V. Narsimha Rao, Manmohan Singh

9. The Shimla agreement was signed between which of the following two countries?

1. India and Pakistan
2. India and Bangladesh
3. India and Nepal
4. India and Sri Lanka

1. 1	**2.** 3	**3.** 3	**4.** 3	**5.** 1	**6.** 3	**7.** 3	**8.** 1	**9.** 1

10. Which one of the following is a Treaty/Agreement not signed by India and Pakistan?

A. The Farakka Treaty
B. The Indus Water Treaty
C. The Shimla Agreement
D. The Tashkent Agreement

Choose the ***correct*** answer from the options given below:

1. A, B and D only 2. B only
3. A only 4. D only

11. Which one of the following is not a part of the 'ASEAN Way'?

1. A form of interaction that respects national sovereignty.
2. A form of interaction that is non-confrontationist.
3. A form of interaction that is cooperative.
4. A form of interaction that is formal.

12. Which of the following statements are correct about the ethnic conflict in Sri Lanka?

A. Sinhala nationalists were hostile to the Tamils and believed that Sri Lanka belongs to the Sinhala people only.
B. India refused to intervene in the conflict, claiming that it was an internal matter of Sri Lanka.
C. The Indian Peace Keeping Force sent to Sri Lanka in 1967 achieved its objective of establishing peace and stability.
D. LTTE demanded a separate country for the Tamils of Sri Lanka.

1. C and D 2. A and B
3. B and C 4. A and D

13. Chronologically, arrange the following Prime Ministers in the order of their tenure.

A. Chandra Shekhar B. P.V. Narsimha Rao
C. A.B. Vajpayee D. V.P. Singh

Choose the ***correct*** answer from the options given below:

1. A, B, C, D 2. A, C, B, D
3. B, A, D, C 4. D, A, B, C

14. The fourth World Social Forum (WSF) meeting was held in _____, India in 2004.

1. New Delhi 2. Mumbai
3. Kolkata 4. Bengaluru

15. Which one of the following is not related to the beginning of an era of coalition government?

1. Rise of regional parties
2. Rise of multi-party system
3. No political party could win a majority of seats
4. Rise of the Congress System

16. Match List-I with List-II.

List-I	List-II
A. Laldenga	I. Sikkim
B. Angami Zapu Phizo	II. Mizoram
C. AASU	III. Nagaland
D. Kazi Lhendup Dorji Khangsarpa	IV. Assam

Choose the ***correct*** answer from the options given below:

1. A-I, B-II, C-III, D-IV
2. A-II, B-III, C-IV, D-I
3. A-I, B-II, C-IV, D-III
4. A-III, B-IV, C-I, D-II

17. In politics, parties or groups are often identified as Left or Right. A party which believes that free competition and market economy alone ensures progress, and opposes unnecessary government intervention in the economy can be categorised as:

1. Leftist 2. Rightist
3. Fascist 4. Communitarian

18. Which of the following statements about the Congress Party are correct?

A. Syndicate was the name given to junior leaders in the Congress party.
B. Syndicate was the informal name given to a group of powerful Congress leaders who were in control of the party's organisation.
C. The Syndicate was led by K.Kamraj, S.K. Patil,S. Nijalingappa, N. Sanjeeva Reddy and Atulya Ghosh.
D. The Syndicate never influenced policy formulation and implementation.

Choose the ***correct*** answer from the options given below:

1. A, B and D only 2. A, B and C only
3. A, B, C and D 4. B and C only

19. Which of the following were not the alternative centers of political and economic power that emerged after disintegration of USSR?

A. European Union
B. African Union
C. Association of South East Asian Nations
D. South East Asian Treaty Organisation

1. A and D 2. B and D
3. A, B and C 4. B, C and D

10. 3	**11.** 4	**12.** 4	**13.** 4	**14.** 2	**15.** 4	**16.** 2	**17.** 2	**18.** 4	**19.** 2

20. Which of the following statements about India's Nuclear Policy are correct?

A. India opposed the Non-Proliferation Treaty (NPT) but supported the Comprehensive Test Ban Treaty (CTBT).

B. India is committed to verifiable and non-discriminatory nuclear disarmament.

C. India's nuclear doctrine of credible minimum nuclear deterrence professes "no first use."

D. India conducted its first nuclear test in 1952 under the guidance of Homi J. Bhabha.

1. B and D 2. A and D
3. A and B 4. B and C

21. Who led the Railway Strike of 1974?

1. Morarji Desai 2. Jayaprakash Narayan
3. George Fernandes 4. Charu Majumdar

22. When did the Constitution of India come into effect?

1. 26th November 1949
2. 26th January 1950
3. 24th January 1950
4. 23rd January 1950

23. The United Nations Conference on Environment and Development was held in June 1992. This was also called the Earth Summit. In which city was it organized?

1. Kyoto 2. New Delhi
3. Porto Alegre 4. Rio de Janeiro

24. In August 1990, the National Front government decided to implement one of the recommendations of the Mandal Commission pertaining to reservations for the OBCs in jobs in the central government and its undertakings. Who among the following challenged this decision in the Supreme Court?.

1. B.P Mandal 2. Kanshi Ram
3. Indira Sawhney 4. V.P. Singh

25. Which plant was patented by American and European firms and generated considerable opposition from those resisting the entry of multinationals into India?

1. Tulsi 2. Ashwagandha
3. Neem 4. Tamarind

26. Match List-I with List-II.

List-I	List-II
A. First Health Minister	I. Jawaharlal Nehru
B. First Minister of Communication	II. Rajkumari Amrit Kaur
C. First Indian to be the Governor General of India	III. Rafi Ahmed Kidwai
D. First Foreign Minister	IV. C. Rajagopalachari

Choose the ***correct*** answer from the options given below:

1. A-II, B-III, C-IV, D-I
2. A-I, B-III, C-II, D-IV
3. A-I, B-II, C-IV, D-III
4. A-III, B-IV, C-I, D-II

27. Which of the following statements about health epidemics as a non-traditional concept of security are correct?

A. There is no difference in how advanced, industrialised countries and poor, backward countries respond to health challenges.

B. Epidemics demonstrate the need for international cooperation due to interdependence of states.

C. One country's success or failure in limiting the spread of diseases does not affect infections in other countries.

D. Health epidemics spread rapidly across countries through migration, business, tourism and military operations.

Choose the ***correct*** statements from the options given below:

1. A, B and D 2. B and D
3. A, C, and D 4. B and C

28. Which of the following statements are correct about the International Atomic Energy Agency (IAEA)?

A. IAEA was established in 1957

B. IAEA came into being to implement the 'Atoms for Peace' proposal

C. IAEA does not inspect nuclear facilities all over the world to prevent the use of nuclear energy for military purposes.

D. IAEA came into being to implement President Dwight Eisenhower's diplomacy.

Choose the ***correct*** answer from the options given below:

1. A, B and D only 2. A, B and C only
3. A, B, C and D 4. A and B only

29. This organ of the United Nations no longer represents contemporary political realities, lacks equitable representation, its decisions reflect only western values and interests, and decision-making is dominated by a few powers.

Identify the organ of the United Nations.

1. Secretariat
2. General Assembly
3. International Court of Justice
4. Security Council

20. 4	**21.** 3	**22.** 2	**23.** 4	**24.** 3	**25.** 3	**26.** 1	**27.** 2	**28.** 1	**29.** 4

30. Which of the following statements are correct regarding military conflict?

A. Only soldiers are injured or killed during a war.
B. In the traditional conception of security, the greatest danger to a country's security is from military threats.
C. Threatening military action endangers the core values of sovereignty, independence and territorial integrity.
D. Military action also endangers the lives of ordinary citizens.

Choose the ***correct*** statements from the options given below:

1. A, B and D only
2. A, B and C only
3. A, B, C and D
4. B, C and D only

31. On the Indian side of the Line of Control, several points in Mashkoh, Dras, Kaksar and Batalik areas were occupied by forces claiming to be Mujahideen. Suspecting the involvement of the Pakistan Army, Indian forces reacted to this occupation. Name the event.

1. Kargil conflict
2. Bangladesh War
3. Kutch war
4. Operation Meghdoot

32. Chronologically arrange the following organizations/ conventions/Treaties according to the year of establishment:

A. International Atomic Energy Agency
B. The Nuclear Non-Proliferation Treaty
C. Chemical Weapons Convention
D. Biological Weapons Convention

Choose the ***correct*** answer from the options given below:

1. A, B, C, D
2. A, B, D, C
3. B, A, D, C
4. C, B, D, A

33. Match List-I with List-II.

List-I (UN Body)	List-II (Composition)
A. Security Council	I. International staff servicing the other principal organs, headed by the Secretary-General, who is appointed by the General Assembly on the recommendation of the Security Council.
B. General Assembly	II. Member states elected by the General Assembly for overlapping three-year terms- 54 seats based on geographical representation.
C. Secretariat	III. Fifteen members - five permanent (with veto rights), ten elected by the General Assembly for two year terms. Decision binding on all UN members.
D. Economic and Social Council	IV. Representatives of all 193 Member States, each with one vote. Major decisions require a two thirds majority; otherwise a simple majority. Decision not binding on UN members.

Choose the ***correct*** answer from the options given below:

1. A-III, B-IV, C-I, D-II
2. A-I, B-II, C-III, D-IV
3. A-I, B-II, C-IV, D-III
4. A-III, B-IV, C-II, D-I

34. The United Nations Conference on Trade and Development (UNCTAD) Report in 1972 deals with:

1. Reform of the global trading system
2. Impact of privatization on least developed countries
3. Sustainable development
4. The New World Order

35. Which of the following is correct regarding the Muslim Women (Protection of Rights on Divorce) Act of 1986?

1. The Act was opposed by orthodox Muslims as an intereference in Muslim Personal Law.
2. The act was supported by most women's organisations.
3. The Act nullified the Supreme Court Judgement in the Shah Bano Case of 1985
4. The Act was passed by the BJP government

36. The welfare goals that democratic politics must achieve is set out in which of the following provisions of the Indian constitution?

1. Fundamental Rights
2. Directive Principles of State Policy
3. Union-State relations
4. Panchayati Raj

37. During which period did the Congress dominance reflect both at the national and the state level?

1. 1952-1967
2. 1967-1969
3. 1969-1971
4. 1977-1980

30. 4	**31.** 1	**32.** 2	**33.** 1	**34.** 1	**35.** 3	**36.** 2	**37.** 1

38. In 1994, a civil war broke out in _____ during which nearly five lakh members of the Tutsi tribe were killed by the rival Hutu tribe.

1. Botswana
2. Rwanda
3. Haiti
4. Serbia

39. Consider the following statements about electoral politics in India.

A. The period after 1989 is characterised as a period of one party dominance.
B. The period after 1989 saw the decline of the Congress and the rise of the BJP.
C. In the elections of 2004, the Congress party formed a pre-election coalition.
D. In the 2004 elections, the BJP led NDA failed to win a majority of seats in the Lok Sabha.

Choose the ***correct*** statements from the options given below:

1. A, B and D only
2. A, B and C only
3. A, B, C and D
4. B, C and D only

40. Which one of the following leaders is known as 'Frontier Gandhi'?

1. Feroz Gandhi
2. Motilal Nehru
3. Jawaharlal Nehru
4. Khan Abdul Gaffar Khan

Directions (Qs. No. 41-45): *Answer the questions based on the passage below:*

British India was divided into what were called the British Indian Provinces and the Princely States. The British Indian Provinces were directly under the control of the British government. On the other hand, several large and small states ruled by princes, called the Princely States, enjoyed some form of control over their internal affairs as long as they accepted British supremacy. This was called paramountcy or suzerainty of the British crown. Princely States covered one-third of the land area of the British Indian Empire and one out of four Indians lived under princely rule. Just before Independence it was announced by the British that with the end of their rule over India, paramountcy of the British crown over Princely States would also lapse. This meant that all these states, as many as 565 in all, would become legally independent. The British government took the view that all these states were free to join either India or Pakistan or remain independent if they so wished. This decision was left not to the people but to the princely rulers of these states. This was a very serious problem and could threaten the very existence of a united India.

41. The above passage talks about which of the following issue faced by the newly independent India?

1. Partition of India.
2. Integration of Princely States with India
3. Struggle between the rulers and the people within the Princely States.
4. The rising conflict between the Princely States.

42. With the end of the British rule in India, the Princely States had which of the following options?

1. The Princely States would remain suzerain under the British Crown.
2. All the Princely States would become legally independent.
3. The Princely States could not join Pakistan.
4. The Princely States could not join India.

43. Which of the following statements is correct with regard to the Princely States?

1. The Princely States enjoyed the same status as the British Indian Provinces during the British Rule.
2. The Princely States enjoyed sovereignty under the British rule.
3. The Princely States covered one-fourth of the land of British Indian empire.
4. The Princely States were not under the direct control of the British Rule.

44. What does the term 'Suzerainty' meant in the context of relation between the British Crown and the Princeley States?

1. Princely States enjoyed complete autonomy in internal matters.
2. Princely States exercised complete autonomy over internal as well as external matters.
3. British Crown followed the policy of non-interference with respect to the Princely States.
4. Princely States had some form of control over internal matters.

45. The political status of the Princely States after the end of British Rule was to be decided by:

1. The people of the Princely States
2. India and Pakistan
3. British Crown
4. The Rulers of the Princely States

38. 2	**39.** 4	**40.** 4	**41.** 2	**42.** 2	**43.** 4	**44.** 4	**45.** 4

Directions (Qs. No. 46-50): *Answer questions based on the picture given.*

46. What was done later to deal with 'Aaya Ram, Gaya Ram' phenomena?

1. An executive order was passed banning floor-crossing.
2. A commission was appointed by the Government of India to look into the phenomena.
3. The Speaker of Lok Sabha convened an all-party convention to develop a code of conduct for the legislators.
4. Parliament brought in a constitutional amendment and an Anti-Defection Law to outlaw defections.

47. The expression "Gaya Ram was now Aya Ram" is attributed to:

1. Rao Birendra Singh
2. Om Prakash Chautala
3. Chaudhari Charan Singh
4. VP Singh

48. What does the country learn from incidents like *Aaya Ram Gaya Ram*?

1. Political parties need more money to satisfy their party leaders.
2. Defection should be declared as a criminal punishable offence.
3. The country needs a strong law to prevent defections.
4. Defection is a democratic process.

49. When an elected representative leaves the party on whose symbol he/she was elected and joins another party this action is known as:

1. Outside Support 2. Issue based support
3. Frequent transfer 4. Defection

50. The expression 'aaya ram gaya ram' originated due to the action of which politcal leader in 1967?

1. Gaya Lal 2. Ram Lal
3. Devi Lal 4. Brijender Singh

EXPLANATORY ANSWERS

1. The Janata Party government (1977–79) appointed the Shah Commission of Inquiry headed by Justice J.C. Shah to investigate allegations of abuse of authority, excesses, and violations of civil liberties during the Emergency period (1975–77). It critically examined the misuse of power by the Indira Gandhi government.

2. Between 1964–66, India faced two crises—war threats and severe food shortages due to failed monsoons. In this context, Prime Minister Lal Bahadur Shastri coined the slogan "Jai Jawan Jai Kisan", highlighting the importance of both soldiers (for defense) and farmers (for food security). It became the nation's call to resilience.

3. In 1972, the Club of Rome, a global think tank, published the report "The Limits to Growth." It warned against unchecked population growth, industrialization, and exploitation of natural resources, predicting ecological collapse if corrective steps were not taken. This was one of the first global alerts about environmental sustainability.

4. In 1944, leading industrialists like J.R.D. Tata, G.D. Birla, and others prepared a proposal for India's economic development known as the Bombay Plan. It advocated state intervention, planned investment, and industrial growth for post-independence India. This plan influenced later economic strategies though not officially adopted.

5. In 1973, Prime Minister Indira Gandhi's government superseded three senior judges (Justices Shelat, Grover, and Hegde) to appoint Justice A.N. Ray as Chief Justice of India. This controversial decision followed the landmark Kesavananda Bharati case ruling, where the Supreme Court limited Parliament's power to amend the Constitution.

6. China has historically claimed NEFA (North-East Frontier Agency, now Arunachal Pradesh) as its territory, calling it "South Tibet." This dispute was one of the root causes of the 1962 Sino-Indian War. Regions like Meghalaya, Tripura, and Sikkim were never formally claimed by China.

7. The 1960s are often described as India's "Dangerous Decade" because the country faced multiple challenges—wars with China (1962) and Pakistan (1965), food shortages, political instability after Nehru's death in 1964, and economic stress. This period tested the strength of Indian democracy.

8. The United Front government was formed in June 1996 with H.D. Deve Gowda as Prime Minister. Later, in April 1997, I.K. Gujral took over as PM after Deve Gowda lost support. They were the two key leaders associated with this coalition.

9. The Shimla Agreement was signed on 2 July 1972 between Indira Gandhi (India) and Zulfikar Ali Bhutto (Pakistan) after the 1971 Bangladesh Liberation War. It reaffirmed peaceful bilateral relations and converted the ceasefire line in Kashmir into the Line of Control (LoC).

46. 4	**47.** 1	**48.** 3	**49.** 4	**50.** 1

10. • The Farakka Treaty (1996) was signed between India and Bangladesh over Ganga river water sharing.

• The Indus Water Treaty (1960), Shimla Agreement (1972), and Tashkent Agreement (1966) were all signed between India and Pakistan.

Hence, the treaty not signed by India and Pakistan is the Farakka Treaty.

11. The ASEAN Way emphasizes informality, consensus-building, non-interference, cooperation, respect for sovereignty, and non-confrontation. Therefore, being formal is not part of the ASEAN Way.

12. • A is correct: Sinhala nationalists claimed Sri Lanka as the land of Sinhalese, marginalizing Tamils.

• B is incorrect: India did intervene by sending the Indian Peace Keeping Force (IPKF).

• C is incorrect: The IPKF was sent in 1987 (not 1967) under the Indo-Sri Lanka Accord, and it failed to establish lasting peace.

• D is correct: The LTTE demanded a separate Tamil state called Tamil Eelam.

13. D. V.P. Singh (1989–90) became PM first.

A. Chandra Shekhar (1990–91) followed.

B. P.V. Narasimha Rao (1991–96) succeeded him.

C. A.B. Vajpayee (1996, 1998–2004) came after Rao.

So, the correct chronological order is D, A, B, C.

14. The fourth World Social Forum (WSF) was held in Mumbai in January 2004. It brought together activists, NGOs, and movements discussing globalization, social justice, and alternatives to neoliberalism.

15. The era of coalition governments began when the dominance of the Congress system declined in the late 1980s. Factors like the rise of regional parties, emergence of multi-party competition, and no single party gaining a clear majority were key reasons. The "Rise of the Congress System" is associated with the 1950s–60s, not with coalitions.

16. A. Laldenga → Mizoram (II): Leader of Mizo National Front who signed the 1986 Mizo Accord.

B. Angami Zapu Phizo → Nagaland (III): Founder of Naga National Council demanding Naga independence.

C. AASU → Assam (IV): All Assam Students' Union, spearheaded the Assam Movement (1979–85).

D. Kazi Lhendup Dorji Khangsarpa → Sikkim (I): First Chief Minister of Sikkim after its merger with India in 1975.

17. A party favouring free competition, market economy, and minimal government intervention is categorized as Rightist. Leftist parties, in contrast, emphasize state control, social equality, and welfare.

18. • A is incorrect: Syndicate was not junior leaders, but senior powerful leaders.

• B is correct: It was an informal name for influential Congress leaders controlling the party.

• C is correct: Leaders included K. Kamaraj, S.K. Patil, S. Nijalingappa, N. Sanjeeva Reddy, Atulya Ghosh.

• D is incorrect: The Syndicate strongly influenced candidate selection and policy decisions.

19. After USSR's collapse (1991), new centers of power included European Union (EU) and ASEAN.

B. African Union (formed in 2002) was not a major global power bloc.

D. SEATO (South East Asian Treaty Organisation) was a Cold War military alliance dissolved in 1977.

Thus, not alternative centers = B and D.

20. • A is incorrect: India opposed both NPT and CTBT, as they were discriminatory.

• B is correct: India supports universal, non-discriminatory nuclear disarmament.

• C is correct: India's nuclear doctrine emphasizes "credible minimum deterrence" with a 'No First Use' policy.

• D is incorrect: India's first nuclear test was in 1974 (Pokhran-I), under Indira Gandhi, not in 1952.

21. The Railway Strike of 1974 was one of the biggest strikes in India, involving around 1.7 million workers. It was led by George Fernandes, the then president of the All India Railwaymen's Federation, demanding better wages and working conditions.

22. The Constitution of India was adopted on 26 November 1949, but it came into effect on 26 January 1950, chosen to honour the date of the 1930 Purna Swaraj Declaration. This marked India's transformation into a Republic.

23. The United Nations Conference on Environment and Development (UNCED), popularly known as the Earth Summit, was held in Rio de Janeiro, Brazil, in June 1992. It focused on sustainable development and produced important agreements like Agenda 21.

24. The Mandal Commission recommendations on OBC reservations (27%) were implemented by the V.P. Singh government in 1990. This was challenged in the Supreme Court by Indira Sawhney, leading to the landmark Indira Sawhney v. Union of India (1992) judgment, which upheld the reservations with some conditions.

25. During the 1990s, American and European firms patented products derived from Neem, which sparked strong opposition in India. Activists and farmers resisted this as "biopiracy," arguing that neem had been traditionally used for centuries in India.

26. A. First Health Minister → Rajkumari Amrit Kaur (II): She was India's first Health Minister, serving from 1947 to 1957.

B. First Minister of Communication → Rafi Ahmed Kidwai (III): Held charge of Posts and Communications in Nehru's cabinet.

C. First Indian Governor-General → C. Rajagopalachari (IV): Took office in 1948 after Lord Mountbatten.

D. First Foreign Minister → Jawaharlal Nehru (I): Held the Foreign Affairs portfolio along with being Prime Minister.

27. • A is incorrect: Responses vary between advanced and poor nations depending on resources.

• B is correct: Epidemics highlight the need for global cooperation, as no state can fight them alone.

• C is incorrect: One country's failure can spread infections to others, as seen with COVID-19.

• D is correct: Diseases spread rapidly through travel, migration, trade, and military activity.

28. • A is correct: IAEA was established in 1957.
• B is correct: It was created to implement the "Atoms for Peace" initiative.
• C is incorrect: IAEA does inspect nuclear facilities worldwide to prevent misuse.
• D is correct: It was tied to U.S. President Eisenhower's 1953 "Atoms for Peace" speech.

29. The UN Security Council reflects outdated power structures (1945 victors), is dominated by P5 (US, UK, France, Russia, China), and lacks equitable representation. Its decisions often mirror Western or great power interests, not global consensus.

30. • A is incorrect: Wars also kill civilians, not just soldiers.
• B is correct: Traditional security concepts emphasize military threats as the main danger.
• C is correct: Threatening military action undermines sovereignty, independence, and territorial integrity.
• D is correct: Civilians are endangered in wars through bombings, displacement, and destruction.

31. In 1999, intrusions occurred in Mashkoh, Dras, Kaksar, and Batalik sectors along the Line of Control. Initially claimed to be Mujahideen, they were later found to be Pakistan Army regulars. The Indian Army launched Operation Vijay, leading to the Kargil conflict.

32. A. IAEA: Established in 1957.
B. Nuclear Non-Proliferation Treaty (B): Opened for signature in 1968.
D. Biological Weapons Convention (D): Signed in 1972, entered into force in 1975.
C. Chemical Weapons Convention (C): Opened for signature in 1993, in force from 1997.
So, chronological order: A, B, D, C.

33. A. Security Council → III: 15 members (5 permanent with veto, 10 elected); binding decisions.
B. General Assembly → IV: 193 members; one country one vote; decisions mostly recommendatory.
C. Secretariat → I: Administrative staff under Secretary-General.
D. ECOSOC → II: 54 members elected for 3-year terms; deals with economic and social issues.

34. The 1972 UNCTAD Report emphasized the need to reform the global trading system to benefit developing countries, addressing inequities in international trade, terms of trade, and market access.

35. The Muslim Women (Protection of Rights on Divorce) Act, 1986, passed by the Rajiv Gandhi government, diluted the Supreme Court's Shah Bano judgment by restricting divorced Muslim women's right to maintenance under personal law, limiting it to the iddat period. It was opposed by women's organisations but supported by orthodox Muslims.

36. The Directive Principles of State Policy (Part IV of the Constitution) lay down the welfare goals that democratic politics must achieve, such as social justice, reducing inequalities, promoting education, health, and livelihoods. They act as guidelines for governance, unlike Fundamental Rights which are enforceable.

37. The period 1952 to 1967 is called the era of Congress dominance both at the Centre and in most states. In the first three general elections (1952, 1957, 1962), the Congress won a clear majority nationally and controlled almost all state governments.

38. In 1994, a brutal civil war took place in Rwanda where about five lakh Tutsis were massacred by the Hutu majority in one of the worst genocides of the 20th century.

39. • A is incorrect: After 1989, India entered a coalition era, not one-party dominance.
• B is correct: The period marked Congress decline and rise of BJP as a national force.
• C is correct: In 2004, Congress formed the UPA coalition before elections.
• D is correct: In 2004, the BJP-led NDA lost majority, and UPA came to power.

40. Known as "Frontier Gandhi", Khan Abdul Gaffar Khan was a Pashtun independence activist from North-West Frontier Province, closely associated with Mahatma Gandhi in the freedom struggle. He founded the Khudai Khidmatgar (Red Shirt Movement).

41. The passage highlights the challenge faced by newly independent India in ensuring the integration of 565 princely states. These states were legally free after the lapse of paramountcy, making their merger with India or Pakistan critical for national unity.

42. With the end of British rule, paramountcy lapsed, and princely states were given three choices — join India, join Pakistan, or remain independent. Thus, all states were legally independent initially.

43. Unlike British Provinces, princely states had autonomy in internal affairs but acknowledged British supremacy. They were not directly ruled by the British government.

44. The term suzerainty meant that while British Crown retained paramount power, princely states could exercise control over their internal matters as long as they accepted British supremacy.

45. The British left the decision of accession or independence to the rulers of the princely states, not to their people. This created serious challenges for integration.

46. To deal with the menace of "Aya Ram, Gaya Ram," the 52nd Constitutional Amendment Act, 1985 introduced the Anti-Defection Law (Tenth Schedule). It disqualified legislators who defected from their parties.

47. The phrase "Gaya Ram was now Aya Ram" was first used by Rao Birendra Singh, then Haryana MLA, in 1967 after repeated floor-crossings by Gaya Lal, who switched parties thrice in a single day.

48. Incidents of frequent defections highlighted the instability of governments and the need for a strict anti-defection law to preserve political stability and party discipline.

49. When an elected representative leaves the party on whose ticket he/she was elected and joins another party, it is termed as defection. This undermines the democratic mandate of voters.

50. The term "Aya Ram, Gaya Ram" originated in 1967 when Gaya Lal, an MLA from Haryana, changed parties thrice in one day, leading to widespread criticism of such opportunistic politics.

Previous Years' Paper

Common University Entrance Test for UG Programmes

CUET–UG—SOCIOLOGY*

Entrance Exam, 2025

(Exam held on 16-05-2025)

Subject Code: 326

1. Which of the following is a structural change that happened in Indian economy due to British rule?

1. Modernisation of thought
2. Sanskritisation of lower castes
3. Dependency on British industrialisation
4. Westernisation of mass media

2. Why is detailed demographic data important?

1. It helps in the planning and implementation of State policies.
2. It is a hallmark of modern nation-state.
3. It helps to have a birds's eye view of the population.
4. It helps to understand demographic transition.

3. What does the word 'dwija' imply?

1. Double standards
2. Twice-born
3. Jajmani system
4. Prejudice

4. The 'Population Explosion' happens in which of the following stages?

1. First Stage
2. Third stage
3. Second stage
4. Developed stage

5. In order to avoid the provisions of the Land Ceiling Act, which among the following strategies was adopted by the landowners?

1. Benami transfers
2. Contract farming
3. Abolition of zamindari system
4. Pay tax

6. What is the purpose of the Pre-natal Diagnostic Techniques (Regulation and Prevention of Misuse) Act?

1. To prevent abortion due to poverty and ignorance.
2. To give incentives to families to raise girl child.
3. To prevent female infanticide.
4. To prevent misuse of technology for selective abortions.

7. Which of the following is an "acquired" trait to classify tribes in India?

1. language
2. livelihood
3. racial features
4. habitat

8. What was "Raiyatwari" system?

1. The tenants could keep two-third of the agricultural produce.
2. A situation of absentee landlords.
3. The cultivators paid agricultural tax directly to the British government.
4. Buying land in the name of others after land ceiling.

9. During 1960's Banshi and his fellow peasant workers organised committees to fight back against the atrocities and oppressions of their landlords. This social movement strived to change the existing social and political arrangement. What is this kind of movement called?

1. Redemptive
2. Reformist
3. Revolutionary
4. Radical

10. Who had given the three aspects to the modern framework of change in colonial India?

1. Satish Saberwal
2. M.S. Rao
3. Keshav Chandra Sen
4. Vishnu Shastri

11. What is the Liberal and Marxist critique of Malthus's theory of population growth?

1. That he disregarded poverty as a social problem.
2. That he only talked about positive and preventive checks.
3. That he did not give a detailed theory of demographic transition.
4. That he failed to give a theory of population explosion.

12. What is the specific purpose of introducing Panchayati Raj governance?

1. To ensure direct grassroot democracy.
2. To act on poverty alleviation.
3. To ensure population control.
4. To ensure effective policy for State.

1. 3 **2.** 1 **3.** 2 **4.** 3 **5.** 1 **6.** 4 **7.** 2 **8.** 3 **9.** 3 **10.** 1 **11.** 1 **12.** 1

13. Which of the following is a correct statement about demography?

1. Demographic change is purely biological.
2. Demographic data is a static data for a population.
3. Population explosion does not happen in every country.
4. Demographic change is based on economic, social and cultural variables.

14. Match List-I with List-II.

List-I (Types of Family)	List-II (Characteristic)
A. Matrilocal Family	I. Consists of one set of parents and their children
B. Patriarchal Family	II. Based on the rule of residence
C. Patrilineal Family	III. Defines men exercise authority and dominance
D. Nuclear Family	IV. It pertains to the rule of inheritance

Choose the ***correct*** answer from the options given below:

1. A-II, B-III, C-IV, D-I
2. A-I, B-III, C-II, D-IV
3. A-II, B-III, C-I, D-IV
4. A-III, B-IV, C-I, D-II

15. Which of the following are features of capitalism as a social system?

A. Commodification of labour power.
B. Caste based networks of trading.
C. Surplus value.
D. Rising inequalities.

Choose the ***correct*** answer from the options below.

1. A, B and D only 2. A, C and D only
3. B, C and D only 4. A, B and C only

16. What is the term given by Jan Breman to migrant workers?

1. Dalit
2. Foot loose labour
3. Circulation of labour
4. Labour force

17. The Nakarattars banking system is based on:

1. Class based banking system
2. Caste based banking system
3. Western banking system
4. Free-Trade system

18. What are the characteristics of social stratification?

A. It is based on natural differences.
B. It is a function of individual differences.
C. It persists over generations.
D. It is supported by patterns of belief/ideology.

Choose the ***correct*** answer from the options given below:

1. A and D only
2. C and B only
3. C and D only
4. A and B only

19. Match List-I with List-II.

List-I (Term/Name)	List-II (Characteristics)
A. Privatisation	I. Work which focuses on providing services like trade, transport, financial services etc.
B. Disinvestment	II. Spread of investment into different types of economic activities in order to reduce risks.
C. Tertiary sector	III. Private companies can invest in sectors earlier reserved for the government.
D. Diversification	IV. The government sells its share in public sector companies.

Choose the ***correct*** answer from the options given below:

1. A-IV, B-II, C-III, D-I
2. A-III, B-IV, C-I, D-II
3. A-I, B-II, C-IV, D-III
4. A-III, B-II, C-I, D-IV

20. Which of the following is correct about unorganised sector work in India?

1. Less number of people work in this sector.
2. It is independent of personal relationships.
3. Lack of proper wages and other working conditions.
4. It is only for women and unskilled labourers.

21. The characteristics of the caste system:

A. Caste is an ascribed status.
B. Caste groups are 'endogamous'.
C. Caste is an achieved status.
D. Castes involve segmental organization.
E. Caste groups are based on choice of individuals

Choose the ***correct*** answer from the options given below:

1. A, B and D only 2. D, B and C only
3. A, B and E only 4. B, C and E only

22. In a democratic state, which of the following is a key actor in governance?

1. Women's groups 2. Status groups
3. Political parties 4. International organisations

23. According to Emile Durkheim, what is the cause of suicide?

1. It is based on individual mindset.
2. It is based on biological anomaly.
3. It is influenced by social causes.
4. It is more prevalent in western countries.

24. Which of the following is an example of the reformist social movement?

1. Right To Information 2. Bolshevik Revolution
3. Naxalite Movement 4. Anti-abortion Movement

25. According to Max Weber, on what basis classes and status groups are differentiated?

1. Social facts 2. Lifestyles
3. Caste system 4. Market economy

13. 4	**14.** 1	**15.** 2	**16.** 2	**17.** 2	**18.** 3	**19.** 2	**20.** 3	**21.** 1	**22.** 3	**23.** 3	**24.** 1	**25.** 2

26. Which among the following statement(s) is/are correct about the Raiyatwari system:

A. Raiyat means cultivator.
B. The actual cultivators were responsible for paying the tax.
C. Zamindars play a dominant role.
D. Colonial government dealt directly with the farmer.

Choose the ***correct*** answer from the options given below:

1. A, B and D only 2. A, B and C only
3. A, C and D only 4. B, C and D only

27. Arrange the following in chronological order:

A. Bengal Revolt B. Champaran Satyagraha
C. Deccan Riots D. Bardoli Satyagraha

Choose the ***correct*** answer from the options given below:

1. C, A, B, D 2. A, C, B, D
3. B, A, D, C 4. C, B, D, A

28. The process by which something which was not a commodity before in market economy and is made into a commodity is known as:

1. Commoditisation 2. Capitalism
3. Labour power 4. Mode of production

29. Match List-I with List-II.

List-I (Name)	List-II (Example)
A. Eenadu	I. Radio Channel
B. Zee TV	II. Soap Opera
C. AIR	III. Telugu Newspaper
D. Buniyad	IV. Satellite Channel

Choose the ***correct*** answer from the options given below:

1. A-II, B-I, C-IV, D-III
2. A-I, B-III, C-II, D-IV
3. A-III, B-IV, C-II, D-I
4. A-III, B-IV, C-I, D-II

30. Match List-I with List-II.

List-I (Book/Theory proposed)	List-II (Author/Thinker)
A. The Three Sermons of Human Nature	I. Begum Rokeya Sakhawat Hussain
B. The City	II. Ralph Ellison
C. Sultana's Dream	III. Bishop Joseph Butler
D. Invisible Man	IV. Daya Pawar

Choose the ***correct*** answer from the options given below:

1. A-II, B-I, C-III, D-IV
2. A-III, B-IV, C-I, D-II
3. A-III, B-IV, C-II, D-I
4. A-I, B-III, C-II, D-IV

31. Prejudices are often grounded in:

1. Direct evidence 2. Logical conclusions
3. Stereotypes 4. Critical thinking

32. Which of the following statements are correct in respect of New Farmer's Movement:

A. It began in Punjab and Tamil Nadu.
B. It was party oriented.
C. Ideology was anti-state and anti-urban.
D. The focus of demand was price and its related issues.

Choose the ***correct*** answer from the options given below:

1. A, B and D only 2. A, B and C only
3. A, C and D only 4. B, C and D only

33. Match List-I with List-II.

List-I (Concept)	List-II (Example)
A. Sanskritisation	I. Dalit groups adopting the use of fork and spoons.
B. Westernisation	II. Dalit groups adopting the practice of dowry.
C. Modernisation	III. Public advertisements for jobs stating qualification only.
D. Secularisation	IV. Public holidays for festivals of all religions.

Choose the ***correct*** answer from the options given below:

1. A-IV, B-III, C-II, D-I
2. A-II, B-I, C-III, D-IV
3. A-II, B-I, C-IV, D-III
4. A-III, B-IV, C-I, D-II

34. The Adi Dharma Movement in India belonged to which category of social movement?

1. Caste Based Movement 2. Worker's Movement
3. Peasant Movement 4. Ecological Movement

35. Arrange the following in chronological order:

A. Caste Disabilities Removal Act
B. First Backward Commission
C. The Scheduled Castes and Scheduled Tribes (prevention atrocities) Act
D. State Reorganization Commission

Choose the ***correct*** answer from the options given below:

1. D, B, C, A 2. A, B, D, C
3. B, A, D, C 4. C, B, D, A

36. The term 'dikus' refers to:

1. Adivasis
2. Dalit
3. Migrant traders and Money lenders
4. Migrant workers

37. Which of the following denotes racial discrimination followed in South Africa?

1. Apartheid 2. Assimilation
3. Reservation 4. Prejudice

38. Arrange the following in order of their year of occurrence:

A. Statehood for Jharkhand
B. All India Trade Union Congress
C. Bihar Provincial Kisan Sabha
D. All India Kisan Sabha

Choose the ***correct*** answer from the options given below:

1. B, C, D, A 2. A, C, B, D
3. B, A, D, C 4. C, B, D, A

26. 1	**27.** 2	**28.** 1	**29.** 4	**30.** 2	**31.** 3	**32.** 3
33. 2	**34.** 1	**35.** 2	**36.** 3	**37.** 1	**38.** 1	

39. Ritu works for an IT firm and is happy that the firm gives her freedom of working hours. She can even work late on Saturday night and come late on Monday, every time her boss gives her a deadline. Also, most meetings happen over a weekend dinner at the office. What is Ritu being subjected to?

1. knowledge economy where her work is in the IT sector
2. 'flexi-time' but in reality expansion of working hours by the management
3. globalisation because her clients are in Japan
4. gender discrimination

40. Arrange the following events in order of their occurrence:

A. Hong Kong Influenza
B. Spanish Flu
C. Asian Influenza
D. First Population Policy in India

Choose the ***correct*** answer from the options given below:

1. B, C, A, D 2. A, C, B, D
3. B, A, D, C 4. C, B, D, A

Directions (Qs. No. 41-45): *Read the passage carefully and answer the questions based on the passage:*

The Right to Information Act 2005 (Act No. 22/2005) is a law enacted by the Parliament of India giving Indians access to government records. Under the terms of the Act, any person may request information from a "public authority" (a body of Government or instrumentality of State) which is expected to reply expeditiously or within thirty days. The Act also requires every public authority to computerize their records for wide dissemination and to proactively publish certain categories of information so that the citizens need minimum recourse to request for information formally. This law was passed by Parliament on 15 June 2005 and came into force on 13 October 2005. Information disclosure in India was hitherto restricted by the Official Secrets Act 1923 and various other special laws, which the new RTI Act now overrides. The Act specifies that citizens have a right to:

- Request any information (as defined)
- Take copies of documents
- Inspect documents, works and records
- Take certified samples of materials of work.
- Obtain information in the form of printouts, diskettes, floppies, tapes, video cassettes or in any other electronic mode.

41. The Right To Information Act came into force on:

1. 15 June, 2005 2. 13 October, 2005
3. 22 October, 2005 4. 17 June, 2005

42. Under RTI who is given accountability?

1. A Public Authority 2. Private Organisations
3. Citizen of India 4. Civil Society

43. Which of the following act is overrided by RTI Act?

1. Prevention of Atrocity Act
2. Official Secrets Act
3. Persons with Disability Act
4. Government of India Act

44. Which of the following statements are correct about the purpose of RTI Act?

1. Gives citizens access to government records.
2. Prohibit public authorities to provide data voluntarily to the public.
3. RTI brings transparency in private organisations too.
4. Put accountability on public for good governance.

45. Within how many days, a public authority is expected to reply under RTI?

1. 20 days 2. 10 days
3. 30 days 4. 41 days

Directions (Qs. No. 46-50): *Read the passage carefully and answer the questions based on the passage:*

There has been greater recognition that both men and women are constrained by dominant gender identities. For instance, men in patriarchal societies feel they must be strong and successful. It is not manly, to express oneself emotionally. A gender-just society would allow both men and women to be free. This, of course, rests on the idea that for true freedom to grow and develop, injustices of all kinds have to end. The idea of a gender-just society is based upon two important factors — educated women with multiple roles and improved sex ratio. The programme of the Government of India, Beti Bachao, Beti Padhao Yojana is an important effort in the actualization of a gender-just society.

46. Patriarchal society refers to:

1. Dominant role of men
2. Dominant role of women
3. Rule of residence
4. Rule of lineage

47. What is the basis for a gender-just society?

1. Gender idenities based on commonsense.
2. Multiple gender roles and conflicts.
3. Presence of dominant gendered identities as role models.
4. Presence of educated women with multiple roles and improved sex ratio.

48. What do men in patriarchal society usually feel?

1. Strong and successful
2. Equal to women
3. Underprivileged
4. Assume secondary role

49. The government scheme of Beti-Bachao, Beti-Padhao is an example of:

1. Gender biasness towards girl child.
2. Changes in patriarchal society.
3. Improved social status of girl child.
4. Actualisation of a gender-just society.

50. What is the situation of women in patriarchal society?

1. Have dominant role in household.
2. Can do all kinds of work.
3. Have equal access to resources.
4. Face discrimination in various spheres.

39. 2	**40.** 1	**41.** 2	**42.** 1	**43.** 2	**44.** 1	**45.** 3	**46.** 1	**47.** 4	**48.** 1	**49.** 4	**50.** 4

EXPLANATORY ANSWERS

1. One of the most significant structural changes brought by British rule in India was the destruction of traditional Indian industries and the integration of the Indian economy into the global capitalist system as a raw material supplier. Indian artisans and craftsmen, particularly in textiles, lost their livelihoods because cheap machine-made goods from Britain flooded Indian markets. Simultaneously, India exported raw cotton, jute, indigo, and other materials to Britain. This led to a structural dependency on British industrialisation, transforming India into a colonial economy.

2. Detailed demographic data is essential for governance because it provides a foundation for planning and implementation of state policies. Governments rely on such data to design programmes related to health, education, employment, housing, and poverty alleviation. Without accurate demographic details—such as age structure, literacy levels, and fertility rates—it would be impossible to allocate resources effectively. Thus, demographic data is not only statistical but also an instrument of policy-making.

3. The term 'dwija', which means 'twice-born', was traditionally applied to the three upper varnas—Brahmins, Kshatriyas, and Vaishyas—after they underwent the upanayana (sacred thread) ceremony. The first birth was biological, while the second symbolised their spiritual and social initiation into education and learning. This distinction reinforced social hierarchies by granting ritual superiority to the "twice-born" over others like Shudras and Dalits, who were excluded from this practice.

4. Population explosion is a characteristic of the second stage of demographic transition. In this stage, birth rates remain very high due to cultural practices and lack of family planning, but death rates fall drastically because of improved sanitation, medicine, and food supply. This mismatch between high fertility and low mortality leads to very rapid population growth. The first stage shows high birth and death rates (stable population), while the third stage sees declining birth rates. Hence, the second stage is the critical phase of explosion.

5. The Land Ceiling Act was introduced to redistribute surplus land from big landlords to the landless poor by setting a limit on the maximum land one could own. To evade this law, landlords resorted to 'benami' transfers', i.e., registering land in the names of relatives, servants, or fictitious persons. This allowed them to retain control over land without legally violating the ceiling limits. Other options like zamindari abolition or paying taxes were unrelated strategies.

6. The Pre-natal Diagnostic Techniques (Regulation and Prevention of Misuse) Act (1994) was passed to regulate the use of diagnostic technologies such as ultrasound and amniocentesis. These were being misused for sex determination, leading to female foeticide and worsening the child sex ratio in India. The Act aimed to prevent selective abortions by penalising both doctors and families involved in illegal practices. Thus, its central purpose was to prevent misuse of technology for sex-selective abortions.

7. Tribal classification often uses ascribed traits like racial features, language, and habitat, which are inherited by birth. However, livelihood is an acquired trait, as it depends on the economic activities pursued by a community. For example, some tribes may shift from hunting-gathering to agriculture or wage labour due to changes in environment or economy. This adaptability makes livelihood an acquired trait, unlike the others which are fixed.

8. The Raiyatwari system was introduced in Bombay and Madras presidencies by the British. Under this system, there were no zamindars or middlemen; cultivators (raiyats) paid land revenue directly to the colonial government. Though this reduced the power of landlords, the heavy burden of revenue fell directly on peasants, often leading to indebtedness. The system was different from the Zamindari system (where zamindars collected revenue).

9. In the 1960s, peasant struggles like those led by Banshi were directed not at minor reforms but at overthrowing oppressive landlord domination and changing the social-political structure itself. Such movements are termed 'revolutionary' because they aim at structural transformation of society rather than gradual improvements. They challenge existing power hierarchies in a radical way, unlike reformist or redemptive movements.

10. Satish Saberwal, an eminent Indian sociologist, provided a modern framework to understand social change in colonial India. He explained change through three aspects: economy, polity, and culture. His analysis showed how British colonialism restructured Indian society by introducing new economic systems, political institutions, and cultural influences. This framework helped sociologists study modernisation in India.

11. Malthus's theory argued that population grows geometrically while food production grows arithmetically, leading to poverty and famine unless checked by natural or preventive means. Liberal and Marxist critics argued that Malthus ignored poverty as a socially created problem arising from exploitation and unequal distribution of resources. By blaming population growth alone, he overlooked structural inequalities in society and economy, making his theory socially insensitive.

12. Panchayati Raj was constitutionally introduced to decentralise democracy and bring decision-making closer to people. Its purpose was not limited to poverty alleviation or policy implementation but to ensure direct participation of villagers in governance. By giving Gram Sabhas and Panchayats powers, it created grassroots democracy and strengthened self-governance in rural India.

13. Demographic change is not purely biological; it is influenced by multiple socio-economic and cultural factors. Fertility patterns depend on education and cultural norms, mortality declines with healthcare access, and migration is driven by economic opportunities.

Thus, demographic change reflects a combination of biological processes and wider social, economic, and cultural variables.

14. A. Matrilocal Family → II. Based on the rule of residence (wife and husband live in the wife's parental home).

B. Patriarchal Family → III. Men exercise authority and dominance.

C. Patrilineal Family → IV. Based on rule of inheritance through the male line.

D. Nuclear Family → I. Parents and their children only.

This sequence matches option 1.

15. Capitalism is characterised by commodification of labour (workers selling their labour as a commodity), surplus value (profits extracted from workers' labour), and rising inequalities (gap between classes). Caste-based trading networks are traditional features of Indian society but not integral to capitalism. Therefore, the correct set of features includes A, C, and D.

16. Jan Breman, a Dutch sociologist, studied the conditions of rural migrant workers in India. He used the term "*foot loose labour*" to describe them. These workers are landless poor who constantly migrate in search of seasonal or casual employment. They do not have stable jobs, fixed employers, or secure income and are often exploited due to their vulnerable position.

17. The Nakarattars (or Nattukottai Chettiars) of Tamil Nadu were a prominent caste-based banking community during the colonial period. Their financial networks extended across South and Southeast Asia. Their banking system was not based on modern Western principles but on caste solidarity and kinship-based trust. Hence, it was a caste-based banking system.

18. Social stratification refers to the hierarchical arrangement of individuals and groups in society. It is characterised by persistence over generations (children inheriting their parents' status) and by being supported through belief systems or ideologies that justify inequalities (like caste or class ideologies).

It is not merely based on natural or individual differences, but on structured inequality. Hence, the correct traits are C and D.

19. A. Privatisation → III. Private companies can invest in sectors earlier reserved for the government.

B. Disinvestment → IV. The government sells its share in public sector companies.

C. Tertiary sector → I. Work focusing on services like trade, transport, financial services etc.

D. Diversification → II. Spreading investment across different activities to reduce risks.

This matches option 2.

20. The unorganised sector in India employs a very large portion of the workforce, but its main characteristic is lack of security and poor working conditions. Workers often face irregular wages, no fixed hours, absence of benefits like healthcare or pensions, and exploitation due to lack of legal protection. Thus, the defining feature is lack of proper wages and working conditions.

21. The caste system has certain defining characteristics. First, caste is an ascribed status, meaning individuals are born into it and cannot change it by choice. Second, caste groups are endogamous, meaning members marry within their own caste. Third, castes follow segmental organisation, meaning society is divided into separate, rigidly demarcated groups with specific roles. It is not an achieved status, nor is it based on free choice of individuals.

22. In a democratic state, the most crucial actors in governance are political parties. They aggregate interests, contest elections, form governments, make policies, and represent citizens. While women's groups and international organisations may influence, political parties are the core institutions through which democracy functions.

23. Emile Durkheim, in his famous work *Suicide* (1897), argued that suicide is not merely an individual or biological act but is deeply influenced by social causes. He classified suicides into types like egoistic, altruistic, anomic, and fatalistic, showing how variations in social integration and regulation influence suicide rates. Thus, the root cause lies in social conditions.

24. A reformist social movement aims at bringing gradual change within the existing system without completely overthrowing it. The Right to Information movement in India is a good example, as it worked within democratic frameworks to demand transparency and accountability from the government, leading to legal reforms. Revolutionary movements like the Bolshevik Revolution or Naxalite movement seek radical structural change, not reform.

25. According to Max Weber, classes are determined by people's position in the market economy (i.e., access to resources and opportunities), while status groups are differentiated on the basis of lifestyles, prestige, and social honour. He distinguished between economic class and social status, showing that they are interrelated but not identical.

26. The Raiyatwari system was introduced by the British in the Madras and Bombay presidencies. In this system:

- Raiyat literally means cultivator.
- The actual cultivators were made responsible for paying land revenue directly to the colonial government, without intermediaries.
- Zamindars did not play a dominant role here; unlike the Zamindari system, they were removed from the revenue chain.
- The colonial state directly dealt with the farmer, assessing and collecting taxes.

Thus, A, B, and D are correct, while C is incorrect.

27. Let us arrange the events in their proper historical sequence:

- Bengal Revolt (1859–60): This was an indigo revolt by peasants against indigo planters in Bengal.
- Deccan Riots (1875): Peasant riots in Maharashtra against moneylenders due to debt burdens.
- Champaran Satyagraha (1917): Gandhi's first satyagraha in India, protesting indigo cultivation system in Bihar.
- Bardoli Satyagraha (1928): Led by Sardar Vallabhbhai Patel against increased land revenue in Gujarat.

So, the chronological order is: A (Bengal Revolt) → C (Deccan Riots) → B (Champaran Satyagraha) → D (Bardoli Satyagraha).

28. Commoditisation refers to the process by which goods, services, or even ideas that were not previously sold in the market are transformed into commodities that can be bought and sold. For example, water, education, or cultural practices becoming marketable commodities is an instance of commoditisation. Capitalism and labour power are broader concepts, while mode of production refers to the economic system.

29. Matching the given media examples:

- Eenadu → III. Telugu Newspaper (a leading Telugu-language daily newspaper).
- Zee TV → IV. Satellite Channel (one of the first Indian private TV channels).
- AIR (All India Radio) → I. Radio Channel (national radio broadcaster).
- Buniyad → II. Soap Opera (a popular TV serial in the 1980s).

So, the correct sequence is A-III, B-IV, C-I, D-II.

30. Matching the books/theories with authors:

- The Three Sermons of Human Nature → III. Bishop Joseph Butler (an 18th-century theologian and philosopher).
- The City → IV. Daya Pawar (a Dalit writer who wrote on urban experiences).
- Sultana's Dream → I. Begum Rokeya Sakhawat Hussain (a feminist utopian text written in 1905 envisioning a world ruled by women).
- Invisible Man → II. Ralph Ellison (a famous novel about race and identity in America).

Thus, the correct pairing is A-III, B-IV, C-I, D-II.

31. Prejudices are preconceived notions about individuals or groups not based on reason or evidence but shaped by fixed ideas. They are usually grounded in stereotypes, which are oversimplified generalisations about social categories like caste, gender, race, or religion. These stereotypes influence perceptions and behaviour without logical or critical evaluation, reinforcing discrimination.

32. The New Farmer's Movements (1980s–90s) emerged mainly in Punjab and Tamil Nadu, focusing on issues of procurement prices, electricity, loans, and state policies affecting farmers. They were not party-oriented; rather, they operated as independent farmers' organisations. Their ideology was anti-state and anti-urban, as they saw urban-based state policies exploiting rural producers. The central focus remained prices and related issues like fair procurement and subsidies. Hence, A, C, and D are correct.

33. Let us match correctly:

- Sanskritisation → II. Dalit groups adopting the practice of dowry (imitating higher caste practices for upward mobility).
- Westernisation → I. Dalit groups adopting the use of fork and spoons (imitating Western cultural habits).
- Modernisation → III. Public advertisements for jobs stating qualification only (focus on merit, rationality, and qualifications).
- Secularisation → IV. Public holidays for festivals of all religions (state neutrality in religion).

So the sequence is A-II, B-I, C-III, D-IV.

34. The Adi Dharma Movement (19th–20th century) was led by Swami Achhutanand and others in North India. It was primarily a caste-based movement of Dalits, seeking equality, dignity, and liberation from the oppressive Hindu caste order. It rejected caste hierarchies, emphasised self-respect, and attempted to create a separate Dalit religious identity.

35. Chronological order of the given legislations/commissions:

- Caste Disabilities Removal Act – 1850 (allowed inheritance rights to those who converted to other religions).
- First Backward Classes Commission – 1953 (headed by Kaka Kalelkar, submitted report in 1955).
- State Reorganization Commission – 1953 (submitted report in 1955, implemented in 1956 for linguistic reorganisation of states).
- SC & ST (Prevention of Atrocities) Act – 1989.

Thus, the correct sequence is A (1850) → B (1953) → D (1956) → C (1989).

36. The term 'dikus' was used by Adivasis to refer to outsiders such as migrant traders, moneylenders, and colonial officials who exploited them economically. These outsiders disrupted traditional ways of life, took control over tribal lands, and trapped Adivasis in debt through unfair moneylending practices. Hence, the word symbolised the exploiters from outside tribal society.

37. In South Africa, the system of apartheid institutionalised racial discrimination from 1948 until the early 1990s. Under apartheid, people were segregated on the basis of race, with laws enforcing separate schools, transport, housing, and restrictions on non-white populations. It was a systematic, state-sponsored form of racial oppression.

38. Chronological order of these organisations/movements:

- All India Trade Union Congress (1920): India's first national trade union organisation.
- Bihar Provincial Kisan Sabha (1929): Formed to mobilise peasants against zamindari exploitation.

- All India Kisan Sabha (1936): National-level peasant organisation formed in Lucknow.
- Statehood for Jharkhand (2000): Became a separate state from Bihar.

Thus, the sequence is B (1920) → C (1929) → D (1936) → A (2000).

39. Ritu's case illustrates a situation where companies offer 'flexi-time' but in reality expand working hours. Although flexible hours are supposed to give freedom, in practice employers often extend the workday by blurring the boundary between personal and professional life, especially in IT sectors. Weekend meetings and late-night work disguised as flexibility point to managerial control rather than real autonomy.

40. Let us carefully analyse each event with dates before arranging them:

B. Spanish Flu: This pandemic broke out in 1918–1919, right after World War I, and is considered one of the deadliest in human history, killing millions worldwide including a huge toll in India.

C. Asian Influenza: Occurred in 1957–1958, starting in East Asia (China) and spreading rapidly across continents. It was caused by an H2N2 virus and resulted in significant global fatalities.

A. Hong Kong Influenza: Emerged in 1968–1969, caused by the H3N2 strain. Originating in Hong Kong, it spread globally and marked another serious influenza outbreak of the 20th century.

D. First Population Policy in India: Introduced in 1976, during the Emergency, under Indira Gandhi's government. It emphasised controlling population growth through family planning programmes and was the first official policy step in India towards population stabilisation.

Hence, the correct chronological sequence is: Spanish Flu (1918) → Asian Influenza (1957) → Hong Kong Influenza (1968) → India's First Population Policy (1976).

41. The RTI Act was passed by Parliament on 15 June 2005 but it officially came into force on 13 October 2005. From this date onwards, Indian citizens legally gained the right to demand information from public authorities.

42. Under the RTI Act, accountability lies with a Public Authority, which refers to any government department, ministry, or institution of the State. These authorities are obliged to maintain records, provide requested information, and proactively publish certain data to ensure transparency.

43. The RTI Act overrides restrictive provisions of the Official Secrets Act, 1923, which previously limited access to government information by treating many documents as classified. With the RTI, transparency became the norm, except in cases involving national security and sensitive information.

44. The primary purpose of the RTI Act is to give citizens access to government records and thereby promote transparency and accountability in governance. It does not apply to private organisations directly, nor does it prohibit voluntary disclosure by public authorities. Its aim is to empower citizens in demanding accountability from the State.

45. The RTI Act specifies that a public authority must respond within 30 days of receiving a request. In urgent cases involving life or liberty of a person, the reply must be given within 48 hours, but the general timeframe remains 30 days.

46. A patriarchal society is one where men occupy the dominant position in family, social, and political life. It enforces male authority while subordinating women, limiting their roles and rights. The passage itself highlights that men are expected to be strong and successful, showing the dominance of male norms.

47. According to the passage, a gender-just society rests on two key elements: the presence of educated women with multiple roles and an improved sex ratio. These conditions create equality, dismantle rigid gender identities, and foster freedom for both men and women.

48. In patriarchal societies, men usually feel compelled to be strong and successful, as weakness or emotional expression is considered "unmanly." This reflects how patriarchal norms restrict men's own identities along with women's freedom.

49. The *Beti Bachao, Beti Padhao Yojana* is a government programme aiming to improve the status of girl children through awareness on education and prevention of female foeticide. It is therefore an initiative towards the actualisation of a gender-just society, not gender bias or mere symbolic changes.

50. In patriarchal societies, women are generally discriminated against in various spheres—economic, political, educational, and even within the household. They often have limited access to resources and opportunities, and their roles are subordinated to men.

Previous Years' Paper

Common University Entrance Test for UG Programmes

CUET-UG—GENERAL TEST

Entrance Exam, 2025

(Exam held on 27-05-2025)

Subject Code: 501

1. Jatin is ninth from the front in a column of boys. There were thrice as many behind him as there were in front. How many boys are there between Jatin and the fifth boy from the end of the column?

1. 33
2. 20
3. 21
4. 19

2. Earth Hour, the voluntary one hour blackout observed by 187 countries on 23rd day of March every year, to mark a battle against global warming, was first organized by which organization of the following:

1. Green Peace
2. World Health Organization
3. World Wildlife Fund for Nature
4. People for Ethical Treatment of Animals

3. Which one of the following is credited as the 'pioneer of rocket technology' in India?

1. Haider Ali
2. Sher Shah Suri
3. Tipu Sultan
4. Alauddin Khilji

4. C is to the East of B, which is to the North of D. If A is to the South of D, then in which general direction of C is A?

1. South
2. South-West
3. North
4. North-East

5. Earthquake refers to the vibration on the earth's surface caused by catastrophic endogenetic forces.

(A) The magnitude or intensity of energy released by an earthquake is not measured by the modified Mercalli Intensity Scale.

(B) The place on the ground surface which is perpendicular to the focus is called the epicenter.

(C) Seismology is the special branch of geology that deals with the study of earthquakes.

(D) Shadow zones are some specific areas where earthquake waves do not occur or occur rarely.

Choose the **correct** answer from the options given below:

1. (A), (B) and (D) only
2. (A), (C) and (D) only
3. (A), (B) and (C) only
4. (B), (C) and (D) only

6. A, B, C, D, E, F and G are sitting around a circular table facing the center. E is second to the right of F, who is sitting on the immediate right of C. A & D are the only persons sitting between G & E.

(A) B is third to the right of G.

(B) C is the immediate right of G.

(C) D is the immediate right of B.

(D) G is second to the left of F.

Choose the **correct** answer from the options given below:

1. (C) and (D) only
2. (A), (B) and (D) only
3. (A), (B) and (C) only
4. (A), (B), (C) and (D)

7. Arrange the sequence of national events in the order of their occurrence.

(A) Inauguration of Prerna Sthal.

(B) Droupadi Murmu takes oath as the 15th President of India.

(C) Karpoori Thakur, referred to as 'Jan Nayak', became the 49th recipient of the Bharat Ratna.

(D) India became the first country to prepare a full list of fauna, called 'Fauna of India'.

Choose the **correct** answer from the options given below:

1. (A), (B), (C), (D)
2. (B), (A), (D), (C)
3. (B), (C), (A), (D)
4. (C), (B), (D), (A)

1. 4 **2.** 3 **3.** 3 **4.** 2 **5.** 4 **6.** 2 **7.** 3

8. A trader sells wheat at 10% profit and uses weight 10% less than the actual measure. What is his actual percentage gain?

1. 18.18%   2. 20%
3. 22.22%   4. 10%

9. Choose the number which is different from the others.

1. 295   2. 552
3. 729   4. 906

10. Which of the following is called the 'Tiger of the Ganges' along with the distinction of being the 'National Aquatic Animal'?

1. Ghariyal   2. Dolphin
3. Royal Bengal Tiger   4. Hippopotamus

11. How many degrees will the hour hand move, in the time within which the minute hand moves 240°?

1. 20°   2. 18°
3. 24°   4. 22°

12. 'Amar Sonar Bangla', the national anthem of present day Bangladesh was written by which of the following poets?

1. Bankim Das Chatterjee
2. Rabindra Nath Tagore
3. Ashfaq Ullah Khan
4. Sarojini Naidu

13. Who among the following emperors fought the 'First Battle of Panipat'?

1. Babur and Sikandar Lodhi
2. Akbar and Hemu
3. Humayun and Sher Shah Suri
4. Babur and Ibrahim Lodhi

14. When seen through a mirror, an analog clock shows quarter to four. The correct time shows by the clock:

1. 9:15   2. 9:45
3. 8:15   4. 8:45

15. If the slant height of a cone is decreased by 15 per cent and the radius of its base is increased by 20 per cent, then by what per cent will its curved surface area change?

1. 2 per cent decrease
2. 2.5 per cent decrease
3. 2.5 per cent increase
4. 2 per cent increase

16. Match the following missions to their respective purposes:

List-I (Mission)	List-II (Purpose)
(A) Chandrayaan-3	(I) Development and launch of a dual-frequency synthetic aperture radar satellite
(B) Gaganyaan-3	(II) Attempt for soft landing on moon
(C) NISAR	(III) Solar Observatory Mission
(D) Aditya-L1	(IV) India's first crewed (human) space mission

Choose the **correct** answer from the options given below:

1. (A) - (II), (B) - (IV), (C) - (I), (D) - (III)
2. (A) - (I), (B) - (III), (C) - (II), (D) - (IV)
3. (A) - (IV), (B) - (I), (C) - (III), (D) - (II)
4. (A) - (III), (B) - (IV), (C) - (I), (D) - (II)

17. Manish is eighteenth from the right end and Rahul is fifth from the left end in a row of boys. If there are seven boys between Manish and Rahul, how many boys are there in the row?

1. 29   2. 30
3. 31   4. 41

18. The partition of Bengal in 1905 was realized during the Viceroyship of:

1. Lord Mountbatten
2. Lord Dalhousie
3. Lord Irwin
4. Lord Curzon

19. Trace out the figure, from among the following options, in which the figure (X) is embedded:

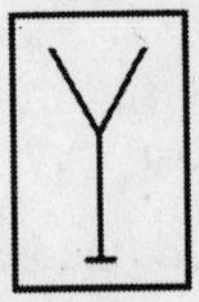

(X)

1. 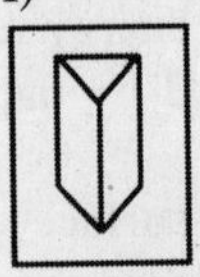   2. 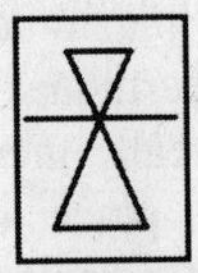

3.    4. 

8. 3	**9.** 1 & 3	**10.** 2	**11.** 1	**12.** 2	**13.** 4
14. 3	**15.** 4	**16.** 1	**17.** 2	**18.** 4	**19.** 4

20. A bag contains 3 red, 2 blue, 5 green and 4 yellow balls. If two balls are picked at random, what is the probability that either both are red or both are blue?

1. 1/7 2. 3/91
3. 4/91 4. 5/91

21. The sum of n terms of the series

$$1+\frac{3}{2}+2+\frac{5}{2}+3+\frac{7}{2}+\ldots\ldots$$

1. $\frac{n(n+1)}{2}$ 2. $\frac{n(n+3)}{4}$
3. $\frac{(n+1)(n+2)}{4}$ 4. $\frac{n(n+3)}{2}$

22. The component of the blood which helps to fight infections is:

1. Erythrocytes 2. Plasma
3. Platelets 4. Leukocytes

23. A boy travels between point A and point B at a speed of 6 km/h and returns at a speed of 9 km/h. If the total time taken by him is 1 hour 15 min, the distance between A and B is:

1. 6.5 km 2. 5.5 km
3. 4.5 km 4. 9 km

24. In the given question, a statement is followed by two assumptions. You have to decide which of the assumptions is implicit in the statement and choose your answer accordingly.

Statement: Over The Top (OTT) platform has become indispensable for the entertainment of people.

Assumptions:

I. People enjoy watching content on OTT.
II. OTT is the only medium of entertainment.

1. Only assumption II is implicit.
2. Only assumption I is implicit.
3. Both I and II are implicit.
4. Neither I nor II is implicit.

25. In the letter series, some of the letters are missing, which are given in the alternatives (A), (B), (C) and (D).

m n o n o p q o p q r _ _ _ _ s t u

(A) r (B) s
(C) q (D) p

Choose the **correct** sequence from the options given below:

1. (C), (B), (D), (A) 2. (A), (B), (C), (D)
3. (B), (A), (D), (C) 4. (B), (D), (C), (A)

26. The value of gravity (g) on the Moon is .... of that on the earth's surface.

1. 1/2 2. 1/3
3. 1/6 4. 1/9

27. In the given question, find out which of the following answer figures completes the figure matrix?

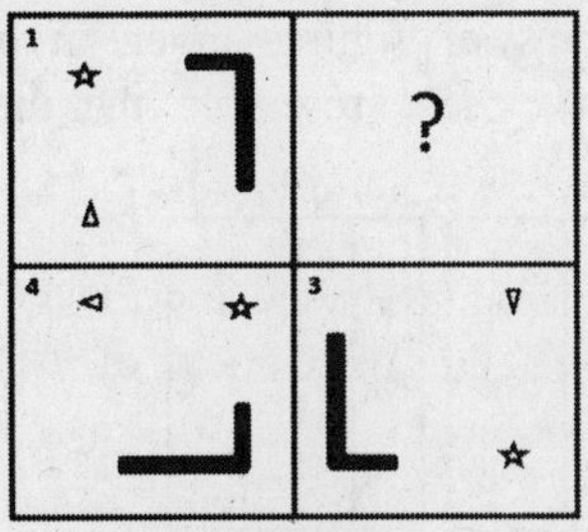

1. 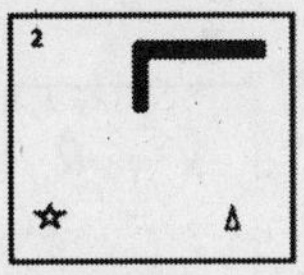
2. 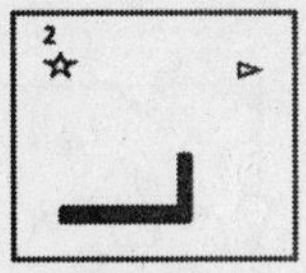
3. 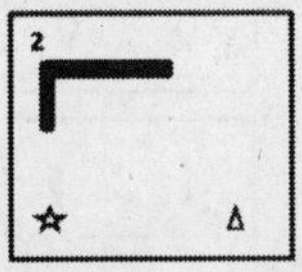
4. 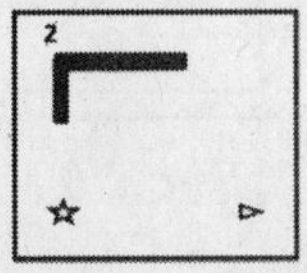

28. P and Q together can do a piece of work in 60 days. Q and R together can do it in 120 days. P and R together can do it in 90 days. In what time can Q alone do the same work?

1. 144 days 2. 720 days
3. 360 days 4. 720/7 days

29. Soap consists of:

1. Alkali salts of higher fatty acids
2. Calcium carbonate, aluminum silicate and gypsum
3. Sodium silicate and silicate of a base, like calcium or lead
4. Sodium silicate and ammonium nitrate

30. Match List-I with List-II.

List-I	List-II
(A) Remainder when 17^{35234} is divided by 8	(I) 0
(B) Remainder when 4444 is divided by 9	(II) 1
(C) Unit's digit of $(34)^{15}+(34)^{16}$	(III) 2
(D) Unit digit of 7^4-9^3	(IV) 7

Choose the **correct** answer from the options given below:

1. (A) - (II), (B) - (IV), (C) - (I), (D) - (III)
2. (A) - (I), (B) - (II). (C) - (III), (D) - (IV)
3. (A) - (II), (B) - (IV), (C) - (III), (D) - (I)
4. (A) - (IV), (B) - (II), (C) - (I), (D) - (III)

20. 3 **21.** 4 **22.** 4 **23.** 3 **24.** 2 **25.** 4 **26.** 3 **27.** 4 **28.** 1 **29.** 1 **30.** 1

31. The number of diagonals in a Hexagon is:

1. 6 2. 7
3. 8 4. 9

32. The figures X, Y and Z given below show a sequence of folding of paper. The fig. (Z) shows the manner in which the folded paper has been cut. Choose from the answer figures given in options which would most closely resemble the unfolded form of fig. (Z).

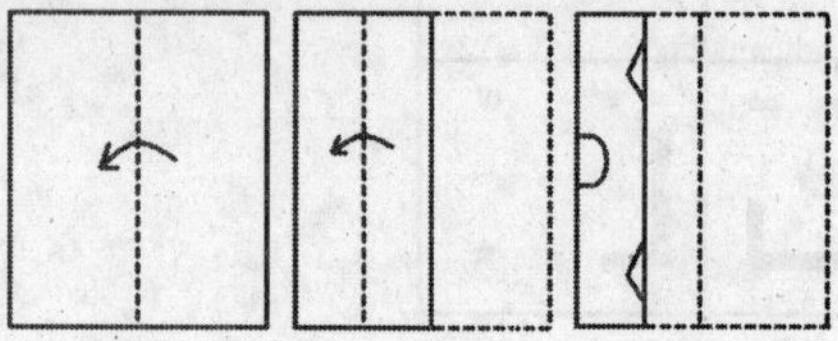

X Y Z

1. 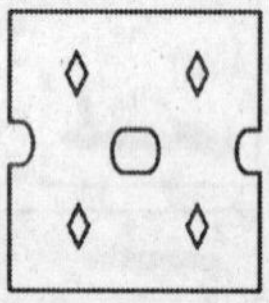 2. 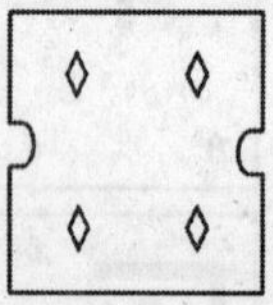

3. 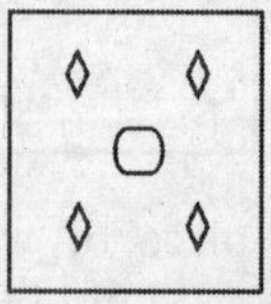 4. 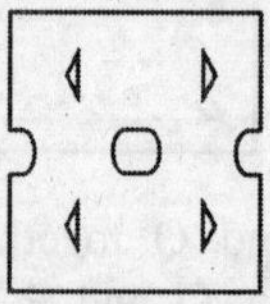

33. If the area of an equilateral triangle is $36\sqrt{3}$ cm^2, then the length of the side is:

1. 12 cm 2. 9 cm
3. 6 cm 4. 3 cm

34. Arrange the sequence of the stages of human progress in order of their occurrence.

(A) The Palaeolithic Age
(B) The Chalcolithic Age
(C) The Neolithic Age
(D) The Mesolithic Age

Choose the **correct** answer from the options given below:

1. (A), (B), (C), (D)
2. (B), (A), (D), (C)
3. (D), (A), (B), (C)
4. (A), (D), (C), (B)

35. Select a suitable figure from the answer figures which will substitute this question mark so that a series is formed in order.

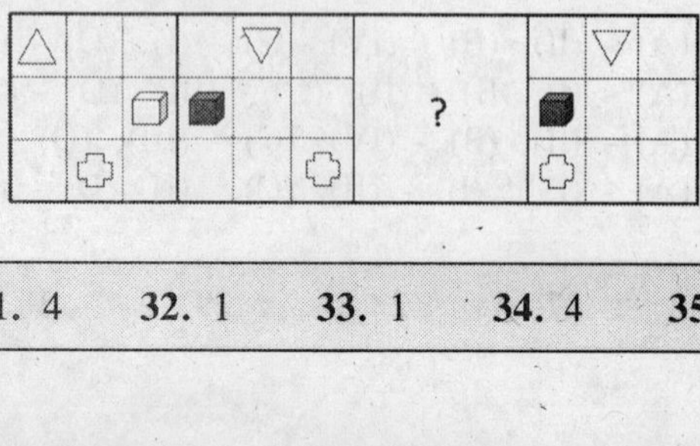

1. 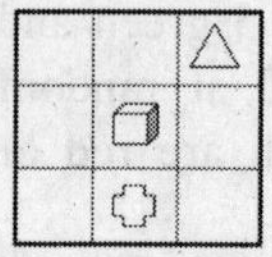 2. 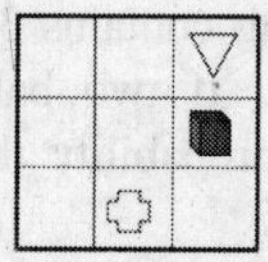

3. 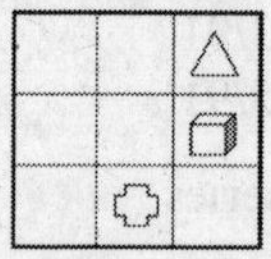 4. 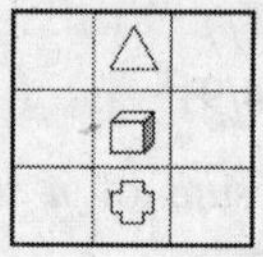

36. The sum of the digits of a 4-digit number is subtracted from the number. The resulting number is always:

1. divisible by 6 2. divisible by 9
3. divisible by 4 4. divisible by 8

37. Trace out the alternative figure from among the following options in which the figure (X) is embedded (rotation is not allowed):

(X)

1.  2. 

3.  4. 

38. 3 men or 15 boys can do a piece of work in 30 days. In how many days will 2 men and 5 boys do this work?

1. 15 days 2. 25 days
3. 30 days 4. 40 days

39. The nearest integer to 6650 which is exactly divisible by 429 is:

1. 6864 2. 6435
3. 6436 4. 6535

40. Which of the following nicknames would you most likely relate to Thailand?

1. Land of Thousand Elephants
2. Land of Morning Calm
3. Land of White Elephants
4. Land of Tigers

41. If 10% of X = 15% of Y = 1/5 of Z, then X : Y : Z is:

1. 6 : 3 : 4 2. 10 : 15 : 18
3. 15 : 10 : 18 4. 6 : 4 : 3

31. 4 **32.** 1 **33.** 1 **34.** 4 **35.** 3 **36.** 2 **37.** 2 **38.** 3 **39.** 1 **40.** 3 **41.** 4

42. In the given question, a statement is followed by two conclusions numbered I and II. You have to assume everything in the statement to be true, then consider the two conclusions together and decide which of them logically follows beyond a reasonable doubt from the information given in the statement.

Statement: Birds of same feather flock together.

Conclusions:

I. Similar people tend to associate with each other.
II. A group of birds have beautiful feathers.

1. Only conclusion I follows
2. Only conclusion II follows
3. Both I and II follow
4. Neither I nor II follows

43. Choose the correct water image of the given figure, amongst the following answer figures:

1. 
2. 
3. 
4. 

44. The relation between Mean, Median and Mode for symmetrical distribution is:

1. Mode = 2 Median – 5 Mean
2. Mode = 4 Median – Mean
3. Mean = Median = Mode
4. Mode = 2 Median = Mean

45. Which one of the following answer figures completes the figure matrix given below:

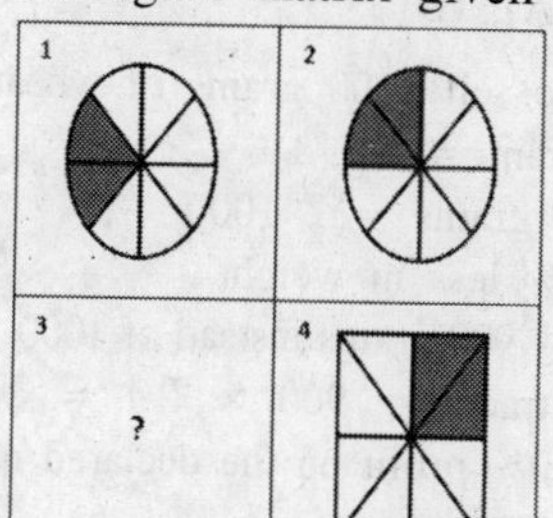

1. 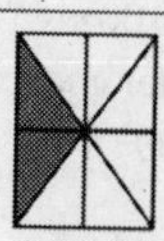
2. 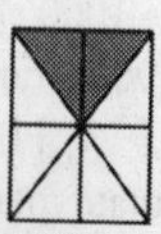
3. 
4. 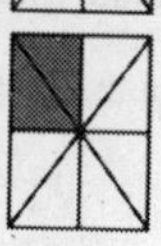

46. Mohiniyattam is a solo female dance form known for its rhythmic and unbroken flow of body movements.

(A) The love and devotion to god Vishnu is usually the theme of this dance form.
(B) This dance form belongs to the state of Andhra Pradesh.
(C) Mohiniyattam has the grace and elegance of Bharatanatyam and the vigor of Kathakali.
(D) The dancers attire in a beautiful white and gold bordered Kasavu sari with distinctive white jasmine flowers around a French bun at the side of her head.

Choose the **correct** answer from the options given below:

1. (A), (B) and (C) only
2. (A), (B) and (D) only
3. (A), (C) and (D) only
4. (B), (C) and (D) only

47. The question below consists of a question and two statements numbered I and II given below it. You have to decide whether the data provided in the statements is sufficient to answer the question.

The last Tuesday of February 2024 fell on which date?

I. The first Tuesday of that month fell on 6th.
II. The last day of that month was Thursday.

1. The data in the statement I alone is sufficient to answer the question.
2. The data in the statement II alone is sufficient to answer the question.
3. The data in both statements I and II together are necessary to answer the question.
4. The data either in statement I alone or in statement II alone are sufficient to answer the question.

48. By looking in a mirror, it appears that it is 6:05 on an analog clock. What is the actual time?

1. 11:30
2. 5:50
3. 5:55
4. 11:28

49. For what value of k, the system of equations $3x - ky - 3 = 0$ and $2x - 3y - 4 = 0$ has no solution?

1. 6
2. 9
3. 5
4. 9/2

50. Paris Olympics 2024 was held in the vicinity of which river?

1. Seine
2. Thames
3. Colorado
4. Nile

42. 1 **43.** 3 **44.** 3 **45.** 2 **46.** 3 **47.** 4 **48.** 3 **49.** 4 **50.** 1

EXPLANATORY ANSWERS

1. Jatin is 9th from the front, so there are 8 boys ahead of him. According to the question, the number of boys behind him is three times the number in front:
$8 \times 3 = 24$ boys behind Jatin.
Therefore, total number of boys
= 8 (in front) + 1 (Jatin himself) + 24 (behind)
= 33 boys.
The fifth boy from the end will be at position number $= 33 - 5 + 1 = 29$ from the front.
Jatin is 9th from the front.
The number of boys between Jatin (9th) and the fifth from end (29th) $= 29 - 9 - 1 = 19$ boys.

2. Earth Hour was first initiated by the World Wide Fund for Nature (WWF) in 2007 in Sydney, Australia. It is observed annually on the 23rd of March in over 180 countries, encouraging individuals, communities, and businesses to turn off non-essential lights for one hour to raise awareness about global warming and environmental conservation.

3. Tipu Sultan is regarded as the pioneer of rocket technology in India. He and his father Haider Ali developed iron-cased rockets which were used effectively during wars against the British, especially in the Anglo-Mysore wars. These Mysorean rockets influenced later European military rocket designs.

4. C is to the east of B, and B is to the north of D, so C is northeast of D. A is to the south of D.
Thus, from C's position (northeast of D), A would lie toward the southwest.
Hence, A is in the south-west direction from C.

5. (B), (C) and (D) only
(A) is incorrect because the Modified Mercalli Intensity Scale does measure the intensity of shaking, not magnitude, so the statement is factually wrong.
(B) is correct: the epicenter is the point on the earth's surface directly above the earthquake's focus.
(C) is correct: seismology is the branch of geology that studies earthquakes.
(D) is correct: shadow zones are regions where seismic waves are not recorded due to the wave refraction and absorption patterns inside Earth.

6. We are given:
- E is second to the right of F,
- F is sitting on the immediate right of C,
- A and D are the only persons sitting between G and E.

Let's fix positions clockwise using the given information.
Start by placing C at position P1, then:
- F is to the immediate right of C ⇒ F at P2
- E is second to the right of F ⇒ E at P4

So far:

P1 – C	P2 – F
P3 – (unknown)	P4 – E

Now use the clue: A and D are the only persons sitting between G and E.
So G _ A D _ E (clockwise), placing A and D between G and E.
Try placing:
- E at P4
- Then P5 = A, P6 = D, P7 = G

Now filled:

P1 – C	P2 – F
P3 – B (only person left)	P4 – E
P5 – A	P6 – D
P7 – G	

Complete clockwise arrangement:
C – F – B – E – A – D – G
Now check each option:
(A) B is third to the right of G
From G (P7), count clockwise:
1st = C (P1), 2nd = F (P2), 3rd = B (P3) ⇒ True
(B) C is immediate right of G
From G (P7), immediate right is P1 = C ⇒ True
(C) D is immediate right of B
From B (P3), immediate right is P4 = E ⇒ False
(D) G is second to the left of F
From F (P2), moving left:
1st left = C (P1), 2nd left = G (P7) ⇒ True
So, only (A), (B), and (D) are correct.
Answer: 2: (A), (B) and (D) only.

7. Let's arrange the events with year:
(B) Droupadi Murmu became President in July 2022
(C) Karpoori Thakur awarded Bharat Ratna in Januar[y] 2024
(A) Prerna Sthal inaugurated in February 2024
(D) 'Fauna of India' list launched in March 2024
Correct sequence of occurrence:
(B) → (C) → (A) → (D)
Answer: 3: (B), (C), (A), (D).

8. Let the trader claims to sell 1000 grams of wheat.
Cost Price (CP) per gram = Re. 1
So, actual CP of 1000 grams = ₹ 1000
However, he gives 10% less in weight.
That means he gives only 900 grams instead of 1000 gram[s]
So, actual cost to the trader = 900 × ₹ 1 = ₹ 900
He sells the wheat at 10% profit on the declared quanti[ty] (1000 grams), not on actual.
So, SP = 1000 × ₹ 1 × (1 + 10/100) = ₹ 1100
Thus, for 900 grams of wheat, the trader receives ₹ 11[00]
His gain = ₹ 1100 – ₹ 900 = ₹ 200
Now calculate percentage gain:

$$\text{Percentage gain} = \frac{\text{Gain}}{\text{Actual CP}} \times 100 = \frac{200}{900} \times 100$$

$$= 22.22\%.$$

9. This question allows for two valid interpretations, ea[ch] highlighting a different number as the odd one out bas[ed] on distinct logical reasoning:

Logic 1 – Perfect Power Logic:

- 729 is a perfect cube (9^3) and also a perfect sixth power (3^6), making it unique among the given numbers.
- 295, 552, and 906 are not perfect squares, cubes, or higher powers.

So, 729 stands out due to its special mathematical structure.

Logic 2 – Divisibility by 5:

- 295 ends in 5 ⇒ divisible by 5.
- 552, 729, and 906 do not end in 0 or 5, so they are not divisible by 5.

Thus, 295 is the only number in the group divisible by 5.

Since both logics are equally valid and highlight different numbers, both 295 and 729 are correct answers, depending on the reasoning applied.

Answer: 1 and 3: 295 and 729.

10. The Ganges River Dolphin is referred to as the 'Tiger of the Ganges' due to its importance in the river ecosystem. It is also officially declared as the National Aquatic Animal of India by the Government.

11. The minute hand of a clock moves 6° per minute (360° in 60 minutes).

To move 240°, time taken = 240 ÷ 6 = 40 minutes.

The hour hand moves 0.5° per minute (360° in 12 hours = 0.5° per minute).

So, in 40 minutes, hour hand moves = 0.5 × 40 = 20°.

12. 'Amar Sonar Bangla' is the national anthem of Bangladesh. It was written by Rabindra Nath Tagore in 1905 during the Swadeshi movement, as a protest against the partition of Bengal by the British. The first ten lines of this song were adopted as the national anthem by Bangladesh in 1971.

13. The First Battle of Panipat took place in 1526 between Babur, the founder of the Mughal Empire, and Ibrahim Lodhi, the last ruler of the Delhi Sultanate.

Babur's victory marked the beginning of Mughal rule in India and the end of the Lodhi dynasty.

14. When a clock shows 3:45 in the mirror, the actual time is calculated by subtracting from 12:00.

12:00 – 3:45 = 8:15

Therefore, the actual time shown by the clock is 8:15.

15. Curved Surface Area (CSA) of a cone

$= \pi \times r \times l$

Let original radius = 100, slant height = 100

Original CSA $= \pi \times 100 \times 100 = 10000\pi$

New radius = 100 + 20% = 120

New slant height = 100 – 15% = 85

New CSA $= \pi \times 120 \times 85 = 10200\pi$

$$\% \text{ change} = \frac{10200 - 10000}{10000} \times 100 = 2\%$$

So, the curved surface area increases by 2%.

16. Let's match the missions correctly:

(A) Chandrayaan-3 → (II) Attempt for soft landing on the moon: Chandrayaan-3 was ISRO's mission to achieve a successful soft landing on the Moon. It succeeded in August 2023.

(B) Gaganyaan-3 → (IV) India's first crewed (human) space mission: Gaganyaan aims to send Indian astronauts (Gagannauts) into space. Gaganyaan-3 is part of this human spaceflight programme.

(C) NISAR → (I) Development and launch of a dual-frequency synthetic aperture radar satellite: NISAR (NASA-ISRO Synthetic Aperture Radar) is a joint Earth observation mission with a dual-frequency radar for climate and disaster monitoring.

(D) Aditya-L1 → (III) Solar Observatory Mission: Aditya-L1 is India's first solar mission, launched to study the Sun's outer atmosphere (corona and solar wind).

Answer: 1: (A) – (II), (B) – (IV), (C) – (I), (D) – (III).

17. Given:

- Manish is 18th from the right end
- Rahul is 5th from the left end
- 7 boys are between them

So, total boys = (Position of Manish from right) + (Position of Rahul from left) + (Number of boys between them) = 18 + 5 + 7 = 30.

18. The Partition of Bengal was carried out in 1905 during the viceroyalty of Lord Curzon. The stated purpose was administrative efficiency, but it was widely seen as an attempt to divide and weaken nationalist sentiments in Bengal. The partition was strongly opposed and later annulled in 1911.

19. The given figure (X) is a "Y" shaped structure — it consists of a vertical line with two diverging arms at the top, forming a symmetric "Y".

Now let's carefully examine each option:

- **Option 1:** Contains a combination of hexagonal lines and verticals, but the structure does not form a Y shape. *(Incorrect)*
- **Option 2:** Has intersecting triangles forming an hourglass or "X" shape, which is not similar to figure (X). *(Incorrect)*
- **Option 3:** Shows a triangle with internal divisions but does not clearly form a Y-shaped structure. The lines do not match the alignment of figure (X). *(Incorrect)*
- **Option 4:** If you closely observe the center, you can clearly identify the "Y" shape embedded within. It consists of a vertical line with two lines diverging upwards, exactly as in figure (X). *(Correct)*

Therefore, figure (X) is correctly embedded in Option 4.

20. Total number of balls in the bag

= 3 red + 2 blue + 5 green + 4 yellow = 14 balls

We are required to find the probability that either both balls are red or both are blue when two balls are drawn at random.

Total number of ways to choose 2 balls out of 14

$$= {}^{14}C_2 = \frac{14 \times 13}{2} = 91$$

Now, Number of ways to choose 2 red balls $= {}^3C_2 = 3$

Number of ways to choose 2 blue balls $= {}^2C_2 = 1$

So, favourable outcomes = 3 + 1 = 4

Therefore, required probability = **4/91.**

21. The given series is: $1+\frac{3}{2}+2+\frac{5}{2}+3+\frac{7}{2}+...$

Observe the pattern:

- Odd-positioned terms: 1, 2, 3, … form an arithmetic sequence of natural numbers
- Even-positioned terms: $\frac{3}{2}, \frac{5}{2}, \frac{7}{2}$, … also form an arithmetic sequence

Let's calculate the sum of first few terms and test the formulas:

For $n = 1 : 1 \rightarrow$ Sum = 1

Check Option 2:

$$1\times\frac{1+3}{2} = \frac{4}{2} = 2 \rightarrow \textit{(Incorrect)}$$

$n = 2$: $1+\frac{3}{2} = \frac{5}{2}$

Option 2: $2\times\frac{2+3}{2} = 2\times\frac{5}{2} = 5 \rightarrow$ *(Incorrect)*

$$n = 4: \quad 1+\frac{3}{2}+2+\frac{5}{2} = \left(\frac{1}{2}\right)+\left(\frac{3}{2}\frac{5}{2}\right)$$

$$= 3 + 4 = 7$$

Option 2: $4\times\frac{4+3}{2} = 4\times\frac{7}{2} = 14 = 14 \rightarrow$ *(Correct)*

$$n = 5: \quad 1+\frac{3}{2}+2+\frac{5}{2}+3 = (1+2+3)+\frac{3}{2}+\frac{5}{2}$$

$$= 6 + 4 = 10$$

Option 2: $5\times\frac{5+3}{2} = 5\times\frac{8}{2} = 20 \rightarrow$ *(Correct)*

Hence, the formula that correctly represents the sum of n terms of the series is: $\frac{n(n+3)}{2}$.

22. The component of blood that helps in fighting infections is known as Leukocytes, or white blood cells (WBCs). They are part of the immune system and function to identify and destroy harmful pathogens like bacteria, viruses, and other foreign invaders.

Other options:

- **Erythrocytes (RBCs):** Carry oxygen
- **Plasma:** Transport medium for cells and nutrients
- **Platelets:** Help in blood clotting

Only leukocytes have the defensive role against infections.

23. Let the distance between A and B be x km.

Time taken to go from A to B at 6 km/h = $\frac{x}{6}$ hours

Time taken to return from B to A at 9 km/h = $\frac{x}{9}$ hours

$$\text{Total time} = 1 \text{ hour } 15 \text{ minutes}$$

$$= 1.25 \text{ hours}$$

So, $\frac{x}{6}+\frac{x}{9} = 1.25$

Take LCM of 6 and 9 = 18

$$\frac{3x+2x}{18} = 1.25 \Rightarrow \frac{5x}{18} = 1.25$$

$$\Rightarrow x = \frac{1.25\times18}{5} = \frac{22.5}{5} = 4.5$$

Therefore, the distance between A and B is 4.5 km.

24. Statement: "Over The Top (OTT) platform has become indispensable for the entertainment of people."

- **Assumption I:** People enjoy watching content on OTT — Implicit, because unless people find OTT entertaining, it wouldn't be considered indispensable.
- **Assumption II:** OTT is the only medium of entertainment — Not implicit, as the statement says OTT is indispensable, not exclusive.

Only the first assumption logically follows from the statement. Answer: 2: Only assumption I is implicit.

25. Given sequence:

m n o | n o p | q o p | q r _ _ _ _ s t u

Break the series into overlapping trios:

- m n o
- n o p
- o p q
- p q r
- q r s
- r s t
- s t u

So, missing letters after "q r" must be:

s, t, p, q ⇒ But needs to fit full letter structure.

However, based on the pattern, after "q r", the correct 4-letter gap to reach "s t u" should be:

s, t, u, v, but that conflicts.

Let's look again:

From "m n o", next trio = shift one forward each time:

n o p

o p q

p q r

q r s

r s t

s t u

So the missing letters are: s, t, u, v — but since the sequence given already ends at "s t u", the missing 4 letters just before that are: r, s, t, u

Therefore: The missing letters are: (B) s, (D) p, (C) q, (A) r.

But reordered correctly, matching pattern: (B), (D), (C), (A).

26. The gravitational acceleration on the Moon is approximately 1/6th of that on Earth.

- Earth's gravity ≈ 9.8 m/s^2
- Moon's gravity ≈ 1.63 m/s^2

$$\frac{1.63}{9.8} \approx \frac{1}{6}$$

27. To solve this figure matrix, let's analyze both shapes and symbols row-wise and column-wise.

Step 1: Analyze arrow shapes (thick L-shapes):

- In the first row, images (1) and (2) both have an L-shape rotated differently.
- In the second row, images (4) and (3) also have L-shapes in different orientations.

Now observe the positions of the thick L-shapes:

- From left to right in the top row: shape rotates 90° clockwise from 1 to 2.

- From left to right in the bottom row: shape rotates 90° clockwise from 4 to 3.

So, following the same logic, the L-shape in the missing figure (top right) must be a 90° clockwise rotation of the shape in cell (2).

Looking at cell (2), the shape is a vertical L. Its 90° clockwise rotation is the horizontal L found in option 4.

Step 2: Analyze the small symbols (triangle, star, etc.):

Each box contains a triangle and a star, and their positions also follow a consistent diagonal symmetry or shifting across rows/columns.

Following the same position trend of symbols (as seen in cells 1, 2, 3, and 4), the triangle and star in the missing cell match the placement seen in option 4.

Thus, both the thick L-shape and the symbol positions match in option 4.

28. Let the total work be 1 unit.

We are given:

- P and Q together can complete the work in 60 days $\Rightarrow$ (P + Q)'s 1-day work = 1/60
- Q and R together can complete the work in 120 days $\Rightarrow$ (Q + R)'s 1-day work = 1/120
- P and R together can complete the work in 90 days $\Rightarrow$ (P + R)'s 1-day work = 1/90

Now, add all three equations:

$$(P + Q) + (Q + R) + (P + R) = \frac{1}{60}+\frac{1}{120}+\frac{1}{90}$$

$$\Rightarrow \quad 2(P + Q + R) = \text{LCM of } 60, 120, 90 = 360$$

Convert each to a common denominator:

$$\frac{1}{60} = \frac{6}{360};\ \frac{1}{120} = \frac{3}{360};\ \frac{1}{90} = \frac{4}{360}$$

$$\Rightarrow \quad \text{Sum} = \frac{6+3+4}{360} = \frac{13}{360}$$

$$\text{So,} \quad 2(P + Q + R) = \frac{13}{360}$$

$$\Rightarrow \quad P + Q + R = \frac{13}{720}$$

Now subtract (P + R)'s work to get Q's work:

$$Q = (P + Q + R) - (P + R)$$

$$= \frac{13}{720}-\frac{1}{90}$$

Convert 1/90 to denominator 720:

$$\frac{1}{90} = \frac{8}{720} \Rightarrow Q = \frac{13-8}{720} = \frac{5}{720}$$

Therefore, Q alone can complete the work in:

$$= \frac{720}{5} = 144 \text{ days.}$$

29. Soap is formed by saponification, where alkali (such as NaOH or KOH) reacts with fatty acids or triglycerides. This forms alkali salts of higher fatty acids, which we commonly call soap.

Other options refer to ingredients used in glass, ceramics, or fertilizers.

30. Let's solve each part of List-I and match with the correct element from List-II:

(A) Remainder when $17^{(35234)}$ is divided by 8:

Use modulo patterns.

Since $17 \equiv 1 \pmod 8$, then $17^n \equiv 1^n \equiv 1 \pmod 8$ for any n.

$\Rightarrow$ Remainder = 1 $\rightarrow$ Matches with (II)

(B) Remainder when 4^{4444} is divided by 9:

Powers of 4 modulo 9 cycle as:

$$4^1 \equiv 4 \pmod 9$$
$$4^2 \equiv 7 \pmod 9$$
$$4^3 \equiv 1 \pmod 9$$

Cycle: 4, 7, 1 (length 3)

Now, 4444 $\div$ 3 gives remainder 1

$\Rightarrow$ So, $4^{4444} \equiv 4^1 \equiv 4 \pmod 9$ $\rightarrow$ Matches with (IV)

(C) Unit digit of $(34)^{15}$ + $(34)^{16}$:

Look at unit digit pattern of 4:

$$4^1 = 4$$
$$4^2 = 16 \rightarrow \text{unit digit } 6$$

Cycle: 4, 6 (length 2)

For 4^{15} $\rightarrow$ odd $\Rightarrow$ unit digit = 4

For 4^{16} $\rightarrow$ even $\Rightarrow$ unit digit = 6

Sum = 4 + 6 = 10 $\Rightarrow$ Unit digit = 0 $\rightarrow$ Matches with (I)

(D) Unit digit of $7^4 - 9^3$:

7^4: powers cycle $\rightarrow$ 7, 9, 3, 1 $\Rightarrow$ 7^4 $\Rightarrow$ unit digit = 1

9^3: powers cycle $\rightarrow$ 9, 1 $\Rightarrow$ 9^3 $\Rightarrow$ unit digit = 9

Now 1 − 9 = -8 $\Rightarrow$ take unit digit = 2

$\rightarrow$ Matches with (III)

Correct matching: (1): (A)-II), (B)-(IV), (C)-(I), (D)-(III).

31. Formula for number of diagonals in an n-sided polygon $= \frac{n(n-3)}{2}$

For a hexagon (n = 6): $= \frac{6(6-3)}{2} = 6 \times \frac{3}{2} = 9$.

32. Let's analyze the folding and cutting step by step:

- **Figure X:** The paper is first folded vertically in half, from left to right.
- **Figure Y:** Then the paper is again folded vertically from right to left, making a total of two vertical folds. So, the paper is folded into quarters (1/4th of its original width).
- **Figure Z:** Shows cuts made on the folded paper: One semicircular cut on the vertical edge (middle of the folded sheet)

  Two diamond-shaped cuts at the top and bottom

Now, when the paper is unfolded, the cuts will mirror along both fold lines.

- The semicircular cut, made at the center fold, will mirror to form two symmetrical semicircles on either side, resulting in two full circular notches on the middle of left and right edges.
- The diamond cuts on the folded sheet will replicate four times upon full unfolding (mirroring across both folds).

Among the options:

- Option 1 shows:
  4 diamond shapes — correctly placed due to mirroring
  2 semicircular edge notches — correct as per the central vertical cut

Thus, the unfolded paper must look like Option 1.

33. We are given that the area of an equilateral triangle is:

$36\sqrt{3}\ \text{cm}^2$

The formula for the area of an equilateral triangle with side length aaa is:

$$\text{Area} = \frac{\sqrt{3}}{4}a^2$$

Substitute the given area into the formula:

$$\frac{\sqrt{3}}{4}a^2 = 36\sqrt{3}$$

Divide both sides by $\sqrt{3}$:

$$\frac{1}{4}a^2 = 36$$

Multiply both sides by 4: $a^2 = 144$

Take the square root of both sides: $a = \sqrt{144} = 12$

Therefore, the length of each side of the equilateral triangle is 12 cm.

34. The correct chronological order of the prehistoric ages of human progress is:

(A) Palaeolithic Age – Old Stone Age: beginning of human tools and hunting

(D) Mesolithic Age – Middle Stone Age: transition phase, microliths used

(C) Neolithic Age – New Stone Age: agriculture, domestication begins

(B) Chalcolithic Age – Copper-Stone Age: early use of metal tools

Therefore, the correct sequence is:

Palaeolithic → Mesolithic → Neolithic → Chalcolithic.

35. Let's analyze the movement and transformation of the three elements in the figure across the series from left to right:

Top row (Triangle) – 1st Item:

Pattern:

- It moves one step forward in each frame (left to right)
- It also alternates its orientation (inverted every time)

Sequence:

1. ▲ in column 1
2. ▼ in column 2
3. ▲ in column 3
4. ? → should be in column 4 and inverted ⇒ ▼
5. ▼ in column 5
6. ?

So, triangle in column 4, facing downward (▼)

Middle row (Cube) – 2nd Item:

Pattern:

- Moves 2 steps at a time, alternating forward and backward
- Also alternates color between white and black

Sequence (position and colour):

1. White cube in column 2
2. Black cube in column 3 (→ moved forward 1 step, and changed colour)
3. ? → Now should move 2 steps back, from column 3 → column 1, and colour switches to white
4. Then black cube reappears in column 2 in the next image

So, cube should be white, placed in column 1

Bottom row (Plus symbol) – 3rd Item:

Pattern:

- Remains in same shape and colour, and moves 1 step forward each time

Sequence:

1. **Column 3**
2. **Column 4**
3. **Column 5**

So, in the missing frame, it should be in column 6

But we are to find the missing figure before that — so before it reaches column 5, it was in column 4

→ It must be in column 4 in the missing image

Final Expected Configuration:

- Top row: ▼ in column 4
- Middle row: White cube in column 1
- Bottom row: White plus in column 4

Check which option matches:

Option 3 shows:

- ▼ (triangle) in column 4
- White cube in column 1
- White cross in column 4

Perfect match.

36. Let the 4-digit number be represented as N.

Let the sum of its digits be S.

We are given: The number N – S is always divisible by a certain number.

General Rule: For any number, if you subtract the sum of its digits from the number itself, the result is always divisible by 9.

Why? Let's prove it algebraically:

Let the number be:

$N = 1000a + 100b + 10c + d$ where a, b, c, d are the digits of the number

Sum of digits $= a + b + c + d = S$

Then,

$N - S = (1000a + 100b + 10c + d) - (a + b + c + d)$
$= 999a + 99b + 9c$

Each term on the right-hand side is divisible by 9:

$999a = 9 \times 111a,\ 99b = 9 \times 11b,\ 9c = 9 \times c$

Hence, $N - S$ is divisible by 9

This is a known divisibility property for all whole numbers.

37. We are given a base figure (X), which consists of two intersecting thin lines forming an 'X' shape, where each line has a small outward bend at its ends. The figure is formed by two clean, curved strokes crossing each other. The task is to identify which of the given options contain this exact figure embedded without rotation.

Let's analyze each option carefully:

Option 1:

- Contains thick, straight overlapping bands.
- The structure is geometrically rigid and lacks the distinctive outward curves found in figure (X).
- No accurate embedding of (X) is observed.

Not a match.

Option 2:

- Among all the lines in the structure, the inner intersecting lines are thin and angled, matching the curved outward strokes of figure (X).
- These lines exactly replicate the direction, style, and bending of figure (X) without rotation.

Perfect match

Option 3:

- Composed of thick, diagonal strips with squared ends.
- The distinctive curving ends of figure (X) are not present.
- The lines do not replicate the gentle bend seen in (X).

Not a match

Option 4:

- Similar to Option 3, features wide angular bands.
- No visible trace of the specific curve-ended X shape from figure (X).

Not a match

Hence, only Option 2 correctly embeds figure (X) without rotation and preserves the exact style, shape, and orientation of the curved intersecting lines.

38. We are given:

3 men or 15 boys can complete the work in 30 days.

From this, we calculate total work:

Work = 3 men × 30 days = 90 men-days

This is the same as 15 boys × 30 days = 450 boys-days

We are asked: In how many days will 2 men and 5 boys complete the same work?

Let's convert all workers into a common unit, say man-days:

From the given, 3 men = 15 boys ⇒ 1 man = 5 boys

So, 1 boy = 1/5 man

Now, 2 men = 2 man

5 boys = 5 × (1/5) = 1 man

Total workforce = 2 + 1 = 3 men

Therefore, 2 men and 5 boys together are equivalent to 3 men, and since 3 men can do the work in 30 days, 2 men and 5 boys will also complete the work in 30 days.

39. We are asked to find the nearest integer to 6650 that is exactly divisible by 429.

Step 1: Divide 6650 by 429

$$6650 \div 429 \approx 15.5$$

So, the two closest multiples of 429 are:

- 429 × 15 = 6435
- 429 × 16 = 6864

Step 2: Compare both with 6650:

- |6650 − 6435| = 215
- |6864 − 6650| = 214

Since 6864 is only 214 away and 6435 is 215 away, 6864 is numerically closer to 6650.

Also, both 6435 and 6864 are divisible by 429, but the question specifically asks for the nearest such number. Among the options, Option 1 is 6864, which is the correct choice.

40. Thailand is commonly referred to as the "Land of White Elephants." This nickname comes from the cultural and historical reverence for white elephants in Thai royal traditions.

Other options:

- Land of Thousand Elephants = Laos
- Land of Morning Calm = South Korea
- Land of Tigers = India (also used loosely for Southeast Asia)

Answer: 3: Land of White Elephants.

41. Given: 10% of X = 15% of Y = 1/5 of Z

Let the common value be k

Then, $10X/100 = k \Rightarrow X = 10k$

$15Y/100 = k \Rightarrow Y = (20k)/3$

$(1/5)Z = k \Rightarrow Z = 5k$

Now find the ratio X : Y : Z

$X = 10k,\ Y = 20k/3,\ Z = 5k$

Now take LCM of denominators (1 and 3): Multiply all by 3:

$X : Y : Z = 30k : 20k : 15k$

Now divide all by 5: = 6 : 4 : 3.

42. Statement: "Birds of same feather flock together."

Meaning: People who are similar in nature or interests stick together.

- Conclusion I: Similar people tend to associate with each other → *True*
- Conclusion II: A group of birds have beautiful feathers → *This is not implied*

Only the first conclusion logically follows.

43. We are asked to find the water image of the given figure — this is a vertical reflection over a horizontal axis. In a water image:

- The top and bottom elements swap places.
- The left and right sides remain unchanged.
- All shapes are also inverted vertically.

Let's break down the original figure (from top to bottom):

- **Top-left:** Small black square
- **Top-right:** White triangle pointing upwards
- **Center:** Spade pointing upwards with a downward-pointing triangle inside it
- **Bottom-center:** (None visible in original, triangle is at the base of the spade)

Applying the water image transformation:

1. Black square (top-left) → moves to bottom-left, remains black square
2. White triangle (top-right, pointing up) → moves to bottom-right, becomes downward-pointing
3. Spade with triangle:
   Spade inverts → now points downward
   Internal triangle (was pointing down) → now becomes pointing up
4. No new elements appear at the top

Now check the options:

- Option 1: Spade triangle is still downward → *(Incorrect)*
- Option 2: White triangle on bottom-right is pointing up → *(Incorrect)*
- Option 3: Spade is correctly inverted
  Internal triangle is now upward — *(Correct)*
  Black square is at bottom-left — *(Correct)*
  White triangle is at bottom-right, pointing downward — *(Correct)*

  Matches all water image rules
- Option 4: Black square is misplaced, triangle is on the wrong side — *(Incorrect)*.

44. In a symmetrical distribution, particularly a normal distribution (bell-shaped curve), the values of Mean, Median, and Mode are all equal and located at the center of the distribution. This is a fundamental property of symmetric distributions, where the data is evenly distributed around a central value.

So, Mean = Median = Mode

This condition does not hold for skewed distributions, but for symmetrical ones, it is always true.

45. We are given a 2 × 2 matrix of figures, where the top row contains circular figures and the bottom row contains square figures, all divided into 8 equal sectors.

Our task is to identify the logical relationship between the figures and determine which figure correctly completes the missing position (Box 3).

Step 1: Analyze the top row (Figures 1 and 2)

- **Figure 1 (Top-Left Circle):** Two adjacent sectors are shaded – they occupy the top-left and bottom-left positions (forming a vertical block on the left side).
- **Figure 2 (Top-Right Circle):** The shaded block has moved one sector clockwise. Now the shaded sectors are in the top-right and bottom-right.

So, the rule in the top row is: "Two adjacent sectors are shaded, and in the next figure, the pair shifts one position clockwise."

Step 2: Analyze Figure 4 (Bottom-Right Square)

- Figure 4 has two adjacent shaded sectors in the square – they are in the top-left and top-right.

To follow the same rule as the top row but in reverse, we should now move one sector backward (counter-clockwise) to determine the shading in Figure 3 (the missing figure).

So, if in Figure 4 the shaded sectors are:

- Top-left and top-right (adjacent on the top side), then in the previous step (Figure 3), the shaded sectors must have been:
- Left and top-left, which is one step back counter-clockwise.

Step 3: Find the matching option

Look for the option where the square has two adjacent shaded sectors in the left and top-left positions.

Option 2 matches this exactly.

46. Let's evaluate each statement:

(A) "The love and devotion to god Vishnu is usually the theme of this dance form."

Correct. Mohiniyattam is based on themes of love and devotion, often associated with Lord Vishnu, especially his female form Mohini, making this statement accurate.

(B) "This dance form belongs to the state of Andhra Pradesh."

Incorrect. Mohiniyattam is a classical dance form of Kerala, not Andhra Pradesh.

(C) "Mohiniyattam has the grace and elegance of Bharatanatyam and the vigor of Kathakali."

Correct. It blends the elegance and lasya (grace) of Bharatanatyam with the drama and energy of Kathakali, both of which are classical dance forms of South India.

(D) "The dancer's attire in a beautiful white and gold bordered Kasavu sari with jasmine flowers..."

Correct. This description accurately reflects the traditional costume worn in Mohiniyattam performances.

Hence, only statements (A), (C), and (D) are correct.

47. The data either in statement I alone or in statement II alone are sufficient to answer the question.

Question: What was the date of the last Tuesday in February 2024?

Statement I: The first Tuesday was on 6th February 2024.

If 6th is Tuesday, then subsequent Tuesdays are:

13th, 20th, and 27th ⇒ So, last Tuesday = 27th February

Statement I alone is sufficient.

Statement II: The last day of February 2024 was Thursday.

2024 is a leap year, so February has 29 days.

If 29th is Thursday, then 27th was Tuesday ⇒ Last Tuesday = 27th February

Statement II alone is also sufficient.

Thus, either statement alone is enough to answer the question.

48. To find the actual time from a mirror image of an analog clock, subtract the given time from 11:60.

Given mirror time = 6:05

Real time = 11:60 – 6:05 = 5:55

So, the actual time is 5:55.

49. We are given two equations:

1. $3x - ky = 3$ 2. $2x - 3y = 4$

The condition for no solution in a system of linear equations is:

$$\frac{a_1}{a_2} = \frac{b_1}{b_2} \neq \frac{c_1}{c_2}$$

Let's apply: $\frac{3}{2} = \frac{k}{3} \Rightarrow k = \frac{3 \times 3}{2} = \frac{9}{2}$

Now check: $\frac{3}{2} = \frac{9/2}{3} = \frac{3}{2}$ But $\frac{-3}{-4} = \frac{3}{4} \neq \frac{3}{2}$

So, the condition is satisfied when $k = 9/2$.

50. The Paris Olympics 2024 are being held in venues located along and near the River Seine, which flows through the heart of Paris, France. Major events and even the opening ceremony are planned along this river.

Previous Years' Paper

Common University Entrance Test for UG Programmes

CUET (UG) B.A. (H.) Political Science/ B.A. (H.) History Entrance Exam, 2024*

ENGLISH

1. Re-arrange the following phrases in the right sequence to form a meaningful sentence.

(*a*) for seven hours but was hardly

(*b*) because of the absence of any motivation

(*c*) able to decide who the murderer was

(*d*) she worked on the case

Choose the **correct** answer from the options given below

A. (*a*), (*c*), (*d*), (*b*) B. (*d*), (*a*), (*c*), (*b*)

C. (*d*), (*c*), (*b*), (*a*) D. (*a*), (*b*), (*c*), (*d*)

2. Fill in the blank with the **correct** option.

The candidate assured the interviewers that the dip in her grades during her second semester was an ____ since she had always been a top scorer in the first semester.

A. anomaly B. allay

C. adage D. abatement

3. Match the words in List-I with their definitions in List-II.

List-I (Words)	List-II (Definitions)
(*a*) Theocracy	I. One who keeps drugs for sale and puts up prescriptions
(*b*) Megalomania	II. One who collects and studies objects or artistic works from the distant past
(*c*) Apothecary	III. A government by divine guidance or religious leaders
(*d*) Antiquarian	IV. A morbid delusion of one's power, importance or godliness

Choose the **correct** answer from the options given below:

	(*a*)	(*b*)	(*c*)	(*d*)
A.	III	IV	I	II
B.	IV	III	II	I
C.	I	III	IV	II
D.	III	IV	II	I

4. Fill in the blank with the **correct** option.

A small ______ between two children ended up as a group fight.

A. altercation B. match

C. contest D. race

5. Replace the underlined word with the most appropriate SYNONYM.

For sometime now, we've been <u>toying</u> with the idea of transferring all our business from physical to online sales only.

A. launch B. showing

C. considering D. careful

6. Select the word opposite in meaning to the underlined word.

At first the workers were agreeable to the proposals of their Manager, but later they were <u>reconciled</u> to the new proposals.

A. resistant B. estranged

C. cooperate D. agreed

1. B **2.** A **3.** A **4.** A **5.** C **6.** A, B

***This Previous Year Paper has been given here as a Combination of CUET (UG) 2024 different exams for the Subjects 'English, History, Political Science, Sociology and General Test', which have been mapped to this course.**

7. Complete the sentences given in List-I with the appropriate words given in List-II:

List-I (Sentences)	**List-II (Words)**
(*a*) She was able to give a ______ explanation in the court for her presence near the crime scene.	I. collaborate/d
(*b*) The Rockland Hospital ______ with AIIMS to conduct a free cancer screening camp.	II. corroborate/ing
(*c*) Though she has shown only 4% improvement in achieving her target yet her efforts are ______.	III. credible
(*d*) The doctors give the prognosis by ______ their diagnosis with several tests.	IV. creditable

Choose the **correct** answer from the options given below:

	(*a*)	(*b*)	(*c*)	(*d*)
A.	I	II	III	IV
B.	I	III	II	IV
C.	III	I	IV	II
D.	II	IV	I	III

8. Fill in the blank with the **correct** option.

Most of the guests arrived for the concert ______ bus.

A. by B. with
C. from D. through

9. Choose the word closest in meaning to the underlined word.

Why did you make that <u>flippant</u> remark about her choice of clothes?

A. sarcastic
B. disrespectful
C. casual
D. indifferent

10. Select the word OPPOSITE in meaning to the underlined word.

The thief <u>showed</u> his disbelief when informed that his partner had been arrested.

A. displayed B. concealed
C. battled D. marked

11. Fill in the blank with the **correct** option.

The President finally had to ______ the demands of the public for his resignation.

A. ignore B. initiate
C. accede to D. condone

12. Re-arrange the following parts of a sentence in their correct sequence to form a meaningful sentence.

(*a*) for organizations which provide
(*b*) services to customers on a face-to-face basis
(*c*) employees with whom they deal is very important
(*d*) the quality of the relationship between customers and

Choose the **correct** answer from the options given below:

A. (*a*), (*b*), (*d*), (*c*) B. (*c*), (*a*), (*b*), (*d*)
C. (*b*), (*d*), (*a*), (*c*) D. (*d*), (*a*), (*c*), (*b*)

13. Re-arrange the following parts of a sentence in their correct sequence to form a meaningful sentence.

(*a*) as a concept fundamental to
(*b*) especially with the injunction to treat equals equally
(*c*) justice is associated with the notion of equity and equality,
(*d*) ethical theory and political philosophy,

Choose the **correct** answer from the options given below:

A. (*d*), (*b*), (*c*), (*a*) B. (*c*), (*a*), (*b*), (*d*)
C. (*b*), (*a*), (*d*), (*c*) D. (*a*), (*d*), (*c*), (*b*)

14. Match the idioms in List-I with their meanings in List-II:

List-I (Idioms)	**List-II (Meanings)**
(*a*) blow the gaff	I. feel unable to deal with something
(*b*) at the end of your tether	II. feel terribly ashamed and embarrassed
(*c*) be full of beans	III. divulge a secret
(*d*) want to curl up and die	IV. be full of energy

Choose the **correct** answer from the options given below:

	(*a*)	(*b*)	(*c*)	(*d*)
A.	III	I	IV	II
B.	II	IV	I	III
C.	IV	I	II	III
D.	III	IV	I	II

7. C **8.** A **9.** B, C **10.** B **11.** C **12.** A **13.** D **14.** A

15. Match the blanks in List-I with the Preposition in List-II:

List-I (Sentences)	List-II (Prepositions)
(*a*) The edited version of her article is indistinguishable ________ her first version.	I. with
(*b*) I just don't feel any affinity ______ his prose style. It's too caustic.	II. to
(*c*) Her ideas are not all that dissimilar ______ mine.	III. for
(*d*) It would be wrong to mistake his diffidence ______ his arrogance or coldness.	IV. from

Choose the **correct** answer from the options given below:

	(*a*)	(*b*)	(*c*)	(*d*)
A.	IV	I	II	III
B.	I	III	II	IV
C.	IV	II	I	III
D.	III	IV	I	II

16. Re-arrange the parts in their correct sequence to form a meaningful sentence:

(*a*) students with tools for critical thinking
(*b*) cooperative learning is an
(*c*) that enhances creativity and provides
(*d*) eclectic and unique teaching method

Choose the **correct** answer from the options given below:

A. (*a*), (*c*), (*b*), (*d*) B. (*b*), (*d*), (*c*), (*a*)
C. (*b*), (*a*), (*d*), (*c*) D. (*c*), (*b*), (*d*), (*a*)

Directions (Qs. No. 17-22): *Read the given passage and answer the six questions that follow.*

When I was in my late teens and still undecided about which language I should write in, he told me that the language one is born into, one's mother tongue, can be the only possible medium of creative expression.

For most of his life, my father, Sripat Rai, had been a Hindi editor and critic. Off and on, he translated writings into English from Hindi. He was fond of saying that a failed writer becomes a critic. The weight of his literary expectation came, eventually, to rest on me. He seemed happy that I was showing an inclination for writing. "She will go far," he told my mother after reading the first story that I sent him from Melbourne.

My father's pronouncement on the mother tongue stayed with me when I later started writing fiction in Hindi. Another thing that I barely acknowledged even to myself was that I felt something like shame whenever I thought of writing in English. It seemed wrong for a granddaughter of Premchand even to be thinking so. Our family had a certain linguistic pride. I knew that Premchand was famous, but I had not at that time realised the extent of his popularity.

The fact that I was the granddaughter of Premchand, followed me everywhere. Everyone had a story to tell about their personal engagement with his fiction—the shopkeeper, the long time cook in my father's Delhi house, a tea vendor, etc. The list was long, for there was practically no one who had not read something by him that had moved them. However, it was this very ubiquity, the reverence and love that he inspired in people, that made of him something too large for me to comprehend in the early years of my life. It led also to the strange feeling that, without having read him and just by being related to him, I had somehow inhaled his writing. The reading happened much later.

17. The author grew up with the expectation that she would take up ________.

Fill in the blank with the **correct** option to complete the sentence.

A. editorship of a magazine.
B. translation of literary pieces.
C. creative writing.
D. the job of a critic.

18. When her father said, "She will go far", he meant that ________.

Fill in the blank with the **correct** option to complete the sentence.

A. she will travel widely.
B. she will achieve great heights in life.
C. she will go too far, one of these days.
D. she will settle in a far-off place.

19. Choose a Statement which is **not** true with respect to the passage:

A. The author felt pressurized to write in Hindi because of her father.
B. She felt obligated to carry on the legacy of Premchand.
C. Her family was chauvinistic about the English language.
D. She was in awe of the extensive reach of her grandfather's writings.

15. A **16.** B **17.** C **18.** B **19.** C

20. Premchand became too large for her to understand mainly because of ______ .

(*a*) his ability to connect with people from all walks of life.

(*b*) the fact that she feared him.

(*c*) the kind of love and reverence that he inspired in people.

(*d*) her constant anxiety of failing him.

Choose the **correct** answer from the options given below:

A. (*a*) and (*d*) only
B. (*a*) and (*c*) only
C. (*b*) and (*c*) only
D. (*c*) and (*d*) only

21. 'Inhaled his writing' refers to:

Choose the **correct** option from the following:

A. imbibing his style subconsciously.
B. being compelled to write like him.
C. being influenced by what people said about him.
D. her father's expectation from her.

22. Choose the correct meaning of the word "Ubiquity" as it appears in the passage:

A. Occasional
B. Restricted
C. Omnipresence
D. Unwanted

Directions (Qs. No. 23-28): ***Read the given passage and answer the six questions that follow.***

Free will is the ability to decide and act free from any influence of past events or environment. It implies complete freedom to make any choice absolutely. We clearly don't have free will. Our decisions and actions are never divorced from our past.

We have a conditioned mind. Our memories, past impressions and experiences bias and shape our thoughts and actions in the present. It is our karmic imprint. Not just what we are born with, but also what we accumulate while living. We can consider it as the result of our genetic code, upbringing and environment. It's our backstory.

The only way to experience free will is to get rid of all such conditioning; to neutralise our karmic imprint; to be independent of our psychological coding. That's possible only if we can purify our mind by letting go of all our ego, attachments and fixed beliefs. Then we can reside in the truth of our being.

The above is an exacting definition of free will. What we commonly mean by free will is that we have a choice in most situations like, who you choose to marry, what profession you pursue or how you react to someone's aggression. Sounds reasonable, But here's the catch. Our ability to make that choice too is significantly restricted, dictated by our predispositions.

This applies even to our ability to bring about change within ourselves. Despite a strong resolve to be calmer, kinder or less anxious, our ability to manifest that change depends, partly on our emotional and mental wiring. That's why some people succeed in such efforts more than the others.

If you wish to expand the scope of your agency, explore ways to engage in sustained inner work, deepen your self-awareness, examine and reform your conditioned beliefs. But then, I wonder if your inclination to embark on that journey too depends on your current karmic coding.

23. The author argues that humans don't have "free will" because ______ .

Fill in the blank with the **correct** option to complete the sentence.

A. our decisions are shaped by past events and environmental influences.
B. we are born with pre-determined choices that we are forced to make.
C. we are always dictated by our mind to make irrational choices.
D. human beings are born slaves of social constructs and expectations.

24. "Karmic imprint" referred to in the passage implies ______ .

Fill in the blank with the **correct** option to complete the sentence.

A. the ability to bring about change in oneself.
B. our genetic code, upbringing and environment.
C. the truth of our being, our individuality.
D. the wrong doings and vices of our past lives.

25. "Free will" can be experienced if ______.

Fill in the blank with the **correct** option to complete the sentence.

A. we embrace our past experiences and conditioning.
B. we make choices without considering the consequences.
C. we let go of our ego, attachments and fixed beliefs.
D. we accumulate more and more karmic imprints.

20. B	**21.** A	**22.** C	**23.** A	**24.** B	**25.** C

26. The author proves that the idea of "free will" is a myth by suggesting that ________ .

Fill in the blank with the **correct** option to complete the sentence.

A. our ability to make a choice is restricted by our predispositions.
B. we are unable to bring a change in ourselves.
C. our choices are solely guided by the current environment.
D. our choices are completely independent of past events and our genetic code.

27. What does the author propose as a means to expand the scope of one's agency?

Choose the **correct** option.

A. Making choices frequently and impulsively.
B. Engaging in sustained inner work and self-awareness.
C. Holding on to fixed beliefs and stringent mindsets.
D. Ignoring one's past experiences and dispositions.

28. What do you think could be a suitable title for this passage?

Choose the **most appropriate** option.

A. Definition of "Free Will".
B. Our backstory—key to a successful life.
C. Do human beings really have "Free Will"?
D. Making Choices—Every Man's Prerogative!

Directions (Qs. No. 29-34): *Read the given passage and answer the six questions that follow.*

On a chilly winter evening, nothing warms you up better than a cup of hot cocoa. Chocolate was first consumed in liquid form by the Olmec people of northwestern Central America around 1500 BCE. It was even enjoyed by the Aztec Emperor Montezuma, and the Aztec word for it (*xocolatl*, pronounced *shoh-kwah-tl*) evolved into the English word Chocolate.

But the Aztecs didn't serve their cocoa hot. And since sugar had not yet arrived from Europe, back then, the drink was often flavoured with peppers and spices. It may not have been quite as indulgent as today's version, but it was more palatable if you believed, as the Aztecs did, that chocolate was a gift from the Gods and had healing properties.

After the Spanish arrived in the Americas in the 1500s, liquid chocolate made its way across the pond, where wealthy Europeans added sugar and drank it warm. In *Chocolate : History, Culture and Heritage,* author Bertram Gordon says hot chocolate became "the beverage of the aristocracy," as sugar was still a luxury.

Soon enough, though, hot chocolate caught on with the masses. Chocolate houses—a cross between cafes and casinos—started popping up around 17th-century Europe. In these lively places, hot chocolate was poured from gilded pots into elegant cups (for a posh experience, one can still find it today at the famed Parisian tearoom Angelina's, which is also in New York City). But by the end of the 18th century, chocolate houses had mostly died off, partly because the cost of chocolate was much higher than that of coffee or tea.

Taking a tour of international cups of cocoa, Italians serve it like a thick pudding. Colombians serve it with a dollop of soft cheese while Mexicans punch it up with vanilla, chilli powder and cinnamon. And Filipinos serve it with mango chunks.

29. Cocoa was first introduced by the:

A. American people B. Olmec people
C. Aztec people D. Spanish people

30. The Aztec people made their cocoa palatable by:

A. serving it cold
B. adding sugar to the drink
C. spiking it with spices
D. drinking it as a medicine

31. Why did hot chocolate become "the beverage of the aristocracy" in Europe?

A. The essential ingredient was out of reach of the commoners.
B. The Queen had a marked chocolate maker.
C. Only wealthy Europeans could buy it.
D. It was being consumed by the pharma companies.

32. The Chocolate Houses didn't survive past the 18th century as:

A. people preferred tea/coffee to hot chocolate.
B. it catered to the not so elite of the society.
C. chocolate was costlier than tea or coffee.
D. the supply of cocoa dwindled over the years.

33. Choose the correct statement from the following:

A. Italians serve hot chocolate flavoured with spices.
B. Mexicans serve hot chocolate topped with a dollop of cream.
C. Colombians serve hot chocolate topped with a dollop of cheese.
D. Filipinos served hot chocolate flavoured with peppers.

26. A **27.** B **28.** A, C **29.** B **30.** C, D **31.** A, C **32.** C **33.** C

34. Choose the correct meaning of the underlined expression in the following sentence:

Soon enough, though, hot chocolate <u>caught on</u> with the masses.

A. was readily available in cafes.
B. became popular among the commoners.
C. hot chocolate did not appeal to people.
D. masses got attracted to the rich experience of drinking hot chocolate.

Directions (Qs. No. 35-40): *Read the given passage and answer the six questions that follow.*

Coffee's genetic make-up is no trivial concern; 10 million tonnes of the crop were grown and sold in 2022-23. The coffee that we drink comes from two species: Coffea Canephora, which is also known as Robusta and Coffea Arabica, known as Arabica. In many cases, beans from the two species are blended to make a brew. But the beans of single species are also roasted and sold. Overall, Arabica beans represent around 56% of all coffee sold.

Most genetic variation in living organisms comes from hybridization with other species. However, this is a relatively rare event for Coffea Arabica because it has more than two copies of each chromosome - a phenomenon called polyploidy. Coffea Canephora has two copies of each chromosome, but Coffea Arabica contains multiple copies. This makes it much more difficult for Arabica to interbreed with other species.

As a result, Coffea Arabica's main source of single nucleotide variation is mutation, which occurs at a steady rate over time. However, the species is also relatively young, having formed as a hybrid of Robusta and Coffea Eugenioides - another coffee species that is not widely cultivated - within the past 50,000 years. From that single plant, which has basically no variation, you create the whole species, and then the variation is only the novel mutations that have occurred since that event.

Despite this, there is substantial variation in the physical characteristics of the Arabica coffee plant, including different flavour profiles in the beans and variations in disease resistance, says emeritus geneticist Juan Medrano at the UC Davis Coffee Center at the University of California, Davis. "We're always talking about low variability fat the DNA level, but there is variability at the structural level, at the chromosomal level, at the level of deletions... and insertions," Medrano says.

35. Which of the following varieties of coffee is the most sold in the world?

A. Coffea Canephora
B. Coffea Arabica
C. Coffea Eugenioides
D. A blend of Coffea Canephora and Coffea Arabica

36. Which of the following species of coffee has more than two copies of each chromosome?

A. Arabica
B. Robusta
C. Coffea Eugenioides
D. A blend of Arabica and Robusta

37. Which of the following statements is true about coffea Arabica?

A. Hybridization is the main source of its genetic variation.
B. It has only two copies of each chromosome.
C. It displays the phenomenon of polyploidy.
D. It is easily interbred with other species.

38. Which of the following species of coffee developed only in the last 50,000 years?

A. Coffea Canephora
B. Coffea Eugenioides
C. Arabica
D. Robusta

39. Which of the following types of variability is not very high for Coffea Arabica?

A. Variability at the structural level.
B. Variability at the chromosomal level.
C. Variability at the level of deletions and insertions.
D. Variability at the DNA level.

40. Choose the statement that is factually **incorrect** from the options given below.

A. It is possible to roast the beans of a single species of coffee.
B. Two species of coffee can be blended to make a brew.
C. Due to its genetic make-up, novel mutations do not occur in the species Coffea Arabica.
D. Variations in disease resistance can be seen in the Arabica coffee plant.

41. Re-arrange the following phrases in correct sequence to form a meaningful sentence.

(*a*) created by human
(*b*) collective cultural heritage
(*c*) all languages
(*d*) communities are our

Choose the **correct** answer from the options given below:

A. (*a*), (*b*), (*d*), (*c*)
B. (*b*), (*a*), (*d*), (*c*)
C. (*c*), (*a*), (*d*), (*b*)
D. (*d*), (*b*), (*c*), (*a*)

34. B, D	**35.** B	**36.** A	**37.** C	**38.** *	**39.** D	**40.** C	**41.** C

42. Fill in the blank with the **correct** option, to form a meaningful sentence.

The Principal addressed us in the assembly and _______ the rumours of an early summer break.

A. defended B. quashed
C. cleared D. rebuked

43. Complete the sentences given in List-I with the appropriate phrasal verbs given in List-II.

List-I (Sentences)	**List-II (Phrasal verbs)**
(*a*) She was very _______ with him for his offensive remarks on women in politics.	I. give away
(*b*) I have plenty of interesting books to _______ to book lovers.	II. cut down
(*c*) Strange that people easily _______ to temptation and ruin their reputation!	III. cut up
(*d*) Rahul is trying to _______ on his smoking.	IV. give in

Choose the **correct** answer from the options given below:

	(*a*)	(*b*)	(*c*)	(*d*)
A.	I	II	III	IV
B.	II	IV	I	III
C.	I	II	IV	III
D.	III	I	IV	II

44. Complete the sentences given in List-I with the appropriate adverbs given in List-II:

List-I (Sentences)	**List-II (Adverbs)**
(*a*) I thought the restaurant would be expensive but it was _______ affordable.	I. badly
(*b*) It was a serious accident. But the car was _______ damaged.	II. reasonably
(*c*) The meeting was a disaster as it was very _______ organized.	III. quickly
(*d*) Mira is gifted, she has the ability to learn any language _______.	IV. hardly

Choose the **correct** answer from the options given below:

	(*a*)	(*b*)	(*c*)	(*d*)
A.	II	IV	I	III
B.	IV	II	III	I
C.	I	II	IV	III
D.	III	IV	I	II

45. Choose the appropriate word pair to complete the sentence:

I didn't know Rahul was in the hospital. If I _______, I would _______ him.

A. knew, go
B. had known, have visited
C. have known, be going
D. know, had gone

46. Identify the option closest in meaning to the underlined word:

The movie star's biography is a glossy, <u>sycophantic</u> portrayal.

A. cowardly
B. domineering
C. flattering
D. insolent

47. Choose the correct ANTONYM of the underlined word:

The Minister unleashed a <u>compliment</u> against the newspaper for its biased editorial on illiteracy among women in his constituency.

A. denunciation
B. endorsement
C. regulation
D. speculation

48. Choose the correct SYNONYM for <u>redoubtable</u> from the options given below.

A. flimsy B. perplexing
C. formidable D. voluble

49. Choose the correct ANTONYM for <u>sullen</u> from the options given below.

A. morose B. reticent
C. timid D. genial

50. Rearrange the following parts in the correct sequence to make a meaningful sentence:

(*a*) are inborn but our
(*b*) constituents of flavour, are learned
(*c*) our responses to basic tastes
(*d*) perceptions of smells, the main

Choose the **correct** answer from the options given below:

A. (*b*), (*d*), (*a*), (*c*)
B. (*a*), (*c*), (*b*), (*d*)
C. (*c*), (*a*), (*d*), (*b*)
D. (*c*), (*b*), (*d*), (*a*)

42. B **43.** D **44.** A **45.** B **46.** C **47.** A **48.** C **49.** D **50.** C

EXPLANATORY ANSWERS

1. **(B):**

(*d*) She worked on the case – introduces the subject and the action.

(*a*) for seven hours – specifies the duration of the action.

(*c*) but was hardly able to decide who the murderer was – describes the result of her effort, indicating difficulty in solving the case.

(*b*) because of the absence of any motivation – provides the reason behind the difficulty faced.

The complete sentence would be: "She worked on the case for seven hours but was hardly able to decide who the murderer was because of the absence of any motivation."

2. **(A):** In the sentence, "anomaly" is the most suitable word because it refers to an irregularity or deviation from what is expected or usual. The candidate is explaining that the drop in her grades during the second semester was unusual compared to her consistent top performance in the first semester.

3. **(A):**

(*a*) **Theocracy:** (*iii*) A theocracy is a system of government where religious leaders control the state, or where the state's policies are governed by divine principles or religious doctrines.

The term reflects a political system where religious authority is central.

(*b*) **Megalomania:** (*iv*) Megalomania is a psychological condition where an individual has an exaggerated sense of their own power, importance, or godliness.

This delusion of grandeur is often marked by a belief in one's supreme abilities or dominance.

(*c*) **Apothecary:** (*i*) An apothecary is a historical term for someone who prepares and sells medicines.

This role is akin to that of a modern pharmacist, who manages prescriptions and medicinal products.

(*d*) **Antiquarian:** (*ii*) An antiquarian is a person who studies, collects, or deals in antiques and historical artifacts.

This term is used to describe someone who has a deep interest in historical objects or artistic works from the past.

4. **(A):** The sentence describes a situation that escalated from a small issue to a bigger conflict. "Altercation" means a noisy argument or disagreement, especially in public. Therefore, the sentence should read: "A small altercation between two children ended up as a group fight."

5. **(C):** The word "toying" in this context means considering or thinking about an idea in a casual or preliminary way. The most appropriate synonym for "toying" is "considering."

6. **(A, B):**

(A) **Resistant:** This term means opposed to or unwilling to accept something. It is opposite to reconciled, which means to become resigned or accepting of a situation.

(B) **Estranged:** This term refers to being alienated or disconnected, which is also opposite to reconciled, as it implies a lack of acceptance or harmony with the situation.

7. **(C):**

(*a*) She was able to give a credible explanation in the court for her presence near the crime scene.

(*iii*) "Credible" means believable or convincing, which fits the context of providing a reliable explanation.

(*b*) The Rockland Hospital collaborated with AIIMS to conduct a free cancer screening camp.

(*i*) "Collaborated" means worked together, which is appropriate for describing joint efforts between organizations.

(*c*) Though she has shown only 4% improvement in achieving her target yet her efforts are creditable.

(*iv*) "Creditable" means deserving praise or recognition, fitting for acknowledging her efforts despite modest improvement.

(*d*) The doctors give the prognosis by corroborating their diagnosis with several tests.

(*ii*) "Corroborating" means confirming or supporting with additional evidence, which is suitable for describing the process of validating a diagnosis.

8. **(A):** The preposition "by" is used to indicate the means or method of transport. Therefore, the sentence should read: "Most of the guests arrived for the concert by bus."

9. (B & C): The word "flippant" means not showing a serious or respectful attitude. "Disrespectful" is the closest in meaning as it directly indicates a lack of respect. "Casual" also fits because a flippant remark can be considered overly casual or not serious. Therefore, both "disrespectful" and "casual" are correct.

10. (B): The word "showed" means to display or exhibit something. The opposite of showing would be to conceal or hide. Therefore, the correct word is "concealed."

11. (C): The phrase needed must indicate yielding to demands. "Accede to" means to agree to a request or demand. Therefore, the correct sentence is: "The President finally had to accede to the demands of the public for his resignation."

12. (A):

(*a*) introduces the context: "For organizations which provide."

(*b*) specifies the type of service provided: "services to customers on a face-to-face basis."

(*d*) continues with the main point: "the quality of the relationship between customers and."

(*c*) concludes the thought: "employees with whom they deal is very important."

The sentence is "For organizations which provide services to customers on a face-to-face basis, the quality of the relationship between customers and employees with whom they deal is very important."

13. (D):

(*a*) introduces the topic: "as a concept fundamental to."

(*d*) specifies the field: "ethical theory and political philosophy."

(*c*) links the topic with the main point: "justice is associated with the notion of equity and equality."

(*b*) adds detail about the application: "especially with the injunction to treat equals equally."

The sentence is "Justice is associated with the notion of equity and equality, as a concept fundamental to ethical theory and political philosophy, especially with the injunction to treat equals equally."

14. (A):

(*a*) blow the gaff - III. divulge a secret: To reveal or disclose something that was supposed to be kept secret.

(*b*) at the end of your tether - I. feel unable to deal with something: To reach the limit of one's patience or endurance.

(*c*) be full of beans - IV. be full of energy: To be very lively, energetic, or enthusiastic.

(*d*) want to curl up and die - II. feel terribly ashamed and embarrassed: To feel extremely embarrassed or ashamed, often wanting to disappear or hide.

15. (A):

(*a*) The edited version of her article is indistinguishable from her first version. IV. from: Used to indicate that two things are not distinguishable from each other.

(*b*) I just don't feel any affinity with his prose style. I. with: Used to express a lack of connection or relationship with something.

(*c*) Her ideas are not all that dissimilar to mine. II. to: Used to show similarity or comparison between two things.

(*d*) It would be wrong to mistake his diffidence for his arrogance or coldness. III. for: Used to indicate a misunderstanding or misinterpretation of something.

16. (B):

(*b*) "Cooperative learning is an": This introduces the subject of the sentence, which is cooperative learning.

(*d*) "eclectic and unique teaching method": This describes what cooperative learning is—an eclectic and unique teaching method.

(*c*) "that enhances creativity and provides": This clause explains what the teaching method does, namely enhancing creativity and providing something.

(*a*) "students with tools for critical thinking": This completes the explanation by specifying what the teaching method provides—tools for critical thinking for students.

The Sentence is "Cooperative learning is an eclectic and unique teaching method that enhances creativity and provides students with tools for critical thinking."

17. (C): The passage indicates that the author grew up with the weight of her father's literary expectations, particularly in creative writing. Her father, a Hindi editor and critic, was happy that she showed an inclination for writing. Therefore, the author grew up with the expectation that she would take up creative writing.

18. (B): When her father said, "She will go far," he meant that she would achieve great heights in life. This interpretation aligns with the context of the father's pride in her writing abilities and his expectations for her future success.

19. (C): The statement "Her family was chauvinistic about the English language" is not true with respect to the passage. The passage mentions that her father had translated writings into English from Hindi and felt that the mother tongue should be the medium of creative expression, which indicates a preference for Hindi rather than chauvinism against English.

20. (B): Premchand became too large for her to understand mainly because of his ability to connect with people from all walks of life (*a*) and the kind of love and reverence that he inspired in people (*c*). The passage describes how everyone had a personal engagement with his fiction and how the reverence he inspired made him difficult for her to comprehend.

21. (A): 'Inhaled his writing' refers to imbibing his style subconsciously. The author felt that just by being related to Premchand, she had somehow absorbed his writing, even before she read his works.

22. (C): The word "ubiquity" in the passage means omnipresence. It refers to the widespread presence and influence of Premchand's writings, as practically everyone the author encountered had read something by him.

23. (A): The author argues that humans don't have "free will" because our decisions are shaped by past events and environmental influences. The passage explains that our memories, past impressions, and experiences bias and shape our thoughts and actions in the present.

24. (B): "Karmic imprint" referred to in the passage implies our genetic code, upbringing, and environment. The passage describes karmic imprint as the result of what we are born with and what we accumulate while living, influenced by our genetic code, upbringing, and environment.

25. (C): "Free will" can be experienced if we let go of our ego, attachments, and fixed beliefs. The passage states that to experience free will, one must get rid of all conditioning and be independent of psychological coding by letting go of ego, attachments, and fixed beliefs.

26. (A): The author proves that the idea of "free will" is a myth by suggesting that our ability to make a choice is restricted by our predispositions. The passage explains that even our ability to bring about change within ourselves is significantly restricted by our emotional and mental wiring.

27. (B): The author proposes engaging in sustained inner work and self-awareness as a means to expand the scope of one's agency. The passage suggests that to expand one's agency, one should engage in inner work, deepen self-awareness, and examine and reform conditioned beliefs.

28. (A & C): The most suitable title for this passage is "Do human beings really have 'Free Will'?" The passage questions the existence of free will and explores how our choices are influenced by past events, conditioning, and predispositions. The title "Definition of 'Free Will'" also fits as the passage provides a detailed explanation of what free will means and its constraints. Therefore, both options A and C are suitable titles.

29. (B): Cocoa was first introduced by the Olmec people. The passage mentions that chocolate was first consumed in liquid form by the Olmec people of northwestern Central America around 1500 BCE.

30. (C & D): The Aztec people made their cocoa palatable by spiking it with spices and believed that chocolate had healing properties. The passage notes that since sugar had not yet arrived from Europe, the Aztecs often flavored their drink with peppers and spices and believed that chocolate was a gift from the Gods with healing properties. Therefore, both options C and D are correct.

31. (A & C): Hot chocolate became "the beverage of the aristocracy" in Europe because the essential ingredient was out of reach of the commoners and only wealthy Europeans could buy it. The passage explains that after the Spanish arrived in the Americas, liquid chocolate made its way to Europe where wealthy Europeans added sugar and drank it warm, as sugar was still a luxury. Therefore, both options A and C are correct.

32. (C): The Chocolate Houses didn't survive past the 18th century as chocolate was costlier than tea or coffee. The passage states that by the end of the 18th century, chocolate houses had mostly died off partly because the cost of chocolate was much higher than that of coffee or tea.

33. (C): Colombians serve hot chocolate topped with a dollop of cheese. The passage describes that Colombians serve hot chocolate with a dollop of soft cheese.

34. (B & D): The underlined expression "caught on with the masses" means became popular among the commoners and masses got attracted to the rich experience of drinking hot chocolate. The passage mentions that soon enough, hot chocolate became popular and chocolate houses started popping up around 17th-century Europe, suggesting it appealed to a wider audience. Therefore, both options B and D are correct.

35. (B): The passage states that Arabica beans represent around 56% of all coffee sold, making Coffea Arabica the most sold variety of coffee in the world.

36. (A): The passage mentions that Coffea Arabica contains multiple copies of each chromosome, a phenomenon called polyploidy, indicating that Arabica has more than two copies of each chromosome.

37. (C): The passage states that Coffea Arabica displays the phenomenon of polyploidy, meaning it has more than two copies of each chromosome, making option C the true statement about Coffea Arabica.

39. (D): The passage highlights that Coffea Arabica has low variability at the DNA level compared to structural and chromosomal levels, as well as levels of deletions and insertions.

40. (C): The passage mentions that novel mutations do occur in the species Coffea Arabica since it has a steady rate of mutation over time.

Therefore, the statement that due to its genetic make-up, novel mutations do not occur in Coffea Arabica is factually incorrect.

41. (C):

(*c*) "All languages" introduces the subject of the sentence.

(*a*) "created by human" provides more detail about the subject, describing what all languages are.

(*d*) "communities are our" explains the relationship between the languages and human communities.

(*b*) "collective cultural heritage" concludes by defining what the languages represent.

The sentence is "All languages created by human communities are our collective cultural heritage."

42. (B): The Principal addressed us in the assembly and quashed the rumours of an early summer break. "Quashed" means to put an end to or suppress, which fits the context of addressing and ending rumours.

43. (D):

(*a*) - (*iii*) Correct phrasal verb: "cut up" (means to be very critical or upset).

So, the sentence should be: "She was very cut up with him for his offensive remarks on women in politics."

(*b*) - (*i*) Correct phrasal verb: "give away" (means to distribute something for free).

So, the sentence should be: "I have plenty of interesting books to give away to book lovers."

(*c*) - (*iv*) Correct phrasal verb: "give in" (means to surrender or yield).

So, the sentence should be: "Strange that people easily give in to temptation and ruin their reputation!"

(*d*) - (*ii*) Rahul is trying to __________ on his smoking.

Correct phrasal verb: "cut down" (means to reduce or decrease).

So, the sentence should be: "Rahul is trying to cut down on his smoking."

44. (A):

(*a*) - (*ii*) Correct adverb: "reasonably" (means moderately or fairly).

So, the sentence should be: "I thought the restaurant would be expensive but it was reasonably affordable."

(*b*) - (*iv*) Correct adverb: "hardly" (means barely or not significantly).

So, the sentence should be: "It was a serious accident. But the car was hardly damaged."

(*c*) - (*i*) Correct adverb: "badly" (means poorly or ineffectively).

So, the sentence should be: "The meeting was a disaster as it was very badly organized."

(*d*) - (*iii*) Correct adverb: "quickly" (means at a fast pace).

So, the sentence should be: "Mira is gifted, she has the ability to learn any language quickly."

45. (B): "Had known" is the past perfect tense, which indicates that the knowledge of Rahul being in the hospital would have been relevant in the past.

"Have visited" is the past perfect conditional form of the verb, meaning that if the condition (knowing Rahul was in the hospital) had been met, the action of visiting him would have occurred.

So, the complete sentence would be: "I didn't know Rahul was in the hospital. If I had known, I would have visited him."

46. (C): Sycophantic means behaving or done in an obsequious way to gain advantage; essentially, it refers to excessively flattering or ingratiating oneself to someone in power. Flattering also means showing excessive praise or admiration, this aligns with the meaning of sycophantic.

47. (A): Compliment refers to an expression of praise or admiration. Denunciation is the action of publicly condemning or criticizing someone or something, which is the opposite of giving praise or admiration.

48. (C): Redoubtable means inspiring fear or awe; having a formidable presence. Formidable similarly means inspiring fear or respect through being impressively large, powerful, intense, or capable.

49. (D): Sullen describes a gloomy, sulky, or brooding mood or demeanor. Genial means friendly and cheerful, which is the opposite of being gloomy or sulky.

50. (C):

(*c*) "Our responses to basic tastes" introduces the subject of the sentence.

(*a*) "are inborn but our" follows logically, describing the nature of these responses.

(*d*) "perceptions of smells, the main" continues by shifting focus to another aspect related to the main constituents of flavour.

(*b*) "constituents of flavour, are learned" completes the thought by contrasting the inborn responses to learned perceptions.

So, the rearranged sentence is: "Our responses to basic tastes are inborn but our perceptions of smells, the main constituents of flavour, are learned."

HISTORY

1. Which of the following statements are correct?

(*a*) Harappan seal was a most distinctive artifact of the Harappan Civilization.

(*b*) Harappan seal motifs conveyed a meaning to those unable to read it.

(*c*) Harappan seals had Sanskrit script on them.

(*d*) Harappan seals had Pali and Prakrit inscriptions on them.

(*e*) Some Harappan seals show wider spacing of script from right and cramping on the left.

Choose the **correct** answer from the options given below:

A. (*a*) and (*d*) only
B. (*c*), (*d*) and (*e*) only
C. (*a*), (*b*) and (*e*) only
D. (*a*), (*c*) and (*d*) only

2. Match List-I with List-II.

List-I	List-II
(*a*) Kushanas	I. Piyadassi
(*b*) Ashoka	II. Devputra
(*c*) Samudragupta	III. Court-poet
(*d*) Harisena	IV. Prayaga Prashasti

Choose the **correct** answer from the options given below:

	(*a*)	(*b*)	(*c*)	(*d*)
A.	II	I	IV	III
B.	I	II	III	IV
C.	IV	III	II	I
D.	III	IV	I	II

3. Name the first site from where the Indus Valley Civilization was discovered.

A. Harappa
B. Rakhigarhi
C. Hulas
D. Sinauli

4. Match List-I with List-II.

List-I	List-II
(*a*) Alexander Greenlaw	I. Documenting the inscriptions on the temple walls
(*b*) John Marshall	II. Visits Vijayanagara in 1800
(*c*) J.F. Fleet	III. Conservation works of Vijyayanagara began under him
(*d*) Colin Mackenzie	IV. Detailed photography at Hampi

Choose the **correct** answer from the options given below:

	(*a*)	(*b*)	(*c*)	(*d*)
A.	III	IV	II	I
B.	IV	III	I	II
C.	IV	I	III	II
D.	I	IV	III	II

5. Match List-I with List-II.

List-I	List-II
(*a*) Duarte Barbosa	I. Morocco
(*b*) Marco Polo	II. Spain
(*c*) Ibn Battuta	III. Portugal
(*d*) Antonio Monserrate	IV. Italy

Choose the **correct** answer from the options given below:

	(*a*)	(*b*)	(*c*)	(*d*)
A.	I	II	IV	III
B.	III	IV	I	II
C.	I	III	IV	II
D.	III	IV	II	I

6. Match List-I with List-II.

List-I	List-II
(*a*) Pataliputra	I. Prakrit name of Rajgir, Bihar
(*b*) Rajgaha	II. Present day Coastal Odisha
(*c*) Kalinga	III. Present day Patna
(*d*) Arthashastra	IV. Kautilya

Choose the **correct** answer from the options given below:

	(*a*)	(*b*)	(*c*)	(*d*)
A.	III	I	II	IV
B.	I	III	II	IV
C.	I	II	IV	III
D.	III	IV	I	II

1. C **2.** A **3.** A **4.** B **5.** B **6.** A

7. Which of the following statements are correct?

(*a*) Mahabharata has over 1,00,000 verses.
(*b*) Mahabharata was written by Valmiki.
(*c*) V.S. Sukthankar is associated with the critical edition of Mahabharata.
(*d*) The critical edition of Mahabharata took 47 years to complete.
(*e*) The critical edition of Mahabharata ran into over 13,000 pages.

Choose the **correct** answer from the options given below:

A. (*a*) and (*b*) only
B. (*b*) and (*e*) only
C. (*a*), (*c*), (*d*) and (*e*) only
D. (*b*) and (*c*) only

8. Match List-I with List-II.

List-I	List-II
(*a*) Kula	I. Larger network of kinfolk
(*b*) Jati	II. Families
(*c*) Vamsha	III. People
(*d*) Jana	IV. Lineage

Choose the **correct** answer from the options given below:

	(*a*)	(*b*)	(*c*)	(*d*)
A.	I	II	III	IV
B.	IV	III	II	I
C.	II	I	IV	III
D.	III	IV	II	I

9. Match List-I with List-II.

List-I	List-II
(*a*) Meghe Dhaka Tara	I. Govind Nihalani
(*b*) Garam Hawa	II. Habib Tanvir
(*c*) Tamas	III. Ritwik Ghatak
(*d*) Jis Lahore Nahin Dekhya O Jamya-e-nai	IV. M.S. Sathyu

Choose the **correct** answer from the options given below:

	(*a*)	(*b*)	(*c*)	(*d*)
A.	IV	III	II	I
B.	III	IV	I	II
C.	I	II	III	IV
D.	II	I	IV	III

10. Who was the first woman to be ordained as bhikkhuni?

A. Sigala
B. Karuni Pajapati
C. Mahapajapati Gotami
D. Punna

11. Who amongst the following were the principal deities of the Vedic pantheon?

A. Brahma, Vishnu, Shiva
B. Vishnu, Shiva, Indra
C. Agni, Indra, Soma
D. Agni, Varuna, Indra

12. Which of the following statements are **not** correct?

(*a*) *Vinay Pitaka* does not describe the rules for monks.
(*b*) Buddhism grew only after the death of Buddha.
(*c*) *Sutta Pitaka* are the verses composed by bhikkunis.
(*d*) Punna was a rich land-lady.
(*e*) The word Chaitya may have been derived from the word chita.

Choose the **correct** answer from the options given below:

A. (*d*) and (*e*) only
B. (*a*), (*b*) and (*d*) only
C. (*c*) and (*e*) only
D. (*b*), (*d*) and (*e*) only

13. Madras, Bombay and Calcutta were the anglicised names of _______ where the British first set up trading posts.

A. Cities
B. Villages
C. Towns
D. Capitals

14. Which of the following statements are correct?

(*a*) Guru Arjan compiled Guru Nanak's hymns in the Adi Granth Sahib.
(*b*) Guru Tegh Bahadur laid the foundation of the Khalsa Panth.
(*c*) Guru Nanak composed the Guru Granth Sahib.
(*d*) Mirabai was a Maratha princess.
(*e*) Mirabai was a Rajput princess.

Choose the **correct** answer from the options given below:

A. (*a*) and (*d*) only
B. (*c*) and (*d*) only
C. (*b*) and (*c*) only
D. (*a*) and (*e*) only

15. Which Sufi teacher was also known as the 'Gharib Nawaz'?

A. Shaikh Nizamuddin Auliya
B. Khwaja Muinuddin
C. Amir Khusrau
D. Shaikh Qutbuddin Bakhtiyar Kaki

7. C **8.** C **9.** B **10.** C **11.** C **12.** * **13.** B **14.** D **15.** B

16. Lord Jagannatha is a form of which God?

A. Surya B. Vishnu
C. Shiva D. Brahma

17. Which among the following travellers visited the city of Vijayanagara during the 15th century?

(*a*) Domingo Paes (*b*) Abdur Razzaq
(*c*) Afanasii Nikitin (*d*) Fernao Nuniz
(*e*) Nicolo de Conti

Choose the **correct** answer from the options given below:

A. (*b*), (*c*) and (*e*) only
B. (*c*), (*d*) and (*e*) only
C. (*a*), (*b*) and (*d*) only
D. (*b*), (*c*) and (*d*) only

18. Match List-I with List-II.

List-I	List-II
(*a*) Terracotta models of plough	I. Kalibangan
(*b*) Ploughed field	II. Shortughai
(*c*) Traces of canals	III. Dholavira
(*d*) Water reservoirs	IV. Cholistan

Choose the **correct** answer from the options given below:

	(*a*)	(*b*)	(*c*)	(*d*)
A.	IV	I	II	III
B.	I	II	IV	III
C.	I	II	III	IV
D.	IV	III	II	I

19. Who amongst the following, founded the Vijayanagara Empire?

A. Krishnadeva Raya
B. Harihara and Bukka
C. Raja Raya
D. Rajendra II

20. Match List-I with List-II.

List-I	List-II
(*a*) Shell	I. Shortughai
(*b*) Lapis-Lazuli	II. Nageshwar
(*c*) Carnelian	III. South Rajasthan
(*d*) Steatite	IV. Lothal

Choose the **correct** answer from the options given below:

	(*a*)	(*b*)	(*c*)	(*d*)
A.	III	IV	I	II
B.	II	I	IV	III
C.	I	II	III	IV
D.	IV	III	II	I

21. Match List-I with List-II.

List-I	List-II
(*a*) Mahals	I. Territorial unit
(*b*) Pahariyas and Santhals	II. Permanent Settlement
(*c*) 1793	III. Rajmahal hills
(*d*) Taluq	IV. Estates

Choose the **correct** answer from the options given below:

	(*a*)	(*b*)	(*c*)	(*d*)
A.	I	II	III	IV
B.	IV	III	II	I
C.	IV	III	I	II
D.	II	I	IV	III

22. Which of the following statements are correct?

(*a*) Moneylenders were called 'dikus'.
(*b*) Zamindars hired the Santhals to reclaim land.
(*c*) Santhals were merchants.
(*d*) Land of the Santhals was demarcated as 'Damin-i-koh'.
(*e*) Santhals charged heavy land revenue from dikus moneylenders.

Choose the **correct** answer from the options given below:

A. (*a*), (*b*) and (*c*) only
B. (*c*) and (*e*) only
C. (*a*), (*b*) and (*d*) only
D. (*c*) and (*d*) only

23. Which of the following statements are true about the zamindars?

(*a*) Milkiyat lands were cultivated for the general use of the people.
(*b*) Zamindars could sell, bequeath or mortgage the milkiyat lands.
(*c*) Zamindars collected revenue on behalf of themselves.
(*d*) Most Zamindars had fortresses as well as armed contingent.
(*e*) Control over military resources was another source of power for the Zamindars.

Choose the **correct** answer from the options given below:

A. (*a*), (*d*) and (*e*) only
B. (*c*), (*d*) and (*e*) only
C. (*a*), (*b*) and (*c*) only
D. (*b*), (*d*) and (*e*) only

16. B **17.** A **18.** A **19.** B **20.** B **21.** B **22.** C **23.** D

24. Kauravas and Pandavas belonged to which ruling family?

A. Kuru B. Panchal
C. Magadha D. Vatsa

25. Which report reproduced zamindars' and ryots' petitions as appendices for consideration of the British Parliament?

A. The First Report
B. The Seventh Report
C. The Sixth Report
D. The Fifth Report

26. The rebel leaders issued Proclamations and few ______ to propagate their ideas during the 1857 revolution.

Fill in the blank with the correct answer from the options given below:

A. Cartridges B. Ishtahars
C. Sepoys D. Taluqdars

27. In 1857 "the life has gone out of the body" was said in reference to which state?

A. Jhansi B. Awadh
C. Kanpur D. Delhi

28. Which of the following statements are correct?

(*a*) Bell of arms was a store room in which weapons were kept.
(*b*) The army of Awadh supported the British.
(*c*) Firangi is a term of Persian origin applied to the British by the rebels.
(*d*) The 7th Awadh Irregular Cavalry accepted the new cartridges in early May.
(*e*) Local leaders emerged, urging peasants, zamindars and tribals to revolt.

Choose the **correct** answer from the options given below:

A. (*a*), (*b*) and (*c*) only
B. (*b*) and (*d*) only
C. (*a*), (*c*) and (*e*) only
D. (*d*) and (*e*) only

29. Match List-I with List-II.

List-I	List-II
(*a*) Nana Sahib	I. Awadh
(*b*) Rani Lakshmi Bai	II. Arrah
(*c*) Kunwar Singh	III. Kanpur
(*d*) Birjis Qadr	IV. Jhansi

Choose the **correct** answer from the options given below:

	(*a*)	(*b*)	(*c*)	(*d*)
A.	I	II	III	IV
B.	I	II	IV	III
C.	III	IV	II	I
D.	II	I	III	IV

30. Who was the leader of the Santhal Revolt of 1855-56?

A. Birsa Munda B. Gonoo
C. Sidhu Manjhi D. Shah Mal

31. Who fought in the famous Battle of Chinhat in which the British forces under Henry Lawrence was defeated?

A. Shah Mal
B. Maulvi Ahmadullah Shah
C. Birjis Qadr
D. Kunwar Singh

32. Who was the Commissioner of Lucknow when the rebels besieged it during the Revolt of 1857?

A. Colin Campbell B. Henry Lawrence
C. James Outram D. Henry Havelock

33. The Sunset Law was associated with:

A. Zamindari System/Permanent Settlement
B. British Navy
C. Imperial Court
D. Freedom Movement

34. During his 'Salt March' Gandhiji began walking towards the ocean from his ashram, located ______.

Fill in the blank with the correct answer from the options given below:

A. Ahmedabad B. Sabarmati
C. Wardha D. Kochrab

35. Mahatma Gandhi's Salt March was notable as the first nationalist activity focused on ______ .

A. Women
B. Lord Irwin
C. Subhas Chandra Bose
D. 15 March, 1930

36. "Purna Swaraj" as the goal of nationalism in India was aimed to achieve ______ .

A. Partial freedom
B. Complete independence
C. Indian identity
D. Partition

24. A **25.** D **26.** B **27.** B **28.** C **29.** C **30.** C **31.** B **32.** B **33.** A
34. A, B **35.** A **36.** B

37. Which of the following statements of Gandhiji made at the opening of Benaras Hindu University are true?

(*a*) Gandhiji charged the Indian elite with a lack of concern for the labouring poor.

(*b*) Gandhiji was not worried about the contrast between the "richly bedecked noblemen" and millions of poor Indians.

(*c*) Gandhiji said, "Our salvation can only come through lawyers, doctors and rich landlords."

(*d*) Gandhiji emphasised that farmers are going to secure the salvation of India.

(*e*) Gandhiji told the privileged invitees, "Strip yourself of this jewellery and hold it in trust for your countrymen."

Choose the **correct** answer from the options given below:

A. (*a*), (*b*) and (*c*) only
B. (*c*), (*d*) and (*e*) only
C. (*b*), (*c*) and (*d*) only
D. (*a*), (*d*) and (*e*) only

38. Match List-I with List-II.

List-I	List-II
(*a*) Khilafat Movement	I. Mahatma Gandhi's biographer
(*b*) Jallianwala Bagh Massacre	II. Turkish ruler
(*c*) Kemal Ataturk	III. 1919
(*d*) Louis Fisher	IV. 1919-1920

Choose the **correct** answer from the options given below:

	(*a*)	(*b*)	(*c*)	(*d*)
A.	I	II	III	IV
B.	I	IV	II	III
C.	III	I	IV	II
D.	IV	III	II	I

39. Who was the Judge who presided over Gandhiji's trial after the withdrawl of the Non-Cooperation Movement?

A. Justice C.N. Broomfield
B. Justice William Hodges
C. Justice Joseph Noel
D. Justice Thomas Barker

40. When were separate electorates first created by the British Colonial Government?

A. 1919 B. 1923
C. 1909 D. 1907

Directions (Qs. No. 41-45): *Read the passage and answer the five questions that follow.*

Mughal chronicles, especially the *Akbar Nama*, written by Abu'l Fazl, have bequeathed a vision of empire in which agency rests almost solely with the emperor, while the rest of the kingdom has been portrayed as following his orders. Yet if we look more closely at the rich information, these histories provide information about the apparatus of the Mughal State from which we may be able to understand the ways in which the imperial organization was dependent on several different institutions to be able to function effectively. One important pillar of the Mughal State was the nobility.

41. Mughal chronicles viewed the emperors as supreme sovereign because:

A. Nobility wanted him to be one.
B. Vision of empire viewed the emperor as the sole ruler.
C. Chronicles were a rich source of history.
D. Imperial administration was weak.

42. Which section of the Mughal Court was viewed as very significant?

A. Imperial vision B. The Empire
C. Nobility D. Mughal Chronicles

43. Which chronicle says that the entire kingdom has to follow the king's orders?

A. *Urdu Akbhar* B. *Badshah Nama*
C. *Akbar Nama* D. *Kitabkhana*

44. The Mughal imperial administrative apparatus was effectively dependent on ________ .

A. Travellers B. Nobles
C. Masses D. Mir Bakshi

45. Who is the author of *Akbar Nama*?

A. Chandrabhan Barahman
B. Muhammad Kazim
C. Lahori
D. Abu'l Fazl

Directions (Qs. No. 46-50): *Read the passage and answer the five questions that follow.*

The Constituent Assembly deliberated upon the Indian Constitution, which came into effect on 26 January, 1950. It has the dubious distinction of being the longest in the world. But its length and complexity are perhaps understandable when one considers the country's size and diversity. At Independence, India was not merely large and

37. D **38.** D **39.** A **40.** C **41.** B **42.** C **43.** C **44.** B **45.** D

diverse, but also deeply divided. A Constitution designed to keep the country together, and to take it forward, had necessarily to be an elaborate, carefully-worked-out, and painstakingly drafted document. For one thing, it sought to heal wounds of the past and the present, to make Indians of different classes, castes and communities come together in a shared political experiment. For another, it sought to nurture democratic institutions.

46. When did the Constitution of India come into force?

A. 26th January, 1950 B. 15th August, 1947

C. 31st January, 1929 D. 6th November, 1949

47. Why is the Constitution of India described as the longest document in the world?

A. It is a painstakingly drafted document.

B. It is carefully workd out.

C. It imbibes culture of hierarchy.

D. The country size and diversity impacted the Constitution length.

48. How can we say that the Constitution of India seeks to unify India?

A. It deals with the country's problems.

B. The area of the subcontinent was under its control.

C. It was designed to keep the country's divided classes, communities and castes together.

D. It was to nurture democratic institutions.

49. In which body was the Constitution of India deliberated upon?

A. Parliament of India

B. Through Newspaper coverage

C. Constituent Assembly

D. Princely States

50. The nature of the Constitution imbibed the right to ______.

A. Cultural Rights B. Educational Rights

C. Equality D. Religion

EXPLANATORY ANSWERS

1. (C): The Harappan seals were a distinctive artifact of the Harappan Civilization, known for their intricate animal motifs and short inscriptions in a script that remains undeciphered. These seals likely served various purposes, including the identification of property and the conveyance of authority. The motifs, recognizable and symbolic, could communicate information even to those who could not read the script, suggesting a form of visual language. There is no evidence that Sanskrit, Pali, or Prakrit was used on these seals; these languages were not in use during the Harappan period. Additionally, some seals show a distinct arrangement of script, typically more spaced on the right and cramped on the left, indicating a stylistic or functional aspect of the script layout.

2. (A): In many inscriptions, the Kushan ruler is also called Devaputra suggesting the divine origin of the king. In adopting this title they were perhaps influenced by the Chinese custom of calling the emperor T'ien-tzu meaning "the son of Heaven". It is interesting to note that an inscription, found at Kamra (Punjab, Pakistan), describes the Kushan ruler Vajheshka not only as "son of god" but also as devatnanuia alluding to god living in the form of man. The Kushan royal statues found at a temple at Mathura and in the small sanctuaries in the Śwat region prove that the Kushan monarchs were actually worshipped as divinities.

In inscriptions, the title "Piyadassi" or "Priyadarsin" is often associated with the title "Devanampriya" ("Beloved of the Gods"). Separately, the title also appears in "Devanampriya" in conjunction with the name "Ashoka" as in the Minor Rock Edict inscription discovered in Maski, associating Ashoka with Devanampriya.

The Allahabad Pillar (now Prayagraj) inscription of Samudragupta is one of the important epigraphic sources for the study of the political history of the Imperial Guptas. It is written in excellent Sanskrit in the form of a panegyric. It popularly called as Allahabad Prashasti in the academic circles. Historians, both ancient and modern, have considered the historical value of Allahabad Prashasti. Allahabad Prashasti is inscribed with ornamental and literary Sanskrit, befitting the taste of the elite class of the time. The inscription is a panegyric praising Samudragupta and Lists the political and military achievements of his reign including his expeditions to the south. It provides a unique snapshot of the

46. A	**47.** D	**48.** C	**49.** C	**50.** A, B, C, D

Gupta Empire and its neighbours and is the source of much of what is known of the geopolitical landscape of that era. Samudragupta court poet and minister Harisena composed the Allahabad pillar Inscription or Prayag Prashasti. The Pillar was an Asokan Pillar erected by Asoka six century before him. This Inscription is a eulogy of Samudragupta and mentions about the conquests of Samudragupta and boundaries of the Gupta Empire. As per this inscription, Samudragupta defeated 9 kings in North, 12 Kings in South, reduced all the Atavika states to vassalage. The stone pillar now situated in the fort of Allahabad built by Akbar the Great now carries the inscriptions of three rulers viz. Ashoka, Samudragupta and Jahangir.

3. **(A):** The Indus Valley Civilization, also known as the Harappan Civilization after its first discovered site, Harappa, was unearthed in the 1920s. Harappa, located in present-day Pakistan, was one of the earliest urban centers of the civilization, prominently featuring the advanced urban planning and sophisticated craftsmanship characteristic of the culture.

4. **(B):** The Vijayanagara Empire was the most dignified and glorious empire of South India. Its Capital was Hampi. Hampi was discovered by Colin Mackenzie, the first Surveyor General of India in 1815. His (Colin Mackenzie's) arduous work, gave a new direction to all the future researcher. Alexander Greenlaw took the first detailed photography of Hampi in 1856, which proved quite useful for the scholar. J.F. Fleet in 1876, began compilation and documentation of the inscription from the walls of the temples in Hampi.

   John Marshall began the conservation of Hampi in 1902. In 1976, Hampi was declared as a site of national importance and in 1986 it was declared as world Heritage centre. Vijayanagara Empire was founded by the two brothers, Harihara and Bukka in 14th century. The ruler of Vijayanagara empire were called Rayas.

   The most powerful ruler of Vijayanagara empire was Krishnadeva Raya. During his tenure, the empire touched its glory. Administration of the Vijayanagara Empire was very good and its people were very happy. The Vijayanagara Empire began to decline by 16th century and this might empire ended in 17th century.

5. **(B):** Duarte Barbosa, a Portuguese writer, is linked to option III, known for his descriptions of Eastern trade routes. Marco Polo, an Italian explorer famous for his travels through Asia, corresponds to option IV. Ibn Battuta, the Moroccan explorer, is known for his extensive travels across the Muslim world and beyond, fitting option I. Antonio Monserrate, a Spanish missionary, is associated with his mission to the court of Akbar in India, aligning with option II.

6. **(A):** Pataliputra, adjacent to modern-day Patna, Bihar, was a city in ancient India, originally built by Magadha ruler Ajatashatru in 490 BCE, as a small fort near the Ganges river. Udayin laid the foundation of the city of Pataliputra at the confluence of two rivers, the Son and the Ganges. He shifted his capital from Rajgriha to Pataliputra due to the latter's central location in the empire.

   Rajagaha (the Prakrit name for present day Rajgir in Bihar) was the capital of Magadha. Interestingly, the old name means "house of the king". Rajagaha was a fortified settlement, located amongst hills. Later, in the fourth century BCE, the capital was shifted to Pataliputra, present-day Patna, commanding routes of communication along the Ganga.

   Kalinga is a historical region of India. It is generally defined as the eastern coastal region between the Ganges and the Godavari rivers, although its boundaries have fluctuated with the territory of its rulers. The core territory of Kalinga now encompasses all of Odisha and some part of northern Andhra Pradesh. The Kalingas have been mentioned as a major tribe in the legendary text Mahabharata. In the 3rd century BCE, the region came under Mauryan control as a result of the Kalinga War.

   The Arthashastra is an Ancient Indian Sanskrit treatise on statecraft, political science, economic policy and military strategy. Chanakya, also identified as Vishnugupta and Kautilya, is traditionally credited as the author of the text. Chanakya was a scholar at Taxila, the teacher and guardian of Mauryan emperor Chandragupta Maurya.

7. **(C):** The Mahabharata is indeed one of the longest epic poems known, with over 100,000 verses, matching option (*a*). V.S. Sukthankar was notably involved in the critical edition of the Mahabharata, which is reflected in option (*c*). This critical edition was a monumental task, taking 47 years to complete, as stated in option (*d*).

   Furthermore, this edition extended to over 13,000 pages, as described in option (*e*). Notably, the Mahabharata was not written by Valmiki, who is actually credited with the Ramayana.

8. (C): In Indian social structure, 'Kula' refers to a group of families, hence matched with II.

'Jati' refers to a larger network of kinfolk or a community group, fitting option I.

'Vamsha' indicates lineage, particularly in terms of hereditary lines, aligning with option IV.

'Jana' indicates a larger group or people collectively, corresponding to option III.

9. (B): Meghe Dhaka Tara is a 1960 film written and directed by Ritwik Ghatak, based on a social novel by Shaktipada Rajguru with the same title. It stars Supriya Choudhury, Anil Chatterjee; Gita Dey, Bijon Bhattacharya, Niranjan Roy, and Gyanesh Mukherjee.

Garm Hawa is a 1973 Indian drama film directed by M. S. Sathyu, with Balraj Sahni as the lead actor. It was written by Kaifi Azmi and Shama Zaidi, based on an unpublished short story by noted Urdu writer Ismat Chughtai. The film score was given by the classical musician Ustad Bahadur Khan, with lyrics by Kaifi Azmi.

Tamas is a 1988 period television film written and directed by Govind Nihalani. It is based on the Hindi novel of the same name by Bhisham Sahni (1974), which won the author the Sahitya Akademi Award in 1975. Set in the backdrop of riot-stricken Pakistan at the time of the partition of India in 1947, the film deals with the plight of emigrant Sikh and Hindu families to India as a consequence of the partition.

Asghar Wajahat's most noted Partition play, **'Jis Lahore Nai Dekhya',** was first performed under the direction of Habib Tanvir in 1989, who subsequently took the play to Karachi, Lahore, Sydney, New York and Dubai. Play has also been performed in several regional languages, a version of it has also been directed by theatre director Dinesh Thakur, Abhijeet Choudhary from Swatantra Theatre, Pune and now veteran Bollywood director Rajkumar Santoshi plans to make a film on it.

10. (C): Mahapajapati Gotami is historically recognized as the first woman to be ordained as a bhikkhuni in the Buddhist tradition. She was the Buddha's stepmother and aunt, playing a crucial role in establishing the Bhikkhuni Sangha for women, thus allowing them the opportunity for ordination similar to monks.

11. (C): In the Vedic pantheon, the principal deities included Agni, the god of fire, Indra, the king of gods and god of rain and thunderstorms, and Soma, associated with a ritual drink and also revered as a deity. These gods were central in Vedic rituals and are frequently mentioned in the Rigveda, the oldest of the Vedas. Brahma, Vishnu, and Shiva, mentioned in option A, are primarily figures in later Hinduism, particularly emphasized in the Puranic texts, not the Vedas.

13. (B): Madras (now Chennai), Bombay (now Mumbai), and Calcutta (now Kolkata) were cities during the British colonial period. These locations were selected by the British East India Company for establishing their initial trading posts due to their strategic coastal locations facilitating maritime trade. They were not villages or mere towns but prominent urban centers during the colonial era and served as pivotal points for British trade and administrative activities in India.

14. (D): Guru Arjan, the fifth Sikh Guru, compiled the hymns of his predecessors including Guru Nanak into the Adi Granth Sahib, which later became the Guru Granth Sahib, fulfilling the role stated in option **(*a*)**. Guru Tegh Bahadur, the ninth Sikh Guru, did not lay the foundation of the Khalsa Panth; that was initiated by Guru Gobind Singh, making option (*b*) incorrect. Guru Nanak did not compile the Guru Granth Sahib; he authored many hymns included within it, refuting option (*c*). Mirabai was indeed a Rajput princess, specifically from Merta, Rajasthan, aligning with option (*e*). She was not a Maratha princess as suggested in option (*d*).

15. (B): Khwaja Muinuddin Chishti, known as Khwaja Gharib Nawaz, was a prominent Sufi saint of the Chishti Order in India. His teachings and spiritual lineage played a significant role in the spread of Islam and the establishment of the Sufi tradition across South Asia. He is celebrated for his compassionate approach to the poor, which earned him the title 'Gharib Nawaz' (Protector of the Poor). His dargah in Ajmer, Rajasthan, remains a major pilgrimage site.

16. (B): Lord Jagannatha is widely regarded as a form of Lord Vishnu. This deity is particularly revered in the state of Odisha, India, where the famous Jagannath Temple is located in Puri. The iconography of Jagannatha, with large round eyes and a symmetric face, is a distinctive representation of Vishnu in regional tradition, especially during the annual Rath Yatra festival.

17. (A): Abdur Razzaq, Afanasii Nikitin, and Nicolo de Conti were travelers who visited the city of Vijayanagara during the 15th century. Their accounts provide valuable insights into the empire's culture, economy, and political landscape. Domingo Paes and Fernao Nuniz, though important chroniclers of Vijayanagara, visited slightly later, thus not aligning with the options specified in choice A.

18. (A): Banawali is located in Fatehabad in Haryana on the left bank of dried up bed of the Saraswati. The excavations have yielded three-fold culture sequence: Pre-Harappan (Early-Harappan), Harappan and Bara (post Harappan). Terracotta models of plough have been found at sites in Cholistan and Banawali (Harayana). A ploughed field is found at Kalibangan (Rajasthan).

Shortugai, in Darqad District of northern Afghanistan, was a trading colony of the Indus Valley civilization (or Harappan Civilization) established around 2000 BC on the Oxus river (Amu Darya) near the lapis lazuli mines. It is considered to be the northern-most settlement of the Indus Valley Civilization. Traces of canals have been found at the Harappan site of Shortughai in Afghanistan. It is also likely that water was drawn from wells was used for irrigation.

Dholavira is an important Harappan site located in Kutch region in Gujarat, India. It is renowned for its water management system, with a great network of stone cut reservoirs and canals which was vital in this rainfall deficient region. Seasonal streams Mansar (in the north) and Manhar (in the south) flowed outside the town.

19. (B): Harihara I and Bukka Raya I are credited with founding the Vijayanagara Empire in the mid-14th century. They established it with the guidance of the sage Vidyaranya, aiming to protect Hindu traditions and culture against the invasions and influence from the northern Muslim sultanates, marking a significant era in South Indian history.

20. (B): Shell artifacts have been notably found at Nageshwar, aligning it with option II for (*a*). Lapis Lazuli, indicative of trade connections with Afghanistan, was found at Shortughai, making option I correct for (*b*).

Carnelian, a semi-precious stone widely used in Harappan sites, was prominently found at Lothal, aligning with option IV for (*c*). Steatite, used particularly for bead making, was significant in South Rajasthan, making option III correct for (*d*).

21. (B): Rajmahal Hills are located in the Santhal Pargana division of Jharkhand. its hills are today inhabited by the Sauria Paharia people whilst its valleys are dominated by the Santhal people. The Rajmahal hills are named after the town of Rajmahal. The River Ganges wanders around the hills changing the direction of flow from east to south. Francis Buchanan-Hamilton travelled through the Rajmahal hills in the early 19th century. He described the hills that seemed impenetrable.

In 1793, Governor-General Lord Cornwallis introduced the Permanent Settlement, also known as the Permanent Settlement of Bengal. This agreement between the British East India Company and Bengal's landlords aimed to set a fixed amount for land revenue.

Mahals were territorial divisions within the Mughal and later British administrative system, aligning with the definition of estates revenue units.

A tehsil, also known as tahsil, taluk, or taluka is a local unit of administrative division in India and Pakistan. It is a subdistrict of the area within a district including the designated populated place that serves as its administrative centre, with possible additional towns, and usually a number of villages. The terms in India have replaced earlier terms, such as pargana and thana.

22. (C): The term 'dikus' was indeed used by tribal groups like the Santhals to refer to outsiders, often moneylenders or traders perceived as exploiters, which matches option (*a*). Zamindars commonly employed tribal groups such as the Santhals to reclaim and cultivate land, aligning with option (*b*). The term 'Damin-i-koh' specifically referred to the hilly region allocated to the Santhals by the British, which fits option (*d*). Santhals were not merchants by traditional occupation, and they did not charge land revenue from dikus, which counters options (*c*) and (*e*).

23. (D): Milkiyat lands were privately owned by zamindars, and they had the rights to sell, mortgage, or bequeath these lands, confirming option (*b*). Many zamindars maintained fortresses and armed contingents, a testament to their authority and need for security, matching with option (*d*). The control over military resources, such as private armies, was indeed another source of power for zamindars, aligning with option (*e*).

Option (*a*) is incorrect as milkiyat lands were not generally used for the public but were private properties of the zamindars. Zamindars did collect revenue, but typically on behalf of the state or as part of the colonial administrative framework, which makes option (*c*) partially accurate but not entirely fitting the traditional role.

24. (A): The Kauravas and Pandavas are central characters in the epic Mahabharata, and both belonged to the Kuru dynasty, which was a significant ruling family in ancient India. This family's stories and conflicts are set in and around the region of Hastinapura, which was the capital of the Kuru kingdom.

25. (D): The Fifth Report of the Select Committee on the Affairs of the East India Company, presented in 1812, is particularly noted for its comprehensive detail on the administration of Indian territories under British control, including extensive appendices that reproduced zamindars' and ryots' petitions. This report was significant for influencing British policy-making and parliamentary oversight regarding the colonial administration in India.

26. (B): During the 1857 revolution, rebel leaders used various means to propagate their ideas and mobilize support. "Ishtahars," which are proclamations or public announcements, were one of the key tools used. These helped to disseminate the revolutionary messages widely among the populace, rallying them against the British administration.

27. (B): The phrase "the life has gone out of the body" was said in reference to the state of Awadh during the 1857 rebellion. This metaphor was used to describe the impact of the British annexation and the subsequent upheaval, capturing the sense of loss and devastation felt by the local populace as their traditional governance structure was dismantled.

28. (C): A "bell of arms" indeed refers to a storeroom where weapons were kept, which aligns with option (*a*). "Firangi," a term of Persian origin, was used by the rebels and local populace to refer to Europeans, specifically the British, during the colonial period, fitting option (*c*). The rebellion of 1857 saw the emergence of various local leaders who encouraged a wide array of social classes including peasants, zamindars, and tribals to join the revolt, which is accurately described in option (*e*). The other options are incorrect as the army of Awadh largely did not support the British, and the 7th Awadh Irregular Cavalry rejected the new cartridges, which were a point of contention due to the grease used being potentially offensive to both Hindu and Muslim troops.

29. (C): The Revolt of 1857 is also called the Sepoy Mutiny or India's First War of Independence. It was started on 10 May 1857 at Meerut, as a mutiny of sepoys of the British East India Company's army. The revolt spread over the entire area from the neighborhood of Patna to the borders of Rajasthan. The main centers of revolt in these regions namely Kanpur, Lucknow, Bareilly, Jhansi, Gwalior, and Arrah in Bihar. Following is a list of important leaders who took part in the revolt from different parts of the country.

Place	Leader
Barrackpore	Mangal Pandey
Delhi	Bahadur Shah II, General Bakht Khan
Delhi	Hakim Ahsanullah (Chief advisor to Bahadur Shah II)
Lucknow	Begum Hazrat Mahal, Birjis Qadir, Ahmadullah (advisor of the ex-Nawab of Awadh)
Kanpur	Nana Sahib, Rao Sahib (nephew of Nana), Tantia Tope, Azimullah Khan (advisor of Nana Sahib)
Jhansi	Rani Laxmibai
Bihar (Jagdishpur)	Kunwar Singh, Amar Singh
Allahabad and Banaras	Maulvi Liyakat Ali
Faizabad	Maulvi Ahmadullah (He declared the Revolt as Jihad against English)
Farrukhabad	Tufzal Hasan Khan
Bijnaur	Mohammad Khan
Muradabad	Abdul Ali Khan
Bareilly	Khan Bahadur Khan
Mandsor	Firoz Shah
Gwalior/Kanpur	Tantia Tope
Assam	Kandapareshwar Singh, Manirama Datta.

30. (C): Sidhu Manjhi, along with his brother Kanhu, were the primary leaders of the Santhal Revolt of 1855-56. This revolt was a significant uprising by the Santhal community against the oppressive practices of landlords and moneylenders in the region, marking an important moment in the history of tribal resistance in India. Sidhu's leadership was crucial in mobilizing the Santhals to fight for their rights and justice.

31. (B): Maulvi Ahmadullah Shah was a prominent figure in the Revolt of 1857 and played a key role in several engagements against the British, including the Battle of Chinhat. In this battle, the forces of Maulvi Ahmadullah Shah were instrumental in defeating the British forces led by Henry Lawrence, marking a significant victory for the rebels during the early stages of the uprising.

32. (B): During the Revolt of 1857, Henry Lawrence was the British Commissioner stationed in Lucknow. He played a crucial role in the defense of the British residency in Lucknow, which was besieged by the rebels. His leadership was pivotal until his death from injuries sustained during the siege.

33. (A): The Sunset Law was associated with the Zamindari System and the Permanent Settlement introduced by the British in India. This law stipulated that land revenue settlements were to be finalized by sunset of the day they were presented, emphasizing the urgency and importance of revenue collection within the administrative framework of British India.

34. (A & B): Gandhiji began his famous Salt March from his ashram, which was located at Sabarmati, near Ahmedabad. This march was a pivotal act of civil disobedience against the British salt laws, starting from the ashram and proceeding towards the sea to make salt, symbolizing resistance against colonial rule.

35. (A): Mahatma Gandhi's Salt March was notable for involving women significantly in a major act of civil disobedience against the British rule for the first time. Gandhi encouraged the participation of women from all walks of life, marking the march as a key moment in the inclusion of women in the national freedom movement, demonstrating their capacity and right to be active participants in efforts to gain independence from British rule.

36. (B): "Purna Swaraj" translates directly to "complete independence." This was declared as the goal of the Indian National Congress in 1930, marking a significant shift from earlier demands for dominion status to an outright pursuit of full sovereignty from British rule.

37. (D): During his speech at the opening of Banaras Hindu University, Gandhiji criticized the Indian elite for their disconnection from the poor, aligning with option (*a*). He never indicated indifference to the disparities between the wealthy and the impoverished, contradicting option (*b*). He did not suggest that salvation would come through the professional elite such as lawyers and landlords, countering option (*c*). Instead, he emphasized the critical role of farmers in India's future, confirming option (*d*). Gandhiji also famously challenged the attendees to consider their wealth and opulence by suggesting they strip off their jewellery for the nation's benefit, fitting option (*e*).

38. (D): The Khilafat Movement, aimed at protecting the caliphate and expressing solidarity with the Ottoman Empire after World War I, occurred around 1919-1920, making option IV correct for (*a*). The Jallianwala Bagh Massacre, a pivotal event in Indian history, occurred in 1919, aligning with option III for (*b*). Kemal Ataturk was indeed a Turkish ruler who reformed Turkey into a secular state, fitting option II for (*c*). Louis Fisher was a noted biographer of Mahatma Gandhi, confirming option I for (*d*).

39. (A): Justice C.N. Broomfield was the presiding judge at the trial of Mahatma Gandhi after the withdrawal of the Non-Cooperation Movement. This trial is notable for Gandhi's own admission of guilt and his eloquent statement on why he felt compelled to disobey the laws of the British colonial government.

40. (C): Separate electorates for Muslims were first introduced by the British Colonial Government in 1909 through the Indian Councils Act, also known as the Morley-Minto Reforms. This legislation provided for the direct election of Indians to various legislative councils and established separate electorates for major religious groups, thereby beginning a policy of communal representation which had long-lasting impacts on the political landscape of India.

41. (B): Vision of empire viewed the emperor as the sole ruler: Mughal chronicles like the Akbar Nama by Abu'l Fazl often presented a vision of the empire where the emperor was depicted as the supreme sovereign. This portrayal was likely due to the chronicler's role in the court and the importance of reinforcing the emperor's central authority in the historical narrative, making the emperor appear as the central figure in the governance and administration of the empire.

42. (C): The nobility was considered a very significant section of the Mughal Court, as indicated in the passage. They were seen as a crucial pillar of the Mughal state, supporting the emperor's authority and helping in the administration and governance of the empire through their roles in various institutional frameworks.

43. (C): The Akbar Nama, written by Abu'l Fazl, explicitly states that the entire kingdom was to follow the king's orders, reinforcing the emperor's authority and central role in the administration of the empire. This chronicle serves as a primary source detailing how the emperor's commands were seen as binding across the Mughal empire.

44. **(B):** The Mughal imperial administrative apparatus was effectively dependent on nobles. These nobility members played crucial roles in governance, military command, and local administration, acting as intermediaries between the emperor and the common masses, and ensuring the execution of imperial decrees across the vast territories of the Mughal empire.

45. **(D):** Abu'l Fazl is the author of the Akbar Nama, a comprehensive chronicle of the reign of Emperor Akbar. Abu'l Fazl was a key court historian and one of the nine gems in Akbar's court, tasked with documenting the emperor's reign and the workings of the empire in detailed accounts, which included not just political events but also cultural and administrative insights.

46. **(A):** The Constitution of India came into force on 26th January, 1950. This date marks the official adoption of the constitution, transforming India into a republic, signifying the complete transfer of governance from British authority to the newly established Indian government.

47. **(D):** The country size and diversity impacted the Constitution length: The Constitution of India is described as the longest document in the world primarily because of the need to address the diverse and complex nature of Indian society. The wide array of cultures, languages, and religions necessitated a detailed and inclusive constitution to ensure fair and effective governance across all segments of the population.

48. **(C):** It was designed to keep the country's divided classes, communities, and castes together: The Constitution of India was crafted with the explicit intent to unify a highly diverse and divided nation. It aimed to forge a common identity and national unity by accommodating the varying interests and needs of different classes, castes, and communities, promoting a cohesive and inclusive framework for all citizens.

49. **(C):** The Constitution of India was deliberated upon in the Constituent Assembly, a body specially convened to draft and shape the constitution. This assembly comprised representatives from various parts of India, reflecting the country's diversity and ensuring that multiple viewpoints were considered in the drafting process.

50. "ALL ARE CORRECT": The nature of the Constitution imbibed the right to Cultural Rights, Educational Rights, Equality, and Religion. The Indian Constitution is comprehensive, providing for a range of fundamental rights that protect the cultural and educational rights of citizens, ensure equality before the law, and safeguard the freedom of religion, thereby embodying the principles of a diverse and democratic society.

POLITICAL SCIENCE

1. Which of the following nations adopted an 'Open Door' policy and economy reforms in 1978?
   A. South Korea B. China
   C. USA D. Japan

2. In 1966, who made the six-point proposal for the greater autonomy of East Pakistan?
   A. Jawaharlal Nehru
   B. Sheikh Mujib-ur-Rahman
   C. General Yahya Khan
   D. Zulfikar Ali Bhutto

3. In which year was Mikhail Gorbachev elected as the General Secretary of the Communist Party of the Soviet Union?
   A. 1982 B. 1983
   C. 1984 D. 1985

4. Which of the following countries have **not** accepted Euro as the common currency?
   A. Denmark and Sweden
   B. Spain and Portugal
   C. Greece and Germany
   D. France and Austria

5. The ASEAN Regional Forum (ARF) established in 1994, is the organization that carries out the coordination of:
   A. Trade and Finance
   B. Friendship and Solidarity
   C. Security and Foreign Policy
   D. Investment and Labour

6. Which of the following countries joined SAARC in the year 2007?
   A. Bhutan B. Nepal
   C. Afghanistan D. Bangladesh

7. Which of the following countries is **not** included in South Asia?
   A. Pakistan B. China
   C. Bangladesh D. Nepal

8. At the Yalta Conference, the 'Big Three' decided to organise a United Nations Conference on the proposed world organisation. The 'Big Three' stood for:
   A. Roosevelt, Churchill and Krushchev
   B. Roosevelt, Churchill and Stalin
   C. Deng Xiaoping, Churchill and Stalin
   D. Kennedy, Attlee and Stalin

9. The International Atomic Energy Agency (IAEA) was established in:
   A. 1951 B. 1953
   C. 1955 D. 1957

10. Which of the following organization provides loans and grants to member countries for human development (education and health), agriculture and rural development infrastructure and environment protection?
    A. WTO B. World Bank
    C. IMF D. UNO

11. What is the full form of START?
    A. Strategic Arms Reduction Toll
    B. Strategic Arms Reduction Treaty
    C. Strategic Arms Reduction Tactics
    D. Strategic Arms Reduction Tax

12. Which of the following is a threat to Global security?
    A. Human Rights B. Arms Control
    C. Terrorism D. Disarmament

13. Match List-I with List-II:

List-I (Indigenous People)	**List-II (Region)**
(*a*) Mapuche	I. East of Panama Canal
(*b*) Kuna Tribe	II. Bangladesh
(*c*) Indigenous people of Cordillera Region	III. Chile
(*d*) Tribal people of the Chittagong Hill Tracts	IV. Philippines

Choose the **correct** answer from the options given below:

	(*a*)	(*b*)	(*c*)	(*d*)
A.	I	II	III	IV
B.	III	I	IV	II
C.	I	II	IV	III
D.	III	IV	I	II

1. B **2.** B **3.** D **4.** A **5.** C **6.** C **7.** B **8.** B **9.** D **10.** B
11. B **12.** C **13.** B

14. When was the Kyoto Protocol signed?

A. 1992 B. 1995

C. 1997 D. 1999

15. When was the Energy Conservation Act passed?

A. 1998 B. 1999

C. 2001 D. 2005

16. Which of the following global platform brings together Human Rights activists, environmentalists, labour, youth and women activists opposed to neo liberal globalization?

A. World Economic Forum

B. World Social Forum

C. World Cultural Forum

D. G-20

17. Which of the statement is true about globalization?

A. Globalization is purely an economic phenomenon

B. Globalization is purely a cultural phenomenon

C. Globalization is a multi-dimensional phenomenon

D. Globalization has had a universal impact on all states and societies

18. When is 'Ambedkar Jayanti' observed in India?

A. January 14 B. February 14

C. March 14 D. April 14

Directions (Qs. No. 19-23): *Study the picture given below and answer the five questions that follow:*

19. Look at the picture and identify the Logo.

A. EU B. SAARC

C. UN D. ASEAN

20. Who was the second Secretary General of UN?

A. U. Thant B. Trygve Lie

C. Dag Hammarskjold D. Kurt Waldheim

21. Which day is celebrated as the UN day?

A. 20th October B. 22nd October

C. 24th October D. 26th October

22. The UN was founded as a successor to which of the following?

A. League of Nations

B. Concert of Europe

C. Council of Europe

D. Hague Conference

23. Write the full form of UNDP.

A. United Nations Development Planning

B. United Nations Development Programme

C. United Nations Design Programme

D. United News Development Programme

Directions (Qs. No. 24-29): *Read the following paragraph carefully and answer the five questions that follow:*

In the North-East, regional aspirations reached a turning point in 1980s. This region now consists of seven States, also referred to as the 'Seven Sisters'. The region has only 4 per cent of the country's population but about twice as much share of its area. A small corridor of about 22 kilometers connects the region to the rest of the country. Otherwise the region shares boundaries with China, Myanmar and Bangladesh and serves as India's gateway to South-East Asia.

The region has witnessed a lot of change since 1947. Tripura, Manipur and Khasi Hills of Meghalaya were erstwhile Princely States which merged with India after Independence. The entire region of North-East has undergone considerable political reorganisation. Nagaland State was created in 1963; Manipur, Tripura and Meghalaya in 1972, while Mizoram and Arunachal Pradesh became separate States only in 1987. The Partition of India in 1947 had reduced the North-East to a land-locked region and affected its economy. Cut off from the rest of India, the region suffered neglect in developmental terms. Its politics too remained insulated. At the same time, most States in this region underwent major demographic changes due to influx of migrants from neighbouring States and countries.

The isolation of the region, its complex social character and its bakwardness compared to other parts of the country have all resulted in the complicated set of demands from different States of the North-East. The vast international border and weak communication between the North-East and the rest of India have further added to the delicate

14. C	**15.** C	**16.** B	**17.** C	**18.** D	**19.** C	**20.** C	**21.** C	**22.** A	**23.** B

nature of politics there. Three issues dominate the politics of North-East: demands for autonomy, movements for secession, and opposition to 'outsiders'. Major initiatives on the first issue in the 1970s set the stage for some dramatic development on the second and the third in the 1980s.

24. North-East region consists of seven States called ________ .

A. Seven Sisters B. Seven Stars
C. Seven Seas D. Seven Brothers

25. Which of the following countries does the North-East region share its boundaries with?

A. China, Nepal and Bangladesh
B. China, Bhutan and Bangladesh
C. China, Myanmar and Bangladesh
D. China, Sri Lanka and Bangladesh

26. In which year was the State of Nagaland created?

A. 1961 B. 1963
C. 1965 D. 1967

27. Khasi tribes, an ethnic group, are the inhabitants of which of the following States?

A. Manipur B. Mizoram
C. Nagaland D. Meghalaya

28. The North-East serves as gateway to which of the regions mentioned below?

A. South-East Asia B. South Asia
C. West Asia D. Europe

29. Who among the following entered into Standstill Agreement with India in November?

A. Maharaja of Manipur
B. Nizam of Hyderabad
C. Nawab of Junagadh
D. Maharaja of Kashmir

30. Which of the following Princely States were reluctant to sign the Instrument of Accession with India?

A. Tamil Nadu, Gujarat, Punjab
B. Kerala, Hyderabad, Bombay
C. Assam, Goa, Tripura
D. Hyderabad, Junagadh, Kashmir

31. The 'two-nation theory' was advanced by which of the following party?

A. Janata Dal
B. Muslim League
C. Socialist Party
D. Swatantra Party

32. Who was known as 'Frontier Gandhi'?

A. Mahatma Gandhi
B. Sardar Patel
C. Khan Abdul Ghaffar Khan
D. Potti Sriramulu

33. Match List-I with List-II:

List-I	List-II
(*a*) S.A. Dange	I. Bharatiya Jana Sangh
(*b*) Shyama Prasad Mukherjee	II. Swatantra Party
(*c*) Minoo Masani	III. Praja Socialist Party
(*d*) Ashok Mehta	IV. Communist Party of India

Choose the **correct** answer from the options given below:

	(*a*)	(*b*)	(*c*)	(*d*)
A.	IV	I	II	III
B.	I	III	II	IV
C.	I	II	IV	III
D.	III	IV	I	II

34. Who was the leader of the anti-caste movement and the founder of Independent Labour Party?

A. Acharya Narendra Dev
B. Rafi Ahmed Kidwai
C. A.K. Gopalan
D. Babasaheb Bhimrao Ambedkar

35. Who among the following was known as the 'Milkman of India'?

A. Arun Krishna B. Muljibhai Patel
C. Verghese Kurien D. M.S. Swaminathan

36. **Statement I:** The Second Five Year Plan stressed on heavy industries.

Statement II: A bulk of industries like electricity, railways, steel could be developed by the private sector.

A. Both Statement I and Statement II are correct
B. Both Statement I and Statement II are incorrect
C. Statement I is correct, but Statement II is incorrect
D. Statement I is incorrect, but Statement II is correct

37. The Second Five Year Plan was drafted under the leadership of ________ .

A. K.N. Raj
B. P.C. Mahalanobis
C. J.C. Kumarappa
D. P.C. Mahapatra

24. A **25.** C **26.** B **27.** D **28.** A **29.** B **30.** D **31.** B **32.** C **33.** A
34. D **35.** C **36.** C **37.** B

38. Which of the following treaty was rejected by India as discriminatory as it prevented only non-nuclear countries from acquiring nuclear weapons?

A. Intermediate Range Nuclear Force Treaty
B. Non Proliferation Treaty
C. Strategic Arms Reduction Treaty
D. Strategic Offensive Reduction Treaty

39. Where was the first summit of the NAM (Non-Alignment Movement) held?

A. Bengaluru B. Belgrade
C. Belgium D. Belarus

40. The Shimla Agreement of 1972 was signed between India and which of the following countries?

A. Nepal B. Pakistan
C. China D. Bangladesh

41. Who proposed in 1963 that all senior Congressman should resign from office to make way for younger party workers?

A. S. Nijalingappa
B. V.V. Giri
C. K. Kamaraj
D. Indira Gandhi

42. Who gave the strategy of 'Non-Congressism'?

A. Ram Manohar Lohia
B. C. Natarajan Annadurai
C. K. Kamaraj
D. Karpoori Thakur

43. The Mandal Commission was appointed by ______ Government at the Centre.

A. Indian National Congress Party
B. Bharatiya Janata Party
C. Janata Party
D. Samajwadi Party

44. In 1974, nationwide strike by all the employees of the Railways was led by which of the following leaders?

A. Jayaprakash Narayan
B. Charu Majumdar
C. George Fernandes
D. Indira Gandhi

45. Which of the following political party led the movement for the formation of Punjabi Suba?

A. Congress B. Lok Dal
C. Akali Dal D. CPI

46. Who among the following led the Anti Brahmin movement, worked for the Justice Party and also found Dravidar Kazhagam?

A. A.K. Gopalan
B. E.V. Ramasami Naicker
C. K. Kamaraj
D. Potti Sriramulu

47. What does BAMCEF stand for?

A. Backward and Muslim Communities Employees Federation
B. Backward and Minority Communities Education Federation
C. Backward and Minority Communities Employees Federation
D. Backward and Majority Communities Employees Federation

48. Match List-I with List-II:

List-I (Prime Minister)	**List-II (Period)**
(*a*) H.D. Deve Gowda	I. May 2004–May 2014
(*b*) I.K. Gujaral	II. June 1996–April 1997
(*c*) V.P. Singh	III. April 1997–March 1998
(*d*) Manmohan Singh	IV. December 1989 – November 1990

Choose the **correct** answer from the options given below:

	(*a*)	(*b*)	(*c*)	(*d*)
A.	II	III	IV	I
B.	I	III	II	IV
C.	I	II	IV	III
D.	III	IV	I	II

49. Who was the founder of Bahujan Samaj Party?

A. Mayawati
B. B.R. Ambedkar
C. Jagjivan Ram
D. Kanshi Ram

50. The model of transition in Russia, Central Asia and East Europe that was influenced by World Bank and the IMF came to be known as:

A. Current Therapy
B. Shock Therapy
C. Fiscal Therapy
D. Glasnost

38. B **39.** B **40.** B **41.** C **42.** A **43.** C **44.** C **45.** C **46.** B **47.** C
48. A **49.** D **50.** B

EXPLANATORY ANSWERS

1. **(B):** In 1978, under the leadership of Deng Xiaoping, China adopted significant economic reforms and an 'Open Door' policy aimed at opening the country to foreign businesses that wished to invest in China. These reforms marked a shift from a purely socialist economy to a more market-oriented one. The policy was instrumental in sparking rapid economic growth and integrating China into the global economy.

2. **(B):** In 1966, Sheikh Mujibur Rahman, the leader of the Awami League in East Pakistan (now Bangladesh), proposed the six-point plan demanding greater autonomy for East Pakistan. The proposal was crucial in the context of growing disparities and tensions between East and West Pakistan, eventually leading to the independence of Bangladesh in 1971.

3. **(D):** Mikhail Gorbachev was elected as the General Secretary of the Communist Party of the Soviet Union in 1985. His tenure was noted for significant reforms including perestroika (economic restructuring) and glasnost (increased transparency and freedom of speech), which contributed to the eventual dissolution of the Soviet Union.

4. **(A):** Denmark and Sweden, although members of the European Union, have opted not to adopt the Euro as their national currency. Both countries have retained their traditional currencies, the Danish Krone and the Swedish Krona, respectively.

5. **(C):** The ASEAN Regional Forum (ARF) was established in 1994 with the purpose of facilitating coordination on security and foreign policy matters among its members and other interested parties. The forum plays a crucial role in promoting peace and stability in the Asia-Pacific region.

6. **(C):** Afghanistan became a member of the South Asian Association for Regional Cooperation (SAARC) in 2007. SAARC aims to promote economic and regional integration among its member countries in South Asia.

7. **(B):** China is not included in the South Asia region. South Asia typically includes the countries of Afghanistan, Bangladesh, Bhutan, India, Maldives, Nepal, Pakistan, and Sri Lanka. China, being located primarily in East Asia, does not fall within this geographic categorization.

8. **(B):** The 'Big Three' at the Yalta Conference consisted of U.S. President Franklin D. Roosevelt, British Prime Minister Winston Churchill, and Soviet Premier Joseph Stalin. They met in 1945 to discuss the reorganization of post-World War II Europe and the formation of the United Nations.

9. **(D):** The International Atomic Energy Agency (IAEA) was established in 1957. Its primary role is to promote the peaceful use of nuclear energy and to inhibit its use for any military purpose, including nuclear weapons.

10. **(B):** The World Bank is known for providing financial and technical assistance to developing countries for development programs (e.g., education, health, agriculture, and environmental and natural resource management) that are expected to improve the economic prospects and quality of life for people in those countries.

11. **(B):** START, or the Strategic Arms Reduction Treaty, was a series of bilateral treaties between the United States and the Soviet Union (and later its successor states) on the reduction and limitation of strategic offensive arms. The treaty was first signed on July 31, 1991, and was aimed at reducing the nuclear arsenals of both countries.

12. **(C):** Terrorism is considered a significant threat to global security. It involves the use of violence and threats to intimidate or coerce, especially for political purposes. Terrorism aims to create fear, provoke or escalate conflict, and destabilize governments, which can lead to widespread human rights abuses and disruptions in international peace and security.

13. **(B):** Matching the indigenous peoples to their respective regions:
    (*a*) Mapuche are primarily located in Chile.
    (*b*) Kuna Tribe is indigenous to the region east of the Panama Canal.
    (*c*) Indigenous people of the Cordillera Region are found in the Philippines.
    (*d*) Tribal people of the Chittagong Hill Tracts are located in Bangladesh. This alignment helps in understanding the geographical distribution of these indigenous communities.

14. **(C):** The Kyoto Protocol, an international treaty that commits state parties to reduce greenhouse gas emissions, was adopted on December 11, 1997, in Kyoto, Japan. This protocol was one of the first

actionable steps towards global efforts in combating climate change.

15. **(C):** The Energy Conservation Act was passed in 2001 in India. The act provides for the legal framework, institutional arrangement, and a regulatory mechanism at the Central and State level to embark upon energy efficiency drives in the country. The main goal is to reduce energy consumption and promote energy efficiency.

16. **(B):** The World Social Forum is a global platform bringing together various groups including human rights activists, environmentalists, and anti-globalization advocates. It was first held in 2001 as a counter-event to the World Economic Forum and serves as a space for discussing strategies to oppose neoliberal globalization.

17. **(C):** Globalization encompasses various aspects including economic, cultural, political, and technological exchanges that integrate the world. The impacts are vast and varied, affecting different dimensions of society and making it a multi-dimensional phenomenon.

18. **(D):** 'Ambedkar Jayanti' is observed on April 14 each year in India to commemorate the birthday of Dr. B.R. Ambedkar, an Indian jurist, economist, and social reformer who inspired the Dalit Buddhist movement and campaigned against social discrimination. April 14 is celebrated as a public holiday in India in his honor.

19. **(C):** The logo shown in the picture represents the United Nations (UN), identifiable by its emblematic design of a world map surrounded by olive branches, symbolizing peace. The UN is an international organization founded in 1945 to promote international peace and security, develop friendly relations among nations, and coordinate international cooperation.

20. **(C):** Dag Hammarskjöld was the second Secretary-General of the United Nations, serving from April 1953 until his death in September 1961. Hammarskjöld is known for his active role in addressing international crises during his tenure, significantly shaping the role of the UN in global diplomacy.

21. **(C):** UN Day is celebrated on October 24 each year to mark the anniversary of the entry into force of the UN Charter in 1945. This date signifies the official establishment of the United Nations and is celebrated worldwide to highlight the aims and achievements of the organization.

22. **(A):** The UN was founded as a successor to the League of Nations, which was established after World War I but was largely ineffective in preventing another major conflict. The failure of the League of Nations led to the establishment of the UN with a more comprehensive structure and broader mandate to maintain peace and security.

23. **(B):** UNDP stands for the United Nations Development Programme. It is a UN organization tasked with assisting countries in their sustainable development goals by improving economic policies, governance, and capacity building, providing support across a range of development initiatives.

24. **(A):** The North-East region of India consists of seven states, commonly referred to as the 'Seven Sisters.' These include Arunachal Pradesh, Assam, Meghalaya, Manipur, Mizoram, Nagaland, and Tripura, known for their unique cultural heritage and geographical significance in India.

25. **(C):** The North-East region of India shares its boundaries with China to the north, Myanmar to the east, and Bangladesh to the south-west, making it a strategic gateway to South-East Asia and significant in terms of geopolitical and trade relations.

26. **(B):** The state of Nagaland in India was created in the year 1963, following the signing of the Nagaland Peace Accord between the Indian government and the Naga leaders. This was a significant event in the history of regional autonomy movements in India.

27. **(D):** The Khasi tribes are an ethnic group predominantly inhabiting the state of Meghalaya in India. They are known for their matrilineal society and are one of the major tribal communities in the North-East.

28. **(A):** The North-East region of India serves as a gateway to South-East Asia, facilitating cultural, economic, and political interactions. The region's strategic location enhances its role in India's Act East policy, aimed at strengthening ties with its eastern neighbors.

29. **(B):** Hyderabad, the largest of the Princely States was surrounded entirely by Indian territory. Some parts of the old Hyderabad state are today parts of Maharashtra, Karnataka and Andhra Pradesh. Its ruler carried the title, 'Nizam', and he was one of the world's richest man. The Nizam wanted an independent status for Hyderabad. He entered into what was called the Standstill Agreement with India in November 1947 for a year while negotiations with the Indian government were going on.

30. **(D):** Hyderabad, Junagadh, Kashmir: These three princely states were initially reluctant to sign the Instrument of Accession with India following independence in 1947. Hyderabad and Junagadh were influenced by their Muslim rulers, while Kashmir's strategic location and diverse population led to its contested accession.

31. **(B):** The two-nation theory, proposing the creation of separate nations for Muslims and Hindus, was advanced by the Muslim League under the leadership of Muhammad Ali Jinnah. This ideology was a fundamental driving force behind the partition of India and the creation of Pakistan in 1947.

32. **(C):** Khan Abdul Ghaffar Khan is known as 'Frontier Gandhi' due to his close association with Mahatma Gandhi and his adoption of non-violent struggle. Khan Abdul Ghaffar Khan was a Pashtun leader from the North-West Frontier Province who advocated for the rights of Pashtuns and played a significant role in the Indian independence movement.

33. **(A):**

(*a*) S.A. Dange was associated with the Communist Party of India.

(*b*) Shyama Prasad Mukherjee founded the Bharatiya Jana Sangh.

(*c*) Minoo Masani was a key figure in the Swatantra Party.

(*d*) Ashok Mehta was involved with the Praja Socialist Party. This alignment reflects their respective ideological and political affiliations.

34. **(D):** Dr. B.R. Ambedkar was a prominent leader of the anti-caste movement and the founder of the Independent Labour Party in 1936. He was instrumental in campaigning against social discrimination towards the untouchables and played a pivotal role in drafting India's Constitution.

35. **(C):** Verghese Kurien, often called the 'Milkman of India,' was the architect of India's White Revolution, which transformed the country into one of the largest milk producers in the world. His work with the dairy cooperative movement in India, notably with Amul in Gujarat, significantly improved milk production and rural livelihoods.

36. **(C):** Statement I is correct, but Statement II is incorrect: The Second Five Year Plan of India emphasized the development of heavy industries such as steel, electricity, and machinery, under the public sector. The plan did not rely on the private sector for these critical industries, contrary to what Statement II suggests.

37. **(B):** The Second Five Year Plan was drafted under the guidance of P.C. Mahalanobis, a noted Indian statistician and economist. His approach focused on industrialization and played a crucial role in shaping the economic policies during this period.

38. **(B):** India rejected the Non Proliferation Treaty (NPT) as discriminatory because it prohibited non-nuclear states from acquiring nuclear weapons while allowing the established nuclear states to maintain their arsenals. India viewed this as a flawed treaty that did not promote genuine nuclear disarmament.

39. **(B):** The first summit of the Non-Aligned Movement (NAM) was held in Belgrade, Yugoslavia, in 1961. This conference was significant in establishing a group of states that were not formally aligned with or against any major power bloc during the Cold War.

40. **(B):** The Shimla Agreement of 1972 was signed between India and Pakistan following the Bangladesh Liberation War of 1971. This agreement led to the return of prisoners of war and the establishment of new boundaries between the two nations, notably returning captured territory in the west and committing to peaceful resolution of issues.

41. **(C):** K. Kamaraj proposed in 1963 that all senior Congress leaders should resign from their positions to make way for younger, more energetic party workers. This proposal was part of the Kamaraj Plan, which aimed at revitalizing the Indian National Congress and making it more responsive to the needs of the people.

42. **(A):** The strategy of 'Non-Congressism' was given by Ram Manohar Lohia, who was a significant figure in the Indian socialist movement. This strategy aimed to unite all non-Congress parties to create a viable political alternative to the Congress, which was dominant in Indian politics at the time.

43. **(C):** The Mandal Commission, formally known as the Socially and Educationally Backward Classes Commission, was established in 1979 by the Janata Party government under Prime Minister Morarji Desai. The commission was tasked with identifying the socially or educationally backward classes of India to provide them with affirmative action.

44. (C): The nationwide railway strike in 1974, one of the largest strikes in India, was led by George Fernandes. This strike was significant in the history of Indian labor movements and highlighted the demands for better wages and working conditions for railway workers.

45. (C): The Akali Dal was the leading political party in the movement for the formation of the Punjabi Suba, a state for Punjabi-speaking people. The demand was driven by cultural and linguistic identity, leading to the reorganization of Punjab and the creation of Haryana and Himachal Pradesh as separate states.

46. (B): E.V. Ramasami Naicker, also known as Periyar, led the Anti-Brahmin movement and was a founder of the Justice Party and later Dravidar Kazhagam. His efforts were pivotal in advocating for social justice and equality, challenging the traditional caste hierarchies in South India.

47. (C): The All India Backward and Minority Communities Employees Federation, abbreviated as BAMCEF, is an organisation for employees of oppressed communities that was established in 1971 by Kanshi Ram, D. K. Khaparde, and Dinabhana. The term got its significance from the Constitution of India, which categories the oppressed and exploited communities into classes on the basis of their status: Scheduled Castes (SC), Scheduled Tribes (ST), Other Backward Class (OBC) and Minority Communities.

BAMCEF started at a convention held in Delhi in 1978, with an official launch on 6 December 1978, the death anniversary of B. R. Ambedkar. The ideology of BAMCEF is to fight against the rooted system of inequality that divides the Indian citizens and to abolish the caste system.

48. (A):

- **H.D. Deve Gowda** is an Indian politician who served as the prime minister of India from 1 June 1996 to 21 April 1997. Deve Gowda was born on 18 May 1933 in Haradanahalli, a village in Holenarasipura Taluk, of the erstwhile Kingdom of Mysore (now in Hassan, Karnataka). His father Dodde Gowda was a paddy farmer and mother, Devamma was a home maker.
- **Inder Kumar Gujral** was an Indian diplomat, politician and freedom activist who served as the prime minister of India from April 1997 to March 1998. Born in Punjab, he was influenced by nationalistic ideas as a student, and joined the All India Students Federation and the Communist Party of India. He was imprisoned for taking part in the Quit India movement.
- **V.P. Singh** was an Indian politician who was the Prime Minister of India from 1989 to 1990. He was educated at Allahabad University and Fergusson College in Pune. In 1969, he joined the Indian National Congress party and was elected as a member of the Uttar Pradesh Legislative Assembly.
- **Manmohan Singh** is an Indian retired politician, economist, academician and bureaucrat who served as the Prime Minister of India from 2004 to 2014. He is the fourth longest-serving prime minister after Jawaharlal Nehru, Indira Gandhi and Narendra Modi.

49. (D): Kanshi Ram was the founder of the Bahujan Samaj Party (BSP), established in 1984. The party was formed to represent and secure the political rights of India's Bahujan Samaj, which includes Dalits, Adivasis, OBCs, and religious minorities.

50. (B): The term "Shock Therapy" refers to the sudden release of price and currency controls, withdrawal of state subsidies, and immediate trade liberalization within a country, to transition from a state-controlled to a capitalist economy. This model was notably applied in Russia, Central Asia, and Eastern Europe during the early 1990s following the advice and influence of the World Bank and the IMF.

SOCIOLOGY

1. The Chipko Movement is an example of:

A. Peasant Movement
B. Workers Movement
C. Ecological Movement
D. Dalit Movement

2. Match the following individuals with their contributions to Indian media.

List-I (Individuals)	List-II (Contributions)
(*a*) Raja Rammohun Roy	I. Started the Bombay Samachar
(*b*) Fardoonji Murzban	II. Encouraged media to act as a watchdog of democracy
(*c*) Ishwar Chandra Vidyasagar	III. Started the Shome Prakash
(*d*) Jawaharlal Nehru	IV. Started the Sambad-Kaumudi

Choose the **correct** answer from the options given below:

	(*a*)	(*b*)	(*c*)	(*d*)
A.	I	II	III	IV
B.	I	III	II	IV
C.	IV	II	I	III
D.	IV	I	III	II

3. Who among the following is credited with the invention of the printing press?

A. Leonardo da Vinci
B. Johann Gutenberg
C. Galileo Galilei
D. Isaac Newton

4. In South Bihar, the locals have a common resentment against migrant traders and moneylenders. What are these migrant groups known as?

A. Nakarattars
B. Adivasis
C. Dikus
D. Oraons

5. According to one of the theories of social movements, social conflict arises when a social group feels that it is worse off than others around it. What is this theory known as?

A. Theory of Relative Deprivation
B. Theory of Reformative Action
C. Theory of Redemptive Action
D. Theory of Resource Mobilization

6. Which of the following characteristics are associated with the Women's Movement of post-1947?

(*a*) Involvement of women in nation building task
(*b*) Growth of autonomous women's movement
(*c*) All women suffer discrimination at uniform level
(*d*) Change in ideology and organizational strategy

Choose the **correct** answer from the options given below:

A. (*a*), (*b*) and (*d*) only
B. (*a*), (*b*) and (*c*) only
C. (*a*), (*b*), (*c*) and (*d*)
D. (*b*), (*c*) and (*d*) only

7. Match List-I with List-II:

List-I (Name of Sociologists)	List-II (Work)
(*a*) Nicholas Dirks	I. Family, Kinship and Marriage in India
(*b*) Louis Dumont	II. Homo-Hierarchicus—The Caste System and its Implications
(*c*) Patricia Uberoi	III. Castes of Mind : Colonialism and the Making of Modern India
(*d*) Andre Beteille	IV. The Reproduction of Inequality: Occupation, Caste and Family

Choose the **correct** answer from the options given below:

	(*a*)	(*b*)	(*c*)	(*d*)
A.	II	I	IV	III
B.	I	III	IV	II
C.	III	II	I	IV
D.	IV	II	I	III

1. C	**2.** D	**3.** B	**4.** C	**5.** A	**6.** A	**7.** C

8. Match the following concepts (List-I) with their appropriate description (List-II):

List-I (Concepts)	List-II (Definition)
(*a*) Fertility Rate	I. Number of live births per 1000 women in the child bearing age group
(*b*) Total Fertility Rate	II. Total number of live births that a hypothetical woman would have during her entire reproductive years
(*c*) Infant Mortality Rate	III. Total number of women who die in childbirth per 1000 live births
(*d*) Maternal Mortality Rate	IV. Number of deaths of babies before the age of one year per 1000 live births

Choose the **correct** answer from the options given below:

	(*a*)	(*b*)	(*c*)	(*d*)
A.	I	II	III	IV
B.	I	III	II	IV
C.	I	II	IV	III
D.	III	IV	I	II

9. The statement "The changes brought about in Indian society and culture as a result of over 150 years of British Rule, the term subsuming changes occurring at different levels...technology, institutions, ideology and values" refers to the process of ________ .

Fill in the blank with the **correct** answer from the options given below:

A. Sanskritisation B. Colonisation
C. Westernisation D. Secularisation

10. In Begum Rokeya Sakhawat's book "Sultana's Dream" we find the following excerpt, "Where are the men? ...., where they ought to be... we shut our men indoors...just as we are kept in the zenana?" What do these lines describe?

A. Double standard imposed by male dominated society
B. Comparison of work done by men and women in a male dominated society
C. Reversal of roles of Gender
D. Challenging patriarchy

11. For which of the following social reasons is the city preferred over village?

(*a*) Decline of common resources in villages
(*b*) Opportunity for earning cash income
(*c*) Sufficient work opportunity
(*d*) Relative Anonymity

Choose the **correct** answer from the options given below:

A. (*a*), (*b*) and (*d*) only
B. (*b*), (*c*) and (*d*) only
C. (*a*), (*b*), (*c*) and (*d*)
D. (*a*), (*c*) and (*d*) only

12. Which of the following factors was **not** responsible for unification of India under Colonial rule?

A. Socio-cultural B. Economic
C. Political D. Administrative

13. Which of the following factors was **not** considered significant during industrialisation in independent India?

A. Development of heavy and machine-making industries
B. Expansion of the public sector
C. Presence of a large cooperative sector
D. Role of coastal cities for trading purpose

14. In which of the following States is Birhor tribe found?

A. Assam B. Bihar
C. Rajasthan D. Nagaland

15. The term "prejudice" refers to ________ .

Fill in the blank with the **correct** answer from options given below:

A. Community identity
B. Social inequality
C. Pre-judgment
D. Individual's life chances

16. Which of the following leaders is not associated with AITUC?

A. M.N. Roy B. S.A. Dange
C. V.V. Giri D. Jayprakash Narayan

Directions (Qs. No. 17-21): *Read the given passage carefully and answer the next five questions.*

In many ways it was a major political change, namely, *the collapse of the erstwhile socialist world* that hastened globalisation and also gave a specific economic and political approach to the economic policies that underpin globalisation. These changes are often termed as neo-liberal economic measures. We have already seen what concrete steps the liberalisation policy took in India. Broadly, these policies reflect a political vision of free enterprise which believes that a free reign to market forces will be both

8. C **9.** C **10.** C **11.** * **12.** A **13.** D **14.** B **15.** C **16.** D

efficient and fair. It is, therefore, critical of both State regulation and State-subsidies. The existing process of Globalisation in this sense does have a political vision as much as an economic vision.

17. What does the term 'liberalisation policy' refer to in the given passage?

A. Regulation of State subsidies
B. Regulation of market forces
C. Regulation of social welfarism
D. De-regulation of market forces

18. What is the central political vision reflected in the economic policies underpinning Globalisation?

A. Free enterprise B. State subsidies
C. Centralised power D. State regulation

19. What is the economic measure that accompanied the collapse of the socialist world and the advent of Globalisation?

A. Conservative measures
B. Welfare measures
C. Neo-liberal measures
D. Protectionist measures

20. What major political change is highlighted in the passage?

A. Collapse of Welfare State
B. Collapse of Capitalist State
C. Collapse of Socialist State
D. Collapse of trade protectionism

21. According to the passage, what is the political vision behind Globalisation?

A. It supports State regulation
B. It is critical of State regulation
C. It advocates for Socialist State
D. It advocates for State subsidies

Directions (Qs. No. 22-26): *Read the given passage carefully and answer the next five questions.*

My grandfather, like most Nagas who had come into close contact with Europeans, was convinced that education was the only way to get ahead in life. He aspired for his children the kind of life he had seen being lived by the British administration and missionaries. He sent my mother away to school, first in neighbouring Assam, then as far as Shimla. My mother was encouraged by one of the more educated men in her village who told her that with an education in these new times, she could even become like the Indian lady who spoke before the world: Vijaylaxmi Pandit, who represented India at the UN. My father, by dint of his own intelligence and hard work, put himself through the local mission school and college in Shillong. All Nagas of my parents' generation who were able to, chose to get educated in English. For them, it was more than a gateway to upward mobility. In a region where tribes that live no more than 20 kms apart speak completely different languages, it was a medium through which they could communicate amongst themselves and with the world. They became the voice of their people and made English the official state language.

22. Which of the following is the main reason for opening up of new opportunities for the people of North-East?

A. Urbanization
B. Sanskritization
C. Western education
D. Modernization

23. According to the passage, which of the following a gateway to upward mobility?

A. Politics B. Education
C. Cultural change D. Social change

24. Name the process through which the movement of individuals takes place from their existing status to improved status.

A. Sanskritization B. Westernization
C. Assimilation D. Upward Mobility

25. Who among the following represented India at the UN?

A. Jawaharlal Nehru
B. Vijaylakshmi Pandit
C. British Missionaries
D. Naga leaders

26. Which of the following is the reason for improved communication among the different factions of the Naga tribes?

A. Use of English language
B. Missionary help
C. Naga leaders
D. Working together in British administration

27. Which of the following Sociologists argued that Sociology helps in understanding the links and connections between "personal troubles" and "social issues?

A. Durkheim B. C.W. Mills
C. Bourdieu D. Weber

17. D	18. A	19. C	20. C	21. B	22. C	23. B	24. D	25. B	26. A	27. B

28. Which programme of the Government of India directly targets at improving sex-ratio?

A. Widow Pension
B. Pre-Natal Diagnostic Techniques (Regulation and Prevention of Misuse) Act
C. Beti Bachao Beti Padhao
D. Sukanya Samriddhi Yojana

29. Which of the following statements is true about Colonialism in India?

A. Parochialism gave birth to Colonialism in India.
B. Colonialism gave birth to Nationalism in India.
C. Urban poor were the main carriers of Nationalism in Colonial India.
D. Capitalist economic changes in India were not related to Colonialism.

30. Match the following terms (List-I) with their description (List-II):

List-I (Terms)	List-II (Descriptions)
(*a*) Varna system	I. Process of adopting higher caste practices
(*b*) Scheduled Castes	II. Four-fold division of society
(*c*) Sanskritisation	III. Opposed to Hindu society
(*d*) Resistance Tribes	IV. Recognised by Govt. of India Act, 1935

Choose the **correct** answer from the options given below:

	(*a*)	(*b*)	(*c*)	(*d*)
A.	I	II	III	IV
B.	II	III	I	IV
C.	IV	II	I	III
D.	II	IV	I	III

31. Which of the following are arguments given by Alfred Gell to explain the significance of market beyond its economic function?

(*a*) Layout of the market symbolises the hierarchical inter-group social relations of that region.
(*b*) Few goods are free in the market for groups lower in the hierarchy.
(*c*) Different social groups are located according to their position in the caste hierarchy and hierarchical market system.
(*d*) Interactions between tribals and non-tribal traders are based on social inequalities.

Choose the **correct** answer from the options given below:

A. (*a*), (*b*) and (*d*) only
B. (*a*) and (*c*) only
C. (*a*), (*b*), (*c*) and (*d*)
D. (*a*), (*c*) and (*d*) only

32. Which of the following principles are applied to maintain caste based restrictions?

(*a*) Birth (*b*) Marriage
(*c*) Food Sharing (*d*) Occupation

Choose the **correct** answer from the options given below:

A. (*a*), (*b*) and (*d*) only
B. (*a*), (*b*) and (*c*) only
C. (*a*), (*b*), (*c*) and (*d*)
D. (*b*), (*c*) and (*d*) only

33. How has national development impacted tribal development?

(*a*) Tribal areas located in mineral rich and forest covered parts of the country paid a disproportionately high price for development.
(*b*) Large dams, factories and mines were built in Nehruvian era.
(*c*) Tribals were dispossessed of their land for setting up hydroelectric power plants.
(*d*) These developments benefitted the tribes at the expense of others.

Choose the **correct** answer from the options given below:

A. (*a*), (*b*), (*c*) and (*d*)
B. (*a*), (*c*) and (*d*) only
C. (*a*), (*b*) and (*c*) only
D. (*b*), (*c*) and (*d*) only

34. Which of the following statements are true about stereotypes?

(*a*) Stereotypes are often applied to ethnic and racial groups.
(*b*) Stereotypes fix whole groups into single entity.
(*c*) Stereotypes refuse to recognise the variation across individuals.
(*d*) Stereotypes are partly colonial constructs.

Choose the **correct** answer from the options given below:

A. (*a*), (*b*) and (*d*) only
B. (*a*), (*b*) and (*c*) only
C. (*a*), (*b*), (*c*) and (*d*)
D. (*b*), (*c*) and (*d*) only

28. C **29.** B **30.** D **31.** D **32.** D **33.** C **34.** C

35. In every society, some individuals have a greater share of valued resources—money, property, education, prestige etc.,—than others. These social resources can be divided into different forms of capital. Identify them from the following.

(*a*) Economic capital
(*b*) Cultural capital
(*c*) Social capital
(*d*) Educational capital

Choose the **correct** answer from the options given below:

A. (*a*), (*b*) and (*d*) only
B. (*a*), (*b*), (*c*) and (*d*)
C. (*a*), (*c*) and (*d*) only
D. (*b*), (*c*) and (*d*) only

36. In which year did the first Backward Classes Commission headed by Kaka Kalelkar submit its report?

A. 1956
B. 1953
C. 1950
D. 1958

37. Which of the following arguments are correct about tribes in India?

(*a*) Adivasis were always the oppressed group, as they are now.
(*b*) Tribes were absorbed in Hindu society through Sanskritisation.
(*c*) Tribes occupied a special trade niche, trading forest produce, salt and elephants.
(*d*) Adivasis often exercised dominance over the plains people through their capacity to raid them.

Choose the **correct** answer from the options given below:

A. (*a*), (*b*) and (*d*) only
B. (*b*), (*c*) and (*d*) only
C. (*a*), (*b*), (*c*) and (*d*)
D. (*a*), (*c*) and (*d*) only

38. What was the opinion of Dr. B.R. Ambedkar about local self-government during the drafting of the Constitution?

A. He believed that local elites and upper castes would exploit the downtrodden masses further.
B. He thought that local self-government will empower the downtrodden masses.
C. He believed that local self-government will ensure equal representation of all social groups.
D. He believed that local self-government will led to economic prosperity.

39. Which of the following is **not** an example of community identity?

A. Membership of family
B. Membership of religious group
C. Membership of a professional group
D. Membership of caste group

40. Which of the following Articles of the Constitution of India, provides for the Right of Minorities to establish and administer educational institutions of their own and that the State shall not discriminate in granting aid to such educational institutions?

A. Article 21
B. Article 29
C. Article 30
D. Article 25

41. Which of the following statements about Commmunalism are correct?

(*a*) Communal means something related to a community.
(*b*) Communalism is about religion, not politics.
(*c*) A devout believer may or may not be communal.
(*d*) Communalism results in constructing identity of large and diverse groups as singular and homogeneous.

Choose the **correct** answer from the options given below:

A. (*a*), (*b*) and (*d*) only
B. (*a*), (*b*) and (*c*) only
C. (*a*), (*c*) and (*d*) only
D. (*b*), (*c*) and (*d*) only

42. On account of which of the following identity markers, do people often face discrimination and exclusion?

(*a*) Gender
(*b*) Ethnicity
(*c*) Disability
(*d*) Caste

Choose the **correct** answer from the options given below:

A. (*a*), (*c*) and (*d*) only
B. (*a*), (*b*) and (*d*) only
C. (*a*), (*b*), (*c*) and (*d*)
D. (*b*), (*c*) and (*d*) only

35. * **36.** B **37.** B **38.** A **39.** C **40.** C **41.** C **42.** C

43. Which of the following are true about Gram Sabha in Panchayati Raj?

(*a*) The Gram Sabha collects central taxes from the village.
(*b*) The Gram Sabha consists of the entire body of citizens in a village.
(*c*) The Gram Sabha is the general body that elects the local government.
(*d*) The Gram Sabha participates in village-level development activities.

Choose the **correct** answer from the options given below:

A. (*a*), (*b*) and (*d*) only
B. (*a*), (*b*) and (*c*) only
C. (*a*), (*b*), (*c*) and (*d*)
D. (*b*), (*c*) and (*d*) only

44. How did the Supreme Court enhance Fundamental Rights, particularly relating to the Right to Life under Article 21?

A. By restricting individual liberty.
B. By narrowing the scope of Article 20.
C. By expanding the interpretation to include various aspects of a quality life.
D. By expanding the scope of Fundamental Duties.

45. Who amongst the following Sociologists remarked that tribal institutions in themselves need not necessarily be democratic in their structure and functioning?

A. Tiplut Nongbri B. Virginius Xaxa
C. Verrier Elwin D. G.S. Ghurye

46. Match List-I with List-II.

List-I (Dominant Caste)	List-II (Region)
(*a*) Rajputs	I. Andhra Pradesh
(*b*) Lingayats	II. Punjab
(*c*) Jat Sikhs	III. Karnataka
(d) Kammas	IV. Uttar Pradesh

Choose the **correct** answer from the options given below:

	(*a*)	(*b*)	(*c*)	(*d*)
A.	IV	III	II	I
B.	III	I	II	IV
C.	I	IV	II	III
D.	II	IV	III	I

47. Which of the following festivals are related to agriculture?

(*a*) Bihu (*b*) Baisakhi
(*c*) Holi (*d*) Pongal

Choose the **correct** answer from the options given below:

A. (*a*), (*b*) and (*d*) only
B. (*a*), (*b*) and (*c*) only
C. (*a*), (*b*), (*c*) and (*d*)
D. (*b*), (*c*) and (*d*) only

48. Which of the following are the indicators of globalisation of agriculture?

(*a*) Contract farming
(*b*) Increased dependence of farmers on fertilisers and pesticides
(*c*) Promotion of indigenous knowledge for agriculture
(*d*) Entry of multinationals into agricultural sector

Choose the **correct** answer from the options given below:

A. (*a*), (*b*) and (*c*) only
B. (*a*), (*b*) and (*d*) only
C. (*a*), (*b*), (*c*) and (*d*)
D. (*b*), (*c*) and (*d*) only

49. Under which of the following systems is all work broken down into its smallest repetitive elements and divided amongst the workers?

A. Binary System
B. Corporate System
C. Flexi System
D. Scientific Management System

50. Match the concepts (List-I) with their respective descriptions (List-II):

List-I (Concepts)	List-II (Descriptions)
(*a*) Liberalisation	I. Economy based on information and technology
(*b*) Transnational Corporations	II. Mixing of global and local culture
(*c*) Glocalisation	III. Companies producing goods and services in multiple countries
(*d*) Weightless Economy	IV. Opening up of the economy to the global markets

Choose the **correct** answer from the options given below:

	(*a*)	(*b*)	(*c*)	(*d*)
A.	I	II	III	IV
B.	IV	II	III	I
C.	IV	III	II	I
D.	III	IV	I	II

43. D **44.** C **45.** A **46.** A **47.** A **48.** B **49.** D **50.** C

EXPLANATORY ANSWERS

1. **(C):** The Chipko Movement, which began in the 1970s in India, is a notable example of an ecological movement. It involved villagers, particularly women, embracing trees to prevent them from being cut down by logging companies. This non-violent protest highlighted the importance of forest conservation and raised awareness about the environmental impact of deforestation.

2. **(D):**

(*a*) **Raja Rammohun Roy - Started the Sambad-Kaumudi (IV):** Raja Rammohun Roy, a prominent social reformer, founded the Sambad-Kaumudi in 1821. This was one of the earliest Bengali newspapers, aimed at promoting social reform and education.

(*b*) **Fardoonji Murzban - Started the Bombay Samachar (I):** Fardoonji Murzban established the Bombay Samachar in 1822. It is one of the oldest newspapers in India that played a significant role in the development of journalism in the country.

(*c*) **Ishwar Chandra Vidyasagar - Started the Shome Prakash (III):** Ishwar Chandra Vidyasagar, a key figure in the social reform movement, founded the Shome Prakash in 1858. It was a Bengali weekly newspaper that focused on social issues and reform.

(*d*) **Jawaharlal Nehru - Encouraged media to act as a watchdog of democracy (II):** Jawaharlal Nehru, India's first Prime Minister, emphasized the role of the media in upholding democratic values and acting as a check on government power, reinforcing its role as a watchdog in a democratic society.

3. **(B):** Johann Gutenberg is credited with the invention of the movable-type printing press around 1440. His innovation revolutionized the production of books by allowing for the mass production of printed materials, which dramatically increased the accessibility of knowledge and contributed significantly to the spread of literacy and ideas during the Renaissance.

4. **(C):** In South Bihar, the term "Dikus" refers to migrant traders and moneylenders who are viewed with resentment by the local population. The term signifies outsiders who come into the region and are perceived as exploiting local resources and economic opportunities.

This resentment often stems from the impact these migrant groups have on local livelihoods, including practices like high-interest money lending and commercial trading that can disadvantage the local communities.

5. **(A):** The Theory of Relative Deprivation posits that social conflict arises when individuals or groups feel they are worse off compared to others in their society. This sense of deprivation is based not on an absolute lack of resources or conditions, but on a relative comparison to the perceived better circumstances of others.

6. **(A):**

(*a*) **Involvement of women in nation-building tasks:** Post-1947, women actively participated in various nation-building activities, including political, social, and economic development.

(*b*) **Growth of autonomous women's movement:** There was a significant increase in independent and autonomous women's organizations advocating for gender equality and women's rights.

(*d*) **Change in ideology and organizational strategy:** The movement evolved in its approach and strategies, reflecting changes in ideological perspectives and adapting to new challenges.

7. **(C):**

(*a*) **Nicholas Dirks - Castes of Mind: Colonialism and the Making of Modern India (III):** Nicholas Dirks explores how colonial rule influenced the development of the caste system in India, focusing on the intersection of caste and colonialism in shaping modern India.

(*b*) **Louis Dumont - Homo-Hierarchicus: The Caste System and its Implications (II):** Louis Dumont's seminal work delves into the hierarchical nature of the caste system in India, examining its social and cultural implications.

(*c*) **Patricia Uberoi - Family, Kinship and Marriage in India (I):** Patricia Uberoi's study provides an in-depth analysis of family structures, kinship, and marital practices in India, highlighting the diversity and dynamics within Indian social systems.

(*d*) **Andre Beteille - The Reproduction of Inequality: Occupation, Caste and Family (IV):** Andre Beteille examines how social inequalities are perpetuated through occupation, caste, and family structures, focusing on the mechanisms that sustain these inequalities.

8. (C):

(*a*) **Fertility Rate - Number of live births per 1000 women in the childbearing age group (I):** This measures the number of live births among women within the childbearing age range (usually 15-49 years) per 1000 women in that age group.

(*b*) **Total Fertility Rate - Total number of live births that a hypothetical woman would have during her entire reproductive years (II):** This indicates the average number of children a woman would have during her lifetime, assuming current age-specific birth rates remain constant.

(*c*) **Infant Mortality Rate - Number of deaths of babies before the age of one year per 1000 live births (IV):** This measures the number of infant deaths per 1000 live births in a given year, reflecting the overall health and quality of healthcare systems.

(*d*) **Maternal Mortality Rate - Total number of women who die in childbirth per 1000 live births (III):** This represents the number of maternal deaths per 1000 live births, indicating the risks associated with childbirth and maternal health care quality.

9. (C): Westernisation refers to the process by which Western ideas, technology, institutions, and values were introduced and integrated into Indian society due to the influence of British colonial rule. This process involved changes at various levels, including technological advancements, institutional reforms, and shifts in ideology and values.

10. (C): These lines illustrate a role reversal where women have taken on the dominant roles traditionally held by men, while men are confined in domestic spaces similar to how women were traditionally confined in the zenana (women's quarters). This reversal highlights the author's critique of gender roles and her envisioning of a society where gender norms are challenged and inverted.

12. (A): The unification of India under British colonial rule was mainly driven by economic, political, and administrative factors. Economically, the British established a unified market and infrastructure like railways, which integrated various regions. Politically, the British consolidated princely states and imposed a central authority, while administratively; they introduced a uniform system of governance and laws across the country. In contrast, socio-cultural factors, although significant in shaping national identity and resistance, were not the primary means through which India was unified under colonial rule.

13. (D): The role of coastal cities in trade, while important, was not a primary factor in the industrialization strategy. Coastal cities facilitated trade by handling imports and exports, but the core objectives were centered around building heavy and machine-making industries and increasing public sector investment. During industrialization in independent India, the emphasis was on developing heavy industries, expanding the public sector, and focusing on large-scale industrial growth.

14. (B): The Birhor tribe is predominantly found in Bihar. They are an indigenous group traditionally engaged in forest-based activities and hunting, reflecting their deep connection with the natural environment. While their presence extends to other neighboring regions, Bihar is one of the key states where they are located, highlighting their traditional habitat and cultural heritage in this part of India.

15. (C): Prejudice involves forming opinions or judgments about individuals or groups based on preconceived notions, often without adequate knowledge or understanding. It typically leads to unfair treatment and discrimination based on characteristics such as race, gender, or religion.

16. (D): M.N. Roy, S.A. Dange, and V.V. Giri were all associated with AITUC, a prominent trade union organization in India. Jayprakash Narayan, on the other hand, was primarily known for his role in the Indian independence movement and his involvement in political reform and the "Total Revolution," but he was not directly linked to AITUC.

17. (D): The passage discusses the collapse of the socialist world leading to globalisation and neo-liberal economic measures, which emphasize free enterprise and minimal state intervention. Therefore, 'liberalisation policy' here means reducing or removing state regulations and subsidies to allow market forces to operate more freely.

18. (A): The passage indicates that the economic policies supporting globalisation are driven by a political vision of free enterprise, which advocates minimal state intervention and relies on market forces to drive efficiency and fairness.

19. **(C):** The passage refers to neo-liberal economic measures as the approach that emerged following the collapse of the socialist world, promoting free enterprise and minimal state intervention. This shift reflects a political vision that emphasizes efficiency and fairness through open markets rather than through state-controlled or subsidized economic policies.

20. **(C):** The passage points out that the collapse of the erstwhile socialist world was a significant political change that accelerated globalisation and influenced the economic and political approach underpinning neo-liberal policies.

21. **(B):** The passage indicates that the political vision underpinning Globalisation is critical of both State regulation and State subsidies, advocating instead for a free enterprise system where market forces operate with minimal interference.

22. **(C):** The passage highlights how the exposure to Western education, encouraged by the British administration and missionaries, provided the Naga people with new opportunities for upward mobility and communication. This education allowed them to interact with the broader world and ultimately influenced the adoption of English as the official state language.

23. **(B):** According to the passage, Education is described as a gateway to upward mobility. The passage emphasizes that the Naga people viewed education, particularly Western education, as a means to improve their social and economic status and to communicate more effectively with others.

24. **(D):** The process through which the movement of individuals takes place from their existing status to an improved status is Upward Mobility. This term refers to the social and economic advancement of individuals or groups, typically through education, employment, or other means that improve their position in society.

25. **(B):** Vijaylakshmi Pandit, a prominent Indian diplomat, represented India at the United Nations. She was renowned for her significant role in international diplomacy, serving as the first female President of the UN General Assembly.

26. **(A):** The use of the English language is the reason for improved communication among the different factions of the Naga tribes. According to the passage, English served as a common medium for communication among tribes with different languages, facilitating interaction and cooperation both within the region and with the outside world.

27. **(B):** C.W. Mills argued that Sociology helps in understanding the links and connections between "personal troubles" and "social issues." Mills introduced the concept of the "sociological imagination," which allows individuals to see how their personal experiences are connected to larger social and historical forces.

28. **(C):** The programme of the Government of India that directly targets improving the sex ratio is Beti Bachao Beti Padhao. This scheme aims to address the declining sex ratio and promote the education and empowerment of girls. It focuses on improving the status of girls through education and ensuring their protection and survival.

29. **(B):** Colonialism in India led to various economic, political, and social changes that contributed to the rise of Indian nationalism. The oppressive nature of British rule and the exploitation of resources fueled the desire for independence and self-rule, which ultimately gave rise to the nationalist movement in India.

30. **(D):**

(*a*) **Varna system is described as the four-fold division of society:** This system categorizes society into four main groups: Brahmins, Kshatriyas, Vaishyas, and Shudras.

(*b*) **Scheduled Castes are those recognized by the Government of India Act, 1935:** These are historically marginalized communities that receive affirmative action benefits.

(*c*) **Sanskritisation refers to the process of adopting higher caste practices:** It involves lower caste individuals or groups emulating the practices of higher castes to gain social prestige.

(*d*) **Resistance Tribes are opposed to Hindu society:** These tribes often resist mainstream social and religious practices and maintain their distinct cultural identities.

31. **(D):**

(*a*) **Hierarchical Layout:** Gell argues that the arrangement of a market often mirrors the social hierarchy of the region. For example, higher-status groups may occupy more prominent or desirable locations within the market, while lower-status groups are positioned less advantageously.

(*c*) **Social Group Placement:** The location of various social groups within the market can indicate their social standing. In hierarchical societies, markets often physically place groups in ways that reinforce their social status, such as segregating traders based on caste or class.

(*d*) **Social Inequality in Interactions:** Gell notes that interactions between different social groups, such as tribals and non-tribal traders, are influenced by existing social inequalities. This dynamic shapes market transactions and reflects broader social relationships.

32. (D):

(*b*) **Marriage:** Caste restrictions often include rules about whom one can marry, typically mandating that individuals marry within their own caste.

(*c*) **Food Sharing:** Caste-based restrictions often govern the sharing of food and participation in communal meals, with certain castes being restricted from sharing food with others.

(*d*) **Occupation:** Specific occupations are traditionally assigned to different castes, and these roles are often restricted based on caste affiliation.

33. (C):

(*a*) **Tribal areas located in mineral-rich and forest-covered parts of the country paid a disproportionately high price for development:** This is true as these areas often faced environmental degradation and displacement due to development projects.

(*b*) **Large dams, factories, and mines were built in the Nehruvian era:** This is correct as the Nehruvian period saw significant industrial and infrastructural development, including large dams and mines in tribal areas.

(*c*) **Tribals were dispossessed of their land for setting up hydroelectric power plants:** This accurately reflects the impact of development, where tribal lands were often acquired for such projects, leading to displacement.

34. (C):

(*a*) **Stereotypes are often applied to ethnic and racial groups:** This is true as stereotypes frequently target specific ethnic and racial groups, generalizing their characteristics.

(*b*) **Stereotypes fix whole groups into a single variation entity:** This statement is correct because stereotypes reduce the complexity of a group to a single set of traits or behaviors.

(*c*) **Stereotypes refuse to recognize the variation across individuals:** This is accurate as stereotypes ignore individual differences within a group, applying a uniform label to everyone.

(*d*) **Stereotypes are partly colonial constructs:** This statement is also true because many stereotypes were reinforced and propagated during colonial times to justify domination and control.

36. (B): The First Backward Classes Commission, also known as the Kaka Kalelkar Commission, submitted its report on 1953. The commission was established by a presidential order under Article 340 of the Constitution of India, which deals with socially and educationally backward classes. The commission was chaired by journalist and social reformer Kaka Kalelkar. The report listed 2,399 backward castes or communities, with 837 of them classified as "most backward".

37. (B):

(*b*) **Tribes were absorbed in Hindu society through Sanskritisation:** This is correct because many tribes have adopted Hindu practices and norms through a process known as Sanskritisation, which involves adopting higher caste practices to improve their social status.

(*c*) **Tribes occupied a special trade niche, trading forest produce, salt and elephants:** This is accurate as many tribes historically engaged in specialized trade, including trading forest products, salt, and elephants.

(*d*) **Adivasis often exercised dominance over the plains people through their capacity to raid them:** This is also correct as some tribal groups exerted influence or control over neighboring plains through raiding and other means.

38. (A): Dr. Ambedkar was concerned that local self-government could reinforce existing social hierarchies and caste-based discrimination. He feared that the power structures at the local level would be dominated by local elites and upper castes, which could perpetuate the oppression of lower castes and marginalized groups. Consequently, he advocated for strong safeguards and protections to prevent the exploitation of the downtrodden by local authorities.

39. (C): Membership of a professional group is not typically considered an example of community identity in the same way as the other options. Community identity often refers to a shared sense of belonging or common characteristics among individuals within a group based on more enduring and inherent aspects such as family, religion, or caste. Membership in a professional group, while important for career and networking, usually pertains more to occupational or interest-based affiliations rather than a deep-rooted sense of community identity.

40. (C): Article 30 of the Indian Constitution safeguards the rights of minorities to establish and manage their own educational institutions. This provision ensures that minorities, whether based on religion or language, can create and run schools and colleges that cater to their communities. Furthermore, it mandates that the State cannot discriminate against these institutions when providing financial assistance or support, thereby promoting equal opportunities for all educational institutions regardless of their minority status.

41. (C):

(*a*) **Communal means something related to a community.** This is correct because the term "communal" indeed pertains to aspects related to communities.

(*c*) **A devout believer may or may not be communal.** This is correct because religious devotion does not automatically make someone communal; communalism specifically refers to the politicization of religion.

(*d*) **Communalism results in constructing identity of large and diverse groups as singular and homogeneous.** This is correct because communalism often involves simplifying complex identities into a single, uniform group identity based on religion.

42. (C):

(*a*) **Gender:** Discrimination and exclusion based on gender are widespread, affecting opportunities, rights, and social standing.

(*b*) **Ethnicity:** Ethnic groups can face discrimination based on cultural, racial, or national differences.

(*c*) **Disability:** People with disabilities often encounter barriers in various areas of life, leading to exclusion and discrimination.

(*d*) **Caste:** Caste-based discrimination, particularly in South Asia, has historically led to significant social and economic exclusion.

43. (D):

(*b*) **The Gram Sabha consists of the entire body of citizens in a village:** This statement is true. The Gram Sabha includes all the registered voters in the village.

(*c*) **The Gram Sabha is the general body that elects the local government:** This statement is true. The Gram Sabha plays a role in electing the members of the Gram Panchayat, which is the local government at the village level.

(*d*) **The Gram Sabha participates in village-level development activities:** This statement is true. The Gram Sabha is involved in discussing and approving plans and projects for the development of the village.

44. (C): The Supreme Court of India has significantly enhanced Fundamental Rights by expansively interpreting the Right to Life under Article 21. Rather than limiting it to mere physical survival, the Court has broadened its scope to encompass various aspects of a quality life, including the right to health, a clean environment, education, and personal liberty. This interpretation ensures that individuals can lead dignified and meaningful lives, reflecting a comprehensive understanding of what constitutes a life of quality and well-being.

45. (A): Tiplut Nongbri, an eminent sociologist, observed that tribal institutions are not inherently democratic in their structure and functioning. This remark highlights that while tribal societies may have unique cultural and social practices, their governance systems do not always align with democratic principles such as equal participation and representation. Instead, tribal governance can be influenced by traditional hierarchies, customs, and leadership patterns that may not fit the conventional democratic framework.

46. (A):

(*a*) **Rajputs:** Rajputs are a dominant caste primarily found in the state of Uttar Pradesh (IV). They are historically known as a warrior class and have significant political and social influence in this region.

(*b*) **Lingayats:** Lingayats are a dominant community in Karnataka (III). They follow a distinct religious tradition within Hinduism and hold considerable socio-political power in the state.

(*c*) **Jat Sikhs:** Jat Sikhs are predominant in Punjab (II). They form a significant part of the agricultural community and have substantial influence in the region's politics and economy.

(*d*) **Kammas:** Kammas are a dominant caste in Andhra Pradesh (I). They are traditionally landowners and farmers and play a key role in the social and political landscape of the state.

47. (A):

(*a*) **Bihu:** This is an agricultural festival celebrated in Assam, particularly marking the Assamese New Year and the spring festival. It is closely associated with farming, especially the sowing season.

(*b*) **Baisakhi:** This is a significant harvest festival in Punjab, marking the beginning of the harvest season for crops like wheat.

(*d*) **Pongal:** This is a major harvest festival in Tamil Nadu, celebrated to thank the Sun God for agricultural abundance.

48. (B):

(*a*) **Contract farming:** This involves agreements between farmers and multinational corporations or large domestic companies for the production and supply of agricultural products, which is a clear indicator of globalization.

(*b*) **Increased dependence of farmers on fertilizers and pesticides:** This can be a result of globalization, as it often involves adopting agricultural practices and inputs from global markets.

(*d*) **Entry of multinationals into the agricultural sector:** This is a direct indicator of globalization, as it involves the participation of global companies in local agriculture.

49. (D): The Scientific Management System, developed by Frederick Taylor, involves breaking down work into its smallest repetitive elements to enhance efficiency and productivity.

By analyzing each task in detail and dividing it into simple, repetitive components, this system allows for the specialization of workers, each focusing on specific tasks.

50. (C):

(*a*) **Liberalisation:** This refers to the process of opening up the economy to global markets, reducing trade barriers, and encouraging free trade. Therefore, it matches with description IV.

(*b*) **Transnational Corporations:** These are companies that operate and produce goods and services in multiple countries. Therefore, it matches with description III.

(*c*) **Glocalisation:** This concept involves the mixing of global and local cultures, adapting global practices to local contexts. Therefore, it matches with description II.

(*d*) **Weightless Economy:** This term refers to an economy that is based on information and technology rather than traditional, physical goods. Therefore, it matches with description I.

GENERAL TEST

1. From the given options, which pass connects Jammu with Srinagar?

A. Banihal Pass
B. Nathu La Pass
C. Niti Pass
D. Rohtang Pass

2. Which of the following is not correctly matched regarding Padma Awards-2024?

A. Padma Vibhushan Award → Shri Konidela Chiranjeevi
B. Padma Shri Award → Mithun Chakraborty
C. Padma Bhushan Award → M. Fathima Beevi
D. Padma Bhushan Award → Sitaram Jindal

3. Match List-I with List-II.

List-I (Person)	**List-II (Area of Work)**
(*a*) Vishakhadatta	I. Medicine
(*b*) Kartikeya Sarabhai	II. Poet
(*c*) Charaka	III. Environmentalist
(*d*) Satyendra Nath Bose	IV. Mathematics

Choose the **correct** answer from the options given below:

	(*a*)	(*b*)	(*c*)	(*d*)
A.	I	III	IV	II
B.	II	III	I	IV
C.	II	I	III	IV
D.	III	IV	I	II

4. If $\sin A = \frac{4}{5}$, then (3 – tan A) (2 + cos A) = ?

A. $\frac{12}{5}$
B. $\frac{13}{3}$
C. $\frac{13}{5}$
D. 3

5. A man can row a boat at 8 km/h in still water. If the speed of the water current is 2 km/h and it takes him 2 hours to row to a place and come back, then how far off (in km) is the place?

A. 7.5
B. 6
C. 9.5
D. 10

6. The following states were formed after 1960. What was the correct sequence of their formation?

(*a*) Haryana (*b*) Sikkim
(*c*) Nagaland (*d*) Goa

Choose the **correct** answer from the options given below:

A. (*c*), (*b*), (*a*), (*d*)
B. (*c*), (*a*), (*b*), (*d*)
C. (*c*), (*d*), (*a*), (*b*)
D. (*d*), (*c*), (*a*), (*b*)

7. Out of the given options, which scheme's objective is to conduct an annual survey at the gram panchayat level to monitor the progress in the development process of the rural areas?

A. Mission Antyodaya (2022-23)
B. Mission Karmayogi (2022-23)
C. Mission Rashtriya Gokul (2022-23)
D. Mission Atmanirbhar Bharat (2022-23)

8. Which one of the following countries is **not** a member of the "Quadrilateral Security Dialogue", also known as "QUAD"?

A. China
B. Japan
C. India
D. Australia

9. Who has become the first woman chairperson of the Railway Board of India Railways in 2023?

A. Jaya Verma Sinha
B. Mita Vashishth
C. Ravneet Kaur
D. Vasudha Gupta

10. Match List-I with List-II.

List-I (Country)	**List-II (Currency)**
(*a*) Myanmar	I. Ruble
(*b*) Russia	II. Ngultrum
(*c*) Malaysia	III. Kyat
(*d*) Bhutan	IV. Ringgit

Choose the **correct** answer from the options given below:

	(*a*)	(*b*)	(*c*)	(*d*)
A.	III	I	II	IV
B.	III	I	IV	II
C.	IV	I	III	II
D.	II	I	IV	III

1. A **2.** B **3.** B **4.** B **5.** A **6.** B **7.** A **8.** A **9.** A **10.** B

11. "Jhulaghat Suspension Bridge" between India and which country has become fully operational now?

A. Bhutan B. Nepal
C. China D. Myanmar

12. Due to ocean acidification when the ocean becomes more acidic, what happens to the pH level of the ocean?

A. The pH level goes down.
B. The pH level stays the same.
C. The pH level goes up.
D. The pH level becomes zero.

13. Who is the first para-athlete to receive the Padma Bhushan award in India?

A. Bhavina Patel
B. Devendra Jhajharia
C. Avani Lekhara
D. Mariyappan Thangavelu

14. Zemu Glacier is located in which state of India?

A. Uttarakhand
B. Himachal Pradesh
C. Sikkim
D. Arunachal Pradesh

15. Who among the following is Chile's first woman President?

A. Mary Robinson
B. Michelle Bachelet
C. Kim Campbell
D. Jennifer Shipley

16. Which organisation developed and launched 'Ugram' Indigenous Assault Rifle for the armed forces?

A. ISRO B. BEL
C. HAL D. DRDO

17. Which of the following substances is a bad conductor of electricity?

A. Diamond
B. Gold
C. Silver
D. Graphite

18. Which of the following disease is caused due to the deficiency of proteins?

A. Arthritis
B. Kwashiorkor
C. Goitre
D. Night Blindness

19. Match List-I with List-II

List-I (Navy–Institution)	**List-II (Place)**
(*a*) INS Chilka	I. Goa
(*b*) INS Hansa	II. Andhra Pradesh
(*c*) INS Satavahana	III. Kerala
(*d*) INS Garuda	IV. Odisha

Choose the **correct** answer from the options given below:

	(*a*)	(*b*)	(*c*)	(*d*)
A.	III	I	II	IV
B.	I	IV	II	III
C.	IV	I	III	II
D.	IV	I	II	III

20. DRDO has conducted the first successful flight test of Agni-5 missile equipped with MIRV technology. What is the full form of MIRV?

A. Multiple Independently Targetable Re-Entry Vehicle
B. Mission India Target Re-Entry Vehicle
C. Multiple Independently Technology Re-Entry Vehicle
D. Multiple Indirect Targetable Re-Entry Vehicle

21. Which Indian has won the "Ramon Magsaysay Award-2023"?

A. Korvi Rakshand
B. Ashwini Kumar
C. Dipti Ranjan Sahoo
D. Dr. Ravi Kannan R.

22. Who has been appointed the Chairman of the 16th Finance Commission of India?

A. Ajay Narayan Jha
B. Smt. Annie George Mathew
C. Pradip Kumar Mohanty
D. Dr. Arvind Panagariya

23. Sri Ranganathswamy Temple which is situated in Tamil Nadu, is dedicated to which deity?

A. Lord Shiva B. Lord Vishnu
C. Goddess Durga D. Goddess Lakshmi

24. The Election Commission of India gets the power to conduct elections from which of the following articles?

A. Article 324 B. Article 280
C. Article 264 D. Article 26

11. B	**12.** A	**13.** B	**14.** C	**15.** B	**16.** D	**17.** A	**18.** B
19. D	**20.** A	**21.** D	**22.** D	**23.** B	**24.** A		

25. Match List-I with List-II.

List-I (Centre of Handicraft)	List-II (State)
(*a*) Mon	I. Arunachal Pradesh
(*b*) Nalbari	II. Assam
(*c*) Pasighat	III. Meghalaya
(*d*) Tura	IV. Nagaland

Choose the **correct** answer from the options given below:

	(*a*)	(*b*)	(*c*)	(*d*)
A.	IV	II	I	III
B.	I	III	IV	II
C.	IV	III	I	II
D.	I	II	IV	III

26. In which state is "Amchang Wildlife Sanctuary" located?

A. Assam B. Rajasthan
C. Odisha D. Manipur

27. India's first 3-D printed Post Office has been inaugurated in:

A. Guwahati B. Kolkata
C. Mumbai D. Bengaluru

28. What should come in the place of the questions mark (?) in the following alphanumeric series?

A1X, B4P, E25J, J100F, ?

A. O289D B. O225E
C. Q289D D. Q225E

29. In the given analogy, choose the word which will replace the question mark :

NEGI : MVTR :: SING : ?

A. TRNS B. TRNT
C. FRMT D. HRMT

30. In a certain code language 'ki ru pi' means 'nobody like cruel', 'ki mi cha' means 'king was cruel' and 'ru pi cha' means 'nobody like king'. What is the code for 'was' in the given code language?

A. ki B. mi
C. cha D. ru

31. Read the following information carefully to choose the best option for the question:

'P % Q' means that 'P is the sister of Q'
'P + Q' means that 'P is the son of Q'
'P × Q' means that 'P is the husband of Q'
'P – Q' means that 'P is the brother of Q'

Which of the following means 'A is the son-in-law of G'?

A. A × U + S × G
B. A + S % U × G
C. A – S + U × G
D. A × U % S + G

32. If 26th January, 2020 was a Sunday, then what day of the week was it on 16th March of that year?

A. Sunday B. Monday
C. Tuesday D. Wednesday

33. What will be the measurement of the angle made by the hour and minute hands of a clock when the time is 'quarter past 3'?

A. $6\frac{1}{2}^\circ$ B. 10°
C. $7\frac{1}{2}^\circ$ D. $8\frac{1}{2}^\circ$

34. If in a certain code language, 'MERCURY' is coded as 'NGUGZXF', then how will 'ENTANGLE' be coded in the same code language?

A. FPXFSMSM B. FPWESMSM
C. FPWESNSN D. FPWFTNSM

35. The problem given below consists of a question and two statements numbered I and II. You have to decide whether the data provided in the statements are sufficient to answer the question.

How many sisters does Sunny have?

I. Sunny is the only son of his parents.
II. Sunny's parents have three children.

A. Only statement I alone is sufficient to answer the question.
B. Only statement II alone is sufficient to answer the question.
C. Statements I and II together are sufficient to answer the question.
D. Either statement I or II alone is sufficient to answer the questions.

36. A boy leaves his house. He travels 6 km towards South, then travels 8 km towards West and further travels 9 km towards South. How far and in which direction is he from his house now?

A. 13 km, South West
B. 17 km, South West
C. 17 km, North West
D. 13 km, West

25. A **26.** A **27.** D **28.** C **29.** D **30.** B **31.** D **32.** B **33.** C **34.** B **35.** C **36.** B

37. Find out which of the answer figures completes the figure matrix:

Problem figure:

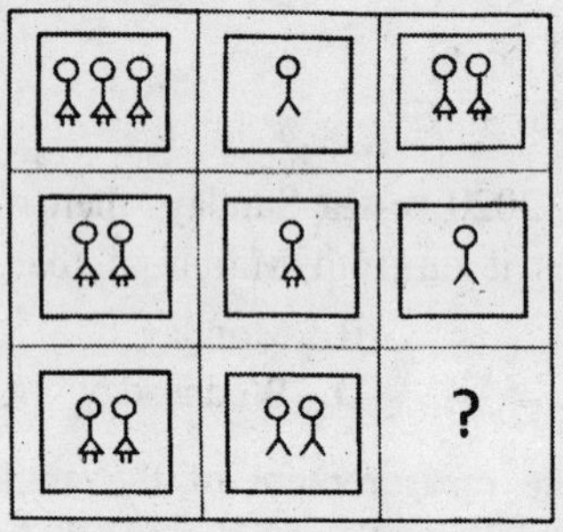

A. 

B. 

C. 

D. 

38. A clock seen through a mirror shows 'quarter to seven'. What is the correct time shown by the clock?

A. 6:15 B. 6:17
C. 5:17 D. 5:15

39. The sequence of folding a piece of paper and the manner in which the folded paper has been cut is shown in the following figures. How would this paper look when unfolded?

A. 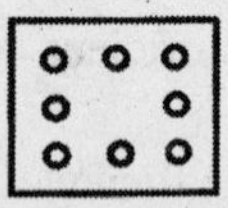

B. 

C. 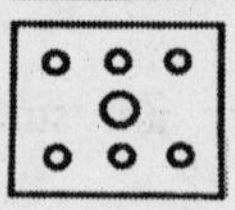

D. 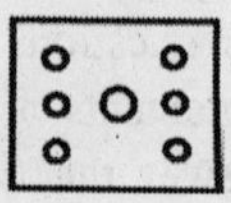

40. Find out the missing (?) number and letter.

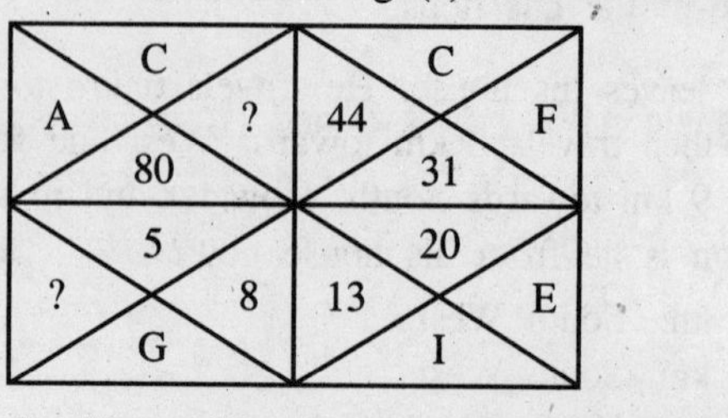

A. 59 and K B. 61 and L
C. 61 and K D. 59 and L

41. What will be the next number of the series

3, 6, 10.5, 17, 26, ?

A. 31 B. 38
C. 40 D. 41

42. In a class of 40 students, Anjali's rank is thrice that of Anita. There are 4 students who have ranks worse than that of Anjali. Anita's rank in the class is:

A. 9th B. 10th
C. 18th D. 12th

43. Six people E, H, K, M, S and U are seated in a circle facing the centre. U and H are immediate neighbours of M. E is the only person sitting between K and S. H is to the immediate right of S. Who is to the immediate right of U?

A. M B. E
C. K D. S

44. Find out which of the answer figures from the options can be formed using all the pieces given in the problem figure.

Problem figure

A. 

B. 

C. 

D. 

45. Read the given statements and conclusions carefully assuming that the information given in the statements is true, even if it appears to be at variance with commonly known facts. Decide which of the given conclusion(s) logically follows from the statements.

Statements:

No keyboard is a mouse
All mouses are computers.
All computers are laptops.

Conclusions:

I. All mouses are laptops.
II. All computers can never be keyboards.

A. Only conclusion I follows
B. Only conclusion II follows
C. Neither conclusion I nor II follows
D. Both conclusions I and II follow

37. B **38.** D **39.** B **40.** B **41.** B **42.** D **43.** C **44.** C **45.** D

46. Simplify: $24 \div 4 \times 2 + 8 - 4 = ?$

A. 1 B. 7
C. 16 D. 56

47. The difference of the greatest and the smallest of the fractions $\frac{1}{2}, \frac{8}{11}, \frac{7}{8}, \frac{7}{9}, \frac{5}{6}$ is:

A. $\frac{3}{8}$ B. $\frac{6}{7}$
C. $\frac{7}{9}$ D. $\frac{1}{3}$

48. The sum of LCM and HCF of two numbers is 854. If the LCM is 60 times the HCF and one of the numbers is 70, then the other number is:

A. 160 B. 164
C. 168 D. 172

49. The present age of Harish is 8 times the sum of the ages of his two sons at present. After 8 years, his age will be 2 times the sum of the ages of his two sons. The present age of Harish (in years) is:

A. 31 B. 32
C. 33 D. 34

50. In an examination, it is required to get 300 marks to pass. A student gets 225 marks and is declared fail by 10% marks. What are the maximum marks of the examinations?

A. 700 B. 750
C. 800 D. 850

51. In a class of 40 students, ratio of boys and girls is 3 : 2 and the average marks scored by boys is 42 and that by girls is 46. Then the average marks scored by the whole class. is:

A. 43.4
B. 43.6
C. 43.8
D. 44

52. The sum of three numbers is 136. If the ratio between the first number and the second number is 2 : 3 and that between the second and third number is 5 : 3, then the first number is:

A. 42 B. 40
C. 36 D. 32

53. An item is sold for ₹ 504 after allowing 20% discount and still a profit of 5% has been earned. The marked price is how much more than the cost price?

A. ₹ 120 B. ₹ 135
C. ₹ 150 D. ₹ 160

54. A certain sum becomes ₹ 2,356 in 3 years and ₹ 2,660 in 5 years on simple interest. The value of sum is:

A. ₹ 1800 B. ₹ 1880
C. ₹ 1900 D. ₹ 1980

55. In a square, lengths of the diagonals are $(4k + 6)$ cm and $(7k - 3)$ cm. The area of the square (in cm^2) is:

A. 144 B. 162
C. 169 D. 172

56. The volume of a cylinder having base radius 3 cm is 396 cm^3. Find its curved surface area (in cm^2). (Use $\pi = 22/7$)

A. 280 B. 301.5
C. 264 D. 320.6

57. A tap can fill a tank in 6 hours. After half the tank is filled, three more similar taps are opened. What is the total time taken to fill the tank completely?

A. 4 hours
B. 5 hours
C. 3 hours 30 minutes
D. 3 hours 45 minutes

58. A train running at the speed of 80 km/h crosses a 350 m long tunnel in 36 seconds. The length of the train (in m) is:

A. 350 B. 380
C. 420 D. 450

59. If the mean of 3, 4, 9, $2k$, 10, 8, 6 and $(k + 6)$ is 8, and mode of 2, 2, 3, $2p$, $(2p + 1)$, 4, 4, 5 and 6 (p is a natural number) is 4, then the value of $(k - 2p)$ is :

A. 0 B. 1
C. 2 D. 3

60. In a triangle ABC, points D and E are on AB and AC respectively such that DE is parallel to BC. If AD = 6 cm, DB = 4 cm, AE = 9 cm, then the length of EC (in cm) is:

A. 7 B. 6.4
C. 6 D. 5.5

46. C	**47.** A	**48.** C	**49.** B	**50.** B	**51.** B	**52.** B	**53.** C
54. C	**55.** B	**56.** C	**57.** D	**58.** D	**59.** C	**60.** C	

EXPLANATORY ANSWERS

1. **(A):** The **Banihal Pass connects** Jammu with Srinagar, playing a **crucial role** in linking the Jammu region with the Kashmir Valley. Located in the Pir Panjal range at an elevation of about 2,832 meters (9,291 feet), it is traversed by the Banihal-Qazigund road tunnel, also known as the Jawahar Tunnel, which ensures all-weather connectivity between the two regions.

2. **(B):** Padma Shri Award — Mithun Chakraborty
The incorrect match regarding the Padma Awards-2024 is Mithun Chakraborty listed as a Padma Shri awardee. In reality, Mithun Chakraborty was honored with the Padma Bhushan for his significant contributions to Indian cinema.

3. **(B):**
(*a*) **Vishakhadatta - Poet (II):** Vishakhadatta was an ancient Indian poet and playwright, known for his work "Mudrarakshasa."
(*b*) **Kartikeya Sarabhai - Environmentalist (III):** Kartikeya Sarabhai is a renowned Indian environmentalist and founder of the Centre for Environment Education (CEE).
(*c*) **Charaka - Medicine (I):** Charaka was an ancient Indian physician, known as the author of the "Charaka Samhita," a seminal text on Ayurveda.
(*d*) **Satyendra Nath Bose - Mathematics (IV):** Satyendra Nath Bose was an Indian physicist and mathematician, best known for his work on quantum mechanics and the Bose-Einstein statistics.

4. **(B):** Given, $\sin A = \frac{4}{5}$

$$\therefore \quad \cos A = \sqrt{1-\sin^2 A} = \sqrt{1-\left(\frac{4}{5}\right)^2}$$

$$= \sqrt{1-\frac{16}{25}} = \sqrt{\frac{9}{25}} = \frac{3}{5}$$

$$\therefore \quad \tan A = \frac{\sin A}{\cos A} = \frac{\frac{4}{5}}{\frac{3}{5}} = \frac{4}{3}$$

$\therefore$ (3 – tan A) (2 + cos A)

$$= \left(3-\frac{4}{3}\right)\left(2+\frac{3}{5}\right)$$

$$= \left(\frac{5}{3}\right)\left(\frac{13}{5}\right) = \frac{13}{3}.$$

5. **(A):** Given, speed of boat in still water = **8 km/h** and speed of current = 2 km/h

$\therefore$ Speed upward = 8 – 2 = 6 km/h

and speed downward = 8 + 2 = 10 km/h

Let, distance = d

$$\text{Then,} \quad \frac{d}{6}+\frac{d}{10} = 2$$

$$\Rightarrow \quad d\left(\frac{1}{6}+\frac{1}{10}\right) = 2$$

$$\Rightarrow \quad d\left(\frac{5+3}{30}\right) = 2$$

$$\Rightarrow \quad d = \frac{2\times 30}{8}$$

$$\Rightarrow \quad d = \frac{15}{2} = 7.5 \text{ km}$$

Hence, required distance = d = 7.5 km.

6. **(B):**
(*c*) **Nagaland:** Formed on December 1, 1963, becoming the 16th state of India. It was created to recognize the distinct identity and culture of the Naga people.
(*a*) **Haryana:** Formed on November 1, 1966, when it was separated from Punjab. This reorganization was based on linguistic lines to cater to the Hindi-speaking population.
(*b*) **Sikkim:** Became the 22nd state of India on May 16, 1975. Before this, Sikkim was a protectorate and then a kingdom under Indian suzerainty.
(*d*) **Goa:** Became the 25th state of India on May 30, 1987, through the 56th Amendment of the Constitution of India. The day is celebrated annually as Goa Statehood Day.

7. **(A):** Mission Antyodaya (2022-23) aims to enhance the living conditions of rural areas by conducting an annual survey at the gram panchayat level. This initiative monitors the progress in the development process, ensuring that various governmental schemes and programs are effectively implemented and yielding the desired outcomes.

8. **(A):** The "Quadrilateral Security Dialogue" (QUAD) is a strategic alliance comprising Japan, India, Australia, and the United States, aimed at enhancing cooperation on security and regional stability in the Indo-Pacific region. China is not a member of this dialogue.

9. (A): Jaya Verma Sinha made history in 2023 by becoming the first woman chairperson of the Railway Board of Indian Railways. Her appointment marks a significant milestone in the history of Indian Railways, reflecting progress towards gender equality in top administrative positions.

10. (B):

(*a*) **Myanmar - The Kyat (III)** is the official currency of Myanmar. It is used for all financial transactions within the country and is represented by the symbol "Ks." The Kyat is subdivided into 100 pyas, though smaller denominations are rarely used.

(*b*) **Russia - The Ruble (I)** is the currency of Russia, symbolized as "₽" or "RUB." It is one of the oldest currencies in the world and has been in use since the 13th century. The Ruble is subdivided into 100 kopecks and is crucial for everyday transactions within Russia.

(*c*) **Malaysia - The Ringgit (IV),** often abbreviated as MYR, is the currency of Malaysia. It is symbolized by "RM" and is subdivided into 100 sen. The Ringgit is used throughout Malaysia and is essential for domestic commerce and trade.

(*d*) **Bhutan - The Ngultrum (II)** is Bhutan's currency, represented by the symbol "Nu." It is pegged to the Indian Rupee and is used in all financial transactions within Bhutan. The Ngultrum is subdivided into 100 chetrum.

11. (B): The "Jhulaghat Suspension Bridge," connecting India and Nepal, has recently become fully operational, enhancing cross-border connectivity and facilitating easier movement of people and goods between the two countries. Located in the Uttarakhand region of India, this bridge is a significant infrastructure development aimed at strengthening bilateral ties and improving access to remote areas on both sides of the border.

12. (A): Ocean acidification occurs when excess carbon dioxide (CO_2) from the atmosphere dissolves in seawater, forming carbonic acid. This process decreases the pH level of the ocean, making it more acidic. As a result, the pH level goes down, which can negatively impact marine life, particularly organisms with calcium carbonate shells or skeletons, such as corals and shellfish, by affecting their ability to form and maintain these structures.

13. (B): Devendra Jhajharia is the first para-athlete to be honored with the Padma Bhushan, one of India's highest civilian awards. Known for his exceptional achievements in para-athletics, Jhajharia is a javelin thrower who has won multiple gold medals at the Paralympic Games, including in 2004 and 2016.

14. (C): The Zemu Glacier is located in Sikkim, India, within the Kanchenjunga range of the Himalayas. It is one of the largest glaciers in the eastern Himalayas and feeds several important rivers in the region. The glacier is renowned for its stunning natural beauty and is a crucial source of water for the surrounding ecosystems.

15. (B): Michelle Bachelet made history as Chile's first woman President, serving two non-consecutive terms from 2006 to 2010 and again from 2014 to 2018. Her presidency marked a significant milestone for gender equality in Chilean politics.

16. (D): The 'Ugram' Indigenous Assault Rifle was developed and launched by the Defence Research and Development Organisation (DRDO), which is India's premier defense research agency. This advanced assault rifle is designed to enhance the capabilities of the Indian armed forces with its modern features and improved performance.

17. (A): While diamond is a form of carbon and has a strong covalent bonding structure, it does not have free electrons or ions to conduct electricity, making it an insulator. In contrast, gold, silver, and graphite are good conductors of electricity.

18. (B): Kwashiorkor is a serious nutritional disorder caused by a deficiency in dietary protein, despite adequate caloric intake. It primarily affects young children and is characterized by symptoms such as swelling of the abdomen and legs (edema), irritability, liver damage, and skin changes. The condition arises when there is not enough protein in the diet to meet the body's needs for growth and repair, leading to severe physical and metabolic disturbances.

19. (D):

(*a*) **INS Chilka - Odisha (IV):** INS Chilka is the premier naval training establishment for the Indian Navy, located near Chilika Lake in Odisha.

(*b*) **INS Hansa - Goa (I):** INS Hansa is a significant naval air station located in Dabolim, Goa, serving as the base for the Indian Navy's aviation operations.

(*c*) **INS Satavahana - Andhra Pradesh (II):** INS Satavahana is a naval submarine training base located in Visakhapatnam, Andhra Pradesh, focusing on training submariners.

(*d*) **INS Garuda - Kerala (III):** INS Garuda is a naval air station situated in Kochi, Kerala, and plays a crucial role in naval aviation operations.

20. (A): MIRV, or Multiple Independently Targetable Re-Entry Vehicle, is a missile technology that enables a single missile to carry multiple warheads, each capable of being directed to a different target independently. This enhances the missile's effectiveness and strategic value, as it allows for a single launch to potentially strike several targets simultaneously, increasing the chances of mission success and complicating defense measures for adversaries.

21. (D): Dr. Ravi Kannan R. was awarded the Ramon Magsaysay Award in 2023 for his exemplary work in delivering quality healthcare to underserved communities in India. As a prominent oncologist, Dr. Kannan has dedicated his career to providing medical services to patients in remote and economically disadvantaged regions.

22. (D): Dr. Arvind Panagariya has been appointed the Chairman of the 16th Financè Commission of India. He is an esteemed economist and former Vice Chairman of NITI Aayog, known for his expertise in economic policy and development.

23. (B): The Sri Ranganathswamy Temple in Tamil Nadu is dedicated to Lord Vishnu, one of the principal deities in Hinduism. Located in Srirangam, it is one of the most significant Vaishnavite temples in India and is renowned for its grandeur and architectural excellence.

24. (A): Article 324 of the Indian Constitution provides for the establishment and powers of the Election Commission of India, empowering it to supervise, direct, and control the entire process of elections to the Parliament and State Legislatures, as well as the office of the President and Vice President of India.

25. (A):

(*a*) **Mon - Nagaland (IV):** Mon is a district in Nagaland known for its rich tradition of tribal crafts, including traditional weaving and basketry, reflecting the diverse cultural heritage of the Naga tribes.

(*b*) **Nalbari - Assam (II):** Nalbari in Assam is renowned for its traditional Assamese handicrafts, particularly handloom products like muga silk and traditional weaving techniques.

(*c*) **Pasighat - Arunachal Pradesh (I):** Pasighat in Arunachal Pradesh is noted for its indigenous crafts, including intricate woodwork and weaving, showcasing the craftsmanship of the local tribes.

(*d*) **Tura - Meghalaya (III):** Tura in Meghalaya is recognized for its traditional handicrafts, including weaving and bamboo crafts, which are integral to the cultural expressions of the Garo tribe.

26. (A): The Amchang Wildlife Sanctuary is located in Assam, near the city of Guwahati. This sanctuary is renowned for its rich biodiversity, including a variety of wildlife such as elephants, tigers, and several species of birds and reptiles. It serves as an important conservation area, protecting the natural habitat and promoting ecological balance in the region.

27. (D): India's first 3-D printed Post Office was inaugurated in Bengaluru, showcasing a groundbreaking approach in construction technology. The building, created using 3-D printing techniques, exemplifies innovation in architectural design and efficiency. This project reflects a move towards modernizing infrastructure and highlights India's commitment to adopting cutting-edge technology in various sectors.

28. (C):

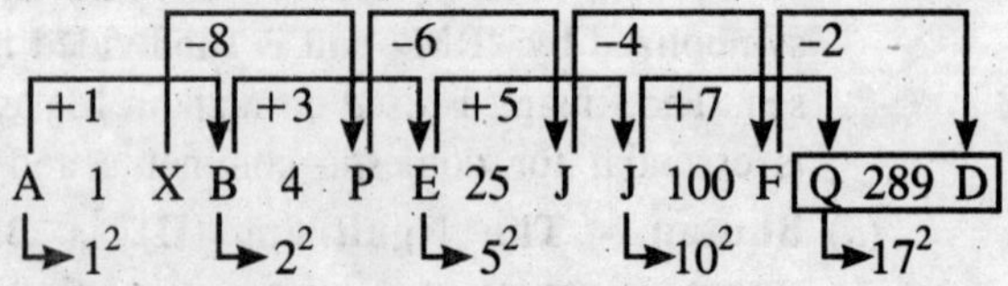

∴ Q289D should come in the place of the question mark in the series.

29. (D): Alphabets in natural series and reverse series

A = Z, B = Y, C = X, ... X = C, Y = B, Z = A

Given, NEGI : MVTR

⇒ N E G I → M V T R

Similarly, S I N G → H R M T

So, NEGI : MVTR :: SING : HRMT.

30. (B): Given, 'ki ru pi' = 'nobody like cruel' ...(*i*)

'ki mi cha' = 'king was cruel' ...(*ii*)

'ru pi cha' = 'nobody like king' ...(*iii*)

From (*i*) and (*ii*),

'cruel' = 'ki'

From (*ii*) and (*iii*),

king = cha

From (*ii*), mi = was

So, 'mi' is the code for 'was' in the given code language.

31. (D): (D) A × U % S + G

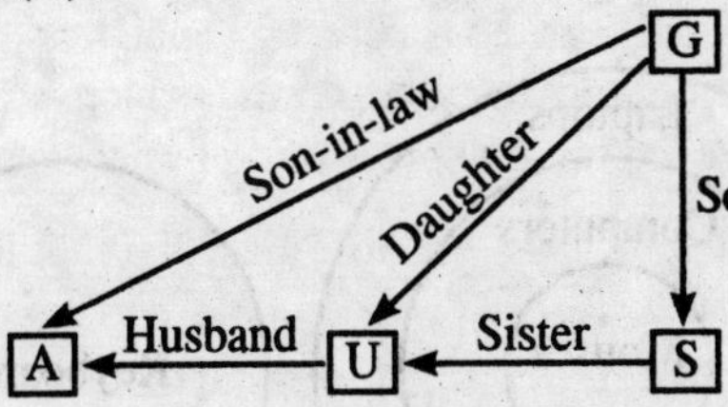

So, option (D) means 'A' is the son-in-law of 'G'.

32. (B): Given, 26 January, 2020 = Sunday

∴ 25 January, 2020 = Saturday

Number of day from 26 January, 2020 to 16 March, 2020

$$= 6 + 29 + 16 = 51 \text{ days}$$
$$= 7 \times 7 + 2 = 2 \text{ odd days}$$

∴ 16 March, 2020 = Saturday + 2 days = Monday.

33. (C): Here, 'quarter past 3' = 3 hours 15 minutes

Angles traced by the hour hand in 12 hours = 360°

Angled traced by hour hand in 3 hours 15 minutes

$$i.e., = \frac{13}{4} \text{ hours}$$

$$= \frac{360°}{12} \times \frac{13}{4} = \frac{195}{2} = 97\frac{1}{2}°$$

Angled traced by minute hand in 60 minutes = 360°

∴ Angle traced by it in 15 minutes

$$= \left(\frac{360°}{60} \times 15\right) = 90°$$

Hence, required angle $= \left(97\frac{1}{2}° - 90°\right) = 7\frac{1}{7}°$.

34. (B): Given,

M E R C U R Y
+1 +2 +3 +4 +5 +6 +7
N G U G Z X F

Similarly,

E N T A N G L E
+1 +2 +3 +4 +5 +6 +7 +8
F P W E S M S M

So, 'ENTANGLE' will be coded as 'FPWESMSM'.

35. (C): From given statements (I) and (II).

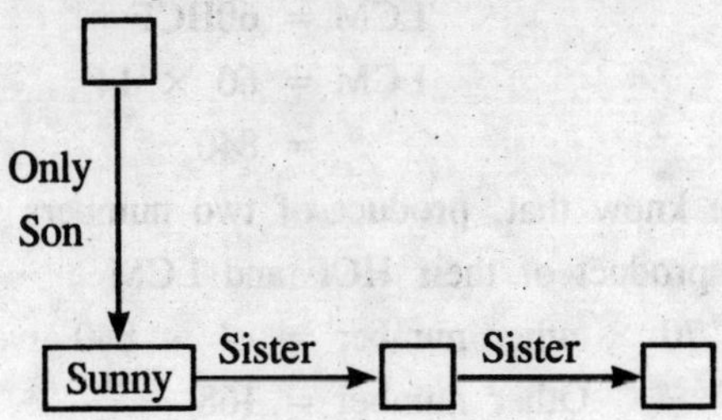

Sunny has 2 sisters.

So, Statements (I) and (II) together are sufficient to answer the question.

36. (B): Here, Starting point = A = house

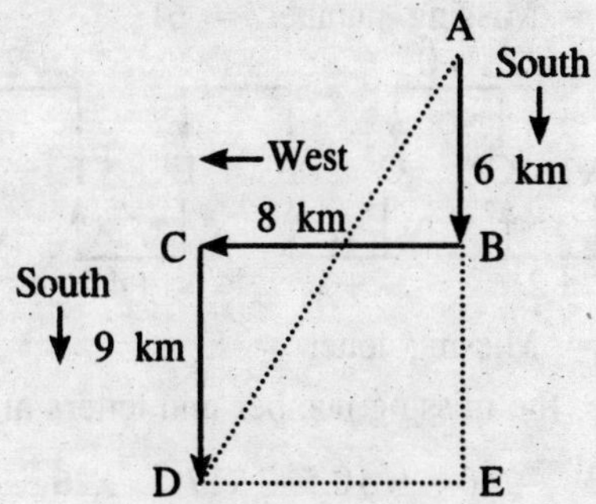

$$AB = 6 \text{ km}$$
$$BC = 8 \text{ km}$$
$$CD = 9 \text{ km}$$

$$\because \quad AB + CD = 6 + 9 = 15 \text{ km} = AE$$

$$\text{and } BC = ED = 8 \text{ km}$$

$$\therefore \quad AD = \sqrt{AE^2 + ED^2}$$
$$= \sqrt{(15)^2 + (8)^2}$$
$$= \sqrt{225 + 64} = \sqrt{289}$$
$$= 17 \text{ km}$$

He (D) is 17 km far and in South-West direction from his house now.

38. (D): A clock seen through a mirror show quarter to seven = 6:45

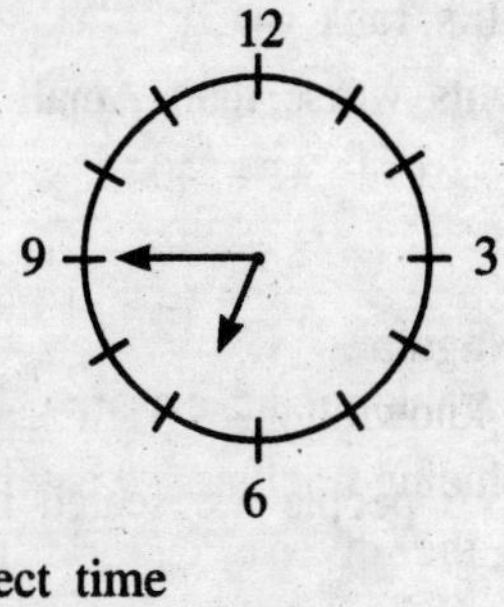

Now, correct time

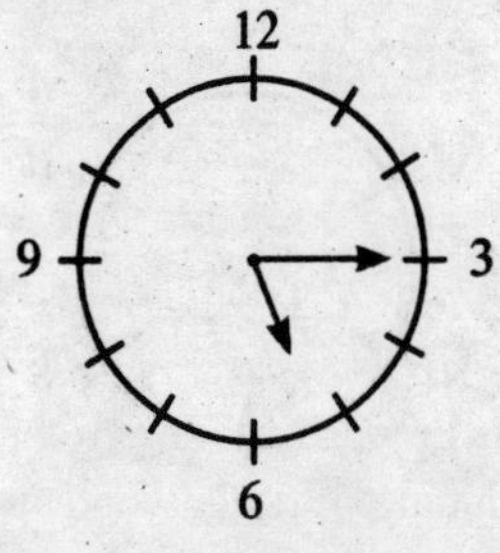

Hence, correct time show by the clock = 5:15.

40. (B): 5 8 13 20 31 44 **61** 80

+3 +5 +7 +11 +13 +17 +19

Here, 3, 5, 7, 11, 13, 17 and 19 are prime numbers.

$\therefore$? = Missing number = 61.

and

+0 −1 −2

A C C F E I G **L**

+2 +3 +4 +5

$\therefore$? = Missing letter = L

Hence, the missing number and letters are 61 and L.

41. (B): 3 6 10.5 17 26 **38**

+3 +4.5 +6.5 +9 +12

+1.5 +2 +2.5 +3

+1/2 +1/2 +1/2

? = the next number of the series = 38.

42. (D): Given, Number of students in a class = 40

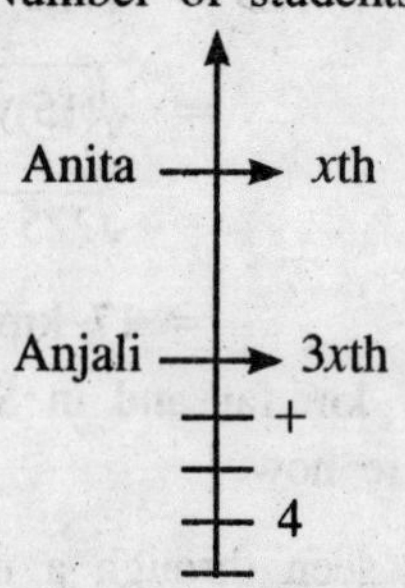

Let Anita's rank = x

Then, Anjali's rank = $3x$

and 4 students worse than Anjali

So, $3x + 4 = 40$

$\Rightarrow$ $3x = 36$

$\Rightarrow$ $x = 12$

So, Anita's rank in the class = 12th.

43. (C): Given, 6 people are seated in a circle facing the centre

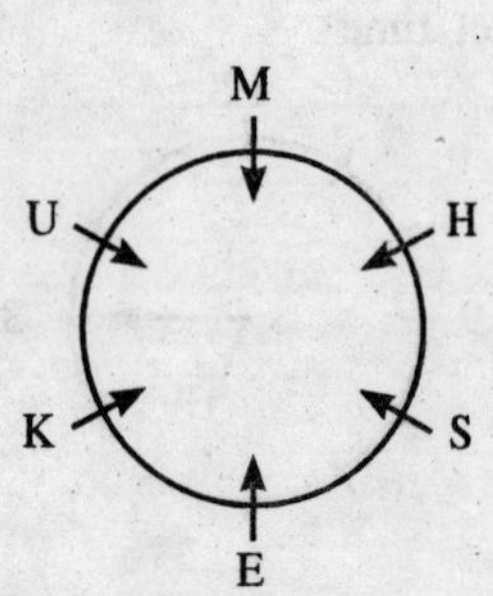

Here, K is the immediate right of U.

45. (D): From given statements:

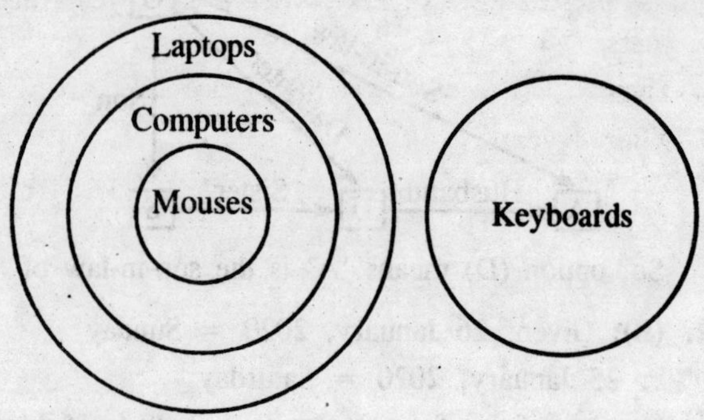

Conclusion:

I. All Mouses are laptops. (True)

II. All Computers can never be keyboards. (True)

Here, Both conclusions I and II follow.

46. (C): $24 \div 4 \times 2 + 8 - 4$

$= 6 \times 2 + 8 - 4$

$= 12 + 8 - 4$

$= 20 - 4 = 16.$

47. (A): $\because$ $\frac{1}{2} = 0.5$ $\frac{8}{11} = 0.72$

$\frac{7}{8} = 0.85$ $\frac{7}{9} = 0.77$

$\frac{5}{6} = 0.83$

$\therefore$ Greatest fraction = $\frac{7}{8}$

and smallest fraction = $\frac{1}{2}$

$\therefore$ Required difference = $\frac{7}{8} - \frac{1}{2} = \frac{7-4}{8} = \frac{3}{8}.$

48. (C): Given LCM + HCF = 854

and LCM = 60 HCF

$\therefore$ 60HCF + HCF = 854

$\Rightarrow$ 61HCF = 854

$\Rightarrow$ HCF = $\frac{854}{61} = 14$

$\Rightarrow$ HCF = 14

$\therefore$ LCM = 60HCF

$\Rightarrow$ LCM = 60×14

= 840

We know that, product of two numbers

= product of their HCF and LCM

$\Rightarrow$ $70 \times$ other number = 14×840

$\Rightarrow$ Other number = 168.

49. (B): Let present age of Harish be z years and present ages of his two sons be x years and y years

Then, $z = 8(x + y)$ ...(*i*)

After 8 years,

$z + 8 = 2(x + y + 8 + 8)$

$\Rightarrow z + 8 = 2(x + y) + 32$ ...(*ii*)

From (*i*) and (*ii*),

$z + 8 = 2\times\frac{z}{8}+32$

$\Rightarrow z + 8 = \frac{z}{4}+32$

$\Rightarrow z-\frac{z}{4} = 32 - 8$

$\Rightarrow \frac{4z-z}{4} = 24$

$\Rightarrow \frac{3}{4}z = 24 \Rightarrow z = 32$ years

Hence, the present age of Harish is 32 years.

50. (B): Let the maximum marks of the examination $= x$

Then, $300 - 225 = x\times\frac{10}{100}$

$\Rightarrow 75 = \frac{x}{10}$

$\Rightarrow x = 750.$

51. (B): Given, number of students in a class = 40

Boys : Girls = 3 : 2

$\therefore$ Number of boys $= 40\times\frac{3}{5} = 24$

and number of girls $= 40\times\frac{2}{5} = 16$

Now, Total marks scored by boys

$= 24 \times 42 = 1008$

and total marks scored by girls

$= 16 \times 46 = 736$

Hence, the average marks scored by the whole class

$= \frac{1008+736}{40} = \frac{1744}{40} = 43.6.$

52. (B): Given, the sum of 3 numbers = 136

First : Second = 2 : 3 = 10 : 15

Second : Third = 5 : 3 = 15 : 9

$\therefore$ First : Second : Third = 10 : 15 : 9

Then, the first number $= 136\times\frac{10}{10+15+9}$

$= 136\times\frac{10}{34} = 4 \times 10 = 40.$

53. (C): Marked price $\times\frac{100-20}{100}$ = ₹ 504

$\Rightarrow$ M.P. $\times\frac{4}{5}$ = ₹ 504

$\Rightarrow$ M.P. $= 504\times\frac{5}{4}$

$\Rightarrow$ M.P. $= 126 \times 5$ = ₹ 630

and cost price $\times\frac{105}{100}$ = ₹ 504

$\Rightarrow$ C.P. $= 504\times\frac{105}{100} = 504\times\frac{20}{21}$

$\Rightarrow$ C.P. $= 24 \times 20 = 480$

So, M.P. − C.P. = 630 − 480 = ₹ 150

Hence, the marked price is ₹ 150 more than the cost price.

54. (C): Given, sum become ₹ 2356 in 3 years and sum become ₹ 2660 in 5 years.

$\therefore$ Simple interest in 5 − 3 = 2 years

= 2660 − 2356 = ₹ 304

$\Rightarrow$ Simple interest in 3 years $= \frac{304}{2}\times 3$

$= 152 \times 3$ = ₹ 456

$\therefore$ The value of sum = 2356 − 456 = ₹ 1900.

55. (B): In a square, length of diagonals are equal

$\therefore 4k + 6 = 7k - 3$

$\Rightarrow 7k - 6k = 6 + 3$

$\Rightarrow k = 9$

$\therefore$ Diagonal $= 4k + 6$

$= 12 + 6 = 18$ cm

and diagonal = Side $\sqrt{2}$

$\Rightarrow 18 = \text{Side}\sqrt{2} \Rightarrow \text{Side} = 9\sqrt{2}$

$\therefore$ Area of the square $= (\text{Side})^2 = \left(9\sqrt{2}\right)^2$

$= 162$ cm^2.

56. (C): The volume of a cylinder = 396

$\Rightarrow \pi r^2h = 396$

$\Rightarrow \pi(3)^2h = 396$

$\Rightarrow \pi h = \frac{396}{9} = 44$

$$\Rightarrow \qquad \pi h = 44$$

Its curved surface area $= 2\pi rh$

$$= 2\pi h \times 3 \quad [\because \pi h = 44]$$
$$= 2 \times 44 \times 3$$
$$= 264 \text{ cm}^2.$$

57. (D): A tap can fill a tank in 6 hours

$\Rightarrow$ A tap can fill $\frac{1}{2}$ tank in 3 hours

and remaining part of tank fill in $\dfrac{\frac{1}{2}}{\frac{4}{6}}$ hours

$$= \frac{1}{2} \times \frac{6}{4} = \frac{3}{4} \text{ hours}$$

$$= \frac{3}{4} \times 60 = 45 \text{ minutes}$$

$\therefore$ The total time taken to fill the tank completely

$$= 3 \text{ hours} + 45 \text{ minutes}$$
$$= 3 \text{ hours } 45 \text{ minutes.}$$

58. (D): Let the length of the train $= x$ m

Then, $\dfrac{x + 350}{80 \times \frac{5}{18}} = 36$

$$\Rightarrow \qquad x + 350 = 36 \times 80 \times \frac{5}{18}$$
$$= 2 \times 80 \times 5$$
$$\Rightarrow \qquad x + 350 = 160 \times 5 = 800$$
$$\Rightarrow \qquad x = 800 - 350$$
$$\Rightarrow \qquad x = 450 \text{ m.}$$

59. (C): Given, mean $= 8$

$$\therefore \quad \frac{3 + 4 + 9 + 2k + 10 + 8 + 6 + (k + 6)}{8} = 8$$

$$\Rightarrow \qquad 46 + 3k = 8 \times 8$$
$$\Rightarrow \qquad 3k = 64 - 46 = 18$$
$$\Rightarrow \qquad k = 6$$

and 2, 2, 3, $2p$, $(2p + 1)$, 4, 4, 5 (p is a natural number)

$\Rightarrow$ 2, 2, 3, 2×2, $(2 \times 2 + 1)$, 4, 4, 5

$\Rightarrow$ 2, 2, 3, 4, 5, 4, 4, 5

Given, Mode $= 4$

$$\Rightarrow \qquad 2p = 4$$
$$\Rightarrow \qquad p = 2$$

Henec, $(k - 2p) = 6 - 2 \times 2$

$$= 6 - 4 = 2.$$

60. (C): Given, in ΔABC,

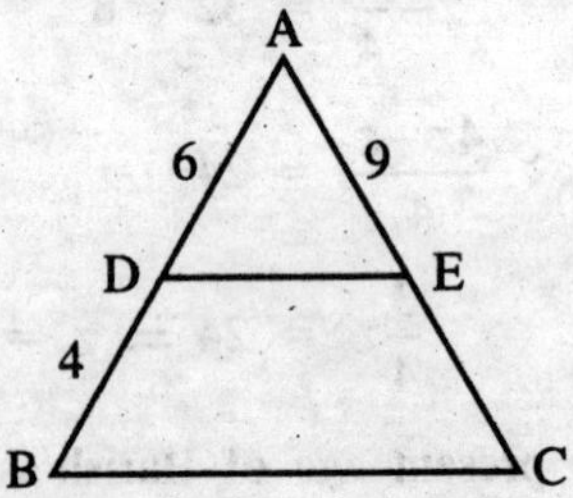

DE || BC

AD = 6 cm

DB = 4 cm

AE = 9 cm

From Thales theorem,

In ΔABC, $\dfrac{AD}{DB} = \dfrac{AE}{EC}$

$$\Rightarrow \qquad \frac{6}{4} = \frac{9}{EC}$$
$$\Rightarrow \qquad 6EC = 9 \times 4$$
$$\Rightarrow \qquad EC = \frac{9 \times 4}{6} = \frac{36}{6} = 6$$
$$\Rightarrow \qquad EC = 6 \text{ cm.}$$

Previous Years' Paper (Solved)

(Common University Entrance Test for UG Programmes)

CUET (UG) B.A. (H.) Political Science/ B.A. (H.) History Entrance Exam, 2023*

ENGLISH

Directions (Qs. No. 1-5): *Read the following passage to answer question:*

The village school was located in a prominent place where apart from the school, there were a few shops, a small temple and a government dispensary. The headmaster of the school was a learned and scholarly man loved by all. The dispensary was looked after by a doctor and a male nurse. The doctor attended the dispensary very punctually and used to retire to his residence after the duty hours and never allowed anyone to visit his residence after the duty hours.

The school was housed in dilapidated building and very often the headmaster used to take the children out to the nearby garden where they could play and take part in various sports and games under the able supervision of the headmaster.

One day a stray dog entered the garden when the children were playing. One of them pelted a stone at the dog and it started barking and all of a sudden became boisterous and bit a child in the leg. The boy was very badly hurt and his leg started bleeding. The children who by this time became panicky rushed to the headmaster who together with a few students, took the child to the nearby dispensary and then to the doctors residence.

The headmaster knocked at the door of the doctor for help. But the doctor refused to open the door and made it clear that he would not attend to anyone howsoever serious he may be, during his leisure hours. However the headmaster continued to knock at the door and finally the doctor opened the door when he saw the headmaster trembling with fear and the student in agony and pain.

The doctor mellowed down now and took the child to the dispensary for bandaging and giving necessary injections and medicines. The doctor was impressed by the dedication and sincerity of the headmaster. He realized his folly and decided to attend to the needy and sick even during his leisure hours.

1. The village school was located near the:

A. Forest B. Market
C. Library D. Pond

2. After the duty hours the government dispensary doctor normally:

A. Slept and dreamt
B. Spent time with his family
C. went to his private clinic
D. Rested at home and never allowed visitors

3. All of a sudden a dog became boisterous and it bit a child in the leg. The dog got angry mainly because:

A. One boy did mischief
B. Dog was feeling hungry
C. Dog saw another dog
D. Boy did not give food to the dog

4. The head master was trembling with fear at the doctor's residence along with the injured boy. The doctor was:

A. afraid of higher officials
B. afraid of student's parents
C. not opening the door
D. impressed with the dedication of the headmaster

5. Find the synonym from a passage which means "To become less extreme in behaviour".

A. Stray B. boisterous
C. mellowed D. Folly

Directions (Qs. No. 6-10): *Read the following passage to answer question:*

The needs of a nations people are bigger and much more important than any other considerations. The mission of parliament is that it has to be alive and dynamic over issues vital to the existence of our very nationhood. Our freedom did not come as a gift. The whole country struggled for decades to achieve the first vision of independence, so

*** This Previous Year Paper has been given here as a Combination of CUET (UG) 2023 different exams for the Subjects 'English, History, Political Science, Sociology and General Test', which have been mapped to this course.**

we have to protect it. There were excellent leaders in all walks of life-science, education and industry. To preserve this freedom from intruders and others who would compromise it is our bounden duty and not a matter of choice and convenience. No ideology is above the security and prosperity of our country. No agenda is more important than harmony among the people. Students should get ready to transform India into a developed nation. Ignite your minds and think big.

A teacher once said, 'Give me a five-year-old child. After seven years, no God or Devil will be able to change the child.' Will all teachers be such gurus? The administrators have a great opportunity to link the people and political leaders. They should always take decisions that are good for the people I believe it is only executives like empowered district collectors who can assist transformation. The state-Central integrated fund has to be deployed in mission mode programmes.

6. We have to protect our nations Independence as we got it after:
A. excellent leader
B. War and Fight
C. Struggle for decades
D. Help from foreign country

7. To transform India into a Developed Nation Dr. A.P.J. Abdul Kalam expects his students to:
A. Ignite the minds B. Fire the mind
C. Use the mind D. Clean the mind

8. The one who can link the people and political leaders even to assist for transformation. They are known as:
A. Leader B. Administrators
C. Manager D. Major

9. The existence of Nation hood is maintained by:
A. Country B. Office
C. Collectorate D. Parliament

10. Find the synonym from the passage which means:
'Trespasser'
Choose the correct option:
A. Leader B. Teacher
C. Intruder D. Collector

Directions (Qs. No. 11-15): *Read the following passage to answer question:*

Village Resource Centres (VRCs) were established by the Indian Space Research Organisation (ISRO) as part of its societal mission of bringing space-based services emanating from Satellite Communication (SatCom) and Earth Observation (EO) to rural society. While SatCom provides the method for an effective delivery of information and services across vast regions, EO provides community-centric information regarding geo-referenced land records; natural resources; the environment; sites for exploiting ground water for potable use and recharging: wasteland and reclamation; watershed profile; and cropping patterns. It can also provide customized local area information. These systems are very useful for predicting disaster, giving early warning and vulnerability-related information.

ISRO has undertaken the mission of assisting the VRC programme with a portfolio of services which are being established in collaboration with forty partner agencies across twenty-two states. A total of 473 VRCs have been set up with plans for rapid expansion in the future. Each VRC essentially has digital connectivity; specialty health care providers enabled via the Indian National Satellite System (INSAT); Spatial information on natural resources facilities for primary health care and distance education.

11. Village resource centres were set up by the ______ to bring space based centres to rural society:
A. Sat com
B. Indian Space Research Organisation
C. Earth observation
D. Indian National Satellite system

12. ISRO has undertaken the mission of assisting the village Resource Centres Programme with forty partner agencies across ______ states.
A. Twenty One B. Twenty Two
C. Twenty Three D. Twenty Five

13. Match List-I with List-II:

List-I	*List-II*
(*a*) SatCom	(*i*) Village Resource Centres
(*b*) VRCs	(*ii*) Indian National Satellite System
(*c*) ISRO	(*iii*) Satellite Communication
(*d*) INSAT	(*iv*) Indian Space Research Organisation

Choose the correct answer from the options given below:

	(*a*)	(*b*)	(*c*)	(*d*)
A.	(*iii*)	(*iv*)	(*i*)	(*ii*)
B.	(*iv*)	(*ii*)	(*iii*)	(*i*)
C.	(*ii*)	(*iv*)	(*i*)	(*iii*)
D.	(*iii*)	(*i*)	(*iv*)	(*ii*)

14. Find a word from the passage that means the same as 'to assume things before it happens'.
A. Communications B. Observations
C. Information D. Prediction

15. Find a word from the passage that is an antonym of the word 'safe/secure'.
A. Exploitation B. Expansion
C. Vulnerable D. Collaboration

16. Fill in the blank with the correct determiner:
The teacher asked him ______ questions.
A. much B. a few
C. any D. every

17. Change the following into direct speech:

He requested me to shut the door.

A. He told, "The door should be shut."

B. He said, "Please shut the door."

C. He said, "Shut the door."

D. He ordered, "Close the door."

18. Fill in the blank with the correct adverb:

I ______ met him at the conference on Sunday but discussed a lot of things.

A. Always B. Never

C. Briefly D. Finally

19. Which of the following sentences does ***not*** use the correct modals.

(*a*) I swim across the river when I was young.

(*b*) It may rain next Friday

(*c*) I expected that I would get a first class

(*d*) One ought to respect the environmental laws

(*e*) This used to be a dense jungle.

Choose the ***correct answer*** from the options given below:

A. (*a*) and (*d*) only B. (*a*) only

C. (*e*) only D. (*c*) and (*d*) only

20. Complete the sentence by choosing the appropriate options:

He gave ______ European ___ one-rupee coin.

A. the, an B. a, a

C. an, an D. the, a

21. Complete the sentence by choosing the appropriate set of prepositions:

He is notoriously mean ______ his treatment ______ his servants.

A. in, of B. with, of

C. of, with D. for, of

22. Synonym of the word "alleviate".

(*a*) worsen (*b*) grow

(*c*) lessen (*d*) increase

(*e*) reduce

Choose the ***correct answer*** from the options given below:

A. (*a*) and (*e*) only B. (*c*) and (*e*) only

C. (*b*) and (*d*) only D. (*a*) only

23. Choose the correct Exclamatory sentence of the given sentence:

The Night is very beautiful.

A. How beautiful is the night!

B. Night is so beautiful!

C. What beautiful night!

D. Night is too beautiful!

24. Choose the option that has been correctly changed from Direct to Indirect speech.

Adesh said, "Please shut the door behind you."

(*a*) Adesh requested me to please shut the door behind me.

(*b*) Adesh said that I request you to shut the door behind you.

(*c*) Adesh said to shut the door behind you.

(*d*) Adesh said to me that I request to shut the door behind you.

Choose the ***correct answer*** from the options given below:

A. (*a*) only B. (*b*) only

C. (*c*) only D. (*d*) only

25. Match the underline phrases with their meanings:

List-I (Phrases)	***List-II (Meanings)***
(*a*) I had so much work to do but the fever <u>got the best of me</u>	(*i*) Peaceful time
(*b*) They spent their <u>halcyon days</u> in a village	(*ii*) Vulnerable/Weak spot
(*c*) He earned really well but ended up penniless. Gambling was his <u>achilles heel</u>	(*iii*) Competent for a work
(*d*) A doctor <u>worth his salt</u> will advise people for healthy eating	(*iv*) Take advantage of something

Choose the ***correct answer*** from the options given below:

	(*a*)	(*b*)	(*c*)	(*d*)
A.	(*iv*)	(*i*)	(*ii*)	(*iii*)
B.	(*iv*)	(*ii*)	(*i*)	(*iii*)
C.	(*i*)	(*iii*)	(*ii*)	(*iv*)
D.	(*iv*)	(*iii*)	(*ii*)	(*i*)

26. Choose the correct meaning of the underlined word from the following sentence:

The minister entered the hall with his <u>entourage</u>.

A. cars

B. belongings

C. following subordinates

D. police

27. Find out the adverbs from the given sentence and tick the correct option given below:

People often complain about foolish things and easily try to escape from the reality.

A. complain, reality
B. often, easily
C. easily, complain
D. often, escape

28. Choose the option with the same meaning:

Camouflage

(*a*) disguise (*b*) cover
(*c*) demonstrate (*d*) fabric

Choose the ***correct answer*** from the options given below:

A. (*a*) only B. (*b*) only
C. (*c*) only D. (*d*) only

29. Complete the sentence using the correct options:

When I reached the station, the train

A. been leaving
B. had been already leaving
C. had already left
D. has left

30. State the kind of clause for the underlined part of the given sentence:

The Children whom I teach in standard 8 are very disciplined.

A. Adverb clause B. Adjective clause
C. Noun clause D. Adverb clause of time

31. Match List-I with List-II to complete the idioms:

List-I	***List-II***
(*a*) At one's	(*i*) tongue
(*b*) Hold one's	(*ii*) fingertips
(*c*) Lose one's	(*iii*) head
(*d*) Win	(*iv*) hands down

Choose the ***correct answer*** from the options given below:

	(*a*)	(*b*)	(*c*)	(*d*)
A.	(*ii*)	(*i*)	(*iii*)	(*iv*)
B.	(*i*)	(*ii*)	(*iii*)	(*iv*)
C.	(*iv*)	(*iii*)	(*ii*)	(*i*)
D.	(*ii*)	(*i*)	(*iv*)	(*iii*)

32. Find the correct Antonym of the word 'Terrible':

A. scaring B. soothing
C. horrible D. frightening

33. Match List I with List II for suitable antonyms:

List-I (Word)	***List-II (Antonym)***
(*a*) Charming	(*i*) Hide
(*b*) Occasional	(*ii*) Miser
(*c*) Generous	(*iii*) Hideous
(*d*) Exhibit	(*iv*) Regular

Choose the correct answer from the options given below:

	(*a*)	(*b*)	(*c*)	(*d*)
A.	(*iii*)	(*iv*)	(*ii*)	(*i*)
B.	(*iv*)	(*ii*)	(*iii*)	(*i*)
C.	(*iii*)	(*ii*)	(*i*)	(*iv*)
D.	(*ii*)	(*i*)	(*iv*)	(*iii*)

34. Arrange the following in the correct sequence:

(*a*) With telling us about
(*b*) has been mainly occupied
(*c*) the finite world has been analysed
(*d*) the elements into which
(*e*) The language of man

Choose the correct answer from the options given below:

A. (*e*), (*b*), (*a*), (*d*), (*c*)
B. (*a*), (*e*), (*b*), (*d*), (*c*)
C. (*e*), (*a*), (*b*), (*d*), (*c*)
D. (*e*), (*d*), (*a*), (*b*), (*c*)

35. Match the phrases with their meaning:

List-I	***List-II***
(*a*) Set in	(*i*) to treat with contempt
(*b*) Wind up	(*ii*) extinguished
(*c*) look down upon	(*iii*) begin
(*d*) put out	(*iv*) bring to an end

Choose the correct answer from the options given below:

	(*a*)	(*b*)	(*c*)	(*d*)
A.	(*ii*)	(*iii*)	(*iv*)	(*i*)
B.	(*iv*)	(*ii*)	(*iii*)	(*i*)
C.	(*iii*)	(*i*)	(*iv*)	(*ii*)
D.	(*iii*)	(*iv*)	(*i*)	(*ii*)

36. Choose the option that gives the correct meaning of the foreign word:

'animus'

A. good intention B. bad intention
C. mean while D. self love

37. Identify the correct passive voice form of the following sentence:

One should keep one's promises.

A. Promises need to be kept.
B. Promises should be kept.
C. Nobody keeps promises.
D. One has kept one's promises.

38. Complete the sentence with suitable option:

You ______ stood by your friends in their bad times.

A. ought to have B. should
C. must D. can have

39. Choose the correct question tag for the given sentence:

She doesn't really know how to get out of the problem?

A. Isn't she? B. doesn't she
C. does she? D. Is it?

40. Choose the correct option to change the following sentence into passive voice.

Your behaviour astonished me.

A. I was astonished by you with your behaviour.
B. You are astonished by me with behaviour.
C. I was astonished by your behaviour.
D. With your behaviour you were astonished

41. Choose one word which can be substituted for the given sentence:

'One who acts against religion'.

A. Egoist B. Heretic
C. Optimist D. Stoic

42. Fill in the blank with the suitable homonym Choose the correct one from the following.

Ravi writes in his note book today.

The marriage is performed as per Hindu ______.

A. Rites B. Wrights
C. Rights D. Raight

43. Parts of a sentence are given in a jumbled order. Arrange the parts in the correct sequence to form a meaningful sentence.

(*a*) the resistance (*b*) of
(*c*) depend on (*d*) what does
(*e*) a conductor

Choose the ***correct answer*** from the options given below:

A. (*d*), (*a*), (*e*), (*c*), (*b*) B. (*d*), (*a*), (*b*), (*e*), (*c*)
C. (*b*), (*a*), (*d*), (*e*), (*c*) D. (*d*), (*a*), (*c*), (*b*), (*e*)

44. Choose the correct idiomatic expression.

The staff agreed to execute the plans.

A. Carry away B. Lay out
C. Turn down D. Carry out

45. Complete the omitted/grammatically correct sentence:

"Asoka two lives, one as ruthless conqueror and the as a compassionate ruler"

(*a*) Asoka led two lives one as the most ruthless conqueror and the as a compassionate ruler.
(*b*) Asoka led two various lives, one ruthless conqueror and the as a compassionate ruler.
(*c*) Asoka led two live one as ruthless conqueror and the as a famous compassionate ruler.
(*d*) Asoka led two lives one as ruthless conqueror and the other as a compassionate ruler.
(*e*) Asoka led two lives one as ruthless conqueror so and the as a compassionate ruler.

Choose the correct answer from the options given below:

A. (*a*) only B. (*b*) only
C. (*e*) only D. (*d*) only

46. Choose the correct subject for a letter of enquiry for a course in Choreography:

A. Enquiry for choreography
B. Course in choreography
C. Enquiry regarding course in choreography
D. Enquiry in course of choreography

47. Choose the correct Assertive sentence of the given sentence:

Alas that youth should pass away!

A. It is sad that youth has passed away
B. It is sad to think that youth should pass away
C. It is sad that youth shall pass away
D. It is sad that youth passes away

48. Complete the sentence in List I with the correct preposition from List II:

List-I	*List-II*
(*a*) ____ the street the piper slept	(*i*) in
(*b*) Little Jack Horner sat ____ a corner	(*ii*) into
(*c*) Old mother Hubbard went ____ the cupboard	(*iii*) over
(*d*) The cow jumped ____ the moon	(*iv*) to

Choose the correct answer from the options given below:

	(*a*)	(*b*)	(*c*)	(*d*)
A.	(*ii*)	(*i*)	(*iv*)	(*iii*)
B.	(*i*)	(*ii*)	(*iv*)	(*iii*)
C.	(*iii*)	(*ii*)	(*i*)	(*iv*)
D.	(*ii*)	(*iii*)	(*iv*)	(*i*)

49. Find out which part of the sentence has an error.

The captain along with his team are practicing very hard for the forthcoming matches.

A. The Captain along with his team
B. are practicing very hard
C. for the
D. forthcoming matches

50. Spot the Error

(*a*) Copernicus proved (*b*) that Earth
(*c*) moves (*d*) round
(*e*) the sun

Choose the ***correct answer*** from the options given below:

A. (*b*) only B. (*c*) only
C. (*d*) only D. (*e*) only

ANSWERS

1. **(B):** The village school's location is mentioned in the passage as being in a prominent place surrounded by some shops, a temple, and a government dispensary. There's no direct mention of the school being near a forest, library, or pond. However, the presence of shops suggests a market-like setting, which makes option B the most likely answer.

2. **(D):** The doctor's routine after his duty hours is clearly stated in the passage. It says that the doctor "used to retire to his residence after the duty hours and never allowed anyone to visit his residence after the duty hours." This directly indicates that he rested at his home and was strict about not entertaining visitors during that time.

3. **(A):** The primary reason the dog became aggressive and bit a child is directly linked to a particular action from one of the children. The passage mentions, "One of them pelted a stone at the dog." This act of mischief from the child triggered the dog's aggressive behavior. In this scenario, pelting a stone can be seen as a direct threat, leading to the dog's defensive reaction.

4. **(D):** The doctor's initial refusal to help was overridden when he saw the headmaster's state of extreme worry and the injured student's pain. The passage says, "the doctor opened the door when he saw the headmaster trembling with fear and the student in agony and pain." Following this, the doctor's subsequent actions and feelings were influenced by the headmaster's dedication. The doctor was "impressed by the dedication and sincerity of the headmaster." The headmaster's commitment to the well-being of his student is evident here, showcasing the strong bond and sense of responsibility educators often feel towards their students.

5. **(C):** The term "mellowed" in the passage refers to the doctor's change in behavior from strict and unyielding to more understanding and compassionate. The phrase "The doctor mellowed down now" indicates a reduction in his earlier stern behavior. In this context, "to mellow" means to become gentler or more lenient, which aligns with the definition of "to become less extreme in behavior."

6. **(C):** India's hard-won independence came after a prolonged "struggle for decades," as stated in the passage. This wasn't a result of wars or direct fights, nor was it a gift from excellent leaders or foreign aid. The mention of the prolonged struggle underscores the sacrifices, non-violent protests, negotiations, and relentless efforts made by the entire nation to free itself from colonial rule.

7. **(A):** Dr. A.P.J. Abdul Kalam, a visionary leader and former President of India, always emphasized on the power of the youth. In the passage, he inspires students to "ignite your minds" as a means to transform India into a developed nation. Igniting the mind symbolizes invoking curiosity, passion, and a thirst for knowledge and innovation.

8. **(B):** "Administrators" are pinpointed in the passage as having a significant role in bridging the gap between the people and political leaders, subsequently aiding in transformation. Administrators, in this context, likely refer to government officials and civil servants who are responsible for implementing policies and ensuring governance at the grassroots level.

9. **(D):** The "existence of our very nationhood" is closely tied to the mission of the "parliament," as highlighted in the passage. A nation's parliament is its supreme legislative body and represents the collective will of its people. It enacts laws, discusses national issues, and holds the government accountable.

10. **(C):** The term "intruder" is synonymous with 'trespasser'. An intruder is someone who enters a place without permission or authorization, often with malicious intent. In the context of the passage, the term is used to emphasize the importance of safeguarding India's hard-won freedom from those who might seek to harm or compromise it. The reference to intruders can be seen as a broader metaphor for any force or ideology that might threaten India's sovereignty, harmony, or security.

11. **(B):** The **Indian Space Research Organisation (ISRO)** is credited with setting up Village Resource Centres (VRCs) to extend space-based services to the rural populace. ISRO, established in 1969, has been instrumental in utilizing space technology for India's development, especially focusing on rural and remote areas.

12. **(B):** The passage clearly mentions that ISRO has collaborated with forty partner agencies spread out across **twenty-two states** for the VRC program. India, with its diverse geography and vast area, has always faced challenges in ensuring that the benefits of technology and development reach even the most remote corners. The initiative to span across twenty-two states shows the program's expansive reach, attempting to bring the advantages of space technology to a broader spectrum of the Indian population.

13. (D): Matching the terms with their respective meanings or representations, we get:

- SatCom (*a*) aligns with Satellite Communication (*iii*), which is a technology for relaying and broadcasting information using satellites.
- VRCs (*b*) stands for Village Resource Centres (*i*), which are centers established in rural regions to provide space-based services.
- ISRO (*c*) is the acronym for Indian Space Research Organisation (*iv*), the space agency of the Government of India.
- INSAT (*d*) matches with Indian National Satellite System (*ii*), a series of multipurpose geostationary satellites commissioned by ISRO to cater to telecommunications, broadcasting, meteorology, and search and rescue operations.

14. (D): The word **'Prediction'** means to foresee or anticipate an event before it takes place. In the realm of space technology and observation, prediction plays a pivotal role, especially in forecasting natural calamities, weather patterns, or any other potential events that could have significant societal implications.

15. (C): The term **'Vulnerable'** denotes a state of susceptibility or being prone to harm, danger, or risk. In contrast to being 'safe' or 'secure,' a vulnerable state means that there's potential exposure to harm. In the context of space-based observations, understanding vulnerabilities becomes vital. By identifying areas, populations, or resources that are vulnerable - be it to natural disasters, climate change, or any other threats - proactive measures can be adopted to mitigate adverse impacts. (B) The correct option is "a few." In this context, "questions" is a countable noun. The determiner "much" is used with uncountable nouns, "any" usually appears in negative or interrogative contexts, and "every" doesn't fit grammatically. "A few" is used to indicate a small number of countable nouns. Therefore, "The teacher asked him a few questions." is the appropriate construction.

16. (B): Direct speech is a direct quotation of what someone else said. The phrase "He requested me to shut the door." can be changed to direct speech as "He said, 'Please shut the door". The word "please" implies a request. The other options do not convey the sense of a request as directly and politely as option B does.

17. (B) **18. (C)** **19. (B)**

20. (B): The correct answer is "a European a one-rupee coin." In this case, "European" is used as a noun referring to a person from Europe. When we refer to a singular, unspecified entity, we use the indefinite article "a" before consonant sounds and "an" before vowel sounds. "European" starts with a "y" sound (a consonant sound) and "one-rupee coin" starts with a "w" sound (also a consonant sound). Therefore, "a" is the appropriate article for both nouns.

21. (A): The correct set of prepositions is "in" and "of." We use "in" to describe a manner or way in which something is done, and "of" to show possession or relation. Therefore, "He is notoriously mean in his treatment of his servants" implies that he treats his servants in a mean manner.

22. (B): The word "alleviate" means to make a situation or a pain less severe. Out of the given options, "lessen" and "reduce" are synonyms to "alleviate" as they both convey the idea of diminishing or decreasing something in intensity, degree, or amount.

23. (A): An exclamatory sentence is one that expresses strong emotion. In this context, "How beautiful is the night!" is the correct exclamatory form of "The night is very beautiful." This structure ("How [adjective] is [subject]!") is a common form of expressing admiration or surprise in English exclamatory sentences.

24. (A): When converting direct speech to indirect speech, the exact words of the speaker are paraphrased and certain changes are made to pronouns, tense, and words showing place and time. The correct conversion of "Adesh said, 'Please shut the door behind you.'" is "Adesh requested me to please shut the door behind me." This captures the essence of the request made by Adesh without directly quoting him.

25. (A): Matching the phrases with their meanings:

- (*a*) "I had so much work to do but the fever got the best of me" corresponds to (*iv*) "Take advantage of something." This phrase implies that the fever overcame or overwhelmed the person, preventing them from working.
- (*b*) "They spent their halcyon days in a village" matches with (*i*) "Peaceful time." "Halcyon days" is an idiom that means a calm, peaceful, or happy period in the past.
- (*c*) "He earned really well but ended up penniless. Gambling was his Achilles heel" aligns with (*ii*) "Vulnerable/Weak spot." An "Achilles heel" refers to a person's main weakness or vulnerability.
- (*d*) "A doctor worth his salt will advise people for healthy eating" pairs with (*iii*) "Competent for a work." The idiom "worth one's salt" means to be competent or deserving of one's salary or position.

26. (C): The word "entourage" refers to a group of people attending or surrounding an important person. In this context, it pertains to the minister's accompanying group, which can be his aides, assistants, or any other group of followers. Hence, the most accurate meaning among the given options is "following subordinates."

27. (B): An adverb is a word that modifies a verb, an adjective, or another adverb. In the given sentence, "often" modifies the verb "complain" and "easily" modifies the verb "try." Therefore, the correct adverbs from the sentence are "often" and "easily."

28. (A): The term "camouflage" means to disguise something, usually to make it blend in with its surroundings. Out of the given options, "disguise" directly captures the essence of "camouflage." Thus, the word "disguise" is synonymous with "camouflage."

29. (C): The sentence indicates a completed action in the past relative to another past action or event. The train had already departed by the time the speaker reached the station. The correct tense to denote this sequence of past events is the past perfect tense, which is formed using "had" + past participle. Therefore, "had already left" is the appropriate completion for the sentence.

30. (B): Clauses in English can function as different parts of speech and can be classified based on their function. In the sentence "The Children whom I teach in standard 8 are very disciplined," the underlined clause "whom I teach in standard 8" provides additional information about "The Children," making it an adjective clause. An adjective clause modifies a noun (in this case, "The Children") and often starts with relative pronouns like "who," "whom," "whose," "which," or "that."

31. (A): Idioms are fixed expressions with meanings not directly deducible from the individual words. For the given idioms: (*a*) "At one's fingertips" means having information or a skill readily available. (*b*) "Hold one's tongue" means to refrain from speaking. (*c*) "Lose one's head" suggests panicking or acting without thinking. (*d*) "Win hands down" means to win easily. Thus, the correct matches are (*ii*), (*i*), (*iii*), and (*iv*) respectively.

32. (B): Antonyms are words that have opposite meanings. The word 'Terrible' denotes something causing fear or dread. Among the given options, "soothing" suggests calmness and comfort, making it the opposite of "terrible."

33. (A): Matching words with their antonyms: (*a*) The opposite of "Charming," which means attractive, is "Hideous" implying ugly. (*b*) "Occasional" means happening from time to time, while "Regular" implies happening frequently. (*c*) "Generous" means giving more than is necessary or usual, while its opposite "Miser" denotes a person who hoards money and avoids spending. (*d*) "Exhibit" means to display or show, while "Hide" means to conceal. So, the correct antonyms are (*iii*), (*iv*), (*ii*), and (*i*).

34. (A): Arranging sentences in a logical order is essential for coherence. The correct sequence forms a comprehensible statement about human language: "The language of man (*e*) has been mainly occupied (*b*) with telling us about (*a*) the elements into which (*d*) the finite world has been analysed (*c*)."

35. (D): Understanding the meaning of phrases is essential for comprehension: (*a*) "Set in" means to begin or commence. (*b*) "Wind up" denotes bringing something to a conclusion or end. (*c*) "Look down upon" signifies treating someone with contempt or considering them inferior. (*d*) "Put out" means extinguished, usually in the context of a light or fire. The correct matches are (*iii*), (*iv*), (*i*), and (*ii*).

36. (B): The Latin word "animus" refers to a feeling of ill will, animosity, or hostility. Thus, the correct meaning of 'animus' in the given context is "bad intention."

37. (B): Changing a sentence to passive voice involves shifting the focus from the doer of the action to the receiver of the action. The sentence "One should keep one's promises" focuses on the act of keeping promises, so in passive form, it becomes "Promises should be kept," which emphasizes the promises themselves.

38. (A): The given sentence implies a sense of obligation or duty in the past that wasn't met. The phrase "ought to have" suggests a missed obligation or something that should have been done in the past but wasn't. Thus, "You ought to have stood by your friends in their bad times" indicates that it was expected or would have been right for the person to stand by their friends, but they didn't.

39. (C): Question tags are short questions at the end of statements. They're used mainly in speech. When the main part of the sentence is negative, the question tag is positive. "She doesn't really know" is negative, so the tag should be positive: "does she?"

40. (C): To form the passive, you use the appropriate form of verb "to be" + the past participle of the main verb. The given sentence, "Your behaviour astonished me," is in the active voice where "me" is the object. In its passive form, "me" becomes the subject and the focus shifts to the feeling, making it "I was astonished by your behaviour."

41. (B): A "heretic" is someone who holds beliefs that are contrary to the accepted beliefs of a particular religion. The definition provided "One who acts against religion" aligns closely with this term. An egoist is someone centered on their own needs, an optimist is someone who looks at the positive side of things, and a stoic is someone who endures pain without showing feelings.

42. (A): Homonyms are words that are pronounced the same but differ in meaning, derivation, or spelling. In this context, the word "Rites" (religious practices or ceremonies) is suitable. "Wrights" refers to makers or builders (like "wheelwright"), "Rights" are entitlements or freedoms, and "Raight" is not a standard English word.

43. (B)

44. (D): Idiomatic expressions are phrases that have a figurative meaning different from their literal meaning. The phrase "carry out" means to execute or perform an action, which aligns with the given statement about executing plans. "Carry away" means to become overly enthusiastic, "Lay out" is to present or explain something in detail, and "Turn down" means to reject or decline.

45. (D): Constructing the sentence, we need to establish a comparison between two types of lives led by Asoka. The sentence "Asoka led two lives one as ruthless conqueror and the other as a compassionate ruler" correctly juxtaposes the two contrasting phases of his life. It also uses correct parallel structure, using "one as" and "the other as" to introduce the two lives.

46. (C): "Enquiry regarding course in choreography" is the most comprehensive and clear subject for a letter of inquiry. It explicitly states that the inquiry is about a course specifically in choreography. While the other options also imply an inquiry about choreography, option C provides the most direct and clear phrasing for the context.

47. (B): An assertive sentence is a declarative statement. The original sentence, "Alas that youth should pass away!", is an exclamatory sentence that conveys a feeling of sadness about the passing of youth. The closest option that captures this sentiment in a declarative way is "It is sad to think that youth should pass away."

48. (A)

49. (B): The phrase "The captain along with his team" requires a singular verb because "along with" doesn't make the noun plural. So, the verb "are" should be changed to "is". The correct statement should be "The captain along with his team is practicing very hard for the forthcoming matches."

50. (A): Copernicus did not just prove "that Earth" but rather "that the Earth." Proper nouns like Earth, when referred to as the planet we live on, often take the definite article "the." The rest of the statement, "moves round the sun," is accurate, as it accurately captures the heliocentric theory that Copernicus is known for.

HISTORY

1. Who among the following traveller was impressed by the fortification of the Vijayanagara and mentioned about seven lines of defense in forts?

A. Duarte Barbosa B. Abdur Razzaq
C. Domingo Paes D. Nicolo de Conti

2. James Prinsep deciphered the .... script.

A. Aramaic B. Greek
C. Kharosthi D. Devnagari

3. Choose the incorrect statement regarding 'Objectives Resolution':

A. It was introduced on 13 December 1946 in the Constituent Assembly.
B. It proclaimed India to be an "Independent Demographic Sovereign Republic".
C. It outlined the defining ideals of the Constitution of Independent India.
D. It provided the framework within which the work of Constitution making was to proceed.

4. In which Harappan site traces of canals have been found?

A. Dholavira B. Kalibangan
C. Rakhigarhi D. Shortughai

5. Match List-I with List-II.

List-I (Symbols)	List-II (Meaning in Buddha's Life)
(*a*) Empty seat	I. Enlightenment
(*b*) Stupa	II. Mahaparinibbana
(*c*) Wheel	III. Meditation of Buddha
(*d*) Bodhi Tree	IV. First sermon of the Buddha

Choose the correct answer from the options given below:

	(*a*)	(*b*)	(*c*)	(*d*)
A.	I	III	II	IV
B.	III	II	IV	I
C.	III	II	I	IV
D.	II	I	IV	III

6. Who among the following said, 'I believe separate electorate will be suicidal to the minorities'?

A. Vallabhbhai Patel
B. Govind Ballabh Pant
C. Jawaharlal Nehru
D. Subash Chandra Bose

7. What is the name of Francois Bernier's book?

A. Travels in India
B. Travels in Asia
C. Travels in the Orient
D. Travels in the Mughal Empire

8. Identify the ***correct*** statements:

(*a*) 'Relief of Lucknow' painted by Fellice Besto.
(*b*) Subsidiary Alliance introduced by Wellesley in Awadh.
(*c*) Summary Revenue Settlements introduced in Awadh by British.
(*d*) 'In Memoriam' was painted by Joseph Noel Paton.
(*e*) 'Khoob Lari Mardani woh to Jhansi wali Rani thi' (like a man she fought, she was the Rani of Jhansi) was written by Shobha Kumari Chauhan.

Choose the ***correct*** answer from the options given below:

A. (*a*), (*b*), (*c*) only B. (*b*), (*c*), (*d*) only
C. (*c*), (*d*), (*e*) only D. (*a*), (*c*), (*e*) only

9. Consider the following statements about the urban core of Vijayanagara city. Mark the ***correct*** statements.

(*a*) There is little evidence of houses of ordinary people.
(*b*) Fine Chinese porcelain have been found in some areas.
(*c*) Tombs, Mosques and Muslim residential quarters have been found.
(*d*) Field excavations do not indicate prevalence of local cults.
(*e*) Wells and tanks were absent.

Choose the ***correct*** answer from the options given below:

A. (*a*), (*b*), (*c*) only
B. (*b*), (*c*), (*d*) only
C. (*c*), (*d*), (*e*) only
D. (*a*), (*c*), (*d*) only

10. Arrange the below given information in a chronological order:

(*a*) Alexander Cunningham publishes 'Bhilsa Topes', one of the earliest works on Sanchi.
(*b*) Sanchi declared a World Heritage Site.
(*c*) John Marshall and Alfred Foucher publish 'The Monument of Sanchi'.
(*d*) Prime Minister Jawaharlal Nehru lays the foundation stone of National Museum, New Delhi.
(*e*) Passing of the Treasure Trove Act, giving government the right to acquire all objects of archaeological interest.

Choose the ***correct*** answer from the options given below:

A. (*e*), (*a*), (*c*), (*b*), (*d*)
B. (*a*), (*e*), (*c*), (*d*), (*b*)
C. (*a*), (*b*), (*c*), (*d*), (*e*)
D. (*c*), (*a*), (*e*), (*d*), (*b*)

11. Arrange the following in a chronological manner:

(*a*) Permanent Settlement was introduced in Bengal.
(*b*) English East India Company acquires 'Diwani' of Bengal.
(*c*) Santhal Revolt in Rajmahal hills.
(*d*) First revenue settlement was started in Bombay Deccan.
(*e*) Ryots rebelled in Deccan villages.

Choose the ***correct*** answer from the options given below:

A. (*e*), (*b*), (*a*), (*c*), (*d*)
B. (*a*), (*b*), (*c*), (*d*), (*e*)
C. (*b*), (*a*), (*d*), (*c*), (*e*)
D. (*d*), (*a*), (*e*), (*b*), (*c*)

12. What did the word 'Tajwiz' mean during the Mughal period?

A. An order to prevent nobles from becoming rebellious.
B. Petition presented by a nobleman to emperor, recommending an applicant be recruited as Mansabdar.
C. Imperial order to bring criminals to the Mughal Court.
D. Petition to decide on justice.

13. The term 'Dikus' was used by the Santhals for ....

A. Fellow Santhals B. Peasants
C. Money lenders D. Their God

14. Who among the following while welcoming the Objectives Resolution said, "The real minorities are the mass of this country".

A. N.G. Ranga
B. Somnath Lahiri
C. Jaipal Singh
D. B.R. Ambedkar

15. While travelling to India, who faced the barrier of languages as he belonged to Khwarizma. Still he cited Indian texts, the Vedas, Bhagvad Gita, Manusmriti, etc., to provide an understanding of Indian society. Who was he?

A. Ibn Battuta B. Abdur Razzaq
C. Al-Biruni D. Abul Fazl

16. Which among the following film is NOT based on 'Partition'?

A. Garam Hawa B. Tamas
C. Meghe Dhaka Tara D. Mother India

17. Which of the following was not a provincial political centre of the Mauryan Empire?

A. Taxila B. Mathura
C. Ujjayini D. Tosali

18. Which Government set up a commission of enquiry to investigate into the causes of the Deccan Riots?

A. Calcutta B. Madras
C. Delhi D. Bombay

19. Who suffered defeat in the battle of Chinhat?

A. French B. Portuguese
C. Dutch D. British

20. Which Harappan site have the evidence of 'water reservoirs'?

A. Banawali B. Kalibangan
C. Harappa D. Dholavira

21. Who was the leader of Santhal Rebellion?

A. Sidhu Manjhi B. Shah Mal
C. Umaji Raje D. Gunoo

22. Who among the following are associated with Revolt of 1857?

(*a*) Shah Mal
(*b*) Nana Sahib
(*c*) V. D. Savarkar
(*d*) Kesari Singh Barahat
(*e*) Danka Shah

Choose the ***correct*** answer from the options given below:

A. (*a*), (*b*), (*d*) only
B. (*a*), (*b*), (*e*) only
C. (*a*), (*b*), (*c*) only
D. (*b*), (*c*), (*d*) only

23. Choose the ***correct*** statements in relation to 'Amuktamalyada'.

(*a*) It is written in Kannada.
(*b*) It is work on Grammar.
(*c*) It was composed by Krishnadeva Raya.
(*d*) It is written in Telugu.
(*e*) Krishnadeva Raya said that 'a king should improve the harbours of his country and so encourage its commerce'.

Choose the ***correct*** answer from the options given below:

A. (*a*), (*b*), (*c*) only
B. (*b*), (*c*), (*d*) only
C. (*c*), (*d*), (*e*) only
D. (*a*), (*d*), (*e*) only

24. Which of the following statements are correct about the Revolt of 1857?

(*a*) The Sepoy Mutiny began at Meerut Cantonment.

(*b*) Shah Mal mobilized Pargana Barout in Uttar Pradesh.
(*c*) In Kanpur, Peshwa Baji Rao II led the uprising.
(*d*) British were not able to capture principalities like Jhansi and Satara.
(*e*) In Chotanagpur, Gonoo, a tribal cultivator became leader of the Kol tribals of the region.

Choose the ***correct*** answer from the options given below:
A. (*a*), (*b*), (*c*) only
B. (*a*), (*c*), (*e*) only
C. (*b*), (*c*), (*e*) only
D. (*a*), (*b*), (*e*) only

25. The 'Vinaya Pitaka' dealt with ....
A. Gautam Buddha's teachings
B. Regional history of Buddhism
C. Rules and regulations for those who joined the 'sangha' or monastic order
D. Philosophical matter of Buddhism

26. A group of rich peasants in North Bengal were known as ....
A. Jotedars B. Zamindars
C. Adhiyars D. Bargadars

27. Which of the following metal was NOT found at Harappan site?
A. Copper B. Bronze
C. Gold D. Iron

28. Match List-I with List-II.

List-I (Sites)	**List-II (Archaeologist)**
(*a*) Dholavira	I. B.B. Lal and B.K. Thapar
(*b*) Kalibangan	II. S.R. Rao
(*c*) Lothal	III. R.S. Bisht
(*d*) Bahawalpur	IV. M.R. Mughal

Choose the ***correct*** answer from the options given below:

	(*a*)	(*b*)	(*c*)	(*d*)
A.	III	I	II	IV
B.	I	II	III	IV
C.	II	I	III	IV
D.	IV	III	II	I

29. Match List-I with List-II.

List-I (Text)	**List-II (Theme/Content)**
(*a*) Ashtadhyayi	I. State craft
(*b*) Arthashastra	II. Dramaturgy
(*c*) Natyashastra	III. Grammar
(*d*) Charak Samhita	IV. Medicine

Choose the ***correct*** answer from the options given below:

	(*a*)	(*b*)	(*c*)	(*d*)
A.	II	I	III	IV
B.	IV	III	I	II
C.	III	I	II	IV
D.	I	II	III	IV

30. 'Amar Katha' (My Story) is the autobiography of:
A. Kalpana Dutt
B. Surya Sen
C. Debendranath Tagore
D. Binodini Dasi

31. Choose the correct chronological sequence:
(*a*) Establishment of Gajapati Kingdom of Orissa.
(*b*) Establishment of Bahamani Kingdom.
(*c*) Establishment of Vijayanagara Empire.
(*d*) Conquest of Goa by the Portuguese.
(*e*) First Battle of Panipat.

Choose the ***correct*** answer from the options given below:
A. (*a*), (*c*), (*b*), (*d*), (*e*)
B. (*c*), (*b*), (*a*), (*d*), (*e*)
C. (*b*), (*a*), (*c*), (*e*), (*d*)
D. (*a*), (*b*), (*c*), (*d*), (*e*)

32. Match List-I with List-II.

List-I (Travellers)	**List-II (Countries)**
(*a*) Nicolo de Conti	I. Persia
(*b*) Afanasii Nikitin	II. Portugal
(*c*) Fernao Nuniz	III. Italy
(*d*) Abdur Razzaq	IV. Russia

Choose the ***correct*** answer from the options given below:

	(*a*)	(*b*)	(*c*)	(*d*)
A.	II	IV	III	I
B.	IV	III	II	I
C.	III	IV	II	I
D.	III	II	IV	I

33. Match List-I with List-II.

List-I (Types of Lands)	**List-II (Period of Cultivation)**
(*a*) Banjar	I. Annually cultivated and never allowed to lie fallow
(*b*) Parauti	II. Left out of cultivation for a time
(*c*) Polaj	III. Left fallow for three or four years
(*d*) Chachar	IV. Uncultivated for five years or more

Choose the ***correct*** answer from the options given below:

	(a)	(b)	(c)	(d)
A.	III	II	I	IV
B.	IV	II	I	III
C.	II	III	IV	I
D.	IV	I	II	III

34. Choose the ***correct*** statements out of the following:

(*a*) Lord Dalhousie described Kingdom of Awadh as 'a cherry will drop into our mouth one day."

(*b*) Nawab Wajid Ali Shah was Nawab of Awadh.

(*c*) By the terms of Subsidiary Alliance, Nawab of Awadh had to strengthen the military forces on his own.

(*d*) By the terms of Subsidiary Alliance, Nawab of Awadh was free to maintain law and order into the kingdom.

(*e*) Due to Subsidiary Alliance, Nawab will no longer assert control over the chiefs and taluqdars.

Choose the ***correct*** answer from the options given below:

A. (*c*), (*d*), (*e*) only
B. (*a*), (*b*), (*e*) only
C. (*a*), (*b*), (*c*) only
D. (*b*), (*c*), (*d*) only

35. Identify the language which is used for most of the Asokan inscriptions.

A. Sanskrit B. Prakrit
C. Pali D. Tamil

36. Arrange the following Harappan sites from North to South direction:

(*a*) Kalibangan (*b*) Rakhigarhi
(*c*) Balakot (*d*) Nageshwar
(*e*) Dholavira

Choose the ***correct*** answer from the options given below:

A. (*a*), (*d*), (*c*), (*b*), (*e*)
B. (*b*), (*a*), (*c*), (*e*), (*d*)
C. (*c*), (*b*), (*a*), (*e*), (*d*)
D. (*b*), (*a*), (*d*), (*c*), (*e*)

37. Identify the article of Indian Constitution that gave the Centre, the powers to take over a state administration on the recommendation of the Governor.

A. Article 365 B. Article 356
C. Article 386 D. Article 368

38. Which among the following sect believes that 'everything is predetermined'?

A. Jainism B. Buddhism
C. Ajivikas D. Lokayatas

39. .... from Madras made a powerful plea for continuing separate electorates.

A. B. Pocker Bahadur
B. R.V. Dhulekar
C. Somnath Lahiri
D. K.M. Munshi

40. Identify the correct statements:

(*a*) Mahabhashya was written by Patanjali.

(*b*) Jatakas are associated with Buddhism.

(*c*) Dharmasutras were written in Pali language.

(*d*) Sutta Pitaka deals with Jainism.

(*e*) Upanishads deals with meaning of life and philosophy.

Choose the ***correct*** answer from the options given below:

A. (*a*), (*b*), (*c*) only B. (*b*), (*c*), (*d*) only
C. (*c*), (*d*), (*e*) only D. (*a*), (*b*), (*e*) only

Directions (Qs. No. 41-45): *Read the passage and answer the questions:*

Read the following verse composed by 'Appar', a Bhakti saint of South India and answer the questions given below:

"O roques who quote the law books. Of what use are your gotra and kula? Just bow to Marperu's lord as your sole refuge".

41. Appar belonged to which tradition?

A. Alvar B. Nayanar
C. Virashaiva D. Tantric

42. Lord of 'Marperu' refers to the following:

A. The Chola kings B. Vishnu
C. Shiva D. Lord Gomatesvara

43. Andal was a saint of which Bhakti tradition?

A. Alvar B. Nayanar
C. Virashaiva D. Lingayat

44. Karaikkal Ammaiyar belonged to which Bhakti tradition?

A. Virashaiva B. Alvar
C. Nayanar D. Tantric

45. Identify the correct statements:

(*a*) The Bhakti saints composed hymns in Tamil in praise of their gods.

(*b*) Bhakti saints identified certain shrines as abode of their gods.

(*c*) Alvar saints composed Tevaram'.

(*d*) The South Indian Bhakti movement atleast attempted to reform the caste system.

(*e*) Relations with Buddhism and Jainism in Alvar hymns was cordial.

Choose the ***correct*** answer from the options given below:

A. (*a*), (*b*), (*c*), (*d*) only B. (*a*), (*b*), (*d*), (*e*) only
C. (*b*), (*c*), (*d*), (*e*) only D. (*a*), (*c*), (*d*), (*e*) only

Directions (Qs. No. 46-50): *Read the passage and answer the questions:*

After the failure of the Cripps Mission, Mahatma Gandhi decided to launch his third major movement against British rule. This was the "Quit India" campaign, which began in August 1942. Although Gandhiji was jailed at once, younger activists organised strikes and acts of sabotage all over the country. Particularly active in underground resistance were socialist members of the Congress, such as Jayaprakash Narayan. In several districts such as Satara in the west and Medinipur in the east, "independent" governments were proclaimed. The British responded with much force, yet it took more than a year to suppress the rebellion.

46. During which Indian Movement against the British rule, underground resistance was provided by Socialist members?

A. Quit India Movement
B. Non-Cooperation Movement
C. Civil Disobedience Movement
D. Khilafat Movement

47. Choose the correct statements:

(*a*) Failure of Cripps Mission was a cause for starting of the 'Quit India' campaign.
(*b*) 'Quit India' campaign began in March 1942.
(*c*) Jayaprakash Narayan participated in 'Quit India' campaign.
(*d*) Quit India was not a 'Mass Movement'.
(*e*) It was during 'Quit India' year that Muslim League began to make a mark in the Punjab and Sindh provinces.

Choose the ***correct*** answer from the options given below:

A. (*a*), (*b*), (*c*) only
B. (*a*), (*d*), (*e*) only
C. (*c*), (*d*), (*e*) only
D. (*a*), (*c*), (*e*) only

48. Who among the following was a 'Socialist' member of the Congress?

A. W.C. Banerji
B. Jayaprakash Narayan
C. Madan Mohan Malviya
D. Dada Bhai Naoroji

49. In which year did Cripps Mission arrive in India?

A. 1941 B. 1946
C. 1943 D. 1942

50. According to the passage, in which districts "independent" governments were established?

A. Satara and Noakhali
B. Medinipur and Manipur
C. Satara and Medinipur
D. Satara and Calcutta

ANSWERS

1. (B): Abdur Razzaq, the Persian ambassador to Calicut from 1442 to 1443, wrote extensively about his observations during his travels. One of the places he visited was Vijayanagara, the capital of the eponymous empire. In his notes, he was particularly impressed by the fortifications of the city, detailing seven concentric lines of walls and fortifications. These fortifications were indicative of the might and grandeur of the Vijayanagara Empire, one of the most powerful empires in South India during the medieval period. These fortifications not only served as defense mechanisms but also as a testament to the engineering capabilities and urban planning skills of the time.

2. (C): James Prinsep, an English scholar and antiquarian, is celebrated for deciphering the Brahmi script. While the options mentioned include various ancient scripts, it was the Brahmi script, used in many of the inscriptions of Ashoka and other ancient Indian texts, that Prinsep successfully deciphered. This was a seminal breakthrough, as it allowed historians and scholars to read and understand the edicts and inscriptions of the Mauryan period, shedding light on the social, religious, and political fabric of ancient India.

3. (B): The Objectives Resolution was introduced by Jawaharlal Nehru on December 13, 1946, in the Constituent Assembly of India. It played a pivotal role in outlining the vision for the future constitution of India. However, the incorrect statement is that it proclaimed India to be an "Independent Demographic Sovereign Republic." Instead, it envisaged India as a "Sovereign Democratic Republic." This resolution provided the guiding principles that shaped the subsequent drafting of the Indian Constitution.

4. (D): Dholavira, located in modern-day Gujarat, India, is a prominent Harappan site. Among its many unique features, what distinguishes Dholavira from other Indus Valley sites is the presence of an advanced water conservation system, including reservoirs and step-wells. However, it's the site of Shortughai in Afghanistan, where traces of canals have been found. Shortughai is unique in that it's far north of the primary Indus Valley civilization territory, reflecting the extensive reach and influence of the Harappan culture.

5. (B): The symbols and their meanings associated with Buddha's life are rich in metaphor and significance.

(*a*) Empty seat represents the meditation of Buddha. It signifies his presence and the meditative phase before achieving enlightenment.

(*b*) Stupa symbolizes Mahaparinibbana, which is the final death after which there is no rebirth. Stupas were initially built to house the relics of Buddha.

(*c*) Wheel or the Dharmachakra represents the first sermon of the Buddha given at Sarnath. It's a symbol of the Buddha's teachings, often referred to as the "Wheel of Law."

(*d*) Bodhi Tree is where Buddha attained enlightenment. It stands as a symbol of enlightenment and the location, Bodh Gaya, is a major pilgrimage site for Buddhists.

6. (B): Govind Ballabh Pant is attributed with the statement, "I believe separate electorate will be suicidal to the minorities." Govind Ballabh Pant was a key figure in the Indian freedom movement and later went on to become the Home Minister of India. He firmly believed in the unity and integrity of the nation. The concept of separate electorates based on religion or ethnicity could create further divisions and fissures in society. Pant, like many other leaders of his time, envisioned an India where all citizens, irrespective of their religion, caste, or ethnicity, had equal rights and were represented under a common electoral system.

7. (D): François Bernier, a French physician and traveller, wrote a book titled "Travels in the Mughal Empire." Bernier's travelogue provides invaluable insights into the Mughal Empire during the reign of Emperor Aurangzeb. His detailed observations of the socio-economic and political conditions of the time are of great historical significance. Through his writings, readers can glimpse the grandeur of the Mughal court, the socio-economic disparities, the state of medicine, and many other aspects of 17th century India.

8. (B): Among the statements, (*b*) Subsidiary Alliance was a policy introduced by Lord Wellesley, the then Governor-General of India. This policy meant that the Indian rulers signing this alliance were not allowed to have their independent armed forces. They were to be protected by the British army. (*c*) Summary Revenue Settlements were introduced in Awadh by the British. This was an effort to streamline revenue collection and ensure stable income from land taxes. (*d*) 'In Memoriam' is indeed a painting by Joseph Noel Paton, a Scottish artist, but it doesn't pertain to the Indian context. The title refers to mourning or memorializing someone.

9. (A): Regarding the urban core of the Vijayanagara city: (*a*) While the grandeur of palaces and temples is evident, not much is known about the houses of the ordinary people from archaeological remains. (*b*) Artefacts, including fine Chinese porcelain, have been found, suggesting trade links or influence from Far East regions. (*c*) Tombs, mosques, and Muslim residential quarters have been discovered, signifying a multicultural society where multiple religions coexisted.

10. (B): Chronologically: (*a*) Alexander Cunningham's "Bhilsa Topes" was one of the first and foremost works detailing the stupas of Sanchi. Published in 1854, it shed light on the Buddhist architecture of the site. (*e*) The Treasure Trove Act was passed in 1878. This act ensured that the government could acquire objects deemed to have archaeological significance. (*c*) "The Monuments of Sanchi" by John Marshall and Alfred Foucher was published later, providing a more detailed study and documentation of Sanchi. (*d*) Jawaharlal Nehru laid the foundation stone of the National Museum in New Delhi in 1955, reflecting India's effort to consolidate and display its rich heritage. (*b*) Sanchi was declared a World Heritage Site by UNESCO in 1989, marking its global recognition as an archaeological and historical treasure.

11. (C): The chronological sequence is as follows: (*b*) The English East India Company acquired the 'Diwani' rights of Bengal in 1765, enabling them to exercise control over the revenue of the region. (*a*) The Permanent Settlement, also known as the Zamindari System, was introduced in Bengal in 1793 by Lord Cornwallis. This was a system of revenue collection where the Zamindars were recognized as landowners and were given the responsibility to collect and pay fixed revenues to the British administration. (*d*) The first revenue settlement in Bombay Deccan began in the early 19th century. The British tried different systems of revenue collection in various parts of India. (*c*) The Santhal Revolt occurred in 1855-56 in the Rajmahal hills of present-day Jharkhand. The Santhals, a tribal community, rebelled against oppressive moneylenders, Zamindars, and the British. (*e*) The ryots (peasants) in the Deccan villages rebelled in the late 19th century, primarily due to high land revenue demands and frequent famines.

12. (B): During the Mughal period, the term 'Tajwiz' referred to a petition presented by a nobleman to the emperor, recommending an applicant be recruited as a Mansabdar (a rank holder). The Mansabdari system under the Mughals was a complex one, where ranks were given based on the number of troops a Mansabdar commanded. These Tajwiz petitions acted as a form of endorsement or recommendation.

13. (C): The term 'Dikus' was used by the Santhals primarily for the moneylenders, traders, and other non-tribal people who exploited them. The Santhals perceived these outsiders as oppressors and exploiters who took away their lands and subjected them to various forms of economic and social injustice.

14. (A): N.G. Ranga, a well-known agrarian leader, made this poignant statement: "The real minorities are the mass of this country." His statement highlighted that the real minority in India was its vast populace of peasants and workers who were subjected to socio-economic inequalities. While welcoming the Objectives Resolution, he emphasized the importance of addressing the concerns of this significant 'minority'.

15. (C): Al-Biruni, who hailed from Khwarizma (in present-day Uzbekistan), faced language barriers when he came to India. However, he made rigorous efforts to learn Sanskrit and thereby acquainted himself with the rich literary traditions of India. His comprehensive work, "Kitab al-Hind" or "The Book of India," provides detailed insights into the socio-cultural, scientific, and religious aspects of India during his time. He cited Indian texts, including the Vedas, Bhagavad Gita, Manusmriti, and others, to present a holistic view of Indian society.

16. (D): "Mother India" is not based on the theme of Partition. Instead, it deals with the life of a poverty-stricken village woman named Radha, who, in the absence of her husband, strives to raise her sons amidst many hardships. Directed by Mehboob Khan, the film is an exploration of the challenges faced by the rural populace of India. On the other hand, "Garam Hawa," "Tamas," and "Meghe Dhaka Tara" delve into the traumatic events and aftermath of the India-Pakistan Partition in 1947.

17. (B): Mathura was not a provincial political center of the Mauryan Empire. The Mauryan Empire, one of the largest empires in the Indian subcontinent, had several provincial centers to ensure efficient administration. These centers included Taxila in the northwest, Ujjayini in the central region, and Tosali in the east. Mathura, while an important city during ancient times, especially as a religious and trade center, was not a provincial administrative center under the Mauryans.

18. (D): The Bombay government set up a commission of inquiry to investigate the causes of the Deccan Riots. The Deccan Riots of 1875 were agrarian disturbances that erupted in parts of the Pune and Ahmednagar districts of the Bombay Presidency. The main reason behind these riots was the exploitation of the ryots (peasants) by moneylenders. The commission's findings highlighted the grave indebtedness of the peasants and led to the introduction of the Deccan Agriculturists' Relief Act in 1879.

19. (D): The British suffered defeat in the Battle of Chinhat. The battle took place in 1857 during the early phase of the Indian Revolt (often referred to as the Sepoy Mutiny or the First War of Independence). In this battle, forces led by the local chieftains and mutineers confronted the British near the town of Chinhat. The British forces, under the command of Henry Lawrence, faced a significant setback.

20. (D): Dholavira, located in the present-day state of Gujarat, India, provides evidence of water reservoirs. Dholavira is one of the most prominent Harappan sites and is renowned for its urban planning and water management systems. The site contains a series of water reservoirs, constructed using stone masonry, which depict the advanced hydro-engineering techniques of the Harappan civilization. The water management system at Dholavira is a testament to the advanced urban planning and architectural skills of the people of the Indus Valley Civilization.

21. (A): The Santhal Rebellion of 1855-56 was led by Sidhu Manjhi and his brother Kanhu Manjhi. This uprising was one of the most significant tribal movements in India during the 19th century. The Santhals, an indigenous tribe, revolted against the oppressive policies and practices of the British government, as well as the exploitation by local landlords and moneylenders. Their resistance stands as a symbol of the indomitable spirit of tribal communities against colonial and external domination.

22. (B): Among the given options, Shah Mal, Nana Sahib, and Danka Shah are associated with the Revolt of 1857. Nana Sahib, the adopted son of the exiled Maratha Peshwa Baji Rao II, played a pivotal role in the uprising at Kanpur. Shah Mal and Danka Shah were lesser-known figures but were connected to the larger fabric of the revolt that engulfed North India. V. D. Savarkar was not directly associated with the revolt; instead, he is well-known for writing a book that characterized the revolt as the "First War of Indian Independence."

23. (C): "Amuktamalyada" is a well-regarded poetic work written in Telugu by the Vijayanagara Emperor Krishnadeva Raya. It is not a grammar work; instead, it is a devotional poem dedicated to the life of the

Andal, a Tamil Alvar saint. Within the text, Krishnadeva Raya delves into the importance of rulers being just and promoting the economic well-being of their kingdoms. He emphasized the significance of harbors and commerce for a prosperous state. The work stands out not just for its poetic brilliance but also as an insight into the political and economic philosophy of a ruling monarch in medieval India.

24. (D): The Revolt of 1857, often referred to as the First War of Indian Independence, saw participation from various sections of Indian society. (*a*) The Sepoy Mutiny did indeed begin at the Meerut Cantonment in May 1857 when sepoys mutinied against their British officers. (*b*) Shah Mal was instrumental in mobilizing the Pargana Barout in Uttar Pradesh. (*c*) However, in Kanpur, it was not Peshwa Baji Rao II (who had already died years before the revolt) but Nana Sahib who led the uprising. (*d*) The British eventually managed to capture principalities like Jhansi, and the assertion that they couldn't is incorrect. (*e*) In Chotanagpur, Gonoo emerged as a tribal leader of the Kol tribals, mobilizing them against the British.

25. (C): The 'Vinaya Pitaka', one of the three main baskets or 'Tipitakas' of Theravada Buddhist scriptures, primarily deals with the rules and regulations for those who joined the 'sangha' or monastic order. These rules dictate the life of a monk or nun in the Buddhist order, guiding their conduct, behavior, and interactions both within the monastic community and with laypeople. It provides a structured framework to ensure the smooth functioning of the monastic community and uphold the sanctity of the Buddhist teachings. The 'Vinaya Pitaka' forms the disciplinary code for monks and nuns, ensuring the longevity and purity of the Buddha's teachings.

26. (A): Jotedars were rich peasants in North Bengal. The term 'Jotedar' is rooted in Bengali society during the British period and signifies a class of rich peasants who emerged with substantial landholdings. These peasants were different from the Zamindars, who were the major landowners, often collecting rents rather than cultivating land themselves. The Jotedars, on the other hand, both owned and cultivated land, sometimes even leasing out parts of their holdings. They played a significant role in rural power dynamics, often acting as intermediaries between the Zamindars and the actual cultivators. Over time, many Jotedars gained considerable influence in local politics and socio-economic matters.

27. (D): Iron was NOT found at Harappan sites. The Harappan or Indus Valley Civilization (approx. 3300 BCE – 1300 BCE) was known for its advanced metallurgical techniques, particularly in copper, bronze, and gold. The art of iron smelting was not known to the Harappans. It was only during the later Vedic period that iron began to be used widely in the Indian subcontinent. The absence of iron in Harappan sites further supports the belief that the civilization existed in the Bronze Age, a period before the widespread use of iron in the region.

28. (A): The correct match is: (*a*) Dholavira - R.S. Bisht (*b*) Kalibangan - B.B. Lal and B.K. Thapar (*c*) Lothal - S.R. Rao (*d*) Bahawalpur - M.R. Mughal. Dholavira, located in Gujarat, is one of the prominent Harappan sites. R.S. Bisht undertook extensive excavations and research here. Kalibangan, in Rajasthan, was explored by B.B. Lal and B.K. Thapar. Lothal, another significant Harappan site located in Gujarat, was excavated by S.R. Rao. Bahawalpur, though not a Harappan site, is significant in the archaeological context of the subcontinent and was explored by M.R. Mughal.

29. (C): The correct match is: (*a*) Ashtadhyayi - Grammar (*b*) Arthashastra - Statecraft (*c*) Natyashastra - Dramaturgy (*d*) Charak Samhita - Medicine

The "Ashtadhyayi" by Panini is a foundational text on Sanskrit grammar. The "Arthashastra", attributed to Kautilya or Chanakya, is an ancient Indian treatise on statecraft, economic policy, and military strategy. The "Natyashastra", believed to be written by Bharata Muni, is a treatise on performing arts, particularly drama, dance, and music. "Charak Samhita" is one of the principal classical Ayurvedic texts, attributed to the ancient physician Charaka, and deals with medicine.

30. (D): 'Amar Katha' (My Story) is the autobiography of Binodini Dasi. Binodini Dasi, often known as "Notee Binodini", was a celebrated actress in Bengali theatre during the late 19th and early 20th centuries. She began her career in acting at a very young age and soon rose to fame. Her autobiography, 'Amar Katha', provides a candid account of her life, her experiences in the theatre world, and the socio-cultural milieu of her time. Through her writings, Binodini Dasi provides a glimpse into the life of a female artist in a male-dominated society and the challenges and adversities she faced.

31. (B): The correct chronological sequence is: (*c*) Establishment of Vijayanagara Empire (1336 CE). (*b*) Establishment of Bahamani Kingdom (1347 CE). (*a*) Establishment of Gajapati Kingdom of Orissa (1434 CE). (*d*) Conquest of Goa by the Portuguese (1510 CE). (*e*) First Battle of Panipat (1526 CE).

The Vijayanagara Empire and the Bahamani Kingdom were two of the major kingdoms in southern India during the medieval period. The Gajapati Kingdom of Orissa came into prominence a little later. The Portuguese, as part of their colonial endeavors, captured Goa, which then remained a Portuguese colony until 1961. The First Battle of Panipat marked the advent of the Mughal Empire in India with Babur's victory.

32. (C): The correct match is: (*a*) Nicolo de Conti - Italy (*b*) Afanasii Nikitin - Russia, (*c*) Fernao Nuniz - Portugal (*d*) Abdur Razzaq - Persia

Nicolo de Conti was an Italian merchant and traveller who visited the Vijayanagara Empire. Afanasii Nikitin was a Russian explorer who documented his travels in the book "A Journey Beyond the Three Seas". Fernao Nuniz, from Portugal, visited and chronicled the Vijayanagara Empire. Abdur Razzaq was a Persian envoy who also visited the Vijayanagara court.

33. (B): The correct match for the types of lands is: (*a*) Banjar - Uncultivated for five years or more (*b*) Parauti - Left out of cultivation for a time (*c*) Polaj - Annually cultivated and never allowed to lie fallow (*d*) Chachar - Left fallow for three or four years.

In traditional agricultural practices of India, lands were classified based on their period of cultivation. Polaj lands were the most frequently cultivated, while Banjar lands represented long-neglected tracts. Understanding these classifications helps in appreciating the agricultural patterns and land use strategies of historic India.

34. (B): The correct statements are: (*a*) Lord Dalhousie described the Kingdom of Awadh as 'a cherry that will drop into our mouth one day'. (*b*) Nawab Wajid Ali Shah was the Nawab of Awadh. (*e*) Due to the Subsidiary Alliance, the Nawab could no longer assert control over the chiefs and taluqdars.

Lord Dalhousie's "Doctrine of Lapse" was a strategy to annex princely states that did not have a legitimate male heir. Awadh was particularly seen as a ripe target. Nawab Wajid Ali Shah was the last Nawab of Awadh before the British annexed it. The Subsidiary Alliance system, introduced by Lord Wellesley, undermined the sovereignty of the princely states and placed them under British control, often limiting their power over local chiefs and landowners.

35. (B): Most of the Asokan inscriptions are in Prakrit.

Emperor Ashoka of the Mauryan dynasty (c. 268-232 BCE) left behind numerous inscriptions carved on pillars, rocks, and caves across his vast empire. These inscriptions are primarily in the Prakrit language, written in Brahmi script. Prakrit was the vernacular language during Ashoka's time and was spoken by the common people, making it an effective medium for communication. The use of Prakrit underscores Ashoka's desire to communicate directly with his subjects, promoting moral values and his policy of Dhamma.

36. (B): The correct arrangement of Harappan sites from North to South is: (*b*) Rakhigarhi, (*a*) Kalibangan, (*c*) Balakot, (*e*) Dholavira, (*d*) Nageshwar.

Rakhigarhi is located in Haryana and is one of the largest Indus Valley Civilisation sites. Kalibangan, in Rajasthan, is renowned for its unique fire altars and a "world's earliest attested ploughed field". Balakot, located in Pakistan, is a coastal site. Dholavira, situated in Gujarat's Rann of Kutch, is known for its impressive urban planning and architectural brilliance. Lastly, Nageshwar, also in Gujarat, is near the Gulf of Kutch. These sites, spread across modern-day India and Pakistan, provide a testament to the extensive reach and intricate urban networks of the Harappan civilization.

37. (B): Article 356 of the Indian Constitution empowers the Centre to take over a state's administration on the Governor's recommendation. This provision, often termed as 'President's Rule', is invoked when the state government is unable to function as per constitutional provisions. It's a controversial provision, often criticized for its misuse, and it underscores the federal structure of India, emphasizing the balance of power between the Center and states.

38. (C): Ajivikas were an ancient sect that believed everything in the universe was predetermined. This sect was contemporaneous with Jainism and Buddhism and was founded by Makkhali Gosala. The central philosophy of Ajivikas, termed as Niyati, or fate, posits that everything is predestined and individuals have no free will. This deterministic philosophy made them distinct from both Jains and Buddhists.

39. (A): B. Pocker Bahadur from Madras made a forceful appeal for the continuation of separate electorates. The debate around separate electorates was a significant issue during the framing of India's constitution. While some leaders believed it would safeguard minority rights, others felt it would perpetuate divisions. B. Pocker Bahadur's stance showcases the complexities and the multifaceted debates around representation and protection of minority rights in post-colonial India.

40. (D): The correct statements are: (*a*) Mahabhashya was written by Patanjali. It's a commentary on Panini's

Ashtadhyayi and is a seminal work in Sanskrit grammar. (*b*) Jatakas are associated with Buddhism. They are stories about the previous births of the Buddha, where he appears as both animals and humans, exemplifying moral lessons. (*e*) Upanishads deal with the meaning of life and philosophy. These ancient texts form the philosophical basis of Hinduism, exploring profound topics like the nature of ultimate reality (Brahman) and the individual soul's relationship with it (Atman).

Collectively, the Upanishads, Jatakas, and Mahabhashya, despite belonging to different traditions and periods, provide profound insights into the rich tapestry of Indian spiritual, philosophical, and linguistic thought.

41. (B): Appar belonged to the Nayanar tradition. The Nayanars were a group of 63 saints in Tamil Nadu who were devoted to Lord Shiva. They played a pivotal role in the Bhakti movement in South India between the 6th and 9th centuries CE. Through their hymns and devotion, they laid the foundation for Saivism, propagating the belief in Lord Shiva as the ultimate savior and the path of love and devotion as a way to attain him.

42. (C): The 'Lord of Marperu' in Appar's verse refers to Shiva. The context of the verse is a critique of the ritualistic Brahmanical traditions, emphasizing that true salvation or liberation is attained not through rigorous adherence to scriptural rituals but through sincere devotion to Lord Shiva. By referencing "Marperu's lord", Appar highlights the importance of heartfelt devotion over traditional lineage or "gotra" and family or "kula".

43. (A): Andal was a saint of the Alvar tradition. The Alvars were a group of 12 saints in Tamil Nadu devoted to Lord Vishnu. Andal, the only female among the Alvars, is especially revered for her intense love and devotion to Lord Vishnu. Her hymns and verses not only express her profound devotion but also provide insights into the society and values of her time. Notably, her "Thiruppavai" and "Nachiyar Thirumozhi" are celebrated compositions that are still recited during the Tamil month of Margazhi.

44. (C): Karaikkal Ammaiyar belonged to the Nayanar tradition. She was one of the earliest and prominent female saints devoted to Lord Shiva. Her life is a testament to intense devotion, where she even prayed to be turned into a ghoul-like form to avoid worldly distractions and be solely devoted to Shiva. Her poetry and hymns are infused with deep mystical experiences and are considered some of the foundational works of Tamil Shaiva Siddhanta tradition.

45. (B): The correct statements are: (*a*) The Bhakti saints composed hymns in Tamil in praise of their gods. Many saints during the Bhakti movement composed hymns and songs in vernacular languages, breaking away from the traditional Sanskrit, making spiritual knowledge accessible to the common people. (*b*) Bhakti saints identified certain shrines as the abode of their gods. These shrines were celebrated as special places of divine presence and became major pilgrimage sites. (*d*) The South Indian Bhakti movement at least attempted to reform the caste system. By emphasizing personal devotion over ritualistic practices and birth-based caste hierarchy, the Bhakti saints challenged and tried to reform the stringent caste divisions. (*e*) Regarding relations with Buddhism and Jainism, the Alvar hymns often criticized these religions as they aimed to establish the superiority of their form of devotion and their deity. The competitive religious environment of the time meant that these saints sought to differentiate and assert their beliefs over others.

46. (A): The Quit India Movement, which commenced in August 1942, saw an intense underground resistance spearheaded by socialist members. This movement, considered one of the pivotal events during India's struggle for independence, was initiated by Mahatma Gandhi, advocating for an immediate end to British rule. The movement saw widespread participation, including strikes and acts of sabotage that took the British administration by surprise. Despite the swift arrest of Gandhi and other leaders, the movement continued to gain momentum and posed a significant challenge to the British.

47. (D): (*a*) The failure of the Cripps Mission, which aimed to secure full Indian cooperation and support for the British war effort during WWII, indeed became a catalyst for the launch of the 'Quit India' campaign. (*b*) Contrary to the statement, the 'Quit India' campaign began in August 1942, not March. (*c*) Jayaprakash Narayan, a key socialist leader, played a crucial role in the movement, particularly in organizing the underground resistance against British rule. (*e*) The year of the 'Quit India Movement' saw the Muslim League further establish its presence, particularly in Punjab and Sindh, and this period marked the beginning of the League's demands for a separate nation, leading to the eventual creation of Pakistan.

48. (B): Jayaprakash Narayan was a prominent socialist member of the Congress. Popularly referred to as JP, he played an influential role during the Quit India Movement. He later became a fierce critic of the Congress government in post-independent India and was an important figure in the formation of the Janata Party, which opposed the Emergency imposed by Indira Gandhi in the 1970s. JP's commitment to democratic values and his vision of a socialist India cemented his legacy as a significant political and social leader.

49. (D): The Cripps Mission arrived in India in 1942. It was led by Sir Stafford Cripps, a member of the British War Cabinet. The mission aimed to secure Indian support for the British war efforts in World War II by promising dominion status to India after the war. However, the vague nature of the proposals and the lack of any immediate concrete steps towards Indian self-governance led to its rejection by the Indian National Congress. The mission's failure further intensified the demand for complete independence from the British.

50. (C): As per the passage, "independent" governments were established in the districts of Satara and Medinipur. This was a unique feature of the Quit India Movement where, in certain areas, local leadership declared themselves free from British rule and attempted to set up parallel governance structures. While these "independent" governments were short-lived due to the might of the British forces, they symbolized the depth of the Indian desire for self-rule and the lengths to which the freedom fighters were willing to go to achieve independence.

POLITICAL SCIENCE

1. Article 370 was recently abrogated in which State?

A. Jammu and Kashmir B. Nagaland
C. Manipur D. Assam

2. Who was known as Frontier Gandhi?

A. Md. Ali Zinnah B. Abdul Gaffar Khan
C. Mahatma Gandhi D. Sardar Patel

3. Under the provision of which article, the government could declare a state of emergency on grounds of external threats?

A. Article 351 B. Article 144
C. Article 352 D. Article 256

4. Which of the following is not an effect of Indo-China war?

A. The USSR remained neutral during the conflict
B. India had to approach South Africa for military assistance
C. Indo-China war induced a sense of national humiliation
D. For the first time, a no-confidence motion against Nehru's government was moved and debated in the Lok Sabha

5. Who launched the Narmada Bachao Andolan?

A. Jyoti Patkar B. Narmada Devi
C. Medha Patkar D. Aamir Khan

6. Given below are two statements:

Statement I: Vladimir Lenin founded the Bolshevik Party.

Statement II: Joseph Stalin was the successor to Lenin and led the Soviet Union during its consolidation.

In the light of the above statements. Choose the correct answer from the options given below:

A. Both Statement I and Statement II are true
B. Both Statement I and Statement II are false
C. Statement I is true, but statement II is false
D. Statement I is false, but Statement II is true

7. Bandung Conference 1955 is important in world political history because ....

A. It marked the zenith of India's engagement with the newly independent of Afro-Asian nations
B. It further led to the established of NAM
C. It suggested Afro-Asian Unity
D. It created a third military block in the world

8. Bharatiya Jana Sangh was founded by:

A. Deen Dayal Upadhyaya
B. Shyama Prasad Mukherjee
C. Balraj Madhok
D. C. Rajagopalachari

9. Ruble is official currency of:

A. China B. India
C. Japan D. Russia

10. Railway Strike of 1974 was called by ....

A. National Coordination Committee for Railwaymen's struggle
B. National Conference Commission for Railwaymen's struggle
C. National Railway Worker Association
D. National Worker Committee for Railwaymen's struggle

11. Match List-I with List-II.

List-I	List-II
(*a*) Karpoori Thakur	I. Chief Minister of Andhra Pradesh (1956)
(*b*) S. Nijalingappa	II. Chief Minister of Madras (Tamil Nadu-1967)
(*c*) N. Sanjeeva Reddy	III. Chief Minister of Maysore (Karnataka)
(*d*) C. Natarajan Annadurai	IV. Chief Minister of Bihar between December 1970 and June 1971

Choose the ***correct*** answer from the options:

	(*a*)	(*b*)	(*c*)	(*d*)
A.	II	III	IV	I
B.	III	I	II	IV
C.	II	I	III	IV
D.	IV	III	I	II

12. According to the Mandal Commission, some Indian States like .... already had high reservations for economically poor people.

A. Punjab B. Bihar
C. Gujarat D. Maharashtra

13. Match List-I with List-II.

List-I	List-II
(*a*) Josip Broz Tito	I. Egypt
(*b*) Jawaharlal Nehru	II. Indonesia
(*c*) Gamal Abdel Nasser	III. Yugoslavia
(*d*) Sukarno	IV. India

Choose the ***correct*** answer from the options:

	(*a*)	(*b*)	(*c*)	(*d*)
A.	I	II	III	IV
B.	III	IV	I	II
C.	IV	III	II	I
D.	II	I	IV	III

14. Who coined the term United Nations (UN)?
A. Richard Nixon B. Ronald Regan
C. Abraham Linchon D. Franklin D. Roosevelt

15. On which date Kargil Vijay Diwas is celebrated in India?
A. 1 August B. 20 June
C. 1 May D. 26 July

16. In the second Lok Sabha general election of 1957, how many seats were won by CPI (The Communist Party of India)?
A. 26 B. 19
C. 27 D. 16

17. The capital of South Korea, Seoul, is situated at the bank of which river?
A. Yellow River B. Han River
C. Yangt-si-River D. Nile River

18. In which year did the India-Sri Lanka Accord for Indian Peace Keeping Force (IPKF) take place?
A. 1986 B. 1987
C. 1988 D. 1989

19. "The United Nations was not created to take humanity to the heaven, but to save it from the hell", Who made this statement?
A. Pt. J.N. Nehru B. Dag Hammerskjold
C. Kofi Annan D. Ban ki Moon

20. Who was the first Secretary General of the United Nations?
A. Kurt Waldheim B. Trygv-lie
C. U. Thant D. Dag Hammarskjold

21. Match List-I with List-II.

List-I (Movement)	List-II (States)
(*a*) Chipko Movement	I. West Bengal
(*b*) Naxalite Movement	II. Western Uttar Pradesh and Haryana
(*c*) Anti Arrack Movement	III. UP (Now Uttarakhand)
(*d*) Bhartiya Kissan Union	IV. Andhra Pradesh

Choose the ***correct*** answer from the options:

	(*a*)	(*b*)	(*c*)	(*d*)
A.	II	III	IV	I
B.	IV	II	I	III
C.	III	I	IV	II
D.	I	II	III	IV

22. Which factor is responsible for constraints on American power?
A. Largest producer of wheat
B. Nuclear weapon's country
C. Permanent member of U.N Security Council
D. Institutional architecture of the American state itself

23. What was the name of the leader who was opposed to the two-nation theory and wanted to form one democratic country?
A. Rafi Ahmad Kidwai
B. Maulana Azad
C. Khan Abdul Gaffar Khan
D. Faiz Ahmed Faiz

24. On which date, Justice Jagmohan Lal Sinha of Allahabad High Court passed a judgement declaring Indira Gandhi's election to the Lok Sabha invalid?
A. 1 May 1974 B. 12 June 1975
C. 22 August 1970 D. 1 March 1962

25. In 1955 a movie Pather Panchali won numerous awards, nationally and internationally. It was directed by:
A. Asit Sen B. Man Mohan Krishna
C. Satyajit Ray D. Harmesh Malhotra

26. The official candidate for the post of President in 1969 was:
A. V.V Giri
B. K. Kamraj
C. N. Sanjeeva Reddy
D. Chaudhary Charan Singh

27. What was the recommended list of development practices issued at the Rio Summit called?
A. Agenda-Rio-20 B. Agenda-21
C. Agenda-22 D. Agenda-23

28. In which year India signed and ratified the Kyoto Protocol?
A. August 2000 B. August 2001
C. August 2002 D. August 2005

29. Match List-I with List-II.

List-I (Years)	List-II (Creation of New States)
(*a*) 1966	I. Nagaland
(*b*) 1963	II. Mizoram
(*c*) 1972	III. Himachal Pradesh
(*d*) 1987	IV. Meghalaya

Choose the ***correct*** answer from the options:

	(*a*)	(*b*)	(*c*)	(*d*)
A.	III	I	IV	II
B.	III	IV	I	II
C.	II	I	III	IV
D.	I	II	III	IV

30. Write the full form of 'WSF'?
A. World Science Forum
B. World Social Forum
C. World Security Forum
D. World Secular Forum

31. Which state was carved out of Assam from the following?
A. Tripura B. Sikkim
C. Meghalaya D. Manipur

32. Choose the correct answer from the options given below:
(*a*) In 1996 a coalition government was formed with the support of congress and left front
(*b*) In 1991 a coalition government was formed with the support of five regional parties and BJP
(*c*) In 1997 a coalition government formed with the support of left and BJP
(*d*) In 1989, a coalition government was formed with the support of BJP and left front
A. (*c*) and (*d*) only B. (*a*) and (*d*) only
C. (*a*) and (*c*) only D. (*b*) and (*d*) only

33. B.R. Ambedkar converted to Buddhism in:
A. 1950 B. 1952
C. 1954 D. 1956

34. Given below are two statements: one is labelled as Assertion (A) and the other is labelled as Reason (R):

Assertion (A): The nuclear Non-Proliferation Treaty NPT of 1968 was an arms control Treaty which regulated the non-acquisition of nuclear weapons, that were tested and manufactured after 1967.

Reason (R): The NPT did not abolish the Nuclear weapons, rather it limited the number of countries that could have them.

In the light of the above statements, choose the most appropriate answer from the options given below.
A. Both (A) and (R) are correct and (R) is the correct explanation of (A)
B. Both (A) and (R) are correct, but (R) is NOT the correct explanation of (A)
C. (A) is correct, but (R) is not correct
D. (A) is not correct, but (R) is correct

35. "With total revolution as our motto, the future belongs to us". This slogan is associated with which movement?
A. Kisan Movement, 1977
B. Bihar Movement, 1994
C. Gujarat Movement, 1975
D. None of the above

36. The economist who proposed an alternative blueprint that put greater emphasis on rural industrialization was:
A. K.N. Raj B. J.C. Kumarappa
C. Jagdish Bhagwati D. Kailash Nath Katju

37. Identify the QUAD member countries from among the following:
A. Australia, Japan, US and India
B. Australia, China, US and India
C. Australia, China, Russia and India
D. Australia, Japan, Russia and India

38. Land Reforms were introduced after Independence but these reforms were not very successful. The main reason for it was:
A. The abolition of the colonial system of zamindari was not successful
B. Bringing small pieces of land together at one place
C. The landowners were very powerful and wielded considerable political influence
D. Many proposals for land reforms were not introduced in all States of India

39. After Second World War the newly independent countries formed to challenge the dominance of the two super powers. They were represented as:
A. SEATO (South Asian Treaty Organisation)
B. NAM (Non-Aligned Movement)
C. LDCs (The least Developed Countries)
D. SAARC (South Asian Association for Regional Cooperation)

40. Rajiv Gandhi-Longowal Accord was signed in:
A. July 1980 B. July 1982
C. July 1984 D. July 1985

Directions (Qs. 41-45): *Look at the given picture (Logo) carefully and answer the questions that follow.*

41. This logo belongs to which International organisation?
A. UN B. ASEAN
C. EU D. SAARC

42. Where is the Headquarter of this International organisation located?
A. Brussels, Belgium B. Frankfurt, Germany
C. Paris, France D. London, UK

43. By which Treaty this International Organisation came into existence?
A. Bangkok Declaration B. Maastricht Treaty
C. SAFTA agreements D. UNFCCC

44. Which currency is used as legal tender among the member countries of this International organisation?
A. Dollar B. Pound
C. Euro D. Ruble

45. Recently, which country has left the membership of this International organisation?
A. USA B. Russia
C. United Kingdom D. Germany

Directions (Qs. 46-50): *Read the passage carefully and answer the following questions.*

The Indian Government is already participating in global efforts through a number of programmes. For example, India's National Auto-fuel Policy mandates cleaner fuels for vehicles: The Energy Conservation Act passed in 2001, outlines initiative to improve energy efficiency. Similarly, the Electricity Act of 2003 encourages the use of renewable energy. Recent trends in importing natural gas and encouraging the adoption of clean coal technologies show that India has been making real efforts. The Government is also keen to launch a National Mission on Biodiesel, using about 11 million hectares of land to produce biodiesel by 2011-2012. India ratified the Paris Climate Agreement on 2 October 2016 and India has one of the largest renewable energy programmes in the world.

A review of the implementation of the agreements at the Earth Summit in Rio was undertaken by India in 1997.

India feels this contravenes the very spirit of UNDCCC. Neither does it seem fair to impose restriction on India when the country's rise in per capita carbon emissions by 2030 is likely to still represent less than half the world average of 3.8 tonnes in 2000. Indian emissions arc predicted to rise from 0.9 tonnes per capita in 2000 to 1.6 tonnes per capita in 2030.

46. In India, the Energy Conservation Act was passed in which year?
A. 2000 B. 2001
C. 2002 D. 2003

47. Electricity Act of 2003 encourages the uses of ....
A. Renewable energy
B. Non-renewable energy
C. No use of coal technology
D. Not importing the natural gas

48. In which year India ratified the Paris Climate Agreement?
A. 2014 B. 2015
C. 2016 D. 2017

49. India emission are predicted to rise 1.6 tonnes per capita in ....
A. 2025 B. 2030
C. 2035 D. 2040

50. Write the full form of UNFCCC?
A. United Nations Framework Convention on Climate Change
B. Union Nations Framework Convention on Climate Change
C. United National Framework Connection on Climate Change
D. United Nations Forum Convention on Climate Change

ANSWERS

1. (A): Article 370 of the Indian Constitution granted special autonomous status to Jammu and Kashmir. It allowed the state to have its own constitution, a separate flag, and autonomy over all matters except foreign affairs, defense, and communications. However, in August 2019, the Government of India abrogated Article 370, effectively revoking the special status of Jammu and Kashmir.

2. (B): Abdul Ghaffar Khan, popularly known as "Frontier Gandhi," was an Indian independence activist and leader in the Indian National Congress. His nickname "Frontier Gandhi" stems from his lifelong commitment to non-violence and his key role in the Indian freedom struggle, much like Mahatma Gandhi, and his roots in the North-West Frontier Province (now in Pakistan). Ghaffar Khan was a staunch supporter of Hindu-Muslim unity and worked extensively in the northwestern frontier regions, advocating for independence from British rule.

3. (C): Article 352 of the Indian Constitution empowers the President of India to declare a state of emergency in the country on the grounds of external threats or armed rebellion. Once an emergency is proclaimed, it empowers the Central government to use all powers vested in the state governments, and the rights of the citizens can be limited or suspended. The period post-independence has witnessed the imposition of a national emergency three times – in 1962 (India-China war), in 1971 (India-Pakistan war), and most controversially in 1975 (declared by then Prime Minister Indira Gandhi citing "internal disturbance").

4. (B): The Indo-China war of 1962 was a significant event that shaped the foreign policy and defense strategies of India. The USSR (Soviet Union) did remain neutral during the conflict. This war indeed induced a sense of national humiliation, as India suffered territorial losses. It also saw a no-confidence motion moved against Prime Minister Jawaharlal

Nehru's government in the Lok Sabha, although it did not succeed. However, India did not approach South Africa for military assistance. Instead, it sought military and diplomatic support from other nations, including the USA.

5. (C): Narmada Bachao Andolan (NBA) is a social movement that started in the 1980s to protest against the construction of large dams across the Narmada river. Medha Patkar, a social activist, is the main figure associated with the NBA. The movement argues that the dams are leading to the displacement of tribals and other communities without proper resettlement and rehabilitation. Over the years, the NBA has organized various protests, marches, and hunger strikes to highlight the plight of the displaced people and to demand justice for them. The movement also underscores the environmental consequences of these large infrastructure projects.

6. (A): Both Statement I and Statement II are true. Vladimir Lenin was indeed a pivotal figure in the founding of the Bolshevik Party. Under his leadership, the Bolsheviks overthrew the Russian Provisional Government during the October Revolution in 1917. After Lenin's death in 1924, Joseph Stalin emerged as his successor. Stalin, through a combination of political maneuvering and purges of rivals, took control of the Soviet Union and led it during a period of rapid industrialization, collectivization, and consolidation of the state. His leadership was marked by significant achievements in making the Soviet Union a global superpower but also involved severe repressions, purges, and the establishment of an authoritarian regime.

7. (B): The Bandung Conference in 1955 holds a crucial position in world political history because it laid the groundwork for the Non-Aligned Movement (NAM). Held in Bandung, Indonesia, it was a gathering of 29 Afro-Asian nations, which sought to promote economic and cultural cooperation and to oppose colonialism. While the conference itself advocated Afro-Asian unity and cooperation, its broader significance lies in the way it highlighted the shared interests of these newly independent nations. These interests eventually crystallized into the Non-Aligned Movement, a group of countries that declared their neutrality during the Cold War era, positioning themselves as an alternative to the Western and Eastern blocs.

8. (B): The Bharatiya Jana Sangh was founded by Shyama Prasad Mukherjee in 1951. The party was established as a response to what Mukherjee and others perceived as the appeasement of Muslims by the Indian National Congress. The Bharatiya Jana Sangh was the predecessor to the modern-day Bharatiya Janata Party (BJP). While Deen Dayal Upadhyaya, Balraj Madhok, and other leaders played significant roles in the party's ideology and growth, Mukherjee is credited as its founder.

9. (D): The Ruble is the official currency of Russia. It has a rich history that traces back to the days of the Russian Empire and has witnessed the vast transformations that Russia underwent during the 20th and 21st centuries. From the Tsarist era to the Soviet period and now in post-Soviet Russia, the Ruble has remained a constant symbol of the country's economic life. Countries like China, India, and Japan have their currencies - the Yuan, Rupee, and Yen respectively.

10. (A): The Railway Strike of 1974 was called by the National Coordination Committee for Railwaymen's struggle. It was one of the largest and most extensive strikes in India, involving over 1.5 million railway employees. The strike, which began in May 1974, went on for 20 days and brought the entire railway network in the country to a halt. The workers were demanding better wages, conditions, and pensions. The government, led by then Prime Minister Indira Gandhi, responded with a crackdown, arresting thousands of workers and union leaders. The strike was eventually called off, but it marked a significant moment in the labor movement of India.

11. (D): The correct matching is:

(*a*) Karpoori Thakur	IV.	Chief Minister of Bihar between December 1970 and June 1971. Karpoori Thakur was a prominent socialist leader in Bihar and served as the Chief Minister of the state.
(*b*) S. Nijalingappa	III.	Chief Minister of Mysore (now Karnataka). S. Nijalingappa played a significant role in the state's politics and was also a key figure in the Indian National Congress.
(*c*) N. Sanjeeva Reddy	I.	Chief Minister of Andhra Pradesh (1956). N. Sanjeeva Reddy had a long political career, including being the President of India.
(*d*) C. Natarajan Annadurai	II.	Chief Minister of Madras (now Tamil Nadu) in 1967. Annadurai was the founder of the Dravida Munnetra Kazhagam (DMK) party and played an essential role in Tamil Nadu's politics.

12. (D): Maharashtra is one of the states in India that already had high reservations for economically disadvantaged people. The Mandal Commission, set up in 1979, was tasked with identifying socially or educationally backward classes in India to ensure affirmative action policies. Several states, including Maharashtra, had already implemented reservations based on economic and social criteria, providing a precedent for the commission's recommendations.

13. (B): The correct matching is:

(*a*) Josip Broz Tito	III. Yugoslavia: Tito was the leader of Yugoslavia and played a significant role in the Non-Aligned Movement, emphasizing neutrality during the Cold War.
(*b*) Jawaharlal Nehru	IV. India: Nehru was the first Prime Minister of independent India and a central figure in Indian politics.
(*c*) Gamal Abdel Nasser	I. Egypt: Nasser was the President of Egypt and played a significant role in the Arab nationalist movement.
(*d*) Sukarno	II. Indonesia: Sukarno was the first President of Indonesia and an influential leader in the country's fight for independence.

14. (D): The term "United Nations" was coined by Franklin D. Roosevelt, the 32nd President of the United States. The name was devised during World War II to describe the Allied countries opposing the Axis powers. Later, the term would be adopted to refer to the international organization established in 1945 to promote peace, security, and cooperation among member countries. The United Nations Charter, outlining the principles and framework of the organization, was signed in June 1945, marking the beginning of the UN's mission to maintain international peace and foster global collaboration.

15. (D): Kargil Vijay Diwas is celebrated in India on 26 July. It marks the day when Indian armed forces successfully recaptured the strategic heights in the Kargil region from Pakistani intruders in 1999. The Kargil War, also known as Operation Vijay, was fought in the rugged terrains of the Kargil district in Jammu and Kashmir. The day is commemorated every year to honor the valour and sacrifice of the Indian soldiers who laid down their lives in the line of duty during the conflict. It is a significant day of national pride and remembrance in India.

16. (C): In the second Lok Sabha general elections held in 1957, the Communist Party of India (CPI) won 27 seats. This election is significant in the history of Indian politics as the CPI emerged as the main opposition party, a position it would maintain till 1967. Though the Congress Party led by Jawaharlal Nehru continued to dominate the political landscape, the CPI's performance highlighted the presence of alternate political voices in the country. Additionally, this election saw the CPI lead the first democratically elected communist government in the state of Kerala under E.M.S. Namboodiripad.

17. (B): Seoul, the capital city of South Korea, is located on the banks of the Han River. The Han River is a major river that runs through the heart of the city and plays an essential role in the cultural and economic life of the region. Historically, the river has been a significant waterway for trade and transportation. Today, the riverbanks are adorned with parks, recreational facilities, and other amenities that make it a favorite spot for both locals and tourists.

18. (B): The India-Sri Lanka Accord was signed in 1987. This agreement between India and Sri Lanka aimed to ensure peace in the region, especially in the northern and eastern parts of Sri Lanka, which had been affected by the civil war between the Tamil militants and the Sri Lankan government. As per the accord, the Indian Peace Keeping Force (IPKF) was introduced in Sri Lanka to ensure the disarmament of the Tamil militant groups and to oversee the establishment of peace. However, the IPKF's presence became controversial and faced significant challenges, leading to its withdrawal in 1990.

19. (B): The statement, "The United Nations was not created to take humanity to heaven, but to save it from hell," was made by Dag Hammarskjöld, the second Secretary-General of the United Nations. His tenure from 1953 to 1961 witnessed several international crises, and his words reflected the primary purpose of the UN: to prevent wars and maintain peace. Hammarskjöld's leadership and his approach towards global diplomacy made him a revered figure in international relations. He tragically died in a plane crash in 1961 during a peace mission to the Congo.

20. (B): The first Secretary-General of the United Nations was Trygve Lie, who served from 1946 to 1952. He was from Norway and played a crucial role in establishing the foundational operations and principles of the UN. His tenure saw the early challenges of the Cold War era, which affected the functioning of the United Nations. Despite the geopolitical tensions and internal pressures within the organization, Trygve Lie worked towards strengthening the UN's role in international peacekeeping and diplomacy.

21. (C): The movements and their respective states match as follows:

- **Chipko Movement:** Originated in the state of Uttarakhand (previously a part of UP). It was an ecological movement where villagers, especially women, embraced trees to prevent their felling by loggers. This non-violent protest sought to draw attention to the environmental and social issues brought on by deforestation.

- **Naxalite Movement:** Began in Naxalbari, West Bengal. This was a radical communist movement that sought to overthrow the government through peasant uprisings, driven by socio-economic disparities.
- **Anti Arrack Movement:** Started in Andhra Pradesh. This grassroots movement, primarily led by women, aimed at the prohibition of the arrack (local alcohol) trade and production to combat the negative social implications tied to alcoholism.
- **Bharatiya Kissan Union:** Established in Western Uttar Pradesh and Haryana. This union represents the interests of farmers and addresses issues like pricing, subsidies, and loan waivers.

22. (D): The Institutional architecture of the American state itself constrains American power. While the U.S. is a global superpower with significant military, economic, and political influence, its system of checks and balances, divided government, and federalist structure can slow decision-making and complicate international negotiations. The separation of powers between the Executive, Legislative, and Judicial branches ensures that no single branch can unilaterally exert unchecked power, domestically or internationally.

23. (C): Khan Abdul Ghaffar Khan, also known as the Frontier Gandhi, opposed the two-nation theory. He advocated for a united India and was a staunch supporter of non-violence. Ghaffar Khan had a deep-seated belief in the idea of composite nationalism, emphasizing Hindu-Muslim unity. He felt that the division of India on religious lines would harm the largely Muslim population of the North-West Frontier Province, which he represented.

24. (B): On 12 June 1975, Justice Jagmohan Lal Sinha of the Allahabad High Court passed a judgment that declared Indira Gandhi's election to the Lok Sabha invalid. This ruling was based on electoral malpractice during her 1971 campaign. The judgment became a significant turning point in Indian politics, leading to the imposition of the Emergency by Indira Gandhi, during which civil liberties were suspended, and the constitution was amended to suit her political needs.

25. (C): Satyajit Ray, a renowned filmmaker, directed the movie "Pather Panchali" in 1955. This film is the first in the Apu trilogy and is considered a milestone in Indian cinema. Based on Bibhutibhushan Bandyopadhyay's novel of the same name, the movie provides a poignant look at rural life and childhood in Bengal. Its international acclaim helped bring Indian cinema to the global stage, winning awards at the Cannes Film Festival and several other international platforms. Ray's unique narrative style and the movie's realistic portrayal made it a classic that continues to influence filmmakers worldwide.

26. (C): N. Sanjeeva Reddy was the official candidate for the post of President in 1969. He was backed by the ruling party, the Indian National Congress. However, the election saw a significant turn of events when then Vice President V.V. Giri, contesting as an independent candidate, emerged victorious. The 1969 Presidential election is particularly notable for the internal rifts it caused within the Congress, eventually leading to its split.

27. (B): The recommended list of development practices issued at the Rio Summit is known as Agenda 21. The Rio Summit, also referred to as the Earth Summit, took place in 1992 in Rio de Janeiro. Agenda 21 is a comprehensive plan of action to be taken globally, nationally, and locally by organizations of the United Nations, governments, and major groups in every area in which humans impact the environment. Its key aim is sustainable development around the world.

28. (C): August 2002 is when India both signed and ratified the Kyoto Protocol. The Kyoto Protocol is an international treaty extending the 1992 United Nations Framework Convention on Climate Change (UNFCCC), which commits its parties to reduce greenhouse gas emissions. India, being a developing country, did not have any mandatory emission reduction targets under the Kyoto Protocol. Instead, it could voluntarily participate in the Clean Development Mechanism to earn emission reduction credits.

29. (A)

30. (B): WSF stands for the World Social Forum. It is an annual meeting of civil society organizations, first held in Brazil, which offers a self-conscious effort to develop an alternative future through the championing of counter-hegemonic globalization. The WSF is a space for dialogue, reflection, and the exchange of experiences and ideas among social movements, networks, NGOs, and other civil society organizations opposed to neoliberalism and imperialism.

31. (C): Meghalaya was carved out of Assam. In 1972, Meghalaya was formed as a result of the Assam Reorganization (Meghalaya) Act and became an autonomous state. Later, it achieved full statehood. This move was aimed at satisfying the cultural and regional aspirations of the tribal populations of the Khasi, Jaintia, and Garo hills of Assam.

32. (B): In 1996, a coalition government known as the United Front was formed. The Congress, not being a part of this coalition, decided to extend external support, allowing the United Front to form the government. The Left Front, a significant constituent of this coalition, played a crucial role. On the other hand, in 1989, the National Front coalition government was supported from the outside by both BJP and Left Front, marking a unique instance in Indian political history.

33. (D): Dr. B.R. Ambedkar converted to Buddhism in 1956. Towards the end of his life, Ambedkar decided to leave Hinduism due to the caste-based discrimination inherent in its practices. On October 14, 1956, in a symbolic gesture, he, along with several of his followers, converted to Buddhism in Nagpur. His conversion initiated a wave of mass conversions among Dalits in India.

34. (D): The Nuclear Non-Proliferation Treaty (NPT) aimed at preventing the spread of nuclear weapons and nuclear weapon technology. The Assertion (A) is not entirely accurate. The NPT did not regulate non-acquisition of nuclear weapons manufactured after 1967 specifically. Instead, it sought to prevent the spread of nuclear weapons altogether, promote peaceful uses of nuclear energy, and work towards disarmament. The Reason (R) is correct in stating that the NPT aimed at limiting the number of countries that could have nuclear weapons, but it did not abolish them. The treaty recognized five states as nuclear-weapon states: the U.S., Russia, China, the U.K., and France. Other signatories committed to not acquiring nuclear weapons.

35. (D): The slogan "With total revolution as our motto, the future belongs to us" is associated with the Bihar Movement led by Jayaprakash Narayan (JP) in the mid-1970s, not 1994 as mentioned. The movement was a mass agitation against corruption, misrule, and authoritarianism, and it called for a "total revolution" in society. This movement culminated in the imposition of the Emergency by then-Prime Minister Indira Gandhi in 1975. JP's call for a peaceful total revolution was against the backdrop of rampant corruption and the failing democratic structure of the time.

36. (B): J.C. Kumarappa was the economist who proposed an alternative blueprint emphasizing rural industrialization. A follower of Mahatma Gandhi's economic thought, Kumarappa believed in a decentralized economy with a focus on village industries. His views contrasted with the modern industrialization strategies which dominated economic planning in post-independence India. Kumarappa argued for self-reliant villages where industries would complement and support the agrarian economy rather than overshadow it.

37. (A): The QUAD, short for Quadrilateral Security Dialogue, consists of four member countries: Australia, Japan, US, and India. Initiated in 2007, the Quad aims to promote peace, stability, and prosperity in the Indo-Pacific region, though it's often viewed as a counter to China's growing influence in the region. Regular dialogues, joint military exercises, and cooperative projects among the Quad members underscore its strategic significance.

38. (C): One of the primary reasons land reforms post-independence weren't very successful is that landowners were very powerful and wielded considerable political influence. Although laws were introduced in various states to bring about land ceilings, redistribution, and tenancy reforms, their implementation was lackluster. In many areas, powerful landowners used their influence to bypass or dilute reforms. There were also issues related to bureaucracy, corruption, and other systemic problems that hindered genuine reform.

39. (B): NAM (Non-Aligned Movement) represented the newly independent countries after World War II. These nations didn't want to align with either of the superpowers, namely the USA or the USSR, during the Cold War. Instead, they desired to take an independent stand on international issues. Established in 1961 in Belgrade, NAM became an important platform for the Third World countries to voice their concerns, aspirations, and shared interests in a world polarized by superpower rivalry.

40. (D): The Rajiv Gandhi-Longowal Accord was signed in July 1985. This agreement, commonly referred to as the Punjab Accord, was signed between the then Prime Minister Rajiv Gandhi and Harchand Singh Longowal, the President of the Shiromani Akali Dal, to bring peace to Punjab. The accord addressed various issues such as water distribution, Chandigarh's transfer to Punjab, and other religious and economic grievances of Sikhs. The accord was seen as a significant step towards restoring normalcy in Punjab after years of militancy and unrest.

41. (C) **42. (A)** **43. (B)**
44. (C) **45. (C)** **46. (B)**
47. (A) **48. (C)** **49. (B)**
50. (A)

SOCIOLOGY

1. Which statement among the following is incorrect regarding Green Revolution?

A. It was a government programme for agricultural modernisation

B. In it pesticides, fertilizers and other inputs were provided to the farmers

C. It was largely funded by national agencies which provided high yielding variety seeds

D. In it primarily the medium and large farmers benefitted from the new technology

2. Arrange the different kinds of social change in chronological order, starting from the oldest to the most recent:

(*a*) Modernisation (*b*) Secularisation

(*c*) Westernisation (*d*) Sanskritisation

Choose the ***correct*** answer from the options given below:

A. (*a*), (*b*), (*c*), (*d*) B. (*c*), (*a*), (*b*), (*d*)

C. (*d*), (*c*), (*a*), (*b*) D. (*d*), (*a*), (*b*), (*c*)

3. The Right of Information Act, 2005 came into force on:

A. 15 January 2005 B. 13 October 2005

C. 25 November 2005 D. 10 December 2005

4. Migrant workers who migrate from drought prone regions and work on farms during agricultural season and work on brick kilns during off season are known as:

A. Temporary work force

B. Permanent workers

C. Substitute workers

D. Footloose labour

5. The majority of the population of India lives in:

A. Cities B. Rural areas

C. Metropolitan cities D. Urban areas

6. Out of the following which state is not based on linguistic aspect?

A. Delhi B. Punjab

C. Uttaranchal D. Rajasthan

7. Match the persons in List-I with their ideas/work in List-II:

List-I (Person)	List-II (Ideas/Work)
(*a*) Emile Durkheim	I. Failure of entitlements
(*b*) Thomas Robert Malthus	II. Mass Sterilisation
(*c*) Amartya Sen	III. Suicide
(*d*) Sanjay Gandhi	IV. Essay on Population

Choose the ***correct*** answer from the options given below:

	(*a*)	(*b*)	(*c*)	(*d*)
A.	III	IV	II	I
B.	III	IV	I	II
C.	II	IV	I	III
D.	IV	III	II	I

8. Match the book in List-I with authors in List-II:

List-I (Book)	List-II (Authors)
(*a*) Communalism in Modern India	I. Rajeev Bhargava
(*b*) Civil Society, Public Sphere and Citizenship	II. David Miller
(*c*) On Nationality	III. Paul Brass
(*d*) Language, Religion and politics in North India	IV. Bipin Chandra

Choose the ***correct*** answer from the options given below:

	(*a*)	(*b*)	(*c*)	(*d*)
A.	IV	I	II	III
B.	IV	II	III	I
C.	I	IV	II	III
D.	III	I	II	IV

9. Match the states in List-I with their type in List-II:

List-I (State)	List-II (Type)
(*a*) Kashmir	I. New State
(*b*) Bombay	II. Princely State
(*c*) Jharkhand	III. Union Territory
(*d*) Pondicherry	IV. Presidency

Choose the ***correct*** answer from the options given below:

	(*a*)	(*b*)	(*c*)	(*d*)
A.	I	II	III	IV
B.	IV	III	II	I
C.	II	IV	I	III
D.	III	IV	II	I

10. Which of the following is not a reason for agrarian distress?

A. Changed cropping pattern

B. Changing pattern of landholdings

C. Heavy migration to cities

D. Shift to cash crops

11. Find the correct statements:

(*a*) Nation is a community of communities.

(*b*) State is a body that successfully claims a monopoly of legitimate force in a particular territory

(*c*) Nations are communities that have a state of their own

(*d*) Members of a nation do not share the desire to be a part of the same political conductivity

Choose the ***correct*** answer from the options given below:

A. (*a*), (*b*), (*d*) only B. (*a*), (*c*), (*d*) only
C. (*b*), (*c*), (*d*) only D. (*a*), (*b*), (*c*) only

12. Who observed that "The expression 'joint family' is not the translation of any Indian word like that. It is interesting to note that the words used for joint family in most of the Indian languages are the equivalent of translation of the English word 'joint family'.

A. A.R. Desai B. I.P. Desai
C. Periyar D. Sri Narayan Guru

13. When one country establishes its rule over another country, it is known as:

A. Capitalism B. Colonialism
C. Socialism D. Communism

14. Read the statements given below and choose the options with the correct sequence.

(*a*) October 1953, Potti Sriramalu dies

(*b*) Map of India redrawn on linguistic lines

(*c*) Indian National Congress reconstituted on linguistic line

(*d*) Jawaharlal Nehru feared a sub division of India.

Choose the ***correct*** answer from the options given below:

A. (*a*), (*b*), (*c*), (*d*) B. (*c*), (*d*), (*a*), (*b*)
C. (*b*), (*c*), (*d*), (*a*) D. (*d*), (*a*), (*b*), (*c*)

15. Match the book/action in List-I with their proponent in List-II:

List-I (Book/Action)	**List-II (Proponent)**
(*a*) The Meghalaya Succession Act	I. Imtiyaz Ahmad
(*b*) Contemporary India: A Sociological View	II. Patricia Uberoi
(*c*) Family, Kinship and Marriage in India	III. Government of India
(*d*) Family, Kinship and Marriage Among Muslims in India	IV. Satish Despande

Choose the ***correct*** answer from the options given below:

	(*a*)	(*b*)	(*c*)	(*d*)
A.	II	I	IV	III
B.	III	IV	II	I
C.	IV	I	II	III
D.	III	II	IV	I

16. Choose the correct statements:

(*a*) Rural population is highly interested in agriculture.

(*b*) Today the rural areas are more closely integrated to consumers market.

(*c*) Some people work in urban areas and live in villages.

(*d*) Non-farm rural occupations are decreasing.

Choose the ***correct*** answer from the options given below:

A. (*b*), (*c*) only B. (*a*), (*b*) only
C. (*b*), (*d*) only D. (*a*), (*d*) only

17. Arrange the following books in order of its publication years.

(*a*) Dipankar Gupta's Social Stratification

(*b*) M.N. Srinivas's The Dominant Caste and Other Essays

(*c*) Alice Thorner's Semi-feudalism or Capitalism

(*d*) Ruten Mario's Farms and Factories

Choose the ***correct*** answer from the options given below:

A. (*b*), (*c*), (*d*), (*a*) B. (*c*), (*b*), (*a*), (*d*)
C. (*c*), (*a*), (*b*), (*d*) D. (*d*), (*b*), (*c*), (*a*)

18. Which amendment led to reservation for the OBCs in institutions of higher education?

A. 92nd Amendment B. 93rd Amendment
C. 94th Amendment D. 72nd Amendment

19. The 'Jeeta' system of bonded labour was prevalent in:

A. Punjab B. Haryana
C. Karnataka D. Tamil Nadu

20. Which of the following is not a mechanism of political collaboration?

A. SAFTA B. WHO
C. ASEAN D. SARC

21. The process by which something which was not a commodity is made a commodity and becomes part of the market economy is known as:

A. Commercialisation
B. Commodification
C. Globalisation
D. Marketisation

22. The ability to reflect upon oneself is called:

A. Subjectivity B. Objectivity
C. Reflexibility D. Socialisation

23. 'Time Slavery' is a very common phenomena in which of the following sector?

A. Agrarian B. IT
C. Government D. NGO

24. The idea of 'imagined community' was given by:

A. Fardoonji Murzban
B. Benedict Anderson

C. Johann Gutenberg
D. Robert Redfield

25. Amrita Bazar Patrika was an:
A. English Newspaper
B. Bengali Newspaper
C. Assamese Newspaper
D. Marathi Newspaper

26. Arrange the various land revenue reforms that occurred in pre-independent colonial India and independent India in chronological order from the oldest to most recent one:
(*a*) Rayatwari System
(*b*) Abolition of Zamindari System
(*c*) Land Ceiling Acts
(*d*) Tenancy Abolition and Regulation Acts
(*e*) Zamindari System

Choose the ***correct*** answer from the options given below:
A. (*a*), (*b*), (*c*), (*d*), (*e*)
B. (*b*), (*a*), (*c*), (*d*), (*e*)
C. (*e*), (*b*), (*c*), (*d*), (*a*)
D. (*e*), (*a*), (*b*), (*d*), (*c*)

27. Several profound transformation in the nature of social relations in rural areas took place in the post-independent era. These included:
(*a*) A shift from payment in kind (grain) to payment in cash.
(*b*) Rise of class of 'free' wage labourers
(*c*) A loosing of traditional bonds or hereditary relationships between land owner and workers
(*d*) Rise of subsistence agriculture
(*e*) Increase in the use of agricultural labours

Choose the ***correct*** answer from the options given below:
A. (*a*), (*b*), (*c*), (*d*) only
B. (*b*), (*c*), (*d*), (*e*) only
C. (*a*), (*b*), (*c*), (*e*) only
D. (*a*), (*c*), (*d*), (*e*) only

28. Contract fanning did not involve:
A. Production of specialized items
B. Provides complete financial security to farmers
C. Indigenous knowledge of agriculture becomes irrelevant
D. Farmer is assured of market

29. How much contribution agriculture sector makes in the Gross Domestic Product of India?

A. $\frac{1}{2}$ B. $\frac{1}{3}$

C. $\frac{1}{5}$ D. $\frac{1}{6}$

30. Match the names of the book in List-I with their authors in List-II

List-I (Book)	List-II (Authors)
(*a*) Invisible Man	I. Harsh Mandar
(*b*) Caste: Its Modern Avatar	II. Bishop Joseph Butler
(*c*) Analogy of Religion	III. Ralph Ellison
(*d*) Unheard voices: stories of forgotten lives	IV. M.N. Srinivas

Choose the ***correct*** answer from the options given below:

	(*a*)	(*b*)	(*c*)	(*d*)
A.	III	IV	II	I
B.	II	I	III	IV
C.	I	III	II	IV
D.	II	III	IV	I

31. The term diversity emphasises on:
A. Differences B. Similarity
C. Inequality D. Equality

32. The 73rd Constitutional Amendment is related to:
A. Land reforms
B. Panchayat Raj Institutions
C. Anti Defection Law
D. National Green Tribunal

33. Who called upon the media to function as the watchdog of democracy?
A. A.P.J. Abdul Kalam
B. Sarvapalli Radhakrishnan
C. Rabindranath Tagore
D. Jawaharial Nehru

34. Characteristics of tribes are:
(*a*) Tribes are social groups
(*b*) They are modem and have sufficient resources
(*c*) Tribes have distinctive habitat in the hill and forest
(*d*) They are marked by poverty, powerlessness and stigma by Indian Constitution

Choose the ***correct*** answer from the options given below:
A. (*a*), (*b*), (*c*) only B. (*a*), (*c*), (*d*) only
C. (*b*), (*c*), (*d*) only D. (*a*), (*b*), (*d*) only

35. On what grounds can the claim be made that Sanskritisation leads to adoption of upper caste rites and rituals?
(*a*) It is inclusive of girls and women
(*b*) Avoids bride price
(*c*) Promotes dowry practices
(*d*) Does not practice caste discrimination

Choose the ***correct*** answer from the options given below:

A. (*a*) and (*d*) only
B. (*b*) and (*c*) only
C. (*c*) and (*d*) only
D. (*d*) and (*b*) only

36. Arrange the following states in an ascending order in context to projected population growth upto 2041.
(*a*) Punjab
(*b*) Maharashtra
(*c*) Bihar
(*d*) Tamil Nadu

Choose the ***correct*** answer from the options given below:
A. (*a*), (*b*), (*c*), (*d*)
B. (*b*), (*c*), (*a*), (*d*)
C. (*a*), (*b*), (*d*), (*c*)
D. (*d*), (*c*), (*a*), (*b*)

37. Which among these is the farmers agricultural unions?
A. FICCI (Federation of Indian Chambers of Commerce & Industry)
B. ASSOCHAM (Association of Chambers and Commerce)
C. Shetkari Sangathan
D. INTUC (Indian Trade Union Congress)

38. Out of the following which was not the issue of concern for women's movement during 1970?
A. Sati
B. Representation of women in popular media
C. Dowry system
D. Rape of women in police custody

39. Who described the change of relationship between landlords and agricultural workers as a shift from 'patronage to exploitation'?
A. E.P. Thompson
B. Amartya Sen
C. Jan Breman
D. M.N. Srinivas

40. The use of machinery actually deskills worker. Identify the sociologist who gave this idea:
A. Harry Braverman
B. Jan Breman
C. F.W. Taylor
D. Clark Kerr

Directions (Q.No. 41-45): *Read the passage given below and answer the questions.*

'Dominant caste' is a term used to refer to those castes which had a large population and were granted land rights by the partial land reforms effected after independence.

Examples of such dominant caste include Yadavs of Bihar and Uttar Pradesh, the Vokkaligas of Karnataka, the Reddys and Khammas of Andhra Pradesh, the Marathas of Maharashtra, the Jats of Punjab, Haryana and Western Uttar Pradesh and Patidars of Gujarat.

One of the most significant yet paradoxical changes in the caste system in the contemporary period is that it has tended to become 'invisible' for the upper caste, urban middle and upper classes. For these groups, who have benefitted the most from the developmental policies of the post colonial era, caste has appeared to decline in significance precisely because it has done its job so well. Their caste status had been crucial in ensuring that these groups had the...

41. Which among these is not a 'dominant caste'?
A. Reddy's of Andhra Pradesh
B. Jats of Punjab
C. Patidars of Gujarat
D. Gonds of Central India

42. Which among these is not a part of the benefits given to upper castes:
A. Subsidised public education
B. Professional education
C. Reservation
D. Management education

43. Which among these is the lowest in caste hierarchy?
A. Brahmin
B. Kshatriya
C. Shudras
D. Vaisyas

44. For the upper caste, caste plays no part in their public lives and is only limited to the personal sphere. In which among these does caste play a role?
A. Marriage, Religion
B. Education, Public officer
C. Politics, Marriage
D. Religion, Education

45. Which among these gave legal recognition to the scheduled castes and scheduled tribes?
A. The Prevention of Atrocities Act
B. The Government of India Act of 1935
C. The ST/SC Act
D. The Constitution

Directions (Q.No. 46-50): *Read the passage given below and answer the questions.*

Factory production began in India in the early part of the 1860s. The general pattern of trade set up by the colonial regime was one under which raw materials were procured from India and goods manufactured in the United Kingdom were marketed in the colony. The factories were established in the port town of Calcutta (Kolkata), Bombay (Mumbai) and later in Madras (Chennai) also. Tea plantations in Assam were established as early as 1839. Labour was cheap as the colonial government did not regulate either wages or working conditions. Though trade unions were established later, workers did protest for increase in wages. For example, jute workers in Calcutta and textile workers in Ahmedabad. The first trade union was established in April 1918 in Madras by B.P. Wadia, a social worker and member of Theosophical Society.

During the same year Mahatma Gandhi founded the Textile Labour Association (TLA). In 1920 the All India Trade Union Congress (AITUC) was formed in Bombay with people from diverse ideologies. The main ideological groups were the communists led by S.A. Dange and M.N. Roy, the moderates led by M. Joshi and V.V. Giri and the nationalists which involved Lala Lajpat Rai and J.L. Nehru. The colonial government became cautious in dealing with labour and passed the fourth Factories Act in 1922. And in 1926, the Trade Unions Act was passed which provided for registration of trade unions and proposed some regulations. In 1966-67 the economy suffered a major recession which lead to a decrease in production and consequently employment. The confrontation between the state and trade unions become active. During emergency in 1975-77 the Government curbed all trade union activities. The worker's movement was very much part of the wider struggle for civil liberties.

46. The first trade union was established by:
A. Mahatma Gandhi B. B.P. Wadia
C. J.L. Nehru D. M.N. Roy

47. The moderate ideology in the All India Trade Union Congress (AITUC) was led by:
A. J.L. Nehru B. V.V. Giri
C. S.A. Dange D. Lala Lajpat Rai

48. The recession in the economy led to:
A. Increase in production
B. Increase in employment
C. Decrease in production
D. Decrease in unemployment

49. The Act that provided for registration of trade unions and proposed regulations:
A. Factories Act
B. Government of India Act
C. Plantation Labour Act
D. Trade Union Act

50. Which of the following is a correct statement?
A. Goods were manufactured in India
B. Goods were manufactured in United Kingdom
C. Raw materials were manufactured in United Kingdom
D. Raw materials were procured from United Kingdom

ANSWERS

1. (C): The Green Revolution, which took place primarily during the 1960s and 1970s, aimed at increasing agricultural productivity in developing countries, particularly in India. The key elements of the Green Revolution were the introduction of high-yielding variety (HYV) seeds, primarily for wheat and rice, accompanied by the extensive use of fertilizers, pesticides, and improved irrigation techniques. While it is true that the Green Revolution led to increased use of pesticides and fertilizers and benefitted primarily medium and large farmers, the initiative was not solely funded by national agencies. International organizations, particularly the Rockefeller Foundation and the Ford Foundation, played significant roles in funding and promoting the Green Revolution. The International Rice Research Institute (IRRI) in the Philippines and the International Maize and Wheat Improvement Center (CIMMYT) in Mexico were pivotal in developing HYV seeds. These international collaborations played a significant role in the proliferation of HYV seeds and agricultural techniques across the developing world.

2. (C): To understand the chronological order of these types of social change, it's crucial to dive into the historical context:

(*d*) **Sanskritisation:** This is an upward social mobility practice in India, where lower castes emulate the customs and rituals of upper castes. The term was popularized by Indian sociologist M.N. Srinivas. This concept predates the others listed here as it's rooted in India's ancient caste dynamics.

(*c*) **Westernisation:** The process began with the advent of British colonialism in India. It refers to the adoption of Western culture, lifestyles, and ideas. This was especially prominent during the 19th and 20th centuries as India came under British rule.

(*a*) **Modernisation:** Post-independence, India embarked on a journey of modernization, seeking economic development, scientific progress, and social reform. This process accelerated in the latter half of the 20th century, particularly after economic liberalization in the 1990s.

(*b*) **Secularisation:** While the idea of secularism is rooted in ancient Indian ethos (the coexistence of multiple faiths), in terms of governance and society, the emphasis on secularism became more pronounced in the post-independence era. Over time, there's been a gradual decline in the influence of religion on state matters, exemplifying secularization.

3. (B): The Right to Information Act, 2005 was passed by Parliament on 15 June 2005 and received the assent of the President on 15 June 2005. However, it came into full force on 13 October 2005. The Act mandates timely responses to citizen requests for government information. It is an essential tool for promoting transparency and accountability in the functioning of the government.

4. (D): "Footloose labour" refers to workers or industries that are free to move and aren't tied to a particular geographical location due to resources, services, or transport. These workers are generally involved in tasks that do not require them to be at a fixed place. Migrant workers from drought-prone regions fit this definition because they shift their work based on seasons and availability, such as working on farms during the agricultural season and on brick kilns during the off-season.

5. (B): The majority of India's population lives in rural areas. Even with rapid urbanization in the past few decades, a significant portion of the Indian populace still resides in villages and small towns. According to data from the 2011 Census, more than 68% of India's population was based in rural regions. While urban areas have seen growth, and there's an increasing migration trend towards cities for better opportunities, the rural population still constitutes a majority. This dynamic shapes India's socio-economic, political, and cultural landscape.

6. (C): Uttaranchal, now known as Uttarakhand, was not created based on linguistic lines. Uttarakhand was carved out of Uttar Pradesh in 2000, primarily due to regional and developmental disparities. Its formation was more about recognizing the unique cultural and geographic identity of the region and ensuring better governance and development opportunities for its people. In contrast, states like Punjab, Rajasthan, and many others were formed on linguistic lines to consolidate speakers of particular languages, ensuring smoother administration and governance. Delhi is not a full state, it is a Union Territory with legislative power.

7. (B): (*a*) **Emile Durkheim:** Durkheim is famously known for his sociological study on suicide. He examined the varying suicide rates among Protestants and Catholics, arguing that stronger social control among Catholics results in lower suicide rates.

(*b*) **Thomas Robert Malthus:** Malthus wrote "An Essay on the Principle of Population," where he argued that population growth would outpace the growth of food supplies, leading to catastrophic consequences unless checked.

(*c*) **Amartya Sen:** A Nobel laureate in Economics, Sen's work on famines is seminal. He argued that famines do not occur due to a lack of food but because of problems in food distribution, or what he termed "failure of entitlements."

(*d*) **Sanjay Gandhi:** Sanjay Gandhi, during the Emergency in India (1975-77), is infamously associated with the mass sterilization program as a measure of population control.

8. (A): (*a*) **Communalism in Modern India:** This book was authored by Bipin Chandra. It delves into the complexities of communalism and its impact on the Indian society, particularly tracing its roots and evolution during the modern era.

(*b*) **Civil Society, Public Sphere, and Citizenship:** This book is associated with Rajeev Bhargava. It explores the ideas of citizenship, democracy, and the role of civil society in the Indian context.

(*c*) **On Nationality:** The book is written by David Miller, which revolves around the concept of nationality and its significance in modern society.

(*d*) **Language, Religion, and Politics in North India:** This was authored by Paul Brass, focusing on the intricate interplay between language, religion, and politics in North India, tracing patterns of change and continuity.

9. (C): (*a*) **Kashmir:** Historically, before becoming an integral part of India, Kashmir was a princely state under British India.

(*b*) **Bombay:** Before the linguistic reorganization of states, Bombay was a presidency. The Bombay Presidency was a former province of British India.

(*c*) **Jharkhand:** Jharkhand was carved out of Bihar in 2000 and is, therefore, one of the newer states in the Indian union.

(*d*) **Pondicherry:** Now known as Puducherry, it is a Union Territory in India.

10. (C): Heavy migration to cities is not a direct reason for agrarian distress. Agrarian distress refers to the myriad challenges faced by the farming community, including but not limited to debt, poor yields, climate change impacts, lack of adequate pricing for crops, and more. While migration can be a result of agrarian distress, as farmers leave rural areas in search of better livelihood opportunities in urban regions, it's not a direct cause. Changing cropping patterns, changing landholding patterns, and a shift to cash crops can all contribute to agrarian distress in various ways, such as making agriculture more vulnerable to market fluctuations or increasing the costs of input.

11. (D): (a) Nation is a community of communities: True. A nation is often understood as a community that is made up of smaller communities or groups. These groups may be based on language, religion, ethnicity, or other cultural factors. Together, they form a larger community that shares a sense of collective identity, history, and often, a desire for self-governance or autonomy.

(b) State is a body that successfully claims a monopoly of legitimate force in a particular territory: True. This definition is attributed to sociologist Max Weber. A state has the recognized power to use and authorize the use of force within its borders.

(c) Nations are communities that have a state of their own: Not necessarily. While many nations have their own states (nation-states), there are nations without states and states that comprise multiple nations. The Kurds, for instance, are a nation without a state of their own.

(d) Members of a nation do not share the desire to be a part of the same political conductivity: False. Generally, members of a nation have a shared sense of identity and often have a collective aspiration for self-governance or autonomy.

12. (B): I.P. Desai observed the nuances regarding the term "joint family." The term "joint family" as understood in the Indian context refers to an extended family system where multiple generations live together, often sharing a household, resources, and responsibilities. It's a key social institution in India and has evolved over time, influenced by socio-economic and cultural changes.

13. (B): Colonialism is the practice by which one country establishes its rule over another country. It is characterized by the establishment and maintenance of colonies in one territory by people from another territory. Historically, European nations established colonies in parts of Africa, Asia, and the Americas, exploiting their resources and often subjugating the native populations.

14. (B): (*c*) Indian National Congress reconstituted on linguistic line: In the early 20th century, Congress began organizing its units based on linguistic regions.

(*d*) Jawaharlal Nehru feared a sub-division of India: After independence, there was a demand to reorganize states based on linguistic lines. However, Nehru initially resisted these demands, fearing it might lead to further subdivision and fragmentation of India.

(*b*) Map of India redrawn on linguistic lines: In the late 1950s, states were reorganized based on linguistic lines. This was a significant change in the administrative map of India.

(*a*) October 1953, Potti Sriramalu dies: Potti Sriramalu's death after a prolonged hunger strike was pivotal in the creation of the state of Andhra Pradesh, which set a precedent for linguistic reorganization of states.

15. (B): (*a*) The Meghalaya Succession Act: This is an Act associated with the Government of India, which looks into matters of succession in the state of Meghalaya.

(*b*) Contemporary India: A Sociological View: Authored by Satish Deshpande, this book provides a sociological perspective on modern India, examining its complexities, contradictions, and socio-political dynamics.

(*c*) Family, Kinship and Marriage in India: This work is by Patricia Uberoi. It delves into the intricate patterns of family, kinship, and marriage across various communities in India, highlighting the cultural and regional diversities.

(*d*) Family, Kinship, and Marriage Among Muslims in India: Imtiyaz Ahmad provides insights into the family structures, kinship patterns, and marital practices among Muslims in India, drawing attention to the nuances and variations within the community.

16. (A): (*b*) Today the rural areas are more closely integrated to consumers market: True. With advancements in transportation, communication, and the expansion of market economy, rural areas are more closely connected to the broader consumer market than ever before. This has changed the consumption patterns in rural areas and has also influenced their socio-economic dynamics.

(*c*) Some people work in urban areas and live in villages: True. This phenomenon is known as "circular migration" where individuals from rural areas work in urban centers but maintain their residence in villages. This can be seen in cases of daily-wage workers, seasonal workers, or those who migrate for short periods for work but return to their villages. These individuals often contribute significantly to the rural economy through remittances.

17. (B): (*c*) **Alice Thorner's Semi feudalism or Capitalism (1982):** Alice Thorner's work on India's agrarian structure discussed the debate of whether India was moving towards capitalism or was still entrenched in semi-feudalism. Her contributions have been seminal in the studies of Indian agrarian economy.

(*b*) **M.N. Srinivas's The Dominant Caste and Other Essays (1987):** M.N. Srinivas introduced and elaborated on many key concepts in Indian sociology, including "dominant caste". His works, including this one, are pivotal in understanding the caste dynamics in rural India.

(*a*) **Dipankar Gupta's Social Stratification (1991):** Dipankar Gupta's contributions have provided deep insights into the caste and class structures in India. His exploration of social stratification offers a nuanced understanding of hierarchies and power dynamics in Indian society.

(*d*) **Ruten Mario's Farms and Factories (1995):** The book is about Social Profile of big/large farmers and Rural Industrilists in West India making an Important contribution to the understanding of class formation in the countryside in India and South Asia.

18. (B): The **93rd Amendment** to the Constitution of India provided for the reservation for the OBCs (Other Backward Classes) in institutions of higher education. This amendment was significant as it aimed to provide better opportunities for education to historically disadvantaged communities, thus aiming to level the socio-economic playing field.

19. (C): The 'Jeeta' system of bonded labour was prevalent in **Karnataka**. Bonded labour refers to the system where laborers are bound to work for a particular employer due to debt or social obligations. The 'Jeeta' system was a regional manifestation of this broader practice and was particularly present in parts of Karnataka. Such practices have been legally abolished, but remnants and newer forms occasionally emerge in various parts of the country.

20. (B): Among the options given, **WHO (World Health Organization)** is not a mechanism of political collaboration. WHO is an international agency concerned with public health and is a specialized agency of the United Nations. On the other hand, SAFTA (South Asian Free Trade Area), ASEAN (Association of Southeast Asian Nations), and SARC (presumably SAARC, which stands for South Asian Association for Regional Cooperation) are regional political and economic organizations aimed at promoting collaboration and integration among member states.

21. (B): Commodification refers to the process through which something that previously was not considered as a marketable product becomes a commodity available for trade in a market economy. This process transforms objects, ideas, or services that may have cultural, personal, or historical value into products that have a standardized commercial value. Over time, many non-material things, like emotions, personal relationships, or even experiences, have been commodified. This phenomenon has been particularly accentuated in the age of the internet and social media, where digital content, personal data, and virtual experiences are now commodities.

22. (C): Reflexivity, in sociology and anthropology, refers to the practice of considering one's own role in and effect upon the research process. It's essentially a self-examination, and in the context of social research, scholars reflect upon their actions, reactions, and the impacts these might have on the study and its subjects. Reflexivity is vital to understand biases, prejudices, and potential power dynamics that might influence the research's outcomes. It's a way of ensuring greater transparency and honesty in research processes, by acknowledging that researchers aren't passive, objective observers but are actively engaged and may influence the situation they are observing.

23. (B): 'Time Slavery' is often associated with the IT (Information Technology) sector. It refers to the idea where employees are constantly tethered to their work, often beyond official working hours, through devices, emails, and other online tools. While the IT industry offers numerous advantages like high pay and perks, the downside often is the blurring of boundaries between personal and professional lives. Employees can feel compelled to respond to work communications or engage in work-related tasks at all times, which can lead to burnout, stress, and diminished work-life balance.

24. (B): The concept of an 'imagined community' was proposed by Benedict Anderson in his seminal work

"Imagined Communities: Reflections on the Origin and Spread of Nationalism." Anderson posits that a nation is an imagined community because its members, even though they will never meet most of their fellow members, still hold an image of their communion. This sense of imagined connection is essential to the concept of nationalism. The "imagined" aspect does not mean the community isn't real, but that it exists primarily as an idea, especially as nations are often constructed around shared cultural, linguistic, or historical traits, even if members don't have direct daily interaction with the entirety of the nation.

25. (A): Amrita Bazar Patrika was an English Newspaper. Initially launched as a Bengali weekly in 1868, it became a daily newspaper in 1871 and switched to English in 1878 to address a broader audience and bypass laws that were more stringently applied to vernacular press by the British colonial administration. Throughout its history, the newspaper played a crucial role in the Indian independence movement, spreading nationalist ideas and rallying support against colonial rule.

26. (D): The chronological order of the land revenue reforms in pre-independent colonial India and independent India is as follows:

(*e*) **Zamindari System:** Implemented by the British colonial rulers through the Permanent Settlement Act of 1793, the Zamindari system made zamindars or landlords intermediaries between the colonial administration and the peasants. They were responsible for collecting rents from the peasants and paying a fixed sum to the colonial administration.

(*a*) **Rayatwari System:** Introduced in the early 19th century in parts of Madras and Bombay Presidencies, this system established a direct relationship between the peasant (or ryot) and the colonial administration. Here, each peasant was recognized as the owner of his plot of land.

(*b*) **Abolition of Zamindari System:** Post-independence, the Indian government took measures to abolish the zamindari system and redistribute land to actual tillers. This was done to break the stronghold of the zamindars and ensure social justice.

(*d*) **Tenancy Abolition and Regulation Acts:** Various states in India passed these Acts to provide security of tenure to tenants, regulate the rent, and confer rights of ownership to tenants who cultivated land.

(*c*) **Land Ceiling Acts:** Enacted in various states from the 1960s onwards, these Acts aimed to fix a maximum size of landholdings that an individual/family could own. Excess land was to be taken by the state and redistributed among landless peasants.

27. (C): Post-independence India witnessed significant changes in rural areas, including:

(*a*) **A shift from payment in kind (grain) to payment in cash:** With monetization of the rural economy and the growth of markets, transactions in kind gave way to cash-based transactions.

(*b*) **Rise of a class of 'free' wage laborers:** As traditional agrarian structures broke down and as land reforms were implemented, many became free wage laborers instead of bonded or attached laborers.

(*c*) **A loosening of traditional bonds or hereditary relationships between landowner and workers:** With social reforms and a focus on egalitarian principles, hereditary relationships, and obligations began to decline.

(*e*) **Increase in the use of agricultural laborers:** With commercialization of agriculture and diversification of crops, there was an increased demand for agricultural laborers.

28. (B): Contract farming involves a pre-agreed price between companies and farmers. While it can assure a market for farmers and sometimes even offer resources or knowledge to produce specialized items, it does **not provide complete financial security to farmers.** Market dynamics, potential failures in crop yield, and other factors can still pose financial risks.

29. (C): The contribution of the agriculture sector to GDP is continuously decreasing. As per the second advance estimates of national income- 2022-23, the share of Gross Value Added (GVA) of agriculture and allied sectors in the total economy and growth of GVA of agriculture and allied sectors, have gone down in the last 2-3 years. However, farmers' income is steadily growing. The Union Minister of Agriculture and Farmers Welfare, Narendra Singh Tomar informed the Lok Sabha. According to the estimates, released by the Ministry of Statistics & Programme Implementation (MoSPI), the GVA of agriculture and allied sectors in 2020-21 was 20.1%, it was 19% in 2021-22 and it again came down to 18.3% in 2022-23.

30. (A): The correct match between books and authors is:

(*a*) Invisible Man — III. **Ralph Ellison:** A novel that explores individual and collective identity in the context of racial discrimination.

(*b*) Caste: Its Modern Avatar — IV. **M.N. Srinivas:** Srinivas is known for his work on caste in Indian society.

(*c*) Analogy of Religion — II. **Bishop Joseph Butler:** An 18th-century religious text arguing for the reasonableness of Christianity.

(*d*) Unheard voices: stories of forgotten lives — I. **Harsh Mandar:** Mandar's book provides insights into the lives of marginalized individuals in India.

31. (A): The term diversity inherently emphasizes differences. In sociological and cultural contexts, diversity refers to the existence of a variety of cultural or ethnic groups within a society. It recognizes and appreciates the differences in ethnicity, gender, age, national origin, disability, sexual orientation, education, and other individual attributes. By acknowledging diversity, societies can foster inclusivity and ensure that every group's unique attributes and experiences are respected and valued. Furthermore, in the modern world, the importance of diversity is increasingly recognized for its role in driving innovation, fostering understanding, and bridging gaps in various spheres of life.

32. (B): The 73rd Constitutional Amendment is related to the Panchayati Raj Institutions. Enacted in 1992, this amendment provided constitutional status to the Panchayati Raj system, an integral part of India's grassroots-level democracy. It emphasized a three-tier system of governance at the village, intermediate, and district levels. The amendment also mandated regular elections to these bodies, reservation for scheduled castes, scheduled tribes, and women, and also enabled states to vest these local bodies with more powers and authority.

33. (D): It was Jawaharlal Nehru who called upon the media to function as the watchdog of democracy. Nehru, India's first Prime Minister, had a keen understanding of the role of the press in a democratic society. He believed that a free and responsible press was crucial for the healthy functioning of democracy. He often emphasized the media's responsibility to inform, educate, and hold those in power accountable, ensuring that the democratic principles upon which India was founded remained intact.

34. (B): Characteristics of tribes are as follows:

(*a*) **Tribes are social groups:** This is an inherent definition of tribes. They are communities that share a common language, territory, and cultural traits.

(*c*) **Tribes have distinctive habitat in the hill and forest:** Historically, tribes in India have been associated with forests and hills, having a symbiotic relationship with their natural surroundings.

(*d*) **They are marked by poverty, powerlessness, and stigma by the Indian Constitution:** While the Constitution does recognize tribal groups and provides special rights and provisions for them, many tribal communities in India face socioeconomic challenges, marginalization, and discrimination.

35. (B): Sanskritisation is a term coined by Indian sociologist M.N. Srinivas to describe the process by which lower castes in India adopt the customs, rituals, and practices of the upper castes to elevate their social status. The following are its characteristics:.

(*b*) **Avoids bride price:** Historically, some tribal and lower caste groups had a system of bride price, where the groom's family would compensate the bride's family. Upper castes typically practiced dowry instead.

(*c*) **Promotes dowry practices:** Sanskritisation often led to the adoption of dowry practices, which are more prevalent among upper-caste groups. This is contrary to the bride price system and is a marker of adopting higher caste norms.

The process of Sanskritisation often meant embracing practices of the dominant upper castes in hopes of improving one's societal status, even if it meant adopting regressive practices like dowry.

36. (*): According to the Census, Sample Registration System, IIPS projections, the projected population growth of the mentioned states upto 2041 in ascending order are as: Tamil Nadu (2.0%), Punjab (5.3%), Maharashtra (5.8%) and Bihar (24.7%). No option matches with this order (*d*), (*a*), (*b*), (*c*).

37. (C): Shetkari Sangathan is an organization dedicated to the cause of farmers. Founded by Sharad Joshi in Maharashtra during the 1970s, the Shetkari Sangathan has been instrumental in championing the rights and causes of farmers against various issues they face, be it price controls, farming subsidies, or rights to technology. On the other hand, FICCI and ASSOCHAM are industrial and commerce bodies, and INTUC is related to trade unions but not specifically agricultural ones.

38. **(A):** During the 1970s, the women's movement in India became particularly active, addressing several issues. Among these were the representation of women in media, dowry-related violence, and the safety and dignity of women, especially concerning incidents like rape in police custody. Sati, though historically a critical concern, was not a central issue of focus for the women's movement specifically in the 1970s.

39. **(C):** Jan Breman is the scholar who described the change in the relationship between landlords and agricultural workers as a shift from 'patronage to exploitation.' He has done extensive work on the agrarian structure, labor, and the informal sector in India, and his research has often highlighted the deep-seated inequalities and exploitative nature of these relations, especially post-independence.

40. **(A):** The idea that the use of machinery actually "deskills" workers is associated with Harry Braverman. In his influential work "Labor and Monopoly Capital," Braverman argued that the division of labor and the introduction of machinery into the production process served to separate workers from the knowledge and control over their work. This "deskilling" led to the reduction of labor to simple, repetitive tasks that require little to no skill, thus diminishing the power and agency of workers in the workplace.

41. **(D): Gonds of Central India** are not typically referred to as a 'dominant caste' in the traditional sociological understanding of the term. The concept of dominant caste was introduced by M.N. Srinivas and pertained to castes that were numerically significant and held substantial economic and political power in a particular region. The Gonds, while being one of the largest tribal communities in India, do not fit into this category in the same way the other castes like Jats, Patidars, or Reddys do. It's important to note that 'dominance' in this context doesn't necessarily imply a higher position in the traditional caste hierarchy, but rather refers to a combination of numerical strength, economic and political power, and social status.

42. **(C):** Reservation is not primarily a benefit given to the upper castes. In India, reservations are affirmative action policies designed to uplift historically marginalized groups, specifically the Scheduled Castes (SCs), Scheduled Tribes (STs), and Other Backward Classes (OBCs). These policies ensure representation in education, government jobs, and legislatures. Upper castes, traditionally having enjoyed a higher socio-economic status and representation, aren't the primary beneficiaries of these policies.

43. **(C): Shudras** are traditionally considered the lowest in the Varna hierarchy of the caste system. The Varna system is a fourfold categorization, and in descending order of hierarchy, it consists of Brahmins (priests and scholars), Kshatriyas (warriors and rulers), Vaishyas (traders), and Shudras (service providers). Over time, this system became more complex with the emergence of numerous castes and sub-castes.

44. **(A):** For the upper caste, especially in urban contexts, caste tends to be more significant in the personal sphere than in public lives. This means that caste often influences personal decisions such as marriage and religious practices more than it does professional or public decisions. However, it's important to note that the influence of caste is pervasive and can be found in various facets of life, both public and personal, but the emphasis in the given passage suggests its role in marriage and religion for the urban upper caste.

45. **(B):** The Government of India Act of 1935 gave legal recognition to the Scheduled Castes and Scheduled Tribes. It was one of the main statutes from which the Constitution of India drew its foundational structure. The Act introduced the concept of SCs and STs, and provisions were made for their representation. Later, the Constitution of India solidified their status, ensuring their rights and welfare through various provisions. While the other Acts like the Prevention of Atrocities Act and the SC/ST Act play crucial roles in protecting the rights of these communities, it was the 1935 Act and subsequently the Constitution that provided the legal recognition.

46. **(B):** B.P. Wadia is credited with establishing the first trade union in India in April 1918 in Madras. This was a significant development in the labor movement in India. Trade unions play an essential role in representing the interests of workers and advocating for better working conditions, wages, and other workers' rights. While Mahatma Gandhi and J.L. Nehru played pivotal roles in the Indian freedom struggle and did support workers' rights, it was B.P. Wadia who set up the first official trade union, marking a milestone in the history of labor rights in India.

47. **(B):** V.V. Giri was one of the key figures who led the moderate ideology in the All India Trade Union Congress (AITUC). The AITUC was a major confluence of differing ideologies, and the moderates were one of its prominent groups. V.V. Giri, later the President of India, always took a conciliatory approach to labor issues, advocating for peaceful negotiations between workers and employers. This was in contrast to other groups within AITUC that had a more confrontational stance or were driven by political ideologies.

48. **(C):** The recession in the economy in 1966-67 led to a decrease in production. A recession typically signals a period of economic downturn, which is characterized by reduced consumer spending, lower industrial production, and increased unemployment. The 1966-67 recession had wide-ranging effects on the Indian economy, including both the industrial and agricultural sectors. With decreased production came the domino effect of reduced employment opportunities, leading to larger confrontations between the state and trade unions.

49. **(D):** The Trade Union Act of 1926 was enacted to provide for the registration of trade unions and proposed various regulations related to their operation. This legislation marked a significant step towards formalizing the operations of trade unions and giving them legal recognition and protection. The Act ensured that trade unions were not arbitrarily deemed illegal and gave workers a more structured platform to voice their grievances.

50. **(B):** The statement that goods were manufactured in the United Kingdom is accurate. The colonial trade pattern established by the British primarily involved procuring raw materials from India and then manufacturing goods in the UK. These manufactured goods were subsequently marketed and sold in the Indian colony. This exploitation-driven trade pattern was one of the ways through which the British economic imperialism functioned. By keeping the manufacturing base in the UK, they ensured that India remained dependent and didn't develop a robust manufacturing sector of its own during much of the colonial period.

GENERAL TEST

1. Ministry of Health and Family Welfare has launched 'Nikshay Poshan Yojana' related to eradication of which of the following disease?

A. Dengue B. Malaria
C. Tuberculosis D. Kala-Azar

2. Match List-I with List-II.

List-I (Important Days)	List-II (Date)
(*a*) National Youth Day	I. 28th February
(*b*) Army Day	II. 12th January
(*c*) National Science Day	III. 15th January
(*d*) National Safety Day	IV. 4th March

Choose the ***correct*** answer from the options given below:

	(*a*)	(*b*)	(*c*)	(*d*)
A.	II	III	IV	I
B.	II	III	I	IV
C.	III	II	I	IV
D.	IV	III	I	II

3. If P(E) = 0.05, what is the probability of 'not E'?

A. 0.05 B. 0.45
C. 0.95 D. 0.55

4. Find the next term in the alpha-numeric series:

Z1A, W8C, T27E, Q64G, N125I, __?__

A. K216L B. K216K
C. L343K D. L343L

5. Which of the following statements are incorrect?

(*a*) Volume of a cone = $\frac{1}{3}\pi r^3 h$

(*b*) Volume of a cone = $\frac{1}{3}\pi r^2 h$

(*c*) Volume of a hemispere = $\frac{2}{3}\pi r^2$

(*d*) Volume of a hemispere = $\frac{2}{3}\pi r^3$

(*e*) Volume of a cylinder = $\frac{1}{3}\pi r^3 h$

Choose the ***correct*** answer from the options given below:

A. (*a*), (*b*) and (*d*) only
B. (*a*), (*b*) and (*c*) only
C. (*a*), (*c*) and (*e*) only
D. (*c*), (*d*) and (*e*) only

6. Five children Arun, Bhuvi, Charu, Deepak and Emmy are sitting along the corners of a pentagonal table facing the centre. Bhuvi is between Emmy and Charu. Deepak is to the right of Emmy. Who is to the left of Charu?

A. Bhuvi B. Arun
C. Charu D. Deepak

7. A man standing on the bank of a river observes that the angle subtended by a tree standing on the opposite bank is 60° on his side of Bank. When he moved away 24 m from the bank, he finds the angle to be 30°. Find the breadth of the river:

A. 12 B. 18
C. 26 D. 20

8. The first satellite in space was launched by:

A. U.S.A.
B. United Kingdom
C. U.S.S.R.
D. France

9. Given below are two statements: one is labelled as Assertion (A) and the other is labelled as Reason (R).

Assertion (A): Polar areas have high atmospheric pressure.

Reason (R): These areas receive minimum sunshine throughout the year.

In the light of the above statements, choose the ***most appropriate*** answer from the options given below:

A. Both (A) and (R) are correct and (R) is the correct explanation of (A)
B. Both (A) and (R) are true, but (R) is not the correct explanation of (A)
C. (A) is true, but (R) is false
D. (A) is false, but (R) is true

10. Which one of the following numbers is not a prime number?

A. 241 B. 337
C. 391 D. 571

11. If the mean of 5 observations x, $x + 2$, $x + 4$, $x + 6$ and $x + 8$ is 11, then value of x:

A. 7 B. 43
C. 51 D. 8

12. Amar is 16th from the left end in a row of boys and Vishal is 18th from the right end. Satish is 11th towards the right of Amar and 3rd towards the right of Vishal side end. How many boys are there is a row?

A. 45 B. 26
C. 39 D. 41

13. Following question is based on the information given below:

(*i*) 'R × S' means 'R is father of S'
(*ii*) 'R – S' means 'R is sister of S'
(*iii*) 'R + S' means 'R is mother of S'
(*iv*) 'R ÷ S' means 'R is brother of S'

In the expression A + B × C ÷ D how is C related to A?

A. Son
B. Grandson
C. Granddaughter
D. Grandmother

14. Given below are two statements:

Statement (I): Right to information has been granted to every citizen of India under Right to information Act, 2005 which came into force on 12th October, 2005.

Statement (II): Right to information is a fundamental Right.

In the light of the above statements, choose the ***most appropriate*** answer from the options given below:

A. Both Statement I and Statement II are true
B. Both Statement I and Statement II are false
C. Statement I is true, but Statement II is false
D. Statement I is false, but Statement II is true

15. Given below are two statements: one is labelled as Assertion (A) and the other is labelled as Reason (R).

Assertion (A): The 73rd Amendment granted constitutional states to the Gram Sabha.

Reason (R): The Balawant Rai Mehta committee mentioned the Gram Sabha.

In the light of the above statements, choose the ***most appropriate*** answer from the options given below:

A. Both (A) and (R) are correct and (R) is the correct explanation of (A)
B. Both (A) and (R) are correct, but (R) is not the correct explanation of (A)
C. (A) is true, but (R) is not false
D. (A) is false, but (R) is true

16. Select the figure from the options which will continue the series established by the problem figure:

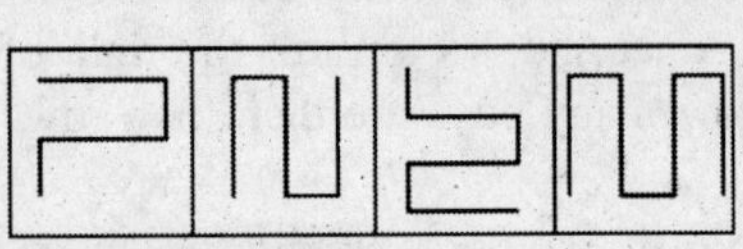

A. 
B. 
C. 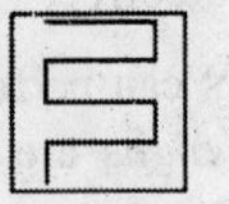
D. 

17. The sum of an Infinite geometric series is 4 and the sum of the cubes of the terms of the same GP is 192. The Common Ratio of the original geometric series is:

A. $\frac{1}{2}$ B. $-\frac{1}{2}$
C. $\frac{1}{4}$ D. $-\frac{1}{4}$

18. A clock is started at noon. By 20 minutes part 6, the hand had has turned through:

A. 175° B. 180°
C. 185° D. 190°

19. Match List-I with List-II.

List-I (World Organization)	**List-II (Headquarters)**
(*a*) BRICS	I. Geneva (Switzerland)
(*b*) NATO	II. Shanghai (China)
(*c*) WTO	III. Kathmandu (Nepal)
(*d*) SAARC	IV. Brussels (Belgium)

Choose the ***correct*** answer from the options given below:

	(*a*)	(*b*)	(*c*)	(*d*)
A.	III	IV	I	II
B.	IV	II	I	III
C.	II	IV	I	III
D.	II	IV	III	I

20. The Credit of inventing soap by using Mustard oil and some alkalies goes to which of the following scientist?

A. Chakrapani
B. Sushruta
C. Nagarjuna
D. Patayjali

21. Given below are two statements, one is labelled as Assertion (A) and the other is labelled as Reason (R).

Assertion (A): Clothes are not washed properly in hard water.

Reason (R): Hard water contains many minerals.

In the light of the above statements, choose the ***most appropriate*** answer from the options given below:

A. Both (A) and (R) are correct and (R) is the correct explanation of (A)

B. Both (A) and (R) are correct, but (R) is not the correct explanation of (A)
C. (A) is correct, but (R) is not correct
D. (A) is not correct, but (R) is correct

22. How many 3 digit even numbers can be formed from the digits (0-9) if repetition of digits are allowed?
A. 350 B. 400
C. 450 D. 1000

23. Which of the planet have no satellite?
(*a*) Mercury
(*b*) Neptune
(*c*) Satrun
(*d*) Venus

Choose the ***correct*** answer from the options given below:
A. (*b*) and (*d*) only
B. (*a*) and (*b*) only
C. (*b*), (*c*) and (*d*) only
D. (*a*) and (*d*) only

24. If CE || DB, what is the value of x:

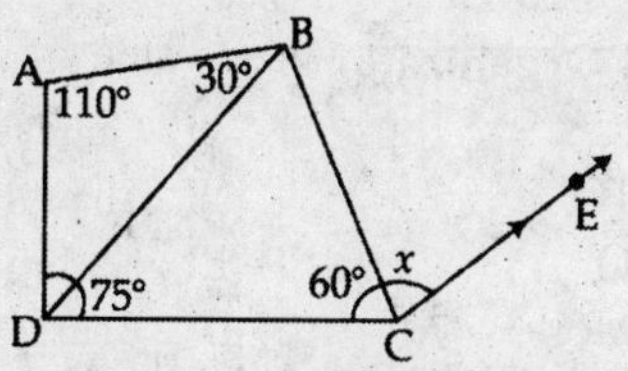

A. 45° B. 30°
C. 75° D. 85°

25. Who was the Chief Justice of India when public interest litigation (PIL) was introduced to the Indian Judicial system?
A. M. Hidayatullah
B. A.M. Ahmadi
C. P.N. Bhagwati
D. A.S. Anand

26. How many cubes are there in a group?

A. 10 B. 16
C. 18 D. 20

27. The only continent through which Tropic of Cancer, Equator and Tropic of Capricorn passes?
A. Asia B. Australia
C. Antarctica D. Africa

28. Facing towards North, Ravi walks 30 m. He then turns left and walks 50 m. He again turns left and walks 30 m. How far is he from his original position and towards which direction?
A. 30 m, North
B. 20 m, East
C. 20 m, South
D. 50 m, West

29. Find out the figure that can be formed from the piece given below:

A.  B. 

C.  D. 

30. Complete the picture series:

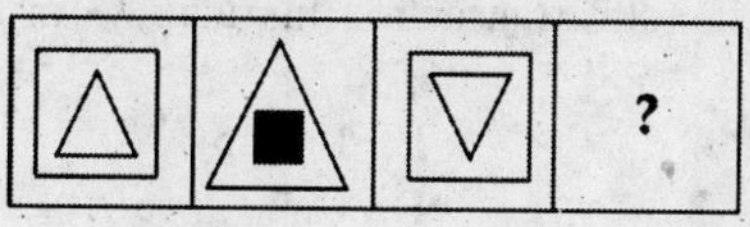

A.  B. 

C.  D. 

31. Find from amongst the figure, the one which resembles the pattern formed when the transparent sheet is folded along the dotted line.

A.  B. 

C.  D. 

32. Who among the following gave the popular slogan "Home Rule is my birthright and I will have it"?
A. Annie Besant
B. Lokamanya Tilak
C. Dadabhai Naoroji
D. Aurobindo Ghose

33. ₹ 800 becomes ₹ 956 in 3 years at a certain rate of simple interest. If the rate of interest is increased by 4%, what will ₹ 800 amount to in 3 years:

A. ₹ 1,020.80 B. ₹ 1,025
C. ₹ 1,052 D. ₹ 1,050

34. Two statements in the following questions, followed by two conclusions I and II. Read the conclusion and decide most suitable answer.

Statements : All horses are goats.
No goat is a donkey.

Conclusions : I. No horse is a donkey.
II. Atleast some goats are horses.

A. If only conclusion I follows.
B. If only conclusion II follows.
C. If both conclusion I and II follows.
D. If none of the conclusion follows.

35. ISRO Launched "GSAT-6A" satellites on:

A. 31 August, 2017 B. 29 March, 2018
C. 05 June, 2017 D. 12 January, 2018

36. A trader sold half of his articles at 60% profit, half of the remaining at 20% loss and the rest was sold at the cost price. In total transaction his gain % or loss % will be:

A. Gain 20% B. Loss 5%
C. Gain 40% D. Gain 25%

37. Match List-I with List-II.

List-I (Name of City)	List-II (Famous for production of)
(*a*) Ahmedabad	I. Machine tools
(*b*) Bangalore	II. Aluminium
(*c*) Bhilai	III. Textiles
(*d*) Renukoot	IV. Steel

Choose the ***correct*** answer from the options given below:

	(*a*)	(*b*)	(*c*)	(*d*)
A.	I	II	III	IV
B.	II	III	IV	I
C.	III	I	IV	II
D.	IV	III	II	I

38. The 36th National Games 2022 was held in which of the following state?

A. Goa B. Gujarat
C. Haryana D. Karnataka

39. Find out the wrong number in the sequence:

40960, 10240, 2560, 640, 200, 40, 10

A. 40 B. 640
C. 200 D. 2560

40. The constitution authorises the president to make provisions for discharge of duties of Governor in extraordinary circumstances under the ______.

A. Article 160 B. Article 162
C. Article 165 D. Article 310

41. The fibre crop which is known as the Golden Fibre?

A. Cotton B. Hump
C. Natural Silk D. Jute

42. The first person to use crystal for radio wave detection was:

A. J.C. Bose B. H.C. Verma
C. S.N. Bose D. C.V. Raman

43. The surface area (in m^2) of a sphere of radius 7 cm is: (Use $\pi = 22/7$)

A. 0.0616 B. 6.16
C. 61.6 D. 0.616

44. By selling on book for ₹ 250, loss percentage is 10%. What is the cost price?

A. ₹ 277.7 B. ₹ 250
C. ₹ 285 D. ₹ 315

45. If $\frac{x}{(b-c)(b+c-2a)} = \frac{y}{(c-a)(c+a-2b)} = \frac{z}{(a-b)(a+b-2c)}$ then value of $x + y + z$ is:

A. $a + b + c$ B. $a^2 + b^2 + c^2$
C. 0 D. 1

46. A completes $\frac{7}{20}$ of a work in 10 days. Then he completes the remaining work with the help of B in 5 days. The time required for A and B together to complete the entire work is:

A. $\frac{100}{29}$ days B. $\frac{100}{13}$ days
C. $\frac{100}{17}$ days D. $\frac{200}{13}$ days

47. Look at the statement and mark the correct answer on the conclusions that follows:

Statements : (*a*) Shubham is my cousin.
(*b*) A cousin may be a aunt's son, uncle's son or son of parent's step-siblings.

Conclusions : I. Shubham is my sisters son.
II. Shubham is my uncle's son.

A. Only conclusion I follows.
B. Only conclusion II follows.
C. Both conclusion I and II follows.
D. Neither conclusion I nor II follows.

48. If Today is Monday, After 62 it will be:

A. Wednesday B. Saturday
C. Sunday D. Thursday

49. The price of rice increases by 30%. A family reduced its consumption so that the expenditure of the rice is up only by 10%. If the total consumption of the rice before the price rise was 10 kg per month, then the consumption of rice per month at present (in kg) is:

A. $7\frac{6}{15}$ B. $8\frac{1}{15}$

C. $8\frac{6}{13}$ D. $8\frac{5}{13}$

50. The volume of a sphere of radius r is obtained by multiplying its surface area with:

A. $\frac{4}{3}$ B. $\frac{r}{3}$

C. $\frac{4r}{3}$ D. $3r$

51. If EFFECTIVE is coded as FEGDDSJUF, then how RELATIVE can be written in that code?

A. TDNZVHXD B. TCNAVGXC

C. SDMZUHWD D. SCMAUGXD

52. A bag contains 6 red, 4 blue and 10 white balls. A ball is picked from the bag at random. What is the probability that it is neither white nor blue?

A. $\frac{20}{6}$ B. $\frac{3}{10}$

C. $\frac{2}{5}$ D. $\frac{1}{2}$

53. Find the area of an equilateral triangle each of whose sides measures 4 cm:

A. $4\sqrt{3}$ cm^2 B. $4\sqrt{3}$ m^2

C. $3\sqrt{3}$ cm^2 D. $3\sqrt{3}$ m^2

54. The difference between two numbers is 24. If one number is 2 times the second, then the two numbers will be:

A. 36, 12 B. 48, 24

C. 32, 8 D. 12, 6

55. Choose the correct mirror image:

A. 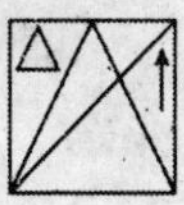 B. 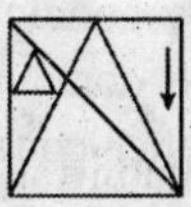

C. 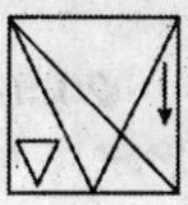 D. 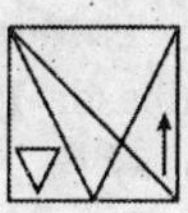

56. Match List-I with List-II.

List-I	List-II
(*a*) First speaker of Lok Sabha	I. Dr. Amartya Sen
(*b*) First Indian to get Bharat Ratna Award	II. G.V. Mavalankar
(*c*) First Indian recipient of Nobel Prize in Economics	III. Dr. S. Radhakrishnan
(*d*) First Indian Nobel Laureate	IV. Rabindra Nath Tagore

Choose the ***correct*** answer from the options given below:

	(*a*)	(*b*)	(*c*)	(*d*)
A.	II	III	I	IV
B.	II	III	IV	I
C.	III	II	I	IV
D.	IV	III	I	II

57. Who has been honoured with the Golden ball award in the FIFA World Cup 2022?

A. Kylian Mbappe B. Luka Modric

C. Lionel Messi D. Enzo Fernandez

58. A boy is running at a speed of p km/h to cover a distance of 1 km but due to slippery ground his speed is reduced by q km/h $(p > q)$. If he takes r hours to cover the distance, which of the following condition is true:

A. $\frac{1}{r} = (p-q)$ B. $r = (p - q)$

C. $r = \frac{1}{p+q}$ D. $r = p + q$

59. What can be placed at '?' if both side of ': :' have same relationship between numbers:

85 : 42 :: 139 : ?

A. 68 B. 69

C. 70 D. 67

60. Commemoration of national days should always be encouraged in schools and colleges. Which of the following statement given below is a strong argument:

(*a*) This type of commemoration gives opportunity to children and youth to value to contribution of people who built our nation.

(*b*) There is nothing wrong in celebrating a day and enjoy once is a while.

(*c*) These events hamper the focus of students from regular study.

A. Argument (*a*) and (*b*) are strong

B. Only argument (*a*) is strong

C. Argument (*b*) and (*c*) are strong

D. Only argument (*c*) is strong

ANSWERS

1. **(C)** **2.** **(B)**

3. **(C):** Required Probability of 'not E'.

$$= 1 - 0.05$$

$$= 1 - \frac{5}{100} = \frac{100 - 5}{100}$$

$$= \frac{95}{100} = 0.95.$$

4. **(B)** **5.** **(C)**

6. **(B):**

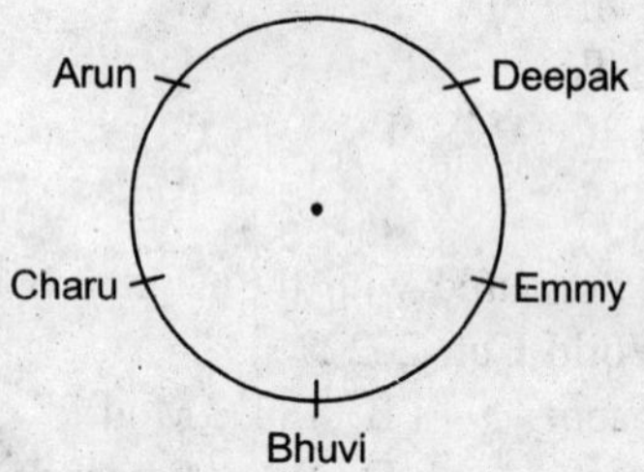

Clearly, Arun is left of Charu.

7. **(A):**

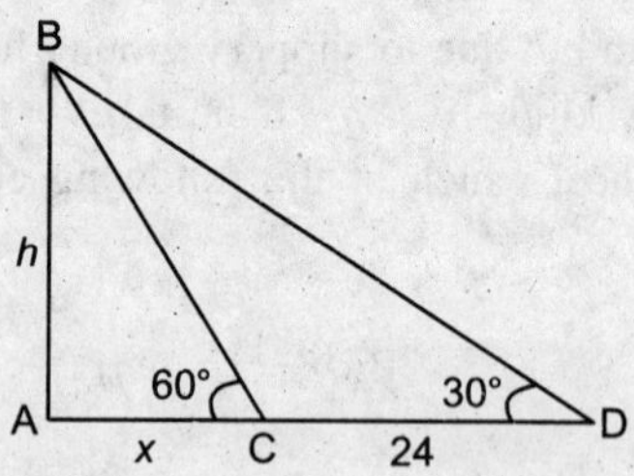

$$\tan 60° = \frac{h}{x}$$

$$\Rightarrow \quad \sqrt{3} = \frac{h}{x}$$

$$\Rightarrow \quad h = \sqrt{3}x$$

$$\tan 30° = \frac{h}{x + 24}$$

$$\Rightarrow \quad \frac{1}{\sqrt{3}} = \frac{h}{x + 24}$$

$$\Rightarrow \quad \sqrt{3}h = x + 24$$

$$\Rightarrow \quad 3x = x + 24$$

$$\Rightarrow \quad 2x = 24$$

$$\Rightarrow \quad x = 12$$

Hence, breadth of the river = 12 m.

8. **(C)** **9.** **(B)**

10. **(C):** 391 is not a prime number because 391 is divided by 17 and 23.

11. **(A):** Total of 5 observations = 11 × 5 = 55

$$\therefore x + x + 2 + x + 4 + x + 6 + x + 8 = 55$$

$$\Rightarrow \quad 5x + 20 = 55$$

$$\Rightarrow \quad 5x = 35$$

$$\Rightarrow \quad x = 7$$

Hence, the value of $x = 7$.

12. **(D)** **13.** **(B)** **14.** **(C)**

15. **(B)** **16.** **(C)**

17. **(B):**

$$S_\infty = \frac{a}{1 - r}$$

$$\Rightarrow \quad 4 = \frac{a}{1 - r}$$

$$\Rightarrow \quad \frac{a}{1 - r} = 4 \qquad ...(i)$$

$$(a)^3 + a^3r^3 + a^3r^6 + ... = 192$$

$$\Rightarrow \quad \frac{a^3}{1 - r^3} = 192 \qquad ...(ii)$$

Divide the cube of (*i*) by (*ii*), we get,

$$\frac{a^3}{(1 - r)^3} \times \frac{(1 - r^3)}{a^3} = \frac{(4)^3}{192} = \frac{64}{192} = \frac{1}{3}$$

$$\Rightarrow \quad \frac{1 - r^3}{(1 - r)^3} = \frac{1}{3}$$

$$\Rightarrow \quad \frac{1^2 + r + r^2}{1 + r^2 - 2r} = \frac{1}{3}$$

$$\Rightarrow \quad r^2 - 2r + 1 = 3(1 + r + r^2)$$

$$\Rightarrow r^2 - 2r + 1 - 3 - 3r - 3r^2 = 0$$

$$-2r^2 - 5r - 2 = 0$$

$$\Rightarrow \quad 2r^2 + 5r + 2 = 0$$

$$\Rightarrow \quad 2r^2 + 4r + r + 2 = 0$$

$$2r(r + 2) + 1(r + 2) = 0$$

$$(2r + 1)(r + 2) = 0$$

$$r = -\frac{1}{2}$$

or

$$r = -2$$

Hence, common ratio = $-\frac{1}{2}$.

18. **(D)** **19.** **(C)** **20.** **(A)**

21. **(B)**

22. (C): For a number to be even, we must have 2, 4, 6, 8, 0 at the unit's place.
Since, digits can be repeated.
Hence, required number of numbers

$$= 5 \times 10 \times 9 = 450.$$

23. (D)

24. (D):

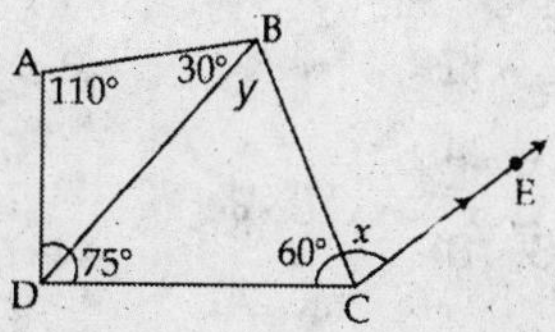

$\because$ CE || DB

$$\angle A + \angle B + \angle C + \angle D = 360°$$
$$\Rightarrow \quad 110° + y + 30° + 60° + 75° = 360°$$
$$\Rightarrow \quad y + 275° = 360°$$
$$\Rightarrow \quad y = 360° - 275° = 85°$$

($\because$ CE || DB $\Rightarrow \angle x = \angle y$)
Hence, $x = y = 85°$.

25. (C) **26. (D)** **27. (D)**

28. (D):

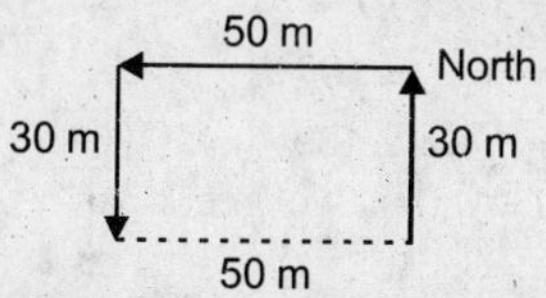

Ravi is 50 m away from his original position and towards west direction.

29. (C) **30. (D)** **31. (C)**

32. (B) **33. (C)** **34. (C)**

35. (B)

36. (D): Let total articles = 100
C.P. of each article = ₹ 100
Total C.P. = 100 × 100 = ₹ 10000

$$\text{S.P. of half articles} = 5000 \times \frac{160}{100} = ₹\ 8000$$

S.P. of half of remaining articles

$$= 2500 \times \frac{80}{100} = ₹\ 2000$$

S.P. of rest articles = ₹ 2500
Total S.P. = ₹ 8000 + 2000 + 2500
= ₹ 12500
Profit = 12500 − 10000
= ₹ 2500

$$\text{Profit \%} = \frac{2500}{10000} \times 100 = 25\%.$$

37. (C) **38. (B)**

39. (C):

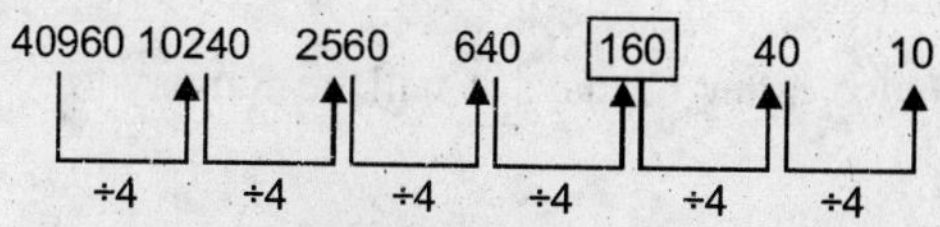

Hence, wrong number = 200.

40. (A) **41. (D)** **42. (A)**

43. (A) Surface area of sphere = $4\pi r^2$

$$= 4 \times \frac{22}{7} \times 7 \times 7 = 616 \text{ cm}^2$$

$$= \frac{616}{10000} \text{ m}^2 = 0.0616 \text{ m}^2.$$

44. (A): Selling price = ₹ 250
Loss = 10%

$$\text{Then, Cost price} = \frac{100}{90} \times 250$$

$$= ₹\ \frac{2500}{9} = ₹\ 277.7$$

45. (C): Let $\frac{x}{(b-c)(b+c-2a)} = \frac{y}{(c-a)(c+a-2b)}$

$$= \frac{z}{(a-b)(a+b-2c)} = k$$

$\therefore$
$$x = k(b-c)(b+c-2a)$$
$$y = k(c-a)(c+a-2b)$$
$$z = k(a-b)(a+b-2c)$$

Now, $x + y + z = k[(b-c)(b+c-2a) + (c-a)(c+a-2b) + (a-b)(a+b-2c)]$
$= k[b^2 + bc - 2ab - bc - c^2 + 2ac + c^2 + ac - 2bc - ac - a^2 + 2ab + a^2 + ab - 2ac - ab - b^2 + 2bc]$
$= k[0] = 0.$

46. (B): $\because \frac{7}{20}$ part of a work A can do in 10 days

$$\text{Remaining part} = 1 - \frac{7}{20} = \frac{13}{20} \text{ part of work}$$

$$\because \text{(A + B)'s 5 days work} = \frac{13}{20} \text{ part}$$

$$\therefore \text{(A + B)'s 1 day work} = \frac{13}{20 \times 5} = \frac{13}{100}$$

Hence, (A + B) can do whole work in $\frac{100}{13}$ days.

47. (D)

48. (C): Today is Monday. After 63 days (7×9) it will be Monday.

Hence, after 62 days it will be Sunday.

49. (C)

50. (B): The Volume of sphere $= \frac{4}{3}\pi r^3$

Surface area of sphere $= 4\pi r^2$

Hence, the volume of sphere of radius r is obtained by multiplying its surface area with $\frac{r}{3}$.

51. (C): As,

E	F	F	E	C	T	I	V	E
+1 ↓	−1 ↓	+1 ↓	−1 ↓	+1 ↓	−1 ↓	+1 ↓	−1 ↓	+1 ↓
F	E	G	D	D	S	J	U	F

Similarly,

R	E	L	A	T	I	V	E
+1 ↓	−1 ↓	+1 ↓	−1 ↓	+1 ↓	−1 ↓	+1 ↓	−1 ↓
S	D	M	Z	U	H	W	D

52. (B): Red ball = 6

Blue ball = 4

White ball = 10

$$\text{Required probability} = \frac{6}{20} = \frac{3}{10}$$

53. (A): Area of an equilateral triangle

$$= \frac{\sqrt{3}}{4}(\text{Side})^2$$

$$= \frac{\sqrt{3}}{4} \times (4)^2 = \frac{\sqrt{3}}{4} \times 16$$

$$= 4\sqrt{3}\ \text{cm}^2.$$

54. (B): Let second number $= x$

$\therefore$ One number $= 2x$

According to the question,

$$2x - x = 24$$

$$\Rightarrow \quad x = 24$$

$$\therefore \quad 2x = 2 \times 24 = 48$$

Hence, number will be 48 and 24.

55. (D) **56. (A)** **57. (C)**

58. (A): Relative speed $= (p - q)$ km/hr

Distance = 1 km

Time = r hours

$$\therefore \quad \text{Speed} = \frac{\text{Distance}}{\text{Time}} = \frac{1}{r}$$

$$\Rightarrow \quad (p - q) = \frac{1}{r}$$

$$\text{Hence,} \quad \frac{1}{r} = (p - q).$$

59. (B): 85 : 42 :: 139 : 69

$85 = \frac{85 - 1}{2} = \frac{84}{2} = 42$ $\quad$ $139 = \frac{139 - 1}{2} = \frac{138}{2} = 69$

Hence, 69 will come at the place of question mark.

60. (B)

Previous Years' Paper (Solved)

(Common University Entrance Test for UG Programmes)

CUET (UG) B.A. (H.) Political Science/ B.A. (H.) History Entrance Exam, 2022*

ENGLISH

Directions (Qs. No. 1-6): *Read the following passage to answer question:*

The first form did not really see very much of Erica because she did not have lessons with them. But even if they met her in a passage or in the art room or gym they looked the other way. In the common-room at night Erica had a miserable time. Not one of the second form girls also would have anything to do with her. Loud remarks about sneaks and cowards were made in her hearing. The only person who ever threw her a word at all was the bad-tempered Margery Fenworthy. Erica did not like Margery any more than the other girls did but she was so grateful to be spoken to even, by the surly first former that she almost began to like the girl.

'I'm surprised you speak to Erica, Margery,' said Pat, when she had heard Margery ask to borrow Erica's stationery said Margery, in her usual rude way. 'You're none of you friendly to me, and I know what it is to have people being beastly to you.' 'But Margery, it's your own fault,' said Pat in surprise. 'You're so rude and sullen. You never smile and joke.' Margery, 'you don't give me a chance.' 'Oh, Margery, what a fib'! Cried Pat. 'It's you who never give us a chance to be decent to you. You scowl and glower and frown all the time.' 'If you're going to pick me to pieces you can save yourself the trouble', said Margery, fiercely. 'I don't care tuppence for any of you. And if I want to speak to that wretched Erica, I shall. Who cares for a pack of silly girls, and a crowd of stuck-up teachers? I don't Pat was astonished. What a strange girl Margery was! Did she really want a chance of being friends with the others? Was she terribly shy? What was behind that funny manner of hers? Pat talked about it with her twin. 'Margery is always making enemies she said.' 'I spoke to her today about it and she accused us of never giving her a chance! Do you think we ought to do something about it?'

1. Match List-I with List-II.

List-I (Part A)	List-II (Part B)
(*a*) Loud remarks about sneaks and cowards were made	(*i*) in the presence of Erica
(*b*) Margery Fenworthy	(*ii*) was very unpopular
(*c*) "Oh Margery ... it's you who never give us a chance to be decent"	(*iii*) said Pat
(*d*) The girl with a twin sister named	(*iv*) Pat

Choose the correct answer from the options given below:

	(*a*)	(*b*)	(*c*)	(*d*)
A.	(*i*)	(*ii*)	(*iv*)	(*iii*)
B.	(*i*)	(*ii*)	(*iii*)	(*iv*)
C.	(*ii*)	(*iv*)	(*iii*)	(*i*)
D.	(*iv*)	(*iii*)	(*i*)	(*ii*)

2. From the given options, choose the one which is correct according to the passage.

The girls mentioned in the passage are:

(*a*) Erica, Margery and Pat
(*b*) Erica and Pat only
(*c*) Only Patricia
(*d*) Joan, Erica and Patricia

A. (*b*) B. (*a*)
C. (*c*) D. (*d*)

3. From the given options, select the one which is right and correct according to the passage:

A. "I am surprised you speak to Margery, Erica" said Pat
B. "I am surprised you speak to Erica, Pat" said Margery

*** This Previous Year Paper has been given here as a Combination of CUET (UG) 2022 different exams for the Subjects 'English, History, Political Science, Sociology and General Test', which have been mapped to this course.**

C. "I am surprised you speak to Margery, Pat" said Erica

D. "I am surprised you speak to Erica, Margery" said Pat

4. From the passage Margaret fenworthy comes across as ______. Select the option which is correct according to the passage.

A. A bad tempered, unpopular girl

B. Heroic and a strong mountaineer

C. Saintly and a recluse

D. A cynical middle aged woman

5. From the passage it may be concluded that Erica was very.

Select the option which is correct according to the passage.

A. Lonely, friendless and timid

B. Dominating and Arrogant

C. Cunning and stupid

D. Brilliant and very popular

6. From the passage it becomes clear that: (choose the correct option).

Not one of the First Form girls would have anything to do with Erica because:

A. She did not have any lessons with them

B. She used to mind her own business

C. She was unfriendly, rude and selfish

D. Erica was away on a holiday in Paris with her family

Directions (Qs. No. 7-12): *Read the following passage to answer question.*

She took me by the hand walked me into the lobby like a five-year old child. Didn't she know I was pushing 15? This was the third home Nancy was placing me in-in a span of eight months! I guess she felt a little sorry for me. The bright fluorescent lights threatened to burn my skin as I walked towards a bouncy-looking lady with curly hair and a sweetly-smiling man. They called themselves Allie and Alex. Cute, I thought.

After they exchanged the usual reams of paperwork, it was off in their Chevy Suburban to get situated into another new home. This time, there were no other foster children and nor another biological child. Anything could happen.

Over the next few weeks, Allie, Alex and I fell into quite a nice routine. She'd make pancakes for breakfast, or he'd fry up some sausage and eggs. They sang a lot, even danced as they cooked. They must have just bought the house because, most weekends, we were either painting a living room butter yellow or staining a coffee table mocha brown.

I kept waiting for the other shoe to drop. When would they start threatening a loss of pancakes if I didn't mow the lawn? When would the sausage and eggs be replaced with unidentifiable slosh because he didn't feel like cooking in the morning? But, it never happened. They kept cooking, singing and dancing like a couple of happy fools.

It was a Saturday afternoon when Allie decided it was time to paint the brick fireplace white. As we crawled closer to the dirty old firepit, we pulled out the petrified wood and noticed a teeny-tiny treasure box! We looked at each other in wonder and excitement. She actually said, "I wonder if the Leprechauns left it!"

7. Over the next few weeks who all fell into a nice comfortable routine?

Select the correct option.

A. Nancy

B. Allie and Nancy

C. The narrator, Allie and Alex

D. Only Alex

8. "She took me by the hand and walked me into the lobby...". The 'me' refers to the:

A. Narrator and the protagonist of the passage

B. Narrator and the footballer

C. A filmstar and a villain

D. The headmaster of an English school

9. On a Sunday afternoon, what did Allie decide to do?

Select the correct option.

(*a*) Crawl towards the dirty old garage

(*b*) Paint the brick firepit white

(*c*) Sing a song

(*d*) Write a letter to the President

Choose the correct answer from the options given below:

A. (*a*) B. (*b*)

C. (*c*) D. (*d*)

10. It appears from the passage that over the next few days the narrator and the other two characters were:

Select the correct option.

A. Relaxed and comfortable

B. Stressed and anxious

C. Depressed and gloomy

D. Plotting revenge

11. Match List-I with List-II:

List-I	*List-II*
(*a*) Nancy	(*i*) Treated the narrator as if he was a 5 year old child
(*b*) Allie	(*ii*) Made pancakes for breakfast
(*c*) Alex	(*iii*) Fried sausages and eggs
(*d*) Narrator	(*iv*) Was placed in the 3rd home

Choose the correct answer from the options given below:

	(a)	(b)	(c)	(d)
A.	(i)	(ii)	(iii)	(iv)
B.	(iv)	(iii)	(ii)	(i)
C.	(iv)	(i)	(iii)	(ii)
D.	(ii)	(iv)	(i)	(iii)

12. From the passage it may be assumed that the narrator was a 15 year old teenager without parents because the passage talks about.

Select the correct option.

A. Foster home for the narrator and other foster children
B. Cleaning firepits
C. Church and Chapels of Great Britain
D. Malls of a Metropolitan city

Directions (Qs. No. 13-18): *Read the following passage to answer question.*

Workers and Slaves

The Pharaohs may have believed that it was their links with the Gods that kept Egypt going, but really it was the hard work of the ordinary people. It was they who dug the soil, worked in the mines and quarries, sailed the boats on the river Nile, marched with the army into Syria or Nubia, cooked food and raised children. Slavery was not very important in ancient Egypt, but it did exist. Most of the slaves were prisoners who had been captured during the many wars Egypt fought with their neighbours in the Near East. Slaves were usually treated well and were allowed to own property. Many Egyptian workers were serfs. This meant that their freedom was limited. They could be bought and sold along with the estates where they worked. Farmers had to be registered with the government. They had to sell crops at a fixed price and pay taxes in the form of produce. During the season of the Nile floods, when the fields lay under water, many workers were recruited into public building projects. Punishment for those who ran away was harsh.

13. From the passage we get to know that a distinct quality of ancient Egypt under the Pharaohs was the fact that.

Select the correct option.

A. Though slavery existed slaves were not treated harshly at all
B. The Pharaohs were very democratic and handsome
C. No Egyptian working in ancient Egypt worked as a serf
D. The river Nile would stop No flowing during the rains in Egypt

14. From the passage we get to know that in ancient Egypt many workers were known as serfs. These were people with:

Select the correct answer.

A. Workers with limited freedom in ancient Egypt
B. Students with limited Intelligence in modern Egypt
C. Nobility with limited power in medieval Egypt
D. Pharaohs with limited connection with the gods of Egyptian Gods

15. What according to the passage was the reason of ancient Egyptian progress and prosperity.

(a) The link the Pharaohs claimed they had with the Gods
(b) The labour and hard work of the ordinary men in ancient Egypt
(c) The mines and quarries full of germs armed with rockets and missiles and jewals in ancient Egypt
(d) The modern smart Egyptian army

Choose the correct answer from the options given below:

A. (a) B. (b)
C. (c) D. (d)

16. From the given passage options, select the one which is true according to the passage.

(a) Pharaohs believed that it was their link with the Gods that favoured Egypt
(b) The ordinary people worked overtime to destroy Egypt
(c) The Pharaohs did not believe they were connected to the Gods
(d) The Pharaohs were the hard working slaves of ancient Egypt

Choose the correct answer from the options given below:

A. (c) B. (b)
C. (a) D. (d)

17. Select the option that is **incorrect** according to the passage.

A. In the Egypt under the Pharaohs, slaves were allowed to own property
B. Most of the slaves were prisoners captured in the many wars Egypt fought with its neighbours in the NEAR EAST
C. Slaves were well treated in ancient Egypt
D. Slavery was extremely important in ancient Egypt

18. Match List-I with List-II.

List-I	*List-II*
(a) Serfs could be	(i) Farmers
(b) Registered with the government	(ii) Recruited workers during the rainy season
(c) Public building projects	(iii) Bought and sold along with the estates were they worked
(d) Harsh punishment	(iv) For those who ran away

Choose the correct answer from the options given below:

	(a)	(b)	(c)	(d)
A.	(i)	(ii)	(iii)	(iv)
B.	(iv)	(iii)	(ii)	(i)
C.	(iii)	(i)	(ii)	(iv)
D.	(ii)	(iii)	(iv)	(i)

Directions (Qs. No. 19-22): *From the given options select the one that is opposite in meaning to the given word:*

19. ACQUITTED
A. Promoted B. Burdened
C. Convicted D. Development

20. RELINQUISH
A. Garbage B. Harmonize
C. Beautify D. Possess

21. CAPACIOUS
A. Limited B. Charming
C. Foolish D. Colourful

22. FRAUDULENT
A. Candid B. Direct
C. Forthright D. Genuine

Directions (Qs. No. 23-26): *From the given options select the figure of speech of the poetic device used in expression.*

23. Both wry with the laboured ease of loss.
A. Simile B. Personification
C. Oxymoron D. Metaphor

24. Far Far from gusty waves.
A. Oxymoron B. Alliteration
C. Simile D. Personification

25. The smiling young trees provided a strange comfort.
A. Personification B. Metaphor
C. Simile D. Oxymoron

26. Like angels from heaven the paratrooper landed on earth.
A. Personification B. Oxymoron
C. Simile D. Pun

Directions (Qs. No. 27-30): *From the given options, select the one which correctly explains the expression.*

27. To be at sixes and sevens.
A. To be a primary school student
B. A state of total confusion and disorder
C. To be certain of batting well in a cricket match
D. To give away secrets

28. Once in a blue moon.
A. Most regularly B. Very often
C. Very rarely D. Once in a fortnight

29. A wild goose chase.
A. A Foolish and useless enterprises
B. To hunt wild life
C. A violent chase of criminals
D. To speak harshly

30. To burn a hole in the pocket.
A. To steal from someone's pocket
B. To destroy someone else's belongings
C. To burn address accidentally
D. To spend money very quickly

Directions (Qs. No. 31-34): *Choose the word from the given options that is closest in meaning to the given word.*

31. PUGNACIOUS
A. Rebellious B. Amusing
C. Quarrelsome D. Desirable

32. CLING
A. Attach B. Detach
C. Release D. Forward

33. ENCHANTING
A. Witty B. Pleasant
C. Comical D. Harmful

34. GIGANTIC
A. Miniature B. Monstrous
C. Diligent D. Awkward

Directions (Qs. No. 35-38): *From the given options, select the one that will rightly substitute the given expression.*

35. Period of 10 years.
A. Decade B. Fortnight
C. Annuity D. Millennium

36. One who loves and collects books.
A. Rockstar B. Bibliophile
C. Bellicose D. Bohemian

37. The killing of a new-born child.
A. Homicide B. Suicide
C. Massacre D. Infanticide

38. Detailed plan of a journey.
A. Passport B. Travelogue
C. Itinerary D. Timetable

Directions (Qs. No. 39-42): *From the given options, select the one that carries the same relation as.*

39. Attach : Detach
A. Barren : Fertile
B. Timid : Coward
C. Ridiculous : Funny
D. Jealous : Envious

40. Medley : Mixture
A. Iterate : Repeat
B. Coarse : Fine
C. Abundance : Scarcity
D. Triumph : Failure

41. Retreat : Advance
A. Garrulous : Talkative
B. Oblivion : Forgetfulness
C. Savage : Civilised
D. Obstinate : Stubborn

42. Meek : Modest
A. Blunt : Sharp
B. Finally : Eventually
C. Clever : Stupid
D. Condemn : Approve

Directions (Qs. No. 43-46): *From the given options, select the rightly spelt word:*

43. A. Katastrophic B. Catestrefic
C. Catastrophic D. Catostrofik

44. A. Kamunism B. Communism
C. Cummonism D. Cumunism

45. A. Cooperative B. Cauperative
C. Koperative D. Coperative

46. A. Pnemonia B. Pneumonia
C. Newmonia D. Nemonia

Directions (Qs. No. 47-50): *Rearrange the following jumbled group of words to make a meaningful sentence.*

47. (*a*) Penetrate the biological tissues
(*b*) Will produce unprecedented amount
(*c*) A large scale exchange of nuclear weapons
(*d*) Of radiation that can

Choose the correct answer from the options given below:
A. (*a*), (*b*), (*d*), (*c*)
B. (*c*), (*d*), (*a*), (*b*)
C. (*c*), (*b*), (*d*), (*a*)
D. (*a*), (*b*), (*c*), (*d*)

48. (*a*) During the last few years
(*b*) People in this area
(*c*) The mission has provided
(*d*) Able service to all the needy

Choose the correct answer from the options given below:
A. (*b*), (*d*), (*c*), (*a*)
B. (*c*), (*d*), (*b*), (*a*)
C. (*a*), (*b*), (*d*), (*c*)
D. (*c*), (*b*), (*a*), (*d*)

49. (*a*) Him to rush to his village immediately
(*b*) An urgent telegram asking
(*c*) He has received
(*d*) No other message other than

Choose the correct answer from the options given below:
A. (*c*), (*d*), (*b*), (*a*)
B. (*b*), (*c*), (*a*), (*d*)
C. (*c*), (*d*), (*a*), (*b*)
D. (*a*), (*b*), (*c*), (*d*)

50. (*a*) He managed to make sense
(*b*) It was the first time when
(*c*) Of the book even though
(*d*) He read anything on the subject

Choose the correct answer from the options given below:
A. (*d*), (*c*), (*a*), (*b*)
B. (*b*), (*a*), (*d*), (*c*)
C. (*a*), (*c*), (*b*), (*d*)
D. (*a*), (*b*), (*c*), (*d*)

ANSWERS

1. (B): The question requires matching statements from List-I with appropriate statements from List-II. (*a*) "Loud remarks about sneaks and cowards were made" can be matched with (*i*) "in the presence of Erica" as the passage mentions that such remarks were made in Erica's hearing. (*b*) "Margery Fenworthy" matches with (*ii*) "was very unpopular" since the passage describes that nobody liked Margery except Erica, which indicates her unpopularity. (*c*) "Oh Margery ... it's you who never give us a chance to be decent" is a statement made by Pat as mentioned in the passage, so it matches with (*iii*) "said Pat". (*d*) The girl with a twin sister is named Pat, so this matches with (*iv*) "Pat".

2. (B): According to the passage, the girls mentioned are Erica, Margery, and Pat. Thus, option (*a*) is the correct answer.

3. (D): In the passage, the exact line reads, "'I'm surprised you speak to Erica, Margery,' said Pat," which directly matches with option (D).

4. (A): Margery Fenworthy is described in the passage as someone with a bad temper. It's mentioned that she is the only one who spoke to Erica and that she is not liked by the other girls. Hence, she comes across as "A bad tempered, unpopular girl".

5. (A): Erica is described as having a miserable time in the common room and no one from the second form girls wanted to have anything to do with her. This suggests that she was lonely and friendless. The fact that she was grateful to Margery, who was known to be bad-tempered, indicates her timidity. Hence, she comes across as "Lonely, friendless, and timid".

6. **(A):** The passage directly mentions "The first form did not really see very much of Erica because she did not have lessons with them". This indicates that the reason for the First Form girls not interacting with Erica was that she didn't have lessons with them. Therefore, the correct option is "She did not have any lessons with them".

7. **(C):** The passage mentions that "Over the next few weeks, Allie, Alex, and I fell into quite a nice routine." This clearly indicates that the narrator, along with Allie and Alex, settled into a comfortable daily pattern. This routine involved cooking breakfast together, singing, dancing, and doing house chores.

8. **(A):** The pronoun "me" in the line "She took me by the hand and walked me into the lobby..." refers to the individual narrating the events of the story. As the passage progresses, the experiences and emotions of this individual are described in the first person. The narrator is the protagonist, or the central character, of this passage.

9. **(B):** The passage states, "It was a Saturday afternoon when Allie decided it was time to paint the brick fireplace white." This clearly indicates that on that particular day, Allie's plan was to paint the fireplace. Thus, the correct answer is that she decided to "paint the brick firepit white."

10. **(A):** The characters' interactions, as depicted in the passage, showcase a harmonious environment. They engage in collaborative activities like cooking and house chores, enjoying music and dance. There's no indication of stress or discomfort, making the atmosphere appear "relaxed and comfortable."

11. **(A):** From the passage, we gather the following: (*a*) Nancy - "She took me by the hand walked me into the lobby like a five-year old child." Thus, Nancy treated the narrator as if he was very young, which matches with (*i*). (*b*) Allie - "She'd make pancakes for breakfast..." clearly aligns with Allie making pancakes or option (*ii*). (*c*) Alex - "or he'd fry up some sausage and eggs". This line directly refers to Alex's cooking activities, indicating (*iii*). (*d*) Narrator - "This was the third home Nancy was placing me in..." which means the narrator was being placed in multiple homes, corresponding with (*iv*).

12. **(A):** The passage's narrative revolves around the experiences of a teenager, presumably without parents, as indicated by mentions of foster care and multiple placements in different homes. The theme of the story underscores the trials and tribulations, as well as the moments of warmth, faced by children in foster care. The recurrent mention of "foster home" and the transition between them makes it evident that the narrator was in the care system, making the option about "foster home for the narrator and other foster children" the most logical inference from the story.

13. **(A):** Slavery existed in ancient Egypt but what set it apart from many other ancient civilizations was the treatment of slaves. The passage specifically states that "Slavery was not very important in ancient Egypt, but it did exist." It further clarifies that slaves were usually treated well and even had the right to own property. This contrasts with many ancient societies where slaves were often treated poorly and had very limited rights, if any at all.

14. **(A):** The term 'serfs' in the context of the passage refers to workers whose freedom was limited. They were tied to the land or estates where they worked, and they could be bought and sold along with these estates. This feudal-like system bound the serfs to the land, making their economic and personal freedoms restricted. In essence, while they weren't slaves, they lacked many of the rights associated with free citizens.

15. **(B):** While the Pharaohs believed that their connections with the Gods were responsible for Egypt's prosperity, it was, in reality, the hard work and labor of ordinary people that drove the nation forward. They worked in various sectors, from agriculture to mining, which contributed to the overall development and sustenance of the ancient Egyptian civilization. The strength of a civilization often rests on the shoulders of its everyday workers, and in ancient Egypt, this was no different.

16. **(C):** The passage clearly mentions that the Pharaohs had a strong belief that their connections with the Gods were what favored Egypt. This belief, however, contrasts with the reality, which was that the ordinary people's hard work and contributions were the actual foundation of Egypt's success.

17. **(D):** The passage explicitly states that "Slavery was not very important in ancient Egypt," which directly contradicts the statement "Slavery was extremely important in ancient Egypt." Thus, the latter statement is incorrect based on the information provided.

18. **(C):** By matching the provided lists: (*a*) "Serfs could be bought and sold along with the estates where they worked," which corresponds to (*iii*). (*b*) The passage says, "Farmers had to be registered with the government," aligning with (*i*). (*c*) During the season of the Nile floods, when fields lay underwater, "many workers were recruited into public building projects," matching with (*ii*). (*d*) The passage mentions a "harsh punishment for those who ran away," which correlates with (*iv*). Therefore, the correct match is (*a*)-(*iii*), (*b*)-(*i*), (*c*)-(*ii*) and (*d*)-(*iv*).

19. **(C):** Acquitted refers to the formal and legal declaration that someone is not guilty of a criminal charge. It is the conclusion of a judicial process that finds the accused innocent. On the other hand, "Convicted" means that a person has been found guilty of a criminal charge. Therefore, it stands as the direct opposite of "Acquitted".

20. **(D):** "Relinquish" means to voluntarily give up or let go of something, especially some rights, title, or possession. It signifies the act of releasing or parting with something one holds. Contrarily, "Possess" implies owning, holding, or having control over something. If you relinquish your right to something, you're giving up your claim or control over it. But if you possess something, it's in your ownership or control. This dynamic displays the contrasting nature of the two terms.

21. **(A):** "Capacious" is an adjective used to describe something that has the ability to contain a lot, often used in the context of a space or container being large in size or volume. Think of a capacious room or a capacious bag—they can hold much. The term "Limited" points towards something being confined, restricted, or not expansive. In the context of space or volume, "Limited" would mean that there's a lack of abundance or room. Thus, it serves as the antonym to "Capacious".

22. **(D):** The term "Fraudulent" relates to deceit, trickery, or wrongful deception with the intention to gain something (often monetary) or deceive someone. It's associated with acts that are not genuine or honest. "Genuine", conversely, denotes authenticity, realness, or being free from pretense, affectation, or deceit. A genuine item is real and not a counterfeit, and a genuine person is sincere and not trying to deceive. Given this contrast in their inherent meanings, "Genuine" stands opposite to "Fraudulent".

23. **(C):** The expression "laboured ease" stands out as a juxtaposition of contradictory terms. "Laboured" typically denotes something that requires effort or hard work, whereas "ease" signifies comfort or lack of difficulty. When combined, these words create an oxymoron, which is a figure of speech that merges contrasting ideas to portray complex emotions or situations. In this case, the oxymoron "laboured ease" conveys the paradoxical feeling of finding comfort or acceptance in loss, even though the process is painful.

24. **(B):** The phrase "Far Far from gusty waves" prominently displays the repetition of the initial sound "f" in both "Far" and "from". This deliberate use of the same initial consonant sound in closely positioned or consecutive words is called alliteration. Alliteration is employed in both prose and poetry to create rhythm, catch the reader's attention, and emphasize particular sections of the text.

25. **(A):** In the statement "The smiling young trees provided a strange comfort," trees are ascribed the human-like quality of "smiling." Trees, in reality, do not smile, but this attribution of a human trait to a non-human entity is called personification. Personification is a figurative device that endows animals, objects, or abstract ideas with human characteristics or behaviors, making them more relatable and allowing writers to create vivid imagery and emotional resonance.

26. **(C):** The phrase "Like angels from heaven the paratrooper landed on earth" draws a direct comparison between the paratrooper and angels using the word "like." This comparative statement that uses "like" or "as" to draw parallels between two dissimilar entities is known as a simile. Similes are a staple of poetic language, enabling poets to conjure imaginative visuals and evoke deeper emotions by juxtaposing familiar concepts with unfamiliar or unexpected ones. Here, the comparison magnifies the gracefulness and perhaps the surprise of the paratrooper's landing.

27. **(B):** The idiom "to be at sixes and sevens" signifies being in a state of confusion or disarray. It traces its origins to a dispute between two London guilds about their precedence in the 14th century. The guilds, the Merchant Taylors and the Skinners, were both founded in close succession, leading to the debate. In various processions, they rotated their positions annually between the sixth and seventh spots, hence the phrase. Over time, the term became more generalized, referring

to any state of confusion or disorder, and not just about specific rankings.

28. (C): The expression "once in a blue moon" denotes an event that happens very infrequently. A blue moon refers to the rare occurrence when there are two full moons in one calendar month. Traditionally, each month has one full moon, but occasionally, the lunar cycle's timing aligns such that a second full moon, termed a "blue moon," appears. Although blue moons are not technically blue, the rarity of the phenomenon has led to the popularization of this phrase in English language, symbolizing something that doesn't happen often.

29. (A): To go on "a wild goose chase" means to pursue something that is unattainable or is a fruitless endeavor. Historically, a "wild goose chase" was a type of horse race in which the lead rider pursued a course of his choosing and others followed at set intervals, much like wild geese flying in formation. Over time, the phrase's meaning shifted, and it began to refer to a pointless or unattainable pursuit, mirroring the futility of chasing after a wild goose.

30. (D): The idiom "to burn a hole in the pocket" refers to the urge to spend money rapidly, especially when one has disposable income or newfound wealth. The visual imagery suggests money being so hot or uncomfortable that it "burns" its way out of one's pocket, emphasizing the impulsive nature of the spending. This expression underlines the human tendency to sometimes act irresponsibly with money, especially when one feels they have more than they're used to.

31. (C): The word "PUGNACIOUS" is derived from the Latin word "pugnare", which means "to fight". It refers to a person who is eager or quick to argue, quarrel, or fight. Thus, the word "Quarrelsome" best captures its essence. Pugnacious individuals are often confrontational and can be challenging to engage with in discussions because of their aggressive nature. Their readiness to dispute can make collaborations difficult, as they may often challenge perspectives aggressively, even if the situation doesn't warrant such a reaction.

32. (A): To "CLING" is to hold on tightly to something or someone. It can also refer to objects that stick closely to surfaces, like wet clothes that cling to the body. The word "Attach" closely resonates with this meaning. In a more abstract sense, people might cling to ideas, memories, or feelings, indicating a reluctance to let go or move on. Attachment can be both physical, like sticking or adhering to a surface, and emotional, like being closely bound or connected to a thought, feeling, or another person.

33. (B): The term "ENCHANTING" is used to describe something that is charming or captivating, often in a delightful or magical way. Something enchanting draws you in and holds your attention because of its beauty or charm. The word "Pleasant" is closely aligned with this sentiment. Enchanting experiences or sights can often evoke feelings of wonder and amazement. They often stand out in memory because of the strong positive emotions they generate. Such moments or things leave a lasting impact, making us want to relive or revisit them.

34. (B): "GIGANTIC" describes something that is very large or enormous in size. It emphasizes an extreme scale or magnitude that often surpasses ordinary standards or expectations. "Monstrous" in this context aligns closely with this meaning, emphasizing the vastness or enormity of something. When we refer to something as gigantic, we often compare it with regular-sized counterparts to underscore its impressive or overwhelming size. The term has its roots in the word "gigant", which historically referred to the Giants of Greek mythology, legendary beings renowned for their immense size and strength.

35. (A): A "Decade" specifically refers to a period of 10 years. Originating from the Greek word 'dekas', which means 'ten', it is commonly used to categorize historical, technological, cultural, or personal events and advancements. For instance, the 1960s is referred to as a decade, and it's often associated with cultural revolutions, civil rights movements, and significant shifts in music and fashion. It's a convenient way to encapsulate years that share common characteristics.

36. (B): A "Bibliophile" is an individual who has a great appreciation for or collects books. The term is derived from the Greek words 'biblion' (book) and 'philos' (loving). A bibliophile often possesses a deep reverence for books, not just for their content, but sometimes also for their physical form, binding, history, and even the art of bookmaking. While all bibliophiles love books, not all of them are collectors. Some might just enjoy reading and surrounding themselves with books without the intent of collecting rare or antique editions.

37. (D): "Infanticide" is the act of killing an infant, usually by a parent. The term comes from Latin 'infans', meaning unable to speak, and 'caedere', which means to kill. Historically and in some cultures, infanticide was practiced for various reasons, including economic distress, the undesirability of the child due to gender or deformities, or societal pressures. Modern societies largely condemn and criminalize infanticide, viewing it as a heinous act. However, it's essential to understand the underlying causes, such as postpartum depression or societal pressures, that might drive someone to commit such an act.

38. (C): An "Itinerary" is a detailed plan or route of a journey. It can be as basic as a list of places one intends to visit or as detailed as specifying dates, times, modes of transportation, and lodging details. People often use itineraries when planning trips to ensure they maximize their time and experiences. Travel agents, tour operators, or even individuals planning their vacations often draft itineraries. In a broader sense, an itinerary can also refer to a planned route or journey for business trips, political campaigns, or any event that requires traveling between multiple locations.

39. (A): "Attach" and "Detach" are antonyms. While "attach" means to fasten or join something to something else, "detach" refers to the act of separating or removing something. Similarly, "Barren" and "Fertile" are antonyms. A barren land is one that cannot produce or is too poor to produce vegetation, while fertile land is rich in nutrients and is conducive for the growth of plants. These terms often describe soil quality in agriculture. Fertile soils are sought after for farming because they can support a diverse range of crops and result in better yields.

40. (A): "Medley" and "Mixture" are synonymous. Both words refer to a combination of different things. For instance, in music, a medley is a blend of several tunes played one after another. Likewise, a mixture refers to a substance made by combining two or more different materials. Similarly, "Iterate" and "Repeat" convey the same idea. To iterate is to say or perform again, often used in the context of computer programming or design processes. Repeat, a more general term, simply implies doing something again.

41. (C): "Retreat" and "Advance" are antonyms. Retreat means to withdraw or move back, often used in military contexts when referring to troops moving away from enemy forces. On the other hand, advance means to move forward or make progress. Similarly, "Savage" and "Civilised" are opposites. A society described as savage is viewed as primitive or lacking the cultural and social refinements of a civilized society. It's essential to approach these terms with caution, as labeling a society "savage" can be ethnocentric and disrespectful. It's always crucial to respect cultural differences without imposing judgments based on one's own cultural standards.

42. (B): "Meek" and "Modest" are similar in their connotations. While meek implies a mild nature or submissive character, modest means having or showing a moderate estimation of one's abilities or achievements. It's about not being boastful or arrogant. Similarly, "Finally" and "Eventually" are synonymous. Both terms denote an outcome that follows a series of events or a period. For instance, "She finally/ eventually arrived at the party" means she arrived after some delay or events. Both words indicate the culmination of waiting or anticipation.

43. (C): The correct spelling is "Catastrophic." The term "catastrophic" refers to something that causes or involves a catastrophe, which is a sudden and widespread disaster. The root word "catastrophe" comes from the Greek "katastrophç," meaning an overturning or a sudden end. In contemporary usage, the word can describe natural disasters like earthquakes or human-made disasters like wars. It's also frequently used in casual speech to refer to significant failures or blunders.

44. (B): The rightly spelt word is "Communism." Communism is a sociopolitical and economic ideology and movement whose ultimate goal is the establishment of a communist society, which is a socioeconomic order structured upon the ideas of common ownership of the means of production and the absence of social classes, money, and the state.

45. (A): "Cooperative" is the correct spelling. A cooperative is a business organization owned and operated by a group of individuals for their mutual benefit. It can also describe a willingness to cooperate with others.

46. (B): "Pneumonia" is the correctly spelt term. Pneumonia is a type of infection that inflames the air sacs in one or both lungs. The air sacs may fill with fluid or pus, causing cough, fever, chills, and difficulty breathing. The "p" at the beginning of the word is silent, which can make the pronunciation and spelling tricky for some.

47. (C): The correct sequence is "(*c*) A large scale exchange of nuclear weapons (*b*) Will produce an unprecedented amount (*d*) Of radiation that can (*a*) Penetrate the biological tissues." From a grammatical perspective, this arrangement forms a subject-predicate-object construction, which is standard in English grammar. Here, "(*c*) A large scale exchange of nuclear weapons" acts as the subject, "(*b*) Will produce" is the verb phrase, and the remaining parts "(*d*) Of radiation" and "(*a*) Penetrate the biological tissues" work as the object and modifier, respectively, providing more details about the consequences of the action.

48. (B): The coherent arrangement is "(*c*) The mission has provided (*d*) Able service to all the needy (*b*) People in this area (*a*) During the last few years." This sequence begins with the main clause "(*c*) The mission has provided (*d*) Able service" which provides the core information. Following this, "(*b*) People in this area" acts as the qualifier, giving specifics about the recipients. Finally, "(*a*) During the last few years" serves as a temporal adverbial phrase, situating the action in time.

49. (A): The proper order is "(*c*) He has received (*d*) No other message other than (*b*) An urgent telegram asking (*a*) Him to rush to his village immediately." Starting with "(*c*) He has received" introduces the subject and the verb. The clause "(*d*) No other message other than" acts as a restrictive modifier, emphasizing the uniqueness of the message. The phrases "(*b*) An urgent telegram asking" and "(*a*) Him to rush to his village immediately" provide further details, functioning as object and purpose clause respectively.

50. (C): The correct sequence is "(*a*) He managed to make sense (*c*) Of the book even though (*b*) It was the first time when (*d*) He read anything on the subject." The main clause is "(*a*) He managed to make sense (*c*) Of the book," where "He" is the subject, "managed" is the verb, and "Of the book" is the prepositional phrase acting as an object. The clause "(*b*) It was the first time when (*d*) He read anything on the subject" is a subordinate clause providing a reason or condition for the main clause, with "It" referring to the act of understanding the book.

HISTORY

1. Which of the following was a class of people in the countryside that lived off agriculture but did not participate directly in the process of agricultural production?

   A. Zamindars B. Mandals
   C. Patidar D. Jotedars

2. Over 95 per cent of the sale of mahals held by the Raja of Burdwan at the auction was fictitious because:

   (*a*) The sale was done by evading the tax.
   (*b*) The Raja was happy on this sale.
   (*c*) The Raja's estates had been publicly sold, but he remained in control of his zamindari.
   (*d*) Many of the purchasers turned out to be servants and agents of the Raja who had bought the lands on behalf of their master.

   Choose the ***correct*** answer from the options given below:

   A. (*a*) and (*b*) Only B. (*b*) and (*c*) Only
   C. (*c*) and (*d*) Only D. (*a*) and (*d*) Only

3. Francis Buchanan, the British official had a visit to the hills of the Paharias in the year:

   A. 1810 B. 1820
   C. 1910 D. 1920

4. One of the main sources of our knowledge about what the rebels wanted is:

   A. The books written by the rebel leaders
   B. The Azamgarh Proclamation, 25 August, 1857
   C. The official records of the British
   D. The British newspapers

5. Which Governor General adopted policies aimed at "reforming" Indian society by introducing English education,

   A. Lord Wellseley B. Lord William Bentinck
   C. Lord Cornwallis D. Lord Irwin

6. Which of the following is not an architectural style of the British buildings in India:

   A. Neo-Gothic style B. Neo-Classical style
   C. Persian style D. Indo-Saracenic style

7. In the context of the Revolt of 1857 the term "revolt" refers primarily to:

   A. The uprising of the civilian population (Peasants, Zamindars, Rajas, Jagirdars)
   B. The uprising of the Sepoys only
   C. The National Movement
   D. The uprising of the tribals

8. The Ain-i-Akbari is made up of several books, choose the correct one:

   A. Three B. Six
   C. Four D. Five

9. Which party announced "Direct Action Day" in British India?

   A. Indian National Congress
   B. Swaraj Party
   C. Muslim League
   D. Hindu Mahasabha

10. Why did people believe in the rumours during the 1857 Revolt of? Arrange the following in sequence:

    (*a*) In situations of uncertainty rumours spread swiftly
    (*b*) Rumours circulated only when they resonated with deeper fears and suspicion
    (*c*) The British established laws to abolish "Sati" and permit widow remarriage
    (*d*) The activities of Christian missionaries aggravated oppressive perceptions

    Choose the ***correct*** answer from the options given below:

    A. (*a*), (*b*), (*c*), (*d*) B. (*d*), (*c*), (*a*), (*b*)
    C. (*b*), (*a*), (*c*), (*d*) D. (*b*), (*c*), (*d*), (*a*)

11. The East India Company set up its trading activities first in:

    A. Madras B. Calcutta
    C. Surat D. Bombay

12. In which year was Bombay given to the British Crown as a part of the dowry of Queen Catherine of Braganza?

    A. 1659 B. 1661
    C. 1663 D. 1665

13. Who was the political guru of Mahatma Gandhi?

    A. Bal Gandadhar Tilak B. Bipin Chandra Pal
    C. Lala Lajpat Rai D. Gopal Krishna Gokhale

14. The judge who presided over the trial of Gandhiji after the Non-Cooperation Movement was:

    A. Louis Fisher B. Lord Irwin
    C. C.N. Broomfield D. George Orwell

15. From the jumbled events, select the correct sequencing:

    (*a*) Mahatma Gandhi attends the Second Round Table Conference at London.
    (*b*) The Dandi March marks the beginning of the Civil Disobedience Movement.
    (*c*) The Quit India Movement takes place.
    (*d*) At the Lahore session of the Indian National Congress "Purna Swaraj" was accepted as the goal.

Choose the ***correct*** answer from the options given below:

A. (*b*), (*d*), (*a*), (*c*) B. (*c*), (*a*), (*b*), (*d*)
C. (*a*), (*b*), (*c*), (*d*) D. (*d*), (*b*), (*a*), (*c*)

16. Find the wrong pair:
(*a*) Labour government in London : 1945
(*b*) Cabinet Mission : 1940
(*c*) Direct Action Day : 1946
(*d*) Partition of India : 1947
(*e*) Quit India Movement : 1941

Choose the ***correct*** answer from the options given below:

A. (*c*), (*d*) only B. (*b*), (*e*) only
C. (*a*), (*b*), (*c*) only D. (*d*), (*e*), (*a*) only

17. Which of the following combination of statements is correct:
(*a*) In 1937, first time Provincial Elections held.
(*b*) The Muslim League failed to win a single seat ir the North West Frontier Province.
(*c*) The Muslim League did very good in reserved constituencies.
(*d*) All the adult population exercised voting right in 1937.

Choose the ***correct*** answer from the options given below:

A. (*b*) and (*c*) only B. (*a*) and (*b*) only
C. (*c*) and (*a*) only D. (*d*) and (*a*) only

18. Find out the arrangement of these statements in sequence:
(*a*) When Jotiba Phule in Maharashtra pointed to the suffering of the depressed castes, he was demanding economic and social justice.
(*b*) When social reformers opposed child marriage, they were pleading for social justice.
(*c*) The National Movement against a government that was oppressive was a struggle for democracy and justice, rights and equality.
(*d*) The Constituent Assembly expressed the aspirations of those who had participated in the movement, for independence.

Choose the ***correct*** answer from the options given below:

A. (*a*), (*b*), (*c*), (*d*) B. (*b*), (*a*), (*c*), (*d*)
C. (*d*), (*b*), (*a*), (*c*) D. (*c*), (*a*), (*b*), (*d*)

19. The notion of minority as defined by N.G. Ranga was:
A. Minorities for Ranga were Hindus in Pakistan
B. Minorities for Ranga were the Sikhs and Muslims
C. Minorities for Ranga were the Hindus, Sikhs, Muslims and Tribals
D. Minorities for Ranga were the poor and the downtrodden

20. Put the following statements in sequence :
(*a*) Dr. B.R. Ambedkar was appointed as the law minister with the recommendation of Gandhiji
(*b*) Vallabhbhai Patel worked mostly behind the scenes, drafting several reports
(*c*) Jawaharlal Nehru declared the "Objectives Resolution", defining ideas of the Constitution
(*d*) Steering constructive discussion in the Constituent Assembly was taken care of by Dr. Rajendra Prasad

Choose the ***correct*** answer from the options given below:

A. (*a*), (*d*), (*c*), (*b*) B. (*d*), (*a*), (*b*), (*c*)
C. (*b*), (*a*), (*c*), (*d*) D. (*c*), (*b*), (*d*), (*a*)

21. In the Vitthala temple, the principal diety was Vitthala, a form of Vishnu it was worshipped in which region?
A. Karnataka
B. Maharashtra
C. Madhya Pradesh
D. Andhra Pradesh

22. Match List-I with List-II:

***List-I* (*Terms used for Ruling Lineages*)**	***List-II* (*The Ruling Lineages for which these terms were used*)**
(*a*) Gajapati	(*i*) The Rayas of Vijayanagara
(*b*) Ashvapati	(*ii*) The Rulers of Orissa
(*c*) Narapati	(*iii*) The Deccan Sultans

Choose the ***correct*** answer from the options given below:

	(*a*)	(*b*)	(*c*)
A.	(*ii*)	(*iii*)	(*i*)
B.	(*i*)	(*ii*)	(*iii*)
C.	(*iii*)	(*ii*)	(*i*)
D.	(*ii*)	(*i*)	(*iii*)

23. The first revenue settlement in the Bombay Deccan was made in:
A. 1850s B. 1840s
C. 1830s D. 1820s

24. Arrange the following events in the correct order of their occurrence:
(*a*) Thousands killed in Amritsar on Independence Day.
(*b*) Tension grew due to the rule of music before the mosque.
(*c*) Pakistan Resolution passed by Muslim League.
(*d*) Riots in Calcutta by people armed with rods and lathis.
(*e*) Meeting between Mahatma Gandhi and Abdul Gaffar Khan in NWFP.

Choose the ***correct*** answer from the options given below:

A. (*a*), (*b*), (*c*), (*d*), (*e*) B. (*b*), (*e*), (*d*), (*a*), (*c*)
C. (*c*), (*b*), (*a*), (*e*), (*d*) D. (*b*), (*e*), (*c*), (*d*), (*a*)

25. Which of the following is an imperial order?

A. Farman B. Salat

C. Fatwa D. Hukum

26. Match List-I with List-II:

List-I *(Different Sufi Terms)*	*List-II* *(Their meanings)*
(*a*) Sama	(*i*) Pilgrimage
(*b*) Zikr	(*ii*) Hospice
(*c*) Khanqah	(*iii*) Audition
(*d*) Ziyarat	(*iv*) Reciting the divine names

Choose the ***correct*** answer from the options given below:

	(*a*)	(*b*)	(*c*)	(*d*)
A.	(*iv*)	(*iii*)	(*ii*)	(*i*)
B.	(*iii*)	(*iv*)	(*ii*)	(*i*)
C.	(*i*)	(*ii*)	(*iii*)	(*iv*)
D.	(*ii*)	(*iii*)	(*i*)	(*iv*)

27. Which of the following travellers wrote about the way silver travelled across the globe to reach India?

A. Duarte Barbosa B. Domingo Paes

C. Giovanni Careri D. Francois Bernier

28. Who among the following was the author of the book "Rihla"?

A. Peter Mundy B. Marco Polo

C. Al Biruni D. Ibn Battuta

29. Match List-I with List-II:

List-I *(Foreign Travellers)*	*List-II* *(Country they came from)*
(*a*) Nicolo de Conti	(*i*) Portugal
(*b*) Abdur Razzaq Samarqandi	(*ii*) Russia
(*c*) Afanasii Nikitin	(*iii*) Italy
(*d*) Domingo Paes	(*iv*) Iran

Choose the ***correct*** answer from the options given below:

	(*a*)	(*b*)	(*c*)	(*d*)
A.	(*iv*)	(*iii*)	(*ii*)	(*i*)
B.	(*iii*)	(*iv*)	(*ii*)	(*i*)
C.	(*iii*)	(*ii*)	(*iv*)	(*i*)
D.	(*iii*)	(*iv*)	(*i*)	(*ii*)

30. The "Peshkash" levied on forest people often included the supply of ______.

A. Grains B. Elephants

C. Woods D. Horses

31. Which of the following is NOT true about Jainsim?

A. The basic philosophy of Jainism was popular even before the birth of Mahavira

B. It believed that entire world is animated

C. It asserted that the cycle of birth and rebirth is shaped through karma

D. Eight vows were taken up by the Jaina monks

32. According to which text, Ashoka distributed portions of the Buddha'a relics to every important town and ordered the construction of stupas over them?

A. Vinayapita B. Ashokavadana

C. Divyavadana D. Sutta Pitaka

33. As the discussion between pro-Hindi and anti-Hindi members of the Constituent Assembly became acrimonious, many members appealed for a spirit of accommodation. One of such member was:

A. R.V. Dhulekar

B. G Durgabai

C. Shri Shankarrao Deo

D. J Nagappa

34. Who was the author of the book "The Other Side of Silence"?

A. Saadat Hasan Manto B. Khushdeva Singh

C. Prakash Tandon D. Urvashi Butalia

35. Brahmi and Kharoshti, two scripts used in earliest inscriptions and coins, were deciphered by:

A. Alexandar Cunningham

B. R.E.M. Wheeler

C. James Prinsep

D. John Marshall

36. Match List-I with List-II:

List-I	*List-II*
(*a*) Silappadikaram	(*i*) Tamil Epic
(*b*) Prayaga Prashasti	(*ii*) Written by Harishena
(*c*) Informs about Sanguttuvan visit to forest	(*iii*) Prayaga Prashasti
(*d*) Praises Samudra Gupta	(*iv*) Silappadikaram

Choose the ***correct*** answer from the options given below:

	(*a*)	(*b*)	(*c*)	(*d*)
A.	(*i*)	(*ii*)	(*iv*)	(*iii*)
B.	(*i*)	(*ii*)	(*iii*)	(*iv*)
C.	(*iv*)	(*iii*)	(*ii*)	(*i*)
D.	(*iii*)	(*iv*)	(*i*)	(*ii*)

37. The Lottery Committee was commissioned in the city of:

A. Madras B. Bombay

C. Calcutta D. Kanpur

38. Ploughing as agriculture technique was practiced in Harappan Civilization.

Which one of the following is **NOT** the evidence to prove the above statement?

A. Terracotta models of plough have been found at the sites of Cholistan and Banawali

B. Motifs of plough displayed on the seals have been found

C. Representation of bull on seals which might have been used for ploughing

D. Evidence of ploughed field at Kalibangan

39. Match List-I with List-II:

List-I	*List-II*
(*a*) Haza-bird	(*i*) Oman
(*b*) Magan	(*ii*) Peacock
(*c*) Dilmun	(*iii*) Harappan region
(*d*) Meluhha	(*iv*) Bahrain

Choose the ***correct*** answer from the options given below:

	(*a*)	(*b*)	(*c*)	(*d*)
A.	(*ii*)	(*i*)	(*iv*)	(*iii*)
B.	(*i*)	(*ii*)	(*iii*)	(*iv*)
C.	(*iv*)	(*iii*)	(*ii*)	(*i*)
D.	(*iii*)	(*ii*)	(*iv*)	(*i*)

40. The British authorities invited the Santhals to settle in the Rajmahal Hills. Choose the correct statements:

(*a*) They were the original inhabitants of the Rajmahal Hills

(*b*) They were eager to adopt settled agriculture

(*c*) They were very powerful zamindars

(*d*) The Santhals forced the Paharias to move deeper into the hills, as the British wanted.

Choose the ***correct*** answer from the options given, below:

A. (*a*) and (*c*) Only B. (*c*) and (*b*) Only
C. (*b*) and (*d*) Only D. (*a*) and (*b*) Only

Directions (Qs. No. 41-45): *Read the following text and answer the following questions:*

Painters too were involved in the production of Mughal manuscripts. Chronicles narrating the events of a Mughal emperor's reign contained, alongside the written text images that described an event in visual form, When scenes or themes in a book were to be given visual expression, the scribe left blank spaces on nearby pages; paintings, executed separately on nearby pages; paintings, executes separately by artists, were inserted to accompany what was described in words. These paintings were miniatures, and could therefore be passed around for viewing and mounting on the pages of manuscripts.

Paintings served not only to enhance the beauty of a book, but were believed to possess special powers of communicating ideas about the kingdom and the power of kings in ways that the written medium could not. The historian Abu'l Fazl described painting as a "magical art": in his view it had the power to make inanimate objects look as if they possessed life.

41. ______, executed separately by artisits, were inserted to accompany the description in words:

A. Manuscripts B. Scribes
C. Paintings D. Writers

42. Chronicles narrated the events of a Mughal Court and alongside the written text ______ described events.

A. Comments on text B. Images
C. Critical notes D. Calligraphy

43. ______ too were involved in the production of manuscripts.

A. Painters B. Publishers
C. Biographer D. Chronicles

44. The painter introduced a new kind of painting for mounting on the page of manuscripts:

A. Illumination with silver and gold foil
B. Elaborate illustration
C. Portrait painting
D. Miniature painting

45. Painting possesses special powers of ______ ideas.

A. Developing B. Generating
C. Communicating D. Conceptualising

Directions (Qs. No. 46-50): *Read the following text and answer the following questions:*

These complexities are reflected in another term used in texts to refer to social categories - *jati*. In Brahmanical theory, *jati*, like varna, was based on birth. However, while the number of *varnas* was fixed at four, there was no restriction on the number of *jatis*. In fact, whenever Brahmanical authorities encountered new groups- for instance, people living in forests such as the *nishadas*- or wanted to assign a name to occupational categories such as the goldsmith or *suvarnakara*, which did not easily fit into the fourfold varna system, they classified them into the fourfold varna system, they classified them as a *jati*, *Jatis* which shared a common occupation or profession were sometimes organised into shrenis or guilds.

We seldom come across documents that record the histories of these groups.

46. In Brahmanical theory Jati was based on ______ like Varna.

A. Birth B. Patriling
C. Community D. Social background

47. The number of Varnas was fixed at four, for number of Jatis there was no ______.

A. Literary information
B. Restriction
C. Exact instruction in the Brahmanical text
D. Evidence

48. Certain communities were assigned a name of occupational category such as ______.

A. Nishada B. Shudras
C. Suvarnakara D. Peasants

49. Jatis which shared a common occupation or profession organised into ______.

A. New Caste B. Varnas
C. Chiefs D. Shrenis

50. People living in forests were named in Brahmanical text, Ekalavya belonged to ______.

A. The hunter gatherer B. Nishadas
C. Mlechchhas D. Yavanas

ANSWERS

1. **(A):** Our history of agrarian relations in Mughal India will not be complete without referring to a class of people in the countryside that lived off agriculture but did not participate directly in the processes of agricultural production. These were the zamindars who were land proprietors who also enjoyed certain social and economic privileges by virtue of their superior status in rural society. Caste was one factor that accounted for the elevated status of zamindars; another factor was that they performed certain services (khidmat) for the state.

   The zamindars held extensive personal lands termed milkiyat, meaning property. Milkiyat lands were cultivated for the private use of zamindars, often with the help of hired or servile labour. The zamindars could sell, bequeath or mortgage these lands at will. Zamindars also derived their power from the fact that they could often collect revenue on behalf of the state, a service for which they were compensated financially. Control over military resources was another source of power. Most zamindars had fortresses (qilachas) as well as an armed contingent comprising unit of cavalry, artillery and infantry.

   Thus, if we visualise social relations in the Mughal countryside as a pyramid, zamindars clearly constituted its very narrow apex. Abu'l Fazl's account indicates that an "upper-caste", Brahmana-Rajput combine had already established firm control over rural society.

2. **(C):** In 1797 there was an auction in Burdwan (present-day Bardhaman). It was a big public event. A number of *mahals* (estates) held by the Raja of Burdwan were being sold. The Permanent Settlement had come into operation in 1793. The East India Company had fixed the revenue that each zamindar had to pay. The estates of those who failed to pay were to be auctioned to recover the revenue. Since the raja had accumulated huge arrears, his estates had been put up for auction. Numerous purchasers came to the auction and the estates were sold to the highest bidder. But the Collector soon discovered a strange twist to the tale. Many of the purchasers turned out to be servants and agents of the raja who has bought the lands on behalf of their master. Over 95 per cent of the sale at the auction was fictitious. The raja's estates had been publicly sold, but the remained in control of his zamindari.

3. **(A):** Francis Buchanan was a physician who came to India and served in the Bengal Medical Service from 1794 to 1815. He was a surgeon to the Governor General of India, Lord Wellesley, for a few years. During his stay in Calcutta (now Kolkata), he organized a zoo that became the Calcutta Alipore Zoo. He was also in charge of the Botanical Gardens for a short time. At the request of the Government of Bengal, he conducted extensive surveys of the areas under the control of the British East India Company.

   Francis Buchanan travelled through Rajmahal hills in 1810 and gave an account about it. Originally in the Rajmahal hills Paharias lived. They lived on hunting, shifting cultivation, food-gathering and was intimately connected to forest. In last decade of 18th century British encouraged forest clearance and Zamindar and Jotedar also started to turn uncultivated land into rice fields. As settled agriculture expanded, the area under forest and pasture contracted. This sharpened the conflict between Paharias and settled cultivators. Around 1780, Santhal came into these areas. They cleared the forest and ploughed land. As the lower hills were taken over by the Santhal Settlers, the Paharias receded interior into the Rajmahal hills.

   He fell ill in 1815 and returned to England. Upon his mother's death, he inherited her property and assumed the name of her family, Hamilton. So as called Buchanan-Hamilton.

4. **(B):** Azamgarh Proclamation is one of the main sources of knowledge about what the rebels wanted during the Revolt of 1857. It was issued on 25th August, 1857.

   It is well known to all, that in this age the people of Hindustan, both Hindus and Mohammedans, are being ruined under the tyranny and the oppression of the infidel and treacherous English. It is therefore the bounden duty of all the wealthy people of India, especially those who have any sort of connection with the Mohammedan Royal families and are considered the pastors and masters of their people, to stake, their lives and property for the well-being of the public.

   The proclamations completely rejected everything associated with British rule of firangi raj as they called it. They condemned the British for the annexations they had carried out and the treaties they had broken. The British, the rebel leaders said, could not be trusted.

5. **(B):** The rumours in 1857 begin to make sense when seen in the context of the policies the British pursued from the late 1820s. As you know, from that time, under the leadership of Governor General Lord

William Bentinck, the British adopted policies aimed at "reforming" Indian society by introducing Western education, Western ideas and Western institutions. With the cooperation of sections of Indian society they set up English-medium schools, colleges and universities which taught Western sciences and the liberal arts.

6. (C): For public buildings three broad architectural styles were used. Two of these were direct imports from fashions prevalent in England. The first was called neo-classical or the new classical. Its characteristics included construction of geometrical structures fronted with lofty pillars. It was derived from a style that was originally typical of buildings in ancient Rome, and was subsequently revived.

Another style that was extensively used was the neo-Gothic, characterised by high-pitched roofs, pointed arches and detailed decoration. The Gothic style had its roots in buildings, especially churches, built in northern Europe during the medieval period. The neo-Gothic or new Gothic style was revived in the mid-nineteenth century in England. This was the time when the government in Bombay was building its infrastructure and this style was adapted for Bombay. An impressive group of buildings facing the seafront including the Secretariat, University of Bombay and High Court were all built in this style.

Towards the beginning of the twentieth century a new hybrid architectural style developed which combined the Indian with the European. This was called Indo-Saracenic. "Indo" was shorthand for Hindu and "Saracen" was a term Europeans used to designate Muslim. The inspiration for the style was medieval buildings in India with their domes, *chhatris, jalis,* arches. By integrating Indian and European styles in public architecture the British wanted to prove that they were legitimate rulers of India. The Gateway of India, built in the traditional Gujarati style to welcome King George V and Queen Mary to India in 1911, is the most famous example of this style.

7. (A): In the context of the revolt of 1857 the term revolt refers primarily to the uprising of the civilian population (peasants, zamindars, rajas, jagirdars) while the mutiny was of the sepoys.

8. (D): Abul Fazl who was one of the nine jewels of Akbar's court and also one of his closest allies wrote a three-volume history of the reign of Akbar. It was titled as Akbar Nama. It was written in the Persian language which was the literary language of the Mughals and included a vivid description of Akbar and his empire. It was produced in the form of a lavish manuscript. It is stated that the book took seven years to complete. It was inspired by the Babur Nama which was written by Babur, founder of the Mughal dynasty. The first volume dealt with the ancestors of Akbar. The second volume recorded all the events that took place during Akbar's reign. The third volume was known as Ain-i-Akbari. It is categorised into five books. The first book is manzil-Abadi, which deals with the imperial household and its maintenance, and the second called sipah-Abadi, which deals with the military and civil matters. The third book dealt with imperial administration, containing provisions about the judiciary and the executive. The fourth book contains information about the customs, traditions, literature, science and Hindu philosophy. The fifth book contains moral sentences said by Akbar, rules of wisdom by the emperor collected by Abul Fazl. The book also contains information about Akbar's ancestors.

Akbar Nama is a very useful source of literary information for the historians as it provides an authentic record of the period during the reign of Akbar. It gave a detailed account of all the aspects of the Mughal Empire.

9. (C): After withdrawing its support to the Cabinet Mission plan, the Muslim League decided on "Direct Action" for winning its Pakistan demand. It announced 16 August, 1946 as "Direct Action Day". On this day, riots broke out in Calcutta, lasting several days and leaving several thousand people dead. By March 1947 violence spread too many parts of northern India.

It was in March 1947 that the Congress high command voted for dividing the Punjab into two halves, one with Muslim majority and the other with Hindu/Sikh majority; and it asked for the application of a similar principle to Bengal.

10. (D): We cannot understand the power of rumours and prophecies in history by checking whether they are factually correct or not. We need to see what they reflect about the minds of people who believed them — their fears and apprehensions, their faiths and convictions. Rumours circulate only when they resonate with the deeper fears and suspicions of people. The rumours in 1857 begin to make sense when seen in the context of the policies the British pursued from the late 1820s. As you know, from that time, under the leadership of Governor General Lord William Bentinck, the British adopted policies aimed at "reforming" Indian society by introducing Western education, Western ideas and Western institutions. With the cooperation of sections of Indian society they set up English-medium schools, colleges and universities which taught Western sciences and the liberal arts. The British established laws to abolish customs like sati (1829) and to permit the remarriage of Hindu widows.

On a variety of pleas, like misgovernment and the refusal to recognise adoption, the British annexed not only Awadh, but many other kingdoms and principalities like Jhansi and Satara. Once these territories were annexed, the British introduced their own system of administration, their own laws and their own methods of land settlement and land revenue collection. The cumulative impact of all this on the people of North India was profound.

It seemed to the people that all that they cherished and held sacred — from kings and socio-religious customs to patterns of landholding and revenue payment — was being destroyed and replaced by a system that was more impersonal, alien and oppressive. This perception was aggravated by the activities of Christian missionaries. In such a situation of uncertainty, rumours spread with remarkable swiftness.

11. (C): The Company had first set up its trading activities in the well-established port of Surat on the west coast. Subsequently the search for textiles brought British merchants to the east coast. In 1639 they constructed a trading post in Madraspatam. This settlement was locally known as Chenapattanam. The Company had purchased the right of settlement from the local Telugu lords, the Nayaks of Kalahasti, who were eager to support trading activity in the region. Rivalry (1746-63) with the French East India Company led the British to fortify Madras and give their representatives increased political and administrative functions. With the defeat of the French in 1761, Madras became more secure and began to grow into an important commercial town. It was here that the superiority of the British and the subordinate position of the Indian merchants were most apparent.

12. (C): Charles II (r. 1660-85) married Catherine of Braganza in May 1662. Part of her large dowry was the Portuguese territory of 'Bom Bahia' (Bombay) on the western coast of India, modern Mumbai. The king agreed to transfer control of Bombay to the East India Company and it soon became their base.

13. (D): Gandhi was deeply influenced by Gopala Krishna Gokhale and referred to him as his political guru. Gokhale encouraged Gandhi to tour India in a third-class railway compartment to understand India. He saw the nation with a very different point of view during his journey.

14. (C): During the Non-Cooperation Movement thousands of Indians were put in jail. Gandhiji himself was arrested in March 1922, and charged with sedition. The judge who presided over his trial, Justice C.N. Broomfield, made a remarkable speech while pronouncing his sentence. "It would be impossible to ignore the fact," remarked the judge, "that you are in a different category from any person I have ever tried or am likely to try. It would be impossible to ignore the fact that, in the eyes of millions of your countrymen, you are a great patriot and a leader. Even those who differ from you in politics look upon you as a man of high ideals and of even saintly life". Since Gandhiji had violated the law it was obligatory for the Bench to sentence him to six years' imprisonment, but, said Judge Broomfield, "If the course of events in India should make it possible for the Government to reduce the period and release you, no one will be better pleased than I".

15. (D): The Purna Swaraj declaration (or complete self-rule independent of the British Empire) was promulgated by the Indian National Congress on 19 December, 1929 in its Lahore session. 26th January 1930 was declared as Purna Swaraj Diwas.

On 12th March, 1930, Gandhiji set out on a March from Dandi to Sabarmati Ashram. The Salt March marked the beginning of the Civil Disobedience Movement.

The second RTC (September-December 1931) was attended by Mahatma Gandhi as the Congress representative. It failed to reach agreement, either constitutionally or on communal representation. The session got deadlocked on the question of the minorities.

On 8 August, 1942 at the All-India Congress Committee session in Bombay, Mohandas Karamchand Gandhi launched the 'Quit India' movement.

16. (B)

17. (B): In 1937, elections to the provincial legislatures were held for the first time. Only about 10 to 12 per cent of the population enjoyed the right to vote. The Congress did well in the elections, winning an absolute majority in five out of eleven provinces and forming governments in seven of them. It did badly in the constituencies reserved for Muslims, but the Muslim League also fared poorly, polling only 4.4 per cent of the total Muslim vote cast in this election. The League failed to win a single seat in the North West Frontier Province (NWFP) and could capture only two out of 84 reserved constituencies in the Punjab and three out of 33 in Sind.

18. (C): The Constituent Assembly was expected to express the aspirations of those who had participated in the movement for independence. Democracy, equality and justice were ideals that had become intimately associated with social struggles in India since the nineteenth century. When the social reformers in the nineteenth century opposed child marriage and demanded that widows be allowed to remarry, they were pleading for social justice. When Swami Vivekananda campaigned for a reform of Hinduism, he wanted religions to become more just. When Jyotiba Phule in Maharashtra pointed to the suffering of the depressed castes, or Communists and Socialists organised workers and peasants, they were demanding economic and social justice. The national movement against a government that was seen as oppressive and illegitimate was inevitably a struggle for democracy and justice, for citizens' rights and equality.

19. **(D):** N.G. Ranga was a socialist who played a significant role in the peasant movement in India. He said that the minorities should be interpreted in economic terms. He believed that the real minorities are the people who are extremely poor and downtrodden. Jaipal Singh belonged to the tribal community so he understood the grievances of the tribals adequately. He said that the tribal groups have been disrespected and confronted for the past 6000 years and now in independent India, they need to be respected and protected. He showed faith in the vision of Nehru's "Objective Resolution", which sought to provide equality of opportunity in India.

The Linguistic minorities wanted the protection of their mother tongue. The religious minorities wanted the right to freely follow their religion without any interference in their faith. The Dalits demanded an end to the discriminatory system of caste-based oppression. The Dalits demanded an end to the discriminatory system of caste-based oppression.

20. **(D):** The Constituent Assembly had 300 members. Of these, six members played particularly important roles. Three were representatives of the Congress, namely, Jawaharlal Nehru, Vallabh Bhai Patel and Rajendra Prasad. It was Nehru who moved the crucial "Objectives Resolution", as well as the resolution proposing that the National Flag of India be a "horizontal tricolour of saffron, white and dark green in equal proportion", with a wheel in navy blue at the centre. Patel, on the other hand, worked mostly behind the scenes, playing a key role in the drafting of several reports, and working to reconcile opposing points of view. Rajendra Prasad's role was as President of the Assembly, where he had to steer the discussion along constructive lines while making sure all members had a chance to speak.

Besides this Congress trio, a very important member of the Assembly was the lawyer and economist B.R. Ambedkar. During the period of British rule, Ambedkar had been a political opponent of the Congress; but, on the advice of Mahatma Gandhi, he was asked at Independence to join the Union Cabinet as law minister. In this capacity, he served as Chairman of the Drafting Committee of the Constitution. Serving with him were two other lawyers, K.M. Munshi from Gujarat and Alladi Krishnaswamy Aiyar from Madras, both of whom gave crucial inputs in the drafting of the Constitution.

21. **(B):** In the Vitthala temple, the principal deity was Vitthala, a form of Vishnu generally worshipped in Maharashtra. The introduction of the worship of the deity in Karnataka is another indication of the ways in which the rulers of Vijayanagara drew on different traditions to create an imperial culture. As in the case of other temples, this temple too has several halls and a unique shrine designed as a chariot. A characteristic feature of the temple complexes is the chariot streets that extended from the temple gopuram in a straight line. These streets were paved with stone slabs and lined with pillared pavilions in which merchants set up their shops.

22. **(A): Gajapati:** Literally means the lord of elephants. This was the name of a ruling lineage that was very powerful in Odisha in the fifteenth century.

Ashvapati: In the popular traditions of Vijayanagara the Deccan Sultans are termed as ashavapati of the lord of horses.

Narapati: In Vijayanagara Empire, the Rayas are called narapati or the lord of men.

23. **(D):** The first revenue settlement in the Bombay Deccan was made in the 1820s. The revenue that was demanded was so high that in many places peasants deserted their villages and migrated to new regions. In areas of poor soil and fluctuating rainfall the problem was particularly acute. When rains failed and harvests were poor, peasants found it impossible to pay the revenue. However, the collectors in charge of revenue collection were keen on demonstrating their efficiency and pleasing their superiors. So they went about extracting payment with utmost severity. When someone failed to pay, his crops were seized and a fine was imposed on the whole village.

24. **(D)**

25. **(A):** The keeping of exact and detailed records was a major concern of the Mughal administration. The mir bakhshi supervised the corps of court writers (waqia nawis) who recorded all applications and documents presented to the court, and all imperial orders (farman). In addition, agents (wakil) of nobles and regional rulers recorded the entire proceedings of the court under the heading "News from the Exalted Court" (Akhbarat-i Darbar-i Mualla) with the date and time of the court session (pahar). The akhbarat contained all kinds of information such as attendance at the court, grant of offices and titles, diplomatic missions, presents received, or the enquiries made by the emperor about the health of an officer. This information is valuable for writing the history of the public and private lives of kings and nobles.

News reports and important official documents travelled across the length and breadth of the regions under Mughal rule by imperial post. Round-the-clock relays of foot-runners (qasid or pathmar) carried papers rolled up in bamboo containers. The emperor received reports from even distant provincial capitals within a few days. Agents of nobles posted outside the capital and Rajput princes and tributary rulers all assiduously copied these announcements and sent their contents by messenger back to their masters. The empire was connected by a surprisingly rapid information loop for public news.

26. (B)

27. (C): Many foreign travellers visited India during the medieval period. They came to India for several motives. Most of the travellers who came to India wrote their accounts. The accounts of these travellers dealt with various aspects. Some travellers accounts deal with the affairs of the court whereas few accounts are focussed on religious issues. Some travellers create about the contemporary style of architecture and monuments, whereas other depicts the social and economic life. The travellers who visited India presented the true picture of Indian civilisation in their accounts. The testimony of an Italian traveller, Giovanni Careri, who passed through India c, 1690, provides a graphic account about the way silver travelled across the globe to reach India.

28. (D): Ibn Battuta's book of travels, called Rihla, written in Arabic, provides extremely rich and interesting details about the social and cultural life in the subcontinent in the fourteenth century. This Moroccan traveller was born in Tangier into one of the most respectable and educated families known for their expertise in Islamic religious law or sharia. True to the tradition of his family, Ibn Battuta received literary and scholastic education when he was quite young. Unlike most other members of his class, Ibn Battuta considered experience gained through travels to be a more important source of knowledge than books. He just loved travelling, and went to far-off places, exploring new worlds and peoples. Before he set off for India in 1332-33, he had made pilgrimage trips to Mecca, and had already travelled extensively in Syria, Iraq, Persia, Yemen, Oman and a few trading ports on the coast of East Africa.

Travelling overland through Central Asia, Ibn Battuta reached Sind in 1333. He had heard about Muhammad bin Tughlaq, the Sultan of Delhi, and lured by his reputation as a generous patron of arts and letters, set off for Delhi, passing through Multan and Uch. The Sultan was impressed by his scholarship, and appointed him the qazi or judge of Delhi. He remained in that position for several years, until he fell out of favour and was thrown into prison. Once the misunderstanding between him and the Sultan was cleared, he was restored to imperial service, and was ordered in 1342 to proceed to China as the Sultan's envoy to the Mongol ruler.

29. (B)

30. (B): The life of forest dwellers in the Mughal era:

- Forest dwellers were termed jangli in contemporary texts. Being jangli, however did not mean an absence of civilization. The term described those whose livelihood came from gathering forest produce, hunting and shifting agriculture.
- These activities were largely season specific that perpetuated mobility which was a distinctive feature of tribes inhabiting these forests.
- For the state, the forest was a subversive place—a place of refuge for troublemakers.
- External forces entered the forest in different ways. The state required elephants for the army so the peshkash levied from forest people often included a supply of elephants.
- The hunt symbolized the overwhelming concern of the state to ensure justice to all its subjects, rich and poor. The hunt was a subject frequently painted by courts artists.
- The spread of commercial agriculture was an important external factor that impinged on the life of those who lived in forests.
- Forest products-like honey, beeswax and gum lac-were in great demand and became major items of overseas export from India.
- Elephants were captured and sold. Trade involved exchange through barter system as well. Some tribed, like the Lohanis in Punjab were involved in overland trade between India and Afghanisthan, and in the two-country trade in Punjab itself.

31. (D)

32. (B): The tradition of erecting stupas may have been pre-Buddhist, but they came to be associated with Buddhism. Since they contained relics regarded as sacred, the entire stupa came to be venerated as an emblem of both the Buddha and Buddhism. According to a Buddhist text known as the Ashokavadana, Asoka distributed portions of the Buddha's relics to every important town and ordered the construction of stupas over them. By the second century BCE a number of stupas, including those at Bharhut, Sanchi and Sarnath, had been built.

33. (A)

34. (D): The partition of India in 1947 caused one of the most harrowing human convulsions in history: over twelve million people were displaced amidst a frenzy of murder, rape and abduction on a massive scale. For decades these violent realities remained buried in silence, even though the memories of brutality never faded. Urvashi Butalia's, The Other Side of Silence, was the first major work to exhume the personal trauma of the Partition. An undisputed classic, it meticulously locates the individual experiences and private pain at the heart of this cataclysmic event. Furthermore, Butalia reveals how people on the margins of history-children, women, ordinary people, the lower castes, the untouchables-were affected by this upheaval. In a passionate and stimulating new introduction, Butalia examines not only recent developments in the expanding field of Partition studies but also the heart-breaking ways in which this colossal tragedy continues to impact our lives and what this means for the future of the Indian subcontinent.

35. (C): Some of the most momentous developments in Indian epigraphy took place in the 1830s. This was when James Prinsep, an officer in the mint of the East India Company, deciphered Brahmi and Kharosthi, two scripts used in the earliest inscriptions and coins. He found that most of these mentioned a king referred to as Piyadassi – meaning "pleasant to behold"; there were a few inscriptions which also referred to the king as Asoka, one of the most famous rulers known from Buddhist texts.

This gave a new direction to investigations into early Indian political history as European and Indian scholars used inscriptions and texts composed in a variety of languages to reconstruct the lineages of major dynasties that had ruled the subcontinent. As a result, the broad contours of political history were in place by the early decades of the twentieth century. Subsequently, scholars began to shift their focus to the context of political history, investigating whether there were connections between political changes and economic and social developments. It was soon realised that while there were links, these were not always simple or direct.

36. (A)

37. (C): After Wellesley's departure the work of town planning was carried on by the Lottery Committee (1817) with the help of the government. The Lottery Committee was so named because funds for town improvement were raised through public lotteries. In other words, in the early decades of the nineteenth century raising funds for the city was still thought to be the responsibility of public minded citizens and not exclusively that of the government. The Lottery Committee commissioned a new map of the city so as to get a comprehensive picture of Calcutta. Among the Committee's major activities was road building in the Indian part of the city and clearing the river bank of "encroachments". In its drive to make the Indian areas of Calcutta cleaner, the committee removed many huts and displaced the labouring poor, who were now pushed to the outskirts of Calcutta.

38. (B): While the prevalence of agriculture is indicated by finds of grain, it is more difficult to reconstruct actual agricultural practices. Were seeds broadcast (scattered) on ploughed lands? Representations on seals and terracotta sculpture indicate that the bull was known, and archaeologists extrapolate from this that oxen were used for ploughing. Moreover, terracotta models of the plough have been found at sites in Cholistan and at Banawali (Haryana). Archaeologists have also found evidence of a ploughed field at Kalibangan (Rajasthan), associated with Early Harappan levels. The field had two sets of furrows at right angles to each other, suggesting that two different crops were grown together.

Most Harappan sites are located in semi-arid lands, where irrigation was probably required for agriculture. Traces of canals have been found at the Harappan site of Shortughai in Afghanistan, but not in Punjab or Sind. It is possible that ancient canals silted up long ago. It is also likely that water drawn from wells was used for irrigation. Besides, water reservoirs found in Dholavira (Gujarat) may have been used to store water for agriculture.

39. (A)

40. (C): At the end of 1810, Buchanan crossed Ganjuria Pahar, which was part of the Rajmahal ranges, passed through the rocky country beyond, and reached a village. It was an old village but the land around had been recently cleared to extend cultivation. Looking at the landscape, Buchanan found evidence of the region having been transformed through "proper application of human labour". He wrote: "Gunjuriya is just sufficiently cultivated to show what a glorious country this might be made. I think its beauty and riches might be made equal to almost any in the universe." The soil here was rocky but "uncommonly fine", and nowhere had Buchanan seen finer tobacco and mustard. On enquiry he discovered that the frontiers of cultivation here had been extended by the Santhals. They had moved into this area around 1800, displaced the hill folk who lived on these lower slopes, cleared the forests and settled the land.

How did the Santhals reach the Rajmahal hills? The Santhals had begun to come into Bengal around the 1780s. Zamindars hired them to reclaim land and expand cultivation, and British officials invited them to settle in the Jangal Mahals. Having failed to subdue the Paharias and transform them into settled agriculturists, the British turned to the Santhals. The Paharias refused to cut forests, resisted touching the plough, and continued to be turbulent. The Santhals, by contrast, appeared to be ideal settlers, clearing forests and ploughing the land with vigour.

The Santhals were given land and persuaded to settle in the foothills of Rajmahal. By 1832 a large area of land was demarcated as Damin-i-Koh. This was declared to be the land of the Santhals. They were to live within it, practise plough agriculture, and become settled peasants. The land grant to the Santhals stipulated that at least one-tenth of the area was to be cleared and cultivated within the first ten years. The territory was surveyed and mapped. Enclosed with boundary pillars, it was separated from both the world of the settled agriculturists of the plains and the Paharias of the hills. After the demarcation of Damin-i-Koh, Santhal settlements expanded rapidly. From 40 Santhal villages in the area in 1838, as many as 1,473 villages had come up by 1851. Over the same period, the Santhal population increased from a mere 3,000 to over 82,000. As cultivation expanded, an increased volume of revenue flowed into the Company's coffers.

41. (C) **42.** (B) **43.** (A)

44. (D) **45.** (C) **46.** (A)

47. (B) **48.** (C) **49.** (D)

50. (B)

POLITICAL SCIENCE

1. Arrange the following in chronological order:
(*a*) Soviet invasion of Afghanistan
(*b*) Fall of Berlin Wall
(*c*) Disintegration of Soviet Union
(*d*) Russian Revolution
(*e*) Warsaw Pact

Choose the ***correct*** answer from the options:
A. (*a*), (*b*), (*c*), (*d*), (*e*) B. (*d*), (*e*), (*a*), (*b*), (*c*)
C. (*b*), (*c*), (*d*), (*a*), (*e*) D. (*d*), (*c*), (*b*), (*e*), (*a*)

2. Indentify the political consequences of disintegration of Soviet Union.
(*a*) Global war on terror
(*b*) End of cold war confrontation
(*c*) Formation of commonwealth of Independent States
(*d*) Gulf war
(*e*) Power relations in world politics changed

Choose the ***correct*** answer from the options:
A. (*b*) & (*c*) only B. (*c*) & (*e*) only
C. (*c*) & (*a*) only D. (*b*), (*c*), (*e*) only

3. Which one of the following statements about the Berlin wall is false?
A. It was built during the cold war
B. It symbolized the division between the capitalist and communist world
C. It marked the unification of the two parts of Germany
D. It was broken by the people on 9 November, 1989

4. Match List-I with List-II.

List-I	List-II
(*a*) Operation Desert Storm	(*i*) 1998
(*b*) Operation Infinite Reach	(*ii*) 1990
(*c*) Operation Enduring Freedom	(*iii*) 2003
(*d*) Operation Iraqi Freedom	(*iv*) 2001

Choose the ***correct*** answer from the options:

	(*a*)	(*b*)	(*c*)	(*d*)
A.	(*ii*)	(*iii*)	(*i*)	(*iv*)
B.	(*i*)	(*ii*)	(*iii*)	(*iv*)
C.	(*iv*)	(*iii*)	(*ii*)	(*i*)
D.	(*ii*)	(*i*)	(*iv*)	(*iii*)

5. Who was the General Secretary of the Communist Party of Soviet Union in 1985?
A. Mikhail Gorbachev B. Nikita Khrushchev
C. Boris Yeltsin D. Leonid Brezhnev

6. Arrange the following events in the correct sequence.
(*a*) Establishment of ASEAN
(*b*) China takeover of Tibet
(*c*) Open door policy adopted in China
(*d*) End of Second World War
(*e*) European Union was established

Choose the ***correct*** answer from the options:
A. (*a*), (*c*), (*d*), (*b*), (*e*) B. (*d*), (*a*), (*b*), (*e*), (*c*)
C. (*a*), (*b*), (*c*), (*d*), (*e*) D. (*d*), (*b*), (*a*), (*c*), (*e*)

7. To introduce a market economy in 1970's, China did not adopt:
A. Open door policy
B. Privatisation of Agriculture & Industry
C. Foreign direct investments & creation of special economic zones
D. The USSR model of Shock Therapy

8. 'Marshall Plan' refers to:
A. South-Asian Trade Act
B. International forum for war criminals
C. America's massive financial help to Europe
D. Co-operation with the developing countries

9. The full form of OECD is:
A. Organization for Export Co-operation and Development
B. Organization for Economic Co-operation and Development
C. Organization for Energy Co-operation and Development
D. Organization for Europe Co-operation and Development

10. ASEAN was established in year:
A. 1965 B. 1967
C. 1970 D. 1972

11. Which of the following is the major issue between the governments of Bangladesh and India?
A. Terrorism B. River water dispute
C. Economic Relations D. Infiltration

12. In 1989, the Indian Peace Keeping Forces pulled out of Sri Lanka without attaing its objective because:
(*a*) India signed an accord with Sri Lanka
(*b*) The Indian Army got into fight with LTTE
(*c*) The Indian government wanted to stabilise relations between the Sri Lankan government and the Tamils
(*d*) Indian troops was not liked by the Sri Lankans
(*e*) Sri Lankan Tamils saw this as interference in the internal affairs

Choose the ***correct*** answer from the options:
A. (*b*), (*d*) & (*a*) only B. (*a*), (*c*) & (*d*) only
C. (*a*), (*b*) & (*e*) only D. (*b*), (*d*) & (*e*) only

13. The Indian Peace Keeping Force (IPKP) was sent to Sri Lanka in:

A. 1985 B. 1987
C. 1988 D. 1989

14. The form of government in Nepal till 2006 was:
A. Capitalist Democracy B. Democratic
C. Communist D. Constitutional Monarchy

15. India's conflict with Pakistan is over strategic issues like:
A. Import natural gas from Afghanistan
B. Role of non regional powers in South Asia
C. India's demand for permanent seat in Security Council
D. Control of the Siachen glacier

16. Indentify the correct statement about World Trade Organization.
A. It was established in 1994
B. All decisions are taken by the five dominant economies in the world
C. It formulates rules for national and international trade
D. It succeded General Agreement on Trade and Tariffs (GATT)

17. Match List-I with List-II.

List-I	List-II
(*a*) Atoms for peace	(*i*) WTO
(*b*) Rules of global trade	(*ii*) ECOSOC
(*c*) Economic & social cooperation	(*iii*) International NGO
(*d*) Advocacy on human rights	(*iv*) IAEA

Choose the ***correct*** answer from the options:

	(*a*)	(*b*)	(*c*)	(*d*)
A.	(*iii*)	(*ii*)	(*i*)	(*iv*)
B.	(*iv*)	(*i*)	(*ii*)	(*iii*)
C.	(*iv*)	(*ii*)	(*iii*)	(*i*)
D.	(*iii*)	(*i*)	(*ii*)	(*iv*)

18. Veto power can be best described as:
A. A special power enjoyed by all the members of the UN Security Council
B. A negative vote which means 'I forbid'
C. Monetary benefits given to the permanent members of the UNO
D. A special power enjoyed by the Secretary General of the UNO

19. Choose the incorrect statement about political consequences of globalisation.
A. It erodes the ability of government
B. Weifare state will be strengthen
C. Minimalist state
D. Capitalist policies

20. Globalization leads to Cultural Homogenisation because:
(*a*) Rise of Uniform Culture
(*b*) External influences enlarge our choices
(*c*) Imposition of Western culture on the rest of the world
(*d*) Modify the culture without overwhelming the tradition

Choose the ***correct*** answer from the options:
A. (*a*) and (*c*) only B. (*b*) and (*d*) only
C. (*b*) and (*c*) only D. (*a*) and (*d*) only

21. Choose the option that correctly represents Political Consequence of globalisation.
A. Law and order increases
B. The state withdrew from many of its welfare function
C. Security of citizen increases
D. Technological innovation declines

22. Jayaprakash Narayan belonged to:
A. Communist Party B. Bharatiya Jan Sangh
C. Socialist Party D. Swatantra Party

23. Match List-I with List-II.

List-I	List-II
(*a*) S.A. Dange	(*i*) Bharatiya Jan Sangh
(*b*) Shyama Prasad Mukherjee	(*ii*) Swatantra Party
(*c*) Minoo Masani	(*iii*) Praja Socialist Party
(*d*) Ashok Mehta	(*iv*) Communist Party of India

Choose the ***correct*** answer from the options:

	(*a*)	(*b*)	(*c*)	(*d*)
A.	(*ii*)	(*i*)	(*iv*)	(*iii*)
B.	(*iii*)	(*ii*)	(*i*)	(*iv*)
C.	(*iv*)	(*i*)	(*ii*)	(*iii*)
D.	(*i*)	(*iv*)	(*iii*)	(*ii*)

24. Indentify the leader who said ______ in 1963 that all senior congressmen should resign from the office to make way for younger Party workers.
A. S. Nijalingappa B. S.K. Patil
C. K. Kamraj D. Neelam Sanjeeva Reddy

25. Match List-I with List-II.

List-I	List-II
(*a*) Instrument of Accession	(*i*) State unites with the Centre
(*b*) Merger agreement	(*ii*) State agreed to become a part of Union of India
(*c*) Vishalandhra Movement	(*iii*) Redrawing of the boundary of States
(*d*) States reorganisation commission	(*iv*) Telugu speaking areas be separated from the Madras Provinces

Choose the ***correct*** answer from the options:

	(*a*)	(*b*)	(*c*)	(*d*)
A.	(*i*)	(*ii*)	(*iii*)	(*iv*)
B.	(*ii*)	(*i*)	(*iv*)	(*iii*)
C.	(*iii*)	(*ii*)	(*i*)	(*iv*)
D.	(*iv*)	(*iii*)	(*ii*)	(*i*)

26. Arrange the following events related to creation of new states in chronological order.

(*a*) Demarcation of bounderies of Jharkhand and Chhattisgarh

(*b*) Formation of Andhra on linguistic lines

(*c*) Creation of Himachal Pradesh on the basis of geographical zones

(*d*) Formation of Maharashtra and Gujarat

(*e*) Formation of Meghalaya

Choose the ***correct*** answer from the options:

A. (*b*), (*d*), (*c*), (*e*), (*a*) B. (*b*), (*c*), (*d*), (*a*), (*e*)

C. (*a*), (*d*), (*c*), (*e*), (*b*) D. (*c*), (*b*), (*d*), (*e*), (*a*)

27. The first state of India to hold elections based on Universal Adult franchise:

A. Maharashtra B. Rajasthan

C. Kerala D. Manipur

28. First five year plan of independent India.

(*a*) It addressed the agrarian sector

(*b*) Investment in dams and irrigation facilities were given priority

(*c*) Planners wanted to raise the national income through rapid industrialization

(*d*) It was formalised by P.C. Mahalanobis

(*e*) It focused on land reforms in agricultural sector

Choose the ***correct*** answer from the options:

A. (*a*), (*c*), (*d*) only B. (*b*), (*c*), *e*) only

C. (*a*), (*c*), (*e*) only D. (*a*), (*b*), (*e*) only

29. Choose the incorrect options with respect to India's Nuclear Policy.

(*a*) Nehru had always put his faith in science and technology

(*b*) Communist China conducted nuclear tests in 1960

(*c*) The five permanent member of UN Security Council did not impose the NPT on the world

(*d*) India wanted to generate atomic energy for its security and use during war

(*e*) A nuclear program was initiated in 1940's under the guidance of Homi J. Bhabha

Choose the ***correct*** answer from the options:

A. (*a*), (*b*), (*c*) only B. (*c*), (*d*), (*e*) only

C. (*b*), (*c*), (*d*) only D. (*a*), (*c*), (*e*) only

30. Arrange the following event in correct sequence.

(*a*) Signing of the Tashkand Agreement

(*b*) China launched a massive invasion on India

(*c*) First nuclear explosion undertaken in India

(*d*) Britain attacked Egypt over Suez Canal

(*e*) Asian Relation Conference

Choose the ***correct*** answer from the options:

A. (*e*), (*d*), (*b*), (*a*), (*c*) B. (*d*), (*e*), (*b*), (*c*), (*a*)

C. (*d*), (*c*), (*a*), (*b*), (*e*) D. (*e*), (*b*), (*a*), (*d*), (*c*)

31. The 'Indian National Army' (INA) was created during the Second World War by:

A. Bhagat Singh

B. Rajguru

C. Netaji Subhash Chandra Bose

D. Chandra Shekhar Azad

32. The first summit of NAM was held in:

A. New Delhi in September 1962

B. Belgrade in September 1961

C. Bangladesh in March 1964

D. Indonesia in February 1965

33. 1960's were labelled as the ______.

A. 'Dangerous decade' B. 'Safe decade'

C. 'Progressive decade' D. 'Regressive decade'

34. What is 'defection'?

A. When an individual migrates to another country

B. Parties with different ideologies

C. A catchy phrase

D. An elected representative leaving the party on whose ticket she/he has been elected

35. The special session of the Constituent Assembly:

"Tryst with Destiny" was addressed by:

A. Maulana Azad B. Mahatma Gandhi

C. Pt. Jawaharlal Nehru D. Rajendra Prasad

36. Match List-I with List-II.

List-I	List-II
(*a*) Politics of consequence	(*i*) Rise of OBCs
(*b*) Caste based parties	(*ii*) Shah Bano case
(*c*) Personal law and Gender Justice	(*iii*) Agreement on Economic policies
(*d*) Growing strength of regional politics	(*iv*) Coalition government

Choose the ***correct*** answer from the options:

	(*a*)	(*b*)	(*c*)	(*d*)
A.	(*iii*)	(*i*)	(*ii*)	(*iv*)
B.	(*ii*)	(*iii*)	(*iv*)	(*i*)
C.	(*iv*)	(*ii*)	(*iii*)	(*i*)
D.	(*iii*)	(*iv*)	(*i*)	(*ii*)

37. Choose the correct option with respect to the development in 1990's.

(*a*) Elections of 1989 marked the end of the congress system

(*b*) Assassination of Rajiv Gandhi by LTTE in 1991

(*c*) New economic reforms were initiated by V.P. Singh

(*d*) In 1989, the UPA formed the government

(*e*) Karpoori Thakur, the then chief minister of Bihar was poineer in introducing the policy of reservation

A. (*a*), (*b*), (*c*) only B. (*a*), (*b*), (*e*) only

C. (*b*), (*c*), (*e*) only D. (*b*), (*c*), (*d*) only

38. Place the statement/events in sequence with regards to expansion of democracy in Nepal.

(*a*) The Maoist of Nepal were successful in spreading their influence in many parts of Nepal.

(*b*) The king was forced to restore the House of Representative
(*c*) Nepal became a democratic republic after abolishing the Monarchy
(*d*) The king accepted the demand for a new democratic constitution
(*e*) The king abolished the parliament and dismissed the government

Choose the ***correct*** answer from the options:

A. (*a*), (*d*), (*b*), (*c*), (*e*) B. (*d*), (*a*), (*e*), (*b*), (*c*)
C. (*c*), (*d*), (*e*), (*b*), (*a*) D. (*b*), (*c*), (*a*), (*d*), (*e*)

39. The General elections of 1967 popularised a saying that one could take a train from Delhi to Howrah and not pass through a single congress ruled state.

Identify the option that does not relate with the saying
A. End of Congress dominance
B. Growing popularity of non congress parties
C. Introduction of Phenomenon of Coalition
D. SVDS formed in different states by the parties having identical ideologies

40. US invaded Iraq under the code name of "Operation Iraqi Freedom" in the year:
A. 2004 B. 2001
C. 2003 D. 2005

Directions (Qs. 41-45): *Read the passage and answer the questions.*

The non-aligned countries were more than merely mediators during the Cold War. The challenge for most of the non-aligned countries - a majority of them were categorised as the Least Developed Countries (LDCs) - was to be more developed economically and to lift their people out of poverty. Economic development was also vital for independence of the new countries. Without sustained development, a country could not be truly free. It would remain dependent on the richer countries including the colonial powers from which political freedom had been achieved.

41. Indentify the country that was not a member of non-aligned group.
A. Pakistan B. Sri Lanka
C. India D. North Korea

42. The Least Developed countries achieved freedom from richer countries. Indentify the correct form of freedom.
A. Economic B. Social
C. Political D. Cultural

43. The main aim of the Least Developed countries was:
A. To provide healthcare facilities to all
B. To promote equality among all
C. To participate in world economic forum
D. To develop economically Uplift people from poverty

44. The countries that were categorised as the Least Developed Countries were:
A. Army rule countries
B. Non-Aligned countries
C. Western bloc countries
D. Eastern bloc countries

45. Indentify the idea that originated to uplift these LDC's countries to the path of development.
A. NIEO B. NAM
C. NATO D. SEATO

Directions (Qs. 46-50): *Read the passage and answer the questions.*

Indian elections in 1971 started with congress 'Garibi hatao' slogans. As oil prices increased in the international markets, India too was captured in the inflation. Rising prices of oil, foodgrains and other essential commodities led to massive protest in many parts of the country. Students' protests in Gujarat and Bihar during 1974 led to the emergence of leaders such as Morarji Desai, Jayaprakash Narayan among others.

Moreover, there was a railway strike organised by George Fernandes to meet the demand of improved working conditions and bonus for the Railway employees. The period also saw the conflict between judiciary and the executive. This conflict culminated in the famous Kesavananda Bharti case, and later into a ruling declaring Indira Gandhi's election invalid. As the Allahabad High Court passed a judgement to this effect, the stage was set for political confrontation between Congress and opposition parties led by Jayaprakash Narayan.

These events finally led to the declaration of emergency by the government on 25th June, 1975.

46. The slogan Garibi Hatao was given by:
A. Morarji Desai B. Indira Gandhi
C. Grand Alliance D. V.V. Giri

47. In which two states students protested against rising food prices, oil etc.?
A. Haryana & Punjab B. Gujarat & Maharashtra
C. Bihar & Gujarat D. Bihar & Rajasthan

48. Who organised the railway strike in 1974?
A. George Fernandes B. Jayaprakash Narayan
C. L.K. Advani D. Atal Behari Vajpayee

49. On what condition did Jayaprakash Narayan led the Bihar Students movement?
A. It will be violent
B. It will be non-violent
C. It will restrict to Bihar
D. It will force the government to bring down food prices

50. The issue of conflict between the executive and judiciary was over:
A. Fundamental Rights of people
B. Decreasing the power of judiciary
C. Amending the criminal laws
D. Appointing the judges of the Supreme Court

ANSWERS

1. **(B):** Russian Revolution-1917
Warsaw Pact-1955
Soviet invasion of Afghanistan-1979
Fall of the Berlin Wall-1989
Disintegration of the Soviet Union-1990

2. **(D):** The end of Cold War resulted in several changes in the International Relations. The concept of bipolar system, which brought the world to fall under the influence of two powerful blocs, was the first victim. It also followed by weakening of the Non-Aligned Movement (NAM). The fall of Berlin Wall in 1989 marked the beginning of the end of Cold War. Soon after that USSR was dismantled in 1991, marking a new era in the history of international relations. The collapse of the USSR led to the death of Warsaw Pact. Many countries took birth in the Baltic, Eastern Europe and Central Asian regions either through civil war or peaceful means. All these events resulted in emergence of the US as the sole super power; and the world became a unipolar system for a while in the 1990s. The international relations in the post-Cold War period have taken a new shape, order and spirit. New actors have emerged, new priorities are identified and new world order has begun. Multiple changes have happened at economic and political fronts at multiple levels - from global to local.

3. **(C):** The Berlin Wall, which had been built at the height of the Cold War and was its greatest symbol, was toppled by the people in 1989. This dramatic event was followed by an equally dramatic and historic chain of events that led to the collapse of the 'second world' and the end of the Cold War. Germany, divided after the Second World War, was unified.

4. **(D):** On 2nd August, 1990 Iraq invaded Kuwait. UN condemned the invasion and demanded withdrawal of Iraqi troops. Massive coalition force of 660,000 troops from 34 countries fought against Iraq and defeated it. The U.N operation was called 'Operation Desert Storm'. It is also known as the first Gulf war.
In 1998, there was bombing at the U.S. embassies in Nairobi, Kenya and Dar-es-Salaam, Tanzania by Al-Qaeda, a terrorist organization. President Clinton ordered 'Operation Infinite Reach' in which Al-Qaeda terrorist targets in Sudan and Afghanistan were attacked.
On 11 September 2001, nineteen hijackers hailing from Arab countries took control of four American commercial aircraft and flew them into important US buildings. President George W. Bush launched 'Operation Enduring Freedom' against Afghanistan to curb terrorism and to crush territories.
On 19th March, 2003 the US launched its invasion in Iraq under the code name 'Operation Iraqi Freedom'.

5. **(A):** In 1985, Mikhail Gorbachev was elected general secretary of the Communist Party of Soviet Union. He proposed the idea of Glasnost, the Russian word for 'openness'. It included the policy of ideological openness and space for criticism of politics and government. He also proposed Perestroika, the Russian word for restructuring. Gorbachev wanted to restructure the economic and political system of the USSR.

6. **(D)** 7. **(B)**

8. **(C):** When World War II ended in 1945, Europe lay in ruins: its cities were shattered; its economies were devastated; its people faced famine. In the two years after the war, the Soviet Union's control of Eastern Europe and the vulnerability of Western European countries to Soviet expansionism heightened the sense of crisis. To meet this emergency, Secretary of State George Marshall proposed in a speech at Harvard University on June 5, 1947, that European nations create a plan for their economic reconstruction and that the United States provide economic assistance.
On December 19, 1947, President Harry Truman sent Congress a message that followed Marshall's ideas to provide economic aid to Europe. Congress overwhelmingly passed the Economic Cooperation Act of 1948, and on April 3, 1948, President Truman signed the act that became known as the Marshall Plan.
Over the next four years, Congress appropriated $13.3 billion for European recovery. This aid provided much needed capital and materials that enabled Europeans to rebuild the continent's economy.
For the United States, the Marshall Plan provided markets for American goods, created reliable trading partners, and supported the development of stable democratic governments in Western Europe. Congress's approval of the Marshall Plan signalled an extension of the bipartisanship of World War II into the post-war years.

9. **(B):** The Organisation for Economic Co-operation and Development (OECD) established in 1961 is an international organisation that works to build better policies for better lives. Its goal is to shape policies that foster prosperity, equality, opportunity and well-being for all. Together with governments, policy makers and citizens, it work on establishing evidence-based international standards and finding solutions to a range of social, economic and environmental challenges. From improving economic performance and creating jobs to fostering strong education and fighting international tax evasion, we provide a unique forum and knowledge hub for data and analysis, exchange of experiences, best-practice sharing, and advice on public policies.

10. (B): ASEAN, in full Association of Southeast Asian Nations, is an international organization established by the governments of Indonesia, Malaysia, the Philippines, Singapore, and Thailand in 1967 to accelerate economic growth, social progress, and cultural development and to promote peace and security in Southeast Asia. Brunei joined in 1984, followed by Vietnam in 1995, Laos and Myanmar in 1997, and Cambodia in 1999.

ASEAN's primary objective was to accelerate economic growth and through that social progress and cultural development. A secondary objective was to promote regional peace and stability based on the rule of law and the principles of the UN Charter. With some of the fastest growing economies in the world, ASEAN has broadened its objective beyond the economic and social spheres.

11. (B): River water dispute is the major issue between the governments of Bangladesh and India. India and Bangladesh share 54 common rivers. The Ganga Waters Treaty signed in 1996 for sharing of waters of river Ganga during lean season. Most recently, the Kushiyara Pact was signed that will benefit people in Southern Assam and the Sylhet region in Bangladesh.

However, there still remain major issues such as river water disputes (Teesta River water sharing), aiding illegal immigrants, and drug trades remain between India and Bangladesh, that must be addressed.

12. (D): The Sri Lankan problem involves people of Indian origin, and there is considerable pressure from the Tamil people in India to the effect that the Indian government should protect the interests of the Tamils in Sri Lanka. The government of India has from time to time tried to negotiate with the Sri Lankan government on the Tamil question. But in 1987, the government of India for the first time got directly involved in the Sri Lankan Tamil question. India signed an accord with Sri Lanka and sent troops to stabilise relations between the Sri Lankan government and the Tamils. Eventually, the Indian Army got into a fight with the LTTE. The presence of Indian troops was also not liked much by the Sri Lankans. They saw this as an attempt by India to interfere in the internal affairs of Sri Lanka. In 1989, the Indian Peace Keeping Force (IPKF) pulled out of Sri Lanka without attaining its objective.

13. (B): The Indian Peace Keeping Force was sent to Sri Lanka in 1987 to end the Sri Lankan Civil War between the Tamil minority groups such as the Liberation Tigers of Tamil Elam (LTTE) and the Sinhalese group. The Indian Peace Keeping Force eventually ended up in a battle with the LTTE to enforce peace - a move that was accepted by neither the Tamils nor the Sri Lankan government. So, it was withdrawn in 1989 and 1990.

14. (D): Till 2006, Nepal was a constitutional monarchy with the danger of the king taking over executive powers. In 2008, the monarchy was abolished and Nepal emerged as a democratic republic. Now we can say that democracy is becoming an accepted norm in the entire region of South Asia.

15. (D): India's conflict with Pakistan is also over strategic issues like the control of the Siachen glacier and over acquisition of arms. The arms race between the two countries assumed a new character with both states acquiring nuclear weapons and missiles to deliver such arms against each other in the 1990s. In 1998, India conducted nuclear explosion in Pokharan. Pakistan responded within a few days by carrying out nuclear tests in the Chagai Hills. Since then India and Pakistan seem to have built a military relationship in which the possibility of a direct and full-scale war has declined.

16. (D): The World Trade Organization (WTO) is an intergovernmental organization that regulates and facilitates international trade. With effective cooperation in the United Nations System, governments use the organization to establish, revise, and enforce the rules that govern international trade. It officially commenced operations on 1 January 1995, pursuant to the 1994 Marrakesh Agreement, thus replacing the General Agreement on Tariffs and Trade (GATT) that had been established in 1948.

The WTO facilitates trade in goods, services and intellectual property among participating countries by providing a framework for negotiating trade agreements, which usually aim to reduce or eliminate tariffs, quotas, and other restrictions; these agreements are signed by representatives of member governments and ratified by their legislatures. The WTO also administers independent dispute resolution for enforcing participants' adherence to trade agreements and resolving trade-related disputes. The organization prohibits discrimination between trading partners, but provides exceptions for environmental protection, national security, and other important goals.

17. (B)

18. (B): A veto is a negative vote and is the most significant distinction between permanent and non-permanent members in the UN Security Council. The power to say no or to stop an official action is called the Veto power. The Security Council of the United Nation provides the veto power to all the five permanent members. These members are the United States of America, France, Britain, China and Russia.

19. (B): Political Consequences of Globalisation:

- At the simple level, globalisation results in the erosion of state capacity i.e., the ability of the government to do what they do. All over the world, the old welfare state is now giving way to minimalist state that performs certain core functions such as the maintenance of law and order and security of its citizens. In place of welfare state, it is the market that becomes the prime determinant of economic and social priorities.

- Secondly it may be stated that globalisation does not always reduce state capacity. The primacy of the state continues to be the unchallenged basis of political community. The old jealousies and rivalries between countries have not ceased to matter in world politics. The state continues to discharge its essential function and conciously withdraws from certain domain which it wishes to.
- Thirdly in some areas the state capacity has received a boost with enhanced technologies available at the disposal of the state. It can now collect different type of the information about its citizens and can rule in a better way. As a result of technology, the states have become more powerful than they were earlier.

20. (A): Cultural homogenization is an aspect of cultural globalization, listed as one of its main characteristics, and refers to the reduction in cultural diversity through the popularization and diffusion of a wide array of cultural symbols—not only physical objects but customs, ideas and values. David E. O'Connor defines it as "the process by which local cultures are transformed or absorbed by a dominant outside culture". Cultural homogenization has been called "perhaps the most widely discussed hallmark of global culture". In theory, homogenization could work in the breakdown of cultural barriers and the global assimilation of a single culture.

Cultural homogenization can impact national identity and culture, which would be "eroded by the impact of global cultural industries and multinational media". The term is usually used in the context of Western culture dominating and destroying other cultures. The process of cultural homogenization in the context of the domination of the Western (American), capitalist culture is also known as McDonaldization, coca-colonization, Americanization or Westernization and criticized as a form of cultural imperialism and neo-colonialism.

21. (B)

22. (C): Jayaprakash Narayan belonged to the Congress Socialist Party. He was born on October 11, 1902, and he passed away on October 8, 1979. In the middle of the 1970s, he led the opposition against Prime Minister Indira Gandhi, whose overthrow he had called for a "total revolution," and for this, he is remembered. Rambriksh Benipuri, a nationalist and author of Hindi literature, wrote his biography, Jayaprakash. In 1999, in honour of his contributions to society, he received the Bharat Ratna, the highest civilian honour in India. The Magsaysay award for Public Service from 1965 is among the other honours.

23. (C)

24. (C): In 1963 K. Kamraj, Congress President and Chief Minister of Madras (Now Tamil Nadu), proposed that all senior Congressmen should resign from office to make way for younger party workers. This proposal is known as 'Kamraj Plan'.

25. (B) **26. (A)**

27. (D): A few days before Independence, the Maharaja of Manipur, Bodhachandra Singh, signed the Instrument of Accession with the Indian government on the assurance that the internal autonomy of Manipur would be maintained. Under the pressure of public opinion, the Maharaja held elections in Manipur in June 1948 and the state became a constitutional monarchy. Thus Manipur was the first part of India to hold an election based on universal adult franchise. In the Legislative Assembly of Manipur there were sharp differences over the question of merger of Manipur with India. While the state Congress wanted the merger, other political parties were opposed to this. The Government of India succeeded in pressurising the Maharaja into signing a Merger Agreement in September 1949, without consulting the popularly elected Legislative Assembly of Manipur. This caused a lot of anger and resentment in Manipur, the repercussions of which are still being felt.

28. (D): The first five-year plan was presented and implemented by Jawaharlal Nehru, India's first Prime Minister. It was launched in 1951, and its objective was to uplift the economic condition of India by mainly focusing on improving the standard of the primary sector. By India's primary sector, we mainly mean agriculture, as it has been the most powerful source of the country's income.

The first five years (1951 - 1956) plan was drafted by the economist K.N Raj and was based on the Harrod-Domar model - a Keynesian model of an economic plan. The plan was to save more of India's capital for bigger future investments and low capital investment in the meantime with a more efficient growth rate and income. The plan aimed to achieve 2.1 % GDP growth that year but ended up growing up to 3.6 %. This success in the initiation of the plan made India believe in it. The first five-year plan wanted to make sure that India becomes self-sufficient, economically strong and thrives in its primary sectors of growth.

29. (C) **30. (A)**

31. (C): The Indian National Army (INA) was formed in 1942, under Mohan Singh, who was an officer in the British army. It was formed with the aid of the

Japanese, in Southeast Asia during the Second World War. After conflicts between the INA leadership and the Japanese military over its function in Japan's war in Asia, the first INA collapsed and was disbanded in December that year. The army was revived under the leadership of Subhas Chandra Bose in 1943. The INA attracted ex-prisoners and thousands of civilian volunteers from the Indians living in Malaya (today known as Malaysia) and Burma under Bose's leadership.

32. **(B):** The first summit of the NAM summit held in 1961 was in Belgrade in Yugoslavia. It was led through an initiative of the Indian Prime Minister Jawaharlal Nehru, Indonesian President Sukarno, Egyptian President Gamal Abdel Nasser and Yugoslavia President Josip Broz Tito and this led to the first conference of the Head of States or Government of Non- Aligned Movement. The conference of the Head of States or Government of the Non- Aligned countries was also called as NAM summits that are the main meeting across the movement and it is held after every few years.

33. **(A):** Prime Minister Jawaharlal Nehru passed away in May 1964. He had been unwell for more than a year. This had generated a lot of speculation about the usual question of succession: after Nehru, who? But in a newly independent country like India, this situation gave rise to a more serious question: after Nehru, what?

The second question arose from the serious doubts that many outsiders had about whether India's democratic experiment will survive after Nehru. It was feared that like so many other newly independent countries, India too would not be able to manage a democratic succession. A failure to do so, it was feared, could lead to a political role for the army. Besides, there were doubts if the new leadership would be able to handle the multiple crises that awaited a solution. The 1960s were labelled as the 'dangerous decade' when unresolved problems like poverty, inequality, communal and regional divisions etc, could lead to a failure of the democratic project or even the disintegration of the country.

34. **(D):** The term 'Defection' implies changing a political party from the party from which he was elected to a different party. The 10th schedule lays down the process by which legislators may be disqualified on the ground of defection by the presiding officer based on a petition filed by another legislator.

35. **(C):** At the hour of midnight on 14-15 August 1947, India attained independence. Jawaharlal Nehru, the first prime minister of free India, addressed a special session of the Constituent Assembly that night. This was the famous 'tryst with destiny' speech that you are familiar with.

36. **(A)** **37.** **(B)**

38. **(B):** The king with the help of the army, retained full control over the government and restricted the expansion of democracy in Nepal. But in 1990, the king accepted the demand for a new democratic constitution, in the wake of a strong pro-democracy movement. However, democratic governments had a short and troubled career. During the nineties, the Maoists of Nepal were successful in spreading their influence in many parts of Nepal. They believed in armed insurrection against the monarch and the ruling elite. This led to a violent conflict between the Maoist guerrillas and the armed forces of the king. For some time, there was a triangular conflict among the monarchist forces, the democrats and the Maoists.

In 2002, the king abolished the parliament and dismissed the government, thus ending even the limited democracy that existed in Nepal.

In April 2006, there were massive, country-wide, pro-democracy protests. The struggling pro-democracy forces achieved their first major victory when the king was forced to restore the House of Representatives that had been dissolved in April 2002. As a result, the transition from monarchy to democracy is nearly complete.

39. **(D)**

40. **(C):** On 19 March 2003, the US launched its invasion of Iraq under the codename 'Operation Iraqi Freedom'. More than forty other countries joined in the US-led 'coalition of the willing' after the UN refused to give its mandate to the invasion. The ostensible purpose of the invasion was to prevent Iraq from developing weapons of mass destruction (WMD). Since no evidence of WMD has been unearthed in Iraq, it is speculated that the invasion was motivated by other objectives, such as controlling Iraqi oilfields and installing a regime friendly to the US.

Although the government of Saddam Hussein fell swiftly, the US has not been able to 'pacify' Iraq. Instead, a full-fledged insurgency against US occupation was ignited in Iraq. While the US has lost over 3,000 military personnel in the war, Iraqi casualties are very much higher. It is conservatively estimated that 50,000 Iraqi civilians have been killed since the US-led invasion. It is now widely recognised that the US invasion of Iraq was, in some crucial respects, both a military and political failure.

41. **(D)** **42.** **(C)** **43.** **(D)**
44. **(B)** **45.** **(B)** **46.** **(B)**
47. **(C)** **48.** **(A)** **49.** **(B)**
50. **(B)**

SOCIOLOGY

1. When population of a particular country rises in the manner of 2, 4, 8, 16, 32, 64, etc. This is explained by Thomas Robert Malthus as:

A. Geometric progression
B. Demographic progression
C. Arithmetic progression
D. Population progression

2. Increase in female infanticide is due to:

A. Famine
B. Pandemics/epidemics
C. Social and cultural prejudices
D. High maternal mortality rates

3. Which policy was introduced by Government of India that could increase the female ratio in the country?

A. Beti Bachao-Beti Padhao
B. Sarva Shiksha Abhiyaan
C. Mahatma Gandhi National Employment Rural Government Act
D. Mid day meal programme

4. The demographic indicator calculated on the basis of data on age specific death rate in a given area over a period of time is called:

A. Fertility Rate B. Demographic Dividend
C. Life Expectancy D. Dependency Ratio

5. Rapid Growth in urbanisation shows that cities act as magnet for rural population. Which of the following are reasons for flow of rural - to urban migration?

(*a*) Decline of Common property
(*b*) For clean environment
(*c*) Lack of Job opportunities
(*d*) Mass transit and mass communication
(*e*) Relative anonymity

Choose the ***correct*** answer from the options given below:

A. (*b*), (*c*), (*d*), (*e*) only
B. (*a*), (*c*), (*d*), (*e*) only
C. (*a*), (*b*), (*d*), (*e*) only
D. (*a*), (*b*), (*c*), (*d*) only

6. Which one of the following is a early political economist who gave the idea of free-market economy?

A. Emile Durkheim B. Max Weber
C. Karl Mark D. Adam Smith

7. Max Weber argued that buying and use of certain commodities enhance/maintain status in society, he called this 'status symbol'. Which of the following represents status symbol?

A. Purchase of Redmi Note 11 mobile phone
B. Purchase non-branded wrist watch
C. Purchase of sunglasses from a hawker
D. Purchase of clothes from roadside stall

8. In which year did Kaka Kalelkar submit the report on OBCs?

A. 1950 B. 1990
C. 1953 D. 1993

9. People perceive disability as:

(*a*) Biologically given
(*b*) Linked with individual's self perception
(*c*) Seen as in need of help
(*d*) Seen as an untouchable
(*e*) Seen as victim

Choose the ***correct*** answer from the options given below:

A. (*a*), (*b*), (*c*), (*d*) only B. (*a*), (*b*), (*c*), (*e*) only
C. (*a*), (*b*), (*d*), (*e*) only D. (*b*), (*c*), (*d*), (*e*) only

10. Classification of social resources into three forms of capital—economic capital, cultural capital and social capital was done by:

A. Emile Durkheim B. P. Bourdieu
C. Max Weber D. Karl Marx

11. The term 'apartheid' is associated with South Africa. It represents:

A. Separation of classes B. Separation of castes
C. Separation of gender D. Separation of races

12. Alternative to 'Nation-state' is:

A. Nation B. State
C. State-Nation D. Multicultural state

13. In 1956, States Reorganisation Commission (SRC) mandated redrawing of map of India ______ on lines.

A. Regional B. Religious
C. Cultural D. Linguistic

14. What is the reason behind raging civil war in Sri Lanka 1983?

A. Denial of majority's linguistic rights
B. Denial of minority's linguistic rights
C. Dis-respect for the sentiments of majority
D. Formation of linguistic states

15. Which among the followings this is NOT a characteristic of a comm-unity?

A. Identify is by birth/ascriptive
B. Members have 'WE' feeling among each other
C. Membership is voluntary in nature
D. It anchors over self-identify

16. Choose the statement that explains the concepts of modernization:

A. It assumes that local ties of modernisation and parochial perspectives give way to universal commitments and cosmopolitan attitudes
B. is based on religious beliefs and attitudes
C. focuses on fatalistic belief
D. emphasises irrationality are rationality

17. Who visualised, independent India to be built on an edifice of giant steel plants and power stations?

A. B.R. Ambedkar B. Mahatma Gandhi
C. Indira Gandhi D. Jawahar Lal Nehru

18. An economic system in which the means of production are privately owned and organised to accumulate profits within a market system is called:

A. Feudalism B. Slavery
C. Capitalism D. Socialism

19. Which of the following is not part of cultural change?

A. Industrialisation B. Sanskritisation
C. Secularisation D. Modernisation

20. Who is the author of the text 'The sources of knowledge'?

A. Sir Sayed Ahmed Khan
B. Jawarharlal Nehru
C. M.K. Gandhi
D. Kandukiri Viresalingam

21. The process of Urbanisation refers to:

A. Increase of Rural areas
B. Migration from village to cities
C. Agricultural production
D. Community Relations

22. Raja Ram Mohan Roy criticized the practice of Sati because:

A. It was against social norms
B. He considered it to be inhuman
C. It challenged the very patriarchal system of India
D. It provided women with lot of freedom

23. In 1938, The National Planning Committee was set up by the Indian National Congress. The Chairman of the Committee was:

A. Bhimrao Ambedkar
B. K.T. Shah
C. Jawaharalal Nehru
D. Rajendra Prasad

24. Who formed Dharma Sabha?

A. Raja Ram Mohan Roy
B. Orthodox members of Hindu Community
C. M.N. Srinivas
D. Ishwar Chandra Vidyasagar

25. Sanskritization as a concept has been criticised as:

(*a*) It does not lead to structural change in society
(*b*) It results in positional change in the society
(*c*) It justifies the model which rests on the idea of purity and pollution
(*d*) It preserves the dalit culture
(*e*) Adoption of upper caste rites results in upheaveal of position of women in society

Choose the ***correct*** answer from the options given below:

A. (*a*), (*d*), (*e*) only B. (*c*), (*d*), (*e*) only
C. (*b*), (*c*), (*d*) only D. (*a*), (*b*), (*c*) only

26. A ______ may be defined as an organisation oriented towards achieving legitimate control of government through an electoral process.

A. Political Party B. Pressure Group
C. Interest Group D. Social Group

27. In the traditional political system of Khasis, each clan had its own council known as:

A. Jaintias B. Garos
C. Durbar kur D. Nongari

28. Agricultural issues have lost importance in public and political dialogue because ______ .

A. Less population is engaged in Agriculture
B. No pressure group to influence policy maker
C. Agricultural society has improved
D. State support increased substantially

29. Arrange the given items (events) in ascending order.

(*a*) Zamindari System
(*b*) Abolition of Zamindari System
(*c*) Rayotwari system
(*d*) Fanner's suicide
(*e*) Green Revolution

Choose the ***correct*** answer from the options given below:

A. (*a*), (*b*), (*c*), (*d*), (*e*) B. (*a*), (*c*), (*b*), (*e*), (*d*)
C. (*a*), (*b*), (*d*), (*e*), (*c*) D. (*e*), (*d*), (*c*), (*b*), (*a*)

30. What do you understand by the term 'feminization of Agricultural' labour force?

A. Women are emerging as the major source of agricultural labour force
B. Women are forced to work in the Agricultural sector
C. Patriarchy excludes women from having land ownership rights
D. The insecurity of women is more as they earn less wages

31. Choose the incorrect options on the Concept of Green Revolution:

A. Process of differentiation
B. Displacements of service caste groups
C. Medium and large farmers were benefitted
D. Reduced regional inequalities

32. Jan Breman described the change in the nature of the relationship between landlords and agricultural workers as:

A. Commercialisation of Labour
B. Footloose Labour
C. A shift from 'patronage to exploitation'
D. Loss of traditional values

33. Who gave the concept of "Nation as an imagined community"?

A. Johann Gutenberg B. Benedict Anderson
C. Ilbert Bill D. Fardoonji Murzban

34. In which of the following ways mass media act as "Watchdog of Democracy"?

(*a*) Spread the spirit of self - reliance
(*b*) Fight against socially oppressive practices
(*c*) Rational Scientific ethos promoted.
(*d*) Documenting Developmental progress
(*e*) Obstruct the development of modern Industrial society

Choose the ***correct*** answer from the options given below:

A. (*b*), (*c*), (*d*), (*e*) only B. (*a*), (*b*), (*c*), (*d*) only
C. (*a*), (*b*), (*e*), (*d*) only D. (*a*), (*b*), (*c*), (*e*) only

35. ______ refer to the mixing of the global with the local.

A. Glocalization B. Globalization
C. Intermixing D. Homogenization

36. Dharma Sabha was an organisation that stalled against the sati campaign led by Brahma Samaj.

Dharma Sabha is an example of:

A. Social movement
B. Revolutionary movement
C. Redemptive movement
D. Counter movement

37. Which of the following is not a feature of old social movements?

A. Related to political party
B. Deals with local/regional Issues
C. Deals with issues pertaining to Global relevance
D. Mostly deals with redistribution of power

38. Match List-I with List-II.

Match the theories/concepts given in List-I with the eminent personalities given in List-II:

List-I (Theories/Concepts)	List-II (Important personalities)
(*a*) theory of collective action	(*i*) Emile Durkheim
(*b*) theory of Relative Resource mobilization	(*ii*) Mancur Olson
(*c*) Division of labour in society	(*iii*) McCarthy and Zald
(*d*) Unquiet woods	(*iv*) Ram Chandra Guha

Choose the ***correct*** answer from the options given below:

	(*a*)	(*b*)	(*c*)	(*d*)
A.	(*i*)	(*iii*)	(*ii*)	(*iv*)
B.	(*i*)	(*ii*)	(*iii*)	(*iv*)
C.	(*ii*)	(*iii*)	(*i*)	(*iv*)
D.	(*iv*)	(*ii*)	(*iii*)	(*i*)

39. Who argued that 'Institution of the state have been captured by elites'?

A. Karl Marx
B. Hary Bramerman
C. Rajni Kothari
D. Gail Omvedt

40. Arrange the following peasant movement in regard to their years from ascending to descending order:

(*a*) Bardoli Satyagrah
(*b*) Bengal Revolt
(*c*) Champaran Movement
(*d*) Telangana Movement
(*e*) Naxalite Movement

Choose the ***correct*** answer from the options given below:

A. (*a*), (*b*), (*c*), (*d*), (*e*)
B. (*b*), (*d*), (*c*), (*a*), (*e*)
C. (*c*), (*b*), (*a*), (*d*), (*e*)
D. (*b*), (*c*), (*a*), (*d*), (*e*)

Directions (Q.No. 41-45): *Read the passage given below and answer the questions.*

The English word 'caste' is actually a borrowing from the Portuguese casta, meaning pure breed. The word refers to a broad institutional arrangement that in Indian languages (beginning with the ancient Sanskrit) is referred to by two distinct terms, varna and jati. Varna, literally 'colour', is the name given to a four-fold division of society into brahmana, kshatriya, vaishya and shudra, though this excludes a significant section of the population composed of the 'outcastes', foreigners, slaves, conquered peoples and other, sometimes referred to as the panchamas of fifth category. Jati is a generic term referring to species of kind of anything, ranging from inanimate objects to plants, animals and human beings. The most commonly cited defining features of caste are the following:

1. Caste is determined by birth.
2. Membership in a caste involves strict rules about marriage.
3. Caste membership also involves rules about food and food-sharing.
4. Caste involves a system consisting of many castes arranged in a hierarchy of rank and status.

The caste system can be understood as the combination of two sets of principles, one based on difference and separation and the other on wholism and hierarchy.

The hierarchical ordering of castes is based on the distinction between 'purity' and 'pollution'.

41. The word 'caste' is derived from Portuguese word casta, meaning:
A. Pure blood
B. Pure Varna
C. Pure Job
D. Pure colour

42. Caste system does not reflect:
A. endogamy
B. ritual purity
C. strict food sharing rules
D. linguistic separation

43. Which of the following is not a feature of caste system?
A. Caste is determined by birth.
B. Membership in a caste involves strict rules about marriage.
C. Caste involves a system of Rank and Status.
D. Caste is division based on gender.

44. Caste system is based on the combination of two sets of principles, please identify the principles.
A. Difference and separation and wholism and hierarchy
B. Purity and pollution
C. Sanskritization and westernization
D. Hierarchy and inequality

45. 'Varna' is the name given to a:
A. Five-fold division of society
B. Six-fold division of society
C. Seven-fold division of society
D. Four-fold division of society

Directions (Q.No. 46-50): *Read the passage given below and answer the questions.*

Thinkers like Karl Marx, Max Weber and Emile Durkheim associated a number of social features with industry, such as urbanisation, loss of face-to-face relationships that are found in rural areas. This was substituted by anonymous professional relationships in modern factory and workplace. Industrialisation involves a detailed division of labour. People often do not see the end result of their work because they are producing only small part of product. The work is often repetitive and exhausting, however it is better than being unemployed. Marx calls this situation alienation where people do not enjoy work and see it as something they have to do in order to survive.

46. Which of the following is not characteristic of industry?
A. anonymous professional relationship
B. division of labour
C. face-to-face relationship
D. alienation

47. Increasing industry production of goods occurs due to:
A. division of labour
B. professional relationship
C. urbanization
D. alienation

48. Match List-I with List-II:

List-I (Concepts/ Sociologists)	List-II (Characteristics/ Counter button)
(*a*) Rural areas	(*i*) Alienation
(*b*) Emile Durkheim	(*ii*) Division of process into several part
(*c*) Karl Marx	(*iii*) Face-to-Face relationship
(*d*) Division of Labour	(*iv*) Sociologist

Choose the ***correct*** answer from the options given below:

	(*a*)	(*b*)	(*c*)	(*d*)
A.	(*i*)	(*ii*)	(*iv*)	(*iii*)
B.	(*i*)	(*iii*)	(*ii*)	(*iv*)
C.	(*ii*)	(*iii*)	(*iv*)	(*i*)
D.	(*iii*)	(*iv*)	(*i*)	(*ii*)

49. Job in industry is not ______.
A. repetitive B. exhaustive
C. enjoyable D. alienating

50. Karl marx, Max Weber and Emile Durkheim talked about:
A. internal features of industry
B. external features of industry
C. economic features of industry
D. social features of industry

ANSWERS

1. (A): Among the most famous theories of demography is the one associated with the English political economist Thomas Robert Malthus (1766-1834). Malthus's theory of population growth—outlined in his Essay on Population (1798)—was a rather pessimistic one. He argued that human populations tend to grow at a much faster rate than the rate at which the means of human subsistence (especially food, but also clothing and other agriculture-based products) can grow. Therefore humanity is condemned to live in poverty forever because the growth of agricultural production will always be overtaken by population growth. While population rises in geometric progression (i.e., like 2, 4, 8, 16, 32 etc.), agricultural production can only grow in arithmetic progression (i.e., like 2, 4, 6, 8, 10 etc.). Because population growth always outstrips growth in production of subsistence resources, the only way to increase prosperity is by controlling the growth of population. Unfortunately, humanity has only a limited ability to voluntarily reduce the growth of its population (through 'preventive checks' such as postponing marriage or practicing sexual abstinence or celibacy). Malthus believed therefore that 'positive checks' to population growth—in the form of famines and diseases—were inevitable because they were nature's way of dealing with the imbalance between food supply and increasing population.

Malthus's theory was influential for a long time. But it was also challenged by theorists who claimed that economic growth could outstrip population growth. However, the most effective refutation of his theory was provided by the historical experience of European countries. The pattern of population growth began to change in the latter half of nineteenth century, and by the end of the first quarter of the twentieth century these changes were quite dramatic. Birth rates had declined, and outbreaks of epidemic diseases were being controlled. Malthus's predictions were proved false because both food production and standards of living continued to rise despite the rapid growth of population.

Malthus was also criticised by liberal and Marxist scholars for asserting that poverty was caused by population growth. The critics argued that problems like poverty and starvation were caused by the unequal distribution of economic resources rather than by population growth. An unjust social system allowed a wealthy and privileged minority to live in luxury while the vast majority of the people were forced to live in poverty.

2. **(C):** Increase in female infanticide is due to social and cultural prejudices. Female foeticide and female infanticide are 2 of the earliest forms of discrimination against female members of our society. Abortion of a girl child in the mother's womb refers to female foeticide and killing a girl child after her birth is referred to as female infanticide. These 2 numbers are under-reported in India, a fact that is proved by a completely skewed sex ratio in India.

3. **(A):** Beti Bachao Beti Padhao Yojana was introduced by Government of India that could increase the female ratio in the country. The Beti Bachao Beti Padhao Yojana is a national initiative run jointly by the Ministry of Women & Child Development (MoWCD), Ministry of Health & Family Welfare (MoH&FW) and Ministry of Education (MoE). Each body is accountable for different aspects of the scheme. Budgetary control and administration of the BBBP falls under the MoWCD's purview. However, capacity building and quality control are responsibilities of the MoH&FW. And community engagement programmes have been allocated under the MoE.

4. **(C):** One concept which is somewhat complicated is that of life expectancy. This refers to the estimated number of years that an average person is expected to survive. It is calculated on the basis of data on age-specific death rates in a given area over a period of time.

5. **(B):** Mass transit and mass communication are bridging the gap between the rural and urban areas. Even in the past, the rural areas were never really beyond the reach of market forces and today they are being more closely integrated into the consumer market.

Considered from an urban point of view, the rapid growth in urbanisation shows that the town or city has been acting as a magnet for the rural population. Those who cannot find work (or sufficient work) in the rural areas go to the city in search of work. This flow of rural-to-urban migration has also been accelerated by the continuous decline of common property resources like ponds, forests and grazing lands. These common resources enabled poor people to survive in the villages although they owned little or no land. Now, these resources have been turned into private property, or they are exhausted. (Ponds may run dry or no longer provide enough fish; forests may have been cut down and have vanished...). If people no longer have access to these resources, but on the other hand have to buy many things in the market that they used to get free (like fuel, fodder or supplementary food items), then their hardship increases. This hardship is worsened by the fact that opportunities for earning cash income are limited in the villages.

Sometimes the city may also be preferred for social reasons, especially the relative anonymity it offers. The fact that urban life involves interaction with strangers can be an advantage for different reasons. For the socially oppressed groups like the Scheduled Castes and Scheduled Tribes, this may offer some partial protection from the daily humiliation they may suffer in the village where everyone knows their caste identity. The anonymity of the city also allows the poorer sections of the socially dominant rural groups to engage in low status work that they would not be able to do in the village. All these reasons make the city an attractive destination for the villagers.

6. **(D):** The most famous of the early political economists was Adam Smith, who in his book, The Wealth of Nations, attempted to understand the market economy that was just emerging at that time. Smith argued that the market economy is made up of a series of individual exchanges or transactions, which automatically create a functioning and ordered system. This happens even though none of the individuals involved in the millions of transactions had intended to create a system. Each person looks only to her or his own self-interest, but in the pursuit of this self-interest the interests of all - or of society - also seem to be looked after. In this sense, there seems to be some sort of an unseen force at work that converts what is good for each individual into what is good for society. This unseen force was called 'the invisible hand' by Adam Smith.

   Thus, Smith argued that the capitalist economy is driven by individual self-interest, and works best when individual buyers and sellers make rational decisions that serve their own interests. Smith used the idea of the 'invisible hand' to argue that society overall benefits when individuals pursue their own self-interest in the market, because it stimulates the economy and creates more wealth. For this reason, Smith supported the idea of a 'free market', that is, a market free from all kinds of regulation whether by the state or otherwise. This economic philosophy was also given the name laissez-faire, a French phrase that means 'leave alone' or 'let it be'.

7. **(A):** One of sociology's founders, Max Weber, was among the first to point out that the goods that people buy and use are closely related to their status in society. He coined the term status symbol to describe this relationship. For example, among the middle class in India today, the brand of cell phone or the model of car that one owns are important markers of socio-economic status. Weber also wrote about how classes and status groups are differentiated on the basis of their lifestyles. Consumption is one aspect of lifestyle, but it also includes the way you decorate your home and the way you dress, your leisure activities, and many other aspects of daily life. Sociologists study consumption patterns and lifestyles because of their cultural and social significance in modern life.

8. **(C):** The Constitution of India recognises the possibility that there may be groups other than the Scheduled Tribes and Scheduled Castes who suffer from social disadvantages. These groups—which need not be based on caste alone, but generally are identified by caste—were described as the 'socially and educationally backward classes'. This is the constitutional basis of the popular term 'Other Backward Classes' (OBCs), which is in common use today.

   Like the category of the 'tribe', the OBCs are defined negatively, by what they are not. They are neither part of the 'forward' castes at the upper end of the status spectrum, nor of the Dalits at the lower end. But since caste has entered all the major Indian religions and is not confined to Hinduism alone, there are also members of other religions who belong to the backward castes and share the same traditional occupational identification and similar or worse socio-economic status.

   For these reasons, the OBCs are a much more diverse group than the Dalits or adivasis. The first government of independent India under Jawaharlal Nehru appointed a commission to look into measures for the welfare of the OBCs. The First Backward Classes Commission headed by Kaka Kalelkar submitted its report in 1953. But the political climate at the time led to the report being sidelined. From the mid-fifties, the OBC issue became a regional affair pursued at the state rather than the central level.

9. **(B):** Some common features central to the public perception of 'disability' all over the world—
   - Disability is understood as a biological given.
   - Whenever a disabled person is confronted with problems, it is taken for granted that the problems originate from her/his impairment.
   - The disabled person is seen as a victim.
   - Disability is supposed to be linked with the disabled individual's self perception.
   - The very idea of disability suggests that they are in need of help.

10. **(B):** According to Pierre Bourdieu social resources can be distinguished between three forms of capital:
    (*i*) **Economic Capital:** It car be divided in the form of material assets and income.
    (*ii*) **Cultural Capital:** It consists of educational qualifications and status.
    (*iii*) **Social Capital:** It is in the form of networks of contacts and social associations.

11. **(D):** Just like caste in India, race in South Africa stratifies society into a hierarchy. About one South African in seven is of European ancestry, yet South Africa's White minority holds the dominant share of

power and wealth. Dutch traders settled in South Africa in the mid-seventeenth century; early in the nineteenth century, their descendants were pushed inland by British colonisation. At the beginning of the twentieth century, the British gained control of what became the Union and then the Republic of South Africa. To ensure their political control, the White European minority developed the policy of apartheid, or separation of the races. An informal practice for many years, apartheid became law in 1948 and was used to deny the Black majority South African citizenship, ownership of land, and a formal voice in government. Every individual was classified by race and mixed marriages were prohibited. As a racial caste, Blacks held low paying jobs; on average, they earned only one-fourth what whites did.

12. (C): In their 2011 book, Crafting State-Nations: India and other Multinational Democracies, political scientists Juan Linz, Alfred Stepan, and Yogendra Yadav argued that ethnically diverse societies have one of two options when balancing the twin objectives of nation-building and democracy-building.

One route is the construction of a nation-state in which the political boundaries of the State mirror the cultural boundaries of the nation. The historian Eugen Weber famously described how French leaders in the wake of the Revolution transformed "peasants into Frenchmen" by moulding a common cultural, linguistic, and national identity that was uniquely—and exclusively—French.

But for societies that possess strong cultural diversity, at least some of which is territorially based and backed by strong sub-national identities, the nation-state model is ineffective at best and counterproductive at worst. For these complex cases, Linz, Stepan, and Yadav suggest an alternative path - what they term a "state-nation". Whereas a nation-state insists on alignment between the boundaries of the State and nation, a state-nation allows for a multiplicity of "imagined communities" to coexist beneath a single democratic roof. It recognises that citizens can have multiple, overlapping identities that need not detract from a larger sense of national unity.

13. (D): In the 1920s, the Indian National Congress was reconstituted on linguistic lines. Its provincial units now followed the logic of language—one for Marathi speakers, another for Oriya speakers, etc. At the same time, Gandhi and other leaders promised their followers that when freedom came, the new nation would be based on a new set of provinces based on the principle of language.

However, when India was finally freed in 1947, it was also divided. Now, when the proponents of linguistic states asked for this promise to be redeemed, the Congress hesitated. Partition was the consequence of intense attachment to one's faith; how many more partitions would that other intense loyalty, language, lead to? So ran the thinking of the top Congress bosses including Nehru, Patel and Rajaji.

On the other side, the rank and file Congressmen were all for the redrawing of the map of India on the lines of language. Vigorous movements arose among Marathi and Kannada speakers, who were then spread across several different political regimes—the erstwhile Bombay and Madras presidencies, and former princely states such as Mysore and Hyderabad. However, the most militant protests ensued from the very large community of Telugu speakers. In October 1953, Potti Sriramulu, a former Gandhian, died seven weeks after beginning a fast unto death. Potti Sriramulu's martyrdom provoked violent protests and led to the creation of the state of Andhra Pradesh. It also led to the formation of the SRC, which in 1956 put the formal, final seal of approval on the principle of linguistic states.

14. (D): The LTTE (Liberation Tigers of Tamil Eelam) was formed in 1976 by Prabhakaran with the intention of acquiring a homeland for the Tamils in Sri Lanka in the north and east parts of the island.

The group first struck in July 1983 when they attacked an army patrol at Tirunelveli in Jaffna. 13 army men were killed which prompted violence on civilian Tamils by the majority community. The initial days of the LTTE were focused on fighting other Tamil factions and consolidating power as the sole representative of the Sri Lankan Tamils. This was achieved by 1986, the same year it captured Jaffna. There were many skirmishes between the government and the insurgents in which civilians were also affected. Many Tamils left their homes for the eastern part of the country.

15. (D)

16. (A): 'Modernity' assumes that local ties and parochial perspectives give way to universal commitments and cosmopolitan attitudes; that the truths of utility, calculation, and science take precedence over those of the emotions, the sacred, and the non-rational; that the individual rather than the group be the primary unit of society and politics; that the associations in which men live and work be based on choice not birth; that mastery rather than fatalism orient their attitude toward the material and human environment;

that identity be chosen and achieved, not ascribed and affirmed; that work be separated from family, residence, and community in bureaucratic organisation (Rudolph and Rudolph, 1967).

17. (D): For Indian nationalists the issue of economic exploitation under colonial rule was a central issue. Images of precolonial fabled riches of India contrasted with the poverty of British India. The Swadeshi movement strengthened the loyalty to the national economy. Modern ideas made people realise that poverty was preventable. Indian nationalists saw rapid industrialisation of the economy as the path towards both growth and social equity. Development of heavy and machine-making industries, expansion of the public sector and holding of a large cooperative sector were considered very important. A modern and prosperous India, as visualised by Jawaharlal Nehru, was to be built on an edifice of giant steel plants or gigantic dams and power stations.

18. (C): An economic system in which the means of production are privately owned and organised to accumulate profits within a market system is called capitalism. Capitalism is often thought of as an economic system in which private actors own and control property in accord with their interests, and demand and supply freely set prices in markets in a way that can serve the best interests of society.

The essential feature of capitalism is the motive to make a profit. As Adam Smith, the 18th century philosopher and father of modern economics, said: "It is not from the benevolence of the butcher, the brewer, or the baker that we expect our dinner, but from their regard to their own interest". Both parties to a voluntary exchange transaction have their own interest in the outcome, but neither can obtain what he or she wants without addressing what the other wants. It is this rational self-interest that can lead to economic prosperity.

In a capitalist economy, capital assets—such as factories, mines, and railroads—can be privately owned and controlled, labour is purchased for money wages, capital gains accrue to private owners, and prices allocate capital and labour between competing uses.

19. (A): Different Kinds of Cultural Change:

- Sanskritisation
- Westernisation
- Modernisation
- Secularisation.

20. (D): Kandukiri Viresalingam's The Sources of Knowledge reflected his familiarity with navya-nyaya logic. At the same time he translated the works of Julius Huxley, an eminent biologist.

21. (B): Urbanisation means the increase in the proportion population of a country who live in urban areas. The most important cause of urbanisation is rural-urban migration. During the late 1990s some 20 to 30 million people were leaving the countryside every year and moving into towns and cities. Developed countries experienced rapid urbanisation during the nineteenth century. Developing countries experienced rapid urbanisation during the second half of the twentieth century.

22. (B): Raja Ram Mohun Roy attacked the practice of sati on the basis of both appeals to humanitarian and natural rights doctrines as well as Hindu shastras. Roy supported women's rights. He was known for his efforts to abolish Sati Pratha (Hindu funeral practice in which widows were compelled to sacrifice themselves with their husband's pyre) and child marriage. Due to his unending efforts, Sati was declared illegal in 1829. He also criticised caste system.

23. (C): Pandit Jawaharlal Nehru was succeeded by Netaji Subhash Chandra Bose as president of the Indian National Congress in 1938 over the 51st session at Haripura. Meghnad Saha had persuaded Netaji Subhash Chandra Bose to set up a national planning committee that can help in planning and developing the economy to eradicate poverty from the country and focus on development of the agriculture sector. Since Netaji Subhash Chandra Bose was made the president of the Indian National Congress, he couldn't take a charge of being a President of the National planning committee. Thus he approached Pandit Jawaharlal Nehru and convinced him to be appointed as the first president of the national planning committee in 1938. After India became independent in 1947 from the British rule, a formal model of planning and planning commission was established and adopted and was reported directly to the prime minister of India, Pandit Jawaharlal Nehru who was the first prime minister of independent India, on 15th of March 1950. Pandit Jawaharlal Nehru was made the chairman of this planning commission. In 1951, the first five year plan was launched that mainly focused on the development of the agriculture sector.

24. (B): The Orthodox members of the Hindu community in Bengal *i.e.,* defenders of sati formed Dharma Sabha and petitioned the British arguing that reformers had no right to interpret holy texts and not to legislate against sati.

25. (D): Sanskritisation as a concept has been criticised at different levels. One, it has been criticised for exaggerating social mobility or the scope of 'lower castes' to move up the social ladder. For it leads to no structural change but only positional change of some individuals. In other words inequality continues to persist though some individuals may be able to improve their positions within the unequal structure. Two, it has been pointed out that the ideology of sanskritisation accepts the ways of the 'upper caste' as superior and that of the 'lower caste' as inferior. Therefore, the desire to imitate the 'upper caste' is seen as natural and desirable.

Third, 'sanskritisation' seems to justify a model that rests on inequality and exclusion. It appears to suggest that to believe in pollution and purity of groups of people is justifiable or all right. Therefore, to be able to look down on some groups just as the 'upper castes' looked down on the 'lower castes', is a mark of privilege. In society where such a world-view exists, imagining an equal society becomes difficult. It shows how such discriminatory ideas become a way of life. Instead of aspiring for an equal society, the exclusion and discrimination seek to give their own meaning to their excluded status. In other words they aspire to be in a position from where they can in turn look down on other people. This reflects an essentially undemocratic vision.

Fourth, since sanskritisation results in the adoption of upper caste rites and rituals it leads to practices of secluding girls and women, adopting dowry practices instead of bride-price and practising caste discrimination against other groups, etc.

Fifth, the effect of such a trend is that the key characteristics of dalit culture and society are eroded. For example the very worth of labour which 'lower castes' do is degraded and rendered 'shameful'. Identities based on the basis of work, crafts and artisanal abilities, knowledge forms of medicine, ecology, agriculture, animal husbandry etc., are regarded useless in the industrial era.

26. (A): In a democratic form of government political parties are key actors. A political party may be defined as an organisation oriented towards achieving legitimate control of government through an electoral process. Political Party is an organisation established with the aim of achieving governmental power and using that power to pursue a specific programme. Political parties are based on certain understanding of society and how it ought to be. In a democratic system the interests of different groups are also represented by political parties, who take up their case. Different interest groups will work towards influencing political parties. When certain groups feel that their interests are not being taken up, they may move to form an alternative party. Or they form pressure groups who lobby with the government. Interest Groups are organised to pursue specific interests in the political arena, operating primarily by lobbying the members of legislative bodies. In some situations, there may be political organisations which seek to achieve power but are denied the opportunity to do so through standard means. These organisations are best regarded as movements until they achieve recognition.

27. (C): Many tribal areas have had a rich tradition of grassroot democratic functioning. We give an illustrative example from Meghalaya. All the three major ethnic tribal groups, namely, the Khasis, Jaintias and the Garos have their own traditional political institutions that have existed for hundreds of years. These political institutions were fairly well-developed and functioned at various tiers, such as the village level, clan level and state level. For instance, in the traditional political system of the Khasis each clan had its own council known as the 'Durbar Kur' which was presided over by the clan headman. Though there is a long tradition of grassroot political institutions in Meghalaya, a large chunk of tribal areas lie outside the provisions of the 73rd Amendment. This may be because the concerned policy makers did not wish to interfere with the traditional tribal institutions.

However, as sociologist Tiplut Nongbri remarks that tribal institutions in themselves need not necessarily be democratic in its structure and functioning. Commenting on the Bhuria Committee Report that went into this issue Nongbri remarks that while the Committee's concern for the traditional tribal institutions is appreciable, it fails to take stock of the complexity of the situation. For notwithstanding the strong egalitarian ethos that characterised tribal societies the element of stratification is not altogether absent. Tribal political institutions are not only marked by open intolerance to women but the process of social change has also introduced sharp distortions in the system, making it difficult to identify which is traditional and which is not.

28. (B)

29. (B)

30. (A): The large scale circulation of labour has had several significant effects on rural society, in both the receiving and the supplying regions. For instance, in poor areas where male family members spend much of the year working outside of their villages, cultivation has become primarily a female task. Women are also emerging as the main source of agricultural labour, leading to the 'feminisation of agricultural labour force.' The insecurity of women is greater because they earn lower wages than men for similar work. Until recently, women were hardly visible in official statistics as earners and workers. While women toil on the land as landless labourers and as cultivators, the prevailing patrilineal kinship system, and other cultural practices that privilege male rights, largely excludes women from land ownership.

31. (D): In most of the Green Revolution areas, it was primarily the medium and large farmers who were able to benefit from the new technology. This was because inputs were expensive, and small and marginal farmers could not afford to spend as much as large farmers to purchase these inputs. When agriculturists produce primarily for themselves and are unable to produce for the market, it is known as 'subsistence agriculture' and they are usually termed 'peasants'. Agriculturists or farmers are those who are able to produce surplus, over and above the needs of the family, and so are linked to the market. It was the farmers who were able to produce a surplus for the market who were able to reap the most benefits from the Green Revolution and from the commercialisation of agriculture that followed.

Thus, in the first phase of the Green Revolution, in the 1960s and 1970s, the introduction of new technology seemed to be increasing inequalities in rural society. Green Revolution crops were highly profitable, mainly because they yielded more produce. Well-to-do farmers who had access to land, capital, technology, and know-how, and those who could invest in the new seeds and fertilisers, could increase their production and earn more money. However, in many cases it led to the displacement of tenant-cultivators. For landowners began to take back land from their tenants and cultivate it directly because cultivation was becoming more profitable. This made the rich farmers better off, and worsened the condition of the landless and marginal holders.

In addition, the introduction of machinery such as tillers, tractors, threshers, and harvesters (in areas such as Punjab and parts of Madhya Pradesh) led to the displacement of the service caste groups who used to carry out these agriculture-related activities. This process of displacement also increased the pace of rural-urban migration.

The ultimate outcome of the Green Revolution was a process of 'differentiation', in which the rich grew richer and many of the poor stagnated or grew poorer. It should be noted that employment and wages for agricultural workers did increase in many areas, because the demand for labour increased. Moreover, rising prices and a shift in the mode of payment of agricultural workers from payment in kind (grain) to cash, actually worsened the economic condition of most rural workers.

32. (C): The change in the nature of the relationship between landlords (who usually belonged to the dominant castes) and agricultural workers (usually low caste), was described by the sociologist Jan Breman as a shift from 'patronage to exploitation'. Such changes took place in many areas where agriculture was becoming more commercialised, that is, where crops were being grown primarily for sale in the market. The transformation in labour relations is regarded by some scholars as indicative of a transition to capitalist agriculture. Because the capitalist mode of production is based on the separation of the workers from the means of production (in this case, land), and the use of 'free' wage labour. In general, it is true that farmers in the more developed regions were becoming more oriented to the market. As cultivation became more commercialised, these rural areas were also becoming integrated to the wider economy. This process increased the flow of money into villages and expanding opportunities for business and employment. But we should remember that this process of transformation in the rural economy, in fact, began during the Colonial period. In many regions in the 19th century, large tracts of land in Maharashtra were given over to cotton cultivation, and cotton farmers became directly linked to the world market. However, the pace and spread of change rapidly increased after Independence, as the government promoted modern methods of cultivation and attempted to modernise the rural economy through other strategies. The state invested in the development of rural infrastructure, such as irrigation facilities, roads and electricity, and on the provision of agricultural inputs, including credit through banks and cooperatives. For regular agricultural growth, uninterrupted power supply to rural India is one of the necessities. The recently launched Deen Dayal Upadhyaya Gram Jyoti Yojana is an effort of the Indian government in this direction. The overall outcome of these efforts at 'rural development' was not only to transform the rural economy and agriculture, but also the agrarian structure and the rural society itself.

33. (B): The first modern mass media institution began with the development of the printing press. Although the history of print in certain societies dates back to many centuries, the first attempts at printing books using modern technologies began in Europe. This technique was first developed by Johann Gutenberg in 1440. Initial attempts at printing were restricted to religious books.

With the Industrial Revolution, the print industry also grew. The first products of the press were restricted to an audience of literate elites. It was only in the mid 19th century, with further development in technologies, transportation and literacy that newspapers began to reach out to a mass audience. People living in different corners of the country found themselves reading or hearing the same news. It has been suggested that this was in many ways responsible for people across a country to feel connected and develop a sense of belonging or 'we feel'. The well known scholar Benedict Anderson has thus argued that this helped the growth of nationalism, the feeling that people who did not even know of each other's existence feel like members of a family. It gave people who would never meet each other a sense of togetherness. Anderson thus suggested that we could think of the nation as an 'imagined community'.

34. (B): In independent India, Jawaharlal Nehru, the first prime minister, called upon the media to function as the watchdog of democracy. The media was expected to spread the spirit of self-reliance and national development among the people. You will recall the general thrust of development in the early years of independence in India from your earlier chapters. The media was seen as a means to inform the people of the various developmental efforts. The media was also encouraged to fight against oppressive social practices like untouchability, child marriages, and ostracism of widows, as well as beliefs of witchcraft and faith healing. A rational, scientific ethos was to be promoted for the building of a modern industrial society. The Films Division of the government produced newsreels and documentaries. These were shown before the screening of films in every movie theatre, documenting the development process as directed by the state.

35. (A): Glocalization is a combination of the words "globalization" and "localization." The term is used to describe a product or service that is developed and distributed globally but is also adjusted to accommodate the user or consumer in a local market.

A common example would be cars that are sold worldwide but adjusted to meet local criteria such as emissions standards or what side the steering wheel is located. It could also focus on more cultural aspects, such as a global fast-food chain offering geographically specific menu items that cater to local tastes.

Often, glocalization campaigns involve culturally friendly media and ad campaigns to encourage the acceptance of foreign products among a local audience.

36. (D): Dharma Sabha was formed as a result of a counter-movement by the defenders of "sati", a practice in the Hindu religion of burning the widow with her husband's body. When Raja Ram Mohan Roy campaigned against sati and formed Brahmo Samaj the supporters of sati started a counter movement against his movement to protect the cruel practice of burning wives alive along with their dead husband.

37. (A): The old social movements often based on class related issues like the trade union or peasant movements different from the new social movements like the environmental or women or tribal movements. The old social movements functioned within the frame of political parties. The Indian National Congress led the Indian National Movement. The Communist Party of China led the Chinese Revolution.

38. (B)

39. (C): Political scientist Rajni Kothari attributes the surge of social movements in India in the 1970s to people's growing dissatisfaction with parliamentary democracy. Kothari argues that the institutions of the state have been captured by elites. Due to this, electoral representation by political parties is no longer an effective way for the poor to get their voices heard. People left out by the formal political system join social movements or non-party political formations in order to put pressure on the state from outside. Today, the broader term of civil society is used to refer to both old social movements represented by political parties and trade unions and to new non-governmental organisations, women's groups, environmental groups and tribal activists.

40. (D): Peasant movements or agrarian struggles have taken place from pre-colonial days. The movements in the period between 1858 and 1914 tended to remain localised, disjointed and confined to particular grievances. Well-known are the Bengal revolt of 1859-62 against the indigo plantation system and the 'Deccan riots' of 1857 against moneylenders. Some of these issues continued into the following period, and under the leadership of Mahatma Gandhi became partially linked to the Independence movement. For instance, the Bardoli Satyagraha (1928, Surat District) a 'non-tax' campaign as part of the nationwide non-cooperation movement, a campaign of refusal to pay land revenue and the Champaran Satyagraha (1917-18) directed against indigo plantations. In the 1920s, protest movements against the forest policies of the British government and local rulers arose in certain regions.

Between 1920 and 1940 peasant organisations arose. The first organisation to be founded was the Bihar Provincial Kisan Sabha (1929) and in 1936 the All India Kisan Sabha. The peasants organised by the Sabhas demanded freedom from economic exploitation for peasants, workers and all other exploited classes. At the time of Independence we had the two most classical cases of peasant movements, namely the Tebhaga movement (1946-47) and the Telangana movement (1946-51). The first was a struggle of sharecroppers in Bengal and in North Bihar for two-thirds share of their produce instead of the customary half. It had the support of the Kisan Sabha and the Communist Party of India (CPI). The second directed against the feudal conditions in the princely state of Hyderabad and was led by the CPI.

Certain issues which had dominated colonial times changed after independence. For land reforms, zamindari abolition, declining importance of land revenue and public credit system began to alter rural areas. The period after 1947 was characterised by two major social movements: The Naxalite struggle and the 'new farmer's movements'. The Naxalite movement started from the region of Naxalbari (1967) in Bengal.

41. (A)	42. (A)	43. (D)
44. (A)	45. (D)	46. (C)
47. (A)	48. (D)	49. (C)
50. (D)		

GENERAL TEST

1. Who got the Major Dhyan Chand Khel Ratna Award 2021 for his excellent performance in cricket?

A. Mithali Raj B. Shikhar Dhawan
C. Virat Kohli D. M.S. Dhoni

2. UNESCO has added this festival to its 2021 list of Intangible Cultural Heritage:

A. Durga Puja B. Diwali
C. Holi D. Kali Puja

3. Which mission has been renamed as Pradhan Mantri Digital health Mission (PM-DHM)?

A. Ayushman Bharat
B. Awaz Health Insurance Scheme
C. Aam Aadmi Bima Yojna
D. National Digital Health Mission (NDHM)

4. The theme of 'Shikshak' Parv-2021 was:

A. Quality and Sustainable Schools: Learning from schools in India
B. Learning Outcomes
C. Quality Teachers for Quality Education
D. Holistic Development

5. Light Combat Helicopters (LCH) are developed by:

A. Bharat Electronics
B. Defence Research and Development Organisation
C. Hindustan Aeronautics Limited
D. Bharat Dynamics

6. Out of the alternatives choose the most appropriate description about the three given words.

Bangle : Anklet : Necklace

A. These are Games product
B. These are jewellery
C. These are metals
D. These are Stationery items

7. From the following pairs select the combination of right pair from the following options.

(*a*) Kuwait : Taka (*b*) Greece : Dinnar
(*c*) Argentina : Peso (*d*) Bangladesh : Taka
(*e*) Sweden : Krona

Choose the correct answer from the options given below.

A. (*c*), (*d*), (*e*) B. (*a*), (*b*), (*c*)
C. (*b*), (*c*), (*d*) D. (*a*), (*d*), (*e*)

8. Arrange the given words in the sequence in which they occur in the dictionary.

(*a*) Firmament (*b*) Finish
(*c*) First (*d*) Fissure
(*e*) Fiscal

Choose the correct answer from the options given below:

A. (*b*), (*c*), (*d*), (*a*), (*e*) B. (*a*), (*b*), (*c*), (*d*), (*e*)
C. (*b*), (*a*), (*c*), (*e*), (*d*) D. (*e*), (*a*), (*b*), (*c*), (*d*)

9. Match List-I with List-II:

List-I	*List-II*
(*a*) Ellora caves	(*i*) Jaipur
(*b*) Amer Fort	(*ii*) Agra
(*c*) Golden Temple	(*iii*) Aurangabad
(*d*) Taj Mahal	(*iv*) Amritsar

Choose the correct answer from the options given below:

	(*a*)	(*b*)	(*c*)	(*d*)
A.	(*i*)	(*iii*)	(*iv*)	(*ii*)
B.	(*iii*)	(*i*)	(*iv*)	(*ii*)
C.	(*iv*)	(*iii*)	(*i*)	(*ii*)
D.	(*iii*)	(*iv*)	(*i*)	(*ii*)

10. Match List-I with List-II.

List-I (River)	*List-II (Continents)*
(*a*) Nile	(*i*) North America
(*b*) Mississippi	(*ii*) South America
(*c*) Ganga	(*iii*) Africa
(*d*) Amazon	(*iv*) India

Choose the correct answer from the options given below:

	(*a*)	(*b*)	(*c*)	(*d*)
A.	(*iii*)	(*i*)	(*iv*)	(*ii*)
B.	(*iii*)	(*ii*)	(*iv*)	(*i*)
C.	(*i*)	(*iii*)	(*iv*)	(*ii*)
D.	(*iii*)	(*iv*)	(*ii*)	(*i*)

11. Among the four options given below three have similarities find the odd one out.

A. Scurvy B. Influenza
C. Beri Beri D. Rickets

12. Match List-I with List-II.

List-I	*List-II*
(*a*) Saina Nehwal	(*i*) Boxing
(*b*) Mary Kom	(*ii*) Wrestling
(*c*) Mithali Raj	(*iii*) Badminton
(*d*) Geeta Phogat	(*iv*) Cricket

Choose the correct answer from the options given below:

	(*a*)	(*b*)	(*c*)	(*d*)
A.	(*iii*)	(*i*)	(*iv*)	(*ii*)
B.	(*iii*)	(*i*)	(*ii*)	(*iv*)
C.	(*iv*)	(*i*)	(*ii*)	(*iii*)
D.	(*iii*)	(*ii*)	(*iv*)	(*i*)

13. Match List-I with List-II.

List-I	*List-II*
(*a*) Hepatitis	(*i*) Blood
(*b*) Pneumonia	(*ii*) Joints
(*c*) Arthritis	(*iii*) Liver
(*d*) Thalassemia	(*iv*) Lungs

Choose the correct answer from the options given below:

	(*a*)	(*b*)	(*c*)	(*d*)
A.	(*iii*)	(*iv*)	(*ii*)	(*i*)
B.	(*iii*)	(*i*)	(*ii*)	(*iv*)
C.	(*iv*)	(*iii*)	(*i*)	(*ii*)
D.	(*ii*)	(*iii*)	(*iv*)	(*i*)

14. In the following questions arrange the given words in the sequence that occur in the dictionary.

(*a*) Whiter (*b*) Wound
(*c*) Writer (*d*) Worked
(*e*) Worst

Choose the correct answer from the options given below:

A. (*a*), (*d*), (*b*), (*e*), (*c*) B. (*a*), (*d*), (*e*), (*b*), (*c*)
C. (*d*), (*a*), (*b*), (*e*), (*c*) D. (*d*), (*a*), (*e*), (*b*), (*c*)

15. Among the four options, three have the same property.. Find the odd one out.

A. Mole Hills B. Nilgiri Hills
C. Aravali Hills D. Shivalik Hills

16. Which of the following is a leap year?

A. 1500 B. 700
C. 1300 D. 2000

17. Which one of the following diagram represents Automobile, Cars, Motorcycle?

A. 
B. 
C. 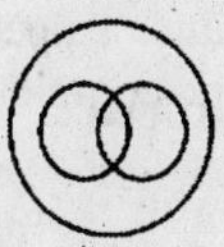
D. 

18. In the given questions select the related word from the alternatives.

Horse : Jockey : Car ______

A. Brake B. Chauffeur
C. Seatbelt D. Steering

19. Among the four options given below three have similar properties. Find the odd one out:

A. Ginger B. Beetroot
C. Carrot D. Cabbage

20. Monu rides his bicycle north wards, then turned left and rides one km and again turned left and rides 2 km. Monu found himself exactly one km west of his starting point. How far did he ride north wards initially?

A. 5 km B. 2 km
C. 3 km D. 4 km

21. Which among the following is the biggest planet of our solar system?

A. Saturn B. Jupiter
C. Mars D. Venus

22. From the given option which word can't be formed from the letters given in:

"PERMANENT"

A. MENTOR B. TRAMP
C. AMPERE D. REMANT

23. Arrange the following words as they occur in the english.

(*a*) Explosive (*b*) Explicit
(*c*) Exponent (*d*) Exposition
(*e*) Explore

Choose the correct answer from the options given below:

A. (*b*), (*e*), (*c*), (*a*), (*d*) B. (*e*), (*b*), (*c*), (*a*), (*d*)
C. (*e*), (*b*), (*a*), (*c*), (*d*) D. (*b*), (*e*), (*a*), (*c*), (*d*)

24. What is meaningful/logical order of the words given below?

(*a*) Type (*b*) Save
(*c*) Open (*d*) Print
(*e*) Close

Choose the correct answer from the options given below:

A. (*c*), (*a*), (*d*), (*b*), (*e*) B. (*a*), (*c*), (*b*), (*d*), (*e*)
C. (*c*), (*a*), (*b*), (*d*), (*e*) D. (*a*), (*c*), (*d*), (*b*), (*e*)

25. The pH value of human's urine in human is about:

A. 2.5 B. 4.0
C. 6.0 D. 9.0

26. HEAVY can be coded as 8, 5, 1, 22, 25, then LIGHT will be coded as.

A. 12, 7, 9, 8, 20 B. 12, 9, 7, 8, 20
C. 7, 8, 9, 12, 20 D. 9, 7, 8, 12, 20

27. Who is known as the 'Father of Green Revolution' in India?

A. Verghese Kurien B. M.S. Swaminathan
C. Dr. Lalji Singh D. Dr. Balram Jakhad

28. Justice is always related to ______.

A. Deceit B. Just
C. Generosity D. Nobility

29. In Rigveda, the river Jhelum is known as:

A. Sutridri B. Parushini
C. Vitasta D. Asikni

30. A person is going towards north in the night and he sees Dhruv tara and sees it on his left side. Which of the following statements justify the fact?

A. Always B. Sometimes
C. Generally D. Never

31. The first Indian women Fighter Pilot to fly a fighter jet is:
A. Avani Chaturvedi B. Gunjan Saxena
C. Shubhangi Swaroop D. Bhawana Kanth

32. Match List-I with List-II.

List-I	*List-II*
(*a*) Pedology	(*i*) Study of muscles
(*b*) Pisciculture	(*ii*) Study of growing old
(*c*) Myology	(*iii*) Study of soils
(*d*) Gerontology	(*iv*) Study of fish

Choose the correct answer from the options given below:

	(*a*)	(*b*)	(*c*)	(*d*)
A.	(*ii*)	(*iv*)	(*iii*)	(*i*)
B.	(*ii*)	(*iii*)	(*i*)	(*iv*)
C.	(*iv*)	(*ii*)	(*i*)	(*iii*)
D.	(*iii*)	(*iv*)	(*i*)	(*ii*)

33. The interest earned on ₹ 25000 in 5 years at simple interest is ₹ 1500. What is the rate of interest?
A. 1.1% B. 1.2%
C. 1.4% D. 1.6%

34. Given that $a : b = 5 : 3$ and $b : c = 2 : 5$

Which of the following is true?
A. $a < b < c$ B. $b < c < a$
C. $b < a < c$ D. $a < c < b$

35. Arrange the given ratios in descending order.
(*a*) 7 : 15 (*b*) 15 : 23
(*c*) 17 : 25 (*d*) 21 : 39

Choose the correct answer from the options given below:
A. (*c*) > (*a*) > (*b*) > (*d*) B. (*a*) > (*d*) > (*c*) > (*b*)
C. (*c*) > (*b*) > (*d*) > (*a*) D. (*d*) > (*a*) > (*b*) > (*c*)

36. A is younger than B by 7 years. If their ages are in the respective ratio of 7 : 9 then how old is A?
A. 31.5 years B. 16.5 years
C. 24.5 years D. 18.5 years

37. Match List-I with List-II.

List-I	*List-II*
(*a*) First country to use Glass	(*i*) New Zealand
(*b*) First country to make Written Constitution	(*ii*) Russia
(*c*) First country to do Artificial Satellite Experiment	(*iii*) USA
(*d*) First Country to impose Carbon Tax	(*iv*) Egypt

Choose the correct answer from the options given below:

	(*a*)	(*b*)	(*c*)	(*d*)
A.	(*iv*)	(*iii*)	(*ii*)	(*i*)
B.	(*iii*)	(*iv*)	(*i*)	(*ii*)
C.	(*ii*)	(*i*)	(*iii*)	(*iv*)
D.	(*i*)	(*ii*)	(*iv*)	(*iii*)

38. The average of 3 odd consecutive numbers is 15. What is the sum of first and last numbers?
A. 30 B. 20
C. 40 D. 35

39. In the formula "W = Fs cos θ", the angle between force and displacement (θ) is equal to 90°, the net work done will be:
A. Double B. Positive but not double
C. Negative D. Zero

40. What is the value of 70% of 420 + 30% of 280?
A. 284 B. 268
C. 368 D. 378

41. 2.56 expressed as a per cent of 1.6 is:
A. 16% B. 25%
C. 160% D. 90%

42. P can do a work in 12 days. Q can do the same work in 10 days. If P and Q come together, both of them can complete the same work in how many days?
A. $2\frac{2}{11}$ days B. $3\frac{3}{11}$ days
C. $5\frac{5}{11}$ days D. $4\frac{4}{11}$ days

43. $\frac{3}{4}$ part of tank is filled by a motor pump in 15 minutes, then the rest part of the tank will be filled in.
A. 3.5 minutes B. 5 minutes
C. 8 minutes D. 20 minutes

44. The ratio of two numbers is 5 : 6 and their HCF is 8. What is the LCM of these numbers?
A. 180 B. 240
C. 280 D. 140

45. A can complete a work in 4 minutes. B in 5 minutes, C in 6 minutes and D in 10 minutes respectively. The average number of units of work completed by them per minute will be:
A. 0.789 B. 0.179
C. 0.501 D. 0.800

46. The value of 2 ÷ 2 – 2.
A. 1 B. –1
C. 0 D. $\frac{1}{2}$

47. The network in the graphical area spread over countries, is known as:
A. LAN B. VAN
C. MAN D. WAN

48. A chair is sold for ₹ 96 at 20% loss. The cost price of the chair is:
A. ₹ 120 B. ₹ 80
C. ₹ 115.20 D. ₹ 76.80

49. The value of $\frac{(8.9)^2 - (2.1)^2}{8.9 - 2.1}$.

A. 8.6 B. 6.8
C. 10.0 D. 11.0

50. The value of $\left(\frac{x}{y}\right)^{2a-3b} \times \left(\frac{x}{y}\right)^{3b-4c} \times \left(\frac{x}{y}\right)^{4c-2a}$.

A. $\frac{x}{y}$ B. 1
C. 0 D. $\left(\frac{x}{y}\right)^{2a+3b+4c}$

51. In parallelogram ABCD, angle A is greater than angle B by 10°, the measure of angle D is:

A. 95° B. 75°
C. 85° D. 65°

52. If the length of diagonals of a rhombus are 10 cm and 24 cm then the side of the rhombus is:

A. 26 cm B. 24 cm
C. 13 cm D. 12 cm

53. In the figure AOB is a straight line then the value of x is:

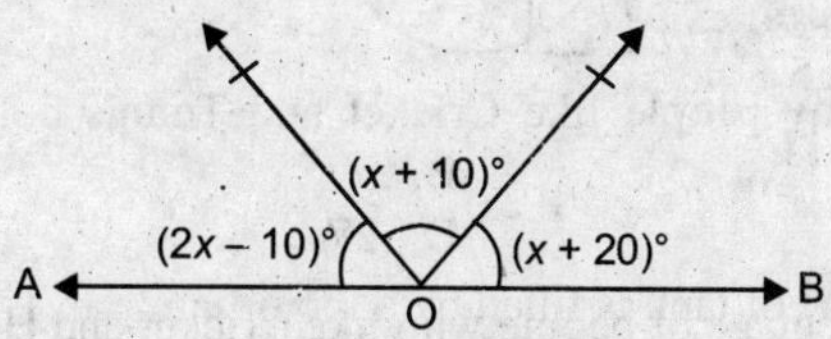

A. 60 B. 50
C. 40 D. 70

54. How much time, the Constituent Assembly took to complete the Constitution?

A. 02 years, 11 months and 18 days
B. 02 years, 18 months and 11 days
C. 03 years, 11 months and 18 days
D. 03 years, 18 months and 11 days

Directions (Qs. No. 55-57): *In the given figure ABCD is a square and radius of semi circle is 7 cm.*

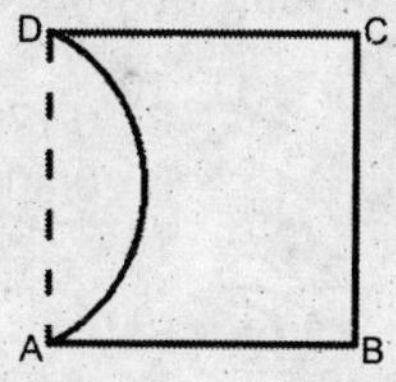

On the basis of the above information answer the questions.

55. The side of the square is:

A. $\frac{7}{2}$ cm B. 7 cm
C. 14 cm D. 12 cm

56. The perimeter of the figure is:

A. 42 cm B. 20 cm
C. 86 cm D. 64 cm

57. Area of the figure is:

A. 119 cm^2 B. 273 cm^2
C. 350 cm^2 D. 42 cm^2

Directions (Qs. No. 58-60): *The marks of 5 students in a unit test are given below:*

$x - 1,\ 2x + 1,\ 2x - 2,\ x - 1,\ 2x + 3$ where $x = 5$.

On the basis of above information answer the questions.

58. The mode of data in numerals is:

A. 11 B. 13
C. 4 D. 8

59. The median of data in numerals is:

A. 11 B. 4
C. 8 D. 13

60. The mean of the data in numerals is:

A. 4 B. 8
C. 13 D. 11

61. Some dens are rooms. All rooms are walls. Some walls are bricks. All bricks are plates.

(*a*) Some plates are walls
(*b*) Some walls are dens
(*c*) Some bricks are rooms
(*d*) Some plates are rooms

Choose the correct answer from the options given below:

A. (*a*) and (*c*) only B. (*b*) and (*c*) only
C. (*a*) and (*b*) only D. (*c*) and (*d*) only

62. If A means '–', B means '÷', C means '+' and D means '×', then 45B3C18A4D6 = ?

A. 179 B. 9
C. 18 D. 152

63. What will be next figure of the series?

A. 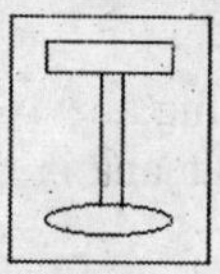

B. 

C. 

D. 

64. Find the next figure of given series:

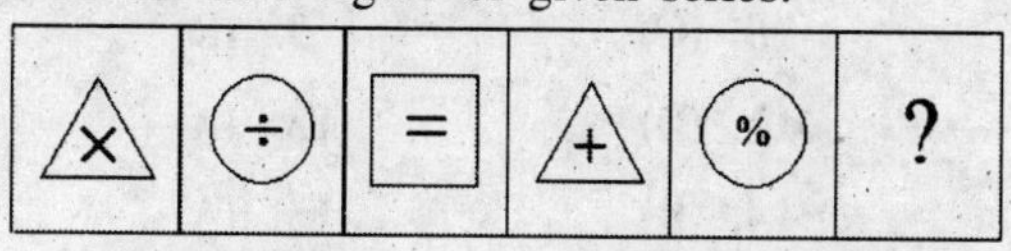

A. 

B. 

C. 

D. 

65. Find the next item of given series.

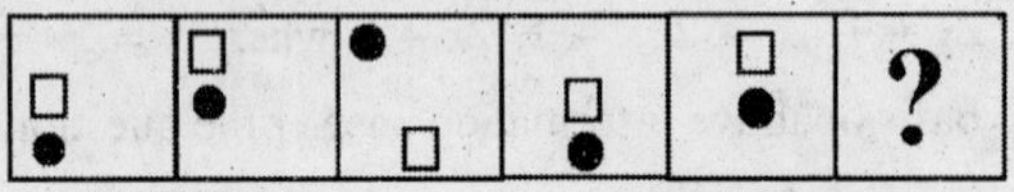

A. 

B. 

C. 

D. 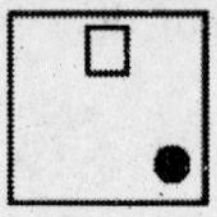

66. Out of the four alternatives choose the most appropriate description about the given words.

Sarnath : Kapilvastu : Sanchi

A. There are places having massive pillars
B. These are linked with lord Buddha
C. These are famous for stone caves
D. These have ancient Universities

67. A meaningful word starting with A is made from the first, the second, the fourth, the fifth and the sixth letters of the word 'CONTRACT'. Which of the following is the middle letter of the word?

A. T B. O
C. C D. R

68. Find the missing number from the following given option:

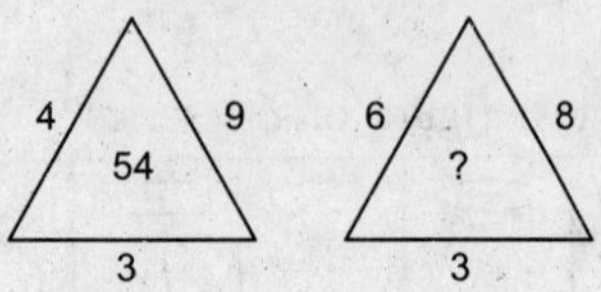

A. 72 B. 17
C. 10 D. 26

69. Forty girls are standing in a row facing the North. Amita is eleventh from left end and Sanjana is thirty first from the right end of the row. How for will Smita, who is third to the right to Amita in the row, be from Sanjana?

A. 3rd B. 4th
C. 2nd D. 5th

70. Find the missing number from the following given options.

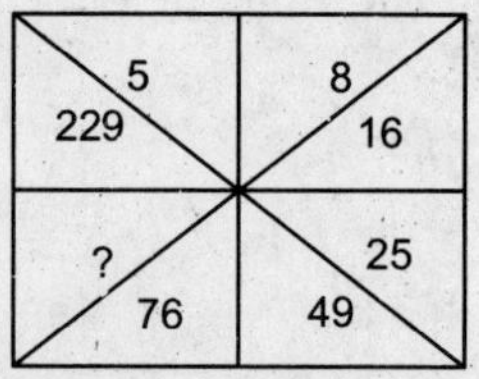

A. 150
B. 53
C. 125
D. 148

71. Among the options given below three have similarities. Find the odd one out.

A. Rice B. Wheat
C. Chick peas D. Corn

Directions (Qs. No. 72-75): *Read details carefully for questions.*

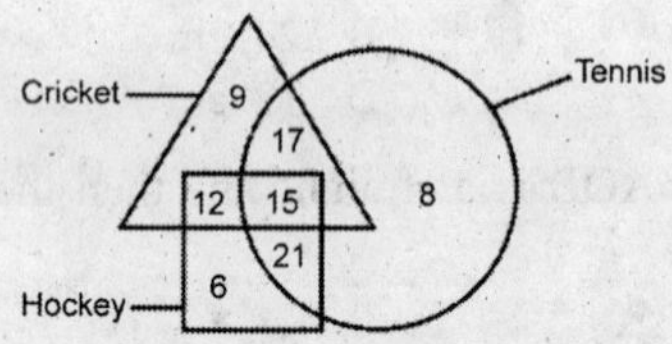

72. How many people like Cricket and Tennis both?

A. 17 B. 32
C. 15 D. 27

73. The percentage of people who like Cricket and Hockey both is ______.

A. 36.36% B. 30.68%
C. 33.3% D. 42.04%

74. Let C, H and T represents number of people who likes Cricket, Hockey and Tennis respectively. The ratio of C : H : T is:

A. 53 : 54 : 61 B. 61 : 54 : 53
C. 54 : 53 : 61 D. 54 : 61 : 53

75. How many people like Cricket, Tennis and Hockey games all together.

A. 21 B. 17
C. 15 D. 12

ANSWERS

1. (A)	**2. (A)**	**3. (D)**	**25. (C)**	**26. (B)**	**27. (B)**
4. (A)	**5. (C)**	**6. (*)**	**28. (*)**	**29. (C)**	**30. (*)**
7. (A)	**8. (C)**	**9. (B)**	**31. (A)**	**32. (D)**	
10. (A)	**11. (B)**	**12. (A)**			
13. (A)	**14. (B)**	**15. (A)**			
16. (D)	**17. (A)**	**18. (D)**			
19. (D)	**20. (B)**	**21. (B)**			
22. (A)	**23. (D)**	**24. (C)**			

33. (B): Rate of interest $= \dfrac{\text{SI} \times 100}{\text{P} \times t}$

$$= \frac{1500 \times 100}{25000 \times 5}$$

$$= \frac{6}{5} = 1.2\%.$$

34. (C): $a : b = 5 : 3$ and $b : c = 2 : 5$

$$a : b : c = 5 \times 2 : 3 \times 2 : 3 \times 5 = 10 : 6 : 15$$

$\therefore b < a < c$ is true.

35. (C): $\frac{7}{15} = 0.466$

$\frac{15}{23} = 0.652$

$\frac{17}{25} = 0.68$

$\frac{21}{39} = 0.538$

$\therefore \frac{17}{25}, \frac{15}{23}, \frac{21}{39}, \frac{7}{15}$ are is descending order.

Hence, $(c) > (b) > (d) > (a)$.

36. (C): Let B's age $= x$ years

$\therefore$ A's age $= x - 7$ years

$$\frac{x-7}{x} = \frac{7}{9}$$

$\Rightarrow 9x - 63 = 7x$

$\Rightarrow 2x = 63$

$\Rightarrow x = \frac{63}{2} = 31.5$

$\therefore$ A's age $= 31.5 - 7 = 24.5$ years.

37. (A)

38. (A): Let three odd consecutive numbers are x, $x + 2$ and $x + 4$

$x + x + 2 + x + 4 = 15 \times 3$

$\Rightarrow 3x + 6 = 45$

$\Rightarrow 3x = 39 \Rightarrow x = 13$

$\therefore$ first no. = 13, last number = 13 + 4 = 17

$\therefore$ Sum of first no. and last no. = 13 + 17 = 30.

39. (D): W = Fs cos 90°

W = 0

$\therefore$ The net work done will be zero.

40. (D): 70% of 420 + 30% of 280

$$= \frac{70}{100} \times 420 + \frac{30}{100} \times 280$$

$= 294 + 84 = 378.$

41. (C): 2.56 = 1.6% of x

$\Rightarrow \frac{256}{100} = \frac{16x}{1000}$

$\Rightarrow x = \frac{256 \times 10}{16} = 160\%.$

42. (C): P's 1 day work $= \frac{1}{12}$

Q's 1 day work $= \frac{1}{10}$

(P + Q)'s 1 day work $= \frac{1}{12} + \frac{1}{10} = \frac{5+6}{60} = \frac{11}{60}$

$\therefore$ (P + Q) can do whole work $= \frac{60}{11} = 5\frac{5}{11}$ days.

43. (B): $\frac{3}{4}$ part of tank is filled in 15 minutes

$\therefore \frac{1}{4}$ part of tank is filled in $\frac{15 \times 4}{3} \times \frac{1}{4} = 5$ minutes.

44. (B): Let numbers are $5x$ and $6x$.

HCF of $5x$ and $6x = x$

$\therefore x = 8$ [HCF = 8 given]

$\therefore$ Numbers are 40 and 48

$$\text{LCM} = \frac{40 \times 48}{8} = 40 \times 6 = 240.$$

45. (B): (A + B + C + D)'s 1 minute work

$$= \frac{1}{4} + \frac{1}{5} + \frac{1}{6} + \frac{1}{10}$$

$$= \frac{15 + 12 + 10 + 6}{60} = \frac{43}{60}$$

$\therefore$ The average no. of units of work

$$= \frac{43}{60 \times 4} = \frac{43}{240} = 0.179.$$

46. (B): $2 \div 2 - 2 = 1 - 2 = -1.$

47. (*)

48. (A): Let C.P. = ₹ 100

Loss $= \frac{20}{100} \times 100 =$ ₹ 20

S.P. = 100 − 20 = ₹ 80

When S.P. ₹ 80 then C.P. = ₹ 100

When S.P. ₹ 96 then C.P. = ₹ $\frac{100}{80} \times 96$

$\therefore$ CP = ₹ 120.

49. (D): $\frac{(8.9)^2 - (2.1)^2}{8.9 - 2.1} = \frac{(8.9 + 2.1)(8.9 - 2.1)}{(8.9 - 2.1)}$

$= 8.9 + 2.1 = 11.0.$

50. (B): $\left(\frac{x}{y}\right)^{2a-3b} \times \left(\frac{x}{y}\right)^{3b-4c} \times \left(\frac{x}{y}\right)^{4c-2a}$

$$= \left(\frac{x}{y}\right)^{2a-3b+3b-4c+4c-2a} = \left(\frac{x}{y}\right)^0 = 1.$$

51. (C):

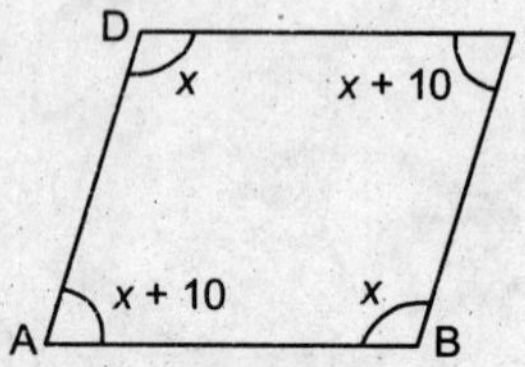

$\because$ ABCD is a $\|$gm

Let $\angle B = x^\circ$

$\therefore$ $\angle A = (x + 10)^\circ$

$\angle A + \angle B + \angle C + \angle D = 360^\circ$

$\Rightarrow x + 10^\circ + x + x + 10 + x = 360^\circ$

$\Rightarrow$ $4x + 20^\circ = 360^\circ$

$\Rightarrow$ $4x = 340^\circ$

$\Rightarrow$ $x = 85^\circ$

$\therefore$ $\angle D = 85^\circ$.

52. (C):

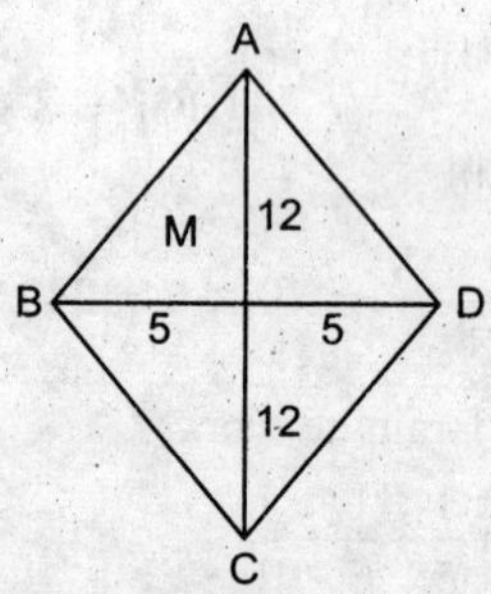

ABCD is a rhombus

In ΔABM,

$(AB)^2 = (12)^2 + (5)^2 = 144 + 25 = 169$

$\Rightarrow$ AB = 13 cm

Hence, the side of rhombus = 13 cm.

53. (C):

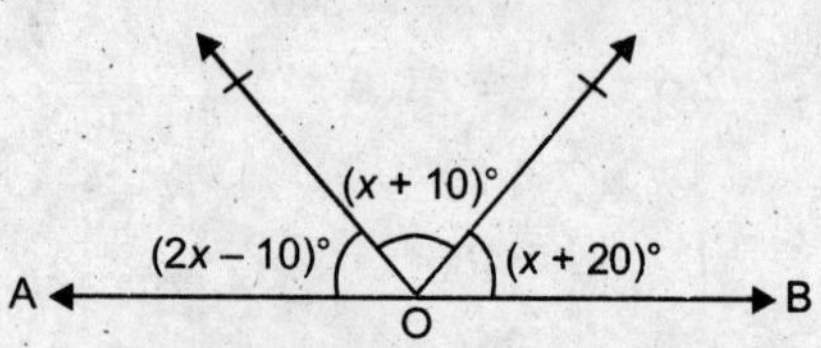

In the given figure, AOB is a straight line

$\therefore (2x - 10)^\circ + (x + 10)^\circ + (x + 20)^\circ = 180^\circ$

$\Rightarrow$ $4x + 20^\circ = 180^\circ$

$\Rightarrow$ $4x = 180^\circ - 20^\circ = 160^\circ$

$\Rightarrow$ $x = 40^\circ$.

54. (A)

55. (C): $\because$ Radius of semi circle = 7 cm

$\therefore$ Side of the square = 7 × 2 = 14 cm.

56. (D)

57. (A): Area of the figure = 119 cm^2.

58. (C): $x - 1, 2x - 1, 2x - 2, x - 1, 2x + 3$

$\because$ $x = 5$, then obtained marks are,

4, 9, 8, 4, 13

Mode of data = 4.

59. (C): First write the data in ascending order,

4, 4, 8, 9, 13

Here $n = 5$ which is odd

$$\therefore \quad \text{median} = \frac{n+1}{2} \text{ th term}$$

$$= \frac{6}{2} \text{ th term}$$

= 3rd term = 8

Hence, median = 8.

60. (B): Mean $= \dfrac{4+4+8+9+13}{5} = \dfrac{38}{5} = 7.6 = 8.$

61. (C)

62. (B): 'A' means –, 'B' means ÷, 'C' means +, 'D' means ×

45 ÷ 3 + 18 – 4 × 6

= 15 + 18 – 24 = 33 – 24 = 9.

63. (A) **64. (C)** **65. (B)**

66. (B) **67. (A)**

68. (A):

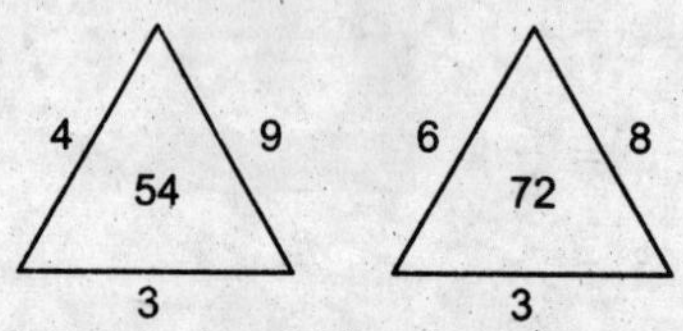

4 × 3 × 9 ÷ 2 = 108 ÷ 2 = 54

6 × 3 × 8 ÷ 2 = 144 ÷ 2 = 72

Hence, 72 will come at the place of question mark.

69. (B)

70. (D):

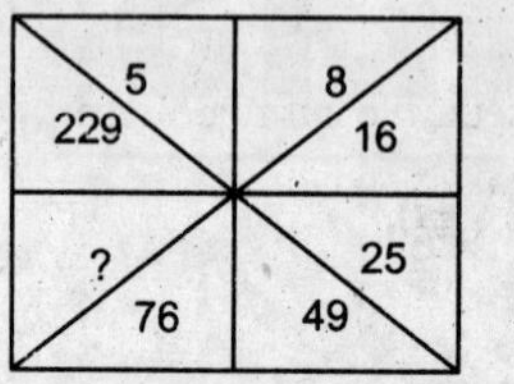

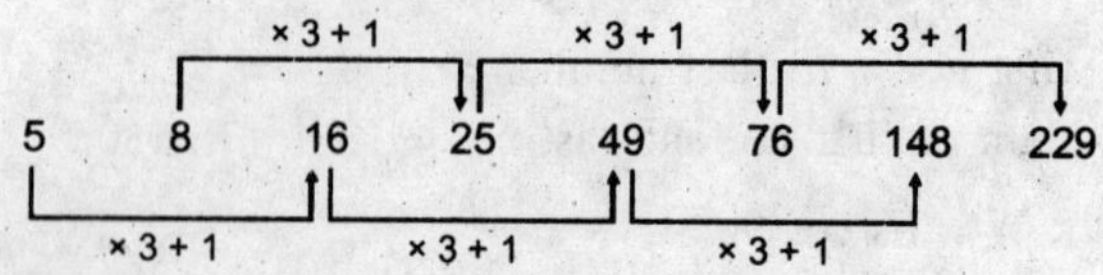

Hence, 148 will come at the place of question mark.

71. (C)

72. (B): 32 people like Cricket and Tennis both.

73. (B): Required % = 30.68%

74. (A): No. of people who likes Cricket

= 27 + 26 = 53

No. of people who likes Hockey = 27 + 27 = 54

No. of people who likes Tennis = 32 + 29 = 61

The ratio of C : H : T = 53 : 54 : 61.

75. (C): No. of people who likes Cricket, Tennis and Hockey all together = 15 which is common in all.

CUET-UG

SECTION-IA

ENGLISH LANGUAGE

Comprehension

Comprehension is a very important part of English paper. The questions on comprehension lay particular stress on understanding a given passage. You are required to read a passage or poem and answer a few questions based on it. Various comprehension questions are set solely with the objectives named below:

1. To test your ability to detect the central idea or the focal point in the given passage.
2. To test your ability to understand and interpret the given passage or poem.
3. To judge your capability to pick out the various arguments put forward by the writer for or against something.
4. To test your accuracy and richness of vocabulary.
5. To test your academic ability to understand the implied and the clearly and fully expressed ideas of the writer of the passage or poem.
6. To test, occasionally, your power of appreciating critically the views contained in the given passage or poem.

While answering comprehension questions, you must comply with the following important points:

1. First, read the whole passage or poem attentively, carefully and quickly.
2. Read it for the second time, slowly but steadily.
3. Work out the probable meaning of new words, from the context in which they have been used.
4. Underline and look for transitional words and phrases as an aid to comprehension.
5. The process of elimination should be used while selecting the correct answer.
6. Your answers should be brief and to the point, where-ever required.

I. CLOZE TEST

A cloze test is a procedure in which a person is asked to supply words that have been removed from a passage as a test of his ability to comprehend text. Practise it regularly to score well.

Directions: *In each of the following passages some numbered blank spaces are given. For each numbered blank space answer choices are given. Pick out the one which is the most appropriate for that blank space. Keep the trend of the passage in mind.*

PASSAGE-1

A drug which has been ....(1).... promoted here for fever and pain ....(2).... has invited medical ....(3).... over its ....(4).... side-effects following adverse reactions and its ....(5).... withdrawal in certain European countries. The scientific advisory committee has issued a ....(6).... advice on the ....(7).... of the drug ....(8).... some serious ....(9).... in the liver. While most doctors in India ....(10).... there is not need to ....(11).... yet, they also admit that they ....(12).... ....(13).... about it as most studies on the drug are industry ....(14).... .

QUESTIONS

1. A. aggressively B. astonishingly C. surprisingly D. immensely

2. A. treatment B. relief C. cure D. removal

3. A. concern B. criticism C. discussion D. debate

4. A. probable B. probably C. possible D. possibly

5. A. unconditional B. immediate C. consequent D. subsequent

6. A. precautionary B. preliminary C. formal D. informal

7. A. sell B. purchase
C. recommendation D. marketing
8. A. reminding B. following
C. thinking D. caring
9. A. complications B. problem
C. complexity D. consequences
10. A. suggest B. insist
C. lay D. say
11. A. worry B. react
C. panic D. exorbitant
12. A. think B. know
C. knew D. known
13. A. a bit B. a little
C. a few D. little
14. A. based B. sponsored
C. surveyed D. experimented

PASSAGE-2

I believe the biggest challenge ....(1).... the world is that of ....(2).... poverty across a large ....(3).... of the ....(4).... population and the continued ....(5).... between the rich and poor nations. The globalisation ....(6).... of the Nineties was ....(7).... to change all that and it has not made a significant impact as yet. Indeed, poverty today is the single biggest ....(8).... of place and democracy. It is high time that even the most ....(9).... rich citizen or indeed all of us ....(10).... people, realise that the only way to ....(11).... prosperity is to defeat poverty.

QUESTIONS

1. A. confronting B. facing
C. spoiling D. destroying
2. A. acute B. continued
C. general D. common
3. A. proportion B. share
C. portion D. fraction
4. A. universal B. en bloc
C. entire D. global
5. A. disputation B. disparity
C. discrimination D. tensile
6. A. struggle B. efforts
C. wave D. air
7. A. considered B. perpetually
C. supposed D. perhaps
8. A. curse B. enemy
C. hurdle D. obstruction
9. A. complacent B. compliant
C. fatuous D. inconsiderate
10. A. well-to-do B. cultured
C. privileged D. developed
11. A. defend B. debilitate
C. protect D. save

PASSAGE-3

What the daily newspapers nowadays ....(1).... carry are the reports of ...(2).... murders, killings, genocides and ....(3).... cleansing all over the world. India is not an exception ....(4)... . For a moment one is sure ....(5).... the principle of religious tolerance, peace and ....(6)...., which were the ....(7).... of Indian society, that are now slowly but steadily ....(8).... hatred, anger, distrust and religious intolerance. Making things worse are the divisive practices being ....(9).... by some ....(10).... minds that have led to the rise of religious fundamentalism. And this is a ....(11)...., which is ....(12)..... in the form of hundreds of innocent lives being lost in all corners of the country.

QUESTIONS

1. A. usually B. generally
C. regularly D. casually
2. A. huge B. massive
C. brutal D. mass
3. A. ethnic B. ethical
C. evasive D. eventual
4. A. to it B. in it
C. for it D. on it
5. A. of thinking
B. to think about
C. to think of
D. thinking about
6. A. conscientious B. compassion
C. rapacity D. sagacity
7. A. heart B. core
C. cornerstones D. milestones
8. A. are replaced with
B. replaced by
C. being replaced by
D. being replaced with
9. A. precluded B. precipitated
C. predisposed D. fabricated
10. A. perverted B. scrupulous
C. nefarious D. ruthless
11. A. calumny B. bane
C. crass D. denouncement
12. A. visible B. coming
C. taking its toll D. resulting its toll.

PASSAGE-4

The outstanding ....(1).... of the development of science and technology can neither be realised nor enriched in an atmosphere with disturbed ....(2).... balance, ...(3).... to pollution hazards. The ....(4).... of pollution and conservation of the natural ecosystems in all the development efforts are ....(5).... not merely for the growth of our ....(6).... but for our very existence on this earth. It demands the ....(7)... that it deserves. Although ....(8).... is expressed in various circles for ....(9).... the environmental balance and ....(10).... of forests, but at the same time there is a large scale ....(11).... of forests, as ....(12).... evidenced in several river valley projects ....(13).... at the national level.

QUESTIONS

1. A. capacity B. potential C. possibility D. advancement
2. A. economical B. natural C. ecological D. polluting
3. A. susceptible B. adversely C. salubrious D. pernicious
4. A. removal B. eradication C. discarding D. evolution
5. A. imperil B. imminent C. impulsive D. imperative
6. A. status B. sociability C. economy D. environment
7. A. importance B. attention C. value D. care
8. A. interest B. enthusiasm C. deep concern D. anxiety
9. A. maintaining B. evolving C. developing D. rising
10. A. growing B. maintaining C. maintenance D. regeneration
11. A. degeneration B. degradation C. deprivation D. dereliction
12. A. blatantly B. vitally C. vividly D. indiscreetly
13. A. executed B. planned C. organised D. undertaken

PASSAGE-5

India is a country where women ....(1).... worshipped and ....(2).... at the same time. If mantras have been chanted to ....(3)... the Goddesses, ...(4).... have also been hurled at a domestic wife questioning her devotion and ....(5).... . Their position has remained more or less the same ....(6).... . Though women have taken ....(7).... since the country achieved independence, they still are a ....(8).... of political, socio-economic and legal neglect. The current year has seen a number of government ....(9).... to empower women. Though these are ....(10)...., much will depend on the ....(11).... implementation of these schemes or else they ....(12).... achieve the targets, they have set for themselves.

QUESTIONS

1. A. are B. were C. has been D. have been
2. A. cursed B. blamed C. crucified D. insulted
3. A. placate B. please C. plead D. respect
4. A. curses B. expletives C. obscenity D. objurgation
5. A. virginity B. purity C. chastity D. fecundity
6. A. till date B. over time C. till now D. until now.
7. A. remarkable progress B. advancement C. rapid strides D. important steps
8. A. object B. subject C. matter D. victim
9. A. machinery B. initiatives C. project D. plannings
10. A. laudable B. languor C. lascivious D. lassitude
11. A. efficient B. thorough C. appropriate D. effective
12. A. would not B. should not C. will not D. cannot

PASSAGE-6

We are ....(1).... about our success and failure in every field. No doubt, we start our actions with ....(2).... but still in a corner of our mind ....(3).... about success and failure and ....(4).... makes us tense. And this tension sometimes ....(5).... that it effects our efficiency and performance. So, we ....(6).... remember that the mind is efficient ....(7).... it is cool, not hot or tense. The tease or excited mind ....(8).... produce rational concepts or ....(9).... thought processes. A calm person has his senses fully ....(10).... with the environment ....(11).... he places himself. A restless person ....(12).... notice anything, consequently he gets into trouble with himself and others and ....(13).... everything.

QUESTIONS

1. A. always worried B. anxious always
C. curious always D. in doubt-always
2. A. over-confidence B. full confidence
C. full enthusiasm D. full effort
3. A. a doubt remains still
B. remains a doubt
C. still remians a doubt
D. a doubt still remains
4. A. intentionally B. unnecessarily
C. necessarily D. unconsciously
5. A. become so intense
B. grow so much
C. become so intensive
D. become so serious
6. A. must B. have to
C. will have to D. shall have to
7. A. when B. when only
C. only then when D. only when
8. A. can never B. could not
C. connot D. possibly
9. A. obnoxious B. obligatory
C. objective D. orderly
10. A. engrossed B. paralleled
C. identified D. sunk
11. A. on which B. in which
C. at which D. where
12. A. do not B. does not
C. did not D. cannot

PASSAGE-7

Great books do not spring from something ....(1).... in the great men who wrote them. They are the ....(2).... of their very core, the ....(3).... of the life itself of the authors. And literature cannot be said to ....(4).... its true purpose. Until it ....(5).... translated into the actual life of him who reads. Literature is the ....(6).... of true ideas and high emotions and life is ....(7).... of ideas and emotions. In a world ....(8).... of literature, the intellectual and emotional activity of all ....(9)... exceptionally gifted men would quickly sink and ....(10).... to a narrow circle. The broad, the noble, the generous would tend to disappear ....(11).... accessible storage. And life would be ....(12).... degraded, because the ....(13).... idea and the pretty emotion would never feel the upward pull of the ideas and emotions of genius.

QUESTIONS

1. A. accidental B. remarkable
C. strange D. superficial
2. A. affluence B. effluence
C. excellence D. magnificence
3. A. outcome B. offspring
C. flow D. expression
4. A. have served B. done
C. achieve D. accomplished
5. A. is B. has been
C. gets D. has
6. A. store B. stock
C. vast reservoir D. huge collection
7. A. expression B. expansion
C. storage D. constituted
8. A. devout B. devolve
C. deterrent D. deprived
9. A. but few B. except
C. but a few D. people
10. A. die B. spoil
C. dissolve D. retract
11. A. for want of B. desiring
C. searching D. for
12. A. altogether B. correspondingly
C. contrarily D. actually
13. A. beautiful B. ornamental
C. stupid D. fallacious

PASSAGE-8

Patriotism is one of the qualities that touches the heart of the ....(1).... countrymen. When a soldier fights and dies in saving his country from the enemy, his sacrifice in this way is termed as ....(2).... and attains the ....(3).... worthy of worship. Thus in a war the soldier gets ....(4).... without surrendering, by which he ....(5).... saved his life, ...(6).... the hearts of his fellow being. This situation is true not only in ....(7).... an enemy but anyone who struggles to acheive a ....(8).... aim without surrendering and ....(9).... his life. He ....(10).... succeeded but he leaves a ....(11).... for others to follow who will definitely win and attain the victory ....(12).... the adversaries..

QUESTIONS

1. A. humble B. rustic
C. fellow D. sophisticated
2. A. intelligent B. virtuous
C. supreme D. courageous

3. A. death B. martyrdom
C. end D. goal

4. A. vanquished B. vanguard
C. reward D. award

5. A. would have had B. would be able to
C. would have D. could have

6. A. attracting B. winning
C. taking D. getting

7. A. struggling B. killing
C. winning D. fighting

8. A. esteemed B. high
C. patriotic D. laudable

9. A. offers B. sacrifices
C. lays D. present

10. A. could have B. could not have
C. may have D. may not have

11. A. trail B. trial
C. goal D. situation

12. A. upon B. over
C. on D. against

PASSAGE-9

Our beautiful sunbright ....(1).... is being systematically damaged by industrial pollution ....(2).... into rivers like the Ganga and Jamuna, ...(3).... wastes from atomic plants ....(4).... into-the world's oceans, and poisonous gases ....(5).... with the ozonosphere. ....(6)...., tropical rain forests and green pastures are ....(7).... under the pressure of a ....(8).... population. Rivers like the Narmada are being dammed to change nature's ....(9).... surface ....(10).... between flora and fauna, and sloping mountain terrain is being ....(11).... into mini oceans to supply electricity to the ....(12).... industrial stomach of our age.

QUESTIONS

1. A. ecology
B. ecosystem
C. environment
D. physical phenomena

2. A. directed B. channelled
C. scattered D. accumulated

3. A. atomic B. scientific
C. nuclear D. bumptious

4. A. diverted B. routed
C. outstretched D. overflown

5. A. channelled B. routed
C. scattered D. mixed

6. A. Besides B. Instead
C. Addition to D. Above all

7. A. diminishing B. reducing
C. minimising D. disappearing

8. A. proliferating B. profiting
C. projecting D. pronounceable

9. A. smooth B. well balanced
C. rough D. unequal

10. A. equilibrium B. equality
C. equation D. equity

11. A. contracted B. convulsed
C. conjured D. converted

12. A. hungry B. greedy
C. vacant D. ever starving

PASSAGE-10

Only ....(1)...., people find a long journey by motor-car ....(2).... . Mostly a long journey by train is much more comfortable and ....(3).... . The tracks, the coaches and the smooth though swift motion ....(4).... the pleasantness of the train journey. ....(5).... at the beautiful countryside from a window seat in a fast moving train has a ....(6).... of its own. A night journey ....(7).... its pleasures too. One can experience a sense of adventure ....(8).... a restful sleep. Modern railway travel being ....(9)... comfortable than in the past, ...(10).... the childhood excitement of ....(11).... the train and its engine as ....(12).... of visual and imaginative delight.

QUESTIONS

1. A. exceptionally B. ordinarily
C. unusually D. abnormally

2. A. disagreeable B. unenjoyable
C. strange D. agreeable

3. A. enjoyable B. suitable
C. appropriate D. enjoying

4. A. hike B. jolt
C. contribute D. all add to

5. A. Observing B. Enjoying
C. To look D. Looking

6. A. comfort B. complacence
C. delight D. satisfaction

7. A. had B. has
C. have D. has have

8. A. alongwith B. together with
C. addition to D. adding to

9. A. highly B. extensively
C. exceptionally D. so much more

10. A. revives B. vibrates
C. regenerates D. enliven

11. A. fancying B. enjoying
C. feeling D. dreaming

12. A. subjects B. objects
C. centre D. focus

PASSAGE-11

Women were earlier considered as the kitchen keepers and house keepers – that was ....(1).... as their ....(2)... field of activity. ....(3)... women began to get educated and came out ....(4)... the social and potitical field and today they are there in all fields and are ....(5)... equal emloyment as the menfolk. Not only this they are ....(6)... themselves in those fields. Two important reasons behind the changed ....(7)... are : firstly, Womens are ....(8)... themselves duly qualified and want to use-their talents to seek an employment; and secondly, with the price-index ....(9).... everyday it is found necessary for the middle class families that the wife having ....(10).... academic qualifications working and ....(11).... the family income. This while giving them a social status, also helps the family to have a better standard of living, which everyone ....(12).... for and rightly too.

QUESTIONS

1. A. recognised B. realized
C. regarded D. looked

2. A. exclusive B. only
C. working D. one

3. A. Day by day B. Slowly
C. Later D. Gradually

4. A. on B. in
C. at D. to

5. A. finding B. seeking
C. enjoying D. sharing

6. A. distinguishing B. proving
C. mastering D. struggling

7. A. scenario B. circumstances
C. society D. culture

8. A. thinking B. finding
C. educating D. proving

9. A. excelating B. intensifying
C. changing D. escalating

10. A. registered B. recognised
C. requisite D. minimum

11. A. substituting B. segment
C. influencing D. suplement

12. A. do crave B. does crave
C. starve D. do starve

PASSAGE-12

Importance of music especially in today's hum drum life cannot be ....(1).... . Today man is surrounded by ....(2).... worries and listening to music ....(3).... his nerves. Music acts as a ....(4).... and soothes the nerves. It is a fine art and groups of all ages ....(5).... to its sweet sound. A person gifted with aesthetic ....(6).... finds music as a food for his soul. Some of the great musicians of the world ....(7).... in high esteem ....(8).... of the kind of they produce western, oriental, classical, pop or light. These musicians ....(9).... concerts which attract people from all walks of life. If people are ....(10).... to balming music, they will definitely find life a rich and healthy ....(11)..... In this way, the importance of music is really ....(12)....

QUESTIONS

1. A. overstated B. understated
C. irrelevant D. relevant

2. A. varied B. innumerable
C. different D. variegated

3. A. calm B. cure
C. soothe D. please

4. A. stimulant B. catalyst
C. machinery D. device

5. A. are attracted B. get attracted
C. are pleased D. feel pleasure

6. A. beauty B. blessing
C. capabilities D. knowledge

7. A. were held B. are held
C. are taken D. are received

8. A. no matter B. considering
C. respectively D. irrespective

9. A. popularize B. organize
C. form D. propagate

10. A. forced B. brought
C. introduced D. exposed

11. A. stage B. experience
C. achievement D. thing

12. A. considerable B. unavoidable
C. imimense D. recognisable

PASSAGE-13

There are groups of people in ....(1).... developing countries who are in poverty line and who became the victims and ....(2).... in a self-fulfilling vicious of poverty. ....(3).... of the parents in the society ....(4).... afford to send their children to school. ....(5)...., the children often go to the labour force ....(6).... in order to ....(7).... the family income and to help the economic ....(8).... of the family. The Indian Government and educational ....(9).... are taking adequate steps for their standard of living and ....(10).... opportunities for schooling with full day food and other required ....(11).... .

QUESTIONS

1. A. each B. all C. whole D. every
2. A. engulfed B. surrounded C. trapped D. fall
3. A. line B. circle C. frame D. structure
4. A. can't B. couldn't C. cannot D. can never
5. A. Though B. Despite C. Instead D. Even so
6. A. at an early age B. in his growing stage C. in his childhood D. at his childhood
7. A. add B. supplement C. hike D. improve
8. A. servility B. survivality C. conditon D. situation
9. A. activist B. executives C. planners D. propagonist
10. A. approving B. alloting C. distributing D. providing
11. A. privileges B. facilities C. necessities D. factors

PASSAGE-14

What is urgently, ...(1).... in our country is a proper survey and a planned assessment of what sort of jobs ....(2).... demand both in the public as well as in the private sector and there ....(3).... a controlled enrolment in institutes and institutions which should be training young men in such needed jobs. It is a ....(4).... task, no doubt, but when the government and the private agencies ....(5).... make large scale survey for so many other problems of the country why cannot this grave problem of unemployment be ....(6).... at a priority basis and money and manpower be invested and ....(7).... to make an assessment of the requirements and then the process of their fulmilment ....(8).... . What is actually needed is not only scheming and planning but actually to have a ....(9)... to find the root of the ....(10).... . Only then can the ....(11).... be found out.

QUESTIONS

1. A. demanded B. needed C. prevalent D. lacking
2. A. are of B. are at C. are most in D. currently
3. A. needs to be B. is C. are D. shall be
4. A. labourious B. Herculean C. time taking D. stupendous
5. A. can B. could C. are out to D. readily
6. A. noticed B. surveyed C. treated D. observed
7. A. used B. employed C. organised D. treated
8. A. be worked out B. be taken up C. be decided D. be developed
9. A. spirit B. will C. motive D. strength
10. A. malady B. grievances C. curse D. paradox
11. A. treatment B. cure C. remedy D. solution

PASSAGE-15

A sudden flood of ....(1).... dangerous toys like swords and bow and arrow make their ....(2)...., in the market during the Dussehra festival. ....(3)...., eyes can and do get injured ....(4).... by these toys and ....(5)...., the victims aare innocent children. ....(6).... by the Ram Lila and similar television serials, children ....(7).... swords at each other or fire arrows from bows which ....(8).... to permanent blindness if ....(9).... to hit the eye. This happens ....(10).... if the injury is servere and not managed properly. Any injury in and around the eye ....(11).... taken seriously land managed on an emergency basis.

QUESTIONS

1. A. potentially B. instantly C. constantly D. inevitably
2. A. arrival B. appearance C. place D. position
3. A. unknowingly B. undoubtedly C. undauntedly D. unfortunately
4. A. advertently B. inadvertently C. unfortunately D. unknowingly
5. A. almost B. almost always C. all the time D. very often

6. A. Motivated B. Inspired
C. Encouraged D. Taught

7. A. attack B. take out
C. brandish D. home

8. A. can lead B. could lead
C. would lead D. lead

9. A. it targets B. it comes
C. they happen D. they are

10. A. usually B. generally
C. commonly D. more often

11. A. are to be B. is to be
C. shall be D. may be

PASSAGE-16

The scientist of today is a man of ....(1).... ambition. He is not contented with ....(2).... he has achieved, but wants to be a creator of new and surprising things so that the common people may ....(3).... at the marvels of his ....(4)...., feel thrilled and go away ....(5).... by his superior wisdom and his ....(6).... inventiveness. The new and challenging scientific forces now ....(7).... by him in the universe will continue to work ....(8).... in ever increasing numbers, to lead mankind to ....(9).... material progress, and to ....(10).... in its hand unlimited power for conquering ....(11).... territories of knowledge and experience.

QUESTIONS

1. A. increasing B. elevating
C. soaring D. diversing

2. A. what B. whatever
C. those D. that

3. A. broad B. work
C. gape D. deride

4. A. invention B. genius
C. life D. achievement

5. A. impressed B. dejected
C. attracted D. motivated

6. A. enviable B. reliable
C. unavoidable D. considerable

7. A. brought B. given
C. let loose D. realised

8. A. fruitfully B. miracles
C. magic D. wonders

9. A. unscathed B. unrelenting
C. unmitigated D. unprecedented

10. A. keep B. allot
C. load D. place

11. A. greater B. varied
C. unknown D. more and more

PASSAGE-17

Education of the future has to ....(1).... human values and see that the human factor is not neglected. The task of education is to help the individual to know himself. ....(2).... as the individual is ignorant of his ....(3)...., his potentialites and his mission of life, he ....(4).... contribute in a creative manner ....(5).... his own growth and development of the society. It is often said that, as education is the ....(6).... of the thinking elite of the nation, ...(7).... the nation's future depends on its system of education. This is true to some ....(8).... .But ....(9)...., the general outlook of society has also a strong ....(10).... on education itself so that education can only be reformed when a ....(11).... change has already begun in society.

QUESTIONS

1. A. consider B. protect
C. care D. preserve

2. A. Till then B. So long
C. Uptill then D. Till that time

3. A. own B. credibilities
C. nature D. real self

4. A. can't B. could not
C. could never D. cannot

5. A. in B. throughout
C. to D. towards

6. A. developing process B. development
C. building up D. guidance

7. A. much of B. many of
C. mostly D. mainly

8. A. limit B. horizon
C. context D. extent

9. A. conversely B. alternately
C. actually D. outwardly

10. A. hearing B. relation
C. opposition D. affinity

11. A. consequent B. corresponding
C. subsequent D. similar

PASSAGE-18

Every action we perform ....(1).... a result. And, naturally, we lay claim ....(2).... the results or fruits ....(3).... from that action in the ....(4).... that it is we who perform the action. This is .....(5).... ignorance because ....(6).... is it the Lord who ....(7).... the result of any action, it is by His will ....(8).... that even the action is accomplished. The will of the Lord ....(9).... whether we cooperate with His will or strive ....(10).... If God wills that an action takes place, he arranges for the ....(11).... for it to happen. It is ....(12).... experience that sometimes despite our best efforts we ....(13).... achieve the results we desire, and at other times the seemingly most ....(14).... situations mysteriously get ....(15).... . ....(16).... way man chooses to act, both the act and the outcome of the cost are dependent ....(17).... on the will of the Lord.

QUESTIONS

1. A. produce B. produces C. causes D. undergoes

2. A. on B. at C. to D. for

3. A. occuring B. obtaining C. deriving D falling

4. A. belief B. hope C. fantasy D. folly

5. A. sheen B. keen C. sheer D. sheathe

6. A. alone B. only that C. not only D. for only

7. A. declares B. decides C. ordains D. ornate

8. A. completely B. entirely C. only D. alone

9. A. prevails always B. prevails everywhere C. is prevalent D. always prevails

10. A. alone B. always C. constantly D. independently

11. A. wherewithal B. whereabouts C. whatsoever D. wherefore

12. A. usual B. general C. universal D. common

13. A. does not B. may not C. do not D. might not

14. A. intractable B. intangible C. internecine D. intricate

15. A. subsided B. resolved C. solved D. converted

16. A. Whatever B. All the C. All those D. Whichever

17. A. mainly B. actually C. entirely D. generally

PASSAGE-19

For centuries, women not only in India but all over the world ....(1).... treated as ....(2).... secondary position to men. ....(3).... human history men ....(4).... far greater power then women to name, classify, and order the worlds in which they both live. ....(5).... studies in various parts of the world point out to a wide ....(6).... in male and female roles ....(7).... cultures and demonstrate the possibility of change in these sex-determined roles. The 20th century in particular ....(8).... the cause of gender justice by internationalizing struggles for equality ....(9).... women and other oppressed people. Women's struggles against their ....(10).... were interwined in ....(11).... degrees with ideologies and movements based on the values of freedom, self-determination, equality, democracy and justice.

QUESTIONS

1. A. has been B. have been C. had been D. were

2. A. occupying B. taking C. possessing D. serving

3. A. All through B. Throughout C. Since D. From

4. A. have B. had C. have had D. enjoy

5. A. Sociological B. Anthropological C. General D. Practical

6. A. concord B. repulsion C. disagreement D. variation

7. A. among B. across C. between D. of

8. A. developed B. envolved C. promoted D. entertained

9. A. for B. to C. among D. by

10. A. subsidiary B. subsequent C. subservience D. subordination

11. A. various B. varying C changing D. differeing

PASSAGE-20

What is required today in our country is ....(1).... of a new political culture based on full respect for human liberty, on pluralism and on a better social deal for all. The major ....(2).... facing us today is to carry out democratic transformation in all the ....(3)...., social, cultural, economic and political. The events of the 20th century ....(4).... one thing absolutely clear that human ....(5)...., everywhere, specially in countries whose political structures were ....(6).... to reflect the revolutionary aspirations of the people ....(7).... not only under stress and strain but are ....(8).... vast upheavals because of the ....(9).... of democracy. At the same time it has also to be understood that democracy cannot be ....(10).... into a static mould.

QUESTIONS

1. A. growing B. developing
   C. creating D. creation
2. A. development B. crisis
   C. challenge D. drawback
3. A. corners B. context
   C. realm D. spheres
4. A. have made B. has made
   C. had made D. made
5. A. travails B. traverse
   C. trapse D. transverse
6. A. supposed B. meant
   C. caused D. forced
7. A. were B. was
   C. are D. have been
8. A. developing B. evolving
   C. experiencing D. faced with
9. A. denial B. rebuff
   C. rebuttal D. absence
10. A. shaped B. flex
    C. frozen D. caused

PASSAGE-21

We are living in very exciting ....(1).... . The ....(2).... change is dizzying and the impact this progress is having on our present and – more importantly – on our future is difficult to ....(3).... in its ...(4).... . This is the age of ....(5).... micro processors, sophisticated software, new hardware technology and high bandwith, high-speed networks. The PC gave us a new way to work, play and ....(6).... . In fact, it brought ....(7).... our desktops computing power, which until a few years ....(8).... had only been available to corporates. With the ....(9).... of the internet, the PC ....(10).... us the most convenient and flexible way to head on to the Net.

QUESTIONS

1. A. periods B. days
   C. phase D. times
2. A. phase B. pace
   C. sphere D. drastic
3. A. guess B. forecast
   C. comprehend D. approximate
4. A. whole B. entirety
   C. fruition D. fullness
5. A. strong B. changing
   C. powerful D. sonorous
6. A. convey B. communicate
   C. entertain D. enjoy
7. A. onto B. to
   C. on D. at
8. A. back B. earlier
   C. behind D. before
9. A. addendum B. adherence
   C. afoot D. advent
10. A. allowed B. privileged
    C. brought D. offered

PASSAGE-22

Visualisation is a strong ....(1).... to memory. Those persons who ...... (2) ..... a powerful memory cannot do so without taking the help of visualisaton. Such persons have developed the .o ....(3).... visualisation even in such ....(4).... tasks as remembering names and numbers. These persons have the names and numbers ....(5).... in their brain even after hearing those names and figues only once. On the other hand those who take the help of revising to memorise ....(6).... to forget it once they have ....(7).... the practice of revising ....(8).... the ones who have applied visualisation to memorise. Psychologists ....(9).... in visualisation a powerful tool for personality development. The more you visualise, the more you are ....(10).... your attitude and behaviour to the blue prints of your vision and ....(11).... more you are inching towards success.

QUESTIONS

1. A. way B. path
   C. aid D. symptom
2. A. command B. master
   C. rule D. enjoy
3. A. use B. apply
   C. put D. place
4. A. trivial B. difficult
   C. mundane D. unscrupulous
5. A. impress B. imprinted
   C. impinge D. store
6. A. bent B. incline
   C. prone d. tend
7. A. dropped B. left
   C. gave up D. given up
8. A. unlike B. opposite
   C. contrary D. not like
9. A. found B. have found
   C. sees D. finds
10. A. shaping B. moulding
    C. making D. attuning
11. A. actually B. factually
    C. subsequently D. consequently

PASSAGE-23

....(1).... people today remember the war that was fought after China invaded India in 1962. Not because the war was never really ....(2).... . Nor because it was ....(3).... almost before it began. The reason is ....(4).... that most of us were yet to be born. The main reason for the Chinese attack seems to ....(5).... to establish the ....(6).... order, expose our ....(7)...., put us in our place. The official reason, ...(8)...., was the territorial dispute, ...(9).... more than 100,000 square kilometres. ....(10).... speaking, India borders Tibet, not China. The McMohan Line ....(11).... the border with Tibet in what is now Arunachal Pradesh was the result of a 1914 treaty ....(12).... British India and Tibet. This was not ....(13).... to the Chinese the result was a .....(14)..... nose. The Chinese attack was ....(15).... fast and furious. ....(16).... brave soldiers ....(17).... down their lives, but India was simply unable to halt the ....(17).... . Panic quickly ....(18)....

QUESTIONS

1. A. A few B. Few C. Fewer D. A little
2. A. joined B. combined C. acted D. approved
3. A. finished B. ceased C. over D. stopped
4. A. simple B. simply C. common D. commonly
5. A. had been B. have C. had D. have been
6. A. pecking B. unavoiding C. powerful D. selfish
7. A. projections B. pretensions C. presumption D. pretending
8. A. more over B. probably C. perhaps D. however
9. A. effecting B. causing C. affecting D. influencing
10. A. Formally B. Informally C. Broadly D. Technically
11. A. relating B. dividing C. defining D. laying
12. A. among B. between C. of D. by
13. A. favourable B. favoured C. acceptable D. accepting
14. A. angry B. bloody C. honed D. blitz
15. A. quick B. prick C. sudden D. unassuming
16. A. Some B. Few C. Many D. A lot of
17. A. onrush B. onset C. omnipotence D. omen
18. A. come in B. gone in C. set in D. set out

PASSAGE-24

Man has always been ....(1).... with flying because it ....(2).... a sense of freedom, of romance and thrill-something too ....(3).... to resist. It is the task of the ....(4).... of the skies to safeguard Indian air-space from unwelcome ....(5)..... . The Indian Air Force ....(6).... a chequered and glorious history. From its ....(7).... days of single-engine aeroplanes like Tempests and Spitfires to the state of the art multi-engine, supersonic MIG and Sukhoi fighters, the Indian Air Force ....(8).... a long way. In addition to the already existing ....(9).... of aircraft and weapon systems, plans are ....(10).... to enhance its air defence power and ....(11).... capability through upgradation and ....(12).... .

QUESTIONS

1. A. fascinated B. moved C. inspired D. fancied
2. A. generates B. cultivates C. reaps D. evokes
3. A. envisaging B. impressing C. enchanting D. laudable
4. A. sentiness B. sedulous C. venturous D. fervid
5. A. emigrants B. intruders C. foreigners D. tourists
6. A. had B. have C. have had D. has had
7. A. early B. undeveloped C. growing D. embryonic
8. A. had come B. has come C. have come D. came
9. A. invention B. inventory C. mechanism D. technique
10. A. progressive B. afresh C. afoot D. affluent
11. A. combat B. increase C. intensify D. ensure
12. A. acquistion B. acknowledgement C. acquiescence D. accumulation

PASSAGE-25

Libraries were never ....(1).... the place to ....(2).... They never will be. But those who've visited libraries for the ....(3).... pleasure of it will testify to the feeling of ....(4).... on entering the labyrinth ....(5).... high with books. Suddenly, a ....(6).... spent reading seems the ideal. It's a similar experience to ....(7).... in a bookshop. The difference : in the second situation, despair ....(8).... you as your eyes zoom ....(9).... on the price; in the first there is the ....(10).... that all these books are yours for the asking. Today, ...(11)...., liberary use is almost ....(12).... necessity-based. The reading room is ....(13).... full with students poring ....(14).... their books..

QUESTIONS

1. A. realised B. seen C. recognised D. considered
2. A. hung out B. hang out C. hang out in D. hung out in
3. A. mere B. sheer C. trivial D. trifle
4. A. exhilaration B. exhaustion C. expedition D. extrapolation
5. A. going B. moving C. pik D. towering
6. A. long time B. whole life C. life time D. life long
7. A. browsing B. move about C. move D. stroll
8. A. swamps B. swab C. swoon D. swoop
9. A. at B. on C. in D. upon
10. A. idea B. surity C. certainty D. knowledge
11. A. although B. however C. in fact D. moreover
12. A. wholly B. partially C. outwardly D. purely
13. A. tight B. completely C. over crowded D. cramped
14. A. into B. onto C. over D. upon

PASSAGE-26

The ....(1).... of a country does not depend on the abundance of its revenue but more ....(2).... by its citizens; its men of education, enlightenment and character. It is for the ....(3).... of higher learning to ....(4).... an academic environment of equity, justice and fair play where those ....(5).... in the ....(6).... task of nation building can ....(7).... their responsibilities in a spirit of sincerity, dedication and commitment. Higher education in India ....(8).... great strides after independence. The ideal of education is to ....(9).... for self-preservation but which also prepares us to recognise and ....(10).... the rights of others and to shoulder our ....(11).... as responsible citizens.

QUESTIONS

1. A. prospects B. fortune C. protrusion D. gaiety
2. A. illustrated B. emancipated C. defined D. apprehended
3. A. institute B. centre C. college D. university
4. A. encourage B. embark C. promote D. polish
5. A. employed B. recruited C. held D. engaged
6. A. paramount B. ardous C. lucrative D. laudable
7. A. dispense B. disburse C. carry D. discharge
8. A. have taken B. had taken C. has taken D. is taking
9. A. evoke B. prepare C. encourage D. cultivate
10. A. concede B. preserve C. coddle D. clung
11. A. obligations B. obduracy C. obsequiousness D. portfolio

PASSAGE-27

Observation is one of the key ....(1).... of modern corporate behaviour. Indeed it has long been the ....(2).... for humans and animals generally. It is essential for every corporate citizen to be able to taste the ....(3).... of what is happening around him all the time, not merely to survive but to ....(4).... . ....(5).... the corporate corridors to check which way the wind is blowing ! Know when it is appropriate to get your ....(6).... in and when it is ....(7).... to maintain a low profile. To ....(8).... a career with the ease and ....(9).... of a winner, you need to be able to ....(10).... a disaster before it happens ! You need to take an advantage before someone else ....(11).... . You need to be at the right place before someone else ....(12).... there. Observation or paying attention to what's happening around us is essential ....(13).... . We need to take the time to ....(14).... the habit of paying attention so that we can make our work ....(15).... and so that we can stand at ease! Career ....(16).... will be the happy outcome!

QUESTIONS

1. A. approach B. method
   C. tactics D. means
2. A. rule B. norm
   C. convention D. technique
3. A. presence B. essence
   C. events D. problem
4. A. thrive B. throb
   C. fare D. blow
5. A. Sniff B. Snuffle
   C. Spin-off D. Splutter
6. A. shore B. oar
   C. objective D. ogle
7. A. correct B. right
   C. prudent D. prudish
8. A. carry B. initiate
   C. continue D. conduct
9. A. caprice B. comfort
   C. over-confidence D. aplomb
10. A. forecast B. apprehend
    C. guess D. foretell
11. A. do B. does
    C. takes D. gets
12. A. come B. comes
    C. get D. gets
13. A. everytime B. alltime
    C. everywhere D. forever
14. A. reap B. sow
    C. cultivate D. grow
15. A. easy B. easier
    C. easiest D. simple
16. A. advancement B. progression
    C. achievement D. cultivation

PASSAGE-28

The ....(1).... Euphoria over the ....(2).... fall in the cost of domestic air travel has ....(3).... to a more realistic appraisal of what is on offer. The aggressive ....(4).... schemes offered since the beginning of July have certainly been good news for certain categories of passengers who probably value ....(5).... above anything else. For them, the heavily discounted fare ....(6).... enables them to afford air travel for the first time. In fact, the ....(7).... of the fare cut ....(8).... such that in specific instances air travel compares ....(9).... to the fares charged by the Railways for upper class travel. Obviously, it ....(10).... for a change in mindset to switch to air travel in ....(11).... to, say, rail transport in India. Economy and affordability will certainly be key ....(12).... but they must be made available ....(13).... a fairly long period. To put it differently, cheaper air travel or at least a ....(14).... fare structure ....(15).... institutionalised in the country.

QUESTIONS

1. A. embryonic B. early
   C. ending D. initial
2. A. casual B. sudden
   C. surprising D. dramatic
3. A. raised B. caused
   C. given way D. gave way
4. A. lucrative B. lofty
   C. laudable D. promotional
5. A. expenses B. affordability
   C. comfort D. time
6. A. scheme B. structure
   C. system D. circular
7. A. portion B. ratio
   C. magnitude D. proportion
8. A. are B. is
   C. has been D. have been
9. A. very slightly B. very favourably
   C. specifially D. generally
10. A. causes B. calls
    C. invites D. lures
11. A. choice B. favour
    C. preference D. alternative
12. A. determinants B. detrimenetals
    C. performers D. issues
13. A. over B. for
    C. to D. through
14. A. different B. distinctive
    C. reducing D. differential
15. A. must be B. has to be
    C. ought to be D. have to be

PASSAGE-29

"I need a break" is a common ..... (1) ..... among the ....(2).... middle and elite classes – under ....(3).... pressure to perform, to live up to their own artificial standards, to earn, and earn some more and ....(4).... some more. But in this vortex, time is at a ....(5)...., and the much needed break ....(6).... materialises because harried professionals are unable to stay away from work long enough ....(7).... from the city and breathe in some fresh air—metaphorically and literally. And weekends? They are ....(8).... lazing at home, ...(9).... on chores, or may be watching some mind numbing television programme. Because it would be hard to think of a place you ....(10).... escape to that was far enough from the city to be ....(11).... and yet close enough to ....(12).... as a weekend break.

QUESTIONS

1. A. restrain B. refrain C. remark D. saying
2. A. hurried B. harried C. worried D. busy
3. A. continuous B. consequent C. constant D. stable
4. A. even B. add C. farther D. then
5. A. premium B. minimum C. limitation D. restriction
6. A. never often B. often never C. although never D. sometimes do not
7. A. to stay away B. to escape C. to go away D. to get moved
8. A. there B. for C. those D. some
9. A. getting B. catching C. catching up D. catching down
10. A. can B. ever C. would D. could
11. A. refreshed B. refreshing C. resting D. rejoining
12. A. consider B. anticipate C. contemplate D. meditate

PASSAGE-30

Every monsoon I'm reminded of an incident that ....(1).... many years ago when I was a young man ....(2).... my first job in Mumbai. I was staying with my sister in those days. On one wet and windy night I ....(3).... with friends, and as it happens when you are in pleasant company, the ....(4).... . It was past ten when I finally bid goodby to my companions and moved towards my sister's house. It had rained the whole day, and it ....(5).... to drizzle again. The rain had ....(6).... people indoors earlier than usual and the dimly-lit street I was walking along was ....(7).... . I had heard that the road was ....(8).... . They said one could hear a woman calling for help on some nights. As I proceeded, I suddenly saw a figure walking ....(9).... me. A bandicoot chose to ....(10).... across my path, just then she seemed to have ....(11).... into thin air. Then I heard a faint ....(12).... for help. This frightened me and as such I turned and fled. The next morning I came to know from my sister that the bandicoot was no other but her friend who had mistakenly thought she was being ....(13).... . Out of fear she was looking behind and walking when she ....(14).... into a ditch. Now every monsoon, I'm reminded of my ....(15).... on that wet night.

QUESTIONS

1. A. happened B. occured C. took place D. had taken place
2. A. in B. on C. working at D. working with
3. A. had been out B. went for outing C. had gone D. was out
4. A. time passes B. time runs C. time flies D. time files
5. A. has B. was C. began D. had begun
6. A. pushed B. sent C. send D. driven
7. A. calm B. peace C. lonely D. deserted
8. A. mysterious B. ghostly C. haunted D. devilish
9. A. before B. in front of C. a head D. near
10. A. scuttle B. scurry C. scuff D. scrouge
11. A. faded B. vanished C. vaporised D. melted
12. A. sound B. voice C. cry D. whisper
13. A. followed B. chased C. pursued D. caught
14. A. fall B. stumbled C. threw D. jumped
15. A. foolishness B. ignorance C. confusion D. cowardice

PASSAGE-31

Most of India's educational institutions, ...(1).... by hiring people who are ....(2).... qualified to be teachers. They are ....(3).... an unhappy group, which is ill-paid and which commands ....(4).... respect. Sadly, it is these men and women who have the enormous duty of ...(5).... tomorrow's society, a responsibility that remains ....(6).... . Children are ....(7).... in this terrifying circle : they are ....(8).... into submission, their innocence is destroyed and their lives become ....(9).... joyless. What follows is still ....(10).... . A violent childhood ....(11).... a violent adulthood. A child who faces the ....(12).... of an adult grows up ....(13).... that violence is the answer to all problems. They become ....(14).... individuals and often their intellectual development ....(15).... in the absence of congenial peace.

QUESTIONS

1. A. get away B. manage C. run D. go away
2. A. not really B. really not C. virtually not D. not actually
3. A. commonly B. mainly C. specifically D. usually
4. A. scant B. scanty C. scarce D. rare
5. A. forming B. moulding C. framing D. making
6. A. unsatisfied B. unprecedented C. unfulfilled D. unrequited
7. A. taught B. caught C. captured D. chained
8. A. battered B. split C. squeezed D. shaped
9. A. universally B. utterly C. wholly D. complete
10. A. unfavourable B. bad C. not good D. worse
11. A. may lead to B. may grow to C. may reach to D. would develop to
12. A. consequences B. wrath C. grief D. wretch
13. A. thinking B. supposing C. infering D. believing
14. A. complex B. complicated C. rough D. sanguine
15. A. slows down B. moves slowly C. hampers D. brakes

PASSAGE-32

Men ....(1).... the maker of their own destinies and they ....(2).... make the destiny of the society and the nation. Life is a great gift of God to men and man ....(3).... making constant efforts to live a ....(4).... life right from the stone age to the modern one. But it is man who ....(5).... to think out how to live well. The ....(6).... before mankind today is between self-preservation and self-destruction. Science has given men all the powers that they need but the new millennium ....(7).... new challenges. We are ....(8).... what nature has given us—forests are being cut down, slums are being ....(9)...., rivers are being polluted. Medical science has made great ....(10)....; but the population is growing in a geometrical ....(11).... . Our natural resources like coal and oil are being ....(12).... . Atomic energy is our only hope. The ....(13).... welcome of the new millennium lies in our determination and hope for self-preservation ....(14).... self-destruction.

QUESTIONS

1. A. are B. have been C. being D. had been
2. A. unitedly B. ultimately C. conjointly D. co-exist to
3. A. have been B. are C. has been D. have had been
4. A. congenial B. cordial C. congregational D. congruent
5. A. have B. is C. are D. has
6. A. optional B. choice C. possibilities D. probabilities
7. A. presents B. places C. offers D. puts forth
8. A. destroying B. ignoring C. neglecting D. wasting
9. A. developed B. constructed C. created D. manufactured
10. A. advancement B. advances C. achievement D. inventions
11. A. dimension B. angle C. index D. proportion
12. A. deported B. deplored C. depleted D. disposed
13. A. actual B. real C. warm D. innate
14. A. upon B. over C. on D. above

II. PASSAGES

Directions: *Read each of the following passages carefully and choose the best answer to each question out of the four alternatives and mark it in the Answer Sheet.*

PASSAGE-1

Cyber crime is the branded stigma defacing the culture and magnanimity of computer technology. It is up keeping the flag with indomitable triumph against developing computer technology worldwide.

Modern age is striding with marching steps of technology revolution beating the past decade of ancestral belief with ultimate care. Computer invention has unfolded the mystery of quick access with the objective of minimum manpower and cutting the time consumption parameters.

As each coin has dual face of its portrait, likewise computer technology is sick of creeping virus. Synthetic manmade dilemma of site hackers activation is causing setback to the expanding anchor of revolutionary device with great loss of time, economy and data profile as suffered by consumers. A recent report from Internet security firm Websense estimates that 85.6 per cent of all the unwanted e-mails contained links to spam sites. The company's data suggests that the number of malicious sites grew 233 per cent in the last six months and saw 671 per cent growth in the number of malicious sites during the last year. In June alone, the total number of e-mails detected as containing viruses increased by 600 per cent compared to May.

Chat rooms, blogs and message boards where the users post comments have been identified as the top targets of hackers and spammers due to the high traffic these attract. According to Websense, 95 per cent of user-generated comments to blogs, chat rooms and message boards during the first half of 2009 were malicious.

It is advisable not to click on spurious links and stay away from keying in passwords at unknown sites as they are most likely to be spammed. Hackers can steal your passwords and log in to your account and access critical information like account numbers and contact details among other things.

QUESTIONS

1. The above passage is:
A. an advisory for the computer users.
B. an advisory for the Internet users.
C. a warning against possible threat to the Internet users.
D. related to chat rooms, blogs and message boards.

2. People who use chat rooms and blogs,
A. are safe and have no threats from spam.
B. are more prone to malicious e-mails.
C. create virus and hack the accounts of others.
D. are unsafe.

3. According to the writer, it is not safe to:
A. log on to spurious links.
B. access one's own account frequently.
C. have essential information stored in a computer.
D. include data-stealing code.

4. Hackers and spammers, according to the writer, are:
A. a new threat to the Internet users and the economy.
B. only pranksters and not serious threat to the system.
C. trained, professional technocrats who are an asset.
D. not expert professionals.

5. Which word in the passage is synonym of *weblog*?
A. blog B. password
C. site D. e-mail

6. Which agency has assessed the data record with spam sites?
A. Microsoft
B. Internet security from Google
C. Websense
D. Spammers

7. Which month dominates the e-mails detection data record?
A. May B. June
C. Last six months D. Last year

PASSAGE-2

South Asian tropical weather reels valuable geographical aesthetic beauty surrounded by wildlife, mountains, steep elevations with dense forest. Human sapiens has been old and innocent victim of natural calamities branded as flood, hurricane, storm, earthquake and tsunami since ages.

Biological data depicts the loss of valuable men and material suffered by mankind owing to the chain reaction by such fatal natural incidents. Global warming has turned an eyesore to the rapid glory of rising civilsation with great mystery yet to be unfolded. UNO data reveals the rate of mortality owned due to natural disaster with great sway of cruel time factor.

Of the 245 natural disasters in the first 11 months of 2009, 224 or 91.4 per cent were due to weather, a UN study has found.

Of the 58 million people affected, 55 million were affected by weather-related disasters, which accounted for $15 billion (₹ 7,05,000 crore) spent in coping with these disasters.

A study has found that half of these disasters, mainly storms and floods, have taken place in Asia, Debarati Guha Sapir of Brussels-based CRED said.

And this data does not include the loss due to drought because that takes longer to account for. Guha Sapir said, "We have found that this is due to global warming, weak political systems, urbanisation, weak infrastructure, population increase and deforestation."

"We have to cap the emissions of greenhouse gases because they produce greater risk of disasters," WMO head Michel Jerraud said. Greenhouse gases, mainly carbon dioxide, are causing the climate change that is already affecting farm output, making droughts, floods and storms more frequent and more severe, and raising the sea level.

QUESTIONS

1. Mark the correct statement(s).
1. Weather is responsible for most of the natural disasters.
2. There is no need to worry about the climatic changes.
3. All the nations are trying to have a common pact to tackle natural disasters.

A. 1 is correct B. Only 2 is correct
C. Only 3 is correct D. 1 and 2 are correct

2. Which one of the following statements is not true?
A. More than 58 million people have been affected by natural disasters.
B. $15 billion have been spent in coping with these disasters.
C. Most of the natural disasters have taken place in Asia.
D. The report does not include the loss caused by droughts.

3. The main cause of natural disasters is :
A. global warming
B. weak political system
C. deforestation
D. all of these

4. The first priority before the nations and the scientists across the world is :
A. to cap the emission of greenhouse gases.
B. to reach an agreement on the nuclear weapons.
C. to help one another when natural disasters occur.
D. to find out the causes of natural disasters.

5. Which word in the passage means the same as *serious*?
A. Reduce B. Severe
C. Underlined D. Underscore

6. Which region is mainly affected by these disasters?
A. United Nation B. Africa
C. Asia D. Brussels

7. Which statement is true?
A. Sea level rise is an alarming incident.
B. Rapid urbanisation is a curse to the global warming.
C. Deforestation with climatic change is responsible for green house gaseous effect.
D. All of these.

PASSAGE-3

Time has brought forth different classical and instrumental range of device that serves healing element to the aweful and mentally distressed state of affair. Temperament compatibility matching is a reasonable trend of motion adhered with the concept of body movement termed as dance therapy.

Dance has mobilised different acknowledgement of its noted culture proclaimed by experts and sensational aspirants. Vedas describe the dance origin from aryan culture to the creeping span of modern India. Archaeological Survey of India has claimed the civilsation existence issue owing to excavation of past events traced in the stone idols displayed in dance "mudra".

Dance is an art form that generally refers to movement of the body, usually rhythmic and to music, used as a form of expression, social interaction or presented in a spiritual or performance setting. Gymnastics, figure skating and synchronised swimming are sports that incorporate dance, while martial arts Kata are often compared to dances. Motion in ordinarily inanimate objects may also be described as dances (the leaves dance in the wind). Every dance, no matter what style, has something in common. It not only involves flexibility and body movement, but also physics. If the proper physics is not taken into consideration, injuries may occur. Choreography is the art of creating dances. The person who creates (*i.e.* choreographs) a dance, is known as the choreographer. Dance has certainly been an important part of ceremony, rituals, celebrations and entertainment since the birth of the earliest human civilisations. Archaeology delivers trace of dance from prehistoric times such as the 9,000 years old Rock Shelters of Bhimbetka painting in India and Egyptian tomb painting depicting dancing figures from circa 3300 BC. One of the earliest structured uses of dance may have been in the performance and in the telling of myths. Before the production of written languages, dance was one of the methods of passing these stories down from generation to generation.

QUESTIONS

1. Dance does not necessarily involve:
A. movement of the body.
B. face expression.
C. rhythmic movements.
D. costumes.

2. According to the passage, which one of the following sports does not incorporate dance?
A. Figure skating B. Gymnastics
C. Chess D. Swimming

3. Which one, according to the passage, is not common in all the dances?
A. Flexibility B. Body movement
C. Music D. Physics

4. Physics in every dance is an important element to:
A. master the art of dance.
B. to perform it scientifically.
C. to save oneself from injury.
D. to get an award.

5. In prehistoric times dance was:
A. a substitute of written language.
B. a source of entertainment.
C. a necessary ritual.
D. not allowed in royal palaces.

6. Choreographer is a term addressed to:
A. a sports trainer B. a gym coach
C. a painting teacher D. a dance teacher

7. What does the term 'the telling of myths' refer to?
A. Telling the beads B. Vedic convention
C. Spiritual recitation D. Protest march

PASSAGE-4

Personal sentiments exposure portray in sober class of distinct feature with fair and pleasant expression. As the cruelty can be overpowered by the amicable terms likewise, impossible review let with expression can be publically announced by either electronic device or diary writing habit. On line conversation such as chattering, message convey are the rampant tool of the time to manage in communication congestion.

Blogs, online versions of personal diaries, have been a craze for quite some time now. Some of us, before the Internet age, used to maintain a small diary to jot down random thoughts, reflections, sayings, poems and other such stuff. Their online versions, however, are much more than that. The biggest difference between a blog and a personal diary is while the latter was a very private affair accessible not even to family members, a blog is a public account. In fact the whole world connected to the internet gets to read its contents if they come across it.

What a blogger should keep in mind while blogging is that by displaying our thoughts, emotions, opinions and personal life in full public glory, we are revealing a part of our private life. We are giving outsiders, strangers, friends, colleagues and relatives a full view of what's happening inside us and without lives, something we would hesitate to do in real life. Once blogging begins, it's difficult to control, and we end up sharing our personal thoughts and emotions that we would otherwise have kept to ourselves. The blog entices us, and we fall to be bait.

Blogs don't preserve our anonymity. They let us publish our pictures, professional and personal details, physical address and locations, etc. The biggest precaution to be observed therefore is to think twice before publishing anything, and ask oneself if one would like to make such matters public. The blog readers try to judge us, understand us, get information about us and take pleasure while peeping into our private lives without realising it.

QUESTIONS

1. Blogs are __________.
A. diaries B. personal diaries
C. online diaries D. official diaries

2. Earlier the personal diaries were not available even to family members but blog can be read by:
A. family and friends
B. friends only
C. anyone who connects to the Internet
D. relatives

3. Which one of the following statements is not true?
A. Blogging does not affect our privacy.
B. Blogging displays our private life in public.
C. Blogging cannot be controlled easily.
D. Blogging allows outsiders to peep into our personal life.

4. The writer in the above passage:
A. favours blogging.
B. criticises the practices.
C. does not want the reader to become a victim of blogging.
D. favours blogging but with some precautions.

5. Which word in the passage stands for *an account from on point of view*?
A. version B. block
C. affair D. account

6. The word Anonymity in the passage refers to:
A. hostility B. friendship
C. unacknowledged D. differences

7. What precaution is stressed by the narrator while releasing personal information?

A. Suggest Comprehensive issue only
B. Reader friendly blog appreciation
C. Hiding personal facts
D. Diary maintenance

PASSAGE-5

Pleasure and sorrow being twin face of a coin suffers the sign of commend and condemn since long before the historic ages. Warriors outcry with victory decorated with deep throat laugh has marked the sentimental coverage of battle filed victory. Baffled war victims, war widows, dependents are the oppressed classes. They seek relief against those causing sabotage to their established settlement.

The history of literature really began long before man learned to write. Dancing was the earliest of the arts. Man danced for joy round his primitive camp fire after the defeat and slaughter of his enemy. He yelled and shouted as he danced and gradually the yells and shouts became coherent and caught the measure of the dance and thus the first war song was sung. As the idea of God developed, prayers were framed. The song and prayers became traditional and were repeated from one generation to another, each generation adding something of its own. As man slowly grew more civilsed, he was compelled to invent some method of writing by three urgent necessities. There were certain things that were dangerous to forget and which, therefore, had to be recorded.

It was often necessary to communicate with persons who were some distance away and it was necessary to protect one's property by making tools and so on, in some distinctive manner. So man taught himself to write and having learned to write purely for utilitarian reasons, he used this new method for preserving his songs and his prayers. Of course, among these ancient people, there were only a very few individuals who learned to write, and only a few could read what was written.

QUESTIONS

1. Liguistic comment and condemn refers to:
A. physical grudge against sorrows
B. a temporary verbal communication
C. slip of tongue with praise and denounce
D. a communal fury against the joys

2. Which one of the following statements is true?
A. Study reveals the historic onslaught with cruelty only.
B. Suffers pledge to reform the existing tyranny.
C. A permanent code of sympathetic temper is sought by the suffers.
D. Language dominates with great passion during mental aggression.

3. Before man invented writing, ______.
A. literature was passed on by word of mouth
B. prayres were considered literature
C. literature was just singing and dancing
D. all of the above

4. According to the passage, dance originated from
A. literature B. yelling and shouting
C. prayers D. war

5. Writing was invented because
A. there were certain things which had to be remembered.
B. there were certain things which had to be communicated to the people who were away.
C. there were certain rituals which had to be preserved.
D. all of the above

6. Which one of the following statements is not true?
A. Since only a few individuals had learnt to write and a few could read what was written.
B. Prayers were developed after the idea of god developed.
C. People learned writing for utilitarian reasons.
D. Dancing was the earliest form of art.

7. Which one of the following words in the passage stands for *ancient*?
A. primitive B. traditional
C. coherent D. utilitarian

PASSAGE-6

Quality dominates the world ahead of its spherical, classical, racial or any undue discrimination ever exercised by any individual. Physical characteristics of a produce differs its structural attribution in quality from substandard produce with richness of prolong usage features declared by the claimant. Talent Hunt initiated by quality seekers have turned the table of established brand on account of innovative additions presented by their hardships.

The simple message that quality matters because it is cheaper to do things right the first time is yet to sink into the thinking of Indian managers and workers who seem quite content to live in their cloistered world where mediocrity reigns supreme. It is only the ignorant who believe that quality consciousness is a cultural trait. Barely half a century back no one associated Japan with high quality, but today 'Made in Japan' is a symbol of assured quality. The daily drill at school is far more important than the seasonal seminar and an obsession with quality at home is the best way of convincing the world that we value good quality. Indian exports will never be recognised for quality unless Indians are known to insist on good quality at home.

Global appreciation surrounds the exceptional brand by keeping up the physical standard neatly and efficiently. It is designed to meet the international standards' numerous logos and certificates to upkeep the label of quality consciousness. It has prime motto of swaying clean chit observation to the sanctioned produce without any objection. Modern age has been proved a turning point to the old established traditional belief. They are using tiring house hold produce to industrial device responsible to deface the status of rapid development. We breath into the cool and fresh air of healthy surrounding devised by mankind monitored by quality management with rigorous span or struggle tackled with due care.

QUESTIONS

1. The theme of the passage is:
A. quality consciousness
B. export promotion
C. quality management
D. promoting Indian culture

2. According to the passage, the Indian exports will never be recognised for quality:
A. unless there is technical advancement.
B. unless there is competition.
C. unless the Indians are known to insist on good quality.
D. unless government supports the exporters.

3. Which one of the following statements is true?
A. Indians are known for their insistence on quality.
B. Indians are not quality conscious.
C. Japan is not known for its quality product.
D. 'Made in Japan' is not a symbol of assured quality.

4. The best way to convince the world about quality is:
A. to conduct seminars on quality control.
B. to advertise the products.
C. to value for quality products at home.
D. all of the above

5. According to the passage, the main fault with the Indian managers is that:
A. they are not hard-working.
B. they are not quality conscious.
C. they are not well trained in quality control.
D. they lack technical knowledge.

6. How quality consciousness is termed as a cultural trait with the ignorant?
A. The mature opinion of quality.
B. Quality dominates ahead of traditional belief.
C. Cultural trait justifies any quality standard.
D. Quality consciousness leads to management growth.

7. Why 'Made in Japan' is a symbol of assured quality?
A. Traditional belief
B. Quality consciousness
C. Age old negligence suffering
D. High export offer

PASSAGE-7

Creamy outlook with soft speech presentation is a prima facie attraction that brings joy on the withering faces with a mixture of sensational touch. Smile with grace is the ultimate boon to the mankind keeping away any melancholy at bay. Old age is often miscalculated as liability with little attention paid to them. Their talents and learned potential is buried alive with undue care by oblivious approach due to disfigured or deformed physical structure taken over by aged talents of the society.

It happens to us all, however hard we may try to delay the process. We grow old. Cosmetic surgery may remove the wrinkles, skin which has sagged may be tightened by means of a facelift and hair dresser may dye grey hair a more youthful colour, but we cannot remain young forever.

However, what is important is the quality of life. Some people are lucky to be taken care of at home whereas others may have to move to residential homes. The worst part of ageing is that often the mind becomes less alert. As people grow older, they experience short term memory. Later some may suffer from dementia, often in the form of Alzheimer's disease.

By no means all people are in this category. Many senior citizens are in the possession of all their faculties and see retirement as a time of freedom. Not only that if they have a generous retirement pension, they are likely to be quite well off with money to be spent on a holiday and other luxuries. Because of this, both businesses and government have a new respect for what is known as grey power.

It is unfortunate that many people regard old people as geriatrics who have one foot in the grave. Someone should remind them that they too would be old one day!

They are honoured with senior citizen label granted by the authority with due regard paid from distinct possession of living cadres. One should always bear in mind the old saying "Tit for Tat". Which denotes its symbolic regulation of periodical sufferings. The aforesaid misdoings of emotional disparity, done by striding steps is a curse to the mankind.

QUESTIONS

1. Cosmetic surgery :
A. helps in the retention of youth forever.
B. cannot stop the natural process of ageing.

C. is the solution to ageing.
D. is the fancy of the rich.

2. While ageing man's greatest worry is :
A. his growing wrinkles.
B. his short term memory.
C. his quality of life.
D. moving to a residential home.

3. The government considers grey power as :
A. a liability
B. an asset
C. neither an asset nor a liability
D. a spent force

4. Retirement is seen as a time of freedom because people :
A. no longer have to go to office.
B. can enjoy their earnings.
C. can spend time with their families.
D. finally move into residential homes.

5. *geriatrics* in the passage refers to :
A. handicapped people
B. doctors for the aged
C. a branch of medicine
D. aged people

6. What is the theme of the passage?
A. Old is gold
B. The grey power
C. Youth domination in the society
D. Aged suffering

7. What does the phrase 'suffer from dementia' refer to?
A. Harmful
B. Short term memory loss
C. Lunacy
D. Paralysis

PASSAGE-8

1. The world is teemed with different continents and oceans surrounded with settled and manless island as declared by the geographical experts of the world.
2. Pacific island dominates amongst the oceans escorted with wildlife, ecosphere and manageable resources with identified culture of scientific explorations. Man hunt for unseen spheres remains a landmark occasion yearning for lavish search with instrumental approach. Galapagos Islands remind us of such human efforts noted for spherical search with wildhunt.
3. The Galapagos Islands in the Pacific Ocean are a rocky, lonely spot, but they are also one of the most unusual places in the world. The reason is that they are the home of some of the last giant tortoises left on earth.
4. Weighing hundreds of pounds, these tortoises wander slowly around the rocks and sand of the islands. Each of these islands has its own particular kind of tortoise. There are seven different kinds of tortoises on the eight islands.
5. Hundreds of years ago, thousands of tortoises wandered around these islands. All that changed when people started landing there. When people first arrived, their ships had no refrigerators. This meant that fresh food was always a problem for the sailors on board. The giant tortoises provided a solution to his problem.
6. Ships would anchor off the islands, and crew would seize as many tortoises as they could. Once the animals were aboard the ship, the crew would roll the tortoises onto their backs and use them for soups and stews.
7. Human search never ends with seeking variable resources sustainable to their growth-oriented programme. Man hunt with crew supported by voyage turns the pages of historical map to best transformation regions discovered by his hardcore practice. How long 'wants' arrest his peace of mind with the dream of next destination is yet to know with.

QUESTIONS

1. The author calls the Galapagos Islands an unusual place because :
A. they are in the Pacific Ocean.
B. the endangered giant tortoises are found there.
C. they are rocky and lonely spots.
D. they are located off the western coast of South America.

2. Which statement is correct?
A. There is one kind of tortoise found on the seven islands.
B. There are eight kinds of tortoises found on the eight islands.
C. There are seven kinds of tortoises found on the eight islands.
D. All the tortoises are on one island.

3. The giant tortoises provided a solution to the problem of not having refrigerators because :
A. the sailors went looking for refrigerators as they were starving.
B. fresh food was available in plenty as the sea was vast.
C. the fresh giant tortoise could be killed and eaten whenever the sailors were hungry.
D. the sailors seized the tortoise to store in refrigerators.

4. *Ships would anchor off the islands* means that Ships:
   A. would go off
   B. would be near the shore
   C. would be off to another land
   D. would go to another island
5. In paragraph 6 the word crew means:
   A. the new settlers.
   B. the men arriving on Galapagos Islands.
   C. the men working on the ships.
   D. the men catching the tortoises.
6. Mark the True statement which best suits the passage.
   A. Galapagos is the unusual island due to regular plains.
   B. People landed at Island duely in search of tortoises.
   C. Lack of refrigerators made crew turn to tortoises.
   D. Tortoises numbered more than crews on the Island.
7. Soups and stews refers to :
   A. soup apart with flesh.
   B. soup extracted out of tortoise cooking.
   C. tortoise fat.
   D. a synthetic process of vegetation.

PASSAGE-9

The goal of the fair, to be held at the Cervantes Institute in the Indian capital, is to attract the largest number of students in order to present them with information on the educational programmes Spain has to offer, primarily postgraduate. Studying in Spain gives students an added advantage of living and studying in one of the world's most important economies that also aims for an internationalisation of its university system, which plays a decisive role in knowledge-based economy.

In this context, the Spanish universities, both private and public, numbering 77 in total, offer Master degrees and PhD programmes adapted to the European Higher Education Area; a harmonised space between all European countries that have opted to participate in this model. This implies that any student that obtains a postgraduate degree in a Spanish university will automatically have their studies recognised in any participating country and may continue their doctoral studies without needing to validate their degree. In addition, Spanish universities are offering more and more postgraduate degrees in English in order to attract international students. Nevertheless, it is also very common for students to come to Spain intending to complete postgraduate studies in Spanish as well. Students are offered a double advantage from, first, studying in high quality university programmes, and second, studying in a rapidly growing language, that will soon reach 500 million speakers. Spanish is also the official language in more than 20 countries and a second language in important economies such as the United States and Brazil, which gives graduates and edge when entering the workforce.

These are just a few reasons why studying in Spain is such a unique opportunity. On February 19 and 20th, Indian students are invited to visit the Cervantes Institute where they can directly ask the universities any and all questions about studying in Spain as well as get information about programmes that the universities offer.

Another incentive for students to attend will be the prize drawing for six intensive Spanish courses at Spanish universities in summer 2011. The six big winners will have air fare, accommodations, and tuition paid for while attending the month-long course.

QUESTIONS

1. The objective of the fair is ________.
   A. to tell about Spain
   B. to tell about the courses being started in India
   C. to impart information about education in Spain
   D. none of the above
2. Decisive role means ________.
   A. taking decisions   B. important role
   C. key role   D. minor role
3. Spanish Universities are offering programmes in English because ________.
   A. English is a global language
   B. it wants to get students from all over the world
   C. English is easy to understand
   D. it is easy to get professors to teach in English
4. One of the advantages of studying in Spain is that ________.
   A. it is a beautiful country
   B. education there is cheap
   C. courses are easy
   D. Spanish is the second language in some important countries
5. Those who attend the fair ________.
   A. will get to participate in a prize draw
   B. will be given free air ticket to Spain
   C. will get fee waiver for one term
   D. none of the above

PASSAGE-10

An incandescent bulb lights up when electrical power heats a metal filament wire to a high temperature until it glows. You usually get them rated between 15 and 100 watts. Meanwhile, fluorescent lamps (tubes and their newer compact versions, known as CFLs) use inert gases inside to fluoresce and produce light. There are also lamps that use an array of light-emitting diodes (LEDs) working in the way electrons behave, a phenomenon called electro luminescence. Because LED lamps are costly, very few homes use them—and it's best to wait a while before buying for their prices to come down, just as you did with CFLs over the past years.

At about ₹ 20 a piece, incandescent bulbs may look cheap, but they are not. They waste some 90 per cent of the power consumed—as heat. Consumers preferred them to energy-efficient fluorescent tubes not just because they are cheaper, but also because you may place them in choice lamp shades. Or because the bluish-white illumination from tubes can seem harsh and unnatural, and may contribute to glare and eyestrain.

If you don't like the way tube lights look in the hall or bedroom, use them only in passages, verandas and the kitchen.

QUESTIONS

1. Bulbs light up when ______.
A. metal filament burns
B. electricity heats up metal filament
C. electric current is in excess
D. metal comes in contact with heat

2. CFLs use ______.
A. gases like Argon, Krypton, etc.
B. mercury
C. thin metal strips
D. any of the above

3. Electro luminescence is the process where ______.
A. electrons and protons react to emit light
B. diodes function as electrons and emit light
C. light is generated by water
D. light is generated by sun

4. Incandescent bulbs are costly because ______.
A. they cost ₹ 20 a piece
B. they break easily
C. their power consumption is high
D. none of the above

5. Bulbs are used because they ______.
A. are cheap
B. conserve energy
C. you can place them in choice lamp shades
D. none of the above

PASSAGE-11

Conservation of water in the agricultural sector is essential since water is necessary for the growth of plants and crops. A depleting watertable and a rise in salinity due to overuse of chemical fertilisers and pesticides have made matters serious. Various methods of water harvesting and recharging have been and are being applied all over the world to tackle the problem. In areas where rainfall is low and water is scarce, the local people have used simple techniques that are suited to their region and reduce the demand for water. In India's arid and semi-arid areas, the 'tank' system is traditionally the backbone of agricultural production. Tanks are constructed either by bunding or by excavating the ground and collecting rainwater.

Rajasthan, located in the Great Indian Desert, receives hardly any rainfall, but people have adapted to the harsh conditions by collecting whatever rain falls. Large bunds to create reservoirs known as khadin, dams called johads, tanks and other methods were applied to check water flow and accumulate run-off. At the end of the monsoon season, water from these structures was used to cultivate crops. Similar systems were developed in other parts of the country. These are known by various local names *jal talais* in Uttar Pradesh, the *haveli* system in Madhya Pradesh, *ahar* in Bihar, and so on.

QUESTIONS

1. There is an increase in water salinity due to ______.
A. conservation of water
B. depletion of water
C. overuse of chemical fertilisers and pesticides
D. water harvesting

2. 'Depleting watertable' means ______.
A. reduction in the groundwater level
B. measurement of water level
C. recharging of water level
D. usage of fertilisers and pesticides

3. In arid and semi-arid regions, rainwater is collected by ______.
A. using industrial methods
B. constructing tanks
C. harvesting of water
D. adapting to the harsh conditions

4. How much rainfall does Rajasthan, the state in the Great Indian Desert, receive?
A. plenty of rainfall B. no rainfall
C. moderate rainfall D. scanty rainfall

5. Where do farmers of Rajasthan get water from to cultivate their crops after the monsoon season?
A. from tanks, bunds, dams and reservoirs
B. from whatever rain that falls
C. from excess rainwater
D. from the rivers

PASSAGE-12

Every family with two or more children often experiences sibling rivalry at one time or the other. Children in general, fight with each other for their parents' attention. They fight among themselves mostly on trivial issues. If it does not get excessive, this kind of rivalry can, in fact, be a healthy competition that trains children to share, respect one another. They will learn to deal with frustration and displeasures in the maturing process.

The firstborns generally feel that they don't have to share their parents' love and attention. But when the next baby or siblings come along, they feel neglected and that changes everything. The first child starts to feel that he/she is no longer the centre of attraction and that he/she is being sidelined because of the new one. Some children might develop negative feelings and emotional imbalance, which may lead to regressive behaviour.

Such problems could be averted if right moves are taken. One way is to explain the firstborns about the arrival of a new child. They need to establish a connection with the new baby before it is born. Older children should be trained to show a positive attitude towards their siblings. They should be involved, along with their parents, in teaching their siblings social and manual skills, which in turn, helps them to accept them. Sometimes personality differences and parental conflicts too have an impact on the children. Parents have to show patience, understand these issues and should openly communicate with their children to resolve them.

QUESTIONS

1. Sibling rivalry means fight between ______.
A. firstborn and second child
B. children of same parents
C. children born to different parents
D. cousins and relatives

2. 'Why do firstborns feel neglected by the arrival of a new child in the family?
A. because they have to share their parents' love and attention
B. because of their negative attitude
C. because they hate their siblings
D. because parents do not love them

3. What does the word 'regressive' in para 2 mean?
A. emotional imbalance
B. withdraw or shy away
C. negative feeling
D. harsh or rude

4. How can older children develop a positive attitude towards their siblings?
A. by developing sibling rivalry
B. by keeping away from their siblings
C. by their involvement in matters related to the young ones
D. by dominating their siblings

5. What should parents do to control sibling rivalry?
A. allow children to fight among themselves
B. do not allow any communication between children
C. punish the children
D. openly communicate with children to resolve issues

PASSAGE-13

Music can have strong consequences on our feelings. One should try to gain benefits from the power of music. Music, in general, helps one to calm down and feel revitalized. It helps to beat a bad mood or to continue a good state of mind. To cheer up or to enhance vitality, one should listen to music with beats, lots of drumming and a fast tempo. When one wants to relax after a busy day, instrumental music with less percussion and a slower rhythm can help. Listening to soothing music before stressful activities has a lot of benefits and so is always advised. A collection of preferred relaxing tunes help to combat stress at work. One can change one's frame of mind by switching from one kind of music to another. To feel refreshed, it is better to start with something tranquil and soothing and to slowly pick up the pace and the beat. But when one prefers to settle down after a busy schedule, follow the reverse style.

Music is an incredible means that people can use to communicate things, especially their feelings and emotions. When added to speech in a song, it becomes a powerful device of communication. Music generally needs special aptitude, inborn talent and rigorous practice. Also, a person needs to have fine muscular strength in order to sing in tune or play a musical instrument. Recollection of the notes demands good memory power. Besides, many people feel that music and love are connected to each other. A person tries to make an impression on his/her love by way of selecting appropriate music.

QUESTIONS

1. Music with fast beats and lots of drumming __________.
A. boosts up one's energy
B. calms down one's mind
C. is less beneficial
D. leads to stress

2. What does 'percussion' mean?
A. stressful condition
B. tranquil mood

C. thumping or fast beat
D. inborn talent

3. What kind of music is preferred when a person wants to settle down?
A. music with lots of percussion
B. first upbeat music and then soothing music
C. music of string instruments
D. first gentle music and then fast music

4. Why is music considered to be a powerful means of communication?
A. because it helps people to express their emotions
B. because it is an incredible tool
C. because it reduces stress at work
D. because it enhances energy in people

5. What qualities are needed for a person to sing or play a musical instrument?
A. love, talent, speech and memory
B. aptitude, emotion, strength and love
C. knowledge, emotion, love and talent
D. aptitude, talent, practice and strength

PASSAGE-14

In order to heal your emotional baggage and prevent it from possibly costing you yet another relationship, you must recognise the roots of your emotional pain or fears and acknolwedge your accountability in them.

According to psychologists, one should review the event or experience that you think caused you to be hurt and identify your role in the experience. "Allow yourself to learn from that and forgive yourself—often misplaced guilt can be the cause for fear. Acknowledge that your past does not have to dictate your future. Release all the emotional hurt and fears that were weighing you down and standing in the way of your seeing each individual relationship for its own merit and potential. It can be difficult to let go of the security blanket of past behaviours but assure yourself that you no longer need them. Sometimes one may require professional help to be able to identify, draw links, acknowledge, accept and forgive themselves. In the end, it all comes down to trust. Want to leave that baggage behind? Allow yourself to trust again," concludes a psychologist.

QUESTIONS

1. It is important to understand _________.
A. pain
B. emotions
C. cause of emotional pain
D. effect of emotional pain

2. It is advised that we should _________.
A. stop feeling the pain
B. review the event
C. take rest
D. all of the above

3. We should not allow the past _________.
A. to guide our future
B. to bother us
C. actions to make today's decision
D. to affect our present

4. We should learn to let go _________.
A. pain
B. negative emotion
C. fear
D. the security of the past

5. The most important thing in life is _________.
A. trust B. love
C. compassion D. fear

PASSAGE-15

Maintaining work-life balance is necessary because imbalance wreaks chaos in life. Increased pressure on one side will affect the other side too.

After all, the two cannot be completely disconnected! The first step towards this is finding the cause for the imbalance.

Some of the potential causes are—you are genuinely overloaded with work, you are incompetent, your time management skills are poor or you chase conflicting goals.

Once you identify the problem, you should admit it and work towards overcoming it. When you are better organised, your efficiency increases. Make a list of activities and prioritise them. This should be done on daily, weekly and monthly basis.

Plan in advance how you will deal with impending additional responsibilities. If you have to spend extra time at the office, inform your family about it and seek their support. If you have to take leave, inform your boss.

When your organisation is going through a change, there is a crisis or you are vying for a promotion, it can be inevitable to spend more time at work. So explore alternative ways to show your loved ones that you care. When you are with your family and friends, make the most of the time. Do not think about work at least during the 'special' time you allotted for them.

Pay attention to your health. Sleep well. Spend time on activities that can help beat fatigue. Allot time for physical exercises, yoga or sports.

QUESTIONS

1. Chaos here means ________.
A. disturbance B. confusion
C. happiness D. calmness

2. As soon as we identify the problem we should ________.
A. work towards overcoming it
B. forget it
C. overcome it
D. none of the above

3. When there is extra work one should ________.
A. stay up at night B. work from home
C. plan in advance D. all of the above

4. When one is spending time with family ________.
A. one should carry work also
B. one should relax and sleep
C. one should keep thinking about work
D. one should not think about work

5. It is important to take care of one's health because ________.
A. it helps to be positive and chargeable
B. one can do more work
C. work is worship
D. none of the above

PASSAGE-16

You are at a party and want to watch your weight and health. However when the appetisers are served you notice nothing looks healthy. The next thing you know, you go ahead and eat those decorative little morsels and blow your eating plan. Stop!

Those little delicious nuts in that bowl are chock-full of nutrition. They will improve your cardiovascular health; hold cancer prevention properties and help you lose weight. It's hard to believe but it's true!

The idea that something from nuts may actually help weight control seems a little counter-intuitive at first; bearing in mind the reputation nuts have for being both fatty and fattening. Nuts are nutrient-packed, healthy 'primal' food, and something that experience shows satisfy the appetite and prevent overeating at meal time. High in proteins, unsaturated fats may aid in weight loss and other disease-fighting properties.

What do nuts have that is heart-healthy? Nuts are an intensely fatty food, with about 80 per cent of the calories they offer coming from fat. But bear in mind that the type of oils found in nuts such as almonds, cashews, walnuts is predominantly the healthy monounsaturated and polyunsaturated type.

Researchers found that people who eat nuts regularly have lower risk of heart disease. In 1998, a study conducted by the Harvard School of Public Health found that women who ate nuts less than four times a week were 40 per cent less likely to die of heart disease. Further, potential heart health benefits of nuts were also found among men. In 2002, the Physician's Health Study found that men who consumed nuts two or more times per week had reduced risk of sudden cardiac death.

QUESTIONS

1. Nuts possess ________.
A. nutritive value
B. fattening properties
C. oil
D. all of the above

2. During meal time nuts ________.
A. add taste to the food
B. satisfy appetite
C. should not be consumed
D. create an urge for water

3. Nuts contain ________.
A. unhealthy oils B. cholesterol
C. healthy oils D. none of the above

4. People who consume nuts regularly ________.
A. are not prone to heart attacks
B. are prone to heart attacks
C. are not prone to kidney failure
D. are prone to kidney failure

5. Sudden cardiac death means death due to ________.
A. kidney failure
B. sudden heart failure
C. sudden brain malfunction
D. increase in lung pressure

PASSAGE-17

Acupuncture is an ancient form of healing that dates back to Stone Age. It is a technique of inserting and manipulating fine needles into specific points on the body to relieve pain or for therapeutic purposes. Acupuncture originated in China and is most commonly associated with traditional Chinese medicine. As per the traditional Chinese medical theory, acupuncture points are situated on meridians along which 'Qi' (pronounced as 'chee'), the vital energy, flows. Apparently, there is no known histological basis for the existence of acupuncture meridians. Different types of acupuncture such as Classical Chinese, Japanese, Tibetan, Vietnamese and Korean are practised throughout the world.

The practice of acupuncture is based on the understanding that a vital energy flows along channels or meridians throughout our bodies. When this energy becomes blocked or does not flow freely, it causes disharmony or disease. In order to correct this disharmony, the vital force must be stimulated so that it moves freely again. A set of very fine needles are used to stimulate peculiar points located on the flow of energy and the actions of the various acupuncture points to treat diseases and disharmonies in the body. Quite significantly, acupuncture is not usually painful. Acupuncture needles are tiny and are quickly inserted through the skin, where the nerves that transmit pain are located. The sensation of the insertion is like a "quick pinch". In general, there is an agreement that acupuncture is safe when administered by well-trained practitioners using sterile needles and that further research is appropriate.

QUESTIONS

1. Where does vital energy flow through in human bodies?
A. through muscle cells
B. through blood cells
C. through meridians
D. through sense organs

2. How are acupuncture points stimulated?
A. by inserting find needles into specific points on the body
B. by knowing the histological basis
C. by flow of vital energy
D. by going to China

3. A person specialising in the technique of Acupuncture is called __________.
A. a practitioner
B. an acupuncturist
C. a classical Chinese
D. a medical doctor

4. How is a disease caused as per the traditional Chinese medical theory?
A. when one feels a quick pinch
B. when blood does not flow through the vessels
C. when needles are inserted into specific points
D. when vital energy does not flow freely through meridians

5. Where are the acupuncture needles inserted?
A. in the nerve cells where vital energy flows
B. on the upper part of the right or left hand
C. in the skin where the nerves transmitting pain are found
D. in the muscular part of the hip region

PASSAGE-18

While many of India's parks have been developed from the hunting preserves of princely India, Keoladeo, popularly known as Bharatpur Wildlife Sanctuary, is perhaps the only case where the habitat has been created by a maharaja. In earlier times, Bharatpur town used to be flooded regularly every monsoon. In 1760, an earthen dam, called the Ajam Dam, was constructed, to save the town from this annual vagary of nature. The depression created by extraction of soil for the dam was cleared and this became the Bharatpur Lake.

At the beginning of this century, this lake was developed and divided into several portions. A system of small dams, dykes, sluice gates, etc., was created to control the water level in different sections. This became the hunting preserve of the Bharatpur royalty and also one of the best duck-shooting wetlands in the world. But hunting was prohibited by mid-60s and the area was then declared a national park on 10 March 1982. This was later accepted as a World Heritage site in December 1985.

The major attractions of tourists visiting this park are the numerous migratory birds, which come from as far away as Siberia and Central Asia to spend their winters in Bharatpur, before returning to their breeding grounds. The migratory birds at this bird sanctuary include several species of Cranes, Pelicans, Geese, Ducks, Eagles, Hawks, Shanks, Stints, Wagtails, Warblers, Wheatears, Fly catchers, Buntings, Larks and Pipits, etc.

QUESTIONS

1. Bharatpur Wildlife Sanctuary was developed __________.
A. from the hunting preserves of princely India
B. by constructing Ajam dam
C. by the Maharaja of Bharatpur Royalty
D. from the floods of every monsoon

2. What is the reason behind the construction of Ajam dam?
A. to develop a hunting preserve
B. to develop a wildlife sanctuary
C. to bring an end to floods
D. to save the town from being flooded

3. One of the best duck-shooting wetlands of the world is __________.
A. Princely India B. Bharatpur lake
C. Ajam dam D. Bharatpur royalty

4. When was Bharatpur Lake given the status of a national park?
A. 10 March 1982 B. 10 January 1982
C. 10 December 1985 D. 10 October 1985

5. What are migratory birds?
   A. birds from Siberia and Central Asia
   B. birds that travel long distances during some seasons
   C. birds from Bharatpur Wildlife Sanctuary
   D. birds from the hunting preserves of India

PASSAGE-19

Lexicographer : a writer of dictionaries, a harmless drudge, that busies himself in tracing the original, and detailing the signification of words. Thus said Samuel Johnson in his Dictionary, with an ironic swipe at his own work. It wasn't the first dictionary of the English language, but it continued to be regarded as an authoritative if quirky icon of language for more than two centuries. In two volumes and 2,300 pages, Johnson tried to tidy up a notoriously untidy and promiscuous language, though he knew at the same time that it was futile to attempt to straitjacket it. We tend to think of dictionaries as "anonymous" productions, but Johnson's personality is all over the work. In his bitter definition of a patron, "commonly a wretch who supports with insolence, and is paid by flattery", Johnson took care of his own patron, Lord Chesterfield, who had promised to help financially but had not delivered till too late. Since Johnson's Dictionary, which has been reprinted, abridged, and is still written about, there have been books too numerous to count on the English language: Melvyn Bragg's The Adventure of English: The Biography of a Language, the most recent (2004), Raymond Williams' Keywords: A Vocabulary of Culture and Society (1985), one of the most respected. But there are hundreds of others.

QUESTIONS

1. Samuel Johnson made an ironic remark at his own work by calling a lexicographer __________.
   A. a harmless drudge
   B. a writer of dictionaries
   C. one who is busy in tracing the original
   D. all the above
2. Johnson's Dictionary __________.
   A. continues to be regarded as an authority on icons
   B. was one of the first dictionaries of English language
   C. was regarded a quirky icon of language
   D. has been printed for more than two centuries
3. Tick the correct statement.
   A. Since Johnson's dictionary many have been reprinted.
   B. Johnson's dictionary has been reprinted and abridged.
   C. Johnson abridged his dictionary many times.
   D. Johnson abridged Melvyn Bragg's 'The Adventure of English'.
4. Which of the following statements are true?
   (1) Johnson's dictionary has two volumes.
   (2) His dictionary defines 'patron' as commonly a wretch who supports with insolence, and is paid by flattery.
   (3) Lord Chesterfield was Johnson's patron.
   (4) Lord Chesterfield did not help Johnson financially.
   A. (1) and (3) are True, (2) and (4) are False.
   B. All are True.
   C. (1), (2) and (3) are True and (4) is False.
   D. (2), (3) and (4) are True and (1) is False.
5. Find a word in the passage that means the same as 'unsuccessful'.
   A. swipe B. insolence
   C. straitjacket D. futile

PASSAGE-20

Swaminathan went to school feeling that he was the worst perjurer on earth. His conscience bothered him : he wasn't at all sure if he had been accurate in his description of Samuel. He could not decide how much of what he had said was imagined and how much of it was real. He stopped for a moment on the roadside to make up his mind about Samuel.... His cane skinned people's hands. Swaminathan cast his mind about for an instance on this. There was none within his knowledge. Years and years ago he was reputed to have skinned the knuckles of a boy in the First Standard and made him smear the blood on his face. No one had actualy seen it. But year after year the story persisted among the boys.... Swaminathan's head was dizzy with confusion in regard to Samuel's character—whether he was good or bad, whether he deserved the allegations in the letter or not.... he felt an impulse to run home and beg his father to take back the letter. But Father was an obstinate man.

As he approached the yellow building he realised that he was perjuring himself and was ruining his teacher. Probably the Headmaster would dismiss Samuel and then the police would chain him and put him in jail. For all this disgrace, humiliation and suffering who would be responsible? Swaminathan shuddered. The more he thought of Samuel, the more he grieved for him. As he felt the bulge of the letter in his pocket, he felt like an executioner.

As he entered the school gate an idea occurred to him, a sort of solution. He wouldn't deliver the letter to the Headmaster immediately, but at the end of the day—to that extent he would disobey his father and exercise his independence. There was nothing wrong in it, and Father would not know it anyway. If the letter was given at the end of the day there was a chance that Samuel might do something to justify the letter.

Swaminathan stood at the entrance to his class. Samuel was teaching arithmetic. He looked at Swaminathan for a moment, Swaminathan stood hoping that Samuel would fall on him and tear his skin off. But Samuel merely asked, 'Are you just coming to the class?'

QUESTIONS

1. Swami was not comfortable going to school that day because __________.
A. he was not well
B. he had lied about his teacher Samuel
C. he had not done his home work
D. his friend was not there

2. He was not sure about Samuel's character because __________.
A. what he knew was all hearsay
B. what he knew was his imagination
C. other teachers had told him so
D. none of the above

3. Swami's father was not likely to take back the letter because __________.
A. he believed that Samuel was a good teacher
B. his father wanted to help Swami and other children
C. he was a very stubborn man
D. all of the above

4. Swami decided to __________.
A. give the letter to the Headmaster
B. give the letter directly to Mr. Samuel
C. tear off the letter
D. give it to the Headmaster at the end of the school

5. As Swami was late to the school he expected __________.
A. Mr. Samuel to hit him
B. Mr. Samuel will allow him into the class
C. to be shouted at by Mr. Samuel
D. none of the above

PASSAGE-21

Leadership does not exist without followership. A leader has to be accepted by the group which the former is supposed to lead. To gain acceptability the leader should cause an emotive impact on the group members. The character exhibited by leaders make them dear to their followers. A leader is one who effectively inspires employees to achieve worthwhile goals. What character of the leader motivates the followers? It is not pomp and show or flattery or sanctioning more incentives.

Pomp and show creates a sense of awe and the leader is defied rather than emulated. Flattery is unrealistic and cannot serve as a long-term motivational tool.

A leader's style should be one that can be emulated by all irrespective of cadre, class or calibre. Simplicity in one's day-to-day conduct is the only thing that can be adopted by all. When the leader is simple, he is counted as one belonging to the group of which he is the leader. That's to motivate the people. Motivation is the innate quality that enables an individual or group to contribute unlimitedly with limited means. It is the proud prerogative of enlightened human beings.

QUESTIONS

1. Leadership co-exists with __________.
A. obedience B. followership
C. discipline D. incentives

2. The pre-requisite for the success of a leader is __________.
A. obedience by the group
B. simplicity of the leader
C. acceptability by the group he is supposed to lead
D. strict discipline of the group

3. The leader should cause an emotive impact on the group members as __________.
A. to ensure obedience
B. to enforce discipline
C. to control the group
D. to gain acceptability

4. To inspire employees to achieve long term goals, a leader should not use __________.
A. sanctioning more incentives
B. flattery
C. pomp and show
D. all of the above

5. Find a word having the same meaning as 'emotive' from the words given below:
A. Prerogative B. Enlightened
C. Sensitive D. Proud

PASSAGE-22

We first became aware that something unusual was happening when one of the ship's officers came up to the Chief Engineer, who sat at one table and spoke to him on a low voice. The Chief Engineer at once stood up and with a brief excuse which told us nothing, left the dining room. At first we thought that there had been an accident or that a fire had broken out on board ship, but soon the word went round that a man had been floating in the sea. Then we noticed that the ship had slowed down and was beginning to turn round, with a rather violent motion. Some of the passengers did not wait to finish their meal, but at once rushed upon deck. Others crowded round the portholes, making it impossible for us to eat in comfort. There was such confusion in the dining room that we decided to join those who had come up on deck.

There we learnt that one of the crew had seen a man in the sea some distance from the ship. He had informed the captain who at once ordered the ship to be turned round. We were now only two hundred yards or so from the man and a life boat had already been lowered into the sea. In it there were four sailors, who were sitting ready at the oars, an officer and the ship's doctor. The officer shouted an order and the sailors began to row away the ship. But looking in the same direction as the boat was going, we were able to make out the position of the man in the water. He was clinging to a large piece of wood. At last, after what seemed to us an age the life boat reached the man and two of the sailors pulled him on the boat. This was not at all easy for the sea was rather rough. Then the sailors began to row back to the ship again. The life boat was raised out of the water and the rescued man, wrapped in a blanket was helped out on the deck. Leaning on the arm of the ship's doctor, but still able to walk, in spite of his terrible experience he was led off to the ship's hospital. As he passed along the deck everyone cheered loudly.

QUESTIONS

1. 'We' here refers to __________.
   A. the crew members
   B. the sailors
   C. the passengers of the ship
   D. all of the above
2. The Passengers rushed to the back of the ship because ____ _____.
   A. the ship was drowning
   B. a fire had broken out on board ship
   C. a fight had broken up
   D. the crew was trying to save a drowning man
3. It was tough for the crew to save the drowning man as __________.
   A. the weather was rough
   B. the sea was rough
   C. the man was unwilling to come along with the sailors
   D. the ship had moved ahead
4. Everyone cheered the man loudly as _______.
   A. he had saved the drowning man
   B. he had informed about the drowning man
   C. he had survived a terrible experience
   D. he was the doctor who treated the drowning man
5. The words or the phrase in the passage that means 'it came into knowledge' is _________.
   A. seem to us an age
   B. with a rather violent motion
   C. in comfort
   D. the word went round

PASSAGE-23

In this world there is no worse nuisance than a boy at the age of fourteen. He is neither ornamental nor useful. It is impossible to shower affection on him as a smaller boy; and he is always getting in the way. If he talks with a childish lisp he is called a baby, and if in a grown-up way he is called impertinent. In fact, talk of any kind from him is resented. Then he is at the unattractive, growing age. He grows out of his clothes with indecent haste: His voice grows hoars and breaks and quivers; His face grows suddenly angular and unsightly. It is easy to excuse the shortcomings of early childhood, but it is hard to tolerate even unavoidable lapses in a boy of fourteen. He becomes painfully self-conscious, and when he talks with elderly people is either unduly forward, or else so unduly shy that he appears ashamed of his own existence.

Yet, it is at this age that in his heart of hearts, a young lad most craves recognition and love; and he becomes the devoted slave of any one who shows him consideration. But none dare openly love him, for that would be regarded as undue indulgence and therefore bad for the boy. So, what with scolding and chiding, he becomes very much like a stray dog that has lost its master.

His own name is the only paradise that a boy of fourteen can know. To live in a strange house with strange people is little short of fortune; while it is height of bliss to receive the kind looks of women and never to suffer their slights.

QUESTIONS

1. The expression 'he is always getting in the way' means that he is _________.
   A. found/seen everywhere you go
   B. behaving in a different way from expected/desired
   C. always troubling others with his undesired ways
   D. he goes where he is asked to
2. A lad of fourteen years of age is resented because __________.
   A. he behaves too childishly
   B. he acts like a grown-up
   C. his behaviour becomes neither of a child nor of a grown-up
   D. he looks troublesome
3. A fourteen-year-old boy becomes self-conscious when __________.

A. when he is regarded neither as a young nor a grown-up
B. when he is slighted by elders
C. when he is not appreciated for his good actions
D. none of the above

4. The great bliss for such a boy is ________.
A. to be rewarded for his achievements
B. to receive the kind glances of women
C. to have the company of jolly friends
D. to do what he likes to do

5. The writer's own attitude towards the fourteen-year-old boy is ________.
A. satirical B. sympathetic
C. indifferent D. none of the above

PASSAGE-24

For years, Fukuoka was widely known as the closest city that Japan had to Venice. It might not have enjoyed the splendid architecture, piazzas or the Basilica San Marco of the Italian city, but the people of the largest metropolis on Kyushu, Japan's most southerly main island, prided themselves on the carefully maintained network of rivers that emptied into the graceful curve of Hakata Bay and gave Fukuoka its blue credentials. Today, however, the capital of Kyushu is forging a new identity for itself as green complements the blue.

Not satisfied with pioneering a method of semi-aerobic landfill known the world over as "The Fukuoka Method", the city has gone on to implement some highly exacting rubbish-segregating standards for both homes and businesses. And it has ambitious plans to turn itself into the world's first city to be powered by hydrogen, a project that is under way and will eventually evolve into a "corridor" of homes and businesses linking Fukuoka with the larger cities of Osaka, Nagoya and eventually, the mammoth Tokyo, some 900 kilometres to the rest.

All that and yet Fukuoka is still regarded as the most pleasant place to live in Japan and among the best in the world. In its annual quality of life survey in July 2010, Britain's *Monocle* magazine ranked Fukuoka the 14th "most liveable" city on the planet, thanks in part to its air connections with the rest of Asia, its low crime rate, sub-tropical climate, excellent public transport services and cultural opportunities.

City authorities also received high marks for subsidising local residents who want to install solar-energy systems in their homes to the tune US$1.2 million. Elsewhere, funds have been invested in the creation of green spaces.

QUESTIONS

1. The city of Fukuoka is considered ________.
A. closest to Venice B. different from Venice
C. Peaceful city D. close to Rome

2. Green complements the blue means ________.
A. green and blue do not go together
B. green and blue go well with each other
C. If we have green in a place, it is auspicious to have blue there
D. none of these

3. Fukuoka has set very high standards for
A. cleanliness
B. keeping city green
C. separating bash at home as well as work place
D. maintaining clean air

4. Fukuoka is high on the list of the most liveable cities in the world because ________.
A. there is less crime
B. environment is clean
C. excellent connectivity, within and outside the city
D. all of the above

5. Residents of Fukuoka who wish to install solar powered system ________.
A. Know the advantages of the same
B. will be subsidised by the state
C. are encouraged by the government
D. none of these

PASSAGE-25

A tiger relies on stealth to catch its prey. It has excellent eyesight and hearing, which help it track animals in the dark. Tigers hunt large animals such as deer and wild pigs, which will provide food for a few days. They slink up on their prey unseen, only charging when they are within about 20m (65 ft). Tigers kill their prey by biting the back, its neck or throat, then dragging it away into thick cover to feed. When they have eaten enough, they conceal the carcass with leaves so they can return to it later on. Male tigers can eat up to 40 kg (85 lb) of meat in one meal.

Tigers love water and often bathe or cool off in rivers and pools during the heat of the day. They usually hunt at night and rest during the day. Most tigers live alone, although mothers with cubs or young siblings sometimes hunt together. A male tiger roams a territory of up to 100 sq km (60 sq. miles) in area, defining its boundaries with scent markings, droppings and scratch marks on boulders or trees. These signals tell other tigers about its sex and size as well as its territory. Tigers also communicate by roaring and moaning. They defend their territory fiercely against rival males, but will tolerate some overlap with the smaller territories of females.

QUESTIONS

1. Stealth means ________.
A. by cheating

B. secret way
C. attacking from front
D. jumping at the prey

2. Tigers hunt big animals because ________.
A. it is easy to hunt them
B. their meat is tasty
C. the meat will last them a few days
D. they are easily available

3. Tigers drag their prey into the bush ________.
A. so that nobody can disturb them
B. it is cool under a bush
C. other animals may snatch their prey
D. to conceal it

4. During the hot summer season ________.
A. tigers like to cool by staying in water
B. tigers go off to sleep
C. tigers stay under the bush
D. tigers move to cooler areas

5. Tigers prefer to ________.
A. stay in small groups
B. stay alone
C. stay as a family
D. take care of their young one

PASSAGE-26

The Kidneys of nearly five per cent of people under the age of 20 are not functioning normally, a study shows. The youngsters have albumin in the urine, which indicates that they could develop a serious kidney disease later in their lives. Doctors say that more youngsters today are at a risk of kidney malfunction due to lifestyle changes, which includes smoking, consumption of junk food and less physical activity from desk-bound jobs. On the eve of World Kidney Day, doctors are stressing on the early detection of Kidney malfunction as the only way to reduce serious complications and chronic kidney disease.

For the pilot study, the institute of nephrology at a hospital used a home detection kit that is dipped in urine to show presence of protein in the sample. During the study, 1,000 people were given the kits. A total of 265 returned them with feedback. Of this, 5% of the young population had urinary protein.

Doctors say that the main issue with kidney disease is the lack of early detection. If detected early, patients can avoid reaching the stage of dialysis, which indicates irreversible and serious kidney damage. "Simple health screening test comprising urine tests, blood test and ultrasounds are important. Early diagonsis and treatment for kidney disease can significantly delay and even prevent kidney failure and need for dialysis." said doctors. One doctor said home detection kits would help in early detection, and added that they were targeting young people in colleges and IT firms to use this kit.

QUESTIONS

1. As many as ________ of youngsters have kidney problem.
A. 20%
B. 5%
C. 22%
D. 12%

2. This problem is mainly due to ________.
A. obesity in youngsters
B. change in lifestyle
C. poor intake of water
D. none of the above

3. The main problem with kidney related disease is ________
A. it is fatal
B. it cannot be treated
C. it cannot be detected early
D. it is painful

4. Simple tests will help in ________.
A. preventing and delaying kidney failure
B. giving treatment
C. relieving pain
D. all of the above

5. Hospitals are targeting colleges and IT firms because
A. youngsters need it the most
B. these places have only youngsters
C. they want to bring down kidney issue among youngsters
D. all of the above

PASSAGE-27

Global warming this century could trigger a run away thaw of Greenland's ice sheet and other abrupt shifts such as a dieback of the Amazon rainforest, scientists say.

They urged governments to be more aware of "tipping points" in nature, tiny shifts that can bring big and almost always damaging changes such as a melt of Arctic summer sea ice or a collapse of the Indian monsoon.

"Society may be lulled into a false sense of security by smooth projections of global change," the scientists at British, German and American institutes wrote in a report saying there were many little-understood thresholds in nature.

"The greatest and clearest threat is to the Arctic with summer sea ice loss likely to occur long before, and potentially contribute to, Greenland ice sheet melt", they wrote in the journal "Proceedings" of the National Academy of Sciences. "Tipping elements in the tropics, the boreal zone, and west Antarctica are surrounded by large uncertainty", they wrote, pointing to more potential abrupt shifts than seen in a 2007 report by the UN Climate Panel.

A projected drying of the Amazon basin, linked both to logging and to global warming, could set off a dieback of the rainforest. Many of these tipping points could be closer.

Other sudden changes linked to climate change, stoked by human use of fossil fuels, included a dieback of northern pine forests, or a stronger warming of the Pacific under EI Nino weather events that can disrupt weather world-wide, they wrote.

A possible greening of parts of the Sahel and the Sahara, if monsoon rains in West Africa were disrupted, was one of the few positive abrupt shifts identified by the scientists.

Even a moderate warming could set off a thaw of Greenland's ice sheet that could then vanish in 300 years—raising sea levels by 20 ft, or 2 meters a century and threatening coasts, Pacific islands and cities from Bangkok to Buenos Aires. The UN Climate Panel foresees a rise in world sea level ranging up to about 80 cms this century and reckons that a thaw of Greenland would take hundreds of years longer.

The new study said a disappearance of Arctic sea ice in summer time could happen in coming decades—earlier than projected by the UN panel. That could stoke further global warming as dark water soaks up more heat than ice and snow.

QUESTIONS

1. Global warming can cause ________.
   A. thawing of green land
   B. excess rain
   C. severe draught
   D. a green earth
2. Nations should be sensitive to small changes that can cause ________.
   A. famine
   B. melting of Arctic ice
   C. decrease in sea level
   D. chill in polar regions
3. There could be a die-back of the rainforest because of ________.
   A. drying of Amazon Basin
   B. water level
   C. ses level
   D. melting glaciers
4. As a result of rains in West Africa ________.
   A. Sahara will turn into desert
   B. Sahara will turn green
   C. flood will come
   D. none of these
5. According to a UN panel report _____ in this century.
   A. sea level will decrease
   B. sea level will remain same
   C. sea level will rise
   D. none of these

PASSAGE-28

From time immemorial drugs have been used by humans for medical purposes. But never before had the abuse ... (A) ... narcotics caused such unprecedented worldwide concern and posed an alarming menace to the society. According to recent World Health Organization estimates, there are millions of ... (B) ... addicts and abusers of cocaine, opium, barbiturates, sedatives and tranquilizers all over the world. It is now an international problem that ... (C) ... the Indian government. Recent movies like Udta Punjab have highlighted that the consumption of drugs has affected the youth in the state of Punjab adversely. Taking a drug other than for medical reason in amount, strength, frequency or manner that ... (D) ... the physical and mental functioning is drug abuse. Drug abuse is a painful problem for the addict, for the family and for all those who touch their lives. It is mostly the youngsters that fall prey to drugs. At this stage, the youngsters are especially vulnerable to pressure from friends. The future generation is virtually being crippled under the impact of drugs. Due to intake of drugs, the person may lose will power, concentration, memory and judgement capacity. There is a need to create awareness amongst the youth as well as work towards rehabilitation of those trapped in ...(E)... abuse.

QUESTIONS

1. Choose the most appropriate option for (B):
   A. heroin B. heroine
   C. medicine D. work
2. Choose the most appropriate option for (D):
   A. mends B. damages
   C. invigorates D. augments
3. Choose the most appropriate option for (E):
   A. object B. environment
   C. substance D. habitat
4. Choose the most appropriate option for (C):
   A. surprises B. pleases
   C. bothers D. amuses
5. Choose the most appropriate option for (A):
   A. by B. of
   C. from D. through

PASSAGE-29

Once upon a time there was a bird. It was ignorant. It sang all right, but never recited scriptures. It hopped pretty frequently, but lacked manners. Said the Raja to himself: "Ignorance is costly at the long run. For fools consume as much food as others, and yet give nothing in return."

He called his nephews to his presence and told them that the bird must have a sound schooling. The pundits were summoned, and at once went to the root of the matter. They decided that the ignorance of the bird was due to their natural habit of living in poor nest. Therefore, according to pundits, the first thing necessary for this bird's education was a suitable cage. The pundits had their rewards and went home happily. A golden cage was built with gorgeous decorations. Crowds came to see it from all parts of the world. "Culture, captured and caged" exclaimed some, in a rapture of ecstasy and burst into tears. Others remarked: "even if culture be missed, the cage will remain, to the end, a substantial fact. How fortunate for the bird." The goldsmith filled his bag with money and lost no time in sailing homewards.

The pundits sat down to educate the bird. With proper deliberation they took their pinch of snuff, as one of them said: "Text-books can never be too many for our purpose!" The nephews brought together an enormous crowd of scribes. They copied from books, and copied from copies, till the manuscripts were piled up to an uncatchable height. Men murmured in amazement. "Oh, the tower of culture, egregiously high! The end of it lost in the clouds!" The scribes, with light hearts, hurried home, their pockets heavily laden. The nephews were furiously busy keeping the cage in proper trim. As their constant scrubbing and polishing went on, the people said with satisfaction: "This is progress indeed!" Men were employed in large numbers, and supervisors were still more numerous. These, with their cousins of all different degrees of distance, built a palace for themselves and lived there happily ever after. Whatever may be its other deficiencies, the world is never in want of fault-finders; and they went about saying that every creature remotely connected with the cage flourished beyond words, excepting only the bird.

When this remark reached the Raja's ears, he summoned his nephews before him and said: "My dear nephews, what is this that we hear?" The nephews said in answer: "Sire, let the testimony of the goldsmiths and the pundits, the scribes and the supervisors, be taken, if the truth is to be known. Food is scarce with the fault-finders, and that is why their tongues have gained in sharpness." The explanation was so luminously satisfactory that the Raja decorated each one of his nephews with his own rare jewels.

The Raja at length being desirous of seeing with his own eyes how his education department engaged itself with the little bird, made his appearance one day at the great hall of learning. From the gate rose the sounds of conch-shells and gongs, horns, bugles and trumpets, cymbals, drums and kettle drums, tom-toms, tambourines, flutes, fifes, barrel-organs and bagpipes. The pundits began chanting mantras with their topmost voices, while the goldsmiths, scribes, supervisors, and their numberless cousins of all different degrees of distance, loudly raised a round of cheers.

The nephews pleased, the Raja was about to remount his elephant, when the fault-finder from behind some bush, cried out: "Maharaja, have you seen the bird?"

"Indeed, I have not!" exclaimed the Raja. "I completely forgot about the bird. Turning back, he asked the pundits about the method they followed in instructing the bird. It was shown to him. He was immensely impressed. The method was so stupendous that the bird looked ridiculously unimportant in comparison. The Raja was satisfied that there was no flaw in the arrangements. As for any complaint from the bird itself, that simply could not be expected. Its throat was so completely choked with the leaves from the books that it could neither whistle nor whisper. It sent a thrill through one's body to watch the process.

This time, while remounting his elephant, the Raja ordered his state ear-puller to give a thorough good pull at both the ears of the fault-finder. The bird thus crawled on, duly and properly, to the verge of inanity. In fact, its proper was satisfactory in the extreme. Nevertheless, nature occasionally triumphed overt training, and when the morning light peeped into the bird's cage it sometimes fluttered its wings in a reprehensible manner. And, though it is hard to believe, it pitifully packed at its bars with its feeble break. "What impertinence!" growled the Kotwal.

The blacksmith, with his forge and hammer took his place in the Rāja's Department of Education: Oh, what resounding blows! The iron chain was soon completed, and the bird's wings were clipped. The Raja's brother-in-law looked back, and shook their heads, saying: "This bird not only lacks good sense, but also gratitude!" With text-book in hand and baton in the other, the pundits gave the poor bird what may fitly be called lessons!

The Kotwal was honoured with a title for his watchfulness, and the blacksmith for skill in forging chains. The bird died.

(A Parrot's story by Rabindra Nath Tagore)

QUESTIONS

1. The Raja wanted the bird to have sound schooling because

A. the bird was consuming the resources of the state but giving nothing in return.

B. he wanted to eventually kill the bird.

C. he wanted to show his gratitude towards the bird.

D. he wished to set before his subjects an example of love towards nature.

2. 'The tower of culture' symbolizes
   A. money B. raja
   C. manuscripts D. cage
3. The word 'impertinence' refers to
   A. disrespect B. stupid
   C. loyalty D. civility
4. The status of the 'bird' in this story can be compared today with that of a
   A. head of the school
   B. student
   C. teacher educator
   D. teacher
5. The bird died in the end because
   A. it lacked good sense
   B. its cage was dirty
   C. Its natural instincts were suppressed
   D. it was brutally beaten up by the Raja

PASSAGE-30

Rakesh was on his way home from school when he bought the cherries. He paid fifty paise for the bunch. It took him about half-an-hour to walk home, and by the time he reached the cottage there were only three cherries left. 'Have a cherry, Grandfather,' he said, as soon as he saw his grandfather in the garden. Grandfather took one cherry and Rakesh promptly ate the other two. He kept the last seed in his mouth for some time, rolling it round and round on his tongue until all the tang had gone. Then he placed the seed on the palm of his hand and studied it. 'Are cherry seeds lucky?' asked Rakesh.

'Of course.'

'Then I'll keep it.'

'Nothing is lucky if you put it away. If you want luck, you must put it to some use.'

'What can I do with a seed?'

'Plant it.'

So, Rakesh found a small space and began to dig up a flowerbed. 'Hey, not there,' said Grandfather, 'I've sown mustard in that bed. Plant it in that shady corner, where it won't be disturbed.' Rakesh went to a corner of the garden where the earth was soft and yielding. He did not have to dig. He pressed the seed into the soil with his thumb and it went right in. Then he had his lunch, and ran off to play cricket with his friends, and forgot all about the cherry seed.

When it was winter in the hills, a cold wind blew down from the snows and went whoo-whoo-whoo in the deodar trees, and the garden was dry and bare. In the evenings Grandfather and Rakesh sat over a charcoal fire, and Grandfather told Rakesh stories and in turn Rakesh would read to him from the newspaper, Grandfather's eyesight being rather weak. Rakesh found the newspaper very dull – especially after the stories – but Grandfather wanted all the news.

One morning in the garden he bent to pick up what he thought was a small twig and found to his surprise that it was well rooted. He stared at it for a moment, then ran to fetch Grandfather, calling, 'Dada, come and look, the cherry tree has come up!' 'What cherry tree?' asked Grandfather, who had forgotten about it. 'The seed we planted last year –look, it's come up!' Rakesh went down on his haunches, while Grandfather bent almost double and peered down at the tiny tree. It was about four inches high. 'Yes, it's a cherry tree,' said Grandfather. 'You should water it now and then.' Rakesh ran indoors and came back with a bucket of water. 'Don't drown it!' said Grandfather. Rakesh gave it a sprinkling and circled it with pebbles. 'What are the pebbles for?' asked Grandfather. 'For privacy,' said Rakesh. He looked at the tree every morning, but it did not seem to be growing very fast, so he stopped looking at it except quickly, out of the corner of his eye. And, after a week or two, when he allowed himself to look at it properly, he found that it had grown – at least an inch!

The cherry tree grew quickly during monsoon. It was about two feet high when a goat entered the garden and ate all the leaves. Only the main stem and two thin branches remained. 'Never mind,' said Grandfather, seeing that Rakesh was upset. 'It will grow again; cherry trees are tough.' Towards the end of the rainy season new leaves appeared on the tree. Then a woman cutting grass scrambled down the hillside, her scythe swishing through the heavy monsoon foliage. She did not try to avoid the tree: one sweep, and the cherry tree was cut in two. When Grandfather saw what had happened, he went after the woman and scolded her; but the damage could not be repaired. 'Maybe it will die now,' said Rakesh. 'Maybe,' said Grandfather. But the cherry tree had no intention of dying. By the time summer came again, it had sent out several new shoots with tender green leaves.

One day he found a bright green praying-mantis perched on a branch, peering at him with bulging eyes. Rakesh let it remain there; it was the cherry tree's first visitor. The next visitor was a hairy caterpillar, who started making a meal of the leaves. Rakesh removed it quickly and dropped it on a heap of dry leaves. Come back when you're a butterfly,' he said.

Winter came early. The cherry tree bent low with the weight of snow. In February it was Rakesh's birthday. He was nine – and the tree was four, but almost as tall as Rakesh. One morning, when the Sun came out, Grandfather came into the garden to 'let some warmth get into my bones,' as he put it. He stopped in front of the cherry tree, stared at it for a few moments, and then called out,

'Rakesh! Come and look! Come quickly before it falls!' Rakesh and Grandfather gazed at the tree as though it had performed a miracle. There was a pale pink blossom at the end of a branch. 'There are so many trees in the forest,' said Rakesh. 'What's so special about this tree? Why do we like it so much?' 'We planted it ourselves,' said Grandfather. That's why it's special. 'Just one small seed,' said Rakesh, and he touched the smooth bark of the tree that he had grown. He ran his hand along the trunk of the tree and put his finger to the tip of a leaf. 'I wonder,' he whispered. 'Is this what it feels to be God?'

QUESTIONS

1. The plot of the story revolves around the concept(s) of:
A. relation between grandfather and Rakesh
B. hope, responsibility, perseverance and pride
C. how to plant trees
D. how to feel like God

2. The author is an ardent lover of:
A. cherries B. grandfather stories
C. nature and animals D. reading newspaper

3. Why does Rakesh circle the plant with some pebbles?
A. His grandfather asked him
B. He likes to play with pebbles
C. To beautify his garden
D. For privacy

4. In the story, the Cherry tree symbolises:
A. beauty B. innocence
C. birth D. survival

5. The status of 'the cherry tree' in this story can be compared today with that of a:
A. birds B. trees
C. animals D. humans

III. POETRY

Directions: *Read the following poems carefully and choose the best answer to each question out of the four alternatives and mark it in the Answer Sheet.*

POEM-1

It is an ancient Mariner,
And he stoppeth one of three.
'By thy long grey beard and glittering eye,
Now wherefore stopp'st thou me?
The Bridegroom's doors are opened wide,
And I am next of kin;
The guests are met, the feast is set:
May'st hear the merry din.'
He holds him with his skinny hand,
'There was a ship,' quoth he.
'Hold off! unhand me, grey-beard loon!'
Eftsoons his hand dropt he.
He holds him with his glittering eye —
The Wedding-Guest stood still,
And listens like a three years' child:
The Mariner hath his will.

— ST Coleridge

QUESTIONS

1. What is the most potent factor with the Ancient Mariner that enables him to hold the wedding guest?
A. His glittering eye B. His skinny hand
C. His long grey-beard D. His starting words.

2. What is the significance of comparing the wedding guest to a three years' child?
A. A three years' child is innocent.
B. He is afraid of a strange man.
C. He is fond of listening to stories.
D. He cannot run away from a grown-up man.

3. Which among the following is not an argument presented by the wedding-guest?
A. The wedding-guest is a close relative of the Bridegroom.
B. His participation in some ceremonies is essential.
C. Merry-making is already going on.
D. Other guests have already arrived.

4. The Ancient Mariner is:
A. A young man
B. A middle-aged man
C. An old man
D. It is not clear from the text

5. The Mariner's story is related to:
A. A ship B. Giants
C. Fairies D. A forest

POEM-2

Shall I hear the lament of the nightingale, submissively lending my ear?
Am I the rose to suffer its cry in silence year after year?
The fire of verse gives me courage and bids me no more to be faint.

With dust in my mouth, I am abject: to God I make my complaint.

Sometimes You favour our rivals then sometimes with us You are free,

I am sorry to say it so boldly. You are no less fickle than we.

(Iqbal: 'Complaint to God')

QUESTIONS

1. What fault does the poet find in God?
- A. God causes misery to people.
- B. He opposes the poet and his companions and favours their opponents.
- C. He is fickle.
- D. He does not care for the poor.

2. What gives courage to the poet?
- A. The song of the nightingale.
- B. The power of poetry.
- C. The sweet smell of the rose.
- D. God's mercy.

3. What is the present mood of the poet?
- A. He is distraught.
- B. He is in a happy mood.
- C. He is in a contemplating mood.
- D. He is talking only frivolously.

4. Why does the poet use the word "lament" for the song of the nightingale?
- A. The nightingale is sad at poet's miserable condition.
- B. It is only teasing the poet.
- C. It seems sad to the poet only.
- D. Proverbially, the nightingale is said to sing sweet but sad songs.

5. In what situation is the rose placed in the poem?
- A. Very advantageous situation.
- B. Helpless situation.
- C. Confusing situation.
- D. Situation of expectation.

POEM-3

'In vain to me the smiling mornings shine,
And reddening Phoebus lifts his golden fire;
The birds in vain and amorous descant join,
Or cheerful fields resume their green attire.
These ears, alas! for other notes repine;
"A different object do these eyes require;
My lonely anguish melts no heart but mine;
And in my breast the imperfect joys expire;"
Yet morning smiles the busy race to cheer,
And new-born pleasure brings to happier men;
The fields to all their wanted tribute bear;
To warm their little loves the birds complain.
"I fruitless mourn to him that cannot hear,
And weep the more because I weep in vain."

— Thomas Gray

QUESTIONS

1. The poet's object in the given poem cannot hear him because:
- A. He has gone deaf.
- B. He does not care for him.
- C. He is awfully busy.
- D. He is dead.

2. What does nature bring to the poet?
- A. A sense of loss
- B. A feeling of joy
- C. A sense of satisfaction
- D. A feeling of charm

3. Why does the poet use the phrase "in vain" so many times?
- A. To tell about the uselessness of his existence.
- B. To tell about the uselessness of beauties of nature and his wails.
- C. To tell about the uselessness of birds' love.
- D. To tell about waste of morning time.

4. What feeling can a keenly observant reader get from a study of the first twelve lines and the last two lines?
- A. A feeling of harmony.
- B. A feeling of amplitude.
- C. A feeling of dichotomy of sense.
- D. A sense of overall satisfaction.

5. What does the morning bring to the "happier men"?
- A. A sense of loss.
- B. A new joy.
- C. A feeling of sorrow.
- D. A feeling of sympathy.

POEM-4

'Turn on the prudent Ant thy heedless eyes,
Observe her labours, Sluggard, and be wise;
No stern command, no monitory voice,
Prescribes her duties, or directs her choice;
Yet, timely provident, she hastes away
To snatch the blessings of a plenteous day;
When fruitful Summer loads the teeming plain,
She crops the harvest, and she stores the grain.

How long shall sloth usurp thy useless hours,
Unnerve thy vigour, and enchain thy powers?
While artful shades thy downy couch enclose,
And soft solicitation courts repose,
Amidst the drowsy charms of dull delight,
Year chases year with unremitted flight,
Till Want now following, fraudulent and slow,
Shall spring to seize thee, like an ambush'd foe.

— *Dr Samuel Johnson*

QUESTIONS

1. What can be said to be the overwhelming quality of an ant?
   A. Industriousness
   B. Dutifulness
   C. Time-consciousness
   D. Regular routine
2. What will finally overtake a sluggard?
   A. Sloth B. Waste of time
   C. Loss of energy D. Want
3. What does the Ant do in summer?
   A. It enjoys the beauties of nature.
   B. It sits in the shade of trees.
   C. It fills its stores with grain.
   D. It spends time eating summer fruits.
4. Which among the following is not the characteristic of Want?
   A. Fraudulence
   B. Ambush
   C. Springing over the enemy.
   D. Abusing the enemy.
5. What is the main characteristic of summer?
   A. It is a very hot season.
   B. It is a fruitful season.
   C. It expects all to do their duties.
   D. It always comes on time.

POEM-5

On their own feet they came, or on shipboard,
Camel-back, horse-back, ass-back, mule-back,
Old civilisations put to the sword.
Then they and their wisdom went to rack;
No handiwork of Callimachus,
Who handled marble as if it were bronze,
Made draperies that seemed to rise
When sea-wind swept the corner stands:
His long lamp-chimney shaped like the stem
Of a slender palm, stood but a day;
All things fall and are built again,
And those that build them again are gay.

— *WB Yeats*

QUESTIONS

1. Which of the following means of transport was not used by the destroyers of old civilizations?
   A. By sea
   B. By air
   C. On the backs of animals
   D. On foot
2. What is the eternal law of life?
   A. Destruction and recreation
   B. Destruction
   C. Creation
   D. Failure of art
3. Which of the following could Callimachus do?
   A. Make a long thin lamp-chimney last long.
   B. Engrave in bronze.
   C. Make metallic artefacts.
   D. Work with marble without breaking it.
4. Is there no hope for civilizations?
   A. Yes, there is.
   B. No, there's none.
   C. The poet gives no clue to it.
   D. There is only a little hope.
5. Who get real happiness from their activity?
   A. The destroyers. B. The builders.
   C. The observers. D. The sea-creatures.

POEM-6

I lay in sorrow, deep *distressed*:
My *grief* a proud man heard;
His looks were cold, he gave me gold
But not a kindly word,
My sorrow passed—I paid him back
The gold he gave to me;
Then stood *erect* and spoke my thanks
And blessed his *Charity.*
I *lay* in *want,* in grief and pain:
A poor man passed my way;
He bound my head, he gave me *bread*
He watched me night and day.
How shall I pay him back again,
For all he did to me?

Oh, gold is great, but greater far

Is *heavenly* Sympathy!

—Charles Mackey

QUESTIONS

1. The proud man heard the poet
A. crying in sorrow B. sing in joy
C. lying in misery D. crying due to pain

2. The proud man helped the poet by
A. giving him comfort
B. assisting him to lie down
C. his cold looks
D. giving him gold

3. The poet thanked the proud man by
A. speaking nicely to him
B. giving him money
C. praising him
D. blessing his large-heartedness

4. The poor man helped the poet by
A. giving him comfort
B. binding his body
C. giving him food
D. serving him like his own

5. The word 'heavenly' means
A. relating to paradise
B. like that of heaven
C. like angels
D. like gods

POEM-7

The earth was green, the sky was blue;
I saw and heard one sunny *morn*
A *skylark hang* between the two,
A singing *speck* above the corn.
A stage below in gay *accord*,
White butterflies danced on wing,
And still the singing skylark *soared*,
And silent sank and soared to sing.
The *cornfield stretched* a *tender* green
To right and left beside my walks;
I knew he had a nest unseen
Somewhere among the million *stalks*.
And as I *paused* to hear his song
While swift the sunny moments *slid*,
Perhaps his *mate* sat listening long,
And listened longer than I did.

—Christina Rossetti

QUESTIONS

1. The skylark sang when
A. it rained
B. the sun shone
C. the earth was green and the sky without clouds
D. there were clouds

2. The skylark while singing looked like
A. a star B. an insect
C. an eagle D. a small dot

3. The skylark rose upwards and upwards
A. while flying B. while singing
C. as it sang D. as it flew

4. The nest of the skylark was
A. in the fields below
B. among the numberless stems of corn
C. beside other nests
D. among trees

5. The word 'paused' means
A. stopped B. stood erect
C. flew across D. went straight

POEM-8

The Forst *performs* its secret *ministry*,
Unhelped by any wind. The owlet's cry
Came loud—and *hark*, again! loud as before.
The *inmates* of my cottage, all at rest,
Have left me to that *solitude*, which suits
Abstruser musings : save that at my side
My *cradled infant slumbers* peacefully.
Tis calm indeed! so calm, that it disturbs
And *vexes meditation* with its strange
And extreme silentness ......

—S.T. Coleridge

QUESTIONS

1. The 'secret ministry' of the frost is that
A. it is falling on the ground
B. it ministers the earth
C. it has a secret deal with the nature
D. it deals with the air

2. There is silence all round. This is seen in the phrase
A. and hark, again
B. all at rest
C. that solitude
D. Abstruser musings

3. Who is sleeping in the cradle?
A. the poet's son B. the poet's child
C. the poet's nephew D. a stranger baby

4. What disturb(s) the calm?
A. the surroundings B. nature
C. weather D. calmness
5. The word 'meditation' means
A. prayers B. thought
C. deep thought D. deep ideas

POEM-9

She *dwelt* among the *untrodden* ways
Beside the springs of Dove,
A Maid whom there were none to praise
And very few to love :
A *violet* by a *mossy* stone
Half hidden from the eye!
—*Fair* as a star, when one
Is shining in the sky.
She lived unknown, and few could know
When Lucy *ceased* to be;
But she is in *grave,* and, oh,
The difference to me!

—William Wordsworth

QUESTIONS

1. Lucy lived a lonely life because
A. no person loved her
B. no one praised her
C. there was no human population
D. she was born in nature
2. Lucy was like a
A. rose flower B. a star
C. a violet flower D. a daffodil
3. She died on unknown death because
A. no one knew her
B. no one could tell where she died
C. she was never known
D. no one knew when she died
4. That the poet is sad over Lucy's death is clear in the words :
A. she is in grave
B. oh
C. the difference to me
D. Lucy ceased to be
5. The word 'untrodden' means
A. not covered
B. unwalkable
C. not walked over
D. hard to walk

POEM-10

I wandered lonely as cloud
That *floats* on high o'er *vales* and hills,
When all at once I saw a crowd,
A *host* of golden daffodils ;
Beside the lake, beneath the trees,
Fluttering and dancing in the breeze.
Continuous as the stars that shine
And *twinkle* in the milky way,
They *stretched* in never-ending line
Along the *margin* of a *bay* :
Ten thousasnd saw I at a *glance*,
Tossing their head in *sprightly* dance.
The waves beside them danced; but they
Outdid the *sparkling* waves in *glee* :
A poet could not but be gay,
In such a *jocund* company;
I *gazed*—and gazed—but little thought
What wealth the show to me had brought.
For oft, when on my couch I lie
In vacant or in *pensive* mood,
They *flash* upon that inward eye
Which is the bliss of *solitude*;
And then my heart with pleasure fills
And dances with the daffodils.

—William Wordsworth

QUESTIONS

1. The poet compares himself with
A. a cloud that is rainy
B. a cloud
C. a floating cloud
D. a daffodil
2. The daffodils danced
A. like stars
B. beside the lake
C. like twinkling stars
D. in lake water
3. The daffodils made the waves shy in their
A. dancing B. shining
C. sparkling D. shaking
4. The poet's wealth from daffodils is
A. the bliss of solitude
B. their dancing
C. their bright colour
D. his joyful heart

5. The word 'sprightly' means
A. happy B. blissful
C. joyful D. playing

POEM-11

Is this a holy thing to see
In a rich and fruitful land,
Babes reduc'd to *misery,*
Fed with cold and *usurous* hand?
Is that *trembling* cry a song?
Can it be a song of joy?
And so many children poor?
It is a land of poverty?
And their sun does never shine,
And their fields are *bleak and bare,*
And their ways are fill'd with thorns :
It is *eternal* winter there.
For where'er the sun does shine,
And where'er the rain does fall,
Babes can never hunger there,
Nor poverty the mind *appall.*

—William Blake

QUESTIONS

1. 'Rich and fruitful land' stands for
A. U.S.A. B. England
C. India D. China

2. Babies there sing a song with
A. joy B. trembling hands
C. a trembling cry D. sadness

3. If the babies live a miserable life, that country is indeed a country of
A. sick children B. happy children
C. poor children D. hungry children

4. 'It is eternal winter there' means
A. children's life is not happy
B. children's future is bleak
C. winter is all the year around
D. winter is at the peak

5. The word 'usurous' means
A. of zamindar
B. very cruel
C. of money lender
D. of trader

POEM-12

There was a family of rabbits
who lived near a *pack* of wolves.
The wolves *announced* that they did
not like the way the rabbits were
living. One night several wolves were
killed in an earthquake and this was
blamed on the rabbits, for it
is well known that rabbits *pound*
on the ground with their *hind*
legs and cause earthquakes. On
another night one of the wolves was
killed by a bolt of *lightning*
and this also was blamed on the
rabbits. The wolves *threatened* to *civilise* the
rabbits if they didn't behave, and
the rabbits decided to run away
to a desert island. But the other
animals, who lived at a great distance,
shamed then saying, "You must stay where
you are and be brave. This is no world
for escapists. If the wolves attack you,
we will come to your aid, in all
probability." So the rabbits continued
to live near the wolves. And one day
there was a *terrible* flood which
drowned a great many wolves. This was
blamed on the rabbits, for it is
well known that they with long
ears cause floods. The wolves *descended* on
the rabbits for their own good,
and imprisoned them in a dark *cave,*
for their own protection.
When nothing was heard about
the rabbits for some weeks, the other
animals demanded to know what
had happened to them. The wolves
replied that the rabbits had been
eaten and since they had been
eaten the affair was a purely
internal matter.
"They were trying to escape" said
the wolves, "and, as you know, this
is no world for escapists."

—James Thurber

QUESTIONS

1. Rabbits do an activity that is similar to earthquakes. It is
A. moving the soil
B. causing earthquakes
C. shaking their hind legs
D. striking the ground

2. The second time wolves died due to
A. electricity B. lightning
C. floods D. earthquakes

3. The other animals advised the rabbits not to go away because
A. they shouldn't be affraid of wolves
B. there was no fear
C. they must be brave
D. they should oppose the wolves

4. The lesson of the incident is that those who escape
A. can't live
B. can't progress
C. shall be free from danger
D. shall lag behind

5. The word 'announced' means
A. went away B. spoke
C. whistled D. declared

POEM-13

The countryside must *preserved*
(Preferably miles away from me.)
Neat hectares of the *stuff* reserved
For those in need of flower or tree.
I'll make do with *landscape* painting
Film *documentaries* on TV
And when I need to escape, *panting,*
Then open-mouthed I'll head for the sea.
Let others *stroll* and take their *leisure,*
In grasses wade upto their knees.
For I *derive* no earthly pleasure
From the green green *rash* that makes me *sneeze.*

—Roger McGough

QUESTIONS

1. The poet feels that the countryside should look
A. green
B. covered with vegetation
C. full of flowers
D. good with trees

2. The poet would like to satisfy himself of his desire to see nature from
A. films B. documentaries
C. TV D. cable TV

3. The poet gets immense pleasure when he is far from
A. natural beauty
B. countryside
C. villageside
D. film documentaries

4. The poet hates the greenery because it makes him
A. sick B. dissatisified
C. a nature lover D. sneeze

5. The word 'landscape' means
A. a scene of nature
B. physical scene of a place
C. nature beauty
D. vegetation

POEM-14

One infant grows up and becomes a *jockey;*
Another plays basketball or hockey,
This one the prize ring hates to enter
That one becomes a *tackle or center,*
I am just as glad as glad can be
That I'm not them, that they're not me.
With all my heart do I admire
Athletes who *sweat* for fun or hire,
Who take the field in *gaudy pomp,*
And *maim* each other as they *romp,*
My *limp and bashful spirit* feeds
On other people's *heroic deeds.*
Now A runs ninety yards to score,
B knocks the champion to the floor.
C risking *vertebrae and spine,*
Lashes his steed across the line,
You'd think my *ego* it would please
To *swap* positions with one of these.
Well, ego might be pleased enough,
But zealous athletes play so rough,
They do not ever, in their dealings
Consider one another's feelings.
I'm glad that when my struggle begins
Twixt prudence and ego, prudence wins.
Athletes, I'll drink to you
Or eat with you,

Or anything except compete with you,
Buy tickets worth their weight in *radium,*
To watch you *gambol* in a stadium.
And reassure myself anew
That you're not me and I'm not you.

—Ogden Nash

QUESTIONS

1. The poet admires the sportspersons who
A. win the game
B. perspire for goals
C. beat other participants
D. enjoy playing

2. The poet's spirit enjoys
A. the great sport feats of the players
B. seeing them getting injured
C. knocking one another of sportspersons
D. their fighting for the goal

3. What makes the poet not to be a sportsperson?
A. hatred to be a player
B. wisdom to avoid playing
C. fear of injuries
D. careless playing leading to injuries

4. The poet will do anything
A. to see the players playing
B. to go to the stadium
C. for the sportspersons
D. for the well-being of the players

5. The word 'prudence' means
A. athletics B. wisdom
C. skill D. bravery

POEM-15

The *fair breeze* blew, the white foam flew,
The *furrow* followed free;
We were the first that ever burst
Into that silent sea.
Down dropt the breeze, the sails *dropt* down,
T was sad as sad could be;
And we did speak only to break
The silence of the sea!
All in a hot and copper sky,
The bloody Sun, at noon,
Right up above the mast did stand,
No bigger than the Moon.
Day after day, day after day,
We *struck*, nor breath nor motion;
As *idle* as a painted ship
Upon a painted ocean.

—S.T. Coleridge

QUESTIONS

1. The weather became fine and this is clear from
A. the wind blowing very fast
B. the wind blowing leisurely
C. the furrow being free
D. the white foam

2. But soon the weather became very bad as
A. the ship couldn't move
B. the sails couldn't gather wind
C. they became sad
D. they couldn't speak

3. The sky became
A. very hot
B. bloody
C. hot and copper like
D. very perspiring

4. The ship looked like a painted one because it
A. couldn't run B. couldn't move
C. got fully aground D. got anchored

5. The word 'mast' means
A. a pillar
B. sailing prop
C. upright post in a ship
D. upright post of wood in a ship

POEM-16

The old priest Peter Gilligan
Was *weary* night and day;
For half his *flock* were in their beds,
Or under green *sods* lay.
Once while he *nodded* on a chair,
At the *moth-hour* of *eve*,
Another poor man sent for him,
And he began to *grieve.*
"I have no rest, nor joy, nor peace,
For people die and die";
And after cried he, "God forgive!
My body *spake,* not I!"
He knelt, and *leaning* on the chair
He prayed and fell asleep;
And the moth-hour went from the fields,
And stars began to *peep.*

"*Mavrone,* mavrone! The man has died
While I slept on the chair";
He *roused* his horse out of its sleep,
And rode with little care.
He rode now as he never rode,
By rocky *lane and fern;*
The sick man's wife opened the door :
"Father! You come again!"
"And is the poor man dead?" he cried.
"He died an hour ago."
The old priest Peter Gilligan
In grief *swayed to and fro.*
"When you were gone, he turned and died
As merry as a bird."
The old priest Peter Gilligan
He knelt at that word.

—W.B. Yeats

QUESTIONS

1. Peter Gilligan was very tired because he
A. had not slept for long
B. had been serving the people day and night
C. nursed the sick
D. cared much for his own people

2. He worried much because
A. his people were dying
B. he had had no sleep
C. his own people were sad
D. the poor man came to him

3. He regretted that the man died
A. when he had slept
B. when it was midnight
C. when no one was near him
D. when he slept

4. Father Gilligan found when he visited the poor man's house that
A. God had visited in his place
B. God had excused him
C. he was not wanted
D. he couldn't do anything

5. The word 'moth-hour' means
A. late evening B. midnight
C. morning D. mid-day

POEM-17

It takes much time to kill a tree,
Not a simple *job* of the knife
Will do it. It has grown
Slowly *consuming* the earth,
Rising out of it, feeding
Upon its *crust, absorbing*
Years of sunlight, air, water,
And out of its *leprous hide*
Sprouting leaves.
So *hack and chop*
But this alone won't do it.
Not so much pain will do it.
The bleeding *bark* will heal
And from close to the ground
Will rise *curled green twigs,*
Miniature boughs
Which if unchecked will expand again
To former size.
No,
The root is to be pulled out
Out of the *anchoring* earth;
It is to be roped, tied,
And pulled out—*snapped out*
Or pulled out *entirely,*
Out from the earth-cave,
And the strength of the tree *exposed,*
The source, white and wet,
The most sensitive, hidden
For years inside the earth.
Then the matter
Of *scorching* and *choking*
In sun and air,
Browning, hardening,
Twisting, withering,
And then it is done.

—Gieve Patel

QUESTIONS

1. The tree has come out of the earth after
A. taking breath in the atmosphere
B. using the soil
C. feeling the heat of the sun
D. absorbing the crust.

2. If the tree is chopped, it will still
A. live B. wither
C. stand D. heal

3. If the tree is chopped, its leaves will
A. glisten
B. grow to their former size

C. will rise from the ground
D. shine beautifully

4. The 'white and wet' part of a tree when uprooted is its
A. source
B. sensitive part
C. life
D. important part

5. The word 'hidden' means
A. clear B. obscure
C. safe D. concealed

POEM-18

The quality of mercy is not *strain'd*;
It droppeth as the gentle rain from heaven
Upon the place beneath. It is twice blest.
It blesseth him that gives and him that takes.
T is *mightiest* in the mightiest; it *becomes*
The *throned monarch* better than his *crown*;
His *sceptre* shows the force of *temporal* power,
The *attribute* to *awe* and *majesty,*
Wherein doth sit the *dread* and fear of kings;
But mercy is above this sceptred *sway,*
It is enthroned in the hearts of kings,
It is an attribute to God himself;
And earthly power doth then show likest God's
When mercy *seasons* justice.

QUESTIONS

1. Mercy is compared with
A. rain
B. king
C. monarch
D. gentle rain

2. Mercy adds more glory to a
A. king
B. monarch
C. monarch's crown
D. monarch sitting in his throne

3. When does mercy becoem God-like?
A. when it enters a king's heart
B. when it mixes with the king's grace
C. when it is seasoned with justice
D. when mercy seasons a king's justice

4. What shows the temporal power of a monarch?
A. his throne B. his mercy
C. sceptre D. his crown

5. The word 'attribute' means
A. quantity B. quality
C. absolute D. feature

POEM-19

Whose *woods* these are I think I know,
His house is in the village thought,
He will not see me stopping here
To watch his woods fill up with snow.
My little horse must think it *queer*
To stop without a farmhouse near
Between the woods and frozen lake
The darkest evening of the year.
He gives his *harness bells* a shake
To ask if there is some mistake.
The only other sound's the sweep
Of easy wind and *downy flake.*
The woods are lovely; dark and deep,
But I have promises to keep,
And miles to go before I sleep,
And miles to go before I sleep.

QUESTIONS

1. The poet is standing
A. in a village
B. on the bank of a river
C. in a forest
D. by the side of a lake

2. When the poet stands, the horse
A. shakes its harness bells
B. shakes the bells
C. stands silently
D. asks a question

3. What kind of a weather is it?
A. wet and cloudy
B. cold and snowy
C. very cold and windy
D. cold and windy

4. '... before I sleep' means here
A. before I sleep on my bed
B. before I die
C. before I go home and sleep
D. before I 'sleep' at one level and **before I 'die'** at another

5. The words 'downy flake' mean
A. soft particles of snow
B. soft snow
C. fluffy snow
D. soft and fluffy

POEM-20

The little creature
with a hundred feet
was on its journey
to where
only it knew.
My civilised foot
dressed in polished leather
came down upon it
even so gently
there was only a soft sound
signifying
the end
of a creature of God
my Maker
I looked to see
if my *sole* was *spoiled*
and walked away

QUESTIONS

1. '... with a hundred feet' actually means
A. a hundred feet
B. many feet
C. about a hundred feet
D. near about a hundred feet

2. The poet calls his foot 'civilised' because he
A. means it otherwise
B. is civilised
C. is wearing polished shoes
D. looks civilised

3. This poem can be classified as
A. humorous B. religious
C. satirical D. romantic

4. The poet walked away. It means he
A. didn't bother about the death of the centipede
B. remained indifferent towards the centipede's death
C. regetted the centipede's death
D. felt pity for the insect

5. The word 'signifying' here means
A. displacing B. indicating
C. making it important D. proving

ANSWERS

I. Cloze Test

PASSAGE-1

1	2	3	4	5	6
A	B	A	C	D	A
7	8	9	10	11	12
A	B	A	B	C	B
13	14				
D	B				

PASSAGE-2

1	2	3	4	5	6
B	B	A	D	B	C
7	8	9	10	11	
C	B	A	C	A	

PASSAGE-3

1	2	3	4	5	6
C	D	A	A	B	B
7	8	9	10	11	12
C	D	B	A	B	C

PASSAGE-4

1	2	3	4	5	6
B	C	A	B	D	C
7	8	9	10	11	12
B	C	A	D	B	A
13					
D					

PASSAGE-5

1	2	3	4	5	6
D	C	A	B	C	B
7	8	9	10	11	12
C	D	B	A	D	C

PASSAGE-6

1	2	3	4	5	6
A	B	D	B	A	B
7	8	9	10	11	12
D	C	D	C	B	B

PASSAGE-7

1	2	3	4	5	6
A	B	D	A	B	C
7	8	9	10	11	12
D	D	C	D	A	B
13					
D					

PASSAGE-8

1	2	3	4	5	6
C	C	B	A	D	B
7	8	9	10	11	12
D	D	C	D	A	B

PASSAGE-9

1	2	3	4	5	6
B	B	C	B	D	A
7	8	9	10	11	12
D	A	B	C	D	D

PASSAGE-10

1	2	3	4	5	6
A	D	A	D	D	C
7	8	9	10	11	12
B	B	D	A	A	B

PASSAGE-11

1	2	3	4	5	6
C	B	D	A	B	A
7	8	9	10	11	12
A	B	D	C	A	B

PASSAGE-12

1	2	3	4	5	6
A	B	C	A	B	C
7	8	9	10	11	12
B	D	B	D	B	C

PASSAGE-13

1	2	3	4	5	6
D	C	B	C	C	A
7	8	9	10	11	
B	B	C	D	B	

PASSAGE-14

1	2	3	4	5	6
B	C	A	D	C	C
7	8	9	10	11	
D	A	B	A	C	

PASSAGE-15

1	2	3	4	5	6
A	B	D	B	D	B
7	8	9	10	11	
C	A	C	D	B	

PASSAGE-16

1	2	3	4	5	6
C	A	C	B	A	A
7	8	9	10	11	
C	B	D	D	D	

PASSAGE-17

1	2	3	4	5	6
D	B	D	D	D	C
7	8	9	10	11	
A	D	A	A	B	

PASSAGE-18

1	2	3	4	5	6
B	C	B	A	C	C
7	8	9	10	11	12
C	D	D	D	A	D
13	14	15	16	17	
C	A	B	D	C	

PASSAGE-19

1	2	3	4	5	6
B	A	B	C	B	D
7	8	9	10	11	
B	C	D	D	B	

PASSAGE-20

1	2	3	4	5	6
D	C	D	A	A	B
7	8	9	10		
C	C	A	C		

PASSAGE-21

1	2	3	4	5	6
D	B	C	B	C	B
7	8	9	10		
A	D	D	D		

PASSAGE-22

1	2	3	4	5	6
C	A	B	C	B	D
7	8	9	10	11	
A	A	B	D	D	

PASSAGE-23

1	2	3	4	5	6
B	A	C	B	A	A
7	8	9	10	11	12
B	D	C	A	C	B
13	14	15	16	17	18
C	B	C	C	A	C

PASSAGE-24

1	2	3	4	5	6
A	D	C	A	B	D
7	8	9	10	11	12
D	B	B	C	A	A

PASSAGE-25

1	2	3	4	5	6
D	C	B	A	D	C

7	8	9	10	11	12
A	A	C	D	B	D
13	14				
D	A				

PASSAGE-26

1	2	3	4	5	6
A	C	B	C	D	B
7	8	9	10	11	
D	C	B	A	A	

PASSAGE-27

1	2	3	4	5	6
C	B	B	A	A	B
7	8	9	10	11	12
C	A	D	D	B	D
13	14	15	16		
C	C	B	B		

PASSAGE-28

1	2	3	4	5	6
D	D	C	D	B	B
7	8	9	10	11	12
C	C	B	B	C	A
13	14	15			
A	D	C			

PASSAGE-29

1	2	3	4	5	6
B	B	C	D	A	B
7	8	9	10	11	12
A	B	C	D	B	C

PASSAGE-30

1	2	3	4	5	6
B	C	A	A	D	D
7	8	9	10	11	12
D	C	C	B	B	C
13	14	15			
A	B	D			

PASSAGE-31

1	2	3	4	5	6
A	B	D	A	B	C
7	8	9	10	11	12
B	A	B	D	A	B
13	14	15			
D	A	A			

PASSAGE-32

1	2	3	4	5	6
B	C	C	A	D	B
7	8	9	10	11	12
C	A	C	B	D	C
13	14				
B	B				

II. Passages

PASSAGE-1

1	2	3	4	5	6
A	D	A	A	A	C
7					
B					

PASSAGE-2

1	2	3	4	5	6
A	A	D	A	B	C
7					
D					

PASSAGE-3

1	2	3	4	5	6
D	C	D	C	A	D
7					
B					

PASSAGE-4

1	2	3	4	5	6
C	C	A	D	A	D
7					
C					

PASSAGE-5

1	2	3	4	5	6
B	D	D	B	D	C
7					
A					

PASSAGE-6

1	2	3	4	5	6
A	C	B	C	B	C
7					
B					

PASSAGE-7

1	2	3	4	5	6
B	C	C	B	D	B
7					
C					

PASSAGE-8

1	2	3	4	5	6
B	C	C	B	B	C
7					
A					

PASSAGE-9

1	2	3	4	5
C	C	B	D	A

PASSAGE-10

1	2	3	4	5
B	A	B	C	C

PASSAGE-11

1	2	3	4	5
C	A	B	D	A

PASSAGE-12

1	2	3	4	5
A	A	B	C	D

PASSAGE-13

1	2	3	4	5
A	C	B	A	D

PASSAGE-14

1	2	3	4	5
C	B	A	D	A

PASSAGE-15

1	2	3	4	5
B	A	C	D	A

PASSAGE-16

1	2	3	4	5
A	B	C	A	B

PASSAGE-17

1	2	3	4	5
C	A	B	D	C

PASSAGE-18

1	2	3	4	5
B	D	B	A	B

PASSAGE-19

1	2	3	4	5
D	C	B	C	D

PASSAGE-20

1	2	3	4	5
B	A	C	D	A

PASSAGE-21

1	2	3	4	5
B	C	D	D	C

PASSAGE-22

1	2	3	4	5
C	D	B	C	D

PASSAGE-23

1	2	3	4	5
A	C	D	B	A

PASSAGE-24

1	2	3	4	5
A	D	A	D	B

PASSAGE-25

1	2	3	4	5
B	C	D	A	B

PASSAGE-26

1	2	3	4	5
B	B	C	A	D

PASSAGE-27

1	2	3	4	5
A	B	A	B	C

PASSAGE-28

1	2	3	4	5
A	B	C	C	B

PASSAGE-29

1	2	3	4	5
A	C	A	B	C

PASSAGE-30

1	2	3	4	5
B	C	D	D	D

III. Poetry

POEM-1

1	2	3	4	5
A	C	B	C	A

POEM-2

1	2	3	4	5
C	B	A	D	B

POEM-3

1	2	3	4	5
D	A	B	C	B

POEM-4

1	2	3	4	5
B	D	C	D	B

POEM-5

1	2	3	4	5
B	A	D	A	B

POEM-6

1	2	3	4	5
C	D	D	D	B

POEM-7

1	2	3	4	5
C	D	B	B	A

POEM-8

1	2	3	4	5
A	B	A	D	C

POEM-9

1	2	3	4	5
A	C	D	B	C

POEM-10

1	2	3	4	5
C	B	A	A	C

POEM-11

1	2	3	4	5
B	C	C	B	C

POEM-12

1	2	3	4	5
D	B	C	B	D

POEM-13

1	2	3	4	5
B	B	A	D	B

POEM-14

1	2	3	4	5
A	A	D	A	B

POEM-15

1	2	3	4	5
B	B	C	C	D

POEM-16

1	2	3	4	5
B	A	D	A	A

POEM-17

1	2	3	4	5
B	A	B	A	D

POEM-18

1	2	3	4	5
D	D	C	C	B

POEM-19

1	2	3	4	5
C	A	C	D	A

POEM-20

1	2	3	4	5
B	A	C	B	B

English Literature : At a Glance

THE OLD ENGLISH PERIOD (I) (ANGLO-SAXON PERIOD) (450-1050)

Beowulf is probably the oldest epic of the Teutonic world. It is believed to be belonging to the first half of the sixth century.

Some important works of the Anglo-Saxon period (Pre-Christian Era)

Some important works of the Anglo-Saxon period are: *The Ruined Burg, The Lover's Message. The Maiden's Complaint, The Wanderer* and *the Seafarer.*

'The Wanderer is also known as *'Widsith'*. The work is based on the wandering life of the gleeman.

Belonging to this period, we also have *"Deor's Lament"*, which, according to Long is, "much more poetic than *'Widsith,'* and is the one perfect lyric of the Anglo-Saxon period.

In the *Seafarer*, we have glimpses of hard sea life along with the call of the sea, which we, in our times, find more pronouncedly, but perhaps less picturesquely, in Masefield's *"Sea-Fever"*.

Some Christian writers of the Anglo-Saxon period

Whereas the pagan literature of the Anglo-Saxon period was chiefly in the form of oral legends which they had brought with them from the foreign lands which they previously inhabited, the Christian writing mainly came into existence as a result of the teachings of the monks who had come under the influence of two schools—the Augustinian School (from Rome) and Northumbrian School (from Ireland).

While the former, did not produce much lasting works, the latter produced a number of good and great writers, *e.g.,* **The Venerable Bede (673-735), Caedmon (seventh century)** and **Cynewulf (eighth century)**.

Besides the poets mentioned above, we have **Alfred (848-90)** who is chiefly known as a translator.

ANGLO-NORMAN PERIOD (1066-1350)

Some important works of the Anglo-Norman period

One important work of this period is *Geoffrey's "Historic Regum Britanniae"* (1137) commonly known as *"History"*. Geoffrey is believed to have died in 1154.

Geoffrey's work which became immensely popular in his own life, is a mixture of pagan and Christian legends and is based more on lies than on real historical events.

However, the said work has its literary value for its poetry and romance pertaining to king Arthur and his Knights, and hence, it became a source of inspiration and scintillating subject matter for such illustrious authors as Malory, Shakespeare and Tennyson.

Geoffrey's work was in Latin verse. Thereafter appeared *"Layman's Brut"* (c. 1200) which has its main interest in giving Arthur's legends in (Anglo-Saxon) English itself.

Then there appeared what are known as *"Metrical Romances"* which were based on the "matter" of France, Rome and Britain.

While in the *Matter of France,* **Charlemagne's** exploits dominated and in the *Matter of Rome* Alexander's adventures and the war of Troy were the main subjects, in the *Matter of Britain*, exploits of Arthur and his knights of the Round Table were chief subject matter. There were a number of cycles pertaining to the knights of Arthur, among them being **Sir Gawain (1350)** *Quest of the Holy Grail, Death of Arthur, Merlin, etc.*

Besides the above, other works of the period included ballads, lyrics and such poems as the *Owl and the Nightingale, Ormulum, Cursor Mundi (1320), The Pearl, Patience, Cleanness, etc.* Also **Roger Bacon's** *"Opus Majus"* appeared in 1267.

THE AGE OF CHAUCER (1340-1400)

The Hundred years war between England and France had already started in 1338 when **Chaucer** was born in **1340**.

In the earlier years of the war, England was all-powerful and under Edward III it won victories over France at Sluys in 1340 and Crecy in 1346, culminating in the capture of Calais in 1347.

Another thumping victory was won by the Black Prince, Edward III's son in 1356 by defeating the French at Poitiers.

As a result of the English victories, the English foreign trade began to flourish, particularly in the export of wool to Flanders, which filled the coffers of the English king and the people also became richer, as we notice conspicuously in **Chaucer's** *Canterbury Tales* when we consider the lot of so many characters, particularly those belonging to landed aristocracy.

This picture is also graphically depicted in **Trevelyan's** *British History of Six Centuries.*

It was unfortunate for England that in the moment of its glory it was overtaken by plague, the Black Death which took a heavy toll of life all over Europe in 1348-49.

As a result of the Black Death, most of the labourers who escaped death, left the country, and this caused an intense scarcity of the availability of essential commodities at cheap rates. To meet this menace, the Parliament tried to force the labourers to accept the same wages as they were getting before the Black Death, and it all finally precipitated into the well-known Peasants' Revolt during the reign of Richard II.

In spite of the passage of certain statutes purported to safeguard the English clergy against the undue domination of the Pope, the low simmering of wrath among the clergymen for several reasons, there emerged in the "Lollards Movement" under the leadership of the redoubtable Wyclif.

Another prominent feature, this one in the literary world, was the slow advent of the spirit of New Learning from Italy and drastic changes in the structure of the English language which had already been continuing as the inevitable outcome of the Norman conquest at Hastings in 1066.

These were the general conditions in which the most significant writers of the age—**Chaucer, Langland, Dunbar,** etc. lived and flourished, thus heralding a new age slowly, but boldly and surely.

MAJOR AUTHORS AND THEIR WORKS OF CHAUCER'S AGE

Sir Thomas More (1478-1535)
Utopia (English Version)

William Tyndale (1485-1536)
New Testament

Geoffrey Chaucer (1340-1400)
The Boke of the Duchesse
The Romaunt of the Rose
The House of Fame
Troylus Cryseyde
The Canterbury Tales
Legends of Good Women
The Parliament of Fouls

Wyclif (1320-1384)
The Bible

John Heywood (1564-1627)
Four P's

Thomas Sackville and Thomas Norton : (1536-1608) (1532-1584)
Gorboduc

The Seventeenth Century

THE RENAISSANCE (1578-1625)

The Renaissance of English Literature coincides with the Age of Queen Elizabeth I. Hence, in the history of English literature, this period is also called as the *Elizabethan Age*. The inspiration for the great works of this period came from the prolific translations into English of works of ancient Rome and Greece. Thus, Plutarch's *Lives* was translated by **Sir Thomas North (1579)** from the French version. Montaigne's Essays was translated by **John Florio (1603)**. In verse, Ovid's *Metamorphoses* was translated by **Arthur Golding (1565, 1567)**. Among other works of foreign origin translated into English were Ariosto's *Orlando Furioso* by **Harrington (1591)**, and Homer's *Iliad* by **George Chapman (1598)**.

The rising English stage and the English novel borrowed from Boccaccio, Cinthio, Bandello and Straparola — the Italians. Attracted though England was to Italian art, it resisted the evil influences of debauchery, crime and passions that the Italian spirit represented. Yet, the time was ripe in England for the full development of every art and literary form. Renaissance means *a flowering again of art and culture*. It inculcated a sense of wonder in things. England also wanted to rival Spain, France and Portugal in her navigational triumphs. Thus in 1578, Sir Francis Drake circumnavigated the world, and in 1588, the English navy destroyed the Armada. The same spirit of adventure moved literature. In *Apologie for Poetrie*, Sidney described the poet — of all sciences 'the monarch'. Poets were encouraged to innovate new styles and rhythms.

Poetry

Three great men of letters led the Renaissance in England — Spenser, Sidney and Lyly.

Edmund Spenser (1552-1599) wrote the *Sheplieardes Calendar* (1579)—an allegory. The union of line and metre is varied and rich. In *Hymnes In honour of Love and Beautie*, he sets forth his philosophy, the conflict in his mind between paganism and Christianity. He also wrote a satire named, *Mother Hubberd's Tale* to denounce the neglect of arts and letters. His pastoral, *Colin Clout's Come Home Again* describes his stay in London in 1589. His *Amoretti* (1595) are sonnets on love and his *Epithalamion* is an ode, But his masterpiece is the *Faerie Queene* (1589, 1595), an allegory in which characters represent virtues and vices. In it his lyrical quality and colour-effects are at their best. The *Faerie Queene* is Queen Elizabeth. The nine-line stanza he used is now called the *Spenserian stanza.*

Sir Philip Sidney (1554-1586) was a scholar, knight and courtier. In 1580 he wrote *Arcadia* which has a blend of pastoral and heroic elements It is a romance of chivalry and love. The language is characterized by *pathetic fallacy* — endowing inanimate objects with feelings and sensations. William Shakespeare borrowed from this style. His other poem, *Astrophel and Stella* (1591) describes his lost love for the daughter of an Earl. His *Apologie for Poetrie* (1595) written in an unaffected prose, is a plea for poetry.

John Lyly (1554-1606) invented an artistic, flowery style called *euphuism* through his famous romance, *Euphues, the Anatomy of Wit* (1579). This style was adopted by the refined people of the Court. The style is characterized by the use of alliteration and antithesis, fantastic metaphors and similes based on mythology, and natural history of flora and fauna.

The works of these three trail-blazed many poets and sonneteers like Samuel Daniel, Michael Drayton, Thomas Watson, Henry Constable and Thomas Lodge. Notable works from 1590 to 1603 were **Samuel Daniel's (1562-1619)** *The Civil Wars* (1595) describing the *War of the Roses*, **Michael Drayton's (1563-1631)** *Idea, the Shepherd's Garland, The Baron's Wars, England's Heroicall Epistles* (1603) and *Poly-Olbion*, a long description of England in 15,000 alexandrines or lines of twelve syllables. England came to be known as *"a nest of singing birds"* because of the great number of lyrics and poems written in this period. **Thomas Campion (1567-1620)** published an anthology called *Two Books of Ayres* (1612). Many of the best poems are found in plays by Ben Jonson, Thomas Dekker, Beaumont and Fletcher, and Webster. But those of William Shakespeare are probably the most beautiful. In his *Sonnets*, he describes his love for a married woman who betrays him. Other poems of this period are Marlowe's Hero and Leander (1598), Shakespeare's *Venus and Adonis* (1593) and *The Rape of Lucrece* (1594).

After Elizabeth's reign, in James I rule, poetry became religious and didactic. The Protestant spirit dominated the literary works. The poems of George Wither, William Browne, the Fletcher brothers and William Drummond show the influence of Spenser still.

Ben Jonson (1573-1637) was the greatest humanist of the time. He was mainly a playwright but wrote poems also. His poetry is found in collections like Epigrams and The Forest (1616) and The Underwoods (1640). He was a satirist and neo-classicist being influenced by the Latin classics.

John Donne's (1573-1631) poetry is revolut-ionary. He disobeys the laws of rhythm and uses a device called the metaphysical conceit in which strangely opposite ideas are juxtaposed.

Prose

Much of the prose of the period is poetical, influenced by euphuism. Robert Greene, Thomas Lodge, Thomas Nashe, Thomas Deloney, and Thomas Dekker are the major writers. **Robert Greene's (1558-1592)** works include *Mamilia* and *Menaphon* and **Thomas Lodge's (1558-1625)** include *Rosalynde: Euphues Golden Legacie* (1590). **Thomas Nashe (1567-1601)** wrote pamphlets like The *Anatomie of Absurdities* and *The Terrors of the Night*. **Thomas Dekker's (1572-1632)** *The Gils Horne booke* is famous for its picturesque prose. Most of the poets and prose writers of this period were also dramatists. Shakespeare used prose for homely and humorous scenes and verse for tragic ones.

Many writers of the English Renaissance were inspired by the literary criticism of the Continent to write some themselves. Stephen Gosson's *The Schoole of Abuse* (1579) and *Sidney's Apologie for Poetrie* are good examples. Sidney eulogizes the poet as a law-giver. The period also saw works of religious prose. **Richard Hooker's (1554-1600)** pamphlet on the Marlin Marprelate controversy is a famous one. Hooker's *Of the Laws of Ecclesiastical Polity* (1594) is a masterpiece of English prose. The most seminal work of the period is the authorized version of the Bible published in 1611. The work was commissioned by James 1. A beautiful prose minus archaism is used by the revisers. The diction was to influence the English language very deeply. It is the language of daily speech, yet fresh and lofty.

Side by side with religious literature, secular and philosophical literature, mostly written by **Francis Bacon (1561-1626)**, came out. He had taken all knowledge as his province and elaborated his doctrines in his *Novum*

Organum (1620). His ideas influenced the formation of *The Royal Society for Improving Natural Knowledge* in 1645. His most popular work is his *Essays* written on diverse topics in a terse, epigrammatic style. The English writers quote copiously from Bacon today. His sentences are household terms. Take for example, "*He that hath wife and children hath given hostages to fortune*". "*Some books are to be tasted, others to be swallowed and some few to be chewed and digested*".

Another great prose-writer of the period was **Robert Burton (1577-1640)** whose *The Anatomy of Melancholy* (1621) is full of pedantry. He borrowed from numerous sources and is full of melancholy and jests; his style abounds in synonyms and epithets.

Drama

Drama thrived in the Renaissance. Foreign influence, especially of Italy, predominated. Plays were written so that the public would enjoy them and applaud the stage. There was a great variety of plays written — pure tragedy, tragi-comedy, historical drama, romantic comedy, comedy of errors, farce, pastoral, etc. The stage was a simple structure, circular in form with a courtyard open to the sky. A platform projected into the courtyard. Boys played the female roles. The public consisted of groundlings and courtiers on galleries. The unities of time, place and action were disregarded. Farce and tragedy were found in succession.

Several mythological allegories were acted before the court. **John Lyly's** euphuistic romances like *Campaspe* (1584), *Sapho and Phao, Endymion* (1592), *Midas* were praises of the queen. **George Peele (1558-1598)** wrote *The Araygnement of Paris* (1584) and *The Old Wives' Tale*. There were violent plays like **Thomas Kyd's (1558-1594)** The *Spanish Tragedie* (1585) and **Christopher Marlowe's (1564-1593)** *Tamburlaine, the Great* (1587) and *Doctor Faustus* (1592). *Doctor Faustus* is an allegory on the Renaissance love of power. It shows how Doctor Faustus, the scientist, sells his soul to the devil for twenty-four years of full power to satisfy every desire. In the end his agony increases as the devil approaches to claim his soul. Marlowe also wrote *The Jew of Malta*, which shows the unbridled love for wealth, and the historical play Edward II. Marlowe crafted the blank verse (mighty line as Shakespeare called it and used). This was suited to the fiery speeches of his characters.

The towering genius of the age was certainly **William Shakespeare (1564-1616)**. He was versatile and wrote about 36 plays and 144 sonnets. "Shakespeare was not of an age but for all times" and "Poets are born not made", wrote Ben Jonson about him. He created a gallery of nearly 800 characters who typify personalities found through human history. Julius Caesar's pride and ambition, Macbeth's unbridled ambition, King Lear's dotedness, and Othello's susceptibility to suspicion against his wife — are tragic flaws that govern men even today.

Shakespeare was not educated except for a few years at a grammar school. He had 'little Latin and less Greek' and read books in translation from Latin and Greek. He adapted the stories into a World entirely his own, instinct with life and vibrancy. Shakespeare began his career by acting for the stage. Then he wrote plays and staged them, mainly to seek court patronage. His great success made him the envy of his contemporaries like Robert Greene. In his tragedies he depicts the fall of great men owing to a tragic flaw in their character. Although they had the will to change their destiny, a fate controlled them. He used the beliefs of his time like the supernatural powers and phenomena to capture the interest of his audience. Some of his historical plays are *Richard II* (1596) and *King John* (1595). Among the romantic comedies *As You Like It* (1600), *The Merchant of Venice* (1596) and *Twelfth Night* (1601) are popular. *A Midsummer Night's Dream* (1595) is a fairy play. *Romeo and Juliet* (1594) is a tragicomedy. He used prose and blank verse.

His *Henry IV* (I & 2) (1597, 1598) contain much more blank verse than his other plays. In depth of psychological insight, and power of style *Hamlet* (1601), one of Shakespeare's great tragedies, stands supreme. *The Tempest* (161I) is one of his last plays which shows the dramatist's mellowed maturity.

Even after 400 years, Shakespeare's plays are very popular, being translated into almost every important language. *"Age cannot wither her nor custom stale her infinite variety"*; Shakespeare described Cleopatra in these words. The same may be said about his plays also.

Ben Jonson was Shakespeare's antithesis. He borrowed the style of the classics and was very erudite. He carefully studied society and wrote about it. He took the different 'humours' or dominating characteristics of men and satirized them in *Every Man in his Humour* (1598) and *Every Man out of his Humour* (1599), *Volpone, or the Fox* (1605) and *The Alchemist* (1605). He also wrote the historical tragedies, *Sejanus His Fall* (1603)' and *Catiline His Conspiracy* (1611). The plays are very true to history. John Marston, Thomas Dekker, Thomas Heywood and Middleton were other playwrights of the age. John Webster (1580-1625) is famous for horror plays like *The White Devil* (1609-1612) and *The Duchess of Malfi* (1613-1614).

MAJOR AUTHORS AND THEIR WORKS

Edmund Spenser (1552-1599)

The Faerie Queene

The Shepheardes Calendar

Amoretti

Epithalamion
Prothalamion
Mother Hubberd's Tale
The Ruins of Time
The Tears of the Muses
Astrophel

Phillip Sidney (1554-1586)
Arcadia
Astrophel and Stella
An Apologie for Poetrie

Ben Jonson (1573-1637)
Every Man in His Humour
Every Man Out of His Humour
Volpone Or the Fox
Cynthia's Revels
The Alchemist
Bartholomew Fayre
Epicaene or the Silent Women
Sejanus His Fall
Catline His Conspiracy
The Poetaster
The Devil as an Ass
The Masque of Beauty

Samuel Daniel (1562-1619)
Delia
Civil Wars between the Two Houses of Lancaster and York

Michael Drayton (1563-1631)
The Battle of Agincourt
England's heroic Epistles
The Barons' Wars
Polyolbion

William Shakespeare (1564-1616)
The Two Gentlement of Verona
The Merry Wives of Windsor
Measure for Measure
The Comedy of Errors
Love's Labour's Lost
The Taming of the Shrew
All's Well that Ends Well
A Midsummer Night's Dream
The Merchant of Venice
Much Ado About Nothing
As You Like it
Twelfth Night
Romeo and Juliet
Macbeth
Hamlet
King Lear
Othello
Antony and Cleopatra
Julius Caesar
Timon of Athens
Coriolanus
Titus Andronicus
Troilus and Cressida
King John
King Richard the Second
King Henry the Fourth-Part First
King Henry the Fourth-Second Part
King Henry the Fifth
King Henry the Sixth-First Part
King Henry the Sixth-Second Part
King Henry the Sixth-Third Part
King Richard the Third
King Henry the Eighth
Cymbeline
Pericles
The Winter's Tale
The Tempest
Venus and Adonis and Rape of Lucrece (Narrative Poems)
Sonnets (154 in number).

Christopher Marlowe (1564-1593)
Tamburlaine the Great
Edward II
Doctor Faustus
The Jew of Malta
The Tragedy of Dido, Queen of Carthage.

George Peele (1558-1597)
The Araygnement of Paris
The Famous Chronicle of King Edward I

Robert Greene (1560-1592)
Frier Bacon and Frier Bungey
Orlando Furioso
Pandosto

Thomas Nashe (1567-1601)
The Unfortunate Traveller Or The Life of Jack Wilton

Thomas Lodge (1558-1625)
The Wounds of Civil War
Rosalynde

Thomas Kyd (1557-1595)
The Spanish Tragedy

John Lyly (1554-1606)

Euphues, The Anatomy of Wit

Euphues and His England

Endymion

Francis Bacon (1561-1626)

Essays

The Advancement of Learning

The New Atlantis

Novum Organum

John Webster (1580-1625)

The White Devil

The Duchess of Malfi

The Devil's Law Case.

Thomas Heywood (1575-1650)

A Woman Killed with Kindness

The English Traveller

The Captives

Robert Burton (1577-1640)

The Anatomy of Melancholy

Sir Thomas Browne (1605-1682)

Religio Medici

Vulgar Errors

Hydrotaphia or Urne Burriale

Christian Morals

Thomas Hobbes (1588-1679)

Leviathan

Jeremy Taylor (1613-1667)

The Liberty of Prophesying

Holy Living

Holy Dying

END OF THE RENAISSANCE (1625-1660)

Prose

Puritanism set the trend for the literature during the reign of Charles 1. The Bible was the guiding spirit which may be best seen in Milton's works. The zealous Calvinists enforced Presbyterianism. The passionate curiosity for life which characterized the Renaissance gave place to a search for salvation. **Sir Thomas Browne (1605-1682)** was a scientist, but in his *Pseudodoxia Epidemica or Vulgar Errors* (1646), we see his belief in miracles. His *Religio Medici* (1642) speaks of the vanity of earthly life. **George Herbert's (1596-1633)** *The Country Parson* and **Jeremy Taylor's (1613-1667)** *Holy Living* (1650) and *Holy Dying* (1651) are sermons championing religious freedom. **John Milton (1608-1674)**, who is famous as a poet, wrote numerous pamphlets in favour of divorce which are models of beautiful prose. His *Areopagitica* (1644) is a speech for the liberty of unlicensed writing.

Another great prose-writer was **Thomas Hobbes (1588-1679)** whose *Leviathan* (1651) is a famous work. He was an empiricist and realist and believed that sensations and ideas are caused by physical reasons. Numerous works of ethics, sociology and history were written. *The History of the Rebellion and Civil Wars in England* was written by **Edward Hyde (1609-1674). Izaac Walton (1593-1683)** wrote the biographies of John Donne and George Herbert. *The Compleat Angler* (1653) is his famous work on the post-Civil War scene and contains descnptions of the English countryside.

Poetry

Two types of poets existed then — the Cavaliers, who were the Royalists, and the religious or Metaphysical poets. Thomas Carew, Sir John Suckling, John Cleveland, Robert Herrick were Cavalier poets who displayed epicurean tastes. Imagination and sensuous imagery predominate their poems. Among the religious poets, Herbert, Crashaw, Vaughan and Marvell stand out. They were mystics. **George Herbert's (1593-1633)** style is simple and expresses Christian piety in his anthology The Temple (1633). His poems *The Pulley and Love* are very popular. **Richard Crashaw (1613-1649)** used fantastic conceits; e.g. he describes the maudlin St. Mary Magdalene's eyes as "walking baths, compedious oceans", **Henry Vaughan (1622-1695)** was a mystic and his poem The Retreat is a nostalgic longing for the blissful heavenly state of childhood.

John Milton's greatest achievement was his *Paradise Lost* (1667). In theme it deals with the fall of man. In form, it follows the strict unity of the classical epic. His other poems are *L'Allegro* (1632), *Il Penseroso* (1632), *Comus* (1634), *Lycidas* (1637), *Samson Agonistes* (1671), etc.

RESTORATION LITERATURE (1620-1734)

Prose

In 1660, Charles II returned to the throne and the Puritan republic ended. The year is also marked as the beginning of the modem literature. **John Bunyan's (1628-1688)** works, *Grace Abounding* (1666) and *The Pilgrim's Progress* (1678) are the last surviving works of Puritan faith. The Pilgrim's Progress is an allegory describing the trials and tribulations on the way to salvation as faced by a Christian. Bunyan's prose is a blend of common speech and the grandeur of the revised Bible.

The scientific spirit took over the reign. The Royal Society of London for the Improvement of Natural

Knowledge, to which Bacon and William Harvey (who discovered the circulation of blood) had contributed, now had many learned men. **Sir Isaac Newton** published Principia in 1687. He discovered the laws of gravity, of the diffraction of white light and the theory of fluxions.

John Locke (1632-1704) propounded a new philosophy of commonsense and intelligent reasoning in his *An Essay Concerning Human Understanding* (1690). It lays stress on development of character. It was to influence the English thought. Voltaire was one of his French disciples.

Poetry

Restoration literature was derived from pre-Commonwealth national literature and was a reaction against Puritan oppression. It rejected severe moral codes of conduct and was chiefly satiric in nature. **Samuel Butler's (1612-1680)** poem, *Hudibras* published in three parts (1663, 1664 & 1678), is a typical work of this period. It is inspired by *Don Quixote*. He satirizes Sir Hudibras as a grotesque Presbyterian with a squire called Ralpho. It lays bare all the human follies in octosyllabic couplets. Many court poets like **Andrew Marvell (1621-1678)** and **John Oldham (1653-1683)** were veterans of the Republican era and satirize the follies of the new age.

The great poet of the period was **John Dryden (1631-1700)**. He excelled in almost every kind of composition. He wrote a series of heroic stanzas in honour of Cromwell on his death. He was a disciple of the metaphysical poets displaying their far-fetched images and conceits. In *Astraea Redux* (1660), he celebrated the return of Charles II and in *Annus Mirabilis* (1667) he commemorated the Great Fire of London and the war with Holland. He was a staunch Tory and his famous satires are *Absalom and Achitophel* (1681), *The Medal and Mac-Flecknoe*. In this last work he satirizes Shadwell, the Whig poet. *The Hind and the Panther* (1687) is an allegory on Catholicism and Anglicanism. Dryden also translated the classics, chiefly Persuis and Juvenal. He turned Virgil's *Aeneid* into brilliant couplets. His *Alexander's Feast* is an ode in honour of St. Cecilia.

Drama

The dramatic works of the Restoration were licentious and full of cynicism. They regarded the moral code of the Puritans as a matter of ridicule. Scenery now played an important part on the stage and actresses, not boys, played the female roles. The theatre was regarded as a place of vice and evil. Shakespeare's plays were rewritten and his tragedies like *Romeo and Juliet* given happy endings. French influence dominated and extraordinary superhuman feats were described. Heroes were presented as ideals and were made to give pompous speeches.

Dryden wrote many plays like *Aurengzebe* or *The Great Mogul* (1675) and The Conquest of Granada (1669, 1670) which abound in rhetoric.

The tragedians were **Thomas Otway (1651-1685)**, Nathaniel Lee (1653-1692) and **Nicholas Rowe (1674-1718)**. The comedy of this period reflects the gay intrigues of the society. Caricature and farce were used and obscenity also touched it. The main aim was to amuse. **Sir George Etheredge (1635-1691)** was an innovator and **William Wycherley (1640-1715)** was a moralist playwright. **William Congreve (1670-1729)** wrote a series of masterpieces including *The Way of the World* (1700). **John Vanbrugh** (1664-1726) and **George Farquhar (1678-1707)** were other comedy writers of the period.

Criticism

Dryden was the first English critic. *The Essay of Dramatick Poesie* (1668) is his longest single prose work and a major piece of English literary criticism. It is in the form of a discussion between four characters, one of whom is Dryden himself. It deals with topics related to theatre and evaluates the works of the Elizabethan dramatists, especially of Shakespeare.

The Diarists of the Restoration Period

One of the sources of information and genres of prose writing during the Restoration were diaries. The important names are those of John Evelyn, Samuel Pepys and Roger North. **John Evelyn (1620-1706)** was a rich man who had cultured tastes. He was a member of the Royal Society and had wide interests in diverse fields like gardening, forestry, navigation and architecture. His *Diary* which was written almost throughout his lifetime throws a floodlight on the major social and national events of the time like the Galley Slaves and the Great Fire. It is written in a plain, graphic style. **Samuel Pepys (1633-1703)** had a chequered career. Coming from the middle classes, he joined the civil services and rose to be the secretary of the Admiralty. He also became the President of the Royal Society and a member of Parliament. His famous *Diary*, covering a period of ten years, is in the form of confessions. It was written in laconic sentences like the messages of a telegram and was in a sort of code which was deciphered only in 1825. The diary shows him to be a man of versatile interests like music, science and literature. But the most controversial aspect is the detailed confessions of his life. Nobody seemed to guess he was a libertine, a morally debauched character who could stoop to low means. When we read the diary, it seems he is writing of another person. **Roger North** belonged to an elite family. He was a Tory gentleman and was engaged in the politics of the times. His famous work is *North's Lives of the Norths* containing biographies of three relatives and an autobiography. His pen pictures and anecdotes are in colloquial style.

MAJOR AUTHORS AND THEIR WORKS

Robert Herrick (1591-1574)
Noble Numbers
Hesperides

Thomas Carew (1598-1639)
Poems
'He that loves a rosy cheek'

Sir John Suckling (1660-1642)
'Ballad upon a Wedding'
'Why so pale and wan, Fond Lover'?

Andrew Marvell (1621-1678)
'To His Coy Mistress'
'The Rehearsal Transprosed'
'Ode upon Cromwell's Return from Ireland'
New Letters (a Prose Work)

George Herbert (1593-1633)
The Temple
Affliction
Easter Wings
The Collar
Man

Richard Crashaw (1613-1649)
Carmen Deo Nostro
The Infant Morturs
Steps to the Temple

John Milton (1608-1674)
Paradise Lost (in twelve Books)
Paradise Regained
Comus
Lycidas
Samson Agonistes
L'Allegro
Ill Penseroso
Areopagitica (Prose Work)
Ode on the Morning of Christ's Nativity
Sonnets (including) :
'On His Blindness'
'On the Late Massacre in Piedmont'
'When the Assault was Intended to the City'
'On His Having Arrived at the Age of Twenty-three'
A large number of Tracts and Pamphlets in support of the Parliament

John Donne (1573-1631)
Songs and Sonnets
Aires and Angels
A Nocturnall upon Lucies Day
A Valediction : Forbidding Mourning
The Extasie
Devotions (Sermon in Prose)
Ignatius His Enclave (a Prose Work)
Of the Progress of the Soul
Death's Duell

Abraham Cowley (1618-1667)
Pyramus and Thisbe
The Mistress
The Davideis
Pindarique Odes
Constantia and Philetus
Discourse by Way of Vision
Concerning the Government of Cromwell (a Prose Work)

Henry Vaughan (1622-1695)
Poems
Regeneration
The Retreat
Olor Iscanus
Thalia Redivia
Silex Scintillans

John Dryden (1631-1700)
(i) Heroic Stanzas on the Death of Oliver Cromwell
Astraea Redux (on the Restoration of Charles II)
Absalom and Achitophel
Religio Laici
The Hind and the Panther
The Fables
Annus Mirabilis
The Medal
Mac Flecknoe
Alexander's Feast
Prefaces to His Plays (in Prose)
An Essay of Dramatic Poesy
(ii) Dryden's Plays
Tyrannic Love
Conquest of Granada
All for love
The Rival Ladies
The Indian Emperor
Aureng-Zeb
Don Sebastian
Cleomenes
Love Triumphant

John Vanbrugh (1664-1726)
The Relapse
The Provoked Wife
The Confederacy

George Farquhar (1678-1707)

The Recruiting Officer

The Beaux Stratagem

Thomas Otway (1652-1685)

Orphan

Venice Preserved

Don Carlos

Alcibiades

Nathaniel Lee (1653-1692)

Nero

The Rival Queens

Sophonisba

John Bunyan (1628-1688)

The Pilgrim's Progress

Grace Abounding

The Life and Death of Mr. Badman

The Holy War

John Locke (1632-1704)

Essay on the Human Understanding

Treatise on Government

Thoughts on Education

John Evelyn (1620-1706)

Diary

Samuel Pepys (1633-1703)

Diary

The Eighteenth Century

THE AUGUSTAN AGE (1700-1740)

In general, the eighteenth century was the age of understanding and enlightenment. The emphasis was on the advancement of the human mind. Sensibility was the guiding principle. This age borrowed the humour and poetic technique of the previous century.

This age is generally called *The Augustan Age* or *The Age of Queen Anne* because the queen patronized the men of letters. The period is also known as the Classical Age. It Was an age of tolerance and harmony and was guided by reason. Dryden still wrote and was a contemporary of French authors Corneille, Racine and Moliere. Many English works were translated by the French. Poetry was still for aristocrats and the courts, but prose spread among the common public. People demanded instructions and information and practical hints for living. This led writers to use a simple style to be comprehensible to all.

Poetry

Matthew Prior (1664-1721) began by writing a parody of The Hind and the Panther in which he expounded his opinions on politics. **Sir Samuel Garth (1661-1791)** and **Joseph Addison (1672-1719)** used the heroic couplet of Dryden. Addison described Marlborough's victory at Blenheim in his poem *The Campaign* (1704). But the poetical luminary of the period was **Alexander Pope (1688-1744)**. He polished Dryden's couplet and used it as a weapon of satire, like in the famous *An Essay on Man* (1732-1734). His *An Essay on Criticism* (1711) and *The Rape of the Lock* (1712, 1714) are other great works. The latter is in mock-heroic style and describes the anger of a lady whose lock of hair had been cut off. Pope also translated the Iliad. He wrote *The Dunciad* (1728) to castigate bad poets. His *Imitations of Horace* (1733-1737) is highly admired even today.

Jonathan Swift, usually known as a prose writer, also showed a gift or versification like in his poem *On the Death of Dr. Swift*. **John Gay (1685-1732)** was popular for his fables like *The Hare with Many Friends* and his songs in *The Beggar's Opera*. **Edward Young's (1683-1765)** *The Commaint, or Night Thoughts on Life, Death, and Immortality* (1742), is a poet's delight in meditation underlining the vanity of all earthly glory.

Prose

This period saw an increasing demand for the circulation of facts and ideas among the public. **Daniel Defoe (1659-1731)** was a trail-blazer as a Journalist and his popular works are *The True-Born Englishman* (1701) and *The Shortest way with the Dissenters* (1702). Defoe wrote the first English nove! Robinson Crusoe (1719), which is a children's classic or collection of adventure stories. He cultivated the art of reporting and presented his stories as historical narratives which are precise and practical.

Steele, Addison, Swift, Arbuthnot were the other great prose-writers of the time. They introduced a style adorned by figures of speech. The periodicals of Steele and Addison contain essays which deal with practical moral questions and reflect the morals of the time.

Richard Steele (1672-1729) led a dissipated life and was full of remorse for it. He extols the Bible as a guide in life in his work *The Christian Hero*. He launched the journal *The Tatler* in 1709. **Joseph Addison** propagated rational and moderate ideas He collaborated with Steele on *The Tatler*. Steele then founded *The Spectator* in 1711 and

Addison again collaborated. Here they were merely the spectators of the society and its foibles. It epitomizes the whole nation. The character of Sir Roger de Coverley is a masterpiece, a comic personality with eccentricities. Other characters, Sir Andrew Freeport. Will Honeycomb, Captain Sentry capture the imagination of the readers.

Jonathan Swift (1667-1745) enjoyed ridicule rather than correction. He lays bare all the vices of man as something that are beyond correction. He ridiculed the modern authors in his The *Battle of the Books* (1704) and attacked the Papists and Presbyterians in *The Tale of a Tub* (1704). His most popular work is a children's classic, *Gulliver's Travels* (1726), which is also a satire on politics, religions, science and nature of man.

John Arbuthnot (1667-1735) was another humanist and man of wit and is known for his *The History of John Bull* (1712), an amusing allegory on the politics of the time.

During this period a number of deists like Locke, Collins and Tindal propounded a philosophy advocating reasoning rather than superstitious beliefs as advocated by orthodox Christians. Earl of Shaftesbury (1671-1713), Lord Bolingbroke (1678-1751) and Mandeville were other rationalists of the time who wrote many prose works.

THE AGE OF TRANSITION (1740-1800)

Like all other periods of transition, this age was also disturbed and confused Two movements can be clearly observed in the writings of the time: (*i*) the allegiance to the old order of classicism, and (*ii*) the search after the new order of Romanticism. The period was marked by new learning, new philosophy, growth of historical research and new realism.

This period is also known as the *Age of Johnson* because **Samuel Johnson (1709-1784)**, the greatest English man of letters, flourished during this period. Samuel Johnson was a versatile man of letters translator, journalist, commentator, critic, novelist, biographer and poet. He created two satirical poems, *London* (1738) and *The Vanity of Human Wishes* (1749). He had a supple style and describes his personal reflections in his essays *The Rambler* (1750-1752) and *The Idler* (1758-1760). His *Dictionary of English Language* (1747-1755) shows remarkable precision in definition and a feeling for the correct use of words. Besides the novel *Rasselas, Prince of Abyssinia* (1759) his best works are biographical and literary studies and his edition of *Shakespeare* (1765). His *Lives of the Poets* (1777-1781) is a biographical work. His admirer James Boswell's famous biography of Johnson has made him immortal. He is described here in candid details. His prejudices, excellences and demerits are all laid bare.

Poetry

Poetry showed the influence of Dryden and Pope. It was mainly didactic and satirical and the couplet still was the major form.

Oliver Goldsmith's (1728-1774) *Deserted Village* (1770) is a masterpiece of the period. **James Thomson's (1700-1748)** *The Seasons* (1730) is a praise of the beauties of Nature in all her diversity. Other noteworthy poems of the period are **William Collins' (1721-1759)** *Ode to Evening*, a delightful lyric, and **Thomas Gray's (1716-1771)** *Elegy Written in a Country Churchyard* (1751).

A general belief in human liberty was seen as the French Revolution proceeded. **William Cowper** (1731-1800) who wrote *The Ballad of John Gilpin,* **George Crabbe (1754-1832)**, the Scotsman **Robert Burns (1759-1796)** and the mystic **William Blake (1757-1827)** echoed the sentiments of the period. Burns was a farmer and wrote in original racy dialect thus causing a break from convention. Blake was a visionary and his poems are collected in *Songs of Innocence* (1789) and *Songs of Experience* (1794). In *The Tyger,* he uses the Lamb as a symbol of innocence and of Jesus, and the Tiger as the symbol of evil in the world, of the evil seen in the French Revolution where thousands were sent to the guillotine.

Novel

The period saw the development of the novel. A series of masterpieces came out. In the novel, the author could describe events in detail. Defoe's novels so far were based on strange subjects. Now they concentrated on commonplace events of family life and society. Adventure of earlier novels gave place to character portrayal. The novels were very long and filled with minute details. **Samuel Richardson (1689-1761)** wrote *Pamela, or Virtue Rewarded* (1740) and *Clarissa Harlowe* (1747-1748). **Henry Fielding (1707-1754)** is famous for *Joseph Andrews* (1742) and *Tom Jones* (1749), **Tobias Smollet (1721-1771)** wrote *The Adventures of Roderick Random* (1748) and *The Expedition of Humphry Clinker* (1771), **Laurence Sterne (1713-1768)** wrote *Tristram Shandy* (1760), and **Oliver Goldsmith** *The Vicar of Wakefield* (1766).

Letter

There were famous letter writers also, like **Lord Chesterfield (1694-1773). Horace Walpole (1719-1797), Thomas Gray and Richardson**. Frequently, a series of letters was bound into book-form. Collections of this kind were the letters of **Lady Mary Wortley Montagu (1689-1762)**, written to Pope from Constantinople, and of Thomas Gray, from the Lake District. Chesterfield's letters to his son contain comments on political and social matters. Richardson's *Pamela* is entirely in letter-form.

Drama

The century was the age of the great novels. Drama lost originality and talent. People saw Shakespeare's plays enacted, but what attracted them was the genius of the actors. However, there were a few good plays written. For instance, Johnson's *Irene* (1749), Fielding's *The Miser*, Goldsmith's anti-sentimental comedy *She Stoops to Conquer* (1773), and Sheridan's *The School for Scandal* (1777) and *The Rivals* (1775).

Historical Work

Towards the last part of the century the history of England was rocked by many revolutionary changes the impact of which were felt in English literature. Till the mid-18th century Victorian England reigned supreme. She was mistress of the seas and her imperial rule covered many colonies. In 1776, America declared her independence and the British Parliament was divided on the issue. Many Britishers favoured the American claims. In 1789, the French Revolution broke out and here too the Britishers were divided into two camps. Inspired by the writings of Rousseau, many believed the Revolution was being fought for the right causes. The Parliament resounded with the speeches of the famous. Some even accused Warren Hastings for his extortion policies in India and some others were against slave-trade.

Treatises on philosophy by **David Hume (1711-1776)** and histories by **William Robertson (1721-1793)** and political economy (*Wealth of Nations*) by **Adam Smith (1723-1790)** came out.

Edmund Burke (1729-1797) read law and began writing to propound his views on human feelings and emotions. His language is as oratorical in Parliament at the trial of Warren Hastings as in his famous writing *A Philosophical Inquiry into the Origin of our Ideas of the Sublime and the Beautiful* (1756).

Other orators who expressed themselves in writing were Tom Painè, Godwin and Jeremy Bentham. **William Godwin (1756-1836)** advocated the elimination of government in *Enquiry Concerning Political Justice* (1793). He proscribed law, marriage, gratitude, everything that limited liberty. His monumental work is *The Decline and Fall of the Roman Empire* (1776-1788) in which he describes the growth of Christianity and his belief in reason rather than the divine. At the same time **William Paley (1743-1805)** wrote *A View of the Evidences of Christianity* (1794) to prove the existence of miracles by logic.

MAJOR AUTHORS AND THEIR WORKS

Alexander Pope (1688-1744)

Pastorals
An Essay on Criticism
Windsor Forest
The Rape of the Lock
Dunciad
Translation of Iliad and Odyssey
To Lord Bathrust
On the Use of the Riches
An Essay on Man
Epistle to Dr. Arbuthnot
Of the Knowledge and Characters of Men
Of the Characters of Women
The Messiah
Satires and Epistles of Horace Imitated

Matthew Prior (1664-1721)

Solomon on the Vanity of the World
Alma : or the Progress of the Mind
The Town and Country Mouse

John Gay (1685-1732)

Fables
The Shepherd's Week
The Rural Sports
Trivia
The Beggar's Opera
The Streets of London

Edward Young (1683-1765)

Night Thoughts

Dr. Samuel Johnson (1709-1784)

The Vanity of Human Wishes
London
The Lives of the Poets
Preface to Shakespeare
Dictionary of the English Language
A journey to the Western Islands of Scotland
The Rambler
Rasselas
Prince of Abyssinia
The Life of Savage
The Adventurer
The Idler

Daniel Defoe (1661-1731)

Robinson Crusoe
Mall Flanders

Colonel Jack
The Memoirs of a Cavalier
Captain Singleton
Journal of the Plague Year
Roxana

Jonathan Swift (1667-1745)
The Battle of the Books
A Tale of a Tub
Gulliver's Travels
Journal to Stella
The Drapier's Letters
Cadenus and Vanessa

Joseph Addison (1672-1719)
The Spectator
The Campaign
Public Credit
The Vision of Mirza
Cato
Rosamond
The Drummer

Richard Steele (1672-1729)
The Tatler
The Guardian
The Funeral
The Lying Lover
The Tender Husband
The Conscious Lover

Thomas Gray (1716-1771)
Elegy Written in a Country Churchyard
On a Distant Prospect of Eton College
On the Death of a Favourite Cat
The Bard
The Progress of Poesy
The Fatal Sisters
The Descent of Odin

The Nineteenth Century

THE ROMANTIC AGE (1798-1830)

The eighteenth century literature of England was inspired by reason, but the nineteenth century was the age of imagination. The Preface to the *Lyrical Ballads* by William Wordsworth and Samuel Taylor Coleridge in 1798, heralds the period of English Romanticism. The authors of this work were disgusted with the excesses of the French Revolution, they condemned the Rationalist Movement. England turned away from the literature of France and transferred her sympathies to Germany. The philosophical doctrine of Romanticism was inspired by Germany. Romanticism was essentially poetic. Although poles apart in their political beliefs, Wordsworth and Shelley both considered the poet as the guide, prophet and seer of mankind.

Poetry

For the great Romantics — Wordsworth, Shelley, Keats, Byron — the study of the wondrous world of feelings, senses, instincts, of Man' relation to Nature, were of prime importance. Romanticism is shot with *metaphysics.* As M. Lanson puts it, *tout traverse de frissons metaphysique* Alexander Pope had used poetry to depict the thoughts of the philosophers in his *Essay on Man.* The Romantics, dedicated to Romantic imagination — *the esemplastic imagination* as Coleridge called it — were convinced that what was revealed to their poetic intuitions, was right, the Truth. Mysterious forces divine in origin moved the earth, not cold rationalist cause and effect. Pope's couplet was dull and too precise governed by convention. The Romantics sought a lyrical form using unusual images and association of words. They found models for these in the Renaissance and the old popular poetry.

William Wordsworth (1770-1850) is aptly called the "High Priest of Nature". He saw Nature as the *'Stern Daughter of the voice of God',* man's conscience whose balmy presence never disappointed. He was born in 1770 in the picturesque Lake District of England. Here he spent happy years of his childhood in communion with God and Nature. After study at Cambridge, he went to France in 1791 and was enthused by the cause of the Revolution. But when the Reign of Terror came and thousands died at the guillotine, his fine sensibilities, his search for human equality and peace received a rude shock. He engaged himself in the philosophy of William Godwin for sometime. Finding no solution to the problem of human pain, he finally turned to the study of Nature. In the poems of the Lyrical Ballads he describes the mundane happenings of country life, the activities of humble people. He used their common dialect with its flawed grammar as his style. He decries the coming of the industrial era which mechanized English life. With no ornament, his poetry draws its power from the intensity of his feelings and imagination, In The Prelude (1805), a long poem, Wordsworth set out to look back and retrospect on his life. He follows the growth, the turnings of his poetic genius since childhood, ruminates on his errors and recalls the corrective lessons of Nature. In his great moral poem, The Excursion (1814), he uses a philosophy to refute the pessimism that the Revolution had brought.

Samuel Taylor Coleridge (1772-1834) was Wordsworth's "Spirits Brother". He was guided by the same philosophy of the imagination. While Wordsworth's imagination gave him a special vision of the common things of rustic life, Coleridge stirred up the supernatural. To apprediate his poetry peopled with strange, translunary beings like the Ancient Mariner, one needs *'that willing suspension of disbelief that constitutes poetic faith'*, In *The Rime of the Ancient Mariner*, Coleridge describes tne strange adventures of a sailor in a ship. Having killed an albatross, the mariner suffers from hallucinations. The poem, with strange rhythm and cadences, creates a wondrous world. Coleridge was a master of lyrical style. His other famous poems are *Christabel* (1816), and *Kubla Khan* (1816). *Kubia Khan* was written as a result of an opium dream and described the wonderful, strange palace of the Chinese king, Kubla Khan. Coleridge certainly fulfils the meaning of *'Renaissance'* as *'a renascence of wonder'*.

Robert Southey (1774-1843) wrote poetry based on outlandish settings and myths like *Thalaba, the Destroyer* (1801), *The Curse of Kehama* (1810), and *Roderick, the Last of the Goths* (1814). His descriptions are rich and graphic and he uses a great variety of verse forms. He wrote a number of poems in ballad form.

Walter Scott (1771-1832) also had an interest in ballad poetry. He translated the *Lenore* from German (1796). His *The Minstrelsy of the Scottish Border* (1802) shows a great romantic interest in the Middle Ages and the days of chivalry.

The second generation of great Romantic poets include Shelley, Keats and Byron.

Percy Bysshe Shelley (1792-1822) gave up his title and wealth to write poetry. His aim was to awaken mankind to the millenium, the coming future, which would remove human anguish and sorrow. His famous ode, *Ode to the West Wind* is an impassioned exhortation — *Make me thy lyre eu'n as the forest is ...... If Winter comes, can Spring be far behind?* He came under the influence of William Godwin, the philosopher. He proclaimed himself an atheist at the age of 21. His works include *Queen Mab* (1813), *Prometheus Unbound* (1818-1819), which shows human revolt against false gods, *To a Skylark, Adonais* (1821), which is an elegy to Keats, and The Cenci (1819). Shelley's style is a mixture of abstractions and visual images.

John Keats (1795-1821) was the most sensuous of the great Romantic poets. As we read his poems, richly laden with imagery and associations, all the senses are stirred up the visual, olfactory, auditory and tactile. It is said he tasted pepper in wine to describe certain lines. His famous odes are *To a Nightingale, To Autumn* and *On a Grecian Urn.*

Lord George Gordon Byron (1788-1824) was a wealthy nobleman who shunned the popular beliefs of his times. He was notorious as a dilletante. At the age of 19, he wrote Hours of Idleness (1807). With the publication of *Childe Harold's Pilgrimage* (1812) he became famous. Childe Harold was Byron himself, the figure of the disillusioned man, the hero fed up of pleasures and debauches. He lives an outlawed life and is rebellious in spirit. He took on more incarnations in his poems, *The Giaour* (1813), *The Corsair* (1814), *The Siege of Corinth* (1815). In these he displayed his own passions and eccentricities. In 1816, divorced from his wife, he retired to Switzerland and then to Italy. He wrote a number of plays — *Manfred* (1817), *Cain* (1821) and *The Deformed Transformed* (1824). The crowning work was his lyrical, satirical *Don Juan* (1819-1823). He went to Greece to fight for its independence, but died of illness. His satire is political, against England and also against English hypocrisy and cant. His licentious descriptions caused scandals. Don Juan, his magnum opus, is written in ottava rima or eight-line stanzas and is full of wit and mockery.

Thomas Moore (1779-1852), Thomas Campbell (1777-1844), Samuel Rogers (1763-1855), Jamess Hogg (1770-1835), Walter Savage Landor (1775-1864) and **Leigh Hunt (1784-1859)** were other poets of the time.

Novel

Novels of terror and mystery prospered from 1800 to 1830. **Matthew Gregory Lewis** (1775-1818) wrote *Tales of Terror* (1800) and *Tales of Wonder* (1801). **Charles Lamb's (1775-1834)** *Tales from Shakespeare* (1807) is very popular even today. *Mrs Shelley,* the poet's wife, wrote the classic *Frankenstein* in which a scientist creates a monster that turns on its creator and destroys his most beloved ones. It is a novel of prophetic fear. **Miss Mary Mitford** wrote on country life and **Maria Edgeworth (1767-1849)** brought out educational novels like Belinda (1801) and *Tales of Fashionable Life* — novels for children.

Jane Austen (1775-1817) produced half a dozen novels which are drawing-room comedies of life. They study the passion and distress of young ladies and the life of country-folk. The novels — *Pride and Prejudice* (1813), *Sense and Sensibility* (1811), *Emma* (1816), *Persuasion* (1818), *Mansfield Park* (1814), *Northanger Abbey* (1818) — are realistic and witty, full of bracing dialogue.

Walter Scott was Scotland's greatest novelist recreating the past of his country's myths and ballads with rich humour. *Waverly* (1814), *Guy Mannering* (1815), *The Heart of Midlothian* (1818) contain history and direct observation. In *Ivanhoe* (1820), he describes the history of England in the days of the legendary Richard, the Lion Heart. *Kenilworth* (1821), *Quentin Dunward* (1823) were his other famous historical novels. He imbued the Romantic era with a love for the Middle Ages.

Prose/Criticism

The Romantic Age saw a number of reviewers and critics like **Jeremy Bentham (1748-1832)**, who expounded utilitarian doctrines, **Sydney Smith (1771-1845)**, and **William Cobbett (1762-1835)**. Coleridge, the poet, interpreted the doctrines of Kant and Schelling which show the distinction between pure reason and practical reason.

Lamb, Hazlitt, De Quincey and Leigh Hunt were Romantic critics of literature. **Charles Lamb's** essays on Shakespeare's tragedies state that we cannot do justice to them by staging them since the passions which are to be felt in their intensity are torn to tatters by the gimmickry of the actors. **William Hazlitt's (1778-1830)** criticism of some of Shakespeare's characters like Falstaff — *he laughs three inches below the flesh* — is a masterpiece. Coleridge's famous work of criticism, *Biographia Literaria* (1817), marvellously analyses Wordsworth's poetry. The Romantics believed that Shakespeare's art was organic like a work of Nature and *"esemplastic"* — able to blend different elements by imagination. **Thomas De Quincey's (1785-1859)** style is penetrating and incisive when criticizing the poets in *The Confessions of an English Opium Eater* (1821).

MAJOR AUTHORS AND THEIR WORKS

William Wordsworth (1770-1850)

The Lyrical Ballads
The Prelude
The Excursion
Tintern Abbey
Ode on Intimations of Immortality
Michael
The Solitary Reaper
Loadamia
Ode to Duty
To Milton
The Leech-Gatherer
Upon Westminster Abbey
The Rainbow
We Are Seven
The World Is Too Much with Us
To the Cuckoo
The Daffodils
Lucy Gray
Simon Lee
Early Spring
Strange Fits of Passion Have I Known

Walter Scott (1771-1832)

The Bride of Lammermoor
Ivanhoe
Quentin Durward
The Heart of midlothian
Old Mortality
The Antiquity
Guy Mannering
Waverly
Rob Roy
Kenilworth
Red Gauntlet
The Black Dwarf
The Monastery
The Abbot
The Pirate
The Fortunes of Night
The Betrothed
The Talisman
Woodstock
Lives of the Novelists
Life of Napoleon
Tales of Grandfather
The Lay of the Last Minstrel
The Minstrelsy of the Scottish Border
Marmion
The Lady of the Lake
Rockeby

Robert Southey (1774-1843)

Joan of Arc
Wat Tyler
After Blenheim
The Holly Tree
The Scholar
A Vision of Judgement
Madoc
Life of Nelson
Thalaba the Destroyer
Roderick
The Curse of Kehama

S.T. Coleridge (1772-1834)

Biographia Literaria
Table Talk
Aids to Reflection
Christabel
Kubla Khan
The Rime of the Ancient Mariner
France : An Ode
Destiny of Nations
Frost at Midnight
Dejection : An Ode
Youth and Age
Religious Musings

Lord Byron (1788-1824)

Childe Harold's Pilgrimage
Don Juan
The Bride of Abydos
Manfred
The Giaour
Hours of Idleness
The Vision of Judgement
The Prisoner of Chillon
Lara
Marino Faliero
English Bards and Scotch Reviewers
The Siege of Corinth
The Corsair
Cain

P.B. Shelley (1792-1822)

On the Necessity of Atheism
The Revolt of Islam
Prometheus Unbound
The Mask of Anarchy
Hellas
The Cenci
The Witch of Atlas
The Indian Serenade
Ozymandias of Egypt
Epipsychidion
Alaster
Queen Mab
Adonais
Ode to the West Wind
The Cloud
Ode to a Skylark
O World! O Life! O Time!
Defence of Poetry (a Prose Work)
To Night
The Sensitive Plant
A Lament

John Keats (1795-1821)

Endymion
Lamia
Hyperion
The Eve of St. Agnes
Isabella
The Eve of St. Mark
La Belle Dame Sans Merci
Ode to a Nightingale
Ode to Autumn
Ode On a Grecian Urn
Ode to Psyche
On Melancholy
On First Looking into Chapman's Homer
Bright Star

Jane Austen (1775-1871)

Sense and Sensibility
Pride and Prejudice
Mansfield Park
Emma
Persuasion
Northanger Abbey

Charles Lamb (1775-1834)

Essays of Elia
The Last Essays of Elia
John Woodvil
Tales from Shakespeare
Specimens of English Dramatic Poets
The English Comic Writers
The Old Familiar Faces

William Hazlitt (1778-1830)

Characters of Shakespeare's Plays
The English Poets
The English Comic Writers
The Dramatic Literature of the Age of Elizabeth
The Round Table : A Collection of Essays
Table Talk on Men and Manners
The Spirit of the Age

Thomas De Quincey (1785-1859)

Confessions of an English Opium Eater
Joan of Arc
English Mail Coach
Dream Fugue
Murder Considered as One of the Fine Arts
Suspiria de Profundis

Samuel Rogers (1763-1855)
Pleasures of Memory
Italy

James Hogg (1770-1835)
Kilmeny
The Queen's Wake

Thomas Campbell
Pleasures of Hope
Theodoric
Gertrude of Wyoming
Lachiel
Lord Ullin's Daughter
The Last Man
Ye Mariners of England
Hohenlinden
The Battle of Baltic

Thomas Moore (1779-1852)
Lalla Rookh
Irish Melodies

Leigh Hunt (1784-1859)
Story of Rimini
Autobiography

Walter Savage Landor (1775-1864)
Gebir
Hellenics
Imaginary Conversations
The Citations of William Shakespeare
Pericles and Aspasia

THE VICTORIAN ERA (1830-1880)

During this era, the conflict between religion and science, mysticism and rationalism, became intense. There were those who, influenced by Darwin's theory of evolution as expounded in his *On the Origin of Species,* lost their faith in the biblical explanation of man's descent from Adam and Eve. They wanted to shun dogma and accept the scientific spirit. Others lamented the loss of faith and the rising consumer values. Mat thew Arnold in his poem *Dover Beach* writes:

"The Sea of Faith was once too at the full.....

But now I only hear its long withdrawing melancholy roar......"

Prose

Carlyle and Ruskin echoed the prophecies of the Romantic era in their prose works. **Thomas Carlyle (1795-1881)**, the Scotsman, abandoned orthodoxy and came under the influence of the German writers Schiller, Novalis, Richter and Goethe. His work *Sartor Resartus* (1833-1834) is a sort of allegory based on a German professor who has written a treatise on clothes. He penetrates through the clothes to the essence of the man's being. Carlyle was also a historian. His historical works are *The French Revolution* (1837) and *The History of Frederich II of Prussia, called frederik the Great* (1858-1865). These are satirical and prophetic, expounding how man and society are organized. He was against materialism and praised the Magi and prophets of the past. He advocates strength and power.

John Ruskin (1819-1900) was indignant about the ugliness of existence brought in by industrialism and the machine. *Unto This Last* (1860), which influenced Gandhiji's economic theories, describes his disgust for soulless labour. He was a student of arts. *Modern Painters* (1843, 1860) is about landscape painters like Turner. He also wrote *The Seven Lamps of Architecture* (1849) and *The Stones of Venice* (1851-1853), praising Gothic art.

Matthew Arnold (1822-1888), the poet, wanted his countrymen to inculcate classical qualities to become harmonious in morals and in ereative works. The English must break away from their insular moorings by imbibing the teachings of Greece and the French. He is *the detector-general of the intellectual failings of his own nation.* Poetry, according to him, is important in character formation, and culture is *"the minister of the sweetness and light essential to the perfect character"*. His works include *On translating Homer, The Study of Celtic Literature and Essays in Criticism* (1865, 1889). He wrote St. Paul and Protestantism advocating that dogma should be removed from Christianity and it should adjust itself to the findings of science.

A number of philosophers, historians and scholars wrote in this period. Charles Darwin's theory of evolution dramatically affected human thought. **John Stuart Mill (1806-1873)** expounded the processes of logic and political economy. **Herbert Spencer (1820-1903)** and **Thomas Henry Huxley (1825-1895)** were scientists. **Thomas Babington Macaulay (1800-1859)** was a poet, essayist and historian who advocated English education in India. The Oxford Movement gave rise to religious writers like **John Keble (1792-1866)** and **John Henry Newman (1801-1890)**. Newman's famous work is *Apologia pro Vita Sua* (1864) in which he explains why he had converted to the Roman Church.

Novel

The transition from Walter Scott's novels to Charles Dicken's first novel in 1836 is a great one. When Queen Victoria ascended the throne, **Frederick Marryat (1792-1848)** produced sea-stories; **Edward Bulwer Lytton (1803-1873)** wrote about Byronic heroes, attractive criminals and historical novels like *The Last Days of Pompeii* (1834); **Benjamin Disraeli** (1804-1881), the Prime Minister of England, wrote *Coningsby: or The New Generation* (1844) and *Sybil: or The Two Nations* (1845) to show that the aristocrats of the society had a duty towards the unfortunate ones. In Disraeli's novels, one finds the politics of Queen Victoria's reign.

Perhaps the greatest Victorian novelist is **Charles Dickens (1812-1870)**, whose identification with the underdog in society was unmatched by any writer. One reason for this is his own troubled childhood led in penury under the shadow of a father who was in debtor's prison. The part of his life comes through vividly in his novel *David Copperfield* (1849-1850) which is also an indictment of the cruel, unimaginative schools of his times. He was a master craftsman in character delineation. A host of characters and their dialogues have become household in the English-speaking world. Thus the incorrigible optimist Micawber, Geakle, Pickwick, Fagin and others are types of characters that may be seen all around us anywhere. Dickens had a forgiving sense of humour. He never let bitterness creep into his recreations of painful events of the past. Among his famous novels are: *Pickwick Papers* (1836; in the picaresque style), *Barnaby Rudge* (1841) and *A Tale of Two Cities* (1859; based on the French Revolution), *Oliver Twist* (1837) and *Hard Times* (1854); novels exposing social conditions. He has a picturesque style and concrete imagination.

William Makepeace Thackeray (1811-1863) made a penetrating analysis of upper middle class and aristocratic society. He was a master of irony. In *The Book of Snobs* (1849), he ridicules the tendency to fawn on nobility and to imitate their manners. *Vanity Fair* (1847-1848), *History of Pendennis* (1848-1850), *The Newcomes* (1853-1855), *The History of Henry Esmond* (1852) and *The Virginians* (1857-1859) are pictures of contemporary life in which he depicts human eccentricities and follies. He was adept at reproducing jargon and idiolects.

The Romantic spirit was still alive in the works of the Bronte sisters. **Charlotte Bronte (1816-1855)** wrote *Jane Eyre* (1847), the story of a governess in a terrifying house. Her sister **Emily Bronte (1818-1848)** wrote *The Wuthering Heights* (1847), set in a wild landscape. Powerful passions and characters have made this one of the greatest novels of all times.

George Eliot (1819-1880), a pen-name for Mary Ann Evans, wrote Adam Bede (1859), the story of a girl who was forced to murder her own baby. *The Mill on the Floss* (1860) and *Romola* (1863) are other novels by her. In *Middlemarch, a Study of Provincial Life* (1871-1872), the novelist builds up, from the lives of a great number of deeply studied characters, the complex picture of the life of a small town.

Poetry

The poetry of this period still shows the influence of the Romantic Era. **Alfred, Lord Tennyson (1809-1892)** was an eclectic, selecting the best of his forerunners. He was first interested in style and metre, but later on ideas started interesting him. A great many poems by him are flawlessly beautiful. If *The Lotus Eaters* is softly languorous, *Ulysses* has a striking severity. Tennyson also experienced the intellectual crisis of his times and shared its anxieties. For instance, *The Princess* (1847) is occupied with the question of feminism. *In Memoriam* (1850) is one of his most beautiful poems. It is an elegy on the premature death of his friend Arthur Hallam. It concerns itself with the belief in immortality, the conflict between the hopes of Christianity and the rationalism of science. It is composed of octosyllabic quatrains. He shows a type of Byronic revolt in Locksley Hall (1886) and Maud (1855). In *Idylls of the King* (1859, 1869, 1889) he took Arthurian legends as his theme.

Robert Browning (1812-1889) was famous for using the technique of dramatic monologue in his poems. Through the protagonists of his poems he gives vent to his feelings, passions and aspirations. Thus in *Paracelsus* (1835), he describes the highly ambitious hero who wanted to transform man's life. We find here Browning's views on truth and philosophy. His other poems include *Sordello* (1840), *Pippa Passes* (1841), *My Last Duchess, Porphyria's Lover* and his masterpiece, *The Ring and the Book* (1868-1869). In his works we find an excess of thought and a rare vocabulary. He uses blank verse dexterously. His brusque speech, broken syntax and uneven rhythm are in contrast to Tennyson's. As Pound and Eliot have said, Browning brought verse nearer to modem colloquial speech. Browning's characters are remote in time and culture. Some of these are Rabbi Ben Ezra, Fra Lippo Lippi and Andrea del Sarto. In *The Ring and the Book* he takes as his subject an Italian crime and explores the minds of all his characters. He strikes a note of hope in his poems. The lines *"God's in his heaven/And all's well with the world"* lay bare his beliefs. But in general, Browning is considered a difficult poet.

Matthew Arnold (1822-1888) was a reflective poet with a melancholic bent. A deep brooding pensiveness informs his poetry. Dover Beach shows his concern with the loss of faith in a world of science. His epic poem *Sohrab and Rustum, Tristram and Iseult, The Scholar Gypsy* are other famous works.

Dante Gabriel Rossetti, William Morris and Algernon Charles Swinburne together are known as the Pre-Raphaelite poets. They affected Raphael, the Renaissance painter, in their desire to paint sonorous wordpictures which may not have much content to conveyor any philosophy to reveal. It was in accordance with the aestheticism of Ruskin. In fact Rossetti and Morris were painters as well as poets. They worshipped beauty like John Keats did. Robert Buchanan attacked these poets as belonging to *the fleshly school of poetry.*

Dante Gabriel Rossetti (1828-1882) translated the Italian poet Dante's *Vita Nuova*. His *The Blessed Damozel* is an exquisite poem and his best sonnets are contained in *The House of Life* in which he extols his young and beautiful wife. They are full of rich sounds and images and mystic symbols. Rossetti was inspired by the ballads of the Middle Ages. Like the primitive Italian painters, he uses rich colours and depicts warm sensuous feelings.

William Morris (1834-1896) was enchanted by Gothic art of the Middle Ages. His poems drew inspiration from those of Froissart, Chaucer and Malory. He borrowed stories from Scandinavia and Iceland. His poems are like frescoes and are very lyrical in quality. The famous ones are *The Earthly Paradise* (1868-1870) and *The Life and Death of Jason* (1867). These works show rhythm and use of archaism. He strove to bring civilization back to art from the utilitarian industrialization.

Algernon Charles Swinburne (1837-1909) was a prodigy. He was a musician, and a sonority of rhymes filled his poetry. He took romantic themes like revolt against society, hatred of monarchy and struggle against traditional morality. His *Atalanta in Calydon* (l865) is his masterpiece and is known for its choral passages.

To these poets of the Victorian Age must be added the name of **Edward Fitzgerald (1809-1883)** whose **The Rubaiyat of Omar Khayyam (1859)** is a classic.

MAJOR AUTHORS AND THEIR WORKS

Alfred Lord Tennyson (1809-1892)

The Princess
In Memoriam
Maud
Enoch Arden
Idylls of the King
Queen Mary
Harold
Backet
Akbar's Tomb
Crossing the Bar
Locksley Hall
Locksley Hall Sixty Years After
Dora
Poems by Two Brothers
The Falcon
The Cup
Poems Chiefly Lyrical
Ulysses
Poems Chiefly Lyrical
Ulysses
The Lotos-Eaters
The Death of Oenone and Other Poems

Robert Browning (1812-1889)

Pauline
Paracelsus
Strafford
Sordello
Bells and Pomegranates
Christmas Eve and Easter Day
Men and Women
Dramatis Personae
The King and the Book
Asolando
Pippa Passes
Fra Lippo Lippi
Andrea del Sarto
King Victor and King Charles
Dramatic Lyrics
Dramatic Romances and Lyrics

Matthew Arnold (1822-1888)

Sohrab and Rustum
Tristram and Iseult
Balder Dead
Empedocles on Etna
Stanzas from the Grande Chartreuse
The Strayed Reveller and Other Poems
Dover Beach
Thyrsis
Scholar Gypsy
On Translating Homer
New Poems
On the Study of Celtic Literature
Essays in Criticism

Culture and Anarchy
Literature and Dogma
Mixed Essays
Friendship's Garland
God and the Bible

D.G. Rossetti (1828-1882)

The Blessed Damozel
World's Worth
Ave
The White Ship
Sister Helen
Eden Bower
The House of Life
Ballads and Sonnets

Christina Georgina Rossetti (1830-1894)

The Goblin Market
The Prince's Market
A Pageant and Other Poems

William Morris (1834-1896)

The Defence of Guenevere
The Life and Death of Jason
The Earthly Paradise
A Dream of John Bull
News from Nowhere
A Tale of the House of the Wolfings
The Roots of the Mountains
The Story of the Glittering Plain
The Sundering Flood
Hope and Fears for Art
Signs of Change

A.C. Swinburne (1837-1909)

Atalanta in Calydon
Erechtheus
Tristram of Lyonesse
Chasteland
Bathwell
Mary Stuart
William Blake : A Critique
A Study of Shakespeare
A Study of Ben Jonson
Songs Before Sunrise

Edward Fitzgerald (1809-1883)

Euphranor : A Dialogue on Youth
Translation of Rubaiat

Thomas Carlyle (1795-1881)

Sartor Resartus
The French Revolution
Heroes and Hero-Worship
Past and Present
The Letters and Speeches of Oliver Cromwell
Latter-day Pamphlets
Life of John Sterling
History of Frederick the Great
Chartism

John Ruskin (1819-1900)

The Modern Painters
Salsette and Elephanta
The Seven Lamps of Architectur
The Stones of Venice
The Two Paths
Unto This Last
Munera Pulveris
Time and Tide by Wear and Tyne
Fors Clavigera
Sesame and Lilies
The Crown of Wild Olive

T.B. Macaulay (1800-1859)

History of England from the Accession of James II
Lays of Ancient Rome

Charles Dickens (1812-1870)

Pickwick Papers
Nicholas Nickleby
Martin Chuzzlewit
Dombey and Son
David Copperfield
Bleak House
A Tale of Two Cities
Great Expectations
Our Mutual Friend
Edwin Drood
Oliver Twist
Little Dorrit
Baraby Rudge
The Uncommercial Traveller
A Christmas Carol
Hard Times
Old Curiosity Shop

William Makepeace Thackeray (1811-1863)

Vanity Fair

Barry Lyndon
Pendennis
Henry Esmond
The New Comes
The Virginians
Adventures of Philip
The Book of Snobs
The History of Pendennis
Lovel the Widower
The Round about Papers
The English Humorists of the Eighteenth Century
The Four Georges
Rebecca and Rowena
The Rose and The Ring
Ivanhoe—the Legend of the Rhine

George Meredith (1828-1909)

The Ordeal of Richard Feveral
Evan Harrington
Emilia in England
Rhoda Fleming
Vittoria
The Adventures of Harry Richmond
Diana of the Crossways
One of Our Conquerous
The Amazing Marriage
The Egoist
Beauchamp's Career
The Tragic Comedians

Charlotte Bronte (1816-1855)

Jane Eyre
Shirley
The Professor
Villette

Emily Bronte (1818-1848)

Wuthering Heights

George Eliot (1810-1880)
(Mary Ann Evans)

Adam Bede
The Mill on the Floss
Silas Marner
Scenes of Clerical Life
Life of Jesus
Romola
Fleix Holt the Radical
Daniel Deronda
Middlemarch

Benjamin Disraeli (1804-1881)

Vivian Gray
Sybil : Or the Two Nations
The Voyage of Captain Popavilla
Henrietta Temple
Coningsby : or the New Generation
Tancred : or the New Crusade
The Wondrous Tale of Alroy and the Rise of Iskander
Contarini Fleming : A Psychological Auto-biography

R.L. Stevenson (1850-1894)

Travels with a Donkey in the Cevennes
An Inland Voyage
Virginibus Pueresque
New Arabian Nights
Treasure Island
The Strange Case of Dr. Jackyll and Mr. Hyde
Kidnapped
The Black Arrow
The Master of Ballantrae
Catriona
Underwords
A Child's Garden of Verses

Thomas Hardy (1840-1828)

Under the Greenwood Tree
Desperate Remedies
A Pair of Blue Eyes
Two on a Tower
Far From the Madding Crowd
The Return of the Native
The Mayor of Casterbridge
Tess of the D'Urbervilles
Jude the Obscure
The Hand of Ethelberta
The Trumpet Major
The Woodlanders
The Well-beloved
A Laodicean
A Group of Noble Dames
Life's LIttle Ironies
Wessex Poems
The Dynasts
A Changed Man
Winter Words
The Waiting Supper and Other Tales

The Modern Age (1880 Onwards)

As the 20th century dawned, new values replaced the old ones and shaped the literature of Great Britain. England fast lost its imperial image as her colonies revolted and fought for independence. Industrialization progressed by leaps and bounds and the two World Wars brought economic depression. All this affected the content of literature. Writers sought new vehicles of expression. The findings of **Sigmund Freud** in the realms of psychology took novelists to the subconscious mind. A great number of writers who became famous men of letters in English came from Ireland **(G.B. Shaw, W.B. Yeats, James Joyce and Samuel Beckett)** and from America (**T.S. Eliot and Ezra Pound**). Socialism became a practising creed and feminism raised her head. Dogmatic Christianity was more or less ignored. Although great strides were made in scientific inventions, science could not provide suitable answers to the deep questioning of the human mind resulting in ethical philosophy. The age saw the end of feudalism. Victorian reticence and prudery gave way to decadence in literature. English writers came under the influence of the French Parnassians and Symbolists. Scandinavia and Russia represented by **Ibsen** and **Tolstoy** also influenced the British men of letters. Many a poet wished to fight free from the fixed rules of versification and wrote in free verse. Many imitated the American poet **Walt Whitman**. English literature became more expansive in its concerns. The life and culture of foreign lands were depicted. Although **Kipling** was an imperialist, his works go beyond England. Being born in India, his works give a graphic view of the country. The great Celtic Revival under Yeats brought a new strain to English literature. Finally, the theatre, lying dormant for a century, now woke up with renewed vigour.

Criticism

The Age began with scholarly works in literary history. **Leslie Stephen (1832-1904)** wrote biographical and critical essays. He produced *The English Utilitarians and the Dictionary of National Biography*. He was an agnostic and rationalist. **A.C. Bradley (1851-1935), H.J.C. Grierson (1866-1960)** and **Edward Dowden (1843-1913)** were other famous critics. Bradley is famous for his critical work on Shakespeare's tragedies.

Walter Horatio Pater (1839-1894) propounded the literary doctrine *Art for Art's Sake* which was a quest for the most refined pleasure. The exquisite in art came from a reflection of the past. He eulogized the accomplishments of the Renaissance. His prose style was rich, musical and classical. His works include *Studies in the History of the Renaissance* (1873) and *Marius the Epicurean* (1885).

John Addington Symonds (1840-1893) was another admirer of the Renaissance. **Oscar Wilde (1856-1900)**, more known as a novelist and dramatist, gave a wider dimension to the theory of Art for Art's Sake by spicing it with wit and paradox. **George Saintsbury (1845-1933)** and **Sir Walter Raleigh (1861-1922)** were other famous critics.

Poetry

Most of the poetry written in this period are the works of those more renowned as novelists: Robert Louis Stevenson, Rudyard Kipling and Thomas Hardy. William Butler Yeats, who pioneered the Celtic Revival, Thomas Steams Eliot, whose *Wasteland* is a watershed leading to modern poetry, Gerard Manley Hopkins, the Catholic poet, are the famous poets of this period.

Rudyard Kipling (1865-1936) wrote on imperialist themes in *Barrack Room Ballads* (1892), *The Seven Seas* (1896) and *Five Nations* (1903). These poems were aimed by their rugged music to rouse people to protest. He combined folk-music with music-hall chorus. It had the sound of drum beats and bugle-calls and even the refinements of chamber music. The poetry of imperialism, heroism of national policy, contained slang and even biblical allusions. In fact, his popularity was that of Walt Whitman, the national poet of America. Many of his subjects were from India, like the poem *Gunga Din*.

W.E. Henley (1849-1903) also wrote poetry which praised Britain's colonial power. *The Song of the Sword, For England's Sake* and *London Voluntaries* are some of his better-known poems.

There were also a group of poets called the Decadents. They were aesthetes and their doctrine was 'Art for Art's Sake'. **Oscar Wilde** was the leading poet of the group. *The Ballad of Reading Gaol* (1898) is his famous work inspired by his crime and imprisonment.

A group of poets had a pessimistic view of life. **John Davidson (1857-1909), Ernest Dawson (1867-1900)** and **A.E. Housman (1859-1936)** are some of these poets. But the leading pessimist of the age was **Thomas Hardy (1840-1928)**, better known as a novelist. He published *Wessex Poems* (1898) after the novel *Jude the Obscure* failed to receive public acclaim. His poetry was musical and highly individual. He had a disillusioned view of life. From 1903 to 1908, he produced the vast poetical work *The Dynasts*, written under the background of Napoleon's struggle against Europe combining real history with symbolic flashes. His poem, *To an Unborn Pauper Child*, reveals his utter dejection with life: *'Breathe : hid heart'*, it begins.

Francis Thompson (1859-1907) and **Gerard Manley Hopkins (1844-1889)** were religious poets of the beginning of the twentieth century. Thompson's poem, *The Hound of Heaven* is a masterpiece. It describes God as a Heavenly Hound chasing man to capture his soul and man fleeing Him in the pleasures of life. The Jesuit, Hopkins invented a new type of verse called *'sprung rhythm'*. It was filled with strange word coinages and is difficult for the ordinary reader to understand. His poetry reflects the conflirt within him between his attraction to Roman Catholicism and his joy tor the beautiful creation. He wrote a number of religious poems of which *The Wreck of the "Deutschland"* is one of the best. It describes the death of five Franciscan nuns on board the ship, *Deutschland*.

Irish, English and Continental influences met in **W.B. Yeats (1865-1939)**. He Was born in Ireland but came to live in London. He was influenced by the strange mystical visions of William Blake, by pre-Raphaelite refinement and even the mysticism and occultism of the Orient, especially of India. His poetry is an attempt to revive Celtic mysticism and Irish mythology. Apparently it Was Yeats who introduced Rabindra Nath Tagore to the West. He also came under the influence of Verlaine, a French symbolist poet. His best poetry is in *The Wild Swans at Coole* (1919), *The Tower* (1928) and *The Winding Stair* (1933). Some of his well-known poems are: *Easter* (1916), *The Second Coming, Byzantium, A Prayer for my Daughter, Leda and Swan, Sailing to Byzantium, Meru, Lapis Lazudili, Among School Children,* etc. His progress as a poet can be assessed by comparing the beautiful but simple *Lake Isle of Innisfree* with the beautiful and profound *Byzantium*.

The towering poet of the 20th century is **Thomas Steams Eliot (1888-1965)**. Eliot came on to the scene when the West was passing through tremendous upheavals — belief in religion, especially of the Church was fading, democracy was the new experiment in politics, and many modernist trends were noticeable in literature. Eliot proclaimed himself "a royalist in politics, an Anglo-Catholic in religion and a classicist in literature". Tradition, according to him, was not the dead past but the past living in the present. In his essay *Tradition and the Individual Talent*, he states that "the talent of an artist shows itself not where he differs from the ancients but where, in his work, they assert their immortality". Eliot's poetry shows metaphysical, symbolist and imagist strains, but his individual talent shines forth unmistakeably. An eclectic philosophy, borrowed from his own Christianity and Buddhism and the Upanishads informs his poetry. His poetry, especially *The Wasteland* (1922) is a poem that describes the zeitgeist (spirit of the times) and the *angoisse metaphysique* (metaphysical anguish) of life in post-World War Europe. It begins with the sentence *"April is a cruel month"* and this sets the strain lor the whole poem. A brooding sense of futility and human inanity pervades modern life. Eliot achieves this effect by a combination of literary allusions to the past which stirs associations, and by what is called as the *objective correlative*. This last technique means that images are described which call up an emotion or a feeling. His other poems are *The Lave Song of J. Alfred Prufrock* and *Four Quartets* (1944). These lines from the *Four Quartets* may sum up the disillusionment of the times: *"Footfalls echo in the memory/Down the passage one could not take / To the door one could not open"*. Eliot was a poet of spiritual regeneration.

As the century proceeds, a host of poets make their mark **Stephen Spender (1909-1995), W.H. Auden (1907-1973), C. Day Lewis (1904-1972), Louis MacNeice (1907-1963)** — all of them wrote with a Social awareness, exposing the horror of the bourgeois culture and capitalist exploitation and the terror of totalitarianism.

We cannot end this section of the early modern twentieth century without a reference to **Rupert Brooke (1887-1915), Wilfred Owen (1893-1918)** and **Siegfried Sassoon (1886-1967)** popularly known as the "War poets". They had served the Armed Forces in the First World War, and after 1918, disillusioned by the horrors they had witnessed took their pens to write against the war. The poem *The Soldier* is one of the finest lyrics in the English language. It describes the poet's sense of impending death in battle and his love for his country: *"If I should die/Think only this of me/That there is a part of England/Buried in some foreign land"*. Another poem is Sassoon's *Everyone Sang,* which describes the exultation felt by the soldiers returning home after the General Armistice was signed. They are described as *freed birds*.

Novel

Just like poetry, the novel of this century reflects the great passions and strivings of the age. The discoveries of **Sigmund Freud (1856-1939)** revealed the relationship of man's behaviour to his subconscious mind. The subconscious contains impressions of past experiences which influence a person's attitudes and behaviour. These discoveries led not only to new methods of psychiatric treatment but also to new dramatic techniques in the art of the novel. The stream-of-consciousness method used by James Joyce and Virginia Woolf spring from these discoveries. The modem novel is more and more concerned with an analysis of human behaviour. The focus shifts from a description of the external atmosphere to the thoughts of the characters.

Thomas Hardy's works are tinged with a gloomy pessimism reminiscent of Schopenhauer, and an analogy may be found in his works to Flaubert and Zola from

France. Hardy's country Dorsetshire and the surroundings become the 'Wessex' of his novels. His work is full of realistic descriptions of the countryside. The places, full of pre-historic and Roman remains, heaths, have a character, and influence the people living there. The pre-historic past presses on the life of today. He is adept at delineating rustic characters. Man is a puppet of fate and an uncontrollable destiny drives him along life. A bitter helplessness pervades his novels *Far from the Madding Crowd* (1874), *The Return of the Native* (1878), *The Mayor of Casterbridge* (1886), and *Jude the Obscure* (1895). His success reached a climax with *Tess of the d'Urbervilles* (1891). His *Tess of the D'UrberviUes* and *Jude the Obscure,* because of their frank handling of sex and religion, aroused the hostility of the reading public. These two books, however, present Hardy's most moving indictments of the human situation.

The works of George Robert Gissing (1857-1903) produce a sense of absolute dejection. He worked as an ill-paid hack in the poor districts of London and described these places vividly in his books. Although impressed by Charles Dickens, his writings show none of Dickens' humour. One bitter, wretched world, a miserable London, exists in his works. Thus *Demos, a Story of English Socialism* (1886) describes the futility of socialist agitation, *The Nether World* (1889), the wretchedness of the London slums, *New Grub Street* (1891), the hopeless lot of a penniless writer, and *The Odd Women* (1893), the plight of unmarried women. His style is as bare and unaffected as his ideas.

Robert Louis Stevenson (1850-1894) stands in contrast to Hardy and Gissing in his recreation of the life of action and adventure. Although he suffered from an incurable malady, he did not lose faith in himself. He brought out *An Inland Voyage* (1878), *Travels with a Donkey in the Cevennes* (1879), *The Silverado Squatters, Treasure Island* (1833), *Kidnapped* and *The Master of Ballantrae* (1889) among others. The last three are very popular among children the world over. He also wrote children's adventure classics like *The Treasure Island* (1883), *Dr Jekyll and Mr. Hyde* (1886) and *Kidnapped* (1886). In *Dr. Jekyll and Mr Hyde* he touches upon the dual nature of man his good and evil aspects. His style is vivid and full of interesting details.

Another great novelist was the Pole, **Joseph Conrad (1857-1924)**, who perfected his knowledge of English and wrote in a vivid style with a strong foreign accent. His experience of sailing life and work in the English merchant service gave him the ideas to write masterpieces like *The Nigger of the Narcissus* (1897), and *Lord Jim: A Tale* (1900). Like the Slavs he was preoccupied with the problem of human misery. *Lord Jim* and *The Heart of Darkness* (1902) show his anger at what the white man had done to exploit Africa and other nations. A trait of his narrative technique is the gradual picture of his character formed from fragmentary descriptions of witnesses. He has a rich, sensuous prose style full of striking imagery.

Rudyard Kipling wrote stories about Indian life: *Plain Tales from the Hills* (1888) and *Soldiers Three* (1888). *Plain Tales from the Hills* depicts an Englishman's encounter with the strange East. Kipling was born in Bombay and spent his early life in India. He knew the land and its customs, its people and languages. His best book is *Kim* (1901), the story of a half-Irish boy, who speaks the language of the rustics of India and accompanies a Buddhist Lama on his search for "Nirvana" or Salvation. Kipling is adept at describing the sights and smells of India and its colourful people with their racy dialects. He also wrote two animal epics entitled, *The Jungle Book* (1894) and a series of short stories for children like *Captains Courageous* (1897), just *So Stories* (1902) and *Puck of Pook's Hill* (1906). Kipling was influenced by Carlyle's doctrine of energy. As a spokesman of the Imperialist theme he believed that it was ideal for a person to sacrifice himself for his tribe. He believed that especially the white man was ordained to rule and lead nations. His works praise Britain's hegemony over her colonies.

Shortly after Kipling, came H. G. Wells and John Galsworthy who were Socialists and criticized the English society. **H.G. Wells** (1866-1946) began by writing stories with a semi-scientific flavour like *The Time Machine* (1895), *The Island of Dr Moreau* (1896), *The Invisible Man* (1897) and *The War of the Worlds* (1898). The stories are ingenuously plotted and thrill and disturb the readers. Later on Wells' interest shifted to social problems. He became a member of the Fabian Society. He wrote *Mankind in the Making* (1903) describing how society would look like when reformed by socialism. He also satirized the society in *Love and Mr Lewisham* (1900), *Kipps* (1905). *Tono-Bungay* (1909) and *Marriage* (1912). He does not glorify Britain's past and he scorns the existing institutions of his country. He wrote a number of remarkable books after the outbreak of World War I in 1914. These show his restless self-examining spirit. Some of these are *Mr Britling Sees it through* (1916) and *The Undying Fire* (1919).

In the works of **John Galsworthy (1867-1933)** we find an artistic conscience. Like Wells, he also attacked the concept of property and commercialism in his novels. He too exposed and criticized national prejudices, especially those existing among his own class, the landed gentry. He was widely read in Continental Literature and was especially influenced by France and Russia. Turgenev with his noble realism was his ideal. He is a detached and impartial observer of his country's decadent values. He advocates a fearless search for truth. *In The Island Pharisees* (1904) he exposes the stagnation of thought among English privileged classes. A similar theme is touched in other novels like *The Country House* (1907), *The Patrician* (1911) and *The Dark Flower* (1913) where country squires, aristocracy and artists are critically studied. *The Forsyte Saga* (1922) is his masterpiece. It is a natural history of the rich upper-middle class family. He describes their attitude to events like the Great War, the growth of socialism, unemployment and the coal strike.

Enoch Arnold Bennett (1867-1931) wrote a number of different types of novels presenting a detailed picture of an industrial district in the provinces. He is a realist like the French nationalists. His masterpiece is *The Old Wives' Tale* (1908).

G.K. Chesterton (1874-1936) was a champion of tradition and he refuted and opposed the attacks of his contemporaries against English society in *Orthodoxy* (1908), *The Napoleon of Notting Hill* (1904). He believed in tradition sanctified by ages of experience and even in the religious bond between men. His style is effective with the use of imagery and comparison and he spices it with plenty of humour.

James Joyce (1882-1941) pioneered a new type of novel with the *stream-of-consciousness* technique. Characters in *Ulysses* (1922) unreel themselves by a sort of interior monologue. Speech is mimicked and styles are parodied. *Ulysses* is modelled on the *Odyssey* of Homer and set in the slums of Dublin. The thousand pages of this novel cover just one day in the life of Leopold Bloom and Stephen Dedalus. Joyce coined words from several languages and was a master craftsman with wit and conceits. His other famous work is the autobiographical *A Portrait of the Artist as a Young Man* (1916) which describes his adolescence and sensuous tendencies.

Virginia Woolf (1882-1941) continued the stream-of-consciousness technique. Her works *To the Lighthouse* (1927) and *Mrs Dallaway* (1925) reveal the hidden inner life of her characters.

E.M. Forster (1879-1970) was the novelist of cultural relations. In **A Passage to India** (1924) he studies the conflict between the west and the east and takes a favourable stand for the latter. *Where Angels Fear to Tread* (1905) studies how the cultural divide between an Italian girl and her English husband leads to the ruination of their marriage and life.

D.H. Lawrence (1885-1930) was a prolific writer. His outspoken views on sexual relations raised much hue and cry. He considered sex the religion of the blood. His novels were dubbed pornographic. He believed in the free expression of human personality, in being guided by unrestrained primitive instincts. In *Sons and Lovers* (1913) he studies the relationship of son and mother and the social disparity of a father, a coalminer and a mother, a teacher. The novel is autobiographical. Other works by him are *The Rainbow* (1915), *Women in Love* (1921), and *The Plumed Serpent* (1926). *The Rainbow,* suppressed as obscene, treats the conflict between man and woman. *Lady Chatterley's Lover* (1928) was canned for being obscene.

George Orwell (1903-1950) wrote novels which were an indictment of totalitarian government: *Animal Farm* (1945) and *Nineteen Eighty-Four* (1949). **Aldous Huxley's** *Brave New World* (1932) is a prophetic book about the future of civilization in the context of scientific advancement.

Drama

After Shakespeare, **George Bernard Shaw (1856-1950)** is the great playwright whose works enlivened the British stage. Shaw, like Ibsen, believed in drama as a vehicle for ideas. He had a rich Irish sense of humour and his plays are satires on various social and philosophical themes. His general technique was to discuss the problem of his play first in its preface. Often this preface is longer than the play itself. *Widowers' Houses* (1892) was his first play. In this he discusses the problem of Housing. In *Mrs Warren's Profession* (1894) he lays bare the profession of a prostitute. In *Arms and the Man* (1894) the theme is the chocolate-cream soldier. Shaw was an iconoclast breaking well-established idols or myths. Thus this play disillusions us of the romantic image of a soldier. He is not one who is willing to die for his country, but one who loves his life. When the enemy is weak, he attacks, but withdraws and takes to his heels if the enemy is strong. George Bernard Shaw had a keen interest in the English language and formulated a standard pronunciation for it. He studies the theme of how language can influence one's rise in the social ladder. Professor Higgins succeeds in teaching a flower-girl to rid herself of a cockney accent and to speak well enough to pass for royalty! In *Man and Superman* we see Shaw as a master conversationalist. Ideas are discussed without much action taking place in the play. *The Apple Cart* (1929) shows the weaknesses of democracy. Although an Irish man, Shaw did not write on Irish themes as such.

Oscar Wilde reminds one of the Restoration playwrights Sheridan and Congreve in his comedy of manners. His style is full of paradox and verbal wit. Some of his famous plays are *Lady Windermere's Fan* (1892), *A Woman of No Importance* (1893) and *The Importance of Being Ernest* (1895).

John Galsworthy's plays *Sfrife* (1909), *Justice* (1910) and *Loyalties* (1922) were based on the theme of class exploitation.

W.B. Yeats contributed to the Irish drama. His Celtic theme comes through in *The Countess Cathleen* (1892) and *The Land of Heart's Desire* (1894). **Sean O'Casey** (1884-1964) and **J. M. Synge** (1871-1909) were other noted Irish playwrights. The latter's plays, *The Playboy of the Western World* (1907) and *Riders to the Sea* (1904) are famous.

T.S. Eliot's contribution to the modern theatre were religious and moral plays. He uses the Greek "chorus" style in *Murder in the Cathedral* (1935) to heighten the dramatic effect of the murder of Thomas Becket by the Archbishop of Canterbury's men. *The Family Reunion* (1939) is a play about sin and expiation. Eliot pruned verse to sound like prose. This is done dexterously in *The Cocktail Party* (1949) and *The Confidential Clerk* (1953) where characters speak verse which sounds like prose.

A group of playwrights came to be known as the "Angry Young Men". **John Osborne (1929-1994)** was the most prominent of them. His play *Look Back in Anger* (1956) catches the mood of the frustrated youth in post-War England. In his plays, he exposes the wretchedness of the working class.

Harold Pinter (1930-2008) mixes comedy and horror in his plays like *The Birthday Party* (1958).

Another group of dramatists drew their inspiration from France. *The Absurd Theatre*, as it was called, began in France with Albert Camus, Jean Genet anJ Ionesco as its pioneers. In England, **Samuel Beckett (1906-1989)** was the Irish dramatist of this school. His plays *Endgame* (1955), *Krapp's Last Tape* (1958) and *Waiting For Godot* (1906) show the meaninglessness of human action and the unrelieved gloom of existence.

MAJOR AUTHORS AND THEIR WORKS

George Bernard Shaw (1856-1950)

Widowers' Houses
Candida
You Never Can Tell
Man and Superman
Back to Methuselah
Saint Joan
Heartbreak House
The Philanderer
Mrs. Warren's Profession
Caesar and Cleopatra
John Bull's Other Island
Major Barbara
The Doctor's Dilemma
Getting Married
The Apple Cart
Pygmalion
The Dark Lady of the Sonnets
Plays Pleasant and Unpleasant
The Millionaire
The Intelligent Woman's Guide to Socialism
Everybody's Political What is What
Cashel Byron's Profession
Love Among the Artists
Androcles and the Lion
The Devil's Disciple
The Man of Destiny

W.B. Yeats (1865-1939)

The Land of Heart's Desire
The Countess Cathleen
The Shadowy Waters
The Hour-glass
The Resurrection
The King's Threshold
On Baile's Strand
The Cat and the Moon
Ideas of Good and Evil
Discoveries
The Wind among the Reeds
The Wanderings of Oisin
The Tower
The Winding Stair and Other Poems
Lake Isle of Innisfree
Byzantium

John Galsworthy (1867-1933)

The Silver Box
Strife
The Skin Game
The Man of Property
Justice
Loyalties
Escape
The Inn of Tranquility
The Forsyte Saga
The Country House
Fraternity
The Patrician
The Dark Flower
Saint's Progress
Maid in Waiting
Flower Wilderness

Rudyard Kipling (1865-1936)

Kim

The Jungle Book
Barrack-room Ballads
Departmental Ditties
The Seven Seas
The Five Nations
Tales from the Hills
Soldiers Three
Life's Handicap
The Phantom Rickshaw
Many Inventions
The Day's Work
Just-so Stories for Little Children
Rewards and Fairies
Debits and Credits

H.G. Wells (1866-1946)

The Time Machine
Love and Mr. Levisham
Kipps
The History of Mr. Polly
Mr. Britling Sees It Through
Christina Albertas Father
The Wonderful Visit
The Island of Dr. Moreau
The Invisible Man
The War of the Worlds
The First Men in the Moon
The Food of the Goas
Marriage
Experiment in Autobiography
The Contemporary Novel

Joseph Conrad (1857-1924)

The Nigger of the 'Narcissus'
Typhoon
Lord Jim
Victory
Almayer's Folly
An Outcast of the Islands
Youth
Heart of Darkness
The Secret Agent
The Shadow of Line
Suspense-A Napoleonic Novel

Arnold Bennett (1867-1931)

The Old Wives' Tale
Clayhanger
Riceyman Steps
Buried Alive
Hilda Lessways
These Twain
Sacred and Profane Love
The Pretty Lady
The Love Match
The Author's Craft

Walter de la Mare (1873-1956)

Peacock Pie
Memoirs of a Midget
Songs of Childhood
Bells and Grass
The Traveller
Early the Morning
Love

T.S. Eliot (1888-1965)

The Waste Land
Prufrock and Other Observations
Gerontion
The Hollow Men
Ash Wednesday
Four Quartets
Sweeney Agonistes
Murder in the Cathedral
The Rock
The Family Reunion
The Cocktail Party
The Confidential Clerk
The Sacred Wood
After Strange Gods
The Elder Statesman
The Idea of a Christian Society
What is a Classic?
For Lancelot Andrews
The Use of Poetry and the Use of Criticism
Elizabethan Essays
Points of View

Virginia Woolf (1882-1941)

The Voyage Out
Jacob's Room
Mrs. Dalloway
To The Light House
The Waves
Flush
Orlando : A Biography
The Common Reader
Roger Fry
The Death of the Moth
Mr. Bennett and Mrs. Brown

A Room of One's Own
Between the Acts (Unfinished)

E.M. Forster (1879-1970)
Abinger Harvest
Two Cheers for Democracy
A Passage to India
Howard's End
The Hill of Devi
The Celestial Omnibus
Collected Short Stories
Where Angels Fear to Tread
The Longest Journey
The Story of the Siren
A Room with a View
The Eternal Moment

James Joyce (1882-1941)
Ulysses
Portrait of the Artist as a Young Man
Finnegans Wake
Dubliners

D.H. Lawrence (1885-1930)
Sons and Lovers
Woman in Love
Lady Chatterly's Lover
The Rainbow
The White Peacock
Kangaroo
The Plumed Serpent

Aldous Huxley (1894-1963)
Point Counter Point
The Burning Wheel
Those Barren Leaves
Brave New World
After Many a Summer
Eyeless in Gaza
Antic Hay
Time Must Have a Stop
Crome Yellow
The Defeat of Youth
The Perennial Philosophy
The Devils of Loudun

George Orwell (1903-1950)
The Animal Farm
The Road to Wigan Pier
Nineteen Eighty-Four
Burmese Days
Keep the Aspidistra Flying

Oscar Wilde (1854-1900)
The Sphinx
The Ballad of Reeding Gaol
The Canterville Ghost
De Profundis
The Duchess of Padua
The Importance of Being Earnest
An Ideal Husband
Lady Windermere's Fan
Salome
The Picture of Dorian Gray
The Happy Prince and the Other Tales

Harold Pinter (1930-2008)
The Birthday Party
The Dumb Waiter
The Care Taker
A Night Out
The Home Coming
Old Times
Silence

Indian Writing in English

ANAND, MULKRAJ (1905-2004)

He was greatly influenced by Premchand on the one hand and Tagore on the other.

Works

Some of his famous novels are :

1. The Village (1939)
2. Across the Black waters (1940)
3. The Sword and the sickle (1942)
4. Untouchable (1933) (his first novel)
5. Seven summers (1951)
6. Private Life of an Indian Prince (1953)
7. The Big Heart (1945)
8. Coolie (1936) (It was recast in seventies)
9. Two Leaves and a Bud (1937)
10. The Old Woman and the Cow (1960)
11. The Road (1961)
12. Death of a Hero (1963)
13. Confession of a Lover (1976)
14. Morning Face (1968)

AUROBINDO, GHOSE (1872-1950)

- He was known as the "firebrand" of India.
- He was a poet, a saint, a philosopher, statesman, yogi and a prophet.
- He is one of the pre-Independence Titanic trio of Indian poets—Tagore, Aurobindo and Sarojini Naidu.
- He is chiefly known for his
  - *(i)* Savitri (1953) a poetic epic on a grand scale.
  - *(ii)* The Life Divine (1939-40)
  - *(iii)* Essays on Gita
- He is a great exponent and proponent of ancient Indian thought.
- According to R. K. Singh, "Aurobindo is sympathetic to the modernist trends in writing and study of poetry and, in fact, himself adopts some of the methods followed by the modern poets."
- To quote Mr. Singh again, "In Aurobindo's literary order, poetry is a means of spiritual expression that helps to open the consciousness..."

CHATTERJEE, BANKIM CHANDRA (1838-94)

- He is generally called 'The Father of Bengali fiction.'
- Today he is most known for his patriotic bent of mind.
- In all he wrote 14 novels.
  - *(i)* Some of them are historical.
  - *(ii)* Others are social.
  - *(iii)* Still others are philosophical with stress on renunciation and non-attachment.
- Some of his novels are :
  - *(i)* *The Poison Tree (1884):* It is a story of Hindu life in Bengal of the period
  - *(ii)* Kapalkundala (1885)
  - *(iii)* Durgeshnandini (1890)
  - *(iv)* Krishnakanta's Will (1895)
  - *(v)* The Two Rings (1897)
  - *(vi)* Rajmohan's Wife (1904) (published posthumously)
  - *(vii)* Anand Math (1884)

CHAUDHURI, NIRAD, C. (1897-1999)

- He came into limelight with the publication of his "The Autobiography of an Unknown Indian." (1951).
- His other important works are:
  - *(i)* A Passage to India (1959)
  - *(ii)* Continent of Circe (1966)
    (He received the Duff Cooper Memorial Prize).
  - *(iii)* The Intellectual in India (1967)
  - *(iv)* To Live or Not to Live (1970)
- He is known for his most correct and chaste prose for which he has earned much acclaim from the scholars and critics, including Khushwant Singh.

DESAI, ANITA (Born-1937)

- She is a renowned novelist and short story writer.
- Some of her famous novels are :
  - *(i)* Cry, the Peacock (1963)
  - *(ii)* Voices in the City (1965)
  - *(iii)* Bye-Bye, Blackbird (1971)
  - *(iv)* Fire on the Mountain (1977)
  - *(v)* Clear Light of Day (1980)
- Her collection of short stories is captioned "Games at Twilight" (1978)

GANDHI, M.K. (1869-1948)

1. His famous work in English is "My Experiments with Truth."
2. The work is an important autobiographical writing which is held in high esteem for its truthfulness, frankness, simplicity and directness of expression in non-ornamental effective English.

MARKANDAYA, KAMALA (1924-2004)

1. She is one of the modern novelists and is known for her:
   - *(i)* Nectar in a Sieve (her first novel) (It is a novel on miserable rural life).
   - *(ii)* Some Inner Fury (1955)
     (It is a novel of violence and destruction)
   - *(iii)* A Silence of Desire (1960)
     (It is a novel urging the readers to speak out frankly to unburden their hearts).
   - *(iv)* Possession (1963)
     (The problem of possession is discussed in this novel).
   - *(v)* A Handful of Rice (1966)
     (It depicts the life of the poor classes in Madras).
   - *(vi)* The Coffer Danus (1969)
   - *(vii)* The Nowhere Man (1972)
   - *(viii)* Two Virgins (1973)
   - *(ix)* The Golden Honeycomb (1977)
   - *(x)* Pleasure City (1982).

KHUSHWANT SINGH (Born-1915)

- He is known for his novels :
  - *(i)* Train to Pakistan (his masterpiece)
  - *(ii)* I Shall Not Hear the Nightingale (1959). (It describes the social life of a Sikh family during the pre-Independence period).
- "The Mark of Vishnu" is another of his well-known works.
- Some of his known stories
  - *(a)* Karma
  - *(b)* When Sikh Meets Sikh
  - *(c)* The Rape, etc.
- He is also known for his:
  - *(i)* A History of the Sikhs
  - *(ii)* Translation of Japji Sahib, etc.
- His regular columns appear weekly in some dailies, *e.g.* :
  - *(i)* 'With Malice Towards One And All'—The Hindustan Times.
  - *(ii)* 'This Above All'—The Tribune.
- Mulk Raj Anand is stated to have said that Khushwant Singh's "Train to Pakistan" is likely to last, while about his other creative literary work, one may have some doubts.
- Among his latest work is "Truth, Love and Little Malice."

MULLER, MAX (1823-1900)

- He was a famous Indologist, German orientalist and linguist, who unearthed a lot of ancient Indian history and Sanskrit scriptures, the Rig Veda, in particular, of which he published six colossal volumes, for which he had got an assignment from the East India Company in 1847.
- Actually he was a student of Sanskrit, who started comparative study of languages and "Avesta" (in 1845) which is the renowned sacred book of the Zoroastrians.
- He gave seven lectures on Indian and ancient Indian philosophy at Cambridge University, which have now been published by Rupa & Co. under the caption: "India: What Can it Teach Us?"
- He distinguishes the highest wisdom of Greece and India by using the terms "to know ourselves" and "to know our self", respectively.
- Muller makes very appreciative comments on the Rig Veda and the Vedic Religion.

NAIDU, SAROJINI (1879-1949)

- She is a well-known Indian English poet who started writing poetry at a very early age and she was inspired by Edmund Gosse to choose Indian themes and scenery rather than imitating the English classics.
- She is now known as 'The Nightingale of India.'
- She took a keen interest in India's struggle for freedom.

  Some of her works are :
  1. The Golden Threshold (1905)
  2. The Bird of Time (1912)
  3. The Broken Wing (1917)
  4. The Sceptred Flute (1946)
  5. The Feather of the Dawn (1961) (It appeared posthumously)

  Some of her famous poems are :
  1. The Queen's Rival
  2. Palanquin Bearers
  3. To My Fairy Fancies
  4. The Pardah Nashin
  5. Awake
  6. Village Song
  7. The Soul's Prayer
  8. Fishermen of Coromondel
  9. It You Call Me
  10. Caprice
  11. Summer Woods
  12. Songs of Radha
  13. The Bird Sanctuary, etc.

NANDY, PRITISH (Born-1951)

- He was the editor of the 'Illustrated Weekly of India' and has now Telecast a T.V. serial over the Doordarshan: "Hungama Unlimited."
  - *(i)* He is a prolific poet, though he is still not considered one of the best.
  - *(ii)* Most of his poetry has been dismissed by critics as mere experimental gimmickry. Such was Saleem Peeradina.
  - *(iii)* Even Nissim Ezekiel dubbed him to be a poetaster.
- Some of his works are :
  - *(i)* Gods and Olives (1967)
  - *(ii)* On Either Side of Arrogance (1968)
  - *(iii)* From the Outer Bank of the Brahmputra (1969)
  - *(iv)* Riding the Midnight River (1975)
  - *(v)* In secret Anarchy (1979), etc.
- He has written a number of anthologies and translated a number of poets including Agyeya, Amrita Pritam, Kaifi Azmi etc.
- He has also written some short stories and a verse play.

NARAYAN, R.K. (1906-2001)

- Of the three great novelists, Narayan, Anand and Rao, it is Narayan who has won the maximum accolade both in India and abroad.
- One of his great achievements is his creation of the famous town of Malgudi like Hardy's Wessex.
- Narayan is the true master of humour, irony, realism, romance and artistry.
- Most of his novels and stories depict the life of people of South India.
- It is sometimes held that Narayan lacks true pathos, genuine depth of feeling, realistic description of poverty and misery, the elements which go in for making a novelist a great one.
- However, he has earned much popularity as a novelist, and within the range of his own art, he cannot be taken except with due regard and attention.

Some of his famous novels are :

1. Swami and Friends (1935)
2. Bachelor of Arts
3. The English Teacher
4. The Financial Expert
5. Mr. Sampath (1949)
6. The Guide (1958)
7. The Man-eater of Malgudi
8. The Dark Room (1939)
9. Waiting for the Mahatma
10. The Vendor of Sweets
11. The Painter of Signs (1976)

(He won the Sahitya Akademi Award for 'Guide' in 1961)

R.K. NARAYAN (as a short story writer)

- Some of his stories have appeared in the following collections:
  - *(i)* Malgudi Days
  - *(ii)* Dodu and Other Stories
  - *(iii)* Cyclone and Other Stories
  - *(iv)* Gods, Demons and Others

Narayan has written a few hundred stories, most of them quite interesting and highly readable:

Some of his famous short stories are :

1. The Golden
2. A Career
3. The Snake Song
4. Man Hunt
5. A Willing Slave
6. An Astrologer's Day
7. The Doctor's word
8. God of Troubles, etc.

NEHRU, JAWAHARLAL (1889-1964)

- He needs no introduction as a freedom fighter, statesman and first Prime Minister of India.
- Some of his literary works are :
  - *(i)* An Autobiography (1936)
  - *(ii)* Glimpses of World History (1939)
  - *(iii)* Discovery of India (1946)
- Children enjoy reading his "Letters from Father to His Daughter."
- He is known for his simple, chaste, poetic English which is a model of natural style.

PRITAM, AMRITA (1919-2005)

- She is the most famous Punjabi Author.
- She won the Jnanpith Award for her "Kagaj Te Kenvas" in 1981.
- Her best known autobiographical work which appeared in the seventies is "Rasidi Ticket."
- *(i)* Her "Shadows of words : An Auto-biography" (a transcreation of the Hindi original by Jyoti Sabharwal) has been published by Macmillan in 2002.

  (ii) The book presents "an inner journey down the memory lane" presented by the author, who considers old age the best part of her life, like the last sips of tea, which are "usually the sweetest."

RADHAKRISHAN, SARVAPALLI (1888-1975)

- He is known as an outstanding educationist and a philosopher who presented the Hindu/Indian viewpoint to the world.
- His works include
  - *(i)* An Idealist View of Life (Lectures)
  - *(ii)* Indian Philosophy (1923,1927)
  - *(iii)* The Hindu View of Life (1932)
  - *(iv)* An Idealist View of Life (1932)
  - *(v)* Eastern Religious and Western Thought (1939)
- He wrote in a very simple, intelligible prose-style.

RAO, RAJA (1908-2006)

- His famous works are:
  - *(i)* The Serpent and the Rope (1960)
  - *(ii)* Kanthapura (1938)
  - *(iii)* The Cat and Shakespeare (1965-66)
- *(i)* He was awarded the Sahitya Akademi Award for his 'The Serpent and the Rope' in 1964.

  (ii) He was also decorated with Padma Bhushan in 1969.

Raja Rao as a short story writer

- He is also a well-known short story writer.
- His first collection of short stories was "Jauni" which was published in France in 1930.
- The collection: "The Cow of the Barricades" was published in 1947

Some of his famous short stories are :

1. Akkayya
2. The Little Gram-shop
3. Kanaka Pal
4. Narsiga

ROY, ARUNDHATI (Born-1961)

She made her debut with her novel: "The God of Small Things" which won her the Booker Prize in 1997, besides a handful amount running into crores as royalty for less than four hundred pages which comprise the said novel.

DE, SHOBHA (Born-1948)

- She is a renowned contemporary Indian English novelist and T.V. serial script writer.
- Some of her novels are prescribed in universities in England and Australias.
- Her T.V. serial "Swabhiman" which ran into numerous episodes was telecast over the Doordarshan.
- *(i)* She has become even more popular with her serial "Kittie Party" telecast over the Zee T.V.

  (ii) According to the Tribune, it "is a clever insight into the mind of today's urban Indian women poised at the crossroads of modernity and tradition."

TAGORE, RABINDRANATH (1861-1941)

Tagore was a versatile genius. He was a :

(i) poet
(ii) novelist
(iii) short story writer
(iv) dramatist
(v) musician
(vi) actor (in dramas)
(vii) painter
(viii) statesman and a host of other things.

Some of his famous novels are :

1. The House and the World (1919)
2. The Wreck (1921)
3. Gora (1923)

VIVEKANANDA, SWAMI (1863-1902)

He is a well-known Indian seer, prophet, recluse preacher, lecturer and poet, who:

(i) made the ancient Indian philosophy known to the whole world at the Parliament of Religious in Chicago, USA.

(ii) Brought about a wave of resurgence among the Indian masses through his stirring spiritually inspired speeches which were also full of:

(a) patriotic fervour
(b) love for universal brotherhood.
(c) spirit of social uplight, etc.

Glossary of Literary Terms

Abridged edition

Condensed or shortened version of a work.

Absence

1. It is a modern term which is used to explain a work of art on the basis of aspects which are absent rather than those which are manifestly present in the work.

Acronym

1. A word formed from the initial letters of other words, *e.g.*

   NOIDA for New Okhla Industrial Development Authority.
2. The word may be considered synonymous to 'acrostic'.

Acrostic

1. It is a form of literary exercise in which the first letters of each line in a poem form a word as we read downwards.
2. Here are two Acrostics by H.S. Bhatia :

   (i) "Wait, O little child, wait!
   In the wind lies thy message,
   Not in the hubbub of the worldly;
   Else you may repent, says the sage."
   (The word formed is "WINE"

Act

Major division in a dramatic work.

Adage

Maxim or proverb.

Addendum

Addition or appendix to a book.

Aesthetic Realism

1. *(i)* According to Hudson, "Esther Waters" by George Moore was a landmark in this movement toward aesthetic realism.
   (ii) This movement was the vehicle of the new realists of which Moore and Gossing were representatives.
   (iii) According to Hudson, "they mistook mere ugliness for frankness and "seeing life steadily and seeing it whole."

Alexandrine

1. It is a line of six iambic feet instead of five.
2. It is not known for certain how this line originated.
3. It appears that it was evolved by Spenser by adding the Alexandrine to the eight-line stave (a b a b b c b c) of Chaucer that he used in the Monkeys Tale.

Alienation Effect

It was a term devised by the famous German playwright, Bartolt Brecht, who wanted to bring home the need, for realization of a kind of 'alienation' of the audience and the actors from the stage during the performance of a play, as the play being a play and not a part of real life.

Allegory

1. When the abstract or spiritual ideas are presented through living images, the result is the allegory.

Examples of Allegorical Works

1. The Pilgrim Progress
2. The Scarlet Letter
3. The Faery Queene
4. Morality Plays, such as "Everyman".
5. Seven Deadly Sins in Dr. Faustus, etc.

Alliteration

1. It signifies the repetition of initial consonant sounds, *e.g.*

   The furrow followed free.

Almanac

Book or table comprising a calendar of days, weeks and months indicating special occasions or events.

Anagnorisis

It means Discovery or Reversal in a Tragedy.

Anagram

Letters or word or phrase which, when re-arranged, form a new word.

Anapaest

It comprises two unaccented syllables followed by an accented one:

(i) Redeploy

(ii) Introduce

(iii) Camouflage

Androcentrism

The term implies the predominance of man in all social and intellectual activities.

Anecdote

Brief account or story about an individual.

'Angry Young Men'

It was a movement which came into existence in the second half of the twentieth century, mainly as a result of Osborn's play: "Look Back In Anger."

Annotation

Textual comment on a book.

Anthology

Collection of poetry or prose from diverse sources.

Anticipated Future

See 'Prosopopaeia'

Antithesis

1. It signifies the setting of one thing against another, often of opposite sense *e.g.*

   'A *friend never* betrays, an *enemy always* does.
2. 'Antithesis' can be expressed in literature also by presenting two aspects (of life) side by side, *e.g.* the real and the marvellous.

Aphorism

Short statement of a truth or dogma couched in memorable terms.

Apostrophe

It implies an exclamatory address to a person. (usually a dead one), some inanimate object or an abstract idea, *e.g.*

"Milton! thou shouldst be living with us at this hour..."

Archaism

It is a word or phrase which is no longer in use, *e.g.* loon, quoth, yclept, eftsoon(s), etc.

Archetypal Approach to Criticism

1. This Approach is also called Mythological, Ritualistic or Totemic Approach.
2. It endeavours to study literature on the basis of myth.

Areopagitica

This is the name of Milton's famous prose pamphlet, pleading for freedom, freedom of the press, in particular.

Argot

Slang or coarse vernacular language.

Aside

1. It is a kind of device similar to "soliloquy" (being probably comparatively brief) when a character speaks to himself.
2. The best example of an "aside" may be Shylock's words : "How like a fawning publican he looks" in Act, I sc. 3 of The Merchant of Venice.

Assonance

Unlike the alliteration (which signifies the repetition of consonant sounds), it signifies the repetition of vowel sounds, *e.g.*

1. I *hear* him *bear* the mark of a *seer* on his head.

Autobiography

An account of a person's life by himself or herself.

Avant-garde

Without going into historical aspects of the word, one can say that it implies those (persons) who support or create the newest ideas, fashions (generally literary or artistic), techniques, styles, etc. in an art, piece of literature, etc.

Ballad

1. Broadly-speaking, there are two kinds of ballads:
   (i) Traditional Ballads such as those pertaining to Robin Hood, Chevy Chase, etc.
   (ii) Modern Ballads, such as The Rime of Ancient Mariner, etc.

Bathos

1. It is a term to denote anticlimax.
2. It is generally used when there is sudden descent or fall from the sublime to the trite or ridiculous, *e.g.*

   Delay not thine departure hence,

   For thou mightst have a hot pudding, Awaiting thee.

Belles lettres

Essays on literary studies and the aesthetics of literature.

Bibliography

List of works on a particular subject or author.

Biography

An account of a person's life.

Blank verse

Poetry with unrhymed line endings (usually written in iambic pentameters).

Blurb

These are the words of praise or description of a book in a nutshell, inserted usually by the publisher on the cover page or jacket of the book, to attract the reader's eye.

Bound verse

Verse based on metrical pattern.

Burlesque

It is a way of writing which generates irony, humour and satire, *e.g.* Cervantes' Don Quixote, Samuel Butler's Hudibras, etc.

Bowdlerize

To 'cleanse' a work by omitting or cutting out indecent passages, phrases or words.

Cacophony

When the excessive use of high sounding words is made such that the meaning is lost or diminished in value in the sound, the result is cacophony instead of euphony.

Cadence

Rhythm and phrasing of language.

Caesura

1. In classical prosody, 'Caesura' means "break between words within a metrical foot." (Concise Oxford).
2. In English prosody, it means "pause about middle of line." (ibid.).
3. A Caesura "which does not immediately follow the ictus" is known as 'Feminine Caesura" (Chambers 20th century).

   (**Note :** In modern connotation, Caesura implies natural pause in a line of verse and not an unnatural or forced one)

Canon

Collection of works established as genuine.

Canto

Division of an epic or narrative poem.

Caption

Short description accompanying an illustration.

Caricature

The chief characteristics of characters are sometimes so exaggerated by the author that the characters look like some humorous or even funny creatures. The result is the creation of caricatures. This is what Dickens (more than any other author) has done.

Catalogue

List of books or works.

Catastrophe

1. It signifies the complete (often sudden) devastation of the fortunes of a character (often the hero and/or the heroine) in a play or piece of fiction.

Catharsis

This is the term used for the ousting of the emotions of pity and fear in the tragedy.

Chronicle Plays

1. These are the plays based on (English) History.
2. Such plays became very popular among the people in the sixteenth century.
3. These plays contain almost every important character, real or legendary, in the period of the times concerned.

Cipher

Writing that employs sub-stitution or transposition of letters.

Classic

(i) A classic (in reality, any book) is "the expression of man" as an individual.

(ii) It is also the expression of his mindset and the stance taken by him.

Cliche

Any word, phrase or expression that has lost its real effect for having been too frequently used by authors or laymen is called a cliche which may otherwise be quite lovable, *e.g.*

(i) The news is too good to be true.

(ii) The sorrow was too deep for tears.

(iii) Thanking you in anticipation, etc.

Climax

1. It is the main point of interest in a play or novel which is reached usually in the third act (or sometimes 4th of a 5 act of a play) or towards the end.
2. The resolution often takes place after the Climax or the forces for it start working or increase their intensity after it.

Colloquial

1. In speech, we sometimes make use of certain words and phrases which are not acceptable in standard speech
2. Such colloquial expressions should be avoided in all formal speech or writing.

Colonialism

1. The term differs from 'colonization' as the term may imply political or economic control of policies in a political unit without real annexation of land.

Colonisation

Literarily, the most significant modernist theories in the matter of

(i) colonisation

(ii) post colonisation

(iii) decolonisation, and

(iv) neo-colonisation have been provided and practised by—

(a) Ngugiwa Thiong'o

(b) Soyinka

(c) Achebe Chinua, etc.

Comedy

Humorous dramatic piece; *high comedy* has welldrawn characterization and witty dialogue; *low comedy*, or *slapstick* has absurd situations and boisterous action; *farce* is exaggerated comedy; *tragi-comedy* is a blend of the tragic and comic; *satire* uses sarcasm and wit to ridicule people's follies and vices (originally in verse).

Comic Relief

1. It is the name given to the brief light or comic dramatic action within the performance of a regular serious play to bring about a relief to the spectators to regain their real selves, for a short while to relax their strained nerves and prepare for further action, often more serious and culminating into breath-taking, gasping climax before denouement.

Conceit

1. A conceit is a far-fetched or highly complex and even obscure or unintelligible comparison between two, often dissimilar, persons or objects.
2. It was commonly used by the Elizabethans particularly the Metaphysical poets, especially Donne.

Concordance

Alphabetical index of words in a work, or works by a single author.

Confidant/Confidante

1. In a play when a character takes upon himself/herself the task of some secret or information characteristic about a character to another, the character indulging in such an activity is known as a "confidant" (mas.) or "confidante" (fem.)
2. Such information or secret is generally in the matter of love.
3. A good example of a 'confidante' is Nerissa in the Merchant of Venice.

Connotation

1. It signifies the suggested or implied meaning of word as against the transparent or literary meaning.
2. Connotative devices are brought into play by the artists, poets in particular to enhance pleasure and acceptability conveyed by words and other expressions.
3. Poets like Keats and T.S. Eliot frequently resort to the device of suggestiveness which is akin to connotation.

Consummation

1. When a work achieves complete satisfaction on all counts-literary as well as artistic, it is consummation that results.
2. An artist who has the knack, calibre or skill to make this achievement, is a consummate artist.

Copyright

Protective law to prevent pirating or plagiarism of an author's work.

Couplet

Two successive rhyming lines in poetry.

Court Comedy

1. It is opposed to the Domestic Comedy in the sense that instead of domestic scenes it contains other elements which attract a different kind of audience, *e.g.*
   (i) endless play of words
   (ii) elaborate dialogues
   (iii) repartees, jests, retorts, etc.

Cycle

Group of works united by an overall theme.

Dactyl

1. Dactyl means one accented syllable followed by two unaccented ones, e.g.
   (i) Lazily
   (ii) Separate
   (iii) Unspoken.

Decayed (or Constant) Metaphor

See Metaphor

Deism

1. A "deist" is a theist who believes in the existence of God but rejects the idea of a revealed religion.

Denouement

1. It is the final resolution of the problem in a piece of dramatic performance.
2. The best document comes about when it arises naturally out of the action of the play and not through the 'Deus ex machina'.

Detonation

When a word refers to its literal meaning independent of the meaning which the author may intend to convey, it is the device of "Detonation" which is at play.

Diabolus Ex Machina

1. The term literally means "devil out of the machine".
2. When all of a sudden a person or an event spoils the whole good game, causing unmitigated misery, it is the work of "Diabolus Ex Machina".
3. Thus, the term signifies sudden, unexpected turn of events for a plightful situation.

Dialect

Manner of speaking pertaining to a particular class or geographical region.

Dialectic

1. It was used originally to refer to the nature of a logical argument.
2. Later, it began to be linked to Kant, Hegel and Marx in varying forms.
3. The three generally accepted aspects of 'dialectic' are:
   (i) Thesis: It is akin to the (original) idea.
   (ii) Antithesis: It implies the inherent opposition in the thesis, which may operate after some time.
   (iii) Synthesis: It implies the resolution of the conflict to evolve a higher (or final) truth.

Dialogue

1. Dialogue is something very important in any poetic or prose play or a piece of prose fictions.
2. *(i)* The nature of the dialogue, including its language depends upon the kind of the play—a tragedy, comedy, romance, etc. or the kind of the scene prevailing there at the time and place of the dialogue.

(ii) Much also depends upon the taste of the spectators or audience which again is related to the spirit of the age :

A Dialogical Novel

1. It is a kind of novel in which a number of voices, interactive in the scheme, operate in work, resulting in a kind of dialogue (or series of dialogues) as against the Monologic Presentation.

Diary

Sequential private record of personal and other events kept by an individual.

Diction

1. It refers to the selection, arrangement and order of words.
2. The term which has become more popular in literary world is "Poetic Diction" to which a lot of space has been devoted by Wordsworth in his "Preface to Lyrical Ballads."

Dictionary

Book containing the words of a language, and their definitions, alphabetically; two-language dictionaries contain the corresponding words of both languages and their meanings, also alphabetically; any book that gives words and phrases about a particular subject, arranged alphabetically.

Didactic

A work is didactic in nature when it undertakes to teach a moral, *e.g.* much of Wordsworth's poetry.

Digest

Publication where works are abridged.

Digression

1. When a writer, instead of carrying on the main plot or incident, starts indulging in a side story, dialogue or descriptive narration, it is digression that results.
2. Digression gives extraneous pleasure which is not inherent in or indispensable to the main story.
3. Digression can sometimes enhance the value of a work but more often it mars its spirit.

Documentary

Form of fiction or drama based on documentary evidence provided by newspapers, recent historical reports or other contemporary or recent factual evidence.

Doggerel

Rough, ill-constructed verse.

Domestic Comedy

1. One of the earliest examples of the Domestic Comedies is "Gammer Gurton's Needle" (Cir. 1562)
2. It presents realistic life of the peasant class of its times.
3. It is full of fun and coarse humour.

Double entendre

Ambiguity in a word or expression, one of whose meanings is usually bawdy or frivolous.

Drama

Work to be performed on a stage by actors.

Dramatic Irony

It is a device occurring in a drama when a character on the stage is unaware of a fact which the audience know and understand.

Dramatic Monologue

1. It is a kind of drama or piece of dramatic poetry in which only one character speaks out throughout the performance and script.

Dramatis Personae

Characters in a play.

Duologue

Conversation between two characters in a play, story or poem.

Edition

Total number of copies of a book printed from unchanged set of type.

Electicism

The term implies the gleaning of facts or ideas from different sources instead of depending on just one source (or a few sources).

Elegy

Serious meditative poem; often lamenting death.

Empathy

In a play or novel, when the reader or spectator begins to feel like the hero/heroine or some particular character as if he/she were that character, it is "empathy" which is at play.

Empiricism

Empiricism implies the importance of experiment and experience in the matter of gaining knowledge,

Encyclopedia

Comprehensive work encompassing and describing many aspects of knowledge; specialist work covering comprehensively a subject or discipline.

Epic

Long narrative poem incorporating myth, legend, folklore and history, about the deeds of heroes, warriors, important people; a grandiose treatment of an individual's or nation's story.

Epic Style

1. It is a style which is dignified and exalted (as grand style is), as:
   (i) Paradise Lost by Milton
   (ii) Aeneid by Virgil
   (iii) Iliad by Homer
   (iv) Hyperion by Keats, etc.
2. Sometimes, it is, also referred to as 'heroic' style.'

Epigram

1. It signifies some brief, witty word, saying or piece of writing.
2. Pope's work, for instance, is a model of "Epigrammatic" style.
3. Bacon's essays are a bundle of Epigrams.

Epilogue

It is the last item in a work of art (as in a drama) which often declares or comments upon the conclusion of the work.

Epistle

Direct address to another person, a 'letter' in the form of verse.

Epitaph

Valediction to dead person or persons; inscription on a tomb or grave.

Epithet

1. It comprises a word or group of words to describe the chief characteristics of a person, *e.g.*
   (i) Alexander the Great
   (ii) The Holy Bible.

Eponymous

Person whose name becomes the title of the work.

Erastianism

1. It implies the doctrine that the state should have supremacy over the church in ecclesiastical matters.
2. Erastianism was one of the doctrines which was vehemently opposed by the followers of the Oxford Movement
3. The doctrine is probably wrongly ascribed to Erastus.

Essay

Short composition, usually in prose, discussing a topic or variety of topics.

Euphemism

1. When an unpleasant expression has to be made in a comparatively pleasant or less harsh way, the mellowed or toned down words which are used express euphemism, *e.g.*
   (i) Instead of saying about a person "He acted foolishly, we can say, "He should have acted more wisely."
   (ii) Instead of saying about a person that he has died, we sometimes say, "God Almighty has called him" or "He has left for his heavenly abode."

Euphony

1. It signifies the pleasant combination of words which create desirable rhythms and tonal effects without interfering with the intended meaning.
2. An excessive use of such devices can lead to tautology or bombasticism and sound superficial or facile.
3. The generally accepted antonym of euphony is "Cacophony".

Euphuism

1. An ornate, floral style of writing popularized by Lyly.

Exposition

It signifies a way of writing where explanations are not withheld or suppressed but manifestly made clear to the reader for immediate response based on clarity.

Fable

A short narrative in prose or verse, often with animals, that points a moral.

Fiction

General term for an imaginative work, usually in prose.

Figure of Speech (or of Rhetoric)

It signifies the unusual use of words to heighten their effect.

First person

Style of novel, etc., in which narrator is a character.

Flashback

1. When a writer while presenting a situation suddenly refers to a past situation or event, it is the device of "flashback" that he exploits.
2. Browning, T.S, Eliot and Stream of consciousness novelists, in particular, take advantage of this device.

Folk tale

Story handed down by word of mouth from generation to generation.

Foot

In poetry, rhythmic unit of two or three syllables.

Foreshadowing

1. It is a device in which the author himself prepares the spectators (or readers) for the catastrophe or some important event which may be on the cards.
2. Such a device checks the readers, etc. from suffering from the malady of disbelief.
3. Shakespeare is probably one of the greatest masters of this device, and it is sometimes believed that one of the main reasons of Shakespeare's grand success was his convincing mastery over the technique of foreshadowing.

Foreword

Short introduction to a work.

Free verse (vers libre)

Poetry free from mechanical restrictions such as metre and rhyme, cadenced according to meaningful stress.

Fustian

It means the use of pompous, ornate, Euphuist or bombastic language.

Gazetteer

Geographical dictionary or index.

Ghost writer

Person who undertakes literary work for another who takes the credit.

Glossary

Alphabetical list of unfamiliar or uncommon words, usually appended to work in which they appear.

Haiku

According to Oxford Dictionary, "A Haiku is a Japanese poem of seventeen syllables, in three lines of five, seven and fine traditionally evoking images of the natural world."

Haplology

"Omission in utterance of a sound resembling a neighbouring sounds (as 'idolatry' for 'idololatry') (ibid.)

Haplography

"The inadvertent writing once of what should have been written twice." (Chambers 20th Century Dictionary)

Heroic Couplet

1. A couplet written in iambic pentametre is known as a 'heroic couplet'.

Heroic verse

1. A poem written in heroic couplets is known as 'heroic verse,' *e.g.* Pope's poems such as:
   (i) Essay Man
   (ii) Essay in Criticism
   (iii) The Rape of the Lock, etc.

Homily

1. It is a term pertaining to a work which instead of laying stress on artistic or aesthetic standards, undertakes to urge the readers on to a high moral life.
2. It is just like a sermon in a church.
3. Such are the most of the poems of Longfellow.

Homograph

1. It implies a word which has the same spelling and pronunciation as another, but is different in meaning and origin from the other, *e.g.* :
   (i) bear (*n*) an animal
   (ii) bear (*v*) (to) tolerate
   (iii) bear (*v*) (to) carry

Homonym

1. *(i)* It is "a word having the same sound and perhaps the same spelling as another, but a different meaning and origin" (Chambers.....)
   (ii) Hence, *Homonymous* means: " having the same name : having different *significations* and origin but the same sound." (ibid.)

Hurd, Bishop

1. He aroused great interest in the Gothic and imaginative literature with his "Letters on Chivalry and Romance" (1762)

Hyperbole

1. It is a figure of speech which expresses an exaggerated statement to heighten the effect of a rhetorical statement, *e.g.*
   (i) O child, may you never die!
   (ii) Child is Father of the Man

Idiom

Form of expression of phrase peculiar to its language and possessing a meaning other than its literal one.

Idolatry

1. It means the worship of an image which is believed to be the abode of a superhuman being.

Idyll

Short pastoral poem conveying mood of happy innocence.

Imagism

School of poetry (early 1900s) concerned with precise language, direct treatment, and freedom of form.

Imperialism

1. It means the state policy for a country (as of England and certain other European countries, in particular during certain periods of history) to expands its area by annexing foreign lands and sub-during the natives.

Impersonality

1. It means that the author himself should not be palpably visible in a piece of literature, in other words, the work should be done on highly objective lines.

Indianism

When an expression is commonly used in India but is not used by the English, it is called an "Indianism," *e.g.*

(i) 'demise' instead of 'death'

(ii) 'bearer' instead of 'waiter'

(iii) 'left for his heavenly abode' instead of 'died,' etc.

Interior Monologue

1. It is a device, as used by James Joyce in Ulysses, to express the thoughts, feelings and emotions of a character on usually more than one levels of consciousness.
2. It is a sort of inner debate which may or may not be conflict in essence.

Interludes

1. Just as Miracles passed into Moralities, the latter gradually passed into Interludes, as the people wanted entertainment along with instruction.

Introduction

Essay stating author's intention to reader.

Inversion

It is the figure of speech (much used by Milton but ridiculed by many modern critics) in which words are presented in their unnatural order, *e.g.*

O God's glory I sing,

And to His Mercy I pray.

Irony

1. It is a device used to convey a meaning which is the opposite of the apparent meaning, *e.g.* What a brave son of India Jai Chand was!

Jingle

Verse or verses with strong rhyme and rhythm.

Journal

Paper, periodical or magazine.

Judicial Criticism

1. It is the kind of criticism which is a sort of judgement on a writer or his work of art.
2. Such kind of best example is Pope's "Essay on Criticism".

Legend

Story about a particular person containing myth and historical fact; explanation of symbols on a map or chart.

Lexicon

Dictionary, especially for Classical and Middle Eastern languages.

Limerick

1. It is a kind of humorous verse written in five jingling lines.
2. The form seems to have derived "from a refrain formerly used, referring to 'Limerick' in Ireland." (Chambers 20th Century Dictionary)

Linguistics

The scientific study of language.

Litotes

1. It is akin to "understatement" which is sometimes used by writers to emphasise the desired meaning, *e.g.* India is not lagging in Information Technology.
2. However, more often it is an "understatement used ironically, especially using a negative to express the category as :

   'I shan't be sorry when it's over' meaning 'I shall be very glad', or 'It was no easy matter' for 'It was very difficult.'"

   (Advanced Learner's Dictionary)

Lyric

Usually short, song-like poem in which the poet expresses personal feelings.

Manuscript

Book or work written by hand.

Maxim

Short statement or even sentence containing a general truth about human conduct and human nature.

Melodrama

1. It was a crude form of drama which appealed to the groundings who were not much interested in the artistic minuteness such as the plot, characterization, etc.
2. They wanted only entertainment through striking scenes and absorbing movement of incidents and situations.

Metaphor

1. It is a kind of simile when a comparison is suggested rather than explicitly stated, such that 'as' or 'like' is not used in such a case, *e.g.*
   (i) Lala Lajpat Rai was the Lion of Punjab.
   (ii) I see a lily on thy face.

Meter

Patterns of stressed and unstressed syllables in verse.

Metonymy

1. It implies the use of the name of some person or thing for another person or thing, *e.g.*
   (i) Have you studied 'Milton'?
   (Milton here means Milton's works).
   (ii) In the 'light' of these remarks:
   ('light' here means in view of....)
   (iii) Sceptre and Crown (i.e. monarchy)
   Must tumble down.

Metre

It may not be possible or even necessary to describe it here in full detail, but we can have a cursory look at the following :

1. *Monometre :* It means a line (or verse) with a single iamb (foot)
2. *Dimetre:* It means a line with two iambs.
3. *Trimetre:* It means a line with three iambs.
4. *Tetrametre:* It means a line with four iambs.
5. *Penta metre:* It means a line with five iambs.
6. *Hexta metre:* It means a line with six iambs.
7. *Hepta metre:* It means a line with seven iambs.

Miracle and Mystery Plays

1. These plays were sponsored by the church and were originally held within the premises of the church, but later, as the number of audience swelled, the boundaries of the church seemed too limited and the plays began of be held outside the church.
2. *(i)* The Miracle plays represented the lives of saints, and later for any biblical theme.
   (ii) The Mystery plays represented scenes from the life of Jesus Christ.

Mock Heroic

When an apparent epic is presented in a light vein, it is known as a "mock heroic" poem piece of fiction, etc., *e.g.*

(i) The Rape of the Lock

Modernism

1. Towards the close of the 20th century, a movement against such modes as realism and naturalism started in all forms of literature and art such as poetry, drama, novel, music, painting, architecture, sculpture, etc. which continued unabated during the first world war period and partly upto the middle of the century.

Modulation

1. Of necessity poetry is musical.
2. As in music, to avoid poetry from falling into "monotony," there is the system of "modulation" which here means, changing the key or tone, to introduce the element of variety to give or enhance pleasure.

Monologue

Single person addressing an audience alone, in drama, verse or prose. *Interior monologue*: unspoken but thought speech in verse or prose.

Moralities or Morality Play

1. They were basically allegories on the same lines as Miracles, or Mysteries but without direct represent of scriptural or Christ-concerned events or personages.
2. In Moralities abstract virtues and vices like Wisdom, Goodness, Justice, Evil, Vice, Greed, Lethargy, Lust, etc. were personified and presented on stage as persons.

Myth

Non-factual story that embodies explanation of how something comes to exist, usually involving supernatural or superhuman creatures.

Narrative

Story or tale in prose or verse.

Narratology

1. It means the study of different forms and structures of a narrative work in the matter of its various syntactical, literary and grammatical frameworks.

Neoclassicism

Movement of late 17th and 18th century reviving classical values in English literature, emphasizing discipline, reason and clarity.

Neologism

Newly-coined word.

New Wave (la Nouvelle Vague)

Movement in literature and cinema originating in France in late 1950s that attempted to eschew fixed values, revealing a character by the way he experienced objects and events, which were often meticulously described.

Nom de plume

Term used to indicate a fictitious name used by a writer to represent his work.

Novel

Extended piece of prose fiction.

Novelette

Long short story of some 15,000 words.

Novella

Prose fiction longer than a short story, shorter than a novel (about 30,000 words), concentrating upon a single event.

Obscurity

1. When a writer's language is not (or not easily) intelligible to the reader, the work concerned is termed as obscure.

Ode

Lyric poem describing an event or feelings about a person, object or event. *Pindaric Ode* (Greece) written for choral recitation in units of three stanzas; *Horatian Ode* (Rome) consisted of succession of stanzas following pattern of first one.

Omniscient Author

It is a device used by some outstanding modern novelists to move freely from the objective narrative to the internal or subjective psyche of a character or characters and then comment freely and apparently unattached on the significance, possibility or outcome of any or some events.

Onomatopoeia

When the very sound (pronunciation) of a word conveys the sense of the object producing such sound, the use of onomatopoeia becomes clear *e.g.,*

(i) The *lashing* of waves on the sea-shore

(ii) The *rustle* of leaves

(iii) The *hissing* of the snake

(iv) The *jungle* of coins

(v) The *clanging* of arms.

Oxymoron

1. It is a figure of speech in which two apparently contradictory words or terms are used to convey, a paradoxical sense, e.g.
   (i) 'busy-idle days' (Lamb in Dream children)
   (ii) Life in Death (Coleridge in 'Rime.....').

Pantomime

1. Pantomimes became popular in England particularly in the first quarter of the 18th century.
2. A Pantomime is a dramatic representation pertaining to some myth, legend or traditional tale (or it may have some fairy element in it).

Parable

A story which conveys a moral lesson is known as a parable, as for instance, the biblical parables.

Paradox

It is a figure of speech in which a truth is brought home through the use of self-contradictory statement, *e.g.*

(i) Cowards die many a time before their death.

(ii) Discretion is the better part of valour.

(iii) After death, we awake into an eternal life.

Parallelism

1. It is a rhetorical device where balancing sentences, phrases or words are used to enhance effect, e.g.

   What is important is not what you say, but what is important is what you mean.
2. Excessive use of this device leads to monotony and superficiality.

Parody

Comic imitation of serious words, style, sense, subject of a writer to make them appear ridiculous.

Pastoral

Literature depicting idealized rural life.

Pathetic Fallacy

When nature is shown as sympathising with human lot, the device used is called "pathetic fallacy," *e.g.*

(i) Byron's description of the battle of Waterloo in Childe Harold's Pilgrimage.

(ii) The behaviour of slow-moving nature in Tennyson's "Lotos-eaters".

Pedantry

1. The term refers to the excessive display of knowledge such as:
   (i) Foreign words and phrases

(ii) Allusions
(iii) Archaic words
(iv) high sounding and sesquipedalian words
(v) cataloguing, etc.

when these are not strictly needed within the context of the work.

Periodic Sentence

A sentence in which the Principal clause occurs at the end when it is preceded by one or more subordinate clauses, such that the sense is clear only when the whole sentence is read, is known as a 'periodic sentence'.

Periodical

Magazine or journal published regularly.

Periphrasis

1. It means a round about way of saying a thing, *e.g.* An idle singer of an empty day, etc.
2. The term is close to circumlocution and euphemism in sense and effect.

Personification

1. It is a device where inanimate objects are shown as those having life and behaving likewise, *e.g.*

   "But yonder comes the powerful *king* of day."

   —*Thomson*

Pessimists

Although in English literature, we have a number of pessimist poets or a good number of poets expressing at times pessimistic ideas or writing sometimes in a pessimistic mood, yet two of the poets are known in particular, as "Pessimists." They are:

(i) Thomas Hardy
(ii) A.E. Housman

Philology

Study of literature. language and linguistics.

Picaresque

Chronicle of adventures of a rogue; originated in 16-century Spain.

Plagiarism

Wrongful appropriation and publication of another's work as one's own.

Platitude

It means a truth or generalization which is too well-known mainly because of its overuse, *e.g.*

Truth is evergreen.

Pleonasm

(a) It means the use of words more than those which are absolutely necessary, *e.g.*
   1. He sat *down* on the ground.
   2. He looked up *high* towards the sky.
   3. He has got *sole* monopoly over such kind of business.

(b) In essence, it is akin to Tautology or circumlocution.

Plot

Plan or organization of events and characters in a play, work of fiction or poem as to induce curiosity and suspense in the audience or reader.

Poem

Literary work which may be in rhyme, blank verse or a combination of the two.

Poetic Diction

1. Diction stands chiefly for choice of words.
2. In poetry, poetic diction is unavoidable as mere metre is not enough to make a poem a literary piece of work.
3. In other words, mere versification or combination of words in rhyme or any other verse form does not make poetry.
4. The poets resort to several devices in this regard, some of which are :
   (i) Use of similes, metaphors, symbols, inversions, and other figures of speech as such as hyperbole, irony, antithesis, personification, etc.
   (ii) Omission of some parts of speech or grammatical rules.
   (iii) Use of archaic or uncommon words.
   (iv) Change in order of words, etc.
   (v) Use of picturesque phrases and expressions
   (vi) Use of other ornamental devices such as epithets
   (vii) Use of highly musical lies, fanciful flights etc.

Poetic Justice

1. It means the reward or punishment handed down to the characters at the end of a work of art according to their deeds.

Poetry

Any kind of metrical composition in a literary work.

Pornography

Work in which there is a deliberate emphasis on the sexual behaviour of characters, in order to arouse sexual excitement.

Potboiler

Work written essentially to gain the author a livelihood.

Precis

Concise statement; short summary of a work.

Preface

Introduction to a work.

Prologue

It is often the original statement by the writer (as in a drama) which highlights the chief aim of the work which is going to be unfolded or staged.

Propaganda

Work devoted to the dissemination of an idea or belief, usually biased.

Prose

Writings not in verse.

(Modern) Prose Style

1. The English prose style started by Bacon, flourished in the hands of Addison and Steele and numerous essayists and prose stylists that followed.
2. As a fine example of the latest modern prose style, Naipaul who won the Nobel Prize for Literature in 2001 deserves to be mentionéd.

Prosody

Study of the handling of language in poetry.

Prosopopaeia

1. This figure of speech is used when:
   (i) The past (called the Historic Present) is written in the present tense:
   Sohrab and Rustam clash with their full might.
   (ii) The (anticipated) future is written in the present tense:
   Here, we go to our new house tomorrow with all our belongings carried in a lorry and then tucked in elegant mahogany almirahs.

Pseudonym

Name other than the true one used by an author to represent his work.

Psychological Process

It is the process applied to the study of a piece of literature to penetrate another's mind and to study the activities, utterances, etc. of various characters, as, for instance, to arrive at the exact nature of Hamlet's madness whether there was "method" in it or not.

Pun

1. When a word gives several meanings (often for fun) as in a play, it is the "pun" that is used.
2. Shakespeare is a great master of this device.
3. **Example :**
   (i) This is the *book.*
   (ii) It means
   (a) any book
   (b) a holy book, often the Bible.

Realism

Literature that attempts to depict life objectively and faithfully.

Refrain

Phrase, line or lines repeated at intervals or at the end of a stanza in poetry.

Review

Notice or critical article on musical, artistic or literary work.

Revue

Theatrical entertainment made up of sketches, dances, songs, recitals and improvised pieces, usually humorous, satirical or topical.

Rhetoric

Art of using language, in speaking or writing, to persuade. The persuasive style (rather than the content) of a work.

Rhythm

1. It signifies the measured regular beat or movement of sounded words in language.
2. Rhythm is a must in poetry as well as prose, as it introduces or enhances the element of pleasure, interest and curiosity.

Rhyme

Echoing sound or audible similarity in two or more words, especially at endings. Device used to construct much poetry.

Riddle

Puzzle, question or enigma; conundrum.

Roman a clef

Novel based upon actual people under disguised names.

Romance

Tale of chivalry, originally written in verse (Medieval times); term applied now to any wonderful or mysterious tale far removed from reality.

Romance Languages

1. Languages which have emerged straightaway from Latin and/or Greek, are called Romance Languages.

Romanticism

Movement originating in late 18th century as revolt against neoclassicism, emphasizing imaginative style.

Saga

Lengthy prose work, sometimes in several parts, describing the history and events surrounding medieval kings, warrriors and, recently, fictitious families.

Satire

Any work in which wickedness, folly, vice and corruption in individuals and society is exposed by ridicule and scorn.

Science fiction

Literature based on scientific fact or fantasy, on earth or on other worlds in space, often set in periods in the distant future.

Semantics

Branch of linguistics dealing with meaning, and the change of meaning, in words.

Semiology

General study or science of signs with which humans communicate with each other (including words and their use in every context).

Sermon

Verbal instruction of some length, usually religious.

Short story

Work of fiction usually revolving around single event.

Sic

Included in brackets after a printed word or quoted passage to indicate that it is quoted accurately, however actually incorrect.

Simile

1. When we draw comparison between two persons by using (usually 'like', as-so or as) it is the 'simile' that we make use of, *e.g.*
   (i) As red as a rose
   (ii) As happy as a lark
   (iii) She looked like a violet, half-hidden behind the rock.
2. *An Exaggerated Simile:* It is a simile in which the sense is clearly exaggerated, *e.g.*
   (i) He ran as fast as lightning
   (ii) He has in himself the force as much as there is in ten horses.

Slang

Colourful and vernacular language of the street, marketplace, barrackroorn, workplace, sportsplace and playground.

Soliloquy

Kind of monologue in which a stage character expresses his thoughts and feelings.

Song

Poem or verse set to music.

Sonnet

14-line poem of set rhyme-scheme; Elizabethan (Shakespearean) *ababcdcdefefgg*, Italian *abbaabba cdcdcd* (or *cdecde*).

Stanza

Group of lines of verse in definite pattern, usually repeated in a poem.

Strophe and Anti Strophe

1. Strophe is "the song sung by the chorus (in a Greek play) as it moved towards one side, answered by an exact counterpart." (Chambers 20th Century Dictionary)
2. Anti-Strophe is the term for the Strophe, "as it returned: part of any ode thus answered..." (*ibid.*)

Style

Characteristic manner of expression in prose or verse; the way in which a thing is written by an author.

Stock Material

Material necessary for a writer to write.

Stock Characters

Characters that are commonly found in most of pieces of dramas or fiction.

Stock Situations

Situations which are frequently presented byauthors in their works.

Synthesis, Poetry of

The term "Poetry of Synthesis" is referred to by I.A. Richards, and it has been thus explained by Cleanth Brooks—

"... a poetry which does not leave out what is apparently hostile to its dominant tone, and which, because it is able to fuse the irrelevant and disordant, has come to terms with itself and invulnerable to irony."

Structure

"The structure meant is a structure of meaning, evaluations and interpretations : and the principle of unity which informs it seems to one of balancing and harmonizing connotations, attitudes and meanings."

Tragedy of Blood (And Thunder)

1. It was basically a melodramatic presentation of horrible, gory scenes.
2. The first famous tragedy of this kind is Kyd's "Spanish Tragedy".

Sublimity

1. It is a term which is used to describe inexplicable beauty which is beyond any rules to describe or measure.

Symbolism

French poetic movement of late 19th century that developed as revolt against realism, concentrating on evoking emotions by use of indirect suggestion (symbol and metaphor); flourished in Russia at turn of century as literary movement, and later in British novel.

Synecdoche

1. This figure of speech is used when the understanding of one thing by means of another is employed.
2. This can be done in several ways, some of which are mentioned below :
   (i) When a part stands for a whole or genus, e.g. We have fifty *hands* in our factory. (hands = workers)
   (ii) When a whole or genus stands for a part, e.g. He belongs to a different *world* from yors (world = category, social set-up, economic status, etc.)
   (iii) When an individual represents a class, *e.g.*
   He is the *Nestor* of our village.
   (Nestor = the oldest man)

Syntax

It means :

(i) The way a sentence is constructed
(ii) Arrangement of words in writing (or in speech) according to the rules of grammar
(iii) Rules pertaining to this system or arrangement.

Synonym

A word similar in meaning to another.

Synopsis

Outline of the main points of a work; a summary.

Tale

Spoken or written narrative.

Tautology

Overuse of synonyms or repetition of ideas in sentence.

Theme

Central idea of a work, rather than its subject.

Thesis

Long essay or treatise on a subject, usually expository; work presented to examiners for academic qualification.

Third person

Style of novel, etc., in which narrator is outside action.

Tract

Short printed treatise on religious or political subject.

Tragedy

It is "a drama in which the principal characters are involved in desperate circumstances or led by overwhelming passions. It is invariably serious and dignified. The movement is always stately, but grows more and more rapid as it approaches the climax ; and the end is always calamitous, resulting in death or dire misfortune of the principals."

Tragic Flaw

1. In Shakespeare's tragedies, in particular, we often find a particular flaw in the character of the hero which ultimately leads to the fall of his destiny, along with the fall of his state or estate.

Transferred Epithet

When an epithet is transferred from a person to a thing, it is known as a 'transferred epithet', *e.g.*

(i) It is a *foolish* idea
(ii) Let *happy* days come.

Translation

Rendering of a work into another language.

Treatise

Formal work examining a subject and the principles underlying it.

Trochaic Line Metre

1. A line in verse is known as a *"trochaic" line* when the first, third and other odd syllables in it are accented (as in the 'Iambic metre') irrespective of the length of the line.
2. A poem comprising such lines is known as having been written in the "Trochaic" metre.

Understatement

1. It is practically the opposite of hyperbole and is sometimes used by the writers to emphasise indirectly the desired meaning.

Vade mecum

Manual or handbook carried for frequent reference.

Verisimilitude

It is the likeness of truth presented in a work of art that makes it similar to the characteristics or situation in real life and that enables the readers to accept it ungrudgingly as truth (and may be, sometimes, more than real happening in life).

Vernacular

Domestic or native language.

Versification

Study of how traditional verse is constructed.

Wit

(*i*) Dryden defines (in "Annus Mirabilis") wit as "delightful imagining of persons, actions, passions or things."

Yarn

Story or tale, sometimes improbable and far-fetched.

Literary and Media Knowledge

NOBEL PRIZE FOR LITERATURE 2000–2021

Year	Laureate	Country	Language	Genre(s)
2000	Gao Xingjian	China, France	Chinese	novel, drama, literary criticism
2001	V. S. Naipaul	United Kingdom Trinidad & Tobago	English	novel, essay
2002	Imre Kertesz	Hungary	Hungarian	novel
2003	J. M. Coetzee	South Africa	English	novel, essay, translation
2004	Elfriede Jelinek	Austria	German	novel, drama
2005	Harold Pinter	United Kingdom	English	drama
2006	Orhan Pamuk	Turkey	Turkish	novel, screenplay, essay
2007	Doris Lessing	United Kingdom	English	novel, drama, poetry, short story, memoirs
2008	J. M. G. Le Clezio	France Mauritius	French translation	novel, short story, essay
2009	Herta Muller	Germany Romania	German	novel, poetry
2010	Mario Vargas Llosa	Peru Spain	Spanish drama	novel, short story, essay
2011	Tomas Transtromer	Sweden	Swedish	poetry, translation
2012	Mo Yan	China	Chinese	novel, short story
2013	Alice Munro	Canada	English	short story
2014	Patrick Modiano	France	French	novel
2015	Svetlana Alexievich	Belarus (Born in Ukrainian SSR)	Russian	history, essay
2016	Bob Dylan	United States	English	poetry, songwriting
2017	Kazuo Ishiguro	United Kingdom (born in Japan)	English	novel
2018	Olga Tokarczuk	Poland	Polish	novel

Year	Laureate	Country	Language	Genre(s)
2019	Peter Handke	Austria	German	novel
2020	Louise Gluck	United States	English	poetry
2021	Abdulrazak Gurnah	United Kingdom (born in Tanzania)	English	novel

MAN BOOKER PRIZE (2000–2021)

Year	Winner	Book	Genre	Country
2000	Margaret Atwood	The Blind Assassin	Novel	Canada
2001	Peter Carey	True History of the Kelly Gang	Historical novel	Australia
2002	Yann Martel	Life of Pi	Fantasy novel	Canada
2003	DBC Pierre	Vernon God Little	Novel	Australia, Mexico
2004	Alan Hollinghurst	The Line of Beauty	Historical novel	United Kingdom
2005	John Banville	The Sea	Novel	Ireland
2006	Kiran Desai	The Inheritance of Loss	Novel	India
2007	Anne Enright	The Gathering	Novel	Ireland
2008	Aravind Adiga	The White Tiger	Novel	India
2009	Hilary Mantel	Wolf Hall	Historical novel	United Kingdom
2010	Howard Jacobson	The Finkler Question	Novel	United Kingdom
2011	Julian Barnes	The Sense of an Ending	Novel	United Kingdom
2012	Hilary Mantel	Bring Up the Bodies	Historical novel	United Kingdom
2013	Eleanor Catton	The Luminaries	Historical novel	New Zealand
2014	Richard Flanagan	The Narrow Road to the Deep North	Historical novel	Australia
2015	Marlon James	A Brief History of Seven Killings	Historical/ experimental novel	United Kingdom
2016	Paul Beatty	The Sellout	Satirical novel	United States of America
2017	George Saunders	Lincoln in the Bardo	Historical/ experimental novel	United States of America
2018	Anna Burns	Milkman	Novel	United Kingdom
2019	Margaret Atwood	The Testaments	Novel	United Kingdom
2019	Bernardine Evaristo	Girl, Woman, Other	Experimental Novel	United Kingdom
2020	Douglas Stuart	Shuggie Bain	Novel	United Kingdom & United States
2021	Domon Galgut	The Promise	Novel	South Africa

SAHITYA AKADEMI AWARDS–2021

Name	Language	Name	Language
Anuradha Sarma Pujari	Assamese	Namita Gokhale	English
Bratya Basu	Bengali	Daya Prakash Sinha	Hindi
Mwdai Gahai	Bodo	DS Nagabhushana	Kannada
Raj Rahi	Dogri	Wali Mohd Aseer Kashtawari	Kashmiri

Name	Language	Name	Language
Sanjiv Verenkar	Konkani	Meethesh Nirmohi	Rajasthani
George Onakkoor	Malayalam	Vindeshwariprasad Mishr "Vinay"	Sanskrit
Kiran Gurav	Marathi	Niranjan Hansda	Santali
Chhabilal Upadhyaya	Nepali	Arjun Chawla	Sindhi
Hrushikesh Mallick	Odia	Ambai	Tamil
Khalid Hussain	Punjabi	Gorati Venkanna	Telugu

JNANPITH AWARD WINNERS (2000-2021)

Award Winners	Year	Award Winners	Year
Dr. Indira Goswami (Assamese)	2000	Pratibha Ray (Odiya)	2011
Rajendra Keshav Lal Shah (Gujarati)	2001	Ravuri Bharadhwaja (Telugu)	2012
D. Jayakanthan	2002	Kedarnath Singh (Hindi)	2013
Vinda Karandikar (Marathi)	2003	Bhalchandra Nemade (Marathi)	2014
Rehman Rahi (Kashmiri)	2004	Raghuveer Chaudhari (Gujarati)	2015
Kunwar Narain (Hindi)	2005	Shankha Ghosh (Bengali)	2016
Ravindra Kelekar (Konkani) and Satyavrat Shastri (Sanskrit)	2006	Krishna Sobti (Hindi)	2017
O.N.V. Kurup (Malayalam)	2007	Amitav Ghosh (English)	2018
Akhlaq Khan Shahryar (Urdu)	2008	Akkitham Achuthan Namboothiri (Malayalam)	2019
Amar Kant & Shrilal Shukla (Hindi)	2009	Nilamani Phookan (Assamese)	2020
Chandrasekhar Kambar (Kannada)	2010	Damodar Mauzo (Konkani)	2021

Famous Books and Authors

Book	Author
A Secular Agenda	Arun Shourie
A Suitable Boy	Vikram Seth
Accession of Extinction	D.R. Mankekar
Adam Beda	George Eliot
Adhe Adhure	Mohan Rakesh
Adonis	P.B. Shelley
Adventures of Huckleberry Finn	Mark Twain
Adventures of Sherlock Holmes	Arthur Conan Doyle
Adventures of Tom Sawyer	Mark Twain
Advise and Consent	Allen Drury
Affluent Society	J.K. Galbraith
After the Dark Night	S.M. Ali
Age of Reason	Jean Paul Sartre
Agni Pariksha	Acharya Tulsi
Agni Veena	Kazi Nazrul Islam
The Agony and the Ecstasy	Irving Stone
Ain-i-Akbari	Abul Fazal
Ajat Shatru	Jai Shankar Prasad

Book	Author
Akbarnama	Abul Fazal
Alchemist, The	Ben Jonson
Alice in Wonderland	Lewis Carroll
All is Well that Ends Well	William Shakespeare
All things Bright and Beautiful	James Herroit
Amar Kosh	Amar Singh
Ambassador's Journal	J.K. Galbraith
Ambassador's Report	Chester Bowles
An American Tragedy	Theodore Drieser
An Autobiography	Jawaharlal Nehru
An Eye to China	David Selboume
An Idealist View of Life	Dr. S. Radhakrishnan
An Unknown Indian	Nirad C. Choudhury
Anandmath	Bankim Chandra Chatterjee
Ancient Mariner	Samuel Taylor Coleridge
And Quiet Flows the Don	Mikhail Sholokhov
Androcles and the Lion	George Bernard Shaw
Animal Farm, The	George Orwell

Book	Author
Anna Karenina	Count Leo Tolstoy
Another Life	Derek Walcott
Answer of History	Mohammed Raza Pahlavi
Antony and Cleopatra	William Shakespeare
Ape and Essence	A. Huxley
Apple Cart	George Bernard Shaw
Arabian Nights	Sir Richard Burton
Area of Darkness	V.S. Naipaul
Arms and the Man	George Bernard Shaw
Around the World in Eighty days	Jules Verne
Arrangement, The	Elia Kazan
Arrival and Departure	Arthur Koestler
Arrowsmith	Sinclair Lewis
Arthashastra	Kautilya
As You Like It	William Shakespeare
Ascent of the Everest	Sir John Hunt
Ashtadhyayi	Panini
Asian Drama	Gunnar Myrdal
Asia and Western Dominance	K.M. Panikkar
Atoms of Hope	Mohan Sundara Rajan
August 1914	Alexander Solzhenitsyn
August Coup, The	Mikhail S. Gorbachev
Autumn Leaves	O. Pulla Reddi
Avanti Sundari	Dandi
Babur Nama	Zaheeruddin Mohammed Babur
Babbit	Sinclair Lewis
Back of Methuselah	George Bernard Shaw
Backward Place, A	Ruth P. Jhabwala
Bandicoot Run	Manohar Malgonkar
Bang-i-Dara	Mohammed Iqbal
Bangla Desh The Unfinished Revolution	Lawrence Liftschultz
Banyan Tree, The	Hugh Tinker
Beast and Man	Murry Midgely
Beginning of the Beginning	Acharya Rajneesh
Betrayal of Pearl Harbour	James Rusbridge and Eric Nave
Bend in the Ganges, A	Manohar Malgonkar
Ben Hur	Lewis Wallace
Bermuda Triangle	Charles Berlitz
Berry Patches	Yevgeny Yevtushenko
Best and the Brightest, The	David Halberstan
Between the Lines	Kuldip Nayar
Beyond Modernisation, Beyond Self	Sisir Kumar Ghose
Bharat Bharati	Maithili Sharan Gupta
Bharatiya Parampara Ke Mool Swar	Govind Chandra Pande
Big Breach, The	Richard Tomlinson
Big Fisherman, The	Lloyd C. Douglas

Book	Author
Biopgraphia Literaria	Samuel Taylor Coleridge
Bisarjan	Rabindra Nath Tagore
Birth and Death of Sun	George Gamow
Bitter Sweet	Noel Coward
Black Arrow, The	Robert Louis Stevenson
Blind Ambitions	John Dean
Blind Beauty	Boris Pasternak
Blind Men of Hindustan ! Indo-Pak Nuclear War	General K.S. Sundarji
Bliss was it in that Dawn	Minoo Masani
Bloodline	Sidney Sheldon
Blue Bird	Maurice Macterlink
Bone People, The	Kerl Hulme
Born Free	Joy Adamson
Bread, Beauty and Revolution	Khwaja Ahmed Abbas
Breakthrough	Gen. Moshe Dayan
Bride for the Sahib and other Stories, A	Khushwant Singh
Bride's Book of Beauty, The	Mulk Raj Anand
Broken Wings	Sarojini Naidu
Brothers Karamazhov	Fyodor Dostoevsky
Bubble, The	Mulk Raj Anand
Bhudha Charitam	Ashvaghosha
Bunch of Old Letters, A	Jawaharlal Nehru
Butterfield-8	John O' Hara
By Love Possessed	James Cozzens
Caesar and Cleopatra	George Bernard Shaw
Cancer Ward	Alexander Solzhenitsyn
Candida	George Bernard Shaw
Candide	Voltaire
Canterbury Tales	Geoffery Chaucer
Cardinal, The	Henry M. Robinson
Centennial	James Michener
Chandalika	Rabindra Nath Tagore
Chemmeen	Thakazhi Sivasankar Pillai
Cherry Orchard	Anton Chekov
Chesaplake	James A. Michener
Chidambara	Sumitra Nandan Pant
Chikaveera Rajendra	Masti Venkatesh Iyengar
Children of Gebelawi	Naguib Mahfouz
Childe Herolds Pilgrimage	Lord Byron
China Passage, A	J.K. Galbraith
China's Watergate	Leo Goodstadt
Chinese Betrayal	B.N. Mullick
Chitra	Rabindra Nath Tagore
Chittirappaval	P.V. Akilandam
Chomas Drum	K. Shivaram Karnath
Chronicle of a Death Foretold	Gabrel Garcia Marquez
Class, The	Eric Segal
Climate of Treason	Andrew Boyle

Book	Author
Comedy of Errors	William Shakespeare
Common Sense	Thomas Paine
Comus	John Milton
Communist Manifesto	Karl Marx
Confessions	J.J. Rousseau
Confessions of a Lover	Mulk Raj Anand
Confessions of an Opium Eater, The	Thomas Dequicey
Confidential Clerk	T.S. Eliot
Conquest of Self	M.K. Gandhi
Conservationist, The	Ms. Nadine Gordimer
Continent of Circle	Nirad C. Choudhury
Coolie	Mulk Raj Anand
Coup, The	John Updike
Count of Monte Cristo	Alexander Dumas
Court Dancer	Rabindra Nath Tagore
Covertly Papers	Joseph Addison
Cresent Moon	Rabindra Nath Tagore
Crescent over Kashmir	Anil Maheshwari
Crime and Punishment	Fyodor Dostoevsky
Crisis into Chaos	E..M.S. Namboodiripad
Crisis in India, The	Ronald Segal
Critique of Pure Reason, A	Immanuel Kant
Crown and the Loincloth, The	Chaman Nahal
Crown of Wild Olive, The	John Ruskin
Cry My Beloved Country	Alan Patan
Culture in the Vanity Bag	Nirad C. Choudhury.
Curtain Raisers	K. Natwar Singh
Dangerous Summer, The	Ernest Hemingway
Darkness at Noon	Arthur Keostler
Dark Room, The	R.K. Narayan
Dashkumar Charitam	Dandi
Das Kapital	Karl Marx
Daughter of the East	Benazir Bhutto
David Copperfield	Charles Dickens
Day in Shadow, The	Nayantara Sehgal
Days of His Grace	Eyvind Johnson
Dean's December	Saul Below
Death of a City	Amrita Pritam
Death of a Patriot	R.E. Harrington
Death of a President	William Manchester
Death, The Supreme Friend	Kakasaheb Kalelkar
Debacle	Emile Zola
Decameron	Giovanni Boccaccio
Decline and Fall of the Roman Empire	Edward Gibbon
Decline and Fall of Indira Gandhi	D.R. Mankekar and Kamala Mankekar
Decline of the West	O Spengier
Deewan-i-Ghalib	Mirza Ghalib
Delhi	Khushwant Singh

Book	Author
Democracy Means Bread and Freedom	Piloo Mody
Democracy Redeemed	V.K. Narsimhan
Descent of Man	Charles Darwin
Deserted Village	Oliver Goldsmith
Devdas	Sharat Chandra Chatterjee
Die Blendung	Elias Canetti
Dilemma of our Time	Harold Joseph Laski
Diplomacy in Peace and War	J.N. Kaul
Discovery of India	Jawaharlal Nehru
Distant Drums	Manohar Malgonkar
Distant Neighbours	Kuldip Nayar
Divine Comedy	A. Dante
Divine Life	Swami Sivananda
Doctor's Dilemma	George Bernard Shaw
Dolls's House, A	Ibsen
Don Juan	Lord Byron
Don Quixote	Saavedra Miguel de Cervantes
Double Helix, The	J.D. Watson
Dragon's Teeth	U.B. Sinclair
Dream in Hawaii, A	Bhabani Bhattacharya
Dream of Fair to Middling Women	Samuel Beckett
Dreams Roses and Fire	Eyvind Johnson
Dr. Jekyll and Mr. Hyde	Robert Louis Stevenson
Durgesh Nandini	Bankim Chandra Chatterjee
Dynamics of Social Change	Chandra Shekhar
Earth	Emile Zola
Earth Mother, The	Pupul Jayakar
Economic Planning of India	Ashok Mehta
Economics of the Third World	S.K. Ray
Eduction of Public Man	Hubert Humphery
Eight Lives	Raj Mohan Gandhi
Elegy Written in a Country Church Yard	Thomas Grey
Emile	J.J. Rousseau
Emma	Jane Austen
End of Era	C.S. Pandit
Ends and Means	Aldous Huxley
Envoy to Nehru	Escott Reid
Essays for Poor to the Rich	John Kenneth Galbraith
Essays of Elia	Charles Lamb
Essays on Gita	Sri Aurobindo Ghosh
Eternal Himalayas	Major H.P.S. Ahluwalia
Eternal India	Indira Gandhi
Executioner's Song	Norman Mailer
Expanding Universe	Arthur Stanley Eddington
Eye of the Storm, The	Patric White
Face to Face	Lasse & Mrs. Lisa Berg
Faces of Everest	Maj. H.P.S. Ahluwalia
Facts are Facts	Khan Abdul Wali Khan

Book	Author
Fall of a Sparrow, The	Salim Ali
Family Reunion	T.S. Eliot
Far From the Madding Crowd	Thomas Hardy
Far Pavilions, The	M.M. Kaye
Faraway Music, The	Svetlana Allilueva
Farewell the Trumpets	James Morris
Farewell to Arms, A	Ernest Hemingway
Farm House	George Orwell
Father and Sons	Ivan Turgenev
Faust	J.W. Von Goethe
Fidelio	L. Beethoven
Fifth Horseman, The	Larry Collins and Dominique Lapierre
Final Days, The	Bob Woodward and Carl Bernstein
Finding a Voice-Asian Women in Britain	Amrit Wilson
Fire Next Time, The	James Balbwin
First Circle	Alexander Solzhenitsyn
Flames form the Ashes	P.D. Tandon
Flounder, The	Gunter Grass
Food Nutrition and Poverty in India	V.K.R.V. Rao
For Whom the Bell Tolls	Ernest Hemingway
Forbidden Sea, The	Tar Ali Baig
Forsyte Saga	John Galsworthy
Forty Nine Days	Amrita Pritam
Freedom At Midnight	Larry Collins and Dominique Lapierre
French Revolution	Thomas Carlyle
Friends and Foes	Sheikh Mujibur Rehman
Friends not Masters	Ayyub Khan
From Here to Eternity	James Jones
From India to America	L. S. Chandrashekhar
From Raj to Rajiv	Mark Tully & Zaheer Masani
Ganadevata	Tara Shanker Bando-padhyay
Gandhi and Stalin	Louis Fisher
Gardener	Rabindra Nath Tagore
Gathering Storm	Winston Churchill
Geeta Govinda	Jaya Dev
Ghasiram Kotwal	Vijay Tendulkar
Gita Rahasya	Bal Gangadhar Tilak
Glimpses of World History	Jawaharlal Nehru
Godan	Munshi Prem Chand
Godfather, The	Mario Puzzo
God of Small Things, The	Arundhati Roy
Gold Bat, The	P.G. Wodehouse
Golden Gate	Vikram Seth
Golden Threshold, The	Sarojini Naidu
Gone with the Wind	Margaret Mitchel
Good Earth	Pearl S. Buck

Book	Author
Gora	Rabindra Nath Tagore
Grammar of Politics	Harold Joseph Laski
Grapes of Wrath	John Steinbeck
Great Challenge, The	Louis Fishcer
Great Depression of 1990, The	Ravi Batra
Great Expectations	Charles Dickens
Great Gatsby	F. Scott Fitzgerald
Great Illusion	Norman Angel
Great Tragedy	Z.A. Bhutto
Guide, The	R.K. Narayan
Gulag Archipelago	Alexander Solzhenitsyn
Gul-i-Naghma	Raghupati Sahai (Firaq) Gorakhpuri
Gulistan and Bostan	Sheikh Saadi
Gulliver's Travels	Jonathan Swift
Gurusagaram	O.P. Vijayan
Hamlet	William Shakespeare
Handful of Dust, A	Evelyn Waugh
Harry Potter*	J.K. Rowling
Harsha Charita	Ban Bhatt
Heat and Dust	Ruth P. Jhabwala
Heir Apparent	Dr. Karan Singh
Henderson, the Rain King	Saul Below
Henry Esmond	William Thackeray
Hero of our Times	Richard Hough
Heroes and Hero Worship	Thomas Carlyle
Higher than Hope	Fatima Meer
Himalayan Blunder	Brigadier J.P. Dalvi
Hindu Civilization	J.M. Barrier
Hinduism	Nirad C. Choudhury
Hindu View of Life	Dr. S. Radhakrishnan
Hounds of Baskervilles, The	Arthur Conan Doyle
House Divided	Pearl S. Buck
House for Mr. Biswas, A	V.S. Naipaul
Huckieberry Finn	Mark Twain
Human Factor	Graham Greene
Humboldt's Gift, The	Saul Bellow
Humour	Ben Johnson
Hunchback of Notre Dame	Victor Hugo
Hungary Stones	Rabindra Nath Tagore
I Am Not an Island	K.A. Abbas
I Follow the Mahatma	K.M. Munshi
Idiot, The	Fyodor Dostoevsky
Idols	Sunil Gavaskar
Idylls of the King	Alfred Teennyson
If I am Assassinated	Z.A. Bhutto
Illiad	Homer
Importance of Being Earnest	Oscar Wilde
In Afghanistan's Shadow	Salig S. Harrison
In Evil Hour	Gabriel Garcia Marquez

Book	Author
In a Free State	V.S. Naipaul
In Memorium	Alfred Lord Tennyson
In Search of Gandhi	Richard Attenbrough
In Search of Identity	Anwar-al-Sadat
India A Wounded Civilization	V.S. Naipaul
India Changes	Taya Zinkin
India Discovered	John Keay
India Divided	Rajendra Prasad
India from Curzon to Nehru and After	Durga Das
India Remembered	Percival and Margaret Spear
India of Our Dreams	M.V. Kamath
India, The Critical Years	Kuldip Nayar
India Today	Rajni Palme Dutt
India We Left	Humphry Trevelyan
India Wins Freedom	Maulana Abul Kalam Azad
Indian Home Rule	M.K. Gandhi
Indian Muslims	Mohammed Mujeeb
Indian Muslims The Need For a Positive Outlook	Wahiduddin Khan
Indian Philosophy	Dr. S. Radhakrishnan
Indian War of Independence	V.D. Savarkar
India's China War	Neville Maxwell
India's Priceless Heritage	N.A. Palkhivala
India	Magasthenes
Indira's India	S. Nihal Singh
Indira Gandhi's Emergence and Style	Nayantara Sehgal
Inheritance of Loss, The	Kiran Desai
Inner Circle, The	Jonathan Frost
Inside Asia (also, Inside Europe and Inside Africa)	John Gunter
Inside Third Reich	Albert Spencer
Intimacy	Jean Paul Sartre
Invisible Man	H.G. Wells
Iron in the Soul	Jean Paul Sartre
Isabella	John Keats
Islamic Bomb	Stev Weissman and Herbert Krounsney
Island in the Steams	Ernest Hemingway
Is Paris Burning	Larry Collins And Dominique Lapierre
Ivanhoe	Sir Walter Scott
Jane Eyre	Charlotte Bronte
Jazz	Toni Morison
Jean Christopher	Roman Rolland
Jinnah-India-Partition Independence	Jaswant Singh
Jobs for Millions	V.V. Giri
Judgement, The	Kuldip Nayar

Book	Author
Judge's Miscellany, A	M. Hidayatullah
Jullius Caesar	William Shakespeare
Jungel Book	Rudyard Kipling
Justice of Peace Ke Aansu	Janardan Prasad Singh
Kadambari	Bana Bhatt
Kagaz te Kanwas	Amrita Pritam
Kali Aandhi	Kamleshwar
Kamayani	Jai Shanker Prasad
Kamasutra	S.J. Vatsyayan
Kanthapura	Raja Rao
Kapal Kundala	Bankim Chandra Chatterjee
Kashmir-Behind the Vale	M.J. Akbar
Kaya Kalp	Munshi Prem Chand
Kayar	Thakazhi Sivasankara Pillai
Ken Attendant Godot	Samuel Backett
Kenilworth	Sir Walter Scott
Khak-i-Dil	Jan Nissar Akhtar
Kidnapped	Robert Louis Stevenson
Killer Angels	Michael Shaara
Kim	Rudyard Kipling
King of Dark Chamber	Rabindra Nath Tagore
King Lear	William Shakespeare
Kipps	H. G. Wells
Kissinger Years, The	T.N. Kaul
Kitni Navon Main Kitni Bar	S.H. Vatsyayan
Kore Kagaz	Amrita Pritam
Kublai Khan	Samuel Taylor Coleridge
Kulliyat-i-Iqbal	M. Iqbal
Kumar Sambhava	Kalidas
L'Allegro	John Milton
La Divine Comedia	A. Dante
Lady Chatterley's Lover	D.H. Lawrence
Lady of the Lake	Sir Walter Scott
Lajja	Ms. Taslima Nasreen
Last Days of Pompeii	Edward George Lytton
Last Maharaja, The	Jean Louis Nou and Jacques Pouchepadass
Last Thing	C.P. Snow
Laws Versus Justice	V.R. Krishna Iyer
Lead Kindly Light	Vincent Shean
Le Contract Social (The Social Contract)	J.J. Rousseau
Leaders	Richard Nixon
Leaves of Grass	Walt Whiteman
Letters from the Field	Margaret Mead
Les Miserables	Victor Hugo
Leviathan	Thomas Hobbes
Life Divine	Aurbindo Ghosh
Life of Dr. Johnson	James Boswell
Light that Failed	Rudyard Kipling

Book	Author
Lines of Fate	Marek Kharitonov
Lipika	Rabindra Nath Tagore
Living Room	Graham Greene
Lolita	V. Nabokov
Long Walk to Freedom	Nelson Mandela
Look Back in Anger	John Osborne
Lord of the Files	William Golding
Lost Child	Mulk Raj Anand
Lost Honour	John Dena
Lotus Eaters	A Tennyson
Love Story	Eric Segal
Lycidas	John Milton
Macbeth	William Shakespeare
Magic Mountain	Maharishi Ved Vyas
Main Street	Sinclair Lewis
Major Barbara	George Bernard Shaw
Making of a Midsummer Night's Dream, The	David Selbourne
Malgudi Days	R.K. Narayan
Malti Madhav	Bhavabhuti
Malavikagnimitra	Kalidas
Man and Superman	George Bernard Shaw
Man Eaters of Kumaon	Jim Corbett
Man of Destiny	George Bernard Shaw
Mankind and Mother Earth	Arnold Toynbee
Man, The Unknown	Lewis Carroll
Man for All Seasons, A	Robert Bolt
Man for Moscow	G. Wynne
Many Worlds	K.P.S. Menon
Marriage and Morals	Bertrand Russel
Masters, The	C.P. Snow
Mati Matal	Gopinath Mohanty
Maurice	E.M. Forster
Mayor of Casterbridge	Thomas Hardy
Meghdoot	Kalidas
Mein Kampf	Adolf Hitler
Memories of Hope	Charles de Gaulle
Memories of Malgudi	R.K. Narayan
Men who Kept the Secrets	Thomas Powers
Men who Killed Gandhi, The	Manohar Malgonkar
Merchant of Venice	William Shakespeare
Middle Ground, The	Margaret Drabble
Middle March	George Eliot
Midnight's Children*	Salman Rushdie
Midsummer Night's Dream, A	William Shakespeare
Mill on the Floss	George Eliot
Miser, The	Moliere
Mistaken Identify	Nayantara Sehgal
Moby Dick	Hermann Melville
Modern Painters	John Ruskin
Moon and Six Pence	W. Somerset Maugham

Book	Author
Moonlight Sonata	L Beethoven
Mookhajiva Kanasugalu	K. Shivram Karnath
Mother	Maxim Gorky
Mother India	Katherine Mayo
Mountbatten and Independent India	Larry Collins & Dominique Lapierre
Mountbatten and The Partition of India	Larry Collins & Dominique Lapierre
Mrinalini	Bankim Chandra Chatterjee
Mrs. Gandhi's Second Reign	Arun Shourie
Much Ado About Nothing	William Shakespeare
Mudra Rakshasa	Vishakhadatta
Murder in the Cathedral	V.S. Eliot
Muslim Dilemma in India	M. K. A. Baig
My Days	R.K. Narayana
My Early Life	M.K. Gandhi
My Experiments with Truth	M.K. Gandhi
My India	S. Nihal Singh
My Life and Times	V.V. Giri
My Music, My Love	Ravi Shankar
My Own Boswell	M. Hidayatullah
My Presidential Years	R.Venkata Raman
My Struggles	E.K. Nayanar
My Truth	Indira Gandhi
Mysterious Universe	James Jens
Naked Came the Stranger	Penelope Ashe
Naked Face, The	Sidney Sheldon
Naked Triangle, The	Balwant Gargi
Naku Thanthi	D.R. Bendre
Nana	Emile Zola
Nature of Mass Poverty, The	J.K. Galbraith
Natya Shastra	Bharat Muni
Neela Chand	Shiv Prasad Singh
Nehru Family and Sikhs	Harbans Singh
Netaji Dead or Alive	Samar Guha
New Dimensions of India's Foreign Policy	Atal Behari Vajpayee
Nine Days' Wonder	John Mansfield
Nineteen Eighty-four	George Orwell
1999-Victory Without War	Richard Nixon
Nisheeth	Uma Shanker Joshi
Niti-Sataka	Bharatrihari
Nixon in White House	Seymour M. Hersh
Non-Violence in Peace and War	M.K. Gandhi
Nuclear India	G.G. Mirchandani and P.K.S. Namboodari
O'Jerusalem	Larry Collins and Dominique Lapierre
Occasion for Loving	Nadine Gordimer
Oddakkuzal	G. Shankara Kurup
Odyssey	Homer

Book	Author
Of Human Bondage	W. Somerset Maugham
Old Man and the Sea	Ernest Hemingway
Oliver Twist	Charles Dickens
Omeros	Derek Walcott
One Day on the Life of Ivan Denisovich	Alexander Solzhenitsyn
One Hundred Years of Solitude	Gabriel Marquez
One World	Wendell Wilkie
One World to Share	Sridath Ramphal
Origin of Species	Charles Darwin
Oru Desattinte Katha	S.K. Pottekkatt
Oscar and Lucinda	Peter Carey
Othello	William Shakespeare
Other Side of Midnight, The	Sidney Sheldon
Our Films, Their Films	Satyajit Ray
Paddy Clarke Ha Ha Ha	Roddy Doyle
Pakistan Papers	Mani Shankar Aiyer
Painted Veil	W. Somerset Maugham
Painter of Signs	R.K. Narayan
Pair of Blue Eyes, A	Thomas Hardy
Pakistan Crisis	David Loshak
Pakistan Cut to Size	D.R. Mankekar
Pakistan, The Gathering Storm	Benazir Bhutto
Panchatantra	Vishnu Sharma
Paradise Lost	John Milton
Paradise Regained	John Milton
Passge to England, A	Nirad C. Choudhury
Passage to India, A	E.M. Forster
Past and Present	Thomas Carlyle
Pather Panchali	Bibhuti Bhushan Bandhopadhayaya
Patriot, The	Pearl S. Buck
Personal Adventure, A	Theodore H. White
Peter Pan	J. M. Berrie
Pickwick Papers	Charles Dickens
Pilgrim's Progress	John Bunyan
Pinjar	Amrita Pritam
Plans for Departure	Nayantara Sehgal
Portrait of India	Ved Mehta
Post Office	Rabindra Nath Tagore
Power and Glory	Graham Greene
Power That Be	David Halberstan
Pratham Pratishruti	Ashapurna Devi
Prelude	William Wordsworth
Prem Pachisi	Munshi Prem Chand
Premonitions	P.N. Haksar
Price of Power	Kissinger
Pride and Prejudice	Jane Austen
Prince	Nicolo Machiaveli

Book	Author
Principla	Issac Newton
Prison and Chocolate Cake	Nayantara Sehgal
Prison Diary	Jaya Prakash Narayan
Prisoner of Zenda	Anthony Hope
Prisoner's Scrapbook, A	L.K. Advani
Prithviraj Raso	Chanda Bardai
Professor, The	Charlotte Bronte
Promises to Keep	Chester Bowels
Pygmalion	George Bernard Shaw
Pyramids of Sacrifice	Peter L. Berger
Radharani	Bankim Chandra Chatterjee
Rage of Angels	Sidney Sheldon
Raghuvansha	Kalidas
Ragtime	E.L. Doctorow
Rainbow, The	Pearl S. Buck
Rains Came	Louis Bromefield
Rajtarangini	Kalhana
Ram Charita Manas	Tulsidas
Ramayana	Maharishi Valmiki
Rangbhoomi	Munshi Prem Chand
Rang-i-Shairi	Raghupati Sahai (Firaq Gorakhpuri)
Rape of Bangladesh	Anthony Mascarenhas
Rape of the Lock	Alexander Pope
Ratnavali	Harsh Vardhan
Razor's Edge	W. Somerset Maugham
Rebel, The	Albert Camus
Rebirth	Leonid Brezhnev
Red and Black, The	Stendhal
Red Badge of Courage	Stephan Crane
Red Star over China	Edgar Snow
Reflections of the French Revolution	Edmund Burke
Reminiscences of the Nehru Age	M.O. Mathai
Reprieve	Jean Paul Sartre
Republic	Plato
Resurrection	Count Leo Tolstoy
Return of the Native, The	Thomas Hardy
Returning to the Source	Acharya Shree Rajneesh
Revenue Stamps, The	Amrita Pritam
Rich Like Us	Nayantara Sehgal
Riding the Storm	Harold MacMillan
Rights of Man	Thomas Paine
Rise and Fall of the Great Powers	Paul Kennedy
Ritu Samhara	Kalidas
Rivals, The	R.B. Shridan
Road to Folly	Leslie Ford
Robe, The	Lloyd C. Douglas
Robinson Crusoe	Daniel Defoe

Book	Author
Romeo and Julliet	William Shakespeare
Rubaiyat	Omar Khayyam
Rubaiyat-i-Omar Khayyam	Edward Fitzgerald
Sadar-i-Riyasat	Karan Singh
Saket	Maithili Sharan Gupta
Sakha Ram Binder	Vijay Tendulkar
Samler's Planet	Saul Bellow
Sands of Time	Sidney Sheldon
Satanic Verses	Salman Rushdie
Sanctuary	William Faulkner
Satyartha Prakash	Swami Dayanand
Savitri	Sri Aurobindo Ghosh
Scarlet Letter	Nathaniel Hawthorne
Scarlet Pimpernal	Baroness Orczy
Sceptred Flute	Sarojini Naidu
Scholar Extraordinary	Nirad C. Choudhury
School for Scandal, The	R.B. Sheridan
Scope of Happiness, The	Vijayalakshmi Pandit
Search for Home, A	Sasthi Brata
Sense and Sensibility	Jane Austen
Sense of Time, A	H.S. Vatsyayan
Sesame and Lilies	John Ruskin
Seven Lamps of Architecture	John Ruskin
Seven Summers	Mulk Raj Anand
Shadow from Ladakh	Bhabani Bhattacharya
Shahnama	Firdausi
Shakuntala	Kalidas
Shalimar	Manohar Malgonkar
Shall We Tell the President	Jeffrey Archer
Shape of Things to Come	H.G Wells
Shame	Salman Rushdie
She Stoops to Conquer	Oliver Goldsmith
Ship of Fools	Katherine Anne Porter
Shivaji, The Great Patriot	Lala Lajpat Rai
Shoes of the Fisherman, The	Morris West
Silas Marner	George Eliot
Six Characters in Search of an Author	Lugi Pirandello
Slave, The	Issac Bashevis Singer
Small Land	Leonid Brezhnev
Sohrab and Rustam	Matthew Arnold
Song of India, The	Sarojini Naidu
Sonnets, The	William Shakespeare
Sons and Lovers	D.H. Lawrence
Sound and the Fury, The	William Faulkner
Soz-i-Watan	Munshi Prem Chand
Spaniard in the Works, A	John Lennon
Spirit of the Age	William Hazlitt
Spy Catcher	Peter Wright

Book	Author
St. John	George Bernard Shaw
Story of My Life	Moshe Dayan
Story of Real Man	Nikolayev Polevol
Strangers and Brothers Omnibus	C.P. Snow
Sunny Days	Sunil Gavaskar
Study of History, A	Arnold Toynbee
Swami and Friends	R.K. Narayan
Swapnavasvadatta	Bhasa
Sword and the Sickle	Mulk Raj Anand
Tale of a Tub, A	Jonathan Swift
Tale of Two Cities, A	Charles Dickens
Tales from Shakespeare	Charles Lamb
Talisman	Sir Walter Scott
Tamas	Bhisham Sahni
Tarzan of the Apes	Edger Rice Burroughs
Tears of D'Urberviles	Thoms Huardy
Tempest, The	William Shakespeare
Thank You, Jeeves	P.G. Wodehouse
The Garden of Life	Naveen Patnaik
The White Tiger*	Arvind Adiga
Thieves in the Night	Arthur Koestler
Thirteenth Sun	Amrita Pritam
Three Musketeers	Alexander Dumas
Thorn Birds	Colleen McCollough
Thousand Days, A	Arthur M. Shlesinger
Through the Indian Looking Glass	David Selbourne
Through the Looking Glass	Lewis Carroll
Times Machine	H.G. Wells
Time to be Happy	Nayantara Sehgal
To Live or not to Live	Nirad C. Choudhury
Tom Jones	Henry Fielding
Train to Pakistan	Khushwant Singh
Traveller, The	Olive Goldsmith
Treasure Island	Robert Louis Stevenson
Trial, The	Franz Kafka
Trinity	Leon Uris
Triumph	John Kenneth Galbraith
Tropic of Cancer	Henry Miller
Tryst with Destiny	L. S. Gopalan
Twelfth Night	William Shakespeare
Twenty Years After	Alexander Dumas
Two Leaves and a Bud	Mulk Raj Anand
Two Women	Alberto Moravia
Ulysses	James Joyce
Uncle Tom's Cabin	H.B. Stowe
Unhappy India	Lala Lajpat Rai
Universe Around Us	James Jeans
Unto this Last	John Ruskin

Book	Author
Untold Story	General B.M. Kaul
Upturned Soil, The	Mikhail Sholokhov
Urvashi	Ramdhari Singh Dinkar
Utopia	Thomas More
Uttar Ramcharita	Bhava Bhuti
Valley of Dolls	Jacqueline Susann
Vanity Fair	William Thackeray
Vendor of Sweets, The	R.K. Narayan
Vicar of Wakefield	Oliver Goldsmith
Victim, The	Saul Bellow
View From Delhi, A	Chester Bowles
View From the UN	U. Thant
Village by the Sea, A	Anita Desai
Village , The	Mulk Raj Anand
Vinay Patrika	Tulsidas
Virangana	Maithili Sharan Gupta
Virginians, The	William Thackeray
Vish Vriksha	Bankim Chandra Chatterjee
Voice of Conscience	V.V. Giri
Voice of Freedom , A	Nayantara Sehgal
Voice of the Voiceless	Ruth Harring
Waiting for Godot	Thomas Becket
Wake up India	Annie Besant
Walls of Glass, The	K.A. Abbas
War and Peace	Count Leo Tolstoy
War of the Worlds, The	H.G. Wells
Waste Land	T.S. Eliot

Book	Author
Way to all Flesh	Samuel Butler
Way of the World, The	William Congreve
Wealth of Nations	Adam Smith
Week With Gandhi, A	Louis Fisher
We Indians	Khushwant Singh
We, the People	N.A. Palkivala
Where the Grass is Greener	David M. Smith
White House Years	Henry Kissinger
Wings of Fire	A.P.J. Abdul Kalam*
Willhelm Meister	J.W. Von Goethe
Without Fear or Favour	Neelam Sanjiva Reddy
Witness to an Era	Frank Moraes
Woman's Life, A	Guy de Maupassant
Wonder That Was India, The	A.L. Basham
Worthy it is	Odysseus Elytis
Wreck, The	Rabindra Nath Tagore
Wuthering Heights	Emile Bronte
Yajnaseni	Pratibha Roy
Yama	Mahadevi Verma
Yashodhara	Maithili Sharan Gupta
Yayati	V.S. Khandekar
Year of the Upheaval	Henry Kissinger
Year of the Vulture, The	Amita Malik
Yesterday and Today	K.P.S. Menon
Zhivago, Dr.	Boris Pasternak
Zulfi, My Friend	Piloo Mody

FAMOUS AUTHORS IN DIFFERENT LANGUAGES

English	William Shakespeare, John Milton, Chaucer, Spenser, Lord Byron, P.B. Shelley, John Keats, Francis Bacon, T.S. Eliot, Cecil Dlay Lewis, Alduous Huxley, W.B. Yeats Bunyan, Dryden, Dr. Johnson, Alexander Pope, Robert Browning, Charles Lamb, Charles Dickens, Thomas Hardy, W.M. Thackeray, George Eliot, Alfred Tennyson, Robert Bridges, George Bernard Shaw, D.H. Lawrence, Oliver Goldsmith, Sheridan, Walter Scott, William Wordsworth, S.T. Coleridge, Henry Fielding, Somerset Maugham, J.K. Rowling.
French	Imile Zola, Gustave Flaubert, Moliere, Proudhon, Jean Paul Sartre, Le Sage, Victor Hugo, Alexander Dumas, Balzac.
German	Goethe, Hoffman, Lessing, Schelling, Schaupenhuer, Heinrich Heine, Guenter Grass
Russian	Tolstoy, Mikhail Solokhov, Turgenev, Dostoevsky, Maxim Gorky, Techov, Alexander Salzhenitsyn, Boris Pasternak
Greek	Homer, Aesop, Aristophanes, Euripedes, Herodotus, Hesoid, Theocritus, Xenophon, Aeschylus, Sophocles
Latin	Dante, Boccacio, Terence, Virgil, Ovid, Horace, Seneca
Norwegian	John Bojer, Ibsen
Persian	Ghalib, Umar Khyyam, Abul Fazal, Amir Khusro, Faiz, Firdausi, Mohd. Iqbal Saddi
Spanish	Juan Valera, Lope De Vega, Cervantes

FAMOUS CHARACTERS AND THEIR CREATORS

Character	Creator	Character	Creator
Adam	Milton	Juliet	William Shakespeare
Alice	Lewis Carroll	Jessica	William Shakespeare
Ancient Mariner	Coleridge	Jean Valjin	Victor Hugo
Ariel	William Shakespeare	Jacques	William Shakespeare
Antonio	William Shakespeare	Jeeves	P.G. Wodehouse
Anna Karenina	Leo Tolstoy	King Arthur	Tennyson
Bassomio	William Shakespeare	Kim	Rudyard Kipling
Bertie Wooster	P.G. Wodehouse	Long John Silver	R.L. Stevenson
Brutus	William Shakespeare	Macbeth	William Shakespeare
Beatrix	Thackery	Micawber	Charles Dickens
Beatrice	William Shakespeare	Miranda	William Shakespeare
Christian	John Bunyan	Mephistopheles	J.W. Von Goethe
Cordelia	William Shakespeare	Mellors	D.H. Lawrence
Cleopatra	William Shakespeare	Malaprop	Sheridian
Clare	Thomas Hardy	Oliver Twist	Charles Dickens
Claudius	William Shakespeare	Peggotty	Charles Dickens
David Copperfield	Charles Dickens	Priyangbada	Kalidas
Dushyanta	Kalidas	Portia	William Shakespeare
Don Quixote	Cervantes	Pip	Charles Dickens
Eliza Doolittle	George Bernard Shaw	Perry Mason	Erle Stanley Gardner
Estella	Charles Dickens	Pickwick	Charles Dickens
Faust	J.W. Von Goethe	Rip Van Winkle	Washington Irving
Gora	Rabindranath Tagore	Sam Weller	Charles Dickens
Hamlet	William Shakespeare	Surpanakha	Valmiki
Harry Potter	J.K. Rowling	Shylock	William Shakespeare
Hyde	R.L. Stevenson	Sherlock Halmes	Arthur Conan Doyle
Hercule Poirot	Agatha Christie	Shakuntala	Kalidas
Hawkins	R.L. Stevenson	Sancho Panza	Cervantes Saavedra
Hector	Homer	Tess	Thomas Hardy
Ivanhoe	Sir Walter Scott	Watson	Arthur Conan Doyle
Iago	William Shakespeare	Zhivago	Boris Pasternak
James Bond	Ian Fleming		

GREAT POETS

Language	Poet
Hindi	Surdas, Tulsidas, Keshav
Sanskrit	Valmiki, Vedvyas, Kalidas
Bengali	Rabindra Nath Tagore
Urdu	Mirza Ghalib
Persian	Sheikh Saadi
Latin	Virgil
Greek	Homer
English	Shakespeare
German	Goethe
Italian	Dante
French	Sully Proudhone
Punjabi	Waris Shah

GREAT INDIAN AUTHORS AND POETS

Language	Authors and Poets
Assamese	Birendra Kumar Bhattacharya; Hem Chandra Barua; Hem Chandra Goswami; Madhavkandali.
Bengali	Ashapoorna Devi; Bankim Chandra Chatterjee; Bibhuti Bhushan Bandopadhyaya; Bishnu Dey; Pramendra Mitra; Rabindra Nath Tagore; R.C. Dutt; Michael Madhusudan Datt; Kazi Nazrul Islam; Tarashankar Bandopadhyaya.
English	Kamala Das; Manohar Malgonkar; R.K. Narayan; Raja Rao; Mulk Raj Anand; Bhabani Bhatacharya; Sasthi Brata; Arun

Language	Authors and Poets
	Joshi; Chaman Nahal; K.A. Abbas; Anita Desai; R. Prawer Jhabwala; Kamla Markandaya; Khushwant Singh; Manoj Dass.
Gujarati	K.M. Munshi; Mirabai; Narmada Sagar; Narsingh Mehta; Govardhan Ram; Uma Shankar Joshi.
Hindi	Tulsidas; Surdas; Kesav Das; Bihari; Kabir; Sumitra Nandan Pant; Jai Shankar Prasad; Maithili Sharan Gupta; Munshi Prem Chand; Upendra Nath Ashk; Suryakant Tripathi 'Nirala', Acharya Chatursen; Mohan Rakesh; Harivansh Rai Bachchan; Mahadevi Verma; Bhagwati Charan Verma; Ramdhari Singh Dinkar.
Kannada	K.V. Puttappa; B.M. Pampan; Panna; Ramchandra Bendre; K.S. Karanth; Purandar Das.
Malayalam	C.V. Raman Pillai; S.K. Pottekkatt; G. Sankara Kurup; Thakazhi Sivasankara Pillai; O. Chandu Menon; Vallathol; Kumaran Asan.

Language	Authors and Poets
Marathi	Hari Narayan Apte. Tikaram Mahay; Tukaram; V.S. Khandekar.
Oriya	Gopalbandhu Das; Gopi Nath Mohanty; Radha Nath Roy.
Punjabi	Sheikh Farid; Bhai Veer Singh; Dhani Ram Chatrik; Amrita Pritam; Nanak Singh; Balwant Gargi; Waris Shah; Bulle Shah.
Sanskrit	Maharishi Valmiki; Maharishi Ved Vyas, Shreeharsh; Ashvaghosh; Shudrak; Bharvi; Jaidev; Bhartrihari; Kalidas; Banabhatta; Bhavabhuti; Dandi.
Tamil	P.V. Akilandam, Subramaniam Bharati; Ramalingam.
Telugu	Lakshmi Narasimhan; Triputi; V. Satyanarayana.
Urdu	Assadulla Khan 'Ghalib'; Mohammed Iqbal; Mir Taqui Mir; Prem Chand; 'Firaq' Gorakhpuri; Rajinder Singh Bedi; Krishan Chander; Qurrat-ul-Ain Hyder; Sardar Jafri; Qazi Abdul Sattar.

WELL KNOWN QUOTATIONS

1. A thing of beauty is a joy for ever; Its loveliness increases; It will never pass into nothingness. — *Keats. Endymion*

2. A little knowledge is a dangerous thing — *Pope*

3. Beauty is truth, truth beauty that is all. Ye know on earth, all all ye need to know — *Keats: Ode on a Grecian urn*

4. All the world is a stage and all the man and women merely players — *Shakespeare: As you like it*

5. Some books are to be tested, others to be swallowed and some few to be chewed and digested —*Bacon*

6. Better to reign in hell than serve in heaven — *Milton: Paradise lost*

7. The child is father of the man — *Wordsworth: My heart leaps up*

8. A single step for man — a giant leap for mankind — *Neil Armstrong*

9. Dilli Chalo — *Netaji Subhash Chandra Bose*

10. To be or not to be — that is the question. — *Shakespeare: Hamlet*

11. Only free men negotiate. I shall never negotiate while I am still a prisoner — *Nelson Mandela*

12. Truth and non-violence are my God — *Mahatama Gandhi*

13. Let a hundred flowers bloom and let a thousand schools of thought contend – *Mao Tse-tung*

14. Jai Jawan, Jai Kisan — *Lal Bahadur Shastri*

15. Eureka! Eureka! — *Archimedes*

16. Some are born great, some achieve greatness and some have greatness thrust upon them — *Shakespeare*

17. Where wealth accumulates, men decay — *Goldsmith*

18. Power tends to corrupt and absolute power corrupts absolutely — *Lord Acton*

19. Man is by nature a political animal — *Aristotle*

20. I have nothing to offer but blood, toil, tears and sweat — *Winston Churchill*

21. I came, I saw, I conquered — *Julius Ceaser*

22. For fools rush in where angels fear to tread — *Pope*

23. Generations to come, it may, will scarce believe that such a one as this ever in flesh and blood walked upon this earth — *Einstein*

24. Government of the people, by the people, for the people — *Lincon*

25. East is east and west is west and never the twain shall meet — *Kipling*

26. Swaraj is my birth right — *Bal Gangadhar Tilak*

27. Cowards die many times before their death: The valiant never taste of death but once

— *Shakespeare: Julius Ceaser*

28. Where ignorance is bliss, It is folly to be wise

— *Grey*

29. I know nothing except the fact of my ignorance

— *Socrates*

30. We are such stuff as dreams are made of and our little life is rounded with a sleep

— *Shakespeare: The Tempest*

31. What's in a name? That which we call a rose By any other name would smell as sweet

— *Shakespeare: Merchant of Venice*

32. Patriotism is the best refuge of a scoundrel

— *Samuel Johnson*

33. Reading maketh a full man; conference a ready man; and writing an exact man — *Francis Bacon*

34. It is excellent to love a giant's strength
but it is tyrannous to use it like a giant

— *Shakespeare: Measure to Measure*

35. Water, water everywhere
Not any drop to drink

— *S.T. Coleridge: The Ancient Mainer*

36. It is strange but true, for truth is always strange

— *Byron: Don Juan*

37. Virtue is its own reward — *Cicero: De Fintibus*

38. Frailty, thy name is woman

— *Shakespeare: Hamlet*

39. We don't fear to negotiate, but we do not negotiate out of fear — *J.F. Kennedy*

40. Give us good mothers and I shall give you good nation — *Napoleon*

41. The woods are lovely, dark and deep
But I have promises to keep
And miles to go before I sleep — *Robert Frost*

42. We have made a tryst with destiny — *Pt. Nehru*

43. Eli, Eli, Lamma Sabcathani (My God, my God, why last thou forsaken me)

— *Jesus Christ at the Cross*

44. If winter comes can spring be for behind

— *Shelley*

45. Man does not live by bread alone — *Bible*

46. Nothing is good or bad, thinking makes it so

— *Shakespeare: Hamlet*

47. Garibi hatao — *Indira Gandhi*

48. Aram haram hai — *Jawaharlal Nehru*

49. Quit India — *Mahatma Gandhi*

50. Jai Jawan, Jai Kisan, Jai Vigyan

— *Atal Behari Vajpayee*

Multiple Choice Questions

THE LAST LESSON
By Alphonse Daudet

1. Assertion (A): Franz was scared to go to school.

Reason (R): He had not learnt his homework and was late for school.

A. Both (A) and (R) are true and (R) is the correct explanation of (A)
B. Both (A) and (R) are true, but (R) is not the correct explanation of (A)
C. (A) is true, but (R) is false
D. (A) is false, but (R) is true

2. Assertion (A): Franz was tempted to stay out of doors.

Reason (R): The weather was warm, birds were chirping and Prussian soldiers were drilling.

A. Both (A) and (R) are true, but (R) is not the correct explanation of (A)
B. Both (A) and (R) are true and (R) is the correct explanation of (A)
C. (A) is true, but (R) is false
D. (A) is false, but (R) is true

3. Assertion (A): Usually there was a great commotion when the school began.

Reason (R): The noise was produced by the opening & closing of desks, lessons repeated in unison by students and the teachers' ruler rapping on the table.

A. Both (A) and (R) are true and (R) is the correct explanation of (A)
B. Both (A) and (R) are true, but (R) is not the correct explanation of (A)
C. (A) is true, but (R) is false
D. (A) is false, but (R) is true

4. Assertion (A): That day everything was as quiet as Sunday morning.

Reason (R): It was indeed a Sunday morning and no one was present in the school.

A. Both (A) and (R) are true and (R) is the correct explanation of A
B. Both (A) and (R) are true, but (R) is not the correct explanation of (A)

C. (A) is true, but (R) is false
D. (A) is false, but (R) is true

5. Assertion (A): M. Hamel was wearing his special dress for the last French class.

Reason (R): The dress comprised of beautiful green coat, frilled shirt & the little black silk cap.
A. Both (A) and (R) are true and (R) is the correct explanation of (A)
B. Both (A) and (R) are true, but (R) is not the correct explanation of (A)
C. (A) is true, but (R) is false
D. (A) is false, but (R) is true

6. Assertion (A): The elderly villagers occupied the back benches on the last day of French lesson.

Reason (R): This fact surprised Franz the most.
A. Both (A) and (R) are true and (R) is the correct explanation of (A)
B. Both (A) and (R) are true, but (R) is not the correct explanation of (A)
C. (A) is true, but (R) is false
D. (A) is false, but (R) is true

7. Assertion (A): The whole school seemed strange and solemn to Franz.

Reason (R): The order had come from Berlin to teach only German in the schools of Alsace & Lorraine. That was their last French class.
A. Both (A) and (R) are true and (R) is the correct explanation of (A)
B. Both (A) and (R) are true, but (R) is not the correct explanation of (A)
C. (A) is true, but (R) is false
D. (A) is false, but (R) is true

8. Assertion (A): Franz was filled with repentance and guilt on the last day of French class.

Reason (R): He did not study French when he had time, he wasted his time in seeking birds' eggs and sliding on the Saar.
A. Both (A) and (R) are true, but (R) is not the correct explanation of (A)
B. Both (A) and (R) are true and (R) is the correct explanation of (A)
C. (A) is true, but (R) is false
D. (A) is false, but (R) is true

9. Assertion (A): The elderly people occupied the back benches.

Reason (R): They were present for thanking M Hamel, for being sorry too for not going to school more, for showing their respect towards the country that was theirs no more.
A. Both (A) and (R) are true and (R) is the correct explanation of (A)
B. Both (A) and (R) are true, but (R) is not the correct explanation of (A)
C. (A) is true, but (R) is false
D. (A) is false, but (R) is true

10. Assertion (A): The teacher is also responsible for poor performance of students in studies.

Reason (R): He often sent them to water his flowers instead of learning their lessons, declared holidays for no reason.
A. Both (A) and (R) are true, but (R) is not the correct explanation of (A)
B. Both (A) and (R) are true and (R) is the correct explanation of (A)
C. (A) is true, but (R) is false
D. (A) is false, but (R) is true

11. Assertion (A): French language was the most beautiful, the clearest and the most logical of all the languages.

Reason (R): As long as the Frenchmen held fast to their language, they had chances of winning freedom.
A. Both (A) and (R) are true and (R) is the correct explanation of (A)
B. Both (A) and (R) are true, but (R) is not the correct explanation of (A)
C. (A) is true, but (R) is false
D. (A) is false, but (R) is true

12. Assertion (A): Will they make them sing in German, even the pigeons.

Reason (R): They had enslaved France, so they could do every impossible act.
A. Both (A) and (R) are true and (R) is the correct explanation of (A)
B. Both (A) and (R) are true, but (R) is not the correct explanation of (A)
C. (A) is true, but (R) is false
D. (A) is false, but (R) is true

13. Assertion (A): When it struck twelve, M. Hamel made a gesture with his hand to everyone that the school was dismissed.

Reason (R): He was too emotional and upset over the Berlin order to speak anything.
A. Both (A) and (R) are true, but (R) is not the correct explanation of (A)
B. Both (A) and (R) are true and (R) is the correct explanation of (A)
C. (A) is true, but (R) is false
D. (A) is false, but (R) is true

14. Look at the statements given below. Choose the option that correctly identifies which statements are fact and which are opinion:
(*a*) By sitting in the class, the elders of Alsace showed their respect for M. Hamel.

(*b*) The elders were regretting that they did not learn their mother tongue.

(*c*) The elders did not appreciate the faithful service of M. Hamel and were only there to bid farewell to the teacher.

(*d*) The teacher was sorrowful as he was to leave not only his students but also the school which he had nurtured.

A. Fact (*a*) and (*d*); opinion (*b*) and (*c*)
B. Fact (*b*) and (*c*); opinion (*a*) and (*d*)
C. Fact (*a*) and (*b*); opinion (*c*) and (*d*)
D. Fact (*b*) and (*d*); opinion (*a*) and (*c*)

15. Statement I: The narrator feels sorry for M. Hamel.

Statement II: Franz could not accept the fact that he won't be learning French any longer.

A. Statement I is true, but Statement II is false.
B. Statement I is false, but Statement II is true.
C. Both these statements can be inferred from the lesson.
D. Neither of the statements can be inferred from the lesson.

Directions: *Read each of the following passages carefully and choose the best answer to each question out of the four alternatives.*

PASSAGE-1

I started for school very late that morning and was in great dread of a scolding, especially because M. Hamel had said that he would question us on participles, and I did not know the first word about them. For a moment, I thought of running away and spending the day out of doors. It was so warm, so bright!

16. Who is the author of these lines?
A. William Douglas B. Selma Lagerlof
C. Alphonse Daudet D. Anees Jung

17. Who was Mr Hamel?
A. Principal B. French teacher
C. Village Sarpanch D. Franz's father

18. Why was Franz in great dread?
A. He had not prepared his grammar lesson
B. He had bunked the class the previous day
C. He had not brought his notebook
D. None of these

19. What did Franz think for a moment?
A. teaching a lesson to his teacher
B. pranking the principal
C. bunking the class
D. joining the Civil movement

PASSAGE-2

I jumped over the bench and sat down at my desk. Not till then, when I had got a little over my fright, did I see that our teacher had on his beautiful green coat, his frilled shirt, and the little black silk cap, all embroidered, that he never wore except on inspection and prize days. Besides, the whole school seemed so strange and solemn.

20. Who is 'I' in the given lines?
A. Franz B. M. Hamel
C. The Mayor D. The Narrator

21. What was unusual about M. Hamel's dress?
A. Wore clean clothes
B. Wore a brand new outfit
C. Wore a traditional French outfit
D. Wore his fancy clothes

22. Why was M. Hamel dressed so unusually?
A. He was retiring
B. It was his last lesson
C. He was leaving the school
D. He was going to be imprisoned

23. Which word in the extract would also mean 'formal and dignified'?
A. Inspection B. Strange
C. Solemn D. Fright

24. 'Got a little over my Fright' means:
A. a bit afraid B. a bit settled
C. being cautious D. all of these

PASSAGE-3

"My children, this is the last lesson I shall give you. The order has come from Berlin to teach only German in the schools of Alsace and Lorraine. The new master comes tomorrow. This is your last French lesson. I want you to be very attentive." What a thunderclap these words were to me!

25. Why does M. Hamel want the students to be attentive?
A. Because it is his last French lesson
B. Because the order has come from Berlin
C. Because he is about to reveal the question paper
D. Because the government officer is on a visit

26. Which order from Berlin is called as 'thunderclap' by Franz?
A. The order of closing schools for a month
B. The order of stopping teaching French
C. The order of executing anyone in Alsace & Lorraine
D. The order of demolishing the school building

27. How would you describe Franz's tone when he says, "What a thunderclap these words were to me"?
A. Angry B. Gloomy
C. Perplexed D. Irritated

28. Statement I: M. Hamel had been subjected to mental torture with the decision to teach only German in Alsace and Lorraine.

Statement II: Nobody except Franz was able to realize the pain in M. Hamel's eyes.

A. Statement I is true, but Statement II is false
B. Statement I is false, but Statement II is true
C. Both Statement I & II cannot be inferred from the passage
D. Both Statement I & II can be inferred from the passage

29. In which of the following options can the underlined words not be replaced with 'wretch'?

A. The beggar has broken my car window.
B. Items like a stick and grenadier are now variable.
C. He is a lonely and miserable rogue.
D. Before the poor knave had time to speak, he was shot.

PASSAGE-4

My last French lesson why I hardly knew how to write I should never learn anymore I must stop there then oh how sorry I was for not learning my lessons for seeking Birds eggs or going sliding on the Saar my books that had seemed such a nuisance a while ago so heavy to carry my grammar and my history of the saints were old friends now that I couldn't give up.

30. Why was it the speaker's last French lesson?

A. because his French teacher was retiring
B. because of a government order to teach only German
C. because the speaker was migrating
D. because French has become a language to be taught in higher classes

31. What is the speaker feeling after getting to know that it is his last French lesson?

A. sad
B. regretful
C. frightened
D. distraught

32. What did Franz do to skip his French lessons?

A. seeking bird eggs
B. going on the slides
C. working on the mill
D. both (A) and (B)

33. How do Franz's feelings regarding his books change?

A. He feels that they were his friends
B. He believes that they were a nuisance
C. He feels that his identity is related to his books
D. He believed that they are of no use to him

PASSAGE-5

Poor man! It was in honour of this last lesson that, he had put on his fine Sunday clothes, and now I understood why the old men of the village were sitting there in the back of the room. It was because they were sorry, too, that they had not gone to school more. It was their way of thanking our master for his forty years of faithful service and of showing their respect for the country that was theirs no more.

34. Why does the narrator refer to M. Hamel as 'poor man'?

A. He empathizes with M. Hamel as he had to leave the village.
B. He believed that M Hamel's 'fine Sunday clothes' clearly reflected that he was not rich.
C. He feels sorry for M. Hamel as it was his last French lesson.
D. He thinks that M. Hamel's patriotism and sense of duty resulted in his poverty.

35. Which of the following idioms might describe the villagers' act of attending the last lesson most accurately?

A. too good to miss
B. too little, too late
C. too many cooks spoil the broth
D. too cool for school

36. Choose the option that might raise a question about M. Hamel's 'faithful service'.

A. When Franz came late M. Hamel told him that he was about to begin class without him.
B. Franz mentioned how cranky M. Hamel was and 'his great ruler rapping on the table'.
C. M Hamel often sent students to water his flowers and gave a holiday when he wanted to go fishing.
D. M Hamel permitted villagers to put their children 'to work on a farm or at the mills' for some extra money.

37. Choose the option that most appropriately fills in the blanks, for the following description of the given extract.

The villagers and their children sat in the class, forging with their old master a (*i*) .... togetherness. In that moment, the class room stood (*ii*) .... It was France itself and the last French lesson a desperate hope to (*iii*) .... to the remnants of what they had known and taken for granted their own (*iv*)......... .

A. (*i*) graceful (*ii*) still (*iii*) hang on (*iv*) country
B. (*i*) bygone (*ii*) up (*iii*) keep on (*iv*) education
C. (*i*) beautiful (*ii*) mesmerised (*iii*) carry on (*iv*) unity
D. (*i*) forgotten (*ii*) transformed (*iii*) hold on (*iv*) identity

PASSAGE-6

But I got mixed up on the first words and stood there, holding onto my desk, my heart beating, and not daring to look up.

38. Who is I here?

A. Mr Hamel
B. Franz
C. Village Sarpanch
D. Not clear from the story

39. What was asked in the classroom from 'I'?
A. Rule of grammar
B. Addition rule
C. Multiplication table of 18
D. Essay on the language

40. Why did he stand holding the desk?
A. He was surprised at the question
B. He had not prepared his lesson
C. He was absent the previous day
D. He did not listen the question clearly

41. What was the reaction of the teacher?
A. Scolded him
B. Shouted at him
C. Sent him out of the class
D. Pitied him

PASSAGE-7

I heard M. Hamel say to me, "I won't scold you, little Franz; you must feel bad enough. See how it is! Every day we have said to ourselves, Bah! I have plenty of time. I'll learn it tomorrow. And now you see where we have come out. That's the great trouble with Alsace; she puts off learning till tomorrow.

42. For what reason Franz could have been scolded?
A. For being late to school
B. for not learning participles
C. for ignoring his lessons
D. for playing all the time

43. Why should Franz be feeling bad?
A. his teacher was retiring
B. he would not learn French now
C. he was rusticated
D. his inability to show his command over friend

44. The given lines indicate how M. Hamel is feeling. Pick the option that correctly states these feelings.

1. angry	2. regretful
3. sad	4. hatred
5. Joyous	6. sympathetic
A. 1 and 4	B. 2 and 3
C. 5 and 6	D. 1 and 3

45. The story 'The Last lesson' highlights which human tendency?
A. male chauvinism B. procrastination
C. courage D. cowardice

PASSAGE-8

M. Hamel went on to talk of the French language, saying that it was the most beautiful language in the world— the clearest, the most logical; that we must guard it among us and never forget it, because when a people are enslaved, as long as they hold fast to their language as it is as if they had the key to their prison. Then he opened a grammar book and read us our lesson. I was amazed to see how well I understood it. All he said seemed so easy, so easy.

46. Which of the following can be attributed to M. Hamel's declaration about the French language?
A. Subjective expertise
B. Nostalgic pride
C. Factual accuracy
D. Patriotic magnification

47. Read the quotes given below. Choose the option that might best describe Hamel's viewpoint.
(*a*) Those who know nothing of foreign languages know nothing of their own.
(*b*) Language is the road map of a culture. It tells you where its people come from and where they are going.
(*c*) A poor man is like a foreigner in his own country.
(*d*) The greatest propaganda in the world is our mother tongue, that is what we learn as children, and which we learn unconsciously. That shapes our perception for life.
A. option (*a*) B. option (*b*)
C. option (*c*) D. option (*d*)

48. "I was amazed to see how well I understood it". Select the option that does not explain why Franz found the grammar lesson 'easy'.
A. Franz was paying careful attention in class this time.
B. M. Hamel was being extremely patient and calm in his teaching.
C. Franz was inspired and had found a new meaning and purpose to learning.
D. Franz had realized that French was the clearest and most logical language.

49. Franz was able to understand the grammar lesson easily because he was:
A. receptive B. appreciative
C. introspective D. competitive

PASSAGE-9

All at once, the church clock struck 12, then the Angelus. At the same moment the trumpets of the Prussians, returning from drill sounded under our windows. M. Hamel stood up very pale in his chair. I never saw him look so tall.

50. What is Angelus?
A. Prayers said in the morning
B. Prayers said in the middle of the day
C. Prayers said in the evening
D. All of these

51. Who are the Prussians?
A. Residents of Germany
B. Residents of Poland
C. Residents of some parts of Austria
D. All of these combined

52. Why was M. Hamel so pale?
A. He was tired by the end of the class
B. He was replaced by the German teacher
C. He was not well
D. He was tired due to the Mischief caused by the students

53. 'I never saw him look so tall' means:
A. Sad B. Excited
C. Lively D. seemed very confident

PASSAGE-10

"Viva La France!" then he stopped and leaned his head against the wall and without a word he made a gesture to us with his hand— "school is dismissed—you may go".

54. The reason for his stopping and leaning against the wall was:
A. because he was unwell
B. because he was emotional
C. because he wanted to teach German too
D. because the students didn't pay attention in his lecture

55. What does 'Viva La France' mean?
A. Good bye France B. Good living France
C. Long live France D. France is the best

56. The phrase 'Viva La France' indicates the speakers:
A. Enthusiasm B. Depression
C. Nostalgia D. Patriotism

57. Why does M. Hamel write Viva La France on the black board:
A. to show his love for French
B. to show his love for teaching
C. to show his love for his country
D. both (A) and (C)

58. French think, "Will they make them sing in German". What does this mean?
A. it means that nothing will be affected
B. it means that when people are deprived their surroundings are also affected
C. it means that a change will be welcome
D. it means that Franz was unaware of what was happening

59. Choose the statement that is not true:
A. Franz did not like going to school
B. He was scared of M Hamel
C. He was excited that he was going to learn German
D. He was regretful on the day of the last lesson

60. What had the narrator counted on to enter the school unnoticed?
A. he counted the leaves of a plant outside the classroom
B. he counted the blessing of God
C. he counted the number of people he met on his way
D. he counted on the hustle and bustle that was usual in the school

61. What did M. Hamel tell the people in the class about French language?
A. French was the most beautiful language in the world
B. French was the most illogical language in the world
C. French was the most logical language in the world
D. Both (A) and (C)

62. Which language was made compulsory to be taught in the schools of Alsace and Lorraine?
A. Portuguese B. French
C. German D. Spanish

63. For how many years had Hamel taught at the school?
A. 10 years B. 20 years
C. 30 years D. 40 years

64. Who were present in the class the last day?
A. all the villagers were present in the class
B. all the students and elderly villagers were present in the class
C. everyone except the teacher were present in the class
D. the Inspector from the neighbouring town was present in the class

65. The word 'rapping' means:
A. singing
B. slapping on the head
C. striking to attract attention
D. teaching strictly

66. "The birds were chirping at the edge of the woods and in the open fields back of the sawmill the Prussian soldiers were drilling."

Which of the following sentences can be said as true after reading the given lines?
A. Alsace bordered Prussia and so Franz could hear the drilling.
B. The Prussian soldiers had started to construct their official building.
C. The people of Alsace like Franz were attracted to the sound of drilling.
D. Prussia had won over Alsace and Lorraine and thus were practicing to settle their authority.

67. Franz saw a huge crowd assembled in front of the bulletin board, but did not stop. How would you evaluate his reaction?
A. Franz was too little to care about the news of lost battles.
B. Nobody in Franz's family was in the army, so it did not matter.

C. Bad news had become very normal, so he went about his task.
D. It was too crowded for Franz to find out what news was up on the board.

68. What did the blacksmith say to Franz?
A. To read the bulletin-board.
B. To get his homework completed.
C. To hurry to the school.
D. To not go so fast.

69. "There was usually great bustle and noise when school began, but it was all very quiet". Which of the following describes Franz's emotions most accurately?
A. Shock and awe
B. Disappointment and anxiety
C. Confusion and distress
D. Curiosity and uncertainty

70. Which of the statements cannot be attributed to Franz?
A. Franz did not like studying; he would rather enjoy nature.
B. Franz loved his teacher a lot.
C. Franz regretted that he did not study French at all.
D. Franz was a naughty student.

71. What does M. Hamel blame the parents for?
A. They preferred children to work in farms.
B. They were not strict.
C. They did not come to M. Hamel's class.
D. They did not love the French language.

72. "It seemed almost as if the poor man wanted to give us all he knew before going away and put it all into our heads at one stroke". Which of the following sentences does not use the phrase 'at one stroke' correctly?
A. The smoke choked the joking man at one stroke.
B. I managed to please both the buyer and the seller at one stroke.
C. Let's settle the matter at one stroke.
D. When the economy crashed, thousands lost their jobs, their homes and their pensions at one stroke.

73. 'They looked like little flags floating everywhere in the school room, hung from the rod at the top of our desks.' In the given sentence, which literary device has been used:
A. Alliteration B. Metaphor
C. Simile D. Both (A) and (C)

74. Choose the term which best matches the tone of statement: "but he had the courage to hear every lesson to the very last".
A. Acceptance B. Neglect
C. Discipline D. Regret

75. "I never saw him look so tall". Which of the following best captures M. Hamel on the last day of school?
A. Cranky, measurable, dedicated, resigned
B. Patient, dignified, emotional, courageous
C. Calm, nostalgic, disappointed, patriotic
D. Proud, reproachful, persistent, heroic

76. What do the marching soldiers under the windows represent?
A. The Dawn of Prussia and the defeat of French people
B. The defeat of Prussia
C. The victory of French
D. None of these

77. Pick a quote that best describes the theme of the story:
A. What is the nation without a mother tongue?
B. The rhythm of my body is the same as my mother tongue. It is in this rhythm where I find sanctity, that I can return to my mother who is everywhere in the universe.
C. Language is the blood of the soil into which thoughts run and out of which they grow.
D. Poetry is the mother tongue of the human race.

78. What did Hauser bring?
A. Sweets B. Children
C. Friends D. Old Primer

79. What made Franz forget M. Hamel's ruler and crankiness?
A. Police Patrolling
B. Strange Quietness
C. Bustle on the streets
D. The idea of his going away

80. When people are enslaved, what key do they have to the prison, according to M. Hamel?
A. Their behaviour B. Power
C. Aggressiveness D. Mother tongue

81. What does the expression "in great dread of scolding" mean?
A. To be happy about it
B. Very badly scared of scolding
C. To be indifferent
D. None of these

82. M. Hamel is introduced as a ruler-wielding teacher. This demonstrates that:
A. he is concerned B. he is adamant
C. he is unfeeling D. he is a hard taskmaster

83. What is the moral that Alphonse Daudet wants to bring out?
A. Not to put off things that one can do that day
B. Old order changed to new
C. One should accept everything that happens
D. Teachers should be respected

84. For the last two years, where did all the bad news come from?
A. The Bulletin Board
B. Town Hall
C. School
D. M. Hamel's House

85. What did Mr. Hamel bring for his class on his last day in the school?
A. New pens B. New notebooks
C. Sweets D. Story books

86. What was Franz expected to be prepared for at school that day?
A. Song B. Dance
C. Essay writing D. Participles

87. Who asked Franz not to hurry to school?
A. Old Hauser B. Former Mayor
C. Former Postmaster D. Blacksmith Watcher

88. The story is set in the days of:
A. Franco–Prussian war (1870-71)
B. Franco–German war (1870-71)
C. Franco–Poland war (1880-81)
D. Franco–Austrian war (1880-81)

89. Prussia then comprised of:
A. Germany, Poland, Parts of Austria
B. Germany, Italy, Poland
C. Germany, England, France
D. France, Austria, Poland

LOST SPRING
By Anees Jung

Directions: *Read each of the following passages carefully and choose the best answer to each question out of the four alternatives.*

PASSAGE-1

"This morning, Saheb is on his way to the milk booth. In his hand is a steel canister. "I now work in a tea stall down the road", he says, pointing in the distance. "I am paid 800 rupees and all my meals". Does he like the job? I ask. His face, I see, has lost the carefree look. The steel canister seems heavier than the plastic bag he would carry so lightly over his shoulder. The bag was his. The canister belongs to the man who owns the tea shop. Saheb is no longer his own master!"

90. "His face, I see, has lost the carefree look". This means as per the assumption of the author, in his looks, Saheb is ....
A. Not burdened with responsibility
B. Burdened with responsibility
C. Burdened but without any responsibility
D. Not burdened but feels responsible

91. Choose the appropriate statements for "Saheb is no longer his own master!"
(*i*) Saheb carries his bag for rag picking.
(*ii*) Saheb works in a tea stall.
(*iii*) Saheb is paid 800 rupees.
(*iv*) Saheb carries canister.
A. (*i*), (*ii*) & (*iii*) B. (*i*), (*ii*) & (*iv*)
C. (*i*), (*iii*) & (*iv*) D. (*ii*), (*iii*) & (*iv*)

92. Read the statements given below.
Choose the correct statement to analyse the mental condition of Saheb-e-Alam.
A. He seems to be dignified working at the tea-stall.
B. He seems to be proud collecting milk from the milk booth.
C. He seems to be responsible carrying the steel canister.
D. He seems to be enjoying his freewheel at the tea-stall.

93. Select the option/options that does *not* explain Saheb's nature of thinking in his new job at the tea stall.
(*i*) He thinks collecting milk is a part of his new job.
(*ii*) Canister is heavy, but he thinks he should carry it for survival.
(*iii*) He is earning 800 rupees and all meals, so he should justify the job.
(*iv*) He is a servant now, he can have a carefree life.
A. Only option (*iii*)
B. Both options (*ii*) & (*iv*)
C. Both options (*i*) & (*iv*)
D. Only option (*iv*)

94. Choose the option that most appropriately fills in the blanks, for the following description of the given extract.
People migrate from villages to cities in search of a better life. They want to earn money so that they can lead a good life and (*i*) ________ their children in a better way. As cities have more (*ii*) ________ for work, this makes them migrate from the villages to these big cities. (*iii*) ________ all miseries and challenges of life at young age, Saheb even finds a job in a tea stall, shifting from rag picking to (*iv*) ________ his struggle for survival.
A. (*i*) give; (*ii*) scope; (*iii*) controlling; (*iv*) continue
B. (*i*) rare; (*ii*) opportunities; (*iii*) Accepting; (*iv*) prove
C. (*i*) provide; (*ii*) jobs; (*iii*) Denying; (*iv*) stop
D. (*i*) leave; (*ii*) chances; (*iii*) Chasing; (*iv*) deal

PASSAGE-2

Savita, a young girl in a drab pink dress, sits alongside an elderly woman, soldering pieces of glass. As her hands move mechanically like the tongs of a machine, I wonder if she knows the sanctity of the bangles she helps make. It symbolises an Indian woman's suhaag, auspiciousness in marriage. It will dawn on her suddenly one day when her head is draped with a red veil, her hands dyed red with henna, and red bangles rolled onto her wrists. She will then become a bride. Like the old woman beside her who became one many years ago. She still has bangles on her wrist, but no light in her eyes. "Ek waqt ser bhar khana bhi nahin khaya", she says, in a voice drained of joy. She has not enjoyed even one full meal in her entire lifetime — that's what she has reaped! Her husband, an old man with a flowing beard, says, "I know nothing except bangles. All I have done is make a house for the family to live in." Hearing him, one wonders if he has achieved what many have failed in their lifetime. He has a roof over his head!

95. I know nothing except bangles. Which one of the following best speaks about the character of the old man.

A. (*i*) Cunning; (*ii*) wise; (*iii*) soft; (*iv*) obedient
B. (*i*) Intelligent; (*ii*) irresponsible; (*iii*) caring; (*iv*) simple
C. (*i*) Innocent; (*ii*) foresight (*iii*) responsible; (*iv*) caring
D. (*i*) Impeccable; (*ii*) honest; (*iii*) rude; (*iv*) simple

96. Which option best indicates that the old woman too has sacrificed something in her life for the sake of her family.

(*i*) The old woman has bangles on her wrist, but she can't see them.
(*ii*) She has not even enjoyed one full meal in her life time.
(*iii*) She never supported her husband in bangle making in her life.
(*iv*) She knows nothing expect making bangles which symbolise an Indian woman's suhaag.

A. (*i*) & (*iv*) B. (*ii*) & (*iii*)
C. (*iii*) & (*iv*) D. (*i*) & (*ii*)

97. "Ek waqt ser bhar khana bhi nahin khaya", the grand mother says. Her voice indicates that she is ....

A. Undergoing an emotion of great happiness.
B. Going through an emotion which lacks happiness.
C. Undergoing an emotion of anger and frustration.
D. Experiencing an emotion which reflects her fear and anxiety.

98. Which of these statements is *ture* about the husband of the elderly woman?

A. He says he knows nothing about making bangles in Firozabad.
B. He did not enjoy even one full meal in his entire life for the sake of his family.
C. He says he knows only bangle making and nothing else in his life.
D. All he has done in his life for the sake of his wife is making bangles for her.

99. "I wonder if she knows the sanctity of the bangles she helps make". In this statement, "I wonder reflects" the author's ....

A. Curiosity B. Anxiety
C. Embarrassment D. Restlessness

100. The narrator asks Saheb to go to school. What is the intension of the narrator here?

A. Narrator wants Saheb to enjoy in the school.
B. Narrator wants Saheb to go for rag picking and school as well.
C. Narrator wants Saheb to go to school instead of rag picking.
D. Narrator seriously encourages him to go to school.

101. "It takes longer to build a school" says the narrator to Saheb. What does the narrator really mean here?

A. There is a possibility to build a school.
B. It takes very long time to build a school.
C. There is a way to build a school.
D. There is no intention to build a school.

102. "After months of knowing him, I ask him his name. "Saheb-e-Alam", he announces. He does not know what it means. If he knew its meaning — lord of the universe — Saheb would have a hard time believing it" because ....

A. He was too poor to bear such a big name.
B. He was not suitable to bear such a big name.
C. His name was opposite to his life.
D. His life was quite suitable to his name.

103. "I like the game", he hums, "content to watch it standing behind the fence". The above sentence refers that Saheb ....

A. Is not satisfied with watching the game standing by the fence of club.
B. Is satisfied with watching the game standing by the fence of the club.
C. Wants to watch the game standing inside the fence of the club.
D. Is not allowed to watch the game even from the fence of the club.

104. "His dream looms like a mirage amidst the dust of streets that fill his town Firozabad, famous for its bangles". For Anees Jung, the dream of Mukesh appears as it is far away from reality. As per the circumstances, she thinks Mukesh would ....

A. Gradually be adjusted with the demands of his family.
B. Gradually be satisfied with his family profession.
C. Gradually be influenced by the societal pressures.
D. All the above

105. "It is his karam, his destiny", says Mukesh's grandmother, who has watched her own husband go blind with the dust from polishing the glass of bangles.

Which one of the following statements appropriately suits to the mind-set or lookout of Mukesh's grandmother.

A. She doesn't like her family members in the business of bangle making.

B. She wants her grandson, Mukesh to find his own destiny.

C. She thinks that her husband has gone blind due to his fate.

D. She doesn't believe in karam and destiny which play a major role in the lives of bangle makers.

106. "I want to be a motor mechanic", Mukesh repeats. Which one of the following best speaks about his repetition.

A. He is thinking to become a motor mechanic if everything is comfortable for him.

B. He wants to be a motor mechanic if his parents permit him.

C. He is strong in his decision of becoming a motor mechanic.

D. He wants to become a motor mechanic to impress the author.

107. The author asks, "Do you know anything about car driving?" Mukesh answers, "I will learn to drive a car". Choose the best efforts from the following which can help Mukesh materialise his dream of becoming a car driver.

A. His dedication and readiness to learn about car driving from the garage.

B. His mental state of uncertainty and lack of conviction to dream of cars.

C. His determination to walk to the garage which is a long way from his home.

D. All the above except (B)

108. Assertion: The children of Seemapuri are living a life of exploitation.

Reason: Extreme poverty forces them to lead such a life.

A. Both (A) and (R) are true and (R) is the correct explanation of (A).

B. Both (A) and (R) are true and (R) is not the correct explanation of (A).

C. (A) is true, but (R) is false.

D. (A) is false, but (R) is true.

109. Assertion: Most of the ragpickers appear walking bare foot in cities and on village roads.

Reason: They were caught in the web of a vicious circle of middlemen.

A. Both (A) and (R) are true and (R) is the correct explanation of (A).

B. Both (A) and (R) are true and (R) is not the correct explanation of (A).

C. (A) is true, but (R) is false.

D. (A) is false, but (R) is true.

110. Assertion: Garbage is wrapped in wonder for the elders in Seemapuri.

Reason: For the elders, it is a means of survival.

A. Both (A) and (R) are true and (R) is the correct explanation of (A).

B. Both (A) and (R) are true and (R) is not the correct explanation of (A).

C. (A) is true, but (R) is false.

D. (A) is false, but (R) is true.

111. Assertion: Saheb was not allowed to play tennis in the neighbourhood club.

Reason: He had proper shoes but no racquet to play tennis.

A. Both (A) and (R) are true and (R) is the correct explanation of (A).

B. Both (A) and (R) are true and (R) is not the correct explanation of (A).

C. (A) is true, but (R) is false.

D. Both (A) and (R) are false.

112. Assertion: Saheb is no longer his own master.

Reason: The tea canister which he carries is his own property.

A. Both (A) and (R) are true and (R) is the correct explanation of (A).

B. Both (A) and (R) are true and (R) is not the correct explanation of (A).

C. (A) is true, but (R) is false.

D. (A) is false, but (R) is true.

113. Statement 1: Mukesh insists on being his own master.

Statement 2: He has no fascination for continuing his family profession.

A. If Statement 1 is the cause, Statement 2 is the effect.

B. If Statement 1 is the effect, Statement 2 is the cause.

C. Both the statements are the effects of a common cause.

D. Both the statements are the effects of independent causes.

114. Statement 1: The children's eyes are more adjusted to the dark than to the light outside.

Statement 2: The boys and girls end up losing their eye sight before they become adults.

A. If Statement 1 is the cause, Statement 2 is the effect.

B. If Statement 1 is the effect, Statement 2 is the cause.

C. Both the statements are the effects of a common cause.

D. Both the statements are the effects of independent causes.

115. Statement 1: The young bangle makers could not organise themselves into a cooperative.

Statement 2: They were caught in a web of vicious circle.

A. If Statement 1 is the cause, Statement 2 is the effect.

B. If Statement 1 is the effect, Statement 2 is the cause.

C. Both the statements are the effects of a common cause.

D. Both the statements are the effects of independent causes.

116. Statement 1: Exemplary punishment should be given by law to those who employ the children to work in hazardous industries.

Statement 2: Child Labour is banned by the law.

A. If Statement 1 is the cause, Statement 2 is the effect.

B. If Statement 1 is the effect, Statement 2 is the cause.

C. Both the statements are the effects of a common cause.

D. Both the statements are the effects of independent causes.

117. Statement 1: Saheb's family left Bangladesh and came to India.

Statement 2: Saheb is no longer his own master.

A. If Statement 1 is the cause, Statement 2 is the effect.

B. If Statement 1 is the effect, Statement 2 is the cause.

C. Both the statements are the effects of a common cause.

D. Both the statements are the effects of independent causes.

DEEP WATER
By William Douglas

Directions: *Read each of the following passages carefully and choose the best answer to each question out of the four alternatives.*

PASSAGE-1

I had not been there long when in came a big bruiser of a boy, probably eighteen years old. He had thick hair on his chest. He was a beautiful physical specimen, with legs and arms that showed rippling muscles. He yelled, Hi, Skinny! How'd you like to be ducked?

118. How did the pool look like when the narrator went there?

A. Pleasant and lively.

B. Thrilling and attractive.

C. Timid and indifferent.

D. Still and clean.

119. Why did the narrator sit on the side of the pool?

A. To enjoy the beauty of the pool.

B. He was afraid of entering the pool alone.

C. To wait for the coach to arrive.

D. To prepare himself mentally to enter the pool.

120. What did the big bruiser of a boy do?

A. He flashed his rippling muscles.

B. He frightened the narrator.

C. He picked the narrator and tossed him into the deep end.

D. He took the narrator along to make him learn swimming.

121. The word 'bruiser' in the extract means:

A. Aggressor B. Genius

C. Gentleman D. Intelligent

PASSAGE-2

I laughed and said, "Well, Mr. Terror, what do you think you can do to me"? It fled and I swam on.

122. Who is 'I' here?

A. William Doughlas B. Anees Jung

C. Khushwant Singh D. Kamala Das

123. Who is being addressed to as Mr. Terror?

A. Coach B. Young boy

C. Water D. None of these

124. Why did the narrator laugh?

A. Happy go lucky nature

B. Mocking Mr. Terror

C. Confident of defeating Mr. Terror

D. All of these

125. Why did Mr. Terror leave?

A. Could intimidate the narrator.

B. Could not make the narrator beg for help.

C. Could brighten up the narrator.

D. Could not frighten the narrator.

PASSAGE-3

It had happened when I was ten or eleven years old. I had decided to learn to swim. There was a pool at the Y.M.C.A in Yakima that offered exactly the opportunity. The Yakima River was treacherous. Mother continually warned against it and kept fresh in my mind the details of each drowning in the river. But the Y.M.C.A pool was safe.

126. Who is 'I' in the above lines?

A. The narrator B. The coach

C. The young boy D. Father of the young boy.

127. Why did mother not allow 'I' to learn swimming in a river?
A. Religion did not allow this.
B. Social barriers to learn swimming
C. Afraid about safety of her child.
D. All of these

128. What was reported to 'I'?
A. Coldness of water in Yakima river.
B. Coldness of water in swimming pool.
C. Drowning cases in Yakima river.
D. Drowning cases in swimming pool.

129. How was Y.M.C.A. a safe pool?
A. It had warm water.
B. It was open only during day time.
C. It had no water in it.
D. It was two to three feet deep at the shallow end.

Directions: *Choose the correct option with reference to the two statements given below:*

130. **Statement 1:** Douglas tried his best to jump out of water.

Statement 2: After a while, Douglas was not anxious in water.
A. If Statement 1 is the cause, Statement 2 is the effect.
B. If Statement 1 is the effect, Statement 2 is the cause.
C. Both the statements are the effect of a common cause.
D. Both the statements are the effects of independent causes.

131. **Statement 1:** The author's father laughed to mock his son's inability to swim.

Statement 2: The author wanted to swim just to prove to his father that he can swim.
A. Statement 1 is true, but Statement 2 is false.
B. Statement 1 is false, but Statement 2 is true.
C. Both Statement 1 and Statement 2 cannot be inferred.
D. Both Statement 1 and Statement 2 can be inferred.

132. **Statement 1:** Douglas had been haunted by fear for many years.

Statement 2: Douglas decided to learn to swim.
A. If Statement 1 is the cause, Statement 2 is the effect.
B. If Statement 1 is the effect, Statement 2 is the cause.
C. Both the statements are the effect of a common cause.
D. Both the statements are the effects of independent causes.

133. **Statement 1:** The narrator's mother warned him against swimming in the Yakima River.

Statement 2: Many people swam safely in the Yakima River.
A. Statement 1 is false, but Statement 2 is true.
B. Statement 1 is true, but Statement 2 is false.
C. Both Statement 1 and Statement 2 are true
D. Both Statement 1 and Statement 2 are false.

134. **Statement 1:** I crossed to oblivion.

Statement 2: The curtain of life fell.
A. If Statement 1 is the cause, Statement 2 is the effect.
B. If Statement 1 is the effect, Statement 2 is the cause.
C. Both the statements are the effect of a common cause.
D. Both the statements are the effects of independent causes.

135. **Statement 1:** The narrator was in the grip of fear of water.

Statement 2: This deprived him of the joys of canoeing, boating, swimming and fishing.
A. Statement 1 is false, but Statement 2 is true.
B. Statement 1 is true, but Statement 2 is false.
C. Both Statement 1 and Statement 2 are true
D. Both Statement 1 and Statement 2 are false.

136. **Statement 1:** At the age of ten or eleven, the narrator decided to learn to swim with water wings at the Y.M.C.A. pool.

Statement 2: The Y.M.C.A. pool was dangerous at the shallow end.
A. Statement 1 is false, but Statement 2 is true.
B. Statement 1 is true, but Statement 2 is false.
C. Both Statement 1 and Statement 2 are true.
D. Both Statement 1 and Statement 2 are false.

137. **Statement 1:** In death there is peace.

Statement 2: There is terror only in the fear of death.
A. If Statement 1 is the cause, Statement 2 is the effect.
B. If Statement 1 is the effect, Statement 2 is the cause.
C. Both the statements are the effect of a common cause.
D. Both the statements are the effects of independent causes.

138 **Statement 1:** The narrator went to different lakes to swim.

Statement 2: He found tiny vestiges of fear still gripped him.
A. If Statement 1 is the cause, Statement 2 is the effect

B. If Statement 1 is the effect, Statement 2 is the cause
C. Both the statements are the effect of a common cause
D. Both the statements are the effects of independent causes

139. Statement 1: The narrator swam up & down the Warm Lake.

Statement 2: He could finally overcome his fear of water.
A. Statement 1 is false, but Statement 2 is true.
B. Statement 1 is true, but Statement 2 is false.
C. Both Statement 1 and Statement 2 are true.
D. Both Statement 1 and Statement 2 are false.

140. Statement 1: As the narrator sank into the pool, light was going out.

Statement 2: There was no more panic.
A. If Statement 1 is the cause, Statement 2 is the effect.
B. If Statement 1 is the effect, Statement 2 is the cause.
C. Both the statements are the effect of a common cause.
D. Both the statements are the effects of independent causes.

141. Statement 1: The narrator was going down into the pool.

Statement 2: He planned to make a big jump upwards and succeeded.
A. Statement 1 is false, but Statement 2 is true.
B. Statement 1 is true, but Statement 2 is false.
C. Both Statement 1 and Statement 2 are true.
D. Both Statement 1 and Statement 2 are false.

Directions: *Read each of the following passages carefully and choose the best answer to each question out of the four alternatives.*

PASSAGE-1

Then I started down a third time. I sucked for air and got water. The yellowish light was going out. Then all effort ceased. I relaxed. Even my legs felt limp; and a blackness swept over my brain.

142. "Then all efforts ceased" What did the author mean by this?
A. He lost all hope.
B. He yielded himself.
C. That he gave in courage to survive
D. All of these

143. Which of the statement is *true* with the reference to the extract?
A. His friend was coming to help him
B. His legs were almost immobilized
C. His arms were moving unceasingly
D. He could see a great light.

144. Which option indicates more accurately narrator's state of mind?
A. His mind was blank
B. He was greatly terrified
C. He was excited
D. He was puzzled

145. Which option indicates that the poet was becoming unconscious?
A. The yellowish light was going out.
B. A blackness swept over my brain.
C. All effort ceased.
D. My legs felt limp.

PASSAGE-2

The belt went through a pulley that ran on an overhead cable. He held on to the end of the rope, and we went back and forth, across the pool, hour after hour, day after day, week after week. On each trip across the pool a bit of the panic seized me. Each time the instructor relaxed his hold on the rope and I went under, some of the old terror returned and my legs froze. It was three months before the tension began to slack

146. "A 'pulley' that ran on an overhead cable". What does this mean?
A. An apparatus with a wheel
B. An apparatus with a rope
C. An apparatus without wheel
D. An apparatus with a wheel and a rope

147. The statement "Back and forth, across the pool" indicates:
A. Moving from one point to another
B. Moving clockwise and anticlockwise
C. Rising and falling
D. Ascending and descending

148. 'Tension began to slack' implies:
A. Fear started multiplying
B. Fear started increasing
C. Stress started decreasing
D. Stress started intensifying

149. 'Panic seized me' refers to:
A. Emancipating with joy
B. Fear gripped him
C. Boundless joy
D. Full of agony

PASSAGE-3

The experience had a deep meaning for me, as only those who have known stark terror and conquered it can appreciate. In death there is peace. There is terror only in the fear of death, as Roosevelt knew when he said, "All we have to fear is fear itself." Because I had experienced both the sensation of dying and the terror that fear of it can produce, the will to live somehow grew in intensity. At last I felt released — free to walk the trails and climb the peaks and to brush aside fear.

150. "In death there is peace" choose the correct option with reference to the above:
A. End of one's existence is happiness
B. That death is solace & comfort
C. That one's final abode is uncertain
D. That there is torment in death

151. The phrase 'Brush aside' refers to:
A. Get closer to B. To finally get rid of
C. Take it for granted D. Not care at all

152. "All we have to fear is fear itself". What does the narrator learn from President Roosevelt's statement?
A. To cancel the fear B. To frighten the fear
C. To dispel the fear D. To prevent the fear

153. "I had experienced both the sensation of dying and terror that fear of it can produce", which of the following idioms might describe the above statement
A. "To be scared to death"
B. "Once in a blue moon"
C. "With a silver spoon"
D. "Hand to mouth"

MY MOTHER AT SIXTY-SIX
By Kamala Das

Directions: *Read the following extract and choose the most appropriate option for each question.*

I saw my mother,
beside me, doze, open mouthed,
her face ashen like that of a corpse and realised with pain
that she was as old as she looked
but soon put that thought away,
and looked out at Young Trees sprinting,

154. Kamala Das turned her attention from her mother, because
A. She was feeling guilty.
B. She was shirking her responsibility.
C. She was trying to escape from pain filled emotions.
D. She didn't like the idea of her mother growing old.

155. The Poetic Device used in the above lines is also found in
A. Leena is the Lata Mangeshkar of Hyderabad.
B. Ayra is as cool as a cucumber to receive the heavy news.
C. The elephant is heavier than many other animals.
D. He is a tiger

156. The words 'doze' and 'ashen' reflect that the mother was:
A. Tired and sleepy
B. Sick and unhealthy
C. Lost strength and vigour as she had grown old
D. Hale and healthy

157. What did the poet realize seeing her mother beside her in the car?
A. That her mother may not survive for long
B. That her mother was suffering
C. That her mother wanted her to be with her
D. That she wanted to go with her daughter

158. 'Thought Away' means:
A. Diverted
B. Escaped
C. Drifted
D. Avoided

159. 'Trees sprinting' contains:
A. Metaphor B. Personification
C. Simile D. Alliteration

160. The Literary Devices used in the above extract are:
A. Simile and Refrain
B. Simile and personification
C. Simile and Alliteration
D. Only simile

Directions: *Read the following extract and choose the most appropriate option for each question.*

I looked again at her,
wan, pale as a late winter's moon and felt that old familiar ache,
my childhood's fear,
but all I said was, see you soon, Amma,
all I did was smile and smile and smile......

161. Kamala Das comparing her mother to winter moon signifies:
A. Human life is as short as that of the moon
B. Though the mother is old, she is still beautiful
C. Winter is the last season of the year
D. Mother is about to die

162. Though she feels painful, Kamala Das smiles on ......
A. To hide her sad feelings and emotions
B. To encourage her mother to smile and feel good
C. Not to dishearten her mother by showing her worried face
D. All the above

163. The tone of the poem is:
A. Pensive and sorrowful
B. Disillusioned and unhappy
C. Happy but discontented
D. Remorseful

Directions: *Study the two statements, in each question, labelled as Assertion (A) and Reason (R).*

164. Assertion (A): Kamala Das was honest and didn't have any hesitation in describing her mother's ageing face.

Reason (R): She compares her mother's face to a corpse.

A. Both (A) and (R) are true and (R) is the correct explanation of (A)
B. Both (A) and (R) are true, but (R) is not the correct explanation of (A)
C. (A) is true, but (R) is false
D. (A) is false, but (R) is true

165. Assertion (A): Kamala Das didn't like her mother growing old.

Reason (R): She turns her attention away from her mother.

A. Both (A) and (R) are true and (R) is the correct explanation of (A)
B. Both, (A) and (R) are true, but (R) is not the correct explanation of (A)
C. (A) is true, but (R) is false
D. (A) is false, but (R) is true

166. Assertion (A): The poet feels the pain of separation at the airport.

Reason (R): She started smiling at her.

A. Both (A) and (R) are true and (R) is the correct explanation of (A)
B. Both (A) and (R) are true, but (R) is not the correct explanation of (A)
C. (A) is true, but (R) is false
D. (A) is false, but (R) is true

167. Assertion (A): The poet gracefully accepts the reality of her mother growing old.

Reason (R): She left for her destination without much difficulty.

A. Both (A) and (R) are true and (R) is the correct explanation of (A)
B. Both (A) and (R) are true, but (R) is not the correct explanation of (A)
C. (A) is true, but (R) is false
D. Both (A) and (R) are false

168. Assertion (A): The poet didn't reveal her sorrow on her face in the airport.

Reason (R): She didn't like to create a scene there.

A. Both (A) and (R) are true and (R) is the correct explanation of (A)
B. Both (A) and (R) are true, but (R) is not the correct explanation of (A)
C. (A) is true, but (R) is false
D. (A) is false, but (R) is true

169. Assertion (A): Kamala Das took her mother to airport.

Reason (R): She wanted to spend some more time with her.

A. Both (A) and (R) are true and (R) is the correct explanation of (A)
B. Both (A) and (R) are true, but (R) is not the correct explanation of (A)
C. (A) is true, but (R) is false
D. (A) is false, but (R) is true

170. Assertion (A): The poet compares her mother to young trees.

Reason (R): Her mother was also young once.

A. Both (A) and (R) are true and (R) is the correct explanation of (A)
B. Both (A) and (R) are true, but (R) is not the correct explanation of (A)
C. (A) is true, but (R) is false
D. (A) is false, but (R) is true

171. Assertion (A): The poet advocates the aged parents should be taken care of by their children.

Reason (R): She looked after her mother by being by her side.

A. Both (A) and (R) are true and (R) is the correct explanation of (A)
B. Both (A) and (R) are true, but (R) is not the correct explanation of (A)
C. (A) is true, but (R) is false
D. Both (A) and (R) are false

172. Assertion (A): The poet compares her mother to a winter moon

Reason (R): Winter moon doesn't shine well like in other seasons.

A. Both (A) and (R) are true and (R) is the correct explanation of (A)
B. Both (A) and (R) are true, but (R) is not the correct explanation of (A)
C. (A) is true, but (R) is false
D. (A) is false, but (R) is true

173. Assertion (A): Kamala Das was scared of losing her mother or her company from her childhood days.

Reason (R): So, kamala Das was expecting this and hence ready for this to happen.

A. Both (A) and (R) are true and (R) is the correct explanation of (A)
B. Both (A) and (R) are true, but (R) is not the correct explanation of (A)
C. (A) is true, but (R) is false
D. (A) is false, but (R) is true

AN ELEMENTARY SCHOOL CLASSROOM IN A SLUM

By Stephen Spender

174. Assertion (A): The slum children's faces are like rootless weeds and their hair unkempt.

Reason (R): The slum children were malnourished.

A. Both (A) and (R) are true, but (R) is the correct explanation of (A)
B. Both (A) and (R) are true, but (R) is not the correct explanation of (A)
C. (A) is false, but (R) is true
D. (A) is true, but (R) is false

175. Assertion (A): The stunted unlucky heir of twisted bones is reciting a father's gnarled disease.

Reason (R): The boy has been born with polio.

A. (A) is true, but (R) is false
B. (A) is false, but (R) is true
C. Both (A) and (R) are true, but (R) is the correct explanation of (A)
D. Both (A) and (R) are true, but (R) is not the correct explanation of (A)

176. Assertion (A): The small boy is dreaming of squirrel's game.

Reason (R): The boy is not interested in the lesson as it is boring.

A. (A) is true, but (R) is false
B. (A) is false, but (R) is true
C. Both (A) and (R) are true, but (R) is the correct explanation of (A)
D. Both (A) and (R) are true, but (R) is not the correct explanation of (A)

177. Statement 1: The slum children were like bottle bits of stones.

Statement 2: The slum children were thin and weak but look beautiful.

A. Statement 1 is true, but Statement 2 is false
B. Statement 1 is false, but Statement 2 is true
C. Both Statement 1 and Statement 2 are true, but Statement 2 is the correct explanation of Statement 1
D. Both Statement 1 and Statement 2 are true, but Statement 2 is not the correct explanation of Statement 1

178. Assertion (A): Ships, Sun and love tempt the children to steal

Reason (R): The slum children have the tendency to steal.

A. (A) is true, but (R) is false
B. (A) is false, but (R) is true
C. Both (A) and (R) are true, but (R) is the correct explanation of (A)
D. Both (A) and (R) are true, but (R) is not the correct explanation of (A)

179. Assertion (A): The slum children should be taken to the green fields outside.

Reason (R): The slum children were forced to stay inside the classroom.

A. (R) is the explanation of (A)
B. (A) is the explanation (R)
C. (A) is the problem and (R) is the solution
D. (R) is the problem while (A) is the solution

180. Assertion (A): The poet wants the children to break barriers and be free.

Reason (R): The poet doesn't want them to be superstitious.

A. Both (A) and (R) are true, but (R) is the correct explanation of (A)
B. Both (A) and (R) are true, but (R) is not the correct explanation of (A)
C. (A) is false, but (R) is true
D. (A) is true, but (R) is false

181. The following words show that the children suffer from 'acute malnutrition':

1. Stunted through 2. Twisted bones
3. Paper-seeming 4. Skin peeped

A. 1 and 2 are true B. 2 and 3 are true
C. 3 and 4 are true D. All are true

182. Assertion (A): The classroom walls are painted in 'sour cream':

Reason (R): The colour symbolizes the bleak future of the slum children.

A. Both (A) and (R) are true, but (R) is the correct explanation of (A)
B. Both (A) and (R) are true, but (R) is not the correct explanation of (A)
C. (A) is false, but (R) is true
D. (A) is true, but (R) is false

183. Assertion (A): The slum children consider Shakespeare wicked.

Reason (R): The slum children are evil and they have malice against him.

A. Both (A) and (R) are true, but (R) is the correct explanation of (A)
B. Both (A) and (R) are true, but (R) is not the correct explanation of (A)
C. (A) is false, but (R) is true
D. (A) is true, but (R) is false

184. Statement 1: The slum children consider map a bad example.

Statement 2: The world in the map has no relation to their world.

A. Statement 1 is true, but Statement 2 is false
B. Statement 1 is false, but Statement 2 is true
C. Both Statement 1 and Statement 2 are true, but Statement 2 is the correct explanation of Statement 1
D. Both Statement 1 and Statement 2 are true, but Statement 2 is not the correct explanation of Statement 1

Directions: *Read the extracts given below and answer the questions that follow.*

POEM-1

Far far from gusty waves these children's faces.
Like rootless weeds, the hair torn around their pallor
The tall girl with her weighed-down head. The paper-seeming boy,
with rat's eyes.

185. What does the poet contrast the children's faces with?
A. Flowers B. Stars
C. Waves D. Plants

186. How do the faces of these children look?
A. beautiful and attractive
B. like rootless weeds
C. ugly and awkward
D. vigorous and refreshing

187. Why are they compared to rootless weeds?
A. because they are healthy
B. because they are malnourished
C. because they are not beautiful
D. because they are from rural background

188. Why is the head of the tall girl 'weighed down'?
A. because she is doing something
B. because she is depressed due to abject poverty
C. she is reading something
D. she is not interested

189. What figure of speech is used in the last line?
A. Alliteration B. Simile
C. Metaphor D. Personification

190. What does 'the paper-seeming boy' imply?
A. he eats papers
B. he sells papers
C. he is lean and thin like a paper
D. he is pure like a paper

POEM-2

............The stunted, unlucky heir
of twisted bones, reciting a father's gnarled disease,
His lesson, from his desk. At the back of the dim class
One unnoted, sweet and young. His eyes live in a dream
Of squirrel's game, in tree room other than this.

191. Why does the poet call the boy 'unlucky heir'?
A. he lost his father
B. his father left her mother
C. his father lost all money
D. he has inherited a disease of twisted bones

192. What is he reciting?
A. devotional songs
B. school lessons
C. his father's gnarled disease
D. folklore

193. Why was the boy unnoted?
A. Because he is small and sitting at the back
B. Because he is not intelligent
C. Because he is illiterate
D. Because he is not fair

194. What does the boy dream of?
A. beautiful world B. squirrel's game
C. owning big house D. riding a bike

195. What similarity do they have with respect to their physical condition?
A. all were neat and tidy
B. all were untidy
C. they were malnourished
D. all were beautiful

POEM-3

On sour cream walls, donations, Shakespeare's head,
Cloudless at dawn, civilized dome riding all cities.
Belled, flowery, Tyrolese valley. Open-handed map
Awarding the world its world.

196. Why were the classroom walls called sour cream walls?
A. because they were painted bright colour
B. because they were painted light yellow colour
C. the colour is pleasant and beautiful
D. it is dark brown colour

197. What things were displayed on the walls of the classroom?
A. medals won by the institution
B. freedom fighters
C. philosophers
D. poets, buildings, world map and valleys

198. What does the world map award?
A. A lot of knowledge
B. a lot of treasure
C. Rich, beautiful world
D. experience

199. Why is Shakespeare called wicked?
A. Because he represents the rich world
B. Because he wrote against them
C. He does not give them happiness and comfort
D. he wrote about their lives

POEM-4

And yet, for these
Children, these windows, not this map, their world.
Where all their future's painted with a fog,
A narrow street sealed in with a lead sky
Far far from rivers, capes, and stars of words.

200. What is the world of slum children?
A. Beautiful fields
B. The windows of the classroom
C. Slum
D. Mountains

201. Why is their future painted with fog?
A. Because they work tirelessly in dark cells
B. Because the room is filled with fog
C. Because they have no clear vision of future
D. They were denied admission

202. How is their world different from the world in the map?
A. Very similar to their world
B. Contrary to the world in the map
C. Not comfortable
D. Does not offer any clues

POEM-5

Surely, Shakespeare is wicked, the map a bad example,
With ships and sun and love tempting them to steal—
For lives that slyly turn in their cramped holes
From fog to endless night?

203. Why is Shakespeare wicked?
A. he wrote about love
B. he didn't write about them
C. he is very wealthy
D. they have no access to love and happiness

204. Why do the slum children consider map a bad example?
A. it is not showing their place
B. it doesn't help them
C. it shows a world which is quite different from their world
D. it is not visible to them

205. Where do the children spend their lives?
A. in foggy slums B. beautiful fields
C. villages D. cities

206. What do you understand by 'from fog to endless night'?
A. they travel through the fog
B. they work at night
C. they spend their entire lives in slums
D. they grope in darkness

207. Which word in the passage means "narrow"?
A. slyly B. steal
C. tempt D. cramped

POEM-6

Unless, governor, inspector, visitor,
This map becomes their window and these windows
That shut upon their lives like catacombs,

208. Who can change the condition of slum children?
A. school teachers
B. The Principal
C. governor, inspector and visitor
D. parents

209. What action does the poet want them to take?
A. to build a new school
B. to take them to the world outside
C. to provide playground
D. to give them money

210. What are 'catacombs'?
A. underground cemetery
B. the caterpillars
C. the mushrooms
D. edible plants

211. What do the 'catacombs' signify?
A. the dead condition
B. the darkness
C. the little narrow homes of the slum dwellers
D. the difficulties they face

POEM-7

Break O break open till they break the town
And show the children to green fields, and make their world
Run azure on gold sands, and let their tongues
Run naked into books the white and green leaves open
History theirs whose language is the sun.

212. What should be shown to slum children?
A. Beautiful pictures B. films
C. green fields D. historical places

213. What would they break?
A. buildings B. dams
C. the barriers which separate them from the world outside
D. their poor huts

214. How can they understand history?
A. by reading the biographies
B. by reading books
C. by observing nature
D. by viewing films

215. Which word in the stanza means "bright blue"?
A. naked B. sands
C. azure D. doom

KEEPING QUIET
By Pablo Neruda

216. **Assertion (A):** The self-introspection is necessary for all literary persons.
Reason (R): Then only they will be able to meditate and save mankind from destruction.
A. Both (A) and (R) are correct and (R) is the correct explanation of (A).

B. Both (A) and (R) are correct, but (R) is not the correct explanation of (A).
C. (A) is true and (R) is false.
D. (A) is false and (R) is true.

217. Assertion (A): The poet wants everyone to remain quiet for sometime.

Reason (R): Silence will allow to listen to the voices of quiet and serene nature.

A. Both (A) and (R) are correct and (R) is the correct explanation of (A).
B. Both (A) and (R) are correct, but (R) is not the correct explanation of (A).
C. (A) is true and (R) is false.
D. (A) is false and (R) is true.

218. Assertion (A): The exercise of counting upto twelve is suggested by the poet.

Reason (R): It helps to sit still and achieve a sense of togetherness.

A. Both (A) and (R) are correct and (R) is the correct explanation of (A).
B. Both (A) and (R) are correct, but (R) is not the correct explanation of (A).
C. (A) is true and (R) is false.
D. (A) is false and (R) is true.

219. Assertion (A): Pablo Neruda desires to stop inhuman activities.

Reason (R): He wants to live in a peaceful atmosphere.

A. Both (A) and (R) are correct and (R) is the correct explanation of (A).
B. Both (A) and (R) are correct, but (R) is not the correct explanation of (A).
C. (A) is true and (R) is false.
D. (A) is false and (R) is true.

220. Assertion (A): The poet wants everyone to learn from the nature to create and not to destroy.

Reason (R): He wants to escape from his duty towards the mankind.

A. Both (A) and (R) are correct and (R) is the correct explanation of (A).
B. Both (A) and (R) are correct but (R) is not the correct explanation of (A).
C. (A) is true and (R) is false.
D. (A) is false and (R) is true.

221. Identify the tone of Pablo Neruda in the following line:

Perhaps the Earth can teach us....

A. Confident and clear about the future events.
B. Dramatic about the prediction he made.
C. Convinced about the sequence of events to follow.
D. Uncertain, yet hopeful about the possibility.

222. Based on the poem, choose the correct option with reference to the two statements given below.

Statement 1: The poet urges his countrymen to stop for a while.

Statement 2: The poet urges all men to stop for a second.

A. Statement 1 is true, but Statement 2 is false.
B. Statement 1 is false, but Statement 2 is true.
C. Both Statement 1 and Statement 2 are true.
D. Both Statement 1 and Statement 2 cannot be inferred.

223. Select the option that best conveys the feelings of the poet corresponding to the following:

"Fishermen in the cold sea
would not harm whales"

A. • fishermen would not kill whales because they did not need them
• fishermen would not kill whales because they were scared of them

B. • fishermen would not kill whales because they realised the damage that they were causing to the ecosystem
• fishermen would stop killing whales for commercial purposes.

C. • fishermen only wished they would not kill whales
• fishermen would not kill whales because they feared that whale population was fast dwindling

D. • fishermen would not kill whales themselves because others were doing that for them
• fishermen would not kill whales because there was a moratorium on killing whales

224. Based on the poem, choose the correct option with reference to the two statements given below.

Statement 1: The poet is in anguish at the plight of the earth and expresses hope that the situation may improve.

Statement 2: The poet's fears of total destruction of the earth are baseless.

A. Statement 1 is true, but Statement 2 is false.
B. Statement 1 is false, but Statement 2 is true.
C. Both Statement 1 and Statement 2 are true.
D. Both Statement 1 and Statement 2 cannot be inferred.

225. Read the statements given below carefully. Choose the option that best describes these statements, with reference to the poem 'Keeping Quiet'.

Statement I: The poem 'Keeping Quiet' calls for change as much in the individual as human society at large.

Statement II: The poem 'Keeping Quiet' implies that individual change will lead to bigger societal change.

Statement III: Neruda believes that when people come together as a community, they will be able to bring a transformation in each person.

A. Statement I is True, Statement II is False, and Statement III cannot be inferred.
B. Statement I and II cannot be inferred, Statement III is True.
C. Statement I is True, Statements II and III cannot be inferred.
D. Statement I cannot be inferred, Statement II cannot be inferred, Statement III is False.

226. Based on the poem 'Keeping Quiet', choose the correct option with reference to the two statements given below.

Statement 1: The poet cautions that one should not mistake doing nothing for total inactivity.

Statement 2: The poet also avers that he does not mean to associate with death.

A. Statement 1 is true, but Statement 2 is false.
B. Statement 1 is false, but Statement 2 is true.
C. Both Statement 1 and Statement 2 are true.
D. Both Statement 1 and Statement 2 cannot be inferred.

227. Classify (1) to (4) as fact (F) or opinion (O), based on your reading of *Keeping Quiet*.

1. The poet wants all humans to introspect themselves by observing silence.
2. The poet says there would no survivors if there were all kinds of wars.
3. The poet says that man can learn from the earth that we still can hope for life even when everything seems dead.
4. Poet says that men are threatening themselves, through their acts, with death.

A. F-1, 3, 4; O-2
B. F-1, 3; O-2, 4
C. F-2; O-1, 3, 4
D. F-3, 4; O-1, 2

Directions (Qs. No. 228-231): *Read the extract to attempt questions that follow:*

For once on the face of the Earth let's not speak in any language, let's stop for one second, and not move our arms so much. It would be an exotic moment without rush, without engines, we would all be together in a sudden strangeness.

228. The poet uses the word "let's" to _______.

A. initiate a conversation between the poet and the readers.
B. invite readers as part of the poem's larger call to humanity.
C. welcome readers into the world of the poem and its subject.
D. address readers as fellow members of the human race.

229. Margaret Atwood said, "Language divides us into fragments, I wanted to be whole". Choose the option that correctly comments on the relationship between Margaret Atwood's words and the line from the above extract – "let's not speak in any language"

A. Atwood endorses Neruda's call to not speak in any language.
B. Atwood justifies Neruda's request to not engage in any speaking.
C. Atwood undermines Neruda's intent to stop and not speak in any language.
D. Atwood surrenders to Neruda's desire for silence and not speak in any language.

230. Why do you think the poet employs words like "exotic" and "strangeness"?

A. To highlight the importance of everyone being together suddenly for once.
B. To emphasize the frantic activity and chaos that usually envelops human life.
C. To indicate the unfamiliarity of a sudden moment without rush or without engine.
D. To direct us towards keeping quiet and how we would all be together in that silence.

231. Choose the option that correctly matches the idioms given in Column-A with their meanings in Column-B.

Column-A	Column-B
1. On the face of the earth	(*i*) In existence
2. What on earth something	(*ii*) To do all possible to accomplish
3. Move heaven and earth	(*iii*) To express surprise or shock
4. The salt of the earth	(*iv*) To be good and worthy

	1	2	3	4
A.	(*i*)	(*iv*)	(*iii*)	(*ii*)
B.	(*i*)	(*iii*)	(*ii*)	(*iv*)
C.	(*ii*)	(*i*)	(*iv*)	(*iii*)
D.	(*iv*)	(*ii*)	(*iii*)	(*i*)

Directions (Qs. No. 232-235): *Read the extract to attempt questions that follow:*

If we were not so single-minded about keeping our lives moving, and for once could do nothing, perhaps a huge silence might interrupt this sadness of never understanding ourselves and of threatening ourselves with death.

232. Look at the images given below. Choose the image to which the above extract can be seen as an appropriate response.

A.  B. 

C.  D. 

233. What do you think is the mood of the poet in the above extract?
A. gloomy, cynical
B. reflective, inspired
C. introspective, aware
D. critical, demotivated

234. Pick the option that does not complete the given sentence suitably, as per the extract. Threatening ourselves with death ______.
A. feeds on the fear of death.
B. challenges finiteness of life.
C. keeps us rushing through life.
D. makes us restless and impatient.

235. What might the "huge silence" signify?
A. melancholy B. understanding
C. discomfort D. flexibility

Directions (Qs. No. 236-239): *Read the extract to attempt questions that follow:*

236. Choose the option that best describes these statements, with reference to the poem.

Statement I: The poem 'Keeping Quiet' calls for change as much in the individual as human society at large.

Statement II: The poem 'Keeping Quiet' implies that individual change will lead to bigger societal change.

Statement III: Neruda believes that when people come together as a community, they will be able to bring a transformation in each person.
A. Statement I is True, Statement II is False, and Statement III cannot be inferred.
B. Statement I and II cannot be inferred, Statement III is True.
C. Statement I is True, Statements II and III cannot be inferred.
D. Statement I cannot be inferred, Statement II cannot be inferred, Statement III is False.

237. "What I want should not be confused with total inactivity". Choose the option that draws the most accurate parallel.

Keeping quiet: total inactivity = ______ : ______
A. reflection and death
B. silence and chaos
C. stagnation and introspection
D. mindfulness and fear

238. What statement does Neruda make about wars?
A. Wars are of varied kinds – internal, green wars, wars with gas, with fire etc.
B. Wars are wasteful and cause irrecoverable loss and damage to property and life.
C. Wars never yield any winners, and the loss is far greater than what can be measured.
D. Wars are unavoidable in the enduring struggle for human dignity and power.

239. "Now I'll count up to twelve and you keep quiet and I will go". Why does the poet wish to go at the end of the poem?
A. The poet does not believe people will be quiet.
B. The poet has already invested enough time.
C. The poet will move on and seek to inspire others.
D. The poet is marking the end of the poem by leaving.

Directions (Qs. No. 240-243): *Read the extract to attempt questions that follow:*

It would be an exotic moment
without rush, without engines,
we would all be together
in a sudden strangeness.

240. The rhyme of the poem is:
A. aabb B. abab
C. acbc D. None of the above

241. The 'exotic moment' that the poet refers to is, when:
A. the whole world is destroyed
B. all the people divided
C. all the people together with oneness
D. all the people speak only in one language

242. Which of the following is an example of anaphora?
A. We would all be together
B. Without rush, without engines
C. It would be an exotic moment
D. All the above

243. The phrase 'sudden strangeness' is an example of
A. Metaphor B. Simile
C. Oxymoron D. Alliteration

Directions (Qs. No. 244-247): *Read the extract to attempt questions that follow:*

Those who prepare green wars,
wars with gas, wars with fire,

victory with no survivors,
would put on clean clothes
and walk about with their
brothers
in the shade, doing nothing.

244. According to the poet wars would result in:
A. the victory of none
B. the death of all
C. complete annihilation of the world
D. above all

245. The phrase 'clean clothes' symbolises:
A. Peace B. Well ironed clothes
C. New clothes D. Spotless clothes

246. _______ walk about in the shade _______.
A. people who hate one another, singing
B. people who love one another dancing
C. people who wage wars, doing nothing
D. none of the above

247. The poetic device used in the fourth line of the extract is
A. Alliteration B. Personification
C. Transferred epithet D. None of the above

Directions (Qs. No. 248-251): *Read the extract to attempt questions that follow:*

What I want should not be
confused
with total inactivity.
Life is what it is about;
I want no truck with death.

248. Which of the following is not correct?
A. The poet wants all people to be idle doing nothing
B. The poet wants all people to keep quiet to introspect
C. The poet wants all people to be like brothers
D. The poet wants all people to love one another

249. The phrase 'Life is what it is about' means:
A. living life miserably
B. living life licentiously
C. living life carefully
D. living life as it is

250. 'I want no truck with death' indicates that the poet:
A. wants a truck for death
B. does not mean that inactivity is death
C. assures people that they would not face death at all
D. does not want a truck

251. The above extract is taken from _______ written by _______.
A. 'Keeping Quiet' by John Keats
B. 'My Mother at Sixty Six' by Pablo Neruda
C. 'Keeping Quiet' by Pablo Neruda
D. 'My Mother at Sixty Six' by John Keats

Directions (Qs. No. 252-254): *Read the extract to attempt questions that follow:*

Perhaps the Earth can teach us
as when everything seems dead
and later proves to be alive.

252. What can we learn from the Earth?
A. No hope for life after such large scale destruction of the planet
B. Hope for life in spite of the wars of all kinds referred to by the poet
C. No scope for life on the planet
D. Hope for life on other planets, after complete destruction of the Earth

253. The words 'everything seems dead' refer to:
A. animals' life B. plants' life
C. flora and fauna D. none of the above

254. The last line of poem ends on a/an _______ note.
A. pessimistic B. optimistic
C. disillusioned D. imaginary

THE THIRD LEVEL
By Jack Finney

255. Choose the option that correctly identifies which statements are facts and which are opinion:
(*i*) Charley is suffering from mental sickness and he is hallucinating.
(*ii*) Charley's wife is concerned and cares for her husband.
(*iii*) Charley's vivid description of the Third level shows he has a strong desire to go to Galesburg.
(*iv*) Charley's friend Sam Weiner cheated Charley and escape from the third level
A. Fact-(*i*) opinion-(*ii*) (*iii*) (*iv*)
B. Fact-(*i*) and (*ii*) opinion-(*iii*) and (*iv*)
C. Fact-(*iii*) and (*ii*) opinion-(*iv*) and (*i*)
D. Fact-(*ii*) and (*iii*) opinion-(*i*) and (*iii*)

256. Assertion (A): Charley wanted to go to Galesburg Illinois.

Reason (R): He has heard many wonderful stories about Galesburg from his grandfather.
A. Both (A) and (R) are true and (R) is the correct explanation of (A)
B. Both (A) and (R) are true, but (R) is not the correct explanation of (A)
C. A is true, but (R) is false
D. A is false, but (R) is true

257. Statement 1: Charley finds it very strange that only he could see the third level.

Statement 2: The third level according to his friend is a place in his mind.
A. Statement 1 is true, but statement 2 is false.
B. Statement 1 is false, but statement 2 is true.

C. Both statement 1 and statement 2 cannot be inferred.
D. Both statement 1 and statement 2 can be inferred.

258. Assertion (A): The clerk refused to accept the money offered by Charley.

Reason (R): He thought the currency was fake.
A. (A) is true, but (R) is false
B. (A) is false, but (R) is true
C. Both (A) and (R) are true and (R) is the correct explanation of (A)
D. Both (A) and (R) are true, but (R) is not the correct explanation of (A)

259. Statement 1: Sam believed Charley was unhappy and looking for an escape. Charley's stamp-collection was a proof of it.

Statement 2: Charley thought all in the modern world are looking for an escape and his hobby of stamp-collection has nothing to do with it.
A. Both statements 1 and 2 can be inferred.
B. Statement 2 is false, but statement 1 is true.
C. Statement 1 is false, but statement 2 is true
D. Both statements 1 and statement 2 are false.

260. Assertion (A): Sam could not go back to his old business in Galesburg Illinois.

He will start a hay and grain business there.

Reason (R): Sam can not start his psychiatric practice there as life is peaceful and no one needs a psychiatrist.
A. (A) is true, but (R) is false
B. (A) is false, but (R) is true
C. Both (A) and (R) are true, but (R) is not the correct explanation of (A)
D. Both (A) and (R) are true and (R) is the correct explanation of (A)

261. Assertion (A): Charley looked at the newspaper. It was The World. He realized he was in a different world.

Reason (R): Charley knew that the world is no longer published in the world he came from.
A. Both (A) and (R) are false, but (R) is the true explanation of (A)
B. Both (A) and (R) are true and (R) is the true explanation of (A)
C. (A) is false (R) is true
D. (A) is true, but (R) is not the true explanation of (A)

262. Assertion (A): Charley bought old style currency to buy two tickets to Galesburg Illinois.

Reason (R): He wanted to start a business there.
A. (A) is true (R) is false
B. Both (A) and (R) are true
C. (A) is false, but (R) is true explanation of (A)
D. Both (A) and (R) are true and (R) is true explanation of (A)

263. Suppose you visit Galesburg Illinois of 1894. Which of the following advertisement is least likely to be found there.
A. Baby food—A life begins with full nutrition.
B. Dress designer-Reclaim yourself.
C. Tea: Refreshing start of your beautiful day.
D. Yoga camp: Stress buster.

264. Assertion (A): Charley idolized the peaceful perfect world of Galesburg Illinois.

Reason (R): Galesburg Illinois of 1894 was a stark contrast to post world war modern world.
A. (A) is true (R) is false.
B. Both (A) and (R) are true and (R) is the true explanation of (A)
C. Both (A) and (R) are true, but (R) is not the true explanation of (A)
D. (R) is true (A) is false

265. Assertion (A): Charley noticed that lights at the station were dim and flickering.

Reason (R): In 1894, open gaslights were used at the railway station.
A. Both (A) and (R) are false, but (R) is the true explanation of (A)
B. (A) is true and (R) is false, but (R) is not the true explanation of (A)
C. (A) is false (R) is true
D. Both (A) and (R) are true and (R) is the true explanation of (A)

266. Assertion (A): Charley believed that the Third Level do exist and his friend Sam Weiner has escaped to Galesburg Illinois.

Reason (R): Sam has disappeared and no one knows where has he gone.
A. (A) is true, but (R) is false
B. Both (A) and (R) are true, but (R) is not the true explanation of (A)
C. Both (A) and (R) are true and (R) is the true explanation of (A)
D. (A) is true, but (R) is not the true explanation of (A)

267. Assertion (A): The third level refers to the third underground level of the grand central railway station.

Reason (R): Sam Weiner's letter states it clearly that the Third level does exist.
A. Both (A) and (R) are true, but (R) does not explain (A)
B. Both (A) and (R) are false
C. Both (A) and (R) are true and (A) can be inferred from (R)
D. (A) is true (R) is False and (A) can not be inferred from (R)

268. Assertion (A): Charley wanted to reach home immediately so he wanted to take a train.

Reason (R): Charley has been in and out of Grand central station hundreds of times.

A. Both (A) and (R) are false, but (R) does explain (A)
B. Both (A) and (R) are true, but (A) can not be inferred from (R)
C. Both (A) and (R) are true and (A) can be inferred from (R)
D. (A) is true (R) is False and (A) cannot be inferred from (R)

269. Assertion (A): Charley's Grandfather lived in a peaceful world in 1894.

Reason (R): The first word war was some 20 years off in future and the Second World War was forty years in future.

A. (A) and (R) both are true and (A) can be inferred from (R)
B. Both (A) and (R) are true, but (A) cannot be inferred from (R)
C. (A) is true, but (R) is false
D. (A) is true, but (R) is false and (A) can be inferred from (R)

270. Assertion (A): Charley was a common man like any other 31 years old with normal life style.

Reason (R): Charley wanted a peaceful life without war and stress.

A. (A) is true, but (R) is false
B. (A) is false, but (R) is true
C. Both (A) and (R) are true and (R) is the true explanation of (A)
D. Both (A) and (R) are false

271. Statement 1: Charley was among the many people who were suffering from mental ennui due to monotony of life.

Statement 2: Louisa, his wife was very happy and contented with her life.

A. Statement 1 can be inferred, but statement 2 can not be inferred
B. Statement 1 and statement 2 both can be inferred.
C. Statement 2 can be inferred, but statement 1 can not be inferred.
D. Statement 1 and 2 can not be inferred.

272. Statement 1: Eggs were thirteen cents a dozens in 1894.

Statement 2: Cost of living was comparatively less in 1894.

A. Statement 2 can be inferred, but statement 1 can not be inferred.
B. Statement 1 and 2 can not be inferred
C. Statement 1 can be inferred, but statement 2 can not be inferred
D. Statement 1 is true and statement 2 can be inferred.

273. Assertion (A): At the stamp and coin store I go to, I found out that Sam bought eight hundred dollars' worth of old-style currency.

Reason (R): That ought to set him up in a nice little hay, feed and grain business; he always said that's what Sam really wished he could do.

A. Both (A) and (R) are wrong and (R) does not explain (A)
B. Both (A) and (R) are true and (R) explains (A)
C. (A) is true, but (R) is false
D. (A) is false, but (R) is true

274 Assertion (A): Charley did not share his thoughts about the tunnel under the city with Sam.

Reason (R): Charley thought his job would be at stake if he shared these thoughts.

A. Both (A) and (R) are true, but (R) does not explain (A)
B. Both (A) and (R) are false and (R) does not explain (A)
C. (A) is true and (R) is false
D. Both (A) and (R) are false

275. Imagine Charley visit India on 25 th March, 2020 to India. Which of the following would be the Lead Story in Indian Newspaper?

A. Indian wins 2 Gold Medals in Japan Olympics.
B. Nifty bulls have a dominant day.
C. Telecom sector is ailing in India.
D. P.M. announces 21 days nation-wide lockdown.

Directions: *Read each of the following passages carefully and choose the best answer to each question out of the four alternatives.*

PASSAGE-1

The paper inside wasn't blank. It read:

941 Willard
Street
Galesburg,
Illinois
July 18, 1894

Charley I got to wishing that you were right. Then I got to believing you were right. And, Charley, it's true; I found the third level! I've been here two weeks, and right now, down the street at the Daly's, someone is playing a piano, and they're all out on the front porch singing Seeing Nelly Home.' And I'm invited over for lemonade. Come on back, Charley and Louisa. Keep looking till you find the third level! It's worth it, believe me!

The note is signed Sam

"Charley I got to wishing that you were right. Then I got to believing you were right"

276. What does the writer wish to believe?

A. That the third level does exist.

B. That Charley was not stable.
C. That the write was there in Galesburg.
D. That the tunnel does exist under the city.

277. Where has the writer been for two weeks?
A. In the third level.
B. In New York.
C. In Galesburg Illinois.
D. In the future where life is peaceful.

278. What does the letter state about the mood of the write?
A. Anxious B. Depressed
C. Excited D. Nonchalant

279. Who are 'THEY' out on the front porch singing 'Seeing Nelly Home'?
A. Sam's friends.
B. People of Galesburg Illinois.
C. A Singers' group.
D. Charley's relatives.

PASSAGE-2

"But I've never again found the corridor that leads to the third level at Grand Central Station, although I've tried often enough. Louisa was pretty worried when I told her all this, and didn't want me to look for the third level any more, and after a while I stopped; I went back to my stamps. But now we're both looking, every weekend, because now we have proof that the third level is still there. My friend Sam Weiner disappeared! Nobody knew where, but I sort of suspected because Sam's a city boy, and I used to tell him about Galesburg — I went to school there — and he always said he liked the sound of the place. And that's where he is, all right. In 1894."

280. Why do you think the speaker is looking for The Third Level?
A. He wanted to meet his grandfather.
B. He wanted to go to Galesburg Illinois.
C. He wanted to meet his friends in the third level.
D. He wanted to prove to everyone that Third level does exist.

281. What is being referred by Sam's *a city boy?*
A. Life in a city is peaceful
B. Life in a city is very challenging and stressful.
C. Boys in cities are carefree and happy
D. City boys are smart and would not believe in fantasy.

282. How would you describe the speaker's vision of Galesburg Illinois?
A. Wishful escapism
B. Idealized sentimentality
C. Nostalgic simplicity
D. Dream like fantasy

283. Which word from the following can be used in place of Suspected'?
A. Doubted B. Trusted
C. Confined D. Accused

PASSAGE-3

Have you ever been there? It's a wonderful town still, with big old frame houses, huge lawns, and tremendous trees whose branches meet overhead and roof the streets. And in 1894, summer evenings were twice as long, and people sat out on their lawns, the men smoking cigars and talking quietly, the women waving palm-leaf fans, with the fire-flies all around, in a peaceful world. To be back there with the First World War still twenty years off, and World War II over forty years in the future... I wanted two tickets for that.

284. Who is speaking to whom in the given extract?
A. Charley to Louisa
B. Charley to the reader
C. Sam to Charley
D. Charley to Sam

285. The given extract is **NOT** an example of:
A. Analogy B. Metaphor
C. Imagery D. Allegory

286. "Men smoking cigars and women waving palm-leaf" refers to a society:
A. Orthodox B. Conservative
C. Liberal D. Modern

287. Which word from the extract is an antonym of small?
A. Huge B. Tremendous
C. Long D. Both (A) and (B)

PASSAGE-4

Well, maybe, but my grandfather didn't need any refuge from reality; things were pretty nice and peaceful in his day, from all I hear, and he started my collection. It's a nice collection too, blocks of four of practically every U.S. issue, first-day covers, and so on. President Roosevelt collected stamps too, you know".

288. What collection is referred in the extract?
A. Money collection B. Coin collection
C. Toys collection D. Stamp Collection

289. Which word from the following is an antonym of 'Refuge'?
A. Escape B. Furnish
C. Deny D. Sanction

290. What does the narrator mean by 'My grandfather started my collection':
A. His grandfather helped him collect coins.
B. His grandfather was a philanthropist.
C. He picked the hobby of stamp collection from his grandfather.
D. His grandfather loved planting trees.

291. Which other story from your text-books has a reference to President Roosevelt.

A. Deep Water B. Lost Spring
C. Last Lesson D. None of the above

PASSAGE-5

There were brass spittoons on the floor, and across the station a glint of light caught my eye; a man was pulling a gold watch from his vest pocket. He snapped open the cover, glanced at his watch and frowned. He wore a derby hat, a black four-button suit with tiny lapels, and he had a big, black, handlebar mustache. Then I looked around and saw that everyone in the station was dressed like eighteen-ninety-something.

292. What caused the glint of light?

A. The bras spittoons
B. The gold watch
C. The sun
D. The chimneys

293. The above extract is an example of:

A. Allusion B. Enjambment
C. Metaphor D. Imagery

294. The word in the extract which means 'to look angry and serious' is:

A. Frown B. Glint
C. Lapels D. Glance

295. Which of the following sentences uses the word 'Snap' as a noun?

A. He shifted his weight and a twig snapped.
B. I think this is too important for a snap decision.
C. He shut the book with a snap and stood up.
D. The brake pedal has just snapped off.

296. 'Dressed like eighteen-ninety-something' which literary device has been used here?

A. Metaphor B. Paradox
C. Anti-thesis D. Simile

PASSAGE-6

The corridor I was in began angling left and slanting downward and I thought that was wrong, but I kept on walking. All I could hear was the empty sound of my own footsteps and I didn't pass a soul. Then I heard that sort of hollow roar ahead that means open space and people talking. The tunnel turned sharp left; I went down a short flight of stairs and came out on the third level at Grand Central Station.

297. The corridor angling left and slanting downward is an example of....

A. A blend
B. An intersection between time and space
C. Hallucination
D. Dizziness

298. What made the narrator think that he was in a 'wrong corridor'?

A. Because it was falling down.
B. Because it was wobbly.
C. Because it was behaving strange.
D. All of the above

299. What is meant by "I didn't pass a soul"?

A. He didn't find any other person there.
B. He didn't cross any ghost.
C. He couldn't see his shadow.
D. None of the above

300. Which of the following does **NOT** mean 'Hollow'?

A. Void B. Empty
C. Vacant D. Solid

PASSAGE-7

But that's the reason, he said, and my friends all agreed. Everything points to it, they claimed. My stamp collecting, for example; that's a temporary refuge from reality.

301. In what context the word 'reason' is referred here?

A. That charley was hallucinating
B. That charley was day dreaming
C. That charley was unhappy and looking for an escape from reality
D. That Charley was not successful in his career.

302. With whom did all Charley's friends agree?

A. Psychiatrist, Sam B. Louisa, his wife
C. His grandfather D. His boss

303. What according to Sam and his friends was a temporary refuse from reality for Charley?

A. His day–dreaming
B. His stamp collection
C. His visits to the third level
D. His nostalgia about Galesburg.

304. The word 'Refuge' from the passage can be best replaced with:

A. Shade B. Rest
C. Leisure D. Shelter

PASSAGE-8

That night, among my oldest first-day covers, I found one that shouldn't have been there. But there it was. It was there because someone had mailed it to my grandfather at his home in Galesburg; that's what the address on the envelope said. And it had been there since July 18, 1894 and I opened it

305. Why should this particular first day cover not be there?

A. Because it was a modern first day cover from the future.
B. Because it was an old first day cover from the past.

C. Because it was not addressed to his grandfather.
D. Because it could not have been collected by his grandfather.

306. Why is Charley not aware of this particular first day cover?
A. Because it appeared recently.
B. It was not meant for him.
C. It was addressed to Louisa, his wife.
D. He was forgetful.

307. The Picture of President Garfield indicates that the first day cover was:
A. New one B. Slightly old
C. Recent one D. Definitely old

308. What can be inferred from the extract regarding this first day cover?
A. That someone from the present travelled to the past.
B. That someone from the future has written this
C. That Charley was followed by secret society
D. That Charley was being tricked.

PASSAGE-9

Now, I don't know why this should have happened to me. I'm just an ordinary guy named Charley, thirty-one years old, and I was wearing a tan gabardine suit and a straw hat with a fancy band; I passed a dozen men who looked just like me. And I wasn't trying to escape from anything; I just wanted to get home to Louisa, my wife.

309. What has happened to the narrator?
A. He got transported to the third level of grand central station.
B. He got transported to Galesburg Illinois
C. He got transported to the future.
D. He recently met an alien.

310. "I passed a dozen men just like me" indicates?
A. Modern fashion
B. Modern Life style
C. Monotony of modern life
D. Lack of variety in fashion

311. Why was the narrator in hurry?
A. He wanted to go for a party with his wife.
B. He wanted to go for a movie with his wife.
C. He had some important meeting.
D. He was already late from office.

312. Which word from the extract means a 'dust coat'?
A. Gabardine B. Straw
C. fancy D. None of the above

PASSAGE-10

The clerk figured the fare he glanced at my fancy hatband, but he figured the fare and I had enough for two coach tickets, one way. But when I counted out the money and looked up, the clerk was staring at me. He nodded at the bills. That ain't money, mister, he said, and if you re trying to skin me, you won't get very far, and he glanced at the cash drawer beside him.

313. Why did the clerk glance at Charley's fancy hatband?
A. Because it was just like his own hat.
B. Because charley's hat was not an ordinary sight for him.
C. Because Charley had a star in his hat band.
D. Because Charley had a mysterious mark on his hat.

314. Why did Charley wanted to buy two tickets?
A. He wanted to go to Galesburg Illinois with his wife.
B. He wanted to go to meet his grandfather with Sam.
C. He wanted to escape in the past with his boss.
D. He wanted to go to the future with his wife.

315 Which of the following does **NOT** explain the expression "If you want to skin me" from the passage.
A. If you want to trick me
B. If you want to cheat me
C. If you want to deceive me
D. If you want to fight with me

316. Which word from the extract means 'take a brief or hurried look'?
A. Nodded B. Stare
C. Glance D. Figure

PASSAGE-11

"Once I got into a tunnel about a mile long and came out in the lobby of Roosevelt Hotel. Another time I came up in an office building on forty-sixth-street, three blocks away":

317. Which of the following statement is true in the given context?
A. The narrator knew about the tunnel and he has been exploring various places.
B. The narrator has been in and out of the third level for quite a few times.
C. The narrator has been visiting his grandfather in Galesburg Illinois frequently.
D. The narrator was aware that he has been wandering here and there quite often.

318. Who is 'I' in the extract?
A. Sam B. Louisa
C. Charley D. None of the above

319. What can be inferred by the 'tunnel' from this extract?
A. A gateway into past.
B. A portal into another planet.
C. A gateway into the future.
D. A portal into an alien world.

320. Which word from the extract means 'An Underground Passageway'?
A. Lobby B. Office
C. Tunnel. D. None of tne above

PASSAGE-12

But I've never again found the corridor that leads to the third level at Grand Central Station, although I've tried often enough. Louisa was pretty worried when I told her all this, and didn't want me to look for the third level any more, and after a while I stopped; I went back to my stamps. But now we're both looking, every weekend.

321 Which corridor the speaker is looking?
A. The corridor leading to the third level.
B. The corridor which was under construction.
C. The corridor that took him to the tunnel.
D. None of the above

322. What made Louisa worried?
A. She knew that the speaker was hallucinating.
B. She was concerned about the well-being of Charley.
C. She thought Charley was fantasizing.
D. All of the above

323. Why did the speaker stop looking for the third level after some time?
A. He was not well.
B. He went to his hobby of stamp-collection.
C. All his efforts couldn't locate the third level.
D. He realized he was fantasizing.

324. 'Now we both are looking' who are WE here?
A. Charley and Louisa.
B. Charley and Sam.
C. Charley and his boss.
D. All of the above

PASSAGE-13

He said I was unhappy. That made my wife kind of mad, but he explained that he meant the modern world is full of insecurity, fear, war, worry and all the rest of it, and that I just want to escape. Well, who doesn't? Everybody I know wants to escape, but they don't wander down into any third level at Grand Central Station.

325. He said I was Unhappy. Identify ***I*** and ***He*** in the sentence.
A. Charley and his boss.
B. Charley and his grandfather.
C. Charley and Sam.
D. Charley and his neighbour.

326. 'That made my wife kind of mad' What does ***Mad*** mean here?
A. Jealous B. Insecure
C. Crazy D. Angry

327. Why was Charley's wife angry?
A. She thought he was going crazy.
B. She thought he was unhappy because of her.
C. She thought Charley was going to Galesburg leaving her alone.
D. None of the above

328. Which of the following does **NOT** mean 'Wander'?
A. Stroll B. Roam
C. Travel D. Cease

329. What was the Third Level?
A. An imaginary discovery of the of Charley's mind.
B. A big tunnel on the grand central station
C. A time-machine on the grand central station.
D. A level in the game that charley had been playing.

330. Why did the narrator go to a psychiatrist?
A. Because he was unhappy and wanted to know why
B. Because he went through an experience no one else did
C. Because he was unhappy and wanted to know why
D. Because he was depressed

331. What is the genre of the lesson "The Third Level"?
A. Historical Fiction B. Tragedy
C. Science Fiction D. Fantasy

332. How frequently the author has been in and out of the grand central?
A. He is a regular visitor
B. He has been in and out of the grand central hundreds of times
C. The author travels every day from grand central.
D. The author visits the grand central occasionally.

333. What does Sam think of Modern Life?
A. That life if full of stress, war and fear.
B. That life is easy and enjoyable
C. That the modern world is full of wonders
D. That the modern world is a great place to be

334. What is a first day cover?
A. It's a stamp issued on the first day of the year.
B. It's a stamp issued in the name of the first citizen of a country
C. An envelope bearing a stamp postmarked on its day of issue.
D. An envelope issued on the first day of the year.

335. As a Metaphor of the title 'The Third Level' which of the following would **NOT** be an appropriate explanation?
A. The bridge between the past and present.
B. The excruciating monotony of the modern life.
C. The convergence of reality and fantasy.
D. The dire need for an alternate plane of understanding

336. What was the date on the newspaper?
A. June 15, 1894 B. June 11, 1894
C. June 10, 1894 D. July 13, 1894

337. Why did Charley visit the Library?
A. To gather more information about the third level.
B. To read more books on Time-Travel.
C. To confirm the main story of the newspaper.
D. To find a book he had seen in the third level.

338. How would you Sam describe Charley?
A. Escapist B. Carefree
C. Happy go lucky D. Workaholic

339. What is the name of Charley's wife?
A. Aliza B. Alisa
C. Louisa D. Lucia

340. What do you call a person who collects stamps?
A. Ticket collector B. Philatelist
C. Stamp-Collector D. Philanthropist

341. What was the name of the newspaper?
A. The Reuters B. The Telegraph
C. The Statesmen D. The world

342. What does the time table mention regarding grand central station?
A. That there are three levels
B. That there are two levels
C. That there is only one level
D. None of the above

343. Why did Charley decide to take sub way from Grand central station?
A. He used to take a train from there everyday
B. He wanted to go to Galesburg Illinois
C. He accidently reached there
D. He was late so he took a train to reach home fast.

344. Who did Charley discuss his strange visit to the third level?
A. His psychiatrist B. His friends
C. His wife D. His grandfather

345. How did Sam interpret charley's visit to the third level?
A. Waking wish fulfillment
B. Escape
C. Dream come true
D. Both (A) and (B)

346. What are some of the things Charley observe at Third Level?
A. Brass spittoons
B. Handlebar moustaches
C. Flickering chimney lights
D. All of the above

347. Why did Charley make a hasty retreat from the Third Level?
A. He came back because he was scared of the experience.
B. He came back hurriedly as he thought he will be arrested.
C. He came back to share this experience with his family.
D. He came back as he was concerned about his wife.

348. Why did Charley withdraw all his savings?
A. To get it exchanged in old style currency
B. To buy a home in Galesburg Illinois
C. To buy a gift for his wife
D. To pay fee to his psychiatrist

349. Why did Louisa become mad at Charley when Sam diagnosed him as unhappy?
A. She thought her husband was fantasizing.
B. She thought she was the reason for his unhappiness.
C. She thought her husband was an escapist.
D. She thought Sam was misguiding her husband.

350. What is Sam's take on Charley's hobby of stamp-collection?
A. Medium of escape
B. Connection between past and present
C. A good part time hobby
D. A good source of information

351. What business would have Sam established in Galesburg for a living?
A. Practice psychiatry
B. Become a flute player
C. Hay and grain business
D. Farming

352. What was the main story about on the first page of *The World?*
A. President Roosevelt
B. President Garfield
C. President Lincoln
D. President Cleveland

353. Why did Sam feel that Charley wanted to escape?
A. He feels charley was stressed because the modern world is full of war and worry.
B. He feels Charley was not happy with his job.
C. He feels that Charley was not happy with his wife.
D. He feels Charley's boss was very demanding.

354. **Explain:** Waking dream wish fulfillment.
A. An experience which takes one to future.
B. An experience which makes one forget the present.
C. An experience which takes one in the past.
D. An experience where one becomes forgetful.

355. What does Charley's letter to Sam signify?
A. A proof of time travel
B. A proof that third level does exist
C. A blend of reality with fantasy
D. A proof that Charley has been to Galesburg Illinois.

356. Why did Charley compare the grand central station with a tree?
A. The shape of the central station is like that of a tree.
B. Like a tree, the grand central station is very high.
C. Like a tree the grand central gives shade to its visitors.
D. Like the roots of a tree the grand central station is expanding.

357. Which US president was a philatelist mentioned in the story?
A. President Garfield
B. President Roosevelt
C. President Cleveland
D. President Jackson

358. What for Sam was invited according to the letter?
A. For a lemonade
B. For a dance party
C. For a birthday party
D. For a rain dance party

359. Why did the clerk at the ticket window refuse to accept Charley's money?
A. Money was insufficient
B. Money was torn
C. Money was old style
D. His money was of modern times

360. Which of the following is apt to justify the story 'the third level'.
A. "I like nonsense; it wakes up the brain cells. Fantasy is a necessary ingredient in living". —Dr. Seuss
B. "Fantasy is hardly an escape from reality. It's a way of understanding it". —Lloyd Alexander
C. "Stories of imagination tend to upset those without one". —Terry Pratchett
D. Fantasy and reality often overlap—Walt Disney

361. With regards to an intersection of time and space in the story, which of the following is **NOT** true?
A. People with side burns, handle-bar moustaches and women in sheep skin coat
B. Open gaslight and smaller booths
C. A large no of ticket windows
D. Broader Currency notes

362. What is the significance of 1894 in the lesson?
A. It represents a utopian world
B. It stands for the past
C. Charley's grandfather lived there
D. All of the above

363. Out of the following which one is the best way to overcome harsh realities of life?
A. Watching TV B. Reading good books
C. Day dreaming D. Fantasizing

THE ENEMY
By Pearl S Buck

Directions: *Read each of the following passages carefully and choose the best answer to each question out of the four alternatives.*

PASSAGE-1

It was at this moment that both of them saw something black come out of the mist. It was a man.

364. Who was watching the mist?
A. The fisherman
B. Doctor Sadao and Hana
C. Tom
D. Hana

365. Who came out of the mist?
A. General Takima B. The fisherman
C. Hana D. A man

366. The word 'both' refers to:
A. The fisherman and the police
B. Dr sadao and Hana
C. The gardener and cook
D. The enemy and General Takima

367. From where did the man come out from the mist?
A. From the black B. From the ocean
C. From the house D. From the tree

PASSAGE-2

His father had taken him often to the islands of those seas, and never had failed to say to the little brave boy at his side, "Those islands yonder, they are the stepping stones to the future of Japan".

368. Who is referred to as "him" in the above extract?
A. Dr. Sadao Hoki B. Hana
C. The gardener D. Dr Sadao's father

369. Who is referred as "the little brave boy" in the above extract? What is his full name?
A. Dr Sadao Hoki B. Hana
C. The General D. Tom

370. Dr. Sadao was ....
A. a psychiatrist B. an engineer
C. a professor D. a surgeon

371. Who is the speaker?
A. Dr. Sadao's father B. Dr. Sadao
C. Hana D. The white man

PASSAGE-3

"A White man!" Hana whispered. Yes, it was a white man. The wet cap fell away and there was his wet yellow hair, long, as though for many weeks it had not been cut and upon his young and tortured face was a rough yellow beard.

372. What did Dr Sadao and Hana mean by 'white man'?
A. the man whose face appeared white due to sand
B. an American prisoner of war
C. a man wearing white shirt
D. none of these

373. Hana's remark "A white man!" on seeing the white man indicated what she was feeling. Pick the option that correctly States the feelings.
1. Horror 2. Shocked
3. Unfamiliar 4. Annoyed
A. 1 and 2 B. 2 and 3
C. 2 and 4 D. 1 and 4

374. How did the white man's face appear?
A. Young C. Fresh
B. Tortured D. Both (A) and (B)

375. Why didn't the white man know the presence of Dr. Sadao and Hana?
A. As he was sleeping
B. As he was pretending to be unconscious
C. As he was unconscious
D. None of these

PASSAGE-4

"Don't faint", he said sharply. He did not put down his exploring instrument. "If I stop now, the man will surely die." She clapped her hands to her mouth and leaped up and ran out of the room. Outside in the garden he heard her retching but he went on with his work.

376. "Don't faint", he said. Who said these words and to whom?
A. Dr Sadao to Hana
B. The cook to the Gardener
C. Dr. Sadao to the patient
D. The patient to Dr. Sadao

377. Who would die? Who was retching?
1. Dr Sadao's wife 2. The General
3. The enemy Soldier 4. The old Gardener
A. 1 and 2 B. 3 and 1
C. 2 and 1 D. 3 and 4

378. Why did Dr. Sadao feel impatient and irritable with the prisoner?
A. It was getting late at night
B. He was tired and sleepy
C. He would not get paid
D. He could not tend to his wife

379. Where was the white man?
A. in the garden
B. on the beach
C. in the room of Sadao's father
D. with the general

PASSAGE-5

"My old master's son knows very well what he ought to do," he now said, pinching a bud from a bush as he spoke. "When the man was so near death why did he not let him bleed?"

380. "When the man was so near-death why did he not let him bleed ?" Who said these words?
A. The cook B. Yumi
C. The gardener D. The General

381. What is the feeling of the speaker?
A. Sarcasm B. Sadness
C. Indignation D. Appreciative

382. How had the man come to be bleeding?
A. He was scratched by the brambles head first
B. He had tripped and fallen
C. His body was torn by the rocks flanking the beach
D. He had been shot

383. Dr. Sadao's helping the white soldier displays which qualities of his?
1. He was above the narrow prejudices.
2. He was a bit selfish when it came to his country's matter.
3. He considered his duty above all the other things.
4. He was cunning and egoist person.
A. 1 and 2 B. 2 and 3
C. 1 and 3 D. 3 and 4

PASSAGE-6

Now Sadao remembered the wound and with his expert finger he began to search for it. Blood flowed freshly at his touch.

384. Who was wounded?
A. Sadao B. Hana
C. The White Soldier D. Yumi

385. Which word best suits 'trained' in the extract?
A. touch B. tended
C. expat D. expert

386. What kind of wound the man had?
A. It was a knife stab
B. It was an injury
C. It was a gun shot
D. The rock had struck the wound

387. What was the dilemma that Dr. Sadao faced?
A. Whether he should marry Hana or not.
B. Whether he should leave Japan and settle in another country.

C. Whether he should study further or start practice
D. Whether he should save the life of the white soldier or let him die.

PASSAGE-7

We must simply tell them that we intend to give him to the police— as indeed we must, Sadao

388. Who is the speaker of the above extract?
A. Hana B. Dr. Sadao
C. Yumi D. The General

389. Who is referred as them in the above extract?
A. The Police B. The Fishermen
C. The Servants D. The Officials

390. Which word in the extract means 'certainly'?
A. Simply B. Intend
C. Indeed D. Give

391. How many of them were employed at the house by the speaker of the extract?
A. Three B. Four
C. Six D. Two

PASSAGE-8

He stood gazing down on the motionless man. This man must have extraordinary vitality or he would have been dead by now. But then he was very young—perhaps not yet twenty five.

392. Who is referred as 'he' in 'he stood gazing'?
A. The police B. The gardener
C. Dr. Sadao D. The General

393. What was the age of the man?
A. Twenty five B. Thirty five
C. Forty five D. Fifty five

394. In whose bedroom the man was lying?
A. In the children's bedroom
B. In the master bedroom
C. The bedroom of the old man
D. The bedroom of the General.

395. Which word in the extract is the synonym of "strength"?
A. Vitality B. Extraordinary
C. Motionless D. Gazing

PASSAGE-9

When she saw him her thick lips folded themselves into stubbornness. "I have never washed a white man", she said, "and I will not wash so dirty a one now".

396. Who is referred as "she" in the above extract?
A. Hana B. The Cook
C. Yumi D. The Girl

397. Who is the listener of the above extract?
A. The Cook B. Hana
C. The Girl D. Yumi

398. Was "the White man" conscious when the above lines is spoken?
A. Yes, he was conscious
B. No, he was unconscious
C. He was sleeping
D. He was pretending sleeping

399. Which phrase is the antonym of "always"?
A. Thick B. Never
C. Will D. Now

PASSAGE-10

"Well, well" the old man said in a tone of amazement, "so I did! But you see, I suffered a good deal. The truth is, I thought of nothing but myself. In short, I forgot my promise to you".

400. Who is referred to as "you" in the above extract?
A. The General B. Doctor Sadao
C. The Assassins D. The Gardener

401. Who is referred to "The old man" in the above extract?
A. The Gardener B. Doctor Sadao
C. The General D. The Assassins

402. Who suffered a good deal in the above extract?
A. The General B. Doctor Sadao
C. The Assassins D. The Gardener

403. Who failed to keep the promise?
A. The Gardener B. Doctor Sadao
C. The General D. The Assassins

PASSAGE-11

"It is very unfortunate that this man should have washed up on your door step". He said irritably.

404. Who is the speaker of the above lines?
A. The Gardener B. Doctor Sadao
C. The General D. The Assassins

405. Who is the listener of the above lines?
A. The General B. Doctor Sadao
C. The Assassins D. The Gardener

406. Who is referred to as "the man"?
A. The General
B. Doctor Sadao
C. The White American soldier
D. The Gardener

407. Which word in the extract is the synonym of "Unlucky"?
A. Irritably B. Washed
C. Unfortunate D. The man

408. **Statement 1:** Those islands yonder, they are the 'stepping – stones' to the future of Japan.

Statement 2: Dr. Sadao Hoki's father had dreamt of a bright future for his son and he hadn't been disappointed.

A. Statement 1 is true, but statement 2 is false
B. Statement 1 is false, but statement 2 is true
C. Both statement 1 and statement 2 cannot be inferred
D. Both statement 1 and statement 2 can be inferred

409. Statement 1: Dr. Sadao had waited to fall in love with Hana until he was sure she believed in traditional Japanese values else his father would never have welcomed her.

Statement 2: Sadao and Hana's chance meeting had turned out to be a very fruitful relationship.
A. Statement 1 is true, but statement 2 is true
B. Statement 1 is false, but statement 2 is true
C. Both statement 1 and statement 2 cannot be inferred
D. Both statement 1 and statement 2 can be inferred

410. Statement 1: Doctor Sadao is not a dedicated surgeon, kind and compassionate towards people in distress.

Statement 2: He faced conflict of duty as a doctor and a citizen of Japan.
A. Statement 1 is true, but statement 2 is false
B. Statement 1 is false, but statement 2 is true
C. Both statement 1 and statement 2 cannot be inferred
D. Both statement 1 and statement 2 can be inferred

411. Statement 1: Hana was a balanced woman.

Statement 2: She was graceful and dignified about the servants when they were leaving the house.
A. Statement 1 is true, but statement 2 is false
B. Statement 1 is false, but statement 2 is true
C. Both statement 1 and statement 2 cannot be inferred
D. Both statement 1 and statement 2 can be inferred

412. Statement 1: The General was selfish by nature, thinks of his treatment only.

Statement 2: He had no faith in Sadao as a doctor.
A. Statement 1 is true, but statement 2 is false
B. Statement 1 is false, but statement 2 is true
C. Both Statement 1 and Statement 2 cannot be inferred
D. Both Statement 1 and Statement 2 can be inferred

413. Statement 1: The gardener felt that Sadao should have let the soldier to die.

Statement 2: He thought that the sea and the gun would take revenge if he saves the soldier.
A. Statement 1 is true, but Statement 2 is false
B. Statement 1 is true, but Statement 2 is true
C. Both Statement 1 and Statement 2 cannot be inferred
D. Both Statement 1 and Statement 2 can be inferred

414. Two statements (Assertion and Reasons) are given below: Choose the option from the one that follow the Statements.

Assertion (A): Dr. Sadao was a true Patriot.

Reason (R): He informed the general about the presence of the white man in his house.
A. Both (A) & (R) are true and (R) is the correct explanation of (A)
B. Both (A) & (R) are true, but (R) is not the correct explanation of (A)
C. (A) is true, but (R) is false
D. (A) is false, but (R) is true

415. Assertion (A): The General sent the assassins to the house of Dr. Sadao.

Reason (R): He himself was in pain and needed Dr. Sadao's help.
A. Both (A) & (R) are true and (R) is the correct explanation of (A)
B. Both (A) & (R) are true, but (R) is not the correct explanation of (A)
C. (A) is true, but (R) is false
D. (A) is false, but (R) is true

416. Who wrote *Don Juan*?
A. Shakespeare B. Tennyson
C. Byron D. T.S. Eliot

417. Who wrote *The Life of Johnson*?
A. Boswell B. Macaulay
C. Churchill D. Sir Walter Raleigh

418. *Priest's Nun's Tale* was written by:
A. Spenser B. Charles Lamb
C. Tennyson D. Chaucer

419. Who is said to have first used the term "Metaphysics"?
A. Matthew Arnold B. Sidney
C. Donne D. Dr. Johnson

420. The writer of *Volpone* is:
A. Johnson B. Milton
C. Jonson D. Shelley

421. Which is the correct chronological sequence?
A. Spenser—Chaucer—Milton—Donne
B. Spenser—Wordsworth—Tennyson—T.S. Eliot
C. Milton—Shakespeare—Philip Larkin—Keats
D. Auden—Eliot—Shelley—Keats

422. *Pilgrim's Progress* was written by:
A. Milton B. Shelley
C. Swinburne D. John Bunyan

423. The writer of the line : *"Stone walls do not a prison make"* is:
A. Lovelace B. Milton
C. W.B. Yeats D. T.S. Eliot

424. *"Monkey's Paw"* is a:
A. Poem B. Drama
C. Short story D. Novel

425. Lyrical Ballads appeared in:
A. 1690 B. 1798
C. 1802 D. 1800

426. The writer of *'A Pair of Blue Eyes'* is:
A. Thackeray B. Dickens
C. George Eliot D. Thomas Hardy

427. *Hard Times* was written by:
A. Thackeray B. Dickens
C. Trollope D. Marquese

428. Which of the following poets was most impressed by the German philosophy?
A. Chaucer B. Wordsworth
C. Coleridge D. Southey

429. The two cities referred to in *"A Tale of Two Cities"* are:
A. London and Paris
B. London and Rome
C. Rome and Paris
D. Moscow and Rome

430. *The Peasant's Bread* is a story by:
A. Maupassant B. Tagore
C. R.K. Narayan D. Tolstoy

431. *The Financial Express* was written by:
A. Raja Rao B. R,K. Narayan
C. Tagore D. Mulk Raj Anand

432. *"Negative Capabiliiy"* is a term associated with:
A. Tagore B. Shelley
C. Keats D. Coleridge

433. The most impressive treatment of "imagination" has been given by:
A. Colcridge B. Shelley
C. Eliot D. Yeats

434. *Lady Chatterley's Lover* was banned because it was considered:
A. obscene B. revolutionary
C. obscurantist D. None of these

435. *For Whom The Bell Tolls* was written by:
A. Marquese B. Hemingway
C. Hawthorne D. None of these

436. The writer of : *"A Pair of Mustachios"* is:
A. Anand B. Tagore
C. Raja Rao D. Anita Desai

437. The writer of *Scarlet Letter* is:
A. Henry James B. James Joyce
C. Hawthorne D. None of these

438. Rousseau is associated with:
A. French Revolution
B. American War of Independence
C. Russian (Bolshevik) Revolution
D. None of these

439. Who wrote *'Train to Pakistan'*?
A. Narayan B. Manohar Malgaon
C. Khushwant Singh D. Anand

440. Who is the writer of *Azadi*?
A. R.K. Narayan B. Khushwant Singh
C. Tagore D. Chaman Nahal

441. *"The God of Small Things"* is written by:
A. R.K. Narayan B. Hemingway
C. Graham Greene D. Arundhati Roy

442. Who wrote the poem *"Listeners"*?
A. Tennyson B. Thomas Hood
C. Goldsmith D. Walter de la Mare

443. In writing *"Canterbury Tales"* Chaucer was influenced by:
A. Decameron B. The Divine Comedy
C. The Holy Bible D. None of these

444. *'Animal Farm'* was written by:
A. James Joyce B. Virginia Woolf
C. George Orwell D. Hemingway

445. Shobha De is a:
A. poet B. dramatist
C. novelist D. an actress

446. Dunciad was written by:
A. Dryden B. Pope
C. Tennyson D. Shelley

447. Bernard Shaw got the Nobel Prize for:
A. Pygmalion B. Man and Superman
C. Saint Joan D. None of these

448. The Victorian Period is marked by:
A. Great political upheavals
B. Great social security
C. Great wars
D. Economic deprivation

449. Swift is known mainly as:
A. an essayist B. a poet
C. a satirist D. a short story writer

450. Who is the writer of the novel *"The Village"*?
A. Khushwant Singh B. Anita Desai
C. Mulk Raj Anand D. R.K. Narayan

451. The most famous writer of the heroic couplet is:
A. Dryden B. Chaucer
C. Spenser D. Pope

452. *Macflecknoe* is a poem written by:
A. Dryden B. Pope
C. Tennyson D. Yeats

453. Who wrote *'Everyman in His Humour'*?
A. Shakespeare B. Jonson
C. Milton D. Keats

454. *'Indian Jugglers'* is an essay by:
A. De Quincey B. Gardiner
C. Hazlitt D. Lamb

455. Who wrote *'The Gropes of Wrath'*?
A. Pearl Buck B. Hemingway
C. Virginia Woolf D. John Steinbeck

456. Who rendered into English the ancient Greek tragedy *"Atlanta in Calydon"*?
A. Swinburne B. Shelley
C. Tennyson D. Arthur Hugh Clough

457. *The Deserted Village* was written by:
A. Cowper B. Goldsmith
C. Keats D. Johnson

458. *'Savitri'* is an epic written by:
A. Tagore
B. Prem Chand
C. Aurobindo
D. Bankim Chandra Chatterjee

459. The anthem *"Vande Mataram"* occurs in
A. Godan B. Anand Math
C. Gora D. Train to Pakistan

460. *'All Fool's Day'* is an essay written by:
A. Charles Lamb B. Hazlitt
C. A.G. Gardiner D. R.C. Stevenson

461. The drama *Tamburlaine* is written by:
A. Shakespeare B. Marlowe
C. Lyly D. Green

462. The book *"Appreciations"* was written by:
A. Morris B. Arnold
C. Walter Pater D. Christina Rossetti

463. *"The Admirable Crichton"* was written by:
A. Steinbeck B. T.S. Eliot
C. Trollope D. James Barrie

464. *"The Death of a Salesman"* was written by:
A. James Barrie B. Eugene O'Neill
C. Arthur Miller D. None of these

465. The Restoration period is said to have started from:
A. 1660 B. 1676
C. 1625 D. 1645

466. Who wrote *"The Lady's Not for Burning"*?
A. Barrie B. Christopher Fry
C. Robert Bridges D. T.S. Eliot

467. Who wrote the poem *"Brahma"*?
A. T.S. Eliot B. Emerson
C. Whitman D. Frost

468. The writer of *Walden* is:
A. Tennyson B. Whitman
C. Thoreau D. Frost

469. In *'Sons and Lovers'* Lawrence has depicted the life of:
A. factory workers B. miners
C. farmers D. animals

470. Who wrote *Kim*?
A. Kipling B. Tagore
C. Lawrence D. Narayan

471. *'The Hairy Ape'* is a famous play by:
A. Barrie B. Eugene O'Neill
C. Christopher Fry D. T.S. Eliot

472. Who is the writer of *Frankenstein*?
A. George Eliot B. Jane Austen
C. Mary Shelley D. Emile Bronte

473. Who wrote the *'Cries of Children'*?
A. Robert Browning B. Elizabeth Barrett
C. Thomas Hood D. Cowper

474. Which poet is known as poet's poet?
A. Shakespeare B. Milton
C. Spenser D. Shelley

475. Who wrote the maximum number of sonnets?
A. Shakespeare B. Milton
C. Sidney D. Wordsworth

476. *Adonais* is the eulogy written on the death of:
A. Coleridge B. Byron
C. Keats D. Wordsworth

477. Who wrote *Mother*?
A. Tolstoy B. Maxim Gorky
C. Chekhov D. Hardy

478. Who is associated with *Malgudi*?
A. Narayan
B. Anand
C. Manohar Malgonkar
D. Anita Desai

479. The author of *Beowulf* is:
A. Bede B. Cynewulf
C. Chaucer D. Unknown

480. The Anglo-Saxon period is often said to be from 450 to ......
A. 900 B. 1000
C. 1050 D. 1100

481. *"To a Mountain Daisy"* is a poem by:
A. Wordsworth B. Shelley
C. Keats D. Burns

482. Who wrote: *"The Devil's Disciple"*?
A. Galsworthy B. Barrie
C. Shaw D. Fry

483. Who wrote *"The Decline and Fall of the Roman Empire"*?
A. Walter Raleigh B. Trollope
C. Smollett D. Edward Gibbon

484. Richard Hooker was a prose writer of the:
A. Victorian period B. Romantic period
C. Elizabethan period D. Chaucerian age

485. Alexander Dumas was:
A. an English writer B. an American writer
C. a French writer D. a German writer

486. Which one was not one of the Lake poets?
A. Shelley B. Wordsworth
C. Southey D. Coleridge

487. *The Theory of Catharsis* is associated with:
A. Plato B. Dryden
C. Aristotle D. Sidney

488. Who wrote *'In Defence of Poetry'*?
A. T.S. Eliot B. Yeats
C. Keats D. Shelley

489. *'The Playboy of the Western World'* is a play by:
A. Barrie B. Synge
C. Fry D. Eliot

490. *'Silent Woman'* is a play by:
A. Marlowe B. Shakespeare
C. Ben Jonson D. Lyly

491. The Scene of *Beowulf* is laid in:
A. England B. France
C. Spain D. None of these

492. *"Kidnapped"* was written by:
A. Dickens B. Thackeray
C. Hardy D. R.L. Stevenson

493. *'The Prisoner of Zenda'* was written by:
A. Sterne B. Trollope
C. Anthony Hope D. George Eliot

494. What was the full name of Cervantes?
A. Jim Cervantes
B. John Cervantes
C. Miguel de Cervantes
D. Sir Roger Cervantes

495. Besides being a poet, Chaucer was:
A. a trader B. a manufacturer
C. a teacher D. a diplomat

496. The name of William Golding's first novel is:
A. The Inheritors B. Lord of the Flies
C. Pincher Martin D. The Pyramid

497. The author of *Erewhon* is:
A. Hardy B. Marquese
C. Samuel Butler D. Cervantes

498. Which of the following is a *Comedy of Manners*?
A. The Way of the World
B. The Duchess of Malfi
C. The Lady's Not for Burning
D. The Hairy Ape

499. Which one among the following is not a pessimist?
A. Gissing B. Browning
C. Hardy D. Thomson

500. Charles Reade's drama *"Drink"* was adapted from a work of:
A. Goethe B. Zola
C. Mallarwe D. Tennyson

501. Which one among the following was not a utilitarian?
A. Rousseau B. James Mill
C. Ricardo D. Bentham

502. *'The Praise of Folly'* was written by:
A. Walter Raleigh B. Thomas Moore
C. Charles Lamb D. Ruskin

503. Who wrote: *"In Praise of Idleness"*?
A. Bertrand Russell B. Thomas More
C. Charles Lamb D. Hazlitt

504. The real name of Saki is:
A. H.H. Munro B. Samuel Butler
C. George Orwell D. The Duke

505. Who started: *"The Tatler"*?
A. Addison B. Swift
C. Steele D. Stevenson

506. The poem *'The Song of the Shirt'* was written by:
A. Mrs. Browning B. Pope
C. Shelley D. Thomas Hood

507. *Sir Roger* was originally the creation of:
A. Addison B. Dryden
C. Steele D. Milton

508. Who wrote: *"Areopagitica"*?
A. Charles Lamb B. Hazlitt
C. De Quincey D. Milton

509. *'The Selfish Giant'* is a story written by:
A. Tagore B. Oscar Wilde
C. Maupassant D. Tolstoy

510. Who wrote : *"Four Quartets"*?
A. T.S. Eliot B. W.B. Yeats
C. W.H. Auden D. Philip Larkins

511. Who wrote : *"Look Back in Anger"*?
A. Steinbeck B. Christopher Fry
C. John Osborne D. Barrie

512. Who wrote : *"The Devils of Loundun"*?
A. Bertrand Russell B. Aldous Huxley
C. J.B. Priestley D. Hazlitt

513. Who wrote : *"Principles of Human Knowledge"*?
A. Milton B. John Bunyan
C. Nash D. George Berkeley

514. Who wrote : *"Liber Amoris"*?
A. Lamb B. Hazlitt
C. Byron D. Wordsworth

515. *"A Railway Clerk"* is a poem by:
A. Keki N. Daruwallah B. Nissim Ezekiel
C. Shiv K. Kumar D. Jayanta Mahapatra

516. Who won The Booker of Bookers?
A. Arundhati Roy B. Khushwant Singh
C. Mulk Raj Anand D. Salman Rushdie

517. Who wrote: *"The Battle of Books"*?
A. Bacon B. Hazlitt
C. Swift D. None of these

518. Who wrote: *"Nectar in a Sieve"*?
A. Mulk Raj Anand
B. Manohar Malgonkar
C. Kamala Markandaya
D. Pearl S. Buck

519. *'The Good Earth'* was written by:
A. Raja Rao B. R.K. Narayan
C. Pearl S. Buck D. Kamala Markandaya

520. The writer of *'The Dove Found No Rest'* is:
A. Pearl S Buck B. Hemingway
C. Raja Rao D. Dennis Stoll

521. Who wrote: *"So Many Hungers"*?
A. Bhabani Bhattacharya
B. Kamala Markandaya
C. Manohar Malgonkar
D. Chaman Nahal

522. Who is the writer of *"The Middleman and Other Stories"*?
A. Mulk Raj Anand B. Bharati Mukherjee
C. Tagore D. Prem Chand

523. Cicero was a Roman:
A. philologist B. physician
C. orator D. None of these

524. Who is the writer of *"Gita Rahasya"*?
A. Tulsi Das B. Vivekananda
C. Shivananda D. B.G. Tilak

525. *'The Rubaiyat of Omar Khayyam'* was translated into English by:
A. Robert Browning B. Tennyson
C. Fitz Gerald D. Hopkins

ANSWERS

1	2	3	4	5	6	7	8	9	10
A	A	A	C	B	B	A	B	A	B
11	**12**	**13**	**14**	**15**	**16**	**17**	**18**	**19**	**20**
B	A	B	A	C	C	B	A	C	A
21	**22**	**23**	**24**	**25**	**26**	**27**	**28**	**29**	**30**
D	B	C	B	A	B	C	C	B	B
31	**32**	**33**	**34**	**35**	**36**	**37**	**38**	**39**	**40**
B	D	A	C	B	C	D	B	A	B
41	**42**	**43**	**44**	**45**	**46**	**47**	**48**	**49**	**50**
D	B	B	B	B	D	B	D	A	D
51	**52**	**53**	**54**	**55**	**56**	**57**	**58**	**59**	**60**
D	B	D	B	C	D	D	B	C	D
61	**62**	**63**	**64**	**65**	**66**	**67**	**68**	**69**	**70**
D	C	D	B	C	D	C	D	B	B
71	**72**	**73**	**74**	**75**	**76**	**77**	**78**	**79**	**80**
A	A	C	C	B	A	A	D	D	D
81	**82**	**83**	**84**	**85**	**86**	**87**	**88**	**89**	**90**
B	D	A	A	B	D	D	A	A	B
91	**92**	**93**	**94**	**95**	**96**	**97**	**98**	**99**	**100**
D	C	D	B	C	D	B	C	A	C

101	102	103	104	105	106	107	108	109	110
D	C	B	D	C	C	D	A	C	D
111	112	113	114	115	116	117	118	119	120
D	C	B	C	B	B	D	D	B	C
121	122	123	124	125	126	127	128	129	130
A	A	C	D	D	A	C	C	D	A
131	132	133	134	135	136	137	138	139	140
C	A	B	A	C	B	D	C	C	A
141	142	143	144	145	146	147	148	149	150
B	D	B	A	B	D	A	C	B	B
151	152	153	154	155	156	157	158	159	160
B	C	A	C	B	C	A	A	B	B
161	162	163	164	165	166	167	168	169	170
B	D	A	A	D	B	D	B	A	D
171	172	173	174	175	176	177	178	179	180
D	C	C	A	C	D	C	A	D	D
181	182	183	184	185	186	187	188	189	190
D	A	D	C	C	B	B	B	C	C
191	192	193	194	195	196	197	198	199	200
D	C	A	B	C	B	D	C	C	B
201	202	203	204	205	206	207	208	209	210
A	B	D	C	A	C	D	D	B	A
211	212	213	214	215	216	217	218	219	220
C	C	C	C	C	D	C	A	A	B
221	222	223	224	225	226	227	228	229	230
D	B	B	C	B	C	B	B	A	B
231	232	233	234	235	236	237	238	239	240
B	D	C	B	B	A	A	C	C	D
241	242	243	244	245	246	247	248	249	250
C	B	D	D	A	C	A	A	D	B
251	252	253	254	255	256	257	258	259	260
C	B	B	B	D	A	D	C	A	D
261	262	263	264	265	266	267	268	269	270
B	A	D	C	D	B	C	B	A	C
271	272	273	274	275	276	277	278	279	280
A	D	B	C	D	A	C	C	B	B
281	282	283	284	285	286	287	288	289	290
B	C	A	B	D	A	D	D	B	C
291	292	293	294	295	296	297	298	299	300
A	B	D	A	C	D	B	C	A	D
301	302	303	304	305	306	307	308	309	310
C	A	B	D	D	A	D	A	A	C
311	312	313	314	315	316	317	318	319	320
D	A	B	A	D	C	D	C	A	C

321	322	323	324	325	326	327	328	329	330
A	B	C	A	C	D	B	D	A	B
331	332	333	334	335	336	337	338	339	340
C	B	A	C	D	B	C	A	C	B
341	342	343	344	345	346	347	348	349	350
D	B	D	A	D	D	B	A	B	A
351	352	353	354	355	356	357	358	359	360
C	D	A	B	C	D	B	A	D	D
361	362	363	364	365	366	367	368	369	370
C	D	B	B	D	B	B	A	A	D
371	372	373	374	375	376	377	378	379	380
A	B	A	D	C	A	B	D	C	C
381	382	383	384	385	386	387	388	389	390
C	C	C	C	D	C	D	A	C	C
391	392	393	394	395	396	397	398	399	400
A	C	A	C	A	C	B	B	B	B
401	402	403	404	405	406	407	408	409	410
C	A	C	C	B	C	C	D	A	B
411	412	413	414	415	416	417	418	419	420
D	A	B	A	D	C	A	D	D	C
421	422	423	424	425	426	427	428	429	430
B	D	A	C	B	D	B	C	A	D
431	432	433	434	435	436	437	438	439	440
B	C	A	A	B	A	C	A	C	D
441	442	443	444	445	446	447	448	449	450
D	D	A	C	C	B	C	A	C	C
451	452	453	454	455	456	457	458	459	460
D	A	B	C	D	A	B	C	B	A
461	462	463	464	465	466	467	468	469	470
B	C	D	C	A	B	B	C	B	A
471	472	473	474	475	476	477	478	479	480
B	C	B	C	D	C	B	A	D	C
481	482	483	484	485	486	487	488	489	490
D	C	D	C	C	A	C	D	D	C
491	492	493	494	495	496	497	498	499	500
D	D	C	C	D	B	C	A	B	B
501	502	503	504	505	506	507	508	509	510
A	B	A	A	C	D	C	D	B	A
511	512	513	514	515	516	517	518	519	520
C	B	D	B	B	D	C	C	C	D
521	522	523	524	525					
A	B	C	D	C					

ENGLISH GRAMMAR & VOCABULARY

Spelling Errors

The most common errors in English are of spellings of words. Even the most learned men are sometimes confused about the correct spellings of some words. One must keep and use a dictionary religiously. Never ignore and let pass a new word casually.

A number of question to test your knowledge of spellings are compiled here. Try to solve as many as you can.

Multiple Choice Questions

Directions: *Find the correctly spelt word out of the four options in each question.*

1. A. Accompalish B. Ackmplesh C. Acomplush D. Accomplish

2. A. Acommodation B. Acomodation C. Accomodation D. Accommodation

3. A. Astonished B. Astronished C. Astoneshed D. Asstonished

4. A. Benefeted B. Benefitted C. Benifited D. Benefited

5. A. Belligerent B. Beligirent C. Belligarant D. Belligerrent

6. A. Chancelery B. Chancellery C. Chancellary D. Chancelary

7. A. Discriminate B. Discremineta C. Discrimenate D. Discriminat

8. A. Damage B. Dammage C. Damaige D. Dammege

9. A. Efficiant B. Effecient C. Efficient D. Eficient

10. A. Extravagant B. Extreragent C. Extreregant D. Extravegent

11. A. Efflorascence B. Eflorescene C. Effllorescence D. Efflorescence

12. A. Equinimity B. Equanimmity C. Equannimity D. Equanimity

13. A. Farmament B. Farmement C. Fermament D. Fremament

14. A. Grieff B. Grief C. Grieef D. Grrief

15. A. Guarantee B. Garuntee C. Guaruntee D. Gaurantee

16. A. Hypocritical B. Hypocretical C. Hypocriticel D. Hypocirticel

17. A. Humurous B. Humorous C. Humoreus D. Humorrous

18. A. Itenerary B. Itinarery C. Itinarary D. Itinerary

19. A. Indipenseble B. Indispansible C. Indispensable D. Indipensable

20. A. Imprecticability B. Impracticebility C. Impracticibility D. Impracticability

21. A. Incradulous B. Incredulous C. Incridulous D. Incredalous

22. A. Juddicious B. Judiceous C. Judicious D. Judiceus

23. A. Kleptomonia B. Kleptemonia C. Kleptomania D. Klaptomania

24. A. Lackdaisical B. Lackadaisical C. Lckadaisicle D. Lackadisical

25. A. Licentious B. Licontious C. Licenttious D. Licientious

26. A. Meddicine B. Medicine C. Medicene D. Medicinne

27. A. Meritricious B. Merefrecious C. Meretricious D. Merritricious

28. A. Missunderstood B. Miesunderstood
C. Misunderstood D. Misunderstod

29. A. Occurad B. Occurred
C. Ocurred D. Occured

30. A. Osttentatious B. Ostentetious
C. Ostentatious D. Ostenttatious

31. A. Obnosious B. Obnoxeous
C. Obnoxious D. Obnoseous

32. A. Omenous B. Ominous
C. Ommineous D. Omineous

33. A. Pecification B. Pacification
C. Pecifacation D. Pecefication

34. A. Prograssive B. Progressive
C. Progresive D. Prograsive

35. A. Pasiveness B. Passiveness
C. Passeveniss D. Passivines

36. A. Polyendry B. Poliendry
C. Pollyendry D. Polyandry

37. A. Puerille B. Puerrile
C. Puerile D. Purrile

38. A. Pesanger B. Passenger
C. Pessenger D. Pasanger

39. A. Querrelsome B. Quarrelsame
C. Quarrelsome D. Querralsome

40. A. Rigourous B. Rigerous
C. Rigorous D. Regerous

41. A. Survellance B. Surveilance
C. Surveillance D. Survaillance

42. A. Schedule B. Schdule
C. Schedale D. Schedeule

43. A. Sepalchrle B. Sepalchral
C. Sepulchrle D. Sepulchral

44. A. Sympathetic B. Smypathetic
C. Sympothetic D. Sympethetic

45. A. Sincerely B. Sencerely
C. Sincerelly D. Sincerrely

46. A. Satellite B. Sattellite
C. Satelite D. Sattelite

47. A. Teracherous B. Treacherous
C. Treacheraus D. Treachereans

48. A. Uncivilized B. Uncevilized
C. Uncivillized D. Uncevelized

49. A. Vainglorious B. Vaniglorious
C. Vaniglerious D. Vaingloreus

50. A. Vulnarable B. Valnerable
C. Velnerable D. Vulnerable

ANSWERS

1	2	3	4	5	6	7	8	9	10
D	D	A	B	A	C	A	A	C	A
11	**12**	**13**	**14**	**15**	**16**	**17**	**18**	**19**	**20**
D	D	C	B	A	A	B	D	C	D
21	**22**	**23**	**24**	**25**	**26**	**27**	**28**	**29**	**30**
B	C	C	B	A	B	C	C	B	C
31	**32**	**33**	**34**	**35**	**36**	**37**	**38**	**39**	**40**
C	B	B	B	B	D	C	B	C	C
41	**42**	**43**	**44**	**45**	**46**	**47**	**48**	**49**	**50**
C	A	D	A	A	A	B	A	A	D

Spotting Errors

The most common errors in English are of spellings, grammar and usage of words. By regular practice, the errors can be easily spotted and minimised.

Common Errors with Nouns and Noun-Phrases

Incorrect	Correct
1. I have bought new *furnitures.*	I have bought new *furniture.*
2. The wages of sin *are* death.	The wages of sin *is* death.
3. She told these *news* to her mother.	She told her mother this *news.*
4. He took *troubles* to do his work.	He took *trouble* (or pains) over his work.
5. The *cattles* were grazing.	The *cattle* were grazing.
6. He showered *many abuses* on me.	He showered *much abuse* on me.
7. I spent the holidays with my *family members.*	I spent the holidays with my *family.*
8. There is no *place* in this compartment.	There is no *room* in this compartment.
9. Write this new *poetry* in your *copy.*	Write this new *poem* in your *note-book.*
10. He took *insult* at this.	He took *offence* at this.
11. Put your *sign* here.	Put your *signatures* here.
12. She is my *cousin sister.*	She is my *cousin.*
13. *Sunil's* my *neighbour's* house was burgled.	*Sunil* my *neighbour's* house was burgled.
14. I lost a *ten-rupees* note.	I lost *a ten-rupee* note.
15. Road closed for *repair.*	Road closed for *repairs.*
16. His house is out of *repairs.*	His house is out of *repair.*
17. What is the *reason* of an earthquake?	What is the *cause* of an earthquake?
18. This building is made of *stones.*	This building is made of *stone.*
19. I disapprove of *these kinds* of games.	I disapprove of *this kind* of games.
20. Veena's and Sheela's father is ill.	Veena and Sheela's father is ill.
21. His *son-in-laws* are doctors.	His *sons-in-law* are doctors.
22. *Alms* is given to the *poor.*	*Alms* are given to the poor.
23. He always keeps his words.	He always keeps his *word.*
24. I carried the *luggages.*	I carried the *luggage.*
25. *Two-third* of the work is left.	*Two-thirds* of the work is left.

Common Errors with Pronouns

Incorrect	Correct
1. Both did not go.	Neither went.
2. We all did not go.	None of us went.
3. Each of these boys play.	Each of these boys plays.
4. Whoever does best he will get a prize.	Whoever does best will get a prize.

	Incorrect	Correct
5.	One should not waste his time.	A man should not waste his time.
6.	I and she are sisters.	She and I are sisters.
7.	He is wiser than me.	He is wiser than I.
8.	Between you and I, Anil is not to be trusted.	Between you and me, Anil is not to be trusted.
9.	Nobody was there but I.	Nobody was there but me.
10.	Who is there ? It is me.	Who is there ? It is I.
11.	Only he and me can use this card.	Only he and I can use this card.
12.	Let you and I go now.	Let you and me go now.
13.	Everyone got one's pay.	Everyone got his pay.
14.	Everyone is frightened when they see a tiger.	Everyone is frightened when he sees a tiger.
15.	These two friends are fond of one another.	These two friends are fond of each other.
16.	I did not like him coming at that hour.	I did not like his coming at that hour.
17.	Who do you think I met?	Whom do you think I met?
18.	You should avail this opportunity.	You should avail yourself this opportunity.
19.	When you have read these books, please return the same to me.	When you have read the books, please return them to me.
20.	They that are humble need fear no fall.	Those that are humble need fear no fall.

Common Errors with Adjectives

	Incorrect	Correct
1.	These all oranges are good.	All these oranges are good.
2.	He held the book in the both hands.	He held the book in both hands.
3.	Both men have not come.	Neither man has come.
4.	That man should do some or other work.	That man should do some work or other.
5.	He is elder than I.	He is older than I.
6.	Shakespeare is greater than any other poets.	Shakespeare is greater than any other poet.
7.	He is a coward man.	He is a cowardly man.
8.	Many villagers cannot write his own name.	Many villagers cannot write their own name.
9.	Each of us loves our home.	Each of us loves his home.
10.	Much efforts bring their reward.	Much effort brings its reward.
11.	He found hundred rupees.	He found a hundred rupees.
12.	He had leave of four days.	He had four days leave.
13.	This is a worth seeing sight.	This is a sight worth seeing.
14.	He will spend his future life here.	He will spend the rest of his life here.
15.	There is a best teacher in that class.	There is a very good teacher in that class.
16.	Of the two plans this is the best.	Of the two plans this is the better.
17.	He is becoming strong every day.	He is becoming stronger every day.
18.	He is worst than I.	He is worse than I.
19.	Jaipur is hot than Delhi.	Jaipur is hotter than Delhi.
20.	In our library the number of books is less.	In our library the number of books is small.

Common Errors with Verbs

	Incorrect	Correct
1.	He asked had we taken our luggage.	He asked if we had taken our luggage.
2.	She asked what are you doing.	She asked what we were doing.
3.	Rama asked to Anil why he is angry.	Rama asked Anil why he was angry.
4.	He does not care for his money.	He does not take care of his money.
5.	He does not care for his work.	He takes no care over his work.
6.	No one cared for him after his mother died.	No one took care of him after his mother died.
7.	He got angry before I said a word.	He got angry before I had said a word.
8.	I met a man who was my tutor 20 years ago.	I met a man who had been my tutor twenty years ago.
9.	I had been for walking yesterday.	I went for a walk yesterday.
10.	If I shall do this I shall be wrong.	If I do this I shall be wrong.
11.	I have left trekking.	I have given up trekking.
12.	I came to know as to how he did this.	I learnt how he did this.
13.	I came to know why he was sad.	I found out why he was sad.
14.	He knows to swim.	He knows how to swim.
15.	The criminal's head was cut.	The criminal's head was cut off.
16.	I said to him to go.	I told him to go.
17.	I told the teacher to excuse me.	I asked the teacher to excuse me.
18.	He is troubling me.	He is giving me trouble.
19.	I have got a hurt on my leg.	I have hurt my leg.
20.	She gave a speech.	She made a speech.

Common Errors in Subject-Verb Agreement

	Incorrect	Correct
1.	The owners of this factory *is* very rich.	The owners of this factory *are* very rich.
2.	The pleasures of nature that one can experience at Shimla *is* beyond description.	The pleasures of nature that one can experience at Shimla *are* beyond description.
3.	There *is* no street lights in our colony.	There *are* no street lights in our colony.
4.	He and I *am* entrusted with the job.	He and I *are* entrusted with the job.
5.	Rice and curry *are* his favourite dish.	Rice and curry *is* his favourite dish.
6.	The honour and glory of our country *are* at stake.	The honour and glory of our country *is* at stake.
7.	Time and tide *waits* for none.	Time and tide *wait* for none.
8.	All the passengers with the driver *was* killed.	All the passengers, with the driver, *were* killed.
9.	The teacher, with her students, *were* going out.	The teacher, with her students, *was* going out.
10.	I as well as they *am* tired.	I as well as they *are* tired.
11.	Not only the soldiers but their captain also *were* captured.	Not only the soldiers but their captain also *was* captured.
12.	Neither you nor I *were* selected.	Neither you nor I *was* selected.
13.	Either of these two applicants *are* fit for the job but neither want to accept it.	Either of these two applicants *is* fit for the job but neither wants to accept it.
14.	One of these students are sure to stand first.	One of these students *is* sure to stand first.
15.	Everyone of these workers want a raise.	Everyone of these workers wants a raise.
16.	None of these letters has been answered so far.	None of these letters *have* been answered so far.
17.	None of the girls were present at the party.	None of the girls *was* present at the party.
18.	Many a battle were fought on Indian soil.	Many a battle *was* fought on Indian soil.
19.	A lot of work remain to be done.	A lot of work *remains* to be done.
20.	The majority of these girls likes music.	The majority of these girls *like* music.

Common Errors in the Use of Modals/Auxiliary Verbs

Incorrect	Correct
1. When I shall see him I shall tell him this.	When I *see* him, I shall tell him this.
2. If I should do wrong, he would punish me.	If I *did* wrong, he would punish me.
3. Until he will have confessed his fault, he will be kept in prison.	Until he *has* confessed his fault, he will be kept in prison.
4. She will obey me.	She *shall* obey me.
5. You would work hard.	You *should* work hard.
6. You shall find him in the garden.	You *will* find him in the garden.
7. He must have died of exposure, but we cannot be certain.	He *might* have died of exposure, but we cannot be certain.
8. You might not show disrespect to your elders.	You *must* not show disrespect to your elders.
9. You may take exercise in order to maintain good health.	You *must* take exercise in order to maintain good health.
10. He must be a crook for all we know.	He *may* be a crook for all we know.

Common Errors in the Use of Adverbs

Incorrect	Correct
1. He is very much angry.	He is *very* angry.
2. She was very good enough to help me.	She was *good enough* to help me.
3. She runs much fast.	She runs *very* fast.
4. She runs very faster than Seema.	She runs *much* faster than Seema.
5. It is bitter cold today.	It is *bitterly* cold today.
6. He is a much learned man.	He is a very learned man.
7. She is thinking very hardly.	She is thinking very hard.
8. To tell in brief the film was boring.	*In short* the film was boring.
9. He told the story in details.	He told the story *in detail.*
10. I did it anyhow.	I *managed to do* it somehow.
11. Aeroplanes reach Europe soon.	Aeroplanes reach Europe quickly.
12. Before long there were dinosaurs on the earth.	*Long ago,* there were dinosaurs on the earth.
13. This book is too interesting.	This book is *very* interesting.
14. He lives miserly.	He lives in *a miserly* way.
15. Just I had gone when she came.	I had just gone when she came.
16. He sings good.	He sings *well.*
17. He sings good than I.	He sings *better* than I.
18. Really speaking it is cold.	*As a matter of fact* it is cold.
19. He is enough tall to reach the ceiling.	He is *tall enough* to reach the ceiling.
20. He went directly to his college.	He went *direct* to his college.

Common Errors in the Use of Conjunctions

Incorrect	Correct
1. As he is fat so he runs slowly.	As he is fat *he* runs slowly.
2. If he is fat then he will run slowly.	If he is fat, he will run slowly.
3. Though he is fat still he runs fast.	Though he is fat, *he runs* fast.
4. *As* I pulled the trigger at the sametime he shook my arm.	As I pulled the trigger, he shook my arm.

Incorrect	Correct
5. No sooner I had spoken than he left.	No sooner *had* I spoken than he left.
6. Not only he will go, but also he will stay there.	Not only *will he* go, but he *will also* stay there.
7. Neither he comes nor he writes.	Neither *does he* come nor *does he* write.
8. Scarcely he entered the room than the telephone rang.	Scarcely *had* he entered the room *when the* telephone rang.
9. Hardly she had left the house than it began to rain.	Hardly *had she* left the house *when* it began to rain.
10. He is the fastest runner and he comes last.	He is the fastest runner *but* he comes last.
11. She is as innocent as if she looks.	She is as innocent as she looks.
12. Until he does not try he must be punished.	He must be punished unless he tries.
13. I want to know as to why you are late.	I want to know why you are late.
14. I am fond of Chinese food as for example sweet and sour prawns.	I am fond of Chinese food, for example, sweet and sour prawns.
15. He was angry therefore I ran away.	He was angry so I ran away.
16. I was trying to work, at that time he was disturbing me.	While I was trying to work, he was disturbing me.
17. Supposing if he is late, what will happen?	Supposing he is late (or if he is late) what will happen?
18. He asked me that why I was late.	He asked me why I was late.
19. Let us catch a taxi lest we should not get late.	Let us catch a taxi lest we should get late.
20. She dresses herself like the teacher does.	She dresses herself as the teacher does.
21. Wait while I come.	Wait *until* (or *till)* I come.
22. Until, there is corruption in India, there can be little progress.	*As long* as there is corruption in India there can be little progress.
23. I have never told a lie nor cheated anybody.	I have never told a lie *nor have I* cheated anybody.
24. Both Mohan as well as Arun are responsible for this action.	Both Mohan *and* Arun are responsible for this action.
25. Hindus and Muslims both are to blame for the riots.	*Both Hindus* and Muslims are to blame for the riots.

Common Errors in the Use of Prepositions

Incorrect	Correct
1. I will not listen him.	I will not listen *to* him.
2. Copy this word by word.	Copy this word *for* word.
3. He enquired from her where she lived.	He enquired *of* her where she lived.
4. Sign here with ink.	Sign here *in* ink.
5. Has she come in train or by foot?	Has she come *by* train or *on* foot?
6. She said this at his face.	She said this *to* his face.
7. Open the book on page one.	Open the book *at* page one.
8. I was invited for lunch.	I was *invited to* lunch.
9. I am ill since three months.	I have been *ill for* three months.
10. This paper is inferior than that.	This paper is inferior *to* that.
11. This resembles to that.	This *resembles* that.
12. My brother is superior than you in strength.	My brother is superior *to* you in strength.
13. He wrote me.	He wrote *to* me.
14. I shall explain them this.	I shall explain this *to* them.
15. Send this letter on my address.	Send this letter *to* my address.
16. He suggested me this.	He suggested this *to* me.
17. He goes *on his* work.	He goes *to his* work.
18. He *reached to* Nagpur.	He *reached* Nagpur.
19. He told *to me* to go.	He told *me* to go.
20. The term begins *from* July 1st.	The term begins *on* July 1st.

Miscellaneous Errors

Incorrect	Correct
1. Many *homes* are lying vacant.	Many *houses* are lying vacant.
2. It is cool in the *shadow* of the tree.	It is cool in the *shade* of the tree.
3. She *keeps* good health.	She *enjoys* good health.
4. My leg is *paining*.	*I am feeling pain* in my leg.
5. *See* this word in the dictionary.	*Look up* this word in the dictionary.
6. The train will arrive *just now.*	The train will arrive *shortly.*
7. They are *pulling* on well.	They are *getting* on well.
8. The river has *over flown* its bank.	The river has *over flown* its banks.
9. He was appointed *on* the post.	He was appointed *to* the post.
10. Last but not *the least,* we have to discuss the problem of over population.	Last but not *least,* we have to discuss the problem of over population.
11. *Cities* after *cities* fell.	*City* after *city* fell.
12. What is the use Munir going there?	What is the use of Munir going there?
13. He *did many mischief.*	He *made much mischief.*
14. It is exact five *in* my watch.	It is exact five *by* my watch.
15. I will dine with them on *next Sunday.*	I will dine with them *Sunday next.*
16. Misfortunes when faced bravely and *manly* become less troublesome.	Misfortunes when faced bravely and *manfully* become less troublesome.
17. I am *laid down* with fever.	I am *laid up* with fever.
18. He is habituated to smoking.	He is *addicted* to smoking.
19. *According to my opinion* he is right.	*In my opinion* (or according *to me)* he is right.
20. Could you please *open* this knot?	Could you please *untie* this knot?

Multiple Choice Questions

Directions: *In this section, each sentence has three parts, indicated by (A), (B) and (C). Read each sentence to find out whether there is an error. If you find an error in any one of the parts (A, B, C), indicate your response by marking the letter related to that part. If a sentence has no error, indicate this by marking '(D)' which stands for "No error". Errors may belong to grammar, usage or idiom. Ignore errors of punctuation, if any.*

1. (A) Beware of/(B) a fair-weather friend/(C) who is neither a friend in need nor a friend indeed/(D) No error.

2. (A) Copernicus proved/(B) that Earth/(C) moves round the Sun./(D) No error.

3. (A) Seldom we have been treated/(B) in such a rude manner/(C) by the police personnel./(D) No error.

4. (A) Some men are born great,/(B) some achieve greatness/(C) and some had greatness thrust on them./(D) No error.

5. (A) The property/(B) was divided/(C) among the two brothers./(D) No error.

6. (A) I am quite certain/(B) that the lady is not only greedy/(C) but miserly./(D) No error.

7. (A) The aircraft overloaded/(B) there was something wrong of the battery/(C) and the engine was making a queer noise/(D) No error.

8. (A) A thorough inquiry of the misappropriation of funds/(B) is now imperative/(C) to bring the guilty to book/(D) No error.

9. (A) The brilliant success in the examination/(B) as well as his record in sports/(C) deserves high praise/(D) No error.

10. (A) While travelling by a train/(B) on a cold winter night/(C) an argument rose between two passengers in our compartment/(D) No error.

11. (A) I cannot find/(B) where has he gone/(C) though I have tried may best/(D) No error.

12. (A) If I was/(B) the Prime Minister of India/(C) I would work wonders/(D) No error.

13. (A) Amit's severe bout of flu/(B) debilitated him so much/(C) that he was too tired to do for work for a week./(D) No error.

14. (A) This is the crux of the entire problem;/(B) everything centres on/(C) it being resolved./(D) No error.

15. (A) One of the major aims of the Air Force/(B) was the complete demolition of all means of transportation/(C) by the bombing of rail lines and terminals./(D) No error.

16. (A) His strong voice cut over/(B) the hum of conversation/(C) like a knife through butter./(D) No error.

17. (A) Even though they weren't expecting us/(B) they managed to knock up/(C) a marvellous meal./(D) No error.

18. (A) The celebrated singer was/(B) surrounded by the usual crowd/(C) of lackeys and hangerons./(D) No error.

19. (A) If it weren't/(B) for you,/(C) I wouldn't be alive today./(D) No error.

20. (A) He looked like a lion/(B) baulked from/(C) its prey./(D) No error.

21. (A) Widespread flooding/(B) is effecting/(C) large areas of the villages./(D) No error.

22. (A) She regards/(B) negotiating prices with customers/(C) as her special preserve./(D) No error.

23. (A) Often in political campaigns, a point is reached at which/(B) the candidates take out their gloves./(C) and start slugging with bare fists./(D) No error.

24. (A) If we really set to/(B) we can get the whole house/(C) cleaned in an afternoon./(D) No error.

25. (A) Pieces of rock plummeted/(B) down the mountainside/(C) in the ground below./(D) No error.

26. (A) Since the two parties each won/(B) the same number of seats,/(C) the minority party holds the balance of power./(D) No error.

27. (A) It's arrogant for you/(B) to assume you'll/(C)win every time./(D) No error.

28. (A) We've paid for our travel and accommod-ation,/(B) so we need only to take/(C) some pocket-money with us./(D) No error.

29. (A) There's no evidence to show/(B) that information technology secrets are more/(C) vulnerable in India than Britain or the US./(D) No error.

30. (A) It is shameful that hunting/(B) is still considered sport/(C) by some unscrupulous people in the civilized world./(D) No error.

31. (A) The Prime Minister's good looks won him/(B)the election but he has still to prove/(C) that he's not a just pretty face./(D) No error.

32. (A) The two books are the same/(B) except for the fact that this/(C) has an answer in the back./(D) No error.

33. (A) He estimated his income tax bill/(B) by extrapolation over figures/(C) submitted in previous years./(D) No error.

34. (A) The modern office block/(B) sticks out like a sore thumb/(C) among the old buildings in the area./(D) No error.

35. (A) I will try to put over/(B) some feelers to gauge/(C) people's reactions to our proposal./(D) No error.

36. (A) A major contribution of Mathura sculptors/(B)of that period were the creation and popularization/(C) of the Buddha's image in human form./(D) No error.

37. (A) Amit has been deceiving Mona/(B) for many years but she/(C) has not still tumbled to it./(D) No error.

38. (A) Mahavira was an advocate of nonviolence and vegetarianism,/(B) who revived and reorganized the Jain doctrine/(C) and established rules for their monastic order. (D) No error.

39. (A) Microwaves are the principle carriers/(B) of television, telephone and data transmissions/(C)between stations on earth and between the earth and satellites./(D) No error.

40. (A) An unit is an abstract idea,/(B) defined either by reference to/(C) a randomly chosen material standard or to a natural phenomenon./(D) No error.

41. (A) With the crisis deepening,/(B) the critics sense an opportunity/(C) about putting in place a more radical strategy./(D) No error.

42. (A) The salesman gave us/(B) a big spiel about why/(C) we should buy his product./(D) No error.

43. (A) I will need several weeks/(B) to invent the lie of the land before/(C) I can make any decision about the future of the business./(D) No error.

44. (A) You should be cautious/(B) and make a few discrete enquiries about/(C) the firm before you sign anything./(D) No error.

45. (A) Your husband doesn't/(B) believe that you are older/(C) than I./(D) No error.

46. (A) We are meeting today afternoon/(B) to discuss the matter/(C) and reach a compromise./(D) No error.

47. (A) Either Ram or/(B) you is responsible/(C) for this action./(D) No error.

48. (A) The student flatly denied/(B) that he had copied/(C) in the examination hall./(D) No error.

49. (A) By the time you arrive tomorrow/(B) I have finished/(C) my work./(D) No error.

50. (A) The speaker stressed repeatedly on/(B) the importance of improving/(C) the condition of the slums./(D) No error.

51. (A) The captain with the members of his team/(B) are returning/(C) after a fortnight./(D) No error.

52. (A) After returning from/(B) an all-India tour/(C) I had to describe about it/(D) No error.

53. (A) The teacher asked his students/(B) if they had gone through/(C) either of the three chapters included in the prescribed text./(D) No error.

54. (A) Although they are living in the country/(B) since they were married/(C) they are now moving to the town./(D) No error.

55. (A) Do you know/(B) how old were you/(C) when you came here?/(D) No error.

ANSWERS

1	2	3	4	5	6	7	8	9	10
D	B	A	C	C	C	B	A	D	C
11	**12**	**13**	**14**	**15**	**16**	**17**	**18**	**19**	**20**
B	A	C	C	B	A	A	C	C	C
21	**22**	**23**	**24**	**25**	**26**	**27**	**28**	**29**	**30**
C	A	A	A	C	A	A	B	D	B
31	**32**	**33**	**34**	**35**	**36**	**37**	**38**	**39**	**40**
C	C	C	D	A	B	C	C	A	A
41	**42**	**43**	**44**	**45**	**46**	**47**	**48**	**49**	**50**
C	D	D	D	C	A	B	D	B	A
51	**52**	**53**	**54**	**55**					
B	C	C	B	D					

Articles

Definite and Indefinite Articles

(*i*) 'A' and 'an' are Indefinite Articles.

(*ii*) 'The' is Definite Article.

(*iii*) 'A' and 'an' modify a noun in a general way.

(*iv*) 'The' particularises it. *e.g.*,

Mohan has **a pen.**

The pen which you gave me was expensive.

Vowel and Consonant Sounds

(*i*) 'A' is used before words starting with the sound of a consonant.

(*ii*) 'An' is used before a vowel sound (vowels a, e, i, o, u) *e.g.*,

a book, a cat, a useful thing, a European girl, a university,

but an FDR, an MA, an honest boy, an hour, an owl, an egg, an umbrella, etc.

Use of Articles 'A' and 'An'

A cat mews. (*i.e.*, every cat)

The cat of my neighbour mews day and night. (*i.e.*, a particular cat)

He gave me **an** egg. (Here 'an' means 'one')

Use of Article 'The'

1. 'The' is used before names of rivers, mountains, seas, oceans:
   The Himalayas, the Ganga, the Yamuna, the Bay of Bengal, the Indian Ocean, the Nile, the English Channel, *etc.*
2. Names of newspapers and magazines:
   The Times of India, the Tribune, The Sun, *etc.*
3. Names of the famous and holy books:
   The Guru Granth Sahib, The Gita, The Ramayana, *etc.*
4. Names of creations of nature:
   the sun, the earth, the moon, the sky, *etc.*
5. While using Adjectives as Nouns:
   The poor should be helped by **the rich.**
6. Sometimes with the Comparative Degree:
   The more you think, **the more** you worry.
7. With the Superlative Degree:
   She is **the most intelligent** girl in our school.
8. Before the imaginary lines and directions:
   The Latitude, The Equator, the east, the west, etc.
9. Before the names of musical instruments:
   the violin, the piano, the flute, etc.
10. While using a Proper Noun as a Common Noun:
    Mohan is **the Sachin** of our team.

Omission of Article 'The'

1. Before some Nouns used to convey general sense, articles are not used but are used to particularise them:
   Man is mortal.
2. Before Proper Nouns:
   Rakesh is an intelligent boy.
3. With Abstract Noun:
   Childhood is the prime time of one's life.
   The childhood of Sohan was full of sorrow.
4. With Material Nouns:
   Milk is an essential food.
   The milk of the cow is sweet.
5. Usually no article is used before names of diseases:
   Cancer is a fatal disease.
   However, when we talk about a disease figuratively, we use an article before its name, *e.g.*
   Corruption is a cancer.
6. Names of games and language:
   I like football.
   I can speak Punjabi, Hindi and English.
7. Gold is a precious metal.

NOTE: As you must have noted above, the definite article 'the' has been used where a noun is particularised.

Double Use of Article 'The'

Read the following sentences carefully to understand this :

1. The poet and novelist has been honoured.
   (The same person is the poet as well as novelist)
2. The poet and the novelist have been honoured.
   (The poet and the novelist are two different persons).
3. I have a black and white dog.
   (that is, one dog)
4. I have a black and a white dog.
   (that is, two dogs)

Multiple Choice Questions

Directions : *Fill in the blanks with suitable articles. Mark 'D' if no article required.*

1. Do you know .... boy in white?
A. a B. an
C. the D. No article

2. She is .... girl I am looking for.
A. a B. an
C. the D. No article

3. Have you read .... Mahabharat?
A. a B. an
C. the D. No article

4. ....rich are not always happy.
A. A B. An
C. The D. No article

5. Oranges are sold by .... dozen.
A. a B. an
C. the D. No article

6. Milk is sold by .... litre.
A. a B. an
C. the D. No article

7. .... Amazon is the longest river in the world.
A. A B. An
C. The D. No article

8. .... higher you climb, the colder it gets.
A. A B. An
C. The D. No article

9. She is .... untidy girl.
A. a B. an
C. the D. No article

10. I am .... M.A. is English.
A. a B. an
C. the D. No article

11. I have already spent .... few rupees I had.
A. a B. an
C. the D. No article

12. .... English are very hard-working.
A. A B. An
C. The D. No article

13. April is the fourth month of .... year.
A. a B. an
C. the D. No article

14. Rice is sold by .... kilogram
A. a B. an
C. the D. No article

15. She is .... best of the three girls.
A. a B. an
C. the D. No article

16. .... man in the car is a friend of mine.
A. A B. An
C. The D. No article

17. Brevity is .... soul of wit.
A. a B. an
C. the D. No article

18. .... thing of beauty is a joy for ever.
A. A B. An
C. The D. No article

19. .... little learning is a dangerous thing.
A. A B. An
C. The D. No article

20. .... best sauce for food is hunger.
A. A B. An
C. The D. No article

21. Birds of .... feather flock together.
A. a B. an
C. the D. No article

22. He makes .... living by begging.
A. a B. an
C. the D. No article

23. It is .... pity that he died so young.
A. a B. an
C. the D. No article

24. What .... nuisance it is?
A. a B. an
C. the D. No article

25. Delhi is .... London of India.
A. a B. an
C. the D. No article

26. Where is .... will, there is a way.
A. a B. an
C. the D. No article

27. Her father is .... physician and surgeon.
A. a B. an
C. the D. No article

28. This will benefit .... poor.
A. a B. an
C. the D. No article

29. ....bird in hand is better than two in a bush.
A. A B. An
C. The D. No article

30. As he is hard-working, he will win .... prize.
A. a B. an
C. the D. No article

31. .... water of this well is dirty.
A. A B. An
C. The D. No article

32. Only .... wearer knows where the shoe pinches.
A. a B. an
C. the D. No article

33. .... action will be taken against you.
A. A B. An
C. The D. No article

34. .... sun rises in the east.
A. A B. An
C. The D. No article

35. She was promoted to .... highest post.
A. a B. an
C. the D. No article

36. Did you see .... Taj Mahal?
A. a B. an
C. the D. No article

37. He is .... one-eyed man.
A. a B. an
C. the D. No article

38. This is .... useful book.
A. a B. an
C. the D. No article

39. Cloth is sold by .... metre.
A. a B. an
C. the D. No article

40. The sun sets in .... west.
A. a B. an
C. the D. No article

41. Amar bought......umbrella yesterday.
A. a B. an
C. the D. No article

42. Surinder is ...... honest boy.
A. a B. an
C. the D. No article

43. She wrote ...... book in French.
A. a B. an
C. the D. No article

44. ...... lion roars.
A. A B. An
C. The D. No article

45. ..... apple a day keeps the doctor away.
A. A B. An
C. The D. No article

46. John bought ...... car yesterday.
A. a B. an
C. the D. No article

47. His father is ..... engineer in the U.S.A.
A. a B. an
C. the D. No article

48. It is hard for ..... owl to fly during the day times.
A. a B. an
C. the D. No article

49. She had ..... rimmed hat.
A. a B. an
C. the D. No article

50. My uncle is ..... heart specialist.
A. a B. an
C. the D. No article

51. He looks as foolish as .... ass.
A. a B. an
C. the D. No article

52. Did you go to .... prison to visit him?
A. a B. an
C. the D. No article

53. I found .... one-rupee note in the market.
A. a B. an
C. the D. No article

54. It is a pleasure to meet such .... efficient man.
A. a B. an
C. the D. No article

55. The Sanyasi lived in a cave in .... Himalayas.
A. a B. an
C. the D. No article

56. There is .... union in our factory.
A. a B. an
C. the D. No article

57. He hit his wife on the head with .... umbrella.

A. a B. an
C. the D. No article

58. I caught him by .... collar.

A. a B. an
C. the D. No article

59. Child is .... father of man.

A. a B. an
C. the D. No article

60. He gazed at .... moon for two hours.

A. a B. an
C. the D. No article

ANSWERS

1	2	3	4	5	6	7	8	9	10
C	C	C	C	C	C	C	C	B	B
11	12	13	14	15	16	17	18	19	20
C	C	C	C	C	C	C	A	A	C
21	22	23	24	25	26	27	28	29	30
A	A	A	A	C	A	A	C	A	A
31	32	33	34	35	36	37	38	39	40
C	C	B	C	C	C	A	A	C	C
41	42	43	44	45	46	47	48	49	50
B	B	A	A	B	A	B	B	A	A
51	52	53	54	55	56	57	58	59	60
B	C	A	B	C	A	B	C	C	C

Prepositions

A Preposition is a word that comes before a Pronoun or a Noun and expresses the relationship between Noun or Pronoun and some part of the remaining sentence.

(*a*) He is busy **with** his work.
(*b*) The boy jumped **into** the river.
(*c*) The birds are chirping **in** the trees.

In these sentences the words **with**, **into** and **in** show the relationship between the verbs **busy, jumped** and **chirping** with the nouns **work, river** and **trees** respectively.

Position of the Preposition

A. A Preposition usually precedes its object.
(*i*) He laughs **at** the poor.
(*ii*) He is angry **with** you.
(*iii*) She agrees **with** me.

B. In the case of Relative Pronouns it comes after the subject.
(*i*) This is the boy whom I was looking **for**.
(*ii*) That is the pen whose mention I was making **of**.

C. In the following cases, the Preposition comes after its object.
(*i*) Where is the boy you were complaining **against**?
(*ii*) What things are there you are looking **for**?
(*iii*) Who is there, you are waiting **for**?

Omission of the Prepositon

In many cases when the sentences contain Nouns of Time or Place, the Prepositions **from, in** and **for** are often omitted.

(*i*) He walked many kilometres.
(*ii*) He came to see me last year.
(*iii*) As I could not find my puppy anywhere, I looked here and there.

Prepositions are small words that show the relationship between one word and another. Prepositions in the following sentences show the position of the paper in relation to the desk, the book, hand and the door.

The paper is **on** the desk.
The paper is **under** the book.
The paper is **in** his hand.
The paper is **by** the door.

Common Prepositions

about	at	by
in	onto	toward
above	before	concerning
inside	out	under
across	behind	despite
into	over	until
after	below	down
like	since	up
against	beneath	during
near	through	upon
along	beside	except
of	throughout	with
amid	between	for
off	till	within
among	beyond	from
on	to	without

Multiple Choice Questions

Directions: *Select the most appropriate preposition from the given alternatives to fill in the blanks and make the sentence meaningfully complete.*

1. Don't try to be an advocate ..... these criminals.
A. for B. with
C. across D. in

2. The audience admired him ..... his sweet voice.
A. to B. on
C. for D. at

3. I want to check your bag ..... fake currency notes.
A. to B. for
C. upon D. on

4. The dew drops clung .... the blades of grass.
A. for B. on
C. to D. in

5. The thief was chased ..... by the police.
A. on B. after
C. into D. at

6. Please carry this bag ..... my room.
A. on B. for
C. to D. in

7. A lorry bumped ..... a car.
A. on B. over
C. into D. to

8. They were begging ..... food.
A. for B. on
C. to D. after

9. She always boasts ..... her wealth.
A. of B. for
C. on D. after

10. She banged ..... the door violently.
A. for B. to
C. on D. down

11. I applied ..... the post of a clerk.
A. for B. on
C. in D. to

12. I applied ..... the Principal for the post of a teacher.
A. to B. on
C. with D. for

13. I begged ..... him not to divulge the secret.
A. for B. of
C. with D. to

14. You had better borrow a pen ..... Rakesh.
A. over B. into
C. from D. by

15. I baked a cake ..... the guests.
A. to B. for
C. on D. of

16. She is confident ..... (her) success.
A. with B. on
C. of D. for

17. The doctor will cure you ..... malaria.
A. of B. with
C. for D. from

18. This law is common ..... all.
A. to B. upon
C. over D. at

19. She was condemned ..... her bad hand writing.
A. on B. for
C. into D. of

20. In summer there will be a great demand ..... desert cooler.
A. on B. with
C. for D. of

21. We shall wait ..... you.
A. on B. for
C. towards D. after

22. Tom displayed his injury ..... all his friends.
A. for B. upon
C. to D. at

23. She distributed the sweets ..... the two brothers.
A. among B. between
C. for D. in

24. Please distribute these apples ..... all.
A. among B. to
C. for D. at

25. It rarely happened that he defended ..... an innocent person.
A. against B. for
C. upon D. at

26. The parents were disappointed ..... the performance of their son.
A. on B. with
C. at D. of

27. Common salt dissolves ..... water.
A. for B. in
C. with D. by

28. This medicare is free ..... sugar.
A. on B. to
C. from D. of

29. The manager granted leave ..... the clerk.
A. to B. on
C. into D. for

30. The air was heavy ..... aroma of perfumes.
A. on B. with
C. into D. from

31. She had a quick glance ..... the magazine.
A. at B. from
C. into D. to

32. The climate of Kashmir is favourable ..... me.
A. with B. in
C. to D. for

33. They hate you ..... your poverty.
A. for B. on
C. in D. of

34. He is eligible ..... this post.
A. for B. to
C. with D. at

35. The smoke was emerging ..... down the foot of the hill.
A. on B. to
C. from D. at

36. The criminal managed to escape ..... the prison.
A. upon B. from
C. with D. of

37. You should educate your friends ..... the benefits of living in villages.
A. on B. towards
C. upon D. in

38. She made a lot of efforts ..... win the match.
A. for B. to
C. upon D. at

39. The new inspector will enquire ..... the murder case.
A. on B. for
C. into D. at

40. The retired soldiers were exempted ..... all taxes.
A. from B. to
C. on D. of

41. She was adept ..... journalism.
A. at B. on
C. with D. in

42. She is afraid ..... snakes.
A. on B. to
C. of D. with

43. I agree ..... your proposal.
A. for B. on
C. to D. with

44. The children were amazed ..... so big a python.
A. at B. on
C. in D. with

45. She was anxious ..... the final match.
A. about B. on
C. with D. for

46. He apologized ..... his being late.
A. towards B. for
C. on D. as

47. The children were amused ..... his jokes.
A. for B. to
C. at D. on

48. She is angry ..... you.
A. to B. with
C. on D. for

49. She is angry ..... your teasing remark.
A. at B. in
C. for D. with

50. A big patch of land was allocated ..... the refugees.
A. to B. for
C. in D. upon

ANSWERS

1	2	3	4	5	6	7	8	9	10
A	C	B	C	B	C	C	A	A	C
11	**12**	**13**	**14**	**15**	**16**	**17**	**18**	**19**	**20**
A	A	B	C	B	C	A	A	B	C
21	**22**	**23**	**24**	**25**	**26**	**27**	**28**	**29**	**30**
B	C	B	A	A	C	B	C	A	B
31	**32**	**33**	**34**	**35**	**36**	**37**	**38**	**39**	**40**
A	C	A	A	C	B	A	B	C	A
41	**42**	**43**	**44**	**45**	**46**	**47**	**48**	**49**	**50**
A	C	C	A	A	B	C	B	A	A

Synonyms & Antonyms

There are thousands of words in English language. No one can remember their meanings easily but with regular practice one can memorise most of them. A number of words with their Synonyms and Antonyms are compiled here. Try to learn as many as you can and answer the questions thereafter.

Words	*Synonyms*	*Antonyms*
Abandon	Cease, Forsake	Continue
Abhor	Hate, Loathe, Detest	Like, Love
Abiding	Enduring, Durable	Fleeting
Able	Proficient, Competent	Incompetent, Unfit
Ability	Skill, Power	Disability, Inability
Abortive	Fruitless, Futile	Fruitful, Successful
Abolish	Destroy, Undo	Restore, Revive
Abridge	Shorten, Curtail	Lengthen, Expand
Absolve	Forgive, Pardon, Excuse	Condemn
Accelerate	Hasten	Retard
Accord	Agreement, Harmony	Discord, Disagreement
Accumulate	Collect, Store, Amass	Distribute, Scatter
Adamant	Hard, Inflexible	Flexible
Adversity	Misfortune, Distress	Prosperity
Adept	Expert, Skilful	Inexpert, Unskillful
Aggravate	Heighten, Intensify	Quell, Suppress
Agile	Nimble	Clumsy, Undeft
Alert	Vigilant	Heedless
Allay	Calm, Soothe, Assuage	Arouse
Ameliorate	Improve, Advance, Amend	Worsen, Deteriorate
Ambiguous	Vague, Unclear	Clear
Amiable	Lovable, Agreeable	Disagreeable
Annihilate	Destroy	Create
Arduous	Hard, Strenuous	Easy
Attacks	Assault	Defend
Audacity	Boldness	Cowardice
Auspicious	Favourable, Propitious, Lucky	Ominous, Inauspicious, Unlucky
Austere	Harsh, Severe, Rigorous	Easy-going
Authentic	True, Genuine	Spurious, False
Avarice	Greed	Generosity
Averse	Unwilling, Loath, Disinclined	Willing, Inclined

Words	*Synonyms*	*Antonyms*
Aversion	Hostility, Hatred	Affinity, Liking
Base	Low, Mean, Ignoble	Noble, Exalted
Boisterous	Noisy, Stormy	Calm, Quiet
Brave	Courageous, Daring, Bold, Plucky	Cowardly, Dastardly, Timid
Brief	Short, Concise, Laconic	Lengthy, Diffuse
Bright	Vivid, Radiant	Dull, Dark
Brutal	Savage, Cruel	Humane, Kindly
Callous	Hard, Cruel, Indifferent	Soft, Tender, Concerned
Cautious	Careful, Wary	Rash, Reckless, Foolhardy
Censure (*n*)	Blame, Condemnation	Praise
Censure (*vb*)	Blame, Condemn	Praise, Commend
Circumscribed	Restricted, Confined, Limited	Unconfined, Unrestricted
Civil	Polite, Courteous, Gracious, Urbane	Rude, Uncivil, Impolite, Ungracious
Coerce	Compel, Force	Volunteer
Compassionate	Pitiful, Sympathetic, Merciful	Unsympathetic, Merciless, Cruel
Compress	Condense, Abbreviate	Expand, Lengthen
Conspicuous	Noticeable, Manifest	Inconspicuous
Constant	Steady, Steadfast, Uniform	Inconstant, Variable
Cordial	Friendly, Warm, Hearty	Cold, Unfriendly
Covert	Hidden, Secret	Overt, Open
Cruel	Savage, Ruthless, Vicious	Kind, Gentle, Benevolent
Cursory	Rapid, Superficial	Thorough, Exhaustive, Intensive
Credible	Believable, Probable, Plausible	Incredible, Unbelievable, Fantastic
Crafty	Cunning, Sly	Artless, Simple, Ingenuous
Costly	Expensive, Dear	Cheap, Inexpensive
Confidence	Trust, Reliance	Distrust, Doubt
Death	Decease, Demise	Existence, Life
Dearth	Scarcity, Lack, Want, Paucity, Shortage	Plenty, Abundance
Decay	Dissolution, Decline, Decomposition, Disintegration	Regeneration
Deference	Respect, Reverence	Disrespect, Irreverence
Deficient	Lacking, Inadequate	Complete, Sufficient
Desolate	Lonely, Deserted	Crowded, Occupied
Destitute	Wanting, Needy	Rich, Affluent
Diligence	Industry, Perseverance	Idleness
Disgrace	Dishonour, Discredit	Honour, Credit
Dwindle	Decrease, Shrink	Grow, Increase
Earthly	Terrestrial, Mundane	Celestial, Heavenly, Unearthly
Eligible	Qualified, Suitable	Ineligible, Unsuitable
Emancipate	Liberate, Free	Enslave
Excited	Impassioned, Stimulated	Composed, Cool, Impassive
Extraordinary	Uncommon, Remarkable, Marvellous	Commonplace, Ordinary
Extravagant	Lavish, Prodigal, Wastrel, Spendthrift	Thrifty, Economical, Frugal
Fabricate	Construct, Make	Destroy
Fabulous	Fictitious, Mythical	Actual, Real
False	Untrue, Mendacious	True, Genuine

Words	*Synonyms*	*Antonyms*
Famous	Well-known, Renowned	Obscure, Unknown
Fantastic	Fanciful, Imaginative, Visionary	Practical, Down to earth
Fearful	Nervous, Anxious, Afraid, Scared	Fearless, Dauntless
Felicity	Happiness	Sorrow
Gaiety	Joyousness, Hilarity	Mourning, Dullness
Garrulous	Talkative, Loquacious	Taciturn, Silent, Reserved
Generous	Liberal, Magnanimous	Stingy, Miserly
Gigantic	Huge, Colossal	Minute, Small
Graphic	Vivid, Pictorial, Meaningful	Vague
Guest	Visitor	Host
Guile	Fraud, Trickery	Artlessness, Ingenuousness
Gratitude	Gratefulness	Ingratitude, Ungratefulness
Gratuitous	Voluntary, Spontaneous, Unwarranted	Involuntary, Forced
Hamper	Hinder, Obstruct	Facilitate, Ease
Haughty	Arrogant, Proud	Humble, Modest
Hazardous	Dangerous, Perilous	Safe, Secure Protected
Headstrong	Obstinate, Stubborn	Weak-willed, Flexible
Hope	Belief, Conviction, Expectation	Despair, Hopelessness
Improvident	Prodigal, Carelessness	Provident, Economical
Incessant	Unceasing, Continuous	Discontinuous
Indolent	Slothful, Lethargic	Active, Energetic
Joy	Delight, Pleasure	Sadness, Gloom
Jolly	Jovial, Merry	Gloomy, Sad
Judicious	Discreet, Prudent	Indiscreet, Injudicious
Knowledge	Enlightenment, Learning	Ignorance, Stupidity
Laborious	Industrious, Assiduous	Slothful, Lazy
Laxity	Slackness, Looseness	Firmness
Lenient	Mild, Forbearing	Strict, Stern
Lethal	Deadly, Fatal, Mortal	Life-giving, Vital, Vivifying
Liberal	Generous, Tolerant	Intolerant, Illiberal
Liberty	Freedom, Independence	Slavery, Bondage
Lively	Animated, Active	Dull, Listless
Loyal	Faithful, Devoted	Treacherous, Disloyal, Unfaithful
Lucky	Fortunate	Unlucky, Unfortunate
Lucrative	Profitable	Unprofitable
Magnanimous	Generous, Largehearted	Ungenerous, Stingy
Malady	Illness, Ailment	Health
Manifest	Noticeable, Obvious	Obscure, Puzzling
Meagre	Small	Plentiful, Large
Mean	Low, Abject	Noble, Exalted
Mendacious	False, Untruthful	Truthful
Misery	Sorrow, Distress	Happiness, Joy
Morbid	Sick, Diseased	Healthy
Mournful	Sorrowful, Sad	Joyful, Happy

Words	Synonyms	Antonyms
Negligent	Careless, Heedless	Careful
Notorious	Infamous, Disreputable	Reputable
Obedient	Submissive, Compliant, Docile	Disobedient, Recalcitrant, Wayward
Obsolete	Antiquated, Out-of-Date	Current, Modern
Opportune	Timely, Seasonable	Inopportune
Opulence	Wealth, Riches	Penury, Poverty
Onerous	Heavy, Burdensome	Light, Easy
Palatable	Tasty, Delicious	Unpalatable
Pathetic	Touching	Joyous, Cheery
Persuade	Urge, Induce	Dissuade
Praise (*vb*)	Applaud, Eulogise	Condemn
Praise (*n*)	Applause, Eulogy	Condemnation
Precarious	Risky, Uncertain	Safe, Certain
Pretence	Pretext, Excuse	Candour, Frankness
Propagate	Breed, Circulate	Terminate, Restrict
Quaint	Odd, Singular	Usual, Ordinary
Quell	Suppress, Subdue	Agitate, Arouse
Rare	Uncommon, Scarce	Common, Ordinary
Refined	Polished, Elegant	Crude, Coarse
Remote	Distant	Near, Close
Renown	Fame, Reputation	Infamy, Notoriety
Rigid	Stiff, Unyielding	Flexible, Yielding
Remorseful	Regretful, Repentant	Unrepentant
Rebellion	Revolt, Mutiny, Insurgency	Loyalty
Scared	Holy, Consecrated	Profane, Unholy
Sane	Sensible, Sound	Insane
Scold	Chide, Rebuke	Praise
Serious	Grave, Earnest	Frivolous
Shy	Bashful	Bold, Impudent
Simple	Plain, Artless	Complex, Cunning, Shrewd
Solitary	Single, Lonely, Secluded	Numerous, Multitude
Shallow	Superficial	Deep
Solace	Comfort, Relief	Discomfort, Grief
Spurious	Sham, False	Genuine, Authentic
Stagnant	Still, Motionless	Moving
Surplus	Excess	Deficit, Shortage
Tame	Gentle, Mild, Domesticated	Savage, Wild
Teacher	Instructor, Educator	Student, Pupil
Tedious	Wearisome, Monotonous	Agreeable, Lively
Temporal	Worldly, Secular	Spiritual
Temperate	Moderate	Immoderate, Intemperate
Tortuous	Winding, Circuitous	Straight, Direct
Tough	Hard, Strong	Tender, Soft, Flexible
Transient	Temporary, Fleeting	Lasting, Durable, Permanent

Words	Synonyms	Antonyms
Trusworthy	Reliable	Unreliable, Untrustworthy
Tranquil	Calm	Agitated
Ugly	Unsightly, Repulsive	Beautiful, Attractive
Useful	Advantageous, Serviceable	Useless
Vehemence	Passion, Force	Apathy, Indifference
Vindictive	Revengeful	Forgiving
Wholesome	Healthy	Unwholesome, Morbid, Unhealthy, Diseased
Wicked	Evil, Impious	Pious, Good
Wise	Sagacious, Erudite	Foolish, Stupid
Wrath	Anger, Fury, Rage	Love, Peace, Calm
Wreck	Ruin, Destroy	Create, Construct
Yield	Surrender, Submit	Resist, Revolt
Yielding	Submissive, Supple	Inflexible, Intractable
Yoke	Oppression, Bondage	Freedom
Zeal	Passion, Fervour	Apathy, Indifference
Zest	Relish, Enthusiasm	Distaste, Disrelish

Multiple Choice Questions

Directions (Qs. 1 to 50): *In the following questions choose the word which best expresses the MEANING of the given word.*

1. TEPID
A. Hot B. Warm
C. Cold D. Boiling

2. MAYHEM
A. Jubilation B. Havoc
C. Excitement D. Defeat

3. TIMID
A. Fast B. Slow
C. Medium D. Shy

4. CANTANKEROUS
A. Quarrelsome B. Rash
C. Disrespectful D. Noisy

5. PRECARIOUS
A. Cautious B. Critical
C. Perilous D. Brittle

6. TACITURNITY
A. Dumbness B. Changeableness
C. Hesitation D. Reserve

7. INEBRIATE
A. Dreamy B. Stupefied
C. Unsteady D. Drunken

8. HARBINGER
A. Massenger B. Steward
C. Forerunner D. Pilot

9. INTIMIDATE
A. To hint B. Frighten
C. Bluff D. Harass

10. IRONIC
A. Inflexible B. Bitter
C. Good-natured D. Disguisedly sarcastic

11. STRINGENT
A. Tense B. Stringy
C. Strict D. Causing to shrink

12. ECSTATIC
A. Animated B. Bewildered
C. Enraptured D. Willful

13. COMMENSURATE
A. Measurable B. Proportionate
C. Beginning D. Appropriate

14. DESTITUTION
A. Humility B. Moderation
C. Poverty D. Beggary

15. ASCEND
A. Leap B. Grow
C. Deviate D. Mount

16. UNCOUTH
A. Ungraceful B. Rough
C. Slovenly D. Dirty

17. LYNCH
A. Hang B. Madden
C. Killed D. Shoot

18. LAUD
A. Lord B. Eulogy
C. Praise D. Extolled

19. CORRESPONDENCE
A. Agreements B. Contracts
C. Documents D. Letters

20. VENUE
A. Place B. Agenda
C. Time D. Duration

21. STERILE
A. Barren B. Arid
C. Childless D. Dry

22. SYNOPSIS
A. Index B. Mixture
C. Summary D. Puzzle

23. GERMANE
A. Responsible B. Logical
C. Possible D. Relevant

24. PONDER
A. Think B. Evaluate
C. Anticipate D. Increase

25. CANNY
A. Obstinate B. Handsome
C. Clever D. Stout

26. ABUNDANT
A. Ripe B. Cheap
C. Plenty D. Absent

27. CONSEQUENCES
A. Results B. Conclusions
C. Difficulties D. Applications

28. SHIVER
A. Shake B. Rock
C. Tremble D. Move

29. DILIGENT
A. Progressive B. Brilliant
C. Inventive D. Hard-working

30. DISTANT
A. Far B. Removed
C. Reserved D. Separate

31. FORAY
A. Excursion B. Contest
C. Ranger D. Intuition

32. FRUGALITY
A. Foolishness B. Extremity
C. Enthusiasm D. Economy

33. GARNISH
A. Paint B. Garner
C. Adorn D. Abuse

34. VIGOUR
A. Strength B. Boldness
C. Warmth D. Enthusiasm

35. CANDID
A. Apparent B. Explicit
C. Frank D. Bright

36. BRIEF
A. Limited B. Small
C. Little D. Short

37. GARRULITY
A. Credulity B. Senility
C. Loquaciousness D. Speciousness

38. FURORE
A. Excitement B. Worry
C. Flux D. Anteroom

39. NEUTRAL
A. Unbiased B. Non-aligned
C. Undecided D. Indifferent

40. LAMENT
A. Complain B. Comment
C. Condone D. Console

41. ADVERSITY
A. Failure B. Helplessness
C. Misfortune D. Crisis

42. TURN UP
A. Land up B. Show up
C. Crop up D. Come up

43. DEIFY
A. Flatter B. Challenge
C. Worship D. Face

44. ERROR
A. Misadventure B. Misgiving
C. Ambiguity D. Blunder

45. SHALLOW
A. Artificial B. Superficial
C. Foolish D. Worthless

46. MASSACRE
A. Murder B. Stab
C. Assassinate D. Slaughter

47. COMBAT
A. Conflict B. Quarrel
C. Feud D. Fight

48. VORACIOUS
A. Wild B. Hungry
C. Angry D. Quick

49. IMPROMPTU
A. Offhand B. Unimportant
C. Unreal D. Effective

50. RABBLE
A. Mob B. Noise
C. Roar D. Rubbish

Directions (Qs. 51 to 100): *In the following questions choose the word which is the exact OPPOSITE of the given words.*

51. STRINGENT
A. General B. Vehement
C. Lenient D. Magnanimous

52. FLIMSY
A. Frail B. Filthy
C. Firm D. Flippant

53. BUSY
A. Occupied B. Engrossed
C. Relaxed D. Engaged

54. ADAPTABLE
A. Adoptable B. Flexible
C. Yielding D. Rigid

55. LOVE
A. Villainy B. Hatred
C. Compulsion D. Force

56. BALANCE
A. Disbalance B. Misbalance
C. Debalance D. Imbalance

57. RELINQUISH
A. Abdicate B. Renounce
C. Possess D. Deny

58. MOUNTAIN
A. Plain B. Plateau
C. Precipice D. Valley

59. FICKLE
A. Courageous B. Sincere
C. Steadfast D. Humble

60. PERENNIAL
A. Frequent B. Regular
C. Lasting D. Rare

61. RARELY
A. Hardly B. Definitely
C. Frequently D. Periodically

62. STARTLED
A. Amused B. Relaxed
C. Endless D. Astonished

63. ADHERENT
A. Detractor B. Enemy
C. Alien D. Rival

64. QUIESCENT
A. Indifferent B. Troublesome
C. Weak D. Unconcerned

65. CONDENSE
A. Expand B. Distribute
C. Interpret D. Lengthen

66. BENIGN
A. Malevolent B. Soft
C. Friendly D. Unwise

67. OBSCURE
A. Implicit B. Obnoxious
C. Explicit D. Pedantic

68. HYPOCRITICAL
A. Gentle B. Sincere
C. Amiable D. Dependable

69. EVASIVE
A. Free B. Honest
C. Liberal D. Frank

70. INDUSTRIOUS
A. Indifferent B. Indolent
C. Casual D. Passive

71. EXTRICATE
A. Manifest B. Palpable
C. Release D. Entangle

72. LUCID
A. Glory B. Noisy
C. Obscure D. Distinct

73. INSIPID
A. Tasty B. Stupid
C. Discreet D. Feast

74. OBEYING
A. Ordering B. Following
C. Refusing D. Contradicting

75. VICTORIOUS
A. Defeated B. Annexed
C. Destroyed D. Vanquished

76. COMMISSIONED
A. Started B. Closed
C. Finished D. Terminated

77. VANITY
A. Pride B. Humility
C. Conceit D. Ostentious

78. ZENITH
A. Acme B. Top
C. Nadir D. Pinnacle

79. TANGIBLE
A. Ethereal B. Concrete
C. Actual D. Solid

80. REPRESS
A. Inhibit B. Liberate
C. Curb D. Quell

81. EPILOGUE
A. Dialogue B. Prelude
C. Post script D. Epigram

82. FRAUDULENT
A. Candid B. Direct
C. Forthright D. Genuine

83. LOQUACIOUS
A. Reticent B. Talkative
C. Garrulous D. Verbose

84. NIGGARDLY
A. Frugal B. Thrifty
C. Stingy D. Generous

85. PERTINENT
A. Irrational B. Irregular
C. Insistent D. Irrelevant

86. FAINT-HEARTED
A. Warm-hearted B. Full-blooded
C. Hot-blooded D. Stout-hearted

87. VIOLENT
A. Humble B. Harmless
C. Gentle D. Tame

88. STATIONARY
A. Active B. Mobile
C. Rapid D. Busy

89. HONORARY
A. Dishonourable B. Reputed
C. Paid D. Official

90. COMMON
A. Rare B. Small
C. Petty D. Poor

91. REPEL
A. Attend B. Concentrate
C. Continue D. Attract

92. ARTIFICIAL
A. Red B. Natural
C. Truthful D. Solid

93. CAPACIOUS
A. Limited B. Caring
C. Foolish D. Changeable

94. PROVOCATION
A. Vocation B. Pacification
C. Peace D. Destruction

95. METICULOUS
A. Mutual B. Shaggy
C. Meretricious D. Slovenly

96. ABLE
A. Disable B. Inable
C. Unable D. Enable

97. COMFORT
A. Uncomfort B. Miscomfort
C. Discomfort D. None of these

98. GAIN
A. Loose B. Fall
C. Lost D. Lose

99. SYNTHETIC
A. Affable B. Natural
C. Plastic D. Cosmetic

100. ACQUITTED
A. Freed B. Burdened
C. Convicted D. Entrusted

ANSWERS

1	2	3	4	5	6	7	8	9	10
B	B	D	A	B	D	D	C	B	D
11	12	13	14	15	16	17	18	19	20
C	C	B	C	D	A	C	C	D	A
21	22	23	24	25	26	27	28	29	30
A	C	D	A	C	C	A	C	D	A
31	32	33	34	35	36	37	38	39	40
A	D	C	A	C	D	C	A	A	A
41	42	43	44	45	46	47	48	49	50
C	B	C	D	B	D	D	B	A	A
51	52	53	54	55	56	57	58	59	60
C	C	C	D	B	D	C	D	C	D
61	62	63	64	65	66	67	68	69	70
D	B	B	A	C	A	C	B	B	B
71	72	73	74	75	76	77	78	79	80
D	C	A	A	A	D	B	C	A	B
81	82	83	84	85	86	87	88	89	90
B	D	B	D	D	D	C	B	C	A
91	92	93	94	95	96	97	98	99	100
D	B	A	B	D	C	C	D	B	C

One Word Substitutions

There are many words in English language which can be perfectly used for a number of words. These words help in expressing ideas in a short and correct manner for the right occasion. Such words not only enhance the vocabulary but also enable you to economise in the use of words to a great extent. Try to learn as many as you can.

Denoting Numbers

- A collection of poems — *anthology*
- A number of merchant ships protected by warships (in war-time) — *convoy*
- A number of stars grouped together — *constellation*
- A number of hired applauders, *i.e.* persons paid to clap — *claque*
- A number of people at church — *congregation*
- A number of people gathered together for some common purpose — *gathering, assembly, society*
- A group of people who get together to work for some cause of common interest — *coterie*
- A number of workmen, prisoners, thieves — *gang*
- A number of sheep — *flock*
- A number of geese — *gaggle*
- A number of leopards — *leap*
- A number of lions, monkeys — *pride, troop*
- A number of herrings, mackerel — *shoal*
- A number of fish taken in a net — *catch, haul*
- A number of whales, porpoises — *school, gam*
- A number of oxen or horses (two or more) harnessed together — *team*
- A number of ships, cars, buses — *fleet*

Denoting Places

- A place where bees are kept — *apiary*
- A place where birds are kept — *aviary*
- A place where fishes are kept — *aquarium*
- A dwelling-place of an animal underground — *burrow*
- A squirrel's home — *drey*
- A nest of a bird of prey — *eyrie, aerie*
- A place where spirituous liquors are produced — *distillery*
- A place where clothes are washed and ironed — *laundry*
- A place where Government records are kept — *archives*
- A place where treasures of art, curiosities, etc. are preserved or exhibited — *museum*
- A place where fruit trees are grown — *orchard*

Pertaining to the Literary Sphere

- A work whose writer is unknown — *anonymous*
- A record of one's life written by oneself — *autobiography*
- The history of the life of a person — *biography*
- The heading or short description of a newspaper article, chapter of a book etc. — *caption*

- A humorous play, having a happy ending — *comedy*
- A list of books in a library — *catalogue, bibliography*
- A book in which the events of each day are recorded — *diary*
- A books containing the words of a language with their definitions, in alphabetical order — *dictionary*
- A book of names and addresses — *directory*
- A short speech by a player at the end of a play — *epilogue*
- A brief summary of a book — *epitome*
- A book containing information on all branches of knowledge — *encyclopedia*
- To remove the offensive portions of a book — *expurgate*
- A speech delivered without earlier preparation — *extempore*
- A noisy or vehement speech intended to excite passions — *harangue*
- A written account, usually in book form of the interesting and memorable experiences of one's life — *memoirs*
- A note to help the memory — *memorandum*
- A declaration of plans and promises put forward by a candidate for election, political party or a sovereign — *manifesto*
- A short speech by a player at the beginning of a play — *prologue*
- Literary theft, or passing off an author's original work as one's own — *plagiarism*
- Speaking aloud to oneself — *soliloquy*
- A play with a sad or tragic end — *tragedy*

Pertaining to Religion

- One who believes that man can have no knowledge of God but only of natural phenomena — *agnostic*
- One who renounces his religious vows or forsakes his religious principles — *apostate*
- One who does not believe in existence of God — *atheist*
- One intolerantly devoted to a particular creed — *bigot*
- To utter profane language against God or anything holy — *blaspheme*
- A breaker of church images — *iconoclast*
- Worship of images or idols — *idiolatory*
- One who believes in God — *theist*
- One who believes in only one God — *monotheist*
- One who believes in many Gods — *polytheist*

Pertaining to Government

- To give up a throne or other office of dignity — *abdicate*
- Absence of government — *anarchy*
- Government by Sovereign of uncontrolled authority — *autocracy, despotism*
- Government by departments of states — *bureaucracy*
- Government of the people, for the people and by the people — *democracy*
- Government by the nobility — *aristocracy*
- The right of self-government — *autonomy*
- Government by a few — *oligarchy*
- Government by the wealthy — *plutocracy*
- Government by divine guidance — *theocracy*
- To decide a political question by the direct vote of the whole electorate — *referendum*
- Sweeping governmental change — *revolution*
- The science of government — *politics*

Pertaining to Professions

- One who attends to the diseases of the eye — *oculist*
- One who tests eyesight and sells spectacles — *optician*
- One who attends to the teeth — *dentist*
- One skilled in the care of hands and feet — *chiropodist*

- A physician who assists women at child-birth — *obstetrician*
- One who drives a motorcar — *chauffeur*
- One who makes or sells candles — *chandler*
- One who preserves the skins of animals and mounts them so as to resemble the living animals — *taxidermist*
- One who compiles a dictionary — *lexicographer*
- One who writes books — *author*
- One skilled in the treatment of diseases of animals — *veterinarian*
- A tradesman who manages funerals — *undertaker*
- One who draws up contracts and lends money on interest — *scrivener*
- One who lends money and keeps goods as security — *pawnbroker*
- A teacher who travels from place to place to give instruction. — *peripatetic*
- One who travels from place to place selling miscellaneous articles — *hawker, pedlar*
- One who collects postage stamps — *philatelist*
- One who lends money at exorbitant interest — *usurer*
- One who takes care of a building — *janitor*
- One who sells sweets and pastries — *confectioner*
- One who works in a coalmine — *collier*
- One who flies an aeroplane — *pilot, aviator*
- One who studies rocks and soils — *geologist*
- One who shoes horses — *farrier*
- A professional rider in horses races — *jockey*
- One who deals in silks, cotton, woollen, and linen goods — *mercer*
- One who deals in wines — *vintner*
- One who deals in fish — *fishmonger*
- One who deals in iron and hardware — *ironmonger*
- One who sells fruits, vegetables, etc. from a barrow — *costermonger*
- One who sets type in a printing office — *compositor*

Pertaining to Medicine

- A substance which destroys or weakens germs — *antiseptic*
- Any medicine which produces insensibility — *anaesthetic*
- A medicine to counteract poison — *antidote*
- Want or poorness of blood — *anaemia*
- A medicine which alleviates pain — *anodyne*
- To cut off a person's body a part which is infected — *amputate*
- One who is recovering from illness — *convalescent*
- To be able to tell the nature of disease by its symptoms — *diagnose*
- A disease affecting many persons at the same place and time — *epidemic*
- A disease confined to a particular district or place — *endemic*
- To disinfect by smoke — *fumigate*
- Free or exempt from infection — *immune*
- A person who is sick — *invalid*
- A cure for all diseases — *panacea*
- A disease widely epidemic — *pandemic*
- Confinement to one place to avoid spread of infection — *quarantine*

Pertaining to Characteristics and Actions

- One who devotes his life to the welfare and interests of other people — *altruist*
- One who can use both hands with equal ease — *ambidexterous*
- One who fishes with a rod — *angler*
- One who kills secretly or by surprise — *assassin*
- A person who collects things belonging to ancient times — *antiquary*
- One who is always finding faults — *censorious*

❑ One living at the same time as another	*contemporary*
❑ One who sneers at the aims and beliefs of his fellowmen	*cynic*
❑ One who delights in speaking about oneself	*egotist*
❑ One who exalts his own opinion	*egoist*
❑ One who dies for a noble cause	*martyr*
❑ One who retires from society to live a solitary life	*recluse, hermit*
❑ One who maliciously sets fire to buildings	*incendiary*
❑ One who is banished from his home or his country	*exile*
❑ One who takes refuge in a foreign country	*refugee, alien*
❑ One who runs away from justice or the law	*fugitive*
❑ One who walks in his sleep	*somnambulist*
❑ One who looks on the bright side of things	*optimist*
❑ One who looks on the dark side of things	*pessimist*
❑ A hater of mankind	*misanthropist*
❑ One who knows everything	*omniscient*
❑ One who is all powerful	*omnipotent*
❑ One who is present everywhere	*omnipresent*
❑ One who devotes his service or wealth for the love of mankind	*philanthropist*
❑ One new to anything	*novice, tyro, neophyte*
❑ One who engages in any pursuit for the love of it, and not for gain	*amateur*
❑ One who journeys to a holy place	*pilgrim*
❑ A leader of the people who can sway his followers by his oratory	*demagogue*
❑ One who has special skill in judging art, music, tastes, etc.	*connoisseur*
❑ One whose reasoning is clever yet false	*sophist*
❑ One who makes a display of his learning	*pedant*
❑ One who is indifferent to pain or pleasure	*stoic*
❑ One who loves his country and serves it devotedly	*patriot*
❑ One devoted to the pleasures of eating and drinking	*epicure*
❑ One who poses to be what he is not	*hypocrite, impostor*
❑ One who foretells events	*prophet*
❑ One who pretends to know a great deal about everything	*mountebank, charlatan, quack*
❑ One versed in many languages	*linguist*
❑ One who cannot pay one's debts	*insolvent*
❑ One who takes over after another in office or employment	*successor*
❑ One who has been before another in office or employment	*predecessor*
❑ One who is opposed to intellectual progress	*obscurant*
❑ One who abstains from alcoholic drinks	*teetotaller*
❑ One who hides away on a ship to obtain a free passage	*stowaway*
❑ One who spends very little	*miser*
❑ One who spends too much	*spendthrift*

Pertaining to War

❑ An unprovoked attack by an enemy	*aggression*
❑ Shells, bombs, military stores	*ammunition*
❑ A place where naval or military weapons are made or stored	*ordnance*
❑ An agreement between belligerents to stop fighting	*armistice*
❑ A general pardon of offenders	*amnesty*
❑ To reduce to nothing	*annihilate*
❑ Nations carrying on warfare	*belligerents*
❑ To surround a place with the intention of capturing	*besiege*
❑ To camp in the open air without tents or covering	*bivouac*

- To seize for military use *commandeer*
- A person who is forced by law to become a soldier *conscript*
- An order prohibiting ships to leave the ports *embargo*
- A number of firearms being discharged continuously *fusillade*
- To make an examination or preliminary survey of enemy territory for military objectives *reconnoitre*

Pertaining to Marriage and Children

- One who marries a second wife or husband while the legal spouse is alive *bigamist*
- One vowed to a single or unmarried life *celibate*
- One engaged to be married *fiancé, fiancee*
- A child whose parents are dead *orphan*
- A hater of marriage *misogamist*
- One who has more than two wives at a time *polygamist*

Pertaining to Death

- Dead and decaying flesh (esp. of animals) *carrion*
- A monument set up for persons who are buried elsewhere *cenotaph*
- To preserve a dead body from putrefaction *embalm*
- Words inscribed on a tomb *epitaph*
- An examination of dead body *postmortem, autopsy*
- An account in the newspaper of the funeral of one deceased *obituary*
- The property left to someone by a will *legacy*
- Occurring after death *posthumous*
- The act of killing a human being *homicide*
- Murder of a new born child *infanticide*
- Murder of a brother *fratricide*
- Murder of a sister *sororicide*
- Murder of a mother *matricide*
- Murder of a father *patricide*
- Murder of a parent *parricide*
- Murder of a king *regicide*

Pertaining to Sciences and Arts

- The study of all heavenly bodies and the earth in relation to them *astronomy*
- The science of land management *agronomics*
- The study of mankind *anthropology*
- The study of physical life or living matter *biology*
- The study of plants *botany*
- The art of beautiful handwriting *calligraphy*
- The science which deals with the varieties of human race *ethnology*
- The study of the origin and history of words *etymology*
- The study of coins *numismatics*
- The study of human face *physiognomy*
- The art of making fireworks *pyrotechnics*
- The study of birds *ornithology*
- The study of languages *philology*
- At home equally on land or in water *amphibious*
- The inside of a nut *kernel*
- The central or innermost part of fruit *core*
- The animals of a certain region *fauna*

- The plants and vegetation of a certain region — *flora*
- Absence of rain for a long time — *drought*
- To supply land with water by artificial means — *irrigate*
- One who studies plant and animal life — *naturalist*
- A cud-chewing animal, *e.g.* the cow — *ruminant*
- A gnawing animal, *e.g.* the rat — *rodent*
- A four-footed animal — *quadruped*
- Animals which carry their young in a pouch, *e.g.* kangaroo — *marsupials*
- Soil composed largely of decayed vegetable matter — *humus*
- A preparation for killing insects — *insecticide*
- A plant or animal growing on another — *parasite*
- Living for many years — *perennial*

Miscellaneous

- Loud enough to be heard — *audible*
- Not distinct enough to be heard — *inaudible*
- Fit for food — *edible*
- Unfit for human consumption — *inedible*
- Fit to be chosen or selected — *eligible*
- Not having the qualities for being chosen — *ineligible*
- Writing that is easy to read — *legible*
- Writing that is difficult to decipher — *illegible*
- Able to read — *literate*
- Unable to read — *illiterate*
- Born of married parents — *legitimate*
- Born of unmarried parents — *illegitimate*
- To send back a person to his own country — *repatriate*
- To banish from one's country — *expatriate*
- To move from one country to another — *migrate*
- One who leaves his country to settle in another — *emigrant*
- One who comes into a foreign country to settle there — *immigrant*
- Incapable of being redeemed from evil, *i.e.* beyond correction — *incorrigible*
- That which cannot be rubbed out or blotted out — *ineffaceable, indelible*
- That which cannot be conquered — *invincible*
- Incapable of making errors — *infallible*
- That which cannot be avoided or prevented — *inevitable*
- Incapable of being burnt — *incombustible*
- That which easily catches fire — *inflammable, flammable*
- That which cannot be seen — *invisible*
- Living for ever — *immortal*
- Increase the gravity of an offence — *aggravate*
- Ordinary or commonplace remark — *platitude*
- That which cannot be satisfied — *insatiable*
- That which cannot be repaired — *irreparable*
- That which cannot be imitated — *inimitable*
- Persons (or efforts) that cannot be wearied — *indefatigable*
- One who eats too much — *glutton*
- To destroy completely — *annihilate*
- A statement open to more than one interpretation — *ambiguous*
- A round about way of speaking — *circumlocution*
- Cautious observation of events, etc. — *circumspection*
- That which cannot be hurt — *invulnerable*

Multiple Choice Questions

Directions: *Below are given some statements each of which is capable of being expressed by one word only. Each statement is followed by four such words of which only one is correct. Out of the given alternatives A, B, C and D choose the correct word which very closely fits each definition.*

1. A set of papers giving information about a person or event:
A. editorial B. agenda
C. dossier D. clippings

2. List and explanations of technical, difficult, etc. terms:
A. preface B. glossary
C. bibliography D. appendix

3. One who pays too much care to his clothes and personal appearance:
A. conscious B. dandy
C. cynosure D. leer

4. A child born after death of father:
A. effeminate B. immature
C. fatherless D. posthumous

5. A person who is hard to please:
A. insensible B. hypocrite
C. egoist D. fastidious

6. Complete failure in something attempted:
A. fiasco B. vain
C. falsies D. flop

7. A word which can be interpreted in any way:
A. confusing B. misnomer
C. ambiguous D. precise

8. A group of persons united by common interests:
A. society B. class
C. clique D. coterie

9. A person who is inexperienced and easily deceived:
A. fool B. immature
C. blackhorn D. greenhorn

10. Instruction by question and answer:
A. interrogatory B. catechism
C. bulletin D. alibi

11. Record of events by someone with first hand knowledge:
A. novice B. report
C. memoir D. itinerary

12. A mode of talk familiar to a particular group or profession:
A. jargon B. colloquial
C. slang D. abuses

13. Person who is crazy:
A. lackadaisical B. tarter
C. scrupulous D. loony

14. A person who readily believes others:
A. hasty B. immature
C. credulous D. credible

15. One who eats human flesh:
A. beast B. cannibal
C. maneater D. carnivorous

16. Intentional destruction of racial groups:
A. genocide B. homicide
C. fratricide D. communal riot

17. One with weakness of mind caused by old age:
A. dastard B. dotard
C. fop D. philanderer

18. Study of insects:
A. zoology B. philology
C. entomology D. etymology

19. A critical judge of any art particularly fine arts:
A. connoisseur B. veteran
C. philistine D. dilettante

20. One who introduces items of an entertainment:
A. consort B. compere
C. director D. introducer

21. A combination of business firms:
A. enterprise B. franchise
C. cartel D. autonomous

22. Freeing of suppressed emotions:
A. catastrophe B. catharsis
C. epilogue D. chagrin

23. One who believes in the power of fate:
A. optimist B. pessimist
C. fearful D. fatalist

24. The murder of brother:
A. genocide B. homicide
C. salvage D. fratricide

25. Additional to proper payment:
A. premium B. overtime
C. ex-gratia D. fringe

26. A person or thing used to tempt somebody into a position of danger:
A. decoy B. provocateur
C. jinx D. scapegoat

27. Custom of having more than one husband at the same time:
A. polygamy B. polyandry
C. bigamy D. sexagenary

28. A person of refined taste in food and drink:
A. emeritus B. epicure
C. glutton D. gourmand

29. A tombstone inscription:
A. epithet B. encomium
C. epistle D. epitaph

30. An office which has no work but high salary:
A. fortuitous B. gratuitous
C. sinecure D. ceremonial

31. One who is indifferent to pains and pleasure of life:
A. stoic B. metaphysical
C. pessimist D. sceptic

32. List of names of persons showing duties to be performed by each in turn:
A. notice B. bulletin
C. roster D. agenda

33. Long angry speech of criticism or accusation:
A. track record B. tirade
C. taut D. outburst

34. One who is in favour of never drinking alcoholic drinks:
A. idealist B. uxorious
C. teetotaller D. unalcoholic

35. Trying to win favour by flattery and charm:
A. smarmy B. shrewish
C. toady D. loquacious

36. A decision on which one cannot go back:
A. incorrigible B. irrevocable
C. rigid D. invulnerable

37. The science that studies the varieties of human race:
A. phrenology B. physiology
C. sociology D. ethnology

38. A person who hates women:
A. philogynist B. philatelist
C. misogamist D. misogynist

39. A group of people in a particular grade in an organisation:
A. colleague B. staff
C. echelon D. commission

40. Honourably discharged from service:
A. emeritus B. latitudinarian
C. infallible D. meritorious

41. One who does not believe in the existence of God:
A. atheist B. altruist
C. agnostic D. flippant

42. The large money paid for an early retirement:
A. goldmine B. golden handshake
C. gratuity D. lion's share

43. A hater of learning and knowledge:
A. misologist B. misogynist
C. philologist D. philanthropist

44. One who lives and acts for the welfare of others:
A. misanthrope B. credulous
C. altruist D. gregarious

45. Mental weariness for want of occupation:
A. desperate B. depression
C. fatigue D. ennui

46. That which makes it difficult to recognise the presence in real of somebody or something:
A. cover B. mask
C. make-up D. camouflage

47. To bear a hand in one's new business:
A. partnership B. interfere
C. assist D. join

48. One who renounces the world and practices self-discipline in order to attain salvation:
A. devotee B. ascetic
C. theist D. parsimonious

49. A place where gambling is practiced:
A. hotel B. motel
C. casino D. stadium

50. A sad song is a:
A. dirge B. elegy
C. ditty D. knell

ANSWERS

1	2	3	4	5	6	7	8	9	10
C	B	B	D	D	A	C	C	D	B
11	**12**	**13**	**14**	**15**	**16**	**17**	**18**	**19**	**20**
C	A	D	C	B	A	B	C	A	B
21	**22**	**23**	**24**	**25**	**26**	**27**	**28**	**29**	**30**
C	B	D	D	D	A	B	B	D	C
31	**32**	**33**	**34**	**35**	**36**	**37**	**38**	**39**	**40**
A	C	B	C	A	B	D	D	C	A
41	**42**	**43**	**44**	**45**	**46**	**47**	**48**	**49**	**50**
A	B	A	C	D	D	C	B	C	A

Idioms and Phrases

- An idiom is a group of words established by usage as having a meaning different from the individual words.
- A phrase is a small group of words standing together as an idiomatic expression.

Learn and practise as may as you can.

Idioms and Idiomatic Phrases

✦ **ABC** (basic principles)
She does not know the ABC of photography.

✦ **At one's beck and call** (ready to obey)
He had a dozen men at his beck and call.

✦ **At sixes and sevens** (in disorder)
The drawing room articles were lying at sixes and sevens on the floor.

✦ **A wet blanket** (a discouraging person)
Don't allow Rakesh to accompany you to the hunting trip because he is a wet blanket.

✦ **A big gun** (an important person)
Mr Smith is a big gun in our city.

✦ **At a stone's throw** (at a short distance from)
My school is at a stone's throw from my house.

✦ **A man of word** (a person who keeps his promise)
Mr Sharma is a man of word.

✦ **A man of a few words** (a remarkable person)
Gandhiji was a man of a few words.

✦ **At arm's length** (to keep away)
We should always keep bad boys at arm's length

✦ **A bolt from the blue** (a sudden and unexpected event)
The news of my friend's death came to me like a bolt from the blue.

✦ **A man of letters** (a scholar)
Radha Krishnan was a man of letters.

✦ **A hard nut to crack.** (a puzzling problem)
To get a win over American basket ball team is a hard nut to crack for India.

✦ **A yeoman's service** (service which is beneficial to the human beings)
He did yeoman's service through his life.

✦ **A snake in the grass** (a hidden foe)
Beware of him because he seems to be a snake in the grass.

✦ **Acid test** (hard test)
The election will be an acid test for the ruling party.

✦ **A wolf in sheep's clothing** (a hypocrite)
You should not keep company with him because he is a wolf in sheep's clothing.

✦ **At the eleventh hour** (at the last moment)
The war was about to start but fortunately at the eleventh hour a messenger came to the PM with a message of peace.

✦ **A great card** (an important person)
Mr Sood is a great card in the ministry of finance.

✦ **A fool of the first water** (one completely foolish)
Being a fool of the first water he could not solve even the simplest sum.

✦ **A bone of contention** (to be the cause of quarrel)
Kashmir is the bone of contention between India and Pakistan.

✦ **A green hand** (not very much experienced)
We shall pay a little to a green hand.

✦ **All in all** (completely)
Rajesh is all in all in this office.

✦ **A bed of roses** (a comfort)
Life is not a bed of roses.

✦ **An apple of discord** (to be the cause of)
Kashmir is an apple of discord between India and Pakistan.

✦ **A white elephant** (of no use)
This sort of glib talker always proves a white elephant in the end.

✦ **A red letter day** (An important day)
15th August is a red letter day for the Indians.

✦ **By hook or by crook** (by any means fair or foul)

✦ **Black sheep** (a traitor)
Later on Mr XYZ proved a black sheep.

- **By dint of** (by means of)
  By dint of hard work, she earned a lot of money.
- **Break ones back** (to work hard to get something)
  He broke his back to earn his livelihood.
- **Break the back of** (accomplish the hardest part of a certain job)
  There is nothing to be worried about as we've already broken the back of the problem.
- **Beat about the bush** (to go on talking on some worthless topic)
  Stop this beating about the bush, come to the main task.
- **Beyond one's means** (beyond one's budget)
  He is living beyond his means, therefore, he is sure to get ruined.
- **Cut loose** (Keep away)
  India should cut loose from bad politics.
- **Chips of the same block** (having the same taste)
  They are the chips of the same block.
- **Cut-throat competition** (a stiff competition)
  There is a cut-throat competition among the publishers in the market.
- **Come what may** (no matter what happens)
  I'll do it come what may.
- **Drop someone a line** (send a letter, etc.)
  Please drop me a line of your well-being.
- **Dull the edge of** (reduce the intensity of)
  Take this pill and it will dull the edge of pain.
- **From hand to mouth** (without any saving)
  The poor factory worker is living from hand to mouth.
- **Fair and square** (clean)
  One must be fair and square in one's dealing.
- **Hard of hearing** (somewhat deaf)
  She is a bit hard of hearing.
- **In the good books of** (be good in one's mind)
  Jack is in the good books of his teachers.
- **In black and white** (in written)
  Don't give him anything in black and white.
- **In cold blood** (mercilessly)
  The old woman was murdered in cold blood.
- **In a crack** (all of a sudden or rapidly)
  The thief left the place in a crack.
- **In full swing** (in full force)
  The studies of the students are going on in full swing.
- **In the twinkling of an eye** (quickly)
  The monkey ate up grams in the twinkling of an eye.
- **Keep the ball rolling** (to maintain the progress of some activity)
  After the death of his father he had to take the charge of his office to keep the ball rolling.
- **Neck and neck** (even)
  There is a neck and neck fight between the two boxers.
- **Once in a blue moon** (seldom)
  She visits her brother once in a blue moon.
- **Slow and steady** (slowly but continually)
  Slow and steady wins the race.
- **To cut a sorry figure** (present oneself in a bad way)
  She cut a sorry figure on the stage.
- **To give a red carpet reception** (to give a warm welcome)
  The PM was given a red carpet reception in America.
- **To dance one's tune** (to follow someone submissively)
  He always dances to his brother's tune.
- **To turn a deaf ear to** (to disregard)
  She turned a deaf ear to her parents' advice.
- **To call a spade a spade** (to speak the truth)
  Gandhiji always called a spade a spade.
- **To bring to book** (to scold)
  The naughty boy was brought to book by the teacher.
- **To cut short** (to reduce)
  Smoking will cut short your life.
  He wants to get money by hook or by crook.
- **To grease the palm of** (to bribe)
  Rohit greased the palm of the clerk and got the file moved.
- **Through thick and thin.** (under all circumstances)
  We'll stand by you through thick and thin.
- **To die by inches** (to die a painful death)
  The old man died by inches.
- **To eat one's words** (to retract one's statement)
  You'll have to eat your words because you have spoken without thinking.
- **To burn the midnight oil** (to work hard)
  You'll have to burn the midnight oil if you want to get good marks.
- **To poke one's nose into** (to meddle with)
  It is bad to poke your nose into others' affair.
- **To fall flat** (to have no effect)
  His father's advice fell flat on him.
- **To make a clean breast of** (to confess)
  He made a clean breast of his involvement in the bomb blast.
- **To get the better of** (overcome)
  Anger got the better of him.
- **To break somebody's back** (to give too much work to him to do)

She broke his back by giving him so much hard work to do.

- **Throw cold water on** (to discourage)
  She tried to throw cold water on his plan but he was well-determined.
- **The long and short of** (in brief)
  The long and short of his lecture is that we should live like brothers.
- **To burn one's fingers** (to get oneself in trouble)
  You have burnt your fingers by speaking against him.
- **To turn over a new leaf** (to change the course of life)
  He has turned over a new leaf in his life.
- **To have one's own axe to grind** (to have vested interest)
  He has his own axe to grind in this matter.
- **To take to one's heels** (to run away)
  The thief took to his heels as soon as he saw the policeman.
- **To move heaven and earth** (to make too much effort)
  The young man moved heaven and earth to find a job.
- **To be caught red handed** (to be caught at the time of committing a crime)
  The clerk was caught red handed when he was accepting bribe from Mr ABC.
- **To receive with open arms** (to give a warm welcome)
  The new president of the club was received with open arms by the members.
- **To be born with a silver spoon in one's mouth** (to be born in a rich family)
  Mr. J. L. Nehru was born with a silver spoon in his mouth.
- **To come to light** (to be known)
  A new disease has recently come to light.
- **To be the apple of one's eye** (be very dear)
  He is the apple of his parent's eye.
- **To make fun of** (laugh at)
  The children made fun of the waiter in the hotel.
- **To let the cat out of the bag** (to divulge secret)
  It was Sohan who let the cat out of the bag by telling the real matter.
- **To open a new chapter** (to start some habit, etc.
  By drinking, you've opened a new chapter in your life.
- **To make the flesh creep** (to terrify)
  The story made my flesh creep.
- **To lose ground** (to retreat)
  After fighting for some time the Pakistani army began to lose ground.
- **To bring to book** (to punish)
  The student was brought to book by the teacher.
- **To show a clean pair of heels** (to run away)
  The thief showed a clean pair of heels as soon as he saw the policeman approaching.
- **To gain ground** (to be established)
  He gained ground in India in a few years.
- **To get wind of** (to get information)
  I got wind of his secret plans.
- **Under a cloud** (be in trouble or in a state of disgrace or suspicion)
  His company seemed to be under a cloud as it had no funds to pay the wages to the workers.

Verbal Phrases

- **Act upon** (to follow)
  I acted upon my father's advice.
- **Act upto** (to perform within limits)
  He acted upto his conscience.
- **Act beyond** (to perform crossing limits)
  We should not act beyond our capacity.
- **Act for** (to perform in place of someone else)
  The vice principal acted for the principal.
- **Back up** (to make a queue)
  The vehicles began to back up.
- **Back down** (withdraw claim in the presence of opposition)
  The leader backed down from his previous statement.
- **Back off** (draw back some plan or action)
  They backed off from building a flyover.
- **Back out** (withdraw from a promise, etc.)
  The government backed out of its promise.
- **Break down** (stop working) My car broke down on the highway.
- **Break into** (enter in certain premises by breaking the door, etc.)
  Last night a thief broke into my neighbour's.
- **Break off** (stop all of a sudden)
  She broke off and began to think over about her/his hand.
- **Break out** (spread)
  Cholera has broken out in the town.
- **Break out of** (escape from)
  A prisoner broke out of the prison last night.
- **Break up** (disperse)
  The cloud of fog began to break up as the sun rose.
- **Break something up** (Cause something to break into small pieces)
  She broke up the chocolate to distribute it among the girls.

✦ **Break with** (Cut off connection after quarrelling with someone)
He has broken with his brother.

✦ **Call on** (pay a visit to somebody)
I'll call on Mohan's today.

✦ **Call out** (to start)
The workers have called out a strike.

✦ **Call off** (to stop the strike etc.)
The workers have called off the strike.

✦ **Call at** (to visit someone's house)
I called at his house yesterday.

✦ **Call in** (send for)
Please call in the doctor.

✦ **Carry on** (continue)
Please carry on your work.

✦ **Carry something out** (perform a task)
Our company is carrying out a big deal with a foreign company.

✦ **Carry something over** (postpone)
The fancy dress competition had to be carried over till Monday)

✦ **Carry someone off** (kill somebody)
Cancer carried her off on the day of her 20th birthday.

✦ **Come of age** (get established)
As our company has come of age, so, there is no problem in selling our goods.

✦ **Come of** (belong to)
She comes of a royal family.

✦ **Come over** (surmount)
We at last came over all our problems.

✦ **Come off** (to take place)
The marriage of my brother comes off in the next month.

✦ **Come round** (agree)
At last he came round to my views.

✦ **Come under** (fall in the category of)
All these animals come under the same species.

✦ **Come down with** (suffer from)
She came down with whopping cough.

✦ **Come from** (be the nature of)
She came from London.

✦ **Come about** (happen)
The explosion came about when the worker struck the match to light a cigarette.

✦ **Cut off** (die)
The princess was cut off in the prime of her life.

✦ **Cut down** (reduce)
The prices of consumer goods should be cut down.

✦ **Cut someone out** (exclude someone)
His father cut him out of his will.

✦ **Fall in**
She fell in love with the prince.

✦ **Fall down** (fail)
The deal fell down for lack of transparency.

✦ **Fall out** (quarrel)
She fell out with his elder brother.

✦ **Fall through** (fail)
The project fell through for lack of funds.

✦ **Get away** (escape)
She got away with her life.

✦ **Get by** (to accomplish something with great difficulty)
She is not rich. She has just enough to get by.

✦ **Get on** (perform)
How are you getting on with your studies?

✦ **Get out** (become known)
The news got out that the PM was paying a visit to Russia.

✦ **Get over** (overcome)
At last I got over all obstacles.

✦ **Get up** (rise)
When do you get up in the morning?

✦ **Give up** (stop)
He gave up smoking.

✦ **Give out** (emit)
Garlic gives out a pungent smell.

✦ **Give in** (collapse)
The bridge gave in under the heavy load.

✦ **Give away** (distribute)
The Principal gave away the prizes.

✦ **Give out** (announce)
It was given out that the President of India would visit the place soon.

✦ **Go off** (explode)
The gun went off suddenly.

✦ **Go on** (continue)
She went on about how she flew the aeroplane.

✦ **Go through** (examine)
I'll go through this book later on.

✦ **Go up** (be built)
The construction of the house is going up.

✦ **Grind on** (continue for a long time in a tedious way)
The discussion over political issues ground on.

✦ **Grind something out** (produce something a tedious way)
She will grind some more short stories.

✦ **Look out** (be careful)
Look out! there is a snake.

✦ **Look down upon** (hate)
We should not look down upon the poor.

✦ **Look at** (watch)
Look at the blackboard.

✦ **Look after** (take care of)
We ought to look after our old parents.

✦ **Look into** (investigate)
The new police inspector will look into the matter.

✦ **Look up** (rise)
The prices of consumer goods are looking up.

✦ **Look back** (think of the past)
It made her feel disolate when she looked back on things of the past.

✦ **Make up** (to fulfil)
I'll make up my deficiency in Mathematics.

✦ **Make out** (understand)
I could not make out what she said.

✦ **Make up one' mind** (to resolve)
I have made up my mind to settle in the USA.

✦ **Make off** (leave hurriedly)
She made off without informing anybody.

✦ **Make something over** (transfer)
She should make her property over to her sons.

✦ **Make over** (hand over)
He made over the charge of the file to Mr Robert.

✦ **Pull back** (retreat)
The government has pulled back from its previous policy.

✦ **Pull something down** (demolish)
The authorities concerned pulled down a few building which were illegally built on government land.

✦ **Pull out** (pluck)
The child pulled out a few petals of the flower.

✦ **Pull through** (recover)
The patient will pull through.

✦ **Push on** (continue a journey)
It was getting darker but we pushed on.

✦ **Push at** (exert force)
He pushed at the bell, but it did not ring.

✦ **Push for** (demand persistently)
The workers have been pushing for the installation of new machines for five years.

✦ **Put out** (extinguish)
She put out the light.

✦ **Put on** (wear)
He put on an overcoat.

✦ **Put off** (postpone)
The plan had to be put off.

✦ **Put by** (spare something for future)
We must put by some money for future.

✦ **Put up with** (stay)
Your aunt is out of town for a couple of days, you may put up with us till she comes.

✦ **Put something down** (record something)
She put a new idea down on the paper.

✦ **Take after** (resemble)
He takes after his father.

✦ **Take off** (remove)
He took off his shoes.

✦ **Take something out** (obtain)
You may take out some money from Rohit if you want to purchase this car.

✦ **Take to** (fall into the habit of)
He took to gambling.

✦ **Turn something down** (reject something)
The judge turned down his appeal.

✦ **Turn on** (attack)
The thief turned on him with a knife.

Multiple Choice Questions

Directions: *Some idioms/phrases are given below with their probable meanings. Select the options with their correct meanings.*

1. Carry out
A. To take from one place to another
B. To continue
C. To obey
D. To make efforts

2. In the same boat
A. A worn out choice
B. Indifferent
C. In identical circumstances
D. Carry off

3. In one's good book
A. A costly book B. A priceless treasure
C. In one's favour D. An enchanting beauty

4. Keep a straight face
A. To do make up
B. To change clothes

C. Assume responsibility
D. To remain serious

5. To be above board
A. To have a good height
B. To be honest in any business deal
C. To have no debts
D. To try to be beautiful

6. On the face of it
A. To agree B. From an action
C. More than enough D. Apparently

7. Let the bygones be bygones
A. In one's favour B. To pretend
C. To forget the past D. Other choice

8. To split hairs
A. Major distinctions
B. Hair with two ends
C. To make minute distinction
D. Without distinction

9. Bread and butter
A. Both bread and butter
B. Something essential
C. Livelihood
D. Relevant things

10. To bell the cat
A. To catch a cat and tie a bell round its neck
B. To make an effort
C. To be quick
D. To face a risk

11. Hard and fast
A. Strict B. Solid
C. Fast moving D. Some hard surface

12. Part and parcel
A. The part of a parcel
B. An essential part
C. A missing parcel
D. Some part of a machine sent by parcel

13. Null and void
A. Something invalid
B. Something that can be avoided
C. Something that can be nullified
D. Something evil

14. To make clean breast of
A. To gain prominence
B. To praise oneself
C. To confess without reserve
D. To destroy before it blooms

15. Trump card
A. A powerful means of achieving an object
B. Resourcefulness
C. The best gamble to attain success
D. None of these

16. Tall talk
A. A discussion continued for a long time
B. A high sounding talk
C. A meaningful talk
D. A useless talk

17. Small talk
A. Gossip
B. A discussion carried on for a long time
C. A brief discussion
D. None of these

18. Throw out of gear
A. To replace B. Hinder, disturb
C. To decide D. Take up tune

19. To and fro
A. Back and forth B. Puzzled
C. Amazed D. Reprove

20. To bell the cat
A. To do an easy job
B. To be indifferent to
C. To undertake a difficult job
D. To clarify

21. To be under cloud
A. Puzzle B. Enjoy the favour
C. Talk thoughtlessly D. To be under suspicion

22. A labour of love
A. A tragic end
B. A funny thing
C. Not fruitful
D. Work done without payment

23. Follow suit
A. Follow an example B. Wear a new dress
C. Irrelevant D. A gay person

24. Foul play
A. Bad intentions
B. A play not well acted
C. A play not liked by the audience
D. None of these

25. To pick holes
A. To find some reason to quarrel
B. To destroy something
C. To criticise someone
D. To cut some part of an item

26. To smell a rat
A. To see signs of plague epidemic
B. To get bad smell of a dead rat
C. To suspect foul dealings
D. To be in a bad mood

27. To put a spoke in one's wheel
A. To encourage
B. Act without restraint

C. Risk something
D. To obstruct one's progress

28. To pull one's leg
A. To give up B. Take care of
C. To befool D. To know

29. To play with fire
A. Grasp the truth
B. To handle something dangerous
C. To ridicule
D. To flee away

30. To reckon with
A. Take up time B. Make an inventory
C. To deal with D. Submit to punishment

31. To run short
A. Talk until one is tired at
B. Apply to oneself
C. To get rid of
D. To have or be too little

32. A man of letters
A. A postman B. A learned man
C. A hypocrite D. An ignorant man

33. A maiden speech
A. A speech made in the parliament
B. A speech made before unmarried girls
C. A speech made by a political leader
D. A speech made for the first time

34. Order of the day
A. An order passed on a particular day
B. A current law
C. Something common or general
D. None of these

35. To end in smoke
A. To make completely understand
B. To ruin oneself
C. To excite great applause
D. None of these

36. To give vent to
A. To allow to flow forth
B. To prove a failure
C. To amass wealth
D. To evade

37. To eat humble pie
A. To apologise or confess
B. To order
C. To flatter
D. To get rid of

38. A black sheep
A. An unlucky person B. A negro
C. An ugly person D. None of these

39. To catch a tartar
A. To trap wanted criminal with great difficulty
B. To catch a dangerous person
C. To meet with disaster
D. To deal with a person who is more than one's watch

40. Sit on fence
A. To remain neutral
B. To show contempt
C. To enjoy the surroundings
D. To become fond of

41. Pay off old scores
A. To repay the debt B. To have revenge
C. To invite D. Secretly

42. Turn turtle
A. To cheat B. To be lopsided
C. To frustrate D. To dance to the tune

43. Wash one's hands of
A. To refuse B. To assist
C. To abuse D. To refuse to be

44. Under duress
A. Under compulsion
B. Willing
C. To elicit information
D. To demand

45. To turn the tables
A. To ruin someone
B. To turn the situation to one's own side
C. To reverse the situation
D. To move from one point to another

46. On the cards
A. Possibly B. Probably
C. Openly D. Likely

47. To leave someone in the lurch
A. To come to compromise with someone
B. Constant source of annoyance to someone
C. To put someone at ease
D. To desert someone in his difficulties

48. To play second fiddle
A. To be happy, cheerful and healthy
B. To reduce importance of one's senior
C. To support the role and view of another person
D. To do back seat driving

49. To yearn for
A. To weep for B. To remember
C. To admire D. To long for intensely

50. Call off
A. To finish B. To withdraw
C. To postpone D. To cry

ANSWERS

1	2	3	4	5	6	7	8	9	10
C	C	C	D	B	D	C	C	C	D
11	**12**	**13**	**14**	**15**	**16**	**17**	**18**	**19**	**20**
A	B	A	C	C	B	A	B	A	C
21	**22**	**23**	**24**	**25**	**26**	**27**	**28**	**29**	**30**
D	D	A	A	C	C	D	C	B	C
31	**32**	**33**	**34**	**35**	**36**	**37**	**38**	**39**	**40**
D	B	D	C	D	A	A	D	B	A
41	**42**	**43**	**44**	**45**	**46**	**47**	**48**	**49**	**50**
B	B	D	A	C	D	D	C	D	B

Narration

Direct and Indirect Narration/Speech

The exact words spoken by the speaker are known as Direct Speech.

The words spoken by somebody and expressed by someone else with some modification are known as Indirect Speech.

(a) Ram says to me, "You do not help me."

(b) Ram tells me that I do not help him.

The sentence (*a*) shows the words spoken by Ram. So, it is a sentence of Direct Speech.

The sentence (*b*) shows the words spoken by Ram and expressed by someone else with certain modification. So, it is a sentence of Indirect Speech.

The following points should be noted while changing Direct Speech into Indirect speech:

1. The verb outside the inverted commas is called the Reporting Verb.
2. The verb or sentence inside the inverted commas is called the Reported Speech.
3. If the Reporting verb is in the Present or Future Tense, there is no change in the tense in the Reported Speech.
4. If the Reporting Verb is in the Past Tense, the Tense in the Reported Speech is changed.
5. The Reporting verb may be in any Tense, in it the Pronouns are changed as under:
   (*i*) First Person according to Subject
   (*ii*) Second Person according to Object
   (*iii*) Third Person, No change.
6. If the Reporting verb is in the Past Tense the Adverb will change as under in the Indirect Speech.

Direct	***Indirect***
now	then
here	there
after	before
today	that day
yesterday	the previous day
these	those
tomorrow	the next day
last week	the previous week
this	that

7. Adjectives/Determiners are changed as under:

Direct	***Indirect***
this	that
these	those

Rules for Change of Tense

Reporting Verb	Reporting Speech	Change of Tense
Present Tense	Any Tense	No change
Future Tense	Any Tense	No change
Past Tense	Present/Future Tense	Change into corresponding Past Tense
Past Tense	Past Indefinite Tense	Change into Past Perfect Tense
Past Tense	Past Continuous Tense	Change into Past Perfect Continuous Tense
Past Tense	Past Perfect/Perfect Continuous Tense	No change
Past Tense	Universal Truth	No change
Past Tense	Proverb	No change

Transformation of Speech Based on Special Rules

1. Rule Related to Interrogative Sentence

- If the answer of an interrogative sentence is possible in yes-no manner.

Illustration.

Dhoni said to Sachin, "Will you help me?"

Dhoni asked Sachin whether he would help him.

(**Note :** The answer of R.S. is possible in yes-no manner)

Rule of Transformation from Direct to Indirect speech

Step I : Change R.V. into ask.

Step II : In place of comma use 'if/whether'.

Step III : Change interrogative sentence into assertive sentence.

- If the answer of an interrogative sentence is not possible in yes-no manner.

Illustration:

Sachin said to Dhoni, "What do you want?"

Sachin asked Dhoni what he wanted.

(**Note :** Only in Step II, you have to avoid comma and inverted comma and rest will be same as mentioned above).

2. Rule related to Imperative Sentence

- Imperative sentence is a sentence which shows Order/ Advice/Request

Illustration:

My teacher said to me, "Go there".

My teacher ordered me to go there.

Rule of Transformation from Direct to Indirect Speech

Step I : Change R.V. as per meaning/sense of R.S. into order/request/advise.

Step II : In place of comma, use 'to'.

Step III : Rest portion will be same.

3. Rule related to Optative Sentence

- Optative sentence is a sentence which expresses the feeling of bless/curse/pray/wish.

Illustration:

Mother said to me, "May you live long!"

Mother blessed me that I might live long.

Rule of Transformation from Direct to Indirect Speech

Step I : Change R.V. as per meaning/sense of R.S. into bless/curse/pray/wish.

Step II : In place of comma, use 'that'.

Step III : Change optative sentence into assertive sentence.

4. Rule related to Exclamatory Sentence

- Exclamatory sentence is a sentence which takes note of exclamatory (!) mark in that sentence showing inner feeling.

Illustration:

She said, "Alas! I am ruined".

She exclaimed with sorrow that she was ruined.

Rule of Transformation from Direct to Indirect Speech

Step I : Change R.V. as per meaning/sense of R.S. into exclaim/exclaims/exclaimed/will or shall exclaim + joy/sorrow/anger/surprise/ applause/contempt.

Step II : Change comma into that.

Step III : Change note of exclamation (!) into full stop (.)

Step IV : Change exclamatory sentence into assertive sentence.

Universal, Historical Truth, etc.

If the Reported Speech expresses a Universal or Historical or Habitual truth, its Tense will not change.

1. The teacher said to the students, "The sun rises in the east."

   The teacher told the students that the sun rises in the east.

2. My father said to me, "The First Battle of Panipat was fought in 1526."

   My father told me that the First Battle of Panipat was fought in 1526.

Multiple Choice Questions

Directions (Qs. 1 to 13): *Select the correct Indirect Speech for the following sentences:*

1. I said to him, "I shall help you."
   - A. I told him that I can help him.
   - B. I told him that I would help him.
   - C. I told him that I will help him.
   - D. I told him that I shall be helping him.

2. My Teacher said to me, "The earth revolves round the sun."
   - A. My teacher told me that the earth revolves round the sun.
   - B. My teacher told me that the earth revolve round the sun.
   - C. My teacher told me that the earth had been revolving round the sun.

D. My teacher told me that the earth has been revolving round the sun.

3. I said to my friend, "My father daily goes for a walk."

A. I told my friend that my father daily goes for a walk.

B. I told my friend that my father daily went for a walk.

C. I told my friend that my father has to go for a walk.

D. I told my friend that my father had gone for a walk.

4. He said to me, "May God bless you!"

A. He requested that God can bless me.

B. He prayed that God can bless me.

C. He prayed that God might bless me.

D. He prayed that God will bless me.

5. The patient said, "Thank you, doctor."

A. The patient thanked the doctor.

B. The patient requested the doctor with thanks.

C. The patient told the doctor thanks.

D. The patient suggested the doctor thanks.

6. Satish said, "No, I shall not talk to him."

A. Satish told that he should not talk to him.

B. Satish suggested that he would not have talked to him.

C. Satish exclaimed with sorrow that he would not talk with him.

D. Satish refused to talk to him.

7. The child said, "What a lovely place!"

A. The child exclaimed with sorrow that it was a lovely place.

B. The child thought that the place was lovely.

C. The child exclaimed with joy that the place was very lovely.

D. The child suggested that the place was lovely.

8. He said, "What a fool I have been!"

A. He told himself with sorrow that he was a fool.

B. He confessed with regret that he had been a great fool.

C. He said himself a fool.

D. He suggested that he could be a fool.

9. He said, "Alas! I am ruined."

A. He told me that he had been ruined.

B. He exclaimed with joy that he had been ruined.

C. He exclaimed with sorrow that he was ruined.

D. He told me that he should not be ruined.

10. The accused said, "I am not guilty."

A. The accused exclaimed with sorrow that I am not guilty.

B. The accused exclaimed with joy that he was not guilty.

C. The accused stated that he was not guilty.

D. The accused told me that he has not been guilty.

11. My teacher said, "The earth is round".

A. My teacher said that the earth was round.

B. My teacher says that the earth is round.

C. My teacher said that the earth is round.

D. My teacher ordered that the earth is round.

12. He said, "What a place it is!"

A. He said that it was a very fine place.

B. He said that is a very fine place.

C. He said that the place is fine.

D. He exclaimed with joy/surprise that it was a very fine place.

13. Ria said, "Shall I thread the needle?"

A. Ria asked if she should thread the needle.

B. Ria asked if she shall thread the needle.

C. Ria ordered if she should thread the needle.

D. Ria says that if she would thread the needle.

Directions (Qs. 14 to 33): *Pick out the correct alternative that completes the incomplete sentence which is changed into Indirect Narration.*

14. She said to me, "I shall see you as soon as I get time."
She told me:

A. that she will see me as soon as she will get time.

B. that she would see me as soon as she would get time.

C. she would see me whenever she got time.

D. that she would see me whenever she gets time.

15. My secretary said to me, "Your plane will leave if you do not go at once."
My secretary told me that:

A. her plane would leave if she did not go at that time.

B. her plane would leave if I do not go at once.

C. my plane would leave if I did not go at that very time.

D. my plane will leave if I did not go at that time.

16. My mother said to me, "Don't quarrel among yourselves".
My mother:

A. forbade me to quarrel among ourselves.

B. asked me not to quarrel among ourselves.

C. asked me that not to quarrel among ourselves.

D. asked me to quarrel not among ourselves.

17. Her father said to her mother, "Excuse the daughter."
Her father:

A. requested her mother to excuse the daughter.

B. asked her mother to excuse the daughter.

C. asked her mother to have excused the daughter.

D. asked her mother to have been excused.

18. He said to his friend, "Wait here till father comes."
He requested his friend:
A. to wait here till father had come.
B. that to wait there till his friend came.
C. to wait there till father came.
D. to wait here until his friend came.

19. She said to her maid, "Run and catch the thief."
She ordered her maid:
A. ran and catch the thief.
B. that to run and to catch the thief.
C. ran and caught the thief.
D. to run and catch the thief.

20. Anita said to Sunita, "What are you doing?"
Anita asked Sunita:
A. what she will be doing.
B. that what she is doing.
C. that what she was doing.
D. what she was doing.

21. She said to me, "Are you meeting me today?"
She enquired of me:
A. whether I am meeting her that day.
B. whether I was meeting her today.
C. whether I was meeting her that day.
D. I was meeting her that day.

22. Nitish said to me, "When did you buy this pen?"
Nitish asked me:
A. when I was to buy that pen.
B. when I would buy that pen.
C. when I had bought that pen.
D. when I was buying that pen.

23. She said to me, "Are you going to market?"
She enquired of me:
A. I am going to market.
B. I was going to market.
C. if I was going to market.
D. if I had been going to the market.

24. Damini said, "Why did not you change your clothes?"
Damini asked me:
A. why I had not changed my clothes.
B. why I did not change my clothes.
C. why I would not change my clothes.
D. why I have not been changing my clothes.

25. Umesh said to me, "Have you read that novel?"
Umesh asked me:
A. if he was reading that novel.
B. if he had read that novel.
C. if I had read that novel.
D. if I was reading that novel.

26. She said to me, "I shall forgive you."
She told me:
A. that she will forgive me.
B. that she was going to forgive me.
C. that she will not forgive me.
D. that she would forgive me.

27. I said to her, "It was very hot last night."
I told her:
A. that it had been very hot the previous night.
B. that it was very hot the previous night.
C. that it has been very hot the last night.
D. that it had been very hot this night.

28. She said to me, "I thank you for the help you have given."
She:
A. told me that she thanked me for the help I had given.
B. thanked me for the help I have given.
C. thanked to me for the help I have given.
D. thanked me for the help I had given.

29. Mohini said to me, "Trust in God."
Mohini advised me:
A. that I should trust in God.
B. should trust in God.
C. trusted in God.
D. to trust in God.

30. I said to him, "Let us go to school."
I told him:
A. we would go to school.
B. we shall go to school.
C. that we would go to school.
D. that we should go to school.

31. Rajni said, "May God bless you?"
Rajni:
A. exclaimed with wish that God might bless me.
B. expressed a wish that God might bless me.
C. asked God to bless me.
D. shouted with joy to bless me.

32. My mother said me, "Do not have so many friends."
My mother forbade me:
A. to have so many friends.
B. not to have so many friends.
C. to have been so many friends.
D. to possess so many friends.

33. Ram said, "Pay attention to me."
Ram asked:
A. pay attention to him.
B. paid attention to him.
C. having paid attention to him.
D. to pay attention to him.

Directions (Qs. 34 to 50): *In questions below, the sentences have been given in Direct/Indirect Speech. Out of the four alternatives suggested select the one which best expresses the given sentence in Indirect/Direct Speech.*

34. She said that her brother was getting married
A. She said, "Her brother is getting married."
B. She told, "My brother is getting married"
C. She said, "My brother is getting married".
D. She said, "My brother was married".

35. "Please don't go away", she said.
A. She said to please her and not go away.
B. She told me to go away.
C. She begged me not to go away.
D. She begged that I not go away.

36. "If you don't keep quiet I shall shoot you", he said to her in a calm voice.
A. He warned her to shoot if she didn't keep quiet calmly.
B. He said calmly that I shall shoot you if you don't be quiet.
C. He warned her calmly that he would shoot her if she didn't keep quiet.
D. Calmly he warned her that be quiet or else he will have to shoot her.

37. I told him that he was not working hard.
A. I said to him, "You are not working hard."
B. I told him, "You are not working hard."
C. I said, "You are not working hard."
D. I said to him, "He is not working hard."

38. She said that she would finish the work the next day.
A. She said, "I will finish the work the next day."
B. She said, "I will finish the work tomorrow."
C. She said, "You will finish the work tomorrow."
D. She said, "I finished the work."

39. She said to him, "Why don't you go today?"
A. She asked him why he did not go that day.
B. She said to him that why he don't go today.
C. She asked him not to go today.
D. She asked him why he did not go today.

40. "Are you alone, my son?" asked a soft voice close behind me.
A. A soft voice asked that what I was doing there alone.
B. A soft voice said to me are you alone son.
C. A soft voice from my back asked if I was alone.
D. A soft voice behind me asked if I was alone.

41. My cousin said, "My room-mate had snored throughout the night."
A. My cousin said that her room-mate snored throughout the night.
B. My cousin told me that her room-mate snored throughout the night.
C. My cousin complained to me that her room-mate is snoring throughout the night.
D. My cousin felt that her room-mate may be snoring throughout the night.

42. He asked Rama if he needed his help then.
A. He said to Rama, "Do you need my help?"
B. He told Rama, "Tell me if you need help."
C. He asked Rama, "Do I need your help?"
D. He said to Rama, "Do you need my help now?"

43. Nita ordered her servant to bring her a cup of tea.
A. Nita told her servant, "Bring a cup of tea."
B. Nita said, "Bring me a cup of tea."
C. Nita said to her servant, "Bring me a cup of tea."
D. Nita said to her servant, "Bring her that cup of tea."

44. He exclaimed with joy that India had won the Sahara Cup.
A. He said, "India has won the Sahara Cup."
B. He said, "India won the Sahara Cup."
C. He said, "How! India will win the Sahara Cup."
D. He said, "Hurrah! India has won the Sahara Cup."

45. The boy said, "Who dare call you a thief?"
A. The boy enquired who dared call him a thief.
B. The boy asked who called him a thief.
C. The boy told that who dared call him a thief.
D. The boy wondered who dared call a thief.

46. The little girl said to her mother, "Did the sun rise in the East?
A. The little girl said to her mother that the sun rose in the East.
B. The little girl asked her mother if the sun rose in the East.
C. The little girl said to her mother if the sun rises in the East.
D. The little girl asked her mother if the sun is in the East.

47. Dhruv said that he was sick and tired of working for that Company.
A. Dhruv said, "I am sick and tired of working for this Company."
B. Dhruv said, "He was tired of that Company."
C. Dhruv said to me, "I am sick and tired of working for this Company."
D. Dhruv said, "I will be tired of working for that Company."

48. He said to his father, "Please increase my pocket-money."
A. He told his father, please increase the pocket-money.
B. He pleaded his father to please increase my pocket-money.
C. He requested his father to increase his pocket-money.
D. He asked his father increase his pocket-money.

49. She said to her friend, "I know where is everyone."
A. She told that she knew where was everyone.
B. She told her friend that she knew where was everyone.
C. She told her friend she knew where is everyone
D. She told her friend that she knows where was everyone.

50. His father ordered him to go to his room and study.
A. His father said, "Go to your room and study."
B. His father said to him, "Go and study in your room."
C. His father shouted, "Go right now to your study room."
D. His father said firmly, "Go and study in your room."

ANSWERS

1	2	3	4	5	6	7	8	9	10
B	A	A	C	A	D	C	B	C	C
11	**12**	**13**	**14**	**15**	**16**	**17**	**18**	**19**	**20**
C	D	A	B	C	A	B	C	D	D
21	**22**	**23**	**24**	**25**	**26**	**27**	**28**	**29**	**30**
C	C	C	A	C	D	A	A	A	D
31	**32**	**33**	**34**	**35**	**36**	**37**	**38**	**39**	**40**
B	A	D	C	C	C	A	B	A	D
41	**42**	**43**	**44**	**45**	**46**	**47**	**48**	**49**	**50**
A	D	C	B	A	B	A	C	B	A

❑❑❑

Voice

A sentence in active voice focuses on the person or thing doing the action. A sentence in passive voice focuses on the person or thing affected by the action. *e.g.*,

The idol was built. (Active voice)
Someone built the idol. (Passive voice)

Transformation of Voice

- Voice and Tense are closely associated with each other.
- Tense plays an important role while transforming the voice.

On the basis of following points, voice can be transformed from active to passive voice.

The Present Indefinite Tense

Active voice: Subject + V_1 + Object

Passive voice: Subject + is, am, are + V_3 + by + Object

1. **Active voice:** He sings sweet songs.
   Passive voice: Sweet songs are sung by him.
2. **Active voice:** She does not cause any hindrance in my work.
   Passive voice: No hindrance in my work is caused by her.
3. **Active voice:** Do they love their country?
   Passive voice: Is their country loved by them?

The Present Continuous Tense

Active voice: Subject + is/am/are + V_1 + ing + Object.

Passive voice: Subject + is/am/are + being + V_3 + by + Object.

1. **Active voice:** She is cooking food.
   Passive voice: Food is being cooked by her.
2. **Active voice:** Rita is not knitting a sweater.
   Passive voice: A sweater is not being knitted by Rita.
3. **Active voice:** Is Meena baking a cake?
   Passive voice: Is a cake being baked by Meena?

The Present Perfect Tense

Active voice: Subject + has/have + V_3 + Object.

Passive voice: Subject + has/have + been + V_3 + by + Object.

1. **Active voice:** I have written an essay.
   Passive voice: An essay has been written by me.
2. **Active voice:** They have not whitewashed the fence.
   Passive voice: The fence has not been whitewashed by them.
3. **Active voice:** Have you cut the cake?
   Passive voice: Has the cake been cut by you?

The Past Indefinite Tense

Active voice: Subject + V_2 + Object

Passive voice: Subject + was/were + V_3 + by + Object

1. **Active voice:** He composed a new song.
   Passive voice: A new song was composed by him.
2. **Active voice:** He did not operate the computer.
   Passive voice: The computer was not operated by him.
3. **Active voice:** Did she catch a fish?
   Passive voice: Was a fish caught by her?

The Past Continuous Tense

Active voice: Subject + was/were + V_1 + ing + Object

Passive voice: Subject + was/were + being + V_3 + by + Object

1. **Active voice:** The farmers were ploughing the fields.
   Passive voice: The fields were being ploughed by the farmers.
2. **Active voice:** He was not administering the new drug to the patient.
   Passive voice: The new drug was not being administered to the patient by him.
3. **Active voice:** Was she sewing a dress?
   Passive voice: Was a dress being sewn by her?

The Past Perfect Tense

Active voice: Subject + had + V_3 + Object.

Passive voice: Subject + had + been + V_3 + by + Object

1. **Active voice:** He had issued me an import licence.
   Passive voice: I had been issued an import licence.
2. **Active voice:** We had not visited the Taj.
   Passive voice: The Taj had not been visited by us.
3. **Active voice:** Who had taught you English?
   Passive voice: By whom had you been taught English?

The Future Indefinite Tense

Active voice: Subject + will/shall + V_1 + Object.
Passive voice: Subject + will/shall + be + V_3 + by + Object.

1. **Active voice:** He will remove the dust from the shelf.
   Passive voice: The dust from the shelf will be removed by him.
2. **Active voice:** He will not open the main gate.
   Passive voice: The main gate will not be opened by him.
3. **Active voice:** Will you help us?
   Passive voice: Shall we be helped by you?

The Future Perfect Tense

Active voice: Subject + will/shall + have + V_3 + Object.
Passive voice: Subject + will/shall + have + been + V_3 + by + Object.

1. **Active voice:** They will have sold their house by then.
   Passive voice: Their house will have been sold by them by then.
2. **Active voice:** He will not have informed the police about it.
   Passive voice: The police will not have been informed about it by him.
3. **Active voice:** Will they have accepted the deal?
   Passive voice: Will the deal have been accepted by them?

Imperative Sentences

1. **Active voice:** Open the window.
   Passive voice: You are ordered to open the window.
   Or
   Let the window be opened.
2. **Active voice:** Please/kindly open the window.
   Passive voice: You are requested to open the window.
3. **Active voice:** Never make a noise.
   Passive voice: A noise should never be made.

Infinitives

1. **Active voice:** It is time to open the shop.
   Passive voice: It is time for the shop to be opened.
2. **Active voice:** He begged the officer to forgive him.
   Passive voice: He begged the officer to be forgiven.
3. **Active voice:** He has to break the door.
   Passive voice: The door has to be broken by him.

Prepositional Verb

1. **Active voice:** She laughed at the beggar.
   Passive voice: The beggar was laughed at by her.
2. **Active voice:** He listened to the news.
   Passive voice: The news was listened to by him.
3. **Active voice:** They called in the doctor.
   Passive voice: The doctor was called in by them.

Double Object

1. **Active voice:** He gave me a pen.
   Passive voice: A pen was given to me by him.
   Or
   I was given a pen by him.
2. **Active voice:** She told us a story.
   Passive voice: A story was told (to) us by her.
   Or
   We were told a story by her.

Use of Preposition other than 'by'

1. **Active voice:** The jug contains juice.
   Passive voice: Juice is contained in the jug.
2. **Active voice:** The audience thronged the hall.
   Passive voice: The hall was thronged with the audience.
3. **Active voice:** I know her.
   Passive voice: She is known to me.

Quasi Passive Verbs

1. **Active voice:** Quinine tastes bitter.
   Passive voice: Quinine is bitter when tasted.
   Or
   Quinine is bitter when it is tasted.
2. **Active voice:** Sugar is sweet (to taste).
   Passive voice: Sugar is sweet when tasted.
   Or
   Sugar is sweet when it is tasted.

Implied Sentences

1. **Active voice:** The driver drove the bus.
   Passive voice: The bus was driven.
2. **Active voice:** Someone read the news.
   Passive voice: The news was read.
3. **Active voice:** They say work is worship.
   Passive voice: It is said that work is worship.

Multiple Choice Questions

Directions (Qs. 1 to 20): *In the following questions, a sentence has been given in Active/Passive Voice. Out of the four alternatives suggested, select the one that Best Expresses the same sentence in Passive/Active Voice.*

1. Circumstances will oblige me to go.
A. I will oblige the circumstances and go.
B. I shall be obliged to go by the circumstances.
C. Under the circumstances, I should go.
D. I shall be obliged by the circumstances to go.

2. We waste much time on trifles.
A. Much time was wasted on trifles.
B. Much time will be wasted on trifles.
C. Much time is wasted by us on trifles.
D. Much time is wasted on trifles.

3. Mohan gave the beggar an old shirt.
A. An old shirt was given to Mohan by the beggar.
B. An old shirt was given to the beggar by Mohan
C. The begger was gave an old shirt by Mohan.
D. An old shirt was gave to the beggar by Mohan.

4. They have made him a king.
A. A king has been made by him.
B. He was made a king by them.
C. They have been made kings by him.
D. He has been made a king by them.

5. Who taught you English?
A. By whom English was taught to you?
B. By whom you were taught English?
C. By whom was English taught to you?
D. By whom are you taught English?

6. Was he knocking at the door?
A. Was the door being knocked at by him?
B. Was the door being knocked by him?
C. Was the door knocked by him?
D. Was the door knocking at him?

7. What was Rani doing?
A. What was done by Rani?
B. What was Rani being done?
C. What was being done by Rani?
D. What was being doing Rani?

8. Why were you wasting your time?
A. Why was your time being wasted?
B. Why was your time being wasted by you?
C. Why was your time wasted by you?
D. Why was your time wasted?

9. She has laid out a small garden.
A. A small garden has been laid by her.
B. A small garden has laid her.
C. A small garden being laid by her.
D. A small garden has been laid out by her.

10. She had already solved all the sums.
A. All the sums had already been solved by her.
B. All the sums have already been solved by her.
C. All the sums have been solved by her.
D. All the sums are solved by her.

11. He will have posted the letter.
A. The letter has been posted by him.
B. The letter will be posted by him.
C. The letter will have been posted by him.
D. The letter is posted by him.

12. They will have sold all the books by 4 P.M.
A. All the books will be sold by 4 P.M.
B. All the books will have been sold by 4 P.M.
C. All the books were being sold by 4 P.M.
D. All the books must be sold by 4 P.M.

13. Do you speak English?
A. Is English spoken by you?
B. Does English spoken by you?
C. Is English being spoken by you?
D. Does English being spoken by you?

14. Had they seen me before?
A. Had myself been seen by them before?
B. Had me being seen by them before?
C. Had I been seen by them before?
D. Had I being seen by them before?

15. May I take this pen?
A. May this pen will be taken by me?
B. May this pen shall be taken by me?
C. May this pen should be taken by me?
D. May this pen be taken by me?

16. Can we send it by air?
A. Can this be sent by air?
B. Can it be sent by air?
C. Can it go by air?
D. Can it be send by air?

17. Who wrote this book?
A. By whom was this book written?
B. By whom is this book written?
C. By whom was this book being written?
D. By whom is this book being written?

18. What did you buy?
A. What is bought by you?
B. What is being bought by you?
C. What was bought by you?
D. What was being bought by you?

19. Whom do you want?
A. Who is wanted by you?
B. Who is being wanted by you?
C. You are wanted by whom?
D. You are being wanted by whom?

20. When will you raise this question?
A. When this question will be raised by you?
B. When will this question be raised by you?
C. When this question is being raised by you?
D. When is this question being raised by you?

Directions (Qs. 21 to 35): *In each of the following questions, a sentence is given in Active Voice. Below it are given four alternatives suggesting the Passive Voice form of the above sentence. Choose the correct alternative.*

21. Who did this?
A. This was done by whom?
B. By whom was this done?
C. Who has done this?
D. By whom this was done?

22. One should keep ones promises.
A. Promises should be kept.
B. Ones promises should be kept by one.
C. Promises must be kept.
D. Ones promises one should keep.

23. Give the order.
A. Order given.
B. Order be given.
C. Let the order be given.
D. Order may be given by you.

24. You will have to do it.
A. It will be done by you.
B. It will have to be done by you.
C. It has to be done by you.
D. It would have to be done by you.

25. Keep to the left.
A. You are ordered to keep to the left.
B. You ought to keep to the left.
C. You are advised to keep to the left.
D. You must keep to the left.

26. They will arrange a party.
A. A party will have to be arranged by them.
B. A party they will have to arrange.
C. A party will be arranged by them.
D. A party by them will be arranged.

27. Someone has picked my pocket.
A. My pocket is picked.
B. My pocket has picked.
C. My pocket has been picked.
D. My pocket was picked.

28. He kept me waiting.
A. I kept waiting for him.
B. I kept waiting by him.
C. I was waiting for him.
D. I was kept waiting by him.

29. Why do you tell a lie?
A. Why is a lie told by you?
B. Why is told a lie by you?
C. Why is told by you a lie?
D. Why has a lie been told by you?

30. I have written a letter.
A. A letter is written by me.
B. A letter has been written by me.
C. A letter was written by me.
D. A letter had been written by me.

31. They will have helped you.
A. You will have helped by them.
B. You will have been helped by them.
C. You will be helped by them.
D. You will be helped by them.

32. Open the door.
A. Door may be opened.
B. Let the door be open.
C. Let the door be opened.
D. Door be opened.

33. I am reading a book.
A. A book is read by me.
B. A book is being read by me.
C. A book has been read by me.
D. A book in been read by me.

34. Why did your brother write such a letter?
A. Why your brother wrote such a letter?
B. Why was by brother written such a letter?
C. Why was such a letter written by your brother?
D. Why was written such a letter by your brother?

35. Did you run a great risk?
A. Was a great risk run by you?
B. Was run a great risk by you?
C. Was by you run a great risk?
D. Had you run a great risk?

Directions (Qs. 36 to 45): *In each of the following questions, a sentence is given in Passive Voice. Below it are given four alternatives suggesting the Active Voice form of the above sentence. Choose the correct alternative.*

36. He was made king.
A. He became king.
B. They made him king.
C. They had made him king.
D. He has been made king.

37. Good news is expected by us.
A. We are expecting good news.
B. We have been expecting good news.
C. We had expected good news.
D. We expect good news.

38. The child must be looked after.
A. The child you must look after.
B. You must look after the child.
C. You must look the child after.
D. You may look after the child.

39. What is wanted by you?
A. What you want?
B. What did you want?
C. What do you want?
D. What you do want?

40. Your father is known to me.
A. I am known to your father.
B. I know your father.
C. I have known your father.
D. I knew your father.

41. She may be told the story by you.
A. The story may be told by you to her.
B. You may tell the story to her.
C. You may tell her the story.
D. You may tell to her the story.

42. Duty ought to be done.
A. Let duty be done.
B. One ought to do one's duty.
C. One should do his duty.
D. Do you duty.

43. Is English spoken by you?
A. Did you speak English?
B. Do you speak English?
C. Have you spoken English?
D. Do you know how to speak English?

44. Gold coins are contained in this box.
A. This box contains gold coins.
B. This box has contained gold coins.
C. This box is containing gold coins.
D. This box has gold coins.

45. Character is revealed by manners.
A. Manners revealed character.
B. Manners reveal character.
C. Manners have revealed character.
D. Manners do reveal character.

ANSWERS

1	2	3	4	5	6	7	8	9	10
D	C	B	D	C	A	C	B	D	A
11	**12**	**13**	**14**	**15**	**16**	**17**	**18**	**19**	**20**
C	B	A	C	D	B	A	C	A	B
21	**22**	**23**	**24**	**25**	**26**	**27**	**28**	**29**	**30**
B	A	C	B	C	C	C	D	A	B
31	**32**	**33**	**34**	**35**	**36**	**37**	**38**	**39**	**40**
B	C	B	C	A	B	D	B	C	B
41	**42**	**43**	**44**	**45**					
C	B	B	A	B					

Sentence Completion

Filling the blanks is such an exercise that starts with the primary schools and continues at the highest level of competitive examinations. One must practise it regularly to score well.

Multiple Choice Questions

Directions: *Pick out the most effective word(s) from the given words to fill in the blanks and make the sentence meaningfully complete.*

1. One requires great .... to teach and handle little children who are restless.
A. patience B. attitude
C. determination D. knowledge

2. The researchers will .... some of the causes of increasing poverty in the state.
A. fund B. investigate
C. promote D. circulate

3. I usually perform .... when nobody is watching me.
A. alone B. good
C. better D. hard

4. It was .... to everyone that the minister had been drinking.
A. observed B. known
C. discovered D. realised

5. I would rather stay indoors .... the rain stops.
A. so B. waiting
C. until D. usually

6. The process should be completed as far as possible within a week, ... which the matter should be brought to notice of the officer concerned.
A. following B. failing
C. realizing D. referring

7. The officers are ..... to regular transfers.
A. free B. open
C. subject D. available

8. All letters received from Government should ..... be acknowledged.
A. suddenly B. obviously
C. immediately D. occasionally

9. Mumbai office ..... a meeting of senior officials to discuss the high incidence of frauds.
A. attended B. convened
C. reported D. registered

10. The note should be ..... to all the concerned departments for their consideration.
A. regulated B. requested
C. carried D. forwarded

11. Your present statement does not .... what you said last week.
A. accord to B. accord in
C. accord with D. accord for

12. I had a vague .... that the lady originally belonged to Scotland.
A. notion B. expression
C. imagination D. theory

13. The prisoner showed no .... for his crimes.
A. hatred B. obstinacy
C. remorse D. anger

14. It is inconceivable that in many schools children are subjected to physical .... in the name of discipline.
A. violation B. exercise
C. violence D. security

15. We have not yet fully realised the .... consequences of the war.
A. happy B. pleasing
C. grim D. exciting

16. Happiness consists in being .... what we have.
A. contented to B. contented with
C. contented for D. contented in

17. His rude behaviour is a .... his organization.
A. disgrace for B. disgrace on
C. disgrace upon D. disgrace to

18. No child is .... understanding. One has to wait and provide proper guidance.
A. dull to B. dull in
C. dull of D. dull for

19. I am fully .... the problems facing the industry.
A. alive with B. alive to
C. alive for D. alive on

20. The Romans were .... science.
A. bad in B. bad to
C. bad for D. bad at

21. Although I was .... of his plans, I encouraged him, because there was no one else who was willing to help.
A. sceptical B. remorseful
C. fearful D. excited

22. You have no business to .... pain on a weak and poor person.
A. inflict B. put
C. direct D. force

23. Her uncle died in a car accident. He was quite rich. She suddenly .... all her uncle's money.
A. succeeded B. caught
C. gave D. inherited

24. There was a major accident. The plane crashed. The pilot .... did not see the tower.
A. likely B. probably
C. scarcely D. hurriedly

25. The car we were travelling in .... a mile from home.
A. broke off B. broke down
C. broke into D. broke up

26. What are you .... in the kitchen cupboard?
A. looking in B. looking on
C. looking to D. looking for

27. I did not see the point of .... waiting for them, so I went home.
A. hanging around B. hang on
C. hang together D. hanging up

28. He lost confidence and .... of the deal at the last minute.
A. backed out B. backed on
C. backed down D. backed onto

29. To the dismay of all the students, the class monitor was ..... berated by the principal at a school assembly.
A. critically B. ignominiously
C. prudently D. fortuitously

30. All attempts to revive the fishing industry were ..... failure.
A. foredoomed to B. heading at
C. predicted for D. estimated to

31. There are ..... parked outside than yesterday.
A. fewer cars B. few cars
C. less cars D. a small number of cars

32. The minister had to ..... some awkward questions from reporters.
A. fend B. fend at
C. fend out D. fend off

33. The ..... of evidence was on the side of the plaintiff since all but one of the witnesses testified that his story was correct.
A. propensity B. force
C. preponderance D. brunt

34. Attention to detail is ..... of a fine craftsman.
A. hallmark B. stamp
C. seal of authority D. authenticity

35. Behaving in a .... and serious way, even in a .... situation, makes people respect you.
A. calm, difficult B. steady, angry
C. flamboyant, tricky D. cool astounding

36. Along with a sharp rise in ...., a recession would eventually result in more men, women, and children living in ....
A. crime, apathy B. fatalities, poor
C. deaths, slums D. unemployment, poverty

37. The government has .... to provide financial aid to the ones ...... by severe floods in the city.
A. desired, troubled B. promised, havoc
C. failed, affected D. wanted, struck

38. An airplane with .... passengers on board made an unscheduled .... as the airport to which it was heading was covered with thick fog.
A. imitable, slip B. faulty, stop
C. variety, halt D. numerous, landing

39. Deemed universities .... huge fees, but have not been successful in providing .... education to our students.
A. collect, maintaining
B. pay, better
C. ask, good
D. charge, quality

40. If the banks desire to .... profit, they should get rid of .... measures.
A. lose, concentrate B. increase, populist
C. earn, unhealthy D. maximise, traditional

41. Leadership defines what the future should look like and ...... people with that vision.
A. aligns B. develops
C. trains D. encourages

42. We upset ourselves by responding in an ...... manner to someone else's actions.
A. unabashed B. irrational
C. arduous D. arguable

43. All the people involved in that issue feel a great ...... to his suggestion.

A. contradiction B. adherence
C. indifference D. repugnance

44. These elections will be remembered as much for its anti-incumbency mood as for its ...... mandate.
A. invincible B. rational
C. unprecedented D. deliberate

45. How do you expect us to stay in such a ...... building even if it can be hired on a nominal rent?
A. scruffy B. disperate
C. fragmented D. robust

46. ...... efforts from all concerned are required to raise the social and economic conditions of our countrymen.
A. Perpetual B. Dynamic
C. Massive D. Exploring

47. Many companies see technology as a ...... for a whole host of business problems.
A. consideration B. preference
C. linking D. panacea

48. Known as devout and serious person, she also has ...... sense of humour.
A. better B. plentiful
C. quick D. good

49. The matter would have become serious if ...... action had not been taken.
A. hasty B. fast
C. timely D. unusual

50. The ...... with which he is able to yield the paint brush is really remarkable.
A. ease B. practice
C. majesty D. sweep

51. You must ensure the correctness of the information before ....
A. drawing B. enabling
C. learning D. jumping

52. The rocket .... the target and did not cause any casualty.
A. sensed B. reached
C. missed D. exploded

53. It is desirable to take .... in any business if you want to make profit.
A. advice B. risk
C. loan D. recourse

54. They wasted all the money on purchase of some .... items.
A. excellent B. important
C. significant D. trivial

55. When he found the wallet his face glowed but soon it faded as the wallet was ....
A. empty B. vacant
C. recovered D. stolen

56. He has served the country by .... many significant positions.
A. appointing B. creating
C. developing D. holding

57. The frequent errors are a result of the student's ....
A. talent B. smartness
C. carelessness D. perception

58. The robbers eventually .... in breaking into the house.
A. succeeded B. decided
C. caught D. trained

59. I finally .... her to stay another day.
A. advised B. persuaded
C. suggested D. called

60. Most of the people who .... the book exhibition were teachers.
A. witnessed B. presented
C. conducted D. attended

ANSWERS

1	2	3	4	5	6	7	8	9	10
A	B	C	A	C	B	C	C	B	D
11	**12**	**13**	**14**	**15**	**16**	**17**	**18**	**19**	**20**
C	A	C	C	C	B	D	B	B	D
21	**22**	**23**	**24**	**25**	**26**	**27**	**28**	**29**	**30**
B	C	C	B	C	C	D	A	B	A
31	**32**	**33**	**34**	**35**	**36**	**37**	**38**	**39**	**40**
A	D	D	A	A	D	C	D	C	B
41	**42**	**43**	**44**	**45**	**46**	**47**	**48**	**49**	**50**
A	A	D	C	A	A	D	D	C	A
51	**52**	**53**	**54**	**55**	**56**	**57**	**58**	**59**	**60**
A	C	B	D	A	D	C	A	B	D

Sentence Improvement

One may use the same words in many ways but the best way is only one that makes the perfect usage of the words and conveys the proper meaning of the expression. Try it yourself in the following questions.

Multiple Choice Questions

Directions: *In these questions, a part of the sentence is bold. Below are given alternatives to the bold part at A, B and C which may improve the sentence. Choose the correct alternative. In case no improvement is needed, your answer is 'D'.*

1. Discreet salience **is extremely important** to create that 'irresistible-yet-unattainable' image for brands that want to take India seriously
   A. was extremely important
   B. is mainly important
   C. was important extremely
   D. No Improvement

2. This, over a designer outfit that he wanted for a friend's party and **that his sensitive** parents refused him.
   A. which his sensitive B. which his insensitive
   C. that his insensitive D. No Improvement

3. Goa was full of non-Goa property hunters **rushing about buying up the place** like tomorrow was an expired lease.
   A. rushing in buying up the place
   B. rushed about buying up the place
   C. rushing about to buy up the place
   D. No Improvement

4. Property hunting is a **tired and hungry** making business.
   A. is a tiresome and hungry
   B. is a tiring and hungry
   C. is a tiring and waste
   D. No Improvement

5. Cultural differences aside, **till luxury need speaks** in a manner that befits.
   A. luxury still needs to speak
   B. luxury still need to speak
   C. luxury till need to speak
   D. No Improvement

6. Indian food—the culinary avatar of the subcontinent's social history presented on a platter—**is without doubt the best food** in the world.
   A. is undoubtedly the greatest food
   B. is without doubt greatest food
   C. is best food without doubt
   D. No Improvement

7. It must retain the language of poetry. **It needed to create** stories, and not statements.
   A. It needed creating
   B. It needs creating
   C. It needs to create
   D. No Improvement

8. This year, Asia-Pacific has become the first region **to reach aggregate profiting** in biotech.
   A. to reach aggregated profitability
   B. to reach aggregate profitability
   C. to reach aggregate of profit
   D. No Improvement

9. India is deviating to embrace the West. If Western luxury brands deviate a little, **albeit selectively**, they will find rich Indian arms open far and wide.
   A. though selectively
   B. however selectively
   C. albeit selectedly
   D. No Improvement

10. China and India continued to attract attention and deals, motivated by the desire to increase access to these **largest and growing** drug markets and by the need to lower the costs of drug development.

A. larger and growing
B. large and growing
C. larger and grown
D. No Improvement

11. Luxury brands are **still above of the** clover curve here, with their elite (small) audiences.
A. still ahead of the
B. still in the
C. still far of the
D. No Improvement

12. Agencies **hence needed to be** sure of returns before investing, say admen.
A. hence needs to be
B. so needs to be
C. hence need to be
D. No Improvement

13. India is still a nascent market and that's the spirit everyone's **looking at it.**
A. looking for it B. looking in it
C. looking with it D. No Improvement

14. Questioning the state's move to allow women to serve liquor but not dance in bars **of the ground that** dancing aroused physical lust.
A. on the grounds that
B. of the grounds that
C. over the grounds that
D. No Improvement

15. For England the positives from their crushing series lose come in the shape of James Anderson and Kevin Pietersen, **both of which** have made significant strides up the rankings.
A. both of which B. both of whom
C. both of who D. No Improvement

16. International campaigns can work well for luxury here, **but context cannot be** ignored.
A. so context cannot be
B. but context cannot
C. but context couldn't
D. No Improvement

17. For one, the Indian luxury context, **while evolved rapidly**, still has its own meaning, and its own implications.
A. while evolved rapid
B. which evolving rapidly
C. while evolving rapidly
D. No Improvement

18. But too much of availability can compromise a luxury brand or **made it lose** its lustre.
A. make her lose B. make him lose
C. make it lose D. No Improvement

19. Still, it's under-the-upper **layers themselves who** are aspiring for slivers of luxury.
A. layers themselves which
B. layer itself who
C. layers themself which
D. No Improvement

20. It is like saying Hindi movies, with skimpily dressed dancers, would **effect public** order.
A. effect your B. affect public
C. affected public D. No Improvement

21. The court held that a few women being involved in prostitution was no **justice to deny other** bar girls the right to livelihood.
A. justification to declare other
B. justification to deny other
C. justice to let other
D. No Improvement

22. All-rounder cricketer has also made some progress **over the** player rankings.
A. above the B. at the
C. up the D. No Improvement

23. Former minister on Sunday **joined hands** with a suspended Lok Sabha member to float a new political outfit.
A. folded hands
B. walked hand in hand
C. shaked hands
D. No Improvement

24. Pakistan's former ministers will meet in London on Monday **to ask** a strategy to return home from exile.
A. to chalk out
B. to negotiate
C. to create
D. No Improvement

25. It's a family potboiler, medical thriller and political drama **all in one**–except that it's all too real and all too grim.
A. all 3 in one
B. all coupled into one
C. all rolled into one
D. No Improvement

26. India's efforts to get international support for its civil nuclear energy programme got **a go ahead on** Sunday as Germany indicated it would not come in the way of the India-US nuclear deal.
A. a life in B. a boost on
C. a boost at D. No Improvement

27. Is it time for old bungalows to **bite the dust**?
A. go down B. get down
C. come down D. No Improvement

28. The bungalows was an outward manifestation of a certain **way in life**, and with that era gone.

A. way for life B. way of life
C. way at life D. No Improvement

29. The builder Mittals will reportedly **raise their money**-raking high-rise behind it.

A. highten their money
B. rise their money
C. raise there money
D. No Improvement

30. The impatient present has usually demolished **more of the** past before we wake up to the irretrievable loss.

A. much of B. much of their
C. much of the D. No Improvement

31. Preservation is a romantic notion; demolition **quiet** more practical reasons.

A. has many, B. had many,
C. have many, D. No Improvement

32. You must get back to your **charming self** and impress the audience with your social skills.

A. own self B. main self
C. own uniqueness D. No Improvement

33. Stay focused on your goals and don't **get disturbed by** non-materialistic possessions.

A. get involved by
B. get betrayed by
C. get distracted by
D. No Improvement

34. You may appear more optimistic than your detractors **may want it to be.**

A. want you to be
B. wish yourself to be
C. seek you be
D. No Improvement

35. There are a number of mineral springs in the Czech territory, which **has been used** for medicinal purposes since the early 15th century.

A. have been used B. had been used
C. has being used D. No Improvement

36. The picturesque mountains **offers** excellent bungee jumping spots.

A. shows B. provides
C. offer D. No Improvement

37. Begin your **meal with** traditional faves like potato soup, beef soup with liver dumplings or dill soup made from sour milk.

A. meals with B. meal in
C. meals of D. No Improvement

38. You can also **go to the** National Museum building and the famous Prague State Opera.

A. went to B. visit the
C. saw D. No Improvement

39. If they close the Gulf for a **length of time** to shipping, then certainly we could look at $150, probably higher.

A. larger amount of time
B. larger duration of time
C. larger amount of hours
D. No Improvement

40. **More of them** are owned by the state and even the privately-owned ones are open to the public.

A. Most of which B. Most of them
C. Most of all D. No Improvement

41. Constructed in the ninth century by the Prince Booivoj, the castle has transformed **oneself** from a wooden fortress surrounded by earthen bulwarks to the imposing form it has today.

A. himself B. herself
C. itself D. No Improvement

42. Apart from frequent art exhibitions, **their are also** permanent collections devoted to archaeology, anthropology, mineralogy, natural history and numismatics.

A. there is also B. there are also
C. their are also D. No Improvement

43. You can visit the Czech Museum of Fine Arts, **at a** permanent exhibition on Czech Kubism.

A. with a
B. for a
C. in a
D. No Improvement

44. Tensions **above** Iran come at a time of strong demand for energy.

A. under B. inside
C. over D. No Improvement

45. Because its shores line the narrow Straits of Hormuz, Iran **could quickly hit** both military and commercial shipping.

A. will quickly hit
B. shall quickly hit
C. will be quick hitting
D. No Improvement

46. For most people who exercise **at the** morning, there is no getting around the question: Eat and run? Or run and eat later?

A. in the B. in
C. at the time of D. No Improvement

47. Are ad agencies even attempting to peer into the keyhole of this indulgence sanctum to garner consumer insights **ahead of** the curve?
A. above
B. over
C. within
D. No Improvement

48. Too many people rush into the world of credit and don't stop to think about how **their actions could affect their** credit score and ability to qualify for credit in the future.
A. their actions may affect their
B. their actions might affect their
C. their actions will affect their
D. No Improvement

49. According to the report, **number of deal with** vaccines were energized by concerns around avian flu, SARS, and biodefence products, while looming patent expirations led to more deals in generics.
A. number of deals in
B. number of deal in
C. number of deals with
D. No Improvement

50. This is how the Bombay High Court responded to the state government's purported **moral stand which** dance bars were causing grave harm to society.
A. moral stand in
B. moral stand at
C. moral stand that D. No Improvement

51. If you have a high credit limit, use **at least a** third of it.
A. atleast a
B. at last a
C. utmost a
D. No Improvement

52. Fitness experts will say that **first eating provides** fuel for a proper workout.
A. eating in the beginning provides
B. first eat provides
C. eating first provides
D. No Improvement

53. One study that examined the claim directly in 1995 found that a group of people did **burned much calories from fat on days** when they exercised on an empty stomach than on days when they had a small breakfast first.
A. burn more calories from fat on days
B. burn more calorie from fat on days
C. burnt more calories from fat on days
D. No Improvement

54. Carefree children spent their afternoons **to run about barefoot**, their clothes dusty, and telltale twigs of the neighbour's mango tree in their hair.
A. running barefoot in the sun
B. run about barefoot in the sun
C. running about barefoot in the sun
D. No Improvement

55. A year ago, a 13-year-old girl attempted suicide because her mother **refuses to pay his** mobile bills.
A. refuses to pay her B. refused to pay her
C. refused to pay his D. No Improvement

ANSWERS

1	2	3	4	5	6	7	8	9	10
D	C	D	B	A	D	C	C	D	B
11	**12**	**13**	**14**	**15**	**16**	**17**	**18**	**19**	**20**
C	C	D	A	C	D	C	C	C	C
21	**22**	**23**	**24**	**25**	**26**	**27**	**28**	**29**	**30**
B	C	C	A	C	B	D	B	D	C
31	**32**	**33**	**34**	**35**	**36**	**37**	**38**	**39**	**40**
A	D	C	A	D	C	A	B	D	B
41	**42**	**43**	**44**	**45**	**46**	**47**	**48**	**49**	**50**
C	B	A	C	D	A	D	C	A	C
51	**52**	**53**	**54**	**55**					
C	C	A	C	B					

Reordering Words & Sentences

Different words form a sentence and convey their meaning only when arranged in a proper order. A Paragraph is formed from sentences, it will convey its true meaning and purpose only when the sentences are arranged in a proper manner. Try and practise it in this exercise.

Multiple Choice Questions

Directions (Qs. 1 to 20): *In the following questions, some parts of the sentence have been jumbled up. You are required to rearrange these parts which are labelled P, Q, R and S to produce the correct sentence. Choose the option with proper sequence.*

1. We are doing
P : to the people
Q : to give relief
R : all we can
S : but more funds are needed
The correct sequence should be
A. P Q R S B. R Q P S
C. Q P R S D. S P Q R

2. The man
P : when he was
Q : in the office last evening
R : could not finish
S : all his work
The correct sequence should be
A. P Q R S B. Q R S P
C. R Q P S D. R S P Q

3. The people decided
P : they were going
Q : how much
R : to spend
S : on the construction of the school building
The correct sequence should be
A. Q P R S B. P Q R S
C. P R Q S D. S Q P R

4. The man said that
P : those workers
Q : would be given a raise
R : who did not go on
S : strike last month
The correct sequence should be
A. P Q R S B. P R S Q
C. Q P R S D. R S P Q

5. I think
P : the members
Q : are basically in agreement
R : of the group
S : on the following points
The correct sequence should be
A. R Q P S B. S Q R P
C. P R Q S D. P Q S R

6. While it was true that
P : I had
Q : to invest in industry
R : some lands and houses
S : I did not have ready cash
The correct sequence should be
A. P Q R S B. P R S Q
C. S Q P R D. Q P R S

7. P : But for your help
Q : to finish this work
R : it would not have been possible
S : in time
The correct sequence should be
A. P R Q S B. S P Q R
C. R P Q S D. P Q R S

8. The boy
P : in the competition
Q : who was wearing spectacles
R : won many prizes
S : held in our college

The correct sequence should be
A. P Q R S B. R P S Q
C. Q R P S D. Q P S R

9. About 200 years ago,
P : in the south of India
Q : an old king
R : ruled over a kingdom
S : called Rajavarman
The correct sequence should be
A. Q S R P B. P Q R S
C. Q P S R D. Q S P R

10. P : his land
Q : a wooden plough
R : the Indian peasant still uses
S : to cultivate
The correct sequence should be
A. R Q P S B. Q P S R
C. S R Q P D. R Q S P

11. He was a man,
P : even if he had to starve
Q : who would not beg
R : borrow or steal
S : from anyone
The correct sequence should be
A. P Q R S B. P R Q S
C. Q R S P D. Q P R S

12. P : in the progress of
Q : universities play a crucial role
R : our civilization
S : in the present age
The correct sequence should be
A. S Q P R B. Q R S P
C. Q R P S D. S Q R P

13. P : far out into the sea
Q : for the next two weeks there were further explosions
R : which hurled
S : ashes and debris
The correct sequence should be
A. Q R P S B. R S P Q
C. Q R S P D. S R P Q

14. William Shakespeare,
P : in his lifetime
Q : the great English dramatist
R : wrote thirty-five plays
S : and several poems
The correct sequence should be
A. P Q R S B. R S P Q
C. Q S R P D. Q R S P

15. Whenever I am,
P : with an old friend of mine
Q : in New Delhi
R : to have dinner
S : I always try
The correct sequence should be
A. S Q P R B. Q S R P
C. R P S Q D. P R Q S

16. P : I don't know
Q : must have thought
R : what people sitting next to me
S : but I came away
The correct sequence should be
A. R S Q P B. R Q S P
C. P Q R S D. P R Q S

17. P : in estimating the size of the earth
Q : but they were hampered by the lack of instruments of precision
R : ancient astronomers
S : used methods which were theoretically valid
The correct sequence should be
A. R P Q S B. P R Q S
C. R S Q P D. R P S Q

18. P : It is a pity that
Q : by offering a handsome dowry
R : a number of parents think that
S : they will be able to ensure the happiness of their daughters
The correct sequence should be
A. S Q R P B. P R S Q
C. P S R Q D. P R Q S

19. The common man
P : in nurturing
Q : a more active role
R : communal harmony
S : should play
The correct sequence should be
A. P R S Q B. S Q P R
C. S Q R P D. P R Q S

20. The doctor
P : able to find out
Q : what has caused
R : the food poisoning
S : has not been
The correct sequence should be
A. S P R Q B. P R Q S
C. P R S Q D. S P Q R

Directions (Qs. 21 to 40): *A number of sentences are given below which when properly sequenced form a coherent paragraph. Each sentence is labelled as abcdef...... Choose the most logical order of sentences from among the given choices to construct a coherent paragraph:*

21. (a) Parts of northern region were pounded by heavy rains today,
(b) Vehicular traffic came to a near halt.
(c) As mid and high altitude areas of Himachal Pradesh were in grip of severe cold wave with snow lashing the tribal areas and mid ranges receiving showers.
(d) As the sky remained heavily overcast with dark clouds reducing the visibility considerably.
(e) A large number of tourists were forced to buy heavy woollens and stay indoors due to inclement weather.
A. ecabd B. adecb
C. edabc D. acbde

22. (a) The idea is that students should be able to find employment for themselves after the course.
(b) The Central Board of Secondary Education is planning a revamp of its vocational courses.
(c) For this it is necessary to tie up with the industry as well as mobilise schools for their support.
(d) While others will be made less academic and more in tune with the needs of the industry.
(e) A number of courses have been identified as 'deadwood' and will be done away with.
A. bedac B. abcde
C. acebd D. baced

23. (a) Clearly, age is not a deterrent in one's choice of learning.
(b) Perhaps, it was because of her childhood desire.
(c) When Rachna came to Delhi eight years back, she had not anticipated a career in the field of art.
(d) She has been successful in the various exhibitions that she has been part of in terms of business.
(e) She had got into expressing her thoughts with the help of a brush and colours only because her daughter refused to get initiated into it.
(f) She feels that her use of colour appeals to people.
A. aedcbf B. cdefba
C. cebadf D. acdebf

24. (a) The rehabilitation record has been dismal.
(b) It has been two years years since the earthquake rudely rattled the people of Gujarat.
(c) And since then, life has been a constant struggle.
(d) The quake set Gujarat's clock back by 10 years.
(e) Things changed forever.
A. bedca B. bcade
C. dbace D. edcba

25. (a) In fact, success in exams depended on rote learning from old notes.
(b) when he was studying civil engineering in a college in Gujarat.
(c) He was detained for lack of attendance.
(d) Lectures were soporific, classes rarely worth attending and 80 per cent attendance compulsory.
(e) The college became a trap he hated.
(f) His is a plight many engineers across India would identify with.
(g) He found the going tough.
A. abcdgef B. bgdacef
C. fabcdge D. abcdefg

26. (a) In a country that has close to 600 recognised engineering colleges, there are only seven IITs.
(b) Barring a few exeptions, the academic atmosphere in these is moribund.
(c) The very best students usually get there.
(d) many waste themselves in frustration.
(e) Most of those who get into engineering are good students.
(f) but about 1.25 lakh others and up in the remaining colleges.
A. aecfbd B. abecdf
C. abcdef D. acfbed

27. (a) Whatever the job market, common wisdom says that IIT graduates will find jobs where others have failed.
(b) The IIT brand name is a ticket to success.
(c) When recruiters go headhunting, the IITs are still top of their list.
(d) Its possessor is understood to have an excellent academic record and the will to succeed.
(e) In the job market, that counts.
A. bdeac B. abcde
C. abdce D. dbace

28. (a) It will pave the way ....
(b) signalling a new beginning in strategic ties......
(c) for a tangible Indian economic presence in Iran and Central Asia.
(d) Iran has offered India valuable road linkages to central Asia ......
(e) aimed at promoting peace and economic cooperation in the region.
A. dbeac B. debca
C. acebd D. abced

29. (a) A good college is essential for a successful career and admissions are based on marks.
(b) The marks-based system followed by all the boards in the country recognises only a small percentage of students as successful.
(c) The marks one scores in the crucial board exams dictate the path his life takes.
(d) Anyone scoring below a certain percentage is automatically branded a 'failure'.
(d) So if you cannot make it into the best college, your career is over even before it has started.

A. abcde B. bcdea
C. bdcae D. abdec

30. (a) The project has already started on an experimental basis in the west district.
(b) A website is soon going to be launched where application forms can be downloaded and submitted.
(c) Standing in a queue at a government office to submit application form will be a thing of the past.
(d) A unique code will be alloted while submitting the form which will help in finding the status of the application.
A. abcd B. dabc
C. cbda D. badc

31. (a) To curb bio-terrorism is a difficult task.
(b) To check these attacks and lessen their impact, we need an impartial team of sincere, strong and dedicated men.
(c) The media can play a strong role in stopping this unnecessary spread of panic.
(d) Since bio-terrorism is not visible or easily detectable, it can be used often.
(e) Men who honour the lives of their fellow countrymen before their own.
A. abcde B. dabce
C. adbec D. acbed

32. (a) He was dying.
(b) No one was ready to touch him as even shifting him from one place to another would lead to profuse bleeding.
(c) He was a five-day old infant, premature and bleeding profusely.
(d) Even if injected one small needle, blood would ooze out and continue to flow for an hour at a stretch.
(e) This small being had haematoma, a thick blood clot in his brain.
A. edbca B. cabde
C. eacdb D. cedba

33. (a) The day I don't treat a patient, I feel ....
(b) I have enough to eat, I crave for blessings now.
(c) But if a financially weak patient gives me only ₹ 50, I don't mind.
(d) Each month I do three to four operations free of cost.
(e) I have lost something in life.
(f) My consultation fee is ₹ 300.
A. fcdeab B. dfcbae
C. fcabde D. bdfcea

34. (a) When he was rushed to the nearby Primary Health Centre after his fall, the doctor referred him to a hospital.
(b) This worsened his injury.
(c) Had a little precaution been exercised after the accident, Tarun would have continued with his gymnastic classes.
(d) He was paralysed from waist downwards when he fell from the vaulting horse while doing gymnastics.
(e) However, the doctor forgot to tell Tarun's parents to take him on a stretcher as he had suffered spinal injuries.
(f) Tarun is wheelchair bound for two years.
A. fdeabc B. abcdef
C. fdcaeb D. fdbcae

35. (a) As the temperature rises, staying hydrated can become a greater challenge for people exercising both indoors and out.
(b) Several things can influence this process, including age, gender, physical conditioning. humidity and a lack of sufficient fluids.
(c) In hot weather, individuals can lose as much as two quarts of sweat per hour.
(d) As we age, we have a lower perceived level of thirst in response to fluid loss and early stages of dehydration.
(e) If not replenished, this can lead to dehydration, heat exhaustion and even heatstroke.
A. abcde B. dbcae
C. cbdea D. acebd

36. (a) The leopard was discovered in the servant quarters of a farmhouse.
(b) The injuries appeared to have been caused by the paws of the leopard, and were not teeth wounds.
(c) It took the wild life officials, Delhi Police and Delhi zoo vets eight hours to capture the leopard that had wandered into a factory in south Delhi.
(d) The leopard then jumped into the factory where the workers managed to lock it in a small generator room before calling in the police.
(e) Before its capture, the leopard attacked two women and a man in the farmhouse.
A. aebdc B. bdaec
C. eadbc D. adbec

37. (a) Police suspect a carpenter working at John's house as he has not reported for work since the day the boy went missing.
(b) John did not return home in the afternoon.
(c) John's mother had herself put the boy on the vehicle in the morning.

(d) John smiled at him and was last seen walking up to him.

(e) His parents called the school and were told John had not been to school at all and had been marked absent.

(f) He was about to enter the school when someone called out his name.

A. cfdbea B. debfca

C. bfdaec D. abcdef

38. (a) However, the mayhem over the last few months is deeply shocking.

(b) Yet I do not agree with the prophets of doom who see nothing but disaster ahead.

(c) When I came back to my motherland India after a stay in Switzerland, I felt I was trading a hotbed of intense religious and political violence for peace and quiet.

(d) I think our nation is searching for an identity.

(e) And a new vision of the future will emerge from this.

A. abcde B. cabde

C. cebad D. bedca

39. (a) An integrated and combined approach was required to reveal the mystery of the brain —its structure, composition and function.

(b) Since the early 80's, scientists were clear that the brain would be the final frontier to conquer.

(c) The initiative was flagged off and came to be known as the Human Brain Project.

(d) But that wasn't easy because understanding the brain involved completely integrating information from the level of the gene to the level of behaviour.

(e) To fulfill this requirement a group of American scientists from various disciplines decided to work together.

A. acbed B. bdaec

C. abdec D. badec

40. (a) A product is something that is made in a factory, a brand is something that is bought by a consumer.

(b) The trick therefore, lies in the brand positioning.

(c) For a consumer, the satisfaction of becoming associated with a name that is the 'best' and the 'leader' is far more important and at times makes him ignore the price factor.

(d) Brands come and go.

(e) Still there are those who manage to stay and develop an affinity with consumers.

A. aebcd B. debac

C. decab D. aecdb

ANSWERS

1	2	3	4	5	6	7	8	9	10
B	D	A	B	C	C	A	C	A	D
11	**12**	**13**	**14**	**15**	**16**	**17**	**18**	**19**	**20**
C	A	C	D	B	D	C	B	B	D
21	**22**	**23**	**24**	**25**	**26**	**27**	**28**	**29**	**30**
D	A	C	A	B	D	A	A	C	C
31	**32**	**33**	**34**	**35**	**36**	**37**	**38**	**39**	**40**
C	D	B	C	D	A	A	B	B	B

Comprehension Passages

Passages

Directions: *Read the following passages and answer the questions given below each.*

PASSAGE-1

In the Roman times, defected enemies were generally put to death as criminals for having offended the emperor of Rome. In the middle ages, however, the practice of ransoming of returning prisoners in exchange for money became common. Though some saw this custom as a step towards a most humane society, the primary reasons behind it were economic rather than humanitarian.

In those times, rulers had only a limited ability to raise taxes. They could neither force their subject to fight nor pay them to do so. The promise of material compensation in the form of goods and ransom was therefore the only way of inducing combatants to participate in a war. In the middle ages, the predominant incentive for the individual soldiers was the expectation of spoils. Although collecting ransom clearly brought financial gain, keeping a prisoner and arranging for his exchange had its cost. Consequently, procedures were devised to reduce transaction costs.

One such device was a rule asserting that the prisoner had to assess his own value. This compelled the prisoner to establish a value *without too much distortion;* indicating too low a value would increase, the captive's chances of being killed, while indicating too high a value would either ruin him financially or create a prohibitively expensive ransom that would also result in death.

1. It can be inferred from the passage that a medieval soldier

A. was less likely to kill captured members of opposing armies than was a soldier of the Roman Empire

B. was similar to a 20th century terrorist in that he operated on a basically independent level and was motivated solely by economic incentives

C. had few economic options and chose to fight because it was the only way to earn an adequate living

D. was motivated to spare prisoners' lives by humanitarian rather than economic ideals

2. Which of the following best describes the change in policy from executing prisoners in Roman times to ransoming prisoners in the middle ages?

A. The emperors of Rome demanded more respect than did medieval rulers and thus Roman subjects went to greater lengths to defend their nation

B. It was a reflection of the lesser degree of direct control medieval ruler had over subjects

C. It became a show of strength and honour warrior of the middles ages to be able to capture and return their enemies

D. Medieval soldiers were not as hum-anitarian as their ransoming practices might have indicated

3. The primary purpose of the passage is to

A. discuss the economic basis of the medieval practice of exchanging prisoners for ransom

B. examine the history of the treatment of prisoner of war

C. emphasize the importance of a warrior's code of honour during the middle ages

D. explore a way of reducing the cost of ransom

4. The author uses the phrase *"without too much distortion"* in order to

A. indicate that prisoners would fairly assess their worth

B. emphasize the important role medieval prisoners played in determining whether they should be ransomed

C. explain how prisoners often paid more than an appropriate ransom in order to increase their chances for survival

D. suggest that captors and captives often had understanding relationships

PASSAGE-2

The world dismisses curiosity by calling it idle or mere idle curiosity—even though curious persons are seldom idle. Parents do their best to extinguish curiosity in their children because it makes life difficult to be faced everyday with a string of unanswerable questions about what makes fire hot or why grass grows. Children whose curiosity survives parental discipline are invited to join our university. With the university, they go on asking their questions and trying to find the answers. In the eyes of a scholar, that is what a university is for. Some of the questions which the scholars ask, seem to the world to be scarcely worth asking, let alone answering. They asked questions too minute specialised for you and me to understand without years of explanation. If the world inquires of one of them why he wants to know the answer to a particular question he may say especially if he is a scientist, that the answer will in some obscure way make possible a new machine or weapon or gadget. He talks that way because he knows that the world understands and respects utility.

But to you who are now part of the university, he will say that he wants to know the answer simply because he does not know it, the way the mountain climber wants to climb a mountain, simply because it is there. Similarly a historian asked by an outsider why he studies history may come out with the argument that he has learnt to repeat on such occasions, something about knowledge of the past making it possible to understand the present and mould the future. But if you really want to know why a historian studies the past, the answer is much simpler, something happened and he would like to know what. All this does not mean that the answers which scholars find to their questions have no consequences. They may have enormous consequences but these seldom form the reason for asking the questions or pursuing the answers. It is true that scholars can be put to work answering questions for the sake of the consequences as thousands are working, now, for example, in search of a cure for cancer. But this is not the primary function of the scholars. For the consequences are usually subordinate to the satisfaction of curiosity.

1. According to the passage, the children make life difficult for their parents
   A. by their ceaseless curiosity
   B. by unceasing bombardment of questions
   C. by asking irrelevant questions
   D. by posing profound questions
2. The common people consider some of the questions that the scholars ask unimportant
   A. as they are too lazy and idle
   B. as they are too modest
   C. as it's beyond their comprehension
   D. as it is considered a waste of time
3. A historian really studies the past
   A. to comprehend the present and to reconstruct the future
   B. to explain the present and plan the future
   C. to understand the present and make fortune
   D. to understand the present and mould the future
4. Children whose curiosity survives parental discipline means
   A. children retaining their curiosity in spite of being discouraged by their parents
   B. children pursuing their mental curiosity
   C. children's curiosity subdued due to parents' intervention
   D. children being disciplined by their parents
5. According to the passage, parents do their best to discourage curiosity in their children
   A. because they have no time
   B. because they have no patience to answer them
   C. because they feel that their children ask stupid questions continuously
   D. because they are unable to answer all their questions

PASSAGE-3

The factor of geographical distribution is equally, possibly even more, significant that English is spoken as first or native language in at least four continents of the world, Russian in two, Chinese and the Indian languages in one. English is without question the closest approach to a world language today. It goes without saying that no two persons ever have an identical command of their common language. Certainly, they have not precisely the same vocabulary. There are at least minor differences in pronunciation, indeed the same individual will not pronounce his vowels and consonants in absolutely identical fashion everytime he utters them. Everyone possesses, in addition, certain individual traits of grammatical form and syntactical order, constituting that peculiar and personal quality of language which we term as style. All of this is implicit in the well-known phrase, 'Style is the man.' No men are identical, no two styles are the same. If this be true of but two persons, the potential of differences resident in a language spoken by more than 200 million truly staggers imagination.

1. The author argues that English is the closest approach to a world language because
   A. there are more native speakers of English than of any other language
   B. English has less number of mutually unintelligible dialects
   C. the geographical distribution of English covers a much greater area
   D. other languages are much too complex to be world languages

2. The fact that the same individual will not pronounce his vowels and consonants identically everytime shows that
   A. literary style varies from person to person
   B. mutual intelligibility is a myth
   C. vocabulary varies from individual to individual
   D. no two persons speak the same language exactly the same way
3. It is evident from the passage that style is
   A. a strange type of language
   B. a language where one does not have to be particular about correctness and grammar
   C. language used in a particular way by an individual
   D. a question of grammatical and syntactic correctness
4. According to some authorities
   A. more people speak Chinese dialect than English
   B. more people speak English as an auxiliary language than as a first language
   C. more people speak English in the UK than in England
   D. about one-fourth of the world's population speaks English
5. The overall implication of the passage is that
   A. to suppose that 230 million people speak English as a native language would certainly be an underestimate
   B. the 55 million inhabitants of the British Isles speak like the 30 million inhabitants of the dominions and colonies
   C. a little less than half the native English speakers in the world live in the US
   D. about one-tenth of the total English-speaking world population lives in British dominions and colonies

PASSAGE-4

What is the future which awaits our children? The underlying assumption of the question, that Indian children have a common future, is itself dubious. It can legitimately be asked whether a student who is well-fed, attending a boarding school in the salubrious climate of the hills and learning to use computers has any future in common with a malnourished child who goes to a school with no blackboards, if indeed he does go to school. The latter may have no worthwhile future at all. And it might be worthwhile to analyse the significance of this marginalisation of more than 75 per cent of the children of this country.

The failure to provide an infrastructure for primary education in the villages of India more than 40 years after independence is in sharp contrast with the sophisticated institutions, for technical institutes of higher education are funded by the government, which essentially means that the money to support them comes from taxes. And, since indirect taxation forms a substantial part of the taxes collected by the government, the financial burden is borne by all the people. L.K. Jha put it graphically when he observed that 25 paise of every rupee spent on educating an IIT student comes from the pockets of men and women whose children may never enter a proper classroom.

1. The author is trying to highlight which of the following?
   A. Faulty system of direct taxes
   B. The greatness of L.K. Jha
   C. Need of sophisticated education for rural poor
   D. Need to have common future for Indian children
2. Which of the following pairs have been termed as 'sharp contrast' by the author?
   (*i*) Infrastructure for technical education
   (*ii*) Lack of infrastructure for rural primary schools
   (*iii*) 25 paise of every rupee earned by Government is spent on education
   (*iv*) The financial burden of higher technical education is borne by all people
   (*v*) 75% of children have limited opportunities
   A. (*ii*) and (*iv*) B. (*ii*) and (*iii*)
   C. (*iii*) and (*iv*) D. (*i*) and (*ii*)
3. Which of the following statements is not true?
   (*i*) The author welcomes Govt.'s initiative on primary education
   (*ii*) 75% of the children have a bright future
   (*iii*) 25% cost of educating a technocrat comes from poor people
   A. Only (*i*) B. Only (*ii*)
   C. Only (*iii*) D. Only (*i*) and (*ii*)
4. According to the author, who among the following does not have a hopeful and prosperous future?
   (*i*) All students from technical institutes
   (*ii*) All students financially supported by the Government
   A. Only (*i*) B. Only (*ii*)
   C. Both (*i*) and (*ii*) D. Neither (*i*) nor (*ii*)
5. What seems to be the likely answer of the author to the question posed by him in the first sentence of the passage?
   (*i*) There is no common future for the Indian children
   (*ii*) The future is worthwhile for majority of Indian children
   (*iii*) The majority may never enter a proper classroom
   A. Only (*i*) B. Only (*ii*)
   C. Only (*iii*) D. Both (*i*) and (*ii*)
6. What seems to be the purpose of the author in writing this passage?

A. Setting goals for children of upper middle class
B. Questioning the legitimacy of public schools
C. Highlighting lack of infrastructural facilities for primary education
D. Focusing on inequality in educational opportunities

PASSAGE-5

Cyber crime is the branded stigma defacing the culture and magnanimity of computer technology. It is upkeeping the flag with indomitable triumph against developing computer technology worldwide.

Modern age is striding with marching steps of technology revolution beating the past decade of ancestral belief with ultimate care. Computer invention has unfolded the mystery of quick access with the objective of minimum manpower and cutting the time consumption parameters.

As each coin has dual face of its portrait, likewise computer technology is sick of creeping virus. Synthetic man-made dilemma of site hackers activation is causing setback to the expanding anchor of revolutionary device with great loss of time, economy and data profile as suffered by consumers. A recent report from Internet security firm Websense estimates that 85.6 per cent of all the unwanted e-mails contained links to spam sites. The company's data suggests that the number of malicious sites grew 233 per cent in the last six months and saw 671 per cent growth in the number of malicious sites during the last year. In June alone, the total number of e-mails detected as containing viruses increased by 600 per cent compared to May.

Chat rooms, blogs and message-boards where the users post comments have been identified as the top targets of hackers and spammers due to the high traffic these attract. According to Websense, 95 per cent of user-generated comments to blogs, chat rooms and message-boards during the first half of the year were malicious.

It is advisable not to click on spurious links and stay away from keying in passwords at unknown sites as they are most likely to be spammed. Hackers can steal your passwords and log in to your account and access critical information like account numbers and contact details among other things.

1. The above passage is:
A. an advisory for the computer users.
B. an advisory for the Internet users.
C. a warning against possible threat to the Internet users.
D. related to chat rooms, blogs and message boards.

2. People who use chat rooms and blogs,
A. are safe and have no threats from spam.
B. are more prone to malicious e-mails.
C. create virus and hack the accounts of others.
D. are unsafe.

3. According to the writer, it is not safe to:
A. log on to spurious links.
B. access one's own account frequently.
C. have essential information stored in a computer.
D. include data-stealing code.

4. Hackers and spammers, according to the writer, are:
A. a new threat to the Internet users and the economy.
B. only pranksters and not serious threat to the system.
C. trained, professional technocrats who are an asset.
D. not expert professionals.

5. Which word in the passage is synonym of *weblog*?
A. blog B. password
C. site D. e-mail

6. Which agency has assessed the data record with spam sites?
A. Microsoft
B. Internet security from Google
C. Websense
D. Spammers

7. Which month dominates the e-mails detection data record?
A. May B. June
C. Last six months D. Last year

PASSAGE-6

Progress in life depends a good deal on crossing one threshold after another. Some time ago, a man watched his little nephew try to write his name. It was hard work, very hard work. The little boy had arrived at an effort threshold. Today he writes his name with comparative ease. No new threshold confronts him. This is the way with all of us. As soon as we cross one threshold, as soon as we conquer one difficulty, a new difficulty appears, or should appear. Some people make the mistake of steering clear of thresholds. Anything that requires genuine thinking and use of energy, they avoid. They prefer to stay in a rut where thresholds are not met. Probably, they have been at their job a number of years. Things are easy for them. They make no effort to seek out new obstacles to overcome. Real progress stops under such circumstances.

Some middle-aged and elderly people greatly enrich their lives by continuing to cross thresholds. One man went into an entirely new business when he was past middle life and made success of it, De Morgan didn't start to write novels until he was past sixty. Psychologists have discovered that man can continue to learn throughout his life. And it is undoubtedly better to try and fail than not to try at all. There one can be placed in the category of the Swiss mountaineer of whom it was said, *"He died climbing"*. When a new difficulty arises to obstruct your path, do not complain. Accept the challenge. Determine to cross this threshold as you have crossed numerous other thresholds in your past. In the words of a poet, do not rest but strive *to pass from dream to grander dream.*

1. What obstructs real progress in life?
A. Remaining at one and the same post
B. Avoiding the thinking and energy
C. Shunning every work
D. Stopping education

2. What does progress in life depend upon?
A. Good habits
B. Hardwork
C. Overcoming one difficulty after another
D. Spirit of service and cooperation

3. What does *'He died climbing'* signify?
A. He died when he was climbing the hill
B. He died before getting at the top
C. He strove hard till the last moment of life
D. He climbed the hill and then died

4. What does *'to pass from dream to grander dream'* mean?
A. Always having greater and greater aspiration in life
B. Seeing one good dream and then greater aspiration in life
C. Making plan after plan
D. Seeing one dream after the other

5. What did the man entering a new business past middle life do of his business?
A. He miserably failed in it
B. He achieved partial success
C. He dropped the business after some time
D. He achieved good success in it

6. How can you accomplish the most difficult tasks?
A. By mobilizing all possible resources
B. By avoiding all obstacles
C. By sticking to hardwork
D. By doing it bit by bit and persisting in the effort

7. What does De Morgan's life teach?
A. That it is futile to learn many things
B. That one is never old in case he has vigour
C. That it is never too late to learn
D. That creative writing can be made even late in life

8. How do middle-aged and elderly people add brilliance to their lives?
A. By overcoming difficulty one after another
B. By getting sycophants to surround them
C. By making fine speeches
D. By acquiring resourcefulness

9. What should we do when a new difficulty obstructs our path?
A. Run away from it
B. Be bold and face it
C. Manoeuvre to get it removed
D. Enlist other people's help to get it over

10. When did De Morgan start to write novels?
A. When he was sixty years old
B. When he was below sixty
C. When he studied psychology
D. None of these

PASSAGE-7

It is *heartening* to know that if one had not had any heart attack earlier and he stops smoking, his chances of having a heart attack *drop* to that of a non-smoker in about six months' time. Stopping of smoking is also the single most effective means of secondary prevention (recurrence of a heart attack) in heart patients.

Smoking leads to pain and stiffness in the legs while walking. No amount of drugs can help. The only remedy is to give up smoking. If women smoke during pregnancy, there is an increased risk of death of the baby in the womb or soon after birth. Even where the baby survives, there is likelihood of delayed physical and intellectual development of the baby till it reaches 11 years of age.

Still worse the fact about smoking is that passive smoking is equally dangerous. Passive smokers are those who do not smoke but being in the company of smokers have to inhale smoke exhaled by the smokers They are equally prone to heart diseases, lung cancer and bronchitis, for no fault of theirs. It is seen that the incidence of these diseases is greater among women whose husbands are *heavy* smokers As such, every non-smoker has a fundamental right to safeguard himself against the danger of passive smoking. "Your smoking is injurious to my health and I have a right to stop you from smoking" could be the slogan against passive smoking. It is a great threat to the health of the individual, the family and the society. In fact one has to choose between health and smoking including passive smoking. *One cannot have both.*

Another matter of *grave concern* about smoking is the long time interval between the start of smoking habit and the manifestation of deadly diseases like cancer, chronic bronchitis and heart attack. People are generally not aware of the link between smoking and the misery they have to undergo years later and younger people often fall victim to this menacing habit under the wrong impression that they are *immune* to its disastrous effects, not realising that they are *heading* towards catastrophe. The prolonged incubation period of many tobacco-related diseases has prevented recognition of the size of the threat and the *grim* picture of chronic and life-threatening diseases.

1. What is "passive smoking"?
   A. Giving up the habit of smoking abruptly
   B. Exhaling smoke by a non-smoker
   C. Unintended intake of smoke exhaled by smokers
   D. Smoking cigarettes which are harmless in nature
2. The effects of passive smoking are more and more prominently observed among
   A. the children
   B. the smokers
   C. the wives of smokers
   D. the non-smokers
3. Which of the following is a heartening thing, according to the author?
   A. People who have had a heart attack stop smoking
   B. It takes only six months for any person to quit smoking
   C. The smoker carries the risk of heart attack for six months
   D. None of these
4. Which of the following statements is/are false in the context of the passage?
   (*i*) Passive smokers are not free from risk of heart diseases
   (*ii*) Intake of certain medicines helps recover pain and stiffness in legs caused by smoking
   (*iii*) Younger people are immune to the disastrous effects if their regular smoking is under control
   A. (*i*) and (*ii*) only B. (*ii*) and (*iii*) only
   C. (*ii*) only D. (*iii*) only
5. Which of the following is not mentioned in the passage as a likely result of smoking by women during pregnancy?
   A. Death of baby before birth
   B. Death of baby after birth
   C. Survival of baby with some abnormality
   D. Abnormal delay in the childbirth
6. Which of the following is considered by the author as a matter of "grave concern"?
   A. Inordinate delay in appearance of symptoms of hazards of smoking
   B. Long time required for giving up the habit of smoking
   C. Manifestation of deadly diseases like cancer, bronchitis, etc.
   D. Lack of awareness of people regarding the hazards of smoking
7. The youth feel that they are immune to the hazardous effects of smoking because
   A. these effects of smoking are not visible within a short time span
   B. they do not realise that they are heading towards disaster
   C. they feel a great thrill in acquiring the habit of smoking
   D. the link between smoking and its disastrous effects cannot be established
8. Which factor prevents people from realising the extent of threat of smoking hazards?
   A. Their lack of awareness of civic responsibilities
   B. Their firm belief that they are not immune to these hazards
   C. The less disastrous effects of tobacco-related diseases
   D. None of these
9. The last sentence of the third para *"One cannot have both"* means
   A. active smoking and passive smoking
   B. smoking and risk of heart diseases
   C. threat to the individual and also to the family
   D. None of these

Directions (Qs. 10 to 12): *Choose the word which is most nearly the **SAME** in meaning as the word given in bold capitals as used in the passage.*

10. **HEADING**
    A. crowning B. marching
    C. adorning D. title
11. **HEAVY**
    A. excessive B. bulky
    C. large D. thick
12. **DROP**
    A. roll B. escape
    C. remove D. reduce

Directions (Qs. 13 to 15): *Choose the word which is most nearly the **OPPOSITE** in meaning of the word given in bold capitals as used in the passage.*

13. **GRIM**
    A. dim B. dark
    C. presentable D. pleasant
14. **IMMUNE**
    A. free B. vulnerable
    C. powerful D. weak
15. **HEARTENING**
    A. cheerful B. miserable
    C. frightening D. dangerous

PASSAGE-8

The happy man is the man who lives objectively, who has free affections and wide interests, who secures his happiness through these interests and affections and through the fact that they, in turn, make him an object of interest and affection to many others. To be the recipient of affection is a potent cause of happiness, but the man who demands affection is not the man upon whom it is *bestowed.* The man who receives affection is, speaking broadly, the man who gives it. But it is useless to attempt to give it as a calculation, in the way in which one might lend money at interest, for a calculated affection is not genuine and is not felt to be so by the recipient.

What then can a man do who is unhappy because he is encased in self? So long as he continues to think about the causes of his unhappiness, he continues to be self-centred and therefore does not get outside the vicious circle, if he is to get outside it, it must be genuine interests, not by simulated interests adopted merely as a medicine. Although this difficulty is real, there is nevertheless much that he can do if he has rightly diagnosed his trouble. If, for example, his trouble is due to a sense of sin, conscious or unconscious, he can first persuade his conscious mind that he has no reason to feel sinful and then proceed, to plant his rational conviction in his unconscious mind, concerning himself meanwhile with some more or less neutral activity. If he succeeds in *dispelling* the sense of sin, it is possible that genuine objective interests will arise spontaneously. If his trouble is self-pity, he can deal with it in the same manner after first persuading himself that there is nothing extraordinarily unfortunate in his circumstances.

If fear is his trouble, let him practise exercises designed to give courage. Courage has been recognised from time immemorial as an important virtue, and a great part of training of boys and young men has been devoted to producing a type of character capable of fearlessness in battle. But moral courage and intellectual courage have been much less studied, they also, however, have their technique. Admit to yourself everyday at least one painful truth, you will find this quite useful. Teach yourself to feel that life still be worth living even if you were not, as of course you are, immeasurably superior to all your friends in virtue and in intelligence. Exercises of this sort prolonged through several years will at last enable you to admit facts *without flinching* and will, in so doing, free you from the empire of fear over a very large field.

1. Who according to the passage is the happy man?
A. who is encased in self
B. who has free affection and wide interests
C. who is free from worldly passions
D. who has externally centre passions

2. According to the passage, calculated affection
A. appears to be false and fabricated
B. makes other pen-on to love you
C. turns into permanent affection over a period of time
D. leads to self-pity

3. Which of the following virtues, according to the passage, has been recognised for long as an important virtue?
A. Patriotism B. Sacrifice
C. Courage D. Self-consciousness

4. Which of the following, according to the passage, has not been studied much?
A. Feeling of guilt and self-pity
B. The state of mind of an unhappy man
C. How to get absorbed in other interests
D. Moral and intellectual courage

5. If a man is suffering from a sense of sin
A. he should invite opinion of others
B. he should admit his sin at once
C. he should consciously realize that he has no reason to feel sinful
D. he should develop a fearless character

6. What happens to a man who demands affection?
A. His feelings are reciprocated by others
B. He tends to take a calculated risk
C. He becomes a victim of a viscious circle
D. None of these

7. What should a man do who is suffering from the feeling of self-pity?
A. He should control his passions and emotions
B. He should persuade himself that everything is alright in his circumstances
C. He should seek affection from others
D. He should develop a feeling of fearlessness

8. How to get out of the viscious circle mentioned in the passage?
A. By practicing skills of concentration
B. By inculcating the habits of self-absorption
C. Being true to others and one's internal circumstances
D. None of these

9. Which of the following statements is not *true* in the context of the passage?
A. Happy man has wide interests
B. Courage has been recognized as an important virtue
C. Unhappy man is encased in self
D. Issue of intellectual courage has been extensively studied

10. Which of the following words is ***SIMILAR*** in meaning of the word **'bestowed'** as used in the passage?
A. Conferred B. Accommodated
C. Trusted D. Withdrawn

11. Which of the following statements is *true* in the context of the passage?
A. All passions stem from unhappiness
B. The happy man lives in subjectively

C. Any virtue has a dark side also
D. One feels happy if one receives affection

12. Which of the following words is ***SIMILAR*** in meaning to the word **'flinching'** as used in the passage?
A. Wincing B. Convincing
C. Explaining D. Debating

13. What happens when you think about cause of your unhappiness?
A. You try to introspect and look critically at yourself
B. You realize that the life can be lived in different ways
C. You try to practice exercise designed to give courage
D. You remain a self-centred person

14. What according to the passage is the real cause of happiness?
A. Material rewards and incentives received
B. Critical analysis of the happy state of mind
C. Affection received from others
D. Calculated risks taken

15. Which of the following words is ***OPPOSITE*** in meaning of the word **'dispelling'** as used in the passage?
A. Giving B. Accumulating
C. Projecting D. Scattering

PASSAGE-9

Education, particularly higher education, is the obvious but crucially important instrument for nation building. As Confucious has said:

"If you are thinking of one year, plant rice. If you are thinking of a decade, plant trees. If you are thinking of a century, educate the people."

When we set about the task of higher education, we should be absolutely clear in our perception of the goals of education in the specific context of our nation's development. No *doubt,* one of the important aims of education would be to create the required range and nature of trained manpower assessed to be needed by different sectors of national growth. The entire educational apparatus must be geared progressively to fulfill the requirements of different phases of our growth in every sector—primary, secondary and *tertiary.* The aim must be to ensure that our country does not experience either *paucity,* or a *surfeit* of trained manpower in any specific segment of our economy. The requirements of our country, as a free, democratic, secular, socialist, nation, *aspiring* for rapid development, *entail* a specific recipe for our educational institutions. Today's educational institutions must therefore be developed accordingly and must regulate themselves to give the country the precise nature and quantum of trained manpower as projected by the requirements of our planned economy.

1. The author has quoted thoughts of Confucious to stress
A. importance of planting trees for human beings
B. the worthless efforts in planting rice
C. the benefits of investing in education
D. the need for assessing manpower requirement

2. Which statement cannot be made on the basis of the passage?
A. Higher education should keep in view the requirements of national economy
B. Higher education has not been employed for nation building
C. All levels of education have a role to play in nation's growth
D. In our country we need to have a specially planned educational system

3. The writer believes that
A. there are no problems related to higher education
B. investment in education is of long-range
C. higher education should be used to assess manpower needs
D. aims of higher education in India are absolutely clear

4. The author's expectations from higher education, are essentially
A. unrealistic B. confusing
C. critical D. vague

5. The writer indicates that
A. higher education did not play any role in national growth
B. primary education did not play any role in national growth
C. our nation experiences paucity of trained manpower in many sectors
D. today's higher education has no precise goals to achieve

6. Author has used the word 'apparatus' to indicate the
A. scientific nature of education
B. complicated organization demanded by education
C. readily visible benefits of education
D. entire equipment of education to perform particular function

7. Which of the following has not been conveyed by the passage?
A. Education at any level can contribute in nation building
B. Manpower needs in many areas can be fulfilled through higher education
C. Rapid development of our nation is possible through higher education
D. Present higher education does not ensure surfeit of trained manpower

8. This passage is likely to be addressed to
   A. politicians only   B. scientists only
   C. students only   D. cannot be said

9. Choose a suitable title to the passage:
   A. Manpower Planning in India
   B. Importance of Higher Education
   C. Demands of Higher Education
   D. Role of Higher Education in India

Directions (Qs.10 to 12): *Choose the word which is most nearly the **SAME** in meaning as the word given in bold capitals as used in the passage.*

10. DOUBT
   A. suspicion   B. certain
   C. definite   D. sure

11. TERTIARY
   A. last   B. important
   C. third   D. terminal

12. ASPIRING
   A. inquiring   B. awaiting
   C. involving   D. striving

Directions (Qs.13 to 15): *Choose the word which is most **OPPOSITE** in meaning as the word given in bold capitals as used in the passage.*

13. PAUCITY
   A. moderate   B. enormity
   C. mediocrity   D. littleness

14. SURFEIT
   A. abundance   B. redundancy
   C. repletion   D. lack

15. ENTAIL
   A. entitled   B. ensure
   C. dismiss   D. retain

PASSAGE-10

Books are a great treasurehouse of knowledge. They are the living examples of man's *march* on the path to higher and higher civilisation. The great men who died long ago, live in their books. We feel their very personality and existence when we read their books. We feel as if they were conversing with us.

Books not only store civilization but also carry it forward. All coming generations get the light of knowledge from the books written by their ancestors and try to improve upon that knowledge. Civilization cannot make much *headway* in a country where there are not many *great* books. We get through books the latest knowledge in the fields of arts, science, commerce, etc. This knowledge is helpful to us and *enables* us to achieve success in the field of our choice.

Books are never failing friends. They never *desert* us, not even when all fair-weather friends have deserted us. They dispel the dark clouds of gloom from our minds and increase our happiness if we are already happy. Through the ages, the scriptures and other great books have provided immeasurable *solace* to the wounded and strife-torn humanity.

There may be books prescribed for some course or profession, but then there are books for general study. The books of literature—poetry, drama, novel, short stories, etc., are generally highly thrilling and inspiring if they are written by a good author. There may be tragic, comical or humorous books. The question is that of an individual's choice.

To be a lover of books, though not to be bookworm, is a sign of good luck. A voracious reader gets much *more pleasure* from reading books than a miser gets in hoarding money. The knowledge embedded in books is valueless; so is pleasure obtained from reading them. A good book absorbs the whole spirit of man; the reader's pleasure is indescribable.

1. Which of the following, according to the passage, is not true about books?
   A. They are source of inspiration
   B. They are source of knowledge
   C. They are source of happiness
   D. They are means of livelihood

2. How do the books help in progress of civilization?
   A. Based on the earlier books new knowledge is obtained
   B. The books provide solution to many problems
   C. The books inspire the scientists
   D. Not mentioned in the passage

3. How do the books make people more happy?
   A. They help the reader to overcome the shadows of uncertainty
   B. They help bring in joy by amusing the reader through their content
   C. They help the reader to understand the darker side of life
   D. Not mentioned in the passage

4. Which of the following is the author's view about the knowledge and pleasure derived from books?
   (*i*) We get more of knowledge and less of pleasure
   (*ii*) We get more of pleasure and less of knowledge
   (*iii*) We get knowledge and pleasure in equal measure
   A. only (*i*)   B. only (*ii*)
   C. either (*i*) or (*ii*)   D. only (*iii*)

5. The high quality of books produced by a country indicates:
   A. it has a high rate of literacy
   B. it has a progressive civilization
   C. it is not an industrialised nation
   D. it has learned ancestors

6. Why are the books, according to the passage, called never-failing friends?
   A. Books do not betray individuals
   B. Books are inanimate
   C. Books always give companionship to the reader
   D. Books are available in the market anytime unlike others
7. How do the books help in bringing peace in the minds of people?
   A. Books provide information about the past civilization
   B. Books help people learn to take correct steps with the help of the recorded information
   C. Books act as a window to the minds of the great men
   D. Not mentioned in the passage
8. Which of the following has been described as a sign of good luck?
   A. Being a miser
   B. Having lot of money
   C. Advancing the culture
   D. A passion for books

Directions (Qs. 9 to 12): *Choose the word which is most nearly the **SAME** in meaning as the word given in bold capitals as used in the passage.*

9. **SOLACE**
   A. peace B. tranquillity
   C. calmness D. console
10. **ENABLES**
   A. helps B. succeeds
   C. promotes D. stops
11. **HEADWAY**
   A. higher B. forge
   C. movement D. improve
12. **MARCH**
   A. move B. progress
   C. pass D. register

Directions (Qs. 13 to 15): *Choose the word which is most **OPPOSITE** in meaning of the word given in bold capitals as used in the passage.*

13. **GREAT**
   A. small B. thin
   C. short D. ordinary
14. **PLEASURE**
   A. displeasure B. pain
   C. happiness D. hardship
15. **DESERT**
   A. waterhole B. bitter
   C. accompany D. propel

ANSWERS

PASSAGE-1

1	2	3	4
A	B	A	A

PASSAGE-2

1	2	3	4	5
A	C	D	A	D

PASSAGE-3

1	2	3	4	5
A	D	C	D	A

PASSAGE-4

1	2	3	4	5	6
D	A	D	A	A	D

PASSAGE-5

1	2	3	4	5	6	7
A	D	A	A	A	C	B

PASSAGE-6

1	2	3	4	5
A	C	C	A	D
6	**7**	**8**	**9**	**10**
D	B	A	B	D

PASSAGE-7

1	2	3	4	5
C	C	D	B	D
6	**7**	**8**	**9**	**10**
A	A	D	D	B
11	**12**	**13**	**14**	**15**
A	D	D	B	C

PASSAGE-8

1	2	3	4	5
B	A	C	D	C
6	**7**	**8**	**9**	**10**
D	B	D	D	A
11	**12**	**13**	**14**	**15**
D	D	D	C	B

PASSAGE-9

1	2	3	4	5
D	D	C	D	D
6	**7**	**8**	**9**	**10**
D	A	D	B	A
11	**12**	**13**	**14**	**15**
C	D	B	D	C

PASSAGE-10

1	2	3	4	5
D	A	D	D	B
6	**7**	**8**	**9**	**10**
A	D	D	D	A
11	**12**	**13**	**14**	**15**
D	B	D	B	C

YOUR SPACE

HISTORY

ANCIENT INDIA

- The Story of the First Cities Harappan Archaeology
- Political and Economic History: How Inscriptions Tell a Story
- Social Histories Using the Mahabharata
- A History of Buddhism: Sanchi Stupa

SET-1

1. Who were the first people to paint the pottery of Indus Valley Civilisation?
A. Chalcolithic B. Mesolithic
C. Iron Age men D. Neolithic

2. The races are arranged taking into account their arrival in India. Pick out the chronologically correct sequence:
A. Aryan, Dravidian, Proto Australoid, Negrito
B. Negrito, Aryan, Proto Austrolaid, Dravidian
C. Negrito, Proto Australoid, Dravidian and Aryan
D. Dravidian, Aryan, Proto Australoid, Negrito

3. Which one of the following may be regarded as a remote possibility for the origin of the Indus Culture?
A. Kulli Culture
B. Nal Culture
C. Sumerian Culture
D. Culture of the Village People of the Punjab

4. Who was the archaeologist who came upon a seal with pictographic writing while excavating a Buddhist establishment at Mohenjo-daro?
A. R.D. Banerjee
B. N.G. Majumdar
C. Alexander Cunningham
D. Daya Ram Sahni

5. What was the political structure of the Indus Valley?
A. Oligarchy B. Federalism
C. Autocracy D. Theocracy

6. Identify the one that is common between Indus and Mesopotamian civilisations among the following:
A. Cylindrical seals
B. Bronze Age Culture
C. Planning towns with chess board system
D. Knives with ribs in the middle

7. Which of the following was not known to the Indus valley people?
A. Seasum B. Cotton
C. Potato D. Wheat

8. The humped Ox or Brahmani bull in the Indus valley was:
A. a monster B. a beast of burden
C. a sacred animal D. an unknown animal

9. What made the Harapans more away from urban settlements?
A. Foreign invasion B. Demographic factors
C. Ecological changes D. Hydrological changes

10. Which crop was the earliest to be cultivated by the people of Indus Valley?
A. Wheat B. Rice
C. Cotton D. Rye

11. The Harappan Civilisation was chiefly concentrated in:
A. Punjab, Rajasthan and Gujarat
B. Sindh, Punjab and Rajasthan
C. Haryana, Rajasthan and Tamil Nadu
D. Punjab, Rajasthan and Assam

12. The mature phase of the Harappan culture spanned aproximately:
A. 500 years B. 700 years
C. 300 years D. 1000 years

13. Indus valley skeletons reveal that the Harappans probably did not belong to one of the following races:
A. Mongoloid B. Alpine
C. Somite D. Proto-Austroloid

14. Which is controversial with regard to the granary in Harappa?
A. The urban non-agricultural population was fed on it.
B. Suggest private ownership.
C. It indicated that there was surplus production.
D. The whole affair was looked after by an agency.

15. "They (the Indus valley people) were not on the whole an artistic people". It has been commented by:
A. Dr. Romila Thapar B. Dr. A.D. Pusalkar
C. Dr. R.D. Mazumdar D. Dr. A.L. Basham

16. "Sindon" was the name given by the Greeks to one of the following items. Which one was it?
A. Jute B. Wool
C. Cotton D. None of these

17. The Indus valley people were:
A. Vegetarian
B. Non-vegetarian
C. Both non-vegetarian and vegetarian
D. Were not beef eaters

18. The Indus valley people were worshippers of:
A. Shiva B. Mitra
C. Varuna D. Mother Goddess

19. Pre-Harappan settlement was discovered in 1981 at the foot of the Bolan pass on the Bolan river at one of the following places. Identify it;
A. Mansa B. Manda
C. Mehergarh D. Alamgirpur

20. One thing is common among the following between the Indus and Mesopotamian civilisation. Identify:
A. Larger urban complex
B. Seals rolled on clay tablets
C. Ornamental architecture
D. Use of potter's wheel

21. Which among the following is not the distinctive pottery of the Indus people?
A. Black and Red ware B. Glazed
C. Painted Grey ware D. Poly chrome

22. What is the approximate area which covered the Indus civilisation?
A. 1,300,000 square kilometres
B. 600,000 square kilometres
C. 600 square kilometres
D. 6000 square kilometres

23. The metal which perhaps not known to the Indus valley people was?
A. Copper B. Iron
C. Tin D. Gold and Silver

24. Which of the following reasons was not a purpose of the Great Bath at Mohenjodaro?
A. community bathing
B. water sports and exercises
C. to store water during draughts
D. used during Rituals and Sacrifices

25. Which one of the following items was not used by the Indus valley people as their staple diet?
A. Dairy Products B. Dates
C. Wheat D. Refined Sugar

26. How many of the known 250 Indus Valley sites can be classified as cities?
A. Eight B. Six
C. Hundred D. Seven

27. The first excavation in the Indus valley at Mohenjo-daro was carried out in the years:
A. 1909 A.D. B. 1920 A.D.
C. 1922 A.D. D. 1955 A.D.

28. Which of the following is not a characteristic feature of the Indus valley pottery?
A. Red and black polished ware
B. Painted black designs
C. Vegetal and geometric patterns
D. None of the above

29. Well planned cities with all their common feature throughout Harappa suggest:
A. A single centralised state
B. Oligarchic commercial republic
C. Theoratic state
D. Free community

30. Kagzi refers to:
A. polychrome pottery B. egg-shell pottery
C. perforated pottery D. special paper for writing

31. Which of the following statement on the Harappan civilisation is controversial?
A. Harappan civilisation may be called peasant urban
B. It is not certain whether there was any closeness between the Indus urban areas and the country-side peasants.
C. Indus cities depended on their existence on food and raw material obtained from the country-side.
D. Indus cities provided marketing centres.

32. Which statement on the Harappan culture is incorrect?
A. The antiquities in all the seven layers at Mohenjo-daro are homogeneous.
B. There is no deterioration of masonary in the later occupation of the cities.
C. It is essentially a riverine culture.
D. Discovery of weapons in the later levels of Mohenjo-daro points to threat to life.

33. The jewellers of the Harappan civilisation primarily used two metals:
1. Bronze 2. Silver
3. Copper 4. Gold
Choose the correct answer from the codes given below:
A. 1 and 2 B. 2 and 3
C. 3 and 4 D. 2 and 4

34. The first concern of the Harappan town planners was:
A. to protect their cities from frequent floods
B. to make citadels to protect themselves from the enemies
C. to produce enough food surplus to feed towns
D. to develop sea-borne trade

35. Which of the the following statement on the men and women of the Indus valley is Not correct?
A. Men wore long hair.

B. Men wore robes but left one shoulder bare.
C. Women wore large necklaces but very light bangles.
D. The coiffeurs of women-were often elaborate.

36. Most unique feature of the Indus valley civilisation, the like of which has not yet been found in any other city of the same antiquity is:
A. weights and measures B. drainage system
C. cultivation of land D. double-story houses

37. Strike out which is not an important feature of Harappan culture.
A. Horse racing
B. Peace-loving community
C. Efficient civic organisation
D. Love for indoor hobbies, jewellery and cosmetics, dancing

38. The most intriguing thing about the Indus valley women is:
A. their jewellery
B. their foundness for handicrafts
C. their vanity
D. the care they bestowed on children

39. Which one of the following arts and crafts was not practised by the Harappans?
A. Masonry B. Seal cutting
C. Carpentry D. Iron-mongering

40. Paint out the incorrect statement:
A. Harappan probably did not practise canal irrigation
B. Whether or not the plough was used is controversial
C. Pesticides were invariably used
D. Enough surplus food was produced to feed the town dwellers

41. Which of the following was not an item of import for the Indus people?
A. Tin B. Copper
C. Textile D. Lapis Liazuli

42. The Harappan culture belongs to the Bronze Age. Which two metals are mixed to make this alloy?
1. Copper 2. Zinc
3. Brass 4. Tin
A. 1 and 2 only B. 1 and 3 only
C. 4 only D. None of these

43. Which of the following was not a feature of internal trade at the Harappans?
A. Trade was multifaceted.
B. It was opened on regional and inter-regional levels.
C. It was purely a barter-trade.
D. It was a guild system coupled with nomadic people.

44. No temples, or public places of worship, or monumental sculptures have been found at Harappan cities. This indicates that:
A. religion was a state or public affair.
B. the Harappans were atheists.
C. religion was more personal and private affair.
D. they were sceptical in disposition.

45. Which one of the following is false with regard to Harappan people?
A. The statues of Mother Goddess were crudely fashioned.
B. Tiny monkeys and squirrels were used as pinhead beds.
C. The statues of women were fully clothed with elaborate head-dresses.
D. For children they made monkeys sliding down a string, whistles and gods were made like birds etc.

46. Which West Asian site is associated with the discovery of a bale of cloth evidently an export from Harappan India?
A. Ur B. Umma
C. Susa D. Lagash

47. Evidence of the horse comes from which of the following Harappan sites?
A. Harappa, Lothal, Kalibangan
B. Lothal, Surkotada
C. Mohenjo-daro, Lothal, Banwali
D. Banwali, Ropar, Surkotada

48. The Indus valley people do not use one of the following weapons. What is that?
A. Swords B. Spears
C. Arrow-heads D. Axes

49. Which cults did the Harappan practise?
1. Fire 2. Female diety
3. Fertility 4. Fetism
A. Only 2 and 3 B. Only 1 and 2
C. 1, 2 and 3 D. All of these

50. The discovery, in the upper levels of a Harappan site, of human skeletons lying bell-mell, with a skull having injury mark, shows the invasion and massacre. What is that site?
A. Mohenjo-daro B. Harappa
C. Banawali D. Kalibangan

51. The main food crops of the Harappan were:
A. Wheat and Barley B. Wheat and Bajra
C. Maize and Wheat D. Wheat and Rice

52. Dwellers of Mohenjo-daro:
A. were utilitarians
B. were expert in carpenter's crafts
C. were aesthetes
D. loved ideas of luxury

53. Which expression does not apply to the Harappan culture?
A. Standardisation
B. Materialistic achievements
C. Homogeneity
D. Desire to emulate others

54. One feature of the Indus valley civilisation was not rivalled by any other civilisation till the time of the Romans. Indentify it.
A. The Great Bath B. Sewage system
C. Use of cosmetics D. Worship of some dieties

55. What is special about the Indus valley urban centres discovered in Saurashtra, Gujarat and Kathiawar?
A. horse known
B. discovery of wood-works
C. ship-building was known
D. cross influence between Harappan culture and local cultures of Chalcolithic nature.

56. Absence of windows in the Harappan houses implied that Harappan women were kept in strict seclusion is:
A. Proved fact B. Disproved
C. Controversial D. None of these

57. That the Indus women used rouge and Lipstick is:
A. Proved B. Disproved
C. Debatable D. None of these

58. The Harappan cultivated the Land with:
A. hoe
B. plough share
C. hoe and plough share
D. either hoe or plough share or some other tool not known to us

59. Which was not a Harappan port?
A. Balakot B. Sutkagendor
C. Sotka Koh D. Kalibangan

60. The Indus valley belonged to:
A. Mediterranean race
B. Proto-Astraloid race
C. Tibetan Mongoloid race
D. Alpine race

61. The important public place discovered at Mohenjo-daro was:
A. the great bath B. the great granary
C. the great cementery D. the acropolis

62. Kalibanga is situated in:
A. Madhya Pradesh B. Rajasthan
C. Karnataka D. Baluchistan

63. Lothal in the Indus valley was famous as a/an:
A. port
B. administrative centre
C. place where graneries have been found
D. religious centre

64. The concept of decimal system as a measuring unit of length was:
A. Known to the Indus valley people due to their contacts with the Egyptians.
B. known to the Indus valley people, and was not borrowed.
C. not known to the Indus valley people
D. none of the above

65. The Indus valley people were not familiar with:
A. Cotton B. Barley
C. Tobacco D. Wheat

66. Where is Lothal situated?
A. Pakistan B. Gujarat
C. Rajasthan D. Haryana

67. Which of the following statement is incorrect?
A. The Indus valley people worshipped linga and yoni
B. The Indus valley people worshipped the pipal tree
C. The Indus valley people worshipped Mother Goddess
D. The Indus valley people performed horse sacrifices

68. Mohenjo-daro is situated in:
A. Sindh province of Pakistan
B. Gujarat State of India
C. Afghanistan
D. Punjab State of India

69. At one of the sites of the Indus valley civilisation a dockyard has been discovered. Which is that site?
A. Rangpur B. Kalibangan
C. Lothal D. Ropar

70. Which one of the following is not one of the Harappan sites related to the maritime activities of the Harappan people?
A. Sotka Koh B. Desalpur
C. Balakot D. Lothal

71. The social group in which the Indus valley people lived were:
A. Peasants, hunters, traders and labourers.
B. The learned ones, warriors, traders, artisans and manual workers.
C. Brahmans, Kshatriyas, Vaisyas and Sudras
D. None of these

72. At how many places have the Indus valley finds been discovered?
A. 250 sites B. 2 sites
C. 10 sites D. 50 sites

73. Which among the following is common design between Mohenjo-daro and Baluchistan pottery?
A. Animal designs
B. Geometrical design
C. Floral designs
D. Svastika

74. Which among the width of the widest streets of the Mohenjo-daro is correct? (Approximately)
A. 10 metres B. 20 metres
C. 15 metres D. 8 metres

75. Some of the streets of the Indus cities ran straight even upto:
A. 200 metres B. 800 metres
C. 400 metres D. 600 metres

76. Which kind of bricks is not found among the Indus cities?
A. Sawn bricks B. Rectangular
C. Wedge shaped D. Square

77. Where was the vanity case found?
A. Harappa B. Lothal
C. Kot Diji D. Mohenjo-daro

78. One of the following structures is not found in Harappa. Identify it:
A. Granary B. Citadel
C. Storied houses D. Great bath

79. The local name of Mohenjo-daro is:
A. mound of the living B. mound of the great
C. mound of the dead D. mound of bones

80. Which statement on Kalibangan is Not Correct?
A. Pre-Harappan phase here shows that fields were ploughed in Rajasthan.
B. It is only here that fire-altars belonging to Harappan period have been discovered.
C. The lower Harappan town at Kalibangan is fortified.
D. Drying of the river Ghaggar caused its decline.

81. In 1958 a cursory digging extended Harappan frontiers in the east upto a place near to Meerut in UP. Identify the place:
A. Alamgirpur B. Banwali
C. Ropar D. Sutkagendor

82. The Harappans imported Lapis Lazuli, jade and turquoise from:
A. Khetri and Kolar
B. Mesopotamia
C. Badakshan, the Pamirs and Khorasan
D. Khorasan and Khetri

83. A terracotta model of ship with a stick impressed socket for the mast and eyeholes for fixing come from:
A. Lothal B. Surkotada
C. Harappa D. Mohenjo-daro

84. "The enemy of the Harappans was nature .... India and the barbarians hordes are exonerated". Whose view is this?
A. M. Wheeler's B. G.F. Dale's
C. Marshall's D. Mackey's

85. The birds worshipped by the Harappans were:
A. dove and pigeon
B. dove and peacock
C. pigeon and peacock
D. pigeon, dove and peacock

86. A scale has been found at which of the Harappan sites?
A. Harappa B. Lothal
C. Mohenjo-daro D. Surkotada

87. In which age were the Copper and Stone implements used?
A. Neolithic B. Chalcolithic
C. Microlithic D. Mesolithic

88. Who is considered as father of Indian Archaeology?
A. Alexander B. Lord Curzon
C. Mortimer Wheeler D. John Marshall

89. The Indus people were probably ruled by:
A. Kings
B. Priests
C. Merchants
D. An assemble of elected elders

90. Which of the following statement regarding the Indus valley people is very revealing?
A. Their script remain unchanged throughout their history.
B. They were in contact with Mesopotamia.
C. Their civilisation was possibly theocratic just like the Egyptains and Mesopotamians.
D. They learnt nothing from Mesopotamia.

91. The terracotta figures of men and women squatting with their arms folded round their knees and wearing round caps on their heads were probably those of:
A. Prisoners B. Slaves
C. Labourers D. Cultivators

92. 'Swastika' is symbol of:
A. Sangam origin B. Indus valley origin
C. Aryan origin D. None of the above

93. Which was the backbone of the Indus economy?
A. agriculture B. trade
C. carpentry D. wheel made pottery

94. Crude ochre colour pottery (though its origin is uncertain), discovered from the Yamuna-Gangetic Doab, has been associated with:
A. the migrant Harappans
B. the early Aryans
C. the later Aryans
D. the Mauryas

95. The most popular form of burial at Mohenjo-daro was:
A. complete burial B. fractional burial
C. post cremation burial D. cremation

96. The disapearance of Indus valley civilisation was most probably because of:
A. diverse reasons B. the floods of the Indus
C. Aryan invaders D. unknown invaders

97. One possible factor you may not accept as responsible for the 'eclipse' of the Indus civilisation is:
A. over population
B. over cultivation hence decrease in fertility
C. fluctuations of salinity because of shift of the riverine situation
D. deforestation

98. According to Dr. S.R. Rao, the Indus script, originally a mixed writing of 62 signs including pictures was disciplind into an alphabetic script of:

A. 22 signs B. 26 signs
C. 30 signs D. 24 signs

99. Indus script is:
A. bonstrophedon B. indeographic
C. cuneiform D. logographic

100. Indus seals:
A. were purely secular in character
B. were used as means of exchange by Harappans
C. reveal their religions character
D. were exported in big numbers

ANSWERS

1	2	3	4	5	6	7	8	9	10
A	C	C	A	D	B	C	C	D	C
11	**12**	**13**	**14**	**15**	**16**	**17**	**18**	**19**	**20**
A	C	C	A	A	C	C	D	C	D
21	**22**	**23**	**24**	**25**	**26**	**27**	**28**	**29**	**30**
C	A	B	C	D	B	C	D	A	B
31	**32**	**33**	**34**	**35**	**36**	**37**	**38**	**39**	**40**
B	B	B	A	C	B	A	C	D	C
41	**42**	**43**	**44**	**45**	**46**	**47**	**48**	**49**	**50**
C	B	C	C	C	B	B	A	D	A
51	**52**	**53**	**54**	**55**	**56**	**57**	**58**	**59**	**60**
A	A	D	B	D	C	A	C	D	A
61	**62**	**63**	**64**	**65**	**66**	**67**	**68**	**69**	**70**
A	B	A	B	C	B	D	A	C	B
71	**72**	**73**	**74**	**75**	**76**	**77**	**78**	**79**	**80**
A	A	D	A	B	D	A	D	C	B
81	**82**	**83**	**84**	**85**	**86**	**87**	**88**	**89**	**90**
A	C	A	B	A	B	B	A	C	D
91	**92**	**93**	**94**	**95**	**96**	**97**	**98**	**99**	**100**
B	B	A	A	A	A	A	B	D	B

SET-2

1. Who applied the name India to our country?
A. Aryans B. Persians
C. Greeks D. English

2. What is Avesta?
A. It is a name of Vedic God
B. It is a place in Iran
C. It is the religious book of the ancient Iranians
D. It is a place in Central Asia

3. The main source of livelihood of the Rigvedic people was?
A. Agriculture B. Cattle breeding
C. Poultry D. Animal husbandry

4. The word "Aryan" derived are in the vedic period meant:
A. superior
B. cultured
C. foreigners or strangers
D. noble

5. Who gave the Siva Cult to India?
A. Mongoloids B. Proto-Australoids
C. Dravidians D. Aryans

6. Who among the following was the first to suggest the similarity between Sanskrit language of Aryans, Greeks and Latin?
A. Sir Williams Jones B. Monier Williams
C. Max Muller D. None of the above

7. Which was not the cause of Aryans Victory over the Dasas or Dasyus?
A. use of chariots in war
B. use of horses in war
C. use of metal armours and helmets
D. use of elephant in war

8. Marriage by Purchase was called:
A. Paisach B. Rakshasa
C. Asura D. Gandharva

9. Initially the Aryans cleared the land by means of:
A. fire B. bronze axe
C. iron axe D. wooden plough

10. "The country that lies North of the ocean and south of the snowy mountains is called Bharata. From which text is this description taken?
A. Rig-Ved B. Ramayana
C. Mahabharata D. Vayu Purana

11. In which records do you find the use of the word Hindu for Sindhu?
A. Greeks B. Persian
C. Sumerian D. Egyptian

12. Probably slavery originated in:
A. Rig vedic period B. Later vedic period
C. Mauryan period D. Post-Mauryan period

13. The discovery of inscriptions at Bogazkoi in Asia Minor is not about.
A. The treaty between the kings of the Hitties and the Mitanis.
B. The vedic gods Indra, Mitra, Varuna and the Asvins who are invoked to uphold the treaty.
C. determining the age of Rig-veda.
D. description of gods worshipped by later vedic age.

14. What is the importance of Avesta for vedic period?
A. The words, phrases, stanzas, myths and legends in it suggest the similarity between Rig veda and Avesta and that the ancestors of the Hindus and the Persians had lived together for a long time.
B. It has no importance to understand vedic culture.
C. It shows the culture exchange between ancient Iranians and Rig-vedic people.
D. It shows close similarity between the physical features of the Iranians-Aryan and the vedic-Aryan.

15. The Brahmis spoke a language similar to the language spoken by:
A. Khasis B. Dravidians
C. Aryans D. Bhutiyas

16. Upanayana, the ceremony of initiation started during:
A. Later vedic-period B. Rig-vedic period
C. The Maurya period D. The Pallava period

17. The caste-system became rigid with the stringent laws on the Shudras which meant restrictions on—
A. the right to learn vedas
B. the sacred thread ceremony
C. the right to own property
D. the right to engage themselves in trade and commerce

18. The varna-based social division first appeared in:
A. 300 BC – 100 BC B. Later vedic period
C. Rig-vedic period D. Mauryan period

19. Which points regarding Rigvedic woman is not correct?
A. She had to perform Symbolic self-immolation at the death of her husband.
B. She enjoyed an honourable position.
C. She had to burn herself on her husband's pyre.
D. She received education.

20. The Rig-vedic society was mainly:
A. a pastoral society B. a food gathering society
C. a migrating society D. a tribal society

21. The two epics, the Ramayana and the Mahabharata are concerned with events which took place between:
A. 300 and 100 B.C. B. 700 and 300 B.C.
C. 1000 and 500 B.C. D. 1000 and 700 B.C.

22. Which of the following was not one of the distinguished tribes of the later vedic-period?
A. Videhas B. Kurus
C. Bharatas D. Panchalas

23. The source of income of the Rig-vedic ruler was primarily:
A. Tributes B. Spoils of war
C. Agriculture taxes D. Pasturage tax

24. Chariot racing formed an important element of which one of the following sacrifices?
A. Rajasuya B. Vajapeya
C. Ashvamedha D. Agnihotra

25. The important characteristics of the vedic religion were:
1. Goddess like 'prithvi', 'Aditi' and 'Usha'
2. Goddess are co-equal to their male-partners
3. Predominance of male dieties.
4. Worship of nature.
Code:
A. only 3 and 4 B. only 2 and 4
C. only 1 and 4 D. only 1 and 3

26. Which of the following statement is not correct regarding Indra?
A. He was the god exclusively associated with sacrifices.
B. He was known as 'Purandara'
C. He killed the evil dragon 'Virata'
D. He was the god of Thunder

27. Which of the following was not a factor responsible for the proliferation of castes in ancient India?
A. Guilds
B. Development of new crafts
C. Tribal affiliations
D. To maintain social purity

28. Which of the following are known as Brahmanas?
A. The original texts of the vedas
B. Explanatory prose manuals relating to prayer and sacrificial ceremony

C. Commentaries appended to the Aryans dealing with philosophic questions.
D. Books dealing with worship and contemplation meant for wood dwelling hermits.

29. Which one of the following abstract deities of the vedic religion has been admired most in the Rig-veda?
A. Sraddha (faith)
B. Apsaras (water-nymphs)
C. Gandharvas (aerial spirits)
D. Usha (goddes of dawn)

30. Which of the following statements about the vedic-king is correct?
A. The Mantri Parishad exercised check over the authority of the king.
B. Samiti and Sabha exercised check over the authority of the king.
C. There was no check on the authority of the king.
D. The people directly exercised control over the king.

31. In which veda do we find reference to locked waters and water wheels?
A. Rig-veda B. Yajur-veda
C. Sam-veda D. Atharva-veda

32. The battle of ten kings is mentioned in which of the chapters of Rig-veda?
A. Book VII B. Book III
C. Book I D. Book X

33. Among amusements the Aryans gave first place to:
A. Dice B. Chariot-race
C. Music D. Dance

34. "In the utmost need I cooked the entrails of a dog among the gods I found no protection, I held my wife in degradation" who said this in the Rig-vedic period?
A. a brahmin B. a kshatriya
C. a vaishya D. a non-Aryan

35. The charioteers or sutas are thought to have spring from the marriage of:
A. Shudras and Brahmin women
B. Kshatriyas and Brahmin women
C. Vaishyas and Kshatriyas women.
D. Vaishyas and Brahmin women.

36. Which of the following propounded the theory of a doubled invasion of India by Aryans at different periods of history?
A. Dr. Giles B. Dr. Hoernle
C. Sir George Grierson D. C.V. Vaidya

37. Which of the following is not correct about Aryan movement towards South?
A. Indo-Aryan conquest of northern India never affected peninsular portion of the country.
B. According to tradition, it was the vedic sage Agastya, who introduced Aryan ideas to the Dravidians.
C. Indo-Aryans made spiritual conquest of the south.
D. By peaceful penetration and not by sword, they succeeded in carrying their ideas and civilization to the farthest Corners of the south.

38. The vedic mountain "Mujavant" was the home of:
A. all gods
B. Indra
C. Soma
D. herbs and medicinal plants

39. Which of the following region was called "Aryavarta"?
A. From Yamuna upto West Bengal
B. Punjab and Delhi Region
C. The whole of northern India
D. The region beyond Vindhya mountain

40. In India Varna law enjoyed:
A. Legal Sanction only
B. Religions Sanction only
C. Economic Sanction only
D. The Sanction of both the state and religion

41. Which of the following god was borrowed by the Aryans from the Indus valley civilization?
A. Pashupti B. Hanuman
C. Ganesh D. Kartikeya

42. Which of the following is an Upanishad?
A. Dhammapada B. Mahabhashya
C. Svetasvatar D. Milindapandha

43. What was the common form of Govt. during the Rigvedic period?
A. Parliamentary form of government
B. Presidential form of government
C. Military Dictatorship
D. Hereditary Monarchy

44. The Purusha-Sukta of the Rigveda contains:
A. Mantras in praise of Rudra
B. Mantras in praise of Usha
C. Rules of horse sacrifice
D. Mantras about the creation of the universe

45. Which of the following statements about the teaching of the Upanishad is incorrect?
A. They believe in the existence of a supreme all pervading universal soul.
B. They believe in rebirth.
C. They believe that moksha can be achieved by means of the knowledge of the ultimate reality.
D. They believe that moksha can be achieved by means of animal sacrifices.

46. Which of the following is correct?
A. The Upnishads denied the existence of an all pervading supreme universal soul.
B. The Upanishads believed in the transmigration of soul.

C. The Upanishads believed in animal sacrifices as means to attaining salvation.
D. The Upanishads did not believe in the theory of karma.

47. The vedic God in charge of right, truth and moral order (Rita) was:
A. Varuna B. Indra
C. Dyaus D. Prajapati

48. What was the centre of Aryan civilization during the later vedic-age?
A. Karnataka
B. Sindhu
C. Rajasthan
D. The territory between the Saraswati and Ganga

49. What was the name of the king to whom all the early Aryan dynasties traced their origin?
A. Parasuram B. Sri Krishna
C. Sri Ram Chandra D. Manu – Vaivaswata

50. The term Sudra is mentioned in the Rig-Veda only once. How many times does the term 'Vaisya appear in the Rig Veda?
A. 9 times B. 10 times
C. 3 times D. Only once

51. Which musical instrument was not known to the Aryans?
A. drum B. tabla
C. flute D. harp

52. The Caste System was prevalent in the vedic age. Which of the following shows the four-fold division of the society?
A. Satpatha Brahmana
B. Atharvaveda
C. Purush-Sukta of Rigveda
D. Yajurveda

53. The term "Jana" is used 275 times in the Rigveda. How many times the term "Janapada" is used in the Rigveda?
A. 275 times B. 300 times
C. only twice D. Not even once

54. Bali was the name of the voluntary offering during Rigvedic period but when it became the compulsory tax?
A. Sangama Period B. Buddhist Period
C. Later Vedic Period D. Mauryan Period

55. The institution of "gotra" appear in:
A. Rigvedic period B. Buddhist period
C. Mauryan period D. Later vedic period

56. Which of the following vedas refers to the roat 'Kri' (to purchase) and 'Vanija' (to merchant) and also mentions haggling in the market?
A. Rig Veda B. Sam Veda
C. Yajur Veda D. Atharva Veda

57. Which Veda mentions the following terms: garments (dursa), coverlets (pavasta), barter (prapana), sale (Vikraya), exchange of merchandise (partipana)?
A. Rigveda B. Samveda
C. Yajurveda D. Atharvaveda

58. The change of "Aryanism" from the "Vedic" stage to Brahamanic stage, was marked by:
A. Incorporation of non-aryan features into Aryan society
B. Evolution of Caste hierarchy
C. Transformation from semi-nomadic pastoral economy to settle agrarian economy
D. All of the above

59. The bards or magadhas descended from:
A. Shudra fathers and brahman mothers
B. Kashtriya fathers and brahman mothers
C. Vaishya fathers and kashtriya mothers
D. Shudra fathers and kashtriya mothers

60. Which was not a primary duty of every Aryan?
A. Adhyayana B. Yajna
C. Dan D. Tapa

61. Which of the following had the most esteemed place in vedic village life and economy?
A. Carpenter B. Bronze-Smith
C. Potter D. Weaver

62. Who was the second in importance during the later-vedic period?
A. Carpenter
B. Metal-worker or iron-smith
C. Tanner
D. Weaver

63. The initiation of a brahman boy ordinarily took place in his:
A. 6th year B. 8th year
C. 10th year D. 12th year

64. The concept of Karma, in course of time, meant maintenance of the:
A. Dharma B. Natural laws
C. Social order D. Caste Laws

65. Which one of the feminine institutions was not rejected by the Aryans?
A. Matriarchy B. Polyandry
C. Worship of goddesses D. None of the above

66. Among the Hindus, marriage is:
A. a sacrament
B. a contract
C. a sacrament as well as a contract
D. violable

67. The 'Rajan' or king during early vedic period could NOT claim or receive.
A. regular taxes
B. portain of war booty

C. voluntary gifts
D. None of the above

68. Who was Ganapati in the vedic period?
A. a god B. priest
C. head of Aryan group D. a demi-God

69. According to the vedic texts like the Rig-Veda and Atharvaveda the king was:
A. Elected B. Chosen by lots
C. Hereditary D. Victor in a great battle

70. In the Rig-Vedic Society, gopa or gopati was the epithet given to the:
A. king B. head of the family
C. wealthy man D. brahmana

71. Abhiseka ceremony replaced which one of the following rites in due course of time?
A. Asvamedha B. Vajapeya
C. Rajasuya D. None of the above

72. With whom did the people in later vedic period deposit the taxes?
A. Bhagadugha B. Gramani
C. Sangrihita D. Prajapati

73. The doctrine of royal divinity was explicitly proclaimed for the first time in:
A. Epics B. Manu-Smriti
C. Vedas D. Six Darshana

74. During the later vedic period the eastern kings were known as:
A. Samrats B. Rajas
C. Bhojas D. Virats

75. The salient feature of the Rig-vedic civilization was the worship of:
A. Nature B. Mother Goddess
C. Trinity D. Pashupati

76. The chief impact of the vedic culture of Indian History was:
A. Progress of philosophy and religion
B. Rise of other wordly outlook
C. Rise of democratic theories
D. Growth of Sanskrit-literature

77. The metals which were used by the later vedic Aryans were:
A. Silver, gold-copper, iron and brass
B. Silver, gold and copper only
C. Silver and gold only
D. Silver and copper only

78. The Aryans came to India from outside and first settled in:
A. Punjab B. U.P.
C. Delhi D. Panchala

79. The original home of the Aryans, according to Lokmanya Balgangadhar Tilak was:
A. Central Asia B. Tibet
C. Arctic region D. Kashmir

80. Brihadaranyaka is:
A. A Smriti
B. An Upanishada
C. A treatise on Political Science
D. A Mahakavya

81. Which of the following are not included in the Vedic-literature?
A. Samhitas B. Aranyakas
C. Smritis D. Upanishadas

82. Which of the following is correct?
A. According to the vedic thinkers, monarch was the ultimate source of law
B. According to the vedic thinkers, people were the ultimate source of law
C. According to the vedic thinkers, the nature was the ultimate source of law
D. According to the vedic thinkers, Dharma, which sustained the world, was the ultimate source of law.

83. The concensus among historians that the vedic age began earliest in:
A. 1200 – 1000 BC B. 2500 – 800 BC
C. 2500 BC D. 1000 BC

84. Which of the following failed to develop into a city during later vedic age?
A. Indraprastha B. Mathura
C. Prayag D. Kashi

85. The most widely accepted dates of the composition of Rig-Veda is:
A. 1500 BC to 1000 BC B. 1500 BC
C. About 45000 BC D. 100 BC

86. According to Bhagavatism, there are .... incarnations of Vishnu:
A. six B. eight
C. ten D. twelve

87. The oldest Indian linguistic text is:
A. Mahabharat B. Ashtadhyayi
C. Ramayana D. Nirukta

88. "War begins in the minds of men." In which of the following books the above statement is stated?
A. Mundaka Upanishad
B. Atharvada (Atharvaveda)
C. Samaveda
D. Rigveda

89. The Caste System during the early vedic age:
A. Prohibited only interdining but not intermarriage
B. Prohibited interdining and intermarriages
C. Did not prohibit interdining and intermarriages
D. None of these

90. The philosophy of Upanishads emphasis on:
A. Bhakti B. Gyan
C. Karma D. Tapa

91. Who was the first poet of India?
A. Valmiki
B. Vyasa
C. Kalidas
D. Vashishta

92. The most common crime during the vedic period was:
A. theft, particularly cattle-stealing
B. murder
C. highway robbery
D. rakshasa marriage

93. The scared thread which the Brahman wore was made of
A. Silk
B. Wool
C. Hemp
D. Cotton

94. Which statement about an asceticism is correct?
A. The Atharva Veda after refers to ascetics as Vratyas
B. By the time of the Upanishads, asceticism was widespread
C. Vratya was a priest of non-vedic fertility cult which involved ritual dancing and flagellation
D. All of the above

95. The speculation of the upanishads centre around one word of the Rig veda which one is that?
A. Prajapati
B. Varuna
C. Brahman
D. Indra

96. Which statements on the status and bringing up of children in ancient India is correct?
A. Three personal ceremonies were performed before birth "garbhadhana" to promote conception, "Pumsavama" to procure a male child, and "Simanton-nayana" to ensure the safety of the child in the womb.
B. The birth ceremony or the "Jatakarma" took place before the cutting of the unbilical cord.
C. Usually during the six months of the child the ceremony of (annaprasana) feeling of solid food was celebrated while the tonsure (culakarma) took place in the third year for only boys.
D. All of the above.

97. Which practices were not in existence during the Rig-vedic period?
A. Dowry
B. Child-marriage
C. Divorce
D. Widow-marriage

98. What is the name of that God, who is known by the name of 'Asura' and is possibly the same as Ahura Mazda in the Zoroastrian religion?
A. Agni
B. Varuna
C. Prajapati
D. Rudra

99. Gold, copper and bronze were found during the Rigvedic age. Which of the following was also known during that age?
A. Nishka
B. Satmana
C. Suvarna
D. Krishnala

100. A God who is described amoral, and object of fear archer God whose arrows caused disease, connected with the storm, and the guardian of healing herbs is known as:
A. Yama
B. Varuna
C. Indra
D. Rudra

ANSWERS

1	2	3	4	5	6	7	8	9	10
C	C	C	D	C	A	D	C	A	D
11	**12**	**13**	**14**	**15**	**16**	**17**	**18**	**19**	**20**
B	A	D	A	B	A	B	B	C	B
21	**22**	**23**	**24**	**25**	**26**	**27**	**28**	**29**	**30**
D	C	B	B	A	A	D	B	D	B
31	**32**	**33**	**34**	**35**	**36**	**37**	**38**	**39**	**40**
A	A	B	A	B	B	A	C	B	D
41	**42**	**43**	**44**	**45**	**46**	**47**	**48**	**49**	**50**
A	C	D	D	D	B	A	B	D	D
51	**52**	**53**	**54**	**55**	**56**	**57**	**58**	**59**	**60**
B	C	D	C	D	A	D	D	C	D
61	**62**	**63**	**64**	**65**	**66**	**67**	**68**	**69**	**70**
A	B	B	D	C	A	A	C	A	A
71	**72**	**73**	**74**	**75**	**76**	**77**	**78**	**79**	**80**
C	A	A	A	A	A	A	A	C	B
81	**82**	**83**	**84**	**85**	**86**	**87**	**88**	**89**	**90**
C	D	D	A	A	C	D	B	C	B
91	**92**	**93**	**94**	**95**	**96**	**97**	**98**	**99**	**100**
A	A	D	D	C	D	B	B	A	D

SET-3

1. According to the Buddhist traditions the four great signs transformed the life of Gautama. Which one of the following is known as the "Four Great Signs"?
A. The "four noble Truths".
B. The sights of old age, disease, death and a medicant.
C. The four heavenly signs which accompanied the birth of the Buddha.
D. None of these.

2. Who said this: "The Buddha would have made a good general if he had not become a monk"?
A. Charles Eliat B. Vincent Smith
C. Rhyas Davids D. Romila Thaper

3. What was the name given to those who gave a demonstration of the incidents mentioned in the plays?
A. Sobhanikas B. Ganikas
C. Sthanikas D. Granthikas

4. What does the Stupa symbolise?
A. Evanescence of this world
B. Piety of the Buddha
C. Sanctity of the Buddha
D. Bhakti

5. Mahayana Buddhism originated in:
A. Andhra Pradesh, 1st Century B.C.
B. Bihar, 1st Century A.D.
C. Kashmir, 3rd Century B.C.
D. Bengal, 2nd Century A.D.

6. Where has the Rummindei Pillar been erected?
A. The birth place of the Buddha
B. The place where he preached his eirmon first
C. The place where the Buddha died
D. The place where he attained enlightenment

7. The third Buddhist council was held at Patliputra during the reign of Ashoka, 236 years after the death of Buddha to revise the Scriptures. Which of the following Pitaka was added to the existing two in this council?
A. Sutta Pitakas B. Abhidhamma Pitakas
C. Vinaya Pitakas D. None of these

8. Which of the following is not one of the "Four Noble Sentiments" that a person aspiring for 'nirvana' should cultivate?
A. Karuna of Compassion
B. Metta or Universal love
C. Mudita or Sympathetic joy
D. Upekkha or equanimity

9. Who said this—"Karma acts as a very pragmatic God".
A. The Buddha B. Mahavira
C. Parsva D. Upnishads

10. Which of the following has the bull capital?
A. Rampurva B. Sarnath
C. Lumbini D. Amaravati

11. Name the Greek ambassador at the court of Bindusara.
A. Megasthenes B. Heliodorus
C. Diamaehus D. Menander

12. Where is the Lomasa Rishi Cave?
A. Barabar Area B. Ellora
C. Bhaja D. Amaravati

13. Who said that the Indians did not drink (liquor) in the age of the Mauryas?
A. Megasthenes B. Arrian
C. Strabo D. Pliny

14. Where is the finest of the toranas found?
A. Kerala B. Sanchi
C. Bedsa D. Nagarjuni hills

15. Which one of the following has the quadripartite semi-lions on top?
A. Rampurva B. Lauriya Nandangarh
C. Sarnath D. Amaravati

16. Name the inscription in which the name of the contemporary rulers of the west are given.
A. Rock Edict XIII B. Rock Edict IX
C. Pillar Edict VII D. Bhabra Edict

17. Mahayanism has faith in:
A. Defication of the Buddha and icon worship.
B. Elaborate rituals
C. The Boddhisattavas and devotion to them
D. All of the above

18. Which one of the following councils made Sanskrit the vehicle of Buddhist scriptures?
A. first B. second
C. third D. fourth

19. Who is regarded as the founder of "Shunyavad"?
A. Vasumitra B. Nagarjuna
C. Ashvaghosha D. Upali

20. Which element of Mahayana Buddhism particularly distinguishes it from the Hinayana?
A. Liberal attitude B. Bodhisattava ideal
C. Absolutist philosophy D. Divinity of Buddha

21. The Buddhist doctrine of "Prittyasamut Pada" or dependent origination contained in the second Noble Truth explains.
A. The path which leads to cessation of suffering.
B. The interconnection between desire, suffering and rebirth.
C. The momentariness of all worldly things.
D. The eight fold path very clearly.

22. Who has called Bindusara as Amitrachates?
A. Athenaeus B. Justin
C. Strabo D. Pliny

23. Match the following :

(*a*) Vijnanavada	1. Hinayana
(*b*) Shunyavada	2. Madhyamika School
(*c*) Syadvada	3. Yogachara
(*d*) Sthavirvada	4. Sapta-bhanginaya

	(*a*)	(*b*)	(*c*)	(*d*)
A.	3	2	4	1
B.	3	4	2	1
C.	1	2	3	4
D.	2	1	3	4

24. Who were described as the Pancha-ratrikas?
A. Bhagbatas B. Pasupatas
C. Digambaras D. Hinayanists

25. What word was used in the 6th century B.C. for a man who attained full holiness?
A. Svargi B. Nirvani
C. Arhant D. Buddha

26. Which one of the following was added to Buddhist canonical texts by the fourth council?
A. Jatakas B. Vibhashas
C. Dhammapada D. Kathavatthu, Prakarna

27. Early Schism in Buddhism divided the Buddhist order into:
A. Sthavirvadins and Mahasanghikas
B. Mahasanghikas Sunyavadins
C. Sunyavadins and Sarvastivadins
D. Sthavirvadins and Sarvastivadins

28. The Bhabru Edict records Ashoka's faith in:
A. Tisaranam
B. Toleration
C. Dharmaviiya
D. Solicitude for the Welfare of the people

29. The term 'Piyadassi' occurring in Mahavamsa is identified with Ashoka. It is also identified with another ruler. Identify.
A. Bindusara B. Samprati
C. Salisuka D. Chandragupta

30. Which God was called Herakles by the Greeks?
A. Krishna B. Indra
C. Rudra D. Brahma

31. Which of the following Buddhist text declares the cattle to be of food, beauty and happiness (Annada, Vannada, Sukhada), and thus pleads for their protection?
A. Suttanipata B. Kathavathonu
C. Milindapanho D. Mahavamsa

32. Among which of the communities did Jainism spread rapidly?
A. Trading Community B. Agrarian tourists
C. Craftsmen D. Warriors

33. Why are the majority of Buddhist caves in India to be found in Western Maharashtra?
A. The caves in this region provided a safe sanctuary away from the marauding hordes of foreign-invaders.
B. There was a long-standing tradition in this region of royal patronage to rock-cut architecture.
C. The Sahayadri mountain in western Maharashtra with its hard trap was best suited for rock-cut architecture.
D. None of these.

34. Name of the greatest Buddhist Commentator of the Buddhist Cononical literature who wrote Visuddhimagga, the first famous systematic and philosophical treatise on Buddhist doctrine.
A. Vasumitra B. Nagarjuna
C. Buddhaghosha D. Ashvaghosha

35. The Buddha had accepted the invitation to dinner from one of the following in preference to that of the lichchavis. Identify:
A. Ajatsatru B. Ambapali
C. Khema D. Visakha

36. Match the following:

(*a*) Kanda	1. Sidhhartha's horse
(*b*) Channa	2. Siddhartha's Charioteer
(*c*) Udraka	3. Chief disciple of the Buddha
(*d*) Ananda	4. Second teacher of Siddhartha
(*e*) Kauthaka	5. The Smith who served the last meal to Buddha

	(*a*)	(*b*)	(*c*)	(*d*)	(*e*)
A.	5	2	4	3	1
B.	1	2	3	4	5
C.	2	3	5	1	4
D.	5	2	3	1	4

36. Match the following:

(*a*) Sutta Pitaka	1. A collection of religious discourses of the Buddha
(*b*) Vinaya Pitaka	2. Contains rules of Monastic discipline
(*c*) Abhidhamma Pitaka	3. Consists of meta physical disquisitions

	(*a*)	(*b*)	(*c*)
A.	2	3	1
B.	1	2	3
C.	3	1	2
D.	2	1	3

38. Mahavira gave up worldly life at the age of:
A. 30 B. 29
C. 40 D. 25

39. Who of the following wrote Madhyamika Karika?
A. Nagarjuna B. Vasubandhu
C. Buddhaghosa D. Adhvaghosa

40. How many years did the Buddha wonder before the enlightenment?
A. Seven
B. Six
C. Twelve
D. forty-five

41. Which one of the following is considered the most important vehicle of Buddhist ethical teachings?
A. Sutta Pitakas
B. Jatakastories
C. Vinaya Pitakas
D. Abhidhamma Pitakas

42. Who headed the Jaina exodus to the Mysore Country?
A. Chandragupta
B. Bhadrabahu
C. Sthulabhadra
D. Jamali

43. How many years did Mahavira spend as a religious teacher?
A. 30
B. 40
C. 35
D. 25

44. Which was the name of the son of the Buddha?
A. Rahula
B. Mara
C. Jamali
D. Sidhartha

45. Mahavira practised severe penance for:
A. 30 years
B. 6 years
C. 10 years
D. 12 years

46. Who was the first pontiff of Jainism after Mahavira?
A. Sudhaman
B. Jamali
C. Sthulabhadra
D. Bhadrababu

47. Which one of the following places can be regarded as the largest monastic establishment in western India (containing 130 caves)?
A. Kanheri
B. Junnair (Near Nasik)
C. Ajanta (Near Aurangabad)
D. Karle

48. Which one of the following statement correctly describe the difference between chaitya and a stupa?
A. Chaityas represented Mahayanism and stupas Hinayanism
B. Chaityas were constructed by the manasteries while stupas were constructed by the kings and the rich merchants.
C. Chaitya is a place of Prayers/Worship while stupa is a movement.
D. Chaitya is a religious term, while stupa is an architectural term for a mend containing a relic of the Buddha and later on of leading Buddhist saints.

49. Who of the following was the most renowned Buddhist scholar of Indian origin to propagate madhyamika Buddhism in China?
A. Fa-hiean
B. Kumarjiva
C. I-tsing
D. Huen-Tsang

50. About 600 B.C. which one of the following was not a republic?
A. Sakyas
B. Koliyar
C. Mallas
D. Panchala

51. Who built the fort at Palaligram (Palimbothra) where the city of Pataliputra grew?
A. Ajatsatru
B. Bimbisara
C. Chandragupta Maurya
D. Dhanananda

52. One of the three Pitakas which deals with the Buddhist Curch discipline is known as:
A. Vinaya
B. Sutta
C. Abidhamma
D. None of the above

53. Which statement on Buddhists in the second half of the first millennium is not correct?
A. Buddhist monks took part in Hindu processions.
B. Buddhist families relied on the services of Brahmanas at births, marriages and deaths.
C. Buddhism denied the validity of the vedas.
D. Buddhism did not develop its own metaphysics and tratricism, as Hinduism.

54. Which feature of Buddhism gave it an edge over Aryanism?
A. Absence of Godhead
B. Acceptance of the cycle of birth and death
C. Homely message
D. The jataka stories

55. Which country still possesses a branch of the original pipal tree, under which the Buddha had received enlightenment?
A. Indonnesia
B. China
C. Ceylon
D. Afghanistan

56. Which statement on the similarities between Buddhism and Jainism is not correct?
A. Both Buddhism and Jainism denied the authority of the vedas and opposed animal sacrifices and the performance of rituals and ceremonies.
B. Both the Buddha and Mahavira belonged to princely families and both taught in the language of the common people.
C. Both of them admitted diciplines from all castes and from both sexes.
D. Both spread in various parts of the world extensively.

57. True goal of Mahayana follower is the achievement of:
A. Arhantship
B. Supreme Buddhahood
C. Perfection
D. Bodhisattvahood

58. Who was/were not a Zealous follower(s) of Buddhism?
A. Pala kings of Bengal
B. Sungas
C. Ashoka
D. Harsha

59. The charvakas, or Lokayat school of materialist philosophy did not believe in one of the following. Identify
A. Peraption (Pratyaksha) is the only means of valid knowledge. All interference is invalid.

B. Earth, Water, Finole and Air are the only elements.
C. There is other world.
D. Sensual pleasure is the summum bonum of life: enjoyment is the only end of human existence.

60. The angas literature is associated with:
A. Vaishnavism B. Saivism
C. Jainism D. Buddhism

61. The mother of Mahavira was:
A. Mahamaya B. Trishala
C. Yasoda D. Yasodhara

62. The event of the fight of Mohammed in 622 A.D. is known as Hijrat. What is Gautam's "Great going forth" (His leaving his father's palace) known as?
A. Mahabhiniskramana B. Parinirvana
C. Mahaparinirvana D. Nibbana-yatra

63. Who wrote Jaina Kalpasutra?
A. Bhadrabahu B. Sthulbahu
C. Mahavira D. Parsvanath

64. Which one forms a bridge or rather a half way house between the old Buddhism and Hinduism?
A. the Hinayana School B. The Mahayana School
C. the Vajrayana School D. None of the above

65. Whose relation with the Buddha began with enmity and ended in complete dexotion?
A. Bimbisara's B. Ajatasatru's
C. Devadatta's D. Pradyota's

66. Which one of the following has been the richest source of the well known smooth images in black state and has also yielded an extensive series of Buddhist bronzes?
A. Amaravati B. Tanjore
C. Nalanda D. Kurkihar

67. At which one of the following places the earliest example of the Buddhist stupa architecture has been found?
A. Sarnath B. Sanchi
C. Lumbini D. Bodha Gaya

68. To which one of the following school of art do the earliest images of Buddha in human form belong?
A. Mathura B. Gupta
C. Gandhara D. Amravati

69. The best images of Prajnaparamita, belongs to:
A. Sumatra B. Java
C. China D. India

70. Name the place where the Colossal figures of the Buddha modelled on an earlier Gandhara type, belonging to the 3rd and 4th centuries A.D. has been found.
A. Bamiyan, Afghanistan
B. Chinese Turkistan
C. Burma (new Myanmar)
D. Sri Lanka

71. Which statement regarding Buddha is true?
A. He was born on the day of full moon.
B. His birth and death took place on the day of full moon.
C. His birth, death and awaking — all the three took place on the day of full moon.
D. He became enlightened on the day of full moon.

72. Which of the following Buddhist philosophers is said to have visited Nepal in the 4th century in order to propagate his own doctrine?
A. Acharya Vasubandhu B. Acharya Shantharakshita
C. Acharya Kamlashila D. Acharya Aitsha

73. Who of the following monarchs of Tibet is credited with introduction of Buddhism in Tibet in the 7th century A.D.?
A. Dpal—hkhor—btsan
B. Khri—ide—sren—btas
C. Mu—ne—btsan—po
D. Sron—btsan—Sangam—po

74. The Shailendra kings of Indonesia were followers of Mahayana Buddhism. They establish monesteris at Nalanda and Nagapatinam and the Pala and the Chola emperors granted village for their maintenance. Which one of the following stupas built by them in Java is most renowned?
A. Singasari B. Borobudur
C. Mendut D. Kalasan

75. Which one of the following nurtured as individualistic traditions in Buddhism?
1. Shudras asseting their rights
2. Growing Urbanisation
3. Decaying Brahmanism
4. Republican background
A. only 2 and 4 B. only 1 and 3
C. only 1, 3 and 4 D. All the four

76. Which one of the following constitutes the chief significance of Korean Buddhism?
A. The role it played as an intermediary between China and Japan
B. The unique synthesis of the orthodox and the Tantric Schools of Buddhism
C. The preservation of Mahayana Buddhism in its purest from
D. None of the these

77. When was Buddhism (Mahayana School) First introduced in Japan?
A. 1st Century A.D. B. 3rd Century A.D.
C. 6th Century A.D. D. 8th Century A.D.

78. Which factor disabled Buddhism from the very beginning to emerge as the triumphant religion of India?
A. Lack of clarity regarding life after death.
B. Pride born out of Royal patronage.

C. Acceptance of some of the well known concepts of Aryanism.
D. Division of Buddhist ranks immediately after the death of Buddha.

79. In the field of religion every major religion of the world is represented in India with the exception of:
A. Confucianism B. Zoroastrianism
C. Judaism D. Latin Chriotianity

80. The 57-foot high statues of Gomateshware at Sravana Belgola in Mysore was erected in about 981 A.D. by the Ganga minister.
A. Chamundraya B. Rachamal
C. Rishala D. Bharata

81. According to Buddhist tradition, who instigated Ajatsatru to kill his father Bimkisara?
A. Buddha's cousin Devadatta
B. Bimbisara's wife Chellana
C. Bimbisara's wife Khena
D. Ajatsatru's wife Padmavati

82. One of the earliest references to Krishna as human hero is to be found in the:
A. Chhandogya Upanishad
B. Ghata Jataka
C. Jaina text Uttradyanana Sutra
D. Jaina Aupapatrika Sutra

83. To the classical *i.e.* Greek writers, Lord Krishna was known as:
A. Heracles B. Souraseni
C. Androkottas D. Sandro Kottas

84. "Para" means:
A. the highest aspect of Lord Vasudeva
B. the emanatory form of Vasudeva
C. the incarnatory form of Vasudeva
D. Vasudeva as the inner Controller of the actions of every individual

85. The fact that Jainas included Vasudeva and Baladeva among the 63 Solaka ----- Purushas or eminent Personalities, who influence the history of the world in various ways is:
A. true B. false
C. not likely D. disputed

86. Who was considered as the 9th Avatar of Vishnu?
A. Kapila B. Dattatreya
C. Vyasa D. the Buddha

87. The monolithic column at Besnagar in honour of Vasudeva was erected by Heliodorus in the:
A. 2nd Century B.C. B. 1st Century B.C.
C. 1st Century A.D. D. 2nd Century A.D.

88. Which statement on Vaishnavism is not correct?
A. Vasudeva — Krishna came to be gradually associated with the vedic deity Vishnu and this process was completed by the time the Bhagvat Gita was composed.
B. The Bhagvata religion is also known as Vaishnava Dharma.
C. Buddhist cannos of the first century B.C. mentioned the worshippers of Vasudeva.
D. The worship of Vishnu was certainly known to Megasthenes.

89. Which statement on Bhagavatism is not correct?
A. It did not encourage image worship among the higher sections of the orthodox Indian people.
B. The Vishnu images of the early post. Christian era are mostly to be found in the Mathura regions.
C. The Bhagavata Shrines are mostly built by foreigners as the one referred to in the mora inscription.
D. A few fragments of the mora shrines are now to be found in the Mathura Museum.

90. Amongest the following who contributed most to the Bhagavat cult?
A. Indo-Greeks B. Seythians
C. Parthians D. Kushans

91. Theist religion means:
A. belief in one God
B. the God would reveal himself to the devotees
C. the opposite of montheism
D. the opposite of pontheism

92. The Gita steers a middle course between the two ideals of nivritti and pravritti:
A. correct B. incorrect
C. controversial D. Do not know

93. Which one is known as the layman's upnishad?
A. The Ramayana B. The Gita
C. Mahabharata D. The Jataka Stories

94. Which practice of early Buddhists largely enabled Buddhists to become a popular religion?
A. Preaching in Pali and the simplicity of the doctrine.
B. The personality of the Buddha
C. Acceptance of worship of trees and funerary practices.
D. The simplicity of the doctrine.

95. The system that must have become the basic doctrine of Buddhism is the:
A. Nyaya system B. Sankhya system
C. Uttar-Mimamsa D. None of these

96. Who listened to the first serman of the Buddha?
A. The five as ascetics or monks
B. Sujata
C. Angulimala
D. Upali

97. Symbol of Buddhism is:
A. four-spoked wheel B. eight-spoked wheel
C. ten-spoked wheel D. Not known

98. The future Buddha may be an incarnation in:
A. Human form B. Semi-human form
C. Animal form D. Acquastic animal form

99. Who was/were not a zealous follower(s) of Buddhism:
A. Harsha B. Kanishka
C. Pala kings of Bengal D. Sungas

100. "Buddhayana" refers to the:
A. First "Vehicle" B. Second "Vehicle"
C. Third "Vehicle" D. None of the above

101. Which sect is similar in thinking or indentical to that of the lokayatas?
A. Jains B. Charavakas
C. Brahmanas D. Sharamanas

102. Who said, "Don't ask the caste, ask the deeds whosoever does the right deals attains nirvana"?
A. Krishna B. Yajuavalkya
C. Mahavira D. Gautama

103. Which evidence does not reveal Ashoka's interest in Buddhism?
A. 6th major pillar inscription
B. Schism edicts
C. Nigalisagar pillar inscription
D. Rumindei's pillar inscription

104. One statement on charavaka philosophy is not correct. Identify that one.
A. Enjoyment is the only end of human life.
B. Gods do not exist.
C. Besides perception there are other means of valid knowledge, important among them being inference.
D. The Lokayat philosophy stated that everything, that exists, is experienced by sensory organs.

105. Which statement on the sect of the Ajivikas is wrong?
A. It attracted only men of humble origin.
B. It found fault with Bhramanas interpretation of Karma doctrine.
C. It criticised the caste-structure.
D. Gosala was its founder.

106. When did China received Buddhism?
A. Second century B.C. B. First century B.C.
C. First century A.D. D. Third century A.D.

107. Which one of the following works of Ashvaghosha is considered to be the oldest dramatic work extant in Sanskrit literature?
A. Shariputraprakarana B. Buddhacharita
C. Samanta Pasadika D. Saundarananda

108. Which one expression for describing the under-current of Indian History is more true than the others?
A. The story of Hinduism
B. Exploitation of the rural areas
C. Frequent invasions by foreigners
D. Elusive search for political unity

109. The only incarnation of Lord Siva as suggested in the Vayu and Linga Puranas is that of:
A. Kakulin B. Basava
C. Gosala D. Shankaracharya

110. Which was the earliest of the saiva seets?
A. Kalamukhas B. Kapalikas
C. Pasupata D. Lingayatas

111. The Garuda Pillar erected by the foreigner is at:
A. Besnagar B. Allahabad
C. Sanchi D. Ujjain

112. Who said: "When religion declines and evil-doers are to be destroyed, I shall be born, at different periods"?
A. Krishna B. The Buddha
C. Rama D. Mahavira

113. The first successful invador who annexed the Punjab territories to his empire was:
A. Cyrus I B. Darius I
C. Alexandar D. Darius III

114. Chandragupta Maurya liberated one of the following parts of India from Selukos. Which one was that:
A. North-Western B. South-Western
C. South-Eastern D. Western

115. Who said "Indians do not know the art of writing?
A. Kautilya B. Pliny
C. Megasthenes D. Plutarch

116. Who was referred to as "Vrishala" and "Kulahina":
A. Ashoka
B. Harsha
C. Chandragupta Maurya
D. Chandragupta

117. During the reign of Chandragupta Maurya the Sudarsan lake near Girnar was constructed by?
A. Suvisakha B. Pushyagupta
C. Tushapa D. Parnadatta

118. Tishyarakshita, who opposed the extraordinary generosity of Ashoka to the Buddhist, was:
A. the queen B. a sister
C. a daughter D. a grand-daughter

119. Who was welcomed by these word: "We neither oppose the prince, nor the king but the wicked ministers who oppress us"?
A. Bindusara B. Samprati
C. Kunala D. Jaluka

120. How many nights did Ashoka spend on his "dhammayatras" (Pilgrimage tours)?
A. 240 B. 256
C. 120 D. 280

121. Who saw Ashoka's statue dressed in a monk's robe?
A. Fahien B. Huen Tsang
C. I-tsing D. Alberuni

122. The essence of Law of Piety or Dhamma is:
A. Layman's version of Buddhism
B. Ashoka's version of religious consciousness
C. Porana Pakiti
D. An ideology to indotrinate people

123. Which points does Not show that Ashoka was against Bramhanism?
A. He looked down supon Sacrifice
B. He had something against the Devas
C. He equalted brahmanas with Ajivikas
D. He held that the goal for people was "Swarga"

124. Who was the only Mauryan Successor whose name appears in an inscription as the donor of a cave in Barabar Hills near Gaya?
A. Dasaratha B. Sampati
C. Kunala D. Jaluka

125. The "Vayu Purana" mentions the total number of kings after Ashoka as:
A. Six B. Ten
C. Seven D. Eight

126. Which of the following did for Buddhism in Japan, what Ashoka had done for it in India?
A. Heina B. Prince Shotoku
C. Emperor Suiko D. Kamakura

127. The stupa constructed at which one of the following places in southern India is not only earliest but also a Mahastupa enshrining the mortal remains of the Buddha?
A. Jaggayyapeta B. Amaravati
C. Nagarjunakonda D. Bhattiprolu

128. The serman of the Turning of the wheel of law was preached by the Buddha after his enlightment. Which statement on it is not correct?
A. It was preached in the Deer Park at Sarnath.
B. It is the basic teaching of all the Buddhist sects.
C. The five monks, Kondana, Vappa, Bhadiya, Mahanama and Assagi listened to it.
D. That was his first and last Serman.

129. The turning of the wheel of law was the centre of Buddhist teaching. Which of the following is not correct?
A. Four noble truths
B. Eight fold path
C. Belief in Bodhisattavas
D. The middle path

130. A Boddhisattva in Hinayana Buddhism is:
A. A being of immeasurable charity and compassion
B. The previous incarnation of Buddha
C. A dissident monk
D. The God on the earth in human form

131. Which among the following was absent from the organisation of Buddhist Sanghas?
A. Democratization
B. A central organisation of Sanghas
C. Separate Sanghas for Nuns (women)
D. Separate Sanghas for the followers of Hinayana and Mahayana sects

132. Which one of the following title was not used for Buddha?
A. Sakyamuni B. Tathagata
C. Jina D. Nayaputta

133. About whom Max Mullar called, "the greatest grammarian the world has ever known"?
A. Nagarjana B. Ashvaghosha
C. Panini D. Nayaputta

134. To which of the following countries Ashoka did not send his missionaries?
A. Egypt B. Sri Lanka
C. China D. Burma

135. By what name did the Greek writers call to the city commissioners?
A. Agronomoi B. Astynomoi
C. Sthanika D. Srenis

136. What is the ancient name for East Bengal?
A. Samatata B. Dhauli
C. Svarnagiri D. Gandhara

137. Which of the Greek writers refers to taking of image of Heracles in front of the Paurava army?
A. Curtius B. Justin
C. Strabo D. Measthenes

138. Who is described as the Indian Machiavelli?
A. Bimbisara B. Chanakya
C. Bana D. Kalidasa

139. Into how many books is Arthasastra divided?
A. 15 B. 20
C. 25 D. 150

140. Which one of the following statements about Yogachara (Founded by Maitrey-anatha), the other branch of Mahayanism, is not correct?
A. It recognises three degrees of knowledge Parikalpila (illusory), Paratantra (empirical), and Parinishpanna (absolute).
B. The school is also known as Vijnanavada on account of the fact that it holds Vijnaptimatra (nothing but consciousness) to be the ultimate reality.
C. As against the qualified realism of Madhyamika School it advocates absolute realism.
D. It emphasises the practice of Yoga (Meditation) as the most effective method for the attainment of the highest truth (bodhi).

141. Who of the following Mahayanist Buddhist writers is regarded as the Kant of India by Dr. Stcharbatoky?

A. Dignaga B. Asanga
C. Dharmakirti D. Vasubandhu

142. Ashoka's Coronation took place in:
A. 261 BC B. 273 BC
C. 264 BC D. 250 BC

143. Tantrik-Sect first grew within:
A. Jainism B. Buddhism
C. Hinduism D. Bhagavatism

144. Which of the following was not one of the schools of Tantric-Buddhism?
A. Pratyeka-Buddhayana B. Mantrayana
C. Vijrayana D. Sahajayana

145. Which one of the following Buddhist scholars has been described as "Poet, Musician, Preacher, Moralist, Philosopher, Play-writer, tale-teller and inventor in all these arts .... he recalls Milton, Goethe, Kant and Voltaire"?
A. Vasubandhu B. Asanga or Aryasanga
C. Ashvaghosha D. Nagarjuna

146. Which one of the following Buddhist scholar enjoys great celebrity all over the Buddhist world as grammarian, philosopher and poet?
A. Vasumitra B. Santideva
C. Chandragomin D. Panini

147. **Assertion (A):** The rise of Buddhism was protest movement against the Aryan-dominated Varna System.
Reason (R): The Buddha was a Kshatriya.
Codes:
A. (A) and (R) are true and (R) is the correct explanation of (A).
B. (A) and (R) are true, but (R) is not the correct explanation of (A).
C. (A) is true but, (R) is false.
D. (A) is false, but (R) is true.

148. **Assertion (A):** The rise of hetrodox religions in the 6th century B.C. was the outcome of a desire to have an intelligible easy, and less expensive way to salvation.
Reason (R): The Buddha and Mahavira introduced those changes in the old religious system as were necessary to satisfy this yearning.
Codes:
A. (A) and (R) are true and (R) is the correct explanation of (A).
B. (A) and (R) are true, but (R) is not the correct explanation of (A).
C. (A) is true, but (R) is false.
D. (A) is false, but (R) is true.

149. **Assertion (A):** The rise of Buddhism was the result of the introduction of nees agricultural economy based in the use of the cattle.
Reason (R): The Buddha was opposed to sacrifice.
Codes:
A. (A) and (R) are true and (R) is the correct explanation of (A).
B. (A) and (R) are true, but (R) is not the correct explanation of (A).
C. (A) is true, but (R) is false.
D. (A) is false, but (R) is true.

150. **Assertion (A):** Mahavira was only a reformer.
Reason (R): Jaina ideas were there even before his advent.
Codes:
A. (A) and (R) are true and (R) is the correct explanation of (A).
B. (A) and (R) are true, but (R) is not the correct explanation of (A).
C. (A) is true, but (R) is false.
D. (A) is false, but (R) is true.

ANSWERS

1	2	3	4	5	6	7	8	9	10
B	A	A	A	A	A	B	C	A	A
11	**12**	**13**	**14**	**15**	**16**	**17**	**18**	**19**	**20**
C	A	A	C	C	A	D	D	B	D
21	**22**	**23**	**24**	**25**	**26**	**27**	**28**	**29**	**30**
B	A	A	A	C	B	A	A	D	A
31	**32**	**33**	**34**	**35**	**36**	**37**	**38**	**39**	**40**
A	A	C	C	B	A	B	A	A	B
41	**42**	**43**	**44**	**45**	**46**	**47**	**48**	**49**	**50**
B	B	A	A	D	A	B	D	B	D
51	**52**	**53**	**54**	**55**	**56**	**57**	**58**	**59**	**60**
A	A	D	C	C	D	D	B	C	C
61	**62**	**63**	**64**	**65**	**66**	**67**	**68**	**69**	**70**
B	A	A	B	B	C	A	C	B	A

71	72	73	74	75	76	77	78	79	80
C	A	D	B	A	A	C	C	A	A
81	82	83	84	85	86	87	88	89	90
A	A	A	A	A	D	A	D	A	A
91	92	93	94	95	96	97	98	99	100
B	A	B	A	B	A	B	C	D	C
101	102	103	104	105	106	107	108	109	110
B	D	A	C	A	C	A	A	A	C
111	112	113	114	115	116	117	118	119	120
A	A	B	A	C	C	B	A	C	B
121	122	123	124	125	126	127	128	129	130
C	C	D	A	B	B	D	D	C	B
131	132	133	134	135	136	137	138	139	140
B	C	C	C	B	A	A	B	A	C
141	142	143	144	145	146	147	148	149	150
C	B	C	A	C	C	D	D	A	A

SET-4

1. Manimekalai is considered:
A. The idyllic of Tamil Poetry
B. The odyssey of Tamil Poetry
C. The Mahabharata of Tamil
D. The Ramayana of Tamil

2. The beginning of *civilized* communities in southern India was not because of one of the following. Identify.
A. The megalithic people moved from upland area into fertile river basins.
B. The coming of Jaina and Buddha missionaries made them aware of Northern material culture.
C. The history of early south India witnessed caste system of the northern type.
D. Roman contacts.

3. By how many Pandyan kings was the first Sangam patronised?
A. 89 B. 59
C. 49 D. 79

4. Which one of the following statements about the religious life of the Sangam age is not correct?
A. During the early Sangam age the Brahmanic vedic rituals had taken deep routs.
B. Chola kings patronised expensive sacrificial rituals.
C. The Samskaras, including the upnayan (Sacredthread ceremony) were not followed.
D. Amongst the higher classes (including merchants) marriages were solemnised according to the vedic rites.

5. There was an administrative unit under cholas name "Kuram". What did it mean?
A. A gram B. A tehsil
C. A district D. A group of village

6. The earliest Tamil literature is termed as Sangam literature because it was:
A. a joint creation of one school of scholars.
B. Patronized by the rulers of the Sangam dynasty.
C. Standardized by an academy (Sangam) of Scholars and poets maintained by Pandya rulers at Madurai.
D. Created at the Sangam of three South Indian rivers.

7. Contracts between northern Aryans and Tamils is conveyed in the tradition of:
A. Valmiki B. Agastya
C. Vishwamitra D. Vashishta

8. Sangam literature was written in:
A. Avadhi B. Tamil
C. Maithili D. Malayalam

9. The radiating point for civilization in the land south of Narmada was:
A. Godavari delta
B. Kaveri delta
C. Tungabhadra and Krisha region
D. Pannar river

10. Which one of the following is false with regard to the religious practices of the Sangam Age?
A. Banyan tree was considered to be the abode of God.
B. People worshipped the local God Murugan, who later came to be known as Subramaniam.
C. The kings performed vedic sacrifices.
D. The people had no faith in omens and astrology.

11. Where was the first Sangam held?
A. Madurai B. Kanchipuram
C. Mahabalipuram D. Kaveri Pattanam

12. The Sangam age dates back to:
A. 1200 BC – 1100 AD B. 900 BC – 500 AD
C. 500 BC – 500 AD D. 280 BC – 185 AD

13. Which Sangam work extols the virtuous wife?
A. Silapappadikaram B. Manimekalai
C. Jivakachintamani D. Kundala Kesi

14. The literature of the Sangam age was mostly in the form of :
A. Prose B. Poetry
C. Drama D. None of the above

15. Which one of the following statements on the Cheras is not correct?
A. The first Chera monarch Uidyanjeral was called Imayavaramban.
B. Their greatest ruler was San-u-Guttuven or Red Chera.
C. They used modified version of Tamil.
D. They were in alliance with the Pandyas.

16. Which one of the following statements regarding Sangam age is not correct?
A. Madurai is the Tamil word for Mathura.
B. Sangam literature is not logically connected.
C. Sangam literature refers to 2 or 3 Pandyan kings.
D. The chola kings patronized the Sangam poetry.

17. What is the acceptable date of the third Sangam?
A. 7th Century AD
B. 500 BC
C. 8th century AD
D. Ist three centuries of the Christian era.

18. Which among the following was not included as a seat of learning of the Sangams:
A. Kanchi B. Madurai
C. Mahabalipuram D. Kaveripattanam

19. What is the name of the Chola king who defeated the Pandya and Chera kings in the famous battle of Venni?
A. Karikala
B. Vijaya
C. Nendunjehyan
D. Tondaiaman Ilandiraiyan

20. Who was the king who formed the third Sangam?
A. Mudattiruraman B. Ugrapperuvaludi
C. Nedunehelian D. Kadungan

21. Which one of the following works belong to the third Sangam?
A. Pari Padal B. Kali
C. Gita Govinda D. Rajatarangini

22. Where did the second Sangam function from?
A. Madurai B. Puhar
C. Kapatapuram D. Kanchi

23. Which one of the following statement on the social life in the Sangam era is not correct?
A. The widows had to cut off their hair, discard all ornaments and eat only the plainest food.
B. Civil and military offices were held by the rich peasants called velalas.
C. Caste distinction existed.
D. Talkappiar calls the commercial community as vaisigas.

24. Which one of the following statement on Sangam literature is not correct?
A. It enables us to trace a connected political history of Tamil Kingdom.
B. It sheds light on socio-religious aspects of Tamil-Kingdom.
C. It sheds light on trade relations with "Yavanas".
D. It sheds light on the pronounced fusion that had occurred between the Sanskrit and the Tamil culture.

25. Who wrote Talkappiyam?
A. Tolkappiyar B. Ravivarman
C. Kamban D. Deva Raya I

26. What find help us to determine the date of the third Sangam?
A. Arikkamedu B. Adichhanallur
C. Paiyampali D. Lothal

27. Pick-out the one which dose not go with the others:
A. Kuruntogai B. Ahananura
C. Paripadal D. Pattinappalai

28. Of the three Tamil monarchies of South India, the Pandyas occupied:
A. the extreme south
B. the Kaveri region
C. western coastal strip
D. undermarcated vast territories

29. The political and cultural centre of the Pandyas was:
A. Vengi B. Madurai
C. Kanchipuram D. Mahabalipuram

30. Which dynasty did not exist during the Sangam age?
A. Chalukyas B. Chera
C. Chola D. Pandya

31. For which line of rulers can we construct anything like a continuous geneology with the help of Sangam Literature?
A. Cheras B. Pandyas
C. Cholas D. Satyaputras

32. Which of the attributes does not refer the megalithic graves of Southern India?
A. Graves were encircled by big pieces of stone.
B. Alongwith the skeletons, objects of daily use were also buried.
C. Arrowheads, spearheads, hoes and sickles were also found in the graves.
D. The only iron implement found in the graves was the plough

33. Match three Sangams with the number of Pandyan Kings they were patronized:

(*a*) First Sangam 1. 49
(*b*) Second Sangam 2. 59
(*c*) Third Sangam 3. 89

	(*a*)	(*b*)	(*c*)
A.	1	2	3
B.	3	2	1
C.	2	1	3
D.	3	1	2

34. Which statement on economic activity of ancient India projected the changing social life of the day?
A. The Sangam poems often referred to Yavanas.
B. The Greeks settle in large numbers at Kaveripattnam
C. The foreigners, in course of time, were known as fallen Kashatriyas
D. The presence of foreigners wielding political and economic power posed a threat to castesystem

35. Which one of the following statements on Sangam age is not corrected?
A. Madurai, the capital city of Pandyas, was the centre of this literacy activity.
B. The main function of the Sangam was to bring together the leading poets, scholars and thinkers for the creative and critical literary works.
C. The term Sangam was popularised in the Tamilkam by the Jaina and Buddhist ascenities.
D. The name of the North Indian Sage Agastya was not referred to in the Sangam Literature.

36. Which of the following works of the Sangam age is considered to be the greatest literary works of ancient Tamil Literature?
A. Tolkappiyam
B. Ettutogai (eight authologies)
C. Perunga dai
D. Muttollayiram

37. Which of the following statements about the maugram, the Sabha of this period, is not correct?
A. It was the highest court of Justice.
B. It was the comman meeting place in the village.
C. According to rural, it was a general assembly dealing with all affairs.
D. It served the purpose of political gathering.

38. Pick out the one which does not go with the others.
A. Mullaippatu B. Nedunalvadai
C. Paripadal D. Kurunjippattu

39. Match of the following works and groups to which they belong:

(*a*) Narrinai 1. Epic
(*b*) Maduraikanchi 2. Ettuthogoi
(*c*) Thirukkural 3. Pathupattu
(*d*) Silappadikaram 4. Padiven Kilkanakku Nool

	(*a*)	(*b*)	(*c*)	(*d*)
A.	2	3	4	1
B.	1	2	3	4
C.	3	2	1	4
D.	4	1	3	2

40. Match the following regions and the people who lived there:

(*a*) Marudam 1. Ayars
(*b*) Mullai 2. Kuravas
(*c*) Kurinji 3. Panadavars
(*d*) Neydal 4. Ulavars

Codes:

	(*a*)	(*b*)	(*c*)	(*d*)
A.	4	1	2	3
B.	1	2	3	4
C.	2	3	4	1
D.	3	4	1	2

41. Who was the president of the first Sangam?
A. Valmiki B. Vedavyas
C. Janaka D. Agastya

42. The last authology or group of Sangam literature known as, "Ten Idylls" is:
A. Kural B. Tolkappiyam
C. Pattupattu D. Manimekalai

43. In all, there were/was:
A. four Sangams B. three Sangams
C. two Sangams D. one Sangams

44. Among the following major epics of Tamil literature which one was produced during the age of the third Sangam?
A. Silappadikaram B. Jinak Chintamani
C. Valayapti D. Kundoolkeri

45. South Indians maintained a favourable trade with the Roman empire up to the:
A. 2nd Century A.D. B. 3rd Century A.D.
C. 2nd Century A.D. D. 3rd Century B.C.

46. The main items of export during Sangam was/were:
A. Medicinal herbs B. Pearls
C. Black peppar D. All the above

47. Primary items of import was/were:
A. Gold B. Wine
C. Horses D. All the above

48. What are the major epics of the Sangam age?
A. Silappadikaram, Manimekhalai, Jivak-chintamani, Valayapati, Kundalakasi
B. Manimekhalai, Kavyam, Nalavenba
C. Naladiyar, Silappadikaram, Palamoli, Nilkasi
D. Pattinappalai, Nedunalvadai, Mullai-prathu

49. Which of the following was the great custom port and artificial harbour?
A. Paduca
B. Uraiyur
C. Puhar or Kaviripattinam
D. Tyndis

50. Which of the following was the important port of Eastern coast in the Sangam age?
A. Colchi B. Tyndis
C. Muziris D. Naura

51. What was the important port on the Western Coast in the Sangam, age?
A. Poduca B. Colchi
C. Balita D. Sopatma

52. Which of the following was a great centre of cotton trade?
A. Korkai B. Muziris
C. Balita D. Uraiyur

53. Which Roman wrote: "In no year does India draw our empire of less than five hundred and fifty millions of sesterces"?
A. Pliny B. Strabo
C. Justin D. Plutarch

54. On which of the following imports from India the Roman senate laid an embargo as it was a menace to the city's morals?
A. Saffron B. Wine
C. Pepper D. Muslin

55. The existence of the monsoon winds, blowing across the Indian ocean was discovered by:
A. Hippalus in 45 A.D. B. Plutarch in 78 A.D.
C. Strabo in 56 B.C. D. Pliny in 58 A.D.

56. The Tamil poetry in Sangam period was divided into two main groups, namely.
A. Palai and Mullani B. Kurinji and Aham
C. Marudam and Puram D. Agam and Puram

57. Match the following regions and their Gods:
(*a*) Marudam 1. Mayen
(*b*) Mullai 2. Indran
(*c*) Kurinji 3. Varuna
(*d*) Neydal 4. Seyon

Codes:

	(*a*)	(*b*)	(*c*)	(*d*)
A.	2	1	4	3
B.	1	2	3	4
C.	3	4	2	1
D.	4	3	1	2

58. Match the following regions and the occupation of the people who lived there.
(*a*) Marudam 1. Fishing
(*b*) Mullai 2. Cultivation
(*c*) Neydal 3. Hunting
(*d*) Kurinji 4. Rearing cattle and sheep

Codes:

	(*a*)	(*b*)	(*c*)	(*d*)
A.	2	4	1	3
B.	1	2	3	4
C.	3	4	2	1
D.	4	1	3	2

59. Who spoke of Pandya Kingdom being ruled by a woman in Sangam period?
A. Megasthenes B. Kautilya
C. Panini D. Patanjali

60. The greatest Pandya ruler was;
A. Nedunjeliyan B. Peruvaludi
C. Ilandiraiyan D. Mudikudumi

61. Which statement on the different eco-types (tinai) refferred to in Sangam Literature is wrong:
A. The mountainous region (Kurinci) was the habitat of hunters and food gatherers like the tribes of the Kuruvars.
B. The tribes of herdsmen like the Ayar lived in the forest (mullai).
C. Robbers withdrew the barren land (Palai).
D. People made a living by fishing in the marutam area.

62. Karikala's greatest achivement was:
A. Victory over the Pandya and the Chera King at Venni
B. Conquest of Ceylon
C. Building of the city of Puhar at the mouth of Kaveri
D. Pioneering of the Grand Aricut at Srirangam.

63. Which of the statements on Sangam period is incorrect?
A. Monarchy was the prevalent form of Government.
B. The Tamil kings looked after their country like nurses tending children in their charge an ideal put before them by Ashoka the great.
C. "Chakravartin" ideal was dear to the Tamil Kings.
D. Brahmin advisers were not known to Tamil Kings.

64. What was the emblem of the Sangam-Cholas?
A. the tiger B. the "Bow"
C. Eight-spoked wheel D. Garuda

65. Two of the most recurring causes of warfare in Sangam period were:
1. Cattle lifting
2. refusal to give princesses in marriages
3. smuggling
4. family feuds

Codes:
A. 1 and 2 B. 1 and 3
C. 2 and 3 D. 4 and 1

66. Which one is supposed to be the fifth veda?
A. Trittondar Puranam B. Akkatiyam
C. Jivak Chintamani D. Tiru Kurul

67. Which of the statements regarding the art of warfare in Sangam period is incorrect.
A. Methods of fortification, and of assaulting and defending fortrsses appear to have been fairly well-developed
B. The traditional four-fold army-chariots, elephants, cavalry and infantry was in use.
C. Body armour made of tiger-skin was in use.

D. Women captured in war were-returned to their parents or husbands.

68. Match the following:

(*a*) Arikamedu	1. Broach
(*b*) Colchi	2. Korkai
(*c*) Tyndis	3. Panuai or Tondi
(*d*) Baryagaza	4. Cannanore
(*e*) Naura	5. Pondichery

Codes:

	(*a*)	(*b*)	(*c*)	(*d*)	(*e*)
A.	5	2	3	1	4
B.	5	3	2	4	1
C.	2	1	3	4	5
D.	5	3	4	2	1

69. Megasthenes refers to the rule of Heracles (Vasudeva Krishna's) daughter who was assigned villages to rule in Southern region, and who was probably the founder of Pandya kingdom. Identify her?

A. Pandia B. Panlavi
C. Maitri D. Pandara

70. Match the following:

(*a*) Puram	1. Pre-marital love
(*b*) Marudam	2. Post-marital love
(*c*) Kurinji	3. Marital heroism
(*d*) Mullai	4. The Lamentation of separated lovers
(*e*) Neydal	5. The wife's patient suffering during her lord's separation, longing for his returns

Codes:

	(*a*)	(*b*)	(*c*)	(*d*)	(*e*)
A.	4	3	2	1	5
B.	3	2	1	5	4
C.	2	3	1	4	5
D.	4	3	1	2	5

71. Say which is false among the following?

A. There were slave markets in Tamilkam in the Sangam age.
B. Kalingam was a famous variety of cotton cloth.
C. Bull fighting was a common pastime of the Sangam people.
D. Sangam people used tali as a symbol of marriage.

72. Pick out that which is false among the following:

A. Madalerudal was a practice connected with lovers
B. There was neither prohibition nor licensing of prostitution.
C. Pulippal tali was wrong as an ornament by boys and girls.
D. Sati was unknown to the Sangam people.

73. Pick out that which is correct.

A. Widows were permitted to remarry in the Sangam Age.
B. Sangam women had no right to choose their partners.
C. The wife was considered the luminary of the home.
D. Sangam women led a secluded life.

74. Match the following places and the cause of their fame:

(*a*) Kanchi	1. Cotton weaving
(*b*) Uraiyur	2. Silk weaving
(*c*) Korkai	3. Seat of Sangam
(*d*) Madurai	4. Port facilities

Codes:

	(*a*)	(*b*)	(*c*)	(*d*)
A.	2	1	4	3
B.	1	2	3	4
C.	3	4	2	1
D.	4	3	1	2

75. Match the following dynasties and the rulers to which they belong:

(*a*) Cholas	1. Gajabahu
(*b*) Cheras	2. Karikala
(*c*) Pandyas	3. Senguttuvan
(*d*) Ceylonese	4. Nedunchelian

Codes:

	(*a*)	(*b*)	(*c*)	(*d*)
A.	2	3	4	1
B.	1	2	3	4
C.	3	1	2	4
D.	4	2	1	3

76. Pick out that which is false:

A. Monarchy was the prevalent form of government among the Sangam people.
B. Succession was determined by the law of perimogeniture.
C. The king was assisted by ministers.
D. The Sangam works refer to the existence of Enberayan collective responsibility.

77. Match the following according to the author of the works:

(*a*) Nedunavadai	1. Kapilar
(*b*) Maduraikkanchi	2. Nathathanar
(*c*) Sirupanatruppadai	3. Maruthanas
(*d*) Kurinchippattu	4. Nakkirar

	(*a*)	(*b*)	(*c*)	(*d*)
A.	4	3	2	1
B.	4	3	1	2
C.	3	1	2	4
D.	1	2	3	4

78. Which one of the following Tamil Kings have sent the earliest embassy, (According to strabo) which was met by Augustus at Athens about 20 B.C.?

A. A Chola King B. A Chera King
C. A Pandya King D. A Pallave King

79. Which of the following kings made a grand anicut on the Kaveri, the water of which is now-a-days drawn off through a new channel called vennar?

A. Karikala B. Peruvaludi
C. Ilandiraiyan D. Nendunjeliyan

80. Which one of the following Chera king is the brother of Ilango, the author of the Sangam epic "Silappadikaram"?
A. Nedunjeral B. Karikala
C. Nedunjjelian D. Senuguttuvan

81. What are the "ma" and "vedi" in Sangam period?
A. The taxes of the period
B. The coinage of the time
C. The measures of land
D. The words for love and war.

82. The division of Sangam society was made according to the region of the Tamil land to which the poem referred. Match the Tamil words with the regions they are associated with:

(*a*) Palai	1.	The jungle and wood land
(*b*) Mullai	2.	The hills
(*c*) Kurinji	3.	The dry lands
(*d*) Neydal	4.	The Coast
(*e*) Marudam	5.	The cultivated plains

	(*a*)	(*b*)	(*c*)	(*d*)	(*e*)
A.	3	1	2	5	4
B.	3	1	5	2	4
C.	2	3	1	4	5
D.	2	1	3	4	5

83. Which one the following is NOT the meaning of the word Karikala?
A. 'the man with the charred leg'
B. 'death to Kali'
C. 'death to the enemy (elephants)'
D. 'Incarnation of death (Jama)'

84. Who were the first to establish their ascendency in the south?
A. Cholas B. Pandyas
C. Cheras D. Satyaputras

85. Who had a mastery of the seven notes of Music?
A. Samudragupta B. Harsha
C. Karikala D. Chandragupta II

86. Basic objects of the conflict among the three Sangam kingdoms were:
1. Control over the fertile deltas.
2. access to the important trading stations along the coasts.
3. desire to become Chakravartin Kings *i.e.* digvijaya.
4. desire to increase the number of woman folk thus increase in population.

Codes:
A. only 1 and 2 B. only 2 and 3
C. only 3 and 4 D. only 2 and 4

87. What was the Capital of the Sangam Chera?
A. Vanji B. Madurai
C. Uraiyur D. Tiruchirappalli

88. What was the Capital of the Chera King Nedunjeral Adam?
A. Marandai B. Saliyar
C. Kaveripattinam D. Ponnani

89. Identify the Ceylonese king who was a contemporary of the Chera king Senguttuvan and who was present in the Chera kingdom at the time of the establishment of the Pattini cult by the latter.
A. Gajabahu B. Paranar
C. Tissa D. Meghavarman

90. Who among the Chera monarchs is said to have fed sumptuonsly both the armies at Kurukshetra?
A. Udiyanjeral B. Nedunjeral Adam
C. Senguttuvan D. Anduvan

91. Who among the chera monarchs took the lead in organising the cult of Pattini, the Divine chaste wife, and was supported in his effort by the centemporary rulers of the Pandya and Chola countries and of Ceylon?
A. Senguttuvan B. Udiyanjeral
C. Nedunjeral Adam D. Anduvan

92. Which of the statements on the social life in the Sangam era is NOT correct?
A. Civilian and military offices were held by the rich peasants called vallalars.
B. Agriculture was carried out by lower class women.
C. There were several outcastes.
D. Caste distinctions existed.

93. Which of the statements on Sangam people is incorrect?
A. They used starch for stiffening clothes.
B. Their children wore necklaces of tiger teeth.
C. They enjoyed the eating of betel leaves with nuts.
D. Only women wore ornaments.

94. Which of the statements on "Sangam" woman is incorrect:
A. Women enjoyed much freedom of movement in Society.
B. 'Sati' system was much disliked.
C. The lot of widows was hard.
D. Widows preferred "Sati" to widowhood

95. The most important industry in Sangam period was:
A. raising of sugar cane B. raising of pepper
C. production of cloth D. arms manufacturing

96. Match the following:

(*a*) Baryagaze	1. Broach
(*b*) Naura	2. Cannanore or Mangalore
(*c*) Tyndis	3. Korkai
(*d*) Arikamedu	4. Pondicherry
(*e*) Colchi	5. Ponnani or Tondi

	(*a*)	(*b*)	(*c*)	(*d*)	(*e*)
A.	1	2	5	4	3
B.	1	2	3	4	5
C.	3	1	2	5	4
D.	4	3	1	2	5

97. Match the following:

(*a*) Camara	1. Pondicherry		
(*b*) Poduca	2. Chaul		
(*c*) Semylia	3. Cranganore		
(*d*) Muziris	4. Kaveripatinam		

	(*a*)	(*b*)	(*c*)	(*d*)
A.	4	1	2	3
B.	1	2	3	4
C.	3	4	1	2
D.	2	3	4	1

98. Match the names of the Sangam ports with their new or other names given in the second column.

(*a*) Balita	1. Verkalai
(*b*) Poduca	2. Pondicherry Arikamedu
(*c*) Sopatma	3. Markanam
(*d*) Camara	4. Kaveripattinam

	(*a*)	(*b*)	(*c*)	(*d*)
A.	1	2	3	4
B.	2	3	4	1
C.	3	4	1	2
D.	4	1	2	3

99. The Tamil name of the Vishnu is:
A. Tirumala
B. Virkal
C. Subramaniam
D. Skanda

100. Who was euraged widow who caused the destruction of the city of Madurai by plucking off her breast and hurling it over the town?
A. Kannagi B. Madhavi
C. Sita D. Savitri

ANSWERS

1	2	3	4	5	6	7	8	9	10
B	C	A	B	D	C	B	B	B	D
11	**12**	**13**	**14**	**15**	**16**	**17**	**18**	**19**	**20**
A	C	A	B	D	D	D	D	A	A
21	**22**	**23**	**24**	**25**	**26**	**27**	**28**	**29**	**30**
A	C	D	A	A	A	D	A	B	A
31	**32**	**33**	**34**	**35**	**36**	**37**	**38**	**39**	**40**
A	D	A	D	D	B	D	C	D	A
41	**42**	**43**	**44**	**45**	**46**	**47**	**48**	**49**	**50**
D	C	B	A	A	D	D	A	C	A
51	**52**	**53**	**54**	**55**	**56**	**57**	**58**	**59**	**60**
C	D	A	D	A	D	A	A	A	A
61	**62**	**63**	**64**	**65**	**66**	**67**	**68**	**69**	**70**
C	D	D	A	A	D	D	A	A	B
71	**72**	**73**	**74**	**75**	**76**	**77**	**78**	**79**	**80**
D	D	C	A	A	D	A	C	A	D
81	**82**	**83**	**84**	**85**	**86**	**87**	**88**	**89**	**90**
C	A	D	A	C	A	A	A	A	A
91	**92**	**93**	**94**	**95**	**96**	**97**	**98**	**99**	**100**
A	D	D	B	C	A	A	A	A	A

SET-5

1. What is pranaya?
A. benevolences B. forced labour
C. marriage rites D. prayer

2. The officer-in-charge of survey and settlements under Ashoka were:
A. Dharma Mahamatya B. Samahartas
C. Rajukas D. Prati-Vedakas

3. Which statement on Arthashastra is not correct?
A. The Arthashastra devised the manufacture of liquor in government controlled breweries and gave several brief and cryptic recipes.
B. It suggests the appointment of a superintendent of liquor to control the scale of alcoholic drinks and also organise their manufacture.

C. Tavernkeepers should be instructed to make their establishment well furnished and comfortable.
D. It does not recognise drinking as an evil.

4. Who was Samaharta?
A. Collector General B. Treasurer
C. Auditor General D. Magistrate

5. The first to issue the coins in India were:
A. the Greeks B. the Mauryas
C. the Janapadas D. the Nandas

6. During whose time differences arose between the King and the Parishad in the Mauryan period?
A. Chandragupta Maurya
B. Samprati
C. Ashoka
D. Bindusara

7. What was the copper coin of Mauryan times?
A. Mashaka B. Nishka
C. Suvarna D. Pana

8. Among the virtues of royalty, Kautilya accords first place to:
A. danda-niti B. practice of Dharma
C. self control D. clan

9. Which one of the following group of people were not exempt from taxes in the Mauryan period?
A. Brahmins B. Hermits
C. Generals D. Priests

10. Which one is not a division of the provinces in the Mauryan period?
A. Janapadas B. Pradeshes
C. Ahars D. Vigitas

11. What was the standard of Mauryan times?
A. Pana B. Mashaka
C. Nishka D. Suvarna

12. What was the language of administration in Mauryan times?
A. Prakrit B. Sanskrit
C. Ardhamagadhi D. Kharoshti

13. What was the other name that used for the Parishad in the Mauryan period?
A. Sabha B. Rajyasabha
C. Mantri Prishad D. Pratinidhis

14. What is Vishti?
A. benevolences B. forced labour
C. marriage rites D. a district

15. What is Kara?
A. forced labour B. a special harsh tax
C. benevolences D. a bangle

16. During the Mauryan period committees were set up in administration which ones?
1. Military
2. Municipal Corporations
3. Provincial administration
4. Village administration

Codes:
A. 1 and 2 only B. 1, 2 and 3 only
C. 1, 2 and 4 only D. 2 and 3 only

17. The term 'ahara' as an administrative united appears in:
A. Arthashastra B. Ashokan inscriptions
C. Rig Veda D. Epics

18. Match the officers with their functions:
(*a*) Samaharta 1. Chief Collector
(*b*) Sannidhata 2. Chief Treasurer
(*c*) Sandhivigrahika 3. Minister of Peace and war
(*d*) Pradvivaka 4. Chief Judge
(*e*) Uparka 5. Governor
(*f*) Rajjuka 6. Land Surveyor or revenue officer

Codes:

	(*a*)	(*b*)	(*c*)	(*d*)	(*e*)	(*f*)
A.	1	2	3	4	6	5
B.	1	2	6	3	5	4
C.	1	3	2	4	5	6
D.	1	2	3	4	5	6

19. In which of the following do we find the rates of interest and regulations governing debt and mortgages for example the sliding scale of interest according to the caste of debtor.
A. Panini's Asthtadhayayi
B. Arthashastra
C. Indica
D. Epics

20. The Arthashastra for the first time gives enormous importance to:
A. Political state craft
B. Diplomacy
C. Origin of kingship
D. Regulation of economic activity

21. Which statement on Mauryan architecture is not correct?
A. Mauryan stone-building were modelled on wooden original.
B. Megasthenes mentions that the palace of Chandragupta Maurya was built of carved and gilded wood.
C. It was during Ashoka's reigon that stone in buildings was used on a greater scale.
D. Mauryan architectural traditions contained for long of India.

22. In the times of emergency, peasants in the Mauryan period were compelled to:
A. Raise more crops B. Join the army
C. Pay more taxes D. None of the above

23. Punishment was severe during the reign of the:
A. Mauryas B. Guptas
C. Sungas D. Chalukyas

24. Which edicts of Ashoka are sometimes called 'separate rock edicts'?
A. The two Kalinga Edicts
B. The Minor Rock Edicts
C. The Edicts at Shahbazgarhi and Mansehra
D. None of the above

25. Arthasastra, composed by Kautilya, is a treatise on:
A. Economics B. Polity
C. Commerce D. Numismatics

26. Which Ashokan Pillar bears the figure of a peacock, pointing to the association of Mauryan with it?
A. Nandangarh B. Sarnath
C. Allahabad D. Rummindei

27. To what primary cause would you assign the responsibility for the decline of Mauryan empire after Ashoka?
A. Pacifism of Ashoka
B. Over centralisation
C. Economic crisis
D. Brahmanical reaction after Ashoka's death

28. Which factor or forces strengthened and supported most the imperial system of the Mauryas?
1. a settled agrarian village economy
2. improvement in trade
3. trade with the Roman World
4. material advancement of the Vaisyas

Codes:
A. only 1 and 2 B. only 1, 2 and 3
C. all the four D. only 1, 2 and 4

29. "In the happiness of the subjects lay his happiness and in their troubles lay his troubles." In which book does the statement appears?
A. Indica B. Arthashastra
C. Mudra Rakshasa D. Mritcmakatika

30. Who is described as the Indian Machiavelli?
A. Bimbisara B. Chanakya
C. Bana D. Kalidasa

31. Which one of the following was not a function of the Parishad in the Mauryan period:
A. To keep a check on the whole of administrative system.
B. To implement the king's orders.
C. To keep a watch on the conduct of wars.
D. To decide matters in the absence of the kings.

32. Chandragupta Maurya was:
A. an autocrat B. a statesman
C. a liberal D. an enlightened despot

33. The most reliable source for fixing the date of Ashoka is:
A. Ceylonese Chronicles B. Pali Canon
C. Indika D. Rock Edicts

34. Who said this "All Indians were free and none of them was a slave". (In Mauryan age):
A. Strobo B. Pliny
C. Justin D. Arrian

35. Chandragupta belonged to the Moriya tribe of:
A. Brahmanas B. Kshatriyas
C. Vaishyas D. Shudra

36. Who said "Indians do not know the art of writing"?
A. Kautilya B. Pliny
C. Megasthenes D. Plutarch

37. Which one of the following is considered to be a controversial part of the treaty of 303 B.C. between Chandragupta and Seleucus?
A. Seleucus surrendered a large territory including, according to some historians' Paropanisadia (Kabul), Aria (Herat); Archosia (Quandhar) and Gedrosia (Baluchistan).
B. Chandragupta made a gift of 500 elephants to Seleucus.
C. Seleucus gave his daughter in marriage to Chandragupta
D. A Greek envoy (Megasthenes) was accredited to the Mauryan Court at Pataliputra.

38. Among the following, which one is false. Identify?
A. Chandragupta Maurya concluded a favourable treaty with the Greeks.
B. Chandragupta became a Jain.
C. Chandragupta got the help of Alexander.
D. Chankya assisted Chandragupta in winning Magadha.

39. "All Indians are free and not one of them is a slave"? who said?
A. Itsing B. Fahien
C. Megasthenes D. Huein Tsang

40. Who conquered Deccan?
A. Ashoka B. Dasratha
C. Samprati D. Bindusara

41. Chandragupta Maurya liberated one of the following parts of India from Seleucus. Which one was that?
A. North-Western B. South-Western
C. South-Eastern D. Western

42. Where is the Lomasa Rishi Cave?
A. Barabar Area B. Ellora
C. Bhaja D. Amaravati

43. After abdication, Chandragupta Maurya probably left for:
A. Modern Andhra Pradesh
B. The white Jain tank
C. Chandragiri Hills
D. The modern City of Chikmagalur

44. Chandragupta Maurya defeated Seleucus in 305 B.C. and presented him:
A. 500 war elephants B. 50 war elephants
C. 100 war elephants D. 200 war elephants

45. Which point on the imperial palace of Chandragupta Maurya is not correct?
A. It was close to the modern village of Kumaharahar.
B. It was designed in inmitation of the Persian palace at Persepolis.
C. The gilded pillars were adorned with golden vines and silver birds.
D. It has a natural cooling system.

46. Who said this? "The Buddha would have made a good general if he had not become a monk".
A. Charles Eliot B. Vincent Smith
C. Rhys Davids D. Romila Thapar

47. Who was Justin?
A. A Greek Poet B. Greek Writer
C. Greek Philosopher D. A Greek King

48. According to Kautilya, King:
A. Should be highly educated
B. Should be a person of integrity
C. Should save himself from hist, anger, greed etc.
D. All the above.

49. Who were described as the Pancharatrikas?
A. Bhagavatas B. Pasupatas
C. Digumbaras D. Hinayanists

50. Which among the following is the incorrect match?
A. Chandragupta — Vrishala
B. Bindusara — Amitraghata
C. The Nandas — Kulahinas
D. Mahavira — Arihant

51. Whom did Ashoka send to conduct missionary work in Ceylon?
A. Mahendra B. Aniruddha
C. Mahanaman D. Jamali

52. Who founded Mauryan dynasty?
A. Chanakya B. Chandragupta Maurya
C. Ashoka D. None of the above

53. According to Brahmanical tradition Chandragupta Maurya was born of:
A. Sudra Woman B. Brahman Woman
C. Kshatriya Woman D. Vaishya Woman

54. About the qualities of the ministers Kautilya lays down that they should be:
A. Men of high character
B. Loyal
C. Wise and brave
D. All the above

55. Which was not responsible for Chandragupta's success?
A. Kautilya's guidance
B. Brilliant generalship
C. Greek aid
D. Weakness of the Nanda ruler

56. Who was Sandrokottos?
A. Chandragupta B. Dasarath
C. Ashoka D. Amitraghata

57. What is the number of Vrishiniviras?
A. Five B. Three
C. Ten D. Four

58. Who said that the Indians did not drink (liquor) in the age of Mauryas?
A. Megasthenes B. Arrian
C. Strabo D. Pliny

59. Who was the author of Indica?
A. Kautilya B. Seleucus
C. Ashoka D. Megasthenes

60. Which God was called Herakles by the Greeks?
A. Krishna B. Indra
C. Rudra D. Brahma

61. One of the following occupations was not common between the Sudras and Vaishyas in the Mauryan period:
A. agriculture B. rearing cattle
C. trade D. teaching

62. "The evil of evils is the poverty of the people", who said this?
A. Mahavir B. Buddha
C. Megasthenes D. Kautilya

63. For how many years did Megasthenes stay in India?
A. Two B. Five
C. Ten D. Fourteen

64. Which of the following was not a part of Chandragupta's Empire?
A. Kashmir B. Kathiawar
C. Kalinga D. Afghanistan

65. Metals most frequently used during Chandragupta reign in minting the coins, were:
A. Gold and Silver B. Silver and Copper
C. Copper and Bronze D. Gold and Copper

66. Ashoka's coronation took place in:
A. 261 BC B. 273 BC
C. 264 BC D. 250 BC

67. When did Chandragupta Maurya ascend the Throne?
A. 321 BC B. 322 BC
C. 323 BC D. 324 BC

68. Punishment was severe during the reign of the:
A. Mauryas B. Guptas
C. Sungas D. Chalukyas

69. Who wrote "Mudrarakshasa"?
A. Kautilya B. Megasthenes
C. Vishakhadatta D. Vishnu Sharma

70. Which inscriptions mention the pilgrimages of the emperor to the holy places of Buddhism?
A. Major Rock Edicts
B. Bhabru Edicts
C. Cave inscriptions
D. Rummindei and Nigliva

71. Under the Mauryan administration:
A. Pataliputra was the capital
B. Administration was carried on by six committees
C. Each committee consisting of five members
D. All are correct

72. The espionage system was very extensive under:
A. Mauryas B. Cholas
C. Cheras D. Priest

73. Who was the first ruler of the world to issue a no war declaration?
A. Chandragupta Maurya
B. Alexander
C. Seleucus
D. Ashoka

74. Who was Chandragupta's successor?
A. Bindusara B. Ashoka
C. Dasratha D. Bimbisara

75. Where did Chandragupta Maurya met Alexander?
A. Greece B. Magadha
C. Punjab D. None of the above

76. The key note of Ashoka's policy of Dhamma was:
A. Charity B. Kindness
C. Self Control D. Moderation

77. Who is the first Indian king to speak directly to the people through his inscriptions?
A. Chandragupta Maurya
B. Bindusara
C. Ashoka
D. Dhana Nanda

78. Which was the most important city under Chandragupta Maurya?
A. Pataliputra B. Kausambi
C. Ujjain D. Taxila

79. The administrative system of Chandragupta consisted of:
A. Autonomous king
B. Decentralisation
C. Centralised bureaucracy
D. Mantri Prishad that had the right to over rule King's decision.

80. The palace of Chandragupta was constructed of:
A. Brick B. Stone
C. Wood D. Mud

81. Which religion did Chandragupta Maurya adopted during last year of his reign?
A. Hinduism B. Jainism
C. Buddhism D. Bhagavatism

82. When did Alexander die?
A. 320 BC B. 321 BC
C. 322 BC D. 323 BC

83. During whose reign did the Buddhist Church underwent recognisation?
A. Chandragupta Maurya
B. Bindusara
C. Ashoka
D. Dasratha

84. The Kalinga war was fought in:
A. 261 BC B. 273 BC
C. 218 AD D. 288 AD

85. Who was the last Mauryan King?
A. Bindusara B. Kanishka
C. Ashoka D. Dasratha

86. Who was the immediate heirs of what remained of the Mauryan empire?
A. Shungas B. Chalukyas
C. Huns D. Rashtrakutas

87. Image worship started during the Maurya Period among:
A. The Hindus
B. The Buddhist
C. The Jains
D. None of the above

88. Who has described the killer of Brihadratha as anarya?
A. Kalhana B. Bana
C. Kautilya D. Visakadatta

89. What was the strong hold of the Digambaras?
A. Gujarat B. Rajasthan
C. Karnataka D. Kathiawar

90. One of the following occupations was not common between the Sudras and Vaisyas in the Mauryan period:
A. agriculture B. rearing cattle
C. trade D. teaching

91. Match the coins with the dynasties which issued them:

(*a*) Mauryas	1. Silver, Karshapana, Gold, Suvrana
(*b*) Indo-Bactrian	2. Silver Pana, Ardha Pana, Pada
(*c*) Satavahnas	3. Gold Double dinara
(*d*) Kushans	4. Gold stalor, Silver tetra-drachm and didrachm
(*e*) Guptas	5. Gold Suvarna

Codes:

	(*a*)	(*b*)	(*c*)	(*d*)	(*e*)
A.	2	4	1	3	5
B.	1	2	3	4	5
C.	2	4	1	5	3
D.	4	1	3	2	5

92. The earliest evidence of the practice of Sati dated 510 A.D. is from the:
A. Aihole Inscription
B. Airan Inscription
C. Nasik Inscription
D. Hathigumpha Inscription

93. Who was the author of Kalpasutra?
A. Bhadrabahu B. Panini
C. Subandhu D. Patanjali

94. To whom does Hathigumpha inscription of Orissa belong?
A. Ashoka B. Bindusara
C. Kanishka D. Kharavela

95. One of the following places was not noted for fine cotton fabrics in Mauryan times. Identify.
A. Varanasi B. Vanga
C. Madurai D. Karle

96. Which among the following was used in most of Ashoka's inscriptions?
A. Kharoshti B. Armaic
C. Brahmi D. Greek

97. Who was the first Shaka King in India?
A. Pushyamitra B. Moga
C. Menander D. None of the above

98. Who came to India in search of the great wealth of knowledge and literature in ancient times?
A. Sakas B. Greeks
C. Parthians D. Chinese

99. In which of the three Pitakas are the Jatakas included?
A. Sutta B. Vinaya
C. Abhidhamma D. None of these

100. Which among the following was not a seat of learning during the age of the Maurya?
A. Patliputra B. Taxila
C. Ujjain D. Varanasi

ANSWERS

1	2	3	4	5	6	7	8	9	10
A	C	C	A	C	A	A	C	C	D
11	**12**	**13**	**14**	**15**	**16**	**17**	**18**	**19**	**20**
A	A	C	B	B	A	B	D	B	D
21	**22**	**23**	**24**	**25**	**26**	**27**	**28**	**29**	**30**
D	A	A	A	B	A	B	A	B	B
31	**32**	**33**	**34**	**35**	**36**	**37**	**38**	**39**	**40**
C	D	D	D	B	C	C	C	C	D
41	**42**	**43**	**44**	**45**	**46**	**47**	**48**	**49**	**50**
A	A	C	A	D	A	B	D	A	C
51	**52**	**53**	**54**	**55**	**56**	**57**	**58**	**59**	**60**
A	B	A	D	C	A	A	A	D	A
61	**62**	**63**	**64**	**65**	**66**	**67**	**68**	**69**	**70**
D	D	B	C	B	B	D	A	C	D
71	**72**	**73**	**74**	**75**	**76**	**77**	**78**	**79**	**80**
D	A	D	A	C	D	C	A	C	C
81	**82**	**83**	**84**	**85**	**86**	**87**	**88**	**89**	**90**
B	D	C	A	D	A	D	B	C	D
91	**92**	**93**	**94**	**95**	**96**	**97**	**98**	**99**	**100**
A	B	A	D	D	C	B	D	A	A

SET-6

1. During the pre-Gupta age, the foreign trade was most extensive with:
A. China
B. Roman Empire
C. South-East Asian Countries
D. Central Asia

2. What was the name of South Indian Money Lenders?
A. Seths B. Banjaras
C. Chettis D. Panis

3. What is not true about the functions of guilds?
A. Organization of production.

B. Guilds controlled the prices of manufactured articles.
C. Guilds were politically amibitious and therefore played an important role in the Political arena.
D. In several cities they seem to have issued coins.

4. What is not true of the guild system of the period:
A. The vast majority of artisans joined the guilds, since it was difficult for them to complete as individuals against the guilds
B. Guilds offered the artisans social status and a degree of general security.
C. Guilds could change their location without the permission from the local authority.
D. Some guilds began to employ hired labour and slaves to meet the growing demand of their products.

5. Which of the following is incorrect?
A. There was no compound interest in pre-Gupta period.
B. A debtor could sell his personal belonging for debt in pre-Gupta period.
C. Loan were given on security of ornaments or debtor's personal property in pre-Gupta period.
D. Money-lending was not in practice in pre-Gupta period.

6. The guilds during the Gupta age were under the control of:
A. the king directly B. autonomous bodies
C. provincial governors D. Vishayapati

7. What was the main reason for the expansion of internal trade during the Gupta period?
A. Greater prosperity of the people
B. Maintenance of law and order and strong Central rule
C. Technological progress
D. Better organisation guilds.

8. The most famous city for the production of cotton cloth during the period of the visit of Hiuen Tsang was:
A. Banaras B. Pataliputra
C. Surat D. Mathura

9. Among the previous stones, the most extensive foreign trade during the Gupta age was in that of:
A. Ruby B. Diamonds
C. Pearl D. Sapphire

10. Which of the following regions was most famous for pearl trade during the Gupta period?
A. Gujarat B. Pandya Country
C. Andhra Pradesh D. West Bengal

11. Imported coins were mostly used as:
A. items of jewellery B. bullion
C. foreign exchange D. currency of circulation

12. Which one of the following statements regarding the trade and commerce of the Gupta period is not correct?
A. The Ganga valley was the principal trade area.
B. The circulation of money expanded extensively.
C. On account of development of roads, the use of rivers as trade-routes declined.
D. Sale of certain commodities was subject to strict state control and there was royal monopoly in certain items of trade.

13. What was the Characteristic of pottery of this period?
A. Northern black polished ware
B. Red ware with a brownship slip
C. Painted grey ware
D. Yellow and red

14. Which one of the following was not a feature of the industrial life of the Gupta period?
A. The artisans were held in high esteem.
B. There were also royal foundries.
C. Liquor was produced throughout the country.
D. Bonded labourers were also employed in the industries.

15. Who were Sarthavata?
A. They were caravan traders
B. They were grain merchants
C. They were money lenders
D. They were brokers.

16. Roman trade declined after 3rd century AD and with the Hun invasion of the Roman empire it came to an end. In which direction did the Indian Traders turn for business activities?
A. Africa B. China
C. Sri Lanka D. South-East Asia

17. Which of the following was not the commercial centre connected with Gupta rulers?
A. Calcutta B. Banaras
C. Kausambi D. Pataliputra

18. Which one of the following Indian commodities was not exported to Rome?
A. Pepper
B. Indian animals such as lions, tiger, apes
C. Ivory
D. Wine

19. Which of the following was not the port of east coast which handled South-East Asian Trade?
A. Chaul B. Tamralipti
C. Ghantashala D. Kadura

20. The merchant group of which one of the following towns did not issue coins?
A. Tripuri B. Kashi
C. Vidisa D. Magadha

21. In which metal, was Karshapana coins issued?
1. Gold 2. Silver
3. Copper 4. Lead

Codes:
A. 1 and 2 B. 1, 2 and 3
C. 3 and 4 D. All four

22. Which one of the following was the most commonly used coin?
A. Nishka (Gold) B. Shatamana (Silver)
C. Kakini (Copper) D. Karshapana

23. The trade and Industry during the pre-Gupta age were well organised into:
A. Srenis B. Eathavana
C. Jethaka D. Karshapana

24. The earliest reference to some sort of guild organisation in ancient India is found in:
A. Epics B. Smriti literature
C. Prasastis D. Vedic literature

25. Which empire opened the Red-Sea trade route of Greeks and Indians?
A. Greek B. Roman
C. Muslim D. None of these

26. The king who captured the famous silk route of Central Asia was:
A. Kanishka B. Harsha
C. Ashoka D. Menander

27. Which was not the cause of general stagnation and decline in trade and commerce between the seventh and tenth centuries in Northern India?
A. Collapse of the Roman empire in the West.
B. Rise of Islam and the Collapse of old empires such as the Sassanid (Iranian) empire.
C. Political confrontation among different dynasties and lack of uniform administration in India.
D. Decline of the guilds.

28. The behaviour of the guild members was controlled through:
A. Council of senior member
B. The Elder
C. Specially appointed supervisors
D. Guild Court

29. Which of the following was not one of the leading guilds of the period?
A. Leather workers B. Metal workers
C. Potters D. Carpenters

30. Which one of the following rules were not fixed by the guilds?
A. Work B. Price
C. Distribution D. Social conduct

31. Which one of the following was the most advanced industry of the period?
A. Metal work B. Jewellery
C. Textile D. Minting of coins

32. Which of the following was not one of the varieties of textiles produced during the period?
A. Cotton B. Velvet
C. Wool D. Muslin

33. Which one of the following towns was not connected by land route from India?
A. Alexandrea B. Susa
C. Persepolis D. Seleucia

34. What became prominent in military tactics during Gupta period?
A. Chariots B. Archery
C. Horse archery D. None of the above

35. Main aim of Samudragupta in attacking the states of South India was:
A. Annexation
B. Plunder
C. Extension of his sphere of influence
D. Acceptance of his suzerainty by their rulers

36. The first Christian missionary entered India in the:
A. 1st Century BC B. 1st Century AD
C. 2nd Century AD D. 3rd Century AD

37. Who was the author of Natyashastra?
A. Vasumitra B. Nagarjuna
C. Asvagosha D. Bhasa

38. Who among the following was the author of Mrichhakatika?
A. Bhasa B. Sudraka
C. Nagarjuna D. Gargacharya

39. The earliest paintings of Ajanta caves date back to:
A. 1st Century BC B. 1st Century AD
C. 2nd Century AD D. 3rd Century AD

40. Choose the wrong one. During pre-Gupta and Gupta period:
A. Attitudes of the people in general were liberal
B. State and people enjoyed prosperity during the rules of Satavahanas
C. Agriculture and trade were the main professions of people
D. The king mostly encouraged Tamil language.

41. Choose the wrong one. During pre-Gupta and Gupta period:
A. The society was divided into four castes
B. It was divided on the basis of profession
C. Women commanded good respect in the society
D. Inter-Caste marriage were not permitted

42. Which of the following was called Yavanapriya in Sanskrit?
A. Ivory B. Indian pepper
C. Indian Cotton D. Pearls

43. Which was the most important item of export from India to the Roman Empire?
A. Spices B. Pearls
C. Muslin D. Precious stone

44. What was the major item of import from Roman Empire to India?

A. Metal B. Pottery
C. Wire D. Coins

45. Which one of the following were the main items of trade with the Roman Empire?
A. Industrial raw materials
B. Luxury goods
C. Agricultural commodities
D. Furniture goods

46. Which one of the following acted as intermediaries in East Roman Trade?
A. Iranian merchants
B. Arabs
C. Roman Merchants settled in India
D. Indian merchants

47. What is "periplus of the Erythrean Sea"?
A. The name of a book
B. The name of a Greek town
C. The name of a Central Asian Tribe
D. The name of a Greek God

48. Where was the port of Barbasicum situated?
A. At the mouth of Ganga
B. At the mouth of Cauvery
C. On the West Coast
D. On the Indus Delta

49. At which one of the following ports a sizable Roman settlement and a Roman factory have been discovered?
A. Tamralipti B. Barygaza
C. Kaveripattinam D. Arikamedu

50. When did Saka era begin?
A. 58 BC B. 78 BC
C. 58 AD D. 78 AD

51. One of the most noticeable feature of the religious life of the Gupta period was:
A. the growing importance of idols in Puja
B. listening to discourses on the Upanishadas
C. recitation of the Vedas
D. acceptance of the Ahimsa concept

52. One of the most flourishing marts during the Gupta times was:
A. Praithar B. Ujjain
C. Vaishali D. Tamralipti

53. Decentralisation of administrative authority in the Gupta period was caused by:
A. increased in grants of land and villages with fiscal and administrative immunities to priests and temples.
B. preponderant authority of provincial governors.
C. weak authority of general government.
D. the belief of the Guptas in provincial autonomy.

54. Out of the following which one was the most extensively practised industrial activity in the pre-Gupta period?
A. Pottery B. Carpentry
C. Cloth weaving D. Ivory work

55. In the pre-Gupta times the Ships heading for the Burma Coast and South India began their voyage at:
A. Tamralipti (Tamluk) B. Bharukaccha
C. Barbaricum D. Sopara

56. Which of the following is said to have introduced Indian Culture in Cambodia?
A. Kaundinya B. Kharavela
C. Fa-hsien D. Kshemeshvara

57. In the pre-Gupta period the ships heading for Burma Coast and South India began their voyage at:
A. Tamralipti (Tamluk) B. Bharukachha
C. Patala D. Sopara

58. Who designated Samudragupta as "Indian Nepoleon"?
A. R.C. Majumdar B. Vincent Smith
C. Max Mueller D. H.C. Raychaudhri

59. Who is depicted in the coins of Gupta dynasty as sitting cross legged on the couch playing the lute (vina)?
A. Srigupta B. Skandagupta
C. Ramagupta D. Samudragupta

60. Who is the author of Allahabad pillar inscription?
A. Sudaraka B. Bana
C. Harisena D. Patanjali

61. When was Gupta era started?
A. 319-20 AD B. 315-16 AD
C. 319-20 BC D. 335-36 AD

62. Arrange the following in an order:
1. Chandragupta I
2. Chandragupta Vikramaditya
3. Samudragupta
4. Kumaragupta

Codes:
A. 1, 2, 3, 4 B. 1, 3, 4, 2
C. 1, 4, 2, 3 D. 1, 3, 2, 4

63. Who was Prabhavati?
A. Samudragupta's daughter
B. Samudragupta's wife
C. Chandragupta's wife
D. Chandragupta's daughter

64. Which was the most important town during the pre-Gupta and Gupta period?
A. Pataliputra B. Ujjain
C. Gandhar D. None of the above

65. During Gupta period land tax collected varied from:
A. One third to one fourth
B. One fourth to one sixth
C. One third of the produce
D. One fourth of the produce

66. Who adopted the title of Vikramaditya amongst the Gupta Kings?

A. Chandragupta B. Samudragupta
C. Chandragupta II D. Skandgupta

67. Why did town prosper in the Kushana and Satavahana empires?
A. because there towns had gold reserves
B. good administration
C. they carried on thriving trade with the Roman empire
D. None of the above

68. Which statement on the guilds in the pre-Gupta period is not correct?
A. They controlled the equality of products as well as distribution.
B. They bought and sold as co-operative societies.
C. They trained apprentices.
D. They organised political opposition.

69. The writing of the Gupta period emphasise that the Brahmana should not have accepted food from the Sudra because:
A. it would reduce his spiritual strength
B. he would have lost his caste
C. he would have to perform prayaschitta
D. he would not attain Swarga

70. Why did the Vaishya cease to cultivate the land in ancient India?
A. They wanted a superior social status
B. They took to trade and commerce
C. They went over to Buddhism and Jainism
D. Sudras out numbered them as cultivators

71. Which inscription gives us a biographical sketch of the King Kharavela?
A. Besnagar B. Ayodhya
C. Hathigumpha D. Junagarh

72. Which one was the earliest Sanskrit Inscription?
A. Gimar Inscription
B. Mathura Inscription
C. Nasik Inscription
D. Hathigumpha Inscription

73. Which literature discouraged outright conquest by kings but encouraged lawful conquest, that is, conquered kingdoms being reduced to vassal status?
A. Early Vedic Literature
B. Later Vedic Literature
C. Epic and Smriti Literature
D. None of the above

74. The earliest reference to some sort of guild organisation in ancient India is found in:
A. Epics B. Smriti Literature
C. Prashastis D. Vedic Literature

75. What is the most important confirmation revealing that the guilds gave dominations to religious causes of all kinds:
A. Smriti Literature B. Inscriptions
C. Cross references D. Archaeological evidence

76. What is the most remarkable thing about the iron pillar of Mehrauli near Delhi:
A. its weight
B. its artistic value
C. it is chemically pure iron
D. the inscription on it

77. The Southern Trade route starting from Ujjain proceeded to the city of:
A. Kanchi B. Madurai
C. Pratisthana D. Malkhad

78. Which source does not speak anything about trade routes of ancient India?
A. Jataka stories
B. Milinda Panha
C. Periplus of the Erythrean Sea
D. Sangam Literature

79. Which fact relating to the post-Gupta period had no direct bearing on the changed agrarian system?
A. The revenue that was paid to the king was no longer partly used for maintaining public works.
B. The peasants were forced to pay more taxes in addition to the land tax.
C. Temples also collected additional dues.
D. Decline of the guilds.

80. The land grants in the Gupta period led to:
A. Institutionalisation
B. Strong Central Government
C. Decline of the Guptas
D. Strengthening of the Guptas

81. One of the following was of marginal value in the emergence of guilds and trade in the pre-Gupta period. Which one was that?
A. The Cowri-Shells and the barter economy was replaced by system of coins.
B. The kings of the north-west issued coins superior to the punchmarked coins of the Mauryans.
C. Usury was accepted as a part of banking.
D. Interest was taken by financiers like Sreshthins according to one's caste.

82. Which statement on trade and commerce in the pre-Gupta period is not correct?
A. The trade with South East Asia was occasioned by the demand of Rome for more and more of spices.
B. Trade grew further when Indian traders settled in South-East Asia.
C. The trade with South East Asia was vigorously pursued by all the Coastal areas of India.
D. While the impact of Greco-Roman ideas was more evident in the North. The South witnessed the impact of Roman trade.

83. Which political event has no bearing on the growth of trade in the pre-Gupta period?
A. The construction of roads and a uniform system of administration by the Mauryas.

B. The occupation of North-Western India by non-Indian people.
C. The establishment of Indian kingdom in South East Asia.
D. Intercine warfare amongst the Indian kingdoms.

84. With regards to the number of trades referred to in a number of works which pair is wrong?
A. Disha Nikaya — two dozen
B. Mahavastu — thirty six
C. Milandapanho — seventy five
D. Divyavadana — one hundred and twenty five

85. Which one triggered off external trade in the pre-Gupta period?
A. agricultural Surpluses
B. building of roads and protection by State
C. emergence of coins and precious metals for exchange
D. demand for Indian goods in the West

86. The king who controlled the famous silk route of Central Asia was:
A. Kanishka B. Harsha
C. Ashoka D. Menander

87. What is the meaning of the Chinese word 'yue-chi'?
A. Moon tribe B. Asian tribe
C. Sun tribe D. Young people

88. Who opened the great silk route to the Indians?
A. Kanishka B. Ashoka
C. Harsha D. Fa-hien

89. Which empire opened the Red-Sea trade route to Greeks and Indians?
A. Greek B. Roman
C. Muslim D. None of these

90. Who performed the Asvamedha Sacrifice for Pushyamitra Sunga?
A. Panini B. Patanjali
C. Badrayan D. Visvamitra

91. In which period was there more emphasis on the doctrine of avatars?
A. Maurya period B. Sunga period
C. The period of Panini D. Gupta period

92. Samudragupta adopted the policy of:
A. digvijaya
B. dharmavijaya
C. digvijaya as well as dharmvijaya
D. neither digvijaya nor dharmvijaya

93. Who issued the lion type of coins?
A. Chandragupta I B. Chandragupta II
C. Samudragupta D. Harsha

94. Which king made use of metonymics?
A. Mauryas B. Guptas
C. Satavahanas D. Pushyabhutis

95. Kushan coins show:
A. Economic isolation of Northern India
B. Growing economic relation between Northern and Southern India
C. Economic links with the Hellenistic and Roman world
D. Economic links with South-East Asia

96. Gupta inscriptions from Bengal show:
A. traders influence on local administration
B. government control on trade
C. decline in trade
D. weakening of trade guilds

97. Work on the Ajanta Caves began in the reigon of:
A. Maurya kings B. Gupta kings
C. Satavahana kings D. Chola kings

98. Tribal or Republican states in India disappeared because of:
A. Aryan invasion
B. Mauryan conquests
C. Inroads of Greeks, Sakas and Kushans
D. Gupta imperialism and Hun incursions.

99. Who were the first to adopt the title which conveyed king's divinity?
A. Greeks B. Sakas
C. Kushans D. Guptas

100. The earliest extant book on the Dharmashastra is:
A. Narad Smriti B. Brihaspati Smriti
C. Manu Smriti D. None of the above

ANSWERS

1	2	3	4	5	6	7	8	9	10
B	C	C	C	D	B	B	B	C	B
11	**12**	**13**	**14**	**15**	**16**	**17**	**18**	**19**	**20**
B	C	B	A	A	B	A	D	A	D
21	**22**	**23**	**24**	**25**	**26**	**27**	**28**	**29**	**30**
D	D	A	D	B	A	D	D	A	C
31	**32**	**33**	**34**	**35**	**36**	**37**	**38**	**39**	**40**
C	B	A	C	D	B	C	B	B	D

41	42	43	44	45	46	47	48	49	50
D	B	A	D	B	D	A	D	D	D
51	52	53	54	55	56	57	58	59	60
A	D	A	C	A	A	A	B	D	C
61	62	63	64	65	66	67	68	69	70
A	D	B	A	B	C	C	D	A	A
71	72	73	74	75	76	77	78	79	80
C	A	C	D	B	C	C	D	D	A
81	82	83	84	85	86	87	88	89	90
D	C	D	D	D	A	A	A	B	B
91	92	93	94	95	96	97	98	99	100
D	A	B	C	B	B	C	D	C	C

SET-7

1. What is the literal meaning of Pallava?
A. Peasant B. Creeper
C. Thief D. None of the above

2. Land grants became frequent in India from the:
A. 2nd Century A.D. B. 3rd Century A.D.
C. 4th Century A.D. D. 5th Century A.D.

3. Post-Gupta period saw more expansion of the agrarian economy. Why?
A. Population increased
B. Large number of foreigners came to India
C. Large number of Land grants were made to the Brahmans
D. None of the above

4. To which group of the people in the following list land grants were not made during the post-Gupta period?
A. Members of the royal family
B. The Brahmans
C. The royal officials
D. The temple priests

5. Which one of the following ruling dynasties made the largest grant of villages to temples and Brahmans?
A. Palas B. Guptas
C. Rashtrakutas D. Prathihars

6. The practice of land grants originated in the:
A. Later Vedic Period B. Mauryan Period
C. Satavahana Period D. Kushan Period

7. In the post-Gupta period when villages were granted in the tribal areas the agriculturists were placed under the Control of:
A. Royal officials
B. Villages headman
C. The religious beneficiaries
D. The tribal chief

8. Kalabhars patronised:
A. Brahmans B. Jains
C. Buddhist monasteries D. None of the above

9. Who were Kalabhars?
A. Peasants B. Untouchables
C. Run away slaves D. Evil rulers

10. Vakataka power was followed by:
A. Rashtrakutas B. Guptas
C. Harshavardhana D. Chalukyas of Badami

11. The world 'agrarian' means:
A. Agriculture
B. Agriculture and irrigation
C. Agriculture and allied sectors
D. Property rights on land

12. Which one was the most important consequence of the ancient Indian feudal system?
A. Self-sufficiency of the village
B. Development of rural economy
C. Stability in the social system
D. Extension of arable land

13. Who overthrew Chalukyas of Badami in 757 A.D.?
A. Rashtrakutas B. Ikshavakus
C. Vakatakas D. Pallavas

14. Who founded the Kadamba kingdom?
A. Simueka B. Mayurasarman
C. Krishna D. None of the above

15. In Northern Maharashtra and Vidarbha the Satavahanas were succeeded by the:
A. Vakatakas B. Chalukyas
C. Pandyas D. None of the above

16. Alvar Saints were great devotees of:
A. Vishnu B. Shiva
C. Tirthankars D. Other Goddess

17. The Ikshvakus were supplanted by the:
A. Chalukyas B. Pallavas
C. Rashtrakutas D. None of the above

18. Where did Pallava set up Capital?
A. Pataliputra B. Kannauj
C. Madurai D. Kanchi

19. Western Ganges made land grants to only:
A. Buddhists B. Jains
C. Brahmans D. None of the above

20. When did the land grants to the temples in South India become a common phenomenon?
A. After the 7th Century B. After the 8th Century
C. After the 9th Century D. After the 10th Century

21. The Dravidan language which got protection from the Rashtrakutas ruler was.
A. Kannada B. Tamil
C. Telugu D. Malayalam

22. In the field of fine arts, Chalukyas contributed most towards:
A. Painting B. Sculpture
C. Music D. Architecture

23. The empire of the chalukyas of Badami was destroyed by:
A. The Pallavas B. The Cholas
C. The Pandyas D. The Rashtrakutas

24. The Upanayana ceremony of children started:
A. During the later Vedic age
B. During the age of Buddha
C. During the age of Maurya
D. During the age of Pandyas

25. Who among the following started the practice of donating lands which finally resulted infeudal system?
A. The Mauryas B. The Sungas
C. The Satavahanas D. The Guptas

26. The Ankorvat Temple located in kaniby is that of:
A. Vishnu B. Brahma
C. Shiva D. Buddha

27. The Barabudur temple in Java is that of:
A. Shiva B. Vishnu
C. Brahma D. Buddha

28. The land revenue during post-Gupta age was:
A. 1/5 to 1/6 of the produce
B. 1/4 of the produce
C. 1/3 of the produce
D. 1/2 of the produce

29. In which of the following regions of India were the village councils most active?
A. East B. South
C. North D. West

30. During the post-Gupta period land revenue was relaised by:
A. The officers of the State
B. The Zamindars
C. Village assembly
D. None of the above

31. Who distributed land among peasant during post-Gupta period?
A. The state B. The fief holders
C. The village assemblies D. The Zamindars

32. The natural resources which were donated by the king during the post-Gupta period were:
A. Forest land B. Mines
C. Water resources D. All the above

33. The land grants in which one of the following parts of India empowered the recipients to punish thieves and other criminals?
A. North B. West
C. South D. None of the above

34. The most important motive behind the grant of land to priests and officials was:
A. To weaken the power of big landlords
B. To ensure the regular flow of land revenue
C. To punish the recalcitrant peasants
D. To meet the deep social crisis that affected the ancient social order in the 3rd and 4th centuries A.D.

35. In the South Crown lands were rented out to:
A. Tenants in chief B. Tenants-famous
C. Tenants-at-will D. Permanent tenants

36. The Pallava rulers of South India were:
A. Shudras B. Vaishyas
C. Kshatriyas D. Brahmans

37. Which one of the following statement regarding the decline in the status of the agrarian classes is not correct?
A. The status of a free Vaishya peasant declined and he begun to be viewed as a Shudra.
B. The dependent peasants, whose number was much larger than that of the free peasants; were share-croppers.
C. The lowest stratum of dependent peasantry was represented by the plough-drivers and other field labourers who were mainly Shudras.
D. There were no restrictions on the practice of taking food from the Shudra share-croppers.

38. What was the range of land revenue in the South during the Pallava period as a proportion of the produce of land?
A. 1/3rd to 1/4th B. 1/4th to 1/6th
C. 1/6th to 1/10th D. 1/10th to 1/12th

39. The term " Vithi" refers to:
A. Dyer's street B. Ivory worker's street
C. Weaver's locality D. Metal-worker's street

40. Which of the following was the common medium of exchange according to Fa-hein?

A. Nishka B. Cowries
C. Karshapana D. Kakini

41. Which fact relating to society in the post-Gupta period has very little relevance to the changed agrarian system?

A. Many of the Brahman holders employed cultivators since cultivation was regarded as a low by occupation
B. Buddhist monasteries admitted women
C. Buddhist monasteries also employed tenants
D. Hereditary kingship was stressed which the divine origin of kingship was theorised

42. 'Sulka' refers to:

A. a coin
B. a guild of weavers
C. tolls on the frontier collected from foreign merchants
D. None of these

43. The traditional view regarding the position of land in ancient India was that:

A. the king owned the land
B. the king was the custodian of land
C. the king was the protector of land and the people living on the land
D. the king had his own crown land while the people had property rights on the land possessed by them

44. Which was the most important means to extend the arable land?

A. Conquest
B. Land grants
C. Encouragement to peasants
D. Emergence of the towns

45. Which one of the following was the basic tax?

A. Bhaga B. Kara
C. Bali D. Hiranya

46. The labourers were paid wages in cash or as a share of the produce. What was their share of the produce if accompanied by food?

A. 1/3rd B. 1/4th
C. 1/5th D. 1/6th

47. What was malla-Karra and turshka-danda?

A. Taxation imposed on foreigners unauthorisedly settled in India.
B. Impost levied by the central government to deal with the menace from marauding tribes.
C. The fine imposed on those tax-payers who were found to have evaded payment of taxes.
D. Public collection for waging war against the Turks.

48. There was a special category of land in the South known as eripatti what was its revenue meant for?

A. Feeding of the poor
B. Maintenance of the village tank
C. Maintenance of village roads
D. Creation of permanent assets

49. Which of the following varieties of land available during the period, was generally donated by the way of salary?

A. Follow or waste land owned by the state and the land in newly-formed villages
B. Cultivated land owned by the state and treated as crown land
C. Privately owned land
D. Royal or Crown lands

50. 'Agrahara grants' were:

A. Those Lands which were donated to a temple for its upkeep
B. Lands granted to secular official in lieu of salary
C. Granted to Brahman and were tax-free
D. Made the intellectual class

51. Regarding the land attached to religious institution in Chola times:

A. It was from land tax
B. It was not free from land tax
C. We can say nothing specific about it
D. It was taxed arbitrarily

52. Which fact was the least responsible for the emergence of feudal or regional loyalities?

A. Minor kings sought impressive geneologies as found in Prithviraja Raso.
B. The king granted rent-free lands to his officers or select holders.
C. The Shudras who cultivated the land were made to hand over a fixed share of their produce to the land owners.
D. The feudatories could assign their lands to cultivators who paid them an agreed upon revenue.

53. In ancient India the condition of the peasants was what it was because:

A. he was made a tenant or share-cropper
B. he cultivated land for the king or his chief
C. he cultivated land as though it was his own
D. he had the right of ownership

54. Which of the consequence of Brahmans being granted land in backward area was of crucial importance for India after the 5th and 6th centuries A.D.?

A. Brahmans took agriculture as well as Ayurveda to tribal area.
B. Writing of Prakrit and Sanskrit was disseminated.
C. The aboriginal peasants became the new Sudras.
D. The land grants in the development area down graded the importance of the Vaishya peasants.

55. Which of the following statements regarding the land grants during the period is not true?

A. The number of land grants considerably increased
B. All types of grants became hereditary and permanent in character

C. Some of the grantees were also given transferred administrative functions
D. Land grants were also made to state officials thus ushering in the process of foundalisation

56. Which one made the life of the peasants most miserable in the post-Gupta period?
A. The peasants paid various taxes like temple tax, and tax on goods produced besides land revenue.
B. On occasions the peasants were made to provide free labour.
C. The feudatories even appropriated the common lands of the villages.
D. There was a proliferation of intermediaries between the king and the peasant.

57. Which feature can you associate with the Indian feudalism?
A. Serfdom
B. Manorial system
C. Knigh Service
D. Zamindars exercised many of the royal powers and peasantry was dependent on them

58. Which fact relating to the post-Gupta period had no direct bearing on the charged agrarain system?
A. The revenue that was paid to the king was no longer partly used for maintaining public works
B. The peasants were forced to pay more taxes in addition to the land tax
C. Temples also collected additional dues
D. Emergences of regional warfares

59. How did the practice of land grants lead to the emergance of serfdom:
A. It aggravated their poverty forcing them to the position of slaves.
B. They were often required to work on the land even when it had been granted to others.
C. The exploitation of private landlords was greater than that of the king.
D. Due to obsentee Landlordism.

60. Identify that of the following feature the one that provides a clue to the understanding of decline of economic prosperity after the Guptas:
A. Decay of towns as witnessed by Huien Tsang
B. Village became self-sufficient
C. Rigid varana system
D. Events that occurred beyond India like the rise of Islam, collapse of Roman Empire and intrusion of China into Indo-China.

61. The practice of land grants started with the:
A. Guptas B. Chalukyas
C. Mauryas D. Satavahanas

62. Which one was the most important consequence of the ancient Indian feudal system?
A. Self-sufficient of the village
B. Development of rural economy
C. Stability in the social system
D. Extension of the arable land

63. In which century did the donor not only transfer all sources of revenues to the grantee but also the rights to govern and punish the inhabitants of the villages?
A. 2nd Century A.D. B. 3rd Century A.D.
C. 5th Century A.D. D. 7th Century A.D.

64. In whose court did Asvogosha live!
A. Harsha B. Samudragupta
C. Kaniskha D. Ashoka

65. Who is the author of Rajatarangini?
A. Harsha B. Kalhana
C. Kalidasa D. Panini

66. Who wrote Ashtadhyayi?
A. Panini B. Hatyayna
C. Jayadeva D. Bharata

67. At whose hands did Harsha suffer a defeat?
A. Pulakesin II B. Mahendravaraman I
C. Rajaraja Chola D. Narasimharaman I

68. Which work recognises first the payment of fiscal officers by grants of land?
A. Kautilya's Arthashastra
B. Manusmriti
C. Megasthene's Indica
D. Harsha's three dramas

69. Which of the following were exempted from taxation according to the sacred law?
A. Student B. Ascetics
C. Learned Brahmans D. All the above

70. Which one of the following categories of merchants appears to be most important according to this inscription?
A. Salt merchants B. Oil merchants
C. Grain merchants D. Cloth merchants

71. That the land grants were made to officers for their military and administrative services is directly evident from the epigraphics records of:
A. Maurya B. Satavahanas
C. Guptas D. Post-Gupta period

72. Which one of the following places was famous for fragment rice?
A. Mathura B. Tanjore
C. Ujjain D. Magadha

73. What was the reason for the Indian visit of Hiuen Tsang?
A. to visit the holy places connected with Buddhism
B. to amass wealth
C. to know the geography of India
D. to establish political ties with India

74. Which among the following is true? Harsha held an assembly at Kannauj:
A. to distribute alms to the poor people
B. to commemorate his victories

C. to honour the visit of Hieun-Tsang
D. to settle the question of successors

75. The seven Pagodas at Mahabalipuram belong to one of the following. Identify:
A. Cholas B. The Chalukyas
C. The Pallavas D. The Rashtrakutas

76. The Aihole inscription records the achievements of one of the following. Identify:
A. Harsha B. Samudragupta
C. Pulakesin II D. Rajendra Chola

77. Who wrote Kadambani?
A. Bana B. Harsha
C. Kalidasa D. Kahana

78. The land grants of which one of the following parts of India empowered the recipients to punish thieves and other criminals?
A. West B. South
C. North D. Central India

79. Which one of the following term was used for the plough drivers who represented the section of field labourers?
A. Malavhaaka B. Karsakaka
C. Kinasa D. All the above

80. Which of the following was one of the services to be performed by the villagers, when royal troops and officials halted at the village?
A. Contributed provisions
B. Contributed money
C. Provide Cattle for transport
D. All the above

81. Which one of the following ruling dynasties made the largest grant of villages to temples and Brahmans?
A. Guptas B. Palas
C. Rastrakutas D. Pratiharas

82. What is said to be the original home of the Sungas?
A. Kalinga B. Vidisa
C. Berar D. Bharhut

83. For how many years did the Sungas rule?
A. 60 years B. 80 years
C. 95 years D. 112 years

84. Who was the leader of the Parthien revolt against Antiochus I?
A. Vonones B. Arsaces
C. Maues D. Euthydemus

85. Pick out the wrong match from the following?
A. Grahavarman — Pushyabhuti
B. Rudrasena — Vakataka
C. Nahapana — Kshaharata
D. Toramane — Huns

86. Who among the following has been described as the second Alexander?
A. Arsaces B. Antiochus
C. Demetrius D. Diodotus I

87. Whose general was Apallodotus?
A. Euthydemus B. Demetrius
C. Diodotus D. Antiochus

88. Permission was granted to a Ceylonese king during Samudragupta's reign to build a Buddhist monastery at one of the following places. Identify:
A. Pataliputra B. Bodh Gaya
C. Ujjain D. Vaisali

89. Who among the following could have started the Saka era?
A. Kanishka B. Kadphises II
C. Vasishka D. Chandragupta II

90. Who was the Kushana king? Who is stated to have taken the title 'Caesar'?
A. Kanishka II B. Vasudeva
C. Wema Kadphises D. Vasudeva I

91. Who wrote Buddha Charita?
A. Vasumitra B. Bana
C. Asvagosha D. Charaka

92. Who among the following was called Siloditya?
A. Kanishka B. Harsha
C. Pulakesin II D. Mahendra Verman I

93. Which school of Artists is said to have the "hand of a Greek but the heart of an Indian"?
A. Hellenistic B. Gandhara
C. Mathura D. Gupta

94. Pick out the wrong match from the following:
A. Agnimitra — Mauryas
B. Pushyamitra — Sungas
C. Kharavela — Kalinga
D. Demetrius — Greeks

95. Pick out the wrong match:
A. Vasudeva — Kanvas
B. Patanjali — Grammarian
C. Susarman — Mathematician
D. Devabhuti — Sunge

96. Pick out the wrong match:
A. Vidisa — Modern Besnagar in Eastern Malwa
B. Heliodorus — Greek Ambassador
C. Antiochus — Greek king of Syria
D. Patanjali — Gargi Samhita

97. The Sunga period saw the growth of one of the following religions. Identify:
A. Bhagavata religion B. Saivism
C. Buddhism D. Nature worship

98. The Kanvas were generally the followers of one of the religions given below. Identify:
A. Buddhism B. Jainism
C. Brahmanism D. Bhagavatism

99. Who among the Sunga rulers was the hero of Kalidas's work?
A. Agnimitra B. Pushyamitra
C. Vasumitra D. Bhagabhadra

100. Who was the last king of the Sunga dynasty?
A. Bhga B. Devabhuti
C. Agnimitra D. Vasumitra

ANSWERS

1	2	3	4	5	6	7	8	9	10
B	C	C	A	C	C	C	C	D	D
11	**12**	**13**	**14**	**15**	**16**	**17**	**18**	**19**	**20**
D	D	A	B	A	A	B	D	B	B
21	**22**	**23**	**24**	**25**	**26**	**27**	**28**	**29**	**30**
A	D	D	A	C	A	D	A	B	C
31	**32**	**33**	**34**	**35**	**36**	**37**	**38**	**39**	**40**
C	D	A	D	C	D	D	C	B	D
41	**42**	**43**	**44**	**45**	**46**	**47**	**48**	**49**	**50**
D	C	C	B	A	C	B	B	A	C
51	**52**	**53**	**54**	**55**	**56**	**57**	**58**	**59**	**60**
B	A	C	D	B	D	D	D	B	D
61	**62**	**63**	**64**	**65**	**66**	**67**	**68**	**69**	**70**
D	D	C	C	B	A	A	B	D	C
71	**72**	**73**	**74**	**75**	**76**	**77**	**78**	**79**	**80**
D	D	A	C	C	C	A	C	D	D
81	**82**	**83**	**84**	**85**	**86**	**87**	**88**	**89**	**90**
C	B	D	B	A	C	B	B	A	A
91	**92**	**93**	**94**	**95**	**96**	**97**	**98**	**99**	**100**
C	B	B	A	C	D	A	C	A	B

SET-8

1. The first ruler of the Cholas, who maintained a strong navy, was:
A. Rajendra I B. Karikala
C. Parantaka D. Rajaraja the Great

2. The Chola administration was primarily based upon:
A. Central Government
B. Provincial administration
C. Local self-Government
D. Military power

3. The executive committee of which one of the following general assemblies was called Variyam?
A. Ur B. Sabha
C. Nagaram D. Mahasabha

4. During the time of Cholas "Valanadu" referred to a:
A. Province
B. Sub-division of a province
C. Village
D. Brahmana Village

5. What was the name of the Chola king who first conquered the whole of the island of Sri Lanka?
A. Rajadhiraja I B. Vijayalaya
C. Karilala D. Rajendra I

6. Identify the Chola king who sent to China in 1077 an embassy of 72 merchants:
A. Kulottunga I B. Rajendra I
C. Rajendra II D. Rajadhiraja I

7. Rajendra Chola attacked the Palas in the North probably in:
A. 1018 A.D. B. 1020 A.D.
C. 1021 A.D. D. 1023 A.D.

8. We know a great deal more about the Cholas than their predecessors because:
A. they appointed court chroniclers
B. many books were written during that period
C. of long inscription on the walls of temples
D. of the abundance of coins

9. Who adopted the title of Gangaikonda Chola?
A. Karikala Chola B. Rajendra I
C. Rajaraja I D. Rajadhiraja

10. Parantaka I established Chola power in:
A. 897 A.D. B. 899 A.D.
C. 905 A.D. D. 907 A.D.

11. The Cholas regained their power after the decline of the:
A. Chalukyas B. Rashtrakutas
C. Pallavas D. Kakatiyas

12. The founder of the Chola empire in the 10th century was:
A. Vijayalaya B. Karikala
C. Parantaka I D. Rajaraja the Great

13. What was the name of the Chola king who performed Asvamedha sacrifice?
A. Rajendra I B. Karikala
C. Parantaka D. Rajadhiraja I

14. Rajaraja Chola ascended the throne in:
A. 1016 A.D. B. 1000 A.D.
C. 985 A.D. D. 953 A.D.

15. Rajaraja and Rajendra I commemorated their victories by:
A. erecting temples
B. erecting pillars
C. ordering inscriptions to be written
D. issuing coins

16. By what other name is Kulattunga I known as?
A. Vikrama Chola B. Gangaikonda Chola
C. Pandit Chola D. Rajendra II Chalukya

17. To become a member of the Variyam, which one of the following was not necessary?
A. Ownership of more than 1/4 of the tax-paying land.
B. Residence in a house built on one's own site.
C. Membership of the first three classes of society.
D. Age between 35 and 70 years.

18. Rajendra Chola ascended the throne in:
A. 1044 A.D. B. 1012 A.D.
C. 985 A.D. D. 1000 A.D.

19. Vishti denoted forced labour in Mauryan times. What is the second word meaning forced labour?
A. Vetti B. Sulka
C. Sondhar D. Kara

20. The primary cause of the prosperity of the Chola empire was:
A. agricultural progress
B. trade with foreign countries
C. industries
D. war-booty

21. One of the following did not from an item of export to China and the The West:
A. Jewellery B. Elephants
C. Perfumes D. Spices

22. What was the most important port of the Chola period (10th Century A.D.)?
A. Sopatma B. Camara
C. Kaveripattinam D. Colchi

23. The meetings of the general assembly were held:
A. under a tree
B. on the bank of a tank
C. in a building specially constructed for the purpose
D. at the village temple

24. Devadasi system had become very popular during the period of the:
A. Pandyas B. Cholas
C. Chera D. Chalukyas

25. What was the name of local merchant guilds in Chola times?
A. Ur B. Sabha
C. Nagaram D. Mahasabha

26. Who was the Chola king who bore the name "Arulmolivarman"?
A. Rajendra I B. Parantaka I
C. Rajaraja I D. Kulottunga I

27. Who build the Brihadesvara temple?
A. Parantaka I B. Rajaraja I
C. Rajendra I D. Rajaraja II

28. Who is the author of Kalingattupparani?
A. Kambar B. Ottakuttar
C. Jayangondar D. Pugalendi

29. Who was the founder of Virasaivism?
A. Appar B. Bijjala
C. Basava D. Sundarar

30. Among the places mentioned below no college existed in the Chola period. Identify.
A. Eunayiram B. Tribhuvanam
C. Tiruvaduthurai D. Tiruchi

31. Who patronised the Kannada poet, Rauna?
A. Satyasraya B. Taila II
C. Vikramaditya VI D. Jayasimha II

32. To which of the following did Kannada literature owe much?
A. Brahmanism B. Jainism
C. Buddhism D. Virasaivism

33. The Cholas charged land-tax at the rate of:
A. 1/2 of the produce B. 1/3 of the produce
C. 1/4 of the produce D. 1/6 of the produce

34. The main source of income to the Cholas was:
A. toll tax
B. land tax
C. taxes an occupations, wines and forests
D. annexation of neighbouring territories

35. Possibly the South Indian Vimanas were copies from the:
A. Mandapas B. Rathas
C. Gopurams D. Viharas

36. Which one is an open Pavilion?
A. Mandapas B. Gopurams
C. Ratha D. Viharas

37. The continued incursions of who among the following people weakened the Cholas?
A. Hoysalas B. Western Gangas
C. Yadavas D. Kakatiyas

38. Which among the follownig did not contribute significantly for the final disintegration of the Cholas?
A. Hoysalas B. Pandyas
C. Kakatiyas D. Yadavas

39. Who was the first Chalukya-Chola ruler?
A. Virarjendra B. Kulottunga I
C. Vijayalaya D. Vimaladitya

40. Name the most eminent images constructed under Chola?
A. Images of Vishnu
B. Images of Kuladevta
C. Images of Natraja
D. Images of King's ancestors

41. Which one was the most important item of import?
A. Horses B. Metal-ware
C. Pottery D. Salt

42. The Chola kings primarily were the worshippers of:
A. Shiva B. Ganesha
C. Vishnu D. Kartikeya

43. What was the basic feature of Chola temple architecture:
A. Garbhagriha B. Mandaps
C. Gopurams D. Vimanas

44. The land revenue under the rule of the Chola was:
A. 1/2 of the produce B. 1/4 of the produce
C. 1/3 of the produce D. 1/5 of the produce

45. The Pallava-Chola style of architecture is commonly known as:
A. Pallava B. Chola
C. Nagar D. Dravida

46. Temple architecture in the South attained its climax under:
A. Cheras B. Pandyas
C. Cholas D. Chalukyas

47. The chief features of the temple constructed by the C... las was their:
... opurams B. Pillars
... sembly halls D. Vimanas

... language is patronised by Chola rulers?
... krit B. Tamil
... u D. Kannada

49. Which among the following did not constitute a part of Chola army?
A. Navy B. War elephants
C. Chariots D. Infantry

50. Who amongst the Chola ruler adopted the title Gangaikonda?
A. Rajaraja B. Rajaraja II
C. Rajendra Chola D. Virarajendra

51. Who destroyed the Cheras navy at Trivandrum?
A. Rajaraja B. Rajendra I
C. Sri Vijaya D. Vijayalaya

52. The primary reason of Rajendra Chola in attacking North India was:
A. to establish his supremacy in entire India
B. to capture territories of the North India
C. to perform Aswamedha Yajna
D. to demonstrate his strength

53. The Cholas ruler mostly patronised:
A. Hinduism B. Buddhism
C. Jainism D. Bhagavatism

54. Vijayalaya, the founder of the Chola dynasty, was a feudatory of:
A. The Pallavas B. The Pandyas
C. The Rashtrakutas D. None of the above

55. What was the name of the Chola King who made conquest in Sumatra and Malay peninsula?
A. Rajendra I B. Rajaraja I
C. Rajadhiraja I D. Virarajendra

56. There was an administrative unit under the Cholas Kurran. What did it signify?
A. A village B. A province
C. A district D. A group of villages

57. What was the most serious set-back to the Chola empire in the 9th century?
A. Cholas were completely uprooted their position against Rashtrakutas
B. Cholas were hard out to defend their position
C. Cholas did not have a strong army
D. None of the above

58. Which one of the following terms stands for the regular royal troops of the Cholas?
A. Kadagams B. Nattupaddi
C. Kaikkolar D. Bhrtaka

59. Under Cholas the local merchant guilds were called:
A. Nagaram B. Manigramam
C. Valanjiyar D. None of the above

60. During the reign of Chola rulers Indian foreign trade flourished most with:
A. Persia B. Arabia
C. South-East Asia D. China

61. The social life of the Cholas was characterised by:
A. An extreme sense of exclusiveness

B. An inter mixture of castes
C. Priestly dominance
D. Social harmony

62. Which one of the Rashtrakuta Kings defeated Parantaka I and caused a temporary eclipse of the Cholas?
A. Amonghvarsha I B. Govinda III
C. Indra III D. Krishna III

63. Chola empire was established on the ruins of:
A. Pandyas B. Pallavas
C. Chalukyas D. Rashtrakutas

64. Which style of architecture came into vogue during this period?
A. Nagara B. Dravida
C. Mandapa D. None of the above

65. What was Mandap in temple?
A. A pillard hall B. Monastery
C. Deity Room D. None of the above

66. Name the Chinese Pilgrim who commented that Chola country was deserted and wild succession of marshes and jungles.
A. I-Tsing B. Hiuen Tsang
C. Fa-hien D. None of the above

67. During the whose reign was Raja-rajesvara temple constructed?
A. Vijayalaya B. Rajendra
C. Rajaraja II D. Rajaraja III

68. Who founded the Capital Gangaikond-acholapuram?
A. Parantaka I B. Rajendra Chola
C. Rajadhiraja I D. Rajaraja I

69. What is a "Garbhagriha" in the Dravida style of architecture?
A. A pillard hall B. Monastery
C. Corridor D. Chief deity's room

70. Where is the Gomateswar temple in the South India situated?
A. Madurai B. Tanjore
C. Halebed D. Sravana belgola

71. Nayanars were devotees of:
A. Shiva B. Vishnu
C. Durga D. Tirthankaras

72. Which among the following represented the local mercantile interests?
A. Ur B. Nagaram
C. Mahasabha D. Sabha

73. Navibe Audar Nambi the famous scholar who arranged the Saiva Canons was a contemporary of:
A. Virarajendra B. Rajendra I
C. Rajaraja I D. Rajendra II

74. Chola style of temple architecture is called:
A. Mandap B. Dravida
C. Mandham D. Gopuram

75. Who wrote Ramayana in Tamil language?
A. Kamban B. Kuttan
C. Rugulendi D. Kalladanar

76. Which among the following was not conquerred by Rajendra Chola I?
A. Pandya and Chera territories
B. Sri Lanka
C. Sailendra Empire
D. Southern provinces of the Chalukyas of Kalyani

77. Sudras or slaves or prisoners of war were employed as a scale to reclaim waste land and clear forests for the first time under the:
A. Mauryas B. Satavahanas
C. Cholas D. Guptas

78. Chau-Ju-Khan, a Chinese author of early thirteenth century left an important account on one of the following dynasty. Identify.
A. Chola dynasty B. Slave dynasty
C. Khilji dynasty D. Yadava dynasty

79. The conquest of Sri Lanka was completed during the reign of:
A. Rajaraja B. Rajendra I
C. Parantaka I D. Aditya I

80. The chief social obligation of the Chola state was:
A. to protect the brahmans
B. to protect the women
C. to maintain peace and security in the society
D. to protect temples

81. In which style were the temples at Bhuvaneshwar, Puri and Khajuraho built?
A. Nagara Style B. Vasara Style
C. Dravida Style D. None of the above

82. Kamban is believed to have lived at the Court of:
A. Pandya king B. Chola king
C. Pallava king D. Chalukya king

83. Devotees of Vishnu were called:
A. Brahmanas B. Nayanars
C. Alvars D. None of the above

84. Capitals, like Tanjore, Gangaikondacholapuram; Kanchi were constructed by:
A. Pratiharas B. Cheras
C. Cholas D. Chalukyas

85. When did the Venetian traveller Marco Polo came to Kerala?
A. 10th Century B. 11th Century
C. 12th Century D. 13th Century

86. The South-Indian King who invaded the overseas kingdom of Shrivijaya in South-east Asia was:
A. Rajadhiraja B. Rajaraja I
C. Rajendra I D. Parantaka I

87. Parantaka I established Chola power in:
A. Century 897 A.D. B. Century 899 A.D.
C. Century 905 A.D. D. Century 907 A.D

88. We know a great deal more about the Cholas than their predecessors because:
A. they appointed Court Chroniclers
B. many books were written during that period
C. of long inscriptions on the walls of temples
D. of the abundance of coins

89. Rajaraja and Rajendra I commemorated their victories by:
A. erecting temples
B. erecting pillars
C. ordering inscriptions to be written
D. issuing coins

90. Regarding religion during the Chola period are point 'is' incorrect. Which is?
A. Cholas were Brahmanical Hindus, and most of them worshipped Vishnu
B. Rajaraja built a temple dedicated to Shiva
C. Royal gifts were normally monopolised by Brahmans
D. Chola kings rarely performed Vedic Sacrifices

91. Who built the world famous temples at Khajuraho?
A. Pratiharas B. Pushyabhnis
C. Chandolas D. Tomars

92. Which style of architecture as mentioned by Silpshastra was popular in the Deccan?
A. Nagara B. Vesara
C. Dravida D. None of the above

93. Ghatika is a sattlement of:
A. Merchants B. Brahmans
C. Buddhist monks D. Jain monks

94. Who was the south Indian Kings, whose troops reached the banks of the Ganges, but did not hold the northern region for long, and whose position was similar to that of Samudraguptas campaign in the south?
A. Rajaraja I B. Rajendra I
C. Rajadhiraja D. Vijayalaya

95. Lokamahadevi, the chief queen of a Chola king performed the "Hiranyagrabha" ceremony. Whose wife was she?
A. Rajaraja I B. Rajendra Chola
C. Rajadhiraja D. Kulotunga Chola

96. The founder of the Chola empire in the 10th century was:
A. Vijayalaya B. Karikala
C. Parantaka D. Rajaraja

97. Which of the facts of the administration of the Cholas is incorrect?
A. The kings adopted high sounding title
B. The statues of the dead rulers were worshipped
C. The rajaguru was both the confident and confessor of the royal family
D. The royal household was maintained in a very austere manner typyfing the southern tradition.

98. Who is the author of Kural which is regarded as the Tamil Veda?
A. Tiruthakathevar B. Ilango
C. Tiruvalluvar D. Sittali Sattana

99. Which one is an open pavillion?
A. Mandapam B. Gopuram
C. Ratha D. Vihar

100. The Chola empire decline in:
A. early 13th century B. early 12th century
C. later 11th century D. middle 12th century

ANSWERS

1	2	3	4	5	6	7	8	9	10
D	C	B	B	D	A	C	A	B	D
11	**12**	**13**	**14**	**15**	**16**	**17**	**18**	**19**	**20**
C	C	D	C	A	D	C	B	A	B
21	**22**	**23**	**24**	**25**	**26**	**27**	**28**	**29**	**30**
C	C	D	D	C	C	B	C	C	D
31	**32**	**33**	**34**	**35**	**36**	**37**	**38**	**39**	**40**
B	D	B	C	B	A	A	D	B	C
41	**42**	**43**	**44**	**45**	**46**	**47**	**48**	**49**	**50**
A	A	D	B	D	C	D	B	C	C
51	**52**	**53**	**54**	**55**	**56**	**57**	**58**	**59**	**60**
A	D	A	A	A	D	B	C	A	D
61	**62**	**63**	**64**	**65**	**66**	**67**	**68**	**69**	**70**
[illegible]	D	B	B	A	B	B	B	D	D
[illegible]	**72**	**73**	**74**	**75**	**76**	**77**	**78**	**79**	**80**
[illegible]	B	B	B	A	C	A	A	B	C
[illegible]	**82**	**83**	**84**	**85**	**86**	**87**	**88**	**89**	**90**
[illegible]	B	C	C	D	C	D	C	A	A
[illegible]	**92**	**93**	**94**	**95**	**96**	**97**	**98**	**99**	**100**
[illegible]	B	A	B	A	C	D	C	A	A

SET-9

1. In the Rashtrakuta Kingdom, the directly administered areas were divided into:
A. Rashtra B. Vaisya
C. Bhukti D. All the above

2. The Vaisya was like:
A. Village B. Province
C. A Taluk D. Modern district

3. What was the basic unit of administration under Rashtrakuta?
A. Province B. Family
C. District D. Village

4. In Northern India the period 500-1200 A.D. is considered as a:
A. Period of cultural uplift
B. Period of social uplift
C. Period of stagnation and decline
D. Continuation of Golden age

5. Who among the following Pratihara rulers, was defeated by the Rashtrakuta ruler Govinda III?
A. Vatsraja B. Nagabhatta II
C. Mihirbhoja D. Mahipala

6. The Rashtrakutas were successors of the:
A. Pallavas of Kanchi
B. Chalukyas of Kalyani
C. Chalukyas of Badami
D. None of these

7. Chalukyas established their empire in:
A. Gujarat B. Malwa
C. Deccan D. Far South India

8. The Palas of Bengal patronised:
A. Hinduism
B. Jainism
C. Hinayana Buddhism
D. Tantrika Buddhism

9. Rashtrakutas rulers patronised:
A. Shaivism B. Vaishnavism
C. Jainism D. All the three

10. Who was the contemporary of Palas in the Deccan?
A. Pratiharas B. Chalukyas
C. Rashtrakutas D. None of the above

11. Who checkmated Bhoja's away on the east?
A. Gopala B. Dharmapala
C. Devpala D. None of the above

12. How did Pratiharas gain prominence?
A. Because they were local officials
B. They were big Zamindars
C. On account of their resistance to Arab incursions
D. None of the above

13. Rulers of Sailendra dynasty were:
A. Buddhist in faith B. Jains
C. Brahmans D. None of the above

14. Which amongst the Pala kings tried to extend their power to Assam?
A. Gopala B. Dharmapala
C. Mahendrapala D. None of the above

15. The Pala empire was founded by:
A. Dharmapala B. Gopala
C. Dhruva D. None of the above

16. Amonghavarsha was a:
A. Parthihara king B. Chalukya king
C. Rashtrakuta king D. Pala king

17. The system of administration in Rashtrakuta empires was based on the ideas and practices of the:
A. Gupta empire
B. Harshas kingdom
C. Chalukyas in the Deccan
D. All the above

18. The author of Gita-Govinda was:
A. Jayadeva B. Bana
C. Dandi D. None of the above

19. The University of Vikramasila was established under the patronage of:
A. The palas B. The senas
C. The pratiharas D. Yosovarman of Kannauj

20. Which one of the following aspects of feudal relationship gradually gained importance during this period?
A. Attendance at court
B. Paying of tribute
C. Hierarchy among the feudatories
D. Military service

21. Where did the Pala king have his seat of authority?
A. Kannauj B. Pataliputra
C. Tamralipti D. Monghyr

22. Name the Pala king who founded the Vikramasila University?
A. Dharmapala B. Devapala
C. Ramapala D. Gopala

23. The Pratihara army was considered to be the best of its kind mainly because of the efficiency of its:
A. Infantry B. Cavalry
C. Chariots D. Elephants

24. The Pratiharas first settled at:
A. Ujjain B. Mandor
C. Kannauj D. Chedi

25. Nagabhatta II established Pratihara Supremacy at:
A. Kannauj B. Ajmer
C. Tripuri D. Anhilwada

26. The main basis of social organisation in India during the early medieval period was:
A. Clan B. Religion
C. Caste D. Kingship

27. Which of the following empires lasted the longest?
A. Chalukya empire B. Pala empire
C. Pratihara empire D. Rashtrakuta empire

28. The Pala empire was founded by Gopala, probably in:
A. 600 A.D. B. 650 A.D.
C. 750 A.D. D. 800 A.D.

29. Who was the founder of Chalukya dynasty of Kalyani?
A. Taila B. Gopala
C. Aditya D. None of the above

30. The history of the Pallavas becomes more definite from the time of:
A. Vishnugopa B. Mahendravarman I
C. Simhavishnu D. Narsimhavarman

31. Which one of the following engaged in a three pronged struggle, was the strongest and lasted out the longest?
A. Palas B. Pratiharas
C. Rashtrakutas D. Chalukyas

32. The contest for the mastery of Kannauj started during the reign of the Pala king:
A. Gopala B. Dharmapala
C. Devapala D. Vigrahapala

33. Which one of the following is the most lasting contribution of the Rashtrakutas?
A. Kailasa temple
B. Pampa, Ponna, Ranna; three writers of Kannada poetry and Kailasa temple
C. Patronage of Jainism
D. Checkmating the Prathiharas

34. From among the following name the greatest Pala king that ever ruled in Bengal:
A. Gopala B. Dharmapala
C. Devapala D. Mahipala

35. Who, among the following Pratihara rulers, was defeated by the Rashtrakuta ruler Govinda III?
A. Vatsaraja B. Nagabhatta II
C. Mihir Bhoja D. Mahipala

36. Who built the first great empire south of the Penner and the Tungabhadra?
A. The early Chalukyas B. The Palas
C. Later Chalukyas D. The Pallavas

37. Who amongst the Pallava Kings bore the epithet of Vichitrachitta?
A. Narsimhavarman I B. Vikramaditya I
C. Mahendravarman I D. Rajsimha

38. Where did Chalukyas have their first Capital?
A. Madurai B. Kanchi
C. Vatapi D. Kannauj

39. Who executed the Kailas temple at Ellora?
A. Dantidurga B. Krishna I
C. Amoghvarsha D. Govinda III

40. Where was the second Capital of Rashtrakutas?
A. Vatapi B. Tanjore
C. Madura D. Manyakheta

41. Name the Rashtrakuta King who defeated the Pratihara ruler, Nagabhatta?
A. Amoghavarsha I B. Govinda III
C. Indra III D. Krishna III

42. The founder of the Rashtrakutas dynasty was:
A. Govinda B. Dhruva
C. Dhantivarman D. Kannara or Krishna I

43. Identify the region where the first invasion of Muhammad of Ghaur was launched.
A. Punjab B. Multan
C. Sindh D. Gujarat

44. Which was the capital of the Hindu Shahiya Kingdom when it was attacked by Mahmud?
A. Kabul B. Peshawar
C. Attock D. Udabhanda or Und

45. Which of the following set up a Kingdom for the Hoyasala dynasty?
A. Vishnuvardhana (Sala)
B. Ballalala
C. Bhillama
D. Harihara

46. Which one of the following were the bitterest enemies of the Chauhans?
A. Chandellas B. Solankis
C. Tomaras D. Gahadavalas of Kannauj

47. In which of the following empires did the Pandyas finally merge?
A. Bahmani B. Chera
C. Vijayanagar D. Delhi Sultanate

48. Dhillika (Delhi) was founded in 736 A.D. by the:
A. Gahadavalas B. Tomaras
C. Paramaras D. Chauhans

49. To which Rajput clan did Jai Chand belong?
A. Chauhans B. Rathors or Gaharwars
C. Kalachuris D. Chandallas

50. Which of Mahmud Gazni's invasions of temple towns was the most famous?
A. Somnath B. Mathura
C. Thaneswar D. Kannauj

51. Which one of the following came to India at the instance of Sultan Mahmud?
A. Al-Masudi B. Sulaiman
C. Al-Beruni D. Ibn Hauqual

52. Which of the following looked after Muhammad Ghuri's affairs in India when he was engaged with the Turks in Central Asia?
A. Bakhtiyar Khalji
B. Ikhtiyar-ud-din Muhammad
C. Qutb-ud-din Aibak
D. Muiz-ud-din Muhammad bin sam

53. Which one of the following defeated the Chalukyas of Vatapi (Badami) and founded the Rashtrakuta empire?
A. Dhruva B. Govinda III
C. Dantidurga D. Amoghavarsha

54. Which of the following were the most important rivals of the Rashtrakutas?
A. Palas B. Chalukyas
C. Pallavas D. Pratiharas

55. Where was the capital of the Rashtrakutas located?
A. Badami B. Kalyani
C. Vengi D. Malkhed

56. Who among the Rashtrakuta rulers, constructed the famous Kailasha temple at Ellora?
A. Krishna I B. Govinda II
C. Dhruva D. Govinda III

57. The Paramara dynasty was founded by:
A. Upendra B. Bhoja
C. Vakpati-Munja D. Sindhuraja

58. Dhara, the Capital of the Paramara dynasty, was raised to a position of a eminence by:
A. Sindhuraja B. Bhoja
C. Upendra D. Vakpati-Munja

59. The dynasty of the Chálukyas of Anhilwada was founded by:
A. Mularaja B. Raji
C. Bhima I D. Karna

60. Jainism was patronised by the:
A. Chalukyas B. Chandellas
C. Rathores D. Kalachuris

61. Who overthrew the last ruler of the western Chalukyas of Badami?
A. Dantidurga B. Taila
C. Gopala D. Bhoja

62. Which two Kings defeated the Arabs of Sind?
1. Dhruva 2. Nagabhatta II
3. Mihira Bhoja 4. Krishna III
Codes:
A. 1 and 2 B. 2 and 3
C. 1 and 3 D. 3 and 4

63. Who founded the Brahmana Shahi Dynasty?
A. Kallar B. Samanta
C. Bhima D. Didda

64. Who was the Ghaznavid ruler who fought against Jayapala at Ghuzak?
A. Alptigin B. Ismail
C. Sabuktigin D. Mahmud

65. Who among the Brahmana Shahu got converted to Islam and later abjured it?
A. Anandapala B. Jayapala
C. Trilochanapala D. Sukhapala

66. Who introduced Kulinism among the Brahmanas?
A. Vijaya Sena B. Hemanta Sena
C. Samanta Sena D. Vallala Sena

67. To which race did Mahmud belong?
A. Arabs B. Afghans
C. Mongols D. Turks

68. Who were the Yaminis?
A. Khaljis B. Ghurida
C. Ghaznavids D. Tughluqs

69. Who said that the Rashtrakutas were the most feared rulers of India?
A. Utbi B. Al-Beruni
C. Al-Kazwini D. Sulaiman

70. The continued incursious of which, among the following people weakened the Cholas?
A. Hoysalas B. Western Gangas
C. Yadavas D. Kakatiyas

71. Who was the Chola King who bore the name "Arulmolivarman"?
A. Rajendra I B. Parantake I
C. Rajaraja I D. Kulottunga I

72. Who built the Brihadisvara temple?
A. Parantaka I B. Rajaraja I
C. Rajendra I D. Rajaraja II

73. Who is the author of Kalingattupparani?
A. Kambar B. Ottakuttar
C. Jayangondar D. Pugalendi

74. Which inscription gives details of the election to village assembly?
A. Tiruvalangadu Plates B. Uttaramerur inscription
C. Velvikkudi grant D. Anbil grant

75. Who used the Traikutaka era?
A. Chandellas B. Kalachuris
C. Paramaras D. Chahamanas

76. Name the Kalachuri who issued coins with his name and figure of Lakshmi:
A. Lakshmi-Karna B. Gangeyadeva
C. Kokalla II D. Yasah-Karna

77. Who established a college for Sanskrit studies at Dhar?
A. Sindhuraja B. Bhoja I
C. Vakpatiraja II D. Arjunavarman

78. In which language was the dictionary "Paiyalachchhi" compiled?
A. Prakrit B. Pali
C. Sanskrit D. Telugu

79. Who among the following assumed the title "Navasahasanka".
A. Bhoja B. Sindhuraja
C. Harsha Siyaka II D. Krishnaraja

80. What is the meaning of Paramara?
A. Conqueror of the enemy
B. Slayer of the enemy
C. A virtuous man
D. An immortal

81. Who founded the Simha era?
A. Mularaja B. Bhimadeva I
C. Karnadeva D. Jayasimha Siddharaja

82. In whose reign were the Gurjara Pratiharas deprived of highly prized Vishnu image?
A. Mahipala B. Mahendapala
C. Devapala D. Vijayapala

83. To which of the original clan did the Chandellas Bundelkhand are said to be related?
A. Gonds B. Santhals
C. Kols D. Mundas

84. Name the Pala who made the Pala dynasty a force in North India Politics:
A. Dharmapala B. Mahipala
C. Gopala D. Vigrahapala

85. In which language was "Karpuramanjari" written?
A. Sanskrit B. Prakrit
C. Pali D. Telugu

86. Who founded the Chandella dynasty of Bundelkhand?
A. Jayasakti B. Yasovarman
C. Dhanga D. Nannuka

87. Who was the founder of Virasaivism?
A. Appar B. Bijjala
C. Basava D. Sundaran

88. To which of the following did Kannada literature much:
A. Brahmanism B. Jainism
C. Buddhism D. Virasaivism

89. Who among the following Kings abdicated?
1. Chandragupta Maurya 2. Chandragupta I
3. Samudragupta 4. Rajyavadhan
Codes:
A. only 1 B. only 2
C. only 1 and 2 D. only 1, 2 and 4

90. The Chola period constitutes the most creative phase of South Indian History and is one during which Tamil culture reached a peak in the field of:
A. Literature
B. Literature, temple building
C. Literature, temple building and bronze-casting
D. Literature, temple-building, bronze-casting and self-government

91. The earliest to be Brahmanished in the Deccan were the:
A. Satavahanas B. Pallavas
C. Cholas D. Pandyas

92. Which point on trade and commerce during 800 and 1200 A.D. is incorrect?
A. Malwa and Gujarat benefited the most
B. The North Indian trade languished
C. Some shrenis emerged as sub-caste
D. No ban on sea travel by the Dharmasastras

93. Which one was the chief factor for the successful establishment of Jainism in Western India?
A. Patronage extended by Rashtrakutas, Chalukyas of Kalyani and Parmaras of Malwa.
B. Prosperity because of trade and commerce
C. Hindu influence was weak in the region
D. None of these

94. The founder of the Rashtrakutas dynasty was:
A. Govinda B. Dhruva
C. Dantidurga D. Krishna

95. Which city was the base of contention between the Rashtrakutas, the Pratiharas and the Palas?
A. Kannauj B. Ujjain
C. Pataliputra D. Paithan

96. Who issued the gold coins first?
A. Mauryas B. Nandas
C. Indo-Bactrians D. Kushans

97. Who is known as the South Indian Manu?
A. Bhadrabahu B. Apasthamba
C. Akkatiyar D. Tiruvalluvar

98. Who among the following Sultans did not take the royal title?
A. Kuhsrav Khan B. Jalal-ud-din Khilji
C. Khizr Khan D. Bahlol Khan Lodi

99. Who patronised the Kannada Poet, Ranna?
A. Satyasraya B. Taila II
C. Vikramaditya VI D. Jayasimha II

100. Where did the Yadavas establish their power?
A. Sevuna B. Godawari delta
C. Dvarasamudra D. Orissa

ANSWERS

1	2	3	4	5	6	7	8	9	10
D	D	D	C	B	C	C	D	D	C
11	**12**	**13**	**14**	**15**	**16**	**17**	**18**	**19**	**20**
C	C	A	B	B	C	D	A	A	D

21	22	23	24	25	26	27	28	29	30
D	A	B	B	A	C	D	C	A	C
31	**32**	**33**	**34**	**35**	**36**	**37**	**38**	**39**	**40**
C	B	B	B	B	D	C	C	B	D
41	**42**	**43**	**44**	**45**	**46**	**47**	**48**	**49**	**50**
B	C	B	D	A	D	C	B	B	A
51	**52**	**53**	**54**	**55**	**56**	**57**	**58**	**59**	**60**
C	C	C	D	D	A	A	B	A	A
61	**62**	**63**	**64**	**65**	**66**	**67**	**68**	**69**	**70**
A	A	A	C	D	D	D	C	D	A
71	**72**	**73**	**74**	**75**	**76**	**77**	**78**	**79**	**80**
C	B	C	B	B	B	B	A	B	B
81	**82**	**83**	**84**	**85**	**86**	**87**	**88**	**89**	**90**
D	C	A	A	B	D	C	D	C	D
91	**92**	**93**	**94**	**95**	**96**	**97**	**98**	**99**	**100**
A	D	B	C	A	D	B	C	B	A

MEDIEVAL INDIA

- Agrarian Relations The Ain-i- Akbari
- The Mughal Court: Reconstructing Histories through Chronicles
- New Architecture: Hampi
- Religious Histories: The Bhakti-Sufi Tradition
- Medieval Society Through Travellers' Accounts

SET-1

1. The immediate successor of Qutub-ud-din Aibak was:
A. Iltutmish
B. Aram Shah
C. Ruku-ud-din Firoz Shah
D. Bahram Shah

2. The cause of the Qutub-ud-din's death was:
A. Fall from a horse while playing polo
B. Assassination
C. Serious illness
D. Due to some unknown reason

3. Who was known as "Lakh Baksh"?
A. Aibak B. Babur
C. Iltutmish D. Raziya

4. Name one of the following who was not a source of information as the history of the Delhi Sultanate:
A. Abbas Khan Sharwani B. Amir Khusrau
C. Isami D. Shams-i-Siraj-Afif

5. Who was the first Sultan of Delhi who strove to make monarchy hereditary?
A. Iltutmish B. Aibak
C. Balban D. Alau'd-din Khalji

6. Who was the first Sultan of Delhi to emphasise the divinity of the king?
A. Aibak B. Iltutmish
C. Balban D. Alau'd-din Khalji

7. Who was the first to adopt the title of Sultan?
A. Mahmud of Ghazni B. Aibak
C. Iltutmish D. Balban

8. In spite of her virtues "Raziya" was not successful because:
A. she married Altuniya
B. she behaved like a man
C. of her Orthodox religious belief
D. the nobles did not like the rule of a woman

9. Raziya was assassinated at:
A. Kaithal B. Delhi
C. Lahore D. Bhatinda

10. Cite one of the following who was not a traveller and therefore not a source of information about events of the period:
A. Ibn Batutah B. Marco Polo
C. Abdur Razzaq D. Athanasisus Nikitian

11. Qutb-ud-din's greatest achievement was:
A. the construction of Qutub Minar
B. establishment of Muslim Power in India
C. ending India's connections with Ghazni
D. his generosity towards his generals

12. The Mongols appeared on the border of India for the first time during the region of:
A. Iltutmish B. Balban
C. Ala-ud-din D. Ghauri

13. Who was the immediate successor of Iltutmish?
A. Ruknuddin Firoz B. Raziya
C. Bahram D. Nasiruddin Mahmud

14. Name the Sultan who refused to speak to conmmon people:
A. Balban B. Alau'd-din-Khalji
C. Mohd-bin-Tughlaq D. Iltutmish

15. Who was extremely social with the nobles and officials?
A. Balban
B. Ala-ud-din-Khalji
C. Ghiyas-ud-din-Tughlaq
D. Mohammad Tughlaq

16. "New Muslims" were the followers of:
A. Changez Khan B. Hulagu
C. Ulugh D. Shah Turkan

17. Name the Sultan who thought of becoming a prophet:
A. Ala-ud-din Khalji B. Balban
C. Mohd-bin-Tughluq D. Firuz Tughluq

18. Which of the following cities was not founded by Firoz Shah Tughlaq?
A. Firozabad B. Hissar
C. Jaunpur D. Meerut

19. To which city did Sikandar Lodi Shift his capital?
A. Dholpur B. Agra
C. Gwalior D. Jaunpur

20. Who were "Munhiyas" during the reign of Ala-ud-din Khalji?
A. They were revenue officers
B. They were body-guards of the kings
C. They were head of the market control organisation.
D. They were secret police services who used to give reports about the rates and working of markets.

21. Who among the following rulers ordered a huge bell to be hung at the gate of his palace so that an aggrieved person could ring it at any time of right?
A. Aibak B. Iltutmish
C. Jahandar D. Shah Jahan

22. Which dynasty during the Sultanate period had minimum numbers of Sultans?
A. Slave B. Khilji
C. Tughluq D. Syed

23. Which one of the following was not one of the agrarian measures of Firoz Tughluq?
A. He abolished many taxes and unjust cesses.
B. He undertook revaluation of land to ascertain its assessment.
C. He allowed the imposition of only four kinds of taxes.
D. He was generous in granting land to civil and military officers and in favouring out land.

24. Ala-ud-din Khalji's greatest contribution to the agrarian condition was that:
A. he brought the peasant in direct relation with the state
B. he tried to curb and check the intermediaries
C. the records of the village accountant were audited
D. he was the first to introduce the system of measurement of land for the assessment of revenue

25. Amongst the draconian measures taken by Ala-ud-din-Khalji to stabilise his authority, which one had most bearing on the agrarian system of the day?
A. Mostly Hindus were made to pay half of their gross produced to the state and even the pasturage taxes were enhanced.
B. The Sultan abolished the privileges which the Hindus, Muquddams and Khuls enjoyed.
C. Hindus were made to pay jizya
D. He compelled the peasants to sell their produce to the grain dealers at fixed rates.

26. Who among the following had a Hindu Kotwal, named Biruathan?
A. Ala-ud-din-Khalji B. Firoz Tughlaq
C. Mohammad Tughlaq D. Balban

27. Which one of the following Sultans had the largest standing army?
A. Ala-ud-din-Khalji
B. Mohammad-bin-Tughlaq
C. Firoz Tughlaq
D. Ibrahim Lodi

28. Iqta was the name given to small plots, whose owners were known as Iqtadar. What was the name given to the holders of very large plots?
A. Amil B. Muqta
C. Wajhdars D. Nadim

29. The most serious sectarian conflict between the Sunnis and the Shias occurred during the reign of:
A. Raziya B. Balban
C. Ala-ud-din Khalji D. Muhd-bin-Tughlaq

30. "Zakat" was:
A. a religious tax levied as muslims only
B. a land tax paid by Hindus only
C. a land tax paid by Muslims only
D. the state's share of 1/5th of the spoils of war

31. "Ushrah" means:
A. Land tax paid by Muslims
B. Land tax paid by Hindus
C. Religious tax levied upon Muslims only
D. Religious tax levied upon Hindus only

32. Who levied irrigation tax as the cultivators?
A. Firoz Tughlaq B. Ala-ud-din-Khalji
C. Muhd-bin-Tughlaq D. Balban

33. "Ratan" a Hindu was appointed as a revenue officer during the reign of:
A. Muhammad-bin-Tughlaq
B. Firoz Tughlaq
C. Sher Shah
D. Akbar

34. "Kham" means:
A. tax levied on Muslims only
B. land tax paid by Hindus
C. land-tax paid by Muslims
D. State's share of 1/5th of the spoils of war.

35. Who is the founder of Muslim rule in India?
A. Muhammad Ghori B. Babur
C. Timur D. Qutub-ud-din Aibak

36. Who declared himself independent ruler of Multan when Iltutmish came to power?
A. Ali Mardan B. Razia
C. Qubacha D. None of the above

37. Who is regarded as the real founder of Turkish conquests in North-India?
A. Aibak B. Mahmud of Ghazni
C. Muhammad Ghori D. Iltutmish

38. The rulers of Lodi dynasty were:
A. Pure Afghans B. Pure Turks
C. Timurid Turks D. None of these

39. Which historian has highlighted the fact that Muhammad invaded India seventeen times?
A. R.C. Majumdar B. K. Dutta
C. Sir Henery Elliot D. Iswari Prasad

40. "Kharaj" was:
A. tax levied as muslims only
B. land tax paid by Hindus
C. land tax paid by Muslims
D. state's share of 1/5th of the spoils of war

41. Alberuni came to India in:
A. 9th Century A.D. B. 10th Century A.D.
C. 11th Century A.D. D. 12th Century A.D.

42. Who was responsible for the destruction of the power of Chandelas?
A. Prithviraj Chauhan B. Jayachandra
C. Qutubuddin D. Balban

43. Who was succeeded by Aibak?
A. Balban B. Alauddin
C. Razia D. Iltutmish

44. Who succeeded Muhammad Ghori in 1206 A.D. in India?
A. Iltutmish B. Babur
C. Qutabuddin Aibak D. Qubacha

45. Who is the author of Shahnama?
A. Faizi B. Badauni
C. Afif D. Firdausi

46. "The interest of Muhammad Ghori were not confined to India." Who said the above line?
A. V.A. Smith B. Tara Chand
C. Ishwari Prasad D. Moreland

47. Ala-ud-din-Khalji believed in:
A. Benevolent despotism
B. Absolute despotism
C. Despotism by consent
D. Rule with the help of nobility

48. When did Mohammad Ghazni carried out his last expedition to India?
A. 1025 A.D. B. 1020 A.D.
C. 1017 A.D. D. 1027 A.D.

49. Which language was patronised by Delhi Sultanate?
A. Arabic B. Turki
C. Persian D. Urdu

50. Who was the first Turk to attack India?
A. Mahmud Ghazni B. Alaptgin
C. Subuktgin D. None of above

51. The famous attack of Sarnath temple by Mohammad Ghori was in _____ century.
A. Seventeenth B. Eleventh
C. Fifteenth D. Fourteenth

52. Balban belonged to the:
A. Ilbari tribe B. Moorish race
C. Khilji dynasty D. None of the above

53. The Sultanate period lasted from:
A. 1091 – 1526 B. 1026 – 1526
C. 1092 – 1530 D. 1398 – 1530

54. Muhammad Ghori's forces defeated Jai Chand in the year:
A. 1192 A.D. B. 1194 A.D.
C. 1195 A.D. D. 1193 A.D.

55. What was the cause of Aibaks death?
A. He fell from his library
B. He fell from his horse
C. He was poisoned by the nobles
D. None of the above

56. When was the raid against Sarnath in Gujarat undertaken?
A. 1017 B. 1018
C. 1025 D. 1030

57. Against whom were the initial raids of Muhammad of Ghazni directed?
A. Tanashani dynasty B. South Indian Rulers
C. Rulers of Gujarat D. Hindustani dynasty

58. Who accompanied Mahmud Ghazni during invasions of India?
A. Muhammad-bin-Qasim
B. Al be runi
C. Utbi
D. Euiot

59. Who was the ruler of Delhi at the time of Timur's invasion?
A. Firoz Shah B. Mahmud Shah
C. Khizr Shah D. Nusrat Shah

60. Who founded the Chandala dynasty?
A. Dhanga B. Nannuka
C. Kokalla D. Upendra

61. The generals who were able to carve out a separate spheres of authority later on assumed the title of:
A. Ghazi B. Amir-ul-Umara
C. Sultan D. Amir

62. "The Indian believe that there is no country but theirs, no nationa like theirs, no king like theirs, no religion, like theirs no science like theirs." Who said this?
A. Al-beruni B. Sulaiman
C. Al-Qaqashaudi D. Al-Kazwini

63. Who is the author of Shahnama?
A. Al-beruni B. Firdausi
C. Utbi D. Unsuri

64. Who amongst the Sultans earned the title of "Butshikan".
A. Muhmud Ghazni B. Muhammad Ghori
C. Alauddin Khilji D. None of the above

65. Attachment to the land family and honour was the chief characteristic of:

A. Chlolas B. Chalukyas
C. Pandoyas D. Rajputs

66. Where did the Chauhans establish themselves?
A. Ajmer B. Kannauj
C. Jabalpur D. Malwa

67. Who among the following sacked Delhi in 1398?
A. Targhi B. Timur
C. Changez Khan D. Hulaqu Khan

68. The first Pathan State in Delhi was established by:
A. Ala-ud-din Alam Shah
B. Bahlul Lodi
C. Balban
D. Khizr Khan

69. Who amongst the following Sultans did not take the royal title?
A. Khusrau Khan B. Jalal-ud-din Khalji
C. Khizr Khan D. Bahlul Khan Lodi

70. Which one of the following was not the work of Amir Khusrau?
A. Tarikhi-i-Alai B. Tarikhi-i-Firozshahi
C. Tughlaq Nama D. Ashiqa

71. Who founded Agra?
A. Sikandar Lodi B. Khizr Khan
C. Ala-ud-din D. Ibrahim Lodi

72. What is Ve Sara?
A. an art Style B. a literary piece
C. a painting D. a work as music

73. Among the places given below one was not touched by Timur. Identify:
A. Meerut B. Jammu
C. Haridwar D. Kannauj

74. Who had been appointed in charge of some areas beyond Banaras?
A. Aibak B. Muizzudin
C. Bakhtiyar Khaliji D. None of the above

75. Name the ruler who stayed away and did not help Prithviraja during the second battle of Tarain:
A. Hemchandra B. Jaichandra
C. Anandpala D. Jaipala

76. Who were the two ambitious contenders in the first battle of Tarain?
A. Mahmud of Ghazni and Ala-ud-din
B. Muhammad Ghori and Ala-ud-din
C. Prithviraja and Mahmud of Ghazni
D. Prithviraja and Muhammad Ghori

77. Who ordered the judicial functionaries to compile census registered for the various quarters of Delhi?
A. Muhd-bin-Tughlak B. Firoz-Tughlaq
C. Sher Shah D. Ala-ud-din Khilji

78. Who among the following Sultans of Delhi was not the son of Hindu mother?
A. Ghiyasuddin Tughlaq B. Firoz Tughlaq
C. Buhlul Lodi D. Shihabuddin Umar

79. What was the nature of the Sultanate?
A. Police state B. Benevolent state
C. Welfare state D. Culture state

80. Who founded Devagiri?
A. Jaitugi B. Bhillama
C. Senuchandra D. Singhana

81. Who were the "Sevunas"?
A. Pallavas
B. Western Gangas
C. Yadavas of Devagiri
D. Eastern Chalukyas of Vengi

82. Who is the author of Zafer Namah?
A. Firdausi B. Alberuni
C. Al-Qalqashandi D. Sharaf-ud-din Ali Yazdi

83. Who was the first Sultan of Delhi born of a Hindu Mother?
A. Shahbuddin Khilji B. Ghiyasuddin Tughlaq
C. Firoz Tughluq D. Nasiruddin Khasrau

84. Who was the only Sultan to ascend the throne of Delhi in spite of the great fact that his father was alive?
A. Ala-ud-din Khilji B. Kaiqubad
C. Firoz Tughluq D. Sikandar Lodi

85. One of the following saw the reigns of eight Sultans of Delhi, Identify him.
A. Zia Barani B. Shams-i-Siraj Afif
C. Amir Khusrau D. Ibn Batuta

86. What was the original name of Muhammad-bin-Tughlaq?
A. Ghiyas-ud-din B. Yanna
C. Firoz Shah D. Tughlaq Shah

87. Who among the following made Agra his capital?
A. Sikandar Lodi B. Ibrahim Lodi
C. Bahlul Lodi D. Khizr Khan

88. Who was the victor at Sripurambiyan?
A. Aparajita B. Aditya
C. Varaguna II D. Govinda III

89. Who was called the Lakh Baksha?
A. Iltutmish B. Qutb-ud-din Aibak
C. Jalal-ud-din Khalji D. Aram Shah

90. Who built Quwwat-ul-Islam?
A. Qutb-ud-din B. Iltutmish
C. Balban D. Raziya

91. Which of the following was the capital of Eastern Gangas?
A. Konarak B. Mukhalingam
C. Bhuvaneswar D. Puri

92. Which one was the built by Ala-ud-din Khalji?
A. Alai Darwaza B. Buland Darwaza
C. Lal Quila D. Qutub Minar

93. Which Sultan's power stretched from Delhi to Palam as per the opinion of the people?
A. Shah Alam B. Muhammad Shah
C. Mubarak Shah D. Khizr Khan Sayyid

94. What was the original name of Ala-ud-din Khalji?
A. Ali Gurshasp B. Jafer Khan
C. Alp Khan D. Chajju

95. One of the following cannot be attributed to Ala-ud-din:
A. Siri Fort B. Hazar Sutun
C. Hauz-i-Khas D. Purana Quila

96. Who were called the New Muslim?
A. Hindu converts to Islam
B. Mongol converts to Islam
C. Turkish converts to Islam
D. Persian converts to Islam

97. Which was the most powerful cause for Ibrahim's defeat?
A. Use of artilley
B. Incompetence of Ibrahim Lodi
C. Babur's generalship
D. Dissensions among the Afghan nobles

98. Harihara and Bukka were originally the notives of:
A. Bellary B. Dwara Samudra
C. Kampili D. None of the above

99. Krishnadeva Raya patronished:
A. one language B. two language
C. three language D. four language

100. Which poet who adorned the court of Krishnadeva Raya is known all over South India for his wit & humour?
A. Purandradasa B. Vediraja
C. Haridass D. Tenali Rama

ANSWERS

1	2	3	4	5	6	7	8	9	10
B	A	A	A	A	C	A	D	A	C
11	**12**	**13**	**14**	**15**	**16**	**17**	**18**	**19**	**20**
B	A	A	A	C	C	A	D	B	D
21	**22**	**23**	**24**	**25**	**26**	**27**	**28**	**29**	**30**
B	D	C	D	B	B	A	B	A	A
31	**32**	**33**	**34**	**35**	**36**	**37**	**38**	**39**	**40**
A	A	A	D	A	C	D	A	C	B
41	**42**	**43**	**44**	**45**	**46**	**47**	**48**	**49**	**50**
C	C	D	C	D	A	B	D	C	A
51	**52**	**53**	**54**	**55**	**56**	**57**	**58**	**59**	**60**
B	A	B	B	B	C	D	B	B	B
61	**62**	**63**	**64**	**65**	**66**	**67**	**68**	**69**	**70**
C	A	B	A	D	A	B	B	C	B
71	**72**	**73**	**74**	**75**	**76**	**77**	**78**	**79**	**80**
A	A	D	C	B	D	A	C	A	B
81	**82**	**83**	**84**	**85**	**86**	**87**	**88**	**89**	**90**
C	D	A	B	C	B	A	A	B	A
91	**92**	**93**	**94**	**95**	**96**	**97**	**98**	**99**	**100**
B	A	A	A	D	B	A	D	D	D

SET-2

1. Match the dynastics of Sultanates with the cities they built:

(*a*) Slaves	1. Siri
(*b*) Khiljis	2. Tughlaqabad, Jahanpanah, Feroz Kotla
(*c*) Tughlak	3. Khizrabad and Mubarakbad
(*d*) Saiyyads	4. Oila-i-Rai Pithura

Codes:

	(*a*)	(*b*)	(*c*)	(*d*)
A.	4	1	2	3
B.	1	2	3	4
C.	2	3	1	4
D.	4	2	1	3

2. Who among the following was an exponent of Sudhadhvaita?

A. Ramanuja B. Vallabhacharya
C. Chaitanya D. Sankar

3. Match the dynastics or kings with the coins they issued:

(*a*) Iltutmish	1. Silver tanka
(*b*) Muhammad-bin-Tughlaq	2. Gold dinar and Silver Adils
(*c*) Sher Shah	3. Silver Rupvah
(*d*) Vijayanagar king	4. Gold Pagoda, Varaha, Kopeki, Fanam and Copper Digital

Codes:

	(*a*)	(*b*)	(*c*)	(*d*)
A.	2	1	3	4
B.	1	3	2	4
C.	1	2	3	4
D.	2	4	1	3

4. What led to the growth of a composite or Indo-Islamic Culture?
A. The important effects of the Arab invasion in India
B. The adaptability of the Turkish rulers of the Delhi Sultanate to the prevailing conditions in India.
C. The fusion of the cultural traditions of the Hinduism and Islam.
D. None of these

5. Which statements is/are correct?
1. The ceremonies connected with the worship of Muslim saints are more Indian than Islamic in details
2. Casteism began appearing in Muslim Society
3. Some aristocratic Muslim families adopted the Hindus Customs of Sati and Jauhar

Codes:
A. 1 only B. 1 and 2 only
C. 2 only D. 1, 2, 3

6. Horse shoe arch is distinctive feature of one of the following building. Identify it:
A. Sultan Gachi B. Tomb of Iltutmish
C. Tomb of Balban D. Alai Darwaza

7. Many temples were converted into mosques. One such was a Jain temple and it is the earliest known mosque in India. Identify it.
A. Arhai Din Ka Jhonpra at Ajmer
B. Badshahi Mosque at Badaun
C. Quwwat-ul-Islam Mosque at Delhi
D. None of these

8. The Qutub Minar was completed by Iltutmish. It was dedicated to:
A. Muhammad Ghori B. Qutb-ud-din Ailbak
C. Qutb-ud-din Bakhtiyar D. None of these

9. What exposed some of the evils of Hinduism?
A. The islamic concept of Jehad or holy war
B. The Islamic tenets of brotherhood and equality
C. The Islamic practice of Secluding women
D. Both (A) and (B).

10. Which of the following customs was followed by both Hindus and Muslims?
A. Celebrating marriages with pump and show
B. The Pardah system
C. The 'arti' ceremony
D. All the above

11. Match the building with their location:

(*a*) Adina Mosqe	1. Pandua
(*b*) Mahud Gawan's Madarsa	2. Bidar
(*c*) Jahaz Mahal	3. Mandu
(*d*) Kalam Masjid	4. Delhi

Codes:

	(*a*)	(*b*)	(*c*)	(*d*)
A.	2	1	3	4
B.	1	3	2	4
C.	1	2	3	4
D.	2	4	1	3

12. Match the following provincial architectural structures with the rulers who built them:

(*a*) Jami Masjid at Gujarat	1. Mahmud Begarha
(*b*) The mosque at Champner	2. Ahmed Shah
(*c*) Jami Masjid at Mandu	3. Hoshung Shah
(*d*) Mosque of Sidi Sayyed	4. Mahmud Khilji

Codes:

	(*a*)	(*b*)	(*c*)	(*d*)
A.	2	1	4	3
B.	2	1	3	4
C.	1	3	4	2
D.	3	1	4	1

13. Where is Arhai Din Ka Jhonpra situated?
A. Delhi B. Jaunpur
C. Agra D. Ajmer

14. Arabs freely borrowed Hindu motifs. Which were they?
A. Bell motif B. Swastika
C. Lotus D. All the above

15. Which was the most magnificient building constructed by the Turks in 13th century?
A. Quwat-ul-Islam Mosque
B. Hauz Khas
C. Qutab Minar
D. Siri

16. Who built the Capital at Siri?
A. Ala-ud-din Khilji B. Balban
C. Aibak D. Muhammad Tughlaq

17. In about AD 1300, a number of works on the Mimamsa were written by:
A. Rupa Goswami B. Parthasarathi Mishra
C. Hemachandra Suri D. Madhawa

18. Who translated the Bhagvat Gita into Bengali?
A. Krithivas B. Kavindra
C. Maladhar Vasu D. Srikar Nandi

19. During the Sultanate period who was the ruling class?
A. Turkish noble B. Muslims
C. Arabs D. Hindus

20. The first contact of Indians with Islam began with the:
A. Arab traders B. Roman traders
C. Turkish Traders D. Turkish invaders

21. Which of the following provinces was a sent of Hindu Craftsmanship?
A. Bengal B. Jaunpur
C. Gujarat D. None of these

22. The tall curved spiral roof and the mandapam (ante room) were features of which style of architecture?
A. Nagara B. Shikara
C. Sharqi D. Bengal

23. Which language was patronised by the rulers of Delhi Sultanate?
A. Hindi B. Urdu
C. Persian D. Turki

24. Which social evil gained impetus with the coming of the Muslims?
A. Purdah System B. Polygamy
C. Polyandry D. Child marriage

25. Ibn-i-Batutah came in the court of:
A. Iltutmish
B. Balban
C. Muhammad-bin-Tughlaq
D. Sikandar Lodi

26. Where is Atala Devi Masjid situated?
A. Lahore B. Padua
C. Jaunpur D. Delhi

27. Firoz Tughlaq was the author of:
A. Tarik-i-Firoz Shahi B. Fatwah-i-Jahandari
C. Futuhat-i-Firoz Shahi D. Sirat-i-Firoz Shahi

28. Octagonal-Shaped tombs are associated with:
A. the Khiljis B. The Tughlaqs
C. The Sayyids D. The Lodis

29. Alai Darwaza was added by:
A. Iltutmish B. Balban
C. Alaudin Khilji D. Muhammad Tughlaq

30. Match the words with their authors:

(*a*) Tarika-i-Yamini	1. Muhammad-al-utbi
(*b*) Tarika-i-Feroz Shahi	2. Shams-i-Siraj Afif
(*c*) Tarika-i-Hind	3. Alberuni
(*d*) Taj-ul-Hassan Masir	4. Hasan Nizami

Codes:

	(*a*)	(*b*)	(*c*)	(*d*)
A.	1	2	3	4
B.	2	1	3	4
C.	4	1	3	2
D.	1	4	3	2

31. Match the following works with their authors who wrote in Sanskrit:

(*a*) Gita Govinda	1. Vallabha
(*b*) Hammira	2. Jimuta Vahana
(*c*) Anubhashya	3. Jayasingh Suri
(*d*) Dharmaratna	4. Jayadev

Codes:

	(*a*)	(*b*)	(*c*)	(*d*)
A.	4	3	1	2
B.	3	2	4	1
C.	2	4	3	1
D.	2	1	3	4

32. Match the following Literary figures with the language in which they wrote.

(*a*) Timmana	1. Gujarati
(*b*) Chandidas	2. Bengali
(*c*) Bhattadeva	3. Kannada
(*d*) Narsimha Mehta	4. Assamese

Codes:

	(*a*)	(*b*)	(*c*)	(*d*)
A.	1	2	3	4
B.	4	2	1	3
C.	4	2	3	1
D.	3	2	4	1

33. Match the following books with their respective authors:

(*a*) Prithviraj Raso	1. Malik Muhd. Jaisi
(*b*) Hamir Raso	2. Chand Bardai
(*c*) Sri Krishna Vijaya	3. Maladhar basu
(*d*) Padmavat	4. Sarangdhar

Codes:

	(*a*)	(*b*)	(*c*)	(*d*)
A.	2	4	3	1
B.	2	3	4	1
C.	3	2	1	4
D.	1	2	3	4

34. Who wrote Fatawa-i-Jahandari?
A. Amir Khusrau B. Ziauddin Barani
C. Afif D. None of these

35. The vocabulary of Urdu has been drawn from:
A. Persian and Hindi
B. Hindi, Tamil, Persian, Oriya
C. Arabic, Persian, Hindi
D. Hindi, Arabic, Persian, Turkish

36. Who got Rajtarangani and Mahabharata translated into Persian?
A. Feroz Shah Tughlaq B. Sikander Lodi
C. Zain-ul-Abidin D. None of these

37. Lakshmidhara wrote Smritikalpataru. Its subject matter is:
A. Philosophy B. Music
C. Law D. Medicine

38. Who was given the title of Nayak or master of both the theory and practice of music?
A. Amir Khusrau

B. Sadi
C. Malik Muhammad Jaisi
D. None of these

39. Where was Amir Khusrau born?
A. Badaun B. Delhi
C. Paliali D. Lahore

40. Who was the author of 'Khazain-ul-Futuh'?
A. Hasan Nizami B. Amir Khusrau
C. Yahya Bin Ahmad D. Abdul Fazal

41. Smriti Literature flourished in Mithila and Bengal. Two of its outstanding authors were:
A. Jai Singh Suri and Gangadhar
B. Jayadeva and Madhava Vidyaratna
C. Vachspati Misra and Raghunandan
D. Kabir and Surdas

42. Who among the following authors translated the Bhagavat Gita into Bengali?
A. Krithivas B. Kavindra
C. Malandhar D. Sirkar Nandi

43. Sanskrit Books on medicine and music were translated into Persian during the reigns of:
A. Muhammad-bin-Tughlaq and Zain-ul-Abidin
B. Muhammad-bin-Tughlaq and Nusrat Shah
C. Feroz Shah Tughlaq and Zain-ul-Abidin
D. Muhammad-bin-Tughlaq and Feroz Shah Tughlaq

44. Which among the following was the most important of the causes for struggle between Begarha and the Portuguese?
A. cutting off the trade of the Muslims
B. establishment of Portuguese settlement on the western coast
C. ill-treatment of the Muslims
D. refusal to pay tributes

45. Who said that with the execution of Mahmud Gawan, all the cohesion and power of the Bahmani Kingdom departed?
A. Firishta B. Sayyid Ali Tabataba
C. Meadows Taylor D. Stanley Lane-Poole

46. Pick out the wrong match:
A. Allasani Peddana – Manucharita
B. Vyasaraya – Nyayamrita
C. Lolla Lakshmidhare – Sarasvathivilasa
D. Krishnadeva Raya – Parvatiparinaya

47. Who is called the Akbar of Kashmire?
A. Shah Mirza B. Jamshid
C. Ali shah D. Zain-ul-Abidin

48. In which respect did Zain-ul-Abidin differ from Akbar?
A. Universal toleration
B. Patronage to art and literature
C. Abstention from eating flesh
D. Contingence

49. Who had put an end to the independance of Sind in about 1514?
A. Babur B. Shah Beg Arghun
C. Mahmud Begarha D. Mohmud of Ghazni

50. Who among the following witnessed the Mahanavami festival?
A. Athanasius Nikitin B. Nicolo Conti
C. Caesar Frederick D. Abdul Razzaq

51. Which of the flesh of the following animals was not consumed by the people in the Vijayanagar period?
A. Oxen B. Sheep
C. Lizard D. Rats

52. Which among the following is not applicable to Vijaynagar period.
A. Sati was prevalent
B. Polygamy was known
C. Dowry system was prevalent
D. Child marriage was unknown

53. Pick out the wrong match
A. Mirat-i-Sikandar-Lodis
B. Burhan-i-Ma'qsir-Bahman
C. Riyaz-us-Salatin-Bengal
D. Rajatarangini-Kashmir

54. Who has been described as the pattern of excellence?
A. Ahmad Shah B. Muhammad Shah
C. Bahadur Shah D. Mahmud Begarha

55. Identify the foreign traveller who speaks about Mahmud Begarha
A. Ludovico di Varthema B. Nicolo Conti
C. Nuniz D. Poes

56. Who among the following has described himself as the Second Alexander on his coins?
A. Ala-ud-din-Khalji B. Ahmad Shah
C. Muhammad Shah I D. Firoz Shah

57. Who made Bidar the capital of the Bahman kingdom?
A. Ala-ud-din Bahman shah
B. Firuz Shah
C. Ahmad Shah
D. Muhammad Shah I

58. Which among the following was the most important achievement of Muhmud Gawan?
A. Education of the king
B. Capture of Goa
C. Getting the support of Gujarat against Malwa
D. Annexation of Bankapur

59. Were did Mahmud Begarha register a naval victory over the Portuguese?
A. Diu B. Daman
C. Goa D. Chaul

60. From whom did the Portuguese obtain permission to build a factor at Diu?

A. Mahmud Begarha B. Ahmad Shah
C. Hushang Shah D. Muhammad Shah

61. What provided the background for the rise of sufi Movement?
A. Jain philosophy
B. Buddhist philosophy
C. Indian and Greek ideas
D. None of the above

62. The Qutab Minar was dedicated to
A. Qutab-ud-din-Aibak
B. The Sufi Saint, Qutab-ud-din Bakhtiyar Kaki
C. Khawaja Moin-ud-din chisti
D. The Chishti Saint, Nizam ud-din Auliya

63. Match the following.
(*a*) Timmana 1. Gujarati
(*b*) Chandidas 2. Bengali
(*c*) Bhattadeva 3. Kannada
(*d*) Narsimha Mehta 4. Assamese

Codes:

	(*a*)	(*b*)	(*c*)	(*d*)
A.	1	2	3	4
B.	4	2	1	3
C.	4	2	3	1
D.	3	2	4	1

64. What was sq. inch?
A. An architectural form
B. A musical instrument
C. A style of writing
D. None of these

65. One of the administrative language of Bahmani Kingdom was
A. Gujarati B. Bengali
C. Marathi D. Sanskrit

66. Prithuviraja Raso was written by
A. Chandra Bardai B. Jayadeva
C. Bana D. Amir Khusrau

67. Which decorative device is generally found in the building of Firoz Shah Tughlaq?
A. Shankh B. Bell
C. Lotus D. Swastika

68. Lodis borrowed enamelled tiles from
A. Persia B. Rome
C. Egypt D. South India

69. Which one of the following is best known for the Persian form of Masnavi?
A. Zai Nakashabi
B. Amir Khusrau
C. Malik Mohammad Jaisi
D. None of these

70. Which ruler of Bengali had the Mahabharata and Ramayana translated into Bengali?
A. Hussian Shah B. Nusrat Shah
C. Bahman Shah D. None of these

71. The decorative device found in all the buildings of Feroz Tughlaq is
A. Swastik B. The lotus
C. The Shankh D. The bell

72. Which one of the following language profited most from the religious reformation movement of the 15-16th Centuries?
A. Urdu B. Hindi
C. Sanskrit D. Persian

73. Which one of the following was not borrowed by Hindu astronomers from the Muslims?
A. Cosmology
B. Calculations of altitude and longitude
C. Technical terms
D. Some item of the Calendar (Zich)

74. Who was given the title of nayak?
A. Amir Khusrau
B. Sodi
C. Malik Muhammad Jaisi
D. None of these

75. Aiman-Ghora and Sanam are Perso-Arabic:
A. Tals
B. Ragas
C. Both (A) and (B)
D. None of these

76. Which one of the following was not borrowed by Hindu astronomers from the Muslims?
A. Cosmology
B. Calculation of altitude and longitude
C. Technical terms
D. Some items of the Calendar (Zich)

77. Which of the following instruments was not brought by the Turks to India?
A. Veena B. Rabab
C. Sarangi D. None of these

78. What was the basic reason for the growth of a beautiful style of Indo-Islamic architecture in Gujarat?
A. Import of foreign architects from Persia
B. Availability of almost an infinite variety of material
C. Presence of a splendid indigenous style before the coming of the Muslims
D. The special interest taken by the rulers of Gujarat

79. The Bhagavata was translated into Bengali by:
A. Rupa Goswami B. Chemdidas
C. Maladhar Basu D. None of these

80. The Tabla is believed to have been invented by:
A. Malik Mohammad Jaisi
B. Amir Khusrau
C. Zain-ul-Abidin
D. None of these

ANSWERS

1	2	3	4	5	6	7	8	9	10
A	B	B	C	D	D	C	C	B	D
11	**12**	**13**	**14**	**15**	**16**	**17**	**18**	**19**	**20**
C	B	D	D	C	A	B	C	B	A
21	**22**	**23**	**24**	**25**	**26**	**27**	**28**	**29**	**30**
C	A	C	A	C	C	C	D	C	A
31	**32**	**33**	**34**	**35**	**36**	**37**	**38**	**39**	**40**
A	D	A	B	D	C	C	A	C	B
41	**42**	**43**	**44**	**45**	**46**	**47**	**48**	**49**	**50**
C	C	C	A	C	D	D	D	B	D
51	**52**	**53**	**54**	**55**	**56**	**57**	**58**	**59**	**60**
A	D	A	D	A	A	C	B	D	A
61	**62**	**63**	**64**	**65**	**66**	**67**	**68**	**69**	**70**
C	B	C	A	C	A	C	A	B	B
71	**72**	**73**	**74**	**75**	**76**	**77**	**78**	**79**	**80**
B	C	D	A	B	A	A	C	C	B

SET-3

1. Which one of the following statements regarding the imperial council is not true?
A. The Prime Minister used to be the President of the Council
B. The king presided over the council when grave matters had to be discussed and decided
C. The members of the council had complete control over the policy of the state
D. The council was extremely powerful and the king was a puppet in its hands

2. Who was the pradhani or Sirah pradhani?
A. Commander-in-chief of the forces
B. The judge at the imperial headquarters
C. An administrative officer incharge of the general administration of the empire
D. Head priests

3. Identify the wrong statement with regard to the Ayagar System
A. The Ayagars could sell or mortgage their offices
B. They were granted tax-free lands (Manyams)
C. These 'Ayagars' had no hereditary rights over their offices
D. The Reddi Karnam, and Karnika were some of the important Ayagar officials.

4. The number of the provinces of the Vijaynagar empire was:
A. Four B. Six
C. Five D. Three

5. Which statement on Vijayanagar village is not correct?
A. The village was the unit of administration
B. The village moot, corresponding to the Panchayat of Northern India, managed its own affairs.
C. The hereditary officer of the village moot was known as Mahanayakacharya.
D. The hereditary officer of the village moot was known as Ayagar?

6. The ruler of Vijayanagar empire was called:
A. Raya B. Raja
C. Mandalesvras D. Mahammandalesvaras

7. Which of the following statement is false with regard to the policy of Vijayanagar empire?
A. The Vijayanagar kings claimed divine origin for their power
B. The selection of the ruler appears to have been made generally with the common consensus of the ministers and nobles
C. There are instances of kings like Krishnadeva Raya abdicating in favour of their sons.
D. The Vijayanagar kings used to sometimes appoint their sons as Yuvaraja to obviate the disputes regarding succession

8. Which of the following was not one of the important officers of the state?
A. Custom of the Jewels B. Chief Treasurer
C. Chief Master of Horses D. Provider of the Harem

9. Which one of the following was the largest administrative division in the Vijayanagar empire?

A. Rajya B. Mandalam
C. Kottam D. Nadu

10. Which one of the following was not the expressions used for provinces?
A. Rajya B. Mandala
C. Rashtra D. Chavadi

11. Locate which one of the following was not one of the provinces of the empire of Vijayanagar?
A. Udayagiri B. Penugonda
C. Padaividu D. Raichur

12. Which one of the following was not provinces of the Vijayanagar empire?
A. Grama
B. Naduka, Valitas or Vanitas
C. Sthala, Sammat or Kampana
D. Sima

13. What was the function of the Mahanayakacharya, one of the king's officer?
A. To supervise the work of the nayaks
B. To exercise general supervision over the village administration.
C. To supervise the observance of dharma
D. None of the above

14. What was Kuttagai?
A. Lease system of cultivation
B. Beneficiary tenures like brahmadeya, devadeya and mathapura
C. Service tenure for military or civil service
D. Grant of land to certain categories of craftsmen such as potters, goldsmith etc.

15. 'Amaram' stands for:
A. It was a tax levied on the Muslims
B. Territory with a fixed revenue to military chiefs
C. Head of the village community
D. Areas which were under the control of subordinate rulers

16. Cite one of the following statements about the position of women in Vijayanagar empire which is not correct?
A. Women in general occupied a high position in society
B. They look active part in the political, social and literary life of the country
C. Some of them were trained in wrestling and handling swords and Shields
D. They were generally married after attaining the age of puberty.

17. Which statement on Vijayanagar society is incorrect.
A. Duelling was recognised method of settling disputes
B. Only non-Brahmans consumed all kinds of meat
C. Even Brahmans ate all kinds of meat
D. The flesh of Cattle was strictly prohibited

18. Which one of the following types of marriage was the most popular?
A. Brahma B. Daiva
C. Arsa D. Prajapatya

19. Which of the following taxes was not impractice in the time of the rulers of Vijayanagar empire?
A. Grazing tax B. Tax on Pilgrims
C. Land tax D. Marriage tax

20. What was known as Varam?
A. The best quality of land
B. The system of sharing of agriculture in come between landlord and the tenant
C. A special method of cultivation which was kept as a closely guarded secret among certain classes of cultivators
D. The dowry given to the bridegroom in terms of land.

21. Which of the statement is justified regarding the high position of the women in the society of Vijayanagar empire?
A. Polygamy was not in practice
B. There was no Sati System
C. There was no child marriage
D. Women were engaged in all types of professions.

22. Amongst the things that were built during the days of Krishnadeva Rays, the outstanding one was.
A. the modern city of Hospet
B. embellishment of the Vittalaswamy temple
C. the statue of Narasimha which was carved out of a single piece of granite
D. the Harzara temple

23. Mention one of the following statements outlining the role played by the temple in the economic life of the people which is incorrect.
A. It was the largest employer in the village
B. It was often the biggest single landowner and consumer in an area
C. It largely controlled rural credit
D. It however did very little to encourage rural development

24. At which place were ships in use for coasting and overseas trade built?
A. Eli B. Quilon
C. Calicut D. Maldiva Islands

25. Krishadeva Raya patronised
A. One language B. Two language
C. Three language D. Four language

26. What was the main source of Income of Vijayanagar Kingdom?
A. Trade B. Industries
C. Land revenue D. War booty

27. Define Kaikkolas?
A. Temple priests
B. A community of acrobats

C. An influential community of weavers living around temple precints
D. An anti-religious group which entertained the people by caricaturing various God heads.

28. Nikitin, a Russian traveller, who visited the Bahamani Kingdom describes
(*a*) That the country was overpopulated
(*b*) Misery of the people
(*c*) Life of Luscury of the nobles
(*d*) Overgrowth of military establishment
(*e*) Armies being maintained by nobles
Codes:
A. (*a*), (*b*) and (*c*) B. (*a*), (*b*) and (*d*)
C. (*a*), (*b*), (*c*) and (*e*) D. All the above

29. Match the foreign travellers and their nationalities?
(*a*) Nicolo Conti 1. Russian
(*b*) Athanasius Nikitin 2. Italian (Venetian)
(*c*) Abdur Razzaq 3. Portuguese
(*d*) Domingos Poes 4. Arab
Codes:

	(*a*)	(*b*)	(*c*)	(*d*)
A.	1	2	4	3
B.	2	1	4	3
C.	3	2	4	1
D.	1	4	2	3

30. Which factors kept the Vijayanagar state survive for 200 years?
(*a*) Fire of Hindu patriotism
(*b*) Threat of Bahamani empire
(*c*) Ability and Courage of the kings
(*d*) Foreign help
Codes:
A. (*a*), (*b*) and (*c*) B. (*a*), (*b*) and (*d*)
C. (*b*), (*c*) and (*d*) D. (*a*), (*c*) and (*d*)

31. Sewell writes 'Goa rose and fell simultaneously with the rise and fall of the Tuluva dynasty' why?
A. Goa was a part of the Vijayanagar empire
B. The City enjoyed protection and trade concession
C. The Tuluva kings always had Goa as the last refuge after losing war
D. None of the above

32. Krishnadeva Raya was a followers of:
A. Vaishnavism B. Shaivism
C. Buddism D. Jainism

33. Virupaksha was a:
A. Shaivite deity
B. Vaishnavite deity
C. A representation of Vallabha
D. A deity popularised by Smartas

34. Which language benefited the most from the patronage of letters by Krishnadeva Raya?
A. Telugu B. Kannada
C. Sanskrit D. Tamil

35. Who was the author of Madhura Vijayam?
A. Tirumalamba B. Tukkadevi
C. Chinnadevi D. Gangadevi

36. "The Forgotten Empire" is a book written by:
A. Domingos Poes B. Sewell
C. Nicoli Conti D. Meadows Taylor

37. Who wrote "What I saw (Vijayanagar) was same what as large as Rome and very beautiful to sight. This is the best provided city in the world"?
A. Poes B. Muniz
C. Abdur Razzaq D. Nikitin

38. Who was the author of Panduranga Mahatyam?
A. Tenali Ramakrishna B. Suranna
C. Peddana D. Tirumalamba

39. Athavana tantram is a:
A. Document on the revenue system of the Vijayanagar empire
B. A book on Music
C. A book on Tantricism
D. A book on concerning Polity

40. Whose words are these "with great care and according to your power you should attend to the work of protecting the good and the punishing the wicked without neglecting anything that you see or hear"?
A. Tirumala B. Vir Narasimha
C. Krishnadeva Raya D. Harihara II

41. "A crowned king should always rule with an eye towards dharma" who authored these lines?
A. Krishnadeva Raya B. Tirumala
C. Achyuta Raya D. Deva Raya II

42. Name the language that Krishnadeva Raya used to write his major work 'Amuktamalyada'?
A. Sanskrit B. Tamil
C. Kannada D. Telgu

43. Name the King during whose rule lord Venkateshwara of Tirupati replaced Virupaksha?
A. Tirumala B. Venkatadri or Venkata I
C. Krishnadeva Raya D. Venkata II

44. Who was the real founder of the independent Sultanate of Gujarat?
A. Zafar Khan B. Tatar Khan
C. Shams Khan D. Ahmad Shah

45. Who built the city of Ahmedabad?
A. Zafar Khan B. Ahmed Shah
C. Mahmud Bengarha D. Muzaffar II

46. Which of the following is described as the Shiraz of India?
A. Gaur B. Agra
C. Jaunpur D. Ikdala

47. Pick out the wrong match.
A. Atala-Masjid – Jaunpur
B. Bara Sona Masjid – Gaur

C. Adina Masjid – Pandua
D. Gol Gumbaz – Ajmer

48. What was the name of the old town near which Ahmedabad was built?
A. Junugarh B. Siri
C. Asawal D. Mandu

49. One of the following factors contributed most to the development of Bengali literature. Identify:
A. Patronage of Muhammadan Emperors and Chiefs
B. The support given by the Hindu Rayas
C. Religious activity
D. Economic properity

50. Jaunpur was hailed as the "Shiraz of India". What could be the most important reason for such a description?
A. Some of the Sharqi rulers were themselves of culture
B. the Sharqi rule was marked by prosperity
C. It was not involved in any war with its neighbour
D. It was nearer to Delhi

51. Pick out the wrong match.
A. Khaljis — Malwa
B. Sharqis — Jaunpur
C. Husain Shahi — Bengal
D. Iliyas Shahi — Gujarat

52. Pick out the correct match.
A. Tower of Victory — Chitor
B. Shiraz of India — Delhi
C. Gol Gumbaz — Bijapur
D. Vittalasvami Temple — Belur

53. Who is the founder of the cult of Satyapir?
A. Husain Shah B. Sikandar II
C. Nasir-ud-din D. Haji Iliyas

54. Pick out the wrong match.
A. Bengal — Haji Iliyas
B. Jaunpur — Khwaja Jahan
C. Malwa — Dilawar Khan Ghuri
D. Gujarat — Tatar Khan

55. One of the following may not be regarded as the cause of external invasions of Gujarat. Identify:
A. fertility
B. wealth due to active commerce
C. natural resources
D. strategic importance

56. Pick out the wrong match:
A. Nusrat Shah — Qadam Rasul
B. Raya Ganesh — Danujamardana Deva
C. Ala-ud-din Hussain Shah — Ikdala
D. Indil Khan — Bengali version of the Mahabharata

57. Which is not a correct pair:
A. Nicolo Conti — Deva Raya I
B. Abdur Razzaq — Deva Raya II
C. Barbosa — Krishnadeva Raya
D. Idn Datula — Ghiyasuddin Tughluq

58. Whom do you regard the ablest of the Muslim ruler of Malwa?
A. Hushang Shah B. Mahmud I
C. Mahmud II D. Nasiruddin

59. Name the ruler who assisted Mahmud II to oust Medini Raj:
A. Rana Sanga B. Ratan Singh
C. Muzaffar Shah D. Chand Khan

60. Who built the Bara Masjid?
A. Nusrat Shah
B. Hussain Shah
C. Jalal-ud-din Muhammad
D. Barbak Shah

61. Urdu whose orders a Bengali version of the Mahabharata was written?
A. Hussain Shah B. Jalal-ud-din Muhammad
C. Nusrat Shah D. Haji Iliyas

62. Pick out the correct sequence:
A. Sangama, Aravidu, Tuluva and Saluva
B. Sangama, Tuluva, Saluva and Aravidu
C. Sangama, Saluva, Tuluva and Aravidu
D. Sangama, Aravidu, Saluva and Tuluva

63. One of the following did not visit the city of Vijayanagar. Identify:
A. Nicolo Conti B. Abdur Razzaq
C. Fernao D. Athanarius Nikitin

64. One of the following did not join the Deccani Sultans against Vijayanagar in the battle of Rakshasa-Tangadi. Identify:
A. Bijapur B. Golkunda
C. Ahmadnagar D. Berar

65. This is the best provided city in the world. Who has said this about — Vijayanagar
A. Domingos Poes B. Nuniz
C. Nicolo Conti D. Edoardo Borbosa

66. Pick out the correct sequence
A. Sangama, Bukka I, Virupaksha II and Devaraya I
B. Sangama, Virupaksha II, Devaraya I and Bukka I
C. Sangama, Bukka I, Devaraya I and Virupaksha II
D. Sangama, Devaraya I, Bukka I and Virupaksha II

67. One of the following was not regarded as one of the four Indians of the state:
A. Diwan-i-Wizarut B. Diwan-i-Insha
C. Diwan-i-Arz D. Diwan-i-Kharisat

68. From whom did the Turks know the association of divinity with kingship?
A. The Hindus B. The Chinese
C. The Sassanians D. The Arbas

69. Which one of the following defects of Vijayanagar empire may be regarded as the most serious one?

A. Independence enjoyed by the Provincial governors
B. Failure to develop a sustained commercial activity in spite of the facilities available
C. Permission given to the portuguese to settle on the west coast
D. Failure to develop a desciplined army

70. The authorship of one of the following is not ascribed to Krishnadeva Raya. Identify:
A. Amuktamalyada B. Ushaparivaya
C. Jambuvati – Kalyana D. Narayana – Vilasa

71. We have reference to the following local divisions in the Karnataka portion under the Vijayanagar rulers. Pick out the correct sequence in descending order
A. Nadu, Sima, Ventha, Village
B. Ventha, Nadu, Sima, Village
C. Sima, Ventha, Nadu, Village
D. Ventha, Sima, Nadu, Village

72. Who was the founder of the city of Zainabad?
A. Malik Nasir B. Adi Khan
C. Malik Raja D. Muzaffar Shah

73. What was the original name of Ahsanabad?
A. Gulbanga B. Badami
C. Kalyan D. Malkhed

74. What was the charge levelled against Mahmud Gawan?
A. Gawan was blind to the interests of the state
B. Gawan was organising a baronial chique against the Sultan
C. Gawan was in treasonable correspondence with the Raya of Vijayanagar.
D. Gawan indulged in tyrannical acts.

75. Which among the following not applicable to Vijayanagar period?
A. bloody sacrifices on festive occasions
B. a ban on prostitutes
C. use of flowers by women
D. sale of animals for food alive

76. Pick out the wrong match.
A. History of Kashmir — Jonaraja
B. History of Bahmani Kingdom — Bushan-i-Massir
C. History of Gujarat — Mirat-i-Sikandar
D. History of Bengal — Chanchnama

77. Pick out the wrong one among the attributes ascribed to Ahmad Shah of Gujarat?
A. Warlike B. Lover of justice
C. Munificent D. Tolerant

78. Who was called the Zar Bakhsha?
A. Ahmad Shah B. Qutab-ud-din Ahmad
C. Muhammad Sha II D. Mahmud Begarbha

79. What was the original name of Muhamm-adabad?
A. Dwaraka B. Junagarh
C. Champanir D. Surat

80. The nature of the rule of the kings of Vijayanagar was:
A. Benevolent despotism
B. Rule by the Council of Minister
C. Oligrachical rule
D. On the principles of democracy

81. When point on Krishnadeva Raya is not correct:
A. He belonged to Tuluga dynasty
B. He ruled from 1509 to 1530
C. He was defeated by the Bijapur Sultan
D. He recaptured Raichur Doob

82. Romantically called "The war of the Goldsmith's Daughter" took place between:
A. Firoz Shah and Deva Raya
B. Firoz Shah and Hari Hara II
C. Ala-ud-din Khalji and Karnadeva
D. Ala-ud-din Khalji and Hamir Deva

83. Which two dynastics came to the throne after the 'First Usurpation' and 'Second Usurpation' respectively?
A. Sangama and Saluva dynastics
B. Saluva and Aravidu dynastics
C. Saluva and Tuluva dynastics
D. Sangama and Aravidu dynastics

84. What was the second capital of Vijaynagar?
A. Chandrajiri B. Pernugoda
C. Kampali D. Mysore

85. Who among the following rulers of Vijayanagar entered into a treaty with the Portuguese Governor, Almedia for purchasing all the horses imported by him?
A. Achyuta Raya B. Vir Narsimha
C. Saluva Narsimha D. Krishnadeva Raya

86. Who was the ruler who participated in war with the Bahamani confederacy?
A. Narsimha Saluva B. Vira Narasimha
C. Krishnadeva Raya D. Rama Raya

87. Which fact regarding the battle of Talikota or Rakshasa-Tangadi is of significance in the history of India?
A. Hussain Nizam Shah personally killed Rama Raya
B. The Aravidu Dynasty continued the traditions of the Vijaynagar empire
C. Bijapur and Ahmadnagar attacked Goa in 1569
D. Shivaji claimed descent from Vijayanagar rulers?

88. Which region constituted the bone of contention between the Vijayanagar and Bahamani rulers?
A. Raichur Doab B. Cauvery Doab
C. Tungabhadra Doab D. Kolar Doab

89. Where from did South India get its ships during the Vijayanagar period?
A. Ceylon B. Portugal
C. Maldives D. Persia

90. During the reign of which Sultan of Delhi did the Vijayanagar Empire come into existence:
A. Ghiyas-ud-din Tughlaq

B. Muhammad-bin Tughlaq
C. Firoz Shah Tughlaq
D. Khizr Khan

91. Match the following dynastics with their founders.

(*a*) Sangama dynasty — 1. Narasimha
(*b*) Saluva dynasty — 2. Harihara
(*c*) Tuluva dynasty — 3. Tirumala
(*d*) Aravidu dynasty — 4. Vir Narasimha

Codes:

	(*a*)	(*b*)	(*c*)	(*d*)
A.	1	2	3	4
B.	2	1	3	4
C.	2	1	4	3
D.	4	3	2	1

92. Who succeeded Krishnadeva Raya after his death?
A. Deva Raya II B. Rama Raya
C. Sadasiva Raya D. Achyuta Raya

93. Who gave permission to the Portuguese Governor Albuquerque to build a fort at Bhatkal?
A. Deva Raya I B. Deva Raya II
C. Krishnadeva Raya D. Rama Raya

94. Who built the Vitthalasvami temple?
A. Bukka I B. Devaraya II
C. Tirumala D. Krishnadeva Raya

95. One of the following was not an important industry during the Vijayanagar period. Identify:
A. Textiles B. Mining
C. Metallurgy D. Perfumery

96. Which of the following is not one of the theories propounded by scholars regarding the origin of Valangai (right hand) and Idangai (left hand) castes?
A. Those who stood on the right hand side of the king were called valangais and other who stood on the left side were called Idangais
B. Valangais were agriculturists and Idangais were traders, the distinction arising on account of foreign trade and contact
C. On account of great animosity between the two classes of people, they got there tables.
D. It had its origin in the method of work *i.e.* those working with right hand came to be known as Valangais and left handers as Idangis

97. Which one of the following statement about the practice of becoming a Sati or Sahagamana is not correct?
A. The Sati's sacrifice was commemorated by erection of Sati Kals
B. There was no compulsion and it was done voluntarily
C. It was very popular and widespread
D. There was no social disabilities attached to widows who did not choose to become Satis

98. The City of Vijayanagar had seven fortified walls one within the other. The palace of the king was located at the centre in the seventh fortress, which one of the following occupied pride of place between the third and the seventh fortress?
A. Gardens
B. Shops and Bazaars
C. Houses of Nobles
D. Quarters of Courtesans

99. Arrange the foreign travellers in choronological order:
(*a*) Nikitin (*b*) Ibn Batuta
(*c*) Marco Polo (*d*) Nicolo Conti
(*e*) Abdur Razzaq (*f*) Barbosa

Codes:

A.	(*c*)	(*b*)	(*e*)	(*d*)	(*a*)	(*f*)
B.	(*a*)	(*b*)	(*c*)	(*d*)	(*e*)	(*f*)
C.	(*b*)	(*c*)	(*d*)	(*e*)	(*a*)	(*f*)
D.	(*c*)	(*b*)	(*d*)	(*e*)	(*a*)	(*f*)

100. The fortress of Vijayanagar was located on the bank of the river:
A. Godavari B. Krishna
C. Tungabhadra D. Kaveri

ANSWERS

1	2	3	4	5	6	7	8	9	10
D	C	C	B	D	A	C	D	B	C
11	**12**	**13**	**14**	**15**	**16**	**17**	**18**	**19**	**20**
D	A	B	A	B	D	C	A	B	B
21	**22**	**23**	**24**	**25**	**26**	**27**	**28**	**29**	**30**
D	C	D	D	D	C	C	D	B	D
31	**32**	**33**	**34**	**35**	**36**	**37**	**38**	**39**	**40**
B	A	B	A	B	B	A	A	A	C
41	**42**	**43**	**44**	**45**	**46**	**47**	**48**	**49**	**50**
A	D	D	D	B	C	D	C	A	A
51	**52**	**53**	**54**	**55**	**56**	**57**	**58**	**59**	**60**
D	A	A	D	D	D	D	B	C	A

61	62	63	64	65	66	67	68	69	70
C	C	D	D	A	C	D	C	B	D
71	72	73	74	75	76	77	78	79	80
B	A	A	C	B	D	D	C	C	A
81	82	83	84	85	86	87	88	89	90
C	A	C	B	B	D	D	A	C	B
91	92	93	94	95	96	97	98	99	100
C	D	C	D	D	D	D	B	D	C

SET-4

1. Who was Sayana?
A. a commentator of Vedas
B. a governor of the Vijayanagar empire
C. father of Krishnadeva Raya
D. the founder of the Aravidu dynasty

2. Who has described the Brahmanas as honest men given to merchandise–but little fit for hard work?
A. Nicolo Conti B. Nuniz
C. Paes D. Barbosa

3. Who has said that the Vijayanagar empire possessed 300 sea ports?
A. Abdul Razzaq B. Nuniz
C. Paes D. Caesar Frederick

4. Pick out the wrong match:
A. Amuktamalyada–Telugu
B. Prabhulingabile–Kannada
C. Kalaviyal–Tamil
D. Madhura Vijayam–Malayalam

5. By what name is Vishnu Cithya known?
A. Markandeya Purana B. Amuktamalayada
C. Jambavati Kalyana D. Parvati Parinaya

6. The assimilation of Muslims into Indian Society was rendered easier by many factors. One of the following may not be correct. Identify:
A. Absence of large scale immigration from Afghanistan and Western Asia
B. Muslim were in a minority
C. Advantages to be gained by conversion were not great
D. Persecution

7. Why did Mahmud attack Multan?
A. The ruler followed the heterodox doctrine of the Qarmatrori Seat
B. The ruler was weak
C. Wealth of Multan
D. Desire to bring it under his control

8. Who was Gangu?
A. founder of Bahmani Kingdom
B. astrologer of Delhi
C. descendant of the Persian hero Bahman
D. Governor of Daulatabad

9. Pick out the wrong match.
A. Nizam Shahi Ahmadnagar
B. Qutub Shahi — Golkunda
C. Barid Shahi — Berar
D. Adil Shahi — Bijapur

10. By what name is the tomb of Muhammad Adil Shah called?
A. Gol Gumbaz B. Bara Gumbaz
C. Shib Gumbaz D. Dadi Ka Gumbaz

11. Which among the following may be regarded on the most significant achievements of Vijayanagar empire?
A. Building up a vast empire
B. Efficient administration
C. Economic prosperity
D. Saving the Hindu religion and culture from being engulfed by the rush of new forces.

12. In what language was Basavapurana written?
A. Sanskrit B. Tamil
C. Telgu D. Prakrit

13. When was the battle of Talikota fought?
A. 1565 AD B. 1526 AD
C. 1556 AD D. 1509 AD

14. Who among the Bahmani Sultans was called the Zalim?
A. Ala-ud-din II B. Humayun
C. Muhammad III D. Ahmad

15. "With him departed all the cohesion and power of the Bahmani kingdom"—about whom was this said?
A. Mahmud Gawan B. Ahmad Shah
C. Muhammad Shah III D. Humayun

16. One of the five Deccani Sultanates was annexed by Ahmadnagar. Identify:
A. Bijapur B. Berar
C. Golkunda D. Bidar

17. Pick out the wrong match.
A. Chaitanya – Bengali
B. Sankara Deva – Assamese

C. Mira Bai – Rajasthani
D. Kabir – Gujarati

18. One of the following was not a Maratha Saint. Identify
A. Jnanesvar B. Ramdas
C. Namadeva D. Vallabha

19. Who composed 'Sursagar'?
A. Jayadeva B. Surdas
C. Bana D. None of the above

20. Where is Quwat-ul-Islam mosque situated?
A. Ajmer B. Agra
C. Fatehpur Sikri D. Delhi

21. One of the foilowing composed verses in praise of God Siva. Identify:
A. Mira Bai B. Surdas
C. Chaitanya D. Lalla

22. Who among the following spoke about achieving union with God through love of God?
A. Shiahs B. Sunnis
C. Sufis D. Ulemas

23. By what name is the philosophy of Ramanuja known?
A. Dvaita B. Advaita
C. Visista Dvaita D. Sankhya

24. Kabir Panthis were the followers of:
A. Meera Bai B. Namdev
C. Kabir D. Nanak

25. Where was Guru Nanak born?
A. Hissar B. Amritsar
C. Talwandi D. None of these

26. Namdeva, a Marathi Saint flourished in:
A. 10th century B. 11th century
C. 13th centure D. 14th century

27. Seeds of Bhakti can be found in:
A. Upanishads B. Shrutis
C. Upredas D. Vedas

28. Who said that the Hindu and the Turks were pots of the same clay?
A. Kabir B. Nanak
C. Lalla D. Vallabha

29. One of the following belonged to the chisti order. Identify:
A. Barani B. Mahmud Gawan
C. Firishta D. Lalla

30. Where was the order of Firdausi popular?
A. Ghazi B. Bihar
C. Delhi D. Sind

31. "Dohas" are:
A. The religious teaching of Sufis
B. The Muslim devotees who emphasised the personal devotion of man to God through love
C. A group of merchants who sent large caravans
D. Couples which Kabir composed and by which he taught his followers

32. The language of Bhakti movement was
A. The language of the reformers
B. Sanskrit/Prakrit
C. Hindi/Perisan
D. Perisan and Urdu

33. The Bhakti teachers delivered their message mainly through:
A. Homely Sermars B. Simple Parables
C. Bhajans D. Public Prayer

34. In one of the following the Bhakti saints differed from the Sufis. Identify:
A. Needs for Union with God
B. Stress on love on the basis of relationship with
C. Acceptance of a Guru or Pir
D. Encouraging mysticism

35. One of the following did not help the rise of the Urdu language. Identify?
A. Arabic B. Sanskrit
C. Persian D. Bengali

36. Pick out the wrong match:
A. Chand Minar Daulatabad
B. Madarasa of Mahmud Gawan — Bidar
C. Mihtar Mahal — Golkunda
D. Shah Bazar Maszid — Gulbarga

37. Who wrote I am neither in Kaaba nor in Kailash?
A. Kabir B. Nanak
C. Eknath D. Chaitanya

38. Who said "God is the breath of all Breath"?
A. Kabir B. Nanak
C. Mira Bai D. Chaitanya

39. Pick out the correct match:
A. Ramdas — Amritanubhava
B. Jnanesvar — Dasabodha
C. Ramanuja — Sri Bashya
D. Krithivasa — Bengali translation of Mahabharata

40. Which saint was a contemporary of Shivaji and Samartha Guru?
A. Tukaram B. Raskhan
C. Narasimha D. Surdas

41. One of the following poets was not a contemporary of the rest of four, Identify:
A. Tulsidas B. Surdas
C. Raskhan D. Mira Bai

42. Rahim composed popular poetry in:
A. Braj Bhasa B. Persian
C. Urdu D. Hindi

43. Nirguna school believes in:
A. Absolute God free from human attributes
B. God who is richly endowed with human virtues
C. God who is omnipresent
D. God who is within each human being

44. Guru Nanak was born in:
A. 1469 AD B. 1470 AD
C. 1450 AD D. 1445 AD

45. The poet Amir Khusrau was a follower of
A. Chisti order
B. Suhrawardi order
C. Qadiria order
D. Was not a follower of any order of Sufis

46. In which field did the Arabs gain from India?
A. Metaphysics, medicine and mathematics
B. System of administration
C. Art of military organisation
D. Literature and arts

47. Kabir was born in:
A. 1440 AD B. 1430 AD
C. 1450 AD D. 1445 AD

48. Who wrote the Telugu version of Mahabharata?
A. Nannaya B. Akkatiyar
C. Tiruvaliuvar D. None of the above

49. Who was the great Acharya, who counselled Surdas teaching of Lord's creative play (Bhagavat Lila)?
A. Vallabhacharya B. Ramananda
C. Ramanuja D. Shankaracharya

50. Which one is not the work of Surdas?
A. Sahitya Lehari B. Sur-Sagar
C. Sur-Saravalli D. Sur-Darshan

51. Ramananda was a philosopher of:
A. Vaishanavism B. Shaivism
C. Jainism D. Buddhism

52. Shankaracharya had explicit — faith in:
A. Vaishnavism B. Shaivism
C. Jainism D. Hinduism

53. According to the legand, Sikandhar Lodi, the Sultan of Delhi tried various means to kill:
A. Kabir B. Nanak
C. Mira D. Chaitanya

54. The script of Sikhs is:
A. Guruvani B. Devanagari
C. Gurutipi D. Gurumukhi

55. The word Sikh means:
A. Simple B. devotee
C. disciple D. fighter

56. The name of the last Sikh Guru is:
A. Guru Amardas B. Guru Tegh Bahadur
C. Guru Govind Singh D. Guru Har Govind

57. Kabir didn't write in one of the following language. Which are:
A. Bhojpuri B. Brajabhasa
C. Awadhi D. Rajasthani

58. Who did not allow his followers to have any kind of social intercourse with women?
A. Chaitanya B. Nanak
C. Ramananda D. Shankaracharya

59. Namadeva and Eknath wrote in:
A. Hindi B. Marathi
C. Tamil D. Gujarati

60. The name of the Guru who compiled the 'Adi Granth' is:
A. Guru Govind Singh B. Guru Tegh Bahadur
C. Guru Arjun Dev D. Guru Nanak

61. Who did not write in Gujarati Language?
A. Mira Bai B. Narasimha
C. Kesavadas D. Kabir

62. Mira did not see one of the following. Identify:
A. Tulsidas B. Akbar
C. Tansen D. Surdas

63. Match the works with their authors:

(*a*) Tarikh-i Hind	1. Muhammad-ul-Utbi
(*b*) Tarikh-i-Yamini	2. Shams-i-Siraj Ali
(*c*) Taj-ul-Ma'asir	3. Alberuni
(*d*) Tarikh-i-Firoz Shahi	4. Hasan Nizami

Codes:

	(*a*)	(*b*)	(*c*)	(*d*)
A.	3	1	4	2
B.	1	2	3	4
C.	2	3	4	1
D.	4	1	3	2

64. Match the works with their authors:

(*a*) Tarikh-i-Firoz Shahi	1. Firoz Shah Tughluq
(*b*) Fatuhat-i-Firoz Shahi	2. Yahaya-bin-Sirhindi
(*c*) Tarikh-a-Alai	3. Zia-ud-din-Barani
(*d*) Tarikh-i-Mubarak Shah	4. Khusrau

Codes:

	(*a*)	(*b*)	(*c*)	(*d*)
A.	3	1	4	2
B.	3	4	1	2
C.	2	1	4	3
D.	4	1	3	2

65. A no. of Sanskrit works were rendered into persian for the first time during the reign of:
A. Balban
B. Muhammad-bin-Tughluq
C. Firu Tughluq
D. Sher Shah

66. Which one of the following was not the saint poet of Maharashtra?
A. Jnaneswar B. Namdev
C. Tukaram D. Mira Bai

67. Name the Sufi Saint whose philosophy greatly influenced Aurangzeb?
A. Shaikh Ahmad Sirhindi
B. Khwaja Bagi Billagh

C. Shau Pir of Meerut
D. Shaikh Qadiri

68. Which Sufi order of saints tried to live like ascetics?
A. Subhrawardi B. Qadiri
C. Chisthi D. Naqsh bandi

69. Though Sufi and Bhakti thoughts converged on several points, one of following was not one of them?
A. Belief in the need to unite with God
B. Stress on love as the basis of relationship with God
C. Belief in mysticism
D. The need for the help of a religious preceptor, at least in the initial stages.

70. Which beliefs were not common to Sufi and Bhakti thoughts?
(*a*) The need to unite with God
(*b*) Stress on love as the basis of the relationship with God
(*c*) Need of the Guru or a Pir in initial stages
(*d*) Mysticism
Codes:
A. only (*a*) and (*d*) B. only (*a*) and (*c*)
C. only (*d*) and (*c*) D. all four

71. The first Muslim building erected in India was the
A. Qutab Minar
B. Adhai-din-ka-Jhonpra
C. Quwwat-ul-Islam Mosque
D. Alai-Darwaza

72. Who claimed their decent from the prophet?
A. Shaikhs B. Sayyids
C. Mughals D. Qarunah Turks

73. School attached to mosque were known as:
A. Madarasa B. Maktab
C. Talimghan D. Persia

74. Balban's monarchial ideals were those of the ancient kings of:
A. Mesopotamia B. Saudi Arabia
C. Turkestan D. Persia

75. Who have been termed as "The Brahmana of Islam"?
A. Sayyids B. Shaikhs
C. Pirs D. Ulema

76. Which are of Sufi orders was at first the most orthodox?
A. Suhrawardi B. Qadiri
C. Naqshbandi D. Chishti

77. Who introduced Qadiri Silsila in India?
A. Shaikh Abdul Quadirisi
B. Sayyid Makhdum Muhammad Gilani
C. Abdul Qadir
D. Shaikh Mir Muhammad

78. Which Sufi Silsila tried to counteract the liberal religious policies of Akbar?
A. Quadiri B. Firdausi
C. Suhrawardi D. Naqshbandi

79. The Theory of Islamic Mysticism (Sufism) was profound by:
A. Muin-ud-din Chisti
B. Hamid-ud-din Nagar
C. Sheikh Muhi-ud-din Ibnual Arabi
D. Nizam-ud-din Auliya

80. Which of the following principles was not preached by the saints of Bhakti movement?
A. Unity of God.
B. Opposed Casteism
C. Idol Worship
D. No need of particular language to worship

81. Shankaracharya had explicit faith in:
A. Vaishnavism B. Shaivism
C. Jainism D. Hinduism

82. Which one of the the Sufi order was at frist the most orthodox?
A. Subhrawardi B. Qadiri
C. Naqshbandi D. Chisti

83. Ramananda was philosopher of:
A. Vaishnavism B. Shaivism
C. Jainism D. Bhuddism

84. Arrange the following sufi saints of the Chisti Silsila Chronologically:
1. Shaikh Farid
2. Shaikh Nizamuddin Auliya
3. Shaikh Bhaktiyar Kaki
4. Shaikh Muinuddin Chisthi
Codes:
A. 1, 2, 3, 4 B. 1, 3, 2, 4
C. 1, 3, 4, 2 D. 4, 3, 1, 2

85. Who was the bridge between the Bhakshi movement of the south and the North?
A. Chaitanya B. Namadeva
C. Ramananda D. Nanak

86. Name one of the Bhakti saints who had twelve disciples belonging to the poorest classes?
A. Vallabhacharya B. Ramananda
C. Kabir D. Surdas

87. Identify one order of the Bhakti Cult who was influenced by Islam?
A. Ramanuja B. Namadeva
C. Chaitanya D. Ramananda

88. Who among the following was not a Chisti Saint?
A. Bakhtiyar Kaki
B. Hamid-ud-din
C. Farid-ud-din Ganj-i-Shallar
D. Baha-ud-din Zakaria

89. Name one of the following who established the Chisti order in India?
A. Shaikh Muniuddin Chishti
B. Khawaja Muinuddin Chishti

C. Nizamuddin Auliya
D. Farid-ud-din Ganj-i-Shakar

90. Match the following Bhakti saints with the theories they preached.

(*a*) Ramanuja		1. Unqualified Monism	
(*b*) Nimvark		2. Qualified Monism	
(*c*) Chaitanya		3. Dualism & Non dualism	
(*d*) Vallabhacharya		4. Pure non-dualism	
(*e*) Shankaracharya		5. Dualistic non-dualism	

Codes:

	(*a*)	(*b*)	(*c*)	(*d*)	(*e*)
A.	2	5	3	4	1
B.	5	4	3	2	1
C.	1	3	4	2	5
D.	4	1	5	3	2

91. Bakhtiyar Kaki, a chishti saint, refused the post of Shaikh-ul-Islam offered to him by:
A. Iltutmish
B. Balban
C. Ala-ud-din Khalji
D. Muhammad-bin-Tughluq

92. Name the Sufi saint whose philosophy greatly influenced Aurangzeb.
A. Shaikh Ahmad Sirhindi
B. Khwaja Bagi Billagh
C. Shah Pir of Meerut
D. Shaikh Qadari

93. In which of the following territories was the Firdausi order popular?
A. In & Around Delhi B. Sind
C. Bihar D. Deccan

94. Who was the Bhakti saint regarded by his followers as an incarnation of Vishnu?
A. Ramananda B. Ramanuja
C. Namadeva D. Chaitanya

95. With which religion do we associate the five k's?
A. Jainism B. Buddism
C. Sikhism D. Islam

96. Who was born at Kalady (Malabar) in 783 AD?
A. Shankaracharya B. Ramanuja
C. Ramananda D. Madhavacharya

97. Which sufi saint remarked "Haur Dilli Dur Ast" (Delhi is still far away)?
A. Nizamuddin Auliya
B. Shaikh Salim Chisthi
C. Nasiruddin Chiragh-i-Delhwi
D. Shaikh Farid

98. Which one of the following was the earliest teacher of Bhakti Cult in Maharashtra?
A. Tuka Ram B. Namadeva
C. Dadu D. Ram Das

99. Who was the most famous disciple of Ramananda?
A. Tuka Ram B. Tulsi Das
C. Kabir D. Dadu

100. Who was the author of Ramacharitamanas?
A. Ramananda B. Mira Bai
C. Kabir D. Tulsi Das

ANSWERS

1	2	3	4	5	6	7	8	9	10
A	B	A	D	B	D	A	B	C	A
11	**12**	**13**	**14**	**15**	**16**	**17**	**18**	**19**	**20**
D	C	A	B	A	B	D	D	B	D
21	**22**	**23**	**24**	**25**	**26**	**27**	**28**	**29**	**30**
D	C	C	C	C	D	A	A	A	B
31	**32**	**33**	**34**	**35**	**36**	**37**	**38**	**39**	**40**
D	A	A	D	D	C	A	A	C	A
41	**42**	**43**	**44**	**45**	**46**	**47**	**48**	**49**	**50**
C	A	A	A	A	A	A	A	A	D
51	**52**	**53**	**54**	**55**	**56**	**57**	**58**	**59**	**60**
A	D	A	D	C	C	D	A	B	C
61	**62**	**63**	**64**	**65**	**66**	**67**	**68**	**69**	**70**
D	D	A	A	C	D	A	C	C	D
71	**72**	**73**	**74**	**75**	**76**	**77**	**78**	**79**	**80**
C	B	B	D	B	C	B	D	C	C
81	**82**	**83**	**84**	**85**	**86**	**87**	**88**	**89**	**90**
D	C	A	C	C	B	B	D	B	A
91	**92**	**93**	**94**	**95**	**96**	**97**	**98**	**99**	**100**
A	A	A	D	C	A	A	C	C	D

SET-5

1. Once Sher Shah exclaimed that he had lost the empire of Hindustan for a handful of bajra. What does this means?
   A. Once he got stranded in the desert of Rajasthan with getting food for 17 days and he would have been killed but for timely supply of bajra rotis by the Rajput kings, Maldev.
   B. Sher Shah never gave such an exclamination.
   C. The troops of Jaila & Kumpa, two famous generals of Maldev, the Rajput king of Jodhpur (Marwar) cut their way to the very heart of Sher Shah's Camp and he would have been killed but for timely help.
   D. One of the Rajput kings served him with bajra rotis containing position and he would have been killed but for timely medical help.
2. What made Bairam Khan rebel against Akbar?
   A. He was the man of masterful personality.
   B. He was increased by the outrageous conduct of Pir Muhammad, his old servant now in Akbar's favour, who wanted to hustle him out the country.
   C. He was stung by the outrageous conduct of Akbar, who dismissed him & asked him to go to Mecca.
   D. He was tempted by the youth of Akbar and wanted the throne for himself.
3. During which period Bairam Khan worked as regent of Akbar?
   A. 1556 A.D. — 1558 A.D.
   B. 1556 A.D. — 1564 A.D.
   C. 1556 A.D. — 1560 A.D.
   D. 1556 A.D. — 1605 A.D.
4. Which of the following was not a result of the Rajput policy of Akbar?
   A. The Rajputs gave cooperation to the administrative machinery of Akbar
   B. The Rajputs gave help to the military achievements of Akbar
   C. It developed the Indo-Islamic culture
   D. The cooperation of the Rajputs changed the minds of the orthodox Muslim Ulemas and they became liberal.
5. Which chronological order of Babur's battles in Hindustan is correct?
   A. Panipat, Ghaghara, Chanderi, Khanua
   B. Panipat, Chanderi, Khanua, Ghaghara
   C. Panipat, Khanua, Chanderi, Ghaghara
   D. Panipat, Khanua, Ghaghara, Chanderi
6. The first Rajput Chief who entered into matrimonial alliance with Akbar was:
   A. The ruler of Ranthambor
   B. The ruler of Marwar
   C. The ruler of Jaipur
   D. The ruler of Kalinjar
7. The only state in Northern India which Akbar failed to annex was:
   A. Kashmir B. Malwa
   C. Mewar D. Gondwana
8. The second battle of Panipat was fought in 1556 A.D. between:
   A. Akbar & Uday Singh B. Akbar & Rana Pratap
   C. Akbar & Hemmu D. Akbar & Raja Surjan Rai
9. Which of the following states of Southern India was completely annexed by Akbar?
   A. Ahmedanagar B. Bijapur
   C. Khandesh D. Golkunda
10. The Mughals were:
    A. Turks B. Mongols
    C. Arabs D. Chaghtais
11. Which Battle did Babur fight against the Afghans?
    A. Panipat B.. Ghaghara
    C. Khanua D. Chanderi
12. Why was Akbar interested in extending his sway to the south of Narmada and which are of the following factors did not shape his Deccan policy in this regard?
    A. His desire to bring the whole of India under his sway and to repeat the experiments of the Sultans of Delhi in the Deccan
    B. For the expulsion of the Europeans, particularly the Portuguese, the annexation of the Deccan was essential.
    C. The Deccan had become the centre of bitter religious controversies, which would have disturbed the religious peace he was trying to restore in the North.
    D. As in the case of Ala-ud-din Khalji, the Wealth of the South was one of the biggest inducements to him
13. Humayun fought his decisive battle against Sher Shah at:
    A. Chausa B. Chunargah
    C. Bilgram D. Panipat
14. The task of initiating the disciple into the new faith (*i.e.* Din-i-Ilahi) was done on
    A. Monday B. Tuesday
    C. Saturday D. Sunday
15. Match the following.

(*a*) Abolition of Jaziya	1. A.D. 1563
(*b*) Abolition of Pilgrims Tax	2. A.D. 1564
(*c*) Abolition of enslaving war prisoner	3. A.D. 1562
(*d*) Fall of Bairam Khan	4. A.D. 1560

Codes:

	(a)	(b)	(c)	(d)
A.	2	1	3	4
B.	4	1	3	2
C.	1	2	3	4
D.	3	4	2	1

16. The infallibility Decree assured to Akbar so far as any written instrument called have such effect, the atmost power that any man could claim to exercise, within the limits of Islam, which of the following historians express the above view about the infallibility decree?
A. Stanley Lane Poole B. V.A. Smith
C. Edwards and Garret D. S.R. Sharma

17. Arrange chronologically.
1. Construction of Ibadat Khana
2. Promulgation of Din-i-Ilahi
3. Insuring of Mazharuama

Codes:
A. 1, 2, 3 B. 3, 1, 2
C. 1, 3, 2 D. 2, 3, 1

18. The first step that Akbar took to make him free from the influence of the Ulemas (religious Jurists of Islam) was to read the Khutaba in his own name from the mosque at Fatehpur Sikri on the:
A. 22nd October, 1573 B. 22nd June, 1579
C. 3rd March, 1574 D. 3rd March, 1580

19. It is generally held that Jahangir as a prince was in love with Mehr-un-nisa when she was a maiden and the emperor arranged the murder of her husband Sher Afghans to marry her. Dr. Beni Prasad attempts to exonerate Jahangir of this charge which of the following reason have not been advanced by Dr. Beni Prasad in support of this thesis?
A. No contemporary chronicler has made the charge against the emperor
B. Contemporary European writers who are otherwise critical of Jahangir do not impute the crime to Jahangir
C. If Jahangir as a prince took Sher Afgan as his rival in love, he would have got him killed when Sher Afghan was placed under Prince Salim
D. The chroniclers of Shah Jahan's reign also make no mention of the affair.

20. Which of the following historians has supported the view that Jahangir was a strange "compound of opposites"?
A. V.A. Smith B. Ishwari Prasad
C. Beni Prasad D. I.H. Quereshi

21. The reading of the Khutba by the emperor caused resentment among the Ulemas to silence them, Akar issued the "Infallibility Decree" (Mahzar) on the:
A. 26th June, 1579 B. 2nd September, 1579
C. 3rd March, 1580 D. 10th December, 1580

22. Which of the following historian described "Din-i-Ilahi" as a movement of Akbar's folly, not of his wisdom"?
A. V.A. Smith B. Stanley-Lave-Poole
C. Beni Prasad D. Eduards and Garret

23. The reconciliation between Akbar and Prince Salim was achieved with the effects of:
A. Salima Sultan Begam
B. Khan Azam
C. Man Singh
D. Hamida Banu Begam

24. Jahangir ascended the throne in the year.
A. 1600 A.D. B. 1605 A.D.
C. 1590 A.D. D. 1627 A.D.

25. Akbar promulgated Din-i-Ilahi in 1582. It was:
A. Islamic doctrine
B. Code of conduct
C. Hindu law influenced by Islam
D. None of the above

26. Which of the following is correct?
A. Shah Jahan conquered Quandhar but lost to the Uzbegs at Balkh
B. Shah Jahan did not conquer Quandhar but defeated the Uzbegs at Balkh
C. Shah Jahan both conquered Quandhar and defeated the Uzbegs at Balkh
D. Shah Jahan failed both in conquering Quandhar and in fighting the Uzbegs at Balkh

27. Todarmal classified the land into from they are:
1. Polaj 2. Parauti
3. Krori 4. Chachar
5. Potadar 6. Banjar

Codes:
A. 1, 2, 4, 6 B. 1, 2, 3, 4
C. 1, 3, 5, 6 D. 2, 3, 4, 5

28. Match the following categories of land with the respective names assigned to them:
(*a*) Polja (1) Land which was cultivated almost every year
(*b*) Paraufi (2) Land which had been follow for one or two year
(*c*) Chachar (3) Fallow hand
(*d*) Banjar (4) Land which had been fallow for three or four year

Codes:

	(a)	(b)	(c)	(d)
A.	1	2	4	3
B.	3	1	4	2
C.	1	3	4	2
D.	2	1	4	3

29. Who was the first Mughal ruler to introduce prohibition?
A. Babur B. Akbar
C. Humayun D. Jahangir

30. The "Chain of Justice" is associated with:
A. Akbar B. Jahangir
C. Nur Jahan D. Shah Jahan

31. Name one of the following who acted as check on Subahdar?
A. Diwan B. Bakhshi
C. Faujdar D. Waqa-i-Navis

32. A faujdar was incharge of:
A. A Pargana B. A Province
C. A Sarkar D. A Village

33. Who was the first to rebel against Jahangir after his accession to the throne?
A. Prince Khusrow B. Rana Raj Singh
C. Prince Shahryar D. Prince Khurram

34. The Mugal empire reached its territorial climax under:
A. Akbar B. Jahangir
C. Shah Jahan D. Aurangzeb

35. Who among the following, was the revenue officer of a Sarkar?
A. Amal Guzar B. Amil
C. Bitikchi D. Khazandar

36. The Yusufzair rose in revolt against Aurangzeb in the year:
A. 1658 A.D. B. 1667 A.D.
C. 1678 A.D. D. 1687 A.D.

37. Aurangzeb reimposed Jaziya in:
A. 1675 A.D. B. 1679 A.D.
C. 1681 A.D. D. 1682 A.D.

38. Among the following who was an illiterate?
A. Babar B. Akbar
C. Jahangir D. Aurangzeb

39. What was the name of the Sikh Guru who was executed by Aurangzeb?
A. Guru Hargovind B. Guru Har Rai
C. Guru Arjun Dev D. Guru Teg Bahadur

40. During the Mughal rule, the chief of the city was:
A. Shiqdar B. Munsif
C. Kotwal D. Muqaddam

41. Match the following government officials with their respective functions:

(*a*) Khan-i-Saman	1. Household department and karkhanas
(*b*) Sadra-Us-Sudur	2. Chief adviser to the emperor on ecclesiastical affairs and chief justice of the empire
(*c*) Wazir	3. Prime Minister and the intermediary between the ruler and the rest of the officials
(*d*) Vakil	4. Finance Minister

Codes:

	(*a*)	(*b*)	(*c*)	(*d*)
A.	1	2	3	4
B.	2	3	1	4
C.	4	3	2	1
D.	1	2	4	3

42. Which one of the following was the auditor general?
A. Mir Alish B. Mustafi
C. Mushriff D. Mir Barr

43. What was Nur Jahan's real name?
A. Arjumand Banu Begam
B. Mehr-un-nisa
C. Hamida Banu Begam
D. Ruqaiya Begam

44. Shalimar garden at Lahore was raised by:
A. Akbar B. Shah Jahan
C. Jahangir D. Aurangzeb

45. The mansab was only:
A. An office B. A post
C. A rank D. Grade of pay

46. The range of the Mansabs as organised by Akbar was:
A. 100 to 5000 B. 10 to 5000
C. 10 to 7000 D. 10 to 10000

47. In what language was Padmavat written?
A. Hindi B. Urdu
C. Sanskrit D. Persian

48. Who wrote Padmavat?
A. Amir Khusrau
B. Muhammad Jaisi
C. Narahari
D. Tulsi Das

49. The most important industry during the Mughal period was
A. Silk B. Sculpture
C. Cotton D. Handicrafts

50. Who was the designer of Taj Mahal?
A. Ustad Ahmed Lahori B. Ali Mardan
C. Abdus Samad D. Sanwal Das

51. Pick out the wrong match
A. Khaljis — Malwa
B. Sharqis — Jaunpur
C. Hussain Shahi — Bengal
D. Iliyas Shahi — Gujarat

52. Pick out the correct match.
A. Tower of Victory — Chittor
B. Shiraz of India — Delhi
C. Gol Gumbaz — Bijapur
D. Vittalasvami Temple — Belur

53. Who is the founder of the cult of Satyapir?
A. Hussain Shah B. Sikandar II
C. Nasir-ud-din D. Haji Iliyas

54. Pick out the wrong match.
A. Bengal — Haji Iliyas
B. Jaunpur — Khwaja Jahan
C. Malwa — Dilawar Khan Ghuri
D. Gujarat — Tatar Khan

55. One of the following may not be regarded as the cause of External invasions of Gujarat. Identify:
A. fertility
B. wealth due to active commerce
C. natural resources
D. strategic importance

56. Pick out the wrong match.
A. Nusrat Shah — Qadam Rasul
B. Raya Ganesh — Danujamardana Deva
C. Ala-ud-din Hussain Shah — Ikadala
D. Indil Khan — Bengali version of the Mahabharata

57. Which is not a correct pair?
A. Nicolo Conti — Deva Raya I
B. Abdur Razzaq — Deva Raya II
C. Barbosa — Krishnadeva Raya
D. Idn Datula — Ghiyasuddin Tughluq

58. Whom do you regard the ablest of the Muslim ruler of Malwa?
A. Hushang Shah B. Mahmud I
C. Mahmud II D. Nasiruddin

59. Name the ruler who assisted Mahmud II to oust Medini Raj
A. Rana Sanga B. Ratan Singh
C. Muzaffar Shah D. Chand Khan

60. Who built the Bara Masjid?
A. Nusrat Shah
B. Hussain Shah
C. Jalal-ud-din Muhammad
D. Barbak Shah

61. Which among the following was completed during the reign of Sher Shah?
A. Padmavat B. Tughlaq-nama
C. Padshah-nama D. Razm-nama

62. The Jama Masjid at Delhi was constructed by:
A. Akbar B. Jahangir
C. Aurangzeb D. Shah Jahan

63. Match the following.
(*a*) Battle of Bahadurpur 1. Fought between Dara and Shuja
(*b*) Battle of Dharmat 2. Fought between Dara and Aurangzeb
(*c*) Battle of Samugarh 3. Fought between Dara and Combined armies of Aurangzeb and Murad

Codes:

	(*a*)	(*b*)	(*c*)
A.	1	3	2
B.	2	3	1
C.	1	2	3
D.	3	1	2

64. The Shalimar garden at Srinagar was raised by:
A. Akbar B. Shah Jahan
C. Aurangzeb D. Jahangir

65. Pick out the wrong match:
A. Jama — Assessed revenue
B. Mal — State's share of the actual crop
C. Desturu' lamal — Schedule of Cash revenue rates
D. Zabti — Simple sharing of the harvested grain

66. Which kind of Revenue system prevailed in Bengal?
A. Muqtai B. Zabti
C. Dausala D. Batai

67. Pick out the wrong match:
A. Batai — Sharing of harvested grain
B. Kaukut — Fixing land revenue on the basis of average produce and average prices.
C. Zabti — Assessment based on measurement
D. Muqtai — Fixed demand

68. Pick out the correct match:
A. Ramdas — Paintings
B. Abdul Samad — Calligraphy
C. Maulana Beqir — Musician
D. Nitam-ud-din — Historian

69. One of the following was not translated into persian during the reign of Akbar. Identify:
A. Quran B. The Bible
C. The Mahabharata D. The Rig Veda

70. Many movements were organised against Aurangzeb, but the causes were different. Identify the wrong match:
A. Rajputs — Successions
B. Marathas — Local independence
C. Jats — Agrarian background
D. Sikhs — Economic factor

71. The leader of various movements against Aurangzeb are given below. Pick out the wrong match:
A. Gokla — Jats
B. Churaman — Satnamis
C. Akmalkhan — Afridis
D. Govind Singh — Sikhs

72. One of the following Mughal emperors did not dream of the conquest of central Asia. Identify:
A. Babur B. Shah Jahan
C. Aurangzeb D. Akbar

73. Who introduced tobacco cultivation in India?
A. Arabs B. Persians
C. The Portuguese D. The Dutch

74. Who built the I'timad-ud-daulah's tomb?
A. Akbar B. Mumtaz Mahal
C. Nur Jahan D. Shah Jahan

75. At what cost was Taj Mahal built?
A. fifty lacs of rupees
B. one hundred lacs of rupees
C. seventy-five lacs of rupees
D. forty lacs of rupees

76. Which among the following was opened by Akbar by keys of gold?
A. Ahmadnagar B. Chittor
C. Surat D. Asirgarh

77. What was the last conquest of Akbar?
A. Ahmadnagar B. Berar
C. Orissa D. Khandesh

78. What was the religion of Tansen?
A. Jainism B. Vaishnavism
C. Islam D. Saivism

79. Pick out the wrong match.
A. Tuka Ram — Marathi
B. Mira Bai — Hindi
C. Madhusudana — Telgu
D. Paranjoti — Tamil

80. The names of the wives of the Mughal rulers are given below, Pick out the wrong match:
A. Akbar — Jodha Bai
B. Jahangir — Mehr-un-nisa
C. Shah Jahan — Arjumand Banu Begam
D. Humayun — Asmat Begam

81. Pick out the correct match:
A. Bajar — Land that was left fallow for a year or two
B. Polaj — Land that was continuously cultivated
C. Banjar — Land that was left fallow for three years
D. Parauti — Land that was left fallow for five years and more

82. The new capital of Akbar was:
A. Lahore B. Delhi
C. Fatehpur Sikri D. Asirgarh

83. Who among the following took the title of Alamgir?
A. Akbar B. Jahangir
C. Shah Jahan D. Aurangzeb

84. Humayun recaptured Qandhar & Kabul in:
A. 1540 A.D. B. 1542 A.D.
C. 1543 A.D. D. 1555 A.D.

85. When was Humayun able to recover Delhi?
A. 1545 A.D. B. 1546 A.D.
C. 1550 A.D. D. 1555 A.D.

86. The fortress belonging to the Mores was:
A. Singarh B. Raigarh
C. Satora D. Javli

87. The headquarters of Shivaji's fleet was at:
A. Daman B. Kolaba
C. Kolhapur D. Cochin

88. Who succeeded Sher Shah after his death?
A. Humayun B. Islam Shah
C. Abbas D. None of the above

89. Who was the founder of Pondicherry?
A. Duplex B. Martin
C. Dumas D. Law

90. The first English "factory" in India was set up in:
A. Cambay B. Bombay
C. Surat D. Cochin

91. Parganas were under the charge of:
A. Shiqdar B. Munsif
C. Amil D. None of these

92. Who built Purana Qila?
A. Akbar B. Humayun
C. Sher Shah D. Babur

93. Vasco-da-Gama reached Calicut in:
A. 1453 A.D. B. 1458 A.D.
C. 1498 A.D. D. 1508 A.D.

94. When Vasco-da-Gama come to India, he was helped by:
A. the ruler of Cochin
B. the Zamorin of Kozhikode
C. the king of Vijayanagar
D. the Sultan of Bijapur

95. Who invited Babur to invade India?
A. Ibrahim Lodi B. Daulat Khan
C. Rana Sanga D. None of the above

96. When was the first battle of Panipat fought?
A. Ist Feb 1526 B. 3rd March 1527
C. Ist May 1526 D. 21st April 1526

97. The Waggouers of the sea were the:
A. English B. French
C. Portuguese D. Dutch

98. Who was defeated and killed in the first battle of Panipat?
A. Sikandar Lodi B. Ibrahim Lodi
C. Rana Sanga D. Rana Kumbha

99. When did Babur die?
A. 1529 B. 1530
C. 1531 D. 1540

100. Shahu was in the imperial palace of the Mughals for:
A. 17 years B. 19 years
C. 21 years D. 7 years

ANSWERS

1	2	3	4	5	6	7	8	9	10
C	B	C	D	C	C	C	C	C	D
11	**12**	**13**	**14**	**15**	**16**	**17**	**18**	**19**	**20**
B	D	C	D	A	B	C	C	C	A
21	**22**	**23**	**24**	**25**	**26**	**27**	**28**	**29**	**30**
B	A	A	D	B	C	A	A	D	B
31	**32**	**33**	**34**	**35**	**36**	**37**	**38**	**39**	**40**
A	C	A	D	A	B	B	B	D	C
41	**42**	**43**	**44**	**45**	**46**	**47**	**48**	**49**	**50**
D	B	B	B	C	D	A	B	C	A
51	**52**	**53**	**54**	**55**	**56**	**57**	**58**	**59**	**60**
D	A	A	D	D	D	D	B	C	A
61	**62**	**63**	**64**	**65**	**66**	**67**	**68**	**69**	**70**
A	D	A	D	D	A	B	D	D	D
71	**72**	**73**	**74**	**75**	**76**	**77**	**78**	**79**	**80**
B	C	C	C	A	D	D	B	C	D
81	**82**	**83**	**84**	**85**	**86**	**87**	**88**	**89**	**90**
B	C	D	C	D	D	B	B	B	C
91	**92**	**93**	**94**	**95**	**96**	**97**	**98**	**99**	**100**
A	C	C	B	B	D	D	B	B	B

MODERN INDIA

- Colonialism and Rural Society: Evidence from Official Reports
- Representations of 1857
- Colonialism and Indian Towns: Town Plans and Municipal Reports
- Mahatma Gandhi through Contemporary Eyes
- Partition Through Oral Sources
- The Making of the Constitution

SET-1

1. Match the following:

List-I	*List-II*
(*a*) First Anglo-Mysore War	1. Sir Eyre Coot
(*b*) Second Anglo-Mysore War	2. General Stuart
(*c*) Third Anglo-Mysore War	3. General Smith
(*d*) Fourth Anglo-Mysore War	4. Major General Medows

Codes:

	(*a*)	(*b*)	(*c*)	(*d*)
A.	3	1	4	2
B.	2	3	4	1
C.	3	2	1	4
D.	1	4	3	2

2. Match the following:

List-I	*List-II*
(*a*) Death of Haider	1. 1782
(*b*) Death of Tipu	2. 1784
(*c*) Treaty of Srirangapatnam	3. 1792
(*d*) Treaty of Mangalore	4. 1799

Codes:

	(*a*)	(*b*)	(*c*)	(*d*)
A.	2	3	1	4
B.	1	3	4	2
C.	2	4	3	1
D.	1	4	3	2

3. Who was the Governor General during Second Anglo-Mysore War?

A. Warren Hastings B. Lord Cornwallis
C. Sir John Shore D. Lord Wellesly

4. Which of the following statements about the First and the Second Anglo-Mysore War are incorrect?

1. The First Anglo-Mysore War began in 1746 and ended in 1750.
2. The Second Anglo-Mysore War began in 1780 and ended in 1784.
3. The first defensive treaty between the British and Mysore was concluded in 1784.
4. One of the causes for the outbreak of the second war was the British capture of Mahe, a French settlement within Haider's Jurisdiction.

Codes:

A. 1 and 2 B. 1 and 3
C. 2 and 3 D. 3 and 4

5. The treaty of Srirangapatnam signed by Tipu and Cornawallis, contained:

1. Surrender of almost Tipu's half of the territories which were to be shared among the English the Nizam and the Marathas.
2. Payment of a war indemnity of about ₹ 3 crores by Tipu.
3. Stationing of a British resident at Srirangapatnam.
4. Sending two of his sons by Tipu as hostages to the British Camp.

Codes:

A. 1 and 2 B. 3 and 1
C. 1, 2 and 4 D. 1, 3 and 4

6. From which of the following countries did Tipu seek help to expel the British from India?

1. France 2. Arabia
3. Afghanism 4. Russia

Codes:

A. 1, 2 and 4 B. 2, 3 and 5
C. 1, 2, 3 and 4 D. 1, 2, 3 and 5

7. Which of the following statements are correct about the Fourth Anglo-Mysore War?

1. The immediate cause of this war was the landing of a small French force at Mangalore in April 1798.
2. Lord Wellesly was the Governor-General during the war.
3. Tipu Sultan was successively defeated at Seda Seer and Malvelley by the British.
4. Tipu was captured and executed by the British after this war.
5. Arthur Wellesly, the future duke of Wellington and the person who later defeated Napolean in the water battle of waterloo, participated in this war.

Codes:

A. 1, 2, 3 and 4 B. 2, 3, 4 and 5
C. 1, 2, 3 and 5 D. 1, 3, 4 and 5

8. Which of the following statements about the state of Mysore are not true?

1. After the Fourth Anglo-Mysore War, a major part of Mysore was annexed by the British.
2. A small portion of it was destored to a minor son of Tipu Sultan.
3. A subsidiary treaty was signed by the British with the new ruler of Mysore.
4. In 1849, Lord Dallousie took over the administration of Mysore because of misgovernment by its ruler.
5. In 1881 Lord Ripon restored it to its ruler.

Codes:

A. 1 and 2 B. 2 and 4
C. 2 and 3 D. 3 and 5

9. Which of the following statement about Ranjit Singh are true?

1. Before his rise into prominence, Punjab was ruled by 12 Sikh 'Misls'.
2. He was born to the chief of Kanhiya Misl.
3. He succeeded to the chieftainship of his 'Misl' as a minor with his mother as the Regant.
4. He assumed full charge.

Codes:

A. 1 and 2 B. 3 and 4
C. 1, 3 and 4 D. 2, 3 and 4

10. Arrange the following conquests of Ranjit Singh in the chronological order:

1. Ludhiana 2. Amritsar
2. Kangra 4. Lahore

Codes:

A. 4, 2, 1 and 3 B. 2, 1, 3 and 4
C. 2, 4, 3 and 1 D. 1, 3, 4 and 2

11. Arrange the following events in the reign of Ranjit Singh in the chronological sequence.

1. Aquisition of the Kohinoor by Ranjit Singh from Shah Suja of Afghanistan.
2. Assumption of the title of Maharaja of Lahore by Ranjit Singh.
3. Meeting between Ranjit Singh and Bentinck.
4. Mission of Metcalf to Ranjit Singh.
5. Occupation of Kashmir by Ranjit Singh.

Codes:

A. 3, 1, 4, 5 and 2 B. 1, 3, 4, 2 and 5
C. 4, 2, 1, 5 and 3 D. 2, 5, 4 and 3

12. Ranjit Singh did:

1. organise his army on western lines with the help of Europeans.
2. cooperate with Zaman Shah of Afghanistan when the latter invaded Punjab in 1799.
3. recruit only Sikhs as soldiers.
4. establish modern foundaries to manufacture Canon.

Codes:

A. 1, 2 and 3 B. 1, 2 and 4
C. 2 and 4 D. 3, 4

13. Pick out the two places which witnessed battles between the England and the Amirs before the formal annexation of Sind?

1. Hyderabad 2. Dabo
3. Miani 4. Mirpur

Codes:

A. 1 and 2 B. 2 and 3
C. 3 and 4 D. 1 and 3

14. Arrange the following successors of Ranjit Singh in the chronological order:

1. Sher Singh 2. Kharak Singh
3. Dalip Singh 4. Nao Nihal Singh

Codes:

A. 2, 4, 1 and 3 B. 2, 1, 4 and 3
C. 1, 3, 2 and 4 D. 1, 4, 3 and 2

15. Which is the correct chronological sequence of the following events?

1. Occupation of Shikarpur by the British
2. Occupation of Ferozpur by the British
3. Succession of Dalip Singh as the ruler of Punjab
4. Appointment of British resident at Ludhiana

Codes:

A. 1, 3, 4 and 2 B. 4, 3, 1 and 2
C. 3, 4, 2 and 1 D. 2, 1, 4 and 3

16. Arrange the following battles of the First Anglo-Sikh War in the chronological order:

1. Buddewal 2. Aliwal
3. Ferozpur 4. Sobroan
5. Mudki

Codes:

A. 1, 3, 5, 4 and 2 B. 5, 3, 1, 2 and 4
C. 2, 4, 3, 5 and 1 D. 3, 2, 1, 4 and 5

17. The treaty of Lahore contained:

1. Ceding of the Jallendar Doab to the British and payment of a war indemnity of about 11/2 crore.
2. appointment of a British resident at Lahore.
3. derecognition of Dalip Singh as the ruler of Punjab.
4. reduction of Sikh army to 20,000 infantry and 12,000 cavalary.
5. permission to the ruler of Punjab to employ any European without the consent of the British.

Codes:

A. 1, 3 and 2 B. 1, 2 and 4
C. 2, 4 and 5 D. 3, 4 and 5

18. Which of the following were the cause for the second Anglo-Sikh War?

A. Desire of the Sikh army to avenge their humiliation in the First Anglo-Sikh War

B. Discontentment of the Sikh Sardars with the British control over Punjab
C. Mistreatment of Rani Jindan by the British
D. Revolt of the Governor of Multan leading to the outbreak of General rebellion by the Sikhs.

Codes:

A. 1, 2 and 4 B. 1, 3 and 4
C. 2, 3 and 4 D. All of them

19. Two English officers sent to Multan to help Sardar Khan Singh, the newly appointed Governor, in taking over its administration were murdered by the Sikhs in April 1848. Who were they?

1. Vans Agnew 2. Herbert Edwards
3. Lt. Nicholson 4. Lt. Anderson
5. Richard Temple

Codes:

A. 1 and 3 B. 2 and 4
C. 1 and 4 D. 3 and 4

20. Who was the founder of the autonomous state of the carnatic?

A. Safdar Ali B. Dost Ali
C. Sadatullah Khan D. Anwaruddin

21. Which of the Lists are correctly matched?

List-I		*List-II*
1. Lal Singh	—	The Prime Minister of Punjab before and during the First Anglo-Sikh War
2. Tej Singh	—	The Commander-in-Chief of Punjab before and during the First war
3. Mulraj	—	The Governor of Multan who resigned and then revolted against the British in 1848
4. Sher Singh	—	The person who was sent by the British to supress the revolt at Multan but who him-self joined the revolt

Codes:

A. 1, 2 and 3 B. 2, 3 and 4
C. 1, 3 and 4 D. All of them

22. Arrange the following battles and events of the Second-Anglo Sikh War in the chronological order:

1. Battle of Gujarat
2. Battle of Ramnagar
3. Surrender of Sher Singh
4. Capture of Multan and Surrender of Mulraj
5. Batte of Chillianwala

Codes:

A. 3, 2, 1, 4 and 5 B. 1, 2, 3, 4 and 5
C. 4, 2, 1, 5 and 3 D. 2, 5, 4, 1 and 3

23. After the annexation of Punjab by the British, a Board of three commissioners was constituted in 1849 to administer Punjab. Who were those three Britishers?

1. Henry Lawrence 2. John Lawrence
3. Walter Gilbert 4. Charles G. Mensel
5. V. Richard Temple

Codes:

A. 1, 3 and 5 B. 1, 2 and 4
C. 2, 3 and 4 D. 2, 4 and 5

24. Which of the following statements about Bahadur Shah are true?

(*a*) He fought a war of succession with his brothers before he became the emperor.
(*b*) After becoming the emperor he assumed the title of Shah Alam-I.
(*c*) His reign lost between 1700 and 1712.
(*d*) His reign witnessed the outbreak of the Maratha Civil war between Shahu and Tara Bai.

Codes:

A. (*a*) and (*b*) B. (*b*), (*c*) and (*d*)
C. (*a*), (*b*) and (*d*) D. (*c*) and (*d*)

25. Bahadur Shah did:

1. execute Govind Singh, tenth Guru of the Sikhs.
2. take Chatrasal, the Bundela chief into his service.
3. release, Sahu, the son of Shambhaji.
4. defeat and kill Churaman, the jat chief.

Codes:

A. 1 and 2 B. 2 and 3
C. 3 and 4 D. 2 and 4

26. Arrange the following Mughal emperors in the chronological order.

1. Alamgir II 2. Akbar II
3. Shah Alam II 4. Bahadur Shah II

Codes:

A. 2, 4, 3 and 1 B. 1, 3, 4 and 2
C. 2, 3, 1 and 4 D. 1, 3, 2 and 4

27. Which of the following statement about the Sayyid brothers is correct?

1. They played a decisive role in the succession of Farruksiyar as the emperor.
2. They are known in Indian history as king makers.
3. Abdullah Khan, the elder of the two brothers, was made the Mir Bakshi by Farruk Siyar.
4. They murdered Faruksiyar in 1719 and made two young princes emperors in quick succession.

Codes:

A. 1, 2, 4 and 5 B. 2, 3 and 4
C. 1, 2, 3 and 5 D. 2, 4 and 5

28. Arrange the following Mughal emperors in the correct chronological sequence.

1. Faruk Siyar 2. Jahandar Shah
3. Ahmed Shah 4. Shah Alam I
5. Muhammad Shah

Codes:

A. 4, 2, 1, 5 and 3 B. 2, 1, 4, 3 and 5
C. 1, 4, 3, 2 and 5 D. 5, 4, 1, 3 and 2

29. Hyder Ali did:
 1. assumed all power by over throwing Nanjaraja.
 2. conquer and annex several territories such as Coorg, Malabar, Bellary, Gooty etc.
 3. Fight the First and Second Anglo-Mysore War against the British.
 4. Get killed by the British in the second Anglo-Mysore War.

 Codes:
 A. 2 and 3 B. 2 and 4
 C. 1, 2 and 4 D. 2, 3 and 4

30. Which of the following statements are not true about Haider Ali?
 1. He began his career as a soldier of the Mysore state, ruled by the rulers of Hindu wodeyar dynasty.
 2. During his term as the faujdar of Dindigul, he established a modern dockyard.
 3. Due to his successful defence of Srirangapattanam against the Marathas in 1759 he was given the title of "Fateh Haider Bahadur" by Nanraja the king of Mysore.
 4. He was not only a capable military leader and efficient administrator, but also a well read man.

 Codes:
 A. 2 and 3 B. 2 and 4
 C. 1, 2 and 4 D. 2, 3 and 4

31. Who was the governor of Madras who concluded the treaty of Mangalore with Tipu Sultan?
 A. Lord Harris B. Lord Hamilton
 C. Lord Macarteney D. Lord Stephenson

32. Tipu Sultan did:
 1. attempt to introduce modern industries in Mysore by inviting foreign experts.
 2. send embassies to France, Turkey, Iran and Pegu to develop foreign trade.
 3. attempt to set-up a state trading company on the European lines.
 4. introduce a new system of coinage, new scales of weights and measures, and a new calendar.
 5. establish modern arsenal at Dindigual with French help.

 Codes:
 A. 1, 3, 4 and 5 B. 1, 2, 3 and 4
 C. 2, 3, 4 and 5 D. 1, 2, 4 and 5

33. Which of the following statements about Tipu Sultan is/are incorrect?
 1. He tried to increase the state income by introducing the practice of revenue farming.
 2. He reduced the hereditary possessions of the poligars.
 3. He checked the collection of illegal cesses from the peasants.
 4. He refused to grant remmission of land revenue to the peasantry even in adverse situations.

 Codes:
 A. 1 only B. 1 and 2
 C. 3 and 4 D. 1 and 4

34. **Assertion (A):** Colonel Clive caused the signature of Admiral Watson to be forged on a duplicate copy of the treaty signed with Mir Jafar and his supporters.

 Reason (R): Clive wanted to cause trouble to Admiral Watson.

 Codes:
 A. (A) and (R) are true and (R) is the correct explanation of (A).
 B. (A) and (R) are true, but (R) is not the correct explanation of (A).
 C. (A) is true, but (R) is false.
 D. (A) is false, but (R) is true.

35. **Assertion (A):** The British won the battle of Plassey without any real fighting.

 Reason (R): The Battle of Plassey gave the British a political foothold in Bengal.

 Codes:
 A. (A) and (R) are true and (R) is the correct explanation of (A).
 B. (A) and (R) are true, but (R) is not the correct explanation of A.
 C. (A) is true, but (R) is false.
 D. (A) is false, but (R) is true.

36. **Assertion (A):** Mir Qasim abolished all duties on internal trade in 1763 after his unsuccessful attempts, to check the misuse of the 'Dastaks' by the Servants of the company.

 Reason (R): He wanted to place the Indian and British traders on the same footing without either group getting an advantage.

 Codes:
 A. (A) and (R) are true and (R) is the correct explanation of (A).
 B. (A) and (R) are true, but (R) is not the correct explanation of (A).
 C. (A) is true, but (R) is false.
 D. (A) is false, but (R) is true.

37. **Assertion (A):** Within a short period of Mir Qasim accession as the Nawab, serious difference arose between him and the British.

 Reason (R): The British got dissatisfied with the inefficient rule of Mir Qasim.

 Codes:
 A. (A) and (R) are true and (R) is the correct explanation of (A).
 B. (A) and (R) are true, but (R) is not the correct explanation of (A).
 C. (A) is true, but (R) is false.
 D. (A) is false, but (R) is true.

38. Assertion (A): From the military point of view, the battle of Buxar was much less important than the Battle of Plassey.

Reason (R): The British won the Battle of Buxar due to their superior military techniques.

Codes:

A. (A) and (R) are true and (R) is the correct explanation of (A).
B. (A) and (R) are true, but (R) is not the correct explanation of (A).
C. (A) is false, but (R) is true.
D. (A) is true, but (R) is false.

39. Assertion (A): The British acquired an effective control over the administration of Bengal from February 1765.

Reason (R): In Feb, 1765 the British concluded a treaty with the new Nawab by which he aggreed to leave the entire administration in the hands of a British nominated Dy. Subedar, who could be removed only with their consent.

Codes:

A. (A) and (R) are true and (R) is the correct explanation of (A).
B. (A) and (R) are true, but (R) is not the correct explanation of (A).
C. (A) is true, but (R) is false.
D. (A) is false, but (R) is true.

40. Assertion (A): Clive was sent to India in 1765 by the home authorities to serve his second term as the Governor of Calcutta and consolidate the gains made by the British after the Battle of Buxar.

Reason (R): He proved himself to be an honest and sincere officer during his first term as the Governor.

Codes:

A. (A) and (R) are true and (R) is the correct explanation of (A).
B. (A) and (R) are true, but (R) is not the correct explanation of (A).
C. (A) is true, but (R) is false.
D. (A) is false, but (R) is true.

41. Assertion (A): The treaty of Allahabad was concluded by the British with the Mughal emperor Shah Alam-II.

Reason (R): The Mughal emperor granted the Diwani of Bengal, Bihar and Orissa to the East India Company in 1765.

Codes:

A. (A) and (R) are true and (R) is the correct explanation of (A).
B. (A) and (R) are true, but (R) is not the correct explanation of (A).
C. (A) is true, but (R) is false.
D. (A) is false, but (R) is true.

42. Assertion (A): In the Dual system of government in Bengal, the British had all the power but no responsibility.

Reason (R): In this system of government, the Nawab had neither power nor responsibility.

Codes:

A. (A) and (R) are true and (R) is the correct explanation of (A).
B. (A) and (R) are true, but (R) is not the correct explanation of (A).
C. (A) is true, but (R) is false.
D. (A) is false, but (R) is true.

43. Assertion (A): The Dual System of Government was an adorit measure of Clive to mark the real position of the company in Bengal.

Reason (R): The serious defects inherent in the Dual Government caused immense misery to the people of Bengal.

Codes:

A. (A) and (R) are true and (R) is the correct explanation of (A).
B. (A) and (R) are true, but (R) is not the correct explanation of (A).
C. (A) is true, but (R) is false.
D. (A) is false, but (R) is true.

44. Who was the first British Governor of Sind?

A. Sir Charles Napier B. Sir John Keane
C. Sir Henry Lawrence D. Robert Montgomery

45. Who was the governor-general of India when Sind was annexed?

A. Lord Auckland B. Lord Ellenborough
C. Lord Dalhousie D. Lord Hardinge-I

46. Who confessed "The defeat of many Bailles and Braith waites will not destroy them". I can ruin their resources by land, but, I cannot dry up the sea?

A. Haider Ali B. Tipu Sultan
C. Sher Singh D. Anwaruddin

47. Who was the Governor-General who remarked what a man is this Lord Macarteny! I yet believe that, in spite of peace, he will effect the loss of the carnatic?

A. Warren Hastings B. Lord Cornawallis
C. Lord Wellesly D. Lord Dalhousie

48. Who declared "However contrary it may be to our past views and to our present views, annexation of Punjab is the most advantageous policy for us to pursue".

A. Lord Hugh Gough B. Sir John Lawrence
C. Lord Ellenborough D. Lord Dalhousie

49. To which place Murshid Ali Khan transfer his Capital from Dacca?

A. Kasim Bazar B. Monghyer
C. Murshidabad D. Gaur

50. Who captured and executed Siraj-ud-Daula after the battle of Plassey?

A. Miran, the son of Mir Jafar
B. Robert Clive, the new Governor of Fort William
C. Mir Jafar, the new Nawab of Bengal
D. Mir Kasim, the son in law of Mir Jafar

ANSWERS

1	2	3	4	5	6	7	8	9	10
A	D	A	B	D	D	C	B	C	A
11	**12**	**13**	**14**	**15**	**16**	**17**	**18**	**19**	**20**
D	B	B	A	D	B	B	D	C	C
21	**22**	**23**	**24**	**25**	**26**	**27**	**28**	**29**	**30**
D	D	B	C	B	D	A	A	C	D
31	**32**	**33**	**34**	**35**	**36**	**37**	**38**	**39**	**40**
C	B	D	C	B	A	C	D	A	C
41	**42**	**43**	**44**	**45**	**46**	**47**	**48**	**49**	**50**
D	C	B	A	B	A	A	D	C	A

SET-2

1. Who was the founder of the line of Peshwas?
A. Shivaji B. Tara Bai
C. Baji Rao I D. Balaji Vishwanath

2. Which Maratha leader revived the Jagir or Saranjanmi System?
A. Sambhaji B. Sahu
C. Raja Ram D. Baji Rao I

3. Which of the following transferred the capital of the Maratha empire from Satara to Poona?
A. Sambhaji B. Sahu
C. Baji Rao I D. Balaji Vishwanath

4. Who was the first Maratha leader to entertain the idea of an all Indian Maratha empire?
A. Sahu B. Raja Ram
C. Baji Rao I D. Balaji Vishwanath

5. Which of the following fought a civil war?
A. Raja Ram and Tara Bhai
B. Sahu and Tara Bhai
C. Raja Ram and Sahu
D. Raja Ram and Baji Rao I

6. The conquests of the Marathas outside their original kingdom was made by the:
A. Central army under the Maratha King
B. Central army under the Peshwa
C. Private armies of Maratha Sardars
D. None of these

7. When did the Mughal invade Bijapur?
A. 1620 AD B. 1650 AD
C. 1657 AD D. 1660 AD

8. When was Afzal Khan killed by Shivaji?
A. 1650 AD B. 1659 AD
C. 1660 AD D. 1662 AD

9. Who was Dabir in Shivaji's Administration?
A. Master of troops:
B. Master of religious ceremonies
C. Master of ceremonies
D. Master of correspondence

10. When did the Peshawa becomes the official head of the Maratha administration?
A. 1740 B. 1745
C. 1746 D. 1749

11. When was Purander beseiged?
A. 1660 AD B. 1662 AD
C. 1665 AD D. 1670 AD

12. Shivaji levied ¼ of land revenue of the neighbouring states which was known as:
A. Surdeshmukhi B. Kharaji
C. Jakat D. Chauth

13. Match the following:
(*a*) Peshawa 1. Nagpur
(*b*) Bhonsles 2. Gwalior
(*c*) Gaekwards 3. Baroda
(*d*) Halkars 4. Poona
(*e*) Scindhias 5. Indore

Codes:

	(*a*)	(*b*)	(*c*)	(*d*)	(*e*)
A.	1	2	3	4	5
B.	4	3	1	2	5
C.	4	1	5	2	3
D.	4	1	3	5	2

14. What was Kesaria?
A. Maratha Flag
B. Maratha guerilla warfare units
C. Maratha Fort in Malwa
D. Maratha oath of revenge

15. When was Shambhuji put to death by Aurangzeb?
A. 1686 AD B. 1689 AD
C. 1690 AD D. 1693 AD

16. When was Shivaji born?
A. 1617 AD B. 1627 AD
C. 1637 AD D. 1647 AD

17. State's share in the produce of the land in the Maratha Kingdom was:
A. 25% B. 16%
C. 35% D. 40%

18. When was the coronation of Shivaji carried out?
A. 1670 AD B. 1672 AD
C. 1674 AD D. 1678 AD

19. When did Shivaji conquer Jawli?
A. 1656 AD B. 1660 AD
C. 1670 AD D. 1676 AD

20. Which of the following helped the Sayyid brother in overthrewing Farrukh Siyar?
A. Baji Rao I B. Balaji Vishwanath
C. Balaji Baji Rao D. None of these

21. Which Maratha Senapati was defeated and killed by Baji Rao I?
A. Sambhaji II B. Trimbak Rao Dhabade
C. Chimnaji Appa D. Narayan Rao

22. Which statement on the Maratha confederacy is correct?
A. It was a combination of autonomous units presided over by man who were as good as rulers though united for certain common purposes like defence and foreign affairs.
B. The Maratha captains established themselves at Indore, Gwalior, Dhar, Baroda and Nagpur.
C. The central authority as represented by the Peshwa was a nominal one.
D. All the above

23. From whom did Shivaji receive Poona as a jagir?
A. The Mughals B. The Adil Shahis
C. The Nizam Shahis D. The Portuguese

24. Match the following.
(*a*) Shivaji's mother 1. Ahilaya Bai
(*b*) Shivaji's guardian 2. Jija Bai
(*c*) Shivaji's guru 3. Dadaji Kondadeo
4. Ram Das

Codes:

	(*a*)	(*b*)	(*c*)
A.	1	4	3
B.	2	4	3
C.	2	3	4
D.	1	3	4

25. Shivaji was born at the Fort of:
A. Jinji B. Shivner
C. Javli D. Champaner

26. Which port on the western coast was attacked and plundered by Shivaji in 1664?
A. Surat B. Chaul
C. Goa D. Bassein

27. Who wrote "We shall hear Shivaji in like the centre of a circle"?
A. Raja Jai Singh B. Shiasta Khan
C. Aurangzeb D. None of these

28. Which of the following was not alive at time of Shivaji's coronation in 1674?
A. Gaga Bhatt B. Tukaram
C. Dadaji Kondadeo D. Ram Das

29. Shivaji was assisted by a council of 8 ministers called the 'Astha Pradhan'. Match the following 4 ministers with their respective functions.
(*a*) Peshwa 1. General administration
(*b*) Amatya 2. Foreign affairs
(*c*) Nyayadhisha 3. Justice
(*d*) Samant 4. Finance

Codes:

	(*a*)	(*b*)	(*c*)	(*d*)
A.	1	2	3	4
B.	1	4	3	2
C.	1	3	2	4
D.	1	4	2	3

30. Shivaji's kingdom was divided into four provinces. Each provice was under the charge of a:
A. Subedar or Mamlatdar
B. Subedar or Deshmukh
C. Subedar or Jamladar
D. None of these

31. What were Saranjams?
A. Hereditary nights in land
B. Cash salaries
C. Revenue grants
D. Tax-free lands

32. Match the following:
(*a*) Deshmukh 1. Loose auxiliaries
(*b*) Silhadars 2. Zamindars
(*c*) Mirasdars 3. Hereditary holder of land
4. Revenue officials

Codes:

	(*a*)	(*b*)	(*c*)
A.	2	3	4
B.	2	1	3
C.	3	4	1
D.	3	2	1

33. What was Paga?
A. Guerilla warfare tactics
B. Regular army
C. Area adjoining a Maratha fort
D. Military expedition

34. What was Mokasa?
A. Jagirs B. Religious ceremonies
C. Cavalry D. None of these

35. In 1680 the Marathas obtained a naval victory over:
A. The French B. The Portuguese
C. The Dutch D. The English

36. What was Shivaji's greatest achievement?
A. He welded together the Maratha race
B. He inflicted crushing defeats on the Mughal armies
C. His land revenue and military administrations were followed by other Deccan powers
D. He popularised guerilla warfare

37. Tara Bai was the widow of:
A. Shivaji B. Sambhaji
C. Sahu D. Raja Ram

38. Kavi Kulash was the brahmin advisor of:
A. Shivaji B. Sahu
C. Shambhaji D. Raja Ram

39. Given below are the 4 Maratha leaders. Arrange them chronologically.
1. Shivaji 2. Shahji
3. Sahu 4. Sambhaji
Codes:
A. 1, 2, 3 and 4 B. 2, 3, 1 and 4
C. 2, 1, 4 and 3 D. 2, 1, 3 and 4

40. Muhammad Quli a Muslim convert was recovered to Hinduism by Shivaji in 1676. What was his real name?
A. Vyankoji B. Ragunath Pant
C. Netaji Palkar D. Nischal Puri Goswami

41. Which of the following fort is not connected with Shivaji's life?
A. Raigarh B. Shivner
C. Jawli D. Lohgarh

42. Which of the following fort is connected with Shivaji's childhood?
A. Shivner B. Troma
C. Jawli D. Panhala

43. Who imprisoned Tara Bai during her struggle against Shahu?
A. Rajas Bai B. Jija Bai
C. Jodha Bai D. Yesu Bai

44. Shivaji II was the son of:
A. Tara Bai B. Yesu Bai
C. Jija Bai D. Jodha Bai

45. Which wife of Shivaji had committed Sati?
A. Sai Bai B. Gunwanta Bai
C. Sakwar Bai D. Putli Bai

46. Which of the following stood on the right side of the throne to pour holy water on the king's head?
A. Peshwa B. Senapati
C. Sachiv D. Mantri

47. The official incharge of the tarfs under Shivaji was designated as:
A. Patel B. Pant
C. Havaldar D. Kulkarni

48. Shivaji introduced a uniform unit of measurement for the purpose of land revenue. This unit was known as:
A. Jarib B. Kathi
C. Gaz D. Tanab

49. The highest rank in the Paga or State cavalry was:
A. One Jumladar B. Five Havaldar
C. Five Hazari D. Ten Jumladar

50. In the infantry of Shivaji, a Havaldar commanded:
A. Five Nayaks B. Ten Nayaks
C. Twelve Nayaks D. Fifteen Nayaks

51. Identify the fort where the Mughals laid seize on Raja Ram for 8 years?
A. Purandhar B. Satara
C. Jinji D. Kolnapur

52. One of the following was in favour of Shahu ascending the throne in place of Shivaji II. Identify him:
A. Paras Ram Timbak B. Dhanji Jadav
C. Ram Chandra Pant D. Shankarji Narain

53. Who was the Peshwa at the time of the third Battle of Panipat fought between the Marathas and Ahmad Shah Abdali?
A. Madhav Rao B. Balaji Baji Rao
C. Baji Rao D. Narayan Rao

54. Who was the ultimate beneficiary of the 3rd Battle of Panipat after the Maratha army had been routed?
A. Ahmad Shah Abdali
B. Shah Alam II, the Mughal Emperor
C. The Marathas
D. The English

55. Which of the following Maratha Chiefs was the cast to join the subsidiary alliance with the British?
A. The Peshwa B. Mokkar
C. Bhonsle D. Scindia

56. Trimbakji was the famous minister of:
A. Narayan Rao B. Baji Rao II
C. Madho Rao Narayan D. Madhav Rao I

57. Who was the governor general during the Poona Settlement?
A. Lord Masting
B. Lord Clive
C. Lord Wellesly
D. Lord Marques of Hastings

58. The Battle of Mukand Dara was fought during the:
A. First Anglo – Maratha war
B. Second Anglo – Maratha war
C. Third Anglo – Maratha war
D. Fourth Anglo – Maratha war

59. The Treaty of Rajput was signed in 1806 between the British and:
A. Holkar B. Gaekward
C. Scindia D. Bhonsle

60. The name of Mustani a dancing girl is associated with:
A. Balaji Vishwanath B. Baji Rao
C. Balaji Baji Rao D. Madhav Rao

ANSWERS

1	2	3	4	5	6	7	8	9	10
D	C	D	C	B	C	C	B	C	D
11	**12**	**13**	**14**	**15**	**16**	**17**	**18**	**19**	**20**
C	D	D	A	B	B	D	C	A	B
21	**22**	**23**	**24**	**25**	**26**	**27**	**28**	**29**	**30**
B	D	C	C	B	A	A	C	B	A
31	**32**	**33**	**34**	**35**	**36**	**37**	**38**	**39**	**40**
C	B	B	A	D	A	D	C	C	C
41	**42**	**43**	**44**	**45**	**46**	**47**	**48**	**49**	**50**
D	A	A	A	D	C	A	B	C	A
51	**52**	**53**	**54**	**55**	**56**	**57**	**58**	**59**	**60**
C	C	B	D	D	C	A	C	A	B

SET-3

1. Which of the following was the Ist proprietory holding of the English in India?
A. Madras B. Surat
C. Masulipatnam D. Hariharpur

2. The lease of Madras in 1639 A.D. was obtained by the English from
A. The ruler of Chandragiri
B. The ruler of Bijapur
C. The ruler of Mysore
D. The ruler of Golkunda

3. Which of the following was not one of the three Villages for which the English were granted Zamindari in Bengal in 1698 and where they built Fort William around their Factory?
A. Sutanati B. Burdwan
C. Kalikata D. Govindpur

4. In which year were factories opened for the first time in Orissa?
A. 1613 A.D. B. 1632 A.D.
C. 1639 A.D. D. 1663 A.D.

5. From which Mugal Emperor did John Middenhall tried to obtain a Farman for trade in Gujarat?
A. Akbar B. Jahangir
C. Aurangzeb D. None of these

6. The battle of 'Swally Hole' was fought in the year
A. 1605 A.D. B. 1612 A.D.
C. 1498 A.D. D. 1526 A.D.

7. Where was the first trading station of the Britishers established in the South?
A. Madras B. Bombay
C. Surat D. Masulipatnam

8. The Dutch had no trading stations at
A. Masulipatnam B. Pulicat
C. Calicut D. Cassimbazar

9. Due to commercial rivalry the Dutch indulged in the massacre of Englishmen at:
A. Malacca B. Amboyna
C. Surat D. Mugli

10. The Dutch company established monopoly of trade with:
A. India B. Egypt
C. China D. Indonesia

11. In 1622 the Portuguese lost Ormuz in the Persian Gulf to:
A. Britain B. Spain
C. Portugal D. France

12. Goa was acquired by Albuquerque from:
A. Ahmadnagar B. Bijapur
C. Golkunda D. Berar

13. Which one of the following was not a portuguese settlement?
A. Mugli B. Dutch
C. Bombay D. Chaul

14. Vasco-da-Gama founded a factory during his 2nd visit to India in 1501 at:
A. Bassein B. Salsette
C. Chaul D. Cannanore

15. Vasco-da-Gama established friendly relations with the Zamorin, who was the ruler of:
A. Calicut B. Goa
C. Travancore D. Cochin

16. Vasco-da-Gama who discovered first the direct sea-route from Europe to India reached Calicut in the year:
A. 1946 A.D. B. 1500 A.D.
C. 1498 A.D. D. 1495 A.D.

17. The Cape of Good Hope was discovered by:
A. Vasco-da-Gama B. De Almeida
C. Albuquerque D. Bartholomew Diaz

18. Which one of the following powers was the first to establish trade links with India?
A. English B. Dutch
C. Portuguese D. French

19. The Portuguese established their Ist business centre at:
A. Calicut B. Surat
C. Goa D. Cochin

20. Who was the first portuguese viceroy in India?
A. Vasco-da-Gama B. Albuquerque
C. Da Almeida D. Duarte Pacheo

21. Who is commonly known as the Navigator?
A. King John II B. Prince Hery
C. King Emmanuel D. Pope Alexander VI

22. The Danish establish a factory in 1620 at:
A. Pondicherry B. Calicut
C. Tranquebar D. Goa

23. The trade links of the Swedish East India Company which was formed in 1731, was exclusively confined to:
A. Indonesia B. China
C. Ceylon D. Malaya

24. Vasco-da-Gama was the native of:
A. Portugal B. Germany
C. France D. Russia

25. Who captured Goa in 1510?
A. Vasco-da-Gama B. William Hawkins
C. Franciscode Almeida D. Albuquerque

26. Who founded the French East India Company?
A. Colbert B. Francois Caron
C. Francis Martin D. Dumas

27. When did East India Company receive a charter from Queen Elizabeth?
A. 1598 A.D. B. 1599 A.D.
C. 1600 A.D. D. 1602 A.D.

28. When did Hawkins reach the court of Jahangir?
A. 1606 A.D. B. 1607 A.D.
C. 1608 A.D. D. 1609 A.D.

29. Who was largely responsible for virtual plunder or loot of India in the early stages of British conquest?
A. Clive B. Warsen Hastings
C. Cornwallis D. Dalhousie

30. The British made vigorous attempts to restrict and crush Indian manufacturers by various measures and internal duties:
A. during the merchantilist period
B. during the beginning of industrial revolution in England
C. during the governor-generalship of Bentinck
D. during the governor-generalship of Dalhousie

31. Who was responsible for the establishment of Portuguese power in India?
A. Vasco-da-Gama
B. Pardo-Carbag
C. Alfonso-d'-Albuquerque
D. Francis Xavier

32. Which European was bigoted in its altitude towards Indian religions?
A. Dutch B. Portuguese
C. French D. English

33. What was the major factor for the British triumph over the French in India?
A. Government support B. Financial Strength
C. British navy D. British diplomacy

34. The Dutch shifted their trading centres from Pulicat to:
A. Nagapattinam B. Tranquebar
C. Salsette D. None of the above

35. What was the nucleus for French power in India?
A. Chandarnagar B. Pondicherry
C. Cochin D. Tranquebar

36. What was the major centre for French trade in the east?
A. Ceylon B. Java
C. Mauritius D. Pondicherry

37. If Dupleix was responsible for the French weakness India, it was due to his:
A. Treachery to local nuclear
B. Incapacity as a general
C. Visionary schemes
D. Over-ambitiousness

38. Who obtained Madras for the East India Company?
A. Francis Drake B. Francis Day
C. Francis D. Lord Francis

39. Which official of the East India company adopted aggressive tactics to further British trading interests?
A. Job Charnock B. Robert Clive
C. Josiah Child D. Thomas Roe

40. Where did the English open their first factories in Eastern India?
A. Bihar B. Orissa
C. Bengal D. Assam

41. From which one of the following Deccan Sultanates did Albuquerque Capture Goa?
A. Berar B. Ahmadnagar
C. Bijapur D. Golkunda

42. In 1602 Dutch Limited East India Company was given an exclusive right:
A. 5 year B. 21 year
C. 25 year D. 50 year

43. Who is connected with the 'Blue water' Policy?
A. Albuquerque B. Dupleix
C. De Almeida D. Robert Clive

44. "The discovery of America and the cape route to India were the two greatest and most important events recorded in the history of mankind." Who wrote these words?
A. G.B. Shaw B. Adam Smith
C. Thomas Stephen D. J.S. Mill

45. By the Cartage system Indian ships sailing to destinations not reserved by an European power for its own trade had to buy passes if it was to avoid seizure and confiscation of its merchandise while European power followed this system?
A. The Portuguese B. The French
C. The English D. The Swedes

46. The first printing press in India was set up by:
A. The Portuguese B. The Dutch
C. The French D. The English

47. Which European power was not organised on Commercial lines?
A. The Portugues B. The Dutch
C. The French D. The English

48. Bengal was well known for the export of:
A. Indigo B. Raw Silk
C. Cotton D. Precious Stones

49. What was the name of the man, whom Dupleix supported for the masnad of Arcot?
A. Muhammad Ali B. Salabat Jung
C. Chanda Sahib D. Muzaffar Jang

50. What was the name of the French, about whom Dupleix said that "He had signed the ruin of the country and dishonours of the nation"?
A. Bussy B. Godhean
C. Dumas D. Lally

51. During whose government the French started dreaming of establishing an Empire in India?
A. Dupleix B. Francois Martin
C. Tenoir D. Dumas

52. Identify the founder of the French East India Company?
A. Cobert B. Francois Martin
C. Delehaye D. Francois Caron

53. Which of the following causes was not responsible for the success of the English against the French in India?
A. Mughal emperors helped the English
B. Expensive financial resources of the English
C. Superior naval power of the English
D. Better support to the English in India from England

54. The Capital and Centre of French activities in India was:
A. Cassim Bazar B. Chandernagar
C. Pondicherry D. Surat

55. Who granted to the French area in Andhra known as Northern Sarkars?
A. Anwar-ud-din B. Asaf Jah
C. Muzzafar Jang D. Salabat Jang

56. The Second carnatic war was different from the other two carnatic wars in the sense that:
A. It did have its origin in Europe
B. In this war the Britishers were defeated
C. This war gave the French a victory in the seas
D. The Britishers won this war by treachery

57. The First Carnatic war ended with:
A. Treaty of Aix-la-Chappale
B. Treaty of Paris
C. Treaty of Ryswick
D. Treaty of Bassein

58. The Battle of Adyar or St. Thomas was fought between:
A. The English and the French
B. The English and the Mughals
C. The French and the Dutch
D. The French and Nawab of Arcot

59. Which one of the following European wars in associated with the third carnatic war?
A. The seven years war
B. The war of the Austrian Succession
C. The war of Roses
D. The Austro-Prussian war

60. Which of the following is incorrect about the failure of Dupleix?
A. He was short of man power
B. He lacked courage and his strategy was inferior to that of the English
C. He lacked money
D. His generals were timid and insincere

ANSWERS

1	2	3	4	5	6	7	8	9	10
A	A	B	D	A	B	D	C	B	D
11	12	13	14	15	16	17	18	19	20
A	B	B	D	A	C	D	C	A	C
21	22	23	24	25	26	27	28	29	30
B	C	B	A	B	A	C	D	A	B

31	32	33	34	35	36	37	38	39	40
B	B	C	A	B	C	D	B	C	B
41	42	43	44	45	46	47	48	49	50
C	B	C	B	A	A	A	B	C	B
51	52	53	54	55	56	57	58	59	60
A	A	A	C	B	A	A	D	A	D

SET-4

1. Who was the President of the Indian Education Commission of 1882?
A. Thomas Releigh B. W.W. Hunter
C. Macualay D. Sadler

2. When did the Indian universities assure teaching functions as well?
A. 1857 B. 1882
C. 1897 D. 1904

3. By which act did education officially came under Indian control for the first time:
A. Indian Councils Act of 1892
B. Indian Councils Act of 1909
C. Government of India Act of 1919
D. Government of India Act of 1935

4. When was the Double Government consisting of the Board of Control and the court of directors created at the Home government level?
A. 1784 B. 1813
C. 1833 D. 1853

5. Which act was responsible for the ultimate death of the presidency system?
A. Regulating Act of 1773
B. Pitt's India Act of 1784
C. Charter Act of 1813
D. Charter Act of 1833

6. Who was the first to attempt decentralisation of Financial administration?
A. Ripon B. Mayo
C. Curzon D. Lytton

7. Who is generally acknowledged as the pioneer of local-self government in modern India?
A. Ripon B. Mayo
C. Lytton D. Curzon

8. Which Act created the official legislature in India?
A. Indian Councils Act, 1861
B. Indian Councils Act, 1892
C. Charter Act, 1833
D. Charter Act, 1853

9. Who among the following did not belong to the so-called "Indian School" which favoured a limited paternalistic role for the collector as opposed to his limited role of the "English school"?
A. Thomas Munro B. Elphistone
C. Cornwallis D. John Lawrence

10. When did the practice of holding I.C.S. examinations simultaneously in England as well as in India begin?
A. 1912 B. 1922
C. 1932 D. 1935

11. During which period did India properly witness the process of Deindustrialisation due to British economic policies?
A. 1600 – 1715 B. 1757 – 1813
C. 1813 – 1860 D. 1860 – 1947

12. Warren Hasting's experiment of actioning the right to collect revenue to the higher bidder is almost similar to:
A. Poligar system of Vijayanagar empire
B. Iqta system of Delhi Sultans
C. Jagir system of Mughals
D. Ijara system of Mughals

13. The British restarted to the "Downward Filtration Theory" till 1854 to justify one of their colonial policies in India?
A. Social policy B. Commercial policy
C. Industrial policy D. Educational policy

14. Who was the president of the Board of Revenue when Lord Cornwallis introduced permanent settlement in Bengal and Bihar?
A. Sir John Shore B. Sir Metcalfe
C. Sir Charles Napier D. Sir Denison

15. Who was mainly responsible for the introduction of the Ryotwari-System in Madras?
A. Eliphinstone B. Thomas Munro
C. Macartny D. John Lawrence

16. Which of the following is not one of the causes responsible for the rise of money-lenders in British India?
A. New Revenue Policy
B. New Legal System
C. New Educational System
D. Commercialisation of Agriculture

17. The proportion of agriculture labourers to agricultural population was:

A. The highest in Zamindari areas and lowest in the Ryotwari areas.
B. The highest in the Mahalwari areas and lowest in the Zamindari areas.
C. The highest in the Ryotwari areas and lowest in the Zamindari areas
D. The highest in Ryotwari areas and lowest in the Mahalwari areas.

18. Which one of the following is not result of the destruction of Indian handicraft industries by the British?
A. Depopulation and ruins of towns and cities
B. Rise of self-sufficient village economies
C. Increase in unemployment
D. Overcrowding agriculture

19. Who was the founder of the "Drain Theory" Which among others, exposed the constant drain of wealth from India to England?
A. Dadabhai Nauroji B. Gokhle
C. R.C. Dutt D. S.N. Banerjee

20. Which one of the following was not one of the earliest-machine based modern industries to come into existence in India?
A. Cotton Textile Industry
B. Jute Industry
C. Iron and Steel Industry
D. Coal-Mining Industry

21. Which of the following was not a plantation industry in British India?
A. Indigo B. Tea
C. Coffee D. Salt-petre

22. The first telegraph line introduced by Lord Dalhousie in 1853 ran between?
A. Bombay and Thana B. Calcutta and Madras
C. Bombay and Agra D. Calcutta and Agra

23. Which of the above are incorrectly matched?

List-I	List-II
(*a*) Queen Victoria's proclamation	1. Lytton
(*b*) Statistical survey of India	2. Canning
(*c*) Strachey Faminine Commission	3. Mayo
(*d*) Repeal of the Vernacular Press Act	4. Ripon

Codes:
A. All of them B. 1, 2, 3
C. 2, 3, 4 D. 1, 3, 4

24. Match the following.

1. Scholarship Scheme	(*a*) Dufferin
2. Scheme of statutory civilians	(*b*) John Lawrence
3. Aitchison Commission	(*c*) Reading
4. Lee Commission	(*d*) Lytton

Codes:

	1	2	3	4
A.	(*a*)	(*c*)	(*d*)	(*b*)
B.	(*c*)	(*a*)	(*d*)	(*b*)
C.	(*d*)	(*b*)	(*c*)	(*a*)
D.	(*b*)	(*d*)	(*a*)	(*c*)

25. Assertion (A): In the mercantile stage of British Colonialism in India, large scale export of British goods to India was absent.

Reason (R): In the first stage of Colonialism the British did not introduce any basic change in India's economy society and culture.

Codes:
A. (A) and (R) are true and (R) is the correct explanation of (A).
B. (A) and (R) are true, but (R) is not the correct explanation of (A).
C. (A) is true, but (R) is false.
D. (A) is false, but (R) is true.

26. Assertion (A): From 1813 onwards the economic as well as non-economic policies of the British in India were determined by the interests of the industrial bourgeoise of England.

Reason (R): In the second stage of British Colonialism, India was made an equal trading partner with England.

Codes:
A. (A) and (R) are true and (R) is the correct explanation of (A).
B. (A) and (R) are true, but (R) is not the correct explanation of (A).
C. (A) is true, but (R) is false.
D. (A) is false, but (R) is true.

27. Assertion (A): The Court of directors established the East India College at Haileybury to replace the College of Fort William at Calcutta.

Reason (R): The Home government did not want to leave the task of establishing and consolidating British rule in India to the Indians.

Codes:
A. (A) and (R) are true and (R) is the correct explanation of (A).
B. (A) and (R) are true, but (R) is not the correct explanation of (A).
C. (A) is true, but (R) is false.
D. (A) is false, but (R) is true.

28. Assertion (A): The British introduced a uniform civil code for all Indians irrespective of their different religions.

Reason (R): (A) law commission headed by Lord Macaulay codified all the available Indian laws.

Codes:
A. (A) and (R) are true and (R) is the correct explanation of (A).

B. (A) and (R) are true, but (R) is not the correct explanation of (A).
C. (A) is true, but (R) is false.
D. (A) is false, but (R) is true.

29. Assertion (A): The British government in India generally followed a policy of only partial transformation and cautions modernisation of Indian society.

Reason (R): All Englishmen, whether they were conservatives or radicals, desired the safety and perpetuation of British rule in India.

Codes:

A. (A) and (R) are true and (R) is the correct explanation of (A).
B. (A) and (R) are true, but (R) is not the correct explanation of (A).
C. (A) is true, but (R) is false.
D. (A) is false, but (R) is true.

30. Assertion (A): English education made good progress in the three presidencies of Bengal, Bombay and Madras after 1844.

Reason (R): Lord Hardinge decided to give government employment to these Indians who were educated in English schools.

Codes:

A. (A) and (R) are true and (R) is the correct explanation of (A).
B. (A) and (R) are true, but (R) is not the correct explanation of (A).
C. (A) is true, but (R) is false.
D. (A) is false, but (R) is true.

31. Assertion (A): Mass education hardly made any real progress all through the period of British rule in India.

Reason (R): The British government in India, generally followed a policy of opening a large number of elementary schools instead of a few Colleges.

Codes:

A. (A) and (R) are true and (R) is the correct explanation of (A).
B. (A) and (R) are true, but (R) is not the correct explanation of (A).
C. (A) is true, but (R) is false.
D. (A) is false, but (R) is true.

32. Assertion (A): Wood's despatch of 1854 is generally known as the "Magna Carta" of English education in India.

Reason (R): It outlined a comprehensive plan for the future development of education system in India.

Codes:

A. (A) and (R) are true and (R) is the correct explanation of (A).
B. (A) and (R) are true, but (R) is not the correct explanation of (A).
C. (A) is true, but (R) is false.
D. (A) is false, but (R) is true.

33. Assertion (A): Under the Zamindari system, the revenue collectors and other intermediaries in revenue administration were overnight converted into landlords.

Reason (R): Under this system, the Zamindar could keep for himself only $1/11^{th}$ of the rental that he got from the peasantry, while paying $10/11^{th}$ of it to the government.

Codes:

A. (A) and (R) are true and (R) is the correct explanation of (A).
B. (A) and (R) are true, but (R) is not the correct explanation of (A).
C. (A) is true, but (R) is false.
D. (A) is false, but (R) is true.

34. Assertion (A): The permanent settlement is said to have intially resulted in increased agricultural production.

Reason (R): In this system, the Zamindar could keep for himself any increase in the rental of his estate.

Codes:

A. (A) and (R) are true and (R) is the correct explanation of (A).
B. (A) and (R) are true, but (R) is not the correct explanation of (A).
C. (A) is true, but (R) is false.
D. (A) is false, but (R) is true.

35. Assertion (A): In the Ryotwari areas, the peasant had to pay land revenue to the government when his produce was totally or partially destroyed.

Reason (R): Under the Ryotwari system the land-revenue demand of the government was fixed.

Codes:

A. (A) and (R) are true and (R) is the correct explanation of (A).
B. (A) and (R) are true, but (R) is not the correct explanation of (A).
C. (A) is true, but (R) is false.
D. (A) is false, but (R) is true.

36. Assertion (A): In the Mahalwari areas each peasant was individualy responsible to the government for the payment of revenue.

Reason (R): In these areas the government resumed the right to revise land revenue demand periodically.

Codes:

A. (A) and (R) are true and (R) is the correct explanation of (A).
B. (A) and (R) are true, but (R) is not the correct explanation of (A).
C. (A) is true, but (R) is false.
D. (A) is false, but (R) is true.

37. **Assertion (A):** Under the new land as well as land revenue systems, the peasant was in constant need of finding ways to get money.

Reason (R): The right of modern industries in England resulted in a growing demand for raw materials from India.

Codes:

A. (A) and (R) are true and (R) is the correct explanation of (A).
B. (A) and (R) are true, but (R) is not the correct explanation of (A).
C. (A) is true, but (R) is false.
D. (A) is false, but (R) is true.

38. Who among the following governor generals created the covenated Civil Service of India, which came to be known as Indian Civil Service from 1861 onwards?

A. Bentinck B. Wellesley
C. Cornwallis D. Warren Hastings

39. Who was responsible for the establishment of the college of Fort William at Calcutta to train the young Civil Servants of India?

A. Wellesley B. Dalhousie
C. Bentinck D. Cornwallis

40. During whose viceroyship did the High Courts came into existence at the three presidential cities of Calcutta, Madras and Bombay?

A. Warren Hastings B. John Lawrence
C. Dalhousie D. Canning

41. Who passed the widow remarriage act?

A. Canning B. Dalhousie
C. Auckland D. Bentinck

42. Johnthan Duncan founded the Sanskrit College in 1792 at:

A. Calcutta B. Allahabad
C. Bombay D. Varanasi

43. When did the British make English the medium of instruction in India?

A. 1813 B. 1833
C. 1835 D. 1844

44. Who among the following gave official Sanction to the educaiton of girls in India?

A. Dalhousie B. William Bentinck
C. Hardinge D. Ellenborough

45. Sir Charles Wood, who drafted the educational dispatch of 1854, was then:

A. Secretary of State for India
B. President of the Court of Directors
C. President of the Board of Control
D. Prime Minister of England

46. **Assertion (A):** The commercialisation of Indian agriculture during the British period adversely affected the economic positon of the peasant.

Reason (R): The commercialisation, besides making the peasants heavily dependant on the middleman for the sale of his product, made him subject to all the viscitudes of the erratic Indian as well as world market.

Codes:

A. (A) and (R) are true and (R) is the correct explanation of (A).
B. (A) and (R) are true, but (R) is not the correct explanation of (A).
C. (A) is true, but (R) is false.
D. (A) is false, but (R) is true.

47. **Assertion (A):** After the acquisition of the Diwani of Bengal, the Company directly organised the "Drain of wealth".

Reason (R): After 1765, the company began to send to England the revenue of Bengal through what are called investments.

Codes:

A. (A) and (R) are true and (R) is the correct explanation of (A).
B. (A) and (R) are true, but (R) is not the correct explanation of A.
C. (A) is true, but (R) is false.
D. (A) is false, but (R) is true.

48. The Charter Act of 1883 did:

1. complete the process of throwing open the Indian trade to all British subjects.
2. rename the Governor-General of Fort William as the Governer-General of India.
3. allow the different presidencies to make laws for themselves.
4. include a law member to the council of the Governor-General.

Codes:

A. 1 and 4 B. 2, 3 and 4
C. 1, 2 and 4 D. 2 and 3

49. Match the followings.

List-I	*List-II*
(*a*) First Governor General of Fort William	1. Lord Macauly
(*b*) First Chief Justice of Supreme Court	2. Lord Canning
(*c*) First law member of the Governor- General's Council	3. Warren Hastings
(*d*) First Viceroy as well as the Governor-General of India	4. Eligah Impey

Codes:

	(*a*)	(*b*)	(*c*)	(*d*)
A.	3	1	4	2
B.	3	4	2	1
C.	2	4	1	3
D.	3	4	1	2

50. Match the followings.

List-I	List-II
(a) Appointment of a separate Lt. Governor for Bengal	1. Charter Act of 1813
(b) Provision of an annual sum of one lakh rupees for the spread of education	2. Charter Act of 1853
(c) Abolition of the Board of Control and Court of Directors	3. Government of India Act of 1858
(d) Introduction of the Portfolio system	4. Indian Councils Act, 1861.

Codes:

	(a)	(b)	(c)	(d)
A.	3	2	4	1
B.	3	1	2	4
C.	1	2	3	4
D.	4	1	3	2

ANSWERS

1	2	3	4	5	6	7	8	9	10
B	D	C	A	D	B	A	D	C	B
11	**12**	**13**	**14**	**15**	**16**	**17**	**18**	**19**	**20**
C	D	D	A	B	C	D	B	A	C
21	**22**	**23**	**24**	**25**	**26**	**27**	**28**	**29**	**30**
D	D	B	D	A	C	B	D	A	A
31	**32**	**33**	**34**	**35**	**36**	**37**	**38**	**39**	**40**
C	A	B	A	C	D	B	C	A	B
41	**42**	**43**	**44**	**45**	**46**	**47**	**48**	**49**	**50**
D	D	C	A	C	A	A	C	D	B

SET-5

1. When was the new Enfield Rifle with greased cartridges introduced in the British Indian Army?

A. November, 1856 B. December, 1857
C. January, 1857 D. February, 1857

2. Which of the following events before the Revolt of 1857 gave jolts to the British armed strength?

1. First Afghan War
2. Anglo-Sikh War
3. First Anglo-Burmese War
4. Grivean War
5. Santhal uprising
6. Third Anglo-Maratha War

Codes:

A. 1, 2, 3 and 6 B. 2, 3, 5 and 6
C. 3, 4, 5 and 6 D. 1, 2, 4 and 5

3. Which of the following were the grievances of the sepoys?

1. Discrimination in payment and pensions.
2. Mistreatment of Sepoys by the British officials.
3. Refusal of the British to pay "Bhatta" while fighting in remote regions.
4. British governments order requiring the sepoys to serve overseas when required.
5. Encouragement given to chirstian missionaries by British army officers.

Codes:

A. 1, 2 and 5 B. 1, 3 and 4
C. 2, 3 and 5 D. All of them

4. Which of the following statements about Mangal Pandey are incorrect?

1. He was a sepoy in the 19th Native infantry stationed at Berhampur.
2. In March 1857, he single handely revolted and killed two English officer.
3. He made a futile attempt to commit suicide when he realised the hopelessness of the situation.
4. He was executed by the British.

Codes:

A. 1 and 2 B. 2 and 3
C. 1 and 4 D. 1 and 3

5. The annexation of some Indian states by Dalhousie was cancelled by the court of Directors. Who were they?

1. Sambalpur 2. Baghat
3. Nagpur 4. Udaipur
5. Jhansi

Codes:

A. 2, 3 and 4 B. 2, 3 and 5
C. 1 and 2 D. 2 and 4

6. What is the chronological sequence in which following places witnessed sepoy revolts?

1. Naushera
2. Delhi
3. Meerut
4. Hoti Mardan

Codes:

A. 2, 3, 1 and 4 B. 3, 2, 1 and 4
C. 4, 3, 2 and 1 D. 1, 3, 4 and 2

7. Which of the following Acts were passed by the British Government in 1856?

1. Hindu Widow Remarriage Act
2. Abolition of Sati
3. Religious Disabilities Act
4. General Service Enlistment Act

Codes:

A. 1 and 2 B. 2 and 4
C. 1, 3 and 4 D. 1, 2 and 3

8. Which of the following statements about Nana Saheb are true?

(*a*) Nana Saheb was the adopted son of the last Peshwa.
(*b*) The original name of Nana Saheb was Dhonda Pandit.
(*c*) The last Peshwa Baji Rao-II, was murdered by Nana Saheb.
(*d*) Dalhousie refused to recognise Nana Saheb as his Peshwa and suspended his pension.

A. (*a*), (*b*), (*c*) B. (*a*), (*b*), (*d*)
C. (*b*), (*c*), (*d*) D. (*a*), (*c*), (*d*)

9. What was the ratio of the Indian Sepoys to the Europeans in the British Indian army on the eve of the outbreak of the revolt of 1857?

A. 4 : 1 B. 5 : 1
C. 6 : 1 D. 7 : 1

10. At Delhi the Mughal Emperor's wife is said to have sabotaged the work of the rebels by acting as the informer to the British. What is her name?

A. Hazarat Mahal B. Zinnat Mahal
C. Mumtaz Mahal D. Fatima Begum

11. Which of the following statements about Maulavi Ahmedullah are correct?

1. He was a native of Delhi.
2. Just before the outbreak of the revolt of 1857, he led a minor revolt of the people against the Birtish at Faizabad.
3. He was one of the main leaders of the rebels at Lucknow and after its fall at Bareilly during the revolt.
4. He was caught and executed by the British after the revolt.

Codes:

A. 2 and 3 B. 1 and 4
C. 1 and 3 D. 3 and 4

12. Which of the following statements about Kanpur during the revolt of 1857 are true?

1. The besieged British surrendered to the rebels after a few days of resistance.
2. Despite Nana Saheb's promise of safe conduct to Allahabad, all the English men were murdered by the rebel sepoys while the former were leaving Kanpur in Boats.
3. After a brief period of confinement, all the English women and children were put to death by the followers of Nana Saheb.
4. The British after defeating Nana Saheb, reoccupied Kanpur in July, 1857.
5. The mutinious Gwalior regiment under Tantia Tope tried to capture it from the British in November 1857 but failed.

Codes:

A. 1, 2, 3 and 4 B. 1, 2, 4 and 5
C. 2, 3, 4 and 5 D. 1, 3, 4 and 5

13. Arrange the following places of revolt in the chronological order:

1. Mathura
2. Jhansi
3. Bareilly
4. Kanpur

Codes:

A. 1, 3, 4 and 2 B. 2, 4, 1 and 3
C. 3, 2, 1 and 4 D. 4, 2, 3 and 1

14. Match the list:

List-I	***List-II***
(*a*) Lt. Baugh	1. The officer who blew up the magazine at Delhi so that would not fall into the hands of sepoys.
(*b*) Colonel	2. The officer who murdered Mughal emperor's sons after the re-capture of Delhi
(*c*) Lt. Willoughby	3. The officer who was severely wounded by Mangal Pandey.
(*d*) Lt. Hudson	4. The commanding officer of the 11th Native Infantry at Meerut and who was killed by the Sepoys.

Codes:

	(*a*)	(*b*)	(*c*)	(*d*)
A.	4	1	2	3
B.	1	2	3	4
C.	3	4	1	2
D.	2	3	4	1

15. Which of the following are correctly matched?

List-I	***List-II***
1. Nana Saheb	Kanpur
2. Begam Hazarat Mahal	Lucknow
3. Rani Lakshmi Bai	Jhansi
4. Khan Bahadur Khan	Arrah
5. Kunwar Singh	Bareilly

Codes:

A. All of them B. 1, 2 and 3
C. 2, 3 and 4 D. 3, 4 and 5

16. Which of the following statements about Bakht Khan are true?

1. He was an ordinary Subedar in the British Army.
2. He led the revolt to the Sepoys at Meerut and brought them to Delhi.
3. He was the defacto leader of the Sepoys at Delhi, the nominal leader being the Mughal Emperor.
4. After the re-capture of Delhi by the British, he went to Awadh and died fighting the British in May, 1859.

Codes:

A. 1 and 2 B. 3 and 4
C. 1, 3 and 4 D. 2, 3 and 4

17. Match the following.

List-I	*List-II*
(*a*) Azimullah Khan	1. A relative of Mughal emperor
(*b*) Ahmad Ullah	2. Nephew of Nana Saheb
(*c*) Amar Singh	3. Adviser of Nana Saheb
(*d*) Firoz Shah	4. Adviser of the Ex-Nawab of Awadh
(*e*) Rao Saheb	5. Brother of Kunwar Singh

Codes:

	(*a*)	(*b*)	(*c*)	(*d*)	(*e*)
A.	3	5	4	2	1
B.	5	4	3	1	2
C.	4	3	5	1	2
D.	3	4	5	1	2

18. Made the following places with the Britishers who recaptured them using the codes given below:

(*a*) Gwalior	1. Sir Colin Campbell
(*b*) Bareilly	2. William Taylor
(*c*) Arrah	3. Brig. General Neil
(*d*) Banaras	4. Sir Hugh Rose
	5. General Nicholson

Codes:

	(*a*)	(*b*)	(*c*)	(*d*)
A.	2	4	3	5
B.	1	3	2	4
C.	5	4	1	2
D.	4	1	2	3

19. Which of the following statements about Tantia Tope are true?

1. He was the brother of Nana Saheb.
2. After the fall of Kanpur to the British, he joined Rani Lakshmi Bai against the British.
3. After losing Gwalior, he escaped to Central India and carried on Guearrilla War for 10 months.
4. He was betrayed and handed over to the British by Man Singh, a feaudotary of Sindhia.
5. He was transported for life by British in April 1859.

Codes:

A. 1, 2 and 5 B. 2, 3 and 4
C. 2, 3 and 5 D. 2, 4 and 5

20. Which of the following were causes for the failure of the rebels in 1857-58?

1. Disorganisation
2. Indiscipline
3. Participation of masses
4. Common interests
5. Decentralised leadership
6. Use of traditional weapon

Codes:

A. 1, 2, 3 and 5 B. 2, 3, 4, 5 and 6
C. 2, 3, 5 and 6 D. 2, 3, 4 and 6

21. Which of the following regions/presidencies did not participate in the revolt of 1857?

1. Bengal 2. Madras
3. Bombay 4. Central India
5. Western Punjab 6. Rajputana

Codes:

A. 1, 2, 3, 5 and 6 B. 2, 3, 4, 5 and 6
C. 2, 3, 5 and 6 D. 2, 4, 5 and 6

22. Which of the following Prime Ministers of Native states cooperated with the British in suppressing the revolt of 1857?

1. Sir Dinkar Rao 2. Sir Khan Bahadur
3. Sir Salar Jang 4. Sir Tang Bahadur

Codes:

A. 1, 2 and 3 B. 2, 3 and 4
C. 1, 3 and 4 D. 1, 2 and 4

23. Which of the following rulers of Indian States cooperated with the British in suppressing the revolt of 1857?

1. Nizam of Hyderabad
2. Sindhia of Gwalior
3. Holkar of Indore
4. Ex-Nawab of Rohilkhand
5. Gulab Singh of Kashmir
6. Raja of Jodhpur

Codes:

A. 1, 2, 4, 5 and 6 B. 1, 2, 3, 4 and 6
C. 1, 3, 4, 5 and 6 D. 2, 3, 4, 5 and 6

24. Which of the following classes did not participate in the Revolt of 1857?

1. Money Lenders
2. Merchants
3. Modern Intelligentsia
4. Agricultural Labourers
5. Urban based absentee landlords

Codes:

A. 1, 2, 3 and 5 B. 2, 3, 4 and 5
C. 1, 3, 4 and 5 D. 1, 2, 3 and 4

25. Which of the following classes participated in the Revolt of 1857?

1. Peasants
2. Capitalists
3. Handicraftsmen
4. Traditional Zamindars
5. Dispossed rulers

Codes:

A. 1, 3 and 5 B. 2, 4 and 5
C. 1, 2, 4 and 5 D. 1, 3, 4 and 5

26. Which of the following British officers lost their lines at Lucknow?

1. General John Nicolson
2. Brig. General Neil
3. Major General Havelock
4. Sir Henry Lawrence

Codes:

A. All of them B. 1, 2 and 3
C. 2, 3 and 4 D. 1, 3 and 4

27. Who among the following British officers lost their lines at Lucknow

1. General John Nicolson
2. Brig. General Neil
3. Major General Havelock
4. Sir Henry Lawrence

Codes:

A. All of them B. 1, 2 and 3
C. 2, 3 and 4 D. 1, 3 and 4

28. Assertion (A): The Sikh army rendered valuable service to the British in the suppression of the revolt of 1857.

Reason (R): Sir Henry Lawrence, the chief Commissioner of Punjab during the revolt, failed to maintain peace in Punjab.

Codes:

A. (A) and (R) are true and (R) is the correct explanation of (A).
B. (A) and (R) are true, but (R) is not the correct explanation of (A).
C. (A) is true, but (R) is false.
D. (A) is false, but (R) is true.

29. Assertion (A): The British remained as perpetual foreigners in India.

Reason (R): Some of the foreign conquerers of India, like Mughals and Delhi Sultans, made India their home.

Codes:

A. (A) and (R) are true and (R) is the correct explanation of (A).
B. (A) and (R) are true, but (R) is not the correct explanation of (A).
C. (A) is true, but (R) is false.
D. (A) is false, but (R) is true.

30. Assertion (A): The Indian middle and upper classes were totally excluded from high administrative and military post by the British.

Reason (R): Many of the traditional Zamindars lost their Zamindaries to the new class of urban based absent landlords.

Codes:

A. (A) and (R) are true and (R) is the correct explanation of (A).
B. (A) and (R) are true, but (R) is not the correct explanation of (A).
C. (A) is true, but (R) is false.
D. (A) is false, but (R) is true.

31. Which of the following were the main factors for the success of the British in supressing the revolt of 1857?

1. Immense resources
2. Superior military weapons and techniques
3. Able leadership
4. Assistance of some of the Indian rulers
5. End of Crimean War which enabled them to concentrate most of their troops in India.

Codes:

A. 1, 2 and 4 B. 2, 3 and 5
C. 1, 3 and 4 D. All of them

32. Assertion (A): The faulty deployment of troops on the eve of the revolt of 1857 may be considered as one of the main causes for the revolt.

Reason (R): Those was only an insignificant number of European soldiers compared to that of the sepoys at important military centres like Delhi and Allahabad on the eve of the revolt.

Codes:

A. (A) and (R) are true and (R) is the correct explanation of (A).
B. (A) and (R) are true, but (R) is not the correct explanation of (A).
C. (A) is true, but (R) is false.
D. (A) is false, but (R) is true.

33. Assertion (A): The British though introduced a unitary or highly centralised system of Government of India, continued to follow up the policy of divide and rule.

Reason (R): The British refused to pay foreign service allowence to the Indian sepoys while they were fighting in the remote regions like Punjab and Sind.

Codes:

A. (A) and (R) are true and (R) is the correct explanation of (A).
B. (A) and (R) are true, but (R) is not the correct explanation of (A).
C. (A) is true, but (R) is false.
D. (A) is false, but (R) is true.

34. Who was the famous Urdu Poet who witnessed the massacare of male civilians of Delhi by the British soldiers after it was recaptured?

A. Firak Gorakhpuri B. Josh Malihabadi
C. Mirza Ghalib D. Mir Babar Ali Anis

35. Assertion (A): In some places artisans and craftsmen participated in the revolt of 1857.

Reason (R): The British policy of "one way" free trade destroyed village industries and handicrafts in India.

Codes:

A. (A) and (R) are true and (R) is the correct explanation of (A).
B. (A) and (R) are true, but (R) is not the correct explanation of (A).
C. (A) is true, but (R) is false.
D. (A) is false, but (R) is true.

36. Assertion (A): The British followed a policy of religious prosecution of Hindus and Muslims in the army in order to forcibly convert them into chirstians.

Reason (R): The British Government gave full protection and encouragement to the christian missionaries in India.

Codes:

A. (A) and (R) are true and (R) is the correct explanation of (A).
B. (A) and (R) are true, but (R) is not the correct explanation of (A).
C. (A) is true, but (R) is false.
D. (A) is false, but (R) is true.

37. Who was the British General who esteemed Rani "Lakshmi Bai of Jhansi as the best and bravest military leader of the rebels"?

A. Sir Colin Campbell B. Major General Havelock
C. Sir James Outram D. Sir Hugh Rose

38. Assertion (A): The immediate cause of the revolt of 1857 was the introduction of the New Enfield Rifle in the British Indian Army.

Reason (R): The sepoys were required to before loading the cartridge into the new rifle, bite off its end which was feared to have been greased with the fat of cows and Pigs.

Codes:

A. (A) and (R) are true and (R) is the correct explanation of (A).
B. (A) and (R) are true, but (R) is not the correct explanation of (A).
C. (A) is true, but (R) is false.
D. (A) is false, but (R) is true.

39. Who wrote the following passage?

"In no instance it is a friendly glance directed to the white man's carriage ____ oh! that language of the eye; who can doubt, who can misinterpret it"?

A. G.B. Malleson B. J.W. Kaye
C. W.H. Russell D. T.R. Holmes

40. Which of the following statement about Rao Bharmal are not true?

1. He was the ruler of Mandu in central India.
2. He revolted due to the frequent interference of the British in the internal affairs of his state.
3. He was defeated and killed in a battle with the British.
4. The British imposed a subsidiary treaty on his successor.

Codes:

A. 1 and 2 B. 3 and 4
C. 1 and 3 D. 2 and 4

41. Which of the following statements about Velu Thambi are true?

1. He was the Raja of Travancore State.
2. He revolted because of British demand for his removal.
3. Despite the stiff resistance put up by his forces, Trivandrum the Capital of Travancore, fell to the British forces.
4. He was caputured and executed by the British.

Codes:

A. 2 and 3 B. 1 and 3
C. 2 and 4 D. 3 and 4

42. Arrange in correct sequence:

1. Revolt of Rao Bharmal
2. Revolt of Velu Thambi
3. Rebellion of Birabhadra Rauze
4. Rebellion of Kattabomman

Codes:

A. 4, 2, 1 and 3 B. 2, 3, 4 and 1
C. 3, 1, 2 and 4 D. 1, 4, 2 and 3

43. Arrange the following revolts in the correct sequence:

1. Satara disturbances
2. Sambalpur outbreak
3. Bundela revolt
4. Gadkhari rebellion

Codes:

A. 2, 3, 4 and 1 B. 4, 2, 1 and 3
C. 1, 3, 2 and 4 D. 2, 1, 3 and 4

44. Which of the following statements about Virapandya Kattaboman are true?

1. He was the ruler of Panchalakurichi in the Tirunelveli district of Tamil Nadu.
2. He revolted because of British attempts to impose their sovereignty over him.
3. In the end he was captured and executed by the British.
4. The territory was restored to one of his minor sons.

Codes:

A. All of them B. 2 and 4
C. 2 and 3 D. 3 and 4

45. Who was the author of the Book, "The Indian War of Independence 1857"?

A. Sir Sayyed Ahmed Khan
B. V.D. Savarkar
C. S.R. Sharma
D. R.C. Majumdar

46. Match the following.

List-I	List-II
(a) Chittur Singh	1. Leader of Kittur revolt
(b) Channama	2. Leader of Satara outbreak
(c) Dhar Rao Pawar	3. Leader of Bundel rebellion
(d) Madhukar Shah	4. Leader of Ramosi revolt

Codes:

	(a)	(b)	(c)	(d)
A.	4	2	1	3
B.	4	1	2	3
C.	1	2	4	3
D.	2	3	1	4

47. Which of the following statements about the Paiks are true?

1. They were a militia class in Orissa occupying rent free land under the Zamindar.
2. After the British occupation of Orrisa, they were also required to pay land revenue to the British.
3. They revolted first under the leadership of the Raja of Parlakimedi.
4. In their second revolt, they defeated the British forces and occupied Puri for a short period.

Codes:

A. 1, 2 and 3 B. 1, 2 and 4
C. 2, 3 and 4 D. 1, 3 and 4

48. Arrange the following revolts in the chronological order?

1. Kittur Rising 2. Ramosi Revolt
3. Paik Rebellion 4. Satavadi Revolt

Codes:

A. 2, 4, 1 and 3
B. 4, 2, 3 and 1
C. 1, 3, 4 and 2
D. 3, 2, 1 and 4

49. Which of the following statements about Ramosis are true?

1. Under the Peshwa they served in the inferior ranks of police.
2. After the annexation of Peshwa's territory, the British despensed with their service.
3. Their revolt created serious disturbances in Poona and the surrounding areas for quite sometime.
4. All the Ramosis who participated in the revolt were finally captured and executed by the British.

Codes:

A. 1, 2 and 3 B. 2, 3 and 4
C. 1, 2 and 4 D. 1, 3 and 4

50. The British attached the Zamindari and property of a number of Zamindars for non-payment of revenue, resulting in the revolt of those Zamindars against the British. Which of the following Zamindars fall under this category?

1. Zamindar of Palkonda
2. Zamindar of Kurnool
3. Zamindar of Parlakimedi
4. Zamindar of Gumsur

Codes:

A. 1, 2, 3 B. 2, 3, 4
C. 1, 2, 4 D. 1, 3, 4

ANSWERS

1	2	3	4	5	6	7	8	9	10
C	D	D	A	D	B	C	B	D	B
11	**12**	**13**	**14**	**15**	**16**	**17**	**18**	**19**	**20**
A	A	A	C	B	C	D	D	B	C
21	**22**	**23**	**24**	**25**	**26**	**27**	**28**	**29**	**30**
A	D	B	A	D	C	C	C	B	B
31	**32**	**33**	**34**	**35**	**36**	**37**	**38**	**39**	**40**
D	A	B	C	A	D	D	A	C	C
41	**42**	**43**	**44**	**45**	**46**	**47**	**48**	**49**	**50**
A	C	D	C	B	B	B	D	A	D

SET-6

1. What was the first and fundamental idea with which the Brahma Samaj was started?

A. monotheism
B. widow remarriage
C. removal of purdah for women
D. university education

2. Where was Brahma Samaj first established?

A. Bengal B. The Punjab
C. Bombay D. Madras

3. In which one of the following regions was the Indian family matrilineal?

A. Kerala B. Bengal
C. Assam D. Andhra

4. Where was the purdah system not practised in the 18th Century?
A. South Indian B. Rajasthan
C. The Punjab D. Gujarat

5. Which one of the following was not known to Raja Rammohan Roy?
A. Sanskrit B. Persian
C. Hebrew D. Malayalam

6. In what language did Rammohan write his Gift to Monotheists?
A. Sanskrit B. Bengali
C. Persian D. Hindi

7. Against which of the following social evils did Rammohan organise the historic agitations?
A. Sati B. Female infanticide
C. Early D. Untouchability

8. Who founded the Hindu College?
A. David Hare B. William Jones
C. Rammohan Roy D. Dayananda

9. Who among the following was not associated with Rammohan?
A. David Hare B. Alexander Duff
C. Annie Besant D. Prasanna Kumar Tagore

10. To which of the following categories of people did Vivian Derozio belong?
A. Irishman B. Anglo-Indian
C. Englishman D. Frenchman

11. Who were discribed by Surendranath Benerji as pioneers of the modern civilisation of Bengal, the conscript fathers of our race?
A. Brahma Samajists
B. Asiatic Society of Bengal
C. Derozians
D. Arya Samajists

12. In which one of the following persons one cannot find a happy blend of Indian and Western culture?
A. Rammohan Roy
B. Ishwar Chandra Vidyasagar
C. Dayananda Saraswati
D. Dwarkanth Tagore

13. Outside Bengal, where did Brahma Samaj take a firm root?
A. Rajasthan B. Andhra
C. Orissa D. Maharashtra

14. Who took the pen-name of Lokahitawadi?
A. G.H. Deshmukh
B. Jyotiba Phule
C. Karsondas Mulji
D. Ishwar Chandra Vidyasagar

15. Who founded the Deccan Education Society?
A. R.G. Bhandarkar B. Kaka Kelkar
C. Jyotiba Phule D. M.G. Ranade

16. Who among the following was the greatest Sanskrit scholar?
A. R.G. Bhandarkar
B. Swami Dayananda
C. Ramakrishna Paramahansa
D. Annie Besant

17. Who was known in early life as Mula Sankara?
A. Dayananda B. Ramakrishna
C. Vivekanand D. Rabindranath Tagore

18. Which among the following started a crusade against other religions?
A. Brahma Samaj B. Prarthana Samaj
C. Theosophical Society D. Arya Samaj

19. Which of the following is said to have contributed to the growth of communalism in India in the 20th Century?
A. Brahma Samaj B. Arya Samaj
C. Prarthana Samaj D. Ramakrishna Mission

20. What was the first association founded by Rammohan Roy?
A. Atmiya Sabha
B. Brahma Sabha
C. Tattvabodhini Sabha
D. Young Bengal Movement

21. Which one of the following does occupy an intermediate position between reform and revivalism?
A. Brahma Samaj B. Arya Samaj
C. Prarthana Samaj D. Ahmadiya Movement

22. Who was the leader of the young Bengal Movement?
A. G.F. Andrews B. Rammohan Roy
C. H.V. Derozio D. Dayananda

23. Where was Paramahansa Mandali started?
A. Bengal B. Gujarat
C. The Punjab D. Maharashtra

24. Who gave the call 'Back to the Vedas'?
A. Swami Vivekananda
B. Ramakrishna Paramahansa
C. Dayananda
D. Raja Rammohan Roy

25. Who said the different creeds are but different paths to reach the same God (yatmat tata path)?
A. Ramakrishna B. Annie Besant
C. Vivekananda D. Dayananda

26. Who wrote 'Ramakrishna — His life and Sayings'?
A. Swami Vivekananda B. Max Muller
C. Rasmani D. Keshab Chandra Sen

27. Who among the following was not a follower of Dayananda?

A. Lala Hansraj B. Pandit Guru Dutt
C. Lala Lajpat Rai D. M.G. Ranade

28. The Gurukul of Haridwar was started as a countermove to
A. Dayananda Anglo-Vedic College of Lahore
B. Muhammedan Anglo-oriental College
C. Sanskrit College
D. Banaras Hindu College

29. When was the parliament of Religions held?
A. 1893 A.D. B. 1902 A.D.
C. 1883 A.D. D. 1913 A.D.

30. Where did the Theosophists establish their headquarters?
A. Calcutta B. Lahore
C. Poona D. Adyar

31. Among the following which one proved to be an important factor in Socio-religious reform movement especially in South India?
A. Arya Samaj B. Prarthana Samaj
C. Brahma Samaj D. Theosophical Society

32. Who said the following words? 'So long as the millions live in hunger and Ignorance, I held every man a traitor'
A. Rammohan Roy
B. Ishwar Chandra Vidyasagar
C. M.K. Gandhi
D. Swami Vivekananda

33. Who said the following words?
'liberty in thought and action is the only condition of life, growth and well-being, where it does not exist, the man, the race and the nation must go down'.
A. Swami Vivekananda B. M.K. Gandhi
C. B.G. Tilak D. Dadabhai Nauroji

34. Whose followers are said to belong to Aligarh school?
A. Sayyid Ahmad Khan
B. Muhammad Iqbal
C. Maulana Abul Kalam Azad
D. Muhammad Ali Jinnah

35. Who invented the term 'Pakistan'?
A. Muhammad Iqbal B. Sayyid Ahmad Khan
C. M.A. Jinnah D. Rahmat Ali

36. Who started the Ahmadiya Movement?
A. Sayyid Ahmad Khan B. Mirza Ghulam Ahmad
C. Ahmad Ullah D. Ahmad Shah of Delhi

37. Who founded the Servants of India Society?
A. G.K. Gokhale B. Surendranath Banerjee
C. B.G. Tilak D. M.G. Ranade

38. Who started the Indian women's university?
A. D.K. Karve B. M.G. Ranade
C. B.G. Tilak D. G.K. Gokhale

39. Who among the following does not belong to the branch of study in which the other three had specialised?
A. J.G. Bose B. C.V. Raman
C. B.N. Seal D. Meghnad Saha

40. Who founded a Sanskrit College at Banaras?
A. William Jones B. Jonathan Duncan
C. Charles Grant D. Warren Hastings

41. Who among the following did not establish an English school?
A. William Carey B. David Hare
C. Rammohan Roy D. Jonathan Duncan

42. Who made a powerful plea in favour of Western education in his minute of 2nd February, 1835?
A. Alexander Duff B. T.B. Macaulay
C. William Bentinck D. Jonathan Duncan

43. Where was the first university established in India?
A. Bombay B. Poona
C. Madras D. Calcutta

44. Who organised the Non-Brahmin Movement in Maharashtra?
A. Jyotiba Govind Phule B. M.G. Ranade
C. B.G. Tilak D. G.H. Deshmukh

45. When was the Non-Brahmin movement started in Tamil Nadu?
A. 1914 A.D. B. 1916 A.D.
C. 1928 A.D. D. 1939 A.D.

46. What was the political party that grew out of the South Indian people's Association limited?
A. D.M.K. B. Dravida Kazhagam
C. Justice Party D. Swarajists

47. Who started the Dravida Kazhagam?
A. E.V. Ramasami (Periyar)
B. C.N. Annadurai
C. T.M. Nair
D. K. Veeramani

48. Who among the following Scheduled caste people launched a spirited depressed classes fight against caste tyranny?
A. B.R. Ambedkar B. M.C. Rajah
C. Jagjivan Ram D. Rao Bahadur Srinivasan

49. Who said the following words?
"Nobody can remove your grievance as well as you can and you cannot remove these unless you get political power into your hands".
A. B.G. Tilak B. M.K. Gandhi
C. Jawaharlal Nehru D. B.R. Ambedkar

50. What was the first labour organisation formed in India?
A. The Bombay Mill hands Association
B. Amalgamated Society of the Railways of India and Burma
C. The Printers Union
D. Bombay Postal Union

51. When did the All-India Trade Union Congress first meet?
A. 1920 A.D. B. 1914 A.D.
C. 1926 A.D. D. 1985 A.D.

52. Whom do you consider as a major curse of the rural people?
A. Zamindars B. Government
C. Money-lenders D. Robbers

53. Who among the following was not among those who came to defend I.N.A. prisoners?
A. Jawaharlal B. Tej Bahadur Sapru
C. Kailash Nath Katju D. Vallabhbhai Patel

54. Who said the following words?
"Long years ago we made a tryst with destiny, and now the time comes when we shall redeem our pledge..."
A. M.K. Gandhi B. Subhas Chandra Bose
C. Jawaharlal Nehru D. M.A. Jinnah

55. What method did the British follow to deal with the boycott of the Simon Commission?
A. Brutal Suppression
B. Bilateral talks with the Congress
C. Concessions
D. Persuasions

56. Who said the following words?
"The Muslims were fools to ask for Safeguards and the Hindus were greater fools to refuse them".
A. Maulana A.K. Azad B. Muhammad Iqbal
C. M.A. Jinnah D. Jawaharlal Nehru

57. How many km did M.K. Gandhi walk to reach Dandi?
A. about 375 km B. about 200 km
C. about 400 km D. about 250 km

58. Who was the first governor-general of Pakistan?
A. Quid-i-Azam M.A. Jinnah
B. Khwaja Nazim-ud-din
C. Ghulam Mohammad
D. Liaquat Ali Khan

59. Who was the first prime minister of Pakistan?
A. Qaid-i-Azam M.A. Jinnah
B. Liaquat Ali Khan
C. Khwaja Nazim-ud-din
D. Z.A. Bhutto

60. Under what Plan/Act was partition of India effected?
A. Wavell's Plan
B. Indian Independence Act of 1947
C. Cabinet Mission Plan
D. Government of India Act of 1935

ANSWERS

1	2	3	4	5	6	7	8	9	10
A	A	A	A	D	C	A	A	C	B
11	**12**	**13**	**14**	**15**	**16**	**17**	**18**	**19**	**20**
C	C	D	A	D	A	A	D	B	A
21	**22**	**23**	**24**	**25**	**26**	**27**	**28**	**29**	**30**
B	C	D	C	A	B	D	A	A	D
31	**32**	**33**	**34**	**35**	**36**	**37**	**38**	**39**	**40**
D	D	A	A	D	B	A	A	C	B
41	**42**	**43**	**44**	**45**	**46**	**47**	**48**	**49**	**50**
D	B	D	A	B	C	A	A	D	A
51	**52**	**53**	**54**	**55**	**56**	**57**	**58**	**59**	**60**
A	C	D	C	A	A	A	A	B	B

SET-7

1. Who among the following Viceroys became a victim of one of the convicts during his visit to Andamans?
A. Lytton B. Ripon
C. Mayo D. Curzon

2. Who are known as the "Liberators of the Indian Press"?
A. Sir Charles Metcalfe B. Lord Minto
C. Sir Thomas Munro D. Lord Macauly

3. The Indian press played an important role in spreading the message of patriotism and modern ideas among the people. Which of the following is/are not true about its activities?
1. Criticising the official policies.
2. Urging the people to unite and work for national welfare.

3. Putting toward the views of Indians as well as those of the British Government.
4. Popularising modern ideas of self-governments democracy etc.
5. Enabling nationalist workers to exchange views with one another.

Codes:

A. 3 B. 1
C. 1, 3 D. 4, 5

4. Which of the following are correctly matched?

1. Hindu Patriot (1853) Girish Chandra Ghosh
2. Rast Goftar (1851) Dadabhai Nauroji
3. Akbar-O-Saidagas (1852) Dadabhai Kavasji
4. Indian Mirrior (1862) Devendra Nath Tagore

Codes:

A. 2, 3, 4 B. 1, 2, 3
C. 1, 3, 4 D. 1, 3, 4

5. Which of the following are correctly matched?

1. Statesman (1875) — Devendra Nath Tagore
2. National Paper (1865) — Rober Knight
3. Tribune (1862) — Dayal Singh Majeethia
4. Bengalee (1881) — Girish Chandra Ghosh

Codes:

A. 1, 2 B. 2, 3
C. 3, 4 D. 1, 4

6. Match the following.

List-I	*List-II*
(*a*) National Indian Association (1867)	1. William Adam
(*b*) Indian Society (1872)	2. Gokhale
(*c*) Servants of India Society (1905)	3. Mary Carpenter
(*d*) British India Society (1839)	4. Anand Mohan Bose

Codes:

	(*a*)	(*b*)	(*c*)	(*d*)
A.	1	3	2	4
B.	3	4	2	1
C.	4	1	2	3
D.	3	1	2	4

7. Which of the following are correctly matched?

(*a*) Second Session of the Congress	1. Pheroz Shah Mehta
(*b*) Third Session (Madras)	2. Dadabhai Nauroji
(*c*) Fourth Session (Allahabad)	3. Sir William Wedderton
(*d*) Fifth Session (Bombay)	4. Badruddin Taiebji
(*e*) Sixth Session (Calcutta)	5. George Yule

Codes:

	(*a*)	(*b*)	(*c*)	(*d*)	(*e*)
A.	2	4	5	3	1
B.	2	1	3	4	5
C.	3	2	1	4	5
D.	1	5	3	2	4

8. Match the following.

List-I	*List-II*
(*a*) Banga-Duta	1. First paper from Bombay
(*b*) Madras Courier	2. First paper from Madras
(*c*) Bombay Herald	3. A weekly paper in four language
(*d*) Bombay Samachar	4. First paper in Gujarat
	5. First paper from Bengal

Codes:

	(*a*)	(*b*)	(*c*)	(*d*)
A.	5	2	4	1
B.	3	2	1	4
C.	4	3	1	2
D.	3	2	1	5

9. Which is the correct chronological sequence of the following associations?

1. Poona Sarvajanik Sabha
2. Indian Association of Calcutta
3. Bombay Presidency Association
4. Madras Mahajan Sabha

Codes:

A. 1, 2, 4, 3 B. 2, 3, 4, 1
C. 1, 4, 2, 3 D. 3, 2, 1, 4

10. Who is the founder of the Amrit Bazar Patrika?

A. Sisir Kumar Ghosh
B. Girish Chandra Ghosh
C. Harish Chandra Mukherjee
D. S.N. Banerjee

11. Who was the Secretary of States for India at the time of the foundation of Indian National Congress?

A. Lord Morley B. Lord Elgin
C. Lord Hamilton D. Lord Cross

12. Which of the following statements is/are true about the Vernacular Press Act, 1878?

1. It was passed by Lord Mayo.
2. It came to be known as the "Gagging Act".
3. It liberated the Indian Press from restrictions.
4. It was replaced by Lord Ripon in 1882.

Codes:

A. 1, 2 B. 2, 4
C. 1, 3 D. 3, 4

13. The administrative and economic unification of India by the British also paved the way for the rise of Indian National Movement. Which of the following statements is/are incorrect in this regard?

1. The British Unified India administratively by introducing a uniform and modern system of government throughout the country.
2. The destruction of local self sufficient economy had increasingly atomised India's economic life.
3. The introduction of modern trade and industries had inter-linked the economic-fate of the people living in different parts of India.

4. The introduction of the modern means of transport and communication had promoted natural contact.

Codes:

A. 2, 3 B. 2

C. 3 D. 3, 4

14. Which of the following statements is incorrect?

A. Amrit Bazar Patrika work originally a Bengali Paper, but became a full-fledged English paper in 1878 in order to escape from the Vernacular Press Act.

B. Hindu was founded by G.S. Aiyar and Viraraghava Chari.

C. Sanjibani, started in 1883, was a Marathi Paper.

D. The Bombay Times became the Times of India in 1861.

15. Who among the following did not attend the first session of Congress at Bombay?

A. W.C. Banerjee B. S.N.Banerjee

C. Badruddin Tayebji D. K.T. Tailong

16. What is the name of Bengali monthly founded and edited by Bankim Chandra Chatterjee from 1873?

A. Somprakasha B. Bangaduta

C. Bangadarsna D. Bengalee

17. Which of the following statements about the Ilbert Bill is/are not true?

1. The controversy around the Ilbert Bill helped Indian nationalism to take up an organised form.
2. According to the original Bill, Indian Judge could try Europeans also.
3. It was passed without any amendment despite the vehement opposition of the British residents in India.
4. The Indians did not organise any campaign in favour of the Bill.

Codes:

A. 1, 4 B. 2, 3

C. 3, 4 D. 4 only

18. Arrange the following organisations in the chronological order:

1. East India Association in London
2. Land holders Society at Calcutta
3. Madras Native Association
4. Bengal British Indian Society
5. British Indian Association

Codes:

A. 2, 3, 1, 4, 5 B. 1, 4, 3, 5, 2

C. 3, 5, 4, 1, 2 D. 2, 4, 5, 3, 1

19. Match the following:

(*a*) Digdarsana (1818)	1. First Paper in Urdu
(*b*) Bengal Gazette (1818)	2. First Bengali Monthly
(*c*) Mirat-ul-Akbar (1822)	3. First Journal in Persian
(*d*) Bombay Samachar	4. First Bengali Newspaper

Codes:

	(*a*)	(*b*)	(*c*)	(*d*)
A.	4	2	1	3
B.	2	4	1	3
C.	4	2	3	1
D.	2	4	3	1

20. **Assertion (A):** The introduction of western system of education and English language was an important cause for the rise and growth of nationalism in India.

Reason (R): The Indian national movement would not have been possible without the English language as a medium.

Codes:

A. (A) and (R) are true and (R) is the correct explanation of (A).

B. (A) and (R) are true but (R) is not the correct explanation of (A).

C. (A) is true but (R) is false.

D. (A) is false but (R) is true.

21. **Assertion (A):** Dadabhai Nauroji organised the East India Association in London.

Reason (R): He wanted to influence the British public opinion.

Codes:

A. (A) and (R) are true and (R) is the correct explanation of (A).

B. (A) and (R) are true but (R) is not the correct explanation of (A).

C. (A) is true but (R) is false.

D. (A) is false but (R) is true.

22. Who was the first woman president of the Indian National Congress?

A. Sarojini Naidu B. Sucheta Kripalani

C. Rajkumari Amrit Kaur D. Annie Besant

23. Who was the first Muslim president of the Indian National Congress?

A. Muhammed Ali Jinnah

B. Badruddin Tayebji

C. Sir Syed Ahmed Khan

D. Abul Kalam Azad

24. The extremist method of "passive resistance" did not include:

1. Refusal to co-operate with the Government.
2. Sending petitions to the Government.
3. Boycott of Government service, courts, schools and Colleges.
4. Refusal to pay rent to the Zamindars.

Codes:

A. 2 B. 1, 2

C. 4 D. 2, 4

25. Which of the following statements about Gokhale are not true?

1. He was a moderate in politics, but a radical in matters of social reforms.
2. He wanted political progress and social reforms to go simultaneously.
3. He was opposed to "passive resistance" in India as well as in South Africa.
4. He was totally opposed to western civilisation.

Codes:

A. 4 B. 3, 4
C. 2, 4 D. 2, 3, 4

26. Who is the first profounder of the Doctrine of "Passive resistance"?

A. B.G. Tilak B. Arubindo Ghosh
C. G.K. Gokhale D. M.K. Gandhi

27. Who described Tilak, as the "Father of Indian unrest"?

A. Valentine Chiro B. Disraeli
C. Minto II D. Chelmsford

28. Who presided over the Surat session of the Indian National Congress?

A. Dadabhai Nauroji
B. Gopal Krishna Gokhale
C. Rashbehari Ghosh
D. S.N. Banerjee

29. Who exclaimed, "when the Queen desires that none should die, what the Governor declares that all should live ..... will you kill yourself by timidity and starvation"?

A. Bipin Chandra Pal B. Dadabhai Nauroji
C. Tilak D. Gokhale

30. Who said "The Congress movement was neither inspired by the people, nor devised or planned by them"?

A. Lala Lajpat Rai B. Sir Syed Ahmed
C. Lord Curzon D. Lord Dufferin

31. Which of the following statements about Tilak are incorrect?

1. Believed that political freedom should precede social reform.
2. Favoured initiative by the Congress in the matter of social reforms.
3. Opposed British Government's initiative in the matter of the social reforms.
4. Did not consider social and political reforms to be interlinked.
5. Separated religions from politics.

Codes:

A. 5 B. 2, 5
C. 2, 4, 5 D. 4

32. When did Tilak declare, "Swaraj is my birthright, and I will have it"?

A. 1905 B. 1909
C. 1914 D. 1916

33. When did the British pass a law it an offence to preach nationalism?

A. 1890 B. 1895
C. 1898 D. 1904

34. Assertion (A): Arya Samajists were responsible for the rise of extremism in the Indian National Congress.

Reason (R): Many of them were in the forefront of the national movement.

Codes:

A. (A) and (R) are true and (R) is the correct explanation of (A).
B. (A) and (R) are true, but (R) is not the correct explanation of (A).
C. (A) is true, but (R) is false.
D. (A) is false, but (R) is true.

35. Assertion (A): British residents in India Vehemently opposed the Ilbert Bill.

Reason (R): The Bill proposed to establish social equality in the administration of Justice.

Codes:

A. (A) and (R) are true and (R) is the correct explanation of (A).
B. (A) and (R) are true, but (R) is not the correct explanation of (A).
C. (A) is true, but (R) is false.
D. (A) is false, but (R) is true.

36. Assertion (A): Dwarka Nath Tagore was one of the founder members of the "Landholders Society" of Calcutta.

Reason (R): The society was the first example of an organised constitutional agitation for redress of grievances.

Codes:

A. (A) and (R) are true and (R) is the correct explanation of (A).
B. (A) and (R) are true, but (R) is not the correct explanation of (A).
C. (A) is true, but (R) is false.
D. (A) is false, but (R) is true.

37. Assertion (A): Raja Rammohan Roy was one of the first Indian leaders to start an agitation for political reforms.

Reason (R): He founded the Landholders Society at Calcutta in 1838.

Codes:

A. (A) and (R) are true and (R) is the correct explanation of (A).
B. (A) and (R) are true, but (R) is not the correct explanation of (A).
C. (A) is true, but (R) is false.
D. (A) is false, but (R) is true.

38. Match List-I with List-II.

List-I	*List-II*
(*a*) Hindu Mahasabha	1. 1906
(*b*) Indian Liberal Foundation	2. 1915
(*c*) Muslim League	3. 1916
(*d*) Home Rule League	4. 1918

Codes:

	(*a*)	(*b*)	(*c*)	(*d*)
A.	2	4	1	3
B.	2	1	4	3
C.	3	2	4	1
D.	4	1	3	2

39. Match the following:

(*a*) Foundation of Women's University	1. Lord Lands Downe
(*b*) Creation of Governorship for Bengal	2. Lord Curzon
(*c*) Ancient Movements Preservation Act	3. Lord Hardinge II
(*d*) Indian Council Act of 1891	4. Lord Chelmsford

Codes:

	(*a*)	(*b*)	(*c*)	(*d*)
A.	2	1	3	4
B.	4	3	1	2
C.	3	4	2	1
D.	4	3	2	1

40. Assertion (A): In the life of Dadabhai Nauroji, there was a slow transition from liberalism and modertism to some form of radicalims and extremism.

Reason (R): He was gradually disallusioned with British Politicians and their policies.

Codes:

A. (A) and (R) are true and (R) is the correct explanation of (A).
B. (A) and (R) are true, but (R) is not the correct explanation of (A).
C. (A) is true, but (R) is false.
D. (A) is false, but (R) is true.

41. Assertion (A): Till the Fag end of the 19th Century, Tilak did not advocate "passive resistance".

Reason (R): Till his death, his idea of self-government meaning to him complete autonomy, did not change.

Codes:

A. (A) and (R) are true and (R) is the correct explanation of (A).
B. (A) and (R) are true, but (R) is not the correct explanation of (A).
C. (A) is true, but (R) is false.
D. (A) is false, but (R) is true.

42. Assertion (A): Gokhale claimed self-government not as a matter of right but as a reward by the display of wisdom, experience, moderation etc.

Reason (R): He was greatly influenced by the British ideas of moderation and peaceful evolution.

Codes:

A. (A) and (R) are true and (R) is the correct explanation of (A).
B. (A) and (R) are true, but (R) is not the correct explanation of A.
C. (A) is true, but (R) is false.
D. (A) is false, but (R) is true.

43. Which of the following was/were not contributed by the revolutionary terrorists?

1. Setting a rare example of death-defying heroism in the cause of motherland.
2. Being the first to demand "Dominian States" much before the Congress did.
3. Production of a wealth of patriotic songs, and creation of a new interest in regional and local history and folk traditions.
4. Establishment of world-wide contacts.

Codes:

A. 2 B. 4
C. 2, 4 D. 3, 4

44. Which of the following persons was/were not involved with the foundation of the Anushilan Samiti of Calcutta in 1902?

1. Promotha Mitter
2. Abani Mukherji
3. Barindra Kumar Ghosh
4. Jatindra Nath Benerji
5. Pulin Das

Codes:

A. 2, 4 B. 3, 5
C. 2, 5 D. 3, 4

45. Which of the following were the causes for the emergence and growth of revolutionary terrorism in India?

1. Frustration of the youth with the constitutional methods of the moderates and the passive resistance of the extremists
2. Failure of the Swedeshi and anti-partition movements to get the partition of Bengal repeated.
3. Protection and co-operation given by the masses to the terrorists.
4. Growing hatred among the youth for foreign rule due to social arrogance of the British and the represive measures adopted by the Government.
5. Influence of the Irish terrorists and the Russian Nihlists.

Codes:

A. 1, 2, 4 B. 2, 3, 5
C. 1, 2, 4, 5 D. 2, 3, 4, 5

46. Which of the following newspaper/journal was not from Bengal?

A. Yugantar B. Kal
C. Bandi Jivan D. Dhumketu

47. Which of the following statements about revolutionary terrorists are not true?
1. They came mainly from the lower classes.
2. Most of them belonged to the upper classes.
3. Most of them came from the rural areas.
4. They neglected the real demands of the peasants and workers.

Codes:
A. 1, 2, 3 B. 2, 4
C. 2, 3, 4 D. 1, 3

48. Which of the following newspaper/journal was from Maharashtra?
A. Kranti B. Atmasakti
C. Sarathi D. Sandhya

49. Who was the revolutionary terrorist who ended his days as Ramkrishna Mission's Swamiji?
A. Aurobindo Ghosh
B. Hemchandra Kanungo
C. Ajit Singh
D. Jatindranath Bandopadhyay

50. Who was the founder of the secret society, "Abhinava Bharat"?
A. Naren Bhattacharji B. Jatin Mukherjee
C. Ganesh Saverkar D. Damodar Chapekar

51. Which of the following are correctly matched?

1. Sandhya	Brahmobandheb Upodhyay
2. Bande Matram	Satish Chandra Mukherjee
3. New Delhi	Bipin Chandra Pal
4. Dawn	Aurobindo Ghosh

Codes:
A. 1, 2 B. 2, 3
C. 3, 4 D. 1, 3

52. Which of the following correctly matched?

A. Punjabee	T. Prakasham & M. Krishna Rao
B. Bharat Mata	Ajit Singh
C. Krishna Patrika	M.G. Ranade
D. Quarterly Journal	Lajpat Rai

53. Which of the following are correctly matched?

(a) Comrade	1. Annie Besant
(b) Al-Hilal	2. Muhammad Ali
(c) Zamindar	3. Abdul Kalam Azad
(d) Commonweal	4. Zafar Ali Khan

Codes:

	(a)	*(b)*	*(c)*	*(d)*
A.	1	2	4	3
B.	3	2	4	1
C.	2	3	4	1
D.	1	3	4	2

54. Match the following.

List-I	***List-II***
(a) Rabindranath Tagore	1. Nil Darpan
(b) Dadabhai Nauroji	2. Economic History of India
(c) Dinbandhu Mitra	3. Gora
(d) R.C. Dutta	4. Poverty and British rule in India

Codes:

	(a)	*(b)*	*(c)*	*(d)*
A.	3	4	2	1
B.	3	2	4	1
C.	3	2	1	4
D.	3	4	1	2

55. Assertion (A): Aurobindo Ghosh was the most typical representative of the extremist nationalism in its intense metaphysical and religious form.

Reason (R): Nationalism to him, is not a mere political programme, but a religion that has come from God.

Codes:
A. (A) and (R) are true and (R) is the correct explanation of (A).
B. (A) and (R) are true, but (R) is not the correct explanation of (A).
C. (A) is true, but (R) is false.
D. (A) is false, but (R) is true.

ANSWERS

1	2	3	4	5	6	7	8	9	10
C	A	A	A	C	B	A	B	A	A
11	**12**	**13**	**14**	**15**	**16**	**17**	**18**	**19**	**20**
D	B	B	C	B	C	C	D	D	A
21	**22**	**23**	**24**	**25**	**26**	**27**	**28**	**29**	**30**
C	D	B	D	B	B	A	C	C	A
31	**32**	**33**	**34**	**35**	**36**	**37**	**38**	**39**	**40**
B	D	C	A	C	D	C	A	D	A
41	**42**	**43**	**44**	**45**	**46**	**47**	**48**	**49**	**50**
C	A	A	C	C	B	B	A	D	C
51	**52**	**53**	**54**	**55**					
D	B	C	D	A					

PASSAGE BASED QUESTIONS

Directions: *Read the following passage from the Arthashastra of Kautilya, and answer the following questions:*

PASSAGE-1

The Superintendent of cattle should know about cattle looked after in return for a wage, tended with a tax and a fixed return, become useless and cast off, entered in the state hards by payment of a shares the total number of cattle in herds, cattle that are lost or have perished, and the total produce of milk and ghee. The cowherd, the buffalo-herdsman, the milker, the churner and the hunter should look after do one hundred milch-cows, receiving a wage in cash. For, if given a wage in milk and ghee, they might do harm to the calves. These are cattle looked after for a wage. One person should look after one hundred animals containing an equal number of aged cows, milch-cows, cows with young, cows with calf for this first time and heifers. He should give eight vasrakas of ghee, one pana per animal and the hide with the mark, every year. This is tending with a tax and a fixed return. Herdsmen looking after one hundred animals divided into an equal number of cows that are diseased that are crippled, that do not allow another person to milk them, that are difficult to milk and that kill their calves, should give a share appropriate to that class. These are cattle become useless and cast off.

1. How many aged cows and how many heifers is one herdsman assigned in the above passage?

A. Twenty and forty respectively
B. Twenty and twenty respectively
C. Thirty and twenty respectively
D. Twenty and thirty respectively

2. For which of the following was there a payment in both kind and cash?

A. The milker and the churner
B. The second category of the responsibilities of the Superintendent
C. The cattle that are lost or have perished
D. Herdsmen looking after crippled cows.

3. Why were those who looked after milch cows not paid in milk and ghee?

A. So that they do not consume milk and ghee excessively
B. Because they would become lazy and careless in their work, if paid in kind
C. So that they do not deprive the calves of their share of milk
D. Because it was more profitable for the state to sell milk and ghee in the market

4. How many categories was the work of the Superintendent of cattle divided into?

A. Four B. Five
C. Six D. Seven

5. What are the work and the entitlement of the hunter in the above passage?

A. Looking after milch cows and payment in kind
B. Looking after aged cows for payment in hide
C. Tending heifers in return for a wage
D. Looking after milch cows in return for a cash wage

PASSAGE-2

The Timariots, Governors and Revenue contractors on their part, reason in this manner. Why should the neglected state of this land create uneasiness in our minds? And why should we expend our money and time to render it fruitful? We may be deprived of it in a single moment, and our exertions would benefit neither ourselves nor our children. Let us draw from the soil all the money we can, though the peasant should starve or abscond and we should leave it, when commanded to quit, a dreary wilderness.

6. The above observation is made by which of the following European traveller?

A. Thomas Bowrey
B. Jean Baptiste Tavernier
C. Francois Bernier
D. Jean de Thevenot

7. By 'Timariots', the traveller refers to which of the following Mughal official?

A. Mansabdar B. Jagirdar
C. Ijaradar D. Subadar

8. On the basis of the above observation which of the following historian has argued that the Mughal system of transfer of Jagirs led to the expolitation of peasantry that in turn created 'crisis' in the Mughal empire?
A. Irfan Habib B. Satish Chandra
C. J.F. Richards D. M. Athar Ali

9. Which of the following was not the characteristic of the Mughal jagir system?
A. Mughal jagirs were frequently transferred
B. Under Aurangzeb jagirs were made permanent and hereditary
C. Jagirdars used to employ their agents to collect the revenue
D. Jahangir instituted altun-tamgha jagirs to be held permanently

10. Which of the following chronicles of Shahjahan's reign mentions that the practice of ijara became very common during Shahjahan's reign and that it was one of the causes of the ruin of the peasantry?
A. Abdul Hamid Lahori
B. Muhammad Salil Kamboh
C. Muhammad Waris
D. Muhammad Sadiq Khan

PASSAGE-3

A different kind of historian was Barani, whose work, written in 1357, is a history of the Delhi Sultanate from the point where Minhaj Siraj ended his narrative. Barani is different from his peers, especially because he takes up aspects of life other than dynastic and political, such as economic, social, intellectual and religious. He is also novel in that he applies to events a distinct historical theory of his own. This theory was premised on a triangular relationship between despotic monarchy, the established nobility and upstarts from the non-aristocratic classes.

11. Which are the elements of triangular relationship described by Barani?
A. Despotic monarchy, established nobility; upstarts from the non-aristocratic classes.
B. Despotic monarchy, new nobility; upstarts from the non-aristoractic classes.
C. Despotic monarchy, established nobility; people from the aristocratic classes.
D. Despotic monarchy, new nobility; groups from non-aristocratic classes.

12. Which of the following is correct about Barani's writing style?
A. Barani has written dynastic history
B. Barani is accurate in providing dates of political events
C. Barani's account ends at Muhammad bin Tughlaq's reign
D. Barani believed in critical analysis of socio-economic and intellectual history

13. Barani's purpose of writing *Tarikh-i-Firuz Shahi* was to:
A. protect *Shariat*
B. please Muhammad bin Tughlaq
C. please Firuz Shah Tughluq
D. highlight the events during Iltutmish-Sikandar Lodi period

14. Name the book of Barani which is a history of the Delhi Sultanate from the point where Minhaj Siraj ended his book:
A. Tajul Ma'asir
B. Tarikh-i Firuzshahi
C. Fathiya Ibriya
D. Tabaqat-i-Mahmud Shahi

15. What is the title of Minhaj Siraj's book?
A. *Tajul Ma'asir*
B. *Fatawa i Jahadari*
C. *Tabaqat i Nasiri*
D. *Tarikh i Mahmud Shahi*

PASSAGE-4

Jahangir twice mentions a tower, tank and pavilion used as a hunting palace about 29 km from Lahore. Today the site is known as Shaikhupura, but Jahangir in 1606 refers to it as Jahangirpura and then in 1620 calls it Jahangirabad, both meaning City of Jahangir, the latter a more Persianate form. Here the emperor's favourite tame antelope died before 1606; it was buried in a grave above which a sculpted antelope and eulogy written by Mulla Muhammad Husain of Kashmir were placed. Adjacent to this gravestone, a tower was constructed around 1606 under the supervision of Sikandar Muin Khan, the landholder of the area. On Jahangir's orders, Sikandar Muin Khan also built a tank and royal residence. Despite Muin's death while the work was in progress, the complex was handsomely completed by 1620, the later stages of construction having been supervised by Iradat Khan. The expenses incurred were sufficiently awesome that the emperor recorded the amount in his memoirs. Jahangir considered the site a 'kingly hunting place', although his successor found the place inadequate and in 1634 spent another sizable sum rebuilding the pavilion.

16. Both the names Jahangirpura and Jahangirabad carry same meaning, *i.e.*, 'City of Jahangir'. From which language the word *Pura* is taken?
A. Marathi B. Urdu
C. Persian D. Sanskrit

17. In which book does Jahangir twice mention the tower, tank and pavilion?
A. *Maasir-i Jahangiri*

B. *Tuzuk-i Jahangiri*
C. *Iqbalnama-i Jahangiri*
D. *Majalis-i Jahangiri*

18. The plan of the Shaikhupura tower resembles to Hiran Minar built during Akbar's reign. In which of the following cities is Hiran Minar situated?
A. Fatehpur Sikri B. Delhi
C. Agra D. Sikandara

19. Who among the following mentioned per-sonalities was also called Shaikhu Baba?
A. Prince Kamran
B. Emperor Humayun
C. Shaikh Salim Chishti
D. Emperor Jahangir

20. In which of the following cities is situated 'Nim Sarai Minar' built during Akbar's reign?
A. Panipat B. Malda
C. Lahore D. Multan

PASSAGE-5

Ancient India has bequeathed to us a vast treasury of texts which represent the intellectual and literary activities of more than two thousand years and cover a wide field. The earliest literary work, the Samhita of the Rigveda, is at least three thousand years old and may be even considerably older. A continuous stream of literature flowing since that remote age, widening in course of centuries and embracing almost all fields of human endeavour excepting political activity throws a light on the civilization of India such as we do not meet with in cases of other ancient cultures. This mass of literature deal with philosophy and religion, including ethics, ritual and ceremonial; cosmogony, cosmology, geography, astronomy and the allied sciences; political and economic doctrines and practices; and in a minor way, with almost all branches of secular life. It includes, besides a mass of religious texts, purely literary works such as epics, lyrics, kavyas (poems), dramas and prose romances, as well as biographies and folk tales. This literature is as bulky in volume as it is varied in its contents. Although it does not help us very much in reconstructing the political history of ancient India, it throws a flood of light on an enables us to trace the various stages in the development of culture and civilization in ancient India, such as is not possible in the case of ancient Egypt, Western Asia and China and even Greece and Rome.

21. The seventh Mandala of the Rigveda is ascribed to the family of:
A. Atri B. Bharadvaja
C. Vasishtha D. Visvamitra

22. The most popular themes of ancient Indian dramas are based on the Ramayana, Mahabharata, courtly love and folk tales. Which of the following dramas, considered to be written by Bhasa, has taken its plot from the Ramayana?
A. Abhisheka B. Avimaraka
C. Balacharita D. Pancharatra

23. The Brahmanas are the texts which throw a flood of light on Vedic rituals and ceremonies. Which of the following pairs of the Brahmanas and Vedic Samhitas is NOT correctly matched?
A. Aitareya Brahmana—Rigveda Samhita
B. Tandya Brahmana—Samaveda Samhita
C. Kausitaki Brahmana—Yajurveda Samhita
D. Gopatha Brahmana—Atharvaveda Samhita

24. Which of the following historical works are authored by Bilhana?
(*a*) Vikramankadeva—Charita
(*b*) Bhuvanabhyudaya
(*c*) Kavi—rahasya
(*d*) Karnasundari

Choose the correct answer from the options given below:
A. (*a*) and (*b*) only B. (*b*) and (*c*) only
C. (*a*) and (*c*) only D. (*a*) and (*d*) only

25. The Indian Philosopher Vedanta Desika wrote a Sandesa Kavya (a form of lyric poem), named:
A. Meghaduta B. Pavanaduta
C. Hamsa-Sandesa D. Siladuta

PASSAGE-6

The Indian National Congress, being a movement and not just a party, included within its fold, individuals and groups which subscribed to widely divergent political and ideological perspectives. It was the mainstream organization but not the only stream. Obviously, the non-Congress movements were never seen as parallel streams, as some have maintained. Though they were outside the Congress, most of them were not really separate from it and at no stage they became alternatives to the Congress. The only ones which may be said to have formed of an alternative stream of politics were the communal and casteist movements which were not national or anti-imperialist. Several Satyagraha campaigns — apart from innumerable mass agitational campaigns — were waged between 1919 and 1942. The movement in its various forms and phases took modern politics to the people. It did not appeal to their pre-modern consciousness based on religion, caste and locality or loyalty to the traditional rulers. Though in some cases caste structure was used in villages to enforce discipline in a movement whose motivation and demands had nothing to do with caste. The social and religious reform movements which developed during the 19th century as part of the defence against colonialization of Indian culture merged with the national movement. As a mass movement, while the Indian national movement was able to tap the diverse energies, talents and capacities of a large varieties of people to fight against the British rule, emphasis was also laid on the constructive programme.

26. In which year women participated in the proceedings of the Indian National Congress?

A. 1885 B. 1889
C. 1898 D. 1926

27. Which among the following were parallel but not alternative streams of agitation?

(*a*) The Ghadar movement
(*b*) The Civil Disobedience movement
(*c*) The Indian National Army
(*d*) The Royal Indian Navy Revolt

Choose the correct answer from the options given below:

A. (*a*) and (*b*) only B. (*a*), (*c*) and (*d*) only
C. (*b*) and (*d*) only D. (*b*), (*c*) and (*d*) only

28. Which one of the following Satyagraha movements was not a part of the Indian National Congress programme?

A. Rowlatt Satyagraha
B. Non-Cooperation movement
C. Mahad Sweet Tank Satyagraha
D. The Quit India Movement

29. Which kind of individuals were not asso-ciated with the Indian national movement?

A. Imperialists B. Moderates
C. Communists D. Swarajists

30. Which one of the following was a non-Congress movement?

A. Extremists
B. All India Trade Union Congress
C. All India Depressed Classes Mission Society of India
D. Kisan Sabhas

PASSAGE-7

"The nationalist movement was from the beginning zealous in defence of civil liberties. Hence, the nationalists fought against the attack by the colonial authorities on the freedom of the press, speech and association, and other civil liberties. He assigned as much importance to them as he did to economic equality and socialism. The resolution on fundamental rights, passed by the Karachi Congress in 1931 and drafted by him, guaranteed the rights of free expression through speech and press. Secularism was from the beginning made a basic constituent of the nationalist ideology and a strong emphasis was laid on Hindu-Muslim unity. Furthermore, it was clearly understood that the objective of unifying the Indian people into a nation would have to be realised by taking into account regional, religious, caste, ethnic and linguistic differences. The cultural aspirations of different linguistic groups were given full recognition in 1921 by organizing provincial and area committee of the Indian National Congress along linguistic lines and not according to British-created multi-lingual provinces. From its earliest Phase, the Indian nationalists accepted, with near unanimity, the objective of complete economic transformation of the country on the basis of modern industrial and agricultural development, with a view to make India economically self-reliant, to be based on independence from foreign capital, creation of an indigenous capital goods, the foundation and development of independent science and technology."

31. Why did the British deny civil liberties to Indians?

A. Indians were not fit for it
B. To project cultural superiority
C. Because Indians were educationally backward
D. For exploiting India economically

32. Which one of the following principle was not advocated by the nationalists to make India self-reliant?

A. Growth of Science and Technology
B. Industrialization of India
C. Inviting foreign capital for the establishment of big industries
D. Creation of indigenous capital goods

33. Which one of the following did Jawaharlal Nehru not believe in?

A. Economic inequality
B. Secularism
C. Freedom of Press
D. Freedom of speech

34. In wielding India into a nation, what was considered by the Indian Nationalists as an essential requisite?

A. End of economic exploitation
B. Preserving its multi-cultural diversity
C. Granting civil liberties
D. Propagating Hindi as a national language

35. How were the cultural aspirations of Indians fulfilled by the Indian National Congress?

A. By advocating Khadi Gramodyog
B. By representing all sections of Indians in the organisation
C. By creating multi-lingual provinces
D. By introducing elections to the organi-sation

PASSAGE-8

Born in 1754, Colin Mackenzie became famous as an engineer, surveyor and cartographer. In 1815, he was appointed as the first Surveyor General of India, a post he held till his death in 1821. He embark on collecting local histories and surveying historic sites in order to better understand India's past and make governance of the colony easier. He says that "it struggled long under the miseries of bad management... before the South came under the benign influence of the British government". By studying Vijayanagara, Mackenzie believed that the East India Company could gain "much useful information on many of these institutions, laws and customs whose influence still prevails among the various Tribes of Natives forming the general mass of the population to this day".

36. Who was Colin Mackenzie?
A. Colin Mackenzie became famous as an engineer, surveyor and cartographer.
B. In 1815, he was appointed as the first Surveyor General of India.
C. Mackenzie collected information about local histories and surveyed historic sites are no benefit for Britishers.
D. Both (A) and (B) correct

37. Mackenzie collected information about local histories and surveyed historic sites, make governance of the colony easier. Who got benefited with this?
A. It helped Britishers to better understand India's past customs and traditions.
B. It helped to East India Company to govern their colony in an easy manner.
C. Both (A) and (B) are correct.
D. Both (A) and (B) are wrong.

38. According to him what benefits would the East India Company gain after studying Vijayanagara?
A. This knowledge certainly helped the government officials to rule the general masses.
B. The East India Company became aware about the various Tribes of Natives forming the general mass of the population of India.
C. Studying the important information about Vijayanagara regarding laws and customs.
D. All the above

39. What were the problems faced by Colin Mackenzie?
A. He says that "it struggled long under the miseries of bad management".
B. He belongs to Germany.
C. He was the famous Navigator.
D. He came to India for study Sanskrit, and he feel Sanskrit was easy subject.

PASSAGE-9

Krishnadeva Raya (ruled 1509-29), the most famous ruler of Vijayanagara, composed a work on statecraft in Telugu known as the Amuktamalyada. About traders he wrote : A king should improve the harbours of his country and so encourage its commerce that horses, elephants, precious gems, sandalwood, pearls and other articles are freely imported. He should arrange that the foreign sailors who land in his country on account of storms, illness and exhaustion are looked after in a suitable manner... Make the merchants of distant foreign countries who import elephants and good horses be attached to yourself by providing them with daily audience, presents and allowing decent profits. Then those articles will never go to your enemies.

40. Who was the most famous ruler of Vijayanagara?
A. Krishnadeva Raya was the most famous ruler of Vijayanagara.
B. Rama Raya was the most famous ruler of Vijayanagara.
C. Bukka Raya was the most famous ruler of Vijayanagara.
D. Amara-nayakas were military commanders, They were most famous

41. Explain the responsibilities of king mentioned by Krishnadeva Raya.
A. He should encourage commerce so that horses, elephants freely imported.
B. A king should improve the harbours of his country. Then he planned good horses will never go to your enemies.
C. Precious gems, sandalwood, pearls and other articles are freely imported.
D. All the above

42. Explain the measures taken by the king to improve the conditions of his country.
A. He encouraged free import of horses, elephants, precious gems,
B. He also gave them precious presents to merchants.
C. He made extensive arrangements could get decent profits.
D. All the above three are correct.

43. Mention the name and theme of the work compiled by him.
A. Krishnadeva Raya composed a work in Telugu known as Amuktamalyada. The main theme of this work was a statecraft.
B. Aliya Rama Raya composed a work in Telugu known as Amuktamalyada.
C. Only (A) correct
D. Only (B) correct

44. The Vijayanagara King, Krishnadeva Raya ruled from _______ to _______.
A. 1509 to 1529 B. 1519 to 1530
C. 1540 to 1551 D. 1531 to 1560

45. Who founded Vijianagara Empire?
A. Harihara
B. Bukka
C. Harihara & Bukka
D. Basava

PASSAGE-10

Although Harappa was the first site to be discovered it was badly destroyed by brick Robbers. As early as 1875, Alexander Cunningham, the First Director General of the Archaeological Survey of India (ASI), often called the Father of Indian Archaeology, noted that the amount of bricks taken from the ancient site was enough to lay bricks for "about 100 miles" of the railway line between Lahore and Multan. Thus, many of the ancient structures at the site were damaged. In contrast, Mohenjodaro was far better preserved.

46. The Harappan site was badly destroyed by ______.
A. Natural Calamities
B. Brick Robbers
C. Engineers
D. Animals

47. Who was Alexander Cunningham?
A. Doctor
B. Engineer
C. Player
D. First Director General of the Archaeological Survey of India (ASI)

48. Who was called as the Father of Indian Archeology?
A. Alexander Cunningham
B. Alexander
C. J.A. Smith
D. Colin Mackenzie

49. Compared to Harappa ______ was far better preserved.
A. Mohenjadero B. Lothal
C. Kalibangan D. Ropar

PASSAGE-11

About the drains, Mackay noted: "It is certainly the most complete ancient system as yet discovered." Every house was connected to the street drains. The main channels were made of bricks set in mortar and were covered with loose bricks that could be removed for cleaning. In some cases, limestone was used for the covers. House drains first emptied into a sump or cesspit into which solid matter settled while waste water flowed out into the street drains. Very long drainage channels were provided at intervals with sumps for cleaning. It is a wonder of archaeology that "little heaps of material, mostly sand, have frequently been found lying alongside drainage channels, which shows ... that the debris was not always carried away when the drain was cleared".

Drainage systems were not unique to the larger cities, but were found in smaller settlements as well. At Lothal for example, while houses were built of mud bricks, drains were made of burnt bricks.

50. Where were the drainage systems found?
A. Larger cities B. Small settlements
C. Huts D. Citadels

51. Lothal is located in ______.
A. Madhya Pradesh B. Gujarat
C. Karnataka D. Andhra Pradesh

52. The drains were built of ______.
A. Burnt bricks B. Clay
C. Dried bricks D. Stones

PASSAGE-12

A large building found at Mohenjodaro was labelled a palace by as archaeologists but no spectacular finds were associated with it. A stone statue was labelled and continues to be known as the "priest-king". This is because archaeologists familiar with Mesopotamian history and its "priest-kings" and have found parallels in the Indus region.

53. With what name was the stone statue identified?
A. Tree B. Lion
C. Buffalo D. Priest King

54. Name the contemporary of Mohenjadaro civilization.
A. Greek B. Mesopotamian
C. Chinese D. Roman

55. Name the site of Bronze age civilization in India?
A. Bombay B. Calcutta
C. Delhi D. Lothal

PASSAGE-13

Here is an excerpt from the account of Megasthenes: Of the great officers of state, some ... superintend the rivers, measure the land, as is done in Egypt, and inspect the sluices by which water is let out from the main canals into their branches, so that every one may have an equal supply of it. The same persons have charge also of the huntsmen, and are entrusted with the power of rewarding or punishing them according to their deserts. They collect the taxes, and superintend the occupations connected with land; as those of the woodcutters, the carpenters, the blacksmiths, and the miners.

56. What is Indica?
A. Indica is an account of Guptas by the Greek writer Megasthenes.
B. Indica is an account of Mauryas by the Greek writer Megasthenes
C. Indica is an account of Kushanas by the Greek writer Megasthenes
D. Indica is an account of Cholas by the Greek writer Megasthenes

57. Who sent Megasthenes to India
A. Seleucus II
B. Seleucus I
C. Alexander the Great
D. None of them

PASSAGE-14

This is an excerpt from the Prayaga Prashasti: He was without an antagonist on earth; he, by the overflowing of the multitude of (his) many good qualities adorned by hundreds of good actions, has wiped off the fame of other kings with the soles of (his) feet; (he is) Purusha (the Supreme Being), being the cause of the prosperity of the good and the destruction of the bad (he is) incomprehensible; (he is) one whose tender heart can be captured only by devotion and humility; (he is) possessed of compassion; (he is) the giver of many hundred-thousands of cows; (his) mind has received ceremonial initiation for the uplift of the miserable, the poor, the forlorn and the suffering; (he is) resplendent and embodied kindness to mankind; (he is) equal to (the gods) Kubera (the god of wealth), Varuna (the god of the ocean), Indra (the god of rains) and Yama (the god of death)...

58. Where does this excerpt is taken from
A. Aihole Prashasti B. Kalinga Prashasti
C. Hatigumpha D. Prayaga Prashasti

59. What is the present name of Prayaga
A. Prayagraj B. Allahabad
C. Ayodhya D. Lucknow

PASSAGE-15

The revolt of 1857 was much more than a mere product of sepoy discontent. It was in reality a product of accumulated grievances against the company's administration, a popular discontent and hatred against foreign rule. The most important cause was the economic exploitation, the complete destruction of its traditional economic fabric, the impoverishment of the vast mass of peasants, artisans and handicraftsmen as also a large number of traditional zamindars and chiefs. As a result of the British land and revenue policies and the system of Judicial administration, a large number of peasant proprietors lost their land to traders and moneylenders and found themselves in utter debt. In addition, the common people were hard hit by corruption even at the lower levels of administration. The complex judicial system enabled the rich to oppress-the poor and the growing poverty made them desperate. The middle and upper classes of Indian society suffered by their exclusion from higher positions in the administration. Displacement of Indian rulers led to the loss of patronage to the men of arts and culture and also to the religious preachers--Pandits and Maulvis, who played an important role in spreading discontent against the government. Besides, Lord Dalhousie's policy of annexations of native states by applying the 'Doctrine of Lapse' was widely resented. Lastly, the conversion activites by the Christian missionaries created fear and suspicion among the general public.

60. Choose the correct option from the following:
A. Due to various land and revenue policies, Indian peasants became rich
B. British land and revenue policies led to the indebtedness of Indian peasants
C. The judicial system helped the poor to rise against their oppressors
D. Traditional Zamindars and chiefs were favourably dealt-with by the British

61. From among the following who adopted the policy of 'Doctrine of Lapse'?
A. Lord Canning B. Lord Curzon
C. Lord Dalhousie D. Lord Wellesley

62. Which one of the following states was ***not*** annexed under the 'Doctrine of Lapse'?
A. Udaipur B. Baghat
C. Sambalpur D. Awadh

63. Who among the following considers the revolt of 1857, merely a 'sepoy mutiny'?
A. Eric Stokes B. John W. Kay
C. R.C. Majumdar D. S.N. Sen

PASSAGE-16

These ships [plying in Arabian Sea] are wretched affairs, and many of them get lost; for they have no iron fastenings, and are only stitched together with twine made from the husk of the Indian nut. They beat this husk until it becomes like horse-hair, and from that they spin twine, and with this stitch the planks of the ships together. It keeps well, and is not corroded with the sea-water, but it will not stand well in a storm. The ships are not pitched, but are rubbed with fish-oil. They have mast, sail and rudder, and have no deck, but only a cover spread over the cargo when loaded. This cover consists of hides, and on the top of these hides they put the horses, which they take (from Hormuz) to India for sale. They have no iron to make nails of, and for this reason they use only wooden tree-nails in their ship-building, and then stitch the planks with twine as I have told you. Hence it is a perilous business to go on a voyage in one of those ships, and many of them are lost, for in the Sea of India the storms are often terrible.

64. According to Marco Polo, Indian ships normally had how many masts?
A. Two B. Five
C. One D. Three

65. Marco Polo complains about the absence of the iron nails. Which of the following seventeenth century traveller also complains of the absence of use of lathe to cut the screw groves?
A. Tavernier B. Manucci
C. Bernier D. Thevenot

66. Marco Polo while complaining that Indian ships had only a cover spread over the cargo when loaded, was complaining about the absence of the following?
A. Gudgeon B. Pintle
C. Steering oar D. Decks

67. In the Indian ships, in joining planks, which of the following techniques was used?
- A. Rabbeting or tongue-and-groove technique
- B. Caulking
- C. Carvelling
- D. Clinker technique

PASSAGE-17

Chaturvedin (Brahmana versed in the four Vedas) and the 'outcaste'

This is an excerpt from a composition of an Alvar named Tondaradippodi, who was a Brahmana: You (Vishnu) manifestly like those 'servants' who express their love for your feet, though they may be born outcastes, more than the Chaturvedins who are strangers and without allegiance to your service.

68. Who was Tondaradippodi?
- A. Alvar B. Nayanar
- C. Buddhist D. Jain

69. Who are Alvars?
- A. Worshippers of Vishnu
- B. Worshippers of Shiva
- C. Worshippers of Buddha
- D. Worshippers of Mahaveera

PASSAGE-18

Rituals and the Real World

Here is a vachana composed by Basavanna:
When they see a serpent carved in stone, they pour milk on it.
If a real serpent comes they say 'kill. Kill.'
To the servant of the god who could eat if served they say: 'Go away! Go away!'
But to the image of the god which cannot eat they offer dishes of food.

70. Who was Basavanna?
- A. Founder of Virashaivism
- B. Founder of Vaishnavism
- C. Founder of Shaivism
- D. Founder of Buddhism

71. With what name were the followers of Virashaivism called?
- A. Monks B. Nayanars
- C. Ulemas D. Lingayats

PASSAGE-19

Love for the Lord

This is part of a song attributed to Mirabai:
I will build a funeral pyre of sandalwood and aloe,
Light it by your own hand
When I am burned away to cinders;
Smear this ash upon your limbs.
... let flame be lost in flame.
In another verse, she sings:
What can Mewar's ruler do to me?
If God is angry, all is lost,
But what can the Rana do?

72. Who was Meera Bai?
- A. Rajput princess from Merta in Marwar
- B. Rajput princess of Gwalior
- C. Rajput princess of Jhansi
- D. Rajput princess of Delhi

73. To which god did she worship?
- A. Lord Krishna B. Lord Shiva
- C. Buddha D. Mahaveera

ANSWERS

1	2	3	4	5	6	7	8	9	10
B	B	C	D	D	C	B	A	B	D
11	**12**	**13**	**14**	**15**	**16**	**17**	**18**	**19**	**20**
A	A	C	B	C	D	B	A	D	B
21	**22**	**23**	**24**	**25**	**26**	**27**	**28**	**29**	**30**
C	A	C	D	C	B	B	C	A	C
31	**32**	**33**	**34**	**35**	**36**	**37**	**38**	**39**	**40**
A	C	A	B	B	D	C	D	A	A
41	**42**	**43**	**44**	**45**	**46**	**47**	**48**	**49**	**50**
D	D	C	A	C	B	D	A	A	B
51	**52**	**53**	**54**	**55**	**56**	**57**	**58**	**59**	**60**
B	A	D	D	D	B	B	D	A	B
61	**62**	**63**	**64**	**65**	**66**	**67**	**68**	**69**	**70**
C	D	B	C	D	D	A	A	A	A
71	**72**	**73**							
D	A	A							

POLITICAL SCIENCE

Political Theory

1. Who among the following defines political science as the study of "the act of human and social control" or the "study of control relationship of wills"?
A. Robson B. Pollock
C. Maitland D. Catlin

2. ______ is the parent science of all the social sciences.
A. Sociology B. History
C. Philosophy D. None of the above

3. Which of the following deals with morality and formulates rules which should influence the behaviour of man while living in society?
A. Philosophy B. Ethics
C. Sociology D. None of the above

4. Ethics is concerned with man as a man and as such, it is prior to:
A. Society B. Science
C. Political Science D. History

5. Who among the following prominent writers has given psychological explanations of almost all the political problems?
A. Le Bon B. Baldwin
C. Graham Wallas D. All of the above

6. Political scientists have borrowed such ideas as 'cultural relativism', 'social evolution', 'cultural diffusion' from:
A. Anthropology B. Sociology
C. Philosophy D. Economics

7. Who among the following said that politics has its roots, psychologically, in the study of mental habits and vocational activities of mankind?
A. Barker B. Plato
C. Bryce D. Wallas

8. Ivor Brown points out that economics deals mainly with _____ and politics is concerned with _____ .
A. wealth, government
B. business, state
C. commodities, human beings
D. production, administration

9. Which of the following theories of the origin of the state was accepted by liberalism?
A. Pluralist theory B. Marxist theory
C. Historical theory D. Institutional theory

10. Which of the following views believes that the state originated with class division and class struggle in society?
A. Liberal view B. Marxist view
C. Pluralist view D. Traditional view

11. "It is not the consciousness of man which determines the material conditions of life but it is material conditions of life which determine their consciousness" – this statement is given by:
A. Gettell B. Karl Marx
C. Galbraith D. Catlin

12. "Politics is that part of social science which treats of the foundations of state and the principles of government". Who made this statement?
A. Willoughby B. Seeley
C. Paul Janet D. S.L. Wasby

13. Guild and Palmer strongly pleaded that the subject of politics should be:
A. The political parties
B. To secure obedience
C. Negative
D. Power instead of the state

14. The Father of modern sociology, A. Comte, portrayed society as a potentially harmonious and ordered structure in which all social classes
A. worked for social change
B. worked for the common good
C. worked for the individual
D. worked for capitalists

15. Socialist states are based on marxian ideology and are known as the:
A. Blue world B. Green world
C. Red world D. Yellow world

16. Who among the following considers Marxism to be an ideology rather than a political theory?
A. Germino B. David Held
C. R.A. Dahl D. G.H. Sabine

17. Arrange the following works of Isaiah Berlin in chronological order of his publications.

Select the correct answer from the codes given below:
(*a*) Concepts and Categories : Philosophical Essays
(*b*) Four Essays on Liberty

(*c*) Vico and Herder : Two Studies in the History of Ideas
(*d*) Karl Marx : His Life and Environment

Codes:

A. (*a*), (*b*), (*c*) and (*d*) B. (*c*), (*b*), (*a*) and (*d*)
C. (*d*), (*b*), (*c*) and (*a*) D. (*b*), (*d*), (*a*) and (*c*)

18. Who among the following said that political theory stands for an abstract model of the political order?

A. T.P. Jenkin B. R.A. Dahl
C. W.T. Bluhm D. Weinstein

19. Which one of the following statements is not true?

A. Classical political theory is qualitative.
B. Behavioural political theory is quantitative.
C. Post-behavioural political theory is both qualitative and quantitative.
D. Behavioural theory is not specially concerned with Anglo-American model.

20. Which one of the following statements is not true?

A. Neo-liberalism refers to significant revival of interest in classical liberalism.
B. Neo-liberal ideas were taken up by the political parties of the New Right in Britain.
C. The revival of classical liberalism occurred as a reaction against the onset of a world recession in the 1970s.
D. T.H. Green accepted the classical liberal notion of liberty only.

21. Who among the following said that ideology should neither be thought of as liberating or oppressive, nor as true or false. It can be any these things?

A. Andrew Heywood
B. John Rawls
C. Andrew Gamble
D. Bill Coxall

22. For Locke, which of the following statements is not true?

(*a*) The state must be a constitutional state.
(*b*) Government must possess discretionary power.
(*c*) It is a tolerant state.
(*d*) The right to property is not a natural right.

Select the correct answer from the codes given below:

A. (*a*) and (*c*) B. (*a*) and (*b*)
C. (*b*) only D. (*d*) only

23. For Rousseau, which of the following statements is not true?

(*a*) Two original instincts *i.e.*, self-love and sympathy make up man's nature.
(*b*) A thinking man is a depraved animal.
(*c*) Family is the only natural society.
(*d*) General will is not a group mind.

Select the correct answer from the codes given below:

A. (*a*) and (*b*) B. (*b*) and (*c*)
C. (*c*) only D. (*d*) only

24. For J.S. Mill, which of the following statements is not true?

(*a*) Pleasures differ in quality as well as in quantity.
(*b*) Mill makes use of the non-utilitarian arguments.
(*c*) The felicific calculus is absurd.
(*d*) Pleasures can be objectively measured.

Select the correct answer from the codes given below:

A. (*b*) and (*c*) B. (*a*) and (*b*)
C. (*a*), (*b*) and (*c*) D. (*d*) only

25. Match the following:

List-I	List-II
(*a*) Modern political thinker	(*i*) Plato
(*b*) Positivist school	(*ii*) Machiavelli
(*c*) Normative political theory	(*iii*) August Comte
(*d*) Scientific/inductive method	(*iv*) Aristotle

Codes:

	(*a*)	(*b*)	(*c*)	(*d*)
A.	(*ii*)	(*iii*)	(*i*)	(*iv*)
B.	(*ii*)	(*iv*)	(*i*)	(*iii*)
C.	(*i*)	(*ii*)	(*iv*)	(*iii*)
D.	(*iv*)	(*i*)	(*iii*)	(*ii*)

26. Match the items of List-I with items of List-II by selecting the **correct** answer from the codes :

List-I (Thinkers)	List-II (Theories)
(*a*) Mao Tse Tung	(*i*) Proletarian Dictatorship
(*b*) Lenin	(*ii*) Cultural Revolution
(*c*) Marx	(*iii*) One Country Socialism
(*d*) Stalin	(*iv*) Communist Party as the Vanguard of the proletariat

Codes:

	(*a*)	(*b*)	(*c*)	(*d*)
A.	(*ii*)	(*iv*)	(*i*)	(*iii*)
B.	(*iii*)	(*i*)	(*iv*)	(*ii*)
C.	(*iv*)	(*ii*)	(*i*)	(*iii*)
D.	(*ii*)	(*iv*)	(*iii*)	(*i*)

27. Rearrange the following works of Karl Marx in sequential order in terms of Publication Year.

(*a*) Critique of Political Economy
(*b*) Poverty of Philosophy
(*c*) Communist Manifesto
(*d*) The Holy Family

Codes:

A. (*d*), (*b*), (*c*) and (*a*) B. (*a*), (*c*), (*d*) and (*b*)
C. (*b*), (*a*), (*d*) and (*c*) D. (*d*), (*c*), (*b*) and (*a*)

28. Communitarian theory lays emphasis on:
A. Community as an inescapable ideal
B. Unlimited freedom of the individual
C. Limited role of the state
D. Partial regulation of market economy

29. Given below are the two statements, one labelled as Assertion (A) and the other labelled as Reason (R). Select the **correct** answer from the codes given below.
Assertion (A) : Behavioural political theory sought to eliminate the role of values and make Political Science a pure science and quantitative.
Reason (R) : Political Science, being a social science, can never be value-free as it deals with human beings who are value-bound.
A. Both (A) and (R) are true and (R) is the correct explanation of (A).
B. Both (A) and (R) are true and (R) is not the correct explanation of (A).
C. (A) is true, but (R) is false.
D. (A) is false, but (R) is true.

30. Which of the following were described by David Easton as intellectual foundations of the System Analysis? Give the correct answer from the codes given below:
(*a*) Regularities (*b*) Verification
(*c*) Techniques (*d*) Quantification
Codes:
A. (*a*) B. (*a*), (*b*)
C. (*a*), (*b*), (*c*) D. (*a*), (*b*), (*c*), (*d*)

31. Who among the following referred to the 'decline' of political theory?
(*a*) David Easton and Alfred Cobbon
(*b*) Lasslett and Robert Dahl
(*c*) Will Durant
(*d*) Nathenial Hawthorn
A. (*b*) and (*c*) B. (*c*) and (*d*)
C. (*a*) and (*c*) D. (*a*) and (*b*)

32. Which of the following statements relating to Mao's theory of contradictions are **true?**
(*a*) Contradictions are universal in all times and in all societies.
(*b*) Antagonistic contradictions exist among the hostile classes in terms of ownership of productive forces.
(*c*) Non-antagonistic contradictions could exist among people which could be resolved without resorting to violence.
(*d*) Contradictions have no place in a socialist system.
Choose the **correct** answer from the below:
A. (*d*) and (*a*) B. (*b*) and (*d*)
C. (*a*), (*b*) and (*c*) D. (*a*), (*b*), (*c*) and (*d*)

33. Given below are two statements one labelled as Assertion (A) and the other labelled as Reason (R).
Assertion (A) : For John Locke, Natural Rights are a product of nature.
Reason (R) : State has to protect and safeguard these rights.
A. Both (A) and (R) are true and (R) is the right explanation of (A)
B. Both (A) and (R) are true, but (R) is not the right explanation of (A)
C. (A) is true, but (R) is false
D. (A) is false, but (R) is true

34. John Locke's contribution chiefly lies in his:
(*a*) Consent theory.
(*b*) Limited Government.
(*c*) Theory of state as a corporate body.
(*d*) Organic conception of state.
Select the **correct** answer from the codes given below:
A. (*a*) and (*d*)
B. (*a*) and (*c*)
C. (*b*) and (*c*)
D. (*a*) and (*b*)

35. Dialectical materialism of Karl Marx postulates that:
(*a*) Matter is in a state of motion.
(*b*) Motion in the matter is due to the pressure of environment.
(*c*) Law of transformation is both quantitative and qualitative.
(*d*) Conflict in matter is continuous and endless.
Identify the **correct** answer:
A. (*a*), (*b*) and (*d*) B. (*a*) and (*c*)
C. (*b*) and (*d*) D. (*c*) and (*d*)

36. Which of the following statement is **correct** regarding J.S. Mill?
(*a*) State is justified in confirming itself to limited functions
(*b*) Welfare policies are more important.
(*c*) State intervention into 'self-regarding' action.
(*d*) State intervention into 'other regarding action' is justified.
Choose the **correct** answer:
A. (*b*) and (*c*) B. (*a*) and (*b*)
C. (*a*) only D. (*d*) only

37. The Magna Carta, the Glorious Revolution and the writings of John Locke all contributed to the strengthening of Great Britain:
A. Absolute Monarchy
B. Ethnic Rivalaries
C. Parliamentary Democracy
D. Imperialist Policies

38. Which one of the following is **not** a factor, for Fukuyama, leading to the triumph of liberal democracy?
A. The struggle for 'recognition'.
B. The logic of science's mastery over nature.
C. The absence of major contradictions in liberal democracy.
D. The triumph of liberalism is more in terms of economics than ideologies.

39. Who among the following said, "Post-behaviouralism was a genuine revolution, not a reaction; a becoming, not a preservation; a reform, not a counter reformation"?
A. James Bryce B. Charles E. Merriam
C. David Easton D. G.A. Almond

40. Who among the following said, 'We can not shed our values in the way we remove our coats'?
A. Leo Strauss B. Alfred Cobban
C. Jean Blondel D. David Easton

41. Who among the following characterised early liberalism as 'possessive individualism'?
A. F.A. Hayek B. Robert Nozick
C. C.B. MacPherson D. Rawls

42. Given below are two statements, one labelled as Assertion (A) and the other labelled as Reason (R). Identify the correct answer.
Assertion (A) : F.A. Hayek portrayed state intervention and collectivism, even in their moderate forms, as inevitably leading to an erosion of Liberty.
Reason (R) : He is a supporter of *laissez faire* and opponent of Keynesian economics and the welfare state.

Codes:
A. Both (A) and (R) are true and (R) is the correct explanation of (A).
B. Both (A) and (R) are true, but (R) is not the correct explanation of (A)
C. (A) is true, but (R) is false
D. (A) is false, but (R) is true

43. Which one of the following statements is not true?
A. Marx drew distinction between 'ideology' and 'science'.
B. Napoleon denounced ideology as cloudy metaphysics that ignored history and reality.
C. de Tracy coined the term ideology.
D. Daniel Bell talked of 'ideology without an end'.

44. For whom, "ideas" and not the "material conditions of production" are the effective causes of revolution?
A. Karl Marx B. Lenin
C. Engels D. Stalin

45. Who of the following said that felicity is "continued success in obtaining those things which a man from time to time desires"?
A. Bentham B. J.S. Mill
C. Hobbes D. Rousseau

46. Which of the following is not an idea of Rousseau?
A. A thinking man is a depraved animal
B. Science is the fruit of idle curiosity
C. Philosophy is mere intellectual frippery
D. General will is the sum total of wills

47. For J.S. Mill which one of the following is not true?
A. Pleasures differ in quality
B. The felicific calculus is absurd
C. The principle of utility is the final end of life
D. Liberty consists in doing what one desires

48. For Karl Marx, who among the following is not a Utopian socialist?
A. St. Simon B. Proudhon
C. Fourier D. Engels

49. Given below are two statements, one labelled as Assertion (A) and other labelled as Reason (R). Select the correct answer from the codes given below:
Assertion (A) : For Gandhiji, Satyagraha is not identical to passive resistance.
Reason (R) : Satyagraha denoted a legitimate, moral and truthful form of political action by the people against the Brutal state power.

Codes:
A. Both (A) and (R) are true and (R) is the correct explanation of (A)
B. Both (A) and (R) are true, but (R) is not the correct explanation of (A)
C. (A) is true, but (R) is false
D. (A) is false, but (R) is true

50. Who coined the slogan "No control, no co-operation"?
A. Mahatma Gandhi B. J.L. Nehru
C. Aurobindo D. Subhash Chandra Bose

51. Who among the following stated that, "Every State is known by the rights that it maintains"?
A. Harold J. Laski B. T.H. Green
C. Immanuel Kant D. Tom Paine

52. The chief exponent of Scientific Socialism is/are?
A. Karl Marx
B. Fredrick Engels
C. Both A & B
D. Neither A & B

53. Who is the author of Grammar of Politics?
A. Mill B. Rousseau
C. Lasswell D. Laski

54. "State is known by the rights that it maintains" who said?
A. Russel B. Woodrow Wilson
C. Janet D. Laski

55. Who is the author of Proposed Roads to Freedom?
A. Russel B. Tolstoy
C. Bryce D. Leacock

56. Maine authored the book
A. The History of Institutions
B. Democracy and Liberty
C. Social Contract
D. Political Science and Government

57. Who defined "Liberty is the opposite of over government"?
A. Seeley B. J.S. Mill
C. Gramsci D. Marx

58. Which is known as the birth place of democracy?
A. Athens B. America
C. India D. Switzerland

59. Direct democracy is now practice in
A. Cantons of Switzerland
B. States of India
C. States of America
D. England

60. Who among the following analyses liberty as a triadic relationship in the defined manner-X is free from Y to do or become (or not to do or become) Z?
A. Gerald Mac Callum B. Milton Friedman
C. Robert Nozick D. Isaiah Berlin

61. Who among the following discussed two types of liberty as Opportunity Concept of Freedom (Negative Liberty) Exercise Concept of Freedom (Positive Liberty)?
A. Robert Nozick B. Milton Friedman
C. Charles Taylor D. Harold Laski

62. The book "The Constitution of Liberty" (1960) is written by who among the following?
A. Isaiah Berlin B. Steven Lukes
C. Ronald Dworkin D. F.A. Hayek

63. Social primary goods according to John Rawls refers to:
A. goods are distributed by the basic structure of a society
B. include rights and liberties, powers and opportunities, and income and wealth
C. distribution of "social primary goods" to all the members of society in a fair or just manner
D. All the above

64. "Original position" is under a "Veil of ignorance" is a concept developed by whom among the following?
A. Robert. A. Dahl B. Gramsci
C. A.B. Hall D. John Rawls

65. Who among the following identifies power with domination in conceptual, methodological and political terms?
A. Michael Foucault B. Steven Lukes
C. Edward Banfield D. V. Pareto

66. Two conclusions emerge from the power perspective: the one who exercises the power had the option or the alternative to act differently; and those on whom the power had the option or the alternative to act differently, if power was not exercised over them-The statement is made by who among the following?
A. Robert Dahl B. Delbert Miller
C. Steven Lukes D. Edward Banfield

67. Social Citizenship refers to
A. right to participate in an appropriate standard of living
B. right to participate in the exercise of political power
C. more than one country and culture
D. the police and defence forces are coercive structures of the state

68. Multiculturalism aims at:
A. accommodating diverse identity groups into a homogeneous society
B. state has been conflated with nation in their conceptualization
C. autonomy and self-governing rights
D. equality before the law

69. Match List-I of Authors with List-II of Books:

List-I (Authors)	List-II (Books)
(*a*) T.H. Marshall	(*i*) Citizenship and Social Class (1950)
(*b*) R. Bendix	(*ii*) Nation-Building and Citizenship (1964)
(*c*) Robert Nozick	(*iii*) Anarchy, State, and Utopia (1974)
(*d*) Willy Kymlicka	(*iv*) Multicultural Citizenship: A Liberal Theory of Minority (1997)

Select the correct code the options given below:

	(*a*)	(*b*)	(*c*)	(*d*)
A.	(*iv*)	(*i*)	(*ii*)	(*iii*)
B.	(*iii*)	(*iv*)	(*i*)	(*ii*)
C.	(*ii*)	(*iii*)	(*iv*)	(*i*)
D.	(*i*)	(*ii*)	(*iii*)	(*iv*)

70. The concept of multiculturalism was prevalent since
A. ancient times
B. medieval times
C. modern times
D. post-modern times

71. Will Kymlicka argues for
   A. group differentiated rights
   B. racism and ethnic cleansing
   C. collapse of the European colonial system
   D. multicultural in a descriptive sense

72. The book "Reflections on the Revolution in France" was written by whom among the following conservative thinker?
   A. Edmund Burke (1993)
   B. Michael Oakeshot (1962)
   C. James Alexander (2014)
   D. Andrew Heywood (2007)

73. Who among the following has written on "Citizenship and Social Class"?
   A. Marshall McLuhan B. T.H. Marshall
   C. Manuel Castells D. Anthoni Giddens

74. The word "citizen" was made popular by which of the following revolution of the world
   A. French Revolution in 1789
   B. Glorious Revolution, 1689
   C. American War of Independence, 1776
   D. None of these

75. Why "Melting Pot" in United States is famous?
   A. all the immigrant cultures are mixed and amalgamated without state intervention
   B. not to facilitate immigrants and others to preserve their cultures
   C. culture is very closely linked to nationalism
   D. resurgence of people's movements against the totalitarian

76. Capitalism is the primary cause of environmental degradation-who said this?
   A. Habermas B. Medha Patkar
   C. Arundhoti Ray D. Anna Hazare

77. The Dialectic of Sex: The Case for Feminist Revolution (1970) is a work of
   A. Shulamith Firestone B. Roxanne Dunbar
   C. Naomi Weisstein D. Judith Brown

78. Radical feminists movement was started in which of the following countries?
   A. United States B. United Kingdom
   C. Australia D. All A, B & C

79. Nation-Building and Citizenship (1964) is a book written by who among the following political philosopher?
   A. R. Bendix B. Bryan S. Turner
   C. Jack Barbalet D. Charles Taylor

80. Burke's 'Reflections on the Revolution in France' has been taken as definitive and fortunate of:
   A. Traditional Conservatism
   B. Medieval Conservatism
   C. Modern Conservatism
   D. None of these

ANSWERS

1	2	3	4	5	6	7	8	9	10
D	A	B	C	D	A	C	C	C	B
11	12	13	14	15	16	17	18	19	20
B	C	D	B	C	A	C	C	D	D
21	22	23	24	25	26	27	28	29	30
A	D	D	D	A	A	A	A	B	D
31	32	33	34	35	36	37	38	39	40
D	C	A	D	A	D	C	D	C	D
41	42	43	44	45	46	47	48	49	50
C	A	D	B	C	D	C	D	A	C
51	52	53	54	55	56	57	58	59	60
A	A	D	D	A	A	A	A	A	A
61	62	63	64	65	66	67	68	69	70
C	D	D	D	A	D	A	A	D	A
71	72	73	74	75	76	77	78	79	80
A	A	B	A	A	A	A	D	A	C

Political Institutions in India

1. A special session of the Constituent Assembly was held at midnight on 14-15 August, 1947 in connection with the:
A. Independence resolution
B. Partition of India
C. Transfer of Power
D. None of the above

2. Which committee was appointed to prepare guidelines for the Constituent Assembly?
A. Drafting Committee
B. Congress Expert Committee
C. Advisory Committee
D. Union Powers Committee

3. Which committee was set up to prepare a draft constitution on August 29, 1947?
A. Staff Committee
B. Union Constitution Committee
C. Drafting Committee
D. Union Powers Committee

4. The elections to the Constituent Assembly were held in:
A. June, 1946 B. July, 1946
C. August, 1946 D. July, 1947

5. Which of the following is included in the Committees on procedural Affairs?
A. Training and Staff Committee
B. Credentials Committee
C. Hindi Translation Committee
D. All of the above

6. The elections to the Constituent Assembly were:
A. Indirect B. Held Twice
C. Direct D. None of the above

7. Fundamental duties have been introduced in the Constitution by:
A. 42nd Amendment Act, 1976
B. 44th Amendment Act, 1978
C. 73rd Amendment Act, 1993
D. None of the above

8. The Dominion Status of India was established under:
A. Government of India Act, 1919
B. Government of India Act, 1935
C. Both A and B
D. Indian Independence Act, 1947

9. Protection of Civil Rights Act, 1955 pertains to:
A. Human Rights B. Citizenship
C. Untouchability D. Freedom of expression

10. According to the Constituent Assembly Debates Directive principles is merely another name for the:
A. Bill of Rights
B. Human Rights Character
C. Instruments of Instructions
D. Governmental Accountability

11. Which Article of the Constitution states that the state shall organise village panchayats as units of self-government?
A. Article 43 B. Article 40
C. Article 45 D. Article 42

12. The case of Gopalan vs. State of Madras was relevant to:
A. Article 21 B. Article 12
C. Article 16 D. Article 14

13. How can a citizen protect his Fundamental Rights?
A. By a writ in the Supreme Court of India
B. By approaching the President of India
C. Through police action
D. They are already protected

14. Which of the following is not a Fundamental Right?
A. Right against exploitation
B. Equal pay for equal work
C. Equality before law
D. Right to freedom of religion

15. An interpretation of the Indian Constitution is based on the spirit of the:
A. Preamble B. Fundamental Duties
C. Fundamental Rights D. None of the above

16. Right to property has been eliminated from the fundamental rights by:
A. 42nd Constitutional Amendment Act of 1976
B. 44th Constitutional Amendment Act of 1978
C. 43rd Constitutional Amendment Act of 1977
D. 24th Constitutional Amendment Act of 1971

17. Fundamental duties enjoin upon a person to respect:
A. Mother Tongue B. National Flag
C. National Anthem D. Both B and C

18. It is a Fundamental Duty of a citizen of India to develop:
A. Her or his economic status and social standing
B. The understanding between different communities
C. Scientific temper and spirit of enquiry
D. All of the above

19. Special provision for the protection of children is made in:
A. Article 23 B. Article 24
C. Article 39(b) D. All of these

20. 'Equality before the law', is an expression of:
A. English Common law
B. French Administrative law
C. American Constitutional law
D. None of the above

21. Which of the following statements are true?
1. The Home Minister is the defacto chairperson of NDMA.
2. NDMA is an agency of the Ministry of Home Affairs.
3. It is a statutory body established by Disaster Management Act enacted by the Government of India in December, 2005.
A. 1, 2 B. 2, 3
C. 1, 3 D. All the above

22. Which of the following statements is/are true?
1. The Finance Act gives effect to financial proposals at the beginning of every Financial Year.
2. The Finance Act for a particular financial year also includes the amendments that have been made with respect to Direct Taxes.
A. Only 1 B. Only 2
C. Both 1 and 2 D. None of these

23. Which of the following statements are true?
1. The Rajya Sabha may amend money bills.
2. Money bill must be returned to the Lok Sabha within 14 days or the bill is deemed to have passed by the both houses in the form it was originally passed by the Lok Sabha.
3. Money bill cannot be returned by the President to the Parliament for its reconsideration, he has to give his assent to the bill or can withhold his assent.
A. 1, 2 B. 2, 3
C. 1, 3 D. All the above

24. Who certifies a bill as a money bill?
A. President
B. Prime Minister
C. Speaker of the Lok Sabha
D. Finance Minister

25. Which of the following statements are incorrect?
1. Jnanpith Award is the most prestigious literary honour in the country along with Sahitya Akademi Award.
2. It is given for a Magnum opus produced by a writer.
3. Any writer who writes in any of the official languages of India is eligible for this honour.
A. 1, 2 B. 2, 3
C. 1, 3 D. All the above

26. Which of the following statements are true?
1. Nai Roshni is a scheme for Leadership Development of Minority Women launched in 2012-13.
2. The scheme would provide minority women support, leadership training, information and confidence to interact with government system, banks and intermediaries at all levels.
3. The scheme is implemented through Panchayati Raj and NGOs.
A. 1, 2 B. 2, 3
C. 1, 3 D. All the above

27. Which of the following statements are correct in context with Transgender Bill?
1. The Bill aims at formulation and implementation of a comprehensive national policy for the upliftment of transgenders.
2. A National Transgender Welfare Commission and a special transgender court will be set up.
3. The bill demands reservation for the community in education, financial assistance and social inclusion.
4. Tamil Nadu was the first State to constitute a welfare board for the transgender community in the country.
A. 1, 2, 3 B. 2, 3, 4
C. 1, 3, 4 D. All the above

28. Which of the following statements is/are correct?
1. The 73rd Constitutional Amendment Act provides recognition to the Urban Local Bodies as the third tier of the Government in urban areas.
2. State Election Commission has a responsibility to conduct elections for urban local bodies.
A. Only 1 B. Only 2
C. Both 1 and 2 D. None of these

29. Which of the following statements is/are correct?
1. Competition Commission of India is a constitutional body.
2. Being a quasi-judicial body so the appointment of the Chairman is nominated by higher Judicial body or the Chief Justice of India.
A. Only 1 B. Only 2
C. Both 1 and 2 D. None of these

30. Which of the following statements related to NJAC is/are correct?

1. NJAC will replace the collegium system for the appointment of judges as mandated in the existing preamended constitution by a new system.
2. NJAC will be a statutory body.
3. It will give the executive equal role in appointments.

A. 1 and 2 B. 1 and 3
C. 2 and 3 D. All of the above

31. Which of the following statements are correct?

1. "Tourist Visa on Arrival-Electronic Travel Authorization (TVoA-ETA)" scheme is renamed as e-Tourist Visa.
2. A tourist visiting India had to obtain the e-Visa before departing from his country.
3. The validity of the Visa is for 30 days from the date-of-arrival.

A. 1 and 2 B. 1 and 3
C. 2 and 3 D. All of the above

32. Which of the following are done under Swaccha Bharat Abhiyan?

A. Construction of individual sanitary latrines for households below the poverty line
B. Conversion of dry latrines into low-cost sanitary latrines
C. Setting up of sanitary marts
D. All of the above

33. Which of the following statements related to Bibek Debroy Committee recommendations are correct?

1. Private entry into running both freight and passenger trains.
2. To progressively phase out the practice of a separate railway budget.
3. To ensure increases in passenger fares.
4. Establishment of an independent body to provide a level-playing field to private players.

A. 1, 2 and 3 B. 2, 3 and 4
C. 1, 3 and 4 D. All of the above

34. Which of the following statements is/are correct?

1. The Union Home Ministry has notified a new set of rules to regulate official visits of Governors outside their States.
2. Now governors need prior permission from the President and putting a cap of 73 days in a year as duration of such visits.

A. Only 1 B. Only 2
C. Both 1 and 2 D. None of these

35. Which of the following statements is/are correct?

1. National Commission for Backward Classes is an Indian statutory body established in 1993.
2. The Commission considers inclusions in and exclusions from the lists of communities notified as backward.

A. Only 1 B. Only 2
C. Both 1 and 2 D. None of these

36. Which of the following statements is/are correct?

1. UNESCO's global education report says that India has reduced its out of school children by over 90% and has achieved universal primary education.
2. India is the only country in South and West Asia to have an equal ratio of girls to boys in both primary and secondary education.

A. Only 1 B. Only 2
C. Both 1 and 2 D. None of these

37. Which of the following statements are incorrect?

1. National Disaster Response Force works under Ministry of Agriculture.
2. States have to keep 25 per cent of the State Disaster Response Fund (SDRF) reserved for local disasters such as heavy rain.
3. Centre links disaster compensation to farmers with annual inflation derived from the Consumer Price Index (CPI).

A. 1 and 3 B. 1 and 2
C. 2 and 3 D. All of the above

38. Which of the following statements are correct?

1. The National Food Securities Act (NFSA) passed in 2013 has been implemented in only 11 states and union territories.
2. The government extended the deadline by 6 months for remaining states to implement NFSA.
3. The law aims to provide legal entitlements to 5 kg of subsidized food-grains per person a month at ₹ 1-3/kg.

A. 1 and 2 B. 1 and 3
C. 2 and 3 D. All of the above

39. Which of the following statements are correct?

1. Rajasthan state government recently tabled Prevention of Witch-Hunting Bill in the Assembly.
2. Bill provides for life imprisonment if Witch-Hunting causes death, and imprisonment up to five years and a fine.

A. Only 1 B. Only 2
C. Both 1 and 2 D. None of these

40. Which among the following is NOT a Standing Committee?

A. Public Accounts Committee
B. Ethics Committee
C. Railway Convention Committee
D. Business Advisory Committee

41. Consider the following statements. Which among them is/are NOT true?

1. A parliamentary committee is appointed or elected by either Lok Sabha or Rajya Sabha or nominated by the Speaker of Lok Sabha or Chairman of Rajya Sabha.
2. A parliamentary committee works under the direction of the Speaker of Lok Sabha or the Chairman of Rajya Sabha.
3. A parliamentary committee is one which presents its report to either Lok Sabha or Rajya Sabha or either to the Speaker or Chairman.
4. A parliamentary committee has a secretariat provided by the Lok Sabha or Rajya Sabha.

A. Only 1 and 3
B. Only 2 and 4
C. Only 1, 2 and 3
D. All are true

42. Consider the following statements. Which among them is/are NOT true?

1. Standing Committees are the permanent committees that are constituted on a regular basis.
2. Ad hoc committees are temporary committees that are dissolved when the task is completed.
3. Committee of Privileges is an ad-hoc committee.
4. Joint Committee on Fertilizer pricing is a standing committee.

A. Only 3 and 4 B. Only 1 and 2
C. Only 1 and 3 D. Only 2 and 4

43. What among the following is NOT true about the Public Accounts Committee?

1. The Committee was first set up in 1921.
2. Its main function is to audit the annual reports of Comptroller and Auditor General of India (CAG).
3. It consists of 15 Lok Sabha members and 7 Rajya Sabha members.
4. The term of the office of the Public Accounts Committee is one year.

A. Only 1 B. Only 2
C. Only 3 D. All are true

44. Which among the following is NOT true about the Estimates Committee?

1. The first Estimates Committee of the post-independence era was first set up in 1950.
2. Estimates Committee has a right to question the policies approved by the Parliament.
3. It consists of members that are both from Lok Sabha and Rajya Sabha.
4. Chairman of the Estimates Committee is always from the Opposition party.

A. Only 4 B. Only 3
C. Only 2 and 4 D. Only 2, 3 and 4

45. Consider the following statements about the Public Undertakings Committee. Which among them is/are not true?

1. Public Undertakings Committee was first created in 1964.
2. It consists of 15 members from Lok Sabha and 7 members from Rajya Sabha.
3. Its Chairman is strictly a member of the Lok Sabha.
4. The main function of the Public Undertakings Committee is to analyze the accounts of Public Undertakings and examine reports of CAG on public undertakings.

A. Only 1, 2 and 3 B. Only 2 and 4
C. Only 3 and 4 D. All are true

46. Consider the following statements about the Ethics Committee. Which among the following is/are NOT true about it?

1. Ethics Committee overlooks the discipline and decorum in the Parliament.
2. It was constituted in Rajya Sabha in 1997, and in Lok Sabha in 2000.
3. Ethics Committee is an ad-hoc committee.
4. Ethics Committee is involved in making sure that everyone conforms with the code of conduct.

A. Only 1 B. Only 2
C. Only 3 D. All are true

47. Consider the following statements about the Committee on Government Assurances. Which among them is/are not true?

1. It was constituted in 1953.
2. Its main function is to examine the assurances and undertakings given by the ministers on the floor of the House and report back on the status of these assurances and promises.
3. For the Lok Sabha, it consists of 15 members.
4. For the Rajya Sabha, it consists of 10 members.

A. Only 1 B. Only 2
C. Only 3 D. All are true

48. When was the first Parliamentary Forum on Water Conservation and Management constituted?

A. 1950 B. 1970
C. 2005 D. 1985

49. When was the first Parliamentary Forum on Youth constituted?

A. 2010 B. 2008
C. 2006 D. 1985

50. When was the first Parliamentary Forum on Global Warming and Climate Change constituted?

A. 2005 B. 2006
C. 2007 D. 2008

51. When was the first Parliamentary Forum on Disaster Management constituted?
A. 2011 B. 2010
C. 2009 D. 2008

52. When was the first Parliamentary Forum on Population and Public Health constituted?
A. 2007 B. 2006
C. 2005 D. 2004

53. When was the first Parliamentary Forum on Children constituted?
A. 2006 B. 2007
C. 2008 D. 2009

54. Which among the following is/are not a part of the State Executive?
1. Governor
2. Chief Minister
3. Council of Ministers (state)
4. Advocate General
A. Only 1 B. Only 4
C. Only 1 and 4 D. All the above

55. Which among the following statement is/are not true about the conditions of a Governor's office?
1. A Governor can simultaneously function as a member of Lok Sabha or Rajya Sabha or State Legislature while discharging his duties as a Governor of other state.
2. The Governor should not hold any office of profit.
3. The same person can be appointed as a Governor of 2 or more states.
4. The Governor has personal immunity from any liabilities regarding his official acts.
A. Only 1 B. Only 2
C. Only 3 D. All are true

56. Which among the following statements is/are not true about the executive powers of the Governor?
1. The Governor appoints the Vice-Chancellor of the universities of the state.
2. The Governor acts as the Chancellor of the universities of the state.
3. The Governor appoints the Chief minister and other state ministers.
4. The Governor appoints the advocate general of the state.
A. Only 1 B. Only 2
C. Only 4 D. All are true

57. Which among the following statements concerning the Chief Minister is/are not true?
1. His role is analogous to that of the Prime Minister.
2. He can recommend the dissolution of the state legislative assembly to the governor.
3. He allocates and reshuffles the portfolios among the state ministers.
4. His salary and allowances are determined by the state legislature.
A. Only 1 B. Only 2
C. Only 3 D. All are true

58. Article 17 of the Indian Constitution provides for:
A. Abolition of titles
B. Equality before law
C. Abolition of untouchability
D. Equality of opportunity in matters of public employment

59. Article 370 of the Constitution of India was for:
A. Temporary provisions for Jammu and Kashmir
B. Special provisions in respect of Nagaland
C. Provisions in respect of the Financial Emergency
D. None of these

60. Who among the following was the President of the Constituent Assembly of India?
A. M.A. Jinnah B. Dr. Rajendra Prasad
C. Jawaharlal Nehru D. Lal Bahadur Shastri

61. The majority of the provisions of Indian Constitution can be amended:
A. By the Parliament alone
B. By the State Legislatures acting together
C. Only on ratification by half of the States
D. With the joint approval of the Parliament and State Legislatures

62. A proclamation of emergency, under Article 352, on account of war or aggression requires approval of the Parliament within:
A. One month B. Two months
C. Four months D. Six months

63. Which Constitutional Amendment gave precedence to the Directive Principles of State Policy over Fundamental Rights?
A. 42nd B. 44th
C. 52nd D. 56th

64. Which of the following expressions does not figure in the Preamble to the Indian Constitution?
A. Secular
B. Federal
C. Socialist
D. Sovereign Democratic Republic

65. The basic features of the Indian Constitution which are not amendable under Article 368 are:
A. Judicial review and the federal system
B. Sovereignty, territorial integrity, federal system and judicial review

C. Sovereignty, territorial integrity and parliamentary system of Government
D. Sovereignty, territorial integrity, federal system and judicial review and parliamentary system of Government

66. 'Cabinet System' and 'Collective Responsibility' are the contributions of:
A. India B. Britain
C. Ireland D. USA

67. The Creamy Layer, concept refers to:
A. The grouping based on social status
B. The grouping based on castes
C. The grouping based on economic status
D. The grouping based on milk consumption

68. In the Constitution of India, the 'Right to Constitutional Remedies' has been provided in Article:
A. 30 B. 31
C. 32 D. 35

69. Which amendment to the constitution provides for the reservation of 1/3 seats in the Municipal Boards and village panchayats for women?
A. 73rd & 74th Amendments
B. 82nd & 83rd Amendments
C. 72nd & 73rd Amendments
D. 74th & 75th Amendments

70. By which constitutional amendment political defections were banned?
A. The 50th Amendment of 1984
B. The 53rd Amendment of 1986
C. The 54th Amendment of 1986
D. The 52nd Amendment of 1985

71. The system of Privy Purses in respect of former rulers of Indian states before independence was abolished by the Constitution through:
A. 26th Amendment Act, 1971
B. 27th Amendment Act, 1971
C. 38th Amendment Act, 1975
D. 42nd Amendment Act, 1976

72. What is meant when the Constitution declares India a "Secular State"?
A. Religious worship is not allowed
B. Religions are patronized by the state
C. The state regards religions as private affairs of the citizen and does not discriminate on this basis
D. None of these

73. Under which Article of the Constitution is the President's Rule introduced in a State due to the failure of the constitutional machinery?
A. 352 B. 356
C. 360 D. 350

74. Who said that "Oh! Disrespectable democracy! I love you"?
A. G.B. Shaw B. Lord Bryce
C. Carpenter D. Appa Dorai

75. The final authority to interpret our Constitution is the:
A. President B. Parliament
C. Prime Minister D. Supreme Court

76. A secular State is one which:
A. Is irreligious
B. Is anti-religion
C. Has no religion of its own
D. Takes into consideration the religious sentiments of the people

77. Which among the following article is associated with the amending of the Constitution of India?
A. Article 443 B. Article 308
C. Article 368 D. Article 321

78. The Constitution of India describes the country as a:
A. Federation B. Union of States
C. Confederation D. Unitary State

79. Indian Constitution has divided the powers and function of the state into:
A. Two lists B. Three lists
C. Four lists D. Five lists

80. The concept of Constitution first originated in:
A. Japan B. USA
C. Britain D. Switzerland

81. Evaluate the following statements:
1. The legal interpretation of equality is chiefly influenced by equality before law and equal protection of law.
2. Equality before law means rule of law.
A. 1 is correct, but 2 is incorrect
B. 2 is correct, but 1 is incorrect
C. Both are correct
D. Both are incorrect

82. Which Articles in the Constitution give provisions for the electoral system in our country?
A. Articles 124-128 B. Articles 324-329
C. Articles 256-259 D. Articles 274-279

83. What is the maximum allowed duration between the last session of the dissolved Lok Sabha and the recalling of the Lok Sabha?
A. 2 months B. 4 months
C. 5 months D. 6 months

84. Who designated the first Indian voting machine?
A. S.K. Thorat B. Narendra Jadhare
C. M.B. Haneefa D. A.G. Rao

85. Which was the first Indian state to go for Internet voting?

A. Gujarat B. Punjab
C. Karnataka D. Andhra Pradesh

86. Which is the largest Lok Sabha constituency in General Elections by area?

A. Ladakh B. Barmer
C. Arunachal West D. Delhi Sadar

87. Which is the smallest Lok Sabha constituency in General Elections by area?

A. Delhi Sadar B. Mumbai South
C. Kolkata North West D. Chandni Chowk

88. Which is the largest Lok Sabha constituency in General Elections by population?

A. Malkajgiri B. Sasaram
C. Unnao D. Daman & Diu

89. Which is the smallest Lok Sabha constituency in General Elections by population?

A. Buxar B. Lakshadweep
C. Ghaziabad D. Bangalore North

90. The objectives of Indian Planning are:

A. Increasing national income
B. Elimination of poverty
C. Reducing inequalities in income and wealth
D. All of the above

91. The term "Fourth Estate" is used for:

A. Parliament
B. Judiciary
C. The Executive
D. The Press and Newspaper

92. Through which Constitutional Amendment was the Nagarpalika Bill passed?

A. 70th B. 72nd
C. 73rd D. 74th

93. Who can legislate on those residual matters which are not mentioned in Central/State/Concurrent lists?

A. Parliament alone
B. State legislatures exclusively
C. Parliament or State legislatures as adjudicated by the Supreme Court
D. Parliament after State legislatures concur

94. Which schedule of the Constitution deals with the disqualification of elected members on the ground of defection?

A. 8th B. 9th
C. 10th D. 11th

95. According to the Article 75(3) of the Constitution of India the Council of Ministers are collectively responsible to the:

A. Rajya Sabha B. Parliament
C. President D. Lok Sabha

96. The two words that were inserted by the 42nd Amendment to the Preamble to the Constitution are:

A. Secular, Democratic B. Sovereign, Democratic
C. Socialist, Secular D. Secular, Republic

97. Which among the following statements is/are false?

1. For qualifying to the Lok Sabha, a person must be at least 25 years of age.
2. A person can be a member of both Lok Sabha and Rajya Sabha at the same time.
3. A person belonging to SC or ST can contest elections from a general seat also, and not just the reserved seat.
4. If a member of either of the Houses votes against the directions given by his party, he can be deemed to be disqualified.

A. Only 1 B. Only 2 and 4
C. Only 3 D. Only 2

98. Which among the following statements concerning the Chief Minister is/are not true?

1. At his time of appointment, the Chief Minister need not be a member of the state legislature.
2. Chief Minister must always prove his majority in the legislative assembly before his appointment.
3. It is the governor who does the final appointment of the Chief Minister.
4. The Chief Minister can recommend the dissolution of the legislative assembly to the governor.

A. Only 1 B. Only 2 and 4
C. Only 2 D. Only 2 and 3

99. Which of the following roles/functions/responsibilities are not under the purview of the Financial Commission?

1. Sharing of net proceeds of taxes between the Centre and the States
2. Recommending principles for governing the grants-in-aid to the states by the centre.
3. Recommendations on matters referred to it by the President for the interest of sound finance.
4. Preparation and periodical revision of electoral rolls.

A. Only 1 B. Only 2
C. Only 3 and 4 D. Only 4

100. The 14th Finance Commission of India, whose chairman is Y.V. Reddy, has allocated what % of central tax revenues that were shared by the Centre with the States?

A. 56% B. 50%
C. 70% D. 42%

101. Chief Minister of a state is the sole channel of communication between:

A. Ministers and the Governor
B. Ministers and the Legislature
C. Both A and B
D. Governor and the Legislature

102. Whips are maintained by the parties to:

A. Discuss matters of national interest
B. Discipline the members of legislature belonging to respective parties
C. Act as a precautionary measure in case of an imminent threat of defection from the party
D. Both B and C

103. Which of the following has not been specified in the constitution?

A. Size of the Council of Minister
B. Salaries of the Council of Minister
C. Both A and B
D. Powers of the Chief Minister

104. Which Article of the constitution makes a mention of the Advocate-General for the state?

A. Article 157 B. Article 167
C. Article 177 D. Article 187

105. Which Article of the Constitution provides the procedure for the abolition of the second chamber of the Legislature (Legislative Council) in a state where it exists as well as for the creation of such a chamber in a state where there is none at present?

A. Article 139 B. Article 231
C. Article 169 D. None of these

106. Of the total number of members of the Legislative Council in State what is the proportion of members nominated by the Governor of the State?

A. One-fourth B. One-fifth
C. One-sixth D. One-seventh

107. All decisions of the Council of ministers in a state relating to the administration of the state of affairs and proposals of legislation are communicated to the Governor by:

A. Secretary of the Legislative Assembly
B. Chief Minister
C. Advisor to the Chief Minister
D. None of the above

108. Which Article confers upon the Governor the power to reserve a Bill pertaining to the state for consideration of the President?

A. Article 100 B. Article 201
C. Article 111 D. Article 179

109. The States having Bicameral Legislatures are:

A. Bihar, Rajasthan, Uttar Pradesh and Odisha
B. Bihar, Maharashtra, Karnataka, Uttar Pradesh, and Andhra Pradesh
C. Rajasthan, Assam, Madhya Pradesh, Uttar Pradesh, Bihar, West Bengal
D. Tamil Nadu, Punjab, Kerala and Bihar

110. Which Article of the Constitution confers upon the Governor of a state the power to make ordinances?

A. Article 123 B. Article 213
C. Article 93 D. None of the above

111. With reference to regionalism, consider the following statements:

1. Regionalism is a disintegrating force unlike nationalism which is a unifying force.
2. Regionalism is not conducive with the idea of federalism.

A. Only 1 B. Only 2
C. Both 1 and 2 D. Neither 1 nor 2

112. The election process in India follows the first past the post system. This system offers many advantages like:

1. Providing a proportionate outcome of seats based on votes.
2. Less wastage of votes.
3. Establishing a clear link between representatives and constituencies.

Select the correct answer using the codes given below.

A. Only 1 and 2 B. Only 1 and 3
C. Only 3 D. Only 2 and 3

113. The major benefits of federalism is/are:

1. It helps in quick decision making.
2. It gives voice to regional interests.
3. It creates a network of checks and balances.

Select the correct answer using the codes given below.

A. Only 1 and 2 B. Only 1 and 3
C. Only 2 D. Only 2 and 3

114. Match List-I with List-II and select the correct answer using the codes given below:

List-I (Parties)	List-II (Trade Unions)
(*a*) Indian National Congress	(*i*) C.I.T.U.
(*b*) Bhartiya Janata Party	(*ii*) A.I.T.U.C.
(*c*) Communist Party of India	(*iii*) B.M.S.
(*d*) Communist Party of India (Marxist)	(*iv*) I.N.T.U.C.
	(*v*) B.K.S.

Codes:

	(*a*)	(*b*)	(*c*)	(*d*)
A.	(*iii*)	(*iv*)	(*ii*)	(*i*)
B.	(*iv*)	(*iii*)	(*i*)	(*v*)
C.	(*iii*)	(*iv*)	(*i*)	(*v*)
D.	(*iv*)	(*iii*)	(*ii*)	(*i*)

115. Which of the following statements is/are correct?
1. The National Integration Council is a recommendatory body.
2. The National Integration Council is a constitutional body.

A. Only 1 B. Only 2
C. Both 1 and 2 D. Neither 1 nor 2

116. Communalism in Indian context means:
A. Serving the community in a befitting manner
B. Using communal identity for political gains
C. A group of people bound by ethnic feelings
D. Creating friendly relations with the other communities

117. In which of the following years, was the National Integration Council constituted first?
A. 1950 B. 1956
C. 1961 D. 1963

118. Which of the following states/union territories have a common High Court?
A. UP and Bihar
B. Punjab and Jammu & Kashmir
C. Punjab, Haryana and Chandigarh
D. Assam and Bengal

119. Panchayati Raj is organised at the:
A. Block level
B. Village and Block level
C. Village, Block and District level
D. Village, Block, District and State level

120. Which of the following courts is responsible for the enforcement of Fundamental Rights?
A. Supreme Court B. High Court
C. District Court D. Both A and B

121. Which of the following statements is/are correct?
1. In Part IX of the Constitution of India, there is no provision of reservation for women in any seat to be filled by direct election in every Panchayat.
2. The 11th schedule of the Constitution of India distributes power between the state legislature and the panchayat just as the 7th schedule distributed powers between the centre and the states.

A. Only 1 B. Only 2
C. Both 1 and 2 D. Neither 1 nor 2

122. Which of the following statements is/are correct?
1. The Governor of a state may reserve a bill for consideration of the President of India.
2. The Governor of a state is competent to withdraw an ordinance issued in the state at any time.

A. Only 1 B. Only 2
C. Both 1 and 2 D. Neither 1 nor 2

123. Which of the following Constitution Amendment Acts seeks that the size of the Councils of Ministers at the centre and in a state must not exceed 15% of the total no. of members in the Lok Sabha and the total no. of members of the Legislative Assembly of that state respectively?
A. 91st B. 93rd
C. 95th D. 97th

124. Which of the following statements is/are correct?
1. The mode of removal of a judge of a High Court in India is same as that of removal of a judge of the Supreme Court.
2. After retirement from the office, a permanent judge of a High Court cannot plead or act in any court or before any authority in India.

A. Only 1 B. Only 2
C. Both 1 and 2 D. Neither 1 nor 2

125. Which of the following statements about the state Governor is not true?
A. He is a part of the state legislature
B. He can pardon a sentence of death
C. He appoints Judges of the State High Court
D. He has no emergency powers

126. To be officially recognised by the speaker of the Lok Sabha as an opposition group, a party or coalition of parties must have at least:
A. 55 members
B. 60 members
C. 80 members
D. 1/3 of total members of the Lok Sabha

127. The entire concept of community development was conceived by the:
A. State Government B. Local Government
C. Union Government D. None of the above

128. Which of the following committees was appointed by the government to review the working of the community development programme?
A. Balwant Rai Mehta committee
B. Ashok Mehta committee
C. Santhanam committee
D. None of the above

129. Which of the following is the main source of income of the panchayats?
A. Grants from Government
B. Taxes on buildings
C. Tax on commercial crops
D. All of the above

130. The Chief Executive of the Panchayat Samiti is the:
A. Block Development Officer
B. Chairman

C. Sarpanch
D. None of the above

131. Consider the following features of the 73rd Constitutional Amendment Act.
1. Panchayati Raj bodies will receive finance from the state government in the form of grants.
2. One-third seats of the total seats in the Panchayati Raj bodies will be reserved for women.
3. Mostly states will have three-tier Panchayati Raj system.
4. Panchayati Raj bodies will prepare plans for economic development, social justice and social welfare.

Which of the above are correct? Choose the correct answer using the given codes:
A. 1, 2, 3 and 4 B. 2 and 4
C. 1 and 2 D. 1, 2 and 3

132. L.M. Singhvi suggested that Panchayati Raj should primarily be viewed as the:
A. Rural self-government system
B. Local self-government system
C. Urban self-government system
D. Political self-government system

133. Municipalities have which of the following authorities?
A. The Council and its committees
B. Chairman/President
C. Chief Executive Officer/Chief Municipal Officer
D. All of the above

134. Urban areas where troops are stationed are known as:
A. Cantonments B. Tents
C. Camps D. Dormitories

135. Seventy-Third Amendment Act is extremely important for political empowerment of:
A. Women B. Scheduled Castes
C. Scheduled Tribes D. All of these

136. Which of the following parts of the constitution envisages a three-tier system of panchayats?
A. Part IX B. Part VII
C. Part XI D. Part VI

137. Which of the following amendments inserted parts IX and IX A in the Constitution?
A. 72nd and 73rd B. 70th and 71st
C. 73rd and 74th D. 18th and 19th

138. Part IX A which has come into force in 1993 gives a Constitutional foundation to the local self-government units in:
A. Villages
B. Rural areas
C. Urban areas
D. None of the above

139. Institutions of self-government, called by a general name "municipalities", are:
A. Nagar panchayats, for transitional areas, *i.e.*, an area which is being transformed from a rural area to an urban area
B. Municipal councils for smaller urban areas
C. Municipal corporations for larger urban areas
D. All of the above

140. Which of the following states first resorted to reservation of women in Panchayati Raj Institutions?
A. Andhra Pradesh
B. Karnataka
C. Maharashtra
D. All of the above

141. What is the minimum age that a person must attain to be eligible to be a member of a panchayat?
A. 18 years B. 21 years
C. 25 years D. 30 years

142. Who among the following constitute the National Development Council?
1. The Prime Minister
2. The Chairman of Finance Commission
3. Ministers of the Union Cabinet
4. Chief Ministers of the States

Select the correct answer using the codes given below:
A. 1, 2 and 3 only B. 1, 3 and 4 only
C. 2 and 4 only D. 1, 2, 3 and 4

143. Which of the following statements is/are correct?
1. National Development Council is an organ of the Planning Commission.
2. The economic and social planning is kept in the concurrent list in the Constitution of India.
3. The Constitution of India prescribes that Panchayats should be assigned the task of preparation of plans for economic development and social justice.

A. 1 only B. 2 and 3 only
C. 1 and 3 only D. 1, 2 and 3

144. The Government enacted the Panchayat Extension to Scheduled Areas (PESA) Act in 1996. Which one of the following is not identified as its objective?
A. To provide self-governance
B. To recognize traditional rights
C. To create autonomous region in tribal areas
D. To free tribal people from exploitation

145. Which among the following countries does **not** have a Central Civil Service Commission charged with the responsibility for recruitment to the higher civil service?
A. Canada B. UK
C. USA D. France

146. Which of the following was **not** identified by the Santhanam Committee as a major cause of corruption in India?
A. Administrative delays
B. Scope for personnel discretion in the exercise of powers
C. Cumbersome procedures
D. Absence of regulatory functions of the government

147. Mayor-in-Council form of Municipal Corporation is:
A. Brought by the 74th Constitutional Amendment Act
B. Based on the theory of Separation of Powers
C. Akin to cabinet form of government
D. Based on the American local government pattern

148. Globalisation means:
A. Financial market system is centred in a single state
B. The growth of a single unified world market
C. Geographical location of a firm is of utmost importance
D. Foreign capitalist transactions

149. Which one of the following is **not** the function of NDC?
A. Review of National Plans
B. Review of Socio-Economic Policies
C. Suggestions to achieve Plan Targets
D. Review of Union-State Relations

150. The programme aimed at enabling illiterate women to acquire functional skills, better awareness of health, hygiene and child care is:
A. National Female Literacy Mission
B. Functional Literacy for Adult Women
C. Female Farmers Functional Literacy and Training
D. Total Literacy Programme

151. HDI is entrusted with reference to:
1. Life expectancy at birth
2. Real GDP per capita
3. Infant mortality
4. Morbidity

Codes:
A. 1 and 2 are correct B. 2 and 3 are correct
C. 3 and 4 are correct D. All the above

152. Which Article of the Constitution of India provides for the District Planning Committee?
A. Article 242 ZD B. Article 243 ZA
C. Article 243 ZD D. Article 244 ZA

153. Assertion (A) : The National Rural Health Mission (NRHM) has been successful in improving health condition of the poor couples living in the villages.

Reason (R) : The Accredited Social Health Activist (ASHA) is playing a significant role in providing healthcare services to the needy couples.
A. Both (A) and (R) are true and (R) is the correct explanation of (A)
B. Both A and R are true, but R is not the correct explanation of A
C. A is true, but R is false
D. A is false, but R is true

154. Assertion (A) : Education of girls and women in India has reinforced gender role, specially motherhood.

Reason (R) : In India, women's education was neglected for many years.
A. Both A and R are true, but R is not the correct explanation of A
B. Both (A) and (R) are true and (R) is the correct explanation of (A)
C. R is true, but A is false
D. R is false, but A is true

155. Assertion (A) : Corruption is the cause of poverty and underdevelopment.

Reason (R) : The poor are corrupt and underdeveloped.
A. Both A and R are correct and R is the correct explanation of A
B. Both A and R are correct, but R is not the correct explanation of A
C. A is true, but R is false
D. A is false, but R is true

156. Assertion (A) : Social Welfare Administration generates awareness about the challenges of a society in transition where negative use of technologies and practices is impacting on the well being of women and children.

Reason (R) : Social Welfare Administration is the summation of social welfare institutions, policies and programmes.
A. Both A and R are correct and R is the correct explanation of A
B. Both A and R are correct, but R is not the correct explanation of A
C. A is true, but R is false
D. A is false, but R is true

157. India that is Bharat shall be a "union of states". From which Constitution was adopted the words "union of states"?
A. USA B. France
C. Switzerland D. Canada

158. The Objective Resolution in the Constituent Assembly was moved by:
A. Dr Rajendra Prasad
B. B.R. Ambedkar
C. Jawaharalal Nehru
D. Alladi Krishnaswamy Iyer

159. The procedure for amending the Constitution is in:
A. Article 368 B. Article 360
C. Article 367 D. Article 371

160. Some of the basic philosophy developed over time that embody the concept of constitutionalism are:
A. separation of powers
B. judicial control and
C. accountable government
D. All of these

161. Separation of powers divides the mechanism of governance into branches *i.e.*, as:
(*a*) Legislature
(*b*) Executive
(*c*) Judiciary
(*d*) Parliamentary Committee

Select the correct code from the options given below:
A. (*a*) & (*b*) B. (*c*) & (*d*)
C. (*c*) & (*b*) D. (*a*), (*b*) & (*c*)

162. Who among the following is the exponent of Rule of Law?
A. A.V. Dicey B. Barker
C. Seeley D. Montesquieu

163. Dicey lays down three essential components of Rule of Law as:
(*a*) Nobody is to be punished except for a specific breach of law that is established in an ordinary legal manner before ordinary courts of law.
(*b*) No one is above the law.
(*c*) Courts play a vital role in protecting the rights and freedoms of an individual
(*d*) The separation of the judiciary from the Executive under Article 50

Select the correct code from the options given below:
A. (*a*) & (*b*) B. (*c*) & (*d*)
C. (*c*) & (*b*) D. (*a*), (*b*) & (*c*)

164. Constitutionalism can be governed with the help of various provisions of constitution that are:
(*a*) Rule of law
(*b*) Separation of power
(*c*) Checks and balances
(*d*) Comptroller and Auditor General

Select the correct code from the options given below:
A. (*a*) & (*b*) B. (*c*) & (*d*)
C. (*c*) & (*b*) D. (*a*), (*b*) & (*c*)

165. The outstanding phenomena of Democratic Consolidation are mainly on;
(*a*) Judicial activism & RTI
(*b*) The recent work of the Election Commission of India
(*c*) The new panchayatiraj or the consolidation of the institutions of local governance
(*d*) An inclusive civil service

Select the correct code from the options given below:
A. (*a*) & (*b*) B. (*c*) & (*d*)
C. (*c*) & (*b*) D. (*a*), (*b*) & (*c*)

166. The RTI Act (2005) attempts to consolidate democracy in India by:
(*a*) Strengthening the notion of equality between the governing and the governed
(*b*) It also works to offset the imperialist culture of governance
(*c*) It is created by the provisions of the Indian Evidence Act (1872)
(*d*) Sharing of power with politico-administrative units

Select the correct code from the options given below:
A. (*a*) & (*b*) B. (*c*) & (*d*)
C. (*c*) & (*b*) D. (*a*), (*b*) & (*c*)

167. The multifaceted process of deepening democracy in India necessarily involves the kinds of actors as:
(*a*) the State as well as
(*b*) non-State actors
(*c*) non electoral means
(*d*) abolition of the caste system

Select the correct code from the options given below:
A. (*a*) & (*b*) B. (*c*) & (*d*)
C. (*c*) & (*b*) D. (*a*), (*b*) & (*c*)

168. Democracy works on the principle of:
A. Checks and balances
B. Intervention of the state
C. Dictatorial Nature of the state
D. None of these

169. Who among the following developed Cultural Lag with special reference to social change?
A. William Fielding Ogburn
B. MacIver and Page
C. Karl Marx
D. Herbert Spencer

170. Which among the following constitutional amendment provided for the establishment of the National Judicial Appointments Commission as ultra-vires?
A. 99th constitutional amendment
B. 82nd constitutional amendment
C. 73rd constitutional amendment
D. 74th constitutional amendment

ANSWERS

1	2	3	4	5	6	7	8	9	10
C	B	C	B	D	A	A	D	C	C
11	12	13	14	15	16	17	18	19	20
B	A	A	B	A	B	D	C	B	A
21	22	23	24	25	26	27	28	29	30
B	C	B	C	B	D	D	B	D	B
31	32	33	34	35	36	37	38	39	40
D	D	D	C	C	C	D	D	C	C
41	42	43	44	45	46	47	48	49	50
D	A	D	D	D	C	D	C	C	D
51	52	53	54	55	56	57	58	59	60
A	B	A	B	A	D	D	C	A	B
61	62	63	64	65	66	67	68	69	70
A	A	A	B	D	B	A	C	A	D
71	72	73	74	75	76	77	78	79	80
A	C	B	A	D	C	A	B	B	B
81	82	83	84	85	86	87	88	89	90
C	B	D	C	A	A	D	A	B	D
91	92	93	94	95	96	97	98	99	100
D	D	A	C	D	C	D	C	D	D
101	102	103	104	105	106	107	108	109	110
B	B	C	C	C	C	B	B	B	B
111	112	113	114	115	116	117	118	119	120
D	C	D	D	A	B	C	C	C	D
121	122	123	124	125	126	127	128	129	130
D	C	A	C	B	A	C	A	D	A
131	132	133	134	135	136	137	138	139	140
A	B	D	A	D	A	C	C	D	D
141	142	143	144	145	146	147	148	149	150
B	B	B	C	B	D	D	B	D	B
151	152	153	154	155	156	157	158	159	160
D	C	A	A	C	B	D	C	A	D
161	162	163	164	165	166	167	168	169	170
D	A	D	D	D	D	A	A	A	A

• • •

Politics in India Since Independence

1. The extra constitutional body who is authorised to make assessment of national wealth is:
   A. Finance Commission
   B. Comptroller and Auditor General
   C. Planning Commission
   D. National Development Council

2. National Development Council comprises of:
   A. All Governors of states
   B. All Chief Ministers of states
   C. All Central ministers
   D. Central Cabinet ministers only

3. Mixed Economy means:
   A. Mixed form of production and distribution
   B. Co existence of Public sector and Public sector
   C. Economies of third world
   D. Emerging economies.

4. Development Planning is:
   A. Change Oriented B. Hierarchical
   C. Centralism D. Bureaucratic

5. The Great depression was an economic phenomena took place during:
   A. 1940s B. 1950s
   C. 1930s D. 2010s

6. HDI means:
   A. Human Development Item
   B. Human Development Index
   C. Housing Development Bank of India
   D. None of the above

7. Chairman of NITI AAYOG of India is:
   A. President of India
   B. Prime Minister of India
   C. Vice President of India
   D. Home Minister

8. MGNREGA stands for:
   A. Mahatma Gandhi National Rural Employment Guarantee Act
   B. National Rural Integration Progremme
   C. A project under UN
   D. None of these

9. The Stages of Economic Growth was written by:
   A. W.W Rostow B. G B Shaw
   C. Kuznets D. Adam Smith

10. Development in socialism doesn't mean:
    A. Equal distribution of resources
    B. Egalitarianism
    C. Competition
    D. Common ownership of resources

11. Capitalist model of development relates to:
    A. Co-operative model of development
    B. Individual development
    C. Equality of all
    D. None of these

12. Public Sector denotes:
    A. Individual enterprise for people
    B. Government controlled firms
    C. Communication facilities
    D. Industries

13. Market Mechanism is a feature of:
    A. Mixed economy B. Capitalism
    C. Socialism D. Marxism

14. Development Planning Indian economy before 1990 was known for its style of functioning as a:
    A. Socialist economy B. Planned economy
    C. Mixed economy D. Capitalist economy

15. The pillar of economic development for Mahatma Gandhi was:
    A. Grama Swaraj B. Trusteeship
    C. Decentralisation D. Sarvodaya

16. The amendment which made state planning boards mandatory:
    A. 73rd constitutional amendment
    B. 61st amendment
    C. 42nd amendment
    D. None of these

17. The Five Year plans launched in India in:
    A. 1950 B. 1951
    C. 1965 D. 1947

18. The reasons for Economic reforms introduced in India are mainly on:
    (*a*) Public sector was given an important role in development policies during 1951–1990
    (*b*) The performance of the majority of public enterprises was disappointing

(*c*) They were incurring huge losses because of inefficient management
(*d*) Policy changes were proposed to go public sector underatkings

Select the correct code of the options given below:
A. (*a*), (*b*) & (*c*) B. (*a*) & (*b*)
C. (*c*) & (*d*) D. (*a*) & (*c*)

19. The most urgent problem which prompted the introduction of New Economic Policy in 1991 was:
A. Poor performance of public sector
B. High tax rate leading to tax evasion
C. Foreign exchange crisis
D. All of these

20. Reason which gives importance to privatization:
A. Decline in private monopoly
B. Favour the objective of social welfare
C. Reduce the cost by minimising wastages
D. Increase employment due to exit policy for sick public enterprises

21. The main changes in fiscal policy are:
A. Quantitative restrictions on import and exports reduced
B. System of fixed exchange rate converted into market determined exchange rate
C. Use of foreign exchange made more liberal
D. All of these

22. The new economic policy seeks to replace:
A. LLP raj B. LPG raj
C. LQG raj D. LQP raj

23. Which of the following is not the one of those steps taken in financial sector reforms?
A. Lifting of regulations on interest rate of deposit
B. Liberalisation of branching regulations for both private and public sector banks
C. Delicensing of industries
D. Reduction of barriers for entry of private banks

24. Liberalisation leads to some limitation:
A. Lesser participation of foreign investors
B. It neglects the social welfare
C. No improvement in productivity
D. No improvement in financial sector

25. Poverty in less developed countries is largely due to:
A. Voluntary idleness
B. Income inequality
C. Lack of cultural activities
D. Lack of intelligence of people

26. The best indicator of economic development of any country is:
A. Its agriculture
B. Its transport
C. Its gross production
D. Its per capita income

27. The Gandhian Plan was presented by:
A. M.N. Roy B. Nehru
C. Shriman Narayan D. 8 leading economist

28. Which of the following is not a feature of Indian Planning?
A. Physical Planning
B. Indicative Economic Planning
C. Decentralised Planning
D. None of these above

29. 'Twenty point programme' was launched in the year:
A. 1969 B. 1975
C. 1977 D. 1980

30. Mahalanobis model has been associated with which five year plan?
A. 1st five year plan B. 2nd five year plan
C. 3rd five year plan D. 4th five year plan

31. The annual growth rate of India's population according to 2011 census is:
A. 1.9% B. 1.76%
C. 2% D. None

32. Among the Indian state which has the highest density:
A. Bengal B. Kerala
C. Punjab D. Bihar

33. As per the 2011 census literacy rate in India was:
A. 94% B. 74.04%
C. 88.8% D. 100%

34. Globalization of Indian Economy means:
A. Increasing External borrowing
B. Larger FDI
C. Import Substitution
D. Minimum possible restrictions on economic relation with other countries

35. Which one of the following statements about globalization is not correct?
A. All economies are closed
B. Secular economies
C. Open economies with trade liberalization
D. None of these are correct

36. What is the full form of Niti Aayog?
A. National Institute to Transform India
B. National Institute for Transforming India
C. National Institution to Transform India
D. National Institution for Transforming India

37. The book "Planning Economy for India" was written by:
A. V.K.R.V. Rao B. M. Visvesvaraya
C. K.N. Rai D. Manmohan Singh

38. India's economic planning cannot be said to be:
A. Indicative B. Imperative
C. Limited D. Democratic

39. How many tribes are there in India?
A. 645 B. 565
C. 345 D. None of these

40. In which state of India resides the maximum number of tribes?
A. Madhya Pradesh B. Nagaland
C. West Bengal D. None of these

41. Which is the largest tribe in India?
A. Bhil B. Gond
C. Baiga D. None of these

42. In which state Garo, Khasi and Jaintia tribes are located?
A. Assam B. Meghalaya
C. Madhya Pradesh D. None of these

43. Daphla and Lampo tribes are found in which state?
A. Madhya Pradesh B. Arunachal Pradesh
C. Rajsathan D. None of these

44. Which state has the largest population of Santhals?
A. Jharkhand B. Arunachal Pradesh
C. Rajsathan D. None of these

45. Which caste is largest in Tamil Nadu by population?
A. Vanniyar B. Raji
C. Saharya D. None of these

46. Find out the odd one:
A. Poumai – Manipur B. Garo – Mizoram
C. Dafla – Uttar Pradesh D. None of these

47. In which year the Forest Right Act was passed?
A. 2000 B. 2006
C. 2005 D. None of these

48. What is the name of the tribe that is battling against Vedanta for preservation of Niyamgiri hills?
A. The Kondha or Kandha
B. Kandha Gauda
C. Oriya Munda
D. Dongria Kondh

49. Which of the following is/are true?
1. Article 244 in Part X of the Constitution envisages a special system of administration for certain areas designated as 'scheduled areas' and 'tribal areas'.
2. The Fifth Schedule of the Constitution deals with the administration and control of scheduled areas and scheduled tribes in any state.

Select the correct answer
A. Only 1 B. Only 2
C. All of the above D. None of the above

50. The National Commission for Schedule Caste was established under........of Indian Constitution.
A. Article 338 B. Article 250
C. Article 180 D. Article 142

51. Which of the following is not matched correctly?
A. National Commission for Women: 1992
B. National Minorities Commission: 1993
C. National Backward Classes Commission: 2002
D. National Child Rights Protection Commission: 2007

52. Who appoints the Chairman of the National Commission for Scheduled Castes?
A. President
B. Prime Minister
C. Lok Sabha Speaker
D. None of the following

53. Which of the following is not the function of the National Commission for Scheduled Castes?
A. Providing Constitutional protection to Scheduled Castes
B. To investigate any case that violates the interests of Scheduled Castes
C. To submit the report to the Prime Minister related to the protection of Scheduled Castes
D. None of the above

54. Which constitution amendment has recommended the establishment of a commission for Scheduled Castes and Scheduled Tribes?
A. 41st Constitutional Amendment
B. 65th Constitutional Amendment
C. 82nd Constitutional Amendment
D. 76th Constitutional Amendment

55. Which amongst the following is/are correct?
1. Indian society during nineteenth century was marred by religious superstitions and social obscurantism.
2. Social conditions of women were good but some vices like sati, child marriage prevailed in the society
3. Raja Ram Mohan said "Sati is murder according to every shastra".
4. People at lower ladder of the society were called untouchables, who formed about 20 per cent of population.

Select the correct code:
A. Only 1 B. Only 2 is incorrect
C. All of the above D. None of the above

56. Which amongst the following is/are correct?
A. The Hindu Widow Remarriage Act came in 1856.
B. Vishnu Shastri Pandit founded Widow Remarriage Association in the 1850s.

C. Indian Women University was set up in 1916 at Bombay by Professor Karve.
D. All are correct

57. Who among the following started dalit movement in India?
A. Dr. B.R. Ambedkar B. Bal Gangadhar Tilak
C. Jyotiba Phule D. None of these

58. According to Dr. B.R. Ambedkar the dalits and marginalised in this country will have struggle against two adversaries. Which are they?
1. Brahmanism 2. Capitalism
3. Socialism 4. Communalism

Codes:
A. 1 and 2 B. 1 and 4
C. 2 and 3 D. 3 and 4

59. Which of the following matches is not correct?
A. Louis Dumont — Caste based on purity and pollution
B. B.R. Ambedkar — Caste as graded form of inequality
C. M.N. Srinivas — Dominant caste
D. G.S. Ghurye — Racial origin of caste

60. Name the online platform launched by the Ministry of Women and Child Development to support women entrepreneurs?
A. Digital India
B. Mahila E-haat
C. One Stop Centre Scheme
D. None of the above

61. In which year the Central Social Welfare Board was established?
A. 1950 B. 1951
C. 1952 D. 1953

62. Which of the following scheme provide education to girls and their welfare?
A. One Stop Centre Scheme
B. UJJWALA
C. SWADHAR Scheme
D. Beti Bachao Beti Padhao

63. Support to Training and Employment Programme for Women scheme is:
A. SWADHAR B. STEP
C. Nari Shakti Puraskar D. RMK

64. Priyadarshini scheme provides:
A. Women Empowerment
B. Livelihood in Mid-Gangetic plains
C. Empower to address women legal, political and health problems
D. All the above are correct.

65. National Mission for Empowerment of Women was launched on:
A. 15 August, 2010
B. 15 August, 2011
C. 15 October, 2010
D. 15 October, 2011

66. Which scheme promotes community participation through involvement of Students Volunteers for empowerment of rural women?
A. NAND-GHAR YOJANA
B. eSamvad Portal
C. Pradhan Mantri Mahila Shakti Kendra scheme
D. She-Box Portal

67. Arrange the following initiatives with regard to Women's Studies in chronological order:
1. Establishment of Indian Association of Women's studies.
2. First National Conference on Women's Studies.
3. Publication of 'Towards Equality Report'
4. Second National Education Policy

Code:
A. (1), (3), (2), (4) B. (1), (2), (3), (4)
C. (3), (2), (1), (4) D. (4), (2), (3), (1)

68. What is the common focus of most feminist therapies today?
A. Improving living conditions for women around the world.
B. Creating a more gentle, loving, woman centred world.
C. Showing how society's view of treatment of non-dominant groups impacts mental health.
D. Seeking balance in the un-equal power relationships between women and men.

69. For which of the following reasons early feminist approaches to development have been criticised?
(*a*) Only looking at women
(*b*) Not engaging with development agencies
(*c*) Having unrealistic aims
(*d*) Ignoring women's roles in production

Select correct code of the options given below
A. (*a*), (*c*) & (*d*) B. (*c*), (*b*) & (*a*)
C. (*b*), (*a*) & (*d*) D. (*a*) & (*b*)

70. Assertion (A) : In patriarchal society, all economic development causes the marginalization and devaluation of women's labour.

Reason (R) : In patriarchal society, the nature of house work and women's responsibility for carrying it out are unchangeable *i.e.*, constant.

Code:

A. Both (A) and (R) are wrong
B. Both (A) and (R) are correct and (R) is the correct explanation for (A)
C. (A) is correct, but (R) is wrong
D. Both (A) and (R) are correct, but (R) is not the correct explanation for (A)

71. As the women's suffrage movement emerged from the abolition movement, the women's liberation movement grew out of the struggle for:
A. civil rights
A. political power
B. dominance in the family
C. challenge against livelihoods

72. Which of the following is correct with regard to 'identity politics' in the feminist context in India?
A. Minority, caste and dalit issues
B. Race and ethnicity
C. Gender, race, caste, class and minorities
D. Gender, race, caste, minorities

73. Which among the following book reveals that the white hetrosexual, middle class women were discontented and unhappy despite living the "Ideal" female life but were unable to explain why is "the problem that has no name"?
A. The second sex B. Feminine mystique
C. The second stage D. The subjection of women

74. Which among the following feminist identified "alienation" as the concept that will provide us with a theoretical framework to accommodate main insight of Marxist, radical, psychoanalytic and even liberal feminist thought?
A. Iris young B. Alison Jagger
C. Juliet Mitchell D. Mary Daly

75. Among the following feminists who has analysed 'Reproduction through the lens of male alienation' while criticizing Shulamith Firestone's views on female biology as the cause of women's oppression:
A. Mary O' Brien B. Mary Dally
C. Kate Millet D. Juliet Mitchell

76. Consider the incorrect statement regarding New Farms Act, 2020:
A. The Farmers' Produce Trade and Commerce (Promotion and Facilitation) Act, 2020
B. The Farmers (Empowerment and Protection) Agreement of Price Assurance and Farm Service Act, 2020
C. The Farmers Protection Act, 2020
D. The Essential Commodities (Amendment) Act, 2020

77. The epicenter of farmers protest is:
A. Punjab & Haryana
B. Punjab & Madhya Pradesh
C. Bihar & Uttar Pradesh
D. Punjab & Rajasthan

78. Consider the following statement regarding Farmers Fear in new farms Act:
1. MSP will stop
2. APMC will end
3. Big Companies will exploit farmers in the name of contract

Choose correct code from given below:
A. 1 and 3 Only B. 2 and 3 Only
C. 1 and 2 Only D. 1, 2 and 3

79. Indian farmer was goaded into cultivation of opium by:
A. promise of high prices
B. system of advances
C. the village headman
D. revenue concessions

80. Strip cultivation was practiced by:
A. peasants in England B. tribals
C. nomadic pastoralists D. shifting cultivators

81. For poorer farmers machines brought misery because of:
A. displacement B. banks refused loans
C. banks gave loans D. indebtedness

82. Which of the following was an important factor in farmers investing in threshing machines?
A. Labour shortage
B. Insolence of labourers
C. High wages demanded by labour
D. To reduce dependence on labour

83. In which Farmers' movement did Mahatma Gandhi participate first of all?
A. Kheda B. Champaran
C. Bardoli D. Baroda

84. Which among the following Farmer's revolt are not correctly matched?
A. Deccan Peasant Revolt (1875)
B. Mopilla Revolt (1921)
C. Bardoli (1927)
D. Kheda (1918)

85. Farmers' movement led by rich farmers in:
A. Uttar Pradesh B. Karnataka
C. Maharashtra D. All of these

86. The beginning of the New Farmers' Movement in general is seen from the decade of:
A. 1980s B. 1970s
C. 1960s D. 1940s

87. Some of the most important Farmer's struggles that were carried till the beginning of 1980s.Which of the following struggles are not correctly matched?

A. Anti-Single Food Zone, 1972
B. Struggle against Power Tariff, 1975
C. Struggle against increasing water rates, increasing commercial tax, 1975
D. Agitation against defective tractors, 1979

88. The Uttar Pradesh movement under Mahendra Singh Tikait organised many rallies, agitations as well as struggles. Some of the major well known struggles are as:

(*a*) Struggle against Power Tariff, 1986
(*b*) Meerut Struggle, 1988
(*c*) Agitation for Payment of Arrears, 2007
(*d*) Sit-in Dharna at Jantar Mantar, 2008

Codes:

A. Both (*a*) & (*b*) B. Both (*c*) & (*d*)
C. Both (*b*) & (*a*) D. All of the above

89. Shetkari Sangathana of Maharashtra also carried couple of struggles. Which of the following are correctly matched?

(*a*) Nasik Agitation of 1980
(*b*) Nippani Agitation of 1981
(*c*) Rail and Rasta Roko agitation of 1981, 1986
(*d*) Pandharpur Rally of 1983

Codes:

A. Both (*a*) & (*b*) B. Both (*c*) & (*d*)
C. Both (*b*) & (*a*) D. All of the above

90. The new strategies "Gav Bhandi" is associated with the farmer's movement of:

A. Maharashtra B. Madhya Pradesh
C. Karnataka D. West Bengal

91. Civil society can be understood as:

A. the whole population of a state
B. the people within a state who behave in a politically civilised way
C. a social organization made up of retired civil servants.
D. a framework within which people who lack political authority conduct their lives.

92. Why did the term 'civil society' become popular in the 1980s?

A. At that time there was growing disenchantment with the perceived dishonesty of governments, especially as recipients of aid
B. The downfall of many totalitarian regimes was attributed to movements generated by civil society
C. It seemed to offer the possibility of peaceful change in other states
D. All of the above

93. Why has the term 'civil society' aroused suspicion in some Islamic states?

A. In those countries the state denies civil rights to its citizens.
B. It can be seen as part of a project of 'Westernization'.
C. The term is difficult to translate into Arabic.
D. It failed to recognize that brutal violence is the only way to facilitate change

94. What does 'infrapolitics' denote?

A. Relations between sovereign states
B. Relationships between key decision-makers
C. The way in which seemingly powerless people subvert the authority of the powerful
D. The disengagement of many people nowadays from the political process

95. A positive view of the political role of the media sees it as:

A. a way of keeping people harmlessly amused when times are hard.
B. a way of promoting constructive 'role models' for young people
C. much more trustworthy than politicians
D. at its best, a potential check on executive power

96. What is civil Society?

A. The society considered as a community of citizens linked by common interests and collective activity is a civil society.
B. It is the aggregate of non-governmental organizations and institutions that manifest interests and will of citizens.
C. It is referred to as the third sector of the society distinct from government and business.
D. All of the above

97. Which one of the following statements is not correct about civil society organisations?

A. They are sovereign bodies
B. They are voluntary but nonprofit-making agencies
C. They work in close proximity with people
D. They create awareness; educate and sensitise people on common issues and act as catalysts of social change

98. Value of the programme in Social action group work lies in?

A. Establishing satisfying affective (love) relationship
B. Enhancing knowledge of possible alternative activities.
C. Giving expression to creative dynamics drives
D. Increasing proficiency in the chosen programme activity.

99. Social action group work as a method of social work aims at:
A. Development of democratic life style
B. Development of leadership qualities
C. Development of capability of adjustment
D. All the above

100. Which of the following is NOT a principle of social group work?
A. Confidentiality
B. Guided group interactions
C. Progressive programme development
D. Evaluation of the progress made by the group

101. The book "Social Group Work – A Helping Process" is authored by?
A. H.B. Trecker B. G. Konopka
C. G.H. Mead D. Peter Samuel

102. The Mutual Aid Model of group work practice has its roots in the practice theory proposed:
A. H.B. Trecker B. G. Konopka
C. William Schwartz D. Naiper

103. Regional Disparity means:
A. It refers uneven economic achievement in different geographical regions
B. It is reflected by the indicators like per capita income
C. It refers to the proportion of population living below the poverty line
D. All of these

104. Government Interventions to reduce Regional Disparities are:
A. Higher resource transfers from the Centre to the Backward States
B. Planning Commission (before 2014) mainly in the form of plan transfers
C. Finance Commission in the form of non-plan transfers
D. All of these

105. Among the following, which countries have high participation of women in public life?
A. Sweden and India B. Norway and Sri Lanka
C. Nepal and Finland D. Sweden and Africa

106. Identify the statements which suggest that it is not politics that gets caste-ridden, it is the caste that gets politicised.
(*a*) When governments are formed, political parties take care that representatives of different castes find a place in it.
(*b*) Each caste group incorporates neighbouring castes which were earlier excluded.
(*c*) Various caste groups enter into a coalition with other castes.
(*d*) Political parties and candidates in elections make appeals to caste sentiments.

Codes:
A. (*a*), (*b*) and (*d*) B. (*b*), (*c*) and (*d*)
C. (*b*) and (*c*) D. (*a*) and (*d*)

107. Identify two reasons that state that caste alone cannot determine elections in India:
(*a*) No party wins the votes of all the voters of a caste or community.
(*b*) Some political parties are known to favour some castes and are seen as their representatives.
(*c*) No parliamentary constituency in the country has a clear majority of one single caste.
(*d*) Mobilising and securing political support has brought new consciousness among the lower castes.

Codes:
A. (*a*) and (*c*) B. (*a*) and (*d*)
C. (*b*) and (*c*) D. (*b*) and (*d*)

108. When we speak of gender divisions, we usually refer to:
A. Biological difference between men and women
B. Unequal roles assigned by the society to men and women
C. Unequal child sex ratio
D. Absence of voting rights for women in democracies.

109. In India seats are reserved for women in:
(*a*) Lok Sabha
(*b*) State legislative assemblies
(*c*) Cabinets
(*d*) Panchayati Raj bodies

Codes:
A. (*a*), (*b*) and (*d*) B. (*b*), (*c*) and (*d*)
C. (*b*) and (*c*) D. (*a*) and (*d*)

110. Which among the following statements about India's Constitution is wrong? It:
A. prohibits discrimination on grounds of religion.
B. gives official status to one religion.
C. provides to all individuals freedom to profess any religion.
D. ensures equality of citizens within religious communities.

111. In India, the representation of women in legislature has been:
A. moderate B. high
C. low D. very low

112. The emergence of political parties has accompanied with:
A. Grow of parliament as an institution
B. Diversification of political systems
C. Growth of modern electorate
D. All of the above

113. Political parties are responsible for maintaining a continuous connection between:
A. People and the government

B. President and the Prime Minister
C. People and the opposition
D. Both A and C

114. Rajni Kothari prefers to call the Indian party system as:
A. Congress system
B. One party dominance system
C. Multi-party systems
D. Both A and B

115. During which of the following years the Congress party has faced serious electoral reverses?
A. 1967 B. 1977
C. 1989 D. All of these

116. What is the most appropriate meaning the term secularism in the Indian context?
A. Seperation of religion from politics
B. Freedom of religion
C. There shall not be any religion of the state
D. Equality of all religions

117. Which of the following are the important socio-economic factors of regional imbalance in India?
A. per capita income
B. regional location of industries
C. population
D. below poverty line

118. Which of the following can play a vital role in removing regional disparity?
A. Bureaucracy B. State
C. Civil servants D. Judiciary

119. As a political strategy, communalism is opposed to:
A. Nationalism B. Regionalism
C. Localism D. Internationalism

120. Identity the correct chronological order in which the following came into existence.
Use the codes given below:
1. Swatantra Party
2. Muslim League
3. Bharatiya Janata Party
4. Communist Party of India

Code:
A. 4, 3, 1, 2 B. 1, 3, 2, 4
C. 2, 4, 1, 3 D. 3, 1, 4, 2

121. A political party is recognized as a regional party, if:
A. It gets 4 per cent votes in the state either in the Lok Sabha or the Assembly elections
B. It gets 5 per cent votes in the state either in the Lok Sabha or the Assembly elections
C. It gets 6 per cent votes in the state either in the Lok Sabha or the Assembly elections
D. It gets 7 per cent votes in the state either in the Lok Sabha or the Assembly elections

122. The issue of adequate participation of women in Panchayati Raj institutions was first raised by:
A. Santhanam Committee Report
B. Ashok Mehta Committee Report
C. Balwant Rai Mehta Committee Report
D. All of the above

123. The term 'Stasiology' refers to:
A. Party politics
B. Scientific study of party politics
C. Study of pressure group politics
D. None of the above

124. Who among the following divided the non-competitive party system into one party authoritarian, one-party pluralistic and one-party totalitarian?
A. Alan Ball
B. La Palaombara and Myron Weiner
C. Harry Eckstein
D. James Jupp.

125. The Dalit panther movement was launched in:
A. West Bengal B. Bihar
C. Odisha D. Maharashtra

126. Political parties are registered as per the provision of:
A. Article 324 of the Constitution
B. The Election Commission
C. The Election Commission in consultation with the govt.
D. Representation of Peoples Act 1951

127. Which of the following is one of the salient features of the coalition governments?
A. Lack of polarization
B. Political opportunism
C. Political defections
D. All of the above

128. Which of the following is not the type of coalition categorized on the basis of interaction of Infrastructure and Politics?
A. Few party governmental coalition
B. Secular coalition
C. Post election coalition
D. Infrastructure dominated coalition

129. Birsa Munda was associated with tribal struggle of:
A. North East Region B. Jharkahand
C. Nagar Division D. Deccan

130. In the first decade following independence, which of the following legislations transformed the legal status of women?
A. The Hindu Marriage Act, 1955
B. The Succession
C. The Adoption Act, 1956
D. All of the above

ANSWERS

1	2	3	4	5	6	7	8	9	10
C	B	B	A	C	B	B	A	A	D
11	**12**	**13**	**14**	**15**	**16**	**17**	**18**	**19**	**20**
B	B	B	C	A	A	B	A	C	C
21	**22**	**23**	**24**	**25**	**26**	**27**	**28**	**29**	**30**
A	C	C	B	B	C	A	A	B	B
31	**32**	**33**	**34**	**35**	**36**	**37**	**38**	**39**	**40**
A	B	B	D	C	D	B	B	A	A
41	**42**	**43**	**44**	**45**	**46**	**47**	**48**	**49**	**50**
A	B	B	A	A	C	B	D	A	A
51	**52**	**53**	**54**	**55**	**56**	**57**	**58**	**59**	**60**
C	A	C	B	B	D	A	A	D	B
61	**62**	**63**	**64**	**65**	**66**	**67**	**68**	**69**	**70**
D	D	B	D	B	C	B	D	A	A
71	**72**	**73**	**74**	**75**	**76**	**77**	**78**	**79**	**80**
A	C	B	B	A	C	A	D	B	A
81	**82**	**83**	**84**	**85**	**86**	**87**	**88**	**89**	**90**
D	D	B	C	D	A	D	D	D	A
91	**92**	**93**	**94**	**95**	**96**	**97**	**98**	**99**	**100**
D	D	B	C	D	D	A	A	D	A
101	**102**	**103**	**104**	**105**	**106**	**107**	**108**	**109**	**110**
B	B	C	D	D	C	A	B	A	B
111	**112**	**113**	**114**	**115**	**116**	**117**	**118**	**119**	**120**
D	C	D	D	D	D	D	B	A	C
121	**122**	**123**	**124**	**125**	**126**	**127**	**128**	**129**	**130**
C	C	B	B	D	D	D	C	B	D

●●●

India's Foreign Policy

1. Which among the following is not a philosophical base of the Indian Foreign policy?
   A. Containment of Communism
   B. Anti-imperialism
   C. Non Alignment
   D. Anti-colonialism
2. Who among the following is the chief architect of India's Foreign policy?
   A. Gandhiji B. Jawaharlal Nehru
   C. Indira Gandhi D. Sardar Vallabhai Patel
3. Which agreement was signed between India and Pakistan after Indo-Pakistani War of 1965?
   A. Tashkent Agreement
   B. Bangkok Agreement
   C. Panchasheel Agreementd
   D. None of the above
4. Simla Agreement was signed in:
   A. 1971 B. 1972
   C. 1974 D. 1975
5. Simla Agreement was signed between:
   A. Jawaharlal Nehru and Muhammad Ali Jinnah
   B. Benazir Bhuto and Indira Gandhi
   C. Indira Gandhi and Zulfiqar Ali Bhutto
   D. Jawaharlal Nehru and Zulfiqar Ali Bhutto
6. Simla Accord signed in 1974 is related to:
   A. Status of Tibet
   B. Liberation of Bangladesh
   C. Ending the war between India and Pakistan in 1971
   D. None of the Above
7. SAARC was established in the year:
   A. 1975 B. 1980
   C. 1985 D. 1990
8. Which among the following Decade is designated by SAARC as the SAARC Decade of the Rights of the Child?
   A. 1991-2000 B. 2001-2010
   C. 2011-2010 D. 2006-2015
9. SAFTA agreement came in to force on:
   A. 5 September, 1990 B. 30 January, 2005
   C. 10 December, 1985 D. 1 January, 2006
10. First SAARC summit was held at:
    A. Dhaka B. New Delhi
    C. Colombo D. Islamabad
11. India is part of:
    A. SAARC B. NAFTA
    C. CER S. European Union
12. Which among the following is not a South Asian Country?
    A. Sri Lanka B. Afghanistan
    C. Pakistan D. China
13. India conducted its first Nuclear Test in the year:
    A. 1974 B. 1978
    C. 1998 D. 1996
14. Chakmas are the ethnic groups in which of the following country?
    A. Sri Lanka B. Afghanistan
    C. Pakistan D. Bangladesh
15. India declared LTTE to be a terrorist outfit after the assassination of who among the following Prime Minister of India?
    A. Indira Gandhi B. Rajiv Gandhi
    C. Lal Bahadur Shastri D. None of these
16. Which among the following is associated with the liberation of Bangladesh?
    A. LTTE
    B. Mukti Bahini
    C. NATO
    D. International Court of Justice
17. Bangladesh was liberated from Pakistan in the Year:
    A. 1971 B. 1972
    C. 1980 D. 1985
18. In which year China conducted its first Nuclear explosion:
    A. 1960 B. 1962
    C. 1964 D. 1974
19. What is India's position regarding Iran in the International Atomic Energy Agency in 2005:
    A. India favoured
    B. India abstained from voting
    C. India Voted against
    D. None of these

20. Which among the following is not a principle of India's Nuclear Doctrine today?
A. No first use
B. Credible Minimum deterrent
C. Civilian Control
D. First use

21. Which treaty is a bilateral agreement and governance treaty between India and Pakistan, signed on February 21, 1999?
A. Delhi Declaration B. Colombo Declaration
C. Beijing Declaration D. Lahore Declaration

22. In 1992 India signed which of the following Convention (CWC), stating that it did not have chemical weapons and the capacity or capability to manufacture chemical weapons?
A. NPT B. Biological weapon
C. Chemical Weapons D. Disarmament

23. India's Strategic Nuclear Command was formally established in the year ....
A. 2006 B. 1998
C. 2003 D. 2010

24. The National Security Council (NSC) of India is the apex agency looking into the country's political, economic, energy and strategic security concerns. It was established by who among the following Prime Minister of India?
A. Man Mohan Singh B. Indira Gandhi
C. Atal Behari Vajpayee D. Rajiv Gandhi

25. Which among the following is a principle of US foreign policy during the time of Cold War?
A. Non Alignment
B. Socialism
C. Containment of Communism
D. None of these

26. Who among the following is not associated with NAM?
A. Jawaharlal Nehru
B. Kwame Nkumrah of Ghana
C. Gamel Abdel Nasser
D. Mao- Tse Tung

27. In which year the Bandung Conference was held?
A. 1950 B. 1955
C. 1960 D. 1965

28. Which of the following is a military alliance?
A. SAARC B. EU
C. NATO D. NAM

29. The NAM summit which demanded expansion of the United Nations Security council had met at:
A. Tehran B. Cairo
C. Akarta D. Harare

30. Where does the European Commission have its offices?
A. Brussels B. London
C. Washington DC D. New York

31. Which of the following treaty established the European Union under its current name in 1993?
A. Washington B. Maastricht
C. Utrecht D. None of these

32. IAEA stands for:
A. International Atomic Energy Agency
B. International Alliance of Economic Agencies
C. Indian Atomic Energy Agency
D. None of these

33. In which year ASEAN was formed?
A. 1965 B. 1978
C. 1979 D. 1967

34. Where is head quarters of ASEAN located at?
A. Beijing B. Jakarta
C. Brunei D. None of these

35. Which among the following statement regarding Terrorism is right?
A. There is no universally accepted definition for terrorism
B. There is a universally accepted definition for terrorism
C. United Nations definition on Terrorism is accepted by all the nations
D. None of these

36. Which among the following is not a Panchasheel Principle?
A. Mutual non-aggression
B. Peaceful co-existence
C. No first use of nuclear weapons
D. Equality and mutual benefit

37. The Millenium Development Goals are supposed to be achieved by the year:
A. 2020 B. 2015
C. 2030 D. 2050

38. The 'Blue helmet' refers to:
A. Red Cross
B. UNICEF
C. UN Peace Keepers
D. Human Right volunteers

39. Dumbarton Oaks conference of 1944 emphasis on:
A. Promotion of peace
B. International brotherhood
C. Equality
D. Promotion of human right and fundamental freedom

40. Which decade is known as UN Literacy decade?
A. 1970's B. 1993-2003
C. 2013-2023 D. 2003-2012

41. Camp David Peace Treaty is related to:
A. The developmental practices in the third world countries
B. Korean problem
C. Pakistan problem
D. Palestine problem

42. Prisoner's dilemma is a phenomenon that fuels:
A. arms race B. arms control
C. disarmament D. peace

43. Seventh Chapter of UN charter deals with:
A. Amendment of UN charter
B. Collective Security
C. Trusteeship
D. NIEO

44. Which article of the UN charter permits military action against aggression?
A. 42 B. 44
C. 16 D. 15

45. The Korean issue was in the year:
A. 1950 B. 1947
C. 1991 D. 2001

46. Which of the following decisions in General Assemblies of United Nations requires two-third majority?
A. Peace and security
B. Admission of new members
C. Budgetary matters
D. All the above

47. The Resolution 678 (1990) of UN Security Council deals with:
A. Disarmament B. Kashmir Issue
C. Korean Issue D. Iraque Issue

48. Which one doesn't belong to the methods of peaceful settlement of disputes provided by the U.N?
A. Negotiation
B. Arbitration
C. Judicial settlement
D. Force

49. The Human Rights Council was established in:
A. 2012 B. 1948
C. 1999 D. 2006

50. The 'Third Committee' is associated with:
A. Collective security
B. Trusteeship
C. Human Rights
D. None of the above

51. The main policy-making body of UN dealing with human rights issues is:
A. Security Council
B. The Human Rights Council
C. UNESCO
D. Human Rights Commission

52. The International Convention on the Elimination of All Forms of Discrimination against Women was adapted in the year:
A. 1977 B. 1952
C. 1997 D. 1981

53. The International Covenant on Civil and Political Rights was adapted in the year:
A. 1966 B. 1952
C. 1997 D. 2005

54. The United Nations advisory services programme is related to:
A. UN reforms B. Financial aid
C. Human Rights D. Development

55. The First International tribunal to deal with terrorism as a crime was:
A. Special Court for Sierra Leone
B. International Criminal Tribunal for Rwanda
C. Nuremburg tribunal
D. None of the above

56. The Permanent court of International Justice was established in
A. 1919 B. 1922
C. 1945 D. 1950

57. The treaty of Westphalia was signed in the year:
A. 1648 B. 1957
C. 1888 D. 1216

58. The UNO tries to solve the problems of the world by:
A. oppression
B. using its military force
C. co-operation
D. reducing financial aids preventing import and export

59. "Veto" in UN security council is:
A. the positive vote of all the members
B. the negative vote by a permanent member
C. the negative vote for a central country
D. the negative vote for the security council

60. The United Nations charter contains the:
A. Aims of organization
B. Rates of membership fee
C. Amount of aid to be granted to each country
D. Financial gain for its members

61. The United Nations Organization came into existence as a result of:
A. Two world war
B. A desire of nations to have durable peace
C. Efforts to make world free from wars
D. All the above

62. Which are the specialized agencies of UN known as Breton world sisters?
A. UNESCO and UNICEF
B. IMF and WHO
C. IBRD and UNESCO
D. IMF and World Bank

63. The First International tribunal to deal with terrorism as a crime was:
A. Special Court for Sierra Leone
B. International Criminal Tribunal for Rwanda
C. Nuremburg tribunal
D. None of the above

64. Who is currently appointed as Secretary-General of Gulf Cooperation Council?
A. Fahim bin Sultan Al Qasim
B. Jamil Ibrahim Hejailan
C. Nayef Falah Mubarak Al Hajraf
D. Abdullah Bishara

65. In which year the Charter of the GCC was signed formally establishing the institution?
A. 25 May, 1981 B. 25 May, 1980
C. 25 May, 1985 D. 25 May, 1987

66. Who among the following Prime Minister launched Look East policy in 1992, to give a strategic push to India's engagement with South-East Asia region?
A. P.V. Narasimha Rao B. Narendra Modi
C. Manmohan Singh D. Atal Behari Vajpayee

67. Act East Policy is the successor of:
A. Look West Policy B. Look East Policy
C. Neither A nor B D. Both A & B

68. Prime Minister of India highlighted which of the 4C's of Act East Policy:
(*a*) Culture
(*b*) Commerce
(*c*) Connectivity
(*d*) Capacity building

Select the correct code the options given below:
A. (*a*) & (*b*) B. (*c*) & (*a*)
C. (*b*) & (*d*) D. (*a*), (*b*), (*c*) & (*d*)

69. What is an important dimension of India's Act East Policy?
A. Connectivity B. Capacity building
C. Security D. None of these

70. What is Quad?
A. Quad is an informal strategic dialogue of like-minded democracies
B. It is converging across the Indian and Pacific oceans
C. It comprises of the US, Japan, India and Australia.
D. All of these

71. How many union consisting The African Union (AU) as a continent?
A. 55 countries B. 60 countries
C. 70 countries D. 80 countries

72. In which year the African bloc was founded?
A. On 26 May, 2001 in Addis Ababa
B. On 26 May, 2003 in Addis Ababa
C. On 26 May, 2008 in Addis Ababa
D. On 26 May, 2009 in Addis Ababa

73. Which among the following is not correctly matched?
A. The intention of the AU is to replace the Organisation of African Unity (OAU)
B. It was established on 25 May 1963 in Addis Ababa by 32 signatory governments
C. The AU's secretariat, the African Union Commission, is based in Addis Ababa
D. To achieve greater unity and solidarity in the middle east.

74. In which of the following, a person is constantly followed/chased by another person or group of several peoples?
A. Phishing B. Bulling
C. Stalking D. Identity theft

75. Which of the following usually observe each activity on the internet of the victim, gather all information in the background, and send it to someone else?
A. Malware
B. Spyware
C. Adware
D. All of the above

76. Which of the following refers to stealing one's idea or invention of others and use it for their own benefits?
A. Piracy
B. Plagiarism
C. Intellectual property rights
D. All of the above

77. Which of the following refers to exploring the appropriate, ethical behaviors related to the online environment and digital media platform?
A. Cyber law
B. Cyberethics
C. Cybersecurity
D. Cybersafety

78. Which of the following are famous and common cyber-attacks used by hackers to infiltrate the user's system?
A. DDos and Derive-by Downloads
B. Malware & Malvertising
C. Phishing and Password attacks
D. All of the above

79. In Wi-Fi Security, which of the following protocol is more used?
A. WPA B. WPA2
C. WPS D. Both A and C

80. Which of the following statements is correct about the firewall?
A. It is a device installed at the boundary of a company to prevent unauthorized physical access.
B. It is a device installed at the boundary of an incorporate to protect it against the unauthorized access.
C. It is a kind of wall built to prevent files from damaging the corporate.
D. None of the above

ANSWERS

1	2	3	4	5	6	7	8	9	10
A	B	A	B	C	A	C	B	D	A
11	12	13	14	15	16	17	18	19	20
A	D	A	D	B	B	A	C	C	D
21	22	23	24	25	26	27	28	29	30
D	C	C	C	C	D	B	C	C	A
31	32	33	34	35	36	37	38	39	40
B	A	D	B	A	C	B	C	A	D
41	42	43	44	45	46	47	48	49	50
D	A	B	A	A	A	D	D	D	C
51	52	53	54	55	56	57	58	59	60
B	D	A	D	A	B	A	C	B	A
61	62	63	64	65	66	67	68	69	70
D	D	A	C	A	A	B	D	C	D
71	72	73	74	75	76	77	78	79	80
A	A	D	C	B	D	B	D	B	B

●●●

Governance and Public Policy in India

1. The rise in the popularity of the term governance is closely linked with the:
A. redefinition of the role of state
B. redefinition of the role of civil society organizations
C. redefinition of the role of public undertakings
D. None of these

2. In which of the following report redefined the role of state?
A. World Development Report, 1994
B. World Development Report, 1992
C. World Development Report, 1990
D. World Development Report, 1991

3. Governance refers to:
A. the complex set of institutions and actors
B. the blurring of boundaries and responsibilities for tackling social and economic issues
C. the autonomous self, governing networks of actors
D. All of these

4. World Bank has employed major dimensions to construct measures of governance. These dimensions are:
1. Voice and Accountability—measuring political, civil and human rights
2. Instability and violence—measuring the likelihood of violent threats to or changes in government, including terrorism
3. Government effectiveness—measuring the competence of the bureaucracy and the quality of public service delivery
4. Regulatory burden—measuring the incidence of market, unfriendly policies
5. Rule of law—measuring the quality of contract enforcement, the police, and the courts, as well as the likelihood of crime and violence

Select the correct codes:
A. 1, 2 & 3 B. 3, 4 & 5
C. 1, 2, 3, & 5 D. 1, 2, 3, 4 & 5

5. In which year the term governance gained currency in India with the realization of the Indian economy?
A. 1991 B. 1992
C. 1995 D. 1998

6. Which among the following five year plans explicitly took upon the issue of governance by indicating that governance has in the recent times emerged at the forefront of the development agenda?
A. Fifth Five Year Plan B. Sixth Five Year Plan
C. The Tenth Plan D. 12th Five Year Plan

7. The state comprises the various institutions of:
1. Government 2. Bureaucracy
3. Military 4. Police
5. Courts 6. Social security system

Select the correct codes:
A. 1, 2, 3 & 4 B. 1, 2, 3, 4 & 5
C. 2, 3, 5 & 6 D. 1, 2, 3, 4, 5 & 6

8. Governance was first used by the World Bank in its report on
A. Sub-Saharan Africa in 1989
B. Sub-Saharan Africa in 1990
C. Sub-Saharan Africa in 1998
D. Sub-Saharan Africa in 1994

9. Which of the following is the distinguishing characteristic of State, as compared with other associations?
A. Population B. Territory
C. Government D. Sovereignty

10. Which of the following are the four characteristics of state?
A. Government, territory, population, association
B. Association, sovereignty, territory, population
C. Army, territory, population and sovereignty
D. Population, territory, government and sovereignty

11. The term state has often been confused with:
A. Sovereignty B. Association
C. Nation D. Government

12. Which of the following is not true about difference between the State and the Government?
A. The will of the State is expressed through Government
B. The State is concrete while the Government is abstract
C. The State has original whereas Government has delegated powers
D. The State is large whereas Government is a small body

13. The relationship between civil society and state refers to:

1. The civil society is an integral part of governance
2. Civil society also mediates the relationship between the state and the market
3. The state mediates the relationship between civil society and the market for the welfare of people
4. The state provides an institutional framework within which civil society can prosper and flourish

Select the correct codes:

A. 1, 2 & 3 B. 2, 3 & 4
C. 1, 3 & 4 D. 1, 2, 3 & 4

14. Civil society can be understood as:

A. the whole population of a state.
B. the people within a state who behave in a politically civilised way
C. a social organization made up of retired civil servants.
D. a framework within which people who lack political authority conduct their lives.

15. Why did the term 'civil society' become popular in the 1980s?

A. At that time there was growing disenchantment with the perceived dishonesty of governments, especially as recipients of aid
B. The downfall of many totalitarian regimes was attributed to movements generated by civil society
C. It seemed to offer the possibility of peaceful change in other states
D. All of the above

16. Why has the term 'civil society' aroused suspicion in some Islamic states?

A. In those countries the state denies civil rights to its citizens
B. It can be seen as part of a project of 'Westernization'
C. The term is difficult to translate into Arabic
D. It failed to recognize that brutal violence is the only way to facilitate change

17. The periphery of participation should enlarge to include:

A. the civil society B. the state
C. the sovereignty D. None of these

18. Good government should aim at sustainable human development, participation of civil society organizations and fair and free elections. The statement is made by:

A. ILO B. General Assembly
C. UNDP D. IMF

19. Good governance is associated with:

A. accountability of political leadership
B. enlightened policy-making
C. a civil service imbued with a professional ethos
D. All of these

20. Good governance incorporates features like:

1. equity 2. participation
3. transparency 4. accountability and
5. rule of law

Select the correct codes:

A. 1, 2, 4 & 5 B. 2, 3, 4 & 5
C. 1, 3, 4 & 5 D. 1, 2, 3, 4 & 5

21. Good Governance Day (Susasan Divas) was established in India in 2014, to be observed annually on 25-December, the birth anniversary of:

A. former Prime Minister Shri Atal Bihari Vajpayee
B. former Prime Minister Shri P.V. Narsimha Rao
C. former Prime Minister Shri V.P. Singh
D. former Prime Minister Dr. Manmohan Singh

22. Good Governance as "the manner in which power is exercised in the management of a country's economic and social resources for development". This definition is made by:

A. 1992 report entitled "Governance and Development" of the World Bank
B. 1992 report entitled "Governance and Development" of the IMF
C. 1992 report entitled "Governance and Development" of African Union
D. None of these

23. The Principles of Good Governance defined by United Nations, are mainly on:

1. Participation, Rule of Law
2. Consensus Oriented, Equity and Inclusiveness
3. Effectiveness and Efficiency
4. Accountability, Transparency & Responsiveness

Select the correct codes:

A. 1, 2 & 3 B. 2, 3 & 4
C. 1, 3 & 4 D. 1, 2, 3 & 4

24. The Initiatives for Good Governance in India are mainly on:

1. Right to Information
2. E-Governance
3. Ease of Doing Business
4. Decentralization
5. Police Reforms

Select the correct codes:

A. 1, 2, 3 & 5 B. 2, 3, 4 & 5
C. 1, 3, 4 & 5 D. 1, 2, 3, 4 & 5

25. The Model Police Act as a part of good governance initiatives was implemented in the year:
A. 2015 B. 2017
C. 2018 D. 2019

26. The Aspirational Districts Programme (ADP) was launched in January 2018 to:
1. transform the lives of people in the under-developed areas of the county
2. Anchored in NITI Aayog, the programme is aimed at transforming 115 most backward district
3. Focused interventions in the field of health and nutrition,
4. Focused interventions in education, agriculture and water management,
5. Focused interventions in financial inclusion and skill development

Select the correct codes:
A. 1 & 2 B. 4 & 3
C. 3 & 5 D. 1, 2, 3, 4 & 5

27. The Good Governance Index was launched on the occasion of Good Governance Day on:
A. 25 December, 2019 B. 25 December, 2020
C. 25 December, 2018 D. 25 December, 2017

28. The Good Governance Index is a uniform tool across States to assess:
1. the Status of Governance and impact of various interventions taken up by the State Government
2. the Status of Governance and impact of various interventions taken up by the Union Territories
3. to provide quantifiable data to compare the state of governance in all states and Union Territories
4. to improve governance and shift to result oriented approaches and administration.

Select the correct codes:
A. 1, 2 & 3 B. 2, 3 & 4
C. 1, 3 & 4 D. 1, 2, 3 & 4

29. Objective of probity in governance:
1. To ensure accountability in governance
2. To maintain integrity in Public Service
3. To ensure compliance with the process
4. To preserve public confidence in Govt process
5. To avoid the potential for misconduct, fraud, and corruption

Select the correct codes:
A. 1, 2, 3 & 4 B. 2, 3, 4 & 5
C. 1, 3 & 5 D. 1, 2, 3, 4 & 5

30. The ethical concern of governance has been given in both eastern and western literature like:
1. Bhagavad Gita 2. Arthashastra
3. Confucius 4. Plato
5. Mill, etc

Select the correct codes:
A. 1, 3 & 5 B. 2, 3, 4 & 5
C. 1, 3, 4 & 5 D. 1, 2, 3, 4 & 5

31. The Chairman of First Administrative Reforms commission:
A. Venkidachellaya B. Fasal Ali
C. Hanumanthaya D. None of these

32. MGNREGA stands for:
A. Mahatma Gandhi National Rural Employment Guarantee Act.
B. National Rural Integration Progremme.
C. A project under UN
D. None of these

33. Sevottam associated with:
A. Ombdusman
B. Lok Ayukta
C. Grievances Redress Cell
D. Supreme Court

34. In India Omudsman is known as:
A. Sessions Judge B. Municif Judge
C. Lok Ayukta D. Lok Pal

35. In which one of the following kinds of a public undertaking ministerial control is all pervasive?
A. Government company
B. Departmental undertakings
C. Government corporation
D. Joint undertaking

36. Of all controls over public administration the one which is more continuous and self-corrective is:
A. Control by the legislature
B. Control by the executive
C. Control by the judiciary
D. Control by the media

37. What is about Accountability and the Right to Information Act in governance?
1. The Right to Information Act, 2005 has introduced a huge element of transparency in the decision-making in the government
2. Digitisation of various services to the citizens has not only facilitated faster delivery of services
3. It also provided a clear trail of transactions for any analysis by an oversight agency.

Select the correct codes:
A. 1 & 2 B. 2 & 3
C. 1 & 3 D. 1, 2 & 3

38. Accountability and the Citizen's Charter are meant for:
1. The Citizen's Charter also clearly spelt out the responsibilities of various agencies of the government.

2. The Citizens Charter of the Central Board of Direct Taxes (CBDT) provides for inter-alia service delivery standards
3. Includes the specified timelines for issue of refunds or redressal of grievances

Select the correct codes:

A. 1 & 2 B. 2 & 3
C. 1 & 3 D. 1, 2 & 3

39. The role of Vigilance in Accountability:
1. The institutional mechanisms existence of strong and independent accountability institutions is a necessary condition for good governance.
2. These institutions can detect the violations and deviations from prescribed norms as well as the instances of poor administration
3. They can indicate the abuse of power and unconstitutional conduct

Select the correct codes:

A. 1 & 2 B. 2 & 3
C. 1 & 3 D. 1, 2 & 3

40. Which of the following article of the Indian Constitution says, the Union Budget of a year is referred to as the Annual Financial Statement (AFS)?

A. Article 112 B. Article 114
C. Article 115 D. Article 116

41. Judicial control over administration refers to:

A. The control exercised by the Courts over the administration is called judicial control
B. The power of the court to keep the administrative acts within the limits of law
C. It also implies the right of an aggrieved citizen to challenge the wrongful act of administration in the court of law
D. The primary purpose of judicial control over administration is the protection of the rights and liberty of citizens

42. Which among the following Instruments of Checks & Balances are in the democratic set up in the country?

1. Legislature 2. Executive
3. Judiciary 4. Civil society groups

Select the correct codes:

A. 1 & 2 B. 2 & 3
C. 1, 2 & 3 D. 1, 3 & 4

43. The Legislative control over executive are mainly on:
1. Power to assess works of the executive through the question hour and zero hour
2. Impeachment of the President
3. The executive acting through Ministers cannot raise money by taxation
4. The executive borrowing or otherwise without the authority of Parliament

Select the correct codes:

A. 1, 2, 3 & 4 B. 2, 3 & 4
C. 1, 2 & 3 D. 1, 3 & 4

44. The major Legislative Control over executive are mainly on:
1. Question Hour
2. Adjournment Debates
3. Debates on Enactment of Acts and Amendments
4. Budget Discussion
5. President's Speech
6. Audit

Select the correct codes:

A. 1, 2, 3, 5 & 6 B. 1, 2, 3, 4, 5 & 6
C. 1, 2, 3, 4 & 5 D. 2, 3, 5 & 6

45. The Administrative control over the executive are mainly on:
1. The administration performs the policymaking function concerning finance
2. Government decides the policy of expenditure
3. Acceptance of provision in the budget estimates
4. Questions like pay, pension and provident fund to the officials are all determined by the government

Select the correct codes:

A. 1, 2 & 4 B. 1, 2, 3 & 4
C. 1, 2 & 3 D. 2, 3 & 4

46. The Administrative Reforms Commission in its report on "Finance Accounts and Audit" highlighted the problem and observed that: "The Control of the Finance Minister" over public expenditure is exercised, in the main, three stages: What are these?
1. Approval of programmes or policies in principle
2. Acceptance of provision in the budget estimates, and
3. Prior sanction to incurring of expenditure subject to such power as have been delegated to the administrative ministries
4. Administration has to provide the machinery

Select the correct codes:

A. 1, 2 & 3 B. 1, 2, 3 & 4
C. 2, 3 & 4 D. 1, 3 & 4

47. The advantages of Budgetary Control System refers to:
1. The extent by which actual results have varied from defined objective
2. The centralized control with delegated responsibility
3. Budget under various functional units indicates the limits for expenses and results to be achieved
4. Budgetary system helps managers to learn from past experience

Select the correct codes:

A. 1, 2 & 3 B. 1, 2, 3 & 4
C. 1, 2 & 4 D. 2, 3 & 4

48. Control through Parliamentary Committees refers to:

1. control over revenue
2. expenditure
3. borrowing
4. accounts

Select the correct codes:

A. 1, 2 & 3 B. 1, 2, 3 & 4
C. 1, 2 & 4 D. 2, 3 & 4

49. Judicial control over legislature and executive are mainly on:

A. Impeachment and the removal of the judges
B. Unamendability of the constitution under the basic structure doctrine
C. The power to review executive action to determine if it violates the Constitution
D. All of these

50. Administrative culture means:

1. improving the Performance and Integrity of the Public Services
2. the civil servants are to adhere to ethical standards
3. committed to basic principles of the Constitution
4. to regulate the relationship between the politicians and the civil servants

Select the correct codes:

A. 1, 2 & 3 B. 1, 2, 3 & 4
C. 1, 2 & 4 D. 2, 3 & 4

51. Which of the following measures were taken up by the GOI in administrative reforms is/are correct?

A. Secretariat Reorganization Committee, 1947
B. Shri N. Gopalaswamy Ayyangar Report, 1950
C. A.D. Gorwala Committee, 1951
D. Committee on Plan Projects, 1958

52. Who was the chairman of the Administrative Reforms Commission (ARC), 1966?

A. K Hanumanthaiya B. Veerappa Moily
C. Shri Dharam Vira D. L K Jha

53. In which year "The Second Administrative Reforms Commission" (ARC) was constituted as a Commission of Inquiry, under the Chairmanship of Veerappa Moily?

A. 31 August, 2005 B. 30th July, 2007
C. 30th March, 2007 D. 30th April, 2006

54. In which year at the central level the Right to Information Act was passed by the Parliament?

A. 2008 B. 2007
C. 2005 D. 2006

55. The Right to Information in India is governed by two major bodies. What are these?

1. Central Information Commission (CIC)
2. State Information Commissions (SIC)
3. Consumer Commission (CC)
4. National Human Rights Commission (NHRC)

Select the correct codes:

A. 1 & 2 B. 1 & 4
C. 2 & 3 D. 3 & 4

56. Which of the following porovisions regarding "National Water Policy, 2012" is/are correct?

1. Envisages to establish a standardized national information system with a network of data banks and data bases
2. Guidelines for the safety of storage dams and other water-related structures.
3. Regulate exploitation of groundwater
4. Resource planning and recycling for providing maximum availability.

Select the correct codes:

A. 1, 2, 3 & 4 B. 2, 3 & 4
C. 1, 2 & 3 D. 1, 3 & 4

57. State Public Information Officer is directly under the corresponding:

A. State Governor
B. State Chief Minister
C. Cabinet Ministers
D. President of India

58. Consumer Protection Act aims at:

1. to provide better and all-round protection to consumers
2. applies to the whole of India
3. applies to all goods and services unless otherwise expressly notified by the Central Government
4. has no jurisdiction over the State Information Commission

Select the correct codes:

A. 1, 2 & 3 B. 1, 2 & 4
C. 2, 3 & 4 D. 3 & 4

59. Consumer Protection act:

1. provides for a three-tier consumer grievance redressal machinery with the District Forums
2. provides for a three-tier consumer grievance redressal machinery
3. provides for a three-tier consumer grievance redressal machinery at the base
4. provides for a three-tier consumer grievance redressal machinery at the middle level
5. provides for a three-tier consumer grievance redressal machinery at the National Commission at the apex level

Select the correct codes:
A. 1, 2 & 3 B. 1, 2, 3, 4 & 5
C. 1, 2, 3 & 5 D. 2, 3 & 4

60. In which year "The Consumer Protection act" was passed?
A. 1986 B. 1987
C. 1988 D. 1999

61. In which among the following act is/are correct?
1. The Essential Commodities Act, 1955
2. The Prevention of Food Adulteration Act, 1955
3. MRTP Act, 1970

Select the correct codes:
A. 1 & 2 B. 1, 2 & 3
C. 1 & 3 D. 2 & 3

62. In which country The concept of Citizens Charters originated?
A. Britain B. France
C. Poalnd D. Austarlia

63. The Right of Citizens for Time Bound Delivery of Goods and Services and Redressal of their Grievances Bill, 2011 (Citizens Charter):
1. Seeks to create a mechanism to ensure timely delivery of goods and services to citizens
2. It requires every public authority to publish a CC within six months of the commencement of the Act
3. Levies a penalty of up to ₹ 50,000 for failure to render services
4. Emphasised on citizens as customers

Select the correct codes:
A. 1, 2 & 4 B. 1, 2, 3 & 4
C. 1, 2 & 3 D. 2, 3 & 4

64. Which is the oldest known system designed for the redressal of citizen's grievance?
A. Ombudsman System B. Lokpal
C. Lokayukta D. None of the above

65. Which was the first Commonwealth country in the world to adopt the Ombudsman system?
A. India B. Sweden
C. New Zealand D. United Kingdom

66. The 'Procurator system' is still running in which of the following countries?
A. India B. Sweden
C. New Zealand D. Russia

67. Consider the following three statements:
1. The judiciary is within the purview of Lokpal/ Lokayukta in India
2. In New Zealand, the judiciary is NOT within the purview of the Parliamentary Commissioner for Investigation
3. In Sweden, the judiciary is NOT within the purview of the Ombudsman system

Which of the above statement/s is/are true?
A. Only 1 and 3 B. Only 2 and 3
C. Only 2 D. All are true

68. Which was the first Indian state to establish the institution of Lokayukta?
A. Bihar B. Uttar Pradesh
C. Andhra Pradesh D. Maharashtra

69. Which state's Lokayukta's office is considered to be the strongest in terms of power and scope?
A. Bihar B. Karnataka
C. Andhra Pradesh D. Maharashtra

70. When did The Lokpal and Lokayuktas Act, 2013 came into force?
A. June 2013 B. May 2013
C. December 2013 D. January 2013

71. Who appoints the Lokayukta and Upalokayukta?
A. Governor
B. Chief Minister
C. Speaker of Lok Sabha
D. Judge of High Court

72. Which of the following committee recommended for Panchayati Raj System in India?
A. Punchhi Samiti
B. Balwantrai Mehta Committee
C. Singhvi Committee
D. None of the following

73. How many tiers are there in the Panchayati Raj system of India?
A. One-tier B. Two-tier
C. Three-tier D. Four-tier

74. Which of the following system is established on the basis of the direct election?
A. Gram Panchayat B. Block Committee
C. Zila Parishad D. Both B and C

75. Which of the following statements is not correct?
A. Panchayati Raj was established in India by Jawahar Lal Nehru
B. Madhya Pradesh was the first state which implemented The Panchayati Raj system in India
C. 73rd Constitutional amendment was implemented in 1992
D. Tamil Nadu has adopted the bicameral method

76. Which of the following Article is related to Panchayati Raj?
A. Article 243 B. Article 324
C. Article 124 D. Article 73

77. Which schedule was added to the Constitution by the 73rd Constitutional Amendment?
A. 6th B. 7th
C. 9th D. 11th

78. How many posts are reserved for women at all levels in the Panchayati raj system.
A. 1/3 B. 1/2
C. 2/3 D. 1/4

79. Who gives the final approval to the five-year plans of India?
A. National Development Council (NDC)
B. Ministry of Finance
C. Planning Commission (now NITI Aayog)
D. President of India

80. The very first five-year plan of India was based on the model of:
A. Mahalanobis model B. Harrod Domar Model
C. Bombay Plan D. None of these

81. Which programme gave the slogan of Garibi Hatao?
A. 7th five-year plan B. 3rd five year plan
C. 6th five year plan D. 5th five-year plan

82. Jawahar Rojgar Yojna was launched in:
A. 5th five year plan B. 6th five year plan
C. 8th five year plan D. 7th five year plan

83. Which statement depicts the best definition of sustainable development?
A. It means optimal utilization of natural resources.
B. Sustainable use of natural resources without considering the need of the future generation.
C. Present generation fulfills its needs while considers the needs of the future generation as well.
D. None of the above

84. The concept of sustainable development is recommended by the:
A. Brundtland Commission
B. Brettonwoods Commission
C. World Bank
D. World Economic Forum

85. Which of the following is considered as the three pillars of the sustainability?
A. Economic development
B. Social development
C. Environment protection
D. All of the above

86. Which of the following statement/s is true about the sustainable development?
1. It was introduced in early 1980's in particular through the publication of the World Conservation Strategy by IUCN, UNEP and WWF.
2. It was introduced in early 1992's on the recommendation of Brettonwoods commission.
3. It was introduced in early 1980's on the recommendation of Brundtland commission.
4. It means that Present generation should fulfill its needs while considering the needs of the future generation as well.

Codes:
A. 1, 2 & 3 B. 1, 2, 3 & 4
C. 1, 2 & 4 D. 2, 3 & 4

87. Which among the following component is the foundation of participatory development?
A. Good Governance B. Governance
C. State D. Judicial review

88. The Banking Ombudsman Scheme 1995 was framed by the Reserve Bank of India under the:
A. Banking Regulations Act, 1949
B. Banking Regulations Act, 1959
C. Banking Regulations Act, 1969
D. Banking Regulations Act, 1979

89. Participatory Development means:
1. It is top-down participation in the sense that the management of the project defines where, when and how much the people can participate
2. It is more dominant in terms of resources available
3. It means conventional project practice in a more participatory and sensitive manner
4. It is bottom up participation

Select the correct codes:
A. 1 & 2 B. 1, 2, 3 & 4
C. 1, 2 & 3 D. 3 & 4

90. Participation in Development means:
1. It is bottom up participation in the sense that the local people have full control over the processes and the project provides for necessary flexibility
2. It is more prevalent with NGOs then with the governments
3. It entails genuine efforts to enage in practices which openly and radically encourage people's participation
4. It is top-down participation

Select the correct codes:
A. 1, 2 & 3 B. 1, 2, 3 & 4
C. 1, 3 & 4 D. 3 & 4

91. 'NAMASTE' is a portal of which Union Ministry of India?
A. Ministry of Defence
B. Ministry of Communications
C. Ministry of AYUSH
D. Ministry of External Affairs

92. The Agriculture trading portal e-NAM (National Agriculture Market) was launched on April 14, in which year?

A. 2010 B. 2012
C. 2016 D. 2018

93. Mukhyamantri Yuva Yogayog Yojana', that was seen in news, is an initiative of which Indian state/UT?

A. Madhya Pradesh B. Uttar Pradesh
C. Haryana D. Tripura

94. The Prime Minister recently launched 10000 FPOs all over the country. What does FPO stand for?

A. Farmer Priority Organisations
B. Farmer Produce Organisations
C. Farmer Productivity Organisations
D. Farmer Primary Organisations

95. What is the objective of the 'covid19.odisha.gov.in' portal launched by Odisha in tackling the crisis faced due to Covid-19?

A. Provide official data on positive cases
B. Registration of migrant workers
C. Registration for Public Distribution System
D. Provide tele-medicine facility

96. Which of the following provision of houses to every family is /are correct?

1. The President's clarion call to ensure the provision of houses to every family
2. It remains the key objective of the 'Housing for All' scheme.
3. The government has made it clear that one of its key priorities is to ensure safe and affordable housing for all.
4. This mandate also includes upgradation of slums

Codes:

A. 1 & 2 B. 1, 2, 3 & 4
C. 2 & 4 D. Only 2

97. PMAY-G is converged with Swachh Bharat Mission (Gramin) and Mahatma Gandhi National Rural Employment Guarantee Scheme (MGNREGS) for the:

1. construction of sanitary toilets
2. unskilled wage component
3. support provided to homeless families
4. or to those who live in kutcha houses as per the Socio-Economic Caste Census (SECC), 2011 data.

Codes:

A. 1 & 2 B. 1, 2, 3 & 4
C. 2 & 4 D. Only 2

98. Under the Pradhan Mantri Awas Yojana "Urban-PMAY-U), the mission aims to:

1. achieve the objective of 'Housing for All' by 2027
2. achieve the objective of 'Housing for All' by 2035
3. achieve the objective of 'Housing for All' by 2022
4. achieve the objective of 'Housing for All' by 2024

99. The mission aims to achieve the objective of "Housing for All' by 2022 through its four pillars. What are these?

1. in-situ slum redevelopment
2. affordable housing through a credit linked subsidy scheme
3. affordable housing in partnership between public and private agencies
4. subsidy for beneficiary led individual house construction or enhancement

Codes:

A. 1, 2, 3 & 4 B. 1, 2, 3
C. 2 & 4 D. Only 2

100. The 'Housing for All' scheme faces the following key constraints: Which are correctly matched?

1. Lack of access to finance from formal financial institutions.
2. Long-drawn out, multi-level approval system in urban areas in a large majority of municipal jurisdictions.
3. For several categories of houses or those in particular locations, these delays are common even where a single window system has reportedly been introduced
4. Limited private sector participation in affordable housing schemes in urban areas.

Codes:

A. 1, 2, 3 & 4 B. 1, 2, 3
C. 2 & 4 D. Only 2

101. What was the theme of the economic survey 2021?

A. COVID-19 warriors
B. COVID 19 Pandemic
C. Doctors and Health Workers
D. None

102. The Swachh Bharat Mission (SBM) was launched on October 2, 2014, to make India open defecation free by 2019. It has two sub missions. What are these?

A. Swachh Bharat Mission (Gramin) for rural areas under the Ministry of Drinking Water and Sanitation (MDWS)
B. Swachh Bharat Mission (Urban) for urban areas under the Ministry of Housing and Urban Affairs
C. Neither A nor B
D. Both A & B

103. In which year the government of India launched "Namami Gange" scheme clean and rejuvenate the River Ganga to maintain "Aviral" and "Nirmal Dhara" and ensure its ecological and geological integrity?

A. 2014-15 B. 2017-18
C. 2018-19 D. 2010-11

104. Under Ayushman Bharat, scale-up a new vision for comprehensive primary health care across the country, built on the platform of health and wellness centres (HWCs), to:

1. Provide quality ambulatory services for an inclusive package of diagnostic, curative, rehabilitative and palliative care, close to the people
2. Deliver preventive and promotion services, and action on the ground to tackle determinants of ill health locally
3. Create a mass movement for Healthy India (Swasth Bharat Jan Andolan)
4. None of these

Codes:

A. 1, 2, 3 & 4 B. 1, 2 & 3
C. 1, 2 & 4 D. 2, 3 & 4

105. The key features of New India's primary health care system will be:

1. Primary health care nucleus comprising five to six upgraded sub-centres
2. Coupled with a primary health centre, and population outreach
3. Planning of health facility distribution in districts
4. Digitization of family records and information from the community to the facility level

Codes:

A. 1, 2, 3 & 4
B. 1, 2 & 3
C. 2, 3 & 4
D. 1 & 2

106. On the strong platform of Pradhan Mantri – Jan Arogya Yojana (PM-JAY), the objectives of the schme are to:

1. Attain a coverage of at least 75 per cent of the population with publicly financed health insurance (covering most secondary and tertiary care procedures) by 2022-23
2. Reduce by 50 per cent the proportion of households facing catastrophic health expenditure from the current levels
3. Quality of health care delivered to citizens and population health outcomes.

Codes:

A. 1 & 2 B. 1, 2 & 3
C. 2 & 3 D. 1 & 3

107. Which among the following scheme is coming under Universal Health coverage?

A. PM-JAY under Ayushman Bharat
B. Rashtriya Swasthya Bima Yojana (RSBY)
C. Pradhan Mantri Bhartiya Janaushadhi Pariyojana
D. RSBY scheme

108. Which of the following statements regarding Ek Bharat Shrestha Bharat programme is/are correct?

1. It aims to actively enhance interaction between people of diverse cultures living in different States and UTs in India.
2. Ministry of culture is the nodal agency for coordination of the programme.

Select the correct answer using the code given below:

A. 1 only B. 2 only
C. Both 1 and 2 D. Neither 1 nor 2

109. Recently The State of Food Security and Nutrition in the World, 2019 was released. In this context consider the following statements: Which of the statements is/are correct?

1. It is a biannual report issued by FAO, IFAD, UNEP, WEP, and WHO.
2. For the first time, the report comes with estimates of the prevalence of moderate or severe food insecurity based on the Food Insecurity Experience Scale (FIES).
3. The report highlights that hunger is declining.

Select the correct code:

A. 1 and 2 only B. 1 and 3 only
C. 2 only D. 1 only

110. Which of the following are the features of PM Formalization of Micro Food Processing Enterprises Scheme?

1. Adoption of One District One product Approach
2. Focus on waste to wealth products and minor forest produce
3. Credit-linked capital subsidy for setting new micro food processing units
4. Focus on capacity building and research

Select the correct answer using the code given below:

A. 1, 2 and 3 only B. 1, 2 and 4 only
C. 1, 3 and 4 only D. 2, 3 and 4 only

111. Consider the following statements regarding the POSHAN Abhiyaan. Which of the statement are correct?

1. It is a multi-ministerial convergence mission with the vision to ensure attainment of malnutrition free India by 2022.
2. The Ministry of Health and Family Welfare (MoHFW) is implementing POSHAN Abhiyaan.

3. Its objective is to reduce stunting in identified Districts of India with the highest malnutrition burden by improving utilization of key Anganwadi Services and improving the quality of Anganwadi Services delivery.

Select the correct code:
A. 1 and 2 only B. 2 and 3 only
C. 1 and 3 only D. 1, 2 and 3

112. Consider the following statements regarding Pradhan Mantri Kisan Maan Dhan Yojana (PM-KMY): Which of the following statements is/are correct?
1. It is a Central Sector Scheme administered by the Department of Finance, Ministry of Finance.
2. The Life Insurance Corporation of India (LIC) is the Pension Fund Manager for the scheme and responsible for Pension pay out.

Select the correct code:
A. 1 only B. 2 only
C. Both 1 and 2 D. Neither 1 nor 2

113. Consider the following statements about Jan Soochna Portal. Which of the statements is/are correct?
1. It is the first ever public information portal launched by the government of Rajasthan.
2. It will not require citizens to submit RTI application for seeking information.
3. The portal will prevent anomalies and corruption in government.

Select the correct code:
A. 1, 2 and 3 B. 1 only
C. 2 and 3 only D. 2 only

114. Consider the following statements regarding National Nutrition Survey. Which of the statements is/are correct?
1. Comprehensive national nutrition survey was conducted by Ministry of women and child development (MoWCD) in partnership with UNICEF.
2. Clinical development services was the monitoring agency for the survey.

Select the correct code:
A. 1 only B. 2 only
C. Both 1 and 2 D. Neither 1 nor 2

115. Consider the following statements regarding the Right to Information Act (RTI) 2005. Which of the statements is/are correct?
1. A non-government organization financed indirectly by the funds of Government is a public authority under the act.
2. While the institution of the Supreme Court falls under the ambit of the act, the office of Chief Justice of India (CJI) has been exempted.

Select the correct code:
A. 1 only B. 2 only
C. Both 1 and 2 D. Neither 1 nor 2

116. Consider the following statements regarding the Bharatiya Poshan Krishi Kosh (BPKK): Which of the statements is/are correct?
1. It was launched by Ministry of Agriculture with support from Bill & Melinda Gates Foundation.
2. It aims to reduce malnutrition through a multi-sectoral results-based framework.

Select the correct code:
A. 1 only B. 2 only
C. Both 1 and 2 D. Neither 1 nor 2

117. With reference to Shala Darpan Portal, consider the following statements: Which of the statements are correct?
1. It provides an integrated platform to meet the educational and administrative needs of all stakeholders.
2. It has been launched by Union Ministry of Human Resource Development for Kendriya Vidyalaya Samiti.
3. It is a duplex communication system capable of sending and receiving effective dialogue between every stakeholder.

Select the correct code:
A. 1 and 2 only B. 2 and 3 only
C. 1 and 3 only D. 1, 2 and 3

118. Which of the following statements is/are correct regarding Swachh Survekshan?
1. Ministry of Drinking Water and Sanitation released Swachh Survekshan League in New Delhi.
2. In the category of population between one lakh and 10 lakhs, Jamshedpur occupied the 1st spot.

Select the correct answer using the code given below:
A. 1 only B. 2 only
C. Both 1 and 2 D. Neither 1 nor 2

119. Consider the following statements regarding Sustainable Development Goals India Index: Which of the statements is/are correct?
1. Ministry of Health and Family Welfare has released the second edition of the Sustainable Development Goals (SDG) India Index.
2. India's composite score improved from 57 in 2018 to 60 in 2019-20

Select the correct code:
A. 1 only B. 2 only
C. Both 1 and 2 D. Neither 1 nor 2

120. Consider the following statements regarding 'Swachh Paryatan' mobile app: Which of the statements are correct?

1. The app facilitates general public to communicate their complaints about any unclean area/garbage piles in and around tourist destinations.
2. It has been launched by Ministry of Drinking Water and Sanitation.
3. Only the Adarsh Smarak Monuments have been identified for inclusion in this app.

A. 1 and 2 only B. 2 and 3 only
C. 1 and 3 only D. 1, 2 and 3

121. The 3rd version of Bhuvan Panchayat web portal was recently launched. Consider the following statements in this regard: Which of the statements is/are correct?

1. It aims to provide geo-spatial services to aid gram panchayat development planning process.
2. It has been launched by Ministry of Panchayati Raj.

Select correct code:
A. 1 only B. 2 only
C. Both 1 and 2 D. Neither 1 nor 2

122. Consider the following statements regarding UMANG App: Which of the above statements is/are correct?

1. It is developed by National e-Governance Division (NeGD) to fast-track mobile governance in India.
2. It provides major services offered by only Central and State Government departments.
3. Presently, it supports only English language.

Select the correct code:
A. 1 only B. 1 and 2 only
C. 2 and 3 only D. 1, 2 and 3

123. Consider the following statements regarding Good Governance Index (GGI): Which of the above statements is/are correct?

1. Ministry of Housing and Urban Affairs has launched the 'Good Governance Index'.
2. The objectives of GGI are to provide quantifiable data to compare the state of governance in all states and UTs.

Select the correct code:
A. 1 only B. 2 only
C. Both 1 and 2 D. Neither 1 nor 2

124. Essential Commodities Act (ECA), 1955 was in news recently. Which of the following statement(s) is/are incorrect about ECA?

1. ECA was enacted to ensure the easy availability of essential commodities to consumers.
2. Government intervention through ECA can increase price volatility of essential Commodities
3. ECA incentivises storage infrastructure development

Select the correct code:
A. 1 and 2 only B. 1 and 3 only
C. 3 only D. 1, 2 and 3

125. The Mahatma Gandhi National Rural Employment Guarantee Act (MGNREGA) is the world's largest:
A. Anti-poverty programme
B. Housing for all Program
C. Water for all Program
D. None of these

126. In the cash benefits transferred in 2019-20 under the Direct Benefits Transfer Scheme, the largest head under which DBT transfers were made was:
A. Fertilizer Subsidy
B. PAHAL – LPG Subsidy
C. MGNREGA
D. Farmer compensations for drought, calamity, etc.

127. Which of the following is/are true regarding Pradhan Mantri Awaas Yojana — Gramin?

1. Cost of unit assistance to be shared between Central and State Governments in the ratio 75:25 in plain areas.
2. The beneficiary will be entitled to 90 days of unskilled labour from MGNREGA.

Select the correct code:
A. Only 1 B. Only 2
C. Both 1 and 2 D. Neither 1 nor 2

128. National Mission for a Green India is merged with:
A. Swachha Bharat Abhiyan
B. National River Conservation scheme
C. National Afforestation Program
D. MGNREGA

129. Which of the following statements are correct?

1. MGNREGS fulfills the constitutional rights in India.
2. MGNREGA is to be implemented mainly by gram panchayats.
3. The places where the recent unseasonal rain and hailstorms have affected crops the government will increase the number of work days under the Mahatma Gandhi National Rural Employment Guarantee Scheme to 200 from 100.

Select the correct code:
A. 1 & 2 B. 1 & 3
C. 2 & 3 D. 1, 2 & 3

130. With reference to National Rural Health Mission (NRHM), which of the following are the jobs of 'ASHA' a trained community health worker?

1. Accompanying women to the health facility for antenatal care checkup
2. Using pregnancy test kits for early detection of pregnancy
3. Providing information on nutrition and immunization
4. Conducting the delivery of baby

Select the correct answer using the codes given below:

A. 1, 2 and 3 Only B. 2 and 4 Only
C. 1 and 3 Only D. 1, 2, 3 and 4

131. Who is the current CEO oı the NITI Aayog?

A. Rajeev Kumar B. Arvind Subramanyam
C. Amitabh Kant D. Narendra Modi

132. Which of the following statement is correct about the NITI Aayog?

A. NITI Aayog was on formed 25 January, 2016
B. NITI Aayog comes under the Ministry of Commerce and Industry
C. The full form of NITI Aayog is National Institute for Transforming India
D. The NITI Aayog is a policy think tank of the Government of India

133. When was NITI Aayog established?

A. 1 January, 2015 B. 25 January, 2016
C. 14 May, 2014 D. 1 July, 2015

134. Which of the following statement is/are correct about the NITI Aayog?

1. The aim of NITI Aayog is to achieve Sustainable Development Goals and to enhance cooperative federalism in the country.
2. The Prime Minister of India is the ex-officio Chairperson of the NITI Aayog
3. There are 8 full time members in the NITI Aayog

Select the correct code:

A. Only 2 & 3 B. Only 2
C. Only 1 D. Only 1 & 2

135. Who of the following is the part of Governing Council of NITI Aayog?

A. All Chief Ministers of the states
B. Chief Ministers of Delhi and Puducherry
C. Lieutenant Governor of Andaman & Nicobar Island
D. All of the above

136. Which of the following is not the function of the NITI Aayog?

A. To evolve a shared vision of national development priorities sectors and strategies
B. To foster cooperative federalism
C. To give final approval to the Five Year Plans of India
D. To create a knowledge, innovation and entrepreneurial support system

137. Which of the following district topped the rank of Aspirational district for the period of June 1, 2018, and October 31, 2018.

A. Virudhunagar (Tamil Nadu)
B. Mewat (Haryana)
C. Pakur (Jharkhand)
D. Hailakandi (Assam)

138. Which of the following is true about the Aspirational district initiative of NITI Aayog?

A. Aspirational ranking of districts is based on 10 parameters
B. The first delta ranking for aspirational districts was released in June 2018.
C. The aspirational district programme was launched by Prime Minister Narendra Modi on January 5, 2016.
D. All of the above statements are true

139. Which of the following is not matched correctly about NITI Aayog?

A. NITI Aayog head office: Delhi
B. Narendra Modi: Chairman
C. Parent Agency: Government of India
D. NITI Aayog replaced: National Development Council

140. Right to Education Act (RTE) provided free and compulsory education to children in 2009 and enforced it as a fundamental right under which article?

A. Article 21-A
B. Article 22-A
C. Article 23-A
D. Article 24-A

141. In which part Originally, Article 45 and Article 39 (f) of DPSP, had a provision for state funded as well as equitable and accessible education?

A. Part IV of Indian Constitution
B. Part III of Indian Constitution
C. Part II of Indian Constitution
D. None of these

142. The first official document on the Right to Education was with which of the following committee?

A. Ramamurti Committee Report in 1990
B. R.S. Sarkaria Commission
C. Tapas Majumdar Committee
D. None of these

143. In which of the following Committee (1999) was set up, which encompassed insertion of Article 21A.

A. Ramamurti Committee
B. Tapas Majumdar Committee
C. Both A & B
D. Neither A nor B

144. The Government has also launched an integrated scheme, for school education named as Samagra Shiksha Abhiyan, which subsumes the three schemes of school education: which of the following is/are correct?

1. Sarva Shiksha Abhiyan (SSA)
2. Rashtriya Madhyamik Shiksha Abhiyan (RMSA)
3. Centrally Sponsored Scheme on Teacher Education (CSSTE)

Select the correct code:

A. Only 2 & 3 B. 1, 2 & 3
C. Only 1 D. Only 1 & 2

145. Which among the following achievements of Right to Education Act, 2009 is/are correct?

1. The RTE Act has successfully managed to increase enrolment in the upper primary level (Class 6-8)
2. Stricter infrastructure norms resulted in improved school infrastructure, especially in rural areas
3. More than 3.3 million students secured admission under 25% quota norm under RTE
4. It made education inclusive and accessible nationwide

Select the correct code:

A. Only 2 & 3 B. 1, 2, 3 & 4
C. Only 1 D. Only 1 & 2

ANSWERS

1	2	3	4	5	6	7	8	9	10
A	B	D	D	A	D	D	A	D	D
11	**12**	**13**	**14**	**15**	**16**	**17**	**18**	**19**	**20**
A	B	D	D	D	B	A	C	D	D
21	**22**	**23**	**24**	**25**	**26**	**27**	**28**	**29**	**30**
A	A	D	D	A	D	A	D	D	D
31	**32**	**33**	**34**	**35**	**36**	**37**	**38**	**39**	**40**
C	A	C	C	B	B	D	D	D	A
41	**42**	**43**	**44**	**45**	**46**	**47**	**48**	**49**	**50**
A	C	A	B	B	A	B	B	D	B
51	**52**	**53**	**54**	**55**	**56**	**57**	**58**	**59**	**60**
D	A	A	C	A	A	A	A	B	A
61	**62**	**63**	**64**	**65**	**66**	**67**	**68**	**69**	**70**
A	A	C	A	C	D	C	D	B	D
71	**72**	**73**	**74**	**75**	**76**	**77**	**78**	**79**	**80**
A	B	C	A	B	A	D	A	A	B
81	**82**	**83**	**84**	**85**	**86**	**87**	**88**	**89**	**90**
D	D	C	A	D	B	A	A	A	A
91	**92**	**93**	**94**	**95**	**96**	**97**	**98**	**99**	**100**
C	C	D	B	B	B	B	C	A	A
101	**102**	**103**	**104**	**105**	**106**	**107**	**108**	**109**	**110**
A	D	A	B	A	B	A	A	C	B
111	**112**	**113**	**114**	**115**	**116**	**117**	**118**	**119**	**120**
C	B	A	B	A	D	C	B	B	C
121	**122**	**123**	**124**	**125**	**126**	**127**	**128**	**129**	**130**
A	A	B	C	A	B	B	D	A	A
131	**132**	**133**	**134**	**135**	**136**	**137**	**138**	**139**	**140**
C	D	A	D	D	C	A	B	D	A
141	**142**	**143**	**144**	**145**					
A	A	B	B	B					

●●●

Comparative World Politics

1. According to which theory, participation represents the process by which goals are set and means are chosen in relation to all sorts of social issues?
   A. Socialist theory
   B. Marxist theory
   C. Democratic theory
   D. None of the above

2. Which of the following are the major types of participation, exercised by citizens in the decision-making process in government and administration?
   1. Democratic
   2. Administrative
   3. Social
   4. Community Development

   Select the correct answer using the codes given below:
   Codes:
   A. 1, 2 and 3 B. 2, 3 and 4
   C. 1, 3 and 4 D. 1, 2, 3 and 4

3. Which book published in 1908, is the first study of pressure groups?
   A. The Process of Government
   B. Comparative Politics
   C. The Politics of the Developing Areas
   D. Political Behaviour

4. Who among the following made the famous statement: "England does not love coalitions"?
   A. K.C. Wheare B. Bertrand Russell
   C. Disraeli D. Churchill

5. Coalition governments continue to be:
   A. Stable B. Undemocratic
   C. Unstable D. None of the above

6. Who initiated the systematic study of pressure groups?
   A. Powell B. Lenin
   C. Grazia D. Bentley

7. Which of the following is not the main feature of the economic philosophy of sarvodaya as emphasised by Vinobaji?
   A. Elimination of poverty
   B. Helping world peace
   C. Cooperation of all political parties
   D. Revival of the old social order

8. Which of the following personalities are associated with Reformation, the great religious movement of the sixteenth century Europe which resulted in the establishment of Protestantism?
   A. Martin Luther B. Machiavelli
   C. Louis XIVth D. Garibaldi

9. The socio-cultural economic force/forces which made cardinal contribution of the birth and development of liberalism were:
   A. Renaissance and Reformation
   B. Enlightenment
   C. Scientific and Industrial Revolutions
   D. All of the above

10. The idea of 'possessive individualism' is given by:
    A. Hannah Arendt
    B. C.B. Macpherson
    C. Karl Popper
    D. None of the above

11. A theory of 'social engineering' or 'piecemeal engineering' is advanced by:
    A. Ernest Gellner B. L.T. Hobhouse
    C. Charles Taylor D. Karl Popper

12. Who among the following attached utmost importance to human dignity?
    A. Hegel B. Kant
    C. Marx D. Green

13. Which of the following is not a dimension of the 'felicific calculus' propounded by Bentham?
    A. Intensity B. Duration
    C. Probability D. Purity

14. Contributing significantly to the doctrine of utilitarianism, he said, "each to count as one, and no one for more than one". He is:
    A. J.S. Mill B. Jeremy Bentham
    C. James Mill D. David Hume

15. Which of the following pairs is not correctly matched?
    A. Democratic theory : C.B. Macpherson
    B. Freedom : Maurice Cranston
    C. The Tyranny of Majority : L.T. Hobhouse
    D. Problems of Political Philosophy : D.D. Rapheal

16. Which of the following are corollaries of the rule of law?

1. Ruling elite of society must adhere to the dictates of law and steer clear of any arbitrariness in governance.
2. Law of the land should be properly notified so that the citizens know as to how it will effect them.
3. Laws should be 'general' in form so that they are uniformly applicable to all the citizens; there should be no separate laws for any specific category of the people.
4. Rights and duties of the citizens and ruler alive should be laid down in the form of a legal code.

Select the correct answer using the codes given below:

Codes:

A. 1 and 2 B. 2 and 3
C. 3 and 4 D. 1, 2 and 3

17. Match List-I with List-II and select the correct answer using the codes given below the lists:

List-I	List-II
(*a*) A.V. Dicey	1. Law and Opinion in England in the Twentieth Century
(*b*) Roscoe Pound	2. Law in a Changing Society
(*c*) Morris Ginsberg	3. Introduction to the Study of the law of the Constitution
(*d*) W. Friedmann	4. The Spirit of the Common law

Codes:

	(*a*)	(*b*)	(*c*)	(*d*)
A.	3	4	1	2
B.	4	3	2	1
C.	3	4	2	1
D.	4	3	1	2

18. "Whenever any form of Government becomes destructive to these ends, it is the Right of the People to alter or abolish it, and to institute new Government."—The American Declaration of Independence, 1776.

Which of the following is implied in the above statement?

A. Right to recall
B. Right to carry out armed insurrection
C. Right to electoral boycott
D. Right to revolution

19. Match List-I (Forms of Democracy) with List-II (Description) and choose the correct answer from the codes given below the lists:

List-I (Forms of Democracy)	List-II (Description)
(*a*) Social Democracy	1. It is basically a Guild socialist idea and Cole was its exponent. Its aim is the management of industry by workers on self-governing lives
(*b*) People's Democracy	2. Its central idea is economic equality. Karl Marx used it in place of political democracy and called it the determining factor of politics
(*c*) Industrial Democracy	3. It is neither capitalist nor socialist. It is partly liberal and partly socialist. It aims at social equality and welfare of the people.
(*d*) Economic Democracy	4. It is commonly used by communist states. It is intended to put emphasis in the politico-economic, macro-micro and suprainfra nature of their democracy.

Codes:

	(*a*)	(*b*)	(*c*)	(*d*)
A.	2	4	1	3
B.	4	3	1	2
C.	4	1	3	2
D.	3	4	1	2

20. There are certain mechanisms to secure direct democracy. Which of the following pairs is/are not correctly matched in this connection?

1. Referendum : A special procedure of referring a particular billon constitutional amendment for popular vote. If a majority votes in its favour, the bill becomes law
2. Recall : A devise to enable to a people's representative to call the popular assembly consisting of all the adult members of the electorate of his or her constituency in order to listen to their grievances and redress them
3. Initiative : A devise which enables a specified number of people to draft a bill and send it to the legislature for its consideration. It is a positive power in the hands of the people to initiate a law which they desire to be passed

4. Plebiscite : A mode of securing opinion of the people's representatives in an assembly. It is a negative power of the representatives to put a check on undesirable legislation by the government

Select the correct answer from below:

A. 1 and 2 B. 2 and 3
C. 2 and 4 D. Only 2

21. Match List-I (Scholars) with List-II (Works) and select the correct answer from the codes given below the lists:

List-I (Scholars)	**List-II (Works)**
(*a*) Political Parties: A Sociological Study of the Oligarchical Tendencies of Modern Democracy	1. Maurice Duverger
(*b*) Political Parties: A Genuine case for Discontent	2. Giovanni Sartori
(*c*) Parties and Party Systems: A Frame-work for Analysis	3. Robert Michels
(*d*) Political Parties: Their Organisation and Activity in the Modern State	4. Jean Blondel

Codes:

	(*a*)	(*b*)	(*c*)	(*d*)
A.	2	3	1	4
B.	2	3	4	1
C.	3	2	1	4
D.	3	4	2	1

22. The main characteristics of the party implied in Lenin's conceptualization are:

1. The party is in possession of a unique type of knowledge as well as a distinctive method. Its knowledge base is Marxism and its method is dialectic.
2. The party is in principle a rigidly disciplined and carefully selected small group. It claims intellectual superiority because of the possession of unique knowledge.
3. The party has to be territorialy all pervasive in the sense that its branches should spread in all the parts and regions of the country.
4. The party is, by design, a highly centralised organization. Autonomy of local units is thus ruled out. The rank and file would be subject to strict discipline and rules of obedience.

Select the correct answer from the following:

A. 1 and 2 B. 1, 2 and 3
C. 1, 2 and 4 D. 1, 2, 3 and 4

23. Assertion (A) : The existence of a single political party is antithetical to democracy.

Reason (R) : The essence of democracy is its hospitality to all kinds of opinions and so one party state is diametrically opposite to the democratic system.

A. Both (A) and (R) are true and (R) is the correct explanation of (A).
B. Both A and R are true, but R is not the correct explanation of A.
C. A is true, but R is false.
D. A is false, but R is true.

24. Match List-I (Confederations) with List-II (Duration) and select the correct answer from the codes given below the lists:

List-I (Confederation)	**List-II (Duration)**
(*a*) German Confederation	1. 1991 – Continuing
(*b*) Swiss Confederacy	2. 1815 – 1866
(*c*) American Confederacy	3. 1781 – 1789
(*d*) Commonwealth of Independent States	4. 1815 – 1840

Codes:

	(*a*)	(*b*)	(*c*)	(*d*)
A.	1	4	3	2
B.	1	3	4	2
C.	2	4	3	1
D.	2	3	4	1

25. Though the country is divided into administrative units called 'Departments' which are divided into cantons, arrondissements and communes, each having its organs for local administration, but the general opinion is that it is almost misleading to talk about local governments.

The country referred to above is:

A. USA B. Switzerland
C. France D. Italy

26. Consider the following points about the Presidential system of government of the American model:

1. The President and his ministers cannot become the members of the legislature. In case the President appoints somebody as his minister who is also a member of the legislature, he will have to resign his legislative membership before accepting the ministerial assignment.
2. Ministers do not attend the sessions of the legislature and though they may go and also speak in the House, they cannot vote. Again, the legislature cannot censure the conduct of the ministers, it can only initiate proceedings of impeachment against the President.

3. The President may send his messages to the legislature and the latter may, and may not, act according to the wishes of the Head of the State.
4. The bills passed by the legislature are subject to the veto power of the President who may exercise this power in case of bills not pertaining to his choice. The budget prepared by the President is submitted to the legislature that may pass it, or cut it wherever it so chooses.

Which of the above are valid? Select the correct answer from the following:

A. 1 and 2
B. 2 and 4
C. 1, 2 and 3
D. 1, 2, 3 and 4

27. Assertion (A) : The most important merit of a parliamentary form of government is harmony and cooperation between the legislature and executive.

Reason (R) : Under the parliamentary system the acts of omission and commission of the government can be criticised without any loss of time as the legislature is sitting most of the time and the ministry or the executive also sits in the legislature. There is no difficulty in asking the questions.

A. Both (A) and (R) are true and (R) is the correct explanation of (A).
B. Both A and R are true, but R is not the correct explanation of A.
C. A is true, but R is false.
D. A is false, but R is true.

28. Assertion (A) : A Presidential system is suitable for emergencies.

Reason (R) : All powers are concentrated in the hands of the President and he can afford to take prompt decisions to meet a crisis.

A. Both (A) and (R) are true and (R) is the correct explanation of (A).
B. Both A and R are true, but R is not the correct explanation of A.
C. A is true, but R is false.
D. A is false, but R is true.

29. Assertion (A) : A federal system is a poor device as far as harmonization of national unity with local autonomy is concerned.

Reason (R) : In the federal system, there is always the danger of secession of units from the federal government. As the units enjoy autonomy, there can develop a spirit of defiance and independence and that can ultimately result in a revolt against the federal government.

A. Both (A) and (R) are true and (R) is the correct explanation of (A).
B. Both A and R are true, but R is not a correct explanation of A.
C. A is true, but R is false.
D. A is false, but R is true.

30. Which of the following statements is false?

A. Pressure groups are an important channel of communication for transmission of political ideas from the mass of the citizen to the rulers
B. Pressure groups are influence groups organised to influence policies. They attempt to exert influence over the government or parliament or local authorities
C. Pressure groups are non-political entities. They are involved in the political process but are not willing to assist in forming a government.
D. None of these.

31. Anomic Pressure Groups are those groups.

A. Which perform the role of interest articulation by publicising protests in order to exert pressure on policy-makers for changing particular policies and decisions
B. Which perform the role of interest articulation by associating themselves with certain political parties
C. Which perform the role of interest articulation from the political platform.
D. None of the above

32. The Weberian model of bureaucracy has been criticised from a variety of stand points. Consider the following points in this regard:

1. The Weberian model appears to be a 'machine theory' and a closed system model taking little account of organisational interactions with the environment.
2. The structural features of bureaucracy as laid down by Weber might be suitable for routine and repetitive tasks but these would produce dysfunctional consequences in terms of human behaviour if the jobs would involve innovation and creativity.
3. Weberian model has not been found to respond adequately to the tasks of socio-economic transformation in the developing countries. These tasks require quick changes whereas the capacity of the Weberian model for adaptation to change is rather slow.
4. Weber's model is confined to the study of formal bureaucratic structure and fails to take notice of the informal structure of bureauracy such as informal relations, informal norms and values, an

informal power hierarchy and informal power struggles.

Which of the above points make a valid criticism of the Weberian model? Select the correct answer from below:

A. 1 and 3 B. 2 and 3
C. 1, 2 and 3 D. 1, 2, 3 and 4

33. Match List-I with List-II and select the correct answer using the codes given below the lists:

List-I	List-II
(*a*) Kaplan	1. Comparative Politics
(*b*) Freeman	2. Political Science and Government
(*c*) Garner	3. Power and Society
(*d*) Gilchrist	4. Principles of Political Science

Codes:

	(*a*)	(*b*)	(*c*)	(*d*)
A.	1	2	3	4
B.	2	3	1	4
C.	3	1	2	4
D.	3	1	4	2

34. Who among the following is one of the advocates of the Power theory in politics?

A. Catline B. Kaplan
C. Lasswell D. All of the above

35. Political Socialisation is the process of induction into the political culture and the psychological dimension of the:

A. Socio-economic system
B. Political system
C. Economic system
D. Social system

36. Who defines the political system as the 'institutions, processes and interactions through which values are authoritatively allocated in a society'?

A. Almond B. Easton
C. Aptev D. Pye

37. Who was one of the first among the modern political scientists to challenge the traditional approaches?

A. Freud B. Lasswell
C. Bernard Crick D. Charles Merriam

38. Traditional study of politics was dominated by:

A. Behavioural approach
B. Normative approach
C. Marxist approach
D. Power approach

39. Who is the chief exponent of Communication Theory Approach?

A. Almond B. Karl Deutsch
C. Marx D. Coleman

40. According to the Marxist point of view, politics is only a part of:

A. Structure B. Substructure
C. Superstructure D. Class structure

41. Marx, Engels and Lenin argued that political systems should be compared and contrasted with reference to their respective:

A. Substructures B. Class structures
C. Superstructures D. Caste structures

42. Who propounded the Elitist theory?

A. Mosca B. Robert Dahl
C. Lasswell D. Catlin

43. Besides common law and the statute law, the English courts apply a certain type of rules which is known as:

A. Rationality B. Veracity
C. Equity D. None of the above

44. In which book Dicey developed the idea of Rule of law, published in 1885?

A. The British Constitution
B. Law and the Constitution
C. An Introduction to the British Constitution
D. None of the above

45. Who said that "rule, predominance or supremacy of the law" is an outstanding feature of the British Constitution?

A. Dicey B. Harvey
C. Tocqueville D. Barther

46. The distinction between Constitutional law and Administrative law is very clear in countries like:

A. USA B. Germany
C. India D. Both (A) and (C)

47. The doctrine of the Rule of law was enunciated by:

A. Rawls B. Dicey
C. Bryce D. Barker

48. The law made by the King-in-Council or by the King-in-Parliament is known as the:

A. Common law
B. Statutory law
C. Civil law
D. None of the above

49. Which among the following cannot be reckoned as or associated with political participation?

A. Citizen's attitudes, perceptions or knowledge or interest in politics
B. Electoral activities such as voting campaigning individually or collectively
C. The activities of professionals such as government officials, party officials, political candidates etc.
D. Both (A) and (C)

50. Which among the following scholars draw a distinction between 'participation' and 'mobilization'?
A. Myron Weiner
B. Norman H Nie
C. Sidney Verba
D. All of the above

51. Who elaborated the theory of separation of powers which had a great democratic appeal and influenced the making of American constitution?
A. Bentham B. Mill
C. Locke D. Montesquieu

52. The statement that "Balance in the structure of society is a pre-requisite to the maintenance of democracy," is made by:
A. Gaetano Mosca B. Karl Mannheim
C. C. Wright Mill D. Ernest Barker

53. The "Iron Law of Oligarchy" was propounded by:
A. James Burnham B. Robert Michels
C. Gaetano Mosca D. Graham Wallas

54. Who doveloped a model of the democratic process and described it as 'polyarchy'?
A. Giovanni Sartori B. S.M. Lipset
C. Robert Dahl D. None of the above

55. Who has described democracy as "government by the poorest, the most ignorant, the most-incapable who are necessarily the most-numerous"?
A. Talleyrand B. G.D.H. Cole
C. Lecky D. Bryce

56. Who differentiated parties from authoritarian groups on the basis of the criterion that genuine parties rest upon "formally free recruiting"?
A. Laski B. Max Weber
C. Carl Friedrich D. None of these

57. Who pointed out that, "the party system was in particular the mechanism by which the class state was transformed into the nation state"?
A. Burke B. MacIver
C. Laski D. None of these

58. In his study of political parties Robert Michels focussed on:
A. Organisation B. Cadre
C. Structure D. Leadership

59. The demarcation of parties as those of Left and those of Right can be traced in its origin to:
A. Soviet Political Parties
B. American Constituent Assembly
C. Custom followed in the legislatures of European Continental Countries
D. None of the above

60. Who stated that "a realistic survey of the British Constitution today must begin and end with parties and discuss them at length in the middle"?
A. K.C. Wheare B. W.B. Munro
C. Ivor Jennings D. None of the above

61. Who has opined that a political party "is held together, primarily by its ideology and organisation"?
A. Laski B. Edmund Burke
C. Roucek Huszar D. Carl Friedrich

62. Pressure groups were referred to as 'anonymous empire' by:
A. MacIver B. Almond
C. S.E. Finer D. None of the above

63. Who says that victory is "the first commandment of a political party"?
A. Alan Ball B. Barker
C. Finer D. None of the above

64. Decentralisation may be:
A. Political B. Administrative
C. Moral D. Both (A) and (B)

65. Without decentralisation ______ is impossible.
A. Comparative administration
B. Financial administration
C. Grass-roots administration
D. Personnel administration

66. The cabinet under a Presidential system is:
A. Part of the legislature
B. Controls the lower judiciary
C. A tool of the President
D. Both (B) and (C)

67. Who among the following opines that Federalism, when successful, has generally been a stage towards a Unitary government?
A. Wheare B. Laski
C. Dicey D. All of the above

68. Who defines the term bureaucracy as the systematic organization of tasks and individuals into a pattern which can most effectively achieve the ends of collective efforts?
A. Gladden B. Pfiffner
C. Max Weber D. Marx

69. Who among the following identified bureaucracy with institutions and large scale organisations in society?
A. Karl Marx B. Engels
C. Harold Laski D. Marshall E. Dimock

70. Which of these statements about how to study the American presidency would be supported by an advocate of institutional analysis?
A. Focus on the occupant

B. Focus on public opinion
C. Focus on the office
D. None of these

71. The behavioural approach emphasizes:
A. Behaviour rather than attitudes
B. Individuals rather than instiutions
C. Contemporary events rather than history
D. Social structure rather than rational choices.

72. Which method is associated with the behavioural approach?
A. Sample surveys
B. Participant observation
C. Comparative history
D. Elite interviews

73. Which is a central concern of the structural approach?
A. Power within a group
B. Relationships between group
C. Group leaders
D. Group culture

74. Which of the following comes closest to Almond and Verba's notion of a civic culture?
A. A culture in which most people are active in civic affairs
B. A culture which blends an active majority with a passive minority
C. A culture which blends an active minority with a passive majority
D. A culture which gives priority to civil over personal affairs

75. According to Almond and Verba, the civic culture:
A. Inhibits the stability of liberal democracies
B. Is unconnected to the stability of liberal democracies.
C. Contributes to the stability of liberal democracies.
D. Is incompatible with the stability of liberal democracies.

76. Social capital is based on:
A. Eastern Europe's 'third way'
B. Widespread acceptance of the market economy
C. Start-up funding for voluntary organizations
D. A culture of trust and cooperation

77. Which one of these countries is a consociational democracy?
A. Belgium B. U.K.
C. USA D. Sweden

78. Which one of the following is not an example of one of Huntington's civilizations?
A. The West B. Islam
C. Communism D. Hindu

79. Who said, 'The empires of the future will be empires of the mind'?
A. Winston Churchill B. Karl Marx
C. Gabriel Almond D. Franklin Roosevelt

80. An opinion poll is:
A. A measure of what public opinion would be if everyone were fully informed about an issue.
B. A moderated discussion about a particular topic among a small group.
C. A lobbying campaign aimed at the general public.
D. A series of questions asked in a standard way of a systematic sample of the population.

81. Which of the following is true for social movements?
A. They focus on a specific issue.
B. They operate only at national level.
C. They seek to become the government.
D. They stand for public office.

82. In most communist states, political participation:
A. was more extensive and more regimented than in liberal democracies.
B. was more extensive and less regimented than in liberal democracies.
C. was less extensive and more regimented than in liberal democracies.
D. was less extensive and less regimented than in liberal democracies.

83. In most liberal democracies, the most common channel through which interest groups seek to influence public policy is:
A. the legislature B. the courts
C. the bureaucracy D. the political executive

84. Over the last few decades, the significance of promotional groups in most liberal democracies has:
A. increased B. stabilized
C. declined D. disappeared

85. Which type of group exerts most influence on the European Commission?
A. Political parties B. Promotional groups
C. Protective groups D. Social movements

86. Over the last few decades, the importance of party members in selecting party leaders in liberal democracies.
A. shows no clear trend
B. has stayed the same
C. has decreased
D. has increased

87. The purpose of primary elections is to allow a party's supporters to:
A. Choose which candidate will represent their party in a general election.

B. Choose the party leader.
C. Decide on party policy.
D. Ratify changes to the party's constitution.

88. Michels' iron law of oligarchy states that:
A. Party members always dominate the party leaders
B. Power within parties rests with a single oligarch
C. The pursuit of power is an end in itself
D. Who says organization, says oligarchy

89. In Western Europe, several green parties have:
A. Formed a single party majority government
B. Formed a single party minority government
C. Participated in coalition governments
D. Repositioned themselves as far right parties

90. Which of these electoral systems is most commonly used in elections to the legislatives of Western European countries?
A. The alternative vote
B. Plurality systems
C. Majority system
D. Party list proportional representation

91. Which of the following is generally true for proportional representation?
A. It is used mainly for presidential elections.
B. It leads to single-party government
C. It is based on single-member consti-tuencies
D. It often leads to government by coalition

92. Which of these countries employs the mixed member proportional system?
A. Finland B. France
C. Germany D. United States

93. Duverger argued there was 'an almost complete correlation' between:
A. The plurality method and a two-party system.
B. The plurality method and a multiparty system.
C. Proportional representation and a two-party system.
D. Mixed member proportional representation and a multiparty system.

94. In the 21st century, turnout in American presidential elections:
A. Always increased
B. Usually increased
C. Usually decreased
D. Always decreased

95. A referendum is:
A. A no confidence vote
B. A vote of the assembly on a constitutional issue
C. A form of proportional representation
D. A vote of the electorate on an issue of public policy

96. According to Weber, the bureaucracy is:
A. A disciplined hierarchy in which civil servants are subject to the authority of their superior.
B. A loose network in which work is negotiated through business-style contracts
C. The personal office of the head of state
D. A device for distributing patronage and the spoils of office.

97. In a spoils system:
A. public servants seek to dilute politicians' proposals.
B. public servants are recruited by competitive examination.
C. elected politicians distribute government jobs to their own supporters.
D. an Ombudsman monitors public appointments.

98. An Ombudsman is a public official who:
A. offers political advice to ministers
B. investigates allegations of maladministration.
C. makes judgements on administrative law.
D. supervises recruitment of the bureaucracy.

99. The first Ombudsman was established in:
A. Denmark B. Finland
C. Norway D. Sweden

100. E-government refers to the use of information and communication technology in:
A. Administering elections
B. Communicating between states
C. Providing public services
D. All of the above

101. Who said, 'there is only one way to deal with Congress, and that is continuously, incessantly and without interruption'?
A. Bill Clinton
B. Ronald Reagan
C. Lyndon Johnson
D. Abraham Lincoln

102. In Parliamentary government:
A. One person serves as head of both government and state.
B. The cabinet is directly elected by the voters.
C. The government cannot be brought down by the assembly.
D. Governing parties emerge from the assembly.

103. Semi-presidential government employs both:
A. A Prime Minister and a strong elected president.
B. A Prime Minister and a ceremonial monarch.
C. Military and civilian heads of government.
D. An elected president and a ceremonial Monarch.

104. Which one of these countries employes semi-presidential government?
A. USA B. UK
C. France D. Germany

105. Substantive representation is when:
A. Representatives give priority to policy issues.
B. Representatives give priority to serving their party.
C. Representatives resemble their constituents in given characteristics such as gender.
D. Representatives act in the interests of their constituents.

106. Who said, 'Parliament is not a congress of ambassadors from different and hostile interests .... but parliament is a deliberative assembly of one nation, that of the whole'?
A. J.S. Mill B. John Locke
C. James Madison D. Edmund Burke

107. Which one of the following is traditionally seen as a debating legislature?
A. America's Congress
B. Britain's House of Commons
C. Germany's Bundesrat
D. Sweden's Riksdag

108. The incumbency effect refers to:
A. The electoral bonus accruing to members standing for re-election
B. The tendency for governments to win no-confidence votes.
C. The growing prevalence of career politicians.
D. The growing significance of parliamentary committees.

109. Which of these functions of legislatures in liberal democracies has generally grown in importance in recent decades?
A. Holding emergency debates
B. Initiating bills
C. Shaping foreign policy
D. Overseeing (scrutinizing) the executive.

110. 'Stages of Economic Growth: A Non-Communist Manifesto" was most clearly elaborated in the writings of:
A. W.W. Rostow B. Max Weber
C. Talcott Parsons D. Andre Gunder Frank

111. Dependency theory arose in the late fifties and the sixties as an extended critique of which of the following perspective?
A. Traditional Perspective
B. Medieval Perspective
C. Ancient Perspective
D. Modernization Perspective

112. Paul Baran's "The Political Economy of Growth, Monthly Review Press, 1957" work is also very important. Baran argued that the economic relationships that existed between Western Europe (and later Japan and United States) and the rest of the world were based on:
A. Conflict and exploitation
B. Coordination and Monitoring
C. Social impact assessment
D. None of these

113. Who among the following developed the idea of world capitalist economy in the "World System Analysis"?
A. Paul Baran
B. Andre Gunder Frank
C. Colin Leys
D. Immanuel Wallerstein

114. Who among the following developed "New institutionalism" as an approach to the study of institutions?
A. John Meyer B. Colin Leys
C. Petras D. G.W. Domhoff

115. Which of the following is not a character of Comparative Politics?
A. Comparative politics is the modern way of studying politics
B. Comparative Politics has a very wide and comprehensives cope
C. Comparative Politics depends upon scientific-empirical methods of study
D. Comparative politics has a very narrow scope

116. Which of the following subject is not included in the scope of Comparative Politics?
A. Study of selected structures
B. Study of political behaviours
C. Analysis of the similarities and differences, among political processes.
D. Study of political cultures

117. Which of the following subject is not included in the scope of Comparative Politics?
A. Study of all political systems
B. Study of environment and infrastructure of politics
C. Study of political socialization
D. Study of selected structures

118. Decolonization refers:
A. The transfer of political authority from colonial rulers to indigenous leaders
B. European countries lacked the wealth
C. Economic policies were definitely an impetus for the start of colonization
D. European settlers met labour requirements

119. The Effects of Colonialism are based on which of the following?
A. Slave Trade
B. Columbian Exchange
C. Boost to Mercantilism
D. All the above

120. In which year the General Assembly of United Nations adopted its landmark Declaration on the Granting of Independence to Colonial Countries?
A. 1960 B. 1987
C. 1970 D. 1980

121. In which year the General Assembly proclaimed the "International Decade for the Eradication of Colonialism"?
A. 1980 B. 1990
C. 1960 D. 1970

122. The debate on Advanced Capitalist State according to Gramsci consists of:
A. the coercive apparatus comprising of the police, army and judiciary
B. the other includes various institutions of civil society such as media, church, schools
C. power is distributed and shared by many groups
D. Both (A) and (B)

123. The State in Capitalist Society (1969) is written by whom among the following political scientists?
A. Ralph Miliband B. Althusser
C. Poulantaz D. Marcuse

124. Poulantaz (1973) relates the view of State Theory (1973) refers to the major function of capitalism namely:
A. stress the ideological and structural mechanisms
B. the reproduction of the capitalist society in its totality
C. the concepts of ruling class or the power elite
D. None of these

125. Which among the following is not correctly matched?
A. A.M. Carnoy (1983) - The State and Political Theory
B. R.A. Dahl (1965) - A Preface to Democratic Theory
C. S.M. Lipset (1963) - Social Man
D. R. Miliband (1969) - The State in Capitalist Society

126. Edward Said is famous for his theory of:
A. Orientalism Theory B. Dependency Theory
C. World System theory D. Realistic theory

127. The Changing Nature of Post Colonial State referred as:
A. Consolidation B. Disintegration
C. Globalization D. All the above

128. State system suffered a setback due to:
A. Growing interdependence
B. The rise of nuclear weapons
C. The growing role of public opinion in recent years
D. All the above

129. The Welfare State has often been described as a state that takes responsibility in providing:
A. basic economic and social security for its citizens
B. basic economic and cultural integration for its citizens
C. basic economic and civil security for its citizens
D. only basic economic security for its citizens

130. What is the amalgamation and rapid unification between countries identified as?
A. Globalisation B. Liberalisation
C. Socialisation D. Privatisation

131. Globalisation has improved the living structure of which of the following?
A. All the people
B. Workers in developing countries
C. People in developed countries
D. None of the above

132. Which of the following is the main reason behind the investments of MNCs?
A. To benefit foreign countries
B. To provide financial support to the country's government
C. For the welfare of underprivileged people
D. To increase the assets and earn profits

133. In which year Universal adult franchise was introduced in Germany?
A. 1919 B. 1915
C. 1920 D. 1930

134. The liberal democratic regimes in the developed states have been categorized as:
A. Totalitarian regimes
B. Democratic regimes
C. Polyarchical regimes
D. None of these

135. The liberal democratic or polyarchical regimes are to be found in which of the following states?
A. North America, Western Europe and Australia
B. Japan and South Africa
C. Latin America, Poland and South Africa
D. Both (A) & (B)

136. In which year France introduced universal adult franchise?
A. 1924 B. 1987
C. 1945 D. 1939

137. 'Oligarchy: Participation and Opposition' is a work of:
A. Robert A. Dahl B. Karl Manheim
C. Burnham D. Vilfredo Pareto

138. Lijphart distiniguishes the democratic regimes between:
A. majority democratic regimes and the pluralist democratic regimes
B. majority democratic regimes and the organised parliamentary lines
C. Both (A) and (B)
D. None of these

139. Pluralist democratic regimes based on the US model represent:
A. the separation of power
B. the tradition of authoritarianism
C. the conventions of British Parliament
D. None of these

140 'Clash of Civilisations' is a work of who among the following political scientists in comparative political analysis?
A. Almond and Powell B. Samuel P. Huntington
C. S.M. Lipset D. None of these

141. The tradition of classification of political regimes goes back to the Greek city states in the:
A. 4th Century BC B. 5th Century BC
C. 6th Century BC D. None of these

142. Jellenick is a German writer who classified political regimes into which one of the following categories?
A. monarchical and republican
B. democratic and totalitarian
C. primary and representative
D. unitary and federal

143. Which among the following is correctly matched according to Classification of Political Regimes?
A. Tutelary democracy — Edward Shils
B. Aristocracy — Almond & Powell
C. Plutocracy — Jean Blondel
D. Limited Monarchy — Thomas Hobbes

144. "Political Development in the New States" is a book written by who among the following political scientist?
A. David Apter B. S.E. Finer
C. Edward Shils D. David Apter

145. Almond and Powell have also given a triple classification of political systems based upon structural differences and functions, and cultural secularisation. They are:
A. Primitive B. Traditional
C. Modern D. All of these

146. Patrimonialism regimes are autocratic or oligarchic and exclude which among the following groups?
A. lower, middle and upper classes from power
B. mobilized modern systems are those based upon structuralisation
C. primitive bands
D. None of these

147. Authoritarian regimes have been mostly established in the developing states of:
A. Latin America, the Middle East Africa and South East Asia
B. Developed states of the West like Spain, Portugal and Greece,
C. Neither (A) nor (B)
D. Both (A) & (B)

148. What does the idea of constitutionalism capture?
A. The idea of a limited government
B. Rule of law principle
C. Common Welfare
D. None of these

149. Federal government has an agreement and there are certain essential features that ensure its proper working. They are:
A. a written constitution
B. division of powers
C. independence of judiciary
D. All the above

150. Which among the following is not correctly matched?
A. A.R., Ball, (1971) — Modern Politics and Government
B. Gabriel Almond and Powell (1964) — Comparative Politics : A Developmental Approach
C. Robert Dahl (1964) — Modern Political Analysis
D. Jean Blondel (1970) — Democracy

ANSWERS

1	2	3	4	5	6	7	8	9	10
C	D	A	C	C	D	D	A	D	B
11	**12**	**13**	**14**	**15**	**16**	**17**	**18**	**19**	**20**
D	B	C	B	C	B	A	D	D	C

21	22	23	24	25	26	27	28	29	30
D	C	A	C	C	D	B	A	D	D
31	32	33	34	35	36	37	38	39	40
A	D	C	D	B	B	B	B	B	C
41	42	43	44	45	46	47	48	49	50
B	A	C	B	C	D	B	B	D	D
51	52	53	54	55	56	57	58	59	60
D	B	B	C	C	B	B	D	C	C
61	62	63	64	65	66	67	68	69	70
C	C	C	D	C	C	C	B	D	C
71	72	73	74	75	76	77	78	79	80
B	A	B	B	C	D	A	C	A	D
81	82	83	84	85	86	87	88	89	90
A	A	C	A	C	D	A	B	C	D
91	92	93	94	95	96	97	98	99	100
D	C	A	B	D	A	C	B	D	C
101	102	103	104	105	106	107	108	109	110
C	D	A	C	D	D	B	A	D	A
111	112	113	114	115	116	117	118	119	120
D	A	D	A	A	B	A	A	D	A
121	122	123	124	125	126	127	128	129	130
B	D	A	B	C	A	D	D	A	A
131	132	133	134	135	136	137	138	139	140
B	D	A	C	D	C	A	A	B	A
141	142	143	144	145	146	147	148	149	150
A	A	A	C	D	A	D	A	D	D

• • •

International Relations & International Organisation

1. Political realism is contrary to the _______ approach to international politics.
A. Pragmatic B. Legalistic
C. Moralistic D. Both B and C

2. According to Morgenthau, the laws by which man moves in the social world are :
A. Man-made B. Eternal
C. Temporary D. Obscure

3. Which theory is the result of the behavioural revolution in social sciences?
A. The Systems theory B. The Realist theory
C. The Idealist theory D. The Pluralist theory

4. Who treats equilibrium mainly in the context of balance of power system?
A. Fox B. Kaplan
C. Liska D. Merriam

5. Charles McClelland's concept of system comes from:
A. Geography B. Biology
C. Economics D. History

6. Who treats six models of major international system?
A. Rosenau B. Lasswell
C. Kaplan D. None of the above

7. According to Kaplan, the most likely transformation of the balance of power system is into a :
A. Bipolar System B. Unipolar System
C. International System D. None of the above

8. Who produced formulations of the decision-making theory in 1738?
A. Anthony Downs B. Daniel Bernouli
C. David L. Sills D. Robinson

9. Who was the chief exponent of the realist theory?
A. Kennan B. Hans Morgenthau
C. Watkins D. Easton

10. Erich Kaufmann wrote in a book that the essence of the state was:
A. Increase of power B. Development of power
C. Display of power D. All of the above

11. Who said that the study of politics is the study of influence and the influential in his work on politics?
A. Kennan B. Lasswell
C. Morgenthau D. Watkins

12. Who gave theoretical orientation to realism?
A. Bross B. Burton
C. Morgenthau D. Lasswell

13. The two most vital concepts in which the inconsistency of Morgenthau's theory is most clearly revealed are:
A. Power and Society
B. Power and Statesmanship
C. Diplomacy and Society
D. Diplomacy and Statesmanship

14. According to Morgenthau, the best means of preserving peace in a society of sovereign nations is:
A. National interest B. Diplomacy
C. Foreign trade D. Autonomy

15. Who believes that a theory of International politics is "but a specific instance of a general theory of politics"?
A. Tucker B. Morgenthau
C. Kennan D. Wasserman

16. The new Economic policy of India comprises the various policy measures and changes introduced since:
A. June 1992 B. July 1991
C. May 1990 D. July 1992

17. What does NAFTA stand for?
A. North Asian Free Trade Association
B. North African Free Trade Association
C. North Atlantic Free Trade Association
D. North American Free Trade Association

18. The World Trade Organisation (WTO) is the successor to which one of the following institutional arrangements?
A. World Trade Community
B. International Trade and Development Association
C. General Agreement on Trade and Tariffs
D. Association for Economic and Social Reconstruction

19. What does TRIMs stand for?
A. Trade-Related Investment Measures
B. Tariff-Related Investment Measures
C. Technology-Related Investment Measures
D. Training-Related Investment Measures

20. After the New Economic Policy, 1991 who opined that India would recover from her crisis and carry out adjustment programmes within a short duration itself, unlike other economies in a similar situation?

A. America B. World Bank
C. United Nations D. None of the above

21. As a part of SAP (Structural Adjustment Policies), the economy was being ______ *i.e.*, opened up to foreign goods and capital.

A. Systematised B. Globalised
C. Capitalised D. None of the above

22. Who said that due to New Economic Policy India will find itself at the receiving end?

A. Sethi B. Khushro
C. Jagmohan D. Halleiner

23. Which of the following is the largest open market in the world?

A. ECM B. TRIPs
C. NAFTA D. TRIMs

24. Which of the following countries has open economy?

A. Hong Kong B. Taiwan
C. Singapore D. All of these

25. Which act was passed in India to prevent restrictive trade practices?

A. GATT B. MRTP
C. MFA D. TRIMs

26. Which agreement encompasses a comprehensive overhaul of GATT'S dispute settlements, rules and procedures aimed at ensuring the prompt and efficient resolution of disputes?

A. Seattle agreement B. Durban agreement
C. Montreal agreement D. None of the above

27. Who among the following personalities coined the phrase 'global village'?

A. James Rosenau B. Fucuyama
C. Ledley Bull D. Marshall McLuhan

28. Who among the following scholars asserted that – "Globalization does not simply refer to the objectiveness of increasing inter-connectedness. It also refers to cultural and subjective matters [namely, the scope and depth of consciousness of the world as a single place"]?

A. Raland Robertson B. Romain Rolland
C. Ernest Gelner D. None of the above

29. Who among the following argued that 'realism is likely to remain the single most useful instrument in our intellectual toolbox'?

A. Holsti B. E.H. Carr
C. Hans Morgenthau D. Stephen Walt

30. Which of the following is not the basic norm of the balance of power system that are clear to each of the state actors engaged in the process of balancing?

A. Any actor or coalition that tries to assume dominance must be constrained.
B. States want to increase their capabilities by acquiring territory, increasing their population or developing economically.
C. Negotiating is better than fighting.
D. Other states are viewed as potential enemies.

31. Match List-I with List-II and select the correct answer from the codes given below:

List-I (Scholar)	List-II (Statement)
(*a*) McLean and McMillan	1. It is not so much the absolute power of a state as its power position in relation to other states that counts.
(*b*) Morgenthau	2. Defined power as the capacity to impose one's will on others by reliance on effective sanctions in the case of non-compliance.
(*c*) George Schwarzer-berger	3. Defined power as man's control over the minds and actions of other men.
(*d*) Van Dyke	4. Power is the ability to make people do what they would not otherwise have done.

Codes:

	(*a*)	(*b*)	(*c*)	(*d*)
A.	4	3	2	1
B.	4	3	1	2
C.	4	1	2	3
D.	1	2	3	4

32. Given below are two statements, one labelled as Assertion (A) and the other labelled as Reason (R). Select the correct answer from the codes given below:

Assertion (A) : End of Cold War signified a shift from ideological politics in International relations.

Reason (R) : Religious fundamentalism is posing a threat to security.

Codes:

A. Both (A) and (R) are true, and (R) is the correct explanation of (A).
B. Both (A) and (R) are true, but (R) is not the correct explanation of (A).
C. (A) is true, but (R) is false.
D. (A) is false, but (R) is true.

33. Match List-I with List-II and select the correct answer from the codes given below:

List-I (Writer)	List-II (Idea)
(*a*) Immanual Wallerstein	1. Game theory
(*b*) Von Newmann	2. End of history
(*c*) Morgenthau	3. Realism
(*d*) Francis Fukuyama	4. Dependency theory

Codes:

	(*a*)	(*b*)	(*c*)	(*d*)
A.	2	3	1	4
B.	3	2	4	1
C.	4	1	3	2
D.	1	4	2	3

34. Given below are two statements, one labelled as Assertion (A) and the other labelled as Reason (R). Select the correct answer from the codes given below:

Assertion (A) : Non-alignment policy was more relevant during cold war period.

Reason (R) : Non-aligned countries are divided on ethnic and religious differences.

Codes:

A. Both (A) and (R) are true, and (R) is the correct explanation of (A).
B. Both (A) and (R) are true, but (R) is not the correct explanation of (A).
C. (A) is true, but (R) is false.
D. (A) is false, but (R) is true.

35. Given below are two statements, one labelled as Assertion (A) and the other labelled as Reason (R). Select the correct answer from the codes given below:

Assertion (A) : American foreign policy supported the democratic regimes.

Reason (R) : At times the military systems were also supported by America.

Codes:

A. Both (A) and (R) are true, and (R) is the correct explanation of (A).
B. Both (A) and (R) are true, but (R) is not the correct explanation of (A).
C. (A) is true, but (R) is false.
D. (A) is false, but (R) is true.

36. "Uniting for Peace Resolution" is also called as:

A. Truman plan B. American plan
C. Achieson plan D. Eisenhower plan

37. 'Balance of Power' is an important principle of:

A. Liberal thought in international politics.
B. Marxist thought in international politics.
C. Traditional thought in international politics.
D. Realist thought in international politics.

38. According to Iris L Calude Jr. which of the following is not a device for the management of power?

A. Arms control B. Collective security
C. Balance of power D. World Government

39. The modern state system with its territorial sovereignty came into existence first in Europe in the wake of the

A. Treaty of Versailles B. Congress of Vienna
C. Treaty of Westphalia D. Congress of Berlin

40. According to Karen A. Mingrt, which of the following conditions is not essential to make first generation peacekeeping operations most effective?

A. A clear and practical mandate or purpose for the operation.
B. US. forces must also be present in the peace-keeping operations.
C. Consent of the parties involved as to the mandate and composition of the force.
D. Strong financial and logistical support of the members of the UN Security Council.

41. Match List-I with List-II and select the correct answer from the codes given below:

List-I (Term)	List-II (Contents)
(*a*) Preventive diplomacy	1. It is like classical peace-keeping. It refers to the deployment of a UN force in the field with the consent of all parties.
(*b*) Peace making	2. It involves developing social, political and economic infrastructure to prevent further violence and consolidate peace.
(*c*) Peace keeping	3. It involves confidence-building measures, fact finding and preventive deployment of UN authorised forces.
(*d*) Post-conflict peace building	4. It is designed to bring hostile parties to agreement essentially through peaceful means.

Codes:

	(*a*)	(*b*)	(*c*)	(*d*)
A.	3	4	1	2
B.	3	4	2	1
C.	1	2	3	4
D.	4	3	2	1

42. Match List-I with List-II and select the correct answer from the codes given below :

List-I (Book)	List-II (Author)
(*a*) International Relations Theory: The Three Traditions	(*i*) Gerhard Wahlers

(*b*) The North South Divide and the International System	(*ii*) Tadjbaksh Shakbanon and Anuradha Chenoy
(*c*) Human Security	(*iii*) N.B. Adams
(*d*) India and the European Union	(*iv*) Martin Wright

Codes:

	(*a*)	(*b*)	(*c*)	(*d*)
A.	(*iv*)	(*iii*)	(*ii*)	(*i*)
B.	(*ii*)	(*iv*)	(*i*)	(*iii*)
C.	(*iii*)	(*i*)	(*iv*)	(*ii*)
D.	(*i*)	(*iii*)	(*ii*)	(*iv*)

43. Which one of the following can be regarded as the currency of power?

A. Food
B. Nuclear Weapons
C. Industrial Capacity
D. Military Preparedness

44. Who was of opinion that, "the end of cold war represented the victory of ideal state", and liberal capitalism?

A. Michael Doyle B. Thomas Dunne
C. Francis Fukuyama D. Samuel Huntington

45. Which world leader gave a special concept of 'Development' after the Second World War?

A. Franklin Delano Roosevelt
B. Harry Truman
C. Jawaharlal Nehru
D. Winston Churchill

46. Match List-I with List-II and select the correct answer from the codes given below:

List-I (Authors)	**List-II (Books)**
(*a*) B. Buzan	(*i*) Man, the State and War
(*b*) I. Hansen	(*ii*) Social Theory of International Politics
(*c*) K.N. Waltz	(*iii*) The Evolution of International Security Studies
(*d*) A. Wendt	(*iv*) People, States and Fear

Codes:

	(*a*)	(*b*)	(*c*)	(*d*)
A.	(*iv*)	(*iii*)	(*i*)	(*ii*)
B.	(*iv*)	(*iii*)	(*ii*)	(*i*)
C.	(*i*)	(*ii*)	(*iii*)	(*iv*)
D.	(*iv*)	(*i*)	(*ii*)	(*iii*)

47. Which country is the example of Latent Nuclear Capacity?

A. India B. Japan
C. China D. North Korea

48. Match List-I with List-II and select the correct answer from the codes given below:

List-I	**List-II**
(*a*) Counter force strategy	(*i*) Types of nuclear strategy that threatens assets that are valuable to an adversary, such as cities with industrial assets and large populations.
(*b*) Counter-proliferation	(*ii*) International lawyers who argue that there is a legal right of humanitarian intervention in both UN charter law and customary international law.
(*c*) Counter-restrictionist	(*iii*) Term used to describe a variety of efforts to obstruct slow, or roll back nuclear weapons programmes and nuclear proliferation.
(*d*) Counter value strategy	(*iv*) Type of nuclear strategy that targets an adversary's military and nuclear capabilities.

Codes:

	(*a*)	(*b*)	(*c*)	(*d*)
A.	(*iv*)	(*iii*)	(*ii*)	(*i*)
B.	(*iv*)	(*iii*)	(*i*)	(*ii*)
C.	(*ii*)	(*i*)	(*iii*)	(*iv*)
D.	(*iii*)	(*iv*)	(*i*)	(*ii*)

49. Who is given credit to coin the term—Soft Power?

A. Joseph Nye
B. N. Alarcon
C. A.J. Bellamy
D. S. Chesterman

50. According to K.J. Holsti, which one of the following is not a feature of the contemporary state system?

A. The rise in the number and type of states.
B. The great potential for destruction by those who possess nuclear weapons and modern delivery systems.
C. The predominant position of influences that has been achieved by the three essentially non-European states : Russia, China and the United States.
D. The large number of states are keen to join political and economic alliances.

51. The Principal purpose of India's foreign policy vis-a-vis the UN is to pursue three closely related goals.

Which of the following is not included among them?

A. A significant role in the shaping of international relations in the 21st century.
B. A movement towards a non-violent and humane international system.

C. The promotion of conditions for a sustainable and relatively equitable pattern of international development.
D. To help UN to develop its own financial resources.

52. The roots of newly emerging forces of globalisation have been traced in specific economic and political developments in the late 1980s or early 1990s. Which of the following can not be included in this category?
A. The end of Cold War.
B. Testing of nuclear devices by India and Pakistan in 1998.
C. Dismantling of state socialism in the USSR.
D. The collapse of the Berlin wall.

53. Who among the following is associated with Democratic Peace Theory?
A. Kenneth Waltz B. Michael Doyle
C. Jackson and Sorenson D. John Mearsheimer

54. Who among the following regards International Politics as an autonomous discipline?
(*a*) C.A.W. Manning (*b*) Karlin M. Copper
(*c*) Martin Wright (*d*) Hoffson

Select the correct answer from the codes given below:
A. (*a*), (*b*) and (*c*) B. (*b*), (*c*) and (*d*)
C. (*c*), (*d*) and (*a*) D. (*a*), (*b*) and (*d*)

55. Which of the following pairs are correctly matched. Choose your answer from the codes given below:
(*a*) The control of the Arms Race – Hedley Bull
(*b*) Some Economic Aspects of Disarmament – L. Gromoo and V. Strigachow
(*c*) The challenge of the Nineteen sixties – James P. Warbarg
(*d*) Winning without war – Emile Benoit

Codes:
A. (*a*), (*b*) and (*c*) B. (*b*), (*c*) and (*d*)
C. (*d*), (*c*) and (*a*) D. (*b*), (*d*) and (*a*)

56. Who among the following is not related to Bargaining Theory?
A. Kenneth Waltz B. J.F. Nash
C. Thomas Schelling D. Roger Fisher

57. Which one of the following was not feature of Old Diplomacy?
A. Limited
B. Aristocratic
C. Transparency
D. Freedom of Action for Ambassadors

58. In which year Brezhnev had propounded the concept of Asian Collective Security System?
A. 1967 B. 1968
C. 1969 D. 1970

59. Which of the following Articles of the Charter of United Nations Organisation are related to Regional Organisations?
(*a*) Article 51 (*b*) Article 52
(*c*) Article 53 (*d*) Article 54

Select the correct answer from the codes given below:
Codes:
A. (*b*), (*c*) and (*d*) B. (*a*), (*c*) and (*d*)
C. (*a*), (*b*) and (*d*) D. (*a*), (*b*) and (*c*)

60. Which of the following country is not a member of ASEAN?
A. Laos B. Combodia
C. Vietnam D. North Korea

61. Originally what was the total strength of security council of United Nations?
A. 9 B. 10
C. 11 D. 15

62. Bachract and Baratz have mentioned about the three classes of International Relations to control the conduct of states. Which of the following are the three classes?
(*a*) Influence Relationship
(*b*) Force Relationship
(*c*) Legitimate Relationship
(*d*) Power Relationship

Select the correct answer from the codes given below:
A. (*b*), (*c*) and (*d*) B. (*a*), (*c*) and (*d*)
C. (*d*), (*c*) and (*b*) D. (*b*), (*c*) and (*a*)

63. Which one of the following books was written by E.H. Carr?
A. The open society and its enemies
B. Twenty years crisis
C. Political Realism and Political Idealism
D. The Realities of American Foreign Policy

64. Which of the following pairs is not correctly matched?

	Author		Book
A.	William C. Olson	:	The Growth of a Discipline
B.	G.F. Kennan	:	American Diplomacy
C.	Russel H. Fifield	:	The Introductory Course in International Relations
D.	Robert Strausz-Hupe and Stefan Possony	:	International Relations : A General Theory

65. Who among the following are supporters of Realistic Approach in International Politics?
(*a*) Couloumbis and Wolfe
(*b*) Fredrick Schuman
(*c*) Nicholas Spykman
(*d*) E.H. Carr

Select the correct answer from the codes given below:

A. (*b*), (*c*) and (*d*) B. (*a*), (*c*) and (*d*)
C. (*a*), (*b*) and (*d*) D. (*a*), (*b*) and (*c*)

66. Who among the following had declared that arms race in itself is experience of terror?

A. Hadley Bull B. Arnold Toynbee
C. Kenneth Boulding D. Lynn Miller

67. Which of the following countries was a part of recently concluded P5+1 Nuclear Argument?

A. Japan B. Australia
C. India D. Germany

68. Which of the following is not a form of National Power?

A. Social Power
B. Military Power
C. Psychological Power
D. Economic Power

69. Which of the following scholars of International Politics did not subscribe to this view that no social science can survive without idealistic aspects?

A. Herbert Butterfield
B. E.H. Carr
C. Reinhold Niebuhr
D. Arnold Wolters

70. Which of the following is also called as Total Disarmament?

A. Qualitative Disarmament
B. Quantitative Disarmament
C. General Disarmament
D. Comprehensive Disarmament

71. Who stated, "International Politics includes analysis of political relations and problems of peace among nations"?

A. Charles Scheichar B. Norman Padelford
C. Harold Sprout D. H.J. Morgenthau

72. Game theory owes a heavy debt to the seminal work entitled, "The Theory of Games and Economic Behaviour". It has been written by

A. Mortan Kaplan
B. John Von Neumann and Oskar Morgenstern
C. Karl Deutsch
D. Michael Hass

73. Who among the following has remarked that, power in a political context means "the power of man over the minds and actions of other men"?

A. George Schwarzenberger
B. Herman Heller
C. Hans Morgenthau
D. Bertrand Russell

74. Match List-I with List-II and select the correct answer from the codes given below:

List-I (Treaties/Proposals)	List-II (Year)
(*a*) SALT II (Strategic Arms Limitation Talks)	(*i*) 1987
(*b*) PTBT (Partial Test Ban Treaty)	(*ii*) 1979
(*c*) Atom for Peace Proposal	(*iii*) 1963
(*d*) INF Treaty (Intermediate Nuclear Force Treaty)	(*iv*) 1953

Codes:

	(*a*)	(*b*)	(*c*)	(*d*)
A.	(*i*)	(*ii*)	(*iii*)	(*iv*)
B.	(*ii*)	(*iii*)	(*iv*)	(*i*)
C.	(*iv*)	(*ii*)	(*i*)	(*iii*)
D.	(*iii*)	(*ii*)	(*i*)	(*iv*)

75. Which one of the following factors contributed to the emergence of 'New Detente' after Cold War?

A. Pressure by the Non-aligned Movement
B. The signing of INF Treaty by Reagan and Gorbachev.
C. Emergence of Namibia as a free African Nation
D. Deployment of RDF (Rapid Deployment Force) in Persian Gulf

76. The demand for New International Economic Order was first made at

A. Tehran Summit
B. Durban Summit
C. Kuala Lumpur Summit
D. Algiers Summit

77. Which one of the following is not correct about Association of South East Asian Nations (ASEAN)?

A. First India ASEAN Summit was held in November, 2002.
B. ASEAN declared South East Asian Nuclear Weapon free zone in 1995.
C. ASEAN is working to remove trade barriers and develop economic relationship with China, Japan and South Korea.
D. India became full dialogue partner of ASEAN in 1991.

78. Who among the following used the phrase– The United Nations is 'sharing in the name of solidarity' for underlining the necessity of the UN?

A. Winston Churchill B. Dag Hammarskjold
C. Trygve Lie D. Woodrow Wilson

79. Which one of the following is not a feature of 'Shopkeeper diplomacy'?

A. It is based on peaceful approach
B. It is a means of diplomacy for maintaining peace through compromise

C. It is based on the sound business principles of moderation
D. It tries to safeguard national interest through war only

80. Positive peace implies
A. a ceasefire
B. stopping the formation of death squads
C. transformation of relationship
D. social construction of war

81. Wilson's idealism was a precursor to
A. liberal international relations theory
B. radical international relations theory
C. neither liberal nor radical international relations theory
D. None of these

82. The Twenty Years' Crisis (1939) is a work of who among the following idealists in international relations?
A. E.H. Carr B. John A. Hobson
C. David Davies D. Lester Pearson

83. Idealism is also marked by the prominent role played by international law and international organizations in its conception of
A. Policy formation
B. Welfare policies
C. Social impact Assessment
D. Neo-Conservatism

84. One of the most well-known tenets of modern idealist thinking is
A. Democratic peace theory
B. Human rights theory
C. Authoritarian mindset
D. Realistic theory

85. Neo-conservatism has drawn from historical liberalism its intense focus on the promotion of
A. Universal values
B. International institutions
C. Minority protections
D. Both A & C

86. Structural Marxism is an approach to Marxist philosophy based on structuralism, primarily associated with the work of the French philosopher
A. Louis Althusser
B. Nicos Poulantzas
C. Thompson
D. Eric Hobsbawm

87. Parliamentary Socialism in 1961 is a work of
A. Miliband B. E.P. Thompson
C. John Saville D. C. Wright Mills

88. As a development model, Neo-liberalism in international relations refers to the
A. rejection of structuralist economics in favour of the Washington Consensus.
B. denotes a conception of freedom as an overarching social value
C. involves the privatization of public economic sectors
D. All of these

89. "An Inquiry into the Principles of the Good Society" is a book written by who among the following political philosopher?
A. Walter Lippmann
B. Alexander Rüstow
C. Ludwig von Mises
D. Louis Rougier

90. Neo-liberalism began accelerating in importance with the establishment of the
A. Mont Pelerin Society in 1947
B. Communitarian Society 1960
C. Post Modern Society 1970
D. None of these

91. Neoliberal ideas were first implemented in which of the following country?
A. West Germany B. East Germany
C. North korea D. South Korea

92. Power and Interdependence: World Politics in Transition (2008) is written by who among the following neo-liberals?
A. Robert Keohane B. Joseph Nye
C. Milton Friedman D. Both A & B

93. The critical theory was developed within the modern discipline of IR with the help of
A. Antonio Gramsci and his influence over Robert Cox and the paradigm of production
B. Frankfurt school – Jürgen Habermas in particular
C. Habermas over Andrew Linklater and the paradigm of communication
D. All of these

94. The perspective of critical theory inquires
A. global economic forces and related hierarchies of power
B. in monitoring the chaos and insecurity
C. forcing people to leave their homes in different parts of the world
D. All of these

95. The first comprised women's suffrage movements of the 19th and early 20th centuries, promoting women's
A. Political right B. Civil liberty
C. Social right D. Economic right

96. The second wave of feminism the women's liberation movement, began in the

A. 1960s B. 1980s
C. 1950s D. 1940s

97. The fourth wave feminism from around 2012 used social media to

A. combat sexual harassment
B. violence against women
C. rape culture
D. All of these

98. Which of the following act is not correctly matched?

A. Custody of Infants Act -1839
B. Married Women's Property Act -1870
C. Representation of the People Act-1918
D. All-white Senate Judiciary Committee-1920

99. Postmodernism is a broad movement that developed in the

A. mid- to late 20th century
B. mid- to late 19th century
C. mid- to late 18th century
D. mid- to late 17th century

100. Who among the following are associated with the philosophy of Post-modernism?

A. Jean-François Lyotard,
B. Jacques Derrida
C. Fredric Jameson
D. All of these

101. Postmodernism is often associated with schools of thought such as

A. deconstruction, B. post-structuralism
C. institutional critique D. All of these

102. The term postmodern was first used in

A. 1870 B. 1860
C. 1850 D. 1840

103. In 1996, Walter Truett Anderson described postmodernism as belonging to one of typological world views which he identified as:

A. Postmodern-ironist B. Scientific-rational
C. Social-traditional D. All of these

104. Postmodernism, or, the Cultural Logic of Late Capitalism (1991) is associated with the work of

A. Fredric Jameson B. Douglas Kellner
C. Jean Baudrillard D. Jean-François Lyotard

105. US policy toward international terrorism contains a significant of

A. Military component B. Political component
C. Neither A & B D. Both A & B

106. Domestic terrorism is defined as activities that

A. involve acts dangerous to human life by assassination
B. to affect the conduct of a government by mass destruction, or kidnapping
C. to intimidate or coerce a civilian population;
D. Both A, B and C

107. Which of the following about terrorist activities is not correct?

A. Red Army Faction from 1970 to 1998
B. Revolutionary Cells from 1973 to 1983
C. National Socialist Underground from 2000 to 2006
D. The murder of Walter Lübcke

108. Political warfare means

A. use of political means to compel an opponent to do one's will
B. coercive nature leads to destroying an opponent's political will
C. political warfare is to alter an opponent's actions in favour of one state's interests
D. All of these

109. After World War II, the threat of Soviet expansion brought two new aims for American political warfare: what are these?

A. To restore Western Europe through military, economic, and political support
B. To weaken the Soviet hold on Eastern Europe through propaganda
C. To embrace a political warfare philosophy as both a defensive necessity
D. Both A & B

110. President Harry S. Truman established a government political warfare capability in

A. The National Security Act of 1947
B. The National Security Act of 1948
C. The National Security Act of 1950
D. The National Security Act of 1960

111. Jihadist extremism in the United States (or Islamist extremism in the United States) refers to

A. Islamic extremism B. Eurasian Policy
C. Freedom of religion D. All of these

112. A non State actor is an entity that falls into one of the following groups:

A. non-governmental organizations (NGOs)
B. business associations
C. philanthropic foundations
D. All of these

113. Transnational organized crime groups and terrorist movements are obviously

A. non-state actors
B. state actors
C. neither non-state nor state actors
D. None of these

114. Under this paradigm, the traditional Westphalian nation-state experiences an erosion of power and sovereignty, and tick out which of the following is coming under the jurisdiction of the cause?
A. Non-state actors are part of the cause
B. state actors are part of the cause
C. Fourth World societies
D. Both A & B

115. The term Non State Actors is widely used in development cooperation, particularly under which of the following agreement?
A. the Cotonou Agreement
B. Centre on Housing Rights and Evictions
C. Human Rights Council
D. International Campaign to Ban Landmines

116. The traditional security paradigm reached a peak during the
A. Cold War B. Look West
C. Look East D. None of these

117. In the traditional security, the greatest danger to a country is from
A. Military threats B. Political threats
C. Social threats D. Cultural threats

118. The non-traditional security consists of dangers such as:
A. terrorism B. human rights
C. global poverty D. All of these

119. External threats of The "Traditional Notion of Security" consist of which of the following components:
A. military threats B. threat of war
C. balance of power D. Both A, B & C

120. How many countries are in the United Nations?
A. 194 B. 198
C. 193 D. 197

121. Each of the Member States of the United Nations has how many seat in the General Assembly?
A. Two seats B. Four Seats
C. One Seat D. Five seats

122. Which of the following members ate and date of admission is not correctly matched?
A. United Republic of Tanzania-14 December 1961
B. United Kingdom of Great Britain-24 October 1945
C. United States of America-24 October 1950
D. Uruguay-18 December 1945

123. The main purposes of the UN are documented under the UN Charter as
A. To keep peace throughout the world
B. To develop friendly relations among nations
C. To help nations work together
D. All of these

124. Who is the last member of UN?
A. South Sudan became the 193rd member of the United Nations
B. Russia became the 193rd member of the United Nations
C. Afghanistan became the 193rd member of the United Nations
D. Poland became the 193rd member of the United Nations

125. Which among the following as the most powerful organ of the United Nations?
A. United Nations Security Council
B. United Nations General Assembly
C. United Nations Economic and Social Council
D. United Nations International Court of Justice

126. As of 2019, who among the following countries are permanent non-member observer states in the General Assembly of the United Nations?
A. The Holy See and Palestine
B. Canada and Japan
C. France and Great Britain
D. None of these

127. The difference between the ICC and the International Court of Justice are mainly on:
A. The International Court of Justice (ICJ) is a civil court that hears disputes between countries
B. The International Court of Justice (ICJ) is the principal judicial organ of the United Nations (UN).
C. The ICC is a criminal court that prosecutes individuals
D. All A, B & C

128. The Bretton Woods Agreement and System created a collective international currency exchange regime that lasted from
A. the mid-1940s to the early 1970s
B. the mid-1950s to the early 1970s
C. the mid-1930s to the early 1940s
D. the mid-1940s to the early 1950s

129. The Bretton Woods system was the first system used to control
A. the value of money between different countries
B. the political system between different countries
C. the social system between different countries
D. None of these

130. Bretton Woods failed due to
A. the US decision to suspend gold convertibility
B. collapse was the inflationary monetary policy
C. consolidation of the world political system
D. Botha A & B

131. North-South relations begin with
A. decolonialization after World War II
B. colonization of the country during 1st world War
C. anti-colonial struggles among the developed countries
D. None of these

132. Globalization has largely displaced the North–South divide as the theoretical underpinning of the development efforts of international institutions such as
A. the IMF B. World Bank
C. WTO etc D. All A, B & C

133. The North–South divide is popularly called as
A. Global North and Global South
B. Global East and Global West
C. Neither A nor B
D. Both A & B

134. The North is mostly correlated with the Western world called as
A. First World plus much of the Second World
B. Called third world
C. Called Eastern world
D. None of these

135. The Sustainable Development Goals (SDGs,) set in 2015 by the United Nations General Assembly and intended to be achieved by the year 2030, are part of a UN Resolution called
A. The 2030 Agenda B. The 2025 Agenda
C. The 2024 Agenda D. The 2022 Agenda

136. Who among the following country hosted the most recent 12th BRICS summit on 17 November 2020 virtually due to the COVID-19 pandemic?
A. Russia B. Poalnd
C. South Africa D. India

137. In which year there policy decisions in the induction of South Africa in BRIC?
A. 2014 B. 2010
C. 2017 D. 2020

138. The New Development Bank (NDB), formally referred to as the
A. BRICS Development Bank
B. World Bank
C. International Monetary Fund
D. Structural adjustment Program

139. How many countries comprises as G20
A. 19 countries and the European Union
B. 20 countries excluding European union
C. 20 countries and the African belt
D. None of these

140. Which among the following policy making body of G20 enriched participation of key international organizations?
A. World Bank, International Monetary Fund,
B. International Labour Organization, World Trade Organization
C. United Nations, etc.
D. All A, B & C

141. Which of the following reasons lead to climate change?
A. People burn fossil fuels and convert land from forests to agriculture
B. Burning fossil fuels produces carbon dioxide
C. Human activity produces indirect effect
D. All of these

142. In which year under the Paris Agreement, nations collectively agreed to keep warming "well under 2.0°C (3.6°F)" through mitigation efforts.?
A. 2011 B. 2010
C. 2015 D. 2021

143. Which among the following international environmental agreements is not correctly matched?
A. Convention on Long-Range Transboundary Air Pollution (LRTAP), Geneva, 1979.
B. Paris Agreement, 2010
C. Kyoto Protocol, 1997
D. Framework Convention on Climate Change (UNFCCC)

144. Internal migration refers to
A. moving within a state
B. moving to a different state, country
C. moving into a new country
D. moving back to where you came from

145. The major forms of migration relates to
(*a*) Invasion
(*b*) Conquest
(*c*) Colonization and
(*d*) Emigration/immigration

Select the correct code given below:
A. (*a*), (*b*) & (*c*) B. (*b*) & (*a*)
C. (*d*) & (*a*) D. (*a*), (*b*), (*c*) & (*d*)

146. The term identity politics may have been used in political discourse since at least the
A. 1970s B. 1960s
C. 1950s D. 1940s

147. Who among the following Historian discussed identity politics extensively in his 1991 book "The Disuniting of America"?
A. Brendan O'Neill
B. Owen Jones
C. Arthur Schlesinger Jr.
D. Judith Butler

148. Which among the following is not correctly matched?
A. ethnic racial identity politics dominated American politics in the 19th century
B. racial identity has been the central theme in Southern politics since slavery was abolished
C. racial identity politics utilizes racial consciousness or the group's collective memory
D. All of these

149. Arab identity politics concerns the identity-based politics derived from
A. the racial or ethno-cultural consciousness of Arab people
B. the personal is political
C. identities of gender, class, and race
D. None of these

150. "The Case for Identity Politics: Polarization, Demographic Change, and Racial Appeals" is written by who among the following political scientists?
A. Mike Gonzales B. Christopher T. Stout
C. Ross Douthat D. Ezra Klein

ANSWERS

1	2	3	4	5	6	7	8	9	10
D	B	A	B	B	C	A	B	B	D
11	**12**	**13**	**14**	**15**	**16**	**17**	**18**	**19**	**20**
B	C	D	B	B	B	D	C	A	B
21	**22**	**23**	**24**	**25**	**26**	**27**	**28**	**29**	**30**
B	C	C	D	B	C	D	A	D	D
31	**32**	**33**	**34**	**35**	**36**	**37**	**38**	**39**	**40**
A	B	C	B	B	C	D	A	C	B
41	**42**	**43**	**44**	**45**	**46**	**47**	**48**	**49**	**50**
A	A	B	C	B	A	B	A	A	D
51	**52**	**53**	**54**	**55**	**56**	**57**	**58**	**59**	**60**
D	B	B	D	A	A	C	C	A	D
61	**62**	**63**	**64**	**65**	**66**	**67**	**68**	**69**	**70**
C	B	B	D	A	A	D	A	D	D
71	**72**	**73**	**74**	**75**	**76**	**77**	**78**	**79**	**80**
D	B	C	B	B	D	D	B	D	C
81	**82**	**83**	**84**	**85**	**86**	**87**	**88**	**89**	**90**
A	A	A	A	D	A	A	D	A	A
91	**92**	**93**	**94**	**95**	**96**	**97**	**98**	**99**	**100**
A	D	D	D	A	A	D	D	A	D
101	**102**	**103**	**104**	**105**	**106**	**107**	**108**	**109**	**110**
D	A	D	A	D	D	B	D	D	A
111	**112**	**113**	**114**	**115**	**116**	**117**	**118**	**119**	**120**
D	D	D	D	A	A	A	D	D	C
121	**122**	**123**	**124**	**125**	**126**	**127**	**128**	**129**	**130**
C	C	D	D	A	A	D	A	A	D
131	**132**	**133**	**134**	**135**	**136**	**137**	**138**	**139**	**140**
A	D	D	A	A	A	B	A	A	D
141	**142**	**143**	**144**	**145**	**146**	**147**	**148**	**149**	**150**
D	C	B	A	D	A	C	D	A	B

●●●

Miscellaneous MCQs

1. The end of the Cold War is usually seen as the beginning of ______________.
   A. Contemporary era in world politics.
   B. Indian Politics.
   C. Political History
   D. Western Political Thought

2. The dominance of two superpowers, the of________ and ________ the was central to the Cold War.
   A. Soviet Union
   B. United State of America
   C. Both A and B
   D. None of the above

3. New Internal Economic Order (NIEO) as a means of attaining ________ and ______.
   A. Freedom and Equality
   B. Economic development
   C. Political Independence
   D. Both B and C

4. In which year the leaders of the Union of Soviet Socialist Republics were worried that the United States of America would invade communist ruled Cuba.
   A. April 1961 B. April 1916
   C. April 1996 D. April 1960

5. Who was the president of a small island ______ nation of the United States?
   A. John F Kennedy
   B. Fidel Castro
   C. Nikita Khrushchev
   D. George Bush

6. _______ as an ally of the Soviet Union and received both diplomatic and financial aid from it.
   A. USA B. Cuba
   C. Russia D. Britain

7. Who decided to convert Cuba into a Russian base?
   A. American President Kennedy
   B. Fidel Castro
   C. Nikita Khrushchev
   D. Stalin

8. In which year nuclear missiles was placed in Cuba?
   A. 1962 B. 1926
   C. 1965 D. 1960

9. After how many weeks USA became aware of Missile in Cuba?
   A. Four weeks B. Two weeks
   C. Three weeks D. One week

10. A clash seemed imminent in what came to be known as the_______.
    A. Cuban Missile Crises
    B. Cuban Crises
    C. Missile Crises
    D. Cuba Missile Crises

11. The Cuban Missile Crises was a high point of what came to be known as the _____ .
    A. Hot War B. Cold War
    C. World War 1 D. World War 2

12. __________ referred to the competition, the tensions and a series of confrontations between the United States and Soviet Union, backed by their respective allies.
    A. Hot War B. Cold War
    C. World War 2 D. Cuban Missile Crises

13. The Cold War included ________.
    A. Peace, competition and understanding.
    B. Rivalries, military alliance and the balance of power.
    C. Unity, competition and rivalries
    D. Peace, competition and unity.

14. The Cold War was accompanied by a ______ conflict as well.
    A. Monetary Conflicts B. Ideological Conflicts
    C. Personal Conflicts D. All of the above.

15. Who was the leader of Western Alliance?
    A. US B. Russia
    C. USSR D. Allied powers

16. The Western Alliance represent ideology of:
    A. Socialism
    B. Liberalism, Democracy and Capitalism
    C. Communalism
    D. Marxism

17. Who was the leader of Eastern Alliance?
    A. Soviet Union B. USA
    C. Russia D. Britain

18. The Eastern Alliance represent the ideology of:
A. Capitalism
B. Marxism
C. Socialism and Communalism
D. Socialism and Marxism

19. Allied forces led by the __________.
A. Germany, Italy and Japan
B. US, Soviet Union, Britain and France
C. US, Soviet Union, Italy and Japan
D. USA, USSR

20. The World War Two spread up to which regions?
A. Asia, India, China and Burma
B. South east Asia, China, Burma and parts of India's Northeast
C. Northeast Asia, China, Burma and part of India's northeast.
D. Northeast Asia, China, Burma and parts of India's north.

21. Why did the critics said it was unnecessary to drop bombs?
A. Japan was innocent
B. Japan was about to surrender
C. Japan was week
D. Japan was stronger

22. According to critics, what was the reasons for American Bombing Japan?
A. To stop the Soviet Union from making military and political gains in Asia
B. To show Moscow that the United States was supreme
C. To end the war quickly
D. Both A and B

23. According to the US supporters have USA Dropping of the atomic bombs was necessary to:
A. To stop the Soviet Union from making military and political gains in Asia
B. To stop further loss of American and Allied lives.
C. To end war quickly and to stop
D. Both B and C

24. Atomic Bomb of US on Hiroshima was code named.
A. The bomb was code-named "Little Boy"
B. Fat man
C. Little baby
D. Little girl

25. Atomic Bomb on Nagasaki was code named as:
A. Fat man
B. Fat boy
C. Fat women
D. Fatty man

26. The yield of Little Boy and Fat man were ________ respectively.
A. 15 and 26 kilotons B. 15 and 29 kilotons
C. 15 and 21 kilotons D. 14 and 21 kilotons

27. By the early 1950s the US and the USSR were already making thermonuclear weapons hat had a yield between _______.
A. 10 and 15 kilotons
B. 10 and 15 thousand kilotons
C. 15 and 20 kilotons
D. 100 thousand kilotons.

28. When two rival powers are in possession of nuclear weapons capable of inflicting death and destruction uncapable to each other, a full-fledged war is:
A. unlikely B. likely
C. must D. possible

29. What happens in Logic of deterrence situation?
A. Both sides have the capacity to retaliate against an attack
B. Cause so much destruction that neither can afford to initiate war
C. Neither side would want to risk war
D. Both A and B

30. In spite being an in tense form of rivalry between great powers—remained a "cold and hot or shooting war due to:
A. Logic of War B. Logic of peace
C. Logic of deterrence D. All of the above

31. The deterrence relationship prevents war but not ________.
A. Fighting
B. Ideological conflict
C. Rivalry between powers
D. None of the above

32. In the deterrence relationship both blocks led by the superpowers were respected to behave as _______ actors.
A. Rational and responsible
B. Responsible and vigilant
C. Careful honest
D. None of the above

33. When two superpowers and the blocks led them are in a ______ relationship, fighting wars will be massively destructive?
A. Friendly B. Deterrence
C. Peaceful D. Neutral

34. Cold War managed to ensure ________.
A. Peace B. Human lives
C. Human survival D. None of the above

35. The Western alliance was formalized into an organization, the ______, which came into existence ________.

A. NATO, In April 1949
B. SEATO, In April 1948
C. CENTO, In April 1994
D. TANTO, In April 1947

36. NATO is an association of ________ states.

A. 23 B. 30
C. 18 D. 25

37. The Eastern alliance, known as the __________ was led by the Soviet Union.

A. Warsaw pact B. SEATO
C. CENTO D. NATO

38. The Eastern alliance was created in _______ and its principal function was to counter _____ forces in Europe.

A. 1954, CENTO B. 1955, NATO
C. 1955, SEATO D. None of the above

39. In East and Southeast Asia and in West Asia, the United States built an alliance system called______ and ______.

A. CENTO and NATO B. NATO and SEATO
C. SEATO and CENTO D. None of the above

40. The Soviet Union and Communist China responded by heaving close relations with regional countries such as:

A. India, Pakistan and Nepal
B. North Vietnam, North Korea and Iraq
C. Iraq, Pakistan and Bhutan
D. North Vietnam, North Korea and Pakistan

41. Name the movement which gave newly independent countries a way staying out of the alliance.

A. NAM B. NATO
C. CENTO D. SEATO

42. Which among the following statements about the Cold War is wrong?

A. It was a competition between the US and Soviet Union and their respective allies
B. It was an ideological war between the superpowers
C. It triggered of an arms race
D. The US and USSR were engaged in direct wars.

43. Which among the following statements does not reflect the objectives of NAM?

A. Enabling newly decolonized countries to pursue independent policies.
B. Not joining any military alliances.
C. Following a policy of neutrality on global issues.
D. Focus on elimination of global economic inequalities.

44. Which of the following is not a member of NATO?

A. The US B. England
C. France D. None of these

45. Which of the following was not a member of SEATO?

A. USSR B. New Zealand
C. Pakistan D. Australia

46. Which of the followings statement about the NIEO is false?

A. Give the LDCs control over their natural resources
B. Obtain access to Western markets
C. Reduce the cost of technology from the Western countries.
D. Provide the developed countries with a greater role in international economic institutions.

47. In 1945 the allied forces included the US, _____ USSR and ______.

A. US, Britain, USSR and France
B. US, Japan, USSR and France
C. US, France, USSR and Italy
D. US, Italy, USSR and Japan

48. The event that took place in 1961 was

A. The construction of the Berlin wall.
B. Soviet intervention in Afghanistan.
C. Vietnamese intervention in Cambodia.
D. The Unification of Germany

Directions (Qs. No. 49-53): *Read the passage carefully and answer the question that follow:*

In April 1961, the leaders of the Union of Soviet Socialist Republics (USSR) were worried that the United States of America (USA) would invade communist-ruled Cuba and overthrow Fidel Castro, the president of the small island nation off the çoast of the United States. Cuba was an ally of the Soviet Union and received both diplomatic and financial aid from it. Nikita Khrushchev, the leader of the Soviet Union, decided to convert Cuba into a Russian base. In 1962, he placed nuclear missiles in Cuba. The installation of these weapons put the US, for the first time, under fire from close range and nearly doubled the number of bases or cities in the American mainland which could be threatened by the USSR.

49. Who were worried that the United States of America would invade communist ruled Cuba?

A. The leaders of Cuba
B. The leaders of USSR
C. The leaders of Cuba
D. None of the above

50. Who was Fidel Castro?

A. President of USSR B. President of USA
C. President of Cuba D. President of Britain

51. Cuba was an ally of the Soviet Union and received both:
A. Technical and Financial aid
B. Diplomatic and Financial aid
C. Political and Technical aid
D. None of the above

52. Nikita Khrushchev, the leader of the Soviet Union, decided to convert Cuba into a:
A. USA base B. Cuba base
C. Russian base D. Britain base

53. In which year nuclear missile was placed in Cuba?
A. 1962 B. 1926
C. 1965 D. 1960

Directions (Qs. No. 54-58): *Read the passage carefully and answer the question that follow:*

Three weeks after the Soviet Union had placed the nuclear weapons in Cuba, the Americans became aware of it. The US President, John F. Kennedy, and his advisers were reluctant to do anything that might lead to full-scale nuclear war between the two countries, but they were determined to get Khrushchev to remove the missiles and nuclear weapons from Cuba. Kennedy ordered American warships to intercept any Soviet ships heading to Cuba as a way of warning the USSR of his seriousness. A clash seemed imminent in what came to be known as the Cuban Missile Crisis. The prospects of this clash made the whole world nervous, for it would have been no ordinary war. Eventually, to the world's great relief, both sides decided to avoid war. The Soviet ships slowed down and turned back.

54. After____ weeks the Soviet Union had placed the nuclear weapons in Cuba.
A. One week B. Four weeks
C. Three weeks D. Two weeks

55. Who were reluctant to do anything that might lead to full-scale nuclear war between the two countries?
A. Fidel Castro and Nikita Khrushchev
B. John F. Kennedy and Fidel Castro
C. John F. Kennedy and his Advisers
D. Nikita Khrushchev and his advisers

56. To whom Kennedy ordered to intercept any Soviet ships heading to Cuba.
A. Russian warships B. American warships
C. Cuban warships D. None of the above

57. What was the greatest relief to the whole world?
A. Soviet ships heading to Cuba.
B. Cuban Missile crise was high point.
C. Both sides decided to avoid war.
D. All the above.

58. A _______ seems imminent in what came to be known as the Cuban Missile Crises.
A. War B. Clash
C. Nuclear War D. Social Life

Directions (Qs. No. 59-63): *Read the passage carefully and answer the question that follow:*

The end of the Second World War is a landmark in contemporary world politics. In 1945, the Allied Forces, led by the US, Soviet Union, Britain and France defeated the Axis Powers led by Germany, Italy and Japan, ending the Second World War (1939-1945). The war had involved almost all the major powers of the world and spread out to regions outside Europe including Southeast Asia, China, Burma (now Myanmar) and parts of India's northeast. The war devastated the world in terms of loss of human lives and civilian property. The First World War had earlier shaken the world between 1914 and 1918.

59. Which incident is a landmark in contemporary world politics?
A. The end of the First World War.
B. The end of the Second World War.
C. The end of Cold of War.
D. All the above.

60. In 1945, _______ forces, led by the US, Soviet Union, Britain and France defeated the Axis Powers led by Germany.
A. Axis Power B. Allied Power
C. Soviet Power D. Union Power

61. The war had involved almost all the major powers of the world and spread out to regions outside ______.
A. Europe, Asia, China, Pakistan and Burma.
B. Europe, Southeast Asia, China, Burma and parts of India's northeast.
C. China, India, Burma and Pakistan
D. All the above

62. Which war had earlier shaken the world between 1914 and 1918?
A. Second World War B. Cold War
C. First World War D. None of the above

63. The War devastated the World in terms of loss of ____ and _____.
A. Freedom and Finance
B. Human lives and civilian property
C. Ideology and Political life
D. Economy and Freedom

Directions (Qs. No. 64-68): *Read the passage carefully and answer the question that follow:*

The end of the Second World War was also the beginning of the Cold War. The world war ended when the

United States dropped two atomic bombs on the Japanese cities of Hiroshima and Nagasaki in August 1945, causing Japan to surrender. Critics of the US decision to drop the bombs have argued that the US knew that Japan was about to surrender and that it was unnecessary to drop the bombs. They suggest that the US action was intended to stop the Soviet Union from making military and political gains in Asia and elsewhere and to show Moscow that the United States was supreme. US supporters have argued that the dropping of the atomic bombs was necessary to end the war quickly and to stop further loss of American and Allied lives. Whatever the motives, the consequence of the end of the Second World War was the rise of two new powers on the global stage.

64. What was also the reason for beginning of the Cold War?
A. The end of the First World War
B. The end of the Second World War
C. The end of the Cold War
D. All the above

65. When was the Second World War ended?
A. Both sides decided to avoid war
B. Mutual understanding by both
C. USA dropped atomic bombs on Hiroshima and Nagasaki
D. All the above

66. Who suggested that the US action was intended to stop the Soviet Union for making military and political gains in Asia and elsewhere?
A. US critics B. US supporters
C. Both A and B D. None of the above

67. Who have argued that the dropping of the atomic bombs was necessary to end the war quickly?
A. US critics B. US supporters
C. Both A and B D. None of the above

68. According to critics, what was the reasons for American Bombing Japan?
A. To stop Soviet Union from making military and political gains in Asia.
B. To stop further loss of America and Allied lives.
C. To end war quickly and to stop
D. Both A and C

Directions (Qs. No. 69-73): *Read the passage carefully and answer the question that follow:*

The western alliance was formalised into an organisation, the North Atlantic Treaty Organisation (NATO), which came into existence in April 1949. It was an association of twelve states which declared that armed attack on any one of them in Europe or North America would be regarded as an attack on all of them. Each of these states would be obliged to help the other. The eastern alliance, known as the Warsaw Pact, was led by the Soviet Union. It was created in 1955 and its principal function was to counter NATO's forces in Europe.

69. In which year the NATO came into existence?
A. In April 1948
B. In April 1949
C. In April 1984
D. In April 1947

70. The Eastern Alliance was led by whom?
A. USA B. Britain
C. Soviet Union D. None of the above

71. What was the principal function of Warsaw pact?
A. To defend Western Alliance.
B. To defend Europe and North America
C. To counter NATO's forces in Europe
D. All the above

72. NATO was an association of __________ states.
A. Eleven B. Twelve
C. Thirteen D. Fourteen

73. Western Alliance was led by whom?
A. Britain B. USA
C. USSR D. Cuba

Directions (Qs. No. 74-78): *Read the passage carefully and answer the question that follow:*

The Cold War threatened to divide the world into two alliances. Under these circumstances, many of the newly independent countries, after gaining their independence from the colonial powers such as Britain and France, were worried that they would lose their freedom as soon as they gained formal independence. Cracks and splits within the alliances were quick to appear. Communist China quarrelled with the USSR towards the late 1950s, and, in 1969, they fought a brief war over a territorial dispute. The other important development was the Non-Aligned Movement (NAM), which gave the newly independent countries away of staying out of the alliances.

74. What was threatening of the cold war to the whole world?
A. Destruction of the world.
B. Division of the world.
C. Division into two alliances.
D. All the above

75. Why did many newly independent countries worry after gaining independence?
A. Getting more facilities
B. Loss of freedom
C. More independence
D. None of the above

76. What was reason behind the quarrel between China and USSR?

A. Territorial disputes B. Financial disputes
C. Military disputes D. All the above

77. What was the prospective of the newly independent countries?

A. Cooperate to alliance
B. Stay away from the alliance
C. Stay with USSR
D. Stay with US

78. In which year China ad USSR fought a brief war over a territorial dispute?

A. 1969 B. 1968
C. 1967 D. 1996

Directions (Qs. No. 79-82): *Read the passage carefully and answer the question that follow:*

Sometimes, countries outside the two blocs, for example, the non-aligned countries, played a role in reducing Cold War conflicts and averting some grave crises. Jawaharlal Nehru — one of the leaders of the NAM — played a crucial role in mediating between the two Koreas. In the Congo crisis, the UN Secretary-General played a key mediatory role. By and large, it was the realisation on a superpower's part that war by all means should be avoided that made them exercise restraint and behave more responsibly in international affairs. As the Cold War rolled from one arena to another, the logic of restraint was increasingly evident. However, since the Cold War did not eliminate rivalries between the two alliance, mutual suspicions led them to arm themselves to the teeth and to constantly prepare for war. Huge stocks of arms were considered necessary to prevent wars from taking place.

79. Which countries played a crucial role in reducing Cold War?

A. Allied countries B. Non-Aligned countries
C. Western countries D. Foreign countries

80. Who was an Indian played crucial role in mediating between the two Koreas?

A. Mahatma Gandhi
B. Jawaharlal Nehru
C. Netaji Subash Chandra Bose
D. Motilal Nehru

81. Who played a crucial role in mediating in the Congo Crises?

A. Jawaharlal Nehru B. NAM countries
C. UN Secretary General D. Western countries

82. What were considered necessary to prevent wars for taking place?

A. International affairs B. Logic of restraint
C. Huge stock of arms D. Non-aligned countries

Directions (Qs. No. 83-94): *In the question below, there are two statements marked as Assertion (A) and Reason (R). Read the statements and choose the correct option.*

Options:

A. If both (A) and (R) are true, and (R) is the correct explanation of (A).
B. If both (A) and (R) are true, but (R) is not the correct explanation of (A).
C. If (A) is true but (R) is false.
D. If (A) is false but (R)is true.

83. Assertion (A) : The end of the Second World War also the beginning of the Cold War.

Reason (R) : The world war ended when the United States dropped two atomic bombs on the Japanese cities Hiroshima and Nagasaki.

84. Assertion (A) : The Western alliance was formalised into an organisation, NATO which came into existence in 1949.

Reason (R) : The Eastern alliance, was led by the Soviet Union and it was created in 1955.

85. Assertion (A) : The Cuban Missile Crises was a high point of what came to be known as the Cold War.

Reason (R) : The Cold War referred to the competition, the tension and a series of confrontations between the United States and Soviet Union.

86. Assertion (A) : Cuba was an ally of the Soviet Union and received both diplomatic and financial aid from it.

Reason (R) : Three weeks after the USA had placed the nuclear weapons in Cuba.

87. Assertion (A) : The Cold War was not simply a matter of power rivalries, of military alliance, and of the balance of power.

Reason (R) : These were accompanied by a real ideological conflict as well, a difference over the best and the most appropriate way of organising political, economic, and social life all over the world.

88. Assertion (A) : Economic development was also vital for the independence of the new countries.

Reason (R) : Without sustained development, a country could not truly free. It would remain dependent on the richer countries including the colonial powers from which political freedom had been achieved.

89. **Assertion (A) :** The Cuban Missile Crises was a high point of what came to be known as the Cold War.

Reason (R) : The war devastated the world in terms of loss of human lives and civilian property.

90. **Assertion (A) :** The Second World War ended when the United States dropped two atomic bombs on the Japanese cities.

Reason (R) : The end of the Second World War is a landmark in contemporary world politics.

91. **Assertion (A) :** Since the Cold War did not eliminate rivalries between the two alliances, mutual suspicious led them to arm themselves to the teeth and to constantly prepare for war.

Reason (R) : The non-aligned countries were more than merely mediators during the Cold War.

92. **Assertion (A) :** The Cold War was an outcome of the emergency of the US and the USSR as two superpowers rival to each other.

Reason (R) : When two rival powers are in possession of nuclear weapons capable of inflicting death and destruction unacceptable to each other, a full-fledged war is unlikely.

93. **Assertion (A) :** The two superpowers were not keen on expanding their spheres of influence in different parts of the world.

Reason (R) : The smaller states in the alliances used the link to the superpowers for their own purpose.

94. **Assertion (A) :** The consequence of the end of the Second World War was the rise of two new powers on the global stage.

Reason (R) : With the defeat of Germany and Japan, the devastation of Europe and in many other parts of the world, the United State and the Soviet Union became the greatest powers in the world.

95. The Berlin War symbolized the division between the _________world.
A. capitalist and communist
B. rich and poor
C. developed and developing.
D. East and West

96. The Berlin Wall was more than _____ kilometer long.
A. 100 km B. 150 km
C. 175 km D. 200 km

97. The USSR group was also known as the ______ bloc.
A. Capitalist bloc
B. Socialist bloc
C. Democratic bloc
D. Developed bloc

98. Warsaw pact signed by mainly by the countries of _____ Europe.
A. Eastern B. Central
C. Southern D. Western

99. When Mikhail Gorbachev became General secretary of the communist party of Soviet Union?
A. 1981 B. 1985
C. 1989 D. 1990

100. The Soviet Union invaded Afghanistan in _____.
A. 1969 B. 1979
C. 1989 D. 1999

101. _______ was the successor of Lenin.
A. Putin B. Gaubachev
C. Stalin D. Trotosky

102. Collectivisation of agriculture was done by ______ in the USSR.
A. Stalin B. Lenin
C. Yeltsin D. Putin

103. Who among the following is not a Baltic republic?
A. Estonia B. Lithuania
C. Latvia D. London

104. What is the meaning of Perestroika?
A. Rejecting B. Recounting
C. Restructuring D. Reopening

105. What is the meaning of Glasnost?
A. Transparency B. Openness
C. Lockdown D. Strick

106. ________ became the first republic to declare its independence from USSR?
A. Lithuania B. Liberia
C. Georgia D. Azerbaijan

107. Yeltsin became the President of Russia in the year _____.
A. 1998 B. 1991
C. 1994 D. 1995

108. In 1991 _______ signed as the President of the Soviet Union.
A. Gorbachev B. Yeltsin
C. Kruschev D. Breznev

109. Czechoslovakia was split into _______ parts after 1945.

A. 5 B. 4
C. 3 D. 2

Directions (Qs. No. 110-119): *The following questions consist of two statements—Assertion (A) and Reason (R). Answer these questions selecting the appropriate option given below:*

A. Both (A) and (R) are true and (R) is the correct explanation of (A).
B. Both (A) and (R) are true, but R is not the correct explanation of (A).
C. (A) is true, but (R) is false.
D. (A) is false, but (R) is true.

110. Assertion (A) : USSR came into being after 1917 Revolution.
Reason (R) : It was inspired by socialism and opposed capitalism.

111. Assertion (A) : After Second World War, the world was divided into Eastern Block and Western Block.
Reason (R) : Western countries joined Eastern Block.

112. Assertion (A) : Vladimir Lenin died in 1924.
Reason (R) : Stalin came to power in 1924.

113. Assertion (A) : Joseph Stalin period saw the rapid industrialisation of USSR.
Reason (R) : His period was known as the Great Terror of 1930's.

114. Assertion (A) : Cold War came to an end with the collapse of Soviet Union.
Reason (R) : USA became only the powerful country in the world.

115. Assertion (A) : Many western European countries joined NATO.
Reason (R) : It was a military alliance formed by USA.

116. Assertion (A) : Shock therapy was the transition of communism to capitalism.
Reason (R) : The collapse of communism resulted in shock therapy.

117. Assertion (A) : Due to shock therapy the value of Russian Ruble declined.
Reason (R) : Ruble is not the currency of USSR.

118. Assertion (A) : India's Relations with Russia are an important aspect of India's foreign policy.
Reason (R) : India maintained good Relations with all the post-communist countries.

119. Assertion (A) : The Berlin wall was built in 1961.
Reason (R) : Germany was the friend of allied countries.

Directions (Qs. No. 120-124): *Read the following passage and answer these questions.*

The Berlin Wall symbolised the division between the capitalist and the communist world. Built in 1961 to separate East Berlin from West Berlin, this more than 150 kilometre long wall stood for 28 years and was finally broken by the people on 9 November 1989. This marked the unification of the two parts of Germany and the beginning of the end of the communist bloc.

120. Berlin wall symbolises the division between _______ and _________.

A. Capitalism and Secularism
B. Capitalism and Democracy
C. Capitalism and Communism
D. Communism and Socialism

121. Berlin wall was built in _________ year.

A. 2020 B. 2021
C. 1961 D. 1999

122. The Berlin Wall Separates _____________.

A. East Berlin from North Berlin.
B. East Berlin from North West Berlin
C. East Berlin from West Berlin
D. East Berlin from South Berlin

123. The Berlin Wall stood for __________ years.

A. 10 B. 21
C. 20 D. 28

124. The Berlin Wall was broken on ___________.

A. 9th November 1989
B. 10th November 1989
C. 11th November 1989
D. 12th November 1989

Directions (Qs. No. 125-130): *Read the following passage and answer these questions.*

After the Second World War, the east European countries that the Soviet army had liberated from the fascist forces came under the control of the USSR. The political and the economic systems of all these countries were modelled after the USSR. This group of countries was called the Second World or the 'socialist bloc'. The Warsaw Pact, a military alliance, held them together. The USSR was the leader of the bloc.

125. The second world war ended in __________ year.

A. 1942
B. 1943
C. 1944
D. 1945

126. USSR stands for __________.
A. Union of Soviet
B. Soviet Republic
C. Union of Soviet Socialist Republic
D. Union of Republic

127. After second world war, the East European countries came under the control of:
A. USA B. USSR
C. UK D. France

128. The military alliance of Warsaw was created by __________.
A. USA B. USSR
C. Britain D. China

129. The western Block was controlled by __________.
A. China B. USA
C. USSR D. India

130. Arrange the following in the chronological order of occurrence:
I. Disintegration of USSR
II. Berlin wall collapse
III. February Revolution
IV. Gorbachev became the General Secretary of USSR
A. I, II, III and IV B. II, I, III and IV
C. III, IV, II and I D. IV, III, II and I

131. Which among the following statements that describe the nature of Soviet economy is wrong?
A. Socialism was the dominant ideology
B. State ownership/control existed over the factors of production
C. People enjoyed economic freedom
D. Every aspect of the economy was planned and controlled by the state.

132. Which among the following is not an outcome of the disintegration of USSR?
I. End of the ideological war between USA and USSR
II. Birth of CIS
III. Change in the balance of power in the world
IV. Crisis in the Middle East

Select the correct answer using the four given above:
A. IV only B. II, I and III
C. III, II and IV D. II and IV

133. Which among the following statements is false?
A. Russian revolution was inspired by the ideals of socialism.
B. Lenin was the leader of Russian revolution.
C. The transition from socialism to capitalism is known as shock therapy
D. India was responsible for the disintegration of USSR.

134. The communist party was not accountable to the people, Ordinary people were exploited by rampant corruption.They were given no representation in the state machinery:
I. USSR started the five year plan
II. People were subjected to lot of difficulties
II. India adopted five year plan copying from USSR
IV. USA and USSR remained to be powerful after disintegration.

Read the following options mention which sentence is wrong?
A. I only B. I and II
C. I, II and III D. IV only

135. Russia had good relationship with India because:
A. India purchases its arms
B. India imports oil from India
C. India had very good cultural relations with it
D. All of the above

136. Consider the following statements. Find the wrong statement
A. Lenin was the leader of Bolshevik party
B. Stalin was not the immediate successor of Lenin
C. Gorbachev was blamed for the disintegration of USSR
D. Boris Yelstin was the first elected president of Russia

137. The Berlin wall was toppled on ______.
A. 9th November 1989
B. 8th November 1989
C. 7th November 1989
D. 6th November 1989

138. Soviet political system was based on _____ ideology.
A. Mixed economy
B. Socialism and communism
C. Capitalism
D. Private sector

139. USSR stands for _______.
A. Union of Socialist Russia
B. Union of Soviet
C. Union of Soviet Socialist Republic
D. United States Russia

Directions (Qs. No. 140-144): *Read the following passage and answer the questions..*

The UN was founded as a successor to the League of Nations. It was established in 1945 immediately after the Second World War. The organization was set up through the signing of the United Nations Charter by 51 states. It tried to achieve what the League could not between the two world wars. The UN's objective is to prevent international conflict and to facilitate cooperation among states. It was founded with the hope that it would act to stop the conflicts between states escalating into war and, if war broke out, to limit the extent of hostilities. Furthermore, since conflicts often arose from the lack of social and economic development, the UN was intended to bring countries together to improve the prospects of social and economic development all over the world.

140. _______ was the founded as a successor to league of Nations.

A. UNESCO B. The UN
C. The USA D. The USSR

141. The UN was established in the year:

A. 1942 B. 1946
C. 1945 D. 1940

142. The UN's objective is:

A. to prevent international conflict and to facilitate cooperation among states
B. to start war
C. to create war like situation
D. to encourage conflicts

143. How many states signed to set up the organization?

A. 50 B. 45
C. 51 D. 52

144. How do often conflicts arise?

A. lack of social and economic development
B. lack of culture
C. lack of knowledge
D. lack of faith

Directions (Qs. No. 145-149): *Read the following passage and answer the questions.*

IMF—The International Monetary Fund is an International organization that oversees these financial institutions and regulations that act at the International level. The IMF has 189 member countries (as on 12 April 2016) but they do not enjoy an equal say. The top ten countries have more than 52 per cent of the votes. They are the G-8 members (The US, Japan, Germany, France, the UK, Italy, Canada and Russia), China and Saudi Arabia. The US alone has 16.54 per cent voting rights.

145. What is IMF?

A. International Monetary Fund is an international organization that it oversees those financial institutions and regulations that act at the international level
B. Indian Making Form is an international organization that it oversees those financial institutions and regulations that act at the international level.
C. International marking Fees is an international organization that it oversees those financial institutions and regulations that act at the international level.
D. International Money Fund is a international organization that it oversees those financial institutions and regulations that act at the international level.

146. Write about the membership and voting procedure of the International Monetary Fund.

A. The IMF has 189 member countries, but they do not enjoy an equal say. The US alone has 16.54 per cent voting rights.
B. The IMF has 189 member countries, but they are enjoying equal rights.
C. The US alone has 16.54 per cent voting rights because it is the permanent member country in the Security Council.
D. None of these

147. Why has the US alone held 16.54 per cent voting rights?

A. The US alone has 16.54 per cent voting rights because it is the poorest country. The US providing less amount for it's funding.
B. The US alone has 16.54 per cent voting rights because it is the richest member country of the organization. The US provides maximum for its funding.
C. The US alone has 16.54 per cent voting rights because it is the sole superpower in the world.
D. The US alone has 16.54 per cent voting rights because it is the permanent member country in the Security Council.

148. Which are the following G-8 member countries?

A. US, Japan, India, Russia, Nepal, Germany.
B. US, Germany, Japan, France, UK, Italy, Canada, Russia, China and Saudi Arabia.
C. US, Pakistan, Bhutan, Nepal, Singapore, Canada, China and Saudi Arabia.
D. US, Japan, Netherlands, Bhutan, Afghanistan, Italy, Iraq.

149. What is the voting per cent of the top ten countries?

A. 65% B. 75%
C. 85% D. 52%.

150. The UN Security Council have ______ Permanent members and ______ non-permanent members.

A. Ten permanent and fifteen non-permanent member countries
B. Ten permanent and ten non-permanent member countries
C. Ten permanent and five non-permanent member countries
D. Five permanent and ten non-permanent countries

151. The present Secretary General of the UN is:
A. Ban Ki-moon B. Kofi A. Annan
C. Antonio Guterres D. U Thant

152. The prime objective of UN is:
A. To maintain peace and security
B. It is the major financial contributor of the world
C. To encourage conflicts
D. None of these

153. The total number of members represented in General assembly is:
A. 191 B. 195
C. 193 D. 197

154. The World Trade Organization (WTO) formed on 1st January:
A. 1994 B. 1995
C. 1996 D. 1997

155. Check which is not an agency of UN?
A. International Committee of Red Cross
B. UNDP
C. IMF
D. ILO

156. India became a member of the UN in:
A. 1945 B. 1947
C. 1950 D. 1962

157. Which of the following organizations is meant for Children?
A. UNESCO B. UNICEF
C. UNHCR D. UNHRC

158. The office of the UN General Assembly:
A. New York B. Washington DC
C. San Francisco D. Zurich

159. Currently in 2016 UN peacekeeping operations are:
A. 15 B. 14
C. 17 D. 16

160. Which of the following has veto power in the Security Council?
A. India B. Pakistan
C. Brazil D. America

161. The United Nations was not created to take humanity to the heaven, but to save it from the hell. Who made this statement?
A. Pt. Jawaharlal Nehru B. Kofi Annan
C. Ban Ki-moon D. Dag Hammarskjold

162. Expand IAEA?
A. International Atomic Energy Act
B. International Atomic Energy Accord
C. International Atomic Energy Agency
D. International Atomic Eastern Agency

163. The International Court of Justice popularly known as the
A. Supreme Court B. World Court
C. Criminal Court D. Subordinate Courts

164. The largest international human rights organization in ________ .
A. Russia B. Germany
C. Canada D. US

165. What is the full form of NGO?
A. Non-gazette office
B. Non-Governmental Organization
C. Nation governing organization
D. None of these

166. The more weightage to India's proposal for permanent membership in the Security Council is:
A. Nuclear capability
B. Located in Asia
C. India's membership in the UN
D. India's growing economic power and stable political system

167. How many judges are there in the International Court of Justice?
A. Fifteen judges B. Sixteen judges
C. Seventeen judges D. Eighteen judges

168. Which one of the following is not a permanent member of the UN Security Council?
A. Russia B. India
C. China D. France

169. The highest functionary of the UN is called ________.
A. General Assembly B. Secretariat
C. Security Council D. None of these

170. How many countries are members of the UN?
A. 188 B. 190
C. 192 D. 193

171. What is Amnesty International?
A. it is an NGO (Non Governmental Organization) at international forum
B. it is an organization
C. it is a government organization
D. None of these

172. Who has a right to vote in the UN?
A. Each member nation of UN
B. Only five permanent member countries
C. Only non-permanent member countries
D. None of these

173. The UN agency concerned with the safety and peaceful use of nuclear technology:
A. The UN Committee on Disarmament
B. International Atomic Energy Agency

C. UN International Safeguard Committee
D. None of these

174. Which of the following oversees those financial institutions and regulations that act at the international level?
A. WTO B. IAEA
C. IMF D. WHO

175. Which of the following is suggestion for becoming a new member of the Security Council?
A. A major economic power
B. A major military power
C. A substantial contributor to the UN budget
D. All of the above

176. Name any two member states of the European Union who are permanent members of the UN Security Council?
A. India and Brazil
B. Britain and France
C. Singapore and Malaysia
D. Andaman and Lakshadweep

177. Where are the head quarters of WTO?
A. New York
B. Washington DC
C. Geneva (Switzerland)
D. New Zeeland

178. The number of principal organs of UNO is ______.
A. 3 B. 4
C. 5 D. 6

179. Which organization of United Nations has ceased to be operational?
A. Trusteeship Council
B. Secretariat
C. International Court of Justice
D. Economic and Social Council

180. Which of the following countries is not a member of the G-8 group?
A. Germany B. France
C. Italy D. Spain

181. The head quarters of International Court of Justice are at:
A. Geneva B. Rome
C. The Hague D. Vienna

182. What is the purpose of 'United Nations Conference on UNCTAD?
A. Promotes International Trade with a view to accelerate economic growth of developing countries
B. Set rules for World Trade
C. Promotes International Monetary cooperation and expansion of International Trade
D. None of the above

183. The term of office of the UN Secretary-General is:
A. Three years B. Four years
C. Five years D. Six years

184. Which of the following is Human Rights Organisation?
A. The French Community
B. The Arab League
C. The organization of African Unity
D. Amnesty International

185. Which of the following organizations is meant for Children?
A. UNESCO B. UNICEF
C. UNHCR D. UNHRC

186. Which of the following is a genuine contender for becoming a permanent member of Security Council?
A. China B. France
C. India D. Pakistan

187. Arrange the following in the chronological order:
(*a*) Establishment of Human Rights Council
(*b*) Yalta Conference
(*c*) Atlantic Charter
(*d*) India joins the UN
A. (*b*), (*d*), (*a*), (*c*) B. (*c*), (*b*), (*d*), (*a*)
C. (*a*), (*b*), (*c*), (*d*) D. (*b*), (*c*), (*d*), (*a*)

188. Arrange the following in the chronological order of their establishment:
(*a*) The WTO
(*b*) Amnesty International
(*c*) League of Nations
(*d*) World Bank
A. (*c*), (*d*), (*a*), (*b*)
B. (*d*), (*c*), (*b*), (*a*)
C. (*d*), (*c*), (*b*), (*a*)
D. (*a*), (*b*), (*c*), (*d*)

189. Assertion (A) : The World Bank was created during the Second World War in 1944.
Reason (R) : The Soviet Union has collapsed.
In the context of the above two statements which one of the following is correct?
A. Both (A) and (R) are true and (R) is the correct explanation of (A)
B. Both (A) and (R) are true, but (R) is not the correct explanation of (A)
C. (A) is true, but (R) is false
D. (A) is false, but (R) is true

190. Assertion (A) : US and other western countries want improvements in the UN's budgetary procedures and its administration.
Reason (R) : The UN consists of many different structures and agencies.

In the context of the above two statement which one of the following is correct?

A. Both (A) and (R) are individually true, but (R) is not the correct explanation of (A)
B. Both (A) and (R) are individually true and (R) is the correct explanation of (A)
C. (A) is true, but (R) is false
D. (A) is false, but (R) is true

191. Assertion (A) : In the Security Council, there are five permanent members and ten non-permanent members.

Reason (R) : Charter gave the permanent members a privileged position to bring about stability in the world.

In the context of the above two statements which one of the following is correct?

A. Both (A) and (R) are true and (R) is the correct explanation of (A)
B. Both (A) and (R) are true, but (R) is not the correct explanation of (A)
C. (A) is true, but (R) is false
D. (A) is false, but (R) is true

192. Assertion (A) : We should keep in mind that the membership of the UN Security Council was expanded from 11 to 15 in 1965.

Reason (R) : UN General Assembly members now are developing countries.

In the context of the above two statements which one of the following is correct?

A. Both (A) and (R) are individually true and (R) is the correct explanation of (A)
B. Both (A) and (R) are true, but (R) is not the correct explanation of (A)
C. (A) is true, but (R) is false
D. (A) is false, but (R) is true

193. Assertion (A) : The International Atomic Energy Agency (IAEA) was established in 1957.

Reason (R) : IAEA teams did not inspect nuclear facilities all over the world to ensure that civilian reactors are not being used for military purposes.

In the context of the above two statements which one of the following is correct?

A. Both (A) and (R) are true and (R) is the correct explanation of (A)
B. Both (A) and (R) are true, but (R) is not the correct explanation of (A)
C. (A) is true, but (R) is false
D. (A) is false, but (R) is true

194. Assertion (A) : The biggest discussion has been on the functioning of the Security Council.

Reason (R) : The organization was setup through the signing of the United Nations Charter by 51 states.

In the context of the above two statements which one of the following is correct?

A. Both (A) and (R) are true and (R) is the correct explanation of (A)
B. Both (A) and (R) are true, but (R) is not the correct explanation of (A)
C. (A) is true, but (R) is false
D. (A) is false, but (R) is true

195. Assertion (A) : UN Created for peaceful building Commission.

Reason (R) : To prevent World Wars.

In the context of the above two statements which one of the following is correct?

A. Both (A) and (R) are true and (R) is the correct explanation of (A)
B. Both (A) and (R) are true, but (R) is not the correct explanation of (A)
C. (A) is true, but (R) is false
D. (A) is false, but (R) is true

196. Assertion (A) : World Trade Organisation is an international organisation.

Reason (R) : It sets the rules for global trade.

In the context of the above two statements which one of the following is correct?

A. Both (A) and (R) are true and (R) is the correct explanation of (A)
B. Both (A) and (R) are true, but (R) is not the correct explanation of (A)
C. (A) is true, but (R) is false
D. (A) is false, but (R) is true

197. Assertion (A) : Only the permanent members of the Security Council posses the veto power.

Reason (R) : One veto can stall a Security Council resolution.

In the context of the above two statements which one of the following is correct?

A. Both (A) and (R) are true and (R) is the correct explanation of (A)
B. Both (A) and (R) are true, but (R) is not the correct explanation of (A)
C. (A) is true, but (R) is false
D. (A) is false, but (R) is true

198. Assertion (A) : Humanitarian policies are implemented by the main organs and specialized agencies spread across the globe.

Reason (R) : The members of the General Assembly are automatically the members of all other principal organs and specialized agencies of the UN.

In the context of the above two statements which one of the following is correct?

A. Both (A) and (R) are true and (R) is the correct explanation of (A)
B. Both (A) and (R) are false
C. (A) is true, but (R) is false
D.. (A) is false, but (R) is true

Directions (Qs. No. 199-208): *The following questions consists of two statements—Assertion (A) and Reason (R). Answer these questions. Selecting the appropriate option given below.*

A. Both (A) and (R) are true and (R) is the correct explanation of (A)
B. Both (A) and (R) are true and (R) is not the correct explanation of (A)
C. (A) is true, but (R) is false
D. (A) is false, but (R) is true

199. Assertion (A) : The partition of the country proved everyone's worst tears. There were serious questions about the future of India.

Reason (R) : British government decided to give independence to India

200. Assertion (A) : There were no single belt of uniform Muslim majority areas in British India. There were two areas of concentration one in the west and in the east.

Reason (R) : Not all Muslim majority areas wanted to join with Pakistan.

201. Assertion (A) : Writers, poets, and film makers in India and Pakistan have often used the phrase division of hearts to describe partition.

Reason (R) : Muslim league put forward the Two nation theory that British did not consist of one but two people.

202. Assertion (A) : The ruler of Travancore decided to remain independent and Nizam of Hyderabad made a similar announcements the next day.

Reason (R) : With the end of British rule in India, paramountcy of the British crown over princely rulers also came to an end.

203. Assertion (A) : India was divided into 14 states and 6 union territories by the state Reorganisation Act 1956.

Reason (R) : The creation of linguistic provinces has helped a lot in instilling the fellings of regionalism in the Indian public.

204. Assertion (A) : Nehru, believing in secularism, supported the declaration of India as a secular state. A secularist state means that the state will not have any religion of its own and will treat all religions equally.

Reason (R) : Nehru believed that a strong nation can be built by making India a secular state.

205. Assertion (A) : The first deputy prime minister and home minister of India, Sardar Vallabhbhai Patel, emerged as a Iron man of India.

Reason (R) : Sardar Vallabhbhai Patel faced key challenges of integration of Hyderabad, Junagarh, Kashmir.

206. Assertion (A) : Partition of India was the outcome of the "two-nation theory".

Reason (R) : Punjab and Bengal were the two provinces divided on the basis of religion.

207. Assertion(A) : Princely states covered one third of the land area of the British Indian Empire.

Reason (R) : Some of the princely states clearly wanted to become part of the Indian Union.

208. Assertion (A) : Nehru, the architect of India's nation-building had clearly specified that India was not a mere geographical or historical entity. According to him India had a unique capability to synthesise alien culture and this had been the secret of India's unity in diversity.

Reason (R) : In the 21st century, the whole world has woken up to the facet of this diversity. Selfish and petty politicians have sowed seeds of disintegration by using ethnic, lingual and cultural factionalism for narrow political gains.

Directions (Qs. No. 209-213): *Read the following passage and answer the questions.*

Patel faced key challenges of integration from three states, viz., Hyderabad, Junagarh and Kashmir. It was under his leadership that Indian forces compelled Hyderabad and Junagarh to merge with India. Keeping well-versed with Pakistan's intentions from jinna's divisive "Two Nation theory", Sardar Patel's opinion on Kashmir was different from other leaders. Like Hyderabad, he also wanted Kashmir's integration with India through military operations. But due to political decisions of some prominent leaders, Sardar could not Succeed in integrating Kashmir fully with India which later turned into a major historical blunder for the country.

However, Sardar will always remain as an astounding leader who combined himself the features of a true 'Nationalist', 'Catalyst' and 'Realist'—popularly characterized as NCR in Indian political history.

209. In which form Sardar Patel is known as?

A. VCR B. NCR
C. MCR D. NRC

210. Which state of India could not be unified due to some major leaders' short-sighted political decision?

A. Manipur
B. Junagarh
C. Hyderabad
D. Kashmir

211. In which states, Sardar Patel had to face challenges to unite with Indian Union?

A. Hyderabad, Manipur, Goa
B. Hyderabad, Junagarh, Goa
C. Goa, Puducherry and Junagarh
D. Hyderabad, Junagarh, Kashmir

212. Sardar Patel was a ____.

A. Nationalist B. Changer
C. Realistic D. All the above

213. In the matter of which state of India committed blunder mistake?

A. Kashmir B. Hyderabad
C. Manipur D. Goa

Directions (Qs. No. 214-218): *Read the following passage and answer the questions.*

Most important is that with linguistic states permission was given to 'doctrine of diversity'. When we say that India has opted democracy. There its broader meaning in Indian democ acy. Democracy was chosen for recognising diversities and accepting them. Besides we also have to accept that in diversities, there might be conflicts in them. In other words, democracy in India is related to ideas, life methods and their multiplicity.

214. With which democracy is aligned?

A. In ideas and life method
B. Politics and government
C. Social and economic life
D. None of the above

215. What is meaning of choosing democracy?

A. To recognise unity and accepting it
B. To recognise diversity and not accepting it
C. To recognise diversity and accepting it
D. All of the above

216. For linguistic states reorganisation, which principle was permitted?

A. Unity
B. Diversity
C. Culture
D. Civilisation

217. In diversity there may be mutual ______

A. Protest B. Support
C. War D. None of the above

218. What is the meaning of will of the people?

A. democracy B. autocracy
C. monarchy D. None of the above

219. Which one of the following is a princely states of India initially resisted to join the Indian Union?

A. Baroda B. Hyderabad
C. Mysore D. Gwalior

220. When Gujarat was carved out of Bombay?

A. 1950 B. 1960
C. 1970 D. 1980

221. Amrita Pritam was a prominent poet from:

A. Punjab B. Gujarat
C. Mumbai D. Punjab

222. The cities that were divided into "communal zones" during the partition violence were.

A. Lahore, Amritsar and Calcutta
B. Kashmir, Lucknow and Allahabad
C. Madras, Hyderabad and Mysore
D. Delhi, Mumbai and Gwalior

223. The states created in 1960 were:

A. Maharashtra and Gujarat
B. Odisha and West Bengal
C. Rajasthan and Gujarat
D. Punjab and Haryana

224. The interim government formed under the cabinet mission plan was headed by:

A. Dr. Rajendra Prasad
B. Jawaharlal Nehru
C. Sardar Vallabhbhai Patel
D. Rajagopalachari

225. How many princely states existed at the time of Independence of India?
A. 560 B. 562
C. 563 D. 565

226. When Meghalaya was carved out of Assam?
A. 1970 B. 1971
C. 1972 D. 1973

227. Who is called "Iron man of India"?
A. Jawaharlal Nehru B. Vallabhbhai Patel
C. Rajendra Prasad D. Muhammad Ali Jinnah

228. Which among the following statements about the partition is incorrect?
A. Partition of India was the outcome of the 'Two Nation Theory.'
B. Punjab and Bengal were the two provinces divided on the basis of religion.
C. East Pakistan and West Pakistan were not contiguous.
D. The scheme of partition included a plan for the transfer of population across the border.

229. Match the principles with the instances:

(*a*) Mapping of boundaries of religious grounds	(*i*) Pakistan and Bangladesh
(*b*) Mapping of boundaries on grounds of a different language	(*ii*) India and Pakistan
(*c*) Demarcating boundaries within a country by geographical zones	(*iii*) Jharkhand and Chhattisgarh
(*d*) Demarcating within a country on administrative and political grounds	(*iv*) Himachal Pradesh and Uttarakhand

Codes:

	(*a*)	(*b*)	(*c*)	(*d*)
A.	(*ii*)	(*i*)	(*iv*)	(*iii*)
B.	(*i*)	(*iv*)	(*ii*)	(*iii*)
C.	(*iii*)	(*i*)	(*ii*)	(*iv*)
D.	(*iv*)	(*iii*)	(*ii*)	(*i*)

230. Arrange the following the chronological order of occurrence.
(*a*) Birth of Pakistan
(*b*) Join of Hyderabad in Indian Union
(*c*) Carving out of Arunachal Pradesh from Assam
(*d*) Appointment of State Re-organisation commission
A. (*a*), (*b*), (*d*), (*c*) B. (*d*), (*a*), (*c*), (*b*)
C. (*d*), (*b*), (*a*), (*c*) D. (*a*), (*b*), (*d*), (*c*)

231. Which of the following statement is not false?
A. Mahatma Gandhi wanted to become the Prime Minister of India
B. The year 1947 was a year of unprecedented violence and the year of displacement
C. Mohammed Ali Jinnah : Wanted to remain with Indian Union
D. All are True

232. How many kinds of challenges that Independent India faced?
A. 1 B. 2
C. 3 D. 5

233. Identify the wrongly matched :

A. Dr. B.R. Ambedkar	–	Chairman of drafting committee
B. Moulana Abdul Kalam Azad	–	First Education Minister
C. Sardar Vallabhbhai Patel	–	First Finance Minister
D. Dr. Babu Rajendra Prasad	–	First President of India

234. The state which has achieved nearly total literacy in India is:
A. Tamil Nadu B. Andhra Pradesh
C. Kerala D. Manipur

235. Who said, "Planning is a way of organizing and utilizing resources to maximum advantage in terms of defined social ends"?
A. K.T. Shah
B. Planning commission of India
C. Dr. Rajendra Prasad
D. None of these

236. The idea of Five Year Plan was adopted in India from:
A. United States of America
B. Japan
C. United Soviet Socialist Republics
D. Australia.

Directions (Qs. No. 237-239): *Read the following passage and answer the questions.*

Based in Anand, a town in Gujarat, Amul is a dairy cooperative movement joined by about 2 and half million milk producers in Gujarat. The Amul pattern became a uniquely appropriate model for rural development and poverty alleviation, spurring what has come to be known as the White Revolution. In 1970 the rural development programme called Operation Flood was started. Operation Flood organised cooperatives of milk producers into a nationwide milk grid, with the purpose of increasing milk production, bringing the producer and consumer closer by eliminating middlemen, and assuring the producers a regular income throughout the year. Operation Flood was, however, not just a dairy programme. I'll saw dairying as a path to development, for generating employment and income for rural households and alleviating poverty. The number of members of the cooperative has continued to increase with the numbers of women members and Women's Dairy Cooperative Societies also increasing significantly.

237. In which pace was Amul Diary Co-operative movement-blasted?
A. Anand, Gujarat
B. Porbandar, Gujarat
C. Gandhinagar, Gujarat
D. Ahmedabad, Gujarat

238. In which year was Operation Flood started?
A. 1971 B. 1972
C. 1970 D. 1973

239. Operation flood is related to ____________
A. Green Revolution B. White Revolution
C. Russian Revolution D. French Revolution

Directions (Qs. No. 240-241): *The following questions consist of two statements—Assertion (A) and Reason (R). Answer these questions selecting the appropriate option given below:*
A. Both (A) and (R) are true and (R) is the correct explanation of (A)
B. Both (A) and (R) are true, but R is not the correct explanation of (A)
C. (A) is true, but (R) is false
D. (A) is false, but (R) is true

240. Assertion (A) : The Green Revolution benefited all the sections of Indian society.
Reason (R) : The rich peasants and the iarge landholders were the major beneficiaries of the process.

241. Assertion (A) : Land reforms did not take place effectively in most parts of the country.
Reason (R) : Political Power remained in the hands of land-owning classes.

242. Arrange the following in chronological order of their occurrence.
I. The first five year plan
II. The great economic depression of Europe
III. Partition of India
IV. The second five year plan
A. I, II, III, IV B. IV, II, III, I
C. I, IV, III, II D. II, III, I, IV

243. The three major objectives of first five year plan were:
I. Agriculture
II. Dams
III. Irrigation
IV. Education
Select the correct answer using the four given above:
A. I, II, III B. II, III, IV
C. III, II, IV D. IV, III, I

244. Which one of the following statements about Bombay plan is incorrect?
A. It was a blue print for Indias economic future
B. It supported state ownership of industry
C. It was made by some leading industrialists
D. It supported strongly the idea of planning

245. During Nehru era, parties and groups in the country believed that India should become friendly with block led by USA.
I. Because that bloc claimed to be pro democracy.
II. Dr Ambedkar also supported this idea. Some political parties opposed communism
III. Some political parties opposed communism
IV. India joined Warsaw pact.
Select the correct answer choosing the four given above:
A. II, III B. I, II, IV
C. I, III, IV D. I, II only

246. What considerations should be kept in mind to set up an industry?
A. Profit making
B. Role of environmentalists
C. Not to ask local people where it will be set up
D. Approval of USA

247. Consider these statements about White Revolution. Find the Wrong statement.
A. It is a revolution in the field of milk production
B. It is also known as operation flood
C. Amul diary is located in Gujarat
D. It is not helping the local villagers

248. Consider these statements about POSCO Plant. Find the wrong statement:
A. Odisha has one of the largest resources of untapped iron ore in the country
B. POSCO plant may displace local tribals
C. Odisha villagers protested against this
D. Odisha is located to the north west of India

249. Green Revolution benefited only few states.
Identify correct option:
A. Punjab, Haryana, Western Uttar Pradesh
B. Andhra Pradesh, Madhya Pradesh, Uttar Pradesh
C. Odisha, West Bengal, Madhya Pradesh
D. Kerala, Karnataka, Tamilnadu

250. Article 51 of the Indian Constitution lays down some provisions regarding:
A. Powers of Prime Minister
B. Fundamental Rights
C. Promotion of International peace and security
D. Fundamental Duties

251. When was Britain attacked Egypt over the Suez Canal issue?
A. In 1965 B. In 1956
C. In 1966 D. In 1955

252. When was USSR invaded Hungary?
A. In 1976 B. In 1955
C. In 1956 D. In 1965

253. The Afro-Asian conference held in the Indonesian city of Bandung in:
A. In 1955 B. In 1956
C. In 1965 D. In 1954

254. Which Conference marked the zenith of India's engagement with newly independent Asian and Africa nations?
A. Malaysian Conference B. Egyptian Conference
C. Singapore Conference D. Bandung Conference

255. The First Summit of the NAM was held in Belgrade in:
A. September 1916 B. September 1960
C. September 1963 D. September 1961

256. Who was the Architect of Non-alignment Movement?
A. Indira Gandhi B. Atal Behari Vajpayee
C. Jawaharlal Nehru D. Mahatma Gandhi

257. After the Chinese revolution in 1949, which country was the first to recognize the Communist Government?
A. India B. Pakistan
C. Bangladesh D. USSR

258. In the Nehru cabinet who was apprehensive of the future attack from China?
A. Jawaharlal Nehru B. Vallabhbhai Patel
C. Jagjivan Ram D. C. Rajagopalachari

259. The Panchsheel agreement was signed between India and:
A. Pakistan B. China
C. Bangladesh D. USA

260. When was the Panchsheel agreement signed between India and China?
A. On 29 April 1954 B. On 28 April 1955
C. On 30 April 1056 D. On 29 June 1954

261. In _________, China took over control of Tibet.
A. 1951 B. 1950
C. 1952 D. 1949

262. Who accompanied the Tibetan spiritual leader Dalai Lama during the official Chinese visit to India in 1956?
A. Hua Guofeng
B. Chinese Premier Zhou Enlai
C. Li Peng
D. Zhao Ziyang

263. The Tibetan spiritual leader, the Dalai Lama, sought and obtained political asylum in India in:
A. 1956 B. 1959
C. 1960 D. 1958

264. After Nehru, the first Prime Minister to visit China was:
A. Lal Bahadur Shastri B. Indira Gandhi
C. Rajiv Gandhi D. V.P. Singh

265. When was the Communist Party of India spilt into two, (CPIM & CPI):
A. In 1965 B. In 1964
C. In 1963 D. In 1966

266. The Indus Waters Treaty was signed between by:
A. Lal Bahadur Shastri & Imran Khan
B. Nehru & Ayub Khan
C. Indira Gandhi & Musharaf
D. Vajpayee & Mushrid Khan

267. Expand NEFA:
A. North Eastern Far Agency
B. North Eastern Frontier
C. North Eastern Fullest Agency
D. North Eastern Frontier Agency

268. The Treaty assured India of Soviet support if the country faced any attack:
A. Treaty of Peace B. Water Treaty
C. Panchsheel Treaty D. Tashkent Agreement

269. Which agreement was signed between Indira Gandhi and Zulfikar Ali Bhutto on 3 July 1972?
A. Water Treaty B. Treaty of Peace
C. Tashkent Agreement D. Shimla Agreement

270. Which among the following is not a principle of India's Nuclear Doctrine today?
A. Not first use
B. Credible Minimum deterrent
C. Civilian Control
D. First Use

271. When did India and Israel establish full diplomatic relations in?
A. In January 29, 1990 B. In January 29, 1992
C. In January 29, 1991 D. In January 29, 1989

272. The period when the nuclear test was conducted was a difficult period in:
A. Domestic Politics B. Foreign Politics
C. Military dominance D. Financial world.

273. India has developed self-sufficiency in _________ technology.
A. Atomic B. Nuclear
C. Electricity D. Scientific

274. Five principles of peaceful co-existence are called ________.

A. Punchsheel
B. SAARC
C. India's foreign policy
D. Treaty Peace

275. Sri Lanka is member of ________.

A. UNESCO B. WHO
C. G7 D. SAARC

276. Both domestic and international environment influence the ______ policy of nation.

A. Nuclear B. Foreign
C. Peaceful D. Deterrence

Directions (Qs. No. 277-281): *Read the following passage and answer the questions that followed.*

Under leadership of Jawaharlal Nehru, India convened the Asian Relations Conference in March 1947, five months ahead of attaining its independence. India made earnest efforts for the early realisation of freedom of Indonesia from the Dutch colonial regime by convening an international conference in 1949 to support its freedom struggle. India was a staunch supporter of the decolonisation process and firmly opposed racism, especially apartheid in South Africa. The Afro-Asian conference held in the Indonesian city of Bandung in 1955, commonly known as the Bandung Conference, marked the zenith of India's engagement with the newly independent Asian and African nations. The Bandung Conference later led to the establishment of the NAM. The First Summit of the NAM was held in Belgrade in September 1961. Nehru was a co-founder of the NAM.

277. Under whose leadership, India convened the Asian Relations Conference in March 1947?

A. Jawaharlal Nehru
B. Indira Gandhi
C. Lal Bahadur Shastri
D. Vallabhbhai Patel

278. In which city the Afro-Asian conference held?

A. Belgrade B. Indonesia
C. Bandung D. Africa

279. Where was the first Summit of NAM held?

A. Indonesia B. Bandung
C. Belgrade D. Dutch

280. Who was the co-founder of NAM?

A. Indira Gandhi B. Jawaharlal Nehru
C. Vallabhbhai Patel D. Lal Bahadur Shastri

281. Which country made earnest efforts for the early realization of freedom of Indonesia?

A. Pakistan B. India
C. Dutch D. Belgrade

Directions (Qs. No. 282-286): *Read the following passage carefully and answer the questions that follows:*

India has opposed the international treaties aimed at non-proliferation since they were selectively applicable to the non-nuclear powers and legitimised the monopoly of the five nuclear weapons powers. Thus, India opposed the indefinite extension of the NPT in 1995 and also refused to sign the Comprehensive Test Ban Treaty (CTBT). India conducted a series of nuclear tests in May 1998, demonstrating its capacity to use nuclear energy for military purposes. Pakistan soon followed, thereby increasing the vulnerability of the region to a nuclear exchange. The international community was extremely critical of the nuclear tests in the subcontinent and sanctions were imposed on both India and Pakistan, which were subsequently waived. India's nuclear doctrine of credible minimum nuclear deterrence professes "no first use" and reiterates India's commitment to global, verifiable and non-discriminatory nuclear disarmament leading to a nuclear weapons free world.

Foreign policy is always dictated by ideas of national interest. In the period after 1990, Russia, though it continues to be an important friend of India, has lost its global pre-eminence. Therefore, India's foreign policy has shifted to a more pro-US strategy.

282. Which of the following nuclear treaties were rejected by India?

A. NPT, CTBT
B. Kyoto Protocol
C. Panchsheel Agreement
D. None of the above

283. When did India conduct series of nuclear tests?

A. June 1998 B. May 1998
C. April 1998 D. March 1998

284. Why India's foreign policy shifted to become more pro-US?

A. Because Russia betrayed India
B. Because Russia attacked India
C. Because US derived more profit to India
D. Because Russia lost its global pre-eminence

285. Which one of the following is India's stand for the use of nuclear weapon?

A. No use of nuclear weapon at all
B. No first use of nuclear weapon
C. Use nuclear weapon in case of war
D. None of the above

286. In which year India opposed the indefinite extension of the NPT.

A. In 1996 B. In 1995
C. In 1994 D. In 1993

Directions (Qs. No. 287-293): *The following questions consists of two statements—Assertion (A) and Reason (R). Answer these questions by Selecting the appropriate option given below.*

A. Both (A) and (R) are true and (R) is the correct explanation of (A)
B. Both (A) and (R) are true and (R) is not the correct explanation of (A)
C. (A) is true, but (R) is false
D. (A) is false, but(R) is true

287. Assertion (A) : The first UN General Assembly Resolution of 1946 called for elimination of atomic weapons and weapons of mass destruction.

Reason (R) : In 1948 India called for elimination of all nuclear weapons and use of nuclear energy only for peaceful purposes.

288. Assertion (A) : India opposes the NPT (1968) because the treaty is unequal.

Reason (R) : In 1974 India had carried out underground nuclear tests for peaceful purposes.

289. Assertion (A) : In 1964 China conducted its nuclear test. In 1962 China had attacked India.

Reason (R) : The decision to go ahead and manufacture the atomic bomb given by Prime Minister Indira Gandhi in 1974.

290. Assertion (A) : Non-alignment allowed India to gain assistance both from USA and USSR.

Reason (R) : The cold war has affected the relationship between India and Pakistan.

291. Assertion (A) : The Indo-Pak war of 1965 was the culmination of a series of disputes between India and Pakistan. Within the first year of independence both the countries witnessed tension over the issue of Kashmir and refugee exchange due to partition.

Reason (R) : In 1965 Soviet Union started developing close relations with Pakistan. Despite the efforts of Shastri, Indian Prime Minister, Soviet Union was not convinced. Using this opportunity, on 5th August, 1965 Pakistan stationed troops along the LOC.

292. Assertion (A) : Since 1947, India has been following an independent foreign policy of non-alignment and this policy is in perfect accord with the policy of friendly relations with all the countries of the world.

Reason (R) : The term 'Panchsheel' is related to the five moral principles of Lord Buddha. Lord Buddha made the five principles obligatory for the life of an individual. In international life, the term Panchsheel was used in 1954 when India recognised the sovereignty of China over Tibet.

293. Assertion (A) : Six-point proposal of Sheikh Mujib – ur Rehman for greater autonomy to East Pakistan.

Reason (R) : India and Bangladesh sign the Farakka Treaty for sharing of the Ganga waters in 1996.

Directions (Qs. No. 294-298): *Read the passage and answer the questions.*

From this perspective of democracy, representation can help or hurt democracy, even if representation cannot be democratic since it cannot replicate the *demos.* But the phenomenon of representation reflects an emotional roller - coaster - great hopes during an election campaign, great disappointment from the work of governments in office. This problem stems in part from the fact that representative government and, the *demos* potentially operate at cross - purposes. The office of a representative results from elections, which elevate a set of political rulers above the ruled in order to make the laws. In office, they make compromises to get legislative business done. Representatives may feel proud of what they accomplished, because they made the decisions that led to the compromise. But citizens can't take pride in legislative work, and they mostly suffer the consequences required by the compromise. That doesn't mean representatives always will be scorned, as mentioned above, their office-enables them to undertake political initiatives not viable during an election campaign or to protect minorities whose needs may have been neglected. That said, the necessary activity of legislative compromise takes place above the heads and behind the backs of the people. As such, it contradicts the 'Athenian and Aristotelian understanding of democracies as political orders that depend on the deliberative and decisive power of citizens (i.e., the *demos*) acting with authoritative power. Citizens of the Athenian democracy were said to rule and be ruled in turn, but in every case their power required the political presence and deliberative action of citizens.

294. Which of the following is reflected in the phenomenon of representation?

A. Great hopes during an election campaign
B. Great appreciation for the work of government in office
C. Great promises from the representative democracy
D. Great challenges from liberalization, privatisation and globalisation

295. What is the obvious outcome of an election?

A. Career of a leader
B. Ministerial birth of a politician
C. Office of a representative
D. Future prospects of a budding activist

296. Athenian and Aristotelian understanding of democracies means:

A. Political orders depending on the deliberative powers of citizens
B. Political system rooted in grassroot politics
C. System of government prevalent in Greek city states
D. Western conceptualization of democracy

297. What takes place above the heads and behind the backs of the people?

A. Executive arrogance
B. Judicial activism
C. Parliamentary sovereignty
D. Legislative compromise

298. Why could have representatives felt proud of what they accomplished?

A. They made the decisions for their followers
B. They made the decisions that led to the compromise
C. They made a level jump in their career progression
D. They made their adversaries compromise with their core values

Directions (Qs. No. 299-303): *Read the passage and answer the questions.*

Ronald Dworkin's thesis is that some of the rights people have fundamental, but many are not. They are fundamental because they are 'the rights against the state'. Dworkin says that the notion of rights as trumps "marks the distinctive conept of an individual right against the state which is the heart ... of constitutional theory in the United States." In the special supplement, Dworkin argued that the concept of right against the government becomes most useful particularly when the society is divided on racial lines into majority and minority. The right to freedom of speech and religious freedom belong to this category. Therefore, they are strong rights. He asserts that these rights should be permitted and they should not be interfered or banned. These freedoms are to be allowed even if the welfare of the collectivity is infringed.

On the contrary, he also presupposes a large area of rights where the state can make legislations curtailing those rights to achieve common welfare. They can be called weak rights. Right to liberty for example becomes a weak right against right to equality, a strong right. This at the outset may look contradictory, but it is not. For example, restraining the movement on the roads for safety and smooth traffic movement does not mean restraining the rights, on the other hand, putting a restriction on publication or restraining the freedom of speech will infringe the rights even if it enhances general welfare. Thus, even though in both cases rights are involved, curtailment of one is justified, whereas the other is not.

299. The rights claimed against the state are considered as:

A. Fundamental rights B. Human rights
C. Natural rights D. Legal rights

300. The idea of right against the government becomes very useful when the society is divided into majority and minority on the basis of:

A. Caste B. Class
C. Race D. Religion

301. The strong rights need to be:

A. inferred B. permitted
C. borrowed D. ordained

302. Which of the following is a weak right?

A. Right to property
B. Right to equality
C. Right to liberty
D. Right to religious freedom

303. The rights that can be curtailed to achieve common welfare may be called as:

A. Strong rights B. Fundamental rights
C. Human rights D. Weak right

304. 'All aspects of luck, including natural ability, should be irrelevant to distributive justice'— This statement refers to the concept of:

A. Meritocracy B. Plutocracy
C. Luck egalitarianism D. Aristocracy

305. Which among the following is NOT a salient feature of 'individualist anarchism'?

A. Private property B. Ultra liberalism
C. Civil disobedience D. Organicism

306. The theory that 'the Earth is best understood as a living entity that acts to maintain its own existence' is known as:

A. Tragedy of commons B. Sustainability
C. Social ecology D. Gaia hypothesis

307. Which among the following countries have no written constitution?

A. Australia B. New Zealand
C. Spain D. France

308. Which among the following forms of government is ideal for Machiavelli?

A. Republic B. Aristocracy
C. Democracy D. Hereditary Monarchy

309. Which of the following thinkers did not believe in women equality?
A. Plato and Mill
B. Aristotle and Hegel
C. Mill and Mary Wollstonecraft
D. Plato and Mary wollstonecraft

310. In "The Considerations on Representative Government", J.S. Mill did not elaborate upon:
A. Ideal government based on proportional representation
B. Protection of minoritie
C. Institutions of self-government
D. Political Economy

311. Aristotle's "ideal state is always Plato's second best:" Who said this?
A. G.H. Sabine B. W. Ebenstein
C. J.A. Dunning D. C.L Wayper

312. Which one of the following is not the function of State, according to Kautilya?
A. Acquisition of that which is not under its control and possession
B. Preservation of what has been acquired
C. Accentuation of what has been preserved
D. Empire building only

313. 'Agganasutta' is related with:
A. Hindu Philosophy B. Buddhist Philosophy
C. Jain Philosophy D. Vedanta Philosophy

314. Which one of the following party firstly joined by E.V. Ramasami Periyar?
A. Bharatiya Janata Party
B. Indian National Congress
C. Justice Party
D. Communist Party of India

315. The concept of 'credible minimum deterrent' relates to which of the follwing types of weapons?
A. Chemical B. Biological
C. Nuclear D. Space-based

316. Who gave the idea of 'the New Northern Concert of Power' (NNCP) to analyse the relevance of non-aligned movement in post-cold war era?
A. M.S. Rajan
B. S.D. Muni
C. A.P. Rana
D. Muchkund Dubey

317. In which of the following subjects, Rajya Sabha has got more power than Lok sabha?
A. Ratification of President's rule in a state
B. Creation of a new All India Service
C. Creation of Legislation Council in a state
D. Alteration in the boundary of a state

318. Which article of the Indian Constitution is associated with judicial activism?
A. 14 B. 18
C. 21 D. 25

319. Who among the following was strongly opposed to the idea of Panchayati Raj system in India?
A. B.R. Ambedkar
B. Jaya Prakash Narayan
C. Ram Manohar Lohia
D. Mahatma Gandhi

320. Which of the following statement is false about the Indian federalism?
A. it is a good example of 'holding together' federation
B. it has a tendency of strong Central Government
C. it reflects the spirit of 'coming together' federation
D. it has been referred to as 'quasi federal' system

321. Who has given originally the idea of 'Hindu Rashtra'?
A. V.D. Savarkar B. K.B. Hedgewar
C. B.S. Moonje D. M.S. Golwalkar

322. Who among the following characterized the Indian polity as being stable not in the sense of a stationary unresponsive state but in terms of a 'regulated movement'?
A. Myron Weiner B. W.H. Morris Jones
C. James Manor D. Atul Kohli

323. Who among the following was not a member of the 'Syndicate' group of the Congress party?
A. M.N. Nijalingappa
B. Morarji Desai
C. K. Kamaraj
D. Y.V. Chavan

324. A formal organization, according to Chester Bernard, comes into existence when:
A. There are persons who are willing to contribute action
B. There are persons with different goals and purpose
C. There are prsons willing to communicate through informal channels only
D. Executive is unwilling to handle the economy of incentives within an organisation

325. The concept of 'traditional' authority involves:
A. Use of authority by virtue of their inherited status by persons
B. The exercise of power subject to rules and regulations
C. The use of power based on the basis of magical qualities by a person
D. The use of power/authority as per inherited status as well as extraordinary contribution to the history of advanced business organisation

326. Which of the following factors did not contribute to the evolution of the scientific management theory?
A. lack of effective standards of work
B. lack of clear understanding of worker-management responsibilities
C. rule-of-thumb based decisions by the management
D. proper job design and economic incentives to workers

327. Which of the following statements about the 'Consumer Protection Act 2019' is NOT true?
A. It has widened the definition of consumer
B. It provides for E-filing of complaints
C. It establishes Central Consumer Protection Authority
D. It ignores mediation as an alternate disputes resolution mechanism

328. 'Consumer Protection Bill 2019' was passed by the Indian Parliament on:
A. 13th July 2019 B. 25th July 2019
C. 6th August 2019 D. 9th August 2019

329. 'Hegemony' refers to:
A. economic exploitation
B. structural inequality
C. the capacity of bourgeoisie to displace rival views and become, in effect, the common sense of the age
D. military domination

330. Who among the following rejected 'scientific determinism' and advocated political and intellectual struggle?
A. Antonio Gramsci B. Karl Marx
C. V.I. Lenin D. Friedrich Engels

331. Which of the following indicates the nature of planning in India in Contemporary times?
A. Annual Planning
B. Centralised Planning
C. Perspective Planning
D. Five year Planning

332. Who among the following was/is the first chairman of NITI Aayog in India?
A. Amitabh Kant B. Arvind Pangariya
C. Narendra Modi D. Manmohan Singh

333. Who among the following has presented the incremental model of public policy?
A. Henry Fayol B. Charles E. Lindblom
C. Fred W. Riggs D. David Easton

334. Which one of the following is not a theory or model of representation?
A. Trusteeship B. Delegation
C. The Mandate D. Consensus

335. According to Greek system of classification of regimes, the degenerative form of rule by many is known as:
A. Tyranny
B. Aristocracy
C. Anarchic democracy (mob rule)
D. Oligarchy

336. Who among the following is often portrayed as the 'father' of cultural nationalism?
A. Guisseppe Mazzini
B. Charles Maurras
C. Frantz Fanon
D. Johann Gottfried Herder

337. Which one of the following is NOT a cause of Democratic Shift in the context of Democratisation?
A. Crisis of import-substitution
B. Loss of popularity and legitimacy by military regimes
C. Social change
D. Media

338. Who among the following reformulated Hans Morgenthau's 'six principles of political realism' from a feminist perspective?
A. Judith Butler B. J.Ann Tickner
C. Helen M. Kinsella D. Betty Friden

339. 'The combination of liberal democracy and the market had drawn a finishing line in the history of political and social development'. Who made this statement?
A. Samuel P. Huntington
B. Benjamin Barber
C. Francis Fukuyama
D. Alexander Wendt

340. Which of the following is the executive-bureaucratic arm of the European Union?
A. The European Council
B. The European Commission
C. The Council
D. The European Parliament

341. Which of the following is not a principle of jus ad bellum (just recourse to war)?
A. just cause B. legitimate authority
C. proportionality D. humanity

342. Who among the following is NOT a key figure of 'Conservatism'?
A. T.H. Green B. Edmund Burke
C. Michael Oakshott D. Friedrich Von Hayek

343. In which one of the following countries, 'consociationalism' as a power-sharing mechanism is not practiced?
A. Germany B. Netherlands
C. Switzerland D. Belgium

344. Which Article of the Indian Constitution provides power to the President to promulgate ordinances?

A. Article 123 B. Article 221
C. Article 222 D. Article 223

345. Which of the following pairs are correctly matched?

(*a*) John Rawls – Egalitarian
(*b*) Plato – Idealist
(*c*) Mary Wollstonecraft – Communist
(*d*) Gramsci – Feminist

Choose the correct answer from the options given below:

A. (*a*) and (*b*) B. (*b*) and (*c*)
C. (*c*) and (*d*) D. (*c*) and (*a*)

346. Who had formed the "Society for right to die with dignity"?

A. Jai Prakash Narayan B. Minoo Masani
C. Krishna Ayyar D. Medha Patkar

347. Arrange the following four reports of Second Administrative Reforms Commission in their sequential order:

(*a*) Right to Information
(*b*) Unlocking Human capital
(*c*) Crisis Management
(*d*) Ethics in Governance

Choose the correct option:

A. (*a*), (*b*), (*c*), (*d*) B. (*d*), (*c*), (*b*), (*a*)
C. (*a*), (*d*), (*b*), (*c*) D. (*c*), (*a*), (*d*), (*b*)

348. Who is not a supporter of Libertarianism?

A. Robert Nozick B. Milton Friedman
C. Robert Dahl D. F.A. Hayek

349. Who defined leadership as "the ability of a manager to induce subordinates to work with zeal and confidence"?

A. Koontz and O'Donnell
B. Chester Bernard
C. M.P. Follet
D. Peter Drucker

350. When did International Labour Organization become a specialized agency of the United Nations Organization?

A. 1945 B. 1946
C. 1947 D. 1948

ANSWERS

1	2	3	4	5	6	7	8	9	10
B	C	D	A	B	B	C	A	C	A
11	**12**	**13**	**14**	**15**	**16**	**17**	**18**	**19**	**20**
B	B	B	B	A	B	A	C	B	B
21	**22**	**23**	**24**	**25**	**26**	**27**	**28**	**29**	**30**
B	B	D	A	A	C	B	A	D	C
31	**32**	**33**	**34**	**35**	**36**	**37**	**38**	**39**	**40**
C	A	B	C	A	B	A	B	C	B
41	**42**	**43**	**44**	**45**	**46**	**47**	**48**	**49**	**50**
A	D	C	D	A	D	A	A	B	C
51	**52**	**53**	**54**	**55**	**56**	**57**	**58**	**59**	**60**
B	C	A	C	C	B	D	B	B	B
61	**62**	**63**	**64**	**65**	**66**	**67**	**68**	**69**	**70**
B	C	B	B	C	A	B	D	B	C
71	**72**	**73**	**74**	**75**	**76**	**77**	**78**	**79**	**80**
C	B	C	C	B	A	B	A	B	B
81	**82**	**83**	**84**	**85**	**86**	**87**	**88**	**89**	**90**
C	C	A	B	A	C	A	A	B	A
91	**92**	**93**	**94**	**95**	**96**	**97**	**98**	**99**	**100**
B	A	D	A	A	B	B	B	B	B
101	**102**	**103**	**104**	**105**	**106**	**107**	**108**	**109**	**110**
C	A	D	C	B	A	B	A	D	A
111	**112**	**113**	**114**	**115**	**116**	**117**	**118**	**119**	**120**
C	A	B	A	A	A	C	A	C	C

121 C	122 C	123 D	124 A	125 D	126 C	127 B	128 B	129 B	130 C
131 C	132 A	133 D	134 D	135 D	136 B	137 A	138 B	139 C	140 B
141 C	142 A	143 C	144 A	145 A	146 A	147 B	148 B	149 D	150 D
151 D	152 A	153 C	154 B	155 A	156 A	157 B	158 A	159 D	160 D
161 D	162 C	163 B	164 D	165 B	166 D	167 A	168 B	169 B	170 D
171 A	172 A	173 B	174 C	175 D	176 B	177 C	178 D	179 A	180 D
181 C	182 A	183 C	184 D	185 B	186 C	187 B	188 A	189 B	190 A
191 A	192 A	193 C	194 B	195 A	196 A	197 A	198 B	199 B	200 A
201 B	202 A	203 A	204 A	205 A	206 B	207 B	208 B	209 B	210 D
211 D	212 D	213 A	214 A	215 C	216 C	217 B	218 A	219 B	220 B
221 A	222 A	223 A	224 B	225 D	226 D	227 B	228 D	229 A	230 A
231 B	232 C	233 C	234 C	235 B	236 C	237 A	238 C	239 B	240 C
241 A	242 D	243 A	244 A	245 A	246 B	247 D	248 D	249 A	250 C
251 B	252 C	253 A	254 D	255 D	256 C	257 A	258 B	259 B	260 A
261 B	262 B	263 B	264 B	265 B	266 B	267 B	268 A	269 D	270 D
271 B	272 D	273 B	274 A	275 D	276 B	277 C	278 C	279 C	280 D
281 B	282 A	283 B	284 D	285 B	286 B	287 B	288 B	289 A	290 C
291 A	292 B	293 B	294 A	295 C	296 A	297 D	298 B	299 A	300 C
301 B	302 C	303 D	304 C	305 D	306 D	307 B	308 A	309 B	310 D
311 A	312 D	313 B	314 B	315 C	316 C	317 B	318 C	319 A	320 C
321 A	322 B	323 D	324 A	325 A	326 D	327 D	328 C	329 C	330 A
331 C	332 C	333 B	334 D	335 C	336 D	337 D	338 B	339 C	340 B
341 D	342 A	343 A	344 A	345 A	346 B	347 A	348 C	349 A	350 B

● ● ●

SOCIOLOGY

Structure of Indian Society

1. In a good social structure each group and institution is expected to perform:

A. Specific functions
B. Un-scheduled functions
C. No function of any consequence
D. Only few limited functions

2. Who was the first thinker to highlight the structure of society?

A. Darwin B. Durkheim
C. Spencer D. August Comte

3. Who of the following is not associated with the ideas expounded by social system:

A. Max Weber B. Durkheim
C. Robert F. Bales D. Rousseau

4. Social structure is a ________ structure which is created, maintained for a time and changes.

A. Living B. Flexible
C. Tangible D. New

5. Who has differentiated between "actual structure" and 'general structure'?

A. Ginsberg B. Redcliffe Brown
C. Merton D. Parsons

6. In the case of ________, it is not the body but 'ego' or self which acts.

A. Actor B. Action
C. Social structure D. Social system

7. According to Parsons which one of the following is not a structural element?

A. Social stratification B. Social disorganisation
C. Family D. Marital relations

8. Which of the following is not covered under 'element of social structure'?

A. deviation B. observance
C. sanction D. group action

9. ________ refers to the functional aspect of social structure.

A. Role B. Status
C. Social system D. Social organization

10. Social structure is an ________ entity.

A. Legal B. Abstract
C. Absolute D. Informal

11. ________ is an abstract and intangible phenomenon.

A. Group B. Community
C. Social Structure D. Association

12. ________ system refers to the statuses and roles of the individual.

A. Ideational B. Positional
C. Cultural D. Normative

13. Which one of the following is true of cast system?

A. A person finds his place on the basis of his ability
B. It is not a narrow area
C. One gets one's social place on the basis of heredity
D. People can marry outside the cast

14. Normative system, which is an element of social structure refers to ________

A. Ideals and values B. Rules and regulations
C. Folkways D. Economic pursuits

15. Manifest function are those which are:

A. intended B. un-intended
C. un-organised D. None of the above

16. Latent functions are those which are:

A. un-intended B. intended
C. recognised D. all of the above

17. Which of the following is dysfunction in a growing organisation?

A. security of service
B. technological advancement
C. competitive market
D. research facilities

18. According to ________, social system has passed through three stages, viz, savagery, barbarian and civilized.

A. Tylor B. Morgan
C. Durkheim D. Grabner

19. Who has talked of social act, status-role and actor, as elements of social system?

A. Radcliffe Brown B. Tylor
C. Parsons D. Loomie

20. The distribution of various roles among the actor in a social system is called ________ by Parsons.

A. Stratification B. Division of labour
C. Allocation D. Role-set

21. Symbol and language are ________ of a social system.
A. Biological Pre-requisites
B. Functional Pre-requisites
C. Cultural Pre-requisites
D. Idealistic Pre-requisites

22. Who has classified social system into 'organic solidarity' and 'mechanical solidarity'?
A. Durkheim B. Weber
C. Morgan D. Tylor

23. Classification of social system into hunting, pastoral, agricultural and industrial social system, has been made by
A. Marxists B. Idealists
C. Evolutionists D. Diffusionists

24. Adaptation and goal attainments are:
A. related to each other
B. opposed to each other
C. partly related to each other
D. in no way related to each other

25. ________ has classified the cultural system into sensate, ideational and idealistic.
A. Sorokin B. Ginsberg
C. Linton D. Mead

26. Socialisation takes place through various motivational processes which may be called too ________ of socialization.
A. Ends B. Mechanisms
C. Modes D. Elements

27. Lack of division of labour is characteristic of social system based on ________.
A. Achieved Values
B. Mechanical Solidarity
C. Organic Solidarity
D. Caste System

28. Who has classified social system on the basis of solidarity
A. MacIver B. Morgan
C. Kingsley Davis D. Durkheim

29. Which one of the following is not functional problem of social structure?
A. pattern of maintenance
B. adaptation
C. environment
D. integration

30. The ________ is the root cause which weaves the web of social relationship and sets the social structure in motion.
A. Action B. Goal
C. Normative pattern D. Economic system

31. Johnson has classified functions in social structure as:
A. involved and relative
B. latent and manifest
C. dormant and manifest
D. None of the above

32. Which one of the following is true of social structure?
A. its units are individuals
B. its units are institutions
C. its units are associations
D. none of the above are its units

33. Redcliffe Brown classified social structure into:
A. social and economic B. political and social
C. general and social D. general and actual

34. The stability of a social structure depends upon the effectiveness of its ________ system.
A. Legal B. Normative
C. Economic D. Sanction

35. The social classes are large groups of people who differ from each other by their relation to the means of social production. Whose view is this?
A. Marx B. Weber
C. Lenin D. Ralph Dahrendorf

36. Find out the incorrect match
A. Spencer — organic view of society
B. Durkheim — organic solidarity and mechanical solidarity
C. Redcliffe Brown — allocation of roles
D. Sorokin — sensate, ideational and idealistic

37. Which one of the following is not the function of social system?
A. to maintain continuity
B. to ensure social stability
C. to help in maintaining economic self-sufficiency
D. to promote social integration

38. According to ________, both the social structure and the human organism are prove to change, yet they are stable
A. Redcliffe Brown B. Spencer
C. Malinowski D. Parsons

39. Social organisation and social groups:
A. are not different from each other
B. quite different from each other
C. are closely linked with each other
D. always work in close cooperation with each other

40. In a social organization of today most important is:
A. Coordinate activity of institutions
B. Coordination of priests and the holy
C. Financial aid
D. Political patronage

41. It is now fully well accepted that for maintaining social structure:
A. latent functions have no role
B. manifest functions alone are responsible
C. latent functions have their own role to play
D. manifest functions have no place

42. _______ must motivate the actors adequately to the performances, necessary for the social system to develop or persist.
A. Social structure
B. Social system
C. Gratificational system
D. Need disposition system

43. In a good social structure roles are:
A. more important than role occupants
B. less important than role occupants
C. both role and occupants are equally important
D. neither role nor role occupants are important

44. H.M. Johnson believed that "The structure of anything consists of the relative inter-relationship among its parts which are:
A. unstable B. fluctuating
C. rigid and hard D. stable

45. Under _______ system, material happiness is given primary importance where as under _______ system spritual happiness is regarded more important.
A. Marxist, Idealistic B. Sensate, Ideational
C. Ideational, Idealistic D. Sensate, Idealistic

46. During middle ages the king
A. Had no problems with the estate holders
B. Had to fight wars with the feudal lords
C. Was successful in persuading the estate holders to accept his supremacy
D. Tried to win the loyalty of the estate holders by giving them donations

47. Formal social structure is one:
A. which is indicated by informal groupings
B. which indicates division of functions
C. which includes plans and groupings
D. which gives prominence to grouping over plans

48. Norms when institutionalised are:
A. always followed on every occasion
B. cannot be followed on every occasion
C. partially followed every occasion
D. all the above statements are true

49. Specialization of labour and disappearance of mental and moral homogeneity of individuals, according to Durkheim, is associated with _______.
A. Organic Solidarity
B. Corporate Society
C. Mechanical Solidarity
D. Primitive Society

50. Which of the following is not true of the role occupant?
A. he must do certain social things
B. he must not do certain social things
C. he may decide what social things to do and what not to do
D. he is above all social obligation

51. Who has mentioned five mechanisms of socialization, viz. reinforcement, extinction inhibition, substitution, imitation and identification?
A. Redcliffe Brown B. Nadel
C. Parsons D. Merton

52. When role occupants divided themselves into sub groups, the latter:
A. live shorter life than the individual members
B. live longer life than the individual members
C. has as much life as the individual members
D. has nothing to do with the life of individual members

53. When Universalism is combined with achievement values, it produces a social structure of _______ pattern.
A. Universalistic — Ascription
B. Particularistic — Achievement
C. Universalistic — Achievement
D. Particularistic — Ascription

54. _______ Social values favour status determination on the basis of generalized rules independent of one's achievement.
A. Universalistic
B. Particularistic
C. Achieved
D. None of the above

55. If selection is made on the basis of caste, religion, state, etc. it means that in such societies — social values are considered more important.
A. Universalistic B. Achieved
C. Particularistic D. Ascribed

56. Manifest and latent functions are:
A. always linked with each other
B. always opposed to each other
C. sometimes close to each other
D. none of the above is true

57. The concepts of aristocracy and ethnic superiority are found in _______ type of social structure.
A. Universalistic — Achievement
B. Particularistic — Achievement
C. Particularistic — Ascription
D. Universalistic — Ascription

58. Under universalistic — Achievement pattern the choice of goal by the individual must be in accord with the ________.

A. Universalistic values B. Particularistic values
C. Legal values D. Community values

59. ________ denotes functional aspect of the actor, whereas ________ denotes his place in the social system.

A. Role, status
B. Social system, social structure
C. Gratificational system, status
D. Orientation system, role

60. 'The components of social structure are human beings, the structure it self being an arrangement of persons in relationships institutionally defined and regulated. Who has said this?

A. Durkheim B. Nadel
C. Parsons D. Redcliffe Brown

61. Who of the following has said about latent and manifest functions that "the distinction enables us to pose the question, what difference does the manifestness or latency of a mechanism make to the effectiveness of mechanism for good or bad"?

A. H.M. Johnson B. Merton
C. Parsons D. Durkheim

62. ________ does not consist only of adhoc responses to a particular situation stimuli but also of a system of expectations relative to individual's own need disposition.

A. Status B. Social system
C. Action D. Actor

63. There are four types of social values for the classification of social structure, which one of the following is not covered under these values?

A. described B. achieved
C. ascribed D. particularistic

64. ________ is a process in the actor situation system which motivates the individual or individuals in the case of a group.

A. Action B. Integration
C. Gratification D. Co-operation

65. Parsons has kept the Indian and the Chinese social structures under ________ category

A. The Particularistic — Achievement
B. The Universalistic — Ascription
C. The Particularistic — Ascription
D. The Universalistic — Achievement

66. Who has described four types of social structure on the basis of four social values, viz. universalistic, particularistic, achieved and ascribed social value?

A. Redcliffe Brown B. Morton
C. Parsons D. Durkheim

67. Social organisation and social groups are:

A. neutral to each other
B. complementary to each other
C. contradictory to each other
D. diametrically opposed to each other

68. Which of the following statements is true?

A. Class is more open than cast
B. The Cast system is believed to have been divinely ordained whereas classes are not founded on religious dogmas
C. Caste is more open than class
D. Both (A) and (B) are true

69. In our modern social organisation process is going on in which:

A. small groups are only disintegrating
B. small groups are only combining
C. big groups are only disintegrating
D. big groups are only combining

70. According to ________ social structure is concerned with the forms of inter relationship between various units rather than with the units.

A. MacIver B. Parsons
C. Spencer D. Redcliffe Brown

71. In a good social organisation the people should be:

A. reluctant to accept any status
B. prompt in accepting some status
C. allowed to accept equal status
D. made to realise that all have equal capabilities

72. Which of the following statements is true?

A. Social Structure is an abstract and intangible phenomenon
B. Redcliffe Brown considers 'Social structure' as real as are individual organisms.
C. None of the above
D. Both (A) and (B) are true

73. Social organisation is replaced by social disorganisation when:

A. imposition is replaced by willingness
B. willingness is replaced by imposition
C. there is unanimity among the people
D. none of the above is true

74. The integration and co-ordination of the different parts of social structure depend upon ________ to social norms.

A. Deviation
B. Attachment
C. Conformity
D. None of the above

75. For proper social organisation it is essential that:
A. Society should have full control over its members
B. Society should have only partial control over its members
C. Society should forget excessive control over its members
D. Social controls should be rigid and tight

76. Who of the following has defined social organisation as "the totality of cultural institutions and their inter-relationship together with the body of unorganised activities and characteristic"?
A. Earnest Jones B. Merton
C. Reuter and Hart D. Lundberg

77. Which one of the following is not a reason for maintaining distinction between manifest and latent functions?
A. manifest functions are everything in social structure
B. manifest functions alone are not everything in social structure
C. both the functions are needed for introducing social reforms
D. both help in knowing the effectiveness of mechanism.

78. In Sociology, characteristics of dysfunction is that:
A. it is subjective
B. it is objective
C. it is neither subjective nor objective
D. it is partly subjective and partly objective

79. Main characteristic of purpose and function is that:
A. Purpose is objective and function is subjective
B. Both are objective
C. Both are subjective
D. Purpose is subjective, function is objective

80. Dysfunctions are those functions which:
A. help in the accomplishment of task
B. help in accelerating certain tasks
C. hinder fulfilment of tasks
D. have nothing to do with goals

81. The social structure of Nazi Germany was ________
A. Universalistic — Achievement
B. Particularistic — Ascription
C. Particularistic — Achievement
D. Universalistic — Ascription

82. What is not true of 'function' in society?
A. it contributes of the fulfilment of one or more tasks
B. it contributes to the fulfilment of one task alone
C. it does not hinder fulfilment of tasks
D. it is not opposed to task achievements

83. Universalistic - Achievement type of social structure is ________ where as universalistic ascription type is ________ .
A. Individualistic, collectivistic
B. Legal, rational
C. Flexible, rigid
D. Non-Contractual, Contractual

84. Which of the following is the functional problem of social structure?
A. Pattern of maintenance
B. Adaptation
C. Integration
D. All of the above

85. In a good social structure groups and sub-groups
A. try to adapt themselves
B. merge with each other
C. oppose each other
D. cooperate with each other in a limited sense

86. Which is one of the primary means of social control through which different activities and relationships are co-ordinated to minimize conflicts on the social level
A. Institutionalization
B. Integration
C. Co-operation
D. Substitution

87. An informal social structure is one of which
A. groups are subordinated to plans
B. groups and plan get equal place
C. groups have prior place over plans
D. groups and plans are nothing do with each other

88. Social structure:
A. has nothing to do with social deviation
B. helps indefining social deviation
C. gives no place to social deviation
D. can exist with social deviations only

89. In a good society, about social structure it is:
A. desirable that it should be rigid
B. proper that in it institutions must not yield
C. wanted that in it institutions must change with the changing times
D. desirable that every institutional change should be resisted

90. In a good social structure for goal attainment it is essential that resources must be mobilised in an effective manner
A. according to specific nature of the task
B. without consideration for the task
C. according to unspecified task
D. task and goal have no relevance

ANSWERS

1	2	3	4	5	6	7	8	9	10
A	C	D	A	B	A	D	C	C	B
11	**12**	**13**	**14**	**15**	**16**	**17**	**18**	**19**	**20**
C	B	C	A	A	A	A	B	C	C
21	**22**	**23**	**24**	**25**	**26**	**27**	**28**	**29**	**30**
C	A	C	A	A	B	B	D	C	A
31	**32**	**33**	**34**	**35**	**36**	**37**	**38**	**39**	**40**
B	A	D	A	A	C	C	A	B	A
41	**42**	**43**	**44**	**45**	**46**	**47**	**48**	**49**	**50**
C	B	A	D	B	B	B	B	A	D
51	**52**	**53**	**54**	**55**	**56**	**57**	**58**	**59**	**60**
C	B	C	A	C	C	D	A	A	D
61	**62**	**63**	**64**	**65**	**66**	**67**	**68**	**69**	**70**
A	C	B	A	A	C	B	D	D	B
71	**72**	**73**	**74**	**75**	**76**	**77**	**78**	**79**	**80**
B	D	C	C	A	C	A	B	D	C
81	**82**	**83**	**84**	**85**	**86**	**87**	**88**	**89**	**90**
D	B	A	D	A	A	C	B	C	A

●●●

Social Institutions : Continuity and Change

1. Which of the following is an institution?
A. Family B. Leadership
C. Social movements D. Movements

2. Which of the following is a Political Institution?
A. State B. Political Parties
C. Idealism D. Individualism

3. Which of the following is an economic institution?
A. Division of labour B. Price-level
C. Standard of living D. Economic structure

4. Which of the following is not a familiar institution?
A. Marriage
B. Family
C. Variability of structure
D. Kinship of society

5. Institutions are the, "established forms of conditions of procedure characteristic of group activity." This definition has been given by:
A. MacIver B. Ginsberg
C. Gillin and Gillin D. None of the above

6. Individuals are the members of the:
A. Community B. Institutions
C. Both of them D. None of them

7. Institution is:
A. Abstract
B. Concrete
C. Abstract as well as concrete
D. None of the above

8. Who of the following is of the view that in sociological partance an institution is not of folkways and mores?
A. Ginsberg B. H.E. Barnes
C. Maxwell D. Gillin and Gillin

9. "Social institutions are sets of organised human relationships established by common will" was said by:
A. C.H. Cooley B. E.A. Ross
C. Kingsley Davis D. Sheriff and Sheriff

10. Who of the following has said that "A social institution is a functional configuration of culture pattern"?
A. Kampbell Young B. MacIver
C. Ginsberg D. Gillin and Gillin

11. An institution represent:
A. Human aspect
B. Is a 'Social condition of behaviour'
C. Is human aspects as well as is a social condition of behaviour
D. Is concerned with the social life.

12. Pick up one of the following which is not an essential element of community?
A. Community Sentiments B. Locality
C. Individual interests D. Common way of life

13. Which one of the following is not concerned with the institution of family?
A. marriage B. child
C. kinship D. family business

14. Manifest functions of a institution are those which are:
A. unstable B. unorganised
C. unplanned D. unanticipated

15. Ritual of church for worship is:
A. an institution B. a community
C. an association D. a society

16. A common method used for the study of social institution is:
A. evolutionary method B. analytical method
C. historical method D. case study method

17. For the study of institution like family and religion dependable method of study is:
A. Interview method B. Questionnaire method
C. Schedule method D. Historical method

18. Individuals are the members of the:
A. Community B. Institution
C. Both of them D. None of them

19. In India the institution of family has a trend towards
A. Joint family B. Single family
C. Patriarchal family D. Matriarchal family

20. Who among the following does not fall under the Category of Community?
A. Keralites in Delhi
B. Trade union movement
C. The people of U.S. origin
D. None of the above

21. Industry is institutional structure of an institution which by nature is:
A. political B. cultural
C. economic D. social

22. Institutional structure of religion is:
A. Religious scriptures B. Priest
C. Church D. Rituals

23. Who has tried to divide the functions of an institution as manifest and latent?
A. K. Davis B. MacIver
C. Gillin and Gillin D. Morton

24. "Social institutions are the very heart of a culture and culture of a community undoubtedly its proud" was said by:
A. MacIver B. Ginsberg
C. K. Young D. K. Davis

25. Which one of the following is not true of the functions of the guilds?
A. These performed religious and political functions
B. These were often instrumental in making Laws
C. These had considerable power in medieval courts
D. These had nothing to do with religious and political functions

26. "An institution is a net of folkways and mores that centre in the achievement of some human end or purpose". This definition has been given by:
A. Green B. Summer
C. Max Webar D. Ginsberg

27. Which one of the following is not strictly a function of Social institution?
A. Setting up social norms
B. Regulating social activity of individual
C. Promoting social culture
D. Imposing morality and ethics

28. What does institution mean?
A. It means the place where only technical education is imparted
B. It means the place where some education is imparted
C. It is a special term denoting those social units which are established and are necessary for the social development
D. Where admission is restricted to a certain types of people

29. Which of the following statement is correct?
A. Institutions are the system of life which regulate it from their different positions.
B. Institution is confined to the economic life of the individuals
C. Institution is confined to family only
D. None of the above

30. A Political institution means:
A. The institution which gives education of politics
B. The institution which is based on certain political ideas
C. The institution owned by some political party
D. The institution which looks after the political affairs of the individuals

31. Which of the following statements is correct regarding the institutions?
A. Institutions are always based on certain established forms of rules, conventions and usages.
B. Institutions are the artificial products of the society.
C. It is the familial factors which exclusively give birth to institutions
D. None of the above

32. Which one of the following was not the characteristic of merchant guilds?
A. These promoted economic interest of the merchants
B. These tried to keep monopoly of the trade
C. These brought pressures on the rulers
D. These ensured that activities of the guilds were confined to the village

33. One of the following mentioned characteristics is not a characteristic of institution. Point out such a sentence:
A. Through institutions the individuals activities are controlled
B. Collective activities of men form the basis of the institution
C. Every institution is based on certain rules which are to be observed by everyone
D. No institution has a symbol, may be material or non-material

34. Who of the following has stressed that social institutions come into existence when material and non-material cultures are elaborated around fundamental human functions?
A. Gillin and Gillin
B. MacIver
C. Ogburn
D. None of the above

35. Who of the following has defined institution by saying that, "Institution is definite organisation pursuing some specific interest in a specific way"?
A. R.M. MacIver B. Ogburn
C. Ginsberg D. E.A. Ross

36. Which of the following is not the characteristic of an institution?
A. It must follow some well established rules
B. Its strength is based on obedience to rules
C. These grow with the society
D. These have no definite objectives

37. Pick up one which is not true of an institution:
A. it is least concerned with customs and mores
B. customs and mores are its distinguishing feature
C. it meets primary needs of the people
D. it is very stable

38. Which of the following is not a significant advantage of social institutions?
A. Diversified human behaviour is simplified
B. These help in providing social controls
C. These help in removing controls
D. These help in fulfilling natural instinct of men

39. Which of the following is true of an institution but not of an association?
A. It is optional for members to accept its rules
B. It is compulsory for the members to accept its rules
C. It can be created at any time
D. It has evolutionary character

40. Pick up one of the following which does not signify the advantage of social institutions:
A. individual gets special status
B. individual gets special role
C. energies are properly channelised
D. role and status of individual is regulated

41. Which one of the following is true of an association but not of an institution?
A. In it, there is much of rationalism and less of dogmatism
B. In it there is less of rational and more of dogmatism.
C. It comes into being for specific purpose
D. It comes into existence to meet secondary needs of the people

42. Which one of the following is true of institution but not of community?
A. It has spontaneous origin
B. It has concern with society as a whole
C. It has no spontaneous origin
D. It deals with social life of the people

43. Which of the following is true of a community but not of institution?
A. It does not indicate procedures
B. It indicates procedures
C. It deals with one aspect of social life
D. It grows with the passage of time

44. Which of the following is true of an association but not of an institution?
A. It represents human aspect
B. It is abstract
C. It is mode and nothing else
D. It does not represent human aspect

45. Which one of the following is not true of an institution?
A. It reforms foundational functions
B. It is not concerned with foundational functions
C. It is needed for maintaining social order
D. It grows automatically

46. Society can be properly studied if latent and manifest functions are:
A. kept separate from each other
B. allowed to come closer to each other
C. are made contradictory to each other
D. are not allowed to interfere with each other

47. Which one of the following is not true of institutional structures?
A. These are definite entries for social operation
B. These exist in concrete form
C. These exist in discrete form
D. These give expression to institutionalised complexes

48. Institutional structure of a political institution is:
A. form of government
B. participation behaviour of voters
C. extent of judicial impartiality
D. relationship of executive with judiciary

49. Which one of the following is not correct about institutional structure?
A. There is rule to codify its working
B. There are no codified rules of its working
C. There are symbols which synthesize relationship
D. It is bound with the others

50. These days in India the institution of marriage is weakening because:
A. our religious leaders are becoming rigid
B. women are becoming economically self-sufficient
C. less number of people are liking to marry
D. people prefer small size family

51. A Nambudri family is called:
A. Tarwad B. Machong
C. Illom D. Deling Son

52. Who has made the distinction between family of orientation and family of procreation?
A. Murdock B. MacIver
C. Warner D. Morgan

53. In the Garo family the heir is called:
A. Karnavan B. Ling
C. Pelingson D. Nokna

54. The Joint family is a characteristic peculiar to:
A. Muslims B. Christians
C. Jews D. Hindus

55. Which family was founded upon the inter marriage of several Sister, own and collateral, with each other's husbands in a group?
A. Punkan B. Conjugal
C. Consarguineal D. Polygamous

56. Who has given the concept of 'atomistic family?
A. Murdock B. Warner
C. Durkheim D. Zimmer man

57. Who has written the book 'Social structure'?
A. MacIver B. Kapadia
C. Murdock D. Redcliffe Brown

58. ________ is the family into which an individual is born and in which he is socialized.
A. Nuclear family B. Conjugal family
C. Family of orientation D. Family of procreation

59. The Khasi family is known as:
A. Ling B. Tarward
C. Nokna D. Delingson

60. If in a family, the off springs inherit the mother's name, the family is called:
A. Matronymic B. Patronymic
C. Matri-potestal D. Matrilineal

61. Which family is formed by an individual when he marries and has children?
A. family of orientation
B. family of pro-creation
C. nuclear family
D. conjugal

62. The eldest male member of the Tarwad is known as:
A. Patriarch B. Karnavan
C. Nokna D. None of the above

63. When the off springs inherit the father's name, the family is called:
A. Patronymic B. Patrilined
C. Patriarchal D. Conjugal

64. Who among the following follow the matrilinal family system?
A. Nairs of Kerala B. Bhils
C. Kadars D. Muslims

65. In ______ family the husband goes to live in the house of his wife.
A. Matrilineal B. Matriarchal
C. Joint family D. Matripotestal

66. In ______ family, the wife goes and lives in the house other husband.
A. Patrilocal B. Patrilineal
C. Bilateral D. Joint family

67. The extended family of Garos is called:
A. Machong B. Tarwad
C. Ling D. None of the above

68. A Nairs family is called:
A. Gotul B. Nokna
C. Tarward D. Tavazhis

69. Find out the incorrect match.
A. Garos — Machong B. Nairs — Tarwad
C. Khasis — Ling D. Gonds — Ka Khadduh

70. When the descent is traced through the mother it is ______ family.
A. Matrilineal B. Matrilocal
C. Matriarchal D. Matripotestal

71. Sir Henry Maine's name is associated with:
A. Sex communism theory
B. Patriarchal theory
C. Matriarchal theory
D. Theory of polygamy

72. When husband and wife live alternately at each other's residence the marriage system is known as:
A. matrilocal B. patrilocal
C. changing D. None of the above

73. I.H. Morgan's name is associated with:
A. patriarchal theory
B. matriarchal theory
C. primitive promiscuism theory
D. none of the above

74. The type of family in which after marriage husband moves to the residence to wife is known as:
A. matrilocal residence B. patrilocal residence
C. changing residence D. matrilineal family

75. Which of the following is not a salient feature of the family?
A. it is universal
B. it is found in all societies
C. in it members have primary emotions only for each other
D. it is a small sized organisation

76. Whose name out of the following is not associated with the theory of polygamy?
A. Darwin B. Zukerman
C. Malinowsky D. E.A. Ross

77. Type of the family in which descent starts with the mother is known as:
A. Conjugal B. Procreation
C. Extended D. Matronymic

78. A family in which individual gets married is known as:
A. Orientation family B. Procreation family
C. Patronymic family D. None of these

79. Which one of the following theories believed that the family started with patriarch?
A. Polygamy B. Patriarchal
C. Matriarchal D. Multi-factor

80. "The mother" was written by:
A. I.H. Morgan B. Briffault
C. Sidquick D. Gillin and Gillin

81. A family in which an individual is born is known as:
A. Procreation family B. Monogamous family
C. Orientation family D. Extended family

82. The type of the family in which father is the source of authority is known as:
A. Patrilocal B. Patriarchal
C. Patronymic D. Patrilineal

83. Type of the family in which mother is the basis of all authority is known as:
A. Matrilineal B. Matrilocal
C. Matronymic D. Procreation

84. The family in which there is only one couple with children is known as:
A. immediate family B. conjugal family
C. consanguine family D. procreation family

85. When one man married one woman only with definite regulations, the system was known as:
A. extended B. monogamous
C. patriarchal D. None of these

86. When after marriage husband lives in the residence of his wife the system is known as:
A. Patronymic family
B. Patriarchal family
C. Orientation family
D. Patrilocal residence family

87. The system under which woman can many more than one husband and keep all of them with herself is known as:
A. Polyandrous B. Polygamous
C. Patronymic D. Procreation

88. The system in which one husband could marry one wife but married relations were not definite was known as:
A. syndas B. orientation
C. procreation D. None of these

89. In our times the family system is under heavy strains because of:
A. Urbanisation B. Democracy
C. Small family size D. Religious intoleration

90. Family system in which sex relationship was not definite was known as:
A. Matrilinal B. Patronymic
C. Punaduant D. Patrilineal

91. Out of the following whose name is associated with polygamy theory about the origin of family?
A. Sir Henry Maine B. Herbert
C. Kingsley Davis D. Burgess

92. Whose name is associated with the theory of primitive promiscuism?
A. L.H. Morgan B. J.G. Frazer
C. R. Briffault D. Bliss

93. The systems under which marriage between blood relations was not forbidden is known as:
A. Concanguine B. Matri-local
C. Syndas D. Conjugal

94. In the traditional family the head of the family:
A. was most democratic
B. was more or less autocrat
C. had no control over the family
D. was obeyed as and when liked by the members of the family

95. Which of the following acted as a cause of the decay of the patriarchal family?
A. Economic factor
B. Effect of scientific discoveries
C. Cultural factors
D. All of the above

96. Which one of the following was not a solid factor in giving birth to family life?
A. Individuals needed family for procreation
B. Sexual urge
C. Economic needs compelled them to live in family
D. To develop common language

97. Which of the following is not a characteristic of modern family?
A. Less religious control
B. Separation of non-essential functions
C. Smaller family
D. Anti-filio centric family

98. In a type of family where children's wishes dominate and direct the family policy is called:
A. Filo centric family B. Complicated family
C. Ultra family D. Weak family

99. Which of the following is a factor leading to divorce?
A. Decline and decay of social values
B. Falling social protection
C. Unbalanced marriage
D. All of the above

100. Which of the following is not a characteristic of the joint family?
A. Large size of the family
B. Joint property
C. Individual residence
D. Co-operative organisation

101. Which of the factors mentioned below can be held as the merit of Joint family?
A. Social Insurance B. Ideal of Socialism
C. Social Virtues D. All of the above

102. Which of the following is an example of the patriarchal type of family?
A. The Greeks B. The Romans
C. The Aryans of India D. All of the above

103. Which of the following is a nuclear type of family?
A. The Hindu family B. The American family
C. The Muslim family D. None of the above

104. Which of the following is not a type of family if classified on the basics of residence?
A. Matrilocal B. Patrilocal
C. Matrilineal D. None of the above

105. The Family in which spouses, their off spring and other relatives through marriage, live together, is called as:
A. Conjugal family
B. Consanguinous family
C. Monogamous family
D. Polyandrous family

106. Who of the following classified the functions of family into essential and non-essential?
A. MacIver B. Ginsberg
C. Lundberg D. Durkheim

107. What type of co-operation in found in family, neighbourhood and peer group?
A. Friendly B. Secondary
C. Primary D. All the above

108. In which one of the following tribes fraternal polyandry is prevalent?
A. Nayar B. Khasi
C. Gango D. Santhal

109. Which of the following is an extended family?
A. The Hindu family B. Polyandrous family
C. Polygynous family D. American family

110. When child-bearing is deliberately avoided, the family is called:
A. An arrested family
B. A companionate family
C. Unfortunate family
D. None of these

111. Which of the following is a function of family according to Lundberg?
A. Regulation of behaviour relating to sex and reproduction
B. Co-operation
C. Care and training of children
D. All of the above

112. Which one of the following is not a family if classified on the basis of marriage system?
A. Polygamous family
B. Polyandrous family
C. Monogamous family
D. Matrileneal as well as patrileneal family

113. Which of the following is an essential function of family according to MacIver?
A. Stable satisfaction of sexual need
B. Production of rearing of children
C. Provision of a home
D. All of the above

114. From among the following, who has introduced the concept 'ethnocentrism'?
A. W.G. Sumner B. F.H. Giddings
C. C.H. Cooley D. E. Durkheim

115. The term 'family' has been derived from:
A. Greek word 'familiarte'
B. Roman word 'famulus'
C. Latin word 'familine'
D. None of the above

116. ________ families are comparatively short lived.
A. Extended family
B. Conjugal family
C. Consanguine family
D. Joint family

117. Family is "a system of relationship existing between parents and children" according to:
A. Elliot and Merrill B. Clare
C. Ginsberg D. Tonnies

118. Family is, "the biological social unit composed of husband, wife and children", was said by:
A. Elliot and Merrill B. Johnson
C. Holmes D. MacIver

119. When the woman is considered to be the ancestor of the mainly, it is known as:
A. Patrilineal family B. Matrilineal family
C. Feministre family D. Matriarchal family

120. When a woman marries many men but lives with them alternatively, the family is called:
A. Patrilocal B. Matrilocal
C. Polyandrous D. Polygamous

121. Which of the following is a function of family as classified by Prof. Reed?
A. Socialization
B. Regulation and satisfaction of sexual needs
C. Race perpetuation
D. All of the above

122. Who among the following has applied the term 'rol bargaining' in the study of family?
A. Elliot and Merrill B. William J. Goode
C. G. Lundberg D. L.H. Morgan

123. In traditional village the head of the village used to be one who was:
A. The eldest person in the family
B. The eldest person in the village
C. The wisest person in the family
D. The wisest person in the village

124. What is hypogamy?
A. Marriage of a girl to a man of lower class or caste
B. Marriage outside caste
C. Marriage of one women with one man
D. Marriage of a girl to a man of higher class or caste

125. Who has made the distinction between family of orientation and family of procreation?
A. Murdock B. MacIver
C. Warner D. None of these

126. Who is the author of the book 'Urbanization and Family Change'?
A. David Cooper B. Michael Anderson
C. A.M. Shah D. M.S. Gore

127. Among whom of the following the matriarchal system did not exist?
A. South American Indians
B. North American Indians
C. People of Malabar
D. Nairs of Kerala

128. The youngest daughter called ______ in a khasi family is in charge of the family religion and gets the lion's share of the family property.
A. Noknja B. Kakhadduh
C. Heir apparent D. Delingson

129. Who of the following is a supporter of theory of primitive promiscuism of the origin of society?
A. J.L. Lubbock B. L.H. Morgan
C. J.G. Fraser D. All the above

130. Which one of the following theories believed that family started with the patriarch?
A. Polygamy B. Patriarchal
C. Matriarchal D. Multi-factor

131. Which one of the following was not a stage of family life, as suggested by Morgan?
A. Consanguine family B. Punaluant family
C. Syndamian family D. Matriarchal family

132. Which of the following is not a type of family if classified on the basis of structure?
A. Patriarchal B. Matriarchal
C. Monogamous D. None of the above

133. On the basis of ______ we can divide family into nuclear and extended.
A. Organization B. Descent
C. Marriage D. Place

134. A ______ family comprises of a nucleus of blood relatives surrounded by a fringe of wives and others who are only incidental to the maintenance of the family unit.
A. Consanguine B. Conjugal
C. Joint D. Nuclear

135. A family is said to be ______ when it is socially compulsory to marry within the larger group to which the family belongs.
A. Endogamous B. Exogamous
C. Matriarchal D. None of the above

136. On the basis of ______ family can be divided into matriarchal and patriarchal.
A. Decent B. Authority
C. Residence D. Organisation

137. Problem of inheritance is acute in:
A. Extended family system
B. Conjugal family system
C. Neolocal family system
D. Nuclear family system

138. The marriage relations in the matriarchal type of family are:
A. Transient in nature
B. Permanent in nature
C. Of double coincidence in nature
D. Similar to that of the patriarchal society

139. Match both the groups:
(*a*) Ralph Linton 1. Atomistic family
(*b*) Zimmerman 2. Family of orientation
(*c*) Warner 3. Punaluan family
(*d*) Morgan 4. Conjugal and consan guine family

Codes:

	(*a*)	(*b*)	(*c*)	(*d*)
A.	1	2	3	4
B.	4	1	2	3
C.	3	2	4	1
D.	2	3	1	4

140. Who has defined family as a group governed by a sex-relationship sufficiently precise and enduring to provide for the procreation and upbringing of children?
A. Murdock B. MacIver
C. Tylor D. Briffault

141. ________ is a conjugal family in which single relatives, such as unmarried or widowed brother, sister or the cousin of the husband or wife, live with the family.
A. Compound family B. Conjugal family
C. Expanded family D. Extended family

142. ________ is the type of family resulting from the practice of polygyny or polyandry, in which two or more nuclear families are united through a common husband or wife.
A. Atomistic family B. Compound family
C. Bilateral family D. Extended family

143. Peasant family is mainly characterised by:
A. Hunting and food gathering
B. Agriculture as a way of life
C. Settled cultivation
D. None of the above

144. Which type of family was founded upon marriage between single pairs, with the married couple having exclusive cohabitation with one another?
A. Monogamian B. Patriarchal
C. Consanguineal D. None of the above

145. Which family was founded upon marriage between single pairs, without giving the right of exclusive cohabitation to any person over another?
A. Punaluan B. Syndyasmian
C. Extended D. Polyandrous

146. Which family consisted of a group which was founded upon the intermarriage, in a group of siblings, own and collateral, i.e. of brothers and sisters and cousins?
A. Conjugal B. Consanguine
C. Punaluan D. Polyandrous

147. Which one of the following theories about the origin of the family believed that in the past offering of wife or daughter to a guest was considered as a mark of hospitality?
A. Matriarchal B. Patriarchal
C. Polygamy D. Sex Communism

148. Which one of the following theories believed that origin of family is based on the philosophy of possession of women by men?
A. Multi-factor theory
B. Patriarchal theory
C. Polygamy theory
D. Theory of sex communism

149. Which of the following is not a feature of modern family?
A. Change in man-women relationship
B. Diluted control of the marriage contract
C. Laxity in the sex relationship
D. Bigger family structure

150. Joint family system is weakening because:
A. government is now favouring it
B. the people have started disliking it
C. the religious leaders are propagating it
D. the land does not need man power.

151. Who has used the concept of 'quasi group' in the study of Indian society?
A. K.N. Sharma B. Y.B. Damhe
C. A.C. Mayer D. None of the above

152. Which one of the following is the practical solution for the reconstruction of the modern family?
A. Process of modernisation should be checked.
B. There should be bomon urbanisation
C. Only agreeable changes should be brought in the family
D. Members of the family should be over-sensitised

153. Which one of the following is not an important cause of instability of modern family?
A. romantic marriages
B. arranged marriages
C. disassociation of religion from marriage
D. shortening of child bearing period

154. Which one of the following is not true of joint family system?
A. family has a combined kitchen
B. gods and goddesses are worshipped at one place
C. ownership of sources of production belong to the whole family
D. ownership of production but not that of consumption belongs to the whole family.

155. Which one of the following is not a direct cause of dis-integration of Joint family system?
A. means of transportation have quickened
B. means of communication have developed
C. women have been given the right to lives separately
D. the hold of aged over family has gradually increased

156. Which theory is based on the 'Psychic unity of mankind?
A. Evolutionism
B. Diffusionism
C. Functionalism
D. Neo-diffusionism

157. Which one of the following is not a characteristic of Joint family system?
A. all members live together under one roof.
B. members may or may not be related to each other
C. property belongs to the whole family
D. family income is pooled together

158. Which one of the following is not the optional but compulsory function of family?
A. it develops cultural activities.
B. it provides recreation to members
C. it arranges education for the children
D. it gives protection to the young

159. Which one of the following is not a disadvantage of Joint family system?
A. it encourages idleness
B. it stands in the way of development
C. it leads to quarrels
D. it makes leisured difficult

160. Which one of the following is not an important advantage of joint family system?
A. it provides social security
B. it encourages savings
C. it makes leisure possible
D. it helps in the development of good virtues

161. Who has written the book Modernization of Indian Tradition?
A. M.N. Srinivas B. Yogendra Singh
C. G.S. Ghurye D. M.S. Gore

162. Joint family system is on the decline, which is not the main cause for its disintegration?
A. there is change from agricultural to industrial economy
B. there is increased western influence
C. there is increased pressure on land
D. there is increased agricultural production

163. Which one of the following is not the essential function of the family?
A. it gives its members love and sympathy
B. it tries to socialise its members
C. it helps in the preservance of social customs
D. it tries to promote religious feelings

164. Which one of the following is not a salient feature of the family?
A. it is a nucleus of all social activities.
B. it is only a closed group
C. in it all work in the spirit of give and take
D. it is an open group

165. Which one of the following is not an important cause of weakness of modern family?
A. there is considerable technological advancement
B. there is rapid industrialisation
C. there is trend towards urbanisation
D. the society has under-estimated the need of regulation of marriage.

166. Which of the following is not a feature of the joint family system?
A. in it family size is very large
B. in it each unit of the family has its own head
C. in it the head of the family commands high respect
D. in it all the members have common kitchen

167. J.L. Lubbock's name is associated with one of the following theories. Identify it:
A. theory of primitive promiscuism
B. patriarchal theory
C. multi-factor theory
D. matriarchal theory

168. In the traditional family the head of the family used to be one who was:
A. the eldest person in the family
B. the eldest person in the village
C. the wisest member of the family
D. the wisest person of the village

169. Which one of the following is not true about the disintegration of joint family system?
A. there is increased urbanisation
B. people have desire to live in glamorous cities
C. cities provide more facilities than the villages
D. it has failed to develop social virtues

170. Which one of the following is not the characteristic of family?
A. it is based on mating relationship
B. it is essentially based on duration of the marriage
C. it pre-supposes institution of marriage
D. each family has some nomenclature

171. Transitional growth means:
A. high birth rate and high death rate
B. low birth rate and low death rate
C. high birth rate and low death rate
D. low birth rate and high death rate

172. Which of the following mentioned factors can be held as the merit of joint family?
A. Rapid economic progress
B. Division of labour
C. Economy in expenditure
D. Opportunity for leisure.

173. Which one of the following statements is correct?
A. There is not race of the origin of the family
B. Divine inspiration has led to the origin of the family
C. Social contract made the families exist
D. None of the above

174. The family is a patriarchal when:
A. Father of the house arranges for everything
B. One husband keeps more than one wife
C. Children bear their father's family name
D. The patriarch decides everything

175. What is a polyandrous family?
A. A family in which one of woman marries several men and lives with them alternately
B. A family in which several men marry two women collectively
C. A family in which one man marries one woman
D. A family in which all the brothers marry more than one women

176. Mark the correct statement (inreference to patriarchal family):
A. After marriage the husband lives with the parents of his wife.
B. After marriage the wife goes to live in her husband's house
C. It was essential for wife as well as the husband to build a separate house for their dwelling
D. None of the above

177. What is matrilocal family?
A. A family in which the wife is chosen from the local caste
B. A family in which the wife is chosen from the local village
C. A family in which the husband lives at his wife's parent's house
D. A family belonging to one locality

178. Which one of the following is the family unit of Kodavas?
A. Ghar B. Chulah
C. Okka D. Biradari

179. The social group in which a person is born is referred to as which one of the following?
A. The family of socialization
B. The family of procreation
C. The family of orientation
D. The family of recreation

180. "Family is more or less durable association of husband and wife with or without children, or of a man or woman alone, with children," is a definition given by:
A. Nimkoff B. MacIver
C. Lundberg D. Rousseau

181. Family has been defined as, "a group of persons whose relations to one another based upon consanguinity and who are therefore kin to one another?
A. Davis B. Sumner and Keller
C. Burgess and Locke D. None of the above

182. Family is "aminiature social organisation, including at least two generations and is characteristically formed upon the blood bond". Who, out of the following gave this definition?
A. Sumner and Keller
B. Elliot and Merrill
C. The American Bureau of census
D. None of the above

183. Regarding the development of life, following words have been said, "the societies have not followed a single, consistent line of evolution, but a multitude of diverging lines," by:
A. Lowie B. Linton
C. Max Weber D. G. Almond

184. Which of the following is not an essential of family?
A. A systematic form of marriage
B. A system of putting up names (i.e. nomen clature)
C. A common cohabitation
D. No requirement of an economic provision

185. Which one of the following is not an essential of family?
A. A common shelter to live in
B. A common belief in god and godesses
C. A mating relationship
D. A common political and economic ideology

186. Mark the correct statements out of the following:
A. family is a biological unit embodying sexual relationship between wife and husband
B. family is a social unit
C. family is a cultural unit
D. family is a social as well as a cultural unit

187. An endogamous family is the type of family:
A. In which marriage within the group is allowed.
B. In which marriage from outside is allowed
C. In which one member does not belong to the same group
D. None of the above

188. Which of the following is a feature of family?
A. Universality
B. There is no need of emotional attachment among the members
C. No prescribed size can be guessed
D. None of the above

189. Which of the following is a nuclear family?
A. A family in which one husband, wife and their children live together
B. A family in which all the brothers of the husband as well as their wives and children live together
C. A family in which only wife and husband live together
D. None of the above

190. Point out the features of the family:
A. Family has emotional basis
B. Family is inhabited by some limited number of members
C. Family is the nucleus of all groups
D. All of the above

191. Mark the correct statement:
A. Family is formulated by customs and conventions
B. Every member of the family need not own responsibility
C. Family as an association is permanent
D. family as an institution is temporary

192. Which one of the following is a concrete suggestion for reducing instability of modern family?
A. Marriage should be kept as a social arrangement only
B. Members should not be allowed to waste time in discussions
C. Areas of arrangement should be widened
D. Younger members should be kept away from hard realities of life.

193. Which of the following tribes practice polygyny?
1. Masai 2. Yoruba 3. Bantu

Select the correct answer using the code given below:
A. 1 and 2 only B. 2 and 3 only
C. 1 and 3 only D. 1, 2 and 3

194. An exogamous family is the family which:
A. Permits marriage with the individuals from the other groups
B. Which does not permit marriage with the members of an out group.
C. Which does not permit marriage
D. Which is based on the monolithic social structure

195. Which is correct?
A. Sibs are generally exogamous and therefore a family contains members of several sibs.
B. Sibs are generally endogamous and therefore a family contains members of several sibs.
C. Sibs are generally endogamous and therefore a family contains members of one sib.
D. Sibs are generally exogamous and therefore a family contains members of one sib

196. What is a patriarchal family?
A. A family which is looked after by the father of the children
B. A family in which a child bears his father's family name
C. A family in which the inclusive powers are with the male head of the family
D. A family based on the concept of fraternity

197. The **Nayar** taravad system was based on which one of the following?
A. Virilocal residence patterns
B. Uxorilocal residence patterns
C. Neolocal residence patterns
D. Natolocal residence patterns

198. According to Briffault what led to the decay of the matriarchal at type of family:
A. The change in the psychological conditions.
B. The change in the way of thinking.
C. The growth of agriculture and handicraft as the occupation of livelihood.
D. The change in the religious idea of the primitive people.

199. An extended family may be defined as:
A. A family in which all brothers, their wives and children live together
B. A family in which only elder brother, his wife and his bachelor brothers live together
C. A family which is extended due to social upliftment
D. A family extended due to legal injecture

200. The matriarchal type of families grew because:
A. Males were not interested in the family life.
B. Males were in small number
C. Males were dominated by religious and cultural intelligence of goddess
D. Males went out for bunting and collecting means for livelihood and thus were generally away from the family

201. According to Morgan, which of the following is the correct order of evolution of family?
A. Monogamian family, Consanguine family, Punaluan family Syndasmian family and patriarchal family
B. Punaluan family, Syndyasmian family, consanguineal family, patriarchal family and monogamian family
C. Consanguine family, punaluan family, syndyasmian family, patriarchal family and monogamian family
D. None of the above

202. Which one of the following is not a serious problem of modern family?
A. there is problem of proper development of the children
B. there is problem of proper administration of family
C. there is problem of meeting economic needs of the family
D. there is problem of finding suitable matches by the head of the family

203. Which one of the following statement is true?
A. Family is an old institution but its origin can be traced
B. Though family is new institution yet its origin cannot be found
C. family is of course a new institutional and its origin has been traced
D. family is an old institution and its origin is in obscurity

204. Children learn the ways of adults, perpetuating the values, norms and social practices of their culture. What is this process called?
A. Natural selection B. Social interaction
C. Socialization D. Evolution

205. Which of the following can be a feasible suggestion for the reconstruction of modern family?
A. process of industrialisation should be slowed down
B. family should be run on democratic lines
C. head of the family should be given all powers
D. Single family system should be ended

206. Which one of the following is not true of the joint family system?
A. it raises living standards of the members
B. it perpetuates orthodoxy in society
C. it leads to litigation among the members
D. it makes the conditions of women in the family miserable

207. Why has the functionalist approach to the study of the institution of family been criticised by many sociologists?
1. Functionalist perspective assume the middle class families to be the ideal nuclear families.
2. Functionalist approach does not consider class, regional and religious variations in studying the institution of family.
3. Functionalist view does not explore alternatives to the family.

Select the correct answer using the code given below:
A. 1 and 2 only B. 2 and 3 only
C. 1 and 3 only D. 1, 2 and 3

208. Which one of the following is not a feature of modern family?
A. its members are not economically dependent on the head of the family
B. girls have become economically self-sufficient
C. women are partners in all walks of life
D. its members even today look towards elders for guidance

209. Which one of the following is not an important cause for the weakness of the family of today?
A. bonds of marriage are considered breakable
B. joints family is being replaced by single family system
C. there is shortage of accommodation
D. there are legal protections for the distribution of property

210. Which one of the following is not the case of instability of modern family?
A. women are becoming economically self-sufficient
B. keen struggle is going on to inherit parental property
C. there is absence of social mores
D. there is constraining influence of the elders

211. ________ terms refer more to relationship rather than to kin.
A. Classificatory B. Descriptive
C. Exploratory D. Expressive

212. Primitive Societies are characterised more by _____ terms in kinship.
A. Classificatory B. Ambiguous
C. Descriptive D. Deceptive

213. The descendants of common male ancestor are called ________.
A. Agnates B. Cognates
C. Lineal kins D. Collateral Kins

214. Who calls 'clan' a compromise Kingroup?
A. Murdock B. Frazer
C. Boas D. Elwin

215. Joking relationship in society is found between:
A. Father and son-in-law
B. Daughter and father-in-law
C. Son and father
D. Devar and Bhabhi

216. The two phratries viz. Tartharol and Teivaliol are found among ________
A. Todas B. Melanesiantribes
C. Nuers D. Kadars

217. Inpopular Hindi ________ is a classificatory term.
A. Samadhin B. Tab
C. Chacha D. Ami

218. The relatives connected through blood ties are called ________.
A. Affinal Kin B. Consanguineal Kin
C. Tertiary Kin D. Agnates

219. When a group of clans get marged together, it is called ________.
A. Phratry B. Moitey
C. Sections D. Clan-set

220. ________ may be indicative of equality and mutual reciprocity.
A. Amitate B. Avoidance
C. Joking relationship D. Couvade

221. The system under which one relative is supposed to avoid the other is known as:
A. Alunclate B. Amitate
C. Avoidance D. Couvade

222. The system under which maternal uncle gets prominent place in Kinship is known as:
A. Couvade B. Amitate
C. Alunclate D. Takanonymy

223. According to Redcliffe Brown, ________ may be kind of friendliness expressed through a show of hostility.
A. Avoidance B. Joking relations
C. Couvade D. Amitate

224. Which of the following is not clearly indicated by Kinship?
A. Lineage B. Affinity
C. Status D. Relationship

225. One's father is one's ________ .
A. Primary affinal Kin
B. Tertiary Kin
C. Primary consanguineal kin
D. Secondary kin

226. Nature of Kinship created by marriage is called ________ .
A. Affinal B. Consanguineous
C. Monogamous D. Reproductive

227. Frazer has reported brother-sister avoidance from ________ .
A. Todas B. Nuers
C. Veddas of ceylon D. Andaman Islanders

228. The distance maintained between daughter-in-law and her parents-in-law, is called ________ in sociology.
A. avoidance B. social distance
C. social isolation D. None of the above

229. When a Kinis referred to indirectly through another kin, the system is known as:
A. avunclate B. tekanonymy
C. amitate D. couvade

230. What is not the indicative of kinship change pattern in our modern society?
A. inter-caste marriage system
B. changing affinity
C. less stress on residence
D. means of transportation and communication

231. Kinship:
A. is always related to sex
B. is occasionally related to sex
C. is unlinked with sex
D. may or may not be related to sex

232. Uncle is a ________ term in Kinship.
A. classificatory B. related
C. descriptive D. deceptive

233. The reverse of avoidance is:
A. joking relationship B. anitate
C. couvade D. teknonyony

234. In primary kinship relationship is:
A. direct and close B. indirect
C. permanent D. hereditary

235. Kinship and descent are essential for maintaining:
A. social system B. marriage
C. communal harmony D. None of the above

236. Secondary kin of the primary kinis called ________ .
A. distant kin B. third degree kin
C. secondary kin D. tertiary kin

237. Which one of the following was not an important factor of kinship in ancient India?
A. birth in the family B. willing adoption
C. marriage D. legal adoption

238. Which one of the following is not one of the three basic rules of decent?
A. Patrilineal B. matrilineal
C. bilateral D. fraternal

239. One's wife's brother is one's ________ .
A. Primary kin B. tertiary kin
C. affinal secondary kin D. secondary kin

240. The Sema Naga use ________ for mother, father's, brother's wife and mother's sister.
A. hepu B. aja
C. ami D. shi

241. Out of the following who has divided Kinship into primary and secondary Kinship?
A. Elliot and Merill B. Ginsberg
C. Gillin and Gillin D. R.M. MacIver

242. Kinship is:
A. biological relationship only
B. biological relationship of sexual union
C. biological relationship without sexual union
D. Unrelated to biological relationship.

243. Double descent produces bilineal kin groups known as ________ .
A. Moities B. Phartries
C. Sections D. Sects

244. ________ in Latin means sociological father.
A. Pater B. Paternity
C. Genitor D. Peter

245. ________ is the rule where by the married couple establish their own residence.
A. Neolocal residence
B. Bilateral residence
C. Individual residence
D. Patrilocal residence

246. The first significant contribution to the study of kinship terms was made by________.
A. Tylor B. Morgan
C. Malinowski D. Redcliffe Brown.

247. The Practice of convade is reported from ________.
A. Khasi tribe B. Oraon tribe
C. Jhangs D. Santhals

248. Genitor in Latin means ________.
A. Biological father hood
B. Sociological father hood
C. Creator
D. None of the above

249. Any Kin related to ego through primary Kin is called ________.
A. secondary Kin B. indirect Kin
C. tertiary Kin D. None of the above

250. In an avunculate system, maternal uncle's authority is known as ________.
A. Avuncupotestality B. Maternal geniter
C. Patri-matrimony D. None of the above

251. Kinship by nature is:
A. always specific
B. always unspecific
C. never specific
D. in some cases specific, while others not

252. One of the factor which has effected Kinship more these days is:
A. economic pattern B. residence
C. religion D. culture

253. Those kin, who branch out from main 'lineal kin' like uncles and cousin, are called ________.
A. Collateral Kin B. Tertiary Kin
C. Ulterine Kin D. Patrimatri lineal kin

254. ________ always prescribes some extent of inheritance of property.
A. Rules of residence B. Descent
C. Marriage D. Clan

255. Clan is basically an ________ group.
A. exogamous B. endogamous
C. indivisible D. None of the above

256. Those Kin who are related to each other directly through descent are called ________.
A. agnatic Kin
B. collateral Kin
C. lineal Kin
D. None of the above

257. The descendants of a common female ancestress are called:
A. Cognates B. Agnates
C. Uterine Kin D. Collateral Kin

258. Father is a ________ term in Kinship.
A. Classificatory B. descriptive
C. ambiguous D. much used

259. ________ is a bilaternal consanguineal Kin group.
A. Family B. Kindred
C. Clan D. Lineage

260. If a common ancestor is the binder among a people, they are called ________.
A. Agnates B. Cognates
C. Sections D. Phratries

261. In which of the following tribes, clan does not exist?
A. Kadar B. Nuer
C. Oraon D. Santhal

262. Among the Kuki clans ________ is used for father's father, mother's wife brother's Son.
A. hepu B. aja
C. ani D. shi

263. ________ is usually associated with totemism.
A. Lineage B. Clan
C. Family D. Section

264. Primary Kin of the secondary Kin is called ________.
A. secondary Kin B. tertiary Kin
C. informal Kin D. indirect Kin

265. ________ term describes speaker's exact relationship.
A. Descriptive B. Classificatory
C. Exploratory D. Expressive

266. ________ is a kind of Kinship usages.
A. Avoidance B. Promiscuity
C. Incest Taboo D. Seduction

267. The practice of teknonymy is found among ________.
A. Khasi tribe B. Oraon tribe
C. Kadar tribe D. Santhal tribe

268. The most important characteristic of Kinship relationship:
A. Between the members of a family.
B. Created by bonds of blood.
C. Of affection.
D. Where the rule of head of family is preponderant

269. The System under which one term refers to only one system is known as:
A. Classificatory B. Descriptive
C. Biological D. None of the above

270. The bond between the blood relatives is called ________.
A. Affinal Kinship B. Consanguineal Kinship
C. Primary Kinship D. Secondary Kinship

271. If a person is related to 'ego' directly, then he is ego's ________.
A. Secondary Kin B. Direct Kin
C. Primary Kin D. First Kin

272. Which one of the following is not the basic rule of descent?
A. Patrilineal B. Matrilineal
C. Bilateral D. Hereditary

273. The primitive Kinship system is a ______ system.
A. narrow range B. broad range
C. flexible D. limited

274. Which one of the following falls under the category of tertiary Kinship?
A. father of the daughter-in-law
B. father of the wife
C. father of the mother
D. father of the uncle

275. The bond between the spouses and their relatives on the either side is called ______.
A. Kinship B. Affinal Kinship
C. Ritual Kinship D. Primary Kinship

276. Which among the following is not a Kinship relation?
A. wife's brother B. sister's husband
C. friend's wife D. father's mother

277. The instance of joking relationship has been reported from ______.
A. Vedda tribe of Ceylon B. Nuers of Sudan
C. Matrilineal hopi D. Andaman Islanders

278. According to Levistrauss, no society is ________, if by that, total neglect of one side in favour of the other is implied.
A. Bilateral B. Unilateral
C. Patrilineal D. Matrilineal

279. When in Kinship special role is given to father's sister, the system is known as:
A. Amitate B. Couvade
C. Avunclate D. Avoidance

280. The modern western kinship system is a ______ system.
A. narrow range B. broad range
C. limited D. flexible

281. ________ says that 'avoidance' is a mechanism to preserve peace.
A. Tylor B. Turney-High
C. Frazer D. Freud

282. Consanguineous Kinship is the one which is between:
A. mother-in-law and father-in-law
B. uncle and nephew
C. husband and wife
D. lover and beloved

283. Children of the same parents are called ______.
A. off springs B. cousins
C. brothers D. siblings

284. The relatives by marriage are called ________.
A. tertiary Kin B. primary Kin
C. secondary Kin D. affinal Kin

285. In our times one of the causes of weakness in Kinship is:
A. heredity
B. weakness in culturalist
C. living away from the relatives
D. losing effect of morality

286. The term 'matri-patrilocal residence' has been coined by:
A. Murdock B. Tylor
C. Malinowski D. Morgan

287. Ego's father's brother is ego's ______
A. Primary Kin B. Secondary Kin
C. Tertiary D. None of the above

288. Which one of the following fall under the category of secondary Kinship?
A. father and daughter
B. mother and son
C. mother and daughter
D. mother-in-law and daughter-in-law

289. Which one of the following falls under the category of primary Kin?
A. daughter and mother-in-law
B. uncle and aunt.
C. mother and daughter
D. son-in-law and mother-in-law

290. Affinal Kinship indicates relationship between:
A. sister and brother
B. father and mother
C. brother and brother
D. mother-in-law and father-in-law

291. Which among the following is not a primary Kin?
A. mother B. father
C. uncle D. brother

292. Which among the following is a tertiary Kin?
A. uncle (mama)
B. wife of brother-in-law (sala)
C. brother's son
D. father

293. Which among the following is not a secondary Kin?
A. wife of brother-in-law (sala)
B. sister's husband
C. brother's wife
D. wife's brother

294. Which among the following is not included among the affinal kin?
A. father-in-law B. mother-in-law
C. brother-in-law D. younger sister

295. Where father's sister is given more respect than the mother,the relationships called:
A. Couvade B. Amitate
C. Avunclate D. Teknonymy

296. Usage of avoidance is common in some society, Which among the following comes under this category in our society?
A. Jija-Sali relationship
B. Dever-Bhabhi relationship
C. Father-Sister relationship
D. Son-in-law and Mother-in-law relationship

297. ________ is the rule or pattern by which the married couple establish residence with or quite near the parents of the groom.
A. Matrilocal residence B. Rule of residence
C. Patrilocal residence D. Patriliny

298. When the wife of a person calls her husband through son or daughter in Hindus society the system is known as that of:
A. avoidance B. teknonymy
C. couvade D. amitate

299. Find out the incorrect match:
A. Tylor — Classificatory and descriptive Kinship terms.
B. Pater — Social father hood.
C. Avoidance — Son-in-law and mother-in-law
D. Couvade — Khasi tribe

300. Which one of the following statements is not true about Kinship?
A. it is universal
B. it is recognised in every society
C. relationship nomenclatures are uniform
D. it is deep rooted in every society

301. ________ consists in making a husband lead the life of an invalid along with his wife when ever she gives birth to a child.
A. Couvade B. Avunculate
C. Amitate D. Avoidance

302. Kinship terms have been broadly divided into ________.
A. expressive and expansive
B. latent and manifest
C. classificatory and descriptive
D. classificatory and exploratory

303. A ________ group is said to be a 'broad range' or' narrow range', according to the number of persons it includes.
A. family B. clan
C. bilateral descent D. kinship

304. Which one of the following is not major task of kinship usage?
A. it creates group
B. it governs the role relationship between kins
C. it provides guidelines for interaction between the persons
D. it avoids social stratification

305. When a person is referred to as the father or the mother of his or her child, the Kinship usage is called ________.
A. amitate B. avoidance
C. couvade D. teknonymy

306. In the world there are societies in which:
A. only classificatory system is found
B. only descriptive system is found
C. none of above is found
D. both are found

307. Find out the incorrect match:
A. Unilinear con-anguineal Kin group – clan
B. clan – Exogamy
C. Unilateral descent – Kindred
D. Matri-patrilocal residence – Murdock

308. A ________ consists of descendants in one live, either matrilineal or patrilineal. Who know their exact geneological relationship and who recognize obligations to one another.
A. lineage B. class
C. clan D. unilateral descent

309. According to Red cliffe Brown, action is a ________ but its members do not share a common residence.
A. Unilateral group B. Affinal group
C. Consanguineal group D. Collateral group

310. Which of the following statements is true?
A. Affinal Kins are relataed by marriage
B. In 'Amitate', father's sister is assigned a special role
C. The principles by which ego's Consan guineal relatives are determined is known as rules of descent

D. All the above statements are true

311. Who have pointed out the 'avoidance' is a social fact and must therefore have a social explanation?
A. Durkheim B. Redcliffe Brown
C. Malinowski D. Tylor

312. Which one of the following is not the advantage of rule of descent?
A. rights about inheritance of property are conveniently laid down
B. family feuds are easily settled
C. rules about sexual relations are laid down
D. rights of each person are defined

313. If in a kinship system, maternal uncle enjoys apreeminent place in the life of his nephew and niece as a matter of convention, the kinship usage is called ____.
A. avunculate B. amitate
C. couvade D. matriliny

314. Which one of the following statements about Kinship is not true?
A. it is usages create group of Kins
B. it creates relationship structure
C. it defines role of different relationships
D. it indicates expected behaviour of Kins

315. The principle or set of principles by which ego's consanguineal relatives are determined is technically known as:
A. rules of residence B. rules of kinship
C. rules of descent D. none of the above

316. Who of the following has said that "kinship systems are changing all the times. The change in structural parts are usually slow l.e. they usually emerge clearly in the course of generations"?
A. H.M. Johnson B. A. Dumont
C. Elliot and Merill D. Burgess

317. Who of the following has classified kinship on the basis of classificatory system and descriptive system?
A. Murdock B. Morgan
C. Ginsberg D. Merton

318. Which one of the following is the advantage of rules of descent?
A. Net work of social positions is established
B. Kinship system is strengthened
C. Kinship hierarchy is established
D. Kinship and social relationships are linked

319. The system under which a person inherits some but not all of his father's consanguineal relatives is known:
A. patrilineal descent B. matrilined descent
C. bilateral discent D. None of the above

320. Within each kin group, there are certain types of coactive behaviour patterns which exhibit a regularity, a more or less permanent definite structure. Such types of behaviour are called ________.
A. Normative pattern B. Kinship usages
C. Kinterms D. Rules of descent

ANSWERS

1	2	3	4	5	6	7	8	9	10
A	A	A	C	A	A	B	C	B	D
11	12	13	14	15	16	17	18	19	20
B	C	D	C	A	C	D	A	B	A
21	22	23	24	25	26	27	28	29	30
C	C	D	A	D	B	D	C	A	D
31	32	33	34	35	36	37	38	39	40
A	D	D	C	A	A	A	C	B	D
41	42	43	44	45	46	47	48	49	50
B	C	A	A	A	B	C	A	B	B
51	52	53	54	55	56	57	58	59	60
C	D	D	D	A	D	C	B	A	C
61	62	63	64	65	66	67	68	69	70
C	B	A	A	B	A	A	C	D	A
71	72	73	74	75	76	77	78	79	80
B	C	B	A	C	D	D	D	B	B

81	82	83	84	85	86	87	88	89	90
C	B	A	A	B	D	A	A	A	C
91	92	93	94	95	96	97	98	99	100
D	D	A	B	D	D	D	A	D	C
101	102	103	104	105	106	107	108	109	110
D	D	B	D	A	A	C	A	A	A
111	112	113	114	115	116	117	118	119	120
D	D	D	A	B	B	D	A	B	C
121	122	123	124	125	126	127	128	129	130
D	B	B	A	C	D	A	B	D	B
131	132	133	134	135	136	137	138	139	140
B	C	C	A	A	B	C	B	B	B
141	142	143	144	145	146	147	148	149	150
C	B	B	A	B	B	D	C	D	D
151	152	153	154	155	156	157	158	159	160
C	C	B	D	D	A	B	D	D	B
161	162	163	164	165	166	167	168	169	170
B	D	D	D	D	B	A	A	D	B
171	172	173	174	175	176	177	178	179	180
C	B	D	C	A	B	C	B	C	A
181	182	183	184	185	186	187	188	189	190
A	A	B	D	C	C	A	A	C	D
191	192	193	194	195	196	197	198	199	200
A	C	B	A	A	C	D	A	A	D
201	202	203	204	205	206	207	208	209	210
C	C	D	C	B	A	B	D	C	B
211	212	213	214	215	216	217	218	219	220
A	A	A	A	D	A	A	B	A	C
221	222	223	224	225	226	227	228	229	230
C	C	B	C	C	A	C	A	B	C
231	232	233	234	235	236	237	238	239	240
A	A	A	A	A	D	D	D	D	B
241	242	243	244	245	246	247	248	249	250
D	B	C	A	A	B	A	A	A	A
251	252	253	254	255	256	257	258	259	260
D	B	A	B	A	C	C	B	B	B
261	262	263	264	265	266	267	268	269	270
A	A	B	B	A	A	A	B	B	B
271	272	273	274	275	276	277	278	279	280
C	D	B	A	B	C	C	B	A	A
281	282	283	284	285	286	287	288	289	290
B	B	D	D	C	A	B	D	C	D
291	292	293	294	295	296	297	298	299	300
C	B	A	D	C	D	C	B	A	C
301	302	303	304	305	306	307	308	309	310
A	C	D	D	D	D	C	A	C	D
311	312	313	314	315	316	317	318	319	320
B	B	A	C	C	A	B	C	C	B

Social Inequality and Exclusion

1. Who has given the concept 'status-set'?
   A. MacIver B. Kingsley Davis
   C. Robert Merton D. Weber
2. A person is evaluated to high—if he receives rewards which others have not:
   A. Prestige B. Status
   C. Esteem D. Position
3. "A person's status is his group standing or ranking in relation to others" was said by:
   A. Sheriff and Sheriff B. Ginsberg
   C. Ogburn and Nimkoff D. Kingsley Davis
4. Status of an individual in the society is something which is:
   A. permanent
   B. temporary
   C. does not change with changing time
   D. does not change with changing situations
5. Role of an individual comes to prominance in a society in which there is:
   A. division of labour
   B. no division of labour
   C. no social complexity
   D. no difficult social organisation
6. Which one of the following cannot be placed under the category of achieved status?
   A. head of an office
   B. manager of a firm
   C. director of an organisation
   D. recipient of some money
7. A first born child may be given a special treatment by his parents. How do you describe it?
   A. The manner of introducing him to society
   B. It shows the esteem of the parents
   C. Child enjoys the prestige
   D. Status is ascribed to him
8. The Personal Manager in a corporation is an example of ________ .
   A. informal status B. bureaucratic status
   C. legal status D. formal status
9. ________ is a state of relative isolation of the occupants of a role.
   A. Role-insulation B. Role-discontinuity
   C. Ambiguous role D. Role-isolation
10. The status like husband-wife and doctor-patient can be called ________
    A. Perceived statuses B. Polar statuses
    C. Status-set D. Paired-status
11. Which one of the following cannot be placed under the category of role?
    A. bride groom
    B. basket making
    C. traffic policeman
    D. evaluation of answer books
12. ________ refers to a pattern of behaviour expected of the occupant of the status.
    A. Position B. Personality
    C. Character D. Role
13. Usually in a society who of the following occupy high social status?
    A. An engineer B. A scholar
    C. Petty Shopkeeper D. A painter
14. Which of the following has not much relevance with status?
    A. His allotted duty B. His birth
    C. His hard labour D. His ecology
15. The changes from the courtship to the marriage is referred to as
    A. Role-discontinuity B. Perceived role
    C. Internalized role D. Role-continuity
16. Achieved status, means:
    A. The status achieved during the process of cultural diffusion
    B. The status acquired during the process of personality cult
    C. The status acquired by the individuals during the process of socialisation, on the basis of talent etc.
    D. The status acquired through the culture traits
17. ________ refer to a set of roles that centres around a particular social status.
    A. Dual status B. Polar status
    C. Role set D. Role continuity

18. Which one of the following can be placed under the category of ascribed status?
A. an engineer B. book writer
C. caste person D. social reformer

19. Which one of the following will you categorise as achieved status?
A. sex B. age
C. caste D. social work

20. A status primarily refers to:
A. evaluated position B. prestigious position
C. functional position D. group position

21. The Precedence of one role over another is called:
A. Role superiority B. Role-Primacy
C. Role-Precedent D. Role-model

22. ________ refers to taking of the role of another by viewing one self from the point of view of the other.
A. Role insulation B. Role-model
C. Reflexive role taking D. None of the above

23. According to Secrad and Buckman which one is not the basis of status?
A. Capacity of a person for proper rewarding
B. Extent of receiving awards
C. His investments
D. His incomes

24. ________ refers to statuses that exist in pairs by virtue of the fact that each is defined in terms of its relationship to the other.
A. Polar status B. Status-set
C. Pair-status D. None of the above

25. Age is considered an important cause of role differentiation because:
A. of physical strength of the person concerned
B. of supposed capability for handling serious jobs
C. of increased social relationship
D. of high social status

26. One of the major problems of modern society is:
A. To harmonise conflicts
B. To focus attention on social conflicts
C. To under-estimate social conflicts
D. To over-estimate social conflicts

27. Social roles are responsible for:
A. smooth working of society
B. disorganising of society
C. bringing social stratification
D. claiming more rights

28. In modern industrialised society the status of women in industry:
A. has considerably gone down
B. is gradually rising
C. has remained unchanged
D. has not been assigned

29. Role may be called:
A. As the behaviour of an individual which is expected by the community
B. The particular post assigned to an individual to be played
C. The contribution of the individual in innovating a culture
D. The performance of certain duties by an individual in his interest

30. In a democratic society role of a leader is not:
A. to take unilateral decision
B. to involve people in decision
C. to encourage decentralisation
D. to decrease social tensions

31. In Indian society who of the following ususally is considered a person with low status?
A. An office clerk B. A good musician
C. A good painter D. A university teacher

32. Achieved status is one which is:
A. thrust upon a person
B. inherited by a person
C. based on the birth of a person
D. obtained by a person after struggle

33. Role decides the manner in which:
A. rights should be claimed
B. obligations should be discharged
C. rights should not be claimed
D. obligations should not be discharged

34. ________ means the location of individual in the social network of reciprocal obligations and privileges, i.e. rights and duties.
A. Prestige B. Position
C. Status D. Role

35. When a status is derived from the membership of an involuntary group that is called?
A. Crystallization status B. Ascribed status
C. Achieved status D. Consistency status

36. In a competitive society, which one of the following does not matter in status formation?
A. knowledge B. education
C. expertise D. family

37. Who has given the concept of "Reflexive role taking"?
A. Merton B. Linton
C. Cooley D. G.H. Mead

38. Who has given the concept of 'Role set'?
A. Linton B. Merton
C. MacIver D. Tylor

39. Which one of the following is not a cause of role conflict?
A. Inadequate wage
B. Improper recognition of work
C. Indifferent attitude of the employer
D. Less production in the factory

40. Which one of the following is not covered under the category of investments in rewards?
A. Race
B. Ethnicback ground
C. Physical environments
D. Family

41. Which one of the following is an important factor of role differentiation?
A. Knowledge
B. Length in service
C. Gentlemen
D. Human approach to problems

42. Who has referred to 'role' as the dynamic aspect of status?
A. MacIver B. Ralph Linton
C. Merton D. Cooley

43. Status of an individual is decided by the position of an individual on account of:
A. Physical environments
B. Neighbourhood
C. Sccial relationship
D. Social stratification

44. Office and status, in our modern day society are:
A. Closely linked with each other
B. Not linked with each other
C. Loosely related to each other
D. Opposed to each other

45. In primitive societies, greater emphasis is laid on ________.
A. Division of labour B. Ascribed status
C. Perceived status D. Polar statuses

46. The evaluation of status is ________ where as evaluation of an individual's role behaviour in a status is ________.
A. Prestige, esteem
B. Esteem, privilege
C. Privilege, personality
D. Position, esteem

47. Individual's talent and effort are manifest in his ________.
A. Achievement of status
B. Ascription of status
C. Gratification of needs
D. Getting a good job

48. Which of the following is not covered under the category of status?
A. Bride B. Ticket examiner
C. Factory manager D. Travelling

49. Find out the incorrect match:
A. Polar status — Husband and wife
B. Status-set — Merton
C. Ascribed status — A district magistrate
D. Achieved status — A bank officer

50. Status of an individual indicates his:
A. Economic placement
B. Political achievement
C. Literary accomplishments
D. Integrated personality

51. The role that a person believes, others expect his to play is called ________.
A. Perceived role B. Internalized role
C. Formal role D. Functional role

52. The changes from occupational role to retirement role is known as ________.
A. Role-discontinuity B. Role conflict
C. Transitional role D. Role insulation

53. The type of status, which a social class or individual enjoys, depends upon the ________.
A. Material benefits
B. Social evaluation
C. Educational qualification
D. Proper fulfilment of role-expectation

54. In an industrial society, all occupational statuses are:
A. Achieved statuses B. Polar statuses
C. Functional statuses D. Ascribed statuses

55. Shamsher Singh belongs to fighting tribe of the Northwest frontier. This is an example of ________.
A. Achieved status B. Functional status
C. Formal status D. Ascribed status

56. Pick up one of the following as a factor in role differentiation:
A. Knowledge B. Sense of hatred
C. Geography D. None of the above

57. Sibling rivalry is a major example of ________.
A. Status comparison B. Internalized status
C. Perceived status D. Status-set

58. ________ places the right persons in the right place in a society.
A. Achieved status B. Competition
C. Ascribed status D. None of the above

59. Author of the book 'The study of Man' was:
A. MacIver B. Tylor
C. Ralph Linton D. Kingsley Davis

60. Who has distinguished between status and role?
A. MacIver B. Ralph Linton
C. Kingsley Davis D. Sumner

61. ________ refers to a location in a system of social relationship while ________ refers to the behaviour associated with that location.
A. Status, role
B. Position, personality
C. Privilege, character
D. None of the above

62. ________ is always related to the expectation a position where as ________ is attached to the position as such.
A. Personality, status B. Status, role
C. Esteem, prestige D. Prestige, role

63. Who has distinguished between achieved status and ascribed status?
A. Ralph Linton B. Simmel
C. Le Bon D. MacIver

64. ________ refers to formally designated position in a group with officially specified rights and duties.
A. Formal status B. Legal status
C. Role making D. Functional status

65. Which one of the following is not a contributory factor in deciding status?
A. Office B. Family
C. Physical ability D. Tastes

66. Status is something which is:
A. Comparable B. Non-comparable
C. Concrete D. Absolute

67. Ascribed status in society is one which an individual gets:
A. after hard labour
B. after some labour
C. of his own
D. on the basis of his ability

68. In fancy is an ________ status.
A. Achieved B. Integrated
C. Ascribed D. Absolute

69. A statue was raised in honour of a dead leader it indicates that the people had for him:
A. Prestige
B. esteem
C. to remind the posterity of his deeds
D. a status is ascribed to him

70. Which one of the following is not an achieved status?
A. engineer B. land lord
C. brahmin D. priest

71. "The manner in which a person actually carries out the requirements of his position", called:
A. role B. status
C. culture D. office

72. The term ________ is used to refer to the total catalogue of social roles played by an individual.
A. role set B. role repertoire
C. multiple roles D. status sequence

73. The precedence of one role over another is called:
A. role superiority B. role-primacy
C. role-precedent D. role-model

74. ________ refers to set of roles that centres around a particular social status.
A. dual status B. polar statuses
C. role-set D. role-continuity

75. ________ refers to taking of a role of another by viewing one self from the point of view of the other.
A. role insulation B. role-model
C. reflexive role taking D. none of the above

76. Who has given the concept of "Reflexive role taking"?
A. Merton B. Linton
C. Cooley D. G.H. Mead

77. The role that a person believes, others expect him to play is called ________.
A. perceived role B. internalized role
C. formal role D. functional role

78. The changes from the countership to marriage is referred to as ________.
A. role-discontinuity B. perceived role
C. internalized role D. role-continuity

79. Which of the following is not an achieved status?
A. Professor B. Minister
C. Engineer D. Old age

80. Which of the following is an achieved status?
A. Age B. Sex
C. Kinship D. Doctor

81. Who has referred to 'role' as the dynamic aspect of status?
A. MacIver B. Ralph Linton
C. Merton D. Cooley

82. According to ________, "Status is a place in a particular system which a certain individual occupies at a particular time".
A. Mazumdar B. MacIver
C. Linton D. Kingsley Davis

83. Small children are taught to play with dolls, to play house, to play doctor and soon. This is an example of:
A. role expectations B. role playing
C. playing-at-a-role D. role taking

84. A woman imagines her self in the position of her significant other an sees herself through their eyes, this is an example of:
A. role expectations B. role playing
C. playing-at-a-role D. role taking

85. Bureaucratic organisations are designed to acquaint inductees with their rights and obligations. This is an example of:
A. role B. role expectation
C. role performance D. role enactment

86. ________ is a state of relative isolation of the occupants of a role.
A. role-insulation B. role-discontinuity
C. ambiguous role D. role-isolation

87. Individual's talent and effort are manifest in his:
A. achievement of status
B. ascription of status
C. gratification of needs
D. getting a good job

88. What is the term used for statuses which are arranged in such a manner that individuals occupy them in regular sequence?
A. Status inheritance B. Status multiplication
C. Status sequence D. Status set

89. Every man in the society occupies a number of statuses. Different status associated with a single person is known as:
A. Status inconsistency B. Status sequence
C. Status set D. Status succession

90. Among the following mark out the one who enjoys prestige:
A. A rich businessman
B. A doctor in private practice
C. A broker
D. A magistrate

91. Who does not have the esteem among the following?
A. A successful dentist
B. A popular police officer
C. A high official charged for corruption
D. A brilliant student

92. Among the following, which do not indicate status?
A. Bharat Ratna
B. Labourer
C. The title of Knighthood
D. Use of the prefix "Pandit"

93. In our modern society a scribed status:
A. Is replacing achieved status
B. Controlling achieved status
C. Is being replaced by achieved status
D. Has not been at all affected by achieved status

94. Which statement on roles is wrong?
A. An individual in the course of his life performs a number of different roles, successfully or simultaneously
B. The synthesis of all the social roles that an individual has performed from birth to death constitutes his social personality
C. A person cannot perform his role without the co-operation of his social circle
D. Roles do not figure in the process of socialisation

95. What is not the social role in the following?
A. A priest performing a ceremony
B. A politician preaching the cult of violence
C. A lawyer preparing his witness
D. An actor involved in an act of violence on the screen

96. Indicate out of the following which of the offices held by 'A' from time to time was prestigious to him?
A. 'A' was highly successful as an advocate
B. 'A' had been an esteemed member of parliament
C. 'A' remained a minister but had to resign
D. 'A' as the head of a statutory body

97. What does not constitute a social role in the following?
A. A worker on the field
B. A person committing a dacoity
C. A police man pursuing a dacoit
D. A teacher in his class

98. Which one of the following cannot be placed under the category of achieved status?
A. head of an office
B. manager of a firm
C. director of an organisation
D. recipient of some money

99. Which one of the following is not the characteristic of status?
A. It is permanent
B. It has no permanency
C. It changes with time
D. It changes with place

100. Which one of the following is not the characteristic of status?
A. It changes from individual to individual
B. It changes from office to office
C. It changes with the circumstances
D. It is not influenced by the circumstances

101. Social status of an individual is formed through:
A. Aspiration alone
B. Achievement alone
C. None of the both
D. Both combined together

102. The people who enjoy high status in society wish:
A. The others to come up to them
B. The others to go down
C. To maintain the status quo
D. To bring revolutionary changes

103. In our modern society which one of the following is not relevant factor in status?
A. Extent of distribution of rewards
B. Hereditary position of the ancestors
C. Accumulated wealth
D. Influence in administration

104. Who of the following has said that "role is the manner in which a person actually carries over the requirements of his position?
A. Sheriff and Sheriff
B. Kingsley Davis
C. MacIver and Page
D. Ogburn and Nimkoff

105. When incompatibility arises between two or more roles an individual is expected to perform in a griven situation, the situation is called ________.
A. incompatibility of roles
B. counterfeit role
C. role-conflict
D. antagonised role

106. Which of the following is not true of the role of a leader of a group?
A. He serves as a model for the others
B. He provides cognitive focus for unity
C. He is prime figure for his followers
D. He controls groups relations

107. Match both the groups:

Group-1	*Group-2*
(*a*) Polar statuses	1. Sibling rivalry
(*b*) Status comparison	2. G.H. Mead
(*c*) Reflexive role taking	3. Doctor-Patient
(*d*) Linton	4. Achieved Status and Ascribed Status

Codes:

	(*a*)	(*b*)	(*c*)	(*d*)
A.	2	1	3	4
B.	3	1	2	4
C.	4	3	2	1
D.	1	4	3	2

108. Role conflict does not arise when a person is given a role:
A. Which one does not like to perform
B. Which is not conducive to his environment
C. Which conflicts with the interests of the others
D. When each one works under a well planned system

109. Which one of the following is appplicable to 'achieved status'?
A. One which is acquired through competition
B. One which is acquired through cultural diffusion
C. Acquired through personality development
D. All of these

110. ________ refers to taking of the role of another by viewing one self from the point of view of the other.
A. Role insulation
B. Role-model
C. Reflexive role taking
D. None of the above

111. Who of the following has said that "a social role is pattern of behaviour expected of an individual in certain group or situation"?
A. MacIver
B. K. Young
C. Kingsley Davis
D. Lundberg

112. The ________ of citizenship, religious affiliation and community membership is in most cases a matter of identificaltion with the parents.
A. Achievement
B. Ascription
C. Conferral
D. Right

113. The urban conditions of life and the extreme division of labour has made possible the:
A. Ascription of status
B. Institutionalization of status
C. Achievement of status
D. Status comparison

114. ________ tends to reinforce individual's own particular role perspective and decrease his under standing of others points of view:
A. Ethnocentrism
B. Role-insulation
C. Ethical role
D. Role-model

115. The emphasis on ascription or achievement criteria in a particular society depends very much on the whole package of ________ of that society.
A. social values
B. gratification as system
C. economic values
D. political values

116. Status is essential:
A. For an individual only
B. For the society as a whole
C. Neither for the individual nor for the society
D. Both for the individual and the society

117. When incompatibility arises between two or more roles an individual is expected to perform in a given situation, the situation is called:
A. incompatibility of roles
B. counterfeit role
C. role-conflict
D. antagonized role

118. In our modern society which one of the following is not relevant factor in status?
A. extent of distribution of rewards
B. hereditary position of the ancestors
C. accumulated wealth
D. influence in administration

119. Only adults are allowed to see a particular movie that is being shown in the city theatre. Here, 'Adult hood' can be referred to as
A. Ascribed status B. Confered status
C. Achieved status D. Polar status

120. Role indicates what:
A. individual owes to the society
B. society owes to the individual
C. are the privileges of individuals in his society
D. what individuals owes to the society and what individual expects from it

121. Who has said in relevance to status that, "Every society, no matter how simple or complex, must differentiate persons interms of both prestige and esteem."
A. Ginsberg B. Gillin and Gillin
C. Kingsley Davis D. Merton

122. Which one of the following is not relevant to status?
A. It helps in specialisation of functions
B. It is essential for promotion of responsibility
C. It is needed for balanced personality development
D. It helps in developing honesty and integrity

123. A person's ________ in any situation is defined by the set of expectations for his behaviour held by others and by the person himself.
A. Status B. Responsibility
C. Role D. Position

124. A little boy pushes out his undeveloped belly and pompously swings an imaginary club in copy of the policeman who walks past his house everday. Which of the following explains this best?
A. Role set B. Role playing
C. Role D. Socialization

125. A person with a relatively low status in a formal hierarchy of status position may achieve prestige because of another status outside that group such type of status is called:
A. Involuntary status B. Achieved status
C. Informal status D. Potential Status

126. ________ refers to a role that an individual pretends to be his own, but in reality that has been assumed as a cover to protect him from the penalties associated with his actual role.
A. Dual role B. Counter feit role
C. Ambiguous role D. Unethical role

127. What typed of role, out of the following a woman is not supposed to perform in a diveloping society:
A. To take care of the household
B. To attend to field
C. To perform strenuous job
D. To do immoral work

128. In a modern advanced society role of one of the following is more important than that of the following is more important than that of the others. Pick up one:
A. Those who enjoy political power
B. Those who are law abiding
C. Those who are law violators
D. Those who are close to the centre of power

129. Who of the following has said that, "A role is a set of socially expected and approved behaviour pattern consisting of both duties and privileges"?
A. Ogburn and Nim Koff
B. Kingsley Davis
C. MacIver
D. None of the above

130. Kinship is considered an important factor for Role differentiation because of fact that those who have links with good people:
A. Can create social problems
B. Can help in solving social problems
C. Can discharge important obligations
D. Can't discharge any significant obligation

131. Officer may have a functionally more important and dominant role than a higher ranking line officer. Here, the status of the medical officer is called ________ .
A. rational status B. functional status
C. utility status D. informal status

132. Who of the following has said that, "Since each person has but so much time, energy and ability and since his activities must achieve results and satisfy needs, his system of statuses must be integrated"?
A. MacIver B. K. Young
C. Kerton D. Kingsley Davis

133. Bihari Lal, who has amassed a lot of wealth out of black marketing, is constructing a house for the mentally retarded children, and posing as a saviour of the down trodden his present role can be called ________ .
A. Role insulation B. Counterfeit-role
C. False role D. Role-set

134. One of the following has said that "status is social position that determines for its possessor a part from his personal attributes or social service, a degree of respect, prestige and influence. Pick up the one:
A. Merton B. C. North
C. MacIver and Page D. Gillin and Gillin

135. Justice Ghosh has been appointed to investigate into the corruption charges against his son, who happens to be the director of a public company. The situation of justice Ghosh can be referred to as:

A. Role-conflict B. Dual Role
C. Status-set D. Perceived role

136. Point out the condition under which status comparison cannot be made:

A. Person must be able to observe rewards
B. Person must have approximately same power
C. Person should be capable of ignoring rewards
D. Persons whose rewards and costs are not much different from his own.

137. Role of authoritative group leader does not include one of the following. Pick up that:

A. he takes maximum responsibility
B. he undertakes absolute functions
C. he dictates all activities
D. he promotes people's participation in activities

138. In a society role conflicts arise when:

A. people are not aware of their proper role
B. people know but do not perform their role properly
C. role of everyone is not clear
D. the poeple are not rewarded for performing their role.

139. In our modern society which one of the following is supposed to be performing more important role?

A. Those who are engaged in production
B. Those engaged in distribution
C. Those who are consumers of goods
D. None of the above

140. Who of the following has said that, "A role is a set of socially expected and approved behaviour pattern consisting of both duties and privileges"?

A. Ogburn and Nim Koff
B. Kingsley Davis
C. MacIver
D. None of the above

141. According to ________, "status is a place in a particular system which a certain individual occupies at a particular time."

A. Mazumdar B. MacIver
C. Linton D. Kingsley Davis

142. ________ refers to an individual whose behaviour in a particular role provides a pattern upon which another individual bases his behaviour in performing the same role.

A. role-model B. ideal role
C. internalized role D. perceived role

143. When the old Testament prop het Abraham was commanded by God to slay his son, his role as a father conflicted with his role as god's servant. This is an example of:

A. role set
B. role conflict
C. role performance
D. role playing

144. A little boy pushes out his undeveloped belly and pompously swing an imaginary club in copy of the policeman who walks past his house everyday. Which of the following explains this best?

A. role-set
B. role-playing
C. role
D. socialization

145. Role of authoritative group leader does not include one of the following. Pick that up:

A. he takes maximum responsibility
B. he undertakes absolute functions
C. he dictates all activities
D. he promotes people's participation in activities

146. In democratic society role of a leader is not:

A. to take unilateral decision
B. to involve people in decision making
C. to encourage decentralisation
D. to decrease social tensions

147. Age is considered an important cause of role-differentiation because:

A. of physical strength of the person concerned
B. of supposed capability for handling serious jobs.
C. of increased social relationship
D. of high social status

148. In our modern society which one of the following is supposed to be performing more important role?

A. those who are engaged in production
B. those who are engaged in distribution
C. those who are consumer of goods
D. none of the above

149. Which is not the way to achieve a status?

A. Manifestation of unusual talent
B. High class professional education
C. High appreciation gained for the work done
D. Raising a fortune by uncivic means and giving away a good part of it as charity

150. "Status is the social position that determines for its possessor a part from his personal attribute or social services, a degree of respect, prestige and influence"— this definition has been given by:

A. Green B. Ginsberg
C. MacIver D. Davis

151. Article ________ provides for a Commissioner/ Chairman for scheduled castes.
A. 338 B. 339
C. 340 D. 342

152. Which Article of the constitution deals with specifying a particular tribe as a scheduled tribe?
A. Art. 342 B. Art. 343
C. Art. 344 D. Art. 345

153. Which Article of the constitution deals with the appointment of a minister in charge of tribal welfare?
A. Art. 164 B. Art. 165
C. Art. 166 D. Art. 167

154. In India which of the following was true about caste system in the past?
A. it was based on birth
B. it was based on religion
C. it was based on the ability of the persons
D. it was based on feudal system

155. Under the constitution the President shall include a caste in the schedule on the recommendation of:
A. State legislature
B. Parliament
C. Governor
D. Chief Justice of India

156. Power to include or exclude a caste from the schedule has been given under our constitution to the:
A. President B. State Governor
C. State legislature D. Parliament

157. Which Article of the constitution deals with the claims of the scheduled castes and the scheduled tribes to services and posts?
A. Art. 335 B. Art. 336
C. Art. 337 D. Art. 338

158. Which Article of the constitution defines scheduled castes and scheduled tribes?
A. Art. 364 B. Art. 365
C. Art. 366 D. Art. 367

159. Under the constitution for which of the following states a provision has been made for appointing a minister incharge of tribal welfare?
A. U.P. B. Jharkhand
C. Tamil Nadu D. West Bengal

160. Of the following who was the staunchest champion of the cause of the scheduled castes and scheduled tribes?
A. Rafi Ahmed Kidwai
B. Gobind Ballabh Pant
C. Mahatma Gandhi
D. Dr. Zakir Hussain

161. During freedom struggle our national leaders made it clear that after independence they will:
A. not touch caste system
B. radically change caste hierarchy
C. abolish caste system
D. strengthen caste system

162. Which Article of the constitution has made it obligatory on the state to protect the people of the S.C. and S.T. from all forms of exploitation?
A. Art. 44 B. Art. 45
C. Art. 46 D. Art. 47

163. Under which Article of the constitution has untouchability been abolished?
A. Art. 15 B. Art. 16
C. Art. 17 D. Art. 18

164. Articles 330, 332 and 334 provide for reservation of seats for SCs and STs in the ________ .
A. House of people and state legislature
B. Services
C. State legislatures
D. House of parliament

165. The article ________ provides for reservation for scheduled castes and scheduled tribes in the services.
A. 335 B. 336
C. 338 D. 339

166. Current thinking about revision of schedules is that:
A. those should be revised
B. these should not be touched
C. more people should be included in the schedule
D. none of the above is true

167. Under ________ Governor of a state has been given special powers in relation to scheduled tribes.
A. Fifth schedule B. Seventh schedule
C. Ninth schedule D. Article 17

168. The people are not prepared to come out of the schedule because that:
A. will reduce their social prestige
B. will increase their privileges
C. will redicule them in society
D. will deprive them of certain privileges

169. Article ________ provides for a Commissioner/ Chairman for scheduled tribes.
A. 337 B. 337A
C. 338 D. 338A

170. Which of the following constitutional amendment provided a separate commission for scheduled castes and scheduled tribes?
A. 89th B. 90th
C. 95th D. 97th

ANSWERS

1	2	3	4	5	6	7	8	9	10
C	B	C	B	A	D	D	D	A	B
11	**12**	**13**	**14**	**15**	**16**	**17**	**18**	**19**	**20**
A	D	A	D	A	C	C	C	D	C
21	**22**	**23**	**24**	**25**	**26**	**27**	**28**	**29**	**30**
B	C	D	A	B	A	A	B	A	A
31	**32**	**33**	**34**	**35**	**36**	**37**	**38**	**39**	**40**
A	D	B	C	D	D	D	B	D	C
41	**42**	**43**	**44**	**45**	**46**	**47**	**48**	**49**	**50**
A	B	C	A	B	A	A	D	C	D
51	**52**	**53**	**54**	**55**	**56**	**57**	**58**	**59**	**60**
A	A	B	A	D	C	A	A	C	B
61	**62**	**63**	**64**	**65**	**66**	**67**	**68**	**69**	**70**
A	C	A	A	D	A	C	C	B	C
71	**72**	**73**	**74**	**75**	**76**	**77**	**78**	**79**	**80**
A	A	B	C	C	D	A	A	D	D
81	**82**	**83**	**84**	**85**	**86**	**87**	**88**	**89**	**90**
B	C	C	D	B	A	A	C	C	D
91	**92**	**93**	**94**	**95**	**96**	**97**	**98**	**99**	**100**
C	B	C	D	B	C	B	D	B	D
101	**102**	**103**	**104**	**105**	**106**	**107**	**108**	**109**	**110**
D	C	B	B	C	D	B	D	D	C
111	**112**	**113**	**114**	**115**	**116**	**117**	**118**	**119**	**120**
D	B	C	B	A	D	C	B	C	D
121	**122**	**123**	**124**	**125**	**126**	**127**	**128**	**129**	**130**
C	D	C	B	C	B	D	A	A	C
131	**132**	**133**	**134**	**135**	**136**	**137**	**138**	**139**	**140**
B	D	B	C	A	C	D	C	A	A
141	**142**	**143**	**144**	**145**	**146**	**147**	**148**	**149**	**150**
C	A	B	B	D	A	B	A	D	C
151	**152**	**153**	**154**	**155**	**156**	**157**	**158**	**159**	**160**
A	A	A	A	C	D	A	C	B	C
161	**162**	**163**	**164**	**165**	**166**	**167**	**168**	**169**	**170**
C	C	C	A	A	A	A	D	D	A

• • •

The Challenges of Unity in Diversity

1. ________ is a form of deviance.
A. Praise B. Falttery
C. Delinquency D. Playing cricket

2. According to Merton, ________ are most likely to select the process of innovation to deviate.
A. lower social strata B. intelligentsia
C. whitecollar workers D. bureaucrats

3. The Hindu society regards polygyny as a form of:
A. integration B. punishment
C. disequilibrium D. deviation

4. ________ consists of deviant acts before they are publicly labelled.
A. Primary deviation B. Initial deviation
C. Latent deviation D. Secondary deviation

5. Drug-addicts follow the path of ________ according to Merton.
A. ritualism B. frustration
C. retreatism D. rejectionism

6. Faulty socialization very often leads to________ .
A. deviant behaviour B. conformity
C. rebellion D. retreatism

7. Find out the incorrect match:
A. Merton — Deviant sub culture
B. Hippie Culture — Deviant sub culture
C. Walter Miller — Labelling theory
D. Deviation — Institutionalised evasion

8. Who among the following had propounded the biological theory of the origin of deviance?
A. Cesare Lombnso B. Durkheim
C. Merton D. Ogburn

9. ________ is action that is oriented to social norms and falls within the band of behaviour permitted by the norm.
A. Value B. Conformity
C. Integration D. Accommodation

10. ________ occurs when conformity to customary norms of the society does not take place.
A. Conformity B. Deviation
C. Conflict D. Disintegration

11. Any conflict in norms that apply to the same actor, inevitable results in deviation. This is called ______ .
A. Insulation B. Socialization
C. Conformity D. Integration

12. ________ refers to motivated violation.
A. Conformity B. Value-difference
C. Deviation D. Accommodation

13. Who has written the seminal essay, 'social structure and Anomie'?
A. Durkheim B. Dahrendorf
C. Albert cohen D. None of the above

14. Who has said that 'Crime is inevitable in normal aspect of social life'?
A. Merton B. Durkheim
C. Cesare Lombroso D. Marx

15. Deviant behaviour is ________ for the group in which it occurs.
A. functional B. necessary
C. motivational D. dysfunctional

16. The ________ trace the source of deviance in the nature of society.
A. Marxists
B. Functionalists
C. Evolutionists
D. Symbolic-Interactionists

17. Merton has studied 'Anomie' in ________ .
A. American society B. British society
C. Spanish society D. Chinese society

18. When an individual deviates from the norms of his sub-culture, he is ________ .
A. an individual deviant
B. a dishonest
C. to be ostracized
D. conforming to group norms

19. ________ is Institutionalise deviasion.
A. Deviation B. Rebellion
C. Retreatism D. Innovation

20. Homo-sexual culture is an example of ________ .
A. deviant sub-culture B. insulation
C. unethical behaviour D. anti-social behaviour

21. Deviation is
A. absolute B. functional
C. relative D. integrative

22. Durkheim regarded some crime as an ______ .
A. anticipation of the morality of the future
B. unstable system of society
C. unwarranted phenomenon
D. none of the above

23. ______ is the response of the group to the societal reaction.
A. Primary deviation B. Rebellion
C. Secondary deviation D. Innovation

24. Who has written the famous book 'Forty-four Juvenile thieves'?
A. Cesare Lombroso B. Ogburn
C. John Bowlby D. None of the above

25. Who has given the 'Labelling theory of deviation?
A. Howard J. Becker B. Walter Miller
C. Clifford shaw D. Albert Cohen

26. According to ______, deviance has certain positive functions to perform.
A. Durkheim B. John Bowlby
C. Merton D. Malinowski

27. Hippie Culture is an example of ______ .
A. deviant sub-culture B. western influence
C. drug-addiction D. escapism

28. Who has distinguished between 'Primary deviation and secondary deviation'?
A. Walter Miller B. Edwin Lemert
C. Becker D. HonryMckay

29. Annomic means:
A. norm lessness B. norm strictness
C. norm laxity D. norms consciousness

30. Which one of the following can be treated as a sanction against a deviant person?
A. Imprisonment
B. Punishment
C. Elevation in a social function
D. Social boycott

31. Annomic arises due to:
A. norm less confusion in norms
B. rigidity of norms
C. group harshness
D. individual strictness

32. The theory of "id", "ego" and "super-ego" about deviant behaviour was expounded by:
A. Freud B. Merton
C. Durkheim D. Max Weber

33. Which one of the following is not a sanction behind norms?
A. Religion B. Education
C. Property D. Customs

34. Deviant behaviour is linked with certain situations; which one of the following is not true?
A. Circumstances B. Attitudes
C. Interests D. Individual norms

35. Which one of the following is not covered under the category of overt force as a form of sanction?
A. Fine B. Punishment
C. Imprisonment D. Flattery

36. Which one of the following is not covered under the category of symbolic sanction?
A. Satire B. Commands
C. Threats D. Censure

37. Sanctions can be in the form of:
A. Rewards
B. Punishments
C. Neither rewards nor punishments
D. Both rewards and punishments

38. Which one of the following is not covered under the category of symbolic sanctions?
A. Prasie B. Promise
C. Fine D. Persuasion

39. Sanctions are means for controlling:
A. Human behaviour
B. Elite behaviour
C. Behaviour of the people
D. Behaviour of middle class people

40. ______ is acquired and learnt.
A. Custom B. Law
C. Habit D. Etiquette

41. ______ is more idealistic than custom.
A. Folkways B. Convention
C. Law D. Mores

42. People very often violate ______ .
A. norms B. values
C. economy D. the dictator

43. The Jains do not take any curd. This is an example of
A. custom B. folkways
C. habit D. convention

44. _____ imply a value judgement about the ______ .
A. Custom, habits B. Conventions, etiquettes
C. Mores, folkways D. Folkways, mores

45. To enforce norms, society takes resource to ______ .
A. military power B. ostracization
C. sanctions D. religion

46. ______ are related to group welfare.
A. Mores B. Customs
C. Conventions D. Habits

47. Mores are ________ in nature.
A. changeable B. rigid
C. ethical D. cultural

48. The sanctions of folkways are:
A. formal B. by the govt.
C. informal D. very rigid

49. ________ of Nazi Germany condemned democracy.
A. Mores B. Politics
C. Convention D. Oligarchy

50. What is called the repository of social heritage?
A. Fashion B. Conventions
C. Mores D. Custom

51. When fashion remains confined to an individual, it is called ________ .
A. style B. pattern
C. punkish D. symbolic

52. Sanctions in a society take the form of ________ .
A. rewards
B. punishment
C. both rewards and punishment
D. non-conformity of norms

53. Which of the following is not covered under the category of formal sanction?
A. Customs B. Mores
C. Public opinion D. Punishment

54. Which one of the following is not covered under the category of informal sanctions?
A. Physical torture B. Public opinion
C. Imprisonment D. Death

55. Which one of the following cannot be covered under the category of positive sanctions?
A. Prasie
B. Promotion
C. Medals
D. Disapproval of opponent's action

56. ________ prescribes the detailed formalities to be observed on ceremonious occasions.
A. Convention B. Etiquette
C. Fashion D. Ritual

57. ________ fade away without formal abolition, where as ________ are abolished by a recognized authority.
A. customs, laws
B. conventions, mores
C. culture, habits
D. mores, fashions

58. ________ means an acquired facility to act in a certain matter without resorting to deliberation or thought.
A. Custom B. Habit
C. Convention D. Etiquette

59. Shaking hands, eating four meals a day, etc. are examples of:
A. folkways B. customs
C. habits D. etiquette

60. The Chinese of Cochin China eat the livers of slain enemies. This is an example of ________ .
A. mores B. habits
C. necessity D. economic pursuit

61. ________ maintains soical order where as ________ facilitates individual activity.
A. custom, habits
B. folkways, fashion
C. culture, style
D. mores, fashion

62. ________ are related to the survival and growth of the group.
A. folkways B. customs
C. habits D. conventions

63. ________ change with one's social status and occupational positions but ________ do not change that way.
A. mores, folkways B. folkways, mores
C. customs, habits D. fashion, etiquette

64. The Hindus condemn polygamy. This is an example of ________ .
A. folkways B. mores
C. convention D. law

65. ________ related to the fundamental needs of the society.
A. Mores B. Folkways
C. Habits D. Fashions

66. ________ is democratic and totalitarian both at the same time.
A. Custom B. Law
C. Fashion D. Culture

67. In society unless the people live up to the expected ________ the social organization may not be effectively maintained.
A. values B. norms
C. status D. economy

68. People of certain communities squat on the ground while eating. This is an example of:
A. folkways B. custom
C. statute D. value

69. According to Karl Mannheim, money economy disintegrates ________ because they are too slow in their working.
A. economy B. fashion
C. custom D. political system

70. ________ make it right for the Eskimos to kill their old people.
A. Folkways B. Religion
C. Mores D. Law

71. ________ is spontaneous, ________ is artificial.
A. Fashion, culture B. Mores, custom
C. Custom, fashion D. Culture, habit

72. Wearing a nylon sari, putting on high heeled shoes, etc. are examples of:
A. fashion B. etiquette
C. convention D. necessity

73. According to Sumner laws are
A. transitional
B. absolute
C. permanent
D. dependent on folkways

74. Conflict in the mores is always ________.
A. transitional B. absolute
C. permanent D. dependent on folkways

75. ________ are spontaneous in origin.
A. Fashions B. Folkways
C. Statutes D. Laws

76. Law is a ________ custom is a ________
A. make, growth
B. regulation, convention
C. growth, social heritage
D. none of the above

77. ________ prescribes those forms which social relations in given situations must follow.
A. Convention B. Etiquette
C. Fashion D. Norms

78. ________ are the recognised or accepted ways of behaving in society.
A. Values B. Roles
C. Role-set D. Folkways

79. ________ identify the individual with the group.
A. Customs B. Habits
C. Mores D. Conventions

80. ________ cannot be violated without incurring severe punishment.
A. Folkways B. Mores
C. Conventions D. Fashions

81. Which of the following is a positive sanction?
A. flattery B. social ostracization
C. law D. imprisonment

82. The westerners lift hats off to show respect. This is an example of:
A. folkways B. habits
C. mores D. conventions

83. From which Latin word is the term "Mores derived ________.
A. Mos B. Mor
C. Mon D. None of the above

84. ________ are the result of deliberate design.
A. Law B. Customs
C. Etiquettes D. Habits

85. The concept of 'folkways' was introduced by ________.
A. Sumner B. Simmel
C. Mead D. Cooley

86. ________ are inherited where as ________ are learnt.
A. culture, customs B. custom, habits
C. habits, fashion D. mores, etiquettes

87. ________ need not be rational.
A. Folkways B. Mores
C. Conventions D. Law

88. MacIver has described ________ as the socially approved sequence of variation on a customary theme.
A. conventions B. fashion
C. etiquette D. culture

89. ________ are regulators of behaviour.
A. folkways B. mores
C. habits D. fashions

90. ________ is an individual phenomenon.
A. Habit B. Fashion
C. Style D. Convention

91. ________ in the "struggle for survival"?
A. Parasites B. Dropouts
C. Escapists D. Failures

92. The basis for Emile Durkheim's theory of deviance was:
A. Ritualism B. Anomie
C. Conformity D. Retreatism

93. According to Thomas and Zaniecki the "Perfect Conformist" would be the:
A. Philistine B. Bohemian
C. Retreatist D. Innovato

94. The theorist who developed labelling theory is:
A. David Meetza B. Erving Goffman
C. Howard Becker D. Robin Williams

95. The "Born loser" Merton's theory who remains honest despite a lack of success is called the:
A. Ritualist B. Rebel
C. Bohemian D. Retreatist

96. Which of the following theorists would most likely be in aggreement with the adage "Laws make criminals"?
A. W.I. Thomas B. D.B. Cooper
C. Howard Berker D. Edwin Sutherland

97. People who kill others, usually one at a time, over a long period of time are called:
A. Mass murderers B. Respectable deviants
C. Folkways violators D. Serial murders

98. Like Shakespeare, Sociologist ________ views society as a theatre stage.
A. Emile Durkheim B. Talcott Parsons
C. Robert Merton D. Erving

99. White collar crime is committed by those whom the rest of society views as:
A. Delinquents B. Respectable people
C. Murderers D. Drun kards

100. Which of the following cannot be called as the deviant individuals?
A. Delinquent B. Saint
C. Miser D. Tlippie

101. ________ is spontaneous, ________ is artificial.
A. Fashion, culture B. Mores, custom
C. Custom, fashion D. Culture, habit

102. Which of the following is not a sanction behind the norms?
A. Law
B. Religion and morality
C. Education
D. Customs and public opinion

103. Any conflict in norms that apply to the same actor, inevitable results in deviation. This is called:
A. Insulation B. Socialization
C. Conformity D. Integration

104. To a considerable extent the norms that apply to a particular actor are ranked in some order of procedure. This built-in-arrangement is called:
A. Conformity B. Deviation
C. Hierarchy D. Socialization

105. ________ is action that is oriented to socia norms and falls within the band of behaviour permitted by the norm.
A. Value B. Conformity
C. Integration D. Accommodation

106. Who of the following was a social deviant?
A. Socrates B. Christ
C. Galileo D. All of the above

107. Which of the followiing type o activities are the products of deviant behaviour?
A. Activities of cheating and malingering
B. Unfair activities
C. Immorality
D. Activities not leading to betrayal of any kind

108. The mores change more rapidly in ________ than in ________.
A. tribal society, modern society
B. simple society, complex society
C. civilization, pre-literate culture
D. none of the above

109. The basic purpose of ________ is to bring about conformity, solidarity and continuity of a particular group.
A. integration B. law
C. sanctions D. culture

110. "If the alpha and omega of human existence are to be found anywhere, it is in the folkways. For we begin with them and always come back to them." who has said this?
A. Sumner B. Kingsley Davis
C. MacIver D. Weber

111. Whether a particular behaviour is to be praised or condemned depends upon the values of:
A. economic system B. cultural norms
C. political norms D. elite standards

112. Which one of the following does not fall under the category of deviant behaviour?
A. Quarrel of a child with his father
B. Addiction of drugs
C. Prostitution
D. Vaga bondy

113. Pick out the thinker whose name is associated with Psycho-analytical theory about deviant behaviour:
A. Parsons B. Lamberso
C. Max Weber D. Freud

114. Who of the following is not associated with the subject matter of sanctions in sociology?
A. W.G. Summer B. A.R. Radcliffe
C. G. Duncan Mitchell D. Machiavelli

115. Deviant behaviour:
A. has nothing to do with legends
B. has nothing to do with myths
C. is usually opposed by legends
D. is sometimes supported by legends and myths

116. According to ________, deviance confunction as a safety value, providing a relatively harmless expression of discontent.
A. Durkheim B. Albert Cohen
C. Merton D. Dahrendorf

117. If the positive sanctions for conformity and the negative ones for deviation are weak ________ occurs.
A. rebellion B. deviation
C. conflict D. insulation

118. ________ explanations of deviance argue that particular individuals are move prone to deviance than others because of their genetic make up.

A. Sociological B. Cultural
C. Biological D. Physiological

119. Cocktail functions of these days can be categorised as:

A. deviant behaviour
B. accepted social norms
C. institutionalised evasion
D. cultural disorganisation

120. ________ refer to those rewards, objectives and ambitions which the individual is encouraged to regard as worth while ends through socialization.

A. Cultural goals B. Material goals
C. Spiritual goals D. Ethical goals

121. Clifford Shaw and Henry Mackay who formed the Chicago school in 1920s' applied ________ approach to explain deviance.

A. Sub-cultural B. Functional
C. Ecological D. Integrational

122. ________ theories argue that certain groups develop distinctive norms and values which deviate from the mainstream culture of society.

A. Sub-cultural B. Biological
C. Psychological D. Interactionist

123. ________ argues that deviance result not from Pathological Personalities but from the culture and structure of society itself.

A. Merton B. Parsons
C. Durkheim D. Tylor

124. The ________ perspective on deviance examines how and why particular individuals and groups are defined as deviant and the effects of difinition upon their future sections.

A. Interactionist B. Structural
C. Sub-cultural D. Ecological

125. People become deviant because they have largely abandoned the commonly held success goals. Merton has called this process:

A. innovation B. insulation
C. ritualism D. retreatism

126. Lemert argues that studies of deviance should focus on ________ which has major consequences for the individual's self-concept, his status in community and his future actions.

A. Secondary deviation
B. Primary deviation
C. Gratification
D. Socialization

127. When the deviants have strongly internalized both the cultural goals and the institutionalized means, yet they become unable to achieve, success: Merton calls it:

A. Retreatism B. Innovation
C. Ritualism D. Rebellion

128. Match both the groups and tick the most correct combination:

Group-1	*Group-2*
(*a*) Edwin lemert theives	1. Forty-four juvenile
(*b*) John Bowlby	2. Labelling theory
(*c*) Merton	3. Social theory and social structure
(*d*) Becker	4. Primary deviation and secondary deviation

Codes:

	(*a*)	(*b*)	(*c*)	(*d*)
A.	4	1	3	2
B.	4	3	2	1
C.	2	3	1	4
D.	1	2	3	4

129. According to Merton, ________ is a form of response which means a rejection of both the success goals and the institutionalized means and their replacement by different goals and means.

A. rebellion B. revivalism
C. retreatism D. ritualism

130. According to ________ theory of deviance, the deviant's abnormally is learned rather than genetically determined.

A. Psychological B. Cultural
C. Sociological D. Biological

131. Who defined 'Anomie', 'as a break down in the cultural structure, occuring particularly where there is an acute disjunction between cultural norms and goals and the socially structured capacities of member of the group to act in accordance with them'?

A. Durkheim B. Marx
C. Merton D. Parsons

132. To a considerable extent the norms that apply to a particular actor are ranked in some order of procedure. This built-in-arrangement is called:

A. conformity B. deviation
C. hierarchy D. socialization

133. Among the following, who has contributed much towards the development of modern theories of deviant behaviour?

A. Durkheim B. Albert Cohen
C. Merton D. John Bowlby

134. According to Merton which of the following rejects normative means of achieving success and terms to deviant means, in particular crime?
A. Retreatism B. Innovation
C. Revivalism D. Insulation

135. According to Durkheim, the function of punishment is to:
A. remove crime in the society
B. establish law and order
C. to socialize the culprit
D. to maintain the collective sentiments at their necessary level of strength.

136. The deviant is one to whom the label has successfully been applied. This is called _________ theory of deviation.
A. Sub-cultural B. Structural
C. Labelling D. Psychological

137. Who among the following, has done much work in the field of delinquency and argues that delinquency is a collective rather than an individual response?
A. John Bowlby B. Cesare Lombroso
C. Albert Cohen D. Merton

138. The structural pressures towards deviance arise from discrepancies between culturally determined goals, on the one hand, and the availability of legitimate means for attaining them on the other: whose view is this?
A. Durkheim B. Redcliffe Brown
C. Merton D. Parsons

139. Who ________ incorporated the 'cultural transmission approach' into Merton's theory of anomie and sought to provide a coherent frame work for the analysis of deviant behaviour?
A. John Bowlby B. Cesare Lombroso
C. Richard Cloward D. Albert Cohen

140. Physical theory about social deviant behaviour believes that deviant behaviour is due to:
A. certain types of defects in the body
B. social pressures and the group leaders
C. social rigidity and caste attitude
D. none of the above

141. Deviant behaviour is found more in a:
A. Slow changing society
B. rapidly changing society
C. stagnant society
D. a society which is not in touch which other societies

142. According to modern thinking a person with a deviant behaviour?
A. Should be socially boycotted
B. Should be severely punished
C. Should be treated as a lunatic
D. Should be convinced about observance of social norms

143. In our modern Indian society which one is çonsidered as a deviant behaviour?
A. favouring of child marriage
B. favouring of widow remarriage
C. propagating of inter caste marriage
D. propagating of five year plans

144. Normalessness today means a society in which:
A. there are all norms
B. many sets of clear norms
C. many sets of norms but none clearly binding upon any body
D. one set of norms clearly binding of few

145. New norms:
A. emerge from daily behaviour of the individuals
B. deliberrate assembly of the individuals
C. deviant behaviour of few individuals
D. strained family relations

146. Beginning of new norms is usually due to:
A. unhappy family relations
B. resentment against existing socio-economic system
C. deviant behaviour of few individuals
D. outdated educational system

147. Physical theory about socially deviant behaviour makes one believe that:
A. all types of bodies are equally receptive to deviant behaviour
B. no body is inclined towards deviant behaviour
C. some bodies are more exposed to deviant behaviour than the others
D. Some type of bodies will be receptive to deviant behaviour in the same manner

148. About social deviant behaviour it is believed that:
A. it has direct relationship with family atmosphere
B. family atmosphere has nothing to do with it
C. it has indirect relationship with parent-child relationship
D. none of the above statements is true

149. Deviant behaviour of one generation:
A. is usually same for the other generation as well
B. can become norm for the other generation
C. is usually norm of another generation
D. cannot become norm of another generation

150. Institutionalised evasion is one is which:
A. deviation is approved by the society
B. deviant behaviour is approved by few well placed individuals
C. deviation is approved by the group
D. deviation does not lose its moral censure

151. Psycho-analytical theory about soical behaviour makes us believe that deviant behaviour is due to:
A. inequality in physical strength
B. varying degree of socialisation
C. conflict in human personality
D. conflict in economic and political system

152. Deviant behaviour sometimes proves useful because:
A. it helps in adapting a culture to social change
B. it is indicative of threats to soical stability
C. it saves the society from cultural disorganisation
D. it helps in checking social change

153. Deviation means behaviour of a member in a society which:
A. does not conform to norms of morality
B. does not conform to social norms
C. is socially dangerous and harmful
D. injures the interests of an individual member

154. A deviant behaviour at one time:
A. will remain so at all times to come
B. in one society will always be so in all other societies
C. can be come a standard norm at another time.
D. Reward can not become a standard behaviour at any time

155. Which one of the following is not true about deviation?
A. It is seen more in a complex society.
B. It disturbs social equilibrium.
C. It is something relative and not absolute.
D. It is not subjected to rigid norms.

156. Which one of the following is not a cause of deviant behaviour? It can be:
A. the result of physical defect.
B. the result of mental defect.
C. the result of social rigidity.
D. due to involvement in social life.

157. Which one of the following is not a characteristic of deviant sub-culture?
A. It gives emotional protection to group members.
B. It helps in the reinforcement of social norms.
C. It helps in providing legal protection.
D. It emotionally discourages the members.

158. By deviant sub-culture we mean:
A. norms of a group of deviant persons.
B. it has nothing to do with normal deliquent behaviour in a society.
C. it usually constitutes an individual.
D. it has nothing to do with the group.

159. Deviation is relative to:
A. Pattern of particulat behaviour at specified time.
B. Pattern of particular behaviour at all times.
C. Pattern of particular behaviour at all places.
D. None of the above.

160. Overt force, as sanction is used:
A. By legitimate authority in the name of an individual
B. As moral force in the name of whole Society.
C. As moral force in the name of an individual.
D. By legitimate authority in the name of whole society.

161. Which one of the following is not a characteristic of deviant behaviour?
A. It disturbs social equilibrium.
B. It contravenes social norms.
C. It is a departure from usual mode of behaviour.
D. It is a departure from newly developed set of behaviour

162. Deviant behaviour is one in which:
A. there is failure to conform to norms of the society.
B. here is failure to accept newly set norms of the society.
C. failure to accept newly set norms of the elities of the society.
D. None of the above

163. Which one of the following is not true of deviant behaviour?
A. It increases when society becomes more complex.
B. It is never socially useful.
C. Certain groups are more prone than the others.
D. It is related to personal attitudes.

164. Norms of one society:
A. do not differ from those of another.
B. can differ radically from those of another society.
C. slightly differ from other societies.
D. have no relevance with the other society.

165. In our society a normal individual:
A. can never be deviant.
B. is usually deviant to a degree.
C. is always deviant to a degree.
D. is formed to became deviant by society.

166. Sanctions are needed:
A. more in primary groups.
B. more in small societies.
C. more in secondary groups and large societies.
D. none of the above.

167. Which of the following is not the purpose of sanctions?
A. These make possible prediction of behaviour.
B. These brings about social conformity.
C. These help in competition.
D. These foster integration and solidarity.

168. Sanctions help in
A. Maintaining continuity with the past.
B. Creating social in security.
C. Promoting impersonality.
D. Disassociating people from society.

169. Basic purpose of sanctions are:
A. To weaken solidarity of a strong group.
B. To strengthen solidarity of a weak group.
C. Not to disturb groups.
D. To brings solidarity in a particular group.

170. Those folk ways that persist ove-- -elatively long periods of time so as to all in a degree of formal recognition and so as to be passed down from one generation to another are called:
A. mores B. customs
C. conventions D. habits

171. A city girl who wears a skirt in a remote village is likely to be criticized. Here ________ .
A. the criticism will be effective.
B. the criticism may not be effective, for the girl does not value the criticism of the village people.
C. the girl will retaliate
D. none of the above

172. ________ refers to practices that have been repeated by a multitude of generations, practices that tend to be followed simply because they have been followed in the past.
A. Custom B. Culture
C. Fashion D. Conventions

173. According to Sutherland's theory there is little chance of a teenager's becoming an embezzler because of:
A. Anomic
B. Stigma
C. Differential association
D. Retreatism

174. The progress from aninitial deviant act to full participation in an area of deviance has been referred to by Becker as:
A. Stigmatization
B. Anomie
C. The deviant evolution
D. The deviant career

175. Sociology of deviant behaviour is concerned with:
A. A detailed study of prostitution, drug-addition and other deviant behaviours.
B. The reasons for the occurrence of such behaviours in situations where they are interdicted or disvalued by normative rules.
C. The cure of prostitution, drug-addiction and other such behaviour.
D. None of the above

176. When the participants of deviant acts are from upper classes and cannot see themselves as being deviant, the acts are usually referred to as:
A. Non-deviant B. Socially acceptable
C. White-coller crimes D. Serial crimes

177. Which of the statement is correct?
A. Definitions of deviance change over time.
B. Definitions of deviance never change.
C. Deviance is not culturally determined.
D. Deviance is non-relative.

178. The"________ man" was the perfect combination of personality characteristic in a theory devised by W.I. Thomas and Florian Znaniecki.
A. Imaginative B. Mechanistic
C. Creative D. Utopian

179. Mark the correct statement out of the following:
A. If the process of socialisation fails the individual becomes more deviant.
B. If the process of socialisation fails the individuals become less deviant.
C. The process of socialisation is not related to deviance at all
D. None of the above

180. If cultural conflicts arise:
A. The cases of deviance may also increase.
B. The cases of deviance may also decrease.
C. It has no effect on deviance.
D. The individual's tendency to conformity with norms increases.

181. "When there is a sudden change, the normative structure of the regulating norms of society is slackened, hence man does not know what is wrong and what is right, his impulses are excessive, to satisfy them he seeks anomie," is a definition given by:
A. Durkheim B. Hellace
C. Tonnies D. Weber

182. When lord Buddha renounced his crown, showed deviant behaviour. It was due to:
A. Personal factors
B. Anomie
C. The causes explained by the physical type theories.
D. Failures in the process of socialization.

183. What is institutionalised evasion?
A. The evasion of norms established by some institution?
B. The evasion which is imported by some institution.
C. When norms of evasion are recognised and sanctioned by a group it is institutionalised norm.
D. When an institution is established to train the individuals to evade some norms.

184. Which of the following is not a good point in deviant behaviour?
A. Deviant behaviour helps in creating new norms.
B. Deviant behaviour helps in adopting a culture.
C. Deviant behaviour shown by preceding generation may become the norms of the succeeding generation.
D. Deviant behaviour helps in creating reshuffle which may be useful for a group.

185. Select the correct statement out of the following:
A. Deviant behaviour helps in creating new norms.
B. All forms of deviations are socially useful.
C. Deviance from norms makes the society up to date.
D. Deviance should be encouraged to the maximum.

186. The behaviour that departs significantly from the values, norms and folkways of a society is called:
A. Determinism B. Discrimination
C. Deviance D. Dysfunction

187. A motivated tendency of an actor to behave in contravention of one or more institutionalised normative patterns is a definition of:
A. Deviant Behaviour B. Customary obedience
C. Refused-tendency D. None of the above

188. "The tendency on the part of one or more of the component factors to behaviour in such a way as to disturb the equilibrium of interactive process", is the definition given by:
A. W.G.Sumner B. Emile Durkheim
C. R.K Merton. D. Talcott Parsons

189. A group organized on the basis of the common ancestry of its members is called:
A. Primary group B. Secondary group
C. In-group D. Descent group

190. Which of the following statements is correct?
A. Deviance is in contradiction to social norms.
B. Deviance is the negation of the social behaviour and decency.
C. Deviance means the performance of activities which are not approved by the society.
D. All of the above.

191. Mark the correct statement out of the following:
A. Deviation is absolute
B. Deviation is relative
C. Deviation is less absolute and more relative.
D. Deviation is relative and not absolute.

192. Mark the correct statement out of the following:
A. When the society changes norms also change.
B. When norms change society is bound to change.
C. Change in society has nothing to do with the change in norms.
D. None of the above.

193. If a person is deviant in certain activities:
A. He will be deviant in all other activities.
B. He will not be deviant in all other activities.
C. He will be hold as an anti-social element.
D. He will become a saint.

194. A person who is completely deviant:
A. May live in society without worries.
B. May be a very spirited individual.
C. May find it difficult to live in society.
D. May 'run the show of life'.

195. Mark the correct statement out of the following:
A. Nearly everyone is deviant in society.
B. Leaders are not deviant people.
C. Thinkers are never deviant in the absolute sense of the world.
D. Deviance does not cause and damage to the society.

196. Who held the view that group size, homo-geneity and segregation affect the group behaviour?
A. Peter M. Blau B. Kingsley Davis
C. Robert K. Merton D. G.C. Homans

197. Public opinion as a means of social control is:
A. A weak sanction.
B. An uncertain sanction, since no one can be sure of its unified stand.
C. Useless since nobody is ready to follow it.
D. Has no relation with social control.

198. It is believed that conformity with the customs is:
A. An automatic process.
B. An indifferently imposed process.
C. An artificial process in the sense that people follow customs to show off.
D. With some conceivable amout of deviation.

199. Customs are those sanctions:
A. Which are relegated by a single authority.
B. Which are regulated by the eldest person in the group.
C. Which are simply accepted by the members of the society.
D. Which are regulated by law.

200. According to Durkheim all — begins with some form of deviance:
A. revolution
B. social change
C. social solidarity
D. collective representation

201. Norms are of several types. Which one of the following is not the type of social norms?
A. formal B. informal
C. persuasive D. positive

202. What are cultural standards that indicate the general good deemed desirable for organized social life?
A. Norms B. Goal pattern
C. Values D. Beliefs

203. Social values indicate:
A. group standards B. institutional standards
C. community standards D. cultural standards

204. Social values are:
A. abstract sentiments B. positive ideals
C. concrete ideals D. concrete sentiments

205. Norms can be placed under the category of:
A. idealism B. liberalism
C. neutralism D. realism

206. ________ is widely considered to be a desirable end in itself.
A. culture B. goal
C. value D. belief

207. Money, power and prestige are the instances of ________.
A. Social values B. Cultural values
C. Individual values D. Group values

208. ________ includes folkways, mores and institutional ways of determining behaviour.
A. Values B. Custom
C. Norms D. Culture

209. "Equality of opportunity" is an example of:
A. value B. goal
C. norm D. right

210. Norms regulate human behaviour through:
A. informal controls
B. social force
C. physical force
D. well established standards

211. The ethos of any culture are a reflection of its basic:
A. values B. norms
C. standards D. beliefs

212. Sanctions about social norms are needed comparatively more in groups which are in nature:
A. spatial B. primary
C. secondary D. temporary

213. ________ incorporate value judgements.
A. values B. norms
C. custom D. mores

214. ________ provide the ultimate meaning and legitimacy for social arrangements and social behaviour.
A. culture B. custom
C. norms D. values

215. In a society conflict to norms occurs when:
A. There is deep roted class struggle
B. Some norms are considered more important than other
C. There is no interpretation of norms
D. Groups tend to conform to different norms

216. We conform to norms for ________ .
A. indoctrination
B. material benefits
C. it is a fundamental duty
D. None of the above

217. ________ are those norms that pervade the entire society.
A. communal norms B. operative norms
C. associational norms D. social norms

218. ________ is always qualified in view of the socially defined situation in which they apply.
A. Conformity to norms B. Regulation of norms
C. Conflict in norms D. Adesired norms

219. The ________ in social values result in ________ social structures and patterns of expected behaviour.
A. equality, different B. differences, divergent
C. mutuality, weird D. differences, equal

220. Conformity to norms depends largely upon ________ as to just what the norm demands.
A. agreement B. regulation
C. deviation D. None of the above

221. Conformity to norms will differ according to the varying ________ different persons in the group.
A. money power of
B. role of
C. pressures exerted upon
D. legal status of

222. The more ________ the group, the more uniform the attitudes and behaviour of its members and the more conformity to the norms.
A. cohesive B. solid
C. flexible D. powerful

223. Utility of norms is that these help in regulating:
A. inter-social relations
B. observing social controls
C. neighbourly relations
D. ultra social relations

224. ________ are standards of group behaviour.
A. Pattern B. Values
C. role D. none of the above

225. There are certain norms that prevail only in certain groups. They are called ________ .
A. Communal norms B. regulative norms
C. associational norms D. selected norms

226. Without ________, behaviour would be unpredictable.
A. norms B. socialization
C. values D. goals

227. ________ refers to all more or less agree upon and expected behaviour.
A. Values B. Pattern
C. Norms D. Custom

228. Norms are ________ .
A. prescriptive
B. prohibitive
C. proscriptive
D. both prescriptive and proscriptive

229. Some norms are so important that they persist inspite of their ________ .
A. regulation
B. deviation
C. weak enforcement
D. approval by the groups

230. Norms are related to the ________ world.
A. factual B. cultural
C. primitive D. None of the above

231. Some groups are able to impose severe sanctions upon its members because the members have no:
A. power B. alternatives
C. status D. prestige

232. In the absence of social norms there will be no:
A. community B. marriage
C. associatioin D. society

233. ________ impinge directly upon a person's self conception.
A. Values B. Customs
C. Norms D. Folkways

234. It is a mistake to suppose that ________ is essential to society.
A. absolute fidelity to norms
B. deviation from norms
C. no proscriptive norms
D. no operative norms

235. A normless society is an ________ .
A. impossibility B. insulation
C. inequality D. isolation

236. Which one of the following is not a cause for violation of social norms?
A. Society may not be keen about their observance
B. Some norms are self-contradictory
C. Some norms are more important than the others
D. People have sufficient wealth to control the society, if norms are violated

237. Sociologists are interested mainly in ________ norms, that is norms that are sanctioned in such a way that violators suffer penalties in the group.
A. ideal B. cultural
C. social D. operative

238. A student who sees a friend cheating in an examination must choose between ________ .
A. conflicting norms
B. communal norm and associational norm
C. ethical norms and social norm
D. norms and values

239. Which of the following is a belief system?
A. Magic B. Tolemism
C. Fetishism D. All of these

240. Which among the following is an informal method of social control?
A. Belief B. Coercion
C. Law D. Education

241. What among the following invests an image, idea, myth or a statement with the super natural attributes?
A. Beauty B. Truth
C. Character D. Faith

242. Which of the following belief system hold that evil is the result to unrealistic desire?
A. Confucianism B. Buddhism
C. Judaism D. Islam

243. Which among the following is a part of the Hindu belief system?
A. Karma and sanskara
B. Transmigration of soul
C. Endless wheels of incarnations
D. All of these

244. Beliefs are:
A. Primitive knowledge
B. Tested emperical knowledge
C. Neither true nor false
D. Practical knowledge

245. Which one of the following is not true of social norms? These help in:
A. Maintaining social cohesion
B. Maintaining social controls
C. Preserving social structure
D. Strengthening spatial groups

246. Social norms are normally responsible for:
A. bringing discontentment in society
B. social disintegration
C. unhealthy competition
D. social integration

247. Which among the following is a part of catholic belief system?
A. concept of Trinity
B. no asceticism, no mysticism
C. salvation of mankind at the end of the world after the coming of the Messiah
D. shadowy gods

248. Prayer and meditation are:
A. man's pleasure
B. man's confession
C. the ideal propaganda
D. the solemn vaneer of a crooked man

249. One of the methods of punishment for a person who violates social norms is that:
A. he is not-cooperated with by others
B. his honour is taken away
C. his prestige is lowered
D. his wealth is snatched

250. In which of the following lies the strength of the belief system?
A. Rituals
B. Rites
C. Ceremonies
D. Confession to the system

251. Which among the following indicates a correct expression of faith?
A. Truth is god
B. God is truth
C. Beauty is truth
D. One's confession to one's belief

252. Mark among the following what you think is a correct meaning of belief:
A. Faith in the supreme
B. Belief in truth
C. The things believed
D. Assent of mind to the truth of a declaration

253. Belief system is a fact of life. Which among the following has contributed to its development?
A. The feeling of fear
B. The desire to under stand the supernatural
C. Man's experiment with truth
D. All of these

254. Which among the following is a part of the Buddhist belief system?
A. Noble Eightfold Path
B. Monastic mysticism
C. Reincarnation
D. All of these

255. With out ________ behaviour would be unpredicable.
A. norms B. socialization
C. values D. goals

256. Man's dependence on society is derived from ________.
A. innate responses to mechanical stimuli
B. values
C. norms
D. learned responses to meaningful stimuli

257. Social values can be most effectively promoted with the help of:
A. Pressure groups B. Trade unions
C. Socialisation D. Fear of the superior

258. Basic values reflect:
A. ethos of a culture
B. fundamentals of behaviour
C. basis of institutions
D. None of the above

259. The degree of ________ may be in part a function of the extent to which norms of other group are in congruous with them.
A. regulation B. integration
C. cohesion D. conformity to norm

260. Who believed that strict adherence to the norms of society it self produces a type of deviance?
A. Robert K. Merton B. Robin M. Williams
C. Durkheim D. MacIver

261. Belief system is concerned with:
A. only religion B. only politics
C. only culture D. all aspects of social life

262. Which among the following has influenced man's faith and belief most?
A. the habitats
B. levels of culture achieved
C. the expanding experience
D. the in-born feeling

263. Belief system in every religious system:
A. has some symbolic expressions
B. has nothing to do with symbols
C. adopts symbols when necessary
D. discards symbols at will

264. Institutional belief system is one which is:
A. adopted by only one institution
B. adopted by few institutions
C. adopted by a particular society
D. discarded by all institutions

265. Institutional belief system:
A. cannot at all be changed
B. can be changed easily
C. can be changed rarely
D. can be changed only when few powerful in the society like that

266. Which of the following is true of the Christian belief system?
A. it believes in worship in the open
B. it believes in the unity of God
C. it believes in the worship of God
D. it believes in Karma theory

267. Belief system of the individual:
A. must be the same as that of the society
B. must be opposite of the society
C. can be different from that of the society
D. none of the above is true

268. Belief system in a society:
A. never creates conflicts
B. always creates conflicts
C. only encourages conflicts
D. partly creates as well as partly settles conflicts

269. In the Hindu belief system transmigration of soul means:
A. after death soul also dies
B. after death soul remains in the same body
C. after death it gets into another body.
D. after death it gets destroyed.

270. In the Hindu belief System,Salvation means:
A. Temporary relief from life and death circle.
B. Permanent relief from life and death circle.
C. Struggle for better life.
D. Struggle for becoming human beings again.

271. Social change and belief System:
A. are loosely linked with each other.
B. are closely linked with each other.
C. are not linked with each other.
D. are indirectly linked with each other.

272. Religious belief system are usually based on:
A. materialistic approaches.
B. are closely linked with each other.
C. moral approaches to the problems.
D. None of the above.

273. When religious belief system come in conflict with each other, the result is:
A. Violent religious out bursts.
B. Changes in trade system.
C. Changes in marriage system.
D. Changes in materialistic outlook.

274. Mark out the incorrect statement:
A. Beliefs do exist outside the sphere of institutional religion
B. Beliefs in one form or the other exist in all types of societies
C. Beliefs are informal means of social control
D. Beliefs do not exist outside the sphere of institutional religion

275. Social norms refer to:
A. all types of behaviour.
B. the most frequently observed behaviour in a society.
C. right type of behaviour.
D. those Standards or rules which specify appropriate and inappropriate behaviour.

276. Norms is:
A. actual behaviour.
B. a culturally shared definition of desirable behaviour.
C. behaviour desired by majority of the individuals
D. Standards of behaviour.

277. Belief system in all the societies:
A. is imposed on the people by the rulers.
B. is imposed on the people by the feudal lords.
C. develops gradually and slowly.
D. is exchanged between the societies.

278. Belief system is usually:
A. linked with super natural power.
B. not linked with super natural power.
C. disassociated from the super natural power.
D. none of the above is true

279. In belief system the Hindus:
A. believe in Karma theory.
B. do not believe in Karma theory.
C. believe but only partially in Karma theory.
D. completely disown Karma theory.

280. In the religious belief system of the Hindus which of the following is not true?
A. it believes in transmigration of the Soul.
B. it believes in Karma theory.
C. it believes in Salvation.
D. it does not believe in the theory of transmigration of Soul.

281. Religious belief System:
A. does not create frustrations at all.
B. always create frustrations.
C. at times creates frustrations.
D. has nothing to do with frustration.

282. In religious belief system which one of the following is not true about Muslim system:

A. it believes in one supreme God.
B. it believes in the theory of held and heaven.
C. it believes in truth and falsehood.
D. it believes in transmigration of Soul.

283. Which one of the following cannot be the cause of frustration in the belief system?
A. untimely death of a relation.
B. heavy loss of property.
C. failure in meeting a group of friends.
D. more reward for less work.

284. Which of the following punishments cannot be awarded to the violators of a norm?
A. withdrawal of friendly and co-operative interaction by others.
B. loss of honour and prestige.
C. ridicule and fines.
D. expulsion from the Society.

285. Those member who have important satisfactions out side the group will frequently ________ from the norms than those who do not have such satisfactions.
A. deviate B. disintegrate
C. integrate D. None of the above.

286. Which one of the following is not true about norms?
A. these promote value judgements.
B. these encourage value free judgements.
C. these have nothing to do with judgements.
D. these do not deal with ideal judgements.

287. Norms in sociology mean:
A. Standardisation of social behaviour.
B. normally accepted mode of behaviour.
C. high ideals of society.
D. regulating human desire to compete with the other.

288. ________ arise in the areas of behaviour where members have become more dependent for the satisfaction of their needs.
A. Normative controls
B. Regulation
C. Folkways
D. Mores.

289. Social norms are most effectively observed when:
A. there is effective sanction behind them.
B. group is integrated.
C. group is homogeneous.
D. there is ideal character of norms.

290. By and large deviation to norms occurs when:
A. Society is not yet mature.
B. members are not prepared to accept norms.
C. members are unwilling to follow norms.
D. few individuals control the whole Society.

291. The extent to which a group can secure conformity to its norms depends on the________ .
A. Cohesiveness of the group.
B. group behaviour.
C. group status.
D. monetary power of the group.

292. Conformity to norms in a society can be maintained when:
A. norms all over are uniform.
B. norms of one society are accepted by the others.
C. norms are flexible.
D. norms are absolute.

293. ________ is compelled by norms to a greater extent than one's ________ .
A. Private behaviour, public behaviour.
B. Role, status.
C. Public behaviour, Private behaviour.
D. Value, role.

294. Which of the following is not a reason for which individuals conform to norms?
A. habituation
B. indoctrination
C. group identification
D. scope to rise in the social ladder

295. The degree of ________ may be in part a function of the extent to which norms of other groups are congruous with them.
A. regulation
B. integration
C. cohesion
D. conformity to norms.

296. There is no uniformity in the conformity of norms on the part of individuals because:
A. Pattern of socialisation is not the same.
B. of heredity differences.
C. of differences in income.
D. individuals have different capacities to resist pressures.

297. Sometimes social norms are not obeyed because the violator:
A. Knows that he will not be ridiculed.
B. Wants to become a popular figure.
C. Knows that society is not keen to get those observed.
D. is sure that no body can do him any harm.

298. Conformity to norms in a society can be maintained when these are:
A. flexible but applied rigidly.
B. rigid and applied rigidly.
C. flexible and applied with flexibly.
D. based on religion.

299. Conflict in the norms happens when:
A. The members of a group clash with each other for the exact interpretation of a norm
B. The individuals of the different group of different norms interact with each other
C. The norms are different for different groups
D. There is class struggle in the society only

300. Social values are important because these:
A. give legitimacy to social behaviour.
B. promote group harmonies.
C. promote happy life.
D. do not touch social arrangements.

301. Which one of the following is not correct about norms?
A. these are formed for all situations
B. these are not formed for all situations.
C. scope of norms varies from one group to the other.
D. group norms have relevance to purpose.

302. Social values are organised:
A. out side the personality of the individuals.
B. within the personality of the individuals.
C. neither outside nor within the personality of the individuals.
D. both within and out side the personality of the individuals.

303. Second and Buckman feel that norms is a standard of behavioural expectation:
A. of society as a whole.
B. not shared by group members.
C. shared by group members.
D. pointed out by outsiders.

304. Brown and Sitznick are of the view that the norms:
A. have nothing to do with behaviour.
B. are blue prints of behaviour.
C. are unrelated to alternate ways.
D. none of the above is true.

305. Ideal norms are those which each society sets:
A. in the hope that these will be obeyed.
B. hoping that these may or may not be obeyed.
C. knowing well that these will not be obeyed.
D. that only few selected will obey these.

306. Deviation from norms means:
A. The phenomenon which explains that a members behaviour is not giving away the behaviour expected from them
B. Unwillingness of the members to follow certain norms
C. Repulsion of the norms from the behaviour of a member
D. Member's incapability to follow certain norms

307. Which one of the following is the characteristic of social norms:
A. these have relevance to sex and status.
B. these are formed for all situations.
C. their scope does not vary from group to group.
D. norms operative in one system can be applied to another system.

308. Which one of the following is not true about norms?
A. these are standards of social behaviour.
B. these are accepted to avoid disintegration.
C. these uphold individuals freedom.
D. these bring diffusion in society.

309. Which one of the following does not contribute in the observance of social norms?
A. fear of public ridicule.
B. fear of going against public opinion.
C. fear of loss of wealth.
D. fear of violation of customs.

310. Social values primarily concern themselves with:
A. organised social life as a whole.
B. disorganised social life.
C. organised social groups.
D. organised institutions.

311. Most effective way of making the group to observe social norms is:
A. to give rewards to the observers.
B. to impose fines on the violators.
C. to create awareness in the minds of the people.
D. to educate people about their necessity.

312. Practical norms are those, about which society hopes that:
A. these may or may not be accepted.
B. only few will accept these.
C. these will be accepted by all in the society.
D. these are the cherished goals.

313. Which of the following statements is true in the case of norms?
A. these are based on value judgements.
B. these are value neutral.
C. these cannot be standardised.
D. these have no links with expected standards.

314. Which of the following is characterised as negative sanction about social norms?
A. imposition by conscience.
B. imposition by denial of incentive.
C. imposition by force.
D. imposition by a group of people.

315. Positive sanctions about social norms are those which are:
A. imposed by the elite of the society.
B. imposed by the political party in power.

C. Which imposed by some legal authority.
D. Which imposed by the conscience of the individual.

316. As far as the individual attitudes are concerned:
A. they are never influenced by the norms.
B. they are always influenced by the norms.
C. the norms are always affected by the individual's influence.
D. they have nothing to do with norms.

317. Which among the following is not a part of Islamic belief system?
A. Salvation of mankind at the end of the world, after the coming of the Messiah.
B. A day of judgement is to come.
C. One supramundane God, called Allah.
D. Concept of hell and heaven.

318. Existence of a society without norms:
A. is impossible
B. is possible only when they are of monolithici structure.
C. is possible only when people are un educated.
D. is possible only when the people interact with each other.

319. The estate system is a feature of:
A. Post-Industrial European Society
B. Feudal European Society
C. Ancient Indian Society
D. Ancient Egyption Society

320. Who has given the concept 'hierarchy' in the context of caste stratification?
A. T.N. Madan B. S.C. Dube
C. D.F. Pocock D. Luis Dumont

ANSWERS

1	2	3	4	5	6	7	8	9	10
C	A	D	A	C	A	C	A	B	B
11	**12**	**13**	**14**	**15**	**16**	**17**	**18**	**19**	**20**
A	C	D	B	D	B	A	A	A	A
21	**22**	**23**	**24**	**25**	**26**	**27**	**28**	**29**	**30**
C	A	C	C	A	A	A	B	A	C
31	**32**	**33**	**34**	**35**	**36**	**37**	**38**	**39**	**40**
A	A	C	D	D	C	D	C	A	C
41	**42**	**43**	**44**	**45**	**46**	**47**	**48**	**49**	**50**
C	A	B	C	C	A	A	C	A	D
51	**52**	**53**	**54**	**55**	**56**	**57**	**58**	**59**	**60**
A	C	D	B	D	B	A	B	A	A
61	**62**	**63**	**64**	**65**	**66**	**67**	**68**	**69**	**70**
A	B	B	B	A	A	B	A	C	C
71	**72**	**73**	**74**	**75**	**76**	**77**	**78**	**79**	**80**
C	A	C	A	B	B	A	D	C	B
81	**82**	**83**	**84**	**85**	**86**	**87**	**88**	**89**	**90**
A	C	A	A	A	B	B	B	B	A
91	**92**	**93**	**94**	**95**	**96**	**97**	**98**	**99**	**100**
B	B	A	C	A	C	D	D	B	C
101	**102**	**103**	**104**	**105**	**106**	**107**	**108**	**109**	**110**
C	C	D	C	B	D	D	C	C	B
111	**112**	**113**	**114**	**115**	**116**	**117**	**118**	**119**	**120**
B	A	D	D	D	B	B	D	C	A
121	**122**	**123**	**124**	**125**	**126**	**127**	**128**	**129**	**130**
C	A	A	A	C	A	A	A	A	A
131	**132**	**133**	**134**	**135**	**136**	**137**	**138**	**139**	**140**
C	C	C	B	D	C	C	C	C	B

141	**142**	**143**	**144**	**145**	**146**	**147**	**148**	**149**	**150**
B	D	A	C	A	C	C	C	B	C
151	**152**	**153**	**154**	**155**	**156**	**157**	**158**	**159**	**160**
C	A	B	C	D	D	D	A	A	D
161	**162**	**163**	**164**	**165**	**166**	**167**	**168**	**169**	**170**
D	A	B	C	B	C	C	A	D	B
171	**172**	**173**	**174**	**175**	**176**	**177**	**178**	**179**	**180**
B	A	C	D	B	C	A	C	A	A
181	**182**	**183**	**184**	**185**	**186**	**187**	**188**	**189**	**190**
A	A	C	D	A	C	A	D	D	D
191	**192**	**193**	**194**	**195**	**196**	**197**	**198**	**199**	**200**
D	A	B	C	A	D	B	A	C	B
201	**202**	**203**	**204**	**205**	**206**	**207**	**208**	**209**	**210**
C	C	A	A	D	C	C	C	A	D
211	**212**	**213**	**214**	**215**	**216**	**217**	**218**	**219**	**220**
A	C	B	D	D	A	A	A	B	A
221	**222**	**223**	**224**	**225**	**226**	**227**	**228**	**229**	**230**
C	A	B	D	C	A	C	D	B	A
231	**232**	**233**	**234**	**235**	**236**	**237**	**238**	**239**	**240**
B	D	C	A	A	D	D	A	D	B
241	**242**	**243**	**244**	**245**	**246**	**247**	**248**	**249**	**250**
D	D	D	A	D	D	D	D	A	A
251	**252**	**253**	**254**	**255**	**256**	**257**	**258**	**259**	**260**
D	D	D	D	A	D	C	A	D	B
261	**262**	**263**	**264**	**265**	**266**	**267**	**268**	**269**	**270**
D	D	A	C	C	D	C	D	C	B
271	**272**	**273**	**274**	**275**	**276**	**277**	**278**	**279**	**280**
B	C	A	D	C	A	C	A	A	D
281	**282**	**283**	**284**	**285**	**286**	**287**	**288**	**289**	**290**
C	D	C	C	A	B	B	A	D	C
291	**292**	**293**	**294**	**295**	**296**	**297**	**298**	**299**	**300**
A	C	C	D	D	D	C	C	C	A
301	**302**	**303**	**304**	**305**	**306**	**307**	**308**	**309**	**310**
A	B	C	B	A	B	A	C	C	A
311	**312**	**313**	**314**	**315**	**316**	**317**	**318**	**319**	**320**
D	C	A	C	D	B	A	A	B	D

●●●

Process of Social Change in India

1. Find the odd man out:
   A. Hegel B. Hobbes
   C. Dahrendorf D. Durkheim

2. The essence of communicative interaction is called ________.
   A. integration B. insulation
   C. isolation D. alienation

3. Which of the following is not included as a type of conflict?
   A. War B. Feud
   C. Litigation D. Collective bargaining

4. If individuals perform a task jointly, it is called:
   A. Primary cooperation
   B. Direct cooperation
   C. Secondary cooperation
   D. Indirect cooperation

5. In its extreme form competition results in:
   A. disorganisation B. conflict
   C. anarchy D. totalitarianism

6. Accommodation is the natural result of:
   A. Competition B. Integration
   C. Isolation D. None of the above

7. ________ is an expression of social equilibrium.
   A. Competition B. Integration
   C. Accommodation D. Conflict

8. ________ is a Conscious action.
   A. Conflict B. Competition
   C. Value D. Organic isolation

9. ________ creates provisions for integration in society.
   A. Dishonesty
   B. Material desires
   C. Cultural heterogenity
   D. Dictatorship

10. Cooperation means working together for achieving:
    A. individual ends B. collective ends
    C. national ends D. ends of family feuds

11. Which of the following is not contained in Robert E. Park's Social classification?
    A. Conflict B. Cooperation
    C. Competition D. Accommodation

12. Adjustment to a new social milieu, i.e. new folkways, mores, and institutions is called:
    A. adaptation B. accommodation
    C. naturalisation D. integration

13. Competition results in:
    A. emotional adjustment B. emotional disturbance
    C. physical pains D. mental satisfaction.

14. War is a type of conflict which implies:
    A. antagonistic impulse in man
    B. antagonistic impulse among the groups
    C. conflict of ideals
    D. conflict to establish truthfulness

15. ________ always implies inhibition of certain egocentred drives.
    A. co-operation B. conflict
    C. competition D. accommodation

16. ________ is marked by both love and hatred.
    A. accommodation B. conflict
    C. integration D. acculturation

17. Which one of the following is not one of the kinds of social Contacts?
    A. positive and negative
    B. temporary and permanent
    C. formal and informal
    D. personal and impersonal

18. When the conflicting parties try to adjust to each other it is called:
    A. surrender B. adjustment
    C. accommodation D. assimilation.

19. ________ is an intermittent process, ________ is a continuous process.
    A. Conflict, Competition
    B. Competition, conflict
    C. Conflict, accommodation
    D. Integration, isolation

20. Racial riot is an instance of:
    A. Latent Conflict B. Corporate conflict
    C. Personal conflict D. Indirect conflict.

21. As pointed out by Giddings, _____ tends to endanger conflicts inimical to group cohesion.
    A. competition B. struggle
    C. isolation D. accommodation.

22. The process of assimilation, as pointed out by _____, involves both denationalisation and renationalisation.
A. MacIver B. Kingsley Davi's
C. Merton D. Fair child

23. ________ is a Conflict theorist.
A. Durkheim B. Merton
C. Mead D. Ralph Dahrendorf

24. As a process, Conflict is ________ of cooperation.
A. mutual B. antithesis
C. synthesis D. supportive

25. ________ is a form of interaction without contact.
A. Conflict B. Competition
C. Accommodation D. Assimilation

26. Conflicts are characterised as modified form of:
A. competition B. struggle
C. cooperation D. resistance

27. ________ helps in the assignment of individuals to proper places in Society.
A. Conflict B. Competition
C. Accommodation D. Integration

28. Competition is an ________ .
A. unusual activity B. unethical activity
C. impersonal struggle D. unwanted action

29. ________ refers to an identity of interests between the individual and the group.
A. Primary co-operation
B. Indirect co-operation
C. Secondary co-operation
D. Formal co-operation

30. Accommodation is a process which obviously follows:
A. assimilation B. conflict
C. acculturation D. adaptation

31. In accommodation, acclimatization change is characterised by:
A. psychology B. physiology
C. religion D. caste

32. In naturalisation, accommodation change is known as:
A. cultural B. physiological
C. psychological D. political

33. The process under which one culture merges it self with the other is called:
A. adaptation B. accommodation
C. assimilation D. acculturation

34. In economics competition is not primarily covered under:
A. Production B. Distribution
C. Consumption D. Name and fame

35. The process of assimilation on the whole is called:
A. Evolutionary
B. Revolutionary
C. Partly evolutionary and partly revolu-tionary
D. Biological

36. 'Closely woven' type of integration is common in:
A. Communistic Societies
B. Theocracies
C. Bureaucracies
D. Liberal democracies

37. Stage through which two cultures pass before they get completely merged is known as:
A. Adaptation B. Accommodation
C. Assimilation D. Acculturation

38. Acculturation means:
A. Cultural modification B. Cultural lag
C. Cultural absorption D. Cultural revolution

39. Which one of the following is true about accommodation but not of assimilation?
A. The process can be sudden
B. It must pass through stages
C. It is a slow process
D. It is not deliberate

40. In our modern society isolation is:
A. hypothetical thinking B. a solid reality
C. practical proposition D. only organic

41. The type of isolation in which a criminal is kept isolated is known as:
A. organic B. spatial
C. social D. cultural

42. Which one of the following is not covered under the category of organic isolation?
A. Limping B. Privacy
C. Dumbness D. Deafness

43. Social value of isolation is:
A. Positive
B. Negative
C. Both positive and negative
D. Neither positive nor negative

44. Who of the following will cherish isolation?
A. A business manager B. An office goer
C. A saint D. An engineer

45. Which among the following involves Competition?
A. Wrestling match
B. Football match between Mohan Bagan and Modammedan sporting club.
C. A tribal archery Competition
D. Candidates taking the IAS examination

46. When a conflict arises due to the claim of one party on the basis of the factors objective in nature it is called:
A. Conflict of impersonal ideas
B. Conflict of litigation
C. Personal conflict
D. Political conflict

47. Which of the following types of conflict was not suggested by Gillin and Gillin?
A. Personal conflict B. Racial conflict
C. Class conflict D. Intra-group conflict

48. Which one of the under mentioned conflicts was suggested by Gillin and Gillin?
A. International conflict B. Ideal conflict
C. Abnormal conflict D. Non-political conflict

49. If a conflict arises between two individuals belonging to the same group, it is called:
A. Personal conflict
B. Intra-group conflict
C. Fructra-structure conflict
D. Negative conflict.

50. If a conflict arises due to the feeling of superiority on the basis of race, it is termed as:
A. Racial conflict B. Anti-racial conflict
C. Non-racial conflict D. Inter-racial conflict

51. "There is no possibility of having a group in front of any feelings of conflict. This was held by:
A. Simmel B. Gumplowicz
C. Mack and Young D. Thomas Green

52. At which of the following levels competition may not be found:
A. Cultural
B. Economic and Social
C. Political and Social
D. Geographic and Demographic

53. If the competition is unfair, it may lead to:
A. Disintegration B. Integration
C. Supplementation D. Co-ordination

54. Which of the following is not a type of cooperation?
A. Armoury co-operation
B. Indirect co-operation
C. Primary co-operation
D. Tertiary co-operation

55. If the individuals co-operate with each other or do something together it is called:
A. Primary co-operation
B. Direct co-operation
C. Indirect co-operation
D. Secondary co-operation

56. The co-operation which is found among members of a family is called:
A. Primary co-operation
B. Secondary co-operation
C. Tertiary co-operation
D. All of the above

57. The co-operation which is found in group like Church is called:
A. Secondary co-operation
B. Primary co-operation
C. Religious co-operation
D. Direct co-operation

58. If the contacts between the groups is primary in its nature, the process of assimilation?
A. will be rapid
B. will slow down
C. will not be affected at all
D. nothing can be said

59. Which of the following factors retard the process of assimilation?
A. Equal economic opportunity
B. Toleration
C. Sympathetic attitude of the dominating group
D. Restrictions on the expansion of the dominant culture

60. Mark the correct statement out of the following:
A. Conflict is anti-thesis of co-operation.
B. Conflict is not an anti-thesis of co-operation.
C. Conflict has no relation with co-operation.
D. All of the above

61. Which of the following is a correct statement?
A. Conflict is deliberate
B. Conflict is not international
C. Conflict is passive
D. Conflict is in contradiction to assimilation

62. According to Darwin the cause of conflict is:
A. The struggle of existence and the survival of the fittest
B. Biological disintegration
C. Degration of the members from the biological standard
D. Scarcity of the sources of subsistence

63. Which one of the following mentioned factors is not a cause of conflict?
A. Difference between individuals
B. Differences in the culture of the individuals
C. Clash of interests
D. Loss of the feelings of out smarting the opponent among the competing groups of individuals

64. Which of the following types of conflict has not been suggested by Simmel?
A. War
B. Racial conflict
C. Conflict of litigation
D. Conflict of ideas which are impersonal

65. The intra-group war arising due to the injustice of one group over another is called:
A. War B. Racial war
C. Group conflict D. Feud

66. When the groups show solidarity, it is called:
A. Integration B. Fusion
C. Diffusion D. Erosion

67. Assimilation is essentially:
A. Political process B. Historical process
C. Social process D. Psychological process

68. Immigrants in all societies are at first:
A. Avoided B. Accommodated
C. Accepted D. Assimilated

69. Integration of a community is:
A. Acceptance B. Assimilation
C. Accommodation D. A matter of adjustment

70. In which of the following the principle of co-operation is not involved?
A. Co-operative society
B. United Nations
C. Family planning
D. 'A' intending to organise opposition against the cricket club

71. Which among the following is based on direct co-operation?
A. Family B. Government
C. Parliament D. General Assembly

72. The stage in which one cultural group borrows some cultural elements from another cultural group and which adds to its leading to the modification of its own culture is called:
A. Cultural-bond B. Modification
C. Adoption D. Acculturation

73. Which among the following does not involve secondary co-operation?
A. Religious organization
B. Industry
C. Trade union
D. Teacher-student relations

74. Which among the following involves secondary co-operation?
A. Trade union
B. Countries which joined to defeat Hitler in the second world war
C. The referee, players and spectators on the play ground
D. All the above

75. If in social set up, people are working against each other unrestrained by any mutually accepted norms, they are said to have:
A. Conflict B. Competition
C. Contravention D. None of the above

76. When there are feelings of conflict which have not found proper expression, the conflict is called:
A. social conflict B. personal conflict
C. caste conflict D. latent conflict

77. When conflict has actually occured and one of the two parties is ready to take advantage, it is called:
A. latent conflict B. class conflict
C. overt conflict D. race conflict

78. ________ generally means working together in the pursuit of common interest.
A. Co-operation B. Integration
C. Unity D. Solidarity

79. Which one of the following is not covered under the category of corporate conflicts?
A. Race riots B. Family feuds
C. Communal riots D. Religious persecutions

80. Under which of the following categories can conflict between the rich and the poor be placed?
A. Caste conflict B. Political conflict
C. Class conflict D. Personal conflict

81. ________ means isolation caused by certain organic defects of the individual, such as deafness or blindness.
A. Spatial isolation B. Organic isolation
C. Physical isolation D. Individual isolation

82. ________ is the harmonizing process whereby the various structural components of society are properly organized.
A. Assimilation B. Integration
C. Co-operation D. Accommodation

83. When carpenters, plumbers and masons co-operate with each other to build a house, the type of co-operation is ________ .
A. indirect B. direct
C. profit oriented D. contractual

84. Who labelled the condition where the continuity of society has broken down to some degree as a 'strain towards anomie?
A. Merton
B. MacIver
C. Durkhein
D. Kingsley Davis

85. ________ refers to an enforced deviation of contacts as for criminals, when somebody is banished from the community or put to solitary imprisonment.
A. Spatial isolation B. Isolation
C. Organic isolation D. Individual isolation

86. ________ is permanent, ________ is non-permanent.
A. Assimilation, accommodation
B. Accommodation, assimilation
C. Conflict, integration
D. Co-operation, assimilation

87. The conflicts which occur among groups within a society or between two societies are called:
A. Class conflicts B. Caste conflicts
C. Corporate conflicts D. Latent conflicts

88. Accommodation through ________ involves plausible excuses for one's behaviour instead of acknowledging the real defect in one's own self.
A. rationalisation B. toleration
C. arbitration D. compromise

89. ________ denotes acquired changes in the behaviour of individuals which enable them to adjust to their environment.
A. Assimilation B. Adaptation
C. Accommodation D. Insulation

90. Secondary co-operation is found among the members of:
A. Primary groups
B. those who live in isolation
C. those in the process of accommodation
D. secondary groups

91. Which one of the following is not the essential of social interaction?
A. social contracts B. communication
C. mores and customs D. None of these

92. To the classification given by Robert E. Park, one social process has been added by MacIver, which one of the following is that?
A. Conflict B. Competition
C. Co-operation D. Accommodation

93. ________ is found in the interaction between the various big and small groups to meet a particular situation.
A. Primary co-operation
B. Tertiary co-operation
C. Secondary co-operation
D. Informal co-operation

94. ________ is a social process in which individuals or groups seek their ends by directly challenging the antagonist by violence or threat of violence.
A. Competition B. Feud
C. Conflict D. Rivalry

95. When the conflict has existed in a hidden form in social tension and dissatisfaction long before it erupts in hostile action it is called ________ .
A. overt B. indirect
C. latent D. primary

96. MacIver has defined ________ as a form of struggle in which men contend against one another for any objective.
A. Competition B. Conflict
C. Feud D. Accommodation

97. "In one sense accommodation is the basis of all formal Social organisation" was said by:
A. Ogburn and Nim Koff B. Sheriff and Sheriff
C. Kingsley Davis D. K. Young

98. "Accommodation is a process in which man attain harmony with their environment" was said by:
A. Biesanz B. Durkheim
C. MacIver D. Max Weber

99. Which of the following is not a kind of accommodation?
A. Co-ordination and subordination
B. Superiority and inferiority
C. Like and dislike
D. Acclimatization and naturalisation

100. When parties to the conflict are on equal footing but willing to adjust to each other, this type of accommodation is called:
A. Co-ordination B. Subordination
C. Liking D. Disliking

101. When accommodation is on the basis of high and low, this type of accommodation may be called:
A. Co-ordination B. Subordination
C. Naturalisation D. Acclimatization

102. When accommodation is on the basis of natural conditions, this type of accommodation is known as:
A. Co-ordination B. Acclimatization
C. Naturalisation D. None of the above

103. When accommodation is on the basis of social conditions, we call it:
A. Naturalisation B. Acclimatization
C. Coordination D. Superiority

104. Which of the following is the most important contributory factor in the process of integration?
A. Quick means of communication
B. High economic standard
C. Emotional unity
D. Political integration

105. In India which of the following is not an important factor which hinders national integration?
A. Regionalism B. Lingualism
C. Lack of wealth D. Casteism

106. In developed societies the success of national integration by a developed country is viewed:
A. As a matter of satisfaction
B. As a matter of concern
C. As a cause of condemnation
D. With indifference

107. War, in which one party to the conflict is near victory and the other agrees to a settlement the accommodation is one of:
A. Compromise B. Pressure
C. Rationalisation D. Conversion

108. Accommodation under which both the parties to the conflict make certain concessions and find consolation in their disappointment is known as:
A. Compromise B. Arbitration
C. Toleration D. Conversion

109. ________ is that form of social action in which individual strive against each other for the possession of or use of some limited material or non-material good.
A. competition B. conflict
C. accomtiodation D. struggle

110. A method in which conflicting parties adjust to each other on the basis of the decision of a third party is called accommodation:
A. under pressure B. compromise
C. conversion D. arbitration

111. The aim of competition is:
A. To banish the opponent
B. To out to the competitor
C. To coerce the competitor to accept something
D. To restrict the scope of the conflict

112. Which of the following is not true of competition?
A. It is entirely unrestricted
B. It aims at banishing or destroying the enemy
C. It is not coercion
D. It helps in the elimination of force of fraud

113. Which of the following is not the characteristic of competition?
A. It is found among all the species
B. It is an inborn tendency
C. It differs in degree from one society to the other
D. Its degree is determined by social values

114. Which one of the following is not an important function of competition? It helps:
A. In determining the status of an individual in the hierarchy
B. To stimulate economy
C. In promoting monopoly conditions
D. In inventiveness

115. Which of the following is not a true statement about competition?
A. It enhances one's ego
B. It is conductive to efficiency
C. It prevents undue concentration of powers
D. It creates respect for rules of the game

116. Which one of the following has not been characterised as a negative function of competition by H.T. Mazumdar?
A. It may lead to neurosis
B. It may lead to monopoly
C. It may lead to conflicts
D. It may lead to social disharmony

117. In modern times:
A. Every society is exclusively competitive
B. Every society is exclusively cooperative
C. Some societies are exclusively competitive
D. No society is either exclusively competitive or exclusively cooperative

118. Which of the following is not a characteristic of competition?
A. It means survival of the fittest
B. It is study of achievements
C. It is unconscious action
D. It is found in all societies

119. According to MacIver, ________ is the manner in which the relations of the members of a group, once brought together, acquire a certain distinctive character.
A. Society B. Social structure
C. Social process D. Social system

120. "Assimilation is a process where by attitudes of many persons are united, and this develop into a united group". Who has given this definition of assimilation?
A. MacIver B. Weber
C. Bogardus D. None of the above

121. Which of the following statements is true of conflict?
A. It always stands in the path of progress
B. Social and individual conflicts are different from each other
C. It is an unconscious behaviour
D. It must go with co-operation

122. Which of the following statements is false?
A. Assimilation is a slow process, accommod-ation may be a sudden process

B. Assimilation is unconscious, accommod-ation is deliberate
C. Conflict is impersonal, competition is personal
D. All the above statements

123. Which one of the following is true of competition?
A. It is essential for economic progress
B. It is a great source of motivation
C. It is the basis of socialist societies
D. It is dangerous at national level

124. Which one of the following is not a very important factor for national integration?
A. Equal opportunities in economic sphere
B. Balanced economic development
C. Strong central authority
D. Oneness of political interests

125. National integration in a multi-racial society can be achieved when:
A. Minority is forced to accept view point of majority
B. Minority is allowed to go its own way
C. Ruling parties appease minorities
D. Minority flows in thé national stream on its own

126. Which one of the following is the most important contributory factor in the process of integration?
A. Equal treatment to all major regional languages
B. Awakening of consciousness for common objectives
C. Effectiveness of media
D. Raising living standard of the people

127. 'A' adopts an infant to make him his own. What is he expected to do?
A. To look after him properly
B. To give him the best education
C. To make him obedient
D. To make his future as a part of his adopted child without any reference to his past

128. Which of the following is not an important hindrance in the way of national integration in developing societies?
A. Low capital formation
B. Inadequate transport system
C. Economic differences
D. Poor international relations

129. In developing societies which of the factors is not a good sign of healthy competition?
A. Using imported technology
B. Employing foreign experts
C. Leaking national secrets for getting technology
D. Stressing on high percentage in profits after winning in competition

130. Which one of the following is not the usual cause of conflict?
A. Survival of the fittest
B. Inborn aggressive nature of human beings
C. Shortage of supply of articles
D. Similar demands on social norms

131. Which of the following statements is incorrect?
A. Conflict leads to intergroup tension
B. Conflict diverts member's attention from group objectives
C. Conflicts is an impersonal struggle
D. Conflict defines issues

132. Which one of the following is the advantage of Social interaction? It helps:
A. in understanding reaction of individual against social forces
B. in the study of the groups
C. in social disorganisation
D. in removing social cleavages

133. Which among the following is not right?
A. Accommodation leads to assimilation
B. Accommodation is appeasement of an adamant group
C. Accommodation is a step towards integration
D. Accommodation eliminates conflict

134. Competition generally occurs:
A. Because there is a feeling of antagonism among the members
B. Because the members do not want that anyone form any other group
C. Because of the scarcity of the thing for which people are competing
D. Because it is in the spirit of the human society

135. Which of the following is not true of social conflicts?
A. These arise due to cultural differences.
B. These are the outcome of differences in the attitudes.
C. These emerge out of clashing interests.
D. These are deliberate creation of the states.

136. Which one of the following in your opinion is not one or the main cause of conflict?
A. Separate demand on Social norms
B. Differences of opinion or ideology
C. Social disequilibrium
D. Excessive supply of articles of subsistence

137. Causes of conflicts are several. Which of the following is not a cause of conflict?
A. It is the outcome of the desire of one to dominate over others.
B. Clash of interests within groups.

C. Clash of interests between the individuals and the individuals.
D. Stagnancy in moral norms of the society.

138. By isolation we mean that a person:
A. is kept aloof from the society.
B. is not allowed to speak in the meetings.
C. is not allowed to attend social functions.
D. is Socially boycotted and condemned.

139. ________ is the process where by persons and groups acquire the culture of other group in which they come to live, by adopting its attitudes and values, its pattern of thinking and behaving.
A. Integration B. Assimilation
C. Accommodation D. Cooperation

140. By assimilation we mean that:
A. the people belonging to two groups merge with each other.
B. the people of two cultures suddenly merge with each other.
C. the people of two cultures slowly merge with each other.
D. the two societies decide to go away from each other.

141. In direct Cooperation is more visibly found in societies:
A. which by the nature are primitive.
B. which are essentially agriculturists.
C. which are tradition ridden.
D. which are industrialised and advanced.

142. In the case of indirect Cooperation which of the following statements is not correct?
A. It is essential that all must gain equally.
B. It is not essential that all must gain equally.
C. All members are supposed to cooperate equally.
D. All have common objectives to achieve.

143. Which of the following statements is true?
A. Accommodation may be achieved through yielding to coercion or admitting to one's defeat.
B. Accommodation is mainly an unconscious activity.
C. Accommodation can be done through arbitration and conciliation.
D. All the above statements are true.

144. Simmel had distinguished four types of conflict. They are:
A. War, feud, litigation and conflict of impersonal ideas.
B. War, racial conflict, personal conflict, feud.
C. Rebellon, coup, Strike and litigation.
D. None of the above

145. Which of the following statements is not correct about conflict?
A. These are essential to make the society dynamic.
B. These make cooperation meaningless.
C. These make cooperation purposeful.
D. These help society to come out of stagnancy.

146. Which one of the following is not a social utility of cooperation? It is needed for:
A. rearing and bringing up of the children.
B. the very survival of the people.
C. socialization.
D. organising trade union movements.

147. Which one of the following is not a characteristic of society?
A. It occurs at all times and at all places.
B. It is a continuous process.
C. It is confined to modernised societies.
D. It is something universal.

148. Which one of the following statements is not true of competition?
A. It helps in violating social norms.
B. It causes personal conflicts.
C. It is conducive to progress.
D. It can be an unconscious activity.

149. Which one of the following is not a characteristic of conflict?
A. It is a conscious action.
B. It is a personal activity.
C. It is a collective social behaviour.
D. It is an integral part of social activities.

150. Social interaction is a process through which members of a group:
A. penetrate each other's mind.
B. develop a sense of healthy competition.
C. help strengthening social customs.
D. save each other from social ridicule.

151. Which of the following statements is false?
A. Conflict involves contact, competition does not.
B. Conflict takes place on a conscious level.
C. Competition involves personal interaction.
D. Conflict disregards Social norms, where as competition cares for those.

152. One of the essentials of cooperation os that the people should:
A. belong to the same nation.
B. have same religious faith.
C. have similar economic status.
D. have desire to achieve common objectives.

153. Conflict is a process which:
A. occurs only in complex societies.
B. is a part of only simple and primitive societies.
C. is witnessed in modern and primitive societies.
D. occurs on human society and is never ending.

154. Conflicts in society occur:
A. unintentionally without any effort of the individuals.
B. by deliberate efforts of the society so as to make it healthy.
C. for achieving Social objectives.
D. for preserving Social interests.

155. Which one of the following is not the element of cooperation?
A. Cooperative organisations have common purpose to achieve.
B. Efforts for achieving objectives can be organised or disorganised.
C. Efforts for achieving objects must be planned.
D. It can be both in the case of states and individuals.

156. In modern Industrialized society the status of women in industry:
A. Has gradually risen
B. Has considerately gone down
C. Has remained unchanged
D. Has not been defined

157. In a method in which one party to the conflict tries to convince the others of his fault and bring them round to his own view point, this type of accommodation is called ________ .
A. Compromise B. Rationalisation
C. Conversion D. Tolerlation.

158. In accommodation, rationalisation is a method in which:
A. one party tries to convince the other of his fault.
B. one acceots the view-point of the other.
C. one agrees to the view-point of the other under pressure.
D. one adjusts by giving some imaginary excuses justifying withdrawal from dispute.

159. In a situation in which one party to the dispute accepts the view point of the other without giving up its own basic policies, this type of accommodation is known as
A. Rationalisation B. Toleration
C. Conversion D. Compromise

160. Which of the following is true of competition?
A. It is not a continuos process
B. It is personal
C. It is impersonal
D. For this deliberate efforts are needed

161. Which one of the following is not a significant feature of a accommodation?
A. It is out of conflict
B. It is as a result of competition
C. It is needed at all levels
D. It is universal in nature and character

162. According to Kropotkin:
A. Co-operation is a disturbance in the smooth running life of an individual
B. Co-operation is not necessary for the modern society
C. No individual can survive without co-operation
D. Nothing can be burdensome than co-operation in the way of individual

163. Which of the following is true of accommodation but does not apply to adaptation?
A. It is more concerned with biology.
B. It is social phenomenon.
C. It is a evolutionary process.
D. It is an outcome of natural competition.

164. Which one of the following is not one of the causes of competition?
A. To earn bread for one self.
B. To lead a luxurious life.
C. To wield more and more power.
D. To provide between services.

165. Which one of the following has not been given as a cause of competition by May and Doob?
A. Competition starts to achieve some goal that is scarce.
B. When the people are not prevented by the rules of situation for achieving goals competition begins.
C. People perform better when goals can be achieved.
D. When people have relatively few psychologically affiliative contracts with each other competition starts.

166. Which one of the following is not covered under the category of nature of competition?
A. It is directly concerned with the people.
B. It is not directly concerned with the people.
C. It is an unconscious process.
D. It is interaction without social contracts.

167. Which one of the following is covered under the category of nature of competition?
A. It is an impersonal action and a continuous process.
B. It is found only in complex societies.
C. It is not universal.
D. It is found in selected communities and classes.

168. The feeling of culture alpluralism:
A. Is a mere hypothesis
B. Has no relation with the process of assimilation
C. Promotes the process of cultural assimilation
D. Acts adversely on the process of cultural assimilation

169. Which one of the following is not the function of competition?
A. It has provided a stimulus to technological innovations.
B. It is responsible for providing stimulus to organisational innovations.
C. It creats desire to excel over others.
D. It is directly concerned with the individuals.

170. Competition when used in an unfair manner:
A. Can have disintegrating effect.
B. Can eliminate monopoly conditions.
C. Avoids social conflicts.
D. Checks exploitation of the weak by the rich.

171. Which of the following statements is not true in the case of Competition and Conflict?
A. Both are continuous process.
B. Competition is impersonal but conflict is personal.
C. Competition is unconscious, conflict is Conscious.
D. Competition is non-violent, conflict is violent.

172. Which of the following statements is not true?
A. In competition both parties gain but not in conflict.
B. competition is productive, conflict is non productive.
C. In competition social norms are respected but in conflict these are violated.
D. In competition hardwork does not pay as much as it pays in conflict.

173. In a large society:
A. It is easy to achieve complete assimilation
B. Complete assimilation is hypothetical only
C. There are no chances of assimilation
D. Nothing can be done

174. Competition is the result of human desire:
A. To survive in society.
B. Arising out of the insufficient supply of anything valuable.
C. To ensure that all are socially benefitted.
D. To promote steel frame work of laws.

175. Integration essentially involves:
A. Similarity of various structural parts.
B. Commonly accepted values.
C. Newly altered but developed values.
D. New social norms to adjust to altered values.

176. Which one of the following is not a serious problem in the process of social integration.
A. Complex social structure.
B. Problem of coordination of structural parts of the society.
C. Extent of Socialization.
D. Trade union system.

177. Point out which one of the following is not an important hindrance in the process of social integration:
A. Cultural heterogeneity
B. Class differentiation
C. Political homogeneity
D. Religious disharmony

178. Which one of the following is not an important cause of hindrance on the path of social integration?
A. Existence of several sub-cultures.
B. Rapidity of social change.
C. Cultural lags.
D. Political system in operation in the country.

179. A 'loosely woven' society is one:
A. Which is not integrated.
B. Which is poorly integrated.
C. In which there are no rigid social norms.
D. In which people do not have wide range of alternative modes.

180. Those who follow philosophy of 'new order' in integration believe in the:
A. Abolition of existing social system.
B. Improvement of existing social order
C. Method of half-way improvement.
D. None of the above

181. A Complex and rapidly changing society's most important method of achieving social integration is:
A. Economic planning
B. Observance of social customs
C. Religious harmony
D. Social planning

182. In India it is difficult to achieve integration because:
A. The country is inhabited by poor people.
B. There are many economic pressure groups.
C. India is a multi-racial society.
D. The country has adopted the system of universal adult franchise.

183. Which one of the following is not true regarding the nature of assimilation?
A. It is evolutionary
B. It is a slow process
C. It is a quick and fast process.
D. It is the outcome of coming into contact with outsiders.

184. Which one of the following is not the nature and character of assimilation?
A. It is complete Social integration.
B. It is partial Social integration.
C. It is not confined to cultures alone.
D. It covers family life.

185. Acculturation of culture starts when meetings are of:
A. Continuous but of short duration.
B. Continuous and of long duration.
C. Occasional and of short duration.
D. Occasional but of long duration.

186. "Acculturation is a process where by societies of different cultures are modified through fairly close and long continued contacts but without complete blending of two cultures". This was said by:
A. Gillin and Gillin B. Sheriff and Sheriff
C. Merill and Eldrege D. Dowson and Gettys

187. Which one of the following is not the basic condition responsible for promoting assimilation?
A. Toleration B. Political ideology
C. Social contacts D. Cultural similarity

188. Which one of the following is not the basic condition for promoting assimilation?
A. Appreciation of each other's Cultural heritage.
B. Coming together on a platform.
C. Favourable climatic conditions.
D. Equal economic standards.

189. Which one of the following is not an important hindrance on the path of social integration?
A. Conditions existing at the time of entry in society.
B. Number of persons involved.
C. Physical growth of the immigrants.
D. Approach to current political problems.

190. "Competition is a contest to obtain something which does not exist in a quantity sufficient to meet the demand". Who is the author of these words?
A. E.S. Bogardus
B. H.T. Mazumdar
C. Biesanz and Biesanz
D. Sutherland, Woodward and Maxwell

191. Which one of the following is not an important hindrance in the process of assimilation?
A. Feeling of superiority by one Community.
B. Inferiority Complex of one Community.
C. Desire to exist as a Semi-Community.
D. Desire to achieve high-living standard.

192. Which one of the following is true about assimilation but not of accommodation?
A. More or less permanent arrangement.
B. It is a temporary arrangement.
C. Whole process can be sudden.
D. It is a conscious process.

193. Physical isolation these days is becoming meaningless. Which one of the following is not an important cause?
A. Developed means of transportation.
B. Net-work of Communication.
C. Universal political ideology.
D. Mass media.

194. Isolation is not liked because of several reasons. Which of the following is not a reason?
A. Because it provides time for serious thinking.
B. Because it helps in meditation.
C. Because it provides opportunities to hoodwink the people.
D. Because, it is used by the state for isolating criminals.

195. Integration of a group depends upon certain factors. One of the following mentioned factors does not belong to this category. Point out such a factor:
A. Common enterprise
B. Frequency of interaction
C. Variety of the interacting members
D. Emotional quality of the interacting members

196. Which among the following does involve conflict?
A. Candidates preparing for I.A.S examination.
B. Workers demonstrating for share in the management of the factory.
C. Spectators waiting for the military parade.
D. Crowd waiting for the procession to move out of the ground.

197. According to A.W. Green conflict is the deliberate attempt to oppose, resist or coerce the will of another or others. In view of this which among the following involves conflicts?
A. Bullion merchants acting in a manner which resulted in shooting up of the gold price.
B. The hustling at the bus stop.
C. Door crashing by the mob at the football stadium.
D. Racial discrimination enforced in South Africa.

198. Which of the following defines latent conflict?
A. When a conflict exists but there is no open declaration.
B. When a conflict is openly declared.
C. When the conflict becomes more hostile.
D. None of the above

199. Which of the following gives an explanation of an overt conflict?
A. When a conflict erupts among the rival groups.
B. When a long age averted conflict reappears.
C. When a conflict is forgotten by all.
D. When a conflict is openly declared.

200. Which of the following statements is correct?
A. A Latent Conflict always becomes an overt conflict.
B. An overt Conflict always becomes a latent conflict.
C. A latent Conflict can never be an overt conflict.
D. None of the above

201. 'Synergism' stands for:
A. The primordial feelings which reminds the members that they belong to each other in Society.
B. The feelings of the groups in strife.
C. The feeling of the tribe in Africa which acted as a hostile tribe.
D. None of the above

202. Mark the correct statement out of the following:
A. Competition helps in determining the status of the individual as well.
B. It facilitates the location of members in a hierarchical System.
C. Competition helps in stimulating economy.
D. Adopting high class of efficiency and encourages inventions.

203. Which one of the following statements is correct?
A. Competition helps in avoiding concentration of power in individual or group of individuals.
B. It ruins the feeling of rule of the game.
C. It acts against enhancing one's ego.
D. It leads to the concentration of power among a few individuals.

204. "Competition performs the broad function of assigning to each individual his place in his social world. Competition is a progressive force which fulfils and does not necessarily destroy". This view has been expressed by:
A. MacIver B. Ginsberg
C. Kroptoksy D. E.A. Ross.

205. "Conflict is the Social process in which individuals of groups seek their ends by directly challenging the antagonist by violence or threat of violence".
A. A.W. Green B. Gillin and Gillin
C. Malthus D. Parsons

206. "As Competition becomes more personal, it shades into Conflict the more disruptive, disjustive social process," is said by:
A. Sutherland Woodward and Maxwell
B. Gillin and Gillin
C. Ginsberg
D. Max Weber

207. "When the common interests of the group are symbolised for the members in the appealing forms of music, ritual, distinctive names, titles, banners, slogans and insignals then:
A. The changes of integration are more.
B. The changes of integration are less.
C. It has no relation with the process of integration.
D. Nothing can happen in the group.

208. "Competition is a correct method to obtain something which does not exist in a quality sufficient to meet the demand. Who of the following gave this definition?
A. Bogardus B. Sutherland
C. Durkheim D. Tonnies

209. "Competition is the striving of two or more persons for the same goal which is limited so that all can share it". This definition has been given by:
A. Bogardus B. Max Weber
C. MacIver D. Biesanz and Biesanz.

210. The process that the dominant group-determines the norms and cultures to be adopted by the dominated group is known as:
A. Interjection B. Acquisition
C. Competition D. Assimilation

211. Which of the following is not an agency of socialization?
A. Family B. Church
C. Environment D. State

212. Socialization process in human beings takes place:
A. during childhood
B. during young age
C. for the whole life
D. at different intervals

213. Whose work is 'mind, self and society'?
A. Elton Mayor B. Pareto
C. G.H. Mead D. Margaret Mead

214. The notion of the "I-me-generalised other" was developed by:
A. Mead G.H. B. Cooley Charles
C. Thomas William D. Merton Robert

215. Which is most appropriate? Social order is maintained largely by:
A. Socialization B. Community
C. Social Sanctions D. Law

216. Most prominent agent of socialization is:
A. family B. community
C. in-group D. association

217. Conforming, passive part of the self is:
A. I B. Me
C. Id D. None of these

218. Which does not belong to Herbert Mead?
A. significant others
B. generalised others
C. I and me
D. the Id, Ego and Superego

219. Which among the following is odd one?
A. Toys B. Wood
C. Teacher D. Radio

220. Who among the following was first who gave socialization theory?
A. Cooley B. Mead
C. Parsons D. Durkheim

221. Which among the following is self-centered stage according to Jean Piagel's view?
A. 2 to 5 years B. 2 to 7 years
C. 5 to 7 years D. 9 to 13 years

222. Who viewed expectation and inspiration as the two main bases of socialization and learning?
A. Parsons B. Mead
C. J. Piaget D. Cooley

223. A society which achieves social unity through a complex of highly specialized roles is based on:
A. Dependency
B. Intimate social relationship
C. Mechanical solidarity
D. Organic solidarity

224. Suggestion is one of the basic principles of:
A. human behaviour B. class
C. socialization D. social process

225. When the child is able to judge the response of a group as a whole he is responding to a:
A. significant others B. generalised others
C. insignificant others D. None of the above

226. An individual starts learning from:
A. mother's womb B. childhood
C. adulthood D. adole scence

227. Socialization is a process of converting a biological organism into:
A. modern man B. primitive man
C. human being D. social man

228. Socialization is a process involving:
A. gradual changing of organism
B. training to adopt to the society
C. setting up of social norms
D. declaring everything as belonging to society

229. According to whom, "suggestion is the cognitive aspect of the gregarious instincts"?
A. Ross B. MacIver
C. Thouless D. Parsons

230. Adult socialization in primitives societies as compared to modern societies is:
A. more complex B. less complex
C. of similar complexity D. None of the above

231. 'Significant others' are:
A. friends B. peer group
C. parents D. police

232. 'Generalized others' are:
A. community B. friends
C. peer group D. parents

233. The process of socialization ends with:
A. adulthood B. youth
C. childhood D. death

234. Sociologist who called the self-image of the looking glass self was:
A. M. Mead B. G.H. Mead
C. S. Freud D. Cooley

235. Kroeber suggested the term ________ as an alternative term for socialization.
A. Culturalization B. Acculturation
C. Enculturation D. Social control

236. Socialization process helps in maintaining:
A. social norms B. social behaviour
C. social attitudes D. none

237. The maximum contribution to the process of socialization, in general, comes from:
A. school B. teacher
C. community D. family

238. Freud found that untamed passions and instinctive desires are represented by:
A. Ego B. Self
C. Id D. Super ego

239. There is more conformity and togetherness among ants than among men this is due to:
A. moral pressure B. social control
C. heredity D. socialization

240. A young adult of 30 years learning the new role of parents is an example of:
A. primary socialization B. secondary socialization
C. adult socialization D. resocialization

241. As compared to sociality, morality is:
A. less extensive B. more reliable
C. more extensive D. less intensive

242. Name the orientation that emphasizes individual choice and decision making in determining behaviour?
A. Zin coism B. Voluntarism
C. Altruism D. Individuality

243. According to Weber which one stems from an individual's emotional stage at a particular time:
A. Affective action B. Reflective action
C. Spring action D. Rational action

244. The socialization process of the individual does not include:
A. the environment
B. culture
C. army
D. the physical, psychological heritage of the individual

245. 'Socialization' implies the process of:
A. an individual becoming an active member of society a social being
B. establishing a social group
C. social control
D. social evolution

246. Who among the following talked about 'play stage' and 'game stage' in the process of socialization?
A. M. Mead B. G.H. Mead
C. S. Freud D. Cooley

247. Who gave the four stages: oral stage, anal stage, oedipal stage and adolescent stage in the process of socialization?
A. Cooley B. G.H. Mead
C. M. Mead D. S. Freud

248. As an individual becomes socialized, he learns:
A. to play a variety of roles
B. skills for a variety of activities
C. to discipline his behaviour
D. all of the above

249. Who put forward the concept of the 'looking-glass self'?
A. Cooley B. Lewis Mumford
C. Bergel D. Hans Kohn

250. Who said "Man is not only a social animal that can develop into an individual only in society"?
A. Hegal B. J.M. Keynes
C. Marx D. Kardiner and Linton

251. Sigmund Freud is founder of:
A. Psychology B. Historicism
C. Psycho-analysis D. Political Sociology

252. Which one of the following is not strictly speaking, one of S. Freud's stages of psychic-sexual development?
A. Oral B. Genital
C. Oedipal D. Anal

253. Mead's generalised 'others' and 'significant others' are creator of:
A. I B. Me
C. Super-ego D. Ego

254. Most sociologists believe that one's self concept:
A. When once formed never changes
B. Can change later in life although childhood experiences are more durable
C. Changes all the time as circumstances change
D. None of the above

255. 'Significant others' in the process of socialization is:
A. Community members B. Peer group
C. Parents D. Children

256. Which of the following does not influence the process of the socialization of an individual?
A. institution of marriage
B. political and economic institutions
C. geographical environment
D. language

257. Rehabilitation of criminals is:
A. Socialization B. Resocialization
C. Desocialization D. Primary socialization

258. Primary socialization take place during infancy, usually within:
A. Family B. Community
C. Out group D. Mother's care

259. The over socialized conception of man was given by:
A. D.H. Wrong B. G.H. Mead
C. C.H. Cooley D. M. Mead

260. Who used the term enculturation for socialization?
A. Hers Kovits B. Kroeber
C. Veblen D. Tylor

261. The 'looking glass self' means that we learn who we are:
A. byself feeling
B. by an act of imitation
C. by other people's experience with us
D. by imagining ourselves to be some one else

262. Single 'savage self', as introduced by Mead is:
A. I B. Super ego
C. Id D. None of these

263. The super ego, according to Freud represents the part of an individual's personality that was created:
A. Through socialization during the formative years
B. Through socialization
C. Through socialization process which occurs throughout one's life
D. None of the above

264. Which among the following ideas are not connected with socialism?
A. That private property should be abolished
B. That there should be a stateless society
C. That the means of production and distribution must be in the hands of the community
D. None of the above

265. Social relationship involves:
A. Co-operation
B. Face to face conflict
C. Conflict
D. Co-operation and conflict

266. 'Social control' more or less, has become the activity of the specialized agencies in:
A. New townships B. Cities
C. Villages D. None of these

267. Who said that socialization takes place through two major mechanism: identification and repression?
A. M. Mead B. Tonnies
C. S. Freud D. Sumner

268. Anticipatory socialization is a preparation for:
A. Present role B. Future role
C. Resocialization D. None of the above

269. Who differentiated 'ego' and 'alter' in the interaction system?
A. T. Parsons B. R. Brown
C. M. Weber D. S. Freud

270. One of the following is not an explanation of Freud's stages of development of self?
A. Anal B. Oral
C. Id D. Oedipal

271. The term 'political socialization' was used by:
A. Almond Powell B. Easton and Dannis
C. Herbert Hyman D. Herbert Spencer

272. Freud's 'Id' can best be translated as _______ .
A. Reason B. Hostility
C. Desire D. Social Conscience

273. Whose name is associated with the process of socialization?
A. C.H. Cooley B. G.H. Mead
C. Sigmund Freud D. All the above

274. According to G.H Mead, the child firstly learns to responds to his:
A. Generalised others B. Significant others
C. Himself D. Society as a whole

275. 'Generalized others'of Mead is meant:
A. Parents of the children.
B. Family members.
C. Community as a whole.
D. Nothing can be said of it.

276. Which among the following is true of socialization?
A. It socializes the individuals.
B. It makes society above individual.
C. It brings individuals into the social.
D. All the above.

277. According to Cooley, the concept of ________refers to an individual perception of self as determined by the way one imagines one appears to others or as others perceive us:
A. Significant others B. Generalised others
C. Looking-glass self D. None of the above

278. To such socialisation, which among the following factors is a must?
A. Process of imitation
B. Process of suggestion
C. Process of identification
D. Language comprehension

279. Who among the following defines irritation as self conscious assumption of author's acts or roles?
A. Margaret Mead B. G.H. Mead
C. C.H. Cooley D. S. Freud

280. Which among the following factors were as an agent of socialisation process.
A. Family B. School
C. Peer group D. Religious institutions

281. Which among the following elements work efficiently in the process of socialization?
A. Environmental Condition
B. Physical and Psychological heritage.
C. Cultural heritage
D. Family pattern in which one is born.

282. Socialisation is a learning process in which a child is influenced by:
A. Cognitive learning B. Evaluative learning
C. Effective learning D. All the above

283. Talking of different stages of socialization who among the following has brought the notion of oral stage, anal stage, oedipal stage and adole scence?
A. Sigmund Freud B. G.H. Mead
C. C.H. Cooley D. R.K. Merton

284. What name is associated with the theory of looking glass self?
A. C.H. Cooley B. G.H. Mead
C. S. Freud D. MacIver

285. The concept of looking glass self means:
A. A man's seeing himself in to a mirror.
B. Self evaluation in the period of crisis.
C. The individual's imagination of how others see him or her.
D. All the above

286. Whose name associated with the concept of generalized others?
A. G.H. Mead B. C.H. Cooley
C. MacIver D. S. Freud

287. Whose name is associated with concept of significant others?
A. C.H. Cooley B. G.H. Mead
C. S. Freud D. MacIver

288. Who has tabled the process of socialization through the process of playing at a role?
A. G.H. Mead B. C.H. Cooley
C. S. Frued D. T. Mazumdar

289. The Concept of 'I' and 'Me' is attributed the name of:
A. C.H. Cooley B. G.H. Mead
C. Sigmund Freud D. T. Mazumdar

290. Who among the following has brought the concept of Id, Ego and Super ego?
A. Sigmund Freud B. G.H. Mead
C. C.H. Cooley D. MacIver

291. Which is true of Freudian?
A. It is raw, unorganised and irritational.
B. It is blind and seeks immediate release of tension.
C. It follows pleasure principle.
D. All the above

292. Which among the following is conventional part of individual's self whose responses fall under the expectations of others?
A. I B. Me
C. Us D. We

293. Which is true of 'I' of G.H. Mead?
A. It is the active and creative part of an individual.
B. It brings social change or process.
C. 'I' resembles to the Freudian concept 'ID'
D. All the above

294. Which is true of 'Me' of G.H. Mead?
A. It is the part with the individual which is socialised.
B. It is the passive and conforming part of the individual.
C. It brings coherence in social order.
D. All the above

295. Which among the following is a true statement?
A. The Id and Super ego fight in the battle field of ego.
B. Ego is governed by the reality principle.
C. Ego fulfills the social demands.
D. All the above

296. The child when become aware of his membership in the family and his social roles assigned to and expected of him is according to Freud:
A. Oral stage B. Anal stage
C. Oedipal stage D. Adolescence.

297. When the secondary sexual characters appear in boys and girls showing as inclination of freedom indication towards opposite sex and a feeling they ensure parental case is that of his:
A. Oral stage B. Anal stage
C. Oedipal stage D. Adolescence

298. Which among the following is true of super ego?
A. It is the internalization of custom and culture as a whole.
B. It speaks of morality and social order.
C. Super ego is the roughly developed by parental rewards and parents
D. All the above

299. Which is true of socialization?
A. It high lights values and manners within individuals.
B. Socialisation includes both learning of new things and unlearning of maladaptive behaviours.
C. Socialization is both intentional and unintentional.
D. All the above

300. Identify reference group from the following:
A. membership group.
B. a group from which one draws one's norms and values.
C. non-membership group.
D. a group often referred to in conversation.

301. 'Id' refers to the instantaneous desire to grateful passions. 'Ego' is the condensed image of the person; while 'Super-ego' includes the aspects of morality. Whose classification is this?
A. G.H. Mead B. Charles Cooley
C. Erving Goff man D. Freud

302. Which of the following is the sufficient condition for the development of self?
A. Social interaction.
B. Satisfaction of biological and emotional needs of the child.
C. Rearing of child in circumstances of near isolation.
D. All the above

303. Socialization refers to:
A. the process of growth from infancy to childhood.
B. the process of personality development in the family only.
C. a life-long process where by person learns social roles and values.
D. the formality of enrollment as a member of a society.

304. Arrange the following stages of socialization Identify:
1. Anticipatory 2. Child
3. Infant 4. Adult
5. Adolescent

Codes:

A. 1, 3, 2, 5, 4 B. 5, 3, 2, 4, 1
C. 3, 2, 5, 4, 1 D. 2, 3, 4, 5, 1

305. Who among the following believe that the age between five and seven is important in the development of the child?

A. Parsons B. Mead
C. J. Piaget D. None

306. 'Looking glass self' is a socialization process which essentially means:

A. a self perception of what other think of us
B. a true Judgement of approval and disapproval.
C. to attract attention and seek praise.
D. a true reflection of one's personality.

307. A student of sociology can study a child when scolded under controlled conditions by applying the technique of:

A. Interview B. Observation
C. Questionnaire D. None the above

308. Whose words are these? "self and society are twin-born, we know one as immediately as we know the other and the notion of a separate and independent ego is an illusion".

A. W.G. Sumner B. A. Wober
C. C.H. Cooley D. G.H. Mead

309. What is the main object of Socialization?

A. Creating affection in the mind of the child.
B. Seeking cooperation from the child.
C. Development of the self.
D. Imparting linguistic knowledge.

310. Which is most appropriate?

A. Animal do not learn.
B. Learned behaviour is highly limited among animals and when it does occur it dies with the individual organism, and each generation must learn all over again.
C. Learned behaviour is quite common among animals and is easily imparted through generations.
D. None of these

311. Three steps in the process of development of self (i) how I appear to others (ii) their valuation of what they see and (iii) self feeling based upon steps one or two. This explain the concept of:

A. 'Generalized other'
B. 'Super ego'
C. 'I'
D. The 'looking-glass self'

312. Which of the following statement do you think is correct?

A. Man's behaviour pattern are only biologically conditioned.
B. In crucials situation man is guided by a hereditary patterns.
C. Man has automatic maturation process.
D. Man has little or no in born control of his behaviour in relation to other.

313. A child, after his birth, starts learning from the automatic and rigid response of the organism to a given stimulus. These processes are termed in Sociology as:

A. Reflexes B. Sentiments
C. Instincts D. Feelings

314. Industrial sociology as a distinct discipline is connected with the research in:

A. Bureaucracy
B. Human relations approach
C. Scientific management school
D. Professionalization

315. This aspect of self, when it operates at conscious level is called the conscience. It develops, largely unconsciously as the individuals incorporates the values and norms of the society into the personality.

A. Id B. Ego
C. Super ego D. All of above

316. The 'Id' consists of biological drives that release energy and it is activated by what Freud called:

A. Socialization
B. Ethnocentrism
C. The pleasure principle
D. The reality principle

317. In the process of socialization, which among the following is the battle ground on the basis of Sigmund Freud's explanation?

A. I B. Id
C. Ego D. Super ego

318. "A Social problem is any deviant behaviour in a disapproved direction of such a degree that it exceeds the clearance limit of the community." Who gave this definition?

A. MacIver B. Weber
C. Page D. Lundberg

319. Who among the following says that socialization is the process by which the child acquires a cultural content, along with self hood and personality?

A. A.W. Green B. MacIver
C. Ogburn D. H.T. Mazumdar

320. Which one of the following statements is correct in respect of a society and a group?

A. Both group and society are equally organized
B. Society is better organized than a group
C. A group is better organized than society
D. Both group and society are disorganized

ANSWERS

1	2	3	4	5	6	7	8	9	10
D	C	D	B	B	D	D	A	C	B
11	**12**	**13**	**14**	**15**	**16**	**17**	**18**	**19**	**20**
B	C	D	A	A	A	C	C	A	B
21	**22**	**23**	**24**	**25**	**26**	**27**	**28**	**29**	**30**
C	D	D	B	B	B	B	C	A	B
31	**32**	**33**	**34**	**35**	**36**	**37**	**38**	**39**	**40**
B	C	C	D	A	A	D	A	A	A
41	**42**	**43**	**44**	**45**	**46**	**47**	**48**	**49**	**50**
B	A	B	C	D	B	D	A	A	A
51	**52**	**53**	**54**	**55**	**56**	**57**	**58**	**59**	**60**
A	D	A	A	B	A	A	C	D	A
61	**62**	**63**	**64**	**65**	**66**	**67**	**68**	**69**	**70**
A	A	D	B	D	A	C	A	B	D
71	**72**	**73**	**74**	**75**	**76**	**77**	**78**	**79**	**80**
A	D	D	D	A	D	C	A	B	C
81	**82**	**83**	**84**	**85**	**86**	**87**	**88**	**89**	**90**
B	B	A	A	A	A	C	A	C	D
91	**92**	**93**	**94**	**95**	**96**	**97**	**98**	**99**	**100**
C	C	B	C	C	B	C	C	C	A
101	**102**	**103**	**104**	**105**	**106**	**107**	**108**	**109**	**110**
B	B	A	C	A	B	C	A	A	D
111	**112**	**113**	**114**	**115**	**116**	**117**	**118**	**119**	**120**
B	B	B	C	C	D	D	C	C	C
121	**122**	**123**	**124**	**125**	**126**	**127**	**128**	**129**	**130**
D	C	B	D	D	B	D	D	C	D
131	**132**	**133**	**134**	**135**	**136**	**137**	**138**	**139**	**140**
C	A	B	C	D	D	D	A	B	C
141	**142**	**143**	**144**	**145**	**146**	**147**	**148**	**149**	**150**
D	A	D	A	C	D	C	B	C	A
151	**152**	**153**	**154**	**155**	**156**	**157**	**158**	**159**	**160**
C	D	D	B	B	A	C	D	B	C
161	**162**	**163**	**164**	**165**	**166**	**167**	**168**	**169**	**170**
B	C	B	D	B	A	A	A	D	A
171	**172**	**173**	**174**	**175**	**176**	**177**	**178**	**179**	**180**
A	D	B	B	B	D	C	D	C	A
181	**182**	**183**	**184**	**185**	**186**	**187**	**188**	**189**	**190**
D	C	C	B	B	A	B	C	D	A
191	**192**	**193**	**194**	**195**	**196**	**197**	**198**	**199**	**200**
D	D	C	C	A	B	D	A	D	C
201	**202**	**203**	**204**	**205**	**206**	**207**	**208**	**209**	**210**
A	D	A	D	B	A	A	A	D	A

211	212	213	214	215	216	217	218	219	220
C	C	C	A	A	A	B	B	B	D
221	222	223	224	225	226	227	228	229	230
A	A	D	C	B	B	D	B	A	B
231	232	233	234	235	236	237	238	239	240
C	A	D	D	C	A	D	A	C	C
241	242	243	244	245	246	247	248	249	250
C	B	A	C	A	B	D	C	A	C
251	252	253	254	255	256	257	258	259	260
C	B	B	B	C	C	B	A	A	A
261	262	263	264	265	266	267	268	269	270
A	A	A	B	D	B	C	B	A	C
271	272	273	274	275	276	277	278	279	280
A	C	D	B	C	D	C	A	C	C
281	282	283	284	285	286	287	288	289	290
A	C	A	C	C	B	B	A	B	A
291	292	293	294	295	296	297	298	299	300
B	B	D	D	D	C	D	D	D	B
301	302	303	304	305	306	307	308	309	310
D	A	C	C	C	A	B	C	C	B
311	312	313	314	315	316	317	318	319	320
D	D	D	C	C	C	C	D	A	C

●●●

Social Change and the Polity

1. According to Pareto, all elites ________ .
   A. decay in quality
   B. increase their quality
   C. become more stable with the lapse of time
   D. gradually gain power

2. Which one of the following is not a valid criticism against Syndicalist philosophy?
   A. it is unscientific
   B. it is vague
   C. it is negative in nature
   D. it provides guarantee against misuse of authority

3. Wright mills explains elite rule in ________ terms rather than in ________ terms.
   A. institutional, psychological
   B. economical, psychological
   C. institutional, economical
   D. none of the above

4. In the past kingship mostly used to be:
   A. elected B. heredity
   C. nominated D. on the basis of ability

5. The ________ provide an example of simple govt. in bands.
   A. Eskimo B. Kadar tribs
   C. Nuers D. Australian aboriginals

6. Among the Bantus tribes ________ is prevalent.
   A. band B. commune
   C. democracy D. state system

7. ________ always concerns goal or benefits for which there is competition.
   A. Economy B. Religion
   C. Politics D. War

8. Which one of the following is not the most important characteristic of the state?
   A. territory B. population
   C. government D. political system

9. Who among the following has worked on the 'Nuers of Sudan'?
   A. Evans Pritchard B. Durkheim
   C. Tylor D. Kluckohn

10. Politics is ________ rather than ________ in nature.
    A. private, public
    B. public, private
    C. profit oriented, philanthropic
    D. secular, communal

11. The concept of ________ is at the center of any treatment of politics.
    A. profit B. power
    C. wealth D. prestige

12. ________ refers to the capacity to take independent action in the face of resistance and confrontation.
    A. Economy B. Power
    C. Authority D. None of the above

13. Even though a/an ________ has a single ruler it is not necessarily a dictatorship.
    A. acephalous B. stateless
    C. state system D. band

14. Which one of the following is not a true feature of Anarchism? It is opposed to the:
    A. state B. representation system
    C. religion D. trade unionism

15. Weber's view of power is known as ________ concept of power.
    A. idealistic B. idiosyncratic
    C. constant sun D. rationalistic

16. According to Karl Marx value of a community is created by:
    A. capital investment
    B. machines installed capacity
    C. labour put in
    D. socially useful labour put in

17. One of the primitive legal mechanisms of Eskimos to control aggression is ________ .
    A. song-duel
    B. street-duel
    C. arrow competition
    D. staying out side the Iglo

18. During middle ages the most powerful authority in Europe use to be:
    A. economically prosperous persons
    B. the church fathers
    C. the kings
    D. the feudals

19. The Nuer of Sudan illustrates the political role of ________ .

A. religion
B. youth dormitory
C. segmentary line age system
D. war

20. In simple society political institutions were based on the principle of:

A. division of powers
B. judicial review
C. written code of conduct
D. supremacy of the ruler

21. According to Wright Mills, elite comprise those who hold ________ in an institutional hierarchy.

A. prestigious occupation
B. command posts
C. military power
D. political power

22. In a simple society it was believed that state was the:

A. product of force
B. divine origin
C. expansion of families
D. none of those

23. Before the British with drew from this country, which among the following did we not possess?

A. Population B. Territory
C. Government D. Sovereignty

24. Which among the following is generally the basis of political institution in simple societies?

A. Kingship B. Kinship
C. Folkways D. Mores

25. Which among the following is a state?

A. YMCA B. Punjab
C. India D. UN

26. Elite theory was given by ________ .

A. Marx B. Weber
C. Pareto D. August Comte

27. The system of city-state in the past was quite common under the:

A. Greek B. Romans
C. Turks D. Indians

28. In a simple society the most effective check on the authority used to be:

A. religious institutions B. economic institutions
C. social institutions D. political institutions

29. Since the society is plural, the authority must also be plural is the slogan of the:

A. Syndicalists B. Marxists
C. Pluralists D. Anarchists

30. Theory which believes that the state was given to man by God is known as:

A. force theory
B. matriarchal theory
C. evolutionary theory
D. divine origin theory

31. Who maintained that 'consent' forms the psychological basis of leadership?

A. Evans Pritchard B. Levistrauss
C. Weber D. Fascists

32. Who of the following believes that the state is only a necessary evil?

A. Individualists B. Socialists
C. Marxists D. Fascists

33. The myth of "General strike" in political system has been created by:

A. Guild socialists B. Fabian socialists
C. Syndicalists D. Fascists

34. In Gandhian philosophy the wealthy person:

A. will emerge stronger and powerful
B. will wither away
C. will remain as he is
D. will considerably weaken himself

35. ________ is a form of government in which ruling power belongs to only a few persons.

A. political democracy B. oligarchy
C. tutelary democracy D. None of the above

36. The Fascists believe that the real power should be vested in the:

A. State B. Church
C. Individuals D. Feudal lords

37. Marx believes that the state has always been the champion of the cause of:

A. middle class
B. the bureaucrats
C. the poor and the down trodden
D. the rich and the powerful

38. Who of the following has raised the state to the highest pedestal?

A. Anarchists B. Fascists
C. Individualists D. Socialists

39. Which among the following names belonged to the utilitarian school of thinkers?

A. R.M. MacIver B. Herbert Spencer
C. John Stuart Mill D. H.J. Laski

40. Who among the following writers has recognized that the nation is distinctly a historical phenomenon?

A. Hans B. Karl Marx
C. Frnest Renan D. All of these

41. Nation is a:
A. Racial Community
B. Tribal Community
C. Religious group of people
D. Territorial Community

42. Which among the following is a nation?
A. United Nations B. Common Wealth
C. People of Africa D. India

43. What differentiates Nation from other groups?
A. common territory
B. common pattern of living
C. common sentiment
D. political independence

44. Mark out among the following the reasons that made Jawaharlal the great leader:
A. His parentage
B. His brahaminical heritage
C. His headship of the Congress
D. His personal qualities

45. What is repugnant to the Gandhian state?
A. To follow the laws
B. Not to follow the laws
C. Not to accept the supremacy of state
D. To submit to the bad laws

46. What distinguishes the state from other associations?
A. Membership
B. Land under its control
C. The binding nature of its rules and regulations
D. The absoluteness and in alienability of its supremacy

47. Which is the most important element of nationality?
A. Common religion B. Common language
C. Common race D. Corporate sentiment

48. Bureaucracy in modern times is indispensable because:
A. It has long traditions
B. It is powerful
C. It fulfils the needs of mass administration
D. It serves the needs of politicians

49. Mark out the incorrect statement: Bureaucracy is a profession calling demanding:
A. Devotion to job B. Devotion to office
C. Devotion to rules D. Devotion to person

50. Which among the following is a positive aspect of bureaucratic administration?
A. Red Tapism
B. Mechanical adherence to rules
C. Its being objective oriented
D. Indifference towards feeling of individuals

51. Which among the following is not a source of law?
A. Custom
B. Religion
C. Habits and family practices
D. Judicial decision

52. Which among the following is not a source of law?
A. Scientific commentaries
B. Manners as "those are more important than laws"
C. Equity
D. Legislations

53. Which among the following is not correct?
A. custom is at the vanishing point of its existence
B. custom is conservative
C. custom is adjustable
D. custom and progress do not always agree

54. The supporter of the matriarchal theory was:
A. Sir J.G. Frazer B. Sir Henry Maine
C. Maclennan D. Manu

55. Who among the follwing is not connected with the matriarchal theory?
A. J.G. Frazer B. Maclennan
C. Morgan D. Jenks

56. In sociology, what is the position of state? Mark out the correct answer:
A. State is supreme
B. It is one among the many associations
C. It is the first of the associations
D. State is omnipotent

57. Which among the following do you think is not a limitation of sovereignty?
A. Constitution of the country
B. Laws of nature
C. The international law
D. Public opinion

58. Among the following mark out the most correct meaning of Dharma?
A. It means law
B. It is synonymous with Hinduism
C. It is the balancing element in all activity
D. It is righteous omnipotent of conduct

59. Among the following mark out what thing is the Gandhian state?
A. Theocracy
B. Democracy
C. Cooperative decentralization
D. Swaraj

60. Which among the following do you think is the true basis of Gandhian state?
A. Non-violence B. Force
C. Satya D. Cooperation

61. Why should the sphere of state activity be limited?
A. State is omnipotent
B. State is omnicompetent
C. State is not omnicompetent
D. State is omnipresent

62. Force is:
A. The basis of state
B. The element of state
C. The end of state
D. The origin of state

63. What differentiates State from Nation?
A. Territory and people
B. Government
C. Sovereignty
D. Consciousness of political unity

64. Which among the following operates as a limit on the functions of the State?
A. The means at it disposal
B. The customs of the community
C. The fear of resistance
D. All of these

65. What is the state of nature? Mark out the correct answer?
A. Supremacy of might on right
B. A state of equality for all men
C. The state, where Devas were troubled by Asura
D. Such a state did not exist historically

66. What is the aim of political institutions? Mark out the correct answer:
A. To sustain law and order
B. To enforce authority
C. To expand the authority of the state
D. To serve the individual best

67. Who among the following is the author of the book, "what is property"?
A. Karl Marx B. Godwin
C. Proudhon D. Bakunin

68. Among the following, markout the propounder of the patriarchal theory:
A. Jenks B. Maclennan
C. Sir Henry Maine D. Frazer

69. Who among the following thinkers has not accepted that the state has an ethical purpose?
A. Laski B. Gandhi
C. Aristotle D. Marx

70. Who among the following thinkers is not associated with the theory of social contract?
A. Hobbes B. Locke
C. Rousseau D. Kautilya

71. Which among the following names is not an Anarchist thinker?
A. Hegel B. Proudhon
C. Bakunin D. Kropotkin

72. In which of the following works the theory of social contract was first propounded?
A. Social contract
B. Leviathan
C. Two treatises of civil government
D. Mahabharata

73. By means of social contract man:
A. Lost his freedom
B. Gained his freedom
C. Become part of the whole
D. State came into existence

74. Historical analysis indicate that the early kings were:
A. wise men
B. god fearing religious priests
C. war lords
D. the founding fathers of the diplomacy

75. For an offence by an individual in simple societies, which of the following sanctions can be applied?
A. Penal sanctions B. Moral sanctions
C. Ritual sanctions D. All

76. Which of the following simple societies possess distinct political institutions?
A. The Zulu B. The Ba Mangwato
C. The Ba Nyankole D. All

77. Which among the following do you think are the essential attributes of a state?
A. Population B. Government
C. Sovereignty D. All

78. What was 'a loose congeries of semi-independent states'?
A. The oriental empire B. The city states
C. The roman empire D. The feudal states

79. Which of the following is not an essential characteristic of the state?
A. Population B. Definite territory
C. Government D. Army

80. In a political system:
A. People are made to conform
B. People conform willingly
C. The individual conforms
D. None of the above

81. Which among the following operates as a limit on the functions of the state?
A. The means of its disposal
B. The customs of the community

C. The fear of resistance
D. All of the above

82. Which among the following does Gandhi Ji think is the most important constituent of a state?
A. The state B. The body politic
C. Law D. Individual

83. According to Gandhi, one can be slave to the state, when:
A. One disobeys the laws
B. By not participating in the body politic
C. By not expressing his views
D. By submitting to the laws which are against, one's conscience

84. "Society is held together by the states and if it were thus held together, it could not exist." This view has been expressed by:
A. MacIver B. E. Barker
C. Lowie D. Terry

85. Rights which are given to the citizens by the constitution but which can not be touched by the state are known as:
A. legal rights B. moral rights
C. political rights D. fundamental rights

86. ________ in a political system is base on the expectations that those who make the decisions will meet certain obligations:
A. Legitimacy B. Prestige
C. Power D. Mobility

87. According to Pareto ________ type of elite achieve power because of their ability to take direct and incisive action and tend to rule by force.
A. lions B. foxes
C. tigers D. stable

88. Find out the incorrect match:
A. Paretolions and foxes elites
B. Marxpower elite
C. Weberlegal, traditional and charismatic authority
D. Evans Pritchard-study of Nuers of Sudan

89. ________ is institutionalized and involves the right to take certain actions, including decisions to issue commands.
A. Authority B. Force
C. Power D. Economy

90. In the past fore most duty of the ruler used to be to:
A. promote religion
B. promote welfare of the people
C. undertake public works activities
D. increase agricultural production

91. In ancient times all over the world, to begin with the popular form of Government used to be:
A. bureaucracy B. dictatorship
C. monarchy D. theocracy

92. ________ provide an example of lions, type of governing elite, according to Pareto.
A. Military dictatorship B. Oligarchy
C. Chiefdom D. Tutelary democracy

93. From ________ point of view, the source of power in society lies in the economic infrastructure.
A. Marx's B. Weber's
C. Parson's D. Wright Mill's

94. According to Pareto ________ provide an example of 'fox' type of elite.
A. military dictatorship
B. political democracy
C. Europeon democracies
D. industrial elites

95. According to Pareto, ________ type of elite, rule by cunning and guile and by diplomatic manipulation.
A. lions B. foxes
C. feeble D. unstable

96. Which of the following is not true of the state?
A. it is all comprehensive
B. it is abstract
C. it is something concrete
D. it enjoys loyalty of the citizens

97. For Aristotle state was an agency for:
A. strengthening political ideology
B. giving good life
C. promoting economic interests
D. promoting religion

98. Which one of the following is not an opticnal function of the state?
A. to provide civic facilities
B. to open educational institutions
C. to arrange for higher education
D. to promote international relations

99. Where do the Guild socialists and syndicalists differ from each other? Both believe that:
A. state is an evil
B. there should be a stateless society
C. state is squeezing the blood of the poor
D. the capital is theft

100. According to Pareto, there are two main types of governing elite they are ________ .
A. ruler and ruled
B. capitalist and proletariat
C. lions and foxes
D. None of the above

101. Which one of the following, if not present, will not make a state in the technical sense of the term:
A. Sovereignty B. Population
C. Territory D. Government

102. ________ saw Marxism as an ideology rather than an objective analysis of society.
A. Elite theory B. Weber
C. Durkheim D. Ralph Dahrendorf

103. Among the Kwakiuti Indians of North American pacific coast, 'Potalath' means ______.
A. war of property B. war of prestige
C. war of blood D. war of power

104. Find out the incorrect match:
A. Bantu tribes–state system
B. A cephalous system–Nuers of Sudan
C. Potlatch–war of property
D. Wright Mills–circulation of elites

105. The sovereign who does not exercise powers but in whose name power is exercised is known as:
A. de–facto sovereign B. de–jure sovereign
C. popular sovereign D. real sovereign

106. A political system in which constitution can be easily amended is known as:
A. flexible constitution
B. rigid constitution
C. partly flexible and partly rigid constitution
D. None of the above

107. The laws which may or may not be obeyed and for which the state does not punish are known as:
A. moral laws B. fundamental rights
C. international laws D. municipal laws

108. Which one of the following is not a limitation on the authority of the states?
A. international treaties
B. respect for public sentiments
C. labours laws
D. moral laws and obligations

109. Major change in society occurs when one elite replaces another, a process Pareto calls ________.
A. circulation of elites B. interchange of elites
C. fixation of elites D. decaying of elites

110. According to Weber, the three forms of authority are ________ meaning that they are not usually found in their pure forms.
A. superficial B. unreal
C. ideal types D. ideological types

111. The leader of a military coup may have ________ but little ________.
A. authority, power B. authority, prestige
C. power, authority D. prestige, power

112. Distinction between compulsory and optional functions of the state is:
A. gradually widening
B. slowly narrowing down
C. continues to be what it was in the past
D. has now practically ended

113. Wright Mills maintained that ________ involves the coincidence of economic, military and political power.
A. real elite B. power elite
C. psychological elite D. economic elite

114. "The structuring of social relations across time and space as the result of the interaction of pre-existing structure and individual agency" can be described as:
A. Structuration
B. Post-structuralism
C. Structuralism
D. None of these

115. The aim of all governmental activities should be the greatest good of the greatest number of people was the philosophy of:
A. Marxists B. Socialists
C. Guild Socialists D. Anarchists

116. A system of government in which real power is vested in the hands of an elected head of the state is known as:
A. parliamentary form of government
B. presidential form of government
C. elected monarchy
D. limited monarchy

117. According to Marx, if the ruling class power is accepted as legitimate by the subject class this is an indication of ________.
A. false class consciousness
B. alienation
C. revolution
D. coercion

118. Who of the following believes that capitalism is sowing the seeds of its own degeneration?
A. Marxism B. Individualism
C. Guild socialism D. Anarchism

119. According to Karl Marx dialectic is the out come of:
A. capital industry conflict
B. action and reaction
C. employer-employee conflict
D. conflict of workers among themselves

120. The system under which a heredity monarch is the head of the state with practically no powers is known as:
A. absolute monarchy B. limited monarchy
C. dictatorship D. bureaucracy

121. Which of the following is associated with the slogan "workers of the world unite, you have nothing to lose but your chains"?
A. Capitalism B. State socialism
C. Marxism D. Guild socialism

122. A system of government which believes that the real powers should be vested in the hands of the proletariat is known as:
A. Anarchism
B. Syndicalism
C. Guild socialism
D. Communism

123. A system of government in which real authority and power is vested in the hands of civil servants is known as:
A. polity B. monocracy
C. pluralism D. bureaucracy

124. A political system which allows free economic competitions without any interference from the state is known as:
A. individualism B. socialism
C. capitalism D. anarchism

125. Of the state in these days, it is expected that it should perform:
A. only compulsory function
B. only optional functions
C. partly compulsory and partly optional function
D. both compulsory and optional functions

126. In the past the king usually had:
A. the cooperation of the feudal lords
B. the cooperation of the church
C. bitter opposition from the feudal lords
D. opposition from his courtiers

127. In the past the aim of the conquest used to be to:
A. spread religion
B. culturally up lift the people
C. socially integrate the world
D. economically raise their standard

128. In a simple society one of the most important function of the king was to:
A. collect taxes
B. maintain charitable institutions
C. financially assist educational institutions
D. dig canals for agriculturalists

129. The Marxists believe that in order to end the state:
A. violence is the only way
B. non-violence is the only way
C. violence needs be used when necessary
D. violence should never be used

130. "The most important outward factor in the formation of nationalities is the state". To whom do you attribute those words?
A. Karl Marx B. Hans Kohn
C. Ramsay Muir D. MacIver

131. Who first introduced the concept of alienation in to sociological theory?
A. Hegel B. August Comte
C. Marx D. Herbert Spencer

132. Vertical mobility involves ________ .
A. change in role
B. change in occupation
C. change in group
D. change in social class position.

133. Subjective class concept locates individuals in the statification hierarchy according to judgements of:
A. analyst B. society
C. individual himself D. community

134. The Caste system is ________ in nature.
A. hierarchical B. symmetrical
C. contradictory D. None of the above

135. If a person became a minister from an ordinary shop keeper, the mobility is called ________ .
A. upward mobility B. downward mobility
C. horizontal mobility D. None of the above

136. According to Weber, communal division is an example of ________ .
A. Status groups B. Class
C. Party D. Caste

137. According to ________ Caste are the modified forms of guilds.
A. Occupational theory B. Political theory
C. Evolutionary theory D. None of the above

138. Interdependence among castes is termed as________ by Srinivas.
A. Jajmani ststem B. Vertical unity
C. Horizontal unity D. Mutuality

139. According to ________ class is determined by a person's market situation.
A. Marx B. Weber
C. Ralph Dahrendorf D. Lenin

140. According to ________ class is a historical category.
A. Weber B. Engels
C. Marx D. Ralph Dahrendorf

141. Jajmani system is ________ .
A. achieved
B. hereditary
C. contractual in nature
D. None of the above

142. _______ argues that stratification system derive from common values.
A. Talcott Parsons B. Weber
C. Davis and Moore D. Tumin

143. Which of the following is employed to mean the numerous sub-divisions of a Varna?
A. Jati B. Caste
C. Gotra D. None of the above

144. According to Marx's classic phrase, the proletariat area:
A. Class in themselves
B. Class for themselves
C. Class by themselves
D. Class through themselves

145. According to _______, social stratification originated on account of religious principles and customs.
A. Hocart B. Risley
C. Ghurye D. Senart

146. The word 'Caste' owes its origin to _______ word 'Caste'.
A. Spanish B. German
C. Latin D. Polynesian

147. Who maintained that basically, alienation involves compulsive conformity to norms?
A. Weber B. Functionalists
C. Marx D. Durkheim

148. Membership in the Caste is _______ .
A. Ascribed B. Given by the govt.
C. Achieved D. God's gift

149. Self-identification is important in determining _______ .
A. Objective status B. Accorded status
C. Subjective status D. Status

150. According to _______, when a class is some what strictly hereditary, we may call it a Caste.
A. MacIver B. Weber
C. Sorokin D. Cooley

151. Caste is an _______ group.
A. exogamous B. utilitarian
C. endogamous D. indispensable

152. Objective class concept locates individuals in the stratification hierarchy according to judgements of:
A. analyst B. society
C. community D. individual himself

153. In which of the following the first literary traces of caste system are found?
A. Rigveda B. Atharvaveda
C. Yajurveda D. Samaveda

154. Who wrote the book, "Class struggle in France"?
A. Marx
B. Lenin
C. Marcuse
D. Ralph Dahrendorf

155. If a teacher leaves one school to work in another this is called _______ .
A. downward mobility B. horizontal mobility
C. vertical mobility D. None of the above

156. Who wrote the book, "Eighteenth Brumaire of Louis Bonaparte"?
A. Lenin B. Engels
C. Herbert Marcuse D. Marx

157. Jajmani relations are _______ .
A. temporary
B. permanent
C. contractual
D. depend on Jajman's will

158. Only when _______ attitudes develop does the class struggle really emerge.
A. 'for sich' B. ansick
C. nationalistic D. capitalistic

159. Alienation for Marx is a/an _______ .
A. objective condition B. subjective condition
C. individual condition D. class condition

160. Status groups, according to Weber are identified by:
A. education B. occupation
C. styles of life D. family back ground

161. Who first used the term 'Rites de passage"?
A. Marx B. Weber
C. A. Van Gennep D. Cooley

162. Marx differentiated various classes in _______ .
A. Objective terms
B. Subjective terms
C. Both subjective and objective terms
D. Absolute terms

163. From Marxian perspective, political power derives from:
A. economic power B. social prestige
C. landed property D. religious sanction

164. The person who gives service to the Jajman is called:
A. Parjan B. Kamin
C. Karmin D. Purohit

165. Marx perceived petty bourgeoisie as _______ .
A. a well integrated class
B. a class in it self
C. a transitional class
D. he did not mention any

166. ________ refers to a social stratum less closed and rigid, than a caste but more closed than a social class.
A. Commune B. Status group
C. Estate D. None of the above

167. The feeling of class consciousness is necessary to constitute a ________ but not ________.
A. Class, Caste B. Caste, Class
C. Status group, Class D. Caste, Status group

168. In the Marxian terminology the institutions and value system form the ________ of society.
A. Foundation B. Super structure
C. Core D. Base

169. The practice of Pratiloma and Anuloma marriages indicates:
A. That the intercaste marriages were not completely unknown
B. That the caste system was rigidly followed
C. That inter caste marriage were discouraged
D. That marriage was not sacramental

170. Who wrote the Communist Manifesto?
A. Marx B. Lenin
C. Engels D. None of the above

171. The choice of mates in caste system is generally ________.
A. exogamous B. endogamous
C. limited D. open

172. Basis of Social stratification is:
A. Social inequality B. Social harmony
C. Social understanding D. Social problems

173. In feudal society one factor which was responsible for social stratification was:
A. estate
B. religion
C. approach to the centre of power
D. none of the above

174. Which of the following does not fall under the category of community disorganisation?
A. divorce B. poverty
C. unemployment D. competition

175. Which of the following is not the cause of crime?
A. defective marriage B. love marriages
C. news and cinema D. change in values

176. Which one of the following is not a major cause of social stratification?
A. sudden crisis
B. cumulative crisis
C. natural calamities
D. absence of change in social values

177. Social stratification means breaking up of relationship between:
A. two individuals
B. two societies
C. two nations
D. group of individuals

178. Which one of the following is not usually the case of social disorganisation?
A. non-adjustment of old order with the new one
B. over population
C. over employment
D. crime

179. Social disorganisation is a process which is:
A. Static B. Continuous
C. One time D. None of these

180. Which one of the following is not the main cause of crime?
A. poverty B. unemployment
C. industrialisation D. achievements

181. Which one of the following is not the main cause of crime in modern societies?
A. poverty B. population explosion
C. war D. joint family

182. Which of the following does not fall under the category of individual social disorganisation?
A. insanity B. divorce
C. suicide D. drunkedness

183. Which of the following schools of thought lays stress on heredity as a cause of crime?
A. economic B. geographical
C. sociological D. typological

184. According to ecological school of thought main cause of crime is:
A. Social conditions
B. Physical environments
C. Heredity
D. Economic needs

185. Which of the following is not the major cause of social disorganization?
A. Urbanisation
B. Industrialization
C. Lack of faith in God
D. Break up of joint family system

186. What among the following you think, keeps caste in alive?
A. The practice of petty loyalty
B. Unhealthy social standards of behaviour
C. A perverse under standing of the caste
D. All of the above

187. Which factors among the following had not weakened the caste system?
A. Industrialization and urbanization
B. The quick means of transport
C. The constitution
D. The policy of reservations

188. The Indian Society has been described as static. Do you agree?
A. Yes
B. No
C. The development of castes and subcaste hindered its development
D. Classes did exist in the Indian society

189. Which among the following do you think discouraged the growth of class system?
A. The miserable economic condition of the people
B. Decline in town life
C. Limited Commercial operations
D. All the above

190. Which among the following do you think is Contributory to the development of capitalist class?
A. Poverty and misery
B. Foreign domination
C. The attitude of the rulers
D. Free enterprise and profit accumulation

191. In which of the following systems of stratifications, flexibility of mobility exist?
A. Estate system B. Caste system
C. Class system D. Social system

192. Mark out among the following the unique feature of Estate system:
A. Legalised inequalities
B. Created disparities of wealth
C. Encouraged hereditary occupations
D. Denial of political rights to the multitudes

193. How many Estates were there under the Estate system?
A. Two B. Three
C. Four D. Five

194. Mark out the privileges enjoyed by church and nobility under Estate system:
A. Complete or partial exemption from taxes
B. Right to tax the residents of Estate
C. Hunting rights
D. All the above

195. Which among the following conclusion you think is correct?
A. Untouchability is the direct consequence of the cast system
B. The absence of the appropriate Brahmanical leadership, the rigid insistence of caste led to the disintegration of the society
C. Casteism destroyed the social flexibility
D. All the above

196. While discussing stratification which of the following has/have referred to effective role allocation and performance?
A. Parsons B. Tumin
C. Davis and Tumin D. Davis and Moore

197. In feudal society one factors which was responsible for social stratification was:
A. Estate
B. Religion
C. Approach of the centre of power
D. None of the above

198. Weber's introduction of the notion of status and status groups into stratification theory was intended to serve as ________.
A. A supplement to pure class analysis
B. An antidote to pure class analysis
C. A rejection of pure class analysis
D. None of the above

199. ________ constitutes the primary model of the estate system.
A. Medieval European feudal society
B. Spanish society
C. Ancient Greek society
D. Medieval Indian society

200. ________ are stratified according to the principles of their consumption of goods as represented by special styles of life.
A. Classes B. Status groups
C. Parties D. Castes

201. Which of the following terms has been identified as a dimension of accorded status by most sociologists?
A. Status B. Social class
C. Class D. Caste

202. Which one of the following has not been included as a characteristic of caste system by N.K. Dutt?
A. Ban on inter-caste marriage
B. Group hierarchy
C. Restrictions on eating habits
D. Fixed occupation

203. In the primitive society the basis of social classification was:
A. Birth of a person
B. Possession of wealth by him
C. Political power they enjoyed
D. Control which they had over religion

204. Private estate is a sort of fundamental right for the people was an idea which developed:
A. During ancient times
B. During middle ages
C. With the down of democracy
D. With the coming of the Marxists

205. Social stratification is an indication of:
A. Process of ranking in society
B. Backwardness of society
C. Competitive capacity of the society
D. International understanding of society

206. How do you explain the causes responsible for social stratification?
A. It is due to the inherited difference among men
B. It is due to the incentives, that society provided to the social position
C. The fittest in conflict and war acquired privileges, against the dominated
D. The origin is not clear

207. Social stratification is guided mainly by:
A. Religious feelings of the person
B. The extent of socialisation
C. Economic considerations of the people
D. Extent of contacts

208. Which one of the following is a factor which does not hinder social mobility?
A. Superstitions B. Narrow outlook
C. Old traditions D. Spread of literacy

209. Private property is given the fullest recognition under:
A. Capitalism B. Marxism
C. Socialism D. Anarchism

210. Private property everywhere has helped in the rise of:
A. Feudalism B. Communism
C. Socialism D. Anarchism

211. Who has given the concept 'hierarchy' in the context of caste stratification?
A. T.N. Madan B. Luis Dumont
C. S.C. Dube D. D.F. Pocock

212. According to Karl Marx Proletariat is:
A. Homogeneous B. Heterogeneous
C. Diversified D. Semi-homogeneous

213. In the Marxian perspective ________ forms the infrastructure of the society.
A. Economy B. Religion
C. Politics D. Belief systems

214. The third estate performs vital role in:
A. Democracy B. Dictatorship
C. Theocracy D. Aristocracy

215. Which of the following theories makes us believe that caste system is not of human but of Divine origin?
A. Racial theory B. Political theory
C. Occupational theory D. Traditional theory

216. In our times most acceptable theory about the origin of the caste system is:
A. Evolutionary theory B. Religious theory
C. Political theory D. Occupational theory

217. Which of the following classes included the 'Serf bound to soil'?
A. Cottars and Villeins B. Theow
C. Theow and Cottars D. Villeins

218. As a basis for conflict with the dominant class what did Marx wish to see created among the depressed strata?
A. A closeness of spirit
B. Harmony
C. Awareness of their pathetic state
D. A sense of identical class interest

219. Who has maintained that the modern caste groups are 'associations' while the ancient castes where communities?
A. Tonnies B. Max Weber
C. Durkheim D. Raymond Mack

220. There is a vertical unity among the castes. This has been maintained by:
A. G.S. Ghurye B. Andre Beteille
C. Mackim Marriot D. M.N. Srinivas

221. The untouchables are not coming forward because of:
A. Lack of knowledge
B. Illiteracy
C. Their inferiority complex
D. Due to their traditional outlook

222. Private property come into the society as a serpent, was said by:
A. Plato B. Hobbes
C. Rousseau D. Machiavelli

223. Which of the following is bigger in organisation?
A. State B. Caste
C. Class D. Community

224. In the medieval society (Roman) there were three classes. Which of the following was not such a class?
A. Theow B. Villeins
C. Cottars D. Plebian

225. Manu's idea of caste's functional differentiation is comparable to our present day:
A. Trade unionism B. Anarchism
C. Occupationalism D. Syndicalism

226. Which of the following castes was known as Padjaa?
A. Sudra B. Brahmin
C. Vis D. Kahatriya

227. The most acceptable belief about the origin of private estate is believed to be:
A. Religion B. Family
C. Education D. Political awakening

228. 'If a 'man' violated a Brahmin female he was to be burnt a live. This punishment was suggested by:
A. Raja Ram Mohan Roy
B. Kautilya
C. Banabhatta
D. Manu

229. The Guild Theory was supported by:
A. Denjil Ibbetson B. Kautilya
C. Pānini D. None of the above

230. In which of the following is the first literanytraces of caste system found?
A. Rigveda B. Atharvaveda
C. Yajuraveda D. Samaveda

231. Changes in social positions with regard to variations in occupations, prestige, income, wealth, power and social class is referred to as:
A. Social change
B. International moblility
C. Social mobility
D. Migration

232. Who said this? 'The differential distribution of authority leads to class formation and class conflict?
A. Karl Popper B. Ralph Dahrendorf
C. Karl Marx D. C. Wright Mills

233. The difference between the 'Dasa' and 'Arya' is reflected through:
A. Rigvedic literature
B. Kautilya's Arthashastra
C. Writings of foreign travellers
D. Mahabharata

234. Class consciousness "Counts in the realization of Similarity of attitude and behaviour with members of other classes", is the view of:
A. Mannheim B. Ginsberg
C. MacIver D. Durkheim

235. A 'Pulayam' must keep himself from a brahmin in kerala at a distance of:
A. Ninety sixpaces B. Thirty sixpaces
C. Twenty-sixpaces D. Seven paces

236. Which of the following caste was known as ekahati?
A. Sudra B. Kshatriya
C. Vis D. Brahmins

237. A Tiyan must keep himself away from a Brahmin. At a distance of:
A. Thirty-six steps B. Nine steps
C. An arm's length D. Forty miles

238. Which of the following is not the main cause responsible for the promotion of class consciousness?
A. Rivalry B. Conflicts
C. Common traditions D. Religious fedings

239. Which one of the following factors contributes to the development of social classes?
A. Population explosion
B. Population control
C. Better health facilities
D. High mortality rate

240. The main factor responsible for distinguishing a social and economic class is not on the basis of:
A. Heredity
B. Social links
C. Possession of wealth
D. Attainments in the field of education

241. According to Karl Marx the main cause responsible for the emergence of social class was:
A. Economic B. Social
C. Political D. Religious

242. According to MacIver the basis of social class formation was:
A. Economic
B. Education
C. Class consciousness
D. Technological advancement

243. Occupation of a person is:
A. Closely linked with his social status
B. Quite separate from his social status
C. Some what linked with his social status
D. None of the above

244. Changes in social positions with regard to variations in occupations, prestige, income, wealth, power and social class if referred to as:
A. Social change
B. International mobility
C. Social mobility
D. Migration

245. One of the important advantages of social class is that it:
A. Enables the society to allocate work to each person in the society
B. Helps in increased production in industry
C. Helps in locating competent persons for manning important jobs in society
D. Helps in urban-rural population migration process

246. The functionalists are primarily concerned with the ________ of social stratification, with the contribution to the maintenance and well being of society.
A. Function B. Aims
C. Value D. Nature

247. According to ______, a social class is any portion of a community marked off from the rest by the social status.
A. MacIver and Page B. Weber
C. Marshall D. Sorokin

248. According to Weber, as the division of labour becomes more complex, class ______
A. becomes more advanced
B. becomes more heterogeneous
C. remain essentially the same
D. none of the above

249. According to Weber, the status order tends to be:
A. Universalistic and achievement oriented
B. Particularistic and ascriptive
C. Particularistic and achievement oriented
D. Universalistic and ascriptive

250. Due to financial problems at home, a landless labourer from a village moved to city to work as a factory labourer. This is an example of:
A. Horizontal mobility
B. Vertical downward mobility
C. Vertical mobility
D. Social mobility

251. 'Social stratification is the mechanism which attaches unequal rewards and privileges to the different positions in society. Whom is this statement attributed to?
A. Parsons
B. Tumin
C. Weber
D. Davis and Moore

252. While discussing stratification who of the following has/have referred to effective role allocation and performance?
A. Parsons
B. Tumin
C. Davis and Tumin
D. Davis and Moore

253. Function and function alone is responsible for the origin of caste structure in India. Who said this?
A. Majumdar B. Ghurye
C. Nesfield D. Risley

254. Who has pointed out three sets of characteristics used as a basis of ranking, viz, possessions, qualities and performances?
A. Max Weber B. Functionalists
C. Talcott Parsons D. R.K. Merton

255. The Concept of ________ is fundamental to the caste system and every type of caste relation is governed by it.
A. Rites B. Pollution
C. Power D. Prestige

256. According to Sir Herbert Risley, Caste system originated in India due to ________
A. an artificial creation by the clever priesthood for permanent division and subjection
B. racial differences and hypergamy
C. specialization of religious duties
D. hereditary occupations and endogamy

257. Who, for the first time, has used the concept of 'Social Structure' in sociology?
A. Karl Marx
B. Herbert Spencer
C. Emile Durkheim
D. Max Weber

258. According to ________, the origin of caste system can be found in the nature and quality of social work performed by the various groups of people.
A. Guild theory B. Political theory
C. Occupational theory D. Racial theory

259. According to ________, when status is wholly predetermined, so that men are born to their lot without any hope of changing it, then class takes the extreme form of caste.
A. Weber B. Marx
C. MacIver D. Davis

260. Weber defines ________ as groups which are specifically concerned with influencing policies and making decisions in the interests of their membership.
A. Statues groups B. Classes
C. Parties D. Castes

261. Weber posits the views that ________ reach their most developed form in the caste system of traditional Hindu Society.
A. Status groups B. Castes
C. Jajmani system D. None of the above

262. ________ refers to movement in any or all of the three areas of living class, occuption and power.
A. Horizontal mobility
B. Vertical mobility
C. Migration
D. Downward mobility

263. ________ may be defined as a hereditary, endogamous group having a traditional association with an occupation.
A. Class B. Caste
C. Estate D. Status group

264. As a basis for conflict with the dominant class what did marx wish to see created among the depressed strata?

A. a closeness of spirit
B. harmony
C. awareness of their pathetic state
D. a sense of identical class interest

265. According to Marx, when a class becomes award of its interests and organizes itself, it becomes a:

A. class in itself B. revolutionary class
C. class for itself D. bourgeoisie

266. Under ________, each group within a village is expected to give certain standardised services to the other castes.

A. Commensality B. Jajmani system
C. Prescriptions D. Mutuality

267. According to Weber ________ within each of the main classes would forestall any move in the direction of internal unity and coherence.

A. Pressure groups B. Power blocks
C. Status groups D. Parties

268. Which of the following terms has been identified as a dimension of accorded status by most sociologists?

A. Status B. Social class
C. Class D. Caste

269. Who said this? 'The differential distribution of authority leads to class formation and class conflict'.

A. Karl Popper B. Ralph Dahrendorf
C. Karl Marx D. Wright Mills

270. Social stratification is the indication of:

A. Process by which a person gets ranks in his society
B. Backwardness of society
C. Competitive capacity of the society
D. International understanding of society

271. ________ refers to the rules and prescriptions about inter caste relations, particularly to eating and drinking of water.

A. Prohibition B. Common sality
C. Regulations D. Prescriptions

272. The "history of all hither to existing society is a history of class struggle". To whom is this statement attributed?

A. Engels B. Lenin
C. Ralph Dahrendorf D. None of the above

273. Weber's introduction of the notion of status and status groups into stratification theory was intended to serve as ________.

A. a supplement to pure class analysis
B. an antidote to pure class analysis
C. a rejection of pure class analysis
D. None of the above

274. According to Marx, a class which has come into being but which is not yet conscious of its fundamental interests is a ________

A. class in itself B. class for itself
C. bourgeoisie D. None of the above

275. Which one of the following is not the main cause of social disorganisation?

A. war
B. cumulative crisis
C. natural calamities
D. absence of social tensions

276. The Upanyana ceremony was:

A. It was a sacrament meant for women
B. It was a ritual performed by a Sanyasi
C. With this ceremony one was initiated a student
D. Initiating a person in the varna

277. Social disorganisation is a problem concerned primarily with:

A. developed societies
B. developing societies
C. under developed societies
D. all the societies

278. Which of the following does not fall under the category of family disorganisation?

A. Venereal diseases
B. Drunkenness
C. Low income
D. Urbanisation

279. Which one of the following is not one of the important causes of social disorganisation?

A. Conflict between the old and the new order
B. Urbanisation
C. Industrialisation
D. Rigidity in social organisation

280. Which one of the following is not the main cause of crime?

A. Lack of family control
B. Strict family controls
C. Use of intoxicating drinks
D. Religion

281. Kingsley Davis's name is associated with one of the following theories about the origin of social stratification. Which one is that?

A. force theory
B. war theory
C. reward theory
D. ransom theory

282. Which one of the following helps us in identifying social structure of rural society in India?

A. Occupation B. Family size
C. Caste D. Skin Colour

283. Who of the following maintains that the classification of people into classes in a device for simplifying the world to which we must respond?

A. W. Lloyd Warner B. Lundberg
C. Ginsberg D. Hobhouse

284. Which one of the following is not true about caste system?

A. One cannot change caste
B. It is a very narrow area
C. Inter-caste marriage is difficult
D. There is class consciousness among the members of the caste

285. When a member of the same generation changes over to a new occupation the type of mobility is called:

A. Intra-generational mobility
B. Inter-generational mobility
C. Educational mobility
D. Occupational mobility

286. Which one of the following is not true of social stratification?

A. It is in the form of hierarchy
B. It indicates only differences in society
C. It indicates rank and status of a person
D. It is based on the division of society into groups

287. Which one of the following is a significant factor responsible for the development of social class?

A. Rapid progress made by the society in urbanisation
B. Lack of social communication
C. Increase in social contacts
D. Decrease in distances

288. In feudal society stratification was on the basis of:

A. Caste of a person
B. Whether one was a slave or a free person
C. Whether one lived in a city or an urban area
D. Whether one was educated or uneducated

289. Markout the correct statement:

A. Estate system existed in Indian feudal society
B. Estate system is a product of feudal Europe
C. Estate and class system are similar
D. Estate and caste system are similar

290. Which among the following statements do you think is correct?

A. Class consciousness is factional in character
B. It is manipulated by the upstart leader
C. It is a sentiment that just determines the conduct of individuals
D. It is a corporate consciousness

291. Which of the following statements is true?

A. Class is more open than caste
B. The caste system is believed to have been divinely ordained where as classes are not founded on religious dogmas
C. Caste is more open than class
D. Both (A) and (B) are true

292. Pre-revolutionary Russia, as a/an ________ society in which the clergy, the nobility, merchants and peasants were separated into social strata that depended on birth and were controlled by law.

A. classless B. caste ridden
C. estate D. agricultural

293. Who maintained that those who perform successfully in terms of society's values will be ranked highly and they will be likely to receive a variety of rewards.

A. Parsons B. Davis
C. Durkheim D. Redcliffe Brown

294. According to Marx, various forms of exploitative made of production have been ________.

A. Slavery, feudalism, and capitalism
B. Slavery, barbarism and capitalism
C. Slavery, bourgeoisie, and capitalism
D. None of the above

295. According to Weber, ________ refers to the unequal distribution of economic rewards where as ________ refers to the unequal distribution of social honour.

A. Class, caste B. Power, prestige
C. Class, status D. Caste, class

296. According to Weber

A. Status and class are always co-related
B. Status and class are co-related but there are many cases in which they are not co-related
C. Class determines status
D. Status determines class

297. The status orders, according to Weber, operates:

A. to encourage social mobility up or down
B. to discourage social mobility up or down
C. to encourage upward social mobility but discourage downward social mobility
D. to encourage group mobility up or down

298. 'Caste is a Brahmanic of Indo-Aryan culture cradled in the land of the Ganges and hence transferred to other parts of India. 'Who has said this'?

A. MacIver B. Majumdar
C. Ghurye D. Risely

299. The social classes are large groups of people who differ from each other by their relation to the means of social production. Whose view is this?
A. Marx B. Ralph Dahrendorf
C. Weber D. Lenin

300. Point out which one of the following does not apply in the case of social disorganisation?
A. there is no clarity in situation
B. bonds of social control are weak
C. there is no adjustment between the individual and the society
D. Members lay stress on duties rather than on rights

301. Which one of the following is not the characteristic of social problem?
A. it results in change of existing social order
B. it exists, whether people like it or not
C. it is related to consciousness
D. it is always desired that its solution be found out

302. Which one of the following is not a salient feature of social disorganisation?
A. it is conflict between the old and the new order
B. it is out come of transfer of functions from one group to the other
C. it results inchange in social structure
D. it is the outcome of rigid political party system

303. Which one is not true of social disorganisation?
A. it is a malady
B. it is a process
C. it is relative to social organisation
D. Social organisation of today can be disorganisation of tomorrow

304. Which of the following classification of social problems has been given by Harold A. Phelps?
A. physical, cultural and economic
B. heritage—physical, biological and cultural
C. system—social, economic and political
D. customs—new, outdated, continuing

305. Social problem may be defined as conditions which:
A. effect a group of people
B. effect a class of people
C. favourable effect large number of people
D. adversely effect large number of people

306. Point out which one of the following is not the characteristic of social organisation?
A. the members of the society have hedonistic behaviour
B. there is similarity of interests and attitudes
C. members lay stress on duties
D. there is strong social control

307. Who recognized the existence of the petty bourgeoisie who not only own the means of production but also contribute their labour power, like the proletariat, as one of the classes in modern capitalist society?
A. Marx B. Engels
C. Marcuse D. None of the above

308. Marx believed that western society had developed through the following main epochs. They are ________.
A. Primitive communism, ancient society, feudal society and capitalist society
B. Savagery, feudalism and capitalism
C. Slavery, barbarism and feudalism
D. Feudalism, capitalism and socialism

309. ________ refers to the division of a population into strate one on top of another, on the basis of the possession of certain characteristics which the society regards as desirable or less desirable.
A. Social inequality B. Social stratification
C. Caste D. Hierarchy

310. Which one of the following is not true about social problem?
A. social harmony is disturbed
B. hostility and suspicion is created
C. there is large scale social dissatisfaction
D. it is permanent in nature and character

311. Which one of the following does not apply to social disorganisation?
A. ostentation is replaced by sincerity
B. social interests are subordinated by individuality
C. there is conflict of more
D. there is conflict among different parts of society

312. Which one of the following is the main cause of social disorganisation?
A. industrialisation
B. breaking up of joint family system
C. change in religious feelings of the people
D. change in political system

313. Which one of the following is not a functional utility of social stratification?
A. it provides different statuses to different persons
B. it is needed freliminating competition
C. it is needed for performance of proper roles
D. it is unavoidable for social advancement

314. Today it is believed that:
A. People commit crime as a matter of habit
B. Society has nothing to do with crimes
C. Criminals are born and not made
D. Criminals are made by the society and they are not born

315. The wars cause crime because:
A. the govrnment becomes tax in administration
B. the people becomes conscious about crimes
C. there are excessive controls
D. there is social disharmony

316. Which one of the following factors does not count much in social status?
A. Occupation of a person
B. Social needs of person
C. Availability of personnel in the society for particular occupations
D. Availability of natural resources to the society

317. In the past in India the Brahmins were considered at the top of the society and also a superior class because they had:
A. A lot of wealth in their possession
B. Political authority and power
C. Control over trade and commerce
D. Education and purity of heart and character

318. In ancient India maximum respect was enjoyed by those who:
A. Held maximum private estate
B. Were spiritually high and did not possess estate
C. Had maximum wealth
D. None of the above

319. Which one of the following is true of caste system?
A. It helps in the promotion of social integration
B. It results in social disintegration
C. It encourages sense of social responsibility
D. It promotes educational equality

320. According to Prof. Srinivas theory of Sanskritisation the word "Sanskritisation" stands for:
A. Study of sanskrit language
B. Study of classical works
C. Desire of the low caste people to go up
D. Attempt by the upper caste to condemn the low caste people

321. Importance of real estate increased when:
A. Hold of religion over society increased
B. Hold of religion over society decreased
C. Hold of religion over society remained what it was
D. Religion become weak

322. Mark out among the following what is correct?
A. Social stratification is the cause of conflict
B. It is the social cover of ugly exploitation
C. It is antisocial in operation
D. It is a constantly changing phenomenon

323. The main cause of crime due to population explosion is:
A. earning capacity of the family comes down
B. social values radically change
C. the people lose faith in religion
D. the state feels helpless in providing facilities

324. Which group of thinkers advocate the Cyclical theories of social change?
A. Comte, Spencer, Morgan
B. Sorokin, Pareto, Toyanbee
C. Comte, Marx, Pareto
D. Spencer, Veblen, Marx

325. Point out which of the following is not the characteristic of social organisation?
A. the members have mutual trust in each other
B. there is a perfect adjustment among the members
C. there is a variety of differing interests and attitudes
D. there is a synthesis between status and functions

326. Which one of the following is not a functional utility of social stratification?
A. it helps in providing opportunities
B. it develops a spirit of struggle
C. it helps in the deciding responsibility of every one in the society
D. it helps identifying unsuitable persons in society

327. The concepts: children of the soil, the minority interest etc. are:
A. Derogatory to the National interest
B. Anti-national in character
C. Indicative of the lack of social mobility
D. The sign of class consciousness

328. Which of the following does not come under corporate class consciousness?
A. People share a similar social status
B. People develop uniting sentiments
C. The people share socially similar status but not uniting sentiments
D. The people share both similar social status and uniting sentiments

329. Corporate class consciousness may be defined as "a sentiment uniting a whole group sharing a similar social status". These words belong to:
A. Page
B. Karl Mannheim
C. Tonnies
D. MacIver

330. Name the Indian Sociologist who made important contribution to the study of social values:
A. D.N. Majumdar
B. Ram Krishna Mukherjee
C. Radha Kamal Mukherjee
D. S.C. Dube

ANSWERS

1	2	3	4	5	6	7	8	9	10
A	D	A	B	A	D	C	A	A	B
11	12	13	14	15	16	17	18	19	20
B	B	C	D	C	D	A	D	C	B
21	22	23	24	25	26	27	28	29	30
B	C	D	B	C	C	B	A	C	D
31	32	33	34	35	36	37	38	39	40
A	A	C	B	B	A	D	B	C	D
41	42	43	44	45	46	47	48	49	50
D	D	D	D	D	D	D	C	A	C
51	52	53	54	55	56	57	58	59	60
C	B	C	C	C	B	C	C	D	D
61	62	63	64	65	66	67	68	69	70
C	A	C	D	D	D	C	B	D	D
71	72	73	74	75	76	77	78	79	80
D	B	D	C	D	D	D	A	D	A
81	82	83	84	85	86	87	88	89	90
D	D	D	B	D	A	A	B	A	A
91	92	93	94	95	96	97	98	99	100
C	A	A	C	B	C	A	D	B	C
101	102	103	104	105	106	107	108	109	110
D	A	A	D	B	A	A	C	A	C
111	112	113	114	115	116	117	118	119	120
C	B	B	A	C	B	A	A	B	B
121	122	123	124	125	126	127	128	129	130
C	D	D	C	D	A	B	D	C	B
131	132	133	134	135	136	137	138	139	140
C	D	C	A	A	A	D	B	B	C
141	142	143	144	145	146	147	148	149	150
B	A	A	A	A	A	A	A	C	D
151	152	153	154	155	156	157	158	159	160
C	A	A	A	B	D	B	A	A	C
161	162	163	164	165	166	167	168	169	170
C	A	A	A	C	C	A	B	A	A
171	172	173	174	175	176	177	178	179	180
B	A	A	A	B	D	D	C	B	A
181	182	183	184	185	186	187	188	189	190
D	B	D	A	D	D	D	B	D	D
191	192	193	194	195	196	197	198	199	200
C	A	B	D	D	A	A	B	A	B
201	202	203	204	205	206	207	208	209	210
B	D	B	B	A	D	C	D	A	A

211	212	213	214	215	216	217	218	219	220
B	A	A	A	D	A	A	D	A	D
221	**222**	**223**	**224**	**225**	**226**	**227**	**228**	**229**	**230**
C	C	A	D	C	A	D	B	A	A
231	**232**	**233**	**234**	**235**	**236**	**237**	**238**	**239**	**240**
C	B	A	B	A	A	A	D	A	B
241	**242**	**243**	**244**	**245**	**246**	**247**	**248**	**249**	**250**
A	A	A	C	A	A	A	B	B	A
251	**252**	**253**	**254**	**255**	**256**	**257**	**258**	**259**	**260**
D	D	C	C	B	B	B	C	C	C
261	**262**	**263**	**264**	**265**	**266**	**267**	**268**	**269**	**270**
A	B	B	D	C	B	C	B	B	A
271	**272**	**273**	**274**	**275**	**276**	**277**	**278**	**279**	**280**
A	D	B	A	D	C	D	B	D	B
281	**282**	**283**	**284**	**285**	**286**	**287**	**288**	**289**	**290**
B	C	D	D	A	B	B	B	B	D
291	**292**	**293**	**294**	**295**	**296**	**297**	**298**	**299**	**300**
D	C	A	A	C	B	B	C	A	D
301	**302**	**303**	**304**	**305**	**306**	**307**	**308**	**309**	**310**
B	D	A	A	D	A	A	A	B	D
311	**312**	**313**	**314**	**315**	**316**	**317**	**318**	**319**	**320**
A	A	B	D	D	D	B	B	B	C
321	**322**	**323**	**324**	**325**	**326**	**327**	**328**	**329**	**330**
B	D	A	B	C	D	A	C	D	C

Social Change and the Economy

1. Kula exchange system is a classic example of:
A. redistribution B. negative reciprocity
C. reciprocity D. tribal market exchange

2. ________ is a price setting mechanism and is characterised by bargaining behaviour.
A. Reciprocity B. Potlatch
C. Market exchange D. Capitalism

3. Division of labour into occupation is called ______ .
A. Social division of labour
B. Occupational division of labour
C. Technical division of labour
D. Territorial division of labour

4. Division of labour within a particular enterprise is called .
A. Social division of labour
B. Technical division of labour
C. Occupation division of labour
D. Territorial division of labour

5. ________ is possible only if surplus is large enough to make it worthwhile.
A. Reciprocity B. Redistribution
C. Gimwali D. Market economy

6. ________ refers to goods, services or assistance freely given to kin, friends and neighbours without any explicit statement that anything is expected in return.
A. Reciprocity B. Generalized reciprocity
C. Balanced reciprocity D. Mutual exchange

7. While the basis of ________ is the exchange of gifts, any gift carries with it an obligation of return, either expressed or implied.
A. redistribution B. reciprocity
C. barter D. none of the above

8. The intra-tribal economic relations are mostly based on ________ .
A. shell money B. jajmani system
C. barter and exchange D. stone money

9. In ______ society, the notion of property is closely related to display and expenditure of wealth rather than to its accumulation.
A. primitive B. modern
C. communist D. industrial

10. The two items, that are circulated in the kula exchange have ________ .
A. high value
B. no value
C. high value but no practical use fullness
D. practical utility but no value

11. The temporary possession of kula article brings ________ to its owner but so does the way in which he gives it away.
A. material benefits B. prestige
C. utility D. wealth

12. ________ refers to the expectation of goods or services of roughly equal value in return for what one gives.
A. Generalized reciprocity
B. Redistribution
C. Gift exchange
D. Balanced reciprocity

13. An economy which has various media of exchange is called ________ .
A. Unicentric B. Multicentric
C. Bicentric D. None of the above

14. Who described the 'kula' exchange system of Eastern New Guinea?
A. Redcliff Brown B. Polyani
C. Evans Pritchard D. Malinowski

15. ________ is the process where by persons receiving goods are obligated to reciprocate by giving goods in return.
A. Distribution B. Reciprocity
C. Exchange D. Mutuality

16. In small scale economies, money may exist, but its purpose is limited. Such money is called ______ .
A. special purpose money
B. general purpose money
C. shell money
D. stone money

17. ________ refers to the process where goods or services are obtained through force or deception.
A. Balanced reciprocity
B. Material exchange
C. Negative reciprocity
D. War

18. ________ refers to the manner in which goods are divided among members of the society.
A. Distribution B. Separation
C. Accumulation D. Exchange

19. ________ requires only two parties where as ________ requires a social centre.
A. Redistribution, reciprocity
B. Reciprocity, redistribution
C. Gimwali, soulva
D. Mwali, woulva

20. ________ has pointed out that various kinds of exchange included in 'reciprocity can be arranged on a continuum according to the degree of balance involved.
A. Karl Polyani B. Marshall Sahlins
C. Tylor D. Wright Mills

21. Primitive economic organisations are of ________ type.
A. production B. subsistence
C. production-selling D. market-oriented

22. The presence of redistribution implies the existence of ________.
A. a value system
B. a stable social relationship
C. a hierarchy
D. a king

23. ________ means giving up self-interest or hostility for the sake of mutual benefit.
A. Negative reciprocity
B. Balanced reciprocity
C. Generalized reciprocity
D. Exchange of gifts

24. Kula exchange consists of the circulation of two items, i.e. ________ and ________.
A. shell armbands and mwali
B. mwali and soulva
C. shell disc necklace and soulva
D. None of the above

25. ________ tend to create generalized reciprocity.
A. Kinties B. Material benefits
C. Religious sanctions D. None of the above

26. Localization of industries is called ________ .
A. Territorial division of labour.
B. Technical division of labour
C. Social division of labour
D. Occupational division of labour

27. The Potlatch system of North West pacific coast Indians is a significant example of ________ .
A. Reciprocity B. Redistribution
C. Gimwali D. Mwali

28. Polyani termed the modern tax institutions as the example of the principal of ________ .
A. market exchange B. reciprocity
C. redistribution D. None of the above

29. Which of the following is not a characteristic of capitalism?
A. Large scale production
B. Private property
C. Competition
D. No-profit

30. ________ in an occupational group.
A. Trade-union B. Peer group
C. Play group D. Conjugal family

31. The theory of Heresy first appeared in the writings of:
A. Adam Smith B. Francois Quesney
C. Ricardo D. None of the above

32. In the primitive days trade was carried on with the help of:
A. coins B. currency
C. exchange of goods D. exchange of women

33. Which of the following is not true labour the aim of lower hunter's economy?
A. hunting reptiles B. collecting fruits
C. preparing sweets D. living in caves

34. Which of the following has been called as the twin brother of industrialism?
A. marketing B. consumption
C. capitalist system D. None of these

35. In complex economy of today the welfare of the workers is:
A. completely ignored
B. partly taken care of
C. given the highest priority
D. None of the above true

36. Karl Marx believed that in the production process maximum role is played by:
A. capital B. machine equipment
C. labour D. government

37. In the feudal system in production maximum stress was laid on:
A. labour B. capital
C. machine D. trade unions

38. According to Marxian philosophy the industrial workers can find an end to their problems if:
A. they destroy the machine
B. they unite
C. they raise capital
D. they set up their own machines

39. Economic development of the societies has been:
A. The outcome of scientific discoveries
B. A long continuous growth
C. The product of the invention of money
D. A sudden change in the life of the people

40. Which of the following statements is true about property?
A. Property is no-human in the usual sense of the word
B. Poperty owner possesses power
C. Property rights alwף.. and necessarily imply the use in actual way and enjoyment of object by the owner of the property
D. Property can be transferred

41. Money provided greater freedom to:
A. employers only
B. workers only
C. employers as well as workers
D. the market mechanism

42. Which of the following is not a feature of capitalism?
A. Private property B. Large scale production
C. Profit institution D. Absence of competition

43. Which of the following is an evil effect of capitalism?
A. Great for wealth
B. Protection of traditional human values
C. A way to materialism
D. No show of artificiality

44. People started leading a more settled life in the:
A. Agricultural stage B. Pastoral stage
C. Hunting stage D. None of the above

45. Agriculture was the leading occupation till:
A. mid eighteenth century
B. mid nineteenth century
C. mid seventeenth century
D. end of nineteenth century

46. The feeling to lead settled life established:
A. The village communities
B. The urban communities
C. The semi-rural communities
D. The semi-urban communities

47. With the specialization due to the division of labour in the agriculture stage:
A. More industries expanded
B. Volume of trade increased
C. Level of employment went up
D. More conflict arose in the society

48. The feudal type of evolved into:
A. socialism B. capitalism
C. syndicalism D. communism

49. Who of the following made a fundamental study of the human division of labour?
A. MacIver B. Durkheim
C. Max Weber D. Karl Mannheim

50. The presence of redistribution implies the existence of:
A. A value system
B. A stable social relationship
C. A hierarchy
D. A king

51. On which of the following principles is the institution of division of labour based?
A. Co-operation B. Independence
C. Individualism D. Disintegration

52. In beginning the domestication of:
A. Big cats came into practice
B. Big animals came into practice
C. Small animals came into practice
D. Dangerous animals came into practice

53. Which of the following is a theory of property?
A. The occupation theory
B. The labour theory
C. The Individualistic theory
D. All of the above

54. Which of the following is not a method adopted by trade unions?
A. Collective bargaining
B. Arbitration
C. Strikes
D. Destruction of the factory

55. Which of the following ideologies supports the institution of private property?
A. Syndicalism B. Socialism
C. Communism D. None of the above

56. Trade union is:
A. An occupational group
B. A business group
C. A competitive group
D. A familial group

57. Trade unions grew:
A. In industrialized societies
B. In the ruralized societies
C. In the illiterate societies
D. In the primitive societies

58. Which one of the following does not hold good in the case of new industrialism?
A. Considerable economic stability
B. Trade fluctuations
C. Waste of land
D. Waste of raw material

59. "The Puritan wanted work to be his vocation; we are forced to want it," who said these words?
A. Ginsberg B. Max Weber
C. W.E. More D. J.A. Schumpeter

60. According to which theory property is essential for the complete development of the human beings?
A. The occupation theory
B. The labour theory
C. The Idealistic theory
D. The socialistic theory

61. Which of the following is not a form of division of labour?
A. Social division of labour
B. Technical division of labour
C. Territorial division of labour
D. Decentralized division of labour

62. Which of the following is another name of the territorial division of labour?
A. Social division of labour
B. Technical division of labour
C. Forced division of labour
D. Socialization of industries

63. When division is made into different occupations it is know as:
A. Technical division of labour
B. Social division of labour
C. Territorial division of labour
D. All of the above

64. When the division is made within a particular enterprise it is known as:
A. Technical division of labour
B. Forced division of labour
C. Specialised division of labour
D. Regulated division of labour

65. Which of the following is a demerit of the corporate form of business enterprise?
A. A corporation is a legal entity
B. It is owned by stock holders
C. A small fraction attend the company's annual meeting
D. All of the above

66. Which of the following is the Latin word from which the word property has been derived?
A. Propriatas B. Proprietoes
C. Proposes D. Prosperity

67. Who of the following is the author of the book "Economy and Society"?
A. A. Comte B. Anderson and Parker
C. E. Durkheim D. Max Weber

68. Due to the rise of agriculture men:
A. Changed the flesh diet of nomadism to the diet of more vegetables
B. Did not change the diet at all
C. Started eating roasted flesh
D. Abandoned flesh eating and started eating milk products

69. Some trades were developed during the agricultural stage of development. Which of the following is such a trade?
A. Pottery making
B. Weaving of wool
C. Wearing of cotton
D. All of the above

70. Which of the following become the centers of trade owing to the industrial revolution?
A. Villages B. Cities
C. Towns D. Dales

71. Specialization based on specially acquired specific technical abilities is ________ in all pre-urban societies.
A. present B. absent
C. very rare D. None of the above

72. ________ is sometimes viewed as simply a process of balancing values.
A. Reciprocity B. Redistribution
C. Barter D. None of the above

73. ________ has divided the systems of exchange into three types, viz reciprocity, redistribution and market exchange.
A. Karl Ployani B. Ogburn
C. Tylor D. Wiser

74. In the broadest sense ________ may be defined as the economic system which market the widest used capital in the process of production.
A. capitalism B. socialism
C. market exchange D. corporation

75. Viewing the geographic area covered by the system as a circle, the travel only clockwise and ________ travel only counter ________ clockwise.
A. soulva, mwali
B. mwali, soulva
C. soulva, shell necklace
D. None of the above

76. Kula exchange system is distinctly different for common barter called ________, since it involves a higher level of trust.
A. mwali B. soulva
C. gimwali D. None of the above

77. ________ is an exchange transaction that involves direct movement of goods or services between parties.
A. redistribution B. barter
C. market exchange D. None of the above

78. In kula exchange ________ item remains in the possession of individual for very long as both items are continually being exchanged.
A. each B. neither
C. only one D. None of the above

79. A/An ________ us a combination of capital groups operating in several countries to control the distribution and prices of particular articles of manufacture.
A. International cartel B. Corporation
C. Multinational D. None of the above

80. The term ________, among Trobrianders means the tribute paid to a chief of subsistence goods.
A. gimloali B. pokala
C. wasi D. sagali

81. Manorial system of economy in England implied:
A. cultivation of land by the owners themselves
B. small scale cultivation
C. feudal system *i.e.* lord employing labourers
D. no control of king over the lords

82. Pre-capitalist system in society came with the:
A. appearance of Eastern commercial routes
B. confiscation of guild property by the kings
C. failure of the crusade
D. appearance of the middle man

83. One of the important effects of the factory system was:
A. improvement in the working conditions of the labourers
B. higher wages for the labourers
C. better housing facilities for all
D. accumulation of capital in just a few hands

84. One of the important ways in which, according to Ginsbert, goods in the past were exchanged was:
A. hospitality and exchange of gifts
B. exchange through animals
C. exchange with the help of food crops
D. exchange of women

85. Industrial system is distinguished from the previous system on the basis of:
A. availability of means of production
B. availability of means of distribution
C. availability of capital
D. application of mechanical power to work machines

86. The Heresy theory believes:
A. man is a corporate being
B. man is an individualistic being
C. man's ultimate aim is collective economic interest
D. man's behaviour is not a process of calculated self-interest

87. Factory system was a quick success on account of:
A. willing cooperation of the people
B. less market competition
C. low prices of the goods produced
D. quick means of transportation of goods

88. Which one of the following is not true of capitalism?
A. capital predominates in economy
B. there is thirst for gains
C. there is desire for profits
D. there is intense desire to look after the welfare of the workers

89. Which one of the following does not apply in the case of complex economy?
A. workers are being given share in the profits
B. workers are being provided more facilities
C. workers are being denied share in the running of industry
D. workers are being allowed to form trade unions

90. In a complex society, which one of the following is not a characteristic of economy?
A. it is linked with other nations of the world
B. it revolves round profits
C. it does not take social needs into consideration
D. it is impersonal in many ways

91. Pick out one of the following which does not hold good in the case of new industrialism:
A. health conditions of the people improved
B. life expectancy increased
C. infant mortality got reduced
D. quality and quantity of diet increased

92. Effect of new industrialism was that the rate of:
A. production of only consumer goods increased
B. production of only producer goods increased
C. neither producer nor consumer goods increased
D. both producer and consumer goods increased

93. In simple economy which of the following did not fit in?
A. there was indentification of labour with his work
B. there was no competition in marketing
C. there was dependence on machines
D. there was no mass production

94. In simple economy which of the following did not fit in?
A. there was identification of labour with his work
B. there was no competition in marketing
C. there was dependence on machines
D. there was no mars production

95. In a simple society which one of the following is the characteristic of economy?
A. there is urbanised economy
B. there is no identification of producer with the produce
C. there is division of labour
D. None of these

96. Of a society with simple economy, which of the following is not true?
A. materialistic outlook develops
B. religious out look dominates
C. there is not too much of over production
D. there is not tendency towards monopoly

97. Which one of the following is not the characteristic of economy of a complex society?
A. in it labour demands share in management
B. in it trade union system is powerful
C. in it technical expertise plays big role
D. in it labour identifies himself with the product the produces

98. Which of the following does not hold good in the case of state capitalism?
A. all aspects of lie are made subservient to economics
B. state owns all the capital
C. possession of wealth in the hands of individual is encouraged
D. it distrusts the individual

99. Lower hunter implies several things. Which of the following is not covered by that?
A. absence of tools
B. possession of goods to be consumed
C. way of transferring environments
D. absence of making tools and instruments

100. According to Marxian philosophy in the industry the labour accepts less wages because:
A. he has left his home
B. he has no capacity to produce
C. he knows that the employer will not give him alternative job
D. he knows that his labour can not be preserved

101. Which one of the following was not true of new industrialism?
A. there was considerable extension in fine arts
B. generous endowments were made to the centres to learning
C. hours of work very much increased
D. illiteracy disappeared

102. Under state capitalism it is believed that the labour:
A. is source of all economic values
B. has less important role in industry than the capital
C. and capital have almost equal role in industry
D. None of the above

103. Which one of the following was not true of craft guilds?
A. these avoided market competitions
B. these arranged economic fairs
C. these up kept the standards of work man ship
D. these encouraged competition with market guilds

104. The system of industrialism is distinguished from the previous systems on the basis of:
A. adaptation of new inventions
B. employment of number of people
C. qualities of the goods produced
D. marketing of the goods produced

105. New industrialism had several characteristics, which one of the following was not one of those?
A. workers were divorced from possession of the capital
B. workers had no share in the management
C. workers were kept out of market control
D. workers were identified the goods produced

106. Every manor in the past:
A. was almost a self-contained economic unit
B. depended on other manors for everything
C. depended on the king for survival
D. was linked with other manors in social life

107. Which one of the following does not apply to new industrialism?
A. There was concentration of wealth
B. There was increased unemployment
C. There was absence of starvation
D. There was environmental pollution

108. In a complex society which one of the following is not a characteristic of economy?
A. It absolutely undermines labour
B. It gives the highest priority to capital
C. In it middle men play a big role
D. It is competitive in nature

109. A condition which in there was permanent division of labour between labour and capital was known as:
A. Anomic B. Useless
C. Illegiti mate D. Improper

110. 'A condition in which individuals did not freely choose their occupations but were forced into them' this type of division was called by Durkheim as:
A. Anomic B. Forced
C. Temporary D. Authoritarian

111. Pick up one of the following which does not hold good in the case of new industrialism:

A. there was considerable economic stability
B. there were trade fluctuations
C. there was waste of land
D. there was waste of raw material

112. In ________ society, the notion of property is closely related to display and expenditure of wealth rather than to its accumulation.
A. primitive B. modern
C. communist D. industrial

113. "Property consists of the right and duties of one person or group as against all other persons and groups with respect to some scare goods", this definition has been given by:
A. Davis B. Durkheim
C. Park Burgess D. A. Heinman

114. A corporate form of business organisation is one in which:
A. The capital is supplied by a number of persons who are its shareholders
B. The capital is supplied by certain private corporations
C. The capital is issued by the local municipal corporations
D. The capital is issued by public corporations

115. Which of the following is not an essential characteristic of capitalism?
A. No restriction on the use of resources
B. Lack of state control over population
C. Class-struggle
D. Production for the public welfare and not for maximizing the profit

116. Invention of money:
A. provided a fillip to the development of trade and commerce
B. strengthened the barter system
C. discouraged the people interested in hoarding and storing
D. helped the 'black, marketeers'

117. Adam Smith explained four principles of capitalism: which of the following is not such a principle?
A. Doctrine of self-interest
B. Laissez-faire policy
C. Theory of competition
D. Concept of regularisation

118. Which of the following was a good effect of capitalism on the social life of the people?
A. High standard of living
B. Rapid economic progress
C. Civilization achieved progress
D. All of the above

119. Which of the following statements are correct in the case of capitalism?
A. Capitalism led to the ruin of human values
B. Materialism was nourished by capitalism
C. Capitalism transformed modern culture into mere artificiality
D. None of these

120. In the agricultural stage of development the people were:
A. Award of the group activity and joint work
B. Not aware of the group activity but not joint work
C. Aware of the group activity but not joint work
D. Not aware of the group activity but worked jointly

121. Increase in population:
A. Developed the era of scientific agriculture
B. Developed the era of intensive cultivation
C. Did not affect the old techniques of agriculture
D. Had nothing to do with the life of individuals

122. In the large scale unit:
A. The relationship between labour and employer became more sweet
B. The relationship between the labour and employer became more impersonal
C. The relationship between the employer and employees did not undergo any change
D. None of the above things happened

123. Under barter system:
A. The people were award of profit
B. The idea of profit did not exist
C. People tried their bast to accumulate gold
D. None of the above

124. A condition of extreme specialization of labour in which the individual became isolated in his specialism is called:
A. Anomic division of labour
B. Forced division of labour
C. Specialised division of labour
D. All of the above

125. Which of the following is a merit of the division of labour?
A. Proper man at the proper place
B. Specialization of a worker in his work
C. Machines undertake the heavy work
D. Better chances of new inventions

126. Mark out the correct statement:
A. Private property is owned by a person or group of persons exclusively
B. Private property is used for one's own good
C. Private property is subjected to the state regulations from time to time
D. All of the above

127. The day today management of a corporate form of business is undertaken by:
A. The Board of Directors
B. The Manager elected by the Board of Directors
C. Officials appointed by the shareholders
D. The person appointed by the concerned government

128. According to Polyani:
A. Few empirical economies display more than one principle of allocation
B. Most empirical economies display more than one principle of allocation
C. No economy displays more than one principle of allocation
D. None of the above

129. According to which theory the 'occupier' of a thing is held as the 'owner' of the said property?
A. The socialistic theory
B. The occupation theory
C. The individualistic theory
D. The legalistic theory

130. Which of the following is an object of the trade unions?
A. To look after the interest of its members
B. To unite the working force to fight against exploitation
C. To pressurize law making
D. All of the above

131. There is a negative relationship between urbanization and ________.
A. Industrialization
B. Modernization
C. Commercialization
D. Agricultural population density

132. Slums are often as ________ as suburbs.
A. homogeneous
B. culturally barren
C. large
D. peculiar

133. Which one of the following is a feature of Indian village community?
A. the people are literate
B. the people are god fearing
C. the people are politically conscious
D. the people are less orthodox

134. Which one of the following is not a feature of Indian village community?
A. orthodoxy
B. lack of scientific approach
C. superstition
D. wide spread literacy

135. In India an urban area is treated as one which has a population of more than:
A. 7500 B. 10000
C. 12500 D. 15000

136. The larger the city the greater is the ______.
A. specialization
B. religious sanction
C. jajmani system
D. incidence of joint family

137. Which among the following is not included in topography?
A. land B. climate
C. people D. water

138. ________ is a narrow loyalty to local interests and historic sentiment.
A. Regionalism B. Sectionalism
C. Nationalism D. Communalism

139. The ________ feeling within a region is called regionalism.
A. we B. in-group
C. community D. none of the above

140. 'Urbanism is a way of life, whereas Urbanisation is a process', who said this?
A. Galpin B. Wirth
C. Burgess D. Fisher

141. Who gave the 'sub-cultural theory' on urbanisation?
A. Galpin B. Gane
C. Burgess D. Fisher

142. Mark out the incorrect answer. In ancient period cities were:
A. Industrial centres B. Commercial centres
C. Religious centres D. Political centres

143. Which type of town was termed as Matha?
A. Commercial town
B. The royal capital
C. Town organized around educational activities
D. Industrial town

144. Social distance in a city is due to:
A. The size of the city
B. The distance between one's residence and the working place
C. The social heterogeneity
D. The transport problem in the city

145. The impact of urbanization during medieval period worked through:
A. Artisans in the towns
B. Army on move
C. Nobles, chiefs and jagirdars
D. Petty government officials

146. Mark out among the following, what Topography is?
A. An intimate description of a place
B. A description of climatic conditions
C. Water
D. Land

147. A study of relations between organism and their environment is called:
A. Topography B. Geography
C. Ecology D. Zoology

148. Some believe that humanistic values are lost when cities as communities become ________.
A. structured B. polymorphic
C. large D. small

149. ________ is more rampant in a city life.
A. Social mobility B. Migration
C. Religious grouping D. Jajmani system

150. With whom is the 'compositional theory' an urbanisation associated?
A. Homer Hyot B. Galpin
C. Burgess D. Gane

151. Who gave the 'central place theory' on the process of urbanisation?
A. MacIver B. Walter Christaller
C. Homer Hyot D. Iban Khaldan

152. Who described cities as the "sinks of civilization"?
A. Rousseau B. Oswald Spengler
C. Lewis Numford D. Henry S. Churchill

153. Regional community aims at:
A. Economic co-operation
B. Balanced development
C. Cultural exchange
D. All of these

154. Which of the following features is not common in a town and a city?
A. Multiplicity of functions
B. Quick means of transport
C. Uniformity all over the country
D. Majority of occupants are engaged in non-agricultural activities

155. Which among the following was not the imperial city of the mughals?
A. Delhi B. Shahjahanabad
C. Agra D. Fatehpur Sikri

156. Which among the following is a political center?
A. New Delhi B. Mumbai
C. New York D. Srinagar

157. Which among the following is recreation centre?
A. New York B. Washington
C. Jerusalem D. Srinagar

158. What among the following does not contribute to the rural economy?
A. Cottage industry
B. Animal husbandry
C. Availability of better equipments
D. Private money lending practice

159. Which of the following factors is not responsible for growth of cities?
A. Surplus resources
B. Industrialization and commercialization
C. Economic pull of the city
D. Jajmani system

160. Which one of the following was one of the important causes for the growth of urban life?
A. Kinship
B. Religion
C. Educational institutions
D. Industrialization

161. Generally speaking, ________ are identified as large, dense and heterogeneous.
A. village communities B. urban communities
C. city neighbourhood D. None of the above

162. With whom is the 'sector theory' on urbanisation associated?
A. Homer Hyot B. Walter Christaller
C. Burgess D. None of the above

163. As compared with the urban communities, village communities are susceptible to:
A. more changes
B. less changes
C. equal changes
D. changes are practically non-existent

164. Which of the following is a feature of urban community?
A. Namelessness B. Class extremes
C. Social heterogeneity D. All of the above

165. In which of the following countries more population is living in the urban areas but their way of life is rural?
A. Japan B. China
C. India D. Chile

166. Over the decades in so far as living standard of the village folk is concerned:
A. it is increasing
B. it is decreasing
C. status quo has been maintained
D. it has seen sudden down fall

167. Which among the following is not a cultural centre?
A. Mecca B. Varanasi
C. Tirupati D. Chandigarh

168. Which among the following is a symbolic city?
A. Rome B. Kolkata
C. Chennai D. New Delhi

169. What has made the agricultural communities in Europe economically more prosperous and socially advanced than our village communities?
A. Good climate
B. Literacy
C. Application of science to agriculture
D. All of these

170. Who among the following are pessimistic about the future of urban life?
A. Oswald Spengler B. Henry S. Churchill
C. Lewis Mumford D. All of these

171. In the developed countries, in the urban areas women:
A. are economically self-sufficient
B. are orthodox
C. are dependent on men
D. are by and large shy

172. Which one of the following is true of women in an urban community?
A. individualisation
B. absence of regard
C. enforcement of strict code of conduct
D. taboo on inter-mixing

173. In the cities joint family system is on the decline because the people:
A. do not like to gain sympathies
B. dislike their relatives
C. have developed materialistic out look
D. have individualistic out look

174. Who of the following has laid stress on namelessness as the characteristic of urban community life?
A. MacIver and Page B. Ogg and Zine
C. Young Mack D. Rose Hume Lee

175. Which one of the following is a serious problem of city life?
A. Shortage of wealth
B. Good neighbourly relations
C. Shortage of accommodation
D. Shortage of recreational facilities

176. The period of true urban revolution is considered to be:
A. 17th century B. 18th century
C. 19th century D. 20th century

177. Occupation as criteria for making a distinction between the urban and the rural communities has been made by:
A. MacIver
B. P. Gisbert
C. Sorokin and Zimmermani
D. None of the above

178. Who has authored the book entitled urbanisation away of life?
A. Rose Hume Lee B. Young Mack
C. N.P. Gist D. Bogardus

179. Which of the following is the true characteristic of urban community?
A. there is constant touch with nature
B. nature is treated as friend
C. there is impersonality of law
D. there is strong attachment to the rituals

180. Which one of the following is not true of city life?
A. it is heterogeneous
B. in it there is loneliness
C. in it there are class extremes
D. it is known for social equality

181. Which one of the following is not covered under the classification of cities given by Gistard Halbert?
A. Production centres B. Defence centres
C. Trade centres D. Political centre

182. The combined influences of the urban scene stimulate what may be termed as ______.
A. associative individualism
B. revolutionary spirit
C. spiritual emancipation
D. None of the above

183. Death rate in the urban community is very high because the people:
A. have no medical facility
B. live a life of tension
C. can not afford medical facilities
D. work at an extraordinary speed

184. In the primitive society man invented weapons and tools for:
A. The sake of curiosity
B. Protecting his family from the wild animals
C. Killing the animals because of hunting habits
D. Satisfying his hunger

185. Which one of the following is not true of urban community?
A. Individuals approach
B. Joint family system
C. Out wards show of life
D. No fear of god

186. In the past which one of the following helped the maximum in the growth of village community?
A. Kinship B. Method of worship
C. Economic standard D. Common heritage

187. ________ is the largest effective community.
A. Nation B. City
C. Tribe D. Neighbourhood

188. Which one of the following is called a culture of poverty?
A. Slums B. Rural areas
C. Suburbs D. Inner cities

189. In the United States all places are treated as urban which have a population of more than:
A. 2500 B. 3000
C. 3500 D. 4000

190. In primitive village community land was the property of:
A. the individual who possessed it
B. the whole family
C. the village temple
D. all in the village

191. Which one of the following does not encourage regionalism?
A. Casteism B. Linguilism
C. Education D. Cultural superiority

192. Regionalism implies to Indian villages:
A. Sectionalism
B. Separatism
C. Integrated development of community
D. All of the above

193. Which one of the following is not one of the features of urban community?
A. face to face contacts
B. complex life
C. materialistic approach
D. glamour in life

194. Which among the following was not a temple town?
A. Gaya B. Tirupati
C. Puri D. Srirangam

195. Which among the following was an exclusive university town?
A. Taxila B. Pataliputra
C. Nalanda D. Kashi

196. Which among the following is not a cause of growth of cities?
A. Trade and commerce
B. Industrialization
C. Development of transport
D. Hygienic out look of the people

197. Who has suggested 'principal activity' as the basis of classifying the cities?
A. Spengler B. Mumford
C. Bogardus D. E.E. Muntz

198. In primitive village community most important part was played by:
A. the money-lenders
B. kinship
C. religion
D. common way of living

199. ________ usually combines rural and urban communities into one unit.
A. City B. Neighbourhood
C. Region D. Community

200. Which of the following is not a feature of a region? It should have separate:
A. Culture B. Area
C. Interests D. Trade unionism

201. Which one of the following has not helped in the growth and development of urban community?
A. Religion
B. Marketing facilities
C. Occupation followed by the people
D. Industrialization

202. Which one of the following is not true of modern village?
A. Common kinship bond
B. Mobility of population
C. Modernisation
D. Collective ownership of land

203. Classification of cities on the basis of principal activity has been given by:
A. MacIver B. Kingsley Davis
C. Gist and Halbert D. E.E. Murtz

204. In India in the urban areas the women try to:
A. be economically self-sufficient
B. be old fashioned
C. keep orthodoxy
D. remain within the four walls of the house

205. Which one of the following is not the modern trend in industrial relations?
A. Industry is being transferred from a complex of industrial relations into a system of political relations
B. The performance of industry is to be measured in terms of social good
C. New conceptions of labour is emerging
D. Industry is being transferred from a complex of industrial relations into a system of social relations

206. A village community is characterised by ________ contacts among the neighbours.
A. less B. rare
C. immediate D. formal

207. _______ is subjective where as _______ is objective.
A. Nationality, statehood
B. Statehood, nationality
C. Regionalism, sectionalism
D. None of the above

208. Modern village community has been very much influenced by:
A. religion B. political system
C. urbanisation D. economic system

209. Who gave the 'concentric zone hypothesis' while discussing the process of urbanisation?
A. Walter Christaller B. Homer Hyot
C. Burgess D. MacIver

210. The size and density of urban society has increased primarily because of ________ .
A. natural increase
B. migration from other cities
C. migration from non-urban areas
D. None of the above

211. Who gave the 'Axiate hypothesis' while discussing the process of urbanisation?
A. Homer Hyot B. Burgess
C. Galpin D. Walter Christaller

212. In India urban community:
A. was existing in the long past
B. came into existence in the recent past
C. came into existence only very recently
D. is existing only nominally

213. A ________ as an integrate area of social life exhibits a balanced state of dynamic equilibrium between its various parts.
A. region B. community
C. neighbourhood D. city

214. ________ is a condition of mind ________ is a condition of law.
A. Statehood, nationality
B. Regionalism, patriotism
C. Nationality, statehood
D. Patriotism, sectionalism

215. Which of the following is not the characteristic feature of urban life?
A. Impersonal relationship
B. Competition
C. Loss of humanistic
D. Informal relationships

216. Cities dominate nations in one way. Which one?
A. As food producer
B. As seats of power
C. As propagators of tradition and custom
D. As centres of ascriptive stratification

217. These days in India one of the following is not the cause of regionalism. Pick that up:
A. narrow political considerations
B. stress on regional language
C. stress on local culture
D. trade unionism

218. Which among the following is a political metropolis?
A. Mumbai B. Kolkata
C. Moscow D. Chicago

219. In the past the most impressive dwelling is believed to have existed in:
A. Switzerland B. Japan
C. United States D. Russia

220. Migrants from rural to urban areas seem to adjust to city life more smoothly if they ________.
A. maintain kinties
B. maintain rural life
C. maintain agriculture
D. maintain village hierarchy

221. Suburbs often have all the features of a city except:
A. crime and delinquency B. slums
C. specialization D. isolation

222. Which of the following is not the feature of village community?
A. Community consciousness
B. Role of neighbourhood
C. Joint family
D. Slums

223. Village community life in the past was common feature in:
A. Asia B. America
C. Europe D. The world over

224. Which among the following factors do you think influences the social organization of the villages?
A. The caste system
B. Its closeness to the town
C. The existence of good means of communication and transport
D. All of these

225. Sophistication of city-dwellers is a feature of urban community. Mark out what it means?
A. Superficial manners of politeness
B. Simple living
C. Glamourous living
D. None of these

226. Mark out the metropolis from among the following:
A. Ghaziabad B. Kanpur
C. Shimla D. Mumbai

227. Communities and association are types of:
A. social groups B. social category
C. aggregate D. society

228. Which is an example of a community?
A. Youth B. Men
C. A band of gypsies D. Muslims

229. Which is in appropriate? A community consists of people who:
A. live in a local area
B. come together because of common interest
C. must co-operate and organize
D. share a community sentiment

230. Which one is not correct? A social class consists of those people in a community who are essentially similar in their:
A. economic status
B. attitude and ways of living
C. educational attainments
D. race

231. Who, of the following has said about community that, 'The mark of a community is that one's life may be wholly lived within it?
A. MacIver B. C.F. Child
C. Kingsley Davis D. G.D.H. Cole

232. Who has defined community 'as an area of social living marked by some degree of social coherence'?
A. Kingsley Davis B. MacIver
C. Linton D. Parsons

233. Which one of following is the basis of the community?
A. Common locality
B. Common living standard
C. Common political ideology
D. Common habits of members

234. Which one of the following is considered as a foreign factor in community life?
A. Increase in wealth
B. Community sentiments
C. Common political ideology
D. Absence of common residence

235. Which one of the following is not a basis of community life?
A. Common locality
B. Common thinking
C. Community sentiments
D. Common way of life

236. An immigrant group in a foreign land staying together is an example of an/a:
A. association B. primary group
C. community D. secondary group

237. Cooley called the small rural communities as:
A. primary groups B. secondary groups
C. formal groups D. informal groups

238. Sociologists have most of ten classified communities on the basis of:
A. their political ideologies
B. their size
C. their principal economic activities
D. their major religions

239. Which of the following is not a type of community?
A. Resort communities
B. Mining centres
C. Health-centres
D. All the above are types of communities

240. Tribe is an example of:
A. association B. exogamous group
C. community D. social group

241. Which of the following is not a community?
A. Monastery
B. Immigrant group which cherishes its own customs and speaks its own language
C. Social caste
D. Tribe

242. Who among the following consists of a community?
A. The people of Indian origin
B. The Indian society
C. Trade union movement
D. The Bengali Brahmins in Allahabad

243. Who among the following do not constitute a community?
A. The group in which 'X' was born
B. The group which 'X' joined after paying the admission fee
C. The religious group which 'A' joined after being converted
D. Aggarwals of Ambala

244. Which one of the following is not the main factor responsible for the development of community?
A. Socialization
B. Community sentiments
C. Education
D. Character

245. In large cities, the neighbourhood is largely a group of ______ characterised chiefly by the fact that the member side within a geographical area.
A. Loose families B. Neigh-dwellers
C. Close-relatives D. slum dwellers

246. A scientific distinction between the urban and the rural community can be made on the basis of:
A. density of population
B. area covered
C. occupation followed by the people
D. None of the above

247. Which one of the following is not one of the features of urban community?
A. Contacts are non-segmental
B. In it there is anonymity
C. In it there is homelessness
D. In it there is social heterogeneity

248. A fundamental aim of ________ is the closer integration of the rural civilization and urban civilization.
A. sectionalism B. regionalism
C. nationalism D. communalism

249. Which one of the following is not covered in the classification of cities given by Murtz?
A. Defence cities B. Commercial cities
C. Political cities D. Diversified cities

250. Which of the following terms was used for an ordinary fortified town where in land trade was an important activity?
A. Pattana B. Neagara
C. Rajdhani D. Kheta

251. The ________ of the urban community is the source of social groupings both vertical and horizontal.
A. economic differentiation
B. social differentiation
C. caste
D. social prestige

252. Which among the following conditions primarily contribute to the development of village community?
A. Good climate
B. Application of science
C. A proper application of intelligence and labour
D. The police of the government

253. Which one of the following is not true of village community in India?
A. The people are conservative
B. The villagers are custom ridden
C. The people are illiterate
D. The villagers have come out of the clutches of money lenders

254. Which one of the following did not play an important role in the growth of village community in the very beginning?
A. Land B. Water resources
C. Climate D. Religion

255. Which one of the following is not true of an Indian village?
A. The people are conservative
B. The people are politically conscious
C. The villagers believe in simplicity
D. The villagers are god fearing

256. Which of the following is not a region?
A. United states of America
B. Organisation of American States
C. The western hemisphere
D. Scandinavian countries

257. Who defined 'city' as a relatively large, dense and permanent settlement of socially heterogeneous individuals?
A. Le Play B. Louis Wirth
C. Murdock D. Burgess

258. Which one of the following was one of the binding forces of rural folk for the medieval village community?
A. Occupational unity
B. Common possession of land
C. Common cultivation
D. Common places of worship

259. Which one of the following contributed the maximum to the growth of urbanisation?
A. Availability of educational facilities
B. Availability of more houses
C. Availability of more land for dwelling
D. Growth in the means of transportation and communication

260. Which one of the following is true of caste system in Indian villages?
A. Its hold has considerably gone up
B. Its hold is going down
C. The system has not come under any pressures
D. The people are prepared to give up caste system

261. Which one of the following is not a feature of village community?
A. The people are religious minded
B. There is dependence on vagaries of nature
C. There is attitude of fear towards nature
D. There is tendency for living a simple life

262. By regional imbalance we mean that a region:
A. should be more balanced than the others
B. has out grown the other
C. is being developed intentionally at the cost of the other region
D. None of the above

263. Since independence in India, trend is towards:
A. discouraging regionalism
B. indifference towards regionalism
C. status quo in regionalism
D. encouragement of regionalism

264. In India in an urban setting:
A. main occupation of the people is agriculture
B. the people prefer trading over agriculture
C. the men break with their past completely
D. the people prefer to have joint family system

265. Regional imbalances can be created by several factors. Which one is not the contributory cause?
A. Availability of natural resources
B. Cultural advancement
C. Economic development of the people
D. Better transport facilities

266. In a developing country in the urban area at the women:
A. have completely forgotten the past
B. are on the war path against social evils
C. refuse to be dependent on men
D. accept by and large social norms

267. In our modern times the trend is towards:
A. giving more rights to the village community
B. curtailing the rights of the village community
C. shaking the village community from its foundations
D. maintaining status quo in the villages

268. Mark out the correct statement:
A. urban life produces greater emotional tension than rural life
B. urban life produces greater insecurity than rural life
C. urban life is faster than rural life
D. All of these

269. ________ has been defined as an area within which the people and the different constituent communities are conspicuously more inter dependent than those within other areas.
A. Region B. Neighbourhood
C. Community D. City

270. Which one of the following is one of the serious problems being faced by today's urban community?
A. Shortage of job opportunities
B. Shortage of money
C. Maintenance of law and order
D. Craze for winning sympathy of the people

271. Which one of the following is not a characteristic of urban population?
A. Large size of the area
B. Greater density of population
C. Heterogeneousness of the population
D. Homogeneous character of the population

272. By lower hunter economy which was supposed to be prevailing in primitive times, we mean an economy in which there was:
A. Indirect utilisation of nature's products
B. Direct utilisation of products of nature
C. Direct utilisation of natural products without alteration
D. Indirect utilisation of nature's products and that too with alterations

273. Urban community came into existence due to several reasons. Which one of the following was the main cause?
A. Desire to live together
B. Desire to own common property
C. Desire to obey a common superior
D. Desire to utilise properly surplus resources

274. Which of the following is true about village community of a developed country?
A. The people are illiterate
B. The people are orthodox
C. The people are god fearing
D. The people are politically awake

275. The most important factor which has led to political awakening in the Indian villages is:
A. too much interest of social reformers
B. spread of education in the villages
C. panchayati raj system
D. desire of the people to become political minded

276. Which one of the following is not true of village community of today's India?
A. There is desire to stay in the villages
B. There is formation of village cooperative societies in good numbers
C. Per capita income is increasing
D. Farmers get good prices for their produce

277. Which of the following does not fall within the concept of regionalism?
A. Uniform development of all regions
B. Development of only one region
C. Economic growth of the region alone
D. Industrialisation of a particular region

278. Which one of the following is not true of politicalisation of Indian villages?
A. It has divided the people into groups
B. It has ended group rivalries from the villages
C. It has decreased community feelings
D. It has given rise to individualism

279. Which one of the following is not true of Indian village of today?
A. Community consciousness on the decrease
B. Politics has made in roads into the villages
C. Joint family system is on the decrease
D. Village is divided into groups on political lines

280. Which of the following is not an essential characteristic of property?
A. Social sanction
B. Possession or ownership
C. Rights and duties regarding ownership
D. All of the above

281. Markout the correct statement:
A. A town is just an over sized village
B. A town serves only its rural customers
C. A town has neither political, cultural nor economic influence over the surrounding farm land
D. A town is multi functional unit

282. Which one of the following is not a significant feature in the task of village reconstruction?
A. More irrigation facilities have been provided to the cultivators
B. Villages have been linked with the cities
C. Village are supplied more electricity
D. Community consciousness in the villages has much increased

283. Regional imbalances are created by various cases. Which one is not the causes?
A. Mineral wealth of the region
B. Better means of transportation
C. Quality of political leadership
D. Awakened citizenry

284. Regional imbalances can be avoided provided:
A. caste system is strong
B. regional language is enriched
C. local leadership is powerful
D. nationalist feelings are strong

285. Which one of the following is not the cause of regional imbalances?
A. Industrialisation of one region above
B. Better trade facilities of a region
C. Urbanisation of a region
D. Strong hold of national leadership

286. The nerve centre in a village is the temple. Indicate its importance:
A. it is a place of individual and family worship
B. it is a place of community worship
C. it is the place to celebrate the festivals
D. All of the above

287. Development of industry has greatly contributed to urban growth. Which among the following denotes this?
A. Multiplicity of non-agricultural occupations
B. Specialisation of jobs
C. Concentration of population
D. All of these

288. In India, in the past, which one was not the feature of the villages:
A. the people did not live a complex life
B. they had not been influenced by city life
C. they believed in simplicity
D. they were too much dazzled by the glamours of city life

289. In India in the past, one of characteristics of the village was that:
A. it too much depended on out side assistance
B. it was a self-sufficient unit
C. the people had too much of mixing with others
D. the people had desire to cooperate with other villages

290. Which one of the following is not true of the marriage system in villages of India?
A. Old family status is given great weightage
B. Child marriage is on the increase
C. Expenditure on marriage is on the decrease
D. Education of the couple is being given due weightage

ANSWERS

1	2	3	4	5	6	7	8	9	10
C	C	A	B	B	B	B	C	A	C
11	12	13	14	15	16	17	18	19	20
B	D	B	D	C	A	C	A	B	B
21	22	23	24	25	26	27	28	29	30
B	C	B	B	A	A	A	C	D	A
31	32	33	34	35	36	37	38	39	40
B	C	C	C	B	C	B	B	B	C
41	42	43	44	45	46	47	48	49	50
C	B	A	A	A	A	B	B	B	C
51	52	53	54	55	56	57	58	59	60
A	A	D	D	D	A	A	A	B	C
61	62	63	64	65	66	67	68	69	70
D	D	B	A	B	A	D	A	D	B

71	72	73	74	75	76	77	78	79	80
B	A	A	A	A	C	D	B	A	B
81	**82**	**83**	**84**	**85**	**86**	**87**	**88**	**89**	**90**
C	D	D	A	D	B	D	D	C	C
91	**92**	**93**	**94**	**95**	**96**	**97**	**98**	**99**	**100**
D	D	C	D	B	A	D	C	D	D
101	**102**	**103**	**104**	**105**	**106**	**107**	**108**	**109**	**110**
C	A	D	C	D	A	C	A	A	B
111	**112**	**113**	**114**	**115**	**116**	**117**	**118**	**119**	**120**
A	A	A	A	D	A	D	D	B	A
121	**122**	**123**	**124**	**125**	**126**	**127**	**128**	**129**	**130**
A	B	B	A	C	D	B	B	B	D
131	**132**	**133**	**134**	**135**	**136**	**137**	**138**	**139**	**140**
D	A	B	D	D	A	C	B	C	B
141	**142**	**143**	**144**	**145**	**146**	**147**	**148**	**149**	**150**
D	A	C	C	C	A	C	B	A	D
151	**152**	**153**	**154**	**155**	**156**	**157**	**158**	**159**	**160**
B	A	D	C	A	A	D	D	D	D
161	**162**	**163**	**164**	**165**	**166**	**167**	**168**	**169**	**170**
B	A	B	D	D	A	D	A	B	D
171	**172**	**173**	**174**	**175**	**176**	**177**	**178**	**179**	**180**
A	A	D	D	B	C	C	D	C	D
181	**182**	**183**	**184**	**185**	**186**	**187**	**188**	**189**	**190**
B	A	B	D	B	A	A	A	A	D
191	**192**	**193**	**194**	**195**	**196**	**197**	**198**	**199**	**200**
D	C	A	D	C	D	D	B	C	D
201	**202**	**203**	**204**	**205**	**206**	**207**	**208**	**209**	**210**
A	D	D	A	B	C	A	C	C	C
211	**212**	**213**	**214**	**215**	**216**	**217**	**218**	**219**	**220**
C	A	A	C	D	B	D	C	A	A
221	**222**	**223**	**224**	**225**	**226**	**227**	**228**	**229**	**230**
B	D	D	C	B	C	A	D	B	D
231	**232**	**233**	**234**	**235**	**236**	**237**	**238**	**239**	**240**
A	B	A	B	B	C	A	B	D	C
241	**242**	**243**	**244**	**245**	**246**	**247**	**248**	**249**	**250**
C	D	B	D	A	D	A	B	D	B
251	**252**	**253**	**254**	**255**	**256**	**257**	**258**	**259**	**260**
A	A	D	D	B	A	B	A	D	D
261	**262**	**263**	**264**	**265**	**266**	**267**	**268**	**269**	**270**
B	B	D	A	B	D	A	D	A	C
271	**272**	**273**	**274**	**275**	**276**	**277**	**278**	**279**	**280**
D	C	D	C	C	A	A	B	A	D
281	**282**	**283**	**284**	**285**	**286**	**287**	**288**	**289**	**290**
A	A	D	D	D	D	D	D	B	B

●●●

Arenas and New Arenas of Social Change

1. The mass media are educates and propagandists. Which theory of the press support this ideology?
   A. Libertarian B. Communist
   C. Authoritarian D. Social responsibility
2. When was Samachar created?
   A. 1977 B. 1981
   C. 1975 D. 1976
3. The 1948, the conference on freedom of information was held in:
   A. New York City B. Colombo
   C. Davos D. Geneva
4. The tabloid, The Sun, is published from:
   A. Lucerne B. Paris
   C. London D. Rome
5. During the 19th century, most of the newspapers of Britian were owned by:
   A. The government
   B. Families
   C. Private share holders
   D. Foreign firms of the West but not belonging
6. What is the full form of CANA?
   A. Canadian news agency
   B. Caribbean news agency
   C. Cambodian news alliance
   D. None of these
7. The AFP belongs to which country:
   A. The Netherland B. Belgium
   C. France D. Mexico
8. Which news agency was providing news to the Indian newspapers during the pre-independence era?
   A. The AFP B. The CANA
   C. Reuters D. The IRNA
9. Who set up the Free Press of India?
   A. S. Sadanand, 1930
   B. Bal Gangadhar Tilak, 1932
   C. B.V. Karanth, 1948
   D. James Augustus Hickey, 1948
10. The newspaper published by M.K. Gandhi when he was in South Africa was:
    A. Reformer B. Harijan
    C. Indian opinion D. The Hindu
11. Who is the head of the News Service Division?
    A. Editor in charge B. Directorial officer
    C. Director General D. Managing Director
12. According to Wilbur Schramm, which one of the following is a value free asset?
    A. Culture B. Religion
    C. Technology D. None of these
13. Which of the following countries progressed economic term, but did not change her cultural values?
    A. India B. The USA
    C. England D. Canada
14. The first implementation exercise of the package Programme Model was initiated in:
    A. The philipians
    B. India (IADP)
    C. Mexico (Pueba project)
    D. None of these
15. Which of the following models emphasis on the strengthening of Democratic process and redistribution of power?
    A. The Shannon and Weaver model
    B. The old model Schramm
    C. The participatory model
    D. The alternative paradigm
16. Which reporting goes behind the news and bring out the truth?
    A. Objective B. Interpretative
    C. Investigative D. Crime
17. When was the 2nd Press Council set up?
    A. December, 1972 B. October, 1971
    C. October, 1970 D. August, 1975
18. Sadharanikaran is a social process, which can be achieved only among:
    A. Common people B. Sahridayas
    C. Culture D. Children
19. The word Global Village is defined by:
    A. Marshall Mc Luhan B. Wilber Schramm
    C. Daniel Leanear D. None of these
20. Tabloid journalism is frequently termed:
    A. Cheque book journalism
    B. Yellow journalism
    C. Investigative journalism
    D. None of these

21. Which was the first newspaper in India?
A. Bengal Gazette B. Calcutta journal
C. Samachar Darpan D. None of these

22. Which is the title of Mac Bride Report?
A. Many voices one world
B. Global village
C. Communication
D. None of these

23. The term agenda setting was coined by:
A. McCombs and Donald Shaw
B. Shannon and Weaver
C. Dennis McQueen
D. None of these

24. What is encoding?
A. It is the vehicle through which a message is carried from the communicator to the receiver
B. It is the formulation of message in the communicators mind
C. It is one who initiates communication process
D. Other end of communication

25. .... is an informal communication.
A. News letter
B. Grapevine
C. Interpersonal communication
D. Intrapersonal communication

26. Oral media dominates the .... flow of communication.
A. Downward B. Upward
C. Horizontal D. Lateral

27. The influence of a group on the attitude of an individual is generally treated in terms of the concept of:
A. Psychological group B. Physical group
C. Corporative group D. Reference group

28. Mass media place a crucial role in forming and reflecting:
A. Public opinion B. Societies image
C. Self image D. Journalistic idea

29. Mass culture is referred to as:
A. Popular culture B. Mass media culture
C. Cultural imperialism D. None of these

30. The role of mass media in correlation function was termed as:
A. forum B. information
C. motivation D. None of these

31. Theories of effects to media violence:
A. Socialisation and hearing
B. Catharsis
C. Aggressive cue
D. Reinforcement

32. The term media comes from the Latin:
A. mode B. middle
C. communis D. communico

33. According to William Stephenson mass media serves the basic purpose of providing entertainment, escape and release this theory was called:
A. Learning theory B. Play theory
C. Reinforcement theory D. Aggressive theory

34. Which one is the highly circular model of communication?
A. Shannon and Weaver model
B. Lasswell's model
C. Osgood's model
D. Schramm's model

35. Which one is the triangle model of communication?
A. New comb's model B. Gate keeping model
C. Gerbner's model D. Schramm's model

36. Modulation index of an AM signal:
A. depends upon the peak amplitude of the modulating signal and the carrier.
B. depends upon the peak amplitude of modulating signal.
C. is a function of carrier frequency.
D. None of these

37. In amplitude modulation:
A. the amplitude of the carrier remains constant.
B. the amplitude of the carrier varies in accordance with the amplitude of the modulating signal.
C. the amplitude of carrier varies in accordance with the frequency of the modulating signal.
D. None of these

38. In modulation process, radio frequency wave is termed as:
A. modulating wave B. modulated wave
C. carrier wave D. None of these

39. Digital signals:
A. represent values as discrete steps.
B. utilise binary code system.
C. do not provide a continuous set of values.
D. All of these

40. The most commonly employed analog modulation technique in satellite communication is the:
A. amplitude modulation B. frequency modulation
C. phase modulation D. All of the above

41. Satellite transponders:
A. Use a high frequency for reception and a lower frequency for retransmission of information to and from earth
B. Use a lower frequency for reception and a higher frequency for retransmission of information to and from earth.

C. Use a single frequency for reception and retransmission of information to and from earth.
D. None of the above

42. For television transmission, the frequency employed is normally in the range:
A. 30-300 Hz B. 30-300 kHz
C. 30-300 MHz D. 30-300 GHz

43. Which of the following is invariably found on all communication satellites as a payload?
A. Transponder B. Photographic camera
C. Optical telescope D. None of these

44. An antenna is:
A. capacitive
B. reactive
C. inductive above its resonance frequency
D. None of these

45. Optical communication uses the frequency range of:
A. 10^9 to 10^{10} Hz B. 10^5 to 10^6 Hz
C. 10^{14} to 10^{15} Hz D. 10^{16} to 10^{17} Hz.

46. Audio signals have frequency range.
A. 20 Hz to 20 kHz B. 20 kHz to 20 MHz
C. 20 MHz to 20 GHz D. All of these

47. What is the amalgamation and rapid unification between countries identified as?
A. Globalisation B. Liberalisation
C. Socialisation D. Privatisation

48. Globalisation has improved the living structure of which of the following?
A. All the people
B. People living in developing countries
C. People living in developed countries
D. None of the above

49. Which Indian industries have been hit by globalisation?
A. Cement
B. Jute
C. Toy making
D. Information technology (IT)

50. Which of these organisations emphasises on the liberalisation of foreign investment and foreign trade?
A. International Monetary Fund
B. World Health Organisation
C. World Trade Organisation
D. International Labour Organisation

51. Tax on imports is considered as an example of:
A. Collateral B. Trade barriers
C. Foreign trade D. Terms of trade

52. Which of the following is the main reason behind the investments of MNCs?
A. To benefit foreign countries
B. To provide financial support to the country's government
C. For the welfare of underprivileged people
D. To increase the assets and earn profits

53. Which of these institutes supports investments and foreign trade in India?
A. International Monetary Fund (IMF)
B. World Trade Organisation (WTO)
C. World Bank
D. International Labour Organisation (ILO)

54. When did the government remove the barriers for investment in India?
A. 1990 B. 1991
C. 1992 D. 1993

55. **Assertion (A) :** The correlation function of mass media is vital for any society.
Reason (R) : The interpretational aspects that include advertising and public relations shape and influence public opinion.

Choose the correct answer from the codes given below:
A. Both (A) and (R) are true, and (R) is the correct explanation of (A)
B. Both (A) and (R) are true, but (R) is not the correct explanation of (A)
C. (A) is true, but (R) is false
D. (A) is false, but (R) is true

56. Some of the barriers to effective communication are:
(*a*) Polysemy
(*b*) Simple language
(*c*) Use of Cliche's
(*d*) Easy construction of sentences

Choose the correct answer from the given below:
A. (*a*) and (*b*) B. (*b*) and (*c*)
C. (*c*) and (*d*) D. (*a*) and (*c*)

57. Which of the following are barriers to effective communication?
(*a*) Physical noise (*b*) Semantic noise
(*c*) Psychological noise (*d*) Non-semantic noise

Choose the correct answer from the options given below:
A. (*a*), (*b*) and (*d*) B. (*a*), (*b*) and (*c*)
C. (*a*), (*c*) and (*d*) D. (*a*) and (*d*) only

58. 'Non-content behaviours such as rate of speaking, loudness, tendency to interrupt and pronunciation peculiarities' are referred to as ____ behaviour.
A. Extra-personal B. Animated
C. Extra-linguistic D. Involuntary

59. In analog communication, contents are considered to be:
A. Convergent B. Static
C. Physical D. Ethereal

60. Match the following:

Set-I (Communication elements)	Set-II (Description of process part)
(*a*) Sender	(*i*) Brain
(*b*) Receiver	(*ii*) Electro-magnetic impulses
(*c*) Message	(*iii*) The central nervous system
(*d*) Medium	(*iv*) Sensory organs

Choose the correct answer from the options given below:

	(*a*)	(*b*)	(*c*)	(*d*)
A.	(*i*)	(*iii*)	(*ii*)	(*iv*)
B.	(*iii*)	(*i*)	(*iv*)	(*ii*)
C.	(*iv*)	(*i*)	(*ii*)	(*iii*)
D.	(*ii*)	(*iv*)	(*iii*)	(*i*)

61. The cognitive domain of communication involves matters related to:
A. Emotions B. Knowledge
C. Fantasy D. Escapism

62. Since most interactions with other people take place at a highly superficial level, making good ______ becomes difficult.
A. Course corrections B. Predictions
C. Deeds D. Announcements

63. Assertion (A) : No enculturisation takes place with resistance.
Reason (R) : People have their own values and self-interest that filter communicated messages.

Choose the correct answer from the options given below:
A. Both (A) and (R) are true and (R) is the correct explanation of (A)
B. Both (A) and (R) are true, but (R) is not the correct explanation of (A)
C. (A) is true, but (R) is false
D. (A) is false, but (R) is true

64. Semantic barrier of communication is implied when the:
A. signal is lost before reaching the receiver
B. message transmitted by the source is unclear
C. receiver's attention is diverted
D. receiver does not understand the meaning of the message

65. Which of the following signifies non-verbal communication in an essential way?
A. Instructions written on a question paper
B. Learner attending an online class
C. The dress code followed by an individual
D. Yoga instructor teaching yoga poses to the pupils

66. Assertion (A) : Communication presupposes a shared, symbolic environment, a social relationship even among non-participants.
Reason (R) : It leads to social interaction, which in combination with other factors contributes to a sense of community.

Choose the correct option given below:
A. Both (A) and (R) are true and (R) is the correct explanation of (A)
B. Both (A) and (R) are true, but (R) is not the correct explanation of (A)
C. (A) is true, but (R) is false
D. (A) is false, but (R) is true

67. Which of the following is a stage of intrapersonal communication?
A. Phatic stage
B. Intimate stage
C. Personal stage
D. Transcendental communication

68. Which of the following is a characteristic of modern mass media?
A. Capital intensive B. Labour intensive
C. Sustainable D. Developmental

69. The dance of the honeybees conveying to other bees where nector will be found is an example of:
A. Mass communication
B. Group communication
C. Interpersonal communication
D. Intrapersonal communication

70. Choose the correct sequence of communication from the options given below:
A. Information – Exposure – Persuasion – Behavioural change
B. Persuasion – Information – Behavioural change – Exposure
C. Exposure – Information – Persuasion – Behavioural change
D. Behavioural change – Information – Persuasion – Exposure

71. Which of the following is a function of mass media?
A. To transmit culture
B. To formulate national policies
C. To help the judiciary take its decisions
D. To stabilise the share market

72. Today's media-society equation is largely:
A. Mystical B. Morally bound
C. Consumer conscious D. Tradition centric

73. Assertion (A) : Media entertainment does not enhance the cultural level of society.
Reason (R) : Most media entertainment encourages escapism, not content quality.

Choose the correct answer from the options given below:

A. Both (A) and (R) are true, and (R) is the correct explanation of (A)
B. Both (A) and (R) are true, but (R) is not the correct explanation of (A)
C. (A) is false, but (R) is false
D. (A) is false, but (R) is true

74. Communication through colours can result in:

(*a*) Aesthetic codes (*b*) Cultural codes
(*c*) Semantic codes (*d*) Binary codes

Choose the correct answer from the options given below:

A. (*a*) and (*d*) B. (*b*) and (*c*)
C. (*b*) and (*d*) D. (*a*) and (*b*)

75. In the communication process, signs derive meanings through:

A. The subjectivity of various components
B. The objectivity of the decoder
C. The network of inter-relations
D. The neutrality of the channel

76. Language of communication also constitutes:

A. The random world B. The social world
C. The divine world D. The unsanctified world

77. Mass media do not have pre-determined functions for everyone and people use them the way they like. This is suggestive of the fact that,

A. Audiences are active
B. Content is of little significance
C. Content lacks plurality
D. Audiences are homogeneous

78. Match List-I and List-II:

List-I (Media)	List-II (Transmission/Communication)
(*a*) Audio	(*i*) Bandwidth
(*b*) Advertising	(*ii*) Linear communication
(*c*) Internet	(*iii*) Non personal communication
(*d*) Newspaper	(*iv*) Frequency modulation

Choose the correct answer from the options given below:

	(*a*)	(*b*)	(*c*)	(*d*)
A.	(*iii*)	(*iv*)	(*ii*)	(*i*)
B.	(*i*)	(*ii*)	(*iii*)	(*iv*)
C.	(*iv*)	(*iii*)	(*i*)	(*ii*)
D.	(*ii*)	(*i*)	(*iv*)	(*iii*)

79. A communication process can be considered complete when:

A. The sender transmits the message
B. The message enters the channel
C. The message leaves the channel
D. The receiver understands the message

80. Which of the following will help overcome communication barriers?

A. Focused listening
B. Neglecting semantic noise
C. Top-down command structure
D. Use of cliched idioms

ANSWERS

1	2	3	4	5	6	7	8	9	10
C	C	D	C	B	B	C	C	A	C
11	**12**	**13**	**14**	**15**	**16**	**17**	**18**	**19**	**20**
C	C	C	B	C	C	C	B	A	B
21	**22**	**23**	**24**	**25**	**26**	**27**	**28**	**29**	**30**
A	A	A	B	B	A	C	A	A	A
31	**32**	**33**	**34**	**35**	**36**	**37**	**38**	**39**	**40**
B	B	B	C	A	A	B	C	D	B
41	**42**	**43**	**44**	**45**	**46**	**47**	**48**	**49**	**50**
A	C	A	C	C	A	A	B	C	C
51	**52**	**53**	**54**	**55**	**56**	**57**	**58**	**59**	**60**
B	D	B	B	A	D	B	C	B	C
61	**62**	**63**	**64**	**65**	**66**	**67**	**68**	**69**	**70**
B	B	D	D	C	D	D	A	B	C
71	**72**	**73**	**74**	**75**	**76**	**77**	**78**	**79**	**80**
A	C	A	D	C	B	A	C	D	A

●●●

Social Movements

1. A type of Social structure where power is in hand of oldest member is known as:
   A. Gerontocracy B. Political system
   C. State system D. Country head
2. Pick the answer that correctly lists the progressive stages in the social movement's life cycle.
   A. Coalescence, Bureaucratization, Emergence & Decline
   B. Decline, Bureaucratization, Coalescence & Emergence
   C. Bureaucratization, Coalescence, Emergence & Decline
   D. Emergence, Coalescence, Bureaucratization & Decline
3. Two explanations of collective behaviour are emergent norm theory and:
   A. Resource mobilization
   B. Social contagion
   C. Relative deprivation
   D. Marxist
4. According to Marxists, revolts to bring about a major overhaul of society are ________.
   A. Peasant revolts B. Gender revolts
   C. Tribal Revolts D. Bourgeois revolts
5. The political opportunity approach emphasizes the way social movements are shaped by ________ .
   A. Forces beyond the control of members
   B. Ideologies
   C. Social contagion
   D. Relative deprivation
6. The collective action perspectives are best to study ___________.
   A. Collective behaviour
   B. Social breakdown
   C. Relative deprivation
   D. New social movements
7. The new social movement approach is based on ______ and post-industrial literature.
   A. Comte B. Weber
   C. Durkheim D. Postmodern
8. The Quiet Revolution occurred in the ________.
   A. 1930s B. 1970s
   C. 1960s D. 1950s
9. Maoists are people who believe in:
   A. Absolute monarchy
   B. Constitutional monarchy
   C. Rule of peasants through armed revolt
   D. Democratically elected government
10. The Bardoli satyagraha was led by which of the following leaders?
    A. R.C. Dutt
    B. Madan Mohan Malviya
    C. Sardar Patel
    D. Jawahar Lal Nehru
11. Because of a socio-cultural phenomenon, death rate registers a sharp fall at times but, _______ does not.
    A. Birth rate
    B. Maternal mortality rate
    C. Life expectancy
    D. Dependency ratio
12. Which of the following is incorrect in the context of the Caste system's imposed rules?
    A. Endogamous Caste groups
    B. A hierarchical system
    C. Open occupational choices
    D. Restrictions on food sharing
13. How did the British understand the caste system's complexity?
    A. Interview
    B. Survey
    C. Participant Observation
    D. Interview and Participant Observation
14. What are the two broad sets of issues that have been most important in giving rise to tribal movements?
    A. Control over vital economic resources and issues relating to matters of ethnic-cultural identity
    B. Control over vital economic resources and globalisation
    C. Control over vital economic resources and colonialism
    D. Control over vital economic resources and secularisation
15. How can be the ideas of inclusive nationalism can be built to be effective?
    A. Constitution B. Parliament
    C. Supreme Court D. Legislature

16. Minority in the sociological sense can be defined by:
A. Privilege
B. Only numerical distinction
C. Solidarity due to experience of disadvantage
D. Individualism

17. What is the type of governance/rule, that often limit or abolish civil liberties?
A. Authoritarian B. Democratic
C. Civil Society D. Libertarian

18. Who wrote Stree Purush Tulana?
A. Tarabai Shinde B. Savitribai Phule
C. Annie Besant D. Anita Ghai

19. Inequalities between men and women according to the Scholars are not ______ but ______.
A. Natural, Social B. Social, Natural
C. Desirable, undesirable D. Economic, racial

20. Which of the following is not a factor related to low child sex ratio?
A. Illiteracy B. Socio-cultural beliefs
C. Economic condition D. Preference for girl child

21. Which among the following is a process involving our significant others is important in developing a sense of community identity:
A. Socialisation B. Secularisation
C. Globalisation D. Marketisation

22. What does the population reach, when the growth rate is 0?
A. Replacement level B. Negative growth
C. Positive growth D. High birth rate

23. The demographic indicators not used to calculate the total fertility rate is:
A. Number of live births in the reproductive age group
B. Age-specific fertility rate
C. Sex ratio
D. Number of women in the child-bearing age group

24. Who was the leader of the Justice Movement?
A. C.N. Mudaliar
B. E.V. Ramaswamy Naicker
C. Sri Narayana Guru
D. Tulsi Ram

25. Which of the following religious revivalist organizations influenced Shahu Maharaj the most?
A. Arya Samaj B. Satyashodhak Samaj
C. Brahmo Samaj D. Prarthana Samaj

26. Which one among the following was demanded by the All India Depressed Classes Leaders' Conference at Bombay in 1931?
A. Universal adult suffrage
B. Separate electorates for untouchables
C. Reserved seats for the minorities
D. A unitary State in India

27. Dr. B.R. Ambedkar published three periodicals for the safeguard of Dalit rights. Which of the following is not one of them?
A. Mook Nayak B. Bahishkrit Bharat
C. Bahishkrit Samaj D. None of these

28. Who wrote the following comments regarding social change in the nineteenth century?
"All progress in social liberation tends to be a change from the law of status to the law of contract, from the restraints of family and caste, customs to the self-imposed restraints of the free will of the individual"
A. Keshub Chandra Sen
B. Swami Vivekanand
C. Sri Narayana Guru
D. Mahadev Govind Ranade

29. Which campaign was launched in 2005, in which 25000 people travelled 350 km, to pressurize the government to take some specified steps for land reform to preserve the land rights of the poorest sections?
A. Swadesh B. LAFTI
C. Janadesh D. Pardhi

30. On which date the 'Telangana Sayuda Porata committee' withdrew its armed struggle?
A. 21st October, 1951 B. 4th August, 1951
C. 20th January, 1951 D. 15th December, 1950

31. When was Channar women given the right to cover their breast?
A. 1841, July 26 B. 1869, July 26
C. 1859, July 26 D. 1861, July 26

32. Which among the following statements are correct with reference to the Paika Rebellion?
A. It was an armed rebellion that took place in Odisha
B. It was led by Bakshi Jagabandhu
C. It took place in the year 1817
D. All cf the above

33. _____ fought for the rights of the Dalit community.
A. Bipin Chandra Pal
B. Subhash Chandra Bose
C. Krishnaji Gopal Karve
D. Bhimrao Ambedkar

34. During the 1920s, the 'Self-respect movement' took place in which state of India?
A. Tamil Nadu B. Uttar Pradesh
C. West Bengal D. Maharashtra

35. Which of the following is incorrectly matched?
A. Satyashodhak Samaj - Jyotiba Phule
B. S.N.D.P. Yogam - Periyar Ramaswamy Naikar
C. Bahishkrit Bharat - B.R. Ambedkar
D. Sadharan Brahmo Samaj - Pandit Shivanata Shastry

36. The 'Kochi Pulaya Maha Sabha' was founded in 1913 under whose leadership?
A. K.P. Karuppan B. Ayyankali
C. Sahodaran Ayyappan D. Kumaran Asan

37. From where did the Bhil related activities of Motilal Tejawat through the Eki movement start?
A. Dungarpur B. Jhadole
C. Udaipur D. Neemda

38. The peasant movement named 'Bijolia Movement' was associated with which state of India?
A. Gujarat B. Rajasthan
C. Uttar Pradesh D. Madhya Pradesh

39. Which among the following is not a social movement?
A. Enviornmental movements
B. Gender movements
C. Human right movements
D. None of the above

40. Who are organic intellectuals?
A. Ordinary people B. Middle class leaders
C. Party leaders D. Authorities

41. Who is the father of social movements in England?
A. Lord Bute B. King John
C. Thomas Hobbes D. John Wilkes

42. The Treaty of Paris was related:
A. Seven Years war B. Glorious revolution
C. League of nations D. UDHR

43. The Treaty of Paris was signed in the year:
A. 1747 B. 1850
C. 1763 D. 1970

44. The book Socialist and Communist Movements since the Third French Revolution is authored:
A. Karl Marx B. Lorenz von Stein
C. Harold Laski D. Frederick Engels

45. The book Socialist and Communist Movements since the Third French Revolution was written:
A. 1848 B. 1777
C. 1912 D. 1949

46. The green parties deal with _____?
A. Human rights B. Environment
C. Direct democracy D. Gender issues

47. The anti nuclear movements emerged during _____ ?
A. Napoleonic wars B. Post first world war
C. Hundred years war D. Post second world war

48. NSM stands for:
A. National Strategic mission
B. New social movements
C. New state modalities
D. Natural social movements

49. New social movements rejects:
A. Parliamentary democracy
B. UN system
C. Multi Polarism
D. Organized politics

50. The solidarity movements originated in:
A. Poland B. USA
C. England D. Germany

51. Who among the following is associated with solidarity movement?
A. Martin Luther B. Karl Marx
C. Le Valeski D. Lenin

52. Which among the following was a peaceful movement?
A. French revolution B. Solidarity movement
C. American revolution D. None of the above

53. 26/11 is related with which country?
A. Iraq B. India
C. Palestine D. Russia

54. The old social movements were _____ movements.
A. Class B. Issues
C. Development D. Caste

55. Which was the tribal movement occurred outside Bihar?
A. Kali Revolt B. Tomar Revolt
C. Kharwar Revolt D. Chuar movement

56. Who was the leader of revolt of the Mundas in 1899-1900?
A. Shambhudan B. Birsa Munda
C. Buddhu Bhagat D. Siddhu

57. Who of the following founded Ahmedabad Textile Labour Association?
A. J.B. Kriplani
B. N.M. Joshi
C. Sardar Vallabhbhai Patel
D. Mahatma Gandhi

58. Who founded All India Harijan Sevak Sangh?
A. Mahatma Gandhi B. Raj Narayan
C. Jay Prakash Narayan D. B.R. Ambedkar

59. The Kuka movement started in mid-nineteenth century in:
A. Bengal B. Madhya Bharat
C. Maharashtra D. Western Punjab

60. Where was the first All India Kisan Sabha formed?
A. Patna B. Lucknow
C. Madras D. Calcutta

61. The first Indian Factory Act (1881) was passed by:
A. Lord Ripon B. Lord Cornwallis
C. Lord Wellesley D. Lord Curzon

62. The militant phase of the trade union movement in India was:
A. 1914-18 B. 1918-26
C. 1926-39 D. 1939-45

63. Who was the leader of Champaran Indigo Movement?
A. Ram Singh B. Baba Ramchandra
C. Birsa Munda D. Mahatma Gandhi

64. Siddhu was associated with:
A. Santhal Rebellion B. Sanyasi Rebellion
C. Munda Rebellion D. Kol Rebellion

65. Which Forest Act defined environment as the sum total of water, air, and land, their inter-relationship among themselves and with the human beings, other living beings and property?
A. Environmental Protection Act, 1986
B. Environmental Protection Act, 1987
C. Environmental Protection Act, 1988
D. Environmental Protection Act, 1989

66. Who wrote 'A Dictionary of Environmental History'?
A. Madhav Gadgil B. Ramachandra Guha
C. Ian D. White D. J.R. MacNeill

67. Environmental History as a field of research evolved in the:
A. 1930s B. 1940s
C. 1950s D. 1960s

68. Environmental History as a field of research evolved firstly in:
A. North America B. China
C. Japan D. the Middle East

69. The American Society for Environmental History was established in:
A. 1970 B. 1973
C. 1975 D. 1983

70. Who wrote the book 'Nature's Economy: A History of the Ecological Ideas'?
A. Alfred W. Crosby B. James C Malin
C. Marc Bloch D. Donald Worster

71. Who wrote the book 'Ecological Imperialism: The Biological Expansions of Europe'?
A. Donald Worster B. Alfred W. Crosby
C. Roderick Nash D. W.P. Webb

72. Which among the following was the book written by Rachel Carson?
A. This Fissured Land B. Ecological Imperialism
C. Nature's Economy D. Silent Spring

73. 'Silent Spring' is written by:
A. Ramachandra Guha B. K. Sivaramkrishnan
C. Rachel Carson D. Richard White

74. Who introduced the concept 'Mode of Resource Use'?
A. Madhav Gadgil C. Marc Bloch
C. Karl Marx D. Ramachandra Guha

75. The concept 'Mode of Resource Use' is first introduced in the work titled:
A. This Fissured Land
B. Nature's Economy
C. Ecological Imperialism
D. In the Belly on the River

76. From the long sweep of human history, according to Ramachandra Guha, we can discern .... distinct modes of resource use.
A. 2 B. 4
C. 6 D. 8

77. The largest period of human history has been spent in the .... mode of resource use.
A. Hunting-Gathering B. Nomadic Pastoralism
C. Settled Agriculture D. Industrial

78. The size of the social groups among hunting-gatherers is ....
A. Small B. Medium
C. Big D. Bigger

79. In which year the Ministry of Environment and Forests formulated the National Forest Policy which to give added importance to Joint Forest Management?
A. 1980 B. 1982
C. 1988 D. 1990

80. Which among the following modes of resource use had the lowest ecological impacts?
A. Hunting-Gathering B. Nomadic Pastoralism
C. Settled Agriculture D. Industrial

81. In which mode of resource use, the elements of private property began to emerge?
A. Hunting-Gathering B. Nomadic Pastoralism
C. Settled Agriculture D. Industrial

82. Who wrote the work 'Deforestation: Problems and Prospects'?
A. Ramachandra Guha B. Raymond Williams
C. Richard White D. Madhav Gadgil

83. Who wrote 'State Forestry and Social Conflict in British India'?
A. Bina Agarwal B. Lucien Febvre
C. Ramachandra Guha D. Raymond L. Bryant

84. Who introduced Sir Dietrich Brandis in India to look into the processes of forest resource management and to establish a systematic forest management system in India?
A. Lord Dalhousie B. Lord Wellesley
C. Dr. Wallich D. Dr. Gibson

85. Who issues the 'Charter of Indian Forests' in 1855?
A. Dr. Heifer B. Cleghorn
C. Lord Dalhousie D. Lord Wellesley

86. In which year Lord Dalhousie issued the 'Charter of Indian Forests'?
A. 1855 B. 1858
C. 1864 D. 1865

87. Who was the first Inspector General of Forests under the British-Indian administration?
A. Cleghorn B. Dietrich Brandis
C. Dr. Gibson D. Sir Richard Temple

88. What was the first nationwide regulation of the Indian forests?
A. Forest Act of 1856
B. Forest Act of 1878
C. Government of India Act, 1935
D. Government Forest Act of 1865

89. Which forest act of colonial period was clarified the rights and duties of forest officials for the first time?
A. Government Forest Act, 1865
B. Forest Act of 1878
C. Indian Forest Act, 1927
D. Forest Policy Resolution, 1894

90. What was the last reformulation of Indian forest policy under the British?
A. Government of India Act, 1935
B. Indian Forest Act, 1927
C. Forest Policy Resolution
D. Sir Herbert Howard's Reformulation of 1894 Resolution

91. Who wrote 'In the Belly of the River'?
A. Ramachandra Guha B. Bina Agarwal
C. Amita Baviskar D. None of these

92. Whose vision of development was centred on the revival of village economy?
A. Mahatma Gandhi B. Subhash C. Bose
C. Jawaharlal Nehru D. Sardar Patel

93. Tehri Dam was constructed on the river:
A. Bhageerathi B. Alakananda
C. Koyna D. Thungabhadra

94. The veteran freedom fighter who led the movement against Tehri dam was:
A. Senapati Bapat B. Chandi Prasad Bhatt
C. Virendra Dutt Saklani D. Smt. Sarla Devi

95. Virendra Dutt Saklani founded a forum to oppose dam construction named:
A. Tehri Baandh Virodhi Sangharsh Samiti
B. Friends of the Doon
C. Kumaun Sangharsh Samiti
D. Save Mussoorie

96. Which river valley project has termed the world's greatest planned environmental disaster?
A. Tehri Dam B. Bakra Nangal Dam
C. Koel Karo D. Narmada

97. The tribal population who inhabited in the Mandla, Balaghat and Bilaspur districts of Madhya Pradesh was:
A. Chenchu B. Saora
C. Baiga D. Kadar

98. Who made the first attempt to put an end to jhum cultivation?
A. Lord Dalhousie B. Sir Richard Temple
C. Lord Anton D. Sir Herbert Howard

99. Who led the Rampa rebellion of 1879-80?
A. Tammam Dora B. Kumra Bhimu
C. Bhimu Gond D. Raji

100. The concept of the hugging of trees had its roots in the ________ community.
A. Saora B. Chenchu
C. Bishnoi D. Baiga

101. The modern chipko movement was inspired by the true story of a brave lady called:
A. Sunita Narain B. Madhu Kishwar
C. Sarla Devi D. Amrita Devi

102. In which year, the modern chipko movement originated in the Himalayan region of Uttarakhand?
A. 1970 B. 1973
C. 1980 D. 1984

103. Under whose leadership, the Dashauli Gram Swarajya Sangh.was established to oppose large scale industries in the Alakananda Valley?
A. Chandi Prasad Bhatt
B. Sunderlal Bahuguna
C. Gaura Devi
D. Ghanashyam Raturi

104. Which village in the Alakananda valley witnessed the first Chipko protest in 1973?
A. Phata B. Kumaon
C. Mandal D. Garhwal

105. Sunderlal Bahuguna was awarded .... in the year 2009 for his services to human kind and for the protection of environment.
A. Magsaysay B. Padma Bhushan
C. Padma Vibhushan D. Padma Shri

106. Chandi Prasad Bhatt was awarded _______ in the year 1982 for his contributions in the protection of environment.
A. Padma Shri B. Padma Vibhushan
C. Padma Bhushan D. Magsaysay

107. Which among the following was the biggest project to be constructed in the Narmada river?

A. Sardar Sarovar B. Bhakranangal
C. Bedthi D. Koel Karo

108. Baba Amte first achieved national prominence for his work on dams with the publication of ______.

A. In the Belly of the River
B. Cry O Beloved Narmada
C. Ganga: The Many Pasts of a River
D. Land of Two Rivers

109. Who inaugurated the first protest march against Coca-Cola plant at Plachimada?

A. Mayilamma
B. Arundhati Roy
C. K.P.S. Menon
D. C.K. Janu

110. The Silent Valley Project was to erect a hydro-electric dam across:

A. Kunthipuzha B. Periyar
C. Bharathapuzha D. Pambaar

ANSWERS

1	2	3	4	5	6	7	8	9	10
A	D	B	D	A	D	D	C	C	C
11	**12**	**13**	**14**	**15**	**16**	**17**	**18**	**19**	**20**
A	C	B	A	A	C	A	A	B	D
21	**22**	**23**	**24**	**25**	**26**	**27**	**28**	**29**	**30**
A	A	C	A	A	B	B	D	C	A
31	**32**	**33**	**34**	**35**	**36**	**37**	**38**	**39**	**40**
C	D	D	A	B	A	B	B	D	B
41	**42**	**43**	**44**	**45**	**46**	**47**	**48**	**49**	**50**
D	A	C	B	A	B	D	B	D	A
51	**52**	**53**	**54**	**55**	**56**	**57**	**58**	**59**	**60**
C	B	B	A	A	B	D	A	D	B
61	**62**	**63**	**64**	**65**	**66**	**67**	**68**	**69**	**70**
A	C	D	A	A	C	D	A	C	D
71	**72**	**73**	**74**	**75**	**76**	**77**	**78**	**79**	**80**
B	D	C	D	A	B	A	A	C	A
81	**82**	**83**	**84**	**85**	**86**	**87**	**88**	**89**	**90**
B	D	C	A	C	A	B	D	C	B
91	**92**	**93**	**94**	**95**	**96**	**97**	**98**	**99**	**100**
C	A	A	C	A	D	C	B	A	C
101	**102**	**103**	**104**	**105**	**106**	**107**	**108**	**109**	**110**
D	B	A	C	C	D	A	B	D	A

GENERAL INTELLIGENCE & REASONING

VERBAL

CHAPTER 1

Analogies

NUMBER ANALOGY

In number analogy also, the relationship between the given numbers is detected and then applied to the second part to find the missing numbers. This relationship between the numbers can be based on any of the following patterns : *(i)* numbers can be odd/even/prime numbers; *(ii)* numbers can be multiples of one number; *(iii)* numbers can be squares/cubes of different numbers; *(iv)* some numbers can be added to/subtracted from/multiplied to/divided into the first number to get the second number; *(v)* the second number can be the sum/product/difference of the digits of first number; and *(vi)* combinations of any mathematical calculations given above can apply to the relationship between the two given numbers.

SOLVED EXAMPLES

Directions : *Which number will come in the place of question mark?*

1. 25 : 81 : : 36 : ?

(*a*) 121 (*b*) 93 (*c*) 65 (*d*) 103

Ans. (*a*) : All the numbers are squares of different numbers.

25	:	81	: :	36	:	121
↓		↓		↓		↓
5^2		9^2		6^2		11^2

2. 36 : 18 : : 72 : ?

(*a*) 164 (*b*) 134 (*c*) 94 (*d*) 14

Ans. (*d*) : The second number is the product of digits of the first number.

36 : 18 : : 72 : 14

3×6 7×2

MULTIPLE CHOICE QUESTIONS

Directions : *In the following questions, select the number from the given options which follows the same relationship as shared between the first two numbers.*

1. 1 : 11 : : 2 : ?

(*a*) 20 (*b*) 22
(*c*) 24 (*d*) 44

2. 18 : 27 : : 22 : ?

(*a*) 42 (*b*) 39
(*c*) 33 (*d*) 54

3. 14 : 20 : : 16 : ?

(*a*) 23 (*b*) 10
(*c*) 48 (*d*) 32

4. 8 : 27 : : 64 : ?

(*a*) 277 (*b*) 125
(*c*) 250 (*d*) 99

5. 0.16 : 0.0016 : : 1.02 : ?

(*a*) 10.20 (*b*) 0.102
(*c*) 0.0102 (*d*) 1.020

6. $\frac{1}{7} : \frac{1}{14} :: \frac{1}{9} : ?$
(a) $\frac{1}{88}$ (b) $\frac{1}{80}$
(c) $\frac{1}{81}$ (d) $\frac{1}{18}$

7. 5 : 24 : : 8 : ?
(a) 65 (b) 63
(c) 62 (d) 64

8. 23 : 53 : : 8 : ?
(a) 66 (b) 57
(c) 27 (d) 19

9. 6 : 9 : : 7 : ?
(a) 4 (b) 14
(c) 10 (d) 28

10. 7 : 28 : : 2 : ?
(a) 8 (b) 16
(c) 24 (d) 12

EXPLANATORY ANSWERS

1. (b) : The first number is repeated to obtain the second number.

2. (c) : In the given set, the numbers are multiples of 9 and in the second set, multiples of 11.

18 : 27 : : 22 : 33
↓ ↓ ↓ ↓
9 × 2 9 × 3 11 × 2 11 × 3

3. (a) : The relationship between the numbers is :

14 : 20 : : 16 : 23
↓ ↓ ↓ ↓
7 × 2 (7 × 3) −1 8 × 2 (8 × 3) −1

4. (b) : The numbers are cubes of different numbers.

8 : 27 : : 64 : 125
↓ ↓ ↓ ↓
2^3 3^3 4^3 5^3

5. (c) : The decimals are divided by 100.

6. (d) : The first fraction is multiplied by half to obtain the second fraction.

$\frac{1}{7} : \frac{1}{14} :: \frac{1}{9} : \frac{1}{18}$
$\times\frac{1}{2}$ $\times\frac{1}{2}$

7. (b) : The second number is square of first number minus 1.

5 : 24 : : 8 : 63
$(5^2) - 1$ $(8^2) - 1$

8. (d) : All the numbers are prime numbers.

9. (c) : The second number is three more than the first number.

6 : 9 : : 7 : 10
+3 +3

10. (a) : The second number is four times the first.

7 : 28 : : 2 : 8
× 4 × 4

LETTER ANALOGY

In this type of analogy the relationship between two given set of letters is established and then applied to the other set to obtain the required set of letters as the answer. These letters can be moved some steps backward or forward; reversed in whole or in sections or have some common identity between each other.

SOLVED EXAMPLES

Directions : *Which set of letters will come in the place of question mark?*

1. JILK : KLIJ : : MNPQ : ?
(a) QNPM (b) MPQN (c) QPNM (d) PNMQ

Ans. (c) : The letters are written in reverse order to get the related set of letters.

JILK : KLIJ : : MNPQ : QPNM

2. FLO : DOL : : RDP : ?

(*a*) PGM (*b*) MGP (*c*) GMP (*d*) MPG

Ans. (*a*) : The first and third letters are moved two and three steps backwards respectively and the second letter three steps forward.

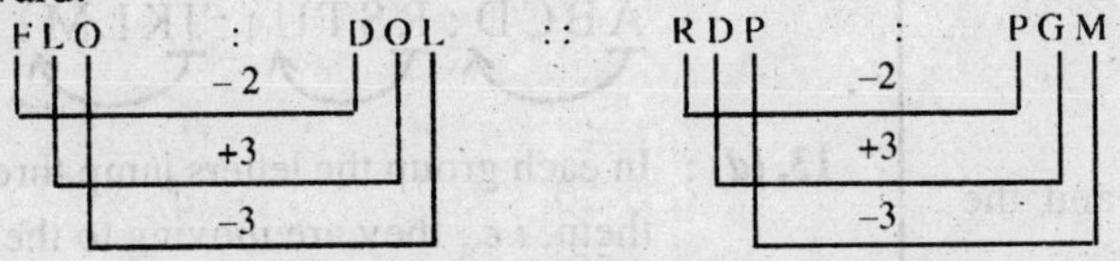

MULTIPLE CHOICE QUESTIONS

Directions : *In the questions given below one term is missing. Based on the relationship of the two given terms find the missing term from the given options.*

1. GFC : CFG : : RPJ : ?
(*a*) JRP (*b*) JPR
(*c*) PJR (*d*) RJP

2. BCF : DEG : : MNQ : ?
(*a*) OPR (*b*) PQS
(*c*) OPP (*d*) QRT

3. NATION : ANITNO : : HUNGRY : ?
(*a*) HNUGRY (*b*) UNHGYR
(*c*) YRNGUH (*d*) UHGNYR

4. SSTU : MMNO : : AABC : ?
(*a*) GGHH (*b*) IJKK
(*c*) XXYZ (*d*) NOOP

5. ACE : FGH : : LNP : ?
(*a*) QRS (*b*) PQR
(*c*) QST (*d*) MOQ

6. UVW : SXU : : LMN : ?
(*a*) JOL (*b*) KNM
(*c*) JKL (*d*) MLO

7. EIGHTY : GIEYTH : : OUTPUT : ?
(*a*) UTOPTU (*b*) UOTUPT
(*c*) TUOUTP (*d*) TUOTUP

8. TSR : FED : : WVU : ?
(*a*) CAB (*b*) MLK
(*c*) PQS (*d*) GFH

9. CJDL : FMGR : : IKJR : ?
(*a*) OQPT (*b*) RSTU
(*c*) OQRT (*d*) KRMO

10. BOQD : ERTG : : ANPC : ?
(*a*) DQSF (*b*) FSHU
(*c*) SHFU (*d*) DSQF

11. BaBy : TaTa : : LiLy : ?
(*a*) PooL (*b*) ROse
(*c*) HaNd (*d*) DoWN

12. BCDA : STUR : : KLMJ : ?
(*a*) VWXU (*b*) EFHG
(*c*) SRTU (*d*) QSRP

13. AEI : LPT : : CGK : ?
(*a*) OSV (*b*) RUY
(*c*) TXC (*d*) FJN

14. RUX : TRP : : BEH : ?
(*a*) SQN (*b*) QON
(*c*) QOM (*d*) QNL

15. CART : ART : : FOUR : ?
(*a*) RUN (*b*) TWO
(*c*) QUE (*d*) OUR

EXPLANATORY ANSWERS

1. (*b*) : The letters of the first group are reversed.

2. (*a*) : The three letters are moved 2, 2 and 1 steps forward respectively.

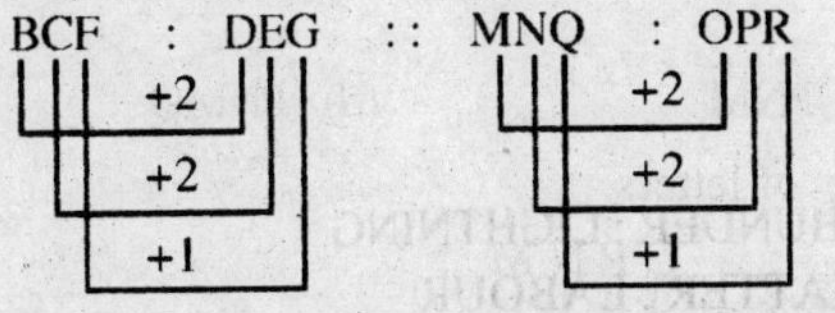

3. (*d*) : The word is divided in sections of two letters and the letters are reversed.

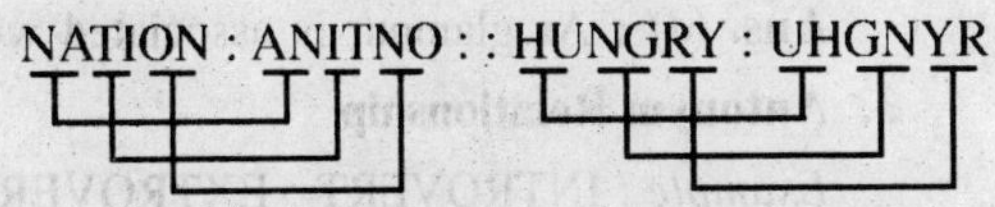

4. (*c*) : The first letter in each group is repeated and followed by two consecutive letters.

5. (*a*) : The three letters are moved 5, 4, and 3 steps forward respectively.

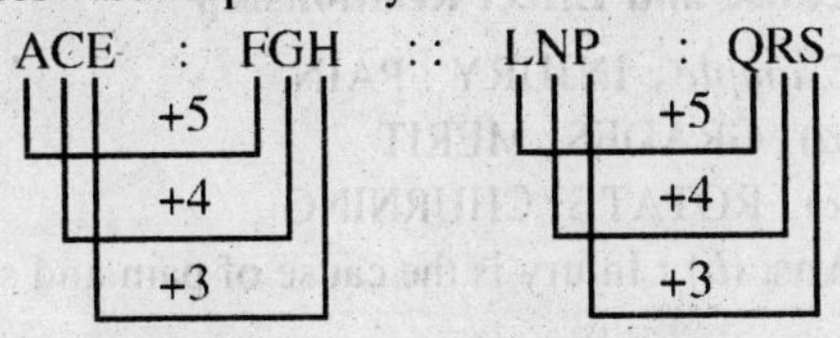

6. (*a*) **:** The three letters are moved –2, +2 and –2 steps respectively.

UVW : SXU :: LMN : JOL

–2   +2   –2   –2   +2   –2

7. (*d*) **:** The word is divided into two sections and the letters are written backwards.

EIGHTY : GIEYTH :: OUTPUT : TUOTUP

8. (*b*) **:** The letters are consecutive and written in reverse order.

9. (*a*) **:** In each set of letters, the 1st and 3rd letters are consecutive.

CJDL : FMGR :: IKJR : OQPT

10. (*a*) **:** In each group, the first and fourth letters are jumping one letter and the second and third letters are also jumping one letter.

BOQD : ERTG :: ANPC : DQSF

P C   S F   O B   R E

11. (*c*) **:** In each group the alternate letters are capitals.

12. (*a*) **:** In each group the first three letters are consecutive and they follow the fourth letter.

ABCD : RSTU :: JKLM : UVWX

13. (*d*) **:** In each group the letters jump three letters between them, *i.e.*, they are moving to the fourth letter.

AEI : LPT :: CGK : FJN

+4 +4   +4 +4   +4 +4   +4 +4

14. (*c*) **:** The letters in first set are jumping two letters, *i.e.*, moving three steps forward and in the second they are jumping one letter, *i.e.* moving two steps backward.

RUX : TRP :: BEH : QOM

+3 +3   –2 –2   +3+3   –2 –2

15. (*d*) **:** The first set of letters drop the first letter to get the second set.

CART : ART :: FOUR : OUR

SEMANTIC ANALOGY

In Analogy Tests the relationship between two given words is established and then applied to the other words. The type of relationship may vary, so while attempting such questions the first step is to identify the type of relationship, which can be any one of the following.

SOLVED EXAMPLES

1. Action Object Relationship

Example : Shoot is to Gun as Eat is to.....

(*a*) Hunger   (*b*) Thirst   (*c*) Dinner   (*d*) Fruit

Ans. (*d*) : The relationship between the given words is that 'shoot' is the action and 'Gun' is the specified object of action. Similarly 'eat' is the action and 'fruit' is the specified object.

2. Association Relationship

Example : Glamour is to Stardom as Colour is to.....

(*a*) Rainbow   (*b*) Shades   (*c*) Art   (*d*) Painting

Ans. (*d*) : As glamour is associated with stardom so is colour with painting.

3. Antonym Relationship

Example : INTROVERT : EXTROVERT

(*a*) ANGLE : TANGENT   (*b*) EXTREME : INTERIM

(*c*) AGAINST : FAVOUR   (*d*) ACTION : LAW

Ans. (*c*) : The related words are opposite in meaning.

4. Cause and Effect Relationship

Example : INJURY : PAIN

(*a*) GRADES : MERIT   (*b*) THUNDER : LIGHTNING

(*c*) ROTATE : CHURNING   (*d*) MATTER : LABOUR

Ans. (*b*) : Injury is the cause of pain and so is thunder the cause of lightning.

5. Degree Relationship

Example : Tepid is to Hot as... is to Wail.

(*a*) Sob (*b*) Shout (*c*) Smile (*d*) Calm

Ans. (*a*) : Tepid is less hot and so also the lower degree of wail is sob.

6. Grammatical Relationship

Example: Clever is to Beautiful as Sour is to ...

(*a*) Lemon (*b*) Cunning (*c*) Loathing (*d*) Taste

Ans. (*b*) : The related words are Adjectives.

7. Obvious Relationship

Example : Mt. EVEREST : NEPAL

(*a*) MEXICO : SOUTH AMERICA (*b*) K2 : CHINA

(*c*) BIG BEN : RUSSIA (*d*) AHMEDABAD : GUJARAT

Ans. (*d*) : Mt. Everest is in Nepal and so is Ahmedabad in Gujarat.

8. Part Whole Relationship

Example : MAN : MAMMAL

(*a*) HAIL : SNOW (*b*) NATIVE : INHABITANT

(*c*) OFFSPRING : FAMILY (*d*) LIBERTY : LITERATE

Ans. (*c*) : Man is a part of the whole species of mammal so is an offspring of the whole family.

9. Purpose Relationship

Example : INSTITUTION : EDUCATION

(*a*) WAR : PEACE (*b*) HEALTH : OBESITY

(*c*) MEDICATION : RECUPERATION (*d*) BUILDING : URBANISM

Ans. (*c*) : The purpose of institution is to impart education and the purpose of medication is quick recuperation (recovery).

10. Sequence Relationship

Example : .... is to Dusk as Summer is to Monsoon.

(*a*) Evening (*b*) Dawn (*c*) Night (*d*) Noon

Ans. (*a*) : Summer season is immediately followed by monsoon (rainy season) and evening is immediately followed by dusk.

11. Synonym Relationship

Example : INDENT : REQUEST

(*a*) REPLICA : CHEAT (*b*) DOLE : ALMS

(*c*) DISMAL : DUNCE (*d*) EXACT : CHECK

Ans. (*b*) : The related words have the same meaning.

12. Volume Relationship

Example : GALLONS : SWIMMING POOL

(*a*) SPECTATORS : AUDITORIUM (*b*) CURRENCY : SHARES

(*c*) DUST : MOUNTAIN (*d*) BOOKS : CATALOGUE

Ans. (*a*) : Gallons of water is needed to fill a swimming pool and large number of spectators can be admitted into an auditorium.

MULTIPLE CHOICE QUESTIONS

Directions : *In the questions given below establish the relationship between the two words. Then from the given options select one which has the same relationship as of the given two words.*

1. HUNGER : FOOD : : THIRST : ?

(*a*) Water (*b*) Drink

(*c*) Tea (*d*) Coffee

2. HUNTER : GUN : : WRITER : ?

(*a*) Book (*b*) Pen

(*c*) Poem (*d*) Page

3. WOOL : SHEEP : : SILK : ?

(*a*) Saree

(*b*) String

(*c*) Silkworm

(*d*) Moth

4. FOOD : STOMACH : : FUEL : ?
(*a*) Engine (*b*) Automobile
(*c*) Rail (*d*) Aeroplane

5. WATER : SAND : : OCEAN : ?
(*a*) Island (*b*) River
(*c*) Desert (*d*) Waves

6. ADULT : BABY : : FLOWER : ?
(*a*) Seed (*b*) Bud
(*c*) Fruit (*d*) Butterfly

7. WRITER : READER : : PRODUCER : ?
(*a*) Creator (*b*) Contractor
(*c*) Creature (*d*) Consumer

8. ENTRANCE : EXIT : : LOYALTY : ?
(*a*) Treachery (*b*) Patriotism
(*c*) Fidelity (*d*) Reward

9. MOTHER : MATERNAL : : FATHER : ?
(*a*) Eternal (*b*) Detrimental
(*c*) Paternal (*d*) Formidable

10. PEARL : NECKLACE : : FLOWER : ?
(*a*) Plant (*b*) Garden
(*c*) Petal (*d*) Bouquet

11. ALPHABET : WORD : : WORD : ?
(*a*) Sound (*b*) Music
(*c*) Sentence (*d*) Dictionary

12. LIFE : DEATH : : HOPE : ?
(*a*) Cry (*b*) Pain
(*c*) Despair (*d*) Sad

13. GOOD : BAD : : VIRTUE : ?
(*a*) Blame (*b*) Sin
(*c*) Despair (*d*) Vice

14. BIRD : FLY : : SNAKE : ?
(*a*) Timid (*b*) Clatter
(*c*) Crawl (*d*) Hole

15. CAT : MOUSE : : BIRD : ?
(*a*) Cage (*b*) Trap
(*c*) Eagle (*d*) Worm

16. STATE : EXILE
(*a*) Police : Arrest
(*b*) Judge : Convict
(*c*) Constitution : Amendment
(*d*) Church : Excommunicate

17. CAPRICIOUSNESS : RELIABILITY
(*a*) Extemporaneous : Predictability
(*b*) Unreliable : Inhuman
(*c*) Tenacious : Practicality
(*d*) Arbitrary : Whimsical

18. LOATH : COERCION
(*a*) Detest : Caressing (*b*) Irritate : Caressing
(*c*) Irate : Antagonism (*d*) Reluctant : Persuasion

19. SCALES : FISH
(*a*) Lady : Dress (*b*) Tree : Leaves
(*c*) Bird : Feather (*d*) Skin : Man

20. TREE : SAPLING
(*a*) Hut : Mansion (*b*) Giant : Dwarf
(*c*) Horse : Foal (*d*) Ant : Elephant

EXPLANATORY ANSWERS

1. (*a*) : Hunger is satiated by food, thirst by water.

2. (*b*) : Weapon of a hunter is a gun, weapon of a writer is a pen.

3. (*c*) : Wool is obtained from sheep, silk is obtained from silkworm.

4. (*a*) : Food is consumed in stomach, fuel is consumed in engine.

5. (*c*) : The related words are near opposites.

6. (*b*) : The youngone of an adult is a baby and that of a flower is a bud.

7. (*d*) : A writer aims to please the readers by his writings, a producer aims to please the consumers by his products.

8. (*a*) : The related words are opposites.

9. (*c*) : Relations on the mother's side are maternal and on the father's side paternal.

10. (*d*) : Many pearls make a necklace, many flowers make a bouquet.

11. (*c*) : More than one alphabet make a word, more than one word make a sentence.

12. (*c*) : The related words are opposites.

13. (*d*) : The related words are opposites.

14. (*c*) : Birds fly, snakes crawl.

15. (*d*) : Cat chases the mouse, bird chases the worm.

16. (*d*) : Punishment of leaving the State is exile, punishment of leaving the Church is excommunication.

17. (*c*) : The related words are antonyms

18. (*d*) : Loathing is the result of constant coersion, reluctance is the result of constant persuasion.

19. (*d*) : Covering of the fish is scales, covering of man is skin.

20. (*c*) : Young tree is a sapling, young horse is a foal.

CHAPTER 2

Number Classification

ODD ONE OUT—NUMBERS

In this type of classification, different numbers are given as options. These numbers have some commonness; except one which is the odd one. One has to identify the similarity and then strike the odd one out as answer option. The number can be odd/even/consecutive, prime numbers, multiple of some number, single, square or cubes of different numbers, plus/minus of some other number or combinations of any mathematical calculation.

SOLVED EXAMPLES

Directions : *Find the odd number from the given options.*

1. (*a*) 62 (*b*) 121 (*c*) 36 (*d*) 256

Ans. (*a*) : The other numbers are squares of :
11, (= 121), 6 (= 36) and 16 (= 256)

2. (*a*) 27 (*b*) 132 (*c*) 93 (*d*) 154

Ans. (*d*) : All other numbers are divisible by 3.

MULTIPLE CHOICE QUESTIONS

Directions : *In each of the following questions, there are four options. Three numbers, in these options, are alike in certain manner. Only one number does not fit in. Choose the one which is different from the rest.*

1. (*a*) 1948 (*b*) 2401 (*c*) 966 (*d*) 1449

2. (*a*) 182 (*b*) 169 (*c*) 130 (*d*) 158

3. (*a*) 129 (*b*) 130 (*c*) 131 (*d*) 132

4. (*a*) 3215 (*b*) 9309 (*c*) 4721 (*d*) 2850

5. (*a*) 1776 (*b*) 2364 (*c*) 1976 (*d*) 3776

6. (*a*) 64 (*b*) 84 (*c*) 16 (*d*) 36

7. (*a*) 24 (*b*) 90 (*c*) 54 (*d*) 36

8. (*a*) 7658 (*b*) 1234 (*c*) 9876 (*d*) 6543

9. (*a*) 3 (*b*) 9 (*c*) 5 (*d*) 7

10. (*a*) 6450 (*b*) 1776 (*c*) 2392 (*d*) 3815

11. (*a*) 24 (*b*) 48 (*c*) 42 (*d*) 12

12. (*a*) 616 (*b*) 252 (*c*) 311 (*d*) 707

13. (*a*) 18 (*b*) 12 (*c*) 30 (*d*) 20

14. (*a*) 3730 (*b*) 6820 (*c*) 5568 (*d*) 4604

EXPLANATORY ANSWERS

1. (*a*) : Other numbers are divisible by 7.
2. (*d*) : Other numbers are multiples of 13.
3. (*c*) : 131 is a prime number.
4. (*b*) : In other numbers, no digit is repeated.
5. (*b*) : In other numbers the last two digits are same.
6. (*b*) : All other numbers are perfect squares.
7. (*a*) : In other numbers, the sum of both the digits is 9.
8. (*a*) : In others, the digits are consecutive in natural or reverse series.
9. (*b*) : All others are prime numbers.
10. (*d*) : All other numbers are divisible by 2.
11. (*c*) : All other numbers are multiples of 12.
12. (*c*) : In other numbers, the first and last digits are same.
13. (*a*) : The other numbers are $3^2 + 3 = 12$, $5^2 + 5 = 30$, $4^2 + 4 = 20$, $6^2 + 6 = 42$
14. (*b*) : In all other numbers, two digits are same.

ODD ONE OUT—LETTERS

In this classification of letters, four groups of letters or a series of letters is given as options. One has to select the option as answer which does not share the commonness of the others.

SOLVED EXAMPLES

Directions : *Find the odd one out in the following letters :*

1. (*a*) NOP (*b*) RTU (*c*) JKL (*d*) EFG
Ans. (*b*) : In each group the letters are consecutive. In this option the first two letters jump one letter (S) inbetween.

2. (*a*) RUX (*b*) CFI (*c*) BDG (*d*) FIL
Ans. (*c*) : In each group, the difference between the letters is same. In this option B and D jump one letter and D and G jump two letters.

MULTIPLE CHOICE QUESTIONS

Directions : *In each of the following questions, four out of five alternatives contain alphabet placed in a particular form. Find the one that does not belong to the group.*

1. (*a*) BXCW (*b*) OTPS (*c*) GQHR (*d*) JNKM
2. (*a*) BVPS (*b*) OLMZ (*c*) RPSR (*d*) XTCD
3. (*a*) RNJH (*b*) SOKG (*c*) QMIE (*d*) MIEA
4. (*a*) QLJS (*b*) GVTI (*c*) KRPM (*d*) ONMP
5. (*a*) PEAR (*b*) TORE (*c*) REAP (*d*) TEAR
6. (*a*) ECA (*b*) JHF (*c*) OMK (*d*) UWY
7. (*a*) ACE (*b*) PRT (*c*) UWY (*d*) MNO
8. (*a*) WVU (*b*) NML (*c*) HGF (*d*) DBA
9. (*a*) ABD (*b*) FGI (*c*) LMO (*d*) STU
10. (*a*) CDE (*b*) JKL (*c*) PQS (*d*) TUV

EXPLANATORY ANSWERS

1. (*c*) : In all other groups, first and third letters are consecutive and second and fourth letters are in reverse alphabetical order.
2. (*c*) : No letter is repeated in any other group.
3. (*a*) : In all other groups, there is a gap of three letters between two consecutive letters.
4. (*d*) : In all other groups, first and third letters are moved two steps forward to obtain fourth and second letters respectively.
5. (*b*) : All other groups contain E, A and R.
6. (*d*) : All other groups contain alternate letters from right to left.

7. (*d*) : All other groups contain alternate letters from left to right.

8. (*d*) : In all others, the three letters are consecutive but in reverse order.

9. (*d*) : In all others, the first two letters are consecutive and third letter is obtained by skipping one letter from the second.

10. (*c*) : In all other, the three letters are consecutive.

ODD ONE OUT—WORDS

In this type of classification, five words are given out of which four are almost same in matter or meaning and only one word is different from the common four. One has to find out the word which is different from the rest.

SOLVED EXAMPLES

Directions : *In the following questions spot the odd one out.*

1. (*a*) Father (*b*) Mother (*c*) Friend (*d*) Brother

Ans. (*c*) : All other are blood relations.

2. (*a*) Water (*b*) Jelly (*c*) Lemonade (*d*) Coffee

Ans. (*b*) : All other are liquids.

MULTIPLE CHOICE QUESTIONS

Directions : *In each of the following questions, four words are alike in some manner. Spot the odd one out.*

1. (*a*) Green (*b*) Red (*c*) Colour (*d*) Orange

2. (*a*) Stable (*b*) Hole (*c*) Canoe (*d*) Sty

3. (*a*) Nose (*b*) Eyes (*c*) Skin (*d*) Teeth

4. (*a*) Venus (*b*) Moon (*c*) Pluto (*d*) Mars

5. (*a*) Happy (*b*) Gloomy (*c*) Lively (*d*) Cheerful

6. (*a*) Cone (*b*) Circle (*c*) Triangle (*d*) Rectangle

7. (*a*) Lead (*b*) Mercury (*c*) Copper (*d*) Iron

8. (*a*) Kite (*b*) Bird (*c*) Radar (*d*) Jet

9. (*a*) Knee (*b*) Shoulder (*c*) Ankle (*d*) Palm

10. (*a*) Deluge (*b*) Calamity (*c*) Catastrophe (*d*) War

11. (*a*) Cub (*b*) Chicken (*c*) Pig (*d*) Pup

12. (*a*) Rabbit (*b*) Crocodile (*c*) Earthworm (*d*) Snail

13. (*a*) Tree (*b*) Leaf (*c*) Bush (*d*) Herb

14. (*a*) Doctor (*b*) Teacher (*c*) Engineer (*d*) Diver

15. (*a*) Trot (*b*) Equestrian (*c*) Derby (*d*) Grunt

EXPLANATORY ANSWERS

1. (*c*) : All others are types of colour.

2. (*c*) : Canoe is a boat. Others are resting places of birds/animals.

3. (*d*) : All others are sense organs.

4. (*b*) : All others are planets.

5. (*b*) : All others are expressions of joy

6. (*a*) : All others are geometrical figures.

7. (*b*) : All others are solid metals.

8. (*c*) : All others are flying objects. Radar traces the objects in sky.

9. (*d*) : All others are joints in human body.

10. (*d*) : All others are nature-bound. Only war is man-made.

11. (*c*) : All others are young ones of animals.

12. (*a*) : All others are crawling animals.

13. (*b*) : All others are types of vegetation.

14. (*d*) : All others are professions, but only Diver's profession comprises of diving under water.

15. (*d*) : All other terms are related with activities of a horse.

CHAPTER 3

Small & Capital Letters/ Numbers Coding-Decoding and Classification

TYPE - I

Coding is a secretive language which is used to change the representation of the actual term/word/value. This coded language can be framed by *(i)* moving the letters one or more steps forward or backward; *(ii)* substituting numbers for letters and vice–versa; *(iii)* writing the letters of the given word in reverse order in part or in whole; and *(iv)* replacing the letters in their natural series by the same positioned letters in their reverse series.

Alphabet in natural series are :

A B C D E F G H I J K L M N O P Q R S T U V W X Y Z

A ↓ 1st, E ↓ 5th, J ↓ 10th, O ↓ 15th, T ↓ 20th, Y ↓ 25th

Alphabet in reverse series are :

Z Y X W V U T S R Q P O N M L K J I H G F E D C B A

Z ↓ 1st, V ↓ 5th, Q ↓ 10th, L ↓ 15th, G ↓ 20th, B ↓ 25th

Note : On reaching Z, the series restarts from A and on reaching A, it restarts from Z.

SOLVED EXAMPLES

1. If FACE is coded as GBDF, then BADE will be coded as :

(a) CBEF *(b)* CEBF *(c)* CFBE *(d)* CBFE

Ans. *(a)* : The word is coded by moving the letters one step forward.

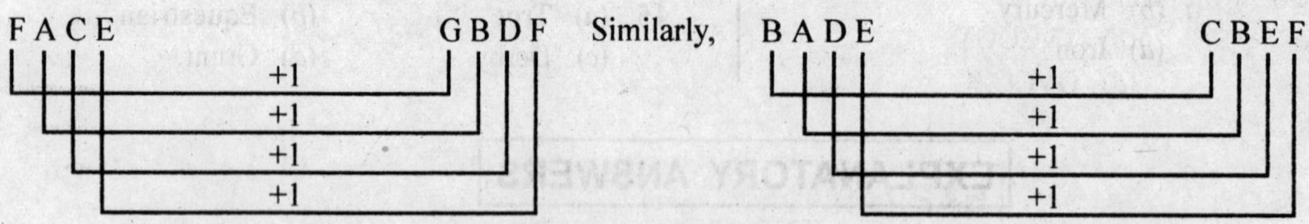

2. If RESULT is coded as 798206, LET will be coded as :

(a) 680 *(b)* 092 *(c)* 096 *(d)* 086

Ans. *(c)* : The letters are coded by numbers, and to code the given word, select the respective coded numbers.

R E S U L T → letters
7 9 8 2 0 6 → code

So, code for LET will be

L E T → letters
0 9 6 → code

MULTIPLE CHOICE QUESTIONS

Directions : *In the following questions select the right option which indicates the correct code for the word or letter given in the question.*

1. If CHAIR is coded as FKDLU then RAID is coded as :
(*a*) ULGD (*b*) ULKG
(*c*) ULDG (*d*) UDLG

2. If CONDEMN is coded as CNODMEN, then TEACHER is coded as :
(*a*) TEACHER (*b*) TAEECHR
(*c*) TCAEEHR (*d*) TAECEHR

3. In a code language COME is written as XLNV and ABLE as ZYOV. How will MOLLY be written in that code?
(*a*) NLOBO (*b*) NLBOO
(*c*) LNOOB (*d*) NLOOB

4. In a certain code PROFESSION is written as EFORPNOISS. In the same code DICTIONARY will be written as :
(*a*) YRANOITCID (*b*) ITCIDYRANO
(*c*) ITCIDYRNAO (*d*) ITCDIYARNO

5. JUNE is coded as NXPF, how will STAY be coded in the same manner?
(*a*) WWCZ (*b*) WVCZ
(*c*) WWDB (*d*) VWZC

6. If in a certain code GENIUS is coded as IGPKWU, then IDIOT will be written in the same code as :
(*a*) JEJPU (*b*) KFKQV
(*c*) LGLRW (*d*) HCHNS

7. If ACTION is coded as ZXGRLM, then HEALTH will be coded in the same way as :
(*a*) SVZOGS (*b*) TVZOGT
(*c*) RUZPGR (*d*) QVGOZQ

8. If THOUSAND is coded as SGNTRZMC, then FUMING will be coded as :
(*a*) GVNJOH (*b*) ETHLMF
(*c*) EVLJMH (*d*) ETLHMF

9. If EARTHQUAKE is coded as MOGPENJOSM, then EQUATE will be coded as :
(*a*) MENOPM (*b*) MENOMP
(*c*) MJOGPM (*d*) MNJOPM

10. In a certain code language HJIZT code is deciphered as MONEY, in the same way NOVGZ will be deciphered as :
(*a*) STUMP (*b*) STALE
(*c*) STICK (*d*) SPIRE

11. If in a certain code JOSEPH is coded as FKOALD, then GEORGE will be coded in the same way as :
(*a*) CBJNCA (*b*) CANKCA
(*c*) CAKNCA (*d*) CAKCNA

12. If COUNTRY is coded in a certain way as EMWLVPA, ELECTORATE will be coded in the same manner as :
(*a*) CJCEVQPYWC (*b*) GJGERQTYVG
(*c*) CNCERQPCRG (*d*) GJGAVMTYVC

13. In a certain code PORTUGESE is written as ESEGUTROP, MALAYALAM will be written in the same code as :
(*a*) MALAYALAM (*b*) MALYALAM
(*c*) MALAYALM (*d*) MALAYLAM

14. If PHILOSOPHY is coded as HPLISOPOYH, ORNAMENTAL will be coded as :
(*a*) ROANEMNTLA (*b*) ONRAMNEALT
(*c*) ROANEMTNLA (*d*) ROANEMNATL

15. If SABOTAGE is coded as UADOVAIE, how will EMERGENCY be coded in the same manner?
(*a*) GMGRIEPCA (*b*) GMGRGEPCA
(*c*) BNBQFDOBZ (*d*) EOETGGNEY

EXPLANATORY ANSWERS

1. (*d*) : The word is coded by moving the letters three steps forward.

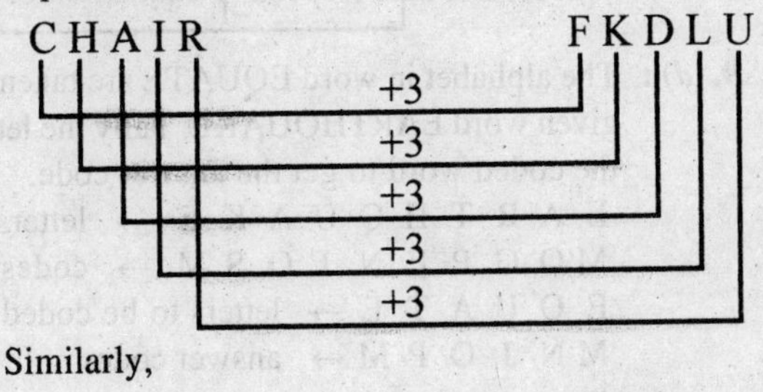

Similarly,

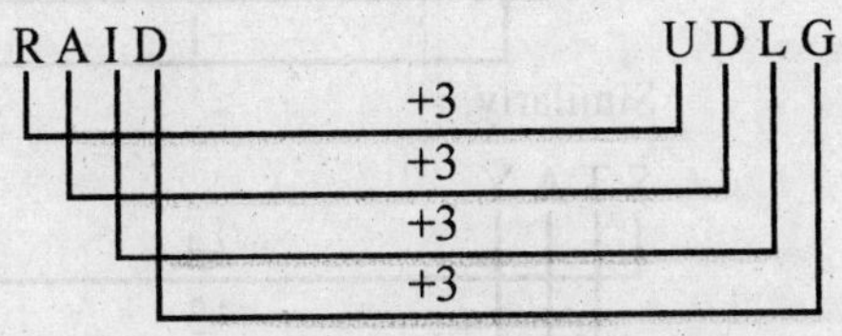

2. (*d*) : In this word, the second and third letters interchange their places and the fifth and sixth letters do the same. Other letters retain their position.

CONDEMN CNODMEN

Similarly,

TEACHER TAECEHR

3. (*d*) : The letters of the word are coded by their represented letters in the reverse series.

C O M E → letters in natural series
X L N V → letters in reverse series
↓ ↓ ↓ ↓
3rd 15th 13th 5th → position of letters
A B L E → letters in natural series
Z Y O V → letters in reverse series
↓ ↓ ↓ ↓
1st 2nd 12th 5th → position of letters

Similarly,

M O L L Y → letters in natural series
N L O O B → letters in reverse series
↓ ↓ ↓ ↓ ↓
13th 15th 12th 12th 25th → position of letters

4. (*b*) : The word is divided into two equal parts and the letters of each part are written backwards.

PROFE SSION EFORP NOISS

Similarly,

DICTI ONARY ITCID YRANO

5. (*a*) : The word is coded by moving the letters +4, +3, +2, and +1 steps respectively.

JUNE NXPF
+4
+3
+2
+1

Similarly,

STAY WWCZ
+4
+3
+2
+1

6. (*b*) : The word is coded by moving the letters two steps forward, *i.e.*,

GENIUS IGPKWU
+2
+2
+2
+2
+2
+2

Similarly,

IDIOT KFKQV
+2
+2
+2
+2
+2

7. (*a*) : The letters of the word are coded by their represented letters in the reverse series.

A C T I O N → letters in natural series
Z X G R L M → letters in reverse series
1st 3rd 20th 9th 15th 14th position of letters

Similarly,

H E A L T H → letters in natural series
S V Z O G S → letters in reverse series
8th 5th 1st 12th 20th 8th → position of letters

8. (*d*) : The word is coded by moving the alphabet one step backwards, *i.e.*,

THOUSAND SGNTRZMC
−1
−1
−1
−1
−1
−1
−1
−1

Similarly,

FUMING ETLHMF
−1
−1
−1
−1
−1
−1

9. (*d*) : The alphabet in word EQUATE are taken from the given word EARTHQUAKE. Tally the letters from the coded word to get the answer code.

E A R T H Q U A K E → letters
M O G P E N J O S M → codes
E Q U A T E → letters to be coded
M N J O P M → answer codes

10. (*b*) : The coded alphabet are deciphered by moving five steps forward, *i.e.,*

HJIZT → MONEY (+5, +5, +5, +5, +5)

Similarly,

NOVGZ → STALE (+5, +5, +5, +5, +5)

11. (*c*) : The word is coded by moving the alphabet four steps backward, *i.e.,*

JOSEPH → FKOALD (–4, –4, –4, –4, –4, –4)

Similarly,

GEORGE → CAKNCA (–4, –4, –4, –4, –4, –4)

12. (*d*) : The word is coded by moving the alphabet two steps forward and two steps backward alternately, *i.e.,*

COUNTRY → EMWLVPA (+2, –2, +2, –2, +2, –2, +2)

Similarly,

ELECTORATE → GJGAVMTYVC (+2, –2, +2, –2, +2, –2, +2, –2, +2, –2)

13. (*a*) : The coded word is the alphabet of the word written backwards.

PORTUGESE → ESEGUTROP

Similarly,

MALAYALAM → MALAYALAM

14. (*c*) : The places of two consecutive letters in the word are interchanged to form the coded word.

PH IL OS OP HY → HP LI SO PO YH

Similarly,

OR NA ME NT AL → RO AN EM TN LA

15. (*a*) : The word is coded by moving only the alphabet at odd positions two steps forward.

SABOTAGE → UADOVAIE (+2, +2, +2, +2)

Similarly,

EMERGENCY → GMGRIEPCA (+2, +2, +2, +2, +2)

TYPE - II

Column coding is a very complex form of coding. It needs a lot of attention and swift eye movement to decode the code for each letter of the given words. Proper words in capital letters are given in one column and the codes in small letters are given in another column. Based on the information given in both columns the candidate has to arrive at the correct answer option.

MULTIPLE CHOICE QUESTIONS

Directions: *The following questions are based on the column pattern. Understand the coding pattern and answer the questions.*

	Column I		Column II
(1)	FAMOUS	(a)	jcqhxp
(2)	SATIRE	(b)	hqdbyn
(3)	FRIGHT	(c)	ybcnke
(4)	TANGLE	(d)	zewhnd
(5)	ROVING	(e)	epbmyw
(6)	HUNTER	(f)	wdnbxk

1. What is the code used for the letter U?
(*a*) d (*b*) n
(*c*) b (*d*) x

2. What is the code used for the letter N?
(*a*) e (*b*) p
(*c*) m (*d*) w

3. What is the code used for the letter A?
(*a*) h (*b*) q
(*c*) b (*d*) n

4. What is the code used for the letter F?
(*a*) w (*b*) p
(*c*) d (*d*) c

5. What is the code used for the letter E?
(*a*) d (*b*) n
(*c*) b (*d*) k

	Column I		Column II
(1)	WRONG	(a)	cklxd
(2)	GRANT	(b)	pdqkc
(3)	STEAM	(c)	qpuns
(4)	CROWS	(d)	lxnvk
(5)	CEMET	(e)	usqvs
(6)	TERMS	(f)	nukqs

6. What is the code used for the letter N?
(*a*) c (*b*) x
(*c*) l (*d*) n

7. What is the code used for the letter M?
(*a*) v (*b*) q
(*c*) u (*d*) s

8. What is the code used for the letter W?
(*a*) d (*b*) x
(*c*) c (*d*) p

9. What is the code used for the letter G?
(*a*) k (*b*) c
(*c*) s (*d*) d

10. What is the code used for the letter S?
(*a*) n (*b*) s
(*c*) d (*d*) k

	Column I		Column II
(1)	HOUSE	(a)	lfyqx
(2)	PAGES	(b)	pyfgm
(3)	LUNGS	(c)	nhmzf
(4)	PHONE	(d)	xqygh
(5)	LANDS	(e)	hofzp
(6)	HOUND	(f)	qnoxh

11. What is the code used for the letter O?
(*a*) h (*b*) g
(*c*) q (*d*) x

12. What is the code used for the letter E?
(*a*) n (*b*) y
(*c*) p (*d*) m

13. What is the code used for the letter G?
(*a*) p (*b*) o
(*c*) f (*d*) m

14. What is the code used for the letter N?
(*a*) l (*b*) y
(*c*) x (*d*) h

15. What is the code used for the letter D?
(*a*) o (*b*) z
(*c*) g (*d*) p

EXPLANATORY ANSWERS

1. (*d*) : From statements (1) and (6), U = X.

2. (*d*) : From statements (5) and (6), RN = bw. From statement (4), N = w.

3. (*a*) : From statements (2) and (4), ATE = hdn. From statement (6), TE = dn. Therefore, A = h.

4. (*d*) : From statements (1) and (3), F = c.

5. (*a*) : From statements (2) and (4), ATE = hdn. From statement (6), TE = dn. From statement (3), T = n. Hence E = d.

6. (*a*) : From statements (1) and (2), N = C.

7. (*c*) : From statements (3), (5) and (6), M = u.

8. (*b*) : From statements (1) and (4), W = x.

9. (*d*) : From statements (1) and (2), G = d.

10. (*a*) : From statements (3), (4) and (6), S = n.

11. (*d*) : From statements (1), (4) and (6), O = x.

12. (*b*) : From statements (1), (2) and (4), E = y.

13. (*d*) : From statements (2) and (3), G = m.

14. (*d*) : From statements (3), (4), (5) and (6), N = h.

15. (*a*) : From statements (5) and (6), D = o.

TYPE - III

There is variety in ways of coding. Coding language is not only for words and numbers but also for hiding a group of words, statements or even sentences. This form of coding pattern may appear to be confusing but after solving only a few questions it is very easy to understand. Questions based on this coding pattern require no moving of steps or straining efforts of calculations, but only quick tallying or comparing ability. The codes can be letters or numbers.

SOLVED EXAMPLE

In a certain code 'ra mei ket' means 'he is rich'; 'rui pha jeu' means 'run for money'; and 'pha rui ket' means 'money for rich'. Which of the following is the code for 'rich'?

(*a*) ra (*b*) pha
(*c*) ket (*d*) jeu

Ans. (*c*) : The given information is :

Code	*Sentence*
1. ra mei *ket*	he is *rich*
2. rui pha jeu	run for money
3. pha rui *ket*	money for *rich*

After comparing codes and sentences 1 and 3, it is clear that word 'rich' is common and so is the code 'ket'.

MULTIPLE CHOICE QUESTIONS

Directions : *In the following questions study the coded patterns and then select the right option from the given alternatives.*

1. In a certain language, (a) 'go ju mi' stands for 'plenty of money'; (b) pao ju go nei vu' for 'money creates lots of problems'; (c) 'kol vu nei' for 'problems create tension'; and (d) 'sol tun ju haw' for 'still money is needed'. Which of the following words stand for 'money'?

(*a*) nei (*b*) ju
(*c*) haw (*d*) go

2. In a certain language, (a) 'FOR' stands for 'old is gold'; (b) 'ROT' stands for 'gold is pure'; (c) 'ROM' stands for 'gold is costly'. How will 'pure old gold is costly' be written?

(*a*) TFROM (*b*) FOTRM
(*c*) FTORM (*d*) TOMRF

3. In a certain code '415' means 'milk is hot'; '18' means 'hot soup'; and '895' means 'soup is tasty'. What number will indicate the word 'tasty'?

(*a*) 9 (*b*) 8
(*c*) 5 (*d*) 4

4. In a certain code '643' means 'she is beautiful', '593' means 'he is handsome', and '567' means 'handsome meets beautiful'. What number will indicate the word 'meets'?

(*a*) 5 (*b*) 3
(*c*) 7 (*d*) 6

5. In a certain code language, (a) 'dugo hui mul zo' stands for 'work is very hard'; (b) 'hui dugo ba ki' for 'Bingo is very smart'; (c) 'nano mul dugo' for 'cake is hard', and (d) 'mul ki qu' for 'smart and hard'. Which of the following words stand for 'Bingo'?

(*a*) jalu (*b*) dugo
(*c*) ki (*d*) ba

6. In a certain code language, (a) 'pic vic nic' stands for 'winter is cold'; (b) 'to nic re' for 'summer is hot'; (c) 're pic boo' for 'winter and summer' and (d) 'vic tho pa' for 'nights are cold'. Which of the following word is the code for 'summer'?

(*a*) nic (*b*) boo
(*c*) to (*d*) re

7. In a certain language, (a) 'mx das sci' means 'good little frock'; (b) 'jm coz sci' means 'girl behaves good'; (c) 'ngv drs coz' means 'girl makes mischief'; and (d) 'das gp coz' means 'little girl fell'. What is the code for 'frock' in this language?

(*a*) mx (*b*) das
(*c*) sci (*d*) gp

8. In a certain language 'mu mit es' means 'who is she' and 'elb mu es' means 'where is she'. What is the code for 'where' in this language?

(*a*) es (*b*) elb
(*c*) mu (*d*) mit

9. In a certain code language '069' means 'grapes are sweet', '476' means 'very sweet fruit' and '509' means 'grapes are ripe'. Which of the following digits means 'ripe' in that language?

(*a*) 0 (*b*) 5
(*c*) 9 (*d*) 7

10. In a certain code language 'roi ja kyo twa' means 'Moody is writing letters', 'pok ju ja twa' means 'Woody is writing cards', 'trn kyo pos un' means 'they are writing letters', and 'koi rus pok' means 'gifts and cards'. What is the code word for 'Moody'?

(*a*) ja (*b*) twa
(*c*) roi (*d*) kyo

EXPLANATORY ANSWERS

1. (*b*) :

Code	Sentence
1. go *ju* mi	plenty of *money*
2. pao *ju* go nei vu	*money* creates lots of problems
3. kol vu nei	problems create tension
4. sol tun *ju* haw	still *money* is needed

In 1st, 2nd and 4th codes and their sentences the word 'ju' is repeated and so is 'money'.

2. (*a*) :

Code	Sentence
1. FOR	old is gold
2. ROT	gold is pure
3. ROM	gold is costly

Therefore,

F stands for old
O stands for is
R stands for gold
T stands for pure
M stands for costly

So, 'pure old gold is costly' will be written as 'TFROM'.

3. (*a*) :

Code	Sentence
1. 415	milk is hot
2. 18	hot soup
3. 895	soup is *tasty*

From 3rd code and its sentence neither number '9' is repeated nor the word 'tasty'.

4. (*c*) :

Code	Sentence
1. 643	she is beautiful
2. 593	he is handsome
3. 567	handsome *meets* beautiful

From 3rd code and its sentence, neither number '7' nor the word 'meets' is repeated.

5. (*d*) :

Code	Sentence
1. *dugo hui* mul zo	work *is very* hard
2. *hui dugo* **ba** *ki*	**Bingo** *is very smart*
3. nano mul *dugo*	cake is *hard*
4. mul *ki* qu	*smart* and hard

From 2nd code and its sentence, neither 'ba' nor 'Bingo' is repeated.

(Words repeated are in italics)

6. (*d*) :

Code	Sentence
1. pic vic nic	winter is cold
2. to nic *re*	*summer* is hot
3. *re* pic boo	winter and *summer*
4. vic tho pa	nights are cold

The word 'summer' is common in 2nd and 3rd sentences and so is the code 're'.

7. (*a*) :

Code	Sentence
1. **mx** *das sci*	*good little* **frock**
2. jm coz *sci*	girl behaves *good*
3. ngv drs coz	girl makes mischief
4. *das* gp coz	*little* girl fell

Word 'frock' is only in the 1st sentence. The code word 'das' is repeated in 4th sentence and 'sci' in 2nd sentence. So, 'mx' is the code for 'frock'.

8. (*b*) :

Code	Sentence
1. *mu* mit *es*	who *is she*
2. **elb** *mu* es	**where** *is she*

The code words 'mu' and 'es' are repeated in Ist sentence. The only code left is 'elb' which means 'where'.

9. (*b*) :

Code	Sentence
1. *069*	*grapes are* sweet
2. 476	very sweet fruit
3. *5*09	*grapes are* **ripe**

The code numbers '0' and '9' are repeated in 1st and 3rd sentences. The only code remaining is '5' which stands for 'ripe'.

10. (*c*) :

Code	Sentence
1. **roi** *ja kyo twa*	**Moody** *is writing letters*
2. pok ju *ja twa*	Woody *is writing* cards
3. trn *kyo* pos un	they are writing *letters*
4. koi rus pok	gifts and cards

'Moody' is in 1st sentence only. The code words 'ja' and 'twa' are repeated in 2nd sentence and 'kyo' in 3rd sentence. Only code word 'roi' remains which stands for 'Moody'.

CHAPTER 4

Semantic Series

MULTIPLE CHOICE QUESTIONS

1. ADG, XVT, BEH, WUS, ?
(*a*) VTR (*b*) CFI
(*c*) DFJ (*d*) STU

2. GMSY, IOUA, KQWC, ?
(*a*) MSYE (*b*) NSYE
(*c*) MTYE (*d*) MSYF

3. ADG, GJM, ?, SVY
(*a*) MPS (*b*) MQR
(*c*) MQS (*d*) SPM

4. KNQ, TWZ, CFI, ?
(*a*) KOR (*b*) LOR
(*c*) MNQ (*d*) JLM

5. AEI, BFJ, CGK, ?
(*a*) DLH (*b*) EGF
(*c*) EFL (*d*) DHL

6. CFI, IKM, OPQ, ?
(*a*) UUU (*b*) UST
(*c*) VUS (*d*) TUV

7. LAZ, NEX, PIV, ?
(*a*) SLS (*b*) QNS
(*c*) RMT (*d*) RMS

8. DED, EFE, FGF, ?
(*a*) HGH (*b*) GHG
(*c*) EFE (*d*) FHF

9. XYZ, UVW, ?, OPQ
(*a*) RST (*b*) STU
(*c*) QRS (*d*) TUV

10. VCL, UEI, TGF, ?
(*a*) SJC (*b*) THI
(*c*) SIC (*d*) RHD

11. ABC, EFG, HIJ, ?
(*a*) IJK (*b*) KLM
(*c*) LMN (*d*) JKL

12. PQR, HIJ, DEF, ?
(*a*) DEF (*b*) CDE
(*c*) ABC (*d*) BCD

13. KNQ, TWZ, CFI, ?
(*a*) MNQ (*b*) LOR
(*c*) LPR (*d*) KOR

14. JOBS, KMEO, LKHK, ?, NGNC
(*a*) MJLH (*b*) LIKG
(*c*) MIKG (*d*) MNGM

15. ABC, ACE, ADG, ?
(*a*) AEG (*b*) AFH
(*c*) AFG (*d*) AEI

16. IOU, JKL, PQR, ?
(*a*) UVW (*b*) XYZ
(*c*) TUV (*d*) VWX

17. AZ, GT, MN, ?, YB
(*a*) KF (*b*) TS
(*c*) RX (*d*) SH

18. BMY, DNW, FOU, ?
(*a*) HPT (*b*) HPS
(*c*) HQS (*d*) GPS

19. ADG, GJM, MPS, ?
(*a*) SVW (*b*) SVY
(*c*) SUW (*d*) SWY

20. AZ, CX, EV, ?
(*a*) HU (*b*) GS
(*c*) GT (*d*) HT

EXPLANATORY ANSWERS

1. (*b*) : There are two alternate series.

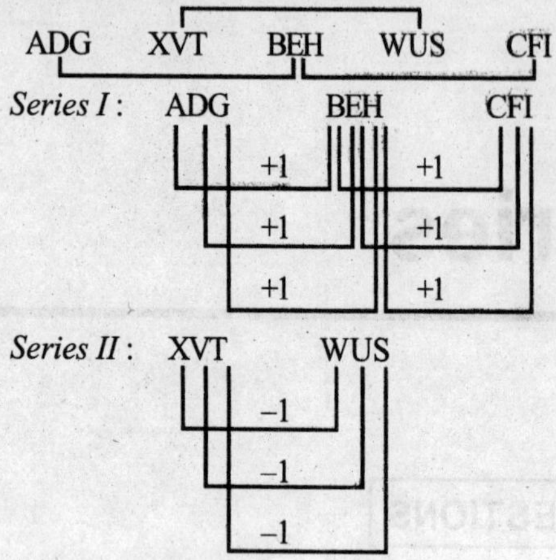

2. (*a*) : The series is formed by moving each letter two steps forward from one group to the next.

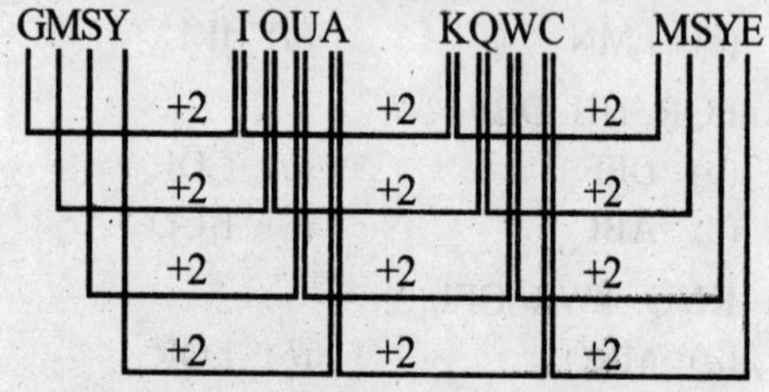

(The series restarts from A on reaching Z)

3. (*a*) : In each group of three letters the alphabet is in the succession of +3. The next group begins with the last alphabet of the previous group.

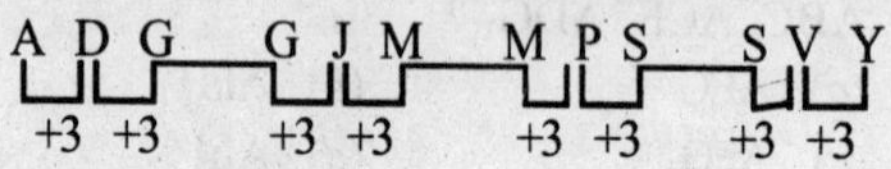

4. (*b*) : All the alphabet in this group series is in succession of +3. The alphabetical series repeat from 'A' on reaching 'Z'.

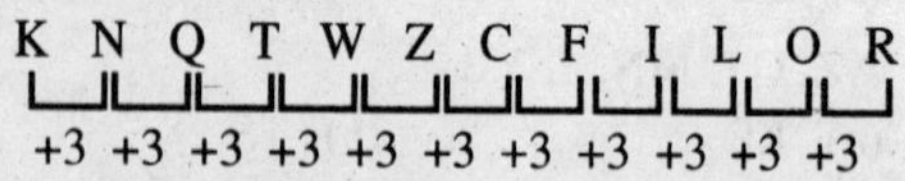

5. (*d*) : Each of the three alphabet in one group corresponds to the alphabet in the next group in the succession of +1, *i.e.,*

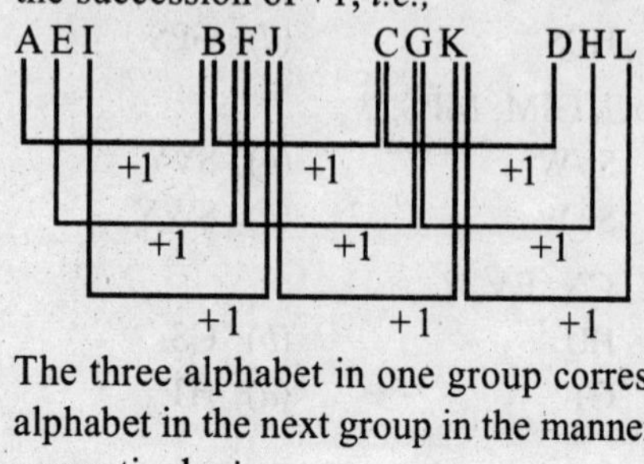

6. (*a*) : The three alphabet in one group correspond to the alphabet in the next group in the manner +6, +5, +4 respectively, *i.e.,*

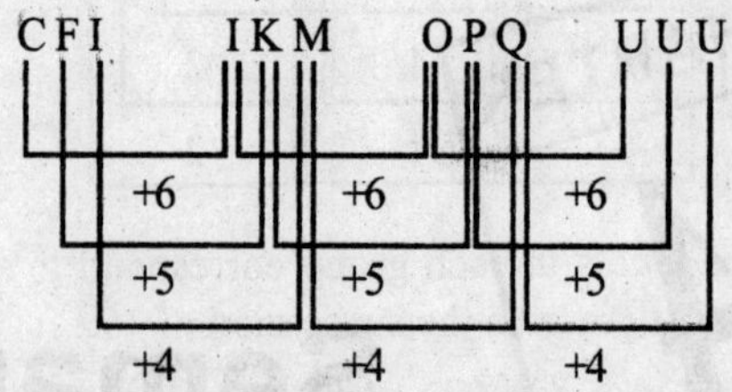

7. (*c*) : The three alphabet in one group correspond to the alphabet in the next group in the manner +2, +4, –2 respectively, *i.e.,*

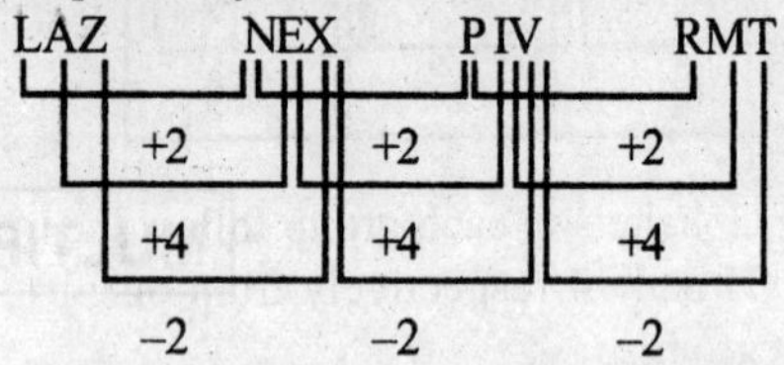

8. (*b*) : The alphabet from one group to the next are in succession of +1, *i.e.,*

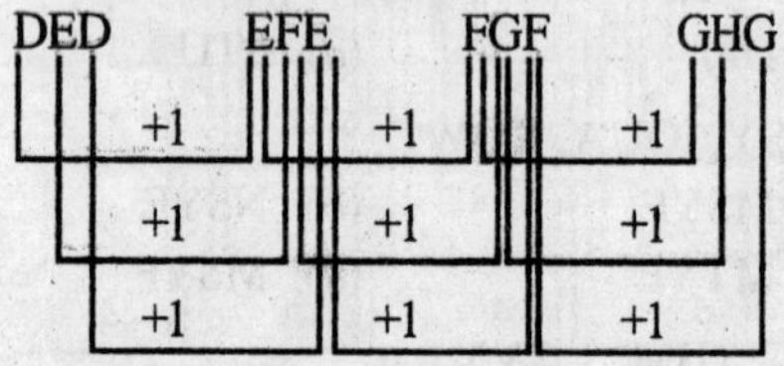

9. (*a*) : The alphabet from one group to the next are in recession of –3, *i.e.,*

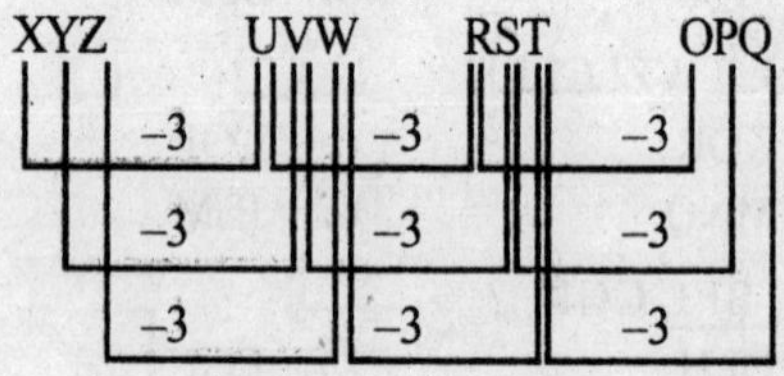

10. (*c*) : The alphabet in one group correspond to the alphabet in the next group in the manner –1, +2, –3 respectively, *i.e.,*

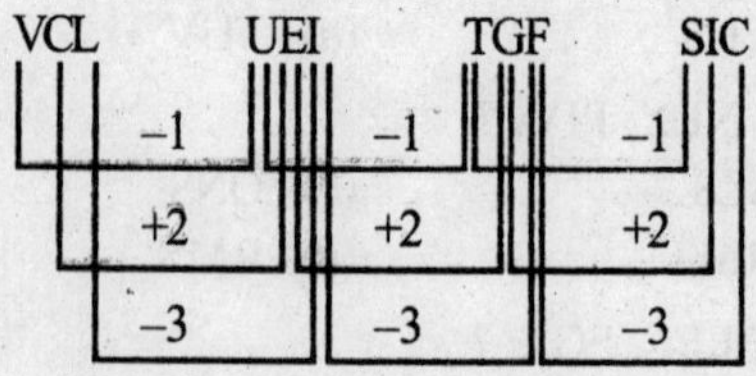

11. (*d*) : The difference between the last letter of the preceding group of alphabet and the first letter of the next group is decreasing by 1, *i.e.,*

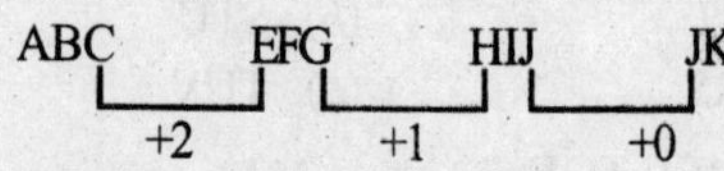

Otherwise the three letters in each group are in their natural order.

12. (*d*) : The letters in each group of alphabet are in the recession of –8, –4, –2 respectively.

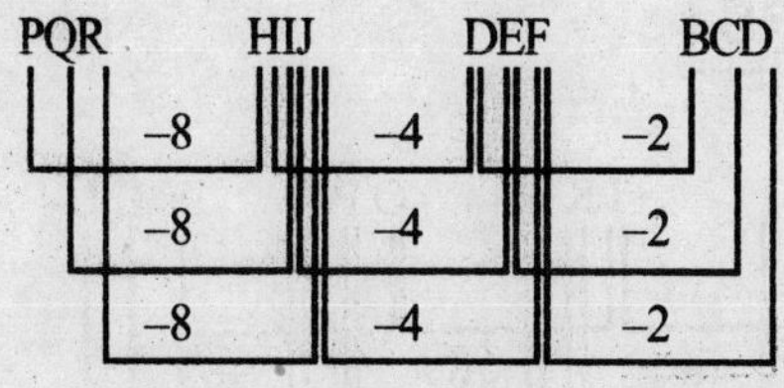

13. (*b*) : The letters in each group correspond to the letter in next group in the succession of +9.

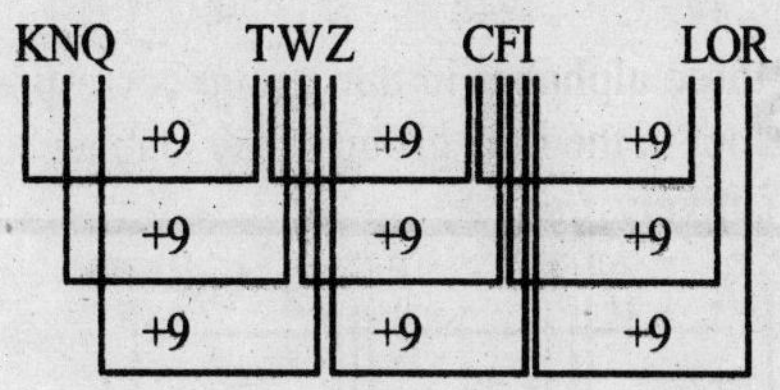

14. (*c*) : The alphabets in each group follow the pattern +1, –2, +3 and –4 respectively from one group to the next group.

15. (*d*) : The difference between the letters in each group is increased by one.

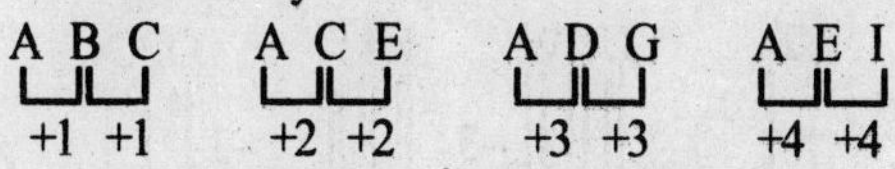

16. (*d*) : The series is formed in this manner :

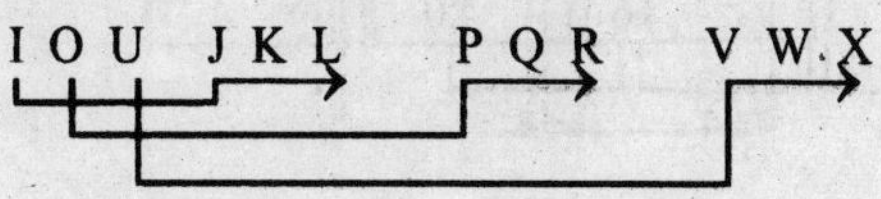

Three consecutive letters to each letter in the first group forms the other groups in the series.

17. (*d*) : The letters in one group correspond to the letters in the next group in the manner +6, –6 respectively, *i.e.*,

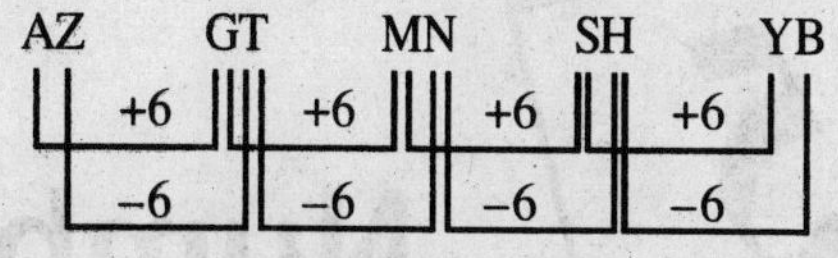

18. (*b*) : The letters in one group correspond to the letters in the next group in the manner +2, +1, -2 respectively, *i.e.*,

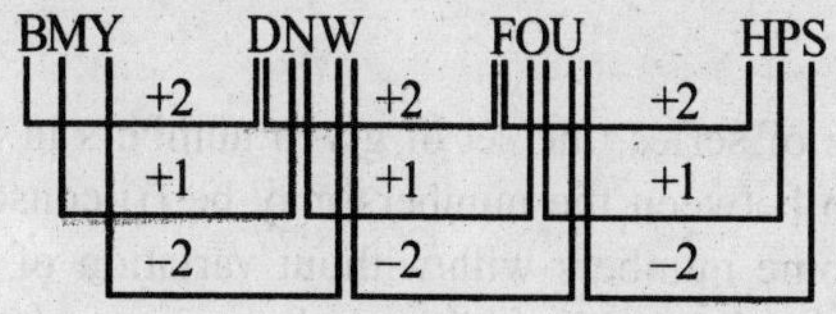

19. (*b*) : The letters in each group are moved six steps forward, *i.e.*,

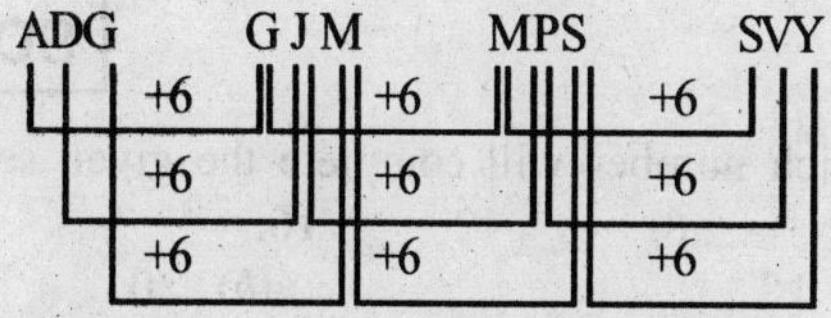

20. (*c*) : The letters in each group correspond to the letters in the next group in the manner +2, –2 respectively, *i.e.*,

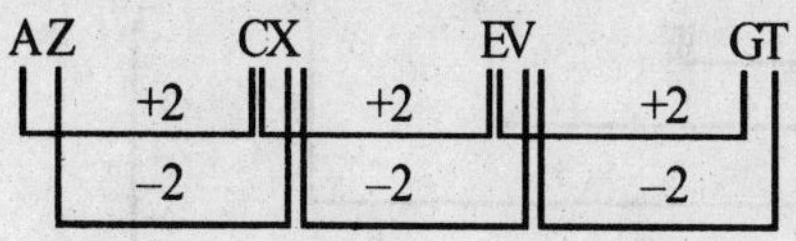

CHAPTER 5

Number Series

In this type of series, the set of given numbers in a series are related to one another in a particular pattern or manner. The relationship between the numbers may be (i) consecutive odd/even numbers; (ii) consecutive prime numbers; (iii) squares/cubes of some numbers with/without variation of addition or subtraction of some number; (iv) sum/product/difference of preceding numbers; (v) addition/subtraction/multiplication/division by some number; and (vi) many more combinations of the relationships given above.

SOLVED EXAMPLES

1. Which number will complete the given series?

4, 8, 12, 16, ?

(*a*) 18 (*b*) 20 (*c*) 22 (*d*) 24

Ans. (*b*): The series is made of numbers which are multiples of 4. Other explanation can be that the difference between the two consecutive numbers is 4.

4 8 12 16 20

4 → 8: × 2; 4 → 12: × 3; 4 → 16: × 4; 4 → 20: × 5

Or

4 +4 8 +4 12 +4 16 +4 20

2. Complete the given series.

2, 14, 98, 686, ?

(*a*) 1976 (*b*) 2548 (*c*) 980 (*d*) 4802

Ans. (*d*) : The numbers are multiplied by 7 to obtain the next numbers.

2 ×7 14 ×7 98 ×7 686 ×7 4802

The given series may also comprise of two alternate series merged as one.

MULTIPLE CHOICE QUESTIONS

Directions: *In the following questions, select the number(s) from the given options for completing the given series.*

1. 3, 9, 27, 81, 243, ?

(*a*) 486 (*b*) 729

(*c*) 972 (*d*) 359

2. 1, 6, 12, 19, 27, ?

(*a*) 38 (*b*) 35

(*c*) 36 (*d*) 54

3. 2, 6, 14, 30, 62, ?

(*a*) 126 (*b*) 128

(*c*) 120 (*d*) 130

4. 8, 48, 16, 96, 32, ?
(*a*) 192 (*b*) 150
(*c*) 64 (*d*) 288

5. 2, 8, 14, 24, 34, 48, ?
(*a*) 66 (*b*) 62
(*c*) 58 (*d*) 64

6. 4, 9, 19, 34, 54, ?, 109
(*a*) 89 (*b*) 84
(*c*) 74 (*d*) 79

7. 3, 15, 35, 63, 99, ?
(*a*) 144 (*b*) 143
(*c*) 121 (*d*) 169

8. 2, 3, 6, 18, 108, ?
(*a*) 1944 (*b*) 1658
(*c*) 648 (*d*) 1008

9. 1, 2, 3, 2, 3, 5, 4, 5, ?
(*a*) 9 (*b*) 6
(*c*) 10 (*d*) 7

10. 7776, 1296, 216, 36, 6, ?
(*a*) 6 (*b*) 0
(*c*) 3 (*d*) 1

11. 1, 8, 27, 64, 125, ?
(*a*) 172 (*b*) 176
(*c*) 216 (*d*) 189

12. 2, 3, 5, 7, 11, 13, ?
(*a*) 19 (*b*) 57
(*c*) 31 (*d*) 17

13. 80, 64, 48, 32, 16, ?
(*a*) 4 (*b*) 0
(*c*) 8 (*d*) 1

14. 3, 8, 13, 24, 41, ?
(*a*) 65 (*b*) 75
(*c*) 70 (*d*) 80

15. 9, 81, 90, 810, 819, ?
(*a*) 7371 (*b*) 900
(*c*) 8100 (*d*) 1638

16. 0, 8, 24, 48, 80, ?
(*a*) 110 (*b*) 96
(*c*) 120 (*d*) 140

17. 2, 4, 8, 3, 9, 27, 4, 16, ?
(*a*) 64 (*b*) 32
(*c*) 48 (*d*) 24

18. 27, 28, 25, 25, 23, 22, 21, ?
(*a*) 20 (*b*) 21
(*c*) 19 (*d*) 18

19. 80, 63, 72, 72, 64, 81, 56, ?
(*a*) 96 (*b*) 98
(*c*) 89 (*d*) 90

20. 0, 5, 22, 57, ?, 205
(*a*) 198 (*b*) 116
(*c*) 172 (*d*) 92

EXPLANATORY ANSWERS

1. (*b*) : The numbers in the series are multiplied by 3 to get the next numbers.

2. (*c*) : The difference between the numbers in the series increases by 1, after beginning from 5, *i.e.*,

1 6 12 19 27 36
+5 +6 +7 +8 +9

3. (*a*) : The difference between the numbers in the series doubles each time, after beginning from 4, *i.e.*,

2 6 14 30 62 126
+4 +8 +16 +32 +64

4. (*a*) : *Explanation I* : The sequence in the series is × 6, ÷ 3 which is repeated.

8 48 16 96 32 192
×6 ÷3 ×6 ÷3 ×6

Explanation II : There are two alternate series and the numbers are multiplied by 2.

×2 ×2
8 48 16 96 32 192
×2 ×2

Series I : 8, 16, 32
Series II : 48, 96, 192

5. (*b*) : The sequence in the series is :

2 8 14 24 34 48 62
+6 +6 +10 +10 +14 +14

The difference increases by 4 at alternate step.

6. (*d*) : The difference between the numbers increases by 5, after beginning from 5, *i.e.*,

4 9 19 34 54 79 109
+5 +10 +15 +20 +25 +30

7. (*b*) : The series follows the sequence of the squares of even numbers beginning from 2, minus 1.

8. (*a*) : Every third number in the series is the product of previous two numbers.

2 3 6 18 108 1944
2 × 3
3 × 6
6 × 18
18 × 108

9. (a) : In this series three numbers form a set. The first two numbers of each set are in natural order and the third number is the sum of first and second numbers. The first number of the next set begins with double the first number of the previous set.

× 2   × 2

1 2 3   2 3 5   4 5 9

1 + 2   2 + 3   4 + 5

10. (d) : The numbers in this sequence are divided by 6 each time.

11. (c) : The sequence in the series is cube of numbers in their natural order.

12. (d) : The series consists of prime numbers in increasing order.

13. (b) : The numbers in the series are decreasing with the difference of 16 at each step.

14. (c) : The sequence in the series is (number + next number) + addition of natural number increasing by 1 at each step, after beginning from 2.

3   8   13   24   41   70

(3+8) + 2

(8 + 13) + 3

(13 + 24) + 4

(24 + 41) + 5

15. (a) : The sequence in the series is × 9, + 9 which is repeated.

16. (c) : The sequence of the series consists of the product of 2 even numbers in natural order, *i.e.,*

0	8	24	48	80	120
↓	↓	↓	↓	↓	↓
(0 × 2)	(2 × 4)	(4 × 6)	(6 × 8)	(8 × 10)	(10 × 12)

17. (a) : In this series 3 numbers form a set. The first number is in natural order. The second number is the square of above number. The third number is the cube of first number.

18. (c) : There are two alternate series :

−2   −2   −2

27   28   25   25   23   22   21   19

−3   −3   −3

Series I : 27, 25, 23, 21 (following −2 pattern)

Series II : 28, 25, 22, 19 (following −3 pattern)

19. (d) : There are two alternate series :

−8   −8   −8

80   63   72   72   64   81   56   90

+9   +9   +9

Series I : 80, 72, 64, 56 (following −8 pattern)

Series II : 63, 72, 81, 90 (following +9 pattern)

20. (b) : The series follows this sequence : cube of natural numbers starting from 1 minus odd numbers starting from 1.

0	5	22	57	116	205
↓	↓	↓	↓	↓	↓
1^3-1	2^3-3	3^3-5	4^3-7	5^3-9	6^3-11

CHAPTER 6 Arithmatical Reasoning

MULTIPLE CHOICE QUESTIONS

Directions (1–5) : *The following questions are based on the information given below :*

Data of 450 candidates, who took part in an examination in Social Science, Mathematics and Science is given below:

Passed in all the subject	167
Failed in all the subject	60
Failed in Mathematics	199
Failed in Social Science	175
Failed in Science	191
Passed in Science only	52
Passed in Mathematics only	48
Passed in Social Science only	62

1. How many passed in at least one subject?
(*a*) 450 (*b*) 390
(*c*) 304 (*d*) 167
(*e*) None of these.

2. How many failed in two subjects only?
(*a*) 56 (*b*) 61
(*c*) 152 (*d*) 162
(*e*) None of these.

3. How many passed in Mathematics and at least in one more subject?
(*a*) 210 (*b*) 203
(*c*) 170 (*d*) 94
(*e*) None of these.

4. How many failed in Social Science only?
(*a*) 15 (*b*) 21
(*c*) 30 (*d*) 42
(*e*) None of these.

5. How many failed in one subject only?
(*a*) 152 (*b*) 144
(*c*) 61 (*d*) 56
(*e*) None of these

6. A, B, C, D and E play a game of cards. A says to B, "If you give me three cards, you will have as many as E has and if I give you three cards, you will have as many as D has." A and B together have 10 cards more than what D and E together have. If B has two cards more than what C has and the total number of cards be 133, how many cards does B have?
(*a*) 22 (*b*) 35
(*c*) 25 (*d*) 23
(*e*) None of these

7. A bus starts from city X. The number of women in the bus is half of the number of men. In the city Y, 10 men left the bus and five women entered. Now, number of men and women is equal. In the beginning, how many passenger entered the bus?
(*a*) 15 (*b*) 30
(*c*) 36 (*d*) 45
(*e*) None of these

8. I have a few sweets to be distributed. If I keep 2, 3 or 4 in a pack, I am left with one sweet. If I keep 5 in a pack, I am left with none. What is the minimum number of sweets I can have to pack and distributed?
(*a*) 25 (*b*) 37
(*c*) 54 (*d*) 65
(*e*) None of these

9. A, B, C, D and E play a game of cards. A says to B, "If you give me 3 cards, you will have as many as I have at this moment while if D takes 5 cards from you, he will have as many as E has", A and C together have twice as many cards as E has B and D together also have the same number of cards as A and C taken together. I all together they have 150 cards, how many cards has C got.
(*a*) 28 (*b*) 29
(*c*) 31 (*d*) 35
(*e*) None of these

10. At the end of a business conference, ten people present shake hands with each other once. How many handshakes will be there all together?
(*a*) 20 (*b*) 45
(*c*) 90 (*d*) 55
(*e*) None of these.

11. Jayesh is as much younger to Anil as he is older to Prashant. If the sum of the ages of Anil and Prashant is 48 years. What is the age of Jayesh?
(*a*) 30 years
(*b*) 24 years
(*c*) 20 years
(*d*) Can't be determined
(*e*) None of these.

12. Five years ago Vinay's age was one-third of the age of Vikash and now Vinay's age is 17 years. What is the present age of Vikash?
(*a*) 9 years (*b*) 36 years
(*c*) 41 years (*d*) 51 years

13. The sum of ages of a father and son is 45 years. Five years ago the product of their ages was 4 times the father's age at that time. The present age of the father and son respectively are.
(*a*) 25 years, 10 years (*b*) 36 years, 9 years
(*c*) 39 years, 6 years (*d*) None of these.

14. Out of a total 120 musicians in a club, 5% can play all the three instruments – guitar, violin and flute. It so happens that the number of musicians who can play any two and only two of the above instruments is 30. The number of musicians who can play the guitar alone is 40. What is the total number of those who can play violin alone or flute alone?
(*a*) 30 (*b*) 38
(*c*) 44 (*d*) 45
(*e*) None of these.

15. In a group of persons travelling in a bus, 6 persons can speak Tamil, 15 can speak Hindi and 6 can speak Gujarati. In that group, none can speak any other language. If 2 persons in the group can speak two languages and one person can speak all the three languages, then how many persons are there in the group?
(*a*) 21 (*b*) 22
(*c*) 23 (*d*) 24
(*e*) None of these.

16. There are 50 students admitted to a nursery class. Some students can speak only English and some can speak only Hindi. Ten students can speak both English and Hindi. If the number of students who can speak English is 21, then how many students can speak Hindi, how many can speak only Hindi and how many can speak only English?
(*a*) 39, 29 and 11 respectively.
(*b*) 37, 27 and 13 respectively.
(*c*) 28, 18 and 22 respectively.
(*d*) 21, 11 and 29 respectively.

17. A shephard had 17 sheep. All but nine died. How many was he left with?
(*a*) Nil (*b*) 17
(*c*) 9 (*d*) 8
(*e*) None of these.

18. 10 years ago, Chandravati's mother was 4 times older than her daughter. After 10 years, the mother will be twice older than the daughter. The present age of Chandravati is:
(*a*) 5 years (*b*) 10 years
(*c*) 20 years (*d*) 30 years
(*e*) None of these.

19. Pushpa is twice as old as Rita was two years ago. If difference between their ages be 2 years, how old is Pushpa today?
(*a*) 6 years (*b*) 8 years
(*c*) 10 years (*d*) 12 years

20. Mr. Sohan Lal is four times as old as his son. Four years later sum of their age will be 43 years. The present age of the son is:
(*a*) 5 years (*b*) 7 years
(*c*) 8 years (*d*) 10 years
(*e*) None of these.

21. 15 years ago the difference between the age of two persons is 10 years. The elder one was twice as old as the younger one. The present age of the elder person is:
(*a*) 15 years (*b*) 35 years
(*c*) 65 years (*d*) 45 years
(*e*) None of these.

22. Consider the diagram given below:

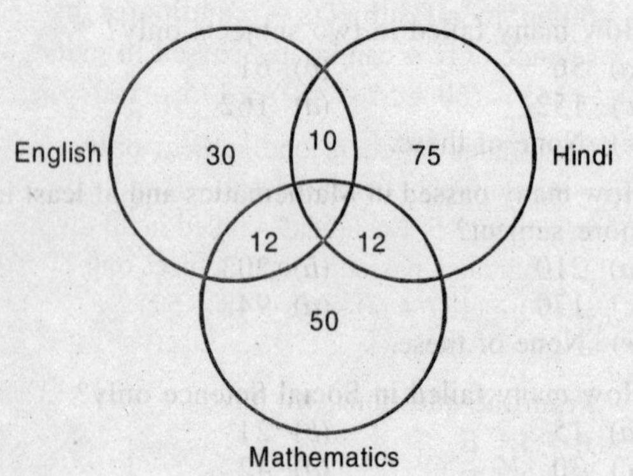

Five hundred candidates appeared in the examination conducted for the tests in English, Hindi and Mathematics. The diagram gives the number of candidates who failed in different tests. What is the percentage of candidates who failed in at least two subjects?

(*a*) 0.078 (*b*) 1.0
(*c*) 6.8 (*d*) 7.8
(*e*) None of these.

23. The sum of the ages of a son and father is 56 years. After four years, the age of the father will be three times that of the son. Their ages respectively are:
(*a*) 12 years, 44 years (*b*) 18 years, 36 years
(*c*) 16 years, 42 years (*d*) 16 years, 48 years
(*e*) None of these.

24. The number of boys in a class are three times the number of girls. Which one of the following numbers cannot represent the total number of children in the class?
(*a*) 48 (*b*) 44
(*c*) 42 (*d*) 46
(*e*) None of these.

25. In 10 years, A will be twice as old as B was 10 years ago. If at present A is 9 years older than B, the present age of B is:
(*a*) 19 years (*b*) 29 years
(*c*) 39 years (*d*) 49 years
(*e*) None of these.

EXPLANATORY ANSWERS

1. (*b*) : Candidates passed at least in one subject = (Candidates passed in only one subjects) + (Candidates passed in only two subjects) + (Candidates passed in only all subjects). (Candidates failed in only two subjects) + (Candidates failed in only one subject) + (Candidates passed in all the subject) = 162 + 61 + 167 = 390.

2. (*d*) : Candidates failed in two subjects only = Candidates passed in one subjects only = 62 + 48 + 52 = 162.

3. (*b*) : Candidates failed in science only =191 – (62 + 60 + 48) = 21
Candidates failed in one social science only = 15
Therefore, candidates passed in maths and at least one more subject
= (21 + 15 + 167) =203

4. (*a*) : Candidates failed in social science only = (candidates failed in social science) – (candidates failed in all subjects + candidates passed in science only + candidates passed in maths only)
= 175 – (60 + 52 + 48) = 175 – 160 = 15.

5. (*c*) : Candidates failed in one subject only
= (total number of candidates) – (candidates passed in all subjects + candidates failed in all the subjects + candidates passed in one subject only)
= 450 – (167 + 60 + 62 + 48 + 52)
= 450 – 389 = 61.

6. (*c*) : From the questions, we have
B – 3 = E ...... (i)
B + 3 = D ...... (ii)
A + B = D + E + 10 ...... (iii)
B = C + 2 ...... (iv)
A + B + C + D + E = 133 ...... (v)
From (i) and (ii)
B – E = D – B ⇒ E + D = 2 B ...... (vi)
From (iii) and (vi)
A + B = 2B + 10 ⇒ B = A – 10
or, A = B + 10 ...... (vii)
From (v), (vi), (iv) and (vii) we have
(B + 10) + (B) + (B – 2) + 2B = 133
5B = 133 – 8 = 125
= 25.

7. (*d*) : In the city X let the number of men be x
Then the number of women be $\frac{x}{2}$.
In the city y, $x-10=\frac{x}{2}+5$
or, $\frac{x}{2}=15$ or, $x=30$ and $y=15$.
Therefore, total number of passenger at the beginning were 30 + 15 = 45.

8. (*a*) : The required number will be obtained by taking LCM of 2, 3 and 4 and adding 1 into it. The number so obtained is 25.

9. (*a*) : From the questions it is clear that
B – 3 = A ...... (1)
D + 5 = E ...... (2)
A + C = 2 E ...... (3)
A + C = B + D ...... (4)
A + B + C + D + E = 150 ...... (5)
From (3), (4) and (5) we get
5E = 150 ∴ E = 30
Now from (2) D = 30 – 5 = 25
and from (4) A = 32
Now from (3) 32 + C = 2 × 30
C = 60 – 32 = 28.

10. (*b*) : Total number of handshakes = (9 + 8 + 7 + 6 + 5 + 4 + 3 + 2 + 1) = 45

11. (*b*) : Let the age of Anil and Prashant be x and (48 – x) years.
Let the age of Jayesh be y years then
(x – y) = y – (48 – x)
x – y = y – 48 + x
2y = 48, y = 24 years
So, Age of Jayesh is 24 years.

12. (*c*) : Vinay's present age is 17 years.
Five years ago Vinay's age was 12 years. and that of Vikash = 36 years
Present age of Vikash = 36 + 5 = 41 years.

13. (*b*) : Let the present age of father be x years and that of son be $(45 - x)$ years.
Five years ago the age of son was $(45 - x - 5) = (40 - x)$.
and that of father $(x - 5)$ years
$(x - 5)(40 - x) = 4(x - 5)$
$40x - x^2 - 200 + 5x = 4x - 20$
or, $41x - x^2 - 180 = 0$
$x = 36.$
$x^2 - 41x - 180 = 0$
$x^2 - (36 + 5)x + 180 = 0$
or, $x^2 - 36x - 5x + 180 = 0$
$x(x - 36) - 5(x - 36) = 0$
$(x - 36)(x - 5) = 0$
$x = 36 \mid x = 5$ unacceptable
Therefore, the present age of father and son are 36 years and 9 years respectively.

14. (*c*) : Let the circles x, y, z represent the musicians who can play guitar, violin and flute respectively.
P + Q + R + S + T + U + V = 120 ...... (1)
Number of musicians who can play all the three instruments = S = 5% of 120 = 6
S = 6 ...... (2)
Number of musicians who can play guitar only = P = 40 ...... (3)
Number of musicians who can play any two and only two of the instruments
= Q + T + U = 30 ...... (4)
Now, from equations (1), (2), (3) and (4) we get
P + Q + R + S + T + U + V = 120
P + (Q + T + U) + S + R + V = 120
40 + 30 + 6 + R + V = 120
R + V = 120 – 76
= 44
Total number of musicians who can play violin alone or flute alone
= (R + V)
= 44

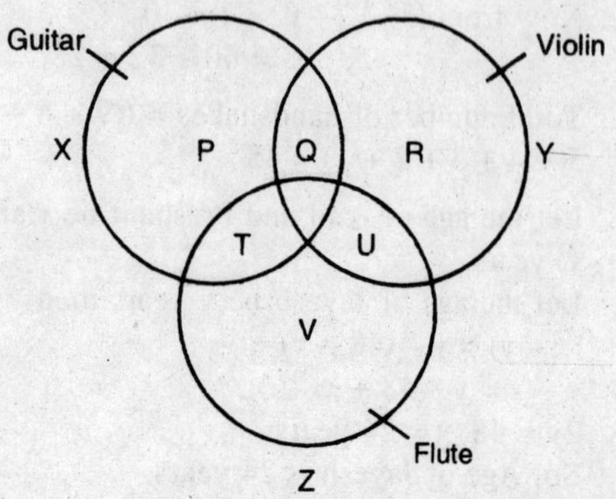

15. (*c*) : Let circles x, y and z represent persons who can speak Tamil, Hindi and Gujarati respectively.
Persons who speak Tamil
= A + B + D + E = 6 ... (1)
Persons who speak Hindi
= B + C + E + F = 15 ... (2)
Persons who speak Gujarati
= D + E + F + G = 6 ... (3)
Persons who speak two languages

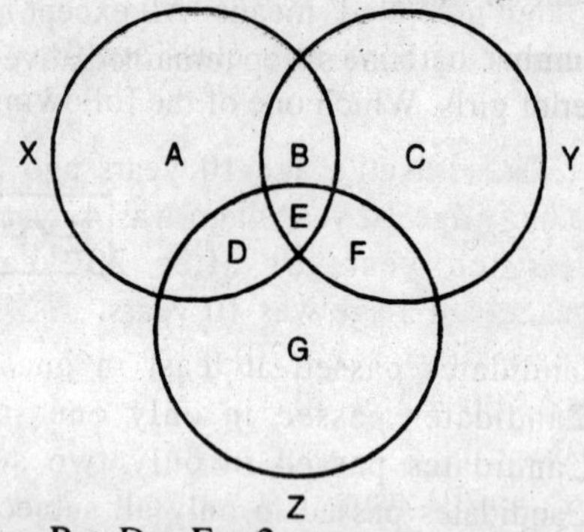

= B + D + F = 2 ... (4)
Persons who speak all the three language
= E = 1 ... (5)
Substituting the value of E in equations (1), (2) and (3) we get
A + B + D = 5 ... (6)
B + C + F = 14 ... (7)
D + F + G = 5 ... (8)
Subtracting (4) from (6), we get
A – F = 3 ... (9)
Adding (7) and (8) we get
B + C + 2F + D + G = 19 ... (10)
Adding (9) and (10) we get
A + B + C + D + F + G = 22 ... (11)
Adding (5) and (11) we get
A + B + C + D + E + F + G = 23 ... (12)
Therefore, total number of person = 23.

16. (*a*) :

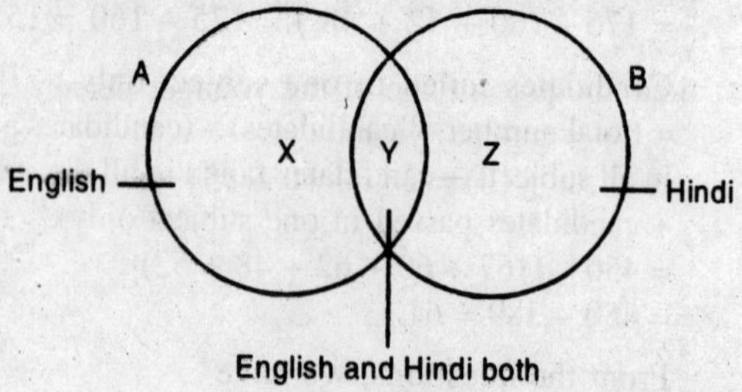

Circle A and B represent the students who speak English and Hindi respectively. Now as per information given in the question total number of students
$= x + y + z = 50$ ... (1)
$y = 10$ ... (2)
$x + y = 21$ ... (3)
From (2) and (3) $x = 11$
Number of students who can speak Hindi is $(y + z)$

From (1) we get

$y + z = 50 - 11 = 39$ ... (4)

Now, number of students who can speak Hindi only is z.

From (4), $y + z = 39$, $z = 39 - y = 39 - 10 = 29$

Therefore, number of the students speaking Hindi = 39, number of students speaking Hindi only = 29 and number of students speaking English only = 11.

17. (*c*) : 'All but nine died' means 'All except nine died'. It means that nine sheep remained alive and other died.

18. (*c*) : Let Chandravati's age 10 years ago be x year mother's age 10 yeags ago was $4x$ year.

After ten year, or after 20 years when Chandravati's age was 10 years.

$(4x + 20) = 2(x + 20)$

$4x + 20 = 2x + 40$

$2x = 20$

or, $x = 10$ years

Present age of Chandravati = 20 years.

19. (*b*) : Let the present age of Pushpa be x year. The present age of Rita would be $(x - 2)$ year.

Now as per question, $x = 2(x - 2 - 2)$

or, $x = 2x - 8$

or, $x = 8$

Therefore, present age of Pushpa is 8 years.

20. (*b*) : Let the present age of the son be x years then, the age of Sohanlal would be $4x$ years. Four years later their age would be $(x + 4)$ and $(4x + 4)$ years.

Now, as per questions,

$(x + 4) + (4x + 4) = 43$ years

$5x + 8 = 43$ years

$5x = 35$ years

or, $x = 7$ years.

Therefore, the present age of son is 7 years.

21. (*b*) : Let the present age of the elder persons be x years.

then, the present age of the younger person $= (x - 10)$ years.

$(x - 15) = 2(x - 10 - 15)$

or, $x = 35$ years.

$\therefore$ The present age of the elder person is 35 years.

22. (*d*) : From the diagram it is clear that number of candidates who failed in at least two subjects = number of candidates who failed in two or more subjects.

$= (10 + 12 + 12 + 5) = 39$

Therefore, required percentage

$$\left(\frac{39}{500} \times 100\right)\% = 7.8\%$$

Therefore, option (*d*) is our answer.

23. (*a*) : Let the age of the father be x, then the age of the son would be $(56 - x)$.

After four years, the age of father would be $(x + 4)$ and that of son would be $(56 - x + 4)$

Now from the information given in the questions. We have

$(x + 4) = 3(56 - x + 4)$

$x + 4 = 168 - 3x + 12$

$4x = 168 + 12 - 4 = 176$

$x = 44$ years

Therefore, the age of father and son is 44 years and 12 years respectively.

24. (*c*) : Let the number of girls be x, then from the question it is clear that number of boys are $3x$.

Therefore, total number of students

= Number of Boys + Numbers of girls

$= x + 3x = 4x$.

Now, the total number of children in the class must be a multiple of 4.

Out of the four options (c) does not qualify this condition. Hence 42 does not represent the total number of children in the class.

25. (*c*) : Let the present age of B be x years

The present age of A would be $(x + 9)$ years.

After ten years the age of A would be $(x + 9 + 10) = (x + 19)$ years. and before ten years the age of B was $(x - 10)$ years.

Now from the information given in the question,

$(x + 19) = 2(x - 10)$

$x + 19 = 2x - 20$

$x = 19 + 20 = 39$ years.

CHAPTER 7

Problem Solving

Number problems consists of number sequences, problems with algebraic expressions, mathematical calculations and other compatiable problems.

SOLVED EXAMPLES

1. How many such 7s are there in the following number sequence which are immediately followed by 4 but not immediately preceded by 8?

5 4 7 8 9 7 4 3 8 7 5 7 4 8 7 4 1 2 7 4 5 7 9 4

(*a*) Two (*b*) Three (*c*) Four (*d*) Five (*e*) None of these

Ans. *(b)* : Number of 7s which are immediately followed by 4 but not immediately preceded by 8 are :

5 4 7 8 9 7 4 3 8 7 5 7 4 8 7 4 1 2 7 4 5 7 9 4

1 2 3

2. A number is 9 times twice the other number. The sum of two numbers is 133. The two numbers are :

(*a*) 9, 124 (*b*) 11, 122 (*c*) 17, 166 (*d*) 7, 126 (*e*) 27, 136

Ans. *(d)* : If the smaller number is x, then

$$x + (2x \times 9) = 133$$
$$x + 18x = 133$$
$$19x = 133$$
$$x = 133 \div 19 = 7$$

If one number is 7, the other number is :

$$133 - 7 = 126$$

3. If all the numbers from 1 to 28 which are exactly divisible by 3 are arranged in descending order, which would come at the sixth place from the top?

(*a*) 12 (*b*) 21 (*c*) 15 (*d*) 18 (*e*) 24

Ans. *(a)* : The numbers divisible by 3 in descending order are : 27, 24, 21, 18, 15, 12, 9, 6, 3 and the number at the sixth place is 12.

MULTIPLE CHOICE QUESTIONS

1. How many 6's are there in the following series of numbers which are preceded by 7 but not immediately followed by 9?

6 7 9 5 6 9 7 6 8 7 6 7 8 6 9 4 6 7 7 6 9 5 7 6 3

(*a*) One (*b*) Two
(*c*) Three (*d*) Four

2. In a chess tournament each of six players will play every other player exactly once. How many matches will be played during the tournament?

(*a*) 12 (*b*) 15
(*c*) 30 (*d*) 36

3. How many 4's are there in the following series which are preceded by 7, but are not preceded by 8?

3 4 5 7 4 3 7 4 8 5 4 3 7 4 9 8 4 7 2 7 4 1 3 6

(*a*) 1 (*b*) 2
(*c*) 3 (*d*) 4

4. How many even numbers are there in the following series of numbers, each of which is immediately preceded by an odd number, but not immediately followed by an even number?

5 3 4 8 9 7 1 6 5 3 2 9 8 4 3 5

(*a*) Nil (*b*) 1
(*c*) 2 (*d*) 3

5. If all the numbers from 1 to 51 which are exactly divisible by 3 are arranged in descending order, which of the following numbers will come at the seventh and tenth places from the top?

(*a*) 33 & 27 (*b*) 33 & 21
(*c*) 21 & 30 (*d*) 33 & 24

6. Nitin was counting down from 32. Shasank was counting upwards, the numbers starting from 1 and he was calling out only the odd numbers. Which common number will they call out at the same time if they were calling out at the same speed?

(*a*) 21
(*b*) 22
(*c*) 19
(*d*) They will not call out the same number

7. In the following list of numerals, how many 3s are followed by 3, but NOT preceded by 3?

2 4 6 3 3 1 5 7 8 3 3 3 4 6 2 3 3 3 3 3 9 7 2 3

(*a*) 1 (*b*) 2
(*c*) 3 (*d*) 4

8. If in a given number 5 8 9 4 3 2 7 6 1 4, we interchange the first and the second digits, the third and the fourth, the fifth and the sixth and so on, then counting from the right end, which digit will be sixth?

(*a*) 3 (*b*) 2
(*c*) 4 (*d*) 5

9. Aparna cuts a cake into two halves and cuts one-half into smaller pieces of equal size. Each of the small pieces is twenty grams in weight. If she has seven pieces of the cake in all with her, how heavy was the original cake?

(*a*) 140 grams (*b*) 280 grams
(*c*) 240 grams (*d*) 120 grams

10. In the following number sequence how many such even numbers are there which are exactly divisible by its immediate preceding number but not exactly divisible by its immediate following number?

3 8 4 1 5 7 2 8 3 4 8 9 3 9 4 2 1 5 8 2

(*a*) Two (*b*) Three
(*c*) Four (*d*) More than four

11. How many 7s are there in the following series which are not immediately followed by 3 but immediately preceded by 8?

8 9 8 7 6 2 2 6 3 2 6 9 7 3 2 8 7 2 7 7 8 7 3 7 7 9 4

(*a*) Nil (*b*) One
(*c*) Two (*d*) Three

12. How many 9's are there in the following sequence which are neither preceded by 6 nor immediately followed by 3?

9 3 8 6 9 9 5 9 3 7 8 9 9 9 3 9 6 3 9

(*a*) One (*b*) Two
(*c*) Three (*d*) Four

13. If a number is five times as great as another number which is four less than forty, then the number is :

(*a*) 220 (*b*) 180
(*c*) 144 (*d*) 200

14. If 2/3rd of a number is 96, what will be the 3/4th of that number?

(*a*) 108 (*b*) 198
(*c*) 128 (*d*) 48

15. If such numbers which are divisible by 5, and also those which have 5 as one of the digits are eliminated from the numbers 1 to 60, how many numbers would remain?

(*a*) 53 (*b*) 47
(*c*) 40 (*d*) 45

16. How many 8's are there in the following number series which are exactly divisible by its immediately preceding and also exactly divisible by immediately succeeding numbers?

8 2 4 5 1 7 2 8 4 8 4 2 2 8 2 6 9 8 4 5 4 8 3 2 8 4 3 1 8 3

(*a*) 1 (*b*) 2
(*c*) 3 (*d*) 4

17. Jagan was to either get one-seventh of a milk chocolate or one-fourteenth of a bigger fruit chocolate. Which chocolate would give him the larger piece if the fruit chocolate is three times as large as the milk chocolate?

(*a*) Milk chocolate
(*b*) Fruit chocolate
(*c*) The pieces will be of the same size
(*d*) Information inadequate

18. How many such 3's are there in the following number sequence which are immediately preceded by an odd number and immediately followed by an even number?

5 3 8 9 4 3 7 2 3 8 1 3 8 4 2 3 5 7 3 4 2 3 6

(*a*) One (*b*) Two
(*c*) Three (*d*) Four

19. Count each 7 which is not immediately preceded by 5 but is immediately followed by either 2 or 3. How many such 7's are there?

5 7 2 6 5 7 3 8 3 7 3 2 5 7 2 7 3 4 8 2 6 7 8

(*a*) 2 (*b*) 3
(*c*) 4 (*d*) 5

20. A number is four less than two times the other number. If their difference is 21, what is the greater number?

(*a*) 50 (*b*) 46
(*c*) 31 (*d*) 21

EXPLANATORY ANSWERS

1. (*c*) : 6795697687678694677695763
1 2 3

2. (*b*) : When all the players have to play with each other then the method of calculating the number of matches to be played is $\frac{n(n-1)}{2}$ where '*n*' is the number of players playing the match. So, the number of matches played will be :
$(6 \times 5) \div 2 = 30 \div 2 = 15$

3. (*d*) : 345743748543749847274136
1 2 3 4

4. (*c*) : 534897165329843 5
1 2

5. (*d*) : The numbers divisible by 3 in descending order are: 51, 48, 45, 42, 39, 36, 33, 30, 27, 24, 21, 18, 15, 12, 9, 6, 3.
(33 — 7th, 24 — 10th)

6. (*d*) : When Nitin is on count 22, Shasank is on 21 and when Nitin is on count 21, Shasank is on 23.

7. (*c*) : 24633157833346233339723
1 2 3

8. (*b*) : The new number after interchanging the digits is :
8549236741
6th

9. (*c*) : There is one bigger piece and six smaller pieces. One small piece weighs 20 gm. Total weight of six smaller speices is 120 gm.
∴ Weight of the bigger piece = 120 gm
∴ Weight of the original cake = 240 gm

10. (*a*) : 38415728348939421582
1 2

11. (*c*) : 8987622632697328727787377794
1 2

12. (*d*) : 938699593789993963 9
1 2 3 4

13. (*b*) : Number four less than forty is $40 - 4 = 36$
Five times the number is $= 36 \times 5 = 180$

14. (*a*) : If the number is *x*, then

$$\frac{2}{3}x = 96$$

$$x = \frac{96 \times 3}{2} = 144$$

$\frac{3}{4}$ th of the number is $144 \times \frac{3}{4} = 108$

15. (*c*) : The eliminated twenty numbers are : 5, 10, 15, 20, 25, 30, 35, 40, 45 and 50 to 60. The remaining numbers are $60 - 20 = 40$.

16. (*d*) : 824517284842282698454 8
1 2 3
32843183
4

17. (*b*) : If fruit chocolate (F) is equal to three times as milk chocolate (M) then —

$$F = 3M$$

or $$\frac{F}{M} = 3$$

$$\therefore \frac{1/14\,F}{1/7\,M} = \frac{3/14}{1/7}$$

When 3/14 > 1/7, then F (Fruit chocolate) will give him the larger piece.

18. (*c*) : 5389437238138423573423 6
1 2 3

19. (*a*) : 57265738373257273482678
1 2

20. (*b*) : If smaller number is *x*, then

$$(2x - 4) - x = 21$$
$$2x - x = 21 + 4$$
$$x = 25$$

The greater number is
$$(25 \times 2) - 4 = 46$$

CHAPTER 8

Numerical Operations/ Symbol Substitution

Questions in this category are easy to attempt. Candidates must be quick in substituting symbols and calculations. The common pattern of questions asked are given below.

SOLVED EXAMPLES

1. If '+' stands for '×'; '×' stands for '÷'; '÷' stands for '–' and '–' stands for '+' then
$2 - 8 \times 2 + 6 \div 7 = ?$

(*a*) 32 (*b*) 19 (*c*) 23 (*d*) 9

Ans. (*b*) : After substituting the symbols in the given expression the new expression will be :

$2 + 8 \div 2 \times 6 - 7$

The solving steps will be :

$2 + 4 \times 6 - 7$

$2 + 24 - 7$

$26 - 7 = 19$

2. If ▲ stands for '+'
■ stands for '–'
● stands for '÷'
✱ stands for '×' then
13 ▲ 5 ✱ 20 ● 10 ■ 9 = ?

(*a*) 26 (*b*) 37 (*c*) 14 (*d*) 55

Ans. (*c*) : After substituting the symbols the new expression will be :

$13 + 5 \times 20 \div 10 - 9$

The solving steps will be :

$13 + 5 \times 2 - 9$

$13 + 10 - 9$

$23 - 9 = 14$

MULTIPLE CHOICE QUESTIONS

Directions : *Each of the following questions is followed by four alternatives. Select the most appropriate answer.*

1. If "+" means "–"; "–" means "×"; "×" means "÷" and "÷" means "+", then
$15 \times 5 \div 10 + 5 - 3 = ?$

(*a*) 9.5 (*b*) 0
(*c*) – 2 (*d*) 24

2. If "+" means "–"; "–" means "×"; "×" means "÷" and "÷" means "+", then
$15 \times 3 \div 15 + 5 - 2 = ?$

(*a*) 0 (*b*) 10
(*c*) 20 (*d*) 6

3. If "+" means "÷"; "×" means "–"; "÷" means "+" and "–" means "×", then
$16 \div 8 \times 6 - 2, + 12 = ?$

(*a*) 22 (*b*) 24
(*c*) 23 (*d*) 20

4. If "+" means "×"; "–" means "÷"; "÷"means "+" and "×" means "–", then what will be the value of $20 \div 40 - 4 \times 5 + 6 = ?$
(*a*) 60 (*b*) 1.67
(*c*) 150 (*d*) 0

5. If "+" means "×"; "–" means "÷"; "×"means "–" and "÷" means "+", then
$5 + 8 - 4 \times 2 \div 9 = ?$
(*a*) 15 (*b*) 13
(*c*) 17 (*d*) 11

6. If × stand for addition, ÷ stands for subtraction, + stands for multiplication and – stands for division, then $(20 \times 6 \div 6 \times 4)$ is equal to
(*a*) 5 (*b*) 24
(*c*) 25 (*d*) 80

7. If "+" means "×"; "÷" means "–"; "×"means "÷" and "–" means "+", what will be the value of the following expression?
$4 + 11 \div 5 - 50 = ?$
(*a*) 79 (*b*) –11
(*c*) 91 (*d*) 89

8. If "+" means "÷"; "÷" means "–"; "–"means "×" and "×" means "+", then
$10 \div 2 - 15 + 3 \times 5 = ?$
(*a*) 10 (*b*) 15
(*c*) 25 (*d*) 5

9. If A stands for add, B for subtract, C for multiply and D for divide, then for what does 4A 3B 3A 2 stand?
(*a*) 2 (*b*) 4
(*c*) 6 (*d*) 8

10. If × stands for add, *y* stands for subract, *z* stands for divide and *p* stands for multiply, then what is the the value of (7 p 3) y 6 × 5?
(*a*) 5 (*b*) 10
(*c*) 15 (*d*) 20

11. If "+" means "÷"; "÷" means "–"; "–"means "×" and "×" means "+", what will be the value of $8 + 2 \div 3 - 4 \times 6 = ?$
(*a*) –2 (*b*) $-15\frac{1}{3}$
(*c*) 12 (*d*) 15

12. If "+" means "÷"; "×" means "–"; "÷"means "×" and "–" means "+", what will be the value of the following expression?
$9 + 3 \div 4 - 8 \times 2 = ?$
(*a*) $6\frac{3}{4}$ (*b*) $-1\frac{3}{4}$
(*c*) $-6\frac{1}{4}$ (*d*) 18

13. If "–" means "÷"; "+" means "×"; "÷"means "–" and "×" means "+", then which of the following must be true?
(*a*) $1 \div 2 + 3 \times 6 - 8 = 12$
(*b*) $2 + 3 - 5 \times 8 \div 4 = 7$
(*c*) $5 + 6 \times 8 - 2 \div 3 = 31$
(*d*) $6 \div 1 + 2 - 8 \times 4 = 31$

14. If "÷" means "+"; "+" means "×"; "–"means "÷" and "×" means "–", then
$5 + 8 - 4 \times 2 \div 9 = ?$
(*a*) 13 (*b*) 15
(*c*) 11 (*d*) 17

EXPLANATORY ANSWERS

1. (*c*): $15 \div 5 + 10 - 5 \times 3$
$3 + 10 - 15 = -2$

2. (*b*): $15 \div 3 + 15 - 5 \times 2$
$5 + 15 - 10 = 10$

3. (*c*): $16 + 8 - 6 \times 2 \div 12$
$16 + 8 - 1 = 23$

4. (*d*): $20 + 40 \div 4 - 5 \times 6$
$20 + 10 - 30 = 0$

5. (*c*): $5 \times 8 \div 4 - 2 + 9$
$10 - 2 + 9 = 17$

6. (*b*): $20 + 6 - 6 + 4 = 24$

7. (*d*): $4 \times 11 - 5 + 50$
$44 - 5 + 50 = 89$

8. (*d*): $10 - 2 \times 15 \div 3 + 5$
$10 - 10 + 5 = 5$

9. (*c*): $4 + 3 - 3 + 2 = 6$

10. (*d*): $(7 \times 3) - 6 + 5$
$21 - 6 + 5 = 20$

11. (*a*): $8 \div 2 - 3 \times 4 + 6$
$4 - 12 + 6 = -2$

12. (*d*): $9 \div 3 \times 4 + 8 - 2$
$12 + 8 - 2 = 18$

13. (*c*): (*a*) $1 - 2 \times 3 + 6 \div 8 = 12 \Rightarrow \frac{-17}{4} = 12$
(*b*) $2 \times 3 \div 5 + 8 - 4 = 7 \Rightarrow \frac{26}{5} = 7$
(*c*) $5 \times 6 + 8 \div 2 - 3 = 31 \Rightarrow 31 = 31$
(*d*) $6 - 1 \times 2 \div 8 + 4 = 31 \Rightarrow \frac{-39}{4} = 31$

14. (*d*): $5 \times 8 \div 4 - 2 + 9$
$10 - 2 + 9 = 17$

CHAPTER 9

Word Building

These are spellings, word order and dictionary related questions. The candidate is given a word and asked to select the word that can/cannot be formed from its spellings. He/she may be asked to decide the meaningful order of the given words. He/she may also be asked to arrange the given words in the sequence in which they occur in the dictionary.

MULTIPLE CHOICE QUESTIONS

Directions (Qs. No. 1 to 12): *From the given alternatives select the word which **cannot** be formed using the letters of the given word.*

1. REPUBLICAN
(*a*) CLIP (*b*) PURE
(*c*) ANKLE (*d*) BANE

2. ESTRANGE
(*a*) GENERATE (*b*) SERGEANT
(*c*) REAGENTS (*d*) GREAT

3. DETERMINATION
(*a*) DETENTION (*b*) DESTINATION
(*c*) TERMINATE (*d*) DOMINATE

4. CHRISTMAS
(*a*) CHRIST (*b*) SMART
(*c*) CRUST (*d*) HARM

5. LEGALIZATION
(*a*) ALERT (*b*) ALEGATION
(*c*) GALLANT (*d*) NATAL

6. CHARACTER
(*a*) CRATE (*b*) CHARTER
(*c*) HEARTY (*d*) TRAÇER

7. ADMINISTRATION
(*a*) Station (*b*) Minister
(*c*) Ration (*d*) Mind

8. ORGANISATION
(*a*) ORGAN (*b*) ORGANISE
(*c*) NATION (*d*) ORATION

9. PERAMBULATOR
(*a*) RAMPANT
(*b*) LABOUR
(*c*) MARBLE
(*d*) RAMBLE

10. POSSESSION
(*a*) SESSION
(*b*) POSE
(*c*) POISE
(*d*) OBSESS

11. PRINTINGS
(*a*) SAINT (*b*) PRINT
(*c*) STING (*d*) RINGS

12. QUALIFICATION
(*a*) LIAR (*b*) FIAT
(*c*) LION (*d*) FICTION

13. From the given alternatives select the word which can be formed using the letters given in the word.
ULTRANATIONALISM
(*a*) ULTRAMONTANE
(*b*) ULTRAMODERN
(*c*) ULTRAIST
(*d*) ULULATE

14. A meaningful word starting with R is made from the first, second, fourth, fifth and eighth letters of the word CREATIVE. Which of the following is the middle letter of the word?
(*a*) E (*b*) T
(*c*) C (*d*) A

Directions (Qs. No. 15 to 18): *Which one of the given responses would be a meaningful order of the following words?*

15. 1. Amoeba 2. Oyster
3. Worm 4. Cow
(*a*) 1, 3, 2, 4 (*b*) 1, 2, 3, 4
(*c*) 4, 3, 2, 1 (*d*) 3, 2, 4, 1

16. 1. Birth 2. Death
3. Childhood 4. Infancy
5. Adolescence 6. Adulthood
7. Old age
(*a*) 2, 6, 7, 5, 4, 3, 1 (*b*) 1, 4, 3, 5, 6, 7, 2
(*c*) 1, 4, 3, 6, 5, 7, 2 (*d*) 2, 7, 6, 4, 5, 3, 1

17. 1. Police 2. Punishment
3. Crime 4. Judge
4. Judgement
(*a*) 3, 1, 2, 4, 5
(*b*) 1, 2, 4, 3, 5
(*c*) 5, 4, 3, 2, 1
(*d*) 3, 1, 4, 5, 2

18. 1. Orange 2. Indigo
3. Red 4. Blue
5. Green 6. Yellow
7. Violet
(*a*) 7, 2, 4, 5, 6, 1, 3 (*b*) 7, 2, 4, 6, 5, 1, 3
(*c*) 7, 2, 6, 4, 5, 1, 3 (*d*) 7, 2, 6, 4, 1, 5, 3

Directions (Qs. Nos. 19 and 24): *Arrange the given words in the sequence in which they occur in the dictionary.*

19. 1. Clone 2. Climate
3. Clutter 4. Create
5. Clapped
(*a*) 52143 (*b*) 51234
(*c*) 52134 (*d*) 53124

20. 1. Lasted 2. Loop
3. Lake 4. Litter
5. Listed
(*a*) 31542 B. 31254
(*c*) 31245 (*d*) 31452

21. 1. Intricate 2. Interview
3. Intransigent 4. Interrogation
5. Intravenous
(*a*) 2, 4, 5, 3, 1 (*b*) 5, 3, 1, 2, 4
(*c*) 4, 2, 3, 5, 1 (*d*) 3, 5, 2, 1, 4

22. 1. Forge 2. Forget
3. Forgo 4. Forgive
5. Format
(*a*) 1, 2, 4, 3, 5
(*b*) 5, 2, 4, 3, 1
(*c*) 1, 4, 3, 2, 5
(*d*) 3, 4, 5, 2, 1

23. 1. Forecast 2. Forget
3. Foreign 4. Forsook
5. Force
(*a*) 3, 5, 1, 2, 4 (*b*) 5, 1, 3, 2, 4
(*c*) 5, 1, 3, 4, 2 (*d*) 5, 1, 2, 3, 4

24. 1. Fenestration 2. Feather
3. Feed head 4. Feature
5. Feminine
(*a*) 2, 4, 3, 5, 1 (*b*) 4, 2, 3, 1, 5
(*c*) 2, 4, 1, 5, 3 (*d*) 4, 2, 3, 5, 1

25. Arrange the given words in the sequence in which they occur in the Dictionary and locate the last word.
(*a*) Frankenstein (*b*) Frankincense
(*c*) Frankalmoign (*d*) Frauendienst

26. Grouping of words are given. Choose the next word in the series from the given options.
AFGHAN, INDEFINITELY, SYNOPSIS, STUPENDOUS, BURST
(*a*) GLACIAL (*b*) COMPANION
(*c*) RESCRIPT (*d*) HIJACKER

ANSWERS

1	2	3	4	5	6	7	8	9	10
(c)	(a)	(b)	(c)	(a)	(c)	(b)	(b)	(a)	(d)
11	**12**	**13**	**14**	**15**	**16**	**17**	**18**	**19**	**20**
(a)	(a)	(c)	(d)	(a)	(b)	(d)	(a)	(c)	(d)
21	**22**	**23**	**24**	**25**	**26**				
(c)	(a)	(b)	(a)	(d)	(d)				

CHAPTER 10

Relationship Concept

While attempting questions on blood relations, one should be clear of all the relation patterns that can exist between any two individuals. These type of questions are given mainly to test one's relationship ability.

Very well known relations are :

Mother	Grandmother
Father	Grandfather
Son	Grandson
Daughter	Granddaughter
Brother	Brother-in-law
Sister	Sister-in-law
Niece	Father-in-law
Nephew	Mother-in-law
Uncle	Son-in-law
Aunt	Daughter-in-law
Husband	Cousin
Wife	

The patterns of some relationships which help in solving questions in these tests are :

Father's *or* Mother's Father	—	Grandfather (Paternal *or* Maternal)
Father's *or* Mother's Mother	—	Grandmother (Paternal *or* Maternal
Father's *or* Mother's Son	—	Brother
Father's *or* Mother's Daughter	—	Sister
Father's Brother	—	Paternal Uncle
Father's Sister	—	Paternal Aunt
Mother's Brother	—	Maternal Uncle
Mother's Sister	—	Maternal Aunt
Uncle *or* Aunt's Son *or* Daughter	—	Cousin
Son's Wife	—	Daughter-in-law
Daughter's Husband	—	Son-in-law
Husband's *or* Wife's Brother	—	Brother-in-law
Husband's *or* Wife's Sister	—	Sister-in-law
Brother's Wife	—	Sister-in-law
Sister's Husband	—	Brother-in-law
Brother's Son	—	Nephew
Brother's Daughter	—	Niece

MULTIPLE CHOICE QUESTIONS

Directions : *In each of the following questions keenly study the relationship mentioned between the persons, and then from the given options select the right relationship as the answer.*

1. 'A' is the father of 'B' and 'C'. 'B' is the son of 'A' but 'C' is not the son of 'A'. What is 'C's' relation with 'A'?
(*a*) Daughter (*b*) Son
(*c*) Niece (*d*) Nephew

2. A lady said, "The person standing there is my grandfather's only son's daughter". How is the lady related to the standing person?
(*a*) Sister (*b*) Mother
(*c*) Aunt (*d*) Cousin

3. Ravi is the brother of Amit's son's son. What is Amit's relation to Ravi?
(*a*) Cousin (*b*) Father
(*c*) Grandfather (*d*) Son

4. Mayank said, "My mother is the sister of Rajat's brother." What is Rajat's relation with Mayank?
(*a*) Cousin (*b*) Maternal uncle
(*c*) Uncle (*d*) Brother-in-law

5. Introducing Lily, Raghav said, "Her father is my mother's only son". How is Lily related to Raghav?
(*a*) Aunt (*b*) Daughter
(*c*) Mother (*d*) Sister

6. Ajay is the brother of Vijay. Mili is the Sister of Ajay. Sanjay is the brother of Rahul and Mehul is the daughter of Vijay. Who is Sanjay's Uncle?
(*a*) Rahul (*b*) Ajay
(*c*) Mehul (*d*) Data inadequate

7. Adity is Bhavi's brother, Bharat is Jayant's father. Ella is Bhavi's mother. Aditya and Jayant are brothers. What is Ella's relationship with Bharat?
(*a*) Sister (*b*) Mother
(*c*) Daughter (*d*) Wife

8. A man introduced the boy coming with him as "He is son of the father of my wife's daughter". What relation did the boy bear to the man?
(*a*) Son-in-law (*b*) Son
(*c*) Brother (*d*) Father

9. A and B are two brothers. C is sister of B. D is sister of E. E is son of A. Who is D's uncle?
(*a*) D (*b*) E
(*c*) B (*d*) C

10. Varun said pointing towards Arun, "He is my sister's only brother's son". How is Arun related to Varun?
(*a*) Son (*b*) Brother
(*c*) Nephew (*d*) Data insufficient

11. Pointing to a man, a lady said, "His brother's father is my grandfather's only son." How is the lady related to the man?
(*a*) Mother (*b*) Sister
(*c*) Daughter (*d*) Aunt

12. Vidya is the wife of Gopi and Gopi is the brother of Akhil. Akhil is the uncle of Vijay. What is Vijay's relation with Vidya?
(*a*) Son (*b*) Nephew
(*c*) Brother-in-law (*d*) Brother

13. If Amit's father is Billoo's father's only son and Billoo has neither a brother nor a daughter, what is the relationship between Amit and Billoo?
(*a*) Uncle - Nephew
(*b*) Father- Daughter
(*c*) Father - Son
(*d*) Cousins

14. A is the sister of B. B is the son of C, and E is the daughter of D, and sister of A. What is D to C?
(*a*) Brother (*b*) Husband
(*c*) Wife (*d*) Data is inadequate

15. A Man said to a lady, "Fagu's mother is the only daughter of your father". How is the lady related to Fagu?
(*a*) Daughter (*b*) Sister
(*c*) Wife (*d*) Mother

16. Pointing to a man, a woman said, "He is the only son of my mother's mother". How is the woman related to the man?
(*a*) Aunt (*b*) Daughter
(*c*) Niece (*d*) Sister

17. If B's mother was A's mother's daughter, how was A related to B?
(*a*) Uncle (*b*) Aunt
(*c*) Sister (*d*) Data is insufficient

18. Pointing to a woman in the photograph a man said, "She is the daughter of my grandmother's only son. How is the woman related to the man?
(*a*) Mother (*b*) Daughter
(*c*) Sister-in-law (*d*) Sister

19. A man and a woman are sitting in a room. Man's mother-in-law and woman's mother-in-law are mother and daughter respectively. Man is the .... of the woman.
(*a*) Father (*b*) Father-in-law
(*c*) Uncle (*d*) Grandfather-in-law

20. Pointing to Suman, Amit said, "He is my sister's only brother's son". How is Suman related to Amit?
(*a*) Grandson
(*b*) Son
(*c*) Nephew
(*d*) Cannot be determined

EXPLANATORY ANSWERS

1. (*a*) :

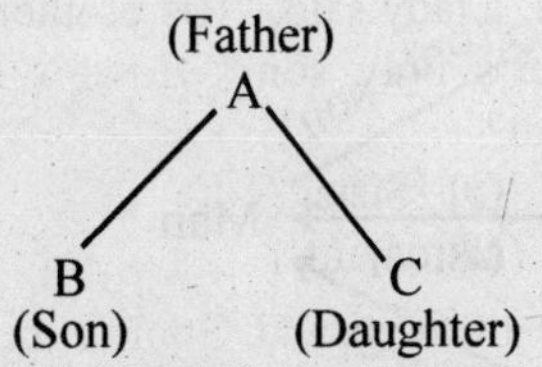

'C' is not the son of 'A', but 'A' is the father of 'C'. So, 'C' is the daughter of 'A'.

2. (*a*) :

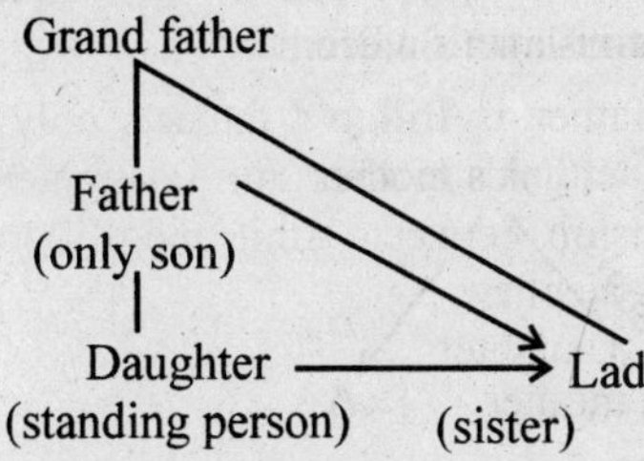

Lady's grandfather's son is lady's father and father's daughter will only be lady's sister.

3. (*c*) :

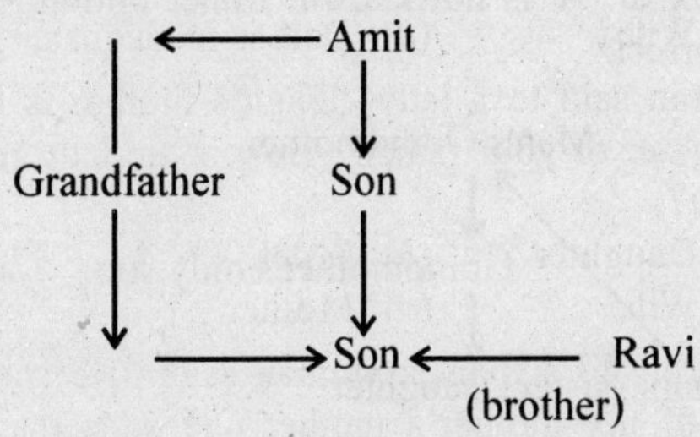

Amit's son's son is Amit's grandson. Ravi is the brother of Amit's son's son. So, Amit is also the grandfather of Ravi.

4. (*b*) :

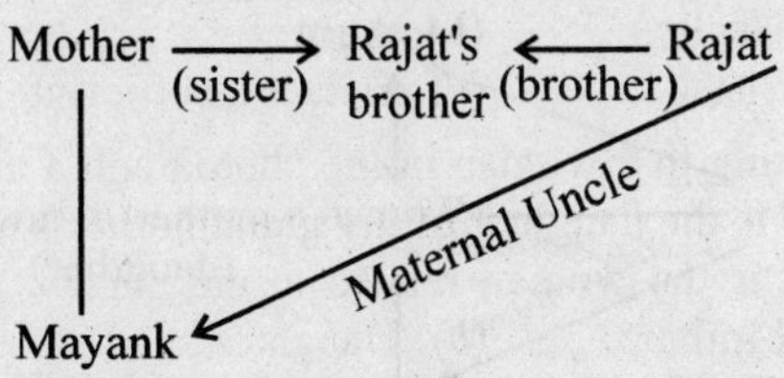

Mayank's mother is the sister of Rajat's brother. So Rajat is also the brother of Mayank's mother. Relation of the brother with his sister's child is maternal. So Rajat is Mayank's maternal uncle.

5. (*b*) : The relation is : Mother
↑ (Son)
Raghav
↓ (Father)
Lily (Daughter)

'My mother's only son' means Raghav himself. 'Her father' means Lily's father; *i.e.* Raghav and so, Lily is Raghav's daughter.

6. (*d*) : 1. Mili (sister) > Ajay (brother) > Vijay ↓ Mehul (daughter)

2. Sanjay (brother) > Rahul

There are two sets of relationship. Information given is incomplete and no relation can be established between the two sets.

7. (*d*) : The relationship chart based on problem is :

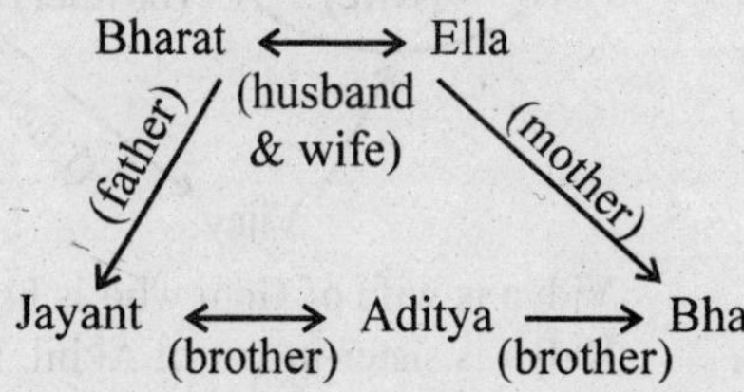

Jayant and Aditya are brothers. If Aditya is Bhavi's brother, then Jayant is also Bhavi's brother. If Bharat is Jayant's father, then he is also the father of Aditya and Bhavi. If Ella is Bhavi's mother, then she is also the mother of Aditya and Jayant. This means Bharat and Ella are husband and wife and the parents of three.

8. (*b*) : The relationship chart based on problem is :

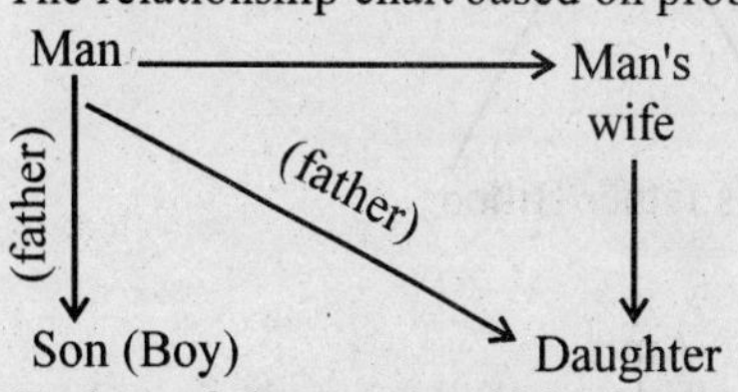

'Father of the man's wife's daughter' is the man himself and the boy in question is the man's son.

9. (*c*) : The relationship chart based on the problem is :

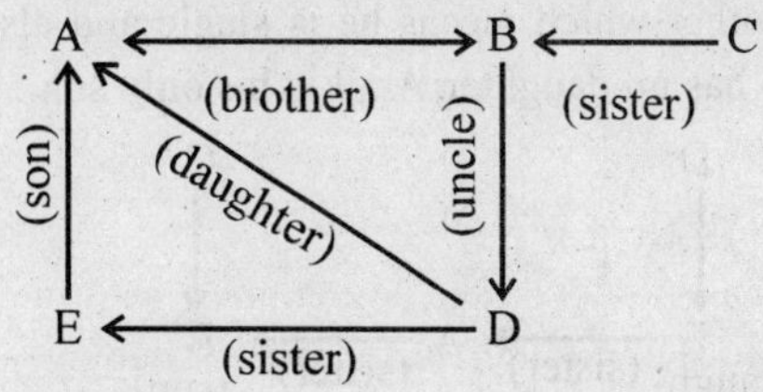

When D is sister of E, who is son of A then D is daughter of A. Brother of A is B and so, B is D's uncle.

10. (*a*) :

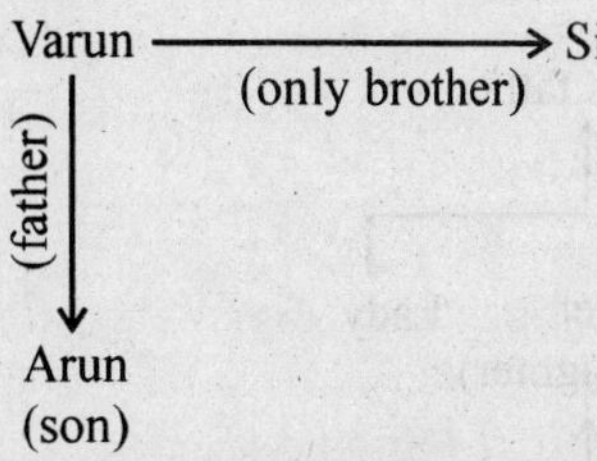

Varun's sister's only brother is Varun himself and Arun is his son.

11. (*b*) :

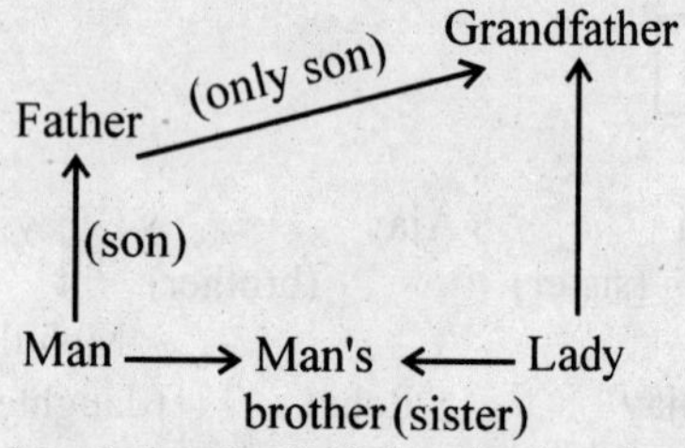

Man's brother's father is also the lady's father as he is the only son of lady's grandfather. So, the lady is man's sister.

12. (*b*) : The relationship chart based on problem is :

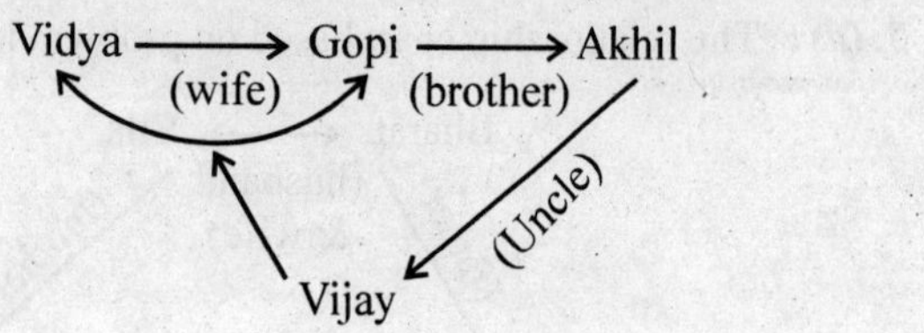

Vidya is wife of Gopi who is brother of Akhil. So, Vidya is sister-in-law of Akhil. If Akhil is uncle of Vijay then Gopi will naturally be the uncle of Vijay as it is not specified that any of the mentioned persons are Vijay's parents. Now, when Vijay is Gopi's nephew then he will also be Vidya's nephew.

13. (*c*) : The relationship chart based on problem is :

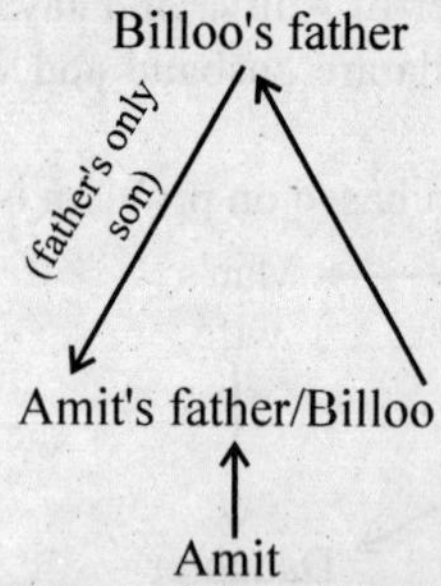

Amit's father is Billoo's father's only son means Billoo is the only son in question also, he is the father of Amit. It must be noted that Billoo has no brother which means he is single and also, when he has no daughter, Amit is his only son.

14. (*d*) :

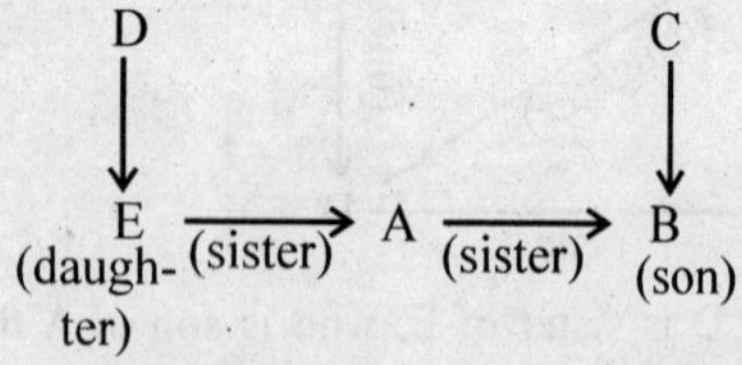

Information about 'D' and 'C' is not given as such no relation can be specified.

15. (*d*) :

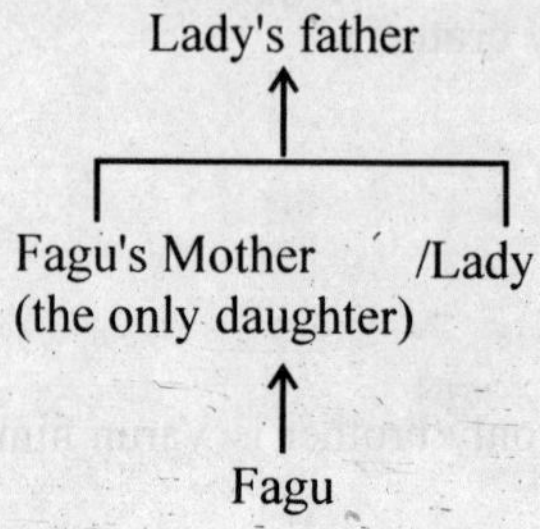

The only daughter of Lady's father is Fagu's mother.

16. (*c*) :

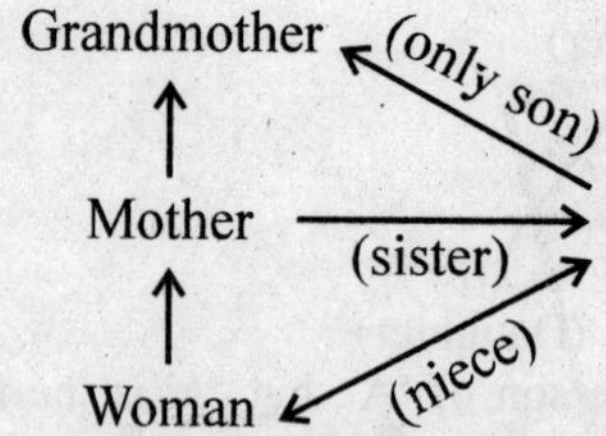

The man is the brother of the woman's mother. So, the woman is man's niece.

17. (*d*) :

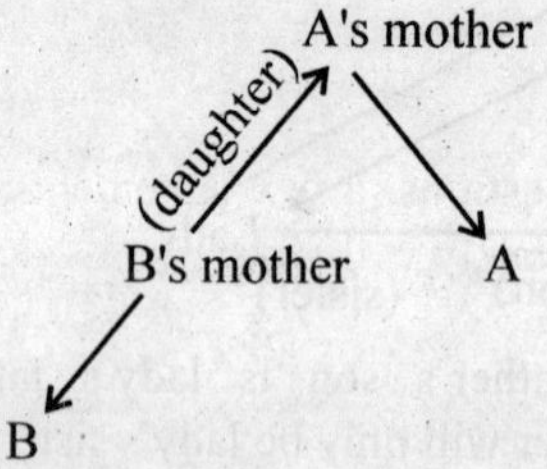

Sex of 'A' is not known. Either option A or B is correct.

18. (*d*) :

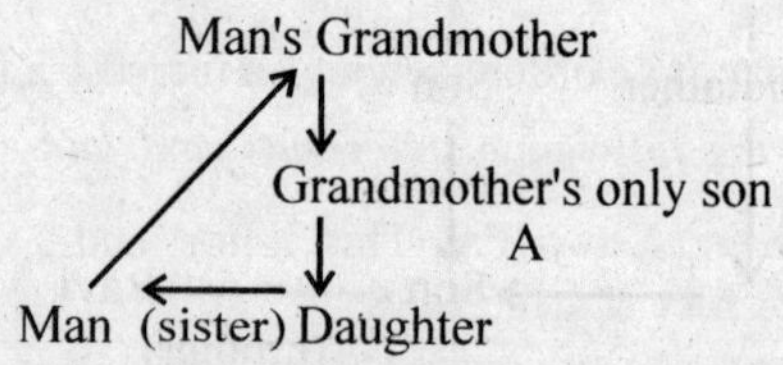

'My grandmother's only son' is the father of the man, and 'daughter of my grand-mother's only son' is the sister of the man.

19. (*b*) :

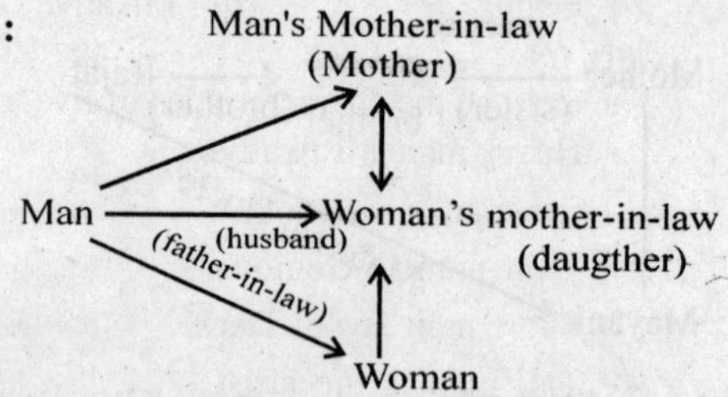

Woman's mother-in-law is the daughter of Man's mother-in-law. So, the man is the husband of woman's mother-in-law and the father-in-law of the woman.

20. (*b*) : Amit ⟵⟶ Amit's Sister
(only brother)
↓
Son (Suman)

'My sister's only brother's is Amit himself and 'Sister's only brother's son' is the son of Amit *i.e.*, Suman is the son of Amit.

CHAPTER 11

Analysis

In these type of questions, a few statements are given. Certain facts are broken up and mentioned in these statements. What is required is to analyse the statements, arrange and sort out the given facts and then answer the questions related to the given statements.

SOLVED EXAMPLES

1. Icecream is as cold as snow. Ice is not as cold as hail. Flakes are not as cold as ice but colder than icecream. What is the coldest?

(*a*) Hail (*b*) Icecream (*c*) Flakes (*d*) Ice (*e*) Snow

Ans. *(a)* : The order showing an increase in coldness, is Icecream/Snow, Flakes, Ice, Hail.

2. *Read the following statements and answer the questions a and b.*

Five men Heavy, Fat, Thin, Short and Tall are running one behind the other. Of the Heavy and the Tall man one is an Artist and the other is Talkative. Thin man who is a Genius is in the centre. Short man is not Dark and the one who is Fair is ahead of Thin man. The Heavy man, who is not an Artist, is in front of the Fat man.

a. Who is Fair?

(*a*) Tall man (*b*) Fat man (*c*) Short man (*d*) Heavy man (*e*) Thin man

Ans. (*b*)

b. What is the Tall Man?

(*a*) Genius (*b*) Talkative (*c*) Artist (*d*) Dark (*e*) Fair

Ans. (*c*)

The chart of the characteristics of five men is :

Heavy man is Talkative.

Fat man is Fair.

Thin man is Genious.

Short man is not Dark.

Tall man is the artist.

MULTIPLE CHOICE QUESTIONS

1. Among five friends, A is heavier than B; C is lighter than D; B is lighter than D but heavier than E. Who among them is the heaviest?

(*a*) B (*b*) C

(*c*) A (*d*) Can't say

2. Pune is bigger than Jhansi, Sitapur is bigger than Chittor. Raigarh is not as big as Jhansi, but is bigger than Sitapur. Chittor is not as big as Sitapur. Which is the smallest?

(*a*) Jhansi (*b*) Pune

(*c*) Chittor (*d*) Sitapur

3. Ajay works more than Ram. Alok works as much as Raju. Pankaj works less than Alok. Ram works more than Alok. Who works the most of all?

(a) Ajay (b) Ram
(c) Alok (d) Raju

4. Vipul is taller than Hans. Hans is taller than Anand. Alok is taller than Ashok. Ashok is taller than Hans. Who among them is the tallest?
(a) Vipul (b) Alok
(c) Ashok (d) Cannot be determined

5. Pramod is taller than Gopal. Gopal is shorter than Madhu. To find out who among them is the tallest, which of the following further informations is necessary?
(a) Madhu is taller than Gopal.
(b) Madhu is shorter than Pramod's brother
(c) Pramod is taller than Madhu.
(d) Pramod is taller than Madhu's brother.

6. Among five friends P, Q, R, S and T, who is the youngest? To arrive at the answer which of the following information given in the statements (A) and (B) is sufficient?
(A) R is younger than P and T.
(B) S is younger than Q.
(a) Only A alone is sufficient
(b) Either A or B is sufficient
(c) Both A and B together are needed
(d) Both A and B together are not sufficient

7. Sushma is richer than Rashmi whereas Anand is richer than Priya. Arun is as rich as Rashmi. Shoba is richer than Sushma.
Which of the following statements is correct according to the above propositions?
(a) Rashmi is poorer than Priya.
(b) Priya is richer than Arun
(c) Arun is poorer than Sushma.
(d) Anand is richer than Rashmi

8. A is elder to B while C and D are elder to E who lies between A and B. If C be elder to B, which one of the following statements is necessarily true?
(a) E is elder to B (b) A is elder to C
(c) C is elder to D (d) D is elder to C

9. Vikram is taller than Rajan but shorter than Annie. Jamal is taller than Annie. Sita is taller than Vikram. Rajan is shorter than Sita. Who is the shortest of all in the group?
(a) Sita (b) Rajan
(c) Vikram (d) Cannot be determined

10. Suresh is as much older than Kamal as he is younger than Prabodh. Navin is as old as Kamal. Which of the following statements is wrong?
(a) Suresh is older than Navin
(b) Kamal is younger than Suresh
(c) Prabodh is not the oldest
(d) Navin is younger than Prabodh

11. Ashok is heavier than Gopal. Mahesh is lighter than Jayesh. Prashant is heavier than Jayesh but lighter than Gopal. Who among them is the heaviest?
(a) Gopal
(b) Jayesh
(c) Prashant
(d) Ashok

12. Subodh's marks in English are as much more than Gopal's marks in History as less than Pramod's marks in English. To find out Subodh's marks in English, which of the following informations given in the statements (A) and (B) is/ are sufficient?
(A) Gopal's marks in History.
(B) Pramod's marks in History.
(a) Both A and B together are needed
(b) Only B is sufficient
(c) Either A or B is sufficient
(d) Both A and B together are not sufficient

13. Pramod is older than Jayesh and Sudhir. Vikas is younger than Anil. To find out who among them is the oldest, which of the following further information will be required, if any?
(a) Sudhir is older than Jayesh
(b) Anil is older than Jayesh
(c) Vikas is older than Pramod
(d) Vikas is younger than Pramod

14. Ashok is younger than Prabir and Gopal. Sohan is younger than Prabir but older than Gopal. Which of the following statements is definitely true?
(a) Ashok is older than Sohan
(b) Sohan is the oldest among them
(c) Gopal is younger than Ashok
(d) Gopal is next to the youngest among them

15. Among five boys, Vasant is taller than Manohar, but not as tall as Raju. Jayant is taller than Datta, but shorter than Manohar. Who is the tallest in their group?
(a) Raju
(b) Manohar
(c) Vasant
(d) Cannot be determined

16. A and D study in the same class. K and L study in the same class. In which class does D study? To answer the above question, which of the following informations given in the statements A and B is/are necessary?
(A) D studies one standard below L.
(B) A's elder brother studies with K.
(a) Both A and B together are not sufficient
(b) Both A and B together are needed
(c) Only A is sufficient
(d) Only B is sufficient

Directions (Qs. 17-18) : *(A) Gopal is shorter than Ashok but taller than Kuhav; (B) Navin is shorter than Kuhav; (C) Jayesh is taller than Navin; (D) Ashok is taller than Jayesh.*

17. Who among them is the tallest?
(*a*) Gopal (*b*) Ashok
(*c*) Jayesh (*d*) Navin

18. Which of the following informations is not necessary to answer the above question?
(*a*) A (*b*) B
(*c*) C (*d*) D

Directions (Qs. 19-20) : *Five men A, B, C, D and E read a newspaper. The one who reads first gives it to C. The one who reads last had taken from A. E was not the first or last to read. There were two readers between B and A.*

19. B passed the newspaper to whom?
(*a*) E (*b*) B
(*c*) A (*d*) None of these

20. Who read the newspaper last?
(*a*) E (*b*) B
(*c*) D (*d*) Cannot be determined

EXPLANATORY ANSWERS

1. (*d*) : The five friends in descending order of weight are : A/D, B/C, E or A/D, B, C/E. Either A or D is the heaviest.

2. (*c*) : The order of cities in descending order of size is : Pune, Jhansi, Raigarh, Sitapur, Chittor.

3. (*a*) : On the basis of doing work, the descending order will be : Ajay, Ram, Alok/Raju, Pankaj.

4. (*d*) : On the basis of height, the descending order will be Vipul/Alok, Ashok, Hans, Anand. Either Vipul or Alok is the tallest.

5. (*c*) : According to the information both Pramod and Madhu are taller than Gopal. Option (c) decides who is the tallest.

6. (*d*) : Statements are not inter-related.

7. (*c*) : On the basis of wealth, the descending order will be :
1. Shobha, Sushma, Rashmi/Arun
2. Anand, *and* Priya
(The two statements are not inter-related.)

8. (*a*) : The order in descending seniority will be : A/C/D, E, B.

9. (*b*) : On the basis of height the descending order will be :
Jamal/Sita, Annie, Vikram, Rajan.
or
Jamal, Sita/Annie, Vikram, Rajan.

10. (*c*) : On the basis of age the descending order will be : Prabodh, Suresh, Kamal/Navin.

11. (*d*) : On the basis of weight, the descending order will be : Ashok, Gopal, Prashant, Jayesh, Mahesh.

12. (*d*) : Comparison in marks do no clarify Subodh's marks in a subject.

13. (*c*) : On the basis of age the descending order will be :
1. Pramod, Jayesh/ Sudhir
and
2. Anil, Vikas
Option (c) connects these two statements.

14. (*d*) : On the basis of age the descending order will be : Prabir, Sohan, Gopal, Ashok.

15. (*a*) : The boys in descending order of height will be: Raju, Vasant, Manohar, Jayant, Datta.

16. (*a*) : There is no useful information in either of the two statements.

17. (*b*) : On the basis of height the descending order will be :
Ashok, Gopal/Jayesh, Kuhav, Navin
or
Ashok, Gopal, Kuhav/Jayesh, Navin.

18. (*c*)

19. (*d*) : The men read the newspaper in this order : B, C, E, A, D, and B passed the newspaper to C.

20. (*c*) : See answer 19 explanation.

CHAPTER 12

Judgement

MULTIPLE CHOICE QUESTIONS

1. Eileen is planning a special birthday dinner for her husband's 35th birthday. She wants the evening to be memorable, but her husband is a simple man who would rather be in jeans at a baseball game than in a suit at a fancy restaurant. Which restaurant below should Eileen choose?

(*a*) Alfredo's offers fine Italian cuisine and an elegant Tuscan decor. Patrons will feel as though they've spent the evening in a luxurious Italian villa.

(*b*) Pancho's Mexican Buffet is an all-you-can-eat family style smorgasbord with the best tacos in town.

(*c*) The Parisian Bistro is a four-star French restaurant where guests are treated like royalty. Chef Dilbert Olay is famous for his beef bourguignon.

(*d*) Marty's serves delicious, hearty meals in a charming setting reminiscent of a baseball clubhouse in honor of the owner,Marty Lester, a former major league baseball all-star. Answer & Explanation

2. The film director wants an actress for the lead role of Lucy who perfectly fits the description that appears in the original screenplay. He is not willing to consider actresses who do not resemble the character as she is described in the screenplay, no matter how talented they are. The screenplay describes Lucy as an average-sized, forty something redhead, with deep brown eyes, very fair skin, and a brilliant smile. The casting agent has four actresses in mind.

1. Actress #1 is a stunning red-haired beauty who is 5'9" and in her mid-twenties. Her eyes are brown and she has an olive complexion.
2. has red hair, big brown eyes, and a fair complexion. She is in her mid-forties and is 5'5".
3. is 5'4" and of medium build. She has red hair, brown eyes, and is in her early forties.
4. is a blue-eyed redhead in her early thirties. She's of very slight build and stands at 5'.

(*a*) 1, 2 (*b*) 2, 3
(*c*) 1, 4 (*d*) 2, 4

3. The school principal has received complaints from parents about bullying in the school yard during recess. He wants to investigate and end this situation as soon as possible, so he has asked the recess aides to watch closely. Which situation should the recess aides report to the principal?

(*a*) A girl is sitting glumly on a bench reading a book and not interacting with her peers.

(*b*) Four girls are surrounding another girl and seem to have possession of her backpack.

(*c*) Two boys are playing a one-on-one game of basketball and are arguing over the last basket scored.

(*d*) Three boys are huddled over a handheld video game, which isn't supposed to be on school grounds. Answer & Explanation

4. Mrs. Carson took a taxi to meet her three friends for lunch. They were waiting for her outside the restaurant when she pulled up in the car. She was so excited to see her friends that she left her tote bag in the taxi. As the taxi pulled away, she and her friends took notice of the license plate number so they would be able to identify the car when they called the taxi company.

1. The four women seem to agree that the plate starts out with the letter J.
2. Three of them agree that the plate ends with 12L.
3. Three of them think that the second letter is X, and a different three think that the third letter is K.

The four license plate numbers below represent what each of the four women thinks she saw. Which one is most likely the license plate number of the taxi?

(*a*) JXK 12L (*b*) JYK 12L
(*c*) JXK 12I (*d*) JXX 12L

5. Zachary has invited his three buddies over to watch the basketball game on his wide-screen television. They are all hungry, but no one wants to leave to get food. Just as they are arguing about who should make the food run, a commercial comes on for a local pizze-ria that delivers. The phone number flashes on the screen briefly and they all try to remember it. By the time Zachary grabs a pen and paper, each of them recollects a different number.

1. All of the men agree that the first three numbers are 995.
2. Three of them agree that the fourth number is 9.
3. Three agree that the fifth number is 2.
4. Three agree that the sixth number is 6; three others agree that the seventh number is also 6.

Which of the numbers is most likely the telephone number of the pizzeria?

(*a*) 995-9266 (*b*) 995-9336
(*c*) 995-9268 (*d*) 995-8266

6. Mark is working with a realtor to find a location for the toy store he plans to open in his town. He is looking for a place that is either in, or not too far from, the center of town and one that would attract the right kind of foot traffic. Which of the following locations should Mark's realtor call to his attention?

(*a*) a storefront in a new high-rise building near the train station in the center of town whose occupants are mainly young, childless professionals who use the train to commute to their offices each day.
(*b*) a little shop three blocks away from the town's main street, located across the street from an elementary school and next door to an ice cream store
(*c*) a stand-alone storefront on a quiet residential street ten blocks away from the town's center
(*d*) a storefront in a small strip mall located on the outskirts of town that is also occupied by a pharmacy and a dry cleaner

7. The neighborhood block association has received many complaints about people knocking on doors and soliciting money for an unknown charity organization even though door-to-door solicitation is prohibited by local laws. Three residents have provided descriptions individuals who have come to their door asking for money.

Solicitor #1 is a white male, 20-25 years old, 5'9", 145 pounds, with very short brown hair. He was wearing a dark blue suit and carrying a brown leather briefcase.

Solicitor #2 is a white male, 25-30 years old, 6'2", 200 pounds, with a shaved-head. He was wearing a red T-shirt and jeans.

Solicitor #3 is a white male, approximately 23 years old, 5'10", slight build, with short brown hair. He was wearing a blue suit.

Three days after the block association meet- ing, a resident noticed a man knocking on doors in the neighborhood and phoned the police to report the illegal activity. This solic- itor was described as follows:

Solicitor #4 is a white male, 22 years old, 140 pounds, about 5'10", with short brown hair. He was carrying a briefcase and wearing a dark suit.

Based on this description, which of the three solicitations was also likely carried out by Solicitor #4?

(*a*) #1, #2, and #3
(*b*) #1, but not #2 and #3
(*c*) #1 and #3, but not #2
(*d*) #1 and #2, but not #3

8. Rita, an accomplished pastry chef who is well known for her artistic and exquisite wedding cakes, opened a bakery one year ago and is surprised that business has been so slow. A consultant she hired to conduct market research has reported that the local population doesn't think of her shop as one they would visit on a daily basis but rather a place they'd visit if they were celebrating a special occasion. Which of the following strategies should Rita employ to increase her daily business?

(*a*) making coupons available that entitle the coupon holder to receive a 25% discount on wedding, anniversary, or birthday cakes
(*b*) exhibiting at the next Bridal Expo and having pieces of one of her wedding cakes available for tasting
(*c*) placing a series of ads in the local newspaper that advertise the wide array of breads
(*d*) moving the bakery to the other side of town

9. Dr. Miller has a busy pediatric dentistry practice and she needs a skilled, reliable hygienist to keep things running smoothly. The last two people she hired were recommended by top dentists in the area, but they each lasted less than one month. She is now in desperate need of a hygienist who can competently handle the specific challenges of her practice. Which one of the following candidates should Dr. Miller consider most seriously?

(*a*) Marilyn has been a hygienist for fifteen years, and her current employer, who is about to retire, says she is the best in the business. The clientele she has worked with consists of some of the wealthiest and most powerful citizens in the county.

(*b*) Lindy recently graduated at the top of her class from one of the best dental hygiene programs in the state. Prioı to becoming a dental hygienist, Lindy spent two years working in a day care center.

(*c*) James has worked as a dental hygienist for three years in a public health clinic. He is very interested in securing a position in a private dental office.

(*d*) Kathy is an experienced and highly recommended dental hygienist who is also finishing up a degree in early childhood education, which she hopes will get her a job as a preschool teacher. She is eager to find a job in a pediatric practice, since she has always wanted to work with children.

10. Mrs. Jansen recently moved to Arizona. She wants to fill her new backyard with flowering plants. Although she is an experienced gardener, she isn't very well-versed in what plants will do well in the Arizona climate. Also, there is a big tree in her backyard making for shady conditions and she isn't sure what plants will thrive without much direct sunlight. Her favorite gardening catalog offers several backyard seed packages. Which one should Mrs. Jansen choose?

(*a*) The Rainbow Collection is ideal for North-east gardens. It includes a variety of colorful perennials that thrive in cool, moist conditions.

(*b*) The Greenhouse Collection will blossom year after year if planted in brightly lit locations and watered regularly.

(*c*) The Treehouse Collection will provide lush green plants with delicate colorful flowers that thrive in shady and partially shady locations.

(*d*) The Oasis Collection includes a variety of perennials that thrive in dry climates and bright sunlight.

EXPLANATORY ANSWERS

1.(*d*) : Since Eileen's husband does not enjoy fancy restaurants, choices a and c can be ruled out. Choice b, although casual, doesn't sound as though it would be the kind of special and memorable evening that Eileen is looking for. Choice d, which is owned by a former baseball star and is described as "charming" and "reminiscent of a baseball clubhouse", sounds perfect for Eileen's husband, who is described as a baseball fan and a man with simple tastes.

2.(*b*) : 2 and 3 possess most of the required traits. They both have red hair and brown eyes, are average-sized, and are in their forties. 1 is very tall and is only in her mid-twenties. She also has an olive complexion. 4 is of very slight build and is in her early thirties. She also has blue eyes.

3.(*b*) : Seeing four girls surrounding another girl, while in possession of her backpack, is the most suspicious of the incidents described.

4.(*a*) : The four women seem to agree that the plate starts out with the letter J. Three of them agree that the plate ends with 12L. Three of them think that the second letter is X, and a different three think that the third letter is K. The plate description that has all of these common elements is "Option A".

5.(*a*) : All of the men agree that the first three numbers are 995. Three of them agree that the fourth number is 9. Three agree that the fifth number is 2. Three agree that the sixth number is 6; three others agree that the seventh number is also 6. "Option A" is the best choice because it is made up of the numbers that most of the men agree they saw.

6.(*b*) : This option is both near the center of town and in a location (near a school and an ice cream store) where children and their parents are sure to be around. This is the only option that meets both of Mark's requirements.

7.(*c*) : The solicitor described as #2 has a shaved head and is much taller and heavier than the solicitors described as #1 and #3. Therefore, choices a and d, which include #2, can be ruled out. Solicitors #1, #3, and #4 have such similar descriptions that the correct answer is clearly choice c.

8.(*c*) : This is the only option that would encourage people to think of the bakery as a shop they would visit regularly and not just on special occasions.

9.(*b*) : The situation described indicates that Dr. Miller's practice presents some specific challenges, namely that it is a busy environment with a child clientele. There is also some indication that even highly recommended, experienced hygienists might not be cut out for Dr. Miller's office. There is nothing to suggest that Marilyn (choice a) or James (choice c) would be a good fit for Dr. Miller's practice. Kathy (choice d) has experience and she is also interested in working with children. However, the fact that she hopes to become a preschool teacher in the not-too-distant future indicates that she might not be the kind of committed, long-term employee that Dr. Miller needs. Lindy (choice b), with her hands-on experience working with children as well as a degree from a prestigious dental hygiene program, is the most attractive candidate for the position based on the situation described

10.(c) : The Treehouse Collection is the only package that can thrive in shady locations. Choice a requires a Northeastern climate. Choices b and d require bright sunlight.

In this type of tests certain categories of information are given followed by certain criteria. Further, the candidates are given a few cause that needs to be analysed. They are required to take the right decision, from the given options, after comparing the information in each case with the given information and criteria.

DECISION MAKING

MULTIPLE CHOICE QUESTIONS

Directions (Qs. 1 to 5) : *Read the following information carefully and answer the questions given below it.*

Following are the criteria for admitting a student in the first year engineering course in a college.

The student must—

(i) have passed XII standard examination in science with at least 80% marks.

(ii) not be more than 20 years old as on 1. 8. 1998.

(iii) have secured at least 90 marks in the entrance test out of a total of 150 marks.

(iv) be able to pay Rs. 15,000 as tuition fees for the first semester and Rs. 5,000 admission charges at the time of taking admission.

In the case of a candidate, who satisfies all other criteria except at—

(a) *(iv)* above but can pay at least 60% of the stipulated fees, the case may be referred to the Admission Committee.

(b) *(iii)* above but has secured more than 95% marks in the XIIth standard examination, the case may be referred to Chairman–Admissions.

You are given the following cases as on 1. 8. 1998. Depending upon the information provided in each case and based on the criteria mentioned above, recommend your decision. You are not to assume anything. If the information provided is not adequate to take a decision, mark 'Data inadequate' as the answer.

1. Subodh Mohaptara was 19 years old as on 20th December, 1997. He has secured 98% marks in XIIth standard examination with science and 80 marks in the entrance test. He can pay the requisite tuition fees and admission charges.

(a) Admit
(b) Refer to Admission Committee
(c) Data inadequate
(d) Do not admit
(e) Refer to Chairman–Admissions

2. Reema Jaiswal was born on 20th July, 1978. She has secured 85% and 75% marks in XIIth standard with science and entrance test respectively. She can pay the requisite tuition fees and admission charges.

(a) Refer to Chairman–Admission
(b) Refer to Admission Committee
(c) Data inadequate
(d) Do not admit
(e) Admit

3. Ashok Dubey was born on 27th November, 1978. He has secured 90% marks in the XIIth standard examination with science and 95 marks in the entrance test. He can pay Rs. 10,000 tuition fees and Rs. 3,500 admission charges.

(a) Admit
(b) Data inadequate
(c) Refer to Admission Committee
(d) Do not admit
(e) Refer to Chairman–Admissions

4. Sudha Mirchandani has secured 95% marks in XIIth standard science stream and 70% marks in the entrance test. She can pay only 65% of the requisite tuition fees and admission charges.

(a) Do not admit
(b) Admit
(c) Data inadequate
(d) Refer to Chairman–Admissions
(e) Refer to Admission Committee

5. Salil Malhotra was born on 25th September in 1979. He has secured 85% and 95% marks in the XIIth standard examination in science stream and entrance test respectively. He can pay the requisite tuition fees and admission charges.

(a) Admit
(b) Do not admit
(c) Refer to Chairman–Admissions
(d) Refer to Admission Committee
(e) Data inadequate

Directions (Qs. 6 to 12) : *Read the following information to answer the given questions :*

Following are the criteria for selecting candidates for Research Fellowship :

The candidate must—

(i) be a post–graduate with minimum of 65% marks.

(ii) not be more than 30 years as on 15. 10. 1993.

(iii) have at least 3 years research experience.

(iv) have diploma in Statistics.

(v) have secured at least 50% marks in the entrance test.

(vi) have finalised the topic for research.

However, in case a candidate who fulfills all other criteria except

(a) *(iii)* above, but has M. Phil degree, should be referred to Dean.

(b) *(iv)* above, should be referred to Chairman.

(c) *(i)* above, but has at least 55% marks in post–graduation and 65% in the entrance test, should be given fellowship.

(d) *(v)* above, but has at lest 45% marks, should be wait–listed.

Based on these criteria and information provided below, decide the course of action in each case. You are not to assume anything. If the data provided is not adequate to decide the given course of action, your answer will be "data inadequate". These cases are given to you as on 15. 10. 1993.

6. 26 years old, Mamta Deo is a post graduate with 58%. She has got four years' research experience and has finalised topic for research. She got 70% marks in diploma in Statistics and 54% marks in the entrance examination.

(a) Fellowship not to be granted
(b) Refer to Dean
(c) Refer to Chairman
(d) Grant Fellowship
(e) Data inadequate

7. Shushila Nair has 65% marks in her post–graduation and is M. Phil. She has 5 years research experience. She has secured 65% in the entrance test and has finalised the research topic. Her date of birth is 11. 8. 65.

(a) Grant fellowship
(b) Wait–list
(c) Refer to Dean
(d) Refer to Chairman
(e) Data inadequate

8. Ameer Khan has got 58% in the entrance test. He has 68% in his post-graduation and 55% in M. Phil. He has got diploma in Statistics and has also finalised the topic for research.

(a) Grant Fellowship
(b) Refer to Dean
(c) Refer to Chairman
(d) Wait-list
(e) Data inadequate

9. 28 years old Neetu Singh is M. Phil with 60% marks. She has secured 70% marks in entrance examination and has finalised the topic for research. She has also got diploma in Statistics.

(a) Grant Fellowship
(b) Fellowship not to be granted
(c) Refer to Chairman
(d) Refer to Dean
(e) Data inadequate

10. Sadhana Suman has got diploma in Statistics with 60% marks and post-graduation with 56% marks. Her date of birth is 12. 12. 1968. She has got one year research experience and is still doing her M. Phil. She has secured 65% marks in entrance exam and has also finalised the research topic.

(a) Grant Fellowship
(b) Fellowship not to be granted
(c) Refer to Dean
(d) Data inadequate
(e) Wait-list

11. Amar Sikka is 28 years old and has got 65% marks in post-graduation and 60% marks in M. Phil. He has got 65% marks in entrance examination and has finalised the topic for research. He also has a diploma in Statistics.

(a) Grant Fellowship
(b) Fellowship not to be granted
(c) Refer to Dean
(d) Refer to Chairman
(e) Data inadequate

12. Madan Paul has got 5 years' research experience and has finalised the research topic. He has got 56% marks in post-graduation. His date of birth is 15. 2. 1966. He has also got diploma in Statistics. He got 70% marks in the entrance test.

(a) Grant Fellowship
(b) Fellowship not to be granted
(c) Refer to Dean
(d) Data inadequate
(e) None of these

Directions (Qs. 13 to 19) : *Read the following information to answer the given questions :*

Following are the conditions for selecting candidates for Research Fellowship :

The candidate must—

(i) be a post-graduate with minimum of 60% marks.

(ii) not be more than 30 years as on 1. 9. 1993.

(iii) have at least 3 years' research experience.

(iv) have diploma in statistics.

(v) have secured at least 55% marks in the entrance test.

(iv) have finalised the topic for research.

However, in the case of a candidate who fulfills all other criteria except—

(a) (iii) above but has M. Phil degree, should be given fellowship.

(b) (iv) above should be referred to Dean.

(c) (i) above but has atleast 55% marks in post–graduation, should be wait-listed.

(d) (v) above but has atleast 50% marks, should be referred to Chairman.

Based on these criteria and information provided below, decide the course of action in each case. You are not to assume anything. If the data provided is not adequate to decide the given course of action, your answer will be "data inadequate". These cases are given to you as on 1. 9. 1993.

13. Vijay Gupta is 24 years old and has got 58% marks in the entrance examination. He has secured 63% marks in his post-graduation and 55% marks in M. Phil. He has got diploma in Statistics and has also finalised the topic for research.
(a) Grant Fellowship
(b) Refer to Dean
(c) Refer to Chairman
(d) Wait-list
(e) Data inadequate

14. Ajoy Dwivedi has secured 65% marks in the post-graduation and has secured 5 years research experience. He has secured 65% marks in the entrance test and has finalised the research topic. His date of birth is 11. 8. 1965.
(a) Grant Fellowship
(b) Wait-list
(c) Refer to Dean
(d) Data inadequate
(e) None of these

15. Madan Soren has got diploma in Statistics with 60% marks and post-graduation with 56% marks. His date of birth is 12. 12. 1968. He has got 1 year research experience and is still doing his M. Phil. He has secured 60% marks in the entrance exam and has also finalised the research topic.
(a) Grant fellowship
(b) Fellowship not to be granted
(c) Refer to Dean
(d) Data inadequate
(e) Wait-list

16. 26 years old Mamta Kulkarni is M. Phil with 60% marks. She has secured 70% marks in the entrance examination and has finali-sed the topic for research. She has also got diploma in Statistics.
(a) Grant Fellowship
(b) Fellowship not to be granted
(c) Refer to Chairman
(d) Refer to Dean
(e) Data inadequate

17. Chander Manoj has got 5 years' research experience and has finalised the research topic. He has got 56% marks in post-graduation and 60% marks in the entrance test. His date of birth is 15. 2. 1966. He has also got diploma in Statistics.
(a) Grant Fellowship
(b) Fellowship not to be granted
(c) Refer to Dean
(d) Data inadequate
(e) None of these

18. Raman Hooda is 28 years old and has got 65% marks in Post-graduation and 60% marks in M. Phil. He has got 65% marks in the entrance examination and has finalised the topic for research. He also has a diploma in Statistics.
(a) Grant Fellowship
(b) Fellowship not to be granted
(c) Refer to Dean
(d) Refer to Chairman
(e) Data inadequate

19. 26 years old Janaki Deo is a post-graduate with 58% marks. She has got four years research experience and has finalised the topic for research. She got 70% marks in the diploma in Statistics and 54% marks in the entrance examination.
(a) Fellowship not to be granted
(b) Refer to Dean
(c) Refer to Chairman
(d) Grant Fellowship
(e) Data inadequate

Directions (Qs. 20 to 27) : *Read the following information carefully and answer the questions given below :*

Following are the criteria of promotion from Junior Officer's Cadre to Senior Officer's Cadre in an organisation :

The candidate must—

(a) have completed atleast 5 years in the organisation.

(b) have secured 65% marks in the written test for promotion.

(c) have secured 60% marks in the Group Discussion.

(d) have secured 70% marks in the interview.

(e) have good record of his work performance.

(f) have good communication skill and get along well with his colleagues.

(g) not be more than 40 years and less than 30 years as on 1. 9. 93.

(*h*) have good academic record with an average of at least 65% marks.

However, in the case of a candidate who—

(*i*) satisfies all other conditions except (*d*) above but has secured 75% marks in the written test and 65% marks in he Group Discussion, the case is to be referred to the General Manager (Personnel)–GM(P) for the decision.

(*j*) satisfies all other criteria except (*h*) above but has secured an average of more than 60% marks, the case is to be referred to the Managing Director (MD) of the organisation.

Now read the information provided in the case of each candidate in each of the questions given below and decide on the basis of the information provided and based on the above conditions, which of the courses of action you would suggest. These cases are given as on 5. 9. 1993. (Remember you are not to assume anything which is not provided in the question). If complete information is not provided, the answer would be Data inadequate.

20. 38 years old Rajesh has secured 65% marks in the written test for promotion, 73% marks in interview and 62% marks in Group Discussion. He has good record of his work performance, good communication skills and gets along well with his colleagues. He has good academic record with an average of 61% marks and has completed 7 years in the organisation.

(*a*) Refer to GM(P)
(*b*) Refer to MD
(*c*) Promote
(*d*) Do not promote
(*e*) Data inadequate

21. 34 years old Sudha has secured 60% marks in the written test for promotion, 72% marks in interview and 69% marks in Group discussion. She has good communication skill and gets along well with her colleagues. Her record of work performance is good and she has completed 6½ years in the organisation.

(*a*) Refer to MD
(*b*) Do not promote
(*c*) Refer to GM(P)
(*d*) Promote
(*e*) Data inadequate

22. Surekha has secured 70% marks in written test for promotion, 69% marks in Group Discussion and 72% marks in the interview. She has a good academic record with an average of 67% marks. She has good record of work performance and gets along well with her colleagues. She has good communication skill and has completed 7 years in the organisation.

(*a*) Do not promote
(*b*) Promote
(*c*) Refer to GM(P)
(*d*) Refer to MD
(*e*) Data inadequate

23. 39 years old Pawan has secured 66% marks in written promotion test and has a good academic record with an average of 62% marks. He has secured 65% marks in Group Discussion and 72% marks in interview. He has good record of his work performance, communication skill and gets along well with his colleagues. He has completed 6 years in the organisation.

(*a*) Do not promote
(*b*) Refer to MD
(*c*) Refer to GM(P)
(*d*) Promote
(*e*) Data inadequate

24. 34 years old Sudhir has secured 76% marks in the written test for promotion, 66% marks in Group Discussion and 67% marks in interview. He has good academic record with an average of 68% marks, good communication skill and gets along well with his colleagues. His work performance is good and he has completed 6 years in the organisation.

(*a*) Promote
(*b*) Refer to MD
(*c*) Refer to GM(P)
(*d*) Do not promote
(*e*) Data anadequate

25. 32 years old Manjula has good academic record with an average of 66% marks. She has secured 67% marks in Group Discussion, 75% marks in interview and 60% marks in written test for promotion. She has good communication skill and gets along well with her colleagues. She has good record of her work performance and has completed 7 years in the organisation.

(*a*) Do not promote
(*b*) Refer to MD
(*c*) Promote
(*d*) Refer to GM(P)
(*e*) Data inadequate

26. 31 years old Krishna secured 65% marks in written test for promotion, 72% marks in interview and 62% marks in Group Discussion. He has good academic record with an average of 67% marks and good communication skill. He has completed 9 years in the organisation. He gets easily annoyed and irritated with his colleagues and his record of work performance since the last two years is just average.

(*a*) Promote (*b*) Refer to GM(P)
(*c*) Refer to MD (*d*) Do not promote
(*e*) Data inadequate

27. 33 years old Neelima has secured 63% marks in Group Discussion, 71% marks in interview and 66% marks in written test for promotion. She hase good academic record with an average of 68% marks and has good communication skill. She gets along well with her colleagues and has good record of her work performance. She has completed 6 years in the organisation.

(*a*) Refer to GM(P)
(*b*) Do not promote
(*c*) Promote
(*d*) Refer to MD
(*e*) Data inadequate

EXPLANATORY ANSWERS

1. (*e*) : Criterion *(iii)* is not satisfied but Criterion *(b)* gives the decision.

2. (*d*) : Both Criterion *(iii)* and Criterion *(b)* are not satisfied.

3. (*c*) : Criterion *(iv)* is not satisfied but Criterion *(a)* gives the decision.

4. (*c*) : Criterion *(ii)* is not given.

5. (*a*)

6. (*a*) : Both Criterion *(i)* and Criterion *(c)* are not satisfied.

7. (*d*) : Criterion *(iv)* is not given but Criterion *(b)* gives the decision.

8. (*e*) : Both Criteria *(ii)* and *(iii)* are not given and Criterion *(a)* alone cannot give the decision.

9. (*e*) : Both Criterion *(i)* and Criterion *(iii)* are not given and criterion *(a)* alone cannot give the decision.

10. (*b*) : Both Criterion *(iii)* and Criterion *(a)* are not satisfied.

11. (*c*) : Criterion *(iii)* is not satisfied but Criterion *(a)* gives the decision.

12. (*a*) : Criterion *(i)* is not satisfied but Criterion *(c)* gives the decision.

13. (*a*) : Criterion *(iii)* is not satisfied but Criterion *(a)* gives the decision.

14. (*c*) : Criterion *(iv)* is not satisfied but Criterion *(b)* gives the decision.

15. (*b*) : Both Criterion *(iii)* and Criterion *(a)* are not satisfied.

16. (*e*) : Criterion *(i)* is not given and Criterion *(c)* is not satisfied.

17. (*e*) : Criterion *(i)* is not satisfied but Criterion *(c)* gives the decision of "wait–list." This option is not given.

18. (*a*) : Criterion *(iii)* is not satisfied but Criterion *(a)* gives the decision.

19. (*a*) : Both Criterion *(i)* and Criterion *(iii)* are not satisfied, Criterion *(c)* and Criterion *(d)* gives different decisions.

20. (*b*) : Criterion *(h)* is not satisfied but Criterion *(j)* gives the decision.

21. (*b*) : Criterion *(b)* is not satisfied.

22. (*e*) : Criterion *(g)* is not given.

23. (*b*) : Criterion *(h)* is not satisfied but Criterion *(j)* gives the desicion.

24. (*c*) : Criterion *(d)* is not satisfied but Criterion *(i)* gives the decision.

25. (*a*) : Criterion *(b)* is not satisfied.

26. (*d*) : Both Criterion *(e)* and Criterion *(f)* are not satisfied.

27. (*c*) :

CHAPTER 13

Statement Conclusion

In this reasoning pattern, a statement is given followed by two conclusions. The statement is to be taken as the fact. Then based on it one has to decide which of the conclusion(s) definitely follows or does not follow from the given statement.

MULTIPLE CHOICE QUESTIONS

Directions (Qs. 1 to 20): *In the following questions, each question has a statement followed by two conclusions. Taking the statement to be true, decide which of the given conclusions definitely follows from the given statement. Indicate your answer as (a) if only I follows; (b) if only II follows; (c) either I or II follows; (d) if neither I nor II follows; and (e) if both I and II follow.*

1. *Statement* : The Principal humiliated the teacher in the presence of students.

Conclusions I: The Principal did not like the teacher.

II: The teacher was not popular amongst his students.

2. *Statement* : Good health is dependent on right eating habits. Most of the people do not follow any rule regarding eating.

Conclusions I: Most of the people have poor health.

II: People are ignorant of proper eating habits.

3. *Statement* : Until our country achieves economic equality and political freedom, democracy would be meaningless.

Conclusions I: Political freedom and democracy go hand in hand.

II: Economic equality leads to real political freedom and democracy.

4. *Statement* : Black cloud follows thunder. Rains follow thunder.

Conclusions I: Thunder is the cause of rain.

II: Black cloud is the cause of thunder.

5. *Statement* : Practice is better than precept. Most doctors are heavy smokers.

Conclusions I: Most doctors cannot advise people not to smoke.

II: Doctors do not regard smoking as injurious.

6. *Statement* : Workers feel highly motivated when they get sense of involvement by participating in the management of companies.

Conclusions I: Workers should be motivated to produce more.

II: Workers should be allowed to participate in the management of companies.

7. *Statement* : Industrial revolution which first of all started in Europe has brought about modern age.

Conclusions I: Disparity between rich and poor results in revolution.

II: Revolution overhauls society.

8. *Statement* : America's defence secretary reiterated that they would continue to supply arms to Pakistan.

Conclusions I: Pakistan is incapable of manufacturing arms.

II: It would ensure peace in the region.

9. *Statement* : Poor people are more trust-worthy as compared to the rich. They can do wonders if they are taken into confidence.

Conclusions I: Poor people are wonderful people.

II: By and large rich people are not trustworthy.

10. *Statement* : Government has spoiled many top ranking financial institutions by appointing bureaucrats as Directors of these institutions.

Conclusions I: Government should appoint Directors of the financial institutes taking into consi-deration the expertise of the person in the area of finance.

II: The Director of the financial institute should have exper-tise commensurate with the financial work carried out by the institute.

11. *Statement* : The Constitutional amendment carried out just last month prohibits the employment of child labour in any organisation.

Conclusions I: The employers must now abide by this amendment to the Constitution.

II: Children below 14 years will now be engaged in acquiring education.

12. *Statement* : People who speak too much against the dowry are those who had taken it themselves.

Conclusions I: It is easier said than done.

II: People have double standards.

13. *Statement* : Vegetable prices are soaring in the market.

Conclusions I: Vegetables are becoming a rare commodity.

II: People cannot eat vegetables.

14. *Statement* : As far as the rate of literacy is concerned, there is hardly any difference between the States of Kerala and West Bengal, but one is ahead of the other in respect of the percentage of population unemployed.

Conclusions I: Unemployment is more in Kerala than in West Bengal.

II: West Bengal has higher unemployment than Kerala.

15. *Statement* : He tirelessly argues for the replacement of the present system of allocating work to the teaching staff in the department by another system which will give the teachers higher job satisfaction.

Conclusions I: No system is free from problems and therefore there should be no system.

II: Any system you may evolve but it should give higher job satisfaction to the teachers.

16. *Statement* : The unequal allocation of funds by the Government for literacy and employment generation programmes stands out clearly when we analyse the attitude of government towards these two areas.

Conclusions I: Government has more favourable attitude towards literacy programmes than employment generation progra-mmes.

II: Government has more favourable attitude towards employment generation programmes than literacy programmes.

17. *Statement* : Amul chocolates sold enough in comparison to all other chocolate brands in India.

Conclusions I: No other chocolate is sold in India.

II: The selling data of every chocolate brand is available in India.

18. *Statement* : Wearing Khadi is not only good for our health but also for our nation.

Conclusions I: Economy of India also depends upon Khadi sector.

II: It is difficult to maintain Khadi clothes.

19. *Statement* : Ideas given by our ancestors that were once discarded as uneconomical and unviable, turn out to be as functional and inevitable in present circumstances.

Conclusions I: In ancient period ideas were considered either completely functional or totally infeasible.

II: Ideas cannot change from time-to-time.

20. *Statement* : The Supreme Court gave a judgement that the maintenance of old age parents is the responsibility of the married girls, if they do not have brothers.

Conclusions I: Constitution is always interpreted to help oppressed people out.

II: Before the Supreme Court gave its verdict, a married girl must have denied to pay for the maintenance of her parents.

Directions (Qs. 21 to 25): *In the following questions, the symbols* $*$, $\underset{=}{*}$,=, @ *and* $\underset{=}{@}$ *are used with the following meanings :*

(*a*) * (*b*) means (*a*) is greater than (*b*),

(*a*) $\underset{=}{*}$ (*b*) means (*a*) is either greater than or equal to (*b*).

(*a*) = (*b*) means (*a*) is equal to (*b*).

(*a*) @ (*b*) means (*a*) is smaller than (*b*) and

(*a*) $\underset{=}{@}$ (*b*) means (*a*) is either smaller than or equal to (*b*).

Answer is given as:

(*a*) If only conclusion I is true;

(*b*) If only conclusion II is true;

(*c*) If either I or II is true;

(*d*) If neither I nor II is true;

(*e*) If both I and II are true.

21. *Statements* : T $\overset{*}{=}$ P, P @ S, P = M

Conclusions : *I.* S * M *II.* T @ S

22. *Statements* : R $\underset{=}{@}$ M, M * P, R $\overset{*}{=}$ L

Conclusions : *I.* M = L *II.* P = L

23. *Statements* : M = T, T $\underset{=}{@}$ Z, S * M

Conclusions : *I.* Z * M *II.* Z = M

24. *Statements* : L @ C, C * Z, Z $\underset{=}{@}$ F

Conclusions : *I.* C * F *II.* F = C

25. *Statements* : Z @ B, N $\overset{*}{=}$ S, B @ N

Conclusions : *I.* B = Z *II.* S $\underset{=}{@}$ B

EXPLANATORY ANSWERS

1. (*a*) : Only conclusion I follows. Conclusion II is not confirmed by the given statement.

2. (*a*) : Conclusion I definitely follows. Conclusion II is not confirmed by the given statement.

3. (*b*) : Only conclusion II follows. Conclusion I cannot be drawn from the given statement.

4. (*b*) : Only conclusion II follows. Conclusion I is wrong as rains are the cause of thunder.

5. (*e*) : Both conclusion I and conclusion II follow from the statements as the doctors who are heavy smokers indicate that they do not regard smoking as injurious and thus, cannot advise people not to smoke.

6. (*e*) : Both conclusions I and II follow from the statement as involvement of workers boosts production and benefits the companies.

7. (*b*) : Only conclusion II follows. Conclusion I is not related the statement.

8. (*d*) : Neither conclusion I nor conclusion II follows. Both the conclusions are unrelated to the statement.

9. (*b*) : Only conclusion II follows. Conclusion I is not related to the statement.

10. (*e*) : Both conclusion I and conclusion II follow.

11. (*a*) : Only conclusion I follows. Conclusion II is not related to the statement.

12. (*e*) : Both conclusion I and conclusion II follow as people who talk too much often do not practise what they say.

13. (*d*) : Neither conclusion I nor conclusion II is confirmed by the statement.

14. (*d*) : Neither conclusion I nor conclusion II follows as the precentage of unemployment in each state is not mentioned.

15. (*b*) : Only conclusion II follows. Conclusion I runs counter to the statement as a system is necessary.

16. (*d*) : Neither conclusion I nor conclusion II is confirmed by the statement.

17. (*b*) : Only conclusion II follows as the data of every chocolate brand shows the comparision of Amul chocolates with other brands. Coclusion I is not confirmed by the statement.

18. (*a*) : Only conclusion I follows. Conclusion II is not related to the statement.

19. (*d*) : Neither conclusion I, nor conclusion II follows; both the conclusions are unrelated.

20. (*b*) : Only conclusion II follows, because the Supreme Court judgement must have come in such a case and not in vacuum.

21. (*a*) : $T \geq P, P < S, P = M$

$\therefore\ S > M$

22. (*d*) : $R \leq M, M > P, R \geq L$

$\therefore\ L \leq R \leq M$

23. (*c*) : $M = T, T \leq Z, Z = M$

If $T = Z$, then $Z = M$

If $T < Z$, then $Z > M$

24. (*d*) : $L < C, C > Z, Z \leq F$

No relation can be established between C and F.

25. (*d*) : $Z < B, N \geq S, B < N$

No relation can be established between B, S and Z.

CHAPTER 14

Syllogistic Reasoning

In this reasoning pattern two statements are followed by few conclusions drawn. Four options (*a*), (*b*), (*c*) & (*d*) are given as answers. Based on the statement the candidate has to select the right answer in each question.

MULTIPLE CHOICE QUESTIONS

Directions (Q. 1–10) : *In each question given below two statements are followed by four conclusions numbered I, II, III and IV. You have to take the two given statements to be true even if they seem to be at variance from commonly known facts. Read the statements and conclusions and decide which of the conclusions logically follows from the two given statements, disregarding commonly known facts.*

1. Statements: All the phones are scales. All the scales are calculators.

Conclusions:

I. All the calculators are scales.
II. All the phones are calculators.
III. All the scales are phones.
IV. Some calculators are phones.

(*a*) Only I and IV (*b*) Only III and IV
(*c*) Only II and IV (*d*) Only I and II

2. Statements: No door is dog. All the dogs are cats.

Conclusions:

I. No door is cat.
II. No cat is door.
III. Some cats are dogs.
IV. All the cats are dogs.

(*a*) Only II and IV (*b*) Only I and III
(*c*) Only III and IV (*d*) Only III

3. Statements: Some tables are T.V. Some T.V. are radios.

Conclusions:

I. Some tables are radios.
II. Some radios are tables.
III. All the radios are T.V.
IV. All the T.V. are tables.

(*a*) Only II and IV (*b*) Only I and III
(*c*) Only IV (*d*) None of the four

4. Statements: All men are vertebrates. Some mammals are vertebrates.

Conclusions:

I. All men are mammals.
II. All mammals are men.
III. Some vertebrates are mammals.
IV. All vertebrates are men.

(*a*) Only IV (*b*) Only II
(*c*) Only III (*d*) Only I

5. Statements: All green are blue. All blue are white.

Conclusions:

I. Some blue are green.
II. Some white are green.
III. Some green are not white.
IV. All white are blue.

(*a*) Only I and II (*b*) Only I and III
(*c*) Only I and IV (*d*) Only II and IV

6. Statements: Some pens are books. Some books are pencils.

Conclusions:

I. Some pens are pencils.
II. Some pencils are pens.
III. All pencils are pens.
IV. All books are pens.

(*a*) Only I and III (*b*) Only II and IV
(*c*) All the four (*d*) None of the four

7. Statements: All the research scholars are psychologists. Some psychologists are scientists.

Conclusions:

I. All the research scholars are scientists.
II. Some research scholars are scientists.
III. Some scientists are psychologists.
IV. Some psychologists are research scholars.

(*a*) Only III and IV (*b*) None of the four
(*c*) All the four (*d*) Only III

8. Statements: All the goats are tigers. All the tigers are lions.

Conclusions:

I. All the goats are lions.
II. All the lions are goats.
III. Some lions are goats.
IV. Some tigers are goats.

(*a*) All the four (*b*) Only I, II and III
(*c*) Only I, III and IV (*d*) Only II, III and IV

9. Statements: All members are students. No student is a girl.

Conclusions :

I. All students are members.
II. No members is a girl.
III. Some students are members.
IV. Some members are girls.

(*a*) Only I follows (*b*) Only I, II and III follow
(*c*) All follows (*d*) Only II and III follows

10. Statements : All soaps are clean. All clean are wet.

Conclusions :

I. Some clean are soaps.
II. No clean is soap.
III. Some wet are soaps.
IV. All wet are soaps.

(*a*) Only I follows
(*b*) Only I and II follow
(*c*) Only either III and IV follow
(*d*) Only I and III follow

Directions (Q. 11–15) : *Every question below has a few statements, followed by four conclusions numbered I, II, III and IV. You have to consider every given statement as true, even if it does not conform to the well known facts. Read the conclusions and then decide which of the conclusions can be logically derived.*

11. Statements: Some keys are staplers. Some staplers are stickers. All the stickers are pens.

Conclusions:

I. Some pens are staplers.
II. Some stickers are keys.
III. No sticker is key.
IV. Some staplers are keys.

(*a*) Only I and II
(*b*) Only II and IV
(*c*) Only II and III
(*d*) Only I and IV and either II or III

12. Statements: All the locks are keys. All the keys are bats. Some watches are bats.

Conclusions:

I. Some bats are locks.
II. Some watches are keys.
III. All the keys are locks.
IV. Some keys are locks.

(*a*) Only I and II (*b*) Only I and IV
(*c*) Only II and III (*d*) Only I and III

13. Statements: All the papers are books. All the bags are books. Some purses are bags.

Conclusions:

I. Some papers are bags.
II. Some books are papers.
III. Some books are purses.
IV. Some papers are purses.

(*a*) Only I and IV (*b*) Only II and III
(*c*) Only I and II (*d*) Only I and III

14. Statements: All the bottles are boxes. All the boxes are bags. Some bags are trays.

Conclusions:

I. Some bottles are trays.
II. Some trays are boxes.
III. All the bottles are bags.
IV. Some trays are bags.

(*a*) Only III and IV (*b*) Only I and II
(*c*) Only II and III (*d*) Only I and IV

15. Statements: Some rats are cats. Some cats are dogs. No dog is cow.

Conclusions:

I. No cow is cat.
II. No dog is rat.
III. Some cats are rats.
IV. Some dogs are cats.

(*a*) Only I and IV (*b*) Only I and II
(*c*) Only I and III (*d*) Only III and IV

EXPLANATORY ANSWERS

1. (*c*)

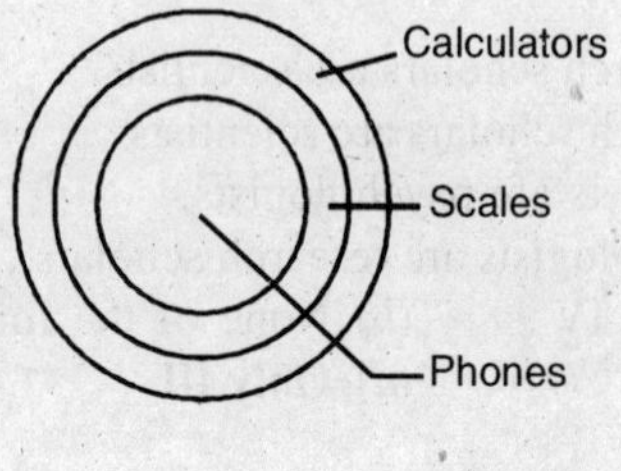

2. (*d*)

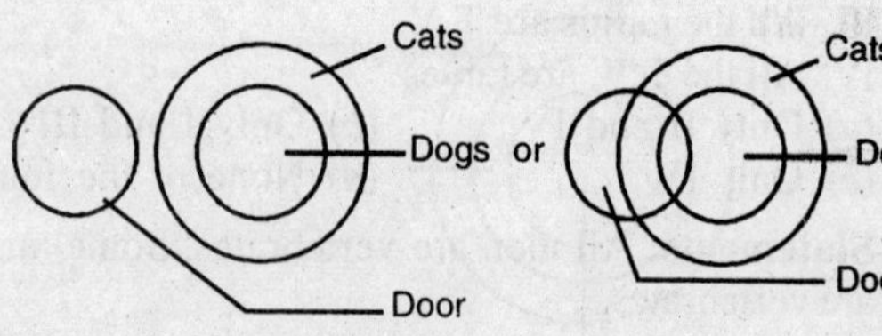

3. (*d*)

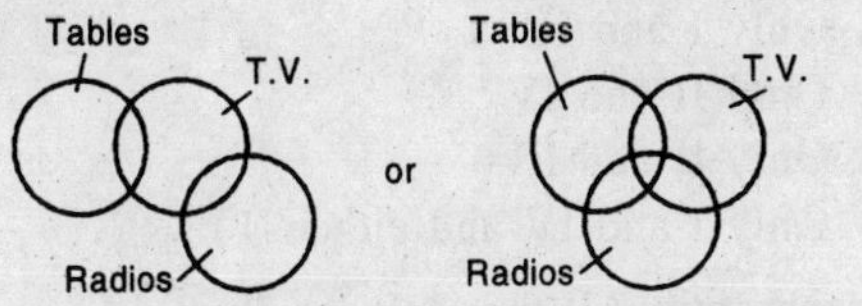

4. (*c*)

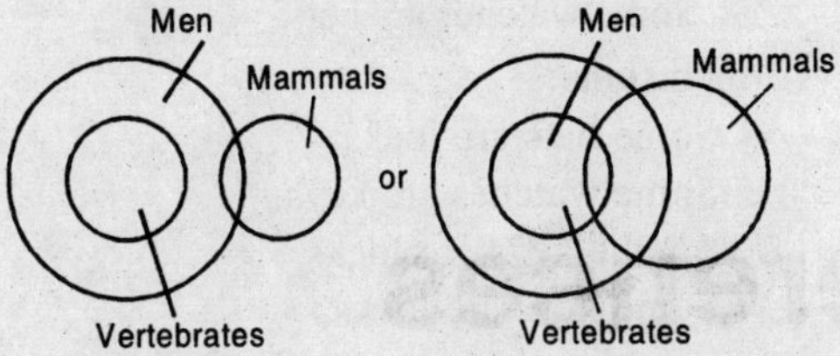

5. (*a*)

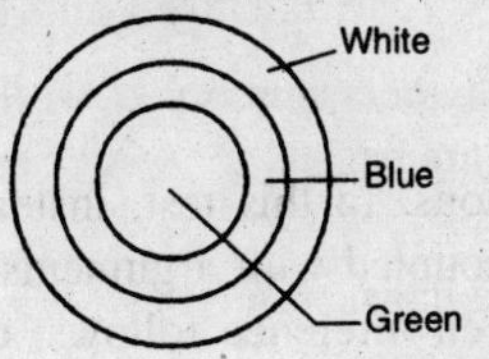

6. (*d*)

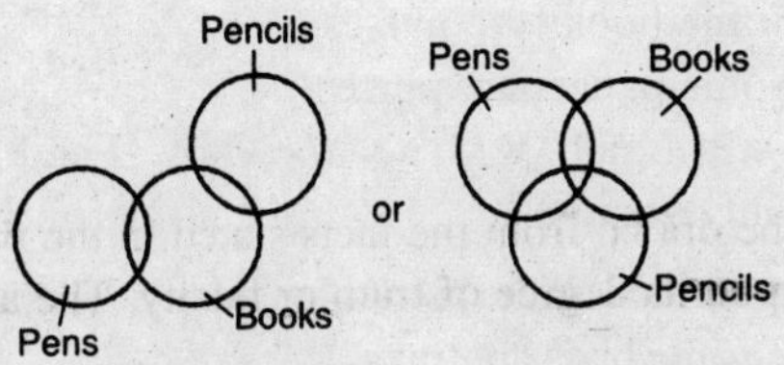

7. (*a*)

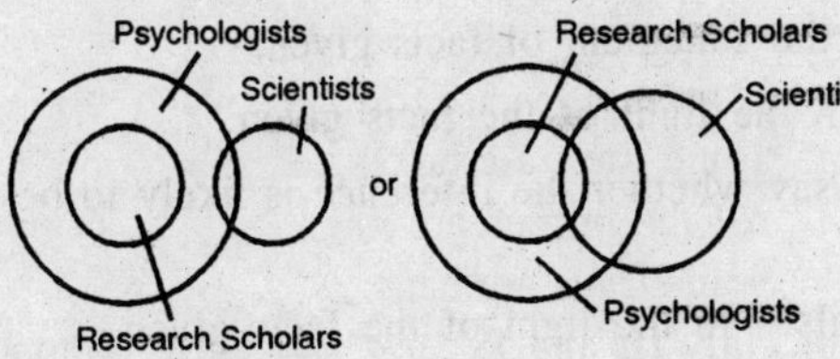

8. (*c*)

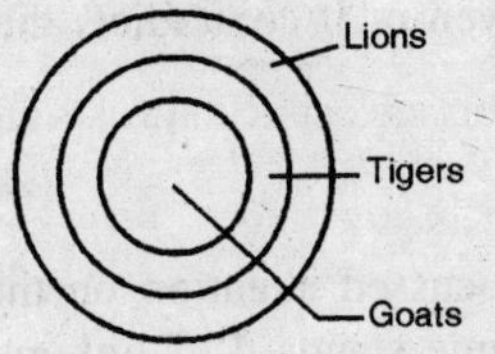

9. (*d*)

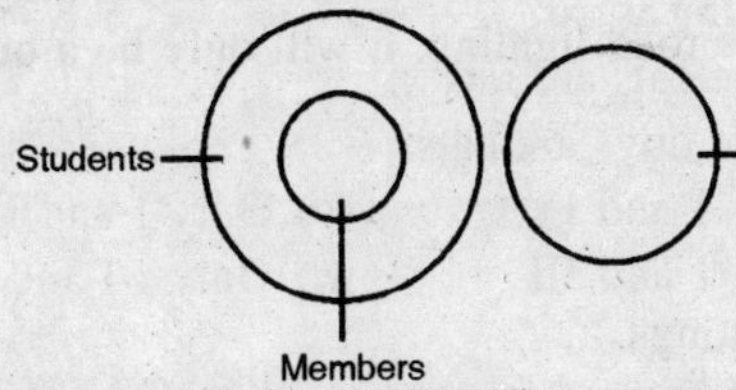

Since Members and Girls are disjoint, it follows that no members is girl. Since Members and Students have a common area, it follows that some student are members.

10. (*d*)

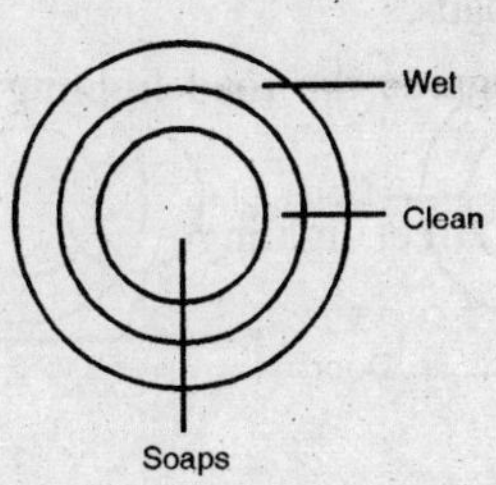

According to diagram, Clean and Soaps have a common area. So, some clean are soaps. Also wet and soaps have a common area. So, some wet are soaps.

11. (*d*)

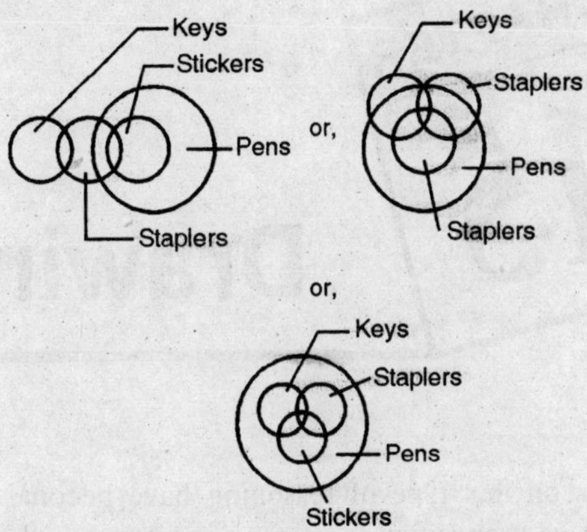

12. (*b*)

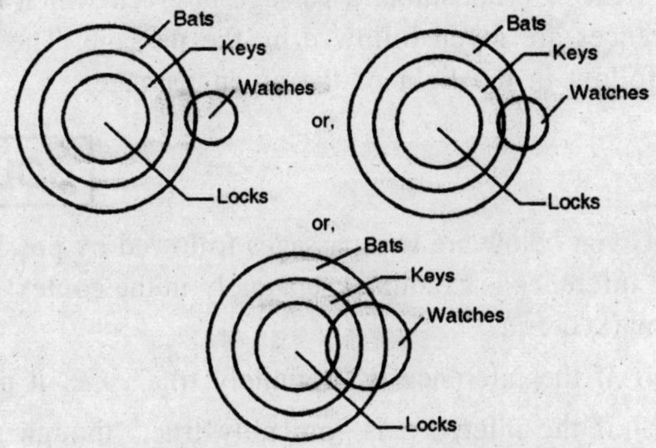

13. (*b*)

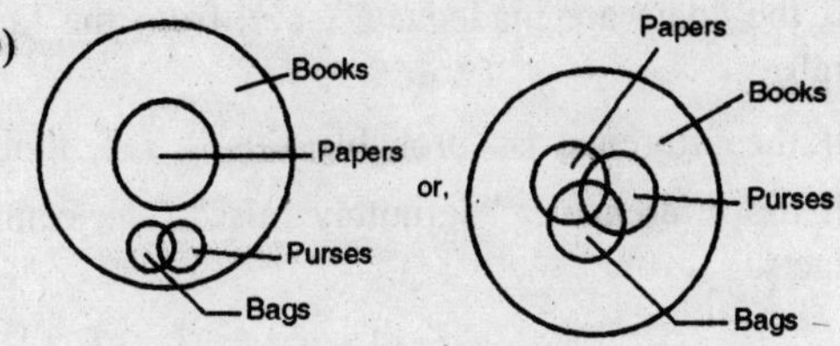

14. (*a*)

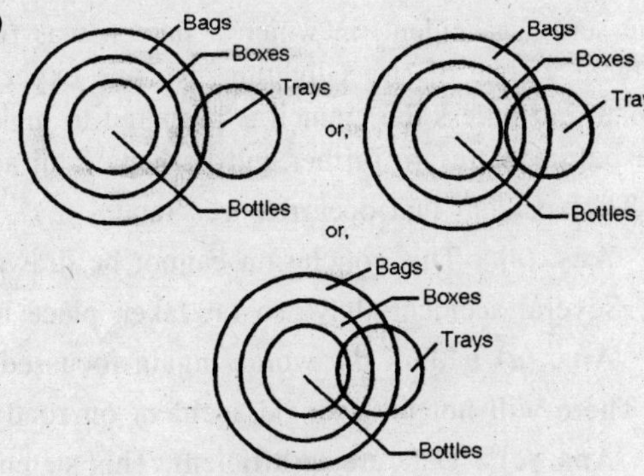

15. (*d*)

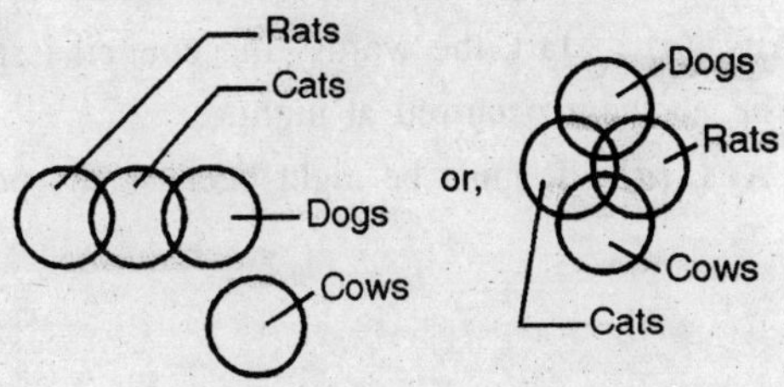

CHAPTER 15

Drawing Inferences

Questions on this type of reasoning have become quite common in competitive examinations. In this test, instead of a statement or proposition, a passage is given which is a congregation of many propositions coupled with arguments. Some inferences are given followed by the passage. The candidate has to decide whether the given inference follows, or does not follow in the light of the given passage.

SOLVED EXAMPLES

Given below are two passages followed by possible inferences which can be drawn from the facts stated in the passage. Each inference is examined separately in the context of the passage to decide upon its degree of truth or falsity. The answers are marked . . . .

(a) if the inference is "definitely true", *i.e.,* it properly follows from the statement of facts given.

(b) if the inference is "probably true," though not "definitely true" in the light of the facts given.

(c) if the "data are inadequate", *i.e.,* from the facts given you cannot say whether the inference is likely to be true or false.

(d) if the inference is "probably false", *i.e.,* though not "definitely false" in the light of the facts given.

(e) if the inference is "definitely false", *i.e.,* cannot possibly be drawn from the facts given or it contradicts the given facts.

PASSAGE I

The serious accident, in which a person was run over by a car yesterday, has again focussed attention on the most unsatisfactory state of street lighting. No one expects side roads to be provided with the same standard of lightings as a main road, but unless the council is prepared to make good its promise as regards road lighting, it will only be a question of time before there are further and perhaps fatal accidents.

1. The accident that occurred was fatal.

Ans. ***(e)*** **:** This conclusion cannot be drawn from the facts given.

2. Several accidents have so far taken place because of unsatisfactory lightings.

Ans. ***(a)*** **:** Mark the words 'again focussed attention on the most . . . lighting'.

3. There will not be a single accident on road if they are satisfactorily illuminated.

Ans. ***(c)*** **:** Data are insufficient. This statement is not confirmed by the paragraph.

4. It seems that the council has promised to improve the state of lighting on side roads.

Ans. ***(a)*** **:** Mark the words "the council is prepared to make good its promise as regards the road lighting."

5. The accident occurred at night.

Ans. ***(a)*** **:** It must be night because the passage deals with unsatisfactory state of street lighting.

MULTIPLE CHOICE QUESTIONS

Directions : *Below are given some passages followed by several possible inferences which can be drawn from the facts stated in each passage. You have to examine each inference separately in the context of the passage and decide upon its degree of truth or falsity.*

Mark Answers	If you think...
(a) "Definitely True"	the inference properly follows from the statement of facts given.
(b) "Probably True"	the inference may be true in the light of the facts given but not definitely true.
(c) "Data Inadequate"	from the facts given it cannot be said whether the inference is likely to be true or false.
(d) "Probably False"	the inference is probably false in the light of the facts given though not definitely false.
(e) "Definitely False"	the inference cannot possibly be drawn from the facts given or it contradicts the given facts.

PASSAGE 1

Indian granite industry is in peril in the absence of a uniform policy from the state governments, despite the thrust given by liberalisation policies of the union government. Compared to the remarkable progress in the field during the last three years, the absence of matching policies by state governments had put granite quarry owners and others involved in the industry on the verge of collapse in the international market. The policies differed from state to state, had created problems as far as loyalty, dead rent and duration of lease were concerned.

1. Each state having granite quarry has set up its own rules which are contrary to the interest of the industry.
2. Till three years ago, granite production in India was not profitable.
3. The granite production is largely controlled by individuals.
4. The granite produced in India does not match with the quality of international level.
5. The union government's liberalisation policy became applicable to granite industry only during the last three years.

PASSAGE 2

Steel production has always been burdened with costs much higher than in comparable plants overseas. On the one hand custom duty on almost all steel imports has been reduced, on the other excise duty has been raised. Domestic steel products are now uncompetitive which in turn has led to the demand that both the custom and excise rates should be reviewed to prevent sickness in the industry.

6. The steel industry in general is making losses as a fall out of the government policy.
7. The cost of production of steel in other countries is less than that in India.
8. India can compete with the foreign countries in re gard to the price of steel with a favourable government policy.
9. Foreign steel has become cheaper comparative to domestic steel.
10. The government is considering lowering of excise duty on steel products.

PASSAGE 3

The annual domestic consumption of plastics in India is expected to grow between 2.5 and 3 million tonnes by the end of the Ist balls of the century from the current level of about one million tonnes. The global consumption of plastics now stands at 100 million tonnes. To sustain the present growth pattern, India would need two additional polymer plants of 1,000 tonnes every year till the turn of the Ist half of this century. Entrepreneurs should now think in lines of globalisation and promote projects of international capacity and they would have to look at technology transfer as well as upgradation and strategic and creative alliances.

11. The total domestic consumption of plastics in India is about one per cent of the global consumption.
12. At present India does not import plastics.
13. India lacks in technological capabilities in producing plastics.
14. There is an expected growth of about .2 per cent in the plastic consumption every year.
15. Potentially India can be one of the major players in the production of plastics in the international market.

EXPLANATORY ANSWERS

1. *(a)* : The policies differed from state to state.

2. *(c)* : Remarkable progress during the last three years is mentioned in the paragraph but nothing suggests that the production was not profitable.

3. *(a)* : There is absence of a uniform policy from the state Governments.

4. *(c)* : According to the paragraph, absence of matching policies had put the quarry owners and others involved in the industry on the verge of collapse in the international market. Nothing is mentioned about the granite quality produced in India or of the international level.

5. (*e*) : The inference does not relate to the facts given in the statement.

6. (*d*) : Government policy alone may not be responsible for the losses. Cost or quality factor may also be responsible.

7. (*c*) : The paragraph mentions that steel production in India has always been burdened with costs much higher than in comparable plants overseas. But nowhere in the paragraph it is mentioned that the cost of production of steel is less in other countries.

8. (*a*) : If the government reviews its policy, India can definitely compete with the foreign countries in regard to the steel price.

9. (*a*) : Customs duty on almost all steel products has been reduced.

10. (*b*) : There is a demand that both the customs and excise rates should be reviewed.

11. (*a*) : The global consumption of plastics is 100 million tonnes and current level of consumption in India is 1 million tonnes.

12. (*c*) : The paragraph does not mention about the import or export of plastics.

13. (*a*) : Entrepreneurs would have to look at technology transfer as well as upgradation and strategic and creative alliances.

14. (*a*) : The expected growth by end of the Ist half of this century is between 2.5 and 3 million tonnes. India needs 2 additional polymer plants of 1,000 tonnes per year.

15. (*a*) : By thinking in lines of globalisation and promoting projects of international capacity India can be one of the major players in the production of plastics in the international market.

CHAPTER 16

Trends

This type of questions are asked to assess the thinking pattern or mental trends of the candidate. These are simple questions but should be answered honestly and carefully.

MULTIPLE CHOICE QUESTIONS

Directions : *In the questions given below four alternatives have been given below each one of them. You have to select the right alternative according to your mind and mark it in your answer sheet.*

1. I like pre-defined rules and regulations.
(*a*) Sometimes (*b*) No
(*c*) Yes (*d*) No idea

2. I found a purse full of money in college premise. I:
(*a*) donated the amount among poor
(*b*) gave it to the principal
(*c*) offered it at temple
(*d*) None of these

3. I am punctual regarding
(*a*) going to bed (*b*) time
(*c*) meals (*d*) dating

4. I was travelling on a boat which capsized. Firstly, I:
(*a*) rescued others (*b*) saved myself
(*c*) closed my eyes (*d*) cursed my luck

5. When someone asks you for help in odd situations then:
(*a*) you give him/her all possible help
(*b*) you promise him/her help
(*c*) you do not help him/her
(*d*) you turn a deaf ear

6. In case my wristwatch is out of order, I:
(*a*) would try to repair it myself
(*b*) would give it to watchmaker
(*c*) would buy a new watch
(*d*) would throw it away

7. Often I change my opinion in the last moment.
(*a*) Yes (*b*) No
(*c*) Sometimes (*d*) No idea

8. Generally I am extrovert and well behaved.
(*a*) Yes (*b*) No
(*c*) Sometimes (*d*) No idea

9. I like to use new technique of work.
(*a*) Yes (*b*) No
(*c*) Sometimes (*d*) No idea

10. When someone considers you wrong then:
(*a*) you do not react
(*b*) you consider him/her wrong
(*c*) you try to ward off the misunderstanding on proper occasion.
(*d*) you pick a fight

11. The secret of my success is:
(*a*) hard labour (*b*) awakening in night
(*c*) gossiping (*d*) luck

12. If you are a female and you are talking with a male:
(*a*) You hide your age
(*b*) You are afraid
(*c*) You talk without hesitation
(*d*) You avoid talks

13. I do like rules and regulations.
(*a*) Yes (*b*) No
(*c*) Sometimes (*d*) No idea

14. Excellent ideas come to my mind:
(*a*) while working alone
(*b*) while working in a group
(*c*) while in sleep
(*d*) while in bathroom

15. Whenever my little baby cries loudly, then I
(*a*) beat him/her
(*b*) feed milk to him/her
(*c*) make him/her sleep
(*d*) ask my husband to handle him/her

16. When I see a mad person, I :
(*a*) approach towards him/her
(*b*) maintain distance from him/her
(*c*) throw stone at him/her
(*d*) start laughing at him/her

17. While driving my car I offer lift to people who ask for lift.
(*a*) Always (*b*) Sometimes
(*c*) Never (*d*) If she is a girl

18. When someone tries to convince you then:
(*a*) You get convinced
(*b*) You do not get convinced
(*c*) You hear him/her passionately
(*d*) You turn a deaf ear

19. Whenever someone knocks on my closed door then firstly I
(*a*) open the door
(*b*) peep through the lens fitted in the door
(*c*) do not open the door
(*d*) yell at him/her

20. I speak to others about my expectation and dreams.
(*a*) Rarely (*b*) Often
(*c*) Sometimes (*d*) Never

21. Any dispute can be solved by :
(*a*) quarrelling (*b*) court
(*c*) dialogue (*d*) money

22. When I do any foolish work then :
(*a*) I feel ashamed (*b*) I feel proud of myself
(*c*) Nothing happens (*d*) I weep

23. If I were correspondent of any newspaper then I would write on the following subject :
(*a*) Cinema and theatre
(*b*) Political events
(*c*) Sports
(*d*) Stock market

24. If I were not human being then :
(*a*) I wish to be a bird (*b*) I wish to be a horse
(*c*) I wish to be God (*d*) Can't say

25. Suppose, you have worn a new shirt and your friend passed a comment that it is not looking good on you. You :
(*a*) will change the shirt immediately
(*b*) will take it lightly as it is your style
(*c*) will not change the shirt but feel offended
(*d*) will start quarrelling

26. I wish to live alone always.
(*a*) Yes (*b*) No
(*c*) Sometimes (*d*) Never

27. I want to spend my spare (extra) time :
(*a*) in reading interesting books
(*b*) in reading comics
(*c*) in viewing films
(*d*) in gossiping

28. Before doing any work I ask myself 'Is it appropriate'?
(*a*) Yes (*b*) No
(*c*) Sometimes (*d*) Never

29. If I see the GOD, I will ask for
(*a*) huge wealth (*b*) honesty
(*c*) love (*d*) heaven

30. People call you selfish.
(*a*) Always (*b*) Sometimes
(*c*) Never (*d*) No idea

31. While talking to friends I do not like to express my very personal matters.
(*a*) Yes (*b*) No
(*c*) Sometimes (*d*) Never

32. Consultation with others helps me to take a decision.
(*a*) Yes (*b*) No
(*c*) Sometimes (*d*) Never

33. After failure:
(*a*) One repents
(*b*) One tries again to succeed
(*c*) Nothing special is happened
(*d*) Nothing in life remains

34. I want to be convinced by arguments.
(*a*) Yes (*b*) No
(*c*) Sometimes (*d*) Never

ANSWERS

1	2	3	4	5	6	7	8	9	10
(*c*)	(*b*)	(*b*)	(*b*)	(*a*)	(*b*)	(*b*)	(*a*)	(*a*)	(*c*)
11	**12**	**13**	**14**	**15**	**16**	**17**	**18**	**19**	**20**
(*a*)	(*c*)	(*a*)	(*a*)	(*b*)	(*b*)	(*b*)	(*a*)	(*b*)	(*a*)
21	**22**	**23**	**24**	**25**	**26**	**27**	**28**	**29**	**30**
(*c*)	(*a*)	(*c*)	(*a*)	(*b*)	(*c*)	(*a*)	(*a*)	(*c*)	(*c*)
31	**32**	**33**	**34**						
(*c*)	(*a*)	(*b*)	(*a*)						

CHAPTER

17

Critical

In this type of reasoning, a statement is given and assumptions are drawn from it. An assumption is something assumed, supposed and taken for granted. The implicity of the two assumptions is in question. The implication means the hidden meaning, something which is derived from and as such based upon the statement.

MULTIPLE CHOICE QUESTIONS

Directions (Qs. 1 to 6): *In each question below are given two statements followed by two conclusions numbered I and II. You have to take the two given statements to be true even if they seem to be at variance from commonly known facts and then decide which of the given conclusions logically follows from the two given statements, disregarding commonly known facts. Read both the statements and—*

Give answer (a) if only conclusion I follows; give answer (b) if only conclusion II follows; give answer (c) if either I or II follows; give answer (d) if neither I nor II follows and give answer (e) if both I and II follows.

1. *Statements* *I* : All tomatoes are red.
II : All grapes are tomatoes.
Conclusions *I* : All grapes are red.
II : Some tomatoes are grapes.

2. *Statements* *I* : All painters are smilling.
II : Some authors are painters.
Conclusions *I* : All smiling authors are painters.
II : Some authors are smiling.

3. *Statements* *I* : All peons in this office are efficient.
II : Ramu is not efficient.
Conclusions *I* : Ramu is not peon in this office.
II : Ramu should be more efficient.

4. *Statements* *I* : All weavers are hard working.
II : No hard working men are foolish.
Conclusions *I* : No weavers are foolish.
II : Some foolish are weavers.

5. *Statements* *I* : All fishes are cars.
II : All cars are vegetables.
Conclusions *I* : Some vegetables are cars.
II : Some vegetables are fishes.

6. *Statements* *I* : Some dogs are pups.
II : All horses are pups.

Directions (Qs. 7 to 10): *In each question below is given a statement followed by three assumptions number I, II and III. An assumption is something supposed or taken for granted. You have to consider the statement along with the assumptions and decide which of the assumptions is implicit in the statement. Then decide which of the alternatives is the correct answer.*

7. *Statement :*

"Use Riya Cold Cream for fair complexion"—an advertisement.

Assumptions :

I. People like to use cream for fair complexion.
II. People are easily fooled.
III. People respond to advertisements.

(*a*) Only I is implicit.
(*b*) Only II is implicit.
(*c*) Only I and III are implicit.
(*d*) Only I and II are implicit.
(*e*) All are implicit.

8. *Statement :*

"Slogans against smoking in office should be put on the notice board"—an employee in an office suggests.

Assumptions :

I. The employee felt that his suggestion will be considered.
II. People smoke in the office.
III. Some people will stop smoking after reading the slogans.

(*a*) Only I is implicit.
(*b*) Only I and II are implicit.
(*c*) Only II and III are implicit.

(*d*) None is implicit.
(*e*) All are implicit.

9. *Statement :*
"I want to present him a book on techniques of yoga on his birthday"—A tells B.
Assumptions :
I. A and B will be invited for the birthday celebrations.
II. The person to whom the book is to be presented, is not keeping good health.
III. Book is the best gift for birthdays.
(*a*) Only I and II are implicit.
(*b*) Only II and III are implicit.
(*c*) Only I and III are implicit.
(*d*) None is implicit.
(*e*) All are implicit

10. *Statement :*
Keeping in view the financial constraint, the management institution has decided to charge at the time of providing employment in various organisations, a placement fee of ₹ 25000 from the organisation in which the student will be provided the employment.
Assumptions :
I. It will help in increasing the demand of the students belonging to the management institution.
II. The amount collected in this way will be purposeful.
III. It may be possible that the organisation providing employment may select less number of students in future.
(*a*) None follows.
(*b*) Only II and III follow.
(*c*) Only I follows.
(*d*) Only I and II follow.
(*e*) None of these

EXPLANATORY ANSWERS

1. (*e*) : When all tomatoes are red and all grapes are tomatoes, then all grapes are also red. When all grapes are tomatoes, then some tomatoes must be grapes. Therefore, both conclusions I and II are correct.

2. (*b*) : When all painters are smiling and some authors are painters, then some authors are smiling. Therefore, only conclusion II is correct.

3. (*a*) : When all the peons of the office are efficient, then Ramu cannot be a peon in this office. Therefore, only conclusion I is correct.

4. (*a*) : When all weavers are hardworking and no hardworking men are foolish, then no weavers are foolish. Therefore, only conclusion I is correct.

5. (*e*) : When all fishes are cars and all cars are vegetables, then all fishes will naturally be vegetables. This means that some vegetables are fishes. And when all cars are vegetables, then some vegetables will be cars naturally. Therefore, both the conclusions I and II are correct.

6. (*d*) : No relationship can be established between the two statements. Therefore, neither conclusion I nor conclusion II is correct.

7. (*c*) : The advertisement itself denotes that people like to use cream for fair complexion and they do respond to advertisements. Advertisements are for awareness of the product not for fooling people.

8. (*e*) : Suggestion for putting up the notice is made because some people must be smoking in office. Notice board is read by people in office and some may stop smoking after reading the slogans.

9. (*c*) : According to A presents are best gifts for birthdays and when A has bought the book he expects to be invited for the birthday celebration. Nothing is mentioned about health of the birthday person.

10. (*b*) : The amount collected will lessen the financial constraint and there is every possibility for selecting less number of students because of the fee charged.

CHAPTER 18

Emotional Intelligence

Emotional intelligence (EI) refers to the ability to perceive, control, and evaluate emotions. Emotional intelligence (EI) is the area of cognitive ability involving traits and social skills that facilitate interpersonal behaviour. Intelligence can be broadly defined as the capacity for goal-oriented adaptive behaviour; emotional intelligence focuses on the aspects of intelligence that govern self-knowledge and social adaptation.

Emotional Intelligence that is also called Emotional Intelligence Quotient or (EQ) narrates the capability, capacity, or deftness to understand. It evaluates and manages one's emotions.

MULTIPLE CHOICE QUESTIONS

Directions: *Answer the following questions by selecting the appropriate option.*

1. In my group of friends, I am generally aware of how each person feels about the other people in our social circle.
(*a*) Strongly Agree (*b*) Agree
(*c*) Disagree (*d*) Strongly Disagree

2. When I am upset, I can usually pinpoint exactly why I am distressed.
(*a*) Strongly Agree (*b*) Agree
(*c*) Disagree (*d*) Strongly Disagree

3. While there are some things that I would like to change, I generally like who I am.
(*a*) Strongly Agree (*b*) Agree
(*c*) Disagree (*d*) Strongly Disagree

4. When I make mistakes, I often berate and criticize myself and my abilities.
(*a*) Often (*b*) Sometimes
(*c*) Rarely (*d*) Almost Never

5. I feel uncomfortable in emotionally charged situations.
(*a*) Strongly Agree (*b*) Agree
(*c*) Disagree (*d*) Strongly Disagree

6. I tend to avoid confrontations. When I am involved in a confrontation, I become extremely anxious.
(*a*) Strongly Agree (*b*) Agree
(*c*) Disagree (*d*) Strongly Disagree

7. I am generally aloof and detached until I really get to know a person.
(*a*) Strongly Agree (*b*) Agree
(*c*) Disagree (*d*) Strongly Disagree

8. I tend to overreact to minor problems.
(*a*) Often (*b*) Sometimes
(*c*) Rarely (*d*) Almost Never

9. I feel confident about my own skills, talents, and abilities.
(*a*) Strongly Agree (*b*) Agree
(*c*) Disagree (*d*) Strongly Disagree

10. I would describe myself as a good judge of character.
(*a*) Strongly Agree (*b*) Agree
(*c*) Disagree (*d*) Strongly Disagree

11. When I am facing an unpleasant task, I tend to:
(*a*) Make a plan and work on it a little each day
(*b*) Get it over with as soon as possible
(*c*) Put it off until the last minute
(*d*) Don't do it at all

12. During a heated argument, I am more likely to:
(*a*) Stop the fight and agree to a short break before resuming the discussion.
(*b*) Shut down and stop responding to the other person.
(*c*) Give in and apologize in order to quickly end the argument.
(*d*) Start insulting the other person.

13. When making an important decision, I tend to:
(*a*) Follow my instincts
(*b*) Rely on direction from other people
(*c*) Go with the easiest option
(*d*) Guess randomly

14. Which of the following statements best describes you?
(*a*) I have an easy time making friends and getting to know new people.
(*b*) I get along well with others, but I have to really get to know someone before they become a true friend.
(*c*) I find it difficult to meet people and make friends.
(*d*) I cannot make friends.

15. You have invested a lot of time and energy into a project for one of your classes. While you feel confident about your work, your instructor gives you a C+ on the project. How do you deal with this situation?
(*a*) Decide the class is stupid and stop putting forth your best efforts.
(*b*) Berate and criticize your own work.
(*c*) Confront the instructor and ask for a better grade.
(*d*) Think about ways you could improve the project and apply these ideas to future schoolwork.

16. One of your best friends has suffered a miscarriage. How do you respond?
(*a*) Allow your friend to express her feelings and offer your support.
(*b*) Spend time with her, but avoid talking about her loss.
(*c*) Convince her to go out with some friends to get her mind off it.
(*d*) Give her some time to herself.

17. One of your co-workers has a habit that annoys you. The problem seems to be getting worse each day. How do you respond?
(*a*) Tell your co-worker what is bothering you.
(*b*) Make a complaint about the behaviour to your supervisor.
(*c*) Talk about your co-worker behind his back.
(*d*) Suffer in silence.

18. You've been feeling stressed out at work and haven't finished projects as quickly as you should. When your boss suddenly assigns you another large project, how do you feel?
(*a*) Anxious about getting all the work done.
(*b*) Overwhelmed by the task before you.
(*c*) Angry that your boss hasn't noticed how overworked you are.
(*d*) Depressed and sure that you can never finish it all.

19. If I am scheduled to meet a loved one at a certain time and that person is late, I get worried and eventually start to panic:
(*a*) Frequently (*b*) Sometimes
(*c*) Rarely (*d*) Never

20. Others do not want to spend time with me in public because my behaviour embarrasses them.
(*a*) Frequently (*b*) Sometimes
(*c*) Rarely (*d*) Never

21. I prevent being in situations where I need to show compassion and affection because I feel uncomfortable comforting others.
(*a*) Frequently (*b*) Sometimes
(*c*) Rarely (*d*) Never

22. When I am angry, I do not care about what I say or do and end up saying and doing things I regret later and need to apologize for.
(*a*) Frequently (*b*) Sometimes
(*c*) Rarely (*d*) Never

23. I feel frequently depressed and unhappy without really knowing why.
(*a*) Frequently (*b*) Sometimes
(*c*) Rarely (*d*) Never

24. If others point out my mistakes or give me negative feedback about myself, I feel ashamed, embarrassed and then become offensive and angry.
(*a*) Frequently (*b*) Sometimes
(*c*) Rarely (*d*) Never

25. Crying makes me feel better so I frequently cry when I am angry, ashamed, or embarrassed.
(*a*) Frequently (*b*) Sometimes
(*c*) Rarely (*d*) Never

ANSWERS

1	2	3	4	5	6	7	8	9	10
(*b*)	(*b*)	(*a*)	(*b*)	(*d*)	(*d*)	(*c*)	(*d*)	(*a*)	(*b*)
11	**12**	**13**	**14**	**15**	**16**	**17**	**18**	**19**	**20**
(*a*)	(*a*)	(*a*)	(*a*)	(*d*)	(*a*)	(*a*)	(*a*)	(*c*)	(*d*)
21	**22**	**23**	**24**	**25**					
(*d*)	(*d*)	(*d*)	(*d*)	(*d*)					

CHAPTER 19

Social Intelligence

Questions on social intelligence are asked to assess the common sense of the candidate in various social situations.

MULTIPLE CHOICE QUESTIONS

Directions : *Each of the following questions is followed by four alternatives. Select the most appropriate answer.*

1. In the examination hall, you find that your question paper is too tough to be answered satisfactorily by you. The best thing you can do is:
(*a*) try cheating from your neighbouring candidate.
(*b*) leave the paper and walk out.
(*c*) try attempting those questions first of which you know something.
(*d*) complain to the examiner about the toughness of the question paper.

2. Your best friend is annoyed with you for certain reasons. You will :
(*a*) try your best to reason out your friend's annoyance.
(*b*) go out and make new friends.
(*c*) show indifference.
(*d*) remind the friend of your good friendship.

3. You were invited to a party, but on the day of the party you are informed that the party has been cancelled. You will :
(*a*) try to find out the reason for its cancellation.
(*b*) decide that you will never go to that place ever again.
(*c*) not discuss the matter with anyone.
(*d*) hold the party at your place instead.

4. You find that the cooking gas cylinder is leaking. The first thing you would do is :
(*a*) switch off the light.
(*b*) close the knob of the cylinder.
(*c*) call the fire brigade for help.
(*d*) alert all the members at home.

5. While returning home from a far away place you find that your pocket has been picked. You will :
(*a*) try to hitch-hike to home.
(*b*) hire a taxi and pay on reaching home.
(*c*) go to the nearest police station and lodge an FIR.
(*d*) call home and ask someone to pick you from the place you made the phone call.

6. Your friend has not invited you to his marriage party, you will :
(*a*) ignore the whole affair.
(*b*) send him your best wishes.
(*c*) attend the ceremony.
(*d*) hold it against him.

7. You are interviewed for a new job. Which of the following questions is most important to you?
(*a*) Remuneration you will be paid.
(*b*) Opportunities for promotion.
(*c*) Scope to develop your ideas and use them to improve the working of the organisation.
(*d*) All the above are equally important.

8. You are walking down the street and suddenly you see two hundred-rupee notes on the pavement. What action will you take?
(*a*) Give the money to beggar.
(*b*) Pocket it yourself.
(*c*) Deposit it in the nearest police station.
(*d*) Leave it as it is.

ANSWERS

1	2	3	4	5	6	7	8
(*c*)	(*a*)	(*a*)	(*b*)	(*b*)	(*b*)	(*d*)	(*c*)

INDEXING ADDRESS MATCHING

Directions : *In each question below a combination of name and address is given in the first column at the left, followed by four such combinations, one each under the columns (a), (b), (c) and (d). You have to find out the combination which is exactly the same as the combination in the first column. The number of that column which contains that combination is the answer. If all the combinations are different, the answer is '(e)'.*

1. Triveni Atma
Opp Lal Banglow
Varanasi -221002

(*a*) Triveni Atma
Opp Lal Bangalow
Varanasi -221002

(*b*) Triveni Atma
Opp Lal Banglow
Varanasi -220012

(*c*) Triveni Atma
Opp Lal Banglow
Varanasi -221002

(*d*) Triveni Athma
Opp Lal Banglow
Varanasi -221002

2. Tara Lal Appa
Javagal street
Calicat 673005

(*a*) Tara Lal Appa
Javagal Street
Calicat 673005

(*b*) Tara Lal Appa
Javagal street
Calicut 673005

(*c*) Tara Lal Appa
Javagal street
Calicat 670035

(*d*) Tara Lal Appa
Javagal streat
Calicat 673005

3. Iqbal Rehman
Bhandri Gali
Post Box No -3097

(*a*) Iqbal Rehman
Bhandri Ghali
Post Box No -3097

(*b*) Iqbal Rehman
Bhandri Gali
Post Box No -3097

(*c*) Iqbal Rehman
Bhandri Gali
Post Box no -3097

(*d*) Iqbal Rahman
Bhandri Gali
Post Box No -3097

4. Jaganpa Shinde
Christ phot co.
Tel no -27363

(*a*) Jaganpa Shinde
Christ photo co.
Tel no -27363

(*b*) Jaganpa Shinde
Christ phot co.
Tel no -27363

(*c*) Jaganpa Shinde
Christ phot co.
Tel no -273633

(*d*) Jaganna Shinde
Christ phot co.
Tel no -27363

5. N.R. Savitri
Giri Girls hostal
Anapuram-167951

(*a*) N.R. Savitri
Giri Girls hostal
Anapuram-167951

(*b*) N.R. Savitri
Giri Girls hostel
Anapuram-167951

(*c*) N.R. Savitri
Giri Girls hostal
Anapuram-167851

(*d*) N.R. Savithri
Giri Girls hostal
Anapuram-167951

6. Madam Brulopher
Jung villa
Banjaram Hills

(*a*) Madam Bruloper
Jung villa
Banjaram Hills

(*b*) Madam Brulopher
Jung villa
Banjaram Hill

(*c*) Madam Brulopher
Jung Villa
Banjaram Hills

(*d*) Madam Brulopher
Jung villa
Banjaram Hills

7. Samartha sen
C 20/05 Guftga Bldg
B. No. - 1631

(*a*) Samartha sen
C 20/05 Guftga Blg
B. No. - 1631

(*b*) Samartha sen
C 200 Guftga Bldg
B. No. - 1631

(*c*) Samartha sen
C 20/05 Guftga Bldg
B. No. - 1631

(*d*) Samartha sen
C 20/05 Guflga Bldg
B. No. - 1631

8. Phiroz Gerabl
Harmit palace
Samaita nagar

(*a*) Phiroz Gerabi
Harmit palace
Samaita nagar

(*b*) Phiroz Gerabl
Harmit place
Samaita nagar

(*c*) Phiroz Gerabl
Harmit palace
Samaita nager

(*d*) Phiroz Gherabl
Harmit palace
Samaita nagar

9. Nitu gajadhar
Shersing Haveli
Jaipur -302006

(*a*) Nitu gajadhar
Shersing Haveli
Jaipur -302006

(*b*) Nitu gajadar
Shersing Haveli
Jaipur -302006

(*c*) Nitu gajadhar
Shersing Haveli
Jaipur -303006

(*d*) Nitu Gajadhar
Shersing Haveli
Jaipur -302006

ANSWERS

1	2	3	4	5	6	7	8	9
(*c*)	(*a*)	(*b*)	(*b*)	(*a*)	(*d*)	(*c*)	(*d*)	(*a*)

CHAPTER 20

Venn Diagrams

In these type of questions diagrammatic representation presents a logical illustration of particular class or statements based on which the questions are asked. A clear view of the diagram makes the concept clear for attempting such questions.

SOLVED EXAMPLE

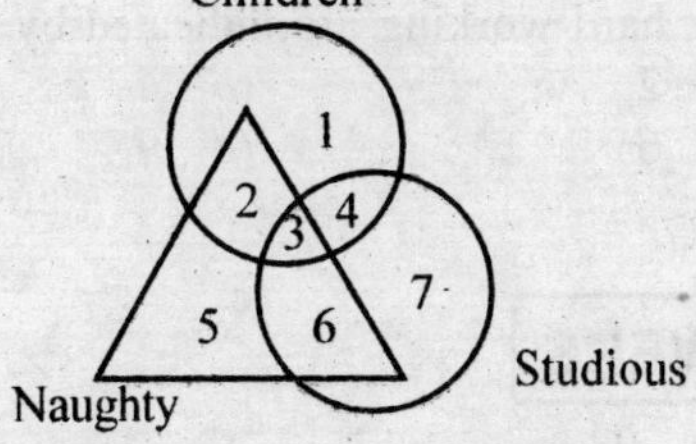

Study the above diagram and specify the region representing children who are naughty as well as studious.

(*a*) 3 and 6 (*b*) 2 and 4
(*c*) only 3 (*d*) only 4

Ans. (*c*) : The explanation depicting children who are naughty as well as studious will be :

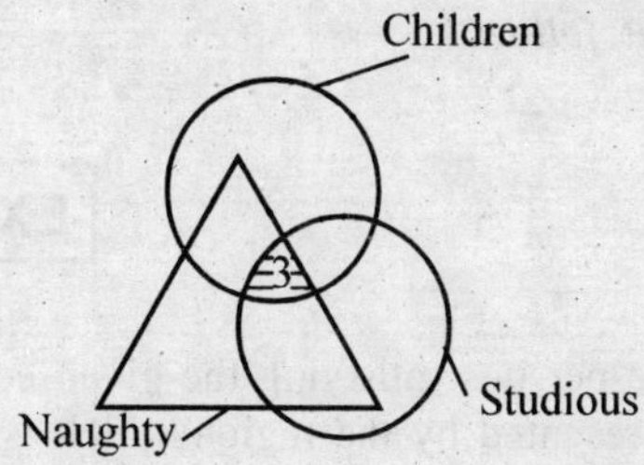

It is now clear that only region 3 represents all the three classes.

MULTIPLE CHOICE QUESTIONS

Directions (Qs. 1–3) : *In the following diagram, there are three figures interlocking each other – a rectangle, a square and a triangle. Each figure represents the class mentioned against it.*

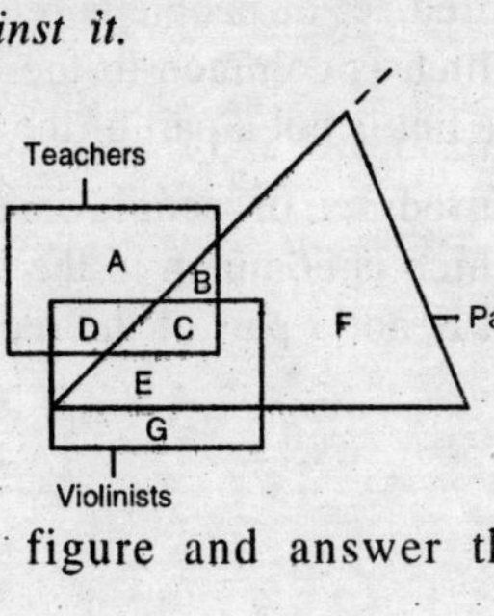

Study the figure and answer the questions that follows.

1. Teachers who are painters but not violinists are represented by

(*a*) B (*b*) C
(*c*) D (*d*) F

2. The region which represents painters and violinists but not teachers, is denoted by

(*a*) B (*b*) D
(*c*) E (*d*) F

3. Which letter represents teachers who are painters as well as violinists?

(*a*) B (*b*) C
(*c*) D (*d*) E

Directions (Qs. 4–6) : *In the figure given below, there are three interesting circles each representing certain section of people. Different regions are marked a-g. Read the statements in each of the following questions and choose the letter of the region which correctly represents the statements?*

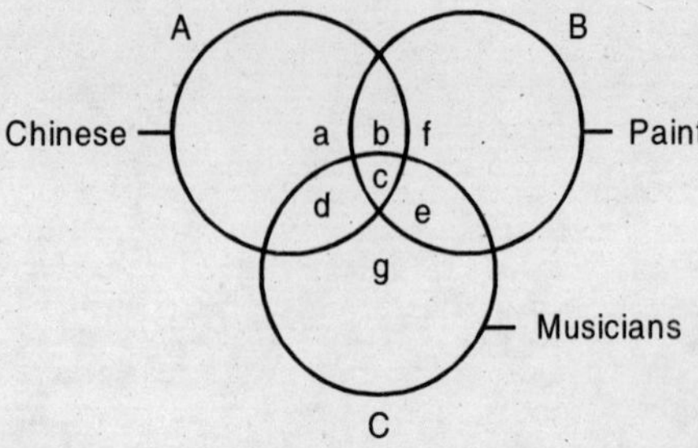

4. Chinese who are painters but not musicians?
(*a*) b (*b*) c
(*c*) d (*d*) g

5. Chinese who are musicians but not painters.
(*a*) d (*b*) c
(*c*) b (*d*) a

6. Painters who are neither Chinese nor musicians.
(*a*) b (*b*) c
(*c*) f (*d*) g

Directions (Qs. 7–10) : *In the following figure, the circle stands for employed, the square stands for hard-working, the triangle stands for rural and the rectangle stands for intelligent. Study the figure carefully and answer the questions that follow.*

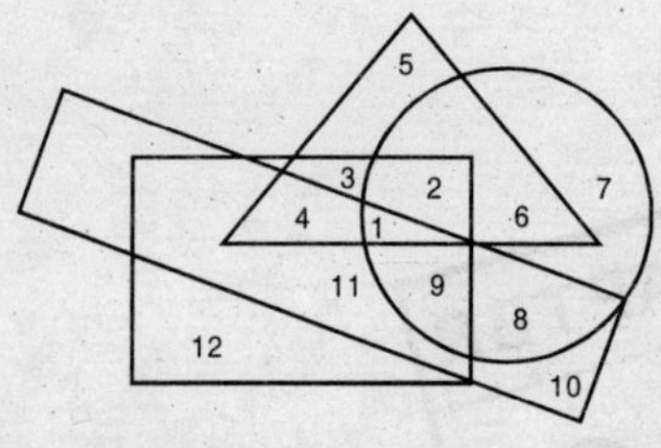

7. Rural employed people who are neither intelligent nor hard-working are indicated by region.
(*a*) 10 (*b*) 9
(*c*) 6 (*d*) 4

8. Unemployed rural hard-working and intelligent people are indicated by region.
(*a*) 1 (*b*) 2
(*c*) 3 (*d*) 4

9. Rural people who are hard-working and employed but not intelligent are indicated by region.
(*a*) 1 (*b*) 2
(*c*) 3 (*d*) 4

10. Rural employed people who are neither intelligent nor hard-working are indicated by region.
(*a*) 2 (*b*) 4
(*c*) 6 (*d*) 9

EXPLANATORY ANSWERS

1. (*a*) : The persons satisfying the given conditions are represented by the region which is common to the rectangle and the triangle but not the square i.e. B.

2. (*c*) : The persons satisfying the given conditions are represented by the region which is common to the triangle and the square but is not a part of the rectangle i.e. E.

3. (*b*) : The required set of persons is represented by the letter denoting the region common to the rectangle, triangle and the square i.e. C.

4. (*a*) : The required region is the one which is common to the circles A and B and lies outside circle C i.e. b.

5. (*a*) : The required region is the one which is common to the circles A and C but is not a part of circle B i.e. d.

6. (*c*) : The required region is the one which lies inside the circle B but is not a part of either circle A or circle C i.e. f.

7. (*c*) : The required set of people is represented by the region which is common to the triangle and circle but is not a part of either the rectangle or the square i.e. 6.

8. (*d*) : The required set of people is represented by the region which lies outside the circle and is common to the triangle, square and rectangle i.e. 4.

9. (*b*) : The required set of people is represented by the region which is common to the triangle, square and circle but is not a part of the rectangle i.e. 2.

10. (*c*) : The required set of people is denoted by the region which is common to the triangle and the circle but is not a part of the rectangle i.e. 2.

CHAPTER 1

Series/Figural Series

MISSING SERIES

This form of series is almost identical to the one mentioned earlier. Here too are given two sets of figures, the Problem Figures and the Answer Figures. The problem figures follow a particular pattern of movement which constitute the series. The only difference from the earlier mentioned set of series is that instead of depicting the last figure that continues the pattern here one of the middle figures needs to be depicted from-the answer figures. This type needs a little more concentration and brain work as the continuity is broken and has to be set right. Understand the set up of elements, pattern and figures in each set and try different styles and rules to find the answer.

SOLVED EXAMPLES

In each question below there are two sets of figures, first problem figures and then follows the answer figures. One of the answer figures should fit into the box where a question mark is placed in the set of problem figures. The letter of the answer figure which should be considered as forming the series and should be placed in the question marked box is the answer.

1. Problem Figures

Answer Figures

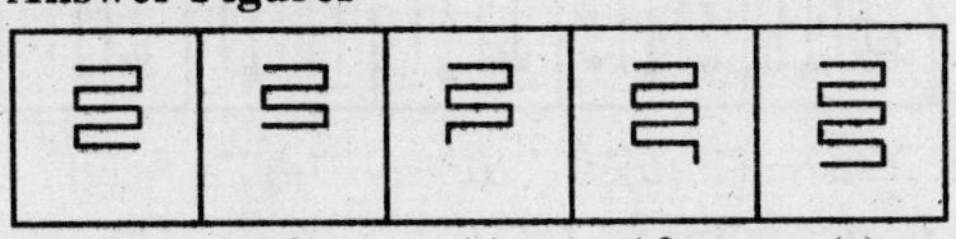

(*a*) (*b*) (*c*) (*d*) (*e*)

Answer (*a*) : Observe the set of problem figures. The design made of straight lines is becoming bigger at each step. In first figure there are two lines segments and in second figure three lines segments are increased. To continue the pattern four line segments should be increased so that further five line segments added in the last figure can complete the series. Answer figure (*a*) contains four more line segments and hence, is the right answer.

2. Problem Figures

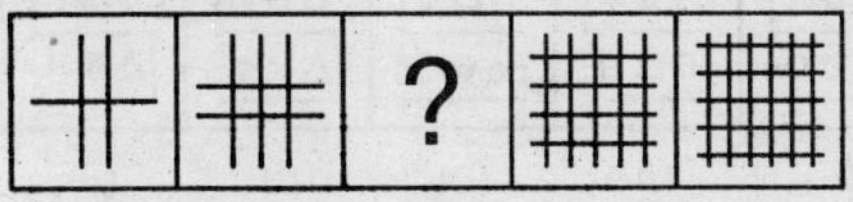

Answer Figures

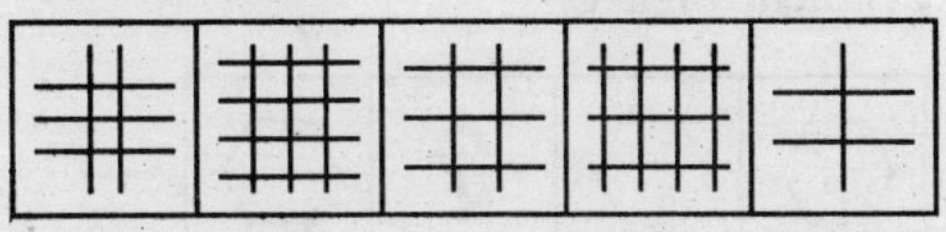

(*a*) (*b*) (*c*) (*d*) (*e*)

Answer (*d*) : Observe that at each step one vertical and one horizontal line is added. By this rule answer figure (*a*) fits in the question marked space. Note that answer figure (*b*) can also be considered in absence of option (*d*), but here the point to be noted is that the number of horizontal lines is one more than the number of vertical lines. So, answer figure (*d*), is the answer.

3. Problem Figures

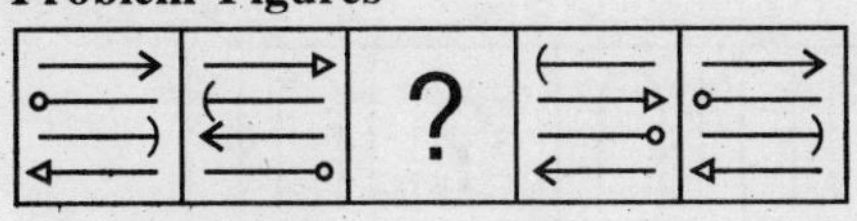

Answer Figures

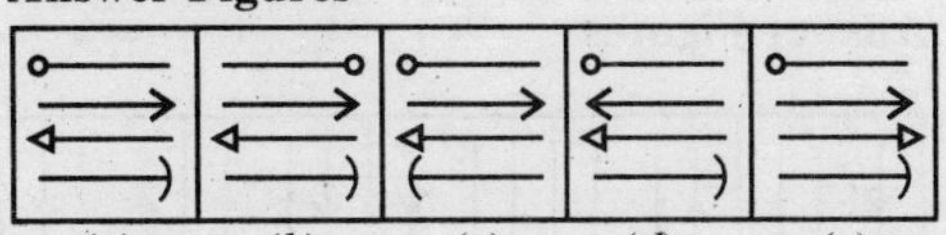

(*a*) (*b*) (*c*) (*d*) (*e*)

Answer (*a*) : Note that the fourth or the bottom element is made the first or the topmost element in the next figure. Similarly, the third element is made the second, the second element made the fourth and the first element made the third. Also, the direction of the elements is changed at each step. By the process mentioned above, answer figure A is the right choice to be considered as forming the series.

MULTIPLE CHOICE QUESTIONS

Directions : *In each of these questions, there are two sets of figures. The figures placed first are Problem Figures, and those follows are Answer Figures indicated by the letters (a), (b), (c), (d) and (e). A series is established if one of the five Answer Figures is placed at the question-marked space. Figures form a series if they change from left to right according to some specific rule. The letter of the Answer Figure which should be placed in the question-marked space is the answer. All the figures, i.e. three Problem Figures and one Answer Figure placed in the question-marked space should be considered as forming the series.*

1. Problem Figures

Answer Figures

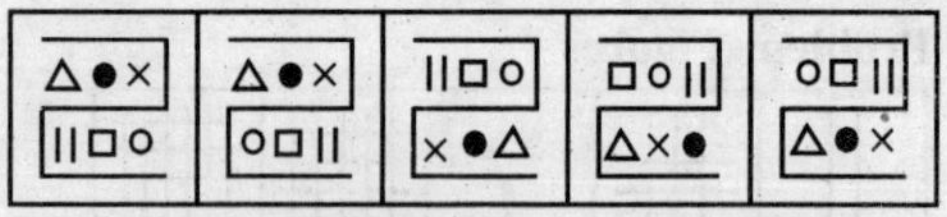

(a) (b) (c) (d) (e)

2. Problem Figures

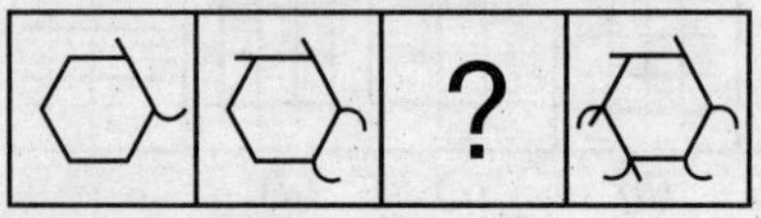

Answer Figures

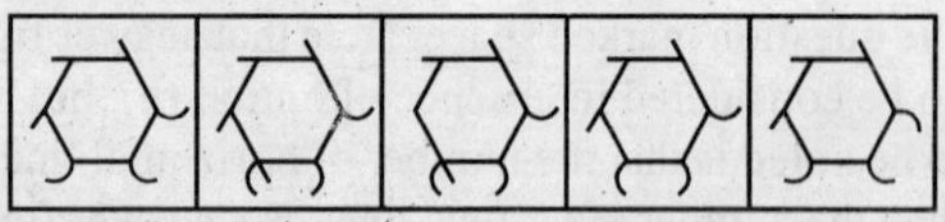

(a) (b) (c) (d) (e)

3. Problem Figures

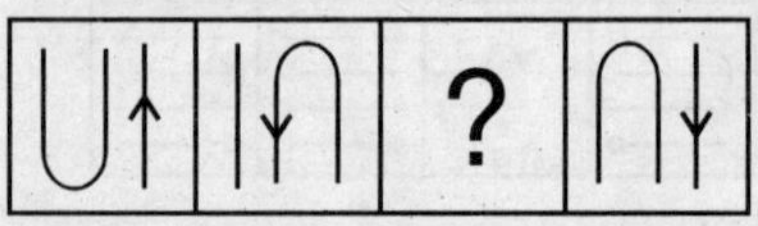

Answer Figures

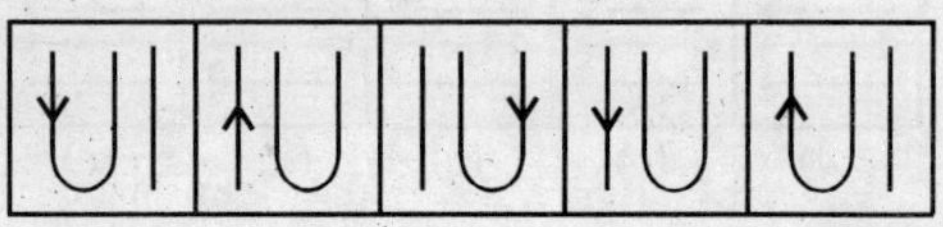

(a) (b) (c) (d) (e)

4. Problem Figures

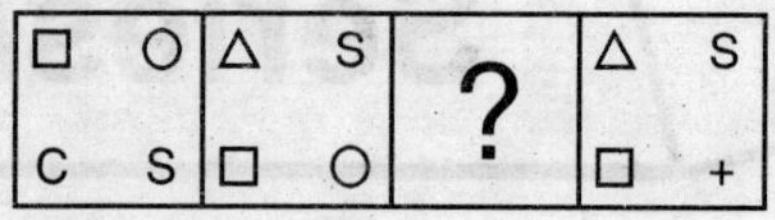

Answer Figures

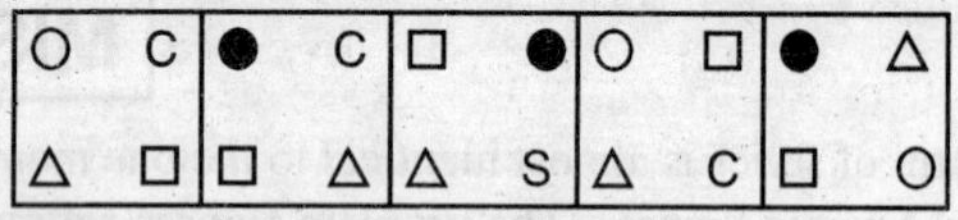

(a) (b) (c) (d) (e)

5. Problem Figures

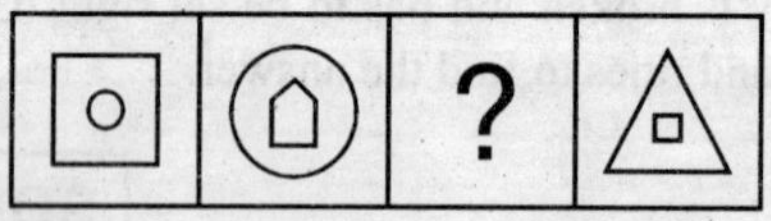

Answer Figures

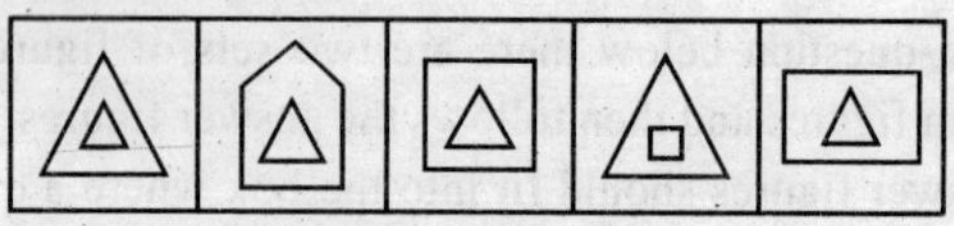

(a) (b) (c) (d) (e)

6. Problem Figures

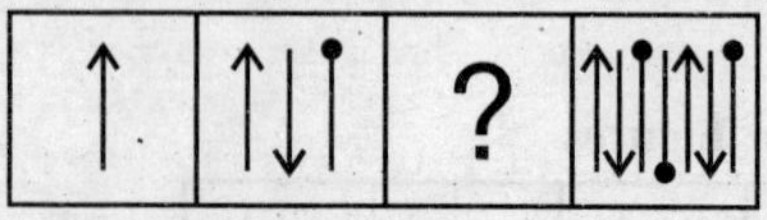

Answer Figures

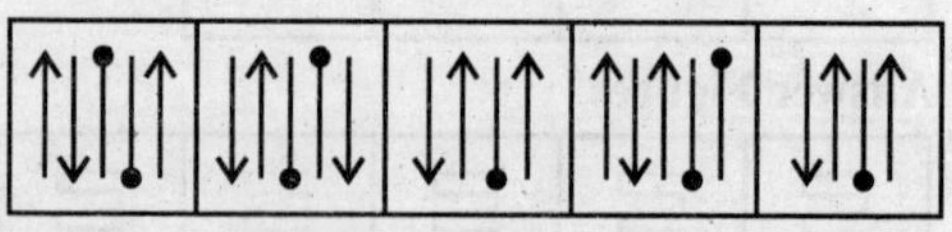

(a) (b) (c) (d) (e)

7. Problem Figures

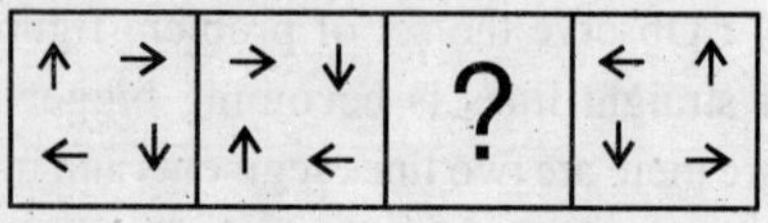

Answer Figures

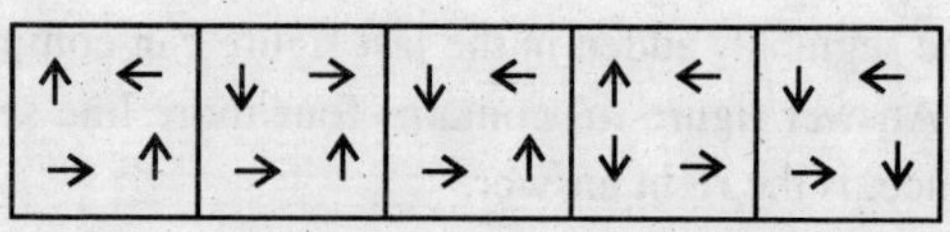

(a) (b) (c) (d) (e)

8. Problem Figures

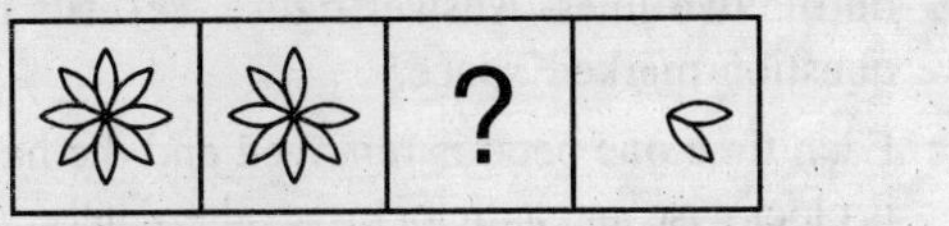

Answer Figures

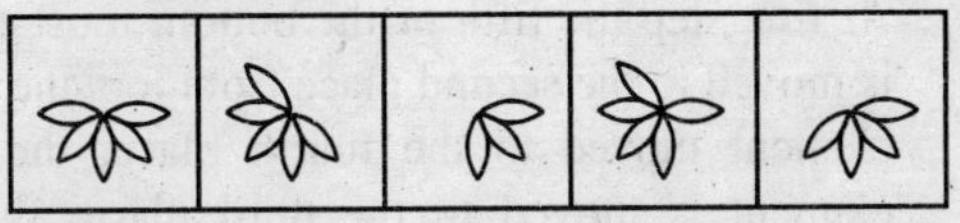

(a) (b) (c) (d) (e)

9. Problem Figures

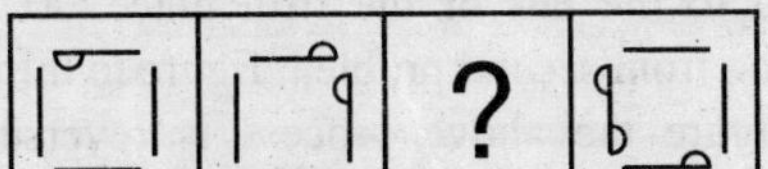

Answer Figures

(a) (b) (c) (d) (e)

10. Problem Figures

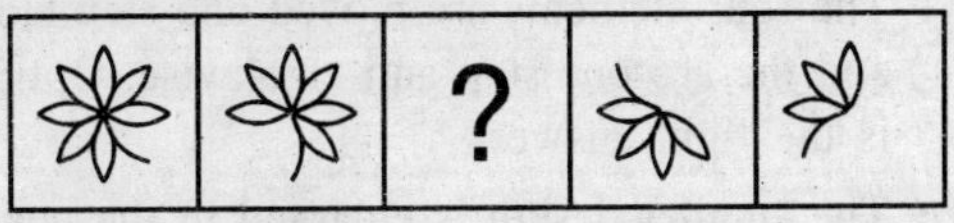

Answer Figures

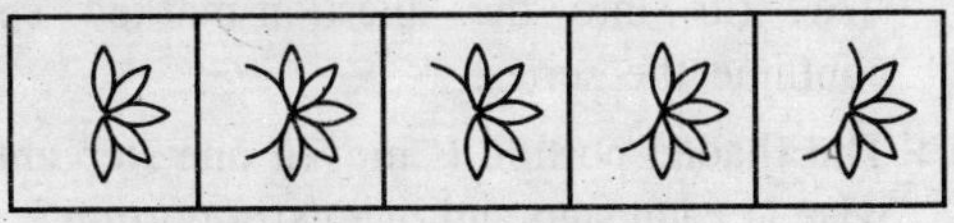

(a) (b) (c) (d) (e)

11. Problem Figures

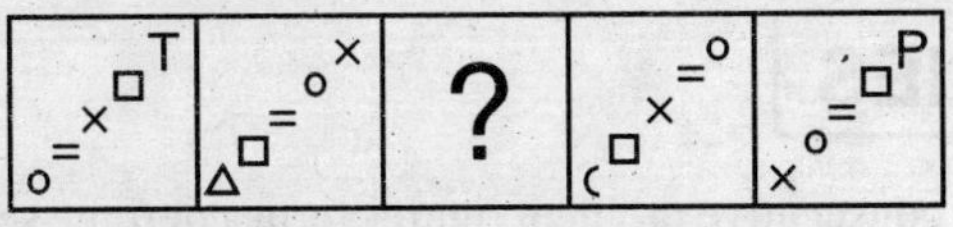

Answer Figures

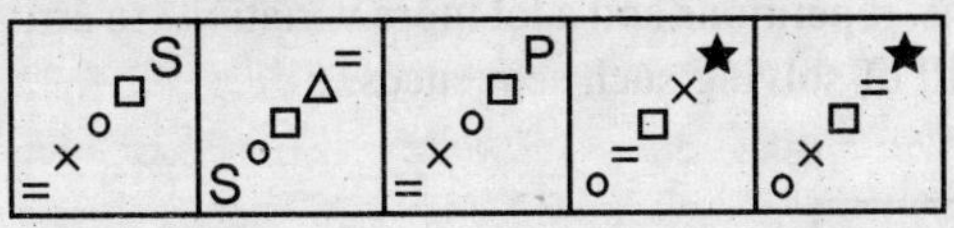

(a) (b) (c) (d) (e)

12. Problem Figures

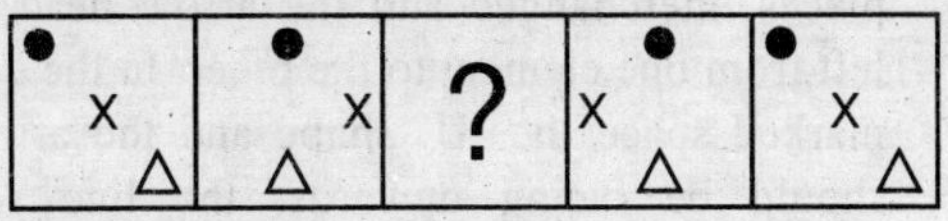

Answer Figures

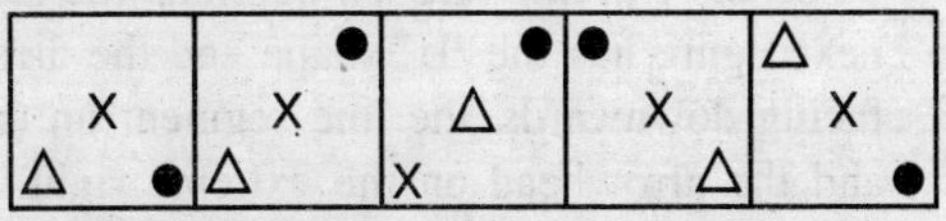

(a) (b) (c) (d) (e)

13. Problem Figures

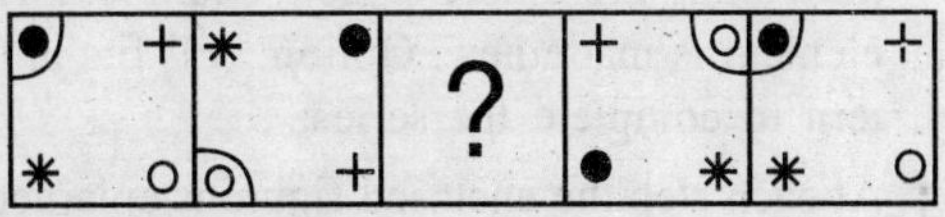

Answer Figures

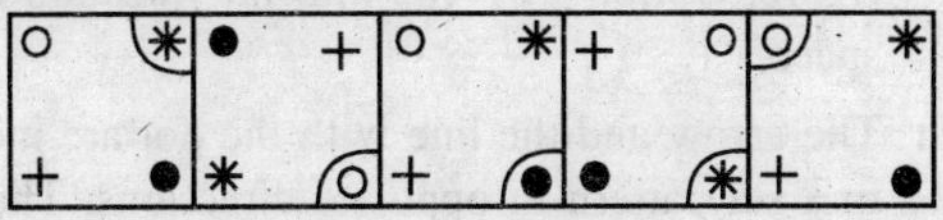

(a) (b) (c) (d) (e)

14. Problem Figures

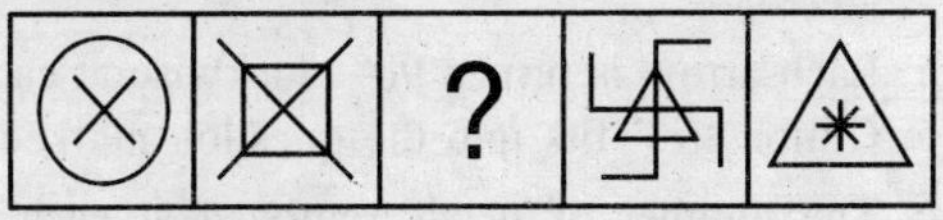

Answer Figures

(a) (b) (c) (d) (e)

15. Problem Figures

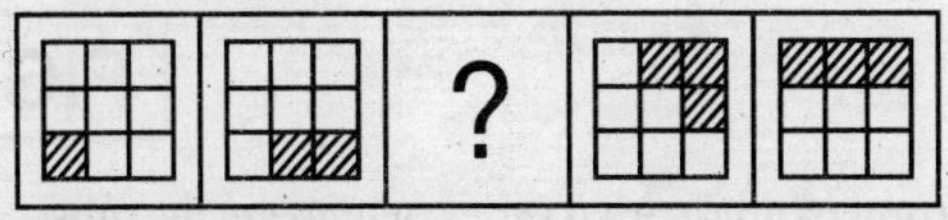

Answer Figures

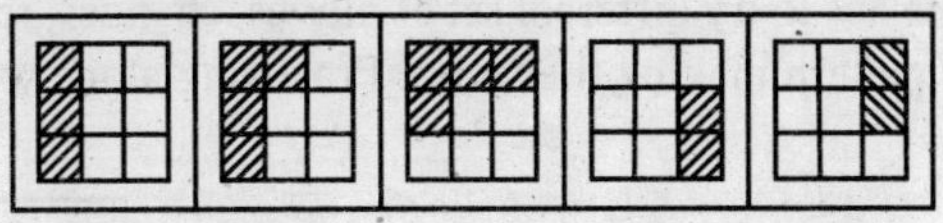

(a) (b) (c) (d) (e)

EXPLANATORY ANSWERS

1. (*c*) : From first problem figure to the second the elements on the top are shifted down and vice versa. In fourth problem figure there are three elements which, as per rule, are also shifted. So, in question marked space only option '(*c*)' can be considered as forming the series.

2. (*d*) : Anticlockwise one of the sides of the hexagon is extended and clockwise one arc is added. The direction of the arc is changed at each step. Answer figure 'D' is the right answer.

3. (*e*) : Both the elements are turned upside down, their places interchanged and the arrow head moved left from one element to the other. In the question marked space the 'U' shape and the arrowhead should be facing upwards, the line segment should be on the right and the arrowhead should be on the extreme left. To continue the series the next figure has the 'U' shape and the arrowhead facing downwards, the line segment on the right and the arrowhead on the extreme right. Option '(*e*)' fits into the question marked space.

4. (*c*) : At each step the places of two elements on the horizontal are interchanged and clockwise one element is made new. Option '(*c*)' fits in the pattern to complete the series.

5. (*b*) : At each step the enclosed figure is enlarged in the next and a new figure is placed inside the enlarged figure. Option '(*b*)' fits into the question marked space.

6. (*a*) : The arrow and the line with the dot are increased in a set pattern in opposite directions. The series they form is two arrows and two lines with the dot which is repeated. Answer figure '(*a*)' is the right choice.

7. (*c*) : Each arrow is turned 90° clockwise at each step. Option '(*c*)' fits into the question marked space.

8. (*a*) : The number of petals removed at each step is increased by one, i.e., the petals are removed in the order of one, two and three, leaving only two petals in the last figure option '(*a*)' is the right answer.

9. (*e*) : The lines are moved clockwise. First a semicircle is added to the adjacent line. Then the semicircles on the opposite sides are added one by one on the two lines. Answer figure '(*e*)' fits into the question-marked space.

10. (*c*) : Each time one petal is removed and the half petal is clockwise and anticlockwise alternately. Answer figure '(*c*)' completes the series.

11. (*a*) : At first step the fifth or the bottom most element is moved to the second place from top, the second element moved to the fourth place, the fourth element is moved to the third place, the third element is moved to the first or the topmost place and the element on the top which is made new is moved to the last or the fifth place. At second step i.e., from second problem figure to third problem figure the above process is reversed. The bottom most element is the first and the top most element is the last or fifth. Hereafter, the process is repeated from the beginning. Option '(*a*)' is the right answer.

12. (*b*) : The three elements are moved half step everytime-first till they reach the extreme right position and then back to the left. Answer figure '(*b*)' fits into the question-marked space.

13. (*c*) : The four elements are moved one step clockwise and the arc one step anti-clockwise. Option '(*c*)' is the right answer.

14. (*b*) : The smaller design is enlarged in the next and a new smaller design is placed in its centre. Option '(*b*)' fits into the question-marked space to continue the series.

15. (*d*) : The shaded portion is moved one step anticlockwise at each step and one extra portion is shaded alternately.

FIGURAL SERIES

In this form of non-verbal series, which are the most common, four or five consecutive problem figures form a definite sequence and one is required to select the one figure from the given set of Answer Figures that will continue the same sequence.

One has to try different set of moves, changes, replacements, rotations, repetitions and a lot more variations to arrive at the logical pattern making the series. Practising alone will sharpen one's skill of solving such sequences.

SOLVED EXAMPLES

In each of the questions given below, which one of the answer figures should come after the problem figure if the sequence were continued?

1. Problem Figures

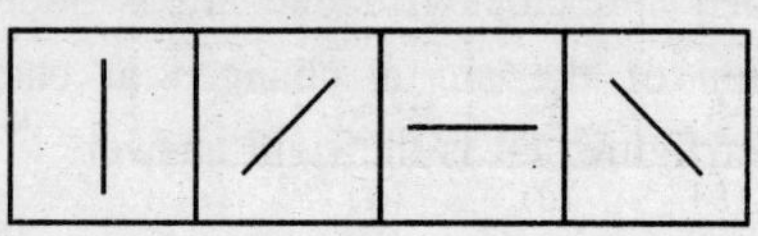

Answer Figures

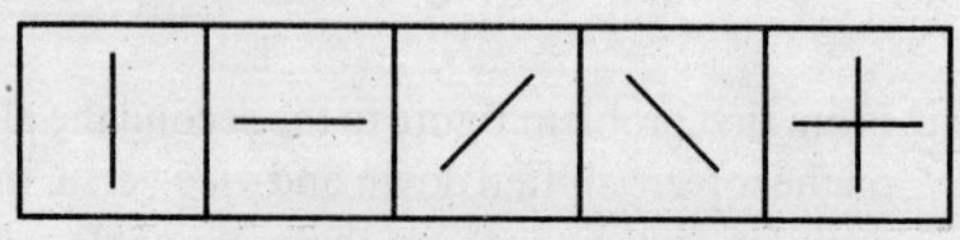

(*a*) (*b*) (*c*) (*d*) (*e*)

Answer (*a*) : All the figures are simple straight lines of the same size. Their directions and positions have changed.

In the first figure, the line is in a vertical position, in the second, the line has moved 45° clockwise, in the third, the line has further moved 45° clockwise, and in the fourth, the line has further moved 45° clockwise. Thus, two facts are brought out: *(i)* the line moves clockwise, and *(ii)* the line moves 45° at each step.

Now the fourth figure (Problem Figures) should be moved 45° clockwise. It will be a vertical line. Thus, the next figure to continue the series will be a vertical straight line.

MULTIPLE CHOICE QUESTIONS

Directions : *In each of the following questions which one of the five answer figures given below should come after the problem figures if the sequence are continued?*

Problem Figures

1. 

Answer Figures

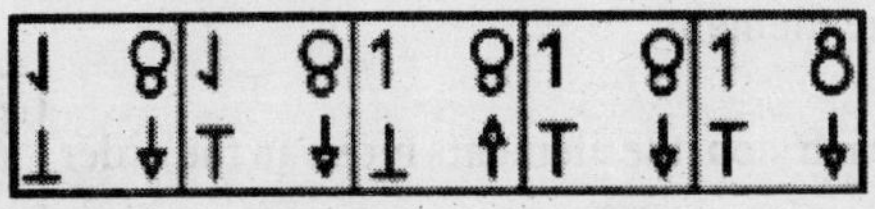

(*a*) (*b*) (*c*) (*d*) (*e*)

Problem Figures

2. 

Answer Figures

(*a*) (*b*) (*c*) (*d*) (*e*)

Problem Figures

3. 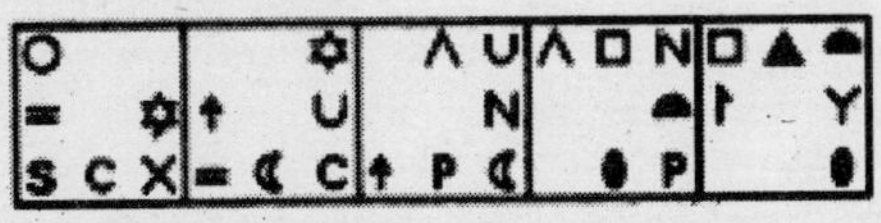

Answer Figures

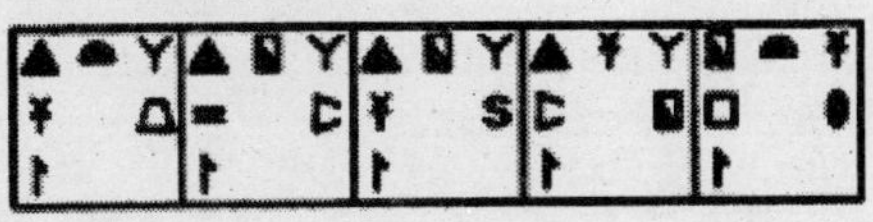

(*a*) (*b*) (*c*) (*d*) (*e*)

Problem Figures

4. 

Answer Figures

(*a*) (*b*) (*c*) (*d*) (*e*)

Problem Figures

5. 

Answer Figures

(*a*) (*b*) (*c*) (*d*) (*e*)

Problem Figures

6. 

Answer Figures

(*a*) (*b*) (*c*) (*d*) (*e*)

Problem Figures

7. 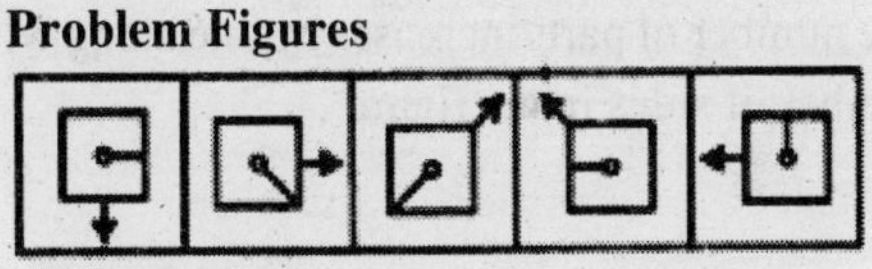

Answer Figures

(*a*) (*b*) (*c*) (*d*) (*e*)

Problem Figures

8. 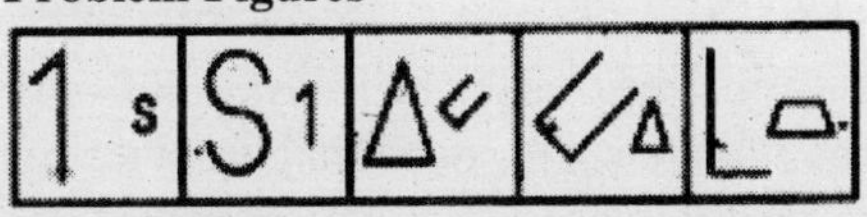

Answer Figures

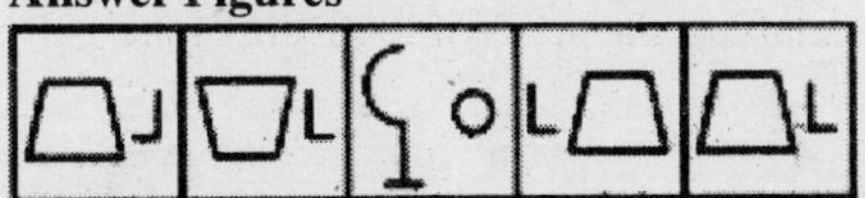

(*a*) (*b*) (*c*) (*d*) (*e*)

Problem Figures

9. 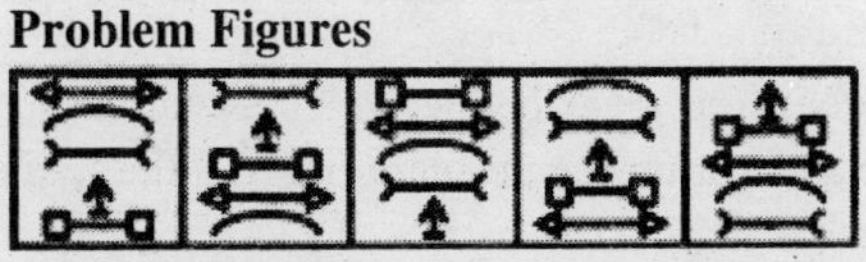

Answer Figures

(*a*) (*b*) (*c*) (*d*) (*e*)

Problem Figures

10. 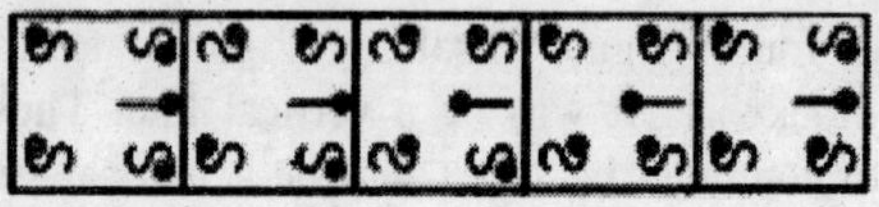

Answer Figures

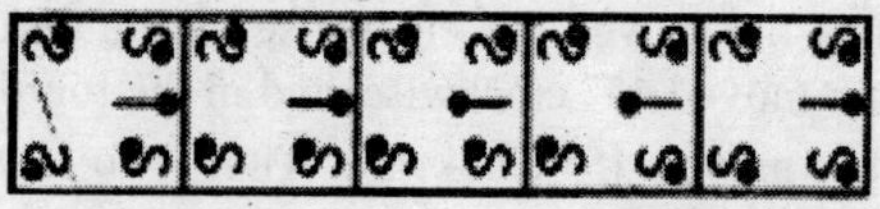

(a) (b) (c) (d) (e)

EXPLANATORY ANSWERS

1. (*d*) : In each step, all the elements move to the adjacent corner (of the square boundary) in a CW direction and the element that reaches the upper-left corner gets vertically inverted.

2. (*c*) : We can label the arcs as shown . The arcs get inverted in the sequence (1 & 2), (3, 4 & 5), (6 & 1), (2, 3 & 4), (5 & 6), ...

3. (*d*) : All the elements move half-a-side of the square boundary in ACW direction in each step. Also, first, third and fifth elements are replaced by new elements in one step and second, fourth and sixth elements are replaced by new elements in the next step. The two steps are repeated alternately.

4. (*a*) : In each step, the dot moves one space CW and the arrow moves two spaces CW.

5. (*c*) : One arc and four arcs get inverted alternately.

6. (*e*) : The number of parts increases by one along with the number of sides in the figure.

7. (*c*) : The pin rotates 45°CW and 90°CW alternately and moves one space (each space is equal to half-a-side of the square) and two spaces CW alternately. The arrow rotates 90°ACW and 45°ACW alternately and moves two spaces and one space.

8. (*e*) : In one step, the two elements interchange positions and the smaller element gets enlarged while the larger element gets reduced in size. In the next step, the smaller element is replaced by a new small element and the larger element is replaced by a new large element.

9. (*c*) : In each step, the elements move in the order .

10. (*b*) : The upper-left element gets laterally inverted in first, third, fifth. .... steps; the upper-right element gets rotated through 180° is first, fourth, seventh,.... steps; the lower-left element gets laterally inverted in second, fourth, sixth, ... steps; the lower-right element gets rotated through 180° in third, sixth,... steps and the pin at the middle-right position gets laterally inverted in every second step.

CHAPTER 2

Semantic Classification

Classification means arranging the given content in groups or classes having qualities of same kind. In classification type questions, the figures or items are sorted out in groups on the basis of their similarities in qualities in shapes, size, pattern, structure, genus, order, species, grade, style, constituents and other specifications, and thus the answer is found out.

TYPE-I

Classification of this type does not have two sets of figures known as Problem Figures and Answer Figures; instead they have only one set of four or five figures known as Problem Figures. One of these Problem Figures is not like the other four figures. In other words, three or four of the Answer Figures belong to a class while one which is the odd figures, does not belong to it.

MULTIPLE CHOICE QUESTIONS

Directions : *In each of the following questions one of the figures is different from the rest. Spot the figure.*

1. 

(a) (b) (c) (d) (e)

2. 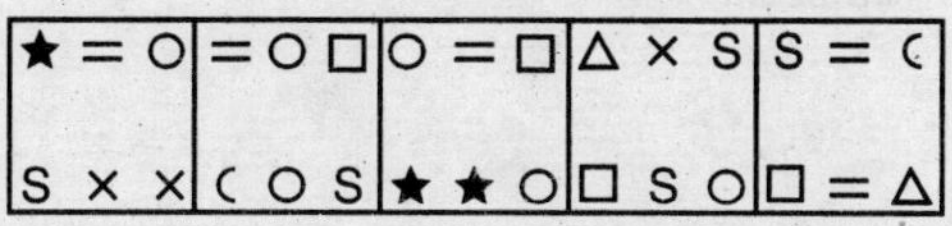

(a) (b) (c) (d) (e)

3. 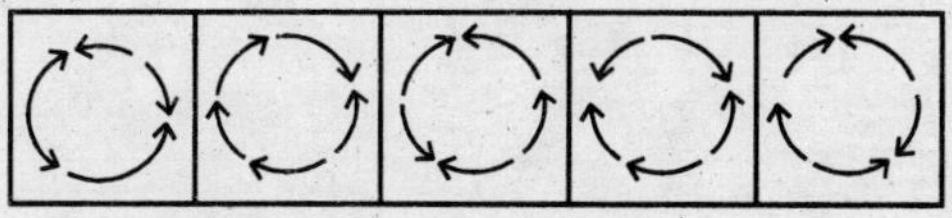

(a) (b) (c) (d) (e)

4. 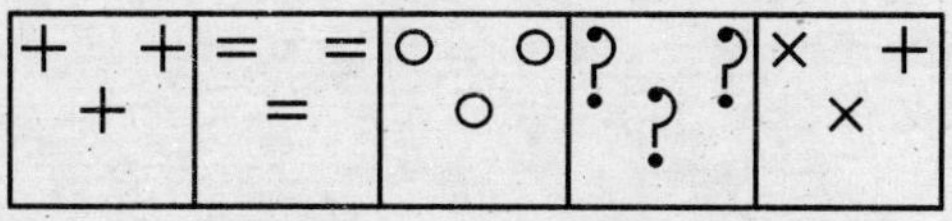

(a) (b) (c) (d) (e)

5. 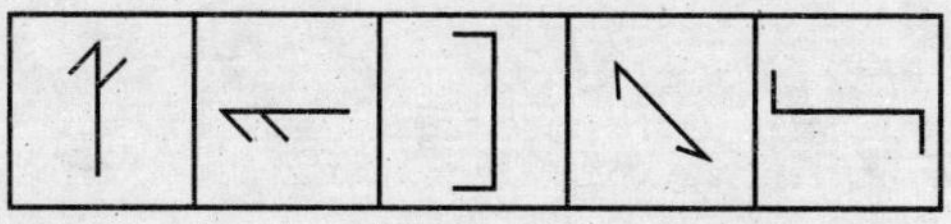

(a) (b) (c) (d) (e)

6. 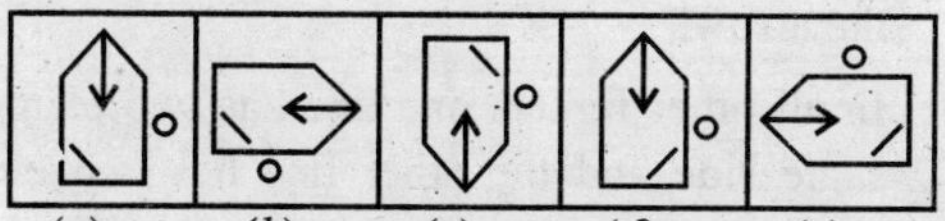

(a) (b) (c) (d) (e)

7. 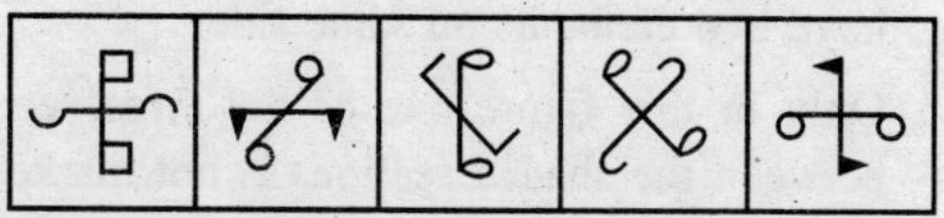

(a) (b) (c) (d) (e)

8. 

(a) (b) (c) (d) (e)

9. 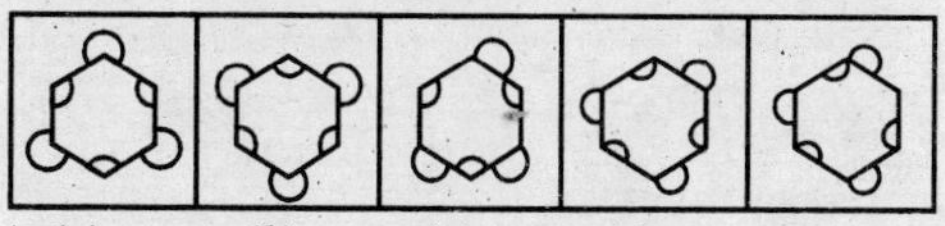

(a) (b) (c) (d) (e)

10. 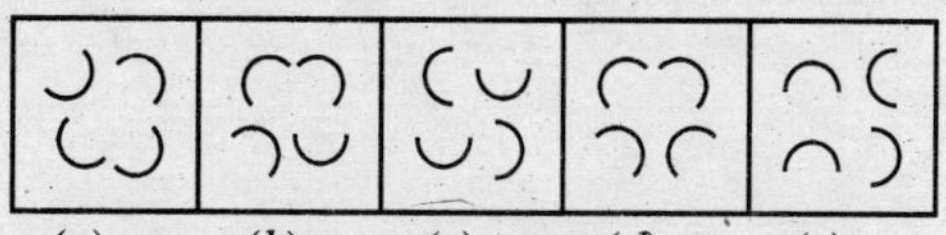

(a) (b) (c) (d) (e)

11. 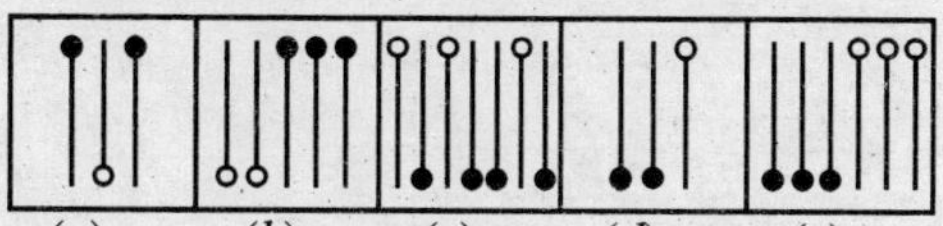

(a) (b) (c) (d) (e)

12.

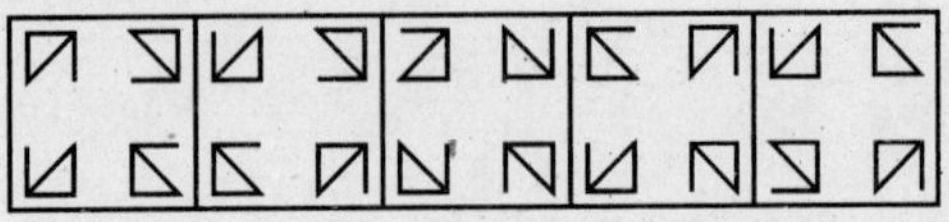

(a) (b) (c) (d) (e)

13.

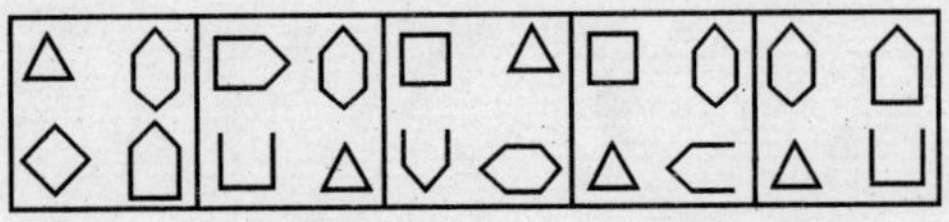

(a) (b) (c) (d) (e)

14.

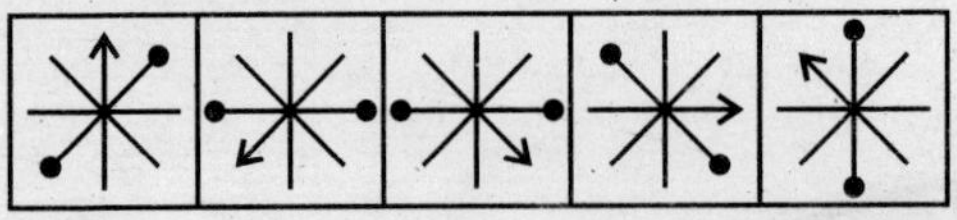

(a) (b) (c) (d) (e)

15.

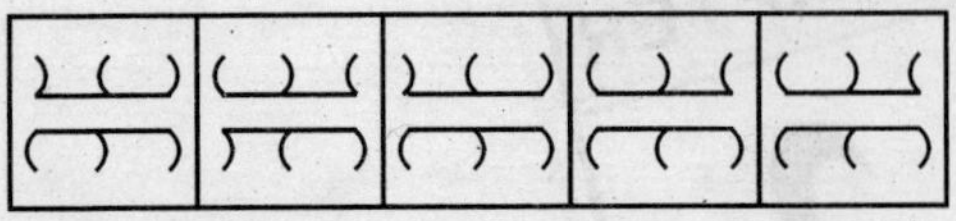

(a) (b) (c) (d) (e)

EXPLANATORY ANSWERS

1. (*d*) : Only in this figure all the lines making the hands and legs of the human shape are drawn downwards.

2. (*c*) : In all other figures only one set of elements is identical.

3. (*b*) : Only in this figure four arrows are pointing in same direction, and one arrow in its opposite direction. In other figures three arrows are in same direction and two in the opposite direction.

4. (*e*) : All other figures have three identical elements.

5. (*d*) : In all other figures two lines are parallelly drawn.

6. (*c*) : In all other figures the circle is on the left side of the arrow.

7. (*c*) : In all other figures one line has two elements on same side and the other line has two elements, one on either side. In this figure both the lines have two elements on same side.

8. (*d*) : Only in this figure one of the three sections in between the shaded sections is not marked.

9. (*e*) : In all other figures the elements inside as well as outside the hexagon are placed at equal distance. In this figure the outside element at the top is wrongly placed (It should be near the other corner of the same line).

10. (*d*) : In all other figures two elements are in same direction and the other two elements are opposite to each other.

11. (*e*) : Only in this figure the two types of elements are equal in number.

12. (*c*) : In all other figures the diagonal line in all other elements is drawn from the right end.

13. (*a*) : In all other figures one of the four elements has one open side.

14. (*c*) : In all other figures the arrow is to the left of the dot.

15. (*b*) : In all other figures two of the three curves on one of the lines are in the same direction and are adjacent.

CHAPTER 3

Figural Analogy

Figural Analogy is a process of reasoning between two parallel cases. It relates to agreement or correspondence in certain respects between two things. It is a process whereby the underlying relationship that exists between two figures, designs or patterns is determined. Under the process, one has to discover the features common to the two figures or designs. This common feature is a model or base. The question seeks solution on the basis of this model or base.

In non-verbal analogy questions, there are two sets of figures which are known as *(i)* Problem Figures, and *(ii)* Answer Figures. The Problem Figures are divided into two parts. The Answer Figures are given below the Problem Figures.

MULTIPLE CHOICE QUESTIONS

Directions : *The second figure in the first unit of the Problem Figures bears a certain relationship to the first figure. Similarly, one of the figures in the Answer Figures bears the same relationship to the first figure in the second unit of the Problem Figures. Locate the figure which would fit the question mark.*

1. Problem Figures

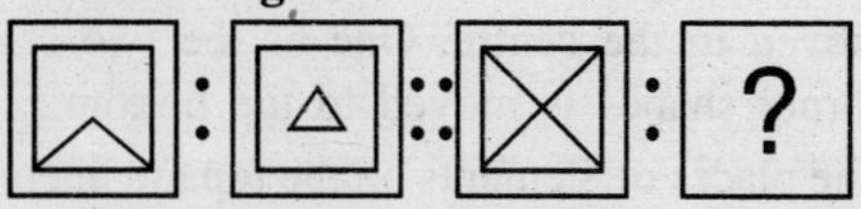

Answers Figures

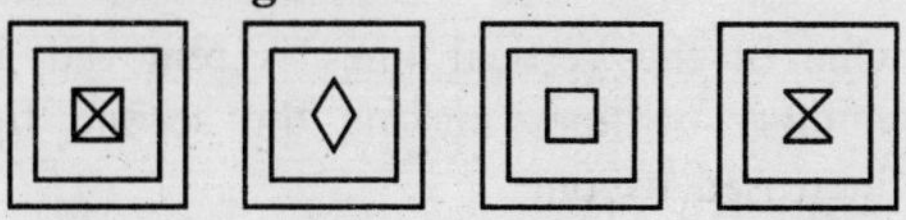

(a) (b) (c) (d)

2. Problem Figures

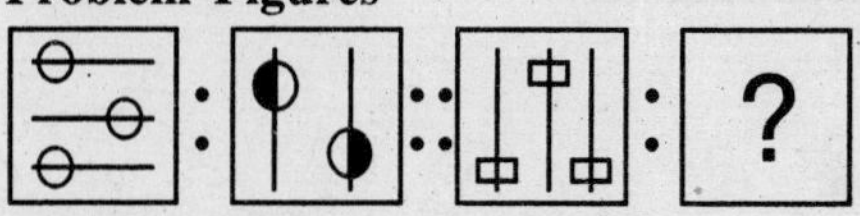

Answer Figures

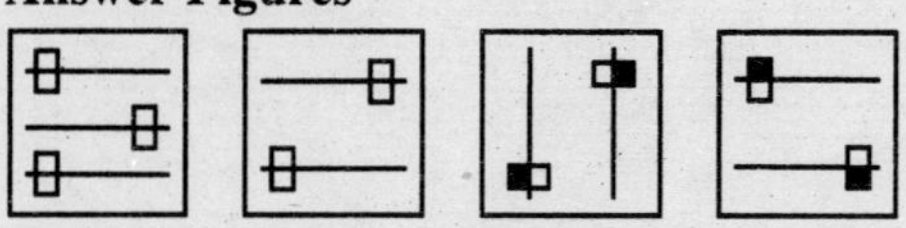

(a) (b) (c) (d)

3. Problem Figures

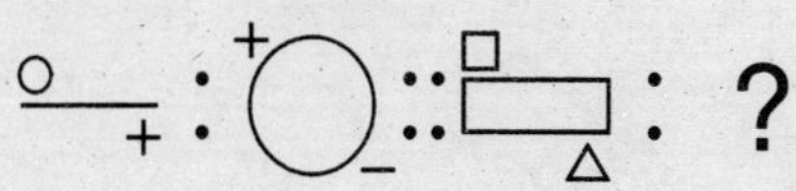

Answer Figures

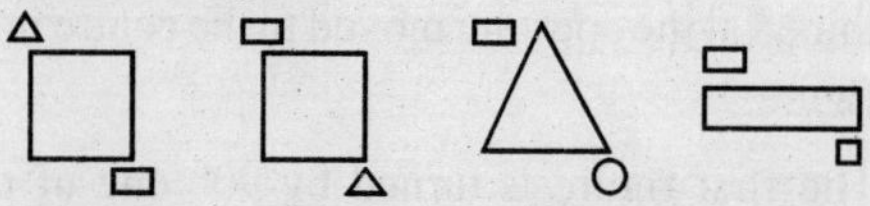

(a) (b) (c) (d)

4. Problem Figures

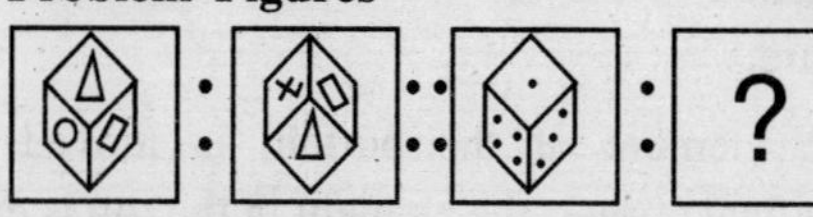

Answer Figures

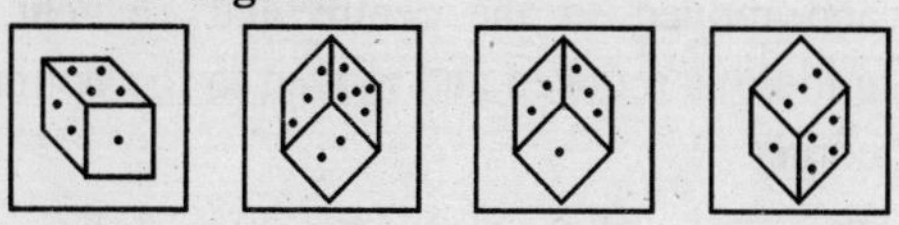

(a) (b) (c) (d)

5. Problem Figures

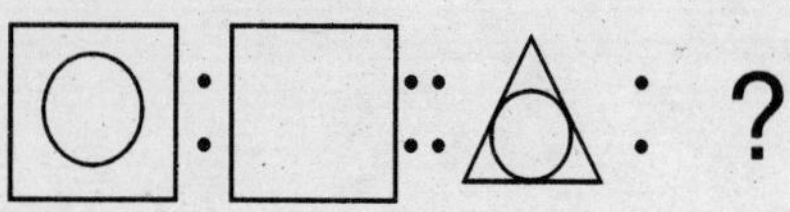

Answer Figures

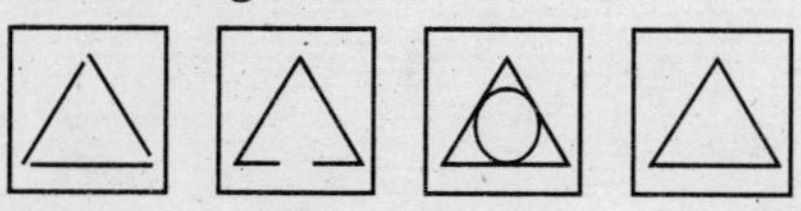

(a) (b) (c) (d)

6. Problem Figures

Answer Figures

(a) (b) (c) (d)

7. Problem Figures

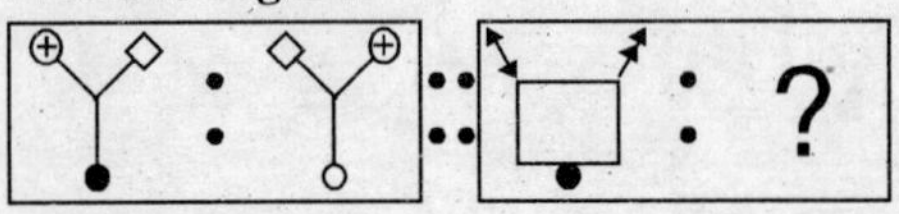

Answer Figures

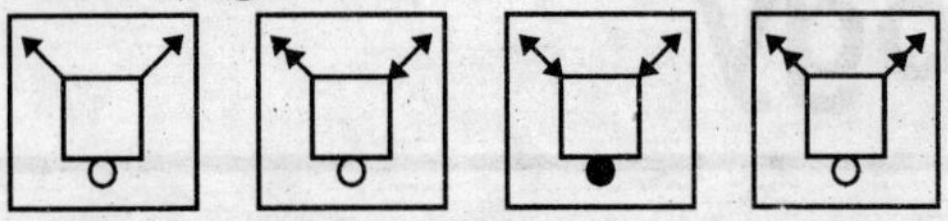

(a) (b) (c) (d)

8. Problem Figures

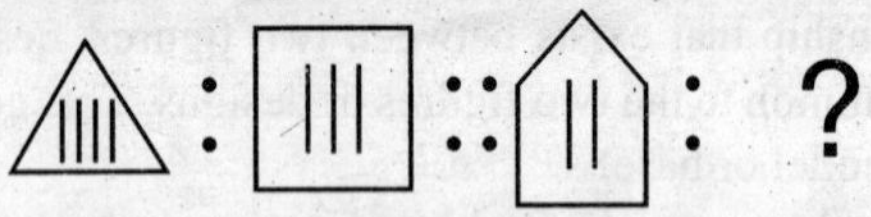

Answer Figures

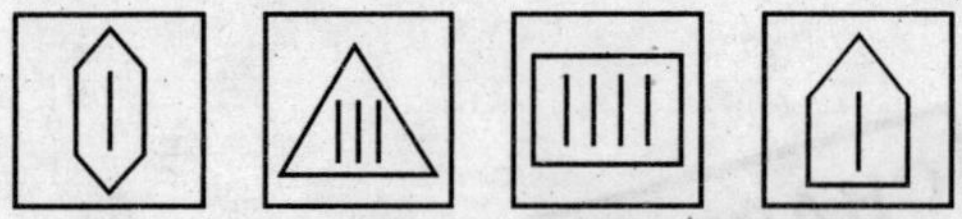

(a) (b) (c) (d)

9. Problem Figures

Answer Figures

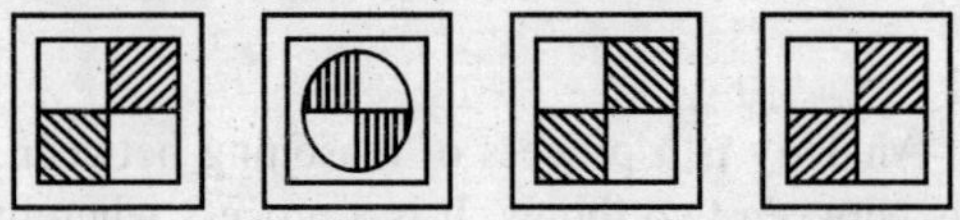

(a) (b) (c) (d)

EXPLANATORY ANSWERS

1. (*d*) : The triangle in the first figure is moved to the centre of the second figure. Similarly, the two triangles joined at the apex are moved to the centre in answer figure.

2. (*d*) : The first figure is turned by 90° one of the bars is removed and opposite sides of the element attached to the bar are shaded to get the second figure.

3. (*a*) : The element at the bottom is moved to the diagonal corner, the element in the top is enlarged and moved to the centre and element in the middle is reduced and moved to the bottom right corner.

4. (*c*) : The view of the cube is changed from top to bottom. The design on the right side remains unchanged while the design on the left side is changed.

5. (*d*) : The inner shape in the first figure is removed to get the second figure.

6. (*b*) : The two half shapes placed vertically are turned upside down and joined, and this new shape is moved to the top. The two curved shapes placed horizontally are joined and this new shape is moved to the centre. One of the two remaining corner shapes is moved to the bottom.

7. (*b*) : The places of elements on the top are interchanged and the shade inside the circle is removed.

8. (*a*) : One of the vertical lines is removed and the number of lines making the second figure is increased by one.

9. (*a*) : First figure is rotated 90° anticlockwise to get the second figure.

CHAPTER

4 Spatial Visualization

In such questions, cut-out pieces are given alongwith the whole figure, that is the figure out of which the figures have been cut. By looking at the cut-out figures one has to find out the figure which may be constituted by putting the pieces together, i.e., one has to find out the figure of which the pieces have been cut. One has to be very imaginative and has to use space perception in finding out the solution. The whole process is mental and requires special skill in visualising different spatial patterns. It is not easy to develop this skill overnight but it can certainly be cultivated by practice and the method of trial and error.

MULTIPLE CHOICE QUESTIONS

Directions (Qs. 1-5) : *Which one figure can be made out of given paper cut-outs?*

1. 

(a) (b) (c) (d)

2. 

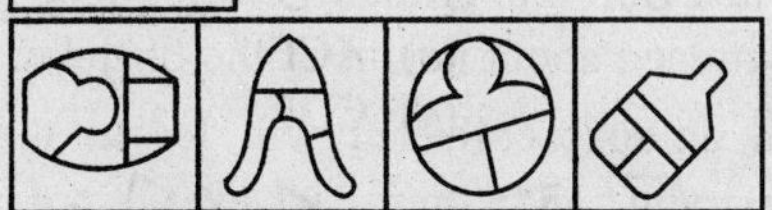

(a) (b) (c) (d)

3. 

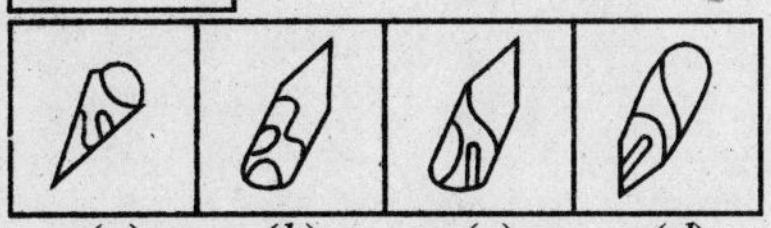

(a) (b) (c) (d)

4. 

(a) (b) (c) (d)

5. 

(a) (b) (c) (d)

Direction (Qs. 6-10) : *In each of the following questions an irregular piece of paper has been cut into two pieces. One piece has been shown on the left while the other piece has been given as one of the four alternatives against it. Find the correct alternative:*

6. 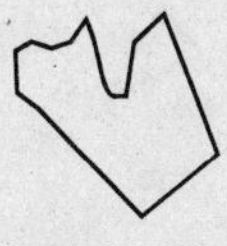

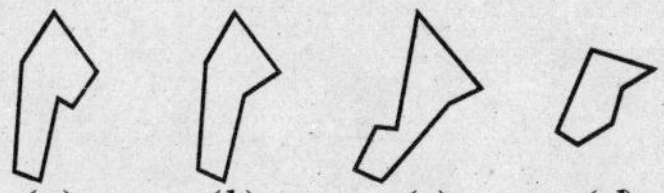

(a) (b) (c) (d)

7. 

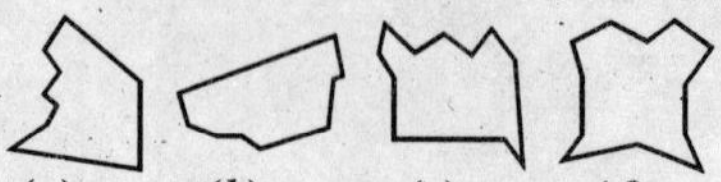

(*a*) (*b*) (*c*) (*d*)

8.

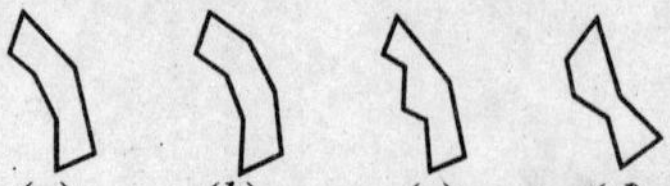

(*a*) (*b*) (*c*) (*d*)

9.

(*a*) (*b*) (*c*) (*d*)

10.

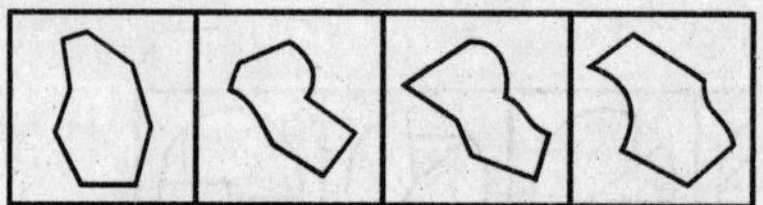

(*a*) (*b*) (*c*) (*d*)

Directions (Qs. 11-15) : *In each of the following questions five diagrams marked A to E are given. Three of these when put together form an equilateral triangle and have been given as one of the four alternatives under the question. Find the correct alternative in each case.*

11.

A B C D E

(*a*) ABE (*b*) BCE
(*c*) ADE (*d*) BDE

12.

A B C D E

(*a*) ABC (*b*) BCD
(*c*) CDE (*d*) BDE

13.

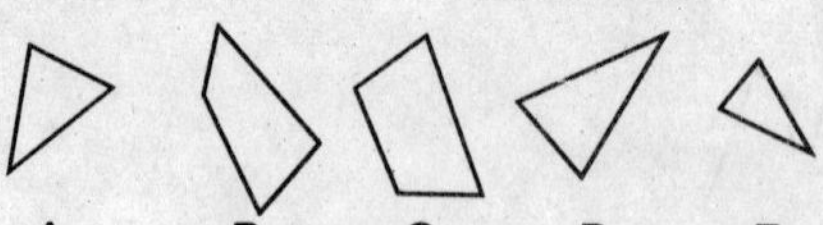

A B C D E

(*a*) BCD (*b*) CDE
(*c*) ABD (*d*) ABE

14.

A B C D E

(*a*) ABD (*b*) ACD
(*c*) BDE (*d*) CDE

15.

A B C D E

(*a*) ABC (*b*) ACE
(*c*) BDE (*d*) CDE

Directions (Qs. 16-20) : *In each of the following questions five diagrams A, B, C, D and E have been given. Three of these diagrams make a complete square which have been given as one of the four alternatives under it. Find the correct alternative in each case.*

16.

A B C D E

(*a*) ABC (*b*) BDE
(*c*) CDE (*d*) BCD

17.

A B C D E

(*a*) ACD (*b*) BDE
(*c*) BCE (*d*) CDE

18.

A B C D E

(*a*) ACD (*b*) BCD
(*c*) ACE (*d*) CDE

19.

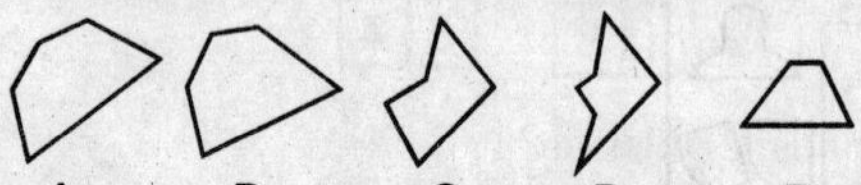

A B C D E

(*a*) ABC (*b*) ACE
(*c*) ADE (*d*) CDE

20.

A B C D E

(*a*) BDE (*b*) ABC
(*c*) ACD (*d*) BCD

ANSWERS

1	2	3	4	5	6	7	8	9	10
(*b*)	(*d*)	(*c*)	(*a*)	(*b*)	(*b*)	(*c*)	(*a*)	(*d*)	(*c*)
11	**12**	**13**	**14**	**15**	**16**	**17**	**18**	**19**	**20**
(*c*)	(*d*)	(*d*)	(*b*)	(*b*)	(*d*)	(*b*)	(*c*)	(*c*)	(*d*)

CHAPTER 5

Space Visualization

In these type of questions, a template or a layout of a cube, dice or a box is given, which can be folded to produce different patterns. To solve these questions what is required is a clear study of the given layout and the selection of one figure, from the alternative patterns which can be made from the given layout. To attempt such problems understand the unfolded patterns given below:

Layout 1. 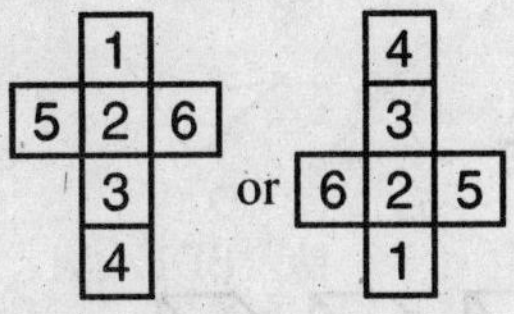

The opposite sides are :
1—3, 2 — 4 and 5 — 6

Layout 2. 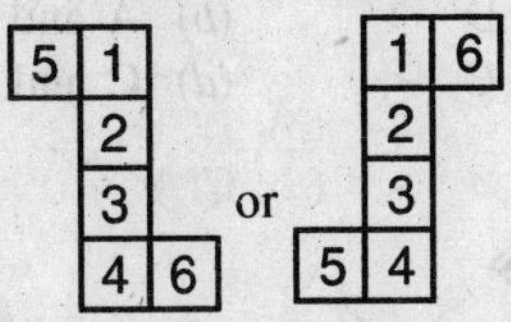

The opposite sides are :
1 — 3, 2 — 4 and 5 — 6

Layout 3. 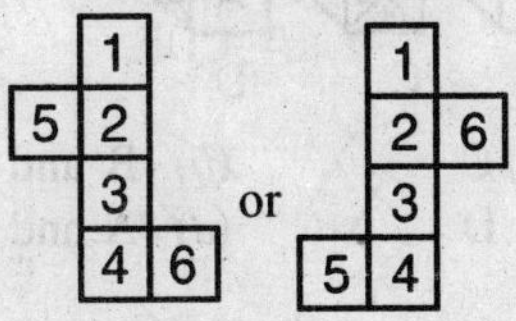

The opposite sides are :
1 — 3, 2 — 4 and 5 — 6.

Layout 4. 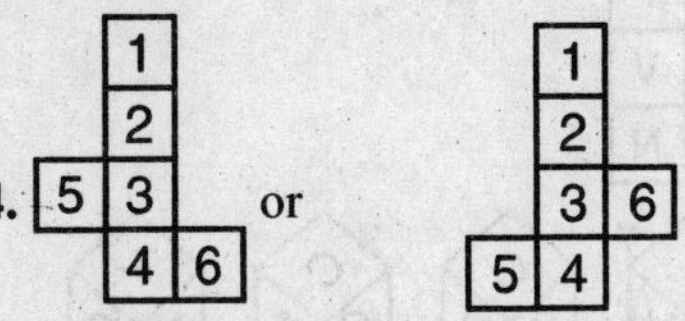

The opposite sides are :
1 — 3, 2 — 4 and 5 — 6

Layout 5. 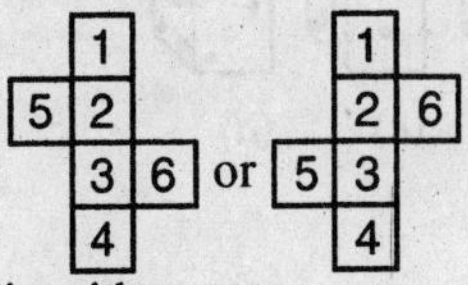

The opposite sides are :
1 — 3, 2 — 4 and 5 — 6

Layout 6. 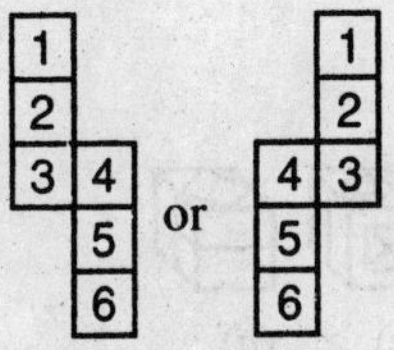

The opposite sides are :
1 — 3, 2 — 5 and 4 — 6

Layout 7. 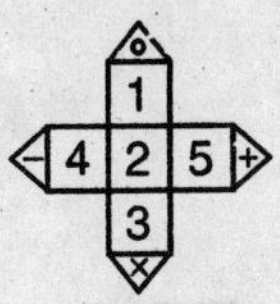

The opposite sides are :

 — 2, 1 — 3 and 4 — 5. Here, side 6 is divided into four parts

Layout 8. 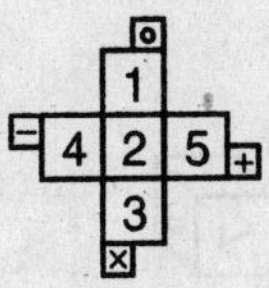

The opposite sides are

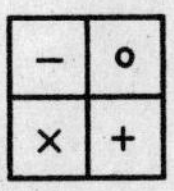 — 2, 1 — 3 and 4 — 5. Here, side 6 is divided into four parts.

Observe from the above layouts that all sides except the opposite side are adjacent sides. Also keep in mind that the three visible sides of the option figures are one of the opposite sides of each opposite pair.

MULTIPLE CHOICE QUESTIONS

Directions : *The figure is folded to produce different box patterns. Study the pattern to know if they can be produced from given figure and select the answer from the alternatives.*

1. 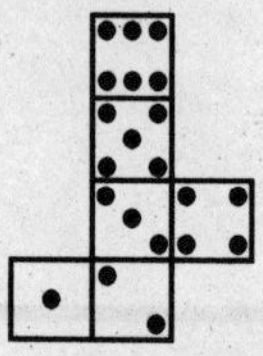

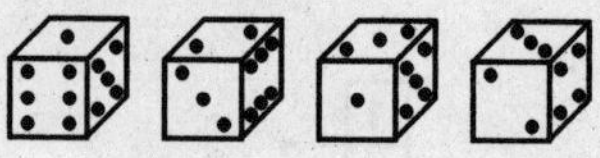

(*a*) (*b*) (*c*) (*d*)

2. 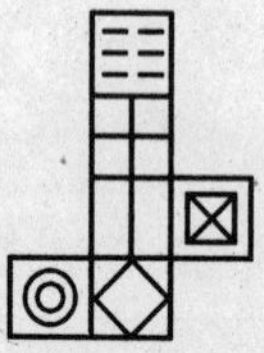

(*a*) (*b*) (*c*) (*d*)

3. 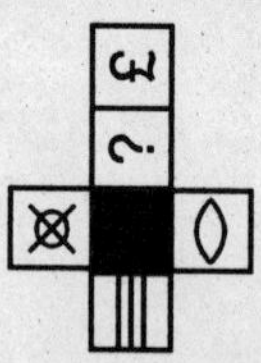

(*a*) (*b*) (*c*) (*d*)

4. 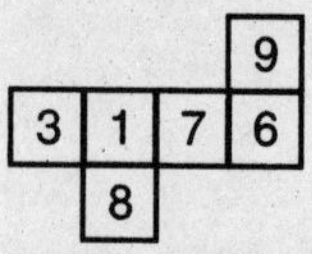

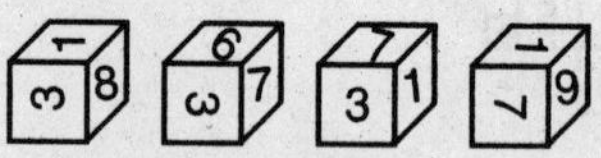

(*a*) (*b*) (*c*) (*d*)

5. 

(*a*) (*b*) (*c*) (*d*)

6. 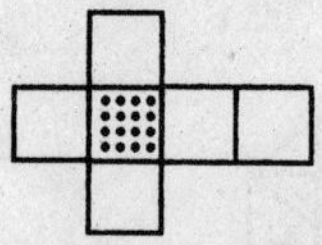

A B C D

(*a*) A, B and D (*b*) B and D
(*c*) B, C and D (*d*) A and D

7. 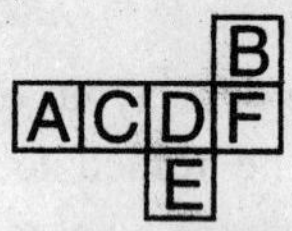

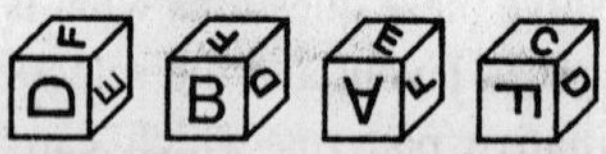

A B C D

(*a*) A and B (*b*) A and D
(*c*) B and C (*d*) All four

8. 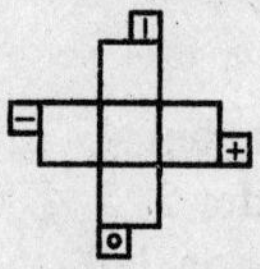

A B C D

(*a*) B and D (*b*) A and D
(*c*) B and C (*d*) C and D

9. 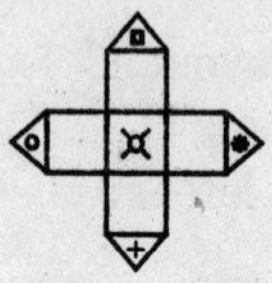

A B C D

(*a*) A and C (*b*) B and C
(*c*) B and D (*d*) A and D

10. 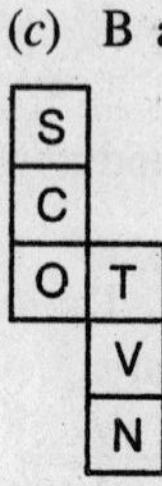

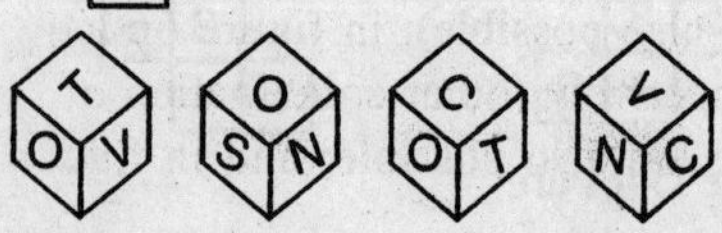

A B C D

(*a*) B and C (*b*) A and D
(*c*) A and C (*d*) All four

11. 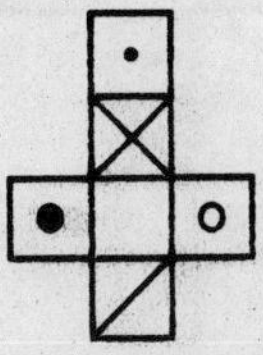

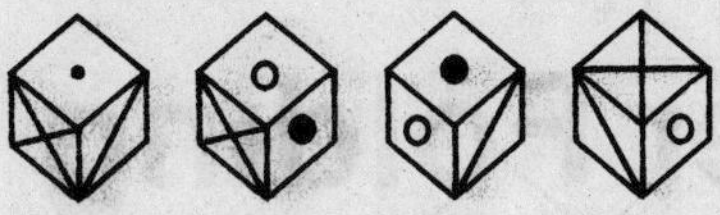

A B C D

(*a*) A and D (*b*) B, C and D

(*c*) All four (*d*) None of the above

12. 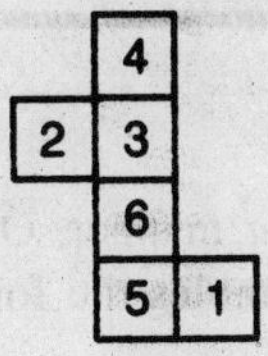

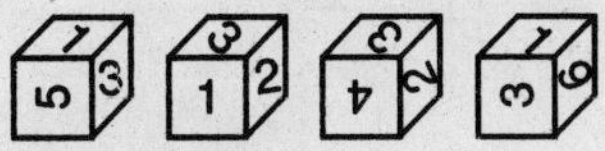

A B C D

(*a*) A and C (*b*) C and D

(*c*) B and C (*d*) B and D

13. 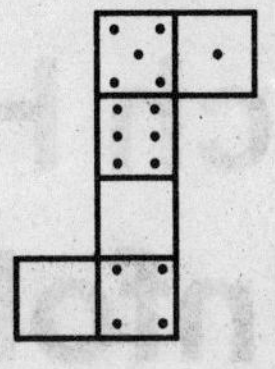

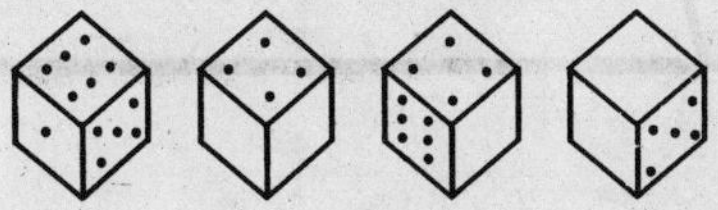

A B C D

(*a*) A and C (*b*) A and B

(*c*) B and C (*d*) B and D

EXPLANATORY ANSWERS

(All answers are based on number pattern of the sides as in the layout given in the beginning of this section)

1. (*d*) : The given figure is same as layout 4. The sides adjacent to top side 3 are in order 2, 5, 4, 6 — of these sides, 4 and 6 are seen on left and right sides respectively.

2. (*b*) : The given figure is same as layout 4. The sides adjacent to top side 5 are in order 4, 3, 2, 1 —of these sides 1 and 4 are seen on left and right sides respectively.

3. (*d*) : The given figure is same as layout 1. The sides adjacent to top side 5 are in order 4, 3, 2, 1 — of these sides 2 and 1 are seen on left and right sides respectively.

4. (*a*) : The given figure is same as layout 3. The sides adjacent to top side 2 are in order 1, 5, 3, 6 — of these sides 1 and 5 are seen on left and right sides respectively.

5. (*c*) : The given figure is same as layout 1. The sides adjacent to top side 6 are in order 1, 2, 3, 4 — of these sides 2 and 3 are seen on left and right sides respectively.

6. (*a*) : The given figure is same as layout 1. The top, left and right sides in figure option (a) are 1, 4 and 5 respectively (other combinations of sides for this figure are also possible); in figure option (b) 2, 1 and 5 respectively (other combination of sides for this figure are also possible; and in figure option (d) 1, 5 and 2 respectively (other combinations of sides for this figure are also possible).

7. (*a*) : The given figure is same as layout 4. In option figure (a) the top side 4 has side 3 on left and side 5 on right. In option figure (b) the top side 4 has side 6 on its left and side 3 on right.

Note : in option figure (c) the sides are correct but the printing of letter on right side is incorrect.

8. (*a*) : The given figure is same as layout 8. Option figures (b) and (d) contain the correct joints of side 6.

9. (*b*) : The given figure is same as layout 7. Option figures (a) and (c) contain the correct joints of side 6.

10. (*c*) : The given figure is same as layout 6. In option figure (a) the top side 4 has side 3 on left and side 5 on right. In option figure (c) the top side 2 has side 3 on left and side 4 on right.

11. (*d*) : The given figure is same as layout 1. None of the figure options can be made from the given figure.

12. (*b*) : The given figure is same as layout 3. In option figure (c) the top side 2 has side 1 on left and side 5 on right. In option figure (d) the top side 6 has side 2 on left and side 3 on right.

13. (*b*) : The given figure is same as layout 2. In option figure (a) the top side 2 has side 6 on left and side 1 on right. In option figure (b) the top side 4 has side 3 on left and side 5 on right.

CHAPTER

6

Pinch Hole/Paper Folding & Unfolding

These type of questions are based on a piece of paper which is folded and cut or punched in a particular manner. One of the option figures either resembles the pattern that would be formed when the paper is unfolded or resembles the form in which the paper is folded and cut or punched.

MULTIPLE CHOICE QUESTIONS

Directions (Qs. 1-5) : *In each one of the following problems, a square transparent sheet with a pattern is given. Figure out from amongst the four alternatives as to how the pattern would appear when the transparent sheet is folded at the dotted line.*

1. 

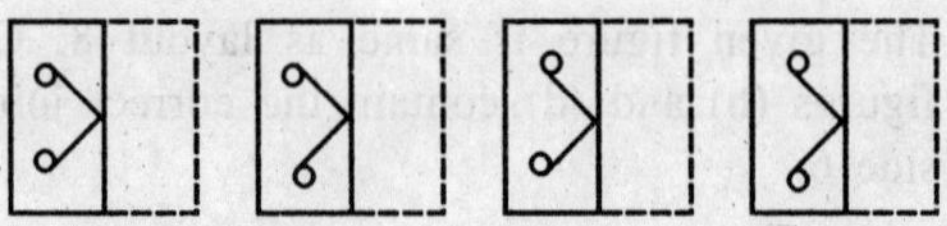

(a) (b) (c) (d)

2. 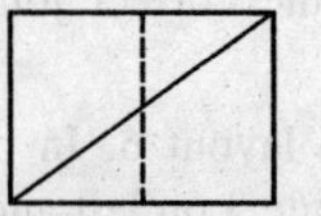

(a) (b) (c) (d)

3. 

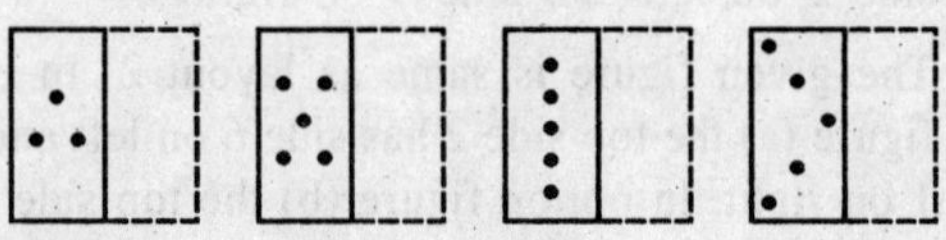

(a) (b) (c) (d)

4. 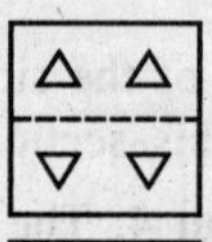

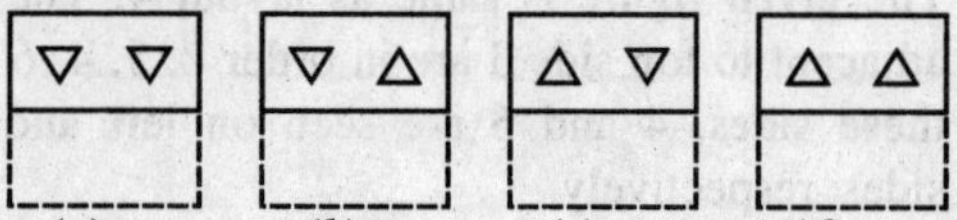

(a) (b) (c) (d)

5. 

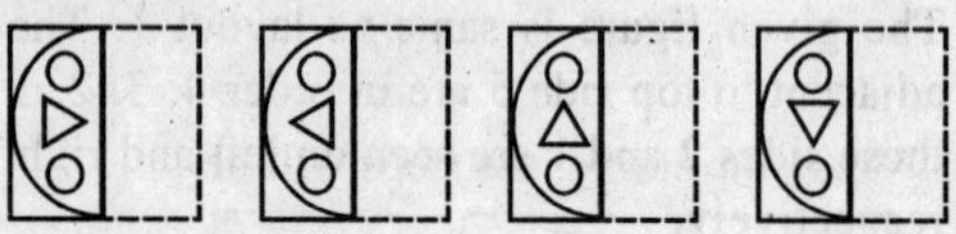

(a) (b) (c) (d)

Directions (Qs. 6-13) : *In each of the following questions a piece of paper has been folded and then punched. From the given options figure out the correct response which shows how it will appear when opened.*

6. 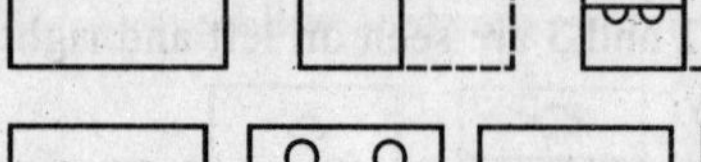

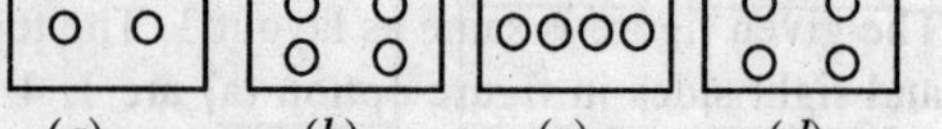

(a) (b) (c) (d)

7. 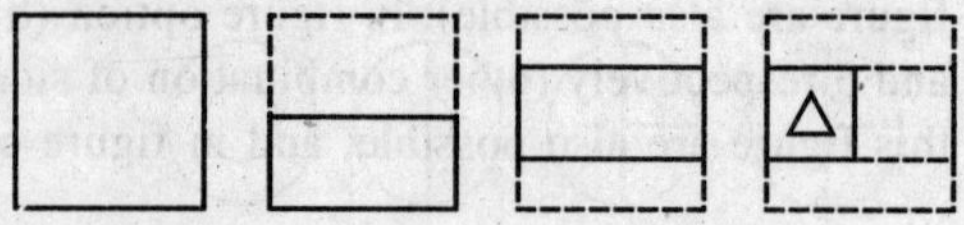

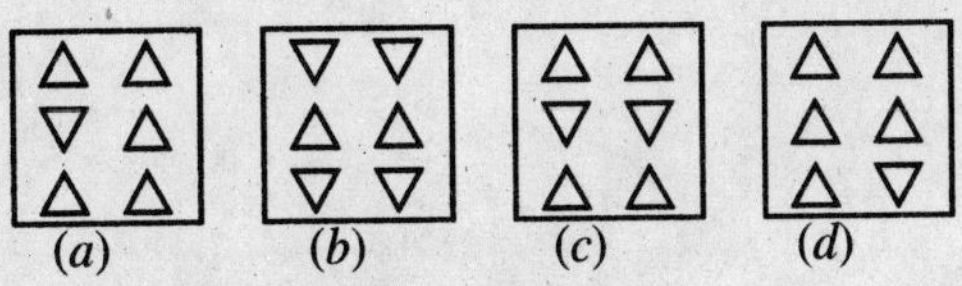

8.

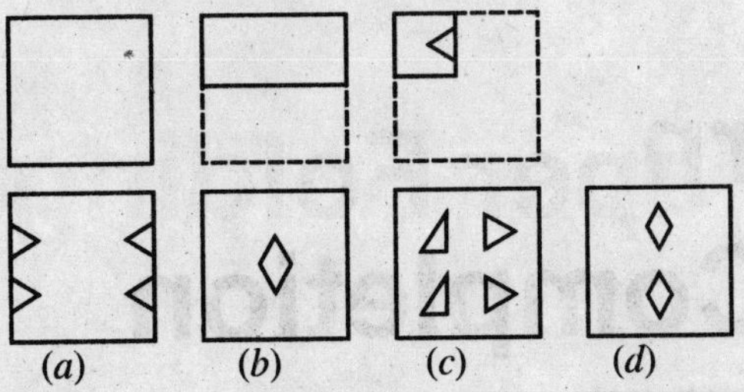

9.

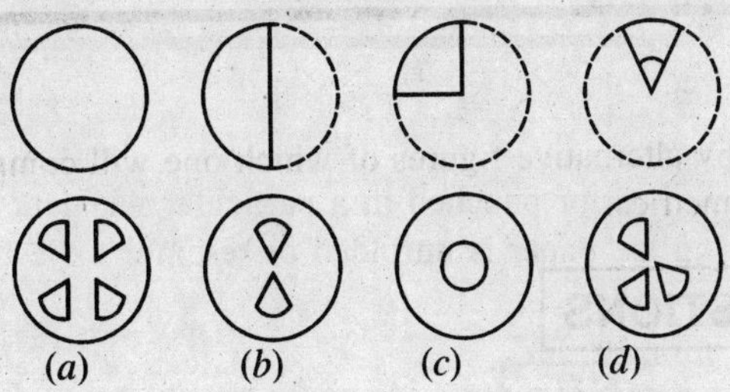

10.

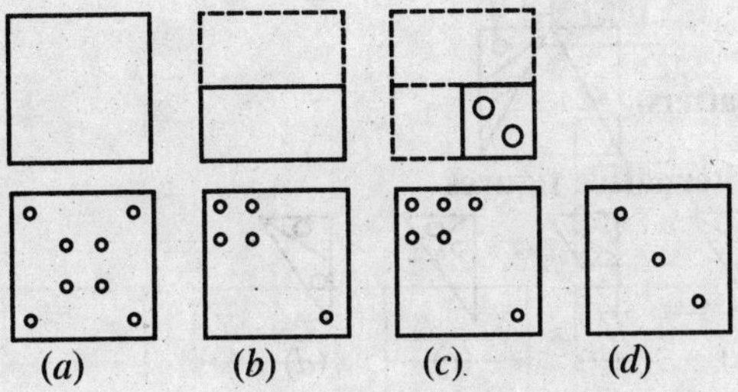

11.

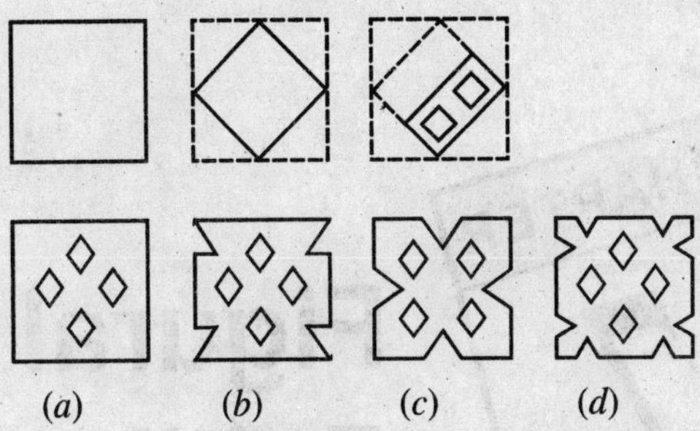

12.

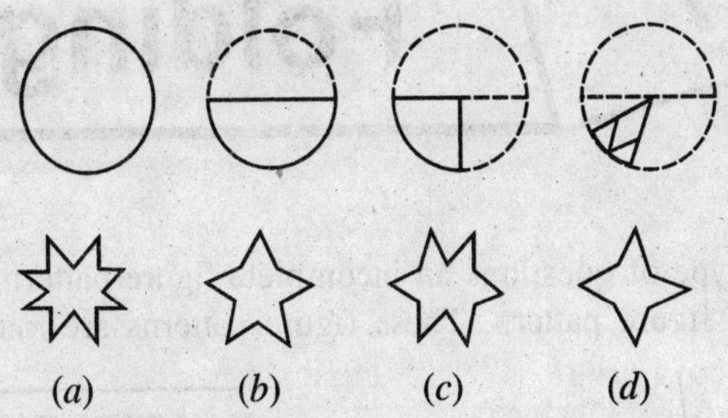

13.

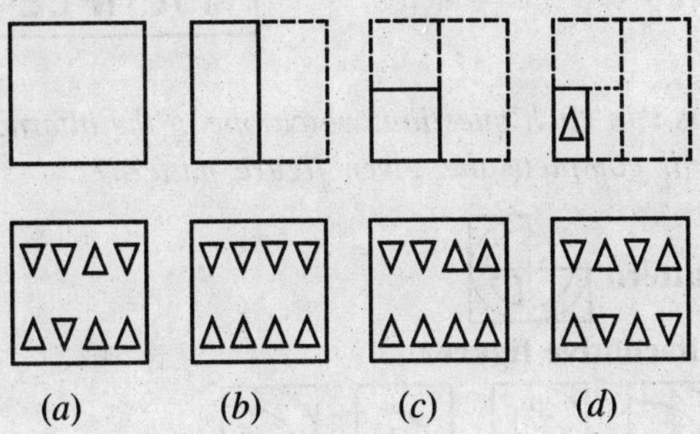

EXPLANATORY ANSWERS

1. (*d*)
2. (*c*)
3. (*b*)
4. (*d*)
5. (*b*)

6. (*c*) **:** When unfolding, the steps will be :

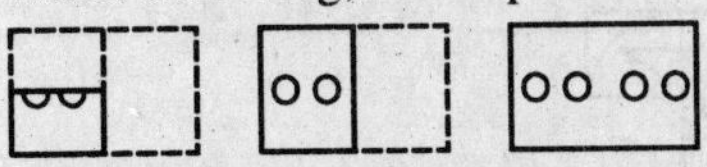

7. (*b*) **:** When unfolding, the steps will be :

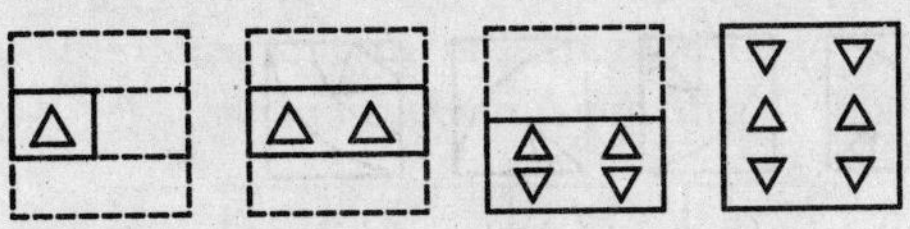

8. (*d*) **:** When unfolding, the steps will be :

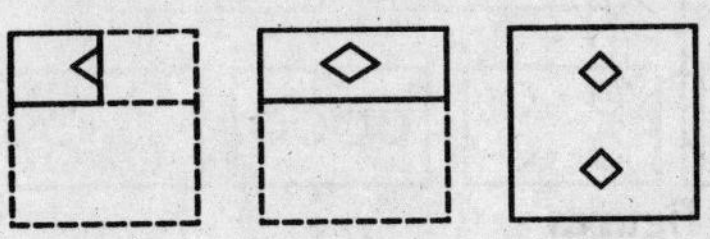

9. (*c*) **:** When unfolding, the steps will be :

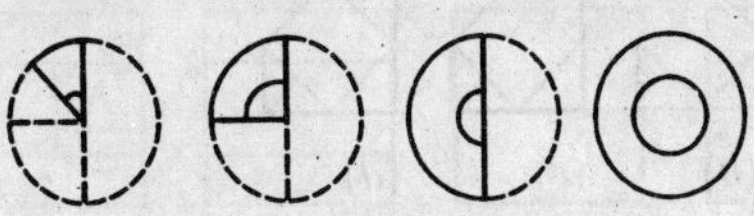

10. (*a*) **:** When unfolding, the steps will be :

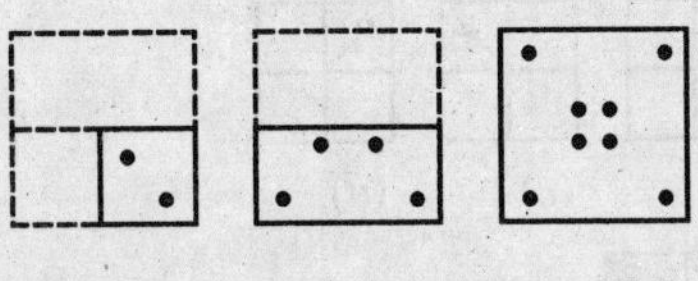

11. (*d*) **:** When unfolding, the steps will be :

12. (*a*) **:** When unfolding, the steps will be :

13. (*b*) **:** When unfolding, the steps will be :

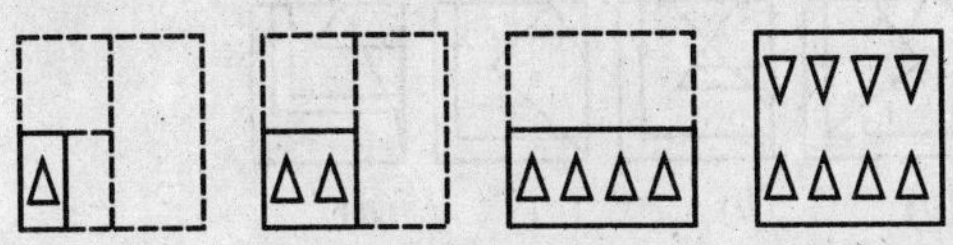

CHAPTER 7

Figural Pattern Folding and Completion

In these type of questions an incomplete figure pattern is given followed by alternative figures of which one will complete the given figure pattern. These figure patterns are mainly based on symmetries.

MULTIPLE CHOICE QUESTIONS

Directions : *In each question, which one of the alternative figures will complete the given figure pattern?*

1. Pattern

Alternative figures

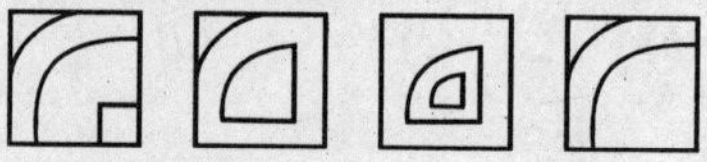

(*a*) (*b*) (*c*) (*d*)

2. Pattern

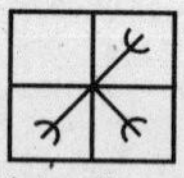

Alternative figures

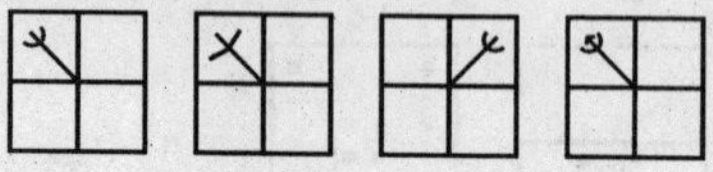

(*a*) (*b*) (*c*) (*d*)

3. Pattern

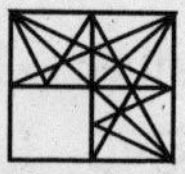

Alternative figures

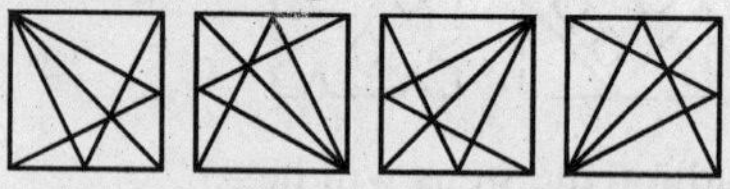

(*a*) (*b*) (*c*) (*d*)

4. Pattern

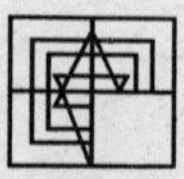

Alternative figures

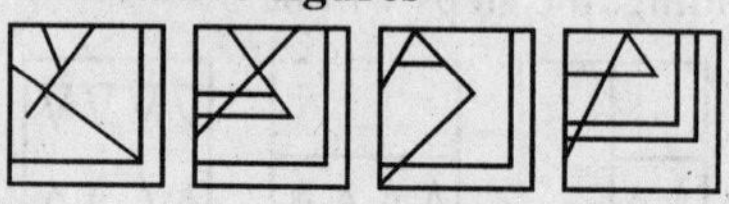

(*a*) (*b*) (*c*) (*d*)

5. Pattern

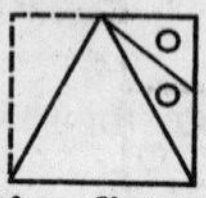

Alternative figures

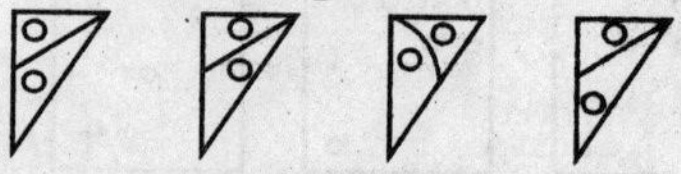

(*a*) (*b*) (*c*) (*d*)

6. Pattern

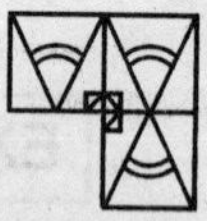

Alternative figures

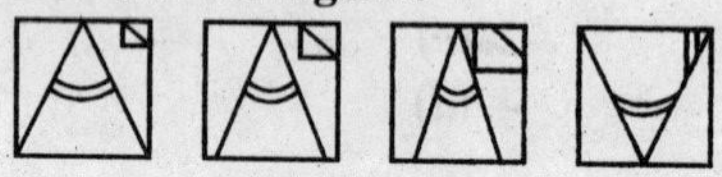

(*a*) (*b*) (*c*) (*d*)

7. Pattern

Alternative figures

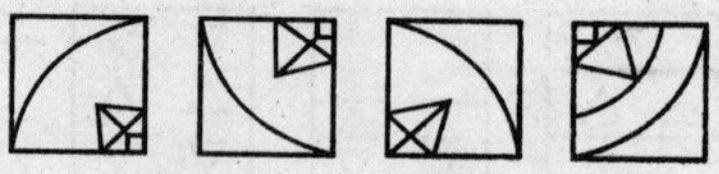

(*a*) (*b*) (*c*) (*d*)

8. Pattern

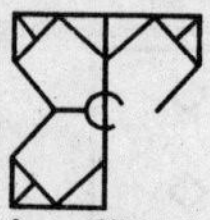

Alternative figures

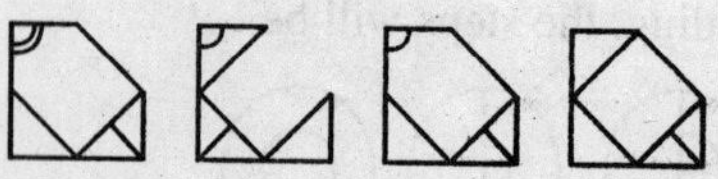

(*a*) (*b*) (*c*) (*d*)

9. Pattern 

Alternative figures

(*a*) (*b*) (*c*) (*d*)

10. Pattern 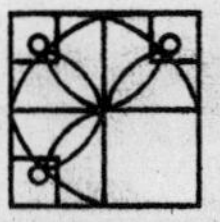

Alternative figures

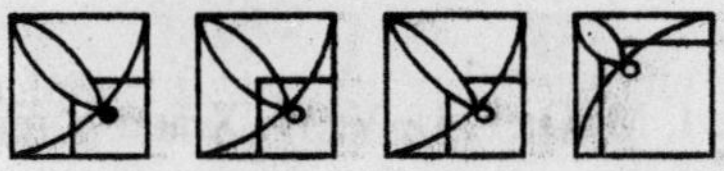

(*a*) (*b*) (*c*) (*d*)

11. Pattern 

Alternative figures

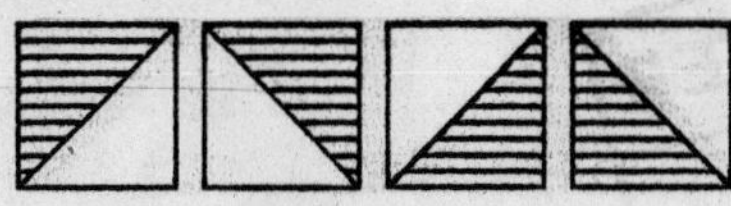

(*a*) (*b*) (*c*) (*d*)

12. Pattern 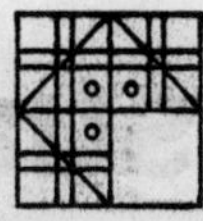

Alternative figures

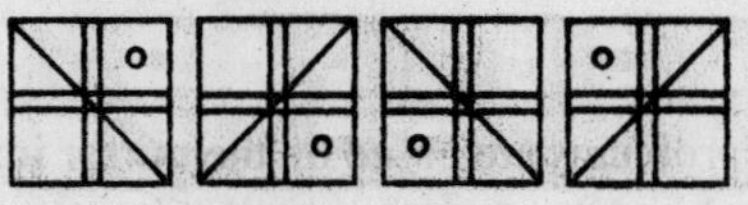

(*a*) (*b*) (*c*) (*d*)

EXPLANATORY ANSWERS

All the completed figures will look like this:

1. (*b*) : 

2. (*a*) : 

3. (*d*) : 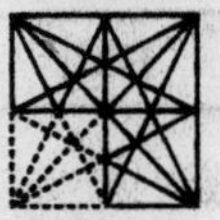

4. (*d*) : 

5. (*a*) : 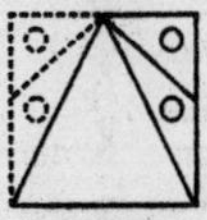

6. (*a*) : 

7. (*b*) : 

8. (*c*) : 

9. (*a*) : 

10. (*b*) : 

11. (*a*) : 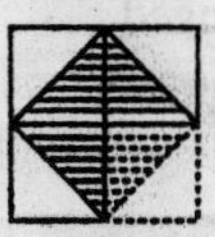

12. (*d*) : 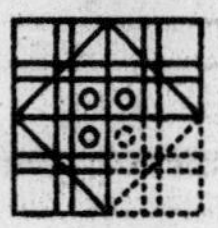

CHAPTER 8

Visual Memory

These type of problems are based on the mirror images or reflections of number, letters and figures. While attempting such questions one must be able to visualise clearly the questioned reflections, be they on vertical plane or on horizontal plane. Study the chart and information given below. The visualisation of letters and numbers is easier than the visualisation of figures for the simple reason that the figures have many forms and all cannot be summed up.

Horizontal Mirror Images (HMI) of Numbers

Number	*HMI*	*Number*	*HMI*
0	0	5	ꙅ
1	I	6	ɓ
2	Ƨ	7	٢
3	Ɛ	8	8
4	ᔭ	9	ɑ

Note : HMI of 0 and 8 remain unchanged

Vertical Mirror Images (VMI) of Numbers

Numbers :	0	1	2	3	4	5	6	7	8	9
VMI :	0	I	Ƨ	3	Ɫ	ꙅ	ɑ	⅃	8	6

Note : VMI of 0, 3 and 8 remain unchanged.
Exceptions in style need caution. Example 3 will be Ɛ, or 8 will be 8.

Horizontal Mirror Images of Capital Letters

Letter	HMI	Letter	HMI	H letter	HMI
A	A	J	Ⴑ	S	Ƨ
B	ꓭ	K	ꓘ	T	T
C	Ɔ	L	⅃	U	U
D	ꓷ	M	M	V	V
E	Ǝ	N	И	W	W
F	ꟻ	O	O	X	X
G	Ꭾ	P	ꟼ	Y	Y
H	H	Q	Ọ	Z	Z
I	I	R	Я		

Note : HMI of A, H, I, M, O, T, U, V, W, X and Y remain unchanged.

Exceptions in style need caution. Example : A will be A, or X will be X.

Vertical Mirror Images of Capital Letters

Letters :	A	B	C	D	E	F	G	H	I	J	K	L	M
VMI :	∀	B	C	D	E	Ⅎ	⅁	H	I	ſ	K	⅂	W
Letters :	N	O	P	Q	R	S	T	U	V	W	X	Y	Z
VMI :	И	O	Ь	Ό	ʁ	ꙅ	⊥	∩	Λ	M	X	⅄	Z

Note : VMI of C, D, E, H, I, K, O and X remain unchanged.

Horizontal Mirror Images of Small Letters

Letter	HMI	Letter	HMI	Letter	HMI
a	ɒ	j	į	s	ƨ
b	d	k	ʞ	t	ɟ
c	ɔ	l	l	u	u
d	b	m	m	v	v
e	ɘ	n	n	w	w
f	ɟ	o	o	x	x
g	ǫ	p	q	y	y
h	ʜ	q	p	z	z
i	i	r	ɿ		

Note : HMI of o, v, w and x remain unchanged.

Vertical Mirror Images of Small Letters

Letter :	a	b	c	d	e	f	g	h	i	j	k	l	m
VMI :	ɐ	p	c	q	ə	ɟ	ƃ	ɥ	!	ɾ	ʞ	l	ɯ
Letter :	n	o	p	q	r	s	t	u	v	w	x	y	z
VMI :	u	o	b	d	ɹ	s	ʇ	n	ʌ	ʍ	x	ʎ	z

Note : VMI of c, o and x remain unchanged. Letter l has exceptions: if it is a straight vertical line – 1 then it remains unchanged.

MULTIPLE CHOICE QUESTIONS

Directions (Qs. 1 to 15) : *In each question below which is the exact horizontal mirror image?*

1. DuST
(*a*) ꓕSuD (*b*) TSnD
(*c*) TSuᗡ (*d*) ᗡuST

2. CHAIR
(*a*) ЯIHAƆ (*b*) ЯIAHƆ
(*c*) ЯIAHC (*d*) ƆHAIR

3. WHOM
(*a*) MOHW (*b*) WOHM
(*c*) ʍHOW (*d*) ʍOHM

4. plaque
(*a*) ǝupalq (*b*) ǝuqblp
(*c*) qlapue (*d*) ǝupalp

5. brows
(*a*) dɿowƨ (*b*) drows
(*c*) ƨword (*d*) sword

6. flying
(*a*) gniylꟻ (*b*) gnilyꟻ
(*c*) gniylf (*d*) gniylꟻ

7. 4379
(*a*) ϱ7Ɛ4 (*b*) 4379
(*c*) ϱ7Ɛ4 (*d*) ϱ7Ɛ4

8. 57182
(*a*) 28175 (*b*) 28175
(*c*) 28175 (*d*) 28175

9. 69430
(*a*) 03496 (*b*) 03496
(*c*) 03496 (*d*) 03496

10. 2JKS
(*a*) SKJ2 (*b*) SKJ2
(*c*) SKJ2 (*d*) SKJ2

11. P9Yf3
(*a*) ƐfY9P (*b*) ƐfY9P
(*c*) ƐfY9P (*d*) ƐfY9P

12. GZ5QRh
(*a*) hRQ5ZG (*b*) hRQ5ZG
(*c*) hRQ5ZG (*d*) hRQ5ZG

13. 2$%CH
(*a*) HC%$2 (*b*) HC%$2
(*c*) HC%$2 (*d*) HC%$2

14. 7↑FN8
(*a*) 8NF↑7 (*b*) 8NF↑7
(*c*) 8NF↑7 (*d*) 8NF↑7

15. yk19G
(*a*) G91ky (*b*) G91ky
(*c*) G91ky (*d*) G91ky

ANSWERS

1	2	3	4	5	6	7	8	9	10
(*c*)	(*b*)	(*a*)	(*a*)	(*c*)	(*d*)	(*b*)	(*a*)	(*d*)	(*c*)
11	**12**	**13**	**14**	**15**					
(*d*)	(*b*)	(*c*)	(*a*)	(*d*)					

CHAPTER 9

Discrimination

In these problems one has to count the geometrical figures in a given complex figure. A little bit of systematic approach is needed to get the correct number of the asked figure. The shapes of all geometrical figures must be clear in mind.

SOLVED EXAMPLES

1. How many straight lines are used to make the figure given below?

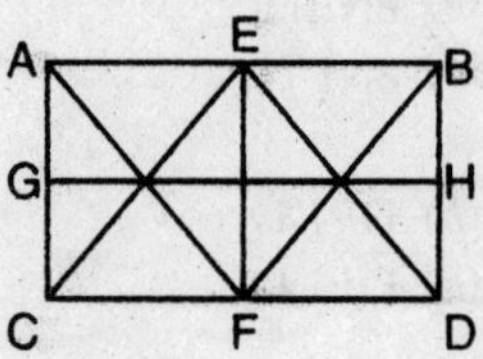

(*a*) 8 (*b*) 6
(*c*) 10 (*d*) 12

Answer (*c*) : The method of counting is given below.

The horizontal lines are AB, GH and CD i.e. – 3 lines, the vertical lines are AC, EF and BD i.e. – 3 lines, the diagonal lines are CE, FB, AF and ED i.e. – 4 lines, therefore the total number of straight lines is

3 + 3 + 4 = 10

2. How many square are there is this figure?

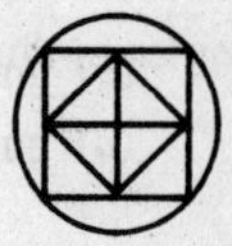

(*a*) 4 (*b*) 6
(*c*) 8 (*d*) 5

Answer (*b*) : The squares are counted in this manner.

There is one main square ABCD divided into four parts by lines EF and GH. So, all the 5 squares are ABCD, AEGI, GICF, EBIH and IHFD. The square in the middle is EGHF. The total number of squares are 5 + 1 = 6

MULTIPLE CHOICE QUESTIONS

1. How many triangles are there in the figure given below?

(*a*) 24 (*b*) 27
(*c*) 25 (*d*) 26

2. How many parallelograms are there in this figure?

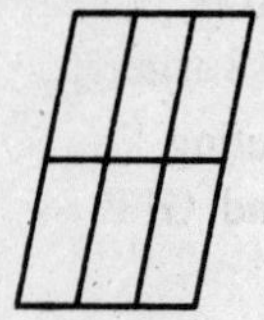

(*a*) 9 (*b*) 13
(*c*) 15 (*d*) 18

3. How many triangles are there in this figure?

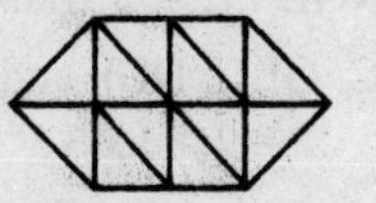

(*a*) 16 (*b*) 17
(*c*) 18 (*d*) 19

4. The number of rectangles in this figure are.

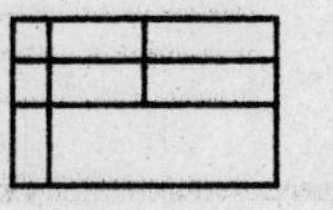

(*a*) 21 (*b*) 24
(*c*) 23 (*d*) 25

5. How many squares are hidden in this figure?

(*a*) 7 (*b*) 8
(*c*) 9 (*d*) 10

6. The number of triangles in this figure are.

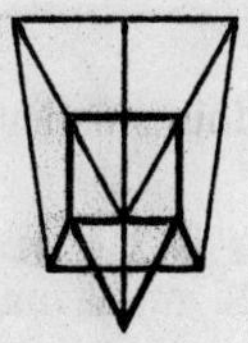

(*a*) 19 (*b*) 16
(*c*) 21 (*d*) 15

7. How many squares are there in the figure given below?

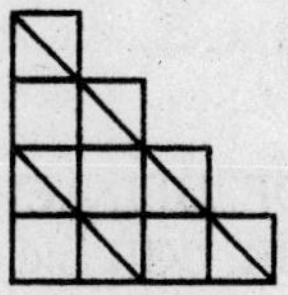

(*a*) 10 (*b*) 11
(*c*) 13 (*d*) 14

8. The number of circles in this figure is

(*a*) 6 (*b*) 5
(*c*) 2 (*d*) 3

9. How many triangles are there in the figure given below?

(*a*) 28 (*b*) 36
(*c*) 24 (*d*) 32

10. How many straight lines are needed to draw the figure in question 9?
(*a*) 10 (*b*) 12
(*c*) 11 (*d*) 13

EXPLANATORY ANSWERS

1. (*a*) :

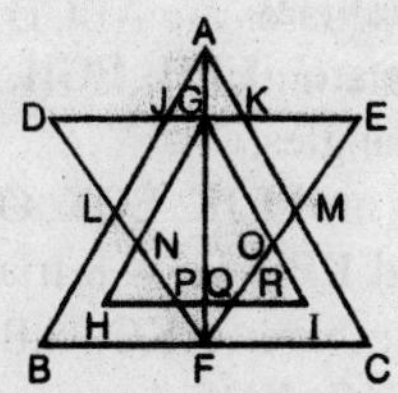

- The main triangles making the figure are ABC, DEF and GHI *i.e.,* – 3 triangles
- The simplest triangles are AJG, AGK, KEM, DJL, NHP, PQF, QFR and ORI *i.e.,* – 8 triangles
- The triangles formed by the bisecting line AF are ABF, AFC, GHQ, GQI, DGF and GFE *i.e.,* – 6 triangles
- The triangles formed inbetween the three triangles AJK, ALF, AMF, DGN, DGF, LBF, MFC, GEO, GNF and GOF – *i.e.,* 10 triangles
- So, the total number of triangles is
  3 + 8 + 6 + 10 = 27

2. (*d*) :

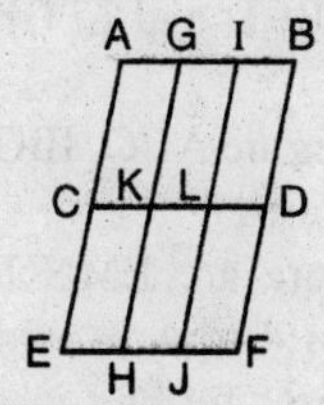

- The main parallelogram is ABEF *i.e.,* 1 parallelogram
- When divided into half by line CD the main figure has ABCD and CDEF *i.e.,* 2 parallelograms
- When further lines GH and IJ are drawn, the parallelograms are AGEH, GIJH and IBJF *i.e.,* – 3 parallelograms.
- The simplest parallelogram are AGCK, CKEH, GIKL, KLHJ, IBLD and LDJF *i.e.* – 6 parallelograms
  Other parallelograms are AICL, CLEJ, GBKD, KDHF, AIEJ and GBHF – *i.e.,* 6 parallelograms
  So, the total number of parallelograms is
  1 + 2 + 3 + 6 + 6 = 18

3. (a) : 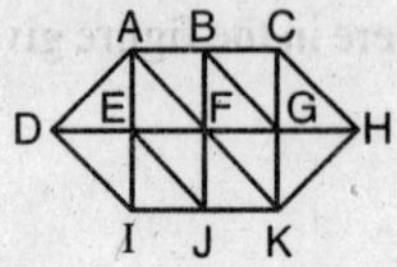

The simplest triangles are ADE, DEI, AEF, ABF, EIJ, EFJ, BFG, BCG, FJK, FGK, CGH and GHK – *i.e.,* – 12 triangles

The bisected triangles are ADI and CHK – *i.e.* – 2 triangles

Other triangles are AIK and ACK *i.e.,* – 2 triangles

So, the total number of triangles is

12 + 2 + 2 = 16

4. (c) : 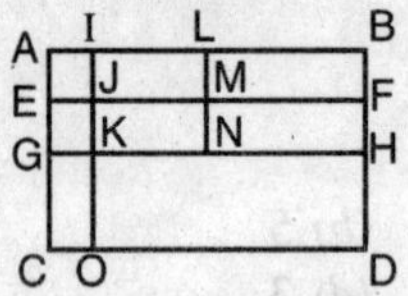

The main rectangle is ABCD – *i.e.,* – 1 rectangle

The simplest rectangles are AIEJ, ILJM, LBMF, EJGK, JMKN, MFNH, GKCO and KHOD *i.e.* – 8 rectangles.

The rectangles which have two parts are ALEM, IBJF, EMGN, JFKH, AIGK, IKLN, LBNH, EJCO and GHCD *i.e.* – 9 rectangles.

The rectangles which have three parts are AICO, ABEF and EFGH *i.e.* – 3 rectangles

The rectangles which have four parts are ALGN and IBKH *i.e.* – 2 rectangles

So, the total number of rectangles

1 + 8 + 9 + 3 + 2 = 23

5. (d) : 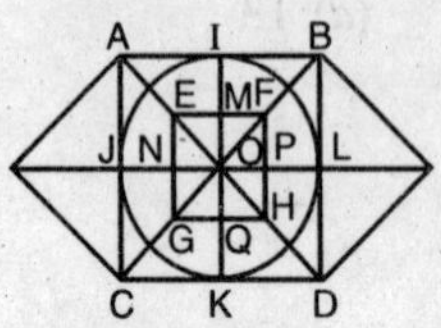

The main squares are ABCD and EFGH *i.e.,* – 2 squares

The simplest outer squares are AIJO, IBOL, JOCK and OLKD *i.e.,* – 4 squares

The simplest inner square are EMNO, NOGQ, MFOP and OPQH *i.e.,* – 4 squares

There are no other squares formed in the figure

So, the total number of squares is

2 + 4 + 4 = 10

6. (b) : 

The main triangles are : ABC, DEF, LNF, and HJC *i.e.* 4 triangles

The simplest triangles are : HIC, IJC, HDC, JCE, DKL, LMF, MFN and NOE *i.e.* – 8 triangles

Other triangles are : AGC, GBC, DCF and CEF – *i.e.* 4 triangles

So, the total number of triangles is 4 + 8 + 4 = 16

7. (c) : 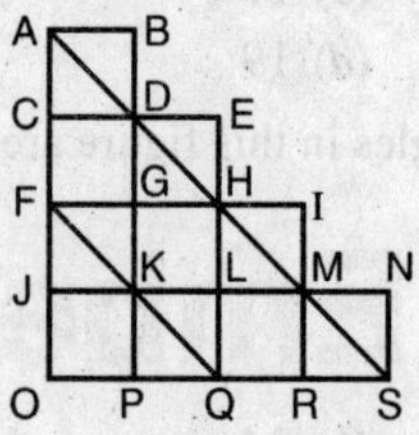

The simplest squares are : ABCD, CDFG, DEGH, FGJK, GHKL, HILM, JKOP, KLPQ, LMQR and MNRS *i.e.* – 10 squares.

Other squares are : CEJL, FHOQ and GIPR *i.e.* – 3 squares

So, the total number of squares is 10 + 3 = 13

8. (a) : 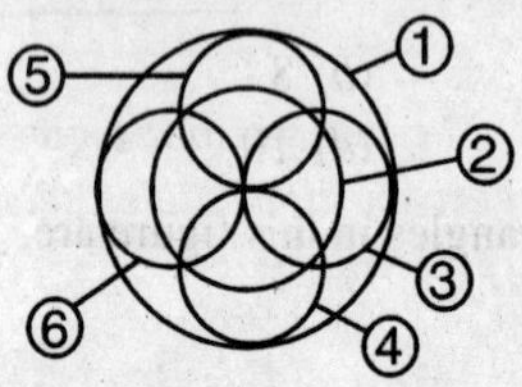

There are two main circles and four smaller circles intersecting each other.

So, the total number of circles is 2 + 4 = 6

9. (d) : 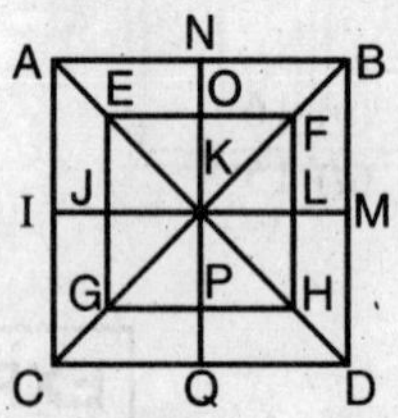

The larger triangles are : ABC, BCD, ABD and ACD *i.e.* – 4 triangles

The smaller triangles are : EFH, EGH, EFG and FGH *i.e.* – 4 triangles.

The simplest triangles are : EJK, EOK, OFK, JKG, FKL, KLH, KGP and KPH *i.e.* – 8 triangles

The bisected triangles are: AKC, ABK, CKD, KBD, EKG, EKF, KHG, KHF, i.e., –8 triangle.

Other triangles are : ANK, NKB, KBM, KMD, KQD, KQC, KCI, IKA *i.e.* – 8 triangles.

So, the total number of triangles is

4 + 4 + 8 + 8 + 8 = 32

10. (b) : The horizontal lines are : AB, EF, KL, GH and CD *i.e.* – 5 lines.

The vertical lines are AC, EG, IJ, FH and BD *i.e.* – 5 lines.

The diagonal lines are : AD and BC *i.e.* – 2 lines.

So, the total number of lines used to draw this figure is 5 + 5 + 2 = 12

CHAPTER

10 Embedded Figures

In these type of questions a figure form is given followed by alternative figures. In one of these figure options the given form is embedded. Practice of visualisation comes handy in attempting such easy questions.

MULTIPLE CHOICE QUESTIONS

Directions (Qs. 1 to 6) : *In the questions given below a figure is given. From the given alternatives select the one in which the given figure is embedded.*

1. 

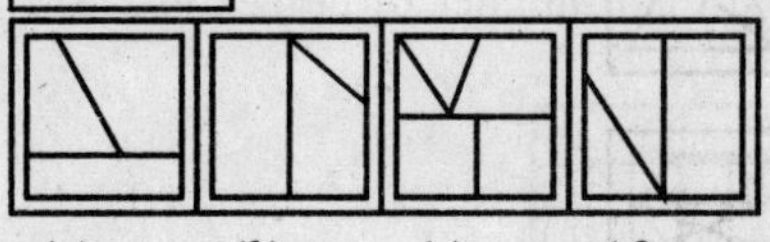

(*a*) (*b*) (*c*) (*d*)

2. 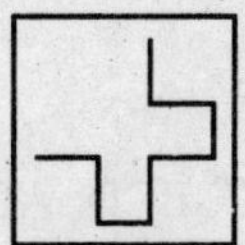

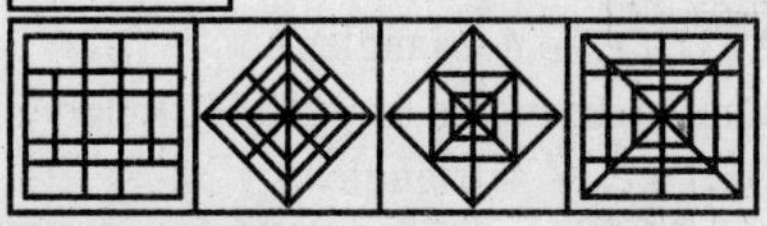

(*a*) (*b*) (*c*) (*d*)

3. 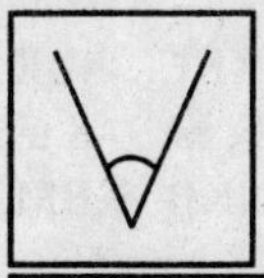

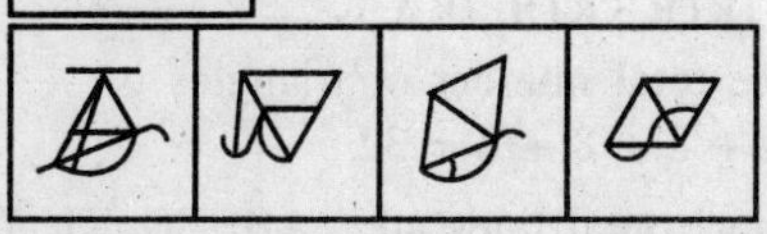

(*a*) (*b*) (*c*) (*d*)

4. 

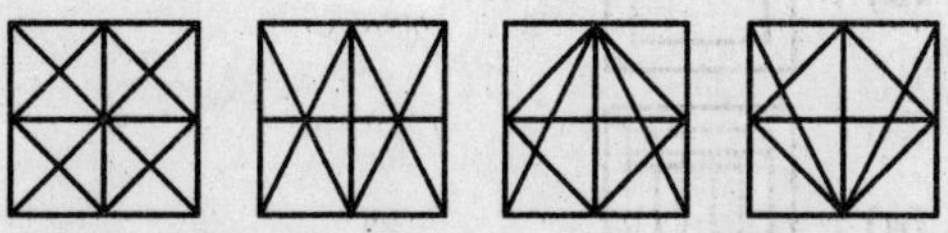

(*a*) (*b*) (*c*) (*d*)

5. 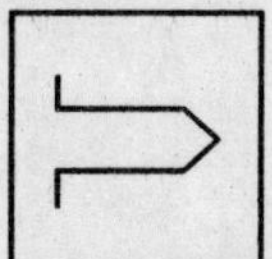

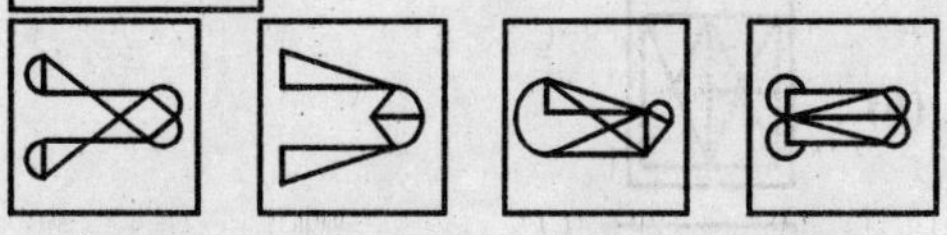

(*a*) (*b*) (*c*) (*d*)

6. 

(*a*) (*b*) (*c*) (*d*)

Directions (Qs. 7 to 10) : *In each question given below find the figure form which is embedded in the given pattern.*

7. 

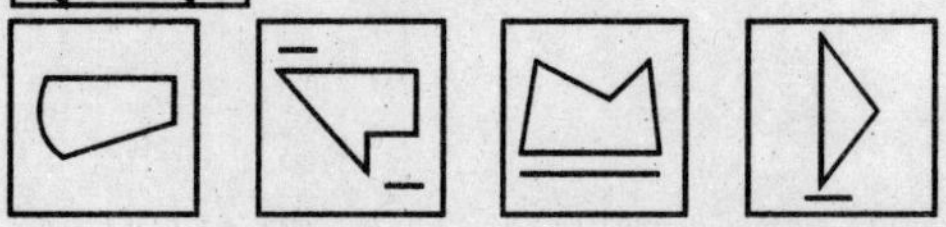

(*a*) (*b*) (*c*) (*d*)

8. 

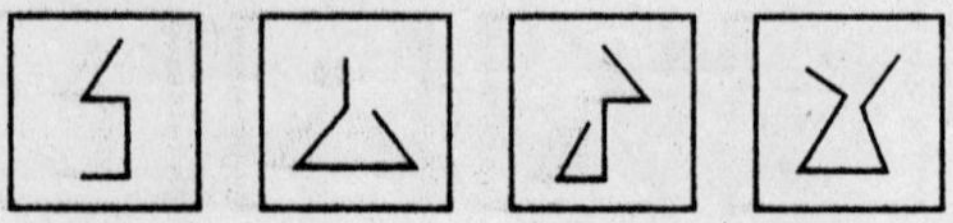

(a) (b) (c) (d)

9. 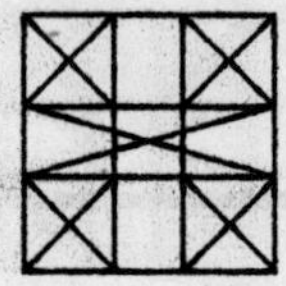

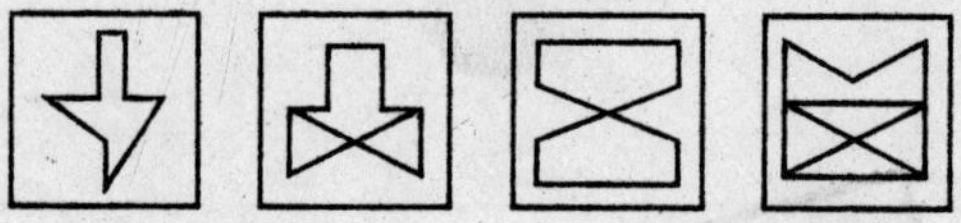

(a) (b) (c) (d)

10. 

(a) (b) (c) (d)

EXPLANATORY ANSWERS

1. (a) : 

2. (a) : 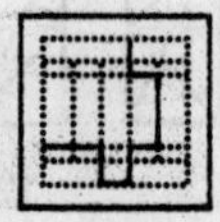

3. (d) : 

4. (b) : 

5. (a) : 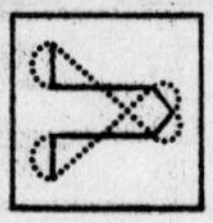

6. (b) : 

7. (d) : 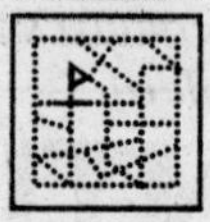

8. (b) : 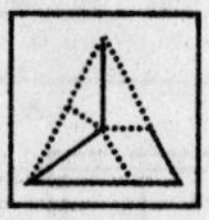

9. (c) : 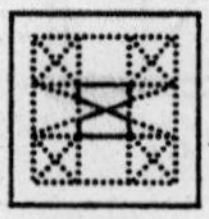

10. (d) : 

QUANTITATIVE APTITUDE

CHAPTER 1

Numbers System

Whole Numbers

In our System of numeration, numbers are written by using the symbols 0, 1, 2, 3, 4, 5, 6, 7, 8 and 9 with each symbol getting a value depending on the place it occupies. These symbols are called digits. A number related to the objects in a collection gives an idea of how many objects are there in the collection.

The number 789345126 can be represented as:

Ten crores	Crores	Ten Lacs (Millions)	Lacs	Ten Thousands	Thousands	Hundreds	Tens	Units
10^8	10^7	10^6	10^5	10^4	10^3	10^2	10^1	10^0
7	8	9	3	4	5	1	2	6

This number can be read as: "Seventy-eight crores, ninety-three lacs, forty-five thousands, one hundred twenty six".

1. **Natural Numbers or Positive Integers (N = 1, 2, 3, 4, 5 .....):** These are also called counting numbers. When two natural numbers are added or multiplied together, the result is always a natural number. Therefore, all positive integers, used for counting objects, are always **natural numbers** whereas zero together with negative integers and fractional numbers are not natural numbers.
2. **Whole Numbers: (W = 0, 1, 2, 3, 4, 5, ...):** The number '0' together with the natural numbers gives us the numbers which are called **whole numbers,** e.g., 0, 1, 2, 3, 4 ..... etc. whereas –10, –15, –12 ..... or $\frac{1}{5}, \frac{2}{9}, \frac{4}{5}$..... etc. are not whole numbers.
3. **Integers: (I = ..., –5, –4, –3, –2, –1, 0, 1, 2, 3, 4, 5, ...):** The negative numbers together with the whole numbers are called integers. The numbers –1, –2, –3, –4, –5, ... are called negative integers and 1, 2, 3, 4, 5, ..., *i.e.,* natural numbers are called positive integers. The number 0 is simply an integer, *i.e.,* it is neither positive nor negative.
4. **Rational Numbers:** A rational number is a number that can be put in the form $\frac{p}{q}$ where p and q are both integers and $q \neq 0$, e.g., 8, $-\frac{7}{5}$, $-\frac{3}{4}$, $\frac{1}{7}$, 0 .... are all rational numbers i.e. a rational number may be positive, zero or negative.
5. **Irrational Numbers:** An irrational number is a number that can not be put in the form $\frac{p}{q}$ where p and q are both integers and $q \neq 0$, e.g., $\sqrt{5}, \sqrt{11}, \sqrt{15}, 3 + \sqrt{5}$ .... etc. are all irrational numbers.
6. **Real Numbers:** All those numbers which are either rational or irrational, are called real numbers, e.g., $\frac{11}{17}$, $\frac{19}{21}$, $-\frac{7}{8}$, $\sqrt{7}$, $8 + \sqrt{3}$ etc. are real numbers.
7. **Even Numbers:** All those numbers which are exactly divisible by 2, are called 'even numbers', e.g., 2, 8, 14, 28, 52 etc. are even numbers.
8. **Odd Numbers:** All those numbers which are not exactly divisible by 2, are called 'odd numbers', e.g., 1, 3, 5, 7, 9, 19 etc. are odd numbers.

9. **Composite Numbers:** The numbers which are divisible not only by 1 or themselves, but by some other numbers also, are called the 'composite numbers'. In other words, the numbers which have more than two factors are called 'composite numbers.', e.g., 4, 9, 15, 18, 27, ... etc. are composite numbers.
10. **Prime Numbers:** The numbers which have only two factors, 1 and the number itself are called 'prime numbers', e.g., 2, 5, 11, 19, 23, 31, ... etc. are prime numbers.
11. **Co-primes:** Two numbers which have only 1 as the common factor are called 'co-primes'. 5 and 7 are co-primes. So are 15 and 16.
12. **Twin Primes:** Two prime numbers which differ by 2, are called 'twin primes', e.g., 3, 5; 5, 7; 11, 13; 71, 73 are some pairs of twin primes.
13. **Consecutive Numbers:** The numbers which are following or coming after other numbers in regular order, are called consecutive numbers. 4, 6, 8, 10 are consecutive even numbers and 9, 11, 13, 15 are consecutive odd numbers. 3, 4, 5, 6, 7 ..... etc. are consecutive numbers in the natural order of the number series.

TESTS FOR DIVISIBILITY OF NUMBERS

1. **Divisibility by 2:** A number is divisible by 2, if its units digit is 0, 2, 4, 6 or 8. For example, each of the numbers 130, 244, 566, 278, ... etc. is divisible by 2.
2. **Divisibility by 3:** A number is divisible by 3, if the sum of its digits is a multiple of 3. For example, each of the numbers 312, 213, 456 is divisible by 3 since sum of digits in each of these numbers is (3 + 1 + 2 = 6), (2 + 1 + 3 = 6) and (4 + 5 + 6 = 15) respectively, each of which is a multiple of 3.
3. **Divisibility by 4:** A number is divisible by 4, if the number formed by its digits in ten's and unit's places is divisible by 4. For example, numbers formed by ten's and unit's digits of 1132, 1312, 1400 and 1348 are 32, 12, 00 and 48 respectively which are divisible by 4. Hence, these numbers also are divisible by 4.
4. **Divisibility by 5:** A number is divisible by 5, if its unit's digit is either 0 or 5. For example, each of the numbers 100, 205, 315, 435 is divisible by 5 since unit's digit in each of these numbers is either 0 or 5.
5. **Divisibility by 6:** A number is divisible by 6, if it is divisible by both 2 and 3.
6. **Divisiblity by 8:** A number is divisible by 8, if the number formed by its digits in hundred's, ten's and unit's places is divisible by 8. For example, numbers formed by hundred's, ten's and unit's digits of 1864, 1024, 2008 and 5000 are 864, 024, 008 and 000 respectively which are divisible by 8. Hence, these numbers also are divisible by 8.
7. **Divisibility by 9:** A number is divisible by 9, if the sum of its digits is a multiple of 9. For example, each of the numbers 23409, 454554, 66636 is divisible by 9 since sum of digits in each of these numbers is (2 + 3 + 4 + 0 + 9 = 18), (4 + 5 + 4 + 5 + 5 + 4 = 27) and (6 + 6 + 6 + 3 + 6 = 27) respectively, each of which is a multiple of 9.
8. **Divisibility by 10:** A number is divisible by 10, if its unit's digit is zero. For example, each of the numbers 50, 80, 1310, 1400 is divisible by 10 since unit's digit in each of these numbers is 0.
9. **Divisibility by 11:** A number is divisible by 11, if the difference of the sum of its digits in even places and the sum of its digits in odd places (starting from unit's place) is either 0 or a multiple of 11. For example, each of the numbers 909183, 540045 and 184712 is divisible by 11 since in each of the numbers difference of the sum of digits in even places and sum of the digits in odd places is [(9 + 9 + 8) – (0 + 1 + 3) = 22], [(5 + 0 + 4) – (4 + 0 + 5) = 0] and [(8 + 7 + 2) – (1 + 4 + 1) = 11] respectively, each of which is either '0' or a multiple of '11'.
10. **Divisibility by 12:** A number is divisible by 12, if it is divisible by 3 and 4 both.

    For example, take a number 769824

    (*i*) Sum of digits = 7 + 6 + 9 + 8 + 2 + 4 = 36, it is divisible by 3.

    (*ii*) The number has 24 as its last two digits, which is divisible by 4.

    Hence, 769824 is divisible by 3 and 4 both, so it is divisible by 12.
11. **Divisibility by 14:** A number is divisible by 14, if it is divisible by 2 and 7 both.
12. **Divisibility by 15:** A number is divisible by 15, if it is divisible by 3 and 5 both.
13. **Divisibility by 16:** A number is divisible by 16, if the number formed by its last four digits is divisible by 16.

    For example, take a number 9877856, the number formed by its last four digits is 7856, which is divisible by 16. Hence, the number 9877856 is divisible by 16.
14. **Divisibility by 24:** A number is divisible by 24, if it is divisible by 3 and 8 both.
15. **Divisibility by 40:** A number is divisible by 40, if it is divisible by 5 and 8 both.
16. **Divisibility by 80:** A number is divisible by 80, if it is divisible by 5 and 16 both.

[**Note:** If a number is divisible by two co-primes separately, then the number will be also divisible by the product of co-primes.]

EXERCISE

1. The difference between the squares of two consecutive numbers is 25. The numbers are—
A. 11, 12 B. 12, 13
C. 15, 14 D. 14, 13

2. The sum of two digits of a number is 15. If 9 is added to the number, the digits are reversed. The number is—
A. 78 B. 87
C. 69 D. 96

3. A number which when multiplied by 11 is as much above 180 as it was originally below it. The number is—
A. 25 B. 30
C. 40 D. 45

4. Divide ₹ 53 among X, Y, Z so that X may receive ₹ 7 more than Y, and Y may receive ₹ 8 more than Z.
A. 10, 15, 18 B. 18, 10, 25
C. 20, 12, 27 D. 25, 18, 10

5. If a = 16 and b = 15, then what is the value of $\frac{a^2+b^2+ab}{a^3-b^3}$ = ?
A. $\frac{1}{2}$ B. $\frac{1}{3}$
C. 1 D. 2

6. Find the number which when multiplied by 16 is increased by 225.
A. 13 B. 14
C. 15 D. 16

7. What is the largest number of four digits which is exactly divisible by 88?
A. 9999 B. 9988
C. 9944 D. 9998

8. If $\frac{a}{b}=\frac{4}{3}$, then $\frac{3a+2b}{3a-2b}$ = ?
A. 2 B. 3
C. 4 D. 5

9. If $\frac{x}{y}=\frac{3}{4}$, then the value of $\frac{6}{7}+\frac{y-x}{y+x}$ = ?
A. 1 B. 2
C. 3 D. 4

10. If the number $(10^n - 1)$ is divisible by 11, then n is—
A. odd number B. even number
C. any number D. multiple of 11

11. $\left(1-\frac{1}{3}\right)\left(1-\frac{1}{4}\right)\left(1-\frac{1}{5}\right)...\left(1-\frac{1}{n}\right)$ = ?
A. $\frac{42}{29}$ B. $\frac{n-1}{n}$
C. $\frac{2}{n}$ D. 0

12. $\left(2-\frac{1}{3}\right)\left(2-\frac{3}{5}\right)\left(2-\frac{5}{7}\right)...\left(2-\frac{997}{999}\right)$ = ?
A. $\frac{997}{999}$ B. ∞
C. $\frac{997}{3}$ D. $\frac{1001}{3}$

13. Divide 48 into two parts such that 7 times the first part added to 5 times the second part is 246. Find the first part.
A. 2 B. 3
C. 4 D. 5

14. The sum of a number and its reciprocal is thrice the difference of the number and its reciprocal. Find the number.
A. $\sqrt{2}$ B. $\sqrt{3}$
C. $\sqrt{5}$ D. $\sqrt{7}$

15. What should be added to the product of four consecutive odd numbers to make it a perfect square?
A. 13 B. 14
C. 15 D. 16

16. A boy was asked to find $\frac{7}{9}$ of a fraction. He made a mistake of dividing the fraction by $\frac{7}{9}$ and so got an answer which exceeded the correct answer by $\frac{8}{21}$. Find the correct answer.
A. 2/3 B. 5/7
C. 7/12 D. 7/15

17. If 40% of a number is 360, what will be 15% of 15% of that number?
A. 11.5 B. 20.25
C. 15.5 D. 21.75

18. The sum of two numbers is 25 and the difference of their square is 75. Find the difference between the numbers.
A. 2 B. 3
C. 4 D. 5

19. Ram eats 8 bananas in the morning, 5 in the afternoon and 2 in the evening. How many dozens of bananas does he eat in a day.
A. $1\frac{1}{4}$ B. $\frac{1}{4}$
C. $\frac{3}{13}$ D. $14\frac{17}{30}$

20. $47^{7.5} \div 47^{\frac{3}{2}} \times 47^{-3} = \left(\sqrt{47}\right)^{?}$ What should come in place of the question mark (?) in the following equation?
A. 5 B. 6
C. 7 D. 8

ANSWERS

1	2	3	4	5	6	7	8	9	10
B	A	B	B	C	C	C	B	A	B
11	**12**	**13**	**14**	**15**	**16**	**17**	**18**	**19**	**20**
C	D	B	A	D	C	B	B	A	B

EXPLANATORY ANSWERS

1. Let the numbers are x and $(x + 1)$

$\therefore \quad (x + 1)^2 - x^2 = 25$

$\Rightarrow \quad x^2 + 1 + 2x - x^2 = 25$

$\Rightarrow \quad 2x + 1 = 25$

$\Rightarrow \quad 2x = 25 - 1 = 24$

$\therefore \quad x = \frac{24}{2} = 12$

$\therefore \quad x + 1 = 12 + 1 = 13$

Hence, the numbers are 12, 13.

2. Let x be the digit in units place. Digit in ten's place is then $15 - x$.

$\therefore$ The number $= 10\,(15 - x) + x$

The new number with reverse digits

$= 10 \times x + (15 - x)$

$\therefore \quad 10(15 - x) + x + 9 = 10x + 15 - x$

$\Rightarrow \quad 150 - 10x + x + 9 = 9x + 15$

$\Rightarrow \quad 18x = 144$

$x = \frac{144}{18} = 8$

The digit of ten's place $= 15 - 8 = 7$

$\therefore$ The required number = 78.

3. Let the number is x

$\therefore \quad 180 - x = 11x - 180$

$\Rightarrow \quad 180 + 180 = 11x + x$

$\Rightarrow \quad 360 = 12x,$

$\Rightarrow \quad x = \frac{360}{12} = 30.$

4. Let Y receives ₹ a. Then X receives ₹ $(a + 7)$ and Z receives ₹ $(a - 8)$

But, $a + 7 + a + a - 8 =$ ₹ 53

$3a - 1 = 53,$

$\Rightarrow \quad 3a = 53 + 1$

$\Rightarrow \quad 3a = 54,$

$\therefore \quad a = \frac{54}{3} =$ ₹ 18. = Y's share

X's share $= a + 7 = 18 + 7 =$ ₹ 25

Z's share $= a - 8 = 18 - 8 =$ ₹ 10.

5. Given $a = 16$ and $b = 15$, then $\frac{a^2 + b^2 + ab}{a^3 - b^3}$

$= \frac{a^2 + b^2 + ab}{(a-b)\left(a^2 + b^2 + ab\right)} = \frac{1}{a-b} = \frac{1}{16-15} = 1$

6. Let the required no. $= x$

then, $\quad 16x - x = 225$

$\Rightarrow \quad 15x = 225 \;\therefore\; x = 15$

7. The greatest no. of 4 digit = 9999

Now, after dividing 9999 by 88, we get Remainder = 55

Hence, the largest 4 digit no. = 9999 – 55 = 9944

8. $\frac{3a+2b}{3a-2b} = \frac{3\frac{a}{b}+2}{3\frac{a}{b}-2} = \frac{3\times\frac{4}{3}+2}{3\times\frac{4}{3}-2} = \frac{6}{2} = 3$

9. $\frac{6}{7} + \frac{y-x}{y+x} = \frac{6}{7} + \frac{1-x/y}{1+x/y} = \frac{6}{7} + \frac{1-3/4}{1+3/4} = \frac{6}{7} + \frac{1}{7} = 1$

10. n is even number.

11. $\frac{2}{3} \times \frac{3}{4} \times \frac{4}{5} \times \ldots \times \frac{n-1}{n} = \frac{2}{n}$

12. $\frac{5}{3} \times \frac{7}{5} \times \frac{9}{7} \times \ldots \times \frac{1001}{999} = \frac{1001}{3}$

13. Let the first part $= x$

then 2nd part $= (48 - x)$

By question, $\quad 7x + 5(48 - x) = 246$

$\Rightarrow \quad 2x = 246 - 240 \;\therefore\; x = 3$

14. Let the no. $= x$

then its reciprocal $= \frac{1}{x}$

By the question, $\left(x + \frac{1}{x}\right) = 3\left(x - \frac{1}{x}\right)$

$\Rightarrow \quad \frac{x^2+1}{x} = \frac{3\left(x^2-1\right)}{x}$

$\Rightarrow \quad x^2 + 1 = 3x^2 - 3$

$\Rightarrow \quad 3x^2 - x^2 = 3 + 1 \;\therefore\; x = \sqrt{2}.$

15. Let the four consecutive odd numbers be $(2x - 3)$, $(2x - 1)$, $(2x + 1)$ and $(2x + 3)$

$\therefore$ Their product $= (2x - 1)(2x + 1)(2x - 3)(2x + 3)$

$= (4x^2 - 1)(4x^2 - 9) = 16x^4 - 40x^2 + 9$

$= (4x^2 - 5)^2 - 16$

Hence, on adding 16, the result will be a perfect square.

16. Let the required fraction = x

then, by the question $x \div \frac{7}{9} - x \times \frac{7}{9} = \frac{8}{21}$

$\Rightarrow \quad x \times \frac{9}{7} - \frac{7x}{9} = \frac{8}{21} \Rightarrow \frac{32x}{63} = \frac{8}{21}$

$\Rightarrow \quad x = \frac{8}{21} \times \frac{63}{32} = \frac{3}{4}$

Hence, the correct answer $= \frac{3}{4} \times \frac{7}{9} = \frac{7}{12}$.

17. Let a number be x

then $\quad 40\%$ of $x = 360$

$\Rightarrow \quad \frac{40}{100} \times x = 360$

$\therefore \quad x = 360 \times \frac{100}{40} = 900$

Now by the question,

15% of 15% of $900 = \frac{15}{100} \times \frac{15}{100} \times 900 = \frac{81}{4} = 20.25.$

18. Let two numbers are a and b

Given, $\quad a + b = 25$

and $\quad a^2 - b^2 = 75$

$\Rightarrow \quad (a + b)(a - b) = 75$

$\Rightarrow \quad (a - b) = \frac{75}{(a+b)} = \frac{75}{25} = 3.$

19. Total dozen of bananas Ram eats in a day

$= \frac{8}{12} + \frac{5}{12} + \frac{2}{12} = \frac{15}{12} = 1\frac{1}{4}$

20. $47^{7.5} \div 47^{\frac{3}{2}} \times 47^{-3} = \left(\sqrt{47}\right)^?$

Let ? = x

then $\quad (47)^{\frac{15}{2}} \div (47)^{\frac{3}{2}} \times (47)^{-3} = (47)^{\frac{x}{2}}$

$\Rightarrow \quad (47)^{\frac{15}{2} - \frac{3}{2} - 3} = (47)^{\frac{x}{2}}$

$\Rightarrow \quad (47)^{\frac{6}{2}} = (47)^{\frac{x}{2}}$

$\therefore \quad x = 6.$

Decimal Fraction

FRACTION

The relation to represent some part of the body to the whole body is known *Fraction*. For example $\frac{2}{5}$ is a fraction where 2 is the numerator and 5 is the denominator.

Important Facts :

(i) A fraction is also called a rational number.

(ii) A fraction is unity when its numerator and denominator are equal.

(iii) When a fraction is reduced in its lowest term, its numerator and denominator are prime to each other, *i.e.*, they have no common factor.

(iv) The value of fraction is not altered by multiplying or dividing the numerator and the denominator by the same number.

Vulgar or Common Fraction : The fraction such as $\frac{2}{9}, \frac{7}{11}, \frac{3}{10}, \frac{9}{100}$ are called vulgar fraction.

Decimal Fraction : Fractions in which denomi-nators are power of 10 are called decimal fractions.

For example : $\frac{1}{10}, \frac{1}{100}, \frac{7}{1000}$ etc.

Here, $\frac{1}{10}$ is 1 tenths, written as .1

$\frac{1}{100} = .01$

$\frac{7}{1000} = .007$

$\frac{13}{100} = .13$ and so on.

Converting a Decimal into a Vulgar Fraction

First of all write down the given number as numerator without the decimal point, and for the denominator write 1 followed by as many zeros as many are there figures after the decimal point. Now reduce the fraction to its lowest terms.

Ex : *(i)* $0.63 = \frac{63}{100}$

(ii) $3.013 = 3\frac{013}{1000} = 3\frac{13}{1000}$

Addition and Subtraction of Decimal Fractions

First of all write down the numbers under one another. Other than the decimal point lies in one column. After arranging in this way, we add or subtract in usual fashion.

An example : Add 521 + 52.1 + 5.21 + 0.521

Sol : 521.000
52.100
5.210
0.521 After adding we get 578.831

Multiplication of decimal fraction

1. To multiply by 10, 100, 1000, etc

Example : *(i)* 63.02 × 10 = 630.2

(ii) 63.02 × 100 = 6302

(iii) 63.02 × 1000 = 63020

2. To multiply of two or more decimal fractions.

An example : (i) 5.91 × 13 = 76.83

(ii) 6.32 × 0.59 = 3.7288

(iii) 63.2 × 0.01 = 0.632

Conclusion: First of all multiply the given numbers assuming them without the decimal point. Now mark off the decimal point from extreme right in the product as many places of decimal as is the sum of the number of decimal places in the given numbers.

DIVISION OF DECIMALS

1. When the divisor is a counting number

Example : (i) 4.309 ÷ 10 = 0.4309

(ii) 0.0182 ÷ 14 = 0.0013

(iii) 9.586 ÷ 100 = 0.09586

(iv) $0.05 \div 10^3 = 0.00005$

(v) 0.49 ÷ 7 = 0.07

Conclusion **:** (i) When divisor is the power of 10, then shift the decimal point to the left by as many places of decimal as is the power of 10, prefixing zero if necessary.

(ii) When divisor is other than power of 10, then divide as in the case of integers, and in quotient, put the decimal point to give as many places of decimal as are there in the dividend.

2. When the divisor is a decimal

Example:

(i) $0.00066 \div 0.11 = \frac{0.00066}{0.11} = \frac{0.066}{11} = 0.006$

(ii) $42 \div 0.07 = \frac{42}{0.07} = \frac{4200}{7} = 600$

(iii) $32.5 \div 0.0064 = \frac{32.5}{0.0064} = \frac{325000}{64} = 5078.125$

Recurring Decimal : If in a decimal number a digit or a set of digits is repeated again and again, the decimal is known as recurring decimal.

For example:

(i) $2.666... = 2.\dot{6}$

(ii) $1.363636... = 1.\dot{3}\dot{6}$ or $1.\overline{36}$

(iii) $7.3424242... = 7.3\dot{4}\dot{2}$ or $7.3\overline{42}$

Recurring decimal numbers are of two types:

(i) **Pure recurring decimals :** A decimal fraction in which all the figures after the decimal point are repeated is called a pure recurring decimal. For example, $0.\overline{3}$, $0.\overline{37}$, $3.\overline{4579}$ etc

(ii) **Mixed recurring decimals :** A decimal fraction in which at least one figure after the decimal point is not repeated is called a mixed recurring decimal. For example, $0.3\overline{59}$, $0.29\overline{54}$, $0.2\dot{7}$ etc.

Conversion of Recurring into Vulgar Fraction

1. Pure recurring decimals

Rule : Put as many 9's in the denominator at the number of digits under recurring and delete the recurring sign.

For example, $0.\overline{5} = \frac{5}{9}$

$$0.\overline{35} = \frac{35}{99}$$

$$0.\overline{24} = \frac{24}{99} = \frac{8}{33}$$

2. Mixed Recurring Decimals

For example,

(i) $0.1\overline{8}$

Here, numerator = 18 − 1 = 17

and denominator = 9 × 10 = 90

$$\therefore \quad 0.1\dot{8} = \frac{18-1}{90} = \frac{17}{90}$$

(ii) $0.2\dot{7}\dot{9}$

Here, numerator = 279 − 2 = 277

and denominator = 99 × 10 = 990

$$\therefore \quad 0.2\overline{79} = \frac{279-2}{990} = \frac{277}{990}$$

(iii) $$0.3\overline{56} = \frac{356-3}{99\times 10} = \frac{353}{990}$$

(iv) $$2.53\dot{6} = 2 + \frac{536-53}{9\times 100} = 2 + \frac{483}{900}$$

$$= 2 + \frac{161}{300} = 2\frac{161}{300}$$

(v) $$0.43\overline{213} = \frac{43213-43}{999\times 100}$$

$$= \frac{43170}{99900} = \frac{4317}{9990}$$

Addition and Subtraction of recurring decimals

Example : (i) Add $3.\overline{76}$ and $1.4\overline{576}$ and subtract also.

3.7	676767	67	
1.4	576576	57	
(+) 5.2	253344	24	⇒ $5.2\overline{253344}$
(−) 2.3	100191	10	⇒ 2.3100191

(ii) Subtract $3.\overline{75}$ from $25.5\overline{473}$

25.5	473473	47
3.7	575757	57
21.7	897715	90

Hence, the required subtract = $21.7\overline{897715}$

Multiplication and Division of Recurring Decimal

Example 1:

(*i*) $7.\overline{63} \times 11 = 7\frac{63}{99} \times 11$

$= 7\frac{7}{11} \times 11 = \frac{84}{11} \times 11 = 84$

(*ii*) $0.\overline{09} \times 7.\overline{3} = \frac{9}{99} \times 7\frac{3}{9}$

$= \frac{1}{11} \times \frac{66}{9} = \frac{6}{9} = 0.\overline{6}$

(*iii*) $0.\overline{6} \times 7.\overline{3} = \frac{6}{9} \times 7\frac{3}{9}$

$= \frac{6}{9} \times \frac{66}{9} = \frac{44}{9} = 4.\overline{8}$

(*iv*) $0.\overline{06} \div 100 = 0.060606... \div 100 = 0.00\overline{06}$

(*v*) $0.73\dot{2} \div 0.02\dot{7} = 0.732\dot{3} \div 0.0277$

$= \frac{7323-73}{99 \times 100} \div \frac{277-2}{99 \times 100}$

$= \frac{7250}{9900} \div \frac{275}{9900} = \frac{7250}{275} = \frac{290}{11} = 26.\overline{36}$

EXERCISE

1. Which of the following is equivalent to $\frac{15}{25}$?

A. $\frac{150}{25}$ B. $\frac{15}{250}$

C. $\frac{3}{5}$ D. $\frac{60}{75}$

2. If $\frac{9*3}{3*7}$ is equivalent to $\frac{9}{7}$, the sign * is replaced by

A. ÷ B. ×

C. + D. –

3. $\frac{5}{6}$ of an hour is equal to

A. half an hour B. 40 minutes

C. 50 minutes D. 55 minutes

4. An aircraft uses 2/5 of its fuel in flying 1,250 kilometres. The distance travelled on remaining fuel is

A. 1875 km B. 2125 km

C. 250 km D. 475 km

5. If $\frac{4}{3} * \frac{3}{4} = \frac{16}{9}$, then * means

A. + B. –

C. × D. ÷

6. Which of the following is the largest fraction?

$\frac{3}{15}, \frac{5}{20}, \frac{8}{64}, \frac{25}{1000}$

A. $\frac{3}{15}$ B. $\frac{5}{20}$

C. $\frac{8}{64}$ D. $\frac{25}{1000}$

7. Six times x increased by 12 is equal to

A. $\frac{x}{2}$ B. $2x$

C. $6x + 12$ D. $12x + 6$

8. Five times y diminished by 20 is equal to

A. $5y - 20$ B. $5y + 20$

C. $y/4$ D. $4y$

9. The number less than 15 by 7 is

A. $15x - 7$ B. 15/7

C. 15 D. 8

10. If 21 is add to four times a number, the result is 57. The number is

A. 7 B. 8

C. 9 D. 10

11. A number, the sum of whose fourth and fifth parts exceeds their third part by 28, is

A. 120 B. 240

C. 220 D. 160

12. Which fraction should be added to the sum of $5\frac{3}{4}$, $4\frac{4}{5}$ and $7\frac{3}{8}$ to make the result a whole number?

A. $\frac{1}{40}$ B. $\frac{2}{40}$

C. $\frac{3}{40}$ D. $\frac{4}{40}$

13. $\frac{1}{15} + \frac{3}{15} + \frac{5}{15} + \frac{6}{15} = ?$

A. $\frac{10}{15}$ B. $\frac{3}{5}$

C. $\frac{4}{5}$ D. 1

14. A number one-sixth of which exceeds its one-ninth by 100 is

A. 600 B. 900

C. 1500 D. 1800

15. The sum of 1/2, 1/4 and 1/8 of a number is 28. The number is

A. 28 B. 32

C. 36 D. 42

16. The sum of 1/9, 1/3, 1/6 and 7/18 of a number is 150. The number is

A. 120 B. 130

C. 140 D. 150

17. Which is the greatest?
.999, .1011, .1995, .9985

A. .999 B. .1011
C. .1995 D. .9985

18. In decimal system, $9\frac{1}{8}$ may be represented as

A. 9.18 B. 9.125
C. 9.025 D. 9.225

19. 2.205 ÷ 0.15 = ?

A. 1.47 B. 14.7
C. 147 D. 0.147

20. G.C.M. of .24, 3.2 and 16.0 is

A. 80 B. 8
C. .8 D. .08

ANSWERS

1	2	3	4	5	6	7	8	9	10
C	B	C	A	D	B	C	A	D	C
11	**12**	**13**	**14**	**15**	**16**	**17**	**18**	**19**	**20**
B	C	D	D	B	D	A	B	B	D

EXPLANATORY ANSWERS

1. $\frac{15}{25} = \frac{3\times5}{5\times5} = \frac{3}{5}$

2. $\frac{9*3}{3*7} = \frac{9}{7}$, or, $\frac{9\times3}{7\times3} = \frac{9}{7}$, ∴ The sign * is ×.

3. $\frac{5}{6}$ of 1 hr. = $\frac{5}{6}\times 60$ minutes = 50 minutes.

4. Remaining fuel = $1-\frac{2}{5} = \frac{5-2}{5} = \frac{3}{5}$

Distance flown by $\frac{2}{5}$ of fuel = 1250 km.

Distance flown by full fuel = $\frac{1250}{2/5} = \frac{1250\times5}{2}$ km.

Distance flown by $\frac{3}{5}$ of fuel

$= \frac{1250\times5\times3}{2\times5} = 1875$ km.

6. $\frac{3}{15} = \frac{1}{5}, \frac{8}{64} = \frac{1}{8}, \frac{5}{20} = \frac{1}{4}, \frac{25}{1000} = \frac{1}{40}$

Now, the fractions are $\frac{1}{5}, \frac{1}{4}, \frac{1}{8}, \frac{1}{40}$

∴ The largest fraction is $\frac{1}{4} = \frac{5}{20}$

7. $x \times 6 + 12 = 6x + 12$

8. $5 \times y - 20 = 5y - 20$

9. $15 - 7 = 8$

10. Let the number be x

∴ $4x + 21 = 57$ or, $4x = 57 - 21 = 36$

Hence, $x = \frac{36}{4} = 9$

11. Let the number be x

∴ $\frac{x}{4}+\frac{x}{5} = \frac{x}{3}+28$

⇒ $\frac{9x}{20} = \frac{x}{3}+28 \Rightarrow \frac{9x}{20}-\frac{x}{3} = 28$

⇒ $\frac{27x-20x}{60} = 28 \therefore x = \frac{28\times60}{7} = 240.$

12. $5\frac{3}{4}+4\frac{4}{5}+7\frac{3}{8} = \frac{23}{4}+\frac{24}{5}+\frac{59}{8} = \frac{717}{40}$

717/40 becomes whole number when 3/40 is added to it, *i.e.*,

$\frac{717}{40}+\frac{3}{40} = \frac{720}{40} = 18$ which is a whole number.

13. $\frac{1}{15}+\frac{3}{15}+\frac{5}{15}+\frac{6}{15} = \frac{1+3+5+6}{15} = \frac{15}{15} = 1$

14. Let the number be x

$\frac{x}{6} = \frac{x}{9}+100$

⇒ $\frac{x}{6}-\frac{x}{9} = 100, \Rightarrow \frac{x}{18} = 100$

∴ $x = 100 \times 18 = 1800.$

15. Let the number be x

∴ $\frac{x}{2}+\frac{x}{4}+\frac{x}{8} = 28 \Rightarrow \frac{7x}{8} = 28$

∴ $x = \frac{28\times8}{7} = 32.$

16. Let the number be x

∴ $\frac{x}{9}+\frac{x}{3}+\frac{x}{6}+\frac{7x}{18} = 150$

⇒ $\frac{2x+6x+3x+7x}{18} = \frac{18x}{18} = 150 \therefore x = 150.$

17. .999 is the greatest.

18. $9\frac{1}{8} = 9+\frac{1}{8} = 9 + .125 = 9.125$

19. $2.205 \div 0.15 = \frac{2.205}{.15} = \frac{2205}{1000}\times\frac{100}{15} = \frac{2205}{150} = 14.7.$

20. G.C.M. of .24, 3.2 and 16.0

= G.C.M. of $\frac{24, 320 \text{ and } 1600}{100} = \frac{8}{100} = 0.08$

Relation Between Numbers

Simplification is a mathematical operation by which a complex expression of numbers or fractions is converted into a simpler or less difficult form. It is erroneous to solve this type of questions on random basis and a very appropriate method is to apply BODMAS Rule for arriving at the solution of such problems. Each of the letters of the word 'BODMAS' when explained serially, has following implications:

1.	B	→	Bracket	[{ (¯) }]
2.	O	→	of	of
3.	D	→	Division	÷
4.	M	→	Multiplication	×
5.	A	→	Addition	+
6.	S	→	Subtraction	–

Therefore, for simplification, we should remove the brackets first. Thereafter operation for 'of', then for 'division', after that the operation for 'multiplication' and thereafter for 'addition' and at last operation for 'subtraction' should be carried out.

Important Notes

A. In mathematical operations the word 'of' indicates multiplication.

B. While removing brackets, first of all bar bracket '–' and after that small bracket '( )' is removed. Thereafter the curly bracket '{ }' and at last square bracket [ ] is removed.

EXERCISE

1. The value of 51 ÷ 17 ÷ 3 is:
A. 9 B. 4
C. 3 D. 1

2. What will be the value of
40 × 2 ÷ 10 + 5 – 4?
A. 5 B. 8
C. 11 D. 9

3. The value of 28 × 104 ÷ (18 + 6) + 3 is:
A. $124\frac{1}{3}$ B. $104\frac{1}{3}$
C. $125\frac{1}{3}$ D. 128

4. If $75^2 - 65^2 = 2x$, then value of x is:
A. 715 B. 700
C. 688 D. 711

5. The value of 99 × 14 ÷ 11 ÷ 0.7 is:
A. 2.9 B. 1.6
C. 1.8 D. 2.8

6. If 45 – [28 – {37 – (15 – ?) }] = 58, then which of the following should replace the sign of interrogation (?)?
A. 18 B. 17
C. 13 D. 19

7. The value of $8\frac{1}{3}+5\frac{1}{4}\times 13\frac{1}{5} \div 6\frac{3}{5}$ is:
A. $19\frac{1}{3}$ B. $18\frac{5}{6}$
C. $21\frac{1}{3}$ D. $22\frac{1}{2}$

8. The value of $\frac{14}{3}$ of $\frac{5}{8}$ of 72 is:
A. 209 B. 217
C. 210 D. 199

9. What will be the value of
10 × 10 × 10 ÷ (20 ÷ 10 × 10 – 10) + 6?
A. 108 B. 111
C. 106 D. 114

10. What will be the value of $\dfrac{\frac{1}{3}\times 20 \div 4}{\frac{1}{4}\times 25 \div 5}$?
A. 7/3 B. 4/3
C. 5/3 D. 10/3

11. Which of the following is the standard form of $\dfrac{(24\times 13)+(28\div 7)}{(24+13)-\left(\frac{14}{3}\text{ of }\frac{5}{8}\right)}$?
A. $\frac{3792}{409}$ B. $\frac{4792}{309}$
C. $\frac{3792}{411}$ D. $\frac{3092}{409}$

12. If $\dfrac{144+32\div ?-8}{35\div \frac{1}{2}\text{ of }\frac{1}{2}}=1$, then which of the following should replace the sign of interrogation?
A. 7 B. 6
C. 10 D. 8

13. What is the value of $\dfrac{2.70\times 2.70+4.30\times 4.30+8.60\times 2.70}{2.70+4.30}$?
A. 6.8 B. 7.0
C. 7.6 D. 8.5

14. What will be the value of $\dfrac{\left(\sqrt{6}+\frac{1}{\sqrt{6}}\right)^2}{\frac{1}{2}\text{ of } 18 + 4}+\frac{2}{3}$?
A. 101/78 B. 104/71
C. 101/88 D. 99/57

15. 1150 ÷ 50 ÷ 23 + 15 = ?
A. 16 B. 20
C. 22 D. 18

ANSWERS

1	2	3	4	5	6	7	8	9	10
D	D	A	B	C	D	B	C	C	B
11	**12**	**13**	**14**	**15**					
A	D	B	A	A					

EXPLANATORY ANSWERS

1. $\because$ $51 \div 17 \div 3 = \dfrac{51}{17} \div 3 = 3 \div 3 = \dfrac{3}{3} = 1$

2. $\because$ $40 \times 2 \div 10 + 5 - 4$

$$= 40 \times \frac{2}{10} + 5 - 4 = 8 + 5 - 4 = 9.$$

3. $\because$ $28 \times 104 \div (18 + 6) + 3$

$$= 28 \times 104 \div 24 + 3$$

$$= 28 \times \frac{104}{24} + 3 = 28 \times \frac{13}{3} + 3$$

$$= \frac{364}{3} + 3 = \frac{373}{3} = 124\frac{1}{3}$$

4. $\because$ $75^2 - 65^2 = 2x$

$\Rightarrow (75 + 65)(75 - 65) = 2x$

$[\because a^2 - b^2 = (a + b)(a - b)]$

$\Rightarrow \quad 140 \times 10 = 2x \Rightarrow x = 70 \times 10 = 700$

$\therefore$ Value of x is 700.

5. $\because$ $.99 \times 14 \div 11 \div 0.7$

$$= .99 \times \frac{14}{11} \div 0.7 = \frac{.99 \times 14}{11 \times 0.7} = 1.8$$

6. $\because$ $45 - [28 - \{37 - (15 - ?)\}] = 58$

$\Rightarrow \quad 45 - [28 - \{37 - 15 + ?\}] = 58$

$\Rightarrow \quad 45 - [28 - \{22 + ?\}] = 58$

$\Rightarrow \quad 45 - [28 - 22 - ?] = 58$

$\Rightarrow \quad 45 - 28 + 22 + ? = 58$

$\Rightarrow \quad 39 + ? = 58$

$\Rightarrow \quad ? = 58 - 39 = 19$

Therefore, the interrogation sign should be replaced by 19.

7. $\because$ $8\frac{1}{3} + 5\frac{1}{4} \times 13\frac{1}{5} \div 6\frac{3}{5}$

$$= \frac{25}{3} + \frac{21}{4} \times \frac{66}{5} \div \frac{33}{5} = \frac{25}{3} + \frac{21}{4} \times \frac{66}{5} \times \frac{5}{33}$$

$$= \frac{25}{3} + \frac{21}{2} = \frac{50 + 63}{6} = \frac{113}{6} = 18\frac{5}{6}$$

8. $\because$ $\dfrac{14}{3}$ of $\dfrac{5}{8}$ of $72 = \dfrac{14 \times 5 \times 72}{3 \times 8} = 210$

9. $10 \times 10 \times 10 \div (20 \div 10 \times 10 - 10) + 6$

$$= 10 \times 10 \times 10 \div \left(\frac{20}{10} \times 10 - 10\right) + 6$$

$$= 10 \times 10 \times 10 \div (20 - 10) + 6$$

$$= 10 \times 10 \times 10 \div 10 + 6$$

$$= 10 \times 10 \times \frac{10}{10} + 6$$

$$= 10 \times 10 \times 1 + 6 = 100 + 6 = 106$$

10. $\because$ $\dfrac{\frac{1}{3} \times 20 \div 4}{\frac{1}{4} \times 25 \div 5} = \dfrac{\frac{1}{3} \times 5}{\frac{1}{4} \times 5} = \dfrac{\frac{5}{3}}{\frac{5}{4}} = \dfrac{4}{3}$

11. $\because$ $\dfrac{(24 \times 13) + (28 \div 7)}{(24 + 13) - \left(\frac{14}{3} \text{ of } \frac{5}{8}\right)} = \dfrac{312 + 4}{37 - \frac{35}{12}} = \dfrac{316}{\frac{409}{12}} = \dfrac{3792}{409}$

12. If $\dfrac{144 + 32 \div ? - 8}{35 \div \frac{1}{2} \text{ of } \frac{1}{2}} = 1 \Rightarrow \dfrac{144 + \frac{32}{?} - 8}{35 \div \frac{1}{4}} = 1 \Rightarrow \dfrac{136 + \frac{32}{?}}{\frac{35}{\frac{1}{4}}} = 1$

$$\Rightarrow \quad 136 + \frac{32}{?} = 35 \times 4 = 140$$

$$\Rightarrow \quad \frac{32}{?} = 140 - 136 = 4 \Rightarrow ? = \frac{32}{4} = 8$$

$\therefore$ Sign of interrogation (?) will be replaced by 8.

13. $\dfrac{2.70 \times 2.70 + 4.30 \times 4.30 + 8.60 \times 2.70}{2.70 + 4.30}$

$$= \frac{(2.70)^2 + (4.30)^2 + 2 \times 4.30 \times 2.70}{2.70 + 4.30}$$

$$= \frac{(2.70 + 4.30)^2}{2.70 + 4.30} \quad [\because a^2 + b^2 + 2ab = (a + b)^2]$$

$$= 2.70 + 4.30 = 7.00$$

14. $\therefore$ $\dfrac{\left(\sqrt{6} + \frac{1}{\sqrt{6}}\right)^2}{\frac{1}{2} \text{ of } 18 + 4} + \dfrac{2}{3} = \dfrac{(\sqrt{6})^2 + \left(\frac{1}{\sqrt{6}}\right)^2 + 2.\sqrt{6}\,\frac{1}{\sqrt{6}}}{9 + 4} + \dfrac{2}{3}$

$$= \frac{6 + \frac{1}{6} + 2}{13} + \frac{2}{3} = \frac{\frac{49}{6}}{13} + \frac{2}{3} = \frac{49}{78} + \frac{2}{3} = \frac{101}{78}$$

15. $1150 \div 50 \div 23 + 15$

$$= \frac{1150}{50} \div 23 + 15 = 23 \div 23 + 15 = \frac{23}{23} + 15$$

$$= 1 + 15 = 16.$$

●●●

CHAPTER

2

Comparing Quantities

Percentage

The word 'per cent' or 'percentage' means 'for every one hundred'. In other words, it gives an indication of rate per hundred. It is denoted by the symbol %.

For example, 5% means 5 out of one hundred or $\frac{5}{100}$.

Remember:

(i) For converting a per cent into a fraction, divide it by 100.

(ii) For converting a fraction into a per cent, multiply it by 100.

(iii) For converting a per cent into a decimal, shift the decimal point two places to the left.

(iv) For converting one given quantity *(x)* as a percentage of another given quantity *(y)*, find $\frac{x}{y}\times 100$.

(v) There is no unit of percentage.

Important Facts—For quickly solving the problems related to percentage, remember following rules:

Rule 1:

(a) Of the given two numbers if the first is $x\%$ more than the second, then the second will be $\left(\frac{100\times x}{100+x}\right)\%$ less than the first.

(b) Of the given two numbers if the first is $x\%$ less than the second, then the second will be $\left(\frac{100\times x}{100-x}\right)\%$ more than the first.

(c) If two numbers are respectively $x\%$ and $y\%$ more than a third number, then the first number will be $\left(\frac{100+x}{100+y}\times 100\right)\%$ of the second.

(d) If two numbers are respectively $x\%$ and $y\%$ less than a third number, then the first number will be $\left(\frac{100-x}{100-y}\times 100\right)\%$ of the second.

Rule 2:

(a) If a number or quantity is increased by $x\%$ then in order to restore its original value it must be decreased by $\left[\frac{100\times x}{100+x}\right]\%$.

(b) If a number or quantity is decreased by $x\%$ then in order to restore its original value it must be increased by $\left[\frac{100\times x}{100-x}\right]\%$.

Rule 3:

(a) If a number is successively increased by $x\%$ and $y\%$ then a single equivalent increase in that number will be $\left(x+y+\frac{xy}{100}\right)\%$

(b) If two successive discounts of $x\%$ and $y\%$ are allowed on a particular amount, then a single discount that is equivalent to the two successive discounts will be $\left(x+y-\frac{xy}{100}\right)\%$

(c) If a number is successively increased by $x\%$, $y\%$ and $z\%$, then a single equivalent increase in that number will be

$$\left[(x+y+z)+\left(\frac{xy+yz+zx}{100}\right)+\frac{(xyz)}{10000}\right]\%$$

(d) If three successive discounts of $x\%$, $y\%$ and $z\%$ are allowed on an amount, then a single discount that is equivalent to the three successive discounts will be

$$\left[x+y+z-\frac{(xy+yz+zx)}{100}+\frac{xyz}{10000}\right]\%$$

Rule 4:

(a) If a number is increased by $x\%$ and thereafter reduced by $x\%$, then the number will be reduced by $\left(\frac{x^2}{100}\right)$ per cent.

(*b*) If a number is reduced by $x\%$ and thereafter increased by $x\%$ then the number will be reduced by $\left(\frac{x^2}{100}\right)$ per cent.

(*c*) If due to an increase of $x\%$ in the selling price of certain commodity the sell/consumption of the commodity decreases by $y\%$, then gross receipts on account of sale of that commodity will be increased or decreased by $\left(x-y-\frac{xy}{100}\right)\%$, where $x > y$ and will be decreased by $\left(y-x+\frac{xy}{100}\right)\%$, where $y > x$.

EXERCISE

1. In the expression xy^2, the values of both variables x and y are decreased by 20%. By this, the value of the expression is decreased by
   A. 40% B. 48.8%
   C. 51.2% D. 80%

2. 15 litres of mixture contains 20% alcohol and rest water. If 3 litres of water be mixed in it, the percentage of alcohol in the new mixture will be:
   A. 15 B. $16\frac{2}{3}$
   C. 17 D. $18\frac{1}{2}$

3. The difference between 70% and 55% of a number is 72. The number is:
   A. 370 B. 460
   C. 480 D. 520

4. 20% of a number is 10% of:
   A. half the number
   B. double the number
   C. ten times the number
   D. twenty times the number

5. 75% of what area is 15 sq. metres?
   A. 10 sq. metres B. 15 sq. metres
   C. 20 sq. metres D. 25 sq. metres

6. In an examination 80% of the students passed in Mathematics and 70% passed in English, while 10% students failed in both the subjects. If 360 students passed in both the subjects, find the total number of students who appeared in the examination.
   A. 400 B. 600
   C. 630 D. 640

7. In an election, there are two candidates. A candidate secured 57% of the total votes polled and elected by a margin of 2100 votes. Find the total number of votes polled.
   A. 15000 B. 17500
   C. 18000 D. 21000

8. Electric tax is increased by 20% and its consumption is decreased by 20%. The change in the expenditure is:
   A. 4% decrease B. 4% increase
   C. 5% decrease D. 5% increase

9. A man loses 10% of his money, after spending 20% of the remainder he is left with ₹ 2160. Initially the man had:
   A. ₹ 1800 B. ₹ 2500
   C. ₹ 3000 D. ₹ 3200

10. In a school 55% of the students are below 9 years of age and the remaining 153 above 9 years of age. The total number of students in the school is:
    A. 296 B. 300
    C. 340 D. 1000

11. The selling price of certain commodity was reduced by 25%. As a result of it, the sales increased by 30%. What was the effect of it on cash collected by daily sales?
    A. 2.5% decrease B. 2.5% increase
    C. 5% decrease D. 5% increase

12. A cooler marked at ₹ 1500 is offered at ₹ 1350 due to off-season discount. Find the rate of off-season discount offered.
    A. 9.5% B. 10%
    C. 10.5% D. 12%

13. The number of Gypsy-cars sold in 2008 was 16,500 and that sold in 2007 was 16580. How much was the percentage decrease in sales of the Gypsy-cars from 2007 to 2008?
    A. less than 1 per cent
    B. more than 1 per cent
    C. zero per cent
    D. cannot be determined

14. A company decided to sell ₹ 50,000 T.V. set for ₹ 48,000 as a world cup offer. What is the percentage discount offered by the company?
    A. 6.5 B. 7
    C. 7.5 D. 4

15. 9% of a number is $\frac{81}{200}$, what is $\frac{2}{7}$ of that number?
    A. $1\frac{1}{5}$ B. $1\frac{2}{7}$
    C. $2\frac{1}{7}$ D. $2\frac{1}{5}$

ANSWERS

1	2	3	4	5	6	7	8	9	10
B	B	C	B	C	B	A	A	C	C
11	12	13	14	15					
A	B	A	D	B					

EXPLANATORY ANSWERS

1. Decrease in expression

$= xy^2 - \frac{80}{100}\times x\left(\frac{80}{100}y\right)^2 = xy^2 - \frac{64}{125}xy^2 = \frac{61xy^2}{125}$

Hence, decrease per cent

$= \frac{61xy^2}{125\times xy^2}\times 100 = 48.8\%$

2. Amount of alcohol $= \frac{20}{100}\times 15 = 3$ litre

Hence, required percentage $= \frac{3}{18}\times 100 = 16\frac{2}{3}\%$

3. Let the number be x; then

$(70 - 55)\times \frac{1}{100}\times x = 72$

$\therefore \quad x = \frac{100\times 72}{15} = 480$

4. Let number be 100, then 20% and 10% of the number be 20 and 10 respectively.

Hence, 20% of a number is 10% of double the number.

5. Let required area be x sq. metre; then

$\frac{75}{100}\times x = 15$

$\therefore\ x = \frac{15\times 100}{75} = 20$ sq metre

6. Here, percentage of students failed in Mathematics and English be 30% and 20% respectively.

Percentage of students failed either one or both subjects $= 30 + 20 - 10 = 40\%$

Hence, percentage of pass students $= 100 - 40 = 60\%$

Now, $60\% = 360$

$\therefore \quad 100\% = \frac{360}{60}\times 100 = 600$

7. Let total number of votes be x; then

$(57 - 43)\times \frac{1}{10}x = 2100$

$\therefore \quad x = \frac{100\times 2100}{14} = 15000$

8. Let initially electric tax is ₹ 100 and consumption = 100 units

Decrease in consumption

= 100 × 100 − 120 × 80 = ₹ 400

Hence, decrease percentage $= \frac{400\times 100}{100\times 100} = 4\%$

9. Let initally the man had ₹ x, then

amount of money loses $= \frac{10}{100}\times x = ₹\frac{x}{10}$

Remaining amount of money $= x - \frac{x}{10} = ₹\frac{9x}{10}$

Money spent $= \frac{20}{100}\times\frac{9x}{10} = ₹\frac{9x}{50}$

Now, $\frac{9x}{10} - \frac{9x}{50} = 2160 \Rightarrow \frac{36x}{50} = 2160$

$\therefore\ x = \frac{2160\times 50}{36} = ₹\ 3000$

10. Let total number of students be x, then

$\frac{45}{100}\times x = 153 \ \therefore\ x = \frac{100\times 153}{45} = 340$

11. Let the selling price of a commodity be ₹ 100 and number of sales = 100 units

Decrease in daily cash

= 100 × 100 − 75 × 130 = ₹ 250

Hence, decrease percentage $= \frac{250\times 100}{100\times 100} = 2.5\ \%$

12. Discount per cent

$= \frac{1500-1350}{1500}\times 100 = \frac{150}{1500}\times 100 = 10\%$

13. Required decrease percentage

$= \frac{16580-16500}{16580}\times 100 = \frac{80}{16580}\times 100 = 0.48\%$

14. Discount per cent $= \frac{2000}{50{,}000}\times 100 = 4\%$

15. Let the number be x; then

$\frac{9}{100}\times x = \frac{81}{200}\ \therefore\ x = \frac{100\times 81}{9\times 200} = \frac{9}{2}$

Hence, $\frac{2}{7}x = \frac{2}{7}\times\frac{9}{2} = \frac{9}{7} = 1\frac{2}{7}$.

Discount

Market Price (M.P.)—The attached price is called the market price (M.P.) or list price (L.P.) of the article and the reduction allowed in the price is called the **discount**.

(*i*) Discount = M.P. – S.P.

(*ii*) Discount % = $\frac{\text{Discount} \times 100}{\text{M.P.}}$

(*iii*) S.P. = M.P. – $\frac{\text{Discount\%} \times \text{M.P.}}{100}$

(*iv*) S.P. = M.P. × $\left(1 - \frac{\text{Discount\%}}{100}\right)$

(*v*) M.P. = $\frac{100 \times \text{S.P.}}{100 - \text{Discount\%}}$

S.P. = M.P. $\left(\frac{100 - \text{Discount\%}}{100}\right)$

M.P. – S.P. = $\frac{\text{M.P.} \times \text{Discount\%}}{100}$

Discount% = $\left(\frac{\text{M.P.} - \text{S.P.}}{\text{M.P.}}\right) \times 100$

EXERCISE

1. A cloth merchant offers 15% festival discount on every saree sold. If a certain saree is sold for ₹ 680, what is its marked price?
A. ₹ 800 B. ₹ 900
C. ₹ 1250 D. ₹ 1300

2. A shopkeeper offers 10% discount on an article and still makes a profit of 20%. What is the C.P. of the article if the marked price is ₹ 350?
A. ₹ 259.20 B. ₹ 262.50
C. ₹ 265.75 D. ₹ 272.5

3. A manufactures marks his goods in such a way that after allowing 20% discount, he makes a profit of 18%. What is the marked price of an item which costs him ₹ 200?
A. ₹ 295 B. ₹ 310
C. ₹ 315 D. ₹ 375

4. The marked price of a brand of coffee is ₹ 35 for 100g. But the shopkeeper gives a cup costing ₹ 7.50 free with it. Even then he gets a gain of 10%. What is the cost price of 100g of coffee?
A. ₹ 15 B. ₹ 25
C. ₹ 35 D. ₹ 65

5. A car is marked at ₹ 2,25,000. The manufacturer gives a discount of 10%. The dealer also gives a discount of 5%. What is the S.P. of the car?
A. ₹ 1,72,369 B. ₹ 1,64,370
C. ₹ 1,52,393 D. ₹ 1,92,375

6. A cycle merchant allows 25% commission on his advertised price and still makes a profit of 20%. If he gains ₹ 60 over the sale of one cycle. What is his advertised price?
A. ₹ 290 B. ₹ 310
C. ₹ 480 D. ₹ 520

7. The marked price of a shirt was ₹ 165 and it was at a discount of 12%. What the selling price of the shirt?
A. ₹ 145.20 B. ₹ 155.30
C. ₹ 165.20 D. ₹ 175.25

8. A trader marks his goods 40% above the cost price and gives a discount of 20% on the marked price. What is his gain per cent?
A. 8% B. 9%
C. 12% D. 15%

9. How much per cent more than the C.P. should a manufacturer mark his goods so that after allowing a discount of 20% on the marked price, he gains 10%.
A. 34.5% B. 27.5%
C. 37.5% D. 38.5%

10. A shopkeeper allows a discount of 10% to his customers and still gains 20%. What is the marked price of an article which costs ₹ 450 to the shopkeeper?
A. ₹ 600 B. ₹ 700
C. ₹ 800 D. ₹ 900

ANSWERS

1	2	3	4	5	6	7	8	9	10
A	B	A	B	D	C	A	C	C	A

EXPLANATORY ANSWERS

1. S.P. = ₹ 680, Discount = 15%

$$\text{M.P.} = \frac{100 \times \text{S.P.}}{100 - \text{Discount\%}}$$

$$= \frac{100 \times 680}{100 - 15} = \frac{100 \times 680}{85} = ₹\ 800$$

2. C.P. = ₹ x, 120% of x = 350 – 350 × 10%

$$\frac{120}{100} \times x = 350 - 35 = 315.$$

$$x = \frac{315 \times 5}{6} = \frac{525}{2},\ \text{C.P.} = ₹\ 262.50.$$

3. Let M.P. = ₹ x

$80\%\ x = 118\%$ of 200

$$\frac{80}{100}\times x = \frac{118}{100}\times 200 \Rightarrow x = \frac{236\times 5}{4} = ₹\ 295.$$

4. Let C.P. of 100 gm coffee = ₹ x

110% of $x = 35 - 7.50 = 27.50$

$$\frac{110}{100}\times x = 27.50$$

$$x = \frac{27.50\times 100}{110\times 100}$$

C.P. = ₹ 25.

5. M.P. = ₹ 225000

$$\text{1st S.P.} = 225000 - 225000\times\frac{10}{100} = 225000 - 22500 = 202500$$

$$\text{2nd S.P.} = 202500 - 202500\times\frac{5}{100} = 202500 - 10125 = ₹\ 192375$$

6. Let M.P. = 100

Commission = 25%

S.P. = 100 – 25 = 75

Profit = 20%

$$\text{C.P.} = \frac{100}{120}\times 75 = \frac{375}{6} = 62.50$$

Gain = 75 – 62.50 = ₹ 12.50

$$\text{M.P.} = \frac{100}{12.50}\times 60 = ₹\ 480$$

7.
$$\text{S.P.} = \frac{\text{M.P.}(100-\text{Discount})}{100} = \frac{165\times(100-12)}{100} = \frac{165\times 88}{100}$$
$$= 33\times 4.4 = ₹\ 145.20$$

8. Let C.P. = 100, M.P. = 140, Discount = 20%

$$\text{S.P.} = 140 - 140\times\frac{20}{100} = 140 - 28 = 112$$

Profit = 112 – 100 = 12

$$\text{Profit \%} = \frac{12\times 100}{100} = 12\%$$

9. Let C.P. = ₹ x, S.P. = 110% of $x = \frac{110}{100}\times x = \frac{11}{10}x.$

Discount = 20%

$$\text{M.P.} = \frac{100\times\frac{11}{10}x}{100-20} = \frac{100\times\frac{11}{10}x}{80} = \frac{11}{8}x.$$

$$\text{Required \%} = \frac{\frac{11x}{8}-x}{x}\times 100 = \frac{3x\times 100}{8x} = 37.5\%$$

10. C.P. = 450, Gain = 20%

$$\text{S.P.} = 450 + 450\times\frac{20}{100} = 450 + 90 = 540$$

Discount = 10%

$$\text{M.P.} = \frac{100\times\text{S.P.}}{100-\text{Discount}} = \frac{100\times 540}{100-10} = \frac{100\times 540}{90} = ₹\ 600$$

Profit & Loss

A consumer who goes to the market and buys certain goods. The buyer is called a customer and the shopkeeper who sells the goods to him is called a retailer. The retailer purchases goods in turn in bulk from a wholesaler who keeps a large stock of good and in this case, the retailer becomes the customer.

1. **Cost price (C.P.):** Cost price is that price at which a particular article is bought. Profit and loss both are marked at cost price.
2. **Selling Price (S.P.):** Selling price is that price at which a particular article is sold.
3. **Overheads:** The expenses incurred on transportation, maintenance, packaging, advertise-ments and the like are included as *Overhead*. These overheads and the profit when added to the cost price determine the selling price.
4. **Profit or Gain** : Whenever a person sells an article at price greater than the cost price he is said to have made a profit or gain.
   Profit or Gain = S.P. – C.P.
5. **Loss** : If S.P. is less than the C.P. there is loss.
   Loss = C.P – S.P

Some Basic Formulae:

(i) Gain = S.P. – C.P.

(ii) Loss = C.P. – S.P.

(iii) $\text{Gain \%} = \frac{\text{Gain}\times 100}{\text{C.P.}}$

(iv) $\text{Loss \%} = \frac{\text{Loss}\times 100}{\text{C.P.}}$

From these we can write direct expressions for S.P. and C.P.

(v) $\text{S.P.} = \left(\frac{100+\text{Gain\%}}{100}\right)\times\text{C.P.}$ in case of gain or profit

(vi) $\text{S.P.} = \left(\frac{100-\text{Loss\%}}{100}\right)\times\text{C.P.}$ in case of loss

These can be rewritten as

$$\text{C.P.} = \frac{100}{100+\text{Gain\%}}\times\text{S.P.} \text{ in case of profit}$$

$$\text{C.P.} = \frac{100}{100-\text{Loss\%}}\times\text{S.P.} \text{ in case of loss}$$

(*vii*) If the C.P. of x goods = S.P. of y goods, then

(*a*) Gain % = $\frac{x-y}{y}\times 100$ [In case of $x > y$]

(*b*) Loss % = $\frac{y-x}{y}\times 100$ [In case of $y > x$]

(*viii*) When a man sells two things at the same price each and in this process his loss on first things is x% and gain on second things is x%, then in such a type question, there is always a loss.

$$\text{Loss \%} = x\% \text{ of } x = \frac{x^2}{100} = \left(\frac{x}{10}\right)^2.$$

$$\text{and Loss} = \frac{2\times \text{S.P.}}{\left(\frac{100}{x}\right)^2 - 1}$$

(*ix*) An article is sold at a profit of x%. Had it been sold for ₹ a some more, y% would have gained. Then, C.P. of an article =

$$\frac{\text{More gain}\times 100}{\text{Difference in percentage profit}}$$

(*x*) A dishonest shopkeeper prefers to sell goods at his cost price but uses a false weight of x grams for each kilogram. Then his gain per cent,

$$\text{gain \%} = \frac{\text{Error}}{\text{True value} - \text{Error}}\times 100$$

$$= \frac{1000-x}{x}\times 100$$

$$\text{or, gain \%} = \frac{\text{True weight} - \text{False weight}}{\text{False weight}}\times 100.$$

EXERCISE

1. Ashok bought 25 kg of rice at the rate of ₹ 6 per kg and 35 kg of rice at the rate of ₹ 7 per kg. He mixed the two and sold the mixture at the rate of ₹ 6.75 per kg. What was his gain or loss in the transaction?

A. ₹ 16 gain B. ₹ 16 loss
C. ₹ 10 gain D. None of these

2. A horse and a cow were sold for ₹ 12000 each. The horse was sold at a loss of 20% and the cow at a gain of 20%. The entire transaction resulted in

A. no loss no gain B. loss of ₹ 1000
C. gain of ₹ 1000 D. loss of ₹ 2000

3. Profit after selling a commodity for ₹ 425 is same as loss after selling it for ₹ 355. The cost of the commodity is :

A. ₹ 285 B. ₹ 390
C. ₹ 295 D. ₹ 400

4. Bhajan Singh purchased 120 reams of paper at ₹ 80 per ream. He spent ₹ 280 on transportation, paid octroi at the rate of 40 paise per ream and paid ₹ 72 to the coolie. If he wants to have a gain of 8%, what must be the selling price per ream?

A. ₹ 86 B. ₹ 86.48
C. ₹ 79 D. ₹ 90

5. Ram bought 4 dozen apples at ₹ 12 per dozen and 2 dozen at ₹ 16 per dozen. He sold all of them to earn 20%. At what price per dozen did he sell the apples?

A. ₹ 14.40 B. ₹ 16.00
C. ₹ 16.80 D. ₹ 16.20

6. Jimmy bought paper sheets for ₹ 7200 and spent ₹ 200 in transport. Paying ₹ 600 he had 330 boxes made, which he sold at ₹ 28 each. What is his profit percentage?

A. 15.5 B. 40
C. 50 D. None of these

7. A owns a house worth ₹ 10000. He sells it to B at a profit of 10% based on the worth of the house. B sells the house back to A at a loss of 10%. In this transaction A gets:

A. no profit no loss B. profit of ₹ 1000
C. profit of ₹ 1100 D. profit of ₹ 1200

8. At what price must Kantilal sell a mixture of 80 kg sugar at ₹ 6.75 per kg with 120 kg at ₹ 8 per kg to gain 20%?

A. ₹ 7.50 per kg B. ₹ 8.20 per kg
C. ₹ 8.35 per kg D. ₹ 9 per kg

9. Subhash purchased a taperecorder at $\frac{9}{10}$ of its selling price and sold it at 8% more than its S.P. His gain is:

A. 8% B. 10%
C. 18% D. 20%

10. A dealer marks his goods 20% above cost price. He then allows some discount on it and makes a profit of 8%. The rate of discount is :

A. 12% B. 10%
C. 6% D. 4%

11. A trader lists his articles 20% above C.P. and allows a discount of 10% on cash payment. His gain per cent is :

A. 10% B. 8%
C. 6% D. 4%

12. Tarun bought a T.V. with 20% discount on the labelled price. Had he bought it with 25% discount, he would have saved ₹ 500. At what price did he buy the T.V.?

A. ₹ 5000 B. ₹ 8000
C. ₹ 10000 D. ₹ 12000

13. While selling a watch, a shopkeeper gives a discount of 5%. If he gives a discount of 7%, he earns ₹ 15 less as profit. The marked price of the watch is :

A. ₹ 697.50 B. ₹ 712.50
C. ₹ 787.50 D. None of these

14. Kabir buys an article with 25% discount on its marked price. He makes a profit of 10% by selling it at ₹ 660. The marked price is :

A. ₹ 600 B. ₹ 700
C. ₹ 800 D. ₹ 885

15. A person bought an article and sold it at a loss of 10%. If he had bought it for 20% less and sold it for ₹ 55 more, he would have had a profit of 40%. The C.P. of the article is :

A. ₹ 200 B. ₹ 225
C. ₹ 250 D. None of these

ANSWERS

1	2	3	4	5	6	7	8	9	10
C	B	B	D	B	A	C	D	D	B
11	**12**	**13**	**14**	**15**					
B	B	D	C	C					

EXPLANATORY ANSWERS

1. C.P. of 60 kg mixture = ₹ (25 × 6 + 35 × 7) = ₹ 395

S.P. of 60 kg mixtire = ₹ (60 × 6.75) = ₹ 405

∴ Gain = ₹ (405 – 395) = ₹ 10

2. Loss % = $\left(\frac{20}{10}\right)^2 = (2)^2 = 4\%$

Total S.P. = ₹ 24000

and Total C.P. = ₹$\left(\frac{100}{96} \times 24000\right)$ = ₹ 25000

∴ Loss = ₹ (25000 – 24000) = ₹ 1000

3. Let C.P. = ₹ x, Then, $425 - x = x - 355$

⇒ $2x = 780$ ∴ x = ₹ 390

4. C.P. of 1 ream = $80 + \frac{280}{120} + \frac{72}{120} + 0.40$

$= 80 + \frac{7}{3} + \frac{3}{5} + \frac{2}{5}$ = ₹ $\frac{250}{3}$

∴ S.P. of 1 ream = ₹$\left(\frac{108}{100} \times \frac{250}{3}\right)$ = ₹ 90

5. C.P. of 6 dozen apples = ₹ (12 × 4 + 16 × 2) = ₹ 80

∴ S.P. = ₹$\left(\frac{120}{100} \times 80\right)$ = ₹ 96

∴ S.P. per dozen = ₹$\left(\frac{96}{6}\right)$ = ₹ 16

6. C.P. of 1 box = $\frac{7200 + 200 + 600}{330}$ = ₹ $\frac{800}{33}$

Hence, Gain% = $\frac{28 - \frac{800}{33}}{800/33} \times 100 = \frac{124}{800} \times 100 = 15.5\%$

7. Final C.P. for A = $\frac{110}{100} \times \frac{90}{100} \times$ ₹ 10000 = ₹ 9900

Hence, profit for A

= $\frac{10}{100}$ × ₹ 10,000 + ₹ (10,000 – 9900) = ₹ 1100

8. C.P. of 1 kg sugar = $\frac{80 \times 6.75 + 120 \times 8}{200}$ = ₹ 7.50

∴ S.P. of 1 kg = ₹$\left(\frac{120}{100} \times 7.50\right)$ = ₹ 9 per kg

9. Let S.P. = ₹ 100;

C.P. for Subhash = $\frac{9}{10} \times 100$ = ₹ 90 and S.P. = ₹ 108

Hence, gain % for Subhash = $\frac{108 - 90}{90} \times 100 = 20\%$

10. Let C.P. be ₹ 100; then Marked price = ₹ 120 and S.P. = ₹ 108

∴ Discount = $\left(\frac{12}{120} \times 100\right)\% = 10\%$

11. Let C.P. be ₹ 100

Then, marked price = ₹ 120

S.P. = ₹$\left(\frac{90}{100} \times 120\right)$ = ₹ 108

∴ Gain % = $\left(\frac{8}{100} \times 100\right)\% = 8\%$

12. Here, 5% = 500

∴ 100% = $\frac{500}{5} \times 100$ = ₹ 10,000

Hence, labelled price = ₹ 10,000

∴ S.P. = $\frac{80}{100}$ × ₹ 10,000 = ₹ 8000

13. Let the marked price = ₹ x

Then, $\frac{7x}{100} - \frac{5x}{100} = 15 \Rightarrow \frac{x}{50} = 15$ ∴ x = ₹ 750

14. C.P. = $\frac{100}{110} \times 660$ = ₹ 600

Hence, M.P. = $\frac{100}{75} \times 600$ = ₹ 800.

Simple Interest

Interest is the money paid for the use of money borrowed, *i.e.*, extra money paid for using other's money is called *interest.*

The sum borrowed is called the principal. The sum of interest and principal is called the *Amount.*

If the interest on a certain sum borrowed for a certain period is reckoned uniformly, then it is called simple interest, denoted by S.I.

Thus, if A = Amount, P = Principal, I = Interest, T = Time (in year), R = Rate per cent per annum, then

(*a*) $I = \frac{P \times R \times T}{100}$ (*b*) $P = \frac{100 \times I}{R \times T}$

(*c*) $T = \frac{100 \times I}{P \times R}$ (*d*) $R = \frac{100 \times I}{P \times T}$

(*e*) $P = \frac{100\,A}{100 + RT}$ (*f*) A = P + I.

EXERCISE

1. If the simple interest on a certain sum of money at 6% per annum for 3 years is ₹ 90, the sum will be:
A. ₹ 500 B. ₹ 450
C. ₹ 525 D. ₹ 560

2. If the simple interest on ₹ 1 for 1 month is 1 paise, the rate per cent p.a. will be :
A. 10% B. 8%
C. 12% D. 6%

3. A sum of money doubles itself in 20 years. In how many years will it triple itself at the same rate of simple interest?
A. 30 years B. 50 years
C. 40 years D. 45 years

4. If the simple interest on ₹ 500 for 4 years is ₹ 40, find the rate per cent p.a.
A. 3½% B. 2%
C. 2½% D. 3%

5. After what time will the sum of ₹ 2000 become ₹ 2240 at 4% per annum simple interest?
A. 3 years B. 2 years
C. 5 years D. 4 years

6. The simple interest on a certain sum of money is $\frac{25}{64}$ of the sum and the number of years equals the rate per cent p.a. The rate per cent p.a. will be :
A. $7\frac{1}{2}\%$ B. $5\frac{1}{4}\%$
C. $6\frac{3}{4}\%$ D. $6\frac{1}{4}\%$

7. A sum of money amounts to ₹ 1150 in 3 years and to ₹ 1250 in 5 years at a certain rate per cent p.a. simple interest. The rate per cent p.a. will be :
A. 5% B. 8%
C. 7% D. 6%

8. The simple interest on a sum of ₹ 892 lent out at 6% p.a. for 8 months will be :
A. ₹ 36.68 B. ₹ 35.68
C. ₹ 48.58 D. ₹ 33.38

9. If the simple interest on a certain sum of money at 6% p.a. for 4½ years is ₹ 81, the sum will be:
A. ₹ 325 B. ₹ 225
C. ₹ 300 D. ₹ 340

10. A sum of ₹ 1850 lent out for 5 years at 3% p.a. simple interest will amount to:
A. ₹ 2227.75 B. ₹ 2127.50
C. ₹ 2137.50 D. ₹ 2086.50

11. A lent a sum of ₹ 1250 to B at a certain rate of interest for 3 years and a sum of ₹ 1500 to C at the same rate of interest for 2 years. If he was paid total ₹ 258.75 as interest in both cases, find the rate of interest at which money was lent by him.
A. $4\frac{1}{6}\%$ B. $6\frac{1}{4}\%$
C. $2\frac{1}{7}\%$ D. $3\frac{5}{6}\%$

12. A invested ₹ 5000 at a certain rate of simple interest and ₹ 4000 for the same period at 1% higher rate of interest. If the interest in both cases is same, the former rate of interest is :
A. 3% B. 4%
C. 6% D. 5%

13. A man lends ₹ 500 for 4 years and ₹ 600 for 3 years at a certain rate of simple interest. If he gets total ₹ 190 as interest in both cases, the rate per cent per annum is:
A. 8% B. 5%
C. 10% D. 4%

14. What annual instalment should be paid to clear the debt of ₹ 645 in 4 years at the rate of 5% p.a. simple interest?
A. ₹ 160 B. ₹ 185
C. ₹ 180 D. ₹ 190

15. If a certain sum of money at simple interest amounts to ₹ 1900 in 3 years and to ₹ 2050 in 5 years, the rate per cent per annum is:
A. 4½% B. 3½%
C. 2½% D. 5¼%

ANSWERS

1	2	3	4	5	6	7	8	9	10
A	C	C	B	A	D	A	B	C	B
11	12	13	14	15					
D	B	B	C	A					

EXPLANATORY ANSWERS

1. $P = \frac{90 \times 100}{6 \times 3} = ₹\ 500$

2. $\text{Rate} = \frac{1 \times 100}{100 \times \frac{1}{12}} = 12\%.$

3. Let principal = ₹ x; Amount = ₹ $2x$;

then $I = 2x - x = ₹\ x$

$\therefore R = \frac{x \times 100}{x \times 20} = 5\%$

Again, if principal = ₹ x;

Amount = ₹ $3x$; then $I = 3x - x = ₹\ 2x$

Hence, $T = \frac{2x \times 100}{x \times 5} = 40$ years

4. $\text{Rate} = \frac{40 \times 100}{500 \times 4} = 2\%$

5. Here, I = 2240 − 2000 = ₹ 240

$\therefore \quad T = \frac{240 \times 100}{2000 \times 4} = 3$ years

6. Let, $R = T = x$; then

$\frac{25}{64}P = \frac{P \times x \times x}{100} \Rightarrow x^2 = \frac{25 \times 100}{64}$

$\therefore \quad x = \frac{5 \times 10}{8} = \frac{25}{4};\ R = 6\frac{1}{4}\%$

7. Here, Simple interest for 2 years

= ₹ 1250 − ₹ 1150 = ₹ 100

$\therefore$ Simple interest for 3 years $= \frac{100 \times 3}{2} = ₹\ 150$

Hence, P = ₹ 1150 − ₹ 150 = ₹ 1000

$\therefore \quad \text{Rate} = \frac{50 \times 100}{1000 \times 1} = 5\%$

8. Here, $I = \frac{892 \times 6 \times \frac{2}{3}}{100} = ₹\ 35.68$

9. $P = \frac{81 \times 100 \times 2}{6 \times 9} = ₹\ 300$

10. $I = \frac{1850 \times 3 \times 5}{100} = ₹\ 277.50$

$\therefore$ Amount = ₹ 1850 + ₹ 277.50

= ₹ 2127.50

11. $\frac{1250 \times R \times 3}{100} + \frac{1500 \times R \times 2}{100} = 258.75$

$\Rightarrow \quad 6750\ R = 25875$

$\therefore \quad R = \frac{25875}{6750} = \frac{23}{6} = 3\frac{5}{6}\%$

12. Here, $\frac{5000 \times R \times T}{100} = \frac{4000 \times (R+1) \times T}{100}$

$\Rightarrow \quad 5R = 4R + 4 \therefore\ R = 4\%$

13. Here, $\frac{500 \times R \times 4}{100} + \frac{600 \times R \times 3}{100} = 190$

$\Rightarrow \quad 38R = 190$

$\therefore \quad R = \frac{190}{38} = 5\%.$

14. Let annual instalment be ₹ x; then

$x + \frac{x \times 3 \times 5}{100} + x + \frac{x \times 2 \times 5}{100} + x + \frac{x \times 1 \times 5}{100} + x = 645 + \frac{645 \times 4 \times 5}{100}$

$\Rightarrow \quad 4x + \frac{3x}{10} = 774 \Rightarrow \frac{43x}{10} = 774$

$\therefore \quad x = \frac{774 \times 10}{43} = ₹\ 180$

15. Simple interest for 2 years

= ₹ 2050 − ₹ 1900 = ₹ 150

$\therefore$ Simple interest for 1 year

$= ₹\ \frac{150}{2} = ₹\ 75$

Since simple interest for 3 years

= ₹ 75 × 3 = ₹ 225

$\therefore$ Principal = ₹ 1900 − ₹ 225 = ₹ 1675

Hence, $\text{Rate} = \frac{75 \times 100}{1675 \times 1} = 4½\%$

Compound Interest

In business transaction if interest as it becomes due is not paid to the lender but is added on to the principal, the money is said to be lent at *compound interest* and the total sum owed after a given time is called the amount at compound interest for that time.

After a certain period, the difference between the amount and the original principal is called the compound Interest (C.I.).

Some Important Formulae :

Let Principal = P, Time = n years

Rate = r% p.a.

then, the amount,

(*a*) when interest is compounded annually:

then, $\text{Amount} = P\left(1+\dfrac{r}{100}\right)^n$

(*b*) when interest is compounded half yearly:

then, $\text{Amount} = P\left(1+\dfrac{r/2}{100}\right)^{2n}$

(*c*) when interest is compounded quarterly :

then, $\text{Amount} = P\left(1+\dfrac{r/4}{100}\right)^{4n}$

(*d*) when time is fraction of a year, say $4\frac{1}{3}$ years,

then, $\text{Amount} = P\left(1+\dfrac{r}{100}\right)^4 \times \left(1+\dfrac{\frac{1}{3}r}{100}\right)$

(*e*) when rates are r_1%, r_2% and r_3% for Ist, IInd and IIIrd year respectively; then,

$\text{Amount} = P\left(1+\dfrac{r_1}{100}\right)\left(1+\dfrac{r_2}{100}\right)\left(1+\dfrac{r_3}{100}\right)$

EXERCISE

1. What will be the compound interest on ₹ 8000 for 3 years at 5% p.a.?

A. ₹ 1361 B. ₹ 1261
C. ₹ 1260 D. ₹ 1250

2. What will be the amount if a sum of ₹ 2500 is invested for 1 year at 4% per annum compound interest, interest being compounded half-yearly?

A. ₹ 2625 B. ₹ 2601
C. ₹ 2830 D. ₹ 2901

3. Find the compound interest on ₹ 2560 for ½ year at 12½% per annum, interest payable quarterly.

A. ₹ 3720.50 B. ₹ 2722.50
C. ₹ 2752.50 D. ₹ 2250.50

4. After how many years will ₹ 3375 become ₹ 4096 at $6\frac{2}{3}$% per annum compound interest?

A. 4 years B. 2 years
C. 2½ years D. 3 years

5. A certain sum of money placed at compound interest amounts to ₹ 110 in 1 year and to ₹ 121 in 2 years. The rate of interest per annum is :

A. 5% B. 10%
C. 8% D. 4%

6. The present population of a city is 80,000. If the rate of growth is 5% per year, find its population after 3 years.

A. 88,100 B. 95,600
C. 92,610 D. 84,600

7. First year's interest on a sum of money placed at compound interest at the rate of 8% per annum is ₹ 72. What will be interest for the second year?

A. ₹ 77.76 B. ₹ 78.66
C. ₹ 85.66 D. ₹ 78.76

8. The difference between compound and simple interest on a certain sum of money for 2 years at 5% per annum is ₹ 21. Find the sum.

A. ₹ 7200 B. ₹ 8400
C. ₹ 9200 D. ₹ 8500

9. In how many years will a sum of ₹ 19200 placed at 10% per annum compound interest yield an interest of ₹ 4032?

A. 1½ years B. 2½ years
C. 2 years D. 3 years

10. The compound interest on a certain sum of money invested for 3 years at 5% per annum is ₹ 1891.50. What will be the simple interest on the same sum at the same rate for 2 years?

A. ₹ 1700 B. ₹ 1200
C. ₹ 1500 D. ₹ 2100

11. The simple interest on a sum of ₹ 4800 for 2 years is ₹ 768. What will be the compound interest on the same sum at the same rate and for the same period?

A. ₹ 798.72 B. ₹ 870.75
C. ₹ 920.69 D. ₹ 884.20

12. A sum of money lent out at a certain rate of simple interest amounts to ₹ 6600 in 2 years and to ₹ 6900 in 3 years. What will be the compound interest on the same sum of money if lent out at the same rate for 2 years?

A. ₹ 605 B. ₹ 715
C. ₹ 615 D. ₹ 595

13. If the first year's interest on a certain sum of money placed at 5% p.a. compound interest is ₹ 1200, what will be the interest for the third year?

A. ₹ 1220 B. ₹ 1323
C. ₹ 1423 D. ₹ 1330

14. If a certain sum of money placed at compound interest amounts to ₹ 960 in 3 years and to ₹ 1000 in 4 years, find the rate of compound interest.

A. $4\frac{1}{6}\%$ B. $5\frac{1}{6}\%$
C. $2\frac{1}{3}\%$ D. 3%

15. What would be the compound interest on ₹ 3200 at 25% per annum for 3 years?

A. ₹ 2050 B. ₹ 2775
C. ₹ 3050 D. ₹ 3180

ANSWERS

1	2	3	4	5	6	7	8	9	10
B	B	B	D	B	C	A	B	C	B
11	**12**	**13**	**14**	**15**					
A	C	B	A	C					

EXPLANATORY ANSWERS

1. ∴ $\text{C.I.} = 8000\left[\left(1+\frac{5}{100}\right)^3-1\right]$

$= 8000\left[\left(\frac{21}{20}\right)^3-1\right] = \frac{8000\times1261}{8000} = ₹\ 1261$

2. $A = 2500\left(1+\frac{2}{100}\right)^2 = 2500\left(\frac{51}{50}\right)^2 = \frac{2500\times51\times51}{50\times50}$

= ₹ 2601.

3. $\text{Amount} = 2560\left(1+\frac{25}{8\times100}\right)^2 = \frac{2560\times33\times33}{32\times32}$

= ₹ 2722.50

4. Here, $4096 = 3375\left(1+\frac{20}{3\times100}\right)^n$

$\Rightarrow \frac{4096}{3375} = \left(1+\frac{1}{15}\right)^n \Rightarrow \left(\frac{16}{15}\right)^3 = \left(\frac{16}{15}\right)^n$

∴ n = 3 years

5. Here, simple interest of ₹ 110 for 1 year = 121 – 110 = ₹ 11

Hence, rate $= \frac{11\times100}{110\times1} = 10\%$

6. Population of the city after 3 years

$= 80{,}000\left(1+\frac{5}{100}\right)^3 = 80{,}000\times\frac{21}{20}\times\frac{21}{20}\times\frac{21}{20} = 92610$

7. Second year's interest = 72 + 8% of 72

$= 72+\frac{72\times8}{100} = 72 + 5.76 = ₹\ 77.76$

8. Here, $P\left[\left(1+\frac{5}{100}\right)^2-1\right]-\frac{P\times5\times2}{100} = 21$

$\Rightarrow P\left[\frac{441}{400}-1\right]-\frac{P}{10} = 21$

$\Rightarrow P\left[\frac{41}{400}-\frac{1}{10}\right] = 21 \Rightarrow P\times\frac{1}{400} = 21$

∴ $P = 21 \times 400 = ₹\ 8400$

9. Amount = ₹ 19200 + ₹ 4032 = ₹ 23232

Now, $23232 = 19200\left(1+\frac{10}{100}\right)^n$

$\Rightarrow \frac{23232}{19200} = \left(\frac{11}{10}\right)^n \Rightarrow \frac{121}{100} = \left(\frac{11}{10}\right)^n$

$\Rightarrow \left(\frac{11}{10}\right)^2 = \left(\frac{11}{10}\right)^n$

∴ n = 2 years

11. $\text{Rate} = \frac{768\times100}{4800\times2} = 8\%$

∴ $\text{C.I.} = 4800\left[\left(1+\frac{8}{100}\right)^2-1\right]$

$= 4800\left[\left(\frac{27}{25}\right)^2-1\right] = \frac{4800\times104}{625} = ₹\ 798.72$

13. Required interest

$= 1200\left(1+\frac{5}{100}\right)^2 = 1200\times\frac{21}{20}\times\frac{21}{20} = ₹\ 1323$

14. Here, simple interest of ₹ 960 for 1 year = 1000 – 960 = ₹ 40

Hence, Rate $= \frac{40\times100}{960\times1} = \frac{25}{6} = 4\frac{1}{6}\%$

15. Compound interest

$= 3200\left[\left(1+\frac{25}{100}\right)^3-1\right] = 3200\left[\left(\frac{5}{4}\right)^3-1\right]$

$= \frac{3200\times61}{64} = ₹\ 3050.$

●●●

CHAPTER 3

Ratio and Proportion

RATIO

In ratio we compare two quantities of the same kind and consider what multiple, part or parts one is of the other. In comparing 8 with 4, observe that it is 2 times 4. This comparison can be represented as $8 \div 4$ or $\frac{8}{4}$.

Hence, *ratio is that relation between two numbers which is expressed by the fraction, the numerator is which is the measure of the first quantity and denominator is the measure of the second quantity.*

If the terms of a ratio be multiplied or divided by the same quantity the value of the ratio remains unaltered.

Thus, 3 : 4 is the same as 9 : 12 and 9 : 12 is the same as 3 : 4.

PROPORTION

The equality of two ratio is called proportion.

Consider the two ratios:

Ist ratio	2nd ratio
5 : 15	7 : 21

Since, 5 is one-third of 15 and 7 is one-third of 21, the two ratios are equal. The equality of two ratios is called proportion and the numbers 5, 15, and 7, 21 are said to be in **proportion.**

The proportion may be written as 5 : 15 : : 7 : 21 (5 is to 15 as 7 is to 21)

$\Rightarrow \quad 5 : 15 = 7 : 21$

$$\Rightarrow \quad \frac{5}{15} = \frac{7}{21}$$

The numbers 5, 15, 7 and 21 are called the terms. 5 is the first term, 15 the second, 7 the third, and 21 the fourth.

The first and fourth terms, *i.e.*, 5 and 21 are called extremes (end terms), and the second and the third terms, *i.e.*, 15 and 7 are called the **means** (middle terms), 21 is called the fourth proportional.

Some Important Facts:

1. If a and b are two quantities, then
   (*a*) Duplicate ratio of $a : b = a^2 : b^2$
   (*b*) Sub-duplicate ratio of $a : b = \sqrt{a} : \sqrt{b}$
   (*c*) Triplicate ratio of $a : b = a^3 : b^3$
   (*d*) Sub-triplicate ratio $a : b = \sqrt[3]{a} : \sqrt[3]{b}$
   (*e*) Inverse or reciprocal ratio of $a : b = \frac{1}{a} : \frac{1}{b}$
   (*f*) Third proportional to 'a' and 'b' $= \frac{b^2}{a}$
2. If A : B = $x : y$ and B : C = $p : q$, then
   (*a*) $A : C = \frac{x \times p}{y \times q}$
   (*b*) A : B : C = $px : py : qy$
3. In what *ratio* the two kinds of tea must be mixed together one at ₹ x per kg and another at ₹ y per kg, so that the mixture may cost ₹ z per kg?
   $$\text{Ratio} = \frac{z - y}{x - z}$$
4. A grey hound persues a hare as takes J_1 leaps for every J_2 leaps of the hare. If K_1 leaps of the hound are equal to K_2 leaps of the hare, then the Ratio of speeds of the hound and hare is
   $$\frac{J_2 \times K_1}{J_1 \times K_2}$$
5. The incomes of two persons are in the ratio of $a : b$ and their expenditure are in the ratio of $x : y$. If the saving of each person is ₹ s, then income of each is ₹ $\frac{as(y-x)}{ay-bx}$ and ₹ $\frac{bs(y-x)}{ay-bx}$ respectively.

6. In a mixture of z litre, the ratio of milk and water is $x : y$. If another p litres of water is added to the mixture, the ratio of milk and water in the resulting mixture $= \dfrac{xz}{yz + p(x+y)}$

7. There are four members a, b, c and d, then formula for

   (a) What should be added to each of these numbers so that the remaining numbers may be proportional $= \dfrac{ad - bc}{(b+c)-(a+d)}$

   (b) What should be subtracted from each of these numbers so that the remaining numbers may be proportional $= \dfrac{ad - bc}{(a+d)-(b+c)}$

8. In a mixture the ratio of milk and water is $a : b$. If in this mixture another K litre of water is added, then the ratio of milk and water in the resulting mixture becomes $a : m$. Then the quantity of milk in the original mixture $= \dfrac{ak}{m-b}$ and quantity of water $= \dfrac{bk}{m-b}$

EXERCISE

1. If A : B = 6 : 7 and B : C = 8 : 9, then A : B : C is:
   A. 24 : 28 : 63 B. 48 : 28 : 63
   C. 48 : 56 : 63 D. None of these

2. The sum of two numbers is 20 and their difference is $2\frac{1}{2}$. What is the ratio of the numbers?
   A. 11 : 7 B. 9 : 11
   C. 9 : 7 D. None of these

3. If 0.7 of one number is equal to 0.075 of another, what is the ratio of the two numbers?
   A. 6 : 14 B. 3 : 28
   C. 5 : 7 D. None of these

4. If 10% of x is the same as 20% of y, then $x : y$ is equal to :
   A. 1 : 2 B. 2 : 1
   C. 5 : 1 D. 10 : 1

5. Two numbers are in the ratio 3 : 5. If each number is increased by 10, the ratio becomes 5 : 7. The numbers are:
   A. 3, 5 B. 7, 9
   C. 13, 22 D. 15, 25

6. The mean proportional between 0.32 and 0.02 is:
   A. 0.34 B. 0.3
   C. 0.16 D. 0.08

7. The sum of three numbers is 98. If the ratio between the first and second be 2 : 3 and that between the second and third be 5 : 8, then what is the second number?
   A. 20 B. 30
   C. 10 D. 40

8. One man adds 3 litres of water to 12 litres of milk and another 4 litres of water to 10 litres of milk. What is the ratio of the strenghts of the milk in the two mixtures?
   A. 15 : 25 B. 25 : 28
   C. 28 : 25 D. None of these

9. ₹ 425 is divided among 4 men, 5 women and 6 boys such that the share of a man, a woman and a boy may be in the ratio of 9 : 8 : 4. What is the share of a woman?
   A. ₹ 34 B. ₹ 24
   C. ₹ 44 D. None of these

10. A vessel contains liquids P and Q in the ratio 5 : 3. If 6 litres of the mixture are removed and the same quantity of liquid q is added, the ratio becomes 3 : 5. What quantity does the vessel hold?
    A. 40 litres B. 50 litres
    C. 30 litres D. None of these

11. A bucket contains a mixture of two liquids P and Q in the proportion 7 : 5. If 9 litres of the mixture is replaced by 9 litres of liquid Q, then the ratio of the two liquid becomes 7 : 9. How much of the liquid P was there in the bucket?
    A. 11 litres B. 21 litres
    C. 31 litres D. None of these

12. Three glasses P, Q and R with their capacities in the ratio 2 : 3 : 4 are filled with a mixture of spirit and water. The ratio of spirit to water in P, Q and R is 1 : 5, 3 : 5 and 5 : 7 respectively. If the contents of these glasses are mixed together, what is the ratio of spirit to water in the mixture?
    A. 14 : 27 B. 23 : 47
    C. 25 : 47 D. None of these

13. A and B are two alloys of gold and copper prepared by mixing metals in proportions 7 : 2 and 7 : 11 respectively. If equal quantities of the alloys are melted to form a third alloy C, the proportion of gold and copper in C will be
    A. 5 : 9 B. 5 : 7
    C. 7 : 5 D. 9 : 5

14. Gold is 19 times as heavy as water and copper 9 times as heavy as water. The ratio in which these two metals be mixed so that the mixtures is 15 times as heavy as water is:
    A. 1 : 2 B. 2 : 3
    C. 3 : 2 D. 19 : 135

15. The contents of two vessels containing water and milk are in the ratio 1 : 2 and 2 : 5 are mixed in the ratio 1 : 4. The resulting mixture will have water and milk in the ratio:

A. 21 : 54 B. 31 : 74
C. 27 : 74 D. None of these

16. One year ago, the ratio between Mahesh and Suresh's salaries was 3 : 5. The ratio of their individual salaries of last year and present year are 2 : 3 and 4 : 5 respectively. If their total salaries for the present year are ₹ 4300, what is the present salary of Mahesh?
A. ₹ 1800 B. ₹ 1900
C. ₹ 1600 D. None of these

17. The ratio of P's and Q's income last year was 3 : 4. The ratio of their own incomes of last year and this year is 4 : 5 and 2 : 3 respectively. If the total sum of their present income is ₹ 4160. What is the present income of P?
A. ₹ 1500 B. ₹ 1400
C. ₹ 1600 D. None of these

18. The monthly salary of A, B, C is in the proportion of 2 : 3 : 5. If C's monthly salary is ₹ 1200 more than that of A, then B's annual salary is:
A. ₹ 14400 B. ₹ 24000
C. ₹ 1200 D. ₹ 2000

19. ₹ 1050 is divided among P, Q and R. The share of P is $\frac{2}{5}$ of the combined share of Q and R. Thus P gets:
A. ₹ 200 B. ₹ 300
C. ₹ 400 D. ₹ 420

20. The ratio between Sumit's and Prakash's age at present is 2 : 3. Sumit is 6 years younger than Prakash. The ratio of Sumit's age to Prakash's age after 6 years will be:
A. 1 : 2 B. 2 : 3
C. 3 : 4 D. 3 : 8

ANSWERS

1	2	3	4	5	6	7	8	9	10
C	C	B	B	D	D	B	C	A	A
11	**12**	**13**	**14**	**15**	**16**	**17**	**18**	**19**	**20**
B	C	C	C	B	A	C	C	B	C

EXPLANATORY ANSWERS

1. A : B = 6 : 7
B : C = 8 : 9
∴ A : B : C = 6 × 8 : 7 × 8 : 7 × 9 = 48 : 56 : 63

2. Ratio $= \dfrac{20 + \frac{5}{2}}{20 - \frac{5}{2}} = \dfrac{22.5}{17.5} = \dfrac{225}{175} = \dfrac{9}{7} = 9 : 7$

3. We have, $0.7x = 0.075\,y$

$\dfrac{x}{y} = \dfrac{0.075}{0.7} = \dfrac{75}{700} = \dfrac{3}{28} = 3 : 28$

4. 10% of x = 20% of y

$\Rightarrow \dfrac{10}{100}x = \dfrac{20}{100}y$

$\therefore \dfrac{x}{10} = \dfrac{y}{5} \Rightarrow \dfrac{x}{y} = \dfrac{10}{5} = \dfrac{2}{1} \Rightarrow x : y = 2 : 1$

5. Let the number be $3x$ and $5x$.

Then, $\dfrac{3x+10}{5x+10} = \dfrac{5}{7} \Rightarrow 7(3x + 10) = 5(5x + 10)$

$\Rightarrow 21x + 70 = 25x + 50 \Rightarrow 4x = 20 \Rightarrow x = 5$

So, the numbers are 15, 25.

6. Mean proportional $= \sqrt{0.32 \times 0.02} = \sqrt{0.0064} = 0.08$

7. The ratio among the three numbers is

2 : 3
5 : 8
and 10 : 15 : 24

∴ The second number $= \dfrac{98}{10+15+24} \times 15 = 30$

8. Strength of milk in the first mixture $= \dfrac{12}{12+3} = \dfrac{12}{15}$

Strength of milk in the second mixture $= \dfrac{10}{10+4} = \dfrac{10}{14}$

∴ The ratio of their strengths $= \dfrac{12}{15} : \dfrac{10}{14}$

= 12 × 14 : 15 × 10 = 28 : 25

9. The ratio of shares of group of men, women and boys = 9 × 4 : 8 × 5 : 4 × 6 = 9 : 10 : 6

∴ Share of 5 women $= \dfrac{425}{9+10+6} \times 10 =$ ₹ 170

∴ Share of 1 woman $= \dfrac{170}{5} =$ ₹ 34

10. Let the vessel contains $5x$ litres and $3x$ litres of liquid P and Q respectively. The removed quantity contains

$\dfrac{16}{5+3} \times 5 = 10$ litres of P

and 16 − 10 = 6 litres of Q.

Now, $(5x - 10) : (3x - 6 + 16) = 3 : 5$

$\Rightarrow \dfrac{5x-10}{3x+10} = \dfrac{3}{5} \Rightarrow 25x - 50 = 9x + 30$

$\Rightarrow 16x = 80 \Rightarrow x = 5$

∴ Vessel contains $8x = 8 \times 5 = 40$ litres.

11. Let the two liquids P and Q are $7x$ litres and $5x$ litres repectively.

Now, when 9 litres of mixture are taken out, P remains

$$7x - 9\left(\frac{7}{7+5}\right) = 7x - \frac{9 \times 7}{12} = \left(7x - \frac{21}{4}\right) \text{ litres}$$

and Q remains

$$5x - 9\left(\frac{5}{7+5}\right) = 5x - \frac{9 \times 5}{12} = \left(5x - \frac{15}{4}\right) \text{ litres}$$

Now, when 9 litres of liquid Q are added,

$$\left(7x - \frac{21}{4}\right) : \left(5x - \frac{15}{4} + 9\right) = 7 : 9$$

$$\Rightarrow \frac{7x - \frac{21}{4}}{5x - \frac{15}{4} + 9} = \frac{7}{9}$$

$$\Rightarrow 63x - \frac{189}{4} = 35x + \frac{147}{4}$$

$$\Rightarrow 28x = \frac{189}{4} + \frac{147}{4} = \frac{336}{4} = 84$$

$$\Rightarrow x = \frac{84}{28} = 3 \Rightarrow 7x = 7 \times 3 = 21 \text{ litres.}$$

12. P : Q : R

2 : 3 : 4

Spirit : Water = 1 : 5, 3 : 5 and 5 : 7

When they are mixed, the ratio of spirit to water

$$= \left(2 \times \frac{1}{1+5} + 3 \times \frac{3}{3+5} + 4 \times \frac{5}{5+7}\right) : \left(2 \times \frac{5}{1+5} + 3 \times \frac{5}{3+5} + 4 \times \frac{7}{5+7}\right)$$

$$= \left(\frac{1}{3} + \frac{9}{8} + \frac{5}{3}\right) : \left(\frac{5}{3} + \frac{15}{8} + \frac{7}{3}\right) = \frac{25}{8} : \frac{47}{8} = 25 : 47$$

13. Gold in C $= \left(\frac{7}{9} + \frac{7}{18}\right) = \frac{21}{18} = \frac{7}{6}$

Copper in C $= \left(\frac{2}{9} + \frac{11}{18}\right) = \frac{15}{18} = \frac{5}{6}$

$\therefore$ Gold : Copper $= \frac{7}{6} : \frac{5}{6} = 7 : 5$

14. Let 1 gm of gold be mixed with x gm of copper to give $(1 + x)$ gm of mixture.

Now, $1G = 19w$

and $1C = 9w$

and mixture $= 15w$

Now, 1 gm gold + x gm copper = $(1 + x)$ gm mixture

$\therefore 19w + 9w \times x = (1 + x) \times 15w$

Thus, $4w = 6wx$

$$\Rightarrow x = \frac{4w}{6w} = \frac{4}{6} = \frac{2}{3}$$

So, the required ratio is $1 : \frac{2}{3}$, *i.e.*, 3 : 2.

15.

	Water	*Milk*
Vessel I	$\frac{1}{3}$	$\frac{2}{3}$
Vessel II	$\frac{2}{7}$	$\frac{5}{7}$

From vessel I, $\frac{1}{5}$ is taken and from vessel II, $\frac{4}{5}$ is taken. Therefore, the ratio of water to milk in the new vessel

$$= \left(\frac{1}{3} \times \frac{1}{5} + \frac{2}{7} \times \frac{4}{5}\right) : \left(\frac{2}{3} \times \frac{1}{5} + \frac{5}{7} \times \frac{4}{5}\right)$$

$$= \left(\frac{1}{15} + \frac{8}{35}\right) : \left(\frac{2}{15} + \frac{20}{35}\right) = \frac{31}{105} : \frac{74}{105} = 31 : 74$$

16. The ratio of Mahesh's salary for the two years = 2 : 3

The ratio of Suresh's salary for the two years = 4 : 5

We have also given that the ratio of their salary during the last year = 3 : 5

Now, we change the antecedents (2 and 4) of the first two ratios so that the antecedents in the first becomes 3 (antecedent of the third ratio) and the antecedent in the second becomes 5 (consequent of the third ratio).

Thus, $2 : 3 = 3 : \frac{9}{2}$ and $4 : 5 = 4\left(\frac{5}{4}\right) : 5\left(\frac{5}{4}\right) = 5 : \frac{25}{4}$

Now, it is clear that the ratio of their salaries for the present year is $\frac{9}{2} : \frac{25}{4} = 18 : 25$

$\therefore$ The present salary of Mahesh

$$= \frac{4300}{18+25} \times 18 = ₹\ 1800$$

17. The ratio of present incomes

$$= 3 \times \frac{5}{4} : 4 \times \frac{3}{2} = \frac{15}{4} : \frac{12}{2} = 30 : 48 = 5 : 8$$

$$\therefore \text{ P's present income } = \frac{4160}{5+8} \times 5 = ₹\ 1600$$

18. Let the monthly salary of A, B, C be $2x$, $3x$ and $5x$

Then, $5x - 2x = 1200$

or, $3x = 1200$

$\therefore$ $x = 400$

B's monthly salary $= 3x = 3 \times 400 =$ ₹ 1200

19. P : (Q + R) = 2 : 5

$\therefore$ P's share $=$ ₹ $\left(1050 \times \frac{2}{7}\right) =$ ₹ 300

20. Let their ages be $2x$ and $3x$ years.

$\Rightarrow$ $3x - 2x = 6 \Rightarrow x = 6$

Sumit's age = 12 years

Prakash's age = 18 years

After 6 years, Sumit's age = 18 years and Prakash's age = 24 years

$\therefore$ Ratio of their ages = 18 : 24 = 3 : 4

CHAPTER

4 Algebra

Square Roots

Points To Remember

- A number n is a perfect square number, if $n = m^2$
- A perfect square number is never negative.
- A square number never ends in 2, 3, 7 or 8.
- The number of zeros at the end of a perfect square is even.
- The square of an even number is even.
- The square of an odd number is odd.
- There are no natural number p and q such that $p^2 = 2q^2$.
- A number m is a square root of n, if $n = m \times m = m^2$. Positive square root of n is written as $\sqrt{n}$.
- If p and q are perfect squares ($q \neq 0$), then
  (*i*) $\sqrt{p \times q} = \sqrt{p} \times \sqrt{q}$
  (*ii*) $\sqrt{\frac{p}{q}} = \frac{\sqrt{p}}{\sqrt{q}}$
- A perfect squares leaves remainder 0 or 1 on division by 3.
  The following table gives the possible remainders for some other prime divisors.

Divisor	Possible Remainders
3	0, 1
5	0, 1, 4
7	0, 1, 2, 4
11	0, 1, 3, 4, 5, 9
13	0, 1, 3, 4, 9, 10, 12

- The unit's digit of the square of a natural number is the unit's digit of the square of the digit at unit's place of the given natural number.

Unit's digit of the number	Unit's digit of the square of the number
0	0
1 or 9	1
2 or 8	4
3 or 7	9
4 or 6	6
5	5

- For every natural number n,
  $(n + 1)^2 - n^2 = (n + 1) + n$
  e.g.; $9^2 - 8^2 = 9 + 8 = 17$
  $19^2 - 18^2 = 19 + 18 = 37$
- The square of a natural number n is equal to the sum of first n odd natural numbers.
  e.g.; $2^2 = 1 + 3$
  $4^2 = 1 + 3 + 5 + 7 = 16$
  n^2 = Sum of first n odd natural numbers.
- A triplet (m, n, p) of three natural numbers m, n and p is called a pythagorean triplet if $m^2 + n^2 = p^2$
- The square root of a perfect square number can be obtained by :
  (*i*) the prime factorization. (*ii*) the division method.
- If n is not a perfect square, then $\sqrt{n}$ is not a rational number.
- Squares of natural numbers having all digits 1 have a following pattern:
  $1^2 = 1$
  $11^2 = 1\,\mathbf{2}\,1$
  $111^2 = 1\,2\,\mathbf{3}\,2\,1$
  $1111^2 = 1\,2\,3\,\mathbf{4}\,3\,2\,1$

$11111^2 = 1\,2\,3\,4\,\mathbf{5}\,4\,3\,2\,1$

$111111^2 = 1\,2\,3\,4\,5\,\mathbf{6}\,5\,4\,3\,2\,1$

$\vdots \qquad \vdots$

$111111111^2 = 1\,2\,3\,4\,5\,6\,7\,8\,\mathbf{9}\,8\,7\,6\,5\,4\,3\,2\,1$

In this pattern the sum of the digits of every number on the right hand side is a perfect square at given below:

$1 + 2 + 1 = 4 = 2^2$

$1 + 2 + 3 + 2 + 1 = 9 = 3^2$

$1 + 2 + 3 + 4 + 3 + 2 + 1 = 16 = 4^2$

. . . .

$1 + 2 + 3 + 4 + 5 + 6 + 7 + 8 + 9 + 8 + 7 + 6 + 5 + 4 + 3 + 2 + 1 = 81 = 9^2$.

- Observe the following pattern

$11^2 = 121$

$101^2 = 10201$

$1001^2 = 1002001$

$10001^2 = 100020001$

- Observe the following pattern

$11^2 = 121$

$101^2 = 10201$

$10101^2 = 102030201$

$1010101^2 = 1020304030201$

$101010101^2 = 10203040504030201$

- **Short Cut Method to find Squares Column Method**

Using $(a + b)^2 = a^2 + 2ab + b^2$.

Make three columns: What is square of 86

$a = 8, b = 6$

Step	Column I (a^2)	Column II $2ab$	Column III b^2
I	$(8)^2 = 64$	$2 \times 8 \times 6 = 96$	$(6)^2 = 36$
II	64	96 + 3 99	**36**
III	64 + 9 **73**	96 + 3 **99**	**36**

The bold digits give the required square $86^2 = 7396$.

Square Root

Square root of a given number is that number which is multiplied by itself is equal to the given number.
For example, square root of 81 is 9 because
$92 = 9 \times 9 = 81$.

Methods of Finding the square root

(a) Prime Factorization Method

(i) Prime Factorization Method

(ii) Group the Factors in Paris

(iii) Take one number from each pair of factors and then multiply them together.

Example: Find the square root of 4761?

Solution: $4761 = \underbrace{23 \times 23} \times \underbrace{3 \times 3}$

$\therefore \quad \sqrt{4761} = 23 \times 3 = 69.$

(b) Method of Division: This method is used when the number is large and the factors cannot be easily determined.

Exar.'ple: Find the square root of 226576?

Solution:

```
         476
    4  226516
        16
   87    665
    7    609
  946    5676
    6    5676
           ×
```

$\sqrt[2]{226576} = 476.$

EXERCISE

1. $\sqrt{53824} = ?$

A. 202 B. 232
C. 242 D. 332

2. The value of $\sqrt{10+\sqrt{25+\sqrt{108+\sqrt{154+\sqrt{255}}}}}$ is:

A. 4 B. 6
C. 8 D. 10

3. Evaluate : $\sqrt{41-\sqrt{21+\sqrt{19-\sqrt{9}}}}$.

A. 3 B. 5
C. 6 D. 6.4

4. $\left(\frac{\sqrt{625}}{11} \times \frac{14}{\sqrt{25}} \times \frac{11}{\sqrt{196}}\right)$ is equal to:

A. 5
B. 6
C. 8
D. 11

5. If $x * y = x + y + \sqrt{xy}$, the value of 6*24 is:

A. 41 B. 42
C. 43 D. 44

6. $\sqrt{\frac{25}{81}-\frac{1}{9}} = ?$

A. $\frac{2}{3}$ B. $\frac{4}{9}$
C. $\frac{16}{81}$ D. $\frac{25}{81}$

7. The value of $\sqrt{0.01}+\sqrt{0.81}+\sqrt{1.21}+\sqrt{0.0009}$ is:

A. 2.03 B. 2.1
C. 2.11 D. 2.13

8. If $\sqrt{18225} = 135$, then the value of $\left(\sqrt{182.25}+\sqrt{1.8225}+\sqrt{0.018225}+\sqrt{0.00018225}\right)$ is:

A. 1.49985 B. 14.9985
C. 149.985 D. 1499.85

9. If $\sqrt{3^n} = 729$, then the value of n is:

A. 6 B. 8
C. 10 D. 12

10. If $\sqrt{1+\frac{x}{169}} = \frac{14}{13}$, then x is equal to:

A. 1 B. 13
C. 27 D. None of these

11. If $\sqrt{1+\frac{55}{729}} = 1+\frac{x}{27}$, then the value of x is:

A. 1 B. 3
C. 5 D. 7

12. The value of $\frac{\sqrt{80}-\sqrt{112}}{\sqrt{45}-\sqrt{63}}$ is:

A. $\frac{3}{4}$ B. $1\frac{1}{3}$
C. $1\frac{7}{9}$ D. $1\frac{3}{4}$

13. Given $\sqrt{2} = 1.414$. The value of $\sqrt{8}+2\sqrt{32}-3\sqrt{128}+4\sqrt{50}$ is:

A. 8.426 B. 8.484
C. 8.526 D. 8.876

14. $\sqrt{\frac{0.081\times0.324\times4.624}{1.5625\times0.0289\times72.9\times64}}$ is equal to:

A. 0.024 B. 0.24
C. 2.4 D. 24

15. The value of $\sqrt{\frac{(0.03)^2+(0.21)^2+(0.065)^2}{(0.003)^2+(0.021)^2+(0.0065)^2}}$ is:

A. 0.1 B. 10
C. 10^2 D. 10^3

16. The square root of $\left(7+3\sqrt{5}\right)\left(7-3\sqrt{5}\right)$ is:

A. $\sqrt{5}$ B. 2
C. 4 D. $3\sqrt{5}$

17. $\left(\sqrt{3}-\frac{1}{\sqrt{3}}\right)^2$ simplifies to:

A. $\frac{3}{4}$ B. $\frac{4}{\sqrt{3}}$
C. $\frac{4}{3}$ D. None of these

18. $\left(\sqrt{2}+\frac{1}{\sqrt{2}}\right)^2$ is equal to :

A. $2\frac{1}{2}$ B. $3\frac{1}{2}$
C. $4\frac{1}{2}$ D. $5\frac{1}{2}$

19. If $3a = 4b = 6c$ and $a+b+c = 27\sqrt{29}$, then $\sqrt{a^2+b^2+c^2}$ is:

A. $3\sqrt{29}$
B. 81
C. 87
D. None of these

20. The square root of $0.\overline{4}$ is:

A. $0.\overline{6}$ B. $0.\overline{7}$
C. $0.\overline{8}$ D. $0.\overline{9}$

ANSWERS

1	2	3	4	5	6	7	8	9	10
B	A	C	A	B	B	D	B	D	C
11	**12**	**13**	**14**	**15**	**16**	**17**	**18**	**19**	**20**
A	B	B	A	B	B	C	C	C	A

EXPLANATORY ANSWERS

1.

```
   2 | 53824 (232
     | 4
  43 | 138
     | 129
 462 |  924
     |  924
     |   ×
```

$\therefore \quad \sqrt{53824} = 232.$

2. Given exp. $= \sqrt{10+\sqrt{25+\sqrt{108+\sqrt{154+15}}}}$

$= \sqrt{10+\sqrt{25+\sqrt{108+\sqrt{169}}}}$

$= \sqrt{10+\sqrt{25+\sqrt{108+13}}} = \sqrt{10+\sqrt{25+\sqrt{121}}}$

$= \sqrt{10+\sqrt{25+11}} = \sqrt{10+\sqrt{36}}$

$= \sqrt{10+6} = \sqrt{16} = 4$

3. Given exp. $= \sqrt{41-\sqrt{21+\sqrt{19-3}}}$

$= \sqrt{41-\sqrt{21+\sqrt{16}}} = \sqrt{41-\sqrt{21+4}}$

$= \sqrt{41-\sqrt{25}} = \sqrt{41-5} = \sqrt{36} = 6$

4. Given exp. $= \frac{25}{11}\times\frac{14}{5}\times\frac{11}{14} = 5$

5. $6*24 = 6 + 24 + \sqrt{6\times 24} = 30+\sqrt{144} = 30+12 = 42$

6. $\sqrt{\frac{25}{81}-\frac{1}{9}} = \sqrt{\frac{25-9}{81}} = \sqrt{\frac{16}{81}} = \frac{\sqrt{16}}{\sqrt{81}} = \frac{4}{9}$

7. Given exp.

$= \sqrt{\frac{1}{100}}+\sqrt{\frac{81}{100}}+\sqrt{\frac{121}{100}}+\sqrt{\frac{9}{10000}}$

$= \frac{1}{10}+\frac{9}{10}+\frac{11}{10}+\frac{3}{100}$

$= 0.1 + 0.9 + 1.1 + 0.03 = 2.13$

8. Given exp.

$= \sqrt{\frac{18225}{10^2}}+\sqrt{\frac{18225}{10^4}}+\sqrt{\frac{18225}{10^6}}+\sqrt{\frac{18225}{10^8}}$

$= \frac{\sqrt{18225}}{10}+\frac{\sqrt{18225}}{10^2}+\frac{\sqrt{18225}}{10^3}+\frac{\sqrt{18225}}{10^4}$

$= \frac{135}{10}+\frac{135}{100}+\frac{135}{1000}+\frac{135}{10000}$

$= 13.5 + 1.35 + 0.135 + 0.0135 = 14.9985$

9. $\sqrt{3^n} = 729 = 3^6$

$\Leftrightarrow \left(\sqrt{3^n}\right)^2 = (3^6)^2$

$\Leftrightarrow 3^n = 3^{12}$

$\Leftrightarrow n = 12$

10. $\sqrt{1+\frac{x}{169}} = \frac{14}{13} \quad \Rightarrow 1+\frac{x}{169} = \frac{196}{169}$

$\Rightarrow \frac{x}{169} = \left(\frac{196}{169}-1\right) = \frac{27}{169}$

$\Rightarrow x = 27.$

11. $\sqrt{1+\frac{55}{729}} = 1+\frac{x}{27}$

$\Rightarrow \sqrt{\frac{784}{729}} = \frac{27+x}{27}$

$\Rightarrow \frac{28}{27} = \frac{27+x}{27}$

$\Rightarrow 27 + x = 28 \quad \Rightarrow x = 1$

12. $\frac{\sqrt{80}-\sqrt{112}}{\sqrt{45}-\sqrt{63}} = \frac{\sqrt{16\times 5}-\sqrt{16\times 7}}{\sqrt{9\times 5}-\sqrt{9\times 7}}$

$= \frac{4\sqrt{5}-4\sqrt{7}}{3\sqrt{5}-3\sqrt{7}} = \frac{4\left(\sqrt{5}-\sqrt{7}\right)}{3\left(\sqrt{5}-\sqrt{7}\right)} = \frac{4}{3} = 1\frac{1}{3}$

13. Given exp.

$= \sqrt{4\times 2}+2\sqrt{16\times 2}-3\sqrt{64\times 2}+4\sqrt{25\times 2}$

$= 2\sqrt{2}+8\sqrt{2}-24\sqrt{2}+20\sqrt{2}$

$= 6\sqrt{2} = 6 \times 1.414 = 8.484$

14. Given exp. $= \sqrt{\frac{81\times 324\times 4624}{15625\times 289\times 729\times 64}}$

$= \frac{9\times 18\times 68}{125\times 17\times 27\times 8} = \frac{3}{125} = 0.024$

15. Given exp. $= \sqrt{\frac{(0.03)^2+(0.21)^2+(0.065)^2}{\left(\frac{0.03}{10}\right)^2+\left(\frac{0.21}{10}\right)^2+\left(\frac{0.065}{10}\right)^2}}$

$= \sqrt{\frac{100\ [(0.03)^2+(0.21)^2+(0.065)^2]}{(0.03)^2+(0.21)^2+(0.065)^2}}$

$= \sqrt{100} = 10$

16. $\sqrt{(7+3\sqrt{5})(7-3\sqrt{5})} = \sqrt{(7)^2-(3\sqrt{5})^2}$

$= \sqrt{49-45} = \sqrt{4} = 2$

17. $\left(\sqrt{3}-\frac{1}{\sqrt{3}}\right)^2 = \left(\sqrt{3}\right)^2 + \left(\frac{1}{\sqrt{3}}\right)^2 - 2\times\sqrt{3}\times\frac{1}{\sqrt{3}}$

$= 3+\frac{1}{3}-2 = 1+\frac{1}{3} = \frac{4}{3}$

18. $\left(\sqrt{2}+\frac{1}{\sqrt{2}}\right)^2 = \left(\sqrt{2}\right)^2 + \left(\frac{1}{\sqrt{2}}\right)^2 + 2\times\sqrt{2}\times\frac{1}{\sqrt{2}}$

$= 2+\frac{1}{2}+2 = 4+\frac{1}{2} = 4\frac{1}{2}$

19. $4b = 6c \Rightarrow b = \frac{3}{2}c$ and $3a = 4b$

$\Rightarrow \quad a = \frac{4}{3}b = \frac{4}{3}\left(\frac{3}{2}c\right) = 2c$

$a + b + c = 27\sqrt{29}$

$2c+\frac{3}{2}c+c = 27\sqrt{29}$

$\Rightarrow \quad \frac{9}{2}c = 27\sqrt{29}$

$\Rightarrow \quad c = 6\sqrt{29}$

$\therefore \sqrt{a^2+b^2+c^2}$

$= \sqrt{(a+b+c)-2(ab+bc+ca)}$

$= \sqrt{\left(27\sqrt{29}\right)^2 - 2\left(2c\times\frac{3}{2}c+\frac{3}{2}c\times c+c\times 2c\right)}$

$= \sqrt{(729\times 29)-2\left(3c^2+\frac{3}{2}c^2+2c^2\right)}$

$= \sqrt{(729\times 29)-2\times\frac{13}{2}c^2}$

$= \sqrt{(729\times 29)-13\times\left(6\sqrt{29}\right)^2}$

$= \sqrt{29(729-468)}$

$= \sqrt{29\times 261} = \sqrt{29\times 29\times 9}$

$= 29 \times 3 = 87$

20. $\sqrt{0.\bar{4}} = \sqrt{\frac{4}{9}} = \frac{2}{3} = 0.666.... = 0.\bar{6}$.

Basic Algebraic Identities of School Algebra & Elementary Surds

Algebric Identies

Some Important Formula

(i) $(a + b)^2 = a^2 + 2ab + b^2$

(ii) $(a - b)^2 = a^2 - 2ab + b^2$

(iii) $a^2 - b^2 = (a - b)(a + b)$

(iv) $(a + b + c)^2 = a^2 + b^2 + c^2 + 2ab + 2bc + 2ca$

(v) $(a + b - c)^2 = a^2 + b^2 + c^2 + 2ab - 2bc - 2ca$

(vi) $(a - b + c)^2 = a^2 + b^2 + c^2 - 2ab - 2bc + 2ca$

(vii) $(-a + b + c)^2 = a^2 + b^2 + c^2 - 2ab + 2bc - 2ca$

(viii) $(a + b)^3 = a^3 + b^3 + 3ab(a + b)$ or

$= a^3 + b^3 + 3a^2b + 3ab^2$

(ix) $(a - b)^3 = a^3 - b^3 - 3ab\,(a - b)$ or

$= a^3 - b^3 - 3a^2b + 3ab^2$

(x) $a^3 + b^3 = (a + b)\,(a^2 + b^2 - ab)$ or

$= (a + b)^3 - 3ab(a + b)$

(xi) $a^3 - b^3 = (a - b)\,(a^2 + b^2 + ab)$ or

$= (a - b)^3 + 3ab\,(a - b)$

(xii) $a^3 + b^3 + c^3 - 3abc$

$= (a + b + c)(a^2 + b^2 + c^2 - ab - bc - ca)$

If $a + b + c = 0$

$a^3 + b^3 + c^3 = 3abc$

(xiii) $(x + a)\,(x + b) = x^2 + (a + b)x + ab$

(xiv) $(a + b)^2 + (a - b)^2 = 2(a^2 + b^2)$

(xv) $(a + b)^2 - (a - b)^2 = 4ab$

(xvi) $(a + b)^3 + (a - b)^3 = 2(a^3 + 3ab^2)$

(xvii) $(a + b)^3 - (a - b)^3 = (2(b^3 + 3a^2b)$

(xviii) If $x+\frac{1}{x}=t$ Then, $x^2+\frac{1}{x^2}=t^2-2$

(xix) If $x-\frac{1}{x}=t$ Then, $x^2+\frac{1}{x^2}=t^2+2$

(xx) $x^3+\frac{1}{x^3}=\left(x+\frac{1}{x}\right)^3-3\left(x+\frac{1}{x}\right)$

(xxi) $x^2-\frac{1}{x^3}=\left(x-\frac{1}{x}\right)^3+3\left(x-\frac{1}{x}\right)$

(xxii) $x+\frac{1}{x}=\sqrt{x^2+\frac{1}{x^2}+2}$

(xxiii) $x-\frac{1}{x}=\sqrt{x^2+\frac{1}{x^2}-2}$

Factorization of Algebraic Expressions

Factorization : The process of writing an algebraic expression as the product of two or more algebraic expressions is called factorization.

Factors : The algebraic expressions that may be multiplied to obtain the given algebraic expressions are called factors of the given expression.

Factor Theorem : If $f(x)$ is completely divisible by $(x - a)$ then $f(a) = 0$, $(x - a)$ is called factor of $f(x)$, if and only if $f(a) = 0$

Remainder Theorem : If an expression $f(x)$ is divided by $(x - a)$ then the remainder is $f(a)$.

e.g., $f(x) = ax^3 + bx + cx + d$

$f(a) = a \cdot a^3 + b \cdot a + c \cdot a + d$ is known as remainder of the given polynomials.

Surds

Given a number, it is not always possible to find some whole number which when multiplied by itself will give the given number. In other words all given numbers are not perfect square numbers. For example, square root of 9, *i.e.*, $\sqrt{9}$ is 3, which is a whole number. But square root of 15, *i.e.*, $\sqrt{15} = 3.873$, which is not a whole number.

Hence square roots of natural numbers which are not perfect squares are not rational numbers. These are irrational numbers and are called **Surds**.

For example, $\sqrt{3}$, $\sqrt{7}$, $2+\sqrt{11}$, $4+\sqrt{13}$ ..... etc. are Surds.

Given below are a few formulas which are quite helpful in solving the problems related to surds:

1. $\sqrt{a} \times \sqrt{a} = a$
2. $\sqrt{a} \times \sqrt{b} = \sqrt{ab}$
3. $\left(\sqrt{a}+\sqrt{b}\right)^2 = a + b + \sqrt[2]{ab}$
4. $\left(\sqrt{a}-\sqrt{b}\right)^2 = a + b - \sqrt[2]{ab}$
5. $x\sqrt{a} + x\sqrt{b} = x\left(\sqrt{a}+\sqrt{b}\right)$
6. $\dfrac{1}{\sqrt{a}+\sqrt{b}} = \dfrac{1}{\sqrt{a}+\sqrt{b}} \times \dfrac{\sqrt{a}-\sqrt{b}}{\sqrt{a}-\sqrt{b}} = \dfrac{\sqrt{a}-\sqrt{b}}{a-b}$
7. $\dfrac{1}{\sqrt{a}-\sqrt{b}} = \dfrac{1}{\sqrt{a}-\sqrt{b}} \times \dfrac{\sqrt{a}+\sqrt{b}}{\sqrt{a}+\sqrt{b}} = \dfrac{\sqrt{a}+\sqrt{b}}{a-b}$
8. $a + \sqrt{b} = c + \sqrt{d} \Rightarrow a = c$ and $b = d$
9. $\sqrt{2} = 1.41421$, $\sqrt{3} = 1.73205$, $\sqrt{5} = 2.23607$, $\sqrt{6} = 2.4494$ $\sqrt{7} = 2.64575$, $\sqrt{8} = 2.82842$, $\sqrt{10} = 3.16227$, $\sqrt{11} = 3.31662$

EXERCISE

1. $(28)^3 + (-15)^3 + (-13)^3 = ?$

A. 16380 B. 16250
C. 16420 D. 16280

2. If $x + \dfrac{1}{x} = 5$, What is the value of $x^3 + \dfrac{1}{x^3}$:

A. 120 B. 210
C. 110 D. 105

3. If $x^2 + \dfrac{1}{x^2} = 83$, what is the value of $x^3 - \dfrac{1}{x^3} = ?$

A. 756 B. 754
C. 856 D. 932

4. $23^3 - 17^3 = ?$

A. 7254 B. 7153
C. 7271 D. 7154

5. If $x + \dfrac{1}{x} = 15$, then the value of $x^2 + \dfrac{1}{x^2}$ will be:

A. 228 B. 230
C. 323 D. 223

6. If $x = 12$ and $y = 4$, the value of $(x+y)^{x/y}$ will be:

A. 4096 B. 3896
C. 4196 D. 5086

7. If $x + y = 2z$, then the value of $\left(\dfrac{x}{x-z} + \dfrac{z}{y-z}\right)$ will be:

A. 1 B. 4
C. 3/2 D. 2

8. If $x + y + z = 0$, then the value of $\dfrac{(x+y)(y+z)(z+x)}{xyz}$ will be:

A. –3 B. –2
C. 0 D. –1

9. If $x + \dfrac{1}{x} = 3$, the value of $x^4 + \dfrac{1}{x^4}$ will be:

A. 49 B. 47
C. 37 D. 42

10. If $\left(x + \dfrac{1}{x}\right)^2 = 0$, then the value of $\left(x^2 + \dfrac{1}{x^2}\right)$ will be:

A. 1 B. –1
C. 2 D. –2

11. If $\left(a + \dfrac{2}{a}\right) = 3$, then the value of $\left(a - \dfrac{2}{a}\right)$ will be:

A. ± 4 B. ± 5
C. ± 2 D. ± 1

12. If $\sqrt{a}+\frac{1}{\sqrt{a}} = 4$, then the value of $a^2 + \frac{1}{a^2}$ will be:

A. 194 B. 199
C. 178 D. 192

13. Factors of $x^2 - 25$ are:

A. $(x - 1)(x - 25)$
B. $(x + 25)(x - 1)$
C. $(x + 5)(x - 5)$
D. $(x - 5)(x - 5)$

14. Square of $\left(x-\frac{1}{x}\right)$ will be

A. $x^2 - 2 - \frac{1}{x^2}$ B. $x^2 - 2 + \frac{1}{x^2}$
C. $x^2 - 4 - \frac{1}{x^2}$ D. $x^2 - 2 + \frac{1}{x}$

15. Factors of $36 - 9x^2$ will be:

A. $(6 + 3x)(6 - 3x)$ B. $(3x - 6)(6 - 3x)$
C. $(3x + 6)(3x - 6)$ D. $(12x - 3x)(3 + 3x)$

ANSWERS

1	2	3	4	5	6	7	8	9	10
A	C	A	A	D	A	A	D	B	D
11	**12**	**13**	**14**	**15**					
D	A	C	B	A					

EXPLANATORY ANSWERS

1. Let $a = 28$, $b = -15$ and $c = -13$. Then

$$a + b + c = 28 - 15 - 13 = 0$$
$$a^3 + b^3 + c^3 = 3abc$$
$$(28)^3 + (-15)^3 + (-13)^3 = 3 \times 28 \times (-15) \times (-13) = 16380$$

2. $$x^3+\frac{1}{x^3} = \left(x+\frac{1}{x}\right)^3 - 3\left(x+\frac{1}{x}\right)$$
$$= (5)^3 - 3 \times 5 = 125 - 15 = 110.$$

3. If $x^2+\frac{1}{x^2} = 83$, what is the value of $x^3-\frac{1}{x^3} = ?$

$$\left(x-\frac{1}{x}\right)^2 = x^2+\frac{1}{x^2}-2$$
$$x-\frac{1}{x} = \sqrt{83-2} = \sqrt{81}$$
$$x-\frac{1}{x} = 9$$
$$\therefore \left(x^3-\frac{1}{x^3}\right) = \left(x-\frac{1}{x}\right)^3 + 3\left(x-\frac{1}{x}\right)$$
$$= (9)^3 + 3 \times 9 = 729 + 27 = 756$$

4. $23^3 - 17^3 = (20+3)^3 - (20-3)^3 = 2(3^3 + 3 \times 20^2 \times 3)$

$[\because (a + b)^3 - (a - b)^3 = 2(b^3 + 3a^2b)]$

$= 2(27 + 3600) = 54 + 7200 = 7254$

5. $\because x+\frac{1}{x} = 15 \Rightarrow \left(x+\frac{1}{x}\right)^2 = (15)^2$

$$\Rightarrow x^2+\frac{1}{x^2}+2.x\frac{1}{x} = 225$$
$$\therefore x^2+\frac{1}{x^2} = 225 - 2 = 223.$$

6. $(x+y)^{x/y} = (12+4)^{12/4} = (16)^3 = 4096.$

$[\because x = 12, y = 4]$

7. $\because x + y = 2z \Rightarrow x - z = z - y = -(y - z)$

$$\therefore \frac{x}{x-z}+\frac{z}{y-z} = \frac{x}{-(y-z)}+\frac{z}{y-z} = \frac{z-x}{y-z} = 1.$$

$[\because x - z = z - y]$

8. $\because$
$$x + y + z = 0 \Rightarrow x + y = -z$$
$$x + y + z = 0 \Rightarrow y + z = -x$$
and
$$x + y + z = 0 \Rightarrow z + x = -y$$
$$\therefore \frac{(x+y)(y+z)(z+x)}{xyz} = \frac{(-z)(-x)(-y)}{xyz} = -1.$$

9. $\because x+\frac{1}{x} = 3 \Rightarrow \left(x+\frac{1}{x}\right)^2 = (3)^2$

$$\Rightarrow x^2+\frac{1}{x^2}+2.x.\frac{1}{x} = 9$$
$$\Rightarrow x^2+\frac{1}{x^2} = 9 - 2 = 7$$
$$\because x^2+\frac{1}{x^2} = 7 \Rightarrow \left(x^2+\frac{1}{x^2}\right)^2 = (7)^2$$
$$\Rightarrow x^4+\frac{1}{x^4}+2.x^2.\frac{1}{x^2} = 49$$
$$\therefore x^4+\frac{1}{x^4} = 49 - 2 = 47.$$

10. $\left(x+\frac{1}{x}\right)^2 = 0 \Rightarrow x^2+\frac{1}{x^2}+2x.\frac{1}{x} = 0$

$$\Rightarrow x^2+\frac{1}{x^2} = -2.$$

11. $\because \left(a-\frac{2}{a}\right)^2 = \left(a+\frac{2}{a}\right)^2 - 4.a.\frac{2}{a} = (3)^2 - 8 = 9 - 8 = 1$

$\therefore \left(a-\frac{2}{a}\right) = \pm\sqrt{1} = \pm 1.$

12. $\because \sqrt{a}+\frac{1}{\sqrt{a}} = 4 \Rightarrow \left(\sqrt{a}+\frac{1}{\sqrt{a}}\right)^2 = (4)^2$

$\Rightarrow a+\frac{1}{a}+2.\sqrt{a}.\frac{1}{\sqrt{a}} = 16 \because \left(a+\frac{1}{a}\right) = 14$

$\Rightarrow \left(a+\frac{1}{a}\right)^2 = (14)^2 \Rightarrow a^2 + \frac{1}{a^2} + 2.a.\frac{1}{a} = 196$

$\therefore a^2 + \frac{1}{a^2} = 196 - 2 = 194.$

13. $x^2 - 25 = (x)^2 - (5)^2$,
[which is of the form $a^2 - b^2$]
$= (x + 5)(x - 5).$

14. According to question:

Square of $\left(x-\frac{1}{x}\right) = \left(x-\frac{1}{x}\right)^2$

$= x^2 - 2.x.\frac{1}{x} + \left(\frac{1}{x}\right)^2$

$= x^2 - 2 + \frac{1}{x^2}.$

15. $36 - 9x^2 = (6)^2 - (3x)^2$ [which is of the form $a^2 - b^2$]
$= (6 + 3x)(6 - 3x).$

Graphs of Linear Equations

Linear Equation in One Variable

Definition: A linear equation in one variable is an equation of the form $ax + b = 0$ or, $ax = c$ where, a, b, c are real numbers, $a \neq 0$ and x is a variable. Its graph is a straight line.

(*i*) If equation is on X-axis, then Y = 0

(*ii*) If equation is on Y-axis, then X = 0

Linear Equation in Two Variables

Definition: An equation of the form $ax + by + c = 0$ or, $ax + by = c$ where, a, b, c are real numbers, $a \neq 0$, $b \neq 0$ and x, y are variables, is called a linear equation in two variables.

For example: (*i*) $2x + 3y = 12$ (*ii*) $x + 2y = 8$

The System of Equations

$a_1x + b_1y + c_1 = 0$ and $a_2x + b_2y + c_2 = 0$ may be either unique solution or no solution or infinitely many solutions.

Unique solution is known as consistent or not parallel. No solution is known as inconsistent or parallel, while many solutions are known as coincident or dependent.

(*a*) **For unique solution:** $\frac{a_1}{a_2} \neq \frac{b_1}{b_2}$

(*b*) **For no solution:** $\frac{a_1}{a_2} = \frac{b_1}{b_2} \neq \frac{c_1}{c_2}$

(*c*) **For many solutions:** $\frac{a_1}{a_2} = \frac{b_1}{b_2} = \frac{c_1}{c_2}$

Graph of linear equations

Graph of a linear equation in two variables x and y *i.e.*, the graph of the equation of the form

$ax + by + c = 0, a \neq 0, b \neq 0$

we consider the equation,

$2x + y = 6$

then, $y = 6 - 2x$

We find different values of this equation

x	0	1	2	3
y	6	4	2	0

Now, we plot these points (x, y) on a graph paper and then join these points

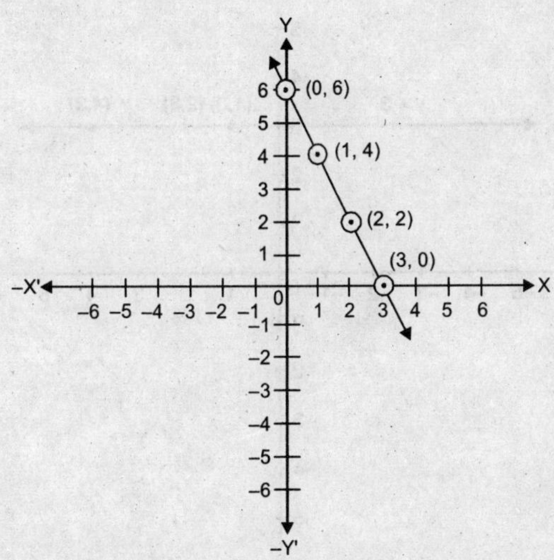

Hence, the line l is called the graph of the equation

$2x + y = 6$

Example 1: Draw the graph:

(*i*) $x = 2$, (*ii*) $y = 3$, (*iii*) $y = 0$

Solution: (*i*) The given equation, $x = 2$ does not contain y

Table of values

x	2	2	2	fixed
y	1	3	4	any value

ploting the points (2, 1), (2, 3) and (2, 4) and joining them

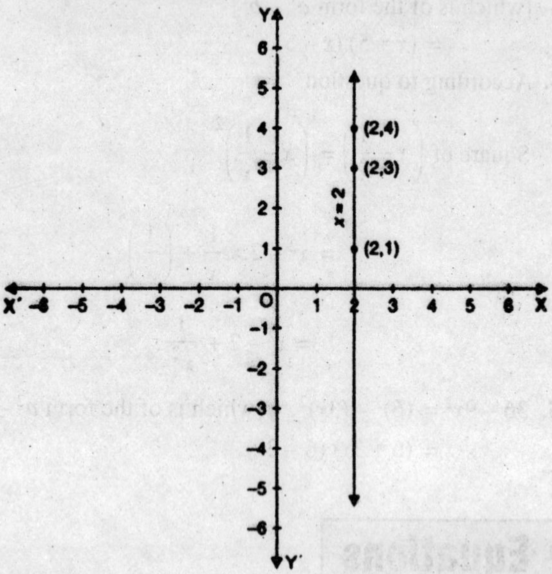

Hence, the graph of the given equation is a line parallel to y-axis

(*ii*) The given equation $y = 3$ does not contain x

Table of values

x	1	2	4	any value
y	3	3	3	fixed

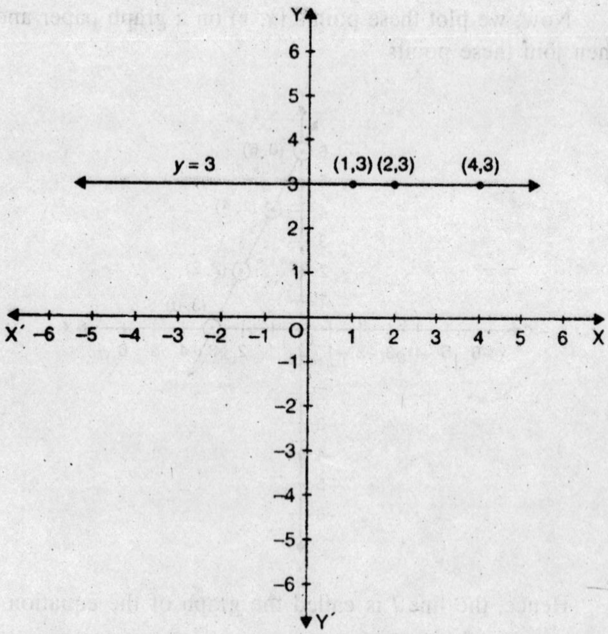

Hence, the graph of the given equation is a line parallel to x-axis.

(*iii*) The given equation is $y = 0$

Table of values

x	1	2	3	any value
y	0	0	0	fixed

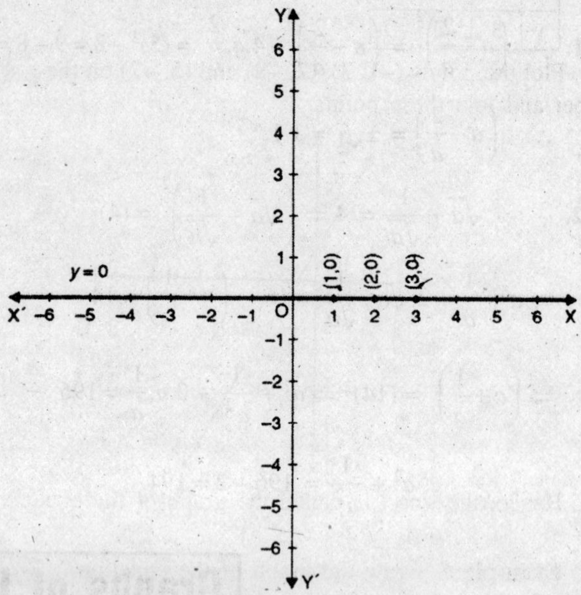

Hence, $y = 0$ is the equation of x-axis.

Example 2. Draw the graph of the line $x - 2y = 3$. From the graph find co-ordinates of the points when (*i*) $x = -5$, (*ii*) $y = 0$

Solution: The given equation is $x - 2y = 3$

Table of value

x	3	5	1
y	0	1	–1

$\because \quad 2y = x - 3$

$\therefore \quad y = \frac{x-3}{2}$

Plotting the points (3, 0), (5, 1) and (1, –1) on the graph paper and joining these points.

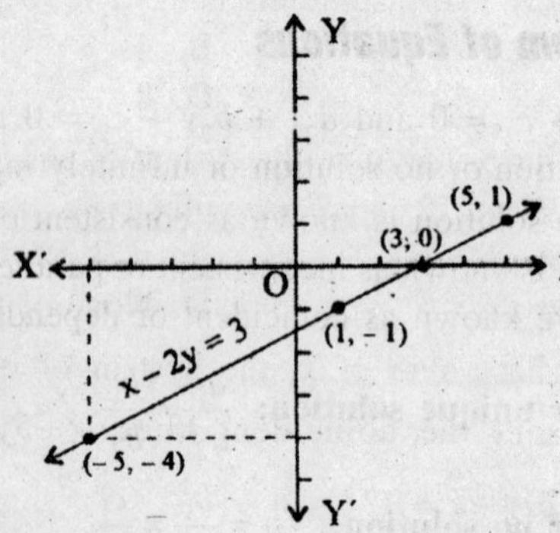

From the graph,

(*i*) when $x = -5$, then $y = -4$

(*ii*) when $y = 0$, then $x = 3$

Example 3. Draw the graph of the equations $5x + 3y = 4$.

Solution: The given equation is $5x + 3y = 4$

$\Rightarrow \quad y = \frac{4-5x}{3}$

Table of values

x	–1	2	5
y	3	–2	–7

Plot the points (–1, 3), (2, –2) and (5, –7) on the graph paper and join these points.

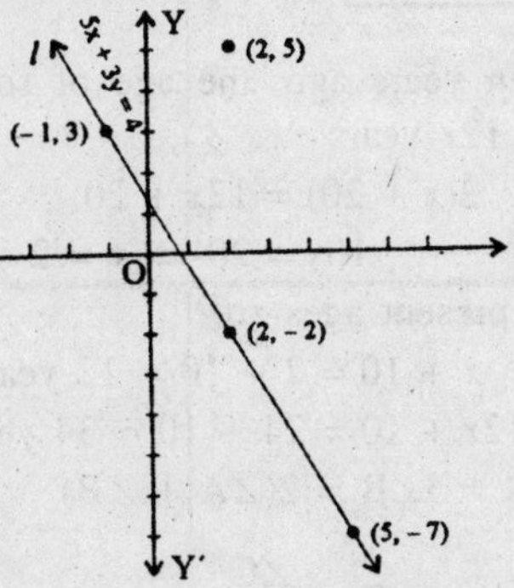

Hence, the line l is called the graph of the equation,

$$5x + 3y = 4$$

Example 4. Draw the graph of the equation

$$2x - 3y = -11.$$

Solution: The given equation is

$$2x - 3y = -11$$

$$\Rightarrow \quad 3y = 2x + 11$$

$$\Rightarrow \quad y = \frac{2x+11}{3}$$

Table of values

x	–1	2	–4
y	3	5	1

plot the points (–1, 3), (2, 5) and (–4, 1) on the graph paper and join these points

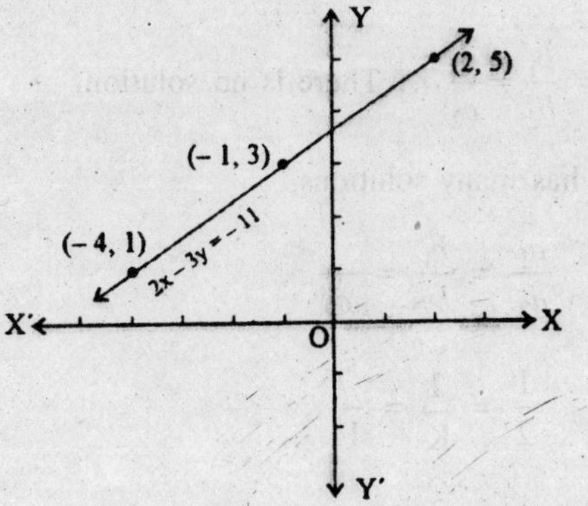

Hence, this line l is called the graph of the equation

$$2x - 3y = -11.$$

EXERCISE

1. The system of linear equations $2x + 3y = 7$ and $4x + 6y = 10$ has:

A. no solution
B. unique solution
C. infinite solution
D. no conclusion can be drawn

2. The value of k for which the system of equations $x + 2y + 7 = 0$ and $2x + ky + 14 = 0$ will have infinitely many solutions is:

A. 2 B. 4
C. 6 D. 8

3. For what value of α, the system of equations $\alpha x + 3y = \alpha - 3$ and $12x + \alpha y = \alpha$ will have a unique solution?

A. $\alpha \neq \pm 6$ B. $\alpha \neq \pm 3$
C. $\alpha \neq \mp 6$ D. None of these

4. For what value of k, the system of equations will represent the coincident lines $x+5y-7=0$ and $4x+20y+k=0$?

A. 28 B. –28
C. –26 D. None of these

5. A lady has 50 paise and ₹ 1 coins in her purse. If in all, she has 40 coins totally ₹ 25.50 how many of each type of coins does she have?

A. 26, 11 B. 11, 29
C. 29, 11 D. None of these

6. A father is three times as old as his son. After twelve years his age will be twice as the age of his son. Find their present ages in years.

A. 12, 26 B. 24, 36
C. 36, 12 D. None of these

7. Ten years ago, father was twelve times as old as his son. Ten years after, he will be twice as old as his son will be. Find their present ages in years.

A. 12, 36 B. 12, 24
C. 12, 34 D. None of these

8. The present age of a father is 3 years more than three times the age of son. Three years hence father's age will be 10 years more than twice the age of son. Determine their present ages in years.

A. 10, 33 B. 33, 10
C. 10, 30 D. None of these

9. In a triangle ABC, $\angle C = 3\angle B = 2(\angle A + \angle B)$. Find three angles in degrees.

A. 20°, 50°, 120° B. 30°, 40°, 120°
C. 20°, 40°, 120° D. None of these

10. The fraction becomes 2 when 1 is added to both the numerator and the denominator, and it becomes 3 when 1 is subtracted from both the numerator and denominator. The given fraction is :

A. 7/3 B. 4/7
C. 3/7 D. 7/4

ANSWERS

1	2	3	4	5	6	7	8	9	10
A	B	A	B	C	C	C	A	C	A

EXPLANATORY ANSWERS

1. $\frac{2}{4} = \frac{3}{6} \neq \frac{7}{10} \Rightarrow \frac{1}{2} = \frac{1}{2} \neq \frac{7}{10}$

$\frac{a_1}{a_2} = \frac{b_1}{b_2} \neq \frac{c_1}{c_2}$ $\therefore$ There is no solution.

2. Since, it has many solutions.

$$\therefore \quad \frac{a_1}{a_2} = \frac{b_1}{b_2} = \frac{c_1}{c_2}$$

$$\frac{1}{2} = \frac{2}{K} = \frac{7}{14}$$

$$\frac{1}{2} = \frac{2}{K} \Rightarrow K = 4.$$

3. Since, the given equations have unique solution.

$$\therefore \quad \frac{a_1}{a_2} \neq \frac{b_1}{b_2}$$

$$\frac{\alpha}{12} \neq \frac{3}{\alpha}$$

$$\Rightarrow \quad \alpha^2 \neq 36 \Rightarrow \alpha \neq \pm 6$$

4. Since, the given set of equations represent coincident lines.

then, $\frac{1}{4} = \frac{5}{20} = \frac{-7}{K} \Rightarrow K = -28$

5. Let, x be the number of 50 paise coins and y be the number of ₹ 1 coins.

According to the question,

$$x + y = 40 \quad \text{...}(i)$$

and $\frac{x}{2} + y = 25.50$

$$\Rightarrow \quad x + 2y = 51 \quad \text{...}(ii)$$

Subtracting equation (*i*) from (*ii*) and solving we get, $x = 29$, $y = 11$

6. Let, age of son = x years.

$\therefore$ age of father = $3x$ years.

According to the question,

$$2(x + 12) = 3x + 12 \Rightarrow x = 12$$

$\therefore$ Son's age = 12 years; Father's age = 36 years.

7. Let ten years ago, the age of son and father were x and $12x$ years.

Then, $2(x + 20) = 12x + 20$

$$\Rightarrow \quad 10x = 20 \Rightarrow x = 2$$

Their present ages are

$$x + 10 = 2 + 10 = 12 \text{ years}$$

$$12x + 10 = 24 + 10 = 34 \text{ years.}$$

9. $\therefore$ $\angle C = 3\angle B = 2(\angle A + \angle B)$

$$\angle A + \angle B = \frac{\angle C}{2}$$

We have, $\angle A + \angle B + \angle C = 180°$

(Sum of angles of a triangle is 180°)

$$\frac{\angle C}{2} + \angle C = 180°$$

$$3\angle C = 2 \times 180°$$

$$\angle C = \frac{2 \times 180°}{3} = 120°$$

$$3\angle B = \angle C$$

$$\angle B = \frac{\angle C}{3} = \frac{120°}{3} = 40°$$

$$\therefore \quad \angle A = 180° - (120° + 40°) = 180° - 160° = 20°.$$

10. Let the fraction be $\frac{x}{y} \Rightarrow \frac{x+1}{y+1} = 2$

$$\Rightarrow \quad x + 1 = 2y + 2$$

$$\Rightarrow \quad x - 2y = 1 \quad \text{...}(i)$$

Again $\frac{x-1}{y-1} = 3$

$$\Rightarrow \quad x - 1 = 3y - 3$$

$$\Rightarrow \quad x - 3y = -2 \quad \text{...}(ii)$$

from (*i*) and (*ii*)

$$\begin{array}{r} x - 2y = 1 \\ x - 3y = -2 \\ - \quad + \quad\; + \\ \hline y = 3 \end{array}$$

Putting the value of y in (*i*) then we get, $x = 7$

$$\therefore \quad \text{fraction} = \frac{x}{y} = \frac{7}{3}$$

●●●

CHAPTER 5

Average

The average of any number of quantities of the same kind can be found by dividing their sum by their number.

Thus,

$$\text{Average} = \frac{\text{Sum of quantities}}{\text{No. of quantities}}$$

Sum of quantities = Their average × Their number

$$\text{Number of quantities} = \frac{\text{Sum of quantities}}{\text{Their average}}$$

When a body coveres the same distance at two different speeds p km/hr and q km/hr, then its average speed for the whole journey is $\frac{2pq}{p+q}$ km/hr.

EXERCISE

1. The average of the fractions $1\frac{1}{2}$, $2\frac{1}{3}$, $3\frac{1}{3}$ and $4\frac{5}{6}$ is:

A. 2 B. $2\frac{1}{2}$
C. 3 D. 4

2. The average of first nine multiples of 3 is

A. 12.0 B. 12.5
C. 15.0 D. 18.5

3. The average of 13 numbers is 68, the average of first 7 numbers is 63 and the average of last 7 numbers is 70. What is the 7th number?

A. 43 B. 45
C. 47 D. 49

4. One-third of a certain journey was covered at the rate of 25 km per hour, one-fourth at the rate of 30 km per hour and the rest at the 50 km per hour. What is the average speed per hour for whole journey?

A. $33\frac{1}{3}$ kmph B. $44\frac{1}{4}$ kmph
C. $22\frac{1}{2}$ kmph D. 33 kmph

5. Nine men went to a hotel. Eight of them spent ₹ 3 for each over their meals and the ninth spent ₹ 2 more than the average expenditure of all the nine. What is the total money spent by them?

A. ₹ 29.25 B. ₹ 29.50
C. ₹ 29 D. ₹ 30

6. An establishment is permitted an average monthly contingency expenditure of ₹ 500 per month during the financial year. When a trial check was made at the end of the first nine months of the year it was found that the average monthly contingency expenditure worked out to be ₹ 511. What average monthly expenditure for the next three months should be aimed at in order to attain the permissible average of ₹ 500 per month for the whole year?

A. ₹ 567 B. ₹ 467
C. 367 D. ₹ 667

7. Average age of 8 persons increased by 2 years, when two men whose ages are 20 and 24 years are replaced by two women. What is the average age of women?

A. 30 years B. 31 years
C. 28 years D. 33 years

8. A man had seven children. When their average age was 12 years, the child who was 6 years of age died. What was the average of the surviving children 5 years after the death of the child?

A. 15 years B. 16 years
C. 17 years D. 18 years

9. The weight of a body, calculated as the average of seven different experiments is 53.735 grams. The average of the first three is 54.005 grams, the fourth was greater than the fifth by 0.004 gram, while the average of the sixth and seventh was 0.010 gram less than the average of the first three. What is the weight of the body as obtained by the fourth experiment?

A. 53.068 gm B. 53.078 gm
C. 53.086 gm D. 53.072 gm

10. A batsman has a certain average of runs for 16 innings. In the 17th innings, he makes a score of 85 runs thereby increasing his average by 3. What is the average after the 17th inning?

A. 33 runs B. 34 runs
C. 37 runs D. 36 runs

11. The average of 50 numbers is 38. If two numbers namely 45 and 55 are discarded, the average of the remaining numbers is

A. 36.5 B. 37
C. 37.5 D. 37.52

12. The average of 6 observations is 12. A new seventh observation is included and the new average is decreased by 1. The seventh observation is

A. 1 B. 3
C. 5 D. 6

13. A man whose bowling average is 12.4 takes 5 wickets for 26 runs and thereby decreases his average by 0.4. The number of wickets, taken by him, before his last match, is

A. 85 B. 78
C. 72 D. 64

14. The average of marks obtained by 120 candidates was 35. If the average of marks of passed candidates was 39 and that of failed candidates was 15, the number of candidates who passed the examination is

A. 100 B. 110
C. 120 D. 150

15. The average of three numbers is 42. The first is twice the second and the second is twice the third. The difference between the largest and the smallest number is

A. 18 B. 36
C. 54 D. 72

ANSWERS

1	2	3	4	5	6	7	8	9	10
C	C	C	A	A	B	A	D	D	C
11	**12**	**13**	**14**	**15**					
C	C	A	A	C					

EXPLANATORY ANSWERS

1. Average $= \frac{1}{4}\left(\frac{3}{2}+\frac{7}{3}+\frac{10}{3}+\frac{29}{6}\right)$

$= \left(\frac{9+14+20+29}{24}\right) = \frac{72}{24} = 3$

2. Average $= \frac{3(1+2+3+4+5+6+7+8+9)}{9} = \frac{135}{9}$

$= 15$

3. Average of 13 numbers = 68

$\therefore$ Total of 13 numbers = 13 × 68 = 884

Average of last 7 numbers = 70

$\therefore$ Total of last 7 numbers = 7 × 70 = 490

$\therefore$ Average of first 6 numbers

= 884 – 490 = 394

$\therefore$ Average of first 7 numbers = 63

$\therefore$ Total of first 7 numbers = 63 × 7 = 441

$\therefore$ 7th number = 441 – 394 = 47

4. Let the total distance covered during journey = 60 km

$\frac{1}{3}$ of the distance covered during journey

$= 60 \times \frac{1}{3} = 20$ km

$\frac{1}{4}$ of the distance covered during journey

$= \frac{1}{4} \times 60 = 15$ km

$\therefore$ The distance covered during the rest of journey = 60 – (20 + 15) = 25 km

Time taken to cover 20 km at 25 km/h

$= \frac{20}{25}$ hours $= \frac{4}{5}$ hour

Time taken to cover 15 km at 30 km/h

$= \frac{15}{30}$ hours $= \frac{1}{2}$ hour

Time taken to cover 25 km at 50 km/h

$= \frac{25}{50}$ hours $= \frac{1}{2}$ hour

Total time taken $= \frac{4}{5}+\frac{1}{2}+\frac{1}{2} = \frac{9}{5}$ hours

Hence average speed per hour

$= 60 \div \frac{9}{5} = \frac{60 \times 5}{9}$

$= \frac{100}{3}$ km/h $= 33\frac{1}{3}$ km/h

5. Let the average expenditure of all the nine $= ₹\ x$

Now amount spent by eight $= ₹\ 3 \times 8 = ₹\ 24$

and total spent by the ninth $= ₹\ x + 2$

$$\Rightarrow \quad \frac{26 + x}{9} = x$$

$\therefore$ Average amount spent by nine $= \frac{26 + x}{9}$

Total amount spent by nine $= 24 + x + 2 = 26 + x$

$\Rightarrow \quad 9x = 26 + x$

or, $\quad 8x = 26$

$$\Rightarrow \quad x = \frac{26}{8} = ₹\ 3.25$$

Hence total money spent

$= ₹\ (3.25 \times 9) = ₹\ 29.25$

6. Average monthly expenditure permitted $= ₹\ 500$

Total expenditure permitted for 12 months

$= ₹\ 500 \times 12 = ₹\ 6000$

Expenditure incurred during the first nine months

$= ₹\ 511 \times 9 = ₹\ 4,599$

Expenditure for the last three month

$= ₹\ (6000 - 4599) = ₹\ 1,401$

$\therefore$ Average monthly expenditure for the three months

$$= ₹\ \frac{1401}{3} = ₹\ 467$$

7. Total increase in the age of 8 persons

$= 2 \times 8 = 16$ years

Total age of two men being replaced

$= 20 + 24 = 44$ years

Total of the age of two women $= 44 + 16 = 60$ years

$\Rightarrow$ The average age of women

$$= \frac{60}{2} = 30 \text{ years.}$$

8. Average age of 7 children $= 12$ years

Total ages of 7 children $= 12 \times 7 = 84$ years

Age of 1 child who died $= 6$ years

Total ages of remaining 6 children

$= 84 - 6 = 78$ years

$\therefore$ Average age of 6 children $= \frac{78}{6} = 13$ years

$\therefore$ Average age of 6 children after 5 years

$= 13 + 5 = 18$ years

9. Total weight of 7 experiments

$= 53.735 \times 7 = 376.145$ gm

Total weight of first three

$= 54.005 \times 3 = 162.015$ gm

The average of the 6th and 7th was 0.010 gm less than that of the first three.

$\therefore$ Average of the 6th and 7th

$= 54.005 - 0.010 = 53.995$ gm

$\therefore$ Total of the 6th and 7th $= 53.995 \times 2 = 107.990$ gm

Thus, total of 4th and 5th

$= 376.145 - (162.015 + 107.990) = 106.140$ gm

The fourth was greater than the fifth by 0.004 gm

$$\therefore \quad \text{The fifth} = (106.140 - 0.004) \times \frac{1}{2} = \frac{106.136}{2}$$

$= 53.068$ gm

Hence, the fourth $= 53.068 + 0.004$

$= 53.072$ gm

10. Average increase in the score of 17 innings

$= 3$ runs

Total increase in the score of 17 innings

$= 3 \times 17 = 51$ runs

$\therefore$ His average of 16 innings

$= 85 - 51 = 34$ runs

Hence, average after the 17th innings

$= 34 + 3 = 37$ runs

11. Total of 50 numbers $= 50 \times 38 = 1900$

Total of 48 numbers

$= 1900 - (45 + 55) = 1800$

$$\therefore \quad \text{Average} = \frac{1800}{48} = 37.5$$

12. Seventh observation

$= (7 \times 11 - 6 \times 12) = 5$

13. Suppose the number of wickets taken before the last match $= x$

$$\Rightarrow \quad \frac{12.4x + 26}{x + 5} = 12$$

$\Rightarrow \quad 12.4x + 26 = 12x + 60$

$\Rightarrow \quad x = 85$

14. Let the number of candidates who passed $= x$

$\Rightarrow \quad 39 \times x + 15 \times (120 - x) = 120 \times 35$

$\Rightarrow \quad 24x = 4200 - 1800$

$$\therefore \quad x = \frac{2400}{24} = 100$$

15. Let the third number $= x$

Then, second number $= 2x$ and first number $= 4x$

$$\therefore \quad \frac{x + 2x + 4x}{3} = 42$$

$$\Rightarrow \quad \frac{7x}{3} = 42 \Rightarrow x = \frac{42 \times 3}{7}$$

$\Rightarrow \quad x = 18$

So, (largest) − (smallest) $= (4x - x) = 3x = 54$

●●●

CHAPTER 6

Partnership Business

When two or more than two persons agree to invest money to run a business jointly, this association or deal is called *partnership* and those who invest money are called *pertners.* The total investment is called the *capital.*

Kind of partners : There are two kinds of partners.

1. **Working or active partner :** When a partner devotes his time for the business in addition to invest his money, he is called a working partner.

   With mutual agreement, the active partners get some fixed percentage of profit as *working allowance.*

2. **Sleeping or non-active partner :** A partner who simply invests money, but does not attend to the business is called a sleeping partner.

Kind of partnership :

(i) **Simple partnership :** If the capitals of several partners are invested for the same period, it is called a simple partnership.

(ii) **Compound or complex partnership :** If the capitals of the partners are invested for diffrent intervals of time, the partnership is called compound or complex.

EXERCISE

1. A and B started a business with the investment of ₹ 80000 and ₹ 60000 respectively. At the end of the year total profit in the business will be divided between them in the ratio of :

A. 2 : 3 B. 3 : 4
C. 2 : 1 D. 4 : 3

2. A and B started a business in partnership with the investment of ₹ 4000 and ₹ 6000 respectively. If at the end of the year total profit is ₹ 2250, what will each of them get?

A. ₹ 900, ₹ 1350
B. ₹ 800, ₹ 1450
C. ₹ 1000, ₹ 1250
D. ₹ 1200, ₹ 1050

3. Sonu, Monu and Mohit together start a business with the investment of ₹ 1800, ₹ 1500 and ₹ 1600 respectively. If at the end of the year, Monu gains a profit of ₹ 900 the total profit in the business is :

A. ₹ 2880 B. ₹ 2940
C. ₹ 3200 D. ₹ 3240

4. Omdutt started a business with a capital of ₹ 8000. After six months, Sanjay joined him with investment of some capital. If at the end of the year each of them gets equal amount as profit, how much did Sanjay invest in the business?

A. ₹ 18000 B. ₹ 17500
C. ₹ 16000 D. ₹ 16500

5. A, B and C buy a farm for ₹ 100000. A contributes ₹ 40000 in it. They sell it, and from the profit B gets ₹ 2750 and C gets ₹ 1750. What would be the profit of A?

A. ₹ 2780 B. ₹ 3000
C. ₹ 3280 D. ₹ 2785

6. A and B jointly invest ₹ 2100 and ₹ 3100 respectively in a firm. A is an active partner and hence he gets 25% of the profit separately. If their business yields them total ₹ 1040 as profit, what will be the gain of each of them?

A. ₹ 415, ₹ 625 B. ₹ 575, ₹ 465
C. ₹ 515, ₹ 525 D. ₹ 560, ₹ 480

7. Two partners invested ₹ 12500 and ₹ 8500 respectively in a business and decided that 60% of the profit incurred from the business will be equally divided between them while remaining profit will be assumed as interest on their capitals. If one of the partners gets ₹ 300 more profit than the other, what is the total profit in the business?

A. ₹ 3937.50 B. ₹ 4940.50
C. ₹ 3936.50 D. ₹ 4156

8. Neeraj and Birju are partners in a business. They divide between them the profit incurred in the business in such a proportion that $\frac{2}{5}$th portion of the profit gained by Neeraj is equal to $\frac{1}{3}$rd portion of the profit gained by Birju. If total profit in the business is ₹ 1210, find the profit earned by Birju.

A. ₹ 780 B. ₹ 660
C. ₹ 680 D. ₹ 590

9. A, B and C together took under lease a pasture ground for ₹ 888. If in this pasture ground A put his 20 sheep out to graze for 2½ months, B put his 30 sheep out to graze for 4 months and C put his 36 sheep out to graze for 3½ months, find the lease amount paid by each of them.

A. ₹ 205, ₹ 315, ₹ 378 B. ₹ 150, ₹ 360, ₹ 378
C. ₹ 170, ₹ 360, ₹ 358 D. ₹ 228, ₹ 360, ₹ 300

10. A, B and C started a business with the investment of ₹ 5000, ₹ 6000 and ₹ 4000 respectively. A is an active partner and therefore he gets 30% of the profit separately. Rest of the profit is divided in the ratio of their capitals. If at the end of year, A's profit is ₹ 200 more than the sum of the profits made by B and C, find the profit made by each of them.

A. ₹ 1620, ₹ 1242, ₹ 1178
B. ₹ 1720, ₹ 1252, ₹ 1228
C. ₹ 1510, ₹ 1187, ₹ 1133
D. ₹ 1600, ₹ 840, ₹ 560

11. Premchand, Nanak and Prabhat together rented a house for 2 years and settled to pay ₹ 1368 as rent. They lived together in this house for 5 months. Then Prabhat left the house and went away. 8 months after Nanak also went away and left the house for Premchand to live alone. How much did Premchand pay as rent of this house?

A. ₹ 1025 B. ₹ 950
C. ₹ 880 D. ₹ 780

12. A started a business with an investment of ₹ 4000. B joined him after 4 months and C joined him after 5 months. At the end of year they get profit in the ratio of 3 : 4 : 7. Find the ratio of capitals invested in the business by B and C.

A. 1 : 2 B. 2 : 1
C. 3 : 2 D. 1 : 3

13. Amit, Sumeet and Suresh started a business with capitals in the ratio of 2 : 3 : 4. Amit took back half of his investment after 3 months and Sumeet took back one-third portion of his investment after 4 months. If at the end of year, Suresh gets a profit of ₹ 3200, what is the total profit in the business?

A. ₹ $6076\frac{2}{3}$ B. ₹ $6066\frac{2}{3}$
C. ₹ 8000 D. ₹ $8333\frac{1}{3}$

14. A, B and C started a business in partnership. A invested ₹ 4000 for 8 months and ₹ 6000 for 4 months. B invested ₹ 3000 for 6 months and ₹ 5000 for next 6 months of the year while C invested ₹ 3000 for whole of the year. If at the end of year, total profit is ₹ 7000, what will be the shares of A, B and C in the profit?

A. ₹ 2800, ₹ 2400, ₹ 1800
B. ₹ 2500, ₹ 2600, ₹ 1900
C. ₹ 2600, ₹ 2500, ₹ 1900
D. ₹ 2000, ₹ 2700, ₹ 2300

15. A, B and C started a business in partnership with respective investment of ₹ 20000, ₹ 18000 and ₹ 12000. A and B are active partners and therefore they get an additional profit of 12% and 8% respectively for supervision and other related work they do for improvement of the trade. Rest of the profit is divided among them in the proportion of their capitals. If profit made by A is ₹ 648 more than B, find the profit earned by each of them.

A. ₹ 3960, ₹ 3312, ₹ 1728
B. ₹ 4960, ₹ 3312, ₹ 1728
C. ₹ 3690, ₹ 3132, ₹ 1820
D. ₹ 5960, ₹ 3600, ₹ 1750

16. Three labourers work for 5 hours, 6 hours and 7 hours respectively in a field and get wages in the proportion of time of working in the field. Three days after they increase their working hours by 1 hour. 4 days after they increase their working hours, work in the field gets finished. If their total wages is ₹ 276, find the share of wages earned by each of them.

A. ₹ 78, ₹ 92, ₹ 106 B. ₹ 88, ₹ 87, ₹ 101
C. ₹ 80, ₹ 90, ₹ 106 D. ₹ 81, ₹ 95, ₹ 100

17. A, B and C together took a pasture ground on rent at ₹ 16 per month with a view to graze their sheep in this ground. A, B and C owned 70, 50 and 40 sheep respectively. After 4 months A sold $\frac{2}{7}$th portion of his sheep to B and 3 month after that C sold $\frac{2}{5}$th portion of his sheep to A. How much will each of them pay as rent after the end of a year?

A. ₹ 70, ₹ 70, ₹ 52 B. ₹ 76, ₹ 76, ₹ 40
C. ₹ 80, ₹ 76, ₹ 36 D. ₹ 40, ₹ 76.30, ₹ 76

18. Samir and Saurabh started a joint firm. Samir's investment was thrice the investment of Saurabh and the period of his investment was two times the period of investment of Saurabh. If Saurabh got ₹ 4000 as profit, then their total profit is:

A. ₹ 16000 B. ₹ 20000
C. ₹ 24000 D. ₹ 28000

19. A, B and C together start a business. The amounts invested by A and B are in the ratio of 4 : 3 whereas the ratio of investments of B and C is 2 : 3. If the total profit earned is ₹ 46000, what is C's share in the profit?

A. ₹ 14000 B. ₹ 15000
C. ₹ 16000 D. ₹ 18000

20. Rani and Nisha started a business initially with ₹ 5100 and ₹ 6600 respectively. If the total profit is ₹ 2730, what is the Rani's share in the profit?

A. ₹ 1190 B. ₹ 1200
C. ₹ 1530 D. ₹ 1540

ANSWERS

1	2	3	4	5	6	7	8	9	10
D	A	B	C	B	B	A	B	B	D
11	**12**	**13**	**14**	**15**	**16**	**17**	**18**	**19**	**20**
B	A	B	A	A	A	B	D	D	A

EXPLANATORY ANSWERS

1. Ratio between their profits = 80000 : 60000 = 4 : 3.

2. Ratio of capitals of A and B = 4000 : 6000 = 2 : 3

A's share in the profit = $\frac{2}{5} \times 2250$ = ₹ 900

B's share in the profit = $\frac{3}{5} \times 2250$ = ₹ 1350

3. Ratio of their capitals
= 1800 : 1500 : 1600 = 18 : 15 : 16
Sum of proportionals = 18 +15 + 16 = 49
Monu's profit = ₹ 900

∴ Total profit in the business = $\frac{900}{15} \times 49$ = ₹ 2940

4. Investment by Omdutt for 1 month
= ₹ 8000 × 12 = ₹ 96000
Let Sanjay invested ₹ x for 6 months
∴ Capital of Sanjay for 1 month = ₹ $x \times 6$ = ₹ $6x$
Now, $6x = 96000$
∴ x = ₹ 16000

5. Here, ratio of capitals of A and (B + C)
= 40000 : 60000 = 2 : 3
Profit of (B + C) = 2750 + 1750 = ₹ 4500

Hence, A's profit = $\frac{4500}{3} \times 2$ = ₹ 3000

6. Separate profit for A = $\frac{1040 \times 25}{100}$ = ₹ 260
Remaining profit = ₹ (1040 – 260) = ₹ 780
Ratio of capitals of A and B = 2100 : 3100 = 21 : 31

A's profit = $\frac{21}{52} \times 780$ = ₹ 315

B's profit = $\frac{31}{52} \times 780$ = ₹ 465

Total profit of A = ₹ (315 + 260) = ₹ 575
Therefore A and B will make profit of ₹ 575 and ₹ 465 respectively.

7. Ratio of their capitals = 12500 : 8500 = 25 : 17
Hence, sum of their ratios = 25 + 17 = 42 and difference of ratios = 25 – 17 = 8
Now total profit taken as interest

= $\frac{300}{8} \times 42$ = ₹ 1575

Hence, total profit in the business

= $\frac{100}{40} \times 1575$ = ₹ 3937.50

8. Let shares of Neeraj and Birju in profit are ₹ x and ₹ y respectively; then,

$\frac{2}{5}x = \frac{1}{3}y$ ∴ $x : y = 5 : 6$

Hence, share of Birju = $\frac{6}{11} \times 1210$ = ₹ 660

9. Ratio of their shares = (20 × 5/2) : (30 × 4) : (36 × 7/2) = 25 : 60 : 63
Sum of proportionals = 25 + 60 + 63 = 148
Total lease amount = ₹ 888

∴ Amount paid by A = $\frac{25}{148} \times 888$ = ₹ 150

Amount paid by B = $\frac{60}{148} \times 888$ = ₹ 360

Amount paid by C = $\frac{63}{148} \times 888$ = ₹ 378

10. Ratio of capitals of A, B and C = 5000 : 6000 : 4000 = 5 : 6 : 4
Let total profit in the business = ₹ x; then

$$\frac{30x}{100} + \frac{5}{15} \times \frac{70x}{100} - \frac{(6+4)}{15} \times \frac{70x}{100} = 200$$

$$\Rightarrow \frac{8x}{15} - \frac{7x}{15} = 200 \quad \therefore x = ₹\ 3000$$

Hence, A's profit = $\frac{8 \times 3000}{15}$ = ₹ 1600;

B's profit = $\frac{6}{15}\times\frac{7\times3000}{10}$ = ₹ 840;

C's profit = $\frac{4}{15}\times\frac{7\times3000}{10}$ = ₹ 560

11. Rent for 1 month = $\frac{1368}{24}$ = ₹ 57

Total rent paid by Premchand

$= 5\times\frac{57}{3} + 8\times\frac{57}{2} + 11\times57$

= 95 + 228 + 627 = ₹ 950.

12. Let, B and C invest ₹ x and ₹ y respectively

∴ Ratio of their capitals = 48000 : $8x$: $7y$

But given ratio of the profits = 3 : 4 : 7

$8x : 7y = 4 : 7 \Rightarrow \frac{x}{y}=\frac{1}{2}$

Hence, $x : y = 1 : 2$

13. Ratio of capitals of Amit, Sumeet and Suresh

= (2 × 3 + 1 × 9) : (3 × 4 + 2 × 8) : (4 × 12)

= 15 : 28 : 48

Sum of the ratios = 15 + 28 + 48 = 91

∴ Total profit in the business

$= \frac{91}{48}\times3200$ = ₹ $6066\frac{2}{3}$

14. Ratio of their capitals

= (4000 × 8 + 6000 × 4) : (3000 × 6 + 5000 × 6) : (3000 × 12)

= 56000 : 48000 : 36000 = 14 : 12 : 9

Sum of proportionals = 14 + 12 + 9 = 35

Share of A in the profit = $\frac{14}{35}\times7000$ = ₹ 2800

Share of B in the profit = $\frac{12}{35}\times7000$ = ₹ 2400

Share of C in the profit = $\frac{9}{35}\times7000$ = ₹ 1800

15. Ratio of their capitals

= 20000 : 18000 : 12000 = 10 : 9 : 6

Let total profit in the business = ₹ x; then

$$\left(\frac{12x}{100}+\frac{10}{25}\times\frac{80x}{100}\right)-\left(\frac{8x}{100}+\frac{9}{25}\times\frac{80x}{100}\right) = 648$$

$$\Rightarrow \frac{11x}{25}-\frac{46x}{125}=648 \Rightarrow \frac{9x}{125}=648$$

$$\therefore \quad x = \frac{648\times125}{9} = ₹\ 9000$$

Hence, share of A = $\frac{11x}{25} = \frac{11\times9000}{25}$

= ₹ 3960;

Share of B = $\frac{46x}{125}=\frac{46\times9000}{125}$ = ₹ 3312

Share of C = $\frac{6}{25}\times\frac{80x}{100}=\frac{6}{25}\times\frac{4}{5}\times9000$ = ₹ 1728

16. Ratio of their working hours

= (5 × 3 + 6 × 4) : (6 × 3 + 7 × 4) : (7 × 3 + 8 × 4)

= 39 : 46 : 53

Sum of proportionals = 39 + 46 + 53 = 138

∴ Wages for the 1st labourer = $\frac{39}{138}\times276$ = ₹ 78

Wages for the 2nd labourer = $\frac{46}{138}\times276$ = ₹ 92

Wages for the 3rd labourer = $\frac{53}{138}\times276$ = ₹ 106

17. Number of sheep of A for 1 month

$= [70\times4 + (70-\frac{2}{7}\times70)\times3 + (70-\frac{2}{7}\times70+\frac{2}{5}\times40)\times5]$

= 280 + 150 + 330 = 760

Number of sheep of B for 1 month

$= [50\times4 + (50+\frac{2}{7}\times70)\times8] = 200 + 560 = 760$

Number of sheep of C for 1 month

$= [40\times7 + (40-\frac{2}{5}\times40)\times5] = 280 + 120 = 400$

Hence, ratio of their sheep

= 760 : 760 : 400 = 19 : 19 : 10

Sum of proportionals = 19 + 19 + 10 = 48

1 year's rent of the pasture ground = 16 × 12 = ₹ 192

∴ Rent to be paid by A = $\frac{19}{48}\times192$ = ₹ 76

Rent to be paid by B = $\frac{19}{48}\times192$ = ₹ 76

Rent to be paid by C = $\frac{10}{48}\times192$ = ₹ 40

18. Ratio of Capitals of Samir and Saurabh

= (3 × 2) : (1 × 1) = 6 : 1

Saurabh's profit = ₹ 4000

Hence, total profit in the business

= 7 × ₹ 4000 = ₹ 28000

19. A : B = 4 : 3 and B : C = 2 : 3,

Therefore, A : B : C = 8 : 6 : 9

Hence, C's profit = $\frac{9}{23}\times46000$ = ₹ 18000

20. Ratio of their Capitals = 5100 : 6600 = 17 : 22

Hence, Rani's profit = $\frac{17}{39}\times2730$ = ₹ 1190

●●●

CHAPTER 7

Mixture and Alligation

Alligation deals with calculation of values or properties of a mixture. Alligation is the rule that enables us—

(1) to find the proportion in which the two or more ingredients at the given prices must be mixed to yield a mixture at the given price. This is termed as "Alligation Alternate".

(2) to calculate the average or mean value of a mixture when the prices of two or more ingredients which are to be mixed together and proportion in which they are to be mixed are given. This is termed as "Alligation Medial".

1. Rule of Alligation:

$$\frac{\text{Amount of Cheaper ingredient}}{\text{Amount of Dearer ingredient}} = \frac{\text{Cost price of Dearer} - \text{Mean Price}}{\text{Mean Price} - \text{Cost Price of Cheaper}}$$

Here cost price of unit quantity of the mixture is called the *Mean Price.*

The above rule may be represented schematically as under:

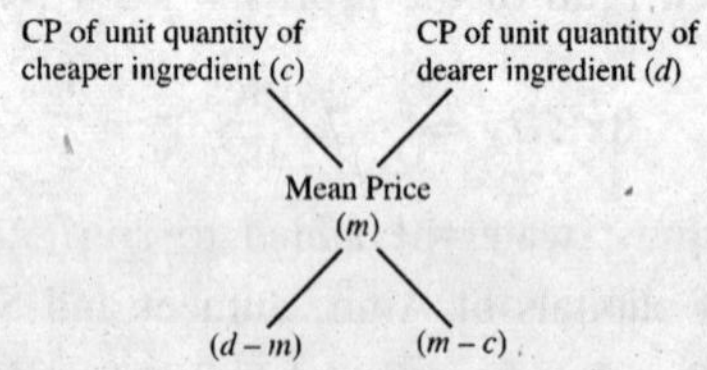

(Cheaper quantity) : (Dearer quantity) $= (d - m) : (m - c)$

This relationship is very helpful in solving problems on mixture involving percentage values, rates, prices, speeds etc.

2. m gm of sugar solution has x % sugar in it. To increase the sugar content in the solution to y %, quantity of sugar need to be added $= \frac{m(y-x)}{100-y}$

3. A vessel contains x litres of liquid A. y litres are withdrawn and replaced by liquid B. Next y litres of the mixture is withdrawn and again replaced by liquid B. This operation is repeated n times.

$$\frac{\text{Quantity of liquid A left after } n\text{th operation}}{\text{Whole quantity of liquid A initially present}} = \left(\frac{x-y}{x}\right)^n \text{ or } \left(1-\frac{y}{x}\right)^n$$

EXERCISE

1. In what proportion must tea at ₹ 62 per kg be mixed with tea at ₹ 72 per kg in order to obtain the mixture worth ₹ 65 per kg?

A. 4 : 6 B. 7 : 3
C. 2 : 3 D. 4 : 7

2. Find the quantity of rice @ ₹ 10 per kg. which should be mixed with 25 kgs of rice @ ₹ 8 per kg, so that on selling the mixture @ 15 per kg there is 80% profit.

A. 6 kgs B. 7 kgs
C. 3 kgs D. 5 kgs

3. A shopkeeper buys 26 kgs of milk @ ₹ 16 per kg. He also buys from another source an inferior quality of milk @ ₹ 10 per kg. How much quantity of the latter should he buy to mix it with the former so that he can sell the mixture @ ₹ 14 per kg without making any loss?

A. 13 kgs B. 12 kgs
C. 14 kgs D. 16 kgs

4. Two vessels A and B contain milk and water in the ratio 7 : 5 and 17 : 7 respectively. In what ratio mixtures from two vessels should be mixed to get a new mixture containing milk and water in the ratio 5 : 3?

A. 1 : 2 B. 2 : 1
C. 2 : 3 D. 3 : 2

5. Two vessels A and B contain mixture of milk and water in the ratio 4 : 1 and 9 : 11 respectively. They are mixed in the ratio of 3 : 2. Find the ratio of milk : water in the resulting mixture.
A. 34 : 16 B. 33 : 17
C. 16 : 34 D. 17 : 33

6. A person has two solutions of sugar with 30% and 50% concentration respectively. In what proportion should he mix two solutions to get 45% concentration in the resulting mixture?
A. 1 : 3 B. 3 : 1
C. 2 : 3 D. 3 : 2

7. 6 litres of milk and water mixture has 75% milk in it. How much milk should be added to the mixture to make it 90% pure?
A. 8 litres B. 9 litres
C. 10 litres D. 12 litres

8. In what ratio must water be added to spirit to gain 25% by selling it at cost price?
A. 1 : 4 B. 4 : 1
C. 3 : 4 D. 4 : 3

9. A shopkeeper has 50 kgs of rice. He sells a part of it at 20% profit and the rest at 40% profit. If he gains 25% on the whole, find the quantity of each part.
A. 12.5 kgs and 37.5 kgs B. 37.5 kgs and 12.5 kgs
C. 23.5 kgs and 21.5 kgs D. 21.5 kgs and 23.5 kgs

10. A shopkeeper has 100 kgs of tea. He sells a part of it at 20% profit and the rest at 5% loss. If his overall profit is 10%, find the quantity for each part.
A. 20 kgs B. 25 kgs
C. 30 kgs D. 40 kgs

11. A merchant has 160 kgs of wheat. He sells a part of it at 10% profit and the rest of 6% loss. If he incurs 4% loss on the whole, find the quantity for each part.
A. 120 kgs B. 140 kgs
C. 150 kgs D. 160 kgs

12. A man bought a certain quantity of sugar for ₹ 8000. He sells one-fourth of it at 20% loss. At what per cent profit should he sell the remainder stock so as to make an overall profit of 20%?
A. 20% B. 30%
C. 35% D. 40%

13. A person has ₹ 5000. He invests a part of it at 3% per annum and the remainder at 8% per annum simple interest. His total income in 3 years is ₹ 750. Find the sum invested at different rates of interest.
A. ₹ 2000 and ₹ 3000 B. ₹ 2500 and ₹ 2500
C. ₹ 3000 and ₹ 2000 D. ₹ 2750 and ₹ 2250

14. A person covers a dista2nce of 100 kms in 10 hours, partly by walking at 7 km/hr and rest by running at 12 km/hr. Find the distance covered in each part.
A. 48 kms B. 72 kms
C. 108 kms D. 124 kms

15. The average monthly salary of employees, consisting of officers and workers, of an organisation is ₹ 3000. The average salary of an officer is ₹ 10,000 while that of a worker is ₹ 2000 per month. If there are total 400 employees in the organisation, find the number of officers and workers separately.
A. 300, 100 B. 50, 350
C. 250, 150 D. 310, 90

16. The average daily wages of staff, consisting of supervisors and labourers, of a company is ₹ 50. The average wages of supervisors is ₹ 150 while that of labourers is ₹ 40 per day. If the number of supervisors is 15, find the number of labourers in the company.
A. 150 B. 175
C. 180 D. 200

17. ₹ 675 was divided among 75 boys and girls. Each boy gets ₹ 20 whereas a girl gets ₹ 5. Find the number of boys and girls.
A. 20, 55 B. 15, 60
C. 25, 50 D. 30, 45

18. A sum of ₹ 70 is divided among 10 children. Each boy gets ₹ 10 whereas a girl gets ₹ 5. If the number of boys is 4, find the number of girls.
A. 6 B. 7
C. 8 D. 9

19. From a cask of wine containing 25 litres, 5 litres are withdrawn and the cask is refilled with water. The process is repeated a second and then a third time. Find the quantity of wine left in the cask and also the ratio of wine to water in the resulting mixture.
A. 61 : 64 B. 16 : 46
C. 46 : 16 D. 64 : 61

20. A vessel contains 80 litres of milk. 16 litres of milk was taken out of the vessel and replaced by water. Then 16 litres of mixture was withdrawn and again replaced by water. The operation was repeated for third time. How much milk is now left in the vessel?
A. 96.40 litres B. 50.36 litres
C. 40.96 litres D. 32.76 litres

ANSWERS

1	2	3	4	5	6	7	8	9	10
B	D	A	B	B	A	B	A	B	D
11	**12**	**13**	**14**	**15**	**16**	**17**	**18**	**19**	**20**
B	B	C	B	B	A	A	A	D	C

EXPLANATORY ANSWERS

1. CP of 1 kg. Cheaper tea ₹ 62   CP of 1 kg. Dearer tea ₹ 72

Mean Price per kg ₹ 65

$d - m = 7$ $m - c = 3$

Using Alligation rule,

$$\frac{\text{Quantity of cheaper tea}}{\text{Quantity of dearer tea}} = \frac{d-m}{m-c} = \frac{7}{3}$$

Therefore, they must be mixed in the ratio of 7 : 3.

3. 16   10

14

4   2

or 2 : 1 $\dfrac{\text{Quantity of milk @ ₹ 10 per kg}}{\text{Quantity of milk @ ₹ 16 per kg}} = \dfrac{1}{2}$

So, quantity of milk @ ₹ 10 per kg. $= \dfrac{26}{2} = 13$ kgs.

5. Fraction is *Milk*   *Water*

A : $\dfrac{4}{5}$ $\dfrac{1}{5}$

B : $\dfrac{9}{20}$ $\dfrac{11}{20}$

(3A + 2B) = A and B : $\left(\dfrac{12}{5}+\dfrac{9}{10}\right)\left(\dfrac{3}{5}+\dfrac{11}{10}\right)$

$\dfrac{33}{10}$ $\dfrac{17}{10}$

So, Ratio of milk : water in the resulting mixture = 33 : 17.

6. 30%   50%

45%

5   15

He should mix 30% and 50% in the ratio 5 : 15 or 1 : 3.

$\dfrac{\text{30\% Solution}}{\text{50\% Solution}} = \dfrac{1}{3}$ or 1 : 3

7. The given solution has 75% milk.

Milk to be added has 100% milk.

75%   100%

90%

10   15

Milk should be added to the given mixture in the ratio 15 : 10 or 3 : 2.

$\therefore$ Quantity of milk to be added $= \dfrac{3}{2} \times 6 = 9$ litres.

8. Let cost price of spirit be ₹ 1 per litre.

Water 0   Spirit ₹ 1

₹ $\dfrac{4}{5}$

$\dfrac{1}{5}$ ₹ $\dfrac{4}{5}$

Then SP of mixture = ₹ 1 per litre

Gain = 25%

So, CP of mixture $= 1 \times \dfrac{100}{125} = ₹\ \dfrac{4}{5}$

We assume that CP of water is zero.

Using alligation rule on cost price,

Water should be mixed to spirit in the ratio $\dfrac{1}{5} : \dfrac{4}{5}$ or 1 : 4.

9. 20%   40%

25%

15   5

or 3 : 1

Quantity sold at 20% profit $= \dfrac{3}{3+1} \times 50 = 37.5$ kgs.

Quantity sold at 40% profit = (50 – 37.5) = 12.5 kgs.

10. +20   –5

+10

10 – (–5) = 15   10

or 3 : 2

Quantity sold at 20% profit $= \dfrac{3}{3+2} \times 100 = 60$ kgs.

Quantity sold at 5% loss = (100 – 60) = 40 kgs.

11.

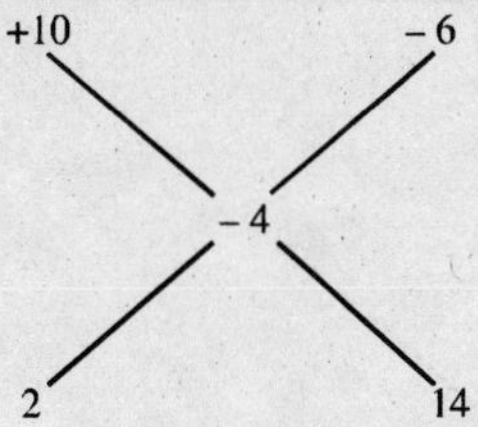

or 1 : 7

Quantity sold at 10% profit = $\frac{1}{1+7}$ × 160 = 20 kgs.

Quantity sold at 6% loss = 160 – 20 = 140 kgs.

12. Let the remainder stock be sold at x% profit.

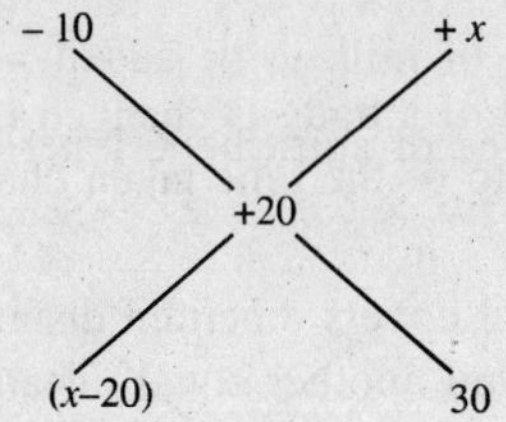

$$\frac{x-20}{30} = \frac{1/4}{3/4} \text{ or } x - 20 = 30 \times \frac{1}{3}$$

or $x = 20 + 10$, $x = 30\%$ profit.

13. Average rate of interest

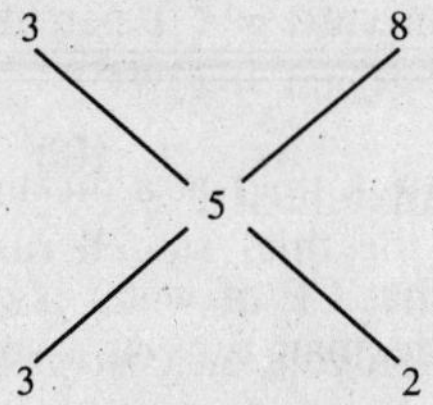

$= \frac{100 \times 750}{5000 \times 3} = 5\%$ per annum

Investment at 3% per annum = $\frac{3}{3+2} \times 5000 =$ ₹ 3000

Investment at 8% per annum = $\frac{2}{3+2} \times 5000 =$ ₹ 2000.

14. Average speed = $\frac{100}{10}$ = 10 km/hr.

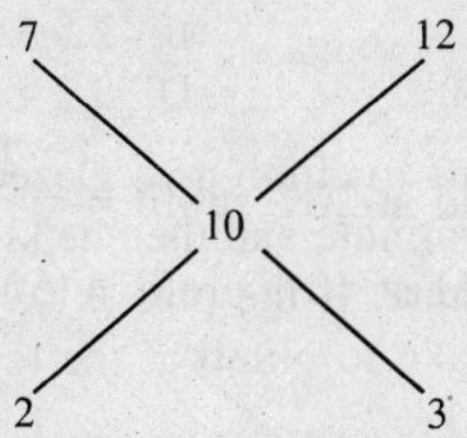

Ratio of time taken at 7 km/hr to 12 km/hr = 2 : 3

Time taken at 7 km/hr = $\frac{2}{2+3}$ × 10 = 4 hrs.

Distance covered at 7 km/hr = 7 × 4 = 28 km.

Distance covered at 12 km/hr = 100 – 28 = 72 km.

15.

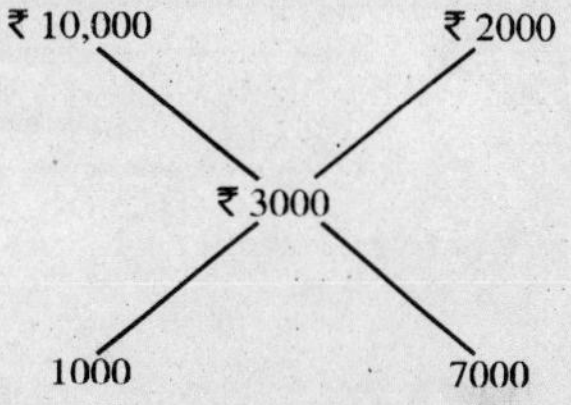

$$\frac{\text{Number of officers}}{\text{Number of workers}} = \frac{1000}{7000} = \frac{1}{7}$$

No. of officers = $\frac{1}{1+7}$ × 400 = 50

No. of workers = 400 – 50 = 350

16.

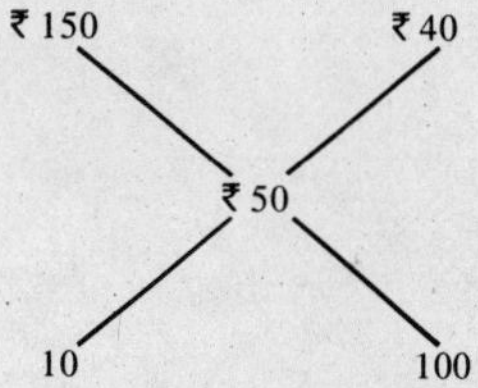

$$\frac{\text{Number of supervisors}}{\text{Number of labourers}} = \frac{10}{100} = \frac{1}{10}$$

Total number of labourers

= Total no. of supervisors × 10

= 15 × 10 = 150.

18.

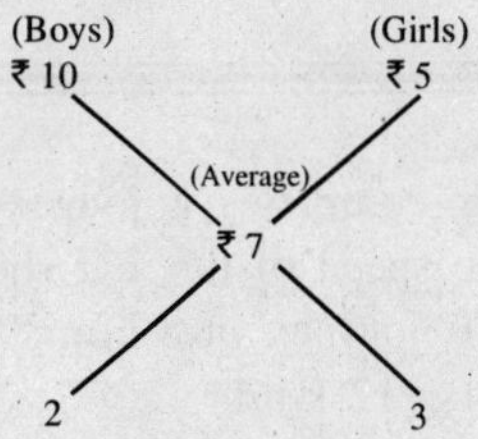

$$\frac{\text{Number of girls}}{\text{Number of boys}} = \frac{3}{2}$$

Number of girls = $\frac{3}{2}$ × 4 = 6

19. Here, quantity of wine left after third operation

$$= \left(1 - \frac{5}{25}\right)^3 \times 25$$

$$= \left(\frac{4}{5}\right)^3 \times 25 = \frac{64}{125} \times 25 = \frac{64}{5} = 12\frac{4}{5} \text{ litres.}$$

Final ratio of wine to water

$$= \frac{(64/125)}{(1 - 64/125)} = \frac{64/125}{61/125}$$

Wine : Water = $\frac{64}{61}$.

20. Amount of milk left

$$= 80\left(1 - \frac{16}{80}\right)^3 = 80\left(\frac{4}{5}\right)^3 = 80 \times \frac{64}{125}$$

= 40.96 litres.

●●●

CHAPTER 8

Time and Distance

Important Formulae:

1. Speed = Distance ÷ Time
2. Distance = Time × Speed
3. Time = Distance ÷ Speed
4. x km/hr = $\left(x \times \frac{5}{18}\right)$ m/sec
5. x metres/sec = $\left(x \times \frac{18}{5}\right)$ km/hr.
6. If the speed of a body is changed in the ratio $m : n$, then the ratio of the time taken changes in the ratio $n : m$.
7. When a man covers a certain distance with a speed of x km/h and another equal distance at the rate of y km/h, then for the whole journey, the average speed is given by

$$\text{Average speed} = \frac{2xy}{x+y} \text{ km/h.}$$

EXERCISE

1. A car moving at 48 km/hr completes a journey in 10 hours. By how much the speed of this car should be increased so as to do this journey in 8 hours?

A. 8 km/hr. B. 12 km/hr
C. 10 km/hr D. 15 km/hr

2. Starting from a point at a speed of 4 km/hr a man reaches at a cerain place and returns back to the point from where he had started journey on bicycle at the speed of 16 km/hr. His average speed during the entire journey will be:

A. 6.4 km/h B. 8.4 km/h
C. 5.4 km/h D. 10 km/h

3. A motorist covers a certain distance at a average speed of 48 km/h in 45 minutes. What speed in km/h he must maintain to cover the same distance in 30 minutes?

A. 66 km/h B. 79 km/h
C. 80 km/h D. 72 km/h

4. Two points A and B are 150 km apart. A man completes his onward journey from A to B in 3 hours 20 minutes and return journey from B to A in 4 hours 10 minutes. His average speed during the entire journey will be less than his average speed during the journey from A to B by:

A. 5 km/h B. 7.5 km/h
C. 9 km/h D. 3 km/h

5. A policeman saw a thief at a distance of 200 m. The policeman and the thief started running at the same time. If the policeman runs at a speed of $4\frac{1}{6}$ m per second and the thief at a speed of $3\frac{1}{3}$m per second, after what time the policeman will catch the thief?

A. 12 min B. 10 min
C. 9 min D. 4 min

6. Kanchan walks from her home at 4 kms per hour and reaches her school 5 minutes late. If she walks at 5 kms per hour, she reaches the school 2½ minutes earlier. How far is the school from her home?

A. 3.5 kms B. 2.5 kms
C. 2.75 kms D. 3.2 kms

7. A monkey wants to climb up a glazed pole. He climbs 12 metres in 1 minute and then he slips back 3 metres in the next minute. If the pole is 63 metre high, how long does he take to climb at the top of the pole?

A. $11\frac{1}{4}$ min B. $12\frac{1}{2}$ min
C. $12\frac{3}{4}$ min D. $14\frac{3}{4}$ min

8. A and B start walking at the same time on a circular path with circumference 35 metre. If they walk in the same direction at 4 km/hr and 5 km/hr respectively, after what time will they meet together?

A. 35 hours B. 27 hours
C. 24 hours D. 40 hours

9. While walking at $\frac{3}{5}$ of his usual speed Kamalkant reaches at his destination late by 30 minutes. His usual time consumed in reaching to his destination is:
A. 32 min B. 40 min
C. 45 min D. 42 min

10. The distance between two stations A and B is 300 km. A train leaves the station A with a speed of 40 km/hr. At the same time another train departs from the station B with a speed of 50 km/hr. How much time will these two trains take to cross each other?
A. 3 hrs 40 min B. 3 hrs 20 min
C. 2 hrs 20 min D. 3 hrs 45 min

11. Gulshan starts from a place P at 2 p.m. and walks to Q at 5 km per hour. Tarun starts from P at 3 p.m. and follows Gulshan on bicycle at 10 km per hour. By when Tarun will catch Gulshan?
A. At 5.30 p.m. B. At 4.00 p.m.
C. At 4.30 p.m. D. At 6.00 p.m.

12. Nilesh goes to school from his village at the speed of 4 km/hr and returns from school to village at the speed of 2 km/hr. If he takes 6 hours in all, then what is the distance between the village and the school?
A. 8 km B. 6 km
C. 5 km D. 4 km

13. A school bus covers a distance from a village to school at the speed of 12 km/hr and reaches the school 8 minute late. The next day the bus covers the same distance at the speed of 20 km/hr and reaches the school 10 minutes early. What is the distance between village and the school?
A. 6 km B. 9 km
C. 12 km D. 15 km

14. By increasing the speed of the bus by 10 km/hr the time of journey for 72 km is reduced by 36 minutes. What was the original speed of the bus?
A. 30 km/hr B. 35 km/hr
C. 40 km/hr D. 45 km/hr

15. A car completes a fixed journey in 8 hours. It covers half distance at the speed of 40 km/hr and rest at the 60 km/hr, the distance of the journey is:
A. 400 km B. 420 km
C. 384 km D. 350 km

16. A car covers four consecutive extensions of 3 km each at the speeds of 10 km/hr, 20 km/hr, 30 km/hr and 60 km/hr. Its average speed of journey is:
A. 30 km/hr B. 25 km/hr
C. 20 km/hr D. 10 km/hr

17. A girl rides her bicycle 10 km at an average speed of 12 km/hr and another 12 km at an average speed of 10 km/hr. Her average speed for the entire journey is approximately:
A. 12.2 km/hr B. 11.2 km/hr
C. 10.8 km/hr D. 10.4 km/hr

18. Raman drove from home to a neighbouring town at the speed of 50 km/hr and on his returning journey, he drove at the speed of 45 km/hr and also took an hour longer to reach home. What distance did he cover each way?
A. 900 km B. 500 km
C. 450 km D. 225 km

19. A man takes 6 hours 35 minutes in walking to a certain place and riding back. He would have taken 2 hours less by riding both ways. What would be the time he would take to walk both ways?
A. 10 hours B. 8 hours 35 minutes
C. 8 hours 25 minutes D. 8 hrs

20. A man covers a distance of 6 km at the rate of 4 km/hr and other 4 km at 3 km/hr this average speed is
A. $3\frac{5}{9}$ km/hr B. $3\frac{9}{17}$ km/hr
C. $5\frac{9}{17}$ km/hr D. $9\frac{3}{17}$ km/hr

ANSWERS

1	2	3	4	5	6	7	8	9	10
B	A	D	A	D	B	C	A	C	B
11	**12**	**13**	**14**	**15**	**16**	**17**	**18**	**19**	**20**
B	A	B	A	C	C	C	C	B	B

EXPLANATORY ANSWERS

1. Let he has to increase his speed by x km/hr for given condition; then,

$$(48 + x) \times 8 = 48 \times 10$$

$$\Rightarrow 48 + x = 60 \therefore x = 12 \text{ km/hr}$$

2. Average speed during the entire journey

$$= \frac{2xy}{x+y} = \frac{2\times4\times16}{4+16} = \frac{8\times16}{20} = 6.4 \text{ km/hr.}$$

3. Let required speed be x km/hr; then

$$x \times \frac{1}{2} = 48 \times \frac{3}{4} \therefore x = 48 \times \frac{3}{4} \times 2 = 72 \text{ km/hr}$$

4. During onward journey from A to B:

$$\text{Average speed} = \frac{150}{10/3} = \frac{150\times3}{10} = 45 \text{ km/hr.}$$

During entire jouney:

$$\text{Average speed} = \frac{300}{\frac{10}{3}+\frac{25}{6}} = \frac{300\times 6}{45} = 40 \text{ km/hr.}$$

Hence, difference of average speed

$= 45 - 40 = 5$ km/hr.

5. Suppose the policeman will catch the thief after t sec

then, $\left(\frac{25}{6}-\frac{10}{3}\right)t = 200 \Rightarrow \frac{5}{6}t = 200$

$\therefore t = \frac{200\times 6}{5} = 240$ sec $= 4$ min.

6. Suppose the distance between her house to the school $= x$ km

Difference of time $= \frac{5}{2} - (-5) = \frac{15}{2}$ min $= \frac{1}{8}$ hr.

$\frac{x}{4}-\frac{x}{5}=\frac{1}{8} \Rightarrow \frac{x}{20}=\frac{1}{8} \quad \therefore x = \frac{20}{8} = 2.5$ km

7. The monkey climbs 12 metres in 1 minute and then he slips back 3 metres in the next minute

$\therefore$ The monkey climbs in the first 2 minutes $= 12 - 3 = 9$ metres

$\therefore$ In the first 12 minutes the monkey climbs $= 9 \times 6 = 54$ metres

Remaining height of the pole to be covered by the monkey $= 63 - 54 = 9$ metre

$\therefore$ The monkey will climb the height of 9 metres in the 13th minute

$\because$ The monkey climbs 12 metres in 1 minute

$\therefore$ The monkey will climb 9 metres in

$\frac{1}{12}\times 9 = \frac{3}{4}$ minute

$\therefore$ Time spent in climbing at the top of the pole

$= \left(12+\frac{3}{4}\right)$ minutes $= 12\frac{3}{4}$ minutes

8. The two persons walk in the same direction

$\therefore$ Their relative speed $= 5 - 4 = 1$ km/hr

Distance covered in 1 round on the circular path = 35 km

$\therefore$ They will meet after $\frac{35}{1} = 35$ hours.

9. Suppose usual speed of Kamalkant is v km/hr and his destination is at a distance of x kms; then usual time taken $= \frac{x}{v}$ hours.

$\frac{x}{3v/5}-\frac{x}{v}=\frac{1}{2} \Rightarrow \frac{2x}{3v}=\frac{1}{2} \quad \therefore \frac{x}{v}=\frac{3}{4}$ hour $= 45$ min.

10. The two trains are moving in the opposite directions

$\therefore$ Relative speed $= 40 + 50 = 90$ km/hr.

$\therefore$ Time taken to cross each other

$= \frac{300}{90} = 3\frac{1}{3}$ hours or, 3 hours 20 minutes.

11. Let Tarun will catch Gulshan after t hours the starting of Tarun; then, $10t = 5(t + 1)$

$\Rightarrow 5t = 5 \therefore t = 1$ hr

Hence, required time = 3 p.m. + 1 hr. = 4 p.m.

12. Let x km be the distance between village and the school; then

$\frac{x}{4}+\frac{x}{2}=6 \Rightarrow \frac{3x}{4}=6 \quad \therefore x = \frac{6\times 4}{3} = 8$ km

13. Let x km be the distance from village to school, then

$\frac{x}{12}-\frac{x}{20} = [8-(-10)] \times \frac{1}{60}$

$\Rightarrow \frac{x}{30}=\frac{18}{60} \therefore x = \frac{18}{60}\times 30 = 9$ km

14. Let original speed of the bus be x km/hr; then

$\frac{72}{x}-\frac{72}{x+10}=\frac{36}{60} \Rightarrow \frac{72(x+10-x)}{x^2+10x}=\frac{3}{5}$

$\Rightarrow \quad 1200 = x^2 + 10x$

$\Rightarrow x^2 + 10x - 1200 = 0$

$\Rightarrow (x + 40)(x - 30) = 0$

$\therefore \quad x = 30$ or $x = -40$

Taking positive value only, so speed of the bus = 30 km/hr.

15. Let the distance of the journey be x km, then,

$\frac{x}{2\times 40}+\frac{x}{2\times 60} = 8 \Rightarrow \frac{5x}{240} = 8$

$\therefore \quad x = 8 \times 48 = 384$ km

16. Total distance of the journey $= 4 \times 3$ km $= 12$ km

Total time taken $= \frac{3}{10}+\frac{3}{20}+\frac{3}{30}+\frac{3}{60}=\frac{36}{60}=\frac{3}{5}$ hr.

Hence, average speed $= \frac{12}{3/5} = \frac{12\times 5}{3} = 20$ km/hr.

17. Average speed

$= \frac{10+12}{\frac{10}{12}+\frac{12}{10}} = \frac{22}{61/30} = \frac{22\times 30}{61} = \frac{660}{61} = 10.8$ km/hr

18. Let his distance of journey of each way be x km; then

$\frac{x}{45}-\frac{x}{50}=1 \Rightarrow \frac{x}{450} = 1$

$\therefore \quad x = 450$ km

19. Here, Walking to a certain place + riding back = 6 hrs 35 min. ...(i)

2 × riding the same distance = 4 hrs 35 min. ...(ii)

Multiplying equation (i) × 2 and subtracting (ii) we get

Time taken in walking both ways = 13 hrs 70 min − 4 hrs. 35 min = 8 hrs. 35 min.

20. His average speed $= \frac{6+4}{\frac{6}{4}+\frac{4}{3}} = \frac{10}{17/6} = \frac{60}{17} = 3\frac{9}{17}$ km/hr

●●●

CHAPTER 9

Time and Work

IMPORTANT FACTS:

1. If A can do a piece of work in n days, then work done by A in 1 day $= \frac{1}{n}$.

2. If work done by A in 1 day $= \frac{1}{n}$; then A can finish the whole work in n days.

3. If A is twice as good a workman as B then; Ratio of work done by A and B = 2 : 1
Ratio of times taken by A and B to finish a work = 1 : 2.

EXERCISE

1. 12 boys can do a piece of work in 16 days. In how many days can 6 boys do the same work?
A. 16 days B. 32 days
C. 23 days D. 24 days

2. A can do a piece of work in 8 days while B can do the same work in 16 days. If they start working together, how long would they take to complete half portion of this work?
A. $2\frac{2}{3}$ days B. $3\frac{5}{7}$ days
C. $4\frac{1}{2}$ days D. $3\frac{1}{2}$ days

3. A can do a piece of work in 4 days. B is 50% more efficient than A. How long would B alone take to finish this work?
A. $3\frac{1}{3}$ days B. $5\frac{1}{4}$ days
C. $2\frac{2}{3}$ days D. $1\frac{2}{3}$ days

4. A and B working together complete a work in 35 days. If A takes 60 days to complete it, how long would B alone take to complete it?
A. 64 days B. 72 days
C. 81 days D. 84 days

5. A few children working together can do a piece of work in 18 days. If the number of children employed on the work is made double, how long would they take to complete half of the work?
A. $4\frac{1}{2}$ days B. $2\frac{1}{3}$ days
C. $8\frac{3}{4}$ days D. $6\frac{1}{2}$ days

6. 10 men or 18 boys can do a piece of work in 15 days. In how many days would 25 men and 15 boys complete the same work working together?
A. $5\frac{1}{2}$ days B. $4\frac{1}{2}$ days
C. $6\frac{2}{3}$ days D. $2\frac{1}{3}$ days

7. A can do a piece of work in 40 days. He starts working, but having some other engagements he drops out after 5 days. Thereafter B completes this work in 21 days. How many days would A and B take to complete this work working together?
A. 15 days B. 16 days
C. 17 days D. 11 days

8. Two persons A and B can complete a piece of work in 8 hours and 16 hours respectively. If they work at it alternately for an hour, A starting first, in how many hours will the work be finished?
A. $9\frac{1}{3}$ hours B. $10\frac{1}{2}$ hours
C. $11\frac{1}{2}$ hours D. $8\frac{1}{2}$ hours

9. 15 men can complete a work in 210 days. They started the work but at the end of 10 days 15 additional men, with double efficiency, were inducted. How many days, in whole, did they take to finish the work?

A. $76\frac{2}{3}$ days B. $84\frac{3}{4}$ days

C. $72\frac{1}{2}$ days D. 70 days

10. A and B working together can complete a piece of work in 12 days and B and C working together can complete the same work in 16 days. A worked at it for 5 days and B worked at it for 7 days. C finished the remaining work in 13 days. How many days would C alone take to complete it?

A. 10 days B. 24 days

C. 32 days D. 40 days

11. A cistern is filled by a tap in $3\frac{1}{2}$ hours. Due to a leak in the bottom of the cistern, it takes half an hour longer to fill the cistern. If the cistern is full, how long will it take the leak to empty it?

A. 28 hours B. 29 hours

C. $31\frac{1}{3}$ hours D. 38 hours

12. A is twice as good a workman as B and thrice as good a workman as C. If C alone can do a piece of work in 24 days, how long would the three persons take to finish the work working together?

A. $3\frac{3}{11}$ days B. $4\frac{4}{7}$ days

C. $4\frac{4}{11}$ days D. $3\frac{4}{11}$ days

13. Two pipes can fill a tank in 8 hours and 12 hours respectively whereas an escape pipe can empty it in 6 hours. If the three pipes are opened at 1 p.m., 2 p.m. and 3 p.m. respectively, at what time will the tank be filled?

A. 7.00 a.m. B. 8.00 a.m.

C. 5.00 a.m. D. 7.30 a.m.

14. Working 7 hours daily 24 men can complete a piece of work in 27 days. In how many days would 14 men complete the same piece of work working 9 hours daily?

A. 32 days B. 31 days

C. 36 days D. 39 days

15. A, B and C undertake to do a piece of work for ₹ 529. If A and B working together do $\frac{19}{23}$ work and B and C working together do $\frac{8}{23}$ work, how should the money be divided among them?

A. ₹ 345, ₹ 102, ₹ 82

B. ₹ 345, ₹ 92, ₹ 92

C. ₹ 330, ₹ 107, ₹ 92

D. ₹ 330, ₹ 92, ₹ 107

ANSWERS

1	2	3	4	5	6	7	8	9	10
B	A	C	D	A	B	A	B	A	B
11	**12**	**13**	**14**	**15**					
A	C	A	C	B					

EXPLANATORY ANSWERS

1. $\because$ 12 boys can do a piece of work in 16 days.

$\therefore$ 1 boy will do the same piece of work in 16 × 12 days.

$\therefore$ 6 boys will do the same piece of work in

$\frac{16 \times 12}{6}$ days = 32 days.

2. (A + B)'s 1 day's work = $\frac{1}{8}+\frac{1}{16}=\frac{3}{16}$

Hence, (A + B) will do the whole work in $\frac{16}{3}$ days

So, they will do the half portion of the work in

$\frac{16}{3 \times 2}$ days = $\frac{8}{3}=2\frac{2}{3}$ days.

3. A's 1 day's work = $\frac{1}{4}$;

Hence, B's 1 day's work = $\frac{150}{100}\times\frac{1}{4}=\frac{3}{8}$

So, B will do the whole work in $\frac{8}{3}=2\frac{2}{3}$ days.

4. (A + B)'s 1 day's work = $\frac{1}{35}$

and also, A's 1 day's work = $\frac{1}{60}$

Hence, B's 1 day's work

$=\frac{1}{35}-\frac{1}{60}=\frac{5}{420}=\frac{1}{84}$

So, B will do the whole work in 84 days.

5. Let number of children be x;

Now x children can do the work in 18 days.

Hence, $2x$ children will do $\frac{1}{2}$ of the work in

$\frac{18 \times x}{2x \times 2} = \frac{9}{2}$ days $= 4\frac{1}{2}$ days.

6. 10 men $\equiv$ 18 boys; 25 men $\equiv \frac{18}{10} \times 25 = 45$ boys

Hence, 25 men + 15 boys = 45 + 15 = 60 boys

Now, 18 boys can do a piece of work in 15 days.

Hence, 60 boys will do a piece of work in

$\frac{15 \times 18}{60} = \frac{9}{2}$ days $= 4\frac{1}{2}$ days.

7. A's 5 days' work $= 5 \times \frac{1}{40} = \frac{1}{8}$

Remaining work $= 1 - \frac{1}{8} = \frac{7}{8}$, which is done by B in 21 days.

Hence, B's 1 day's work $= \frac{7}{8 \times 21} = \frac{1}{24}$

Now, (A + B)'s 1 day's work $= \frac{1}{40} + \frac{1}{24} = \frac{8}{120} = \frac{1}{15}$

Hence, (A + B) will complete the work in 15 days.

8. In 2 hours the part of work $= \frac{1}{8} + \frac{1}{16} = \frac{3}{16}$ will be completed.

Hence, in 5 pairs of hours the part of work

$= 5 \times \frac{3}{16} = \frac{15}{16}$ will be completed

Remaining work $= 1 - \frac{15}{16} = \frac{1}{16}$ which will be done by A.

Time taken by A to complete the $\frac{1}{16}$ work

$= \frac{1/16}{1/8} = \frac{1}{2}$ hour.

Hence, required number of hours

$= 10 + \frac{1}{2} = 10\frac{1}{2}$ hours.

9. 15 men's 10 days' work $= 10 \times \frac{1}{210} = \frac{1}{21}$

Remaining work $= 1 - \frac{1}{21} = \frac{20}{21}$

Now, (15 men + 15 men having double efficiency)'s 1 day's work $= \frac{1}{210} + \frac{2}{210} = \frac{3}{210} = \frac{1}{70}$

Hence, number of days

$= \frac{20/21}{1/70} = \frac{20}{21} \times 70 = \frac{200}{3} = 66\frac{2}{3}$ days

So, required number of total days

$= 10 + 66\frac{2}{3} = 76\frac{2}{3}$ days.

10. Here, A worked for 5 days, B for 7 days and C for 13 days $\equiv$ (A + B) worked for 5 days, (B + C) for 2 days and C for 11 days.

Let C will complete the work in x days,

Now, (A + B)'s 5 days' work + (B + C)'s 2 days' work + C's 11 days' work

$= \frac{5}{12} + \frac{2}{16} + \frac{11}{x} = \frac{13}{24} + \frac{11}{x}$

Again, $\frac{13}{24} + \frac{11}{x} = 1 \Rightarrow \frac{11}{x} = \frac{11}{24}$ $\therefore x = 24$

Hence, C would alone complete the work in 24 days.

11. In 1 hour $\frac{2}{7}$ cistern is filled by the tap.

Hence, in $\frac{1}{2}$ hour $\frac{2}{14} = \frac{1}{7}$ cistern is filled by the tap.

So, $\frac{1}{7}$ cistern is emptied by the leakage in 4 hours.

So, 1 cistern will be emptied by the leakage in 28 hours.

13. Let tank will be filled up after t hours of starting of pipe A;

Then, $t \times \frac{1}{8} + (t-1) \times \frac{1}{12} - (t-2) \times \frac{1}{6} = 1$

$\Rightarrow t\left(\frac{1}{8} + \frac{1}{12} - \frac{1}{6}\right) - \frac{1}{12} + \frac{1}{3} = 1$

$\Rightarrow \quad t \times \frac{1}{24} = 1 - \frac{1}{4}$

$\therefore t = \frac{3}{4} \times 24 = 18$ hours

Hence, required time = 1 p.m. + 18 hours = 7 a.m.

14. Working 7 hours a day 24 men can do the work is 27 days.

Hence, working 9 hours a day 14 men will do the work in $\frac{27 \times 24 \times 7}{9 \times 14} = 36$ days.

15. The part of work is done by B

$= \frac{19}{23} + \frac{8}{23} - 1 = \frac{4}{23}$

The part of work is done by A $= \frac{19}{23} - \frac{4}{23} = \frac{15}{23}$

The part of work is done by C $= \frac{8}{23} - \frac{4}{23} = \frac{4}{23}$

Hence, share of A $= \frac{15}{23} \times ₹\ 529 = ₹\ 345$

share of B $= \frac{4}{23} \times ₹\ 529 = ₹\ 92$

share of C $= \frac{4}{23} \times ₹\ 529 = ₹\ 92$

So, Their shares are ₹ 345, ₹ 92 and ₹ 92.

CHAPTER

10 Geometry

Triangle and Its Various Kinds of Centres

There are 4 very important ways of viewing the center of a triangle. We can look at its CENTROID, ORTHOCENTER, CIRCUMCENTER, and the INCENTER.

Centroid

The centroid is the first center and is obtained by locating the intersection of the three medians of the triangle. The median of a triangle is obtained by joining each vertex with the midpoint of the opposite side.

- It is the point of the intersection of the three median of the triangle. It is denoted by G.
- A centroid divides the area of the triangle in exactly three parts.

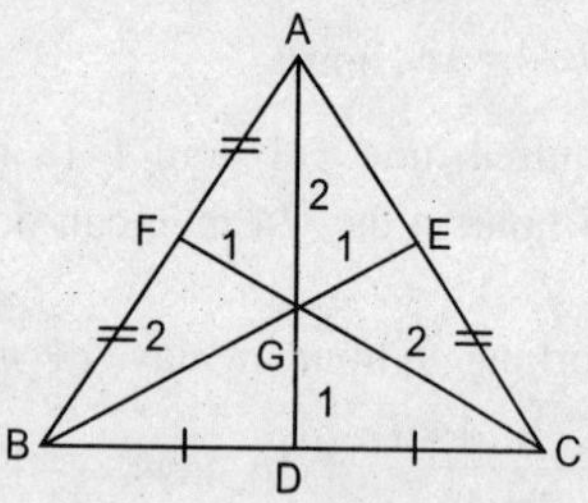

Medians:

- A line segment joining the midpoint of the side with the opposite vertex is called median.
- Median bisects the opposite side as well as divide the area of the triangle in two equal parts.

Orthocenter

The second center of a triangle is the orthocenter. It is obtained by finding the intersection of the 3 altitudes of the triangle. An altitude is found by joining each vertex with the point on the opposite side that creates a perpendicular line with the opposite side.

It is the point of intersection of all the three altitudes of the triangle.

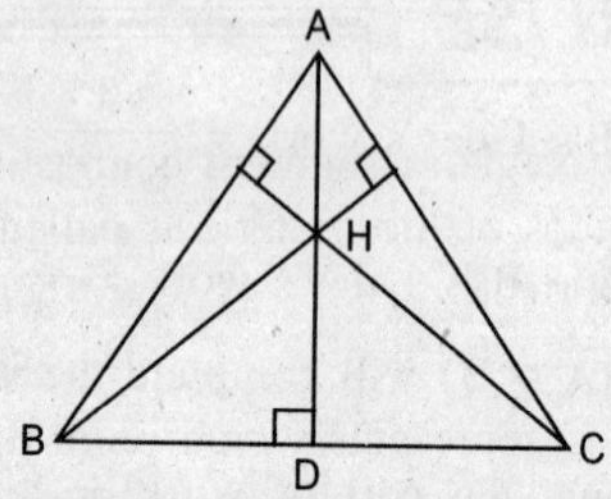

$\angle BHC = 180 - \angle A$

$\angle AHB = 180 - \angle C$

$\angle AHC = 180 - \angle B$

Position of orthocentre inside the triangle:

Acute angled triangle: lies inside the triangle.

Obtuse angle triangle: lies outside the triangle on the backside of the obtuse angle. Orthocentre and circumcentre lie opposite to each other in obtuse angle triangle.

Circumcenter

The third center is the circumcenter. The circumcenter is the intersection of the perpendicular bisectors of each side of the triangle. We can also think of this center as the point that is equidistant from each of the vertices. Since it is equidistant from each vertex, we can also construct a circle that passes through each vertex with the center being the circumcenter.

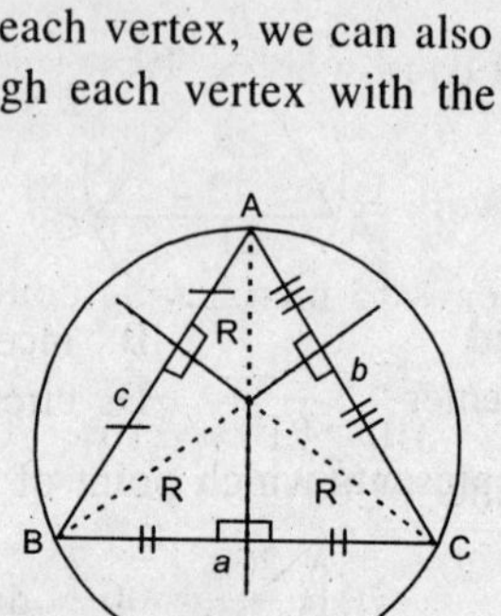

The distance between the circumcentre and the three vertices of a triangle is always equal.

OA = OB = OC = R (circumradius) = $abc/4A$

$\angle BOC = 2\angle A$

$\angle AOC = 2\angle B$

$\angle AOB = 2\angle C$

Location of circumcentre in various types of triangle:

Acute angle triangle: Lies inside the triangle

Obtuse angle triangle: Lies outside the triangle

Right angle triangle: Lies at the midpoint of the hypotenuse.

Incenter

The last center is the incenter. The incenter is found by first constructing the angle bisectors of each of the three angles. The incenter is the intersection of these 3 segments.

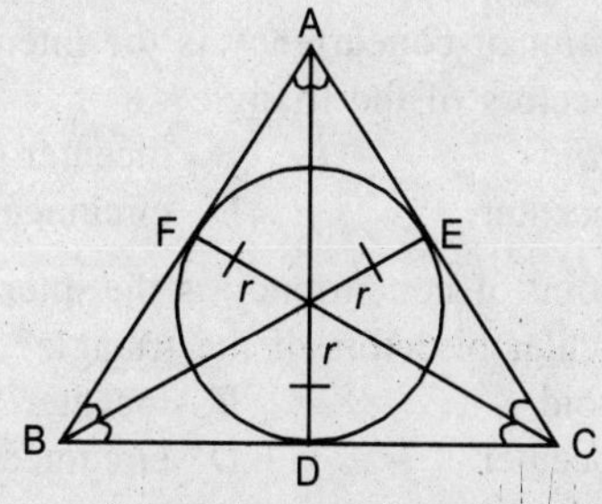

The distance of the in-centre from the all the three sides is equal (ID = IE = IF = inradius "r")

In-radius (r) = Area of triangle/Semiperimetre = A/S

$\angle BIC = 90 + \angle A/2$

$\angle AIC = 90 + \angle B/2$

$\angle AIB = 90 + \angle C/2$

EXERCISE

1. In a triangle, a segment connecting the midpoints of two sides of the triangle is called a _____.

A. shortcut C. centroid
B. midsegment D. vertex

2. Point Q represents which point of concurrency?

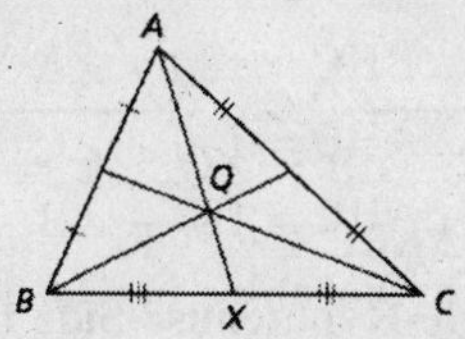

A. centroid C. orthocenter
B. incenter D. circumcenter

3. Point P represents which point of concurrency?

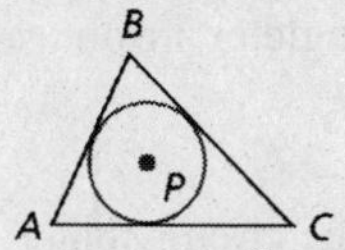

A. centroid C. orthocenter
B. incenter D. circumcenter

4. Point P represents which point of concurrency?

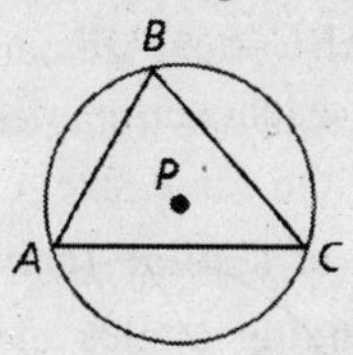

A. centroid B. incenter
C. orthocenter D. circumcenter

5. Point T represents which point of concurrency?

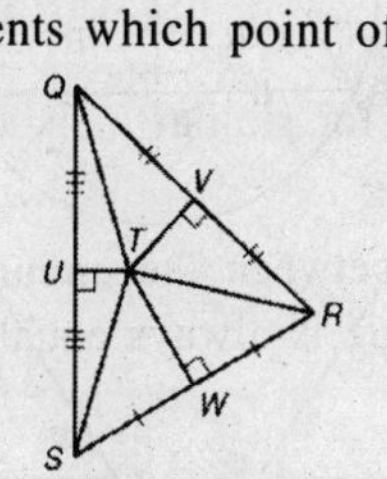

A. centroid B. incenter
C. orthocenter D. circumcenter

6. Point M represents which point of concurrency?

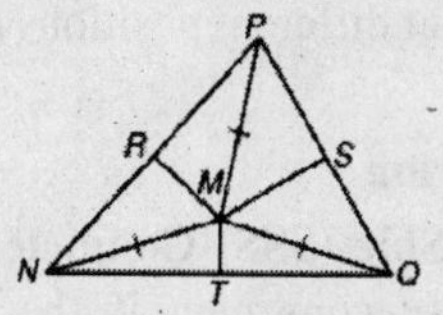

A. centroid B. incenter
C. orthocenter D. circumcenter

7. Point M represents which point of concurrency?

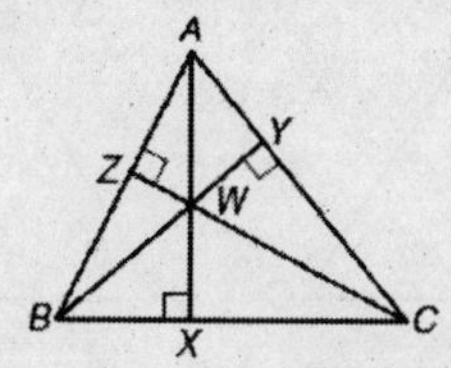

A. centroid B. incenter
C. orthocenter D. circumcenter

8. Point L represents which point of concurrency?

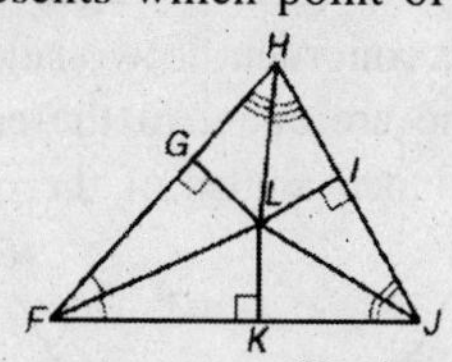

A. centroid B. incenter
C. orthocenter D. circumcenter

9. Which point of concurrency is the intersection of the medians of the triangle?

A. centroid B. incenter
C. orthocenter D. circumcenter

10. Which point of concurrency is the intersection of the altitudes of the triangle?

A. centroid B. incenter
C. orthocenter D. circumcenter

11. Which point of concurrency is the intersection of the angle bisectors of the triangle?

A. centroid B. incenter
C. orthocenter D. circumcenter

12. Which point of concurrency is the intersection of the perpendicular bisectors of the triangle?

A. centroid B. incenter
C. orthocenter D. circumcenter

13. Which point of concurrency is equidistant from the three sides of a triangle?

A. centroid B. incenter
C. orthocenter D. circumcenter

14. Which point of concurrency is equidistant from the three verticies of a triangle?

A. centroid B. incenter
C. orthocenter D. circumcenter

15. Which point of concurrency is the center of gravity of a triangle?

A. centroid B. incenter
C. orthocenter D. circumcenter

ANSWERS

1	2	3	4	5	6	7	8	9	10
B	A	B	D	D	D	C	B	A	C
11	**12**	**13**	**14**	**15**					
B	D	B	D	A					

Congruence and Similarity of Triangles

Congruence of triangle: Two triangles having same shape and measurement but different positions are called congruent triangle.

Congruence criterion

(*i*) **Side-Side-Side (SSS) Congruence criterion:** Two triangles are congruent if the three sides of one triangle are equal to the three sides of the other triangle.

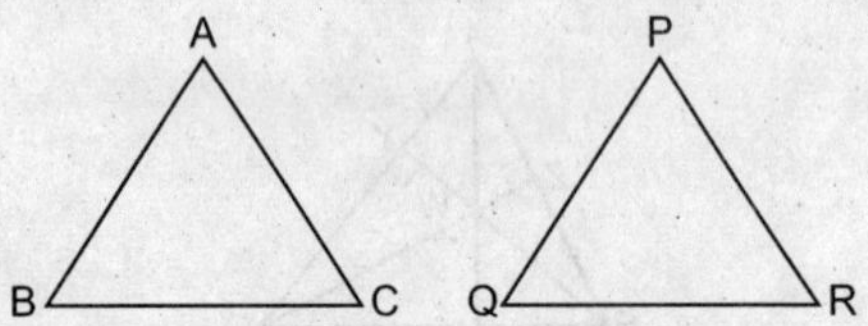

Here, AB = PQ, BC = QR and AC = PR

$\therefore$ $\Delta ABC \cong \Delta PQR$

(*ii*) **Side-Angle-Side (SAS) Congruence criterion:** Two triangles are congruent if two sides and the included angle of one are equal to the corresponding sides and the included angles of the other.

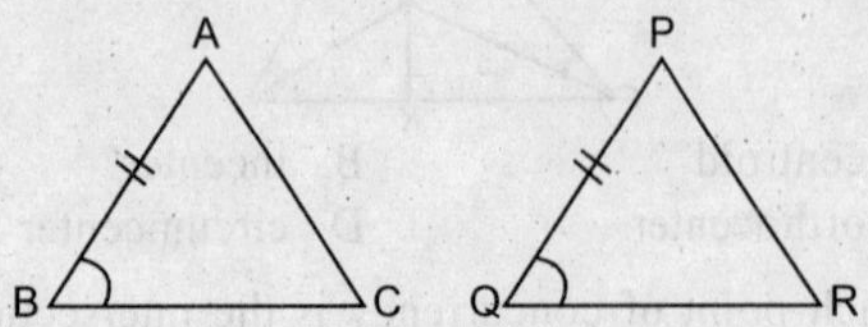

Here, AB = PQ, $\angle B = \angle Q$ and BC = QR

$\therefore$ $\Delta ABC \cong \Delta PQR$

(*iii*) **Angle-Side-Angle (ASA) Congruence criterion:** Two triangles are congruent if two angles and the included side of one triangle are equal to the corresponding two angles and the included side of the triangle.

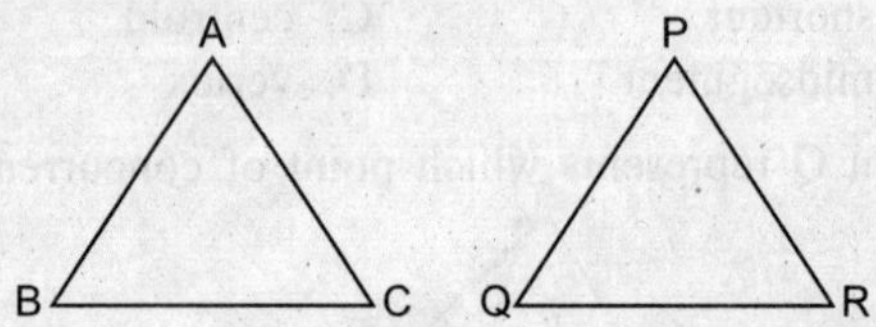

$\because$ $\angle B = \angle Q$, $\angle C = \angle R$ and BC = QR

$\therefore$ $\Delta ABC \cong \Delta PQR$

(*iv*) **Right Angle-Hypotenuse-Side (RHS) congruence criterion:** Two right triangles are congruent. If the hypotenuse and one side of one triangle are respectively equal to the hypotenuse and one side of the other triangle.

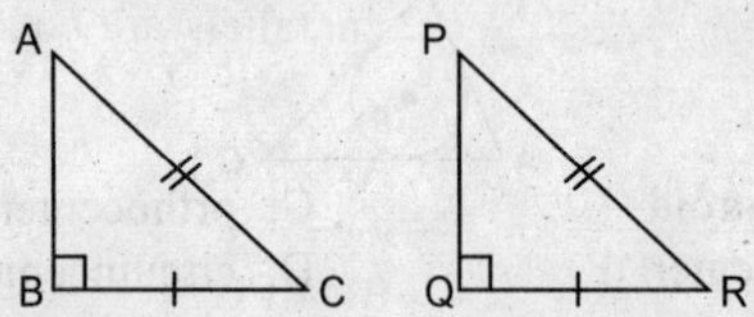

$\because$ $\angle B = \angle Q = 90°$, AC = PR, BC = QR

$\therefore$ $\Delta ABC \cong \Delta PQR$.

Similar Triangles: Two triangles having same shape but not necessarily of the same size, called similar triangle.

Basic properties of similar triangles:

(*i*) The corresponding angles of similar triangles are equal.

(*ii*) The corresponding sides of similar triangles are proportional.

The symbol for similar or is similar to is ~

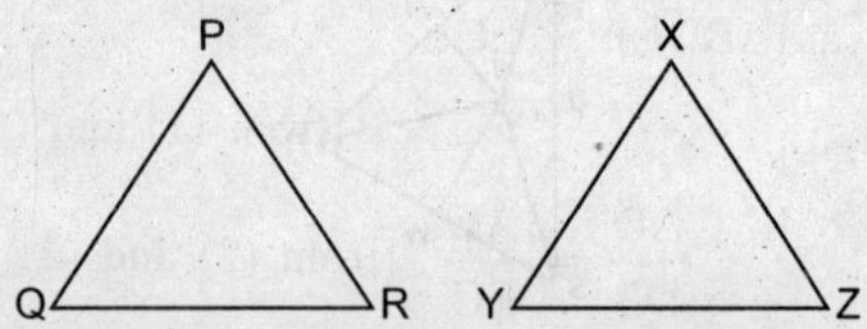

$\angle P = \angle X$, $\angle Q = \angle Y$ and $\angle R = \angle Z$

Then, $\dfrac{PQ}{QR} = \dfrac{XY}{YZ}$ or, $\dfrac{PR}{PQ} = \dfrac{XZ}{XY}$

Thus, $\Delta PQR \sim \Delta XYZ$

→ Congruent triangles are always similar but similar triangles may or may not be congruent.

→ Any two equilateral triangles are always similar triangles.

SOME IMPORTANT THEOREMS

Basic Proportionality Theorem: (Thalse Theorem)

Theorem 1: *In a triangle, a line drawn parallel to one side to intersect the other sides in distinct points divides the two sides in the same ratio.*

Given: A ΔABC in which DE is drawn parallel to side BC.

To prove. $\dfrac{AD}{DB} = \dfrac{AE}{EC}$.

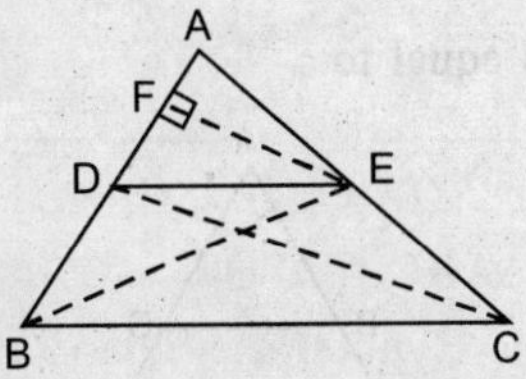

Const.: Join BE and CD. Draw $EF \perp AB$.

Proof: ar.(ΔBDE) = ar.(ΔCDE) ...(1)

[∵ Δs on the same base DE and between the same parallels are equal in area]

$$\frac{ar.(\Delta ADE)}{ar.(\Delta BDE)} = \frac{\frac{1}{2}\times AD\times EF}{\frac{1}{2}\times BD\times EF}$$

[∵ Area of $\Delta = \frac{1}{2}$ base × height]

$$\Rightarrow \quad \frac{ar.(\Delta ADE)}{ar.(\Delta BDE)} = \frac{AD}{DB} \quad ...(2)$$

$$\text{Similarly,} \quad \frac{ar.(\Delta ADE)}{ar.(\Delta CDE)} = \frac{AE}{EC} \quad ...(3)$$

$$\therefore \quad \frac{ar.(\Delta ADE)}{ar.(\Delta BDE)} = \frac{AE}{EC}$$

[from (1) and (3)] ...(4)

$$\therefore \quad \frac{AD}{DB} = \frac{AE}{EC} \quad \text{[from (2) and (4)]}$$

Corollary 1: $\dfrac{AD}{DB} = \dfrac{AE}{EC}$

Adding 1 to both sides, we get

$$\frac{AD}{DB}+1 = \frac{AE}{EC}+1$$

$$\Rightarrow \quad \frac{AD+DB}{DB} = \frac{AE+EC}{EC}$$

Corollary 2: $\dfrac{AD}{DB} = \dfrac{AE}{EC}$

$$\Rightarrow \quad \frac{DB}{AD} = \frac{EC}{AE}$$

Adding 1 to both sides, we get

$$1+\frac{DB}{AD} = 1+\frac{EC}{AE}$$

$$\Rightarrow \quad \frac{AD+DB}{AD} = \frac{AE+EC}{AE}$$

$$\Rightarrow \quad \frac{AB}{AD} = \frac{AC}{AE}.$$

Converse of Basic Proportionality Theorem

Theorem 2: *If a line divides any two sides of a triangle in the same ratio, prove that it is parallel to the third side.*

Given: A ΔABC, DE is st. line such that

$$\frac{AD}{DB} = \frac{AE}{EC}$$

To Prove. DE ∥ BC

Const.: If DE is not ∥ BC, draw BK ∥ DE meeting AC produce in.

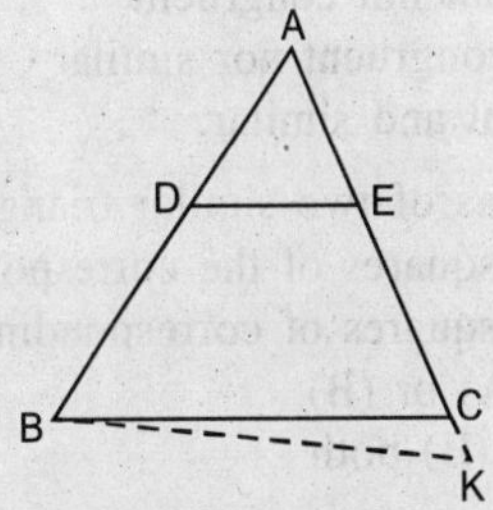

Proof: In DABK, DE ∥ BK

$$\therefore \quad \frac{AD}{DB} = \frac{AE}{EK} \quad ...(1)$$

[∵ A line drawn ∥ to one side of a Δ divides the other two sides in the same ratio]

But, $\dfrac{AD}{DB} = \dfrac{AE}{EC}$ (given) ...(2)

From (1) and (2), we get

$\dfrac{AE}{EK} = \dfrac{AE}{EC}$ or, EK = EC

which is possible only when C and K coincides.

Hence, DE ∥ BC.

EXERCISE

1. Two similar triangles have
A. equal sides B. equal areas
C. equal angles D. None of these

2. Two congruent triangles have
A. proportional sides
B. equal sides
C. equal corresponding sides
D. equal corresponding angles

3. Which of the following is false for two congruent triangles?
A. Corresponding angles are equal.
B. Two sides and included angles are equal.
C. Corresponding sides are equal.
D. Two angles and one side are equal.

4. If the sides of a triangle are 8 cm, 12 cm and 15 cm then the angle is
A. Right angle B. Obtuse angle
C. Acute angle D. None of these

5. If two triangles are on the same base and between the parallel lines then they will be
A. equilaterals B. right angled
C. equal in area D. congruent

6. If the three heights of a traingle are equal then it is
A. right angled triangle B. obtuse angled triangle
C. equilateral triangle D. None of these

7. If two corresponding sides and the angle between them of a traingle are equal to another triangle. Then the angles are :
A. congruent but not similar
B. similar but not congruent
C. neither congruent nor similar
D. congruent and similar.

8. Ratio of areas of two similar triangles is equal to :
A. ratio of squares of the corresponding altitudes
B. ratio of squares of corresponding medians.
C. Either (A) or (B)
D. (A) and (B) both

9. If the areas of two similar triangles are equal then the triangles :
A. are congruent
B. have equal length of corresponding sides
C. (A) and (B)
D. None of these

10. Two isosceles triangles have equal vertical angles and their areas are in the ratio of 9 : 25 then the ratio between their corresponding heights is :
A. 5 : 3 B. 25 : 9
C. 3 : 5 D. 16 : 9

11. If in a Δ DEF, GH || EF and DG : EG = 2 : 3 then the value of $\frac{ar(\Delta DGH)}{ar(\Delta DEF)}$ is :

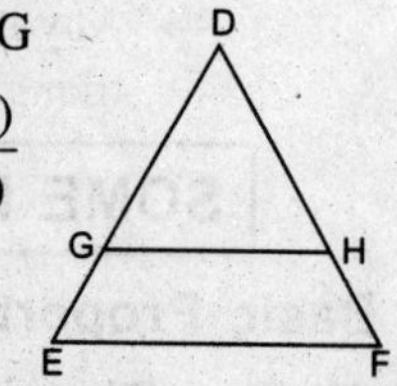

A. $\frac{2}{15}$ B. $\frac{4}{15}$
C. $\frac{4}{25}$ D. $\frac{2}{25}$

12. Sides of two similar triangles are in the ratio of 5 : 11 then ratio of their areas is :
A. 25 : 11 B. 25 : 121
C. 125 : 121 D. 121 : 25

13. If ΔABC ~ ΔADE and ar (Δ ADE) = 9 ar (Δ ABC) then $\frac{BC}{DE}$ is equal to :

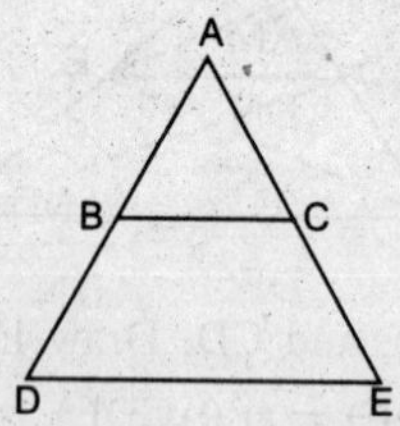

A. $\frac{1}{3}$ B. $\frac{1}{9}$
C. $\frac{3}{4}$ D. None of these

14. In a triangle a line is drawn from the mid-point of one side of and parallel to another side then
A. the line bisects the whole traingle
B. bisects the third side
C. bisects the opposite angle
D. None of these

15. If in a ΔABC, ∠B = ∠C and BD = CE then which of the following is true
A. DE = $\frac{1}{2}$ BC B. DE || BC
C. (A) and (B) D. None of these

ANSWERS

1	2	3	4	5	6	7	8	9	10
C	C	D	C	C	C	C	D	C	C
11	**12**	**13**	**14**	**15**					
C	B	A	B	B					

EXPLANATORY ANSWERS

10. According to equestion

$\angle A = \angle D$ and $\dfrac{ar(\Delta ABC)}{ar(\Delta DEF)} = \dfrac{9}{25}$

Since, $AB = AC$ (given) ....(*i*)

$DE = DF$ (given) ....(*ii*)

Dividing (i) by (ii)

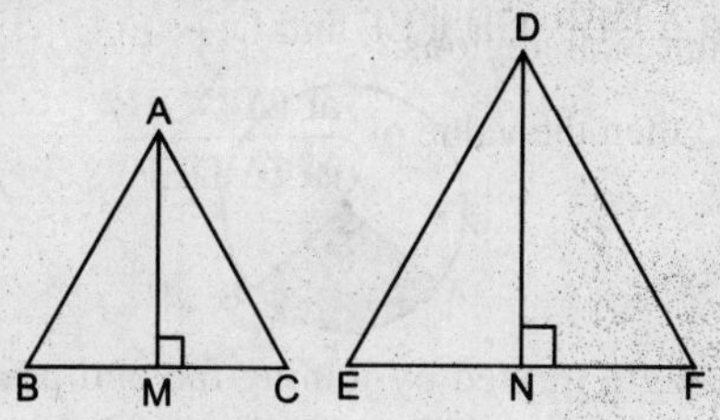

$$\frac{AB}{DE} = \frac{AC}{DF} \quad ...(iii)$$

Hence, $\Delta ABC \sim \Delta DEF$

[By SAS criterion of similar Δs]

In ΔAMC and ΔDNF

$\angle AMC = \angle DNF = 90°$

$\angle C = \angle F$ (because $\Delta ABC \sim \Delta DEF$)

$\therefore \angle AMC \sim DNF$

(By AA Criterion of similar Δs)

$$\therefore \quad \frac{AC}{DF} = \frac{AM}{DN}$$

and, $$\frac{ar(\Delta ABC)}{ar(DEF)} = \frac{AC^2}{DF^2} = \frac{AM^2}{DN^2}$$

$$\therefore \quad \frac{AM^2}{DN^2} = \frac{9}{25}$$

$$\Rightarrow \quad \frac{AM}{DN} = \frac{3}{5}$$

Hence required ratio = 3 : 5

11. $\dfrac{DG}{EG} = \dfrac{2}{3} \therefore \dfrac{DG}{DE} = \dfrac{2}{2+3} = \dfrac{2}{5}$

In ΔDGH and ΔDEF, $\angle D = \angle D$

$\angle DGH = \angle DEF$

(Since, $GH \parallel EF$ and DE is the transversal among corresponding angles)

$\therefore \Delta DGH \sim \Delta DEF$

(By AA criterion of similar triangles)

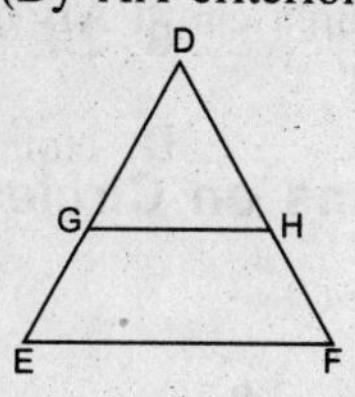

$$\therefore \quad \frac{ar(\Delta DGH)}{ar(\Delta DEF)} = \frac{DG^2}{DE^2} = \frac{2^2}{5^2} = \frac{4}{25}$$

12. Since, ratio of area of two similar traingles = ratio of square of corresponding sides

ratio of sides = 5 : 11

$\therefore$ ratio of their areas $= (5)^2 : (11)^2 = 25 : 121$.

13. From question,

$ar(\Delta ADE) = 9\ ar(\Delta ABC)$

or, $$\frac{ar(\Delta ABC)}{ar(\Delta ADE)} = \frac{1}{9} = \frac{BC^2}{DE^2}$$

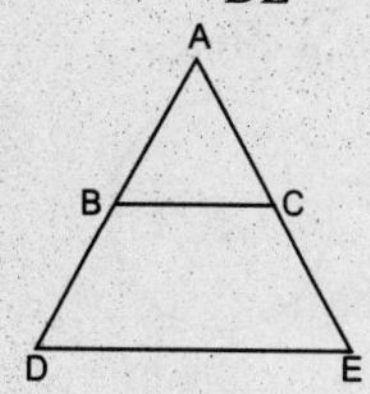

Hence, $$\frac{BC}{DE} = \sqrt{\frac{1}{9}} = \frac{1}{3}$$

14. From question, In ΔABC, D is the mid-point of AB and DE is drawn parallel to BC and it meets at E on AC.

Since, $DE \parallel BC$ (By B.P. Theorem)

$$\frac{AD}{DB} = \frac{AE}{EC} \quad ...(i)$$

also, $AD = DB$ ($\because$ D is mid-point)

$$\therefore \quad \frac{AD}{DB} = 1$$

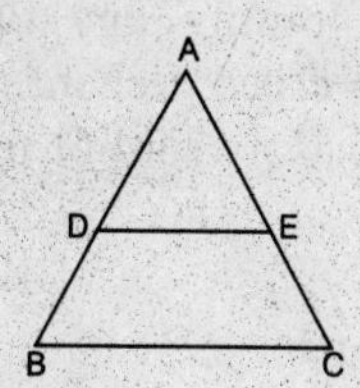

Now, $\dfrac{AE}{EC} = 1$ (From ...(*i*))

$\Rightarrow AE = EC$

Hence, the line bisects the third line

15. According to questions, $\angle B = \angle C$ (given)

$\Rightarrow AB = AC$ (*i*)

and, $BD = CE$ (*ii*)

Subtracting (*ii*) from (*i*), $AB - BD = AC - CE$

$\Rightarrow AD = AE$ (*iii*)

Dividing (*iii*) by (*ii*)

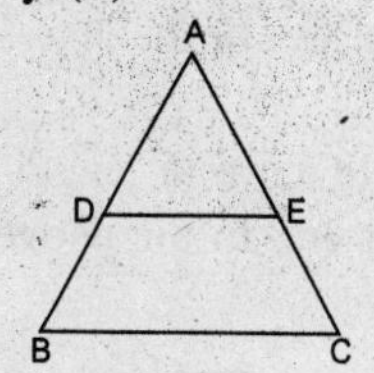

$$\frac{AD}{BD} = \frac{AE}{CE}$$

$\therefore DE \parallel BC$ [By converse of BP Theorem]

Hence, option (B) is true.

Circle and Its Chord

A circle is a set of those points in a plane that are at a given constant distance from a given fixed point in the plane. The fixed point is called the **centre of the circle** and the constant distance of every point on the circle from its centre of called the **radius of the circle**.

Things to Remember

1. Locus of a point moving in a plane such that its distance from a fixed point in the same plane remains constant is called a circle.

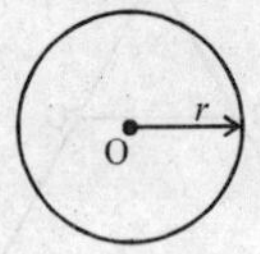

2. The fixed point O is called its centre and the constant distance r is called the radius.
3. The path traced by the moving point as described above is called the circumference of the circle.
4. The part of the plane containing the circle that consists the circle and its interior is called the circular region.

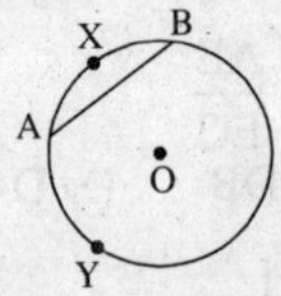

5. Line segment joining any two points on the circumference is called a chord of the circle. In the above figure AB is a chord of the circle.

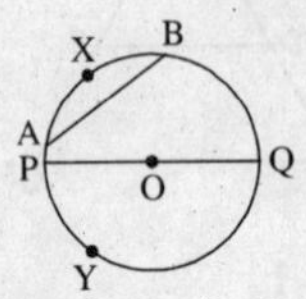

6. The chord passing through the centre of the circle is called its diameter.
   In the above figure PQ is a diameter of the circle.
7. Diameter is the longest chord of the circle.
8. Any fraction of the circumference is called an arc of the circle.
9. The remaining part of the circumference is called the alternate segment of the circle with respect to the arc.
10. An arc of a circle smaller in length than the semicircle is called a minor arc. In the above figure arc AXB is a minor arc.
11. An arc of a circle more in length than the semicircle is called a major arc. In the above figure arc AYB is a major arc.

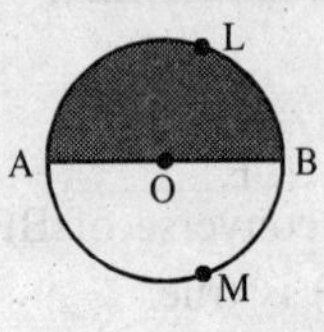

12. Diameter of a circle divides its circumference into two equal arcs. Each of them is called a semicircle.
13. The part of the plane containing the semicircle that consists the semi-circle, the enclosing diameter and its interior is called the semicircular region.
    In the above figure region ALB and region BMA are semicircular regions.

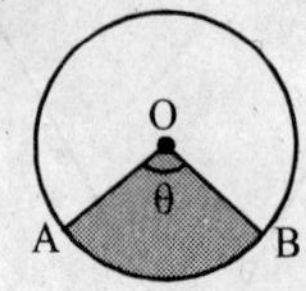

14. The angle formed by joining the end points of an arc to the centre of the circle is said to be the angle subtended by an arc at the centre of the circle. In the above figure, θ is the degree measure of arc AB.
15. The part of the plane containing the circle that consists of the arc enclosing radii and its interior is called the sector of the circle. In the above figure AOB is sector of the circle.
16. A chord of the circle other than a diameter divides the circular region into two unequal parts.
    Each of these parts is called a segment. The larger part is called the major segment and the smaller is called the minor segment.

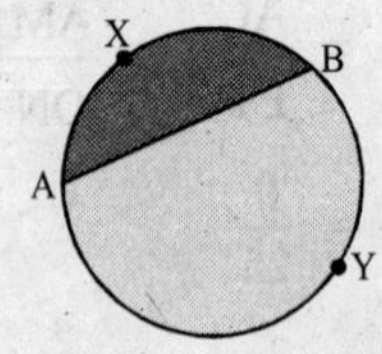

In the above figure segment AXB is a minor segment and segment BYA is the major segment.

17. Two circles in a plane are said to be concentric if they have same centre but different radii.
18. The chord formed by joining the end points of an arc of a circle is called its corresponding chord.

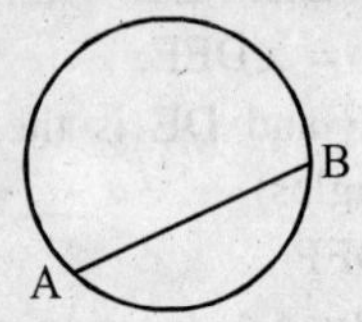

In the given figures chord AB is the corresponding chord of arc AB.

Important Theorems on Circles

1.

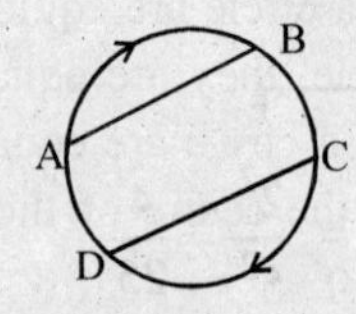

(*a*) If two arcs of a circle are equal then their corresponding chords are also equal.

AB = CD

$\Leftrightarrow$ arcAB = arcCD.

(*b*) If two chords of a circle are equal then their corresponding arcs are also equal.

2.

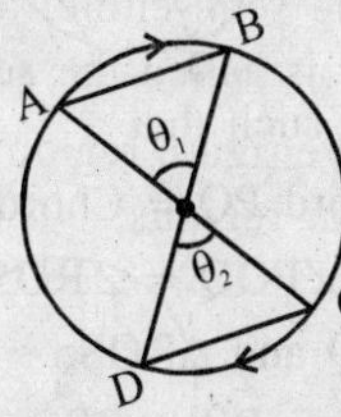

(*a*) If two chords of a circle are equal then they subtend equal angles at the centre of the circle.

(*b*) If two chords of a circle subtend equal angles at the centre of a circle then they are equal

$AB = CD \Leftrightarrow \theta_1 = \theta_2$

3.

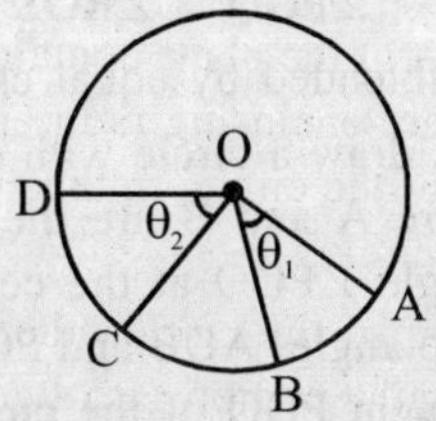

(*a*) If two arcs of a circle have same degree measure then they are equal.

arc AB = arc CD

$\Leftrightarrow \theta_1 = \theta_2$

(*b*) If two arcs of a circle are equal then their degree measures are also equal.

4.

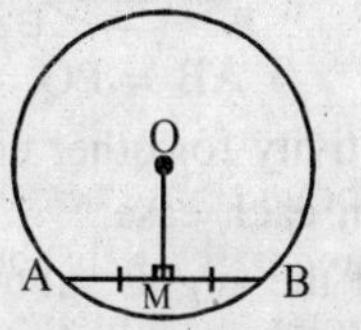

(*a*) Perpendicular to a chord from the centre of the circle bisects the chord.

(*b*) Line segment joining the centre of the circle to the mid point of the chord is perpendicular to the chord.

$OM \perp AB \Leftrightarrow M$ is the mid point of AB.

5.

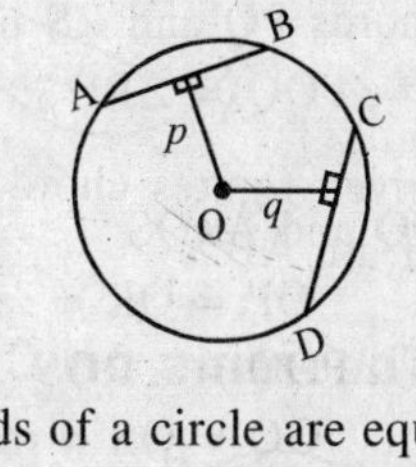

(*a*) If two chords of a circle are equidistant from the centre of the circle, they are equal.

(*b*) If two chords of a circle are equal then they are equidistant from the centre of the circle

$AB = CD \Leftrightarrow p = q$

6.

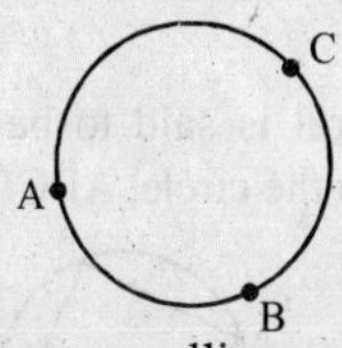

Through any three non collinear points, passes one and only one circle. A, B and C are three non-collinear points in a plane then one and only one circle passes through them.

7. Perpendicular bisector of a chord of a circle passes through the centre of the circle.

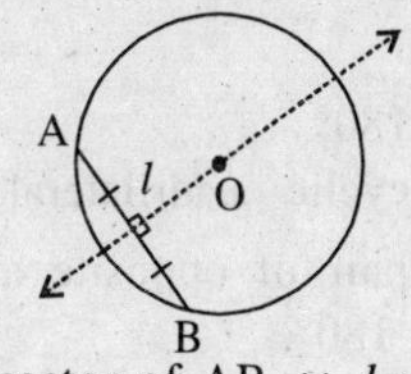

l is the $\perp$ bisector of AB $\Leftrightarrow$ l passes through O.

8.

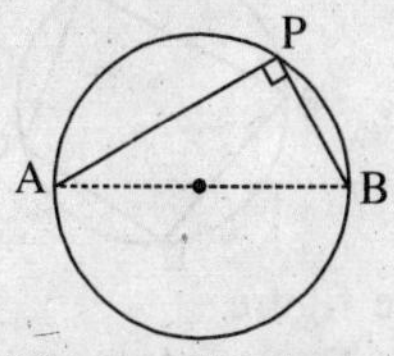

(*a*) **Theorem of Thales:** Angle in a semicircle is a right angle.

(*b*) If an arc subtends a right angle at any point in its alternate segment then it is a semi-circle.

$\overset{\frown}{APB}$ is a semicircle $\Leftrightarrow \angle APB = 90°$

9. Angles in the same segment of a circle are equal

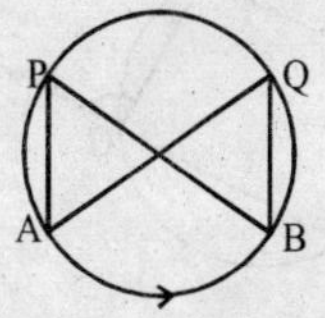

In the above figure $\angle APB = \angle AQB$

10.

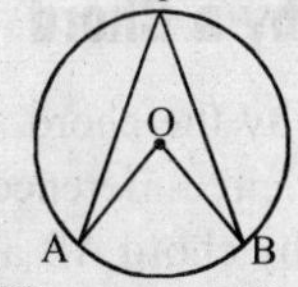

Degree Measure Theorem : Degree measure of an arc is twice the angle subtended by it at any point on the alternate segment of the circle with respect to the arc. In the above figure $\angle AOB = 2\angle APB$

11. If a line segment joining two points subtends equal angles at two other points on same side of the line containing the two points then the four points are concyclic.

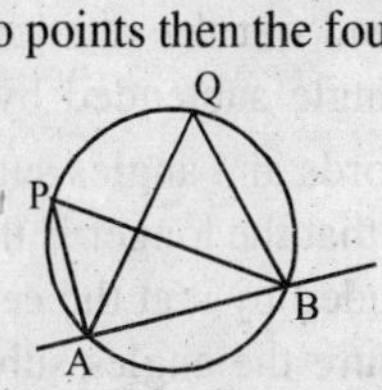

In the above figure $\angle APB = \angle AQB$, then A,B,Q and P are concylic.

Definition

A quadrilateral is said to be cyclic if all of its four vertices lie on the circle, ABCD is a cyclic quadrilateral.

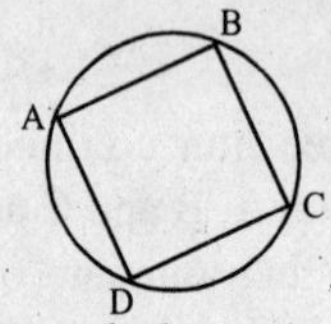

12. If in a quadrilateral the pair of opposite angles is supplementary then the quadrilateral is cyclic.
In the above figure

$\angle A + \angle C = 180°$

or $\angle B + \angle D = 180°$.

$\Rightarrow$ ABCD is cyclic quadrilateral.

13. Sum of each pair of opposite angles of a cyclic quadrilateral is 180°.

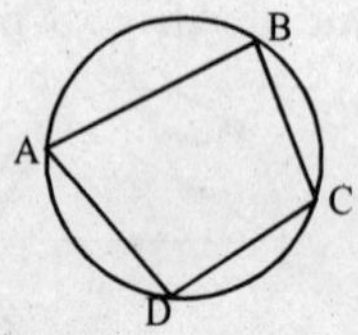

In the above figure
ABCD is cyclic quadrilateral

$\Rightarrow \angle A + \angle C = 180°$

and $\angle B + \angle D = 180°$.

14. Exterior angle of a cyclic quadrilateral is equal to its opposite interior angle.

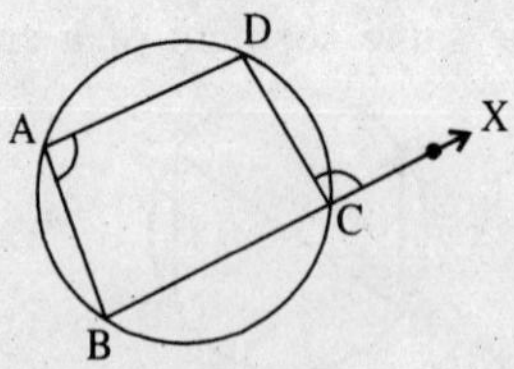

In the above figure, $\angle DCX = \angle A$

Angle subtended by a Chord

The angle subtended by the chord AB at a point C (not on the chord AB) on the circumference of the circle is $\angle ACB$. The angle subtended by chord AB at the centre O is $\angle AOB$.

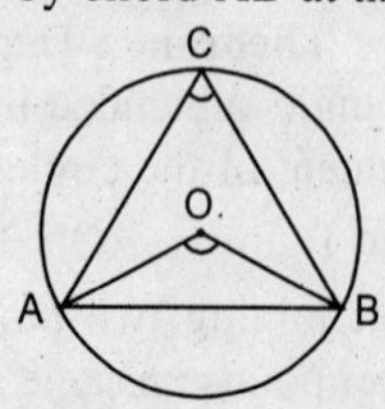

Activity: Let us find out the relation between the size of the chord and the angle subtended by it at the centre.

We draw many chords and angles subtended by them at the centre. We observe that the longer is the chord the bigger will be the angle subtended by it at the centre. We draw two equal chords and measure the angles subtended by them at the centre. We find that the angles subtended by them at the centre are equal.

Theorem 1. Equal chords of a circle subtend equal angles at the centre.

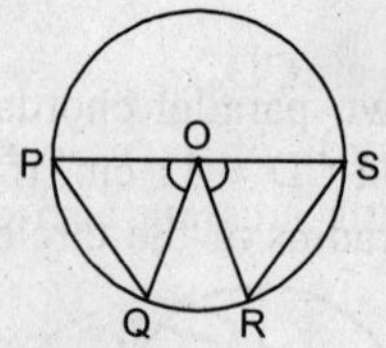

Given. A circle such that

Chord PQ = Chord RS

To prove, $\angle POQ = \angle ROS$

Proof. In ΔPOQ and ΔROS,

$PQ = RS$

$OP = OS =$ radius

$OQ = OR =$ radius

$\therefore \Delta POQ \cong \Delta ROS$

(By SSS Theorem of congruence)

$\Rightarrow \angle POQ = \angle ROS$ (C.P.C.T.)

$\Rightarrow$ Angles subtended by equal chords are equal.

Activity, We draw a circle with centre O and draw an angle AOB, where A and B are the points on the circle. Draw another angle $\angle POQ$ at the centre equal to $\angle AOB$. Separate these two angles AOB and POQ. If we put segment AOB on the segment POQ of the circle, we find that they cover each other.

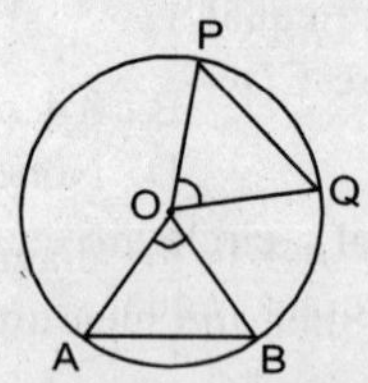

So, AB = PQ

Repeat this activity for other equal angles. We find the chords are equal in each case.

Theorem 2. If the angles subtended by the two chords at the centre of a circle are equal, then the chords are equal.

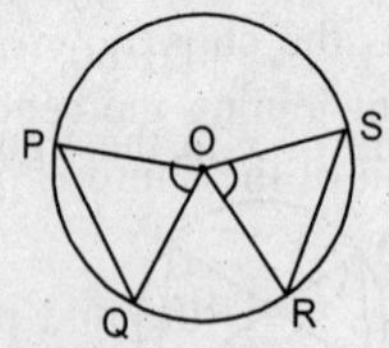

Given. Two chords PQ and RS of a circle in which,

$\angle POQ = \angle ROS$; PQ = RS

To prove.

Proof. In ΔPOQ and ΔROS

$OP = OR =$ radius

$\angle POQ = \angle ROS$

$OQ = OS =$ radius

$\therefore \Delta POQ \cong \Delta ROS$

[By SAS Theorem of congruence]

$\Rightarrow PQ = RS$ (C.P.C.T.)

Hence, Chords are equal.

EXERCISE

1. AB and CD are two parallel chords of a circle such that AB = 5 cm and CD = 11 cm. If distance between them is 3 cm then radius of the circle is

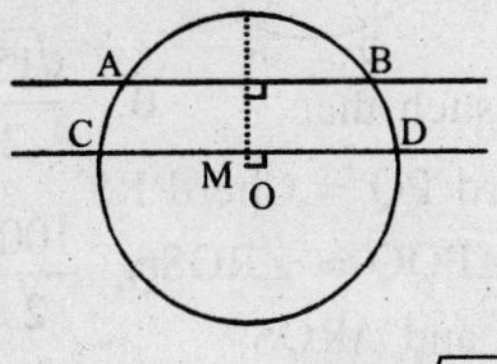

A. $2\sqrt{146}$ cm B. $\sqrt{146}$ cm
C. $\frac{\sqrt{146}}{2}$ cm D. None of these

2. The maximum number of common tangents to any pair of circles in the same plane is :
A. 4 B. 5
C. 2 D. 3

3. Find the length of a chord which is at a distance of 3 cm from the centre of a circle of radius 5 cm.
A. 2 cm B. 6 cm
C. 8 cm D. 10 cm

4. If AB and AC are two chords of a circle of radius 5 cm such that AB = AC = $4\sqrt{5}$ cm then the length of the chord BC is :
A. 8 cm B. 8.4 cm
C. 9 cm D. None of these

5. In the given figure AB is the diameter of the circle, PM bisects ∠APB then the measure of ∠ABM is :

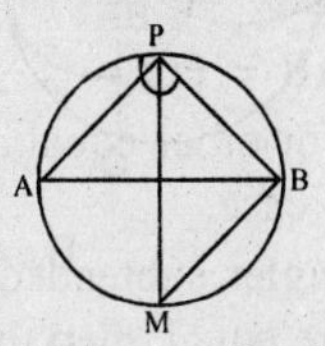

A. 45° B. 30°
C. 15° D. 60°

6. Determine the value of x in the figure given below.

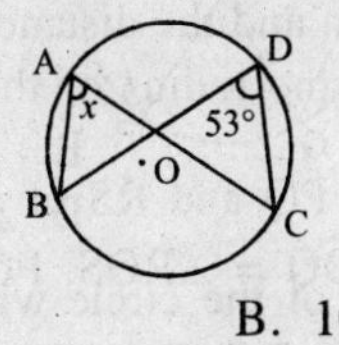

A. 53° B. 106°
C. 26.5° D. 100°

7. Determine the value of x in the figure given below.

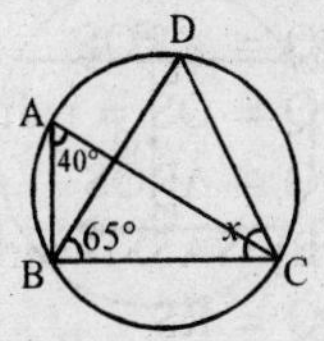

A. 40° B. 75°
C. 65° D. 105°

8. Determine the value of x in the figure given below.

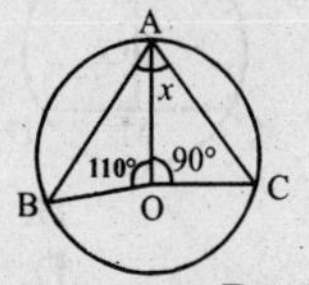

A. 80° B. 100°
C. 90° D. 110°

9. PQ is a diameter and PQRS is a cyclic quadrilateral. If ∠PSR = 150°, then measure of ∠RPQ is :

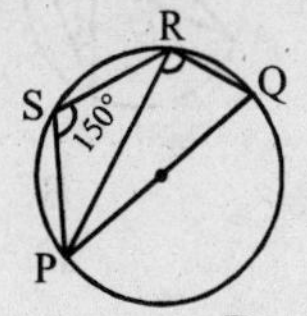

A. 90° B. 60°
C. 30° D. None of these

10. Determine the value of x in the figure given below.

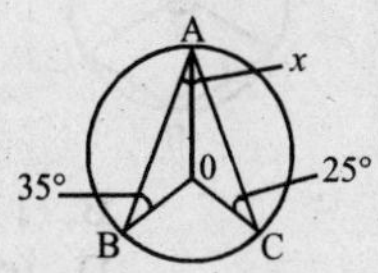

A. 35° B. 25°
C. 30° D. 60°

11. Determine the value of x in the figure given below.

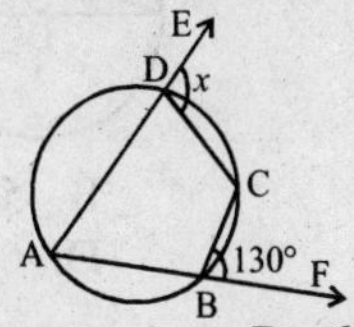

A. 65° B. 60°
C. 50° D. 80°

12. Chords AB and CD of a circle meet inside the circle at D. If PA = 4 cm, AB = 7 cm and PD = 6 cm then length of CD is :

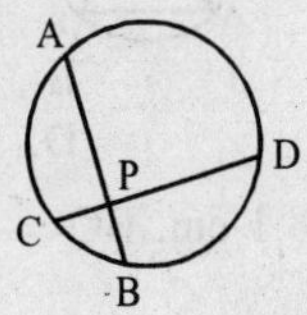

A. 8 cm B. 6 cm
C. 2 cm D. None of these

13. Chords AB and CD of a circle when product meet out side the circle at P, If AB = 4 cm; BP = 3 cm and CP = 14 cm then the length of CD is

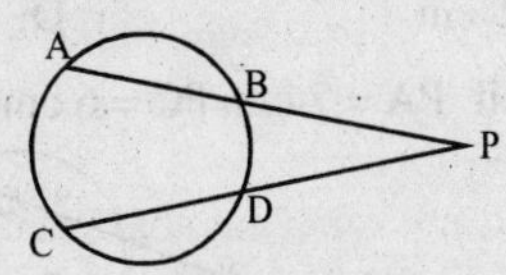

A. 3 cm B. 4.5 cm
C. 6 cm D. None of these

14. AB and CD are two parallel chords of circle such that AB = 10 cm and CD = 24 cm. If LM = 17 cm then the diameter of the circle is

A. 13 cm B. 26 cm
C. 14 cm D. None of these

15. In the given figure determine the value of x.

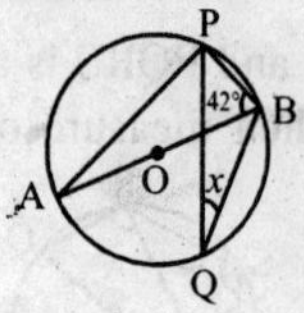

A. 48° B. 42°
C. 60° D. 38°

16. In the given figure determine the value of x.

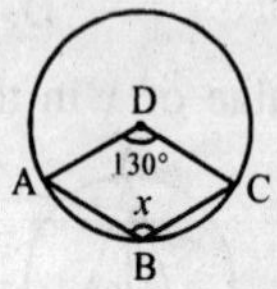

A. 90° B. 115°
C. 130° D. 65°

17. Find x

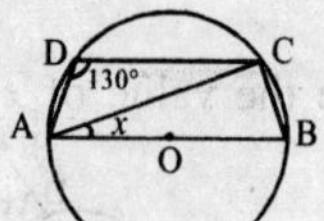

A. 40° B. 50°
C. 30° D. 60°

18. If O is the centre of the circle and ΔAOB is an equilateral triangle, then the measure of ΔACB is

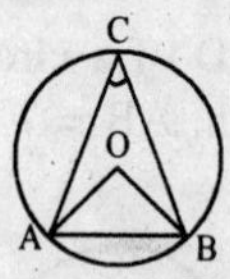

A. 60° B. 30°
C. 90° D. 75°

19. Find x if AO = 8.1 cm, BO = 5 cm, OC = 9 cm and OD = x cm.

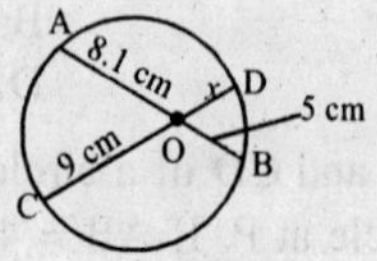

A. 4.1 cm B. 4.1 cm
C. 4.2 cm D. 4.5 cm

20. Find x if PA = 7 cm, PC = 6 cm, AB = 9 cm and CD = x

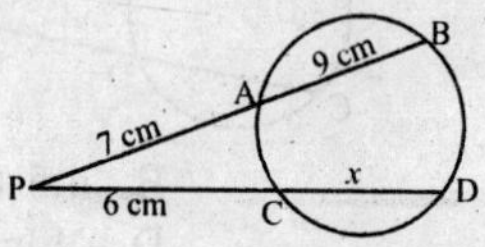

A. 12.0 cm B. 12.6 cm
C. 12.66 cm D. 12.67 cm

21. Two chords AB, CD of lengths 5 cm, 11 cm respectively of a circle are parallel. If the distance between AB and CD is 3 cm, find the radius of the circle.

A. $\frac{\sqrt{146}}{2}$ B. $\frac{\sqrt{150}}{2}$

C. $\frac{150}{3}$ D. $\frac{100}{2}$

22. O is the centre of the circle of radius 5 cm, OP ⊥ AB, OQ ⊥ CD, AB ∥ CD, AB = 6 cm and CD = 8 cm. Determine PQ.

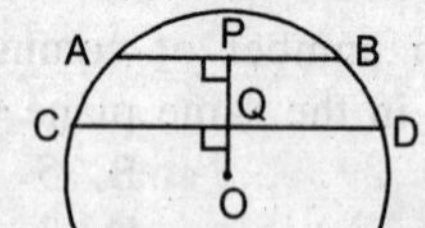

A. 5 cm B. 10 cm
C. 1 cm D. 2 cm

23. Two circle with centres A and B and of radii 5 cm and 3 cm, respectively touch each other internally. If the perpendicular bisector of segment AB meets the bigger circle in P and Q. Find the length of PQ.

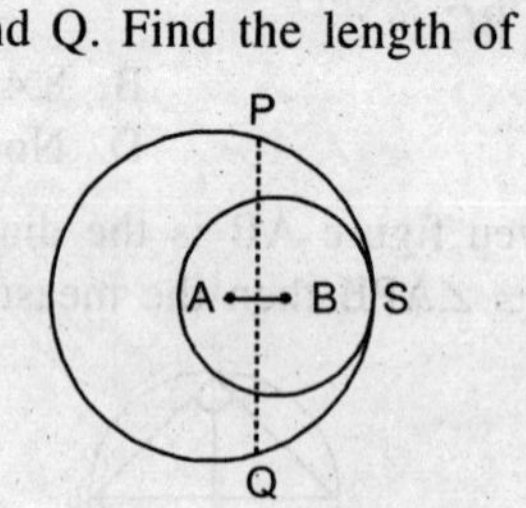

A. $4\sqrt{6}$ cm B. $3\sqrt{2}$ cm
C. $5\sqrt{4}$ cm D. $3\sqrt{5}$ cm

24. AB and CD are two parallel chords of a circle, which are an opposite sides of the centre, such that AB = 10 cm, CD = 24 cm and the distance between AB and CD is 17 cm. Find the radius of the circle.

A. 15 cm B. 13 cm
C. 14 cm D. 20 cm

25. O is the centre of the circle with radius 5 cm. OP ⊥ AB, OQ ⊥ CD, AB ∥ CD, AB = 8 cm and CD = 6 cm. Determine PQ.

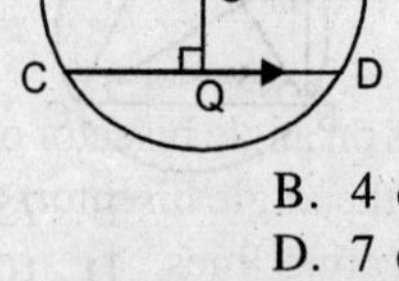

A. 3 cm B. 4 cm
C. 5 cm D. 7 cm

ANSWERS

1	2	3	4	5	6	7	8	9	10
C	A	C	A	A	A	B	A	B	D
11	12	13	14	15	16	17	18	19	20
C	A	D	B	A	B	A	B	D	C
21	22	23	24	25					
A	C	A	B	D					

EXPLANATORY ANSWERS

1. Let OM = x

Then $x^2+\left(\frac{11}{2}\right)^2=r^2$ and $(x+3)^2+\left(\frac{5}{2}\right)^2=r^2$

Then, $x^2+6x+9+\frac{25}{4}=x^2+\frac{121}{4}$

$\Rightarrow 6x = 15 \Rightarrow x = 2.5$ cm

Thus, $r^2=(2.5)^2+\frac{121}{4}=\frac{146}{4} \Rightarrow r=\frac{\sqrt{146}}{2}$ cm

3. Length of chord = $2\sqrt{5^2-3^2}=8$ cm.

4. Let OP = x and BP = y

Then $x^2+y^2=25$ and $(5+x)^2+y^2=80$

Solving these two, we get, y = BP = 4 cm

Thus, BC = 8 cm.

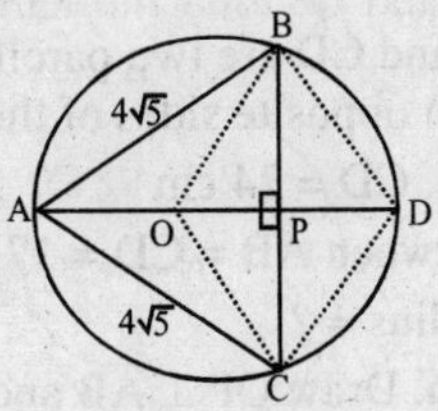

5. $\angle ABM=\angle APM=\frac{1}{2}\angle APB=\frac{1}{2}\times 90°=45°$

6. As angle in the same segment are equal.

$x = 53°$

7. $x+65°+40°=180°$

$x = 75°$

8. $x=\frac{1}{2}\left[(180°-110°)+(180°-90°)\right]$

$=\frac{1}{2}(70°+90°)=80°$

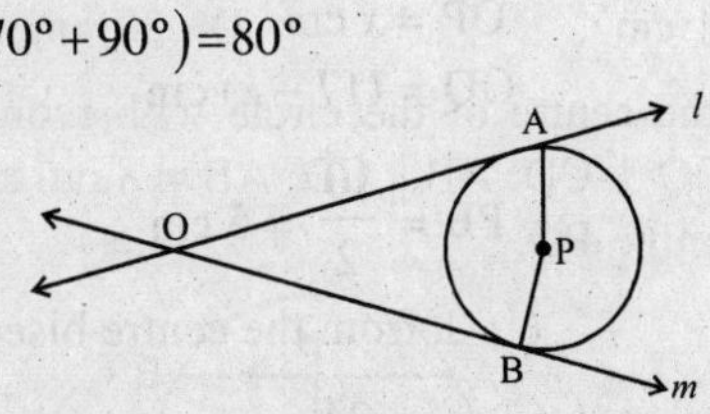

Let P be the centre of a circle touching l and m. Clearly, AP = BP.

Hence, P lies on angle bisector of $\angle$ AOB. Hence, locus of P will be the angle bisectors of the angles formed by these intersecting lines.

9. $\angle PQR=180°-150°=30°$

$\angle PRQ=90°$ (Angle of a semicircle)

$\angle RPQ+90°+30°=180°$

$\Rightarrow \angle RPQ=60°$

10. $\angle OAB=\angle OBA\ (\because OA=OB)$

$\angle OAB=35°$

Similarly, $\angle AOC=25°$

$\therefore \angle x=35°+25°=60°$

12. Use $PA\times PB=PC\times PD$

4 × (7 – 4) = 6 × PC

$\Rightarrow$ PC = 2 cm

CD = PC + PD = 2 + 6 = 8 cm.

13. Use $PA\times PB=PC\times PD$

$\Rightarrow (4+3)\times 3=14\times PD \Rightarrow$ PD = 1.5 cm

$\Rightarrow$ CD = PC – PD = 14 – 1.5 = 12.5 cm.

14. Let OL = x.

Then OM$(17-x)$

Also LB = 5 cm,

MD = 12 cm.

Then $x^2+25=r^2$ and $(17-x)^2+144=r^2$

Solving these we get

x = 12 cm and r = 13 cm

Thus, diameter = 2 × 13 = 26 cm.

15. $x+42°+90°=180° \Rightarrow x=48°$

18. $\angle ACB=\frac{1}{2}\angle AOB=\frac{1}{2}\times 60°=30°$

21. Given, chord AB = 5 cm, chord CD = 11 cm and AB || CD

Perpendicular distance ML between AB and CD = 3 cm

To find. Radius of the circle.

Construction, Join OB, OD and draw perpendicular bisectors OL of AB and OM of CD

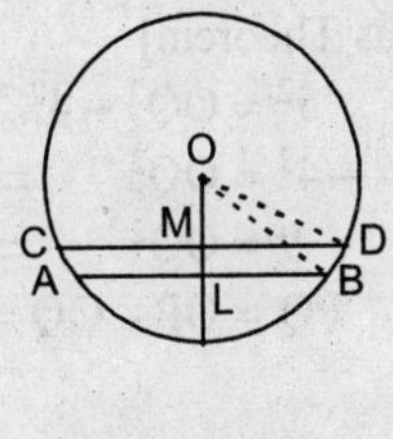

Procedure. In rt. ΔOMD,

$$OD^2 = MD^2 + OM^2$$

(By Pythagoras Theorem)

Let, $OM = x$ cm

$$\therefore \quad r^2 = \left(\frac{11}{2}\right)^2 + x^2 \quad ...(1)$$

And In rt. ΔOLB, $OB^2 = BL^2 + OL^2$

$$\Rightarrow \quad r^2 = \left(\frac{5}{2}\right)^2 + (3+x)^2 \quad ...(2)$$

From (1) and (2), we get,

$$r^2 = \left(\frac{11}{2}\right)^2 + x^2 = \left(\frac{5}{2}\right)^2 + (3+x)^2$$

$$\Rightarrow \quad \frac{121}{4} + x^2 = \frac{25}{4} + 9 + x^2 + 6x$$

$$\Rightarrow \quad x^2 - x^2 + 6x = \frac{121}{4} - \frac{25}{4} - 9$$

$$\Rightarrow \quad 6x = \frac{121 - 25 - 36}{4} = \frac{60}{4} = 15$$

$$\Rightarrow \quad x = \frac{15}{6} \text{ cm} = \frac{5}{2} \text{ cm}$$

From (1), $r^2 = \left(\frac{11}{2}\right)^2 + \left(\frac{5}{2}\right)^2 = \frac{121+25}{4} = \frac{146}{4}$

or $r = \frac{\sqrt{146}}{2}$ cm.

22. Given. A circle with centre O, such that chord AB = 6 cm, chord CD = 8 cm

AB || CD and radius of the circle = 5 cm

$OP \perp AB$ and $OQ \perp CD$

To find. PQ

Construction. Join OA and OC

Procedure. AP = 1/2, AB = 3 cm, CQ = 1/2, CD = 4 cm [Perpendicular from the centre of the circle bisects the chord]

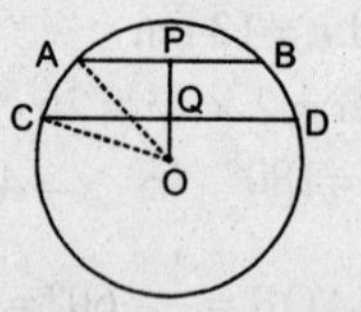

In right Δ OPA, $OA^2 = OP^2 + AP^2$ [By Pythagoras Theorem]

$\Rightarrow \quad 5^2 = OP^2 + 3^2$

$\Rightarrow \quad 5^2 - 3^2 = OP^2 \quad \Rightarrow \quad 25 - 9 = OP^2$

$\Rightarrow \quad 16 = OP^2 \quad \Rightarrow \quad 4 = OP$

In right ΔOQC, $OC^2 = OQ^2 + CQ^2$

[By Pythagoras Theorem]

$5^2 = OQ^2 + 4^2$

$\Rightarrow \quad 5^2 - 4^2 = OQ^2 \quad \Rightarrow \quad 25 - 16 = OQ^2$

$\Rightarrow \quad 9 = OQ^2 \quad \Rightarrow \quad 3 = OQ$

$\therefore \quad PQ = OP - OQ = 4 - 3 = 1$ cm.

23. Given. Two circles touch internally at S, A and B be the centres of the bigger and smaller circles, respectively. The perpendicular bisector PQ bisects AB and meets the circle at P and Q.

To find PQ

Construction. Join PA, ABS

Procedure. With given radii, we find

AS = 5 cm

BS = 3 cm

AB = 5 – 3 = 2 cm and AC = 1 cm [$\perp$ bisector bisects the chord]

PA = radius of bigger circle = 5 cm

In the right triangle ACP,

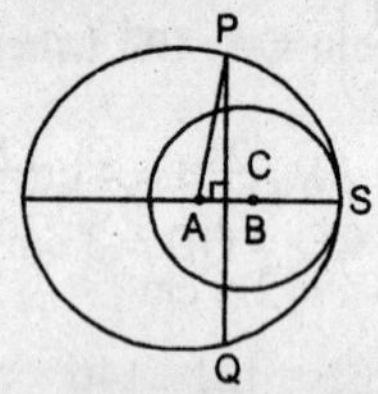

$$PC^2 = PA^2 - AC^2$$

[By Pythagoras Theorem]

$\Rightarrow \quad PC^2 = (5)^2 - (1)^2$

$\Rightarrow \quad PC^2 = 25 - 1 = 24$

$\Rightarrow \quad PC = \sqrt{24} \Rightarrow PC = 2\sqrt{6}$

$\therefore \quad PQ = 2PC = 4\sqrt{6}$ cm.

24. Given, AB and CD are two parellel chords of a circle, which are on opposite sides of the centre.

AB = 10 cm, CD = 24 cm

Distance between AB = CD = 17 cm

To find. Radius = ?

Construction. Draw $OP \perp AB$ and $OQ \perp CD$. Join OB and OD.

Procedure. Since AB || CD and $OP \perp AB$, $OQ \perp CD$

$\therefore$ Points P, O and Q are collinear.

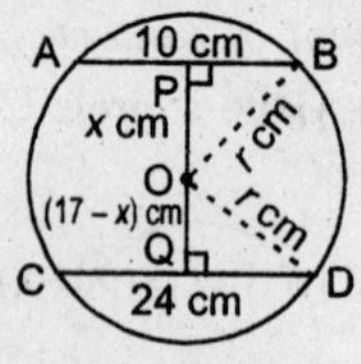

Let, $OP = x$ cm

Then, $OQ = (17 - x)$ cm

$$PB = \frac{10}{2} = 5 \text{ cm}$$

($\because \perp$ from the centre bisects the chord)

$$QD = \frac{24}{2} = 12 \text{ cm}$$

($\because \perp$ from the centre bisects the chord)

In rt. ΔOPB, $r^2 = x^2 + 5^2 \quad ...(1)$

(By Pythagoras Theorem)

In rt. ΔOQD, $r^2 = (17 - x)^2 + 12^2$ ...(2)

From (1) and (2), we have

$$x^2 + 25 = (17 - x)^2 + 12^2$$
$$\Rightarrow \quad x^2 + 25 = 289 + x^2 - 34x + 144$$
$$\Rightarrow \quad x^2 - x^2 + 34x = 289 + 144 - 25$$
$$\Rightarrow \quad 34x = 408$$
$$\Rightarrow \quad x = 12 \text{ cm}$$

Using the value of x in (1), we get,

$$r^2 = 12^2 + 5^2 = 144 + 25 = 169$$

$\therefore$ Radius, $r = 13$ cm. ($\because$ radius can't be –ve)

25. Given, AB and CD are two parallel chords. AB = 8 cm, CD = 6 cm, radius = 5 cm.

To find. PQ

Construction. Join OA, OC, where O is the centre of the circle

Procedure. AP = PB = 4 cm ...[$\because$ AB = 8 cm]

CQ = QD = 3 cm ...[$\because$ CD = 6 cm]

[$\because \perp$ from the centre of a circle on any chord of the circle bisects it]

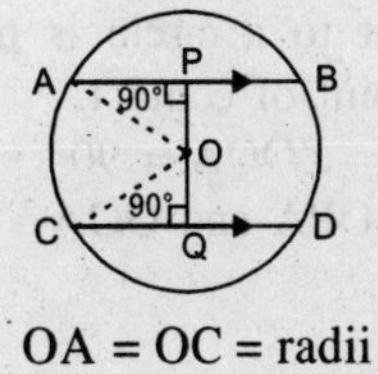

In rt. ΔOAP, OA = OC = radii of the circle = 5 cm

$OP^2 = OA^2 - AP^2$

[By Pythagoras Theorem]

$= (5)^2 - (4)^2 = 25 - 16 = 9$

$\Rightarrow$ OP = 3

In rt. ΔOCQ, $OQ^2 = OC^2 - CQ^2$

[By Pythagoras Theorem]

$(5)^2 - (3)^2 = 25 - 9 = 16$

$\Rightarrow$ OQ = 4

$\therefore$ PQ = PO + OQ = 3 + 4 = 7 cm.

Tangent

Secant

A line which interesects a circle in two distinct points is called a **secant** of the circle. In the fig. the line l intersects the circle in two distinct points A and B. The line l is a secant to the circle.

Tangent

A tangent to a circle is a line that intersects the circle at exactly one point. The point at which it meets the circle is called its point of contact and the line (tangent) is said to touch the circle at this point. In the figure, the line l meets the circle at only point A. Here A is the point of contact.

Some Important theorems on tangent

Theorem 1: *A tangent to a circle is perpendicular to the radius throught the point of contact.*

Given: A tangent AB to a circle C(O, r) with the point P as its point of contact.

To prove: OP $\perp$ AB.

Construction: Let Q be any point other that P, an AB. join OQ.

Proof: $\because$ Q is a point on the tangent AB other than the point of contact P.

$\therefore$ Q lies in the exterior of the circle.

$\therefore$ OQ > OP

i.e., OP < OQ

Thus, of all the segments that can be drawn from the centre O to any point on the line AB, OP is the shortest.

We know that the shortest segment that can be drawn from a given point to a given line perpendicular from the given point to the given line.

Hence OP $\perp$ AB.

Theorem 2: (Converse of theorem 1)

A line drawn through the end of a radius and perpendicular on it is tangent to the circle.

Given: A radius OP of a circle C(O, r) and a line APB perpendicular to OP.

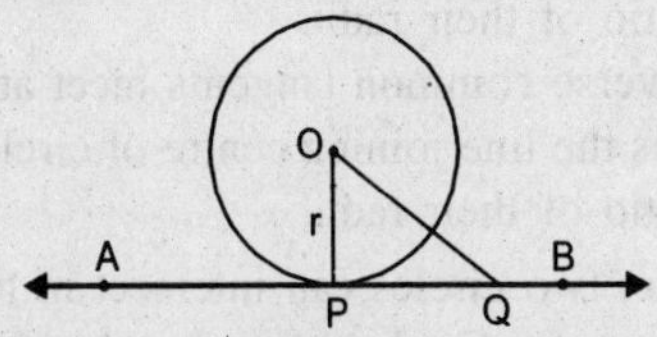

To prove: AB is the tangent to the circle at A.

Proof: Take a point Q, different from P, on line AB, since OP $\perp$ AB, OQ > OP.

$\therefore$ The point Q lies outside the circle (since OP is the shortest line segment from O to AB).

Thus every point on the line AB, other P, lies outside the circle and therefore AB meets the circle only at the point P. Hence AB is a tangent to the circle.

Theorem 3: *The lengths of the two tangents drawn from an external point to a circle are equal.*

Given: A is an external point to the circle C(O, r). AP and AQ are two tangent segments from A to the circle.

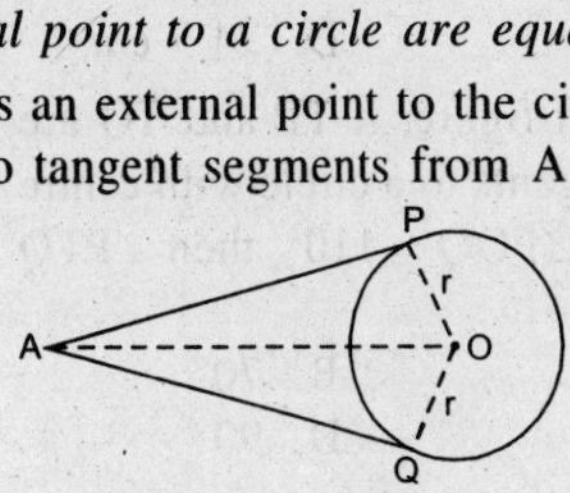

To prove: AP = AQ.

Construction: Draw line segments AP, OP and OQ.

Proof: A tangent to a circle is perpendicular to the radius through the point of contact.

∴ ∠OPA = ∠OQA = 90°

Now in right Δs OPA and OQA,

OP = OQ [each = r]

OA = OA [common]

∴ ΔOPA ≅ ΔOQA [by RHS congruence rule]

∴ AP = AQ [c.p.c.t.c.].

Common Tangents to Two circles

(*i*) Where the two circles neither intersect nor touch each other, there are FOUR common tangents, two of them are transverse & the others are direct common tangents.

(*ii*) When they intersect there are two common tangents, both of them being direct.

(*iii*) When they touch each other:

(*a*) **Externally:** there are three common tangents, two direct and one is the tangent at the point of contact.

(*b*) **Internally:** only one common tangent possible at their point of contact.

(*iv*) Length of an external common tangent & internal common tangent to the two circles is given by:

$$L_{ext} = \sqrt{d^2 - (r_1 - r_2)^2} \ \& \ L_{int} = \sqrt{d^2 - (r_1 + r_2)^2}$$

Where d = distance between the centres of the two circles. r_1 & r_2 are the radii of the two circles.

(*v*) The direct common tangents meet at a point which divides the line joining centre of circles externally in the ratio of their radii.

Transverse common tangents meet at a point which divides the line joining centre of circles internally in the ratio of their radii.

In a plane, two circles can intersect in two points, one point, or no points. Coplanar circles that intersect in one point are called **tangent circles.** Coplanar circles that have a common center are called **concentric.**

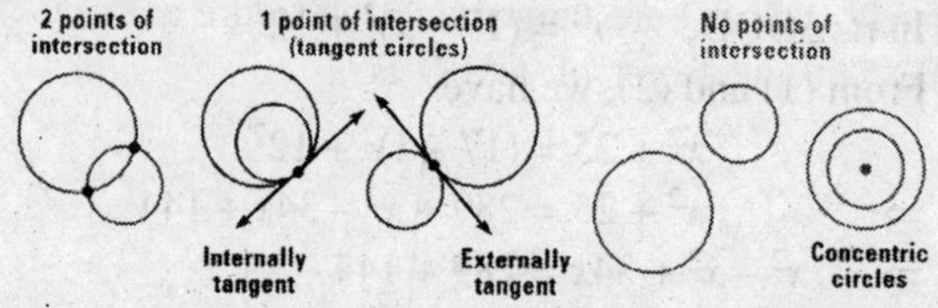

A line or segment that is tangent to two coplanar circles is called a **common tangent.** A *common internal tangent* intersects the segment that joins the centers of the two circles. A *common external tangent* does not intersect the segment that joins the centers of the two circles.

Example: Tell whether the common tangents are internal or external.

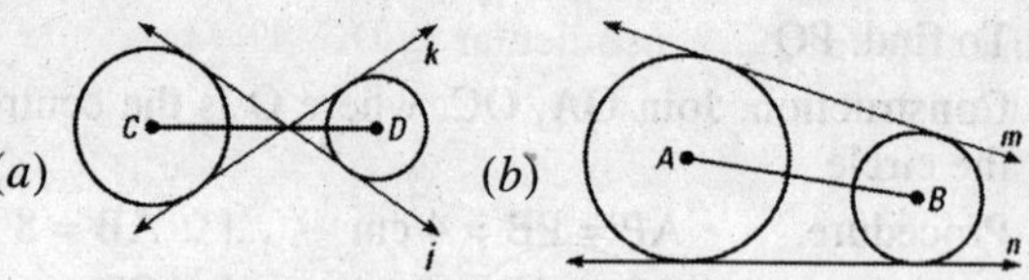

Solution: (*a*) The lines *j* and *k* intersect $\overline{CD}$, so they are common internal tangents.

(*b*) The lines m and n do not intersect $\overline{AB}$, so they are common external tangents.

In a plane, the **interior of a circle** consists of the points that are inside the circle. The **exterior of a circle** consists of the points that are outside the circle.

Example: Give the center and the radius of each circle. Describe the intersection of the two circles and describe all common tangents.

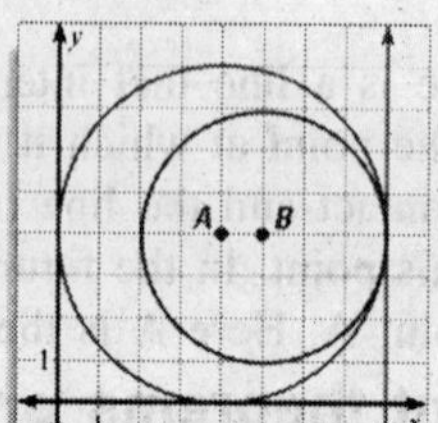

Solution: The center of ⊙A is A(4, 4) and its radius is 4. The center of ⊙B is B(5, 4) and its radius is 3. The two circles have only one point of intersection. It is the point (8, 4). The vertical line x = 8 is the only common tangent of the two circles.

EXERCISE

1. From a point Q, the length of the tangent to a circle is 24 cm and the distance from the centre is 25 cm. The radius of the circle is

A. 7 cm B. 12 cm
C. 15 cm D. 24.5 cm

2. In the given figure, if TP and TQ are the two tangents to a circle with centre O and that ∠POQ = 110°, then ∠PTQ is equal to

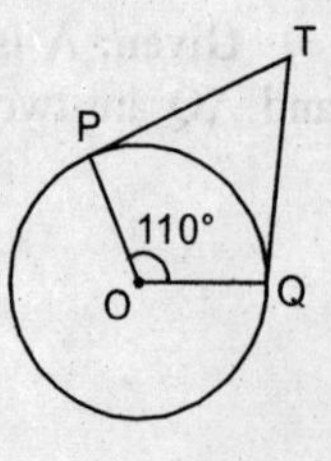

A. 60° B. 70°
C. 80° D. 90°

3. If tangents PA and PB from a point P to a circle with centre O are inclined to each other at angle of 80°, then ∠POA is equal to

A. 50° B. 60°
C. 70° D. 80°

4. In Fig., a circle touches all the four sides of a quadrilateral ABCD whose sides AB = 6 cm, BC = 7 cm and CD = 4 cm. Find AD

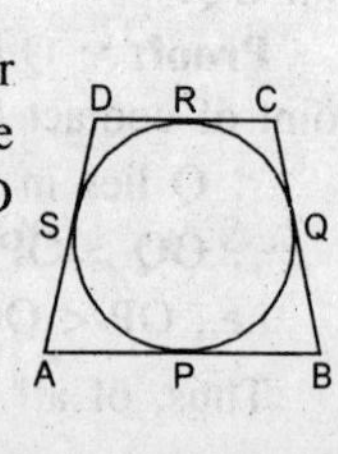

A. 2 cm B. 5 cm
C. 3 cm D. 4 cm

5. If AB, AC, PQ are tangents in the figure and AB = 5 cm. The perimeter of ΔAPQ is

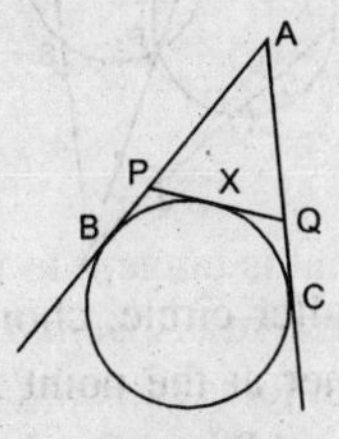

A. 8 cm B. 6 cm
C. 10 cm D. 5 cm

6. In Fig., a circle is inscribed within a quadrilateral ABCD. Given that BC = 38 cm, BQ = 27 cm and DC = 25 cm and that AD is perpendicular to DC. The radius of the circle is

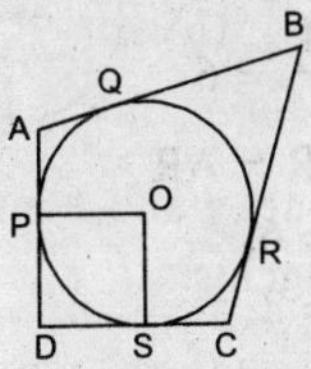

A. 10 cm B. 14 cm
C. 8 cm D. 12 cm

7. Two tangents are drawn to a circle from an external point A, touching the circle at the points P and Q. A third tangent intersects segment AP at B and segment AQ at C and touches the circle at R. If AQ = 10 units, then the perimeter of ΔABC (in units) is
A. 22.0 B. 20.5
C. 20.0 D. 40.0

8. In Fig., two circles intersect each other at points P and Q. From A on line PQ, secant AMD for one circle and secant ASR for the second one are drawn. If AM = 3, MD = 5 and AS = 4, determine SR.

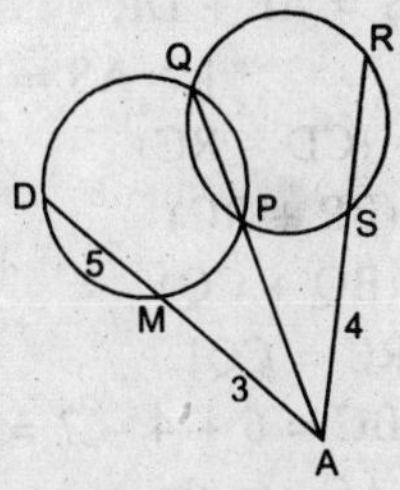

A. 2 cm B. 4 cm
C. 3 cm D. 1 cm

9. In the figure, KLMN is a cyclic quadrilateral and PQ is a tangent to the circle at K. If LN is a diameter of the circle. $\angle$KLN = 30° and $\angle$MNL = 60°. Determine $\angle$QKN

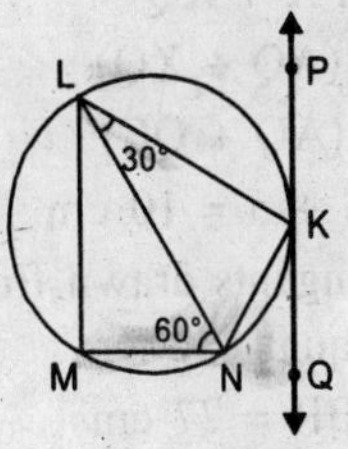

A. 30° B. 60°
C. 90° D. 100°

10. In the given Fig., PQ is tangent and O is the centre of the circle. Find EP is OP = 21, OQ = 9 and OM $\sqrt{80}$.

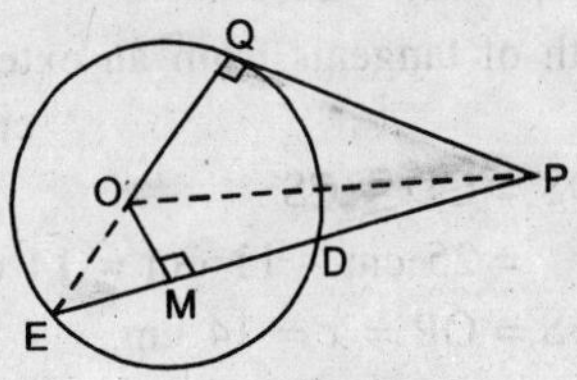

A. 10 B. 20
C. 30 D. 40

ANSWERS

1	2	3	4	5	6	7	8	9	10
A	B	A	C	C	B	C	A	A	B

EXPLANATORY ANSWERS

1. In rt. $\angle d$ ΔOTQ,

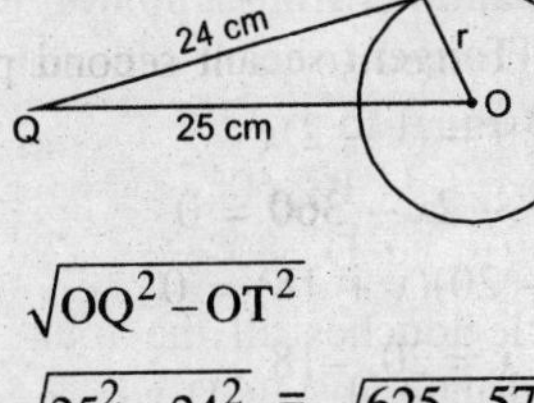

$$OT = \sqrt{OQ^2 - OT^2}$$

$$= \sqrt{25^2 - 24^2} = \sqrt{625-576} = \sqrt{49} = 7 \text{ cm}.$$

2. Since $\angle POQ + \angle PTQ = 180°$

[$\because$ $\angle OPT = 90°$, $\angle OQT = 90°$]

$\Rightarrow$ $110° + \angle PTQ = 180°$

$\Rightarrow$ $\angle PTQ = 180° - 110° = 70°$.

3. Since $\angle APB = 80°$

$\angle AOB = 180° - 80° = 100°$

$\angle PAO = \angle PBO = 90°$

Since OP bisects $\angle AOB$

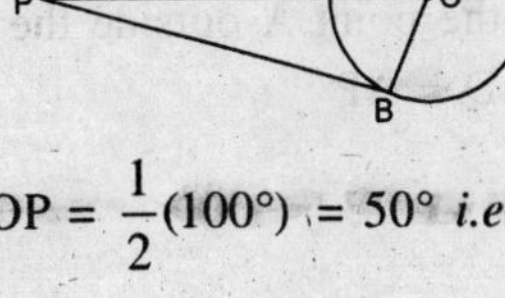

$$\angle AOP = \frac{1}{2}(100°) = 50° \; i.e. \; \angle POA = 50°.$$

4. AD = AS + DS = AP + DR

[∵ AS = AP and DS = DR]

= (AB − BP) + (CD − RC)

= AB + CD − (BP + RC)

= AB + CD − (BQ + CQ)

[∵ BP = BQ, RC = CQ]

= AB + CD − BC = 6 + 4 − 7 = 3 cm.

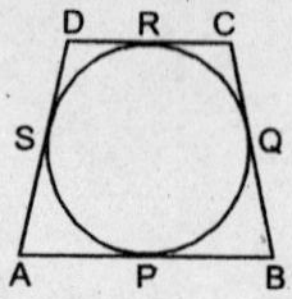

5. Since AB and AC are the tangents from the same point A

∴ AB = AC = 5 cm

Similarly, BP = PX and XQ = QC

Perimeter of ΔAPQ

= AP + AQ + PQ

= AP + AQ + (PX + XQ)

= (AP + PX) + (AQ + XQ)

= (AP + BP) + (AQ + QC)

= AB + AC = 5 + 5 = 10 cm.

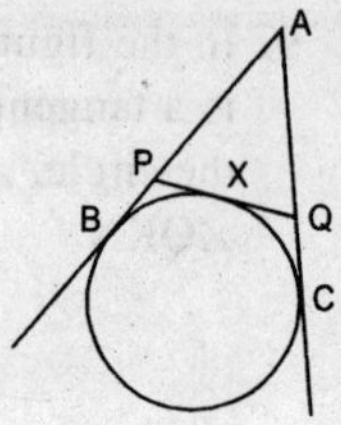

6. ∵ Lengths of tangents drawn from an external point to a circle are equal

∴ BQ = BR = 27 cm

Let x be the radius of the circle

∴ OP = OS = PD = x

CR = BC − BR

= 38 − 27 = 11 cm

Now CS = CR = 11 cm

[∵ Length of tangents from an external point to a circle are equal]

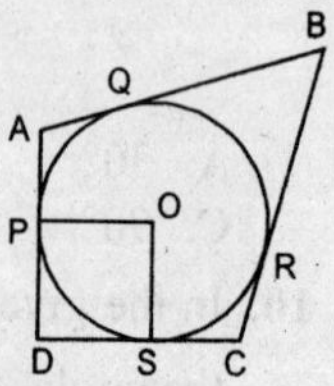

∴ DS = CD − CS

= 25 cm − 11 cm = 14 cm

But DS = OP = x = 14 cm.

Hence radius = OP = 14 cm.

7. Since the tangents to a circle from an external point are equal in length

AP = AQ = 10 units

and BP = BR }
CQ = CR }

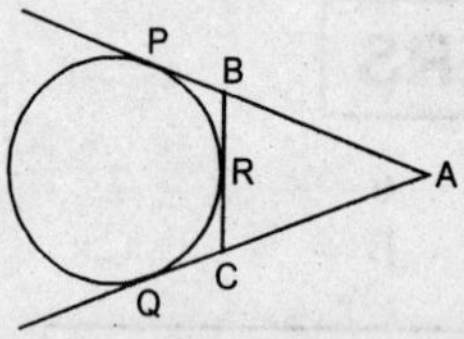

Adding these, we get,

BP + CQ = BR + CR = BC

Adding AB and AC to both sides, we get

BP + CQ + AB + AC = BC + AB + AC

⇒ (BP + AB) + (CQ + AC) = AB + BC + AC

⇒ AP + AQ = Perimeter of ΔABC

⇒ (10 + 10) units = Perimeter of ΔABC

∴ Perimeter of ΔABC = 20 units.

∴ (*iii*) is the correct answer.

8. In the larger circle, chord QP and chord DM intersect each other at the point A outside the circle

∴ AM × AD = AP ...(1)

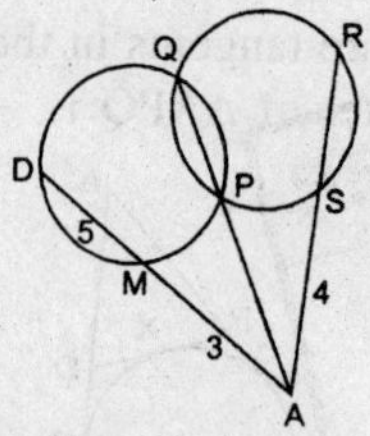

Again in the smaller circle, chord QP and chord RS intersect each other at the point A outside the circle.

∴ AS × AR = AP × AQ ...(2)

∴ AM × AD = AS × AR ...(3)

[From (1) and (2)]

Now AD = AM + MD

= 3 + 5 = 8

∴ From (3), 3 × 8 = 4 × AR

⇒ $AR = \frac{24}{4} = 6$

But AS + SR = AR

∴ 4 + SR = 6,

SR = 6 − 4 = 2.

9. KN is a chord through the point of contact K.

∴ ∠QKN = ∠KLN = 30°

[∠*s* in the alt. segment are equal]

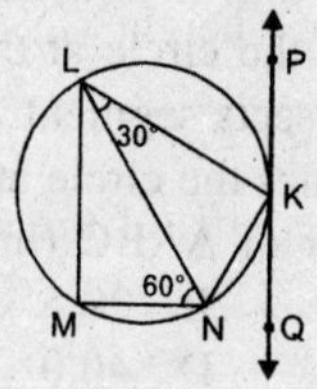

10. Join OQ and OE

In ΔOPQ, *m* ∠OQP = 90°

∴ $OQ^2 + QP^2 = OP^2$ [By Pythagoras Theorem]

⇒ $(9)^2 + QP^2 = (21)^2$

⇒ $QP^2 = (21)^2 - (9)^2 = 360$

In rt. ∠*d* ΔOME,

$OM^2 + EM^2 = OE^2$

⇒ $80 + (EM)^2 = (9)^2$

⇒ $EM^2 = 81 - 80 = 1$

⇒ $EM = +\sqrt{1} = 1$

∴ ED = 2EM = 2 × 1 = 2

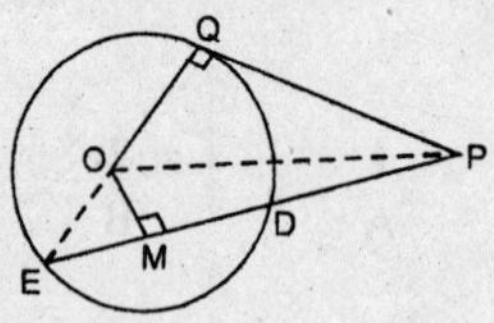

Let EP = x

Then $PQ^2 = PD \times PE$

[Tangent secant second point theorem]

∴ $360 = (x - 2)x$

⇒ $x^2 - 2x - 360 = 0$

⇒ $(x - 20)(x + 18) = 0$

⇒ $x = 20, -18$

But $x \neq -18$

Hence EP = 20.

●●●

CHAPTER 11

Mensuration

Triangle, Quadrilaterals, Regular Polygons

In mensuration we often have to deal with the problem of finding the areas and perimeters of plane figures.

Triangle

1. Perimeter = 3 × side
2. Area = $\frac{1}{2}\times$ base $\times$ height , or

Area = $\sqrt{s(s-a)(s-b)(s-c)}$

where *a, b, c,* are the lengths of the sides of triangle and *s* $=\frac{a+b+c}{2}$

Right Angled Triangle : It is one where one of the angles is right angle, i.e., 90°.

1. $(\text{Hypotenuse})^2 = (\text{Perpendicular})^2 + (\text{Base})^2$
2. Area = $\frac{1}{2}\times$ Base $\times$ Perpendicular

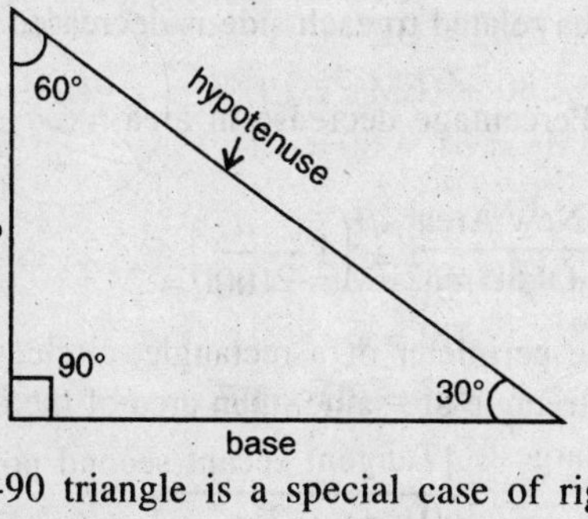

N.B. : 30-60-90 triangle is a special case of right angled triangle, where the three angles are equal to 30°, 60° and 90°.

Here,

3. Side opposite to the angle 30°

$=\frac{1}{2}\times$ Hypotenuse

4. Side opposite to the angle 60°

$=\frac{\sqrt{3}}{2}\times$ Hypotenuse

Equilateral Triangle : All three sides are equal in length and all three angles are equal to 60°

1. Area = $\frac{\sqrt{3}}{4}\times(\text{Side})^2$ 2. Area = $\frac{(\text{Height})^2}{\sqrt{3}}$
3. Height = $\frac{\sqrt{3}}{2}\times$ side 4. Perimeter = 3 × side

Isosceles Triangle : Two sides are equal in lengths.

1. Area = $\frac{b}{4}\sqrt{4a^2-b^2}$

where a = lengths of opposite sides

b = length of unequal side

2. In an isosceles right triangle,

(*a*) Hypotenuse = $\sqrt{2}\times$ congruent side (a)

(*b*) Area = $\frac{1}{2}\times a^2$

(*c*) Perimeter = $\sqrt{2}\times a\left(\sqrt{2}+1\right)$

Quadrilaterals

Rectangle:

1. Area = length(l) × breadth(b)
2. Perimeter = $2(l + b)$
3. Diagonal = $\sqrt{l^2+b^2}$
4. Area of the path (inside of the rectangle)

$= 2x\ (l + b - 2x)$

where, x is the width of path.

5. Area of the path (Outside of the rectangle) = $2x\ (l + b + 2x)$

Square:

1. Area = $(\text{Side})^2$
2. Perimeter = $4 \times$ side
3. Diagonal = side $\times \sqrt{2}$
4. Area of path (outside of square) = $4x \times (a + x)$ [where a = side, x = width of path]
5. Area of path (inside of square) $= 4x \times (a - x)$

Parallelogram: In parallelogram opposite sides are parallel and equal. The two diagonals are not always equal but they bisect each other at the point of intersection.

Area = Base × Height.

Trapezium : It is a quadrilateral whose one pair of opposite sides is parallel. Other two opposite sides are oblique.

1. Area $= \frac{1}{2} \times \text{Height} \times (\text{Sum of parallel sides})$. Here, height is the distance between the two parallel sides.
2. Median $= \left(\frac{1}{2} \times \text{Sum of parallel side}\right)$. Here, median is the segment joining the midpoints of oblique sides.
3. Height $= \frac{2}{K}\sqrt{s(s-k)(s-c)(s-d)}$

   (where $k = a - b$, *i.e.*, the difference between the parallel sides and c and d are the two non-parallel sides.)

   Also $s = \frac{k+c+d}{2}$

Rhombus : It is parallelogram whose all sides are equal and diagonals are bisect each other at right angle.

1. Area $= \frac{1}{2} \times$ Product of diagonals
2. Side $= \sqrt{\left(\frac{d_1}{2}\right)^2 + \left(\frac{d_2}{2}\right)^2}$,

   where d_1 and d_2 are diagonals
3. Perimeter = $4 \times$ side
4. Area of a rhombus (with one side and one diagonal given)

   $= \text{diagonal} \times \sqrt{(\text{side})^2 - \left(\frac{\text{diagonal}}{2}\right)^2}$
5. Other diagonal

   $= 2 \times \sqrt{(\text{side})^2 - \left(\frac{\text{diagonal}}{2}\right)^2}$

Quadrilateral : Area $= \frac{1}{2} \times$ One diagonal ×

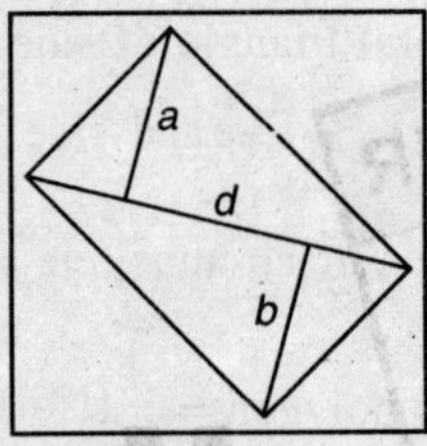

(Sum of perpendicular to it from the opposite vertices)

$= \frac{1}{2} \times d \times (a+b)$

Circle :

1. Diameter = $2 \times$ Radius
2. Area $= \pi r^2 = \frac{\pi}{4}d^2$

   [where d = diameter $= \sqrt{\frac{4A}{\pi}}$
3. Circumference $= 2\pi r = \pi d$
4. Radius $= \frac{\text{Circumference}}{2\pi} = \frac{\sqrt{\text{Area}}}{\pi}$
5. Length of an Arc $= \frac{\theta}{360°} \times 2\pi r$
6. Area of sector $= \frac{\theta}{360°} \times \pi r^2 = \frac{1}{2} \times \text{Arc} \times r$
7. Area of the ring or circular path $= \pi(R + r)(R - r)$

Remember some tricks for plane figures.

(*i*) If area related each side is increased by $a\%$, then

(*a*) Percentage increase in the area $= 2a + \frac{a^2}{100}$

(*b*) $\frac{\text{New Area}}{\text{Old Area}} = \left(1 + \frac{a}{100}\right)^2$

(*ii*) If area related to each side is decreased by $a\%$, then

(*a*) Percentage decrease in area $= 2a - \frac{a^2}{100}$

(*b*) $\frac{\text{New Area}}{\text{Old Area}} = \left(1 - \frac{a}{100}\right)^2$

(*iii*) If the perimeter of a rectangle, circle, quadrilateral and triangle are same, then area of the circle will be the largest.

Polygon

1. Interior angle + Exterior angle = 180°
2. Each interior angle $= \left(\frac{2n-4}{n}\right) \times 90°$

   where n = number of sides
3. Sum of Exterior angles = 360°
4. Perimeter = Number of sides × Length of side.

5. For an equilateral triangle of side '*a*' (*a*) radius of inscribed circle = $\frac{a}{2\sqrt{3}}$ and side of the triangle = $2\sqrt{3}r$, (*b*) radius of circumcircle = $\frac{a}{\sqrt{3}}$

6. Area of regular polygon = $\frac{1}{2}$(No. of sides) (Radius of the incribed circle)

7. Area of regular hexagon

$= \frac{3\sqrt{3}}{2}(\text{side})^2 = 2.598\ (\text{side})^2$

8. Area of a regular octagon

$= 2(\sqrt{2}+1)(\text{side})^2 = 4.828\ (\text{side})^2$

9. Area of cyclic quadrilateral, A

$= \sqrt{s(s-a)(s-b)(s-c)(s-d)}$

where, $s = \frac{a+b+c+d}{2}$ and,

$\angle A + \angle C = \angle B + \angle D = 180°$

10. For circum-circle, if *a* is the length of each side of a regular polygon and R is the circum-radius, then

(*a*) $R = \frac{a}{2}\text{cosec}\left(\frac{180°}{n}\right)$

(*b*) Area of the polygon = $\frac{1}{4}na^2\cot\left(\frac{180°}{n}\right)$, or

(*c*) Area of the polygon

$= nR^2\sin\left(\frac{180°}{n}\right)\cos\left(\frac{180°}{n}\right)$

(*d*) Area of the circum-circle of *n*-sided regular polygon

$= \frac{\pi}{4}a^2\text{cosec}^2\left(\frac{180°}{n}\right)$

11. For in-circle, if *a* is the length of a side of a regular polygon and *r* is the radius of the in-circle, then

(*a*) $r = \frac{a}{2}\cot\left(\frac{180°}{n}\right)$

(*b*) Area of the polygon = $\pi r^2\cot\left(\frac{180°}{n}\right)$

(*c*) Area of the in-circle of an *n*-sided regular polygon

$= \frac{\pi}{4}a^2\cot^2\left(\frac{180°}{n}\right)$

(*d*) Radius of the in-circle of a regular hexagon = $\frac{\sqrt{3}}{4}\times a^2$

(*e*) Area of the in-circle = $\frac{3}{4}\pi a^2$

EXERCISE

1. A rectangle measures 50 cm × 25 cm. Its area is
A. 1150 sq. cm B. 1250 sq. cm
C. 1275 sq. cm D. 1280 sq. cm

2. A field is in the form of a square whose perimeter is 580 m. Area of this field is
A. 20025 sq. m B. 20225 sq. m
C. 30025 sq. m D. 19975 sq. cm

3. Find the area of the square whose each side measures 20 cm.
A. 300 sq. cm B. 380 sq. cm
C. 360 sq. cm D. 400 sq. cm

4. Area of a circle is 154 sq. cm. Its circumference will be
A. 44 cm B. 48 cm
C. 54 cm D. 68 cm

5. The base and the height of a triangle is 8 cm and 10 cm respectively. Its area will be
A. 40 sq. cm B. 20 sq. cm
C. 49 sq. cm D. 64 sq. cm

6. If it is given that the parallel sides of a trapezium are 15 m and 25 m while the distance between them is 10 m. its area will be
A. 150 sq. m B. 225 sq. m
C. 200 sq. m D. 270 sq. m

7. Perimeter of a rectangular field is 760 m and its length and breadth are in the ratio 11 : 8. Area of this rectangular field is
A. 35200 sq. m B. 34700 sq. m
C. 35600 sq. m D. 45200 sq. m

8. If side of a square is reduced by 50%, its area will be reduced by
A. 50% B. 75%
C. 80% D. 60%

9. If area of a square is equal to the area of a rectangle 6.4 m long and 2.5 m wide, then each side of this square measures
A. 8 m B. 5.4 m
C. 3.8 m D. 4 m

10. If perimeter of a right angled triangle is six times its smallest side, then the three sides of this triangle are in the ratio of
A. 13 : 5 : 12 B. 13 : 12 : 5
C. 12 : 5 : 13 D. 13 : 5 : 10

11. The perimeter of a square is 24 m and that of another is 32 m. Find the perimeter of a third square area of which is equal to sum of the areas of these two squares
A. 40 m B. 51 m
C. 37 m D. 42 m

12. If each side of a square is doubled, its area will become
A. double B. four times
C. three times D. eight times

13. The difference between the areas of two squares is 225 sq. metres and each side of the bigger square is 25 metres. The side of the smaller square is
A. 18 m B. 21 m
C. 20 m D. 22 m

14. If the perimeter of an equilateral triangle is 72 cm, its area will be
A. $144\sqrt{3}$ sq. cm B. $142\sqrt{3}$ sq. cm
C. $154\sqrt{2}$ sq. cm D. $144\sqrt{2}$ sq. cm

15. The radii of two circles are 5 cm and 12 cm respectively. Find the radius of a circle which is equal in area to these two circles.
A. 15 cm B. 13 cm
C. 10 cm D. 8 cm

16. If the circumference of a circle is equal to the perimeter of a square, then their areas are in the ratio of
A. 14 : 11 B. 7 : 8
C. 14 : 13 D. 13 : 11

17. Three sides of a triangle are in the ratio of 17 : 15 : 8. If the perimeter of this triangle is 40 m, find its area
A. 50 sq. m B. 49 sq. m
C. 60 sq. m D. 69 sq. m

18. If the length of a rectangle is increased by 20% and width is decreased by 15%, then its area
A. decreased by 4% B. increases by 2%
C. decreases by 2% D. increases by 3%

ANSWERS

1	2	3	4	5	6	7	8	9	10
B	A	D	A	A	C	A	B	D	B
11	12	13	14	15	16	17	18		
A	B	C	A	B	A	C	B		

EXPLANATORY ANSWERS

1. Area of the rectangle
$= l \times b = 50 \times 25 = 1250$ sq. cm

2. Perimeter of the square = 4 × side
According to question :
$4 \times \text{side} = 580 \Rightarrow \text{side} = \frac{580}{4} = 145$ m
$\therefore$ Area = (side)^2 = $(145)^2$ = 20025 sq. m.

3. Area of the square = (side)^2 = $(20)^2$ = 400 sq. cm.

4. Area of the circle= πr^2
$\therefore \quad \pi r^2 = 154$
$\Rightarrow \quad r^2 = \frac{154 \times 7}{22}$
$\Rightarrow \quad r^2 = 7 \times 7 \Rightarrow r = 7$ cm
$\therefore$ Circumference of the circle
$= 2\pi r = 2 \times \frac{22}{7} \times 7 = 44$ cm.

5. Area of the triangle
$= \frac{1}{2} \times \text{base} \times \text{height} = \frac{1}{2} \times 8 \times 10 = 40$ sq. cm.

6. Area of the trapezium
$= \frac{1}{2} \times (\text{sum of the parallel sides}) \times \text{distance between them}$
$= \frac{1}{2} \times (15+25) \times 10 = \frac{1}{2} \times 40 \times 10 = 200$ sq. m.

7. Suppose length and breadth of the rectangular field are $11x$ m and $8x$ m.
$\therefore$ Perimeter of the field
$= 2(11x + 8x) = 2 \times 19x = 38x$ m.
According to question :
Perimeter of the field = 760 m
$\therefore \quad 38x = 760 \Rightarrow x = \frac{760}{38} = 20$
$\therefore$ Length of the field = 11 × 20 = 220 m
Breadth of the field = 8 × 20 = 160 m
$\therefore$ Area of the field = 220 × 160 = 35200 sq.m.

8. Suppose side of the square = x m
In the first case :
Area of the square = x^2 sq. m.
In the second case :
On effecting 50% reduction in the side of the square,
Side of the new square = x – 50% of $x = \frac{x}{2}$ m
$\therefore$ Area of the new square $= \left(\frac{x}{2}\right)^2 = \frac{x^2}{4}$ sq.m.
$\therefore$ Reduction in area of the square
$= x^2 - \frac{x^2}{4} = \frac{3x^2}{4}$ sq. m.
$\therefore$ Percentage reduction $= \frac{3x^2/4}{x^2} \times 100 = 75\%$
Hence, area of the square will be reduced by 75%.

9. Area of the rectangle = 6.4 × 2.5 = 16.00 sq.m.
According to question :
Area of the square = Area of the rectangle
$\therefore$ Area of the square = 16 sq. m.
$\therefore$ Side of the square $= \sqrt{16} = \sqrt{4 \times 4} = 4$ m.

10. Suppose, the three sides of the triangle are a, b and c and a is the largest while c is the smallest side of the triangle.

$\therefore \quad a^2 = b^2 + c^2 \quad$ ... (i)

Perimeter of the triangle = $a + b + c$

According to question :

$(a + b + c) = c \times 6$

$\Rightarrow \quad a + b = 5c \quad$ ... (ii)

From equation (i), $a^2 - b^2 = c^2$

$\Rightarrow (a + b)(a - b) = c^2$

$\Rightarrow \quad 5c(a - b) = c^2$

$\Rightarrow \quad a - b = \frac{c}{5} \; [\because a + b = 5c] \quad$ ... (iii)

From equation (ii) and (iii),

$a + b = 5c, \; a - b = \frac{c}{5}$

$\Rightarrow \quad 2a = 5c + \frac{c}{5}$

$= \frac{26c}{5} \Rightarrow a = \frac{26c}{10} = \frac{13}{5}c$

$\Rightarrow \quad a : c = 13 : 5$

on substituting the value of a in equation (ii)

$b = 5c - \frac{13c}{5} = \frac{12c}{5}$

$\Rightarrow \quad b : c = 12 : 5$

$\therefore \quad a : b : c = 13 : 12 : 5$

Hence, the three sides of the right angled triangle are in the ratio of 13 : 12 : 5.

11. Perimeter of the 1st square = 24 m

$\therefore$ Side of the 1st square = $\frac{24}{4} = 6$ m

Perimeter of the 2nd square = 32 m

$\therefore$ Side of the 2nd square = $\frac{32}{4} = 8$ m

According to question :

Area of the third square = Area of the first two squares

$\therefore$ Area of the third square = Areas of the 1st square + Area of the 2nd square

$= 6^2 + 8^2 = 36 + 64 = 100$ sq. m.

$\therefore$ Side of the third square = $\sqrt{100} = 10$ m

$\therefore$ Perimeter of the third square

$= 4 \times \text{side} = 4 \times 10 = 40$ m.

12. In the first case:

Side of the square = x m

$\therefore$ Area of the square = x^2 sq. m

In the second case:

Side of the square = $2x$ m.

$\therefore$ Area of the square = $(2x)^2 = 4x^2$ sq. m

Hence, it is clear that if side of a square is doubled, its area becomes four times.

13. Suppose side of the smaller square = x m

$\because$ Area of the bigger square = $(25)^2 = 625$ sq. m

And area of the smaller square = x^2 sq. m

According to question :

Differene between the areas of two squares

= 225 sq. m

$\therefore \quad 625 - x^2 = 225$

$\Rightarrow \quad x^2 = 625 - 225 = 400$

$\Rightarrow \quad x = \sqrt{400} = 20$ m

$\therefore$ Side of the smaller side = 20 m.

14. Suppose side of the equilateral triangle = x cm

$\therefore$ Perimeter of the triangle = $3x$ cm

According to question :

$3x = 72 \Rightarrow x = \frac{72}{3} = 24$ cm.

$\therefore$ Area of the equilateral triangle

$= \frac{\sqrt{3}}{4} \times x^2 = \frac{\sqrt{3}}{4} \times (24)^2$

$= 144\sqrt{3}$ sq. cm.

15. $\because$ Radius of the first circle = 5 cm

$\therefore$ Area of the first circle = $\pi \times 5^2 = 25\pi$ sq. cm and

Radius of the second circle = 12 cm

$\therefore$ Area of the second circle

$= \pi \times 12^2 = 144\pi$ sq. cm

According to question :

Area of the new circle

= Sum of the areas of the two circles

$\therefore$ Area of the new circle

$= 25\pi + 144\pi = 169\pi$ sq. cm $= \pi(13)^2$ sq. cm

Hence, it is clear that the radius of the new circle will be 13 cm.

16. Suppose radius of the circle = R cm

And side of the square = x cm

$\therefore$ Circumference of the circle = $2\pi R$ cm

and Perimeter of the square = $4x$ cm

According to question :

$2\pi R = 4x \Rightarrow R = \frac{2x}{\pi}$

$\therefore$ Ratio between the areas of the circle and the square $= \pi R^2 : x^2$

$\Rightarrow x \times \left(\frac{2x}{\pi}\right)^2 : x^2 \Rightarrow \frac{4x^2}{\pi} : x^2 \Rightarrow 4 : \pi : \Rightarrow 4 : \frac{22}{7}$

$\Rightarrow \quad 14 : 11.$

18. Suppose the length and the width of the rectangle are x metre and y metre respectively.

$\therefore$ Area of the rectangle = xy sq. metre

According to question :

On effecting 20% increase in the length and 15% decrease in the width :

Length of the new rectangle

$= x + 20\%$ of $x = 1.2\,x$ metre

Width of the new rectangle

$= y - 15\%$ of $y = .85\,y$ metre

$\therefore$ Area of the new rectangle

$= 1.2x \times .85y = 1.020\,xy$ sq. metre

Prism; Right Circular Cone; Right Circular Cylinder; Sphere; Hemisphere; Right Pyramid; Rectangular Parallelepiped

In mensuration we often have to deal with the problem of finding the volume of solid figure.

Cuboid : A cuboid has six faces, each one a ractangle. It has 12 edges. For example, a rectangular brick.

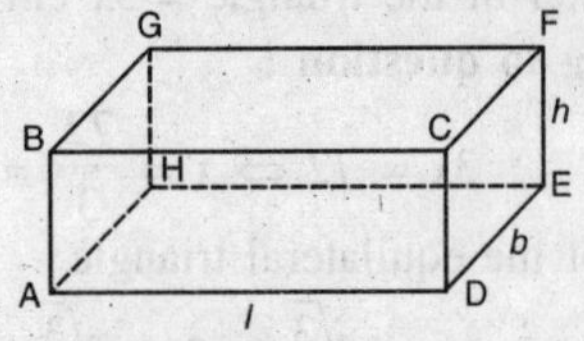

Let length = l, Breadth = b and height = h, then,

1. Volume = (Length × Breadth × Height)
2. Whole surface = $2(lb + bh + lh)$
3. Diagonal = $\sqrt{l^2+b^2+h^2}$
4. Area of 4 walls of a room = $2 \times h\ (l + b)$

Cube : In a cube, Length = Breadth = Height

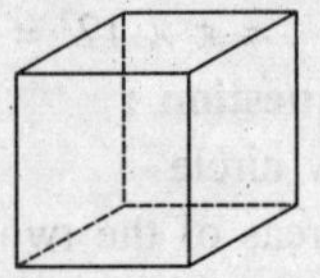

1. Volume = $(l)^3$
2. Length = $\sqrt[3]{\text{Volume}}$
3. Whole Surface area = $6\ l^2$
4. Diagonal = $l \times \sqrt{3}$
5. Lateral surface area = $4\ l^2$

Cylinder :

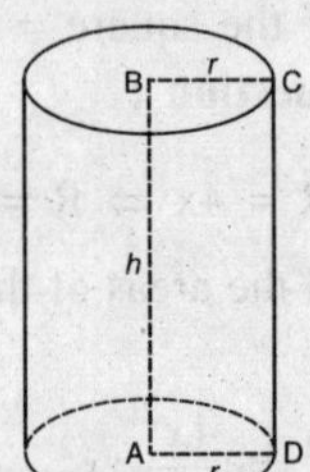

1. Volume = $\pi r^2 h$
2. Curved surface Area = $2\pi rh$
3. Total surface area = $2\pi r(r + h)$
   where r = radius, h = height
4. Curved surface of hollow cylinder
   $= 2\pi h\ (r_1 + r_2)$
5. Total surface of hollow cylinder
   $= 2\pi h\ (r_1 + r_2) + 2\pi\ (r_1^2 - r_2^2)$
6. Volume of hollow cylinder
   $= \pi h\left(r_1^2 - r_2^2\right)$
   where r_1 = outer radius
   r_2 = inner radius

Spherical Cell :

1. Volume = $\frac{4}{3}\pi\left(R^3 - r^3\right)$
2. Total surface area= $4\pi(R^2 - r^2)$
   where R = Outer radius
   r = Inner radius

Sphere

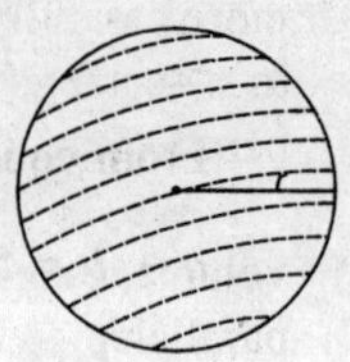

1. Volume = $\frac{4}{3}\pi r^3$
2. Surface area = $4\pi r^2$

Semi-Sphere

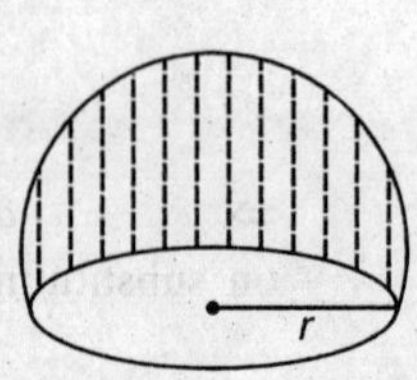

1. Volume = $\frac{2}{3}\pi r^3$
2. Curved surface area = $2\pi r^2$
3. Total surface area = $3\pi r^2$

Cone :

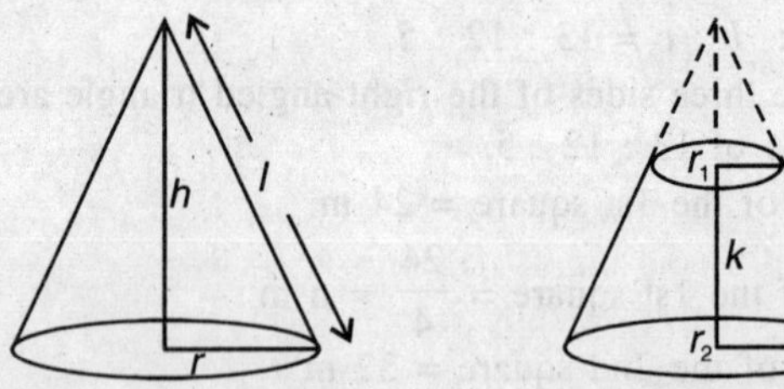

1. Slant height $(l) = \sqrt{r^2 + h^2}$
2. Volume = $\frac{1}{3}\pi r^2 h$
3. Curved surface area = πrl
4. Total surface area = $\pi r\ (l + r)$
5. If the thickness of the frustum of a cone be k and the radii of its ends are r_1 and r_2, then
   (i) Slant height of the frustum of a cone
   $= \sqrt{K^2 + (r_1 - r_2)^2}$
   (ii) Curved surface of the frustum = $\pi(r_1 + r_2)\ l$.
   (iii) Volume = $\frac{\pi K}{3}\left(r_1^2 + r_1 r_2 + r_2^2\right)$

Right Pyramid

1. Volume = $\frac{1}{3}$(area of the base) × height
2. Lateral surface area
   $= \frac{1}{2}$(Perimeter of the base) × Slant height
3. Total surface area = 2 (Area of one end) + Lateral surface area

Right Prism

1. Volume = Area of the base × Height
2. Lateral surface Area = Perimeter of the Base × Height
3. Total surface Area = 2 (Area of one end) + Lateral surface area.

Rectangular Parallelepiped

Sometimes also referred to as "Rhomboid", a parallelepiped is a 3-D shape moulded by 6 parallelograms. If observed more carefully, as a cube relates to a square, a cuboid relates to a rectangle, the same way a parallelepiped is related to parallelogram.

We have the following formula for finding out the volume, lateral surface area and surface area of rectangular parallelepiped.

The formulas are:

$$\text{Volume} = abc$$

$$\text{Surface area} = 2ab + 2bc + 2ac$$

$$\text{Diagonal} = \sqrt{a^2 + b^2}$$

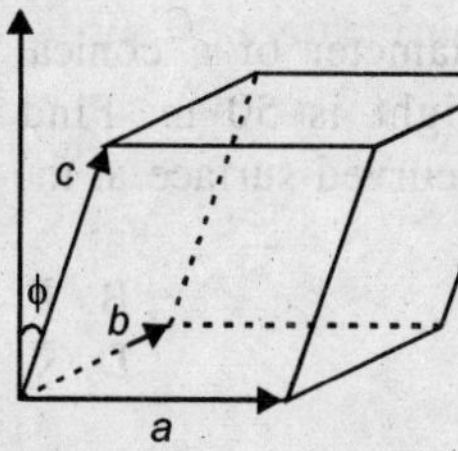

Example: Counting 38 cu. ft. of coal to a ton, how many tons will a coal bin 19 ft. long, 6 ft. wide, and 9 ft. deep contain, when level full?

Solution: The volume of a rectangular parallelepiped is given by the formula

$$V = L \times W \times H$$

Substitute the values of length, width and height of a tin, we have

$$V = L \times W \times H$$
$$V = (19\text{ft})\ (6\text{R.})\ (9\text{ ft.})$$
$$V = 1026\ \text{R}^3$$

The density of a substance is given by the formula

$$\rho = \frac{W}{V}$$

where, ρ is the density, W is the weight, and V is the volume of a substance respectively.

$$W = V \times \rho$$

Therefore, the weight of a coal in a bin is:

$$W = (1026\,\text{R}^3)\left(\frac{1\ \text{ton}}{38\,n^3}\right)$$

$$W = 27\ \text{tons.}$$

Example: The base face of a parallelepiped has opposite sides measuring 5 inches and 10 inches. The height of the parallelepiped is 4 inches. Find the cost of painting its walls from outside at a cost of INR 1.5 per square inch.

Solution: We need to find the lateral surface area first, therefore;

LSA = Perimeter of base × height

LSA = 2 (5 + 10) + 6

LSA = 180 sq. inch

Cost of painting = Lateral surface area × cost per square inch

Cost of painting the walls = 180 × 1.5 = ₹ 270.

EXERCISE

1. A solid in the form of a cuboid is 4 cm × 3 cm × 2 cm. Its volume will be

A. 20 cu cm B. 22 cu cm
C. 28 cu cm D. 24 cu cm

2. A reservoir is 3 m long, 2 m wide and 1 m deep. Its capacity in litres is

A. 8000 litres B. 10000 litres
C. 6500 litres D. 6000 litres

3. Surface area of a cube is 1014 sq. cm. Its volume will be

A. 2197 cu cm B. 2297 cu cm
C. 2179 cu cm D. 2117 cu cm

4. If the volumes of two cubical blocks are in the ratio of 8 : 1, what will be the ratio of their edges?

A. 1 : 2 B. 2 : 1
C. 4 : 1 D. 2 : 3

5. Two spheres have their surface areas in the ratio 9 : 16. Their volumes are in the ratio of

A. 64 : 27 B. 27 : 64
C. 16 : 27 D. 11 : 27

6. The length of the longest rod that can be place in a room 12 m long, 9 m broad and 8 m high is

A. 17 m *(b)* 18 m
C. 25 m D. 16 m

7. The radius and the height of a right circular cone are in the ratio of 3 : 5. If its volume is 120π cu m, its slant height is

A. $3\sqrt{34}$m B. $2\sqrt{28}$m
C. $2\sqrt{44}$m D. $2\sqrt{34}$m

8. Circumference of the base of a cylinder is 88 cm and height of the cylinder is 42 cm. Its volume is

A. 25872 cu cm B. 28572 cu cm
C. 25870 cu cm D. 22584 cu cm

9. It fwo cubes each of 10 cm side are kept close to each other, then the cuboid so formed will have surface area equal to

A. 1200 sq. cm B. 5000 sq. cm
C. 1000 sq. cm D. 1250 sq. cm

10. A rectangular piece of paper is 30 cm long and 20 cm wide. How many ways can be adopted if one wants to give this rectangular piece of paper a cylindrical form?
A. Three B. Two
C. One D. Four

11. In the above question, the cylinders formed will have their volumes in the ratio of
A. 2 : 3 B. 3 : 1 : 1
C. 3 : 2 D. 1 : 3 : 1

12. If a solid sphere of 3 cm radius is melted and recast into a right circular cone whose base radius is same as that of the sphere, the height of the cone will be
A. 8 cm B. 12 cm
C. 6 cm D. 5 cm

13. Diameter of a roller is 2.4 m and it is 1.68 m long. If it takes 1000 complete revolutions once over to level a field, the area of the field is
A. 12672 sq. m B. 12671 sq. m
C. 12762 sq. m D. 11768 sq. m

14. If each edge of a cube is increased by 10%, then by how much percent will the surface area of this cube be increased?
A. 21% B. 18%
C. 15% D. 20%

15. Height and base radius of a solid cylinder are 14 m and 4 m respectively. It is melted and recast into a solid cone of the same base radius as that of the cylinder, what will be the height of the cone?
A. 21 m B. 42 m
C. 48 m D. 54 m

16. A room is in the form of a cube of side 10 m. How many bales of cotton can be kept in it if each bale covers 5 cu m space?
A. 100 B. 175
C. 200 D. 225

17. Three cubes having side 2 cm, 3 cm respectively are melted together to form a new cube. The side of the new cube will be
A. 3.526 cm B. 4.628 cm
C. 4.626 cm D. 4.528 cm

18. If base diameter of a cylinder is increased by 50%, then by how much percent its height must be decreased so as to keep its volume unaltered?
A. 45.56% B. 55.56%
C. 50.16% D. 62.33%

19. The surface area of a cube is 600 sq. m. Its diagonal is
A. $10\sqrt{3}$ cm B. $5\sqrt{3}$ cm
C. $4\sqrt{2}$ cm D. $10\sqrt{2}$ cm

20. The base diameter of a conical tomb is 28 m and its slant height is 50 m. Find the cost of white-washing its curved surface at the rate of 80 paise per sq. m?
A. ₹ 1860 B. ₹ 1760
C. ₹ 1950 D. ₹ 1875

ANSWERS

1	2	3	4	5	6	7	8	9	10
D	D	A	B	B	A	D	A	C	B
11	**12**	**13**	**14**	**15**	**16**	**17**	**18**	**19**	**20**
C	B	A	A	B	C	C	B	A	B

EXPLANATORY ANSWERS

1. Volume of the cuboid
$= l \times b \times h = 4 \times 3 \times 2 = 24$ cu. cm.

2. Volume of the reservoir
$= l \times b \times h = 3 \times 2 \times 1 = 6$ cu. cm
($\because$ 1 cu m = 1000 litre)
$\therefore$ Capacity of the reservoir
$= 6 \times 1000 = 6000$ litre.

3. Surface area of a cube $= 6 \times (\text{side})^2$
$\therefore \quad 6 \times (\text{side})^2 = 1014$
$\Rightarrow \quad (\text{side})^2 = \frac{1014}{6} = 169$
$\Rightarrow \quad \text{side} = \sqrt{169} = 13$ cm
$\therefore$ Volume of the cube $= (\text{side})^3 = (13)^3$
$= 2197$ cu cm.

4. Suppose sides of the two cubical blocks are a_1 and a_2 respectively
$\therefore$ Volume of the two cubical blocks will be $(a_1)^3$ and $(a_2)^3$ rspectively
According to question :
$$a_1^3 : a_2^3 = 8 : 1$$
$$\therefore \quad \frac{a_1^3}{a_2^3} = \frac{8}{1}$$
$$\therefore \quad \left(\frac{a_1}{a_2}\right)^3 = \left(\frac{2}{1}\right)^3 \Rightarrow a_1 : a_2$$
$$= 2 : 1$$
Therefore ratio of their edges = 2 : 1.

5. Suppose radii of the two spheres are r_1 and r_2 respectively.

$\therefore$ Surface areas of the two spheres are $4\pi r_1^2$ and $4\pi r_2^2$ respectively

According to question :

$4\pi r_1^2 : 4\pi r_2^2 = 9 : 16 \Rightarrow r_1^2 : r_2^2 = 9 : 16$

$$\Rightarrow \quad \frac{r_1^2}{r_2^2} = \frac{9}{16} \Rightarrow \left(\frac{r_1}{r_2}\right)^2 = \left(\frac{3}{4}\right)^2$$

$$\Rightarrow \quad r_1 : r_2 = 3:4 \Rightarrow \left(\frac{r_1}{r_2}\right)^3 = \left(\frac{3}{4}\right)^3$$

$$\Rightarrow \quad \frac{r_1^3}{r_2^3} = \frac{27}{64} \Rightarrow r_1^3 : r_2^3 = 27 : 64.$$

Therefore ratio of their volumes

$$= \frac{4}{3}\pi r_1^3 : \frac{4}{3}\pi r_2^3 = r_1^3 : r_2^3 = 27 : 64$$

6. The longest rod that can be placed in the cuboidal room = Length of the diagonal =

$$\sqrt{l^2 + b^2 + h^2} = \sqrt{(12)^2 + (9)^2 + (8)^2}$$

$$= \sqrt{144 + 81 + 64} = \sqrt{289} = 17 \text{ m}$$

7. Suppose the base radius and the height of the right circular cone are $3x$ m and $5x$ m respectively.

$\therefore$ Volume of the cone

$$= \frac{1}{3}\pi r^2 h = \frac{1}{3}\pi(3x)^2 \times 5x \text{ cu m}$$

According to question :

Volume of the cone = 120π cu m (given)

$$\therefore \quad \frac{1}{3}\pi \times 9x^2 \times 5x = 120\pi$$

$$\Rightarrow \quad x^3 = \frac{120 \times 3}{9 \times 5}$$

$$\Rightarrow \quad x^3 = 8 \Rightarrow x^3 = (2)^3$$

$$\Rightarrow \quad x = 2 \text{ m}$$

$\therefore$ The radius and the height of the cone will be $3 \times 2 = 6$ m and $5 \times 2 = 10$ m respectively.

$\therefore$ Slant height of the cone

$$= \sqrt{r^2 + h^2} = \sqrt{(6)^2 + (10)^2}$$

$$= \sqrt{36 + 100} = \sqrt{136} = 2\sqrt{34}\text{m}.$$

8. Suppose the base radius of the cylinder = r cm

$\therefore$ Circumference of the base of the cylinder = $2\pi r$ cm

According to question :

$$2\pi r = 88$$

$$\therefore \quad r = \frac{88}{2\pi} = \frac{88 \times 7}{2 \times 22} = 14 \text{ cm}$$

$\therefore$ Volume of the cylinder

$$= \pi r^2 h = \frac{22}{7} \times (14)^2 \times 42$$

$$= 22 \times 2 \times 14 \times 42$$

$$= 25872 \text{ cu cm.}$$

9. Candidates should note that in such type of questions where two cubes of equal edges are kept close to each other, only the length of the cuboid so form increases and breadth and height of the cuboid remain same as that of the cube.

$\therefore$ Length of the cuboid = Edge of the first cube + Edge of the second cube

$$= 10 + 10 = 20 \text{ cm}$$

$\therefore$ Surface area of the cuboid

$= 2(20 \times 10 + 10 \times 10 + 10 \times 20)$

$$= 2(200 + 100 + 200)$$

$$= 5 \times 500 = 1000 \text{ sq. cm.}$$

10. Obviously, two ways can be adopted if one wants to give the rectangular piece of paper a cylindrical form, *i.e.,*

1. *When the paper is bent towards its length.* In this case, the circumference of the base of the cylinder will be equal to the length of the rectangular piece of paper and the height of the cylinder will be equal to the breadth of the rectangular piece of paper.
2. *When the paper is bent towards its breadth.* In this case, the circumference of the base of the cylinder will be equal to the breadth of the rectangular piece of paper and the height of the cylinder will be equal to the length of the rectangular piece of paper.

11. In the first case :

$$2\pi r = 30$$

$$r = \frac{15}{\pi} \text{ cm and } h = 20 \text{ cm}$$

$\Rightarrow$ volume $(v_1) = \pi r^2 h$

$$= \frac{15 \times 15 \times 20}{\pi} = \frac{4500}{\pi} \text{ cu cm}$$

In the second case :

$$2\pi r = 20 \Rightarrow r = \frac{10}{\pi} \text{ cm and } h = 30 \text{ cm}$$

$\therefore$ Volume $(v_2) = \pi r^2 h$

$$= \frac{10 \times 10 \times 30}{\pi} = \frac{3000}{\pi} \text{ cu cm}$$

$\therefore$ Ratio of the two volumes

$$= v_1 : v_2 = \frac{4500}{\pi} : \frac{3000}{\pi} = 3 : 2$$

12. Volume of the sphere of radius 3 cm

$$= \frac{4}{3}\pi(3)^3 = \frac{4}{3}\pi \times 27 \text{ cu cm}$$

Suppose the height of the cone = h cm

∴ Volume of the cone having base radius equal to that of the sphere = $\frac{1}{3}\pi(3)^2 \times h$

∵ Volume of the cone = Volume of the sphere

∴ $\frac{1}{3}\pi(3)^2 \times h = \frac{4}{3}\pi \times 27 \Rightarrow h = 12$ cm

∴ Height of the cone = 12 cm.

13. Diameter of the roller = 2.4 m

∴ Radius of the roller = 1.2 m

And height (length) of the roller = 1.68 m

∴ Surface area of the roller

$= 2\pi rh = 2 \times \frac{22}{7} \times 1.2 \times 1.68 = 12.672$ sq. m

∴ In one complete revolution, the roller covers 2.672 sq. m.

∴ It will cover in 1000 revolutions = 12.672 × 1000 = 12672 sq. m

∴ Area of the field = 12672 sq. m.

14. The two edges which are included in surface area of the cube are increased by 10%.

∴ $x\% = y\% = 10\%$

and in case of percentage increase, values of x and y are positive

∴ Percentage increase in the surface area of the cube

$= \left(x + y + \frac{xy}{100}\right)\%$

$= \left(10 + 10 + \frac{10 \times 10}{100}\right)\% = 21\%.$

15. Volume of the solid cylinder

$= \pi r^2 h = \pi r^2 \times 14$ cu m

According to question :

Radius of the cone = Radius of the cylinder

$= r$ m = 4 m

and volume of the cone

= Volume of the cylinder

∴ $\frac{1}{3}\pi r^2 \times \text{height} = \pi r^2 \times 14$

∴ Height = 14 × 3 = 42 m

∴ Height of the cone = 42 m.

16. Volume of the cubical room

$= (10)^3 = 1000$ cu m

Number of cotton bales which can be placed in the room

$= \frac{\text{Volume of the room}}{\text{Volume of each cotton bale}} = \frac{1000}{5} = 200.$

17. Edges of the three cubes are 2 cm, 3 cm and 4 cm respectively

∴ Their volumes will be $(2)^3 = 8$ cu cm, $(3)^3 = 27$ cu cm and $(4)^3 = 64$ cu cm respectively.

Volume of the new cube = Total volume of the three cubes

∴ Volume of the new cube

= 8 + 27 + 64 = 99 cu cm

∴ Side of the new cube = $\sqrt[3]{99} = 4.626$ cm.

18. Suppose the height of the cylinder should be decreased by H%

∵ Volume of a cylinder comprises two radii (*i.e.*, two edges) and one height (as the third edge). Radius is increased by 50%.

It means $x\% = y\% = 50\%$ and percentage decrease in the third edge (*i.e.*, height) = H%.

Therefore, $z\%$ = H% and in case of percentage decrease value of z will be negative.

∴ Change in the volume of the cylinder

$= \left(x + y + (-z) + \frac{xy + y(-z) + (-zx)}{100} + \frac{xy(-z)}{100^2}\right)\%$

Since volume of the cylinder remains unchanged.

∴ Change = 0%

∴ $\left(50 + 50 + (-H) + \frac{50 \times 50 - 50H - 50H}{100} + \frac{50 \times 50 \times (-H)}{100^2}\right)\%$

∴ 100 − H + 25 − H − .25H = 0

⇒ 2.25H = 125

⇒ $H = \frac{125}{2.25} = 55.56$

∴ Height of the cylinder should be decreased by 55.56%.

19. ∵ Surface area of the cube = 6 × $(\text{side})^2$

∴ 6 × $(\text{side})^2$ = 600

⇒ $\text{side}^2 = 100$

⇒ side = $\sqrt{100}$ = 10 cm

∴ Diagonal of the cube

$= \sqrt{3} \times \text{side} = \sqrt{3} \times 10 = 10\sqrt{3}$ cm.

20. ∵ Area of the curved surface of the cone = πrl (where r = radius of the cone and l = slant height of the cone)

∴ Area of the curved surface of the cone

$= \frac{22}{7} \times \frac{28}{2} \times 50 = 2200$ sq. m.

∴ Cost of whitewashing at 80 paise per sq. m

$= 2200 \times \frac{80}{100} =$ ₹ 1760.

●●●

CHAPTER 12

Trigonometry

Trigonometrical Ratios; Degree and Radian Measures; Standard Identities; Complementary Angles

Measurement of Angles: In general, the angles are measured in degrees or in radians which are defined as follows:

(a) ***Degrees***: A right angle is divided into 90 equal parts and each part is called a degree. Thus a right angle is equal to 90 degrees. One degree is denoted by 1°.

A degree is divided into sixty equal parts and each part is called a minute and is denoted by 1'.

A minute is divided into sixty equal parts and each part is called a second and is denoted by 1″.

Thus, we have

1 right angle = 90° (read as 90 degrees)

1° = 60′ (read as 60 minutes)

1′ = 60″ (read as 60 seconds)

(b) ***Radians***: A radian is the angle subtended at the centre of a circle by an arc equal in length to the radius of the circle.

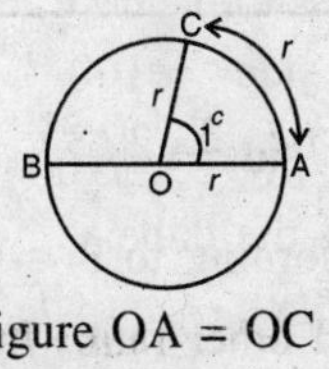

In the adjacent figure OA = OC = arc AC = r = radius of the circle, then measurement of ∠ AOC is one radian and is denoted by 1^c. Thus ∠ AOC = 1^c.

A Constant Number π: The ratio of the circumference to the diameter of a circle is always equal to a constant and this constant is denoted by the Greek letter π.

Thus π = circumference/diameter.

∴ If r is the radius of a circle, then its circumference = $2\pi r$.

The constant π is an irrational number and its approximate value is taken as 22/7.

Relation Between an Arc and an Angle: If s is the length of an arc of a circle of radius r, then the angle θ (in radians) subtended by this arc at the centre of the circle is given by $\theta = s/r$ or $s = r\,\theta$

i.e., arc = radius × angle in radians

Given in the figure,

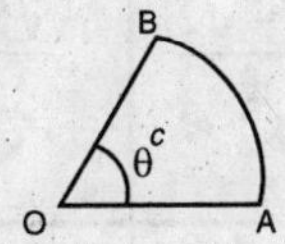

$$\angle \text{AOB} = \frac{\text{arc ACB}}{r} \text{(in radians)}$$

$$= \frac{\pi r}{r} = \pi \text{ radians.}$$

Thus we have, π radians = 180° = 2 right angles

or 1 radian = $\frac{180}{\pi}$ degrees = $\frac{180}{22} \times 7$ degrees = 57° 17' 44.8" (Appr.)

Sectorial Area: Let OAB be a sector having central angle θ^c and radius r. Then area of the sector OAB is given by $\frac{1}{2} r^2\, \theta$.

Trigonometrical Ratios: In a right angled triangle ABC, if ∠ CAB = θ, then BC = side opposite to the angle θ = Perpendicular = p (say), AC = side opposite to the right angle = Hypotenuse = h (say) and AB = b (say).

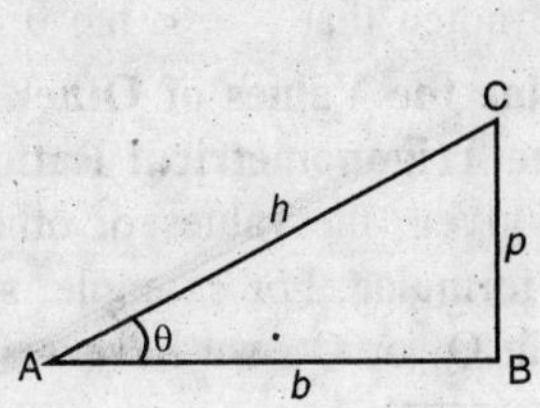

The six trigonometrical ratios are given as follows:
$\sin\theta = p/h$, $\cos\theta = b/h$, $\tan\theta = p/b$.
(Also $\tan\theta = \sin\theta/\cos\theta$, $\text{cosec}\,\theta = 1/\sin\theta$,
$\sec\theta = 1/\cos\theta$, $\cot\theta = 1/\tan\theta$,)

Basic Formulae Connecting Six Trigonometrical Ratios

The formulae connecting the six trigonometrical ratios are:

(i) $\sin^2\theta + \cos^2\theta = 1$ or $\cos^2\theta = 1 - \sin^2\theta$ or $\sin^2\theta = 1 - \cos^2\theta$.

(ii) $1 + \tan^2\theta = \sec^2\theta$ or $\sec^2\theta - \tan^2\theta = 1$

(iii) $1 + \cot^2\theta = \text{cosec}^2\theta$ or $\text{cosec}^2\theta - \cot^2\theta = 1$.

Sign of Trigonometrical Ratios:

1st quadrant $0 < \theta < 90°$,
all trigonometrical ratios +ve,
2nd quadrant $90° < \theta < 180°$,
only $\sin\theta$ and $\text{cosec}\,\theta$, +ve
3rd quadrant $180° < \theta < 270°$,
only $\tan\theta$ and $\cot\theta$, +ve
4th quadrant $270° < \theta < 360°$,
only $\cos\theta$ and $\sec\theta$, +ve.

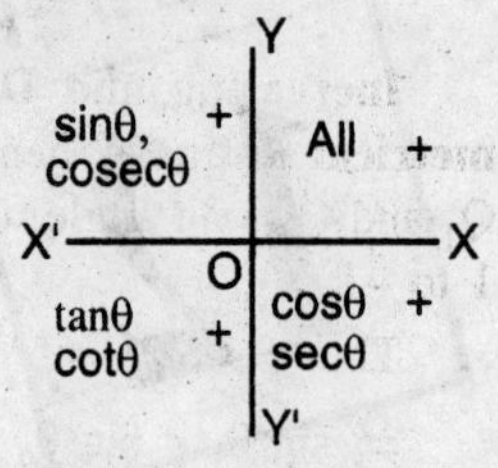

Trigonometrical Ratios of Related Angles:

$\sin(-\theta) = -\sin\theta$	$\cos(-\theta) = \cos\theta$	$\tan(-\theta) = -\tan\theta$
$\sin(90° - \theta) = \cos\theta$	$\sin(180° + \theta) = -\sin\theta$	$\sin(270° + \theta) = -\cos\theta$
$\cos(90° - \theta) = \sin\theta$	$\cos(180° + \theta) = -\cos\theta$	$\cos(270° + \theta) = \sin\theta$
$\tan(90° - \theta) = \cot\theta$	$\tan(180° + \theta) = \tan\theta$	$\tan(270° + \theta) = -\cot\theta$
$\sin(90° + \theta) = \cos\theta$	$\sin(270° - \theta) = -\cos\theta$	$\sin(360° + \theta) = \sin\theta$
$\cos(90° + \theta) = -\sin\theta$	$\cos(270° - \theta) = -\sin\theta$	$\cos(360° + \theta) = \cos\theta$
$\tan(90° + \theta) = -\cot\theta$	$\tan(270° - \theta) = \cot\theta$	$\tan(360° + \theta) = \tan\theta$

Table giving sine, cosine and tangent of some angles less than 90°:

	0°	15°	18°	22.5°	30°	36°	45°	60°	67.5°	90°
sin	0	$\frac{\sqrt{6}-\sqrt{2}}{4}$	$\frac{\sqrt{5}-1}{4}$	$\frac{\sqrt{2-\sqrt{2}}}{2}$	$\frac{1}{2}$	$\frac{\sqrt{10-2\sqrt{5}}}{4}$	$\frac{1}{\sqrt{2}}$	$\frac{\sqrt{3}}{2}$	$\frac{\sqrt{\sqrt{2}+1}}{\sqrt{(2\sqrt{2})}}$	1
cos	1	$\frac{\sqrt{6}+\sqrt{2}}{4}$	$\frac{\sqrt{10+2\sqrt{5}}}{4}$	$\frac{\sqrt{\sqrt{2}+1}}{\sqrt{(2\sqrt{2})}}$	$\frac{\sqrt{3}}{2}$	$\frac{\sqrt{5}+1}{4}$	$\frac{1}{\sqrt{2}}$	$\frac{1}{2}$	$\frac{\sqrt{2-\sqrt{2}}}{2}$	0
tan	0	$2-\sqrt{3}$	$\frac{\sqrt{25-10\sqrt{5}}}{5}$	$\sqrt{2}-1$	$\frac{1}{\sqrt{3}}$	$\sqrt{5-2\sqrt{5}}$	1	$\sqrt{3}$	$\sqrt{2}+1$	not defined

Bounds of T-Ratios: Since $\sin^2\theta + \cos^2\theta = 1$, the absolute values of $\sin\theta$ and $\cos\theta$ can never be greater than 1.

Thus $0 \le |\sin\theta| \le 1$, $0 \le |\cos\theta| \le 1$,
i.e., $-1 \le \sin\theta$; $\cos\theta \le 1$, or $0 \le \sin^2\theta$; $\cos^2\theta \le 1$.

Also $\sec\theta$; $\text{cosec}\,\theta \ge 1$ or ≤ -1
i.e., $\sec\theta$, $\text{cosec}\,\theta$ can never lie between -1 and 1.

It should be noted that $-\infty < \tan\theta$; $\cot\theta < \infty$.

To Determine the Values of Other Trigonometrical Ratios when one Trigonometrical Ratio is given: If one of the *t*-ratio is given, the values of other *t*-ratios can be found by using formulae. For example, $\sin\theta = 1/3$. Since sine is positive in Q_1 or Q_2, we have

$\cos\theta = \sqrt{1-(1/9)}$

or $-\sqrt{1-(1/9)}$, *i.e.,* $2\sqrt{2}/3$

or $-2\sqrt{2}/3$ according to $\theta \in Q_1$ or $\theta \in Q_2$.

We can also find other ratios by forming right angled triangle, *e.g.,* Let $\tan\theta = 1/2$, $\pi < \theta < 3\pi/2$, then since θ in Q_3, sine and cosine both are negative,

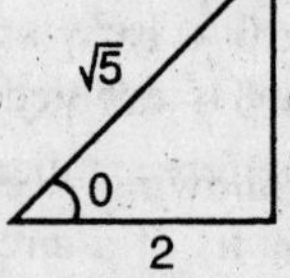

$\therefore$ We have $\sin\theta = -1/\sqrt{5}$,

$\cos\theta = -2/\sqrt{5}$.

Approximate Values of sin θ, cos θ and tan θ when θ is Small: Let θ be small and measured in radians, then sin

$\theta \approx \theta$, $\cos \approx 1$, $\tan \theta \approx \theta$. These are first degree approximations. The second degree approximations are given by

$$\sin \theta \simeq \theta, \cos \theta \simeq 1 - \frac{1}{2}\theta^2, \tan \theta = \theta.$$

Increasing and Decreasing Behaviour of Trigonometrical Ratios: When $-\pi/2 < \theta < \pi/2$, $\sin \theta$ increases in Q_1 and Q_4 with angle while in Q_2, Q_3, $\sin \theta$ decreases from 1 to –1.

Thus $\theta_1 < \theta_2$

$\Rightarrow \sin \theta_1 < \sin \theta_2$ ($\theta_1, \theta_2 \in Q_1$ or Q_4)

$\Rightarrow \sin \theta_1 > \sin \theta_2$ ($\theta_1, \theta_2 \in Q_2$ or Q_3)

We can decide the behaviour of other ratios in a similar manner. If we denote ↑ for increasing and ↓ for decreasing, we have the following chart:

		y		
sin	↓		sin	↑
cos	↓		cos	↓
tan	↑		tan	↑
cot	↓		cot	↓
sec	↑		sec	↑
cosec	↑		cosec	↓
x'		O		x
sin	↓		sin	↑
cos	↑		cos	↑
tan	↑		tan	↑
cot	↓		cot	↓
sec	↓		sec	↓
cosec	↑		cosec	↓
		y'		

EXERCISE

1. The angles of a triangle are in A.P. and the radian measure of the smallest to the degree measure of the mean is $\pi : 200$. The greatest angle in radians is:
   A. $(11/30)\pi$ B. $\pi/3$
   C. $\pi/2$ D. None of these

2. The moon's distance from the earth is 3,50,000 kilometres and its diameter subtends an angle of 31' at the eye of the observer. The diameter of the moon is:
   A. 3157 (11/27) km B. 315 (11/27) km
   C. 3050 (11/27) km D. None of these

3. If $\sin \theta = -3/5$ and θ lies in the third quadrant, then the value of $\cos(\theta/2)$ is:
   A. 1/5 B. $-1/\sqrt{(10)}$
   C. –1/5 D. $1/\sqrt{(10)}$

4. If $\tan \theta = -4/3$, then $\sin \theta$ is:
   A. – 4/5 but not 4/5 B. –4/5 or 4/5
   C. 4/5 but not – 4/5 D. None of these

5. If the angle θ is in the third quadrant and $\tan \theta = 3$, then the value of $\sin \theta$ is:
   A. $1/\sqrt{(10)}$ B. $-1/\sqrt{(10)}$
   C. $-3/\sqrt{(10)}$ D. $3/\sqrt{(10)}$

6. If $(\sec \alpha + \tan \alpha)(\sec \beta + \tan \beta)(\sec \gamma + \tan \gamma) = \tan \alpha \tan \beta \tan \gamma$, then $(\sec \alpha - \tan \alpha)(\sec \beta - \tan \beta)(\sec \gamma - \tan \gamma) = ?$
   A. $\cot \alpha \cot \beta \cot \gamma$
   B. $\tan \alpha \tan \beta \tan \gamma$
   C. $\cot \alpha + \cot \beta + \cot \gamma$
   D. $\tan \alpha + \tan \beta + \tan \gamma$

7. Which of the following is correct?
   A. $\sin 1° > \sin 1$
   B. $\sin 1° < \sin 1$
   C. $\sin 1° = \sin 1$
   D. $\sin 1° = (\pi/180) \sin 1$

8. Which of the following is correct?
   A. $\tan 1 > \tan 2$ B. $\tan 1 = \tan 2$
   C. $\tan 1 < \tan 2$ D. $\tan 1 = 1$

9. The value of $\log \tan 1° + \log \tan 2° + ... + \log \tan 89°$ is:
   A. 0 B. 1
   C. ∞ D. None of these

10. The value of $\cos 105° + \sin 105°$ is:
    A. 0 B. $\sqrt{(3/2)}$
    C. $1/\sqrt{2}$ D. $(\sqrt{3}+1)/2$

11. The value of $\sin\left(67\frac{1}{2}°\right)\sin\left(22\frac{1}{2}°\right)$ is:
    A. $-2\sqrt{2}$ B. $2\sqrt{2}$
    C. $1/2\sqrt{2}$ D. $-1/2\sqrt{2}$

12. The value of $(1 + \cos\pi/8)(1 + \cos 3\pi/8)(1 + \cos 5\pi/8)(1 + \cos 7\pi/8)$ is:
    A. 1/2 B. 1/4
    C. 1/8 D. 1/16

13. The value of $\sin^2\frac{2\pi}{15} - \sin^2\frac{\pi}{30}$ is:
    A. $(\sqrt{5}-1)/4$ B. $(\sqrt{5}-1)/8$
    C. $(\sqrt{5}+1)\sqrt{3}/2$ D. $(\sqrt{5}-1)\sqrt{3}/2$

14. The value of $\sin 50° - \sin 70° + \sin 10°$ is:
    A. 0 B. 1
    C. 2 D. None of these

15. The value of $(\sqrt{3}\,\text{cosec}\,20° - \sec 20°)$ is:
    A. 2 B. $2\sqrt{3}$
    C. 4 D. $\sqrt{8}/2$

ANSWERS

1	2	3	4	5	6	7	8	9	10
A	A	B	B	C	A	B	A	A	C
11	12	13	14	15					
C	C	B	A	C					

EXPLANATORY ANSWERS

1. Let the angles in degrees in A.P. be taken as

$A = \theta - \phi$, $B = \theta$, $C = \theta + \phi$

$\therefore \quad A + B + C = 180° = 3\theta$

$\Rightarrow \quad B = \theta = 60°$

Now $\quad \dfrac{\pi}{200} = \dfrac{\text{A in radian}}{\text{B in degrees}}$

$$= \frac{(60-\phi)(\pi/180)}{60}$$

$\Rightarrow \quad \phi = 6°$

$\therefore$ Greatest angle $C = \theta + \phi = 66°$

$= 66 \times (\pi/180)$

$= (11/30)\ \pi$ radians.

2. Let l be the diameter of moon and a its distance from the earth. If the moon subtends an angle θ at the eye of the observer, then

$$l = a\theta = 350000 \times \left(\frac{31}{60} \times \frac{\pi}{180}\right)$$

$$= \frac{3500 \times 31}{6 \times 18} \times \frac{22}{7} = 3157\ \frac{11}{27} \text{ km.}$$

3. $\because$ θ lies in the third quadrant

$\because \quad \cos\theta$ is –ve

$\because \quad \sin\theta = -3/5$

$\Rightarrow \quad \cos\theta = -\sqrt{(1 - \sin^2\theta)} = -4/5$

Now, $\quad \cos^2 \dfrac{1}{2}\theta = \dfrac{1}{2}(1 + \cos\theta)$

$= \dfrac{1}{2}(1 - 4/5) = 1/10$

$\Rightarrow \quad \cos\dfrac{1}{2}\theta = +1/\sqrt{(10)}$

But given that, $180° < \theta < 270°$

$\Rightarrow 90° < \theta/2 < 135°$

i.e., $\theta/2$ lies in the second quadrant

$\Rightarrow \cos\dfrac{1}{2}\theta$ is –ve

Hence $\cos\dfrac{1}{2}\theta = -1/\sqrt{10}$.

4. $\tan\theta = -4/3$

$\Rightarrow \theta$ lies in 2nd or 4th quadrant.

$\therefore$ $\sin\theta$ is positive or negative according as θ lie in 2nd or 4th quadrant respectively, *i.e.,* $\sin\theta$ may be positive or negative.

Now $\quad \sin\theta = \tan\theta/\sqrt{(1 + \tan^2\theta)} = 4/5$

Hence $\quad \sin\theta = -4/5$ or $4/5$.

5. $\because$ θ is in the third quadrant,

$\because \sin\theta < 0$.

Thus $\quad \sin\theta = -\tan\theta/\sqrt{(1 + \tan^2\theta)}$

$= -3/\sqrt{(10)}$.

6. Multiplying both sides of the given expression by $(\sec\alpha - \tan\alpha).(\sec\beta - \tan\beta).(\sec\gamma - \tan\gamma)$, we get, 1.1.1 $= (\sec\alpha - \tan\alpha).(\sec\beta - \tan\beta).(\sec\gamma - \tan\gamma).\tan\alpha\tan\beta\tan\gamma$

$\Rightarrow (\sec\alpha - \tan\alpha).(\sec\beta - \tan\beta).(\sec\gamma - \tan\gamma)$

$= \cot\alpha.\cot\beta.\cot\gamma$.

7. 1 radian = $(180/\pi)$ Degrees = 57° (appr.)

$\therefore \sin 1° < \sin 57° \Rightarrow \sin 1° < \sin 1$.

8. 1 radian = 57° (appr.)

which lie in first quadrant. $\therefore \tan 1 > 0$,

and 2 radians = 114° (appr.), which lie in second quadrant $\therefore \tan 2 < 0$

Hence $\tan 1 > \tan 2$.

9. $\log\tan 1° + \log\tan 2° + ... + \log\tan 89°$

$= \log[\tan 1°.\tan 2° ... \tan 45° ... \tan 88°.\tan 89°]$

$= \log[\tan 1°.\tan 2° ... \tan 45° ... \tan(90°-2°)\tan(90°-1°)]$

$= \log[\tan 1°.\cot 1°.\tan 2°.\cot 2° ... 1]$

$= \log 1 = 0$

10. $\cos 105° + \sin 105°$

$= \cos(60° + 45°) + \sin(60° + 45°)$

$= \cos 60° \cos 45° - \sin 60° \sin 45°$

$+ \sin 60° \cos 45° + \cos 60° \sin 45°$

$$= \frac{1}{2}.\frac{1}{\sqrt{2}} - \frac{\sqrt{3}}{2}.\frac{1}{\sqrt{2}} + \frac{\sqrt{3}}{2}.\frac{1}{\sqrt{2}} + \frac{1}{2}.\frac{1}{\sqrt{2}}$$

$$= \frac{2}{2\sqrt{2}} = \frac{1}{\sqrt{2}}$$

11. $\sin\left(67\frac{1^\circ}{2}\right)\sin\left(22\frac{1^\circ}{2}\right)$

$= \sin\left(45^\circ+22\frac{1^\circ}{2}\right)\sin\left(45^\circ-22\frac{1^\circ}{2}\right)$

$= \sin^2 45^\circ - \sin^2 22\frac{1^\circ}{2} = \left(\frac{1}{\sqrt{2}}\right)^2 - \frac{1-\cos 45^\circ}{2}$

$= \frac{1}{2} - \frac{1}{2}\left(1-\frac{1}{\sqrt{2}}\right) = \frac{1}{2}\left(1-1+\frac{1}{\sqrt{2}}\right) = \frac{1}{2\sqrt{2}}$

12. $\left(1+\cos\frac{\pi}{8}\right)\left(1+\cos\frac{3\pi}{8}\right)\left(1+\cos\frac{5\pi}{8}\right)\left(1+\cos\frac{7\pi}{8}\right)$

$= (1+\cos\pi/8)(1-\cos\pi/8)$

$(1+\cos 3\pi/8)(1-\cos 3\pi/8)$

$= \sin^2 \pi/8 . \sin^2 3\pi/8 = \frac{1}{4}\left(2\sin\frac{3\pi}{8}.\sin\pi/8\right)^2$

$= \frac{1}{4}\left[\cos\frac{\pi}{4} - \cos\frac{\pi}{2}\right]^2 = \frac{1}{4}\left(\frac{1}{\sqrt{2}}-0\right)^2 = \frac{1}{4}\times\frac{1}{2} = \frac{1}{8}$

13. $\sin^2\frac{2\pi}{5} - \sin^2\frac{\pi}{30} = \sin\left(\frac{2\pi}{15}+\frac{\pi}{30}\right)\sin\left(\frac{2\pi}{15}-\frac{\pi}{30}\right)$

$= \sin\frac{\pi}{6}.\sin\frac{\pi}{10} = \frac{1}{2}\times\frac{\sqrt{5}-1}{4} = \frac{1}{8}(\sqrt{5}-1)$

14. $\sin 50^\circ - \sin 70^\circ + \sin 10^\circ$

$= 2\cos 60^\circ \sin(-10)^\circ + \sin 10^\circ$

$= 2 \times \frac{1}{2} \times - \sin 10^\circ + \sin 10^\circ$

$= -\sin 10^\circ + \sin 10^\circ = 0$

15. $\sqrt{3}\,\text{cosec}\,20^\circ - \sec 20^\circ$

$= \tan 60^\circ\,\text{cosec}20^\circ - \sec 20^\circ$

$= \frac{\sin 60^\circ}{\cos 60^\circ}.\frac{1}{\sin 20^\circ} - \frac{1}{\cos 20^\circ}$

$= \frac{\sin 60^\circ\cos 20^\circ - \cos 60^\circ \sin 20^\circ}{\cos 60^\circ.\sin 20^\circ\cos 20^\circ}$

$= \frac{\sin(60^\circ-20^\circ)}{\frac{1}{2}.\frac{1}{2}(2\sin 20^\circ\cos 20^\circ)} = 4.\frac{\sin 40^\circ}{\sin 40^\circ} = 4$

Heights and Distance

Angle of Elevation and Depression: Let O and P be two points such that P is at higher level than O. Let PQ, OX be horizontal lines through P and O, respectively.

If an observer (or eye) is at O and the object is at P, then ∠XOP is called the angle of elevation of P as seen from O.

This angle is also called the angular height of P from O.

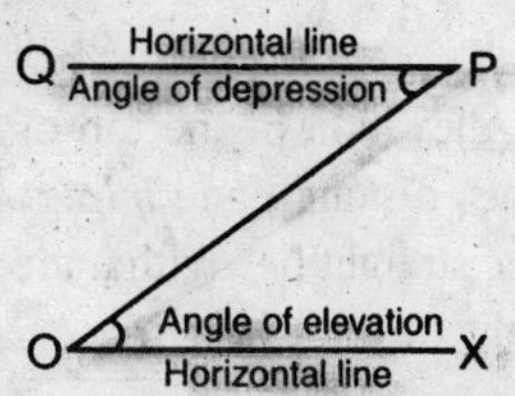

If an observer (or eye) is at P and the object is at O, then ∠QPO is called the angle of depression of O as seen from P.

EXERCISE

1. A person standing on the bank of a river observes that the angle subtended by a tree on the opposite bank is 60°, when he retires 40 metres from the bank he finds the angle to be 30°. Then the breadth of the river is:

A. 40 m B. 60 m
C. 20 m D. 30 m

2. At a point on a level plane a tower subtends an angle θ and a flag-staff *a* ft. in length at the top of the tower subtends an angle ϕ. The height of the tower is:

A. $\frac{a\sin\theta\cos\phi}{\cos(\theta+\phi)}$ B. $\frac{a\sin\theta\cos(\theta+\phi)}{\sin\phi}$

C. $\frac{a\cos(\theta+\phi)}{\sin\theta\sin\phi}$ D. None of these

3. The angle of elevation of the top of a tower standing on a horizontal plane from a point A is α. After walking a distance *a* towards the foot of the tower the angle of elevation is found to be β. The height of the tower is:

A. $\frac{a\sin\alpha\sin\beta}{\sin(\beta-\alpha)}$ B. $\frac{a\sin\alpha\sin\beta}{\sin(\alpha-\beta)}$

C. $\frac{a\sin(\beta-\alpha)}{\sin\alpha\sin\beta}$ D. $\frac{a\sin(\alpha-\beta)}{\sin\alpha\sin\beta}$

4. The angle of elevation of the top of a TV tower from the three points A, B, C in a straight line (in the horizontal plane) through the foot of the tower are α, 2α, 3α respectively. If AB = *a*, the height of the tower is:

A. *a* tan α B. *a* sin α
C. *a* sin 2α D. *a* sin 3α

5. The height of the centre of the round balloon of radius r, which subtend an angle α at the eye of an observer and the elevation of whose centre from the eye is β, is given by:

A. $r \sin \alpha \sin \beta$ B. $r \operatorname{cosec} \frac{1}{2} \alpha \sin \beta$

C. $r \operatorname{cosec} \alpha \sin \beta$ D. None of these

6. ABCD is a square plot. The angle of elevation of the top of a pole standing at D from A or C is 30° and that from B is θ, then $\tan \theta$ is equal to:

A. $\sqrt{6}$ B. $1/\sqrt{6}$

C. $\sqrt{3}/\sqrt{2}$ D. $\sqrt{2}/\sqrt{3}$

7. The angle of elevation of the top of two vertical towers as seen from the middle point of the line joining the foot of the towers are 60° and 30° respectively. The ratio of the heights of the towers is:

A. 2 : 1 B. $\sqrt{3}$: 1

C. 3 : 2 D. 3 : 1

8. ABC is a triangular park with AB = AC = 100 metres. A clock tower is situated at the mid-point of BC. The angles of elevation of the top of the tower of A and B are $\cot^{-1}$ (3.2) and $\operatorname{cosec}^{-1}$ (2.6) respectively. The height of the tower in metres is:

A. 25/2 B. 25

C. 50 D. None of these

9. The angles of elevation of the top of a vertical tower from two points, distant a and b ($a > b$) from the base and in the same straight line with it are complementary. Then the height of the tower is:

A. $\sqrt{(ab)}$ B. $\sqrt{(a^2+b^2)}$

C. $\sqrt{(a^2-b^2)}$ D. $\sqrt{a(a-b)}$

10. From the top of a h metre high cliff the angles of depression of the top and the bottom of a tower are observed to be 30° and 60° respectively. The height of the tower is:

A. $h\sqrt{3}$ B. $2h\sqrt{3}$

C. $h/3$ D. $2h/3$

11. A vertical pole is 75m high. Find the angle subtended by the pole a point 75 m away from its base.

A. 30° B. 45°

C. 60° D. 90°

12. A person standing on the bank of river finds that the angle of elevation of the top of a tower on opposite side bank is 45°. Which of the following statement is correct?

A. Breadth of the river is half of the height of the tower

B. Breadth of the river and the height of the tower are equal

C. Breadth of the river is twice the height of the tower

D. None of these

13. The angles of depression of two ships from the top of a light house are 45° and 30° towards east. If the ships are 200 m apart, find the height of the light house.

A. 100 m B. 173 m

C. 200 m D. 273 m

14. A man 2 m high, walks at a uniform speed of 6 m/min away from a lamp post, 5 m high. Find the rate at which the length of his shadow increases.

A. 4 m/min B. 8 m/min

C. 9 m/min D. 14 m/min

15. Two ships leave a port at the same instant. One sails at 30 km/hr in the direction N 32°E while the other sails at 20 km/hr in the direction S 58° E. After two hours the ships are distant from each other by:

A. $15\sqrt{6}$ km B. 36.5 km

C. $20\sqrt{13}$ km D. 100 km

ANSWERS

1	2	3	4	5	6	7	8	9	10
C	B	A	C	B	B	D	B	A	D
11	12	13	14	15					
B	B	D	A	C					

EXPLANATORY ANSWERS

1. Let A be the position of a person on the bank of a river and OP the tree on the opposite bank and $\angle OAP$ = 60°. When the person retires to the position B, s.t.

AB = 40 m then $\angle$ OBP = 30°

Let OA = x m and OP = h m

In Δ OAP, OP = OA tan 60° = $x\sqrt{3}$

and in Δ OBP, OP = OB tan 30° = $(x + 40)/\sqrt{3}$

$\therefore$ $(x + 40)/\sqrt{3} = x\sqrt{3} \Rightarrow x = 20$ m

2. Let OP be the tower of height h (say) and PQ the flag-staff of height a, such that

$\angle OAP = \theta$ and $\angle PAQ = \phi$

In ΔOAP and ΔOAQ

OA = OP cot θ = $h \cot \theta$

and OA = OQ cot $(\theta + \phi)$

= $(h + a) \cot (\theta + \phi)$

$\therefore$ $h \cot \theta = (h + a) \cot (\theta + \phi)$

$$\Rightarrow h = \frac{a\cot(\theta+\phi)}{\cot\theta - \cot(\theta+\phi)} = \frac{a\sin\theta\cos(\theta+\phi)}{\sin\phi}.$$

3. Let OP be the tower of height h (say) and A and B be the two positions on the horizontal line through O, such that

$\angle$ OAP = α, $\angle$ OBP = β and OB = x

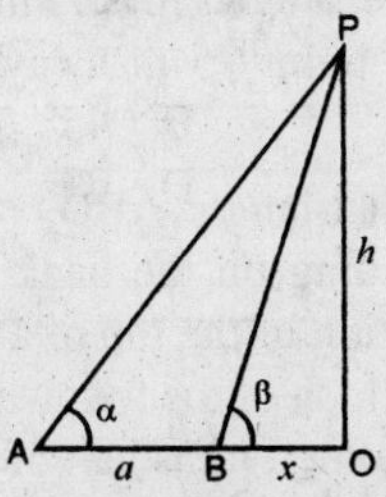

In ΔOBP, OB = $x = h \cot \beta$, and

in ΔOAP, OA = $a + x = h \cot \alpha$

$\therefore a = h(\cot\alpha - \cot\beta)$

$\Rightarrow h = a \sin\alpha \sin\beta / \sin(\beta - \alpha)$

4. OP is vertical tower. The elevations of the top of P from A, B, C are α, 2α, 3α respectively

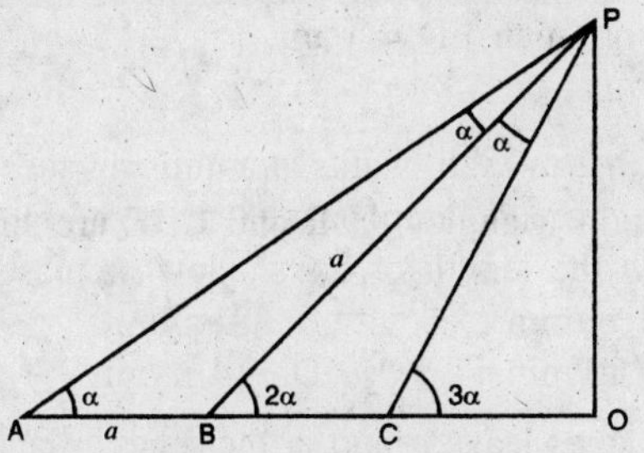

$\angle$OAP = $\angle$APB = α

$\therefore$ AB = PB = a

In ΔOBP, OP = PB sin 2α = $a \sin 2\alpha$

5. Let O be the centre of the balloon of radius r which subtend an angle α at the eye of an observer at E.

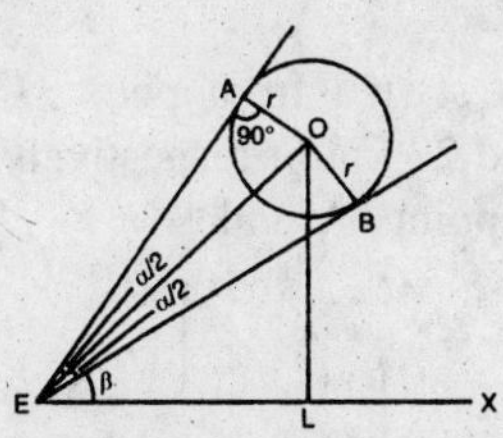

If EA and EB are the tangents to the balloon,

then $\angle$OEA = $\angle$OEB = $\frac{\alpha}{2}$

In ΔOAE, $\sin\frac{1}{2}\alpha$ = OA/OE $\therefore$ OE = r cosec $\frac{1}{2}\alpha$

In ΔOEL, height of the centre of the balloon

= h = OE $\sin\beta$ = r cosec $\frac{1}{2}\alpha \sin\beta$.

6. Let a be the length of a side of square plot ABCD and h, the height of the pole standing at D. Since elevations of P from A or C is 30° and that from B is θ,

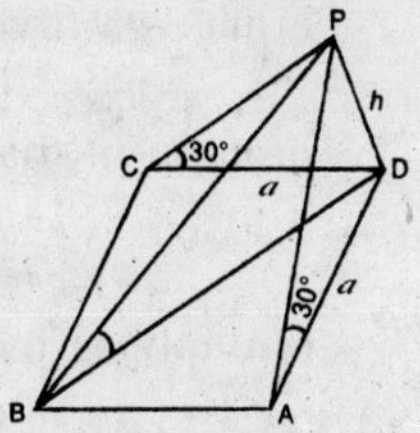

$\therefore$ In ΔPCD, tan 30° = h/a

i.e., $h/a = 1/\sqrt{3}$

And in ΔPBD,

tan θ = PD/BD

= $h/(a\sqrt{2})$

= $1/\sqrt{6}$

$\therefore$ BD = $\sqrt{(AB^2 + AD)^2} = a\sqrt{2}$.

7. Let AB and CD be two towers of heights h_1 and h_2 respectively and O the mid-point of the line joining the foots A and C of the towers.

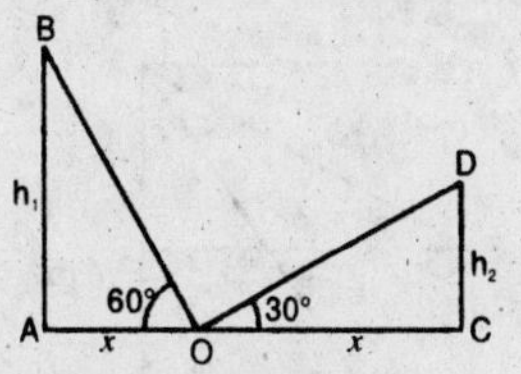

Let OA = OC = x

Then $h_1 = x \tan 60° = x\sqrt{3}$

and $h_2 = x \tan 30° = x/\sqrt{3}$

$\therefore \frac{h_1}{h_2} = \frac{3}{1}$, Hence, $h_1 : h_2 = 3 : 1$.

8. Given $\alpha = \cot^{-1}(3.2)$, $\beta = \text{cosec}^{-1}(2.6)$

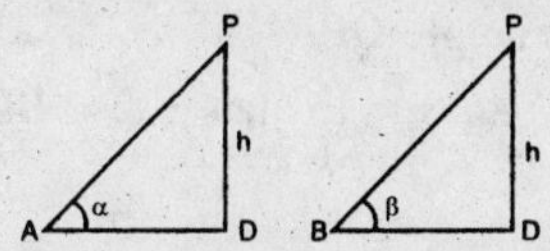

In ΔPAD, AD = $h \cot \alpha$,

In ΔPBD, BD = $h \cot \beta$

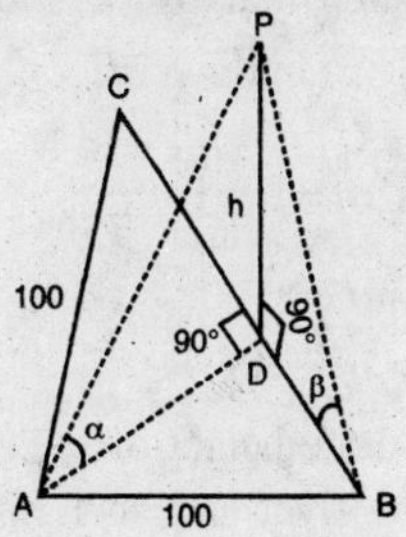

In ΔABD, $AB^2 = AD^2 + BD^2$

$= h^2(\cot^2\alpha + \cot^2\beta)$

$\Rightarrow 100^2 = h^2\{\cot^2\alpha + (\text{cosec}^2\beta - 1)\}$

$\Rightarrow 100^2 = h^2[(3.2)^2 + (2.6)^2 - 1] = 16h^2$

$\Rightarrow h = 25$ m.

9. Let CD = h unit be the height of the tower and A and B be the two points on the ground, such that DA = a; DB = b; $\angle$ DAC = α and $\angle$ DBC = 90° − α

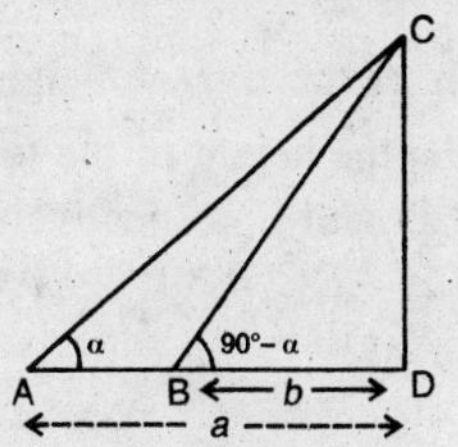

From right triangle ADC,

$$CD = h = a\tan\alpha \qquad ...(i)$$

From right triangle BDC,

$$CD = h = b\tan(90^\circ - \alpha)$$
$$= b\cot\alpha \qquad ...(ii)$$

Multiplying equations *(i)* and *(ii)*, we get

$$h^2 = a\tan\alpha \cdot b\cot\alpha$$

Hence, $h = \sqrt{ab}$

10. Let AB = h m be the height of cliff and CD = x m be the height of the tower and also $\angle ADB = 60^\circ$ and $\angle ACE = 30^\circ$.

Now, from the figure, AE = $(h - x)$m

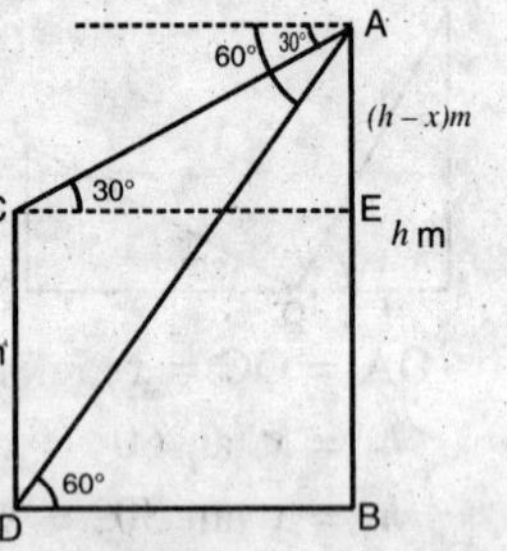

From right triangle ABD,

$$BD = h\cot 60^\circ = \frac{h}{\sqrt{3}}\text{ m}$$

From right triangle CEA,

$$(h - x) = EC\tan 30^\circ = BD\tan 30^\circ$$

$$\Rightarrow \quad h - x = \frac{h}{\sqrt{3}}\cdot\frac{1}{\sqrt{3}} \quad \therefore x = h - \frac{h}{3} = \frac{2h}{3}\,m$$

11. Let AB = 75m be the height of pole and C is a point on the ground such that BC = 75m

Now, from right triangle ABC,

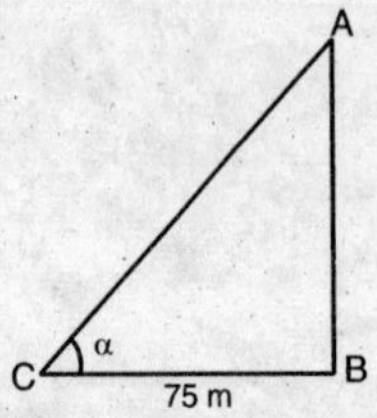

$$\tan\alpha = \frac{AB}{BC} = \frac{75}{75}$$

$$\Rightarrow \quad \tan\alpha = 1$$

$$\therefore \quad \alpha = 45^\circ$$

12. Let AB = h m be the height of the tower; BC = x m be the breadth of the river and also $\angle ACB = 45^\circ$

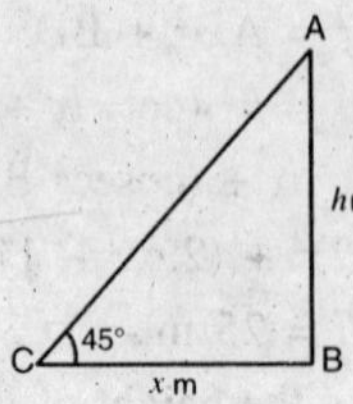

Now from right triangle ABC

$$\tan 45^\circ = \frac{h}{x} \Rightarrow 1 = \frac{h}{x} \therefore x = h$$

Hence, breadth of the river = height of the tower

13. Let AB = hm be the height of the tower and two ships are situated at D and C respectively; such that, CD = 200 m; $\angle ADC = 30^\circ$; $\angle ACB = 45^\circ$ and BC = xm (say)

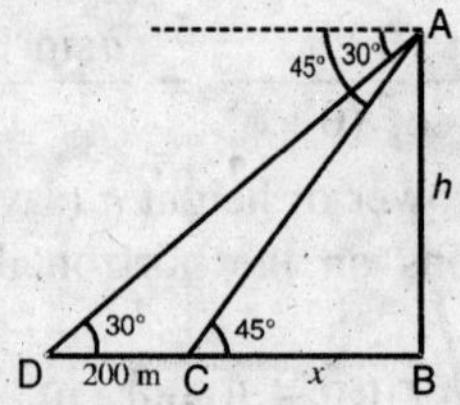

Now from right triangle ABC,

$$\tan 45^\circ = \frac{h}{x} \Rightarrow 1 = \frac{h}{x} \therefore x = h$$

Again from right triangle ABD,

$$\tan 30^\circ = \frac{h}{200 + x}$$

$$\Rightarrow \quad \frac{1}{\sqrt{3}} = \frac{h}{200 + h} \quad (\because x = h)$$

$$\Rightarrow \quad \sqrt{3}h - h = 200$$

$$\Rightarrow \quad h(1.732 - 1) = 200$$

$$\therefore \quad h = \frac{200}{0.732} = 273.2\text{ m} \sim 273\text{ m}$$

14. Let AB = 5m and CD = 2m be the heights of a lamp post and the men respectively. At any time t BD = x m and shadow of man ED = y m.

$$\text{Then,} \quad \frac{dx}{dt} = 6\text{m/min}$$

Now, right triangles ABE and CDE are similar; then

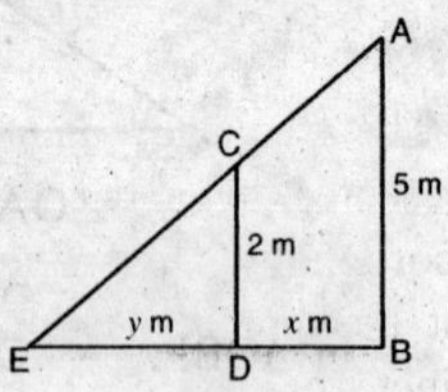

$$\frac{AB}{CD} = \frac{BE}{DE} \Rightarrow \frac{5}{2} = \frac{x + y}{y}$$

$$\Rightarrow \quad 5y - 2y = 2x$$

$$\Rightarrow \quad 3y = 2x$$

$$\Rightarrow 3.\frac{dy}{dt} = 2.\frac{dx}{dt}$$

$$\Rightarrow 3.\frac{dy}{dt} = 2 \times 6 \therefore \frac{dy}{dt} = 4$$

Hence, length of his shadow increases at the rate of 4 m/min.

15. Let two ships started from point O at the speed of 30 km/hr 0 and 20 km/hr respectively, after two hours they reach at points A and B.

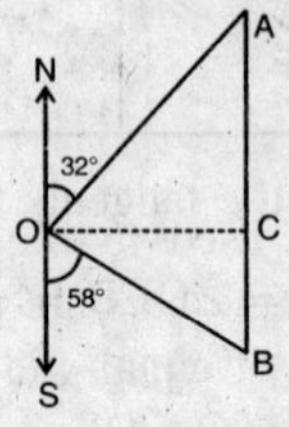

Now, $\angle NOA = 32^\circ$ and $\angle SOB = 58^\circ$,

Then, $\angle AOB = 180^\circ - (32^\circ + 58^\circ) = 90^\circ$

Since Δ AOB is a right triangle in which OA = 2 × 30 = 60 km and OB = 2 × 20 = 40 km

$$\text{Since, } AB = \sqrt{OA^2 + OB^2} = \sqrt{(60)^2 + (40)^2}$$

$$= \sqrt{5200} = 20\sqrt{13}\text{ km}$$

●●●

CHAPTER 13

Data Handling

Histogram; Frequency Polygon; Bar Diagram & Pie-Chart

Graphical Representation of Statistical Data

One of the most convincing and appearing ways in which statistical result may be presented is through diagrams and graphs. The impressions created by diagrams last much longer than those created by the figures presented in a tabular form.

Rather than present data numerically in the form of a table it can sometimes be better to illustrate the information through the use of graphs, charts, diagrams and so on.

The frequency distribution of a discrete value is best represented by a bar diagram. The height of the bars is proportional to the frequency of each variate-value. The bars must be kept distinct to show that the variate-values are distinct.

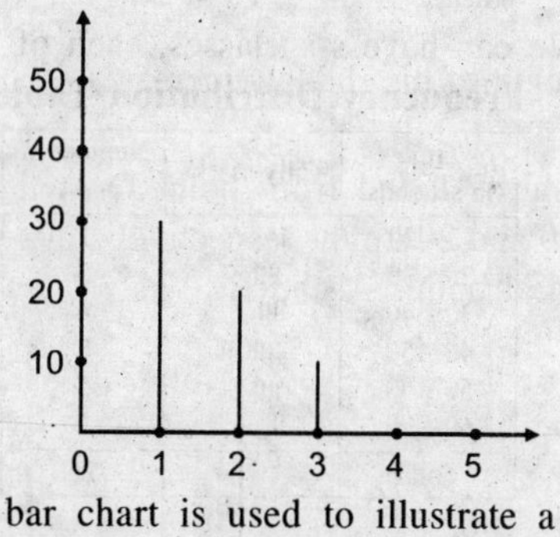

A simple bar chart is used to illustrate a frequency distribution. The lengths of the bars are proportional to the frequency and the bars are of equal width.

Some Important Types of Diagrams and Graphs

The different types of Diagrams and Graphs

(1) Bar diagram

(2) Histogram

(3) Frequency circle

(4) Cumulative frequency curve of the ogive

(5) Pie diagram.

Bar Diagram

Bar diagram is the easiest and most adaptable general purpose chart. In this, bars or rectangles of uniform width are drawn with equal spaces in between on the axis. Along the y-axis is shown, the scale of the height of the rectangles.

Thickness of bars is not taken into account, they should be so constructed that they look attractive and beautiful. This can be done by colouring them or by preparing designs in them.

However, the colour or designs of all bars representing one type of data should be identical. The bars may be vertical or horizontal. Some of the main bar diagrams are:

(*i*) Simple Bar-Diagram

(*ii*) Sub-divided Bar-Diagram

(*iii*) Multiple Bar-Diagram

The following Examples of Illustrate :

Example: The following table gives the population of India (in millions). Draw a bar diagram of the data:

Population (in million) of India 1931-1971

Year	Population (*in millions*)
1931	275.5
1941	312.1
1951	356.9
1961	439.9
1971	546.9

Solution: The above data is represented by a simple bar diagram as follows :

Simple Bar Diagram Showing Population (in Millions)

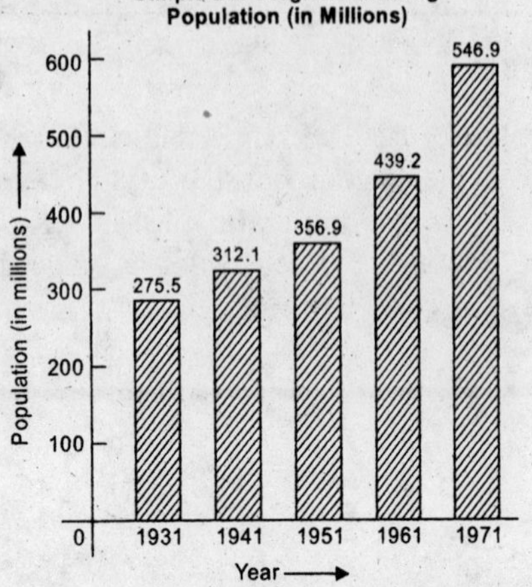

Here years are denoted on the x-axis and population (in millions) on the y-axis. The length of each bar corresponds to the number representing population on the y-axis.

Sub-Divided or Component Bar Diagram

The sub-divided bar diagram is used where the total magnitude of the given variable is to be divided into various parts or sub-classes. The bars are drawn proportional in length to the total and divided in the ratios of their components. Different colours, shades, designs, etc. are used to distinguish the various components.

Example: Represent the following data of sex-wise distribution of students in a school by a bar diagram.

Year	No. of Students		Total
	Male	*Female*	
1978	800	250	1050
1979	900	300	1200
1980	950	375	1325
1981	1000	400	1400
1982	1150	450	1600

Solution: The above data are represented by a sub-divided bar diagram, as follows.

Sub-Divided Bar Diagram showing Sex-wise Distribution of Students

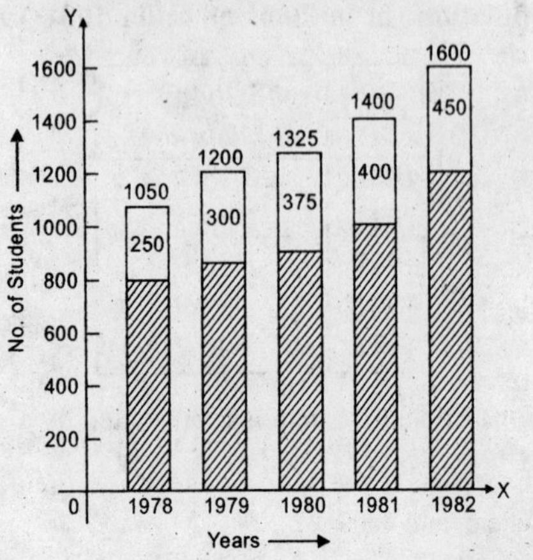

In a multiple bar diagram two or more sets of inter-related data are presented. The technique of drawing such a diagram is basically the same as that of simple bar diagram.

Histograms

The histogram is most popularly used for graphical presentation of a frequency distribution. A histogram is a graph that represents the class frequencies in a frequency distribution by vertical adjacent rectangles. After choosing a convenient scale on the axes, mark off the class intervals along x-axis and the frequencies of the respective class intervals along y-axis. Then construct rectangles with each class intervals as breadth and the respective frequency of the class interval as height. The set of the all adjacent rectangles so constructed form a histogram.

Note : A histogram is a development of the bar chart but remember when drawing a histogram it is the Area of each bar which is proportional to the frequency and there are no gaps between the bars because the classes are usually arranged so that there are no gaps.

The following Examples of Illustrates:

Example: The time taken, in seconds, to solve a problem by each of 25 pupils is as follows: 16, 20, 26, 27, 28, 30, 33, 37, 38, 40, 42, 42, 43, 46, 46, 48, 49, 50, 53, 58, 59, 60, 64, 52, 20.

(*a*) Construct a frequency distribution for these data, using a class interval of 10 seconds.

(*b*) Draw a histogram to represent the frequency distribution.

Solution:

(*a*) Lowest observation = 10

Highest observation = 64

Range = 64 – 10 = 54

We can have six classes, each of width 10.

Frequency Distribution Table

Time (in seconds)	Tally marks	Number of pupils
10 – 20		1
20 – 30	卌	5
30 – 40	IIII	4
40 – 50	卌 III	8
50 – 60	卌	5
60 – 70	II	2
Total		25

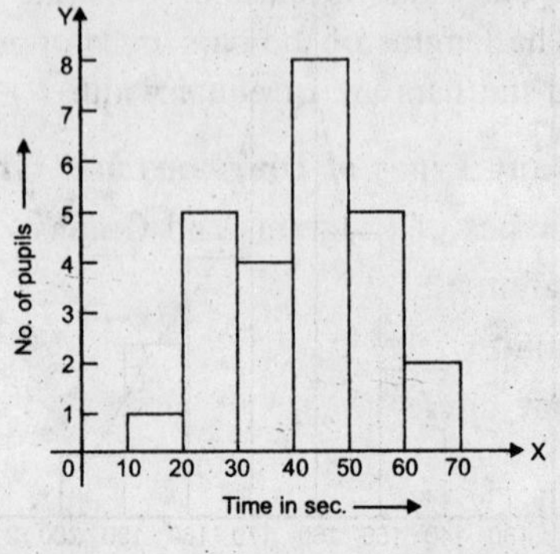

Frequency Polygon

A frequency polygon is a graph of frequency distribution. The steps constructing a frequency polygonal are:

1. Draw a suitable histogram keeping in view all the basic principles.
2. Get the mid-points of the upper horizontal side of each rectangle.
3. Join these mid-points of the adjacent rectangles of the histogram by straight lines taken in order, they form a polygon called frequency polygon.
4. End of frequency polygon preferably extended to the base line.

In a frequency polygon the variables or individuals of each class are assumed to be concentrated at the class-intervals.

Note: If only frequency polygon is to be drawn, first represent the class-marks (x_i) on the x-axis and corresponding frequencies (f_i) on y-axis. Plot all the points (x_i, f_i). Then join these points by line segments. The figure so obtained is known as the frequency polygon. The polygon should be brought down at the ends to the x-axis at each and of the drawn.

The following Examples of Illustrate:

Example: In a city the following weekly observations were made in a study on cost of Living Index for the year 1970–71.

Cost of Living Index	No. of weeks
140 – 150	5
150 – 160	10
160 – 170	20
170 – 180	9
180 – 190	6
190 – 200	2

Draw a histogram and frequency polygon on the same scale.

Solution:

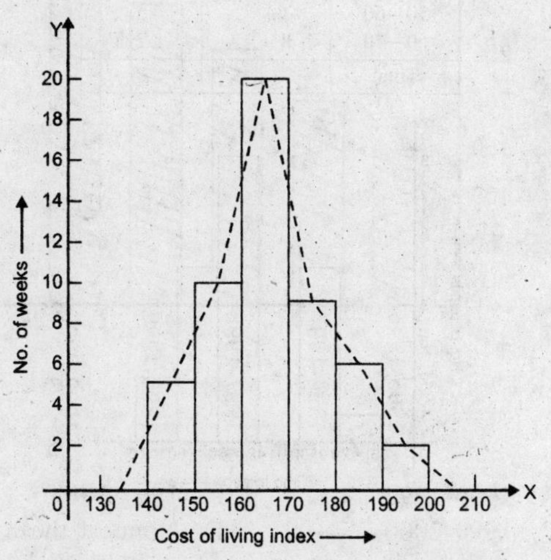

Pie Diagram

Pie-diagrams are used to represent a relative frequency distribution. A pie diagram consists of a circle divided into as many sectors as there are classes in a frequency distribution. The area of each sector is proportional to the relative frequency of the class.

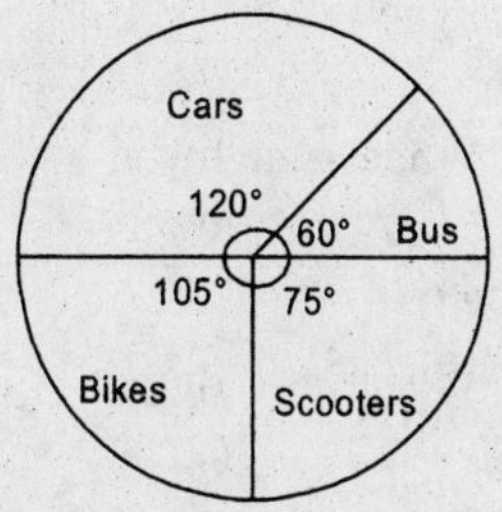

Now we make angles at the centre proportional to the relative frequencies. And in order to get the angles of the disired sectors, we divide 360° in the proportion of the various relative frequencies, *i.e.*,

$$\text{Central angle} = \left[\frac{\text{Frequency} \times 360^\circ}{\text{Total frequency}}\right]$$

Example : The pie-chart provided below gives the distribution of land (in a village) under various food crops. Study the pie-chart carefully and answer the questions that follow.

Distribution of Areas (in Acre) Under various Food Crops

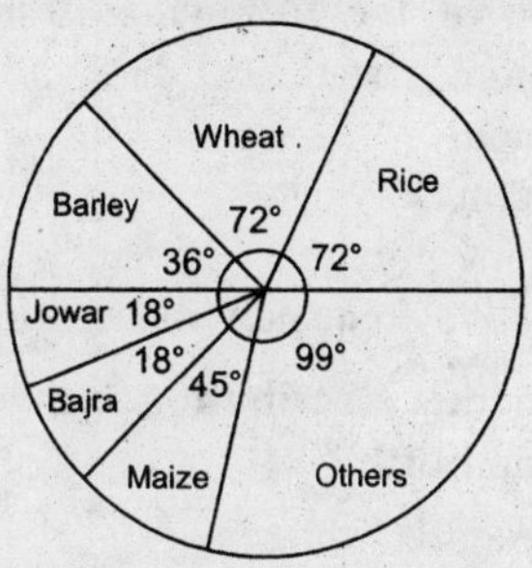

1. Which combination of three crops contribute to 50% of the total area under the food crops?
(*a*) Wheat, Barley and Jowar
(*b*) Rice, Wheat and Jowar
(*c*) Rice, Wheat and Barley
(*d*) Bajra, Maize and Rice

2. If the total area under jowar was 1.5 million acres, then what was the area (in million acres) under rice?
(*a*) 6 (*b*) 7.5
(*c*) 9 (*d*) 4.5

3. If the production of wheat is 6 times that of barley, then what is the ratio between the yield per acre of wheat and barley?
(*a*) 3 : 2 (*b*) 3 : 1
(*c*) 12 : 1 (*d*) 2 : 3

Solution:

1 (*c*): The total of the central angles corresponding to the three crops which cover 50% of the total area, should be 180°. Now, the total of the central angles for the given combinations are:

(*i*) Wheat, Barley and Jowar

$= (72° + 36° + 18°)$

$= 126°$

(*ii*) Rice, Wheat and Jowar

$= (72° + 72° + 18°)$

$= 162°$

(*iii*) Rice, Wheat and Barley

$= (72° + 72° + 36°)$

$= 180°$

(*iv*) Bajra, Maize and Rice

$= (18° + 45° + 72°)$

$= 135°$

Clearly, (*iii*) is the required combination.

2 (*a*): The area under any of the food crops is proportional to the central angle corres-ponding to that crop. Let, the area under rice production be x million acres.

Then, $18 : 72 = 1.5 : x$

$\Rightarrow x = \left(\frac{72 \times 1.5}{18}\right) = 6.$

Thus, the area under rice production = 6 million acress

3 (*b*): Let, the total production of barley be T tonnes and let Z acres of land be put under barley production. Then, the total production of wheat = (6T) tonnes. Also, area under wheat production = (2Z) areas.

$\left[\because \frac{\text{Area under Wheat production}}{\text{Area under Barley production}} = \frac{72°}{36°} = 2 \text{ and therefore, Area under wheat} = 2 \times \text{Area under barley} = (2Z) \text{ acres}\right]$

Now, yield per acre for wheat

$= \left(\frac{6T}{2Z}\right)$ tonnes/acre $= \left(\frac{3T}{Z}\right)$ tonnes/acre

and yield per acre for barley

$= \left(\frac{T}{Z}\right)$ tonnes/acre.

$\therefore$ Required Ratio $= \left(\frac{3T/Z}{T/Z}\right) = 3:1.$

EXERCISE

1. Which one of the following is not the graphical representation of statistical data?

A. Bar graph
B. Histogram
C. Frequency polygon
D. Cumulative frequency distribution

2. In a frequency distribution, ogives are graphical representation of:

A. Frequency
B. Relative frequency
C. Cumulative frequency
D. Raw data

3. A frequency polygon is constructed by plotting frequency of the class interval and the:

A. upper limit of the class
B. lower limit of the class
C. mid value of the class
D. any values of the class

4. In a histogram the area of each rectangle is proportional to:

A. the class mark of the corresponding class interval
B. the class size of the corresponding class interval
C. frequency of the corresponding class interval
D. cumulative frequency of the corresponding class interval

5. In a histogram, each class rectangle is constructed with base as:

A. frequency B. class-intervals
C. range D. size of the class

6. Read the bar graph shown in figure and answer the following question:

In which year is the increase of students maximum?

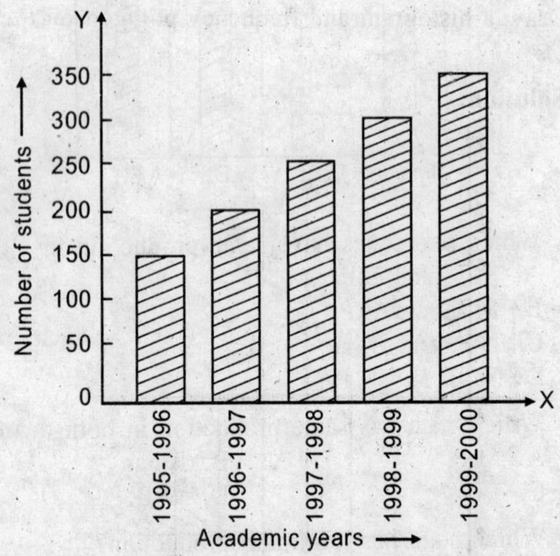

A. 1996-1997 B. 1997-1998
C. 1999-2000 D. None of these

Directions (Qs. 7 to 9) : *Read the following bar graph shown in figure and answer the following questions:*

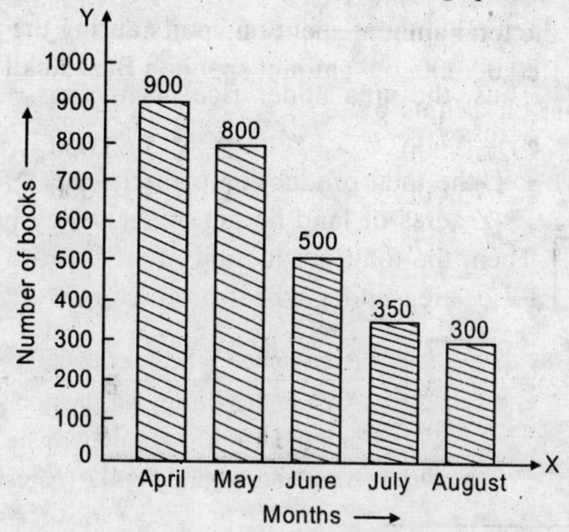

7. In which month was the sale of the books maximum?
A. April B. May
C. June D. August

8. In which month was the sale of the books minimum?
A. April B. May
C. July D. August

9. What is the total sale during these five months?
A. 3800 copies B. 2850 copies
C. 2800 copies D. 2950 copies

Directions (Qs. 10 to 12) : *Read the following bar graph given in figure and answer the following questions:*

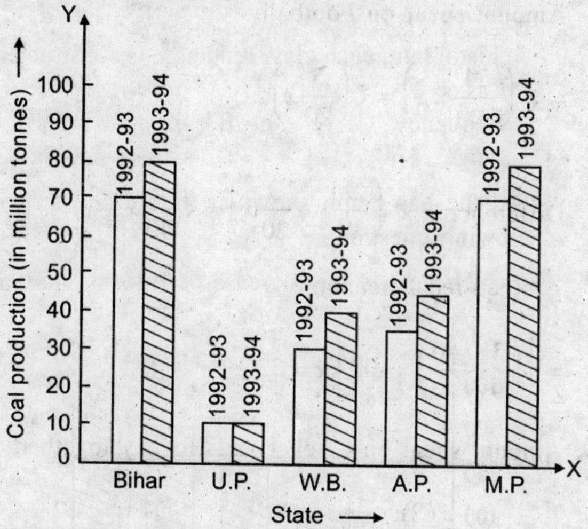

10. Which two states have same production in 1993-94?
A. M.P. and Bihar
B. M.P. and U.P.
C. U.P. and Bihar
D. W.B. and U.P.

11. Which state has same production in both the years?
A. M.P. B. Bihar
C. U.P. D. W.B.

12. Which state has minimum production?
A. M.P. B. A.P.
C. W.B D. U.P.

Directions (Qs. 13 to 15) : *The following bar graph shows the results of an annual examination in a secondary school. Read the bar graph and choose the correct alternative in each of the following.*

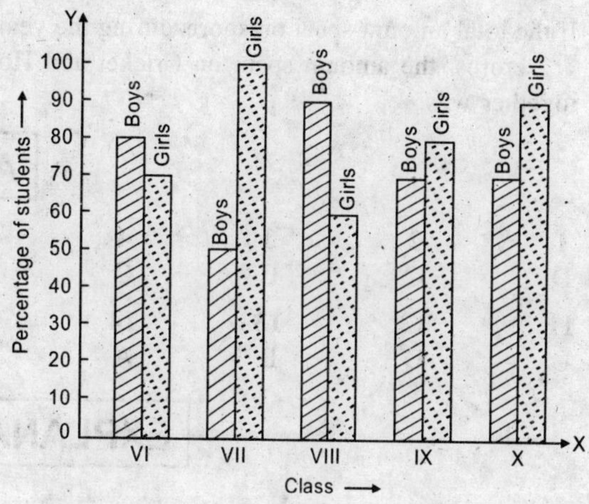

13. The pair of classes in which the results of boys and girls are inversely proportional are:
A. VI, VIII B. VI, IX
C. VIII, IX D. VIII, X

14. The class having the lowest failure rate of girls is:
A. VII B. X
C. IX D. VIII

15. The class having the lowest pass rate of boys is:
A. VI B. VII
C. VIII D. IX

Directions (Qs. 16 to 20) : *The circle-graph given here shows the spendings of a country on various sports during a particular year. Study the graph carefully and answer the questions given below it.*

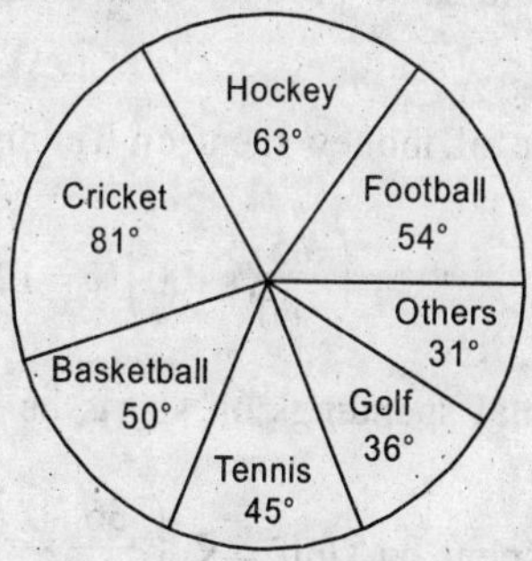

16. What per cent of the total spendings is spent on Tennis?
A. $12\frac{1}{2}\%$ B. $22\frac{1}{2}\%$
C. 25% D. 45%

17. How much per cent more is spent on Hockey than that on Golf?
A. 27% B. 35%
C. 37.5% D. 75%

18. How much per cent less is spent on Football than that on Cricket?

A. $22\frac{2}{9}\%$ B. 27%

C. $33\frac{1}{3}\%$ D. $37\frac{1}{2}\%$

19. If the total amount spent on sports during the year was ₹ 2 crores, the amount spent on Cricket and Hockey together was:

A. ₹ 8,00,000 B. ₹ 80,00,000
C. ₹ 1,20,00,000 D. ₹ 1,60,00,000

20. If the total amount spent on sports during the years be ₹ 1,80,00,000, the amount spent on Basketball exceeds that on Tennis by:

A. ₹ 2,50,000 B. ₹ 3,60,000
C. ₹ 3,75,000 D. ₹ 4,10,000

ANSWERS

1	2	3	4	5	6	7	8	9	10
D	C	C	C	B	D	A	D	B	A
11	**12**	**13**	**14**	**15**	**16**	**17**	**18**	**19**	**20**
C	D	B	A	B	A	D	C	B	A

EXPLANATORY ANSWERS

6. The increase in the number of students is uniform as the increase in the heights of bars is uniform. Hence, in this case the increase is not maximum in any of the year.

7. The sale of the books was maximum in the month of April as the height of the rectangle corresponding to April month is maximum.

8. The sale of the books was minimum in the month of August as the height of the corresponding rectangle is minimum.

9. Total sale of the books during 5 months.

(900 + 800 + 500 + 350 + 300) = 2850 copies.

10. M.P. and Bihar have same production in 1993-1994.

11. U.P. has the same production in both the years.

12. U.P.

16. Percentage of money spent on Tennis

$$= \left(\frac{45}{360} \times 100\right)\% = 12\frac{1}{2}\%$$

17. Let the total spendings on sports be ₹ x. Then,

Amount spent on Golf $= ₹\left(\frac{36}{360} \times x\right) = ₹\frac{x}{10}$

Amount spent on Hockey

$$= ₹\left(\frac{63}{360} \times x\right) = ₹\frac{7}{40}x.$$

$$\text{Difference} = ₹\left(\frac{7}{40}x - \frac{x}{10}\right) = ₹\frac{3x}{40}$$

∴ Required Percentage

$$= \left[\left(\frac{3x/40}{x/10}\right) \times 100\right]\% = 75\%$$

18. Let the total spendings on sports be ₹ x. Then,

Amount spent on Cricket

$$= ₹\left(\frac{81}{360} \times x\right) = ₹\left(\frac{9}{40}x\right)$$

Amount spent on Football

$$= ₹\left(\frac{54}{360} \times x\right) = ₹\left(\frac{3}{20}x\right)$$

$$\text{Difference} = ₹\left(\frac{9}{40}x - \frac{3}{20}x\right) = ₹\frac{3}{40}x$$

∴ Required Percentage

$$= \left[\left(\frac{3x/40}{9x/40}\right) \times 100\right]\% = 33\frac{1}{3}\%$$

19. Amount spent on Cricket and Hockey together

$$= ₹\left[\frac{(81+63)}{360} \times 2\right] \text{ crores}$$

= ₹ 0.8 crores = ₹ 8000000.

20. Amount spent on Basketball exceeds that on Tennis by :

$$= ₹\left[\frac{(50-45)}{360} \times 18000000\right] = ₹\ 250000.$$

●●●

GENERAL KNOWLEDGE & GENERAL AWARENESS

INDIAN HISTORY

ANCIENT INDIA

INDUS VALLEY CIVILISATION (2500-1750 BC)

- The earliest excavations in the Indus valley were done at Harappa in the West Punjab and Mohenjodaro in Sindh. Both places are now in Pakistan.

Important Sites

- The most important sites are Kot Diji in Sindh, Kalibangan in Rajasthan, Ropar in the Punjab, Banawali in Haryana, Lothal, Surkotada and Dhaulavira, all the three in Gujarat.
- Mohenjodaro is the largest of all the Indus cities and it is estimated to have spread over an area of 200 hectares.

Indus Valley Civilisation : An Objective Study

Major Sites	*Excavators*	*Year*	*River*	*Location*	*Important Findings*
1. Harappa	D.R. Sahni	1921	Ravi	West Punjab (Pakistan)	Granaries, Virgin Goddess, Cemetery, Stone symbol of Lingam and Yoni
2. Mohenjodaro	R.D. Banerjee	1922	Indus	Sindh (Pakistan)	Great Bath, Great Granary, Assembly Hall, Proto-Shiva, Brick Kilns, Mesopotamian seals
3. Chanhudaro	N.G. Mazumdar	1931	Indus	Sindh (Pakistan)	Bronze toy cart, Ink-pot, Lipstick, City without a citadel
4. Kalibangan	B.B. Lal & B.K. Thapar	1953	Ghaggar	Ganganagar (Rajasthan)	Decorated bricks, ploughed field surface, Firealtars
5. Lothal	S.R. Rao	1957	Bhogwa	Ahmedabad (Gujarat)	Dockyard, Rice husk, Fire altars, Double burial
6. Banawali	R.S. Bist	1973	Ghaggar	Hissar (Haryana)	Toy plough, Gridiron pattern of Town planning.
7. Dholavira	R.S. Bist	1990	Luni	Kutchh (Gujarat)	A Large well & a bath, A stadium
8. Surkotada	J. Joshi	1964	—	Gujarat	Bones of Horse, Pot burials

Salient Features of the Harappan Culture

- The Harappan Civilization was primarily Urban.
- Mohenjodaro and Harappa were the planned cities.
- The large-scale use of burnt bricks in almost all kinds of constructions are the important characteristics of the Harappan culture.
- Another remarkable feature was the underground drainage system connecting all houses to the street drains which were covered by stone slabs or bricks.
- The most important public place of Mohenjodaro is the Great Bath measuring 39 feet length, 23 feet breadth and 8 feet depth.
- Agriculture was the most important occupation. In the fertile soils, farmers cultivated two crops a year. They were the first who had grown paddy.
- Wheat and barley were the main crops grown besides sesame, mustard and cotton.
- Animals like sheep, goats and buffalo were domesticated. The use of horse is not yet firmly established.
- Bronze and copper vessels are the outstanding examples of the Harappan metal craft.
- A large number of seals numbering more than 2000 have been discovered.

Social Life

- Jewelleries such as bangles, bracelets, fillets, girdles, anklets, ear-rings and finger rings were worn by women. These ornaments were made of gold, silver, copper, bronze and semi precious stones.
- Fishing was a regular occupation while hunting and bull fighting were other pastimes.
- Manufacture of terracotta (burnt clay) was a major industry of the people.
- Figures of animals such as sacred bull and dove were discovered. The figures of Mother Goddesses were used for religious purposes.
- Most of the inscriptions were engraved on seals. It is interesting to note that the Indus script has not yet been deciphered.
- The Pipal tree was used as a religious symbol.
- The origin of the '*Swastika*' symbol can be traced to the Harrapan Civilization.
- The chief male deity was Pasupati, (proto-Siva) represented in seals as sitting in a yogic posture with three faces and two horns.

THE VEDIC PERIOD

RIG VEDIC AGE (1500 - 1000 B.C.)

- The Early Vedic period is known from the *Rig Veda*.
- The *Rig Veda* refers to Saptasindhu or the land of seven rivers. This includes the five rivers of the Punjab, namely, Jhelum, Chenab, Ravi, Beas and Sutlej along with the Indus and Saraswati.
- Historians view that the Aryans came from Central Asia. They entered India through the Khyber pass between 2000 B.C. and 1500 B.C. They first settled in seven places in the Punjab region which they called Sapta Sindhu. Slowly, they moved towards the Gangetic Valley.
- The Aryan Civilisation was a rural civilisation.

Vedic Literature

- The word 'Veda' is derived from the root 'vid', which means to know and signifies 'superior knowledge'.
- The Vedic literature consists of the four Vedas – Rig, Yajur, Sama and Atharva.
- The *Rig Veda* is the earliest of the four Vedas divided into 10 mandalas and it consists of 1028 hymns. The hymns were sung by *Hotri* in praise of various gods.
- The *Yajur Veda* consists of various details of rules to be observed at the time of sacrifice. Its hymns were recited by *Adharvayus*.
- The *Sama Veda* is set to tune for the purpose of chanting during sacrifice. It is called the book of chants and the origins of Indian music are traced in it. Its hymns were recited by *Udgatri*.
- The *Atharva Veda* contains details of rituals.
- Besides the Vedas, there are other sacred works like the Brahmanas, the Aranyakas, the Upanishads, and the epics Ramayana and Mahabharata.

Political Organisation

- During this period, the kingdom was tribal in character. Each tribe formed a separate kingdom.
- The basic unit of political organisation was *kula* or family.
- The highest political unit was called *jana* or tribe.
- There were several tribal kingdoms during the Rig Vedic period such as Bharatas, Matsyas, Yadus and Purus. The head of the kingdom was called as *rajan* or king.
- There were two popular bodies called the *Sabha* and *Samiti*. The former seems to have been a council of elders and the latter, a general assembly of the entire people.

Social Life

- Family was the basis of the society.
- The head of the family was known as *grihapathi*.

Economic Condition

- The Rig Vedic Aryans were pastoral people and their main occupation was cattle rearing. Their wealth was estimated in terms of their cattle.
- Carpentry was another important profession.

RELIGION

- The important Rig Vedic gods were Prithvi (Earth), Agni (Fire), Vayu (Wind), Varuna (Rain) and Indra (Thunder).
- Indra was the most popular among them during the early Vedic period.
- There were also female gods like Aditi and Ushas. There were no temples and no idol worship during the early Vedic period.

Rigvedic Rivers

River	Name in Rigveda
Indus	Sindhu
Jhelum	Vitasta
Chenab	Asikni
Ravi	Parushini
Beas	Vipasa
Sutlej	Sutudri
Gomati	Gomal
Saraswati	Sarasvati
Ghaggar	Prishadavati

LATER VEDIC PERIOD (1000–600 B.C.)

- This age is also called as the Epic Age because the two great epics the Ramayana and Mahabharata were written during this period.

- The Sama, Yajur, Atharva Vedas, Brahmanas, Aranyakas, Upanishads and the two epics are the sources of information for this period.

Political Organisation

- Larger kingdoms were formed during the later Vedic period.
- The king performed various rituals and sacrifices to strengthen his position. They include Rajasuya (consecration ceremony), Asvamedha (horse sacrifice) and Vajpeya (chariot race).
- Kingship became hereditary.
- Kings assumed titles like Ekrat, Samrat and Sarvabhauma.

Economic Condition

- Iron was used extensively in this period and this enabled the people to clear forests and to bring more land under cultivation. Agriculture became the chief occupation.
- Taxes like Bali, Sulk and Bhaga were collected from the people.
- Wealth was calculated in terms of cows.

Social Life

- The four divisions of society (Brahmins, Kshatriyas, Vaisyas and Sudras) or the Varna system was thoroughly established during the Later Vedic period.
- The Ashrama system was formed to attain 4 purusharthas. They were *Dharma*, *Artha*; *Kama* and *Moksha*.

Religion

- Gods of the Early Vedic period like Indra and Agni lost their importance. Prajapathi (the creator), Vishnu (the protector) and Rudra (the destroyer) became prominent during the Later Vedic period.

JAINISM AND BUDDHISM

JAINISM

- Jainism originated in the 6th century B.C. It rejected Vedic religion and avoided its rituals.
- Founded by Rishabha Deva. Rishabha Deva was succeeded by 23 Thirthankaras (prophets). Mahavira was the 24th Thirthankara.

Vardhamana Mahavira (540-468 B.C.)

- Vardhamana was born in a village called Kundagrama near Vaishali in Bihar.
- His father was *Siddhartha*. He was the head of a famous Kshatriya clan.
- His mother was *Trisala*. She was a princess of the Lichchhavi clan. She was the sister of the ruler of Vaishali.
- Vardhamana was married to *Yasoda,* a princess. They had a daughter.
- At the age of 30, he left his home and family. He became an ascetic (monk). He wandered from place-to-place in search of truth for 12 years.
- In the 13th year of his penance, he attained the highest spiritual knowledge called Kevalya or Jnana. Thereafter, he was called Mahavira and Jina. His followers were called Jains and his religion Jainism.
- He died at the age of 72 in 468 B.C. at a place called Pavapuri near modern Rajgir in Bihar.

Teachings of Jainism

- The three principles of Jainism, also known as Triratnas (three gems), are:
  1. right faith.
  2. right knowledge.
  3. right conduct.
- Mahavira preached his disciples to follow the five principles. They are:
  1. Ahimsa—not to injure any living beings
  2. Satya—to speak the truth
  3. Asteya—not to steal
  4. Tyag—not to own property
  5. Brahmacharia—to lead a virtuous life.

Spread of Jainism

- Mahavira preached his religion in Prakrit language which was the language of the masses.
- Chandragupta Maurya, Kharavela of Kalinga and the royal dynasties of south India such as the Gangas, the Kadambas, the Chalukyas and the Rashtrakutas patronised Jainism.
- Jainism was divided into two sects after Vallabhi Council, namely *Svetambaras* (wearing white dresses) under Sthulbhadra and *Digambaras* (naked) under Bhadrabahu.
- The first Jain Council was convened at Pataliputra by Sthulabahu, the leader of the *Digambaras*, in the beginning of the 3rd century B.C.
- The second Jain Council was held at Vallabhi in 5th century A.D. The final compilation of Jain literature called *Twelve Angas* was completed in this council.

BUDDHISM

Gautama Buddha (563-483 B.C.)

- Buddha's original name was *Siddhartha*.
- Siddhartha was born in the Lumbini Garden near Kapilavastu in Nepal. His father was Suddhodana. He was a Sakya chief of Kapilavastu. His mother, Mayadevi, died when Siddhartha was only seven days old. He was brought up by his step mother Mahaprajapati Gauthami.
- At the age of sixteen Siddhartha, married Yasodhara and gave birth to a son, Rahul.
- The sight of an old man, a diseased man, a corpse and an ascetic turned him away from worldly life. He left home at the age of twenty-nine in search of Truth.
- He wandered for seven years and at last, he sat under a bodhi tree at Bodh Gaya in Bihar and did intense penance, after which he got Enlightenment (Nirvana) at the age of

thirty-five. Since then, he became known as the Buddha or 'the Enlightened One'.

- Buddha delivered his first sermon at Sarnath near Banaras (now Varanasi).
- He died at the age of 80 in 483 B.C. at Kushinagar in Uttar Pradesh.

Teachings of Buddha

- The Four Noble Truths of Buddha are:
  1. The world is full of suffering.
  2. The cause of suffering is desire.
  3. If desires are get rid off, suffering can be removed.
  4. This can be done by following the Eightfold Path.
- The Eightfold Path consists of:
  1. Right Thought.
  2. Right Belief.
  3. Right Speech.
  4. Right Action.
  5. Right Living.
  6. Right Efforts.
  7. Right Knowledge.
  8. Right Meditation.

Buddhist Literature

- In Pali language.
- Buddhist scriptures in Pali are commonly referred to as *Tripitakas, i.e.*, 'Three Baskets'.
- ***Vinaya Pitaka:*** Rules of discipline in Buddhist monasteries.
- ***Sutta Pitaka:*** Largest, contains collection of Buddha's sermons.
- ***Abidhamma Pitaka:*** Explanation of the philosophical principles of the Buddhist religion.

Main Buddhist Councils

Buddhist Council	Time	Place	Chairman	Patron
First	483 BC	Rajagriha	Mahakashyapa	Ajatasatru
Second	383 BC	Vaishali	Sabakamuni	Kalashoka
Third	250 BC	Patliputra	Moggaliputta Tissa	Ashoka
Fourth	AD 72	Kundalvana	Vasumitra, Ashwaghosa	Kanishka

The Mahajanapadas

Mahajanapadas	Capital
1. Kashi	Varanasi
2. Kosala	Shravasti
3. Anga	Champanagri
4. Magadh	Girivraj or Rajgriha
5. Vajji	Vaishali
6. Malla	Kushinagar and Pavapuri
7. Chedi	Shuktimati
8. Vatsa	Kaushambi
9. Kuru	Hastinapur, Indraprastha and Isukara
10. Panchal	Ahichhatra and Kampilya
11. Matsya	Viratnagar
12. Surasen	Mathura
13. Asmaka	Paudanya
14. Avanti	Ujjaini
15. Gandhara	Taxila
16. Kamboj	Rajpur (Hatak)

DYNASTIES OF ANCIENT INDIA

HARYANKA DYNASTY

- Bimbisara was the founder of Haryanka Dynasty.
- He was a contemporary of both Vardhamana Mahavira and Gautama Buddha.
- During his rule, Darius I, the Achaemenian emperor, conquered the Indus Valley area.
- Ajatasatru imprisoned his father Bimbisara.
- The first Buddhist Council was convened by Ajatasatru at Rajgir.
- The immediate successor of Ajatasatru was Udayin.
- Udayin laid the foundation of the new capital at Pataliputra situated at the confluence of the two rivers, the Ganges and the Sone.
- Shishunaga was the founder of Shishunaga dynasty.
- After Shishunaga, the mighty empire began to collapse. His successor was Kakavarman or Kalasoka. During his reign, the second Buddhist Council was held at Vaishali.
- Kalasoka was killed by the founder of the Nanda dynasty.

NANDAS

- The fame of Magadha scaled new heights under the Nanda dynasty.
- Mahapadmananda was the founder of Nanda rule in Magadha.
- The last Nanda ruler was Dhana Nanda. Alexander invaded India during his rule.

MAURYAN EMPIRE

CHANDRAGUPTA MAURYA (322–298 B.C.)

- Chandragupta Maurya was the founder of the Mauryan Empire. He overthrew Nanda dynasty with the help of Chanakya.
- Chandragupta defeated Seleukos Nikator, the Greek general of Alexander, in a battle in 305 B.C.
- Seleukos sent Megasthenes as Greek Ambassador to the Court of Chandragupta. Megasthenes wrote *Indica*.
- Chandragupta was a follower of Jainism.
- He came to Sravana Belgola, near Mysore with a Jain monk called Bhadrabahu. The hill in which he lived until his death is called Chandragiri.
- Chanakya served as prime minister during the reigns of Chandragupta and Bindusara.

BINDUSARA (298–273 B.C.)

- Chandragupta Maurya was succeeded by his son Bindusara.
- Bindusara was called by the Greeks as "*Amitraghatha*" meaning, slayer of enemies.

ASHOKA (273–232 B.C.)

- Ashoka was the most famous ruler of the Mauryan dynasty.
- The most important event of Ashoka's reign was his victorious war with Kalinga in 261 B.C.
- Ashoka convened the Third Buddhist Council at Pataliputra around 250 B.C. in order to strengthen the *Sangha*. It was presided over by Moggaliputta Tissa.
- Ashoka's edicts and inscriptions were deciphered by James Prinsep in 1837.
- The last Mauryan king, Brahadratha was killed by his minister Pushyamitra Sunga. It put an end to the Mauryan Empire.

SUNGAS

- The founder of the Sunga dynasty was *Pushyamitra Sunga*, who was the commander-in-chief under the Mauryas.
- He ascended the throne of Magadha in 185 B.C.
- Pushyamitra was a staunch follower of Brahmanism. He performed two asvamedha sacrifices.
- After the death of Pushyamitra, his son Agnimitra became the ruler.
- Agnimitra was a great conqueror. He was also the hero of the play *Malavikagnimitram* written by Kalidasa.

KANVA

- The last Sunga ruler was Devabhuti, who was murdered by his minister Vasudeva Kanva, the founder of the *Kanva dynasty*.
- The Kanva dynasty ruled for 45 years. After the fall of the Kanvas, the history of Magadha was a blank until the establishment of the Gupta dynasty.

SATAVAHANAS

- The founder of the Satavahana dynasty was Simuka.
- The greatest ruler of the Satavahana dynasty was *Gautamiputra Satakarni*.
- The greatest port of the Satavahanas was Kalyani on the west Deccan. Gandakasela and Ganjam on the east coast were the other important seaports.
- The fine painting at Amaravathi and Nagarjunakonda caves belong to this period.

SANGAM AGE (300 B.C. TO A.D. 300)

- The Sangam Age constitutes an important chapter in the history of South India.
- According to Tamil legends, there existed three Sangams (Academy of Tamil poets) in ancient Tamil Nadu popularly called Muchchangam. These Sangams flourished under the royal patronage of the Pandyas.
- *The first Sangam*, held at then Madurai, chaired by Agastya.
- *The second Sangam* was held at Kapadapuram, chaired by Tolkappiyar.
- *The third Sangam* at Madurai was founded by Mudathirumaran.

Political History

- The Tamil country was ruled by three dynasties namely the Chera, Chola and Pandyas during the Sangam Age.

CHERAS

- The Cheras ruled over parts of modern Kerala. Their capital was Vanji and their important seaports were Tondi and Musiris.
- The greatest Chera King was *Senguttuvan*.

CHOLAS

- The Chola kingdom of the Sangam period extended from modern Tiruchi district to southern Andhra Pradesh.
- Their capital was first located at Uraiyur and then shifted to Puhar. Kaveripattinam served as their port.

GUPTA PERIOD

- The Gupta period is considered as the *Golden Age* in the history of India because this period witnessed all round developments in Religion, Literature, Science, Art and Architecture.

CHANDRAGUPTA I (320-334 A.D.)

- In the beginning of the 4th Century A.D., Sri Gupta established a small Kingdom at Pataliputra. He is considered as the founder of the Gupta dynasty.

- The first notable ruler of the Gupta dynasty was Chandragupta I. He assumed the title *Maharajadhiraja*. The Meherauli Iron Pillar inscription mentions his extensive conquests.
- Chandragupta I is considered to be the founder of the Gupta era which starts with his accession in A.D. 320.

SAMUDRAGUPTA (335-380 A.D.)

- Samudragupta was the greatest of the rulers of the Gupta dynasty. The Allahabad Pillar inscription provides a detailed account of his reign.
- Because of his military achievements, Samudragupta was hailed as '*Indian Napoleon*'.

CHANDRAGUPTA II (380-414 A.D.)

- Samudragupta was succeeded by his son Chandragupta II Vikramaditya.
- The greatest of the military achievements of Chandragupta II was his war against the Saka *satraps* of western India.
- The famous Chinese pilgrim, Fahien visited India (A.D. 399 - A.D. 414) during the reign of Chandragupta II.

SUCCESSORS OF CHANDRAGUPTA II

- Kumaragupta (415-455) was the son and successor of Chandragupta II. His reign was marked by general peace and prosperity.
- Kumaragupta was the founder of the Nalanda University.
- Kumaragupta was followed by *Skandagupta* who ruled from A.D. 456 to A.D. 468.
- After Skandagupta's death, many of his successors like Purugupta, Narasimhagupta, Buddhagupta and Baladitya could not save the Gupta empire from the Huns. Ultimately, the Gupta power totally disappeared due to the Hun invasions and later by the rise of Yasodharman in Malwa.

PUSHYABHUTI DYNASTY (600 - 647 A.D.)

- The greatest king was *Harshavardhana*, son of Prabhakar Vardhana of Thaneshwar. He shifted the capital to *Kannauj*.
- *Hieun Tsang* visited during his reign.
- He established a large monastery at Nalanda. Banabhata adorned his court, wrote Harshacharita and Kadambari. Harsha himself wrote three plays–Priyadarshika, Ratnawali and Nagananda.

PALLAVAS

- The Pallavas established their kingdom in Tondaimandalam by Simhavishnu with its capital at Kanchipuram.
- Other great Pallava rulers were Mahendravarman I, Narasimhavarman I, and Narasimhavarman II.
- The *Kailasanatha temple* at Kanchipuram is the greatest architectural masterpiece of the Pallava art.

CHALUKYAS (543-755 A.D.)

- Pulakesin I was the founder of the Chalukya dynasty. He established a small kingdom with Vatapi or Badami as its capital.
- The structural temples of the Chalukyas exist at Aihole, Badami and Pattadakal (Virupaksha temple). Cave temple architecture was also famous under the Chalukyas. Their cave temples are found in Ajanta, Ellora and Nasik.

RASHTRAKUTAS (755-975 A.D.)

- The art and architecture of the Rashtrakutas were found at Ellora and Elephanta.

CHOLAS

- Cholas became prominent in the ninth century and established an empire comprising the major portion of South India. Their capital was Tanjore.
- The founder of the Chola kingdom was Vijayalaya.
- Rajaraja Chola built the famous Brihadeeswara temple at Tanjore.
- *Dancing Figure of Shiva* (Nataraja) belong to Chola period.

MEDIEVAL INDIA

ARAB CONQUEST OF SIND

- In 712 A.D., Muhammad bin Quasim invaded Sind. Quasim defeated Dahir, the ruler of Sind and killed him in a well-contested battle.

Mahmud of Ghazni

- In 1024, Mahmud marched from Multan across Rajaputana, defeated the Solanki King Bhimadeva I, plundered Anhilwada and sacked the famous temple of Somanatha. This was his last campaign in India. Mahmud died in 1030 A.D.
- Mahmud patronized art and literature. *Firdausi* was the poet-laureate in the court of Mahmud.

Muhammad Ghori

- Prithviraj Chauhan defeated Ghori in the first battle of Tarain near Delhi in 1191 A.D.
- In the Second Battle of Tarain in 1192, Muhammad Ghori thoroughly routed the army of Prithiviraj, who was captured and killed.
- After his brilliant victory over Prithviraj at Tarain, Muhammad Ghori returned to Ghazni leaving behind his

favourite general Qutb-ud-din Aibak to make further conquests in India.

SULTANATE PERIOD

SLAVE DYNASTY (1206-1290)

- The Slave dynasty was also called Mamluk dynasty. Mamluk was the Quranic term for slave.

Qutb-ud-din Aibak

- Qutb-ud-din Aibak was a slave of Muhammad Ghori, who made him the Governor of his Indian possessions.
- After the death of Ghori in 1206, Aibak declared his independence. He assumed the title Sultan and made Lahore his capital.
- Muslim writers call Aibak Lakh Baksh or giver of lakhs because he gave liberal donations to them.
- He built the famous Quwat-Ul-Islam mosque at Delhi. He began the construction of the famous Qutb Minar at Delhi but did not live long to complete it. It was later completed by Iltutmish.

Iltutmish (1210-1236 A.D.)

- Iltutmish belonged to the Ilbari tribe and hence his dynasty was named as Ilbari dynasty.
- He shifted his capital from Lahore to Delhi.
- He organised the *Iqta system* and introduced reforms in civil administration and army.

Raziya (1236-1240 A.D.)

- She appointed an Abyssinian slave Yakuth as Master of the Royal Horses.
- In 1240, Altunia, the governor of Bhatinda revolted against her. She went in personally to suppress the revolt but Altunia killed Yakuth and took Raziya prisoner.
- Bahram Shah, son of Iltutmish killed her.

Balban (1266-1286 A.D.)

- Balban introduced rigorous court discipline and new customs such as prostration and kissing the Sultan's feet to prove his superiority over the nobles.
- He also introduced the Persian festival of *Nauroz* to impress the nobles and people with his wealth and power.
- He established a separate military department - *diwan-i-arz* – and reorganized the army.

KHILJI DYNASTY (1290-1320 A.D.)

- The founder of the Khilji dynasty was Jalaluddin Khilji.
- Ala-ud-din Khilji was the greatest ruler of the Khilji Dynasty.
- He was the first Muslim ruler to extend his empire right upto Rameshwaram in the South.
- The Sultan had built a new city called Siri near Delhi.
- Amir Khusrau the great Persian poet, patronised by Balban, continued to live in Ala-ud-din Khilji's court also.
- He introduced the system of *dagh* (branding of horses) and prepared *huliya* (descriptive list of soldiers).
- Ala-ud-din Khilji maintained a large permanent standing army and paid them in cash from the royal treasury.

TUGHLAQ DYNASTY

- Ghiyas-ud-din Tughlaq was the founder of the Tughlaq dynasty.
- To have the capital at the centre of the empire and safe from the Mongol raids, Tughlaq chose Devagiri as his new capital in A.D. 1327. The Sultan renamed the new capital Daulatabad.
- In 1329-30, Muhammad-bin-Tughlaq introduced a token currency.
- Firoz Shah Tughlaq became Sultan after the death of Muhammad-bin-Tughlaq in A.D. 1351.
- He was the first Sultan to impose irrigation tax.
- He had built new towns of Firozabad, Jaunpur, Hissar and Firozpur.
- Timur—Mongol leader of Central Asia, ordered general massacre in Delhi (AD 1398) at the time of Nasiruddin Mahmud (later Tughlaq king).

SAYYID DYNASTY

- Before his departure from India, Timur appointed Khizr Khan as governor of Multan. He captured Delhi and founded the Sayyid dynasty in 1414.
- Mubarak Shah, Mohammed Shah and Alam Shah were some of the other important noteworthy rulers of Sayyid Dynasty.

LODHI DYNASTY

- The Lodhis were Afghans.
- Bahlol Lodhi was the first Afghan ruler while his predecessors were all Turks. He died in 1489 and was succeeded by his son, Sikandar Lodhi.
- In 1504, Sikandar Lodhi founded the city of Agra and transferred his capital from Delhi to Agra.
- Babar marched against Delhi and defeated and killed Ibrahim Lodhi in the first battle of Panipat (1526).

BAHMANI AND VIJAYANAGAR KINGDOMS

- The break up of the Delhi Sultanate provided an opportunity for the rise of a number of kingdoms in the Deccan.
- After the decline of the Tughlaqs, there arose two important kingdoms in the Deccan. They were the Bahmani and Vijayanagar kingdoms.

VIJAYANAGAR EMPIRE

- The Vijayanagar Kingdom was set up in A.D. 1336. Its aim was to check the spread of Muslim power and protect Hindu Dharma in South India.
- Four dynasties – Sangama, Saluva, Tuluva and Aravidu – ruled Vijayanagar from A.D. 1336 to 1672.
- Vijayanagar was founded in 1336 by Harihara and Bukka of the Sangama dynasty.
- The Moroccan traveller, Ibn Batuta, Venetian traveller Nicolo de Conti, Persian traveller Abdur Razzak and the Portuguese traveller Domingo Paes were among them who left valuable accounts on the socio-economic conditions of the Vijayanagar Empire.
- The Hampi ruins and other monuments of Vijayanagar provide information on the cultural contributions of the Vijayanagar rulers.

KRISHNA DEVA RAYA (1509-1530)

- The Tuluva dynasty was founded by Vira Narasimha.
- The greatest of the Vijayanagar rulers, Krishna Deva Raya belonged to the Tuluva dynasty.
- Krishna Deva Raya himself authored a Telugu work, *Amukthamalyadha* and Sanskrit works, *Jambavati Kalyanam* and *Ushaparinayam*.
- He built the famous *Vittalaswamy* and *Hazara Ramaswamy* temples at Vijayanagar.
- Krishna Deva Raya renovated Virupaksha temple in A.D. 1510.
- After his death the enemies of Vijayanagar joined together and defeated the Vijayanagar ruler in the battle of Talaikota.

BAHMANI KINGDOM

- The founder of the Bahmani kingdom was Alauddin Bahman Shah also known as Hasan Gangu in 1347. Its capital was Gulbarga.
- Ahmad Wali Shah shifted the capital from Gulbarga to Bidar.
- *Gol Gumbaj* was built by *Muhammad Adil Shah*; it is famous for the so called '*Whispering Gallery*'.
- *Quli Qutub Shah* built the famous *Golcunda Fort.*

MUGHAL EMPIRE (1526-1707 AD)

BABAR (1526-1530 AD)

- Babar was the founder of the Mughal Empire in India.
- On 21st April, 1526 the first Battle of Panipat took place between Babar and Ibrahim Lodhi, who was killed in the battle.
- Babar was the first one to use guns or artillery in a battle on the Indian soil.
- Babar defeated Rana Sanga of Mewar in the battle of Kanwah in A.D. 1527.
- Babar was a soldier-scholar and wrote his own autobiography called Babar Nama in Turkish language.

HUMAYUN (1530-1556 AD)

- Sher Shah defeated Humayun at Chausa in A.D. 1539 and again at Kannauj in A.D. 1540.
- After losing his kingdom, Humayun became an exile for the next fifteen years.
- In 1555, Humayun defeated the Afghans and recovered the Mughal throne. After six months, he died in 1556 due to his fall from the staircase of his library.
- *Gulbadan Begum*, Humayun's half-sister wrote *Humayun-nama.*

SHER SHAH SURI

- The founder of the Sur dynasty was Sher Shah, whose original name was Farid.
- Sher Shah became the ruler of Delhi in 1540.
- Sher Shah organized a brilliant administrative system. The central government consisted of several departments.
- He built a new city on the banks of the river Yamuna near Delhi. Now the old fort called Purana Quila and its mosque is alone surviving.
- He built a Mausoleum at Sasaram, which is considered as one of the master pieces of Indian architecture.

AKBAR (1556-1605 AD)

- When Akbar ascended the throne in A.D. 1556 he was only 14 years old. His guardian Bairam Khan served him as a faithful minister and tutor.
- Bairam Khan, along with Akbar met Hemu in the second Battle of Panipat in 1556. Hemu was initially successful, but lost his consciousness after an arrow hit him. Akbar killed him.
- The Battle of Haldighati was fought between Rana Pratap of Mewar and Mughal army led by Man Singh and Asif Khan. Some historian say that this battle was indecisive but some say that Rana Pratap was defeated by Akbar.
- Akbar abolished the pilgrim tax and in 1562, he abolished Jaziya.
- Akbar evolved a new faith called Din-i-Illahi or Divine Faith.

JAHANGIR (1605-1627 AD)

- When Akbar died, Prince Salim succeeded with the title Jahangir (Conqueror of World) in 1605.
- Jahangir's eldest son, Khusrau, rebelled against him. He was arrested and put into prison. *Guru Arjun Dev, the fifth Sikh Guru* was executed by Jahangir.
- In 1611, Jahangir married Mehrunnisa who was known as Nurjahan (Light of World).
- Jahangir died in A.D. 1627.

SHAHJAHAN (1628-1658 AD)

- The reign of Shahjahan is generally considered as the *Golden Age* of the Mughal period.
- Shahjahan is called as the *Prince of Builders*. He had built the Jama Masjid and Red Fort in Delhi and Taj Mahal in Agra.
- Fine arts like painting, music and literature reached high level of development during Shahjahan's time.

AURANGAZEB (1658-1707 AD)

- Aurangazeb was the last great Mughal ruler. He ascended the throne after killing his three brothers Dara, Shuja and Murad in a fratricidal war.
- Aurangazeb defeated Sikandar Shah of Bijapur and annexed his kingdom.
- Aurangazeb was against the Sikhs and he executed the ninth Sikh Guru Tegh Bahadur.
- He was called *Darvesh* or a *Zinda Pir*. He forbade *Sati*. Conquered Bijapur (AD 1686) and Golconda (AD 1687) and reimposed Jaziya and Pilgrim tax in AD 1679.
- He built *Biwi ka Makbara* on the tomb of his queen *Rabaud-Durani* at Aurangabad; *Moti Masjid* within Red Fort, Delhi; and the Jami or Badshahi Mosque at Lahore.
- Aurangazeb died in A.D. 1707.

LATER MUGHALS / FALL OF THE MUGHALS

Bahadur Shah (1707-1712)

- Assumed the title of *Shah Alam I*.

Jahandar Shah (1712-1713)

- First puppet Mughal emperor. He abolished *jaziya*.

Farrukhsiyar (1713-1719)

Mohammad Shah (1719-1748)

- Nadir Shah (*of Iran*) defeated him in the Battle of Karnal (1739) and took away *Peacock throne* and *Kohinoor diamond*.

Ahmad Shah (1748-1754)

Alamgir II (1754-1759),

Shah Alam II (1759-1806)

Akbar II (1806-1837)

- He gave Ram Mohan Roy the title '*Raja*'. He sent Raja Ram Mohan Roy to London to seek a raise in his allowance.

Bahadur Shah II (1837-1857)

- He was confined by the British to the Red Fort. During the revolt of 1857, he was proclaimed the Emperor by the rebels. He was deported to Rangoon after that.

Literature of Mughal Period

Author	Work
Babar	Tuzuk-i-Babari
Abul Fazal	Ain-i-Akbari, Akbarnamah
Jahangir	Tuzuk-i-Jahangiri
Hamid	Padshahnama
Darashikoh	Majm-ul-Bahrain
Mirza Md Qasim	Alamgirnama

THE MARATHAS

SHIVAJI (1627-1680 AD)

- Shivaji was born at Shivner in 1627. His father was Shahji Bhonsle and mother Jija Bai.
- His religious teacher was Samarth Ramdas and guardian was Dadaji Kondadev.
- In 1674, Shivaji crowned himself at Raigarh and assumed the title Chatrapathi.
- *Ashtapradhan* (eight ministers) helped in administration. These were Peshwas, Sar-i-Naubat (Military), Mazumdar or Amatya (Accounts); Waqenavis (Intelligence); Surnavis (Corres-pondence); *Dabir* or *Sumanta* (Ceremonies); *Nyayadhish* (Justice); and *Panditrao* (Charity).
- Successors of Shivaji were Shambhaji, Rajaram and *Shahu* (fought at Battle of Khed in AD 1708).

THE PESHWAS

- Balaji Vishwanath was the first Peshwa. He began his career as a small revenue official and became Peshwa in 1713.
- Baji Rao I was the eldest son of Balaji Vishwanath. He was considered as the "greatest exponent of guerilla tactics after Shivaji".
- It was during reign of Balaji Baji Rao (Nanasaheb) when the Marathas lost the Third Battle of Panipat.
- Baji Rao II (last Peshwa) was the first Maratha to have fled from the British attacks instead of fighting with them. Baji Rao II surrendered to Sir John Malcom.

THE SIKH

- Guru Nanak Dev was the founder of Sikhism, the religion that draws its elements from both Hinduism and Islam.
- Name of the ten Sikh Gurus and their works are given below:
  1. **Guru Nanak Dev (1469-1539AD):** The founder of Sikhism.
  2. **Guru Angad Dev (1504-1552AD):** Developed Gurmukhi.
  3. **Guru Amar Das (1479-1574AD):** Struggled against Sati system and Purdah system.
  4. **Guru Ram Das (1534-1581AD):** Founded Amritsar, the holy city of Sikhism.

5. **Guru Arjun Dev (1563-1606AD):** He built the *Swarn Mandir* (Golden Temple).
6. **Guru Hargobind (1595-1644 AD):** Established Akal Takht.
7. **Guru Har Rai (1630-1661 AD)**
8. **Guru Har Krishan (1656-1664 AD)**
9. **Guru Tegh Bahadur (1621-1675 AD)**
10. **Guru Gobind Singh (1666-1708 AD):** Founded the Khalsa and Sikh baptism, composed many poems, and nominated the Sikh sacred text as the final and enduring Guru.

MODERN INDIA

THE ADVENT OF THE EUROPEANS

THE PORTUGUESE

- Vasco-da-Gama, a Portuguese explorer, sailed through the route of Cape of Good Hope and reached near Calicut on 20th May 1498 A.D. during the reign of King Zamorin (Hindu King of Calicut).
- Vasco-da-Gama founded a factory at Cannanore on his second visit to India in 1501. In due course, Calicut, Cochin and Cannanore became the Portuguese trading centres.
- Francisco Almeida came to India in 1505. He was the first Governor of Portuguese possessions in India.
- The real founder of Portuguese power in India was *Alfonso de Albuquerque*. He captured Goa from the rulers of Bijapur in 1510. It was made their headquarters.

THE DUTCH

- The United East India Company of the Netherlands founded a factory at Masulipatnam in 1605. They built their first fort on the main land of India at Pulicut in 1609, near Madras (Chennai). They captured Nagapattinam from the Portuguese.
- They made Agra, Surat, Masulipatnam and Chinsura in Bengal as their trading centres.

THE DANES

- The Danish East India Company was established in 1616 in Denmark.
- They came to South India and founded a factory at Tranquebar (Tharangambadi) in 1620. They also made settlements at Serampore near Calcutta (Kolkata).

THE ENGLISH

- The English East India Company was formed in 1599 under a charter granted by Queen Elizabeth in 1600.
- The East India Company sent Sir William Hawkins to the court of the Mughal Emperor Jahangir in 1609 to obtain permission to erect a factory at Surat.
- In 1615, Sir Thomas Roe, another British merchant, came to Jahangir's court. He stayed for three years and succeeded in getting permission to set up their trading centres at Agra, Surat, Ahmedabad and Broach.
- In 1690, the British got permission from Aurangazeb to build a factory on the site of Calcutta. In 1696 a fort was built at that place. It was called Fort William.

THE FRENCH

- The French East India Company was established in 1664 under the inspiring and energetic leadership of Colbert, the economic adviser of the French King Louis XIV.
- In 1667, the first French factory was established at Surat by Francis Caron who was nominated as Director-General.
- French were defeated by English in the *Battle of Wandiwash* (1760).

EAST INDIA COMPANY

- After the Battle of Plassey in 1757 and the Battle of Buxar in 1764, the East India Company became a political power.
- India was under the East India Company's rule till 1858 when it came under the direct administration of the British Crown.
- Robert Clive was the first Governor of Fort William under the Company's rule.

GOVERNOR-GENERALS OF BENGAL

Warren Hastings (1772-85 AD)

- In 1772, the Company appointed Warren Hastings as the Governor of Fort William.
- The Dual System introduced by Robert Clive was abolished by Warren Hastings.
- Warren Hastings was known for his expansionist policy. His administration witnessed the Rohilla War, the First Anglo-Maratha War and the Second Anglo-Mysore War.
- Pitt's India Act (1784) was passed.

Lord Cornwallis (1786-93 AD)

- Cornwallis inaugurated the policy of making appointments mainly on the basis of merit thereby laying the foundation of the Indian Civil Service.
- Lord Cornwallis introduced Permanent Revenue Settlement.
- Tipu Sultan signed the Treaty of Srirangapatnam in 1792 with the British.

Sir John Shore (1793-98 AD)

- Played an important role in the introduction of Permanent Settlement.
- *Battle of Kharda* between the Nizams and the Marathas (1795).

Wellesley (1798-1805)

- Wellesley came to India with a determination to launch a forward policy that he adopted to achieve his object is known as the 'Subsidiary Alliance'.
- The Fourth Anglo-Mysore War started in 1799. The war was short and decisive. Tipu fought till his capital Srirangapatnam was captured and he himself was shot dead.
- Peshwa Baji Rao II signed the *Treaty* of *Bassein* with the British in 1802. It was a subsidiary treaty and the Peshwa was recognized as the head of the Maratha kingdom.
- The Treaty of Deogaon(1803) was signed between Bhonsle and Wellesley.

Lord Minto (1807-1813)

- Lord Minto concluded the Treaty of Amritsar with Ranjit Singh of Punjab in 1809.
- The Charter Act of 1813 was passed during this period.

Lord Hastings (1813-1823)

- Anglo Nepal War (1814-1816) and Treaty of Sugauli (1816).
- Third Maratha War (1817-18), dissolution of Maratha confederacy and creation of Bombay Presidency.
- He encouraged the freedom of the Press and abolished the censorship introduced in 1799.

GOVERNOR-GENERALS OF INDIA

Lord William Bentinck (1828-1835)

- Charter Act of 1833 was passed and he was made the first Governor-General of India. Before him, the designation was Governor-General of Bengal.
- The social reforms of William Bentinck made his name immortal in the history of British India. These include the abolition of *Sati*, the suppression of Thugs and the prevention of female infanticide.
- The Government Resolution in 1835 made English the official and literary language of India.

Lord Metcalfe (1835-36 AD)

- Known as liberator of press in India.

Lord Auckland (1836-42 AD)

- First Afghan War (1838-42), a disaster for the English.

Lord Ellenborough (1842-44 AD)

- Brought an end to Afghan war. War with Gwalior (1843), *Annexation of Sind* by Charles Napier (1843).

Lord Hardinge (1844-48 AD)

- First Anglo-Sikh War (1845-46) and Treaty of Lahore (1846). Gave preference to English educated persons in employment.

Lord Dalhousie (1848-1856)

- The Doctrine of Lapse was applied by Dalhousie.
- The first railway line connecting Bombay with Thane was opened in 1853.

VICEROYS OF INDIA

Lord Canning (1856-62 AD)

- Lord Canning became the first Viceroy of India in 1858.
- Revolt of 1857, Mutiny took place. Indian Penal Code 1860 was passed.

Lord Elgin (1862 AD)

- Wahabi Movement.

Lord John Lawrence (1864-69 AD)

- Established the *High Courts* at Calcutta, Bombay and Madras in 1865.
- Telegraphic communication was opened with Europe. Created the Indian Forest Department.

Lord Northbrooke (1872-76 AD)

- Kuka Rebellion in Punjab, Famine in Bihar.

Lord Lytton (1876-80)

- In 1878, the Vernacular Press Act was passed. This Act empowered a Magistrate to secure an undertaking from the editor, publisher and printer of a vernacular newspaper that nothing would be published against the English Government. This Act crushed the freedom of the Indian press.
- In 1878, the Arms Act was passed. This Act prevented the Indians to keep arms without appropriate license.
- Lord Lytton also held a Darbar at Delhi in 1877 in which Queen Victoria was declared as the Empress of India. This extravagant Darbar cost millions of ruppes.
- In 1878, the Statutory Civil Service was established exclusively for Indians.

Lord Ripon (1880-84 AD)

- Lord Ripon repealed the Vernacular Press Act and earned much popularity among Indians.
- Ripon appointed a Commission in 1882 under the chairmanship of Sir William Hunter.
- The Commission came to be known as the Hunter Commission. The Commission recommended for the expansion and improvement of the elementary education of the masses.

- Ripon was founder of local self-government in modern India.

Lord Dufferin (1884-88 AD)

- *Third Burmese War* (1885-86 AD). Establishment of the Indian National Congress in 1885.

Lord Lansdowne (1888-94 AD)

- Factory Act of 1891 granted weekly holiday and stipulated working hours for women and children.

Lord Elgin II (1894-99 AD)

- Southern uprisings of 1899. Great famine of 1896-1897 and Lyall Commission on famine was established.

Lord Curzon (1899-1905 AD)

- Curzon instituted in 1902, a Universities Commission to go into the entire question of university education in the country.
- On the basis of the findings and recommendations of the Commission, Curzon brought in the Indian Universities Act of 1904, which brought all the universities in India under the control of the government.

Lord Minto (1905-10 AD)

- Swadeshi Movement (1905-08); foundation of Muslim League (1906); Surat Session and split in the Congress (1907). Morley-Minto Reforms (1909).

Lord Hardinge (1910-16 AD)

- Capital shifted from Calcutta to Delhi (1911); Delhi Durbar; Partition of Bengal was cancelled. The Hindu Mahasabha was founded in 1915 by Pandit Madan Mohan Malaviya.

Lord Chelmsford (1916-21 AD)

- Gandhi returned to India (1915) and founded the Sabarmati Ashram (1916), Champaran Satyagraha, Satyagraha at Ahmedabad (1981), Kheda Satyagraha (1918).
- Rowlatt Act (March, 1919) and the Jallianwala Bagh Massacre (13th April, 1919).
- Khilafat Committee was formed and Khilafat Movement started (1919-20).
- Non-Cooperation Movement started (1920-22).

Lord Reading (1921-26)

- Moplah Rebellion (1921) took place. *Kakori Train* Robbery on 1st August, 1925. *Communal Riots* of 1923-25 in Multan, Amritsar, Delhi etc.

Lord Irwin (1926-31 AD)

- Lahore Session of Congress and *Poorna Swaraj* Declaration (1929).
- Simon Commission visited India in 1927.
- Dandi March (12th March, 1930). Civil Disobedience Movement (1930).
- First Round Table Conference was held in England in 1930. Gandhi-Irwin Pact.

Lord Willingdon (1931-36 AD)

- *Second Round Table Conference* in London in 1931 and *third* in 1932.

Lord Linlithgow (1936-43 AD)

- Congress Ministries resignation celebrated as '*Deliverance Day*' by the Muslim League (1939), the Lahore Resolution (23rd March, 1940) of the Muslim League demanding separate state for the Muslims. (It was at this session that Jinnah propounded his Two-Nation Theory). Outbreak of World War II in 1939. Cripps Mission in 1942. Quit India Movement (8th August, 1942).

Lord Wavell (1943-47 AD)

- Cabinet Mission Plan (16th May, 1946).
- First meeting of the Constituent Assembly was held on 9th December, 1946.
- Arranged the Shimla Conference on 25th June, 1945 with Indian National Congress and Muslim League but failed.

Lord Mountbatten (March to Aug, 1947)

- Last viceroy of British India and the first Governor-General of free India.
- Partition of India decided by the 3rd June Plan or Mountbatten Plan.

NATIONAL MOVEMENT (1885-1947)

INDIAN NATIONAL CONGRESS (1885)

- Allan Octavian Hume, a retired civil servant in the British Government took the initiative to form an all-India organization. Thus, the Indian National Congress was founded and its first session was held at Bombay in 1885. W.C. Banerjee was its first president. It was attended by 72 delegates from all over India.
- The second session was held in Calcutta in 1886 and the third in Madras in 1887.
- Between 1885 and 1905, the Congress leaders were moderates. The Moderates had faith in the British justice and goodwill. They were called moderates because they adopted peaceful and constitutional means to achieve their demands.
- In 1905, Gopal Krishna Gokhale founded the Servants of India Society to train Indians to dedicate their lives to the cause of the country.

Partition of Bengal (1905)

- By Lord Curzon on 16th October, 1905 through a royal proclamation, reducing the old province of Bengal in size by creating East Bengal and Assam out of the rest of Bengal.

- The partition of Bengal in 1905 provided a spark for the rise of extremism in the Indian National Movement.
- Curzon's real motives behind this partition were:
  - To break the growing strength of Bengali nationalism since Bengal was the base of Indian nationalism.
  - To divide the Hindus and Muslims in Bengal.
  - To show the enormous power of the British Government in doing whatever it liked.

Swadeshi Movement (1905)

- The Swadeshi Movement involved programmes like the boycott of government service, courts, schools and colleges and of foreign goods. It was both a political and economic movement.
- Lal, Bal, Pal and Aurobindo Ghosh played an important role.

Muslim League (1906)

- In December 1906, Muslim delegates from all over India met at Dacca for the Muslim Educational Conference.
- Taking advantage of this occasion, Nawab Salimullah of Dacca proposed the setting up of an organisation to look after the Muslim interests. The proposal was accepted.
- The All-India Muslim League was finally set up on December 30, 1906.

Minto Morley Reforms (1909)

- Minto, the Viceroy and Morley, the Secretary of State for India jointly proposed reforms to the Indian Councils. An Act, called the Indian Councils Act or the Minto-Morley Reforms Act was passed in 1909.
- A separate communal electorate was introduced for the Muslims.

The Lucknow Pact (1916)

- During the 1916 Congress session at Lucknow two major events occurred. The divided Congress became united. An understanding for joint action against the British was reached between the Congress and the Muslim League and it was called the Lucknow Pact.
- The signing of the Lucknow Pact by the Congress and the Muslim League in 1916 marked an important step in the Hindu-Muslim unity.

The Home Rule Movement (1916)

- Two Home Rule Leagues were established, one by B.G. Tilak at Poona in April 1916 and the other by Mrs. Annie Besant at Madras in September 1916.
- While Tilak's Movement concentrated on Maharashtra, Annie Besant's Movement covered the rest of the country.

August Declaration

- On 20 August, 1917, Montague, the Secretary of State in England, promised the gradual development of self-governing institutions in India.
- This August Declaration led to the end of the Home Rule Movement.

Rowlatt Act (1919)

- In 1917, a committee was set up under the presidentship of Sir Sydney Rowlatt to look into the militant Nationalist activities. On the basis of its report the Rowlatt Act was passed in March 1919 by the Central Legislative Council. As per this Act, any person could be arrested on the basis of suspicion. No appeal or petition could be filed against such arrests.
- This Act was called the Black Act and it was widely opposed. An all-India hartal was organized on 6 April, 1919.

Jallianwala Bagh Massacre (13 April, 1919)

- On 13th April, the Baisakhi day (harvest festival), a public meeting was organized at the Jallianwala Bagh (garden). Gen. Dyer marched in and without any warning opened fire on the crowd. The firing continued for about 10 to 15 minutes and it stopped only after the ammunition exhausted.
- According to official report 379 people were killed and 1137 wounded in the incident. There was a nationwide protest against this massacre and Rabindranath Tagore renounced his knighthood as a protest.

Khilafat Movement (1920)

- The chief cause of the Khilafat Movement was the defeat of Turkey in the First World War.
- The Muslims in India were upset over the British attitude against Turkey and launched the Khilafat Movement.
- Ali brothers, *Mohd Ali* and *Shaukat Ali* started this movement. It was jointly led by the Khilafat leaders and the Congress.

Non-Co-operation Movement (1920-22)

- Mahatma Gandhi announced his plan to begin Non-Cooperation with the government as a sequel to the Rowlatt Act, Jallianwala Bagh massacre and the Khilafat Movement. It was approved by the Indian National Congress at the Nagpur session in December, 1920.
- The Congress observed the Non-Co-operation movement in 1920. The main aim of this movement was to attain Swaraj through non-violent and peaceful means.
- The whole movement was abruptly called off on 11th February, 1922 by Gandhi following the Chauri-Chaura incident in the Gorakhpur district of U.P. Many top leaders of the country were stunned at this sudden suspension of the Non-Co-operation Movement.

- On 5th February an angry mob set fire to the police station at *Chauri-Chaura* and twenty two police men were burnt to death.

Swaraj Party

- Leaders like Motilal Nehru and Chittranjan Das formed a separate group within the Congress known as the Swaraj Party on 1 January, 1923.
- The Swarajists wanted to contest the council elections and wreck the government from within.

Simon Commission (1927)

- The Act of 1919 included a provision for its review after a lapse of ten years. However, the review commission under the chairmanship of Sir John Simon was appointed by the British Government two years earlier of its schedule in 1927.
- Indian leaders opposed the commission, as there were no Indians in it, they cried *Simon Go Back.*
- The government used brutal repression and at Lahore, *Lala Lajpat Rai* was severely beaten in lathi-charge.

Nehru Report (1928)

- The Secretary of State, Lord Birkenhead, challenged the Indians to produce a Constitution that would be acceptable to all. The challenge was accepted by the Congress, which convened an all party meeting on 28 February, 1928.
- A committee consisting of eight was constituted to draw up a blueprint for the future Constitution of India. It was headed by Motilal Nehru. The Report published by this Committee came to be known as the Nehru Report.

Lahore Session (1929)

- On Dec. 19, 1929, under the Presidentship of J.L. Nehru, the INC, as its Lahore session, declared Poorna Swaraj (Complete Independence) as its ultimate goal.
- On Dec. 31, 1929, the newly adopted tricolour flag was unfurled and Jan. 26, 1930 was fixed as the First Independence Day, which was to be celebrated every year.

Dandi March (1930)

- On 12th March, 1930, Gandhi began his famous March to Dandi with his chosen 79 followers to break the salt laws. He reached the coast of Dandi on 5 April, 1930 after marching a distance of 200 miles and on 6 April formally launched the Civil Disobedience Movement by breaking the salt laws.

Civil Disobedience Movement

- Countrywide mass participation by women.
- The Garhwal soldiers refused to fire on the people at Peshawar.

Round Table Conference

- The first Round Table Conference was held in November 1930 at London and it was boycotted by the Congress.
- On 8th March, 1931 the Gandhi-Irwin Pact was signed. As per this pact, Mahatma Gandhi agreed to suspend the Civil-Disobedience Movement and participate in the Second-Round Table Conference.
- In September 1931, the Second Round Table Conference was held at London. Mahatma Gandhi participated in the Conference but returned to India disappointed.
- In January 1932, the Civil-Disobedience Movement was resumed.

Poona Pact (1932)

- The idea of separate electorate for the depressed classes was abandoned, but seats reserved for them in the provincial legislature were increased.
- Thus, Poona Pact agreed upon a joint electorate for upper and lower castes.

Demand for Pakistan

- *Chaudhary Rehmat Ali* gave the term *Pakistan* in 1933.
- In March 1940, the Muslim League demanded the creation of Pakistan.

Cripps Mission (1942)

- The British Government in its effort to secure Indian co-operation in the Second World War sent Sir Stafford Cripps to India on 23 March, 1942. This is known as Cripps Mission.
- The main recommendations of Cripps was the promise of Dominion Status to India.
- Congress rejected it. Gandhi called Cripp's proposals as a "Post-dated Cheque".

Quit India Movement (1942-1944)

- The All India Congress Committee met at Bombay on 8th August, 1942 and passed the famous Quit India Resolution. On the same day, Gandhi gave his call of 'do or die'.
- On 8th and 9th August, 1942, the government arrested all the prominent leaders of the Congress. Mahatma Gandhi was kept in prison at Poona. Pandit Jawaharlal Nehru, Abul Kalam Azad, and other leaders were imprisoned in the Ahamednagar Fort.
- Quit India Movement was the final attempt for country's freedom.

Indian National Army (INA)

- On July 2, 1943, Subhash Chandra Bose reached Singapore and gave the rousing war cry of *'Dilli Chalo'*. He was made the President of Indian Independence League and soon became the supreme commander of the Indian National Army. He gave the country the slogan of *Jai Hind.*
- INA had three fighting brigades named after Gandhi, Azad and Nehru. Rani of Jhansi Brigade was an exclusive women force. INA headquarters were at Rangoon and Singapore.

Cabinet Mission (1946)

- The Cabinet Mission put forward a plan for solution of the constitutional problem. A proposal was envisaged for setting up an Interim Government, which would remain in office till a new government was elected on the basis of the new Constitution framed by the Constituent Assembly.
- Elections were held in July 1946 for the formation of a Constituent Assembly.
- Muslim league observed the *Direct Action Day* on 16 August, 1946.
- An Interim Government was formed under the leadership of Jawaharlal Nehru on 2 September, 1946.

Mountbatten Plan (1947)

- On 20 February 1947, Prime Minister Atlee announced in the House of Commons the definite intention of the British Government to transfer power to responsible Indian hands by a date not later than June 1948.
- Lord Mountbatten armed with vast powers became India's Viceroy on 24 March, 1947. The partition of India and the creation of Pakistan appeared inevitable to him.
- After extensive consultation Lord Mountbatten put forth the plan of partition of India on 3 June, 1947. The Congress and the Muslim League ultimately approved the Mountbatten Plan.

Indian Independence Act, 1947

- The salient features of this Act was the partition of the country into India and Pakistan would come into effect from 15 August, 1947.
- On 15th August, 1947 India, and on the 14th August Pakistan came into existence as two independent states.
- Lord Mountbatten was made the first Governor General of Independent India, whereas Mohammad Ali Jinnah became the first Governor General of Pakistan.
- C. Rajagopalachari became the first and last Indian Governor-General of India. When India became a Republic on 26 January, 1950 Dr. Rajendra Prasad became the first President of our country.

Socio-Religious Movements and Organisation

Name of the Organisation	*Founder*	*Year*	*Place*
Atmiya Sabha	Ram Mohan Roy	1815	Calcutta
Brahmo Samaj	Ram Mohan Roy	1828	Calcutta
Dharma Sabha	Radhakanta Dev	1829	Calcutta
Tattvabodhini Sabha	Debendranath Tagore	1839	Calcutta
Nirankaris	Dayal Das, Darbara Singh, Rattan Chand etc.	1840	Punjab
Manav Dharma Sabha	Durgaram Manchharam	1844	Surat
Paramhansa Mandli	Dadoba Pandurung	1849	Bombay
Namdharis	Ram Singh	1857	Punjab
Radha Swami Satsang	Tulsi Ram	1861	Agra
Brahmo Samaj of India	Keshab Chandra Sen	1866	Calcutta
Dar-ul-Ulum	Maulana Hussain Ahmed	1866	Deoband
Prarthna Samaj	Atmaram Pandurung	1867	Bombay
Arya Samaj	Swami Dayanand Saraswati	1875	Bombay
Theosophical Society	Madam H.P. Blavatsky and Col. H.S. Olcott	1875	New York (USA)
Sadharan Brahmo Samaj	Anand Mohan Bose	1878	Calcutta
Deccan Education Society	G.G. Agarkar	1884	Pune (Poona)
Muhammadan Educational Conference	Syed Ahmad Khan	1886	Aligarh
Indian National Conference	M.G. Ranade	1887	Bombay
Deva Samaj	Shivnarayan Agnihotri	1887	Lahore
Nadwah-ul-Ulama	Maulana Shibli Numani	1894	Lucknow
Ramakrishna Mission	Swami Vivekananda	1897	Belur
Servents of Indian Society	Gopal Krishna Gokhale	1905	Bombay
Poona Seva Sadan	Mrs. Ramabai Ranade and G.K. Devadhar	1909	Pune (Poona)
Social Service League	N.M. Joshi	1911	Bombay
Seva Samiti	H.N. Kunzru	1914	Allahabad

Newspapers and Journals

- *Bengal Gazette* (1780) (India's first newspaper)—James Augustus Hikky
- *Kesari*—B.G. Tilak
- *Maratha*—B.G. Tilak
- *Sudharak*—G.K. Gokhale

- *Amrit Bazar Patrika*—Shishir Kumar Ghosh and Motilal Ghosh
- *Yugantar*—Bhupendranath Datta and Birender Kumar Ghosh
- *Bombay Chronicle*—Firoze Shah Mehta
- *New India (Daily)*—Annie Besant

Books and Authors

- *Causes of the Indian Mutiny*—Sir Syed Ahmed Khan
- *Ghulam Giri*—Jyotiba Phule
- *Anandmath*—Bankim Chand Chatterjee
- *Satyarth Prakash*—Swami Dayanand
- *Unhappy India*—Lala Lajpat Rai
- *India Divided*—Dr. Rajendra Prasad
- *The Discovery of India*—J.L. Nehru
- *Neel Darpan*—Dinbandhu Mitra
- *Hind Swaraj*—M.K. Gandhi
- *What Congress and Gandhi have done to the untouchables*—Dr. B.R. Ambedkar

Important Sayings

- *'Back to Vedas'*—Dayanand Saraswati
- *'Dilli Chalo!'*—Subhash Chandra Bose's battle cry of *Azad Hind Fauj*
- *'Do or Die'*—Mahatma Gandhi (while launching Quit India movement in 1942)
- *'Give me blood and I will give you freedom'*—Subhash Chandra Bose (in his address to soldiers of *Azad Hind Fauj*)
- *'My ultimate aim is to wipe every tear from every eye'*—Jawaharlal Nehru
- *'Swaraj is my birthright and I will have it'*—Bal Gangadhar Tilak
- *'Inqualab Zindabad'*—Bhagat Singh
- *'Jai Jawan, Jai Kisan'*—Lal Bahadur Shastri
- *'Sarfaroshi ki tamanna Ab Hamare Dil mein Hai'*—Ram Prasad Bismill
- *'Saare Jahan Se Achcha,* Hindustan Hamara'—Dr. Mohammed Iqbal
- *'Hindi, Hindu, Hindustan'*—Bhartendu Harishchandra
- *'Vande Mataram'*—Bankim Chandra Chatterjee

❒❒❒

GEOGRAPHY

WORLD GEOGRAPHY

THE UNIVERSE

- Existing matter and energy are together known as **Universe.**

GALAXY

- A galaxy is a huge system of billions of stars and clouds of dust and gases.
- Our solar system is a part of *Milky Way* galaxy.
- There are millions of galaxies that make the Universe.

STARS

- Stars account for 98 per cent of the matter in a galaxy. The stars nearest to the earth are *Proxima Centauri, Alpha Centauri, Barnard's Star, Sirius* and so on. Of these, *Sirius* is the brightest.

LIGHT YEAR

- Light year is the distance travelled by light in one year at a speed of 2,99,792.5 km. per second.

SOLAR SYSTEM

- The Sun, eight planets, satellites and some other celestial bodies known as asteroids and meteoroids form the solar system.

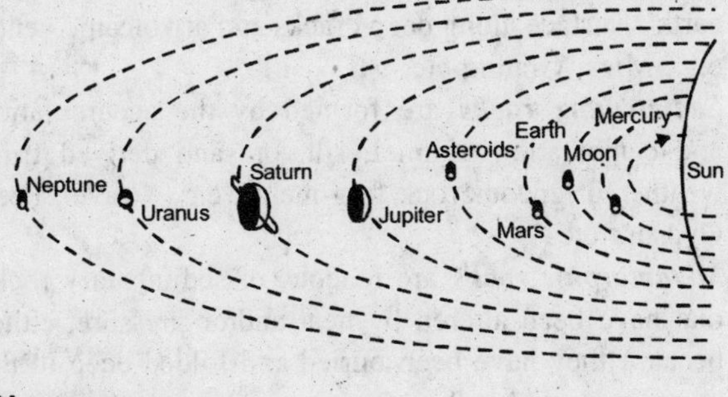

SUN

- The Sun is in the centre of the solar system.
- The Sun is a mixture of gases. It consists of 92% hydrogen, 7.8% helium and 0.2% other gases.
- The Sun is about 150 million km away from the earth.
- The sun is an ultimate source of energy for life on Earth.
- Sunlight takes 8 min 16.6 sec to reach earth.

Facts about Sun

Diameter	— 1.392 × 10^6 km
Volume	— 1.304 × 106 times the volume of earth
Temperature	— 6000°C at surface and 15 million degree C at the centre
Relative density	— 1.4
Gravitational Pull	— 28 times the gravitational pull of the earth

Facts about Planets

Closest to Sun	*Mercury*
Farthest from Sun	*Neptune*
Heaviest	*Jupiter*
Hottest	*Venus*
Inner	*Mercury, Venus, Earth, Mars*
Largest	*Jupiter*
Smallest	*Mercury*
Moons, None	*Mercury, Venus*
Moon; Largest	*Ganymede (Jupiter), larger than Mercury*
Nearest to Earth	*Venus*
Orbits; Order	*Mercury (closest to Sun), Venus, Earth, Mars, Jupiter, Saturn, Uranus, Neptune.*
Rings/largest number	*Saturn*
Spin; Backwards	*Venus (East to West)*

COMETS

- It has a head and a tail. Its tail originates only when it gets closer to the sun. The tail can be 20-30 million km long. It always point away from the sun because of the force exerted by solar wind and radiation on the cometory material.

THE EARTH

- The earth is the third nearest planet to the Sun.
- From the outer space, the earth appears blue because its two-thirds surface is covered by water. It is, therefore, called a blue planet.
- It is the densest of all planets.
- Rotation is the movement of the earth on its axis. Due to this rotation, day and night occur.
- The earth takes about 23 hours 56 minutes and 4 seconds to complete one rotation around its axis.
- Earth takes 365¼ days (one year) to revolve around the sun.

THE EARTH: FACTS AND FIGURES

- *Mass of Earth*—5.972 × 10^{21} tonnes
- *Density of Earth*—5.517 times that of water
- *Volume of Earth*—1.083 × 10^{11} cubic km
- *Equatorial circumference*—4.007 × 104 km
- *Polar Diameter*—12,714 km
- *Equatorial Diameter*—12756 km
- *Polar or Meridional circumference*—4.0 × 10^4 km
- *Estimated Age*—At least 4600 million years
- *Land Surface*—148,951,000 sq km
- *Water Surface*—361,150,000 sq km (71 per cent of total area)
- *Highest Point of the land surface*—Mt. Everest (8,848 metres)
- *Lowest point of the land surface*—Shores of the Dead Sea (396 metres below the sea level)
- *Greatest Ocean depth*—Mariana Trench, East of Philippines (11,033 metres below the sea level)

THE MOON

- Earth has only one satellite, that is, the moon.
- Its diameter is only one-quarter that of the earth. It is about 3,84,400 km away from us.
- The moon moves around the earth in about 27 days. It takes exactly the same time to complete one spin. As a result, only one side of the moon (only 59% of its surface) is visible to us on the earth.
- Moonlight takes 1.3 sec. to reach earth.

LATITUDE

- Imaginary lines drawn parallel to the equator. Measured as an angle whose apex is at the centre of the earth.
- The equator represents 0° latitude, while the North Pole is 90°N and the South Pole 90°S.
- 23½°N represents Tropic of Cancer while 23½°S represents Tropic of Capricorn.

LONGITUDE

- It is the angular distance measured from the centre of the earth. On the globe the lines of longitude are drawn as a series of semicircles that extend from the North Pole to the South Pole through the equator. They are also called meridians.
- The distance between any two meridians is not equal. At the equator, 1 degree = 111 km. At 30°N or S, it is 96.5 km. It goes on decreasing this way until it is zero at the poles.

INTERNATIONAL DATE LINE

- It is the 180° meridian running over the Pacific Ocean, deviating at Aleutian Islands, Fiji, Samoa and Gilbert Islands.
- Travellers crossing the Date Line from west to east repeat a day and travellers crossing it from east to west lose a day.

INDIAN STANDARD TIME (IST)

- Indian Standard Time is calculated on the basis of 82.5°E longitude which passes through Uttar Pradesh, Madhya Pradesh, Odisha, Chattisgarh and Andhra Pradesh.

ECLIPSES

- Sun is the only source of light for both the Earth and Moon. Eclipses occur when the light thus received is either blocked by the earth or by the Moon.
- Eclipses occur when either the Earth moves behind the Moon's shadow or the Moon moves behind the Earth's shadow.

LUNAR ECLIPSE

- Lunar eclipse occur only when the following conditions are met.
  1. The Sun, Earth and Moon must be aligned in a straight line.
  2. The Earth must be positioned between the Sun and the Moon.
  3. The Moon must be in its full phase (Full Moon).

SOLAR ECLIPSE

- Solar eclipses occur only when the following conditions are met.
  1. The Sun, Earth and Moon must be aligned in a straight line.
  2. The Moon must be positioned between the Sun and the Earth.
  3. Must be a New Moon day.

ROCKS

- Rocks are composed of many minerals such as silica, aluminium, iron and magnesium. The nature of the rock is determined by the presence of its minerals.
- Rocks can be classified into three types:
  1. ***Igneous rocks*** are formed by magma that reaches the earth's surface along deep cracks and at volcanic vents. e.g., Mica, Granite etc.
  2. ***Sedimentary rocks*** are formed by the accumulation and cementation of mud, silt, or sand derived from weathered igneous rock frag-ments. e.g., Gravel, Peat, Gypsum etc.
  3. ***Metamorphic rocks*** are igneous or sedimentary rocks that have been altered by heat and/or pressure, either because they have been buried and folded deep in the crust, or because they have come into contact with molten igneous rock, e.g., Gneiss, Marble, Quartzite etc.

VOLCANOES

Sudden eruption of hot magma (molten rock), gases, ash and other material from inside the Earth to its surface.

- ***Active*** which erupts frequently, e.g., Mauna Loa (Hawaii), Etna (Sicily), Vesuvius (Italy), Stromboli (Mediterranean Sea).

- ***Dormant*** Not erupted for quite sometime, e.g., Fujiyama (Japan), Krakatoa (Indonesia), Barren Island (Andamans).
- ***Extinct*** Not erupted for several centuries, e.g., Arthur's Seat, Edinburgh, Scotland.

EARTHQUAKES

- Earthquakes are a form of wave energy that is transferred through bedrock. It is transmitted from the point of the earthquake focus, as spherical seismic waves. They travel in all directions outward.
- The intensity of earthquake waves is recorded by *Seismograph*.

LANDFORMS

- There are three major landforms: mountains, plateaus and plains.

MOUNTAINS

- A mountain can be defined as an area of land that rises abruptly from the surrounding region.
- There are three types of mountains- *Fold Mountains, Block Mountains* and the ***Volcanic Mountains***.
- Himalayas, Alps, Andes, Rockies, Atlas, etc are examples of Fold Mountains.
- The Aravali range in India is one of the oldest **fold mountain** systems in the world.
- The Rhine valley and the Vosges mountain in Europe are examples of such mountain systems.
- Volcanic mountains are formed due to volcanic activity.
- Mt. Kilimanjaro in Africa and Mt. Fujiyama in Japan are examples of such mountains.

Major Mountain Ranges of the World

Range	Location	Highest Peak (m)	Length (km)
Andes	South America	6,960	7,200
Himalayas-Karakoram-Hindukush	South Central Asia	8,848	4,800
Rockies	North America	4,401	4,800
Great Dividing Range	East Australia	2,228	3,600
Western Ghat	Western India	2,637	1,610
Caucasus	Europe	5,642	1,200
Alaska	USA	6,194	1,130
Alps	Europe	4,808	1,050
Apennines	Europe	2,912	—
Ural	Asia	1,895	—
Atlas	North West Africa	—	1,930

PLATEAUS

- A plateau is an elevated flat land. It is a flat-topped table land standing above the surrounding area.

Principal Mountain Peaks of the World

Mountains	Height in Metres
1. Mount Everest	8,848
2. K-2 (Godwin Austen)	8,611
3. Kanchenjunga	8,597
4. Lhotse	8,511
5. Makalu I	8,481
6. Dhaulagiri I	8,167
7. Mansalu I	8,156
8. Chollyo	8,153
9. Nanga Parbat	8,124
10. Annapurna I	8,091
11. Gasherbrum I	8,068
12. Broad Peak I	8,047
13. Gasherbrum II	8,034
14. Shisha Pangma (Gosainthan)	8,014
15. Gasherbrum III	7,952

PLAINS

- A relatively low-lying and flat land surface with least difference between its highest and lowest points is called a Plain.

OCEANS

- Oceans of the world is classified into four groups: the Pacific, the Atlantic, the Arctic and the Indian.
- The Pacific is the largest ocean, being twice the size of the Atlantic. It covers about a third of the Earth's surface, and contains more than half the water on the planet.

Oceans of the World

Names	Area (Sq. Km.)	Greatest Depth
Pacific	166,240000	Mariana Trench
Atlantic	86,560000	Puerto Rico Trench
Indian	73430000	Java Trench
Arctic	13230000	—

Major Rivers of the World

River	Origin	Falls in	Length (Km.)
Nile	Victoria lake	Mediterranean Sea	6,650
Amazon	Andes (Peru)	Atlantic Ocean	6,428
Yangtze	Tibetan Kiang Plateau	China Sea	6,300
Mississippi Missouri	Itaska lake (USA)	Gulf of Mexico (USA)	6,275
Yenisei	Tannu-Ola Mts.	Arctic Ocean	5,539
Hoang Ho	Kunlun Mts.	Gulf of Chibli	5,464
Ob	Altai Mts., Russia	Gulf of Ob	5,410
Congo	Lualaba & Luapula rivers	Atlantic Ocean	4,700
Amur	Northeast China	Sea of Okhotsk	4,444
Lena	Baikal Mts	Laptev Sea	4,400
Mekong	Tibetan Highlands	South China Sea	4,350
Mackenzie	Great Slave Lake	Beaufort Sea	4,241
Niger	Guinea	Gulf of Guinea	4,200

Major Gulfs of the World

Names	Area (Sq. Km.)	Names	Areas (Sq. Km.)
Gulf of Mexico	15,44,000	Gulf of St. Lawrence	2,37,000
Gulf of Hudson	12,33,000	Gulf of California	1,62,000
Arabian Gulf	2,38,000	English Channel	89,900

Important Straits of the World

Straits	Water Bodies joined	Area
Bab-al-Mandeb	Red Sea & Arabian Sea	Arabia & Africa
Bering	Arctic Ocean & Bering Sea	Alaska & Asia
Bosphorus	Black Sea & Marmara Sea	Turkey
Dover	North Sea & Atlantic Ocean	England & Europe
Florida	Gulf of Mexico & Atlantic Ocean	Florida & Bahamas Islands
Gibralter	Mediterranean Sea & Atlantic Ocean	Spain & Africa
Malacca	Java Sea & Bay of Bengal	India & Indonesia
Palk	Bay of Bengal & Indian Ocean	India & Sri Lanka
Magellan	South Pacific & South Atlantic Ocean	Chile
Sunda	Java Sea & Indian Ocean	Indonesia

Important Lakes of the World

Lake	Location	Area (Sq. Km.)
Caspian	Russia and CIS	371000
Superior	Canada and USA	82414
Victoria	Tanzania (Africa)	69485
Huron	Canada and USA	59596
Michigan	USA	58016
Tanganyika	Africa	32892
Baikal	Russia (CIS)	31502
Great Bear	Canada	31080
Malawi	Malawi (Tanzania)	30044
Great Slave	Canada	28438

Highest Waterfalls of the World

Name(s) (Foreign)	Location
Angel (Salto Angel)	Canaima Nat'l Park, Venezuela
Tugela	Natal Nat'l Park, South Africa
Utigord (Utigordsfoss)	Norway
Monge (Mongefoss)	Marstein, Norway
Gocta Cataracts	Chachapoyas, Peru
Mutarazi (Mtarazi)	Nyanga Nat'l Park, Zimbabwe
Yosemite	Yosemite Nat'l Park, California, U.S.
Espelands (Espelandsfoss)	Hardanger Fjord, Norway
Lower Mar Valley (Ostra Mardolafoss)	Eikesdal, Norway
Tyssestrengene	Odda, Norway

Important Cities on River Banks (World)

City	Country	River
Adelaide	Australia	Torrens
Amsterdam	Netherlands	Amsel
Alexandria	Egypt	Nile
Ankara	Turkiye	Kazil
Bangkok	Thailand	Chao Praya
Basra	Iraq	Eupharates and Tigris
Baghdad	Iraq	Tigris
Berlin	Germany	Spree
Bonn	Germany	Rhine
Budapest	Hungary	Danube
Bristol	UK	Avon
Buenos Aires	Argentina	Laplata
Chittagong	Bangladesh	Majyani
Canton	China	Si-Kiang
Cairo	Egypt	Nile
Chung King	China	Yang-tse-kiang
Cologne	Germany	Rhine
Dandzing	Germany	Vistula
Dresden	Germany	Elbe
Dublin	Ireland	Liffy
Hamburg	Germany	Elbe
Kabul	Afghanistan	Kabul
Karachi	Pakistan	Indus
Khortoum	Sudan	Confluence of Blue & White Nile
Lahore	Pakistan	Ravi
Leningrad	Russia	Neva
Lisbon	Portugal	Tagus
Liverpool	England	Messey
London	England	Thames
Moscow	Russia	Moskva
Montreal	Canada	St. Lawrence
Nanking	China	Yang-tse-kiang
New Orleans	U.S.A.	Mississipi
New York	U.S.A.	Hudson
Ottawa	Canada	Ottawa
Paris	France	Seine
Philadelphia	U.S.A	Delaware
Perth	Australia	Swan
Prague	Czech Republic	Vitava
Quebec	Canada	St. Lawrence
Rome	Italy	Tiber
Rotterdam	The Netherlands	New Moss
Stalingrad	Russia	Volga
Shanghai	China	Yang-tse-kiang
Sidney	Australia	Darling
Saint Louis	U.S.A	Mississippi
Tokyo	Japan	Arakava
Vienna	Austria	Danube
Warsaw	Poland	Vistula
Washington D.C.	U.S.A.	Potomac
Yangoon	Myanmar	Irawaddy

World's Geographical Surnames

City of Sky-scrapers—New York
City of Seven Hills—Rome
City of Dreaming Spires—Oxford
City of Golden Gate—San Francisco
City of Magnificent Buildings—Washington D.C.
City of Eternal Springs—Quito (S. America)
China's Sorrow—Hwang Ho
Cockpit of Europe—Belgium
Dark Continent—Africa
Emerald Isle—Ireland
Eternal City—Rome
Empire City—New York
Garden City—Chicago
Gate of Tears—Strait of Bab-el-Mandeb
Gift of the Nile—Egypt
Granite City—Aberdeen (Scotland)
Hermit Kingdom—Korea
Herring Pond—Atlantic Ocean
Holy Land—Jerusalem
Island Continent—Australia
Islands of Cloves—Zanzibar
Isle of Pearls—Bahrein (Persian Gulf)
Key to the Mediterranean—Gibralter
Land of Cakes—Scotland
Land of Golden Fleece—Australia
Land of Maple Leaf—Canada
Land of Morning Calm—Korea
Land of Midnight Sun—Norway
Land of the Thousand Lakes—Finland
Land of the Thunderbolt—Bhutan
Land of White Elephant—Thailand
Land of Thousand Elephants—Laos
Land of Rising Sun—Japan
Loneliest Island—Tristan De Gunha (Mid-Atlantic)
Manchester of Japan—Osaka
Pillars of Hercules—Strait of Gibraltar
Pearl of the Antilles—Cuba
Playground of Europe—Switzerland
Quaker City—Philadelphia
Queen of the Adriatic—Venice
Roof of the World—The Pamirs, Central Asia
Sugar bowl of the world—Cuba
Venice of the North—Stockholm

Windy City—Chicago
Whiteman's grave—Guinea Coast of Africa
Yellow River—Huang Ho (China)
Sickman of Europe—Turkiye

Important Boundaries

Durand Line	Pakistan & Afghanistan
MacMohan Line	India & China
Radcliff Line	India & Pakistan
Maginot Line	France & Germany
Oder Niesse Line	Germany & Poland
Hindenberg Line	Poland & Germany (at the time of First World War)
38th Parallel	North & South Korea
49th Parallel	USA & Canada

Continents: Some Facts

Continent	Biggest Counrty	Highest Peak	Longest River
Asia	China	Mt. Everest (8848 m)	Yangtze Kiang
Africa	Algeria	Mt. Kilimanjaro (5895 m)	Nile
North America	Canada	Mt. Mckinley (6194 m)	Mississippi Missouri
South America	Brazil	Mt. Acancagua (6960 m)	Amazon
Europe	Russia	Mt. Elbrus (5642 m)	Ob
Australia	Australia	Mt. Coscuisco (2228 m)	Darling
Antarctica	—	Vinson Massif (5140 m)	—

INDIAN GEOGRAPHY

AREA AND LOCATION

- India is in the southern parts of the Asian continent. In the west of India lies the Arabian Peninsula while in the east lies the Indo-China Peninsula.
- India extends between 8°4' N and 37°6' N latitudes and between 68°7' E and 97°2' E longitudes.
- India, has a total geographic area of 32,87,263 sq. km. This is only 2.42 % of the total geographic area of the world but holds 17 per cent of the world's population.
- The 23½°N, which is the Tropic of Cancer, runs across the country.
- India has a length of 3214 km from north to south and 2933 km from east to west. It has a land frontier of 15200 km.
- The total length of the coastline of the mainland, Lakshadweep Islands and Andaman and Nicobar Islands is 7,516.6 km.
- India ranks seventh among the countries of the world, in terms of the geographical extent.
- India is bordered on three sides by water and on one by land, it is also a peninsula.
- India shares its common border with Afghanistan and Pakistan in the north-west, China and Bhutan in the north, and Bangladesh in the east. In the south, Sri Lanka is separated from India by a strait, known as the Palk Strait.
- 82°30' E longitude is considered as the Indian Standard Meridian. The local time of this longitude is taken as the Indian Standard Time (IST). This is 5½ hours ahead of the Greenwich Mean Time.

THE INDIAN STATES ON INTERNATIONAL BOUNDARIES ARE:

- ***Bordering Pakistan:*** Jammu and Kashmir, Punjab, Rajasthan, Gujarat.
- ***Bordering China:*** Ladakh, Himachal Pradesh, Uttarakhand, Sikkim, Arunachal Pradesh.
- ***Bordering Nepal:*** Bihar, Uttarakhand, UP, Sikkim, West Bengal.
- ***Bordering Bangladesh:*** West Bengal, Mizoram, Meghalaya, Tripura, Assam.
- ***Bordering Bhutan:*** West Bengal, Sikkim, Arunachal Pradesh, Assam.
- ***Bordering Myanmar:*** Arunachal Pradesh, Nagaland, Manipur, Mizoram.
- ***Bordering Afghanistan:*** Jammu and Kashmir (Pakistan-occupied area).

Important Passes

• Jammu and Kashmir	Burzi-La, Joji-La
• Himachal Pradesh	Bara La, Cha-La, Shipki-La
• Uttarakhand	Niti-La, Lipu-Lekh-La
• Sikkim	Jelep-La, Nathu-La
• Arunachal Pradesh	Bomdi-La

Heighest Mountain Peaks of India

Peaks	Elevation˙ (in mts.)
Godwin Austin (K2)	8611*
Kanchenjunga	8598
Nanga Parvat	8126
Gasherbrum	8068*
Broad Peak	8047*
Dastegil	7885*
Masherbrum (East)	7821
Nanda Devi	7817
Masherbrum (West)	7806*
Rakoposhi	7788*
Kamet	7756
Saser Kangdi	7672

• *Above mean sea level in metres.*

* *Situated in Pak occupied Kashmir (PoK).*

Towns at River Banks

Town	River
Agra	Yamuna
Allahabad	Confluence of the Ganges and the Yamuna
Ayodhya	Saryu
Badrinath	The Ganges
Kolkata	Hooghly
Cuttuck	Mahanadi
Delhi	Yamuna
Dibrugarh	Brahmaputra
Ferozepur	Satluj
Guwahati	Brahmaputra
Hardwar	The Ganges
Hyderabad	Musi
Jabalpur	Narmada
Kanpur	The Ganges
Kota	Chambal
Kurnool	Tungbhadra
Lucknow	Gomti
Ludhiana	Sutlej
Nasik	Godavari
Pandharpur	Bhima
Patna	The Ganges
Sambalpur	Mahanadi
Srinagar	Jhelum
Srirangapattam	Cauveri
Surat	Tapti
Varanasi	The Ganges
Vijaywada	Krishna

Famous Waterfalls of India

Waterfall	Hgt (Mt.)	River	State
Kunchikal	455	Varahi	Karnataka
Dudhsagar	310	Mandvi	Goa
Jog/Gersoppa	255	Sharavati	Karnataka
Rakim Kund	168	Gaighat	Bihar
Chachai	127	Bihad	Madhya Pradesh
Kevti	98	Mahanadi	Madhya Pradesh
Sivasamudram	90	Cauveri	Karnataka

Important Lakes of India

Name of lake	State/UT
Pulicat Lake	Tamil Nadu & Andhra Pradesh Border
Sambhar Lake	Rajasthan
Tso Moriri Lake	Jammu & Kashmir
Vembanad Lake	Kerala
Wular & Dal Lakes	Jammu and Kashmir
Chilka Lake	Odisha
Kolleru Lake	Andhra Pradesh
Loktak Lake	Manipur
Lonar Lake	Maharashtra
Pangong Lake	Ladakh

Rivers of India

Name	Originates From	Falls Into
Yamuna	Yamunotri	Ganga
Chambal	Singar Chouri Peak, Vindhyan escarpment	Yamuna
Ghaghara	Matsatung Glacier	Ganga
Kosi	Near Gosain Dham Peak	Ganga
Sabarmati	Aravalis	Gulf of Khambat
Krishna	Western Ghats	Bay of Bengal
Godavari	Nasik district in Maharashtra	Bay of Bengal
Caurey	Brahmagir Range of Western Ghats	Bay of Bengal
Tungabharda	Western Ghats	Krishna
Ganges	Combines Sources	Bay of Bengal

Name	Originates From	Falls Into
Sutlej	Mansarovar Rakas lakes	Chenab
Indus	Near Mansarovar Lake	Arabian Sea
Ravi	Kullu Hills near Rohtang Pass	Chenab
Beas	Near Rohtang Pass	Sutlej
Jhelum	Verinag in Kashmir	Chenab
Son	Amarkantak	Ganga
Brahmaputra	Near Mansarovar Lake	Bay of Bengal
Narmada	Amarkantak	Gulf of Khambat
Tapti	Betul District in Madhya Pradesh	Gulf of Khambat
Mahanadi	Raipur District in Chhattisgarh	Bay of Bengal
Luni	Aravallis	Rann of Kuchchh
Ghaggar	Himalayas	Near Fatehabad
Betwa	Vindhyanchal	Yamuna

Geographical Surnames

Bengal's Sorrow	Damodar River
City of Palaces	Kolkata
Gateway of India	Mumbai
Pink City	Jaipur
Paris of India	Jaipur
Manchester of India	Ahmedabad
Kashmir of South	Kerala
Son of Sea	Lakshadweep
Queen of Mountains	Mussourie
Iron City	Jamshedpur
Hollywood of India	Mumbai
Scotland of East	Meghalaya
City of Nababs	Lucknow
City of Temples & Ghats	Varanasi
Land of Five Rivers	Punjab
City of Golden Temple	Amritsar
Garden of India	Bangaluru
Spice Garden of India	Kerala
City of Lakes	Srinagar
Twin City	Hyderabad-Secunderabad
City of Seven Islands	Mumbai
Diamond Harbour	Kolkata
Switzerland of India	Kashmir
Rice Bowl	Chhattisgarh
Fruit Bowl	Himachal Pradesh
Ganga of South	Cauvery
Pitsburg of India	Jamshedpur
City of Bridges	Srinagar
Residence of God	Allahabad
A Cross-road (Quadrivial) of National Highways	Kanpur
Heart of India	Delhi
Black River	Sharda
City of Festivals	Madurai
Queen of Deccan	Pune
Sorrow of Bihar	Kosi River

Some Major Irrigational and Multipurpose Projects

S.No.	Name of Project	Related State	River
1.	Bargi Project	Madhya Pradesh	Bargi
2.	Beas	Joint Venture of Haryana, Punjab and Rajasthan	Beas
3.	Bhadra	Karnakata	Bhadra
4.	Bhakra Nangal	Haryana, Punjab and Rajasthan	Sutluj
5.	Bhima I	Maharashtra	Pawana
6.	Bhima II	Maharashtra	Krishna
7.	Chambal	Joint Project of M.P. and Rajasthan	Chambal
8.	Damodar Valley Project	West Bengal and Bihar	Damodar
9.	Dulhasti Power Project	Jammu and Kashmir	Chenab
10.	Farakka	West Bengal	Hooghly

S.No.	Name of Project	Related State	River
11.	Gandak	Bihar and U.P.	Gandak
12.	Ghataprabha	Karnataka	Ghataprabha
13.	Hasdeo Bango Project	Madhya Pradesh, Chhattisgarh	Hasdeo
14.	Hirakud	Odisha	Mahanadi
15.	Jayakwadi	Maharashtra	Godavari
16.	Kakrapara	Gujarat	Tapti
17.	Kangsbati	West Bengal	Kangsbati and Kumari
18.	Karjan	Gujarat	Karjan
19.	Kosi	Bihar	Kosi
20.	Koyana	Maharashtra	Koyana
21.	Krishna Project	Maharashtra	Krishna
22.	Kukadi	Maharashtra	Kukadi
23.	Left Bank Ghagra Canal	Uttar Pradesh	Ghagra
24.	Madhya Ganga Canal	Uttar Pradesh	Ganga
25.	Mahanadi Delta Scheme	Odisha	(The irrigation scheme will utilise releases from Hirakund Reservoir)
26.	Mahi	Gujarat	Mahi
27.	Malaprabha	Karnataka	Malaprabha
28.	Mayurakshi	West Bengal	Mayurakshi
29.	Nagarjunasagar	Andhra Pradesh	Krishna
30.	Panam	Gujarat	Panam
31.	Parambikulam Aliyar	Tamil Nadu and Kerala	Perimbikulam
32.	Pochampad	Andhra Pradesh	Godavari
33.	Pong Dam	Punjab	Beas
34.	Ramganga	Uttarakhand	Ramganga
35.	Ranjit Sagar Dam (Thein Dam)	Punjab	Ravi
36.	Rihand	Uttar Pradesh	Rihand
37.	Sabarmati	Gujarat	Sabarmati
38.	Sharda Sahayak	U.P.	Ghagra
39.	Sone High Level Canal	Bihar	Sone
40.	Tawa	Madhya Pradesh	Tawa
41.	Tehri Dam	Uttarakhand	Bhagirathi
42.	Tungabhadra	Andhra Pradesh and Karnataka	Tungabhadra
43.	Ukai	Gujarat	Tapti
44.	Upper Krishna	Karnataka	Krishna
45.	Upper Penganga	Maharashtra	Penganga
46.	Uri Power Project	Jammu and Kashmir	Jhelum

Major Indian Crops

Crops	Temp(°c)	Water(cm)	States where Produced
Wheat	15°-25°	60-90	Uttar Pradesh, Madhya Pradesh, Punjab, Haryana.
Rice	24°-26°	80-200	West Bengal, Uttar Pradesh, Punjab, Andhra Pradesh, Bihar
Maize	18°-21°	50-60	Karnataka, Madhya Pradesh, Maharashtra
Jowar	20°-35°	40-60	Maharashtra, Madhya Pradesh, Karnataka
Soyabean	25°-27°	50-120	Maharashtra, Madhya Pradesh, Rajasthan
Cotton	20°-30°	80-150	Gujarat, Maharashtra, Telangana, Karnataka, Madhya Pradesh
Tobacco	20°-25°	75-80	Andhra Pradesh, Madhya Pradesh, Gujarat, Karnataka, Maharashtra, Uttar Pradesh
Tea	24°-30°	100-200	Assam, West Bengal, Kerala, Tamil Nadu, Uttar Pradesh
Ground Nut	15°-25°	60-130	Gujarat, Maharashtra

Mineral Wealth at a Glance (Metallic Minerals)

Mineral	Chief Producers
Bauxite	Odisha, Gujarat, Jharkhand
Chromite	Odisha, Karnataka
Coal	Jharkhand, Odisha
Copper	Rajasthan, Madhya Pradesh
Diaspore	Uttar Pradesh, Madhya Pradesh
Gold	Karnataka
Iron	Odisha, Karnataka, Goa
Lead	Rajasthan, Andhra Pradesh
Lignite	Tamil Nadu, Jammu & Kashmir
Manganese	Odisha, Karnataka
Natural Gas	Gujarat, Assam
Petroleum	Gujarat, Assam, Andhra Pradesh
Silver	Rajasthan, Jharkhand, Gujarat
Tungsten	Rajasthan
Zinc	Rajasthan, Maharashtra

Zones and Headquarters of Indian Railways

S.No.	Zone	Headquarters
1.	Central	Mumbai
2.	Eastern	Kolkata
3.	Northern	New Delhi
4.	North-Eastern	Gorakhpur
5.	North-East Frontier	Maligaon, Guwahati
6.	Southern	Chennai
7.	South-Central	Secunderabad
8.	South-Eastern	Kolkata
9.	Western	Mumbai
10.	East Coast	Bhubaneswar
11.	East Central	Hajipur
12.	North Central	Prayagraj
13.	North Western	Jaipur
14.	South Western	Hubballi (Hubli)
15.	West Central	Jabalpur
16.	South East Central	Bilaspur
17.	Metro Railway	Kolkata
18.	South Coast Railway	Vishakhapatnam (Proposed)

Major National Highways

N H	Connects
NH 44	Srinagar to Kanyakumari
NH 27	Porbandar to Silchar
NH 48	Delhi to Chennai
NH 52	Sangrur to Ankola
NH 30	Sitarganj to Ibrahimpatnam
NH 6	Jorabat to Seling
NH 53	Hazira to Paradip
NH 16	East Coast (West Bengal) to Chennai
NH 66	Panvel to Kanyakumari
NH 19	Delhi to Kolkata

Major Ports of Country

1. Syama Prasad Mookerjee (Kolkata)
2. Mumbai
3. J.L. Nehru Port (Nhava Sheva)
4. V.O. Chidambaranar (Tuticorin)
5. Chennai
6. Mormugao
7. New Mangalore
8. Paradeep
9. Deendayal (Kandla)
10. Vishakhapatnam
11. Cochin
12. Kamarajar Port Limited (Ennore).

Major International Airports in India

International Airports	City
Indira Gandhi International Airport	Delhi
Anna International Airport	Chennai
Sri Guru Ram Dass Ji International Airport	Amritsar
Rajiv Gandhi International Airport	Hyderabad
Calicut International Airport	Kozhikode
Chhatrapati Shivaji International Airport	Mumbai
Kempegowda International Airport	Bengaluru
Goa Airport in Vasco di Gama City	Goa
Netaji Subash Chandra Bose International Airport	Kolkata
Thriuvananthapuram International Airport	Thiruvananthapuram
Lokpriya Gopinath Bordoloi International Airport	Guwahati
Sardar Vallabhbhai Patel International Airport	Ahmedabad

❑❑❑

INDIAN POLITY

INDIAN CONSTITUTION

- Demand for a Constituent Assembly composed of the people of India officially asserted by the Congress for the first time in 1935.
- The election for Indian Constitution Assembly held in 1946 according to the *Cabinet Mission Plan.*
- The first session of the Assembly was held in New Delhi on December 9, 1946. *Sachidanand Sinha* was elected provisional chairman of the session.
- On December 11, 1946, Dr. Rajendra Prasad was elected as the Permanent Chairman of the Constituent Assembly.
- The Constitution was framed by the Constituent Assembly of India, set-up in December 1946, in accordance with the Cabinet Mission Plan, under the Chairmanship of Sachidanand Sinha, initially.
- The total membership of Constituent Assembly after partition was 299, among them 70 were representatives from the Indian states and others from British India.
- The Chairman of the Drafting Committee was **Dr. BR Ambedkar**, also called the Father of the Constitution.
- The Constituent Assembly took 2 years, 11 months and 18 days to complete the Constitution.
- The Constitution, adopted on 8th November, 1949, contained 395 Articles and Schedules.
- The Constitution was delayed till 26th January because, in 1929, on this day Indian National Congress demanded Poorna Swaraj in Lahore Session under JL Nehru.
- Indian Constitution is a comprehensive document and it is the lengthiest written Constitution in the World.

THE PREAMBLE

- ***The Preamble of the Constitution:*** "We the people of India, having solemnly resolved to Constitute India into a Sovereign, Socialist, Secular Democratic Republic and to secure to all its citizen:

  Justice, Social, economic and political;

  Liberty of thought, expression, belief, faith and worship;

  Equality of status and of opportunity; and to promote among them all;

  Fraternity assuring the dignity of the individual and the unity and integrity of the nation;

  In our Constituent Assembly, this twenty-sixth day of November, 1949, do hereby adopt, enact and give to ourselves this constitution."

Foreign Sources of Indian Constitution

Foreign Sources	*Subject*
Britain	Parliamentary system, collective responsibilities of Cabinet
America	Fundamental right, Independent Judiciary, Judicial review
Canada	Division of powers
Ireland	Directive principles
Germany	Emergency provisions
Russia	Fundamental duties
Australia	Concurrent list

IMPORTANT ARTICLES

PART - I

UNION AND ITS TERRITORIES (ARTICLE 1 - 4)

- The Constitution says, "India, that is Bharat, shall be a Union of States".
- Parliament has the power to create any State, reduce it, change the name of boundaries of any State.

PART - II

CITIZENSHIP (ARTICLE 5 - 11)

- The Constitution provides for a single Citizenship.
- ***Indian Citizenship can be acquire:***
  1. by birth
  2. by descent
  3. by registration
  4. by naturalisation
  5. by incorporation of territory
- ***Indian Citizenship can be lost by:***
  1. renunciation;
  2. termination — it takes place if a citizen of India voluntary acquires the citizenship of another country; and
  3. deprivation — if the Government terminates the citizenship.

PART - III

FUNDAMENTAL RIGHTS (ARTICLE 12 - 35)

- Following fundamental rights are enjoyed by every Indian citizen, irrespective of caste, colour, creed and sex:
  1. ***Right to Equality:*** No special privileges, no distinction on grounds of religion, caste, creed and sex.
  2. ***Right to Freedom:*** The right to freedom of expression and speech, the right to choose one's own profession, the right to reside in any part of the Indian Union.
  3. ***Right to Freedom to Religion:*** Except when it is in the interest of public order, morality, health or other conditions, everybody has the right to profess, practice and propagate his religion freely.
  4. ***Cultural and Educational Rights:*** The Constitution provides that every community can run its own institutions to preserve its own culture and language.
  5. ***Right against Exploitation:*** Traffic in human beings and forced labour and the employment of children under 14 years in factories or mines, are punishable offences.
  6. ***Rights to Constitutional Remedies:*** When a citizen finds that any of his fundamental rights has been encroached upon, he can move the Supreme Court, which has been empowered to safeguard the fundamental rights of a citizen (Article 32).

PART - IV

DIRECTIVE PRINCIPLES OF STATE POLICY (ARTICLE 36 - 51)

- Directive principles are not enforceable through courts. Main aim of Directive principles is to provide social and economic base of a genuine democracy.

Some Important Directive Principles:

- Provisions for adequate means of livelihood for all citizens (Art. 39).
- Right to work (Art. 41).
- Right to human condition of work and maternity relief (Art. 42).
- Right to a living wage and condition of work ensuring decent standard of life of worker (Art. 43).
- Common Civil Code (Art. 44).
- Prohibit consumption of liquor (Art. 47).
- Prevent slaughter of useful cattle (Art. 48).
- Organise Panchayati Raj (Art. 40).
- Separate the judiciary from the executive (Art. 50).
- Protect and maintain places of historic monuments (Art. 49).
- International peace (Art. 51).

PART - IV A

FUNDAMENTAL DUTIES (ARTICLE 51A)

- The fundamental duties for the Indian citizens have been incorporated in the Constitution through the Constitution (42nd) Amendment Act, 1976. These duties are:
  1. to abide by the Constitution and respect its ideals and institutions, the National Flag and the National Anthem;
  2. to cherish and follow the noble deeds which inspired our national struggle for freedom;
  3. to uphold and protect the sovereignty, unity and integrity of India;
  4. to defend the country and render national service when called upon to do so;
  5. to promote harmony and the spirit of common brotherhood amongst all the people transcending religious, regional or sectional diversities and to renounce practices derogatory to the dignity of women;
  6. to value and preserve the rich heritage of our composite culture;
  7. to protect and improve natural environment including forests, lakes, rivers and wildlife, and to have compassion for living creatures;
  8. to develop the scientific temper, humanism and the spirit of inquiry and reform;
  9. to safeguard public property and to abjure violence;
  10. to strive towards excellence in all spheres of individual and collective activity so that the nation constantly rises to higher levels of endeavour and achievement.
  11. who is parent or guardian to provide opportunities for education to his child or, as the case may be, ward between age of six and fourteen years.

PART - V

UNION (ARTICLE 52 - 151)

THE PRESIDENT

- The President is the Constitutional head of the Republic of India. He is more or less the titular head of the executive.
- He is the constitutional head but not the real executive. The real power is vested in the hands of the Council of Ministers.
- President is the first citizen of India.
- ***Qualifications:*** (i) Indian citizen, (ii) age not less than 35 years, (iii) should have qualification for election to Lok Sabha, (iv) should not hold any office of profit, (v) should not be a Member of Parliament or State Legislature.
- ***Election:*** Indirectly elected through Electoral College consisting of elected members of both the Houses of the Parliament and elected members of the Legislative Assemblies of the States.
- According to the 70th Amendment Act, 1992, the expression 'States' include the National Capital Territory of Delhi and the Union Territory of Puducherry. Members of the Legislative Councils have no right to vote in the Presidential election.

- ***Powers:*** He makes appointments to all the constitutional posts.
- He can address either House of Parliament and dissolve Lok Sabha.
- All Bills passed by Parliament must receive his assent to become an Act.
- He issues ordinances when Parliament is not in session. No Money Bill can be introduced in Lok Sabha without his recommendation.
- He appoints 12 members of special repute in the Rajya Sabha.
- He has the power of *Pardon* to a criminal in special cases.
- The President holds the office for a period of five years. He is eligible for re-election.
- He draws a fix salary per month with various allowances.
- He is also entitled to rent free official residence called Rashtrapati Bhawan.

Vice-President

- ***Article 63*** of the Constitution stipulates a Vice-President for India.
- The Vice-President acts as the ex-officio Chairman of the Council of States (Rajya Sabha).
- He is elected by an electoral college consisting of the members of both Houses of Parliament in accordance with the system of proportional represen-tation by means of the single trans-ferable vote. He must be a citizen of India, not less than 35 years of age, and should be eligible for election as a member of the Council of States.
- Disputes in connection with election of a president or a vice-president are to be a dealt with in accordance with Article-71. Such disputes shall be decided by the Supreme Court.

Council of Ministers

- The Constitution of India provides for a parliament system of government under which the President is only Constitutional ruler and the real power is exercised by the Council of Ministers, headed by the Prime Minister.
- Council of Ministers is composed of all Union Ministers—the Prime Minister, Cabinet Ministers and Ministers of State.
- The Council of Ministers is Collectively responsible to the Lok Sabha.
- The Prime Minister is a link between the President and the Council of Ministers.

Prime Minister

- The Prime Minister is the leader of the majority party in the Parliament.
- He is appointed by the President. Other Ministers are appointed by the president on his advice.
- The Prime Minister is the head of the Government and the head of the Council of Ministers.
- Jawaharlal Nehru was the first Prime Minister and the longest serving so far.

Union Legislature

- The Legislature of the Union, which is called 'Parliament' consists of the President and the two Houses of Parliament known as the Council of states (Rajya Sabha) and the House of the People (Lok Sabha).

RAJYA SABHA

- The Rajya Sabha is the Upper House of the Parliament and it is constituted of representatives from the States or the Constituent units of the Indian Union.
- It is a permanent body, one third of its members retiring after every two years.
- Its maximum strength is 250. Out of these, twelve members are nominated by the President from well-known personalities in the realm of Science, Art, Literature and Social Service. Rest of 238 representatives of the States and Union Territories are elected.
- Currently, the strength of the Rajya Sabha is 245.

LOK SABHA

- The Lok Sabha whose life is five years, is the Lower House of Parliament and comprises of members directly elected by the people.
- The House of the people (Lok Sabha) at present consists of 543 directly elected members from the states and Union Territories.
- Two members of Anglo-Indian Community were nominated by the President, but by the 104th amendment of the constitution this provision have been abolished.
- The House of the People shall continue for five years (unless sooner dissolved) from the date of its meeting and no longer and the expiry of the said period of 5 years shall operate as dissolution of the House.

Parliamentary Committees

- There are several Parliamentary Committees to assist the Parliament in its deliberations.
- These are appointed or elected by the respective Houses of Lok Sabha and Rajya Sabha on a motion made or are nominated by their presiding officers.
- Among the Standing Committees, three are financial Committees:
  (*i*) Public Account Committee;
  (*ii*) Estimate Committee;
  (*iii*) Public undertaking Committee.

Speaker of Lok Sabha

- Speaker is elected by the Lok Sabha from among its members.
- The Speaker will have the final power to maintain order within the House of the People and to interpret its rules of procedure.
- A Deputy-Speaker is also elected to officiate in absence of the Speaker.
- *G.V. Mavlankar* was the first Speaker of the Lok Sabha (1952-1956).

Supreme Court

- The Constitution provides for the Supreme Court, which consists of Chief Justice and 33 judges. They are appointed by the President of India.

QUALIFICATION AND TENURE

- Eligibility conditions for a judge of the Supreme Court are that he must be : (i) a citizen of India; (ii) a judge of a high court for a minimum period of 5 years; or (iii) an advocate of a high court for at least ten years or a distinguished jurist.
- Judges hold office till the age of 65.
- They can resign earlier or can be removed by the President on the recommendation of the two Houses of the Parliament by 2/3rd majority of the members present and voting.

Powers

- *Original jurisdiction:* Cases involving Government of India and the states or cases involving the enforcement of Fundamental Rights fall under original jurisdiction.
- *Appellate Jurisdiction:* In cases which are brought to it in the form of appeals against the judgement of the lower courts—It hears appeals in civil and criminal cases.
- *Advisory functions:* the Supreme Court advises the President on the constitutionality of a particular legal matter. However, its advice is not binding on the President.

Other Powers:

1. it is a court of record and can punish for contempt of itself;
2. it can make rules for regulating the practice and procedure of courts with the approval of the President; and
3. it can recommend to the President the removal of chairman and members of the UPSC. Supreme Court enjoys the power of judicial review (right of the court which declares as unconstitutional, the laws passed by the legislature and orders issued by executive) though it is not specifically mentioned in the Constitution.

- The first Chief Justice of India was H.J. Kania (1950-51).

COMPTROLLER AND AUDITOR GENERAL (CAG) (ARTICLE 148-151)

- The Comptroller and Auditor General of India is guardian of the public purse.
- It is his duty to see that not a *paisa* is spent out of consolidated fund of India or of a state without the authority of the appropriate legislature.
- He is appointed by President of India.
- A person with long administrative experience and knowledge of accounts is appointed.
- Holds office for 6 yrs or till 65 yrs of age.
- The President can remove him only on the recommendation of the 2 houses of Parliament (as in case of judge of Supreme Court).
- The CAG submits its reports to the President (in case of accounts relating to the Union Government) or to the State Governors (for State Government Accounts).
- The first CAG of India was *V Narahari Rao* (1948-1954).
- The CAG is not eligible for further office under the Union or State Governments. The expenses of the office of the CAG is charged to the Consolidated Fund of India.

ATTORNEY GENERAL OF INDIA

- The Attorney General of India is the first law officer of the Government of India.
- Though he is not a member of cabinet he has the right to speak in the House of Parliament, but he has no right to vote.
- The Attorney General of India shall be appointed by the President and shall hold office during his pleasure.
- His duty shall be to give advice on such legal matter from time-to-time as may be referred to him by the President.
- To be appointed as Attorney General, a candidate must be qualified to be appointed as a Judge of the Supreme Court.
- The Attorney General can participate in proceedings of the Parliament without the Right to Vote (Article 88).
- The first Attorney General of Independent India was MC Setalvad (1950-1963).

PART - VI

THE STATES (ARTICLE 152 - 237)

The Governor

- The Governor is appointed by the President and holds office during the pleasure of the President.
- Apart from the power to appoint the council of ministers, if the governor finds that the government of state cannot be carried on in accordance with the provisions of the constitution (Art. 356), he may send his report to the President who may assume to himself the functions of the government of the state. (This is popularly known as 'President's Rule').
- Article 161 gives the Governor the power to grant pardons, reprieves, remission of punishment to persons convicted under the state law.

- Article 171 states that the States where Legislative Councils exists, the Governor can nominate some members from amongst those distinguished in literature, science, arts, cooperative movement and social service.

STATES LEGISLATURE (ARTICLE 168 - 212)

- The state legislature consists of Governor and legislative assembly.
- In some state like *Bihar, Maharashtra, Andhra Pradesh, Karnataka, Uttar Pradesh and Telangana* have a legislative council.
- The membership of the council should not be more than *one-third* of the legislative assembly but not less than 40.
- The legislative assembly of each state shall be composed of members chosen by direct election on the basis of adult suffrage and the number of members shall not be more than 500 or less than 60.
- The assembly of Sikkim, Goa, Puducherry and Mizoram have less than 60 members.

HIGH COURTS (ARTICLE 214-232)

- The High Court stands at the apex of the State Judiciary.
- As per the Constitution, there shall be a High Court in each State. But there may be a common High Court for two or more States and Union Territory, if it is provided by a law of the Parliament. For example, the Madras High Court has its Jurisdiction over the State of Tamil Nadu and the Union Territory of Puducherry.
- The State Government has no control over it.
- There are 25 High Courts in India.
- The Calcutta High Court, established in 1862, is the oldest High Court in India.

THE PANCHAYATS (ARTICLE 243-243 O)

- Panchayati Raj was introduced in India with a view to associate the people with administration at grass-root level.
- It is a three-tier system as recommended by Balwant Rai Mehta Committee.
- Introduced by the 73rd Amendment Act, 1992 which envisaged a three tier system of local governance.

These are:

1. Gram Panchayat at the village level
2. Panchayat Samiti at the block level
3. Zila Parishad at the district level.

Jurisdiction and Seat of High Courts

Name	Territorial Jurisdiction	Seat
Allahabad	Uttar Pradesh	Prayagraj (Bench at Lucknow)
Bombay	Maharashtra, Goa, Dadar and Nagar Haveli and Daman and Diu	Mumbai (Benches at Nagpur, Panaji and Aurangabad)
Calcutta	West Bengal and Andaman & Nicobar	Kolkata (Circuit Benchs at Port Blair and Jalpaiguri)
Chhattisgarh	Chhattisgarh	Bilaspur
Delhi	Delhi	Delhi
Gauhati	Assam, Nagaland, Mizoram and Arunachal Pradesh	Guwahati (Benches at Kohima, Aizawl and Itanagar)
Gujarat	Gujarat	Ahmedabad
Himachal Pradesh	Himachal Pradesh	Shimla
Jammu & Kashmir and Ladakh	Jammu & Kashmir, Ladakh	Srinagar and Jammu
Jharkhand	Jharkhand	Ranchi
Karnataka	Karnataka	Bengaluru (Circuit Benches at Dharwar and Gulbarga)
Kerala	Kerala & Lakshadweep	Ernakulam
Madhya Pradesh	Madhya Pradesh	Jabalpur (Benches at Gwalior and Indore)
Madras	Tamil Nadu & Puducherry	Chennai (Bench at Madurai)
Orissa	Odisha	Cuttack
Patna	Bihar	Patna
Punjab and Haryana	Punjab, Haryana and Chandigarh	Chandigarh
Rajasthan	Rajasthan	Jodhpur (Bench at Jaipur)
Sikkim	Sikkim	Gangtok
Uttarakhand	Uttarakhand	Nainital
Tripura	Tripura	Agartala
Meghalaya	Meghalaya	Shillong
Manipur	Manipur	Imphal
Telangana	Telangana	Hyderabad
Andhra Pradesh	Andhra Pradesh	Amravati

THE MUNICIPALITIES (ARTICLE 243 P-243 ZG)

- Big cities have municipal corporations headed by the elected Mayor.
- For small towns there are elected boards or councils, in turn, elect their Presidents.
- Introduced by the 74th Amendment Act, 1993 which envisages three types of urban local bodies, namely, municipality (nagar palika), city council (nagar panchayat).
- Municipal governance in India was first introduced in Madras in 1688.

PART - XIII

(ARTICLE 301 - 307)

- In this part from Article 301-307 trade, commerce and intercourse within the territory of India are given.

PART - XIV

(ARTICLE 308 - 323)

- In this part services under the union and the states are given.
- ***Article 312: All India Services*** and ***Article 315:*** Public Service Commissions for the Union and for the States.
- The first Public Service Commission was set up in 1926, on the recommendations of the Lee Commission.

UNION PUBLIC SERVICE COMMISSION (UPSC)

- This Commission is responsible for:
  1. recruitment to all civil services and posts, under the Union Government by written examinations, interviews and promotions, and
  2. advising the Government on all matters relating to methods of recruitment, principles to be followed in making promotions and transfers. Its Chairman is appointed by the President.

STAFF SELECTION COMMISSION (SSC)

- The Union Government has constituted a Staff Selection Commission for recruitment to non-technical Class III posts in the central government and in subordinate offices.
- The Administrative Reforms Commission had recommended the setting up of such a Commission.
- The Commission has also been entrusted with the responsibility of making recruitment to Group 'B' services like Assistants' and Stenographers Grade 'C'.
- The Commission has a chairman and two members.

ELECTIONS (ARTICLE 324-329)

- The Constitution provides for an independent election commission to ensure free and fair election to the Parliament, the State legislature and the offices of President and Vice-President.
- Consists of Chief Election Commissioner +2 Election Commissioners. They all enjoy equal powers.
- The Chief Election Commissioner and other Election Commissioners are appointed by the President.
- Election Commissioners are appointed for a term of 5 yrs.
- They are not eligible for re-appointment. Also, they cannot hold any office of profit after their retirement.
- The Election Commission was established on 25th January, 1950 under Article 324 of the Constitution.
- The first Chief Election Commissioner was *Sukumar Sen.*

Functions

- Preparation of electoral rolls and keeping voters list updated.
- Recognition of various political parties and allotment of election symbols.

NITI AAYOG

- The Indian government has replaced Planing Commission with a new institution named **NITI Aayog (National Institution for Transforming India).**
- The Niti Aayog will comprise the following:
  1. Prime Minister of India as the Chairperson.
  2. Governing Council comprising the Chief Ministers of all the States and Lt. Governors of Territories.
  3. Regional Councils will be formed to address specific issues and contingencies impacting more than one state or a region. These will be formed for a specified tenure. The Regional Councils will be convened by the Prime Minister and will comprise of the Chief Ministers of States and Lt. Governors of Territories in the region. These will be chaired by the Chairperson of the NITI Aayog or his nominee.
  4. Experts, specialists and practitioners with relevant domain knowledge as special invitees nominated by the Prime Minister.
- The full-time organizational framework will comprise of, in addition to the Prime Minister as the Chairperson:
  1. Vice-Chairperson : To be appointed by the Prime Minister.
  2. Members : Full-time. : 3
  3. Part-time members : Maximum of 2 from leading universities research organizations and other relevant institutions in an ex-officio capacity. Part time members will be on a rotational basis.
  4. Ex Officio members : Maximum of 4 members of the Council of Ministers to be nominated by the Prime Minister.
  5. Chief Executive Officer : To be appointed by the Prime Minister for a fixed tenure, in the rank of Secretary to the Government of India.
  6. Secretariat as deemed necessary.

FINANCE COMMISSION

- The constitution of the Finance Commission is laid down in Art. 280.
- The chairman must be a person having experience in public affairs; and the other four members also having wide experience in financial matters.
- It consists of Chairman and 4 other members.
- It shall be the duty of the Finance Commission to advice the President on matters such as the distribution between the Union and States of the net proceeds of taxes that is required to be shared.
- The Finance Commission is not a permanent body. It is dissolved after it has submitted its recommendations.

Important Amendments to the Constitution

First Amendment, 1951	:	Added Ninth Schedule.
Twenty-second Amendment, 1969	:	Formation of Meghalaya within the state of Assam was facilitated.
Twenty-sixth Amendment, 1971	:	The privy and privileges of the former rulers of Indian States were abolished.
Thirty-first Amendment, 1973	:	The upper limit of representation of states was raised from 500 to 525. The upper limit for representation of the UTs was reduced from 25 to 20.
Thirty-sixth Amendment, 1975	:	Sikkim was made a full-fledged state of Indian Union and it was included in the First Schedule.
Thirty-eight Amendment, 1975	:	This act led to the amendment of Article 123, Article 213 and Article 352 which stated that the satisfaction of President or of Governor contained in these Articles would be called in question in any court of law.
Forty-second Amendment, 1976	:	This amendment was done in accordance with the recommendations of Swaran Singh Committee and included a number of amendments.
Forty-third Amendment, 1977	:	It provided for the restoration of the Jurisdiction of the Supreme Court and High Courts, curtailed by the enactment of the Constitution (Forty-Second Amendment) Act, 1976.
Forty-fourth Amendment, 1978	:	The right to property was deleted as Fundamental Right and was made a legal right.
Fifty-third Amendment, 1986	:	The Act grants statehood to the Union Territory of Mizoram, thus making it the 23rd State of the Indian Unions.
Fifty-sixth Amendment, 1987	:	The UT of Goa converted into Goa state through this amendment whereas Daman and Diu were organised under a new UT.
Seventy-third Amendment, 1992	:	It is concerning Panchayati Raj.
Seventy-fourth Amendment, 1992	:	It is regarding Municipal Boards and Corporations.
Eighty-ninth Amendment, 2003	:	It provides for constitution of a separate National Commission for Scheduled Tribes. (Earlier, there was a combined National Commission for both SC/STs).
Ninety-first Amendment, 2003	:	It is regarding restricting the total number of Ministers including Prime Minister/ Chief Minister in Lok Sabha and State Legislatures to 15% of the total number of the Union or State Legislatures.
Ninety-ninth Amendment, 2015	:	The amendment is in toto quashed by Supreme Court on 16 October, 2015.
One hundredth Amendment, 2015	:	Exchange of certain enclave territories with Bangladesh and conferment of citizenship rights to residents of enclaves consequent to signing of Land Boundary Agreement (LBA) Treaty between India and Bangladesh.
One hundredth and first Amendment, 2016	:	The act amends the Constitution to introduce "The Goods and Services Tax (GST)."
One hundredth and Third Amendment, 2019	:	The Act providing 10 per cent reservation in government jobs and educational institutions to Economically Weaker Sections (EWS) of General Category, came into effect on January 14, 2019.
One hundredth and Fourth Amendment, 2019	:	This Act ceased the reservation of seats for Anglo-Indians in the Lok Sabha and State Legislative assemblies and extended reservations for SCs and STs for up to ten years.
One hundredth and Fifth Amendment, 2021	:	This Act restores the power of State Governments to identify and specify Socially and Economically Backward Classes (SEBCs).
One hundredth and Sixth Amendment, 2023	:	This Act provides 33% reservation for women in Lok Sabha and State Legislative Assemblies.

NATIONAL SYMBOLS

STATE EMBLEM

- State Emblem of India is an adaptation from the Sarnath Lion Capital of Ashoka. It was adopted by the Government of India on January 26, 1950. In the adapted form, only three lions are visible, the fourth being hidden from the view.
- The wheel (Dharma Chakra) appears in relief in the centre of the abacus with a bull on the right and a horse on the left.
- The bell-shaped lotus has been omitted. The words ''Satyameva Jayate'' meaning ''Truth alone triumphs'' are inscribed below the Emblem in Devanagari script.

NATIONAL FLAG

- The National Flag of India is a horizontal tricolour of deep saffron (Kesari), white and dark green in equal proportion.
- In the centre of the white band there is a wheel in navy blue colour. It has 24 spokes.
- The ratio of the length and the breadth of the flag is 3 : 2. Its design was adopted by the Constituent Assembly of India on July 22, 1947.

NATIONAL ANTHEM

- Rabindranath Tagore's song 'Jana-gana-mana' was adopted by the Constituent Assembly as the National Anthem of India on January 24, 1950.

Jana-gana-mana-adhinayaka jaya he,
Bharata-bhagya-vidhata
Punjab-Sindh-Gujarat-Maratha-
Dravida-Utkala-Banga
Vindhya-Himachala-Yamuna-Ganga
Uchhala-jaladhi-taranga.
Tava subha name jage,
Tava subha asisa mange,
Gahe tava jaya gatha,
Jana-gana-mangala-dayak,
jaya he Bharata bhagya vidhata,
Jaya he, jaya he, jaya he,
Jaya jaya jaya, jaya he.

NATIONAL SONG

- Bankim Chandra Chatterji's 'Vande Mataram' which was a source of inspiration to the people in their struggle for freedom, has been adopted as National Song. It has an equal status with the National Anthem.

Vande Mataram
Sujalam, suphalam, malayaja-shitalam,
Shasya shyamalam, Mataram
Shubhrajyotsna, pulkita yaminim,
Phulla kusumita drumadalashobhinim,
Subhasinim sumadhura—bhashinim,
Sukhadam, Varadam, Mataram.

- **National Bird and Animal of India:** Peacock and Tiger.
- **National Aquatic Animal:** Dolphin
- **National Flower:** Lotus
- **National Calendar:** It was adopted on March 22, 1957. It has 365 days in the year and the first month of the year is Chaitra.

□□□

GENERAL SCIENCE

PHYSICS

PHYSICAL QUANTITIES

- Physical quantities may be divided in two classes: 1. Scalar Quantities 2. Vector Quantities
- A scalar quantity is one which has only magnitude.
- A vector quantity has both magnitude and direction.
- Force, Velocity, Momentum, Acceleration are examples of vector quantities.
- Mass, length, time, volume, speed, energy, work are examples of scalar quantities.

UNITS

- All measurements in physics require standard units.
- In 1960, the General Conference of Weights and Measures recommended that a metric system of measurements called the International System of Units, abbreviated as SI units, be used.

Some Important Units

S.No.	Units	Quantity
1.	Metre	Length
2.	Kilogram	Mass
3.	Second	Time
4.	Ampere	Electric Current
5.	Candela	Luminous Intensity
6.	Newton	Force
7.	Joule	Workdone
8.	Watt	Power
9.	Coulomb	Electric Charge
10.	Volt	Potential Difference
11.	Ohm	Electrical Resistance
12.	Farad	Capacitance
13.	Henry	Inductance
14.	Lumen	Luminous Flux

- Very small distances are measured in micro-meters or (microns) (μm), angstroms (Å), nanometers (nm) and femtometres (fm).

MOTION

- When a body changes its position with respect to something else as time goes on, we say the body is in motion.
- There are two types of motion—translational (linear) and rotational (spin).
- The motion of a car on a road is translational whereas the motion of a top, spinning on its axis is rotational.

SPEED

- It is a scalar form of velocity and is defined as the distance travelled in one second.
- $\text{Speed} = \dfrac{\text{distance travelled}}{\text{time required}}$
- SI unit of speed is m/s.

VELOCITY

- The distance covered by an object in a specified direction in unit time interval is called velocity.
- The SI unit of velocity is m/s.
- Velocity is a vector quantity.

ACCELERATION

- The velocity of a body changes due to change in its speed or direction or both. The rate of change of the velocity of a body is called its acceleration.
- $\text{Acceleration} = \dfrac{\text{change in velocity}}{\text{time taken}}$

FORCE AND MOTION

GRAVITATIONAL FORCE

- It is the force of attraction between two masses.
- It is gravitational force that holds the moon in its orbit round the earth and the earth in its orbit round the sun.
- *Newton's Law of Universal Gravitation* states that every particle in the universe attracts every other particle with a force that is directly proportional to the product of their masses and inversely proportional to the square of the distance between them.
- The value of G is 6.67×10^{-11} SI units.

CENTRIPETAL FORCE

- The force acting towards the centre on a particle executing uniform circular motion is called centripetal force and is given by

$$F = \frac{mv^2}{r}$$

where, m = Mass of the object

v = Speed

r = Radius of the Circular Path

- In case of the moon, gravitational force between the earth and the moon acts as the centripetal force.
- Centripetal force always acts on the particle performing circular motion.

CENTRIFUGAL FORCE

- The pseudo force that balances the centripetal force in uniform circular motion is called centrifugal force.
- Centrifugal force is directed away from the centre along the radius.
- The centrifugal force is zero exactly at the poles and maximum at the equator.

WEIGHT

- The weight of a body is the force with which the earth attracts the body towards its centre.
- The mass of a body is a constant quantity whereas its weight varies slightly from place-to-place on the earth.
- The weight of a body is maximum at the poles and minimum at the equator. This variation in weight is due to:

  1. the shape of the earth.
  2. the rotation of the earth about its axis.
- The weight of an object is less at high elevations than at sea level.
- At the centre of the earth, the weight of a body would be zero.
- On the surface of the moon the value of the acceleration due to gravity is nearly one-sixth of that on earth and, therefore, an object on the moon would weigh only one-sixth its weight on the earth. The mass of an object on the moon would be the same as on earth.
- The weight of a body would be more if the earth stopped rotating. Conversely, if the speed of rotation were higher, the weight would be less.
- A person weighs more in a lift, which is accelerating upward.
- An astronaut feels weightless in a spaceship because he is not pushing against anything.

FRICTION

- Friction is the force which opposes the relative motion of two surfaces in contact.
- It is friction between the ground and the soles of our shoes that makes walking possible and it is lack of friction that makes our feet slip on highly polished surfaces.
- Friction in machines wastes energy and also causes wear and tear. This friction is reduced by using (1) lubricants, and (2) ball bearings.

NEWTON'S LAWS OF MOTION

First Law

- Every object continues in its state of rest or of uniform motion in a straight line if no net force acts upon it. It is also known as *law of inertia*.
- **Examples:** 1. An unwary passenger in a fast-moving bus falls forward when it stops suddenly. This happens because the feet of the passenger come to rest suddenly whereas his upper part of body continues to be in motion. 2. A person getting down from a moving bus has to run some distance, in the direction of the bus, before stopping. If he does not run he is bound to fall because his feet come to rest whereas his body continues to be in motion.

Momentum

- The momentum of a body is defined as the product of its mass and velocity.

Second Law

- This law states that "the rate of change of momentum of a body is proportional to the applied force and takes place in the direction of the force."
- If we express force (F) in Newtons, mass (m) in kilograms and acceleration (a) in metres per second squared, we can write the second law as; F = ma.
- In travelling the same distance, a car consumes more fuel on a crowded road than on a free road. This happens because the car has to stop and start quite often on a crowded road. The repeated acceleration requires a force (second law), which ultimately comes from the fuel. On a free road the car runs at almost uniform speed requiring fewer accelerations and hence less fuel consumption.

Third Law

- This law states that "to every action there is an equal and opposite reaction."
- When a bullet is fired from a gun, equal and opposite forces are exerted on the bullet and the gun.
- The engine in a jet aeroplane works on the same principle as a rocket but there is a difference in the method of obtaining the high velocity as jet.

IMPULSE

- If a force acts on a body for a very short time, then the product of force and time is called the impulse.

  Impulse= Change in momentum

  = Force × Time

Application of Impulse

1. A cricket player draws his hand back while catching.
2. A person jumping on hard cement floor receives more injuries than a person jumping on muddy or sandy floor.

WORK, POWER AND ENERGY

WORK

- Whenever a force acting on a body displaces it, work is said to be done.

  Work = Force × Distance moved in the direction of force.
- Work is a scalar quantity and its SI unit is Joule (J).

POWER

- Power is defined as the rate of doing work.

$$\text{Power} = \frac{\text{Work done}}{\text{Time taken}}$$

- The SI unit of power is Watt (W) and is also measured in horse power.

  1 HP = 746 W

ENERGY

- Energy is defined as the capacity to do work.

Kinetic Energy

- The energy possessed by an object due to its motion is called kinetic energy and is described by the expression

$KE = \frac{1}{2}mv^2$; where, m = mass of the object

v = speed

Potential Energy

- Potential energy is the energy possessed by the body by virtue of its position, configuration or any condition of stress or strain.
- There are many examples of potential energy. A stone held at some height above the ground has potential energy. Water in an elevated reservoir possesses potential energy.

Transformation of Energy

S.No.	Equipment	Transformation
1.	Dynamo	Mechanical energy into electrical energy
2.	Microphone	Sound energy into electrical energy
3.	Loud Speaker	Electrical energy into sound energy
4.	Electric Bulb	Electrical energy into light and heat energy
5.	Battery	Chemical energy into electrical energy
6.	Electrical Motor	Electrical energy into mechanical energy

CENTRE OF GRAVITY

- The centre of gravity of a body is the point where the whole weight of the body can be considered to act.
- Racing cars are build low and with wide wheel bases to reduce the risk of overturning at sharp bends.
- While crossing a river in a boat, passengers are not allowed to stand. This keeps the CG of the system (boat and passengers) low and ensures stability.

ARTIFICIAL SATELLITES

- In the case of a satellite, the centripetal force is provided by the gravitational pull of the earth.
- If the speed of a satellite is more than 11.2 km/s or 25,000 miles/hour, the satellite would escape the earth entirely and would never come back. This is called escape velocity.
- The existence of gaseous atmosphere on the earth is due to the high value of its escape velocity.

Geostationary Satellites

- Geostationary satellites are stationary with respect to an observer on the earth. Their time period is 24-hour. There height above the surface of earth is 36,000 km. They are always in equatorial plane and their orbits are circular. They are also called parking orbits.

DENSITY AND RELATIVE DENSITY

DENSITY

- The mass per unit volume of a substance is called its density.

$$\text{Density} = \frac{\text{Mass}}{\text{Volume}}$$

- The SI unit of density is kilogram per metre cubed (kg/m^3).
- The relative density of a substance is the ratio of the density of the substance to the density of water.
- Relative density has no unit.

PRESSURE

- Pressure is defined as force acting per unit area.

$$\text{Pressure} = \frac{\text{Force}}{\text{Area}}$$

- The SI unit of pressure is newton per metre squared or pascal.
- Broad wooden sleepers are placed below the rails to reduce the pressure exerted by the weight of a train.
- The pressure of water increases with depth, therefore bottom of a dam is made much thicken than the top.
- The pressure exerted on an enclosed liquid at one place is transmitted equally throughout the liquid. This is called Pascal's Principle.
- Hydraulic presses, hydraulic brakes, hydraulic door closers, etc. are applications of the Pascal's Principle.
- At high attitudes where atmosphere pressure is less nose bleeding may occur due to the greater pressure of blood.

- In an aircraft flying at high altitude, normal atmospheric pressure is maintained by the use of air pumps. If this were not done, the crew and passengers would experience difficulty in breathing and consequently face dangers.
- Atmospheric pressure is measured with an instrument called the *Barometer*.

ARCHIMEDE'S PRINCIPLE

- This principle states that when a body is wholly or partially immersed in a fluid, it experiences an upthrust (upward force) equal to the weight of the fluid displaced.
- An iron nail sinks in water whereas a ship made of iron and steel floats. This is due to the fact that a ship is hollow and contains air and, therefore, its density is less than that of water.
- The density of sea water is more than that of river water, due to this a ship sinks less in sea water. It is for this reason that a ship rises a little when it enters a sea from a river.
- It is because of the higher density of sea water that it is easier to swim in the sea.
- A balloon filled with a light gas, such as hydrogen, rises because the average density of the balloon and the gas is less than that of air. The balloon cannot rise indefinitely because the density of the air decreases with increasing altitude. At a certain height, where the density of air is equal to the average density of the balloon, it ceases to rise and drifts sideways with the wind.
- When an ice block floats in water the water level will remain the same when all the ice melts into water.
- A *hydrometer* is an instrument used for measuring the relative density of liquids.
- A special type of a hydrometer called *Lactometer* is used for testing milk by measuring its density.

SURFACE TENSION

- Surface tension is that property of liquids owing to which they tend to acquire minimum surface area.
- Surface tension is caused by molecular attractions.
- When a paint brush is dipped in water all its hair spread out but when it is taken out it is covered with a thin film of water which contracts due to surface tension and pulls the hair together.
- Liquid drops, such as raindrops, oildrops, drops of molten metals, dewdrops etc. are all spherical because their surface tend to contract in order to have minimum surface area. For a given volume, a sphere has the minimum surface area.
- Soaps and detergents lower the surface tension of water. This increases the wetting power of water or its ability to detach dirt particles from clothes and untensils.
- The force of attraction between unlike molecules is called **adhesion** and that between like molecules **cohesion.**
- The melted wax of a candle is drawn up into the wick by capillary action. Oil rises up a lamp wick for the same reason.
- If one end of a sugar cube is dipped into tea, the entire cube is quickly wet on account of capillary action.

VISCOSITY

- The force which opposes the relative motion between different layers of liquid or gases is called viscous force.
- Viscosity is the property of liquids and gases both.

BERNOULLI'S THEOREM

- According to Bernoulli's theorem, in case of streamline flow of incompressible and non-viscous fluid (ideal fluid) through a tube, total energy (sum of pressure energy, potential energy and kinetic energy) per unit volume of fluid is same at all points.

  1. When a bowler spins a ball, it changes its direction (swings) in the air due to unequal pressure acting on it.

HEAT

- Heat is that form of energy which flows from one body to other body due to difference in temperature between the bodies. The amount of heat contained in a body depends upon the mass of the body.

TEMPERATURE

- The temperature of a body is the quantity that tells how hot or cold it is with respect to some standard body.

MEASUREMENT OF TEMPERATURE

- Temperature is measured by a thermometer.
- A thermometer may be graduated in following scales—
  1. The upper and lower points of centigrade scale are 100°C and 0°C.
  2. The upper and lower points of Fahrenheit scale are 212°F and 32°F.
  3. The upper and lower points of Reaumur scale are 80°R and 0°R.
  4. The upper and lower points of Kelvin scale are 373K and 273K.
  5. The upper and lower points of Rankine scale are 672° Ra and 460° Ra.
- At –40 degrees both celsius and Fahrenheit scales will show identical readings.
- Water cannot be used in a thermometer becaues it freezes at 0°C and also because of its irregular expansion.

THERMAL EXPANSION

- Solids, liquids and gases generally expand when heated and contract when cooled.
- Gaps have to be left in railway tracks to make allowance for expansion, otherwise the rails will buckle. Allowance

is made for the expansion of long steel bridges. One end of such bridge is fixed while the other rests on rollers.

- Telephone wires sag more in summer than in winter due to thermal expansion.

EXPANSION OF WATER

- Water has its minimum volume and maximum density at 4°C.

TRANSMISSION OF HEAT

- There are three ways of heat transmission: 1. Conduction; 2. Convection; 3. Radiation.

Conduction

- In this process, heat is transferred from one place to other place by the successive vibration of the particles of the medium without bodily movement of the particles of the medium.
- Conduction takes place mainly in solids.
- Air is a very bad conductor of heat. The good insulating properties of wool, cotton, etc. are mainly due to the air spaces they contain.

Convection

- In this process, heat is transferred by the actual movement of particles of the medium from one place to other place.
- In liquids and gases heat is transmitted by convection.

Radiation

- In this mode of heat transmission heat is transferred from one place to another without effecting the intervening medium.

HEAT CAPACITY

- The heat capacity of a body is defined as the heat required to raise the temperature of the body by 1K. Its SI unit is J/K.

SPECIFIC HEAT CAPACITY

- The specific heat capacity of a substance is the heat required to raise the temperature of a unit mass of the substance by 1K.
- Its SI unit is J/kg K.
- It is because of its high specific heat capacity that water is used as a cooling liquid in car engine.

LATENT HEAT

- It is defined as the amount of heat absorbed or given out by a body during the change of state.
- Each gram of ice that melts absorbs 336 J of heat.

EVAPORATION

- Water can change into the vapour state either by boiling or by evaporation at lower temperatures.
- When sweat evaporates from the skin it draws much heat from the body and produces a cooling sensation.
- In summer, water is stored in pitchers for cooling. Water oozes out of the pores of the pitchers and cools on evaporation.
- The rate of evaporation increases with increase in temperature.

REFRIGERATOR

- In a refrigerator, cooling is produced by the evaporation of a volatile liquid, freon, inside a copper coil (evaporator), which surrounds the freezer.
- The cooling unit (freezer) in a refrigerator is fitted near the top to cool the whole of the interior.

RELATIVE HUMIDITY

- Relative humidity is defined as the ratio of the mass of water vapour in a given volume of air to the mass required for saturating the same volume of air at the same temperature.
- Relative humidity is measured with an instrument called the hygrometer.

PRESSURE COOKER

- The boiling point of a liquid depends on external pressure.
- When the atmospheric pressure is 76 cm of mercury, water boils at 100°C. But when the pressure is increased, the boiling point of water is raised.
- In a pressure cooker, water boils at temperatures higher than 100°C due to increased pressure. The increased boiling temperature allows water to hold more heat which cooks food faster.
- At higher altitudes, atmospheric pressure is reduced. This lowers the boiling point of water and food takes much longer to cook.

WAVE MOTION

- Wave motion may be defined as the transfer of energy without the net transfer of matter.
- If the particles of the medium vibrate perpendicular to the direction of propagation of wave, the wave is called transverse wave.
- Light waves are transverse waves.
- If the particles of the medium vibrate in the direction of propagation of wave, the wave is called longitudinal wave.
- Sound waves are longitudinal waves.

ELECTROMAGNETIC WAVE

- Electromagnetic waves include an enormous range of frequencies—from radio waves with frequencies less than 10^5 Hz to gamma rays having frequencies greater than 10^{20} Hz.

- All electromagnetic wave have the same speed (3×10^8 m/s) in vacuum. The relation $v = n\lambda$ holds good for all electromagnetic waves.

RADIO AND TELEVISION TRANSMISSION

- Radio waves sent out by radio stations are reflected by the ionosphere and can be received anywhere on the earth.
- At night the radio reception improves because the layers of the ionosphere are not exposed to sunlight and are more settled.
- Radar (Radio detection and ranging) employs high frequency radio waves for detecting objects like ships and aeroplanes.
- In microwave oven, when the waves fall on the food, these are absorbed by water, fats, sugars and certain other molecules whose consequent vibrations produce heat. Since heating occurs inside the food, without warming the surrounding air, the cooking time is greatly reduced.
- In microwave oven, food cannot be cooked in metal vessels because the metal blocks out the microwaves.

LIGHT

- Light is a form of energy which is propagated as electromagnetic waves.
- Light is a transverse wave.
- Speed of light in vacuum is 3×10^8 m/s.
- Light takes 8 minute 16.6 second to reach from sun to earth.

REFLECTION

- When light is incident upon a surface, part of it is reflected. But certain surfaces like mirrors and polished metals reflect almost all the light incident upon them.
- The law of reflection states that the angle of incidence is equal to the angle of reflection.
- To see full image in a plane mirror, a person requires a mirror of at least half of his height.

INCLINED MIRROR (NO. OF IMAGES)

- When an object is placed between two inclined mirrors, several images of the object are formed.

CURVED MIRRORS

- There are two types of curved spherical mirrors—1. Concave Mirror, 2. Convex Mirror.
- Concave mirror can concentrate the sun's radiation falling on it at one point, it can be used as a burning glass.
- Concave mirrors are also used in solar cookers.
- Large concave mirrors are used in reflecting telescopes for observing and photographing distant stars and other heavenly bodies.
- Concave mirror is also used as a shaving or make-up mirror.
- Small concave mirrors are used by dentists for examining teeth.
- Concave parabolic mirrors are used in searchlight and headlamps of cars.
- Convex mirrors are also used as rear view mirrors in vehicles.

REFRACTION

- When a ray of light passes from one medium to other it suffers a change in direction at the boundary of separation of two media. This phenomenon is called refraction.
- When a ray passes from one medium to another optically denser medium, e.g., from air to water or glass, it bends towards the normal. Conversely, a ray passing from water or glass into air is bent away from the normal.
- Rivers appear shallow, coin in a beaker filled with water appears raised, due to refraction.
- Another effect of refraction is the apparent upward bending of the immersed portion of a stick when dipped in water.
- It is due to refraction, produced by the earth's atmosphere, that the sun is visible for several minutes after it has set below the horizon. Thus, atmospheric refraction tends to lengthen the day.
- When the sun (or moon) is near the horizon, it appears elliptical, i.e., with the vertical diameter less than the horizontal diameter. This happens because rays from the lower edge of the sun are bent more than those from the upper edge (Atmospheric Refraction).
- One of the most interesting effects of atmospheric refraction and Mirage is a combined effect of atmospheric refraction and total internal reflection.

DISPERSION

- White light consists of seven colours—violet, indigo, blue, green, yellow, orange and red. These colours are called the spectrum of the white light.
- Violet has the minimum wavelength (or maximum frequency) and red the maximum wavelength (or minimum frequency).
- Due to different speeds, the colours are refracted through different angles and therefore, when a narrow beam of white light passes through a glass prism, it is split up into its constituent colours. This separation of light into colours is called dispersion.

COLOUR OF OBJECTS

- We see objects because of the light they reflect.
- When a rose is viewed in white light, its petals appear red and the leaves appear green, because the petals reflect the red part of the white light and leaves reflect the green part. The remaining colours are absorbed. When the same rose is viewed in green light, the petals will appear black

and the leaves green. In blue or yellow light both the petals and leaves will appear black.

- Red, blue and green are primary colours.

LENSES

- There are mainly two types of lenses:
  1. Convex or Converging Lens
  2. Concave or Diverging Lens
- Converging or convex lens is used as a magnifying glass.
- Power of a lens is its capacity to deviate a ray. Power of a lens is measured as the reciprocal of the focal length.

$$P = \frac{1}{f}$$

- SI unit of power of lens is dioptre (D).
- The power of a converging lens is positive and that of a diverging lens is negative.
- For all positions of the object, the images formed by diverging (concave) lens are virtual, erect and diminished.

EYE

- The light entering the eye is focused by the eye-lens to form an image on the retina.
- In front of the eye, lens is the coloured part of eye, called the iris, which automatically adjusts the size of the pupil to the intensity of light falling on it.
- In bright light the iris automatically shuts tighter, reducing the amount of light entering the pupil. This protects the retina from getting damaged.
- When a person enters a dark room after being in bright light, he is not able to see clearly for a while because the iris is unable to dilate the pupil immediately.
- Least distance of distinct vision is 25 cm.

DEFECTS OF VISION

- A person suffering from long sight (hyper-metropia) can clearly see objects at infinity but cannot see near objects clearly. This defect is caused by the eyeball being too short and can be corrected by wearing converging lenses.
- In the case of a person suffering from short sight (myopia), the eye ball is too long and distant objects are focused in front of the retina. This defect can be corrected by wearing diverging lenses.
- ***Astigmatism:*** Curvature of cornea becomes irregular and image is not clear. Cylindrical lens is used.

SCATTERING OF LIGHT

- When light falls on atoms and molecules, it is scattered in all directions.
- Scattering of light is maximum for violet colour and minimum for red colour.
- Blue colour of sky is due to scattering of light.
- In the evening, the sun is lower in the sky and its light has to traverse a longer path through the atmosphere to reach an observer. Thus, at sunset, blue, green and other colours having been scattered only red and some orange light reach us and the sun appears a deep orange-red.
- In outerspace, *i.e.*, beyond the atmosphere, there is nothing to scatter the sunlight and therefore the sky appears dark and stars are visible even in the presence of the sun.

INTERFERENCE OF LIGHT

- The superposition of two (or more) waves of the same kind that pass the same point in space at the same time is called interference.
- Beautiful colours seen in soap bubbles and oil films on water are produced due to the interference of white light reflected by these surfaces.
- LASER (Light Amplification by Stimulated Emission of Radiation) is an optical device which produces an intense beam of coherent monochromatic light.
- Examples of Interference of Light: Holography, Laser.

DIFFRACTION OF LIGHT

- When a beam of light passes through a narrow slit or an aperture, it spreads out to a certain extent into the region of geometrical shadow. This is an example of diffraction, *i.e.*, of the failure of light to travel in a straight line.

SOUND

- Sound waves are longitudinal and cannot travel in vacuum. The transmission of sound requires a medium : air, liquid or solid.
- The longitudinal mechanical waves which lie in the frequency range 20 Hz to 20,000 Hz are called audible or sound waves. These waves are sensitive to human ear.
- The longitudinal mechanical waves having frequencies less than 20 Hz are called Infrasonic. These waves are produced by sources of bigger size such as earthquakes, volcanic eruptions, ocean waves etc.
- The longitudinal waves having frequencies greater than 20,000 Hz are called ultrasonic waves. Human ear cannot detect these waves. But some animals such as cats, dogs, bats can detect these waves.

PITCH

- The pitch (shrillness of a sound) depends on its frequency.
- A sound of higher frequency has a higher pitch.
- The pitch of a woman's voice is higher than that of a man.

LOUDNESS

- The relative loudness of a sound is measured in decibels (db).
- All stringed instruments, such as the violin, sitar, guitar, etc. have sound boxes attached to increase the loudness.

SPEED OF SOUND

- The presence of water vapour in the air increases the speed of sound.
- Sound travels faster through warm air than through cold air. The speed of sound is higher on a hot day than on a cold day.
- Thunder is heard much after the flash of lightning is seen because of the wide difference in the speeds of light and sound.

REFLECTION OF SOUND

- When a sound wave is reflected by a distant obstacle, such as a wall or a cliff, an echo is heard.
- To hear echo, the minimum distance between the observer and reflector should be 17 m.
- Exploration of underwater gas and oil is done by detecting the echoes of shock waves produced by explosions on the water surface.
- Bats emit ultrasonic waves of frequencies up to 80,000. Hz and use the reflection of these waves (echoes) to determine the presence and distance of objects on their way and from them respectively.

DOPPLER EFFECT

- The Doppler effect is the change in frequency of a wave (sound or light) due to the motion of the source or observer.
- It is due to the Doppler effect that the whistle of a train appears shriller when it approaches a listener than when it moves away from him.

ELECTRICITY

- Electricity produced by friction between two dissimilar objects is known as static electricity. Depending on the nature of the objects, one acquires a positive charge and the other an equal negative charge. For example, if a glass rod is rubbed with silk, the rod acquires positive charge and the silk an equal negative charge.
- *Lightning* is a gigantic electric discharge occurring between two charged clouds or between a charged cloud and the earth.

CONDUCTOR

- Conductors are those materials which allow electricity (charge) to pass through themselves.
- Metals conduct electricity because they have a large number of conduction or free electrons.

INSULATORS

- Insulators are those materials which do not allow electricity to flow through themselves. Insulators have no free electrons.

SUPER CONDUCTORS

- The resistance of metals to flow of electricity reduces with decreasing temperature. At temperatures near absolute zero, metals have almost zero resistance and became super conductors.

SEMI-CONDUCTORS

- Certain materials, such as silicon and germanium, have electrical resistivity intermediate between those of conductors and insulators. These materials are termed as semi-conductors.
- Semi-conductors are good insulators in their pure crystalline form but their conductivity increases when small amounts of impurities are added to them.

ELECTRIC CURRENT

- Electric current is simply the flow of electric charge. In solid conductors the flow of electrons and in fluids the flow of ions as well as electrons constitute the current.
- SI units of electric current is Ampere (A).

ELECTRICAL RESISTANCE

- When electric current flows through a conductor, e.g., a metallic wire, it offers some obstruction to the current. This obstruction offered by the wire is called its electrical resistance.
- SI unit of Resistance is ohm.

OHM'S LAW

- If physical conditions like temperature, intensity of light etc. remains unchanged then electric current flowing through a conductor is directly proportional to the potential difference across its ends.

ELECTRIC MOTOR

- In an electric motor, electrical energy is converted into mechanical energy.
- Electric fans, mixers, washing machines, etc. work on electric motors.

INVERTER

- An inverter is a device which converts DC to AC. The inverters used in homes and offices are specially designed to:

  1. Convert DC from a battery to AC, and
  2. Charge the battery.

FUSE

- Electric fuse is a protective device used in series with an electric appliance to save it from being damaged due to high current.
- A fuse is a short piece of wire made of a tin-lead alloy, which has a low melting point.
- Fuses are always connected in the live wire in series.

COST OF ELECTRICITY

- The consumption of electrical energy in a house is measured in the unit kWh.
- Kilowatt hour is equal to the energy consumed in the circuit at the rate of 1 kilowatt for 1 hour.

MAGNETISM

- A magnet attracts and holds pieces of iron but does not attract pieces of copper.
- Iron, cobalt, nickel and certain alloys are strongly magnetic whereas copper, wood, glass, etc. are non-magnetic.
- Our earth behaves as a powerful magnet whose south pole is near the geographical north pole and whose north pole is near the geographical south pole.

ATOMIC & NUCLEAR PHYSICS

- Atom consists of three fundamental particles electron, proton and neutron. All the protons and neutrons are present in the central core of atom called nucleus. Electrons revolve around the nucleus.
- The total number of protons in the nucleus is called atomic number (Z).
- The total number of proton and neutrons in the nucleus is called mass number (A).
- Ernest Rutherford, discovered nucleus by the scattering of α-particles from gold foil.

RADIOACTIVITY

- Henry Bacquerel (1896) observed that a photographic plate blackened, when placed near double sulphate of potassium and uranium. He further observed that uranium emitted special kind of rays. They were called Becqueral rays.
- Pierre and Marie Curie observed that the radiation from pitchblende was four times stronger than uranium. In 1898, they finally discovered two new substances—Polonium and Radium. These newly discovered substances were called radioactive substances and this property of these substances was named radioactivity.
- No radioactive substance emits both α and β particles simultaneously.

X-RAYS

- X-rays are electromagnetic radiations having wavelength from a fraction of an Angestrom to about 100Å. They were discovered by Rontgen during his studies on the electrical discharge phenomena in gases—he found that an unknown radiation was produced when electrons collided with the walls of the tubes.

ATOMIC ENERGY

- India today ranks sixth in the atomic energy programmes. It has developed the required know-how and expertise to manufacture nuclear weapons, but it believes in the peaceful uses of atomic power. The Atomic Energy Commission was set-up in the country in 1948 under the Chairmanship of Dr. H. J. Bhabha.
- ***Bhabha Atomic Research Centre (BARC):*** The Bhabha Atomic Research Centre at Trombay near Mumbai (Maharashtra) has four research reactors: (*i*) APSARA—It is the first atomic reactor in Asia; (*ii*) CIRUS—It is a joint Indo-Canadian project; (*iii*) PURNIMA II—a zero energy fast reactor, and (*iv*) DHRUVA—a high power completely indigenous nuclear research reactor with most advanced laboratories in the world. Another fast breeder reactor KAMINI at Kalpakkam has been constructed. Today India is the seventh country in the world and the first developing nation to have mastered the fast breeder reactor technology.
- **Nuclear Power:** Under Nuclear Power Corporation of India Limited (NPCIL) there are seven nuclear power stations in operation in six States:

  (*i*) Tarapur—Maharashtra, (*ii*) Rawatbhata —Rajasthan, (*iii*) Kalpakkam—Tamil Nadu, (*iv*) Narora—U.P., (*v*) Kakrapara—Gujarat, (*vi*) Kaiga—Karnataka and (*vii*) Kudankulam—Tamil Nadu.
- **Heavy Water:** Heavy water is one of the essential input for Pressurised Heavy Water Reactors (PHWRs) used both as a coolant and moderator. The first heavy water plant was set-up in 1962 in Nangal. Subsequently 7 more plants have been set-up at (*i*) Baroda, (*ii*) Tuticorin, (*iii*) Kota, (*iv*) Talcher, (*v*) Thal, (*vi*) Hazira and (*vii*) Manuguru.
- **Research and Development Centres:** Four research centres namely (*i*) Bhabha Atomic Research Centre, Trombay (Maharashtra), (*ii*) Indira Gandhi Centre for Atomic Research, Kalpakkam (Tamil Nadu), (*iii*) Centre for Advanced Technology, Indore (Madhya Pradesh), (*iv*) Variable Energy Cyclotron Centre at Kolkata (West Bengal) are focal points of research and development work in nuclear energy and related discipline.
- **India's Nuclear Explosions:** On May 18, 1974 India conducted her first underground nuclear explosion at Pokhran (Rajasthan) in the Thar desert, 20 km. away from Jaisalmer, at a depth of more than 100 metres. The successful explosion made India the sixth nuclear nation in the world.
- India conducted 5 nuclear explosion tests at Pokhran in two phases on May 11 and May 13, 1998 and became a nuclear power state.

IMPORTANT INVENTIONS

Name of Invention	Inventor	Nationality	Year
Aeroplane	Orville & Wilbur Wright	U.S.A.	1903
Ball-Point Pen	John J. Loud	U.S.A.	1888
Barometer	Evangelista Torricelli	Italy	1644
Bicycle	Kirkpatrick Macmillan	Britain	1839-40
Bifocal Lens	Benjamin Franklin	U.S.A.	1780
Car (Petrol)	Karl Benz	Germany	1888
Celluloid	Alexander Parkes	Britain	1861
Cinema	Nicolas & Jean Lumiere	France	1895
Clock (mechanical)	I-Hsing & Liang Ling-Tsan	China	1725
Diesel Engine	Rudolf Diesel	Germany	1895
Dynamo	Hypolite Pixii	France	1832
Electric Lamp	Thomas Alva Edison	U.S.A.	1879
Electric Motor (DC)	Zenobe Gramme	Belgium	1873
Electric Motor (AC)	Nikola Tesla	U.S.A.	1888
Electro-magnet	William Sturgeon	Britain	1824
Electronic Computer	Dr. Alan M. Turing	Britain	1943
Film (moving outlines)	Louis Prince	France	1885
Film (musical sound)	Dr. Le de Forest	U.S.A.	1923
Fountain Pen	Lewis E. Waterman	U.S.A.	1884
Gramophone	Thomas Alva Edison	U.S.A.	1878
Helicopter	Etienne Oehmichen	France	1924
Jet Engine	Sir Frank Whittle	Britain	1937
Laser	Charles H. Townes	U.S.A.	1960
Lift (Mechanical)	Elisha G. Otis	U.S.A.	1852
Locomotive	Richard Trevithick	Britain	1804
Machine Gun	James Puckle	Britain	1718
Microphone	Alexander Graham Bell	U.S.A.	1876
Microscope	Z. Janssen	Netherlands	1590
Motor Cycle	G. Daimler	Germany	1885
Photography (on film)	John Carbutt	U.S.A.	1888
Printing Press	Johann Gutenberg	Germany	c.1455
Razor (safety)	King C. Gillette	U.S.A.	1895
Refrigerator	James Harrison & Alexander Catlin	U.S.A.	1850
Safety Pin	Walter Hunt	U.S.A.	1849
Sewing machine	Barthelemy Thimmonnier	France	1829
Ship (steam)	J.C. Perier	France	1775
Ship (turbine)	Hon. Sir C. Parsons	Britain	1894
Skyscraper	W. Le Baron Jenny	U.S.A.	1882
Slide Rule	William Oughtred	Britain	1621
Steam Engine (condenser)	James Watt	Britain	1765
Steel Production	Henry Bessemer	Britain	1855
Steel (stainless)	Harry Brearley	Britain	1913
Submarine	David Bushnell	U.S.A.	1776
Tank	Sir Ernest Swinton	Britain	1914
Telegraph	M. Lammond	France	1787
Telegraph Code	Samuel F.B. Morse	U.S.A.	1837
Telephone (perfected)	Alexander Graham Bell	U.S.A.	1876
Television (mechanical)	John Logie Baird	Britain	1926
Television (electronic)	P.T. Farnsworth	U.S.A.	1927
Thermometer	Galileo Galilei	Italy	1593
Transformer	Michael Faraday	Britain	1831
Transistor	Bardeen, Shockley & Brattain	U.S.A.	1948
Washing Machine (elec.)	Hurley Machine Co.	U.S.A.	1907
Zip-Fastener	W.L. Judson	U.S.A.	1891

Important Discoveries

Discovery	Discoverer	Nationality	Year
Aluminium	Hans Christian Oerstedt	Denmark	1827
Atomic number	Henry Moseley	England	1913
Atomic structure of matter	John Dalton	England	1803
Chlorine	C.W. Scheele	Sweden	1774
Electromagnetic induction	Michael Faraday	England	1831
Electromagnetic waves	Heinrich Hertz	Germany	1886
Electromagnetism	Hans Christian Oersted	Denmark	1920
Electron	Sir Joseph Thomson	England	1897
General theory of relativity	Albert Einstein	Switzerland	1915
Hydrogen	Henry Cavendish	England	1766
Law of electric conduction	Georg Ohm	Germany	1827
Law of electromagnetism	Andre Ampere	France	1826
Law of falling bodies	Galileo	Italy	1590
Laws of gravitation & motion	Isaac Newton	England	1687
Laws of planetary motion	Johannes Kepler	Germany	1609-10
Magnesium	Sir Humphry Davy	England	1808
Neptune (Planet)	Johann Galle	Germany	1846
Neutron	James Chadwick	England	1932
Nickel	Axel Cronstedt	Sweden	1751
Nitrogen	Daniel Rutherford	England	1772
Oxygen	Joseph Priestly, C.W. Scheele	England, Sweden	1772
Ozone	Christian Schonbein	Germany	1839
Pluto	Clyde Tombaugh	U.S.A	1930
Plutonium	G.T. Seaborg	U.S.A	1940
Proton	Ernest Rutherford	England	1919
Quantum Theory	Max Planck	Germany	1900
Radioactivity	Antoine Bacquerel	France	1896
Radium	Pierre & Marie Curie	France	1898
Silicon	Jons Berzelius	Sweden	1824
Special theory of relativity	Albert Einstein	Switzerland	1905
Sun as centre of solar system	Copernicus	Poland	1543
Uranium	Martin Klaproth	Germany	1789
Uranus (Planet)	William Herschel	England	1781
X-rays	Wilhelm Roentgen	Germany	1895

Scientific Instruments

Name of Instrument	Used for
Altimeter	measuring altitude
Ammeter	measuring strength of an electric current
Anemometer	measuring the velocity of wind
Audiometer	measuring level of hearing
Barometer	measuring atmospheric pressure

Name of Instrument	Used for
Callipers	measuring the internal and external diameters of tubes
Calorimeter	measuring quantity of heat
Compass	finding out direction
Dynamo	converting mechanical energy into electrical energy
Galvanometer	detecting and determining the strength of small electric currents
Hydrometer	measuring specific gravity of a liquid
Hygrometer	measuring the humidity in the atmosphere
Lactometer	measuring the purity of milk
Manometer	measuring the gaseous pressure
Micrometer	measuring minute distances, angles, etc.
Microscope	seeing magnified view of very small objects
Photometer	measuring intensity of light from distant stars
Pyrometer	measuring high temperatures
Radar	detecting and finding the presence and location of moving objects like aircraft, missile, etc.
Radiometer	measuring the emission of radiant energy
Rain Gauge	measuring the amount of rainfall
Seismograph	measuring and recording the intensity and origin of earthquake shocks
Sextant	measuring altitude and angular distances between two objects or heavenly bodies
Spectrometer	measuring the refractive indices
Spherometer	measuring the curvature of spherical objects/surface
Sphygmomanometer	measuring blood pressure
Stethoscope	ascertaining the condition of heart and lungs by listening to their function
Stroboscope	viewing objects that are moving rapidly with a periodic motion as if they were at rest
Tachometer	measuring the rate of revolution or angular speed of a revolving shaft
Telescope	viewing magnified images of distant objects
Thermocouple	measuring the temperature inside furnaces and jet engines
Thermometer	measuring human body temperature
Thermostat	regulating constant temperature
Ultrasonoscope	measuring utrasonic sounds
Viscometer	measuring the viscosity of a fluid
Voltmeter	measuring potential difference between two points.

CHEMISTRY

ELEMENTS

- An element may be defined as a substance which is made by same type of atoms and it can neither be broken into, nor built from two or more simpler substances by any known physical or chemical methods, e.g., copper, silver, hydrogen, carbon, oxygen, nitrogen, gold, iron etc.

COMPOUNDS

- A compound may be defined as a substance which contains two or more elements combined in some fixed proportion by weight and which can be decomposed into two or more elements by any suitable method.
- The properties of a compound are entirely different from those of the elements from which it is made.
- Some common examples of compounds are water, sugar, salt, aspirin, chloroform, alcohol and ether.

MIXTURES

- A material containing two or more elements or compounds in any proportion is a mixture.
- The components of a mixture can be separated by physical means like filtration, sublimation and distillation.

ATOMIC STRUCTURE

ATOM

- Atom is the smallest part of the element that takes part in a chemical reaction. Atom of an element can not be changed into that of another element by a chemical or physical means. It does not exist in free state.

MOLECULE

- A molecule is the smallest part of an element or compound that is capable of existing independently.

ATOMIC WEIGHT (OR ATOMIC MASS)

- The atomic mass of an element is the number of times its atom is heavier than 1/12th of the mass of carbon (C^{12}) atom.
- The unit used to measure atomic mass is called atomic mass unit, *i.e.,* amu.

ELECTRON

- The electron is a fundamental particle of an atom which carries a unit negative charge. It was discovered by J.J. Thomson in 1897.

PROTON

- It is a fundamental particle of an atom carrying a unit positive charge. It was discovered by Rutherford and Goldstein in 1886.

NEUTRON

- It is a fundamental particle of an atom carrying no charge. It was discovered by Chadwick in 1932.

ISOTOPES

- The atoms of the same element having different mass numbers are called isotopes.

ISOBARS

- Elements having the same atomic mass but differ in atomic number are called isobars.

ISOTONES

- Elements having the same number of neutrons are called isotones.

OXIDATION AND REDUCTION

- Oxidation is a process in which a substance adds on oxygen or loses hydrogen. In modern terms, oxidation is the process in which a substance loses electrons.
- Reduction is a process in which a substance adds on hydrogen or loses oxygen. In modern terms, reduction is the process in which a substance gains electrons.
- Oxidation and reduction always occur simultaneously. If one substance is oxidised, another is reduced. The reaction in which this oxidation-reduction process occurs is called a redox reaction.
- Oxidising agents are substances which bring about the oxidation of other substances, e.g., Potassium Permanganate, Potassium Dichromate, Nitric Acid, Hydrogen Peroxide, etc.
- Reducing agents are substances which bring about the reduction of other substances, e.g., hydrogen sulphide, hydrogen, carbon, sulphur dioxide, etc.

ACIDS, BASES AND SALTS

ACID

- An acid is any compound that can react with a base to form a salt, the hydrogen of the acid being replaced by positive metallic ion. According to modern theory, an acid is a compound which yields hydrogen ions (protons) to a base in a chemical reaction. In a water solution, an acid tastes sour, turns blue litmus red and produces free hydrogen ions.

Acid	Sources
Citric Acid	Lemons or Oranges (Citrus Fruits)
Lactic acid	Sour milk
Tartaric acid	Grapes
Acetic acid	Vinegar
Maleic acid	Apples
Oxalic acid	Tomato
Formic acid	Red ants

BASES

- Such compounds which gives salt and water with acid known as bases. Bitter in taste, turns red litmus paper into blue, contains replaceable hydroxyl group.
- Some important bases are sodium hydroxide, potassium hydroxide, sodium carbonate and ammonium hydroxide.
- All alkalies are bases but all bases are not alkalies because all bases are not soluble in water.

SALTS

- Salts are ionic compounds containing a positive ion (cation) and a negative ion (anion).
- When an acid reacts with a base, a salt and water are formed. This reaction is called neutralization since the acid and base neutralize each other's effect.

ELECTROLYSIS

- The process of decomposition of an electrolyte by the passage of an electric current through its molten state or its aqueous solution is called electrolysis.
- Device through which electric current is passed known as electrodes.

METALLURGY

- Metals occur in nature, in the native (in free state) as well as in the combined state.
- Naturally occurring materials containing metals are called minerals.
- A mineral from which a given metal is obtained economically is called an ore.
- The process of extraction of a metal in a pure state on a large scale from its ore by Physical and Chemical means is called metallurgy.
- The rocky and siliceous matter that associated with the ore is known as gangue.
- Substance that is added to ore to remove the gangue is known as flux.

- The process of removal of gangue from the ore is known as concentration.
- Calcination is the heating of the ore in the absence of air. This method is employed for obtaining the metal oxides from carbonates and hydroxides.
- Roasting is the heating of the ore in the presence of air. On roasting, part of the ore is oxidised to form an oxide. This oxide is then reduced to the metal.
- The industrial reduction process for obtaining metal from the treated ore is called smelting.

AMALGUM

- An alloy in which one of the component metals is mercury is known as amalgum.

IRON AND STEEL

- Iron is extracted from its ores by the blast furnace process.
- Iron obtained from blast furnace is called pig iron or cast iron containing about 5% carbon.
- Pure iron is called wrought iron which does not contain carbon more than 0.2%, or any other impurities or constituents.
- Steel contains 0.25% – 2% carbon and varying amounts of other elements.

CARBON AND ITS COMPOUNDS

ALLOTROPY

- Such substances which having the same chemical properties, but differ in physical properties, known as allotropes and this property is called allotropy.

DIAMOND

- Diamond is the purest form of carbon.
- It is non-conductor of heat and electricity.
- It is the hardest natural substance.
- It burns in air at 900°C and gives out CO_2.

GRAPHITE (BLACK LEAD)

- It is good conductor of heat and electricity.
- Graphite is used in making lead pencils.
- Graphite is also used as electrodes, lubricant, moderators, electrotyping and carbon arc.

AMORPHOUS FORMS OF CARBON

1. Wood Charcoal – Obtained from wood
2. Sugar Charcoal – Obtained from cane sugar
3. Bone or Animal Charcoal – Obtained from animal bones
4. Coke Charcoal – Obtained from coal

CARBON MONOXIDE (CO)

- Carbon monoxide is an active poison and is very dangerous as it is a colourless and odourless gas and can not, therefore, be easily detected.
- The extremely poisonous nature of carbon monoxide is a result of its combining with the haemoglobin of the blood to form carbo-xyhaemoglobin, which is not decompassed by any of the processes in the body.

HYDROCARBONS

- Compounds of carbon and hydrogen are called hydrocarbon.
- A natural source of hydrocarbon is petroleum obtained from sedimentary rocks.
- Compounds having the same molecular formula but differ in properties due to different structural formula known as isomers and this property is called isomerism.

SATURATED HYDROCARBONS (ALKANES)

- Containing single covalent bonds only.
- Such compounds are, in general, called alkanes for instance, Methane, Ethane, Propane, Butane.

UNSATURATED HYDROCARBONS

- Containing multiple bonds.
- Compounds with double bonds are called alkenes, e.g. ethylene, propyene etc. and triple bond containing compounds are called alkynes, e.g. acetylene, propyne etc.
- Benzene is an unsaturated cyclic hydrocarbon with the structure.
- Compounds derived from benzene are called aromatic compounds.

FUELS

Solid Fuels

- These contain carbon and, during combustion, form mainly carbon dioxide and carbon monoxide with a large amount of heat.
- Examples of solid fuels are wood, coal, coke and paraffin wax.

Liquid Fuels

- These are basically mixtures of several hydrocarbons. During combustion, they form carbon dioxide and water.
- Liquid fuels are obtained as different fractions during the distillation of petroleum.
- Examples of liquid fuels are kerosene oil, petrol, diesel oil and alcohol.

Gaseous Fuels

- Gaseous fuels do not leave ash on burning and have high content of heat.
- The main gaseous fuels are liquefied petroleum gas (LPG, mainly a mixture of propane and butane and used in homes for cooking, water gas ($CO + H_2$), producer gas ($CO + N_2$), coal gas (mixture of hydrogen, methane, ethylene, carbon monoxide, nitrogen, oxygen and carbon dioxide) and natural gas (mixture of methane, ethane, propane and butane with traces of higher hydrocarbons obtained from oil well, above petroleum).

PETROLEUM AND NATURAL GAS

- Natural gas contains about 80% methane and 10% ethane, the remaining 10% being a mixture of higher gaseous hydrocarbons.
- Compressed Natural Gas (CNG) is natural gas filled in cylinders under high pressure.
- The quality of petrol for use in car engines is denoted by their anti-knock properties.
- To increase octane number, tetra ethyl lead (TEL) is added to petrol.

HEAVY WATER

- Chemically heavy water is deuterium oxide.
- Heavy water is used in nuclear reactors as a moderator because it slows the fast moving neutrons.

Hard and Soft Water

- Water which produces lather with soap solution readily is called soft water.
- Water which does not produce lather with soap solution readily is called hard water.
- The hardness of water is due to presence of the bicarbonates, chlorides and sulphates of calcium and magnesium.
- Temporary hardness of water is due to the presence of bicarbonates of calcium and magnesium.
- Permanent hardness of water is due to presence of sulphates, chlorides, nitrates of calcium and magnesium.

GLASS

- Ordinary glass is solid mixture of silica, sodium silicate and calcium silicate.
- Soft glass is a soda-lime silicate glass. It melts at low temperature. It is used in manufacturing of bottles, test tubes etc.
- Hard glass is potash lime silicate and melts at high temperature in comparison to soft glass and is used in manufacturing of flask etc.
- Flint glass is a lead potash silicate and is used in manufacturing of prism, lens and optical instruments.
- Pyrex glass is a mixture of sodium aluminium borosilicates. It is used in manufacturing of high quality equipments in laboratory because it does not melt at very high temperature.
- Safety glass is prepared by placing a layer of transparent plastic glass between two layers of glass by means of a suitable adhesive. It is used in making wind screen of automobiles, aeroplanes, trains etc.

CEMENT

- The approximate composition of Portland cement is:
  1. Calcium Oxide → 62%
  2. Silica → 22%
  3. Alumina → 7.5%
  4. Magnesia → 2.5%
  5. Ferric Oxide → 2.5%
- A small amount of gypsum is added to slow down the setting of cement.
- Cement containing excess amount of lime cracks during setting while cement containing less amount of lime is weak in strength.
- Cement containing no iron is white but hard to burn.

POLYMERS AND PLASTICS

- A polymer is a large molecule, built up from many hundreds of thousands of small unit called monomeric units or monomers.
- The process of formation of polymers from monomers is called polymerization.
- Plastics are cross-linked polymers and very tough.
- Some examples of plastics are — Celluloid, Bakelite and Vinyl Plastics.

RUBBER

- Natural and Synthetic rubbers are examples of polymers.
- Natural rubber is isomer of isoprene.
- When the natural rubber is heated along with sulphur called vulcanisation. The resulting rubber is elastic, hard and strong.
- Synthetic rubbers are made by polymerisation of chloroprene, styrene and butadiene mixtures and isobutylene.

SOAPS

- The soaps are sodium salts of higher fatty acids. They are useful only in soft water as they form an insoluble precipitate in hard water. This precipitate consists of salts of calcium and magnesium of higher fatty acids. No lather or emulsion is formed and washing is not possible.

Some Importants Alloys

Alloys	*Composition*
Brass	Cu, Zn
Bronze	Cu, Sn
Gun metal	Cu, Sn, Zn
Bel metal	Cu, Sn
German silver	Cu, Zn, Ni
Dutch metal	Cu, Zn
Aluminium	Al, Cu
Nichrome	Ni, Fe, Cr, Mn
Chromium steel	Cr, C, Fe

Chemical Formulae, Commercial Name of Chemical Compounds

Commercial Name	Chemical Compounds	Chemical formulae
Common salt	Sodium chloride	$NaCl$
Baking soda	Sodium bicarbonate	$NaHCO_3$
Washing soda	Sodium carbonate	$Na_2CO_3 . 10H_2O$
Caustic soda	Sodium hydroxide	$NaOH$
Chilli salt peter	Sodium nitrate	$NaNO_3$
Soda ash	Sodium carbonate	Na_2CO_3
Hypo	Sodium thiosulphate	$Na_2S_2O_3 . 5H_2O$

BIOLOGY

BRANCHES OF BIOLOGY

(*a*) **Anthropology:** Deals with the scientific study of man and the mankind.

(*b*) **Agronomy:** Deals with the management of farms and science of crop production.

(*c*) **Apiculture:** Deals with the process of bee keeping for commercial purposes.

(*d*) **Entomology:** Deals with the structure, habits and classification of insects.

(*e*) **Eugenics:** Deals with improving the human race.

(*f*) **Pathology:** Deals with the nature of disease, their causes, symptoms, effects, their cure and control.

(*g*) **Physiotherapy:** Deals with the treatment of diseases, body weakness or defects with the help of massage and exercise etc.

(*h*) **Sericulture:** Deals with the production of raw silk from silkworm.

(*i*) **Pharmacology:** Deals with the knowledge and manufacture of drugs.

(*j*) **Occupational therapy:** Deals with treating the physically handicapped or injured persons through exercise etc.

(*k*) **Psychology:** Deals with the study of human mind, its behaviour and mental qualities.

(*l*) **DNA finger printing:** Technique to help identify a person on the basis of genes.

ANIMALS/PLANTS

- The organisms that closely resemble one another are placed in one group, the groups which have similarities are combined together into larger groups, and these into still larger ones. The most inclusive category is kingdom. Other major categories, in descending order are: phylum, class, order, family, genus, and species. Man belongs to Animal kingdom, chordata division or phylum, Mammalia class, Primates order, Hominidae family, Homo genus and Sapiens species.

CELL THEORY

- Cell is the basic unit of structure of all living organisms. According to the cell theory, all organism are composed of cells and cell products and growth and development results from the division and differentiation of cells.
- Cells membrane surrounds all living cells.
- Nucleus is the most important cell organelle which controls and coordinates all cell activities and also concerned with the transmission of heredity characters.
- Mitochondria, ribosomes, lysosomes and dictyosomes are present in plant and animal cells.
- Only plant cells have cell wall, chloroplast and vacuole.
- Viruses constitute a difficulty since in many ways they are intermediate between living and dead matter.
- The cell is said to be made up of a substance called Protoplasm which has two main constituents cytoplasm and nucleus, and is bounded by a cell membrane on outside.
- Cells take up the raw materials for metabolism through the cell membrane from extracellular fluid surrounding them.
- Cytoplasm inside is responsible for maintaining the internal distribution of organelles and also for free cell movements.
- Mitochondria inside provides energy for reactions inside the cell. Ribosomes are responsible for the synthesis of proteins.
- The Endoplasmic Reticulum helps in addition of other sugar units to proteins and their transportation to other parts of the cell.

FOOD

- It is a nutritive substance taken by an organism for growth, work, repair and maintaining life processes. It provides energy to do work and maintain body heat, provides materials for the growth of the body, makes necessary materials for reproduction and provides materials for the repair of damaged cells and tissues of our body.

- **Carbohydrates:** For a normal person, 400 to 500 gms of carbohydrates are required daily but for sportspersons, growing children and nursing mothers, it is on higher side.
- **Proteins:** They are complex organic compounds made up of carbon, hydrogen, oxygen and nitrogen. The building blocks of Protein are Amino acids and there are large number of amino acids.
- Proteins are essential for the growth of children and teenagers, and for maintenance and making good the wear and tear of the body tissues in adults.
- An adult needs about 1 gm of protein per kg of body weight.
- **Fats:** They are esters of long chain fatty acids and an alcohol called glycerol. Fats also contain atoms of carbon, hydrogen and oxygen.
- The main function of fats in the body is to provide a steady source of energy and for this purpose, they are deposited within the body.
- One gm of fat gives 37 kilojoules of energy which is more than double of that given by carbohydrates.
- Fats, the richest source of energy to our body, can be stored in the body for subsequent use. Fats, soluble in organic solvents and insoluble in water, also supply fat-soluble vitamins to our body.
- **Minerals:** Some of the important minerals needed by our body are — iron, iodine, calcium, phosphorus, sodium, potassium, zinc, copper, magnesium, chloride, fluoride and sulphur.
- We get most of the minerals in combined form from plant sources. Deficiency of these minerals causes many diseases.
- **Energy Requirements:** The energy requirement of a body varies according to age, sex, lifestyle, occupation, climate and special situations like pregnancy and lactation.

Age	*Energy requirements*
5 years	6000 kJ per day
11 years	9000 kJ per day
18 years	11000 kJ per day
Adult (normal work)	9600 kJ per day
Adult (heavy work)	12000 kJ per day
Adult (very heavy work)	16000 kJ per day

- **Vitamins:** They act as catalysts in certain chemical reactions of metabolism in our body.
- They don't provide energy to our body nor form body tissues.
- More than 15 types of vitamins are known and only 2 vitamins — D and K can be formed in our body.

Vitamin	*Necessity*	*Source*
Vitamin A	For maintaining healthy eyesight, normal skin and hair	Cod liver oil, fish, eggs, milk, carrot, leafy vegetables.
Vitamin B_1	For growth, carbohydrate metabolism, functioning of heart, nerves and muscles.	Milk, soya-food, meat, whole cereals, green vegetables.
Vitamin C	For keeping teeth, gums and joints healthy, for increasing resistance of body to infection	Citrus fruits, guava, tomatoes.
Vitamin D	For normal growth of bones and teeth	Milk, eggs, butter, cod liver oil, sun light.
Vitamin E	For normal reproduction, functioning of muscles and protection of liver	Green leafy vegetables, milk, butter, tomato.
Vitamin K	For normal clotting of blood and normal functioning of liver	Green leafy vegetables, soyabean, tomato.

- **Roughage:** Though it does not provide any energy to the body, yet keeps the digestive system in order, by helping in retaining water in the body and preserving constitution.
- The main source of roughage are salads, cabbage, corn cob, porridge, vegetables and fruits with stems.

DISEASES

COMMUNICABLE DISEASES

- They are the diseases which can be transmitted from reservoirs of infection or infected person to the healthy but susceptible persons.
- The disease causing agent or the pathogen can be transmitted directly or indirectly.

DEFICIENCY DISEASES

- These occur due to deficiency of some nutrients in the diet or some hormone due to hypo activity or damage to endocrine glands.

Diet Deficiency	*Disease*
Protein	Kwashiorkor
Protein-energy malnutrition	Marasmus
Vitamin A	Night-blindness, Xerophthalmia
Vitamin B_1	Beri-Beri
Vitamin B_2	Cheilosis
Vitamin B_5	Pellagra
Vitamin C	Scurvy

Vitamin D	Rickets (in children), (in adult) Osteomalacia
Vitamin K	Hypothrombinemia
Iron	Anaemia
Iodine	Goitre
Fluoride	Dental caries
Calcium and phosphorus	Affects formation of bones and teeth

Hormone Deficiency	*Disease*
Insulin	Diabetes
Thyroxine	Cretinism (child), Goitre
STH	Dwarfism, Gigantism

ALLERGIC DISEASE

- In these diseases, body becomes hypersensitive to some foreign agents, allergens, which cause inflammation when come in contact with the body or enter inside the body.
- Foreign agents can be dust, pollens, certain-foods, serum, certain drugs or fabrics.
- The unfavourable response of the body to allergens is called allergic reaction. Asthma and hay fever are allergic diseases.

BACTERIAL DISEASES

- Bacteria are minute organisms which are known to cause a number of diseases:

Disease	Incubation period	Spread through
Tuberculosis	2-10 weeks	Air-borne,droplet infection
Diptheria	2-6 days	Air-borne droplet infection
Cholera	6 hours to 2-3 days	Contaminated food and water. House flies are the vectors
Leprosy	Upto 5 years	Prolonged and intimate contact
Whopping cough	7-14 days	Droplet infection
Tetanus	3-21 days	Entry of cysts through any wound made by sharp object, dog bite or fall on the road
Typhoid	1-3 weeks	Directed and Contact
Plague	2-6 days	Rats and bed-bugs transmit the germs
Pneumonia	1-3 days	Air-borne

VIRAL DISEASES

Disease	Incubation period	Spread through
Chicken-pox	12-20 days	Direct contact with infected persons or infected objects
Smallpox	12 days	Droplet infection
Poliomyalitis	7-14 days	Direct and oral
Measles	10 days	Droplet infection
Mumps	12-26 days	Droplet infection
Rabies	1-3 months	Bite of rabied animal like dogs, monkeys, cats
Influenza	24-28 hours	Air-borne

DISEASES CAUSED BY PROTOZOA

- Amoebiasis (Amoebic dysentery), Malaria, Kala-azar, Trypanosomiasis and Giardiasis are main diseases caused by Protozoans.
- Malaria is a parasitic infection.

SYSTEM OF HUMAN BODY

DIGESTIVE SYSTEM

- The digestive system consists of alimentary canal and digestive glands. Alimentary canal is about 8-10 meters long tube of varying diameter. Food is taken in through mouth.
- The tongue helps in ingestion, chewing, tasting and swallowing of food and mixing of food and saliva.
- Salivary glands secret saliva which helps in digestion of starch. Gastric glands present in the mucosa of the stomach, provide acidic medium for the food digestion.
- Liver, the largest sized, reddish brown gland of body, secrets bile. Liver is present in the right upper part of the abdomen. The bile secreted by the liver is stored in gall bladder. It helps in the emulsification and digestion of fats.
- Pancreas is the second largest gland in human body and secretes pancreatic juices. Intestine also secret juices.

RESPIRATORY SYSTEM

- Oxygen is needed for the oxidation and expelling of carbon dioxide is necessary to avoid its-accumulation. This process of exchange of gases between the environment and the body, is called respiration.
- In some unicellular organisms like aerobic bacteria, amoeba, hydra, etc. there is direct exchange of gases between the carbon dioxide of the body and oxygen of water.
- There is no blood for transport of gases. However, in larger and complex form of animals, specialised respiratory organs are developed.
- Amphibians respire through skin, fishes through gills and mammals, birds and reptiles through lungs.
- A normal adult inspires or expires about 500 ml of gas with each breath and about 72 breathes per minutes.

CIRCULATORY SYSTEM

- Main components of the circulatory system are heart, blood vessels and blood.
- Heart is a thick, muscular, contractile and automatic pumping organ. In birds and mammals, heart is divided into four chambers.

- Arteries are thick walled blood vessels which always carry the blood away from the heart to various body parts.
- Veins are thin walled blood vessels which always carry the blood from various parts generally to the heart.
- In an adult healthy person, the normal rate of heart beat at rest is about 70-72 times per minute.

BLOOD

- It is red, opaque, somewhat sticky and viscous fluid in the body of animals.
- It is slightly alkaline (pH = 7.4), heavier than water (sp gr = 1.05) and five times more viscous than distilled water.
- Blood forms 6 to 10% of the body weight.
- An adult, on average, has about 6.8 litres of blood.
- Blood contains plasma and blood corpuscles with the former occupying 55-60% of the volume.
- Plasma transports food components, metabolic wastes and hormones; keeps constant level of pH of blood, maintains body temperature and helps in blood clotting.
- Erythrocytes or red blood corpuscles (RBCs), leukocytes or white blood corpuscles (WBCs) and blood platelets are other parts of the blood.
- Due to the presence of iron containing pigment haemoglobin, RBCs are red in colour. The RBCs are crucial for ex-change of oxygen and carbon dioxide. WBCs are nucleated and non-pigmented cells. They are larger in size than RBCs but far less in number (1 : 600).
- WBCs play an important role in immune system of the body. Blood platelets cause the coagulation of blood and clot formation to prevent excessive bleeding.
- Human blood is divided into four main Groups—A, B, AB and O.
- The plasma of Group A blood contains an anti-B factor and vice-versa, so that people of Groups A and B cannot accept each other's blood.
- Group AB contains neither anti-A nor anti-B factor and people with this group can receive transfusions from both but can give to neither.
- Group O contains both anti-A and anti-B and can receive blood only from Group O but can donate blood to all Groups. Group O is called universal donor because they can donate to all the Groups.
- Group AB is called universal acceptor because they can accept blood from all Groups.

SKELETON SYSTEM

- The frame or the hard structure of the human body is composed from the bones and the organs of making such frame are called skeleton system.

Bones

- Bone is the hardest tissue of the body and form the largest section of the body weight.
- Bones contain organic as well as inorganic matters. With advancing age, the inorganic matter's share increases, causing the bones to become more brittle.
- Long bones such as humerus and femur are hollow while small bones are solid.

EXCRETORY SYSTEM

- In men, excretory system is formed of one pair of kidneys, one pair of ureters, a urinary bladder and a urethra. Kidney is about 10 cm long, bean shaped, dark-red and slightly flattened structure.
- Sweet glands, oil glands, lungs and liver also act as additional excretory organ.
- In case of kidney failure, a man can treated by hemodialysis or transplantation of a kidney from a donor's body.

NERVOUS SYSTEM

- The system which controls and coordinates the body functions, retains memory and receives and sends signals, is called the nervous system.
- The nervous system comprises brain, spinal cord, nerves and nerve fibres.
- Human brain weighs about 1200 to 1400 gm. Main parts of the brain are cerebrum, cerebellum and medulla oblongata.
- Cerebrum controls voluntary function and is site of intelligence, will power, emotions, etc.
- Cerebellum controls involuntary functions like heart beat, respiration, etc.
- Spinal cord is about 45 cm long and about 35 gm in weight. It conducts impulses to and from the brain and controls reflex actions of the body.
- Various cranial (arising from ending into brain) and spinal nerves (arising from spinal cord) control smell, vision, movements of body parts, taste and hearing.

REPRODUCTION SYSTEM

- In this type of reproduction, there is formation and fusion of sex cells, called gametes.
- Organism develops from the zygote through embryo formation.
- It generally involves two parents — male and female.
- The offsprings are different from the parent as variations appear due to new combinations of genes. So, it plays an important role in evolution.
- All higher plants and animals reproduce sexually.

CHROMOSOMES

- Plants and animals have fixed number of chromosomes per cell.
- Genes are located on chromosomes and are responsible for transfer of characteristics from one cell to the next either in the same organism or from parents to offspring.

- Man has 23 pairs of chromosomes, of which one pair is sex chromosomes.
- Males child inherits X chromosomes from the female parent and Y from the male parent.
- Female child receives a X chromosome each from either of its parents.
- Mendel was the first scientist to explain transmission of units from reproductive cells of the parents to the off-springs.

CLONING

- It is the process of producing genetically identical copies of a biological material, starting from a single cell. The original genes are transplanted and thus one can produce organisms of known and desirable characteristics.

GENETIC ENGINEERING

- It is the method of artificial synthesis of new genes and their subsequent transplantation or methods of correcting the defective genes.
- It has helped in producing plants and animals with specific characters.
- So, crippling hereditary diseases can also be cured like hemophilia etc.

DNA FINGERPRINTING

- It consists of examining repetitive DNA in the genome for variations in the lĕngth of restriction fragments.
- Every individual has his own pattern, so that fingerprinting can match blood to a particular person, and patterns are inherited from parent to child, allowing the method to identify relationships between individuals.

IN-VITRO FERTILIZATION

- When a sperm and an egg are made to fertilize outside a living body (usually a test tube), it is called in-vitro fertilization.
- This process has been used to impregnate several females who could not do so through natural means.

Diseases and the Parts of Body they Affect

AIDS—Immune system of body	*Gout*—Joints of bone
Arthritis—Inflammation of joints	*Jaundice*—Liver
Asthma—Lungs	*Meningitis*—Brain or spinal cord
Cataract—Eyes	*Pleurisy*—Pleura (inflammation of)
Conjunctivitis—Eyes	*Polio*—motor neurons
Diabetes—Pancreas	*Pneumonia*—Lungs
Diphtheria—Throat	*Pyorrhoea*—Sockets of teeth
Glaucoma—Eyes	*Tuberculosis*—Lungs
Eczema—Skin	*Typhoid*—Intestine
Goitre—Front of the neck (due to enlargement of thyroid gland)	*Malaria*—Spleen
	Leukaemia—Blood
	Rickets—Bones

SPACE RESEARCH

First in Space

✶ First creator of rules regarding space research	Isaac Newton
✶ First artificial satellite launched in space	Sputnik-1 (1957)
✶ First living being sent in space	Louika (a dog)
✶ Firstever manned spacecraft	Vostok-I
✶ First man in space	Yuri Gagarin U.S.S.R. (1961)
✶ First woman in space	Valentina Tereshkova U.S.S.R. (June 1963)
✶ First man who moved in space out of the spacecraft	Alexi Livonov U.S.S.R. (June 1965)
✶ First person to land on moon	Neil Armstrong, America (21st July, 1969)
✶ First fourwheeled carriage without human being on moon	Leunokhev-I U.S.S.R. (1970)
✶ First space lab in orbit	Skylab (America, 1973)
✶ First space shuttle	Columbia (America, 1981)
✶ First Indian (man) in space	Squadron leader—Rakesh Sharma (13th April, 1984)
✶ First Indian (Woman) in space	Kalpana Chawla (19th Nov., 1997)
✶ First American woman in space	Sailyride (1983)
✶ First spacecraft on Mars	Pathfinder (6 July, 1997)
✶ First woman who lead spacecraft	Allin Collis (America)
✶ First spacecraft without man	Shenzoo, China (20th Nov. 1999)

Indian Space Programme : At a Glance

Satellite	Date	Type	Launch Vehicle	Result
Aryabhatta	19-04-75	Scientific	Cosmos	successful
Bhaskara I	07-06-79	Geosurvey	Cosmos	successful
Rohini	10-08-79	Geosurvey	S.L.V.3	unsuccessful
Rohini D-1	18-07-80	Geosurvey	S.L.V.3	successful
Rohini	31-05-81	Scientific	S.L.V.3	successful
Apple	19-06-81	Communication	Ariane	successful
Bhaskara II	20-11-81	Geosurvey	Cosonos	successful
INSAT-1A	10-04-82	Multipurpose	Delta	unsuccessful
Rohini	17-04-83	Scientific	S.L.V.3	successful
INSAT-1B	30-08-83	Multipurpose	Space Shuttle	successful
SROSS I	24-03-87	Technical	ASLV-D1	unsuccessful
IRS-1A	17-03-88	Remote sensing	Vostok	successful
SROSS II	17-07-88	Technical	ASLV-D2	unsuccessful
INSAT-1C	21-07-88	Multipurpose	Ariane-4	unsuccessful
INSAT-1D	12-06-90	Multipurpose	Delta	successful
IRS-1B	29-08-91	Remote sensing	Vostok	successful
INSAT-2A	10-07-92	Multipurpose	Ariane	successful
IRS-ID	29-09-97	Remote sensing	PSLV	successful
INSAT-3B	22-03-2000	Multipurpose	Ariane	successful
G-SAT-1	18-04-2001	Multipurpose	GSLV-D	successful
MAT SAT	12-09-2002	Meteorology	PSLVC-4	successful
INSAT-3E	28-09-2003	Communication	Ariane-5	successful
Cartosat-1 & hamsat	05-05-2005	Maping and Communication	PSLV-C6	successful
CARTOSAT-2	10-01-2007	Communication	PSLV-C7	successful
Cartosat-2A	28-04-2008	Communication	PSLV-C9	successful
Chandrayaan-I	22-10-2008	Maping and Scientific	PSLV-C11	successful
Oceansat-2	24-09-2009	Remote Sensing	PSLV-C14	successful
CARTOSAT-2B	12-07-2010	Communication	PSLV-C15	successful
RESOURCESAT-2	20-04-2011	Remote Sensing	PSLV-C16	successful
GSAT-12	15-07-2011	Communication	PSLV-C17	successful
Megha-Tropiques	12-10-2011	Maping and Scientific	PSLV-C18	successful
RISAT-1	26-04-2012	Remote Sensing	PSLV-C19	successful
Spot-6	09-09-2012	Remote Sensing	PSLV-C21	successful
Saral	25-02-2013	Scientific	PSLV-C20	successful
GSAT-7	30-08-2013	Defence	Ariane-5	successful
MOM	5-11-2013	Mapping	PSLV-C25	successful
GSAT-14	05-01-2014	Communication	GSLV-D5	successful
IRNSS-1B	04-04-2014	Mapping and Scientific	PSLV-C24	successful
Spot-7	30-06-2014	Remote Sensing	PSLV-C23	successful
GSAT-16	07-12-2014	Communication	Ariane-5	successful
IRNSS-1D	28-03-2015	Mapping and Scientific	PSLV-C27	successful
GSAT-6	27-08-2015	Communication	GSLV-D6	successful
Astrosat	28-09-2015	Mapping and Scientific	PSLV-C30	successful
GSAT-15	11-11-2015	Communication	Ariane-5	successful
TELEOS-1	16-12-2015	Mapping and Scientific	PSLV-C29	successful
IRNSS-1E	20-01-2016	Mapping and Scientific	PSLV-C31	successful
IRNSS-1F	10-03-2016	Mapping and Scientific	PSLV-C32	successful
IRNSS-1G	28-04-2016	Mapping and Scientific	PSLV-C33	successful
Cartosat-2 & others	22-06-2016	Mapping and Scientific	PSLV-C34	successful

Satellite	Date	Type	Launch Vehicle	Result
insat-3DR	08-09-2016	Meteorology	GSLV-F05	successful
Scatsat-1 & others	26-09-2016	Multipurpose	PSLV-C35	successful
RESOURCESAT-2A	07-12-2016	Remote Sensing	PSLV-C36	successful
CARTOSAT-2 & 103 others	15-02-2017	Multipurpose	PSLV-C37	successful
CARTOSAT-2E	23-06-2017	Earth observation Satellite	PSLV-C38	successful
GSAT-17	29-06-2017	Earth observation Satellite	Ariane-5 ECA	successful
Cartosat-2F & others	12-01-2018	Multipurpose	PSLV-C40	successful
GSAT-6A	29-03-2018	Communication	GSLV-F08	successful
GSAT-7A	19-12-2018	Military Satellite	GSLV-MK-II-F11	successful
Chandrayaan-2	22-07-2019	Lunar Exploration	GSLV MK-III M01	—
Cartosat-3	27-11-2019	Earth Imagine Satellite	PSLV-C47	successful
GSAT-30	17-01-2020	Communication	Ariane-5	successful
EOS-01	07-11-2020	Earth Observation	PSLV-C49	successful
Amezonia & 19 others	28-02-2021	Communication	PSLV-C51	successful
EOS-04	14-02-2022	Earth Observation	PSLV-C52	successful
Oceansat-3 & 8 others	26-11-2022	Earth Observation	PSLV-C54	successful
EOS-07	10-02-2023	Earth Observation	SSLV-02	successful
Chandrayaan-3	14-07-2023	Lunar Exploration	LVM-3	successful
Aditya-L1	02-09-2023	Solar Mission	PSLV-C57	successful
XPoSat	01-01-2024	Earth Observation	PSLV-C58	successful

COMPUTER

- The computer is the system of that electronic device through which various informations are processed on the basis of a definite set of instructions called program and mathematical (numerical) and non-mathematical both types of informations are processed.
- The first mechanical computer was composed or fabricated by Blaise Pascal in 1642 and it is called Pascalene.
- But in 1833, Charles Babbage first time conceived an automatic calculator or computer.
- Charles Babbage is called the father of modern computer.
- Herman made an electronic tabulating machine based on punch cards which operates automatically.
- In 1937, first mechanical computer Mark-I was fabricated by Howard Akeen.
- The most outstanding contribution in the development of modern computer goes to John Wan Newmaan who brought the 2nd revolution in the area of computer in 1951.
- He discovered EDVAC (Electronic Discrete Variable Automatic Computer) and utilised the stored program and the binary number system in the computer.

FUNCTIONS OF COMPUTER

- 1. Collection and composition (input) of datas;
  2. Storage of datas.
  3. Processing of datas.
  4. Retrieval or output of the proccessed informations and datas.

UNITS OF COMPUTER

1. Input unit.
2. Central processing unit–CPU.
3. External Memory unit.
4. Output unit.

- The CPU of the computer is called brain of the computer and sometimes CPU is also called Micro Processor of the computer.
- The data is entered through the input unit in the computer and through the central processing unit with the help of External Memory Unit datas are arranged and processed.
- Ultimately by the output unit these datas or informations are issued or released.

PARTS OF COMPUTER

- **Monitor :** The monitor of the computer is like a television in which the picture appears in the form of doted points on the screen and these are called pixels.
- **Hard Disc and Floppy Disc :** The Hard Disc is the permanent disc in the computers while the Floppy Disc is the disc utilised when datas or informations are to be transferred from one computer to another.
- **Mouse :** The mouse of the computer is like the remote control of TV through which computer is directly regulated or controlled without utilising the key-board.
- **Printer :** The printer is a device which prints any documents or processed informations of the computer.

SOME HIGH LEVEL LANGUAGES

1. **FORTRAN :** This language was developed for solving the mathematical formulae very quickly and conveniently.
2. **COBOL :** This language was developed for the commerical purposes. For the processing of this

language a group of sentences is selected called paragraph and all paragraphs composed are called a section, while all sections composed are called a division.

3. **BASIC :** In basic a definite part of the prescribed instruction is only inserted in the computer.
4. **ALGOL :** This was basically fabricated and designed for the complex algebraic calculations.
5. **PASCAL :** It is an amplified and modified form of ALGOL.
6. **COMAL :** This computer language is used for the students of secondary level.
7. **LOGO :** This language is used for children and kids for drawing Graphic line diagrams.
8. **PROLOG :** This language is developed in 1973 in France and is used for Artificial Intelligence which is capable and equivalent to the logical program.
9. **FORTH :** This language was invented by Charles Mure which is frequently used in all types of the works in the computer.

COMPUTER VIRUS

- The computer virus is an electronic code which is used to abolish or erradicate the inclusive informations or programs of the computer.
- Some important computer viruses are Micheleanjalo, Dork Avangor, kilo, filip, Macmug, Scores, Casecade, Jeruslem, Date crime, Coloumbs crime, Internet virus, Pachcom, Pach EXE, COM-EXE, Marizuana, C-brain, bloody, Chenge Mungu and Desi etc.

COMPUTER NETWORKING

- There are two types of networkings which are usually occur—Local Area Networking (LAN) and Wide Area Networking (WAN).

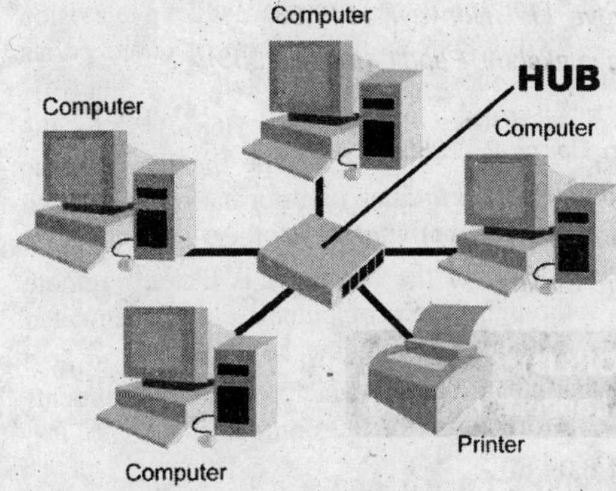

- By LAN all the computers of the same buildings are connected like the computers of university premises, computers of offices etc.
- By WAN all the comptuers of a large area are connected like the computers of all the offices of a city or town etc.
- In India a very large computer network namely INDONET has been installing through which all the main towns and cities has to be interlinked.

COMPUTER TERMINOLOGY

- **Bit :** The bit is a unit of measurement of the electronic data. One bit is either 0 or 1 but not both. On composing 8 bits, 1 byte is formed.
- **Bug :** The Bug is the error in the computer program or system and its eradication is called Debug.
- **Byte :** Total eight bits compose a byte. Thus 8 bits = 1 byte.
- **CD-ROM :** A CD like of music CD in which data can be stored substantially called CD-ROM. In a CD with comparison to floppy extremely more datas can be stored but one problem in it is that one time recorded data can not be deleted or modified.
- **Chip :** It is a thin slice on which by a special mechanism a circuit is designed which is normally made from Silicon.
- **Memory System :** The place where computer data and program are temporarily kept is called Memory system. Usually memory is implied from RAM.
- **Modem :** The device which converts digital signals into analogue signals and vice-versa is called Modem.
- **RAM :** It is Random Access Memory (a place) where datas to be processed are kept temporarily and it is unstable memory.
- **ROM :** It is Read Only Memory and it is stable or Non-valatile memory which doesn't ended after power off.
- **Scanner :** It is a device through which graphic image is transformed to digital image and the scanners are of usually two types one desktop and another hand operating.

PROGRAMING

- Computers perform phenomenal feats of calculation, but they do not do so in a complicated way.
- They actually carry out very simple operations, such as addition and subtraction.
- They achieve their fantastic computing power by carrying out these operations at incredible speed.
- The programme, or set of instructions for operating the computer, is therefore written as a sequence of very simple steps.

  Several computer languages have been developed for different applications, including BASIC, COBOL, FORTRAN and PASCAL. Writing programmes is very skilled and time-consuming work.
- But for most typical computer applications ready-written programmes are available, called "packages".

❐ ❐ ❐

GENERAL KNOWLEDGE

FIRST IN THE WORLD

✶ First Chinese visitor to India	*Fahien*
✶ First foreign invader of India	*Alexander, the Great (Greek)*
✶ First person to climb Mt. Everest	*Tenzing Norgay (India) and Edmund Hillary (New Zealand) (1953)*
✶ First atom bomb dropped at	*Hiroshima (Japan)*
✶ First man in the space	*Yuri Gagarin (former USSR)*
✶ First woman in the space	*Valentina Tereshkova (former USSR)*
✶ First person to walk in the space	*Alexei Leonov (former USSR)*
✶ First person to land on the moon	*Neil Armstrong (USA)*
✶ First and the only woman to have climbed Mt. Everest twice	*Santosh Yadav (Indian; May 12, 1992; May 10, 1993)*
✶ First person on Mt. Everest without oxygen	*Phu Dorjee (Indian; May 9, 1984)*
✶ First person to climb Mt. Everest twice	*Nawang Gombu*
✶ First President of the USA	*George Washington*
✶ First woman Prime Minister	*Sirimavo Bandaranaike (Sri Lanka)*
✶ First person to swim across English Channel	*Mathew Webb*
✶ First woman to swim across English Channel	*Gertrude Caroline Ederle*
✶ First woman to climb Mt. Everest	*Junko Tabei (Japan)*
✶ First woman to climb Mt. Everest alone and without oxygen supplies	*Alison Hargreaves (Britain: May 13, 1995)*
✶ First Aeroplane to fly around the world without refuelling	*Voyager (Dec. 1986)*
✶ First test-tube Baby	*Louise Brown (UK; 1978)*
✶ First all-talking Film	*Jaz Singer (1927)*
✶ First Secretary-General of the UN	*Trygve Lie (Norway: 1946-53)*
✶ First woman President of the UN General Assembly	*Vijayalakshmi Pandit (India: 1953)*
✶ First woman to reach North Pole	*Ann Bancroft (1986)*
✶ First person to reach North Pole	*Robert Peary*
✶ First person to reach South Pole	*Amundsen (1911)*
✶ First woman to command Spacecraft in Space	*Ellin Collins*

SUPERLATIVES (WORLD)
(The Largest, Biggest, Smallest, Longest, Highest)

Animal,	*Tallest*	Giraffe (Average height 6.09 m)
	Largest and Heaviest	Blue Whale (190 tonnes)
	Longest recorded	Boot lace Worm (55 m)
	Fastest	Cheetah (Approximately 100 km/hr)

Bay,	*With max. shore line*	Hudson Bay (Canada: 12268 km)
	With maximum area	Bay of Bengal (India: 217 million hc)
Building,	*Tallest*	Burj Khalifa (Dubai, 818 meter)
Canal,	*Big ship (longest)*	Suez Canal (160 km)
	Busiest	Kiel Canal (North Sea)
City,	*Largest in Area*	Jiuquan Gansu, China (Area 1,67,996 Sq km)
Continent,	*biggest*	Asia
	Smallest	Australia Mainland
Country,	*Largest in Population*	China (over 137 crore)
	Largest in Area	Russia (17,075,400 sq. km)
	With largest electorate	India (over 90 crores)
	Smallest independent	State of Vatican City (0.44 km^2)
Delta,	*Largest*	Sundarban's Ganga-Brahmaputra delta (1,05,000 sq. km)
Desert,	*Largest*	Sahara (N. Africa; maximum length 5,150 km EW; maximum width 3,200 km NS)
Dome,	*Largest*	Singapore National Stadium (310 m)
Epic,	*Longest*	Mahabharata
Film,	*Most Oscars*	Ben Hur (11 Oscars–1959); Titanic (11 Oscars–1998); The Lord of Rings : The Return of the King (11 Oscars—2003).
Fruit,	*Most nutritive*	Avocado (Vitamins A, C, E and Proteins; Central and South America)
	Least nutritive	Cucumber
Gulf,	*Largest*	Gulf of Mexico (1,544,000 sq. km)
Island,	*Biggest*	Greenland (now known as Kalaatdlit Nunaat–2,175,000 sq km)
Lake,	*Largest*	Caspian Sea (Azerbaijan, Russia, Iran border: 37.18 lakh km^2)
	Deepest	Baikal (Siberia)
	Largest (fresh water)	Superior Lake (USA–Canada border: 82,350 km^2)
Library,	*Biggest*	United States Library of Congress (Washington D.C. founded in 1800, contains 101 million items)
	Biggest non-statutory	New York Public Library
Mountain,	*Highest peak*	Mt. Everest (8848 m; Nepal)
	Highest range	Himalayas, Asia (upto 4200 m)
	Greatest mountain range	Himalaya-Karakoram (96 out of 109 peaks over 7315 m are here)
Ocean,	*Largest and Deepest*	The Pacific (Area: 166,240,000 km^2; Depth: 10,924 m)
Peninsula,	*Largest*	Arabia (3.25 million sq. km)
Planet,	*Biggest*	Jupiter (equatorial diameter 142984 km)
	Brightest, hottest and nearest to Earth	Venus
	Nearest to Sun	Mercury
Plateau,	*Highest*	Tibetan Plateau (Central Asia: 4900 m)
Religion,	*Oldest*	Hinduism
Religion,	*Largest*	Christianity
Rivers,	*Longest*	(i) Nile (6650 km) (ii) Amazon (6437 km)
Sea,	*Largest*	South China Sea (2,974,600 sq. km)
	Largest (inland)	Mediterranean
Star,	*Brightest*	Sirius A (also called Dog Star)
Statue,	*Tallest*	Statue of Unity (India) 182 m.

Swimming course,	*Longest recognised*	English Channel
Temple,	*Largest*	Angkor Vat (Cambodia: 402 acres)
Waterfall,	*Highest*	Salto-Angel (in Venezuela on a branch of river Carrao, depth 807 m.)

IMPORTANT CITIES, PLACES, BUILDINGS OF THE WORLD

- **Angkor Vat:** It is a large group of old Hindu temples in Cambodia; a remnant of the Khmer civilisation. The temples were constructed in the first half of the 12th century.
- **Big Ben:** A clock on the tower of the British Parliament building, installed in 1856.
- **Bethlehem:** A town in Jordan; birth place of Christ; a place of pilgrimage.
- **Cape Canaveral:** Situated in Florida (U.S.A.), it is America's spaceship launching centre. Formerly it was known as *Cape Kennedy.*
- **Eiffel Tower:** A tower in Paris (985 ft high); the principal landmark of the city; designed by a French Engineer for the Paris Exposition 1889.
- **Fleet Street:** A street in London, where offices of newspapers are situated.
- **Golden Gate Bridge (U.S.A.):** One of the world's longest suspension bridges, built in 1933-37 across the entrance (Golden Gate) of San Francisco Bay in California. It has a length of 9266 ft.
- **Harappa:** Situated near Montgomery (Pakistan). The famous ruins throw light on 5000-year-old Indus Valley Civilisation.
- **Hiroshima:** A city in Japan; it was the target of the first atom bomb ever dropped on a city (by U.S.A. on August 6, 1945); casualities numbered nearly 1,30,000 and ninety per cent of the city was levelled.
- **India Office Library (London):** A museum of Indian historical works, collected by the British. The library consists of about 3,00,000 books, a large number of manuscripts in Sanskrit, Urdu, Persian and Arabic.
- **Kaaba:** The inner shrine of the great Mosque at Mecca in Saudi Arabia. It is the most sacred place. Muslims face the Kaaba when praying.
- **Karakoram Highway:** It is a 800-km all weather road linking border of China's Sinkiang province with Pakistan.
- **Leaning Tower of Pisa:** A white marble monument (179 feet high) built in the 14th Century in Italy. It is inclined to one side.
- **Mohenjodaro:** Situated in the Larkana District of Sind (Pakistan); ancient ruins throw light on 5,000-year-old Indus Valley Civilisation.
- **Oval, Leeds and Lords (England):** Famous for cricket matches.
- **Panama Canal:** Canal connecting the Atlantic and Pacific Oceans. The canal is 50 miles long and has 12 locks. It was opened to traffic in August, 1914. The canal is administered by the U.S.A.
- **Pentagon (Washington, USA):** It is a five-sided building housing the US Defence Department offices.
- **Burj Khalifa:** It is a 162 storeyed structure built in Dubai having a height of 818 meter. It is now the highest structure of the world. Taipei 101 (508 meter) is now the second highest structure of the world.
- **Pyramids:** Gigantic stone buildings built by the ancient Egyptians in 2700 B.C.; among the seven wonders of the world. The great pyramid at Giza is the largest. These pyramids were tombs for the pharaohs and other important people.
- **Scotland Yard:** Headquarters of the Criminal Investigation Department in London. It is known all over world for its efficient working.
- **Sandhurst (England):** Famous military training institution.
- **Sphinx:** Mythical beast of ancient Egypt; usually represented in art as having a human head and the body of a lion. The most famous one is the great Sphinx, a colossal stone figure at Gizah built in the 26th Century BC.
- **Stonehenge:** Prehistoric monument near Salisbury, England built in between 1800 B.C. and 1500 B.C.
- **Suez Canal:** This canal is an important link between the Mediterranean Sea and the Red Sea. It is about 160 km long and was constructed in 1869 by a French Engineer. It has shortened the distance between Southampton (England) and Bombay (now Mumbai) by about 4,000 miles. The canal was nationalised by Col. Nasser on July 26, 1956. Port Said is the famous port at the entry from Mediterranean Sea.
- **Vatican:** Official residence of the Pope (in Rome). The smallest country. It enjoys a separate entity in the world. (Area 109 acres).
- **Wall Street (New York):** Famous stock exchange market.

CAPITAL & CURRENCIES

Country	Capital	Currency
✶ Afghanistan	Kabul	Afghani
✶ Albania	Tirana	Lek
✶ Algeria	Algiers	Dinar
✶ Angola	Luanda	New Kwanza
✶ Argentina	Buenos Aires	Peso
✶ Armenia	Yeravan	Dram
✶ Australia	Canberra	Dollar
✶ Austria	Vienna	Euro
✶ Azerbaijan	Baku	Manat
✶ Bahrain	Manama	Dinar
✶ Bangladesh	Dhaka	Taka
✶ Barbados	Bridgetown	Dollar
✶ Belarus	Minsk	Ruble
✶ Belgium	Brussels	Euro
✶ Benin	Porto Novo	Franc
✶ Bhutan	Thimphu	Ngultrum[1]
✶ Bolivia	La paz	Dollar
✶ Botswana	Gaborone	Pula
✶ Brazil	Brasilia	Real
✶ Bosnia Herzegovina	Sarajevo	Dinar
✶ Bulgaria	Sofia	Lev
✶ Cambodia	Phnom-Penh	Riel
✶ Canada	Ottawa	Dollar
✶ Chile	Santiago	Peso
✶ China	Beijing	Yuan
✶ Colombia	Bogota	Peso
✶ Congo	Brazzaville	Franc
✶ Croatia	Zagreb	Kuna
✶ Cuba	Havana	Peso
✶ Cyprus	Nicosia	Euro
✶ Czech Republic	Prague	Koruna
✶ Denmark	Copenhagen	Krone
✶ Ecuador	Quito	Sucre
✶ Egypt	Cairo	Pound
✶ Estonia	Tallinn	Euro
✶ Ethiopia	Addis Ababa	Birr
✶ Fiji	Suva	Dollar
✶ Finland	Helsinki	Euro
✶ France	Paris	Euro
✶ Georgia	Tbilisi	Lari
✶ Germany	Berlin	Euro
✶ Ghana	Accra	Cedi
✶ Greece	Athens	Euro
✶ Guatemala	Guatemala City	Quetzal
✶ Guyana	George Town	Dollar
✶ Hungary	Budapest	Forint

Country	Capital	Currency
✶ Iceland	Reykjavik	Krona
✶ India	New Delhi	Rupee
✶ Indonesia	Jakarta	Rupiah
✶ Iran	Teheran	Rial
✶ Iraq	Baghdad	Dinar
✶ Ireland	Dublin	Euro
✶ Israel	Jerusalem	Shekel
✶ Italy	Rome	Euro
✶ Jamaica	Kingston	Dollar
✶ Japan	Tokyo	Yen
✶ Jordan	Amman	Dinar
✶ Kazakhstan	Akmola	Tenge
✶ Kenya	Nairobi	Shilling
✶ Korea (S)	Seoul	Won
✶ Korea (N)	Pyongyang	Won
✶ Kyrgyzstan	Bishkek	Som
✶ Kuwait	Kuwait City	Dinar
✶ Laos	Vientiane	Kip
✶ Latvia	Riga	Euro
✶ Lebanon	Beirut	Pound
✶ Liberia	Monrovia	Dollar
✶ Libya	Tripoli	Dinar
✶ Lithuania	Vilnius	Litas
✶ Luxembourg	Luxembourg	Euro
✶ Macedonia	Skopje	Dinar
✶ Malawi	Lilongwe	Kwacha
✶ Malaysia	Kuala Lumpur	Ringgit
✶ Maldives	Male	Rufiyaa
✶ Mali	Bamako	Franc
✶ Mauritius	Port Louis	Rupee
✶ Mexico	Mexico City	Peso
✶ Moldavia	Chisinau	Leu
✶ Mongolia	Ulan Bator	Tugrik
✶ Morocco	Rabat	Dirham
✶ Mozambique	Maputo	Metical
✶ Myanmar	Nay Pyi Taw	Kyat
✶ Namibia	Winohoek	Dollar
✶ Nepal	Kathmandu	Rupee
✶ Netherlands	Amsterdam	Euro
✶ New Zealand	Wellington	Dollar
✶ Nigeria	Abuja	Naira
✶ Norway	Oslo	Krone
✶ Oman	Muscat	Rial
✶ Pakistan	Islamabad	Rupee
✶ Panama	Panama City	Balboa
✶ Peru	Lima	New Sole
✶ Philippines	Manila	Peso
✶ Poland	Warsaw	Zloty

Country	Capital	Currency
✶ Portugal	Lisbon	Euro
✶ Qatar	Doha	Riyal
✶ Romania	Bucharest	Leu
✶ Russia	Moscow	Ruble
✶ Saudi Arabia	Riyadh	Rial
✶ Senegal	Dakar	Franc
✶ Slovakia	Bratislava	Euro
✶ Spain	Madrid	Euro
✶ Sri Lanka	Colombo	Rupee
✶ Sudan	Khartoum	Dinar
✶ Suriname	Paramaribo	Guilder
✶ Sweden	Stockholm	Krona
✶ Switzerland	Berne	Swiss Francs
✶ Syria	Damascus	Pound
✶ South Africa	Capetown (Legislative) Pretoria *(Administrative)*	Rand
✶ Tadzhikistan	Dushanbe	Ruble
✶ Taiwan	Taipei	Dollar
✶ Tanzania	Dodoma	Shilling
✶ Thailand	Bangkok	Baht
✶ Tunisia	Tunis	Dinar
✶ Turkiye	Ankara	Lira
✶ Turkmania	Ashikabad	Manat
✶ Uganda	Kampala	Shilling
✶ Ukraine	Kiev	Hyrvnia
✶ United Arab Emirates	Abu Dhabi	Dirham
✶ U.K.	London	Pound Sterling
✶ U.S.A.	Washington	Dollar
✶ Uruguay	Montevideo	Peso
✶ Uzbekistan	Tashkent	Som
✶ Venezuela	Caracas	Bolivar
✶ Vietnam	Hanoi	Dong
✶ Yemen	Sana'a	Rial
✶ Zimbabwe	Harare	Dollar
✶ Congo	Kinshasa	Franc
✶ Zambia	Lusaka	Kwacha

GEOGRAPHICAL EXPLORATIONS/DISCOVERIES

Place	Explorer/Discoverer	Nationality	Year
America	Christopher Columbus	Italy	1492
Hawaii Islands (Sandwich Islands)	Captain James Cook	England	1778
Newfoundland	John Cabot	England	1497
New Zealand	Abel Janszoon Tasman	Holland	1642
North Pole	Robert Peary	USA	1909
Sea Route to India (via Cape of Good Hope)	Vasco da Gama	Portugal	1498
South Pole	Roald Amundsen	Norway	1911

NATIONAL MONUMENTS OF SOME FAMOUS COUNTRIES

Monument	Country	Monument	Country
Great Wall of China	China	Pyramid (Giza)	Egypt
Taj Mahal (Agra)	India	Kinder Disk	Denmark
Emperial Palace (Tokyo)	Japan	Leaning Tower of Pisa	Italy
Opera House (Sydney)	Australia	Statue of Liberty (New York)	USA
Eiffel Tower (Paris)	France	Kremlin (Moscow)	Russia

INTELLIGENCE AGENCIES OF SOME PROMINENT COUNTRIES

Country	Intelligence Agency
✶ India	*Research & Analysis Wing (RAW), Intelligence Bureau (I.B.), Central Bureau of Investigation (C.B.I.)*
✶ Pakistan	*Inter Service Intelligence (I.S.I.)*
✶ U.S.A.	*Central Intelligence Agency (CIA), Federal Bureau of Investigation (FBI)*
✶ Britain	*Military Intelligence (M.I.)-5 and 6, Special Branch, Ultra, Joint Intelligence Organisation*

∗ Israel	*Mosad*
∗ Egypt	*Mukhabarat*
∗ Japan	*Nicho*
∗ Russia	*K.G.B. (Komitel Gosudarstvennoy Bezopasnosty) (Committee for State Security)*
∗ Canada	*Security Intelligence Service (SIS)*
∗ S. Africa	*Bureau of State Security (BSS)*
∗ Iran	*Sabak*
∗ Iraq	*Al-Mukhabarat*
∗ Australia	*Australian Security and Intelligence Organisation (ASIO)*
∗ France	*S.D.E.C.E.*
∗ Spain	*C.E.S.I.D.*

MAJOR LANGUAGES OF THE WORLD AND THEIR SPEAKERS

Listing the languages spoken by approximately 1% of humankind (those spoken by more than 60,000,000 people), this table enumerates speakers of each tongue as a primary language.

Language	Speakers (millions)
∗ Chinese	1,322.8
∗ Spanish	471.4
∗ English	369.9
∗ Arabic	349.3
∗ Hindi	342.2
∗ Bengali	228.7
∗ Portuguese	232.4
∗ Russian	153.7
∗ Japanese	126.3
∗ Lahnda	99.6
∗ Marathi	83.1
∗ Telugu	82.6
∗ Turkish	82.2
∗ Malay	81.6
∗ Korean	81.5
∗ French	79.6
∗ Tamil	77.5
∗ Vietnamese	76.1
∗ German, Standard	76.5
∗ Urdu	69.0
∗ Javanese	68.3
∗ Persian	65.7
∗ Italian	64.8
∗ Gujarati	56.9
∗ Pushto	53.1
∗ Bhojpuri	52.3
∗ Hausa	48.6
∗ Kannada	43.6
∗ Yoruba	41.0
∗ Polish	40.0

(**Source:** *The World Almanac-2022*)

NAME OF PARLIAMENTS OF SOME COUNTRIES

Country	Name of Parliament
Afghanistan	Shora
Argentina	National Congress
Australia	Federal Parliament
Austria	National Assembly
Bangladesh	Jatiya Sansad
India	Lok Sabha and Rajya Sabha
Bhutan	Tshogdu (National Assembly)
Britain	House of Commons and House of Lords
Canada	House of Commons and Senate
China	National People Congress
Denmark	Folketing
Iran	Majlis (Islamic Consultative Assembly)
Israel	Knesset
Japan	Diet
Myanmar	Pyithu Hluttaw (People's Assembly)
Nepal	Rashtriya Panchayat
The Netherlands	States-General
Norway	Storting
Poland	Sejm
Russia	Federal Assembly (Council of the Federation and State Duma
South Africa	National Assembly and Senate
Spain	Cortes Generales
Sweden	Riksdag
Switzerland	Federal Assembly (Nationalrat and Standerat)
North Korea	Supreme People's Assembly
South Korea	National Assembly
U.S.A.	Congress (Senate and House of Representatives)
Ethiopia	Federal Council and House of Representatives
Iceland	Alpingi
Bulgaria	National Assembly
Cuba	National Assembly of People's Power

IMPORTANT NEWS AGENCIES OF THE WORLD

Agency	Country	Agency	Country
PTI, UNI, UNIVARTA	India	Reuters, NAFEN	United Kingdom
Antara	Indonesia	Angence France Press (AFP)	France
Tanjug	Serbia		
Associated Press (AP)	America	TASS	Russia

LARGEST AND SMALLEST COUNTRIES (Top 5)

Largest Country (Area-wise)	Largest Country (Population-wise)	Smallest Country (Area-wise)	Smallest Country (Population-wise)
Russia	China	Vatican City	Vatican City
Canada	India	Monaco	Tuvalu
China	USA	Nauru	Palau
United States	Indonesia	Tuvalu	San Marino
Brazil	Brazil	San Marino	Liechstein

RELIGIONS OF THE WORLD

Religion	Member	Percentage	Religion	Member	Percentage
Christianity	2.5 billion	32.2%	Buddhism	545 million	6.9%
Islam	1.9 billion	24.7%	Sikhism	27 million	0.4%
Hinduism	1.07 billion	13.5%			

NATIONAL EMBLEMS OF IMPORTANT COUNTRIES

Country	National Emblem	Country	National Emblem
America	Golden Rod	Australia	Kangaroo
Ireland	Shamrock	Italy	White Lily
Israel	Candelabrum	Iran	Rose
Canada	White Lily	Great Britain	Rose
Chile	Candor and Huemul	Germany	Corn Flower
Japan	Chrysanthemum	Zimbabwe	Zimbabwe Bird
Denmark	Beach	Turkey	Crescent and Star
The Netherlands	Lion	New Zealand	Kiwi, Fern Southern Cross
Norway	Lion	Nepal	Kukri
Pakistan	Crescent	Poland	Eagle
France	Lily	Belgium	Lion
Bangladesh	Water Lily	Mongolia	The Soyombo
Russia	Double headed eagle	Lebanon	Cedar Tree
Sudan	Secretary Bird	Syria	Eagle
India	Lioned Capital		

FIRST IN INDIA

* The first Indian to get the Nobel Prize for Literature — *Rabindra Nath Tagore*
* The first Indian to get the Nobel Prize for Physics — *C.V. Raman*
* The first Indian to get the Nobel Prize for Peace — *Mother Teresa*
* The first Indian to get the Nobel Prize for Economics — *Amartya Sen*
* The first Indian to get Special Oscar award (1992) — *Satyajit Ray*

∗ The first and the last Indian Governor-General of free India	*C. Rajagopalachari*
∗ The first woman to become the Governor of a State	*Smt. Sarojini Naidu*
∗ The first Indian Commander-In-Chief	*General K.M. Cariappa*
∗ The first ever woman to become the Chief Minister of a State	*Smt. Sucheta Kripalani*
∗ The first Indian woman President of UN General Assembly	*Smt. Vijaylakshmi Pandit*
∗ The first Indian to become the President of International Court of Justice	*Dr. Nagendra Singh*
∗ The first Indian woman to swim across the English Channel	*Ms. Aarti Saha*
∗ The first Indian girl to become Miss Universe	*Miss Sushmita Sen*
∗ The first Indian girl to become Miss World	*Rita Faria*
∗ The first Indian to swim across the English Channel	*Mihir Sen*
∗ The first Field Marshal	*S.H.F.J. Manekshaw*
∗ The first Indian recipient of Victoria Cross	*Khudadad Khan*
∗ The first Indian to conquer Mt. Everest	*Sherpa Tenzing (May 29, 1953)*
∗ The first Indian Cosmonaut (man)	*Rakesh Sharma (April 3, 1984)*
∗ The first Indian Cosmonaut (woman)	*Kalpana Chawla (Nov. 19, 1997)*
∗ The first woman to climb Mt. Everest	*Miss Bachendri Pal (May 23, 1984)*
∗ The first ICS	*Satyendranath Tagore*
∗ The first to address the UN General Assembly in Hindi	*Atal Bihari Vajpayee*
∗ The first Newspaper	*Bengal Gazette (Jan 27, 1780)*
∗ The first Postage Stamp issued	*In 1852*
∗ The first Telegraph line laid	*In 1851 (Calcutta-Diamond Harbour)*
∗ The first Railways run	*April 16, 1853 (Bombay-Thane)*
∗ The first Electric Train run	*1925 (Bombay-Kurla)*
∗ The first Atomic Power Station	*Tarapore (Maharashtra)*
∗ The first passenger-cum-cargo ship made in India	*Harshavardhan*
∗ The first Satellite	*Aryabhatta (1975)*
∗ The first President of the Indian National Congress	*W.C. Banerjee*
∗ The first President of Indian Republic	*Dr. Rajendra Prasad*
∗ The first woman judge of the Supreme Court	*Ms Fatima Bibi*
∗ The first to climb Everest without oxygen	*Phu Dorjee (1987)*
∗ The first film (movie)	*Raja Harishchandra*
∗ The first film (talkie)	*Alam Ara*
∗ The first Metro Railway	*Calcutta Metro Railway*
∗ The first Test-tube baby, scientifically documented	*Born on August 6, 1986 at K.E.M. Hospital, Bombay*
∗ The first TV Centre	*At Delhi*
∗ The first Indian to get an Oscar	*Bhanu Athaiya*
∗ The first woman pilot in IAF	*Ms Harita Kaur Deol*
∗ The first woman to get Olympic Medal	*Karnam Malleswari*
∗ The first woman Foreign Secretary	*Chokila Iyer*
∗ First Chief of Defence Staff (CDS)	*General Bipin Rawat*

SUPERLATIVES (INDIA)

Highest, Biggest, Largest and Longest in India

∗ Award for Gallantry, highest	*Param Vir Chakra*
∗ Award, highest civilian	*Bharat Ratna*
∗ Bank, with largest number of branches	*State Bank of India*

* Road Bridge, Longest	*Bhupen Hazarika Bridge, Assam (9.15 km)*
* Road and Rail Bridge, Longest	*Bogibeel Bridge, Brahmaputra River, Assam*
* Cattle Fair, Largest	*Sonepur (Bihar)*
* City, Most Populous	*Mumbai metropolis*
* Corridor, Longest	*Rameshwaram Temple corridor (4,000 ft.)*
* Desert, Largest	*Thar (Rajasthan)*
* Dam, Longest	*Hirakud Dam (Odisha)*
* Delta, Largest	*Sunderban's Delta*
* Dome, Largest	*Gol Gumbaj (Bijapur)*
* Dam, Highest	*Tehri Dam (260 m)*
* Gateway, Highest	*Buland Darwaja at Fatehpur Sikri (176 ft.)*
* Fresh Water Lake, Largest	*Wular Lake (Kashmir)*
* Literacy, Highest	*Kerala (94%)*
* Museum, Largest	*Indian Museum (Kolkata)*
* Mosque, Biggest	*Jama Masjid (Delhi)*
* Peak, Highest**	*K-2 (Pak-Occupied Kashmir)*
* Platform, Longest	*At Shree Siddharoodha Swamiji Railway Station Hubballi, Karnataka, SW Railway (1507 mtrs)*
* Railway Bridge, longest	*Vembanad Bridge, Kerala (4.6 km)*
* River, Longest***	*The Ganges (2525 Km)*
* Rainfall, Highest (annual mean)	*Mowsynram near Cherrapunji (1178 cm)*
* Road Longest	*Grand Trunk Road (1,500 miles)*
* State, with maximum forest cover	*Madhya Pradesh*
* State, with maximum density of population	*Bihar*
* Telescope, Largest in Asia	*Vainu Bappu Telescope (at Kavalur: Chennai) 2.34m*
* Tunnel, Longest (Road)	*Dr. Shyama Prasad Mukherjee Tunnel (9.28 kms, J & K)*
* Tunnel, Longest (Railway)	*T-50 Tunnel, Khari-Sumber section (12.77 kms) Jammu & Kashmir.*
* Tallest Minaret	*Qutub Minar (Delhi 72.5 m.)*
* Waterfall, Highest	*Kunchikal Waterfall (Karnataka: 455 m)*
* Zoo, Largest	*Zoological Gardens (Kolkata)*

** *Highest peak in the world is Mount Everest, which is in Nepal. K-2 is the second highest peak in the world. It is 8,611 metres high.*
*** *Indus and Brahmaputra (each 2900 km). Both of them, however, cover a long distance outside India.*

TABLE OF PRECEDENCE

1. President
2. Vice-President
3. Prime Minister
4. Governors of States within their respective states
5. Former Presidents

5A. Deputy Prime Minister

6. Chief Justice of India, Speaker of Lok Sabha
7. Cabinet Ministers of the Union, Chief Ministers of States within their respective States
   Deputy Chairman NITI Aayog, former Prime Ministers
   Leaders of opposition in Rajya Sabha and Lok Sabha

7A. Holders of the Bharat Ratna Decoration

8. Ambassadors Extraordinary and Plenipotentiary and High Commissioners of Commonwealth Countries accredited to India, Chief Ministers of States outside their respective States
9. Judges of the Supreme Court
10. Deputy Chairman Rajya Sabha, Deputy Chief Minister of States, Deputy Speaker Lok Sabha, Members of the NITI Aayog, Minister of State of the Union and Other Minister in the Ministry of Defence.

BOOKS AND AUTHORS

FOREIGN

Book	Author
✶ As You Like It	*William Shakespeare*
✶ A Tale of Two Cities	*Charles Dickens*
✶ Ben Hur	*Lewis Wallace*
✶ Das Kapital	*Karl Marx*
✶ David Copperfield	*Charles Dickens*
✶ Hamlet	*William Shakespeare*
✶ Iliad	*Homer*
✶ Inferno	*A. Dante*
✶ In Memoriam	*Lord Tennyson*
✶ Ivanhoe	*Walter Scott*
✶ Julius Caesar	*William Shakespeare*
✶ Lady Chatterley's Lover	*D.H. Lawrence*
✶ Lajja	*Taslima Nasreen*
✶ Les Miserable	*Victor Hugo*
✶ Leviathan	*Thomas Hobbes*
✶ Lolita	*V. Nobokov*
✶ Lycidas	*John Milton*
✶ Mein Kampf	*Adolf Hitler*
✶ Moor's Last Sigh	*Salman Rushdie*
✶ Mother	*Maxim Gorky*
✶ Mother India	*Katherine Mayo*
✶ Nana	*Emile Zola*
✶ Odyssey	*Homer*
✶ Origin of Species	*Charles Darwin*
✶ Othello	*William Shakespeare*
✶ Paradise Lost	*John Milton*
✶ Paradise Regained	*John Milton*
✶ Path to Power	*Margaret Thatcher*
✶ Pickwick Papers	*Charles Dickens*
✶ Razor's Edge	*Somerset Maugham*
✶ Republic	*Plato*
✶ The Tempest	*William Shakespeare*
✶ Time Machine	*H.G. Wells*
✶ Tom Sawyer	*Mark Twain*
✶ Treasure Island	*R.L. Stevenson*
✶ Twelfth Night	*William Shakespeare*
✶ Unto This Last	*John Ruskin*
✶ Utopia	*Thomas More*
✶ Wealth of Nations	*Adam Smith*
✶ Wonder that was India	*A.L. Basham*

INDIAN

Book	Author
✶ Ain-i-Akbari	*Abul Fazal*
✶ Anand Math	*Bankim Chandra Chatterjee*
✶ Arthashastra	*Kautilya*
✶ A Suitable Boy	*Vikram Seth*
✶ Bhagwat Gita	*Ved Vyas*
✶ Chidambara	*Sumitranandan Pant*
✶ Devdas	*Sarat Chandra Chatterjee*
✶ Discovery of India	*Jawaharlal Nehru*
✶ Ganadevata	*Tarashankar Bandopadhyaya*
✶ Geet Govind	*Jaya Dev*
✶ Geetanjali	*R. N. Tagore*
✶ Glimpses of World History	*Jawaharlal Nehru*
✶ Godaan	*Prem Chand*
✶ Gul-e-Nagma	*Firaq Gorakhpuri*
✶ Harsh Charita	*Bana Bhatta*
✶ India Divided	*Dr. Rajendra Prasad*
✶ Justice of Peace ke Aansu	Janardan Prasad Singh
✶ The Judgement	*Kuldip Nayyar*
✶ Kadambari	*Bana Bhatta*
✶ Kagaz Te Kanwas	*Amrita Pritam*
✶ Kamayani	*Jai Shankar Prasad*
✶ Kitni Nawon Mein Kitni Bar	*S. H. Vatsyayan*
✶ Kumar Sambhav	*Kalidas*
✶ Mahabharata	*Ved Vyas*
✶ Malgudi Days	*R.K. Narayan*
✶ Meghdoot	*Kalidas*
✶ Mritunjaya	*B.K. Bhattacharya*
✶ Mudrarakshasa	*Vishakhadatta*
✶ Prison Diary	*Jaya Prakash Narayan*
✶ Raghuvansha	*Kalidas*
✶ Rajtarangini	*Kalhana*
✶ Ramayana	*Balmiki*
✶ Ramcharit Manas	*Tulsidas*
✶ Rukh Te Rishi	*Harbhajan Singh*
✶ Satyarth Prakash	*Swami Dayanand*
✶ Sur Sagar	*Surdas*
✶ The Guide	*R.K. Narayan*

IMPORTANT DATES AND DAYS OF THE YEAR

✶ **JANUARY**

5-11 Road Safety Week

12 National Youth Day

15 Army Day

15-21 Pin Code Week

23 National Day of Patriotism

26 Republic Day

30 Martyr's Day

✶ **FEBRUARY**

1-14 Oil Conservation Fortnight

14 Valentine's Day

★ MARCH

4 National Safety Day
8 International Women's Day
15 Consumers' Day
16 Immunisation Day
21 World Forest Day
22 World Day for Water
24 World Meteorological Day
1-7 Preservation of Blindness Week

★ APRIL

7 World Health Day
7-13 Handloom Week
14-20 Fire Service Week
18 World Heritage Day
22 World Earth Day

★ MAY

1 May Day
5 National Labour Day
8 World Red Cross Day
11 National Technology Day
15 International Day of the Family
17 World Telecommunication Day
24 Commonwealth Day
31 World No-Tobacco Day

★ JUNE

5 World Environment Day
21 World Yoga Day
26 International Day against Drug Abuse and Illicit Trafficking

★ JULY

11 World Population Day

★ AUGUST

1-7 World Breast feeding Week
10 Sanskrit Divas
15 Independence Day
20 Sadbhavana Divas

★ SEPTEMBER

1-7 National Nutrition Week
5 Teachers' Day
8 International Literary Day
14 Hindi Diwas
23 World Deaf Day
27 World Tourism Day

★ OCTOBER

2 Gandhi Jayanti
International Day of Non Violence
Anti-Leprosy Day
4 World Animal Day
6 World Habitat Day *(Ist Monday)*
8 Indian Air Force Day
14 World Standard Day
15 International Day of Rural Women
16 World Food Day
24 United Nations Day
27 Infantry Day
28 World Thrift Day
31 Anti-Terrorism Day

★ NOVEMBER

2 All Saints Day
14 Children's Day
15-21 National Cooperative Week
19-25 Quami Ekta Week
20 Child Rights Day
26 Constitution Day

★ DECEMBER

1 World AIDS Day
3 World Day for the Disabled
4 Naval Day
7 Flag Day
8 SMRC Day
10 Human Rights Day
14 National Energy Conservation Day

INDIAN DEFENCE

- The Supreme Command of the Armed Forces is vested in the hands of the President of the Country.
- The responsibility for national defence, however, rests with the Cabinet. All important questions having a bearing on defence are decided by the Cabinet Committee on Political Affairs, which is presided over by the Prime Minister.
- The Defence Minister is responsible to Parliament for all matters concerning the Defence Services.
- All the administrative and operational control of Armed Forces are exercised by the Ministry of Defence. The three services—Army, Navy and Air Force function through their respective service head-quarters headed by the chief of Staff.
- The post of Chief of Defence Staff (CDS) was created in 2019.

Indian Army Commands

Command	*HQ Location*
Eastern Command	Kolkata
Western Command	Chandigarh
Northern Command	Udhampur
Southern Command	Pune
Central Command	Lucknow
Training Command	Shimla
South-Western Command	Jaipur

Indian Air Force Commands

Command	HQ Location
Western Air Command	New Delhi
Sout-Western Air Command	Gandhinagar
Central Air Command	Prayagraj
Eastern Air Command	Shillong
Southern Air Command	Thiruvananthapuram
Training Command	Bengaluru

Indian Navy Commands

Command	HQ Location
Eastern Naval Command	Vishakhapatnam
Western Naval Command	Mumbai
Southern Naval Command	Kochi

Commissioned Ranks in Defence Services

Army	Navy	Air Force
General	Admiral	Air Chief Marshal
Lieutenant-General	Vice-Admiral	Air Marshal
Major-General	Rear-Admiral	Air Vice-Marshal
Brigadier	Commodor	Air Commodor
Colonel	Captain	Group Captain
Lieutenant-Colonel	Commander	Wing Commander
Major	Lt.Commander	Squadron Leader
Captain	Lieutenant	Flight Lieutenant
Lieutenant	Sub-Lieutenant	Flying Officer

Internal Security Organisations of India

S. No.	Name of Organisation	Year of Creation	Headquarters
1.	Assam Rifles (A.R.)	1835	Shillong
2.	Central Reserve Police Force (CRPF)	1939	New Delhi
3.	Territorial Army	1948	In different States
4.	Indo-Tibetan Border Police	1962	New Delhi
5.	Home Guard	1962	In different States
6.	Coast Guard	1978	New Delhi
7.	Border Security Force (B.S.F.)	1965	New Delhi
8.	Central Industrial Security Force (CISF)	1969	New Delhi
9.	National Security Guard	1984	New Delhi
10.	Police	—	In different States

Army Institutes

	Institute	Location
1.	Sainik Schools	33 places in India
2.	Rashtriya Indian Military College (prepare for entrance to N.D.A.)	Dehradun
3.	National Defence Academy (three services)	Khadakwasla, Pune
4.	Indian Military Academy (Army)	Dehradun
5.	Officers Training Academy (3 services) Short Courses	Chennai
6.	National Defence College	New Delhi
7.	The College of Combat	Mhow
8.	The College of Military Engineering	Kirkee
9.	Military College of Telecommunication Engineering	Mhow
10.	The Armoured Corps Centre and School	Ahmed Nagar
11.	The School Artillery	Deolali
12.	The Infantry School	Mhow and Belgaum
13.	College of Material Management	Jabalpur

Air Force Institutions

✶ Air Force Academy	Hyderabad
✶ Flying Instructors School	Tambaram, Chennai
✶ Air Force Administrative College	Coimbatore
✶ Helicopter Training School	Hakimpet
✶ The College of Air Warfare	Secunderabad
✶ Air Force Technical College	Jalahalli

UNITED NATIONS ORGANISATION (UNO)

- The United Nations (UN) is an association of states which have pledged themselves to maintain international peace and security and cooperate in solving international political, economic, social cultural and humanitarian problems towards achieving this end.
- Trygve Lie of Norway (1946-52) was the first Secretary-General of the UN.
- ***Origin:*** UN Charter was signed by 50 members on June 26, 1945. Poland signed the charter later to become one of the original 51 member-states. It officially came into existence on October 24, 1945.
- ***UN Charter:*** The Charter is the Constitution of the UNO and contains its aims and objectives and rules and regulations for its functioning.
- ***Aims and Objectives:*** They are security, welfare and human rights.
- ***Headquarters:*** New York.
- ***Flag:*** The flag is light blue in colour, and emblazoned in white, in its centre is the UN symbol—a polar map of world embraced by twin olive branches open at the top.
- ***Official Languages:*** The official languages of the UN are: English, French, Chinese, Russian, Arabic and Spanish. However, working languages are English and French only.
- ***Present Membership:*** At present 193 countries are members of the UNO. South Sudan is the latest entrant to this world organisation.
- ***Main Organs of the UNO:*** There are six main organs:
  1. General Assembly
  2. Security Council
  3. Economic and Social Council
  4. Trusteeship Council
  5. International Court of Justice, and
  6. Secretariat.

1. *General Assembly:* It consists of representative of all members of the UN. Each member country has only one vote. It meets once a year and passes UN Budget. It is the main place for discussions and policy making in the UN.
2. *Security Council:* It is the Executive body of the UN and is mainly responsible for maintaining international peace and security. It has 15 members, 5 of which (USA, UK, France, Russia and China) are permanent members. The 10 non-permanent members are elected by General Assembly for two-year term and are not eligible for immediate re-election.
3. *Economic and Social Council:* It has 54 members elected by General Assembly.
4. *Trusteeship Council:* It looks after interest of the people in areas not yet independent and leads them towards self-government.
5. *International Court of Justice:* It has 15 judges, no two of whom may be nationals of the same state. They are elected by General Assembly and Security Council for a term of 9 years. The Court elects its President and Vice-President for a 3-year term.
6. *Secretariat:* It is the Secretariat of the UN and is headed by the Secretary General.

Some Important UN Agencies

UN Agencies	Headquarters	Year of Establishment
✶ United Nations Organisations (U.N.O.)	New York	1945
✶ International Monetary Fund (I.M.F.)	Washington	1945
✶ World Health Organisation (W.H.O.)	Geneva	1948
✶ Food & Agricultural Organisation (FAO)	Rome	1943
✶ International Labour Organisation (ILO)	Geneva	1919
✶ UNESCO	Paris	1946
✶ Universal Postal Union (UPU)	Berne	1874
✶ UNIDO	Vienna	1967
✶ International Atomic Energy Agency (IAEA)	Vienna	1957

∗ United Nations Development Programme (UNDP)	New York	1965
∗ UNICEF	New York	1946
∗ International Maritime Organisation (IMO)	London	1948
∗ World Meteorological Organisation (WMO)	Geneva	1951
∗ International Telecommunication Union (ITU)	Geneva	1947
∗ World Trade Organisation (WTO)	Geneva	1995
∗ International Development Association (IDA)	Washington D.C.	1960
∗ World Intellectual Property Organisation (WIPO)	Geneva	1967

Famous International Organisations

International Organisations	Headquarters	Year of Establishment
∗ International Court of Justice	The Hague	1945
∗ International Civil Aviation Organisation (ICAO)	Montreal	1947
∗ International Finance Corporation (IFC)	Washington	1956
∗ Arab League	Cairo	1945
∗ Commonwealth of Nations	London	1931
∗ International Bank for Reconstruction and Development (IBRD)	Washington D.C.	1944
∗ Organisation of Islamic Cooperation (OIC)	Jeddah (Saudi Arabia)	1971
∗ European Economic Community (EEC)	Geneva	1957
∗ Red Cross	Geneva	1863
∗ Interpol	Lyons	1923
∗ Asian Development Bank (ADB)	Manila	1966
∗ North Atlantic Treaty Organisation (NATO)	Brussels	1949
∗ Association of South East Asian Nations (ASEAN)	Jakarta	1967
∗ South Asian Association for Regional Cooperation (SAARC)	Kathmandu	1985
∗ Asia-Pacific Economic Cooperation (APEC)	Singapore	1989
∗ Organisation for Economic Cooperation and Development (OECD)	Paris	1961
∗ Organisation of Petroleum Exporting Countries (OPEC)	Vienna	1960
∗ Commonwealth of Independent States (CIS)	Minsk	1991
∗ International Olympic Committee (IOC)	Switzerland	1894
∗ European Union (EU)	Brussels	Changed form of EEC Established in 1958
∗ Amnesty International (AI)	London	1961
∗ Shanghai Cooperation Organisation (SCO)	Beijing	2001
∗ BRICS Development Bank	Shanghai	2014

AWARDS AND HONOURS

NATIONAL AWARDS

BHARAT RATANA

- Bharat Ratna is India's highest Civilian Award. It was first awarded in 1954.
- The actual award is designed in the shape of a *peepal* leaf with Bharat Ratna inscribed in Devanagri script in the Sun Figure.
- This is India's highest civilian award. It is given for exceptional work on art, literature, science and recognition of public service of the highest order.
- The emblem, the Sun and the rim are of platinum. The inscriptions are in burnished bronze.
- Government servants are not eligible for it. The table shows the recipients of the award:

Bharat Ratna Award Winners

No.	Name	Year
1.	Dr. S. Radhakrishnan	1954
2.	C. Rajagopalachari	1954
3.	Dr. C.V. Raman	1954
4.	Dr. Bhagwan Das	1955
5.	Dr. M. Visvesvaraya	1955
6.	Jawahar Lal Nehru	1955
7.	Govind Ballabh Pant	1957
8.	Dr. D.K. Karve	1958
9.	Dr. Bidhan Chandra Roy	1961
10.	Purushottam Das Tandon	1961
11.	Dr. Rajendra Prasad	1962
12.	Dr. Zakir Hussain	1963
13.	Dr. Pandurang Vaman Kane	1963
14.	Lal Bahadur Shastri	1966
15.	Indira Gandhi	1971
16.	V.V. Giri	1975
17.	K. Kamraj	1976
18.	Mother Teresa	1980
19.	Acharya Vinoba Bhave	1983
20.	Khan Abdul Ghaffar Khan	1987
21.	M.G. Ramachandran	1988
22.	Dr. B.R. Ambedkar	1990
23.	Dr. Nelson R. Mandela	1990
24.	Rajiv Gandhi	1991
25.	Sardar Vallabhbhai Patel	1991
26.	Morarji R. Desai	1991
27.	Maulana Abul Kalam Azad	1992
28.	Jehangir Ratanji Dadabhai Tata	1992
29.	Satyajit Roy	1992
30.	Shri Gulzari Lal Nanda	1997
31.	Mrs. Aruna Asaf Ali	1997
32.	Dr. A.P.J. Abdul Kalam	1998
33.	M.S. Subbalakshmi	1998
34.	C. Subramaniam	1998
35.	Jaya Prakash Narayan	1999
36.	Prof. Amartya Sen	1999
37.	Pt. Ravi Shankar	1999
38.	Gopinath Bardoloi	1999
39.	Lata Mangeshkar	2001
40.	Bismillah Khan	2001
41.	Bhimsen Joshi	2009
42.	C.N.R. Rao	2014
43.	Sachin Tendulkar	2014
44.	Pt. Madan Mohan Malaviya	2015
45.	Atal Bihari Vajpayee	2015
46.	Pranab Mukherjee	2019
47.	Bhupen Hazarika	2019
48.	Nanaji Deshmukh	2019
49.	Karpoori Thakur	2024
50.	L.K. Advani	2024
51.	Charan Singh	2024
52.	P.V. Narasimha Rao	2024
53.	M.S. Swaminathan	2024

REPUBLIC DAY AWARDS

Padma Awards

They fall in line after the Bharat Ratna. They are also discontinued in 1977 along with the Bharat Ratna and award was started again in 1980.

There are three Padma Awards:

- ***Padma Vibhushan:*** This award is given for exceptional and distinguished service in any field, including service rendered by Govt. servants.
- ***Padma Bhushan:*** This award is given for distinguished service of a high order in any field, including service rendered by Govt. servants.
- ***Padma Shri:*** This award is given for distinguished service in any field, including service rendered by Government servants.

Gallantry Awards

- ***Param Vir Chakra:*** The highest award for bravery or some daring and pre-eminent act of valour or self-sacrifice in the presence of the enemy, whether on land, at sea or in the air.
- ***Mahavir Chakra:*** It is the second highest decoration and is awarded for acts of conspicuous gallantry in the presence of the enemy, whether on land, at sea or in the air.
- ***Vir Chakra:*** It is the third in order of awards given for acts of gallantry in the presence of enemy, whether on land, at sea or in the air.
- ***Ashok Chakra:*** This medal is awarded for the most conspicuous bravery or some daring or pre-eminent act of valour or self-sacrifice on land, at sea or in the air but not in the presence of enemy.
- ***Vishishta Sewa Medal:*** It is awarded to personnel of all the three Services in class I, II and III in recognition of distinguished service of the "most exceptional" and "exceptional" and a "high" order respectively. Prefixes Parma and Ati are added before first two categories of medals respectively.
- ***Jeewan Raksha Padak:*** Awarded for meritorious acts or a series of acts of a human nature displayed in saving life from drowning, fire and rescue operations in mines etc.

OTHER NATIONAL AWARDS

SAHITYA AKADEMI AWARDS

- These prizes are awarded annually to the authors of the most outstanding books of literary merit published in each of the 22 languages specified in the Eighth Schedule of the Constitution.
- There are also two awards for Rajasthani and English. The award, in form of a casket containing an inscribed copper plate and a cheque of ₹ 1 lakh is given to the author or his/her heir.

DADA SAHEB PHALKE AWARD

- The award carries a cash prize of ₹ 10 lakh, a Shawl and Swarna Kamal.
- Mrs Devika Rani Roerich was the first person to receive Dadasaheb Phalke Award in 1969.

- The award for 2021 has been given to bollywood actress Waheeda Rehman.

BHARATIYA JNANPITH AWARD

- Instituted in 22nd May, 1961, carries a cash prize of ₹ 11 lakh, a citation and a bronze replica of Vagdevi (Saraswati).
- Instituted by a literary organisation in India.

SARASWATI SAMMAN

- Given for outstanding literary works, value ₹ 15 lakh.

KALINGA PRIZE

- This award is given each year by the UNESCO and founded by former Odisha Chief Minister late Shri Biju Patnaik for popularisation of science.

INTERNATIONAL AWARDS

NOBEL PRIZES

- These Prizes were instituted in 1901 by a Swedish scientist, Dr. Alfred Nobel; the discoverer of Dynamite.
- Six prizes are awarded annually for (i) Chemistry, (ii) Physics, (iii) Medicine, (iv) Literature, (v) Peace and (vi) Economics —started since 1969.
- Indians Honoured with Nobel Prize: So far, following Indians have been honoured with these prizes. Their names are *(i)* Rabindra Nath Tagore for Literature, for his book 'Gitanjali', in 1913, *(ii)* Dr. C.V. Raman for Physics in 1930, for his discovery of 'Raman Effect', *(iii)* Mother Teresa for Peace in 1979, *(iv)* Prof. Amartya Sen in 1998 for Economics and *(v)* Kailash Satyarthi for Peace in 2014. In addition, four non-resident Indians have also been awarded the Nobel Prize. They are: *(i)* Hargobind Khurana for Medicine in 1968, *(ii)* Subramanian Chandrasekhar for Physics in 1983, *(iii)* Venkatraman Ramkrishnan for Chemistry in 2009, *(iv)* Abhijit Vinayak Banerjee for Economics in 2019.

GANDHI PEACE PRIZE

- The government instituted this ₹ 1 crore prize on the lines of the Nobel Peace Prize in 1995.
- It is the highest Civilian International award by the Govt. of India. The award of 2021 have been given to Gita Press, Gorakhpur.

MAN BOOKER PRIZE 2023

- On November 26, 2023, Irish author Paul Lynch won 2023 Booker Prize for his novel, 'Prophet Song' published by Oneworld. He received 50,000 Pound sterling and the Iris Trophy for his award winning novel.

INDIRA GANDHI PRIZE FOR PEACE, DISARMAMENT AND DEVELOPMENT

- The award was instituted in the memory of Mrs. Indira Gandhi to foster creative cooperation among nations of the world.

Highest Honours of Some Countries

Country	*Highest Honour*
India	Bharat Ratna
Pakistan	Nishan-e-Pakistan
Kuwait	Mubarak-Al-kabir Medal
Saudi Arabia	Shah Abdul Aziz Medal
Argentina	The Order of Sona Martin
Nicaragua	Augusto-Caesar Sandino Order
Vietnam	The Order of the Golden Star
Hungary	The Order of Banner
Britain	Member of British Empire, Victoria Cross
Japan	Order of Moulovenice Sun
Denmark	Order of Diana Brog
France	Legend of Honour
America	Presidential Medal of Freedom
Germany	Pore Lee Merit Iron Cross
The Netherlands	Netherlands Lion

SPORTS

OLYMPICS

- First of all these games were held by the Greeks in 776 B.C. on Mount Olympus in honour of the Greek God Zeus. In this way, the history of Olympic Games is about twenty eight hundred years old. These games continued to be held every four years until 394 A.D. when these games were stopped by a royal order of the emperor of Rome.
- The modern Olympic Games which started in Athens in 1896, are the result of the devotion and dedication of a French educator Baron Pierre de Coubertin and the first Olympic meet in the modern series was held in 1896 in Athens, the Capital of Greece. Since then, they are being held every four years except for breaks during world wars.
- The Olympic flag is white in colour with five coloured rings, each ring symbolic of a continent. Summer as well as Winter Olympics are h[...] in the same year.
- The 2020 Olympic Ga[...] held at Tokyo in 2021.
- The official Olympic [...] *Citius, Altius, Swifter, Higher, Stronger*. T[...]ffice of International Olympic Committee [...]ausanne (Switzerland).

COMMONWEALTH GAMES

- The Commonwealth Games are held every four years, in the year in which Asian Games are held. All the Commonwealth Countries (former colonies of Britain) can take part in it.
- The first Commonwealth Games were held in 1930 at Hamilton (Canada).
- There are currently 56 members of the Commonwealth of Nations, and 72 teams participated in the games.
- The 2022 Commonwealth Games officially known as the XXII Commonwealth Games or Birmingham 2022, held in Birmingham, England, between 28 July to 8 August 2022.

ASIAN GAMES

- After the Second World War, most of the Asian Countries gained independence. On the lines of Olympic Games, Asian Games were planned every four years.
- India hosted the first Asian Games in 1951.

WORLD CUP CRICKET

- The first Cricket World Cup was organised in England in 1975. A separate women's Cricket World Cup has been held every 4 years since 1973.

List of Cricket World Cup

Year	Venue	Winner/Runner
1975	England	West Indies beat Australia
1979	England	West Indies beat England
1983	England	India beat West Indies
1987	India & Pakistan	Australia beat England
1992	Australia	Pakistan beat England
1996	India, Pakistan & Sri Lanka	Sri Lanka beat Australia
1999	England	Australia beat Pakistan
2003	South Africa	Australia beat India
2007	West Indies	Australia beat Sri Lanka
2011	India, Sri Lanka, Bangladesh	India beat Sri Lanka
2015	Australia, New Zealand	Australia beat New Zealand
2019	England	England beat New Zealand
2023	India	Australia beat India

HOCKEY WORLD CUP

- The first Hockey World Cup was organised in Barcelona (Spain) in 1971. Women's Hockey World Cup has been held since 1974.

FOOTBALL WORLD CUP

- The Football World Cup is organised by FIFA (Federation of International Football Association). The World Cup is called 'Jules Rimet Cup' named after the name of FIFA President Jules Rimet. The first Football World Cup was organised in Uruguay in 1930.
- In 1942 and 1946, the Football World Cup was not played due to World War II.
- Brazil is the only nation to have participated in every World Cup so far. The 2022 Football World Cup held in Qatar. Argentina on December 18, 2022 emerged Champion of the FIFA World Cup 2022 as it prevailed over France 4-2 on penalties.

IMPORTANT CUPS & TROPHIES

International

- ∗ *American Cup* : Yacht Racing
- ∗ *Ashes* : Cricket
- ∗ *Davis Cup* : Lawn Tennis
- ∗ *Derby* : Horse Race
- ∗ *Grand National* : Horse Streple Chase Race
- ∗ *Jules Rimet Trophy* : World Soccer Cup
- ∗ *King's Cup* : Air Races
- ∗ *Merdeka Cup* : Football
- ∗ *Swaythling Cup* : Table Tennis (Men)
- ∗ *Ryder Cup* : Golf
- ∗ *Thomas Cup* : Badminton
- ∗ *U. Thant Cup* : Tennis
- ∗ *Walker Cup* : Golf
- ∗ *Wightman Cup* : Lawn Tennis
- ∗ *Rothman's Trophy* : Cricket
- ∗ *European Champions Cup* : Football
- ∗ *Grand Prix* : Table Tennis
- ∗ *Edgbaston Cup* : Lawn Tennis
- ∗ *Grand Prix* : Lawn Tennis

National

- ∗ *Agha Khan Cup* : Hockey
- ∗ *Beighton Cup* : Hockey
- ∗ *Bombay Gold Cup* : Hockey
- ∗ *C.K. Naydu Trophy* : Cricket
- ∗ *Deodhar Trophy* : Cricket

* *Duleep Trophy* : Cricket
* *Durand Cup* : Football
* *Dhyan Chand Trophy* : Hockey
* *Dr. B.C. Roy Trophy* : Football (Junior)
* *Ezra Cup* : Polo
* *Guru Nanak Cup* : Hockey
* *Holkar Trophy* : Bridge
* *Irani Trophy* : Cricket
* *Indira Gold Cup* : Hockey
* *Murugappa Gold Cup* : Hockey
* *Nehru Trophy* : Hockey
* *Nixan Gold Cup* : Football
* *Rani Jhansi Trophy* : Cricket
* *Ranji Trophy* : Cricket
* *Rangaswami Cup* : Hockey
* *Ramanujan Trophy* : Table Tennis
* *Rene Frank Trophy* : Hockey
* *Rohinton Baria Trophy* : Cricket
* *Rovers Cup* : Football
* *Santosh Trophy* : Football
* *Subroto Cup* : Football

SPORTS TERMS

* ***Badminton:*** Mixed doubles; Deuce; Drop; Smash; Let; Foot work; Setting.
* ***Base Ball:*** Pitcher; Put out, Strike; Home; Bunt.
* ***Billiards:*** Cue; Jigger; Pot; Break; In Baulk; In Off; Cannons.
* ***Boxing:*** Upper cut; Round; Punch; Bout; Knock down; Hitting below the belt; Ring.
* ***Bridge:*** Finesse; Dummy; Revoke; Grand Slam; Little Slam; No Trump; Rubber.
* ***Chess:*** Bishop, Gambit; Checkmate; Stalemate.
* ***Cricket:*** L.B.W. (leg before wicket); Creases, Popping-creases; Stumped; Bye; Leg-Bye; Googly; Hattrick; Maiden over; Drive; Bowling; Duck; Follow-on; No ball; Leg Break; Silly point; Cover point; Hit-wicket; Late-cut; Slip; Off-spinner; In-swing.
* ***Football:*** Off Side; Block; Drop-kick; Penalty-kick (or goal kick); Corner-kick; Free-kick; Dribble; Thrown-in; Foul.
* ***Golf:*** Boggy; Foursome; Stymic; Tee; Put; Hole; Niblic; Caddie; Links; The green; Bunker.
* ***Hockey:*** Carried; Short Corner; Bully; Sticks; Off side; Roll in; Striking Circle; Under-cutting; Dribble.
* ***Horse racing:*** Jockey; Punter.
* ***Polo:*** Bunker; Chukker; Mallet.
* ***Tennis:*** Back hand drive; Volley; Smash; Half-volley; Deuce; Service; Let; Grand Slam.

Stadiums and Places Associated with Sports

Name of Stadium	Sports	Place
Arun Jaitley Stadium	Cricket	Delhi
Jawaharlal Nehru Stadium	Athletics	Delhi
Shivajee Stadium	Hockey	Delhi
National Stadium	Hockey etc.	Delhi
Ambedkar Stadium	Football	Delhi
Brabourne Stadium	Cricket	Mumbai
Wankhede Stadium	Cricket	Mumbai
Narendra Modi Stadium	Cricket	Ahmedabad
Eden Garden	Cricket	Kolkata
Green Park Stadium	Cricket	Kanpur
Keenan Stadium	Cricket	Jamshedpur
Nehru (Chepauk) Stadium	Cricket	Chennai
Barabati Stadium	Cricket	Cuttack
Lords, Oval, Leeds	Cricket	Britain
Hedingle Manchester	Cricket	Britain
Black Heath	Rugby Football	London
Henley	Boat race	England
Wimbledon	Lawn Tennis	London
Wembley Stadium	Football	London
White City	Dog-race	England
Aintree	Horse-race	England
Tentbridge	Cricket	England
Patnee Martlake	Boat-race	England
Tibankham	Rugby Football	England
Sandy Lodge	Golf	Scotland
Forest Hill	Tennis	New York
Brooklyn	Baseball	New York
Melbourne	Cricket	Australia

Name of Playing Compound of Different Games

Name of Compound	Related Sports
Court	Lawn Tennis, Badminton, Netball, Hand ball, Volleyball, Squash, Kho-Kho, Kabaddi
Diamond	Baseball
Ring	Boxing, Skating, Wrestling, Circus, Riding display
Course	Golf
Board	Table Tennis
Pool	Swimming
Alley	Bowling
Mat	Judo, Karate II
Arena	Horse Riding
Vellodrum	Cycling
Field	Polo, Football, Hockey
Track	Athletics
Pitch	Cricket, Rugby
Rink	Ice Hockey

❑❑❑

Multiple Choice Questions

1. Match List-I with List-II and select the correct answer from the codes given below the lists:

List-I

(*a*) Napoleon Bonaparte
(*b*) Jean Jacques Rousseau
(*c*) Croce
(*d*) Madame Roland

List-II

1. 'A history is contemporary history'
2. 'Liberty what crimes are committed in thy name'
3. 'Man is born free but everywhere he is in chains.'
4. 'I am the Child of Revolution'

Codes :

	(*a*)	(*b*)	(*c*)	(*d*)
A.	1	2	3	4
B.	4	3	1	2
C.	3	4	2	1
D.	3	4	1	2

2. Abraham Lincon was elected the President of United States in:
A. 1862 B. 1860
C. 1875 D. 1855

3. Who was known as the 'Prince of Humanists'?
A. Francisco Petrarch B. Dante
C. Boccacio D. Erasmus

4. D-Day is the day when:
A. Germany declared war on Britain
B. US dropped the atom bomb on Hiroshima.
C. Allied Troops landed in Normandy
D. Germany surrendered to the allies

5. Whose teachings inspired the French Revolution?
A. Locke
B. Rousseau
C. Hegel
D. Plato

6. At a time when empires in Europe were crumbling before the might of Napoleon which one of the following Governor-Generals kept the British flag flying high in India?
A. Warren Hastings B. Lord Cornwallis
C. Lord Wellesley D. Lord Hastings

7. Which one of the following statements regarding Fascism in Italy is *not* true?
A. The Fascists came to power as a result of popular uprising
B. In 1926, all political parties except Mussolini's party were banned
C. The Fascists suppressed the Socialist movement
D. The Fascists were hostile to the Communists

8. The fall of Czar Nicholas-II is known as:
A. Bloody Sunday
B. Bolshevik Revolution
C. February Revolution
D. October Revolution

9. Industrial Revolution took place first in:
A. France B. Germany
C. United Kingdom D. Japan

10. The British Prime Minister at the outbreak of World War II was :
A. Churchill B. Baldwin
C. Attlee D. Chemberlain

11. The 'Great Depression' (1929) economic crisis was met by adopting the policy of
A. Stimulus B. Marshall Plan
C. New Deal D. Open Door

12. The slogan "No taxation without representation" was raised during the:
A. American War of Independence
B. Russian Revolution
C. French Revolution
D. Indian Freedom struggle

13. In the nineteenth century the people of Europe started moving from the villages to the cities due to the impact of :
A. Epidemics
B. War
C. Industrialisation
D. Population explosion in villages

14. The important cause of the Civil War in America was:
A. Abolition of slavery
B. Quest for freedom
C. Industrialisation
D. Rebellion by the native Americans

15. Industrial Revolution could not have come about without:
A. Merchant capitalism
B. The Enclosure Movement
C. The services of the proletariat class
D. An agricultural revolution

16. Consider the following statements :
The French Revolution came about mainly due to the :
1. Extreme poverty of the people
2. Impact of the works of great writers
3. Cruelty of the rulers
4. Impact of impulsive reaction
Which of the above statements are correct?
A. 1, 2 and 4 B. 2 and 3
C. 1, 3 and 4 D. 1, 2, 3 and 4

17. Asia's oldest and largest Buddhist monastery is situated in :
A. Tawang (Arunachal Pardesh)
B. Lhasa (Tibet)
C. Trincomallee (Sri Lanka)
D. Ulan Bator (Mongolia)

18. Who was the main architect of the Russian Revolution?
A. Karl Marx B. Lenin
C. Stalin D. Tolstoy

19. V.I. Lenin is associated with :
A. Russian Revolution of 1917
B. Chinese Revolution of 1949
C. German Revolution
D. French Revolution of 1789

20. Which one of the following statements is *not* correct?
A. Voltaire believed in Natural Religion
B. Rousseau wrote *Social Contract*
C. Montesquieu authored *The Spirit of Laws*
D. Necker believed in 'General Will'

21. 6th April, 1930 is well known in the history of India because this date is associated with..........
A. Dandi March by Mahatma Gandhi
B. Quit India Movement
C. Partition of Bengal
D. Partition of India

22. Which ruler enforced the system of 'Price Control' in India?
A. Mohammad Tughlak
B. Razia Begum
C. Alauddin Khilji
D. Sher Shah Suri

23. The concept of 'Din-e-Elahi' was founded by which king?
A. Dara Shikoh B. Akbar
C. Sher Shah Suri D. Shahjahan

24. Who are supposed to be the earliest inhabi-tants of India? Where did they come from?
A. Aryans from Central Asia
B. Dravidians from Mediterranean
C. Negroids from Africa
D. Bhils and the Santhals from West Asia

25. The one chief characteristic of temple architecture of the Gupta Age was :
A. Absence of dome
B. Huge size
C. Beautiful carvings
D. absence of a covered courtyard for the gathering of worshippers

26. The Rigveda consists of :
A. 1000 hymns B. 2028 hymns
C. 1028 hymns D. 1038 hymns

27. The central point in Ashoka's dharma was :
A. royalty to kings
B. peace and non-violence
C. respect to elders
D. religious tolerance

28. The social evil which was conspicuously absent during ancient India was :
A. *Sati*-System B. *Devadasi*-System
C. Polygamy D. *Purdah*-System

29. Which, among the following, can be accepted as a novelty introduced by Mughal emperors to their buildings?
A. Domes B. Minarets
C. Arches D. Attached gardens

30. The first ruler of India who defeated Muhammud of Ghur was :
A. Mularaja II of Gujarat
B. Prithviraja Chauhan of Delhi
C. Jayachand of Kannauj
D. Parmaldeva of Bundelkhand

31. What important event happened in India in 1911?
A. Bengal was partitioned
B. Non-Cooperation movement was launched
C. India's capital was shifted from Calcutta to Delhi
D. Mahatma Gandhi presided over the Congress session

32. The first phase of the Congress Party (1885-1905) was characterized by its efforts to secure:
A. limited independence
B. complete freedom
C. Indianization of services
D. constitutional reforms

33. The Muslim League demanded a separate homeland for the Indian Muslims openly for the first time at its annual session held in Lahore in the year :
A. 1931 A.D. B. 1936 A.D.
C. 1940 A.D. D. 1941 A.D.

34. Under whose governorship did the East India Company secure the Diwani Rights in Bengal, Bihar and Odisha from Emperor Shah Alam?
A. Lord Cornwallis
B. Lord William Bentinck
C. Lord Clive
D. Lord Wellesley

35. The Simon Commission was generally boycotted by the Indian political parties. What was the reason for this general non-cooperation?
A. the Commission aimed at dividing the people
B. it was an 'all white' Commission
C. it came after the Jallianwala Bagh carnage
D. it was an eye wash

36. Aligarh Muslim University was founded by :
A. Dr. Saifuddin Kitchlu
B. Mohammad Ali Jinnah
C. Sir Syed Ahmed Khan
D. Maulana Mohammad Ali

37. Ibn Batutah was an African traveller visiting India during the time of :
A. Alivardi Khan
B. Ala-ud-din Khalji
C. Iltutmish
D. Mohammad-bin-Tughlaq

38. The battle of Wandiawash was fought in :
A. 1726 B. 1760
C. 1818 D. 1857

39. The abolition of *Sati* by government regulation was at the time of :
A. Warren Hastings B. Lord Wellesley
C. Lord Bentinck D. Lord Ahmerst

40. Pick out the wrong combination :
A. Dilwara Temple : Mt. Abu
B. Pashupati Temple : Kathmandu
C. Padmanabh Temple : Bangalore
D. Minakshi Temple : Madurai

41. Match the following:
(*a*) Chanhudaro (*b*) Kalibangan
(*c*) Lothal (*d*) Surkotada
1. Alleged discovery of the skeleton of horse.
2. Bead making.
3. Traces of a dock and ship on seal.
4. Evidence of ploughing the fields.
The Correct code is :

	(*a*)	(*b*)	(*c*)	(*d*)
A.	2	4	3	1
B.	2	1	3	4
C.	1	2	3	4
D.	2	1	4	3

42. Match the Harappan settlements with the banks of rivers on which they were located :
(*a*) Harappa 1. Ravi
(*b*) Mohenjodaro 2. Indus
(*c*) Ropar 3. Sutlej
(*d*) Kalibangan 4. Ghaggar
(*e*) Lothal 5. Bhogava

Codes :

	(*a*)	(*b*)	(*c*)	(*d*)	(*e*)
A.	1	2	3	4	5
B.	1	2	3	5	4
C.	2	1	3	5	4
D.	2	1	4	3	5

43. The Goddess 'Kannagi' whose many temples were erected during the 'Sangam Age' was the goddess of :
A. Chastity B. Love
C. Prowess D. Wisdom

44. The Jain goal of life is to attain deliverance from the fetters of mudane existence, the way to which lies through three jewels. Which one of the following was not included among the 'three jewels' of Jainism?
A. Right faith B. Right action
C. Right knowledge D. Right conduct

45. The most striking feature of the Ashokan pillar is polish. Name the Ashokan pillar which is considered to be the most graceful of all Ashokan pillars.
A. Sarnath
B. Rampurva
C. Laurya-Nandangarh
D. Rummindei

46. Which are the correct statements?
1. The land grants, started in Satavahana period, paved the way for feudal developments in India.
2. Silk and spices were the Chief Indian export articles of Indo-Roman trade.
3. The Guptas issued the largest number of gold coins in ancient India.
4. The first memorial of a 'SATI' dated 510 A.D. is found at Eran in Madhya Pradesh.
A. 1 and 2 B. 1, 3, and 4
C. 1 and 4 D. 1, 2, 3 and 4

47. Who among the following patronised the 'Gandhara' (Indo-Greek style) School of Art?
A. Ashoka, the Great
B. Harsha Vardhana
C. Kanishka
D. Chandragupta Vikramaditya

48. The Sultanate of Delhi had five ruling dynasties. The dynasty having longest and shortest period were :
A. Ilbari and Khalji
B. Tughlaq and Khalji
C. Tughlaq and Sayyid
D. Ilbari and Lodis

49. Which one of the following events took place at the last during reign of Muhammad-bin-Tughlaq?
A. Introduction of token currency
B. Increase of land-revenue in Doab
C. Transfer of Capital from Delhi to Devagiri.
D. Conquest of Khurasan and Iraq

50. The most learned medieval Muslim ruler who was well versed in various branches of learning including astronomy, mathematics and medicine was :
A. Jalaluddin Khilji
B. Sikander Lodi
C. Ghiyasuddin Tughlaq
D. Muhammad-bin-Tughlaq

51. The 'Sufis' had 12 silsilas. They propounded the idea of Union with God through:
A. Love B. Rituals
C. Fasts D. Prayers

52. Match the following:
(*a*) Peshwa 1. Foreign affairs
(*b*) Panditrao 2. Audit and accounts
(*c*) Amatya 3. Providing grants to scholars
(*d*) Sumant 4. General supervision
5. Military affairs

Select the correct code :

	(*a*)	(*b*)	(*c*)	(*d*)
A.	2	3	4	5
B.	4	1	2	3
C.	4	3	2	1
D.	3	1	4	2

53. The Regulating Act of 1773 can be regarded as the first measure to :
A. assert the right of British Parliament to legislate for India
B. separate the legislature from the executive
C. separate the judiciary from the executive
D. centralise law-making

54. What was the exact constitutional status of the Indian Republic on 26th January, 1950?
A. A Democratic Republic
B. A Sovereign, Democratic Republic
C. A Sovereign, Secular, Democratic Republic
D. A Sovereign, Socialist, Secular, Democratic Republic

55. When the British obtained the grant of Diwani of Bengal, Bihar and Odisha they acquired the right to :
A. maintain law and order in these territories
B. administer civil justice and collect revenue in these territories
C. collect revenue and establish revenue administration in these territories
D. militarily defend these territories

56. Which of the following were responsible for the growth of nationalism in India during the British rule?
1. Economic exploitation of India.
2. Impact of western education.
3. Role of the Press.

Select the correct answer using the codes given below :

Codes:
A. 1, 2 and 3 B. 1 and 2
C. 2 and 3 D. 1 and 3

57. Which one of the following nationalist leaders has been described as being radical in politics but conservative on social issues?
A. G.K. Gokhale
B. B.G. Tilak
C. Lala Lajpat Rai
D. Madan Mohan Malviya

58. Provincial Autonomy in British India was envisaged by the :
A. Act of 1909 B. Act of 1919
C. Act of 1935 D. Act of 1947

59. Dyarchy means :
A. double government
B. a government in which the centre is very powerful
C. a government based on division of power between centre and provinces
D. None of the above

60. The Indian National Congress observed 'Independence Day' for the first time on 26th January in :
A. 1920 B. 1925
C. 1930 D. 1947

61. ....is situated near the banks of Sabarmati River
A. Bhavnagar B. Aurangabad
C. Ahmedabad D. Rajkot

62. Sericulture is:
A. science of the various kinds of serum
B. artificial rearing of fish
C. art of silkworm breeding
D. study of various cultures of a community

63. The most abundant constituents of earth's crust are:
A. Igneous rocks
B. Sedimentary rocks
C. Metamorphic rocks
D. Granite

64. Indian Standard Time is based on:
A. 80°E longitude B. 82½°E longitude
C. 110°E longitude D. 25°E longitude

65. Tides in the oceans are caused by :
A. Gravitational pull of the moon on the earth's surface including sea water
B. Gravitational pull of the sun on the earth's surface only and not on the sea water
C. Gravitational pull of the moon and the sun on the earth's surface including the sea water
D. None of these

66. Nagarjunasagar Project is situated on the river:
A. Tungabhadra B. Cauvery
C. Krishna D. Godavari

67. The difference between the Indian Standard Time and the Greenwich Mean Time is:
A. – 3½ hours B. + 3½ hours
C. – 5½ hours D. + 5½ hours

68. Which of the following dams is not on Narmada river?
A. Indira-Sagar Project
B. Maheshwar Hydel Power Project
C. Jobat Project
D. Koyna Power Project

69. Which of the following statements is **not true** about the availability of water on the earth, the crisis for which is going to increase in the years to come?
A. About 97.5 per cent of the total volume of water available on the earth is salty
B. 80 per cent of the water available to us for use comes in bursts as monsoons
C. About 2.5 per cent of the total water available on the earth is polluted water and cannot be used for human activities
D. Possibility is that some big glaciers will melt in the coming ten-fifteen years and sea level will rise by 3-4 metres all over the earth

70. Which of the following is **not** a cash crop?
A. Jute B. Paddy
C. Cashewnut D. Sugarcane

71. Through which States does Cauvery River flow?
A. Gujarat, M.P., Tamil Nadu
B. Karnataka, Kerala, Tamil Nadu
C. Karnataka, Kerala, Andhra Pradesh
D. M.P., Maharashtra, Tamil Nadu

72. Indian Standard Time is the local time of 82½°E which passes through :
A. Guntur B. Delhi
C. Allahabad D. Kolkata

73. The 17th parallel defines the boundary between:
A. North and South Korea
B. USA and Canada
C. North and South Vietnam
D. China and Russia

74. During the period of south-west monsoon, Tamil Nadu remains dry because:
A. the winds do not reach this area
B. there are no mountains in this area
C. it lies in the rain shadow area
D. the temperature is too high to let the winds cool down

75. Which country does top in producing cocoa?
A. Ivory Coast B. Brazil
C. Japan D. Nigeria

76. The biggest reserves of thorium are in :
A. India B. China
C. The Soviet Union D. U.S.A.

77. The Girnar Hills are situated in which of the following states?
A. Gujarat B. Karnataka
C. Madhya Pradesh D. Maharashtra

78. During December 22nd the sun is vertically over:
A. Tropic of Cancer B. Tropic of Capricorn
C. The Equator D. None of the above

79. Photosphere is described as the :
A. Lower layer of atmosphere
B. Visible surface of the sun from which radiation emanates
C. Wavelength of solar spectrum
D. None of the above

80. Broadly, there are three layers of the earth of the crust, the mantle and the core. The crust forms what percentage of the volume of the earth?
A. 0.5% B. 2.5%
C. 7.5% D. 12.5%

81. The grassland of Argentina is known as :
A. Pampas B. Campos
C. Savanna D. None of the above

82. Different seasons are formed because :
A. Sun is moving around the earth
B. of revolution of the earth around the Sun on its orbit
C. of rotation of the earth around its axis
D. All of the above

83. Eskers and Drumlins are features formed by:
A. underground water
B. running water
C. the action of wind
D. glacial action

84. Match List-I and List-II and select the correct answer using the codes given below the Lists :

List-I *(Rivers)*	List-II *(Towns)*
(a) Ghaghara	1. Lucknow
(b) Brahmaputra	2. Hoshangabad
(c) Narmada	3. Ahmedabad
(d) Sabarmati	4. Guwahati
	5. Ayodhya

	(a)	(b)	(c)	(d)
A.	4	5	1	2
B.	5	4	2	3
C.	5	4	3	1
D.	3	5	2	1

85. Which of the statements as regards the consequences of the movement of the earth is not correct?
A. Revolution of the earth is the cause of the change of seasons.
B. Rotation of the earth is the cause of days and nights.

C. Rotation of the earth causes variation in the duration of days and nights.
D. Rotation of the earth effects the movement of winds and ocean currents.

86. The world is divided into :
A. 12 time zones B. 20 time zones
C. 24 time zones D. 36 time zones

87. The 'Kiel' canal links the :
A. Pacific and Atlantic Oceans
B. Mediterranean Sea and Red Sea
C. Mediterranean Sea and Black Sea
D. North Sea and Baltic Sea

88. Match the following :

List-I	List-II
(*a*) Himadri	1. Outer Himalayas
(*b*) Shivalik	2. Inner Himalayas
(*c*) Himanchal	3. Middle Himalayas
(*d*) Sahyadri	4. Western Ghats

Codes:

	(*a*)	(*b*)	(*c*)	(*d*)
A.	1	2	3	4
B.	4	2	3	1
C.	2	1	3	4
D.	1	2	3	4

89. The term 'Regur' refers to:
A. Laterite soils
B. Black Cotton soils
C. Red Soils
D. Deltaic Alluvial Soils

90. Location of sugar industry in India is shifting from north to south because of:
A. cheap labour
B. expanding regional market
C. cheap and abundant supply of power
D. high yield and high sugar content in sugarcane

91. Consider the following statements :
1. Ozone is found mostly in the Stratosphere.
2. Ozone layer lies 55-75 km above the surface of the earth.
3. Ozone absorbs ultraviolet radiation from the Sun.
4. Ozone layer has no significance for life on the earth.
Which of the above statements are correct?
A. 1 and 3 B. 2 and 4
C. 2 and 3 D. 1 and 4

92. Match List-I with List-II and select the correct answer using the codes given below the Lists :

List-I (*Crops*)	List-II (*Producer*)
(*a*) Banana	1. Brazil
(*b*) Cocoa	2. Cote d'Ivoire
(*c*) Coffee	3. India
(*d*) Tea	4. China

Codes :

	(*a*)	(*b*)	(*c*)	(*d*)
A.	2	3	1	4
B.	3	2	1	4
C.	3	2	4	1
D.	2	3	4	1

93. Darjeeling and Dharamsala would be the right places to visit if one wanted to get a clear view respectively of :
A. Kanchanjunga and Dhauladhar ranges
B. Nandadevi and Dhauladhar ranges
C. Kanchanjunga and Nandadevi ranges
D. Nandadevi and Nanga Parvat

94. Atmosphere exists because:
A. The Gravitational force of the Earth
B. Revolution of the Earth
C. Rotation of the Earth
D. Weight of the gases of atmosphere

95. Victoria lake is located in the continent:
A. Africa
B. Asia
C. North America
D. South America

96. The famous Lagoon Lake of India is :
A. Dal Lake B. Chilka Lake
C. Pulicat Lake D. Mansarover

97. Where are most of the earth's active volcanoes concentrated?
A. Indian Ocean B. Pacific Ocean
C. Aral Sea D. Atlantic Ocean

98. Through which of the following states does the river Chambal flow?
A. U.P., M.P., Rajasthan
B. M.P., Gujarat, U.P.
C. Rajasthan, M.P., Bihar
D. Gujarat, M.P., U.P.

99. Which country is called the sugar bowl of the world?
A. Cuba B. India
C. Argentina D. USA

100. The area covered by forest in India is about:
A. 46% B. 33%
C. 21.71% D. 28%

101. A closed economy is the one which :
A. does not permit emigration or immigration
B. permits emigration but no immigration
C. engages in no foreign trade
D. engages in no foreign and domestic trade or transit

102. In a developed economy the major share of employment originates in the :
A. primary sector B. tertiary sector
C. secondary sector D. any of the above

103. The Economic and Social Commission for Asia and Pacific (ESCAP) is located at :
A. Bangkok B. Kuala Lumpur
C. Manila D. Singapore

104. Commercial vehicles are not produced by which of the following companies in India?
A. TELCO B. Ashok Leyland
C. DCM Daewoo D. Birla Yamaha

105. What is 'Stagflation'?
A. Inflation with growth
B. Deflation with growth
C. Inflation after deflations
D. Inflation with depression

106. The main argument advanced in favour of small scale and cottage industries in India is that:
A. cost of production is low
B. they require small capital investment
C. they advance the goal of equitable distribution of wealth
D. they generate a large volume of employment

107. The most serious economic problems of India are:
A. Poverty and unemployment
B. Stagnation, not poverty
C. Unemployment, not poverty
D. Underdevelopment, not poverty

108. Which of the following is not one of the three central problems of an economy?
A. What to produce
B. How to produce
C. When to produce
D. For whom to produce

109. Gender Responsive Budgeting has been adopted in India in the year:
A. 2017 B. 2004
C. 2014 D. 2005

110. In which of the following industries in India are the maximum number of workers employed?
A. Sugar B. Jute
C. Textiles D. Iron and Steel

111. Terrace Cultivation is practiced mostly:
A. in urban areas
B. on slopes of mountains
C. on tops of hills
D. in undulating tracts

112. Which of the following is a Selective Credit Control method?
A. Bank Rate
B. RBI directives
C. Cash Reserve Ratio
D. Open market operations

113. Which of the following taxes is not shared by the Central Government with the States?
A. Union excise duties
B. Customs duty
C. Income tax
D. Estate duty

114. ICICI is the name of a:
A. Financial Institution
B. Chemical Industry
C. Cotton Industry
D. Chamber of Commerce and Industry

115. Structural Unemployment arises due to
A. Deflationary conditions
B. Heavy industry bias
C. Shortage of raw material
D. Inadequate productive capacity

116. The rate at which RBI gives short-term loan to Commercial banks is called:
A. Reverse Repo Rate
B. Bank Rate
C. Repo Rate
D. Cash Reserve Rate

117. The largest public sector bank in India is:
A. Central Bank of India
B. Punjab National Bank
C. State Bank of India
D. Indian Overseas Bank

118. Which of the following statements best explains the term contraband goods?
A. Goods produced only for exports
B. Goods produced in joint sector only
C. Goods for the trading of which licence is not required
D. Goods that are forbidden, from export, import or even possession, by law

119. Price in the market is fixed by:
A. Stock exchange rates
B. The demand and supply ruling in the market at a particular time
C. The Finance Minister
D. None of the above

120. Devaluation of currency helps to promote:
A. National Income
B. Savings
C. Imports at lower cost
D. Exports

121. Balanced economic growth can be achieved only if:
A. All the sectors of economy grow at the same rate
B. Population growth is arrested
C. All the inter dependent sectors grow in harmony
D. Basic and heavy industries are assigned highest priority

122. 'Blue Revolution' is related to:
A. Fishries B. Poultry
C. Space Research D. Drinking Water

123. What is "hotline"?
A. A telecommunication link
B. An electric wire
C. Hard disk
D. Modem

124. Which of the following banks has launched 'No Q' App?
A. ICICI Bank B. SBI Bank
C. AXIS Bank D. None of the above

125. The term 'devaluation' means:
A. Reducing the value of a currency in terms of another currency
B. Increasing the value of a currency
C. Revising the value of a currency
D. None of the above

126. Per capita net availability of pulses has shown a tendency of:
A. Increase over time
B. Decrease over time
C. Constant over time
D. First increase then decrease

127. National Income is the same as:
A. Net national product at market price
B. Net domestic product at market price
C. Net national product at factor cost
D. Net domestic product at factor cost

128. Which one of the following is not an example of indirect tax?
A. Sales tax B. Excise duty
C. Customs duty D. Expenditure tax

129. The major aim of devaluation is to:
A. encourage imports
B. encourage exports
C. encourage both exports and imports
D. discourage both exports and imports

130. Structural unemployment arises due to:
A. deflationary conditions
B. heavy industry bias
C. shortage of raw materials
D. inadequate productive capacity

131. When was the Family Planning Programme officially started in India?
A. 1950 B. 1952
C. 1956 D. 1962

132. When was the Reserve Bank of India nationalised?
A. 1947 B. 1949
C. 1950 D. 1951

133. Which of the following is *not* a feature of the Indian economy?
A. High rate of population growth
B. Disguised unemployment
C. Lowest rate of adult literacy
D. High rate of exports

134. The 'Relative Deprivation' approach for measuring poverty has been adopted by:
A. developing countries
B. developed countries
C. under-developed countries
D. None of the above

135. One of the main factors that led to rapid expansion of Indian exports is:
A. Imposition of import duties
B. Liberalisation of the economy
C. Recession in other countries
D. Diversification of exports

136. Sustainable economic development means an increase in the rate of growth of real:
A. total and per capita product
B. total and per capita product and level of literacy rate
C. total and per capita product and life expectancy at birth
D. total and per capita product, taking into account the cost of degradation of the quality of environment in this process

137. Functional unemployment occurs when:
A. unemployed have no qualification for job
B. people frequently change their job
C. people were thrown out from job due to recession
D. None of these

138. Which among the following does **not** have a 'free trade zone'?
A. Kandla B. Mumbai
C. Visakhapatnam D. Thiruvanantpuram

139. Sun Belt of USA is important for which one of the following industries?
A. Cotton textile
B. Petrochemicals
C. Hi-tech electronics
D. Food Processing

140. Commercial banking system in India is
A. unit banking B. branch banking
C. mixed banking D. None of the above

141. Who gives recognition to political parties in India?
A. Parliament B. President
C. Supreme Court D. Election Commission

142. The Quorum of the Legislative Council is :
A. one-fourth of its total membership

B. one-third of its membership
C. one-tenth of its membership
D. 25

143. The Indian Constitution is:
A. federal
B. unitary
C. a happy mixture of the federal and unitary
D. federal in normal times and unitary in times of emergency

144. Universal adult franchise implies a right to vote to all:
A. adult residents of the State
B. adult male citizens of the State
C. residents of the State
D. adult citizens of the State

145. When a resolution prefering a charge against the President has been passed by a specified majority in the House, it is sent to the other House for investigation. If, as a result of such an investigation, a resolution is passed through a specified majority by the other House, declaring that the charge has been sustained, the President shall leave his office. The specified special majority must not be less than :
A. two-third of the members present and voting
B. one-third of the members present and voting
C. three-fourth of the members present and voting and two-third of the total membership
D. two-third of the total membership

146. Which one of the following judicial powers of the President of India has been *wrongly* listed?
A. he appoints the Chief Justice and other judges of the Supreme Court
B. he can remove the judges of the Supreme Court on grounds of misconduct
C. he can consult the Supreme Court on any question of law or fact which is of public importance
D. he can grant pardon, reprieves and respites to persons punished under Union Law

147. The Vice-president of India can be removed from his office before the expiry of his term if :
A. the Rajya Sabha passes a resolution by a majority of its members and the Lok Sabha agrees with the resolution
B. if the Supreme Court of India recommends his removal
C. the President so desires
D. None of the above

148. The Chief Justice of a High Court in India is appointed by the :
A. Governor of the State
B. Prime Minister of India
C. Chief Justice of the Supreme Court
D. President of India

149. Which of the following statements is constitu-tionally not true about the passing of the Union Budgets and Finance Bill in India?
1. Under the law, Finance Bill should be adopted by both the Houses of the Parliament within 45 days of its introduction.
2. If the Finance Bill is not adopted within specified period, the government loses its authority to levy the taxes proposed in the budgets.
3. In the absence of full budget, a vote-on-account gives the power to the government to spend.
4. Government cannot raise revenues without a proper approval of the Finance Bill

A. Only 2 B. Only 3
C. Only 4 D. Only 1, 2 and 3

150. Normally, on whose advice the President's Rule is imposed in a State?
A. Chief Minister
B. Legislative Assembly
C. Governor
D. Chief Justice of High Court

151. Which Article of the Indian Constitution deals with Amendment procedure?
A. Article 368 B. Article 358
C. Article 367 D. All of these

152. Government is the agency through which the will of :
A. the state is expressed
B. the people is expressed
C. the head of the state is expressed
D. the majority is expressed

153. In a unitary system of government :
A. The centre is all powerful
B. The centre is weaker than the states
C. The centre and states stand at par
D. The states and centre are supreme in their respective spheres

154. In Cabinet System of Government the real executive authority rests with :
A. The Council of Ministers
B. The Prime Minister
C. The Constitution
D. The Parliament

155. The Head of the State under a parliamentary government:
A. is an elected representative
B. is a hereditary person
C. is a nominated person
D. may be any one of the above

156. In the event of a ministerial proposal being defeated on the floor of the legislature, under the parliamentary system :
A. the government waits for a general no-confidence motion

B. the minister concerned is taken to task by the Prime Minister
C. the minister is forced to resign
D. the whole Council of Ministers resign

157. The "due process of law" is an essential characteristic of the judicial system of:
A. UK B. France
C. USA D. India

158. Under the Constitution it is :
A. obligatory for the President to accept the advice of the Council of Ministers but is not obliged to follow it
B. obligatory for the President to accept the advice of the Council of Ministers
C. not obligatory for the President to seek or accept the advice of the Council of Ministers
D. obligatory for the President to seek the advice of the Council of Ministers if his own party is in power

159. Which one of the following statements is correct?
A. the Presiding Officer of Rajya Sabha is elected every year
B. the Presiding Officer of Rajya Sabha is elected for a term of two years at a time
C. the Presiding Officer of Rajya Sabha is elected for a term of six years
D. the Vice-President of India is the ex-officio Presiding Officer of Rajya Sabha

160. The introduction of "no confidence" motion in the Lok Sabha requires the support of at least:
A. 50 members B. 70 members
C. 60 members D. 80 members

161. The High Court comes under :
A. State List B. Union List
C. Concurrent List D. None of the above

162. Which one of the following has been wrongly listed as a Fundamental Duty of the Indian citizens?
A. to develop scientific temper, humanism and spirit of inquiry and reform
B. to work for raising the prestige of the country in the international sphere
C. to protect and improve the natural environment
D. to strive towards excellence in all spheres of individual and collective activity

163. Which one of the following is not a Fundamental Duty as outlined in Article 51A of the Constitution?
A. to abide by the Constitution and respect its ideals
B. to defend the country and render national service when called upon to do so
C. to work for the moral upliftment of the weaker sections of society
D. to preserve the rich heritage

164. The main characteristics of the Directive Principles of State Policy given in the Indian Constitution are :
A. not enforceable by any court
B. fundamental in the governance of the country
C. 'Like instruments, instructions, political manifesto and a code of moral precepts which have to guide governors of the country'
D. no law can be passed, which is opposed to these principles

165. Of the following which are true?
A. In a State, the Legislative Council is dominant with regard to non-financial bills and the Legislative Assembly with regard to financial (money) bills
B. Vidhan Parishad can virtually block legisla-tion even if the same is passed by the Vidhan Sabha
C. In case of a tie between the two Houses, the Governor is duty-bound to call a joint session of the two Houses to have the issue settled on a majority verdict
D. If a Bill is twice approved by the Vidhan Sabha, it becomes law even if rejected by the Vidhan Parishad

166. Which one of the following types of emergency can be declared by the President?
A. Emergency due to threat of war and external aggresion
B. Emergency due to break-down of constitu-tional machinery in a State
C. Financial emergency on account of threat to the financial credit of India
D. all the three emergencies

167. The chairman of which of the following parliamentary committees is invariably from the members of ruling party?
A. Committee on public undertakings
B. Public accounts committee
C. Estimates committee
D. Committee on delegated legislation

168. Which of the following is not a formally prescribed device available to the members of parliament?
A. Question hour
B. Zero hour
C. Half-an-hour discussion
D. Short duration discussion

169. Which of the following is not a tool of executive control over public administration?
A. Power of appointment and removal
B. Line agencies
C. Appeal to public opinion
D. Civil services code

170. If the Speaker of the State Legislative Assembly decides to resign, he should submit his resignation to the:
A. Judges of the High Court
B. Deputy Speaker
C. Chief Minister
D. Finance Minister

171. Which tax can be levied by Gram Panchayat?
A. Sales Tax
B. Custom Duty
C. Land Revenue
D. Tax on Local Fairs

172. India is a Federal State because of:
A. dual judiciary
B. dual citizenship prevalent here
C. share of power between the Centre and the States
D. rigid Constitution

173. Residuary Subjects are those subjects which are:
A. contained in the State list
B. contained in the Union list
C. contained in the Concurrent list
D. not covered by any of the three lists

174. Which of the following writs can be issued, by the Suprème Court, to enforce Fundamental Rights?
A. Writ of Habeas Corpus
B. Writ of Mandamus
C. Writ of Quo Warranto
D. All of these

175. When the offices of both the President and the Vice-President of India are vacant, who will discharge their functions?
A. Prime Minister
B. Home Minister
C. Chief Justice of India
D. The Speaker

176. The Supreme Court tenders advice to the President of India on a matter of law or fact:
A. on its own
B. only when such advice is sought
C. only if the matter relates to some basic issue
D. only if the issue poses a threat to the unity and integrity of the country

177. Six months shall **not** intervene between two sessions of the Indian Parliament because :
A. it is the customary practice
B. it is the British convention followed in India
C. it is an obligation under the Constitution of India
D. None of the above

178. The States of the Indian Union can be recognised or their boundaries altered by:
A. the Union Parliament by a simple majority in the ordinary process of legislation
B. two-thirds majority of both the Houses of Parliament
C. two-thirds majority of both the Houses of Parliament and the consent of the legisla-tures of concerned States
D. an executive order of the Union government with the consent of the concerned State governments

179. The Basic Feature theory of the Constitution of India was propounded by the Supreme Court in the case of :
A. Minerva Mills Vs. Union of India
B. Golaknath Vs. State of Punjab
C. Maneka Gandhi Vs. Union of India
D. Keshavananda Vs. State of Kerala

180. Which one of the following writs is issued by a court in case of illegal detention of a person?
A. Habeas corpus B. Mandamus
C. Certiorari D. Quo-warranto

181. Name the instrument with the help of which a sailor in a submarine can see the objects on the surface of the sea.
A. Telescope B. Periscope
C. Gycroscope D. Stereoscope

182. 'HEMOPHILLIA' is the disease of ....
A. liver B. blood
C. brain D. bones

183. Vitamin A is abundantly found in ....
A. Brinjal B. Tomato
C. Carrot D. Cabbage

184. .... is not soluble in water.
A. Vitamin A B. Vitamin B
C. Vitamin C D. None of these

185. The blood vessels with the smallest diameter are called ....
A. capillaries B. arterioles
C. venules D. lymphatics

186. Out of the following .... has the greatest elasticity.
A. steel B. rubber
C. aluminium D. annealed copper

187. Cooking gas is a mixture of which of the following two gases?
A. Carbon Dioxide and Oxygen
B. Butane and Propane
C. Carbon Monoxide and Carbon Dioxide
D. Methane and Ethylene

188. The substance most commonly used as a food preservative is:
A. sodium carbonate B. tartaric acid
C. acetic acid D. benzoic acid

189. Normally, the substances that fight against diseases in human systems are known as:
A. dioxyribonucleic acids
B. carbohydrates
C. enzymes
D. antibodies

190. The SI unit of temperature is ....
A. Kelvin B. Celsius
C. Fahrenheit D. None of the above

191. One of the common fungal diseases of man is :
A. plague B. ringworm
C. cholera D. typhoid

192. A clear sky is blue because:
A. red light is scattered more than blue
B. ultraviolet light has been absorbed
C. blue light is scattered more than red
D. blue light has been absorbed

193. Jenner introduced the method of making people immune to :
A. small pox B. rabies
C. cholera D. polio

194. The largest cell in the human body is :
A. Nerve cell B. Live cell
C. Muscle cell D. Kidney cell

195. What is the device that steps up or steps down the voltage?
A. Dynamo B. Conductor
C. Inductor D. Transformer

196. The protein deficiency disease is known as :
A. Kwashiorker B. Cirrhosis
C. Eczema D. Clycoses

197. Iron deficiency causes :
A. rickets B. anaemia
C. cirrhosis D. goitre

198. Blood group of an individual is controlled by :
A. Haemoglobin B. Shape of RBC
C. Shape of WBC D. Genes

199. In a normal man the amount of blood pumped out by the heart per minute is about :
A. 1 litre B. 3 litres
C. 4 litres D. 5 litres

200. Red/green colour blindness in man is known as :
A. Protanopia
B. Deutetanopia
C. Both A and B above
D. Marfan's syndrome

201. The blue colour of the water in the sea is due to :
A. Reflection of the blue light by the impurities in sea water
B. Reflection of the blue sky by sea water and scattering of blue light by water molecules
C. Absorption of other colours by water molecules
D. None of the above

202. The image formed on the retina of the eye is:
A. upright and real
B. larger than the object
C. small and inverted
D. enlarged and real

203. Unit of loudness of sound is:
A. bel B. decibel
C. phon D. none of these

204. Oil rises up the wick in a lamp :
A. because oil is volatile
B. due to the capillary action phenomenon
C. due to the surface tension phenomenon
D. because oil is very light

205. The 'stones' formed in human kidney consist mostly of :
A. calcium oxalate
B. sodium acetate
C. magnesium sulphate
D. calcium

206. We hear the sound later, while the light is seen earlier:
A. because light's speed is more than that of sound
B. because lights travel in a straight direction while sound in a zigzag direction
C. because sound's frequency is lower than light
D. All of the above

207. Which part of an eye is transplanted?
A. Cornea B. Retina
C. Iris D. Sciera

208. The Universal donor group of blood is:
A. O B. A
C. B D. AB

209. The green colour of the leaf is due to :
A. Presence of Chloroplast
B. Presence of Chromium
C. Presence of Nicoplast
D. Presence of excess of oxygen

210. Voice of a child is more shrill than that of an elderly person because:
A. the pitch of the child's voice is higher than that of the person
B. the pitch is lower
C. the child is more energetic
D. None of the above

211. Camel uses its hump for :
A. storing water
B. storing fat
C. for balancing the body
D. temperature regulation

212. A man standing in a free falling lift releases a ball from his hand. The ball would be :
A. moving down
B. moving up
C. stationary
D. moving up and down

213. To change the quality of sound produced by an instrument we need to vary the:
A. pitch B. loudness
C. amplitude D. number of overtonnes

214. The disease caused by Asbestos is:
A. Emphysema B. Paralysis
C. Diarrhoea D. Dysentery

215. Sweetness of a sound depends upon its
A. wavelength
B. frequency
C. amplitude
D. periodicity and regularity

216. Bats can fly in the dark because :
A. they have a better vision in the dark
B. the pupils of their eyes are very big
C. they are guided by ultrasonic waves produced by them
D. any bird can do so

217. Blood is formed in the human adult by the :
A. heart B. spleen
C. kidney D. bone marrow

218. Pencil 'lead' is made up of:
A. graphite B. charcoal
C. lead oxide D. lampblack

219. The deficiency of which one of the following vitamins leads to bleeding of gums and loosening of teeth?
A. Vitamin D B. Vitamin C
C. Vitamin B D. Vitamin A

220. How much blood does a normal person have in his body?
A. 8 litres B. 4 to 5 litres
C. 10 litres D. 2 litres

221. Match List-I with List-II and select the correct answer using the codes given below the Lists :

List-I	List-II
(*a*) Visakhadatta	1. Mrichhakatika
(*b*) Shudraka	2. Ritusamhara
(*c*) Kalidasa	3. Kamasutra
(*d*) Vatsyayana	4. Devichandraguptam

Codes :

	(*a*)	(*b*)	(*c*)	(*d*)
A.	1	4	2	3
B.	4	1	3	2
C.	1	4	3	2
D.	4	1	2	3

222. In which one of the following langauges is the *Dalit* writing more conspicuous?
A. Punjabi B. Assamese
C. Marathi D. Odiya

223. The first writer to use Urdu as the medium of poetic expression was:
A. Amir Khusrau
B. Mirza Ghalib
C. Bahadur Shah Zafar
D. Faiz

224. The religious text of the Zoroastrians is named as:
A. Torah B. The Analects
C. Tripatika D. Zend Avesta

225. Name the music duo which composed music for Raj Kapoor's film 'Bobby'?
A. Laxmikant Pyarelal B. Shankar Jaikishen
C. Kalyanji Anandji D. Nadeem Shravan

226. Raja Harishchandra, an early Indian film, was produced by :
A. D.G. Phalke B. Ashok Kumar
C. Ardeshir Irani D. None of the above

227. All films are certificed by .... before they are publicly exhibited.
A. Films Division
B. National Film Development Corporation (NFDC)
C. Directorate of Advertising and Visual Publicity (DAVP)
D. Central Board of Film Certificate (CBFC)

228. Who among the following was the director of the film 'Taal'?
A. Gulzar B. Shekhar Kapoor
C. Satish Shah D. Subhash Ghai

229. Who amongst the following actresses has played the leading role in the film Elizabeth?
A. Gwyneth Paltrow B. Cate Blanchett
C. Simi Garewal D. Kim Basinger

230. The film 'Train to Pakistan' is based on the novel of the same name, written by:
A. Bhishma Sahani
B. Khushwant Singh
C. Amrita Pritam
D. Khwaja Ahmed Abbas

231. Which of the following is a folk dance form of Jharkhand?
A. Pali B. Jhumar
C. Nati D. Chhau

232. The first feature film (talkie) to be produced in India was:
A. Hatimtai B. Alam Ara
C. Pundalik D. Raja Harishchandra

233. Who directed the film "Bombay"?
A. Shyam Benegal B. Meera Nair
C. Shekhar Kapoor D. Mani Ratnam

234. Late Pankaj Udhas was famous in which of the following fields?
A. Singing B. Acting
C. Music D. Literature

235. Who among the following is the director of the film 'The Kashmir Files'?
A. Subhash Ghai B. Shekhar Kapoor
C. Ramesh Sippy D. Vivek Agnihotri

236. The character played by Jim Carrey in the movie *Man on Moon* is based on:
A. Andy Kaufman B. Edwin Aldrin
C. John Glenn D. Neil Armstrong

237. A popular Hindi film-based on the famous Sanskrit play *Mrichhakatika*, was titled:
A. Meghadoot B. Amrapali
C. Utsav D. Shakuntala

238. Who composed the song 'Zara Yad Karo Kurbani'?
A. Javed Akhtar
B. Pradeep
C. Nusrat Fateh Ali Khan
D. Raghupati Sahay 'Firaq'

239. Who was the producer of the serial 'Mahabharat'?
A. Shyam Benegal B. B.R. Chopra
C. Ramanand Sagar D. Mani Ratnam

240. Which of the following is a folk dance of Rajasthan?
A. Garba B. Dandya
C. Jhumar D. Kathak

241. 'The Colonel' is the nickname of which Indian Test Cricketer?
A. Colonel C.K. Naidu
B. Rahul Dravid
C. Mohinder Amarnath
D. Dilip Vengsarkar

242. The term 'Grandmaster' is used in which of these games?
A. Judo B. Chess
C. Bridge D. Karate

243. The term "Derby" is related with which of the following?
A. Polo B. Swimming
C. Racing D. Horse Racing

244. With which game is Geet Sethi associated?
A. Basketball B. Chess
C. Snooker D. Tennis

245. Beighton Cup is related with which of the following?
A. Hockey B. Polo
C. Cricket D. Soccer

246. Match List-I with List-II and select the correct answer using the codes given below the Lists :

List-I	List-II
(*a*) Basketball	1. Lob
(*b*) Bridge	2. Revoke
(*c*) Golf	3. Pivot
(*d*) Tennis	4. Bunker

Codes :

	(*a*)	(*b*)	(*c*)	(*d*)
A.	2	3	1	4
B.	2	3	4	1
C.	3	2	1	4
D.	3	2	4	1

247. The head office of the International Cricket Council (ICC) is situated in :
A. Zimbabwe B. Australia
C. South Africa D. UAE

248. Match the following :

List-I	List-II
(*a*) Deodhar Trophy	1. Volleyball
(*b*) Durand Cup	2. Football
(*c*) Davis Cup	3. Cricket
	4. Tennis

Codes:

	(*a*)	(*b*)	(*c*)
A.	3	2	4
B.	3	1	4
C.	2	3	1
D.	1	2	4

249. Which of the following is called 'Grand Slam'?
A. Winning the highest number of medals in the Olympic games
B. Winning the men's singles title in Wimbledon Championship
C. Winning the Wimbledon Singles title successively for two years
D. Winning all the four championships Australian, French, Wimblendon and US

250. With which game is the term 'butterfly stroke' associated?
A. Swimming B. Cricket
C. Gliding D. Skiing

251. Who is the first Indian to win the 'International Grand Master' title in Chess?
A. Anupama Abhayankar
B. Bhagyashree Sathe Thipsay
C. Vishwanathan Anand
D. D.V. Prasad

252. The XXII Commonwealth Games were held in 2022 in :
A. Kuala Lumpur B. Bangkok
C. Victoria D. Birmingham

253. The term 'Tee' is associated with which of the following sports?
A. Golf B. Table Tennis
C. Polo D. Judo

254. The famous woman Tennis player who was stabbed during a match, is
A. Steffi Graf B. Monica Seles
C. Mary Pierce D. Martina Navratilova

255. The term 'Baseline' is related to which of the following?
A. Golf B. Hockey
C. Badminton D. Polo

256. In which Indian State did the game of Polo originate?
A. Manipur B. Rajasthan
C. Gujarat D. West Bengal

257. Viswanathan Anand is associated with which sport?
A. Tennis B. Badminton
C. Chess D. Mountaineering

258. Rafael Nadal is the well-known player associated with:
A. Hockey B. Cricket
C. Tennis D. Chess

259. Neeraj Chopra is the well-known player associated with :
A. Javelin Throw B. Golf
C. Table Tennis D. Chess

260. Eden Garden, a famous Cricket stadium, is located in :
A. Kanpur B. Kolkata
C. Jamshedpur D. Pune

261. Maharaja Ranjit Singh Trophy is associated with :
A. Golf B. Hockey
C. Soccer D. Tennis

262. Jaspal Rana is a distinguished athlete in which of the following games?
A. Swimming B. Weightlifting
C. Shooting D. Archery

263. Cricket was an Olympic event at which of the following Olympics?
A. London, 1908 B. Amsterdam, 1928
C. Paris, 1900 D. Melbourne, 1956

264. WISPA competitions are associated with :
A. Squash B. Yatching
C. Boxing D. Billiards

265. Ryder Cup is the famous trophy of :
A. Golf B. Chess
C. Boxing D. Polo

266. Davis Cup is associated with the sport of :
A. Cricket B. Football
C. Tennis D. Hockey

267. 'Volley', 'Chop' and 'Drive Spine' are the term associated with :
A. Lawn Tennis B. Badminton
C. Table Tennis D. Golf

268. Lal Bahadur Shastri Stadium is located at :
A. Hyderabad B. Chennai
C. Ahmedabad D. Varanasi

269. The first winner of "Rajiv Gandhi Khel Ratna Award" (Now Major Dhyanchand Khel Ratna Award) was :
A. Geet Sethi
B. Sachin Tendulkar
C. Viswanathan Anand
D. Karnam Malleswari

270. The winner of 2023 Cricket World Cup is:
A. Australia B. Sri Lanka
C. India D. England

271. The first team event introduced in 1900 at Paris Olympics was :
A. Hockey B. Football
C. Cricket D. Baseball

272. Which of the following international tennis tournaments is held on grass court?
A. US Open B. French Open
C. Wimbledon D. Australian Open

273. Which cricketer is nicknamed as the pied piper of Punjab?
A. Yuvraj Singh
B. Harbhajan Singh
C. Mohinder Amarnath
D. Navjot Singh Sidhu

274. 'Merdeka Cup' is associated with ....
A. Golf B. Football
C. Squash D. Hockey

275. The first time athletes marched into the stadium behind their nation's flag in Olympics:
A. at St. Louis 1904 B. at London 1908
C. at Antwerp 1920 D. at Paris 1924

276. The "Dronacharya Award" is associated with:
A. Eminent Surgeons B. Famous Sports Person
C. Sport Coaches D. Expert Engineers

277. Which cricketer is nicknamed as 'Jumbo'?
A. Venkatesh Prasad B. Anil Kumble
C. Glenn McGrath D. Shane Warne

278. The first time the Olympic Games were organised by a private company at:
A. Montreal, 1976 B. Los Angeles, 1984
C. Atlanta, 1996 D. Rome, 1960

279. In which Asian Games Cricket was played first?
A. Guangzhou, 2010 B. Doha, 2006
C. Busan, 2002 D. Seoul, 1986

280. The term 'Penalty cick' is used in :
A. Hockey B. Football
C. Baseball D. Golf

281. Which of the following countries is not a member of North Atlantic Treaty Organisation (NATO)?
A. Norway B. United Germany
C. Portugal D. Australia

282. Khmer Rouge is a dictatorial party of :
A. Cambodia B. Indonesia
C. Malaysia D. Thailand

283. Which country is not a member of SAARC?
A. Russia B. Bangladesh
C. Nepal D. Pakistan

284. The headquarters of WTO is located at :
A. Geneva B. Paris
C. The Hague D. Washington

285. The main function of the World Trade Organisation (WTO) is:
A. enforcing of Uruguay Round Agreements

B. facilitating multi-lateral trade relations of member countries and reviewing trade policies
C. administering trade dispute settlement procedures
D. None of the above

286. The Secretary-General of the UNO is appointed by the:
A. General Assembly
B. Security Council
C. Trusteeship Council
D. World Bank

287. The United Nations officially came into existence in 1945 on :
A. November 24 B. October 14
C. October 24 D. November 14

288. Which one of the following is true of the International Court of Justice?
A. The Judges of the Court are appointed according to the discretion of the Secretary General
B. No two Judges may belong to the same country
C. The Court consists of 20 Judges
D. The statute of the International Court of Justice is not an integral part of the UN Charter

289. Which of the following was not among the six founding countries of the European Community?
A. Belgium B. France
C. Germany D. UK

290. The smallest country in South America is:
A. Ecuador B. Guyana
C. Surinam D. Uruguay

291. In which year "Human Rights Resolution" was adopted by the U.N.?
A. 1945 B. 1946
C. 1947 D. 1948

292. Where is the headquarters of INTERPOL located?
A. Berlin B. California
C. Lyons D. Montreal

293. Parliament of which of the following countries is known as Great People's Khural?
A. Malaysia B. Mongolia
C. Thailand D. Indonesia

294. Numbers of major organs of United Nations are:
A. 3 B. 4
C. 5 D. 6

295. When is the UN Day celebrated?
A. October 24 B. January 24
C. June 24 D. September 24

296. Which one of the following organ of United Nations is known as the 'Policeman of the World'?
A. Security Council
B. International Court of Justice
C. The Secretariat
D. General Assembly

297. The members of the NAFTA include:
A. USA, Canada and Mexico
B. USA, Canada, Mexico and UK
C. USA, UK, Russia and Mexico
D. USA, Canada and Brazil

298. The sits of International Court of Justice is located at :
A. Vienna B. Paris
C. Hague D. New York

299. Which of the following is known as the Constitution of the UN?
A. UN Charter
B. UN Assembly
C. UN Security Council
D. UN Secretariat

300. The Headquarters of the Amnesty International is located at :
A. New York B. London
C. Geneva D. Addis-Ababa

301. Who is the author of the book 'PRISON DIARY'?
A. Bal Gangadhar Tilak
B. Rajendra Prasad
C. Jai Prakash Narayan
D. Jawahar Lal Nehru

302. Who is the author of 'Satanic Verses'?
A. Lewis Carrol B. Salman Rushdie
C. Parry Mason D. Mulk Raj Anand

303. Who wrote 'Gitanjali'?
A. Kalidas
B. Gopal Das 'Neeraj'
C. Rabindra Nath Tagore
D. Jawahar Lal Nehru

304. Who, among the following, scholars flourishing during the Gupta Age, was the author of *Dasakumara-Charita?*
A. Asanga B. Dignaga
C. Dandina D. Bhattin

305. The author of *Gitagovinda* was:
A. Halayudha B. Jayadeva
C. Kalhana D. Jona-raja

306. "Ingenious Pain" is a book/novel written by:
A. Andrew Miller B. Santa Monica
C. Ben Johnson D. Bill Gates

307. Who amongst the following is the author of the famous book "An Equal Music"?
A. Salman Rushdie B. Shasthivrata
C. Vikram Seth D. Kamla Markandeya

308. The famous Moorti Devi Award is given for excellence in which of the following fields?
A. Medicine
B. Science & Technology
C. Social Service
D. Literature

309. Who has written "Devdas"?
A. Tarasankar Bandyopadhyay
B. Bankim Chandra Chattopadhyay
C. Rabindranath Tagore
D. Sarat Chandra Chattopadhyay

310. "Ain-i-Akbari" is written by:
A. Todar Mal B. Abul Fazal
C. Sheikh Saadi D. Mirza Ghalib

311. "Alice in Wonderland" is written by :
A. Lewis Carrol B. Chester Bowles
C. Charles Dickens D. Jonathan Swift

312. "Mrichchhakatikam" is written by :
A. Vishakhadatta B. Vatsyayana
C. Sudraka D. Bana Bhatt

313. "My Experiments with Truth" is written by :
A. Jawaharlal Nehru
B. M.K. Gandhi
C. Abul Kalam Azad
D. Rajendra Prasad

314. Who wrote the book "India Wins Freedom"?
A. Maulana Abul Kalam Azad
B. Mahatma Gandhi
C. Sir Mohammad Iqbal
D. Abdul Gaffar Khan

315. Match List-I with List-II and select the correct answer using the codes given below the Lists :

List-I	List-II
(a) *Emma*	1. Graham Greene
(b) *Mother India*	2. E.M. Forster
(c) *Human Factor*	3. Jane Austen
(d) *Passage to India*	4. Katherine Mayo

Codes :

	(a)	(b)	(c)	(d)
A.	2	1	4	3
B.	3	4	1	2
C.	3	1	2	4
D.	4	2	1	3

316. 'Poverty and Un British Rule in India' is written by:
A. R.C. Dutt B. J.L. Nehru
C. D.B. Naoroji D. S.N. Sen

317. Name the author of the book *A Passage to England.*
A. E.M. Forster
B. Nirad C. Choudhuri
C. Vikram Seth
D. Eric Segal

318. The author of the book 'The Struggle in My Life' is:
A. Mandela B. J.L. Nehru
C. Tilak D. Gokhale

319. The Shanti Swarup Bhatnagar Award is given by which of the following organisations?
A. Council for Scientific and Industrial Research
B. Indian Council for Agricultural Research
C. Indian National Science Academy
D. Indian Space Research Organisation

320. Which of the following books is not written by Salman Rushdie?
A. The Satanic Verses
B. Shame
C. Naked Face
D. Midnight's Children

321. The different schools of modern socialism derive their strength primarily from the writings of ....?
A. Joseph Stalin B. Leo Tolstoy
C. Mao Tse-tung D. Karl Marx

322. Baba Amte is famous as a ....
A. Painter B. Singer
C. Politician D. Social Worker

323. Central Government says that .... was received well by citizens as 'imandari ka utsav'.
A. Demonetization
B. Goods and Services Tax
C. E-NAM
D. All of the above

324. Mr. Yehudi Menuhin, was a famous:
A. Sitarist B. Cartoonist
C. Journalist D. Violinist

325. Sundarlal Bahuguna, a famous environ-mentalist, is associated with :
A. Chipko Movement
B. Narmada Bachao Andolan
C. Satyagraha Movement
D. Anti-corruption Movement

326. Mother Teressa's native place was :
A. Albania B. France
C. Greece D. Italy

327. The live polio vaccine which can be taken by mouth was developed by :
A. Albert Sabin B. Edward Jenner
C. Jonas Salk D. Selman Waksman

328. Which one of the following authors put forth the theory of the Drain of India's resources to England?
A. Raja Rammohan Roy
B. Bankim Chandra Chatterjee
C. G.G. Agarkar
D. Dadabhai Naoroji

329. The "Last Supper" is a famous renaissance painting. It was a masterpiece of :
A. Michael Angelo B. Leonardo da Vinci
C. Titian D. Raphael

330. Dhyanchand is associated with which sports?
A. Badminton B. Hockey
C. Tennis D. Football

331. 'Man is born free, yet every where he is in chains'. This was said by:
A. Voltaire B. John Stuart Mill
C. Rousseau D. Karl Marx

332. Who among the following was a prominent social reformer?
A. Baba Gurmukh Singh
B. Raja Mahendra Pratap
C. Bipin Chandra Pal
D. Jotiba Govind Phule

333. Whose real name was Gadadhar Chhattopa-dhyaya?
A. Swami Vivekanand
B. Ram Krishna Paramhansa
C. Dayanand Saraswai
D. Raja Ram Mohan Rai

334. Who was known as "Man of Destiny"?
A. Napoleon B. Nehru
C. Hitler D. Mussolini

335. Who discovered that mosquito served as a carrier of malaria?
A. Jonas Salk B. Ronald Ross
C. Louis Pasteur D. Robert Koch

336. Who was the first woman Governor of an Indian State?
A. Sushila Nayar
B. Sucheta Kripalani
C. Sarojini Naidu
D. Sulochana Modi

337. Who among the following founded the Bhartiya Jana Sangh?
A. Deen Dayal Upadhyaya
B. Veer Savarkar
C. Dr. Ram Manohar Lohia
D. Dr. Shyama Prasad Mukherjee

338. Who among the following President of India held his office for two successive terms?
A. V.V. Giri
B. Dr. Rajendra Prasad
C. Dr. S. Radhakrishnan
D. None of these

339. Ustad Amjad Ali Khan is an exponent of:
A. Flute B. Sitar
C. Sarod D. Tabla

340. Who is the first non-Indian to receive the Bharat Ratna?
A. Martin Luther King
B. Zubin Mehta
C. Mother Teressa
D. Khan Abdul Ghaffar Khan

ANSWERS

1	2	3	4	5	6	7	8	9	10
B	C	D	C	B	C	A	C	C	D
11	**12**	**13**	**14**	**15**	**16**	**17**	**18**	**19**	**20**
C	A	C	A	A	D	A	B	A	D
21	**22**	**23**	**24**	**25**	**26**	**27**	**28**	**29**	**30**
A	C	B	C	D	C	B	D	D	B
31	**32**	**33**	**34**	**35**	**36**	**37**	**38**	**39**	**40**
C	D	C	C	B	C	D	B	C	C
41	**42**	**43**	**44**	**45**	**46**	**47**	**48**	**49**	**50**
A	A	A	B	C	D	C	B	B	D
51	**52**	**53**	**54**	**55**	**56**	**57**	**58**	**59**	**60**
A	C	A	B	B	A	B	C	A	C
61	**62**	**63**	**64**	**65**	**66**	**67**	**68**	**69**	**70**
C	C	B	B	C	C	D	D	D	B
71	**72**	**73**	**74**	**75**	**76**	**77**	**78**	**79**	**80**
B	C	C	C	A	A	A	B	B	A
81	**82**	**83**	**84**	**85**	**86**	**87**	**88**	**89**	**90**
A	B	D	B	C	C	D	C	B	D
91	**92**	**93**	**94**	**95**	**96**	**97**	**98**	**99**	**100**
A	B	A	A	A	B	B	A	A	C
101	**102**	**103**	**104**	**105**	**106**	**107**	**108**	**109**	**110**
C	B	A	D	D	D	A	C	D	C

111	112	113	114	115	116	117	118	119	120
B	B	B	A	D	C	C	D	B	D
121	122	123	124	125	126	127	128	129	130
C	A	A	B	A	D	C	D	B	D
131	132	133	134	135	136	137	138	139	140
B	B	D	A	B	D	B	D	D	C
141	142	143	144	145	146	147	148	149	150
D	C	D	D	D	B	A	D	C	C
151	152	153	154	155	156	157	158	159	160
A	B	A	A	A	D	C	B	D	A
161	162	163	164	165	166	167	168	169	170
B	B	C	B	D	D	C	B	B	B
171	172	173	174	175	176	177	178	179	180
D	C	D	D	C	B	C	A	D	A
181	182	183	184	185	186	187	188	189	190
B	B	C	A	A	A	B	D	D	A
191	192	193	194	195	196	197	198	199	200
B	C	A	A	D	A	B	D	D	A
201	202	203	204	205	206	207	208	209	210
B	B	B	B	A	A	A	A	A	A
211	212	213	214	215	216	217	218	219	220
B	A	A	A	D	C	D	A	B	B
221	222	223	224	225	226	227	228	229	230
D	C	A	D	A	A	D	D	B	B
231	232	233	234	235	236	237	238	239	240
D	B	D	A	D	D	C	B	B	C
241	242	243	244	245	246	247	248	249	250
D	B	D	C	A	D	D	A	D	A
251	252	253	254	255	256	257	258	259	260
C	D	A	B	C	A	C	C	A	B
261	262	263	264	265	266	267	268	269	270
B	C	C	A	A	C	C	A	C	A
271	272	273	274	275	276	277	278	279	280
B	C	A	B	A	C	B	B	A	B
281	282	283	284	285	286	287	288	289	290
D	A	A	A	B	A	C	B	D	C
291	292	293	294	295	296	297	298	299	300
D	C	B	D	A	A	A	C	A	B
301	302	303	304	305	306	307	308	309	310
C	B	C	C	B	A	C	D	D	B
311	312	313	314	315	316	317	318	319	320
A	C	B	A	B	C	B	A	A	C
321	322	323	324	325	326	327	328	329	330
D	D	A	D	A	A	C	D	B	B
331	332	333	334	335	336	337	338	339	340
C	D	B	A	B	C	D	B	C	D

❑❑❑

CURRENT AFFAIRS

1. Who is the first Indian to receive an honorary Knighthood under King Charles III?
A. Ratan Tata B. Sachin Tendulkar
C. Sunil Bharti Mittal D. Narendra Modi

2. What is the name of India's first human spaceflight program?
A. Chandrayaan B. Aditya-1
C. Gaganyaan D. LVM3

3. What is the literal meaning of the word "Gaganyaan" in Sanskrit?
A. Lunar Chariot B. Celestial Vehicle
C. Solar Probe D. Orbital Station

4. Who among the following have been awarded the Bharat Ratna in 2024?
(*i*) Karpoori Thakur (*ii*) M.S. Swaminathan
(*iii*) Ch. Charan Singh (*iv*) P.V. Narasimha Rao
(*v*) L.K. Advani
A. (*i*), (*ii*) & (*iii*)
B. (*iii*), (*iv*) & (*v*)
C. (*ii*), (*iv*) & (*v*)
D. (*i*), (*ii*), (*iii*), (*iv*) & (*v*)

5. Who has been appointed as the new Lokpal of India?
A. Justice Lingappa Narayana Swamy
B. Justice AM Khanwilkar
C. President Droupadi Murmu
D. Sushil Chandra

6. When will the provisions of Bharatiya Nagarik Suraksha Sanhita, 2023, Bharatiya Nyaya Sanhita, 2023, and Bharatiya Sakshya Adhiniyam, 2023 come into force?
A. July 1, 2023 B. July 1, 2024
C. January 1, 2023 D. December 31, 2023

7. What is the name of India's first septic tank cleaning robot?
A. Swachhata Atom B. Homosep Atom
C. RoboCleaner 1.0 D. Sanitech Pro

8. Bharat Tex 2024 event, inaugurated by PM Modi in Feb 2024 in New Delhi is related to which sector:
A. Technology B. Agriculture
C. Textiles D. Tourism

9. What is the name of the country's longest signature stayed bridge, recently inaugurated by Prime Minister Narendra Modi in Gujarat?
A. Bharati Setu B. Sudarshan Setu
C. Dwarka Bridge D. Vishwa Setu

10. What is the name of the first private spacecraft to land on the Moon?
A. Apollo 11 B. Odyssey
C. Odysseus D. Artemis

11. Who emerged as the most popular global leader with a 78% approval rating by Morning Consult 2024?
A. President of Mexico
B. Prime Minister Narendra Modi
C. President of Argentina
D. US President Joe Biden

12. What is the theme of the 2024 edition of the Raisina Dialogue?
A. "Tech Frontiers: Regulations & Realities"
B. "Peace with the Planet: Invest & Innovate"
C. "Chaturanga: Conflict, Contest, Cooperate, Create"
D. "Decolonising Multilateralism: Institutions & Inclusion"

13. Who won the women's Badminton Asia Team Championships title 2024?
A. India B. Thailand
C. China D. Indonesia

14. Who has been honored with the 58th Jnanpith Award?
A. Gulzar
B. Jagadguru Rambhadracharya
C. Both A and B
D. None of the above

15. Who has been confirmed as the captain of the Indian cricket team for the 2024 T20 World Cup?
A. Virat Kohli B. Rohit Sharma
C. Ajinkya Rahane D. KL Rahul

16. Where is the 2024 T20 World Cup scheduled to be held?
A. India and Sri Lanka
B. Australia and New Zealand
C. Caribbean and the USA
D. South Africa and Zimbabwe

17. What is the significance of the BAPS Mandir in Abu Dhabi?
A. It is the largest Hindu temple in the Middle East.
B. It is the first traditional Hindu stone temple in the Middle East.
C. It is a modern architectural marvel.
D. It is dedicated to promoting unity in the Indian community.

18. Who emerged victorious in the Tennis Chennai Open ATP Challenger finale held on February 11, 2024?
A. Prajnesh Gunneswaran
B. Roger Federer
C. Luca Nardi
D. Sumit Nagal

19. Which country won the 2024 Under-19 Men's ODI Cricket World Cup?
A. India B. Australia
C. South Africa D. England

20. What is the primary objective of the Aadi Mahotsav 2024?
A. To promote urban art and culture
B. To showcase the rich diversity of India's tribal heritage
C. To celebrate international cuisines
D. To focus on modern technological advancements

21. Which Indian Prime Minister, also having served as Deputy Prime Minister, Chief Minister of Uttar Pradesh, and Union Minister for Home Affairs and Finance?
A. P.V. Narasimha Rao
B. Dr. M.S. Swaminathan
C. Chaudhary Charan Singh
D. Narendra Modi

22. Who won the SAFF U-19 Women's Championship in 2024?
A. Bangladesh B. Nepal
C. Bhutan D. India

23. Who introduced the Finance Bill, 2024, in the Lok Sabha?
A. Prime Minister Narendra Modi
B. Home Minister Amit Shah
C. Finance Minister Nirmala Sitharaman
D. Minister of State for Finance Pankaj Chaudhary

24. Who is the current Prime Minister of Guyana visiting India in February 2024?
A. Justin Trudeau B. Droupadi Murmu
C. Mark Phillips D. Boris Johnson

25. What is the name of the brand launched by government to provide subsidized rice directly to consumers in February 2024?
A. Bharat Grains B. Bharat Rice
C. Bharat Essentials D. Bharat Food

26. With which award will LK Advani be conferred in February 2024?
A. Padma Bhushan B. Bharat Ratna
C. Padma Vibhushan D. Param Vir Chakra

27. What is the name of the woman robot astronaut that will fly into space ahead of ISRO's "Gaganyaan" mission?
A. Vyomnaut B. Gaganyaatri
C. Vyommitra D. Astronautila

28. What is the theme of World Wetlands Day 2024?
A. Wetlands and Climate Change
B. Wetlands and Sustainable Use
C. Wetlands and Human Wellbeing
D. Wetlands and Economic Development

29. What is the fiscal deficit target set in the interim budget for FY 2024-25?
A. 3.5% of GDP B. 4.5% of GDP
C. 5.1% of GDP D. 6.0% of GDP

30. What is the status of income tax slabs or rates in the interim budget 2024-2025?
A. Increased rates B. Decreased rates
C. No changes D. Abolished

31. Which two countries participated in the joint military exercise SADA TANSEEQ in January 2024 in Rajasthan?
A. India and China
B. India and Pakistan
C. India and Saudi Arabia
D. India and Nepal

32. Which pair won the Australian Open Men's Doubles tennis championship in 2024?
A. Rohan Bopanna and Simone Bolelli
B. Matt Ebden and Andrea Vavassori
C. Rohan Bopanna and Matt Ebden
D. Simone Bolelli and Andrea Vavassori

33. Who emerged victorious in the men's singles final of the Australian Open tennis championship 2024?
A. Daniil Medvedev B. Novak Djokovic
C. Jannik Sinner D. Rafael Nadal

34. What is the name of the Indian cricketer who won the ICC ODI Player of the Year award in 2023?
A. Rohit Sharma B. Virat Kohli
C. Shikhar Dhawan D. Hardik Pandya

35. Who was the Chief Guest at the Republic Day parade in 2024?
A. Narendra Modi
B. Droupadi Murmu
C. Emmanuel Macron
D. Virat Kohli

36. What were the twin themes of the Republic Day parade in 2024?
A. Unity in Diversity and Military Strength
B. Viksit Bharat and Bharat – Loktantra ki Matruka
C. Cultural Heritage and Economic Progress
D. Nari Shakti and Global Diplomacy

37. Which countries participated in Exercise Desert Knight alongside the Indian Air Force in January 2024?
A. France and USA B. France and UAE
C. USA and UAE D. France and China

38. Who led the Pran Pratishtha ceremony of Ramlalla in Ayodhya on January 22, 2024?
A. UP Governor Anandiben Patel
B. CM Yogi Adityanath
C. Prime Minister Narendra Modi
D. RSS Chief Mohan Bhagwat

39. Who is the President of the 78th Session of the United Nations General Assembly?
A. Dennis Francis B. Narendra Modi
C. Antonio Guterres D. Joe Biden

40. Who won the gold medal at the Asian Marathon Championships 2024?
A. Huang Yongzheng B. Tiapkin Ilya
C. Man Singh D. Ashvini Jadhav

41. Who lost in the finals of the men's doubles at the India Open Badminton 2024?
A. Satwiksairaj Rankireddy and Chirag Shetty
B. Seo Seung-jae and Kang Min-hyuk
C. Shi Yu Qi and Lee Cheuk Yiu
D. Tai Tzu Ying and Chen Yu Fei

42. Which state is hosting the Khelo India Youth Games 2024?
A. Punjab B. Tamil Nadu
C. Karnataka D. Maharashtra

43. Where will 'Bharat Parv 2024' take place as part of the Republic Day celebrations?
A. India Gate, Delhi
B. Red Fort, Delhi
C. Rajpath, Delhi
D. Feroz Shah Kotla, Delhi

44. Where did the Wings India 2024 event hold in January 2024?
A. Mumbai Airport
B. Begumpet Airport, Hyderabad
C. Palam Airport, New Delhi
D. Safdarjung Airport, New Delhi

45. Who won The Best FIFA Men's Player award at the FIFA Football Awards ceremony in January 2024?
A. Kylian Mbappe B. Erling Haaland
C. Lionel Messi D. Aitana Bonmati

46. Which female football player received the Best FIFA Women's Player Award at the Award ceremony in January 2024?
A. Mary Earps B. Aitana Bonmati
C. Sarina Wiegman D. Kylian Mbappe

47. When does the Pran Pratishtha program for Ram Lala Virajman at Shri Ram Janmabhoomi complex begin?
A. January 21, 2024 B. January 16, 2024
C. January 22, 2024 D. January 15, 2024

48. What is the theme of the 54th annual meeting of the World Economic Forum?
A. Global Challenges
B. Rebuilding Trust
C. Technological Advancements
D. Economic Prosperity

49. Who succeeded Queen Margrethe II as the new King of Denmark on January 14, 2024?
A. Crown Prince Christian
B. Prince Frederik X,
C. King Christian IX
D. Prince Mette Frederiksen

50. Which terrorist group captured a United Nations helicopter in Somalia in January 2024?
A. Taliban B. Al-Shabab
C. ISIS D. Boko Haram

51. Who participated as the Chief Guest in the Vibrant Gujarat Global Summit 2024?
A. President of the Nepal
B. President of the United States
C. Prime Minister of Israel
D. President of the United Arab Emirates

52. Where is the KG-DWN-98/2 block located, where the ONGC starts oil production from Cluster-2 project in January 2024?
A. Arabian Sea B. Bay of Bengal
C. Indian Ocean D. Andaman Sea

53. What was the cause of the nosedive in India-Maldives relations in December 2023?
A. Trade disputes
B. Disparaging remarks about PM Modi's visit to Lakshadweep
C. Military conflicts
D. Economic sanctions

54. Which institute has initiated the country's first smart lab in its OPD block?
A. PGI Chandigarh B. AIIMS New Delhi
C. Apollo Hospitals D. Fortis Healthcare

55. When will the 2024 T20 Men's Cricket World Cup be held in the West Indies and the United States?
A. June 1 to June 15, 2024
B. June 1 to June 29, 2024
C. July 1 to July 15, 2024
D. July 1 to July 29, 2024

56. What is Jain Deemed to be University in Bengaluru awarded for in the Rashtriya Khel Protsahan Puruskar 2023?
A. Encouragement to Sports through CSR
B. Nurturing budding and young talent
C. Promotion of sports at the State level
D. Corporate Social Responsibility initiatives

57. Where is the 16th edition of the India International Jewellery Trade Show taking place?
A. Chennai B. Pune
C. Mumbai D. New Delhi

58. Who received the M.S. Swaminathan Award in 2024?
A. Prof. B.R. Kamboj
B. Thawar Chand Gehlot
C. Chaudhary Charan Singh
D. Rajmata Vijayaraje Scindia

59. What is the name of the Joint Military Exercise conducted between India and UAE in Rajasthan in January 2024?
A. Desert Storm 2024
B. Desert Thunder 2024
C. Desert Cyclone 2024
D. Desert Mirage 2024

60. Who are the new members set to join the Brics group on January 1, 2024?
A. Argentina, Brazil, South Africa
B. Egypt, Ethiopia, Iran, Saudi Arabia, and the United Arab Emirates
C. Mexico, Australia, Turkey
D. Canada, Japan, Germany

61. Which Indian player has been named as FIH Players of the Year 2023?
A. Hardik Singh B. Suraj Karkera
C. SP Raveendran D. Uttam Singh

62. Which state hosted the National Conference on Adventure Tourism in December 2023?
A. Rajasthan B. Maharashtra
C. Madhya Pradesh D. Gujarat

63. Which nation hosted the Indian Ocean Naval Symposium (IONS) Conclave of Chiefs in December 2023?
A. India B. Sri Lanka
C. Myanmar D. Thailand

64. Who has been selected to be conferred with the Major Dhyan Chand Khel Ratna award 2023?
A. Satwiksairaj Rankireddy
B. Chirag Shetty
C. Neeraj Chopra
D. Both (A) & (B)

65. Who was announced as the winner of Sahitya Akademi Award 2023 in Hindi language?
A. Vijay Verma B. Sanjeev
C. Rajasekaran D. Neelam Saran Gour

66. Which nation's space agency has been awarded the Leif Erikson Lunar Prize 2023?
A. USA B. Russia
C. India D. Japan

67. Which state has recently launched the SAANS campaign 2023-24?
A. Assam B. Gujarat
C. Manipur D. Meghalaya

68. UN has declared which year as the 'Year of Camelids'?
A. 2023 B. 2024
C. 2025 D. 2026

69. Which of the following was honoured with Bhutan's National Order of Merit recently?
A. Poonam Khetrapal B. Shambu Prasad Acharya
C. Ruchira Kamboj D. Vikram Doraiswami

70. Which of the following book is the winner of Gaja Capital Business Book Prize 2023?
A. Against All Odds B. Winning Middle India
C. Courting India D. Both (A) & (B)

71. Which team won the U-19 Asia Cup 2023?
A. Sri Lanka B. India
C. Bangladesh D. Nepal

72. Which state has been ranked Second in the latest Agri-marketing reforms Index 2023?
A. Andhra Pradesh B. Tamil Nadu
C. Uttar Pradesh D. Gujarat

73. Which nation was the largest recipient of remittances in 2023?
A. USA B. India
C. China D. Canada

74. Which team won the Vijay Hazare Trophy 2023-24?
A. Tamil Nadu B. Kerala
C. Haryana D. Jharkhand

75. Who won the title of Miss India USA 2023?
A. Rijul Maini B. Nandini Gupta
C. Sheynnis Palacios D. Sini Shetty

76. Prime Minister Narendra Modi inaugurated Diamond Bourse building in which state?
A. Gujarat B. Rajasthan
C. West Bengal D. Odisha

77. Which team won the inaugural edition of Khelo India Para Games in December 2023?
A. Madhya Pradesh B. Rajasthan
C. Maharashtra D. Haryana

78. Which of the following became the first Asian men to be inducted in the International Tennis Hall of Fame?
A. Vijay Amritraj B. Leander Paes
C. Both (A) & (B) D. Rohan Bopanna

79. Which Indian wrestler was named as UWW's 'Rising Star of the Year 2023'?
A. Priya Malik B. Antim Panghal
C. Deepak Punia D. Sakshi Mallik

80. Which of the following is the Oxford's word of the year 2023?
A. AI B. Authentic
C. Hallucinate D. Rizz

81. Which of the following was named as the ICC Women's Player of the month for November 2023?
A. Ashley Gardner B. Nahida Akhtar
C. Smriti Mandhana D. Harmanpreet Kaur

82. As per Southeast Asia Opium Survey 2023, which nation became the largest producer of Opium?
A. Afghanistan B. Laos
C. Indonesia D. Myanmar

83. Which nation's centre was recently awarded with the International Gender Equality Prize 2023?
A. Finland B. Afghanistan
C. Pakistan D. Iran

84. India's largest state-of-the-art Sports Science Centre was inaugurated in which state?
A. Telangana B. West Bengal
C. Tamil Nadu D. Odisha

85. Who was named as 'World Athlete of the Year' 2023?
A. Faith Kipyegon B. Noah Lyles
C. Armand Duplantis D. All of these

86. How many grandmasters are there in India as of December 2023?
A. 80 B. 81
C. 82 D. 84

87. How many medals did India win at the IBA Junior World Boxing Championship 2023?
A. 10 medals B. 16 medals
C. 17 medals D. 19 medals

88. Who was chosen as CEO of The Year 2023 by TIME's magazine?
A. Christiano Ronaldo B. Sam Altman
C. Mary Kom D. Sheetal devi

89. Which nation launched world's first portable hospital in December 2023?
A. China B. Russia
C. India D. USA

90. What was the theme of World Soil Day 2023?
A. Soil and Water: a source of life
B. Soils: Where food begins
C. Halt soil salinization, enhance soil production
D. Keep soil alive, protect soil biodiversity

91. Which of the following topped the Forbes list of 'World's 100 Most Powerful Women' of 2023?
A. Nirmala Sitharaman
B. Christine Lagarde
C. Ursula Von Der Leyen
D. Kamala Harris

92. Who won the 35th Jimmy George Foundation award?
A. Avinash Sable B. Chirag Shetty
C. Murali Sreeshankar D. Tejaswin Shankar

93. Which city hosted the 1st Asian Ranger Forum in December 2023?
A. Guwahati B. Pune
C. Delhi D. Ranchi

94. Which union ministry has recently released the AI based 'Gajraj system'?
A. Ministry of Education
B. Ministry of Home Affairs
C. Ministry of Environment
D. Ministry of Railways

95. As per NSO, what was the GDP growth rate for second quarter (Q2) for FY 2023-24?
A. 7.4% B. 7.2%
C. 6.4% D. 7.6%

96. Who has been appointed as the chairman of World Radio Communication Conference 2023?
A. Sultan Al Jaber B. Mohammad Al Ramsi
C. Zurab Pololikashvili D. Gilbert Houngbo

97. Which city is the host of the 1st Asian Ranger Forum in December 2023?
A. Shillong B. Imphal
C. Guwahati D. Pune

98. Which city is the host of Men's Volleyball Club World Championship 2023?
A. Bengaluru B. Hyderabad
C. Kolkata D. Imphal

99. How many Indians are there in the Forbes list of 'World's 100 Most Powerful Women' of 2023?
A. 1 B. 2
C. 3 D. 4

100. IBA Junior World Boxing Championship 2023 was held in which country?
A. Armenia B. Argentina
C. New Zealand D. South Korea

101. Which team won the ICC Cricket World Cup in 2023?
A. Australia B. West Indies
C. England D. India

102. Who was the highest run scorer in ICC Cricket World Cup 2023?
A. Virat Kohli B. Quinton de Kock
C. Rohit Sharma D. Rachin Ravindra

103. Who took the highest wickets in the ICC Cricket World Cup 2023?
A. Adam Zampa B. Shaheen Afridi
C. Mohammed Shami D. Dilshan Madushanka

104. Which cricketer holds the record for the most sixes in the ICC Cricket World Cup 2023?
A. David Warner B. Rohit Sharma
C. Glenn Maxwell D. Shreyas Iyer

105. Which two teams played in the ICC Cricket World Cup Finale of 2023?
A. India and South Africa
B. India and Pakistan
C. India and Australia
D. South Africa and Australia

06. Which stadium served as the primary venue for the ICC Cricket World Cup Finale 2023?
A. Lord's Cricket Ground
B. Melbourne Cricket Ground
C. Eden Gardens
D. Narendra Modi Stadium

107. Which player among the following earned the title of the "Player of the Tournament" in the ICC Cricket World Cup 2023?
A. Mohammed Shami B. Quinton de Kock
C. Virat Kohli D. Glenn Maxwell

108. What is the total number of medals that India won at the Asian Para Games 2023 in Hangzhou, China?
A. 82 B. 111
C. 303 D. 15

109. Indian Military is conducting the joint military exercise 'Exercise KAZIND-2023' with which country?
A. China B. Kazakhstan
C. Russia D. United States

110. What is the primary purpose of the Asian Women's Hockey Champion's Trophy 2023 that began on October 17, 2023 in Ranchi?
A. To determine the world champion in women's hockey
B. To qualify teams for the upcoming Paris Olympics
C. To promote women's hockey in Asia
D. To raise funds for hockey development

111. Who won the women's singles title at the Abu Dhabi Masters 2023 Badminton tournament on October 24, 2023?
A. Samiya Imad Farooqui
B. Unnati Hooda
C. Saina Nehwal
D. P.V. Sindhu

112. Which film has been selected as the Opening Feature Film of the 54th International Film Festival of India (IFFI) 2023?
A. "Ardhangini" (Bengali)
B. "Aattam" (Malayalam)
C. "Dhai Aakhar" (Hindi)
D. "Kantara" (Kannada)

113. Who received the Dadasaheb Phalke Lifetime Achievement Award at the 69th National Film Awards?
A. R Madhavan B. Waheeda Rehman
C. Vivek Agnihotri D. Pankaj Tripathi

114. Which film was awarded the Best Feature Film for the year 2021 at the 69th National Film Awards?
A. Ek Tha Gaon
B. Rocketry : The Nambi Effect
C. Iravin Nizhal
D. Komuram Bheemudo

115. Which director's film, "Ek Tha Gaon," received the Best Non-Feature Film award?
A. R. Madhavan B. Srishti Lakhera
C. Vivek Agnihotri D. Allu Arjun

116. Which edition of the ASEAN Summit was held in 2023 and in which city?
A. 43rd, Singapore B. 20th, Bangkok
C. 43rd, Jakarta D. 18th, Manila

117. For the assessment year [AY] 2023-24, CBDT has reduced the time taken to process income tax returns to how many days?
A. 41 days B. 52 days
C. 18 days D. 10 days

118. ISRO used which launch vehicle to successfully launch its Solar mission Aditya L1 in September 2023?
A. PSLV C-55 B. PSLV C-54
C. PSLV C-56 D. PSLV C-57

119. Which team has won the 2023 Durand Cup?
A. Kerala Blasters
B. Mohun Bagan Super Giant
C. Indian Army
D. East Bengal

120. Which player has won the 2023 Tata Steel Chess India Women's Rapid Tournament?
A. Divya Deshmukh B. Dronavalli Harika
C. Koneru Humpy D. Vantika Agrawal

121. Which of the following city the G20 summit held in 2023?
A. Brisbane (Australia) B. Osaka (Japan)
C. Antalya (Turkey) D. Delhi (India)

122. What was the inspiration for G20 2023 logo?
A. India's national flag B. Russia's national flag
C. France's national flag D. None of the above

123. What was the theme of the G20 summit 2023 held in India?
A. Shaping an Interconnected World
B. Fighting poverty with rigidity
C. "One Earth-One Family-One Future"
D. Making the world together

124. In which city, India's first 500 Kilo-volt-amperes (kVA) Underground Power Transformer Station was inaugurated in September 2023?
A. Kadapa, Andhra Pradesh
B. Jodhpur, Rajasthan
C. Chennai, Tamil Nadu
D. Bengaluru, Karnataka

125. Which country's Navy, along with Indian Navy (IN) has recently (in September, 2023) conducted a Passage Exercise (PASSEX)?
A. Indonesia B. Sri Lanka
C. Bangladesh D. France

126. When was the United Nations (UN) International Day of Clean Air for Blue Skies 2023 observed across the globe with the theme of 'Together for Clean Air'?
A. 3rd September 2023 B. 4th September 2023
C. 5th September 2023 D. 7th September 2023

127. In which city India's 1st Solar City was inaugurated in September 2023?
A. Chandrapur, Maharashtra
B. Tuni, Andhra Pradesh
C. Churu, Rajasthan
D. Sanchi, Madhya Pradesh

128. Which Railway Station has recently (in September, 2023) certified as "Green Railway Station" with the highest rating of Platinum by IGBC (Indian Green Building Council)-Confederation of Indian Industry (CII)?
A. Mumbai Central Railway Station
B. Vijayawada Railway Station
C. Guwahati Railway Station
D. Chandigarh Railway Station

129. In which state/UT, President Droupadi Murmu unveiled a 12-foot-high statue of the Father of the Nation, 'Mahatma Gandhi' and inaugurated a 'Gandhi Vatika'?
A. Uttar Pradesh B. Maharashtra
C. Gujarat D. Delhi

130. In September 2023, the Indian Men's Hockey Team won the 1st Edition of Men's Hockey Asia Cup Salalah 2023 by defeating (country) in the final held in Salalah, Oman.
A. Bangladesh B. Oman
C. Malaysia D. Pakistan

131. Heath Hilton Streak, Former captain of the _____ (country) Cricket team, passed away in September 2023.
A. Australia B. New Zealand
C. Zimbabwe D. England

132. In August 2023, Neeraj Chopra finished _____ in the men's javelin throw event with _____ metres at the Zurich Diamond League 2023 held in Zurich, Switzerland.
A. 2nd; 84.92 B. 1st; 86.23
C. 2nd; 85.71 D. 1st; 84.92

133. Who has been recently (in August, 2023) appointed as the 1st Women Chairperson & Chief Executive Officer (CEO) of Railway Board?
A. Jaya Varma Sinha B. Madhabi Puri Buch
C. Rekha Sharma D. Mamta Kumari

134. In August 2023, the Indian Women's Hockey Team won the inaugural Women's Hockey Asia Cup by defeating _____ (country) held in Salalah, Oman.
A. Bangladesh B. Indonesia
C. Thailand D. Malaysia

135. The _____ National Sports Day (Rashtriya Khel Divas) 2023 was observed across India on 29th August 2023.
A. 16th B. 12th
C. 14th D. 15th

136. In August 2023, Emmerson Mnangagwa was re-elected as the President of _____ (country) for the second term of 5 years.
A. Rwanda B. Zimbabwe
C. Tanzania D. Ghana

137. In August 2023, Jayanta Mahapatra, who was the first recipient of Sahitya Akademi award for _____ (language) poetry in 1981, passed away.
A. Gujarati B. Malayalam
C. Kannada D. English

138. In which state/UT India's first Artificial Intelligence (AI) school was inaugurated in August 2023?
A. Kerala B. Andhra Pradesh
C. Karnataka D. Delhi

139. What was the theme of World Water Week 2023 that was observed across the globe on 20th to 24th August 2023?
A. Water and Climate Change
B. Building Resilience Faster
C. Seeds of Change: Innovative Solutions for a Water-Wise World
D. Seeing the Unseen: The Value of Water

140. In August 2023, Vinai Kumar Saxena, Delhi Lieutenant Governor (LG) launched Blockchain Technology in the ICJS for electronic-forensic application (eforensic app). What does 'S' stand for in ICJS?
A. Software B. System
C. Storage D. Secondary

141. In August 2023, _____ (state) became the 1st state in India to provide free In Vitro Fertilisation (IVF) therapy.
A. Tamil Nadu
B. Telangana
C. Karnataka
D. Goa

142. In August 2023, Ali Mahaman Lamine Zeine was appointed as the transitional Prime Minister (PM) of _____ (country).
A. Niger B. Guinea
C. Senegal D. Ghana

143. Which of the following cities is set to establish India's first Integrated Theatre Commands (ITC)-South Western Command & Central Command in August 2023?
A. Patna, Bihar
B. Jaipur, Rajasthan
C. Lucknow, Uttar Pradesh
D. Both (B) & (C)

144. Which city topped the 'Swachh Vayu Sarvekshan 2023 Clean Air Survey'?
A. Indore B. Mysore
C. Kochi D. Panjim

145. Which country's central bank Governors topped the 'Global Finance Central Banker Report Cards 2023'?
A. India B. Sri Lanka
C. USA D. UK

146. What is the estimated tiger population in India, as per the report released by the Minister of State for Environment, Forest and Climate Change on Global Tiger Day on 29 July, 2023?
A. 2,500 B. 3,167
C. 3,682 D. 3,925

147. What is the purpose of the 'Meri Mati Mera Desh' campaign ahead of Independence Day 2023?
A. To celebrate Independence Day
B. To honour the martyred men and women
C. To organize Amrit Mahotsav celebrations
D. To build the National War Memorial

148. Which team won the 100th Anniversary Spanish Hockey Federation—International Tournament in July, 2023?
A. England B. Spain
C. India D. Germany

149. What is the primary payload of ISRO's PSLV-C56 rocket launched from Sriharikota on 30 June, 2023?
A. DS-SAR satellite
B. VELOX-AM microsatellite
C. ARCADE microsatellite
D. ST Engineering payload

150. Nisha Biswal, an Indian-American policy expert, has been confirmed to serve as the Deputy Chief Executive Officer (CEO) of which US finance agency?
A. World Bank
B. United States International Development Finance Corporation
C. International Monetary Fund (IMF)
D. Federal Reserve System

151. The main objective of Chandrayaan-3 is to:
A. Establish a human colony on the moon
B. Study the surface and mineralogy of the Moon
C. Conduct a comprehensive study of Mars' atmosphere
D. None of these

152. Who is the director of the Chandrayaan-3 mission?
A. K. Sivan B. M. Vanitha
C. J.J. Robinson D. Ritu Karidhal

153. The Chandrayaan-3 mission's rover known is:
A. Vikram B. Pragyaan
C. Dhruv D. Aditya

154. What is the estimated tiger population in India, as per the report released by the Minister of State for Environment, Forest and Climate Change on Global Tiger Day on 29 July 2023?
A. 2,500 B. 3,167
C. 3,682 D. 3,925

155. What is the purpose of the 'Meri Mati Mera Desh' campaign ahead of Independence Day 2023?
A. To celebrate Independence Day
B. To honour the martyred men and women
C. To organize Amrit Mahotsav celebrations
D. To build the National War Memorial

156. Which team won the 100th Anniversary Spanish Hockey Federation – International Tournament in July 2023?
A. England B. Spain
C. India D. Germany

157. What is the primary payload of ISRO's PSLV-C56 rocket launched from Sriharikota on 30 June 2023?
A. DS-SAR satellite
B. VELOX-AM microsatellite
C. ARCADE microsatellite
D. ST Engineering payload

158. What is the objective of the Khelo India campaign?
A. To enhance sports infrastructure only
B. To nurture and support talented athletes only
C. To provide a platform for identifying talented players and enhance sports infrastructure
D. To provide platforms for different sports competitions

159. The PM SHRI Scheme focuses on nurturing students to become ________ .
A. Wealthy entrepreneurs
B. Engaged, productive, and contributing citizens
C. Government employees
D. Members of the armed forces

160. At the ISSF Junior Shooting World Championships 2023, which country finished in 2nd place on the medals tally?
A. South Korea B. India
C. United States D. China

161. Which organization celebrated its 85th Raising Day on 27th July 2023?
A. Indian Army
B. CRPF (Central Reserve Police Force)
C. BSF (Border Security Force)
D. IAF (Indian Air Force)

162. In which city is the Asian Youth and Junior Weightlifting Championships 2023 being held?
A. Greater Noida B. Mumbai
C. New Delhi D. Kolkata

163. According to the latest report by the International Monetary Fund (IMF), what is the projected Gross Domestic Product (GDP) growth rate for India in the current fiscal year (2023-2024)?
A. 5.9 per cent B. 6.1 per cent
C. 6.3 per cent D. 6.5 per cent

164. Which operation is celebrated as Kargil Vijay Diwas, observed on July 26 every year?
A. Operation Cactus B. Operation Meghdoot
C. Operation Vijay D. Operation Pawan

165. What is the approved interest rate on deposits under the Employees Provident Fund scheme for the financial year 2022-23?
A. 8.10 per cent B. 8.15 per cent
C. 8.20 per cent D. 8.05 per cent

166. What is the recent change made by Twitter in its branding?
A. Changed its name to X Corp.
B. Replaced its blue bird logo with an X.
C. Introduced a new social media platform.
D. Acquired a competitor company.

167. Where will the event "Semicon India 2023" take place from 28th to 30th July 2023?
A. New Delhi B. Bengaluru
C. Hyderabad D. Gandhinagar

168. Who received the National Geoscience Award 2022 for Lifetime Achievement?
A. Dr. Om Narain Bhargava
B. Dr. Amiya Kumar Samal
C. President Droupadi Murmu
D. Banaras Hindu University

169. Which centralized facility was inaugurated by Union Home Minister Amit Shah on July 22, 2023, to address security challenges for 66 civil airports under the CISF's security cover?
A. Central Security Monitoring Centre (CSMC)
B. Air Traffic Control Centre (ATCC)
C. Aviation Security Control Centre (ASCC)
D. Security Operations Command Centre (SOCC)

170. Who won the Korea Open 2023 Badminton men's doubles title in Yeosu?
A. Fajar Alfian and Muhammad Rian Ardianto
B. Liang Wei Keng and Wang Chang
C. Satwiksairaj Rankireddy and Chirag Shetty
D. None of the above

171. The Bhoomi Samman 2023 awards were presented to individuals and teams who excelled in which program?
A. Digital India Education Enhancement Program
B. Digital India Land Records Modernization Programme
C. Digital India Healthcare Access Initiative
D. Digital India Skill Development Scheme

172. Who is the President of the Asian Cricket Council (ACC)?
A. Jay Shah B. Sourav Ganguly
C. Ehsan Mani D. David Richardson

173. Which name has been given to the alliance formed by the opposition parties to contest the 2024 Lok Sabha election?
A. National Democratic Alliance (NDA)
B. Indian National Developmental Inclusive Alliance (INDIA)
C. Congress National Alliance (CNA)
D. Democratic Opposition Front (DOF)

174. Which state in India registered the highest decline in the number of poor according to the National Multidimensional Poverty Index released by NITI Aayog in July 2023?
A. Bihar B. Madhya Pradesh
C. Uttar Pradesh D. Odisha

175. Who did Carlos Alcaraz defeat to win the Men's title at the Wimbledon championship 2023?
A. Roger Federer B. Rafael Nadal
C. Novak Djokovic D. Andy Murray

176. Parul Chaudhary, won a gold medal in which event at the Asian Athletics Championships 2023?
A. Women's 3000 m steeplechase
B. Women's 100 m sprint
C. Women's long jump
D. Women's shot put

177. During his visit to France in July 2023, Prime Minister Narendra Modi announced an agreement to use which flagship instant payment system in France?
A. NEFT (National Electronic Funds Transfer)
B. RTGS (Real Time Gross Settlement)
C. UPI (Unified Payments Interface)
D. IMPS (Immediate Payment Service)

178. Which was the launch site for the LVM3-M4 rocket that carried Chandrayaan-3 to the moon on July 14, 2023?
A. Satish Dhawan Space Centre, Sriharikota
B. Thumba Equatorial Rocket Launching Station
C. Abdul Kalam Island
D. Indian Space Research Organisation, Bengaluru

179. Which rank did the Indian Team secure in the 64th International Mathematical Olympiad (IMO) 2023 out of 112 participating countries?
A. 1st B. 5th
C. 9th D. 12th

180. Which ship, known as India's first indigenously built Guided Missile Destroyer, participated in the seventh edition of the Japan-India Maritime Exercise (JIMEX 23)?
A. INS Delhi B. INS Kamorta
C. INS Shakti D. INS Vikrant

181. Who has been selected as the recipient of the prestigious Lokmanya Tilak Award for 2023?
A. Rajnath Singh B. Dr. Dipak Tilak
C. Amit Shah D. Narendra Modi

182. What is the purpose of the NCC Integrated Software launched in July 2023?
A. To provide debit card facilities to NCC cadets
B. To digitalize the entire process from enrollment to alumni registration
C. To establish an all-India database of Defense Ministry personnel
D. To promote physical fitness among NCC cadets

183. Which state has achieved 100% Open Defecation Free (ODF) plus status?
A. Assam B. Sikkim
C. Manipur D. Meghalaya

184. What is the name of the launch vehicle for Chandrayaan 3?
A. GSLV Mark II B. PSLV-C50
C. GSLV Mark III D. ISRO-XL

185. Which day was recorded as the World's hottest day according to data from the U.S. National Centers for Environmental Prediction?
A. 5 August 2016 B. 3 July 2023
C. 21 August 2022 D. 22 June 2019

186. Which country will host the next meeting of the SCO Council of Heads of State in 2024?
A. China B. Russia
C. India D. Kazakhstan

187. Which Team won the SAFF Championship 2023?
A. Kuwait B. India
C. Lebanon D. Pakistan

188. Where is India's first indigenously developed 700 MW nuclear power reactor, KAPP-3, located?
A. Rawatbhata, Rajasthan
B. Kakrapar, Gujarat
C. Chutka, Madhya Pradesh
D. Gorakhpur, Haryana

189. Who won the Lausanne Diamond League 2023 title in javelin throw?
A. Neeraj Chopra B. Julian Webber
C. Jakub Vadlech D. Shivpal Singh

190. Who won the gold medal in the Asian Mixed Doubles Squash Tournament in June 2023?
A. Dipika Pallikal and Ramit Tandon
B. Harinder Pal Sandhu and Sunayna Kuruvilla
C. Sunayna Kuruvilla and Ramit Tandon
D. Dipika Pallikal and Harinder Pal Sandhu

191. Who has been appointed as the Director of the United Nations Office for Outer Space Affairs (UNOOSA) in Vienna?
A. Antonio Guterres B. Simonetta Di Pippo
C. Aarti Holla-Maini D. None of the above

192. Where will the final match of the ICC Men's Cricket World Cup 2023 be played?
A. Chennai B. Mumbai
C. Kolkata D. Ahmedabad

193. Which city hosted the Special Olympics World Games 2023?
A. Berlin, Germany
B. Delhi, India
C. London, United Kingdom
D. Tokyo, Japan

194. Which Indian women's doubles pair won the World Table Tennis, (WTT) Contender tournament 2023 in Tunis?
A. Sutirtha Mukherjee and Ayhika Mukherjee
B. Sowjanya Bavisetti and Rutuja Bhosale
C. Riya Bhatia and Rutuja Bhosale
D. Sutirtha Mukherjee and Riya Bhatia

195. Diksha Dagar wins Czech Ladies Open 2023 Golf Title. She has overcome which unique challenge or condition?
A. Vision impairment B. Hearing impairment
C. Physical disability D. Language barrier

196. Which Egypt's highest state honor was conferred upon Prime Minister Narendra Modi by President Sisi during his visit to Egypt?
A. Order of the Nile B. Order of Merit
C. Order of Excellence D. Order of the Pharaoh

197. Who won the Bal Sahitya Puraskar 2023 in the Hindi language category?
A. Eknath Avhad B. Suryanath Singh
C. Vishakha Vishwanath D. Sudha Murthy

198. Which company is planning to invest in a chip assembly and testing facility in Gujarat in June 2023?
A. Intel B. Samsung
C. Micron D. TSMC

199. Which country will host the world's fastest motorbike race 'Moto GP' 2023?
A. England B. India
C. Nepal D. Australia

200. Which country blocked the proposal to designate Sajid Mir as a global terrorist at the United Nations on 20th June?
A. China B. United States
C. Pakistan D. India

201. Where was North India's first Skin Bank inaugurated on 20th June 2023?
A. Safdarjung Hospital, New Delhi
B. AIIMS, New Delhi
C. Rajiv Gandhi Hospital, New Delhi
D. Sir Ganga Ram Hospital, New Delhi

202. Who led the yoga session at the United Nations Headquarters in New York on 9th International Yoga Day?
A. Donald Trump B. Angela Merkel
C. Narendra Modi D. Justin Trudeau

203. On 20th June, Who has taken charge as the Chief Executive Officer (CEO) of the Unique Identification Authority of India (UIDAI)?
A. Amit Agarwal B. Subodh Kumar Singh
C. Rupinder Singh D. Akash Tripathi

204. Which Indian athlete has created a new Asian shotput record at the Inter-State Championships in Bhubaneswar, on 19th June 2023?
A. Vikas Gowda
B. Jugraj Singh
C. Tajinderpal Singh Toor
D. Mohd Yasser

205. Which Indian player became the first Indian to win a bronze medal at the Asian Fencing Championships 2023 in China?
A. Karan Singh B. Bhavani Devi
C. Taniksha Khatri D. None of the above

206. Who has been appointed as the chief of the country's external intelligence agency RAW in June 2023?
A. Satyendranath Tagore B. Rameshwar Nath Kao
C. Ravi Sinha D. Vikram Sood

207. Who was confirmed as the first Muslim woman to serve as a federal judge in June 2023?
A. Nusrat Jahan Choudhury
B. Fathima Beevi
C. Nadia Kahf
D. None of the above

208. Which country won the Intercontinental Cup 2023?
A. Lebanon B. Korea
C. India D. None of the above

209. Who has been selected as the recipient of the Gandhi Peace Prize for the year 2021?
A. Geeta Press B. Orient Press
C. Replika Press D. Thomson Press India

210. Which pair won the Indonesia Open 2023 men's doubles title in Badminton?
A. Aaron Chia and Soh Wooi Yik
B. Satwiksairaj Rankireddy and Chirag Shetty
C. Kento Momota and Lee Zii Jia
D. Viktor Axelsen and Anders Antonsen

211. What is the theme of Yoga Day in 2023?
A. Yoga for Swaasthe and Kalyaan
B. Yoga for Peace and Harmony
C. Yoga for Sustainable Development
D. Yoga for Vasudhaiva Kutumbakam

212. What is the title of the song created through the collaboration between Prime Minister Narendra Modi and Grammy Award-winning Indian-American singer Falu?
A. "Millets and Global Hunger"
B. "Harvesting Hope: The Millet Anthem"
C. "Abundance of Millets"
D. "Modi's Melody for Feeding the World"

213. Which state receive the first prize in the best state category in the fourth National Water Awards, 2022?
A. Madhya Pradesh B. Odisha
C. Telangana D. Bihar

214. When was the Pradhanmantri Sangrahalaya, showcasing the journey of all Prime Ministers, opened to the public?
A. 21st April 2022 B. 25th November 2018
C. 01st April 2020 D. 07th April 2019

215. How many gold medals did India win in the U-17 Asian Wrestling Championships 2023 in Bishkek, Kyrgyzstan?
A. One B. Two
C. Three D. Four

216. 'Kheer Bhawani Mela' is a festival celebrated in which Indian state/UT?
A. Kerala B. Ladakh
C. Chhattisgarh D. Jammu and Kashmir

217. Which fintech company has launched "Turbo UPI" in partnership with Axis Bank and the National Payments Council of India (NPCI)?
A. Paytm B. PhonePe
C. Google Pay D. Razorpay

218. Maharashtra government has named which Indian cricketer as 'Smile Ambassador' under the state medical education & drug department's 'Swachh Mukh Abhiyan'?
A. Saurav Ganguly B. Virat Kohli
C. Sachin Tendulkar D. Rohit Sharma

219. Which state government has recently launched Namo Shetkari Mahasanman Yojana?
A. Kerala B. Gujarat
C. Maharashtra D. Rajasthan

220. Which state government launched a new scheme, Mo Ghara (My Home) - a credit-linked housing scheme for rural poor in the state?
A. Assam B. Odisha
C. Chhattisgarh D. Madhya Pradesh

221. Which state government has launched the 'Artificial Intelligence for Youth' initiatives in the state?
A. Kerala B. Tamil Nadu
C. Odisha D. Madhya Pradesh

222. Jude Bellingham has been named Bundesliga Player of the Season for his incredible campaign in season 2022/23. He is associated with which sports?
A. Cricket B. Football
C. Hockey D. Badminton

223. Who has bagged the gold medal in the women's 100 m hurdles event in the T-Meeting 2023 athletics meet in Tilburg, Netherlands?
A. Hima Das B. Dutee Chand
C. Kavita Tungar D. Jyothi Yarraji

224. Rail company Alstom will manufacture 100 aluminum-bodied Vande Bharat trains with sleeper facilities, after bidding the lowest for the tender at a price of Rs 150.9 crores per train. Alstom is the company of which country?
A. France B. Germany
C. Sweden D. Switzerland

225. The Indian G20 Presidency is organizing the third Employment Working Group (EWG) meeting in which city?
A. Geneva B. Paris
C. Berlin D. London

226. Which insurance company has launched a term insurance plan for Type 2 diabetics?
A. SBI General Insurance
B. Bharti AXA General Insurance
C. Bajaj Allianz General Insurance
D. Cholamandalam MS General Insurance

227. Ahmednagar district will be named after warrior queen Ahilyabai Holkar. Ahmednagar is district of which state?
A. Madhya Pradesh B. Gujarat
C. Rajasthan D. Maharashtra

228. Which Card launched country's first mobile-based expense management card?
A. IndusInd Card B. Karbon Card
C. LIC Card D. Citibank Card

229. Which Group has signed an MoU with the Gujarat government to set up a first-ever lithium-ion cell manufacturing gigafactory in Gujarat?
A. Adani Group B. Mahindra Group
C. Aditya Birla Group D. Tata Group

230. Who has been appointed as the first woman Secretary General of the World Meteorological Organisation?
A. Soumya Swaminathan B. Kristalina Georgieva
C. Petteri Taalas D. Celeste Saulo

231. Which Country to host world's largest Conservation Conference in 2025?
A. UAE B. India
C. Bangladesh D. United States

232. Who has launched the Unified Registration Portal for 'GOBARdhan'?
A. Ashwini Vaishnaw
B. Amit Shah
C. Narendra Singh Tomar
D. Gajendra Singh Shekhawat

233. Indian UPI Transactions Reach Record High of How many Trillions in May 2023?
A. ₹ 12.7 Trillion B. ₹ 14.3 Trillion
C. ₹ 15.6 Trillion D. ₹ 16.9 Trillion

234. Which medium-range ballistic missile was successfully test-fired from APJ Abdul Kalam Island?
A. Agni-1 B. Agni-2
C. Agni-3 D. Agni-4

235. India defeated which team to win the Men's Hockey Junior Asia Cup title?
A. Sri Lanka B. Pakistan
C. Nepal D. Bangladesh

236. Prime Minster Street Vendor's AtmaNirbhar Nidhi (PM SVANidhi) Scheme has recently successfully completed how many years?
A. 2 B. 3
C. 4 D. 5

237. Which state police has recently launched a massive state-wide operation named "OP Clean"?
A. Haryana B. Punjab
C. Uttar Pradesh D. Madhya Pradesh

238. Which of the following country has launched its first commercial-grade satellite?
A. North Korea B. South Korea
C. Iran D. Saudi Arabia

239. Which AIIMS has becomes the first of all AIIMS to receive the National Accreditation Board for Hospitals and Healthcare Providers (NABH) accreditation?
A. AIIMS Nagpur B. AIIMS Patna
C. AIIMS Chennai D. AIIMS Bengaluru

240. By which year the city will get the 'Smart City' tag under the Srinagar Smart City Project?
A. 2025 B. 2026
C. 2027 D. 2024

241. Which of the following country has hosted the meeting of BRICS Foreign Ministers?
A. Brazil B. Russia
C. South Africa D. India

242. Who has been appointed as the new Chairman and Managing Director of Steel Authority of India Ltd (SAIL)?
A. Ajit Kumar Saxena B. Amarendu Prakash
C. Rajesh Kumar D. Rajiv Dixit

243. Who has become the first woman from Tamil Nadu to climb the world's highest peak, Mount Everest?
A. Premlata Agarwal B. Krushnaa Patil
C. Malavath Purna D. Muthamizh Selvi

244. The third G20 Health Working Group meeting begins in which city?
A. Bengaluru B. Hyderabad
C. New Delhi D. Mumbai

245. Union Minister for Health and Family Welfare, Dr. Mansukh Mandaviya has inaugurated the state of-the-art National Training Centre for Food Safety and Standards Authority of India (FSSAI) in which city?
A. Patna B. Ghaziabad
C. Visakhapatnam D. Gurugram

246. According to a new report by Standard Chartered, India is set to remain UAE's largest export destination by which year?
A. 2025 B. 2026
C. 2030 D. 2028

247. Who has won the Thailand Open 2023 Women's Singles Title?
A. Iga Swiatek B. Karolína Plíšková
C. Monica Seles D. Ann Se-young

248. Who is the author of the book titled "The Power of One Thought : Master Your Mind"?
A. Zuni Chopra B. Durjoy Dutta
C. BK Shivani D. Samhita Arni

249. Who received 'Climate And Health' award at UITP Awards 2023, Barcelona?
A. CESC Limited
B. Brihanmumbai Electric Supply and Transport (BEST)
C. Indian Railway Catering and Tourism Corporation (IRCTC)
D. Uttar Haryana Bijli Vitran Nigam (UHBVN)

250. President Droupadi Murmu has been awarded the country's highest civilian award Grand Order of the Chain of the Yellow Star. It is the highest civilian award in which country?
A. Fiji B. Nigeria
C. Suriname D. Mauritius

251. Dennis Francis has been elected as the President of the 78th UN General Assembly (UNGA). He is from which country?
A. Trinidad and Tobago B. Suriname
C. Guatemala D. Costa Rica

252. Which state government has announced the launch of 'Mukhyamantri Seekho Aur Kamao' scheme?
A. Madhya Pradesh B. Uttar Pradesh
C. Assam D. Bihar

253. Who has launched a Financial Inclusion Dashboard 'ANTARDRISHTI'?
A. Urjit Patel B. Shaktikanta Das
C. Nirmala Sitharaman D. Droupadi Murmu

254. 'Mission Vatsalya', which was seen in the news, is a scheme implemented by which Union Ministry?
A. Ministry of Rural Development
B. Ministry of Housing and Urban Affairs
C. Ministry of Youth Affairs and Sports
D. Ministry of Women and Child Development

255. The 6th edition of the annual naval exercise 'Ektha' was held between India and which country?
A. Egypt B. UAE
C. Maldives D. Sri Lanka

256. According to the report titled "Tracking SDG7: The Energy Progress 2023", approximately how many people around the world are still using polluting fuels and techniques for cooking?
A. 2.9 billion B. 3.1 billion
C. 2.3 billion D. 1.8 billion

257. Who launched the Girl Empowerment Mission (GEM)-2023?
A. NHPC B. GAIL
C. Coal India D. NTPC Kanti

258. Which of the following has launched the "Addiction Free Amrit Kaal" campaign to promote a healthier & addiction-free India?
A. National Commission for Protection of Child
B. Central Bureau of Investigation
C. National Commission for Women
D. Ministry of Health and Family Welfare

259. Who will inaugurate the integrated Water Resources Action Plan-2023-25 under the Amrit Jal Kranti initiative?
A. Narendra Modi B. Piyush Goyal
C. Nirmala Sitharaman D. Manohar Lal

260. Which company has recently launched a new 'voice chat' feature to its Al-powered Bing Chat on the desktop?
A. Google B. IBM
C. Microsoft D. Tesla

261. Who has inaugurated the first-ever National Training Conclave at the International Exhibition and Convention Centre at Pragati Maidan in New Delhi?
A. Nirmala Sitharaman B. Draupadi Murmu
C. Narendra Modi D. Rajnath Singh

262. Who has released the report highlighting the significant impacts of 'Har Ghar Jal' program on public health and economic savings?
A. World Health Organization
B. World Intellectual Property Organization
C. International Maritime Organization
D. World Meteorological Organization

263. Which Countries Forge 'Atlantic Declaration' to Boost Economic Ties?
A. US and UK B. US and UAE
C. UK and India D. US and Australia

264. Which of the following has approved the First Loss Default Guarantee (FLDG) framework, allowing fintech to partner with banks and non-Banking financial companies (NBFCs)?
A. RBI B. SEBI
C. SIDBI D. IRDAI

265. WBIDC, Amazon and FICCI join hands to promote e-commerce exports from Which State?
A. West Bengal B. Gujarat
C. Tamil Nadu D. Maharashtra

266. Which company has successfully launched pilot study on vehicles using E27 fuel and Ethanol Blended Diesel Fuel?
A. Coal India Limited
B. Bharat Heavy Electricals Limited
C. Steel Authority of India Limited
D. Hindustan Petroleum Corporation Limited

267. Who was given the 'Governor of the Year' award by Central Banking in London?
A. C. Rangarajan B. Urjit Ravindra Patel
C. Shaktikanta Das D. Bimal Jalan

268. Which railway station was recently awarded the 'Eat Right Station' certificate?
A. Varanasi Railway Station
B. Guwahati Railway Station
C. Patna Railway Station
D. Ahmedabad Railway Station

269. India will host the 2025 International Institute of Administrative Sciences (IIAS) Annual Conference at Which State?
A. Gujarat B. Telangana
C. Uttar Pradesh D. Kerala

270. Which has launched mission EVOLVE (Electric Vehicle Operations and Lending for Vibrant Ecosystem) in association with NITI Aayog to finance MSMEs in the EV space?
A. SEBI B. RBI
C. SIDBI D. NABARD

271. A Book titled Rebels Against the Raj : Western Fighters for India's Freedom has won the Elizabeth Longford Prize for Historical Biography 2023. Who is the author of this book?
A. Jhumpa Lahiri B. Vikram Seth
C. Aravind Adiga D. Ramchandra Guha

272. Who joined hands to drive citizen awareness 'G20-Stay Safe Online' campaign?
A. Google and MeitY B. Meta and MeitY
C. Amazon and MeitY D. Microsoft and MeitY

273. NTPC Barauni has achieved a significant milestone by securing the first rank in the Best Industry Category at the 4th National Water Awards. NTPC Barauni is situated in which state?
A. Jharkhand B. Bihar
C. Chhattisgarh D. Rajasthan

274. Which country will rejoin UNESCO in July 2023 four years after leaving due to allegations of bias against Israel?
A. Russia B. Germany
C. Japan D. United States

275. In which country Indian Army is participating in 'Exercise Khan Quest 2023'?
A. France B. Japan
C. Mongolia D. Russia

276. Which state's chief minister has inaugurated "The Tribune Real Estate Expo 2023" in the state?
A. Rajasthan B. Madhya Pradesh
C. Himachal Pradesh D. Uttarakhand

277. Which state's hockey team won the Hockey India Junior Men's National Championship 2023?
A. Uttar Pradesh B. Madhya Pradesh
C. Haryana D. Punjab

278. Which Indian company is included in the list of 100 most influential companies released by 'Time' magazine?
A. Tata Group B. Reliance Industries
C. Bharti Airtel D. NPCI

279. Which City has set a new Guinness World Record in the Yoga event 21st June 2023?
A. Pune B. Surat
C. Indore D. Bengaluru

280. Who organized the 'Ocean Ring of Yoga' on 21st June 2023?
A. US Navy B. Australia Navy
C. Indian Navy D. Indian Coast Guard

281. Who was sworn in as the Central Vigilance Commissioner (CVC)?
A. Praveen Kumar Srivastava
B. Jagdeep Dhankhar
C. Jai Prakash Singh
D. RK Vishwakarma

282. Which player won the Orange Cap in IPL 2023?
A. Nishant Sindhu B. Hardik Pandya
C. Rashid Khan D. Shubman Gill

283. Who has been re-elected as the External Auditor of the World Health Organisation (WHO)?
A. Jim Yong Kim B. Anshula Kant
C. Ajay Banga D. Girish Chandra Murmu

284. Which team won Indian Premier League (IPL) 2023?
A. Chennai Super Kings B. Mumbai Indians
C. Gujarat Titans D. Kolkata Knight Riders

285. Who won the Malaysia Masters badminton title 2023 in men's singles?
A. Priyanshu Rajawat B. Lakshya Sen
C. Sameer Verma D. HS Prannoy

286. Which company carried out the construction of the new Parliament House?
A. Reliance Infrastructure Ltd.
B. Sadbhav Engineering Ltd.
C. Tata Projects Ltd.
D. Dilip Buildcon Ltd.

287. Where was the International Climate Research Meeting (ICRC-2023) held?
A. IIT Kanpur B. IIT Delhi
C. IIT Madras D. IIT Bombay

288. OpenAI launched which app in India for iPhone users on 18 May, 2023?
A. ChatGPT app
B. GPT-3.5 architecture
C. Language model training
D. OpenAI research initiative

289. Who recently took charge as the director of the Central Bureau of Investigation (CBI)?
A. Praveen Sood B. Alok Kumar Verma
C. Rishi Kumar Shukla D. Anil Sinha

290. What was the rank of AI supercomputer "AIRAWAT", in the 61st edition of the Top 500 Global Supercomputing list?
A. 61st B. 75th
C. 80th D. 55th

291. Which author won the 2023 International Booker Prize for his novel "Time Shelter"?
A. Niel Gaiman B. Salman Rushdie
C. Georgi Gospodinov D. None of the above

292. Which team did the Indian junior hockey team defeat in their first match at the Men's Asia Cup 2023?
A. Australia B. Chinese Taipei
C. Japan D. South Korea

293. Who won the gold medal in the men's long jump event at the International Jumping Meeting athletics 2023?
A. Sandeep Singh Maan B. Sanjay Kumar Rai
C. Murali Sreesankar D. Ankit Sharma

294. Where was the 3rd Forum on India-Pacific Islands Cooperation (FIPIC Summit) held?
A. Australia B. New Zealand
C. Papua New Guinea D. Fiji

295. Who is the first Arab female astronaut to go into space?
A. Rayyana Barnawi B. Anousheh Ansari
C. Sara Sabry D. Marsha Ivins

296. In which district of Uttar Pradesh did the 3rd Khelo India University Games start?
A. Agra B. Allahabad
C. Ghaziabad D. Gautam Buddha Nagar

297. Who conferred Fiji's highest honour, the Companion of the Order of Fiji, to Prime Minister Narendra Modi?
A. President of Fiji
B. Prime Minister of Fiji
C. Governor-General of Fiji
D. None of these

298. On 22 May, 2023, who became the world No. 1 player in the men's javelin throw rankings?
A. Anderson Peters B. Rohit Yadav
C. Arshad Nadeem D. Neeraj Chopra

299. In the Italian Open 2023, which player won his first clay court title?
A. Novak Djokovic B. Rafael Nadal
C. Daniil Medvedev D. Holger Roon

300. Which Indian sportsperson won the bronze medal in the women's long jump event at the Golden Grand Prix 2023 Athletics Meet?
A. Shaili Singh B. Reeth Abraham
C. Anju Bobby George D. B Aishwarya

ANSWERS

1	2	3	4	5	6	7	8	9	10
C	C	B	D	B	B	B	C	B	C
11	**12**	**13**	**14**	**15**	**16**	**17**	**18**	**19**	**20**
B	C	A	C	B	C	B	D	B	B
21	**22**	**23**	**24**	**25**	**26**	**27**	**28**	**29**	**30**
C	D	C	C	B	B	C	C	C	C
31	**32**	**33**	**34**	**35**	**36**	**37**	**38**	**39**	**40**
C	C	C	B	C	B	B	C	A	C
41	**42**	**43**	**44**	**45**	**46**	**47**	**48**	**49**	**50**
A	B	B	B	C	B	C	B	B	B

51	**52**	**53**	**54**	**55**	**56**	**57**	**58**	**59**	**60**
D	B	B	B	B	B	C	A	C	B
61	**62**	**63**	**64**	**65**	**66**	**67**	**68**	**69**	**70**
A	D	D	D	B	C	C	B	A	D
71	**72**	**73**	**74**	**75**	**76**	**77**	**78**	**79**	**80**
C	C	B	C	A	A	D	C	B	D
81	**82**	**83**	**84**	**85**	**86**	**87**	**88**	**89**	**90**
B	D	B	D	D	D	C	B	C	A
91	**92**	**93**	**94**	**95**	**96**	**97**	**98**	**99**	**100**
C	C	A	D	D	B	C	A	D	A
101	**102**	**103**	**104**	**105**	**106**	**107**	**108**	**109**	**110**
A	A	C	B	C	D	C	B	B	B
111	**112**	**113**	**114**	**115**	**116**	**117**	**118**	**119**	**120**
B	B	B	B	B	C	D	D	B	A
121	**122**	**123**	**124**	**125**	**126**	**127**	**128**	**129**	**130**
D	A	C	D	B	D	D	B	D	D
131	**132**	**133**	**134**	**135**	**136**	**137**	**138**	**139**	**140**
C	C	A	C	B	B	D	A	C	B
141	**142**	**143**	**144**	**145**	**146**	**147**	**148**	**149**	**150**
D	A	D	A	A	D	B	C	A	B
151	**152**	**153**	**154**	**155**	**156**	**157**	**158**	**159**	**160**
B	D	B	D	B	C	A	C	B	B
161	**162**	**163**	**164**	**165**	**166**	**167**	**168**	**169**	**170**
B	A	B	C	B	B	D	A	C	C
171	**172**	**173**	**174**	**175**	**176**	**177**	**178**	**179**	**180**
B	A	B	C	C	A	C	A	C	A
181	**182**	**183**	**184**	**185**	**186**	**187**	**188**	**189**	**190**
D	B	B	C	B	D	B	B	A	D
191	**192**	**193**	**194**	**195**	**196**	**197**	**198**	**199**	**200**
C	D	A	A	B	A	B	C	B	A
201	**202**	**203**	**204**	**205**	**206**	**207**	**208**	**209**	**210**
A	C	A	C	B	C	A	C	A	B
211	**212**	**213**	**214**	**215**	**216**	**217**	**218**	**219**	**220**
D	C	A	A	A	D	D	C	C	B
221	**222**	**223**	**224**	**225**	**226**	**227**	**228**	**229**	**230**
C	B	D	A	A	C	D	B	D	D
231	**232**	**233**	**234**	**235**	**236**	**237**	**238**	**239**	**240**
A	D	B	B	B	B	B	B	A	D
241	**242**	**243**	**244**	**245**	**246**	**247**	**248**	**249**	**250**
C	B	D	B	B	C	D	C	B	C
251	**252**	**253**	**254**	**255**	**256**	**257**	**258**	**259**	**260**
A	B	B	D	C	C	D	A	D	C
261	**262**	**263**	**264**	**265**	**266**	**267**	**268**	**269**	**270**
C	A	A	A	A	D	C	B	D	C
271	**272**	**273**	**274**	**275**	**276**	**277**	**278**	**279**	**280**
D	A	B	D	C	C	B	D	B	C
281	**282**	**283**	**284**	**285**	**286**	**287**	**288**	**289**	**290**
A	D	D	A	D	C	D	A	A	B
291	**292**	**293**	**294**	**295**	**296**	**297**	**298**	**299**	**300**
C	B	C	C	A	D	B	D	C	A

●●●